THE WORLD BOOK ATLAS

FIELD ENTERPRISES EDUCATIONAL CORPORATION
Chicago London Paris Rome Stuttgart Sydney Tokyo Toronto

1973 EDITION

Printed in the United States of America

ISBN 0-7166-0373-X

Library of Congress Catalog Card Number: 71-654321

PREFACE

The use of maps is essential to a thorough understanding of the world in which man lives. By bringing together maps in a meaningful relationship, an atlas provides a basic educational tool that makes it easier for a user to study a particular area of the earth and compare it with other areas.

Scope of the atlas

THE WORLD BOOK ATLAS has been designed to complement and supplement the 22-volume WORLD BOOK ENCYCLOPEDIA. The atlas contains thematic, historic, and general reference maps that picture all regions of the world of man, both past and present. This edition of the atlas also has a special section dealing with man's exploration of the moon, and a section on car travel in the United States, Canada, and Mexico.

The audience the atlas serves

As with THE WORLD BOOK ENCYCLOPEDIA, this atlas serves the practical needs of the home, the school, and the library. Modern living requires everyone to use maps to find places, to plan trips, to follow news events, and to learn about the world. This atlas has been planned to meet the map reference needs of students, teachers, librarians, and the general public.

Arrangement of the atlas

THE WORLD BOOK ATLAS is conveniently arranged in fourteen sections: *How to Get the Most Out of the World Book Atlas; World; Europe; Asia; Africa; Australia, New Zealand, and Pacific Islands; Polar Regions; Latin America; Canada; United States; Moon; Travel Guide; Population;* and *Index*.

The World section features a unique series of thematic maps dealing with man and the earth. These maps were specially designed by the WORLD BOOK staff to achieve maximum ease of use. They are combined with text, graphs, and photographs to provide the student and general reader with a meaningful picture of the world as the home of man. This section is also designed to teach the unsophisticated map user how to use thematic maps to achieve basic political, social, economic, and geographic understandings.

Each section of the atlas that deals with a major region of the world has several kinds of maps. A shaded relief map of the region—prepared by cartographic artist Richard Edes Harrison—appears in each section's introduction. A physical features map shows the rivers, mountains, seas, and other natural features of the region. A political map shows the boundaries of countries, states, or provinces. Historical maps show the region from ancient times to the present. A series of general reference maps focuses on important areas within the region. These general reference maps are adapted from the Cosmo series of Rand McNally & Company. Color layer-tints show the relief contours of the land.

Ease of use

THE WORLD BOOK ATLAS has been carefully designed to make maps easier to read. The section *How to Get the Most Out of the World Book Atlas* provides special exercises that help readers improve their map-reading skills. In addition, special "What Is Your Atlas I.Q.?" quizzes accompany each major section of the atlas to aid the user in evaluating his own knowledge.

Many other ease-of-use features have been included in THE WORLD BOOK ATLAS. Color-coded thumb tabs on the *Contents* pages help the user find each section of the atlas quickly. The introductory pages to each major section contain a separate index to maps of the countries, states, or provinces in that region.

Population tables and pronouncing gazetteer

The *Population* section in the atlas features the latest population figures for more than 3,000 of the world's major cities plus the population figures from the official census of Canada and the official census of the United States. In addition to giving population statistics, the Major World Cities table also gives the pronunciation for each city. Pronunciations are given by respelling each name in familiar syllables as is done in THE WORLD BOOK ENCYCLOPEDIA. The respellings have been prepared especially for THE WORLD BOOK ATLAS by Clarence L. Barnhart, Editor in Chief of THE WORLD BOOK DICTIONARY and the THORNDIKE-BARNHART Dictionaries.

The Index

The *Index* has been designed for ease of use. It is printed in large, easy-to-read type on green paper. The *Index* has been carefully edited to present only the information the reader needs in order to find what he is looking for quickly and easily. For example, population data is usually a part of such an index. But population data has been assembled in a special section of THE WORLD BOOK ATLAS. The *Index* contains references to both the historic and general reference maps, and it refers the reader to the page that has the best map on a given subject.

Accuracy and authority

The accuracy and authoritativeness of THE WORLD BOOK ATLAS is assured by the combined efforts of three groups of specialists: the Editors of THE WORLD BOOK ENCYCLOPEDIA; the cartographic and research staff of Rand McNally & Company; and the distinguished members of the Cartographic Advisory Board for THE WORLD BOOK ATLAS.

The Editors

STAFF

CARTOGRAPHIC ADVISORY BOARD

LIBRARY COMMITTEE

CONTENTS

HOW TO GET THE MOST OUT OF THE WORLD BOOK ATLAS

X, XI **INTRODUCTION TO THE WORLD BOOK ATLAS**

XII, XIII **HOW TO FIND PLACES ON MAPS**

XIV, XV **HOW TO FIND DIRECTIONS ON MAPS**

XVI **HOW TO FIND DISTANCES ON MAPS**

XVII **HOW TO UNDERSTAND SYMBOLS ON MAPS**

XVIII **HOW TO UNDERSTAND POPULATIONS ON MAPS**

XIX **HOW TO PRONOUNCE NAMES OF CITIES**

XX, 1 **HOW TO UNDERSTAND ABBREVIATIONS AND FOREIGN GEOGRAPHIC TERMS**

WORLD

2, 3 **WORLD INTRODUCTION AND MAP INDEX**

4-11 **THE POLITICAL WORLD**

4, 5 THE COUNTRIES OF THE WORLD

6-11 POLITICAL FACTS AND FIGURES

12, 13 **WORLD TIME ZONES**

14-27 **THE PEOPLE**

14, 15 WHERE DO THE PEOPLE LIVE NOW?

16, 17 HOW FAST IS THE POPULATION GROWING?

18, 19 HOW DO THE PEOPLE MAKE THEIR LIVING?

20, 21 HOW MUCH DO THE PEOPLE HAVE?

22-27 HOW WELL DO THE PEOPLE LIVE?

28-37 **THE EARTH**

28-31 WHAT DOES THE EARTH LOOK LIKE FROM SPACE?

32-33 WHAT DOES THE LAND LOOK LIKE?

34-37 WHAT IS THE WEATHER LIKE?

EUROPE

38, 39 **EUROPE INTRODUCTION AND MAP INDEX**

40 **PHYSICAL FEATURES MAP OF EUROPE**

41 **POLITICAL MAP OF EUROPE**

42-54 **HISTORICAL MAPS OF EUROPE**

42 ANCIENT WORLD (600'S B.C.)

42 CLASSICAL GREECE (ABOUT 450 B.C.)

43 ALEXANDER'S EMPIRE (323 B.C.)

44 ROMAN REPUBLIC (ABOUT 44 B.C.)

45 ROMAN EMPIRE (A.D. 120)

46 ROMAN EMPIRE (A.D. 400)

47 THE CRUSADES (ABOUT 1140)

48 EUROPE ABOUT 1360

49 EUROPE IN 1721

50 EUROPE IN 1810 AND 1815

51 UNIFICATION OF ITALY

51 UNIFICATION OF GERMANY

52 BEFORE WORLD WAR I (1914)

53 AFTER WORLD WAR I (1922 TO 1940)

54 AFTER WORLD II

EUROPE (Continued)

55-73 **MAPS OF COUNTRIES AND DEPENDENCIES**
55 BRITISH ISLES
56 ENGLAND AND WALES
57 SCOTLAND AND NORTHERN ENGLAND
58 FRANCE
59 BELGIUM, NETHERLANDS, AND LUXEMBOURG
60 GERMANY AND AUSTRIA
61 CENTRAL GERMANY
62 DENMARK AND NORTHERN GERMANY
63 NORWAY, SWEDEN, FINLAND, AND ICELAND
64 WESTERN MEDITERRANEAN
65 SPAIN AND PORTUGAL
66 SWITZERLAND AND NORTHERN ITALY
67 ITALY
68 YUGOSLAVIA, HUNGARY, ROMANIA, AND BULGARIA
69 GREECE AND ALBANIA
70 POLAND AND CZECHOSLOVAKIA
71 SOVIET UNION
72 WESTERN SOVIET UNION
73 SOUTH-CENTRAL SOVIET UNION

ASIA

74, 75 **ASIA INTRODUCTION AND MAP INDEX**
76 **PHYSICAL FEATURES MAP OF ASIA**
77 **POLITICAL MAP OF ASIA**
78-83 **HISTORICAL MAPS OF ASIA**
78 PERSIAN EMPIRE (ABOUT 500 B.C.)
79 ANCIENT INDIA (ABOUT 250 B.C. AND 400 A.D.)
79 ANCIENT CHINA (ABOUT 100 B.C.)
80 ASIA ABOUT A.D. 750
81 ASIA ABOUT 1294
82 ASIA ABOUT 1775
83 AFTER WORLD WAR II
84-93 **MAPS OF COUNTRIES AND DEPENDENCIES**
84 ISRAEL AND NORTHERN EGYPT
85 EASTERN MEDITERRANEAN
86 IRAN AND AFGHANISTAN
87 INDIA, PAKISTAN, BURMA, AND CEYLON
88 NORTHERN INDIA AND NEPAL
89 LAOS, CAMBODIA, VIETNAM, MALAYA, AND THAILAND
90 INDONESIA, MALAYSIA, AND THE PHILIPPINES
91 CHINA AND MONGOLIA
92 NORTHEASTERN CHINA
93 JAPAN AND KOREA

AFRICA

94, 95 **AFRICA INTRODUCTION AND MAP INDEX**
96 **PHYSICAL FEATURES MAP OF AFRICA**
97 **POLITICAL MAP OF AFRICA**
98-100 **HISTORICAL MAPS OF AFRICA**
98 ANCIENT EGYPT (1200'S B.C.)

AFRICA (Continued)

99 PARTITION OF AFRICA (1800'S)
100 INDEPENDENCE MOVEMENT

101-107 MAPS OF COUNTRIES AND DEPENDENCIES
101 NORTHEAST AFRICA
102 NORTHWEST AFRICA
103 WEST AFRICA
104 EQUATORIAL AFRICA
105 EAST AFRICA
106 CENTRAL AFRICA
107 SOUTHERN AFRICA AND MADAGASCAR

AUSTRALIA, NEW ZEALAND, AND PACIFIC ISLANDS

108,109 INTRODUCTION AND MAP INDEX
110 PHYSICAL FEATURES MAP OF AUSTRALIA
111 POLITICAL MAP OF AUSTRALIA
112 MAP OF SOUTHEASTERN AUSTRALIA AND NEW ZEALAND
113-115 MAPS OF PACIFIC ISLANDS

POLAR REGIONS

116,117 POLAR REGIONS INTRODUCTION AND MAP INDEX
118 PHYSICAL FEATURES MAP OF THE ARCTIC
119 ARCTIC EXPLORATIONS MAP
120 PHYSICAL FEATURES MAP OF THE ANTARCTIC
121 ANTARCTIC EXPLORATIONS MAP

LATIN AMERICA

122,123 LATIN AMERICA INTRODUCTION AND MAP INDEX
124 PHYSICAL FEATURES MAP OF LATIN AMERICA
125 POLITICAL MAP OF LATIN AMERICA
126-128 HISTORICAL MAPS OF LATIN AMERICA
126 LATIN AMERICA ABOUT 1790
127 AFTER INDEPENDENCE
128 LATIN AMERICA TODAY

129-139 MAPS OF COUNTRIES AND DEPENDENCIES
129 MEXICO
130 CENTRAL AMERICA
131 WEST INDIES
132 PUERTO RICO AND VIRGIN ISLANDS
133 COLOMBIA AND VENEZUELA
134 PERU AND ECUADOR
135 BOLIVIA, PARAGUAY, NORTHERN ARGENTINA, AND CHILE
136 SOUTHERN ARGENTINA AND CHILE
137 URUGUAY AND SOUTHERN BRAZIL
138 NORTHEASTERN BRAZIL
139 NORTHERN BRAZIL AND THE GUIANAS

CANADA

140,141 CANADA INTRODUCTION AND MAP INDEX
142,143 PHYSICAL FEATURES MAP OF CANADA

CANADA (Continued)

144,145 POLITICAL MAP OF CANADA
146,147 HISTORICAL MAPS OF CANADA
146 CANADA TO 1840
147 CANADA AFTER 1867

148-155 MAPS OF CANADIAN PROVINCES
148 ALBERTA
149 BRITISH COLUMBIA
150 MANITOBA
151 NEW BRUNSWICK
152 NEWFOUNDLAND
151 NOVA SCOTIA
153 ONTARIO
151 PRINCE EDWARD ISLAND
154 QUEBEC
155 SASKATCHEWAN

UNITED STATES

156,157 UNITED STATES INTRODUCTION AND MAP INDEX
158,159 PHYSICAL FEATURES MAP OF THE UNITED STATES
160,161 POLITICAL MAP OF THE UNITED STATES
162-164 HISTORICAL MAPS OF THE UNITED STATES
162 COLONIAL AND REVOLUTIONARY PERIOD
163 WESTWARD EXPANSION
164 CIVIL WAR

165 MAP OF THE REGIONS OF THE UNITED STATES
166-213 MAPS OF THE STATES
166 ALABAMA
167 ALASKA
168 ARIZONA
169 ARKANSAS
170 CALIFORNIA
171 COLORADO
172 CONNECTICUT
173 DELAWARE
174 FLORIDA
175 GEORGIA
176 HAWAII
177 IDAHO
178 ILLINOIS
179 INDIANA
180 IOWA
181 KANSAS
182 KENTUCKY
183 LOUISIANA
184 MAINE
173 MARYLAND
185 MASSACHUSETTS
186 MICHIGAN
187 MINNESOTA
188 MISSISSIPPI
189 MISSOURI
190 MONTANA
191 NEBRASKA
192 NEVADA
193 NEW HAMPSHIRE
194 NEW JERSEY
195 NEW MEXICO
196 NEW YORK
197 NORTH CAROLINA
198 NORTH DAKOTA
199 OHIO
200 OKLAHOMA
201 OREGON

UNITED STATES (Continued)

202 PENNSYLVANIA
172 RHODE ISLAND
203 SOUTH CAROLINA
204 SOUTH DAKOTA
205 TENNESSEE
206 TEXAS
207 UTAH
208 VERMONT
209 VIRGINIA
210 WASHINGTON
211 WEST VIRGINIA
212 WISCONSIN
213 WYOMING

MOON

213a, 213b INTRODUCTION AND INDEX
213c MAP OF EARTH SIDE OF THE MOON
213d MAP OF FAR SIDE OF THE MOON
213e-213h THE SURFACE OF THE MOON
213i, 213j FACTS ABOUT THE MOON
213k, 213l LANDING ON THE MOON

TRAVEL GUIDE

214,215 TRAVEL GUIDE INTRODUCTION AND MAP INDEX
216,217 NORTH AMERICAN HIGHWAYS MAP AND DISTANCE TABLE
218,219 NORTHWEST TOURIST REGION MAP
220,221 SOUTHWEST TOURIST REGION MAP
222,223 SOUTHEAST TOURIST REGION MAP
224,225 NORTHEAST TOURIST REGION MAP
226,227 NEW ENGLAND, ALASKA, AND HAWAII TOURIST REGION MAPS

POPULATION

228, 229 INTRODUCTION
230-241 POPULATIONS OF MAJOR WORLD CITIES AND PRONOUNCING GAZETTEER
242-245 THE CENSUS OF CANADA
246-280 THE CENSUS OF THE UNITED STATES

INDEX

281 INTRODUCTION
282-391 INDEX
392 ANSWERS TO QUESTIONS

HOW TO GET THE MOST OUT OF THE WORLD BOOK ATLAS
WORLD
EUROPE
ASIA
AFRICA
AUSTRALIA, NEW ZEALAND AND PACIFIC ISLANDS
POLAR REGIONS
LATIN AMERICA
CANADA
UNITED STATES
MOON
TRAVEL GUIDE
POPULATION
INDEX

HOW TO GET THE MOST OUT

LOOK-IT-UP IN THE WORLD BOOK ATLAS TO LEARN ABOUT:

GEOGRAPHY

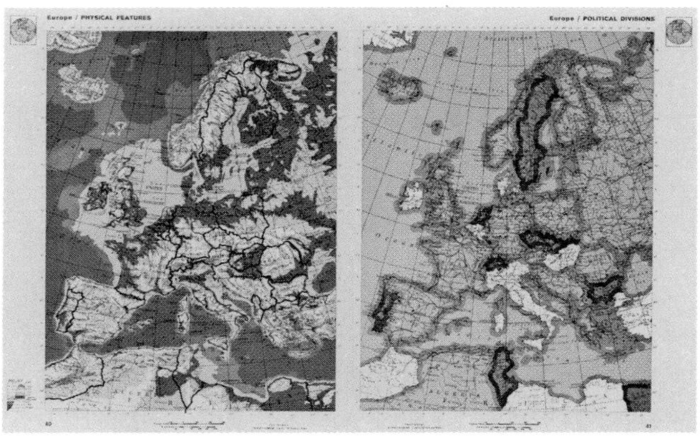

HISTORY

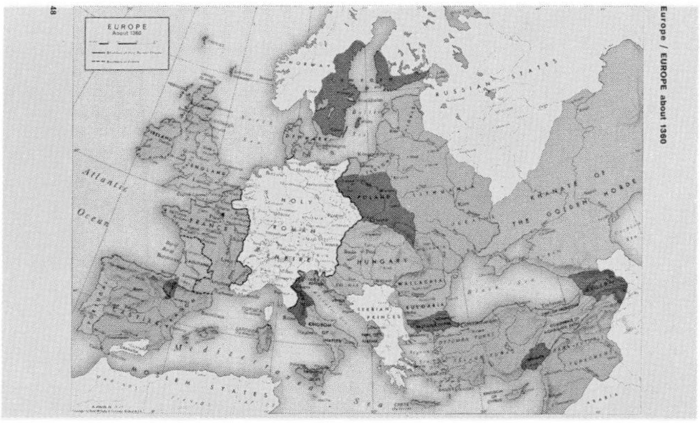

POPULATION

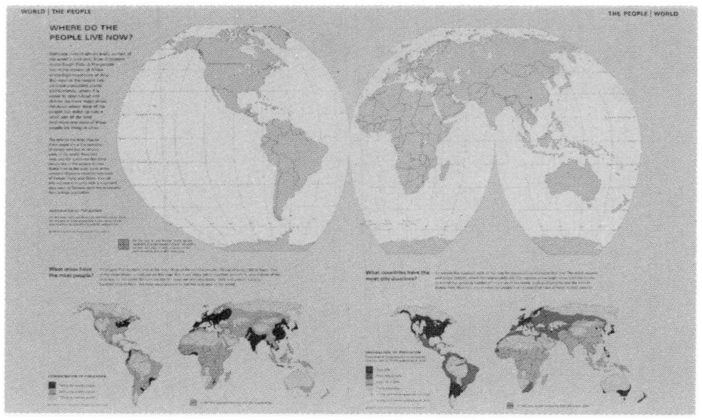

TIME ZONES

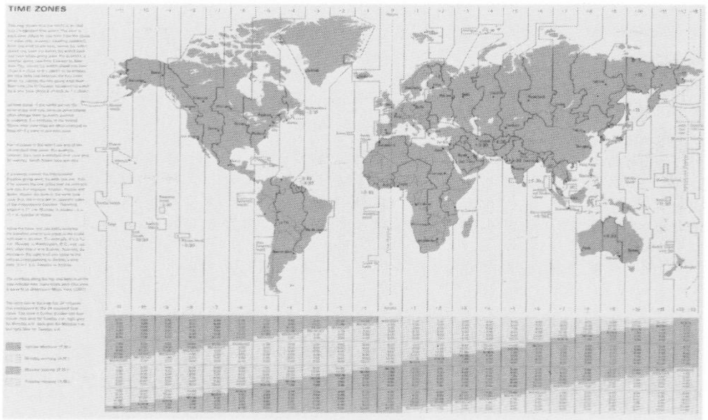

TRAVEL

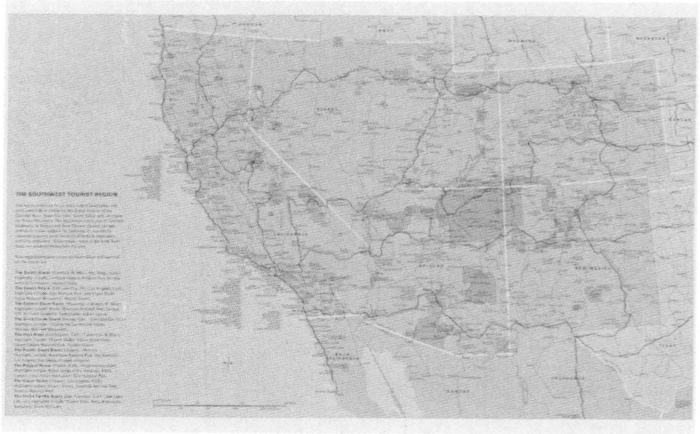

OF THE WORLD BOOK ATLAS

The World Book Atlas brings together in a single volume a wide variety of maps and other reference material. Using the Atlas, the reader can find geographic information about the continents, regions, and countries of the world. The Atlas also contains maps and tables with historical, political, and economic information.

To get the most out of The World Book Atlas, you should first browse through the pages to get a general idea of the kinds of maps and how they are arranged. Next, become familiar with the three ways of finding maps, places, and geographic information in the Atlas. (1) The Contents lists all the maps and other material in the Atlas. Special color-keyed tabs make the Contents especially useful for finding the section of the Atlas you want.

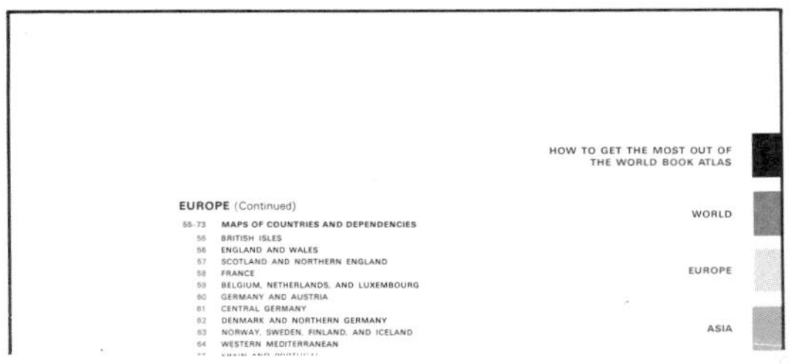

(2) Lists of Maps precede each major section of the Atlas.

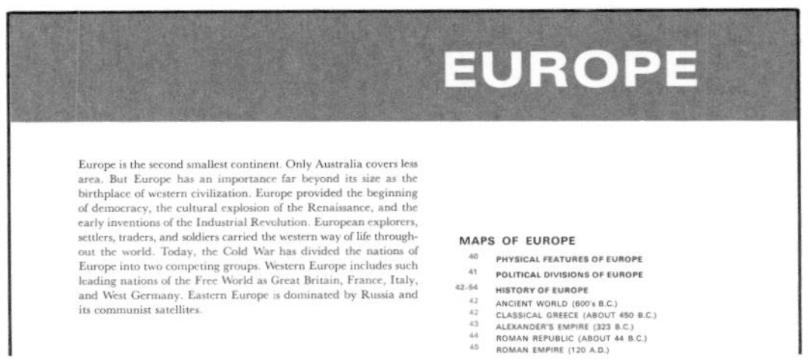

(3) The Index at the back of the Atlas lists 80,000 places in alphabetical order. The Index also refers to the historical maps in the Atlas.

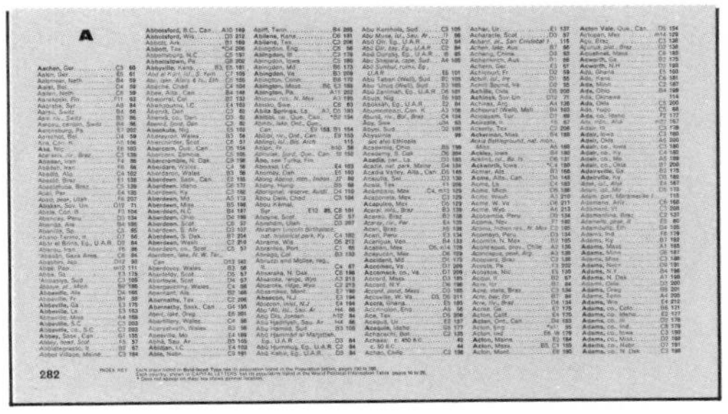

After you become familiar with the contents and organization of the Atlas, study the next ten pages in this section. They explain how to find places on maps, how to find directions and distances, how to understand symbols and populations, how to pronounce names, and how to understand abbreviations and foreign terms on maps. Practice examples will help test your understanding of these important map-reading skills.

Finally, turn to the special Atlas I.Q. sections on the opening pages of each major division of the Atlas. These sections contain questions designed to test your knowledge of the variety of information in The World Book Atlas.

INDEX TO THIS SECTION

XII-XIII HOW TO FIND PLACES ON MAPS
XIV-XV HOW TO FIND DIRECTIONS ON MAPS
XVI HOW TO FIND DISTANCES ON MAPS
XVII HOW TO UNDERSTAND SYMBOLS ON MAPS
XVIII HOW TO UNDERSTAND POPULATIONS ON MAPS
XIX HOW TO PRONOUNCE NAMES ON MAPS
XX-1 HOW TO UNDERSTAND ABBREVIATIONS AND FOREIGN GEOGRAPHIC TERMS

HOW TO FIND PLACES ON MAPS

It is easy to find places on maps in THE WORLD BOOK ATLAS if you follow three simple steps. (1) Look up the name of the place in the green-colored Index in the back of the ATLAS. (2) Find the page number and the coordinates listed next to the name in the Index. (3) Turn to the page numbered in the Index and follow the coordinates across the map to the location of the place.

For example, to find the location of Anping, China, in the ATLAS, first look in the Index. Anping is listed on page 286. The entry reads:

Anping, China.............E6 **92**

The Index tells you that Anping, China, is located on the map on page 92 where the coordinates E and 6 come together.

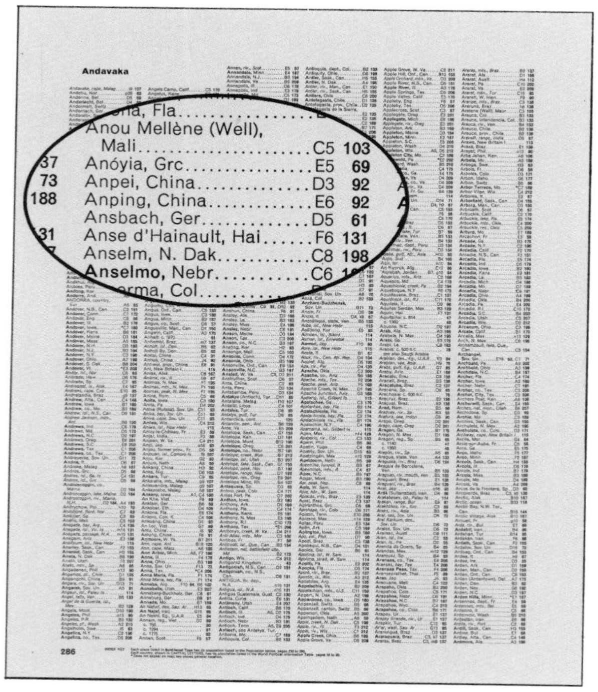

Andavaka

Anou Mellène (Well), Mali....................C5 **103**
Anóyia, Grc................E5 **69**
Anpei, China..............D3 **92**
Anping, China.............E6 **92**
Ansbach, Ger.............D5 **61**
Anse d'Hainault, Hai......F6 **131**
Anselm, N. Dak...........C8 **198**
Anselmo, Nebr...........C6

286

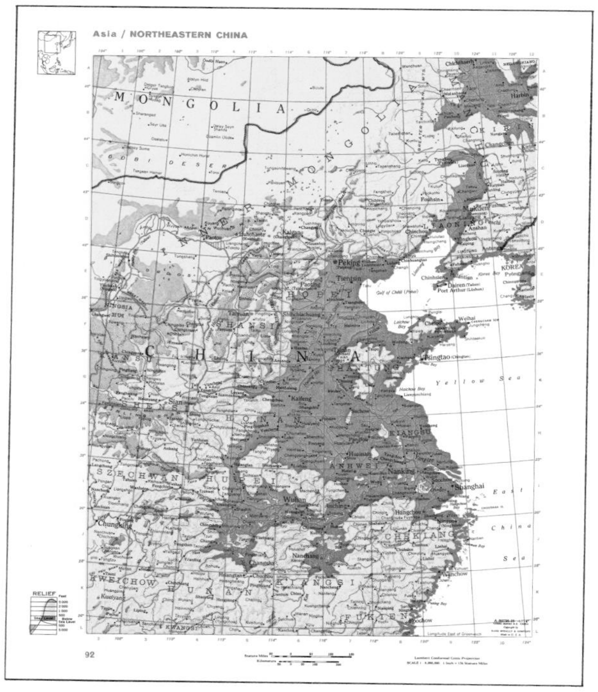

The map of Northeastern China appears on page 92.

Next, turn to page 92 for a map of northeastern China. The coordinates appear along the margins of the map between the longitude and latitude numerals. They are numbered from 1 to 12 across the top of the map, and lettered from A to L down the side of the map. To find Anping, place your left index finger on coordinate E, between the blue 38° and 40° lines of latitude. Then, place your right index finger on coordinate 6, between the blue 114° and 116° lines of longitude. Move your left finger across the map (west to east) and your right finger down the map (north to south). Your fingers will come together in the square formed by the blue longitude and latitude lines. Anping is located in the lower right corner of this square.

TESTING YOUR MAP-READING SKILLS

To gain experience in finding places on maps, answer these 10 questions using the ATLAS as your source. Check your answers by turning to the last page of the ATLAS.

1. To what page would you turn to find the location of Tucumán, Argentina?
2. On what page would you find a map of the Roman Republic in the time of Caesar and Cicero?
3. On what page would you find a map of Nepal?
4. Is Ajaccio, France, located on the eastern or western coast of the island of Corsica?
5. Lead, S. Dak., is located in the western part of the state. In what direction would you travel from Lead to reach Watertown, S. Dak.—north, east, or south?
6. On what river is Newcastle, N.B., located?
7. Iola, Kans., is the seat of what county?
8. Aspen, Colo., is a famous ski resort. Is it north, southwest, or southeast of Denver?
9. On which of New Zealand's islands is Christchurch located?
10. The Atacama Desert is one of the driest places in the world. Where is it located?

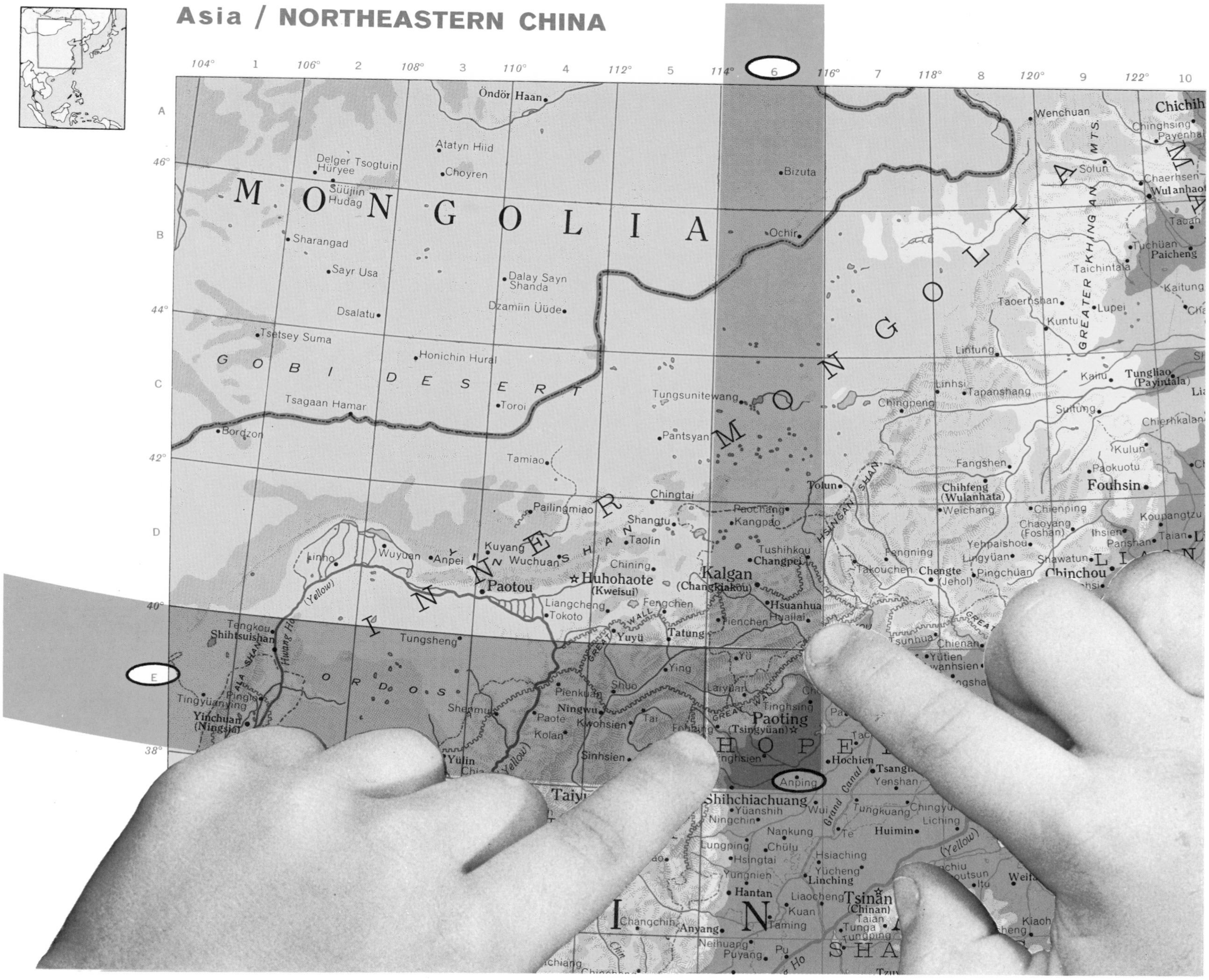

The coordinates appear along the margins of the map between the longitude and latitude numerals. To find Anping, move your left index finger from coordinate E to the center of the map and your right index finger from coordinate 6 to the center of the map. Anping is in the square where the fingers come together.

HOW TO FIND DIRECTIONS ON MAPS

Most of the maps in The World Book Atlas are drawn so that north is at the top of the map, south is at the bottom, west is at the left, and east is at the right. Most maps have a series of lines drawn across them. These are the lines of latitude and longitude. Lines of latitude, or parallels of latitude, are drawn east and west. Lines of longitude, or meridians of longitude, are drawn north and south.

On flat maps, such as those in the Atlas, meridians and parallels may appear as either curved or straight lines. For example, in this section of the map of Europe, the meridians of longitude appear as straight lines coming together toward the top of the map. The parallels of latitude appear as curved lines. The lines appear differently on different types of maps, depending on the kind of map projection.

To determine directions or locations on any particular map, regardless of its projection, you must use the parallels and meridians. For example, suppose you want to know which city is farther north, Paris or Berlin. The map shows that Paris is south of the 50° parallel of latitude and Berlin is north of it. This means that Berlin is farther north than Paris. Now, which city is farther west, Paris or Dublin? By looking at the meridians of longitude, you can see that Dublin is west of the 0° meridian and Paris is east of it. This means that Dublin is farther west than Paris.

Longitude and latitude lines also help locate places on maps. Meridians are numbered in degrees east and west of a line running through Greenwich, England. Parallels are numbered in degrees north and south of the equator. Any place on earth can be located by the longitude and latitude lines running through it.

Parallels of latitude

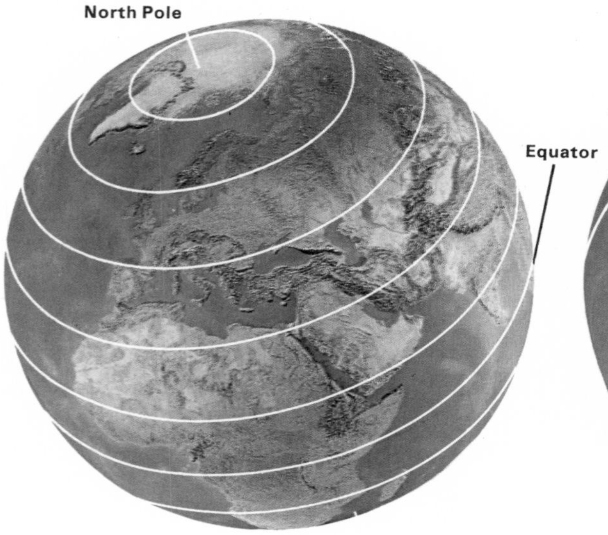

Meridians of longitude

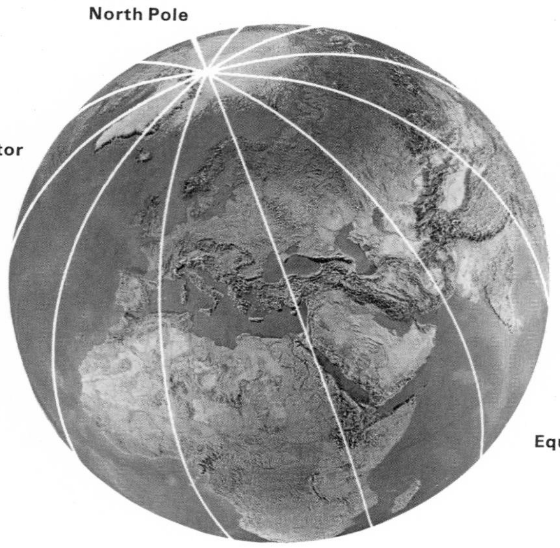

Latitude and longitude

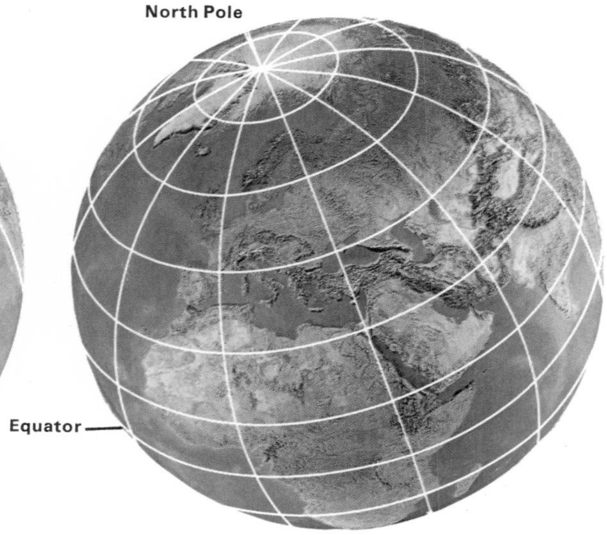

TESTING YOUR MAP-READING SKILLS

To gain experience in finding directions on maps, answer these 10 questions using the Atlas as a source. Check your answers by turning to the last page of the Atlas.

1. On the map of the United States on pages 160 and 161, which is farther west, Chicago or New Orleans?
2. On the map of Asia on page 77, which country is farther east, Japan or the Philippines?
3. On the map of Delaware and Maryland on page 173, which is farther west, Washington, D.C., or Baltimore, Maryland?
4. In what general direction would an airliner fly going from Calgary, Alberta, to Edmonton, Alberta?
5. In what general direction would you travel to go from Cairo, Egypt, to Casablanca, Morocco?
6. Australia's two largest cities are Sydney and Melbourne. Which is farther south?
7. On the map of the Arctic on page 118, which island extends farthest north—Greenland, Novaya Zemlya, or Ellesmere?
8. To fly from Buenos Aires, Argentina, to Rio de Janeiro, Brazil, would you travel south, northeast, or northwest?
9. In what direction is Cleveland from Cincinnati—northeast, northwest, or east?
10. In what direction would you travel going from New York City to Boston?

Europe / PHYSICAL FEATURES

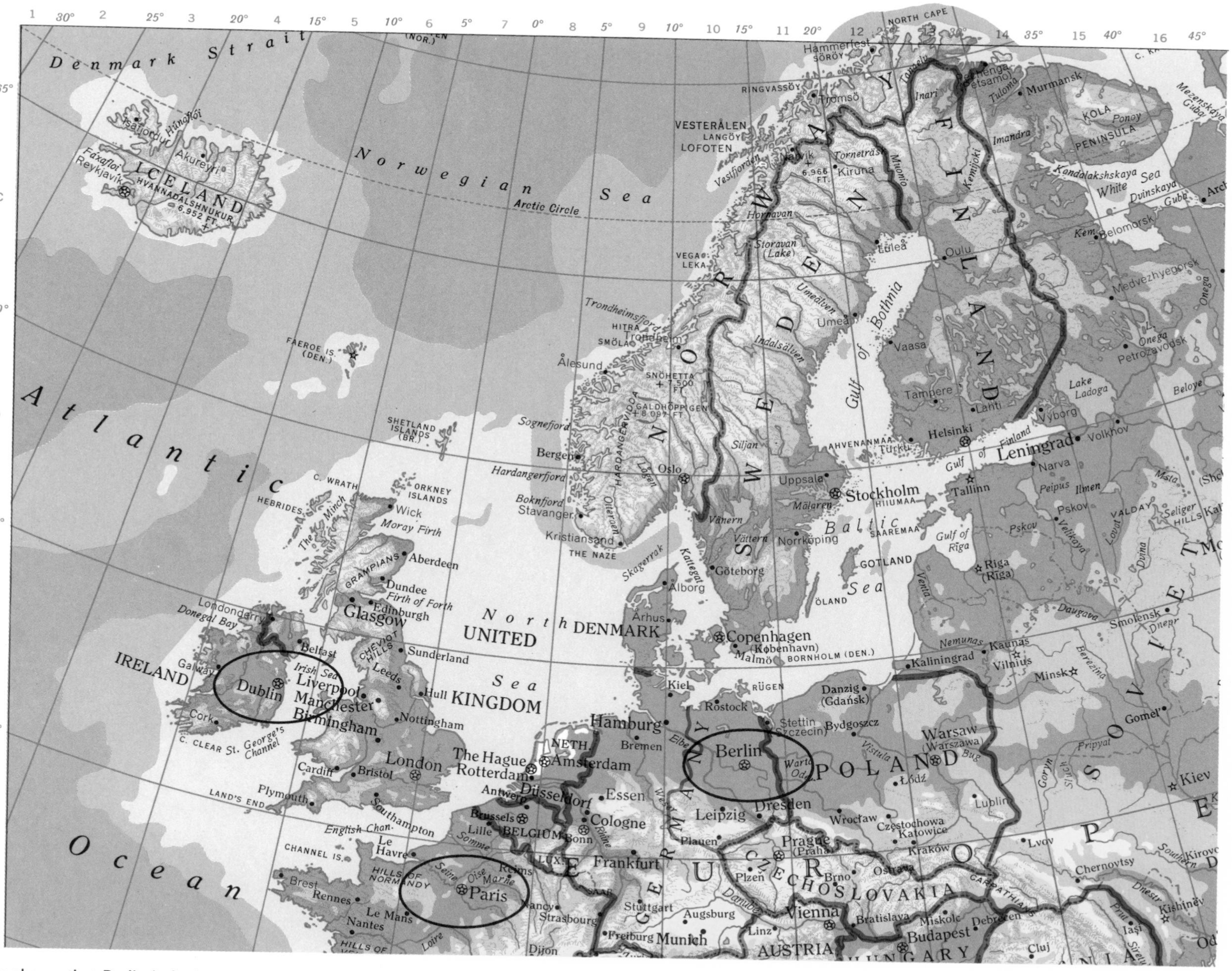

The map shows that Berlin is farther north than Paris and that Dublin is farther west than Paris.

HOW TO FIND DISTANCES ON MAPS

It is easy to find the distance between two places on a map in The World Book Atlas. For example, suppose you want to know the distance between Paris and Rouen. To do so, follow these three steps: (1) Lay a slip of paper on the map so that its edge touches the two cities. Adjust the paper so that one corner touches Rouen. Mark the paper directly at the spot where Paris is located.

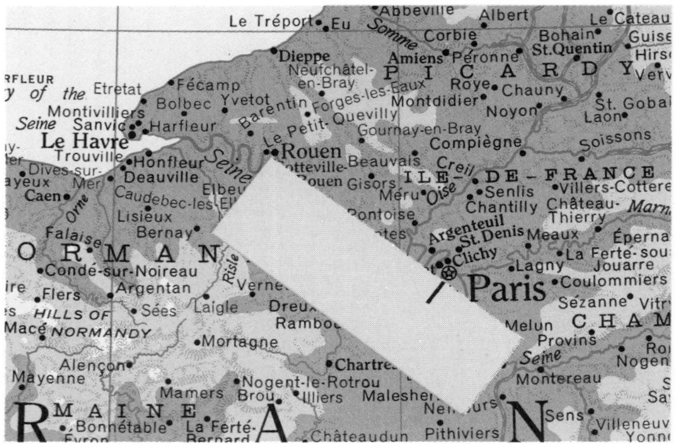

(2) Place the paper along the scale of statute miles beneath the map. Place the corner at 0 and line up the edge of the paper along the scale. The pencil mark on the paper indicates that Rouen is between 50 and 75 miles from Paris.

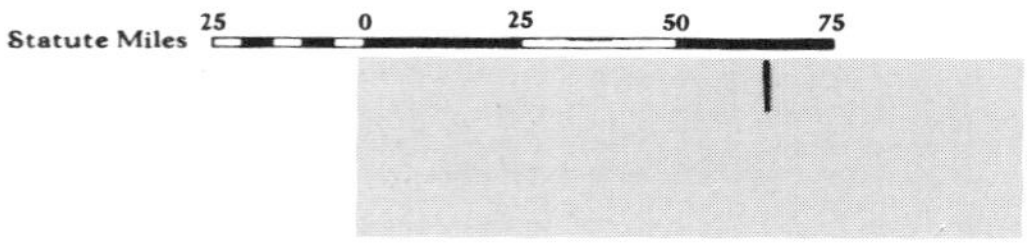

(3) To find the exact distance between Rouen and Paris, move the paper to the left so that the pencil mark is at 50 on the scale. The corner of the paper stands in the fourth five-mile unit. This means that the two towns are 50 plus 15 plus 2, or 67 miles apart.

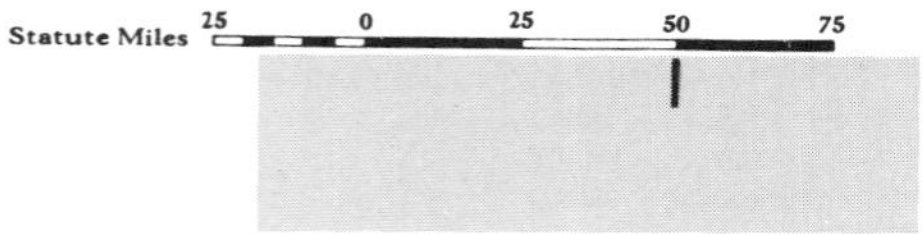

To find the distance between Paris and Rouen, use the scale of statute miles printed along the bottom margin of the page.

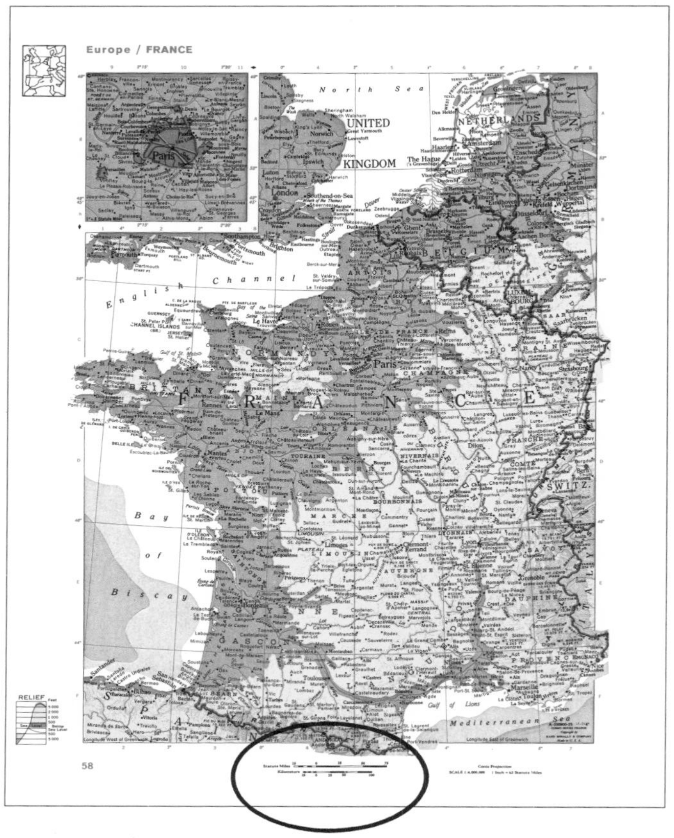

TESTING YOUR MAP-READING SKILLS

To help gain experience in finding distances on maps, answer these 10 questions using the Atlas as your source. Check your answers by turning to the last page of the Atlas.

1. Which city is closer to Baltimore—Washington, D.C., or Annapolis, Md.?
2. About how many miles is it from Cairo, Egypt, to Port Said, Egypt?
3. About how many miles is it from Canberra, Australia, to Sydney, Australia?
4. Using the Iowa map, which distance is greater, Sioux City to Fort Dodge or Des Moines to Cedar Rapids?
5. About how long is the island of Corsica from Cape Corse to Bonifacio?
6. About how many miles would you travel if you flew from Saigon, South Vietnam, to Bangkok, Thailand?
7. About how far would you travel if you made a round-trip between Peking, China, and Mukden, China?
8. An airplane flying from Copenhagen, Denmark, to Helsinki, Finland, stops at Oslo, Norway, and Stockholm, Sweden. About how many miles is each leg of the flight?
9. A boat sailing a straight course from West Palm Beach, Florida, to Nassau, Bahama Islands, would travel how many miles?
10. Is it farther by airplane from Toronto, Ontario, to Quebec, Quebec, or from Vancouver, British Columbia, to Edmonton, Alberta?

HOW TO UNDERSTAND SYMBOLS ON MAPS

All of the terrain maps of continents, countries, states, and provinces in THE WORLD BOOK ATLAS are colored to show the elevation of land and water areas above or below sea level. The maps have a relief key just like the one illustrated below. All land area more than 5,000 feet above sea level is colored brown, those areas between 5,000 feet and 2,000 feet are colored a lighter shade of brown, and so on down to sea level.

This map shows a section of Oregon on page 201. If you drive from Coos Bay to Crater Lake National Park, you would go from an area near sea level through higher elevations until you reached the lake, which lies in an area more than 5,000 feet above sea level.

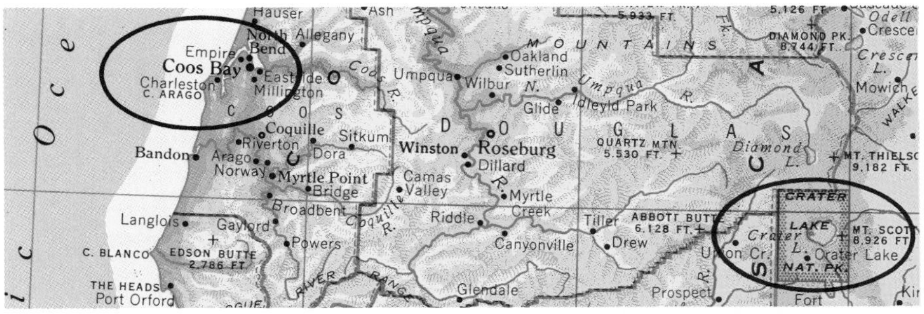

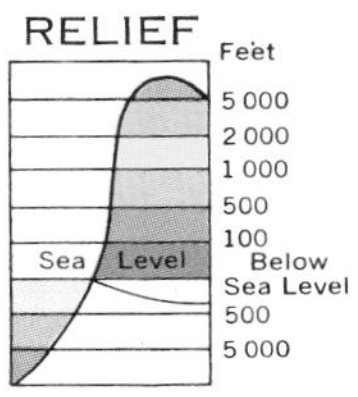

The ocean depths are colored in three shades of blue: light blue for areas from sea level to 500 feet, a medium blue for 500 to 5,000 feet, and a darker blue for all water areas more than 5,000 feet deep.

Besides understanding the colors used on maps, you should understand the most important symbols printed on maps. The three groups of symbols on this page are used on maps in THE WORLD BOOK ATLAS.

TESTING YOUR MAP-READING SKILLS

To gain experience in reading map symbols, answer these 10 questions using the ATLAS as your source. Check your answers by turning to the last page of the ATLAS.

1. If you traveled by car from Kansas City, Kans., to Dodge City, Kans., would your elevation above sea level be increasing, decreasing, or staying about the same?
2. How would you rank these California cities in order of elevation from lowest to highest—Sacramento, El Centro, and San Bernardino?
3. If you took a boat trip downstream from Joliet, Ill., to Peoria, Ill., you would pass four towns that are county seats. Three are Lacon, Hennepin, and Morris. What is the fourth county seat?
4. The Mekong River rises in China and flows through Southeast Asia to the South China Sea. On its way, it passes two national capitals. What are they?
5. Mauna Kea and Mauna Loa are two famous Hawaiian volcanoes. Which one is located in Hawaii Volcanoes National Park?
6. The Hopi Indian Reservation in northeastern Arizona lies in two counties. One is Navajo. What is the other?
7. Using the map of Italy on page 67, which of these three cities has the largest population—Venice, Milan, or Ravenna?
8. The highest point in Nova Scotia has an elevation of 1,747 feet. Where is it located?
9. Minneapolis and St. Paul are the famous Twin Cities of Minnesota. Which one lies farther west?
10. What is the county seat of Schleicher County, Texas?

Topographic symbols

Ranges
Peaks
Passes
Point of elevation above sea level
Escarpments, bluffs, cliffs, and plateaus
Glaciers
Volcanoes
Lava flows
Sand dunes
Deserts

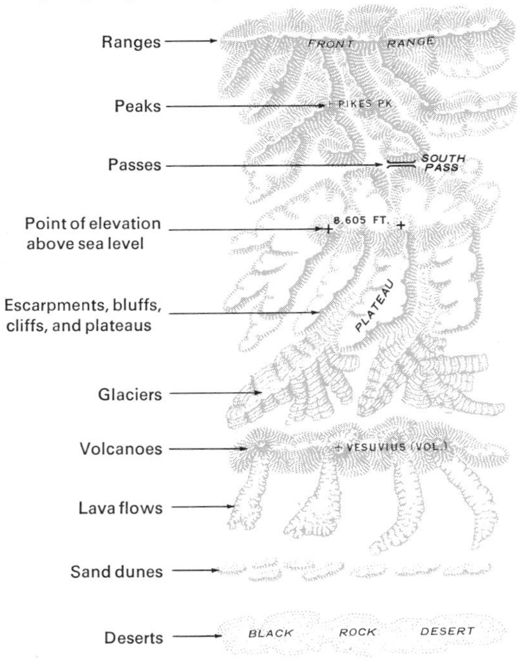

Hydrographic symbols

Coastlines and shorelines
Indefinite or unsurveyed coastlines and shorelines
Lakes and reservoirs
Canals
Rivers and streams
Falls and rapids
Intermittent or unsurveyed rivers and streams
Swamps and marshes
Directional flow arrow
Rocks, shoals, and reefs

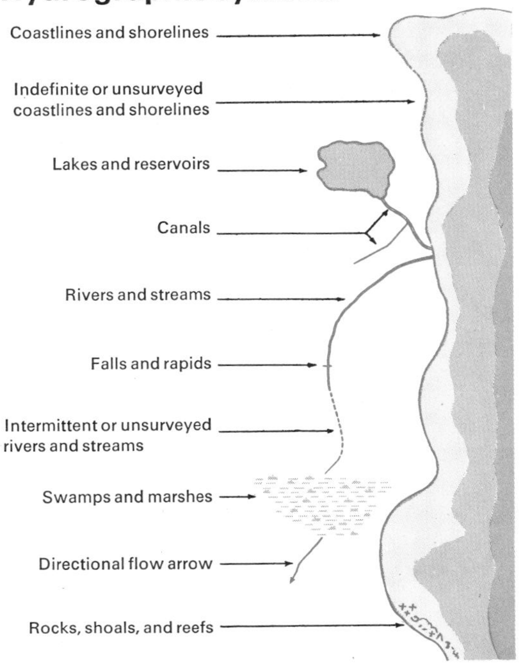

Cultural symbols

Political boundaries

International
State and provincial
County

Major Urban Area

Area of continuous commercial, industrial, and residential development in and around a major United States or Canadian city.

Cities, towns, and villages

Principal cities

• • • • ● Other cities, towns, and villages are indicated by size of type and symbol according to relative population.

○ ○ ○ ◉ County seats are indicated by dot-centered symbol.

○ Communities within a city
⊕ Major capital cities
☆ Minor capital cities

Miscellaneous

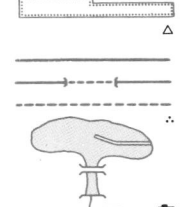

National parks
National monuments
Indian reservations
△ Points of interest
Railroads
Tunnels
Underground or subway
Ruins
Dikes
Bridges
Dams
Race tracks, buildings, etc.

HOW TO UNDERSTAND POPULATIONS ON MAPS

You can tell the relative size of cities and towns on maps in THE WORLD BOOK ATLAS by the size of the lettering in the place name and the size of the dot symbol used to locate it. For example, on this section of the France map you can see that Paris is the largest city because its name has larger letters than the other cities and towns on the map. Rouen, northwest of Paris, is printed in smaller letters, and Dieppe, on the coast, is in still smaller letters. From this difference in the size of lettering, you can tell the relative population of a city or town without actually knowing the population.

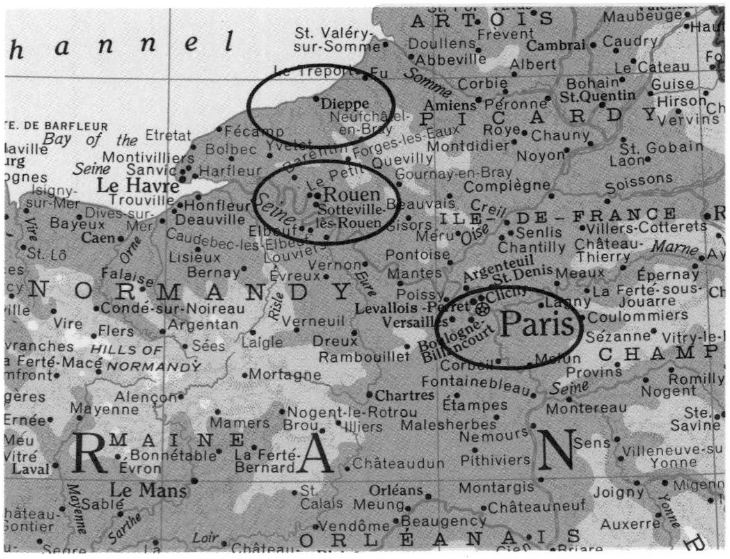

You can find the exact population of thousands of cities in the Population section of the ATLAS. This section is divided into three parts: (1) populations of major cities of the world; (2) populations of Canadian provinces, counties, and cities; and (3) populations of United States states, counties, and cities. The illustration at the right shows the page of the Population section on which Paris is listed.

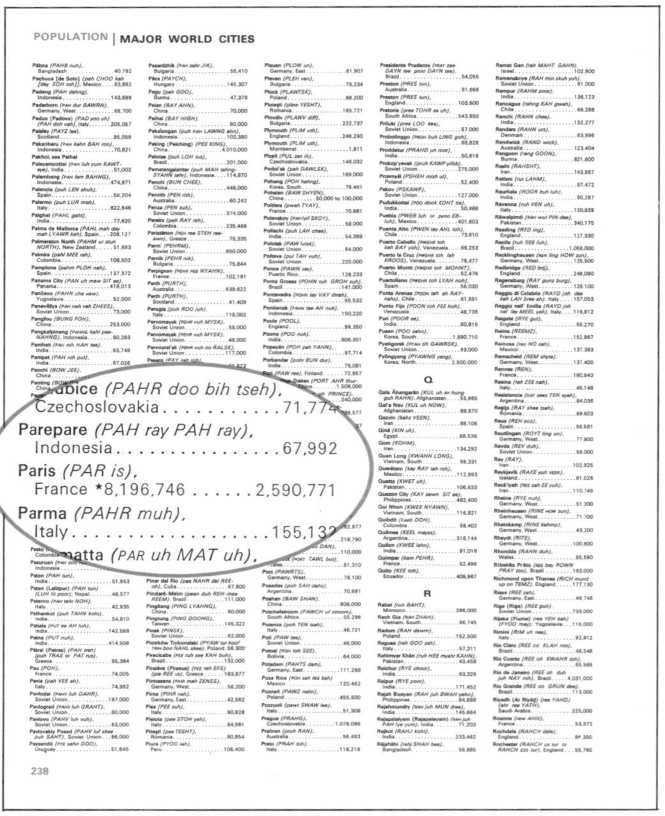
POPULATION | MAJOR WORLD CITIES

Pardubice (PAHR doo bih tseh), Czechoslovakia 71,774

Parepare (PAH ray PAH ray), Indonesia 67,992

Paris (PAR is), France *8,196,746 2,590,771

Parma (PAHR muh), Italy 155,132

Parramatta (PAR uh MAT uh), ...

238

Paris is listed under the Major World Cities in the Population section of the ATLAS.

TESTING YOUR MAP-READING SKILLS

To gain experience in understanding populations in the ATLAS, answer these 10 questions using the ATLAS as your source. Check your answers by turning to the last page of the ATLAS.

1. What is the population of Bern, Switzerland?
2. China and India are the two largest countries in population. What country ranks third?
3. The population of the world was estimated at nearly 3 billion in 1960. What is the estimate for the year 2000?
4. Which Taiwanese city has the largest population—Tainan, Taichung, or Taipei?
5. Plumtree and Bulawayo are towns in Rhodesia. Which place is smaller?
6. Ankara is the capital of Turkey. Using the map on page 85, what city has the largest population in Turkey?
7. What city has the largest population on Mindanao Island, in the Philippines?
8. Which English metropolitan area has more people—Birmingham or Manchester?
9. What city on the Great Lakes has the largest population?
10. Looking at the map on page 176, what is the largest city or town on the island of Hawaii?

HOW TO PRONOUNCE NAMES OF CITIES

In addition to finding out the population for each of the more than 3,000 major world cities listed in the Population section, you can also learn how to pronounce the name of each city. One page of the Population section is illustrated at the right. The pronunciation is given by respelling each city name. The respelling system is easy to use, and is the system used in THE WORLD BOOK ENCYCLOPEDIA. The pronunciation appears in parenthesis after the name of each city.

To pronounce a name, first notice how many syllables it has. You can tell from the size of the letters which syllables to emphasize. When you say the respelled syllables, you have pronounced the name. For example, to pronounce Abidjan *(AB ih JAHN)*, you know that the last syllable receives the greatest emphasis because it appears in large capital letters. The first syllable, in small capital letters, receives less emphasis, and the middle syllable receives the least.

Abakan *(AH buh KAHN)*,
Soviet Union.............90,000
Abeokuta *(AH bay OH koo tah)*,
Nigeria................217,201
Aberdeen *(AB ur DEEN)*,
Scotland...............181,386
Abidjan *(AB ih JAHN)*,
Ivory Coast.............500,000
Abū Zaby *(A boo ZAH bee)*
United Arab Emirates.......46,000
Acapulco *(AH kah POOL koh)*,
Mexico................174,378
Accra *(uh KRAH* or *ACK ruh)*,
Ghana.................521,900
Alcoy *(ahl KOY)*,
Spain...................60,889
Aldridge-Brownhills *(AWL drij BROWN hilz)*, England............86,780
Aleksin *(ah LEK sin)*,
Soviet Union.............61,000
Aleppo (Ḥalab) *(uh LEP oh) (huh LEB)*,
Syria..................578,861
Alès *(ah LESS)*,
France..................42,818
Alessandria *(AH les SAHN dree ah)*,
Italy....................92,760
Alexandria (Al Iskandarīyah)
(AL ig ZAN dree uh) (al is KAHN-duh

Some city names can be pronounced in more than one way. For example, Accra, Ghana, can be pronounced *uh KRAH* or *ACK ruh*. When both pronunciations are important, they both appear.

MAJOR WORLD CITIES

This table includes more than 3,000 cities with populations over 40,000 plus the capital city of each independent country. United States and Canadian cities are listed in special census sections following this list of major world cities. For each of the cities with the largest metropolitan areas in the world, this table includes the population figure for the metropolitan area. This figure is identified by a star (★). In addition to listing the population figure for each city, the pronunciation is given by respelling each city name. For information on how to use this respelling system, turn to the *How to Get the Most Out of the World Book Atlas* section of the ATLAS. The respelling for each name was prepared for THE WORLD BOOK ATLAS by Clarence L. Barnhart, Editor in Chief of THE WORLD BOOK DICTIONARY and the THORNDIKE-BARNHART DICTIONARIES.

230

The pronunciation appears in parenthesis after the name of each city in the Major World Cities tables.

TESTING YOUR MAP-READING SKILLS

To gain experience in pronouncing city names, answer these 10 questions using the ATLAS as your source. Check your answers by turning to the last page of the ATLAS.

1. In pronouncing Borås *(boo ROHS)*, Sweden, the main emphasis is placed on the second syllable. When pronouncing Bremen, West Germany, which syllable receives the main emphasis?
2. Lima *(LEE mah)*, Peru, rhymes with Modena *(MAW deh nah)*, Italy. With which city name does Roubaix, France, rhyme: Szombathely, Hungary, or Sfax, Tunisia?
3. When pronouncing Krasnoyarsk, Soviet Union, do you place greatest emphasis on the first or last syllable?
4. Edinburgh is the capital of Scotland and an important tourist center. How many syllables are pronounced in the name Edinburgh?
5. In pronouncing Nîmes *(NEEM)*, France, the last letter is silent (not pronounced). Which letter is silent in pronouncing Djakarta, Indonesia?
6. Many names are pronounced in a way far different from the way they are spelled. For example, Paochi, China, is pronounced *BOW JEE*, as though the P were a B and the CH a J. How do you pronounce the city of Ise, Japan?
7. Foggia *(FAWD jah)*, Italy, is pronounced as two syllables. How many syllables are pronounced in Prague, Czechoslovakia?
8. Names that are spelled alike are often pronounced differently, as in San Juan *(sahn HWAHN)*, Argentina, and San Marino *(SAN muh REE noh)*. How do you pronounce Santa Cruz, Bolivia, and Santa Maria, Brazil?
9. In pronouncing Chinese names, many T's are pronounced as D's. For example, Tantung, China is pronounced *TAHN DOONG*. How would you pronounce Ping-tung, Taiwan?
10. Graz, Austria, is pronounced *GRAHTS* and Lille, France, is pronounced *LEEL*. How would you pronounce the following names: Seto, Japan; Troyes, France; and Wattenscheid, Germany?

HOW TO UNDERSTAND ABBREVIATIONS AND FOREIGN GEOGRAPHIC TERMS

The table at the right contains the abbreviations and foreign geographic terms that appear on the maps and in the Index of The World Book Atlas. You should become familiar with some of the most common abbreviations, such as "I." for "Island," and "Nat'l" for "National." Foreign geographic terms are part of many place names appearing on maps. For example, "Golfo de Campeche" appears on the map below. If you look up "Golfo" in the list at the right you will find it means "Gulf" in English. Thus, you can translate "Golfo de Campeche" into "Gulf of Campeche." In the same way, you can translate "Cabo Camarón" into "Cape Camarón."

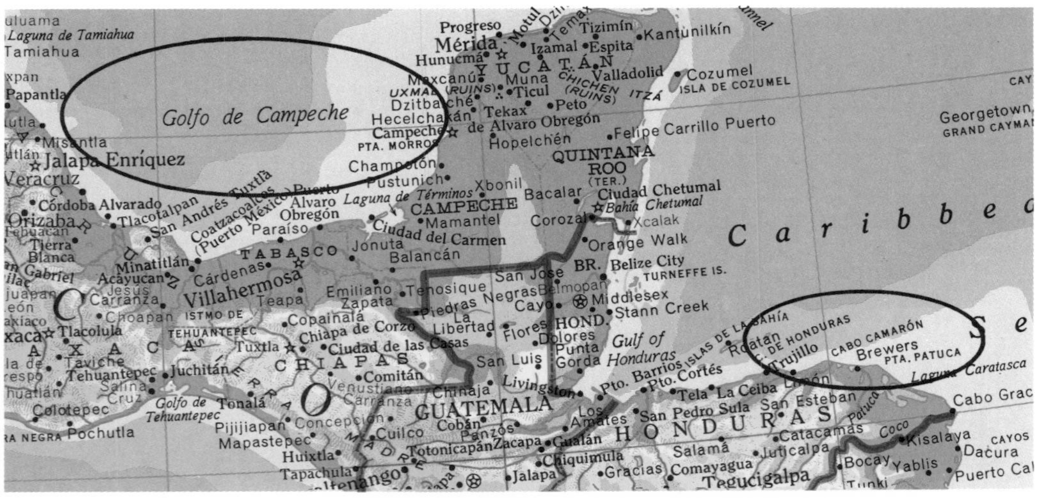

TESTING YOUR MAP-READING SKILLS

To gain experience in reading abbreviations and foreign terms on maps, answer these 10 questions using the Atlas as a source. Check your answers by turning to the last page of the Atlas.

1. In Spanish, "río" means "river." What does the Spanish word "montaña" mean?
2. Georgia is abbreviated "Ga." in the Atlas. For which Canadian province is "P.E.I." the abbreviation?
3. "Monte" is part of many place names in Italy, Spain, and Portugal. What does "Monte" mean?
4. "R." is one of the abbreviations for "River" in English. What does the abbreviation "cr." stand for?
5. "Ozero" means "Lake" in Russian. In which language does "dake" mean "peak" or "mountain?"
6. "Topolnitsa, riv., Bul." is an entry in the Index. To what does this entry refer, and where is it located?
7. "Copenhagen" is "København" in Danish. What does "havn" mean in Danish?
8. Many names in Sweden end in "älven." What does it mean in English?
9. The word "costa" means "coast" in Spanish. What does "costa" mean in Italian?
10. "Norte" means "North" in two languages. One language is Portuguese. What is the other language?

A

Å(a), *Danish, Norwegian, Swedish* . . . river, stream
āb, *Persian* . . . water, river
ābār, *Arabic* . . . wells
acad . . . academy
A.D., *Latin* . . . Anno Domini
admin . . . administration administered
aen, *Norwegian* . . . river, stream
Afg . . . Afghanistan
Afr . . . Africa
Ala . . . Alabama
Alb . . . Albania
Alg . . . Algeria
alp, *German* . . . alpine pasture
Alsk . . . Alaska
Alta . . . Alberta
alto(s), *Spanish* . . . hill(s), mountain(s)
altopiano, *Italian* . . . plateau
älven, *Swedish* . . . stream
A.M., *Latin* . . . Ante Meridian (before noon)
Am . . . American
Am. Sam . . . American Samoa
And . . . Andorra
Ang . . . Angola
anse, *French* . . . cove, bight
Ant . . . Antarctica
approx . . . approximately
Apr . . . April
Arab . . . Arabic
Arc . . . Arctic
arch . . . archipelago
Arg . . . Argentina
Ariz . . . Arizona
Ark . . . Arkansas
arroyo, *Spanish* . . . dry stream bed
ås, *Danish, Norwegian, Swedish* . . . hill, moraine
Atl. O . . . Atlantic Ocean
Aug . . . August
Aus . . . Austria
Austl . . . Australia, Australian
austral, *Spanish* . . . southern
auton . . . autonomous
av., ave . . . avenue
'ayn, *Arabic* . . . waterhole, spring, well

B

B., *Spanish* . . . bahía (bay or harbor)
B . . . bay
baai, *Dutch* . . . bay
bāb, *Arabic* . . . pass
bach, *German* . . . stream, ditch
backe, *Swedish* . . . hill
bahía, *Spanish* . . . bay
bahr, *Arabic* . . . sea, bay
baia, *Italian* . . . bay, gulf
baie, *French* . . . bay, cove
Ba. Is . . . Bahama Islands
baja (bajo), *Spanish* . . . shoal, point
bakke, *Danish* . . . hill
bakken, *Norwegian* . . . mountain, peak
bana, *Japanese* . . . cape
bandar, *Persian* . . . harbor, bay
baños, *Spanish* . . . bathing place, spa
Barb . . . Barbados
batang, *Malay* . . . stream
B.C . . . Before Christ
B.C . . . British Columbia
bdy. (bdry) . . . boundary
beinn, *Gaelic* . . . mountain
Bel . . . Belgium, Belgian
berg, *German, Norwegian, Swedish* . . . mountain, hill
Bhu . . . Bhutan
bir, *Arabic* . . . well
birkat, *Arabic* . . . well, rainpool
Bis. Arch . . . Bismarck Archipelago
bjerg, *Danish* . . . hill, mountain
bldg . . . building
blvd . . . boulevard
Bngl . . . Bangladesh
boca, *Spanish* . . . cove, stream, inlet
bodden, *German* . . . bay, inlet
boğaz, *Turkish* . . . strait
bois, *French* . . . woods
Bol . . . Bolivia
boloto, *Russian* . . . swamp
bord, *French* . . . shore, seaside, bank
boreal, *Spanish* . . . northern
bosch, *Dutch* . . . forest, wood
Bots . . . Botswana
bouche, *French* . . . river mouth
Br . . . Britain, British, branch, bridge
braco, *Portuguese* . . . stream tributary
Braz . . . Brazil
brazo, *Spanish* . . . stream, channel
Br. Hond . . . British Honduras
bros . . . brothers
Bru . . . Brunei
brücke(n), *German* . . . bridge(s)
bucht, *German* . . . bay, channel
bugt, *Danish* . . . bay, gulf
bugten, *Norwegian* . . . bay
bukt (bukten), *Swedish* . . . bay
Bul . . . Bulgaria
Bur . . . Burma, Burmese
burun (burnu), *Turkish* . . . cape

C

C . . . Cape
c., *Latin* . . . circa (about)
cabeza, *Spanish* . . . hill
cabo, *Portuguese, Spanish* . . . cape
cach., *Portuguese* . . . cachoeira (cascade, rapids, waterfall, cataract)
Calif . . . California
Cam . . . Cameroon
Camb . . . Cambodia
campo, *Spanish* . . . field
Can . . . Canada
can . . . canal
Can. Is . . . Canary Islands
cañón, *Spanish* . . . canyon
cap, *French* . . . cape
capo, *Italian* . . . cape, mountain
capt . . . captain
carn, *Gaelic* . . . rocky headland
cat . . . cataract
cath . . . cathedral
caye, *French* . . . key, reef
cayo, *Spanish* . . . rock, key, islet
Celt . . . Celtic
cem . . . cemetery
Cen. Afr. Rep . . . Central African Republic
Cen. Am . . . Central America
cent . . . century
cerro(s), *Spanish* . . . hill(s)
Cey . . . Ceylon
C.H . . . Court House
champ, *French* . . . field
chan . . . channel
chapada, *Portuguese* . . . plateau, upland, hills, range, ridge
chau (chou), *Chinese* . . . island
chāy, *Persian* . . . stream
chiang, *Chinese* . . . stream, channel, bay, sound, lagoon, harbor
ching, *Chinese* . . . well
Chn . . . Chinese
cho, *Japanese* . . . territory
chuan, *Chinese* . . . stream
co . . . county
Col . . . Colombia, college
col, *French* . . . pass
colina, *Spanish* . . . hill, hillock
colline(s), *French* . . . hill(s)
Colo . . . Colorado
Con . . . Congo
concha, *Spanish* . . . bay
confed . . . confederation
Conn . . . Connecticut
cont . . . continent
cord., *Spanish* . . . cordillera
cordillera, *Spanish* . . . mountain range
costa, *Spanish* . . . coast
costa, *Italian* . . . ridge, mountain
côte(s), *French* . . . coast(s)
C.R . . . Costa Rica
cr . . . creek, crater
cuchillar, *Spanish* . . . ridge
C.V. Is . . . Cape Verde Islands
Cyp . . . Cyprus
C.Z . . . Canal Zone
Czech . . . Czechoslovakia

D

dağ, *Turkish* . . . mountain
Dah . . . Dahomey
dake (take), *Japanese* . . . peak
dal, *Danish, Dutch, Norwegian, Swedish* . . . valley
Dan . . . Danish
daqq, *Persian* . . . salt flat, marsh
darya, *Turkic* . . . stream
dasht, *Persian* . . . plain, desert, steppe
D.C . . . District of Columbia
Dec . . . December
deccan, *Hindi* . . . south
Del . . . Delaware
Den . . . Denmark
deniz, *Turkish* . . . sea, bay
dep . . . dependency, dependencies
dept . . . department
des . . . desert
désert, *French* . . . desert
desèrto, *Italian* . . . desert
desierto, *Spanish* . . . desert
détroit, *French* . . . mountain pass
dist . . . district
div . . . division
djebel (jebel), *Arabic* . . . mountain
Dom. Rep . . . Dominican Republic
dr . . . drive
Du . . . Dutch
duinen, *Dutch* . . . dunes
dyk, *Dutch* . . . dam, dike

E

E . . . East
eau, *French* . . . stream
Ec . . . Ecuador
ecuador, *Spanish* . . . equator
Eg . . . Egypt
eiland(en), *Dutch* . . . island(s)
elv, *Norwegian* . . . stream
embalse(s), *Spanish* . . . reservoir(s)
Eng . . . England
ens., *Spanish* . . . ensenada (bay)
entr . . . entrance
Equat. Gui . . . Equatorial Guinea
erg, *Arabic* . . . dune, region of dunes
est, *French, Italian* . . . east
est . . . estuary
este, *Portuguese, Spanish* . . . east
estrecho, *Spanish* . . . strait
étang, *French* . . . pond, lake
état, *French* . . . state
Eth . . . Ethiopia
Eur . . . Europe
exec . . . executive
expwy . . . expressway

F

Falk. Is . . . Falkland Islands
Feb . . . February
fed . . . federation
feld(er), *German* . . . field(s)
fels(en), *German* . . . rock(s)
Fin . . . Finland, Finnish
firth, *Gaelic* . . . inlet
fiume, *Italian* . . . river

fjäll(et), *Swedish* . . . mountain, hill
fjärd(en), *Swedish* . . . bay, fiord
fjell, *Norwegian* . . . mountain, hill
fjord(en), *Danish, Norwegian* . . . fiord, inlet, bay
fjördhur, *Icelandic* . . . fiord, bay, lagoon
fk . . . fork
Fla . . . Florida
fleuve, *French* . . . river
flod, *Danish* . . . lake
flói, *Icelandic* . . . bay, marshland
fluss, *German* . . . stream
foce, *Italian* . . . river mouth
fontein, *Dutch* . . . spring, fountain
forêt, *French* . . . forest
fors(en), *Swedish* . . . waterfall, torrent
forst, *German* . . . forest
foss, *Norwegian* . . . waterfalls
Fr . . . France, French
Fr. Gu . . . French Guiana
Fr. Som . . . French Somaliland
frwy . . . freeway
ft . . . feet, fort
fuente(s), *Spanish* . . . spring(s)
fy . . . ferry

G

g . . . gulf
Ga . . . Georgia
gal . . . gallery
Gam . . . Gambia
gat, *Danish* . . . sound
gawa, *Japanese* . . . stream, channel
gebel, *Arabic* . . . mountain
gebergte, *Dutch* . . . mountains
gebiet, *German* . . . region
gebirge, *German* . . . ridge, mountains
gen . . . general
Geo . . . George
Ger . . . German, Germany
ghat, *Hindi* . . . step
Gib . . . Gibraltar
göl (gölü), *Turkish* . . . lake
golf, *German* . . . gulf
golfe, *French* . . . gulf, bay
golfo, *Italian, Spanish* . . . gulf, bay
gora, *Polish, Russian* . . . mountain
gov., *Portuguese* . . . governador (governor)
gov't . . . government
Gr . . . Great
Grc . . . Greece
Grnld . . . Greenland
Guad . . . Guadeloupe
Guat . . . Guatemala
guba, *Russian* . . . bay, gulf
gunto, *Japanese* . . . archipelago
Guy . . . Guyana

H

hafen, *German* . . . harbor, bay
haff, *German* . . . lagoon
Hai . . . Haiti
hai, *Chinese* . . . sea, lake
hammädat, *Arabic* . . . rocky plain
hamn(en), *Swedish* . . . harbor
hamun, *Persian* . . . swampy lake, plain
haut, *French* . . . high
havn, *Danish, Norwegian* . . . harbor, port
havre, *French* . . . harbor, port
Haw . . . Hawaii
H. B. Co . . . Hudson's Bay Company
hbr . . . harbor
hd . . . head, headland
hdqrs . . . headquarters
hetta, *Norwegian* . . . mountain
hist . . . historical
ho, *Chinese* . . . river
hoek, *Dutch* . . . cape
höfn, *Icelandic* . . . harbor, bay, cove
hoku, *Japanese* . . . north
holm, *Danish, Norwegian, Swedish* . . . island
Hond . . . Honduras
hora, *Czech* . . . mountain
horn, *German* . . . peak
hovden, *Norwegian* . . . peninsula
hoved, *Danish* . . . point, headland
howr, *Persian* . . . lake, marsh
hsien, *Chinese* . . . district
hts . . . heights
hügel, *German* . . . hill
huk, *Danish, Norwegian* . . . point
Hung . . . Hungarian, Hungary
hy . . . highway

I

I . . . island, isle
Ia . . . Iowa
I.C . . . Ivory Coast
Ice . . . Iceland, Icelandic
Ida . . . Idaho
île, *French* . . . island
ilha(s), *Portuguese* . . . island(s)
Ill . . . Illinois
incl . . . includes, including
Ind . . . Indiana
Ind. Res. (I.R.) . . . Indian reservation
Indon . . . Indonesia
ins . . . insular
insel(n), *German* . . . island(s)
inst . . . institute
int . . . interior
I. Q . . . intelligence quotient
Ire . . . Ireland
irmak, *Turkish* . . . stream
is . . . islands
isl . . . island
isla(s), *Spanish* . . . island(s)
isola, *Italian* . . . island
Isr . . . Israel
isth . . . isthmus

It., Ital . . . Italy, Italian
iwa, *Japanese* . . . island

J

Jam . . . Jamaica
Jan . . . January
Jap . . . Japan, Japanese
jar'a', *Arabic* . . . sand area
jct . . . junction
jebel (djebel), *Arabic* . . . mountain
jima (shima), *Japanese* . . . island
jökelen, *Norwegian* . . . glacier
joki, *Finnish* . . . stream
jökull, *Icelandic* . . . glacier, icecap
Jr . . . Junior
Jul . . . July
Jun . . . June

K

kaap, *Dutch* . . . cape
kaikyō, *Japanese* . . . strait
kal, *Persian* . . . stream
kanal, *German* . . . canal
kang, *Chinese* . . . hill, mountain
Kans . . . Kansas
kap, *German* . . . cape
kavir, *Persian* . . . salt desert, waste
kawa, *Japanese* . . . stream, channel
kawr, *Arabic* . . . mountain
kdm . . . kingdom
Ken . . . Kenya
ken, *Japanese* . . . prefecture
khrebet, *Russian* . . . mountain range
köl, *Turkic* . . . lake
kopf, *German* . . . hill, mountain, peak
Kor . . . Korea
kuala, *Malay* . . . bay, river mouth
kūh, *Persian* . . . mountain
kuppe(n), *German* . . . hill(s)
küste, *German* . . . coast, shore
Kuw . . . Kuwait
Ky . . . Kentucky
kyo, *Japanese* . . . gorge

L

l . . . lake
La . . . Louisiana
lac, *French* . . . lake
lag, *Spanish* . . . laguna (lake)
lago, *Italian, Spanish* . . . lake
lagoa, *Portuguese* . . . lagoon
laguna, *Italian, Spanish* . . . lagoon
lahti, *Finnish* . . . bay, gulf
län, *Swedish* . . . administrative division
Leb . . . Lebanon
Le. Is . . . Leeward Islands
Leso . . . Lesotho
Lib . . . Liberia
lib . . . library
Liech . . . Liechtenstein
liman, *Turkish* . . . bay, port
lit . . . little
llanos, *Spanish* . . . plains
loch, *Gaelic* . . . lake, bay
lough, *Gaelic* . . . lake, bay
Lux . . . Luxembourg

M

maa, *Finnish* . . . land
Mala . . . Malaysia
Malag . . . Malagasy Republic
Man . . . Manitoba
mand . . . mandate
Mar . . . March
mar, *Spanish* . . . lake
marais, *French* . . . marsh, lake
mare, *Italian, Romanian* . . . sea
Mart . . . Martinique
Mass . . . Massachusetts
massif, *French* . . . mountain mass
mato, *Portuguese* . . . forest
Maur . . . Mauritania
Md . . . Maryland
med . . . medical
Medit . . . Mediterranean
meer, *Dutch, German* . . . lake, pond
mem . . . memorial
mer, *French* . . . sea
mesa, *Spanish* . . . mesa, hill
Mex . . . Mexico
Mich . . . Michigan
mid . . . middle
mil . . . military
min . . . minute
Minn . . . Minnesota
Miss . . . Mississippi
Mo . . . Missouri
mod . . . modern
mon . . . monument
Mong . . . Mongolia
Mont . . . Montana
mont, *French* . . . mount, mountain
montagne, *French* . . . mountain
montaña(s), *Spanish* . . . mountain(s)
monte, *Italian, Portuguese, Spanish* . . . hill, mountain
Monte . . . Montenegro
Mor . . . Morocco
more, *Russian* . . . sea, sound
morro, *Portuguese* . . . hillock, knoll
morro, *Spanish* . . . bluff, peak
Moz . . . Mozambique
mtn . . . mount, mountain
mts . . . mountains
mun . . . municipality
mund (munde), *German* . . . mouth
mündung, *German* . . . river mouth
muong, *Thai* . . . city
mura, *Japanese* . . . village
mus . . . museum

N

n . . . north, northern
N.A . . . North America
nada, *Japanese* . . . sea
nadi, *Hindi* . . . river, creek
naes, *Danish* . . . cape, peninsula
nafūd, *Arabic* . . . sand hills, desert
nahr, *Arabic* . . . river, stream
najd, *Arabic* . . . plateau
näs, *Swedish* . . . point, peninsula
nat'l. (nat) . . . national
N.B . . . New Brunswick
N.C . . . North Carolina
N.Cal . . . New Caledonia
N.Car . . . North Carolina
N.Dak . . . North Dakota
N.E . . . North East
Nebr . . . Nebraska
Nep . . . Nepal
nes, *Norwegian* . . . point, hill
Neth . . . Netherlands
Neth.W.I . . . Netherlands West Indies
Nev . . . Nevada
Newf . . . Newfoundland
New Hebr . . . New Hebrides
nez, *French* . . . point, cape
N. Gui . . . New Guinea
N.H . . . New Hampshire
Nic . . . Nicaragua
Nig . . . Nigeria
N. Ire . . . Northern Ireland
N.J . . . New Jersey
n.m . . . national monument
N.M . . . New Mexico
N.Mex . . . New Mexico
nong, *Thai* . . . marsh, pond
noorden, *Dutch* . . . north
Nor . . . Norway, Norwegian
nord, *Danish, French, German, Italian, Norwegian, Swedish* . . . north
norte, *Portuguese, Spanish* . . . north
nos, *Russian* . . . cape
n.p . . . national park
N.S . . . Nova Scotia
N.S.W . . . New South Wales
N.T . . . Northern Territory
nuur, *Tibetan* . . . lake
N.W . . . North West
N.W. Ter . . . Northwest Territories
N.Y . . . New York
N.Z . . . New Zealand

O

occ . . . occupied
occidental, *Spanish* . . . western
Oct . . . October
odde, *Danish* . . . point, cape
øen, *Danish, Norwegian* . . . island
oeste, *Portuguese, Spanish* . . . west
off . . . office
ojos, *Spanish* . . . springs
Okla . . . Oklahoma
ön, *Swedish* . . . island
Ont . . . Ontario
oost, *Dutch* . . . east
Oreg . . . Oregon
oriental, *Spanish* . . . eastern
Óros, *Greek* . . . mountain
ost, *German* . . . east
öst, *Danish, Norwegian* . . . east
öster, *Swedish* . . . east
ostrov(a), *Russian* . . . island(s)
ouest, *French* . . . west
øy, *Norwegian* . . . island
ozero, *Russian* . . . lake

P

Pa . . . Pennsylvania
Pää(t), *Finnish* . . . mountain(s)
Pac. O . . . Pacific Ocean
Pak . . . Pakistan
pal . . . palace
pampa, *Spanish* . . . grassy plain
Pan . . . Panama
Pap . . . Papua
Par . . . Paraguay
pas, *French* . . . pass
paso, *Spanish* . . . pass
passo, *Italian* . . . mountain pass
pd . . . pond
P.E.I . . . Prince Edward Island
pen . . . peninsula
peña, *Spanish* . . . mountain
penin . . . peninsula
peresheyek, *Russian* . . . isthmus
Phil . . . Philippines
pic, *French* . . . mountain, peak, hill
picco, *Italian* . . . mountain, peak
pico, *Portuguese, Spanish* . . . peak
piedra, *Spanish* . . . rock, headland
pik, *Russian* . . . peak, mountain
pinar, *Spanish* . . . forest
pk . . . peak, park
pkwy . . . parkway
pl . . . place
planalto, *Portuguese* . . . plateau
plat . . . plateau
playa, *Spanish* . . . beach
P.M., *Latin* . . . Post Meridian (after midday)
P.O . . . Post Office
po, *Chinese* . . . lake
pointe, *French* . . . headland, cape
Pol . . . Poland
polder, *Dutch, German* . . . reclaimed marsh
pol. dist . . . political district
poluostrov, *Russian* . . . peninsula
pont, *French* . . . bridge
ponta, *Portuguese* . . . point
ponte, *Italian* . . . bridge
pop . . . population
Port . . . Portugal, Portuguese
port, *French* . . . harbor, port, haven
Port. Gui . . . Portuguese Guinea
porto, *Italian, Portuguese* . . . harbor
Port. Timor . . . Portuguese Timor
poss . . . possession
P.R . . . Puerto Rico
prado, *Spanish* . . . field, meadow
pref . . . prefecture
presqu'île, *French* . . . peninsula
prin . . . principality
proliv, *Russian* . . . strait
prom . . . promontory
prop . . . proposed
prot . . . protectorate
prov . . . province, provincial
pt . . . point
pta., *Spanish* . . . punta (point)
pu, *Chinese* . . . stream
puerto, *Spanish* . . . port, harbor
punkt, *German* . . . point
punt, *Dutch* . . . point
punta, *Italian, Spanish* . . . point
puy, *French* . . . peak

Q

qal'at, *Arabic* . . . fort
qārat, *Arabic* . . . hill, peak
Qld . . . Queensland
Que . . . Quebec
qur, *Arabic* . . . mountains

R

r . . . river
ra . . . range
rada, *Spanish* . . . anchorage
rann, *Hindi* . . . marshland
ra's, *Arabic* . . . cape
rd . . . road
reg . . . region, regions
reka, *Russian* . . . river
rep . . . republic
represa, *Portuguese* . . . reservoir
res . . . reservoir
rettō, *Japanese* . . . archipelago
Rh . . . Rhodesia
R.I . . . Rhode Island
ría, *Spanish* . . . river mouth
ribeira, *Portuguese* . . . river, stream
rio, *Italian, Portuguese* . . . river, stream
río, *Spanish* . . . river
riv . . . river
rivière, *French* . . . river, stream
Robt . . . Robert
roca, *Spanish* . . . rock in water
Rom . . . Romania
R.R . . . railroad
R.S.F.S.R . . . Russian Soviet Federated Socialist Republic
rūd, *Persian* . . . stream
Rum . . . Rumania
Russ . . . Russia, Russian

S

S., *Spanish* . . . San (Saint)
S . . . South
S.A . . . South America
sa., *Spanish* . . . sierra
saari, *Finnish* . . . island
sabkhat, *Arabic* . . . salt marsh
sable, *French* . . . sand
S. Afr . . . South Africa
sagar, *Hindi* . . . lake
saki, *Japanese* . . . cape, point
Sal . . . El Salvador
salina, *Spanish* . . . salt flat
salto, *Spanish* . . . waterfall
Sam . . . Samoa
sammyaku, *Japanese* . . . mountain range
san, *Japanese* . . . mountain
sanct . . . sanctuary
Sask . . . Saskatchewan
satul, *Romanian* . . . village
Sau. Ar . . . Saudi Arabia
S.C . . . South Carolina
Scot . . . Scotland
S.D . . . South Dakota
sd . . . sound
S. Dak . . . South Dakota
see(n), *German* . . . lake(s)
selva, *Portuguese* . . . forest
sem . . . seminary
Sen . . . Senegal
Sep. (Sept) . . . September
serra, *Italian, Portuguese* . . . hill, mountain ridge
serranía, *Spanish* . . . mountain range
seto, *Japanese* . . . strait, channel
sever, *Russian* . . . north
sha'ib, *Arabic* . . . wadi
shan, *Chinese* . . . range, mountain, hill
shan-tzu, *Chinese* . . . island
shat (chott), *Arabic* . . . salt river or lake
shima, *Japanese* . . . island
shotō, *Japanese* . . . archipelago
shui, *Chinese* . . . stream
shūr, *Persian* . . . stream
si, *Chinese* . . . west, western
sierra, *Spanish* . . . mountain range
sjö, *Norwegian, Swedish* . . . lake
S.L . . . Sierra Leone
sø, *Danish* . . . lake
söder, *Swedish* . . . south
Sol. Is . . . Solomon Islands
Som . . . Somalia
Sopka, *Russian* . . . volcano
source, *French* . . . spring
Sov. Un . . . Soviet Union
Sp . . . Spain
spitze(n), *German* . . . peak(s)
spr. (sprs) . . . spring, springs
sq . . . square
St. (Ste) . . . Saint, Sainte
Sta., *Spanish* . . . Santa (Saint)
sta . . . station
std . . . standard
step', *Russian* . . . treeless plain, steppe
str . . . strait
Straat, *Dutch* . . . strait
strand, *Danish, Dutch, German, Norwegian, Swedish* . . . shore, beach
stretto, *Italian* . . . strait
strom, *German* . . . current, stream
strøm, *Danish, Swedish* . . . channel, lagoon
stroom, *Dutch* . . . current
su (suyu), *Turkish* . . . water, river
Sud . . . Sudan
sud, *French, Spanish* . . . south
süd, *German* . . . south
sul, *Portuguese* . . . south
sund, *Norwegian, Swedish* . . . sound
sungei, *Malay* . . . river, stream, canal
sur, *Spanish* . . . south
Sur . . . Surinam
S.W. Afr . . . South West Africa
Swaz . . . Swaziland
Swe. (Swed) . . . Sweden, Swedish
Switz . . . Switzerland
syd, *Danish, Norwegian* . . . south
Syr . . . Syria

T

tafelland, *German* . . . plateau
Tan . . . Tanzania
tanjong, *Malay* . . . cape, point
tao (tau), *Chinese* . . . island
tell, *Turkish* . . . hill
tem . . . temple
Tenn . . . Tennessee
ter. (terr) . . . territory
Tex . . . Texas
Thai . . . Thailand
thal, *German* . . . valley
tien, *Chinese* . . . lake
tpk . . . turnpike
Trin . . . Trinidad and Tobago
trust . . . trusteeship
tsu, *Japanese* . . . inlet
Tun . . . Tunisia
tung, *Chinese* . . . east, eastern
Tur . . . Turkey

U

U.A.E . . . United Arab Emirates
udd (udde), *Swedish* . . . cape
ufer, *German* . . . river bank
Ug . . . Uganda
U.K . . . United Kingdom
umi, *Japanese* . . . sea, inlet
U.N . . . United Nations
univ. (u) . . . university
Ur . . . Uruguay
ura, *Japanese* . . . bay, shore
U.S . . . United States
U.S.A . . . United States of America
U.S.N . . . United States Navy
U.S.S.R . . . Union of Soviet Socialist Republics
ust'ye, *Russian* . . . river mouth

V

Va . . . Virginia
V.A . . . Veterans Administration
val . . . valley
vale, *Portuguese* . . . valley
vall(en), *Swedish* . . . mountain
valle, *Spanish* . . . valley
vallée, *French* . . . valley
vann, *Norwegian* . . . lake
väst, *Swedish* . . . west
vatten, *Swedish* . . . lake
veld, *Dutch* . . . open plain, field
Ven . . . Venezuela
vest, *Danish, Norwegian* . . . west
Vic . . . Victoria
vidda, *Norwegian* . . . plateau, upland
Viet . . . Vietnam
vik, *Swedish* . . . bay
Vir. Is . . . Virgin Islands
vol . . . volcano
volcán, *Spanish* . . . volcano, mountain
vostok, *Russian* . . . east
Vt . . . Vermont

W

W . . . West
wadi, *Arabic* . . . dry watercourse
wald, *German* . . . forest, woodland
wan, *Chinese, Japanese* . . . bay, gulf
Wash . . . Washington
westersch, *Dutch* . . . western
W.I . . . West Indies
wiek, *German* . . . bay
Win. Is . . . Windward Islands
Wis . . . Wisconsin
Wm . . . William
W. Sam . . . Western Samoa
wüste, *German* . . . desert
W. Va . . . West Virginia
W.W. II . . . World War II
Wyo . . . Wyoming

Y

yama, *Japanese* . . . mountain
yang, *Chinese* . . . channel
Y.M.C.A . . . Young Men's Christian Association
yug, *Russian* . . . south
Yugo . . . Yugoslavia

Z

zaki (saki), *Japanese* . . . cape
zaliv, *Russian* . . . bay, gulf
zapad, *Russian* . . . west
zee, *Dutch* . . . sea
zemlya, *Russian* . . . land
zuiden, *Dutch* . . . south

USE THE MAPS AND OTHER MATERIAL IN THIS SECTION TO FIND OUT ABOUT:

THE POLITICAL WORLD

the locations of countries,
political facts and figures

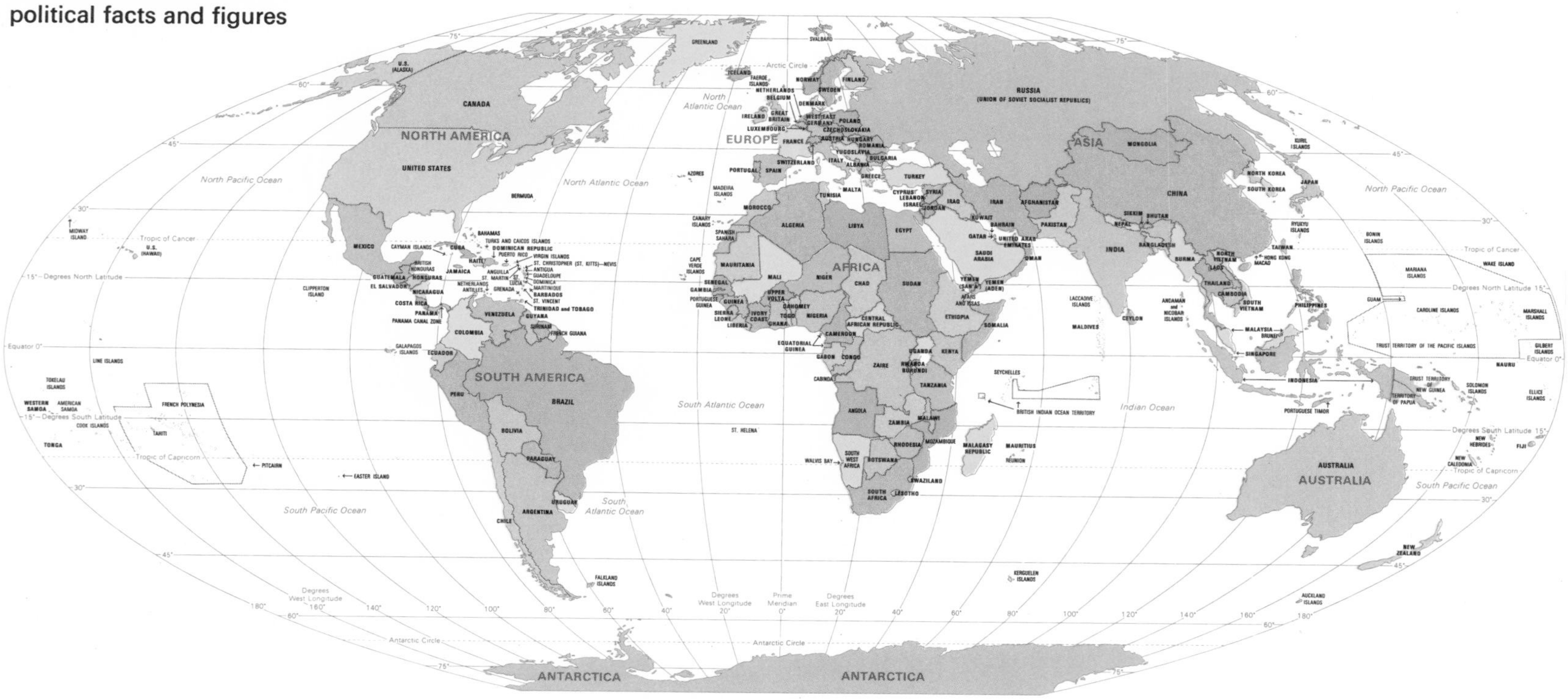

THE PEOPLE OF THE WORLD

where the people live, how fast the population of the world is growing, how the people earn their living, how much of the world's goods they have, and how well they live

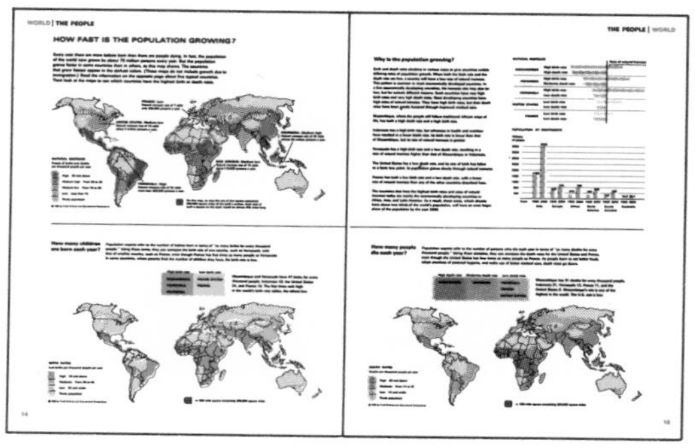

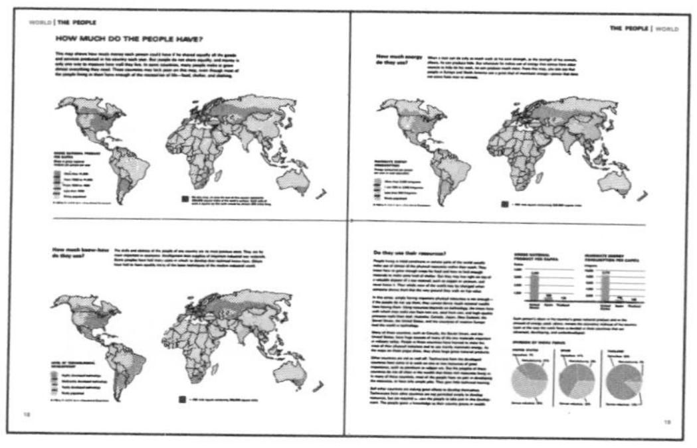

THE EARTH WE LIVE ON

what the earth looks like from space, what the land looks like at ground level, and what the weather is like

WORLD

The maps in this section tell a story—the exciting story of the world and the people who live on it. These maps differ from most maps you might look at. Instead of showing where places are, these maps answer important questions. The answers to the questions illustrate the startling contrasts in our world. They show the great contrasts between rich countries and poor ones, between countries where most of the people have a lot of everything and the countries where most of the people have little of anything. Some scholars speak of these as two worlds, the world of developed countries and the world of developing countries.

You can use these maps in a number of ways. For example, you can simply study a single map to learn how it answers a question about the world. Or you can compare specific countries to learn how they differ and look for the reasons for the differences by studying other maps in this section.

Another important way to use these maps is to study a single country as it appears throughout this section. Take Mexico as an example. You can start by looking up the political information on Mexico on page 8 in the table. Then see how Mexico appears on the map on page 14 that shows where most of its people live. Compare this information with what you can find on such maps as the one showing where farmers grow crops and raise animals, on pages 18 and 19, or the one on pages 32 and 33 showing where the mountains, hills, and plains are.

If you are not sure of the name of a country indicated on one of the maps, or if you have trouble locating a country mentioned in a caption, look for it on the political map on pages 4 and 5.

All these maps are drawn so that you can compare the relative sizes of the countries. To help you judge these sizes, each map has an *area scale* that shows how big an area a little smaller than France appears on the map at the scale used. It looks like this:

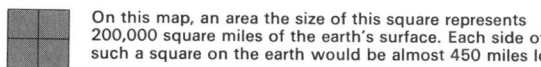

On this map, an area the size of this square represents 200,000 square miles of the earth's surface. Each side of such a square on the earth would be almost 450 miles long.

On maps that deal with people, huge areas appear in light gray as "thinly populated." No information is given about these areas because fewer than one out of every hundred people in the world live in them.

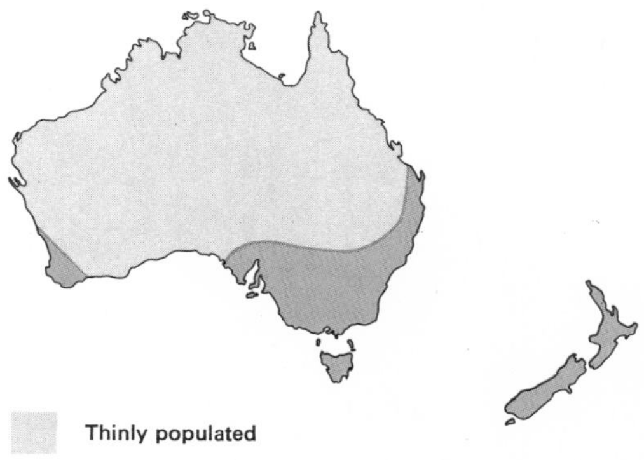

Data and estimates for maps dealing with population from Philip M. Hauser, Director of the Population Research Center at the University of Chicago

WORLD MAPS AND TABLES

4-11	**THE POLITICAL WORLD**
4, 5	THE COUNTRIES OF THE WORLD
6-11	POLITICAL FACTS AND FIGURES
12, 13	**WORLD TIME ZONES**
14-27	**THE PEOPLE**
14, 15	WHERE DO THE PEOPLE LIVE NOW?
16, 17	HOW FAST IS THE POPULATION GROWING?
18, 19	HOW DO THE PEOPLE MAKE THEIR LIVING?
20, 21	HOW MUCH DO THE PEOPLE HAVE?
22-27	HOW WELL DO THE PEOPLE LIVE?
28-37	**THE EARTH**
28-31	WHAT DOES THE EARTH LOOK LIKE FROM SPACE?
32-33	WHAT DOES THE LAND LOOK LIKE?
34-37	WHAT IS THE WEATHER LIKE?

THE COUNTRIES OF THE WORLD

On this map, an area the size of this square represents 200,000 square miles of the earth's surface. Each side of such a square on the earth would be almost 450 miles long.

The names of independent, self-governing countries appear in this kind of type: **BRAZIL**

The names of areas that do not govern themselves appear in this kind of type: ANGOLA

This map shows the world as most persons think of it—the world of separate countries, the world of the United Nations, the world of trade and travel in far-distant lands. You can learn a great deal about the countries of the world from this map. For example, you can easily see that the Soviet Union covers the largest land area of any country in the world, and can probably recognize that it is larger than Canada and China, the next largest countries, put together. Five other countries besides Canada, China, and the Soviet Union cover more than a million square miles apiece. They are Argentina, Australia, Brazil, India, and the United States. But you would have to enlarge this map many times before it could show the smallest countries of the world. Five of these countries are so tiny that they cannot even be named on this map. They are Andorra, Liechtenstein, Monaco, San Marino, and Vatican City. Together, they cover less than 265 square miles.

By tradition, the world has been divided into seven continents: Africa, Antarctica, Asia, Australia, Europe, North America, and South America. But these terms are misleading. For example, you can see from the map that Europe is really only the western part of the great land area that includes Asia. Geographers call this land area *Eurasia.* Africa is actually also joined to Eurasia, and North America is linked to South America. Today, most geographers tend to think in terms of groups of countries related in some other way, such as similar ways of life. For example, they group together the countries of both North and South America where Spanish or Portuguese are the main languages into a region called *Latin America.* But the division into continents is still used.

The shapes of the countries of the world are as different as their sizes. Many of these shapes result from natural barriers, such as great rivers or chains of high mountains. You can see on the map that Ceylon, Cyprus, and Iceland occupy whole islands, and that Australia takes up a

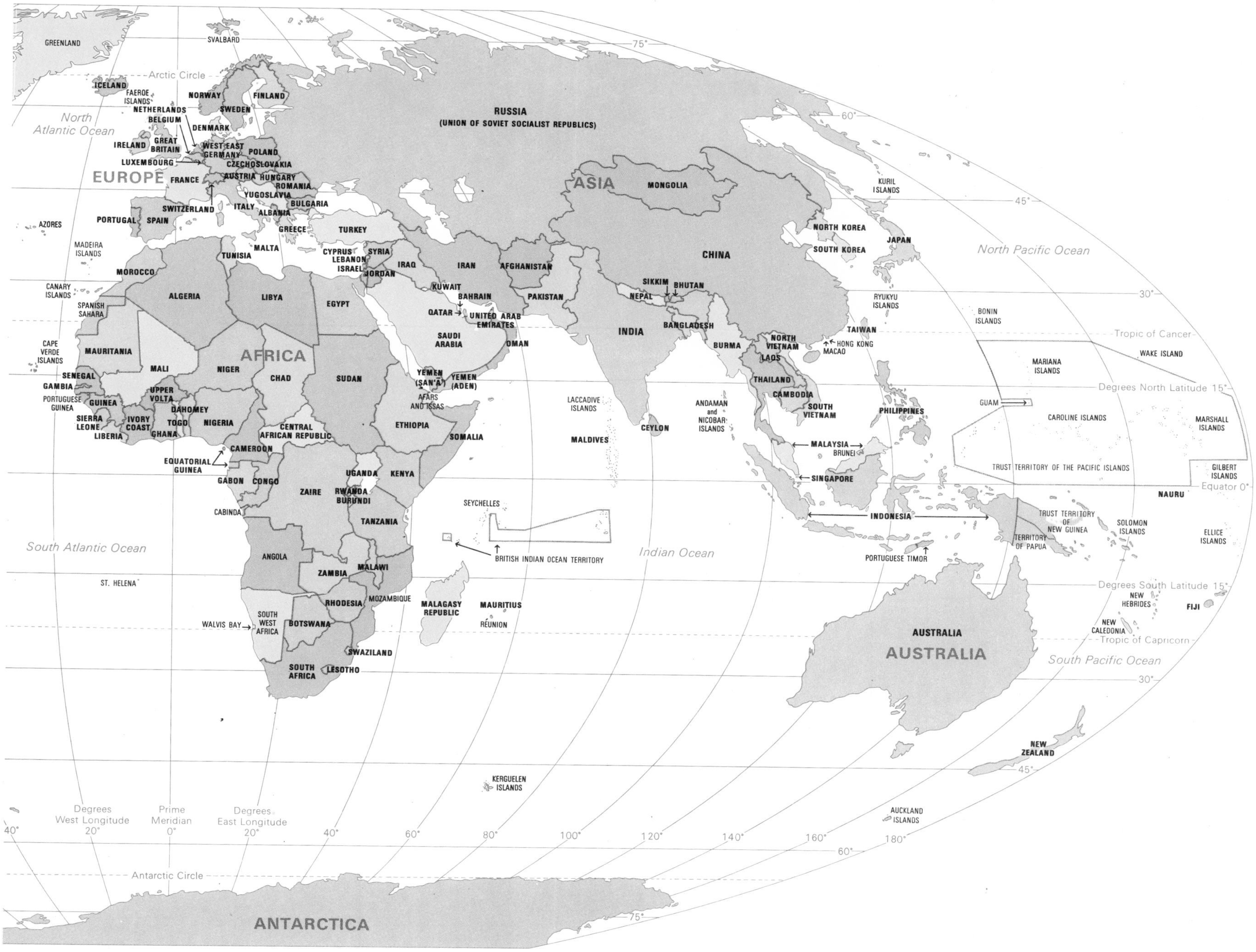

whole island continent. But most countries share land borders with several neighbors. Some of these borders have remained unchanged for hundreds of years, while others have changed many times. Consult the maps of world history on other pages in The World Book Atlas. If you compare them with this map, you can see the changing face of the political world.

This map shows the borders of the world's countries as they exist today, but it cannot show what kinds of borders they are. Some are open and friendly, with signs welcoming visitors as they pass. Others have border posts and strict regulations about who can cross from one country to another. Still others consist of mile after mile of barbed wire and minefields, and almost no one is allowed to cross. Borders vary because the governments that maintain them vary. This fact is something that a map cannot show. But you can gain much political information about the countries of the world from the tables on the next six pages.

There are many facts about the world we live in that this kind of map, called a *political map,* cannot show, but that other maps can. Though the Soviet Union is twice as large as China in area, China is three times as large as the Soviet Union in population. This is just one of the many facts about population that you should keep in mind if you want to understand the political world. It appears in map form, along with many other facts, on pages 14 and 15 of The World Book Atlas. The maps from there to page 27 provide you with much information about the peoples and the world in which they live. They answer such questions as: Why is the population growing? How well do the people live? How many can read and write? You can turn to pages 28 to 31 to see how the earth looks from space, and to the maps and pictures on pages 32 and 33 to see how the various shapes of the land, such as hills and rolling plains, look to travelers on the ground. Finally, before you turn to specific maps of the countries of the world, you can look at maps showing the world's climate on pages 34 to 37.

POLITICAL FACTS AND FIGURES

This table lists all countries and major dependencies in the world, states of the United States, provinces of Canada, and other political subdivisions. Country population figures are 1973 estimates based on the latest United Nations statistics. Figures for the states of the United States are 1970 final census figures. Populations of other political subdivisions are the latest census or other official figures.

The table also gives the Gross National Product (GNP) in U.S. dollars for all countries and subdivisions where this information is available. Most of this data comes from the latest U.S. Department of State or United Nations statistics.

Political division	Area in square miles	Population	*Population density	Gross national product (GNP)	Per capita GNP	Form of government and ruling power	Capital; largest city or town (unless the same)
Afars and Issas	8,494	101,000	12			Overseas Territory (France)	Djibouti
†Afghanistan	250,000	18,388,000	74	$ 1,500,000,000	$ 88	Constitutional Monarchy	Kabul
†Albania	11,100	2,380,000	214	1,200,000,000	571	People's Republic (communist dictatorship)	Tiranë
†Algeria	919,595	15,401,000	17	4,180,000,000	304	Republic	Algiers
American Samoa	76	31,000	408			Unincorporated Territory (U.S.)	Pago Pago
Andorra	175	17,000	97	358,000,000	71	Principality	Andorra
Angola	481,354	5,720,000	12			Overseas Province (Portugal)	Luanda
Anguilla	35	5,850	167			Colony (U.K.) (Commonwealth of Nations)	
Antigua	171	60,000	351	21,000,000,000	871	Associated State (U.K.) (Commonwealth of Nations)	St. John's
†Argentina	1,072,163	25,414,000	24			Republic	Buenos Aires
Ascension Island	34	1,266	37			Dependency of St. Helena (U.K.)	Georgetown
†Australia	2,967,909	13,320,000	4	33,300,000,000	2,664	Constitutional Monarchy (Commonwealth of Nations)	Canberra; Sydney
Australian Capital Territory	939	143,843	153			Federal Territory	Canberra
New South Wales	309,433	4,589,556	15			State	Sydney
Northern Territory	520,280	85,519	0.1			Territory	Darwin
Queensland	667,000	1,823,362	3			State	Brisbane
South Australia	380,070	1,172,774	3			State	Adelaide
Tasmania	26,383	389,874	15			State	Hobart
Victoria	87,884	3,496,161	40			State	Melbourne
Western Australia	975,920	1,027,372	1			State	Perth
†Austria	32,374	7,500,000	232	13,200,000,000	1,786	Federal Republic	Vienna
Azores	893	327,480	367			Province (Portugal)	Ponta Delgada
Bahamas	4,403	180,000	41			Colony (U.K.) (Commonwealth of Nations)	Nassau
†Bahrain	231	235,000	1,017			Protected State (U.K.)	Manama
Balearic Islands	1,936	522,044	270			Province (Spain)	Palma de Mallorca
Bangladesh	55,126	75,840,000	1,376			Republic (Commonwealth of Nations)	Dacca
†Barbados	166	265,000	1,596	160,000,000	618	Constitutional Monarchy (Commonwealth of Nations)	Bridgetown
†Belgium	11,781	9,822,000	834	24,100,000,000	2,487	Constitutional Monarchy	Brussels; Antwerp
Bermuda	21	55,000	2,619			Colony (U.K.) (Commonwealth of Nations)	Hamilton
†Bhutan	18,147	892,000	49	45,000,000	62	Monarchy (Indian protection)	Thimbu
Bismarck Archipelago	18,700	224,964	12			Part of Australian Trust Ter. of New Guinea (3 Districts)	Port Moresby; Rabaul
†Bolivia	424,165	5,326,000	13	983,000,000	201	Republic	Sucre and La Paz; La Paz
†Botswana	231,805	708,000	3	66,000,000	105	Republic (Commonwealth of Nations)	Gaborone; Kanye
†Brazil	3,286,488	101,556,000	31	33,396,000,000	350	Federal Republic	Brasília; São Paulo
British Honduras	8,867	140,000	16	64,000,000	520	Colony (U.K.) (Commonwealth of Nations)	Belmopan; Belize City
Brunei	2,226	135,000	61	82,000,000	1,075	Protected State (U.K.) (Commonwealth of Nations)	Bandar Seri Begawan
†Bulgaria	42,823	8,670,000	202	11,700,000,000	1,375	People's Republic (communist dictatorship)	Sofia
†Burma	261,790	29,445,000	112	2,080,000,000	75	Republic	Rangoon
†Burundi	10,747	3,850,000	358	230,000,000	64	Republic	Bujumbura
†Cambodia	69,898	7,310,000	105	760,000,000	111	Republic	Phnom Penh
†Cameroon	183,569	6,230,000	34	990,000,000	170	Federal Republic	Yaoundé; Douala
†Canada	3,851,809	22,516,000	6	86,634,000,000**	4,047**	Constitutional Monarchy (Commonwealth of Nations)	Ottawa; Montréal
Alberta	255,285	1,627,874	7	3,777,000,000	2,485	Province	Edmonton
British Columbia	366,255	2,184,621	6	5,300,000,000	2,647	Province	Victoria; Vancouver
Manitoba	251,000	988,247	4	2,404,000,000	2,481	Province	Winnipeg
New Brunswick	28,354	634,557	22	1,109,000,000	1,778	Province	Fredericton; Saint John
Newfoundland	156,185	522,104	3	703,000,000	1,392	Province	St. John's
Northwest Territories	1,304,903	34,807	0.03			Territory	Yellowknife
Franklin	549,253	7,167	0.01			District	......; Frobisher Bay
Keewatin	228,160	2,886	0.01			District	......; Baker Lake
Mackenzie	527,490	18,685	0.04			District	......; Yellowknife
Nova Scotia	21,425	788,960	36	1,468,000,000	1,931	Province	Halifax
Ontario	412,582	7,703,106	19	20,852,000,000	2,864	Province	Toronto
Prince Edward Island	2,184	111,641	51	172,000,000	1,568	Province	Charlottetown
Quebec	594,860	6,027,764	10	13,296,000,000	2,245	Province	Québec; Montréal
Saskatchewan	251,700	926,242	4	2,142,000,000	2,233	Province	Regina
Yukon	207,076	18,388	0.09			Territory	Whitehorse
Canary Islands	2,808	1,165,235	415			Two Provinces (Spain)	Santa Cruz and Las Palmas; Las Palmas
Canton & Enderbury Islands	27	(no permanent population)				Condominium (U.K. and U.S.) (Commonwealth of Nations)	Canton Island
Cape Verde Islands	1,557	270,000	173			Overseas Province (Portugal)	Praia; Mindelo
Caroline Islands	463	58,412	126			Part of Pacific Islands Trust Territory (U.S.)	
Cayman Islands	100	12,000	120			Colony (U.K.) (Commonwealth of Nations)	Georgetown

†Member of the United Nations.
*Persons per square mile.

**GNP figures are given for Canada. Personal income figures are given for individual provinces.

Political division	Area in square miles	Population	*Population density	Gross national product (GNP)	Per capita GNP	Form of government and ruling power	Capital; largest city or town (unless the same)
†Central African Republic	240,535	1,620,000	7	$ 200,000,000	$ 135	Republic	Bangui
†Ceylon	25,332	13,397,000	529	2,065,000,000	165	Constitutional Monarchy (Commonwealth of Nations)	Colombo
†Chad	495,755	4,000,000	8	259,000,000	70	Republic	Fort-Lamy
Channel Islands	75	110,649	1,475			Crown dependency (U.K.)	St. Peter Port
†Chile	292,258	10,501,000	36	6,340,000,000	682	Republic	Santiago
†China (excluding Taiwan)	3,691,523	801,380,000	217	121,000,000,000	116	People's Republic (communist dictatorship)	Peking; Shanghai
Christmas Island	55	3,000	55			External Territory (Australia) (Commonwealth of Nations)	
Cocos (Keeling) Islands	5	1,000	200			External Territory (Australia) (Commonwealth of Nations)	
†Colombia	439,737	23,210,000	53	6,610,000,000	313	Republic	Bogotá
Comoro Islands	838	290,000	346	20,000,000	92	Overseas Territory (France)	Moroni
†Congo	132,047	1,010,000	8	233,000,000	249	Republic	Brazzaville
Cook Islands	93	26,000	280			Associated State (New Zealand) (Commonwealth of Nations)	Avarua
Corsica	3,352	269,831	80			Department (France)	Ajaccio; Bastia
†Costa Rica	19,575	1,889,000	97	886,000,000	509	Republic	San José
Crete	3,217	483,258	150			Four Departments (Greece)	Khaniá; Iráklion
†Cuba	44,218	8,900,000	201	4,800,000,000	565	Republic (communist dictatorship)	Havana
†Cyprus	3,572	652,000	183	530,000,000	828	Republic (Commonwealth of Nations)	Nicosia
†Czechoslovakia	49,371	14,685,000	297	32,500,000,000	2,240	Socialist Republic (communist dictatorship)	Prague
†Dahomey	43,484	2,910,000	67	235,000,000	94	Republic	Porto Novo; Cotonou
†Denmark	16,629	5,025,000	302	14,600,000,000	2,920	Constitutional Monarchy	Copenhagen
Dominica	290	79,000	272			Associated State (U.K.) (Commonwealth of Nations)	Roseau
†Dominican Republic	18,816	4,809,000	256	1,351,000,000	332	Republic	Santo Domingo
†Ecuador	109,484	6,736 000	62	1,792,000,000	294	Republic	Quito; Guayaquil
†Egypt	386,662	35,892,000	93	6,580,000,000	200	Republic	Cairo
†El Salvador	8,260	3,952,000	478	988,000,000	288	Republic	San Salvador
†Equatorial Guinea	10,830	310,000	29	76,000,000	270	Republic	Santa Isabel
†Ethiopia	471,778	26,580,000	56	1,693,000,000	67	Constitutional Monarchy	Addis Ababa
Faeroe Islands	540	39,000	72			Self-Governing Territory (Denmark)	Tórshavn
Falkland Islands (excluding dependencies)	4,618	2,172	0.5			Colony (U.K.) (Commonwealth of Nations)	Stanley
†Fiji	7,055	565,000	80	199,000,000	383	Constitutional Monarchy (Commonwealth of Nations)	Suva
†Finland	130,120	4,752,000	37	9,700,000,000	2,068	Republic	Helsinki
Formosa, see Taiwan							
†France	211,208	52,003,000	246	182,100,000,000	3,585	Republic	Paris
French Guiana	35,135	58,000	2			Overseas Department (France)	Cayenne
French Polynesia	1,544	121,000	78			Overseas Territory (France)	Papeete
†Gabon	103,347	521,000	5	309,000,000	630	Republic	Libreville
Galapagos Islands	2,869	3,816	1			Province (Ecuador)	El Progreso; Puerto Baquerizo
†Gambia	4,361	380,000	87	46,000,000	125	Republic (Commonwealth of Nations)	Bathurst
Gaza**	146	356,000	2,438			Military Government	Gaza
Germany, East (including East Berlin)	41,767	17,407,000	417	39,700,000,000	2,320	People's Republic (communist dictatorship)	Berlin (East)
Germany, West (including West Berlin)	95,934	63,454,000	661	186,000,000,000	3,015	Federal Republic	Bonn; Berlin (West)
†Ghana	92,100	9,900,000	107	2,320,000,000	262	Republic (Commonwealth of Nations)	Accra
Gibraltar	2.3	32,000	11,739			Colony (U.K.) (Commonwealth of Nations)	Gibraltar
Gilbert and Ellice Islands	342	59,000	173			Colony (U.K.) (Commonwealth of Nations)	Tarawa
Great Britain, see United Kingdom							
†Greece	50,944	9,100,000	179	9,200,000,000	1,034	Constitutional Monarchy (Military government)	Athens
Greenland	840,000	53,000	0.06			Province (Denmark)	Godthåb
Grenada	133	108,000	812			Associated State (U.K.) (Commonwealth of Nations)	St. George's
Guadeloupe (including dependencies)	687	341,000	496			Overseas Department (France)	Basse-Terre; Pointe-à-Pitre
Guam	212	91,300	431			Unincorporated Territory (U.S.)	Agana; Tamuning
†Guatemala	42,042	5,570,000	132	1,728,000,000	326	Republic	Guatemala City
†Guinea	94,926	4,200,000	44	315,000,000	80	Republic	Conakry
†Guyana	83,000	836,000	10	252,000,000	330	Republic (Commonwealth of Nations)	Georgetown
†Haiti	10,714	5,165,000	482	440,000,000	90	Republic (dictatorship)	Port-au-Prince
†Honduras	43,277	2,854,000	66	675,000,000	249	Republic	Tegucigalpa

†Member of the United Nations.
*Persons per square mile.
**Occupied by Israeli troops in June, 1967.

Political division	Area in square miles	Population	*Population density	Gross national product (GNP)	Per capita GNP	Form of government and ruling power	Capital; largest city or town (unless the same)
Hong Kong	399	4,365,000	10,940	$ 3,620,000,000	$ 885	Colony (U.K.) (Commonwealth of Nations)	Victoria; Kowloon
†Hungary	35,919	10,424,000	290	15,800,000,000	1,530	People's Republic (communist dictatorship)	Budapest
†Iceland	39,769	220,000	6	482,000,000	2,351	Republic	Reykjavík
†India	1,261,817	592,694,000	470	52,700,000,000	90	Federal Republic (Commonwealth of Nations)	New Delhi; Bombay
†Indonesia	735,272	132,681,000	180	12,780,000,000	108	Republic	Djakarta
†Iran	636,296	31,229,000	49	9,910,000,000	345	Constitutional Monarchy	Teheran
†Iraq	167,925	10,376,000	62	2,830,000,000	300	Republic	Baghdad
†Ireland	27,136	3,057,000	113	3,500,000,000	1,196	Republic	Dublin
Isle of Man	227	56,248	247			Crown Dependency (U.K.) (Commonwealth of Nations)	Douglas
†Israel	▲7,992	3,154,000	395	5,273,000,000	1,758	Republic	Jerusalem; Tel Aviv-Yafo
†Italy	116,304	54,970,000	473	109,100,000,000	2,002	Republic	Rome
†Ivory Coast	124,504	4,610,000	37	1,424,000,000	338	Republic	Abidjan
†Jamaica	4,232	2,140,000	506	1,110,000,000	556	Constitutional Monarchy (Commonwealth of Nations)	Kingston
Jammu and Kashmir	86,051	4,625,811	54			In dispute (India & Pakistan)	Srinagar
†Japan	143,751	106,994,000	744	244,800,000,000	2,365	Constitutional Monarchy	Tokyo
†Jordan	37,738	2,600,000	69	575,000,000	286	Constitutional Monarchy	Amman
†Kenya	224,960	11,950,000	53	1,538,000,000	137	Republic (Commonwealth of Nations)	Nairobi
Korea, North	▲▲46,540	15,100,000	324	3,500,000,000	246	People's Republic (communist dictatorship)	Pyongyang
Korea, South	▲▲38,022	34,130,000	898	7,800,000,000	245	Republic	Seoul
†Kuwait	6,178	921,000	149	2,764,000,000	4,006	Emirate	Kuwait
†Laos	91,429	3,180,000	35	216,000,000	73	Constitutional Monarchy	Vientiane and Luang Prabang; Vientiane
†Lebanon	4,015	3,213,000	800	1,525,000,000	529	Republic	Beirut
†Lesotho	11,720	1,170,000	100	94,000,000	90	Constitutional Monarchy (Commonwealth of Nations)	Maseru
†Liberia	43,000	1,240,000	29	352,000,000	231	Republic	Monrovia
†Libya	679,362	2,161,000	3	3,140,000,000	1,670	Constitutional Monarchy	Tripoli and Bengasi; Tripoli
Liechtenstein	61	21,000	344			Principality	Vaduz
†Luxembourg	998	346,000	347	9,000,000	2,720	Constitutional Monarchy	Luxembourg
Macao	6	330,000	55,000			Overseas Province (Portugal)	Macao
Madeira Islands	308	268,937	873			Part of Funchal District (Portugal)	Funchal
†Malagasy Republic	226,658	7,210,000	32	878,000,000	120	Republic	Tananarive
†Malawi	45,747	4,950,000	108	285,000,000	64	Republic (Commonwealth of Nations)	Zomba; Blantyre
Malaya	50,700	9,900,000	195	2,623,000,000	316	Eleven States (Malaysia)	Kuala Lumpur
†Malaysia	128,430	11,740,000	91	3,913,000,000	360	Federation (Commonwealth of Nations)	Kuala Lumpur
†Maldives	115	114,000	991			Republic	Male
†Mali	478,767	5,345,000	11	510,000,000	72	Republic	Bamako
†Malta	122	318,600	2,611	229,000,000	694	Constitutional Monarchy (Commonwealth of Nations)	Valletta; Sliema
Mariana Islands (excluding Guam)	184	9,640	52			Part of Pacific Islands Trust Territory (U.S.)	
Marshall Islands	70	26,848	384			Part of Pacific Islands Trust Territory (U.S.)	
Martinique	425	350,000	824			Overseas Department (France)	Fort-de-France
†Mauritania	397,956	1,250,000	3	180,000,000	154	Republic	Nouakchott
†Mauritius	720	861,000	1,196	189,000,000	226	Constitutional Monarchy (Commonwealth of Nations)	Port Louis
†Mexico	761,604	56,179,000	74	33,176,000,000	676	Federal Republic	Mexico City
Midway Island	2	2,200	1,110			Possession (U.S.)	
Monaco	0.58	25,000	43,103	800,000,000	615	Principality	Monaco
†Mongolia	604,250	1,412,000	2			People's Republic (communist dictatorship)	Ulan Bator
Montserrat	38	16,000	421			Colony (U.K.) (Commonwealth of Nations)	Plymouth
†Morocco	172,414	16,690,000	97	3,254,000,000	205	Constitutional Monarchy	Rabat and Tangier; Casablanca
Mozambique	302,330	7,767,000	26	482,000,000	71	Overseas Province (Portugal)	Lourenço Marques
Nauru	8	9,000	1,125			Republic (Commonwealth of Nations)	
†Nepal	54,362	11,647,000	214	885,000,000	80	Constitutional Monarchy	Katmandu
†Netherlands	14,140	13,493,000	954	29,800,000,000	2,285	Constitutional Monarchy	Amsterdam
Netherlands Antilles	384	230,000	599	250,000,000	1,180	Self-Governing Territory (Netherlands)	Willemstad
New Caledonia	7,336	110,000	15			Overseas Territory (France)	Nouméa
New Guinea	92,160	1,870,000	20			Trust Territory (Australia) (Commonwealth of Nations)	Port Moresby (Papua)
New Hebrides Islands	5,700	91,000	16			Condominium (France-U.K.) (Commonwealth of Nations)	Vila
†New Zealand	103,736	2,936,000	28	6,084,000,000	2,036	Constitutional Monarchy (Commonwealth of Nations)	Wellington; Auckland
†Nicaragua	50,193	2,212,000	44	750,000,000	349	Republic	Managua
†Niger	489,191	4,350,000	9	315,000,000	82	Republic	Niamey
†Nigeria	356,669	59,309,000	166	5,800,000,000	105	Federal Republic (Commonwealth of Nations)	Lagos
Niue Island	100	5,000	50			Territory (New Zealand) (Commonwealth of Nations)	Alofi
Norfolk Island	13	1,000	77			External Territory (Australia) (Commonwealth of Nations)	Kingston
†Norway	125,182	3,973,000	32	10,100,000,000	2,595	Constitutional Monarchy	Oslo
†Oman	82,030	720,000	9	34,000,000	62	Sultanate	Muscat; Maṭraḥ
Pacific Islands Trust Territory	717	94,900	132			Trust Territory (U.S.)	Saipan (Island)
†Pakistan	310,403	64,604,000	208	17,170,000,000	130	Federal Republic	Islāmābād; Karāchi
†Panama	29,209	1,614,000	55	992,000,000	693	Republic	Panama City
Panama Canal Zone	553	56,000	101			U.S. Jurisdiction (Panama sovereignty)	Balboa Heights; Rainbow City
Papua	86,100	730,000	8			External Territory (Australia) (Commonwealth of Nations)	Port Moresby
†Paraguay	157,048	2,630,000	17	582,000,000	245	Republic	Asunción
†Peru	496,225	14,889,000	30	5,380,000,000	396	Republic	Lima
†Philippines	115,830	42,678,000	368	8,545,000,000	222	Republic	Quezon City; Manila
Pitcairn Island	2	92	46			Colony (U.K.) (Commonwealth of Nations)	Adamstown
†Poland	120,725	33,701,000	279	46,100,000,000	1,420	People's Republic (communist dictatorship)	Warsaw
†Portugal (including Azores and Madeira)	35,553	9,990,000	281	6,400,000,000	660	Corporative Republic	Lisbon
Portuguese Guinea	13,948	580,000	42	37,000,000	71	Overseas Province (Portugal)	Bissau

†Member of the United Nations.
*Persons per square mile.

▲Does not include territory occupied by Israel during the Arab-Israeli war of 1967.

▲▲Excludes 487 square miles in Demilitarized Zone between North Korea and South Korea.

Political division	Area in square miles	Population	*Population density	Gross national product (GNP)	Per capita GNP	Form of government and ruling power	Capital; largest city or town (unless the same)
Portuguese Timor	5,763	630,000	109	$ 51,000,000	$ 95	Overseas Province (Portugal)	Dili
Puerto Rico	3,435	3,000,000	873	4,607,000,000	1,648	Commonwealth (U.S.)	San Juan
†Qatar	8,500	92,000	11			Protected State (U.K.)	Doha
Réunion	969	480,000	495	115,000,000	310	Overseas Department (France)	St. Denis
Rhodesia	150,804	5,792,000	38	1,427,000,000	269	Self-governing Colony (U.K.)**(Commonwealth of Nations)	Salisbury
†Romania	91,699	20,929,000	228	24,400,000,000	1,200	Socialist Republic (communist dictatorship)	Bucharest
Russia, see Soviet Union							
†Rwanda	10,169	3,920,000	385	195,000,000	54	Republic	Kigali
Ryukyu Islands	1,464	1,150,000	786	278,000,000	305	Territory (Japan)	Naha
Sabah	29,388	730,000	25	188,000,000	331	State (Malaysia)	Kota Kinabalu
St. Christopher (St. Kitts)-Nevis	103	59,150	574			Associated State (U.K.) (Commonwealth of Nations)	Basseterre
St. Helena	162	6,273	39			Colony (U.K.) (Commonwealth of Nations)	Jamestown
St. Lucia	238	123,000	517			Associated State (U.K.) (Commonwealth of Nations)	Castries
St. Pierre and Miquelon	93	5,000	54			Overseas Territory (France)	St. Pierre
St. Vincent	150	102,000	680			Associated State (U.K.)	Kingstown
San Marino	24	20,000	833			Republic	San Marino
São Tomé and Príncipe	372	62,000	167			Overseas Province (Portugal)	São Tomé
Sarawak	48,342	1,110,000	23	247,000,000	286	State (Malaysia)	Kuching
Sardinia	9,301	1,448,011	156			Three provinces (Italy)	Cagliari
†Saudi Arabia	830,000	8,384,000	10	3,140,000,000	584	Monarchy	Riyadh
†Senegal	75,750	4,220,000	58	700,000,000	178	Republic	Dakar
Seychelles	145	55,000	379			Colony (U.K.) (Commonwealth of Nations)	Victoria
Sicily	9,926	4,809,130	484			Semiautonomous Region (Italy)	Palermo
†Sierra Leone	27,699	2,666,000	96	425,000,000	160	Republic (Commonwealth of Nations)	Freetown
Sikkim	2,744	205,000	75			Monarchy (Indian protection) (Commonwealth of Nations)	Gangtok
†Singapore	224	2,234,000	9,973	1,970,000,000	960	Republic (Commonwealth of Nations)	Singapore
Solomon Islands (Australian)	4,100	73,276	18			Part of Trust Territory of New Guinea (Australia)	Sohano
Solomon Islands (British)	11,500	176,000	15			Protectorate (U.K.) (Commonwealth of Nations)	Honiara
†Somalia	246,200	2,980,000	12	181,000,000	65	Republic	Mogadiscio
†South Africa	471,445	21,596,000	46	16,690,000,000	805	Republic	Pretoria and Cape Town; Johannesburg
South West Africa (Namibia)	318,261	670,000	2			Mandate (United Nations)	Windhoek
†Soviet Union (U.S.S.R.)	8,649,500	250,867,000	29	485,700,000,000	2,000	Federal Soviet Republic (communist dictatorship)	Moscow
in Asia	6,498,500	61,676,000	9				
in Europe	2,151,000	189,191,000	88				
Armenian S.S.R.	11,506	2,493,000	217			Soviet Socialist Republic	Yerevan
Azerbaijan S.S.R.	33,436	5,111,000	153			Soviet Socialist Republic	Baku
†Byelorussian S.S.R.	80,155	9,003,000	112			Soviet Socialist Republic	Minsk
Estonian S.S.R.	17,413	1,357,000	78			Soviet Socialist Republic	Tallinn
Georgian S.S.R.	26,911	4,688,000	174			Soviet Socialist Republic	Tiflis
Kazakh S.S.R.	1,048,306	12,850,000	12			Soviet Socialist Republic	Alma-Ata
Kirgiz S.S.R.	76,641	2,933,000	38			Soviet Socialist Republic	Frunze
Latvian S.S.R.	24,595	2,365,000	96			Soviet Socialist Republic	Riga
Lithuanian S.S.R.	25,174	3,129,000	125			Soviet Socialist Republic	Vilnius
Moldavian S.S.R.	13,012	3,572,000	274			Soviet Socialist Republic	Kishinëv
Russian S.F.S.R.	6,592,850	130,090,000	20			Soviet Federated Socialist Republic	Moscow
Tadzhik S.S.R.	55,251	2,900,000	52			Soviet Socialist Republic	Dushanbe
Turkmen S.S.R.	188,456	2,158,000	11			Soviet Socialist Republic	Ashkhabad
†Ukrainian S.S.R.	233,090	47,136,000	202			Soviet Socialist Republic	Kiev
Uzbek S.S.R.	173,592	11,963,000	69			Soviet Socialist Republic	Tashkent
†Spain (including Balearic and Canary Islands)	194,885	34,299,000	176	32,400,000,000	922	Monarchy (Dictatorship)	Madrid
Spanish Sahara	102,703	63,000	0.6			Overseas Province (Spain)	El Aiún
†Sudan	967,500	17,051,000	18	1,890,000,000	120	Federal Republic	Khartoum; Omdurman
Surinam	63,037	431,000	7	255,000,000	633	Overseas Territory (Netherlands)	Paramaribo
Svalbard (Spitsbergen)	23,958	(no permanent population)				Dependency (Norway)	Longyearbyen
†Swaziland	6,704	458,000	68	90,000,000	215	Monarchy (Commonwealth of Nations)	Mbabane
†Sweden	173,649	8,241,000	47	32,581,000,000	3,655	Constitutional Monarchy	Stockholm
Switzerland	15,941	6,490,000	407	19,600,000,000	3,111	Federal Republic	Bern (Berne); Zurich
†Syria	71,498	6,663,000	93	1,590,000,000	261	Republic	Damascus
Taiwan (Formosa)	13,885	15,160,000	1,092	5,246,000,000	359	Republic	Taipei
†Tanzania	364,900	14,328,000	39	1,265,000,000	98	Republic (Commonwealth of Nations)	Dar es Salaam
†Thailand	198,457	39,249,000	198	6,790,000,000	181	Constitutional Monarchy	Bangkok
†Togo	21,622	2,216,000	102	267,000,000	144	Republic	Lomé
Tokelau (Union) Islands	4	1,687	422			Territory (New Zealand) (Commonwealth of Nations)	.......; Fakaofo (Atoll)
Tonga	270	100,000	370			Monarchy (Commonwealth of Nations)	Nukualofa
†Trinidad & Tobago	1,980	1,140,000	576	836,000,000	800	Monarchy (Commonwealth of Nations)	Port-of-Spain
Tristan da Cunha Islands	81	269	3			Dependency of St. Helena Colony (U.K.)	Edinburgh
†Tunisia	63,379	5,646,000	89	1,198,000,000	98	Republic	Tunis
†Turkey (entire)	301,382	37,941,000	126	8,700,000,000	247	Republic	Ankara; Istanbul
Turkey (in Asia)	292,261	34,731,000	119				
Turkey (in Europe)	9,121	3,210,000	352				

†Member of the United Nations.
*Persons per square mile.

**In 1965, Rhodesia declared its independence, but the United Kingdom refused to recognize the independence of the colony.

Political division	Area in square miles	Population	*Population density	Gross national product (GNP)	Per capita GNP	Form of government and ruling power	Capital; largest city or town (unless the same)
Turks and Caicos Islands	166	6,000	36			Colony (U.K.) (Commonwealth of Nations)	Grand Turk
†Uganda	91,134	10,626,000	117	$ 1,134,000,000	$ 243	Republic (Commonwealth of Nations)	Kampala
†United Arab Emirates	32,278	180,000	6			Federation	Abū Ẓaby
†United Kingdom	94,226	56,551,000	600	102,487,000,000	1,839	Constitutional Monarchy (Commonwealth of Nations)	London
England	50,333	47,091,000	936			Kingdom	London
Northern Ireland	5,462	1,556,000	285			Kingdom	Belfast
Scotland	30,414	5,249,000	173			Kingdom	Edinburgh; Glasgow
Wales	8,017	2,783,000	347			Kingdom	Cardiff
†United States	3,615,122	210,533,000	58	974,100,000,000**	4,756**	Federal Republic	Washington; New York
Alabama	51,609	3,444,165	67	10,610,000,000	3,050	State	Montgomery; Birmingham
Alaska	586,412	302,173	0.5	1,486,000,000	4,749	State	Juneau; Anchorage
Arizona	113,909	1,772,482	16	7,157,000,000	3,871	State	Phoenix
Arkansas	53,104	1,923,295	36	5,902,000,000	3,036	State	Little Rock
California	158,693	19,953,134	126	94,573,000,000	4,677	State	Sacramento; Los Angeles
Colorado	104,247	2,207,259	21	9,263,000,000	4,057	State	Denver
Connecticut	5,009	3,032,217	605	15,503,000,000	5,023	State	Hartford
Delaware	2,057	548,104	266	2,550,000,000	4,570	State	Dover; Wilmington
District of Columbia	67	756,510	11,291	4,446,000,000	6,000	Federal District (U.S.)	Washington
Florida	58,560	6,789,443	116	27,091,000,000	3,848	State	Tallahassee; Jacksonville
Georgia	58,876	4,589,575	78	16,545,000,000	3,547	State	Atlanta
Hawaii	6,450	769,913	119	3,732,000,000	4,797	State	Honolulu
Idaho	83,557	713,008	9	2,490,000,000	3,402	State	Boise
Illinois	56,400	11,113,976	197	53,422,000,000	4,772	State	Springfield; Chicago
Indiana	36,291	5,193,669	143	20,952,000,000	3,973	State	Indianapolis
Iowa	56,290	2,825,041	50	11,053,000,000	3,876	State	Des Moines
Kansas	82,264	2,249,071	27	9,234,000,000	4,090	State	Topeka; Wichita
Kentucky	40,395	3,219,311	80	10,792,000,000	3,288	State	Frankfort; Louisville
Louisiana	48,523	3,643,180	75	11,957,000,000	3,248	State	Baton Rouge; New Orleans
Maine	33,215	993,663	30	3,429,000,000	3,419	State	Augusta; Portland
Maryland	10,577	3,922,399	371	18,055,000,000	4,514	State	Annapolis; Baltimore
Massachusetts	8,257	5,689,170	689	26,044,000,000	4,586	State	Boston
Michigan	58,216	8,875,083	152	38,841,000,000	4,317	State	Lansing; Detroit
Minnesota	84,068	3,805,069	45	15,424,000,000	3,974	State	St. Paul; Minneapolis
Mississippi	47,716	2,216,912	46	6,157,000,000	2,766	State	Jackson
Missouri	69,686	4,677,399	67	18,413,000,000	3,877	State	Jefferson City; St. Louis
Montana	147,138	694,409	5	2,463,000,000	3,479	State	Helena; Great Falls
Nebraska	77,227	1,483,791	19	6,045,000,000	3,998	State	Lincoln; Omaha
Nevada	110,540	488,738	4	2,482,000,000	4,895	State	Carson City; Las Vegas
New Hampshire	9,304	737,681	79	2,826,000,000	3,708	State	Concord; Manchester
New Jersey	7,836	7,168,164	915	35,271,000,000	4,832	State	Trenton; Newark
New Mexico	121,666	1,016,000	8	3,495,000,000	3,394	State	Santa Fe; Albuquerque
New York	49,576	18,241,266	368	92,335,000,000	5,021	State	Albany; New York City
North Carolina	52,586	5,082,059	97	17,427,000,000	3,387	State	Raleigh; Charlotte
North Dakota	70,665	617,761	9	2,115,000,000	3,383	State	Bismarck; Fargo
Ohio	41,222	10,652,017	258	44,775,000,000	4,154	State	Columbus; Cleveland
Oklahoma	69,919	2,559,253	37	9,151,000,000	3,506	State	Oklahoma City
Oregon	96,981	2,091,385	22	8,460,000,000	3,902	State	Salem; Portland
Pennsylvania	45,333	11,793,909	260	49,025,000,000	4,127	State	Harrisburg; Philadelphia
Rhode Island	1,214	949,723	782	3,914,000,000	4,077	State	Providence
South Carolina	31,055	2,590,516	83	8,306,000,000	3,126	State	Columbia
South Dakota	77,047	666,257	9	2,309,000,000	3,446	State	Pierre; Sioux Falls
Tennessee	42,244	3,924,164	93	13,266,000,000	3,325	State	Nashville; Memphis
Texas	267,338	11,196,730	42	42,193,000,000	3,682	State	Austin; Houston
Utah	84,916	1,059,273	12	3,731,000,000	3,395	State	Salt Lake City
Vermont	9,609	444,732	46	1,654,000,000	3,610	State	Montpelier; Burlington
Virginia	40,817	4,648,494	114	18,225,000,000	3,866	State	Richmond; Norfolk
Washington	68,192	3,409,169	50	14,260,000,000	4,135	State	Olympia; Seattle
West Virginia	24,181	1,744,237	72	5,655,000,000	3,228	State	Charleston
Wisconsin	56,154	4,417,933	79	17,366,000,000	3,880	State	Madison; Milwaukee
Wyoming	97,914	332,416	3	1,276,000,000	3,753	State	Cheyenne
†Upper Volta	105,869	5,730,000	54	305,000,000	60	Republic	Ouagadougou
†Uruguay	68,536	2,991,000	44	2,036,000,000	705	Republic	Montevideo
Vatican City	0.17	1,000	5,882			Ecclesiastical State	Vatican City
†Venezuela	352,145	11,595,000	33	10,120,000,000	974	Republic	Caracas
Vietnam, North	61,294	22,643,000	369	1,700,000,000	85	People's Republic (communist dictatorship)	Hanoi
Vietnam, South	67,108	19,799,000	295	3,200,000,000	175	Republic	Saigon
Virgin Islands, British	59	12,000	203			Colony (U.K.) (Commonwealth of Nations)	Road Town
Virgin Islands, U.S.	133	95,000	714			Unincorporated Territory (U.S.)	Charlotte Amalie
Wake Island	3	1,647	549			Possession (U.S.)	
Wallis & Futuna Islands	106	9,600	91			Overseas Territory (France)	Mata-Utu
Western Samoa	1,097	154,000	140			Republic (Commonwealth of Nations)	Apia
Yemen (Aden)	111,075	1,390,000	13	140,000,000	110	People's Republic	Aden; Madīnat ash Sha'b
†Yemen (Ṣan'ā')	75,290	6,210,000	82	460,000,000	80	Republic	Ṣan'ā'
†Yugoslavia	98,766	21,225,000	215	18,500,000,000	902	Socialist Federal Republic (communist dictatorship)	Belgrade
†Zaire	905,568	18,600,000	21	1,800,000,000	101	Republic	Kinshasa
†Zambia	290,586	4,700,000	16	1,682,000,000	405	Republic (Commonwealth of Nations)	Lusaka

†Member of the United Nations.
*Persons per square mile.

**GNP figures are given for the United States. Personal income figures are given for the individual states.

25 LARGEST COUNTRIES OF THE WORLD

IN POPULATION

	Country	Population (1973 estimate)
1.	China (excluding Taiwan)	801,380,000
2.	India	592,694,000
3.	Soviet Union	250,867,000
4.	United States	210,533,000
5.	Indonesia	132,681,000
6.	Japan	106,994,000
7.	Brazil	101,556,000
8.	Bangladesh	75,840,000
9.	Pakistan	64,604,000
10.	Germany, West (incl. West Berlin)	63,454,000
11.	Nigeria	59,309,000
12.	United Kingdom	56,551,000
13.	Mexico	56,179,000
14.	Italy	54,970,000
15.	France	52,003,000
16.	Philippines	42,678,000
17.	Thailand	39,249,000
18.	Turkey	37,941,000
19.	Egypt	35,892,000
20.	Spain	34,299,000
21.	Korea, South	34,130,000
22.	Poland	33,701,000
23.	Iran	31,229,000
24.	Burma	29,445,000
25.	Ethiopia	26,580,000

IN AREA

	Country	Area in square miles
1.	Soviet Union	8,649,500
2.	Canada	3,851,809
3.	China (excluding Taiwan)	3,691,523
4.	United States	3,615,122
5.	Brazil	3,286,488
6.	Australia	2,967,909
7.	India	1,261,817
8.	Argentina	1,072,163
9.	Sudan	967,500
10.	Algeria	919,595
11.	Zaire	905,568
12.	Greenland (Denmark)▲	840,000
13.	Saudi Arabia	830,000
14.	Mexico	761,604
15.	Indonesia	735,272
16.	Libya	679,362
17.	Iran	636,296
18.	Mongolia	604,250
19.	Peru	496,225
20.	Chad	495,755
21.	Niger	489,191
22.	Angola (Portugal)▲	481,354
23.	Mali	478,767
24.	Ethiopia	471,778
25.	South Africa	471,445

▲Greenland, a province of Denmark, and Angola, a province of Portugal, are not independent countries. But they are listed because of their large areas.

THE CONTINENTS

Continent	Area in square miles	Population (1973 estimate)	Population density	Largest city	Highest elevation in feet	Lowest elevation in feet	Highest recorded temperature	Lowest recorded temperature
Asia	16,957,000	2,241,000,000	132	Tokyo	Mt. Everest, China-Nepal, 29,028	Dead Sea, Israel-Jordan, 1,299 below sea level	Tirat Zvi, Israel, 129.2°F.	Oymyakon, Soviet Union, —89.9°F.
Africa	11,707,000	373,000,000	32	Cairo	Mt. Kilimanjaro, Tanzania, 19,340	Qattara Depression, Egypt, 436 below sea level	Al 'Azīzīyah, Libya, 136°F.	Ifrane, Morocco, —11.2°F.
North America	9,416,000	334,000,000	35	New York	Mt. McKinley, Alaska, 20,320	Death Valley, California, 282 below sea level	Death Valley, California, 134°F.	Snag, Yukon, Canada, —81°F.
South America	6,884,000	206,000,000	30	São Paulo	Mt. Aconcagua, Argentina, 22,834	Península Valdés, Argentina, 131 below sea level	Rivadavia, Argentina, 120°F.	Sarmiento, Argentina, —27.4°F.
Antarctica	5,100,000	Uninhabited	. . .	. . . .	Vinson Massif, 16,864	Sea level	Antarctic Peninsula, 58.3°F.	Vostok, —126.9°F.
Europe	4,064,000	666,000,000	164	London	Mt. Elbrus, Soviet Union, 18,481	Caspian Sea, Soviet Union-Iran, 92 below sea level	Seville, Spain, 122°F.	Ust'-Shchugor, Soviet Union, —67°F.
Australia	2,968,000	13,000,000	4	Sydney	Mt. Kosciusko, 7,316	Lake Eyre, 39 below sea level	Cloncurry, 127.5°F.	Charlotte Pass, —8°F.

4,000 YEARS OF WORLD POPULATION GROWTH

(Figures in millions of persons)

Year	World total	Africa	Asia	Oceania	Australia	Europe	North America	South America
2000 B.C.	108	(Regional breakdown unknown)						
1000 B.C.	120							
A.D. 1	138							
1000	275	50	170			42	13	
1100	306	55	186			48	17	
1200	348	61	203			61	23	
1300	384	67	216			73	28	
1400	373	74	224			45	30	
1500	446	82	254			69	41	
1600	486	90	292			89	15	
1700	637	97	405	2		120	1*	12**
1750	728	95	479	2		140	1*	11**
1800	906	90	602	2		187	6*	19**
1850	1,171	95	749	2		266	26*	33**
1900	1,608	120	937	2	4	401	81*	63**
1920	1,862	143	1,044	4	5	461	145**	60*
1940	2,296	191	1,278	5	7	541	185**	89*
1960	2,998	273	1,706	6	10	593	265**	145*
1980	4,457	456	2,645	9	15	696	386**	250*
2000	6,494	815	3,861	14	21	800	562**	421*

*Excludes Mexico and Central America
**Includes Mexico and Central America

TIME ZONES

This map shows that the world is divided into 24 standard time zones. The time in each zone differs by one hour from the zones on either side. A person traveling eastward, from one zone to the next, moves his watch ahead one hour. He moves his watch back one hour when going west. For example, a traveler, going east from Chicago to New York City, moves his watch ahead one hour (from 8 o'clock to 9 o'clock) as he crosses the time zone line between the two cities. When he crosses the line going west from New York City to Chicago, he moves his watch back one hour (from 8 o'clock to 7 o'clock).

All time zones of the world are not the same shape and size, because governments often change them to match political boundaries. For example, in the United States, time zone lines are often changed to keep all of a state in one time zone.

Not all places in the world use one of the 24 standard time zones. For example, Teheran, Iran, uses a standard time zone plus 30 minutes. Saudi Arabia uses sun time.

If a traveler crosses the International Date Line going west, he adds one day. And, if he crosses the line going east, he subtracts one day. For example, Anadyr', Russia, and Nome, Alaska, are both in the same time zone. But the towns are on opposite sides of the International Date Line. Therefore, when it is 11 P.M. Monday in Anadyr', it is 11 P.M. Sunday in Nome.

Using the table, you can easily compare the standard time in one place in the world with that in another. For example, if it is 10 A.M. Monday in Washington, D.C., you can find what time it is in Sydney, Australia, by moving to the right until you come to the column corresponding to Sydney's time zone. It is 1 A.M. Tuesday in Sydney.

The numbers along the top and bottom of the map indicate how many hours each time zone is away from Greenwich Mean Time (GMT).

The table below the map has 24 columns that correspond to the 24 standard time zones. The table is further divided into four colors: dark blue for Sunday P.M., light gray for Monday A.M., dark gray for Monday P.M., and light blue for Tuesday A.M.

- Sunday afternoon (P.M.)
- Monday morning (A.M.)
- Monday evening (P.M.)
- Tuesday morning (A.M.)

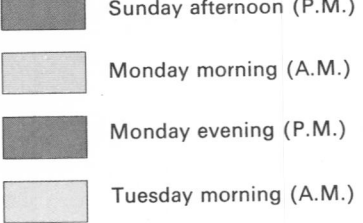

1:00	2:00	3:00	4:00	5:00	6:00	7:00	8:00	9:00	10:00
2:00	3:00	4:00	5:00	6:00	7:00	8:00	9:00	10:00	11:00
3:00	4:00	5:00	6:00	7:00	8:00	9:00	10:00	11:00	MIDNIGHT
4:00	5:00	6:00	7:00	8:00	9:00	10:00	11:00	MIDNIGHT	1:00
5:00	6:00	7:00	8:00	9:00	10:00	11:00	MIDNIGHT	1:00	2:00
6:00	7:00	8:00	9:00	10:00	11:00	MIDNIGHT	1:00	2:00	3:00
7:00	8:00	9:00	10:00	11:00	MIDNIGHT	1:00	2:00	3:00	4:00
8:00	9:00	10:00	11:00	MIDNIGHT	1:00	2:00	3:00	4:00	5:00
9:00	10:00	11:00	MIDNIGHT	1:00	2:00	3:00	4:00	5:00	6:00
10:00	11:00	MIDNIGHT	1:00	2:00	3:00	4:00	5:00	6:00	7:00
11:00	MIDNIGHT	1:00	2:00	3:00	4:00	5:00	6:00	7:00	8:00
MIDNIGHT	1:00	2:00	3:00	4:00	5:00	6:00	7:00	8:00	9:00
1:00	2:00	3:00	4:00	5:00	6:00	7:00	8:00	9:00	10:00
2:00	3:00	4:00	5:00	6:00	7:00	8:00	9:00	10:00	11:00
3:00	4:00	5:00	6:00	7:00	8:00	9:00	10:00	11:00	NOON
4:00	5:00	6:00	7:00	8:00	9:00	10:00	11:00	NOON	1:00
5:00	6:00	7:00	8:00	9:00	10:00	11:00	NOON	1:00	2:00
6:00	7:00	8:00	9:00	10:00	11:00	NOON	1:00	2:00	3:00
7:00	8:00	9:00	10:00	11:00	NOON	1:00	2:00	3:00	4:00
8:00	9:00	10:00	11:00	NOON	1:00	2:00	3:00	4:00	5:00
9:00	10:00	11:00	NOON	1:00	2:00	3:00	4:00	5:00	6:00
10:00	11:00	NOON	1:00	2:00	3:00	4:00	5:00	6:00	7:00
11:00	NOON	1:00	2:00	3:00	4:00	5:00	6:00	7:00	8:00
NOON	1:00	2:00	3:00	4:00	5:00	6:00	7:00	8:00	9:00

WORLD BOOK ATLAS map

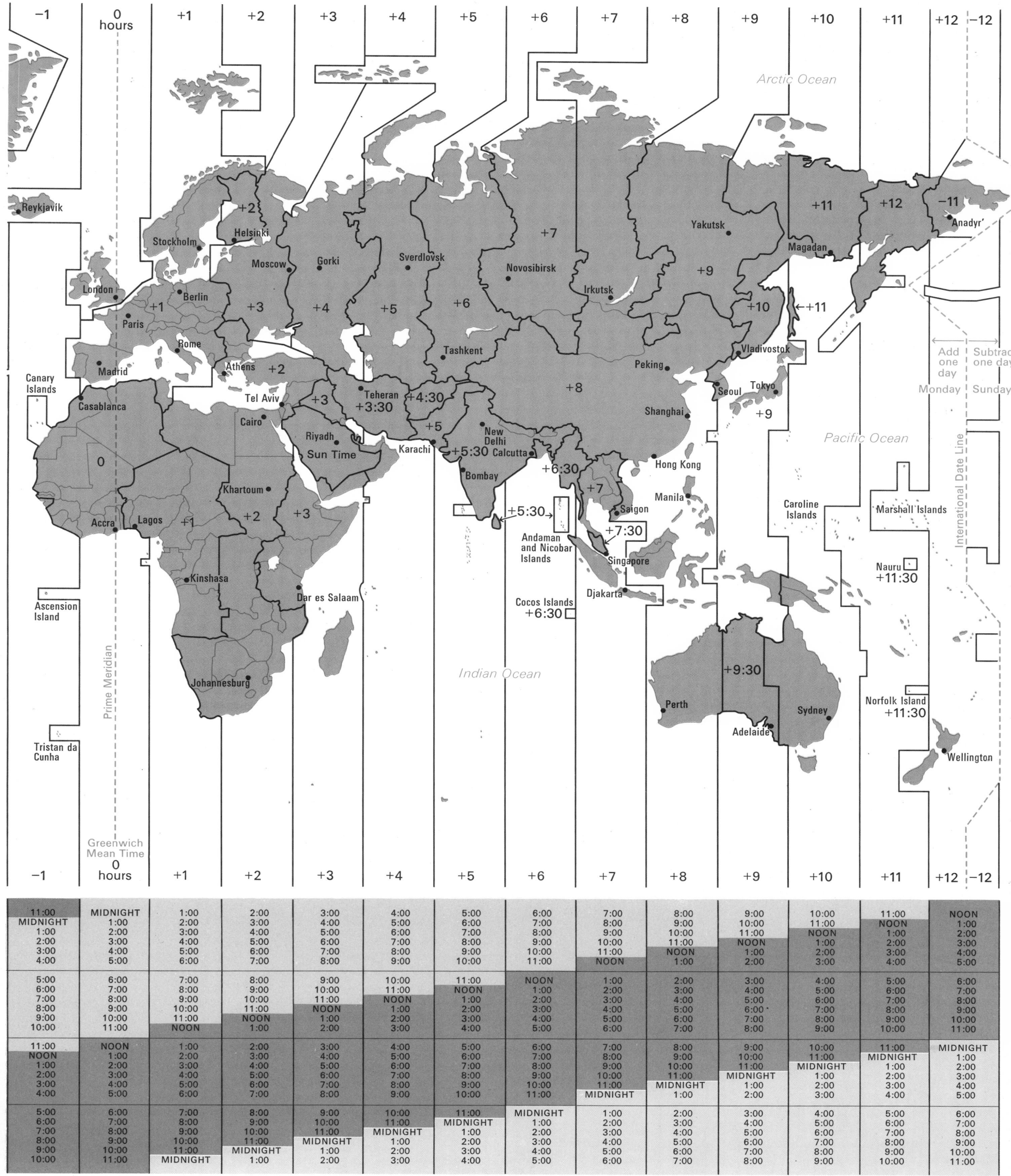

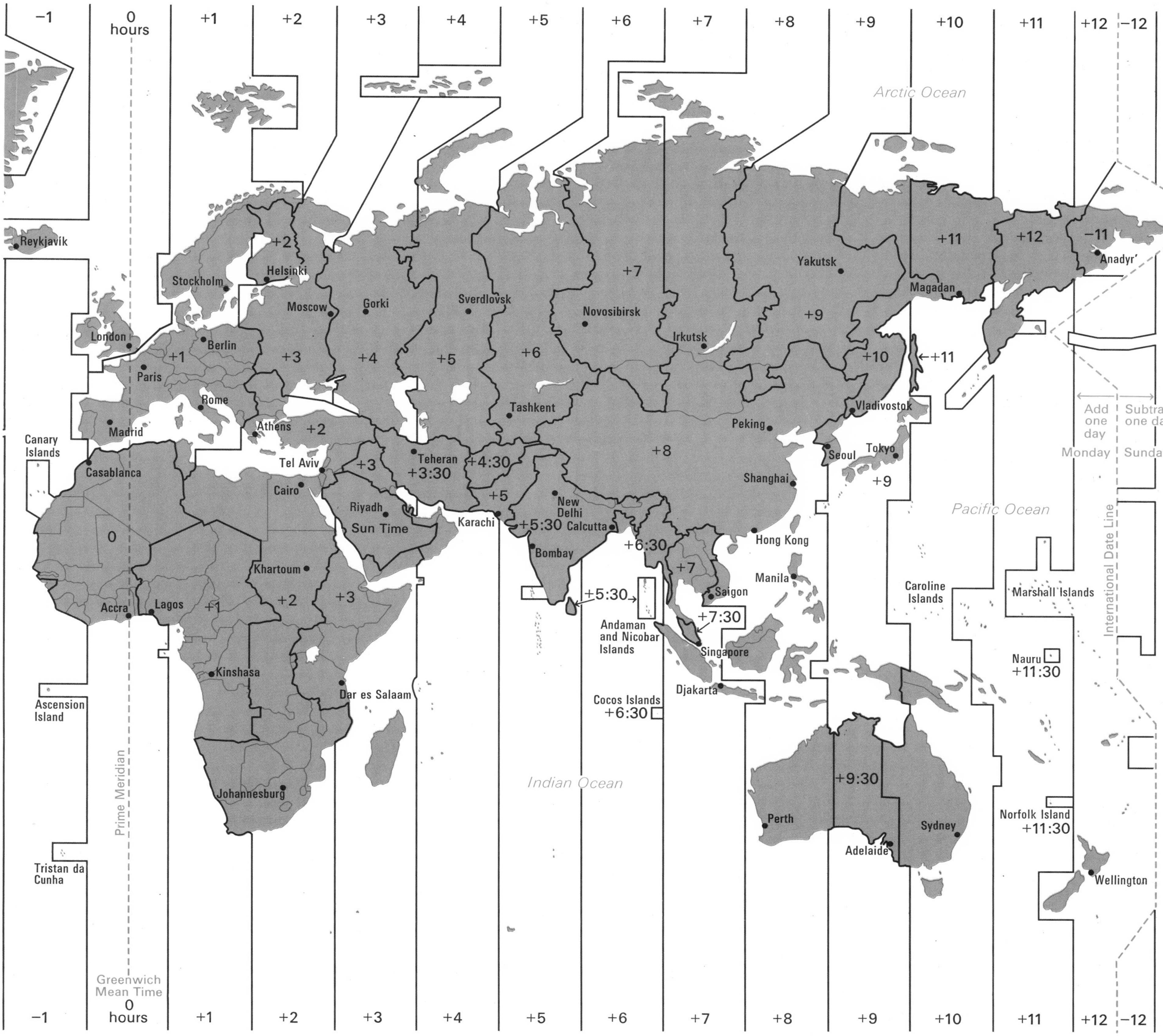

11:00	MIDNIGHT	1:00	2:00	3:00	4:00	5:00	6:00	7:00	8:00	9:00	10:00	11:00	NOON
MIDNIGHT	1:00	2:00	3:00	4:00	5:00	6:00	7:00	8:00	9:00	10:00	11:00	NOON	1:00
1:00	2:00	3:00	4:00	5:00	6:00	7:00	8:00	9:00	10:00	11:00	NOON	1:00	2:00
2:00	3:00	4:00	5:00	6:00	7:00	8:00	9:00	10:00	11:00	NOON	1:00	2:00	3:00
3:00	4:00	5:00	6:00	7:00	8:00	9:00	10:00	11:00	NOON	1:00	2:00	3:00	4:00
4:00	5:00	6:00	7:00	8:00	9:00	10:00	11:00	NOON	1:00	2:00	3:00	4:00	5:00
5:00	6:00	7:00	8:00	9:00	10:00	11:00	NOON	1:00	2:00	3:00	4:00	5:00	6:00
6:00	7:00	8:00	9:00	10:00	11:00	NOON	1:00	2:00	3:00	4:00	5:00	6:00	7:00
7:00	8:00	9:00	10:00	11:00	NOON	1:00	2:00	3:00	4:00	5:00	6:00	7:00	8:00
8:00	9:00	10:00	11:00	NOON	1:00	2:00	3:00	4:00	5:00	6:00	7:00	8:00	9:00
9:00	10:00	11:00	NOON	1:00	2:00	3:00	4:00	5:00	6:00	7:00	8:00	9:00	10:00
10:00	11:00	NOON	1:00	2:00	3:00	4:00	5:00	6:00	7:00	8:00	9:00	10:00	11:00
11:00	NOON	1:00	2:00	3:00	4:00	5:00	6:00	7:00	8:00	9:00	10:00	11:00	MIDNIGHT
NOON	1:00	2:00	3:00	4:00	5:00	6:00	7:00	8:00	9:00	10:00	11:00	MIDNIGHT	1:00
1:00	2:00	3:00	4:00	5:00	6:00	7:00	8:00	9:00	10:00	11:00	MIDNIGHT	1:00	2:00
2:00	3:00	4:00	5:00	6:00	7:00	8:00	9:00	10:00	11:00	MIDNIGHT	1:00	2:00	3:00
3:00	4:00	5:00	6:00	7:00	8:00	9:00	10:00	11:00	MIDNIGHT	1:00	2:00	3:00	4:00
4:00	5:00	6:00	7:00	8:00	9:00	10:00	11:00	MIDNIGHT	1:00	2:00	3:00	4:00	5:00
5:00	6:00	7:00	8:00	9:00	10:00	11:00	MIDNIGHT	1:00	2:00	3:00	4:00	5:00	6:00
6:00	7:00	8:00	9:00	10:00	11:00	MIDNIGHT	1:00	2:00	3:00	4:00	5:00	6:00	7:00
7:00	8:00	9:00	10:00	11:00	MIDNIGHT	1:00	2:00	3:00	4:00	5:00	6:00	7:00	8:00
8:00	9:00	10:00	11:00	MIDNIGHT	1:00	2:00	3:00	4:00	5:00	6:00	7:00	8:00	9:00
9:00	10:00	11:00	MIDNIGHT	1:00	2:00	3:00	4:00	5:00	6:00	7:00	8:00	9:00	10:00
10:00	11:00	MIDNIGHT	1:00	2:00	3:00	4:00	5:00	6:00	7:00	8:00	9:00	10:00	11:00

WHERE DO THE PEOPLE LIVE NOW?

Someone lives in almost every section of the world's land area, from Greenland to the South Pole. A few people live in the deserts of Africa or the high mountains of Asia. But most of the people live on more productive plains and lowlands, where it is easier to obtain food and to move from one place to another. As these maps show, the areas where most of the people live make up only a small part of the land. And more and more of these people are living in cities.

The dots on the large map on these pages show the numbers of people who live in various parts of the world. From this map, you can easily see that more people live in the eastern United States than in the west. Look at the numbers of people crowded into parts of Europe, India, and China. You can also see that a country with a huge land area, such as Canada, does not necessarily have a huge population.

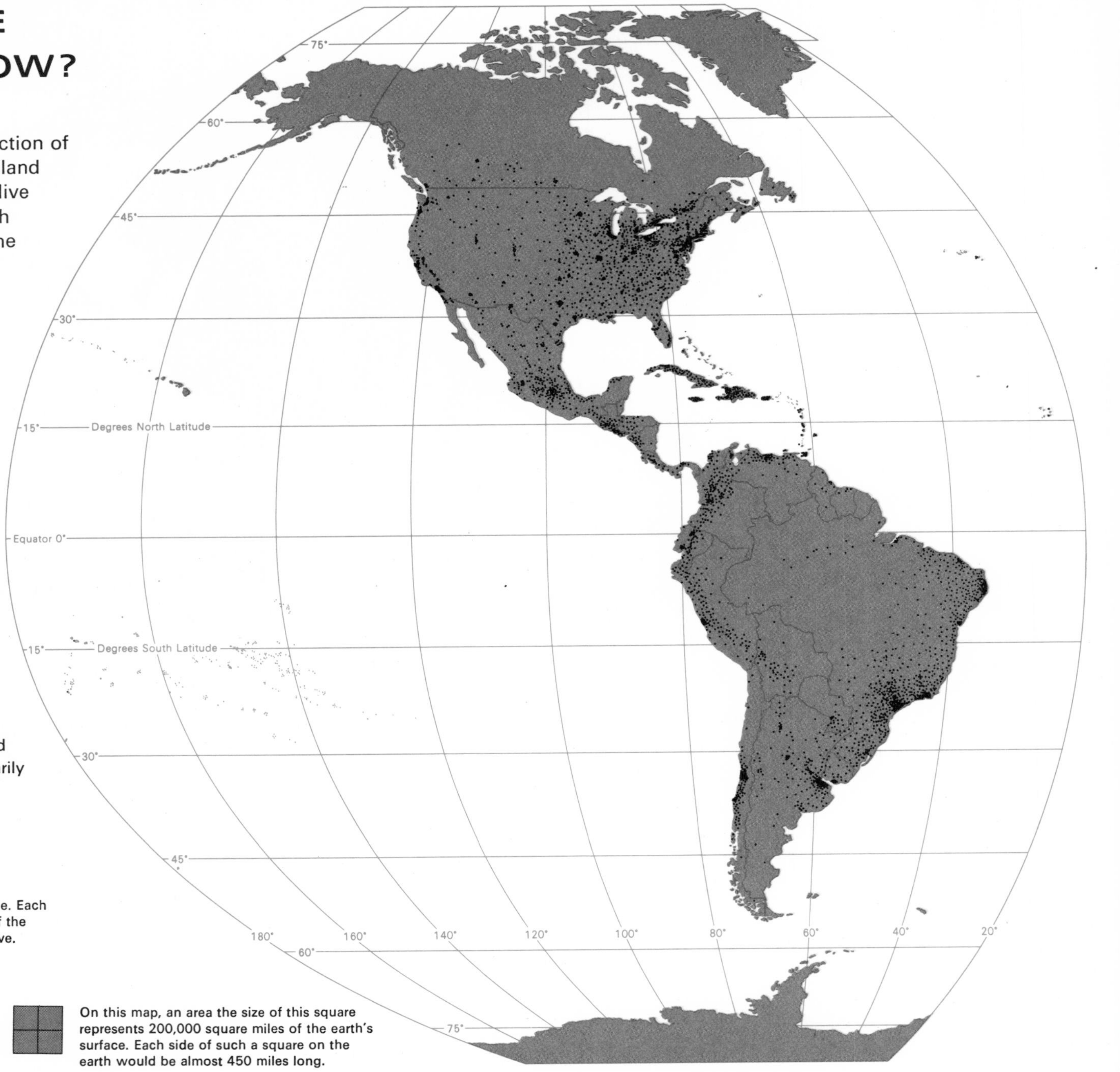

DISTRIBUTION OF POPULATION

On this map, each dot stands for 100,000 people. Each dot appears as close as possible to the center of the area in which the people it stands for actually live.

On this map, an area the size of this square represents 200,000 square miles of the earth's surface. Each side of such a square on the earth would be almost 450 miles long.

What areas have the most people?

To answer this question, look at the map. Most of the world's people—75 out of every 100 of them—live in the areas shown in dark red on this map. But these areas, taken together, amount to only a tenth of the land area of the world. By contrast, the tan areas are relatively empty. Only one person out of a hundred lives in them. Yet these areas amount to half the land area of the world.

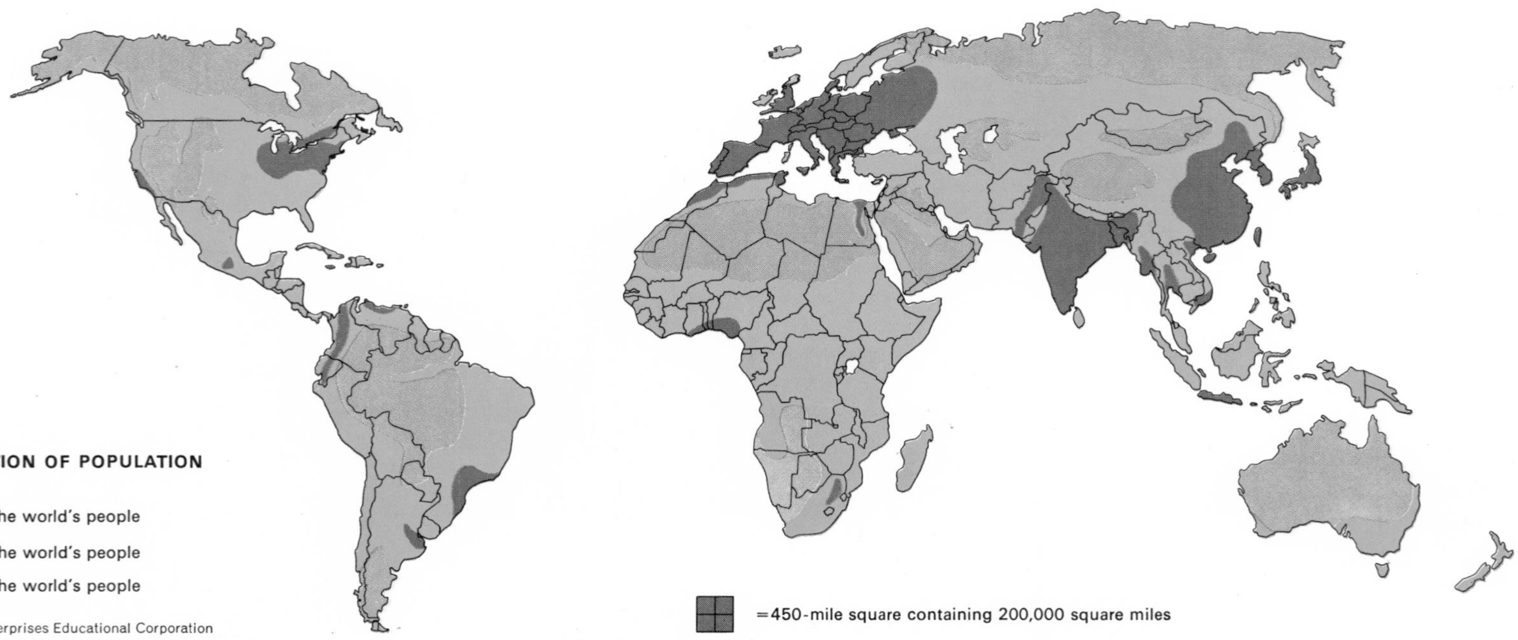

CONCENTRATION OF POPULATION

75% of the world's people

24% of the world's people

1% of the world's people

=450-mile square containing 200,000 square miles

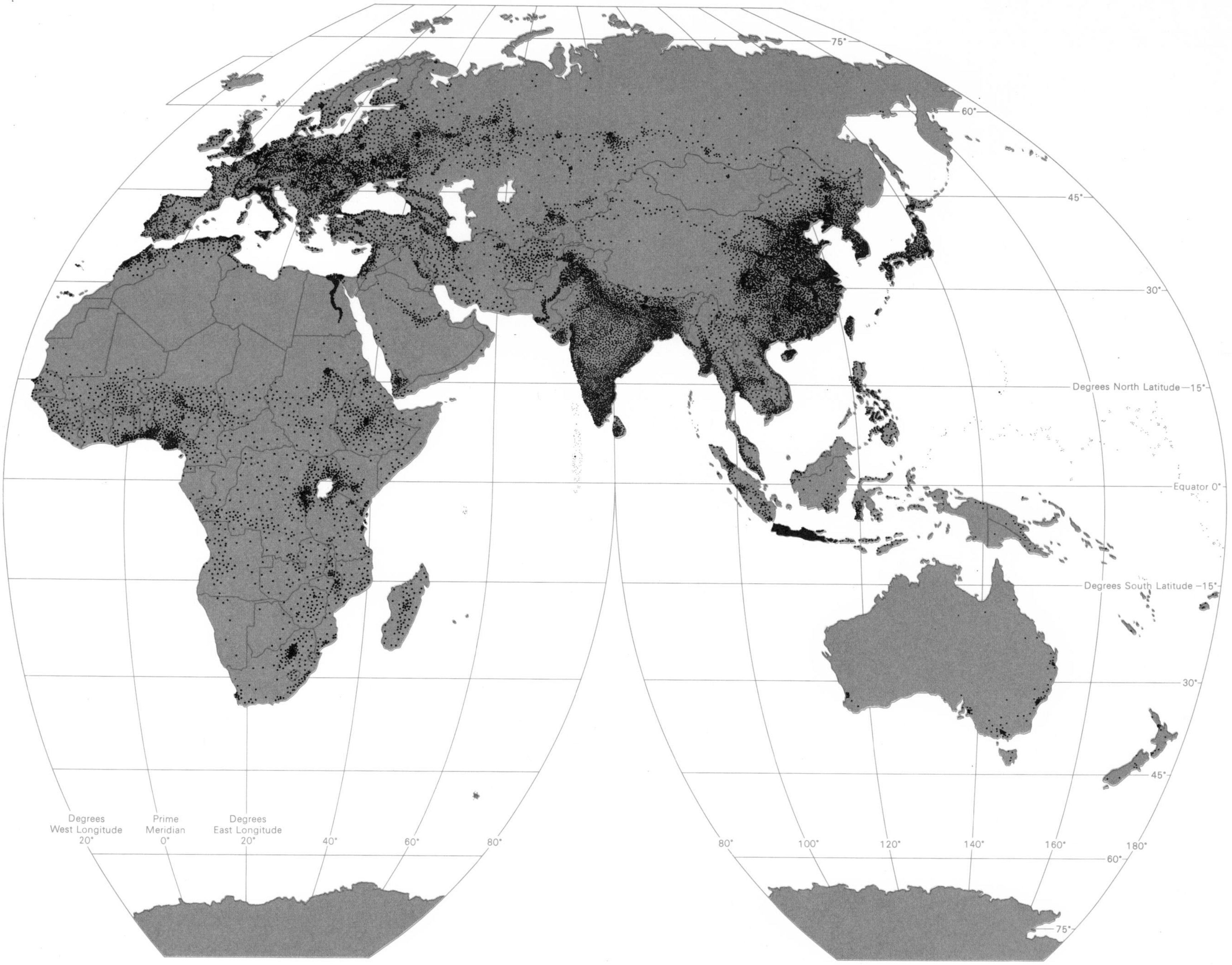

What countries have the most city dwellers?

To answer this question, look at the map for the countries shown in dark red. The black squares and circles indicate where the largest cities are. The squares show larger cities than the circles. In a small but growing number of countries of the world, such as Argentina and the United States, more than seven out of every ten people live in urban areas.

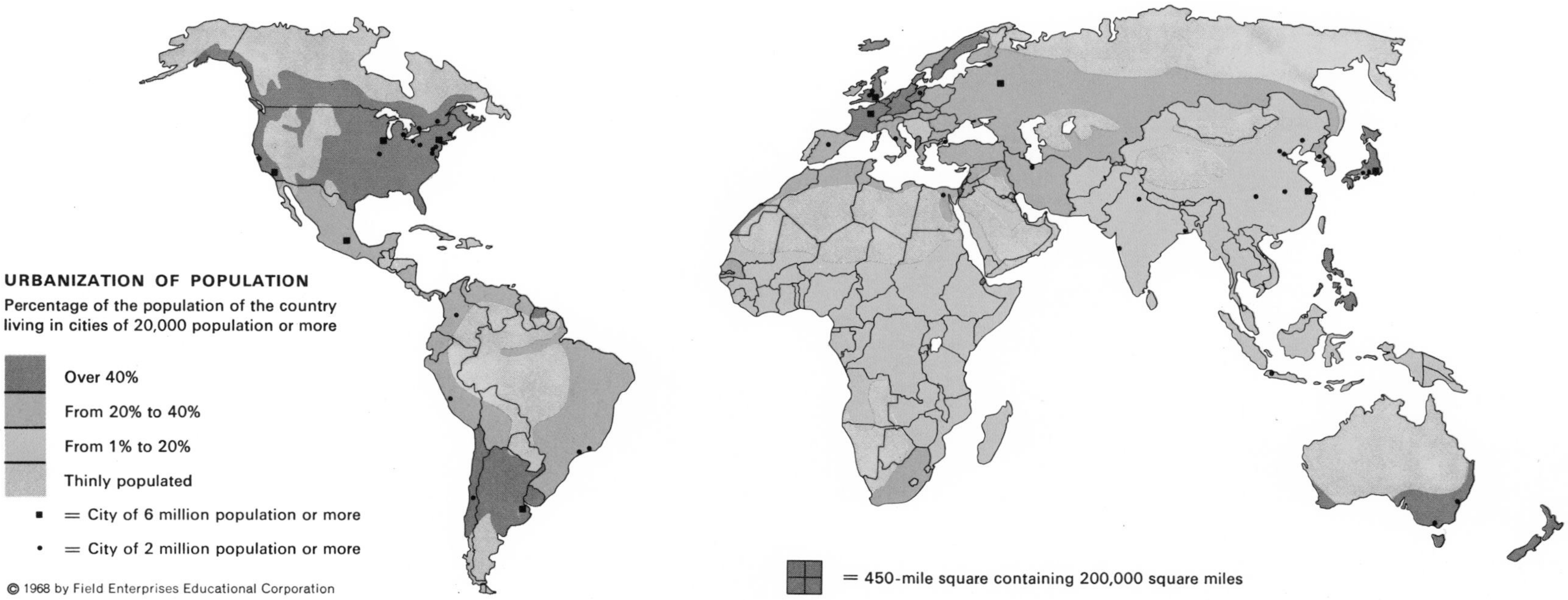

HOW FAST IS THE POPULATION GROWING?

Every year there are more babies born than there are people dying. In fact, the population of the world now grows by about 77 million persons every year. But the population grows faster in some countries than in others, as this map shows. The countries that grow fastest appear in the darkest colors. (These maps do not include growth due to immigration.) Read the information on the opposite page about five typical countries. Then look at the maps to see which countries have the highest birth or death rates.

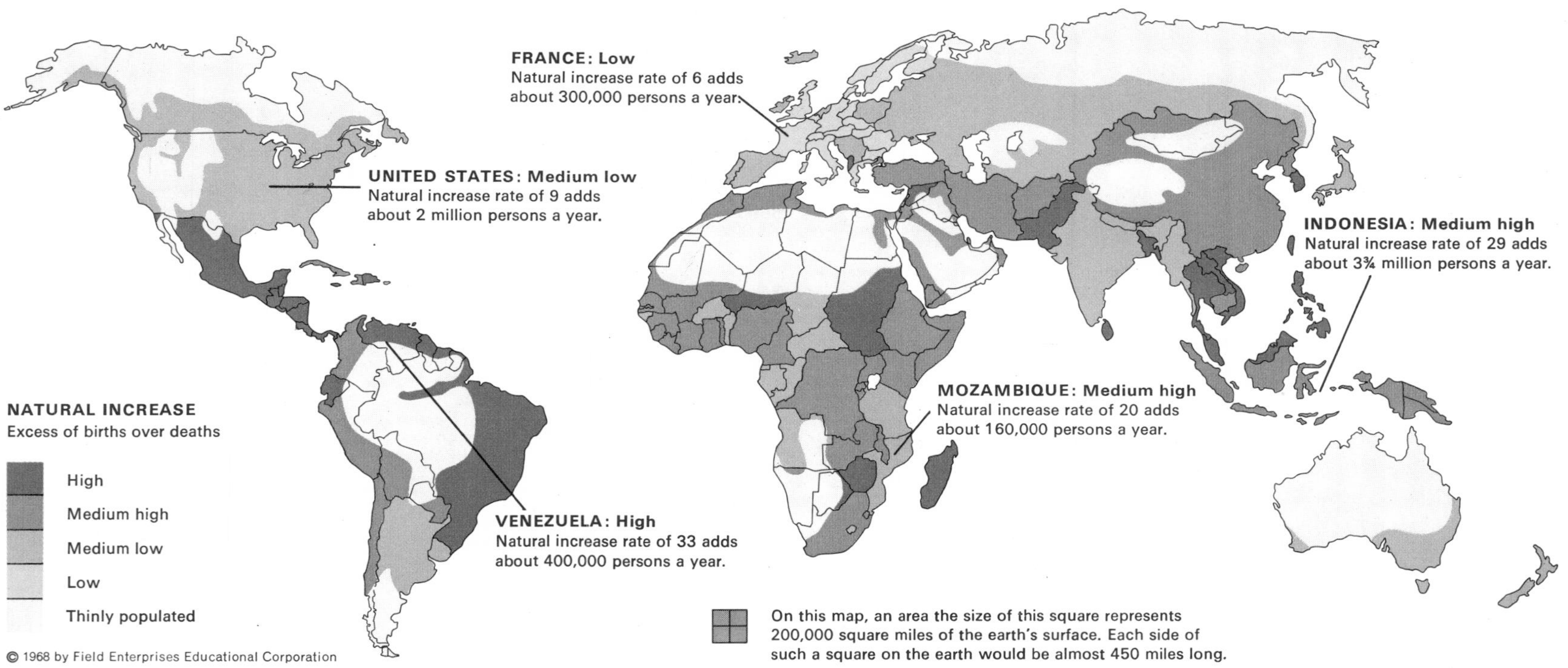
FRANCE: Low
Natural increase rate of 6 adds about 300,000 persons a year.
UNITED STATES: Medium low
Natural increase rate of 9 adds about 2 million persons a year.
INDONESIA: Medium high
Natural increase rate of 29 adds about 3¾ million persons a year.
MOZAMBIQUE: Medium high
Natural increase rate of 20 adds about 160,000 persons a year.
VENEZUELA: High
Natural increase rate of 33 adds about 400,000 persons a year.
NATURAL INCREASE
Excess of births over deaths
High
Medium high
Medium low
Low
Thinly populated
On this map, an area the size of this square represents 200,000 square miles of the earth's surface. Each side of such a square on the earth would be almost 450 miles long.
© 1968 by Field Enterprises Educational Corporation

How many children are born each year?

Population experts refer to the number of babies born in terms of "so many births for every thousand people." Using these terms, they can compare the birth rate of one country, such as Venezuela, with that of another country, such as France, even though France has five times as many people as Venezuela. In some countries, where parents limit the number of children they have, the birth rate is low.

High birth rate	Low birth rate
MOZAMBIQUE	UNITED STATES
VENEZUELA	FRANCE
INDONESIA	

Indonesia has 47 births for every thousand people, Mozambique 43, Venezuela 41, the United States 18, and France 17. The first three rank high in the world's birth-rate tables, the others low.

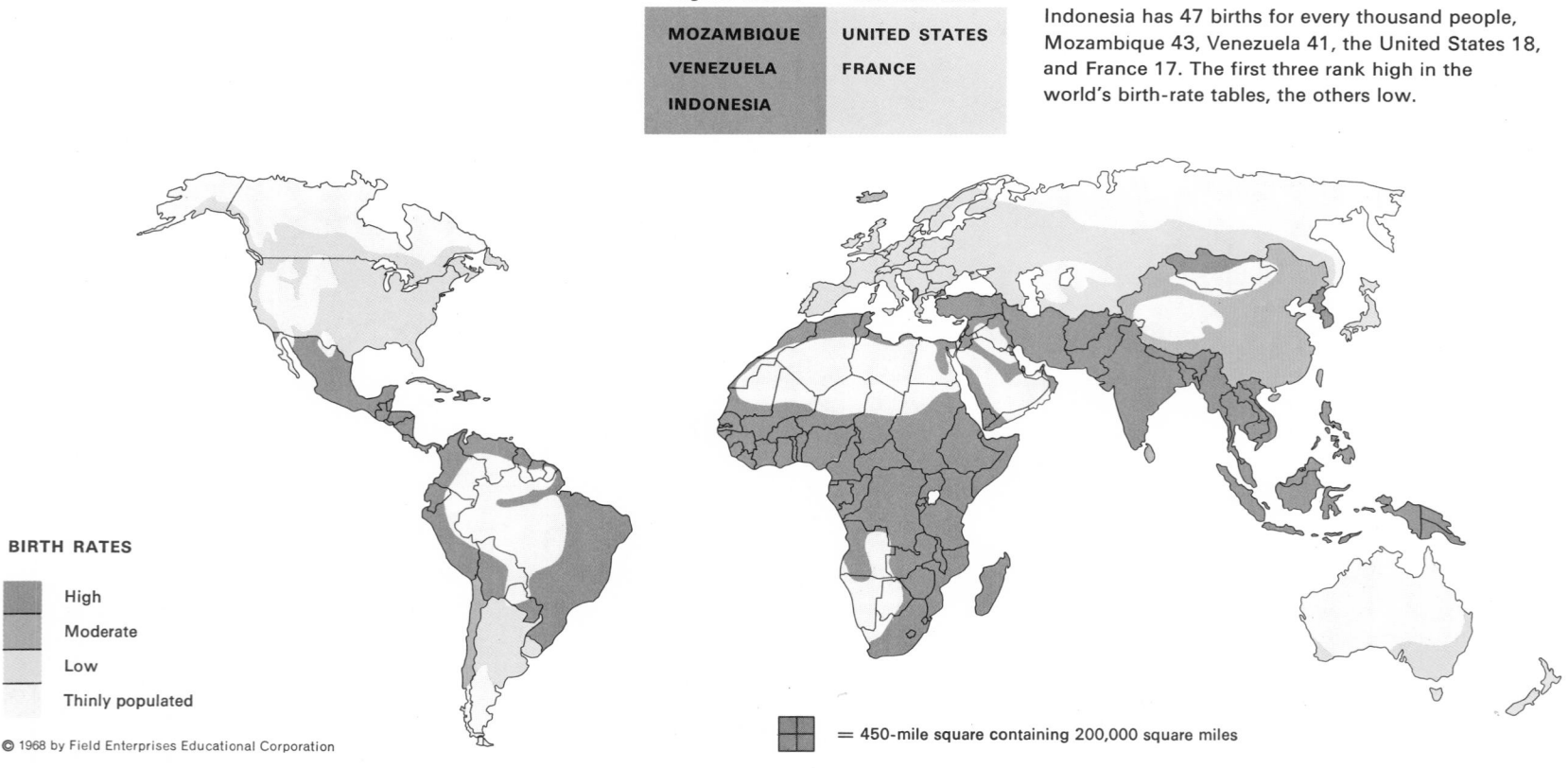

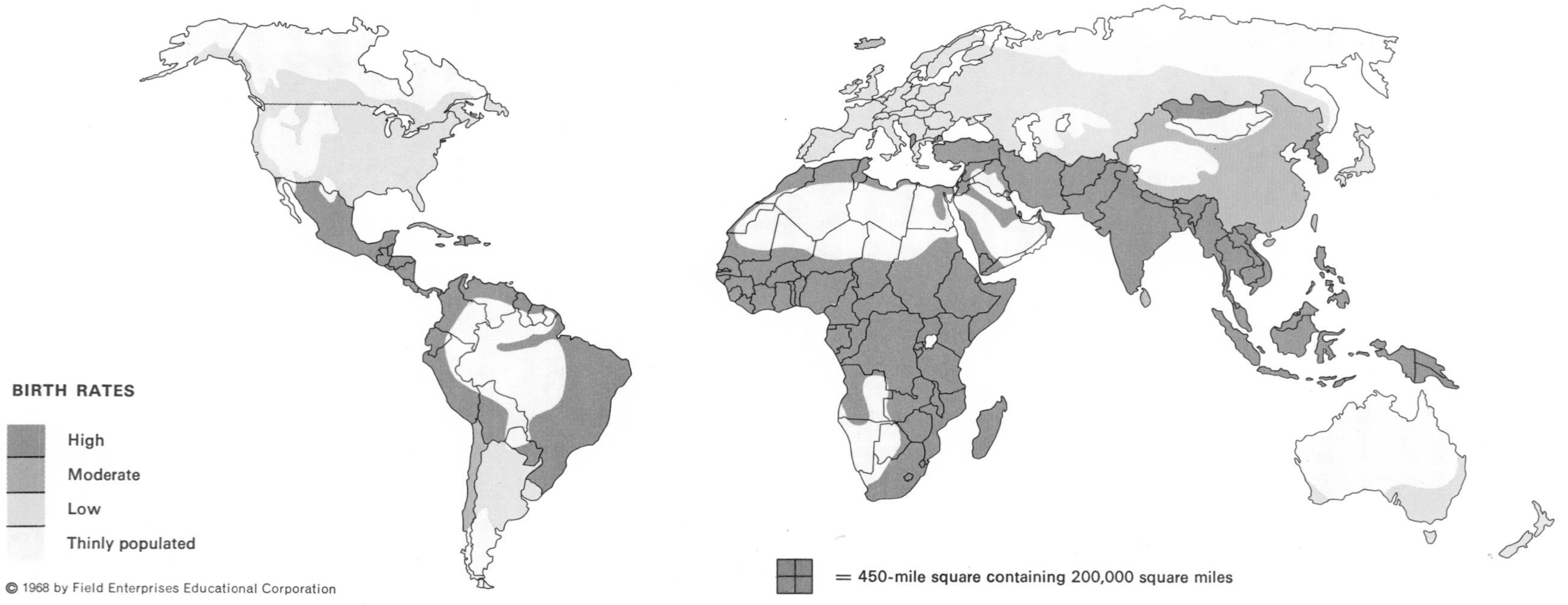
BIRTH RATES
High
Moderate
Low
Thinly populated
= 450-mile square containing 200,000 square miles
© 1968 by Field Enterprises Educational Corporation

Why is the population growing?

Birth and death rates combine in various ways to give countries widely differing rates of population growth. When both the birth rate and the death rate are low, a country will have a low rate of natural increase. This pattern is common in most economically developed countries. In a few economically developing countries, the increase rate may also be low, but for entirely different reasons. Such countries have very high birth rates and very high death rates. Most developing countries have high rates of natural increase. They have high birth rates, but their death rates have been greatly lowered through improved medical care.

Mozambique, where the people still follow traditional African ways of life, has both a high death rate and a high birth rate.

Indonesia has a high birth rate, but advances in health and nutrition have resulted in a lower death rate. Its birth rate is higher than that of Mozambique, and its rate of natural increase is greater.

Venezuela has a high birth rate and a low death rate, resulting in a rate of natural increase higher than that of Mozambique or Indonesia.

The United States has a low death rate, and its rate of birth has fallen to a fairly low point. Its population grows slowly through natural increase.

France has both a low birth rate and a low death rate, with a lower rate of natural increase than any of the other countries described here.

The countries that have the highest birth rates and rates of natural increase today are mainly the economically developing countries in Africa, Asia, and Latin America. As a result, these areas, which already have about two-thirds of the world's population, will have an even larger share of the population by the year 2000.

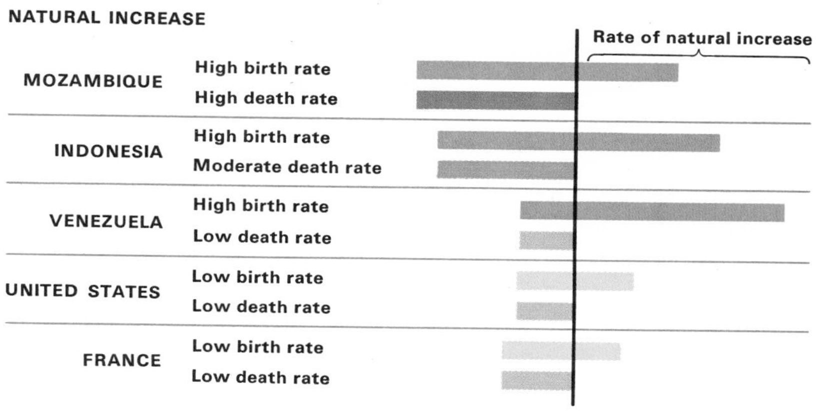

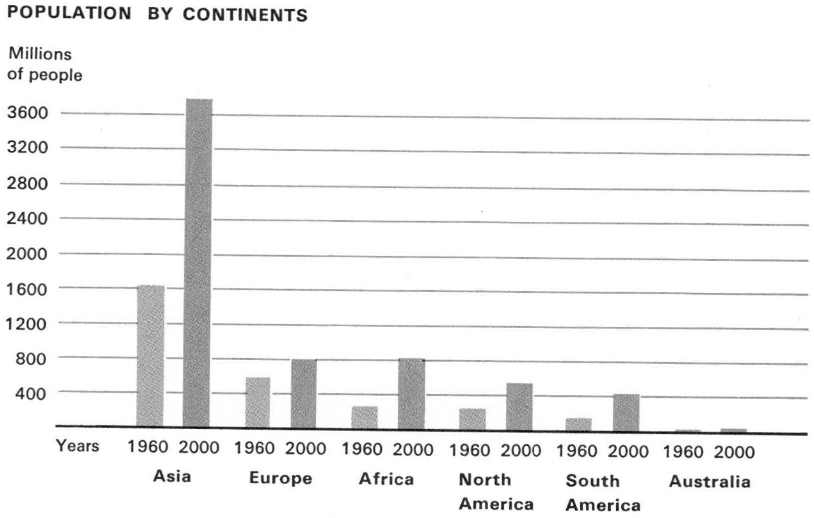

How many people die each year?

Population experts refer to the number of persons who die each year in terms of "so many deaths for every thousand people." Using these statistics, they can compare the death rates for the United States and France, even though the United States has four times as many people as France. As people learn to eat better foods, adopt practices of personal hygiene, and make use of better medical care, death rates go down.

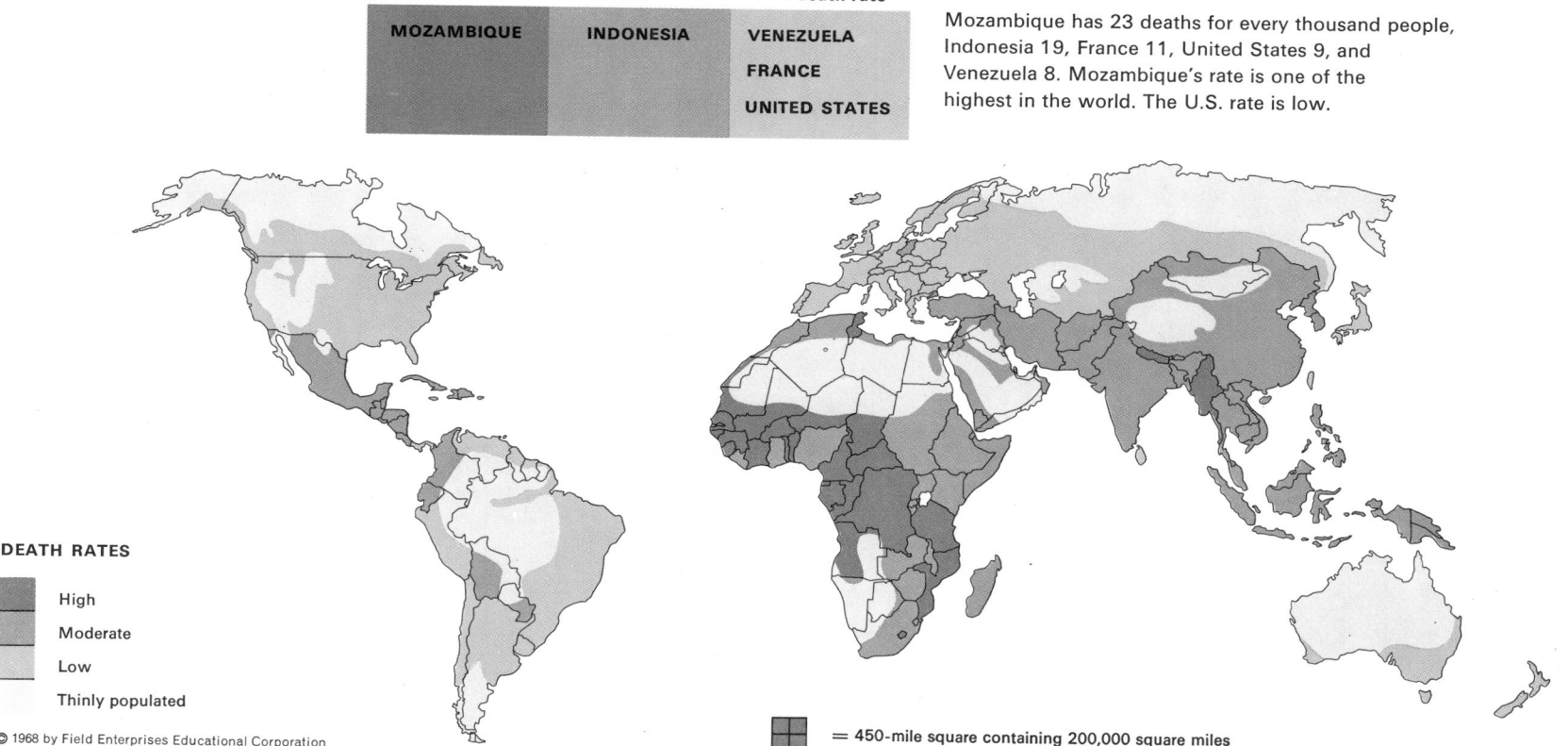

High death rate	Moderate death rate	Low death rate
MOZAMBIQUE	INDONESIA	VENEZUELA FRANCE UNITED STATES

Mozambique has 23 deaths for every thousand people, Indonesia 19, France 11, United States 9, and Venezuela 8. Mozambique's rate is one of the highest in the world. The U.S. rate is low.

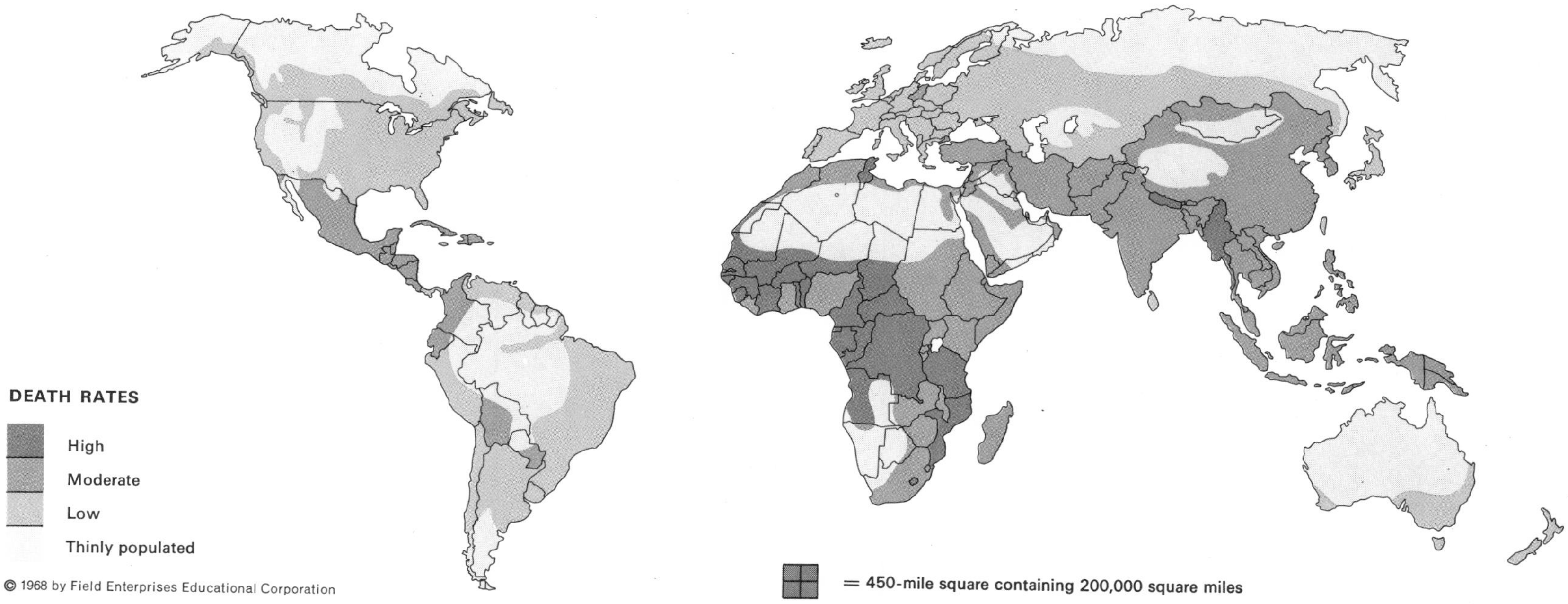

HOW DO THE PEOPLE MAKE THEIR LIVING?

People must work for the food and shelter that they and their families need. Some grow or make what they need themselves. Others work for money with which to buy what they need. In most countries, most of the people work on the land, raising or gathering food and other crops. Only a few countries have more people making a living in other ways than by working on the land.

Where do the people work in agriculture?

To answer this question, look at the map. Farmers in the areas marked in green have fairly good conditions for raising crops—sunshine, water, and fertile soil. Farmers in the areas marked in tan have conditions suitable for grazing animals.

In about 20 countries, including India, more than three out of every four persons have no jobs other than working on the land. These people seldom produce more than just enough to keep their families alive. They have little or no farm machinery and use little or no fertilizer. By contrast, in 10 other countries, no more than one out of every four persons works on the land. Yet farmers in these countries (Australia, Belgium, Canada, Great Britain, Israel, The Netherlands, New Zealand, Sweden, Switzerland, and the United States) produce more than these countries can use of certain kinds of food. This surplus is then traded with other countries that have a need for these foods. In these countries where a food surplus is created, agriculture has become an industry.

MAJOR FARMING AREAS

Dots appear as close as possible to the centers of the areas they represent

. = 4,000 square miles of cropland

. = 4,000 square miles of pastureland

Populated

Thinly populated

© 1968 by Field Enterprises Educational Corporation

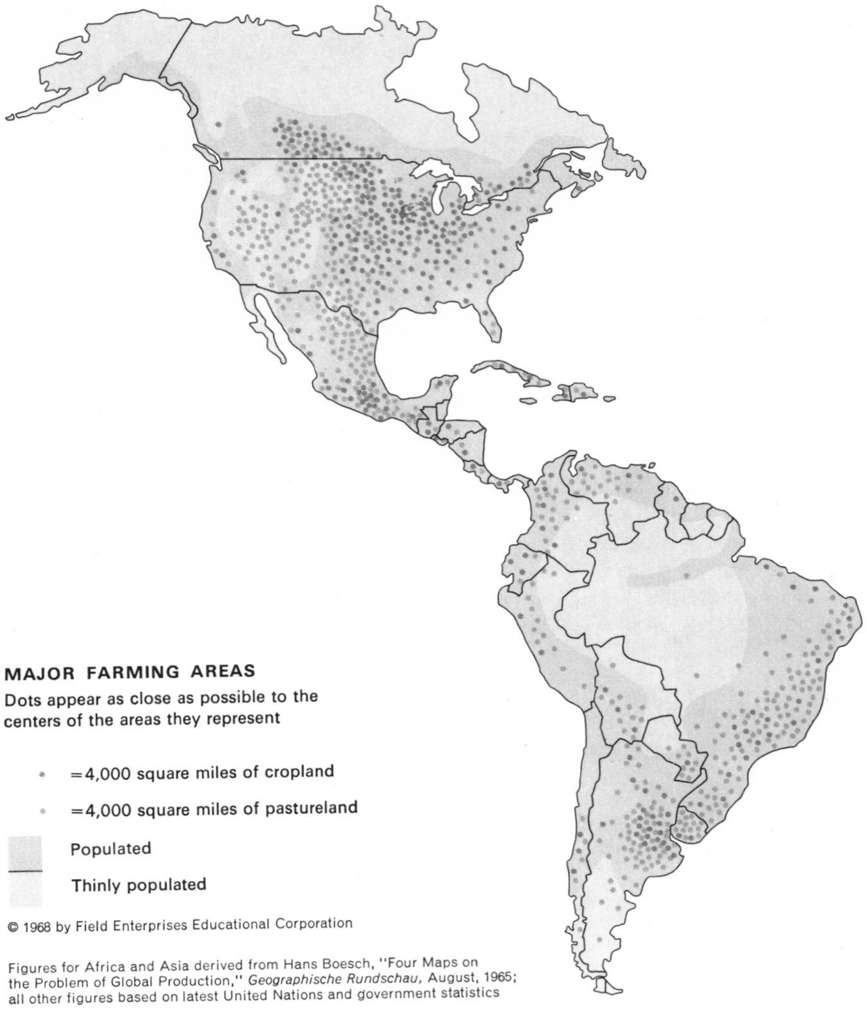

Figures for Africa and Asia derived from Hans Boesch, "Four Maps on the Problem of Global Production," *Geographische Rundschau*, August, 1965; all other figures based on latest United Nations and government statistics

Where do the people work in manufacturing?

To answer this question, look at the map. Most of the factories and workshops of the world are concentrated in small areas of Europe and North America. Smaller industrial areas are growing up in such countries as Argentina, Australia, Brazil, India, and Japan, and even smaller areas in some other countries. In all the industrial areas, most of the workers are employed in manufacturing or in providing services for others, such as teaching, caring for the sick, running stores and restaurants, or manning police and fire forces.

MAJOR INDUSTRIAL AREAS

Areas that contribute most of the value added by manufacture to the gross national product of the country

Heavily industrialized area

Industrialized area

Populated

Thinly populated

© 1968 by Field Enterprises Educational Corporation

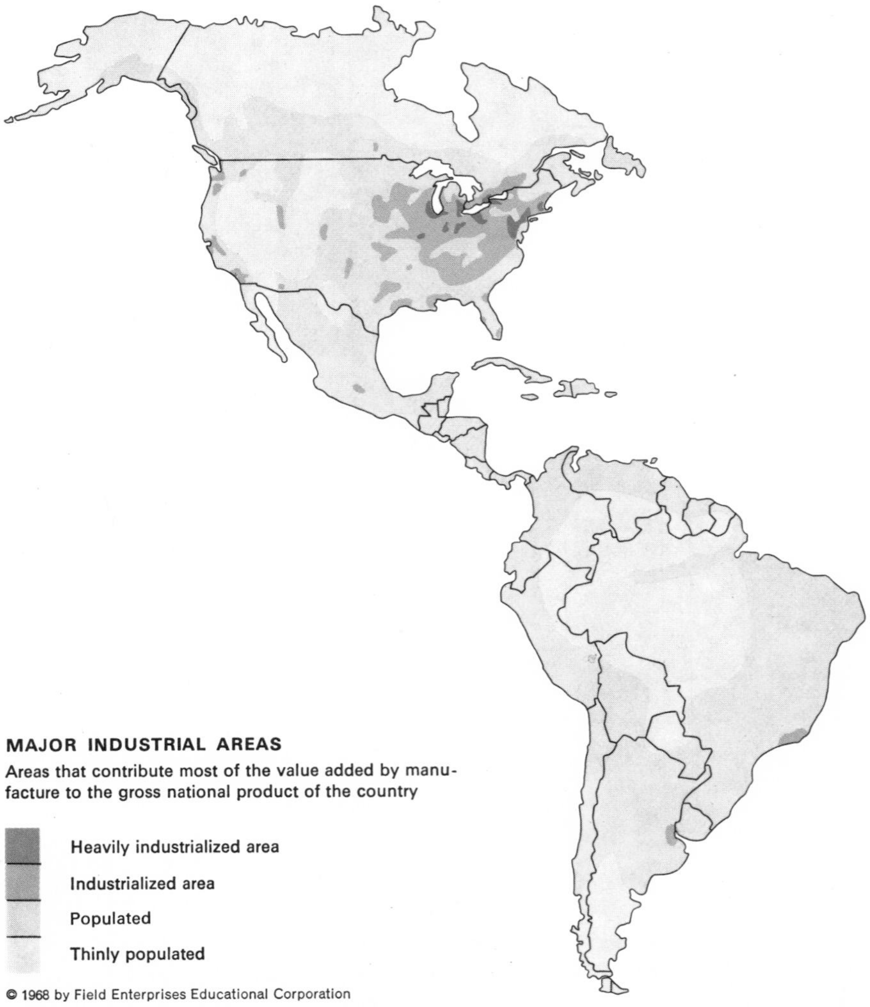

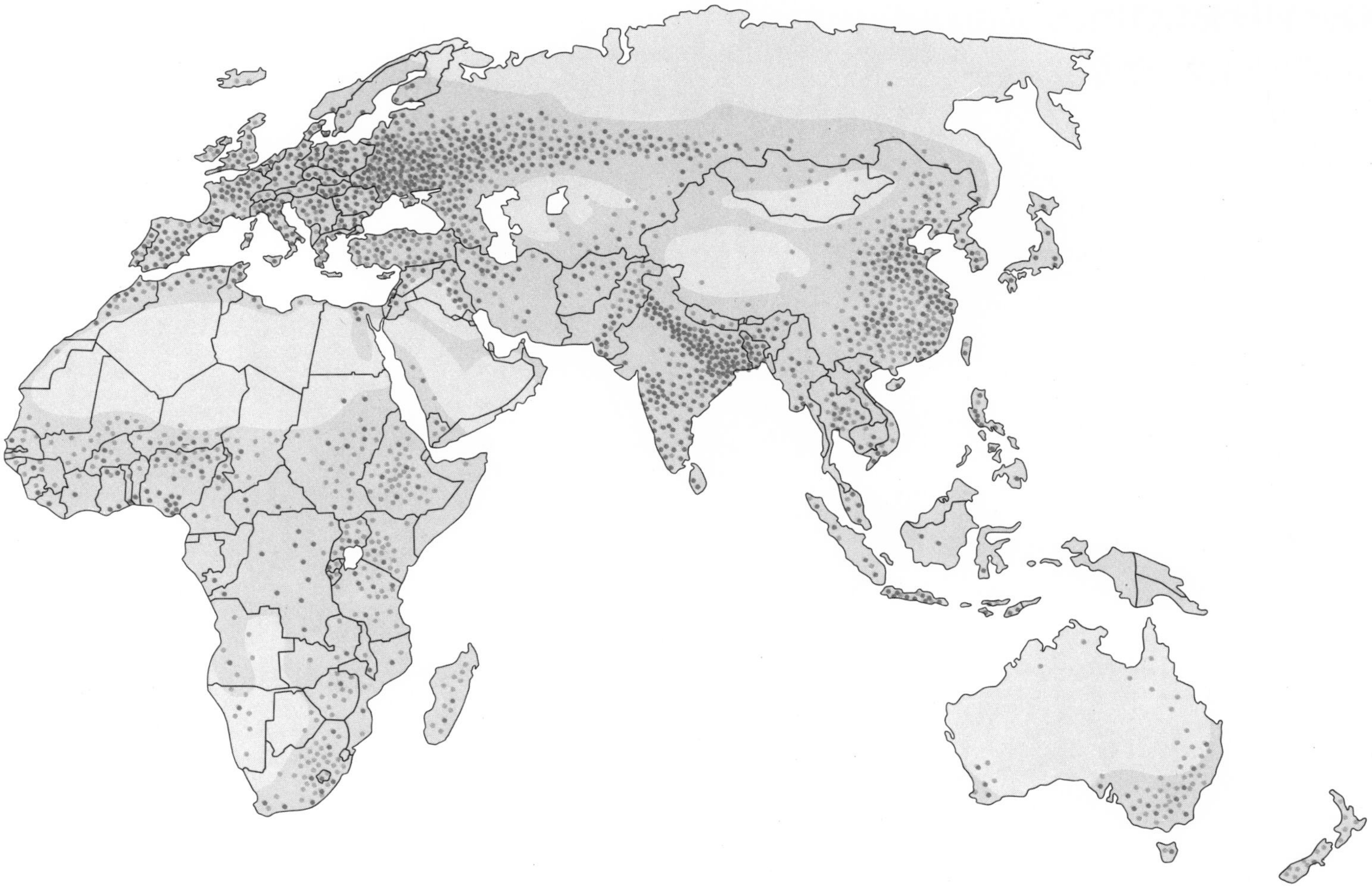

On this map, an area the size of this square represents 200,000 square miles of the earth's surface. Each side of such a square on the earth would be about 450 miles long.

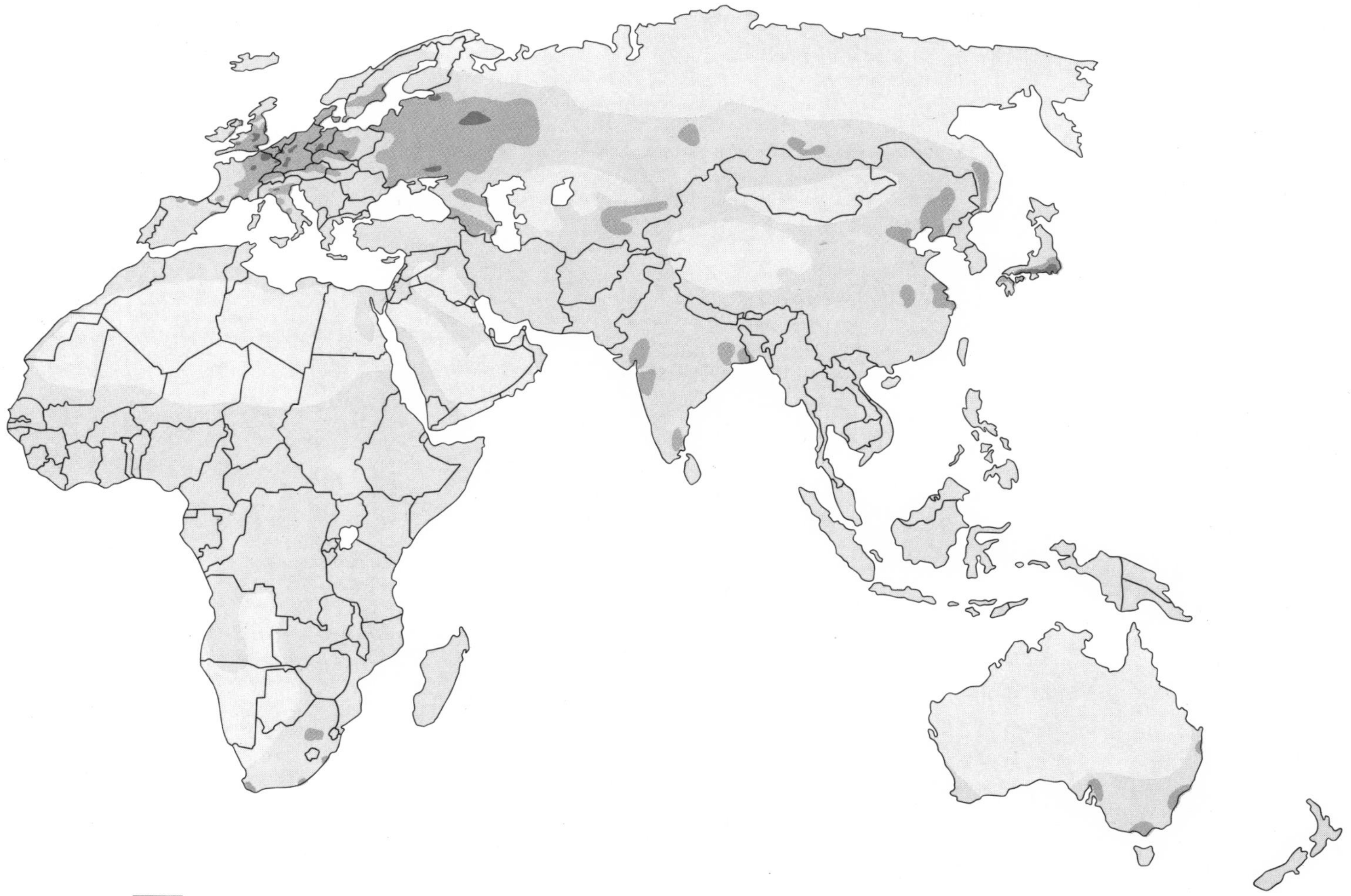

=450-mile square containing 200,000 square miles

HOW MUCH DO THE PEOPLE HAVE?

This map shows how much money each person could have if he shared equally in the value of all goods and services produced in his country each year (gross national product). But people do not share equally, and money is only one way to measure how well they live. In some countries, many people make or grow almost everything they need. These countries may look poor on this map, even though most of the people living in them have enough of the necessities of life—food, shelter, and clothing.

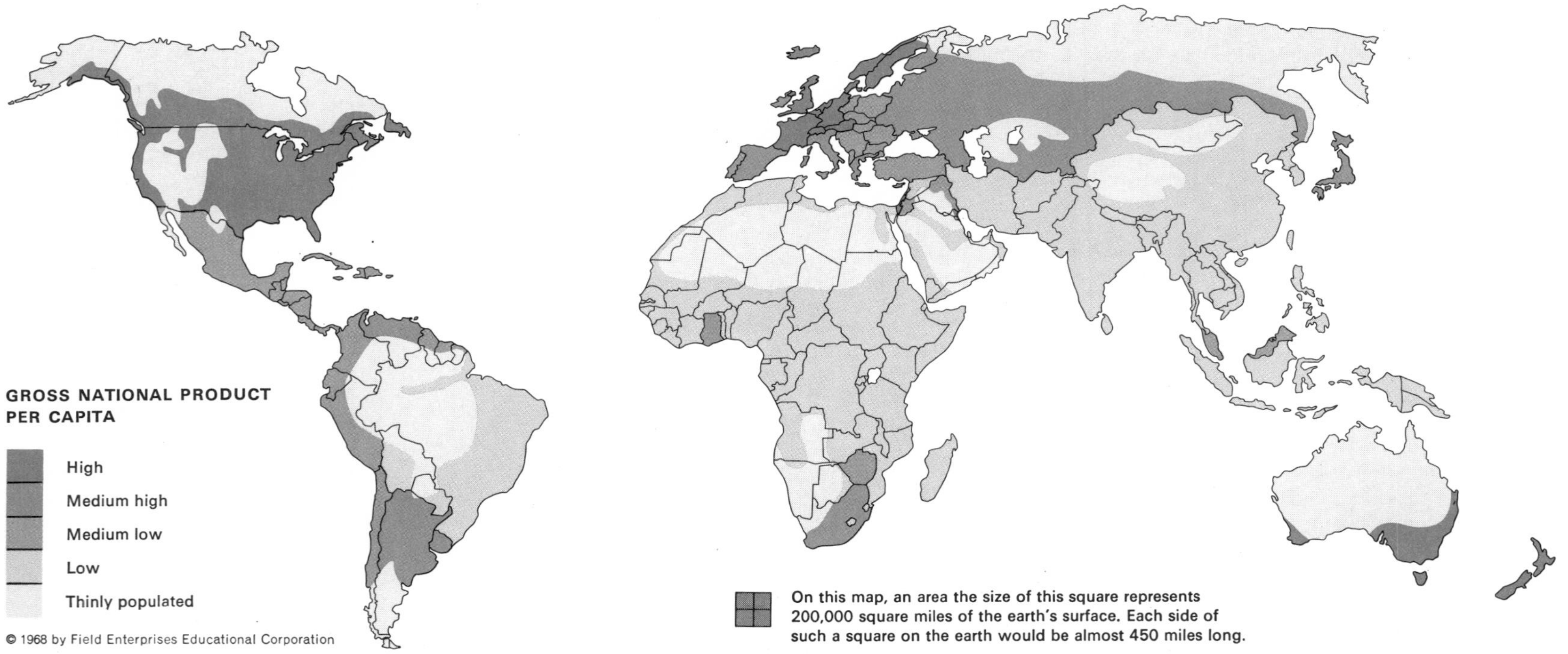

How much know-how do they use?

The skills and abilities of the people of any country are its most precious asset. They are far more important in economic development than supplies of important industrial raw materials. Some peoples have had many years in which to develop their technical know-how. Others have had to learn quickly many of the basic techniques of the modern industrial world.

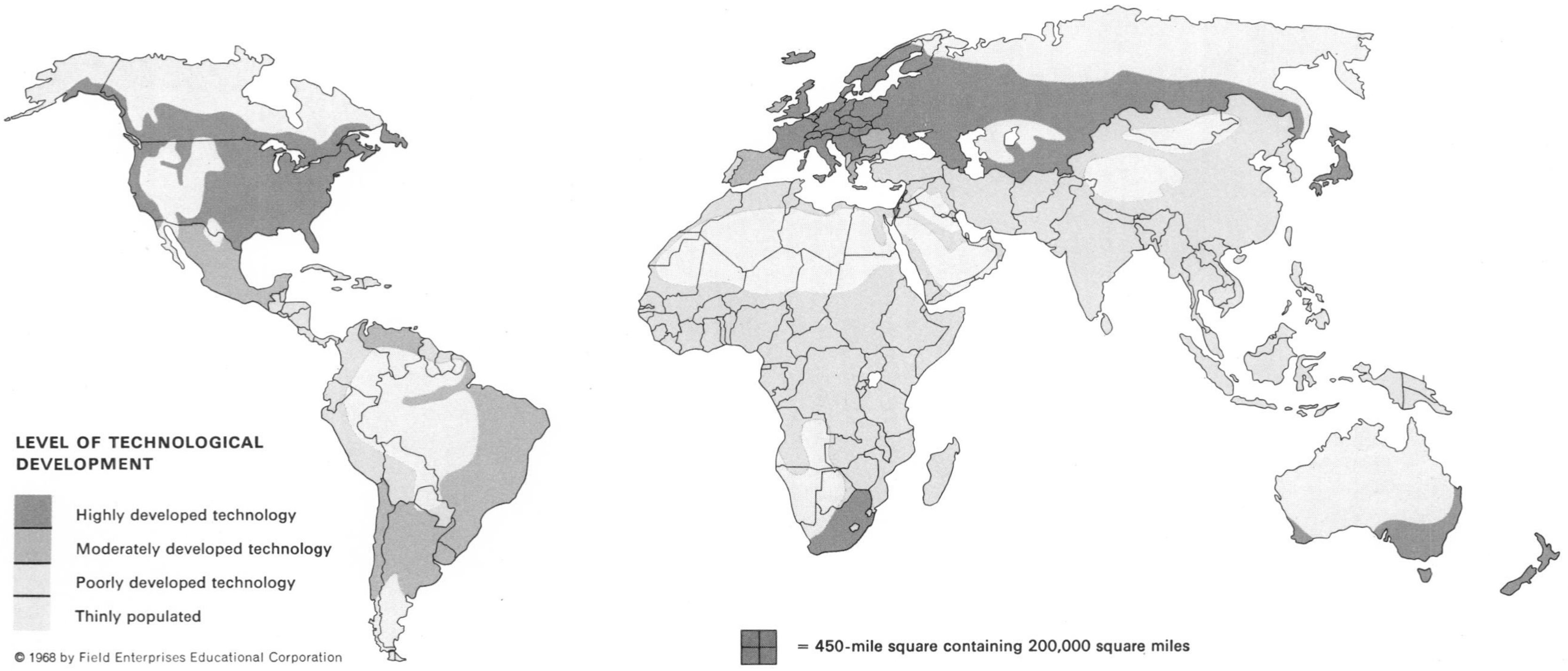

How much energy do they use?

When a man can do only as much work as his own strength, or the strength of his animals, allows, he can produce little. But whenever he makes use of energy that comes from other sources to help do his work, he can produce much more. From this map, you can see that people in Europe and North America use a great deal of *inanimate energy*—power that does not come from men or animals.

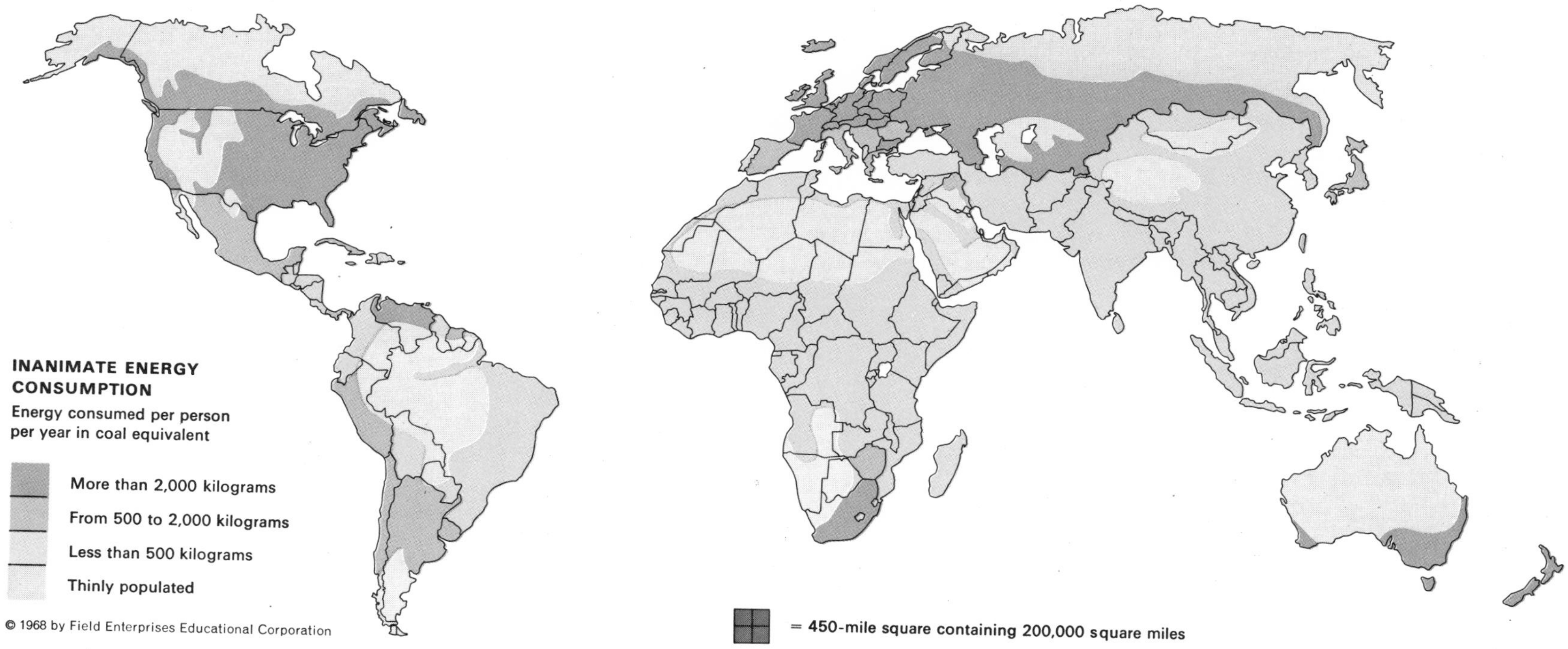

Do they use their resources?

People living in tribal conditions in remote parts of the world usually make use of almost all the physical resources within their reach. They know how to grow enough crops for food and how to find enough materials to make some kind of shelter. But they may live right on top of a valuable deposit of a raw material, such as copper or uranium, and never know it. Their whole view of the world may be changed when someone shows them that the very ground they walk on has value.

In this sense, simply having important physical resources is not enough—if the people do not use them, they cannot derive much national wealth from having them. Using resources depends on *technology,* the know-how with which men make iron from iron ore, steel from iron, and high-quality precision tools from steel. Australia, Canada, Japan, New Zealand, the Soviet Union, the United States, and the countries of western Europe lead the world in technology.

Many of these countries, such as Canada, the Soviet Union, and the United States, have huge sources of many of the raw materials important in industry today. People in these countries have learned to make the most of their physical resources and to use mainly inanimate energy. As the maps on these pages show, they share large gross national products.

Other countries are not so well off. Technicians from the developed countries have come in to work on one or two resources of great importance, such as petroleum or copper ore. But the peoples of these countries do not all share in the wealth that these rich resources bring in. In many of these countries, most of the people have no part in developing the resources, or have only simple jobs. They gain little technical training.

Still other countries are making great efforts to develop themselves. Technicians from other countries are not permitted simply to develop resources, but are required to train the people to take part in this development. The people grow in knowledge as their country grows in wealth.

GROSS NATIONAL PRODUCT PER CAPITA

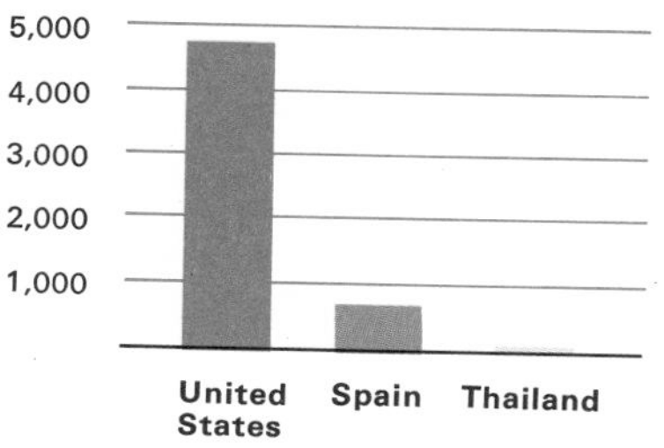

INANIMATE ENERGY CONSUMPTION PER CAPITA

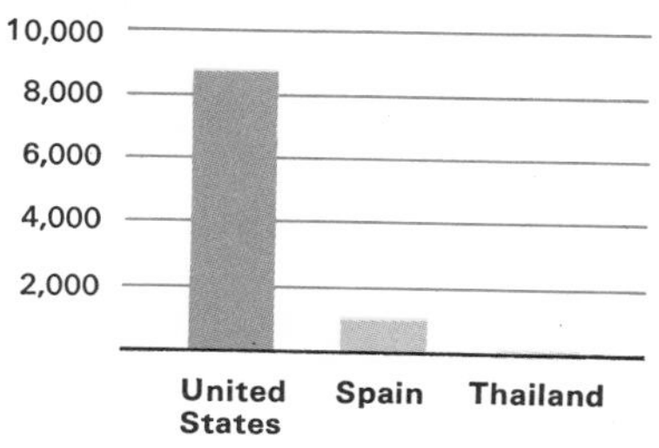

Each person's share in his country's gross national product and in the amount of energy used, *above,* mirrors the economic makeup of his country. Look at the way the work force is divided in three countries that are advanced, developing, and underdeveloped:

DIVISION OF WORK FORCE

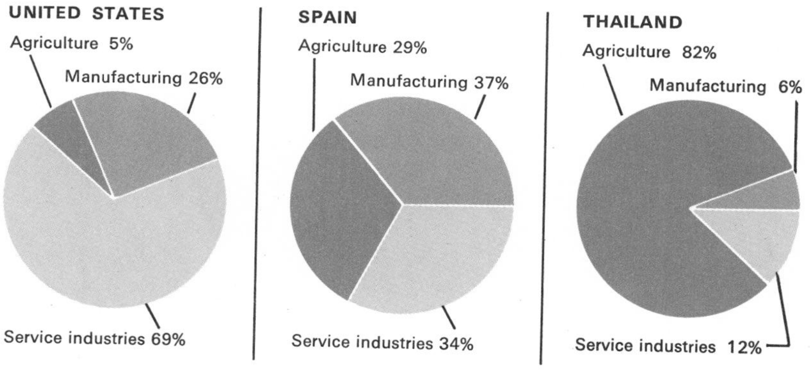

HOW WELL DO THE PEOPLE LIVE?

This question should be asked in several forms: How well-fed are they? (on these pages) How good is their medical care? (on the next two pages) How well-educated and well-informed are they? (pages 26 and 27)

Have they enough to eat?

In most countries, no.
The people may suffer from *malnutrition* (not enough food value in their diet) or from *undernutrition* (not enough food). Although most of them do not starve to death, their food does not give them enough strength to work hard or to recover from diseases. They do not live as long as people with better diets. Infants suffer most, as you can see from the maps on these pages.

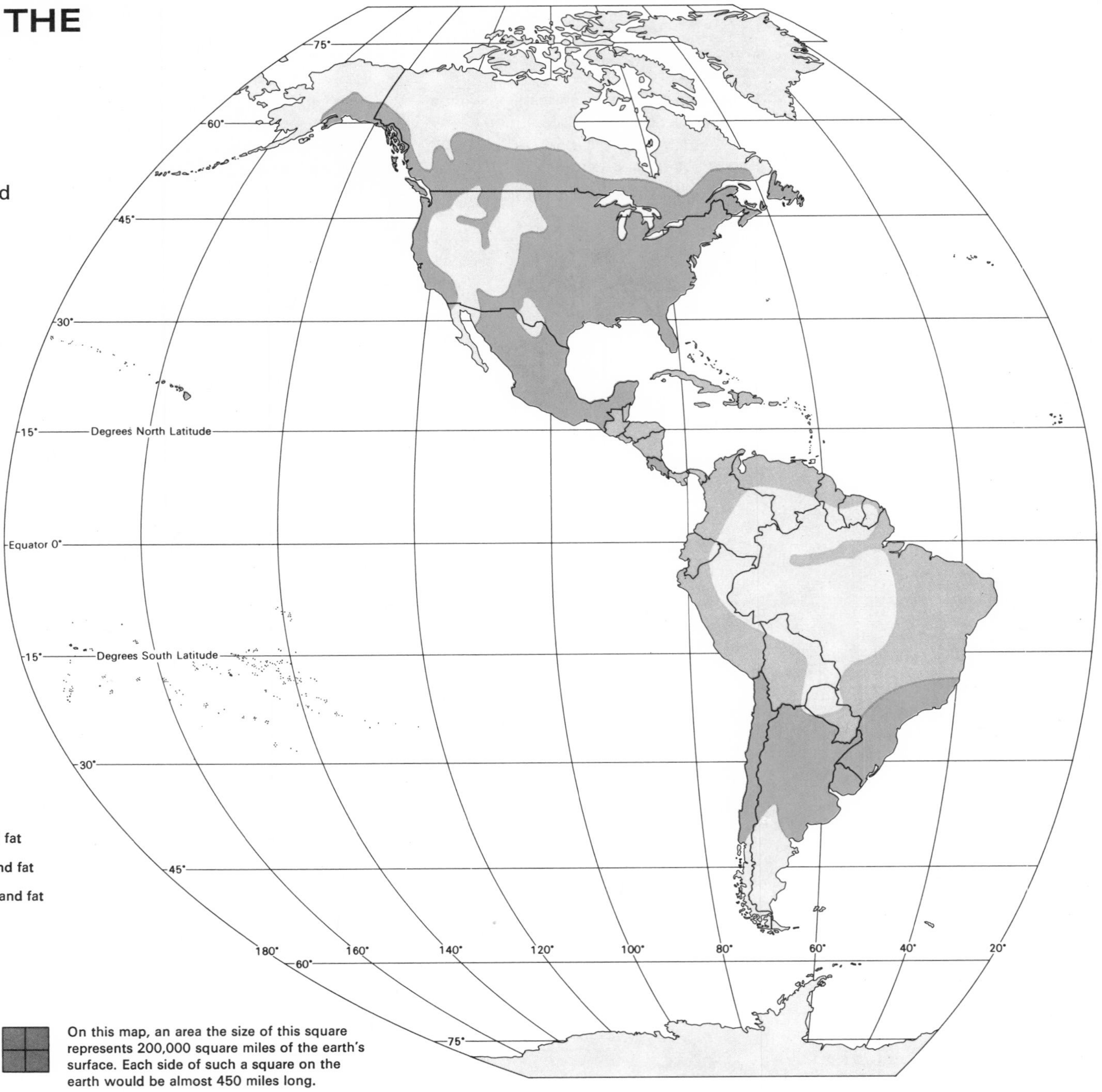

NUTRITIONAL VALUE OF AVERAGE DIET

- Adequate calories, adequate protein and fat
- Adequate calories, inadequate protein and fat
- Inadequate calories, inadequate protein and fat
- Thinly populated

On this map, an area the size of this square represents 200,000 square miles of the earth's surface. Each side of such a square on the earth would be almost 450 miles long.

How long can they expect to live?

The answer to this question depends on where the people live. A person in a central African country such as Gabon is likely to live only about 41 years, while a person in Sweden is likely to live about 75 years. On the average, women live longer than men—to about 45 in Gabon and about 77 in Sweden. In the U.S., men live to about 67, women to about 74.

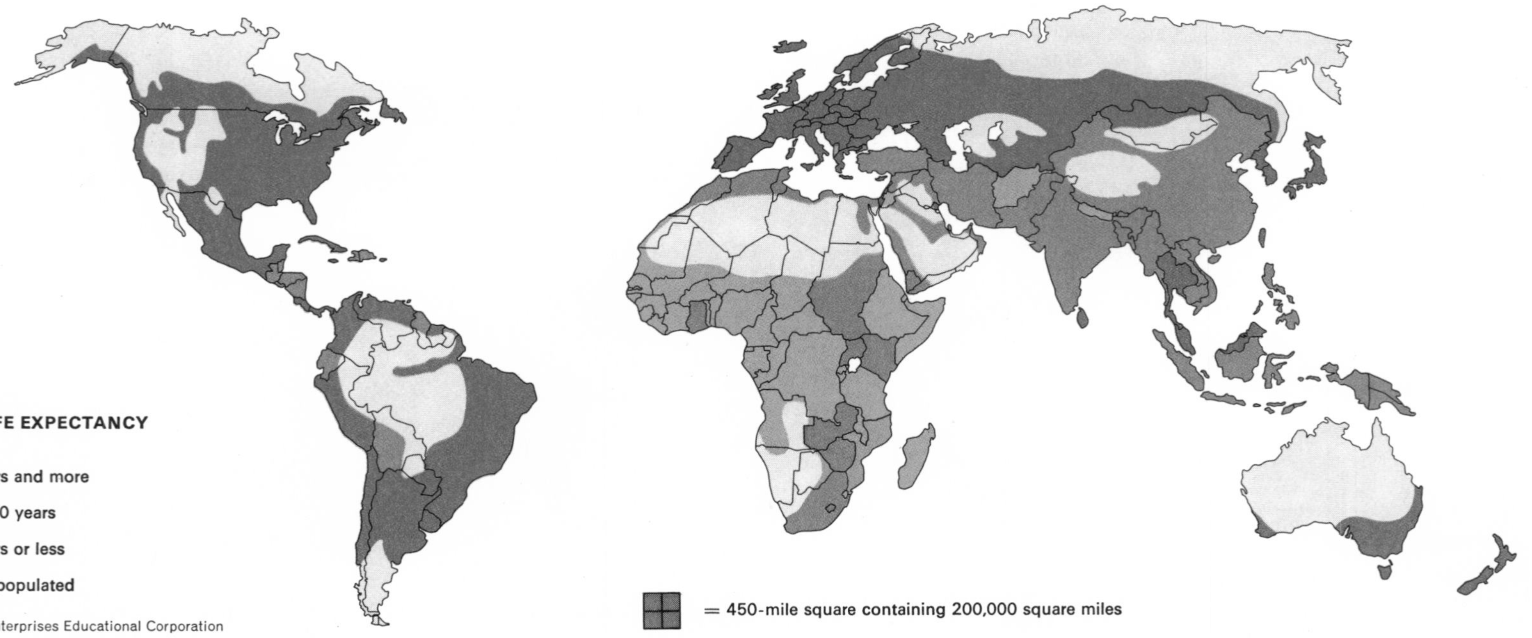

AVERAGE LIFE EXPECTANCY

- 60 years and more
- 45 to 60 years
- 45 years or less
- Thinly populated

= 450-mile square containing 200,000 square miles

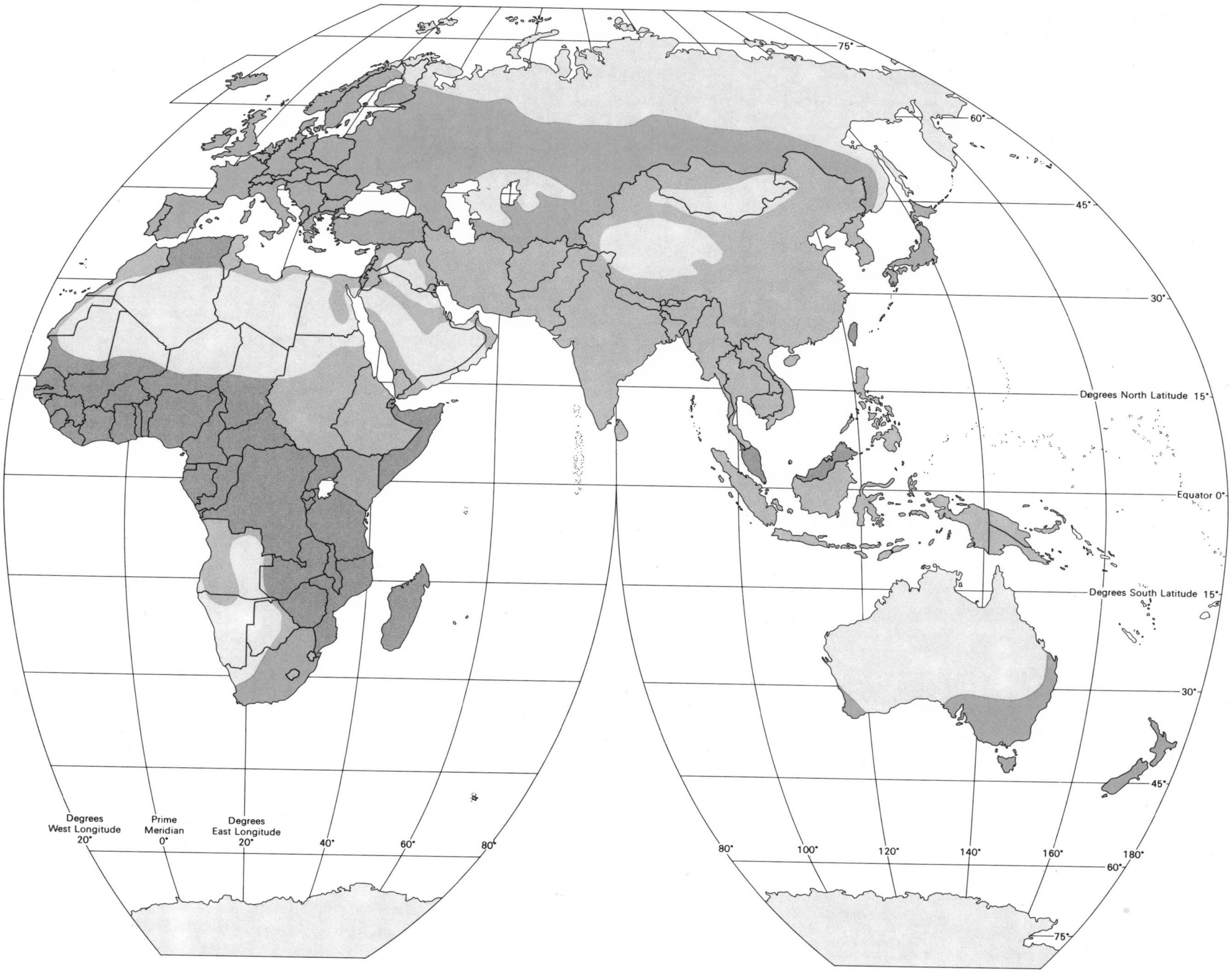

How many infants die?

The answer to this question depends on where the infants are born. In Denmark and Sweden, only 13 or 15 out of every thousand babies will die before their first birthday. In Congo, Zambia, and some other central African countries, more than 10 times that many—between 180 and 260 per thousand—are likely to die within their first year of life.

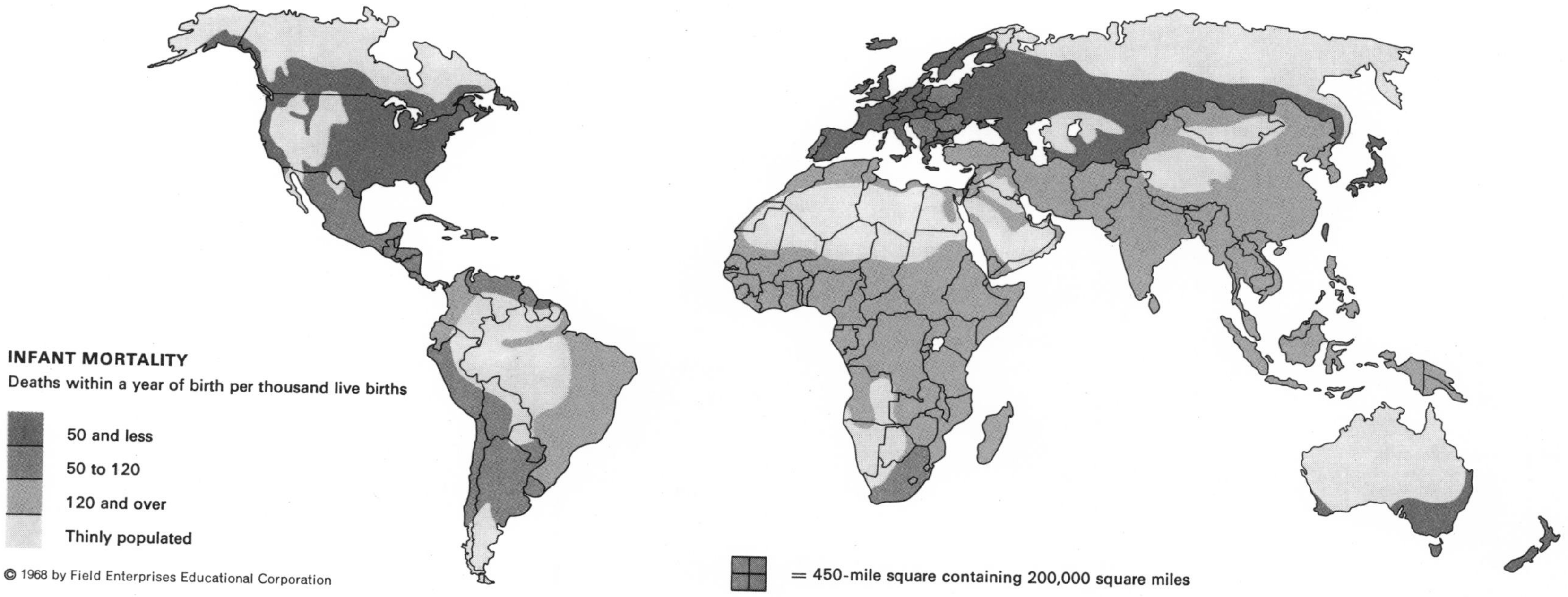

HOW WELL DO THE PEOPLE LIVE?

How good is their medical care?

There are two common ways to measure medical care—the number of physicians and the number of hospital beds. For example, Israel leads the world with one physician for every 430 people, and the Soviet Union comes next with one physician for every 510 people. By contrast, Ethiopia has only one physician for every 90,000 people. Sweden and Ireland have one hospital bed for every 70 people, but Nepal has only one hospital bed for every 7,000 people.

These figures can be compared only with great care, because the definitions on which they are based vary considerably from one country to another. For example, *physician* can mean a university graduate licensed to perform any kind of medical aid without scientific supervision, or it can mean someone with little training licensed to practice with supervision. And a hospital bed can range from a padded bench in the emergency section of a remote country hospital to a complicated piece of equipment surrounded with the latest in medical tools. Some governments count only beds used by short-term patients, while others also count beds used by the chronically ill or the mentally handicapped.

Even when used carefully, these figures are misleading, because most of the physicians and hospital beds in the world are in or near big cities. Many countries have a great deal of medical care available in their large cities, but little or none in the outlying areas. And these figures—the only statistics available—do not tell fully the quality of medical care, which results from many other factors as well, including the attitude of the physician. Dr. Jacques May, author of *Studies in Medical Geography,* compiled the figures for this map and grouped the countries into the patterns you see.

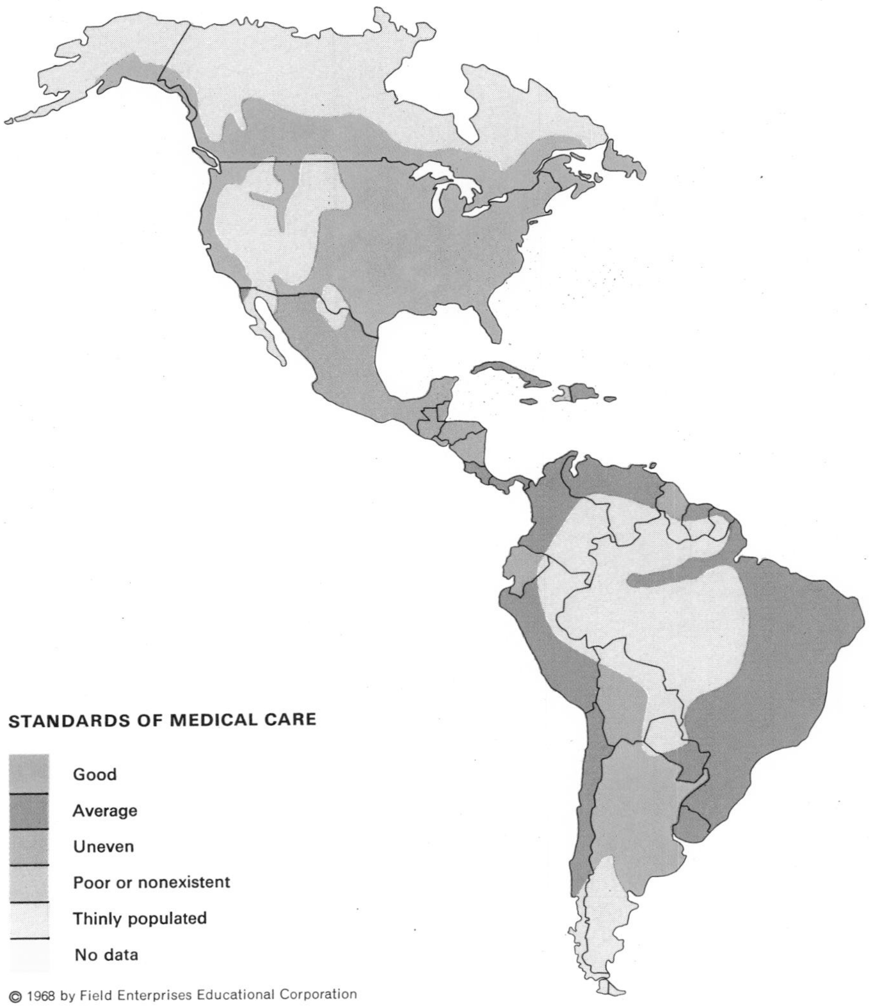

What causes most deaths?

The answer to this question is a good indication of how well the people of various countries have learned to control the conditions in which they live. In the countries shown in dark brown on this map, a large number of the people die each year from *transmissible* diseases—ones caused by bacteria, parasites, viruses, and other agents that enter the body. The most common forms of transmissible diseases are malaria, smallpox, plague, tuberculosis, typhus, yellow fever, and cholera. As the people learn to control parasites and to take precautions against spreading infectious diseases, the number of deaths caused by transmissible diseases goes down. Then, the longer the people live, the more likely they are to die from *degenerative* diseases, such as cancer or heart trouble. These diseases come mostly from internal causes, such as the aging of body tissues.

The task of finding out how many people die from what causes anywhere in the world is a difficult one. Only 50 of the 144 countries shown on this map provide information for the United Nations on the causes of deaths. Even in these countries, the information may be based on inaccurate or incomplete reports. Dr. Jacques May derived the information for the other countries from a number of sources, such as sample studies or hospital records showing the ages at which people died. Those who died fairly young probably died of transmissible diseases, while the others probably died of degenerative ones. Dr. May also took into account reports to the World Health Organization of epidemics of cholera, malaria, plague, smallpox, typhus, and yellow fever. He reasoned that any countries in which these epidemics occur year after year have not gained control over the conditions in which these diseases occur.

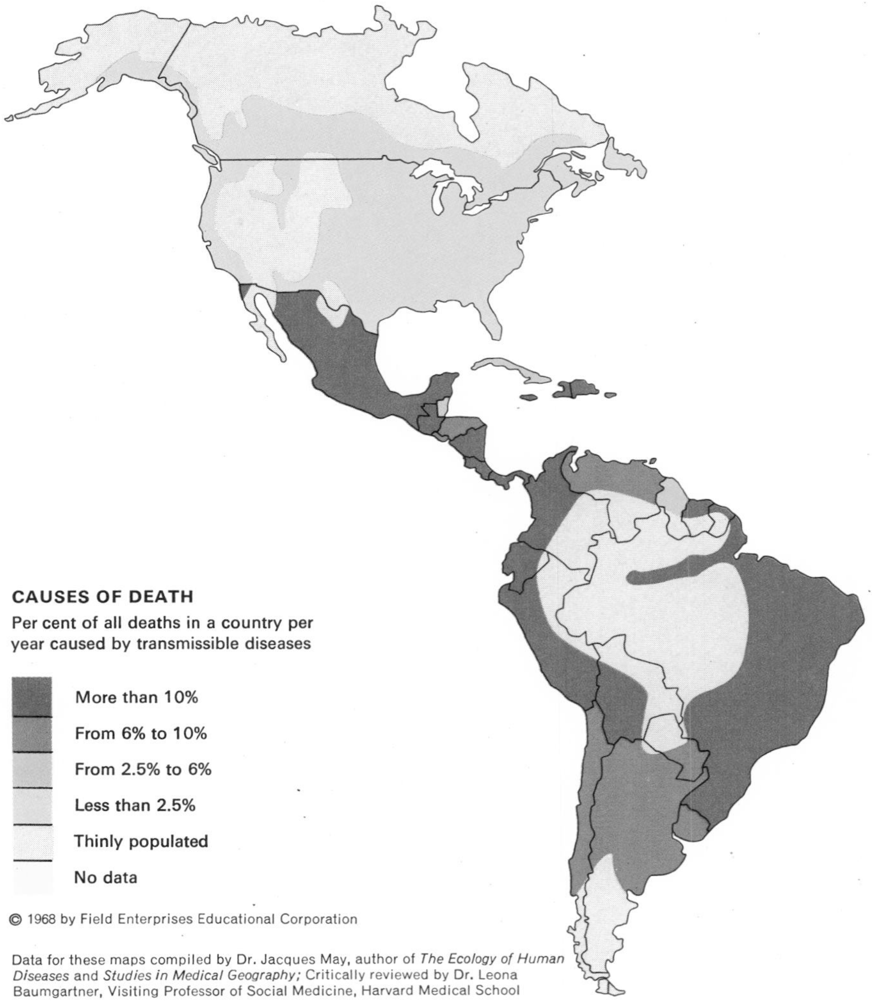

Data for these maps compiled by Dr. Jacques May, author of *The Ecology of Human Diseases* and *Studies in Medical Geography;* Critically reviewed by Dr. Leona Baumgartner, Visiting Professor of Social Medicine, Harvard Medical School

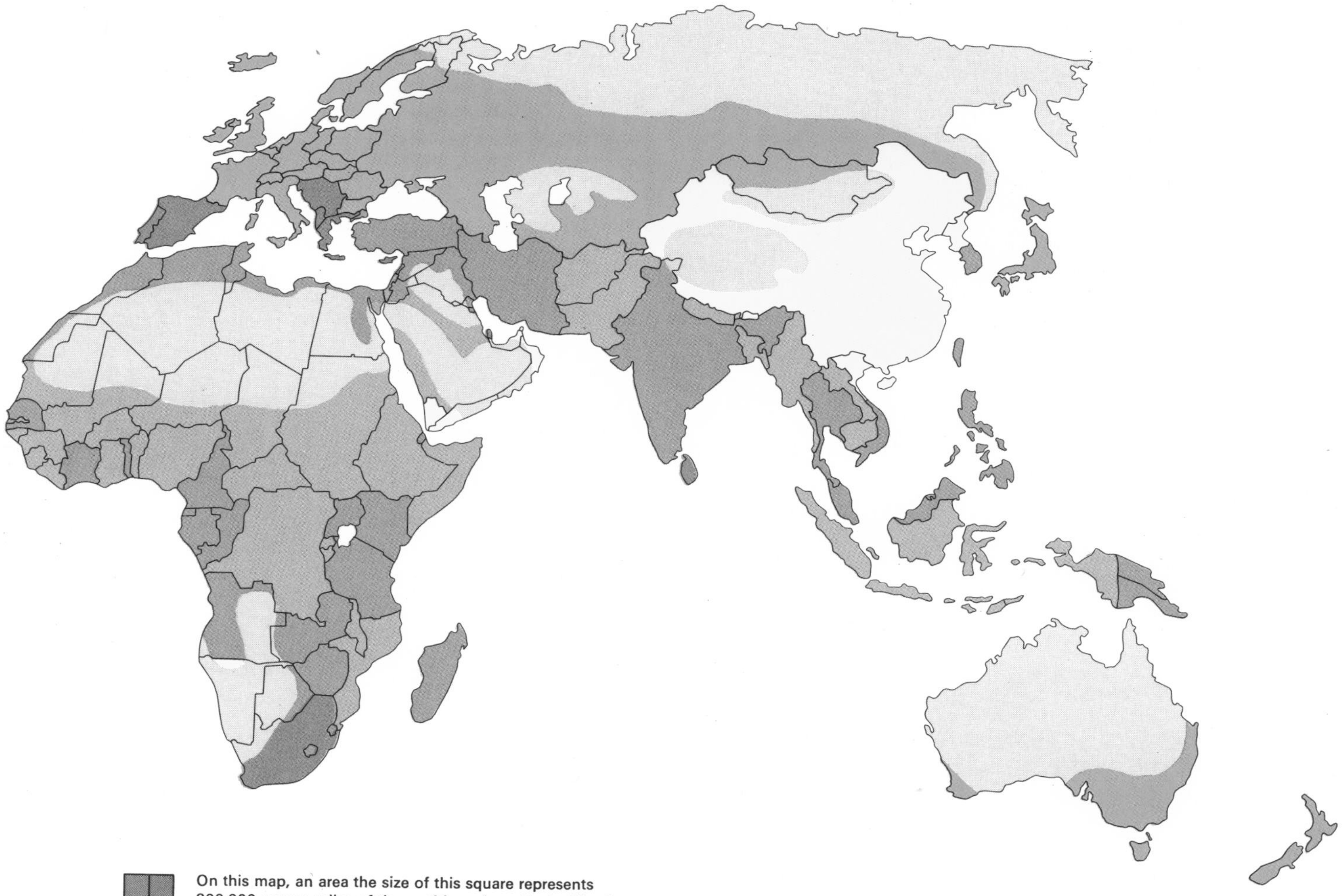

On this map, an area the size of this square represents 200,000 square miles of the earth's surface. Each side of such a square on the earth would be about 450 miles long

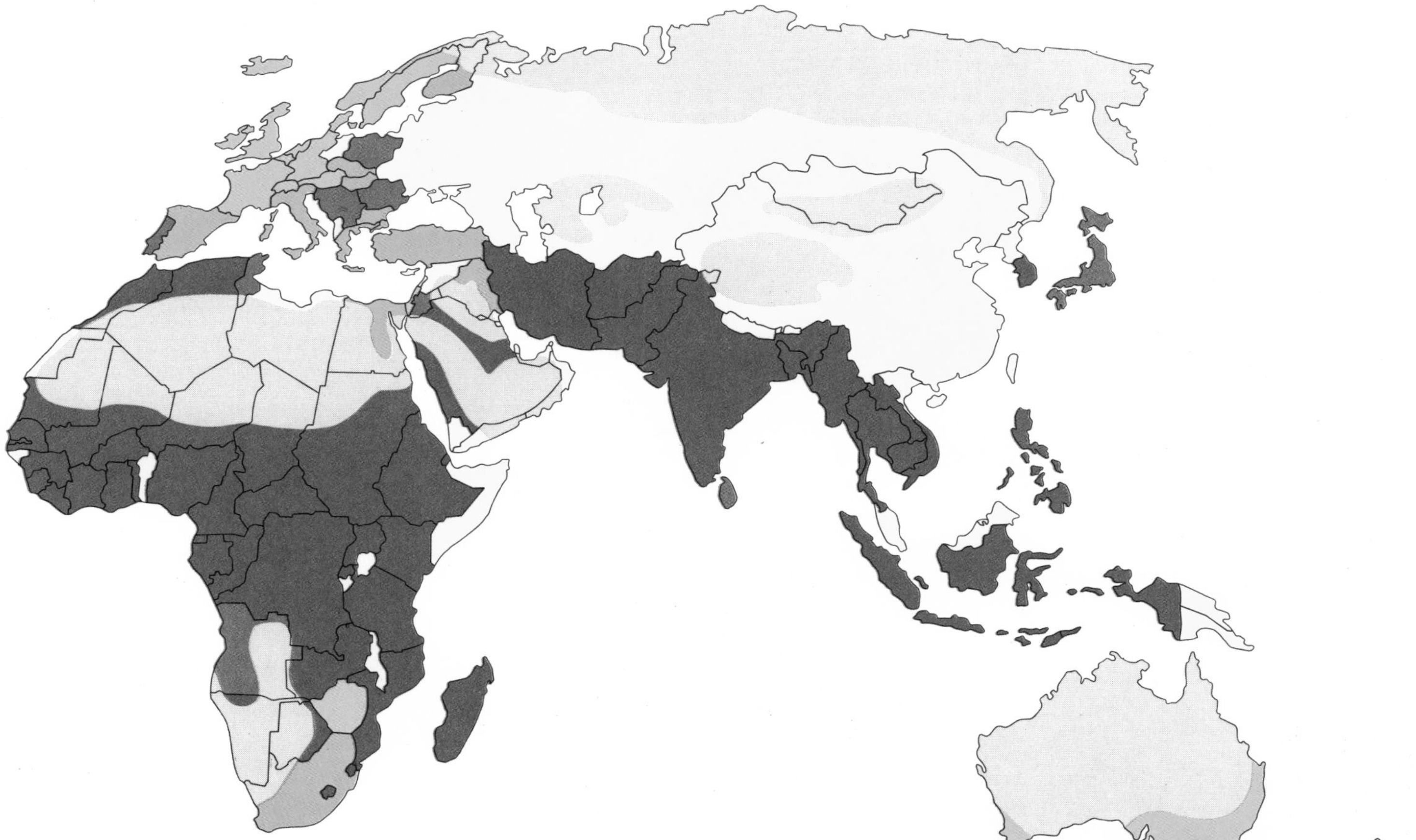

= 450-mile square containing 200,000 square miles

HOW WELL DO THE PEOPLE LIVE?

How many people can read and write?

All people, including those living in tribal groups, have some technical know-how, even if it is only the knowledge of how to hunt, fish, plant crops, and build shelters. But for a country to be able to progress economically, its people must develop their skills and abilities far beyond the tribal stage. The key to this development is education, and one measure of education in any country is the number of people who can read and write. If you compare this map with the map of technological development on page 20; you will see that the countries with highly developed technologies have a high percentage of people who can read and write.

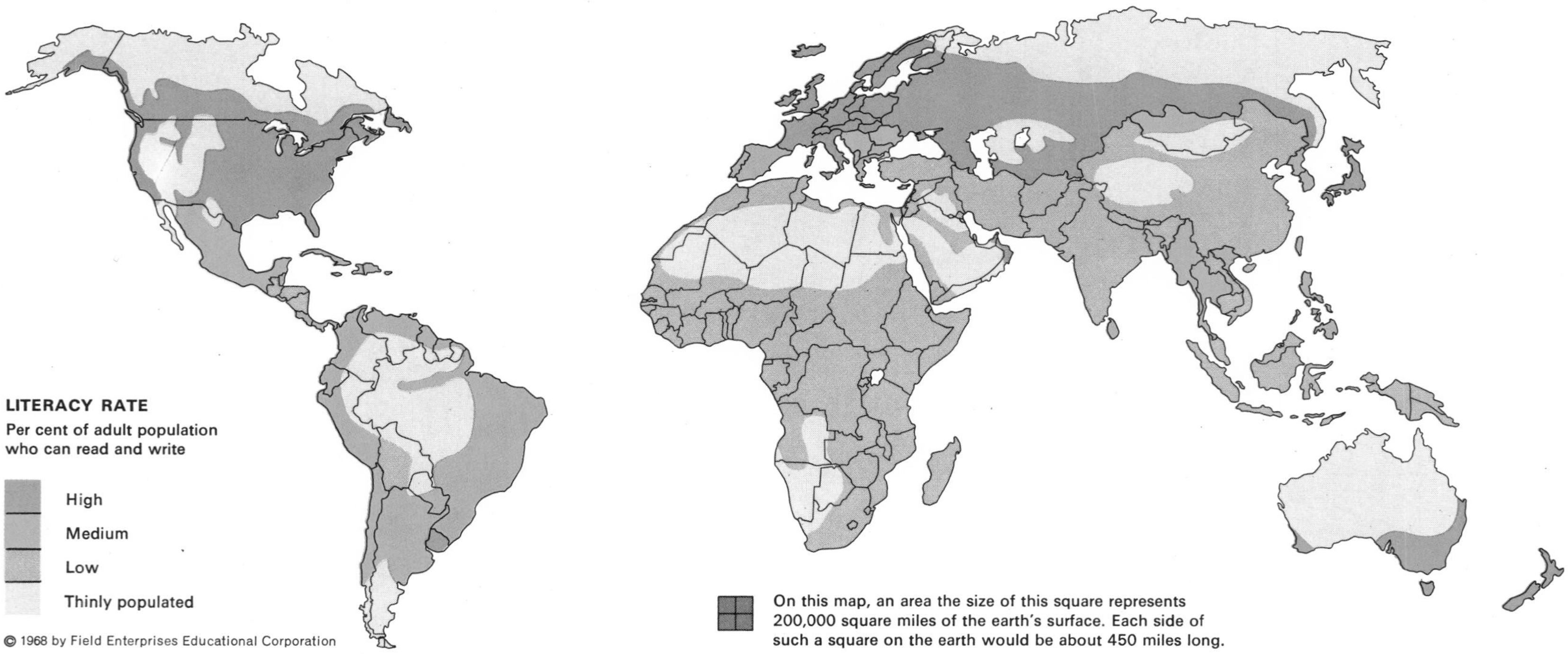

How many people have radios?

One of the great differences between advanced countries and countries with a low level of development is the way the people learn about what is happening in the world around them. In tribal groups, people spread the news by messenger and by signal drums and fires. In highly developed countries, almost everyone can hear about events taking place in all parts of the world by means of radio—and, in many countries, television. This map shows the number of radios per 1,000 people for each of the countries of the world. The figure ranges from a low of one radio for every 500 people in Afghanistan to a high of one radio for each person in the United States.

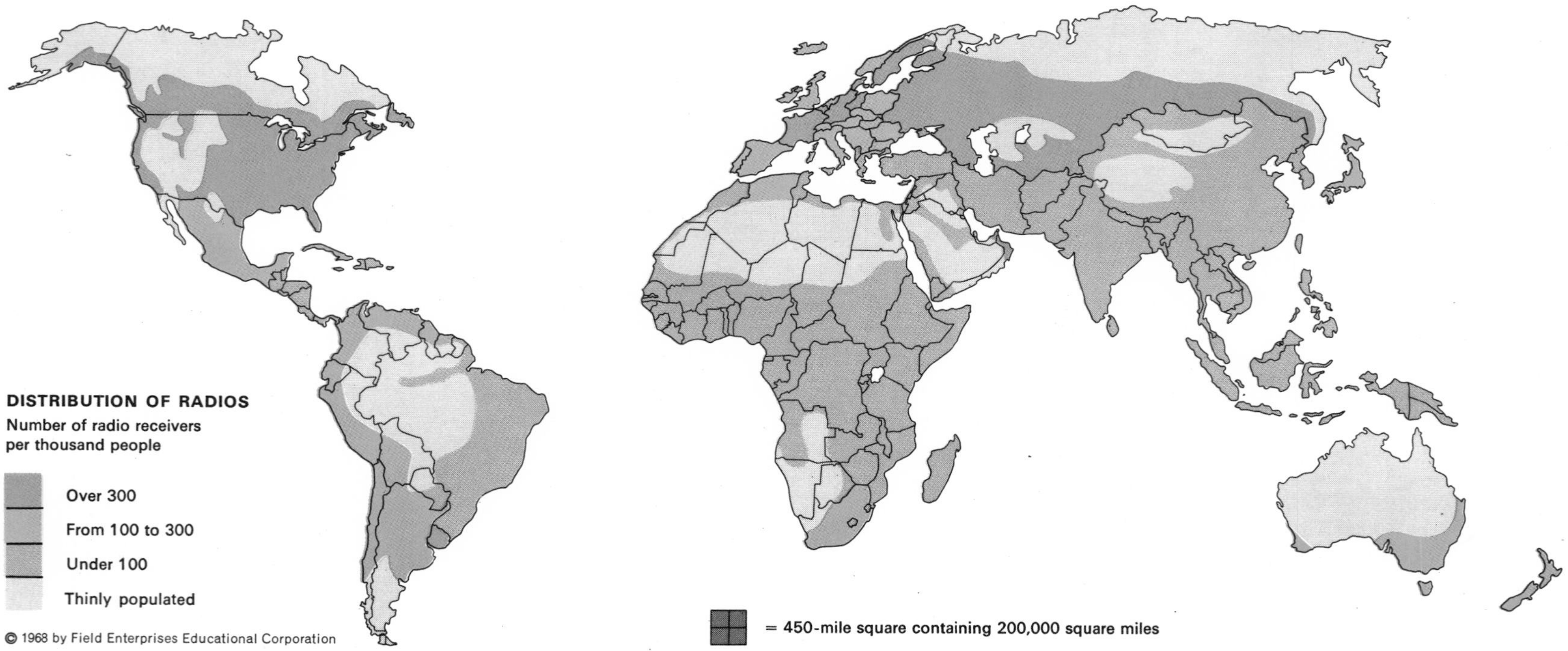

How many people have gone to school?

One of the most serious problems facing underdeveloped countries is the lack of enough wealth to provide the people with an adequate education. Before a country can achieve a high level of technological development, its people must learn many new skills. But the plight of the underdeveloped country is that it cannot afford to spend the money that building and operating schools requires. This map shows you that the countries with the greatest need to build their economies are also the countries with the poorest record of schooling.

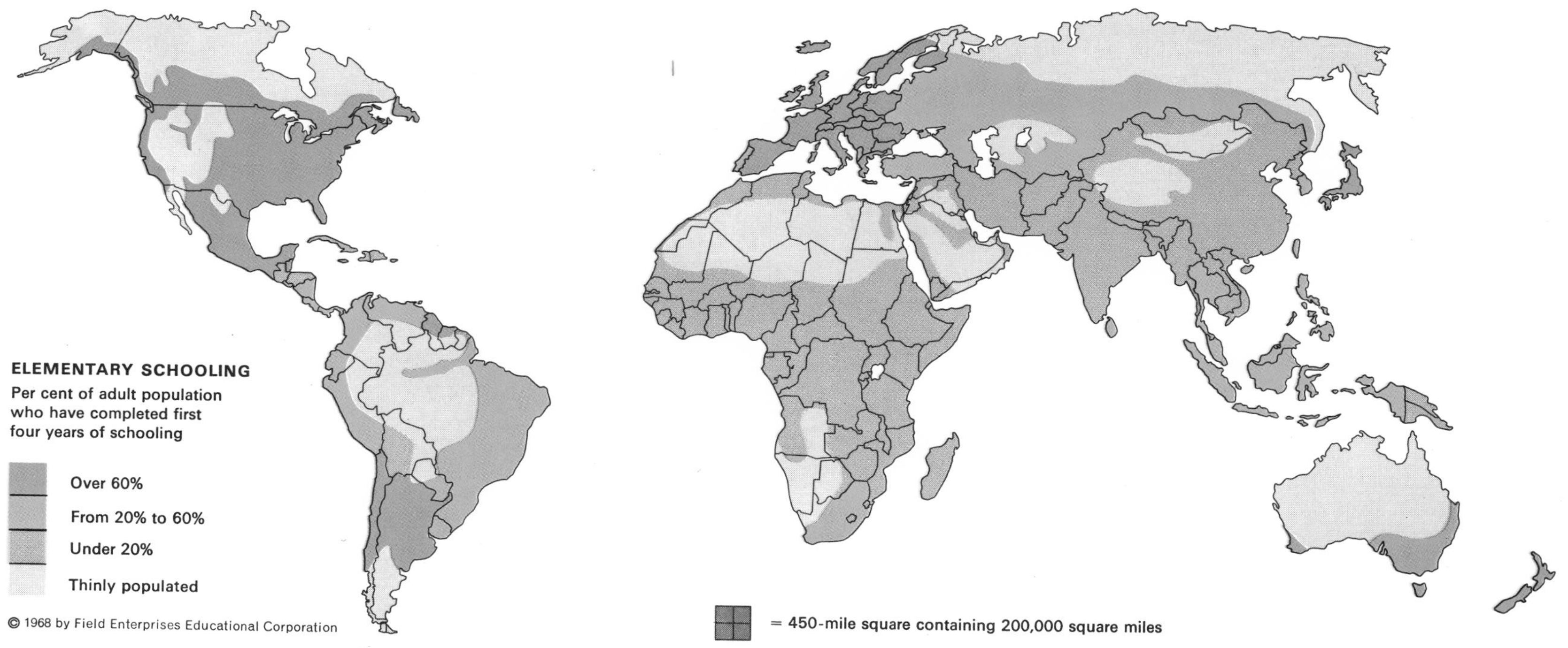

How many people read newspapers?

Newspapers, too, are an indicator of the level of development of any country. As a country becomes more industrialized and as living conditions improve, more and more of the people can and do read newspapers. But widespread newspaper readership is no guarantee of the people's well-being or of the degree of knowledge or information the newspapers contain. An oppressive government may shape newspapers to convey only the information it wants. The final answer to the question, "How well do the people live?" depends to a great extent on whether or not they are free to make the most of their skills, abilities, and resources.

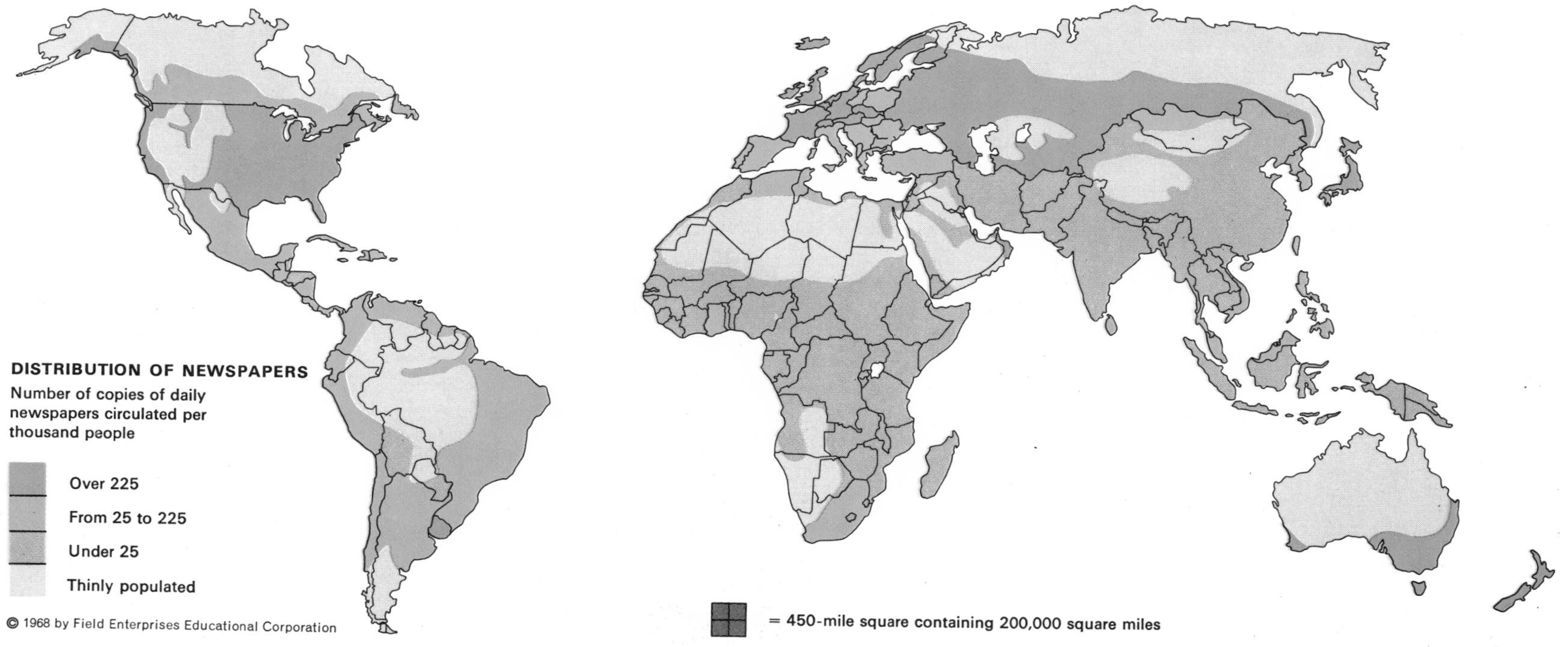

WHAT DOES THE EARTH LOOK LIKE FROM SPACE?

No one could really answer this question until 1961, when men first traveled in space. Astronauts took superb photographs of the earth from their speeding capsules. Photographs like these have given cartographers new tools to check the accuracy of their maps. You can do the same thing with these photographs.

Lake Titicaca lies in a plain between two ridges of the Andes, the Cordillera Oriental to the north and east, *foreground,* and the Cordillera Occidental to the south and west, *background.* The coast of Chile and the Pacific Ocean lie beyond. The *Gemini 9* capsule was about 150 miles above northwestern Bolivia at this point.

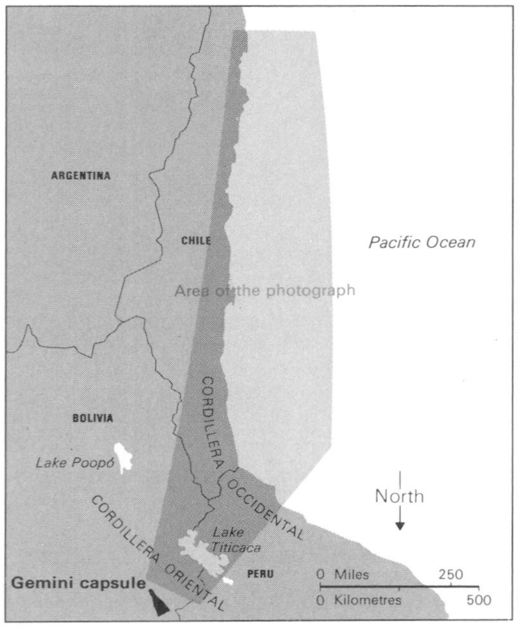

NASA photograph by Thomas P. Stafford and Eugene A. Cernan in *Gemini 9.*

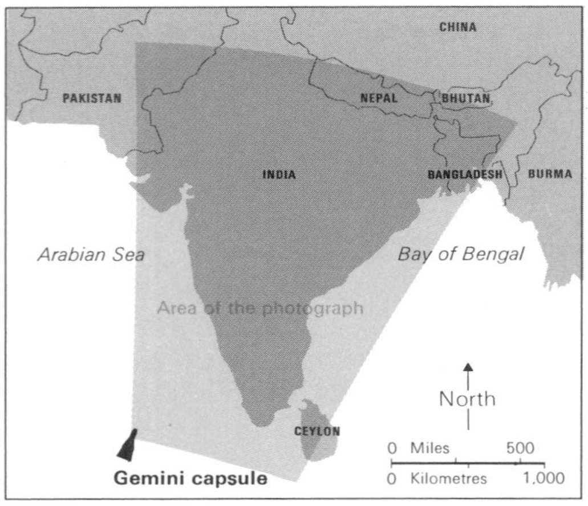

The southern tip of India and the northern tip of Ceylon lie between the Arabian Sea, *left,* and the Bay of Bengal, *right.* Tiny island groups such as the Laccadives and the Maldives are hidden under the clouds scattered over the Arabian Sea. The *Gemini 11* capsule was about 350 miles above the Indian Ocean at this point.

NASA photograph by Charles Conrad, Jr., and Richard F. Gordon, Jr., in *Gemini 11.*

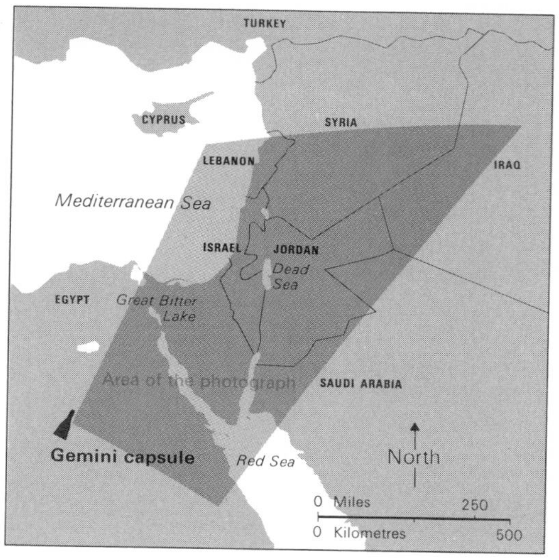

The Sinai Peninsula lies at the northern end of the Red Sea, with the Gulf of Suez, *left*, and the Gulf of Aqaba, *right*. This photograph, taken from *Gemini 11* about 200 miles above the earth, clearly shows the geological formation that includes the Gulf of Aqaba and the Dead Sea, as well as the man-made cut of the Suez Canal.

NASA photograph by Charles Conrad, Jr., and Richard F. Gordon, Jr., in *Gemini 11*.

WHAT DOES THE EARTH LOOK LIKE FROM SPACE?

Photographs taken from space give a vivid, panoramic view of an area. Many space pictures illuminate things that geographers find difficult to show clearly on maps. The photographs on these two pages, taken in 1964 and 1965 by astronauts in *Gemini 4* and *Gemini 5,* are examples of this fact.

The Colorado River drops large quantities of soil as it empties into the Gulf of California in northern Mexico. The San Andreas Fault (a break in the earth's crust) can be seen to the right of the river. This fault runs north for about 600 miles and earthquakes have occurred along it frequently. It separates the flat, sandy Sonora Desert, *right,* from rugged Baja California, *left.*

NASA photograph by James A. McDivitt and Edward H. White in *Gemini 4.*

The Salton Sea, *center,* and the Imperial Valley, *right,* lie below sea level in southern California. The photograph shows the sharp difference between the irrigated farming area of the Imperial Valley and the dry terrain of the surrounding mountains.

NASA photograph by L. Gordon Cooper and Charles Conrad, Jr., in *Gemini 5.*

NASA photograph by L. Gordon Cooper and Charles Conrad, Jr., in *Gemini 5.*

NASA photograph by James A. McDivitt and Edward H. White, Jr., in *Gemini 4.*

Mountain ranges such as the Karakoram, the northwestern extension of the Himalaya, appear as almost impassable barriers to land travel. The valley of the upper Indus River, *foreground,* is almost the only easy route through the rugged area.

Sand dunes in the barren, trackless wastes of southwestern Saudi Arabia present an even more forbidding picture. The Seif Dunes, blown into wave on wave of sand by the prevailing winds of the area, resemble wind-formed waves of water.

WHAT DOES THE LAND LOOK LIKE?

This map shows what the land around you looks like wherever you might be on the earth. Eight classes of land surface are shown. But when an area is given a name to describe what its land surface looks like, the entire area need not look exactly like its name. For example, flat plains are not perfectly flat. Hills may rise from them, and ditches may cut into them. They are called flat plains because they are mostly flat. Most mountain areas have some low hills and even some flat places between the mountains.

The colors on this map do not show how high above sea level any area is. A flat plain in one part of the world may be thousands of feet higher above sea level than a flat plain somewhere else. Yet, to a person who saw them, both plains would look alike. And so, all flat plains are the same color on this map, no matter how high they are.

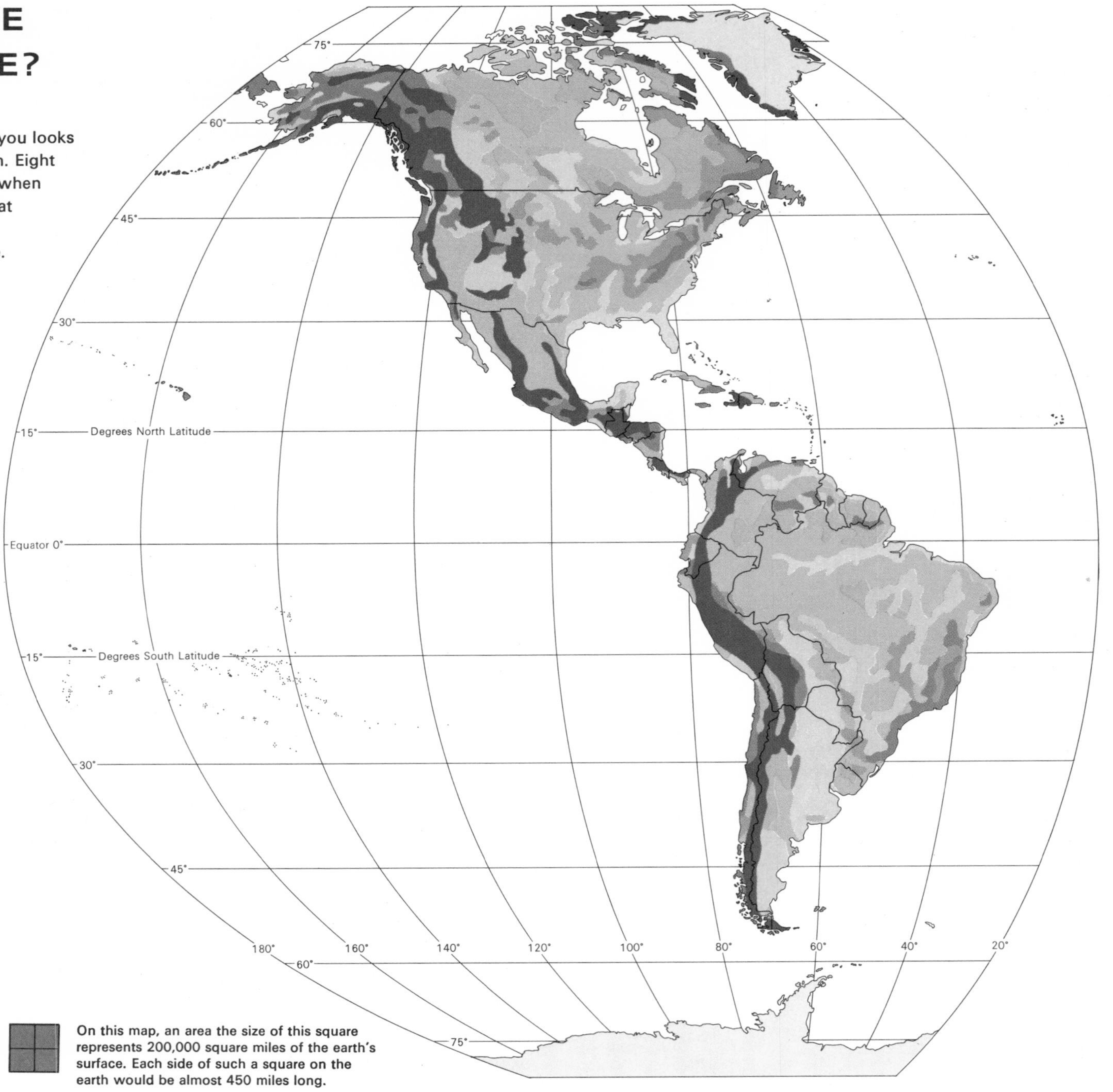

CLASSES OF LAND-SURFACE FORM

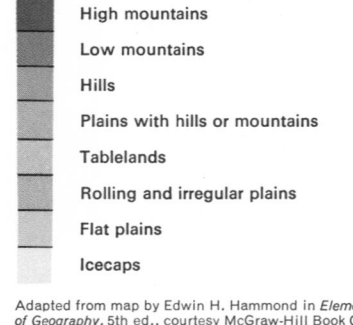

- High mountains
- Low mountains
- Hills
- Plains with hills or mountains
- Tablelands
- Rolling and irregular plains
- Flat plains
- Icecaps

Adapted from map by Edwin H. Hammond in *Elements of Geography*, 5th ed., courtesy McGraw-Hill Book Co.

On this map, an area the size of this square represents 200,000 square miles of the earth's surface. Each side of such a square on the earth would be almost 450 miles long.

Hills and mountains have caused problems for man throughout history. Although some people grow crops on hillsides, most hill and mountain areas are not good for farming. For a long time, an even greater problem was the transportation barrier that man faced when he reached high hills or mountains. Until he found a way around, through, or over the barrier, his movement was stopped. In some areas, the problem was especially difficult because some mountain chains extend across entire continents. The photograph, *lower left,* shows high mountains in Nepal. The photograph, *lower right,* illustrates a plain with hills in Nigeria.

WORLD BOOK photo

Max C. Kirkeberg

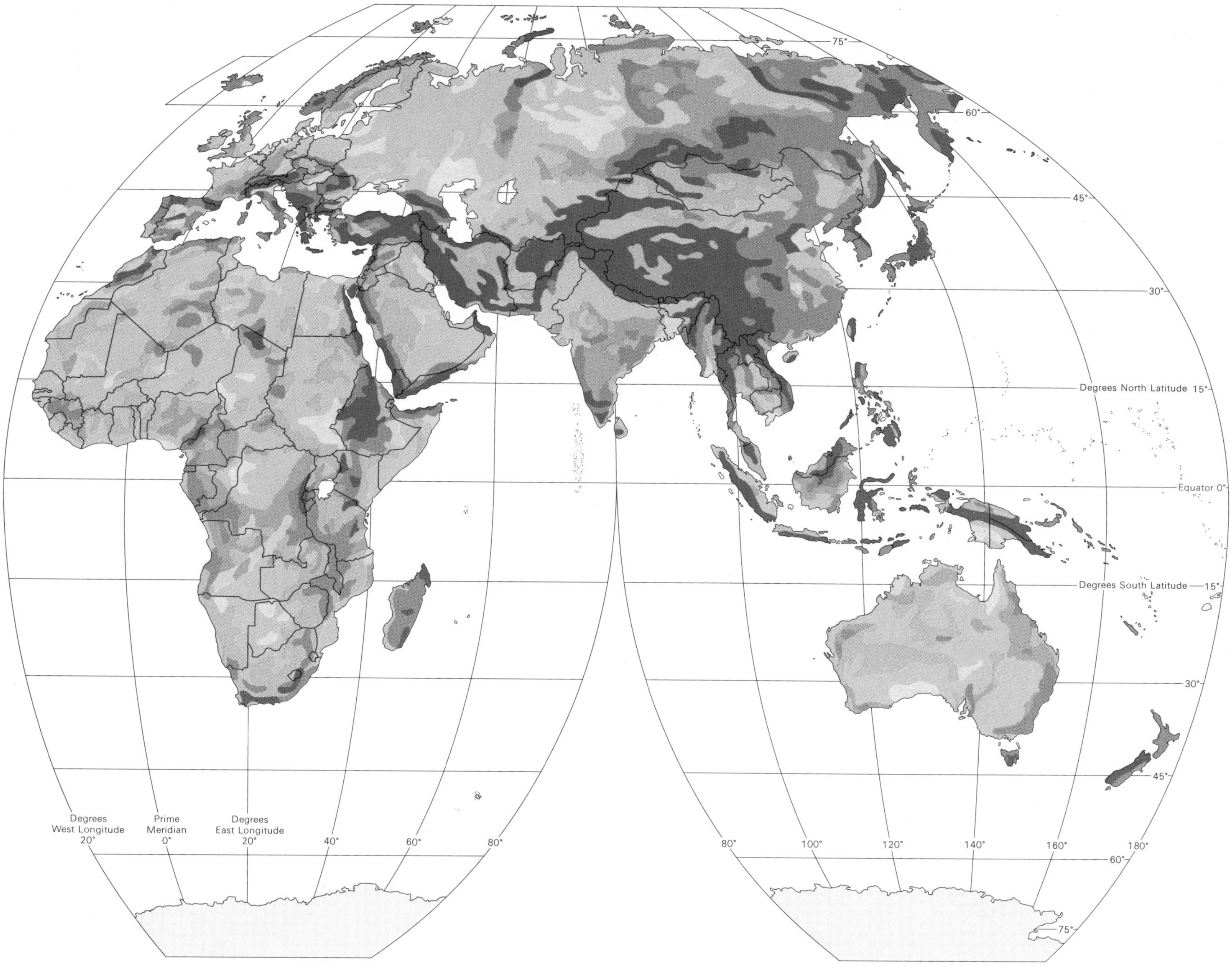

Plains are important to man because they are the easiest land surface on which to farm, build, and move about. But some plains are harder for man to use than others. Some plains are always damp and muddy, others are flooded during certain seasons, and still others are dry and sandy. Some plains are covered with rich soil, but others are rocky. The photograph, *lower left,* shows rolling plains in Wisconsin. These plains combine crop-raising and dairy farming in addition to having scattered wooded sections. The photograph, *lower right,* shows flat plains in Argentina. These plains are used almost exclusively for crop-raising.

Joe Fire, Shostal

Stockpile

WHAT IS THE WEATHER LIKE?

The weather on any day at any place on the earth depends on such things as temperature, moisture, wind, and cloudiness. As these weathermakers change, different types of weather occur. Sometimes very unusual weather occurs. Rain can fall on deserts and very cool days can come in the middle of the hot summer. But most places do not get unusual weather for too long. In most places, weather occurs in a regular pattern that repeats year after year. We call the pattern of weather over a year *climate*.

The colors on the large map on these pages show temperature change from season to season for any place on the earth. In general, temperatures are similar along any given latitude, and they change as latitude changes. You can see that the different colors seem to extend around the earth and that they change as you move away from the equator. But although temperatures are related to latitude, the patterns are not perfectly even. Variations occur because of the effects of bodies of water, mountains, and other surface features.

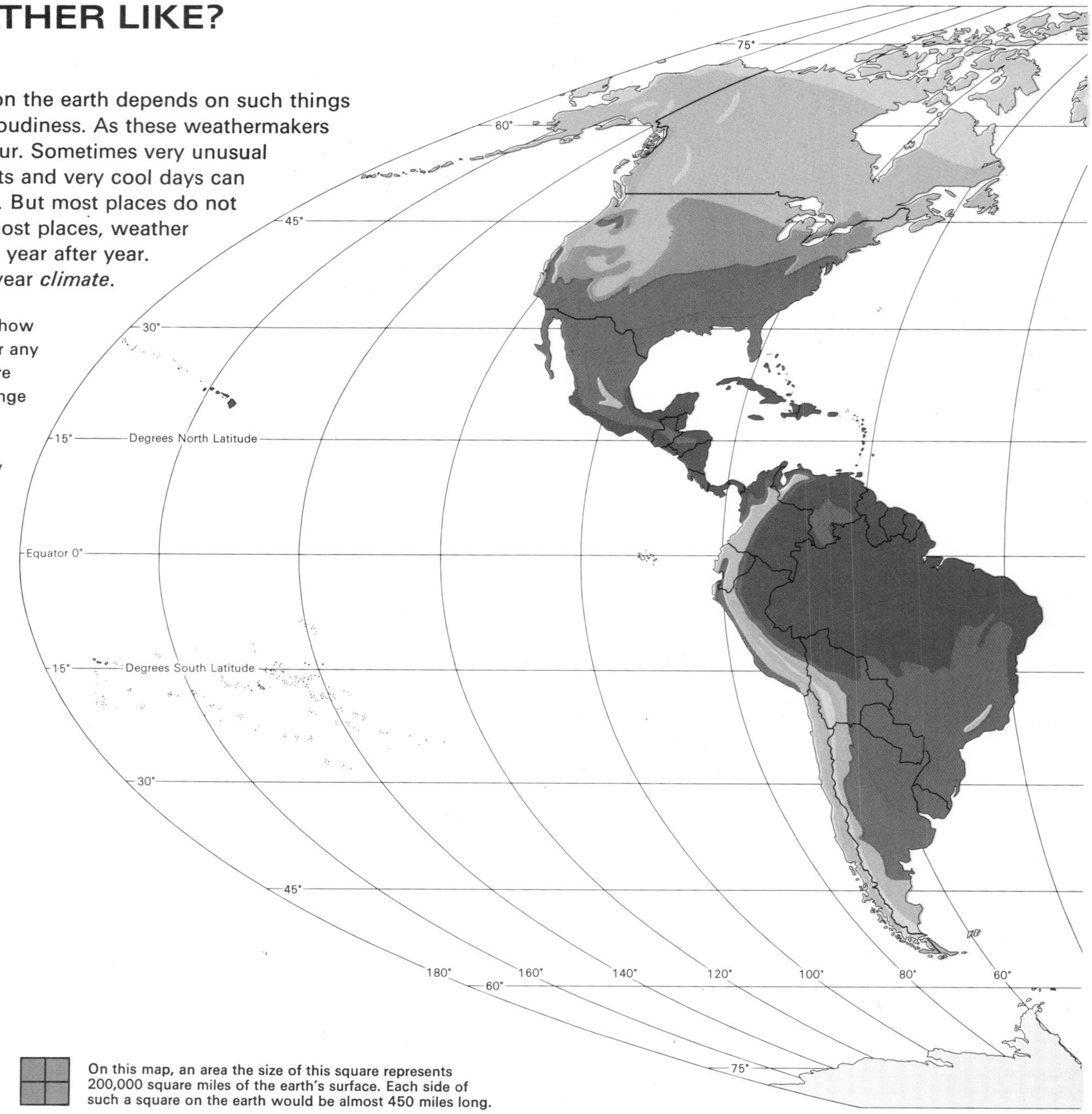

TEMPERATURE REGIONS

The terms *hot*, *mild*, *cool*, and *cold* are determined by the average temperatures for the warmest and coolest months.

Hot = above 68° F. Cool = 32° to 50° F.
Mild = 50° to 68° F. Cold = below 32° F.

- Always hot
- Hot summer, mild winter
- Hot summer, cool winter
- Hot summer, cold winter
- Mild summer, cool winter
- Always mild
- Cold winter, mild summer
- Cold winter, cool summer
- Always cold

From map by A. E. Parkins

On this map, an area the size of this square represents 200,000 square miles of the earth's surface. Each side of such a square on the earth would be almost 450 miles long.

What is the temperature in January?

As the earth revolves around the sun, the sun's most direct rays reach different latitudes at different times of the year. In January, the direct rays have just reached their farthest southern point on the earth. So January is generally the warmest month for people living in the southern half of the earth and the coldest month for people living in the northern half. Notice that, on this map, the area of warmest temperatures is south of the equator.

JANUARY AVERAGE TEMPERATURE

- Above 86° F. (Above 30° C.)
- 68° to 86° F. (20° to 30° C.)
- 50° to 68° F. (10° to 20° C.)
- 32° to 50° F. (0° to 10° C.)
- 14° to 32° F. (–10° to 0° C.)
- –4° to 14° F. (–20° to –10° C.)
- –40° to –4° F. (–40° to –20° C.)
- Below –40° F. (Below –40° C.)

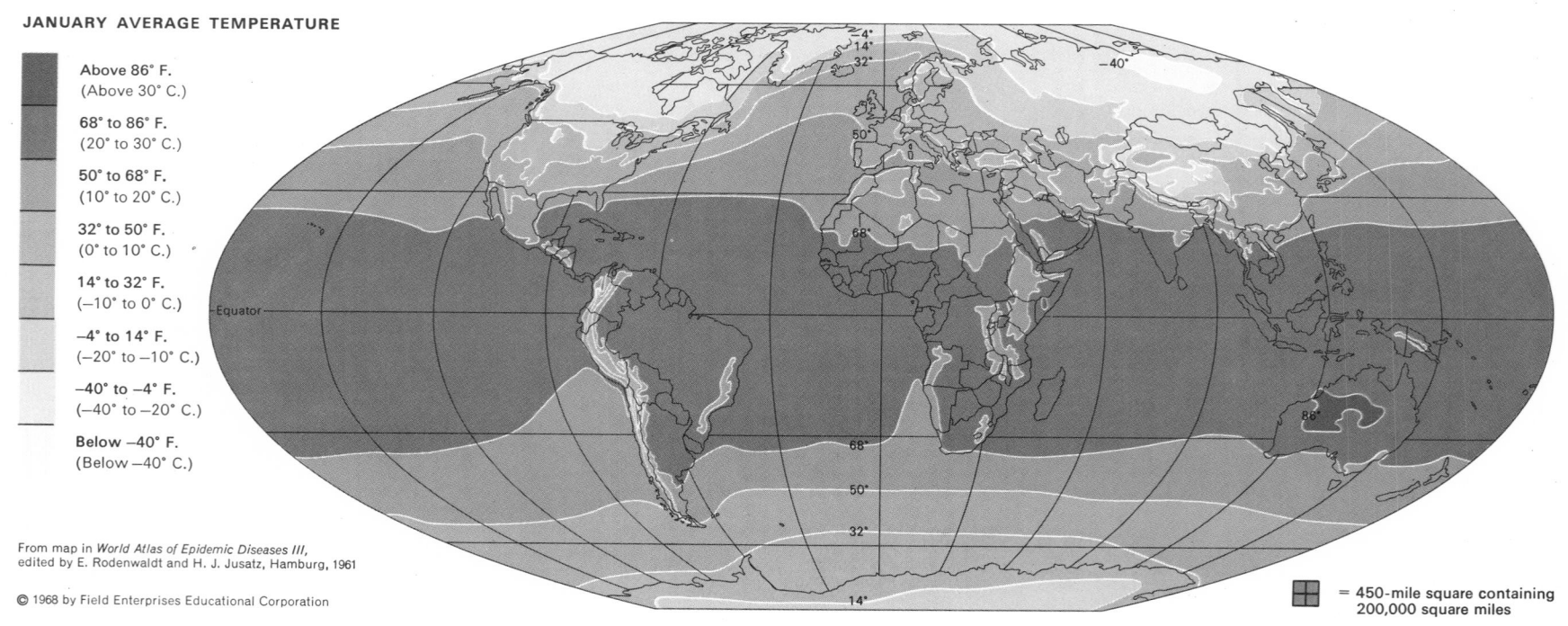

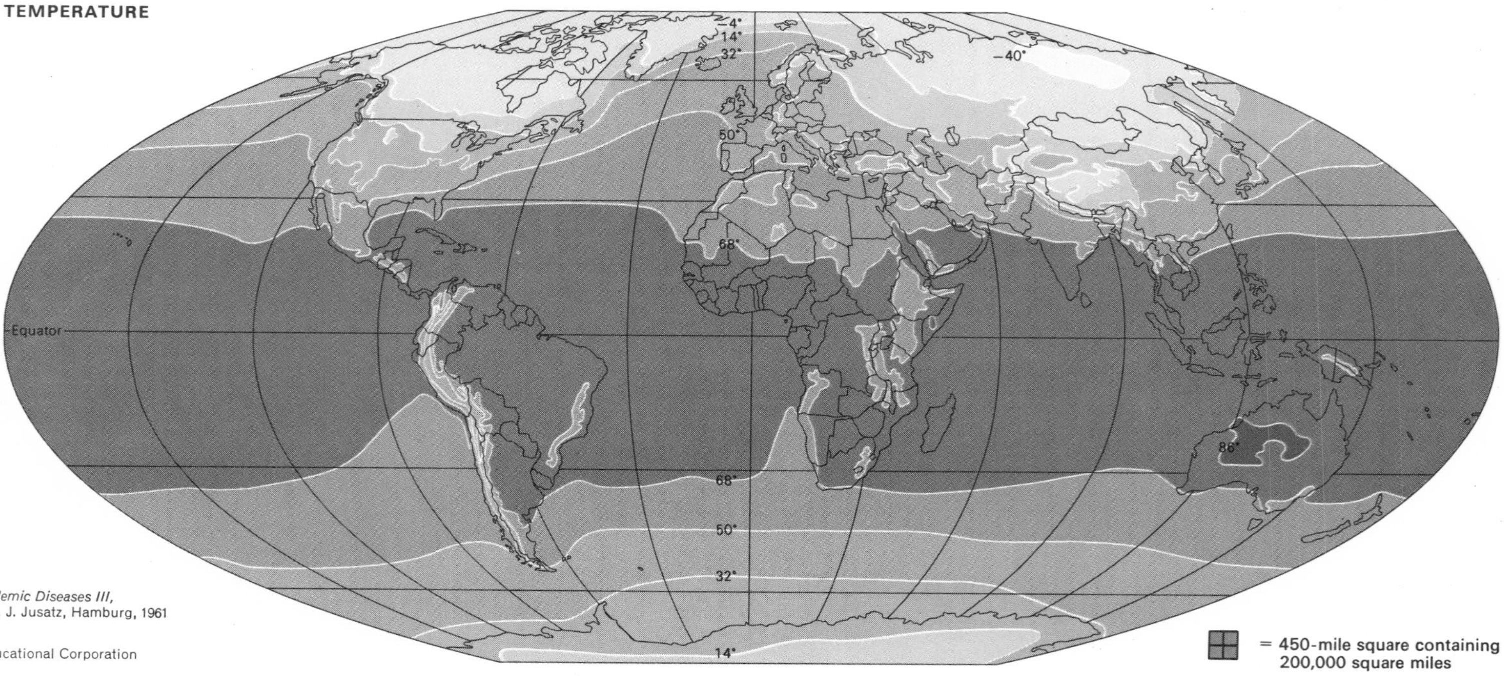

From map in *World Atlas of Epidemic Diseases III*, edited by E. Rodenwaldt and H. J. Jusatz, Hamburg, 1961

= 450-mile square containing 200,000 square miles

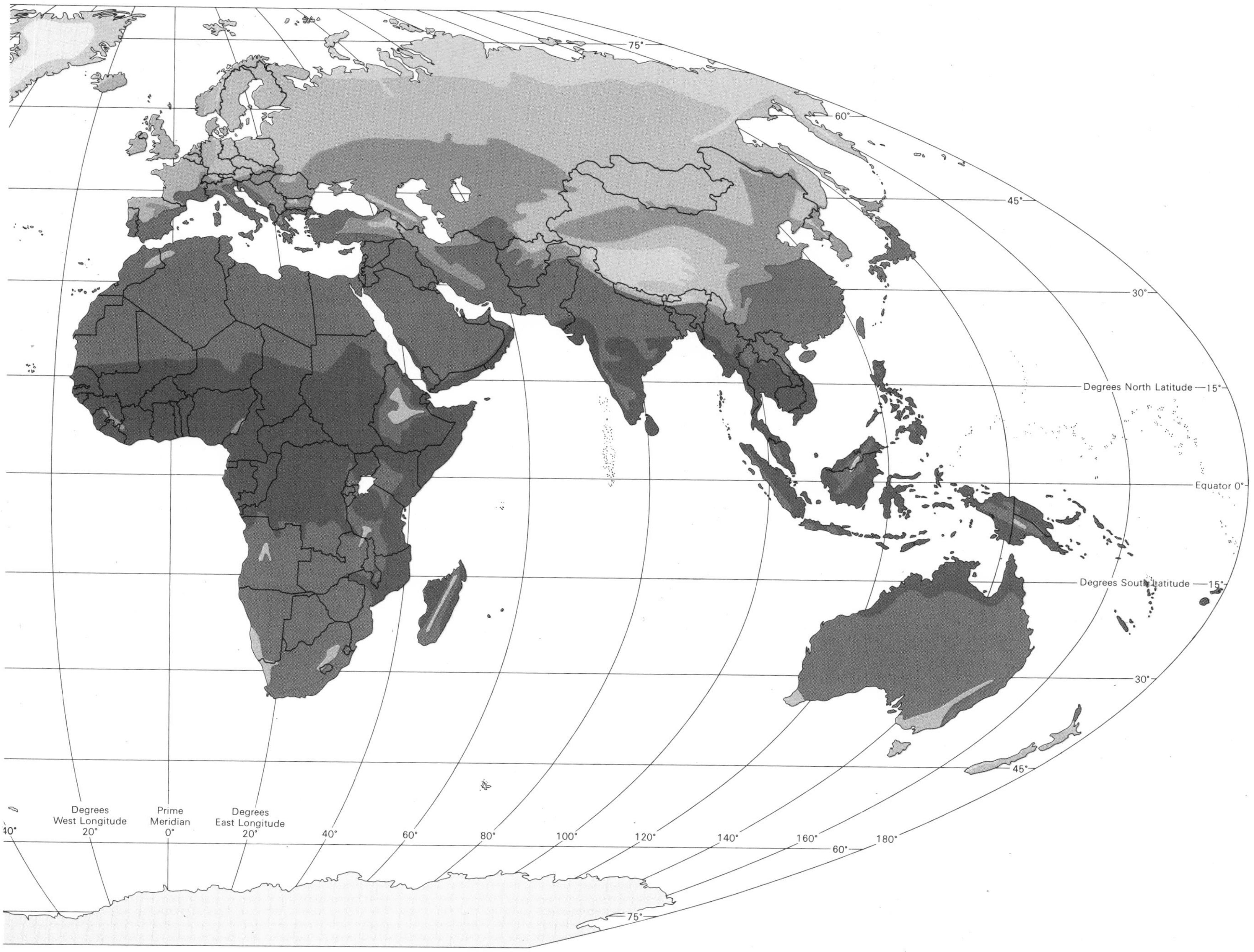

What is the temperature in July?

In July, the direct rays of the sun have just reached their farthest northern point. So July is generally the warmest month for people living in the northern half of the earth and the coldest month for people living in the southern half. Notice that, on this map, the area of warmest temperatures is north of the equator. The area around the equator itself is never far from the sun's direct rays, so it has little temperature change from month to month.

JULY AVERAGE TEMPERATURE

- Above 86° F. (Above 30° C.)
- 68° to 86° F. (20° to 30° C.)
- 50° to 68° F. (10° to 20° C.)
- 32° to 50° F. (0° to 10° C.)
- 14° to 32° F. (−10° to 0° C.)
- −4° to 14° F. (−20° to −10° C.)
- Below −4° F. (Below −20° C.)

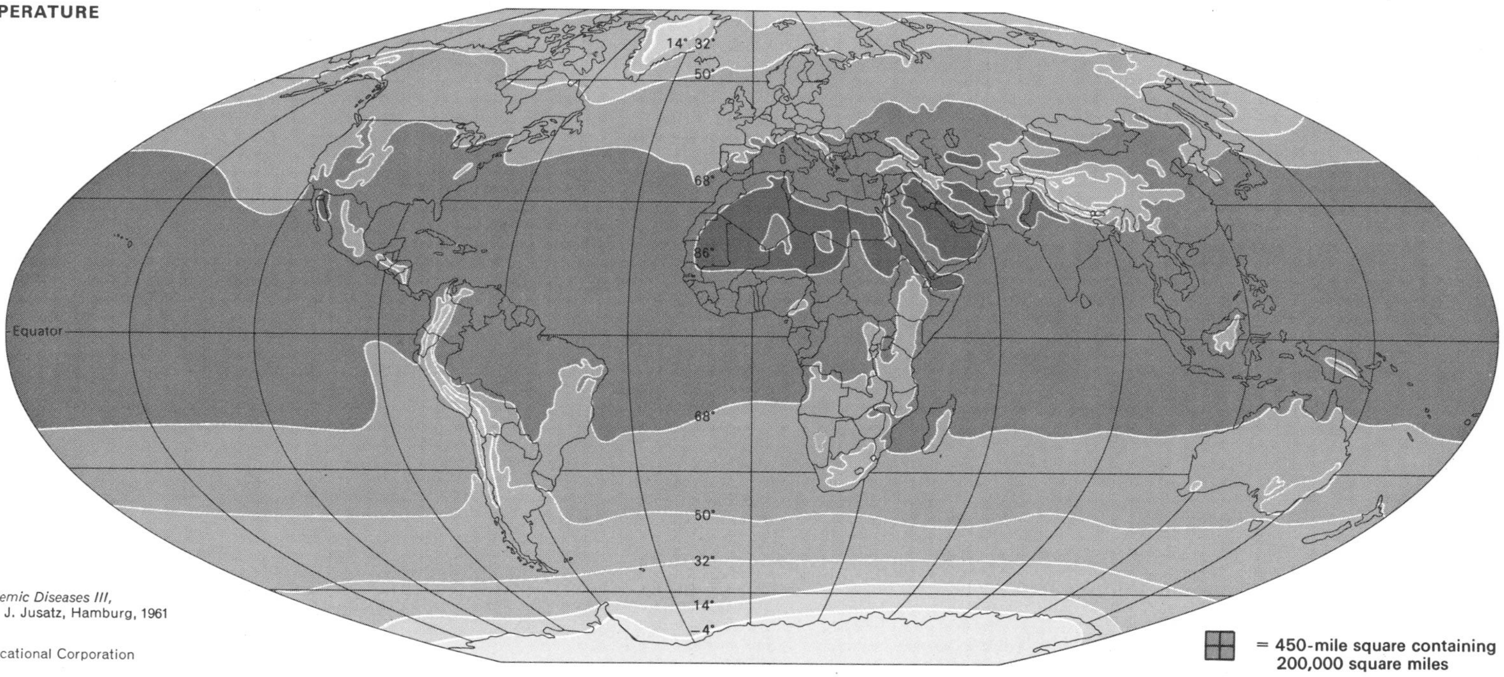

From map in *World Atlas of Epidemic Diseases III*, edited by E. Rodenwaldt and H. J. Jusatz, Hamburg, 1961

= 450-mile square containing 200,000 square miles

WHAT IS THE WEATHER LIKE?

How wet or dry is it?

In order to be able to tell whether an area is a wet area or a dry area, you must first know how much *precipitation* (rain, snow, and other moisture) is likely to fall there during a year. This map shows the total amount of precipitation that falls at any place on the earth during an average year. But this alone does not tell the whole story. Wetness or dryness also depends on how fast the precipitation evaporates, soaks into the ground, or runs into streams and rivers. It is interesting to note that although little precipitation falls at the North and South Poles, the temperatures there are so low that the precipitation cannot evaporate. Instead, snow accumulates on the ground.

Notice on the map that most of the areas of high precipitation lie in a band around the equator. Also, for many areas, precipitation is greatest along coastlines and it decreases as you move inland. If you compare this map with the population map on pages 14 and 15, you will see that most of the world's very dry areas have little or no population.

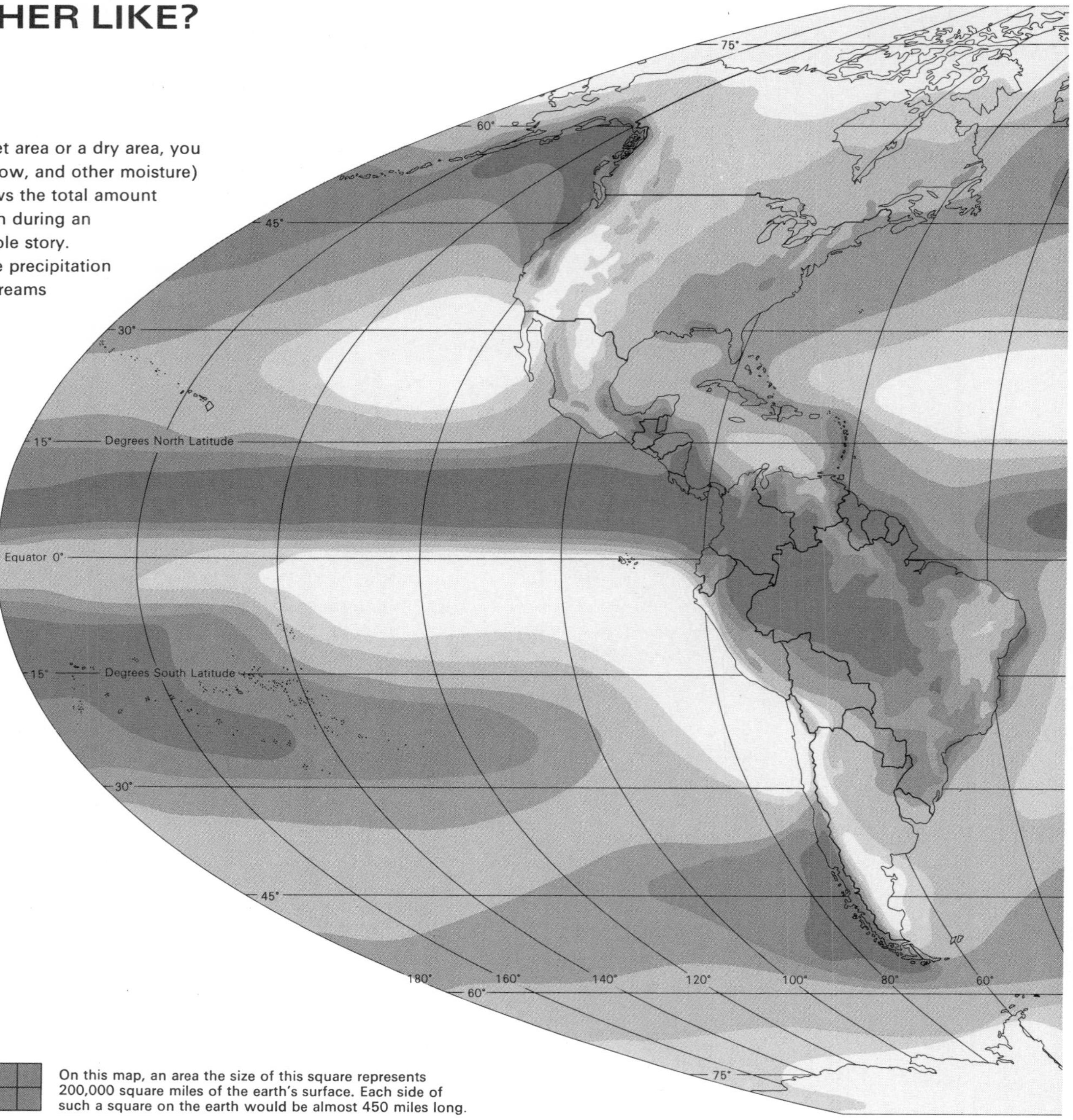

TOTAL YEARLY PRECIPITATION
(Rain, melted snow, and other moisture)

- Over 80 in. (over 200 cm.)
- 60 to 80 in. (150 to 200 cm.)
- 40 to 60 in. (100 to 150 cm.)
- 20 to 40 in. (50 to 100 cm.)
- 10 to 20 in. (25 to 50 cm.)
- Under 10 in. (Under 25 cm.)

From map in *World Atlas of Epidemic Diseases III*, edited by E. Rodenwaldt and H. J. Jusatz, Hamburg, 1961

On this map, an area the size of this square represents 200,000 square miles of the earth's surface. Each side of such a square on the earth would be almost 450 miles long.

When is it wettest?

After precipitation has fallen, it either evaporates, soaks into the ground, or runs off into streams and rivers. But if too much falls, or if it falls too quickly, these ways of eliminating the water may not work well enough, and the area will flood. This explains why sometimes floods occur in a desert following a short, but heavy, rainstorm. This map shows you the seasons when flooding can occur because of too much precipitation.

SEASON OF MAXIMUM RUN-OFF

- Spring
- Summer
- Autumn
- Winter
- Sporadic
- No data

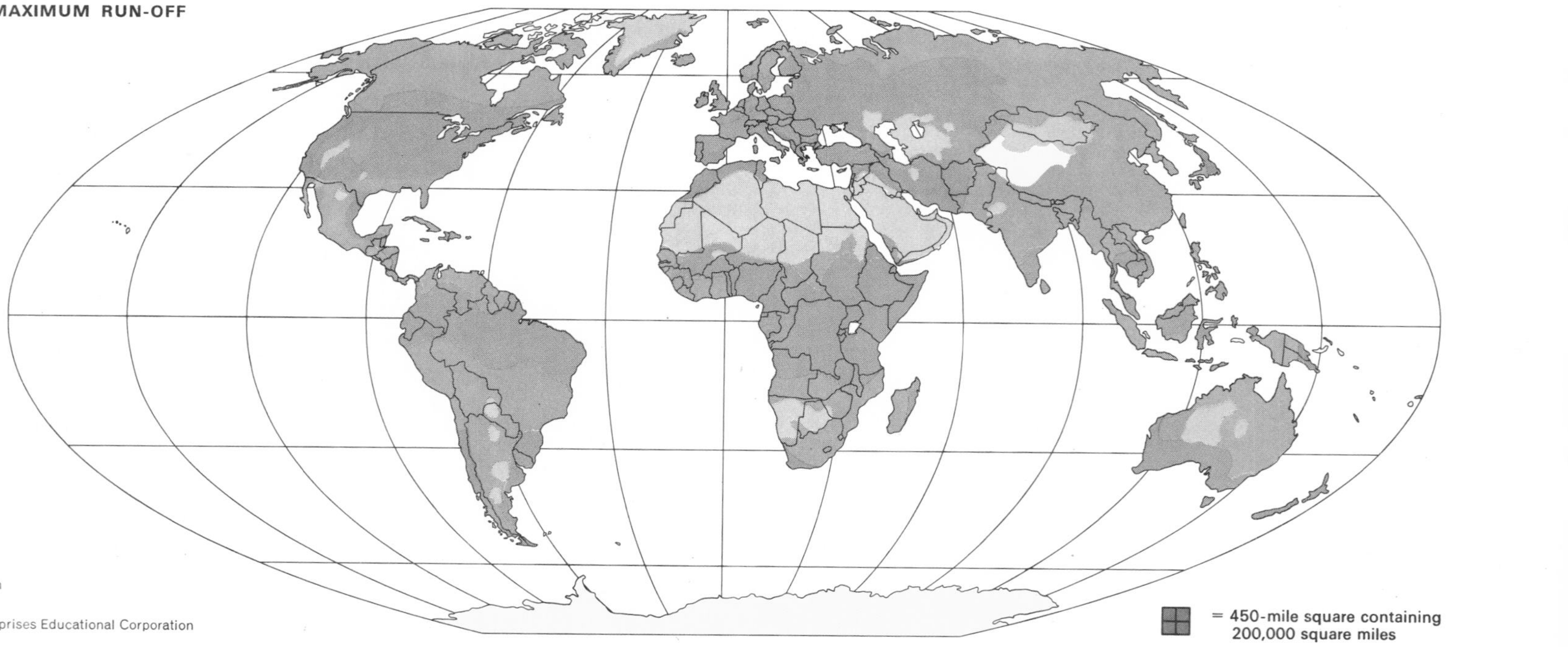

From map by L'vovich

= 450-mile square containing 200,000 square miles

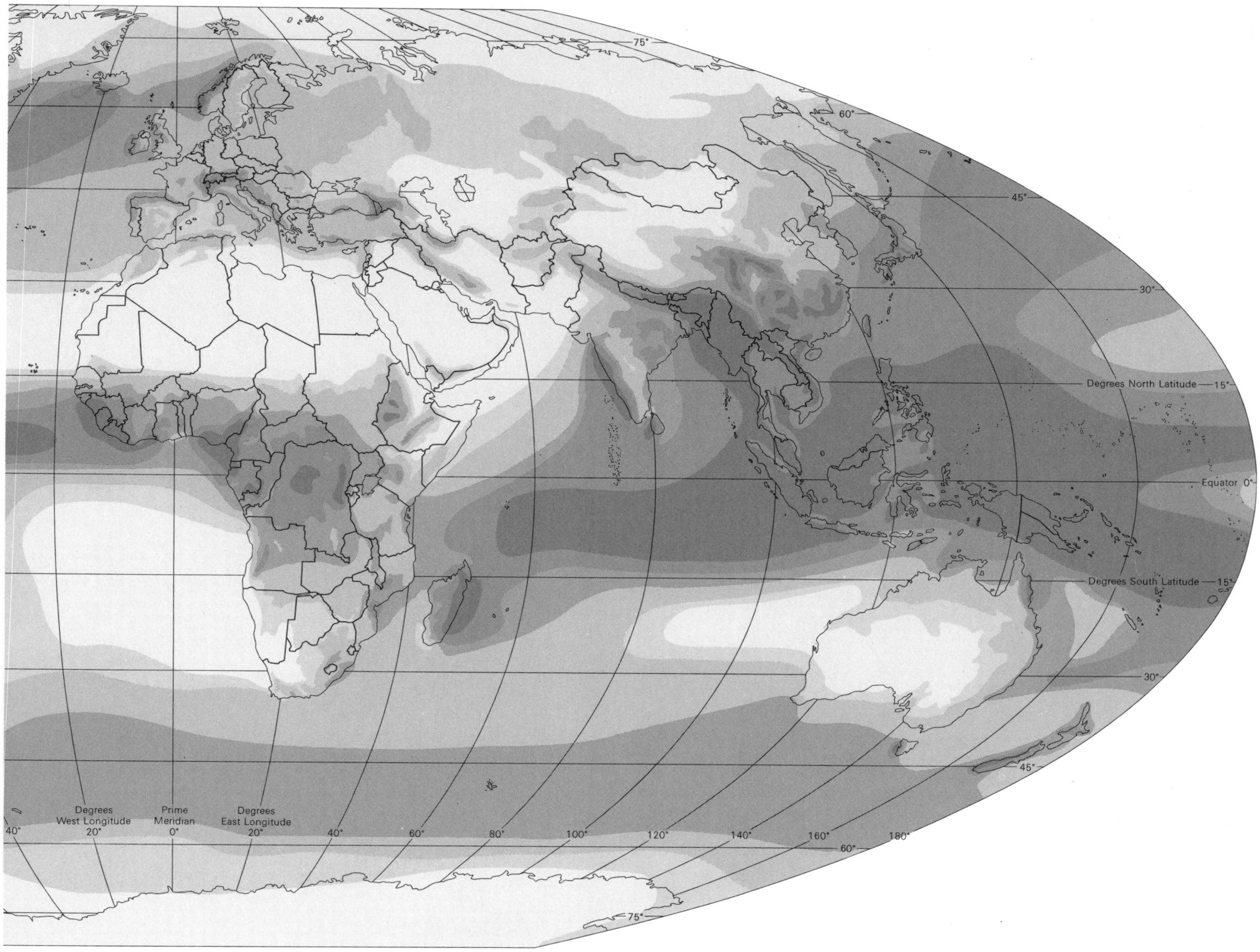

Where is it sunniest?

This map shows you the total number of hours of sunshine any area of the earth is likely to receive during a year. Notice that it is sunniest along the latitudes just north and south of the equator. It is not sunniest at the equator itself, because air conditions often produce clouds there. If you compare this map with the large map *above*, you can see that the areas of greatest sunshine very nearly match the areas of lowest rainfall.

TOTAL HOURS OF SUNSHINE

Number of hours of sunshine per year

- 3,200 to 4,200
- 2,400 to 3,200
- 1,600 to 2,400
- 600 to 1,600

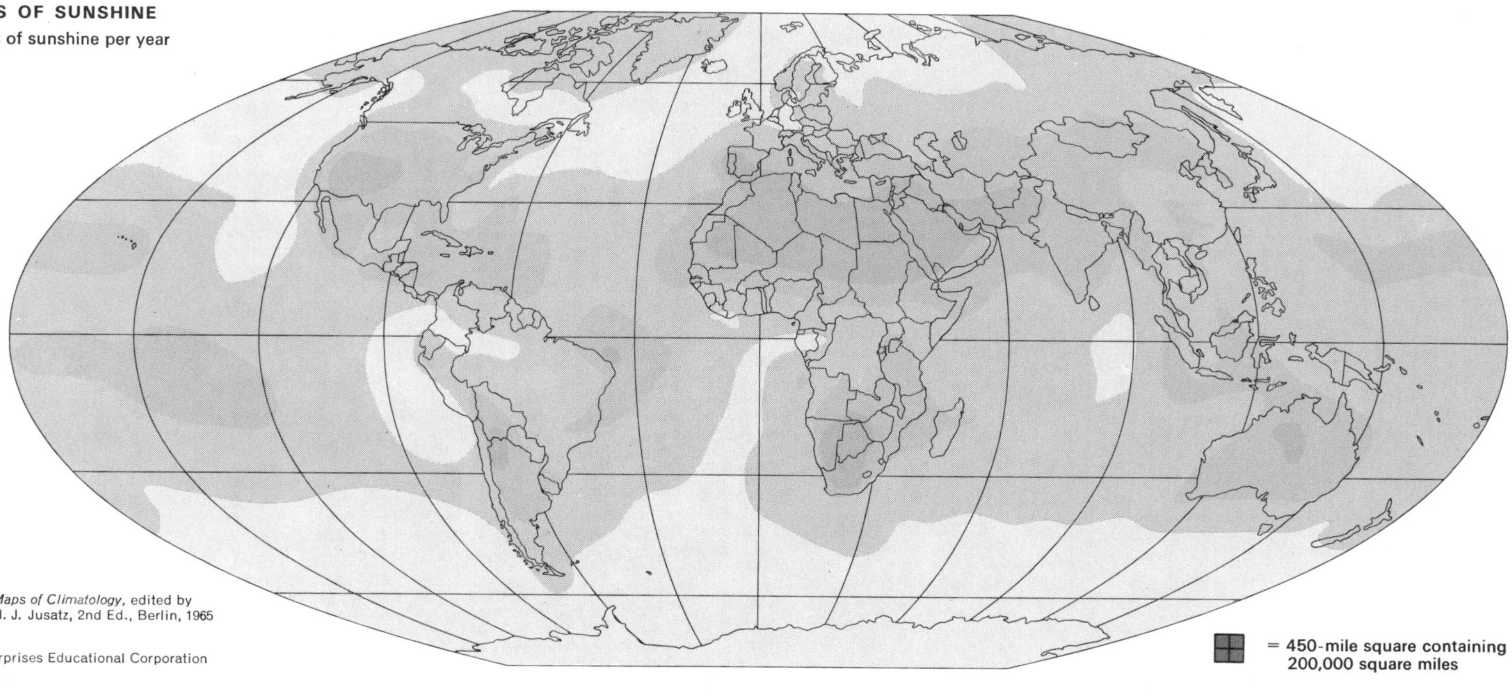

From map in *World Maps of Climatology*, edited by E. Rodenwaldt and H. J. Jusatz, 2nd Ed., Berlin, 1965

= 450-mile square containing 200,000 square miles

NYSTROM map by Richard Edes Harrison

EUROPE

Europe is the second smallest continent. Only Australia covers less area. But Europe has an importance far beyond its size as the birthplace of western civilization. Europe provided the beginning of democracy, the cultural explosion of the Renaissance, and the early inventions of the Industrial Revolution. European explorers, settlers, traders, and soldiers carried the western way of life throughout the world. Today, the Cold War has divided the nations of Europe into two competing groups. Western Europe includes such leading nations of the Free World as Great Britain, France, Italy, and West Germany. Eastern Europe is dominated by Russia and its communist satellites.

WHAT IS YOUR ATLAS I.Q. OF EUROPE?

These questions are designed to test your knowledge of the variety of information about Europe contained in The World Book Atlas. Check your answers by turning to the last page of the Atlas.

Identifying places

1. Four European countries consist entirely of islands. Two are Ireland and Great Britain. What are the other two?
2. Three European countries border on the Adriatic Sea. Two of these are Yugoslavia and Albania. What is the third?
3. The eastern border of France has been crossed many times by invading armies. Four of the countries that border France on the east are Belgium, Luxembourg, West Germany, and Italy. What is the fifth?
4. Western Russia has also been the scene of many historic battles. Which of these countries does *not* lie along Russia's western border—Poland, Finland, Czechoslovakia, or Austria?
5. What mountain range forms the border between France and Spain?

Facts and figures

6. Europe is the second smallest continent in area. But how does it rank among the continents in population?
7. Which of these countries has the largest population—West Germany, Great Britain, or France?
8. Which of these European capitals is farthest west—London, Paris, or Madrid?
9. The famous Strait of Dover between England and France is only 21 miles wide at its narrowest point. Dover is the English city at this point. But what is the French village that lies closest to England?
10. The "beautiful blue Danube" flows through three European capitals. Two of these are Vienna and Belgrade. What is the third?
11. The Volga is another famous European river. Into what body of water does it empty?
12. Stockholm is the capital of Sweden, and Oslo is the capital of Norway. What is the capital of Denmark?

History

13. What is the modern name of the area that the ancient Romans called Gaul?
14. The Battle of Waterloo in 1815 marked the final downfall of Napoleon I. In what present-day country is Waterloo located?
15. During World War I, Germany and its three allies were known as the Central Powers. Two of Germany's allies were Austria-Hungary and Bulgaria. What was the third?
16. The end of World War I saw new nations formed in Europe. Which one of these countries did *not* exist before World War I—Belgium, Romania, or Yugoslavia?
17. The Munich Agreement gave a large part of Czechoslovakia to Hitler's Germany before World War II. In what year was the agreement signed?
18. Estonia, Latvia, and Lithuania lost their independence during World War II. To what country do they now belong?
19. Which of these European countries did not become a member of NATO—Spain, Great Britain, Italy, or Norway?
20. Which one of these European nations does not belong to the United Nations—Switzerland, France, Italy, or Spain?

MAPS OF EUROPE

40 **PHYSICAL FEATURES OF EUROPE**
41 **POLITICAL DIVISIONS OF EUROPE**
42-54 **HISTORY OF EUROPE**
42 ANCIENT WORLD (600's B.C.)
42 CLASSICAL GREECE (ABOUT 450 B.C.)
43 ALEXANDER'S EMPIRE (323 B.C.)
44 ROMAN REPUBLIC (ABOUT 44 B.C.)
45 ROMAN EMPIRE (120 A.D.)
46 ROMAN EMPIRE (400 A.D.)
47 THE CRUSADES (ABOUT 1140)
48 EUROPE ABOUT 1360
49 EUROPE IN 1721
50 EUROPE IN 1810 AND 1815
51 UNIFICATION OF ITALY
51 UNIFICATION OF GERMANY
52 BEFORE WORLD WAR I (1914)
53 AFTER WORLD WAR I (1922 TO 1940)
54 AFTER WORLD WAR II
55-73 **MAPS OF COUNTRIES AND DEPENDENCIES**
69 ALBANIA
65 ANDORRA
60 AUSTRIA
59 BELGIUM
68 BULGARIA
70 CZECHOSLOVAKIA
62 DENMARK
56, 57 ENGLAND
63 FINLAND
58 FRANCE
59-62 GERMANY
55 GREAT BRITAIN
69 GREECE
68 HUNGARY
63 ICELAND
55 IRELAND
67 ITALY
66 LIECHTENSTEIN
59 LUXEMBOURG
64 MALTA
64 MONACO
59 NETHERLANDS
55 NORTHERN IRELAND
63 NORWAY
70 POLAND
65 PORTUGAL
68 ROMANIA
71-73 RUSSIA
67 SAN MARINO
57 SCOTLAND
65 SPAIN
63 SWEDEN
66 SWITZERLAND
69 TURKEY
67 VATICAN CITY
56 WALES
68 YUGOSLAVIA

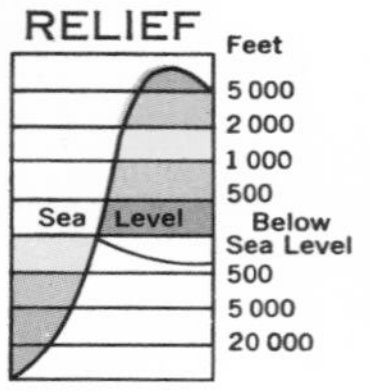

Statute Miles 100 0 100 200 300
Kilometers 100 0 100 200 300 400

Conic Projection
SCALE 1:16,000,000 1 Inch = 252 Statute Miles

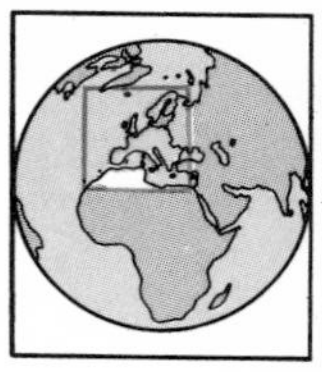

Conic Projection
SCALE 1:16,000,000 1 Inch = 252 Statute Miles

Statute Miles 100 0 100 200 300
Kilometers 100 0 100 200 300 400

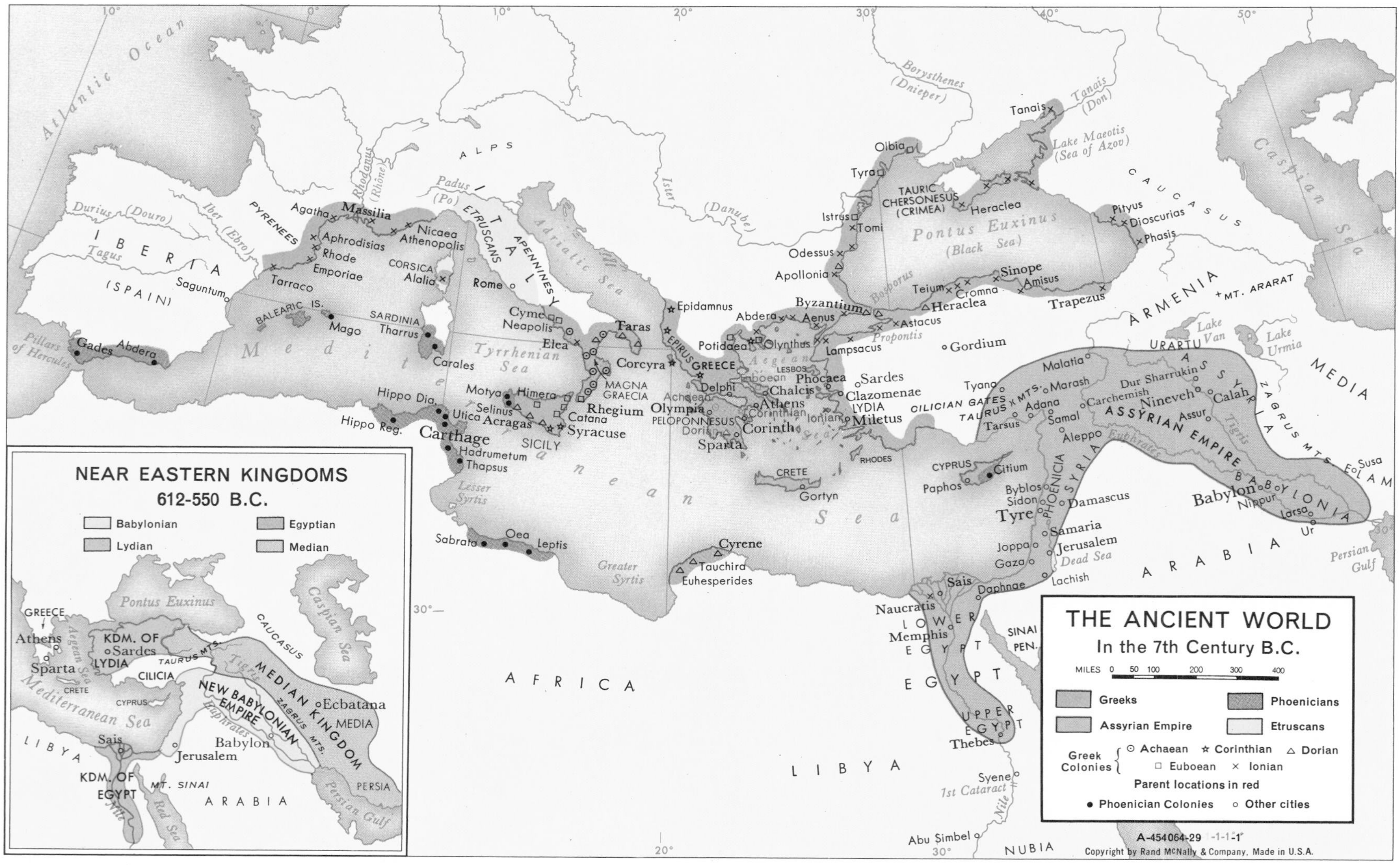
THE ANCIENT WORLD
In the 7th Century B.C.
MILES 0 50 100 200 300 400
Greeks
Assyrian Empire
Phoenicians
Etruscans
Greek Colonies
Achaean
Corinthian
Dorian
Euboean
Ionian
Parent locations in red
Phoenician Colonies
Other cities
NEAR EASTERN KINGDOMS
612-550 B.C.
Babylonian
Lydian
Egyptian
Median
Pontus Euxinus
Caspian Sea
GREECE
Athens
Sparta
KDM. OF LYDIA
Sardes
TAURUS MTS.
CILICIA
CAUCASUS
MEDIAN KINGDOM
Ecbatana
MEDIA
NEW BABYLONIAN EMPIRE
ZAGROS MTS.
Babylon
Jerusalem
Sais
KDM. OF EGYPT
MT. SINAI
ARABIA
PERSIA
Persian Gulf
Red Sea
Nile
LIBYA
Mediterranean Sea
CRETE
CYPRUS
Atlantic Ocean
IBERIA
(SPAIN)
Durius (Douro)
Iber (Ebro)
Tagus
Saguntum
PYRENEES
Pillars of Hercules
Gades
Abdera
Tarraco
Emporiae
Rhode
Aphrodisias
Agatha
Massilia
Nicaea
Athenopolis
Rhodanus (Rhône)
ALPS
Padus (Po)
ETRUSCANS
ITALY
APENNINES
CORSICA
Alalia
Rome
BALEARIC IS.
Mago
SARDINIA
Tharrus
Carales
Tyrrhenian Sea
Cyme
Neapolis
Elea
Taras
Adriatic Sea
Hippo Dia.
Hippo Reg.
Utica
Carthage
Hadrumetum
Thapsus
Motya
Himera
Selinus
Acragas
Catana
Syracuse
SICILY
Rhegium
MAGNA GRAECIA
Corcyra
Epidamnus
EPIRUS
GREECE
Delphi
Olympia
PELOPONNESUS
Doris
Sparta
Corinth
Athens
Chalcis
Euboean
Achaean
Ionian
Potidaea
Abdera
Olynthus
Aenus
Byzantium
Astacus
Propontis
Lampsacus
Phocaea
Sardes
Clazomenae
LYDIA
Miletus
Gordium
Ister (Danube)
Istrus
Tomi
Odessus
Apollonia
Tyras
Olbia
TAURIC CHERSONESUS (CRIMEA)
Heraclea
Borysthenes (Dnieper)
Tanais
Tanais (Don)
Lake Maeotis (Sea of Azov)
Pontus Euxinus (Black Sea)
Bosporus
Teium
Cromna
Heraclea
Sinope
Amisus
Trapezus
Pityus
Dioscurias
Phasis
CAUCASUS
ARMENIA
MT. ARARAT
URARTU
Lake Van
Lake Urmia
Caspian Sea
MEDIA
ASSYRIA
ZAGROS MTS.
Nineveh
Calah
Assur
Dur Sharrukin
Carchemish
Malatia
Marash
Adana
Tarsus
Samal
Tyana
CILICIAN GATES
TAURUS MTS.
ASSYRIAN EMPIRE
Aleppo
Euphrates
Tigris
SYRIA
PHOENICIA
Byblos
Sidon
Tyre
Damascus
Samaria
Jerusalem
Dead Sea
Joppa
Gaza
Lachish
Babylon
BABYLONIA
Nippur
Larsa
Ur
Susa
ELAM
Persian Gulf
ARABIA
CYPRUS
Citium
Paphos
RHODES
CRETE
Gortyn
Mediterranean Sea
Lesser Syrtis
Greater Syrtis
Sabrata
Oea
Leptis
Cyrene
Tauchira
Euhesperides
Sais
Daphnae
Naucratis
Memphis
LOWER EGYPT
SINAI PEN.
EGYPT
UPPER EGYPT
Thebes
Syene
1st Cataract
Nile
Abu Simbel
NUBIA
AFRICA
LIBYA
A-454064-29
Copyright by Rand McNally & Company, Made in U.S.A.

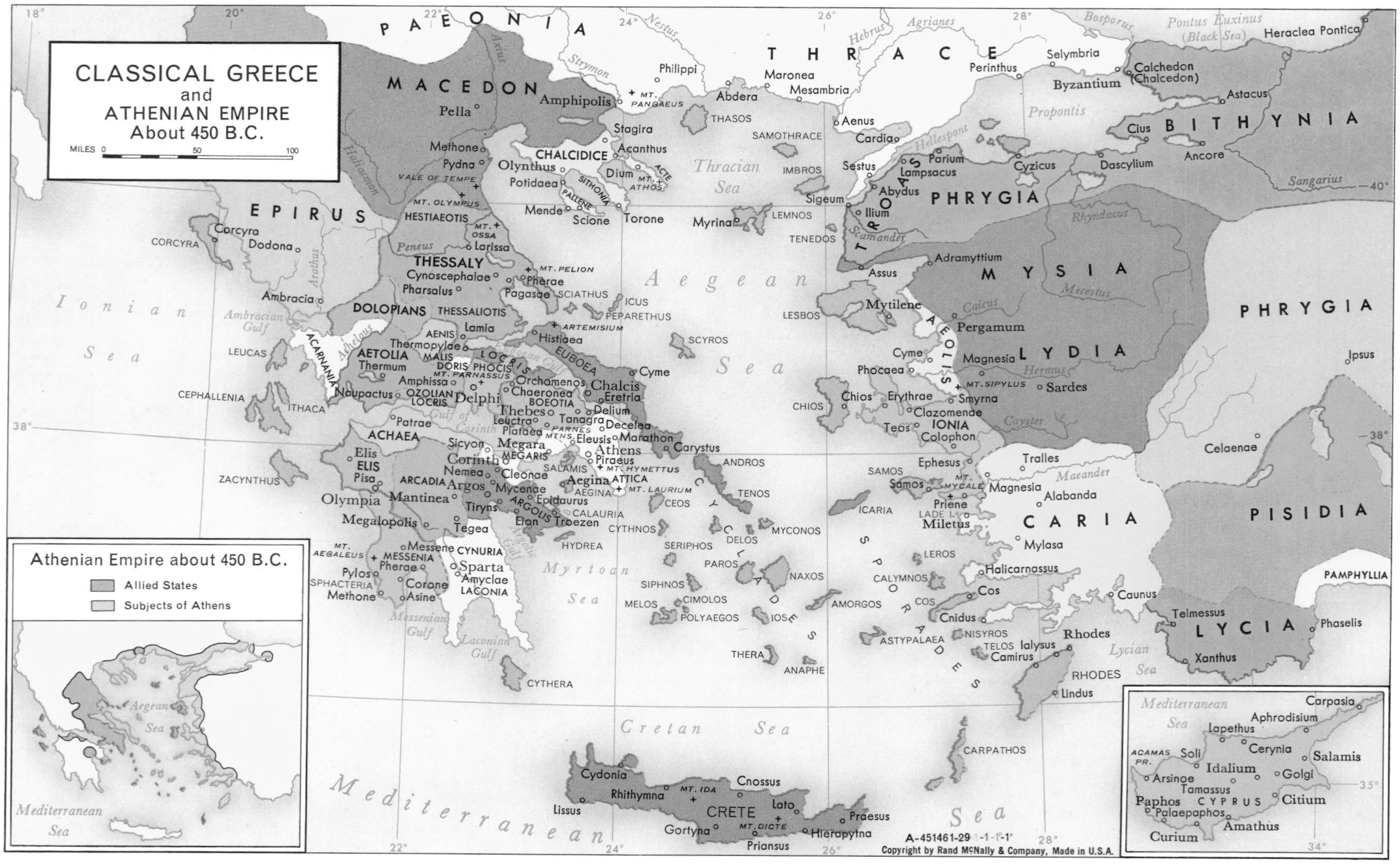
CLASSICAL GREECE
and
ATHENIAN EMPIRE
About 450 B.C.
MILES 0 50 100
Athenian Empire about 450 B.C.
Allied States
Subjects of Athens
Aegean Sea
Mediterranean Sea
PAEONIA
MACEDON
Pella
Amphipolis
MT. PANGAEUS
Philippi
Strymon
Axius
Haliacmon
THRACE
Maronea
Mesambria
Abdera
THASOS
SAMOTHRACE
Aenus
Cardia
Hebrus
Perinthus
Selymbria
Byzantium
Bosporus
Pontus Euxinus (Black Sea)
Heraclea Pontica
Calchedon (Chalcedon)
Astacus
Propontis
BITHYNIA
Cius
Ancore
Sangarius
Dascylium
Cyzicus
Parium
Lampsacus
Hellespont
Sestus
Abydus
Sigeum
Ilium
TROAS
Scamander
PHRYGIA
Rhyndacus
IMBROS
LEMNOS
Myrina
TENEDOS
Adramyttium
Assus
MYSIA
Macestus
Caicus
Mytilene
LESBOS
AEOLIS
Pergamum
Cyme
Phocaea
Magnesia
LYDIA
Hermus
MT. SIPYLUS
Sardes
Smyrna
Erythrae
Clazomenae
IONIA
Teos
Colophon
Cayster
CHIOS
PHRYGIA
Ipsus
Celaenae
Tralles
Maeander
Ephesus
SAMOS
Samos
MT. MYCALE
Priene
Magnesia
Alabanda
ICARIA
LADE I.
Miletus
CARIA
Mylasa
PISIDIA
LEROS
CALYMNOS
Halicarnassus
Cos
COS
Cnidus
Caunus
PAMPHYLLIA
Telmessus
LYCIA
Phaselis
Xanthus
NISYROS
TELOS
Ialysus
Camirus
Rhodes
RHODES
Lindus
Lycian Sea
CARPATHOS
Stagira
Acanthus
CHALCIDICE
Olynthus
Potidaea
SITHONIA
PALLENE
ACTE
MT. ATHOS
Dium
Mende
Scione
Torone
Methone
Pydna
VALE OF TEMPE
MT. OLYMPUS
HESTIAEOTIS
MT. OSSA
Larissa
Peneus
THESSALY
Cynoscephalae
Pharsalus
MT. PELION
Pherae
Pagasae
SCIATHUS
ICUS
PEPARETHUS
DOLOPIANS
THESSALIOTIS
Lamia
AENIS
MALIS
Thermopylae
ARTEMISIUM
Histiaea
EUBOEA
SCYROS
Cyme
Chalcis
Eretria
Carystus
EPIRUS
Corcyra
CORCYRA
Dodona
Ambracia
Ambracian Gulf
Arachthus
Achelous
ACARNANIA
Ionian Sea
LEUCAS
CEPHALLENIA
ITHACA
ZACYNTHUS
AETOLIA
Thermum
DORIS
PHOCIS
LOCRIS
MT. PARNASSUS
Amphissa
OZOLIAN LOCRIS
Naupactus
Delphi
Orchomenos
Chaeronea
BOEOTIA
Thebes
Tanagra
Delium
Decelea
Marathon
Leuctra
Plataea
PARNES MTS.
Eleusis
Athens
Piraeus
MT. HYMETTUS
ATTICA
MT. LAURIUM
Megara
MEGARIS
SALAMIS
Aegina
AEGINA
Patrae
Gulf of Corinth
ACHAEA
Sicyon
Corinth
Nemea
Cleonae
Mycenae
Argos
ARGOLIS
Epidaurus
Tiryns
Troezen
Elon
CALAURIA
Elis
ELIS
Pisa
Olympia
ARCADIA
Mantinea
Tegea
Megalopolis
MT. AEGALEUS
MESSENIA
Messene
CYNURIA
Pherae
Sparta
Amyclae
LACONIA
Pylos
SPHACTERIA
Methone
Corone
Asine
Messenian Gulf
Laconian Gulf
CYTHERA
Myrtoan Sea
HYDREA
CEOS
CYTHNOS
ANDROS
TENOS
MYCONOS
DELOS
SERIPHOS
PAROS
NAXOS
SIPHNOS
MELOS
CIMOLOS
POLYAEGOS
IOS
AMORGOS
THERA
ANAPHE
ASTYPALAEA
CYCLADES
SPORADES
Cretan Sea
CRETE
Cydonia
Rhithymna
MT. IDA
Cnossus
Lato
Praesus
Lissus
Gortyna
MT. DICTE
Hierapytna
Priansus
Mediterranean Sea
Carpasia
Aphrodisium
Lapethus
Ceryneia
ACAMAS PR.
Soli
Salamis
Idalium
Arsinoe
Tamassus
Golgi
Paphos
CYPRUS
Citium
Palaepaphos
Amathus
Curium
A-451461-29
Copyright by Rand McNally & Company, Made in U.S.A.

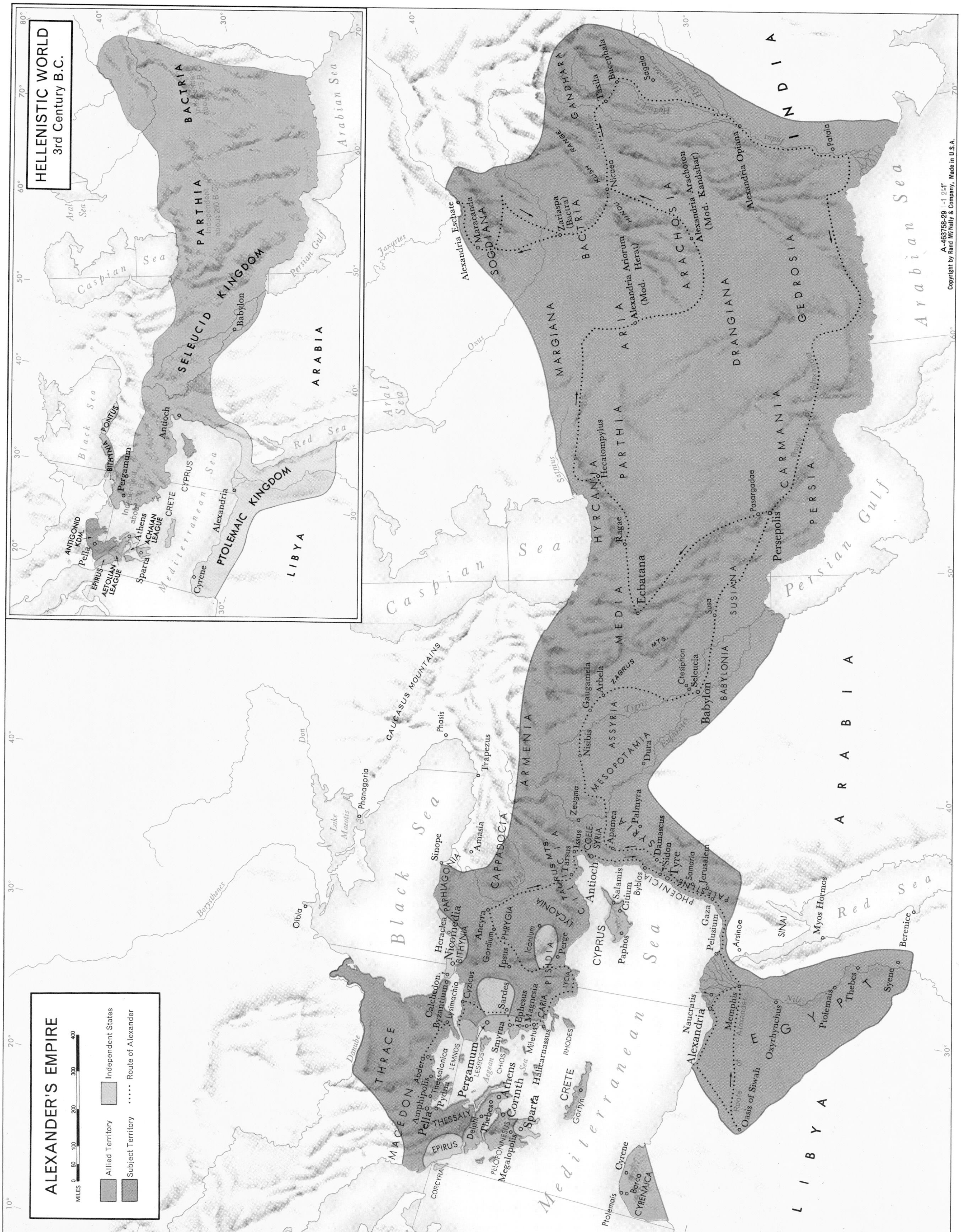
HELLENISTIC WORLD
3rd Century B.C.
BACTRIA
PARTHIA
Independent about 250 B.C.
SELEUCID KINGDOM
Babylon
ARABIA
PONTUS
BITHYNIA
Pergamum
Antioch
CYPRUS
CRETE
Alexandria
PTOLEMAIC KINGDOM
LIBYA
ANTIGONID KDM.
Pella
EPIRUS
AETOLIAN LEAGUE
ACHAIAN LEAGUE
Athens
Sparta
Cyrene
Caspian Sea
Aral Sea
Black Sea
Red Sea
Persian Gulf
Arabian Sea
Mediterranean Sea
ALEXANDER'S EMPIRE
Allied Territory
Subject Territory
Independent States
Route of Alexander
MILES
0
100
200
300
400
THRACE
MACEDON
Pella
Amphipolis
Abdera
Thessalonica
Pydna
THESSALY
EPIRUS
CORCYRA
Delphi
Thebes
Athens
Corinth
Sparta
Megalopolis
PELOPONNESUS
Pergamum
LESBOS
LEMNOS
CHIOS
Smyrna
Sardes
Ephesus
Magnesia
Miletus
Halicarnassus
CARIA
LYCIA
PISIDIA
RHODES
CRETE
Gortyn
Cyrene
Barca
CYRENAICA
Ptolemais
Byzantium
Calchedon
Lysimachia
Cyzicus
Nicomedia
Heraclea
BITHYNIA
PAPHLAGONIA
Sinope
Ancyra
Gordium
Ipsus
PHRYGIA
Iconium
LYCAONIA
CAPPADOCIA
Amasia
Perge
CILICIA
Tarsus
Issus
TAURUS MTS.
CYPRUS
Salamis
Citium
Paphos
Antioch
Byblos
PHOENICIA
COELE-SYRIA
Apamea
Damascus
Sidon
Tyre
Samaria
Jerusalem
PALESTINE
Gaza
Pelusium
Arsinoe
SINAI
Myos Hormos
Berenice
Naucratis
Alexandria
Memphis
Oasis of Siwah
Oxyrhynchus
Ptolemais
Thebes
Syene
EGYPT
LIBYA
ARABIA
Black Sea
Olbia
Borysthenes
Danube
Don
Lake Maeotis
Phanagoria
Phasis
Trapezus
CAUCASUS MOUNTAINS
ARMENIA
Zeugma
Palmyra
SYRIA
MESOPOTAMIA
Dura
Nisibis
Gaugamela
Arbela
ASSYRIA
Tigris
Euphrates
Ctesiphon
Seleucia
Babylon
BABYLONIA
ZAGROS MTS.
MEDIA
Susa
SUSIANA
Ecbatana
Ragae
HYRCANIA
Hecatompylus
PARTHIA
Pasargadae
Persepolis
PERSIA
CARMANIA
GEDROSIA
DRANGIANA
ARIA
Alexandria Ariorum (Mod. Herat)
ARACHOSIA
Alexandria Arachoton (Mod. Kandahar)
Alexandria Opiana
MARGIANA
BACTRIA
Zariaspa (Bactra)
SOGDIANA
Maracanda
Alexandria Eschate
Jaxartes
Oxus
HINDU KUSH
Nicaea
Taxila
Bucephala
GANDHARA
Sagala
Patala
Indus
INDIA
Caspian Sea
Aral Sea
Persian Gulf
Arabian Sea
Red Sea
Mediterranean Sea
A-463758-29 -1-2-1
Copyright by Rand McNally & Company, Made in U.S.A.

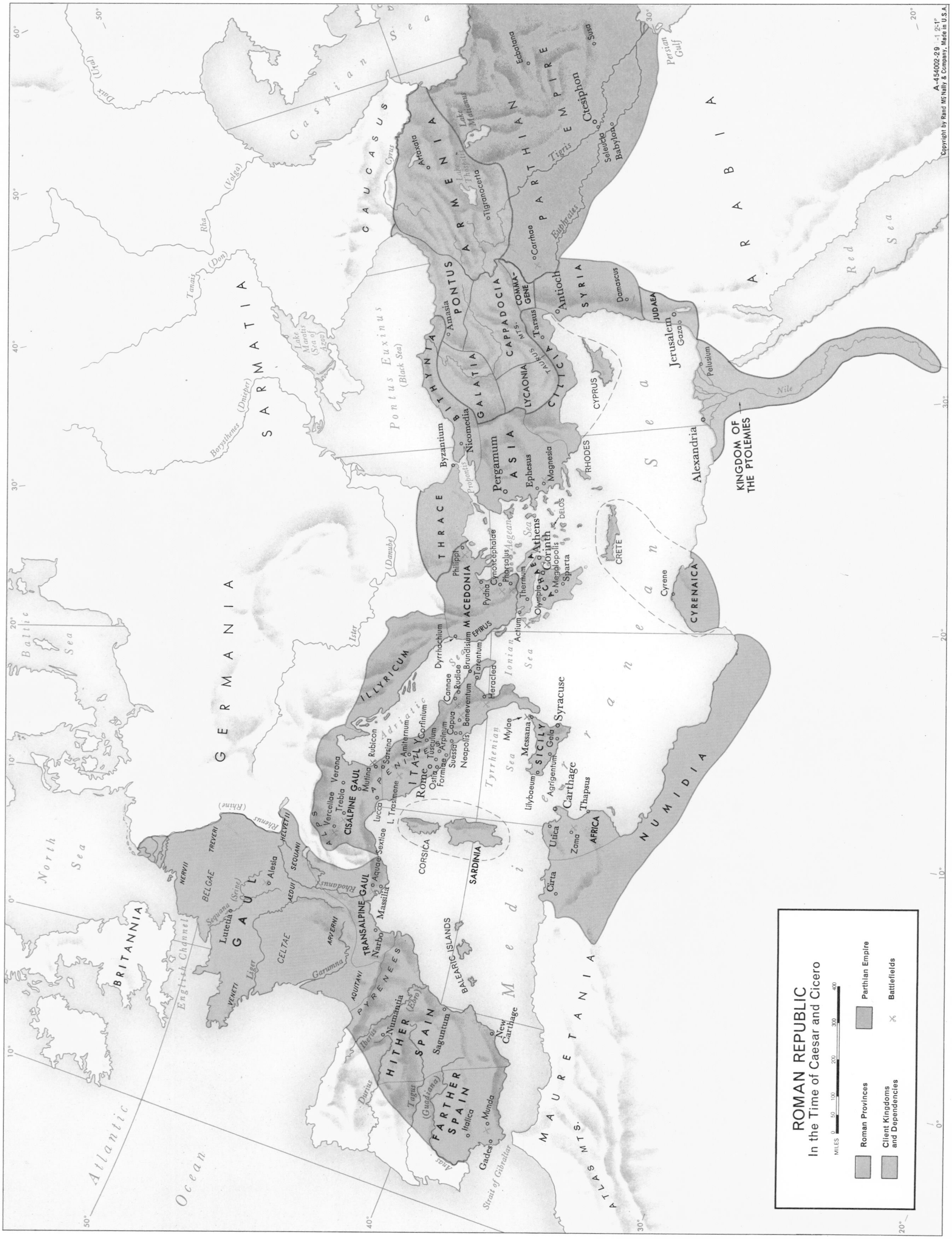
ROMAN REPUBLIC
In the Time of Caesar and Cicero
MILES 0 50 100 200 300 400
Roman Provinces
Client Kingdoms and Dependencies
Parthian Empire
Battlefields
A-454002-29 -1-2-1-
Copyright by Rand McNally & Company, Made in U.S.A.
BRITANNIA
GERMANIA
SARMATIA
CAUCASUS
ARMENIA
PARTHIAN EMPIRE
ARABIA
PONTUS
BITHYNIA
GALATIA
CAPPADOCIA
COMMAGENE
SYRIA
JUDAEA
CILICIA
LYCAONIA
ASIA
CYPRUS
RHODES
THRACE
MACEDONIA
EPIRUS
CRETE
CYRENAICA
KINGDOM OF THE PTOLEMIES
ILLYRICUM
ITALY
SICILY
CORSICA
SARDINIA
AFRICA
NUMIDIA
MAURETANIA
CISALPINE GAUL
TRANSALPINE GAUL
GAUL
BELGAE
HITHER SPAIN
FARTHER SPAIN
BALEARIC ISLANDS
PYRENEES
ALPS
ATLAS MTS.
Atlantic Ocean
North Sea
Baltic Sea
Caspian Sea
Pontus Euxinus (Black Sea)
Mediterranean Sea
Red Sea
Persian Gulf
Strait of Gibraltar
English Channel
Rome
Carthage
Athens
Corinth
Byzantium
Alexandria
Jerusalem
Antioch
Syracuse
Ctesiphon
Pergamum
Nicomedia
Massilia
Narbo
Lutetia
Alesia
Numantia
Saguntum
New Carthage
Gades
Italica
Munda
Utica
Thapsus
Cirta
Zama
Cyrene
Pelusium
Damascus
Tarsus
Ephesus
Magnesia
Sparta
Megalopolis
Olympia
Pharsalus
Philippi
Pydna
Actium
Dyrrhachium
Brundisium
Tarentum
Cannae
Capua
Neapolis
Beneventum
Rubicon
Mutina
Verona
Trebia
Vercellae
Luca
Messana
Agrigentum
Lilybaeum
Carrhae
Tigranocerta
Artaxata
Ecbatana
Susa
Seleucia
Babylon
Amasia

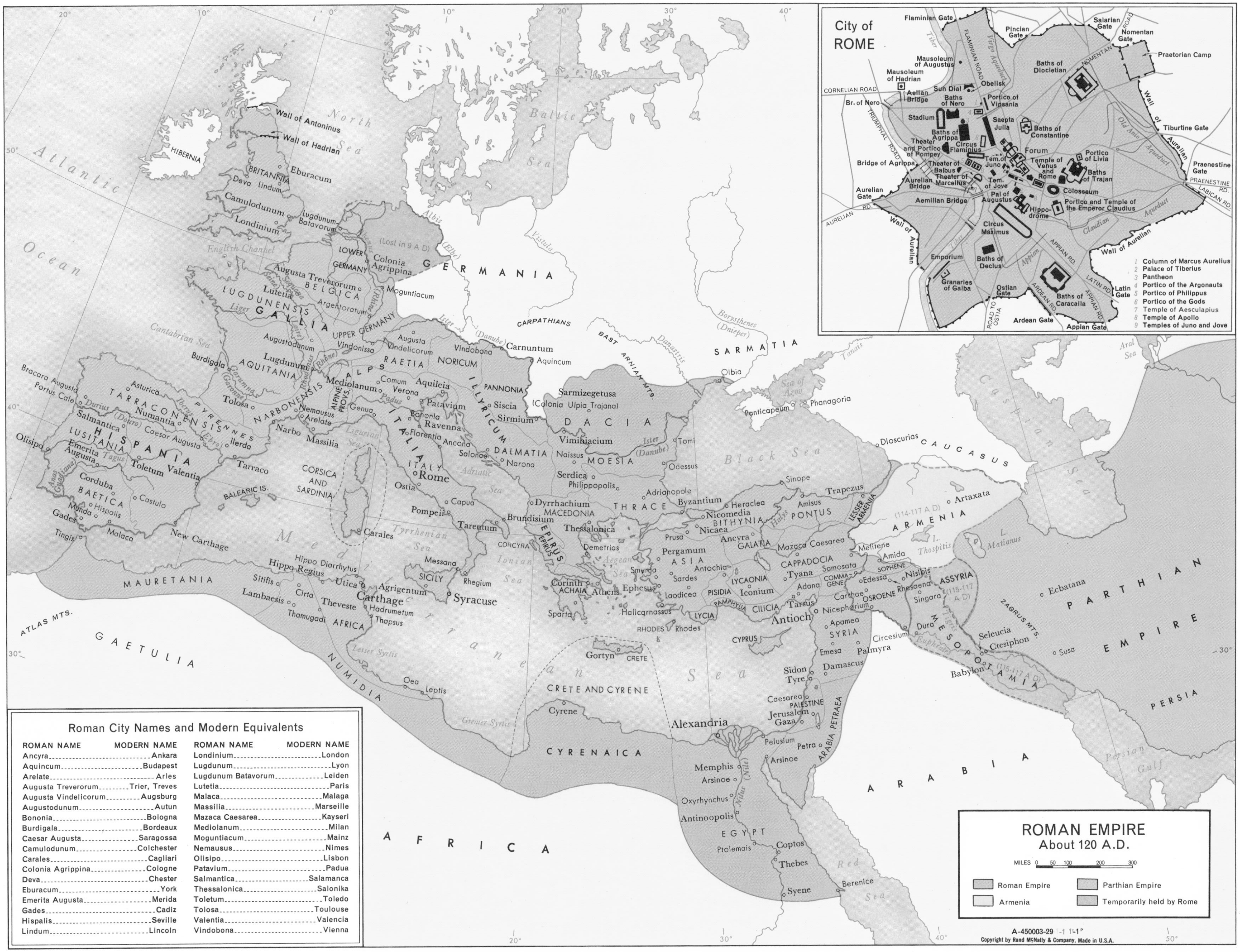

Roman City Names and Modern Equivalents

ROMAN NAME	MODERN NAME	ROMAN NAME	MODERN NAME
Ancyra	Ankara	Londinium	London
Aquincum	Budapest	Lugdunum	Lyon
Arelate	Arles	Lugdunum Batavorum	Leiden
Augusta Treverorum	Trier, Treves	Lutetia	Paris
Augusta Vindelicorum	Augsburg	Malaca	Malaga
Augustodunum	Autun	Massilia	Marseille
Bononia	Bologna	Mazaca Caesarea	Kayseri
Burdigala	Bordeaux	Mediolanum	Milan
Caesar Augusta	Saragossa	Moguntiacum	Mainz
Camulodunum	Colchester	Nemausus	Nimes
Carales	Cagliari	Olisipo	Lisbon
Colonia Agrippina	Cologne	Patavium	Padua
Deva	Chester	Salmantica	Salamanca
Eburacum	York	Thessalonica	Salonika
Emerita Augusta	Merida	Toletum	Toledo
Gades	Cadiz	Tolosa	Toulouse
Hispalis	Seville	Valentia	Valencia
Lindum	Lincoln	Vindobona	Vienna

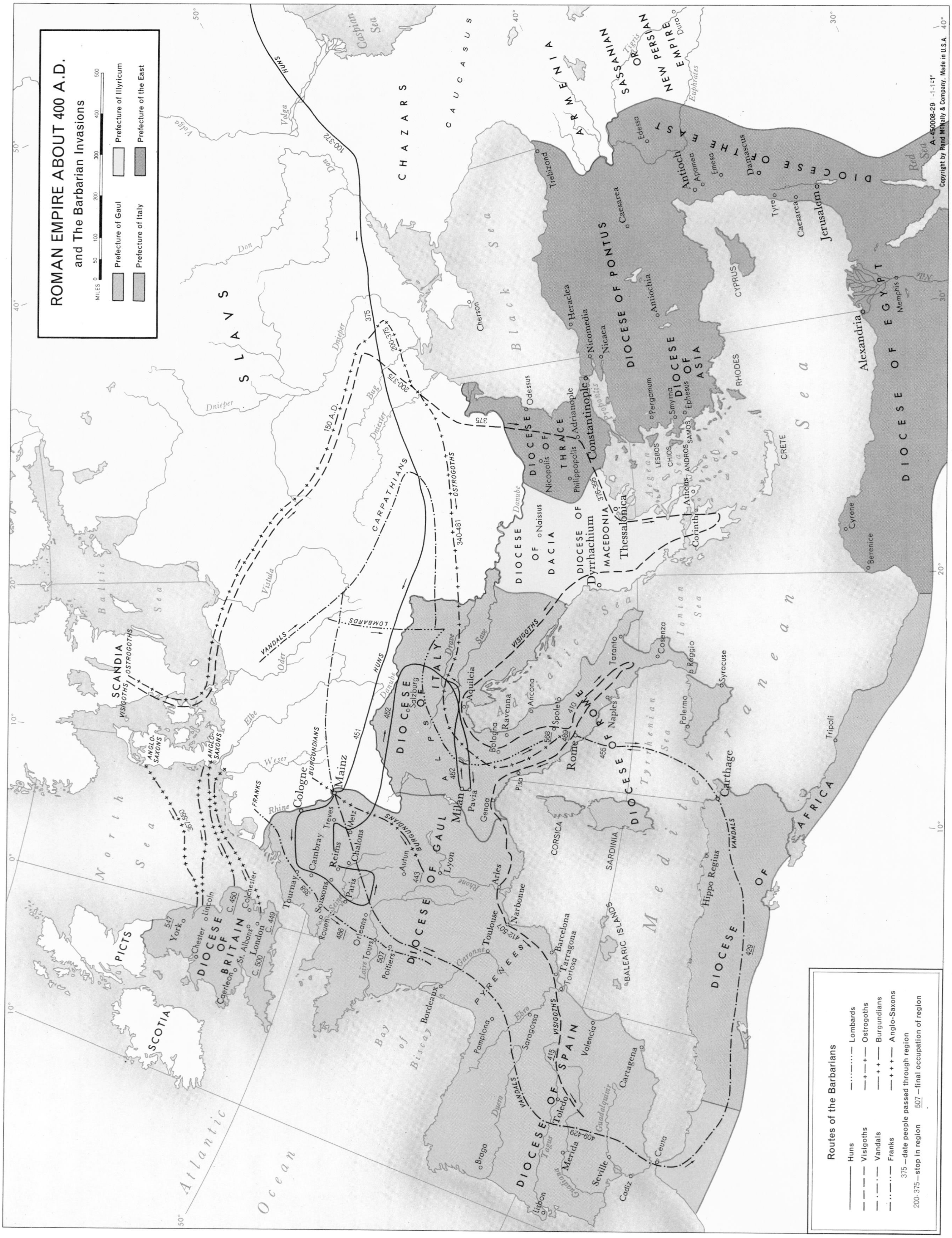
ROMAN EMPIRE ABOUT 400 A.D.
and The Barbarian Invasions
MILES 0 50 100 200 300 400 500
Prefecture of Gaul
Prefecture of Italy
Prefecture of Illyricum
Prefecture of the East
Routes of the Barbarians
Huns
Visigoths
Vandals
Franks
Lombards
Ostrogoths
Burgundians
Anglo-Saxons
375—date people passed through region
200-375—stop in region
507—final occupation of region
A-450008-29 -1-1-1
Copyright by Rand McNally & Company, Made in U.S.A.
SLAVS
CHAZARS
CAUCASUS
ARMENIA
SASSANIAN OR NEW PERSIAN EMPIRE
DIOCESE OF THE EAST
DIOCESE OF PONTUS
DIOCESE OF ASIA
DIOCESE OF THRACE
DIOCESE OF DACIA
DIOCESE OF MACEDONIA
DIOCESE OF ITALY
DIOCESE OF GAUL
DIOCESE OF BRITAIN
DIOCESE OF SPAIN
DIOCESE OF AFRICA
DIOCESE OF EGYPT
DIOCESE OF ROME
SCANDIA
PICTS
SCOTIA
North Sea
Baltic Sea
Black Sea
Caspian Sea
Mediterranean Sea
Atlantic Ocean
Bay of Biscay
Constantinople
Rome
Milan
Carthage
Alexandria
Jerusalem
Antioch
Thessalonica
Dyrrhachium
Cologne
Mainz
HUNS
VISIGOTHS
OSTROGOTHS
VANDALS
LOMBARDS
FRANKS
BURGUNDIANS
ANGLO-SAXONS

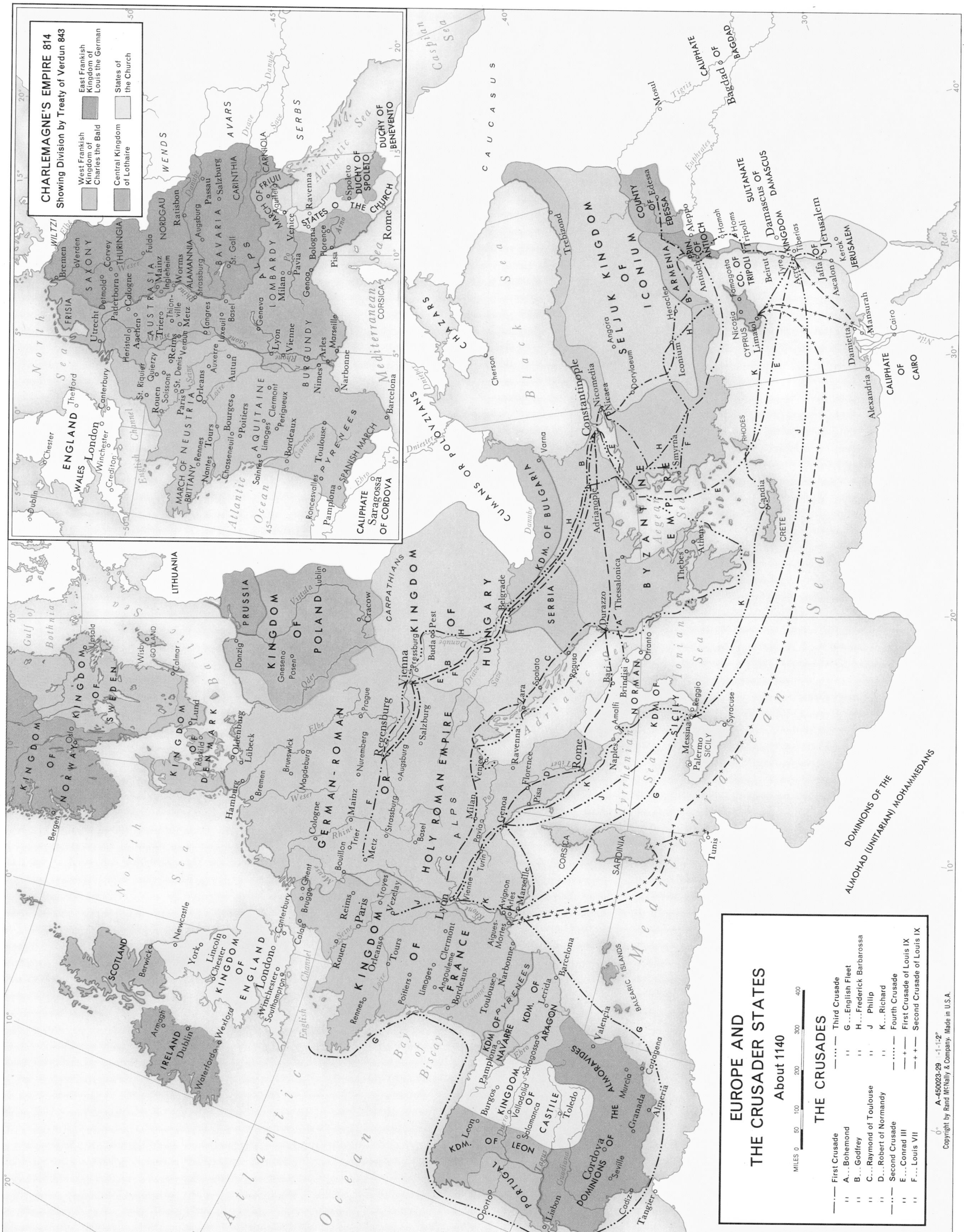
EUROPE AND
THE CRUSADER STATES
About 1140
THE CRUSADES
First Crusade
A...Bohemond
B...Godfrey
C...Raymond of Toulouse
D...Robert of Normandy
Second Crusade
E...Conrad III
F...Louis VII
Third Crusade
G...English Fleet
H...Frederick Barbarossa
J Philip
K...Richard
Fourth Crusade
First Crusade of Louis IX
Second Crusade of Louis IX
MILES 0 50 100 200 300 400
A-450023-29 -1-1-2
Copyright by Rand McNally & Company. Made in U.S.A.
CHARLEMAGNE'S EMPIRE 814
Showing Division by Treaty of Verdun 843
West Frankish Kingdom of Charles the Bald
East Frankish Kingdom of Louis the German
Central Kingdom of Lothaire
States of the Church

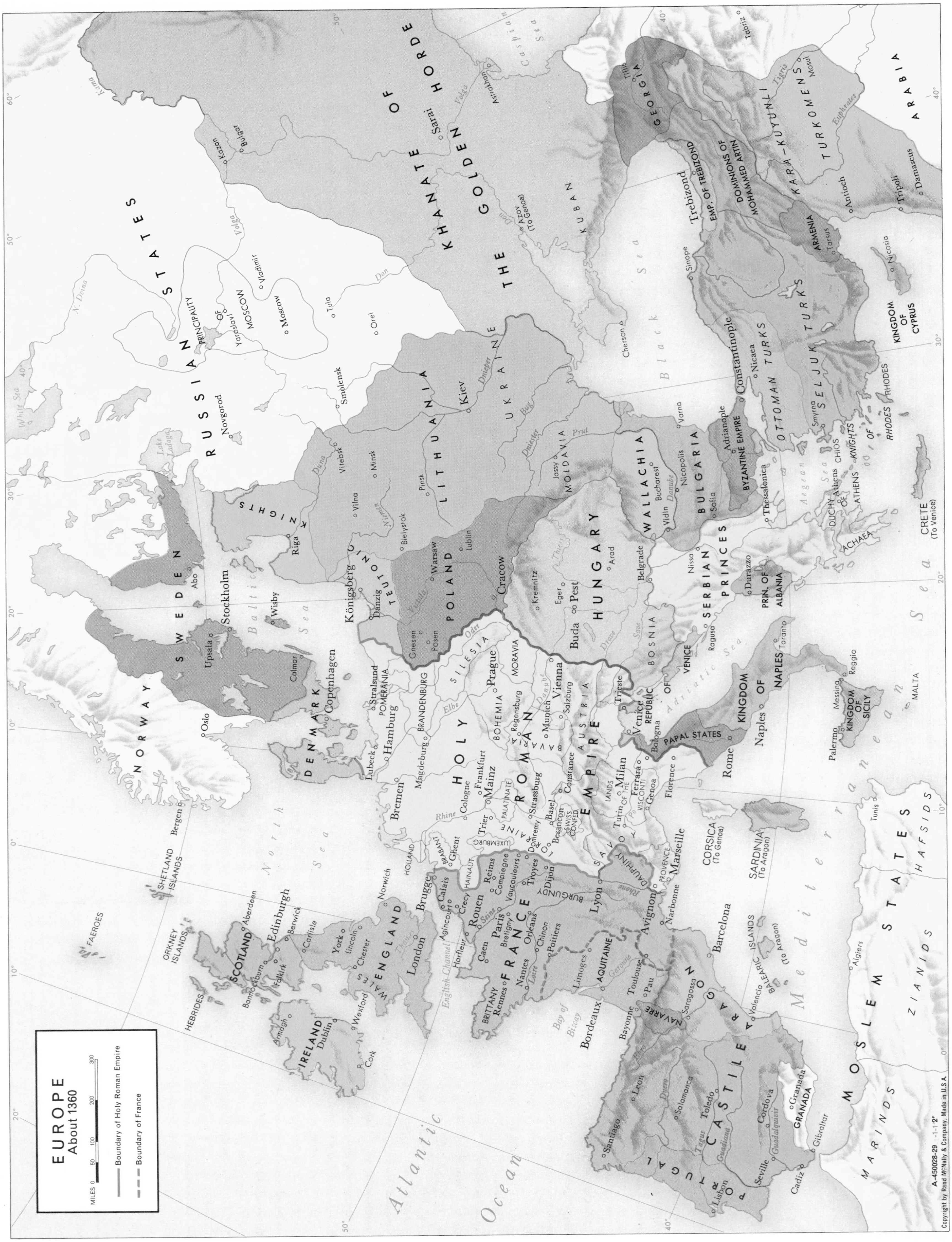
EUROPE
About 1360
MILES 0 50 100 200 300
Boundary of Holy Roman Empire
Boundary of France
RUSSIAN STATES
KHANATE OF THE GOLDEN HORDE
PRINCIPALITY OF MOSCOW
LITHUANIA
UKRAINE
KNIGHTS
TEUTONIC KNIGHTS
POLAND
HUNGARY
MOLDAVIA
WALLACHIA
BULGARIA
BYZANTINE EMPIRE
SERBIAN PRINCES
BOSNIA
PRIN. OF ALBANIA
OTTOMAN TURKS
SELJUK TURKS
KARA-KUYUNLI TURKOMENS
GEORGIA
EMP. OF TREBIZOND
DOMINIONS OF MOHAMMED ARTIN
ARMENIA
KINGDOM OF CYPRUS
ARABIA
KNIGHTS OF RHODES
DUCHY OF ATHENS
ACHAEA
CRETE (To Venice)
SWEDEN
NORWAY
DENMARK
SCOTLAND
ENGLAND
WALES
IRELAND
FRANCE
AQUITAINE
BRITTANY
BURGUNDY
HOLY ROMAN EMPIRE
BOHEMIA
AUSTRIA
SILESIA
MORAVIA
BRANDENBURG
POMERANIA
SAVOY
DAUPHINÉ
PROVENCE
REPUBLIC OF VENICE
PAPAL STATES
KINGDOM OF NAPLES
KINGDOM OF SICILY
CORSICA (To Genoa)
SARDINIA (To Aragon)
BALEARIC ISLANDS (To Aragon)
ARAGON
NAVARRE
CASTILE
PORTUGAL
GRANADA
MOSLEM STATES
HAFSIDS
ZIANIDS
MARINIDS
Atlantic Ocean
North Sea
Baltic Sea
Black Sea
Caspian Sea
Mediterranean Sea
Adriatic Sea
Aegean Sea
Bay of Biscay
English Channel
A-450028-29 -1-1-2
Copyright by Rand McNally & Company, Made in U.S.A.

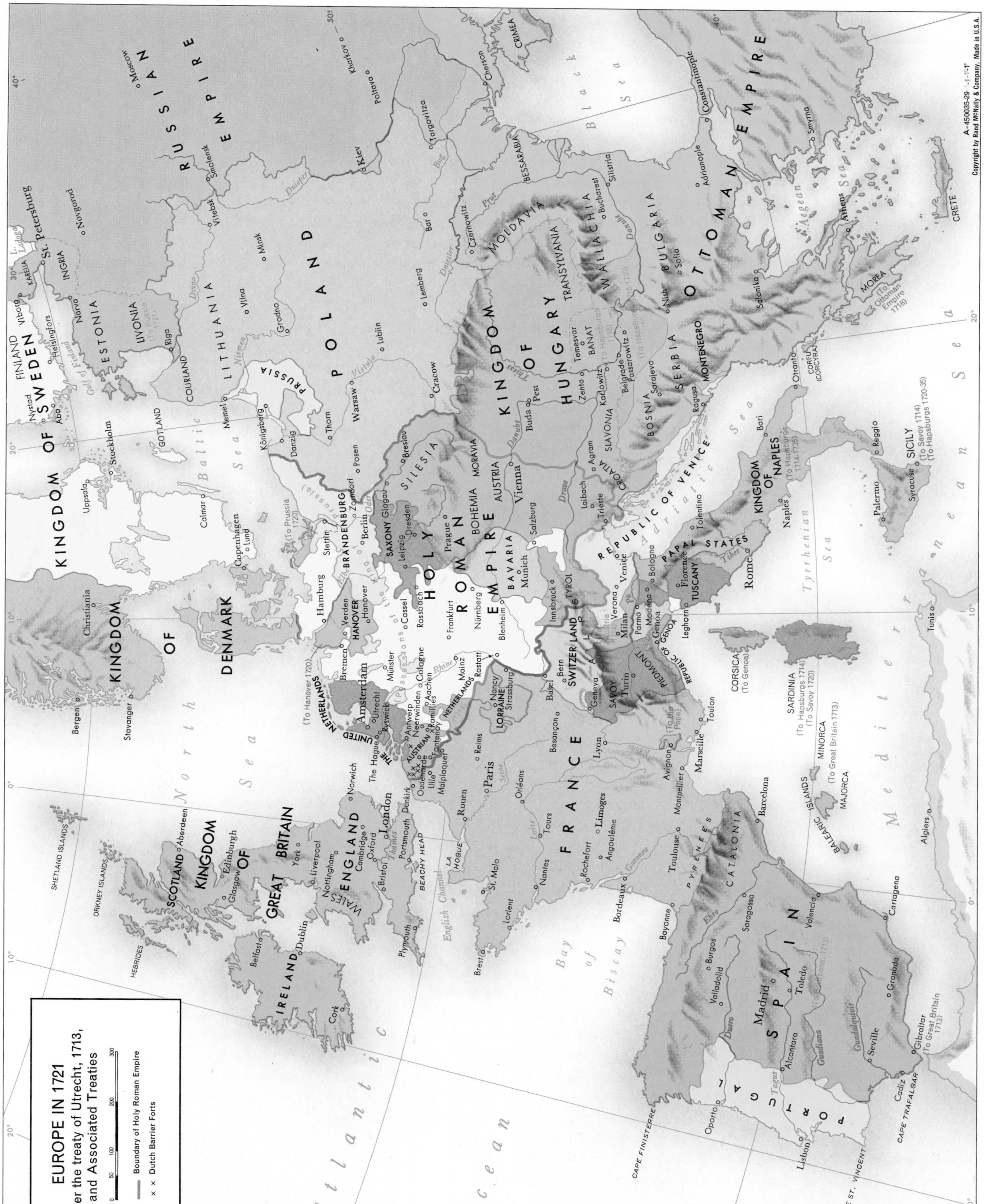
EUROPE IN 1721
After the treaty of Utrecht, 1713, and Associated Treaties
Miles 0 50 100 200 300
Boundary of Holy Roman Empire
x x Dutch Barrier Forts
KINGDOM OF SWEDEN
FINLAND
KINGDOM OF DENMARK
RUSSIAN EMPIRE
POLAND
LITHUANIA
PRUSSIA
KINGDOM OF GREAT BRITAIN
SCOTLAND
ENGLAND
WALES
IRELAND
FRANCE
SPAIN
PORTUGAL
HOLY ROMAN EMPIRE
KINGDOM OF HUNGARY
OTTOMAN EMPIRE
REPUBLIC OF VENICE
PAPAL STATES
KINGDOM OF NAPLES
SICILY (To Savoy 1714) (To Hapsburgs 1720-35)
SARDINIA (To Hapsburgs 1714) (To Savoy 1720)
CORSICA (To Genoa)
MINORCA (To Great Britain 1713)
Gibraltar (To Great Britain 1713)
MOREA (To Ottoman Empire 1718)
THE UNITED NETHERLANDS
AUSTRIAN NETHERLANDS
SWITZERLAND
SAVOY
PIEDMONT
REPUBLIC OF GENOA
TUSCANY
BAVARIA
BOHEMIA
AUSTRIA
SILESIA
SAXONY
BRANDENBURG
HANOVER
LORRAINE
TRANSYLVANIA
WALLACHIA
MOLDAVIA
BULGARIA
SERBIA
BOSNIA
MONTENEGRO
CRIMEA
BESSARABIA
Atlantic Ocean
North Sea
Baltic Sea
Black Sea
Mediterranean Sea
Tyrrhenian Sea
Adriatic Sea
Bay of Biscay
English Channel
A-450035-29
Copyright by Rand McNally & Company. Made in U.S.A.

EUROPE IN 1810
At the Height of Napoleon's Power
MILES 0 50 100 200 300
French Empire ★
"Greater Empire," subject to Napoleon, undergoing internal reform. ★
Nominal Allies of Napoleon. ★
Openly hostile to Napoleon; protected by British fleet.
Hostile to Napoleon.
Battles
Continental System, boycotting British trade.
SCOTLAND
UNITED KINGDOM OF GREAT BRITAIN AND IRELAND
(Act of Union, 1801)
Edinburgh
Dublin
IRELAND
Liverpool
ENGLAND
Hartwell
London
Plymouth
Portsmouth
Bourbon "King of France" in refuge
NORWAY AND DENMARK
SWEDEN
Christiania
Stockholm
Copenhagen
(To Russia 1808) GRAND DUCHY OF FINLAND
Helsingfors
St. Petersburg
Lake Ladoga
RUSSIAN EMPIRE
Moscow
Borodino
Smolensk
Riga
Düna
Tilsit
Vilna
Niemen
UKRAINE
Kiev
Dnieper
Dniester
Bug
Volga
Don
Odessa
King of Prussia in refuge from Berlin
Königsberg
Friedland
1807
PRUSSIA
GRAND DUCHY OF WARSAW (1808-13)
Posen
Warsaw
Berlin
HELGOLAND (Britain)
Hamburg
Amsterdam
WESTPHALIA
CONFEDERATION OF THE RHINE (1806-13)
Leipzig
SAXONY
Dresden
Jena
Cologne
Brussels
Waterloo
1815
Frankfort
BADEN
WÜRT.
BAVARIA
Ulm
Munich
Hohenlinden
Prague
BOHEMIA
Austerlitz
1805
Wagram
1809
AUSTRIAN EMPIRE
(Proclaimed 1804)
Vienna
Buda
Pest
HUNGARY
Lemberg
Vistula
Oder
Elbe
CARPATHIANS
BESSARABIA
MOLDAVIA
Yassy
Prut
WALLACHIA
Bucharest
Danube
Black Sea
English Channel
Brest
Paris
Strassburg
Seine
Loire
FRENCH EMPIRE (1804-14)
Valençay
Bourbon King of Spain in captivity
Bordeaux
Garonne
Bay of Biscay
Lyon
Rhone
SWITZERLAND
Geneva
ALPS
ILLYRIAN PROVINCES (1810-13)
Trieste
Drave
Save
Milan
Turin
Marengo
1800
Savona
Genoa
KDM. OF ITALY (1804-13)
Venice
LUCCA
Florence
Pope in captivity
ELBA
Ancona
Adriatic Sea
Rome
KDM. OF NAPLES (1806-13)
Benevento
Naples
Otranto
Belgrade
MONTENEGRO
OTTOMAN EMPIRE
Sofia
Adrianople
Constantinople
Saloniki
Smyrna
Athens
CORFU (France)
IONIAN ISLANDS (Britain)
CRETE
CYPRUS
Atlantic Ocean
Coruña
Bayonne
PYRENEES
Oporto
KINGDOM OF SPAIN (1808-13)
Madrid
Duero
Ebro
Tagus
Guadiana
Guadalquivir
KDM. OF PORTUGAL
Torres Vedras
Lisbon
Regent of Portugal in refuge in Brazil
Valencia
Bailén
French surrender 1808
Seville
Cape Trafalgar
1805
Gibraltar (Britain)
Marseille
Barcelona
CORSICA (France)
BALEARIC IS.
KDM. OF SARDINIA
King of Savoy in refuge from Turin
Mediterranean Sea
Palermo
KDM. OF SICILY
Bourbon King of Naples in refuge
MALTA (Britain)
A-450037-29 -1-1-1
Copyright by Rand McNally & Company, Made in U.S.A.

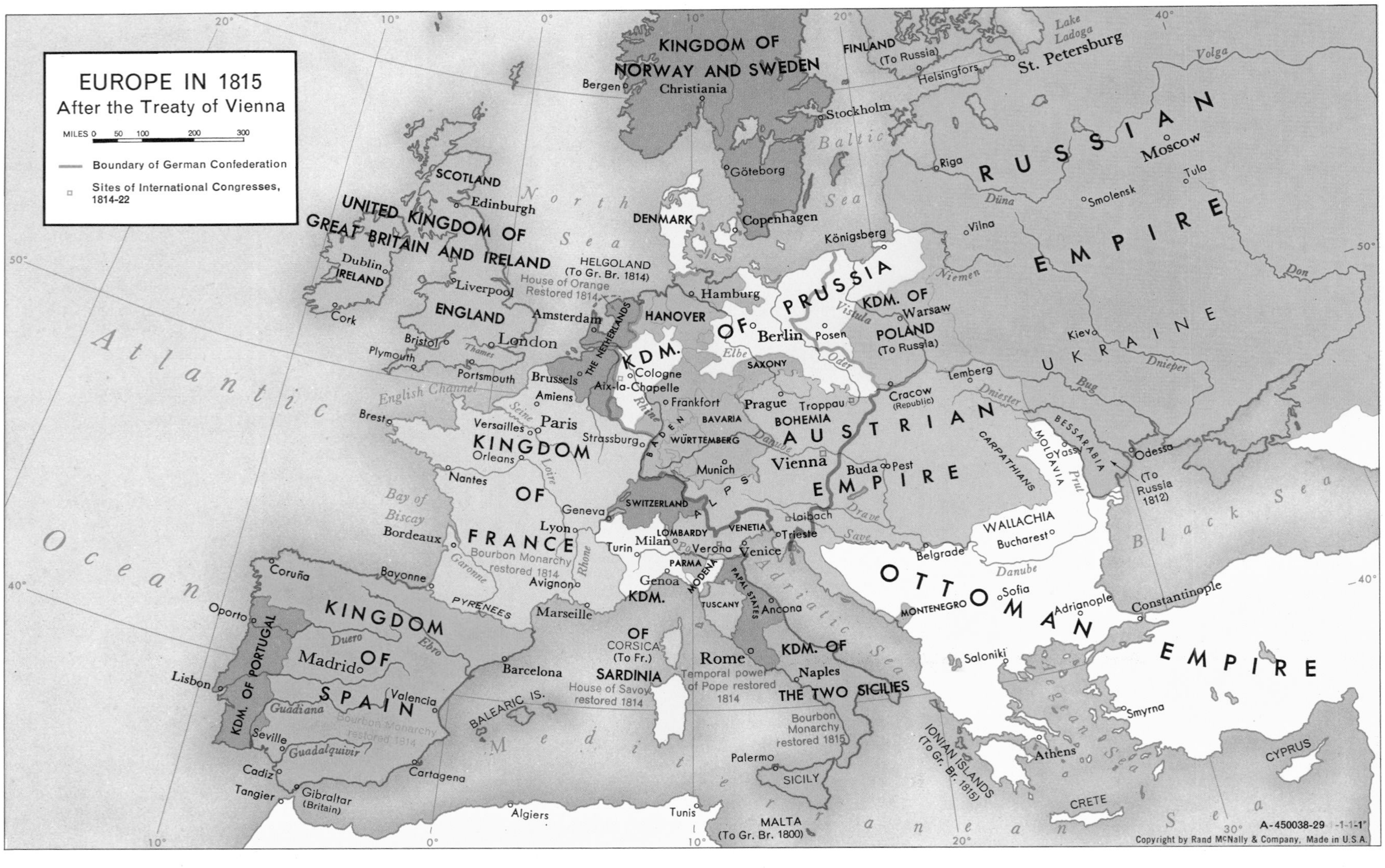
EUROPE IN 1815
After the Treaty of Vienna
MILES 0 50 100 200 300
Boundary of German Confederation
Sites of International Congresses, 1814-22
KINGDOM OF NORWAY AND SWEDEN
Bergen
Christiania
Stockholm
Göteborg
FINLAND (To Russia)
Helsingfors
St. Petersburg
Lake Ladoga
DENMARK
Copenhagen
Königsberg
RUSSIAN EMPIRE
Moscow
Tula
Smolensk
Riga
Düna
Vilna
Niemen
UKRAINE
Kiev
Dnieper
Dniester
Bug
Volga
Don
SCOTLAND
UNITED KINGDOM OF GREAT BRITAIN AND IRELAND
Edinburgh
Dublin
IRELAND
Cork
Liverpool
ENGLAND
Bristol
London
Thames
Plymouth
Portsmouth
HELGOLAND (To Gr. Br. 1814)
House of Orange Restored 1814
THE NETHERLANDS
Amsterdam
Hamburg
HANOVER
KDM. OF PRUSSIA
Berlin
Posen
KDM. OF POLAND (To Russia)
Warsaw
Elbe
Oder
Vistula
SAXONY
Brussels
Aix-la-Chapelle
Cologne
Frankfort
Amiens
Cracow (Republic)
Troppau
Prague
BOHEMIA
Lemberg
BADEN
BAVARIA
WÜRTTEMBERG
Munich
AUSTRIAN EMPIRE
Vienna
Buda
Pest
CARPATHIANS
MOLDAVIA
Yassy
BESSARABIA
Prut
Odessa
(To Russia 1812)
WALLACHIA
Bucharest
Danube
Black Sea
English Channel
Brest
Versailles
Paris
Strassburg
Seine
Orleans
Loire
KINGDOM OF FRANCE
Bourbon Monarchy restored 1814
Nantes
Bay of Biscay
Bordeaux
Garonne
Rhone
Lyon
Geneva
SWITZERLAND
ALPS
Laibach
Trieste
Drave
Save
VENETIA
LOMBARDY
Milan
Turin
Verona
Venice
PARMA
MODENA
Avignon
Genoa
KDM. OF SARDINIA
House of Savoy restored 1814
TUSCANY
PAPAL STATES
Ancona
Adriatic Sea
Rome
Temporal power of Pope restored 1814
KDM. OF THE TWO SICILIES
Naples
Bourbon Monarchy restored 1815
Palermo
SICILY
MALTA (To Gr. Br. 1800)
Tunis
Algiers
CORSICA (To Fr.)
BALEARIC IS.
Mediterranean Sea
Belgrade
MONTENEGRO
OTTOMAN EMPIRE
Sofia
Adrianople
Constantinople
Saloniki
Smyrna
Athens
IONIAN ISLANDS (To Gr. Br. 1815)
CRETE
CYPRUS
Atlantic Ocean
Bayonne
PYRENEES
Marseille
Coruña
Oporto
KINGDOM OF SPAIN
Madrid
Duero
Ebro
Barcelona
Valencia
Bourbon Monarchy restored 1814
KDM. OF PORTUGAL
Lisbon
Guadiana
Guadalquivir
Seville
Cadiz
Tangier
Gibraltar (Britain)
Cartagena
A-450038-29 -1-1-1
Copyright by Rand McNally & Company, Made in U.S.A.

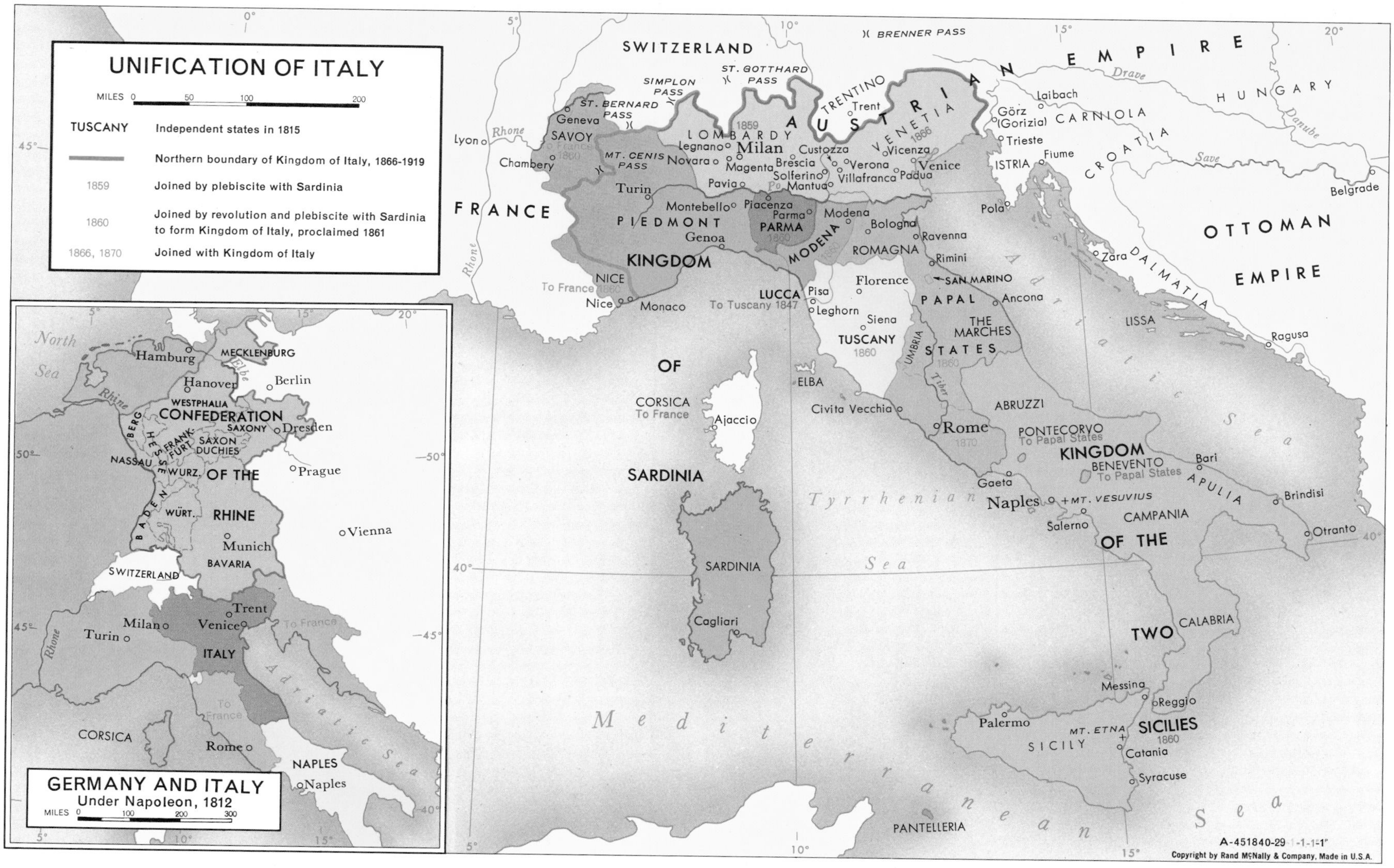
UNIFICATION OF ITALY
MILES 0 50 100 200
TUSCANY Independent states in 1815
Northern boundary of Kingdom of Italy, 1866-1919
1859 Joined by plebiscite with Sardinia
1860 Joined by revolution and plebiscite with Sardinia to form Kingdom of Italy, proclaimed 1861
1866, 1870 Joined with Kingdom of Italy
SWITZERLAND
SIMPLON PASS
ST. GOTTHARD PASS
BRENNER PASS
ST. BERNARD PASS
MT. CENIS PASS
AUSTRIAN EMPIRE
HUNGARY
TRENTINO
Trent
Geneva
SAVOY
Lyon
Chambery
FRANCE
LOMBARDY
Milan
Legnano
Novara
Magenta
Brescia
Custozza
Verona
Vicenza
Venice
Solferino
Villafranca
Padua
Mantua
VENETIA
Görz (Gorizia)
Laibach
CARNIOLA
Trieste
ISTRIA
Fiume
CROATIA
Drave
Danube
Save
Belgrade
Turin
Pavia
Montebello
Piacenza
Parma
PARMA
Modena
PIEDMONT
Genoa
KINGDOM OF SARDINIA
MODENA
Bologna
Ravenna
ROMAGNA
Rimini
Pola
Zara
DALMATIA
OTTOMAN EMPIRE
NICE
To France
Nice
Monaco
LUCCA
To Tuscany 1847
Pisa
Leghorn
Florence
SAN MARINO
PAPAL STATES
Ancona
THE MARCHES
UMBRIA
Siena
TUSCANY 1860
LISSA
Ragusa
CORSICA
To France
Ajaccio
ELBA
Civita Vecchia
Rome 1870
ABRUZZI
PONTECORVO To Papal States
KINGDOM OF THE TWO SICILIES
BENEVENTO To Papal States
Bari
APULIA
Brindisi
Gaeta
Naples
MT. VESUVIUS
Salerno
CAMPANIA
Otranto
Adriatic Sea
Tyrrhenian Sea
SARDINIA
Cagliari
CALABRIA
Messina
Reggio
Palermo
MT. ETNA
SICILY
SICILIES 1860
Catania
Syracuse
Mediterranean Sea
PANTELLERIA
A-451840-29
Copyright by Rand McNally & Company, Made in U.S.A.
GERMANY AND ITALY Under Napoleon, 1812
MILES 0 100 200 300
North Sea
Hamburg
MECKLENBURG
Hanover
Berlin
WESTPHALIA
CONFEDERATION OF THE RHINE
SAXONY
Dresden
BERG
HESSE
FRANKFURT
SAXON DUCHIES
NASSAU
WURZ.
Prague
BADEN
WÜRT.
Munich
BAVARIA
Vienna
SWITZERLAND
Trent
Milan
Venice
To France
Turin
ITALY
Rhone
Adriatic Sea
CORSICA
To France
Rome
NAPLES
Naples

UNIFICATION OF GERMANY
Bismarck's Empire
MILES 0 50 100 200
Boundary of the German Confederation of 1815.
Boundary of the German Empire, 1871—1918
1866 Absorbed by Prussia
1867 Entered North German Confederation, as a member state
1871 Entered German Empire, with preceding, as a member state. Alsace-Lorraine annexed
DENMARK
SWEDEN
Baltic Sea
Copenhagen
Malmö
BORNHOLM
SCHLESWIG
Flensborg
(To Oldenburg)
RÜGEN
Kiel
HOLSTEIN
LÜBECK
LAUENBURG
MECKLENBURG SCHWERIN 1867
MECKLENBURG STRELITZ 1867
POMERANIA
Stettin
Danzig
WEST PRUSSIA
EAST PRUSSIA
Königsberg
Tilsit
North Sea
EAST FRIESLAND
(To Hamburg)
Hamburg 1867
KINGDOM OF HANOVER 1866
OLDEN-BURG
Bremen 1867
Elbe
BRANDENBURG
Berlin
Spree
PRUSSIA
Warta
POSEN
Posen
Thorn
Vistula
Bielostock
ENGLAND
London
Amsterdam
NETHERLANDS
Rotterdam
Rhine
Meuse
Munster
LIPPE
Hanover
BRUNSWICK
Magdeburg
Oder
Neisse
Warsaw
RUSSIAN EMPIRE
Kalisz
Lodz
POLAND
Lublin
Cleves
K D M. OF
Essen
WESTPHALIA
HANOVER
ANHALT
SAXONY
Ruhr
Düsseldorf
WALDECK 1867
Kassel
Leipzig
KINGDOM OF SAXONY 1867
Dresden
Breslau
SILESIA
Ghent
Antwerp
Brussels
Liége
BELGIUM
Lille
Mons
Namur
Cologne
RHINE PROVINCE
Aachen
HESSE-KASSEL 1866
Weimar
SAXON DUCHIES 1867
Coblenz
Bonn
OF PRUSSIA
Wetzlar
NASSAU 1866
Ems
HESSE-DARMSTADT 1867
Frankfurt 1866
REUSS
Karlsbad
Sadowa
Cracow
GALICIA
(Republic of Cracow 1815) (To Austria 1846)
(Neutralized 1867)
Sedan
Luxemburg
(To Prussia 1834)
Mainz
Darmstadt
DARMSTADT 1871
Main
Baireuth
Eger
Prague
BOHEMIA
Pilsen
MORAVIA
Olmütz
Brünn
Reims
Paris
Verdun
Mannheim
BAVARIAN PALATINATE
Würzburg
KINGDOM OF BAVARIA 1871
Nuremberg
Regensburg
AUSTRIAN EMPIRE
Metz
LORRAINE
Strassburg 1871
Nancy
ALSACE
GRAND DUCHY OF BADEN
KINGDOM OF WÜRTTEMBERG 1871
Karlsruhe
Stuttgart
Augsburg
Munich
Danube
Inn
Vienna
HOHENZOLLERN (To Prussia 1849)
FRANCE
Belfort
Constance
Basel
Zurich
SWITZERLAND
Innsbruck
TYROL
AUSTRIA
A-451040-29
Copyright by Rand McNally & Company, Made in U.S.A.
Hamburg and Bremen 1888
GERMAN TARIFF UNITY
The Zollverein
Showing years of adherence of various states to the tariff union initiated by Prussia. The old free cities of Hamburg and Bremen were not brought under the national tariff until long after political unification.

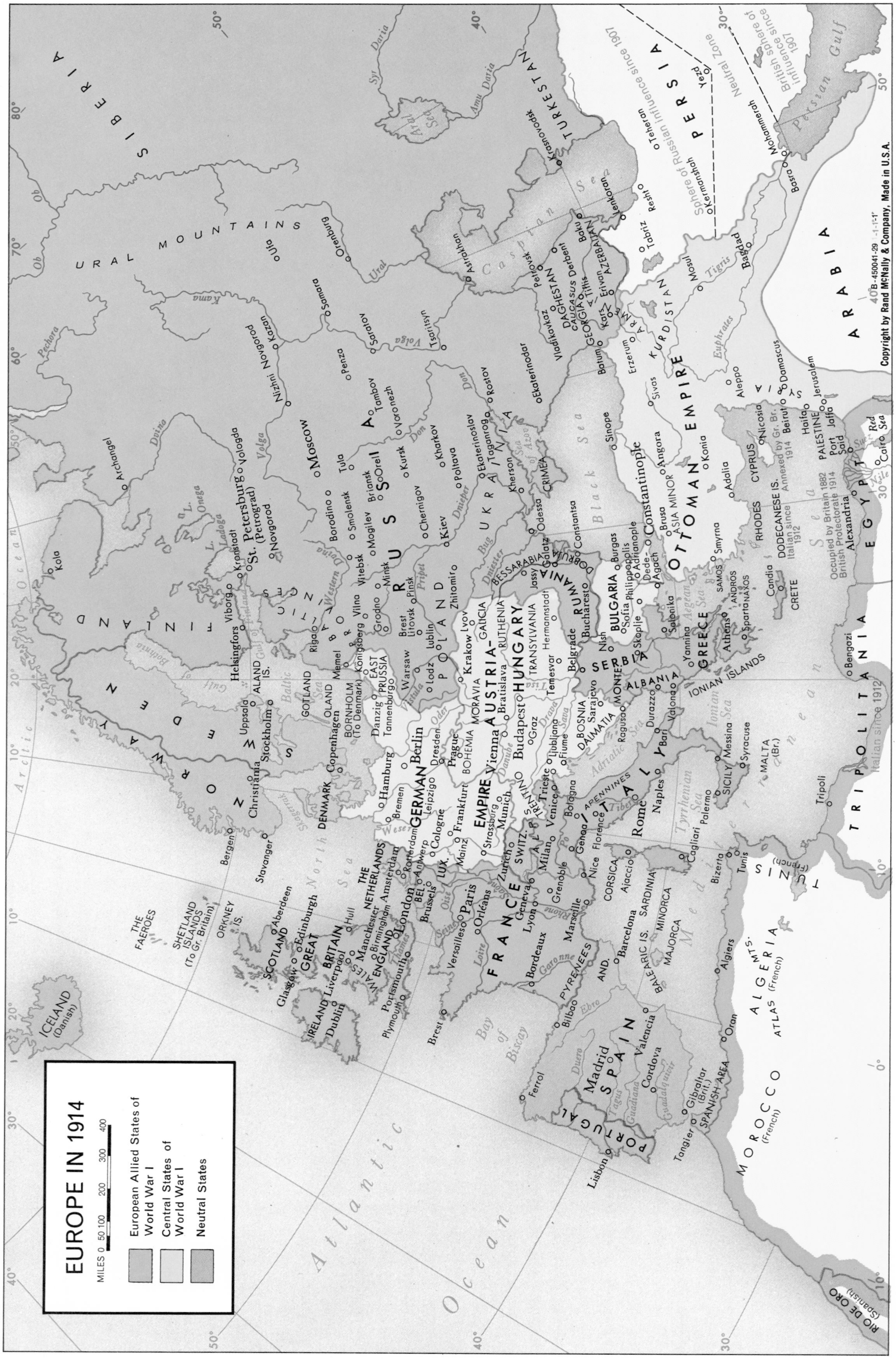
EUROPE IN 1914
MILES 0 50 100 200 300 400
European Allied States of World War I
Central States of World War I
Neutral States
Copyright by Rand McNally & Company, Made in U.S.A.

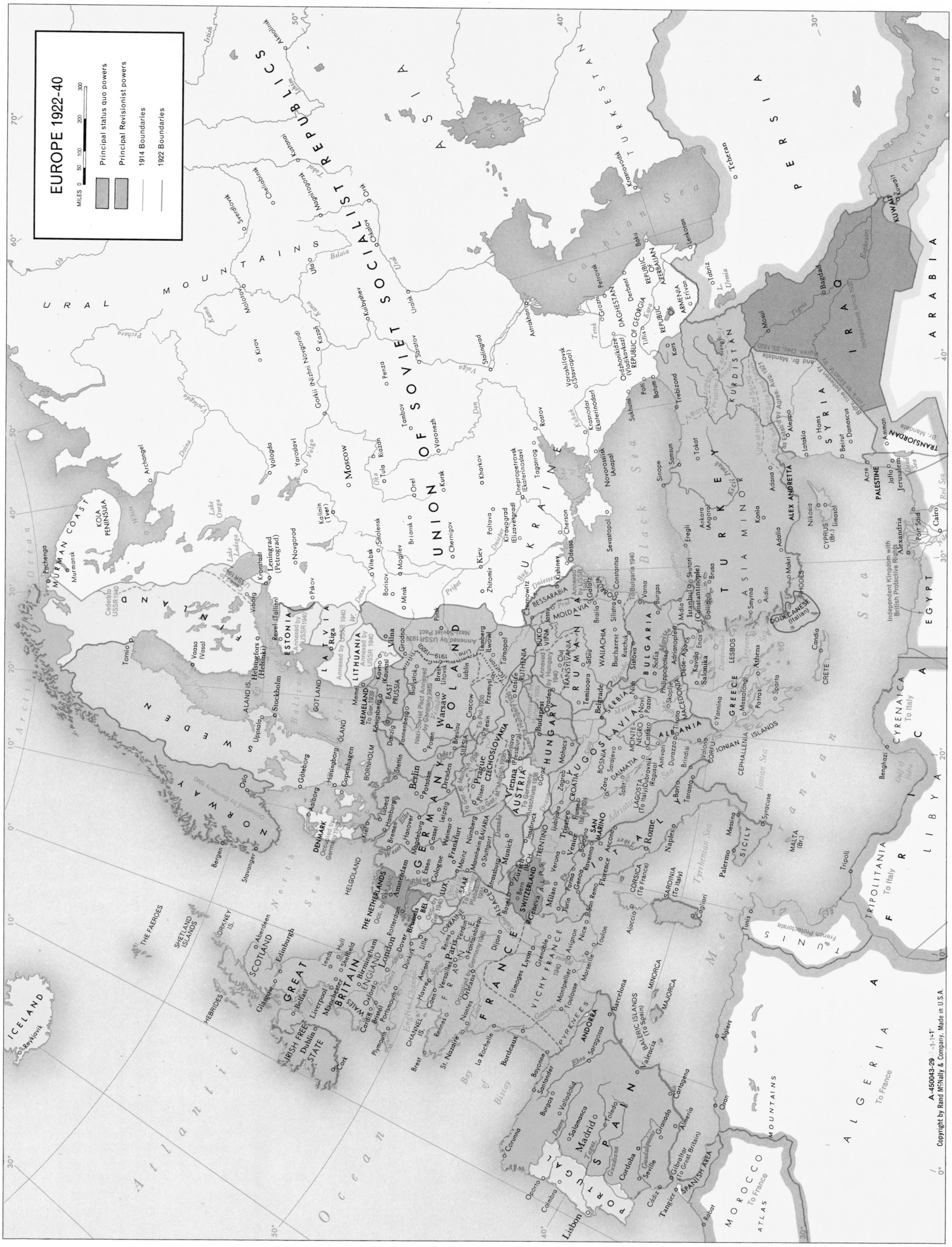
EUROPE 1922-40
MILES 0 50 100 200 300
Principal status quo powers
Principal Revisionist powers
1914 Boundaries
1922 Boundaries
A-450043-29 -1-1-1
Copyright by Rand McNally & Company. Made in U.S.A.

EUROPE
AFTER WORLD WAR II
Showing changes to 1950
MILES 0 50 100 200 300 400 500
North Atlantic Treaty Organization (NATO)
Soviet Russia and People's Democracies
Major Neutral Powers
Yugoslavia-Communist State but Neutral
ICELAND
Reykjavik
IRELAND (EIRE)
Dublin
NORTHERN IRELAND
Belfast
GREAT BRITAIN
London
Glasgow
Edinburgh
Aberdeen
Liverpool
Manchester
Hull
Plymouth
Portsmouth
SHETLAND (Br.)
FAEROE IS. (Den.)
Atlantic Ocean
North Sea
Bay of Biscay
NORWAY
Bergen
Stavanger
Oslo
SWEDEN
Göteborg
Stockholm
Uppsala
GOTLAND
FINLAND
Helsinki
Pechenga
Porkkala—Russia 1946-1956
DEN.
Copenhagen
BORNHOLM (Den.)
NETH.
Amsterdam
The Hague
BELGIUM
Brussels
LUX.
FRANCE
Paris
Le Havre
Cherbourg
Brest
Le Mans
Reims
Bordeaux
Toulouse
Lyon
Marseille
CORSICA
Ajaccio
PYRENEES
SPAIN
Madrid
Barcelona
Valencia
Cartagena
Córdoba
Sevilla
Gibraltar
PORTUGAL
Lisbon
Porto
Coimbra
BALEARIC IS.
WEST GERMAN FEDERAL REP.
Hamburg
Bremen
Cologne
Bonn
Frankfurt
Munich
Nuremburg
EAST GERMANY
Berlin
Leipzig
Dresden
SWITZ.
Zürich
Bern
Geneva
AUSTRIA
Vienna
ITALY
Milano
Genova
Venezia
Trieste
Rome
Napoli
Bari
Palermo
Messina
SICILY
SARDINIA
Cagliari
SAN MARINO
APENNINES
ALPS
CZECHOSLOVAKIA
Prague
HUNGARY
Budapest
YUGOSLAVIA
Belgrade
Zagreb
Sarajevo
Skopje
ALB.
Tirane
GREECE
Athens
Thessaloniki
CRETE
CORFU
CEPHALONIA
DODECANESE
RHODES
BULGARIA
Sofia
Burgas
Stalin
ROMANIA
Bucharest
Cluj
Ploesti
Galatio
Sibiu
Iasi
BUKOVINA
BESSARABIA
Kishinev
POLAND
Warsaw
Lódź
Krakow
Poznan
Gdansk
Szczecin
Lublin
CARPATHIANS
E. PRUSSIA
Kaliningrad
LITHUANIA
Kaunas
Vilnyus
Memel
LATVIA
Riga
ESTONIA
Tallinn
WHITE RUSSIA
Minsk
Brest
UKRAINE
Kiev
Lvov
Odessa
Kharkov
Dnepropetrovsk
SOVIET UNION
Moscow
Leningrad
Novgorod
Pskov
Smolensk
Murmansk
Arkhangelsk
Gorkii
Kazan
Kirov
Kuibyshev
Saratov
Stalingrad
Voronezh
Orel
Rostov
Sevastopol
Yalta
Stavropol
Astrakhan
Tbilisi
Erivan
Baku
Batumi
URAL MTS.
CAUCASUS
Black Sea
Caspian Sea
Aral Sea
Sea of Azov
White Sea
Lake Ladoga
Lake Onega
Baltic Sea
Gulf of Bothnia
TURKEY
Istanbul
Ankara
Izmir (Smyrna)
Konya
Samsun
Trabzon
SYRIA
Aleppo
Damascus
LEBANON
Beirut
IRAQ
Baghdad
IRAN
Tehran
Tabriz
CYPRUS (Br.)
MALTA (Br.)
TUNISIA
Tunis
Bizerte
ALGERIA
Algiers
Oran
MOROCCO
Rabat
Casablanca
Tangier
ATLAS MOUNTAINS
AFRICA
Mediterranean Sea
Tyrrhenian Sea
Ionian Sea
Aegean Sea
Ceded to Russia after W. W. II
To Russia by 1940 peace treaty
Annexed by Russia after W. W. II
Annexed by Poland after W. W. II
Ceded to Czech. after W. W. II
Annexed by Bulgaria after World War II
Annexed by Yugo. after W. W. II
Dodecanese ceded by Italy to Greece after W. W. II
Admitted to NATO after 1950
"Iraq and Iran, members of Baghdad Pact, allied to west"
B-450045-29 -1-1-1
Copyright by Rand McNally & Company, Made in U.S.A.

Conic Projection
SCALE 1:4,000,000 1 Inch = 63 Statute Miles

Statute Miles 25 0 25 50 75
Kilometers 25 0 25 50 100

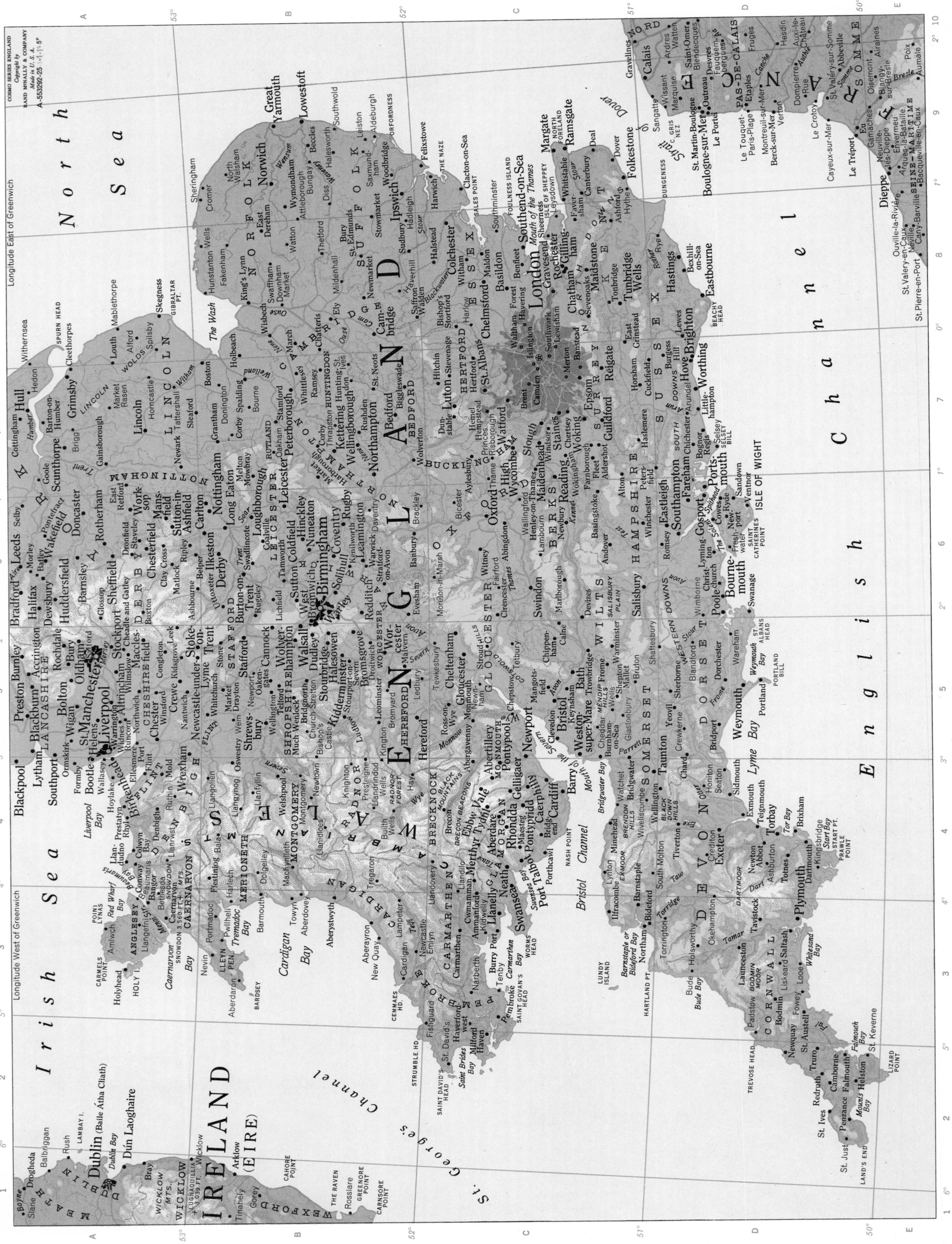

RELIEF

Feet
5 000
2 000
1 000
500
Sea Level
Below Sea Level
500
5 000

Statute Miles 5 0 5 10 20 30 40 50

Kilometers 5 0 5 10 20 30 40 50 60

Lambert Conformal Conic Projection
SCALE 1:2,000,000 1 Inch = 32 Statute Miles

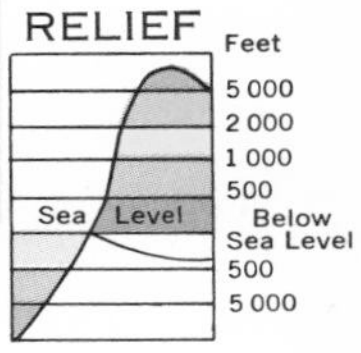

Lambert Conformal Conic Projection
SCALE 1 : 2,000,000 1 Inch = 32 Statute Miles

Statute Miles 5 0 5 10 20 30 40 50

Kilometers 5 0 5 10 20 30 40 50 60

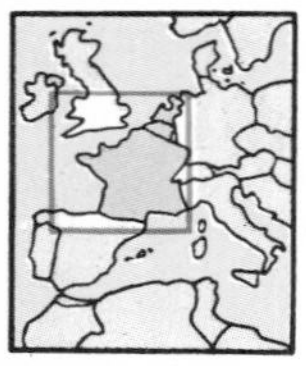

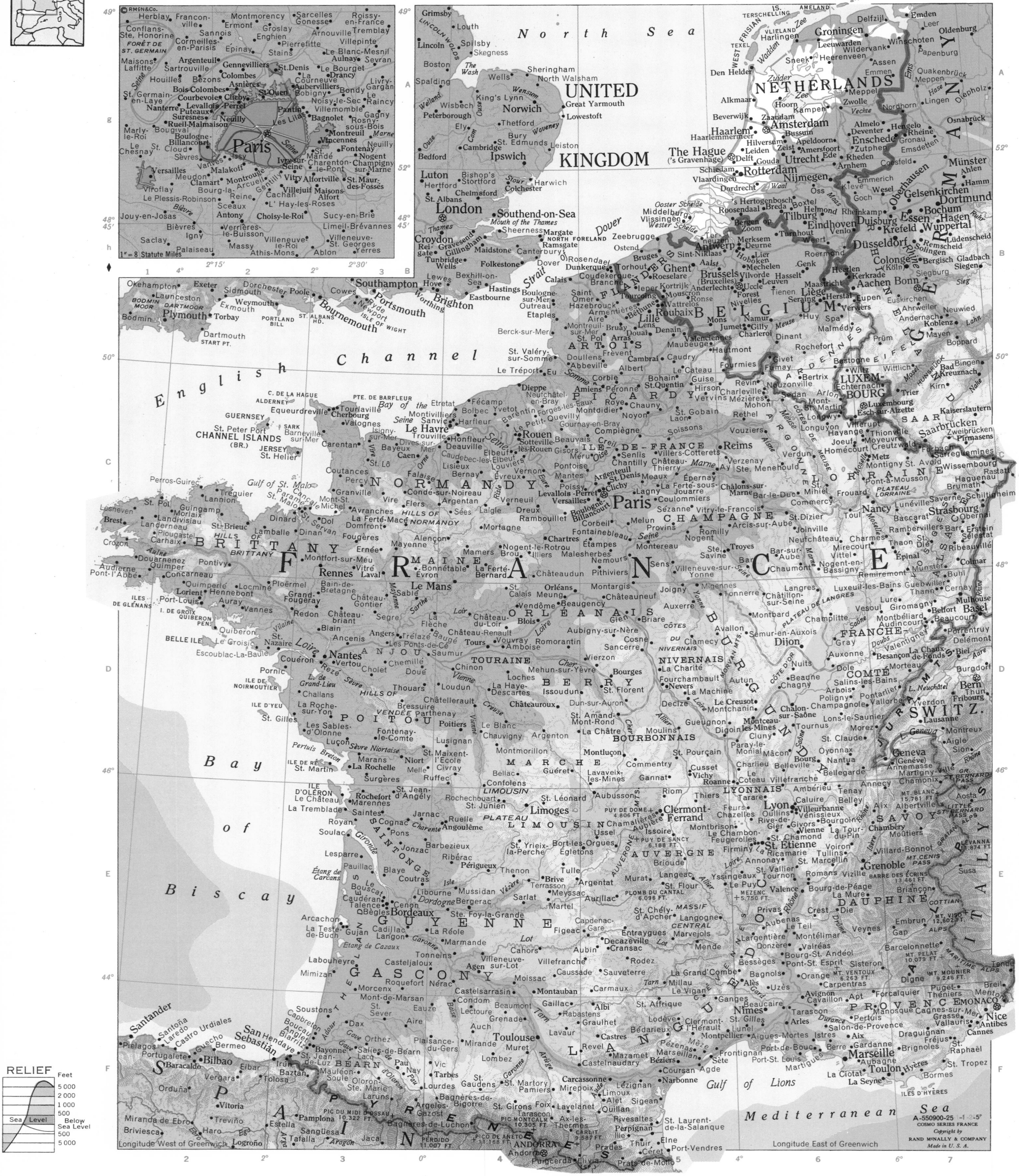

Statute Miles 25 0 25 50 75

Kilometers 25 0 25 50 100

Conic Projection

SCALE 1:4,000,000 1 Inch = 63 Statute Miles

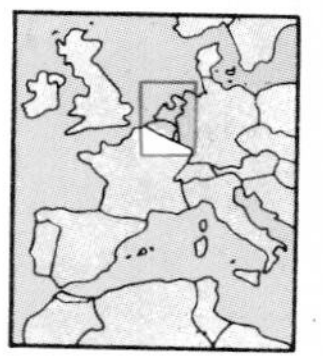

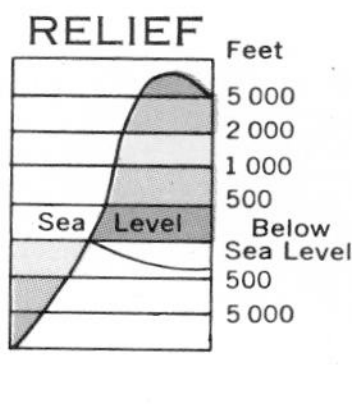

Lambert Conformal Conic Projection
SCALE 1:2,000,000 1 Inch = 32 Statute Miles

Statute Miles 5 0 5 10 20 30 40 50
Kilometers 5 0 5 10 20 30 40 50 60

RELIEF

Feet
5 000
2 000
1 000
500
100
Sea Level
Below Sea Level
500
5 000

60

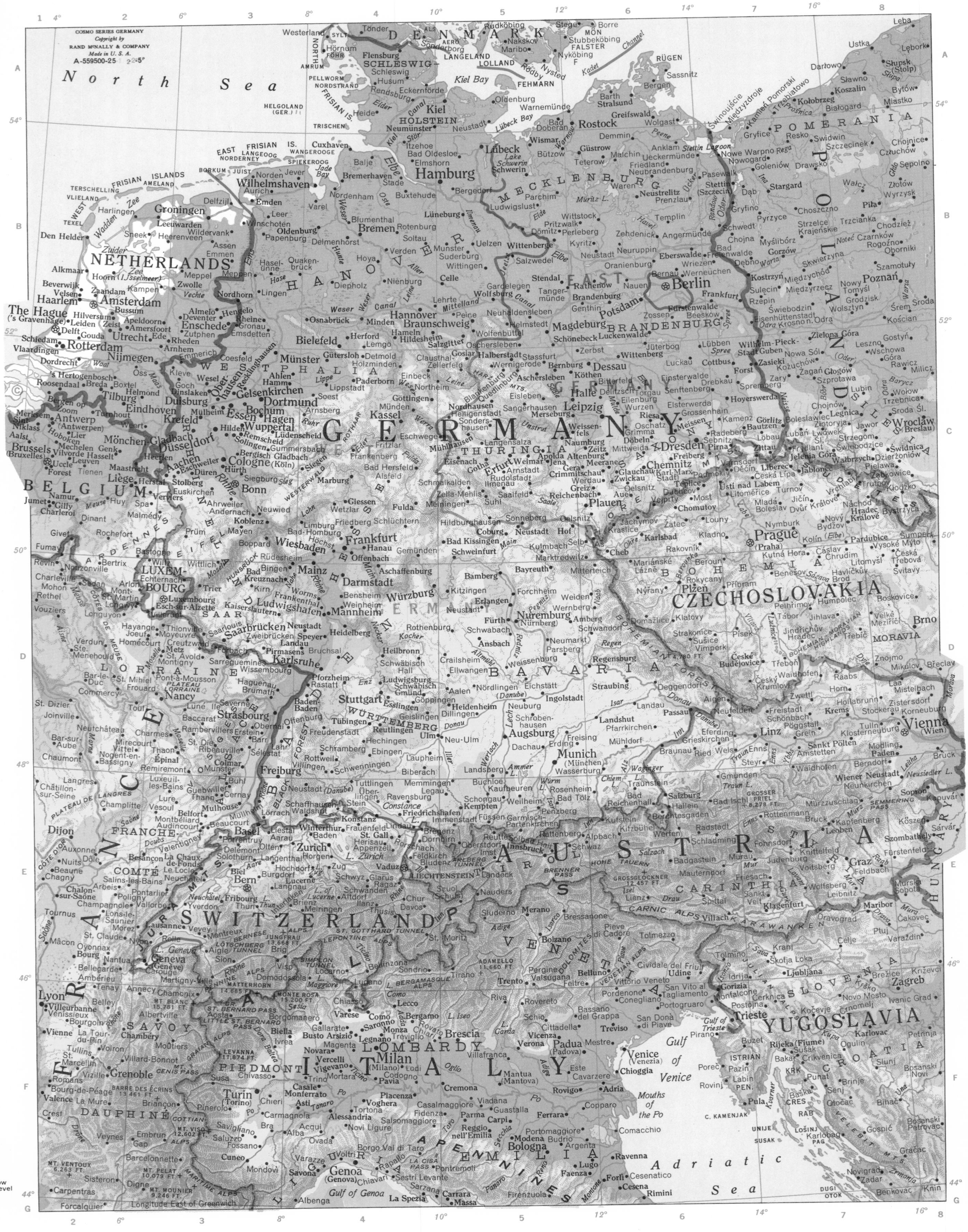

Statute Miles 25 0 25 50 75

Kilometers 25 0 25 50 100

Conic Projection

SCALE 1:4,000,000 1 Inch = 63 Statute Miles

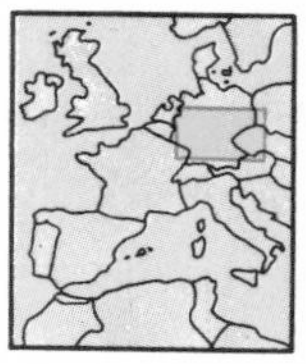

Lambert Conformal Conic Projection
SCALE 1:2,000,000 1 Inch = 32 Statute Miles

Statute Miles 5 0 5 10 20 30 40 50
Kilometers 5 0 5 10 20 30 40 50 60

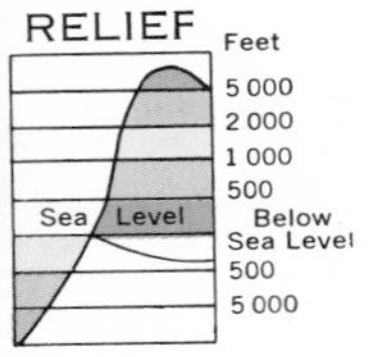

Statute Miles 5 0 5 10 20 30 40 50

Kilometers 5 0 5 10 20 30 40 50 60

Lambert Conformal Conic Projection

SCALE 1:2,000,000 1 Inch = 32 Statute Miles

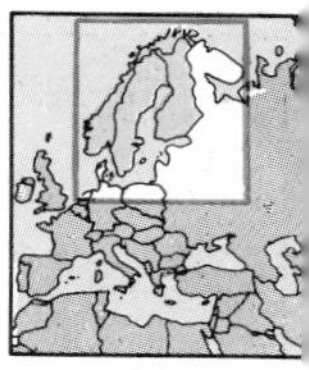

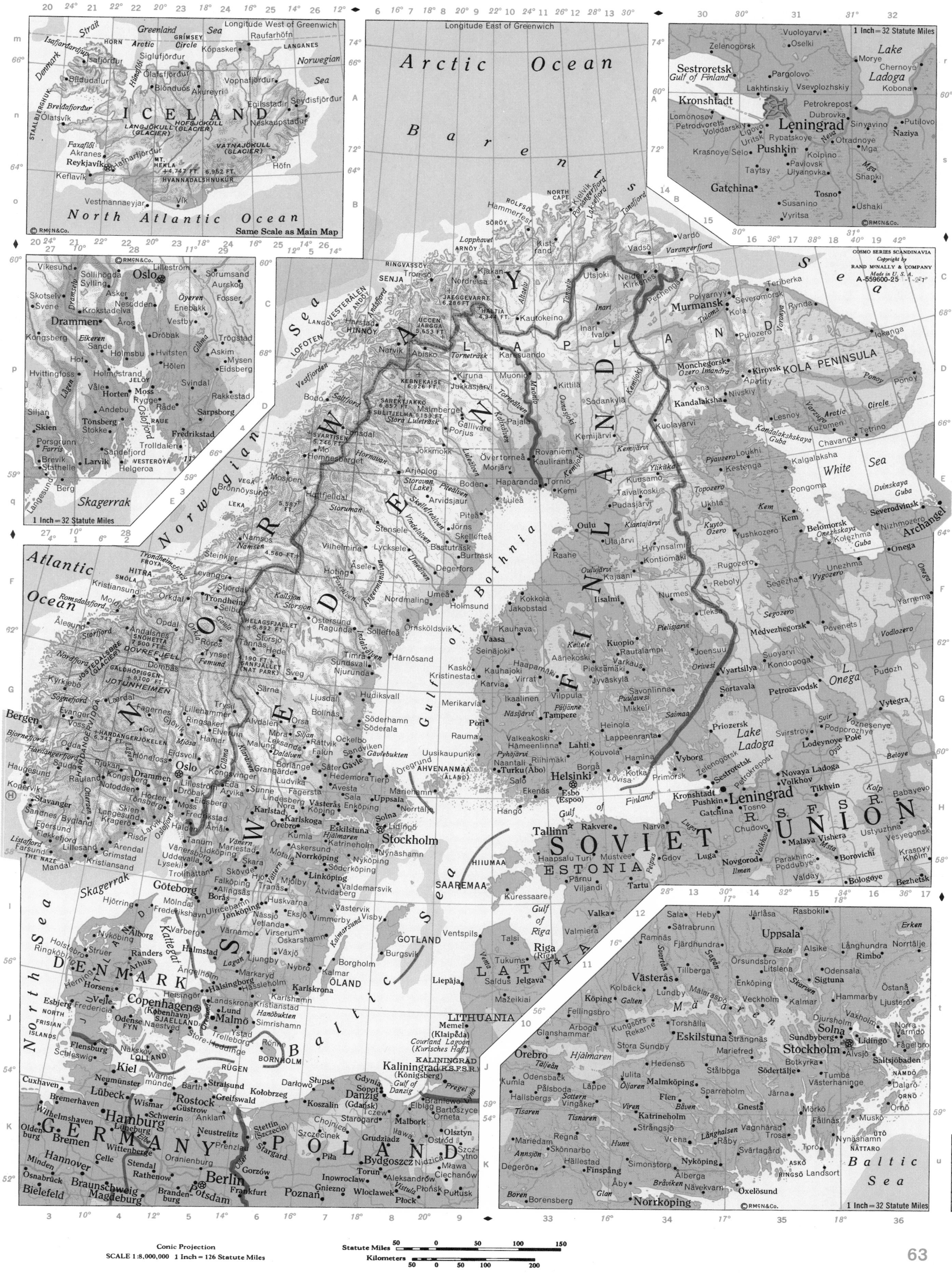
Longitude West of Greenwich
ICELAND
Greenland Sea
Denmark Strait
Arctic Circle
Norwegian Sea
North Atlantic Ocean
Reykjavík
Akureyri
Keflavík
Vestmannaeyjar
LANGJÖKULL (GLACIER)
HOFSJÖKULL (GLACIER)
VATNAJÖKULL (GLACIER)
HVANNADALSHNÚKUR
Same Scale as Main Map
© RMcN&Co.
Oslo
Drammen
Skagerrak
1 Inch = 32 Statute Miles
Longitude East of Greenwich
Arctic Ocean
Barents Sea
Norwegian Sea
Atlantic Ocean
North Sea
NORWAY
SWEDEN
FINLAND
LAPPLAND
DENMARK
GERMANY
POLAND
ESTONIA
LATVIA
LITHUANIA
SOVIET UNION
S. F. S. R.
KALININGRAD (R.S.F.S.R.)
KOLA PENINSULA
White Sea
Gulf of Bothnia
Gulf of Finland
Gulf of Riga
Baltic Sea
Kattegat
Lake Ladoga
L. Onega
Oslo
Stockholm
Helsinki
Copenhagen (København)
Leningrad
Tallinn
Riga
Murmansk
Archangel
Trondheim
Bergen
Göteborg
Malmö
Turku (Åbo)
Tampere
Oulu
Berlin
Hamburg
Gdańsk
Kaliningrad (Königsberg)
Sestroretsk
Kronshtadt
Pushkin
Gatchina
Lake Ladoga
Uppsala
Västerås
Eskilstuna
Norrköping
Mälaren
Hjälmaren
COSMO SERIES SCANDINAVIA
Copyright by RAND McNALLY & COMPANY
Made in U. S. A.
A-559600-25
RELIEF
Feet
5 000
2 000
1 000
500
Sea Level
Below Sea Level
500
5 000
Conic Projection
SCALE 1:8,000,000 1 Inch = 126 Statute Miles
Statute Miles
50 0 50 100 150
Kilometers
50 0 50 100 200

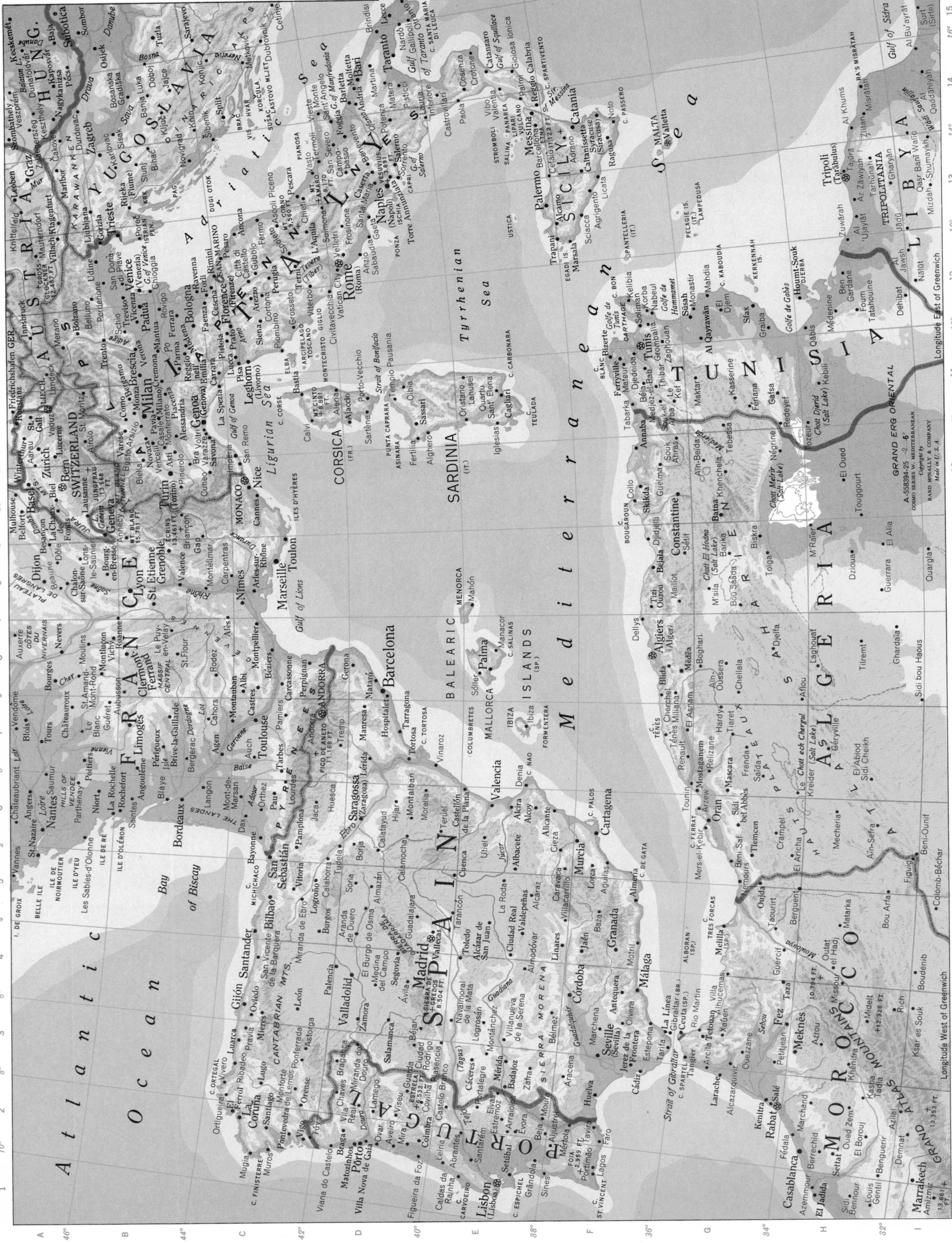

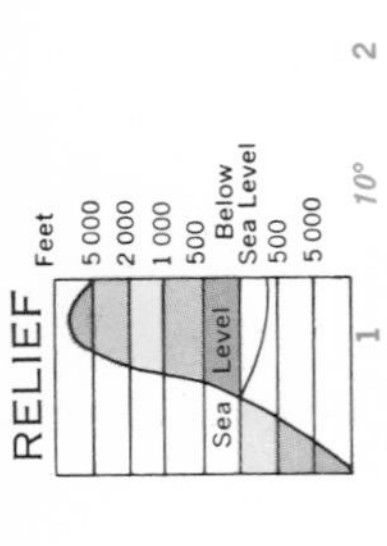

Statute Miles 50 0 50 100 150

Kilometers 50 0 50 100 200

Lambert Conformal Conic Projection

SCALE 1 : 8,000,000 1 Inch = 126 Statute Miles

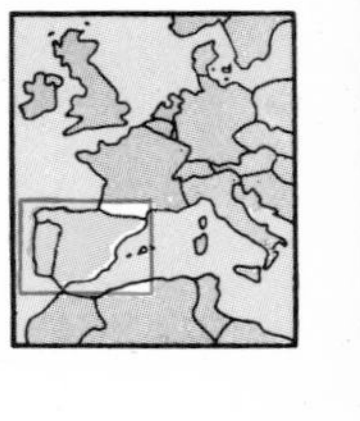

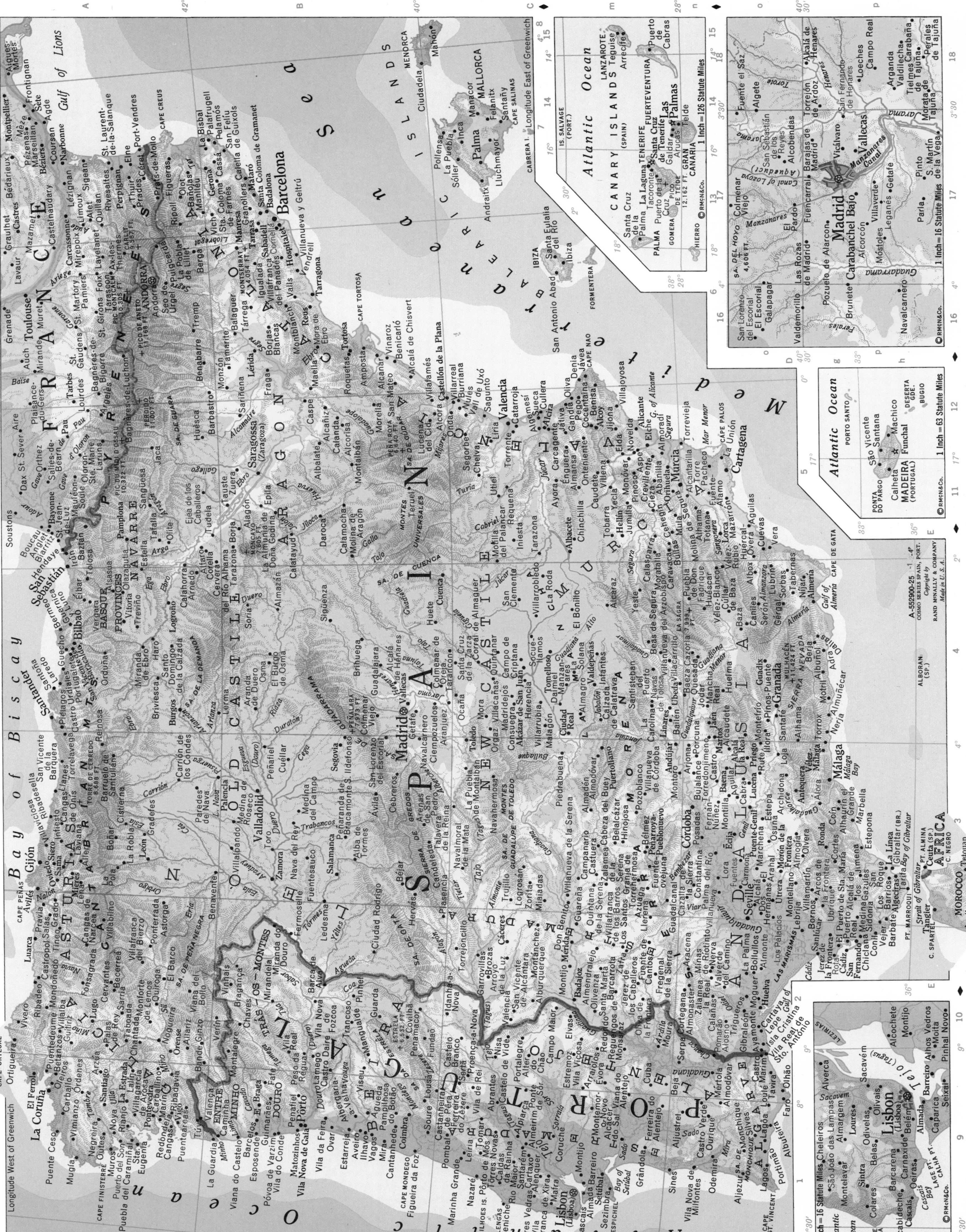

Conic Projection
SCALE 1:4,000,000 1 Inch = 63 Statute Miles

Statute Miles 25 0 25 50 75
Kilometers 25 0 25 50 100

RELIEF

Feet	
5,000	
2,000	
1,000	
500	
Sea Level	
500	Below
5,000	

Gulf of Venice

Adriatic Sea

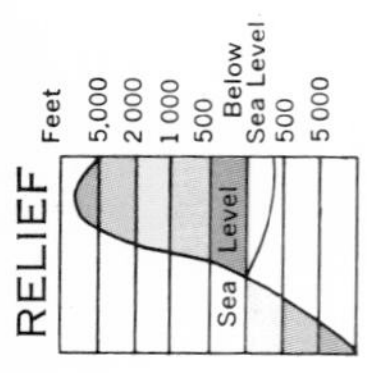

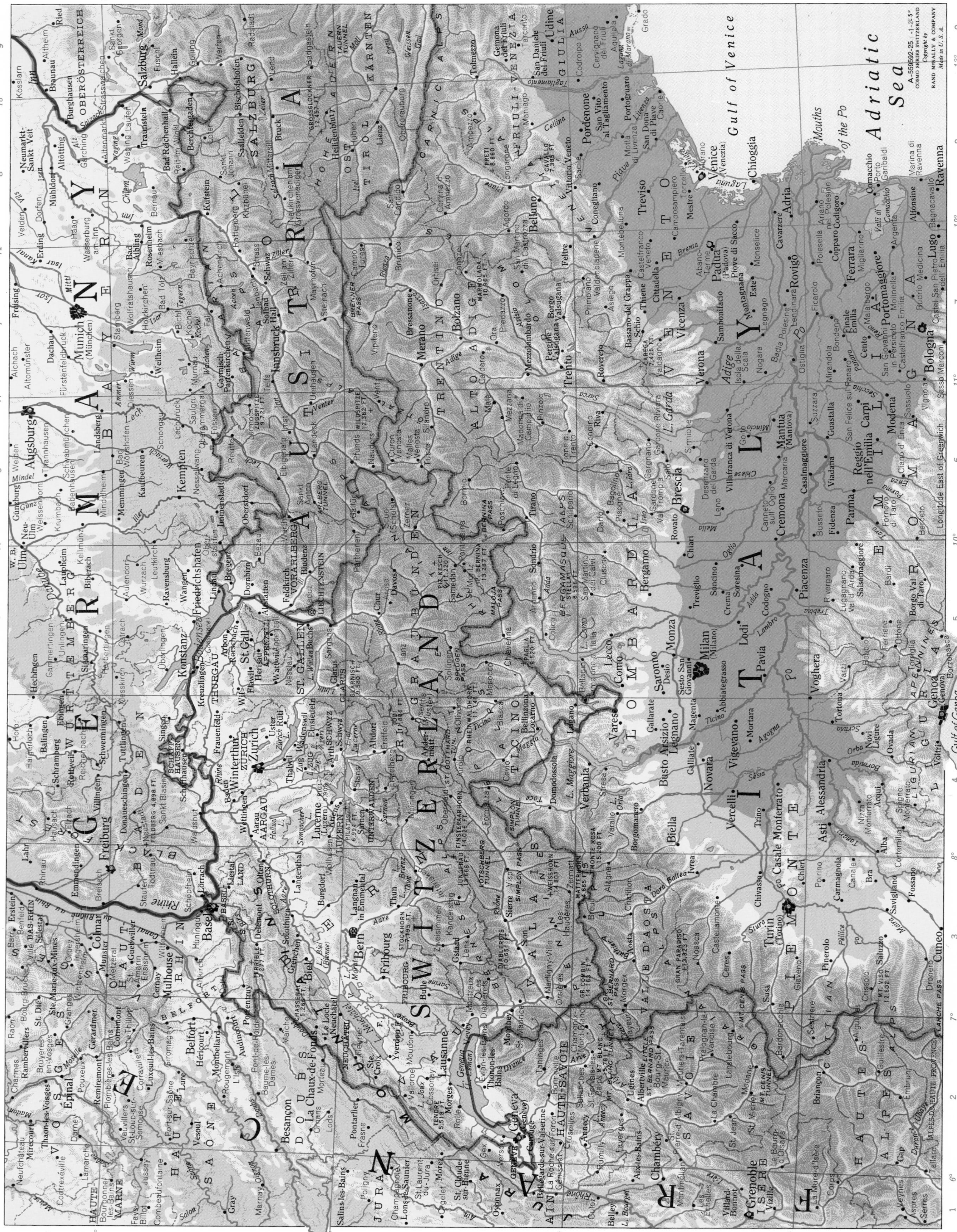

Statute Miles 5 0 5 10 20 30 40 50
Kilometers 5 0 5 10 20 30 40 50 60

Lambert Conformal Conic Projection
SCALE 1:2,000,000 1 Inch = 32 Statute Miles

A-556692-25 -1-25*
COSMO SERIES SWITZERLAND
Copyright by
RAND McNALLY & COMPANY
Made in U.S.A.

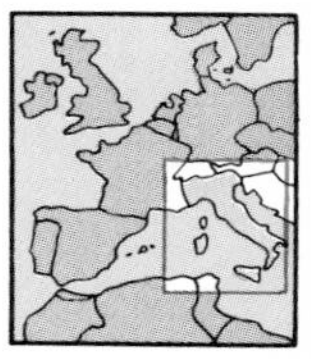

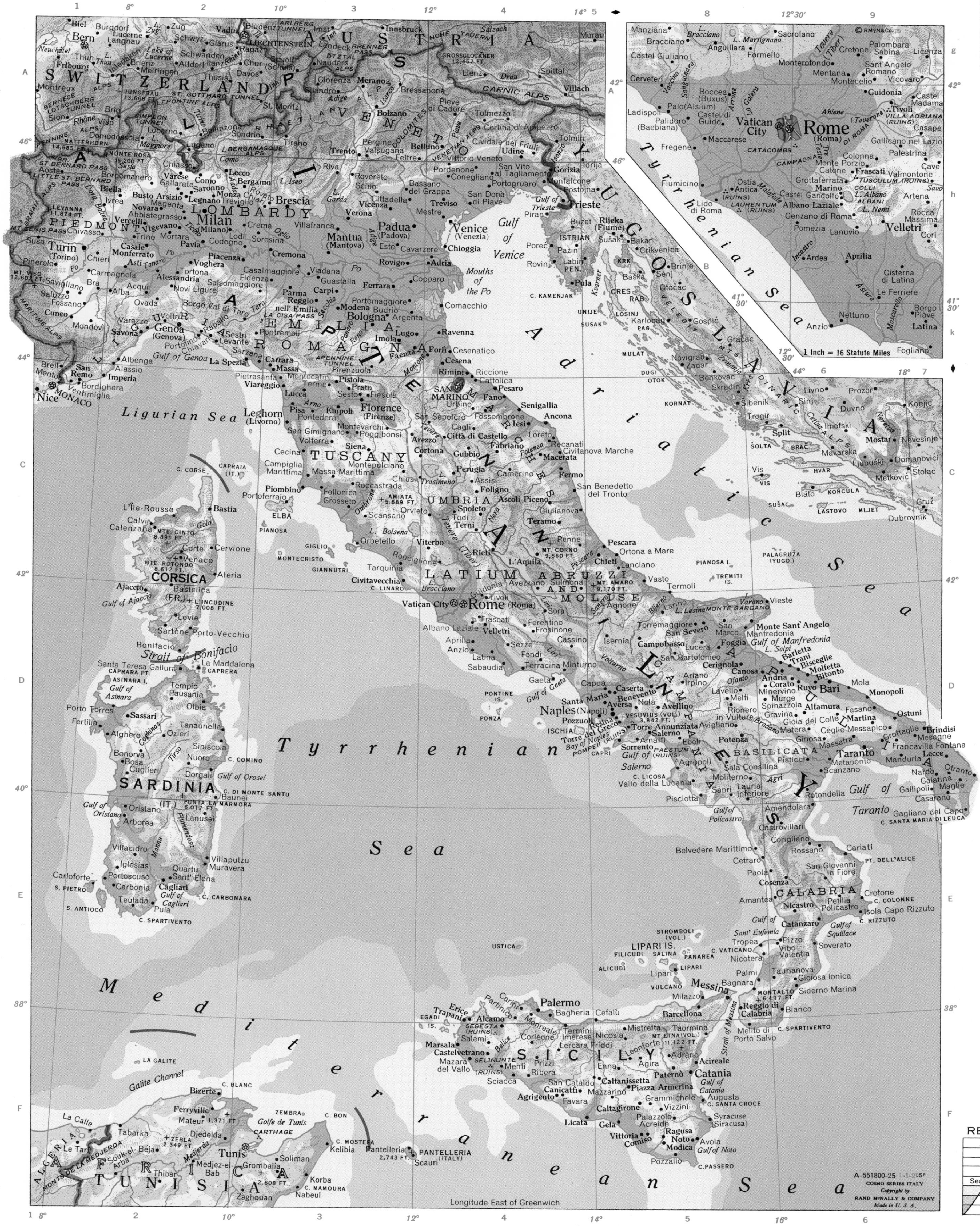

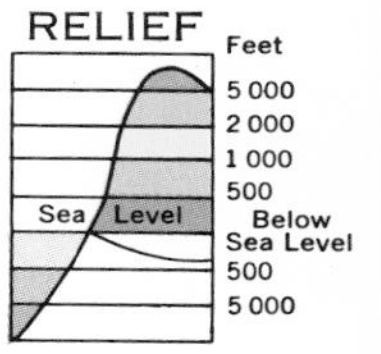

Conic Projection
SCALE 1:4,000,000 1 Inch = 63 Statute Miles

Statute Miles 25 0 25 50 75
Kilometers 25 0 25 50 100

YUGOSLAVIA
HUNGARY
ROMANIA
BULGARIA
ALBANIA
GREECE
TURKEY
ITALY
AUSTRIA
CZECHOSLOVAKIA
SOVIET UNION
Black Sea
Adriatic Sea
Aegean Sea
Sea of Marmara
Budapest
Bucharest (București)
Sofia (Sofiya)
Belgrade (Beograd)
Vienna (Wien)
Istanbul
Conic Projection
SCALE 1:4,000,000 1 Inch = 63 Statute Miles
Statute Miles 25 0 25 50 75
Kilometers 25 0 25 50 100

RELIEF
Feet
5 000
2 000
1 000
500
Below Sea Level
500
5 000
Sea
Level

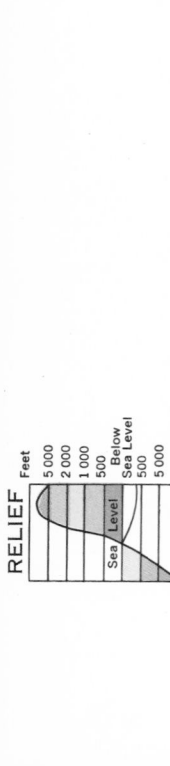

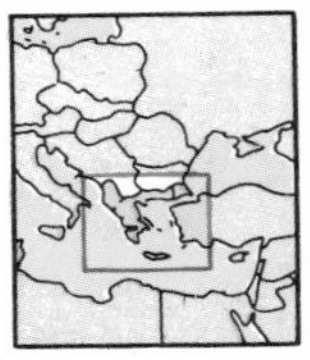

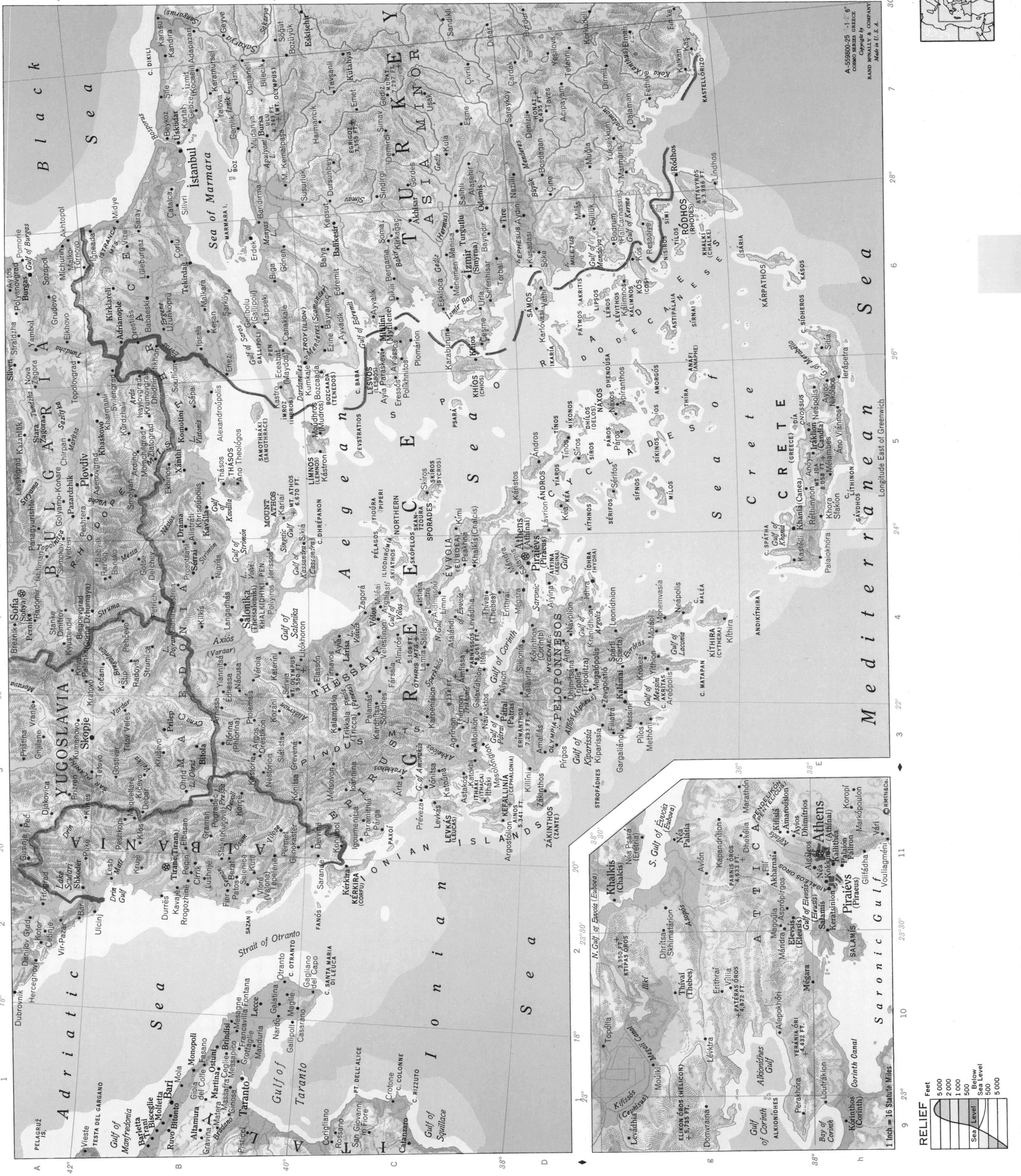

Conic Projection
SCALE 1:4,000,000 1 Inch = 63 Statute Miles

Statute Miles 25 0 25 50 75
Kilometers 25 0 25 50 100

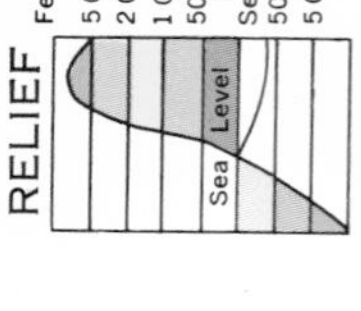

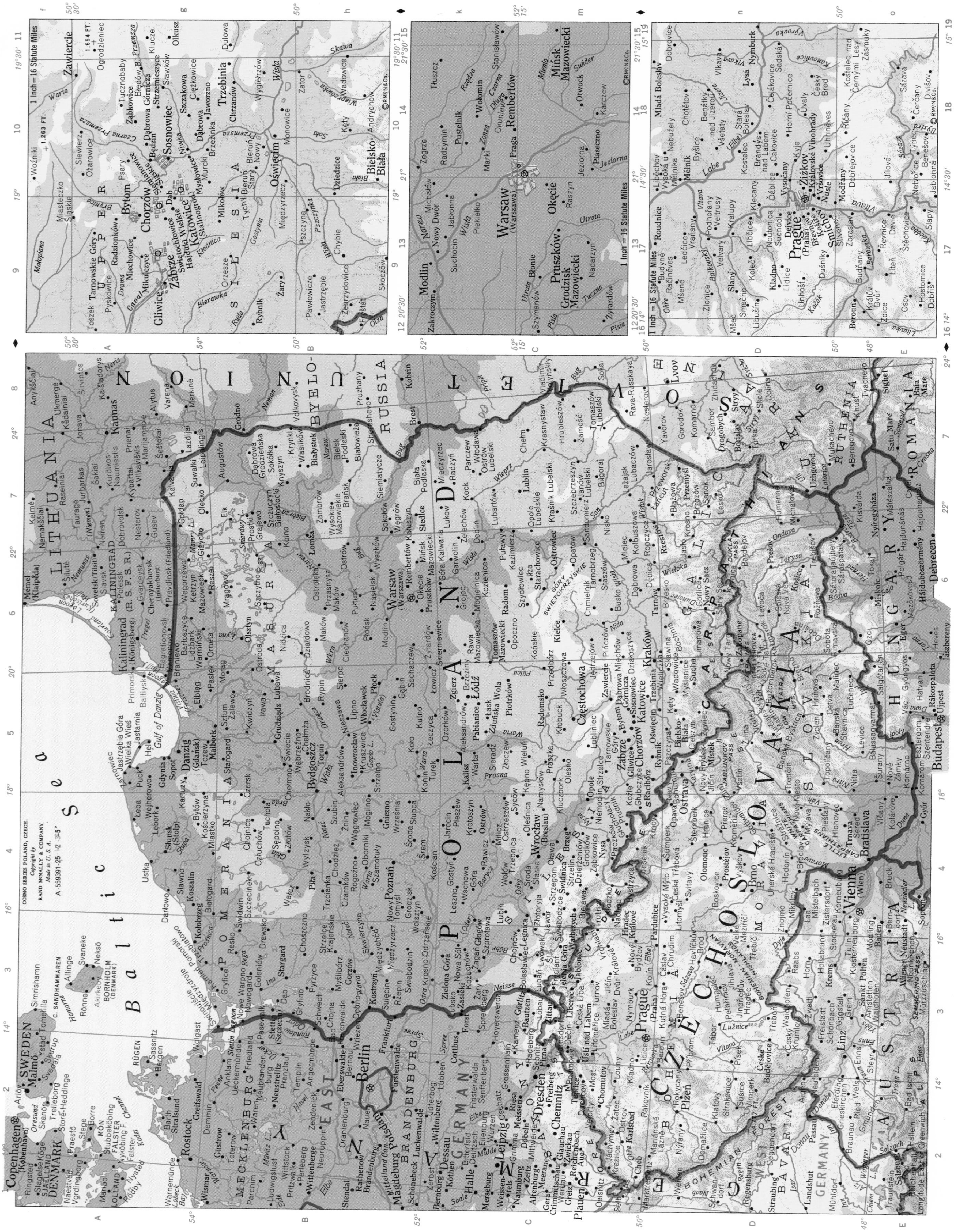

Statute Miles 25 0 25 50 75

Kilometers 25 0 25 50 100

Conic Projection

SCALE 1:4,000,000 1 Inch = 63 Statute Miles

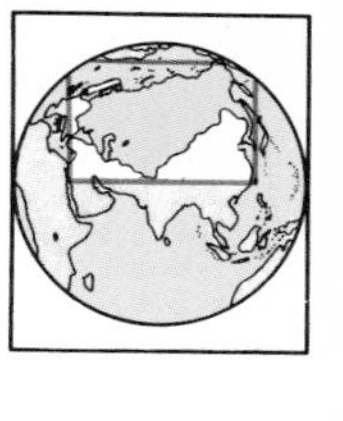

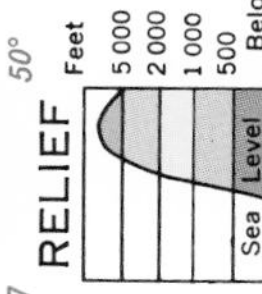

Lambert Azimuthal Equal Area Projection
SCALE 1:28,000,000 1 Inch = 442 Statute Miles

Statute Miles 100 0 100 200 300 400 500
Kilometers 100 0 100 300 500 700

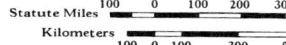

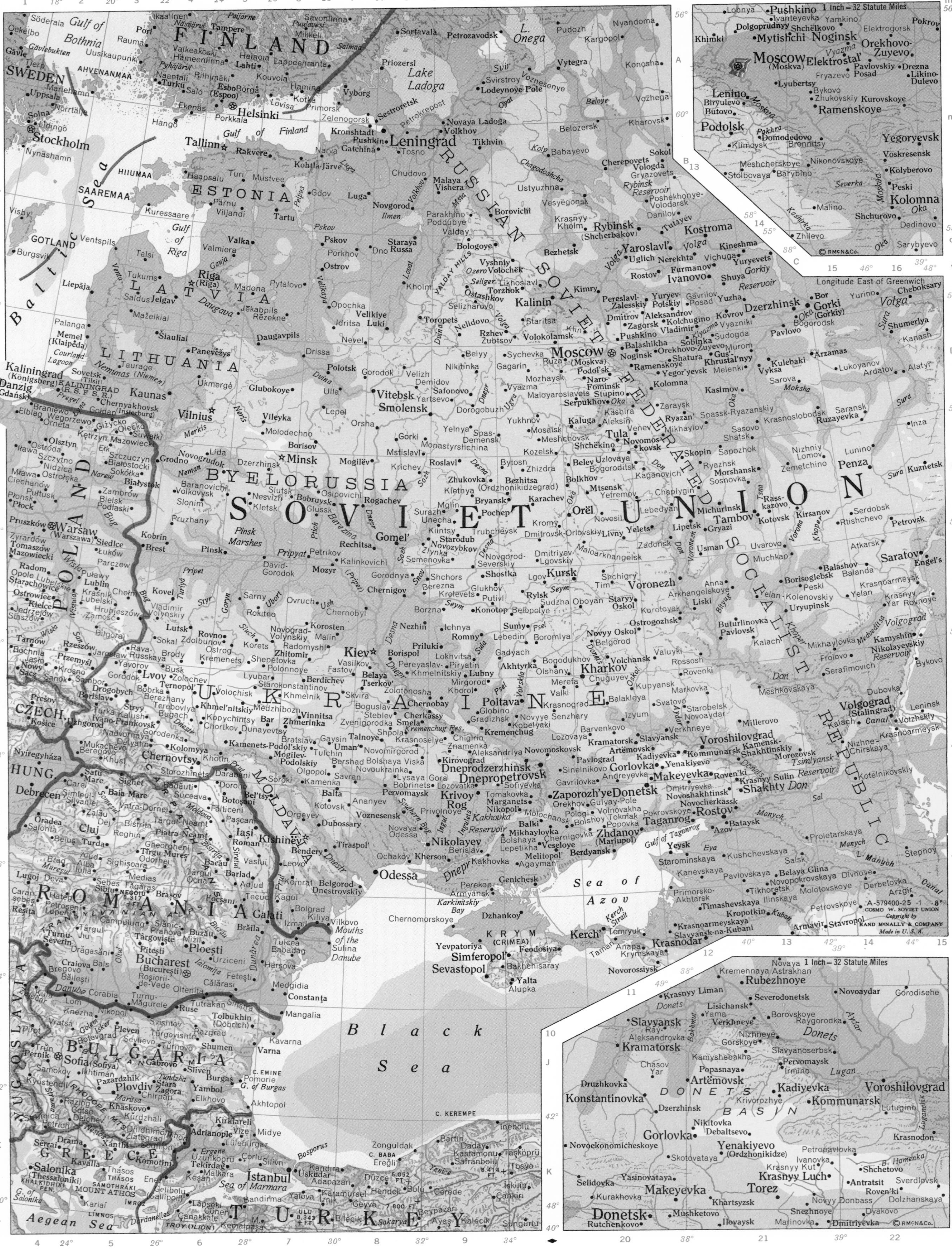

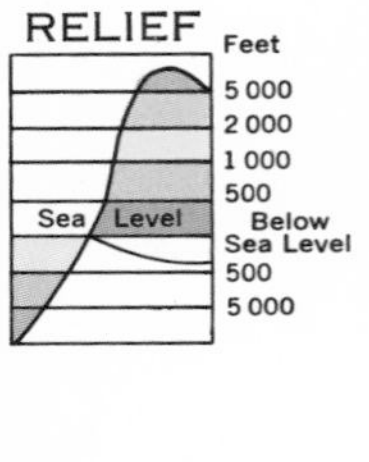

Statute Miles 50 0 50 100 150

Kilometers 50 0 50 100 200

Conic Projection

SCALE 1:8,000,000 1 Inch = 126 Statute Miles

RELIEF

Feet
5 000
2 000
1 000
500
Sea Level
Below Sea Level
500
5 000

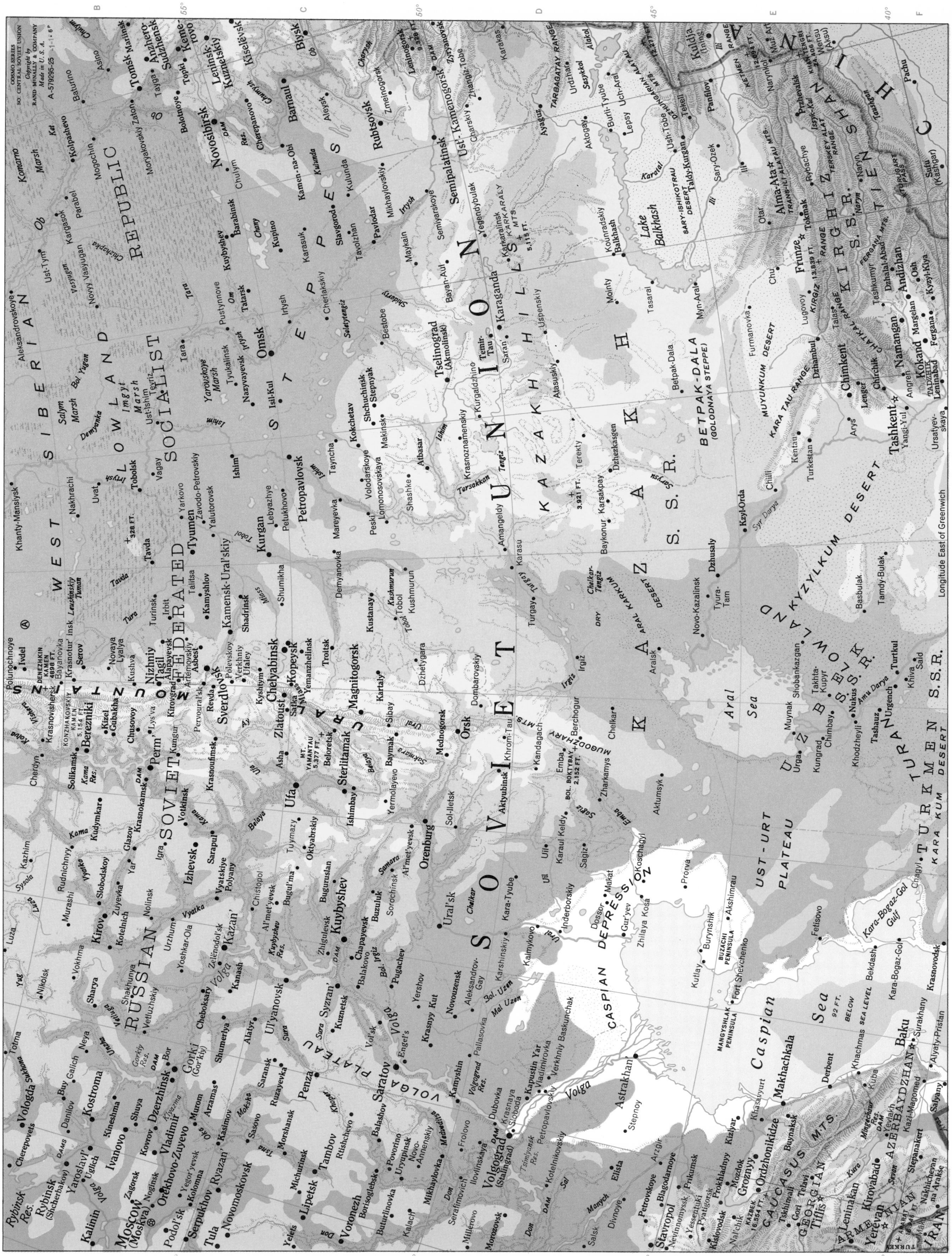

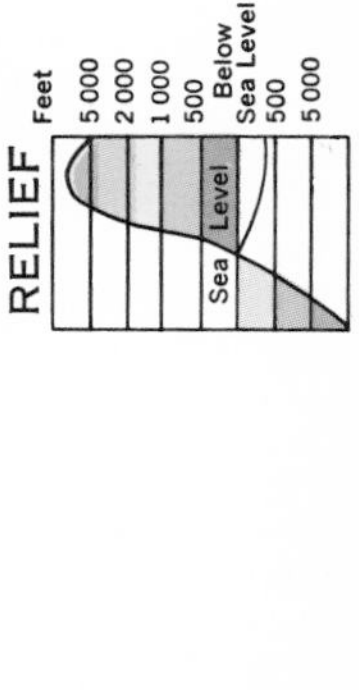

Sinusoidal Projection

SCALE 1: 11,400,000 1 Inch = 180 Statute Miles

Statute Miles 50 0 50 100 150 200 250

Kilometers 50 0 50 100 150 200 250 300

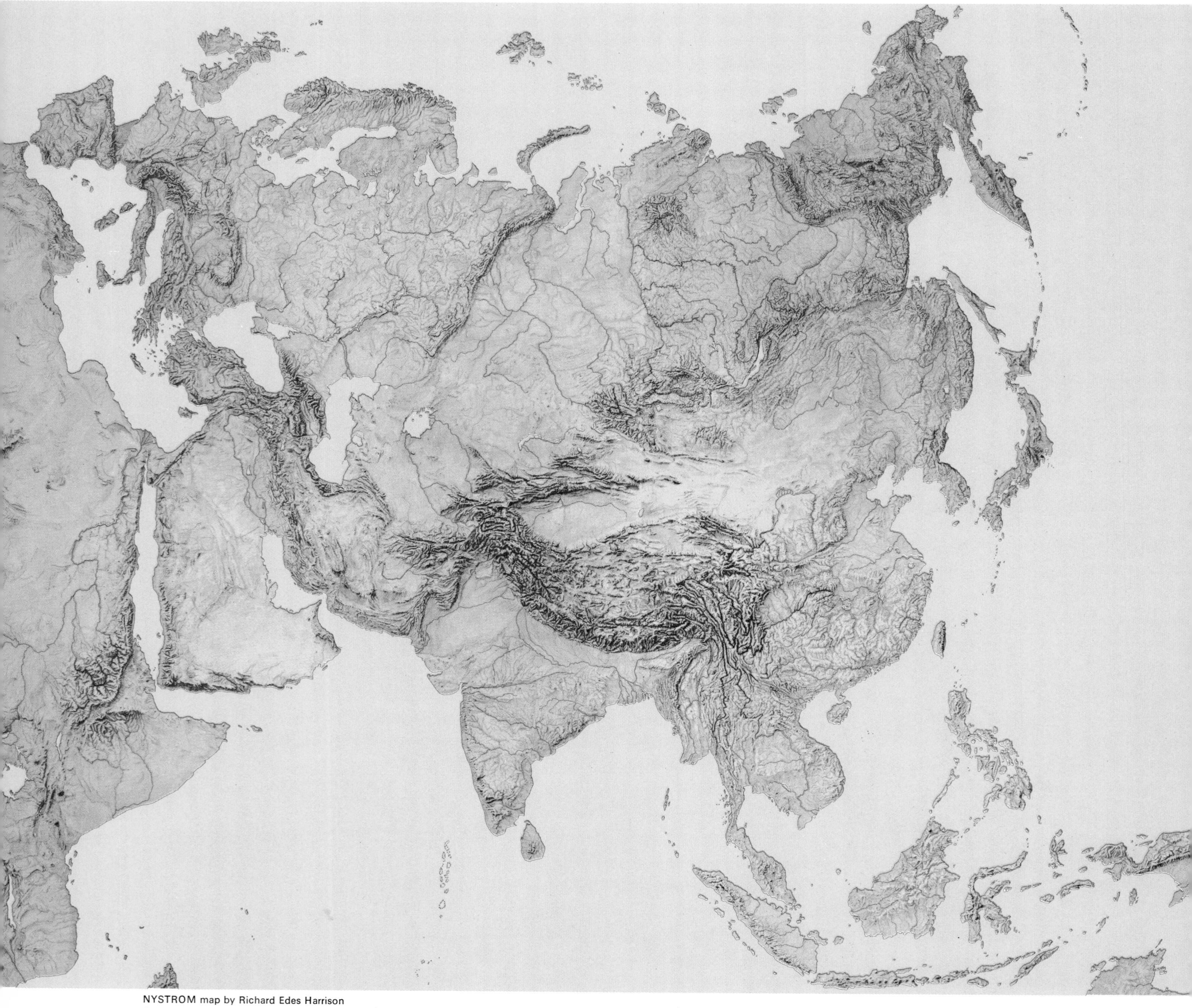

NYSTROM map by Richard Edes Harrison

ASIA

Asia has more land and more people than any other continent. It covers more area than North and South America combined and is one and a half times as large as Africa. Asia extends from the Arctic Circle in the north to the tropics in the south. It wraps nearly halfway around the world from east to west. The ancient civilizations of Asia gave birth to all the world's great religions. Christianity and Judaism began in Palestine in Western Asia. Islam was founded in Arabia, Hinduism and Buddhism developed in India, and Confucianism developed in China. Asia today has industrial centers in Japan, Hong Kong, and the Asian part of Russia, but most Asian nations are still developing.

WHAT IS YOUR ATLAS I.Q. OF ASIA?

These questions are designed to test your knowledge of the variety of information about Asia contained in THE WORLD BOOK ATLAS. Check your answers by turning to the last page of the ATLAS.

Identifying places

1. Lake Baykal, world's deepest fresh-water lake, is in Asia. In what country is it located?
2. The capital of China is Peking. What is the capital of India?
3. Six Asian countries border on the Mediterranean Sea. Four are Egypt, Syria, Cyprus, and Turkey. What are the other two countries?
4. Pakistan, India, Nepal, Burma, Laos, and Vietnam are China's chief neighbors on the south. What countries border China on the north?
5. Mount Everest, the world's highest mountain, is on the border between two Asian nations. One is China. What is the other?
6. The islands of Java, Sumatra, Borneo, and Celebes form the main parts of which Asian nation?
7. Japan is an island country made up of four main islands. The three smallest are Hokkaidō, Shikoku, and Kyūshū. What is the name of the largest Japanese island?
8. The Bosporus, the Sea of Marmara, and the Dardanelles separate the Asian part of Turkey from the European part. With what body of water does the Bosporus connect the Sea of Marmara?

Facts and figures

9. Asia has the two largest countries in the world in population. One is China. What is the other?
10. Three countries lie partly in Asia and in one other continent. Two of these are Russia and Egypt. What is the third?
11. The population of the world is more than 3½ billion persons. About how many persons live in Asia?
12. The British poet Rudyard Kipling wrote a famous poem about Asia called "Mandalay." In what country is Mandalay?

History

13. Several Asian countries have been known by other names. For example, Jordan was once called Transjordan and Thailand was once called Siam. What country was once called Persia?
14. The Bataan Peninsula was the site of a heroic American battle against the Japanese during World War II. Where is the Bataan Peninsula?
15. The Korean War began on June 25, 1950, when North Korean troops invaded South Korea. What parallel of latitude was then the dividing line between the two Koreas?
16. Ancient Mesopotamia was the site of some of the earliest civilizations. What present-day country occupies most of what was once Mesopotamia?
17. The Khyber Pass played a key role in the history of India when it was under British rule. What present-day countries are linked by the Khyber Pass?
18. Marco Polo of Italy was one of the first Europeans to write about the Far East. In what century did he make his famous trip to China?
19. In A.D. 750, Ch'angan was the capital of China. What was the capital of Japan at that time?
20. When Kublai Khan died in 1294, Mongol power stretched across most of Asia. The Mongols conquered Kiev, Russia, in 1240. In what year did they conquer Baghdad?

MAPS OF ASIA

76 PHYSICAL FEATURES OF ASIA
77 POLITICAL DIVISIONS OF ASIA
78-83 HISTORY OF ASIA
78 PERSIAN EMPIRE (ABOUT 500 B.C.)
79 ANCIENT INDIA (ABOUT 250 B.C. AND 400 A.D.)
79 ANCIENT CHINA (ABOUT 100 B.C.)
80 ASIA ABOUT 750 A.D.
81 ASIA ABOUT 1294
82 ASIA ABOUT 1775
83 AFTER WORLD WAR II
84-93 MAPS OF COUNTRIES AND DEPENDENCIES
86 AFGHANISTAN
86 BAHRAIN
87 BANGLADESH
87 BHUTAN
87 BURMA
89 CAMBODIA
87 CEYLON
91, 92 CHINA
85 CYPRUS
91 HONG KONG
87 INDIA
90 INDONESIA
86 IRAN
85, 86 IRAQ
84 ISRAEL
93 JAPAN
85 JORDAN
93 KOREA
86 KUWAIT
89 LAOS
85 LEBANON
91 MACAO
90 MALAYSIA
77 MALDIVE ISLANDS
91 MONGOLIA
88 NEPAL
87 OMAN
87 PAKISTAN
90 PHILIPPINES
86 QATAR
77 SAUDI ARABIA
88 SIKKIM
90 SINGAPORE
85 SYRIA
91 TAIWAN
89 THAILAND
90 TIMOR, PORTUGUESE
85 TURKEY
77 UNITED ARAB EMIRATES
89 VIETNAM
105 YEMEN (ADEN)
105 YEMEN (SAN'Ā')

RELIEF

Feet
5 000
2 000
1 000
500
Sea Level
500
5 000
20 000
Below Sea Level

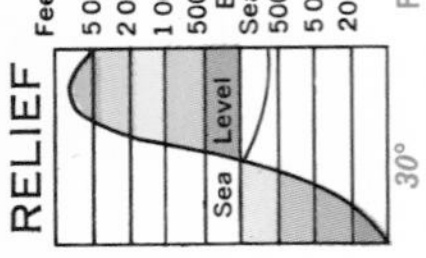

Statute Miles 100 0 100 300 500 700 900

Kilometers 100 0 100 300 700 1100

Lambert Azimuthal Equal Area Projection

SCALE 1:42,000,000 1 Inch = 663 Statute Miles

A-519695-25--5--11"
COSMO SERIES EURASIA
Copyright by
RAND McNALLY & COMPANY
Made in U.S.A.

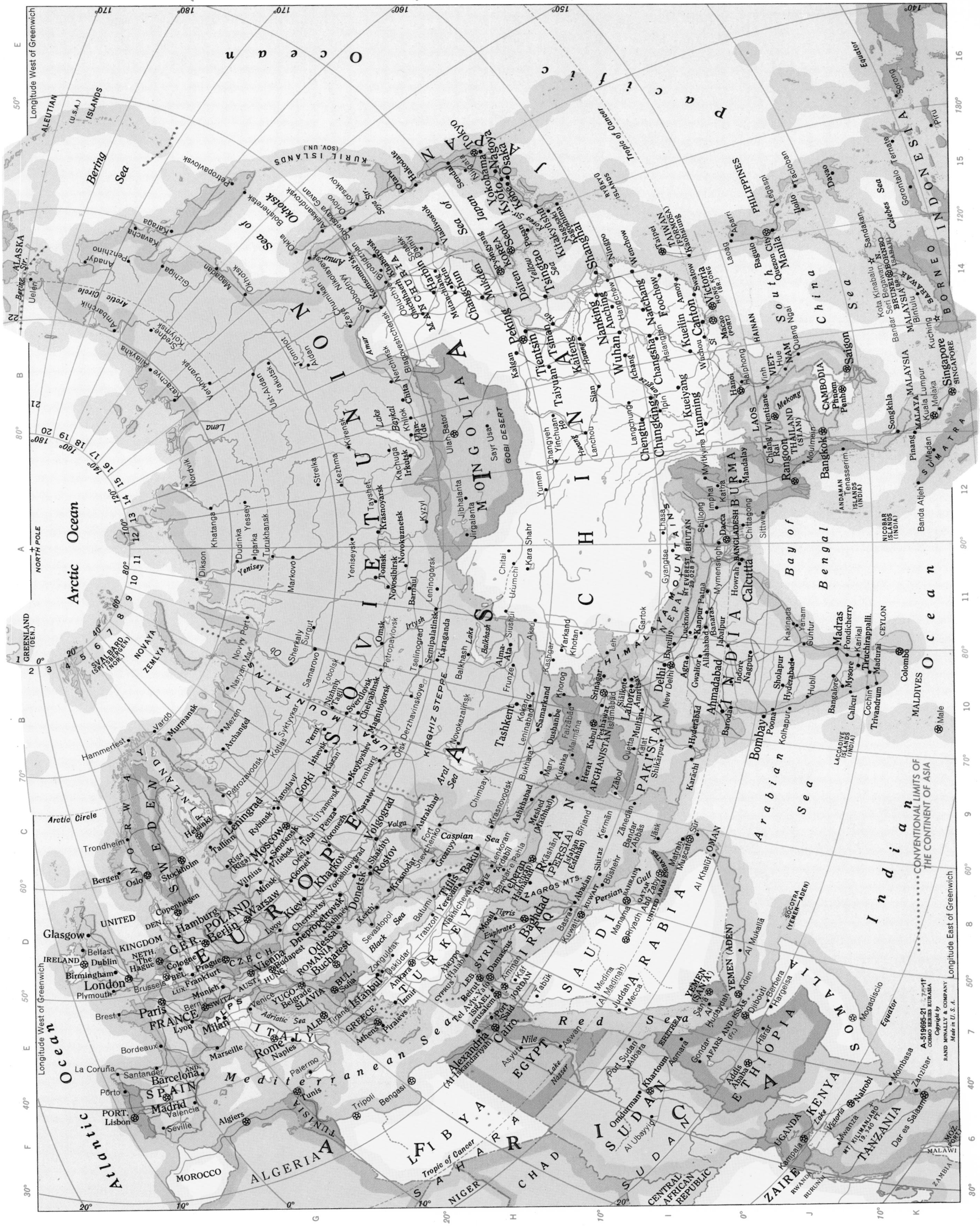

Lambert Azimuthal Equal Area Projection
SCALE 1:42,000,000 1 Inch = 663 Statute Miles

Statute Miles 100 0 100 300 500 700 900
Kilometers 100 0 100 300 700 1100

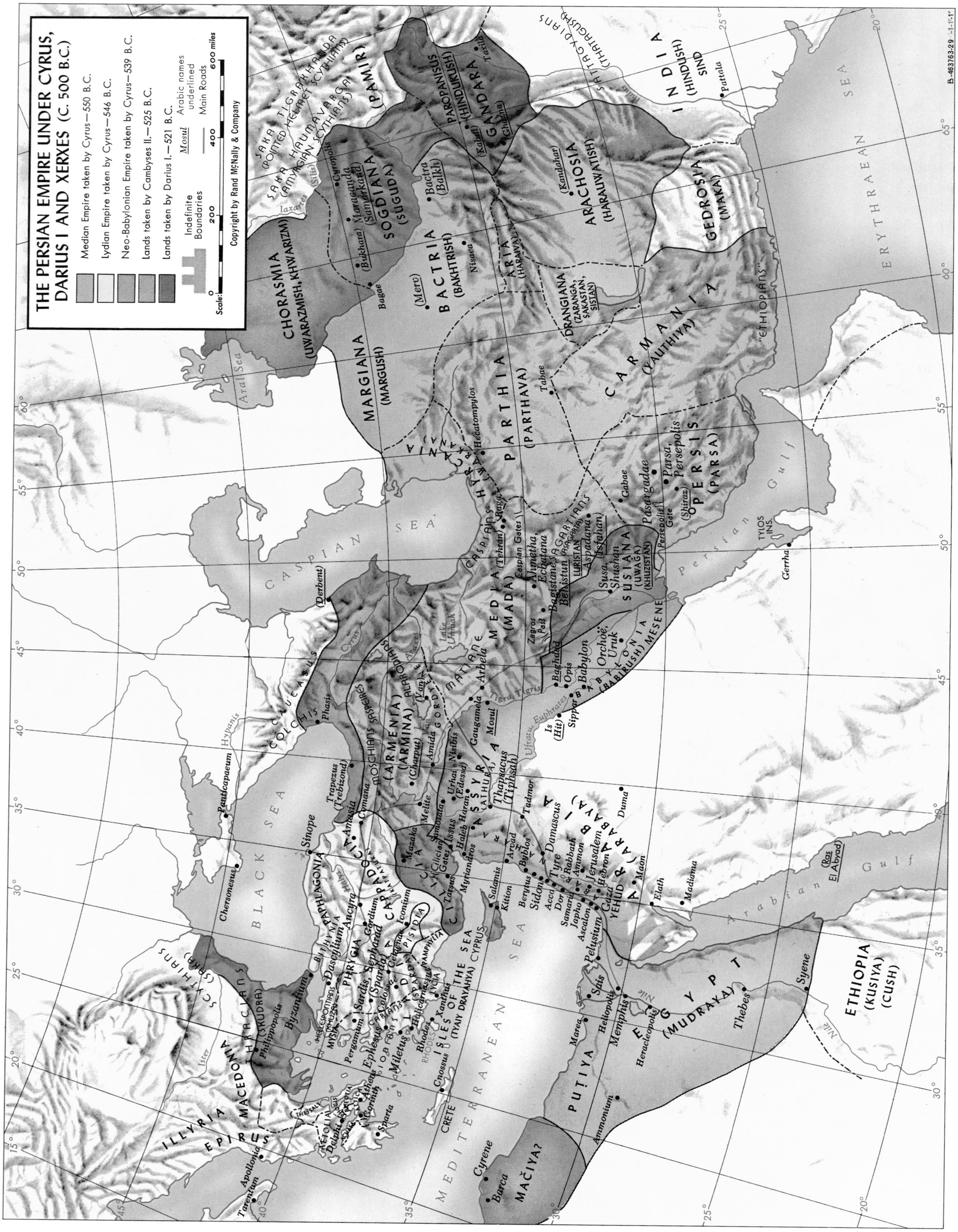
THE PERSIAN EMPIRE UNDER CYRUS, DARIUS I AND XERXES (C. 500 B.C.)
Median Empire taken by Cyrus—550 B.C.
Lydian Empire taken by Cyrus—546 B.C.
Neo-Babylonian Empire taken by Cyrus—539 B.C.
Lands taken by Cambyses II.—525 B.C.
Lands taken by Darius I.—521 B.C.
Indefinite Boundaries
Mosul Arabic names underlined
Main Roads
Scale: 0 200 400 600 miles
Copyright by Rand McNally & Company
CHORASMIA (UWARAZMISH, KHWARIZM)
SOGDIANA (SUGUDA)
BACTRIA (BAKHTRISH)
MARGIANA (MARGUSH)
PARTHIA (PARTHAVA)
ARIA (HARAIVA)
DRANGIANA (ZARANGA, SAKASTAN, SISTAN)
ARACHOSIA (HARAUVATISH)
GEDROSIA (MAKA)
CARMANIA (YAUTHIYA)
PERSIS (PARSA)
SUSIANA (UWAGA) (KHUZISTAN)
MEDIA (MADA)
INDIA (HINDUSH)
SIND
GANDARA
PAROPANISUS (HINDUKUSH)
(PAMIR)
CASPIAN SEA
BLACK SEA
MEDITERRANEAN SEA
Persian Gulf
Arabian Gulf
ERYTHRAEAN SEA
ARMENIA (ARMINA)
ASSYRIA (ATHURA)
ARABIA (ARABAYA)
EGYPT (MUDRAYA)
ETHIOPIA (KUSIYA) (CUSH)
PUTIYA
MAČIYA?
PHRYGIA
PAPHLAGONIA
CAPPADOCIA
CILICIA
LYDIA (SPARDA)
COLCHIS
MACEDONIA
THRACIANS (SKUDRA)
ILLYRIA
EPIRUS
CYPRUS
CRETE
Babylon
Susa
Persepolis
Pasargadae
Ecbatana
Sardis
Memphis
Thebes
Jerusalem
Damascus
Tyre
Byzantium
Bactra (Balkh)
Maracanda (Samarkand)
B-46763-29

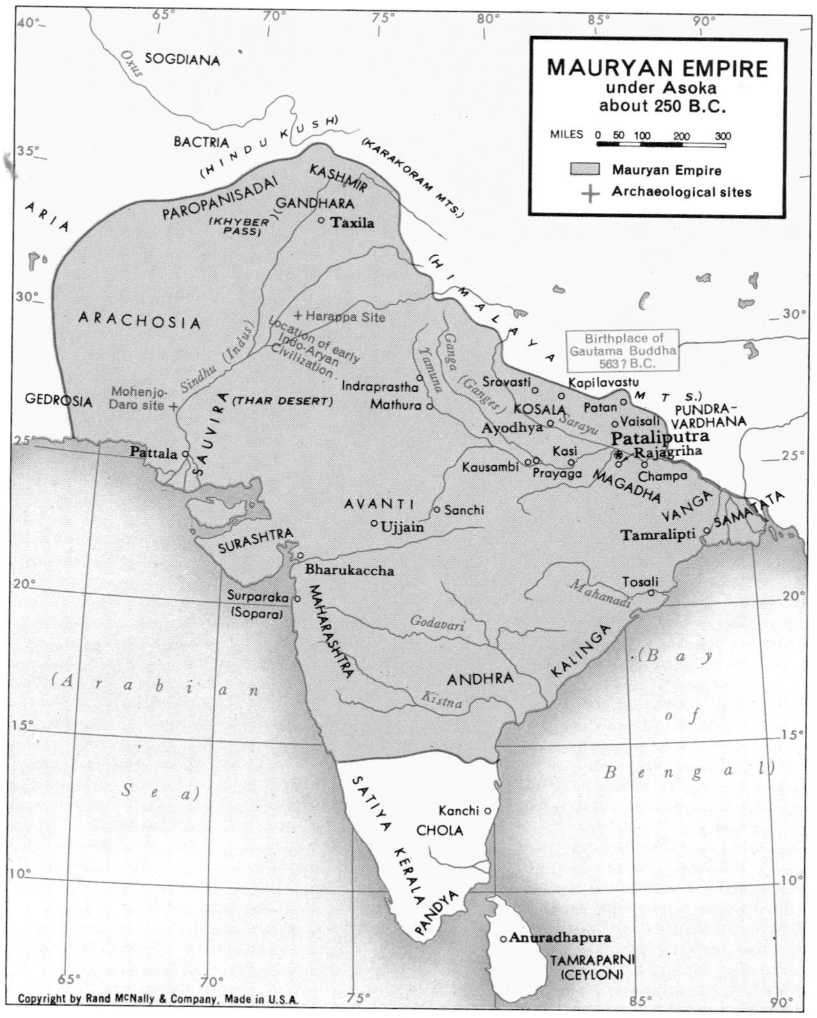
MAURYAN EMPIRE
under Asoka
about 250 B.C.
MILES 0 50 100 200 300
Mauryan Empire
Archaeological sites
SOGDIANA
Oxus
BACTRIA
(HINDU KUSH)
(KARAKORAM MTS.)
ARIA
PAROPANISADAI
KASHMIR
GANDHARA
Taxila
(KHYBER PASS)
ARACHOSIA
Harappa Site
Location of early Indo-Aryan Civilization
Sindhu (Indus)
Yamuna
Ganga (Ganges)
(HIMALAYA MTS.)
Birthplace of Gautama Buddha 563? B.C.
GEDROSIA
Mohenjo-Daro site
(THAR DESERT)
Indraprastha
Mathura
Sravasti
Kapilavastu
Patan
KOSALA
Vaisali
PUNDRA-VARDHANA
Ayodhya
Sarayu
Pataliputra
Rajagriha
Kasi
Kausambi
Prayaga
MAGADHA
Champa
VANGA
SAMATATA
Pattala
SAUVIRA
AVANTI
Sanchi
Ujjain
Tamralipti
SURASHTRA
Bharukaccha
Tosali
Mahanadi
Surparaka (Sopara)
MAHARASHTRA
Godavari
KALINGA
ANDHRA
Kistna
(Arabian Sea)
(Bay of Bengal)
SATIYA
KERALA
PANDYA
Kanchi
CHOLA
Anuradhapura
TAMRAPARNI (CEYLON)
Copyright by Rand McNally & Company, Made in U.S.A.

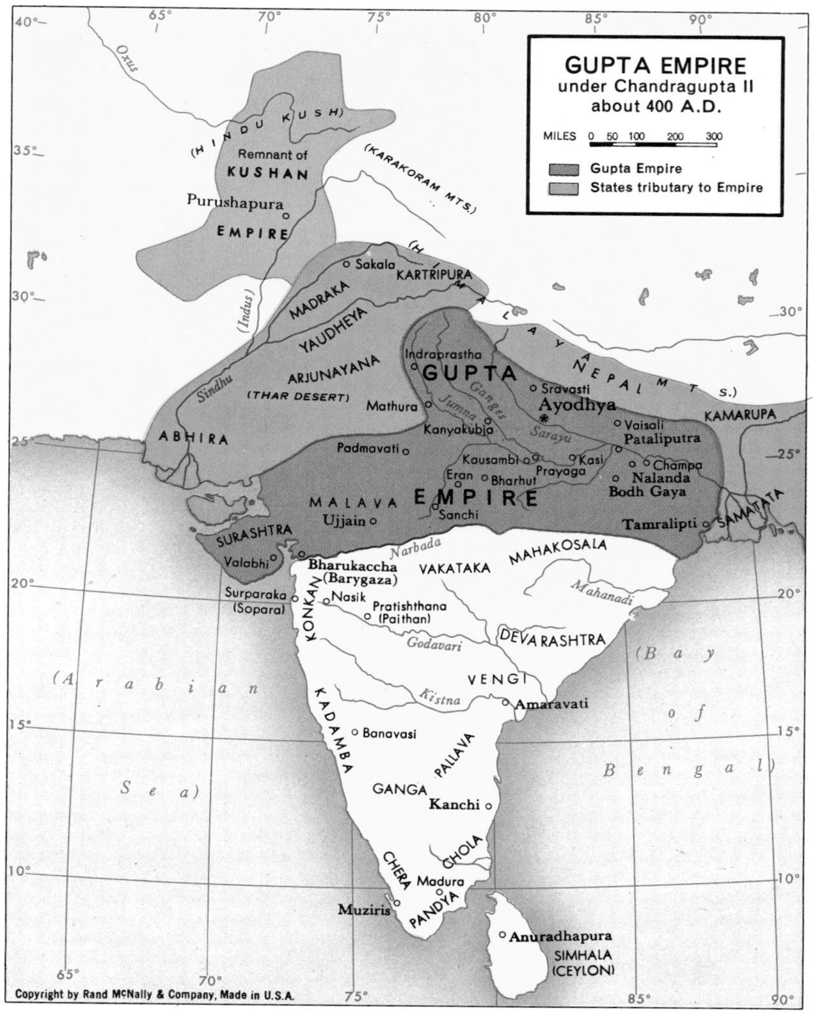
GUPTA EMPIRE
under Chandragupta II
about 400 A.D.
MILES 0 50 100 200 300
Gupta Empire
States tributary to Empire
Oxus
(HINDU KUSH)
(KARAKORAM MTS.)
Remnant of KUSHAN EMPIRE
Purushapura
Sakala
KARTRIPURA
MADRAKA
YAUDHEYA
(Indus)
Indraprastha
GUPTA
ARJUNAYANA
(THAR DESERT)
Sindhu
Mathura
Sravasti
Ayodhya
(NEPAL MTS.)
KAMARUPA
ABHIRA
Kanyakubja
Jumna
Ganges
Sarayu
Vaisali
Pataliputra
Padmavati
Kausambi
Kasi
Champa
Eran
Bharhut
Prayaga
Nalanda
Bodh Gaya
MALAVA EMPIRE
Sanchi
Ujjain
Tamralipti
SAMATATA
SURASHTRA
Valabhi
Narbada
Bharukaccha (Barygaza)
VAKATAKA
MAHAKOSALA
Mahanadi
Surparaka (Sopara)
KONKAN
Nasik
Pratishthana (Paithan)
Godavari
DEVARASHTRA
(Arabian Sea)
(Bay of Bengal)
VENGI
Kistna
Amaravati
KADAMBA
Banavasi
PALLAVA
GANGA
Kanchi
CHOLA
CHERA
Madura
Muziris
PANDYA
Anuradhapura
SIMHALA (CEYLON)
Copyright by Rand McNally & Company, Made in U.S.A.

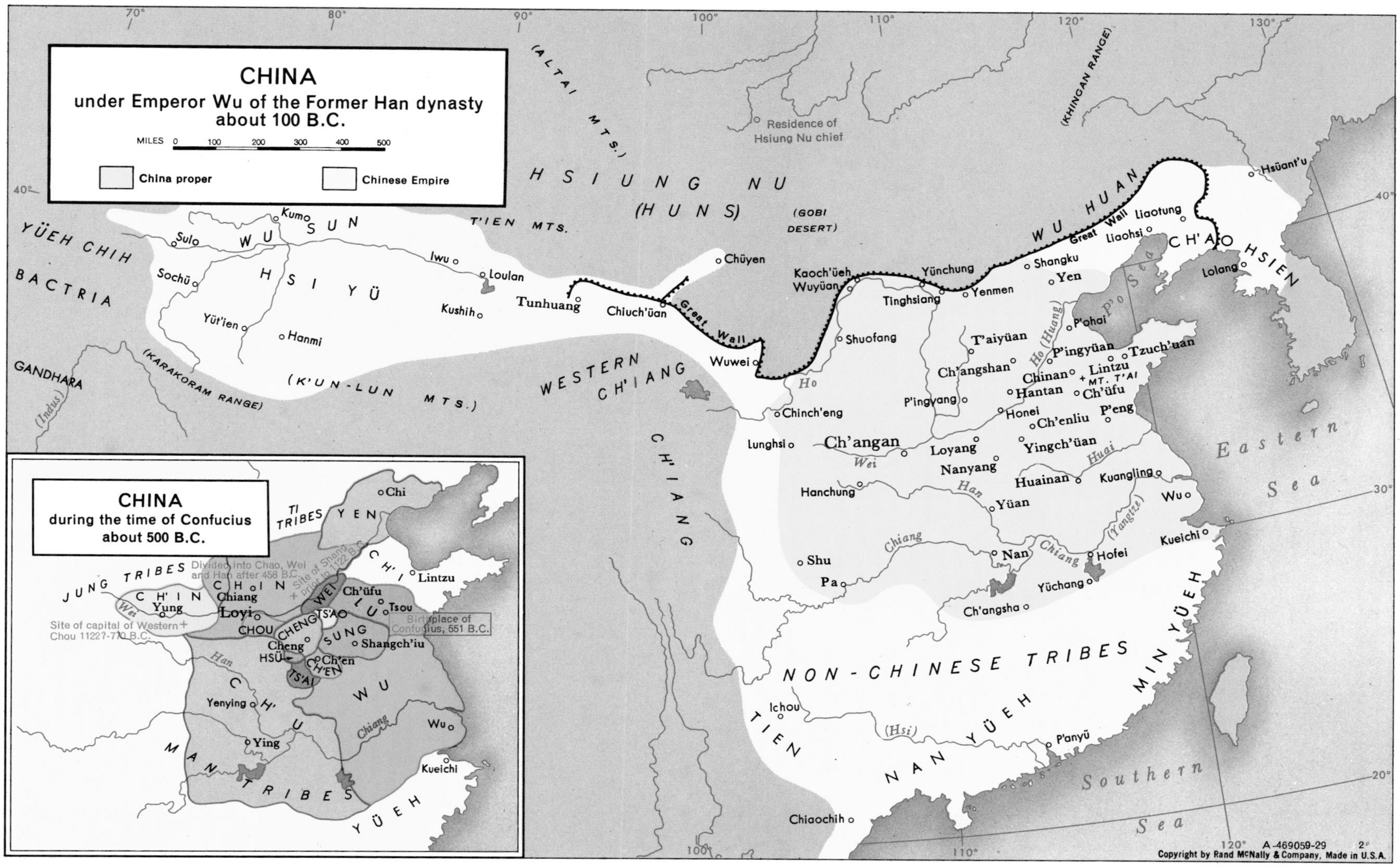
CHINA
under Emperor Wu of the Former Han dynasty
about 100 B.C.
MILES 0 100 200 300 400 500
China proper
Chinese Empire
(ALTAI MTS.)
Residence of Hsiung Nu chief
(KHINGAN RANGE)
HSIUNG NU (HUNS)
(GOBI DESERT)
Hsüant'u
YÜEH CHIH
Sulo
WU SUN
Kumo
T'IEN MTS.
WU HUAN
Great Wall
Liaotung
Liaohsi
CH'AO HSIEN
Lolang
BACTRIA
Sochü
HSI YÜ
Iwu
Loulan
Chüyen
Kaoch'üeh
Wuyüan
Yünchung
Shangku
Yen
Tinghsiang
Yenmen
Yür'ien
Hanmi
Kushih
Tunhuang
Chiuch'üan
Great Wall
Shuofang
T'aiyüan
Ho (Huang)
P'ohai
Po Sea
GANDHARA
(KARAKORAM RANGE)
(K'UN-LUN MTS.)
WESTERN CH'IANG
Wuwei
Ho
P'ingyüan
Tzuch'uan
Ch'angshan
Chinan
Lintzu
MT. T'AI
Ch'üfu
Hantan
(Indus)
Chinch'eng
P'ingyang
Honei
Ch'enliu
P'eng
CH'IANG
Lunghsi
Ch'angan
Wei
Loyang
Yingch'üan
Eastern Sea
Nanyang
Huai
Hanchung
Han
Huainan
Kuangling
Yüan
Wu
Chiang
(Yangtze)
Shu
Nan
Hofei
Kueichi
Pa
Yüchang
Ch'angsha
MIN YÜEH
NON-CHINESE TRIBES
Ichou
TIEN
(Hsi)
NAN YÜEH
P'anyü
Southern Sea
Chiaochih
120° A-469059-29 2°
Copyright by Rand McNally & Company, Made in U.S.A.
CHINA
during the time of Confucius
about 500 B.C.
TI TRIBES
YEN
Chi
JUNG TRIBES
Divided into Chao, Wei and Han after 453 B.C.
Site of Shang capital
CH'I
Lintzu
CH'IN
Yung
CHIN
Chiang
Ch'üfu
Tsou
Loyi
Wei
LU
Site of capital of Western Chou 1122?-770 B.C.
CHOU
CHENG
TSAO
Birthplace of Confucius, 551 B.C.
SUNG
Cheng
Shangch'iu
HSÜ
Ch'en
CH'EN
TS'AI
Han
CH'U
WU
Yenying
Chiang
Wu
Ying
MAN TRIBES
Kueichi
YÜEH

EASTERN AND SOUTHERN ASIA
About 750 A.D.
MILES 0 100 200 400 600 800
A-469015-29 -1-1-1
Copyright by Rand McNally & Company, Made in U.S.A.
The Srivijayan Empire, perhaps under a Sailendran ruler, probably included more of Sumatra and Java and even portions of the Malay peninsula and Borneo by the end of the 8th Century
JAPAN
Nara
Capital from 710-784
Heian
Capital from 794
SILLA
Capital
Hanchow
P'O HAI
Capital
Liaotung
KHITANS
Great Wall
HOPEI
HONAN
HONAN
Taiyüan
Weichow
Loyang
Pien
Sung
Yangchow
Soochow
Yüeh
Hangchow
Hsüan
Chiangling
Kwangchow
Ch'üanchow
Ch'iench'ung
CHINGCHI
Ch'angan
KUANNEI
SHANNAN HSI
SHANNAN TUNG
CHIANGNAN TUNG
CHIANGNAN HSI
HUAINAN
LINGNAN
CHIENNAN
Ch'engtu
Shan
CHINA
East China Sea
Southern Sea
(HAINAN)
NAN CHAO
(TAI)
Tali
Chiaochow
ANNAM
UPPER (LAND) CHENLA
LOWER (MARITIME) CHENLA
CHAMPA
Amaravati
KAUTHARA
Virapura
PANDURANGA
DVARAVATI
Thaton
MON
PYU
Halin
Srikshetra
TAMBRALINGA
LANGKASUKA
KEDAH
(BORNEO)
(SUMATRA)
SRIVIJAYA
Srivijaya
Malayu
BANKA
(JAVA)
SAILENDRAS
TARUMA
MATARAM
Borobodur
Built 772?
UIGHURS
(EASTERN TURKS)
(GOBI DESERT)
Uighur Capital
LUNG YU
T'UYÜHUNS
Tunhuang
TIBET
Lhasa
KAMARUPA
NEPAL
(HIMALAYA MTS.)
FOUR GARRISONS
Lost to Tibetans after 790
TIEN MTS.
KARLUKS
(WESTERN TURKS)
Chinese control lost after 754
Peit'ing
Yenchi
Anhsi
(Kucha)
Yüt'ien
(Khotan)
Chinese garrison 747-751
Tibetan conquest 751
Ch'iasha
(Kashgar)
FERGHANA
Talas
Decisive Battle 751
SOGDIANA
Bokhara
Samarkand
TOKHARISTAN
Balkh
BALTISTAN
Gilgit
KASHMIR
Purushapura
Kabul
Ghazni
Herat
Zaranj
Merv
Kath
Jayhun (Oxus)
Sayhun
MOSLEM CALIPHATE
Omayyad Caliphate until 750
Abbassid Caliphate thereafter
Ray
Isfahan
Hamadan
Baghdad
Tiflis
Tigris
Caspian Sea
GAUDA
(PALAS)
Pataliputra
Nalanda
Tamralipti
Prayaga
Kanauj
Ganges
Jumna
GURJARA
Thanesar
Indraprastha
Ujjain
Anandapura
Broach
VALABHI
(MAITRAKAS)
Nasik
Ajanta
RASHTRAKUTAS
Rise in power from about 752
CHALUKYAS
Manyakheta
(Malkhed)
Vatapi
KALINGA
Amaravati
PALLAVAS
Kanchi
Mamallapuram
CHOLAS
Madura
PANDYAS
SIMHALA
Anuradhapura
Green Sea

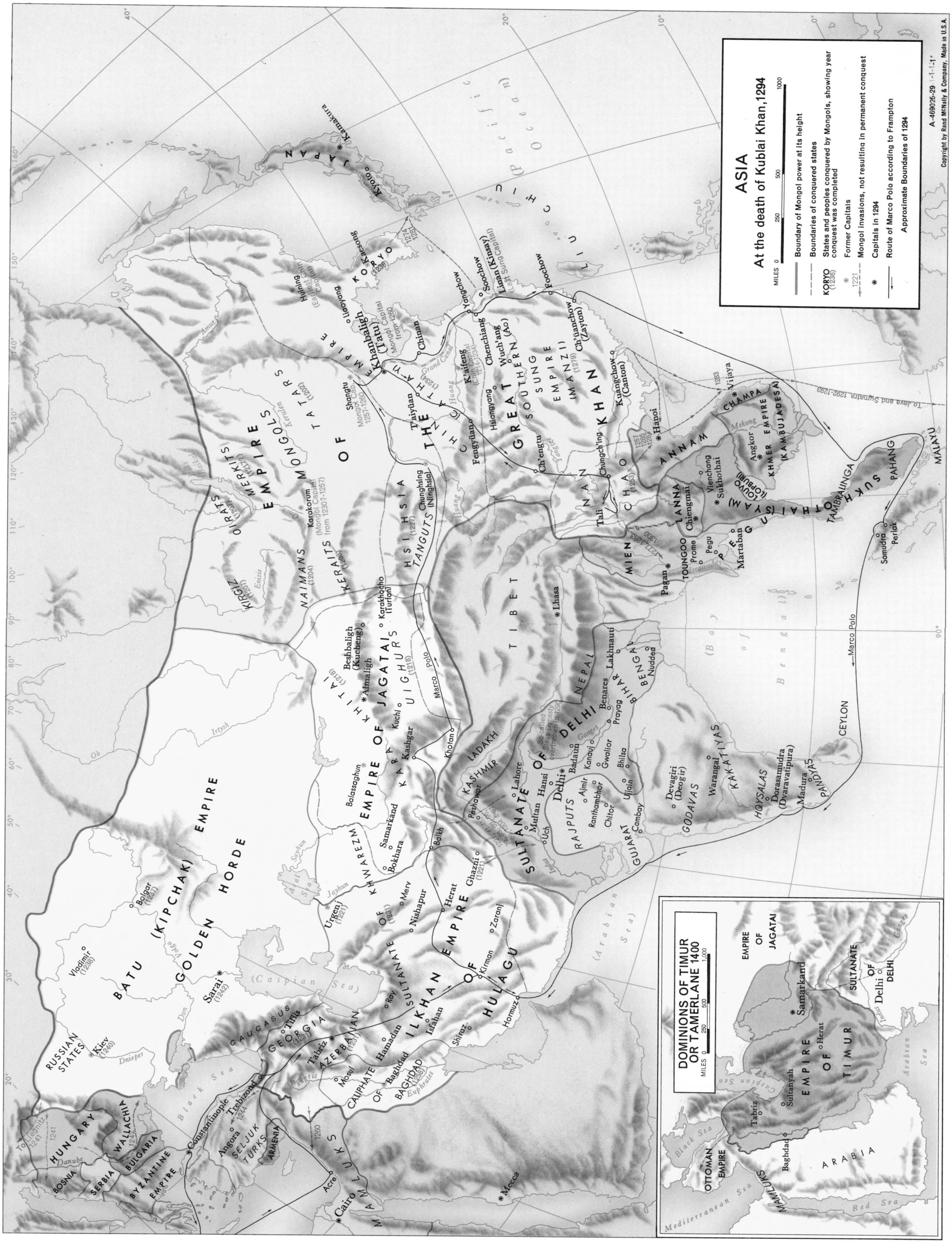
ASIA
At the death of Kublai Khan, 1294
MILES 0 250 500 1000
Boundary of Mongol power at its height
Boundaries of conquered states
KORYO (1236) States and peoples conquered by Mongols, showing year conquest was completed
Former Capitals
1221 Mongol invasions, not resulting in permanent conquest
Capitals in 1294
Route of Marco Polo according to Frampton
Approximate Boundaries of 1294
A-469026-29
Copyright by Rand McNally & Company, Made in U.S.A.
EMPIRE OF THE GREAT KHAN
MONGOLS
TATARS
MERKITS
OIRATS
KIRGIZ
NAIMANS
KERAITS
Karakorum (Mongol Capital from 1230?-1257)
Shangtu
Khanbaligh (Tatu)
HSI HSIA TANGUTS
CATHAY
SOUTHERN SUNG EMPIRE (MANZI)
KORYO
JAPAN
Kyoto
Kamakura
Pacific Ocean
LIU CH'IU
Hanoi
ANNAM
CHAMPA
KHMER EMPIRE (KAMBUJADESA)
SUKHOTHAI (SYAM)
LANNA
NAN CHAO
MIEN
PEGU
TAMBRALINGA
PAHANG
MALAYU
Samudra
Perlak
To Java and Sumatra 1292-1293
TIBET
Lhasa
NEPAL
BENGAL
Bay of Bengal
CEYLON
PANDYAS
HOYSALAS
KAKATIYAS
GODAVAS
SULTANATE OF DELHI
Delhi
RAJPUTS
GUJARAT
KASHMIR
LADAKH
Arabian Sea
EMPIRE OF JAGATAI
KARA KHITAI
UIGHURS
Kashgar
Khotan
Almaligh
Samarkand
Bokhara
KHWAREZM
ILKHAN EMPIRE OF HULAGU
Herat
Ghazni
Baghdad
Tabriz
Hormuz
Caspian Sea
BATU (KIPCHAK) EMPIRE
GOLDEN HORDE
Sarai
Bolgar
Vladimir
Kiev
RUSSIAN STATES
HUNGARY
WALLACHIA
BULGARIA
SERBIA
BOSNIA
BYZANTINE EMPIRE
Constantinople
SELJUK TURKS
ARMENIA
GEORGIA
CAUCASUS
Black Sea
MAMLUKS
Cairo
Acre
Mecca
DOMINIONS OF TIMUR OR TAMERLANE 1400
MILES 0 250 500 1000
EMPIRE OF TIMUR
EMPIRE OF JAGATAI
SULTANATE OF DELHI
OTTOMAN EMPIRE
MAMLUKS
ARABIA
Samarkand
Herat
Delhi
Tabriz
Sultaniyah
Baghdad
Red Sea
Mediterranean Sea

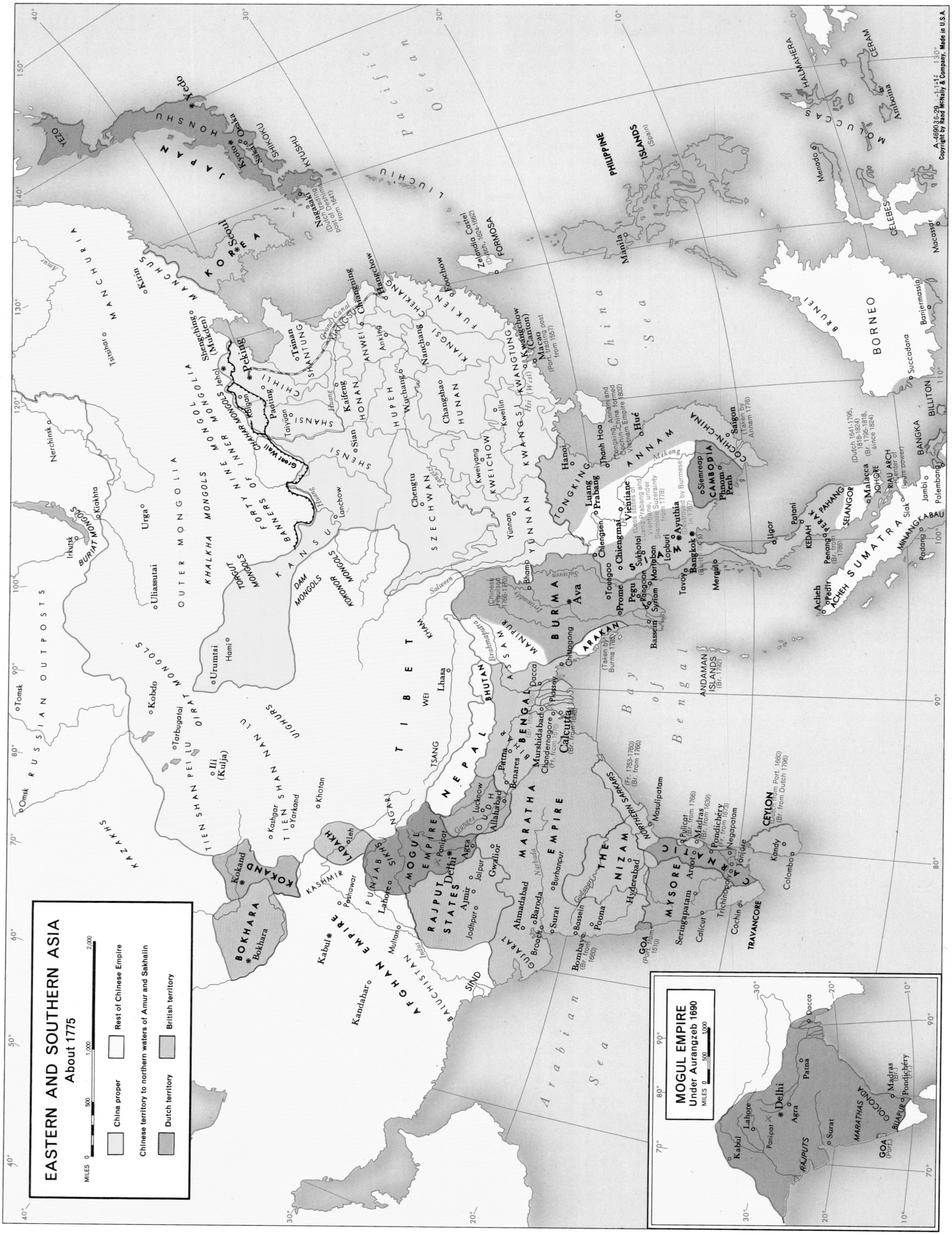
EASTERN AND SOUTHERN ASIA
About 1775
MILES 0 500 1,000 2,000
China proper
Rest of Chinese Empire
Chinese territory to northern waters of Amur and Sakhalin
Dutch territory
British territory
MOGUL EMPIRE
Under Aurangzeb 1690
MILES 0 500 1,000
JAPAN
KOREA
MANCHURIA
OUTER MONGOLIA
TIBET
NEPAL
BHUTAN
BURMA
ANNAM
TONGKING
CAMBODIA
COCHIN-CHINA
MARATHA EMPIRE
MOGUL EMPIRE
RAJPUT STATES
AFGHAN EMPIRE
BOKHARA
KOKAND
MYSORE
THE NIZAM
CEYLON
BENGAL
BORNEO
SUMATRA
PHILIPPINE ISLANDS (Spain)
FORMOSA
Pacific Ocean
South China Sea
Bay of Bengal
Arabian Sea
Peking
Delhi
Calcutta
Canton
Yedo
A-469036-29—1-1-12
Copyright by Rand McNally & Company, Made in U.S.A.

North Pacific Ocean

SAKHALIN (S. Occupation)
KURIL IS. (Russ. Occupation)

J A P A N
HOKKAIDO
HONSHU
Sapporo
Hakodate
Sendai
Vladivostok
Tokyo Yokohama
Allied Occupation
Osaka Kobe
Nagoya
KYUSHU
Nagasaki Fukuoka
SHIKOKU
U.S. Occupation
BONIN IS.

RYUKYU IS.
U.S. Occupation
CAROLINE ISLANDS (U.S. Trust)
NEW GUINEA (Dutch)
AUSTRALIA

M A N C H U R I A
Tsitsihar
Harbin
Kirin
Mukden
Tsinan

Tokchon
KOREA
Seoul
Inchon
Pusan

Sea of Japan

East China Sea

TAIWAN (FORMOSA)
Taipei

PHILIPPINES
REPUBLIC OF THE
LUZON
Manila
SAMAR
LEYTE
NEGROS
PALAWAN
MINDANAO
SULU ARCH
Davao
Zamboanga

S O V I E T U N I O N

Irkutsk
L. Baikal
Ulan Bator
MONGOLIA
GOBI DESERT
ALTAI MTS.
Tihwa

C H I N A
Pekingo
Tientsino
Shanghai
Hankow
Wuchang
Nanking
Kaifeng
Changsha
Chungking
Chengtu
Canton
Hong Kong (Br.)
Macao (Port.)
Hainan

Omsk
Tomsk
Stalinsk

SINKIANG
KUNLUN MTS.
T I B E T
Lhasa

VIETNAM
Hanoi
THAILAND
Bangkok
CAMBODIA
Phnom Penh
Saigon
Associated States of The French Union

BURMA
UNION OF
Mandalay
Rangoon

MALACCA IS.
INDONESIA
UNITED STATES OF
SUMATRA
JAVA
BORNEO
KALIMANTAN (BORNEO)
BRUNEI (Br.)
SARAWAK (Br.)
SULAWESI (CELEBES)
LESSER SUNDAS
TIMOR (Port.)
Djakarta

FEDERATION OF MALAYA
Singapore (Br.)

SOUTH CHINA SEA

NEPAL
BHUTAN
Kathmandu
HIMALAYAS
Dacca
Calcutta
Patna
Howrah

I N D I A
New Delhi
Delhi
Agra
Jaipur
Kanpur
Lucknow
Allahabad
Benares
Nagpur
Hyderabad
Bombay
Poona
Sholapur
Bangalore
Mysore
Madras
Pondichéry (Fr.)
CEYLON
Colombo

Bay of Bengal

KASHMIR AND JAMMU
Srinagar
Amritsar
Lahore
Rawalpindi
P A K I S T A N
Karachi

A F G H A N I S T A N
Kabul
Herat
HINDU KUSH

I R A N
Tehran
Meshed
Isfahan

KIRGHIZ STEPPE
KARA KUM DESERT
KYZYL KUM DESERT
Tashkent
Samarkand
Stalinabad
Alma-Ata
Frunze
TIEN SHAN
Ashkhabad
Aral Sea
Syr Darya
Amu Darya

Caspian Sea
Baku
Tiflis
CAUCASUS
Yerevan
Tabriz

Indian Ocean

Arabian Sea

SOCOTRA (Br.)

T U R K E Y
Ankara
Istanbul
Izmir
CYPRUS (Br.)

S Y R I A
Aleppo
Damascus
LEBANON
Beirut
ISRAEL
Tel Aviv
Jerusalem
JORDAN
Amman

I R A Q
Baghdad
Basra
KUWAIT
BAHRAIN
QATAR
TRUCIAL OMAN
OMAN

S A U D I A R A B I A
Riyadh
Mecca
GREAT SANDY DESERT
YEMEN
ADEN (Br.)
Aden

E G Y P T
Cairo
Alexandria
SUDAN
SYRIAN DESERT
Red Sea
Suez Canal

ETHIOPIA
BR. SOMALILAND
SOMALILAND

GREECE
Athens
CRETE
RHODES
SICILY
Mediterranean Sea
Black Sea
Odessa
Danube
Dnepr
Kharkov
Dnepropetrovsk
Stalingrad
Rostov
Astrakhan
Saratov

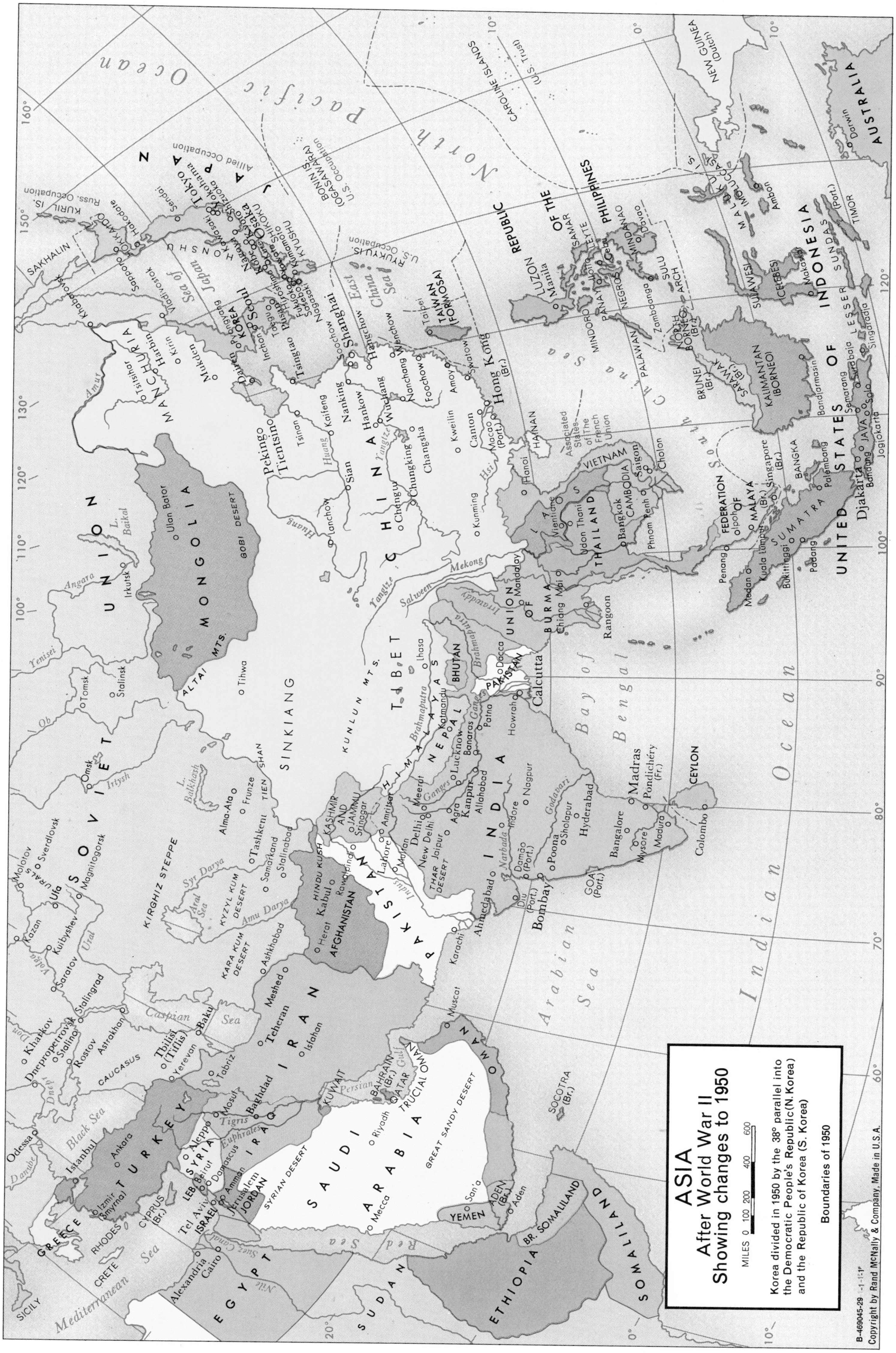

ASIA
After World War II
Showing changes to 1950

MILES 0 100 200 400 600

Korea divided in 1950 by the 38° parallel into
the Democratic People's Republic (N. Korea)
and the Republic of Korea (S. Korea)

Boundaries of 1950

B-469045-29
Copyright by Rand McNally & Company. Made in U.S.A.

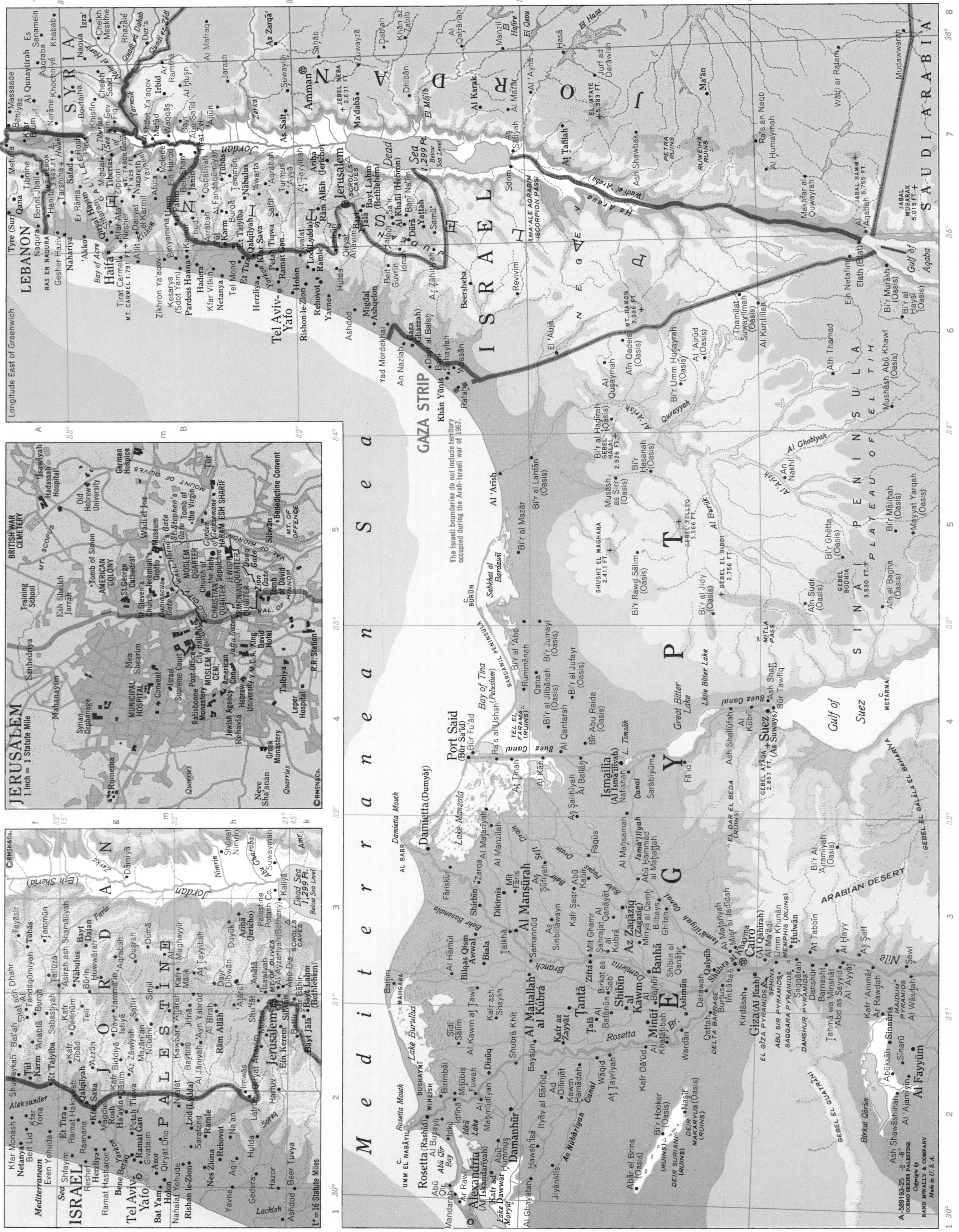

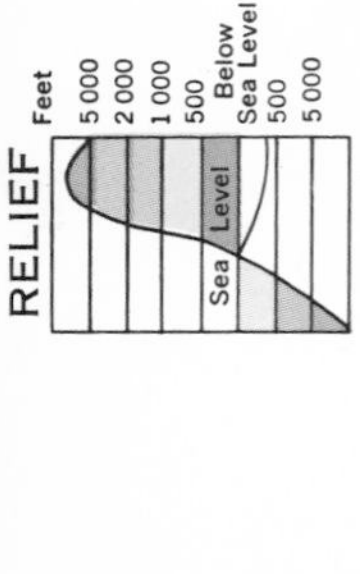

Statute Miles 5 0 5 10 20 30 40 50

Kilometers 5 0 5 10 20 30 40 50 60

Lambert Conformal Conic Projection

SCALE 1:2,000,000 1 Inch = 32 Statute Miles

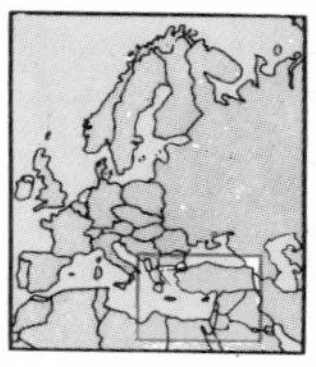

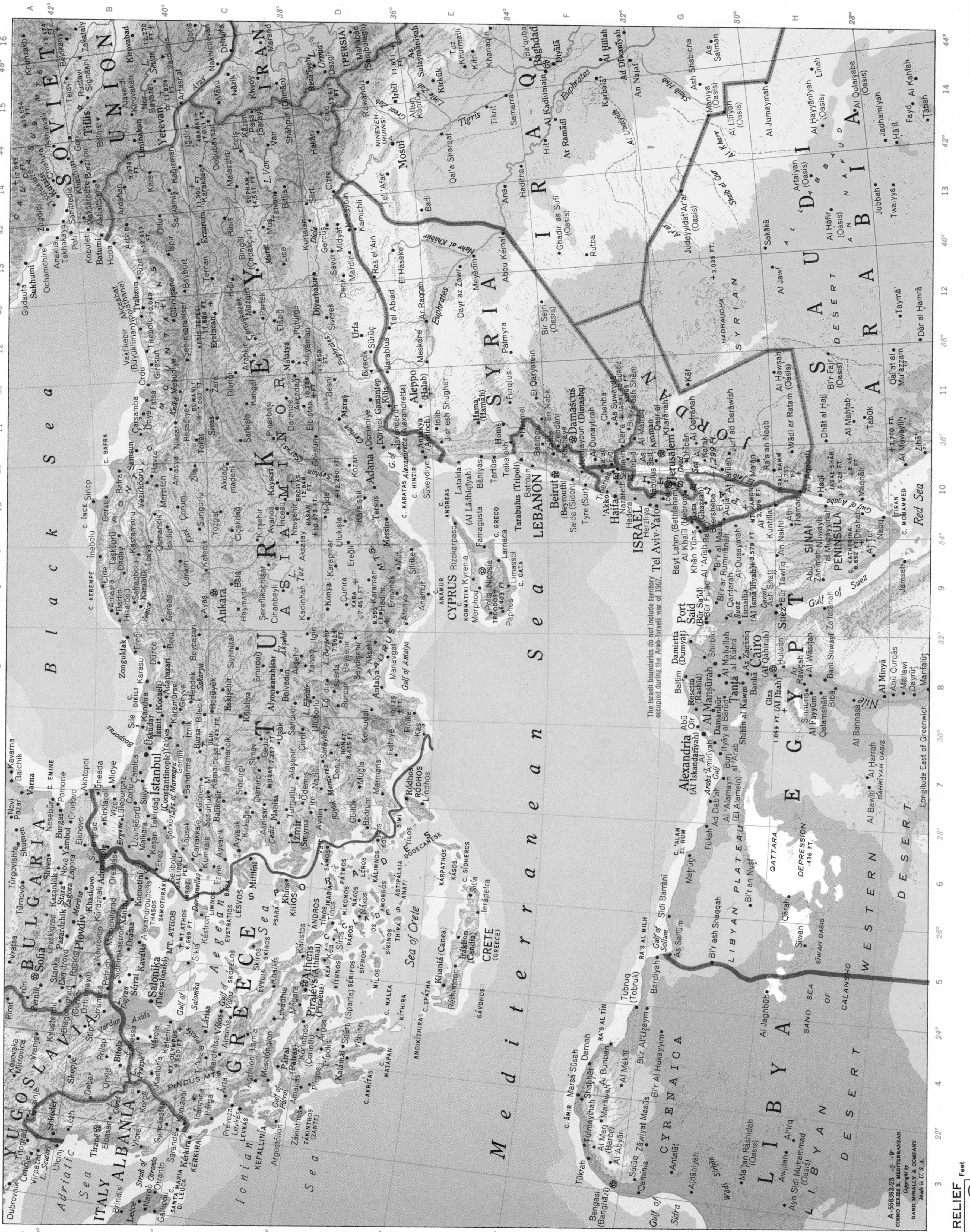

Lambert Conformal Conic Projection
SCALE 1 : 8,000,000 1 Inch = 126 Statute Miles

Statute Miles 50 0 50 100 150
Kilometers 50 0 50 100 200

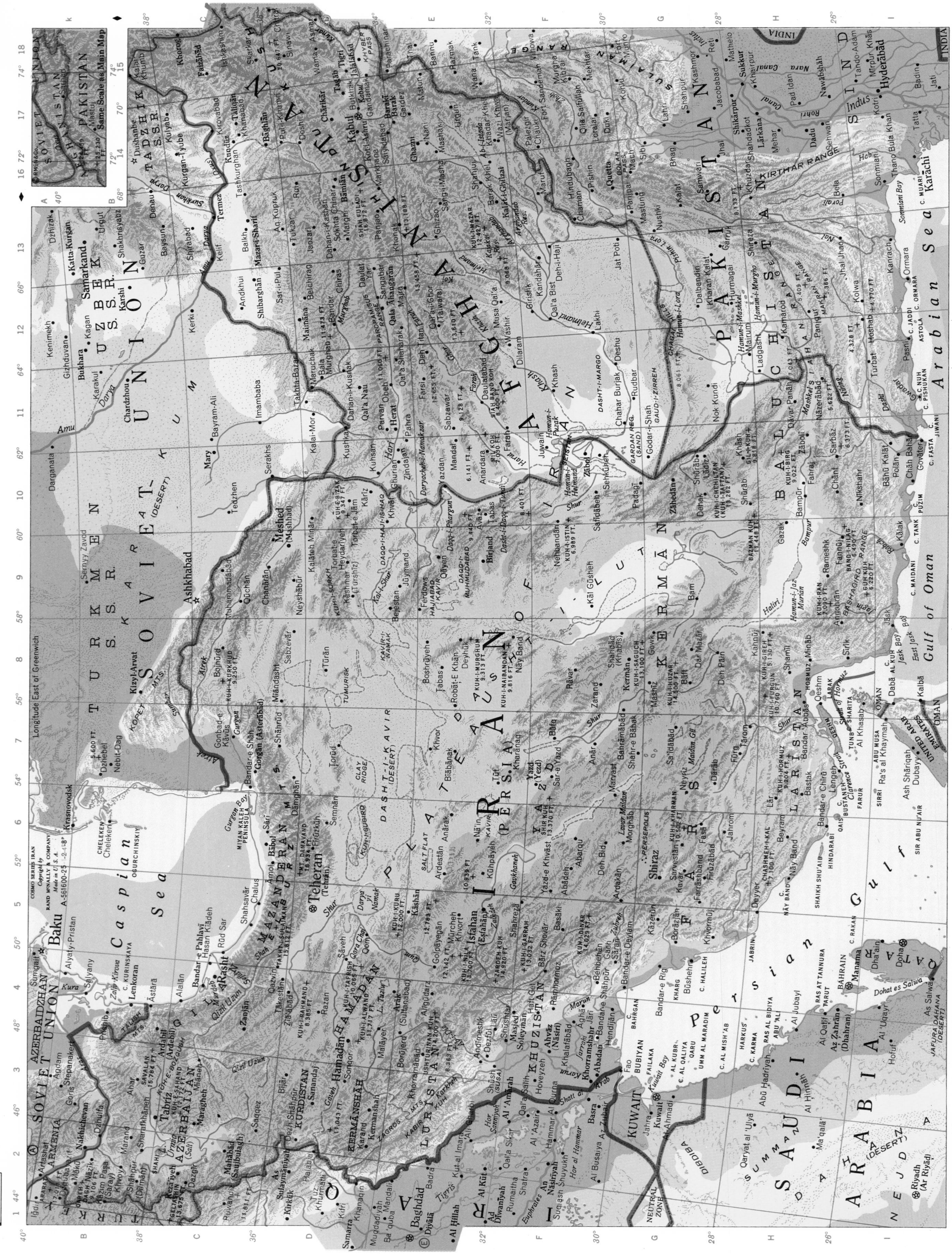

Statute Miles 50 0 50 100 150

Kilometers 50 0 50 100 200

Lambert Conformal Conic Projection

SCALE 1 : 8,000,000 1 Inch = 126 Statute Miles

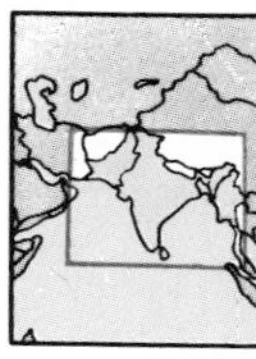

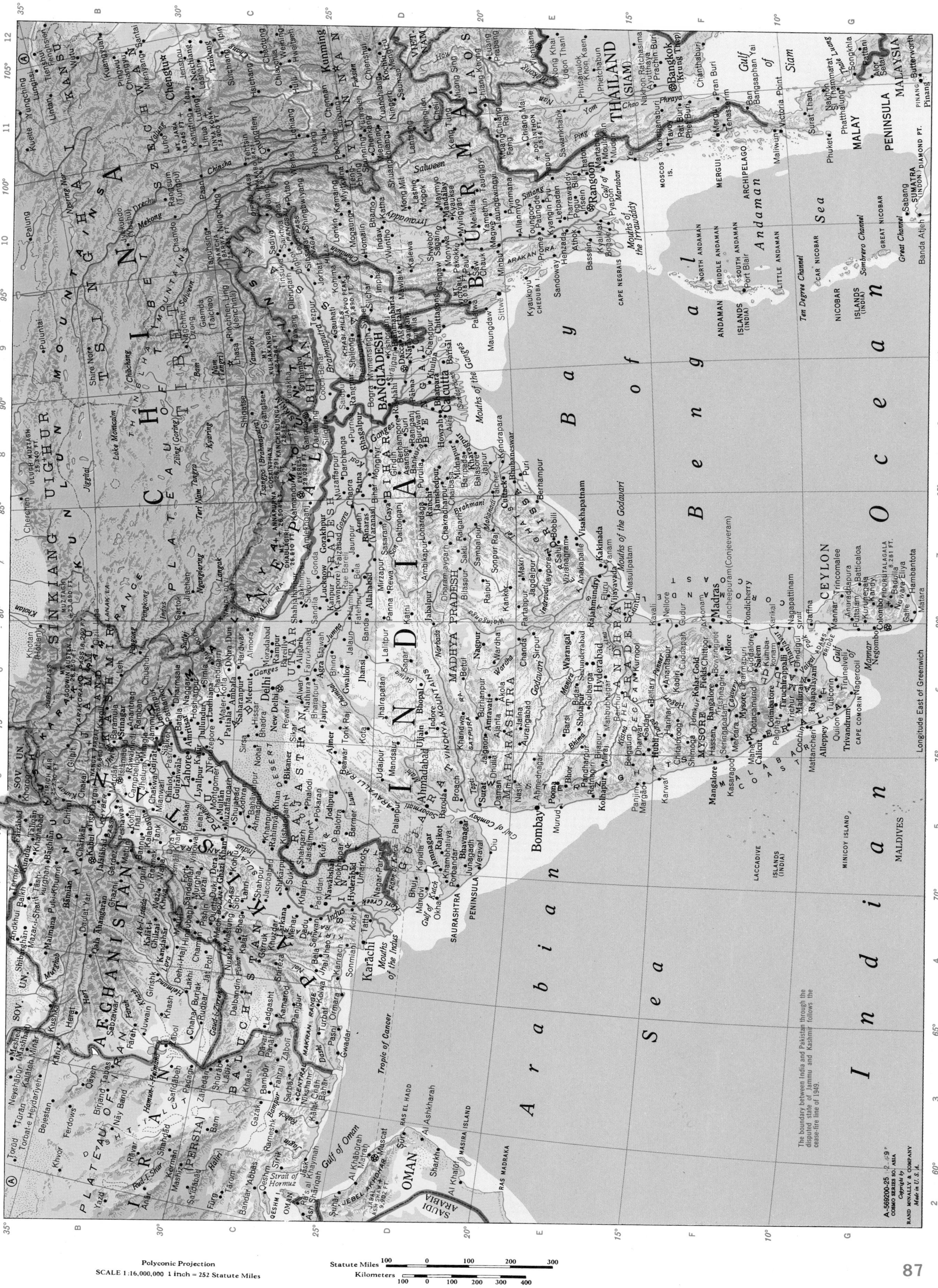

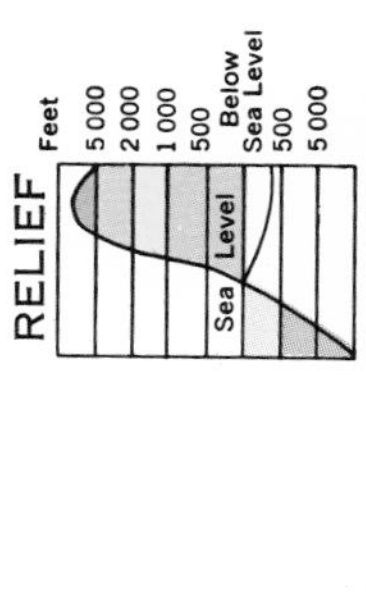

Polyconic Projection
SCALE 1:16,000,000 1 inch = 252 Statute Miles

Statute Miles 100 0 100 200 300
Kilometers 100 0 100 200 300 400

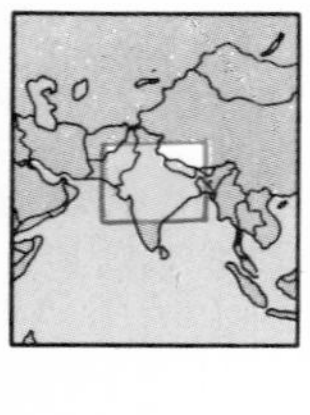

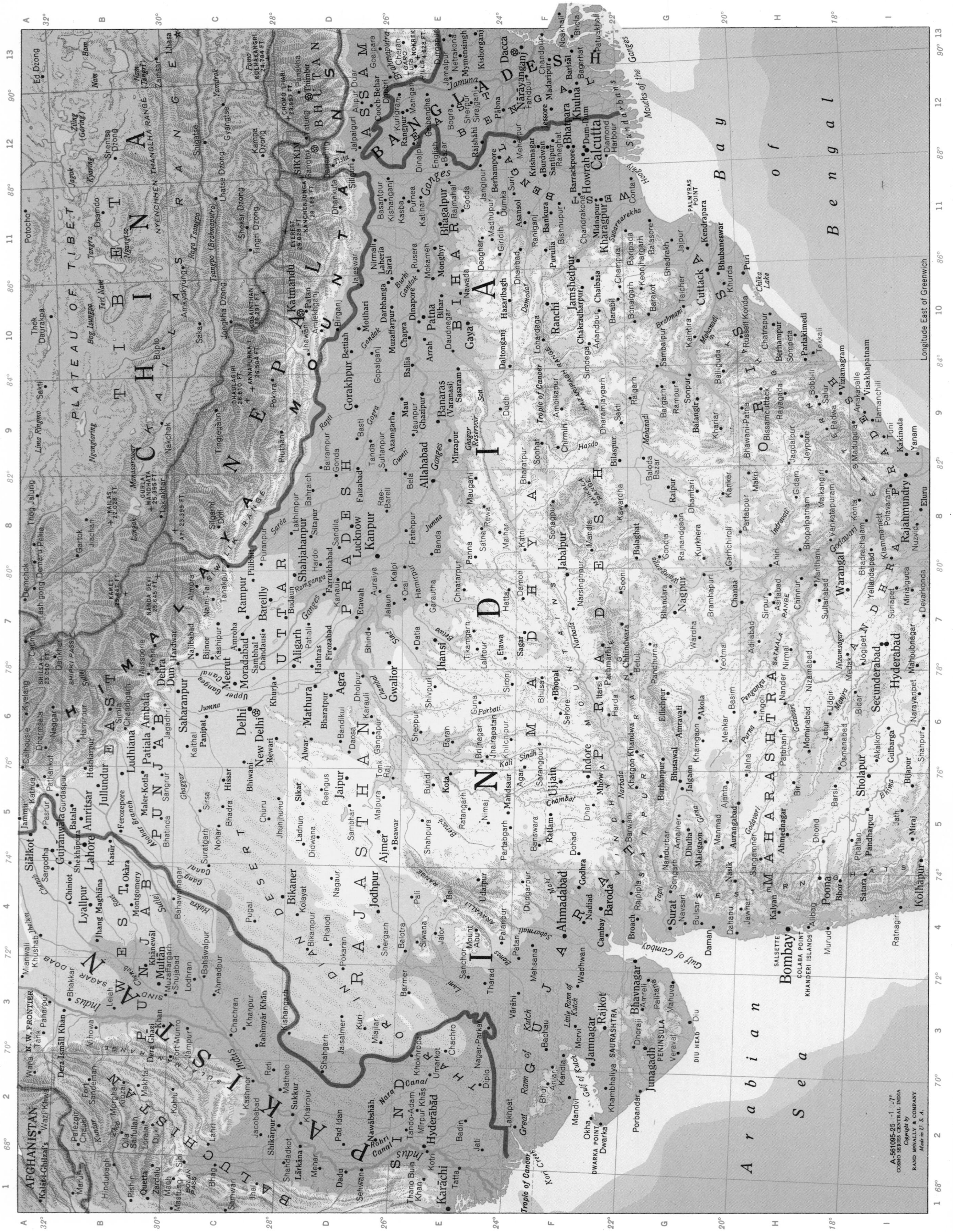

Statute Miles 50 0 50 100 150

Kilometers 50 0 50 100 200

Lambert Conformal Conic Projection

SCALE 1 : 8,000,000 1 Inch = 126 Statute Miles

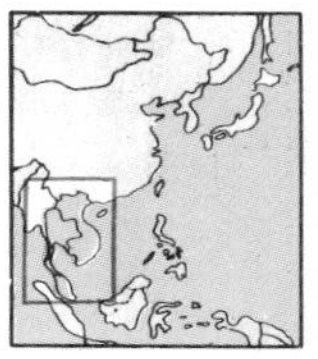

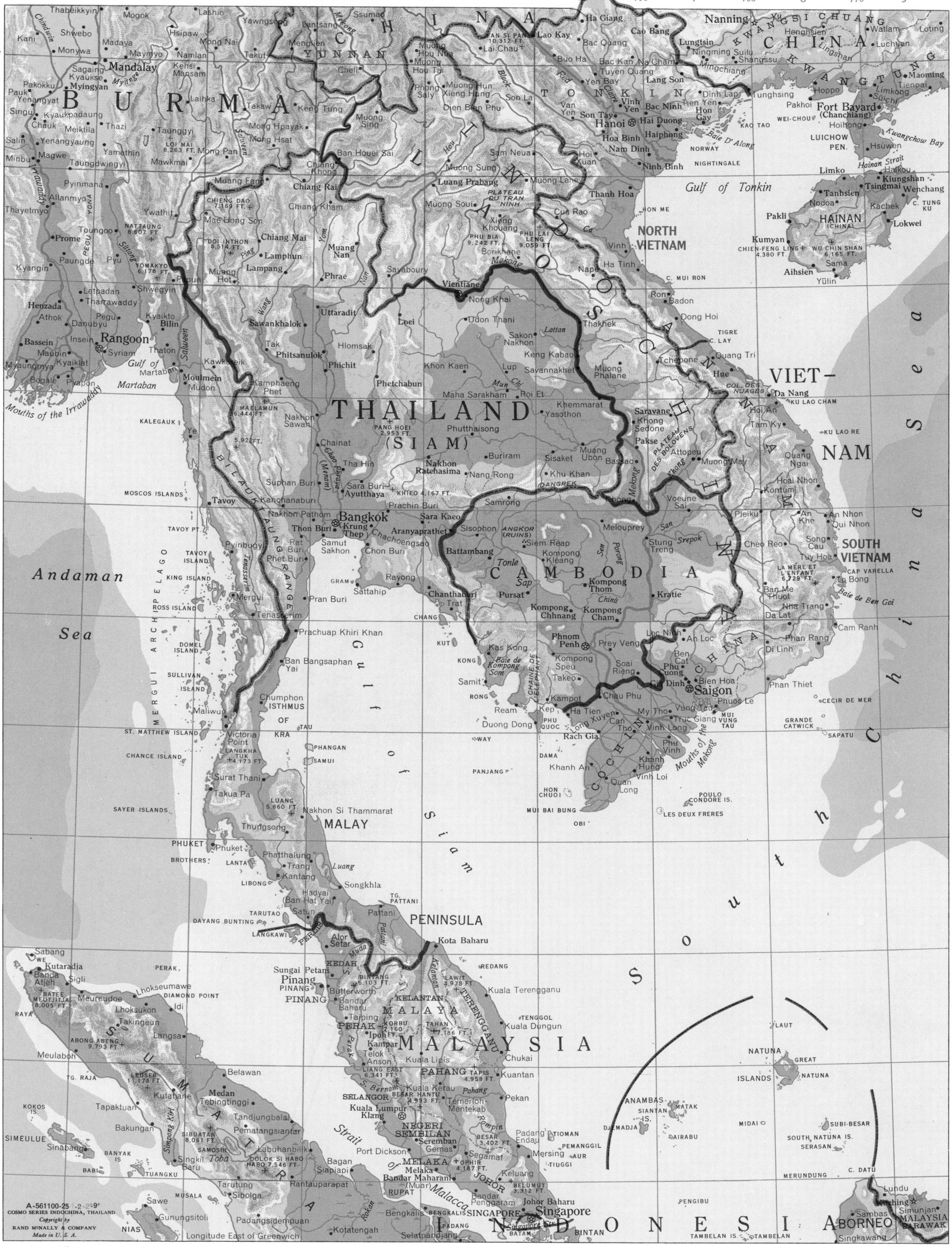

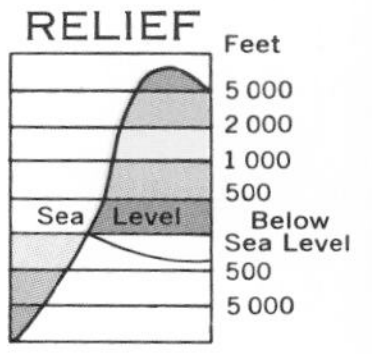

Lambert Conformal Conic Projection
SCALE 1:8,000,000 1 Inch = 126 Statute Miles

Statute Miles 50 0 50 100 150
Kilometers 50 0 50 100 200

Statute Miles 100 0 100 200 300
Kilometers 100 0 100 200 300 400
Polyconic Projection
SCALE 1:16,000,000 1 Inch = 252 Statute Miles

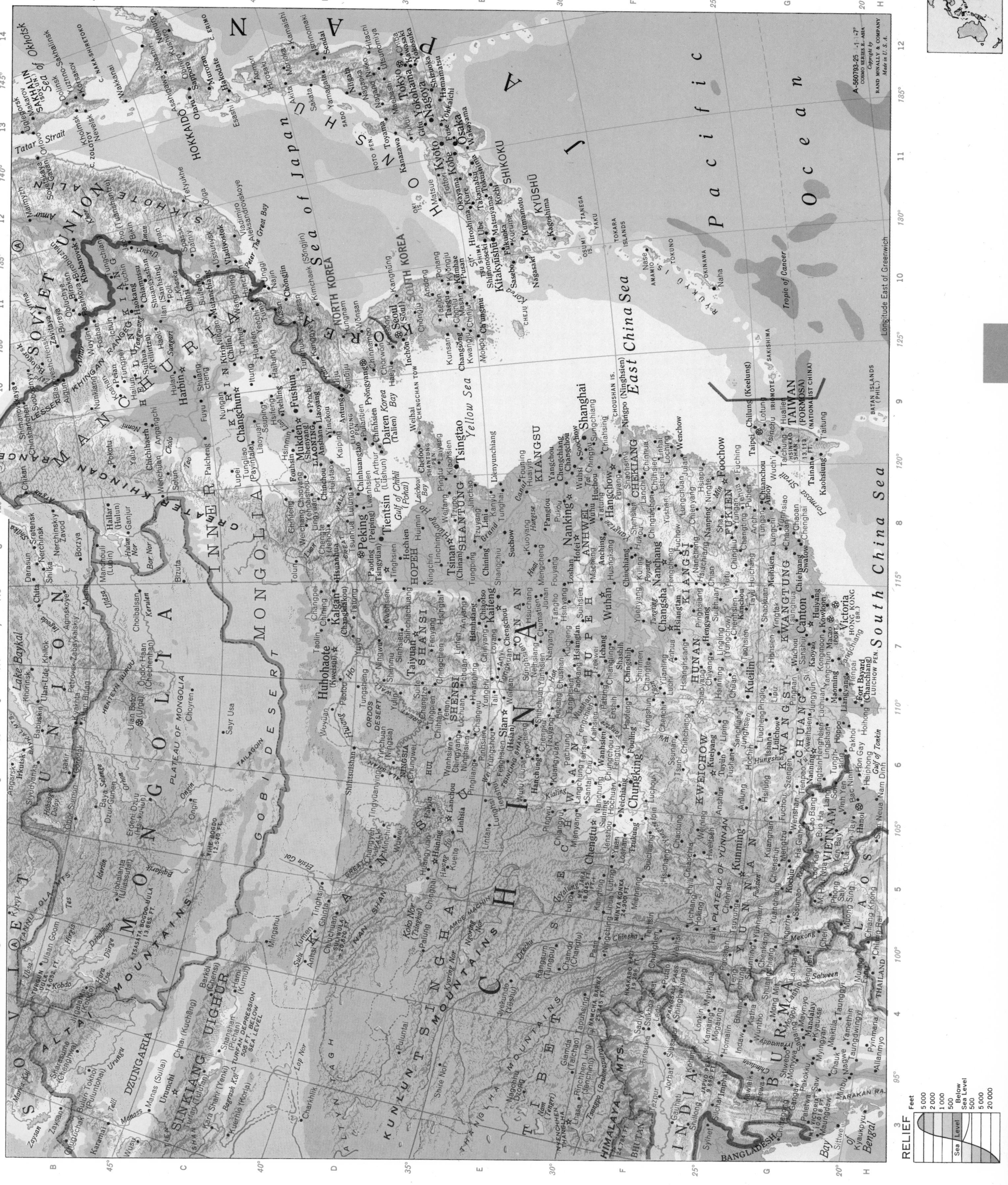

Polyconic Projection
SCALE 1:16,000,000 1 Inch = 252 Statute Miles

Statute Miles 100 0 100 200 300
Kilometers 100 0 100 200 300 400

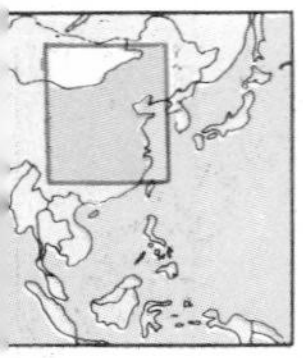

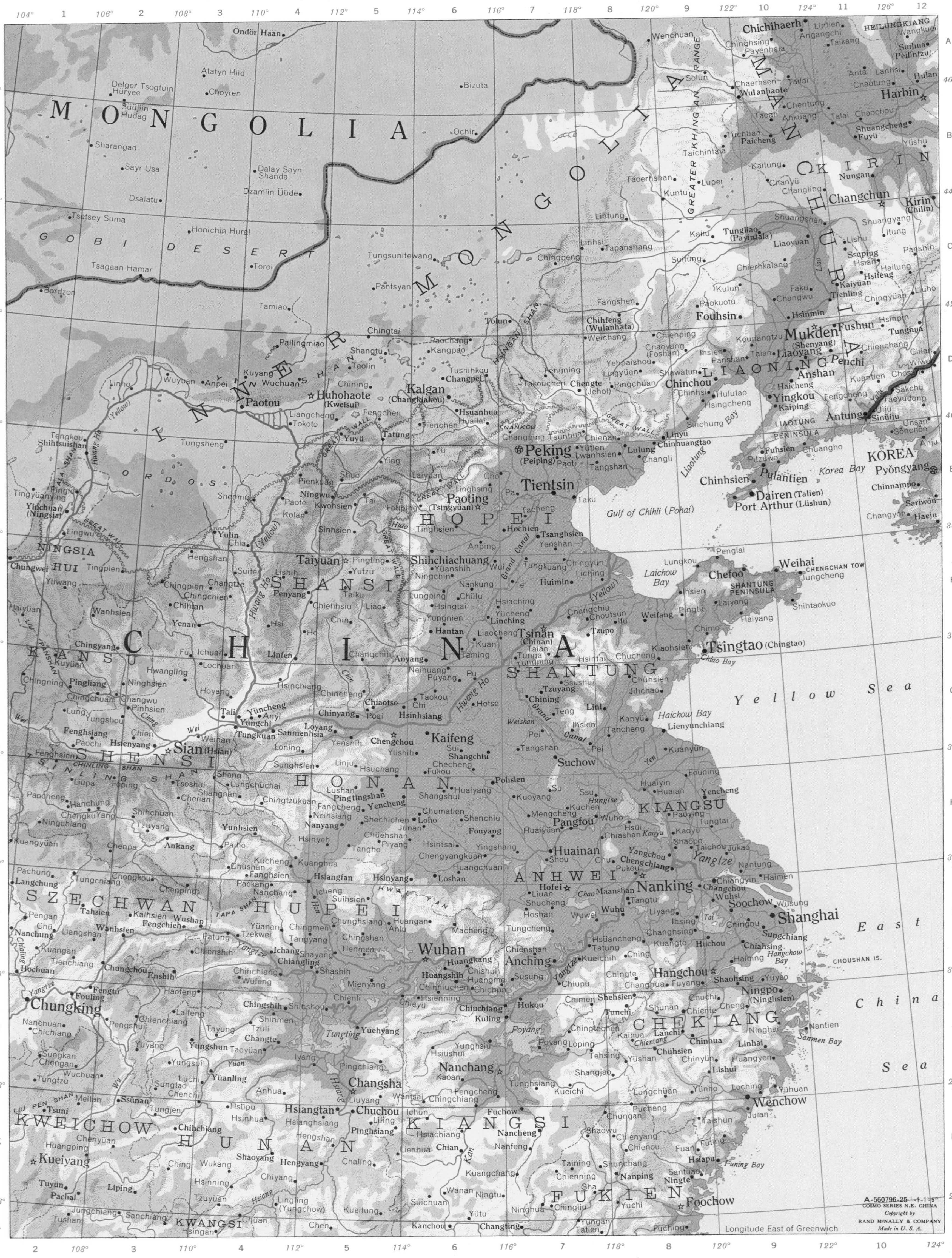
MONGOLIA
GOBI DESERT
INNER MONGOLIA
MANCHURIA
KIRIN
LIAONING
HEILUNGKIANG
KOREA
CHINA
NINGSIA HUI
KANSU
SHENSI
SHANSI
HOPEI
SHANTUNG
HONAN
KIANGSU
ANHWEI
HUPEI
SZECHWAN
CHEKIANG
KIANGSI
HUNAN
KWEICHOW
KWANGSI
FUKIEN
Harbin
Changchun
Kirin (Chilin)
Mukden (Shenyang)
Fushun
Anshan
Dairen (Talien)
Port Arthur (Lüshun)
Antung
P'yŏngyang
Huhohaote (Kweisui)
Paotou
Kalgan (Changkiakou)
Peking (Peiping)
Tientsin
Paoting (Tsingyüan)
Taiyuan
Shihchiachuang
Tsinan (Chinan)
Tsingtao (Chingtao)
Chefoo
Weihai
Sian (Hsian)
Loyang
Kaifeng
Chengchou
Suchow
Nanking
Shanghai
Soochow
Hangchou
Ningpo (Ninghsien)
Wenchow
Wuhan
Nanchang
Changsha
Chungking
Kueiyang
Foochow
Gulf of Chihli (Pohai)
Korea Bay
Yellow Sea
East China Sea
Longitude East of Greenwich
A-560796-25
COSMO SERIES N.E. CHINA
Copyright by RAND McNALLY & COMPANY
Made in U. S. A.
Statute Miles 50 0 50 100 150
Kilometers 50 0 50 100 200
Lambert Conformal Conic Projection
SCALE 1 : 8,000,000 1 Inch = 126 Statute Miles

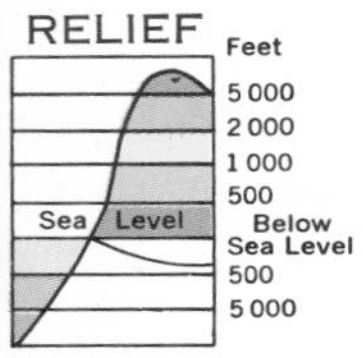
RELIEF
Feet
5 000
2 000
1 000
500
Sea Level
Below Sea Level
500
5 000

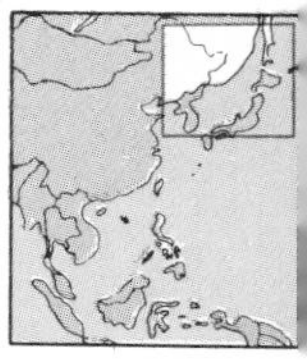

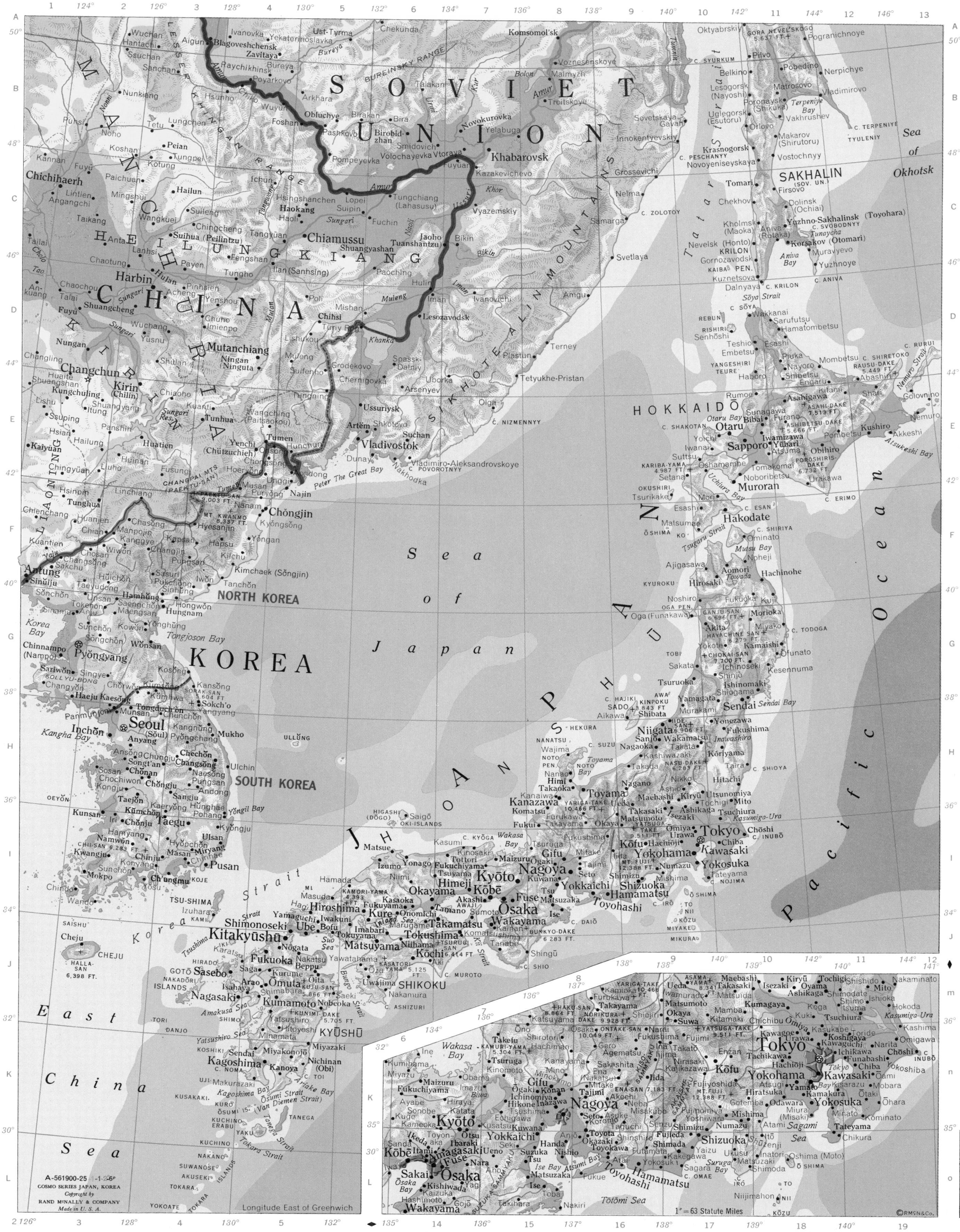

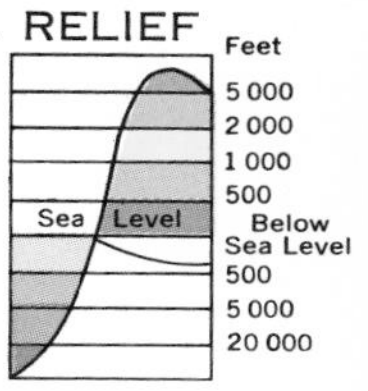

Lambert Conformal Conic Projection
SCALE 1 : 8,000,000 1 Inch = 126 Statute Miles

Statute Miles 50 0 50 100 150
Kilometers 50 0 50 100 200

NYSTROM map by Richard Edes Harrison

AFRICA

Africa, the second largest continent, has more than 30 of the newest nations in the world. For many years, almost the entire continent was under the rule of European countries. Today, most of the former colonies have become self-governing nations that share many of the same problems of health, education, and economic development. They are attacking these problems both on a local basis and in cooperation with their neighbors. The nations of Africa represent a great variety of cultural backgrounds. North of the Sahara, most of the people are Arabs. South of the Sahara, most of the people are Negroes. Relatively small numbers of Europeans and Asians are scattered throughout the continent.

WHAT IS YOUR ATLAS I.Q. OF AFRICA?

These questions are designed to test your knowledge of the variety of information about Africa contained in The World Book Atlas. Check your answers by turning to the last page of the Atlas.

Identifying places

1. Africa is bordered by four large bodies of water. Three of these are the Atlantic Ocean, the Mediterranean Sea, and the Red Sea. What is the fourth?
2. The northernmost country on the African continent is Tunisia. What is the southernmost African nation?
3. Five African nations border on the Mediterranean Sea. Four of these are Egypt, Libya, Tunisia, and Morocco. What is the fifth?
4. If you were to take a trip down the Nile from its source to its mouth, in what general direction would you travel?
5. Cairo is the capital of Egypt and Khartoum is the capital of Sudan. What is the capital of Ethiopia?
6. The largest lake in Africa is named for a famous queen. What is the name of the lake?
7. Africa's highest mountain provides the setting for Ernest Hemingway's famous short story "The Snows of Kilimanjaro." In what country is Kilimanjaro located?
8. The Strait of Gibraltar marks the point where Europe and Africa come closest together. The European country at this point is Spain. What is the African country?
9. One African country lies entirely within South Africa. What is the name of that country?
10. The Suez Canal connects the Mediterranean Sea with what other body of water?

Facts and figures

11. The fourth largest island in the world, with an area about the size of Texas, lies off the east coast of Africa. What is the name of the island?
12. The longest river in the world is found in Africa. What is the name of the river?
13. Africa is the second largest continent in area. Which continent is larger?
14. The largest country in Africa covers more area than Alaska and Texas combined. What is the name of Africa's largest country?
15. Africa ranks third in population among the continents of the world. About how many persons live in Africa?

History

16. Africa had only four independent countries when World War II ended in 1945. Three of these were Ethiopia, South Africa, and Egypt. What was the fourth?
17. Before gaining independence, Algeria was controlled by the French and Tanzania was controlled by the British. From what country did Ghana gain its independence?
18. What is the present name of the African country that was once known as Abyssinia?
19. The Brussels Anti-Slavery Conference of 1889-1890 regulated the import of arms and prohibited the import of intoxicating liquors in what region of Africa?
20. One of the most famous conferences of World War II took place between Prime Minister Winston Churchill and President Franklin D. Roosevelt at Casablanca. In what African country is Casablanca located?

MAPS OF AFRICA

96 **PHYSICAL FEATURES OF AFRICA**
97 **POLITICAL DIVISIONS OF AFRICA**
98-100 **HISTORY OF AFRICA**
98 ANCIENT EGYPT (1200'S B.C.)
99 PARTITION OF AFRICA (1800'S)
100 INDEPENDENCE MOVEMENT
101-107 **MAPS OF COUNTRIES AND DEPENDENCIES**
105 AFARS AND ISSAS
102 ALGERIA
106 ANGOLA
107 BOTSWANA
106 BURUNDI
104 CAMEROON
104 CENTRAL AFRICAN REPUBLIC
104 CHAD
104 CONGO
103 DAHOMEY
101 EGYPT
104 EQUATORIAL GUINEA
105 ETHIOPIA
104 GABON
103 GAMBIA
103 GHANA
103 GUINEA
103 IVORY COAST
106 KENYA
107 LESOTHO
103 LIBERIA
101 LIBYA
107 MALAGASY REPUBLIC
106 MALAWI
103 MALI
103 MAURITANIA
102 MOROCCO
106, 107 MOZAMBIQUE
103 NIGER
103 NIGERIA
103 PORTUGUESE GUINEA
107 RHODESIA
106 RWANDA
103 SENEGAL
103 SIERRA LEONE
105 SOMALIA
107 SOUTH AFRICA
107 SOUTH WEST AFRICA
102 SPANISH SAHARA
105 SUDAN
107 SWAZILAND
106 TANZANIA
103 TOGO
102 TUNISIA
106 UGANDA
103 UPPER VOLTA
106 ZAIRE
106 ZAMBIA

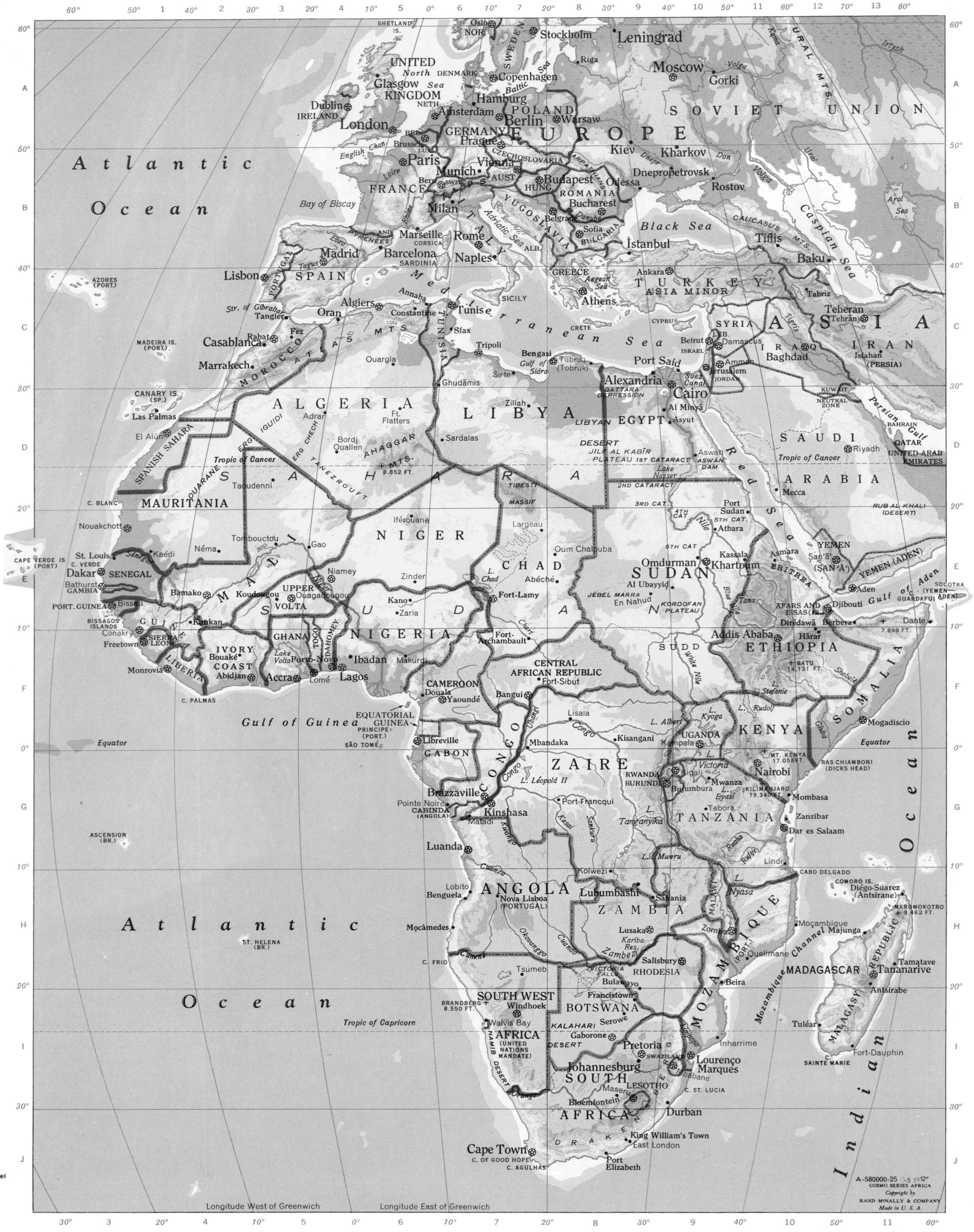

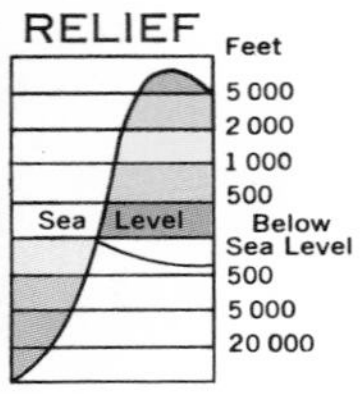

60° 50° 1 40° 2 30° 3 20° 4 10° 5 0° 6 10° 7 20° 8 30° 9 40° 10 50° 11 60° 12 70° 13 80°

A

SHETLAND IS.
Oslo · Stockholm · Leningrad
NOR.
SWEDEN
Moscow · Gorki
UNITED
North DENMARK · Copenhagen
Glasgow Sea
KINGDOM · Hamburg
Dublin
Amsterdam · POLAND · Warsaw
IRELAND · London NETH.
GERMANY · Berlin · EUROPE
Brussels · Prague
CZECHOSLOVAKIA · Kiev · Kharkov
Paris · Munich · Vienna
FRANCE · Budapest · Odessa
ROMANIA · Bucharest
Milan · YUGOSLAVIA · Belgrade
Marseille · Rome · Sofia · BULGARIA
Madrid · Barcelona · ITALY · Naples
SPAIN
Lisbon

Atlantic Ocean

B

Bay of Biscay
PYRENEES
CORSICA
SARDINIA
GREECE · Athens · İstanbul
Black Sea · CAUCASUS MTS · Tiflis · Baku
TURKEY · Ankara
ASIA MINOR

SOVIET UNION
Aral Sea
Caspian Sea

C

AZORES (PORT.)
Algiers · Oran · Constantine · Tunis
TUNISIA · Sfax
Mediterranean Sea
CRETE · CYPRUS · SYRIA · Damascus · IRAQ · IRAN
Beirut · LEB. · Baghdad · Tabriz
ISRAEL · Teheran · Tehran
Casablanca · MOROCCO · Fez · Rabat
Marrakech
Tripoli · Bengasi · Tübruq (Tobruk)
Gulf of Sidra · Sirte
Port Said · Alexandria · Cairo · JORDAN · Amman · Jerusalem · Isfahan (PERSIA)
Suez Canal

D

MADEIRA IS. (PORT.)
CANARY IS. (SP.) · Las Palmas
Ouargla · Ghudāmis
El Aiún
SPANISH SAHARA
Adrar · ALGERIA · Ft. Flatters
LIBYA · LIBYAN DESERT · EGYPT · Al Minyā · Asyut
SAUDI ARABIA · Riyadh · QATAR · UNITED ARAB EMIRATES
KUWAIT · NEUTRAL ZONE · BAHRAIN · Persian Gulf
Mecca · Tropic of Cancer · RUB AL KHALI (DESERT)
MTS. 9,852 FT.
TIBESTI · MASSIF · JILF AL KABIR PLATEAU · Lake Nasser · Aswan · ASWÂN DAM · 1st CATARACT

E

C. BLANC
MAURITANIA · Taoudenni
Nouakchott
CAPE VERDE IS. (PORT.)
C. VERDE · St. Louis
Dakar · SENEGAL · Kaédi · Néma
Iférouane · Largeau · Oum Chalouba · Omdurman · Khartoum · Kassala · Asmara · ERITREA
Port Sudan · Atbara · YEMEN · San'ā' (SAN'Ā')
NIGER · L. Chad · Abéché · SUDAN · Al Ubayyid · JEBEL MARRA · En Nahud · KORDOFAN PLATEAU
YEMEN (ADEN) · Aden · Gulf of Aden · SOCOTRA (YEMEN-ADEN) · C. GUARDAFUI

PORT. GUINEA · Bissau
Tombouctou · Gao · Zinder · MALI · Niamey · Fort-Lamy · CHAD · Fort-Archambault
Bathurst · GAMBIA
BISSAGOS ISLANDS
Conakry · GUINEA · Kankan
SIERRA LEONE · Freetown
Bamako · UPPER VOLTA · Ouagadougou · Koudougou · GHANA · TOGO · DAHOMEY · NIGERIA · Kano · Zaria
Makurdi · CENTRAL AFRICAN REPUBLIC · Fort-Sibut · SUDD
Addis Ababa · BATU 14,131 FT. · ETHIOPIA
AFARS AND ISSAS · Djibouti · Diredawa · Berbera · Harar 7,898 FT.

F

LIBERIA · Monrovia
IVORY COAST · Bouaké · Abidjan · Accra · Lomé · Lagos
C. PALMAS
Lake Volta · Porto-Novo · Ibadan
CAMEROON · Douala · Yaoundé · Bangui
Lisala · L. Albert · UGANDA · Kampala
L. Stefanie · L. Rudolf · SOMALIA · Mogadiscio
L. Kyoga

G (Equator)

Gulf of Guinea
EQUATORIAL GUINEA · PRINCIPE (PORT.) · SÃO TOMÉ
Libreville · GABON
Mbandaka · Kisangani · ZAIRE
MT. KENYA 17,058 FT. · Nairobi · RAS CHIAMBONI (DICKS HEAD)
L. Victoria · RWANDA · Kigali · BURUNDI · Bujumbura · Mwanza · L. Eyasi · KENYA
KILIMANJARO 19,340 FT. · Mombasa
Brazzaville · Pointe Noire · CABINDA (ANGOLA) · Kinshasa · Matadi · L. Léopold II · Port-Francqui · L. Tanganyika · Tabora · TANZANIA · Zanzibar · Dar es Salaam

ASCENSION (BR.)
Luanda
L. Mweru · Lindi

H

Atlantic Ocean
Lobito · Benguela · ANGOLA · Nova Lisboa (PORTUGAL) · Kolwezi · Lubumbashi · Sakania · ZAMBIA · L. Nyasa · CABO DELGADO
COMORO IS. · Diégo-Suárez (Antsirane)
Moçambique · Majunga
ST. HELENA (BR.)
Moçâmedes · Lusaka · Zomba · MALAWI · Quelimane · MOZAMBIQUE · Beira
MAROMOKOTRO 9,462 FT.
C. FRIO · Kariba Res. · Salisbury · RHODESIA · Zambezi · MADAGASCAR · Tamatave · Tananarive
Tsumeb · VICTORIA FALLS · Bulawayo · MALAGASY REPUBLIC · Antsirabe
BRANDBERG 8,550 FT. · SOUTH WEST · Windhoek · Francistown · Inharrime · Tuléar

I (Tropic of Capricorn)

Atlantic Ocean
AFRICA (UNITED NATIONS MANDATE)
Walvis Bay · KALAHARI DESERT · BOTSWANA · Serowe · Gaborone · Pretoria · SWAZILAND · Lourenço Marques
NAMIB DESERT · Johannesburg · SOUTH · Maseru · LESOTHO
Indian Ocean
SAINTE MARIE
Fort-Dauphin
C. ST. LUCIA

J

RELIEF
Bloemfontein · AFRICA · Orange · Durban
DRAKENS · King William's Town · East London
Cape Town · C. OF GOOD HOPE · C. AGULHAS
Port Elizabeth

Longitude West of Greenwich · Longitude East of Greenwich

30° 3 20° 4 10° 5 0° 6 10° 7 20° 8 30° 9 40° 10 50° 11 60°

RELIEF
Feet
5 000
2 000
1 000
500
Sea Level
Below Sea Level
500
5 000
20 000

Statute Miles 100 0 100 300 500 700 900

Kilometers 100 0 100 300 500 700 900 1100 1300

Sinusoidal Projection

SCALE 1:36,313,000 1 Inch = 565 Statute Miles

A-580000-25
COSMO SERIES AFRICA
Copyright by
RAND McNALLY & COMPANY
Made in U.S.A.

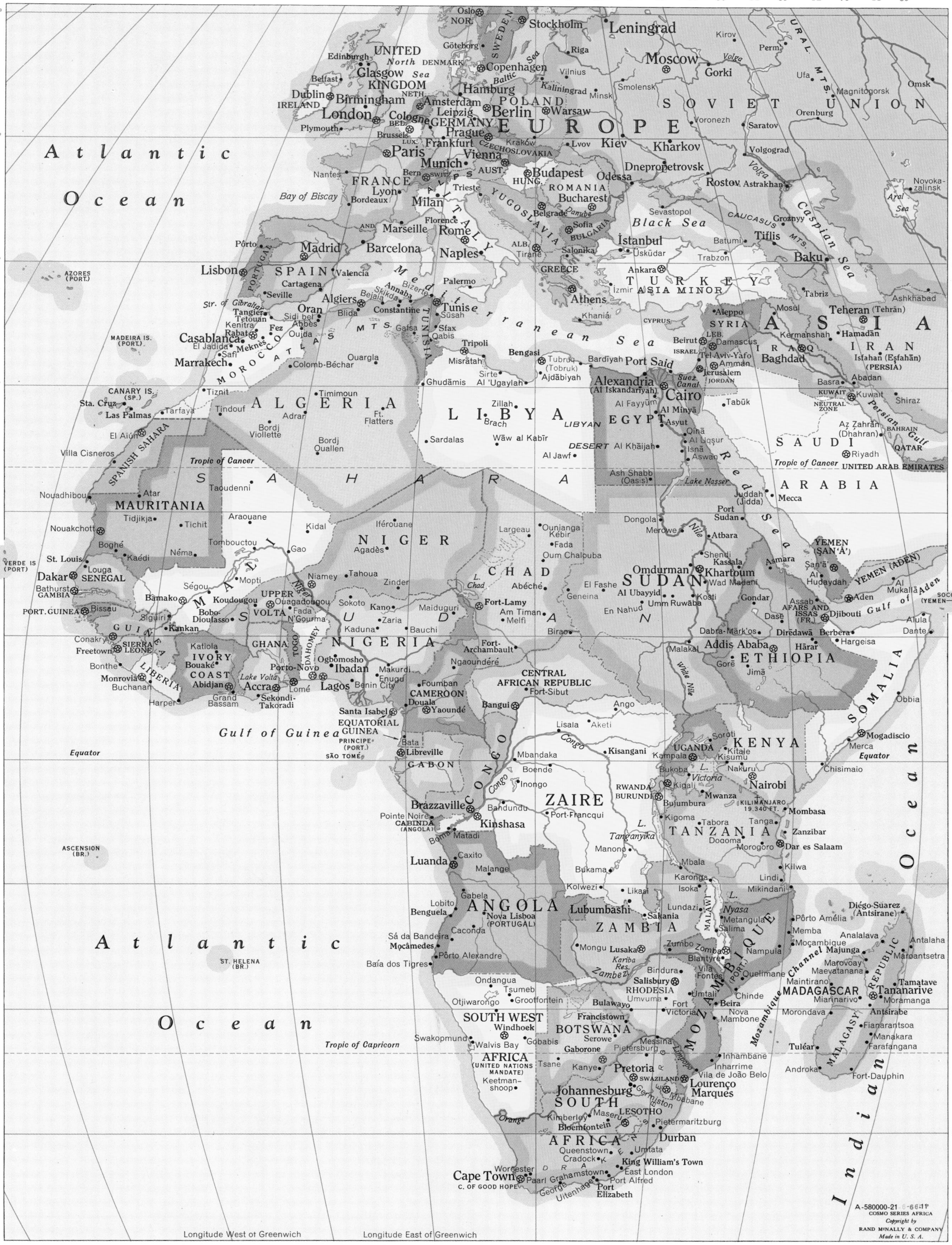

Sinusoidal Projection
SCALE 1:36,313,000 1 Inch = 565 Statute Miles

Statute Miles 100 0 100 300 500 700 900
Kilometers 100 0 100 300 500 700 900 1100 1300

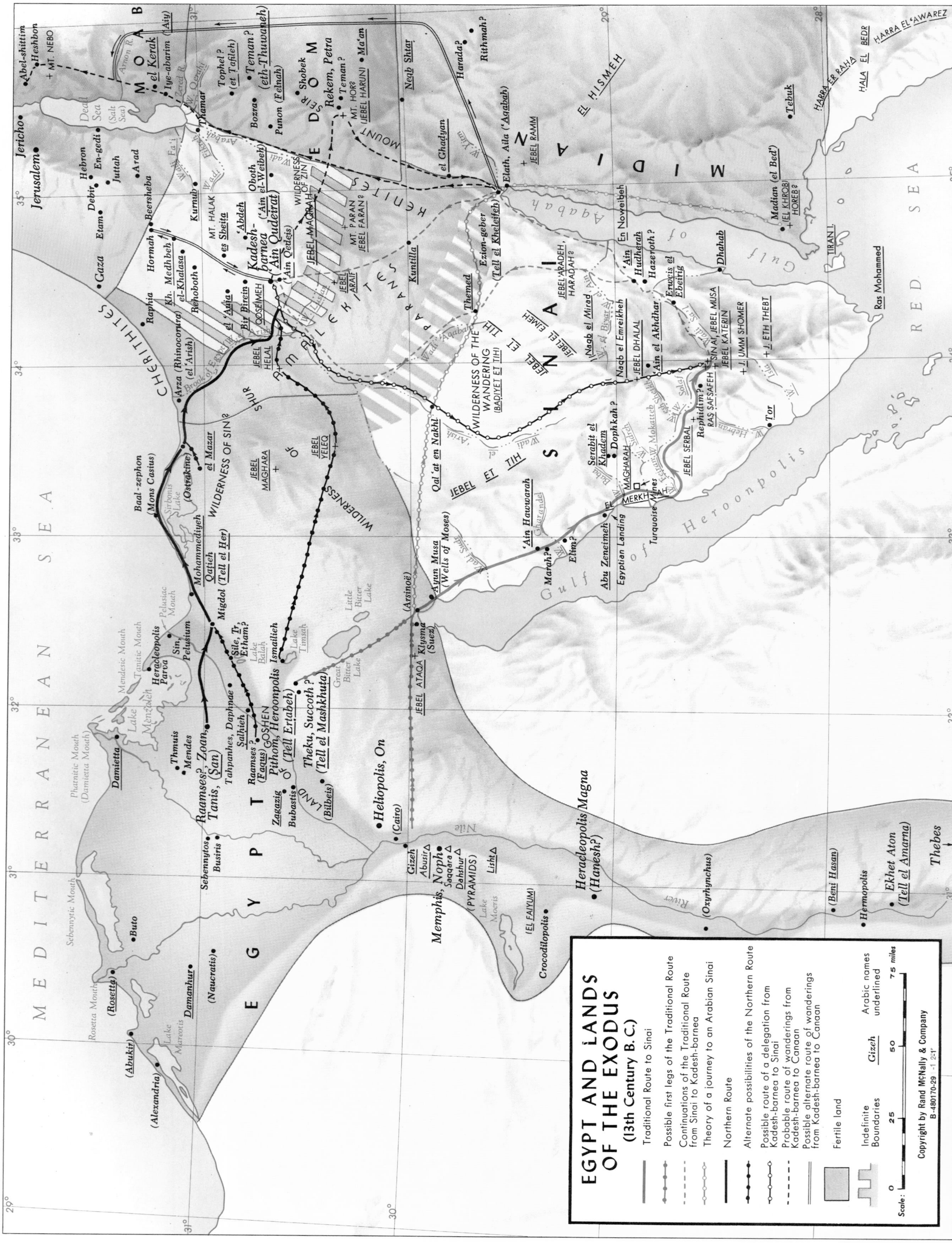
EGYPT AND LANDS OF THE EXODUS
(13th Century B.C.)
Traditional Route to Sinai
Possible first legs of the Traditional Route
Continuations of the Traditional Route from Sinai to Kadesh-barnea
Theory of a journey to an Arabian Sinai
Northern Route
Alternate possibilities of the Northern Route
Possible route of a delegation from Kadesh-barnea to Sinai
Probable route of wanderings from Kadesh-barnea to Canaan
Possible alternate route of wanderings from Kadesh-barnea to Canaan
Fertile land
Indefinite Boundaries
Gizeh Arabic names underlined
Scale: 0 25 50 75 miles
Copyright by Rand McNally & Company
B-480170-29 -1 2-1'
MEDITERRANEAN SEA
EGYPT
SINAI
RED SEA
Gulf of Heroonpolis
Gulf of Aqabah
MIDIAN
EDOM
MOAB

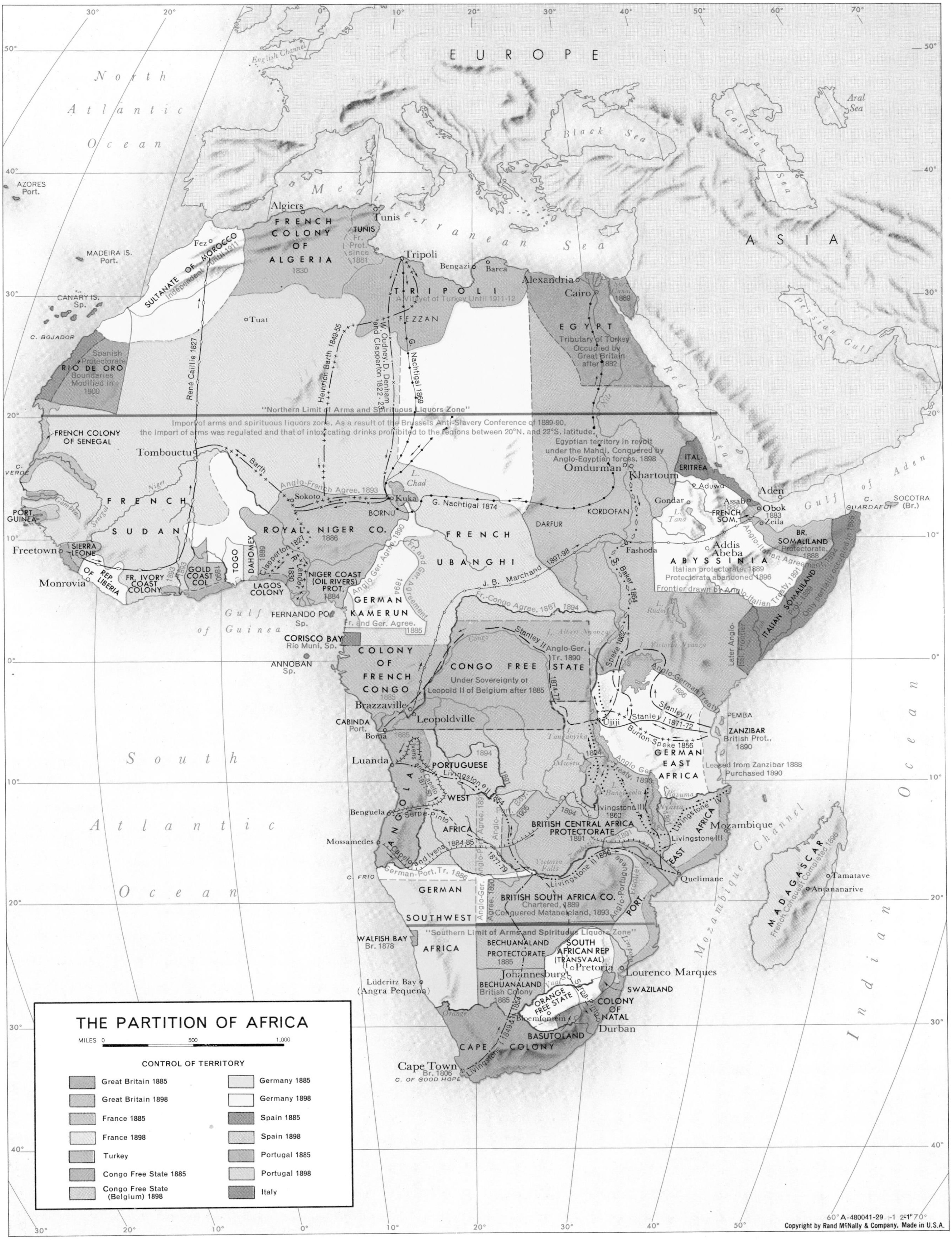
EUROPE
North Atlantic Ocean
AZORES Port.
MADEIRA IS. Port.
CANARY IS. Sp.
C. BOJADOR
Mediterranean Sea
Black Sea
Caspian Sea
Aral Sea
ASIA
Persian Gulf
Red Sea
Gulf of Aden
Algiers
FRENCH COLONY OF ALGERIA 1830
Tunis
TUNIS Fr. Prot. since 1881
Fez
SULTANATE OF MOROCCO Independent until 1911
Tripoli
Bengazi
Barca
TRIPOLI A Vilayet of Turkey Until 1911-12
FEZZAN
Alexandria
Cairo
Suez Canal 1869
EGYPT Tributary of Turkey Occupied by Great Britain after 1882
Tuat
Spanish Protectorate RIO DE ORO Boundaries Modified in 1900
René Caillié 1827
Heinrich Barth 1849-55
W. Oudney, D. Denham and Clapperton 1822-25
G. Nachtigal 1869
"Northern Limit of Arms and Spirituous Liquors Zone"
Import of arms and spirituous liquors zone. As a result of the Brussels Anti-Slavery Conference of 1889-90, the import of arms was regulated and that of intoxicating drinks prohibited to the regions between 20°N. and 22°S. latitude.
FRENCH COLONY OF SENEGAL
Tombouctu
Barth
Anglo-French Agree. 1893
Sokoto
Kuka
L. Chad
BORNU
G. Nachtigal 1874
Egyptian territory in revolt under the Mahdi. Conquered by Anglo-Egyptian forces, 1898
Omdurman
Khartoum
KORDOFAN
DARFUR
ITAL. ERITREA
Aduwa
Assab 1880
Aden
Obok 1883
Zeila
FRENCH SOM.
SOCOTRA (Br.)
C. GUARDAFUI
BR. SOMALILAND Protectorate 1888
Gondar
L. Tana
Addis Abeba
ABYSSINIA Italian protectorate 1889 Protectorate abandoned 1896
Frontier drawn by Anglo-Italian Treaty, 1897
Anglo-Italian Agreement, 1894
ITALIAN SOMALILAND Only partially occupied in 1898
Fashoda
S. Baker 1864
PORT. GUINEA
C. VERDE
Gambia
Senegal
Niger
FRENCH SUDAN
Freetown
SIERRA LEONE
REP. OF LIBERIA
Monrovia
FR. IVORY COAST COLONY
GOLD COAST COL.
TOGO
DAHOMEY 1889
ROYAL NIGER CO. 1886
Clapperton 1827
R. Lander 1830
NIGER COAST (OIL RIVERS) PROT. 1884
LAGOS COLONY
FRENCH UBANGHI
Anglo-Ger. Agree. 1890
Fr. and Ger. Agreement 1894
J. B. Marchand 1897-98
Fr.-Congo Agree. 1887
GERMAN KAMERUN Fr. and Ger. Agree. 1885
Gulf of Guinea
FERNANDO PO Sp.
CORISCO BAY Rio Muni, Sp.
ANNOBAN Sp.
COLONY OF FRENCH CONGO 1885
Brazzaville
Leopoldville
CONGO FREE STATE Under Sovereignty of Leopold II of Belgium after 1885
Stanley II Anglo-Ger. Tr. 1890
L. Albert Nyanza
L. Victoria Nyanza
L. Rudolf
Speke 1862
Later Anglo-Ital. Frontier
Anglo-German Treaty 1886
Stanley II 1871-72
Burton-Speke 1856
Ujiji
L. Tanganyika
PEMBA
ZANZIBAR British Prot., 1890
GERMAN EAST AFRICA
Leased from Zanzibar 1888 Purchased 1890
CABINDA Port.
Boma
Luanda
PORTUGUESE WEST AFRICA
ANGOLA
Livingston II 1854
Benguela
Serpa Pinto
Mossamedes
Capelo and Ivens 1884-85
BRITISH CENTRAL AFRICA PROTECTORATE 1891
Livingstone III 1860
L. Nyasa
Mozambique
EAST AFRICA
Victoria Falls
Livingstone II 1856
Quelimane
C. FRIO
German-Port. Tr. 1886
GERMAN SOUTHWEST AFRICA
BRITISH SOUTH AFRICA CO. Chartered, 1889 Conquered Matabeleland, 1893
PORT.
"Southern Limit of Arms and Spirituous Liquors Zone"
WALFISH BAY Br. 1878
BECHUANALAND PROTECTORATE 1885
SOUTH AFRICAN REP (TRANSVAAL)
Pretoria
Johannesburg
Lourenco Marques
SWAZILAND
BECHUANALAND British Colony 1885
ORANGE FREE STATE
Bloemfontein
COLONY OF NATAL
Durban
BASUTOLAND
CAPE COLONY
Cape Town Br. 1806
C. OF GOOD HOPE
Lüderitz Bay (Angra Pequena)
South Atlantic Ocean
Indian Ocean
Mozambique Channel
MADAGASCAR French Conquest Completed 1896
Tamatave
Antananarive
THE PARTITION OF AFRICA
MILES 0 500 1,000
CONTROL OF TERRITORY
Great Britain 1885
Great Britain 1898
France 1885
France 1898
Turkey
Congo Free State 1885
Congo Free State (Belgium) 1898
Germany 1885
Germany 1898
Spain 1885
Spain 1898
Portugal 1885
Portugal 1898
Italy
A-480041-29
Copyright by Rand McNally & Company, Made in U.S.A.

AFRICA
The Independence Movement
MILES 0 500 1000
Formerly British
Formerly French
Formerly Belgian
Formerly Italian
Independent Before 1945
Formerly Spanish
Not Independent
1966 Year Each Country Gained Independence
A-480046-220
North Atlantic Ocean
South Atlantic Ocean
Indian Ocean
E U R O P E
A S I A
English Channel
Black Sea
Caspian Sea
Aral Sea
Mediterranean Sea
Persian Gulf
Red Sea
Gulf of Aden
Gulf of Guinea
Mozambique Channel
Suez Canal
AZORES (Port.)
MADEIRA IS. (Port.)
CANARY IS. (Sp.)
C. BOJADOR
MOROCCO 1956
Rabat
ALGERIA 1962
Algiers
Adrar
TUNISIA 1956
Tunis
LIBYA 1951
Tripoli
Bengasi
Barca
EGYPT
Alexandria
Cairo
SPANISH SAHARA
El Aiún
MAURITANIA 1960
Nouakchott
MALI 1960
Tombouctou
Bamako
NIGER 1960
Niamey
CHAD 1960
L. Chad
Fort-Lamy
SUDAN 1954
Omdurman
Khartoum
Kodok
C. VERDE
SENEGAL 1960
Dakar
GAMBIA 1965
Bathurst
Bissau
PORT. GUINEA
GUINEA 1958
Conakry
SIERRA LEONE 1961
Freetown
LIBERIA
Monrovia
IVORY COAST 1960
Abidjan
UPPER VOLTA 1960
Ouagadougou
GHANA 1957
Accra
TOGO 1960
Lomé
DAHOMEY 1960
Porto-Novo
Lagos
NIGERIA 1960
Sokoto
Kukawa
CAMEROON 1960
Yaoundé
CENTRAL AFRICAN REPUBLIC 1960
Bangui
Santa Isabel
EQUATORIAL GUINEA 1968
Bata
SÃO TOME (Port.)
Libreville
GABON 1960
CONGO 1960
Brazzaville
Kinshasa
ZAIRE 1960
CABINDA (Angola)
Boma
Luanda
ANGOLA (Port.)
Benguela
Moçâmedes
C. FRIO
ETHIOPIA
Aduwā
Gondar
L. Tana
Addis Ababa
AFARS AND ISSAS (FR)
Assab
Obock
Djibouti
Zeila
C. GUARDAFUI
SOMALIA 1960
Mogadiscio
L. Rudolf
UGANDA 1962
Kampala
KENYA 1963
Nairobi
L. Albert
L. Victoria
Kigali
RWANDA 1962
BURUNDI 1962
Bujumbura
Ujiji
L. Tanganyika
TANZANIA (TANGANYIKA) 1961
PEMBA
(ZANZIBAR) 1963
Dar es Saalem
L. Mweru
L. Bangweulu
Ruvuma
L. Nyasa
MALAWI 1964
Zomba
ZAMBIA 1964
Lusaka
Zambezi
Victoria Falls
Salisbury
RHODESIA 1965
MOZAMBIQUE (Port.)
Moçambique
Quelimane
MALAGASY REPUBLIC 1960
Tamatave
Tananarive
Port Louis
MAURITIUS 1968
SOUTH WEST AFRICA (U.N. Mand.)
Windhoek
Lüderitz
BOTSWANA 1966
Gaberones
Limpopo
Pretoria
Johannesburg
Lourenço Marques
Mbabane
SWAZILAND 1968
Vaal
Orange
Bloemfontein
Maseru
LESOTHO 1966
Durban
SOUTH AFRICA
Cape Town
C. OF GOOD HOPE
Nile
Congo
Niger
Senegal
Gambia
Giuba
Copyright by Rand McNally & Company, Made in U.S.A.

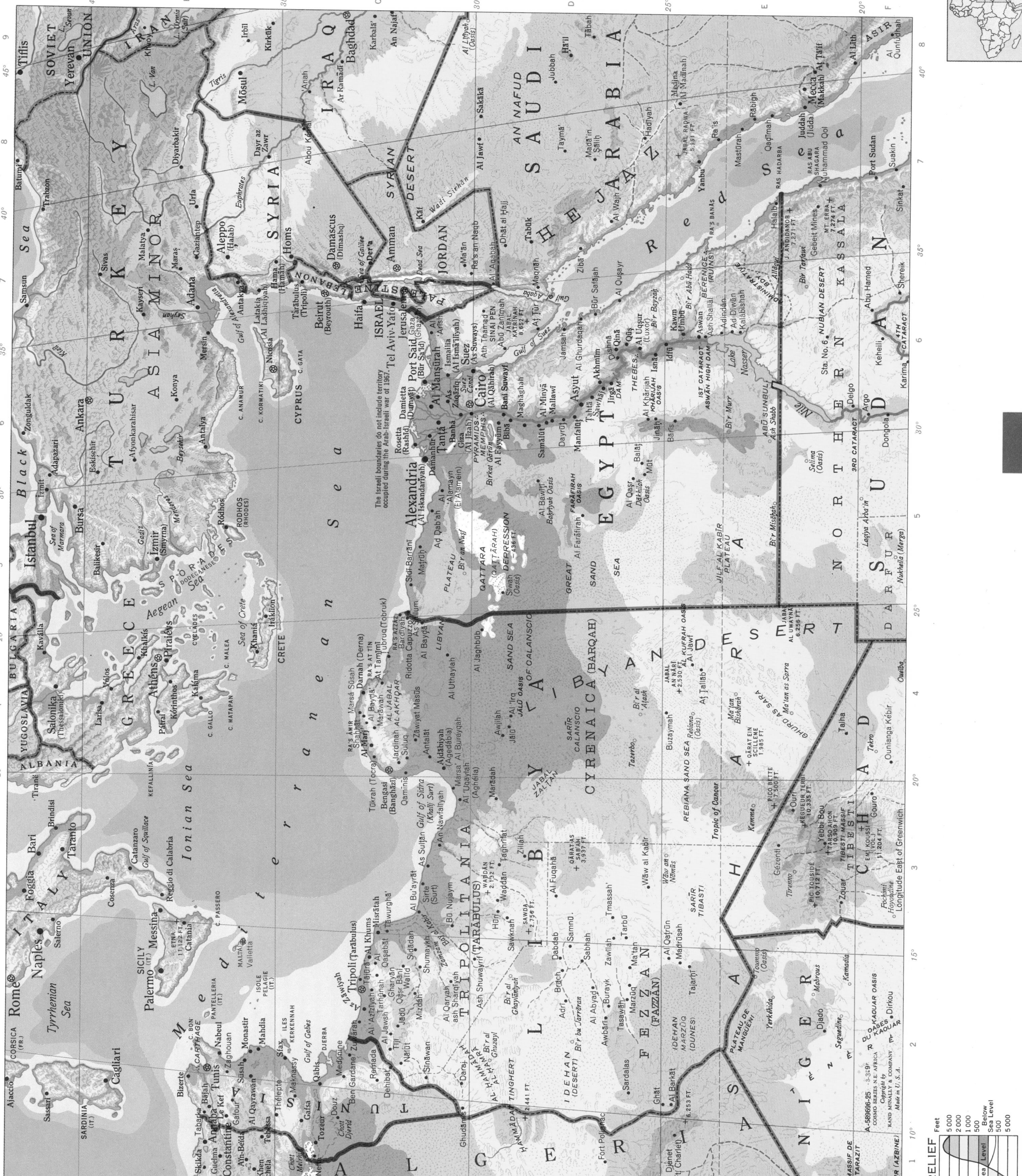

Sinusoidal Projection
SCALE 1: 11,400,000 1 Inch = 180 Statute Miles

Statute Miles 50 0 50 100 150 200 250

50 0 50 100 150 200 250 300

RELIEF
Feet
5 000
2 000
1 000
500
Sea Level
500
5 000
Below Sea Level

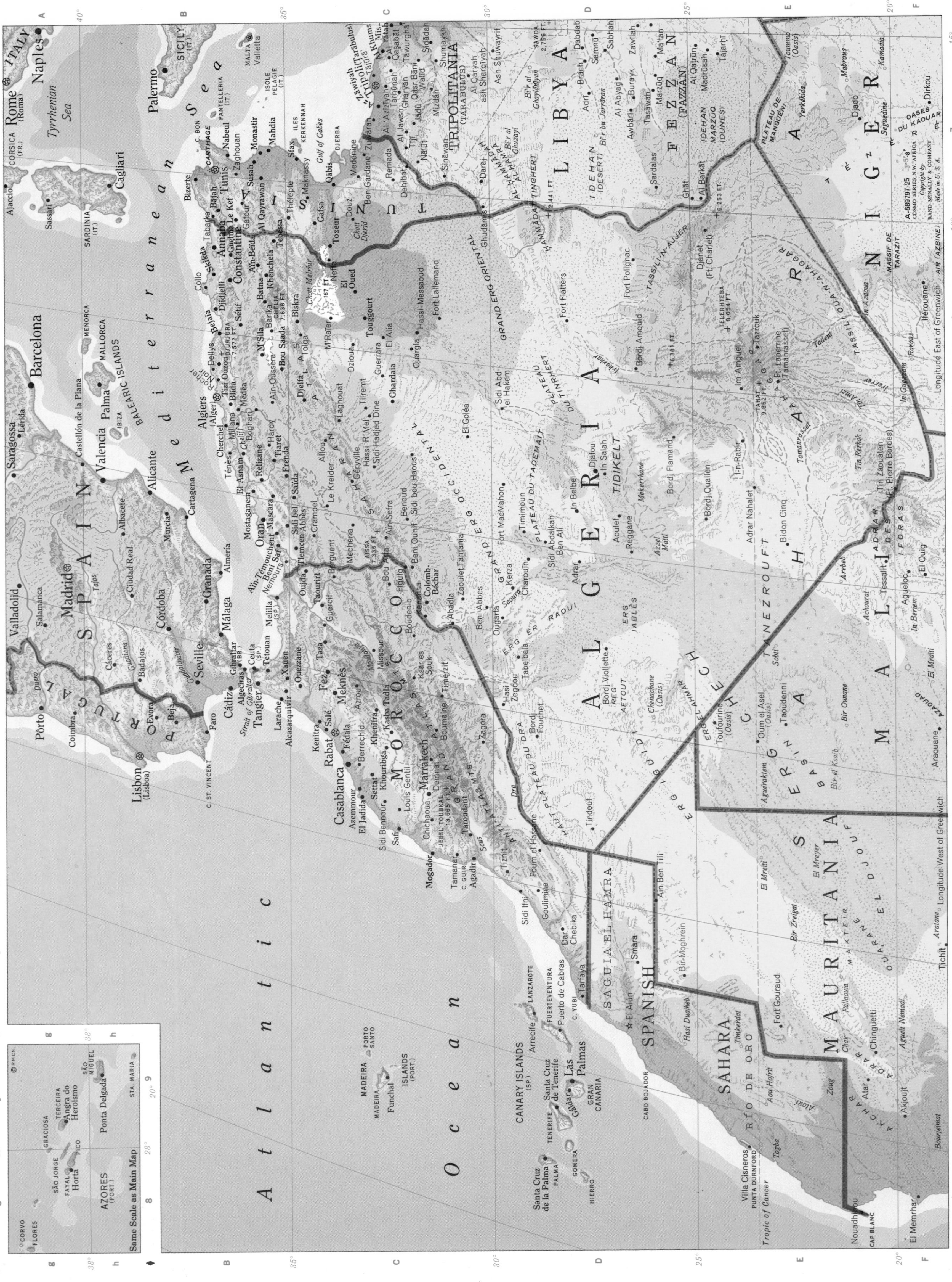

Statute Miles 50 25 0 50 100 150 200 250
Kilometers 50 0 50 100 150 200 250 300

Sinusoidal Projection
SCALE 1 : 11,400,000
1 Inch = 180 Statute Miles

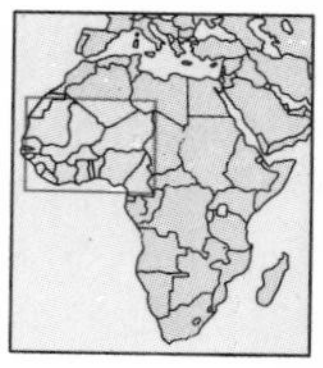

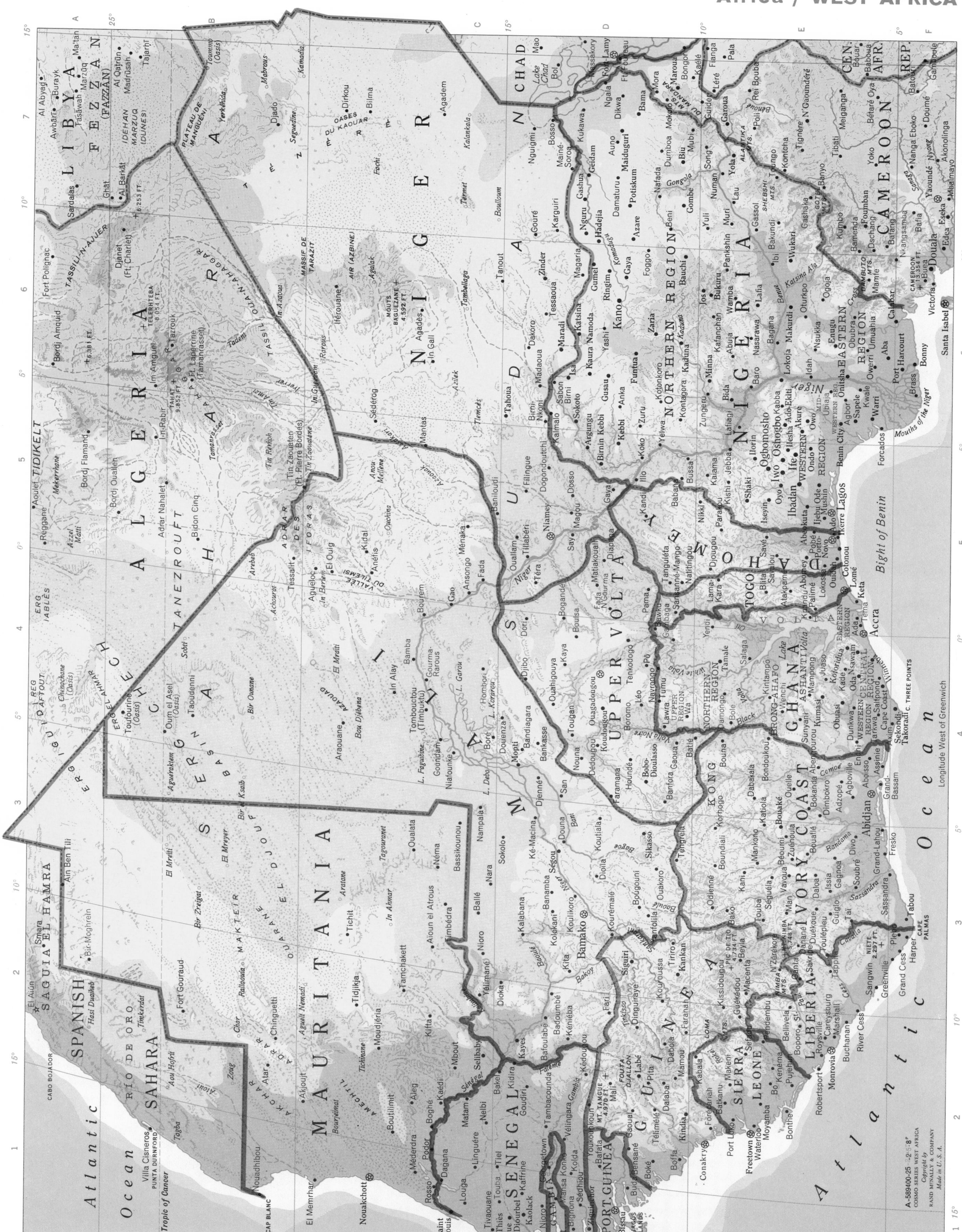

Sinusoidal Projection
SCALE 1: 11,400,000   1 Inch = 180 Statute Miles

Statute Miles 50 25 0 50 100 150 200 250
Kilometers 50 0 50 100 150 200 250 300

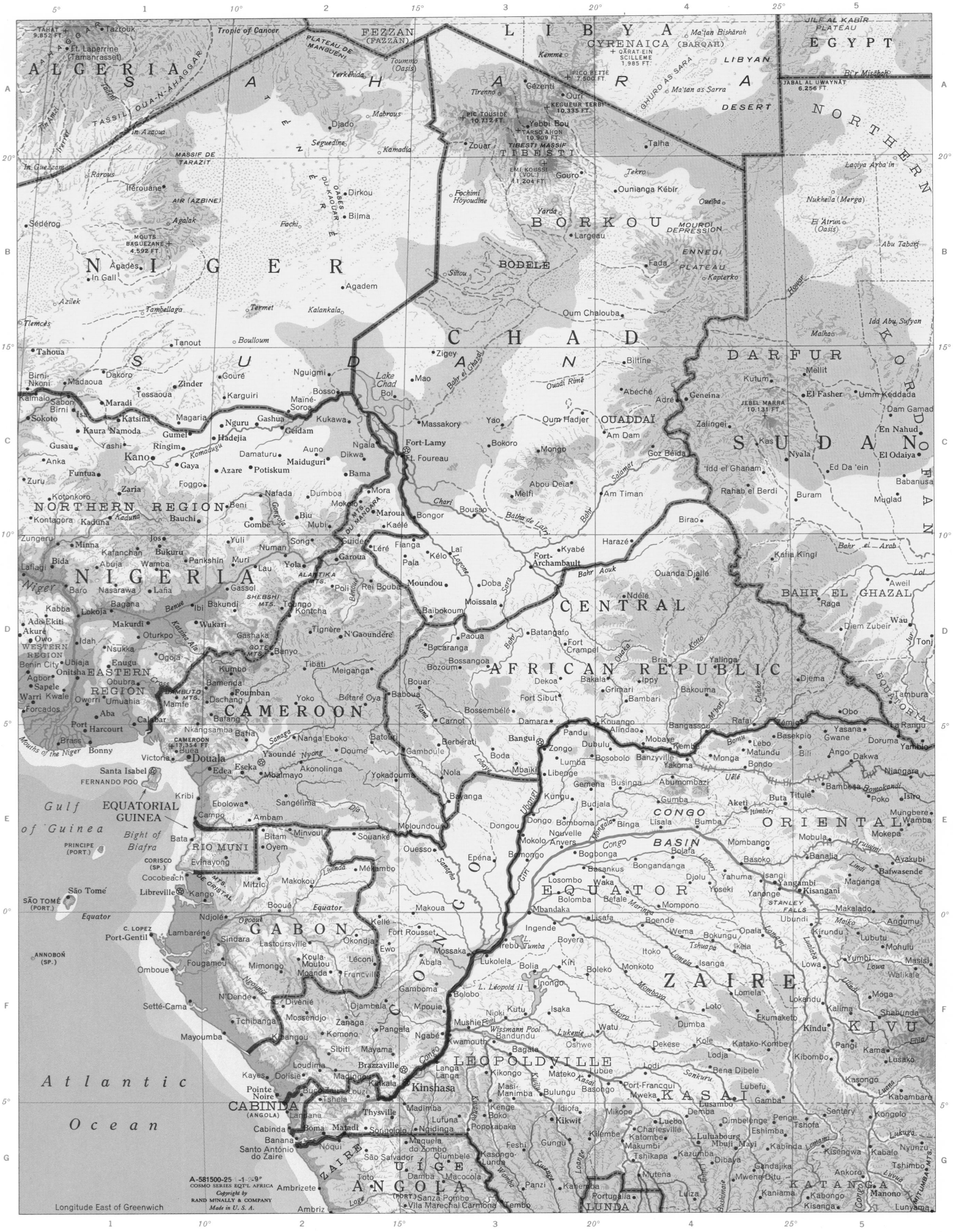

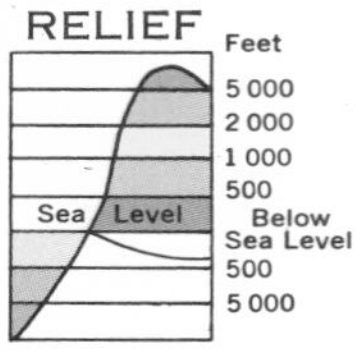

Statute Miles 50 25 0 50 100 150 200 250

50 0 50 100 150 200 250 300

Sinusoidal Projection
SCALE 1: 11,400,000 1 Inch = 180 Statute Miles

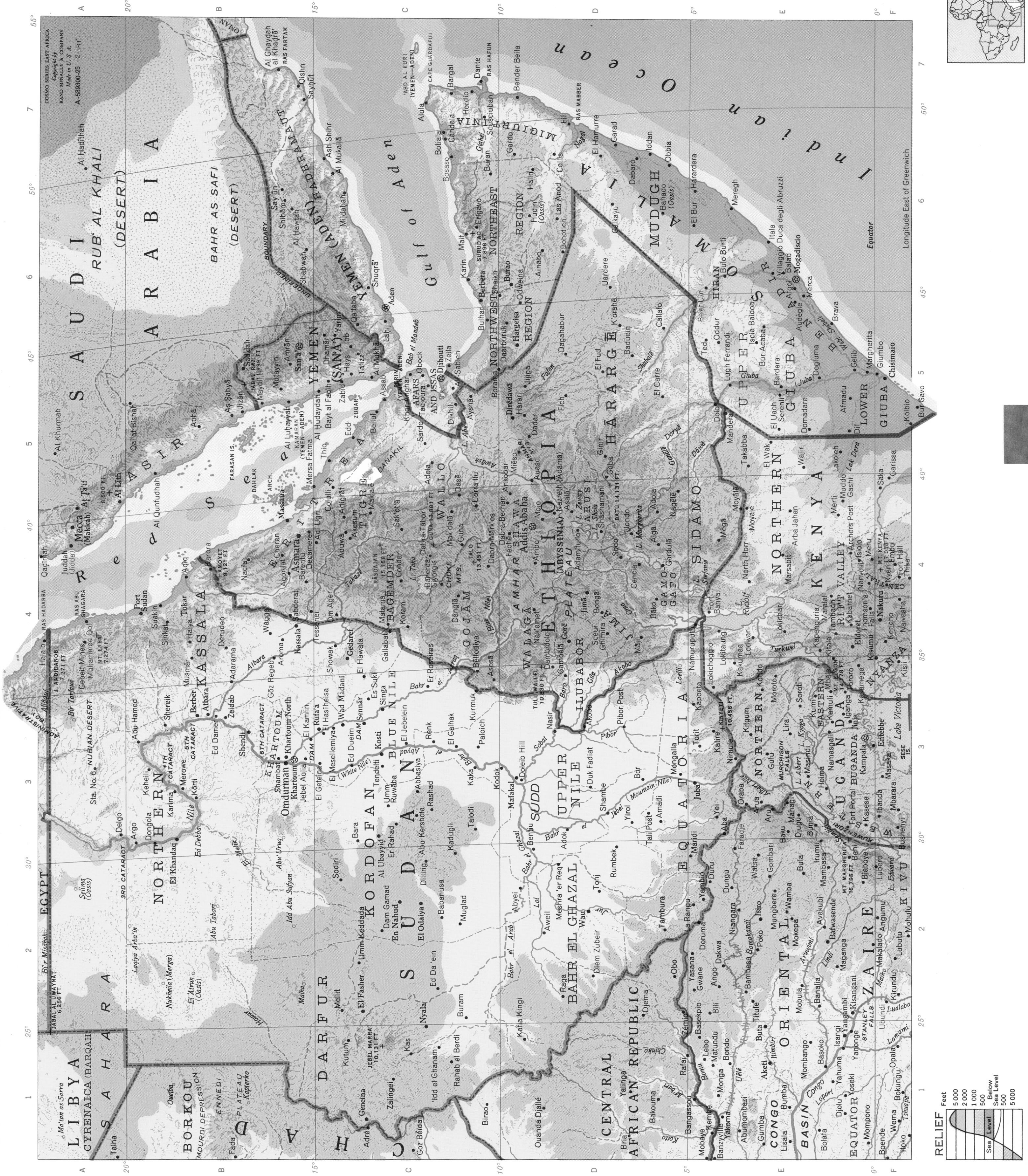

Sinusoidal Projection
SCALE 1: 11,400,000 1 Inch = 180 Statute Miles

Statute Miles 50 25 0 50 100 150 200 250
Kilometers 50 0 50 100 150 200 250 300

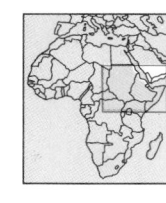

Africa / CENTRAL AFRICA

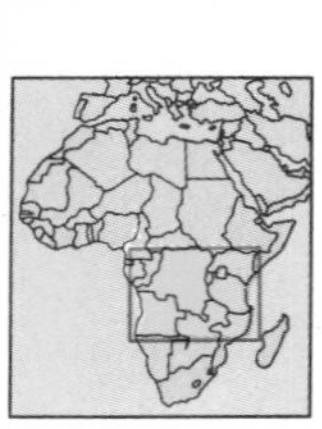

Statute Miles 50 0 50 100 150 200 250

Kilometers 50 0 50 100 150 200 250 300

Sinusoidal Projection

SCALE 1: 11,400,000   1 Inch = 180 Statute Miles

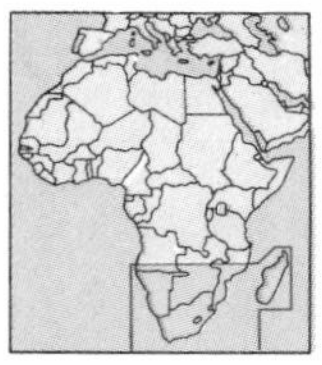

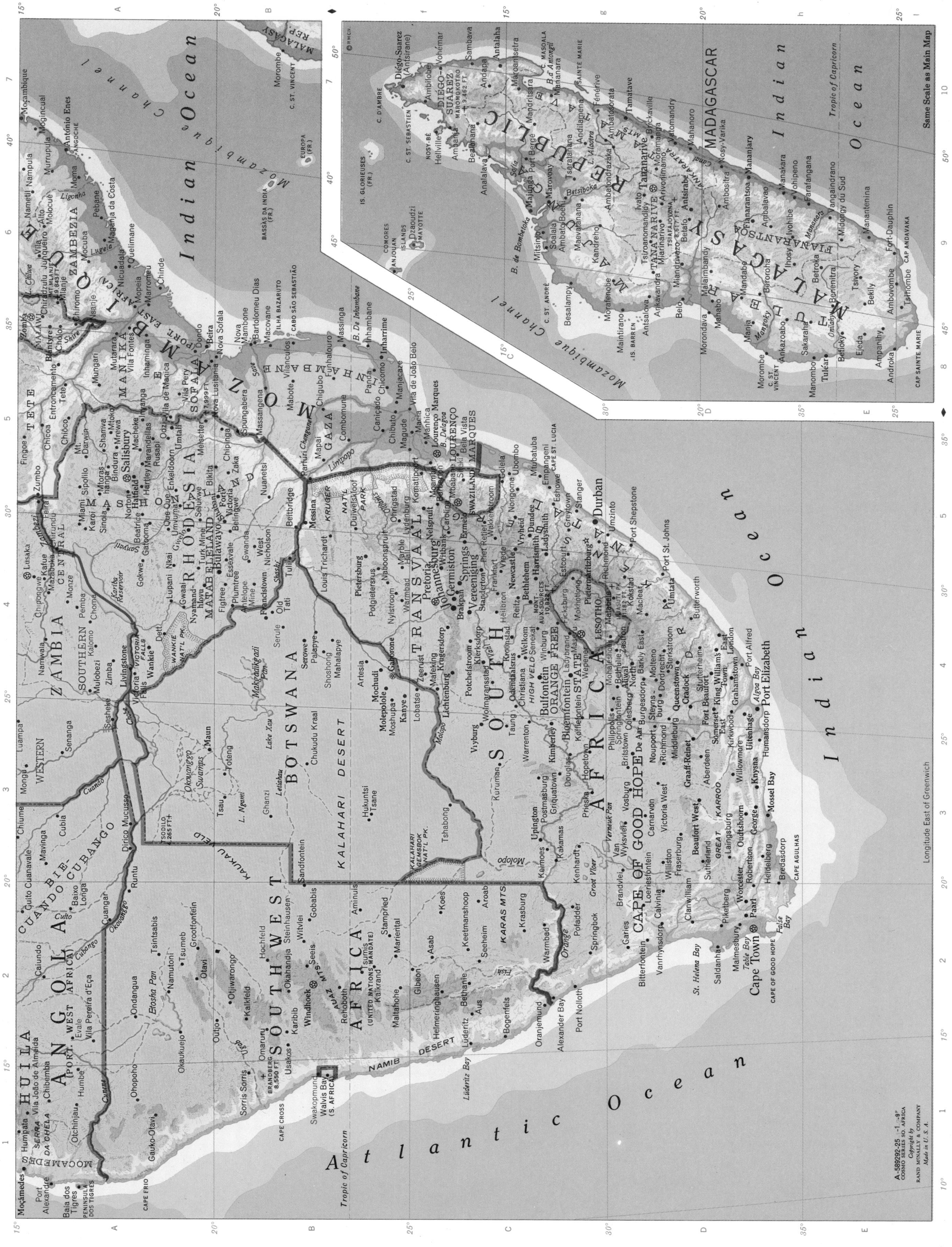

Sinusoidal Projection
SCALE 1: 11,400,000   1 Inch = 180 Statute Miles

Statute Miles 50 25 0 50 100 150 200 250
Kilometers 50 0 50 100 150 200 250 300

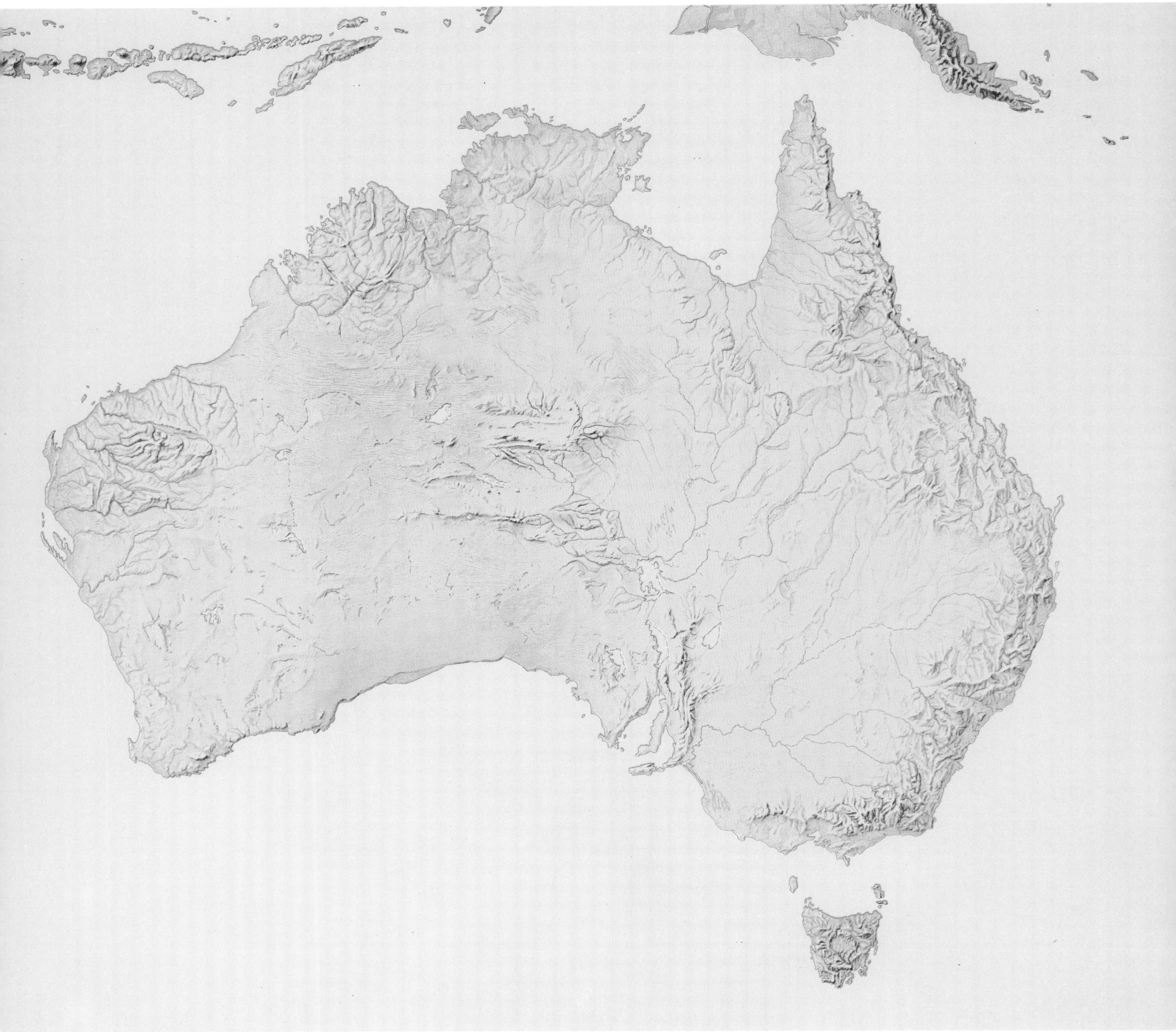

NYSTROM map by Richard Edes Harrison

AUSTRALIA

NEW ZEALAND AND PACIFIC ISLANDS

Australia, New Zealand, and the Pacific Islands are sometimes grouped together under the name Oceania. Among the continents, the Land Down Under is smallest in area; but among the nations of the world, it is the sixth largest. New Zealand, an island country, lies about 1,200 miles east of Australia in the Pacific Ocean. English-speaking Australia and New Zealand are important members of the British Commonwealth. The hundreds of islands in the Pacific are divided into three major groups: (1) Polynesia includes Western Samoa, the Society Islands, and other islands in the central Pacific; (2) Micronesia consists of the Marianas, Marshalls, and other island groups in the western Pacific; (3) Melanesia includes New Guinea, the Solomons, and other nearby islands.

WHAT IS YOUR ATLAS I.Q. OF OCEANIA?

These questions are designed to test your knowledge of the variety of information about Australia, New Zealand, and the Pacific Islands contained in THE WORLD BOOK ATLAS. Check your answers by turning to the last page of the ATLAS.

Identifying places

1. Sydney is the largest city in Australia. But what is the country's capital?
2. The capital of New Zealand is named for a famous British military hero. What is its name?
3. The Pacific Ocean borders Australia to the east. What ocean borders the continent to the west and south?
4. The second largest island in the world lies off the northern tip of Australia. What is its name?
5. The island of Guam is a U.S. territory. To what island group does it belong?
6. Which island is farther west, Wake or Midway?
7. Australia's Great Barrier Reef is the world's largest coral formation. The reef extends for about 1,250 miles along the coast of which of the country's states?

Facts and figures

8. Australia has about the same area as the United States, but it has a much smaller population. About how many million people live in Australia?
9. Which state compares most nearly to New Zealand in area—Colorado, Texas, or Rhode Island?
10. Most Australians live in the southeastern part of the country. Which state has the greater population—Victoria or South Australia?
11. What country is Australia's nearest neighbor?
12. About how many million people live in New Zealand?
13. New Guinea is the second largest island in the world. The eastern half is governed by Australia. Which nation controls the western half?
14. Is New Zealand east or west of the International Date Line?
15. Tahiti is one of the most famous Pacific Islands. To what country does it belong?
16. Into how many main islands is New Zealand divided?
17. Oahu is the economic and cultural center of Hawaii. But what is the largest of the Hawaiian Islands?

History

18. One of the most famous battles of World War II took place on the island of Guadalcanal. To what island group does Guadalcanal belong?
19. On Aug. 2, 1943, Lieutenant John F. Kennedy's patrol boat was run down by a Japanese destroyer in the Blackett Strait. This strait lies between the islands of Kolombangara and Gizo in what large group of islands?
20. Bikini Atoll was the site of atomic bomb tests. To what island group does it belong?

MAPS OF AUSTRALIA, NEW ZEALAND, AND PACIFIC ISLANDS

110 **PHYSICAL FEATURES OF AUSTRALIA**
111 **POLITICAL DIVISIONS OF AUSTRALIA**
112 **PHYSICAL FEATURES OF NEW ZEALAND**
113-115 **MAPS OF PACIFIC ISLANDS**
115 ADMIRALTY ISLANDS
114 BIKINI
115 BISMARCK ARCHIPELAGO
115 BOUGAINVILLE
114 ENIWETOK
114 FIJI
115 GILBERT ISLANDS
115 GUADALCANAL ISLAND
114 GUAM
114 IWO
114 KWAJALEIN
115 LOYALTY ISLANDS
115 MARIANA ISLANDS
115 MARSHALL ISLANDS
114 MIDWAY
113 NAURU
115 NEW BRITAIN
115 NEW CALEDONIA
115 NEW HEBRIDES ISLANDS
115 NEW IRELAND
114 OKINAWA
114 PALAU
114 PONAPE
114 SAIPAN
114 SAMOA
115 SOLOMON ISLANDS
114 TARAWA
114 TINIAN
113 TONGA
114 TRUK
115 VOLCANO ISLANDS
114 WAKE
114 WESTERN SAMOA

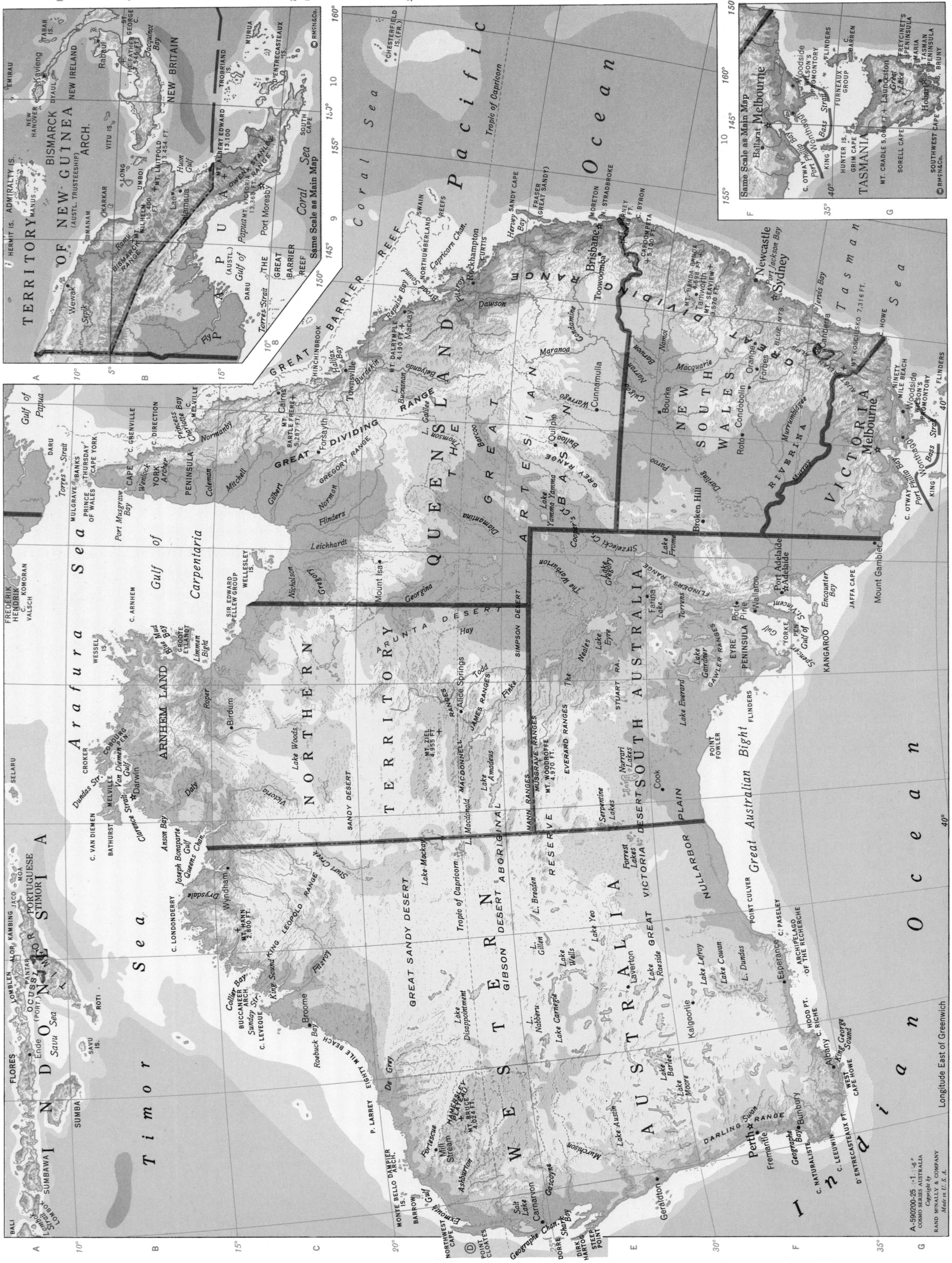

Statute Miles 100 0 100 200 300

Kilometers 100 0 100 200 300 400

Lambert Azimuthal Equal Area Projection

SCALE 1:16,000,000 1 Inch = 252 Statute Miles

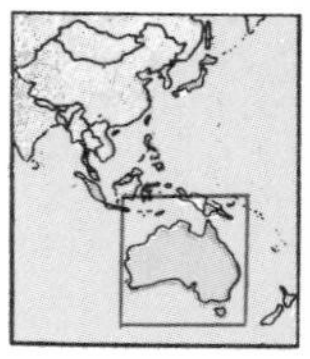

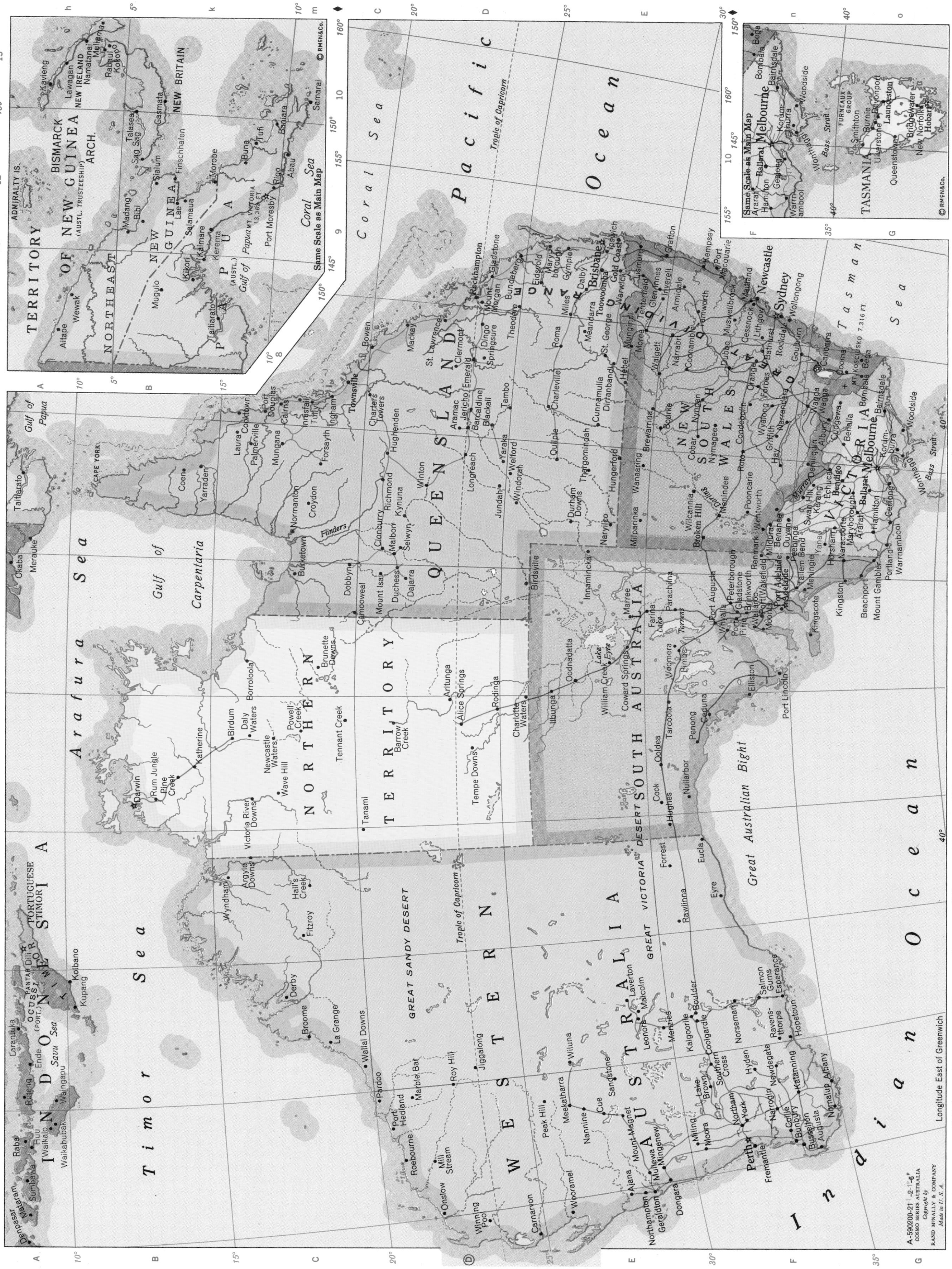

Lambert Azimuthal Equal Area Projection
SCALE 1:16,000,000 1 Inch = 252 Statute Miles

Statute Miles 100 0 100 200 300
Kilometers 100 0 100 200 300 400

A-590200-21 -2- 16
COSMO SERIES AUSTRALIA
Copyright by
RAND McNALLY & COMPANY
Made in U.S.A.

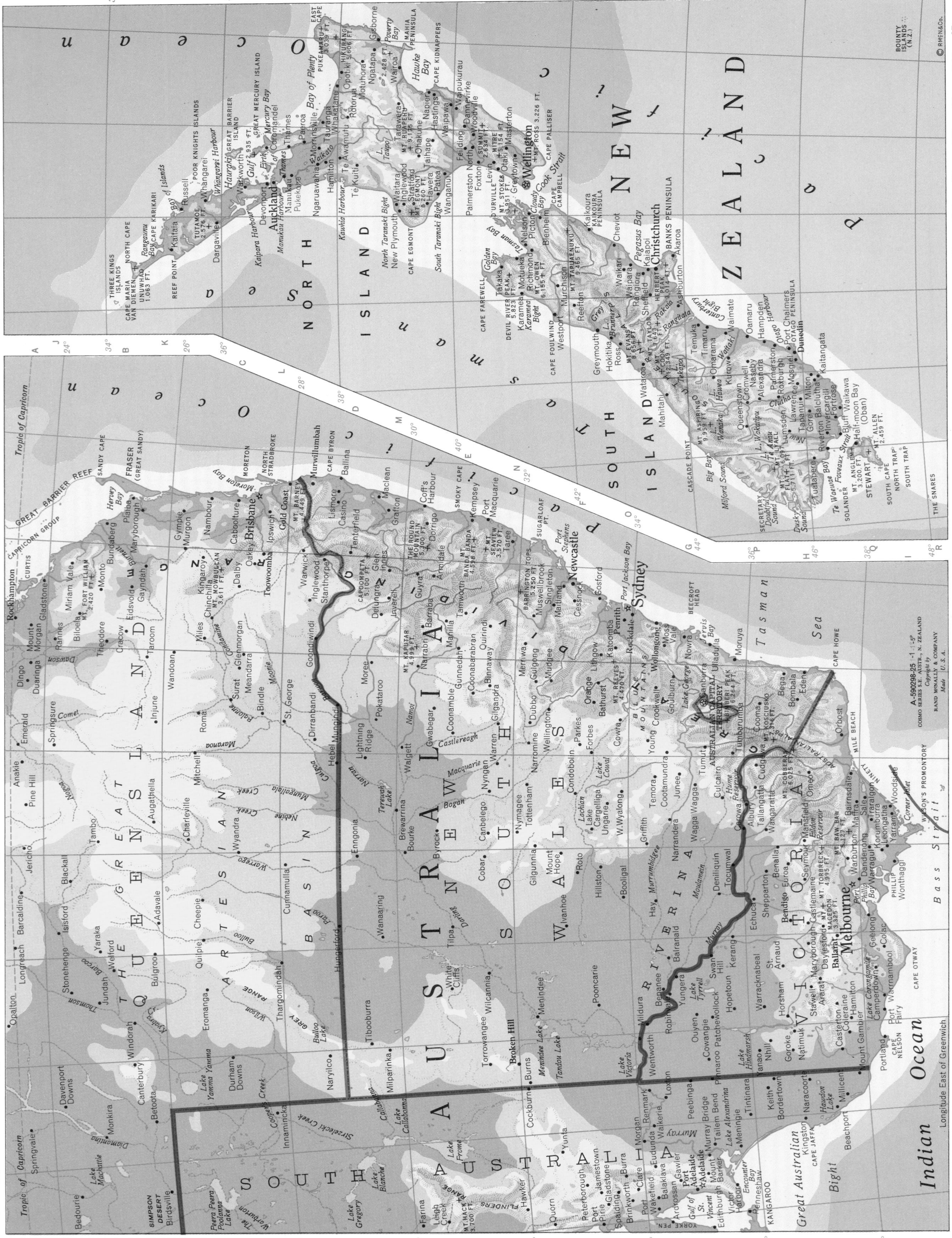

Statute Miles 50 0 50 100 150

Kilometers 50 0 50 100 200

Lambert Conformal Conic Projection

SCALE 1 : 8,000,000 1 Inch = 126 Statute Miles

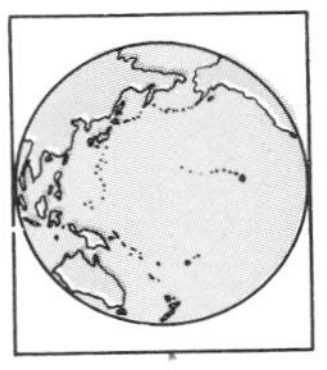

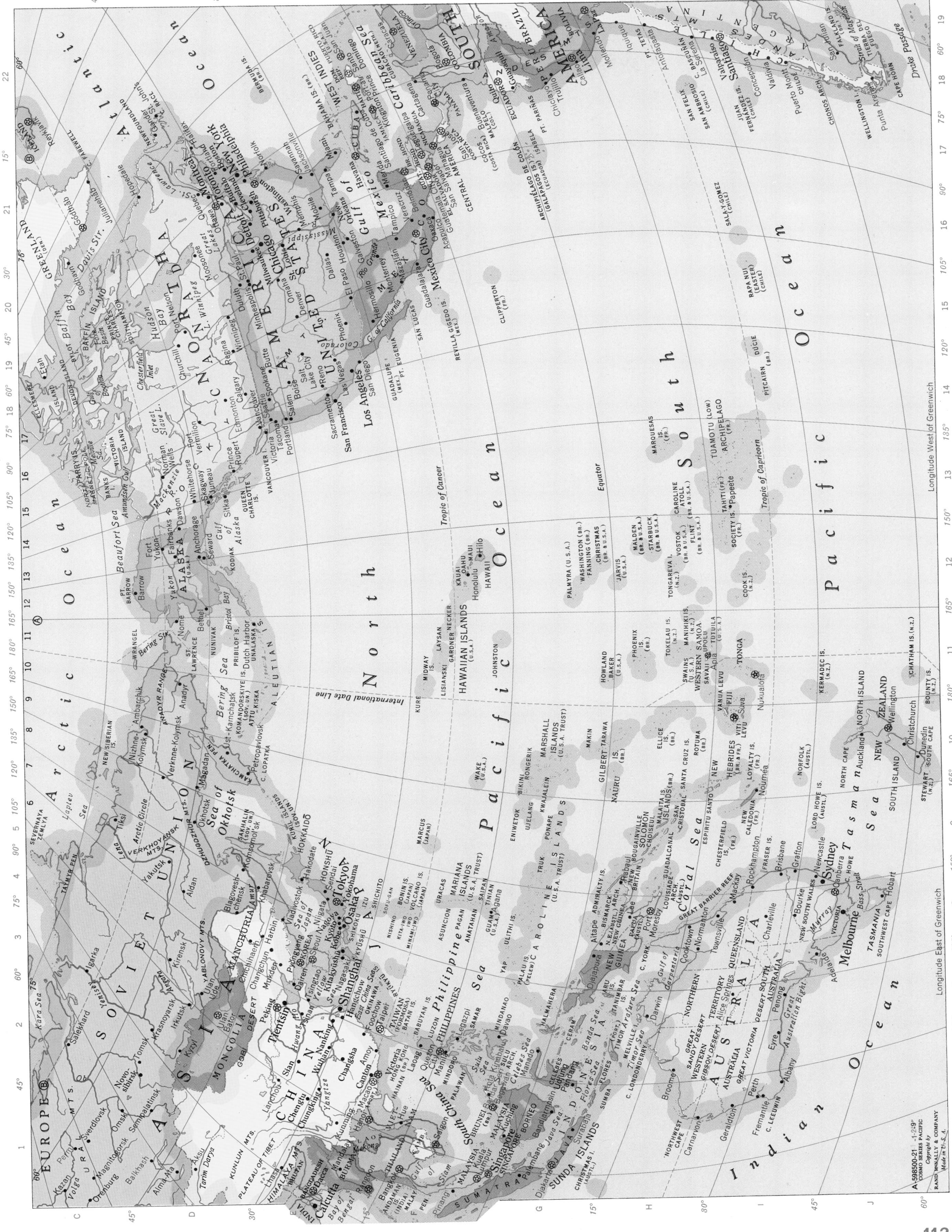

Modified Secant Conic Projection
SCALE 1:66,800,000 1 Inch = 1,040 Statute Miles

Statute Miles 200 0 200 600 1000 1400
Kilometers 200 0 200 600 1000 1400 1800 2200

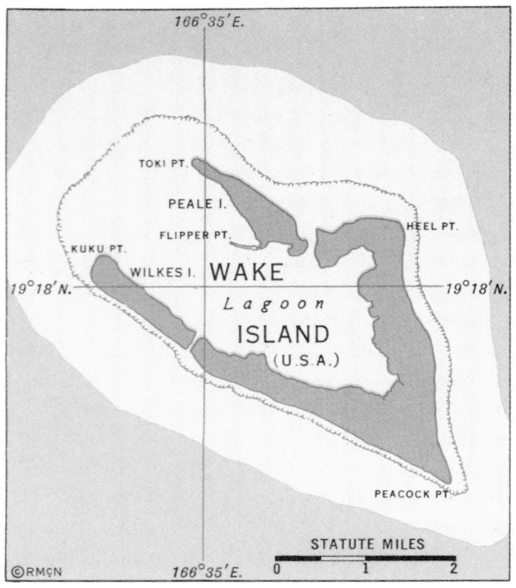
166°35′E.
TOKI PT.
PEALE I.
FLIPPER PT.
HEEL PT.
KUKU PT.
WILKES I.
WAKE
19°18′N.
Lagoon
ISLAND
(U.S.A.)
PEACOCK PT.
STATUTE MILES
0 1 2
©RMcN

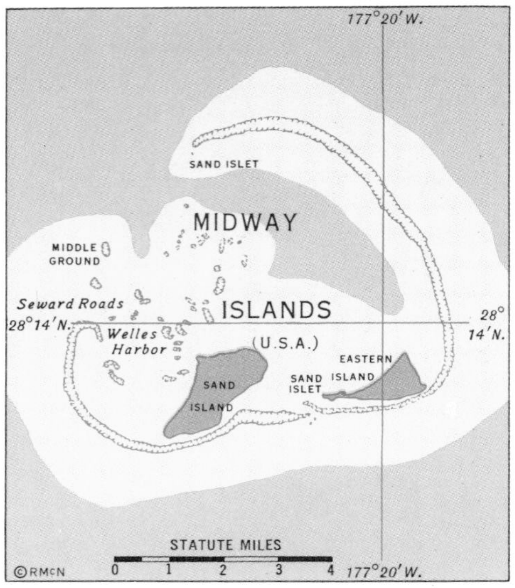
177°20′W.
SAND ISLET
MIDWAY
MIDDLE GROUND
Seward Roads
28°14′N.
Welles Harbor
ISLANDS
(U.S.A.)
SAND ISLAND
SAND ISLET
EASTERN ISLAND
STATUTE MILES
0 1 2 3 4
©RMcN

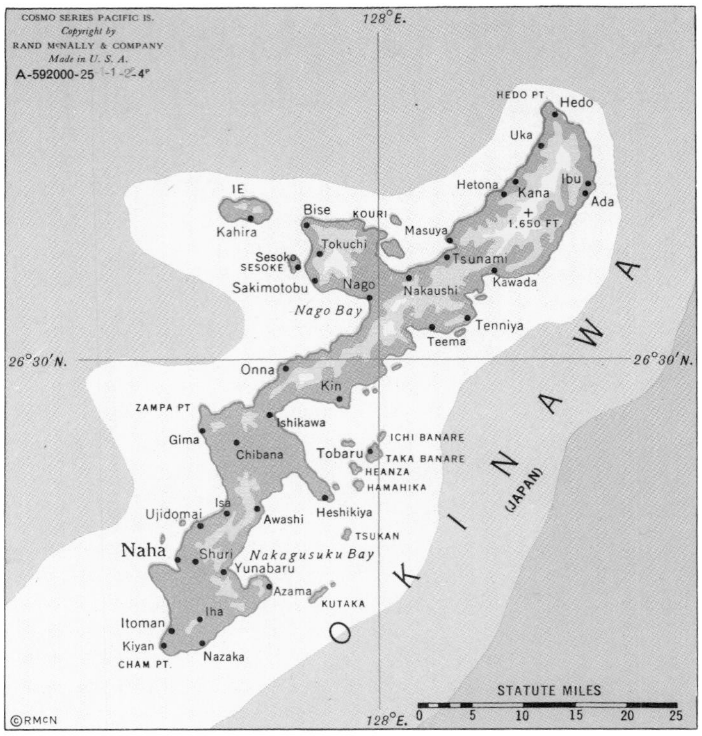
COSMO SERIES PACIFIC IS.
Copyright by
RAND McNALLY & COMPANY
Made in U. S. A.
A-592000-25
128°E.
HEDO PT.
Hedo
Uka
Hetona
Kana
Ibu
Ada
+ 1,650 FT.
IE
Kahira
Bise
KOURI
Masuya
Tokuchi
Sesoko
SESOKO
Tsunami
Sakimotobu
Nago
Nakaushi
Kawada
Nago Bay
Teema
Tenniya
26°30′N.
Onna
Kin
ZAMPA PT.
Ishikawa
Gima
Chibana
Tobaru
ICHI BANARE
TAKA BANARE
HEANZA
HAMAHIKA
Ujidomai
Isa
Awashi
Heshikiya
TSUKAN
Naha
Shuri
Nakagusuku Bay
Yunabaru
Azama
KUTAKA
Iha
Itoman
Kiyan
CHAM PT.
Nazaka
OKINAWA
(JAPAN)
STATUTE MILES
0 5 10 15 20 25
©RMcN

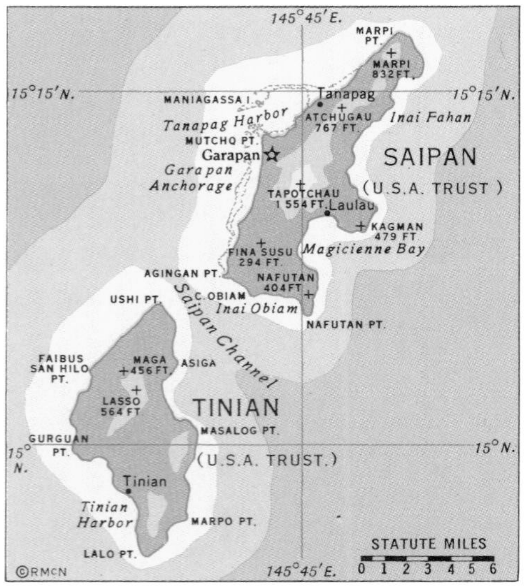
145°45′E.
MARPI PT.
MARPI 832 FT.
15°15′N.
MANIAGASSA I.
Tanapag
Tanapag Harbor
ATCHUGAU 767 FT.
Inai Fahan
MUTCHO PT.
Garapan
SAIPAN
Garapan Anchorage
(U.S.A. TRUST)
TAPOTCHAU 1 554 FT.
Laulau
KAGMAN 479 FT.
FINA SUSU 294 FT.
Magicienne Bay
AGINGAN PT.
NAFUTAN 404 FT.
USHI PT.
C. OBIAM
Inai Obiam
Saipan Channel
NAFUTAN PT.
FAIBUS SAN HILO PT.
MAGA 456 FT.
ASIGA
LASSO 564 FT.
TINIAN
MASALOG PT.
GURGUAN PT.
15°N.
(U.S.A. TRUST.)
Tinian
Tinian Harbor
MARPO PT.
LALO PT.
STATUTE MILES
0 1 2 3 4 5 6
©RMcN

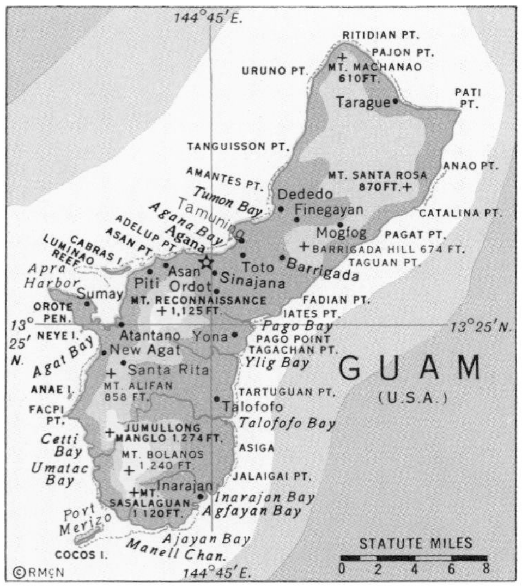
144°45′E.
RITIDIAN PT.
PAJON PT.
MT. MACHANAO 610 FT.
URUNO PT.
PATI PT.
Tarague
TANGUISSON PT.
AMANTES PT.
MT. SANTA ROSA 870 FT.
ANAO PT.
Tumon Bay
Dededo
Tamuning
Finegayan
CATALINA PT.
Agana Bay
Mogfog
PAGAT PT.
CABRAS I.
LUMINAO REEF
ADELUP PT.
ASAN PT.
Agana
BARRIGADA HILL 674 FT.
TAGUAN PT.
Asan
Toto
Barrigada
Apra Harbor
Piti
Ordot
Sinajana
Sumay
MT. RECONNAISSANCE 1,125 FT.
FADIAN PT.
OROTE PEN.
IATES PT.
Pago Bay
PAGO POINT
NEYE I.
Atantano
Yona
TAGACHAN PT.
13°25′N.
New Agat
Ylig Bay
Agat Bay
Santa Rita
GUAM
ANAE I.
MT. ALIFAN 858 FT.
TARTUGUAN PT.
(U.S.A.)
FACPI PT.
Talofofo
Talofofo Bay
JUMULLONG MANGLO 1,274 FT.
Cetti Bay
ASIGA
MT. BOLANOS 1,240 FT.
Umatac Bay
JALAIGAI PT.
Inarajan
Port Merizo
SASALAGUAN 1,120 FT.
Inarajan Bay
Agfayan Bay
COCOS I.
Ajayan Bay
Manell Chan.
STATUTE MILES
0 2 4 6 8
©RMcN

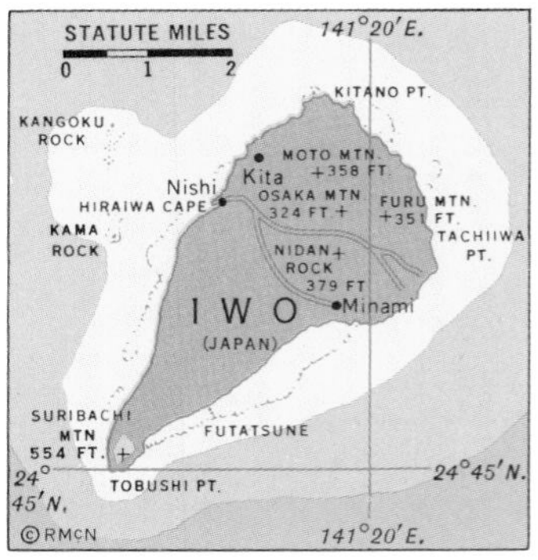
STATUTE MILES
0 1 2
141°20′E.
KITANO PT.
KANGOKU ROCK
MOTO MTN 358 FT.
Nishi
Kita
OSAKA MTN 324 FT.
FURU MTN. 351 FT.
HIRAIWA CAPE
TACHIIWA PT.
KAMA ROCK
NIDAN ROCK 379 FT.
IWO
(JAPAN)
Minami
SURIBACHI MTN 554 FT.
FUTATSUNE
24°45′N.
TOBUSHI PT.
©RMcN

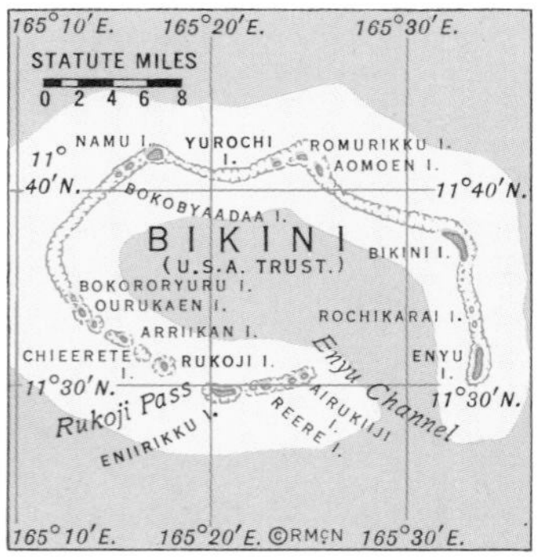
165°10′E.
165°20′E.
165°30′E.
STATUTE MILES
0 2 4 6 8
NAMU I.
YUROCHI
ROMURIKKU I.
AOMOEN I.
11°40′N.
BOKOBYAADAA I.
BIKINI
(U.S.A. TRUST.)
BIKINI I.
BOKORORYURU I.
OURUKAEN I.
ARRIIKAN I.
ROCHIKARAI I.
CHIEERETE I.
RUKOJI I.
ENYU I.
11°30′N.
Rukoji Pass
Enyu Channel
AIRUKIIJI
REERE I.
ENIIRIKKU I.
©RMcN

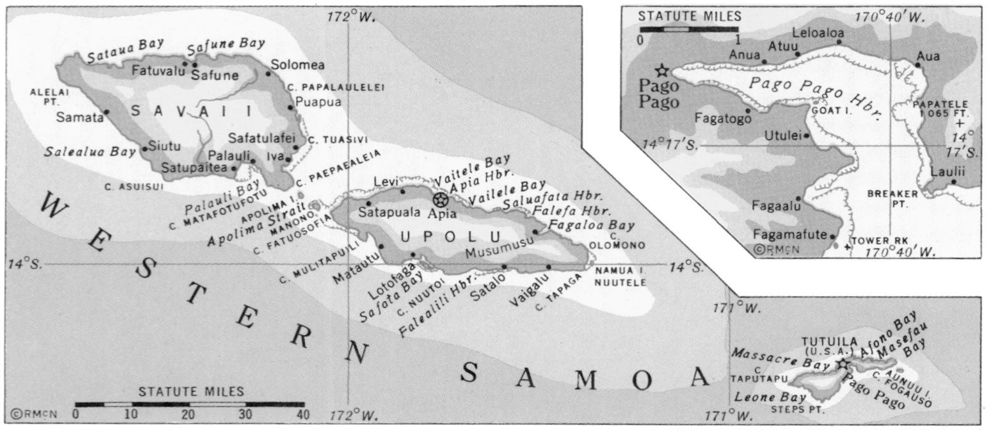
172°W.
Sataua Bay
Safune Bay
Solomea
Fatuvalu
Safune
C. PAPALAULELEI
ALELAI PT.
Samata
SAVAII
Puapua
Safatulafei
C. TUASIVI
Salealua Bay
Siutu
Palauli
Iva
Satupaitea
C. PAEPAEALEIA
C. ASUISUI
Palauli Bay
Levi
Vaitele Bay
Apia Hbr.
C. MATAFOTUFOTU
APOLIMA I.
MANONO I.
Apolima Strait
Apia
Vailele Bay
Saluafata Hbr.
Falefa Hbr.
C. FATUOSOFIA
Satapuala
Fagaloa Bay
UPOLU
Musumusu
OLOMONO
14°S.
C. MULITAPUILI
Matautu
NAMUA I.
NUUTELE
Lotofaga
Safata Bay
C. NUUTOI
Falealili Hbr.
Satalo
Vaigalu
C. TAPAGA
WESTERN SAMOA
STATUTE MILES
0 10 20 30 40
STATUTE MILES
170°40′W.
Leloaloa
Anua
Atuu
Aua
Pago Pago
Pago Pago Hbr.
Fagatogo
GOAT I.
PAPATELE 1,065 FT.
Utulei
14°17′S.
Laulii
BREAKER PT.
Fagaalu
Fagamafute
TOWER RK.
171°W.
TUTUILA (U.S.A.)
Afono Bay
Masefau Bay
Massacre Bay
C. TAPUTAPU
Pago Pago
C. FOGAUSO
LUNUU I.
Leone Bay
STEPS PT.
©RMcN

158°10′E.
STATUTE MILES
0 2 4 6 8
NANKAPENPARAM REEF
Jokaj Harbor
Mant Hbr.
Palikir Pass
PARAM I.
7°N.
JOKAJ
MANT IS.
CAPE U
Ponape
Tapak
TAPAK I.
ARU PT.
PONAPE
PALIKER PT.
(U.S.A. TRUST.)
Tamora
MAJIJO PK. 1,129 FT.
Meilap
Palang
TOLOCOLME PK. 2,576 FT.
6°50′N.
KITI PT.
Tamoroi
Ronkiti
Pok
Lot
Lot Hbr.
Ronkiti Hbr.
ROJ I.
Mutok Hbr.
©RMcN

©RMcN
151°45′E.
RUAC I.
LAMOIL I.
FALALU I.
PIS I.
LAP I.
HOLAP I.
NORTH EAST IS.
QUOI I.
FALAS I.
MOR I.
LELOM REEF
YAWATA I.
TRUK
FALO I.
ULALU I.
(U.S.A. TRUST)
MOEN I.
TOL I.
UDOT I.
PARAM
KUTUA PT.
Piaanu Pass
DUBLON I.
FALA BEGUETS
TARIK
ETEN I.
FEFAN I.
UMAN I.
BERNARD IS.
TSIS I.
7°20′N.
OLLAN I.
Ulifauro Pass
FOURUP I.
UIJEC I.
OTTA I.
MESEGON I.
GIVRY I.
HACO I.
KUOP IS. (ROYALISTS IS.)
SOUTH I.
STATUTE MILES
0 5 10 15

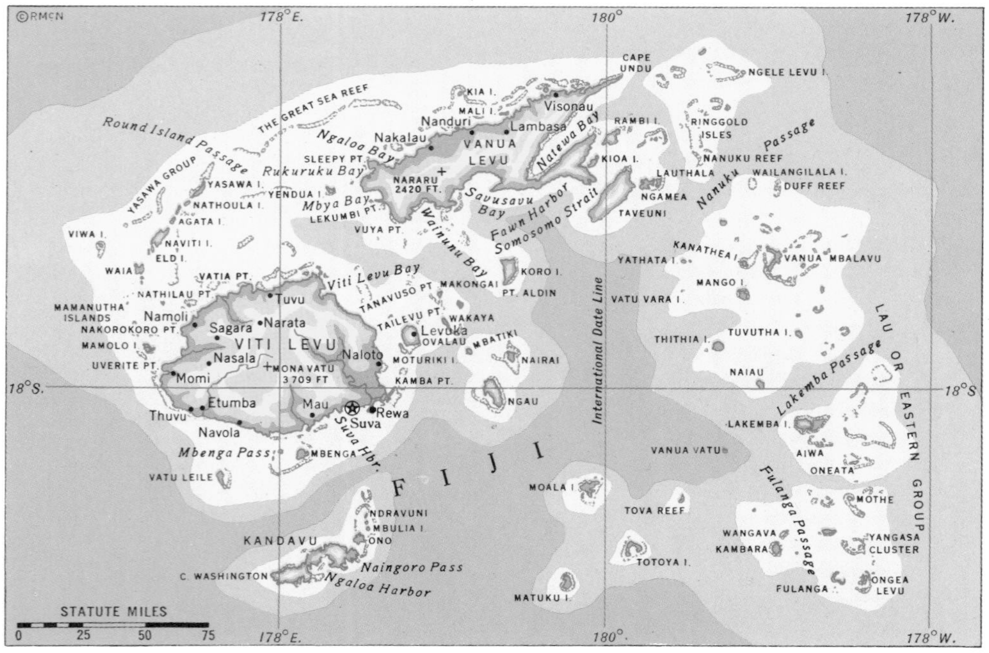
©RMcN
178°E.
180°
178°W.
CAPE UNDU
NGELE LEVU I.
THE GREAT SEA REEF
KIA I.
Visonau
MALI I.
Round Island Passage
Ngaloa Bay
Nakalau
Nanduri
Lambasa
RAMBI I.
RINGGOLD ISLES
VANUA LEVU
Natewa Bay
Nanuku Passage
YASAWA GROUP
SLEEPY PT.
Rukuruku Bay
NARARU 2420 FT.
KIOA I.
NANUKU REEF
YASAWA I.
LAUTHALA I.
WAILANGILALA I.
YENDUA I.
Savusavu Bay
DUFF REEF
NATHOULA I.
Mbyo Bay
NGAMEA
AGATA I.
LEKUMBI PT.
Fawn Harbor
Somosomo Strait
TAVEUNI
VIWA I.
VUYA PT.
NAVITI I.
Wainunu Bay
KANATHEA I.
WAIA I.
ELD I.
YATHATA I.
VANUA MBALAVU
VATIA PT.
Viti Levu Bay
KORO I.
NATHILAU PT.
Tuvu
TANAVUSO PT.
MAKONGAI
PT. ALDIN
VATU VARA I.
MANGO I.
MAMANUTHA ISLANDS
Namoli
TAILEVU PT.
WAKAYA
NAKOROKORO PT.
Sagara
Narata
Levuka
OVALAU
MBATIKI
THITHIA I.
TUVUTHA I.
MAMOLO I.
VITI LEVU
International Date Line
LAU OR EASTERN GROUP
UVERITE PT.
Nasala
MONA VATU 3709 FT.
Naloto
MOTURIKI I.
NAIRAI
NAIAU
Momi
KAMBA PT.
Lakemba Passage
18°S.
Etumba
Mau
Rewa
NGAU
Thuvu
Navola
Suva
LAKEMBA I.
Suva Hbr.
Mbenga Pass
MBENGA
VANUA VATU
AIWA
VATU LEILE
ONEATA
FIJI
MOALA I.
MOTHE
Fulanga Passage
KANDAVU
INDRAVUNI
MBULIA I.
TOVA REEF
ONO
WANGAVA
KAMBARA
YANGASA CLUSTER
C. WASHINGTON
Naingoro Pass
TOTOYA I.
Ngaloa Harbor
ONGEA LEVU
MATUKU I.
FULANGA
STATUTE MILES
0 25 50 75

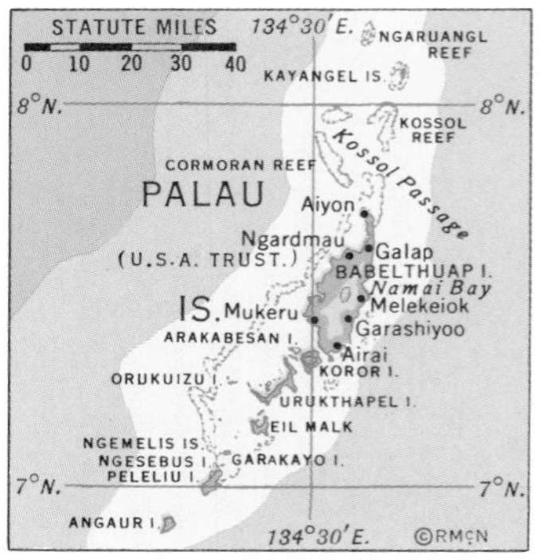
STATUTE MILES
0 10 20 30 40
134°30′E.
NGARUANGL REEF
KAYANGEL IS.
8°N.
KOSSOL REEF
Kossol Passage
CORMORAN REEF
PALAU
Aiyon
Ngardmau
Galap
(U.S.A. TRUST.)
BABELTHUAP I.
Namai Bay
IS.
Mukeru
Melekeiok
ARAKABESAN I.
Garashiyoo
Airai
ORUKUIZU I.
KOROR I.
URUKTHAPEL I.
EIL MALK
NGEMELIS IS.
NGESEBUS I.
PELELIU I.
GARAKAYO I.
7°N.
ANGAUR I.
©RMcN

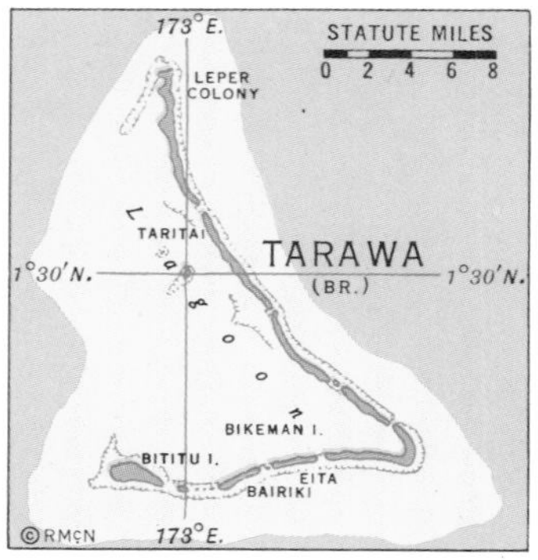
173°E.
STATUTE MILES
0 2 4 6 8
LEPER COLONY
TARITAI
TARAWA
(BR.)
1°30′N.
Lagoon
BIKEMAN I.
BITITU I.
EITA
BAIRIKI
©RMcN

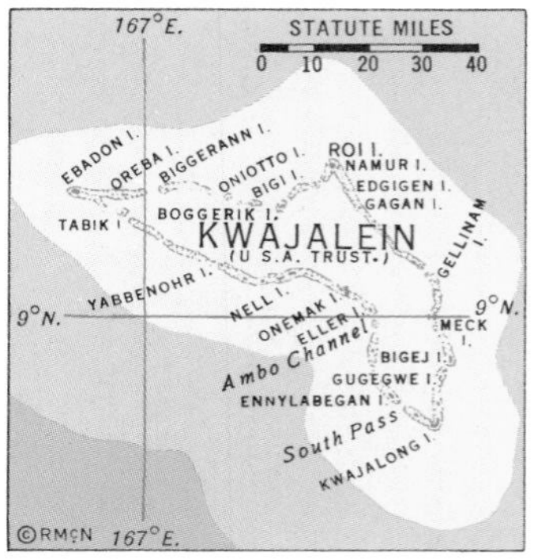
167°E.
STATUTE MILES
0 10 20 30 40
EBADON I.
OREBA I.
BIGGERANN I.
ONIOTTO I.
ROI I.
NAMUR I.
BIGI I.
EDGIGEN I.
BOGGERIK I.
GAGAN I.
TABIK I.
KWAJALEIN
(U.S.A. TRUST.)
GELLINAM I.
YABBENOHR I.
NELL I.
9°N.
ONEMAK I.
ELLEP I.
MECK I.
Ambo Channel
BIGEJ I.
GUGEGWE I.
ENNYLABEGAN I.
South Pass
KWAJALONG I.
©RMcN

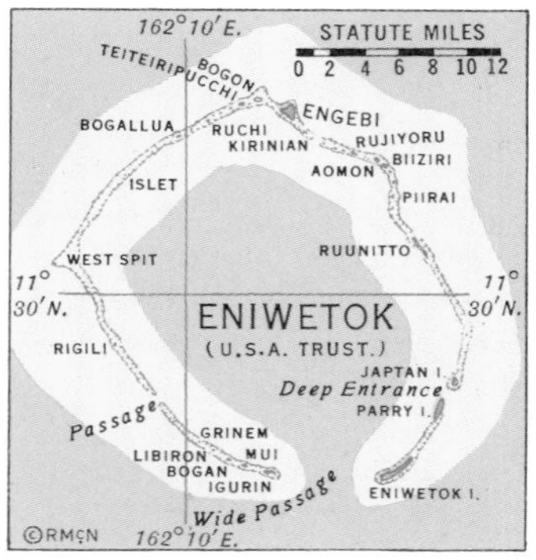
162°10′E.
STATUTE MILES
0 2 4 6 8 10 12
TEITEIRIPUCCHI I.
BOGON I.
ENGEBI
BOGALLUA
RUCHI
RUJIYORU
KIRINIAN
AOMON
BIIZIRI
ISLET
PIIRAI
WEST SPIT
RUUNITTO
11°30′N.
ENIWETOK
(U.S.A. TRUST.)
RIGILI
JAPTAN I.
Deep Entrance
PARRY I.
Passage
GRINEM
LIBIRON
MUI
BOGAN
IGURIN
Wide Passage
ENIWETOK I.
©RMcN

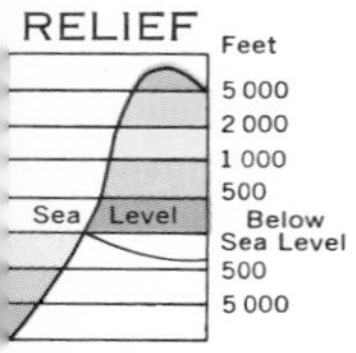
RELIEF
Feet
5 000
2 000
1 000
500
Sea Level
Below Sea Level
500
5 000

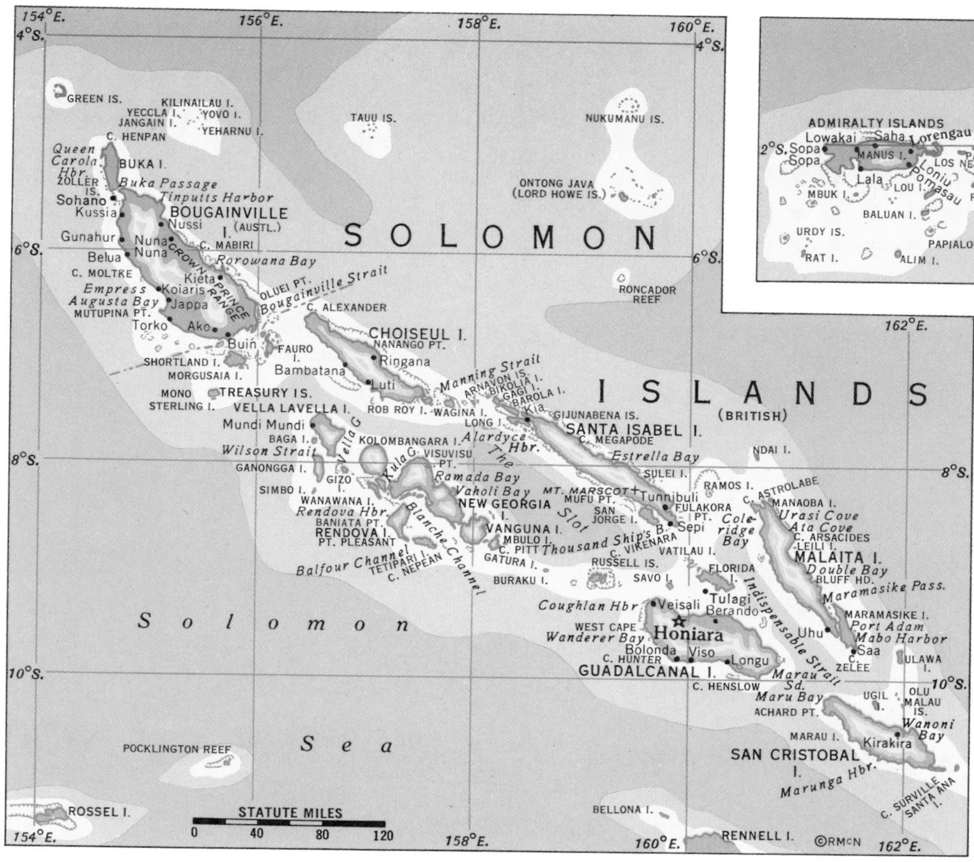
SOLOMON ISLANDS
(BRITISH)
BOUGAINVILLE
(AUSTL.)
BUKA I.
CHOISEUL I.
SANTA ISABEL I.
NEW GEORGIA
MALAITA I.
GUADALCANAL I.
SAN CRISTOBAL I.
Honiara
Solomon Sea
ONTONG JAVA (LORD HOWE IS.)
NUKUMANU IS.
TAUU IS.
GREEN IS.
SHORTLAND I.
TREASURY IS.
VELLA LAVELLA I.
KOLOMBANGARA I.
RENDOVA I.
VANGUNA I.
RUSSELL IS.
FLORIDA
Tulagi
RENNELL I.
BELLONA I.
ROSSEL I.
POCKLINGTON REEF
RONCADOR REEF
SIKAIANA
ULAWA I.
Bougainville Strait
Manning Strait
Indispensable Strait
Kieta
Buin
Kirakira
STATUTE MILES
0 40 80 120
154°E. 156°E. 158°E. 160°E. 162°E.
4°S. 6°S. 8°S. 10°S.
©RMcN

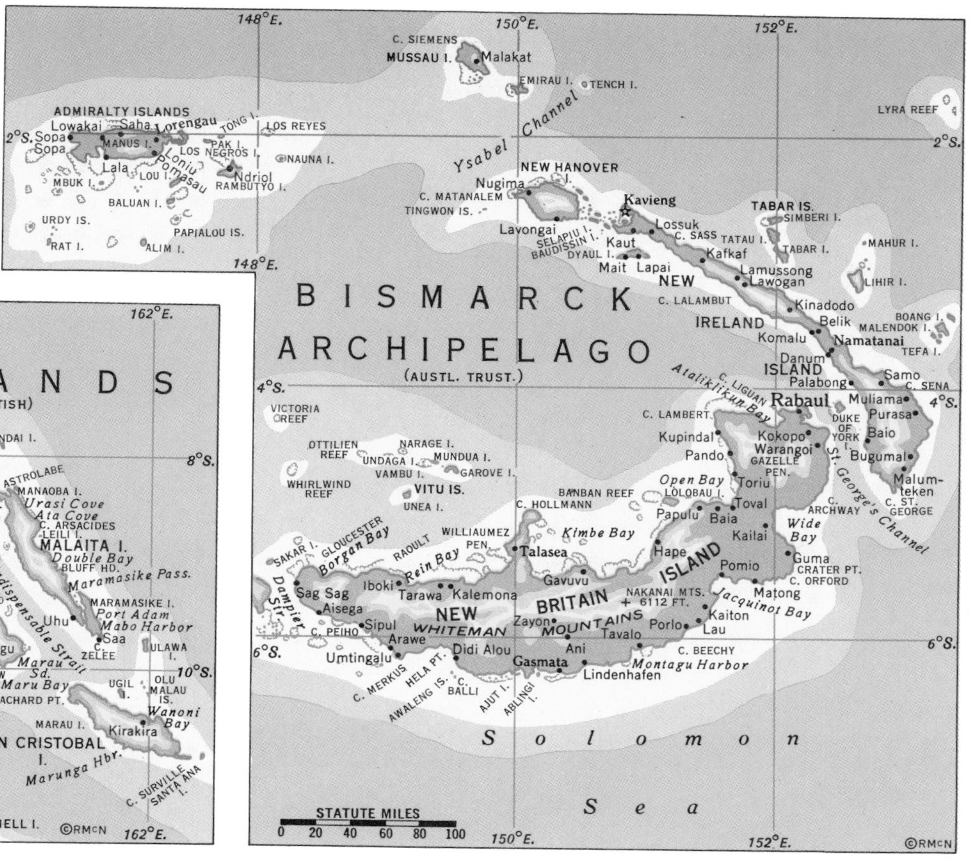
BISMARCK ARCHIPELAGO
(AUSTL. TRUST.)
ADMIRALTY ISLANDS
MANUS I.
Lorengau
MUSSAU I.
EMIRAU I.
NEW HANOVER
NEW IRELAND
Kavieng
Namatanai
TABAR IS.
LIHIR I.
TANGA IS.
FENI IS.
NEW BRITAIN ISLAND
Rabaul
Kokopo
GAZELLE PEN.
Open Bay
Wide Bay
Kimbe Bay
Talasea
Gasmata
UMBOI I.
VITU IS.
DUKE OF YORK
St. George's Channel
Ysabel Channel
Dampier Strait
WHITEMAN MOUNTAINS
NAKANAI MTS.
6112 FT.
Solomon Sea
STATUTE MILES
0 20 40 60 80 100
148°E. 150°E. 152°E.
2°S. 4°S. 6°S.
©RMcN

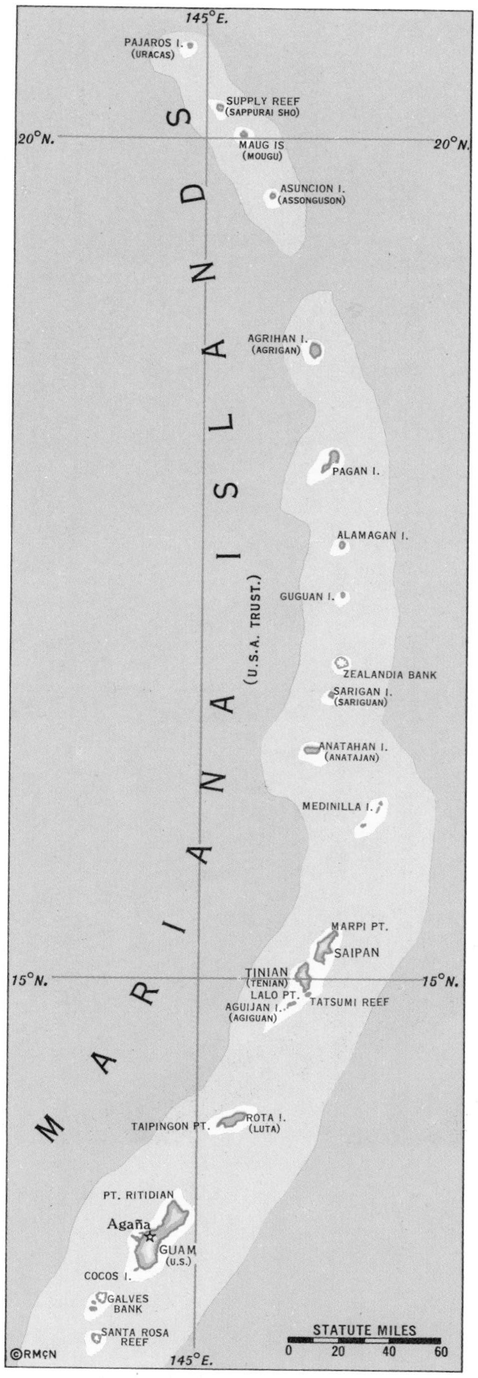
MARIANA ISLANDS
(U.S.A. TRUST.)
PAJAROS I. (URACAS)
SUPPLY REEF (SAPPURAI SHO)
MAUG IS (MOUGU)
ASUNCION I. (ASSONGUSON)
AGRIHAN I. (AGRIGAN)
PAGAN I.
ALAMAGAN I.
GUGUAN I.
ZEALANDIA BANK
SARIGAN I. (SARIGUAN)
ANATAHAN I. (ANATAJAN)
MEDINILLA I.
MARPI PT.
SAIPAN
TINIAN (TENIAN)
LALO PT.
AGUIJAN I. (AGIGUAN)
TATSUMI REEF
TAIPINGON PT.
ROTA I. (LUTA)
PT. RITIDIAN
Agaña
GUAM (U.S.)
COCOS I.
GALVES BANK
SANTA ROSA REEF
STATUTE MILES
0 20 40 60
145°E.
20°N. 15°N.
©RMcN

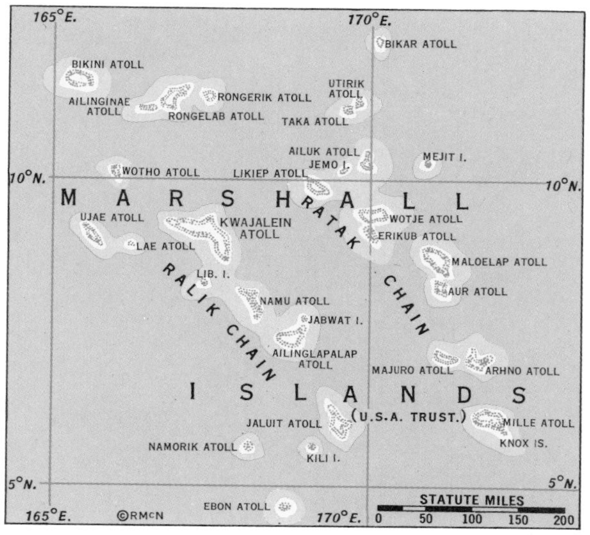
MARSHALL ISLANDS
(U.S.A. TRUST.)
RATAK CHAIN
RALIK CHAIN
BIKINI ATOLL
AILINGINAE ATOLL
RONGERIK ATOLL
RONGELAB ATOLL
UTIRIK ATOLL
TAKA ATOLL
BIKAR ATOLL
AILUK ATOLL
JEMO I.
MEJIT I.
WOTHO ATOLL
LIKIEP ATOLL
UJAE ATOLL
KWAJALEIN ATOLL
LAE ATOLL
WOTJE ATOLL
ERIKUB ATOLL
MALOELAP ATOLL
LIB. I.
AUR ATOLL
NAMU ATOLL
JABWAT I.
AILINGLAPALAP ATOLL
MAJURO ATOLL
ARHNO ATOLL
JALUIT ATOLL
MILLE ATOLL
KNOX IS.
NAMORIK ATOLL
KILI I.
EBON ATOLL
STATUTE MILES
0 50 100 150 200
165°E. 170°E.
10°N. 5°N.
©RMcN

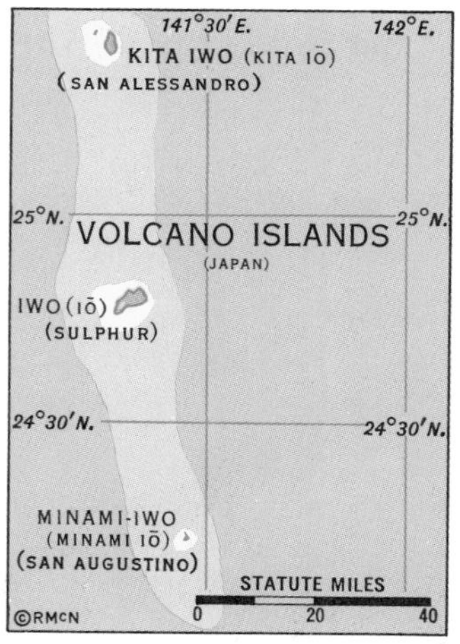
VOLCANO ISLANDS
(JAPAN)
KITA IWO (KITA IŌ)
(SAN ALESSANDRO)
IWO (IŌ)
(SULPHUR)
MINAMI-IWO
(MINAMI IŌ)
(SAN AUGUSTINO)
STATUTE MILES
0 20 40
141°30′E. 142°E.
25°N. 24°30′N.
©RMcN

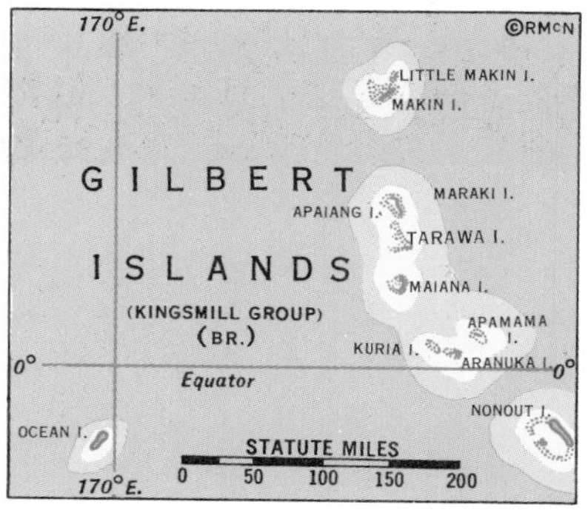
GILBERT ISLANDS
(KINGSMILL GROUP)
(BR.)
LITTLE MAKIN I.
MAKIN I.
MARAKI I.
APAIANG I.
TARAWA I.
MAIANA I.
APAMAMA I.
KURIA I.
ARANUKA I.
NONOUTI I.
OCEAN I.
Equator
STATUTE MILES
0 50 100 150 200
170°E.
0°
©RMcN

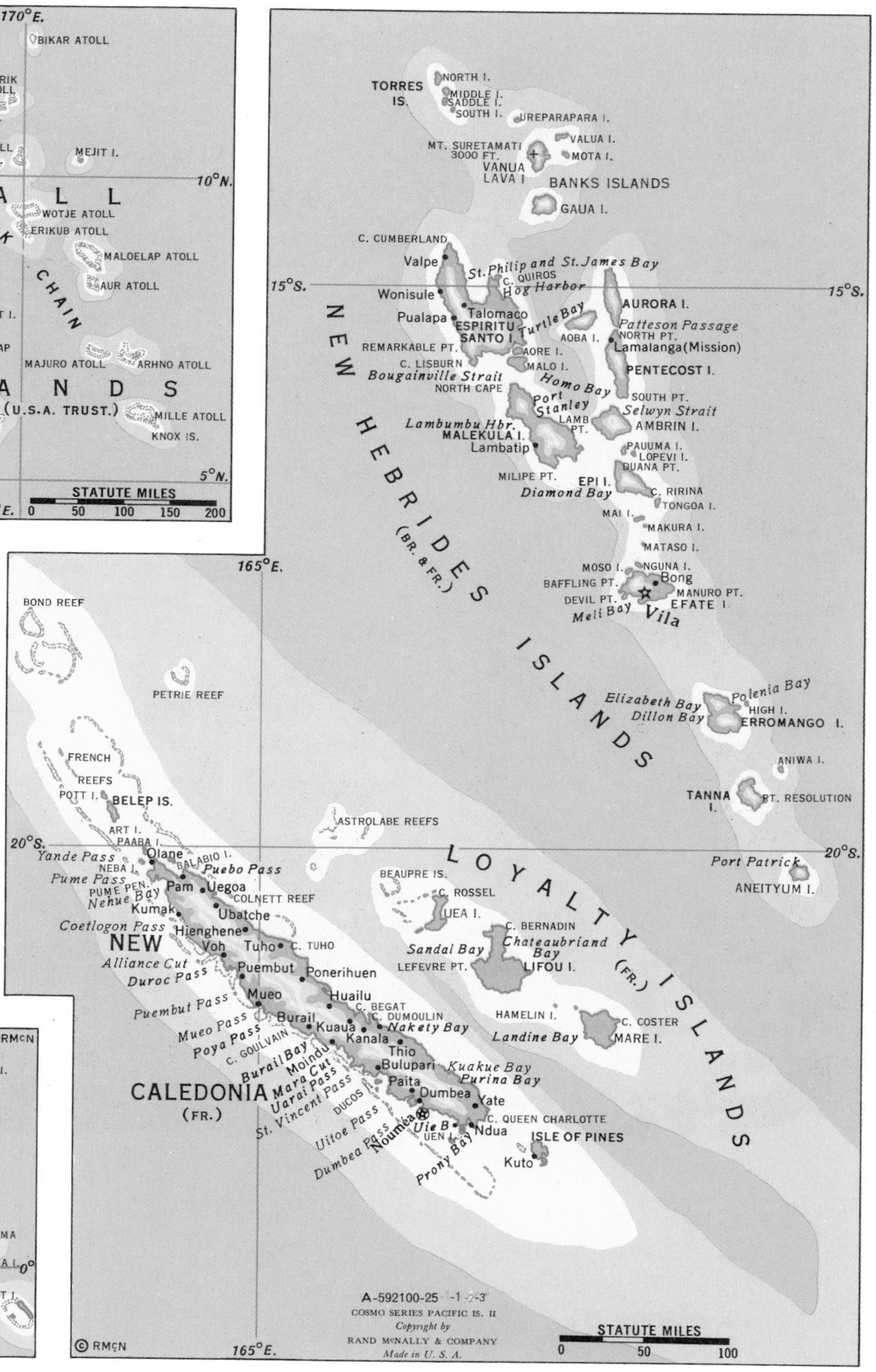
NEW HEBRIDES ISLANDS
(BR. & FR.)
TORRES IS.
BANKS ISLANDS
VANUA LAVA I.
GAUA I.
ESPIRITU SANTO I.
AURORA I.
AOBA I.
PENTECOST I.
MALEKULA I.
AMBRIM I.
EPI I.
EFATE I.
Vila
ERROMANGO I.
TANNA I.
ANIWA I.
ANEITYUM I.
NEW CALEDONIA
(FR.)
LOYALTY ISLANDS
(FR.)
BELEP IS.
Nouméa
ISLE OF PINES
LIFOU I.
MARE I.
UEA I.
BEAUPRE IS.
ASTROLABE REEFS
FRENCH REEFS
PETRIE REEF
BOND REEF
STATUTE MILES
0 50 100
165°E.
15°S. 20°S.
©RMcN
A-592100-25
COSMO SERIES PACIFIC IS. II
Copyright by
RAND McNALLY & COMPANY
Made in U. S. A.

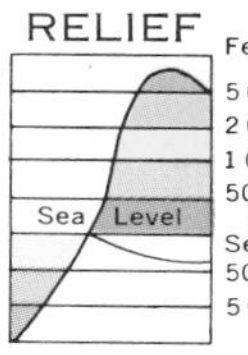
RELIEF
Feet
5 000
2 000
1 000
500
Sea Level
Below Sea Level
500
5 000

Aerial photograph of Victoria Valley, McMurdo Sound, Antarctica.—W. B. Hamilton, U.S. Geological Survey

POLAR REGIONS

Vast regions of continuous cold cap the earth at both the North and South Poles. In the north, the ice-filled waters of the Arctic Ocean cover the North Pole. Surrounding the Arctic Ocean are the northern parts of Europe, Asia, and North America. At the South Pole, the continent of Antarctica is a land covered by a permanent cap of ice and snow. Surrounding Antarctica is a body of water that some scientists call the Antarctic Ocean, and others classify as part of the Atlantic, Pacific, and Indian oceans. The Polar Regions have challenged explorers and scientists for many years. Many have lost their lives in desperate dashes across the ice to the Poles, and others continue to explore these regions in an effort to solve scientific mysteries about the earth and its atmosphere.

WHAT IS YOUR ATLAS I.Q. OF THE POLAR REGIONS?

These questions are designed to test your knowledge of the variety of information about the Polar Regions contained in THE WORLD BOOK ATLAS. Check your answers by turning to the last page of the ATLAS.

Facts and figures

1. Which of these countries does not lie at least partially within the Arctic Circle—the United States, Iceland, Canada, Finland, Sweden, Russia, or Norway?
2. Which of these places lies closest to the North Pole—Barrow, Alaska; Murmansk, Russia; or Thule, Greenland?
3. Antarctica is the continent at the South Pole. What continent is closest to Antarctica?
4. Is Antarctica larger or smaller than the continent of Europe?
5. If you flew in a straight line from Anchorage, Alaska, over the North Pole, which continent would you reach first—Asia or Europe?

Polar exploration

6. An American naval officer led the first expedition to reach the North Pole. What was his name?
7. In what year did he reach the Pole—1932, 1909, or 1921?
8. A Norwegian explorer led the first expedition to reach the South Pole. What was his name?
9. In what year did he reach the Pole—1926, 1943, or 1911?
10. In 1958, a U.S. submarine became the first ship to sail under the North Pole. What was its name?

MAPS OF POLAR REGIONS

118 PHYSICAL FEATURES OF THE ARCTIC
119 ARCTIC EXPLORATIONS
120 PHYSICAL FEATURES OF THE ANTARCTIC
121 ANTARCTIC EXPLORATIONS

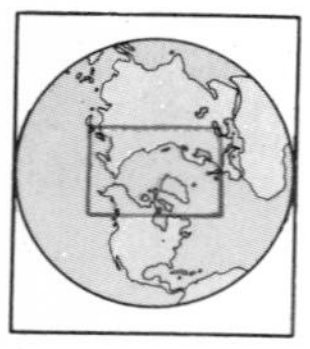

RELIEF
Feet
5 000
2 000
1 000
500
Sea Level
Below Sea Level
500
5 000
20 000

Statute Miles 100 0 100 200 300 400 500

Kilometers 100 0 100 300 500 700

Lambert Azimuthal Equal Area Projection
SCALE 1:28,000,000 1 Inch = 442 Statute Miles

Lambert Azimuthal Equal Area Projection
SCALE 1:28,000,000 1 Inch = 442 Statute Miles

Statute Miles 100 0 100 200 300 400 500
Kilometers 100 0 100 300 500 700

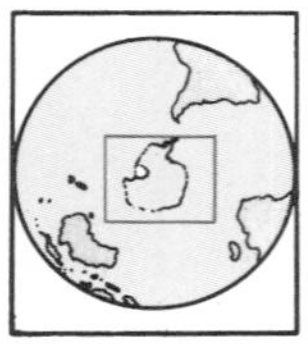

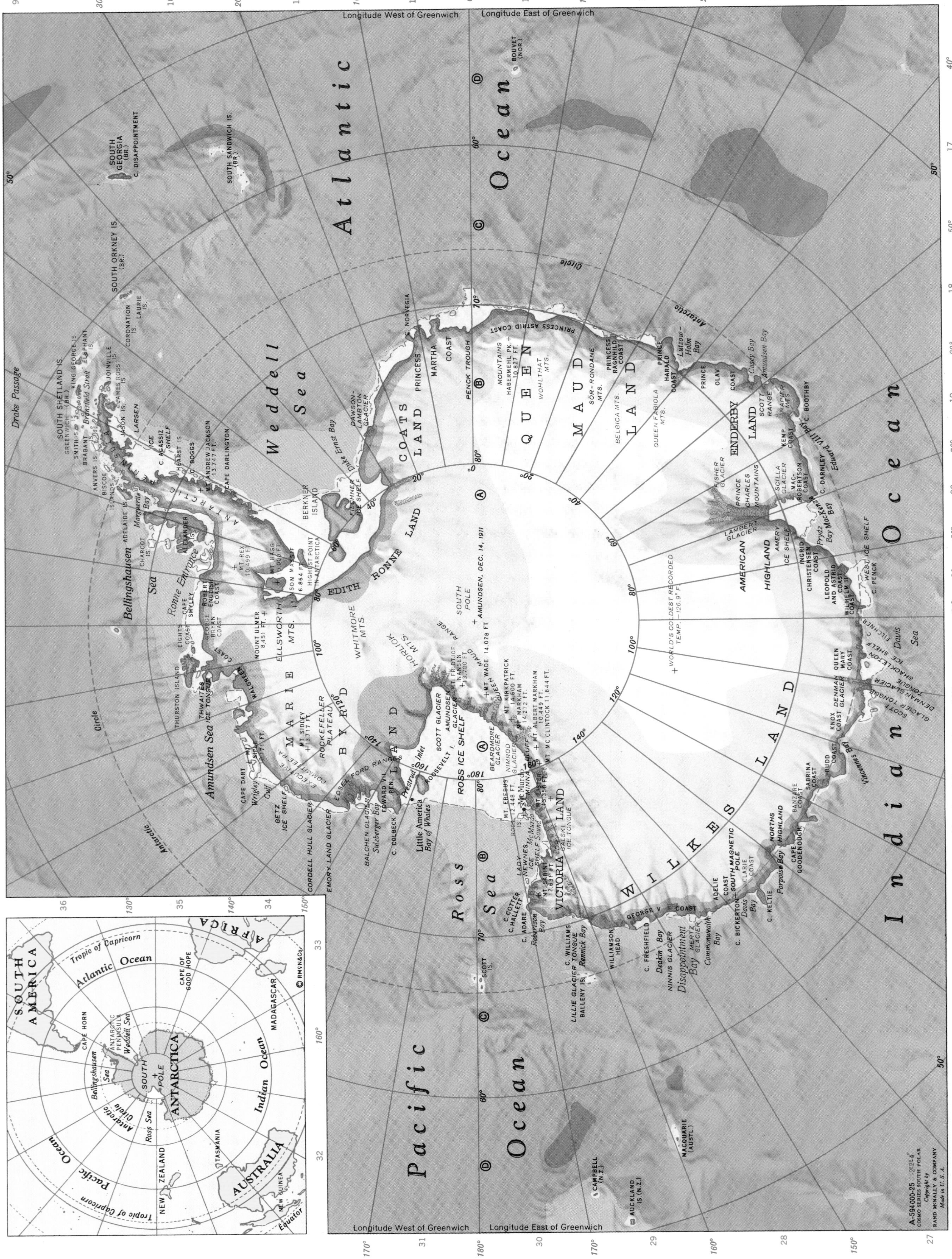

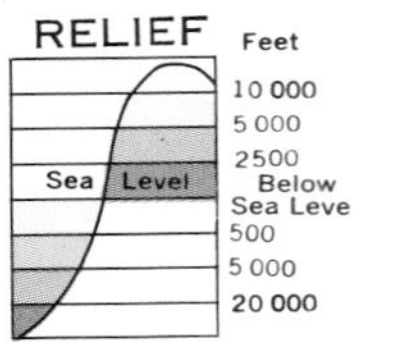

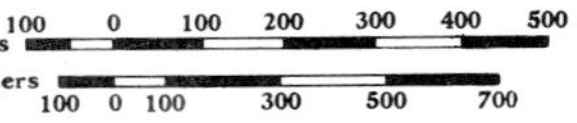

Lambert Azimuthal Equal Area Projection
SCALE 1:28,000,000 1 Inch = 442 Statute Miles

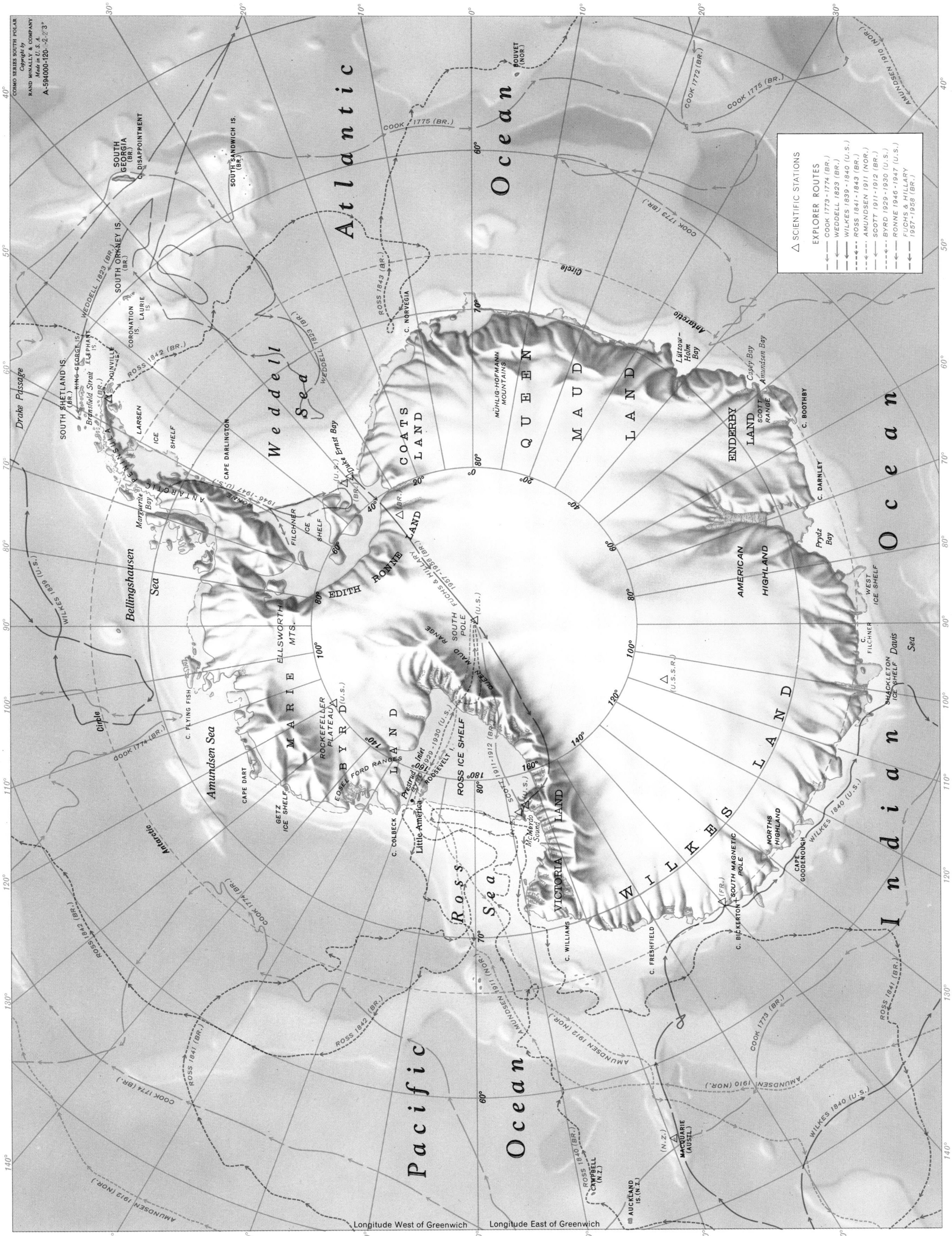

Lambert Azimuthal Equal Area Projection
SCALE 1:28,000,000 1 Inch = 442 Statute Miles

Statute Miles 100 0 100 200 300 400 500
Kilometers 100 0 100 300 500 700

NYSTROM map by Richard Edes Harrison

LATIN AMERICA

Latin America includes the countries of the Western Hemisphere that extend from Mexico to the southern tip of South America. Nearly 300 million persons live in Latin America, sharing a common heritage of language, religion, art, and customs. This cultural heritage was brought to the region by explorers and settlers from Spain, Portugal, and France. Latin America is a major world producer of coffee, meat, petroleum, and many other important agricultural and mineral products. The Latin Americans have built many large, modern cities that are prosperous centers of industry, but they face many difficult social and economic problems. Latin America has one of the fastest rates of population growth in the world, and it lacks the economic means to develop much of its 8 million square miles of area.

WHAT IS YOUR ATLAS I.Q. OF LATIN AMERICA?

These questions are designed to test your knowledge of the variety of information about Latin America contained in THE WORLD BOOK ATLAS. Check your answers by turning to the last page of the ATLAS.

Identifying places

1. The southernmost countries in Latin America are Chile and Argentina. What is the northernmost Latin American nation?
2. Two Latin American countries share the island of Hispaniola in the West Indies. One of these is Haiti. What is the other?
3. What is the capital of Brazil?
4. Six Latin American republics are located in Central America. Five of these are Guatemala, Nicaragua, Costa Rica, Honduras, and El Salvador. What is the sixth?
5. Brazil borders every country in South America but two. One of these is Ecuador. What is the other?
6. Two Latin American nations are completely surrounded by other nations. One of these is Paraguay. What is the other nation?
7. Four U.S. states border Mexico. Three of these are Texas, Arizona, and New Mexico. What is the fourth?
8. Which city is farthest east—(1) St. John's, Newfoundland; (2) New York City; or (3) Recife, Brazil?
9. The largest lake in Latin America is 12,507 feet above sea level on the Peru-Bolivia border. What is the name of this lake?

Facts and figures

10. Aconcagua rises 22,834 feet above sea level and is the highest peak in the Western Hemisphere. In what country is it located?
11. The largest country in Latin America in area is also the largest in population. What is the name of the country?
12. The Amazon River is the second longest river in the world. The river flows about 3,900 miles from its source in Peru to the Atlantic Ocean. Through which other country does most of the river flow?
13. Three Latin American countries lie on the Equator. Two of these are Ecuador and Brazil. What is the third?
14. About how many million persons live in Mexico?
15. If you were on a ship steaming through the Panama Canal from the Caribbean Sea to the Pacific Ocean, in what direction would you be traveling?

History

16. In 1790, two European countries controlled most of Latin America. One was Spain. What was the other country?
17. Spain lost its last two possessions in Latin America as a result of the Spanish-American War in 1898. One of these possessions was Cuba. What was the other?
18. Both Texas and California were once part of Mexico. Texas became part of the United States in 1845. In what year did Mexico cede California to the United States?
19. All of the countries of South America have become independent except two colonies. One of these is French Guiana. What is the other?
20. The treaty establishing the Alliance for Progress was signed at Punta del Este in 1961. In what country is Punta del Este?

MAPS OF LATIN AMERICA

124 **PHYSICAL FEATURES OF LATIN AMERICA**
125 **POLITICAL DIVISIONS OF LATIN AMERICA**
126-128 **HISTORY OF LATIN AMERICA**
126 LATIN AMERICA ABOUT 1790
127 AFTER INDEPENDENCE
128 LATIN AMERICA TODAY
129-139 **MAPS OF COUNTRIES AND DEPENDENCIES**
135, 136 ARGENTINA
131 BAHAMA ISLANDS
131 BARBADOS
135 BOLIVIA
137-139 BRAZIL
130 BRITISH HONDURAS
135, 136 CHILE
133 COLOMBIA
130 COSTA RICA
131 CUBA
131 DOMINICAN REPUBLIC
134 ECUADOR
130 EL SALVADOR
139 FRENCH GUIANA
130 GUATEMALA
139 GUYANA
131 HAITI
130 HONDURAS
131 JAMAICA
129 MEXICO
130 NICARAGUA
130 PANAMA
130 PANAMA CANAL ZONE
135 PARAGUAY
134 PERU
132 PUERTO RICO
139 SURINAM
133 TRINIDAD AND TOBAGO
137 URUGUAY
133 VENEZUELA
132 VIRGIN ISLANDS
131 WEST INDIES ASSOCIATED STATES
ANTIGUA
DOMINICA
GRENADA
ST. KITTS-NEVIS
ST. LUCIA
ST. VINCENT

Gulf of Mexico
Tropic of Cancer
U.S.A.
Miami
C. SABLE
Straits of Florida
BAHAMA IS.
Nassau
ANDROS IS.
WATLING OR SAN SALVADOR I. (COLUMBUS, OCT. 12, 1492)
Havana
CUBA
C. CATOCHE
Yucatán Channel
ISLE OF PINES
WEST INDIES
Windward Passage
MEXICO
GRAND CAYMAN I.
HAITI
DOM. REP.
San Juan
GREATER ANTILLES
Port-au-Prince
Santo Domingo
PUERTO RICO (U.S.A.)
VIRGIN IS.
BARBUDA (BR.)
ANTIGUA (BR.)
GUADELOUPE (FR.)
DOMINICA (BR.)
MARTINIQUE (FR.)
ST. LUCIA (BR.)
ST. VINCENT (BR.)
BARBADOS
GRENADA (BR.)
LEEWARD IS.
WINDWARD IS.
LESSER ANTILLES
JAMAICA
Kingston
Belmopan
BR. HOND.
Gulf of Honduras
GUAT.
Guatemala City
HONDURAS
Tegucigalpa
CABO GRACIAS A DIOS
San Salvador
EL SALVADOR
NICARAGUA
Managua
L. Nicaragua
CENTRAL AMERICA
San Juan del Sur
COSTA RICA
San José
Mosquito Gulf
CANAL ZONE (U.S.A.)
Panama City
PANAMA
Gulf of Panama
Gulf of Darien
PT. NARANJAS
Caribbean Sea
CURAÇAO (NETH.)
PT. GALLINAS
G. of Venezuela
Maracaibo
MARGARITA I.
Caracas
TRINIDAD AND TOBAGO
Port-of-Spain
Barranquilla
Cartagena
Atlantic Ocean
COCOS (COSTA RICA)
C. CORRIENTES
TOLIMA 17,110 FT.
Medellín
Bogotá
Meta
LLANOS
Orinoco
Ciudad Bolívar
VENEZUELA
Caroní
Cuyuní
Georgetown
GUIANA
GUYANA
Paramaribo
SURINAM (NETH. GUIANA)
FRENCH GUIANA
Cayenne
DEVILS ISLAND
C. ORANGE
St. Georges
Essequibo
SIERRA PACARAIMA
GUIANA HIGHLANDS
MALPELO (COL.)
PT. CHARAMBIRÁ
COLOMBIA
Cali
Guaviare
Branco
Oiapoque
MARACÁ I.
C. RASO
ARCHIPIÉLAGO DE COLÓN (GALÁPAGOS IS.) (ECUADOR)
ISABELA I.
Equator
C. SAN FRANCISCO
Quito
Caquetá
Uaupés
Negro
Japurá
Trombetas
Jari
C. MAGOARI
MARAJÓ I.
Pará
Belém
PT. TURÍ
São Luís
ECUADOR
CHIMBORAZO 20,561 FT.
Guayaquil
Gulf of Guayaquil
Putumayo
Napo
Içá
Manaus
Amazonas
(Amazon)
Santarém
Tocantins
PT. CURUMIQUARA
FERNANDO DE NORONHA I.
ROCAS (BRAZIL)
Fortaleza
Pastaza
Iquitos
Marañón
Javari
SELVAS
Purús
Tapajós
Xingú
Parnaíba
Teresina
C. SÃO ROQUE
Natal
PT. MATO
PT. AGUJA
PT. NEGRA
Chiclayo
Juruá
Madeira
Aripuanã
Araguaia
Trujillo
HUASCARÁN 22,205 FT.
Ucayali
Rio Branco
Acre
Pôrto Velho
BRAZIL
Recife
C. YERUPAJÁ 21,765 FT.
Lima
PERU
Madre de Dios
SERRA DOS PARECIS
Guaporé
BRAZILIAN PLATEAU OF MATO GROSSO
Araguaia
Braço Maior
Tocantins
São Francisco
SERRA DO ESPINHAÇO
Paraguaçu
Salvador
PT. MUTÁ
Cusco
Ica
ANDES MOUNTAINS
Mamoré
Lake Titicaca
Brasília
EL MISTI 19,098 FT.
Arequipa
Mollendo
La Paz
BOLIVIA
Paraguay
Taquarí
Paranaíba
PT. SANTO ANTÔNIO
Jequitinhonha
PT. BALEIA
Mucuri
Salar de Coipasa
L. Poopó
Sucre
CHACO
Grande
Belo Horizonte
PT. MONSARÁS
Vitória
Iquique
ATACAMA DESERT
Salar de Uyuni
HIGHLANDS
Tietê
C. DE SÃO TOMÉ
Pacific Ocean
Tropic of Capricorn
PT. ANGAMOS
PT. TETAS
Antofagasta
Pilcomayo
Paranapanema
Paraíba
C. FRIO
São Paulo
Niterói
Santos
Rio de Janeiro
VOLCÁN LLULLAILLACO 22,146 FT.
Salta
PARAGUAY
Asunción
Curitiba
Villarrica
Iguaçu
SAN FELIX
SAN AMBROSIO (CHILE)
Tucumán
GRAN CHACO
Bermejo
Paraná
PT. MORRO
Copiapó
OJOS DEL SALADO 22,590 FT.
Corrientes
Florianópolis
C. BASCUÑÁN
Santiago del Estero
Salinas Grandes
Salado
C. SANTA MARTA GRANDE
Coquimbo
Uruguay
Pôrto Alegre
L. Patos
Córdoba
Santa Fe
Salto
Pampa de Salinas
ACONCAGUA 22,834 FT.
Mendoza
Rio Grande
JUAN FERNÁNDEZ (CHILE)
MÁS AFUERA
MÁS ATIERRA
Valparaíso
Santiago
Rosario
URUGUAY
L. Mirim
PAMPAS
Buenos Aires
La Plata
Montevideo
Río de la Plata
C. SAN ANTONIO
PT. LAVAPIE
ARGENTINA
Neuquén
Mar del Plata
PT. MOGOTES
Colorado
Bahía Blanca
Valdivia
PT. GALERA
Negro
Limay
CHILE
Puerto Montt
PT. RASA
Gulf of San Matías
VALDÉS PEN.
CHILOÉ
Chubut
CHONOS
MAGDALENA I.
ARCHIPELAGO
C. RASO
C. DOS BAHÍAS
Chico
Comodoro Rivadavia
Gulf of St. George
TAITAO PEN.
MT. SAN VALENTÍN 13,314 FT.
C. TRES PUNTAS
PATAGONIA
PT. MEDANOSA
WELLINGTON I.
MT. FITZ ROY 11,600 FT.
C. DESENGAÑO
FALKLAND ISLANDS (GREAT BRITAIN)
Stanley
C. VÍRGENES
Strait of Magellan
Punta Arenas
TIERRA DEL FUEGO
SHAG ROCKS
SOUTH GEORGIA (BR.)
MONTE SARMIENTO 7,546 FT.
NAVARINO I.
CAPE HORN
Longitude West of Greenwich
A-540000-25 -1-1-12
COSMO SERIES SO. AMERICA
Copyright by RAND McNALLY & COMPANY
Made in U. S. A.
RELIEF
Feet
5 000
2 000
1 000
500
Sea Level
Below Sea Level
500
5 000
20 000

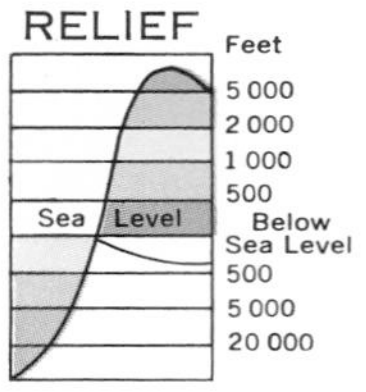

Statute Miles 100 0 100 300 500 700

Kilometers 100 0 100 300 500 700 900 1100

Sinusoidal Projection

SCALE 1: 29,465,000 1 Inch = 465 Statute Miles

Sinusoidal Projection
SCALE 1:29,465,000 1 Inch = 465 Statute Miles

Statute Miles 100 0 100 300 500 700
Kilometers 100 0 100 300 500 700 900 1100

LATIN AMERICA ABOUT 1790
MILES 0 250 500 1,000
European Colonies
Spain
Portugal
Great Britain
France
Netherlands
Seat of Government
1535 Lima Dates indicate year of founding
BRITISH NORTH AMERICA
UNITED STATES OF AMERICA
Disputed by Spain, Russia, and England
Nootka Sound
Claimed by Spain, but unoccupied
INTENDANCY OF NUEVA CALIFORNIA
San Francisco 1776
Monterey 1770
San Luis Obispo 1772
Santa Barbara 1782
Los Angeles 1781
San Diego 1769
WESTERN INTERIOR PROVINCES
San Juan Capestrano 1776
St. Louis 1764
CAPTAINCY-GENERAL OF LOUISIANA
Santa Fé 1609
INTENDANCY OF NUEVO MEXICO
Disputed with U.S. 1783-1795
PRESIDENCY (AUDIENCIA) OF GUADALAJARA
El Paso del Norte 1659
EASTERN INTERIOR PROVINCES
INTENDANCY OF SONORA
Chihuahua
INTENDANCY OF DURANGO
San Antonio 1718
WEST FLORIDA
EAST FLORIDA
New Orleans 1718
Pensacola 1698
St. Augustine 1565
VICEROYALTY OF NEW SPAIN
INTENDANCY OF VIEJA CALIFORNIA
Laredo 1755
Saltillo
INTENDANCY OF SAN LUIS POTOSI
INTENDANCY OF ZACATECAS
Culiacan 1531
La Paz 1535
Queretaro 1550
INTENDANCY OF MEXICO
Mexico City 1325
INTENDANCY OF VALLADOLID
Vera Cruz 1519
INTENDANCY OF VERA CRUZ
INTENDANCY OF PUEBLA
INTENDANCY OF OAXACA
Gulf of Mexico
Atlantic
Tropic of Cancer
Habana
CAPTAINCY-GENERAL OF CUBA
CAPTAINCY-GENERAL OF SANTO DOMINGO Ceded to France 1795
PUERTO RICO
INTENDANCY OF YUCATAN
Belice
Santiago 1514
JAMAICA Br. 1655
Port-au-Prince 1749
Santo Domingo 1496
San Juan 1521
CHIAPAS
CAPTAINCY-GENERAL (AUDIENCIA) OF GUATEMALA
Guatemala
San Salvador 1525
León
Granada 1524
San José 1738
Cartago 1564
Caribbean Sea
Maracaibo
Santa Marta 1525
Cartagena 1533
Portobelo 1584
Panama 1519
La Guaira 1588
Caracas 1567
TRINIDAD Ceded to Great Britain, 1802
CAPTAINCY-GENERAL OF CARACAS
Orinoco
VICEROYALTY OF NEW GRANADA
Established 1717, Refounded 1739
AUDIENCIA OF SANTA FÉ
Bogotá
Magdalena
Stabroek (Georgetown) Approx. 1740
Dutch in 1790
Paramaribo 1640
Cayenne 1664
DUTCH GUIANA
FRENCH GUIANA
Ocean
CAPTAINCY OF PARA
GALAPAGOS IS. Claimed by Spain, but unoccupied
Pacific Ocean
Quito
PRESIDENCY (AUDIENCIA) OF QUITO
Guayaquil 1538
Yapurá
Putumayo
Napo
Negro
Barcelos 1658
CAPTAINCY OF RIO NEGRO
Amazon
Barra do Rio Negro 1660
Tabatinga 1780
Marañón
Belem 1616
São Luís 1612
Fortaleza 1609
CAPTAINCY OF MARANHÃO
CAPTAINCY OF PIAUI
Recife (Pernambuco)
CAPTAINCY OF PERNAMBUCO
CAPTAINCY OF SERGIPE
CAPTAINCY OF BAÍA
Salvador (Baía) 1549
Tapajós
Purús
Madeira
Ucayali
VICEROYALTY OF PERU
AUDIENCIA OF LIMA
Trujillo 1535
Callao 1537
Lima 1535
PRESIDENCY (AUDIENCIA) OF CUZCO
Cuzco
VICEROYALTY OF BRAZIL
Definitively established 1714
Principe de Beira 1760
CAPTAINCY OF MATO GROSSO
Villa Bella (Mato Grosso) 1752
PRESIDENCY (AUDIENCIA) OF CHARCAS
L. Titicaca
La Paz 1548
Chuquisaca 1538
Potosí 1545
Santa Anna (Goiaz) 1736
CAPTAINCY OF GOIAZ
CAPTAINCY OF MINAS GERAIS
Tijuco (Diamantina)
Ouro Preto
CAPTAINCY OF ESPIRITO SANTO
VICEROYALTY OF LA PLATA
Established 1776
Pilcomayo
Salta 1582
Asunción 1537
PARAGUAY
Tucumán 1565
Tropic of Capricorn
CAPTAINCY OF RIO DE JANEIRO
Rio de Janeiro 1567
São Paulo 1554
CAPTAINCY OF SÃO PAULO
Santos 1536
CAPTAINCY OF SANTA CATARINA
CAPTAINCY OF RIO GRANDE DO SUL
Paraná
Uruguay
Abandoned Jesuit Missions
Loosely joined to Peru
CAPTAINCY-GENERAL (AUDIENCIA) OF CHILE
La Serena 1544
Mendoza
AUDIENCIA OF BUENOS AIRES
Santa Fé 1573
Córdoba 1573
Valparaíso 1544
Santiago 1541
BANDA ORIENTAL
Colonia 1680
Buenos Aires 1580
Montevideo 1726
Porto Alegre 1743
Rio Grande 1737
Rio de la Plata
Concepción 1550
Valdivia 1552
CHILOÉ
PATAGONIA
TIERRA DEL FUEGO
MALVINAS (FALKLAND ISLANDS)
CAPE HORN
Drake Passage
A-440037-29
Copyright by Rand McNally & Company, Made in U.S.A.

LATIN AMERICA AFTER INDEPENDENCE
MILES 0 250 500 1,000
UNITED STATES
Columbia
42nd Parallel
Ceded to U.S. 1848
San Francisco
Monterey
Colorado
Santa Fé
Missouri
Mississippi
Ohio
Arkansas
Red
Gila
San Diego
Mesilla Strip Sold to U.S. 1853
TEXAS
Independent 1836
Annexed to U.S. 1845
Rio Grande
LOWER CALIFORNIA
Chihuahua
Monterrey
New Orleans
MEXICO
Independent 1821
Monarchy 1822-23
Republic 1824
Grande de Santiago
Gulf of Mexico
Tampico
Habana
Jalapa
Vera Cruz
Mexico City
Puebla
Acapulco
YUCATAN
Independent 1839-48
CUBA
Sp. until 1898
JAMAICA
(Br. until 1962)
Kingston
Santiago
HAITI
Port-au-Prince
Santo Domingo
DOMINICAN REPUBLIC
United with Haiti until 1844
VIRGIN ISLANDS (Den.)
PUERTO RICO
Sp. until 1898
BRITISH HONDURAS
Belice
CHIAPAS
To Mexico 1823
Guatemala
GUATEMALA
HONDURAS
Tegucigalpa
San Salvador
SALVADOR
NICARAGUA
Managua
MOSQUITO COAST
British Protectorate 1841-50
Caribbean Sea
Maracaibo
CURACAO (Dutch)
TRINIDAD & TOBAGO
(Br. until 1962)
Port-of-Spain
La Guaira
Caracas
VENEZUELA
CENTRAL AMERICA
Independent 1821
United with Mexico 1821
Independent Confederation 1823
Divided into five states 1838
San José
COSTA RICA
Panama
PANAMA ISTHMUS
To Colombia 1821-1903
Magdalena
Orinoco
GREAT COLOMBIA
(1819-1830)
Bogotá
GUYANA
(Br. until 1966)
DUTCH GUIANA
FRENCH GUIANA
Atlantic
Tropic of Cancer
Ocean
GALAPAGOS IS.
Ecuador since 1832
Pacific
Quito
ECUADOR
Guayaquil
Ceded by Ecuador to Brazil 1904
MARAJO I.
Belem
São Luís
Fortaleza
Amazon
Paita
Trujillo
PERU
(1824)
Callao
Lima
Madeira
Tapajós
Tocantins
BRAZIL
Empire of Brazil, Monarchy 1822-1889
United States of Brazil since 1889
Recife (Pernambuco)
CHINCHA IS. (Peru)
Cuzco
Arequipa
Mollendo
Lake Titicaca
La Paz
Ceded to Brazil 1907
São Francisco
São Salvador (Baía)
TACNA
ARICA
Arica
To Chile 1883
To Peru 1929
To Chile 1883
TARAPACÁ
To Chile 1883
Iquique
BOLIVIA
Sucre
Paraguay
ATACAMA
To Chile 1884
Antofagasta
Tropic of Capricorn
CHACO
Claimed by Bolivia and Paraguay
Pilcomayo
Salta
PARAGUAY
Asunción
Paraná
Belo Horizonte
São Paulo
To Brazil 1895
Santos
Rio de Janeiro
Iguassú
To Arg. 1870
Tucumán
ARGENTINA
Ocean
JUAN FERNANDEZ ISLANDS
Chile since 1818
Valparaiso
Santiago
CHILE
Original Republic of Chile 1818
Córdoba
Mendoza
Santa Fé
Rosario
Buenos Aires
URUGUAY
Montevideo
Rio de la Plata
Argentine Nation 1860
PAMPAS
PROVINCE OF BUENOS AIRES
Independent 1853-1859
Bahía Blanca
CHILOÉ
PATAGONIA
Conquered by Argentina 1878-1879
Boundary adjusted by treaty 1881
Strait of Magellan
FALKLAND IS.
Held by Great Britain since 1833
Claimed by Argentina
CAPE HORN
TIERRA DEL FUEGO
Disputed between Argentina and Chile
Divided 1902
Drake Passage
A-440039-29
Copyright by Rand McNally & Company, Made in U.S.A.

LATIN AMERICA TODAY
0 250 500 1,000
MILES
UNITED STATES
Columbia
Colorado
Arkansas
Missouri
Ohio
Red
Mississippi
Rio Grande
Chihuahua
LOWER CALIFORNIA
Monterrey
MEXICO
Gulf of Mexico
Tampico
Grande de Santiago
Mexico City
Puebla
Jalapa
Vera Cruz
Acapulco
Havana
CUBA
Santiago
JAMAICA
Kingston
HAITI
Port-au-Prince
DOMINICAN REP.
Santo Domingo
PUERTO RICO
VIRGIN ISLANDS
BRITISH HONDURAS
Belmopan
GUATEMALA
Guatemala
HONDURAS
Tegucigalpa
EL SALVADOR
San Salvador
NICARAGUA
Managua
MOSQUITO COAST
COSTA RICA
San José
CENTRAL AMERICA
PANAMA
Panamá
Caribbean Sea
Gulf of Maracaibo
CURAÇAO (Neth.)
BARBADOS
TRINIDAD & TOBAGO
Port-of-Spain
La Guaira
Caracas
Orinoco
VENEZUELA
Magdalena
Bogotá
COLOMBIA
Georgetown
GUYANA
SURINAM (Neth. Guiana)
FRENCH GUIANA
TROPIC OF CANCER
Atlantic Ocean
Pacific Ocean
EQUATOR
GALÁPAGOS IS
Quito
ECUADOR
Guayaquil
Paita
Trujillo
PERU
Callao
Lima
Cuzco
CHINCHA IS. (Peru)
Arequipa
Mollendo
Arica
Iquique
Lake Titicaca
La Paz
BOLIVIA
Sucre
MARAJÓ I
Amazon
Belém
São Luís
Fortaleza
Tapajós
Madeira
BRAZIL
Tocantins
Recife
São Francisco
Salvador
Brasília
Belo Horizonte
Paraguai
Paraná
PARAGUAY
Pilcomayo
Asunción
São Paulo
Santos
Rio de Janeiro
Iguaçu
TROPIC OF CAPRICORN
Antofagasta
Salta
Tucumán
Córdoba
Uruguay
JUAN FERNÁNDEZ ISLANDS
Valparaíso
Mendoza
Santiago
Santa Fe
Rosario
Buenos Aires
URUGUAY
Montevideo
Río de la Plata
CHILE
ARGENTINA
PAMPAS
Bahía Blanca
CHILOÉ
PATAGONIA
Strait of Magellan
TIERRA DEL FUEGO
FALKLAND IS
CAPE HORN
A-440046-220 -1-1-5-
Copyright by Rand McNally & Company
Made in U.S.A.

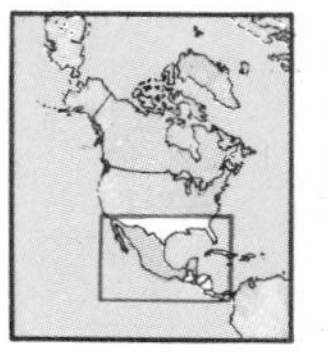

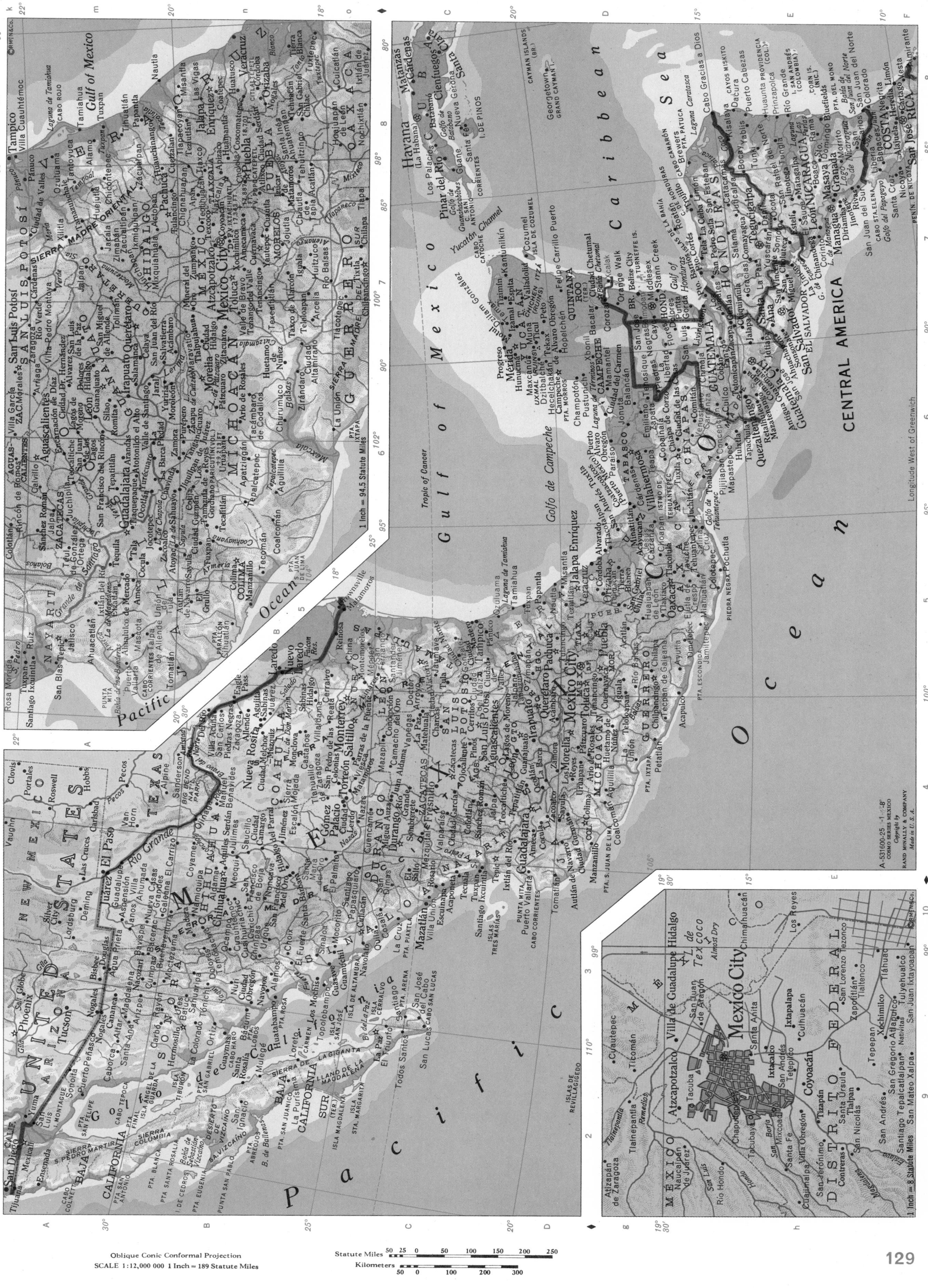

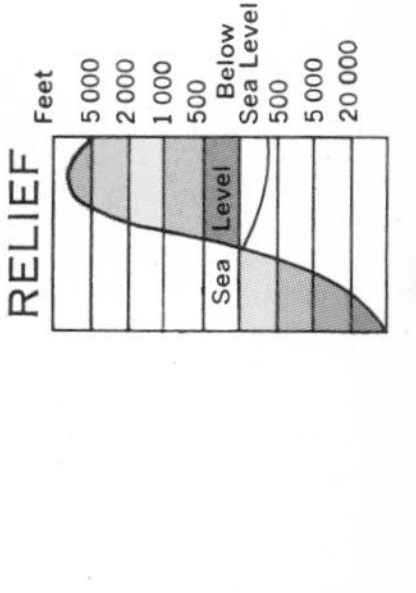

Oblique Conic Conformal Projection
SCALE 1:12,000 000 1 Inch = 189 Statute Miles

Statute Miles 50 25 0 50 100 150 200 250
Kilometers 50 0 100 200 300

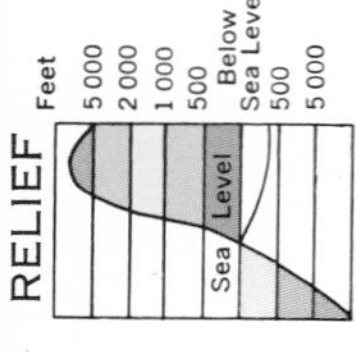

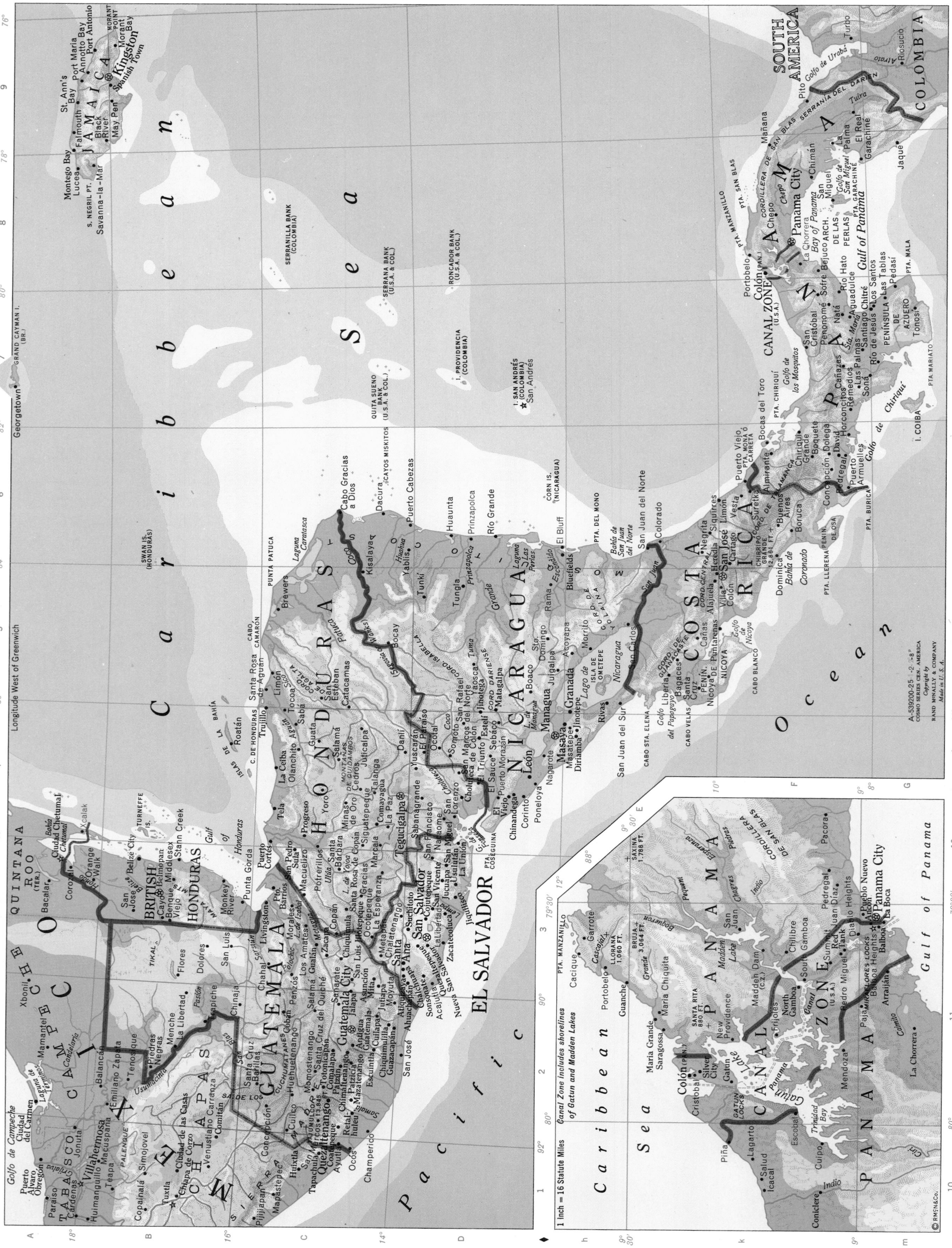

Statute Miles 25 0 25 75 125

Kilometers 25 0 25 75 125 175

Oblique Conic Conformal Projection

SCALE 1:6,000,000 1 Inch = 95 Statute Miles

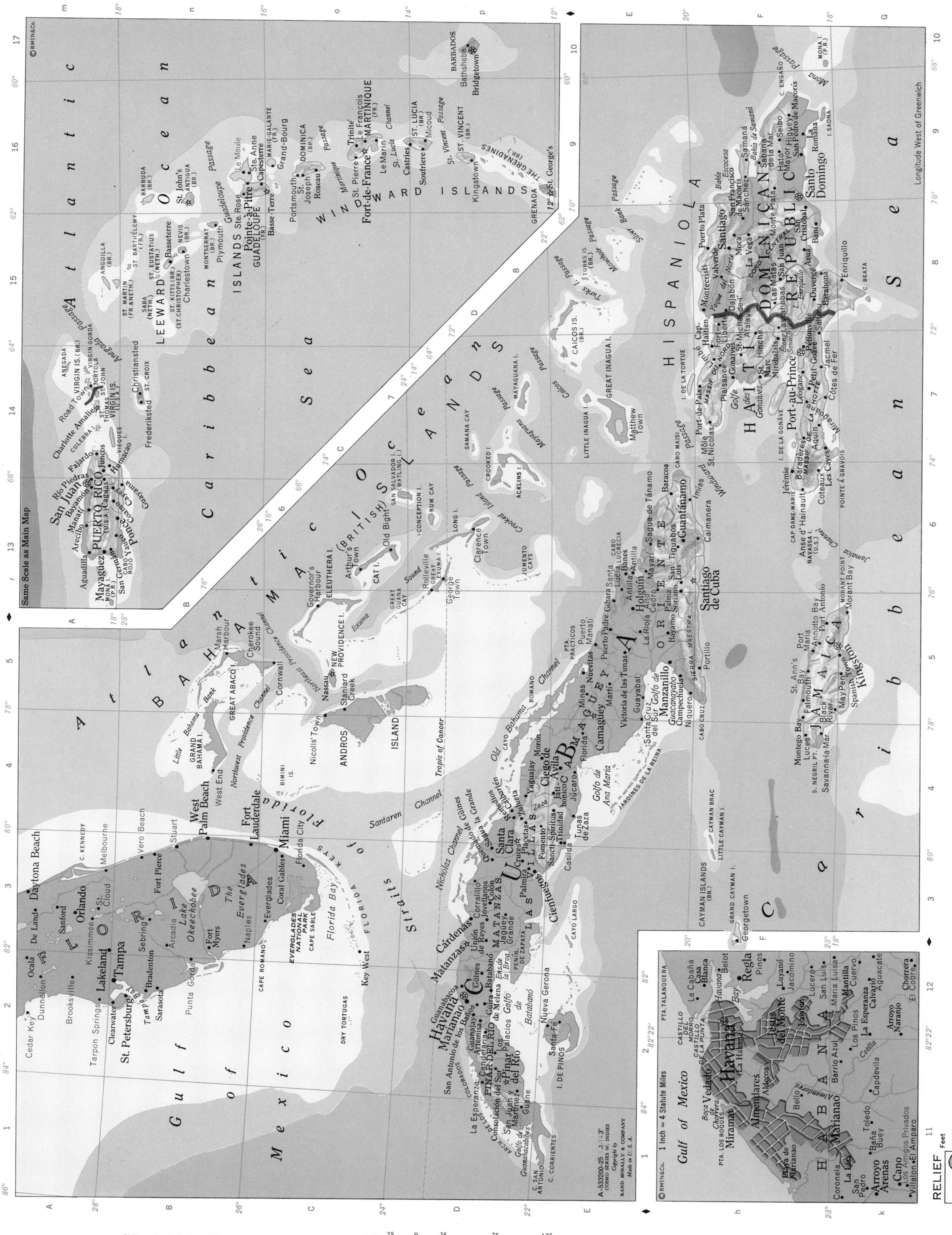

Oblique Conic Conformal Projection

SCALE 1:6,000,000 1 Inch = 95 Statute Miles

Statute Miles 25 0 25 75 125

Kilometers 25 0 25 75 125 175

RELIEF

Feet
5 000
2 000
1 000
500
Sea Level
500
5 000
Below Sea Level

A-532100-25 -1-12"
COSMO SERIES PUERTO RICO
Copyright by
RAND McNALLY & COMPANY
Made in U.S.A.

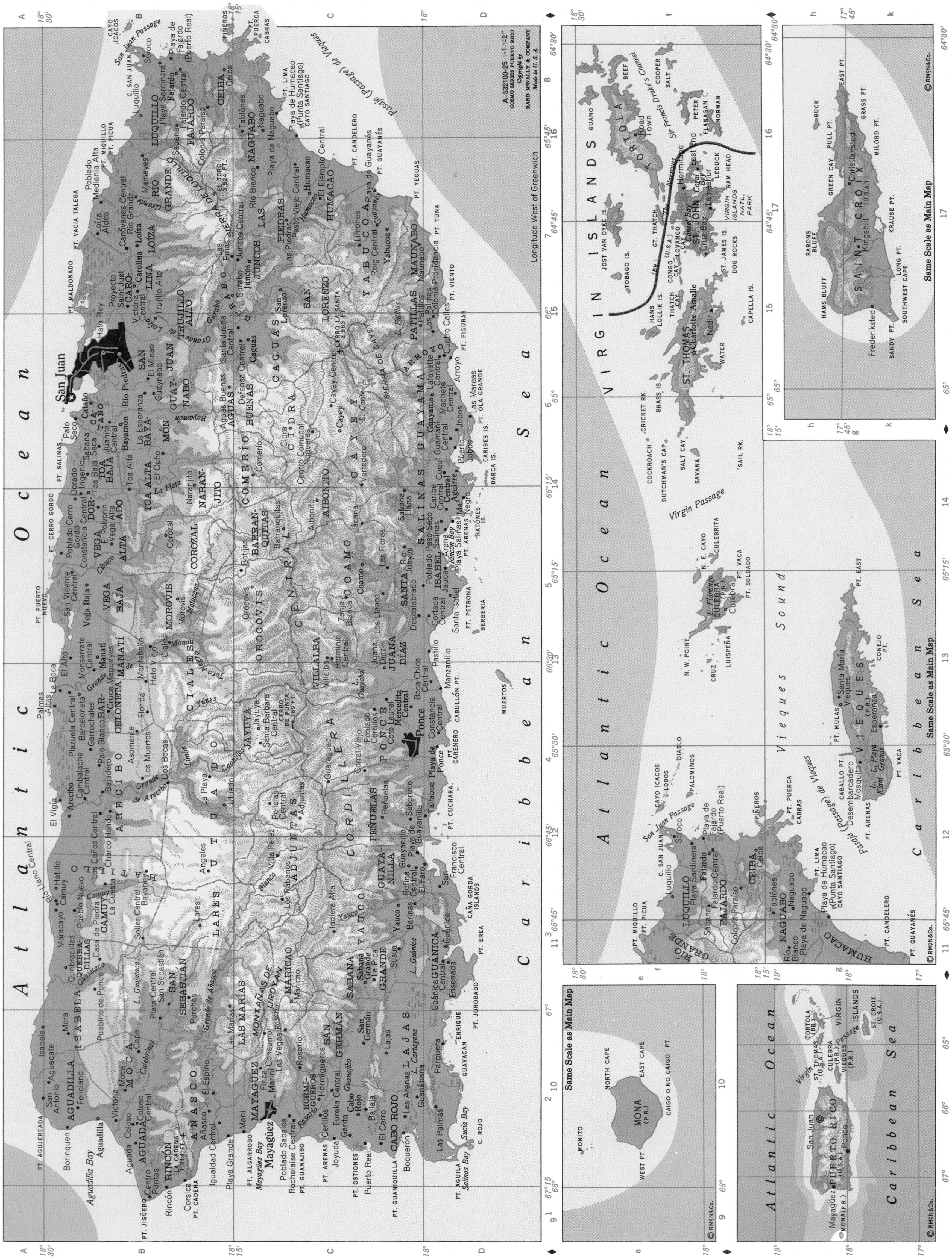

Statute Miles 5 0 5 10
Kilometers 5 0 5 10 15

Lambert Conformal Conic Projection
SCALE 1 : 600,000 1 Inch = 9.5 Statute Miles

Same Scale as Main Map

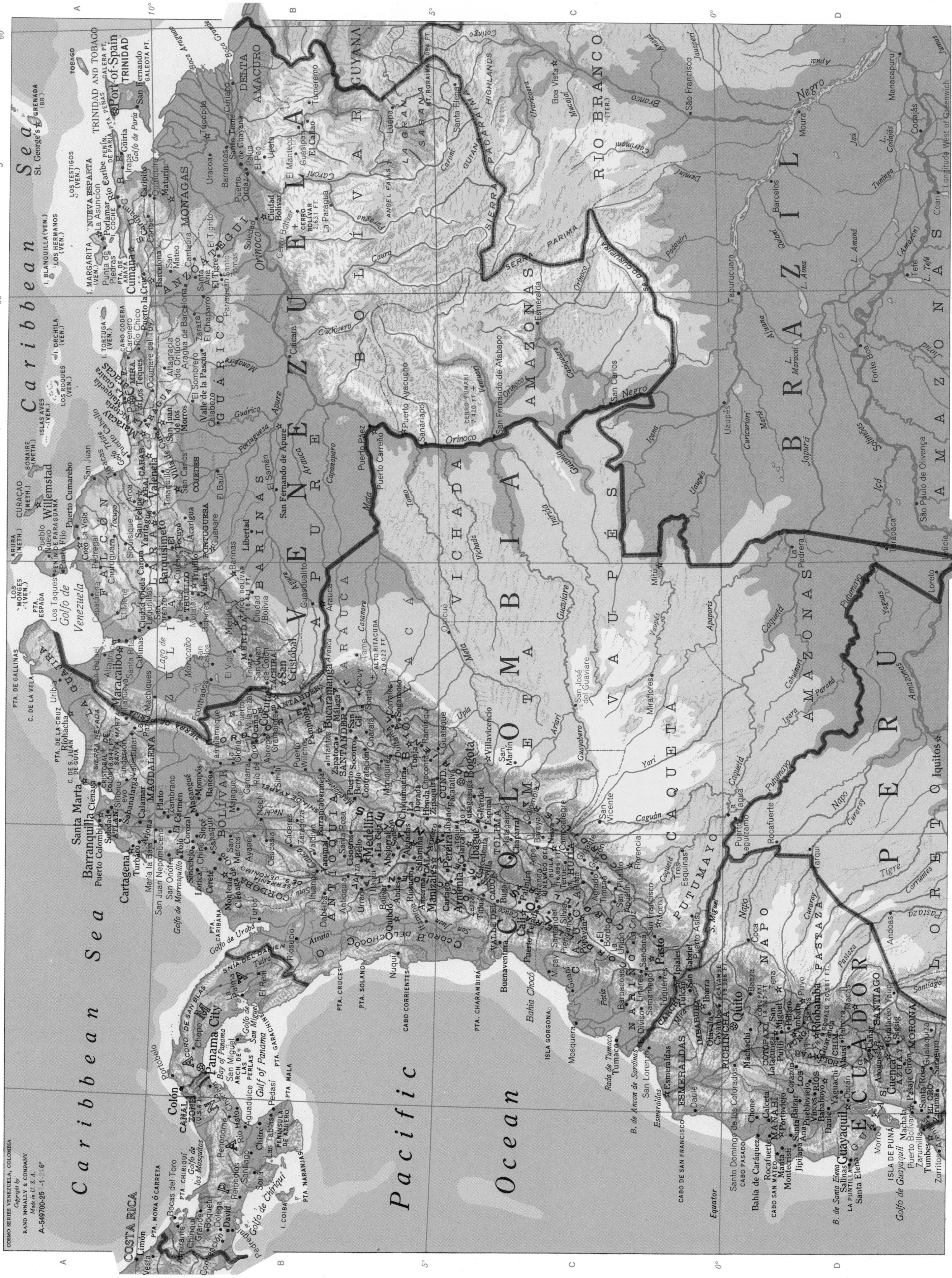

Oblique Conic Conformal Projection
SCALE 1:8,000,000 1 Inch = 126 Statute Miles

Statute Miles 50 0 50 100 150
Kilometers 50 0 50 100 150 200

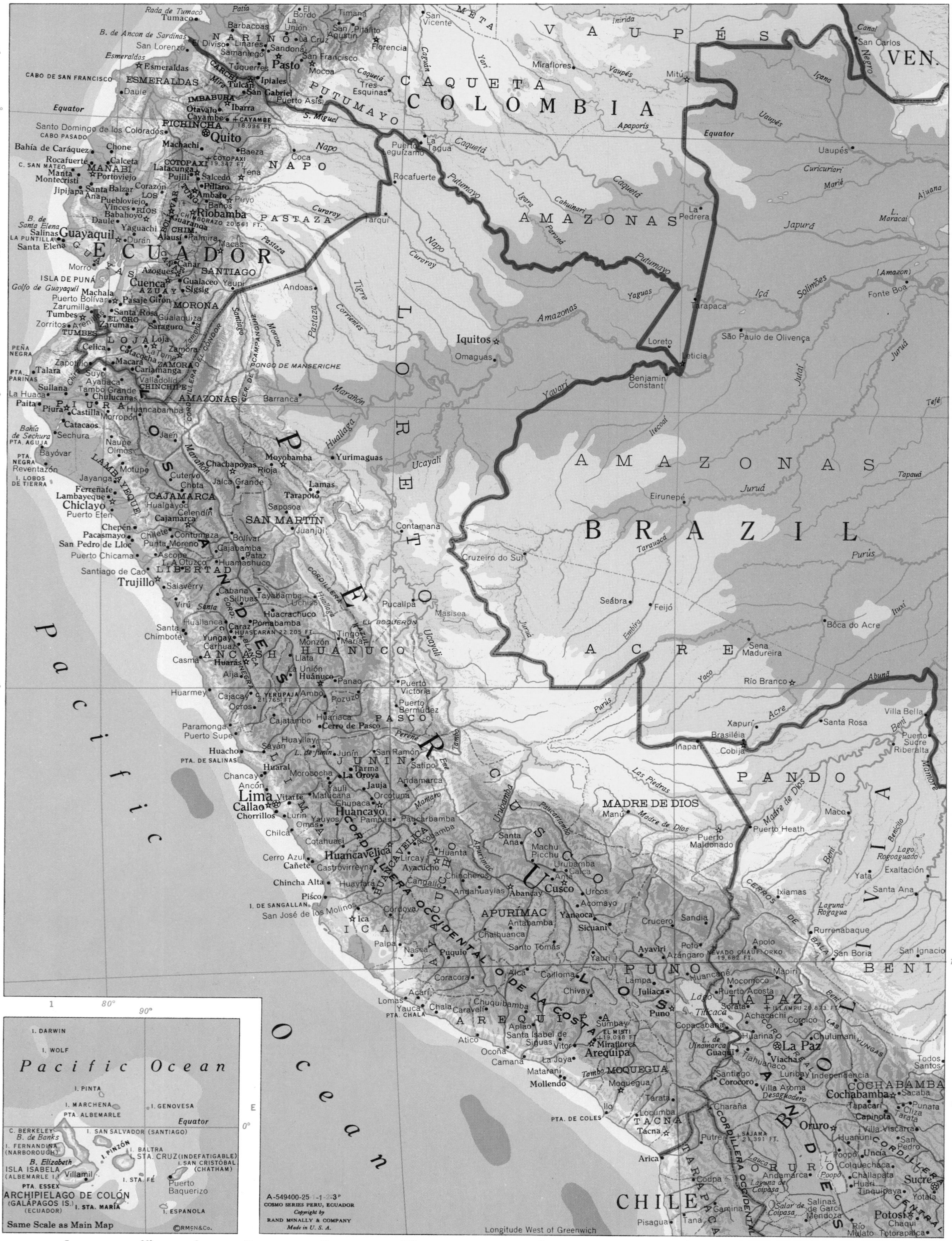

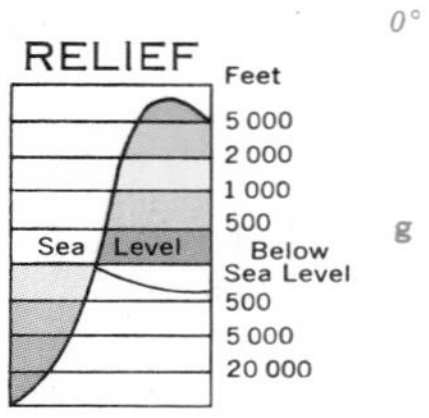

Statute Miles 50 0 50 100 150

Kilometers 50 0 50 100 150 200

Oblique Conic Conformal Projection

SCALE 1:8,000,000   1 Inch = 126 Statute Miles

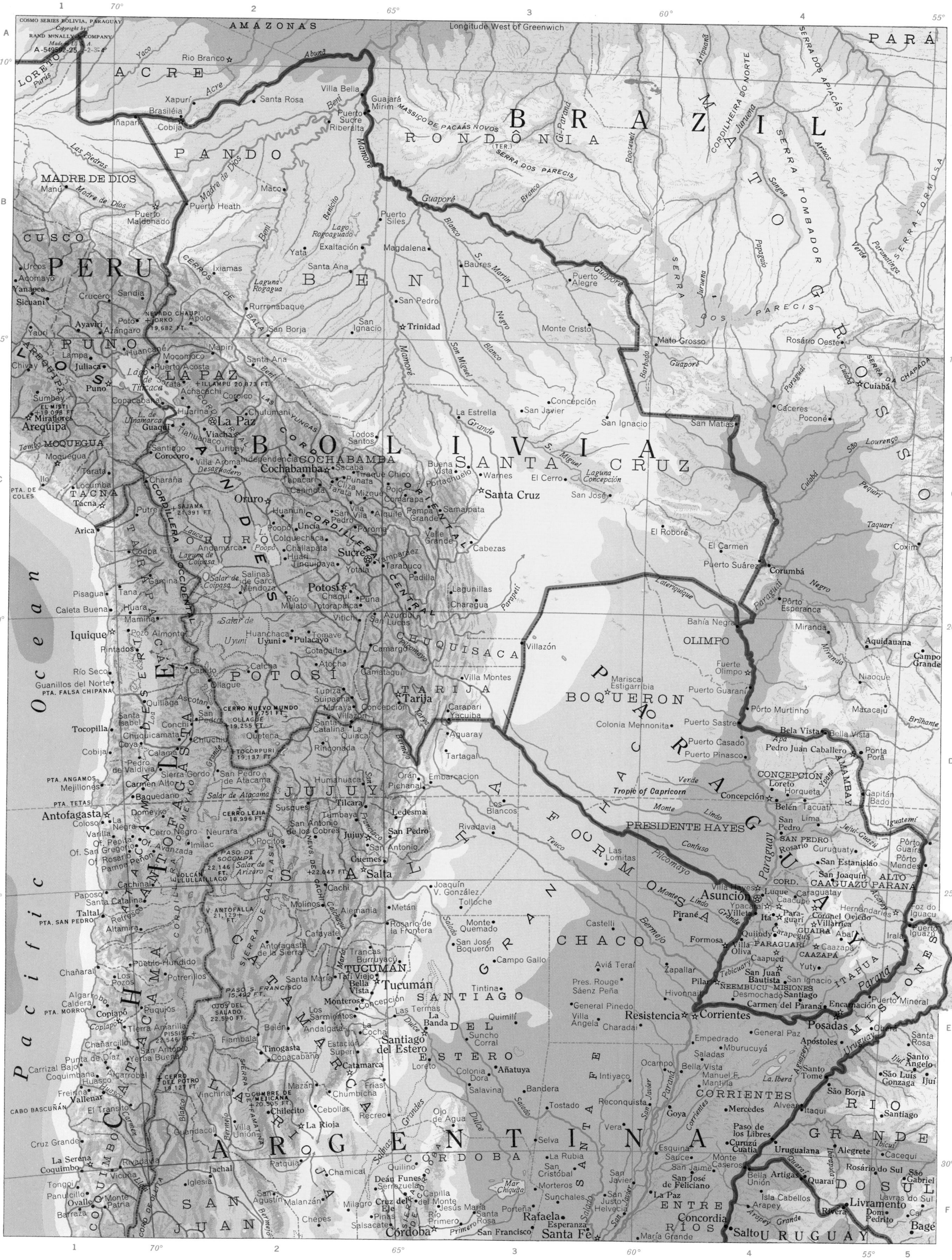

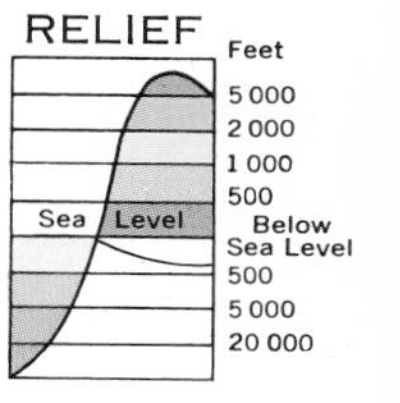

Oblique Conic Conformal Projection
SCALE 1:8,000,000 1 Inch = 126 Statute Miles

Statute Miles 50 0 50 100 150
Kilometers 50 0 50 100 150 200

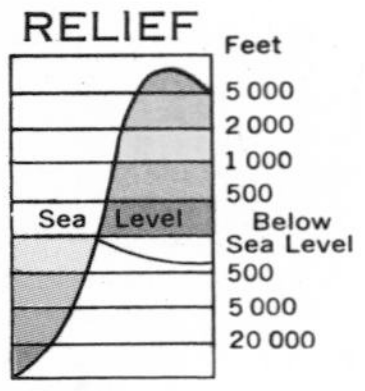

Statute Miles 50 0 50 100 150

Kilometers 50 0 50 100 150 200

Oblique Conic Conformal Projection
SCALE 1:8,000,000 1 Inch = 126 Statute Miles

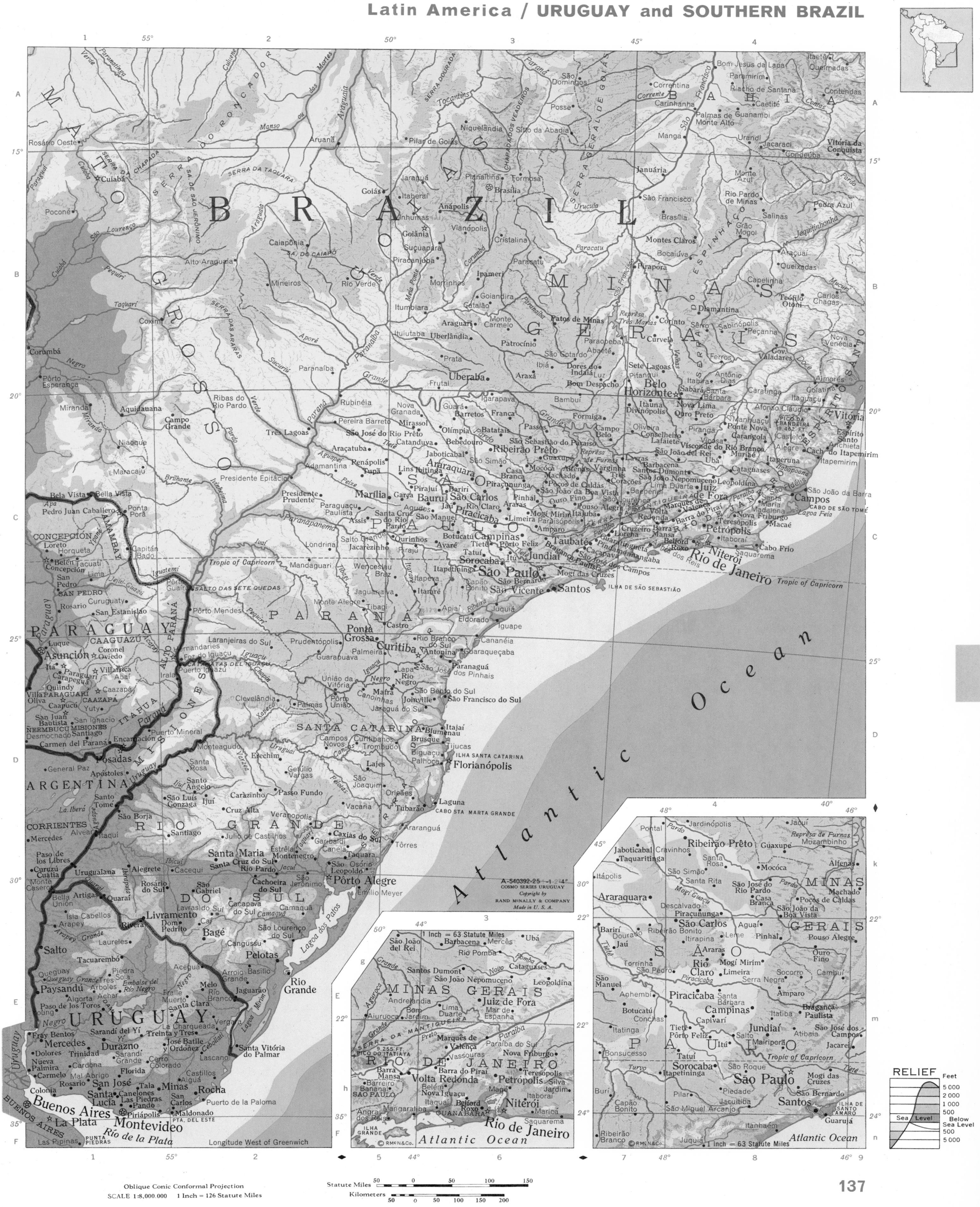
BRAZIL
MATO GROSSO
GOIÁS
MINAS GERAIS
BAHIA
ESPÍRITO SANTO
SÃO PAULO
RIO DE JANEIRO
PARANÁ
SANTA CATARINA
RIO GRANDE DO SUL
PARAGUAY
ARGENTINA
URUGUAY
MISIONES
CORRIENTES
BUENOS AIRES
Atlantic Ocean
Tropic of Capricorn
Brasília
Goiânia
Anápolis
Cuiabá
Belo Horizonte
Uberaba
Ribeirão Prêto
Campinas
São Paulo
Santos
Rio de Janeiro
Niterói
Petrópolis
Juiz de Fora
Vitória
Campos
Curitiba
Paranaguá
Florianópolis
Blumenau
Joinville
Pôrto Alegre
Pelotas
Rio Grande
Santa Maria
Asunción
Concepción
Encarnación
Posadas
Montevideo
Buenos Aires
La Plata
Paysandú
Salto
Río de la Plata
Lagoa dos Patos
Lagoa Mirim
Paraná
Paraguai
Uruguai
São Francisco
Tietê
Iguaçu
SALTO DAS SETE QUEDAS
CATARATAS DEL IGUAÇU
PICO DA BANDEIRA 9,482 FT.
PICO DO ITATIAIA 9,255 FT.
CABO DE SÃO TOMÉ
Cabo Frio
ILHA DE SÃO SEBASTIÃO
ILHA SANTA CATARINA
CABO STA MARTA GRANDE
PTA. DEL ESTE
A-540392-25 -1-2-4
COSMO SERIES URUGUAY
Copyright by
RAND McNALLY & COMPANY
Made in U. S. A.
Longitude West of Greenwich
1 Inch = 63 Statute Miles
RELIEF
Feet
5 000
2 000
1 000
500
Sea Level
Below Sea Level
500
5 000
Oblique Conic Conformal Projection
SCALE 1:8,000,000 1 Inch = 126 Statute Miles
Statute Miles 50 0 50 100 150
Kilometers 50 0 50 100 150 200

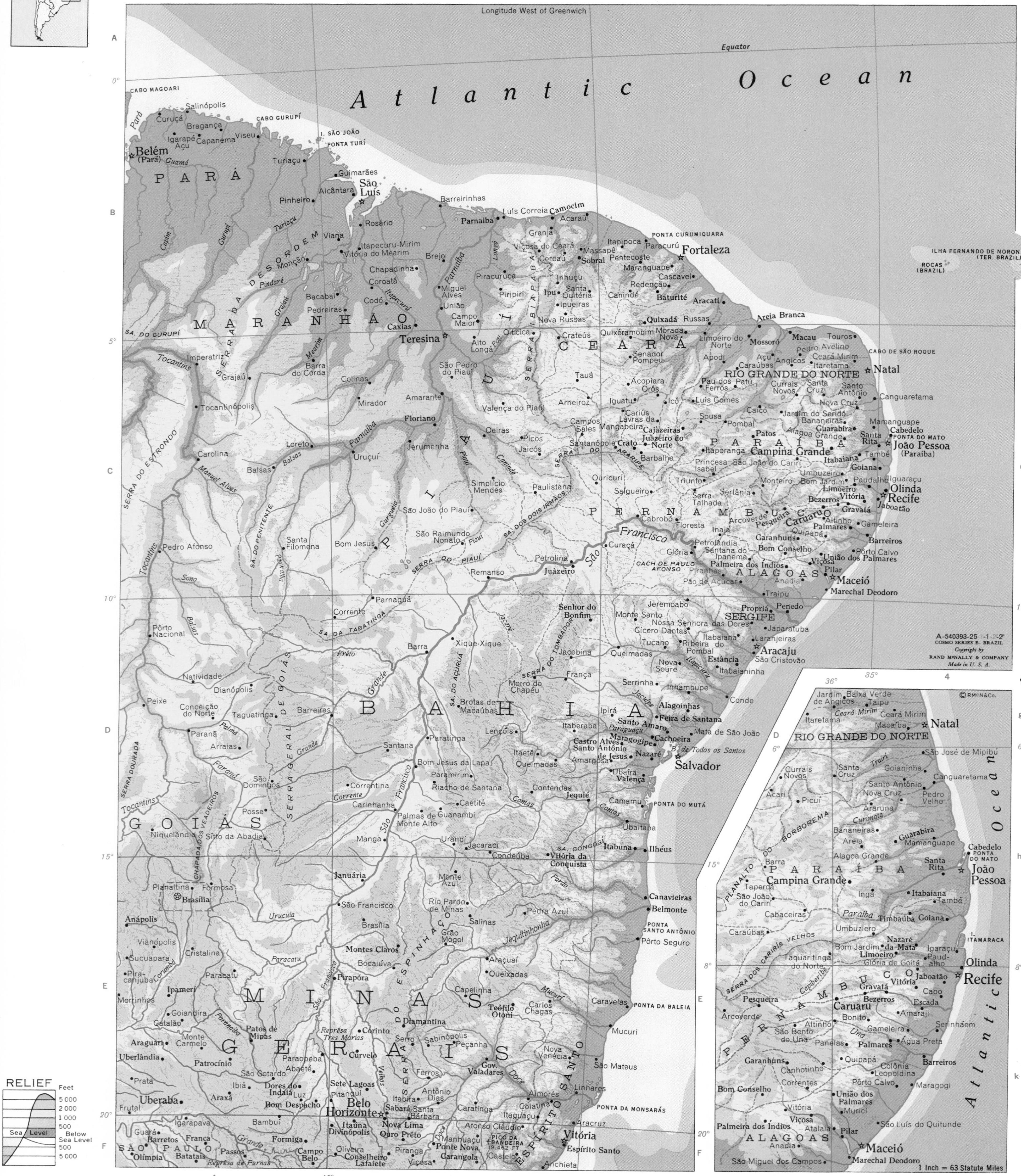

Statute Miles 50 0 50 100 150

Kilometers 50 0 50 100 150 200

Oblique Conic Conformal Projection

SCALE 1:8,000,000 1 Inch = 126 Statute Miles

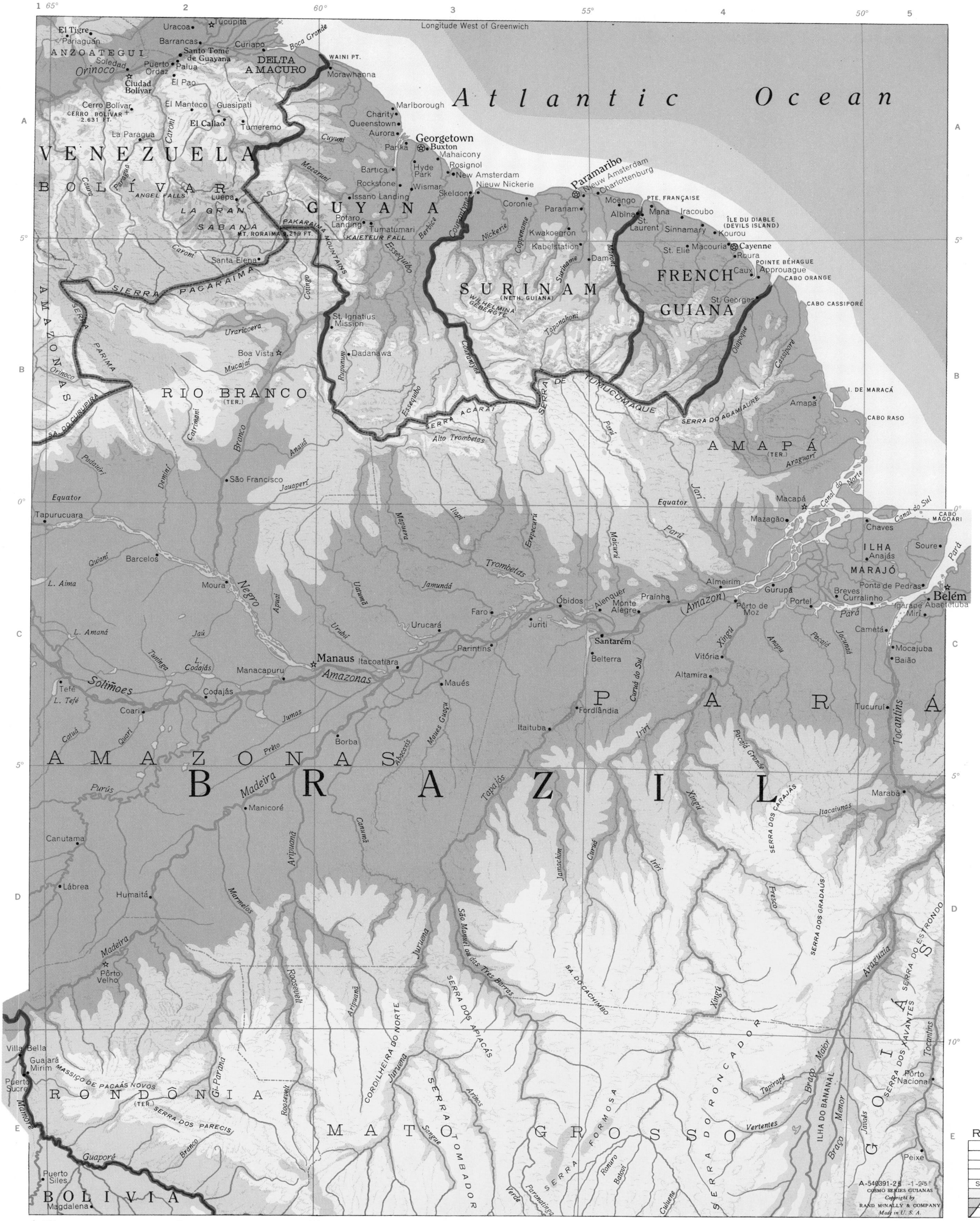

Oblique Conic Conformal Projection
SCALE 1:8,000,000 1 Inch = 126 Statute Miles

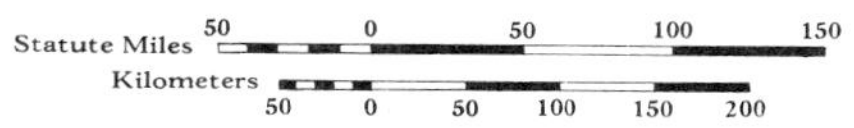

NYSTROM map by Richard Edes Harrison

CANADA

Canada is a giant country about the same size as the entire continent of Europe. Among the nations of the world, only Russia covers more area. In spite of its great size, Canada has a relatively small population. Most of northern Canada is an almost empty wilderness of forests, lakes, and frozen tundra. Almost all of Canada's people live close to the country's southern border, near the United States. Here, the hard-working Canadians enjoy one of the highest living standards in the world. Southern Canada's farms, factories, and mines make the country a rich nation.

WHAT IS YOUR ATLAS I.Q. OF CANADA?

These questions are designed to test your knowledge of the variety of information about Canada contained in THE WORLD BOOK ATLAS. Check your answers by turning to the last page of the ATLAS.

Identifying places

1. Most of the people of Newfoundland live on the island of Newfoundland and many of the people of British Columbia live on the island of Vancouver. In which province do *all* of the people live on an island?
2. What is the largest lake that lies entirely within Manitoba?
3. Alberta, Saskatchewan, and Manitoba are known as the *Prairie Provinces*. Edmonton is the capital of Alberta and Regina is the capital of Saskatchewan. What is the capital of Manitoba?
4. Canada and the United States share Niagara Falls. The American section is in New York State. In what province is the Canadian section?
5. Which city is farthest east—Montreal, Toronto, or Ottawa?
6. The highest mountain in Canada is in the Yukon. What is the name of that mountain?
7. Canada has the longest coastline of any country in the world. Part of this coastline lies along a large bay named for a famous explorer. What is the name of this bay?
8. British Columbia is Canada's westernmost province and Newfoundland is the easternmost province. What province extends farthest south?
9. Which Canadian city is farthest north—Vancouver, Winnipeg, or St. John's?
10. The Canadian Rockies stretch across two provinces. One is British Columbia. What is the other province?

Facts and figures

11. Quebec is the largest province in area, but which is the largest in population?
12. The smallest province in area is also the smallest in population. What is the name of the province?
13. California and New York State each has about as many people as Canada. About how many people live in Canada?
14. What territory of Canada borders Alaska?
15. The Northwest Territories and three provinces border Hudson Bay. Two of the provinces are Quebec and Ontario. Which is the third?

History

16. In 1791, Canada was split into two self-governing regions. Most of the British settlers lived in Upper Canada. What was the region where most of the French settlers lived?
17. During the 1700's and 1800's, large parts of Canada were under the control of a private company. What was the name of the company?
18. The Dominion of Canada was formed in 1867 with four provinces. Three of these were Ontario, Quebec, and New Brunswick. What was the fourth?
19. Alberta and Saskatchewan became provinces in 1905. Which is the only province created since then?
20. During the war of 1812, Ft. Dearborn (Chicago) was captured by British troops in August, 1812. When was York (Toronto) captured by U.S. forces?

MAPS OF CANADA

142-143 **PHYSICAL FEATURES OF CANADA**
144-145 **POLITICAL DIVISIONS OF CANADA**
146-147 **HISTORY OF CANADA**
146 CANADA TO 1840
147 CANADA AFTER 1867
148-155 **PROVINCES OF CANADA**
148 ALBERTA
149 BRITISH COLUMBIA
150 MANITOBA
151 NEW BRUNSWICK
152 NEWFOUNDLAND
151 NOVA SCOTIA
153 ONTARIO
151 PRINCE EDWARD ISLAND
154 QUEBEC
155 SASKATCHEWAN

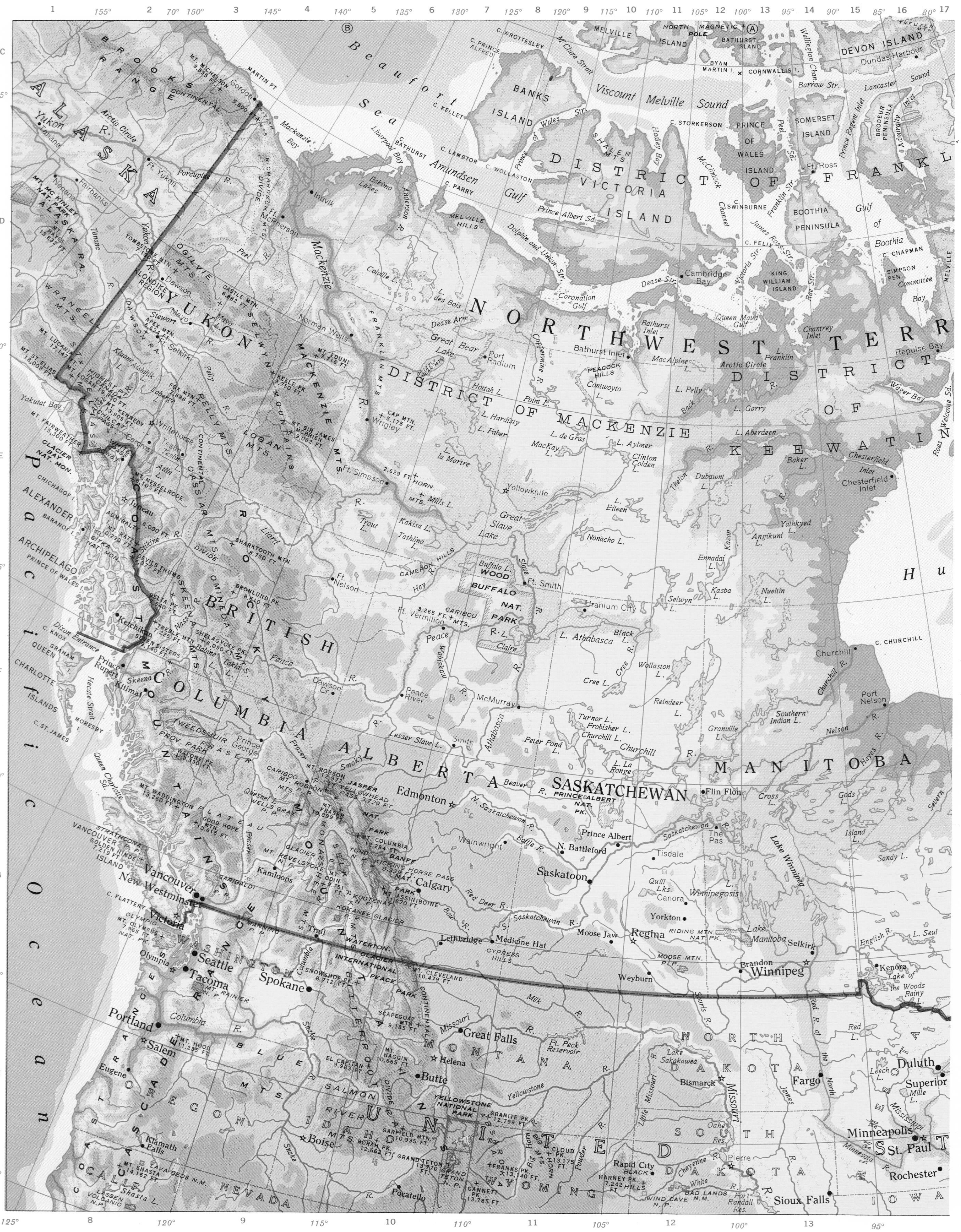
ALASKA
BROOKS RANGE
Beaufort Sea
Arctic Circle
Yukon R.
Fairbanks
MT. MC KINLEY NAT. PARK
ALASKA RA.
WRANGELL MTS.
Porcupine R.
Ft. Yukon
Mackenzie Bay
Inuvik
Ft. McPherson
Amundsen Gulf
Liverpool Bay
BANKS ISLAND
Viscount Melville Sound
MELVILLE ISLAND
NORTH MAGNETIC POLE
BATHURST ISLAND
CORNWALLIS I.
DEVON ISLAND
Dundas Harbour
Lancaster Sound
Barrow Str.
SOMERSET ISLAND
PRINCE OF WALES ISLAND
VICTORIA ISLAND
DISTRICT OF FRANKLIN
BOOTHIA PENINSULA
Gulf of Boothia
KING WILLIAM ISLAND
Cambridge Bay
Coronation Gulf
Queen Maud Gulf
NORTHWEST TERR
Bathurst Inlet
Repulse Bay
DISTRICT OF KEEWATIN
DISTRICT OF MACKENZIE
Great Bear Lake
Port Radium
Norman Wells
Wrigley
Ft. Simpson
Great Slave Lake
Yellowknife
Chesterfield Inlet
Baker L.
Dubawnt L.
Hudson
YUKON
Dawson
Mayo
Stewart
Whitehorse
MACKENZIE MTS.
SELWYN MTS.
OGILVIE MTS.
MT. LOGAN 19,850 FT.
MT. ST. ELIAS 18,008 FT.
Yakutat Bay
Juneau
ALEXANDER ARCHIPELAGO
Ketchikan
Dixon Entrance
Prince Rupert
Kitimat
QUEEN CHARLOTTE ISLANDS
Hecate Strait
Queen Charlotte Sd.
Pacific Ocean
BRITISH COLUMBIA
COAST MOUNTAINS
ROCKY MTS.
Ft. Nelson
Liard
Peace
Dawson Cr.
Prince George
FRASER PLATEAU
MT. ROBSON 12,972 FT.
JASPER NAT. PARK
Kamloops
Vancouver
New Westminster
Victoria
VANCOUVER ISLAND
BANFF NAT. PARK
Calgary
Edmonton
ALBERTA
Peace River
Ft. Vermilion
Lesser Slave L.
McMurray
Athabasca
Ft. Smith
WOOD BUFFALO NAT. PARK
L. Athabasca
Uranium City
SASKATCHEWAN
PRINCE ALBERT NAT. PK.
Prince Albert
N. Battleford
Saskatoon
Regina
Moose Jaw
Medicine Hat
Lethbridge
Yorkton
Weyburn
Flin Flon
MANITOBA
Churchill
Port Nelson
Lake Winnipeg
Lake Manitoba
Winnipegosis
Brandon
Winnipeg
Selkirk
Kenora
Lake of the Woods
Reindeer L.
Wollaston L.
Churchill R.
Nelson
Trail
Spokane
Seattle
Tacoma
Olympia
Portland
Salem
Eugene
Klamath Falls
WASHINGTON
OREGON
IDAHO
MONTANA
WYOMING
NEVADA
CALIF.
CASCADE RANGE
BLUE MTS.
SALMON RIVER MTS.
Boise
Pocatello
Great Falls
Helena
Butte
Missouri
Yellowstone
YELLOWSTONE NATIONAL PARK
GLACIER NAT. PARK
NORTH DAKOTA
SOUTH DAKOTA
Bismarck
Fargo
Pierre
Rapid City
Sioux Falls
Duluth
Superior
Minneapolis
St. Paul
Rochester
IOWA
UNITED STATES
Statute Miles 50 25 0 50 100 150 200 250
Kilometers 50 0 100 200 300

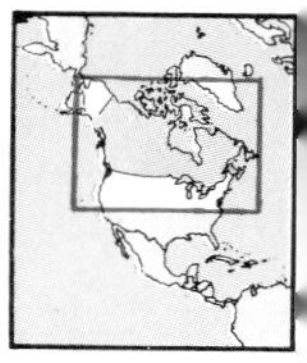

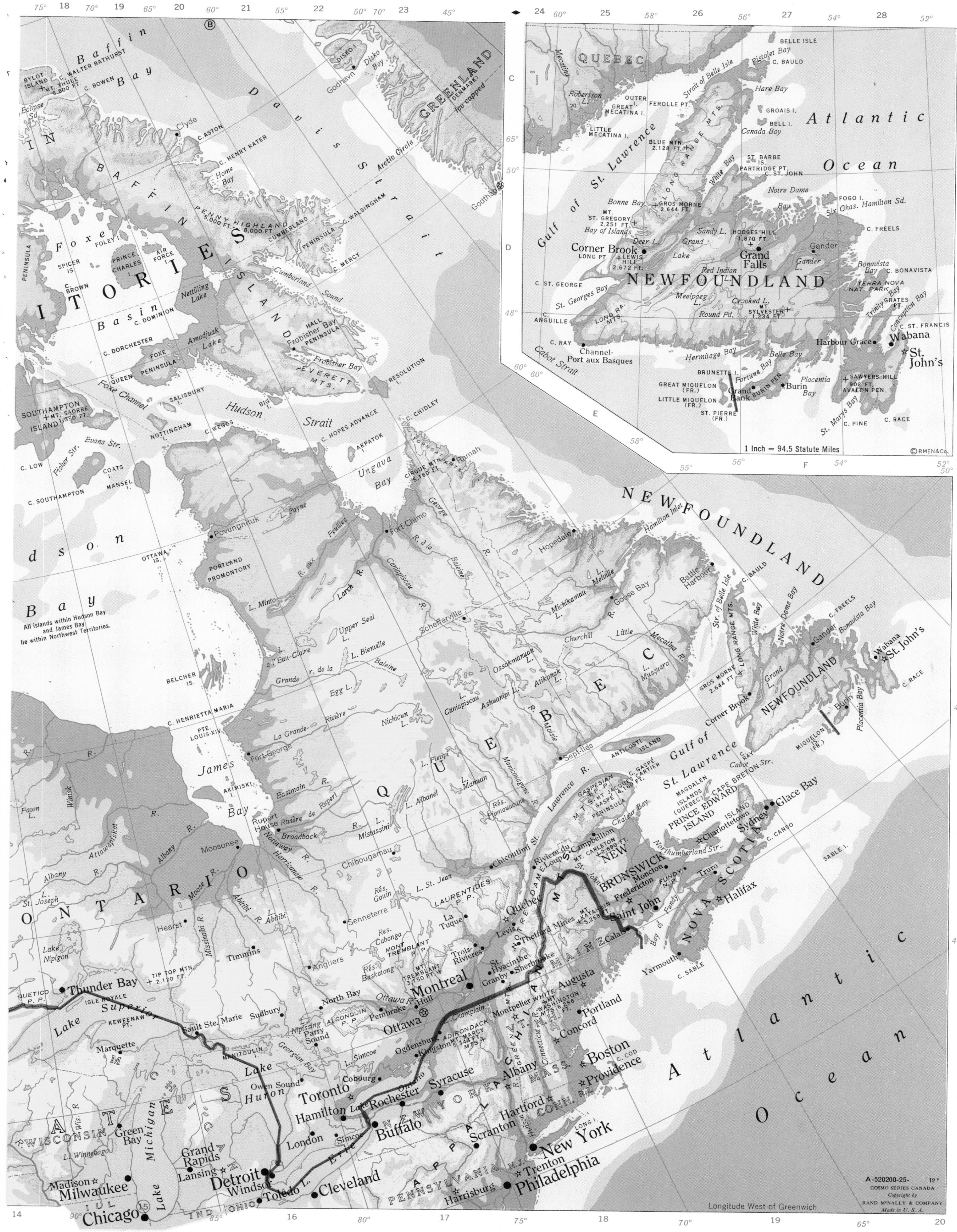
QUEBEC
Strait of Belle Isle
Atlantic Ocean
Gulf of St. Lawrence
NEWFOUNDLAND
Corner Brook
Grand Falls
Gander
Harbour Grace
Wabana
St. John's
Channel-Port aux Basques
Cabot Strait
Burin
Grand Bank
1 Inch = 94.5 Statute Miles
Baffin Bay
Davis Strait
GREENLAND (DENMARK)
Godthaab
BAFFIN ISLAND
Foxe Basin
Hudson Strait
Ungava Bay
Hudson Bay
All islands within Hudson Bay and James Bay lie within Northwest Territories.
James Bay
QUEBEC
ONTARIO
NEW BRUNSWICK
NOVA SCOTIA
PRINCE EDWARD ISLAND
Montreal
Quebec
Ottawa
Toronto
Halifax
Saint John
Thunder Bay
Lake Superior
Lake Huron
Lake Michigan
Detroit
Chicago
Milwaukee
Buffalo
Cleveland
Boston
New York
Philadelphia
Atlantic Ocean
Longitude West of Greenwich
A-520200-25-
COSMO SERIES CANADA
Copyright by RAND McNALLY & COMPANY
Made in U. S. A.

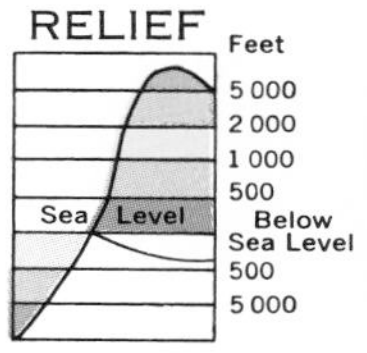
RELIEF
Feet
5 000
2 000
1 000
500
Sea Level
Below Sea Level
500
5 000

Lambert Conformal Conic Projection
SCALE 1:12,000,000 1 Inch = 189 Statute Miles

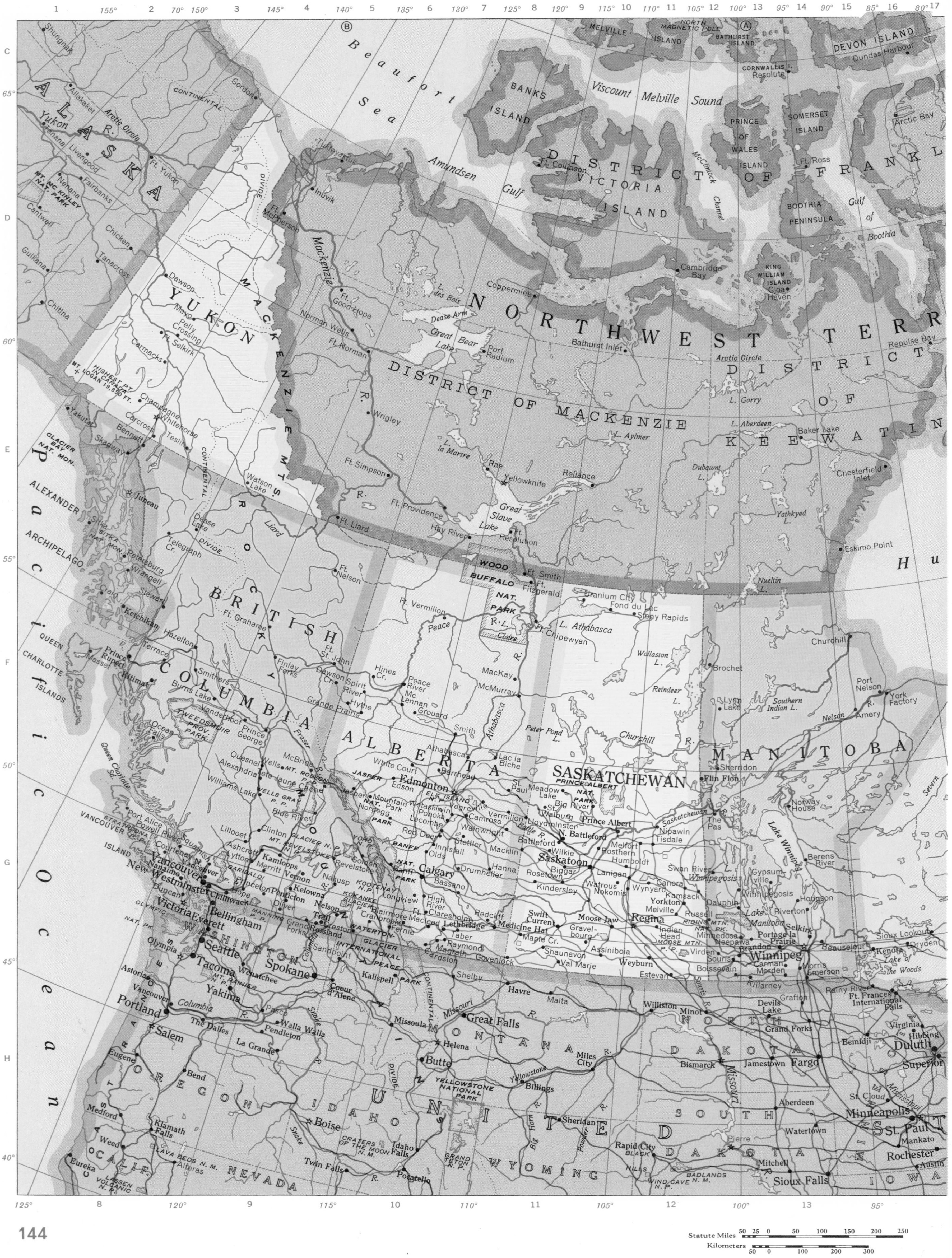
Beaufort Sea
Amundsen Gulf
Viscount Melville Sound
McClintock Channel
Gulf of Boothia
BANKS ISLAND
VICTORIA ISLAND
MELVILLE ISLAND
NORTH MAGNETIC POLE
BATHURST ISLAND
DEVON ISLAND
Dundas Harbour
CORNWALLIS I.
Resolute
PRINCE OF WALES ISLAND
SOMERSET ISLAND
Arctic Bay
BOOTHIA PENINSULA
KING WILLIAM ISLAND
Gjoa Haven
Cambridge Bay
Ft. Ross
Ft. Collinson
DISTRICT OF FRANKLIN
NORTHWEST TERRITORIES
DISTRICT OF MACKENZIE
DISTRICT OF KEEWATIN
ALASKA
YUKON
BRITISH COLUMBIA
ALBERTA
SASKATCHEWAN
MANITOBA
MACKENZIE MTS.
ROCKY MTS.
CONTINENTAL DIVIDE
Arctic Circle
Pacific Ocean
ALEXANDER ARCHIPELAGO
QUEEN CHARLOTTE ISLANDS
Queen Charlotte Sd.
VANCOUVER ISLAND
Tuktoyaktuk
Inuvik
Ft. McPherson
Aklavik
Mackenzie
Ft. Good Hope
Norman Wells
Ft. Norman
Wrigley
Ft. Simpson
Ft. Providence
Ft. Liard
Hay River
Great Bear Lake
Great Slave Lake
L. des Bois
Dease Arm
Port Radium
Coppermine
Bathurst Inlet
L. la Martre
Rae
Yellowknife
Reliance
L. Aylmer
L. Gorry
L. Aberdeen
Baker Lake
Dubawnt L.
Chesterfield Inlet
Yathkyed L.
Eskimo Point
Repulse Bay
Nueltin L.
Churchill
Ft. Resolution
Ft. Smith
Fitzgerald
WOOD BUFFALO NAT. PARK
Uranium City
Fond du Lac
Stony Rapids
L. Athabasca
Ft. Chipewyan
L. Claire
Wollaston L.
Reindeer L.
Brochet
Lynn Lake
Southern Indian L.
Port Nelson
York Factory
Nelson R.
Amery
Churchill R.
Peter Pond L.
Flin Flon
Sherridon
The Pas
Norway House
Lake Winnipeg
Berens River
Gypsumville
Lake Winnipegosis
Lake Manitoba
Selkirk
Winnipeg
Portage la Prairie
Brandon
Dauphin
Swan River
Shungnak
Allakaket
Yukon R.
Tanana
Livengood
Fairbanks
Nenana
MT. MC KINLEY NAT. PARK
Cantwell
Chicken
Tanacross
Gulkana
Chitina
Ft. Yukon
Gordon
Dawson
Mayo
Pelly Crossing
Ft. Selkirk
Carmacks
HIGHEST PT. IN CANADA MT. LOGAN 19,850 FT.
Champagne
Whitehorse
Carcross
Bennett
Teslin
Yakutat
Skagway
GLACIER BAY NAT. MON.
Juneau
Sitka
SITKA NAT. MON.
Petersburg
Wrangell
Craig
Ketchikan
Stewart
Watson Lake
Dease Lake
Telegraph Cr.
Liard
Ft. Nelson
Ft. Grahame
Hazelton
Terrace
Prince Rupert
Masset
Kitimat
Smithers
Burns Lake
Vanderhoof
TWEEDSMUIR PROV. PARK
Ocean Falls
Prince George
Quesnel
Wells
Williams Lake
Alexandria
Finlay Forks
Ft. St. John
Dawson Creek
Spirit River
Hythe
Grande Prairie
Hines Cr.
Peace River
Mc Lennan
Grouard
Ft. Vermilion
Peace R.
MacKay
McMurray
Athabasca R.
Smith
Athabasca
Lac la Biche
White Court
Barrhead
Edmonton
Edson
Jasper
JASPER NAT. PARK
McBride
Tete Jaune Cache
MT. ROBSON
WELLS GRAY P. P.
Blue River
St. Paul
ELK ISLAND NAT. PARK
Vegreville
Wetaskiwin
Ponoka
Camrose
Lacombe
Red Deer
Mountain Park
Nordegg
Vermilion
Lloydminster
Wainwright
Stettler
Innisfail
Olds
Meadow Lake
Big River
St. Walburg
PRINCE ALBERT NAT. PARK
Prince Albert
N. Battleford
Battleford
Macklin
Wilkie
Saskatoon
Biggar
Rosetown
Kindersley
Lanigan
Watrous
Nokomis
Humboldt
Melfort
Rosthern
Nipawin
Tisdale
Wynyard
Canora
Kamsack
Yorkton
Melville
Regina
Moose Jaw
Swift Current
Gravelbourg
Assiniboia
Shaunavon
Val Marie
Weyburn
Estevan
Maple Cr.
Medicine Hat
Redcliff
Lethbridge
Taber
Raymond
Magrath
Cardston
Claresholm
Macleod
High River
Calgary
Banff
BANFF NAT. PARK
Drumheller
Hanna
Bassano
Longview
Blairmore
Fernie
Cranbrook
WATERTON-GLACIER INTERNATIONAL PEACE PARK
Coventry
Golden
Revelstoke
GLACIER NAT. PARK
MT. REVELSTOKE NAT. PARK
Nakusp
KOOTENAY NAT. PARK
YOHO NAT. PARK
Kamloops
Vernon
Kelowna
Penticton
Oliver
Princeton
Merritt
Nelson
Trail
Rossland
Grand Forks
Creston
Clinton
Lillooet
Ashcroft
Lytton
Hope
Chilliwack
Vancouver
New Westminster
North Vancouver
Nanaimo
Duncan
Victoria
Courtenay
Powell River
Squamish
Port Alice
STRATHCONA PROV. PARK
Bellingham
Everett
Seattle
Tacoma
Olympia
OLYMPIC NAT. PK.
WASHINGTON
Wenatchee
Spokane
Sandpoint
Coeur d'Alene
Kalispell
Shelby
Havre
Malta
Yakima
MT. RAINIER NAT. PK.
Columbia R.
Astoria
Vancouver
Portland
Pasco
Walla Walla
Pendleton
The Dalles
La Grande
Salem
Eugene
Bend
OREGON
Medford
Klamath Falls
Weed
Eureka
CALIF.
LASSEN VOLCANIC N. P.
LAVA BEDS N. M.
Alturas
NEVADA
IDAHO
Boise
Snake R.
CRATERS OF THE MOON N. M.
Idaho Falls
Twin Falls
Pocatello
GRAND TETON N. P.
WYOMING
MONTANA
Missoula
Helena
Butte
Great Falls
Missouri R.
Yellowstone R.
YELLOWSTONE NATIONAL PARK
Billings
Miles City
Sheridan
Big Horn R.
Powder R.
Rapid City
BLACK HILLS
WIND CAVE N. P.
BADLANDS N. M.
Pierre
SOUTH DAKOTA
NORTH DAKOTA
Williston
Minot
Bismarck
Jamestown
Fargo
Grand Forks
Devils Lake
Aberdeen
Watertown
Mitchell
Sioux Falls
MINN.
Minneapolis
St. Paul
St. Cloud
Mankato
Rochester
Austin
Duluth
Superior
Hibbing
Virginia
Bemidji
Ft. Frances
International Falls
Rainy River
Kenora
Dryden
Sioux Lookout
Lake of the Woods
Beausejour
Morris
Emerson
Carman
Morden
Killarney
Boissevain
Virden
Souris
Neepawa
Minnedosa
Russell
RIDING MTN. NAT. PK.
MOOSE MTN. P. P.
Indian Head
Grafton
Hudson Bay
Severn R.
UNITED STATES
IOWA
Statute Miles 50 25 0 50 100 150 200 250
Kilometers 50 0 100 200 300

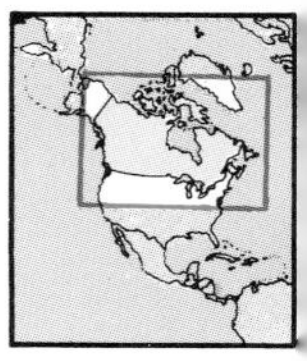

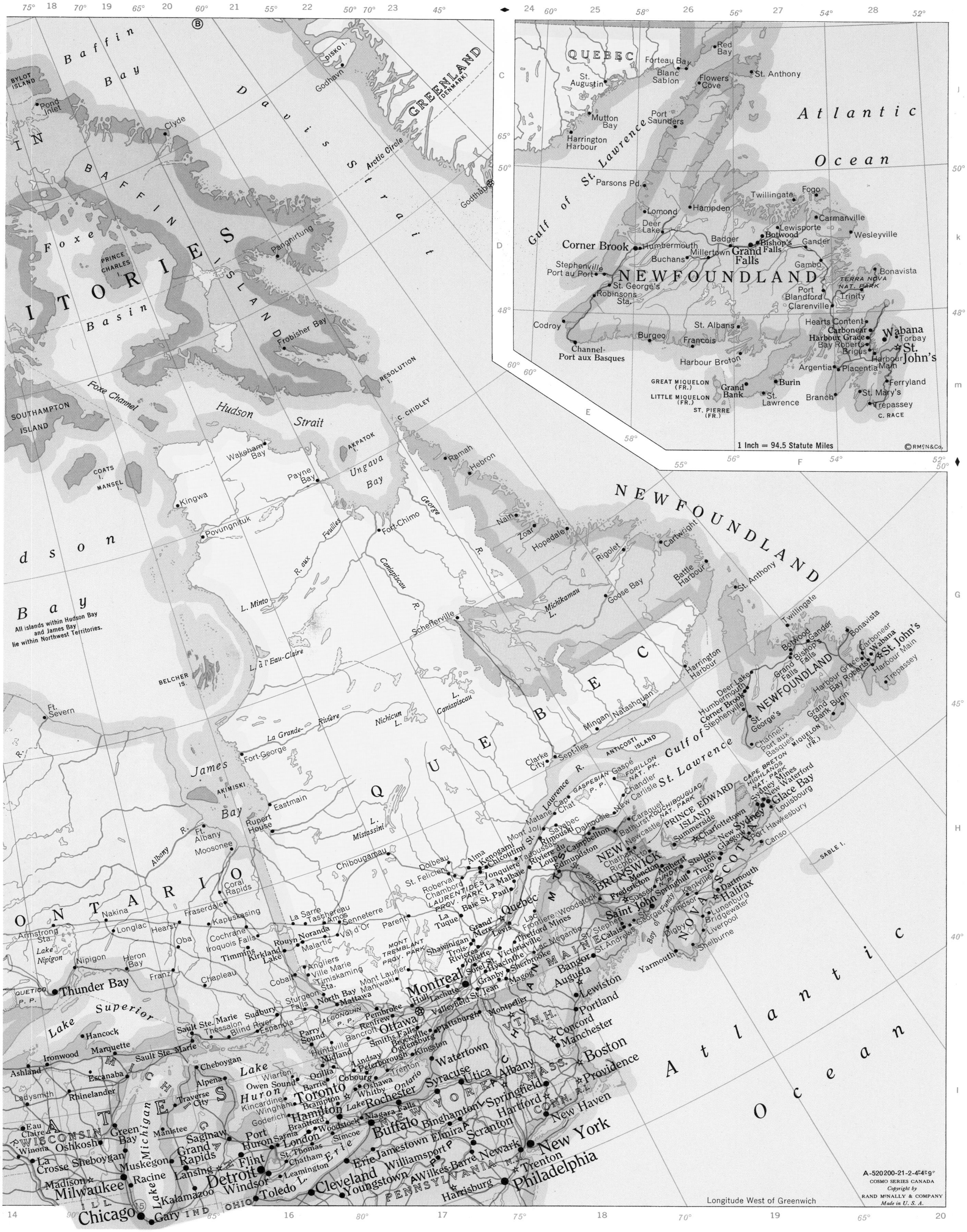

Lambert Conformal Conic Projection
SCALE 1:12,000,000 1 Inch = 189 Statute Miles

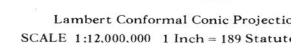

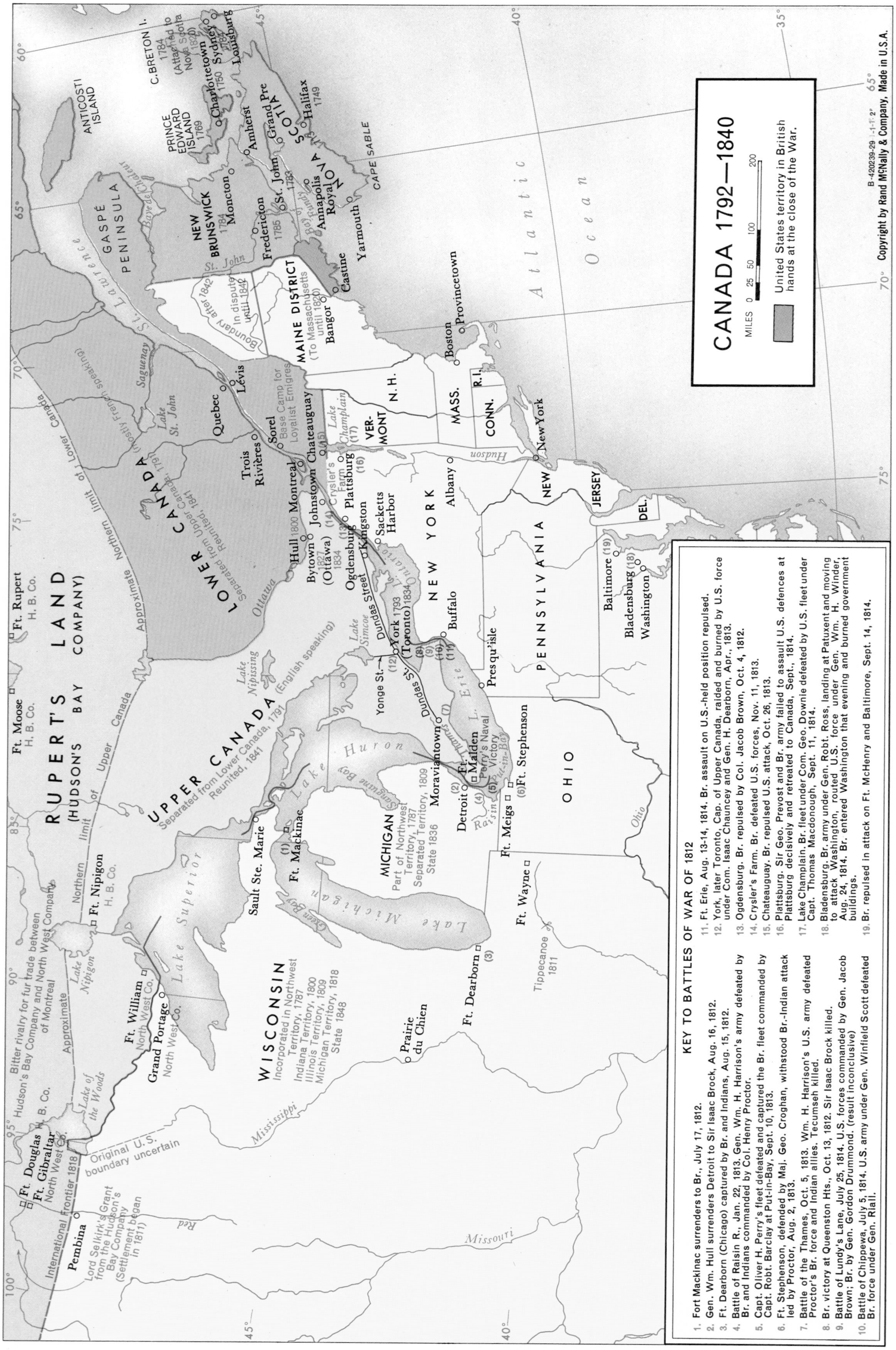
CANADA 1792—1840
MILES 0 25 50 100 200
United States territory in British hands at the close of the War.
KEY TO BATTLES OF WAR OF 1812
1. Fort Mackinac surrenders to Br., July 17, 1812.
2. Gen. Wm. Hull surrenders Detroit to Sir Isaac Brock, Aug. 16, 1812.
3. Ft. Dearborn (Chicago) captured by Br. and Indians, Aug. 15, 1812.
4. Battle of Raisin R., Jan. 22, 1813. Gen. Wm. H. Harrison's army defeated by Br. and Indians commanded by Col. Henry Proctor.
5. Capt. Oliver H. Perry's fleet defeated and captured the Br. fleet commanded by Capt. Robt. Barclay at Put-in-Bay, Sept. 10, 1813.
6. Ft. Stephenson, defended by Maj. Geo. Croghan, withstood Br.-Indian attack led by Proctor, Aug. 2, 1813.
7. Battle of the Thames, Oct. 5, 1813. Wm. H. Harrison's U.S. army defeated Proctor's Br. force and Indian allies. Tecumseh killed.
8. Br. victory at Queenston Hts., Oct. 13, 1812. Sir Isaac Brock killed.
9. Battle of Lundy's Lane, July 25, 1814. U.S. forces commanded by Gen. Jacob Brown; Br. by Gen. Gordon Drummond. (result inconclusive)
10. Battle of Chippewa, July 5, 1814. U.S. army under Gen. Winfield Scott defeated Br. force under Gen. Riall.
11. Ft. Erie, Aug. 13-14, 1814. Br. assault on U.S.-held position repulsed.
12. York, later Toronto, Cap. of Upper Canada, raided and burned by U.S. force under Com. Isaac Chauncey and Gen. H. Dearborn, Apr., 1813.
13. Ogdensburg. Br. repulsed by Col. Jacob Brown, Oct. 4, 1812.
14. Crysler's Farm. Br. defeated U.S. forces, Nov. 11, 1813.
15. Chateauguay. Br. repulsed U.S. attack, Oct. 26, 1813.
16. Plattsburg. Sir Geo. Prevost and Br. army failed to assault U.S. defences at Plattsburg decisively and retreated to Canada, Sept., 1814.
17. Lake Champlain. Br. fleet under Com. Geo. Downie defeated by U.S. fleet under Capt. Thomas Macdonough, Sept. 11, 1814.
18. Bladensburg. Br. army under Gen. Robt. Ross, landing at Patuxent and moving to attack Washington, routed U.S. force under Gen. Wm. H. Winder, Aug. 24, 1814. Br. entered Washington that evening and burned government buildings.
19. Br. repulsed in attack on Ft. McHenry and Baltimore, Sept. 14, 1814.
RUPERT'S LAND
(HUDSON'S BAY COMPANY)
Ft. Moose
H. B. Co.
Ft. Rupert
H. B. Co.
Ft. Douglas
Ft. Gibraltar
North West Co.
H. B. Co.
Bitter rivalry for fur trade between Hudson's Bay Company and North West Company of Montreal
International Frontier 1818
Pembina
Lord Selkirk's Grant from the Hudson's Bay Company (Settlement began in 1811)
Original U.S. boundary uncertain
Approximate Northern limit of Upper Canada
Approximate Northern limit of Lower Canada
Lake of the Woods
Lake Nipigon
Ft. Nipigon
H. B. Co.
Ft. William
North West Co.
Grand Portage
North West Co.
Lake Superior
UPPER CANADA
Separated from Lower Canada, 1791
Reunited, 1841
(English speaking)
LOWER CANADA
Separated from Upper Canada, 1791
Reunited, 1841
(mostly French speaking)
Lake Nipissing
Lake St. John
Saguenay
St. Lawrence
Ottawa
GASPÉ PENINSULA
Baye de Chaleur
ANTICOSTI ISLAND
C.BRETON I.
1784
(Attached to Nova Scotia 1820)
PRINCE EDWARD ISLAND
1769
Charlottetown
1750
Sydney
1784
Louisburg
NEW BRUNSWICK
1784
Moncton
Amherst
Fredericton
1785
St. John
1783
Grand Pre
NOVA SCOTIA
Halifax
1749
Annapolis Royal
Bay of Fundy
Yarmouth
CAPE SABLE
Quebec
Lévis
Trois Rivières
Sorel
Base Camp for Loyalist Emigres
Hull 1800
Montreal
Bytown 1827
(Ottawa) 1834
Johnstown
Chateauguay
Crysler's Farm
Ogdensburg
Kingston
Plattsburg
Sacketts Harbor
Lake Champlain
VER-MONT
N. H.
MAINE DISTRICT
(To Massachusetts until 1820)
Boundary after 1842
In dispute until 1842
St. John
Bangor
Castine
MASS.
Boston
Provincetown
R.I.
CONN.
Hudson
Albany
NEW YORK
New York
NEW JERSEY
DEL.
PENNSYLVANIA
Baltimore
Bladensburg
Washington
Presqu'isle
Buffalo
Lake Simcoe
Yonge St.
Dundas Street
Dundas St.
York 1793
(Toronto) 1834
L. Ontario
L. Erie
Moraviantown
Thames
Detroit
Ft. Malden
Perry's Naval Victory
Put-in-Bay
Raisin
Ft. Meigs
Ft. Stephenson
OHIO
Ohio
Ft. Wayne
Tippecanoe
1811
Lake Huron
Sauguene Bay
Sault Ste. Marie
Ft. Mackinac
MICHIGAN
Part of Northwest Territory, 1787
Separated Territory, 1809
State 1836
Lake Michigan
Green Bay
WISCONSIN
Incorporated in Northwest Territory, 1787
Indiana Territory, 1800
Illinois Territory, 1809
Michigan Territory, 1818
State 1848
Prairie du Chien
Ft. Dearborn
Mississippi
Missouri
Red
Atlantic Ocean
B-420239-29
Copyright by Rand McNally & Company, Made in U.S.A.

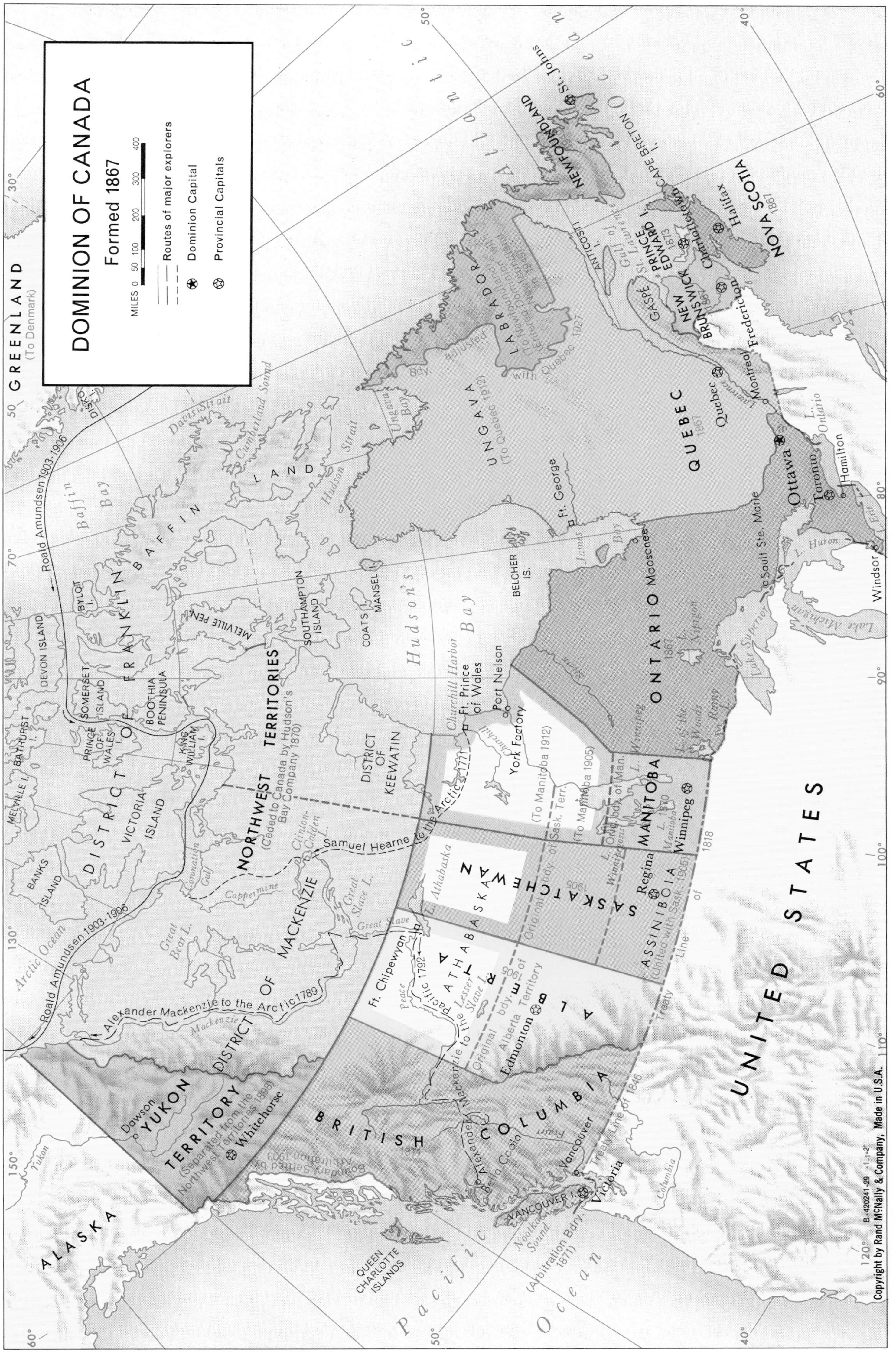
DOMINION OF CANADA
Formed 1867
MILES 0 50 100 200 300 400
Routes of major explorers
Dominion Capital
Provincial Capitals
GREENLAND
(To Denmark)
ALASKA
YUKON TERRITORY
(Separated from the Northwest Territories 1898)
Dawson
Whitehorse
Boundary settled by Arbitration 1903
BRITISH COLUMBIA
1871
Bella Coola
Vancouver
Victoria
VANCOUVER I.
QUEEN CHARLOTTE ISLANDS
Nootka Sound
(Arbitration Bdry. 1871)
Treaty Line of 1846
Pacific Ocean
Arctic Ocean
DISTRICT OF MACKENZIE
DISTRICT OF FRANKLIN
DISTRICT OF KEEWATIN
NORTHWEST TERRITORIES
(Ceded to Canada by Hudson's Bay Company 1870)
Roald Amundsen 1903-1906
Alexander Mackenzie to the Arctic 1789
Alexander Mackenzie to the Pacific 1792
Samuel Hearne to the Arctic 1771
Ft. Chipewyan
Great Bear L.
Great Slave L.
Coppermine
ALBERTA
1905
Edmonton
Original bdy. of Alberta Territory
ATHABASKA
L. Athabaska
SASKATCHEWAN
1905
Regina
ASSINIBOIA
(United with Sask. 1905)
MANITOBA
1870
Winnipeg
(To Manitoba 1912)
York Factory
Port Nelson
Ft. Prince of Wales
Churchill Harbor
Hudson's Bay
ONTARIO
1867
L. Nipigon
Lake Superior
Sault Ste. Marie
Moosonee
Toronto
Hamilton
Windsor
Ottawa
QUEBEC
1867
Quebec
Montreal
UNGAVA
(To Quebec 1912)
Ft. George
LABRADOR
(To Newfoundland, with Newfoundland entered Dominion in 1949)
Bdy. adjusted with Quebec 1927
NEW BRUNSWICK
1867
Fredericton
PRINCE EDWARD I.
1873
Charlottetown
NOVA SCOTIA
1867
Halifax
CAPE BRETON I.
ANTICOSTI I.
GASPÉ
Gulf of St. Lawrence
NEWFOUNDLAND
St. Johns
Atlantic Ocean
BAFFIN LAND
Baffin Bay
Davis Strait
Hudson Strait
Ungava Bay
Cumberland Sound
SOUTHAMPTON ISLAND
COATS I.
MANSEL I.
BELCHER IS.
James Bay
MELVILLE PEN.
DEVON ISLAND
BYLOT I.
SOMERSET ISLAND
BOOTHIA PENINSULA
KING WILLIAM I.
PRINCE OF WALES I.
VICTORIA ISLAND
BANKS ISLAND
MELVILLE I.
BATHURST I.
UNITED STATES
Treaty Line of 1818
L. Huron
Lake Michigan
L. Ontario
L. Erie
B-420241-29
Copyright by Rand McNally & Company, Made in U.S.A.

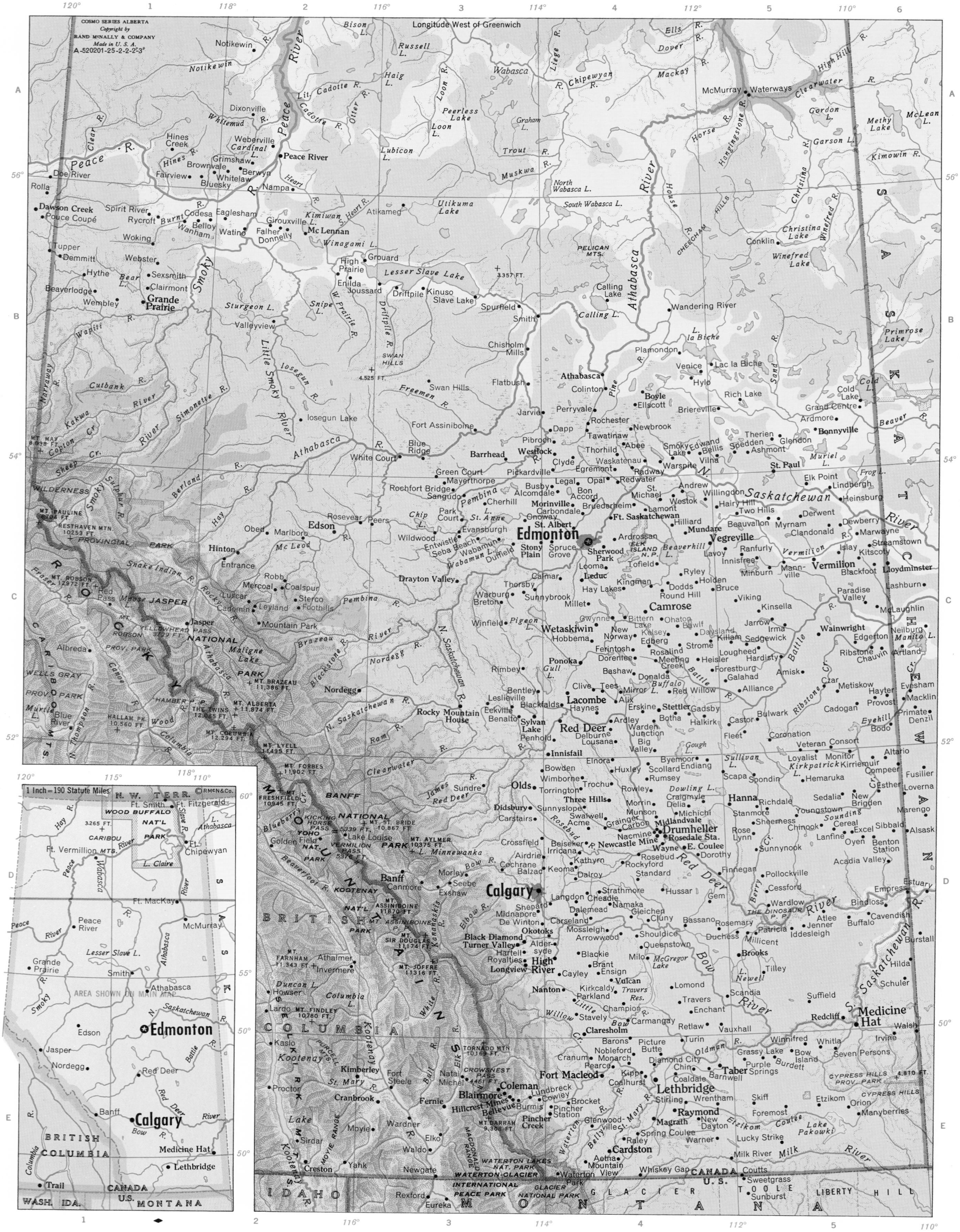

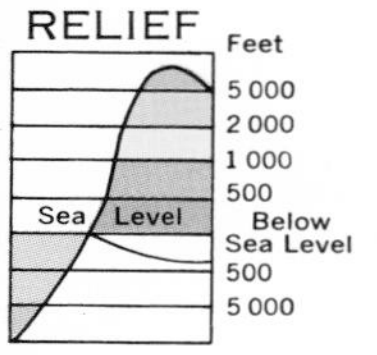

Statute Miles 10 0 10 20 30 40 50 60 70

Kilometers 10 0 10 20 40 60 80 100

Oblique Cylindrical Projection

SCALE 1:3,110,000 1 Inch = 49 Statute Miles

RELIEF

Feet
5,000
2,000
1,000
500
Sea Level
Below
Sea Level
500
5,000

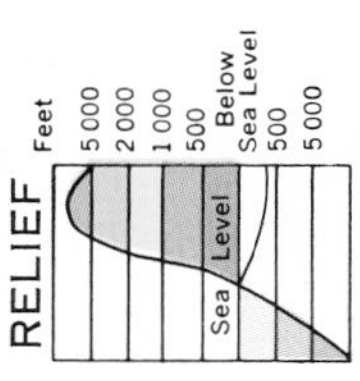

Oblique Cylindrical Projection
SCALE 1:4,255,000 1 Inch = 67 Statute Miles

Statute Miles 10 0 10 20 30 40 50 60 70 80 90 100
Kilometers 10 0 10 20 40 60 80 100 120 140

1 Inch = 315 Statute Miles

1 Inch = 33.3 Statute Miles

Longitude West of Greenwich

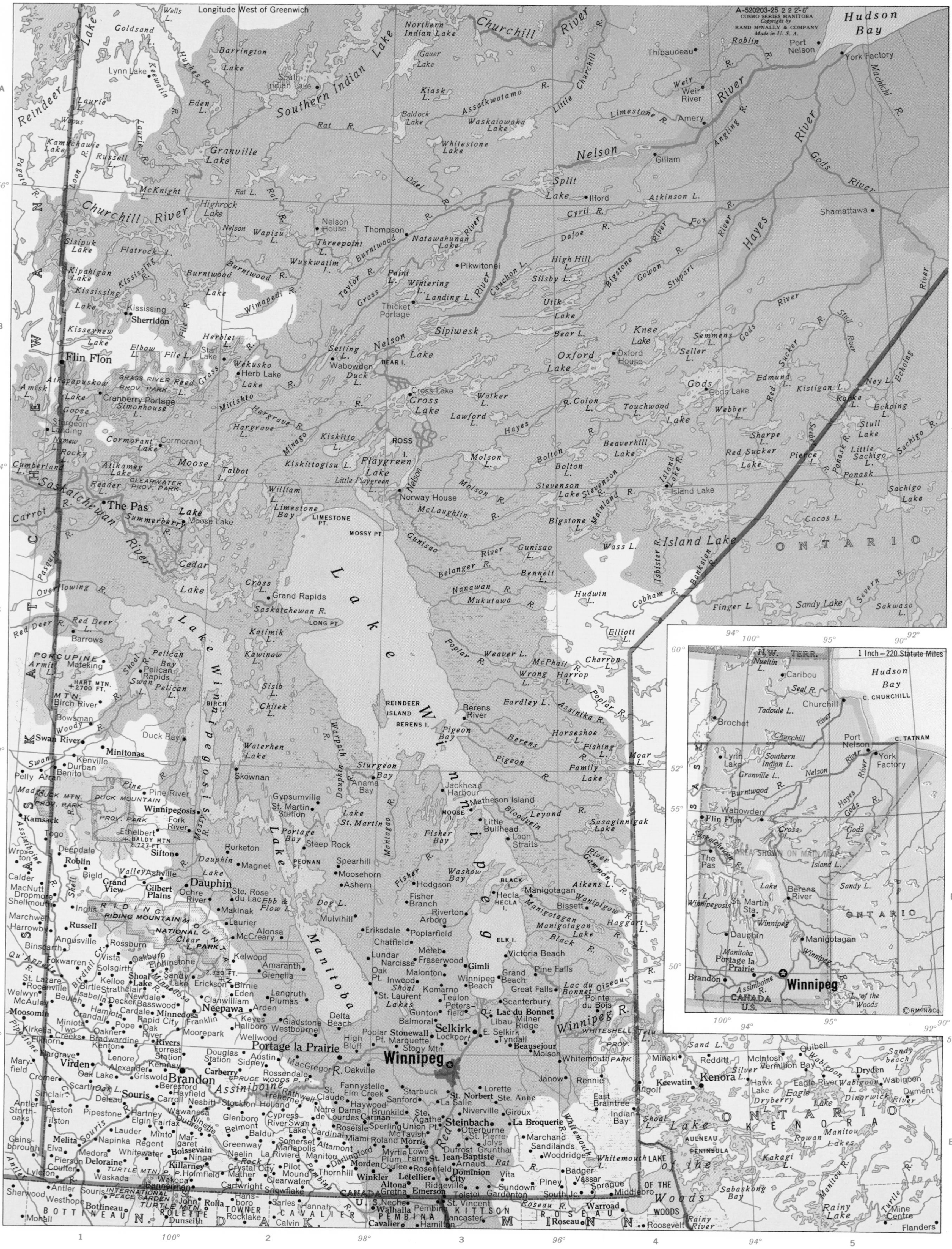

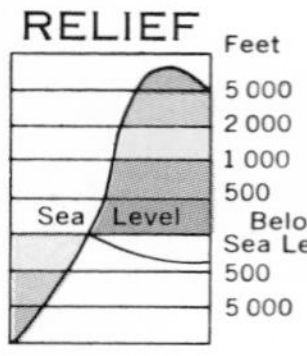

Statute Miles 10 0 10 20 30 40 50 60 70

Kilometers 10 0 10 20 40 60 80 100

Oblique Cylindrical Projection

SCALE 1:3,167,000 1 Inch = 50 Statute Miles

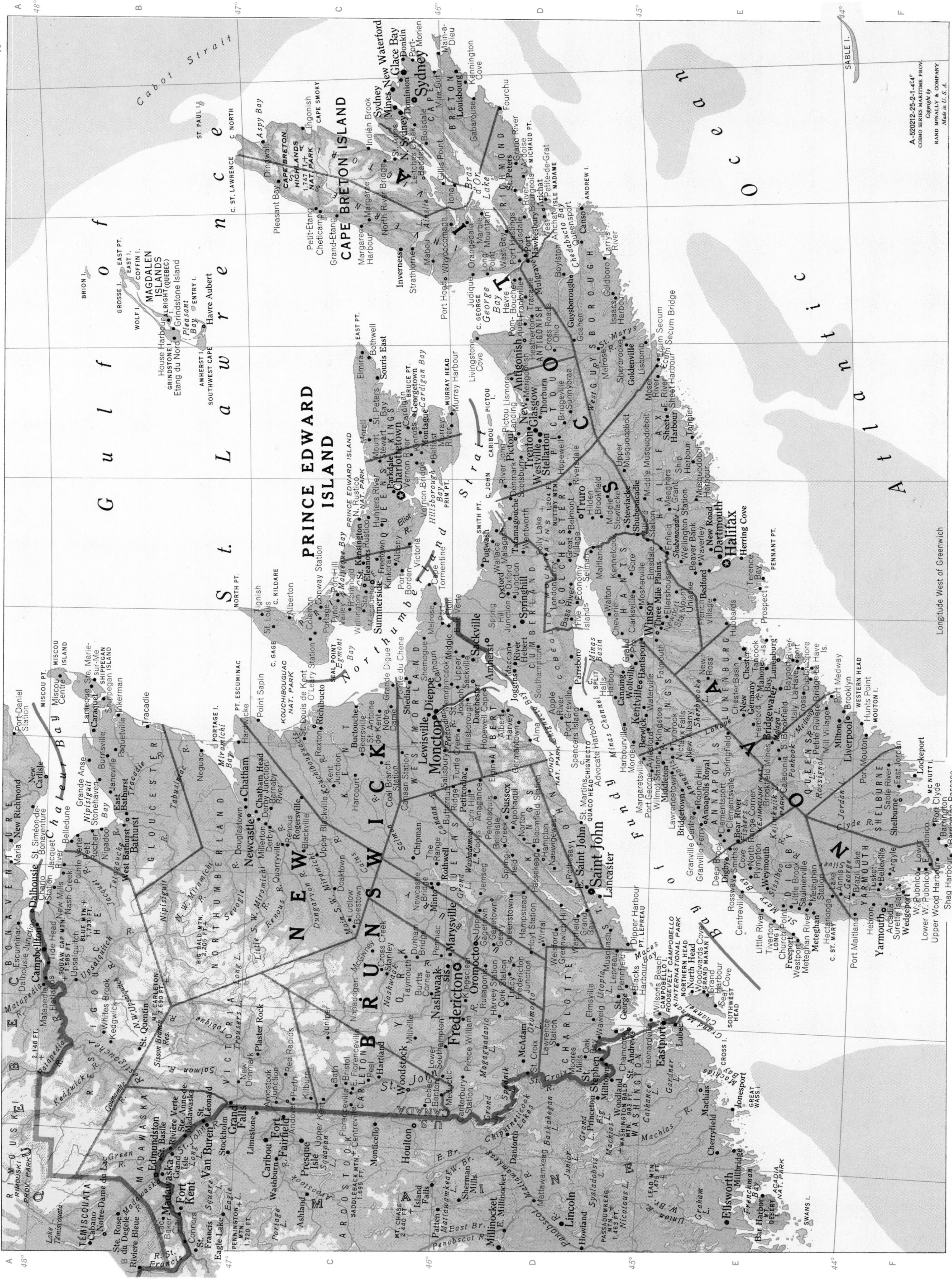

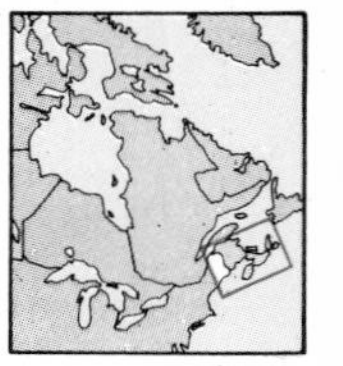

Oblique Cylindrical Projection
SCALE 1:2,312,000 1 Inch = 36.5 Statute Miles

Statute Miles 5 0 5 10 20 30 40 50
Kilometers 5 0 5 15 25 35 45 55 65 75

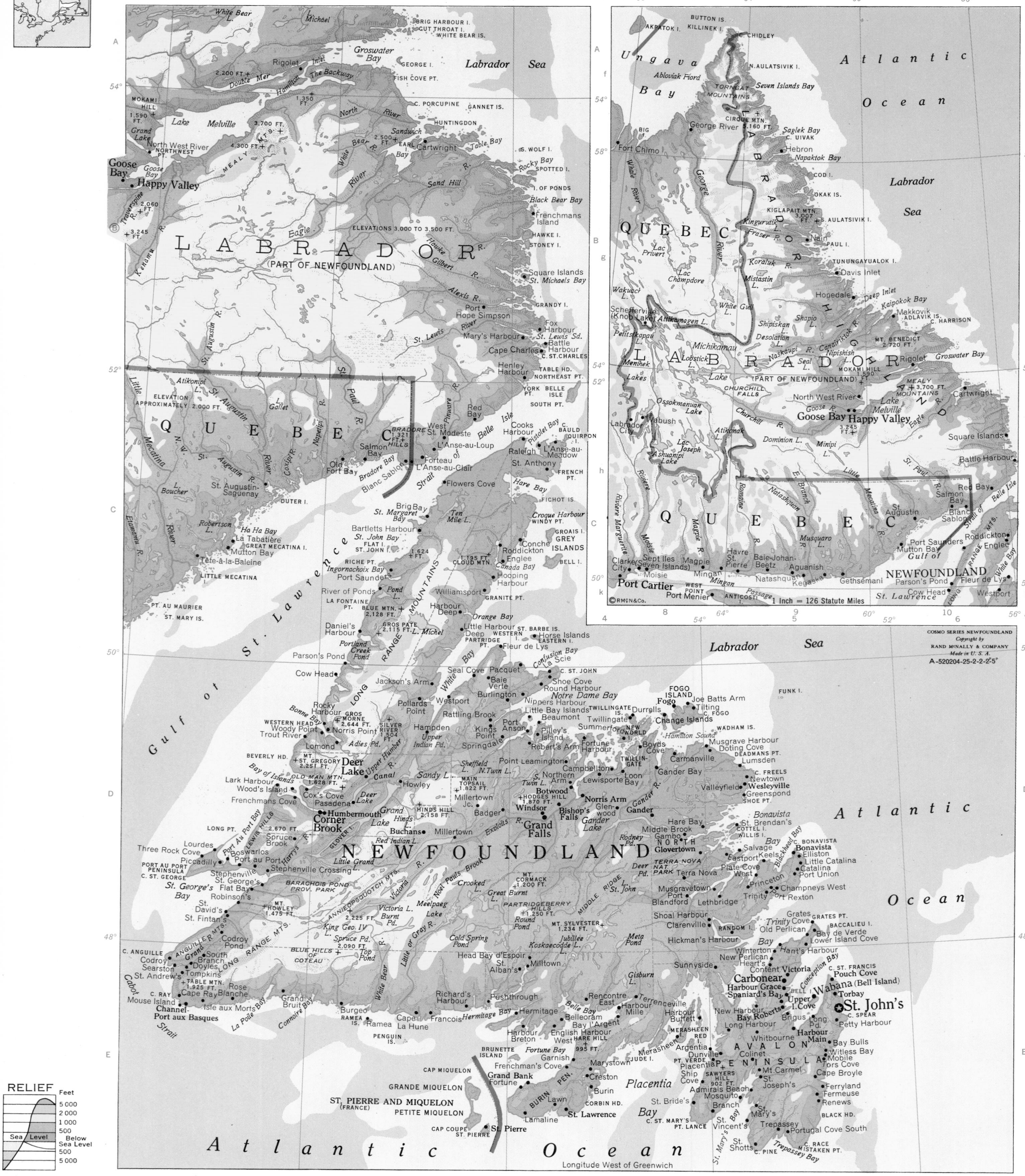

Statute Miles 5 0 5 10 20 30 40 50 60

Kilometers 5 0 5 10 20 30 40 50 60 70 80

Lambert Conformal Conic Projection

SCALE 1 : 3,000,000 1 Inch = 47 Statute Miles

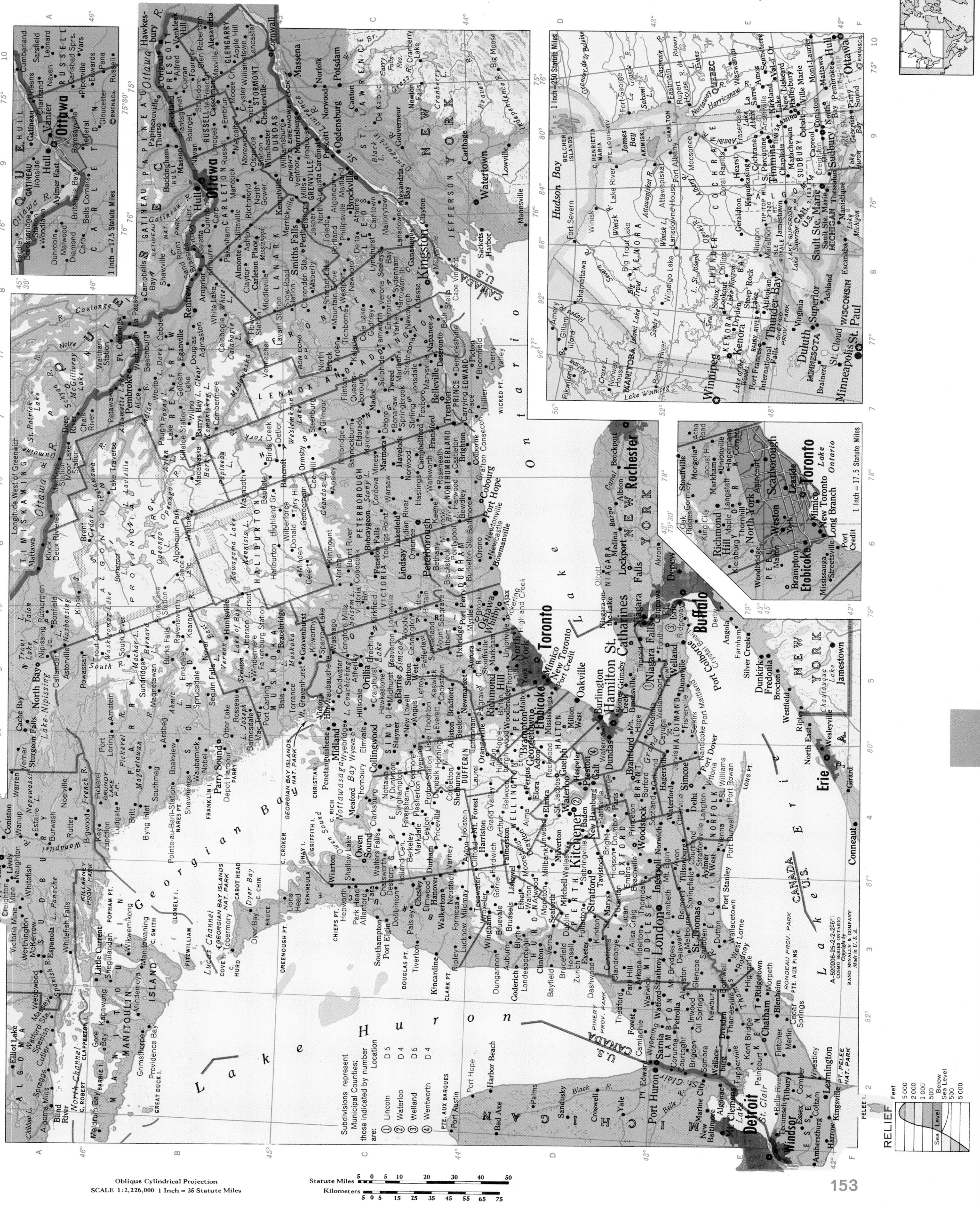
Subdivisions represent Municipal Counties; those indicated by number are:
Location
1 Lincoln D 5
2 Waterloo D 4
3 Welland D 5
4 Wentworth D 4
1 Inch = 17.5 Statute Miles
1 Inch = 250 Statute Miles
RELIEF
Feet
5 000
2 000
1 000
500
Sea Level
Below Sea Level
Oblique Cylindrical Projection
SCALE 1:2,226,000 1 Inch = 35 Statute Miles
Statute Miles
Kilometers
A-520206-25-2-2-
COSMO SERIES ONTARIO
RAND McNALLY & COMPANY
Made in U.S.A.

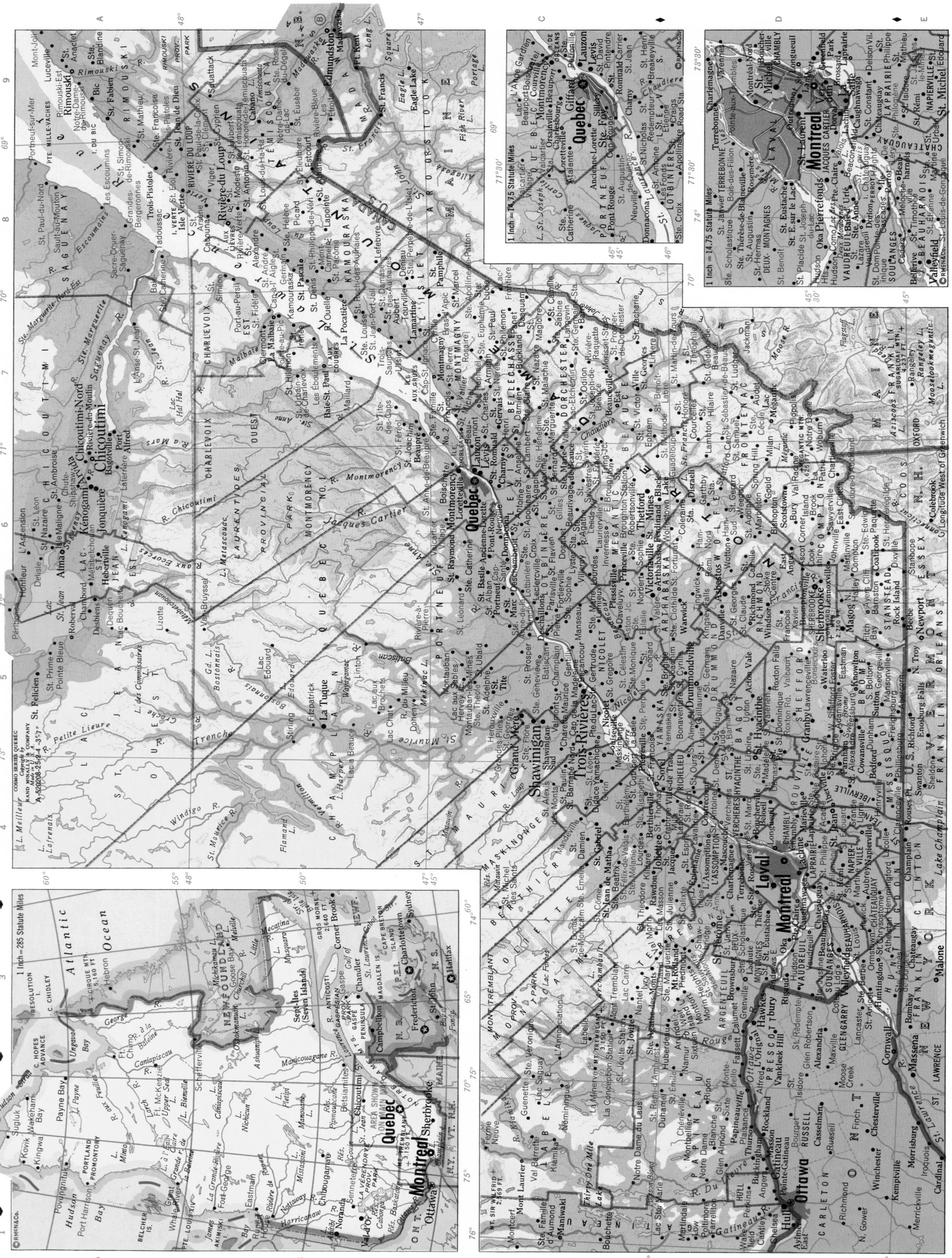

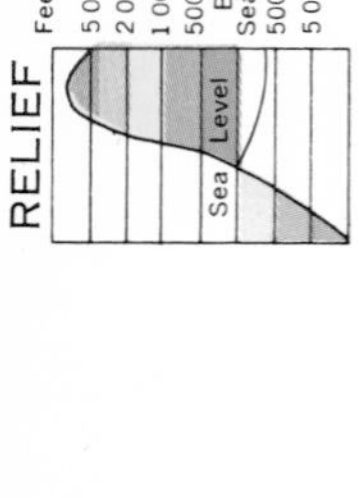

Statute Miles 5 0 5 10 20 30 40
Kilometers 5 0 5 15 25 35 45 55

Oblique Cylindrical Projection
SCALE 1:1,929,000 1 Inch = 30.5 Statute Miles

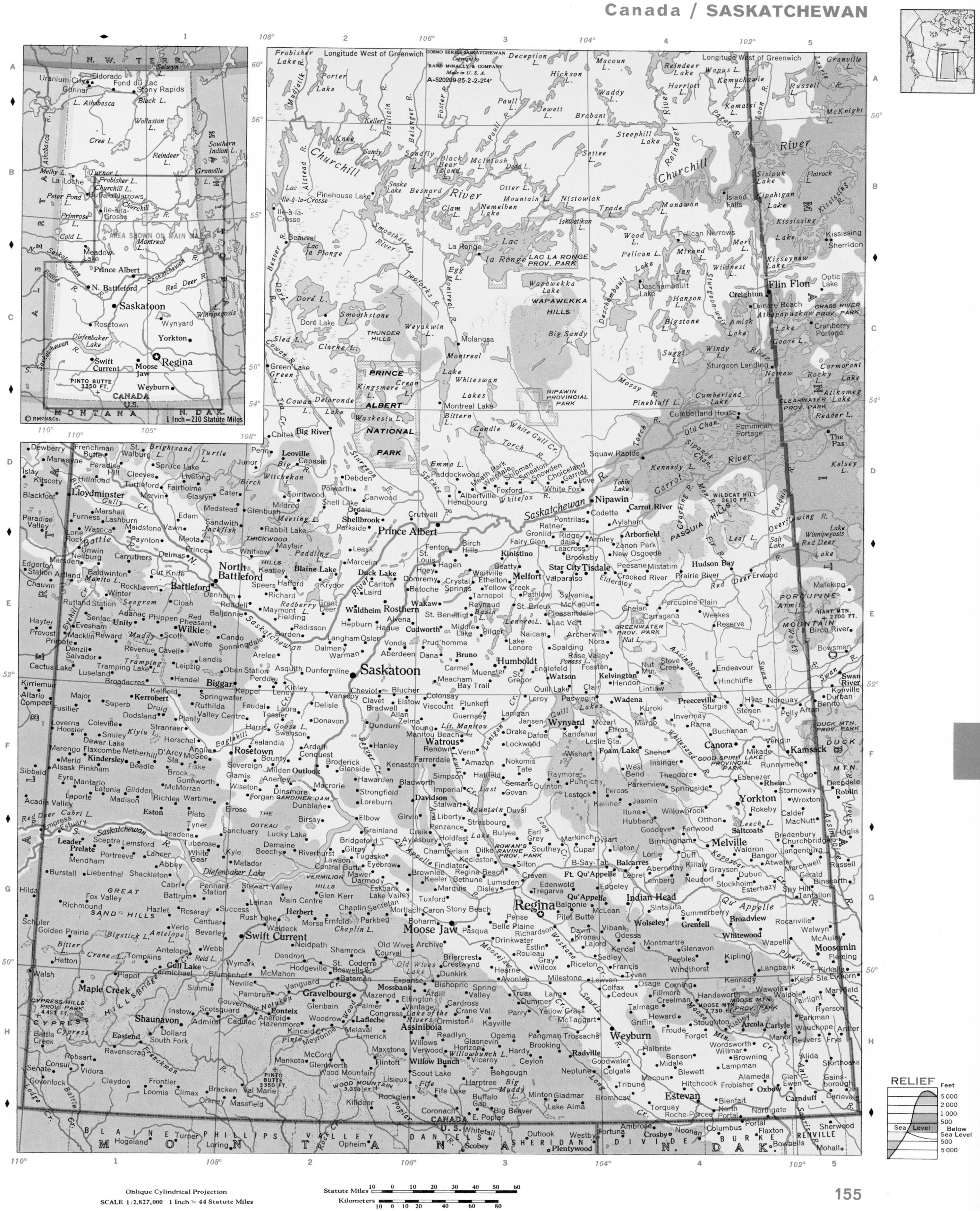
Longitude West of Greenwich
COSMO SERIES SASKATCHEWAN
Copyright by
RAND McNALLY & COMPANY
Made in U. S. A.
A-520209-25-2-2-2-4"
AREA SHOWN ON MAIN MAP
PINTO BUTTE 3350 FT.
CANADA
U.S.
MONTANA
N. DAK.
© RMcN&Co.
1 Inch = 210 Statute Miles
Saskatoon
Regina
Prince Albert
N. Battleford
Swift Current
Moose Jaw
Yorkton
Weyburn
Rosetown
Wynyard
Lake Athabasca
Wollaston L.
Reindeer L.
Churchill
Saskatchewan
PRINCE ALBERT NATIONAL PARK
LAC LA RONGE PROV. PARK
NIPAWIN PROVINCIAL PARK
WAPAWEKKA HILLS
THUNDER HILLS
PASQUIA HILLS
WILDCAT HILL 2610 FT.
GREENWATER PROV. PARK
PORCUPINE MOUNTAIN
HART MTN. 2700 FT.
DUCK MTN. PROV. PARK
GOOD SPIRIT LAKE PROVINCIAL PARK
GRASS RIVER PROV. PARK
CLEARWATER PROV. PARK
ROWAN'S RAVINE PROV. PARK
MOOSE MTN. PROV. PARK
MOOSE MTN. 2,730 FT.
CYPRESS HILLS PROV. PARK 4,453 FT.
CYPRESS HILLS
GREAT SAND HILLS
COTEAU HILLS
VERMILION HILLS
WOOD MOUNTAIN 3,350 FT.
PINTO BUTTE 3,350 FT.
Lloydminster
North Battleford
Battleford
Biggar
Kindersley
Rosetown
Swift Current
Maple Creek
Shaunavon
Gravelbourg
Assiniboia
Moose Jaw
Weyburn
Estevan
Melville
Yorkton
Canora
Kamsack
Humboldt
Melfort
Tisdale
Nipawin
Flin Flon
La Ronge
Wynyard
Watrous
Rosthern
Wilkie
Unity
Indian Head
Carlyle
Oxbow
Carnduff
Moosomin
Hudson Bay
Diefenbaker Lake
Lac la Ronge
Cumberland Lake
Last Mountain Lake
Quill Lakes
Old Wives Lake
MONTANA
NORTH DAKOTA
ALBERTA
MANITOBA
RELIEF
Feet
5 000
2 000
1 000
500
Sea Level
Below Sea Level
500
5 000
Oblique Cylindrical Projection
SCALE 1:2,827,000 1 Inch = 44 Statute Miles
Statute Miles 10 0 10 20 30 40 50 60
Kilometers 10 0 10 20 40 60 80

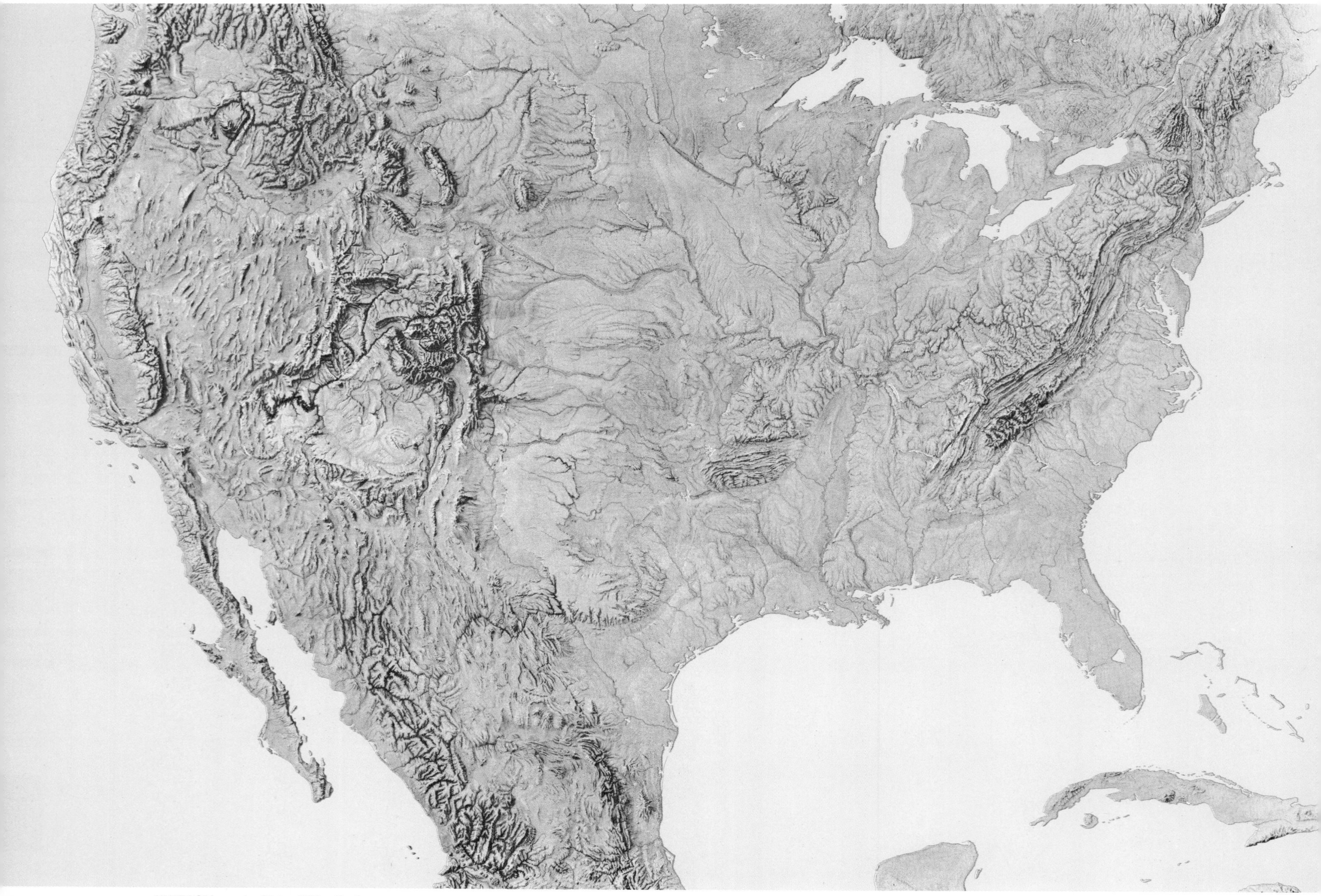

NYSTROM map by Richard Edes Harrison

UNITED STATES

The fifty states of the United States make up the world's leading industrial nation. Forty-nine of the states lie on the mainland of North America, between the Atlantic Ocean on the east and the Pacific Ocean on the west. The fiftieth state, Hawaii, is an island group in the Pacific Ocean about 2,000 miles from the North American mainland. The United States has two great neighbors in North America—Canada to the north and Mexico to the south. The pioneer Americans found a rugged land rich in natural resources. The favorable climate, the fertile soil, the abundant minerals, and the energetic people have combined to make the United States a leader of the free nations of the world.

WHAT IS YOUR ATLAS I.Q. OF THE UNITED STATES?

These questions are designed to test your knowledge of the variety of information about the United States contained in THE WORLD BOOK ATLAS. Check your answers by turning to the last page of the ATLAS.

Identifying places

1. Hawaii is the southernmost state and Alaska is the northernmost state. What state extends farthest west?
2. Texas, Louisiana, Mississippi, and Florida border the Gulf of Mexico. What other state is also on the Gulf?
3. Superior, Huron, Michigan, and Ontario are four of the five Great Lakes. What is the fifth one?
4. The Mississippi River originates in Minnesota. In what state does it enter the Gulf of Mexico?
5. Denver, the *Mile High City*, stands at the eastern side of what great mountain range?
6. Mount McKinley is the highest mountain in the United States. In what state is it located?
7. Which city is farthest west—Detroit, Chicago, or Atlanta?
8. Mexico and Canada border the United States. What foreign country is the next closest neighbor?

Facts and figures

9. Four states border Lake Erie. Two of them are Ohio and New York. What are the other two states?
10. Three countries in the world are larger in area than the United States. Two of these are China and Russia. What is the third?
11. Tennessee shares a common border with eight states. What are the eight states?
12. Alaska is the smallest state in population. What is the smallest state in area?
13. Alaska has the lowest population density of any state—less than one person per square mile. Which state has the highest population density?
14. Only four state capitals were named for Presidents of the United States. Three of these are Jackson, Miss., Madison, Wis., and Jefferson City, Mo. What is the fourth?
15. California and New York rank highest among the states in gross national product. What state ranks third?

History

16. Settlers made several trails famous in their movement to the West—the Oregon Trail, the Santa Fe Trail, and the California Trail. From which town in Illinois did the Mormons start their trail westward in 1846?
17. Two New England states were not included in the original thirteen states. One was Maine. What was the other?
18. The United States obtained Florida from Spain and Louisiana from France. From what country did it obtain California?
19. The Civil War Battle of Bull Run was fought in Virginia and the Battle of Antietam was fought in Maryland. In which state was the Battle of Gettysburg fought?
20. Five slave states did not secede from the Union during the Civil War. Four of these were Delaware, Maryland, West Virginia, and Kentucky. What was the fifth state?

MAPS OF THE UNITED STATES

158-159 PHYSICAL FEATURES OF THE UNITED STATES
160-161 POLITICAL DIVISIONS OF THE UNITED STATES
162-164 HISTORY OF THE UNITED STATES
162 COLONIAL AND REVOLUTIONARY PERIOD
163 WESTWARD EXPANSION
164 CIVIL WAR
165 REGIONS OF THE UNITED STATES
166-213 MAPS OF THE STATES
166 ALABAMA
167 ALASKA
168 ARIZONA
169 ARKANSAS
170 CALIFORNIA
171 COLORADO
172 CONNECTICUT
173 DELAWARE
174 FLORIDA
175 GEORGIA
176 HAWAII
177 IDAHO
178 ILLINOIS
179 INDIANA
180 IOWA
181 KANSAS
182 KENTUCKY
183 LOUISIANA
184 MAINE
173 MARYLAND
185 MASSACHUSETTS
186 MICHIGAN
187 MINNESOTA
188 MISSISSIPPI
189 MISSOURI
190 MONTANA
191 NEBRASKA
192 NEVADA
193 NEW HAMPSHIRE
194 NEW JERSEY
195 NEW MEXICO
196 NEW YORK
197 NORTH CAROLINA
198 NORTH DAKOTA
199 OHIO
200 OKLAHOMA
201 OREGON
202 PENNSYLVANIA
172 RHODE ISLAND
203 SOUTH CAROLINA
204 SOUTH DAKOTA
205 TENNESSEE
206 TEXAS
207 UTAH
208 VERMONT
209 VIRGINIA
210 WASHINGTON
211 WEST VIRGINIA
212 WISCONSIN
213 WYOMING

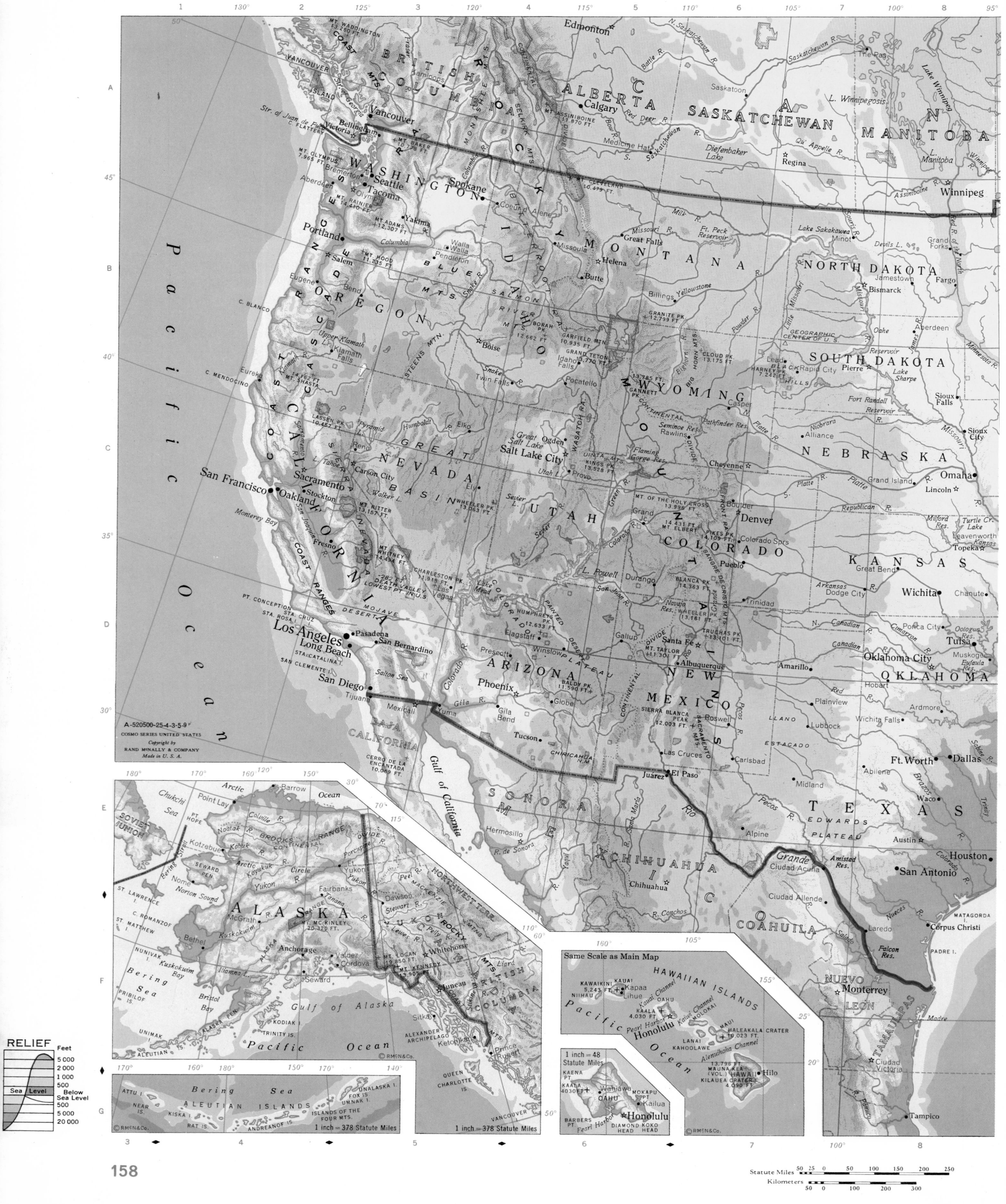

British Columbia
Alberta
Saskatchewan
Manitoba
Washington
Oregon
California
Nevada
Idaho
Montana
Wyoming
Utah
Colorado
Arizona
New Mexico
North Dakota
South Dakota
Nebraska
Kansas
Oklahoma
Texas
Sonora
Chihuahua
Coahuila
Nuevo León
Tamaulipas
Baja California
Pacific Ocean
Gulf of California
Edmonton
Calgary
Saskatoon
Regina
Winnipeg
Vancouver
Victoria
Bellingham
Seattle
Tacoma
Spokane
Yakima
Portland
Salem
Eugene
Boise
Helena
Butte
Missoula
Great Falls
Billings
Bismarck
Fargo
Pierre
Rapid City
Sioux Falls
Casper
Cheyenne
Salt Lake City
Ogden
Provo
Reno
Carson City
Sacramento
San Francisco
Oakland
Stockton
Fresno
Los Angeles
Long Beach
Pasadena
San Bernardino
San Diego
Tijuana
Las Vegas
Phoenix
Tucson
Flagstaff
Prescott
Yuma
Denver
Boulder
Colorado Sprs
Pueblo
Santa Fe
Albuquerque
Las Cruces
El Paso
Juárez
Omaha
Lincoln
Wichita
Topeka
Tulsa
Oklahoma City
Amarillo
Lubbock
Dallas
Ft. Worth
Austin
San Antonio
Houston
Corpus Christi
Laredo
Monterrey
Chihuahua
Hermosillo
Tampico
Great Basin
Great Salt Lake
Columbia R.
Snake R.
Missouri R.
Rio Grande
Coast Mts.
Cascade Range
Sierra Nevada
Coast Ranges
Rocky Mts.
Blue Mts.
Continental Divide
Mojave Desert
Painted Desert
Llano Estacado
Edwards Plateau
Mt. Rainier 14,410 ft.
Mt. Hood 11,235 ft.
Mt. Shasta 14,162 ft.
Mt. Whitney 14,494 ft.
Death Valley −282 ft. Lowest Pt. in U.S.
Mt. Elbert 14,431 ft.
Pikes Pk. 14,109 ft.
Arctic Ocean
Alaska
Anchorage
Fairbanks
Juneau
Nome
Barrow
Mt. McKinley 20,320 ft.
Bering Sea
Gulf of Alaska
Aleutian Islands
Hawaiian Islands
Honolulu
Hilo
Oahu
Mauna Kea 13,796 ft.
Same Scale as Main Map
1 inch = 378 Statute Miles
1 inch = 48 Statute Miles
A-520500-25-4-3-5-9
Cosmo Series United States
Copyright by Rand McNally & Company
Made in U. S. A.
RELIEF
Feet
5 000
2 000
1 000
500
Sea Level
Below Sea Level
500
5 000
20 000
Statute Miles 50 25 0 50 100 150 200 250
Kilometers 50 0 100 200 300

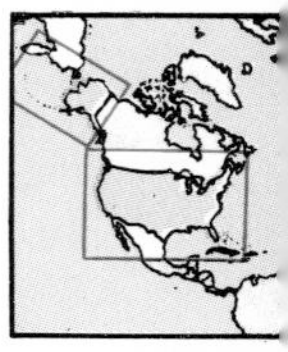

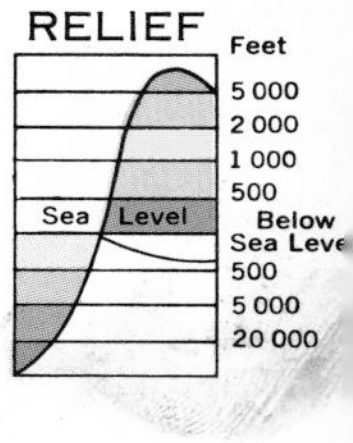

Lambert Conformal Conic Projection
SCALE 1:12,000,000 1 Inch = 189 Statute Miles

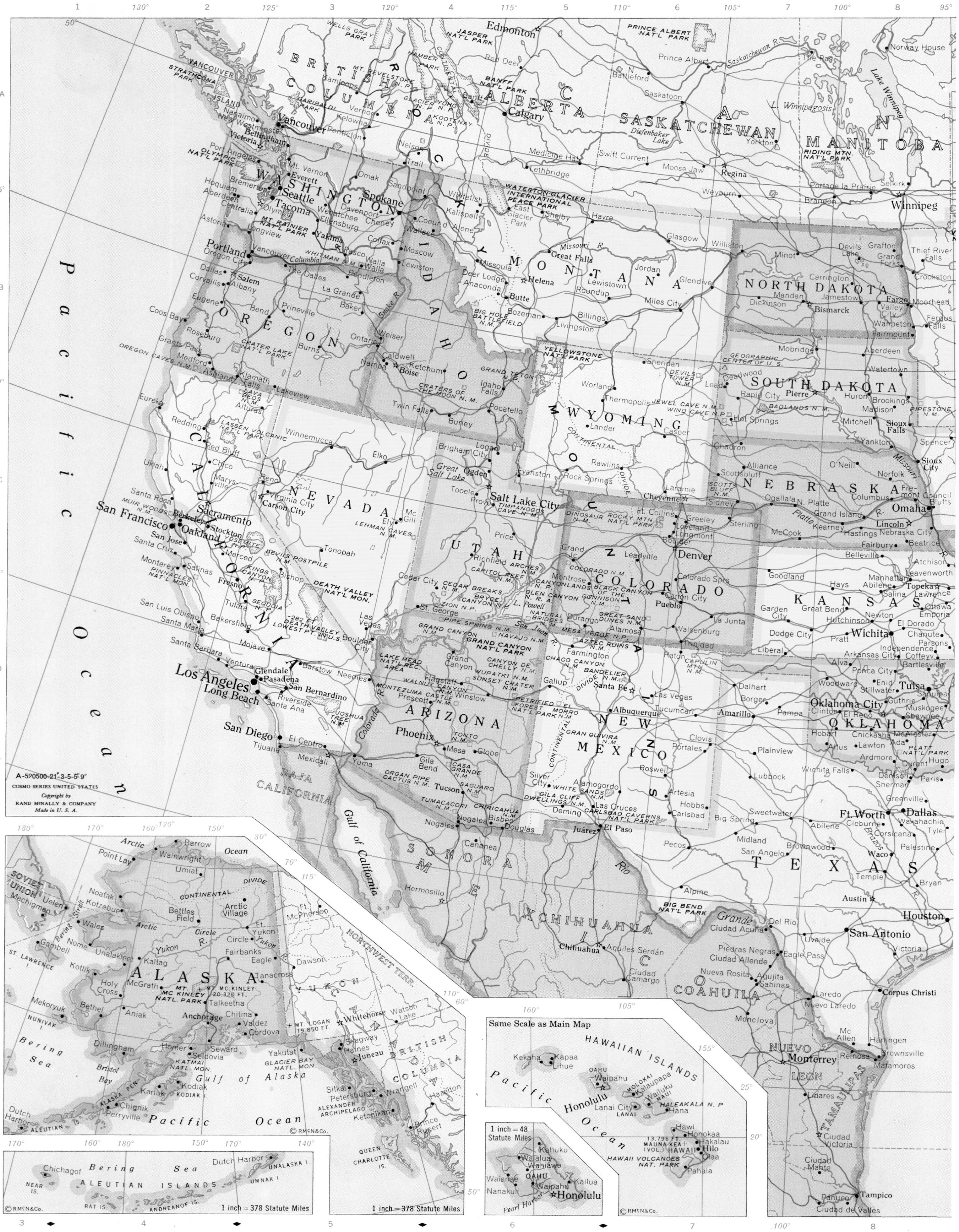

Statute Miles 50 25 0 50 100 150 200 250

Kilometers 50 0 100 200 300

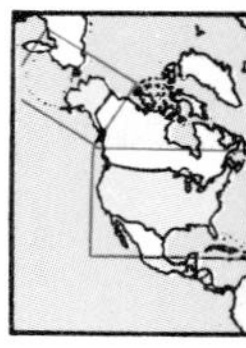

Lambert Conformal Conic Projection
SCALE 1:12,000,000 1 Inch = 189 Statute Miles

BRITISH NORTH AMERICA
After the Seven Years' War
MILES 0 50 100 200 300
Approximate extent of settlement, 1690
Approximate extent of settlement 1760
Boston 1630 Town, with date of first settlement
Proclamation Line of 1763
Limit of British territory
HUDSON'S BAY COMPANY
QUEBEC
LOUISIANA (To Spain)
RESERVED FOR INDIANS
WEST FLORIDA
EAST FLORIDA
MAINE DIST. (MASS.)
NOVA SCOTIA
NEW YORK
PENNSYLVANIA
VIRGINIA
NORTH CAROLINA
SOUTH CAROLINA
GEORGIA
Quebec 1608
Montreal 1642
Port Royal 1605
Halifax
Salem 1626
Boston 1630
Plymouth 1620
Providence 1636
Hartford 1636
New York 1626-64 (Nieu Amsterdam)
Philadelphia 1682
Baltimore 1745
Richmond 1609
Jamestown 1607
Charleston 1672
Savannah 1733
St. Augustine 1565
St. Louis 1764
Kaskaskia
Vincennes
Detroit
Ft. Mackinac
Ft. Pitt
Mobile 1702
Pensacola 1698
New Orleans 1718
Gulf of Mexico
Atlantic Ocean

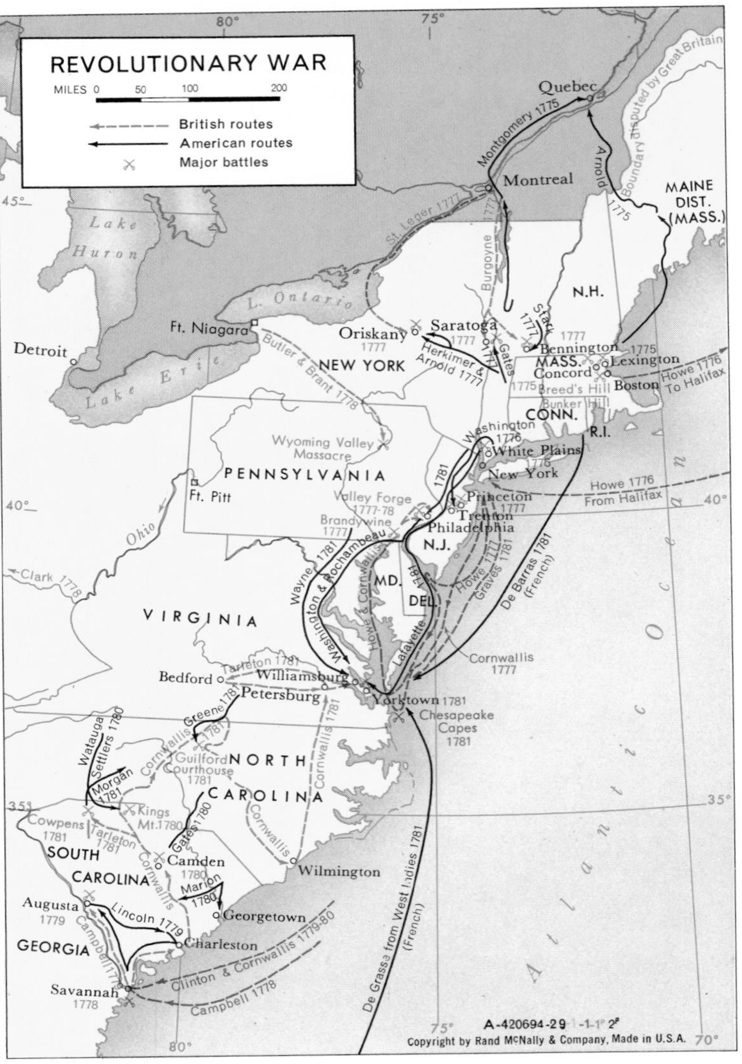
REVOLUTIONARY WAR
MILES 0 50 100 200
British routes
American routes
Major battles
Quebec
Montreal
Montgomery 1775
Arnold 1775
MAINE DIST. (MASS.)
N.H.
NEW YORK
PENNSYLVANIA
VIRGINIA
NORTH CAROLINA
SOUTH CAROLINA
GEORGIA
Saratoga 1777
Oriskany 1777
Bennington 1777
Lexington 1775
Concord 1775
Boston
Bunker Hill
Ft. Niagara
Detroit
Wyoming Valley Massacre
Ft. Pitt
Valley Forge 1777-78
Brandywine 1777
Princeton 1777
Trenton 1776
White Plains 1776
New York
Philadelphia
Yorktown 1781
Chesapeake Capes 1781
Cornwallis 1777
Williamsburg
Petersburg
Bedford
Guilford Courthouse 1781
Kings Mt. 1780
Cowpens 1781
Camden 1780
Wilmington
Georgetown
Charleston
Augusta 1779
Savannah 1778
De Grasse from West Indies 1781 (French)
De Barras 1781 (French)
Howe 1776 From Halifax
A-420694-29
Copyright by Rand McNally & Company, Made in U.S.A.

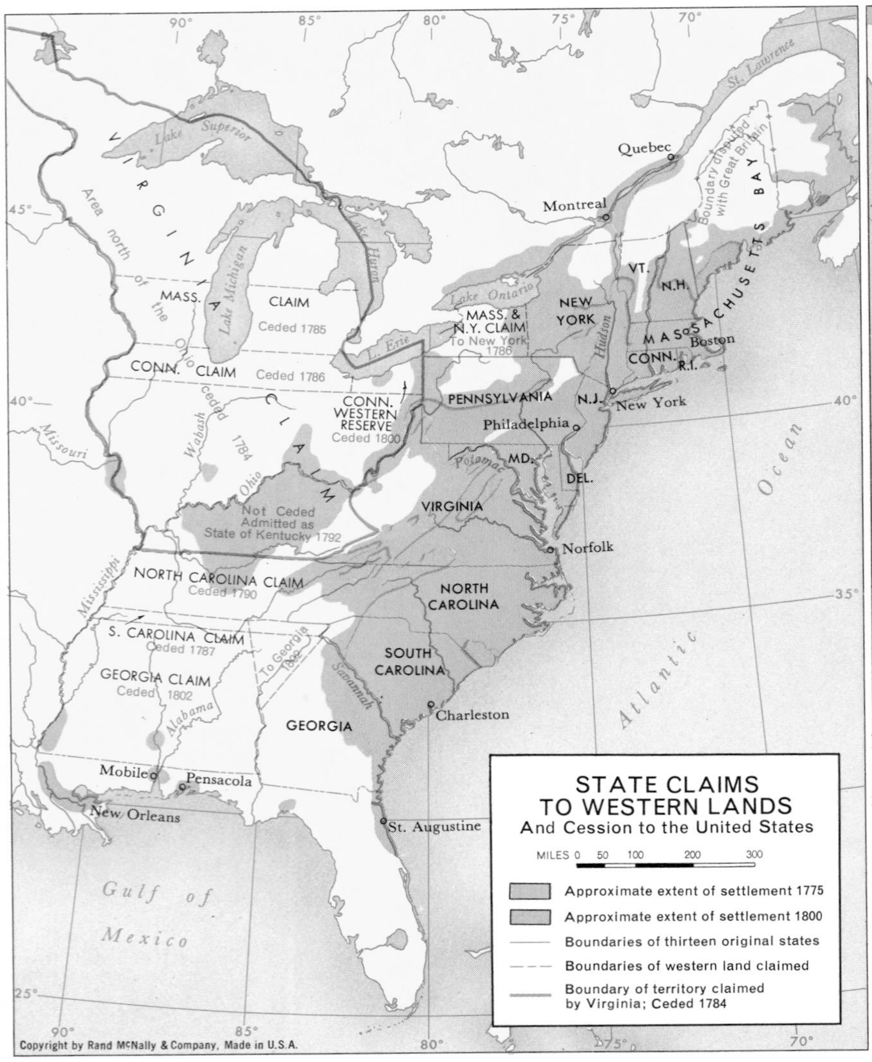
STATE CLAIMS TO WESTERN LANDS
And Cession to the United States
MILES 0 50 100 200 300
Approximate extent of settlement 1775
Approximate extent of settlement 1800
Boundaries of thirteen original states
Boundaries of western land claimed
Boundary of territory claimed by Virginia; Ceded 1784
VIRGINIA CLAIM
MASS. CLAIM Ceded 1785
CONN. CLAIM Ceded 1786
CONN. WESTERN RESERVE Ceded 1800
MASS. & N.Y. CLAIM To New York 1786
Not Ceded Admitted as State of Kentucky 1792
NORTH CAROLINA CLAIM Ceded 1790
S. CAROLINA CLAIM Ceded 1787
GEORGIA CLAIM Ceded 1802
Quebec
Montreal
VT.
N.H.
MASSACHUSETTS
NEW YORK
PENNSYLVANIA
VIRGINIA
NORTH CAROLINA
SOUTH CAROLINA
GEORGIA
Boston
New York
Philadelphia
Norfolk
Charleston
St. Augustine
Mobile
Pensacola
New Orleans
Gulf of Mexico
Atlantic Ocean
Copyright by Rand McNally & Company, Made in U.S.A.

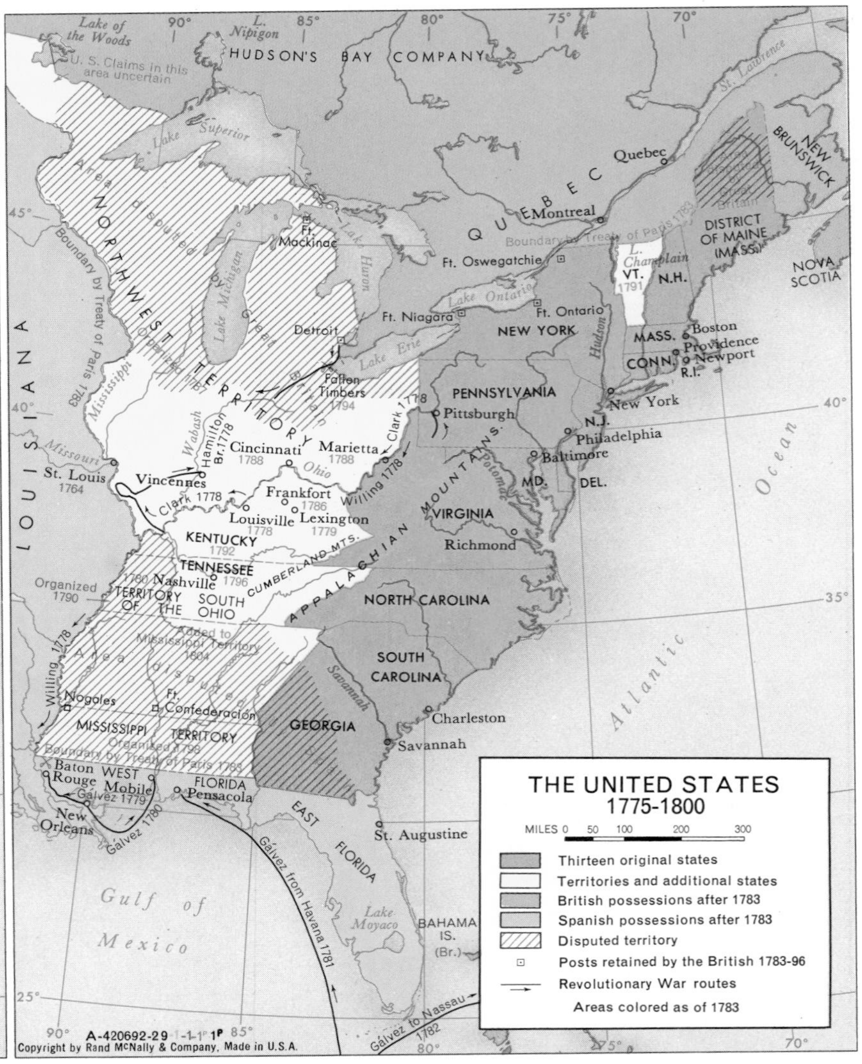
THE UNITED STATES 1775-1800
MILES 0 50 100 200 300
Thirteen original states
Territories and additional states
British possessions after 1783
Spanish possessions after 1783
Disputed territory
Posts retained by the British 1783-96
Revolutionary War routes
Areas colored as of 1783
HUDSON'S BAY COMPANY
QUEBEC
LOUISIANA
NORTHWEST TERRITORY
KENTUCKY 1792
TENNESSEE 1796
TERRITORY SOUTH OF THE OHIO
MISSISSIPPI TERRITORY
WEST FLORIDA
EAST FLORIDA
DISTRICT OF MAINE (MASS.)
NEW BRUNSWICK
NOVA SCOTIA
VT. 1791
N.H.
MASS.
CONN.
R.I.
NEW YORK
PENNSYLVANIA
N.J.
MD.
DEL.
VIRGINIA
NORTH CAROLINA
SOUTH CAROLINA
GEORGIA
Fallen Timbers 1794
Cincinnati 1788
Marietta 1788
Vincennes
St. Louis 1764
Frankfort 1786
Louisville 1778
Lexington 1779
Nashville 1780
Detroit
Ft. Mackinac
Ft. Niagara
Ft. Oswegatchie
Ft. Ontario
Pittsburgh
Baltimore
Philadelphia
New York
Boston
Providence
Newport
Richmond
Charleston
Savannah
St. Augustine
Nogales
Baton Rouge
Mobile
Pensacola
New Orleans
Gálvez from Havana 1781
BAHAMA IS. (Br.)
Gulf of Mexico
Atlantic Ocean
A-420692-29
Copyright by Rand McNally & Company, Made in U.S.A.

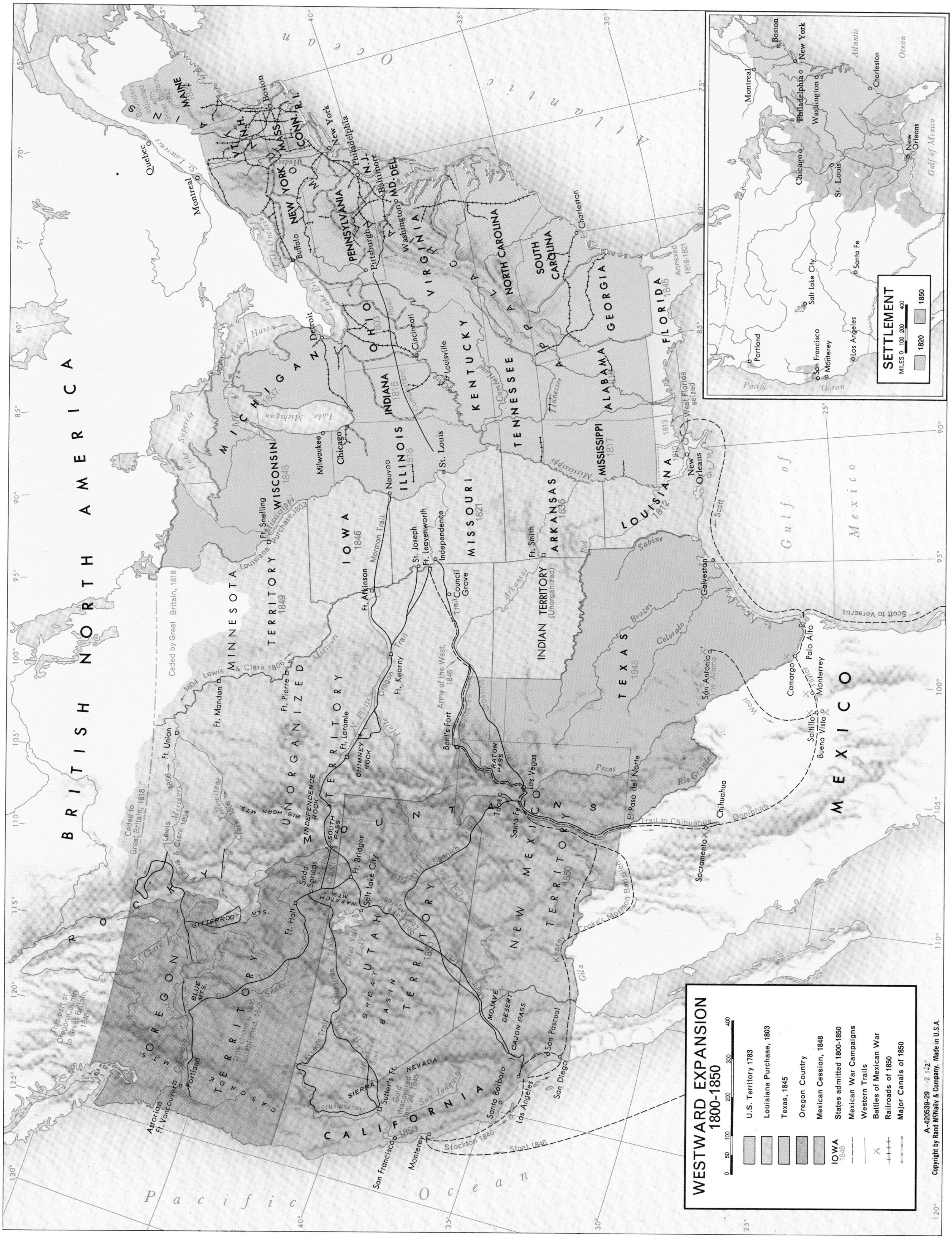
WESTWARD EXPANSION
1800-1850
U.S. Territory 1783
Louisiana Purchase, 1803
Texas, 1845
Oregon Country
Mexican Cession, 1848
States admitted 1800-1850
Mexican War Campaigns
Western Trails
Battles of Mexican War
Railroads of 1850
Major Canals of 1850
SETTLEMENT
1820
1850
BRITISH NORTH AMERICA
MEXICO
Pacific Ocean
Atlantic Ocean
Gulf of Mexico

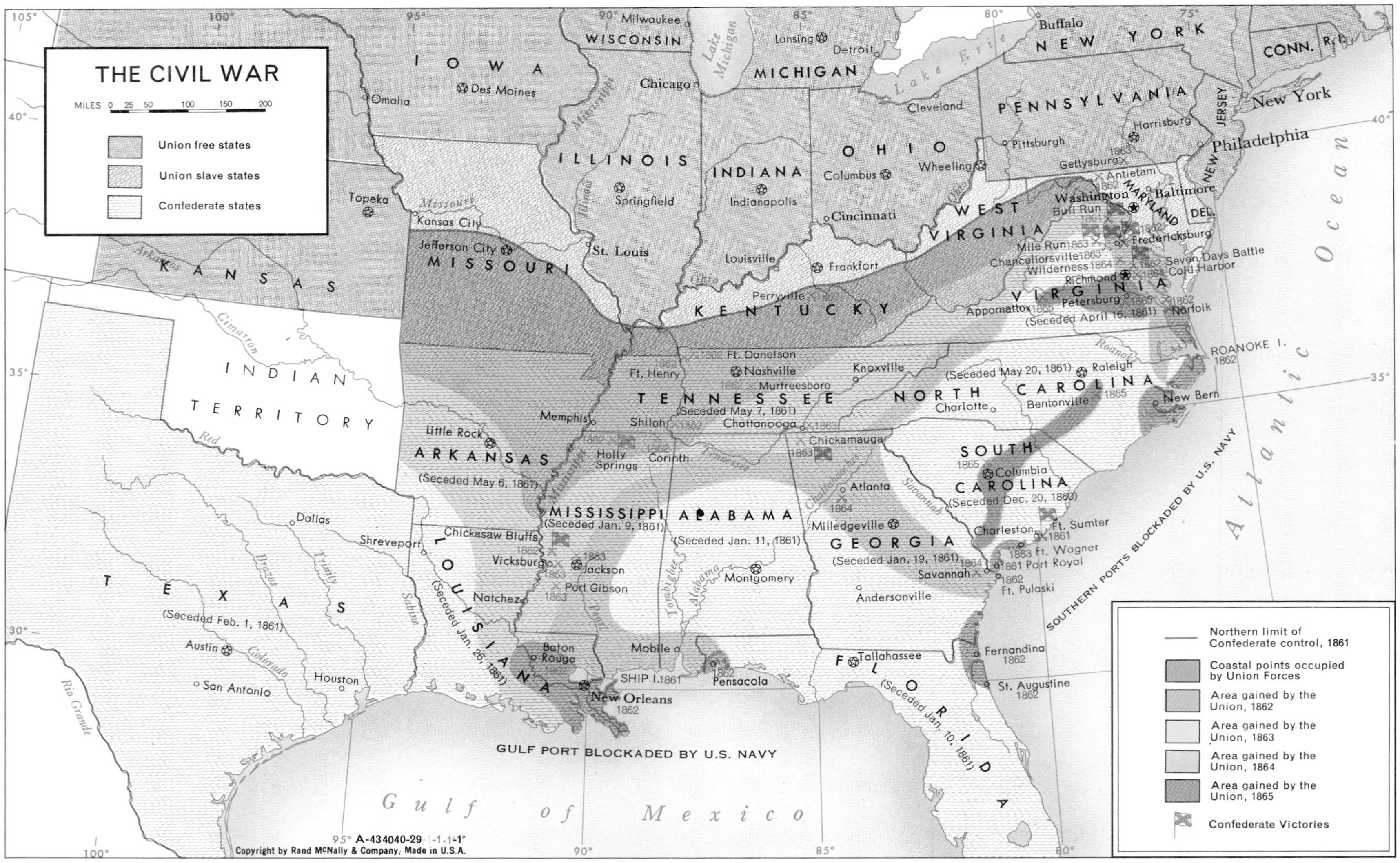
THE CIVIL WAR
MILES 0 25 50 100 150 200
Union free states
Union slave states
Confederate states
Northern limit of Confederate control, 1861
Coastal points occupied by Union Forces
Area gained by the Union, 1862
Area gained by the Union, 1863
Area gained by the Union, 1864
Area gained by the Union, 1865
Confederate Victories
IOWA
Des Moines
Omaha
WISCONSIN
Milwaukee
Chicago
MICHIGAN
Lansing
Detroit
Lake Michigan
Lake Erie
Buffalo
NEW YORK
CONN.
R.I.
New York
PENNSYLVANIA
Cleveland
Pittsburgh
Harrisburg
Philadelphia
NEW JERSEY
ILLINOIS
Springfield
INDIANA
Indianapolis
OHIO
Columbus
Wheeling
Cincinnati
Gettysburg
Antietam
Baltimore
WEST VIRGINIA
Washington
Bull Run
MARYLAND
DEL.
Fredericksburg
Chancellorsville
Wilderness
Mine Run
Seven Days Battle
Cold Harbor
Richmond
VIRGINIA
Petersburg
Appomattox
(Seceded April 16, 1861)
Norfolk
Topeka
Kansas City
Jefferson City
MISSOURI
St. Louis
KANSAS
Louisville
Frankfort
Perryville
KENTUCKY
INDIAN TERRITORY
Ft. Donelson
Ft. Henry
Nashville
Murfreesboro
Knoxville
TENNESSEE
(Seceded May 7, 1861)
Memphis
Shiloh
Chattanooga
Corinth
Holly Springs
Chickamauga
NORTH CAROLINA
(Seceded May 20, 1861)
Raleigh
Charlotte
Bentonville
New Bern
ROANOKE I. 1862
Little Rock
ARKANSAS
(Seceded May 6, 1861)
SOUTH CAROLINA
Columbia
(Seceded Dec. 20, 1860)
Charleston
Ft. Sumter
Ft. Wagner
Port Royal
Ft. Pulaski
Atlanta
Milledgeville
GEORGIA
(Seceded Jan. 19, 1861)
Savannah
Andersonville
MISSISSIPPI
(Seceded Jan. 9, 1861)
ALABAMA
(Seceded Jan. 11, 1861)
Montgomery
Chickasaw Bluffs
Vicksburg
Jackson
Port Gibson
Natchez
Dallas
Shreveport
LOUISIANA
(Seceded Jan. 26, 1861)
TEXAS
(Seceded Feb. 1, 1861)
Austin
San Antonio
Houston
Baton Rouge
New Orleans
SHIP I. 1861
Mobile
Pensacola
Tallahassee
FLORIDA
(Seceded Jan. 10, 1861)
Fernandina
St. Augustine
SOUTHERN PORTS BLOCKADED BY U.S. NAVY
GULF PORT BLOCKADED BY U.S. NAVY
Gulf of Mexico
Atlantic Ocean
A-434040-29
Copyright by Rand McNally & Company, Made in U.S.A.

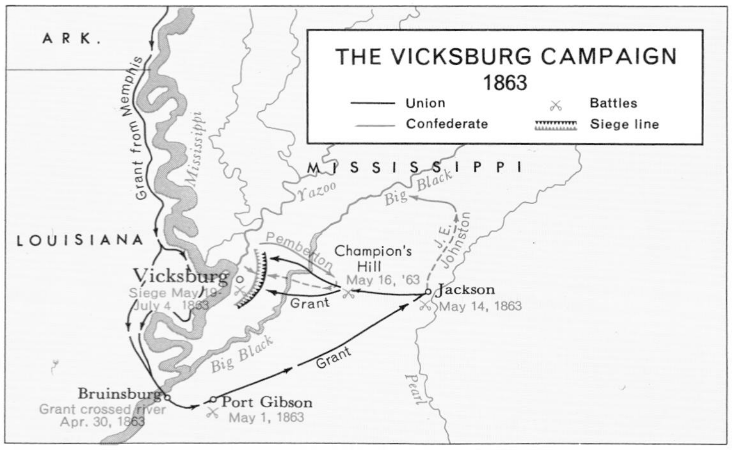
THE VICKSBURG CAMPAIGN
1863
Union
Confederate
Battles
Siege line
ARK.
MISSISSIPPI
LOUISIANA
Grant from Memphis
Vicksburg
Siege May 19-July 4, 1863
Champion's Hill
May 16, '63
Pemberton
J. E. Johnston
Jackson
May 14, 1863
Grant
Big Black
Bruinsburg
Grant crossed river
Apr. 30, 1863
Port Gibson
May 1, 1863

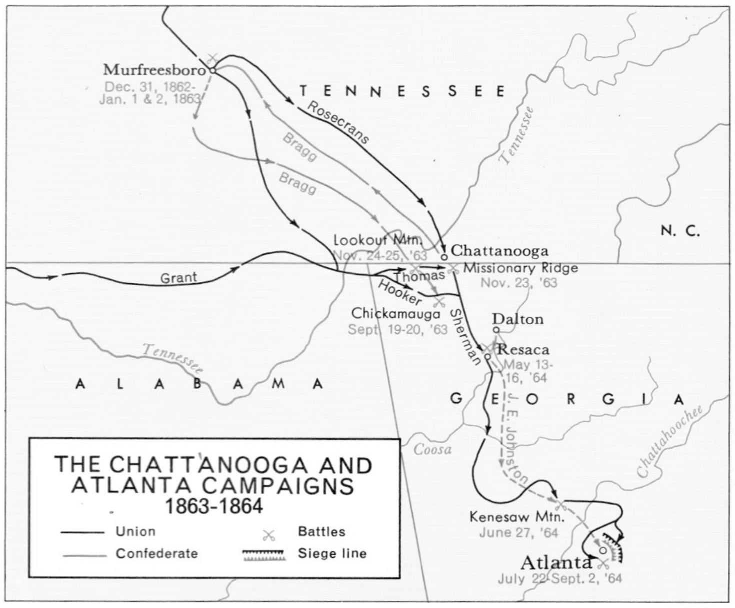
THE CHATTANOOGA AND ATLANTA CAMPAIGNS
1863-1864
Union
Confederate
Battles
Siege line
Murfreesboro
Dec. 31, 1862-Jan. 1 & 2, 1863
TENNESSEE
Rosecrans
Bragg
Lookout Mtn.
Nov. 24-25, '63
Chattanooga
Missionary Ridge
Nov. 23, '63
Thomas
Hooker
Sherman
Grant
N. C.
Chickamauga
Sept. 19-20, '63
Dalton
Resaca
May 13-16, '64
ALABAMA
GEORGIA
J. E. Johnston
Kenesaw Mtn.
June 27, '64
Atlanta
July 22-Sept. 2, '64

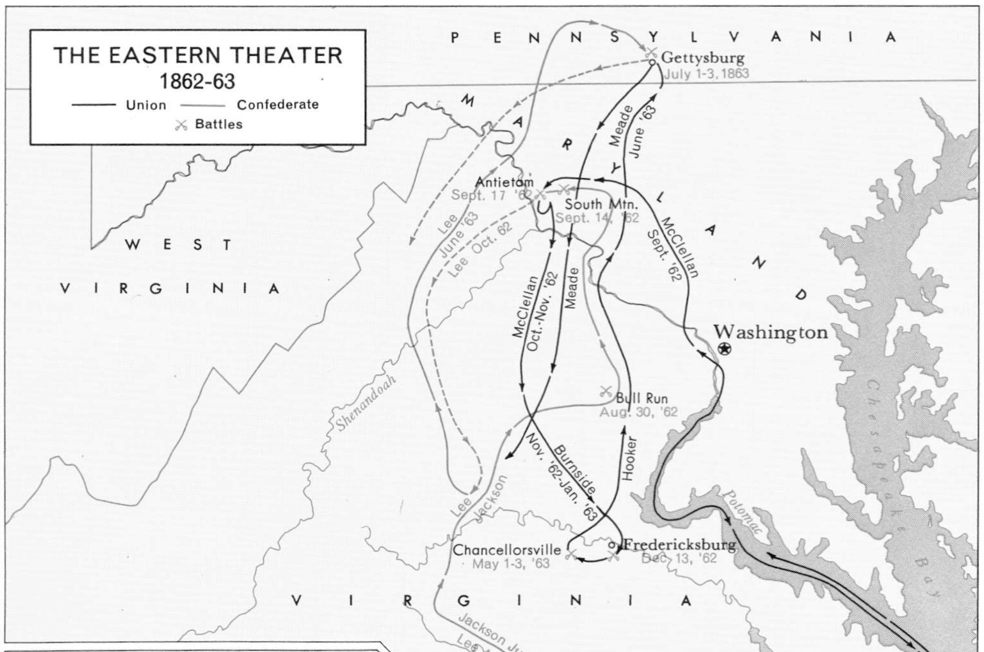
THE EASTERN THEATER
1862-63
Union
Confederate
Battles
PENNSYLVANIA
Gettysburg
July 1-3, 1863
Meade June '63
MARYLAND
Antietam
Sept. 17 '62
South Mtn.
Sept. 14 '62
McClellan Sept. '62
Lee June '63
Lee Oct. '62
WEST VIRGINIA
McClellan Oct.-Nov. '62
Washington
Bull Run
Aug. 30, '62
Burnside Nov. '62-Jan. '63
Hooker
Jackson
Chancellorsville
May 1-3, '63
Fredericksburg
Dec. 13, '62
VIRGINIA
Jackson July '62
Lee Aug. '62
Richmond
Seven Days' Battles
June 26-, '62
McClellan
Johnston May '62
Malvern Hill
July 1, '62
Williamsburg
May 5, '62
McClellan Mar.-May '62
McClellan Aug. '62
Monitor vs. Merrimac
Mar. 9, 1862
A-434340-29
Copyright by Rand McNally & Company, Made in U.S.A.

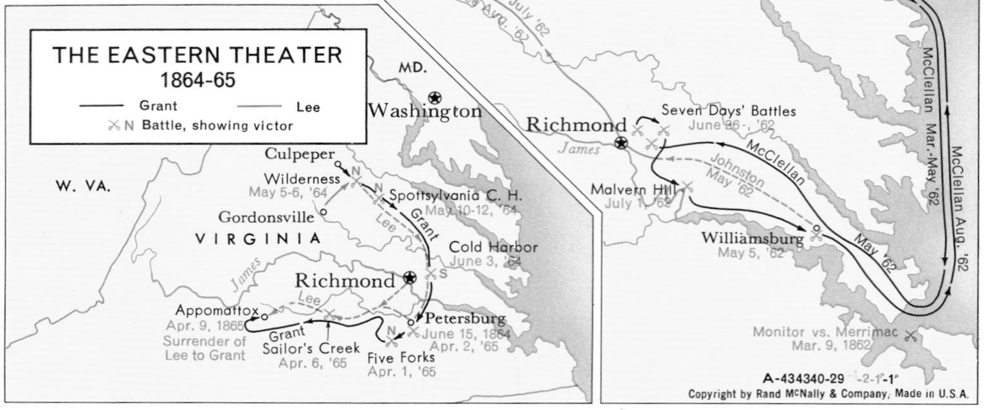
THE EASTERN THEATER
1864-65
Grant
Lee
N Battle, showing victor
MD.
Washington
W. VA.
Culpeper
Wilderness
May 5-6, '64
Spottsylvania C. H.
May 10-12, '64
Gordonsville
VIRGINIA
Cold Harbor
June 3, '64
Richmond
Appomattox
Apr. 9, 1865
Surrender of Lee to Grant
Sailor's Creek
Apr. 6, '65
Petersburg
June 15, 1864-Apr. 2, '65
Five Forks
Apr. 1, '65

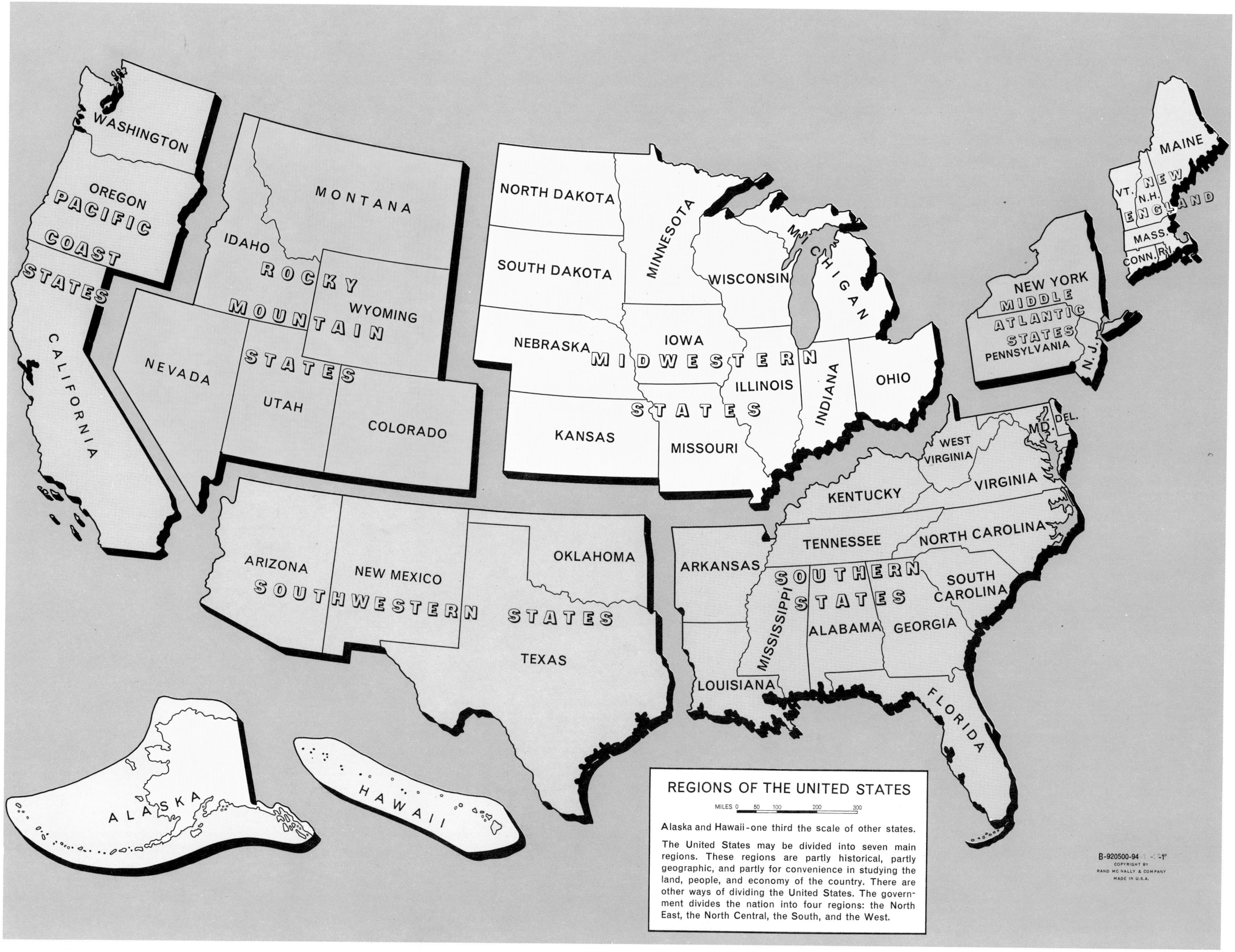

REGIONS OF THE UNITED STATES

MILES 0 50 100 200 300

Alaska and Hawaii-one third the scale of other states.

The United States may be divided into seven main regions. These regions are partly historical, partly geographic, and partly for convenience in studying the land, people, and economy of the country. There are other ways of dividing the United States. The government divides the nation into four regions: the North East, the North Central, the South, and the West.

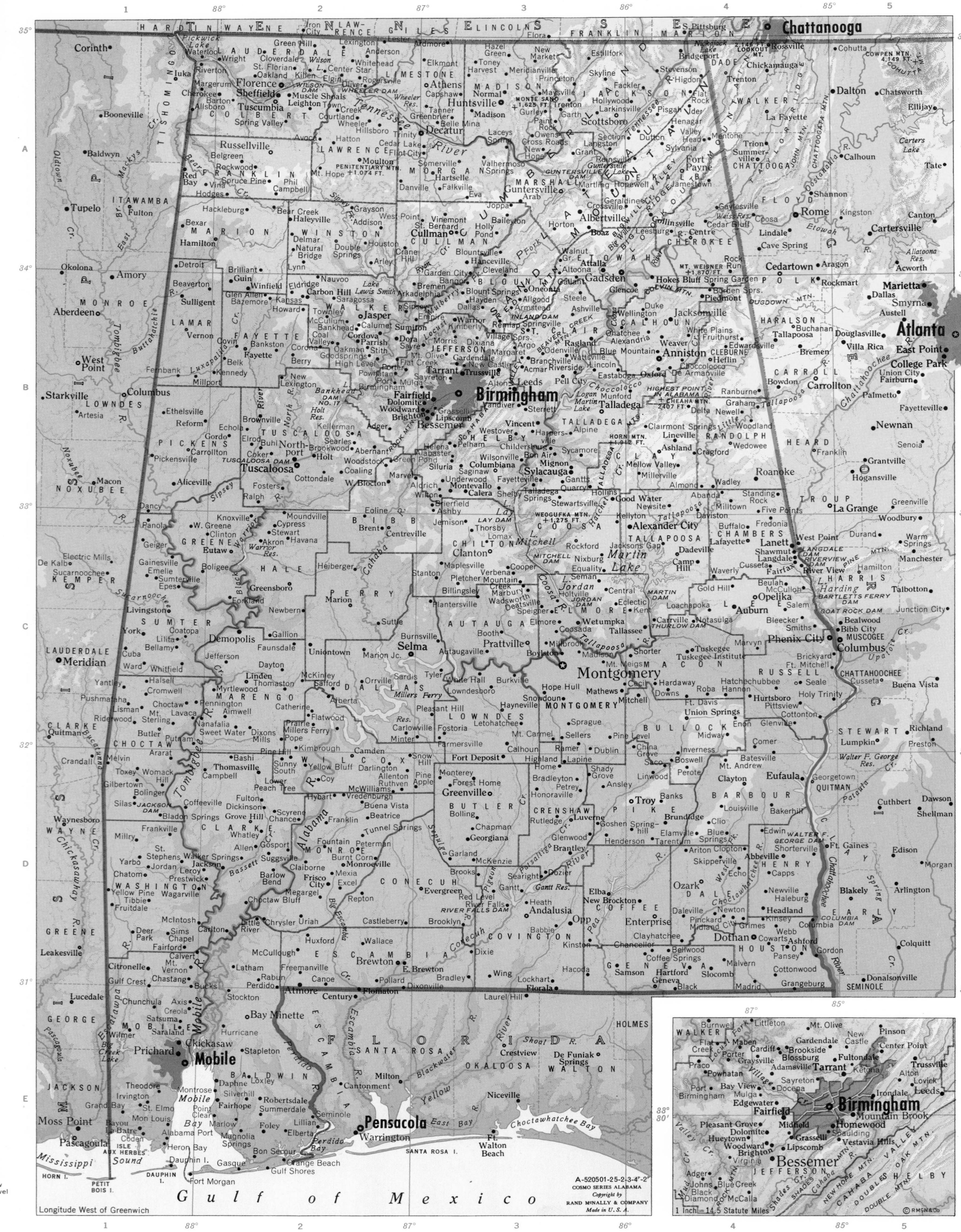

Statute Miles 5 0 5 10 20 30 40

Kilometers 5 0 5 15 25 35 45 55

Lambert Conformal Conic Projection

SCALE 1:1,831,000 1 Inch = 29 Statute Miles

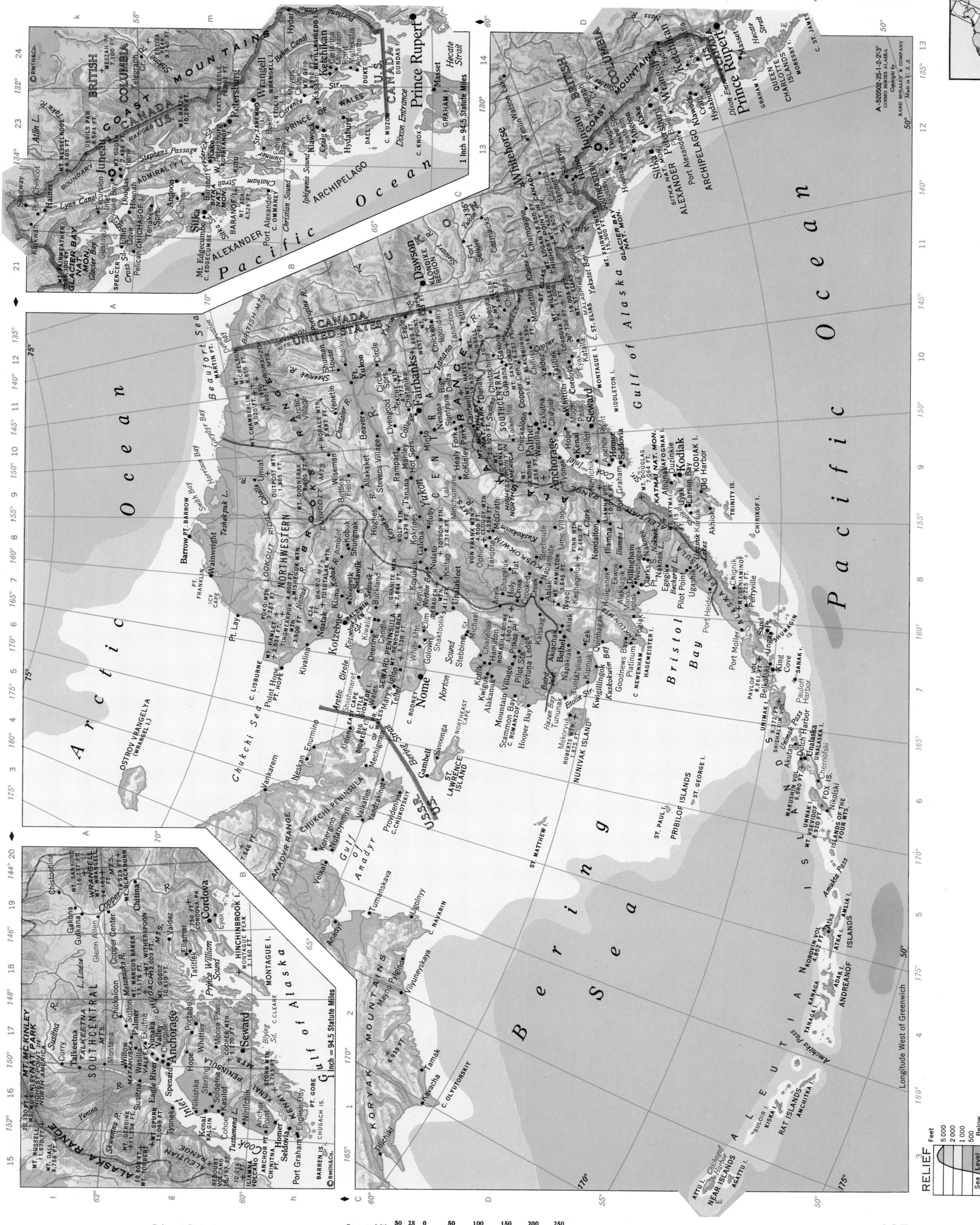

Polyconic Projection
SCALE 1:12,000,000 1 Inch = 189 Statute Miles

Statute Miles 50 25 0 50 100 150 200 250
Kilometers 50 0 100 200 300

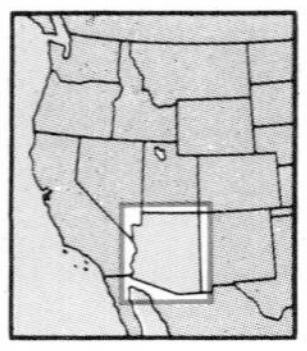

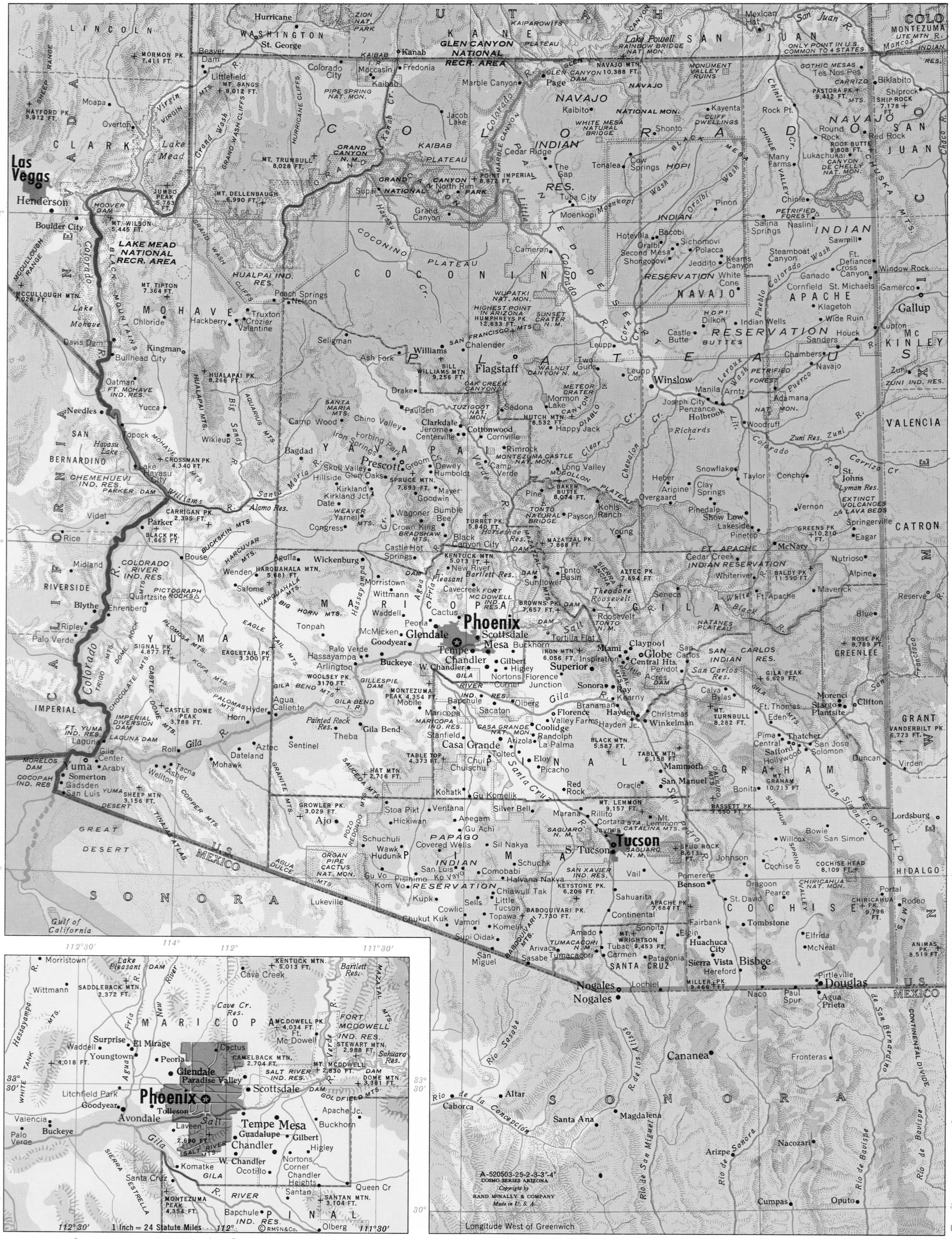

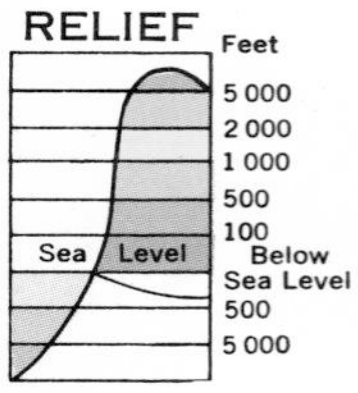

Statute Miles 10 0 10 20 30 40 50 60 70 80 90

Kilometers 10 0 10 20 40 60 80 100 120

Lambert Conformal Conic Projection
SCALE 1:2,725,000 1 Inch = 43 Statute Miles

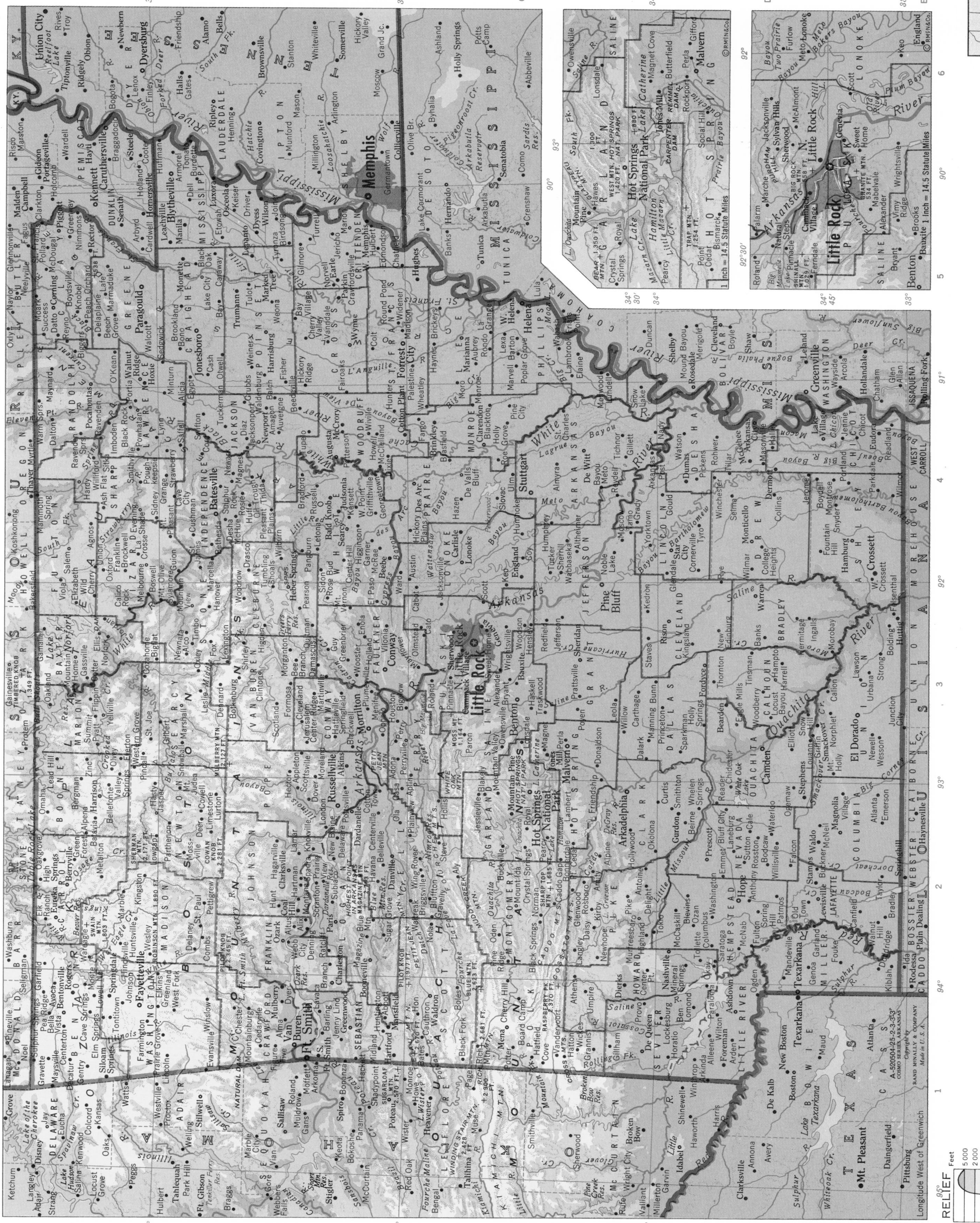

Lambert Conformal Conic Projection
SCALE 1:1,832,000 1 Inch = 29 Statute Miles

Statute Miles 5 0 5 10 20 30 40

Kilometers 5 0 5 15 25 35 45 55

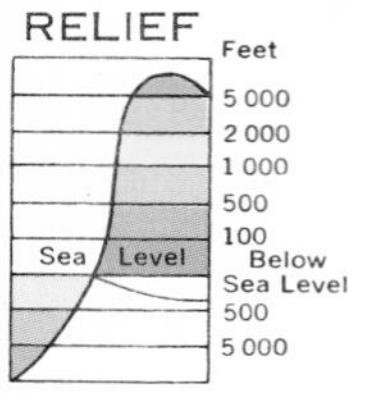

Statute Miles 10 0 10 20 30 40 50 60 70 80 90

Kilometers 10 0 10 20 40 60 80 100 120

Lambert Conformal Conic Projection
SCALE 1:3,733,000 1 Inch = 59 Statute Miles

RELIEF

Feet
5 000
2 000
1 000
500
100
Sea Level
Below
Sea Level
500
5 000

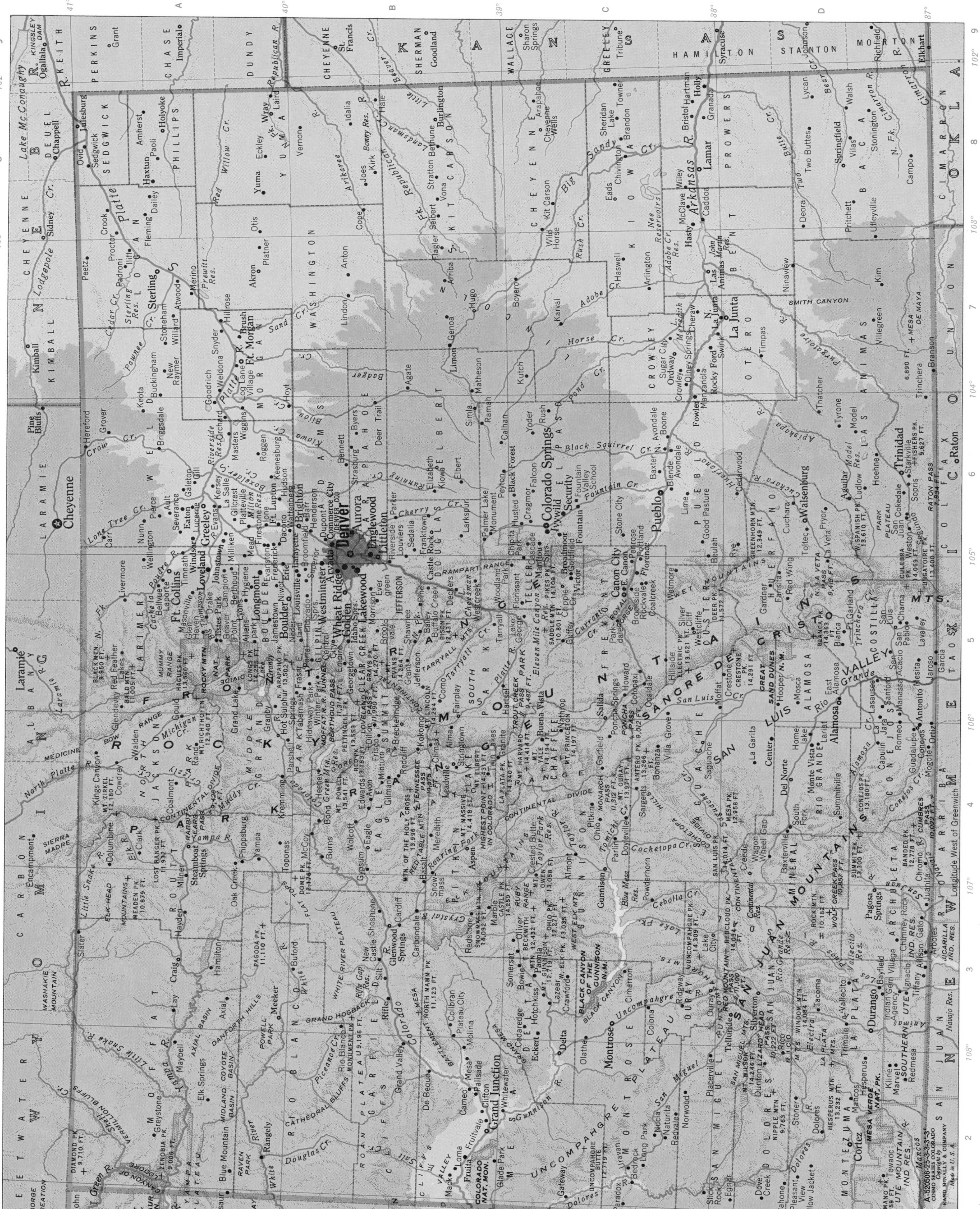

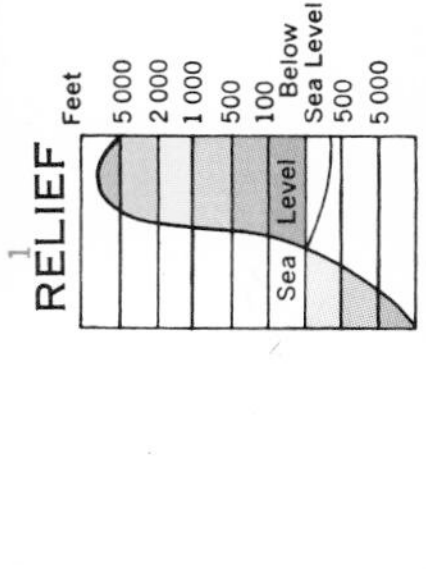

Lambert Conformal Conic Projection
SCALE 1:2.186.000 1 Inch = 34.5 Statute Miles

Statute Miles 5 0 5 10 20 30 40 50
Kilometers 5 0 5 15 25 35 45 55 65 75

RELIEF

Feet	
5 000	
2 000	
1 000	
500	
100	
Sea Level	
500	Below
5 000	Sea Level

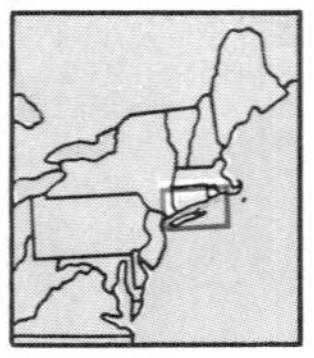

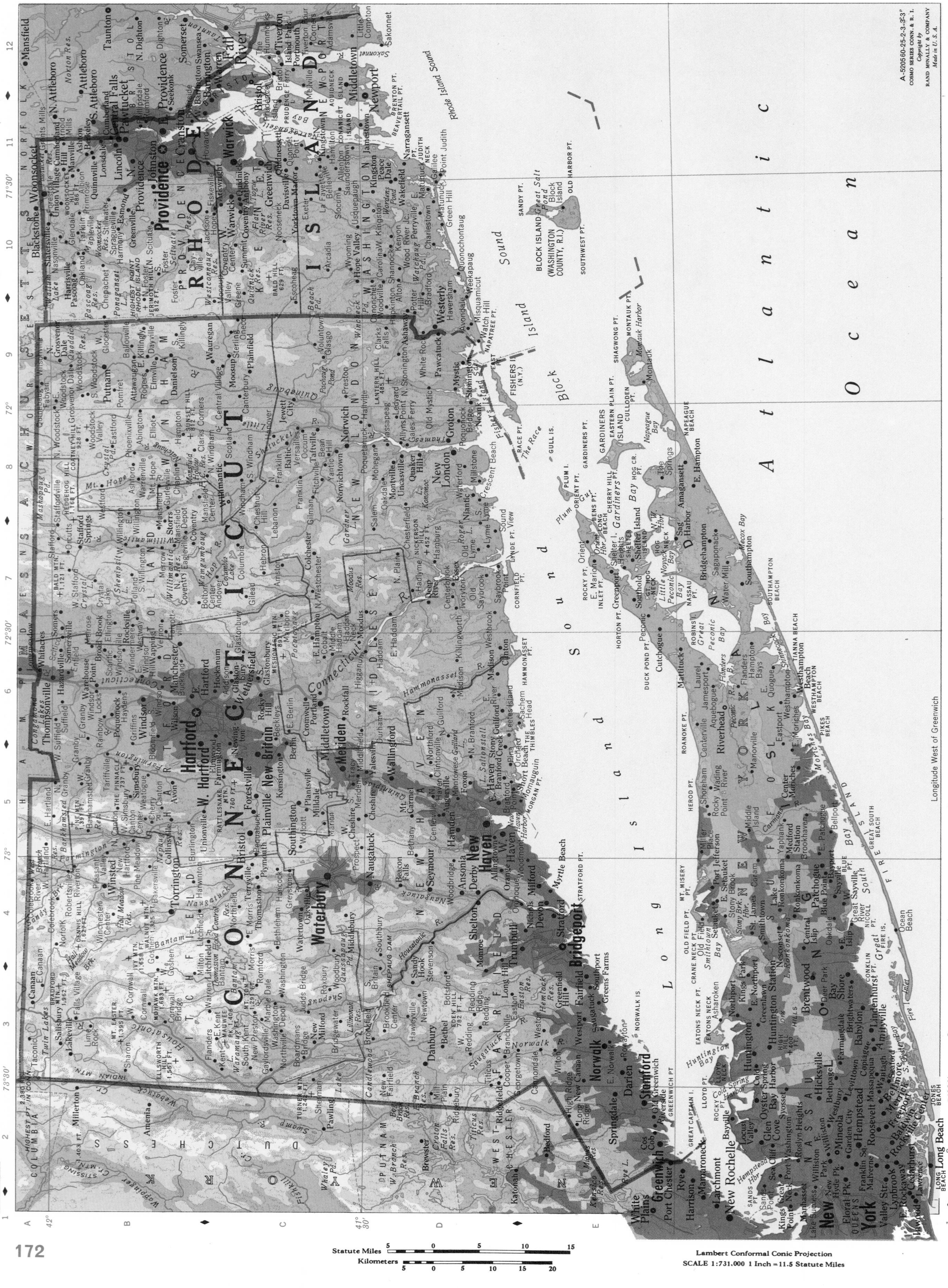

Statute Miles 5 0 5 10 15
Kilometers 5 0 5 10 15 20

Lambert Conformal Conic Projection
SCALE 1:731,000 1 Inch = 11.5 Statute Miles

A-500560-25-2-3-33°
COSMO SERIES CONN. & R. I.
Copyright by
RAND MCNALLY COMPANY
Made in U.S.A.

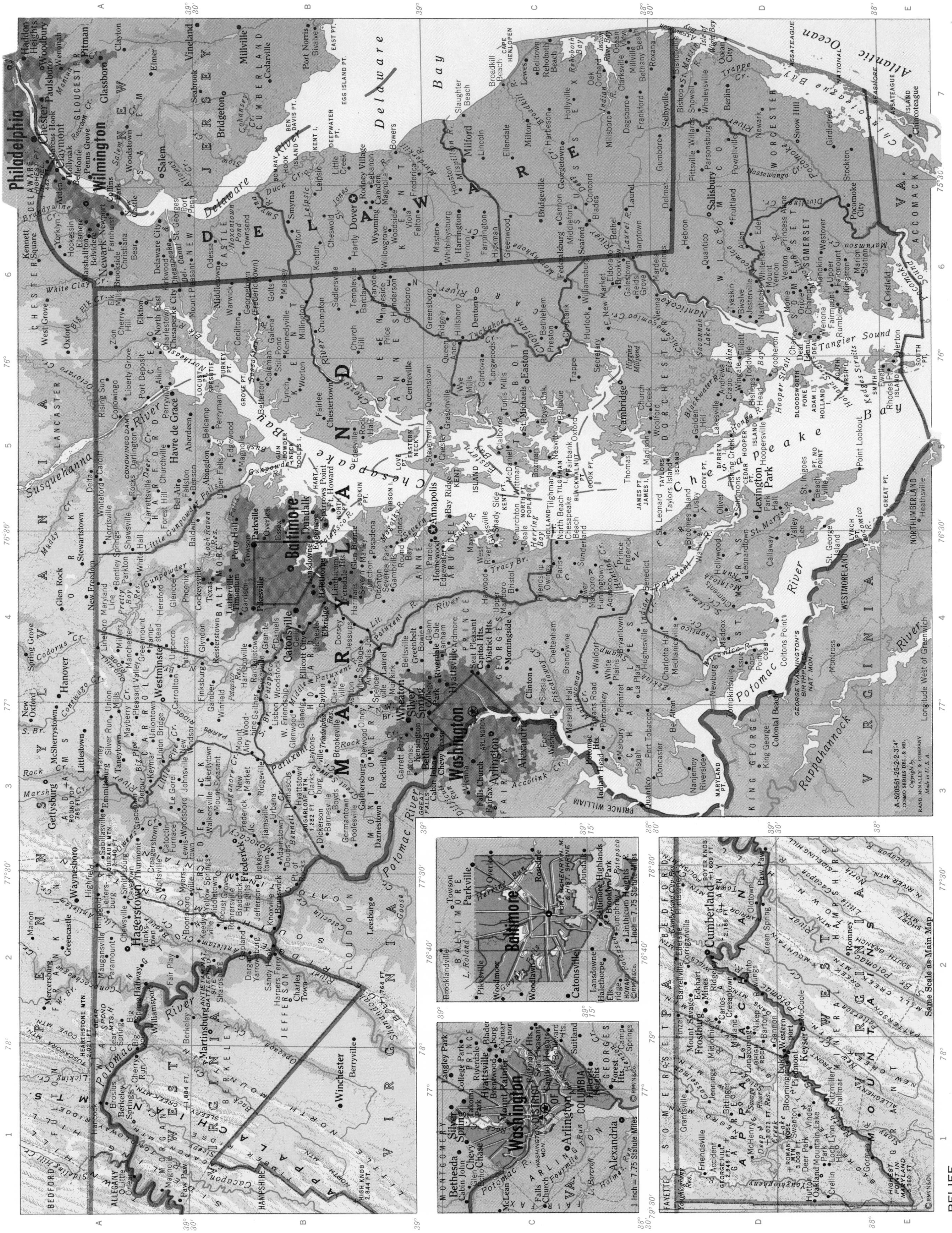

Lambert Conformal Conic Projection
SCALE 1:985,000 1 Inch = 15.5 Statute Miles

Statute Miles 5 0 5 10 15 20
Kilometers 5 0 5 10 15 20 25 30

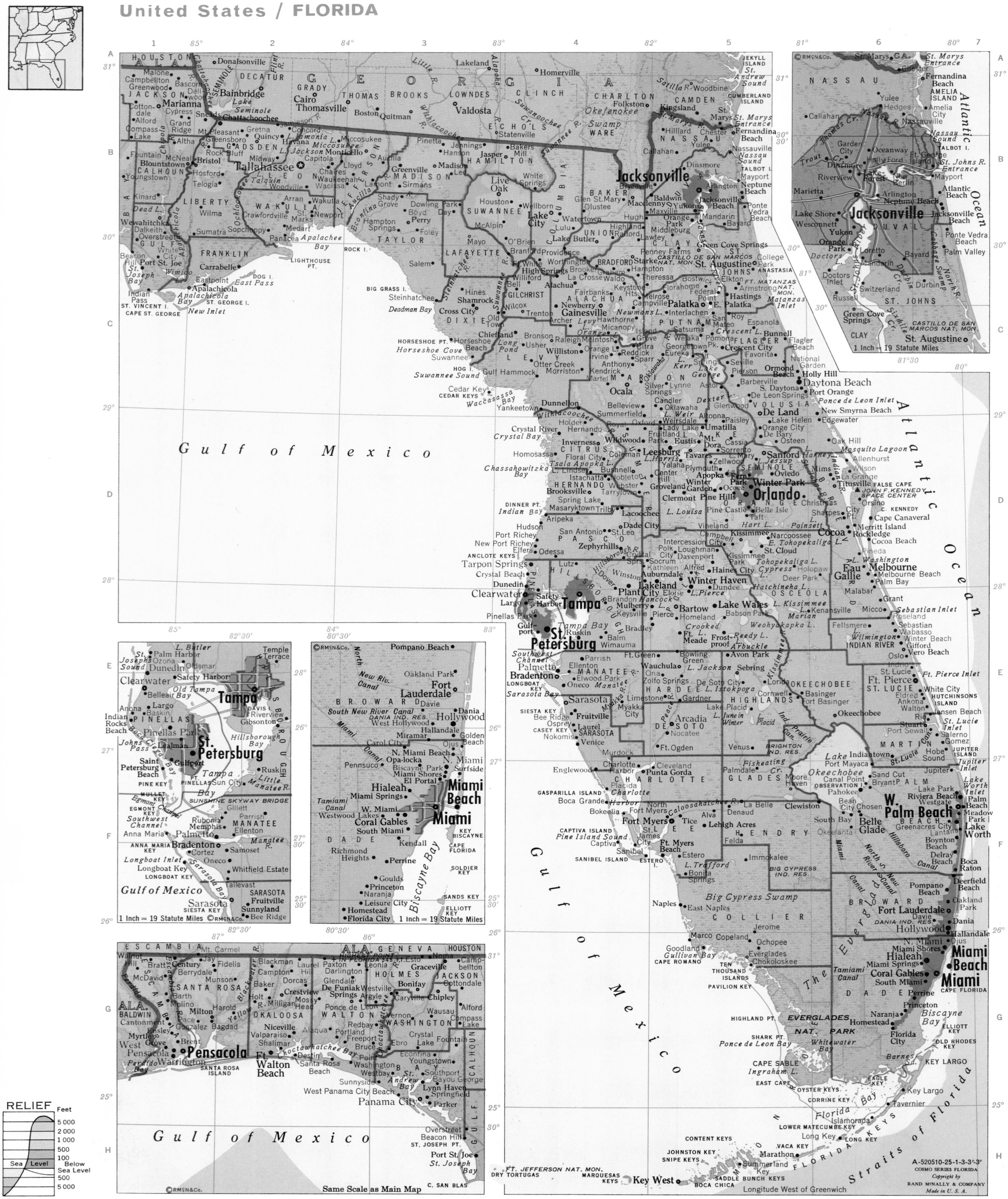

Statute Miles 5 0 5 10 20 30 40 50

Kilometers 5 0 5 15 25 35 45 55 65

Lambert Conformal Conic Projection
SCALE 1:2,425,000 1 Inch = 38 Statute Miles

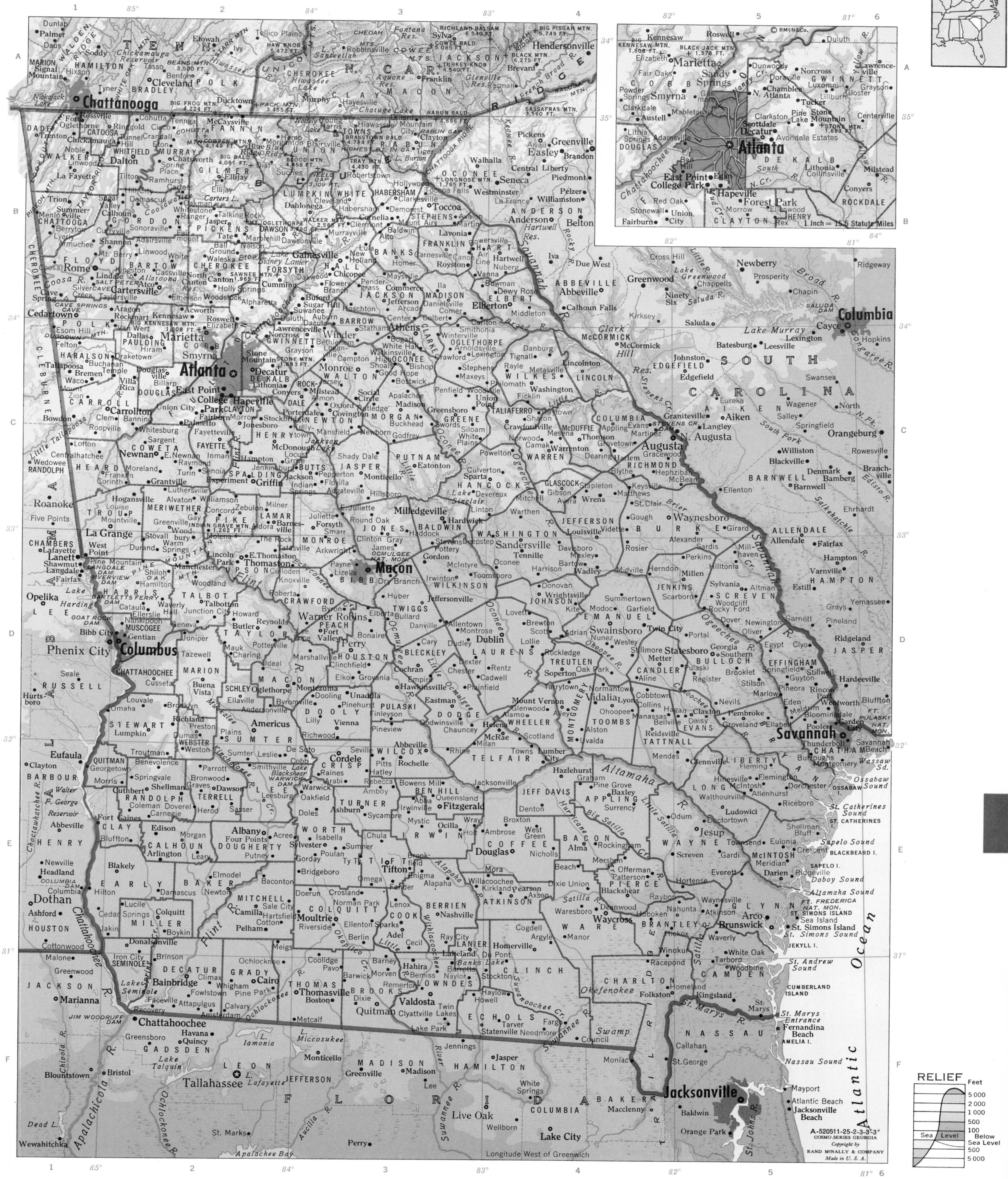

Lambert Conformal Conic Projection
SCALE 1:1,962,000 1 Inch = 31 Statute Miles

Statute Miles 5 0 5 10 20 30 40
Kilometers 5 0 5 15 25 35 45 55

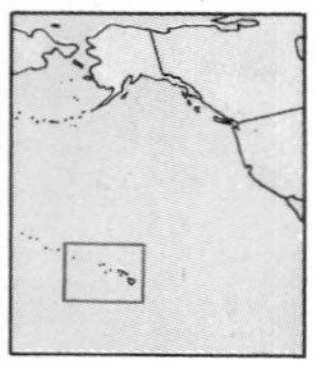

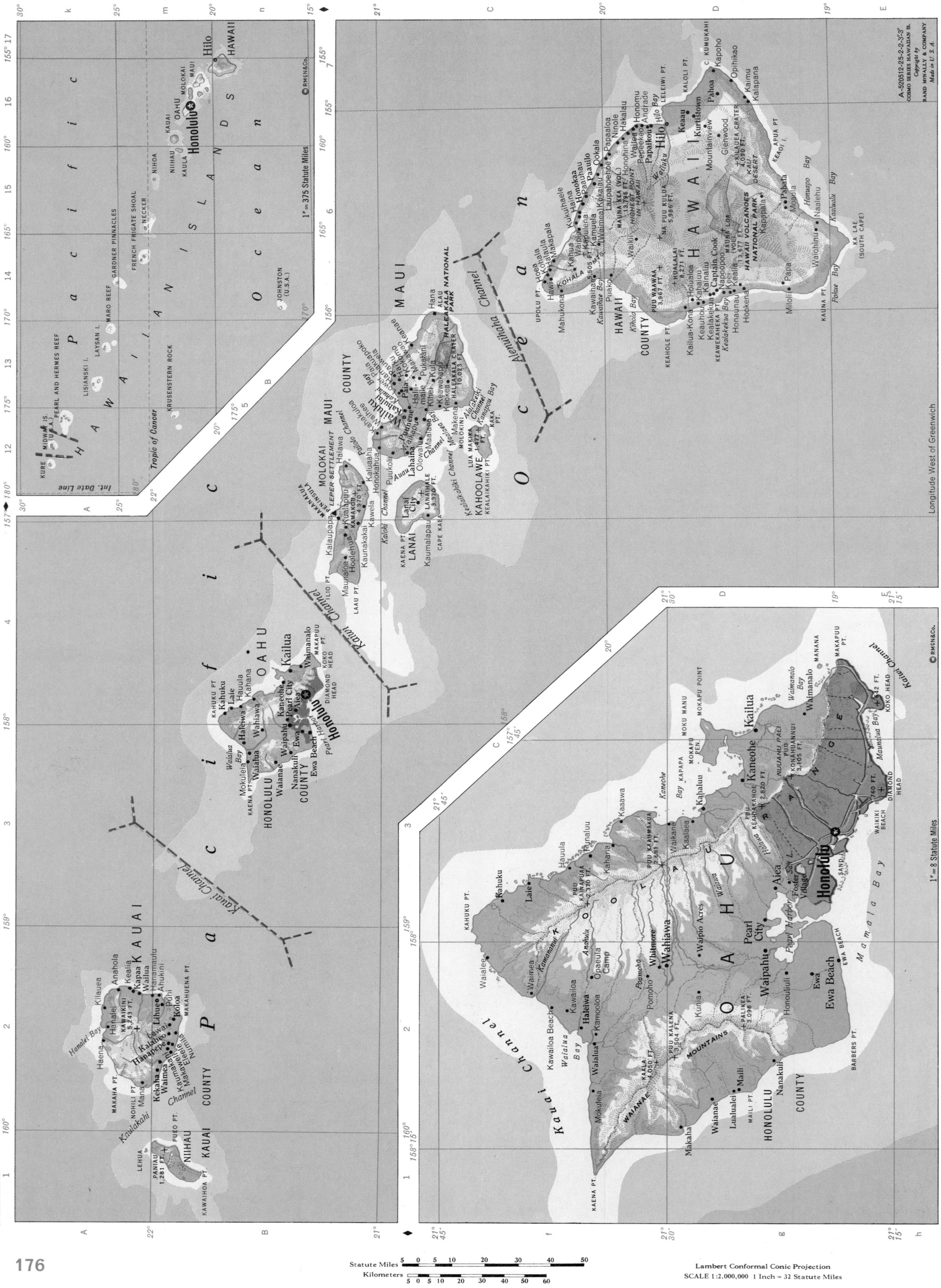

Statute Miles 5 0 5 10 20 30 40 50

Kilometers 5 0 5 10 20 30 40 50 60

Lambert Conformal Conic Projection

SCALE 1:2,000,000 1 Inch = 32 Statute Miles

COSMO SERIES IDAHO
Made in U.S.A.
A-520513-25-2-3-3-5

RELIEF Feet
5 000
2 000
1 000
500
100
Sea Level
Below
Sea Level
500
5 000

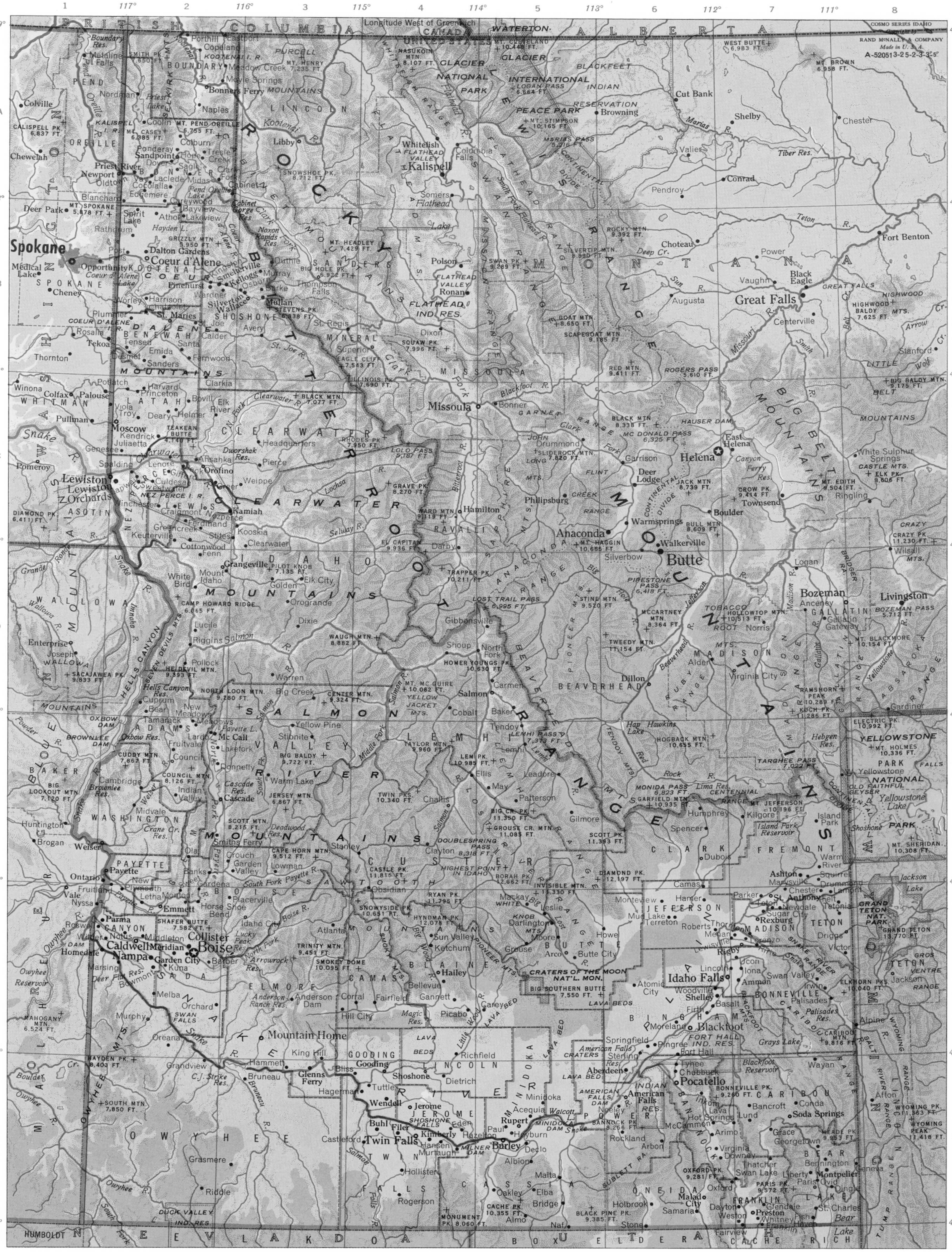

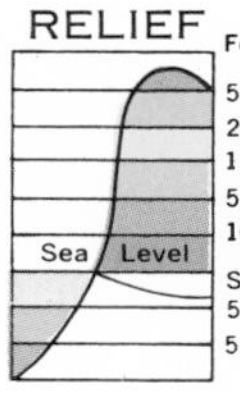

Lambert Conformal Conic Projection
SCALE 1:2,633,000 1 Inch = 41.5 Statute Miles

Statute Miles 5 0 5 10 20 30 40 50 60

Kilometers 5 0 5 15 25 35 45 55 65 75

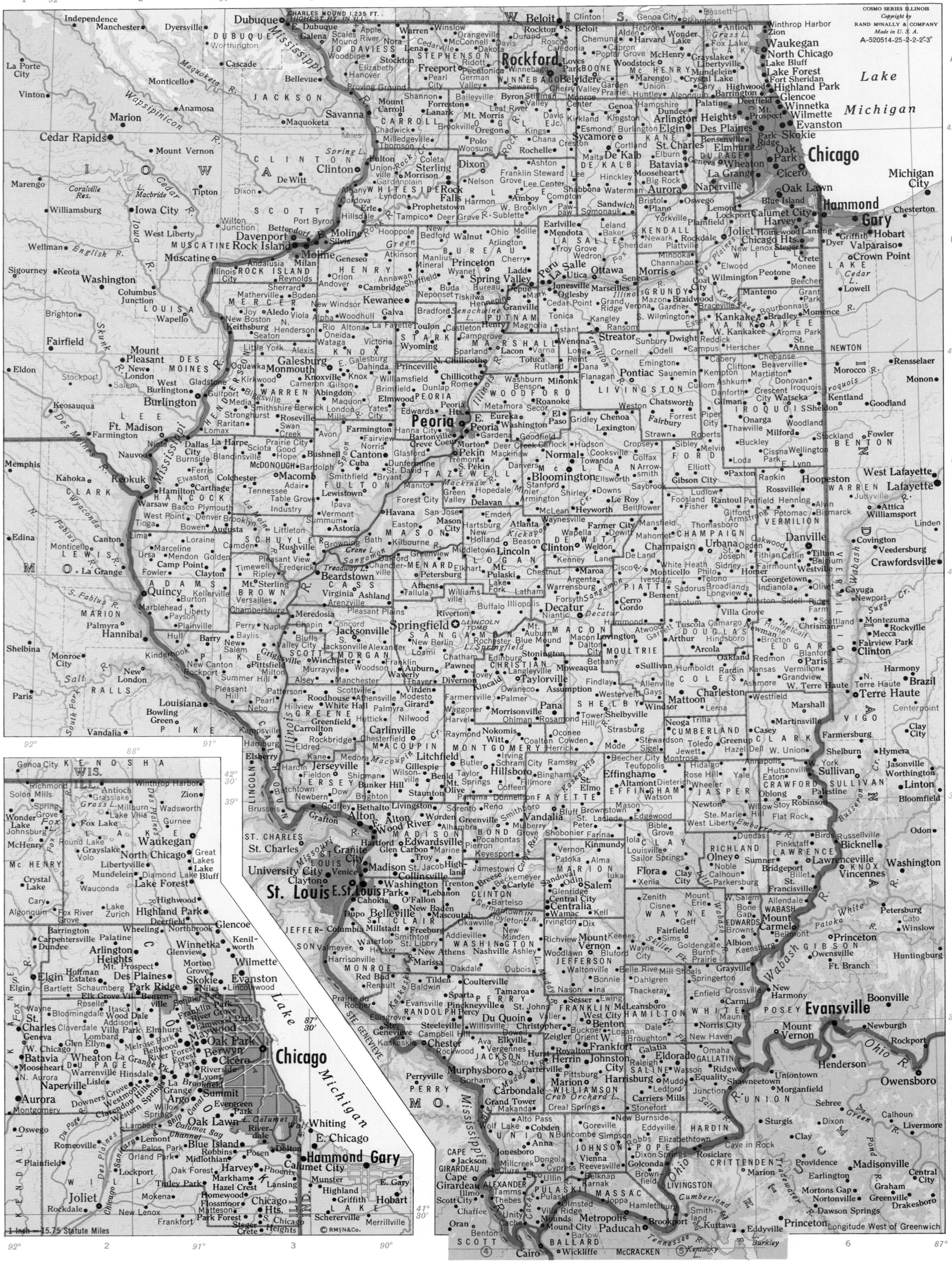

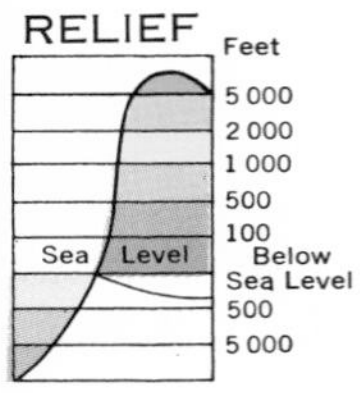

Statute Miles 5 0 5 10 20 30 40

Kilometers 5 0 5 15 25 35 45 55

Lambert Conformal Conic Projection

SCALE 1:1,997,000 1 Inch = 31.5 Statute Miles

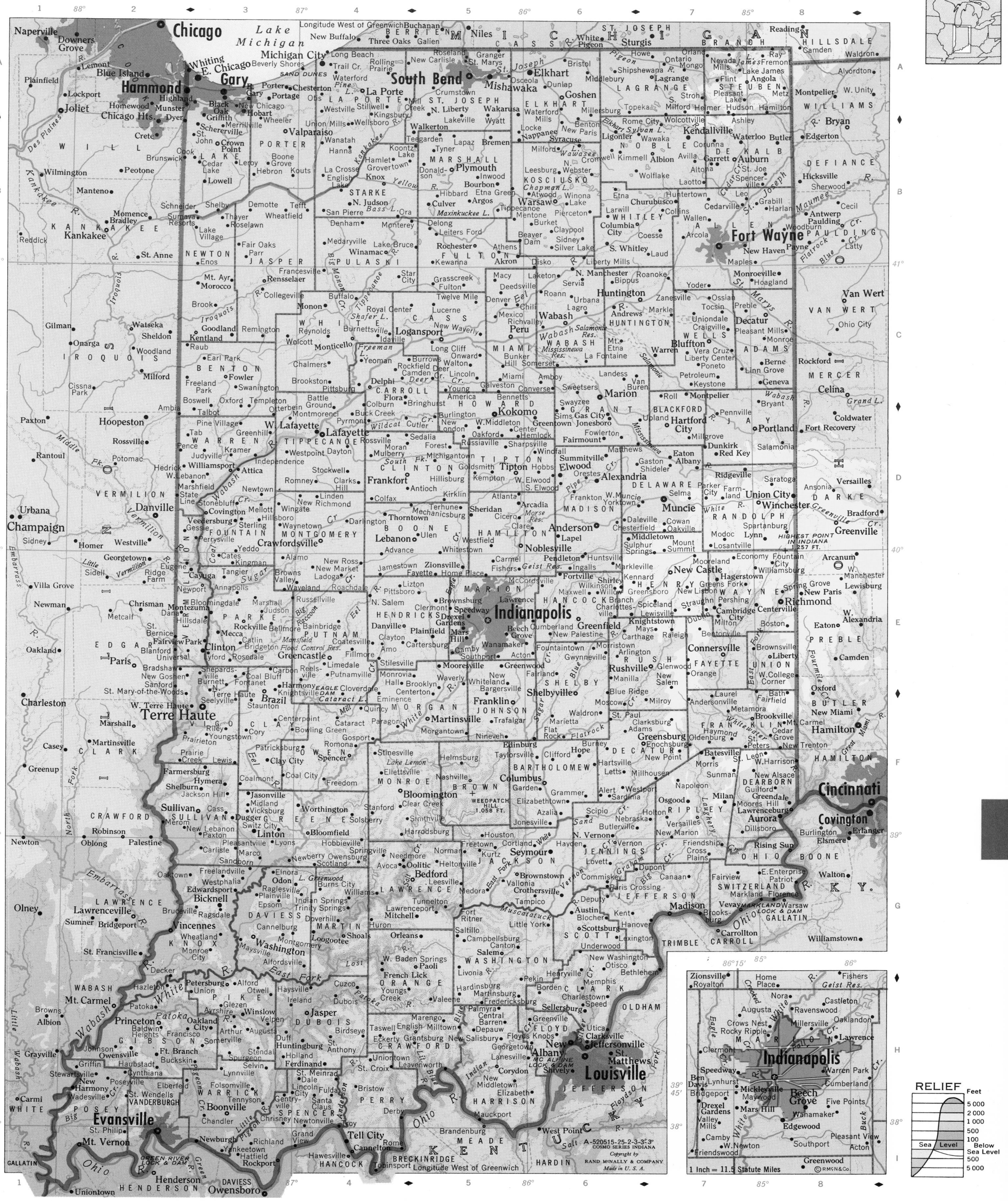
Chicago
Lake Michigan
Gary
Hammond
South Bend
Elkhart
Fort Wayne
Lafayette
Kokomo
Marion
Muncie
Anderson
Indianapolis
Terre Haute
Bloomington
Columbus
Richmond
Evansville
Louisville
Cincinnati
Covington
Champaign
Danville
Kankakee
Joliet
Owensboro
Henderson
HIGHEST POINT IN INDIANA 1,257 FT.
WEEDPATCH HILL 1,058 FT.
Longitude West of Greenwich
A-520515-25-2-3-3'3"
COSMO SERIES INDIANA
Copyright by RAND McNALLY & COMPANY
Made in U. S. A.
1 Inch = 11.5 Statute Miles
RELIEF
Feet
5 000
2 000
1 000
500
200
100
Sea Level
Below Sea Level
500
5 000
Lambert Conformal Conic Projection
SCALE 1:1,465,000 1 Inch=23 Statute Miles
Statute Miles 5 0 5 10 15 20 25 30
Kilometers 5 0 5 15 25 35

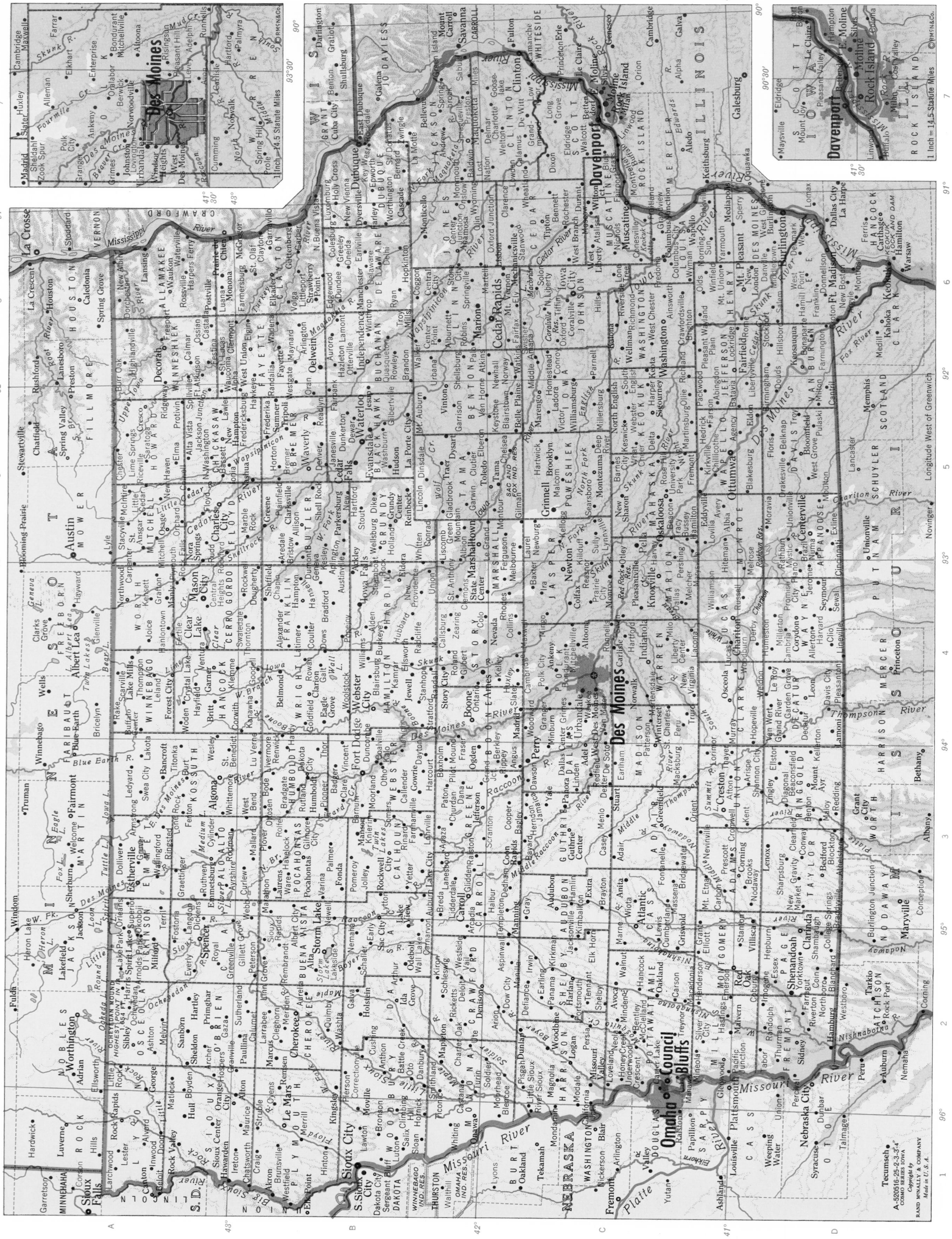

Statute Miles 5 0 5 10 20 30 40

Kilometers 5 0 5 15 25 35 45 55

Lambert Conformal Conic Projection

SCALE 1:1,834,000 1 Inch = 29 Statute Miles

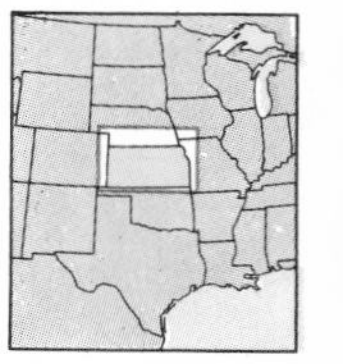

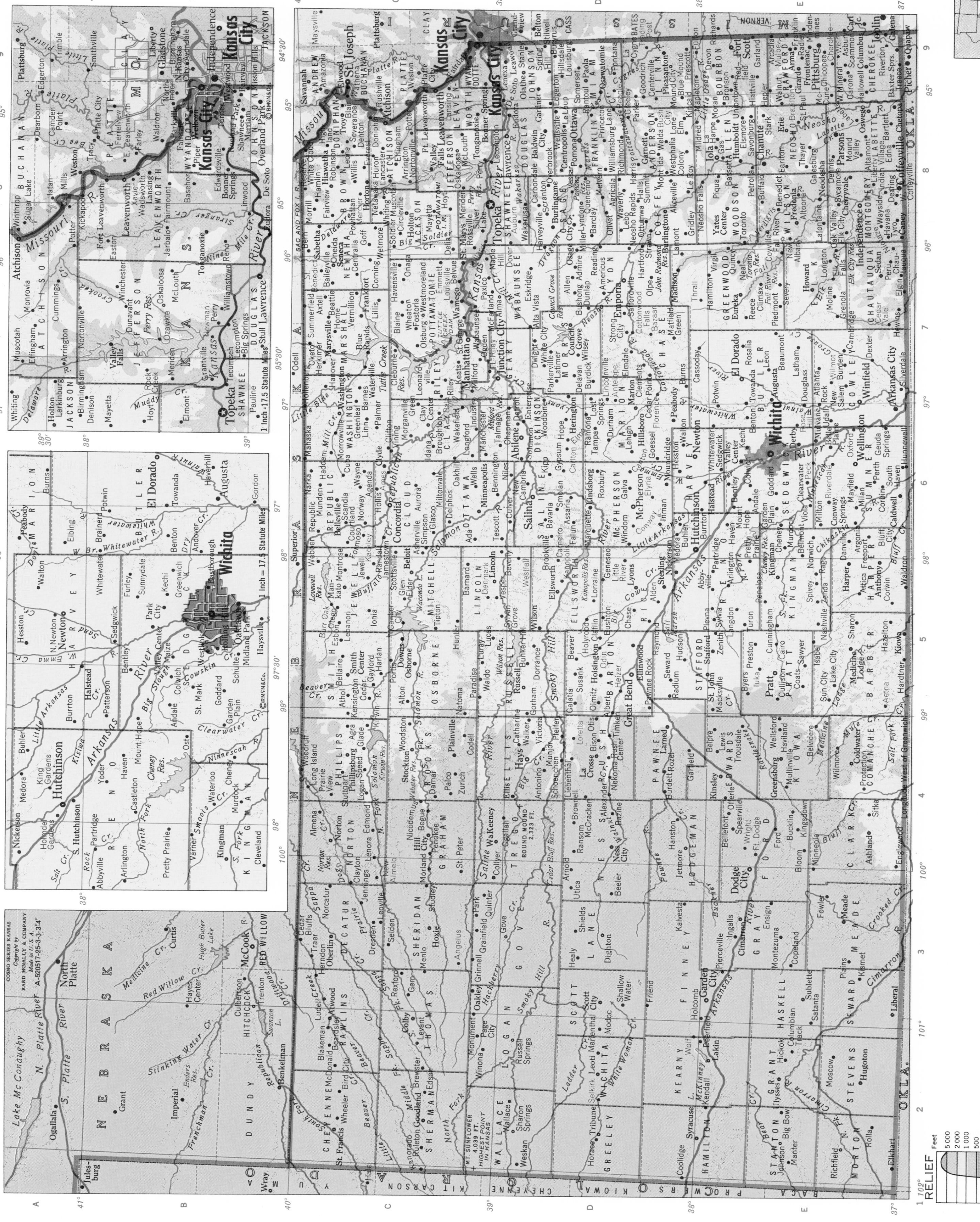

Lambert Conformal Conic Projection
SCALE 1:2,208,000 1 Inch = 35 Statute Miles

Statute Miles 5 0 5 15 25 35 45
Kilometers 5 0 5 15 25 35 45 55 65

RELIEF
Feet
5 000
2 000
1 000
500
100
Sea Level
Below
Sea Level
500
5 000

OHIO

Cincinnati
1 Inch = 13.5 Statute Miles
IND.

Dayton
Cincinnati
Springfield

Louisville
New Albany
1 Inch = 13.5 Statute Miles

Huntington
W. VA.

Louisville
Jeffersonville

Evansville
Mt. Vernon

Owensboro

Paducah
Mayfield

Bowling Green

Hopkinsville

Kingsport
Bristol

LAND BETWEEN THE LAKES
RECREATION AREA
Same Scale as Main Map

182

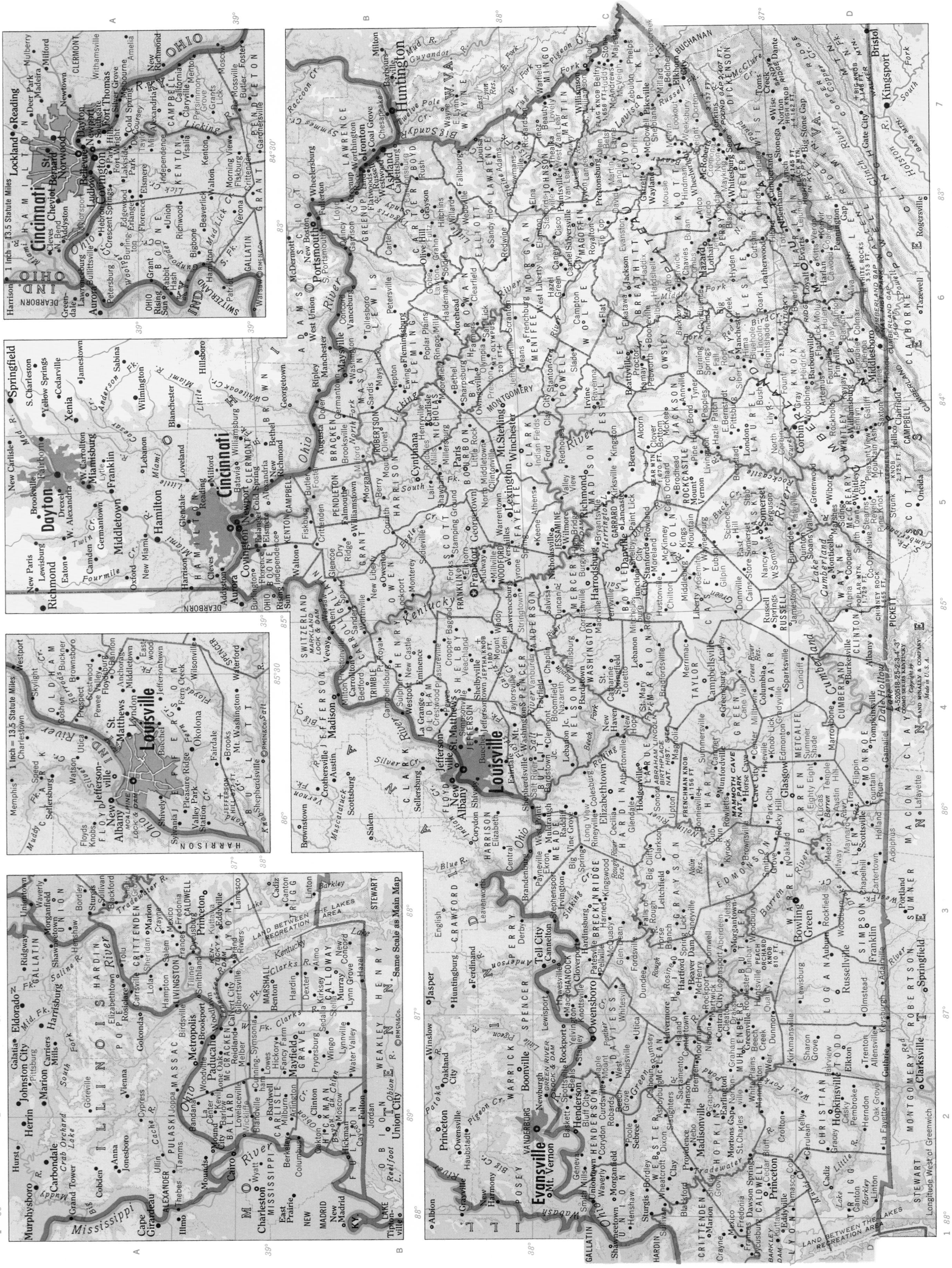

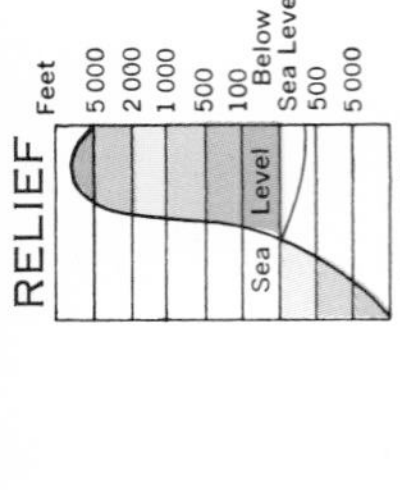

Statute Miles 5 0 5 10 20 30 40
Kilometers 5 0 5 10 20 30 40 50 60

Lambert Conformal Conic Projection
SCALE 1:1,738,000 1 Inch = 27 Statute Miles

RAND M°NALLY & COMPANY
Made in U.S.A.

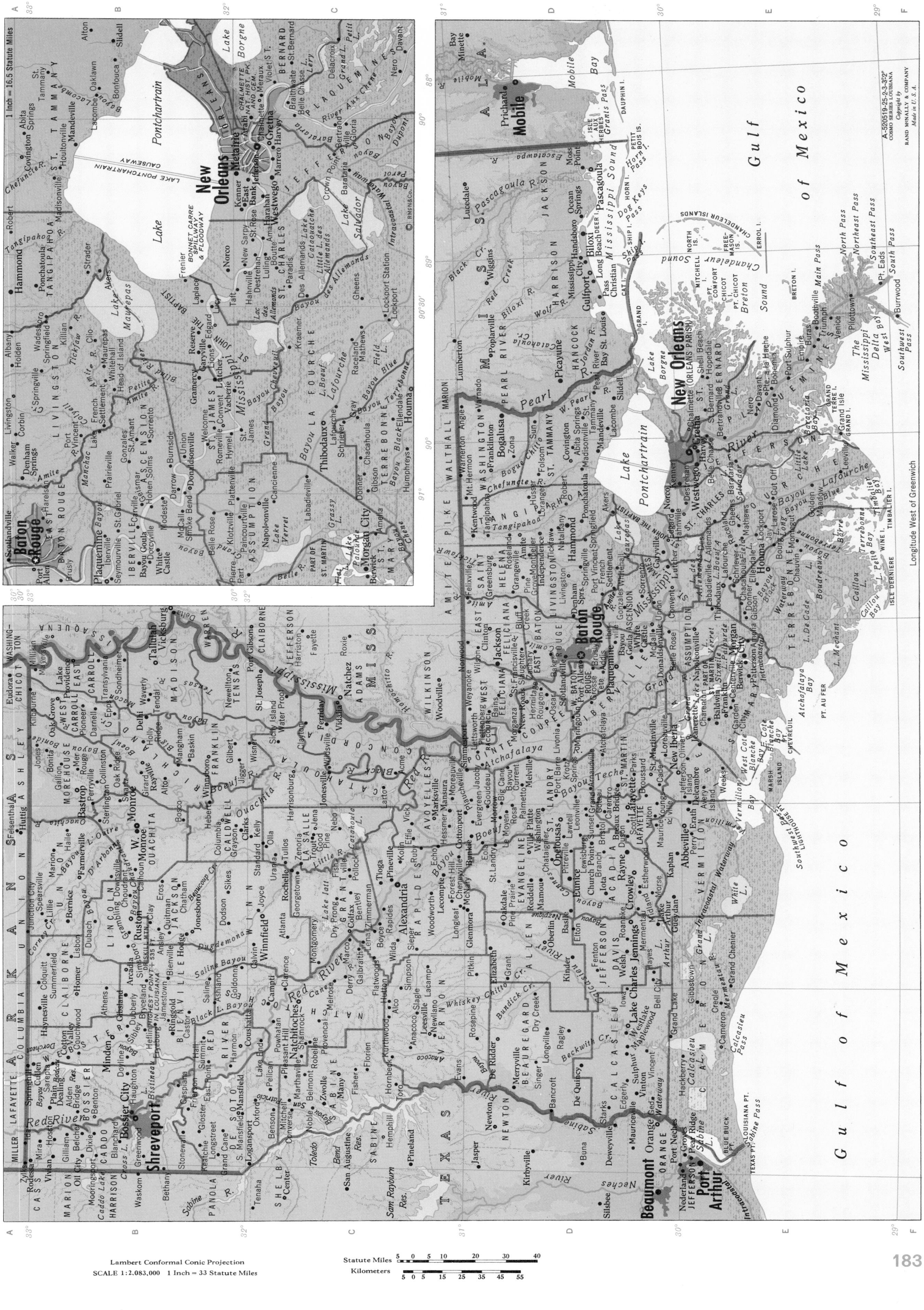

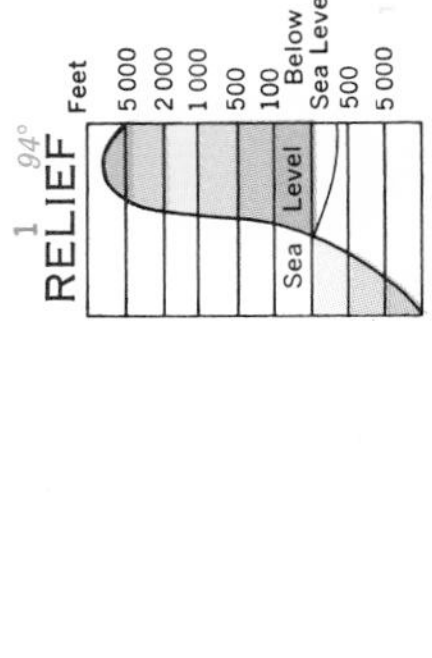

Lambert Conformal Conic Projection
SCALE 1:2,083,000 1 Inch = 33 Statute Miles

Statute Miles 5 0 5 10 20 30 40
Kilometers 5 0 5 15 25 35 45 55

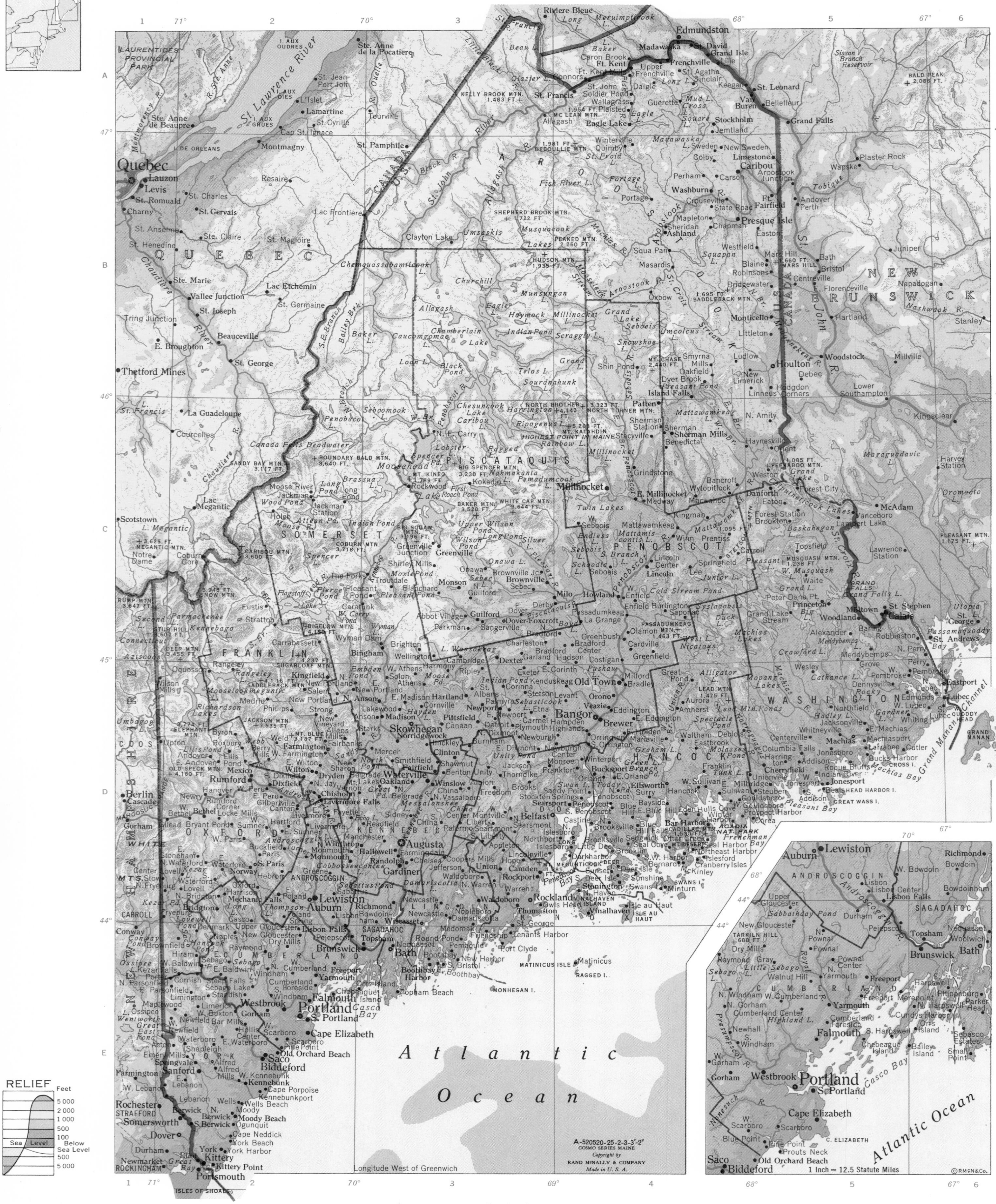

Statute Miles 5 0 5 10 20 30

Kilometers 5 0 5 10 20 30 40

Lambert Conformal Conic Projection

SCALE 1:1,581,000 1 Inch = 25 Statute Miles

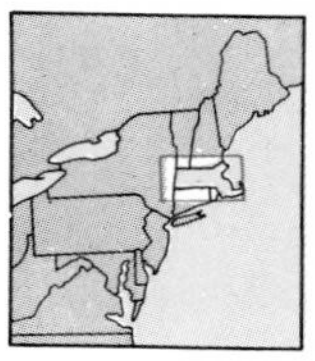

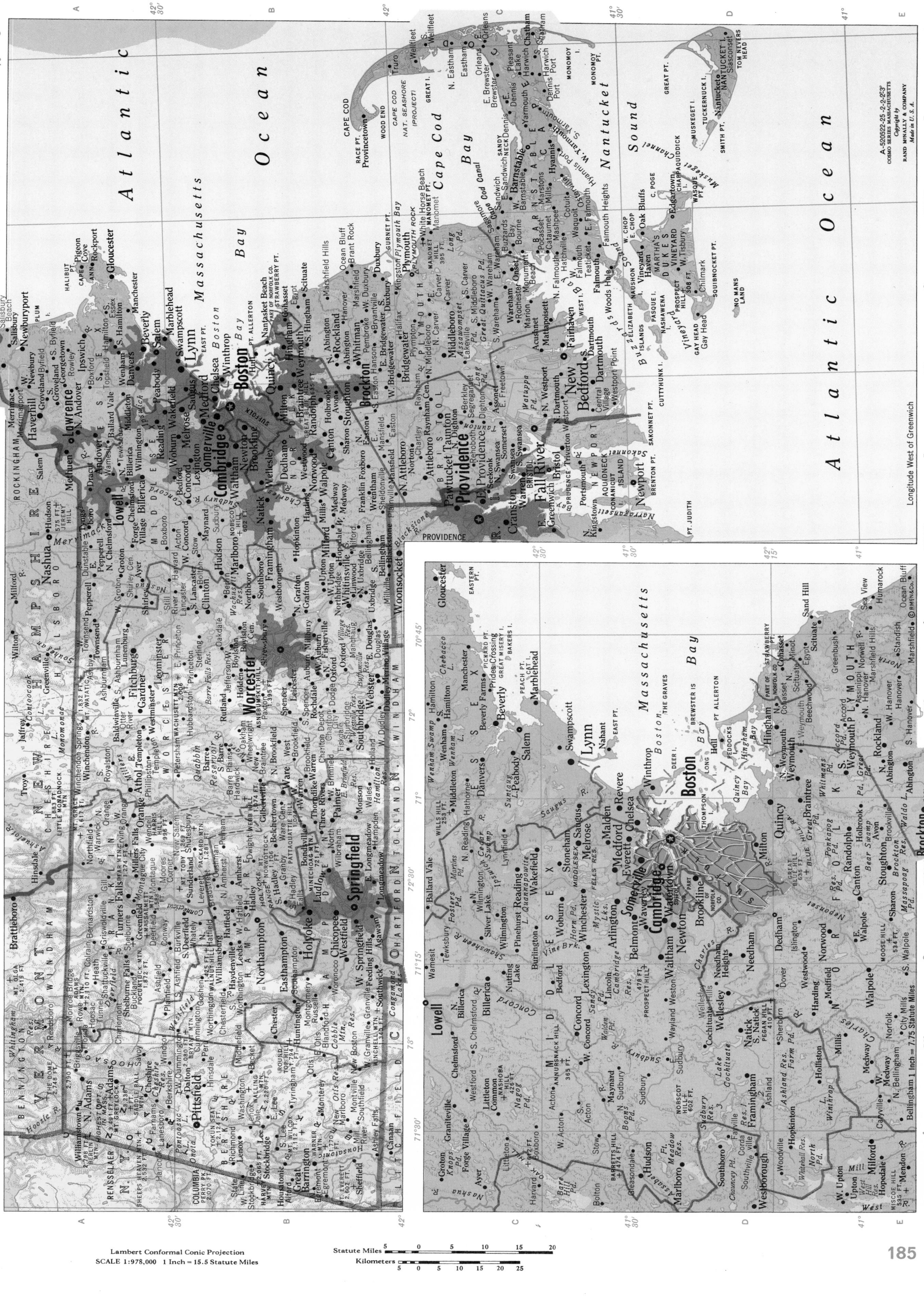

Lambert Conformal Conic Projection
SCALE 1:978,000 1 Inch = 15.5 Statute Miles

Statute Miles 5 0 5 10 15 20
Kilometers 5 0 5 10 15 20 25

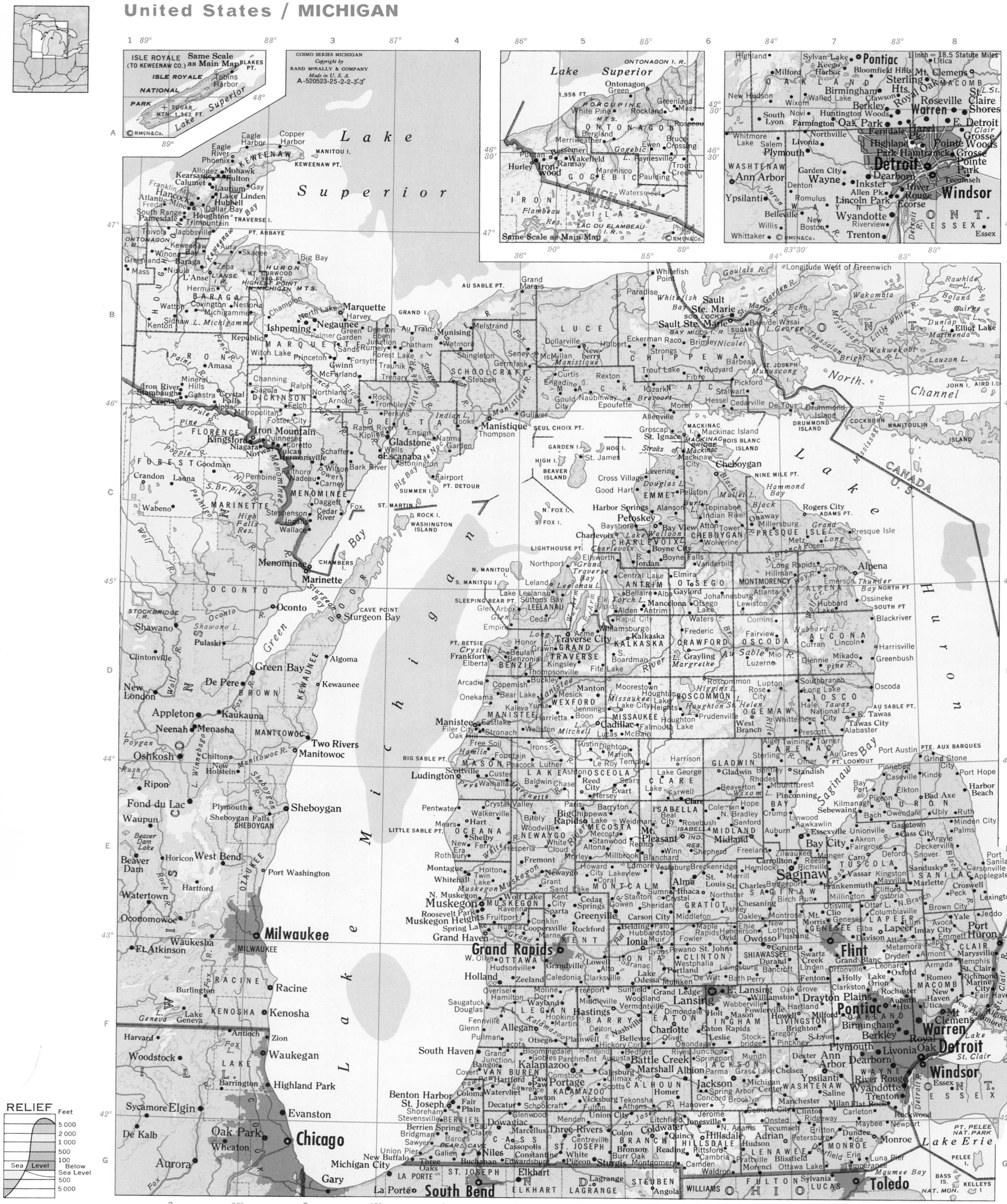

Statute Miles 5 0 5 10 20 30 40 50

Kilometers 5 0 5 15 25 35 45 55 65 75

Lambert Conformal Conic Projection

SCALE 1:2,347,000 1 Inch = 37 Statute Miles

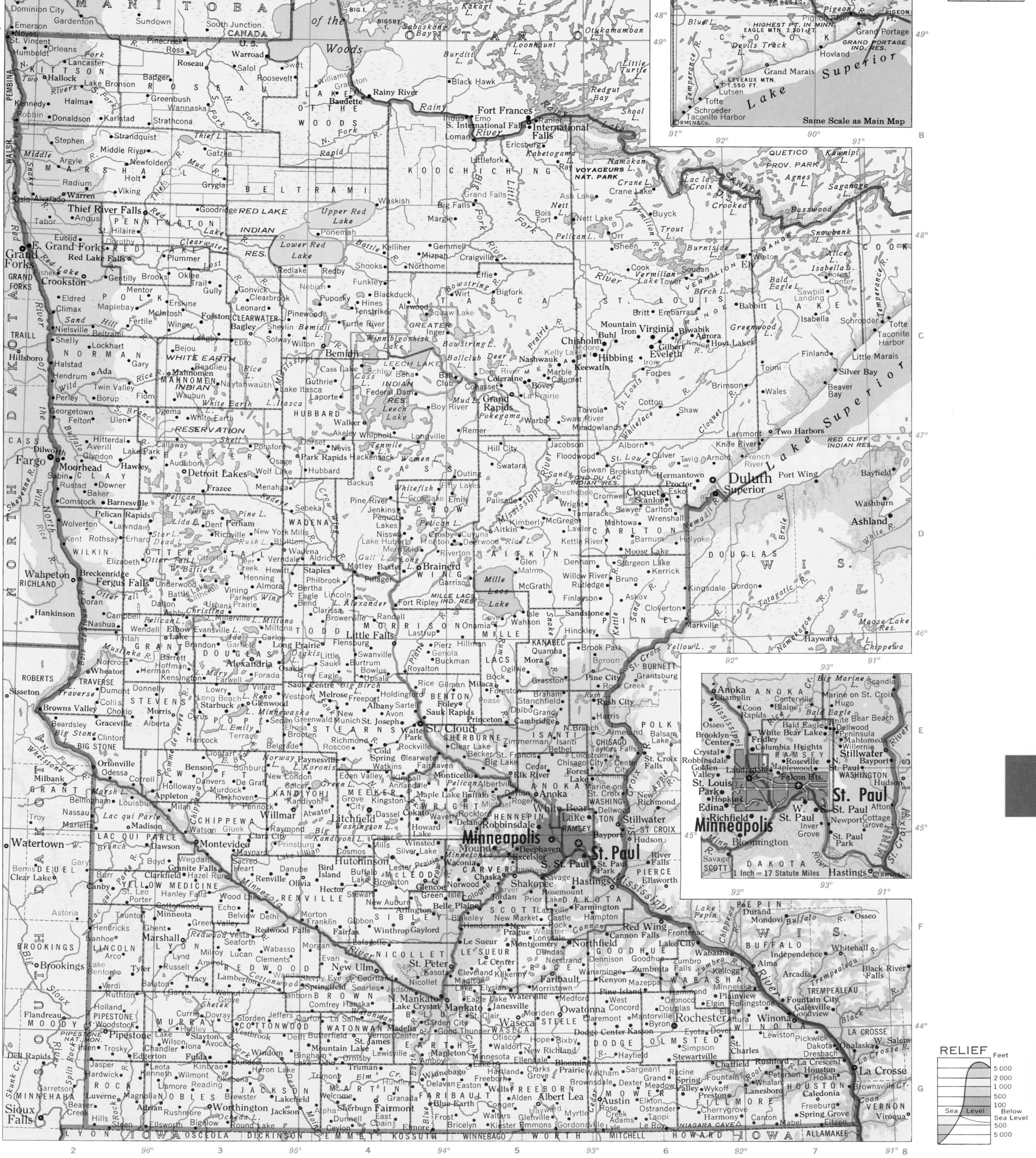

Lambert Conformal Conic Projection
SCALE 1:2,179,000 1 Inch = 34 Statute Miles

Statute Miles 5 0 5 10 20 30 40 50
Kilometers 5 0 5 15 25 35 45 55 65

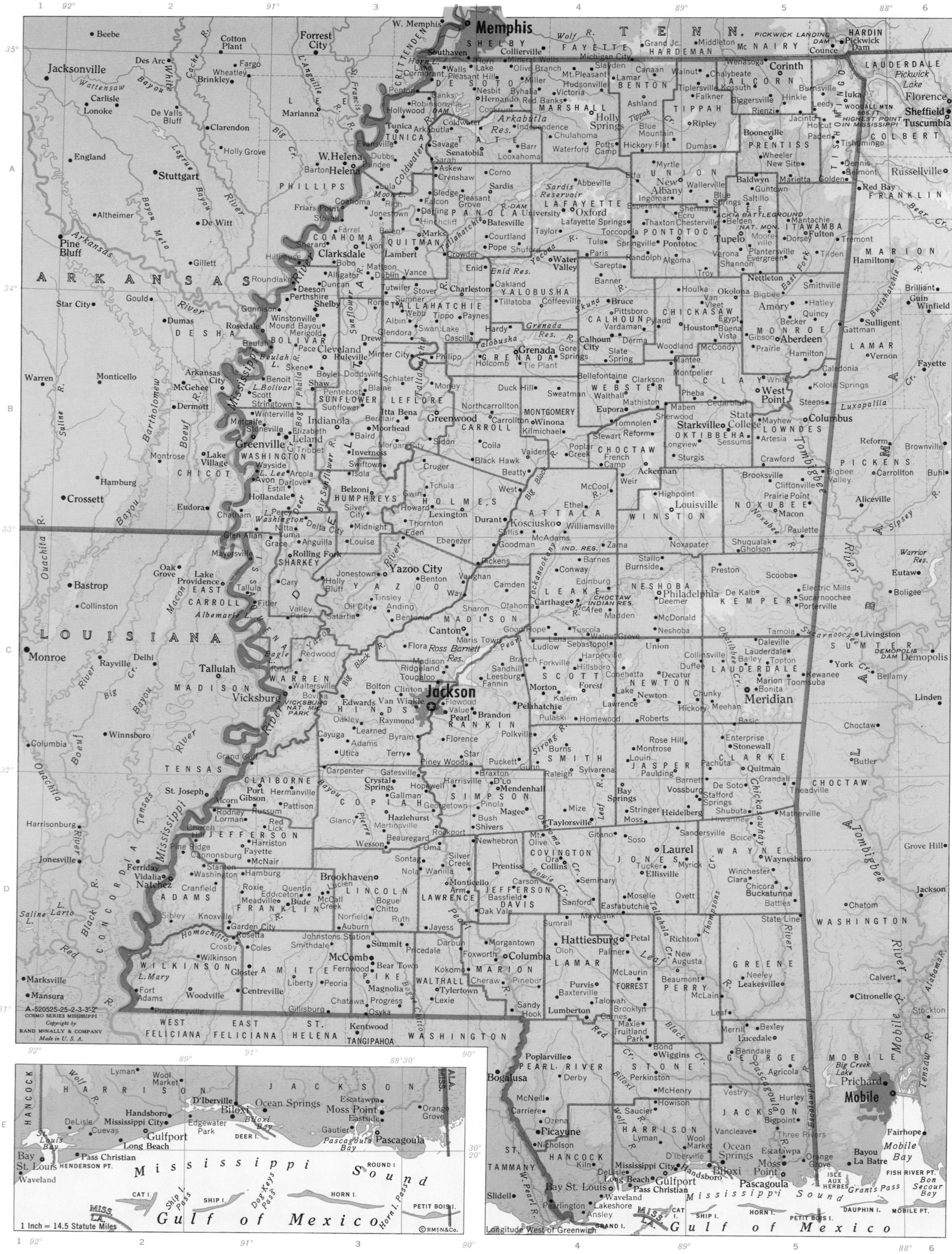

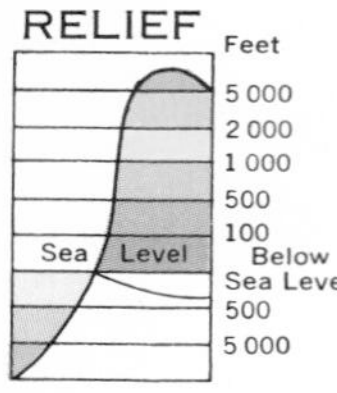

Statute Miles 5 0 5 10 20 30 40

Kilometers 5 0 5 15 25 35 45 55

Lambert Conformal Conic Projection

SCALE 1:1,837,000 1 Inch = 29 Statute Miles

RELIEF

Feet	
5000	
2000	
1000	
500	
100	
Sea Level	
Below Sea Level	500

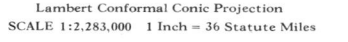

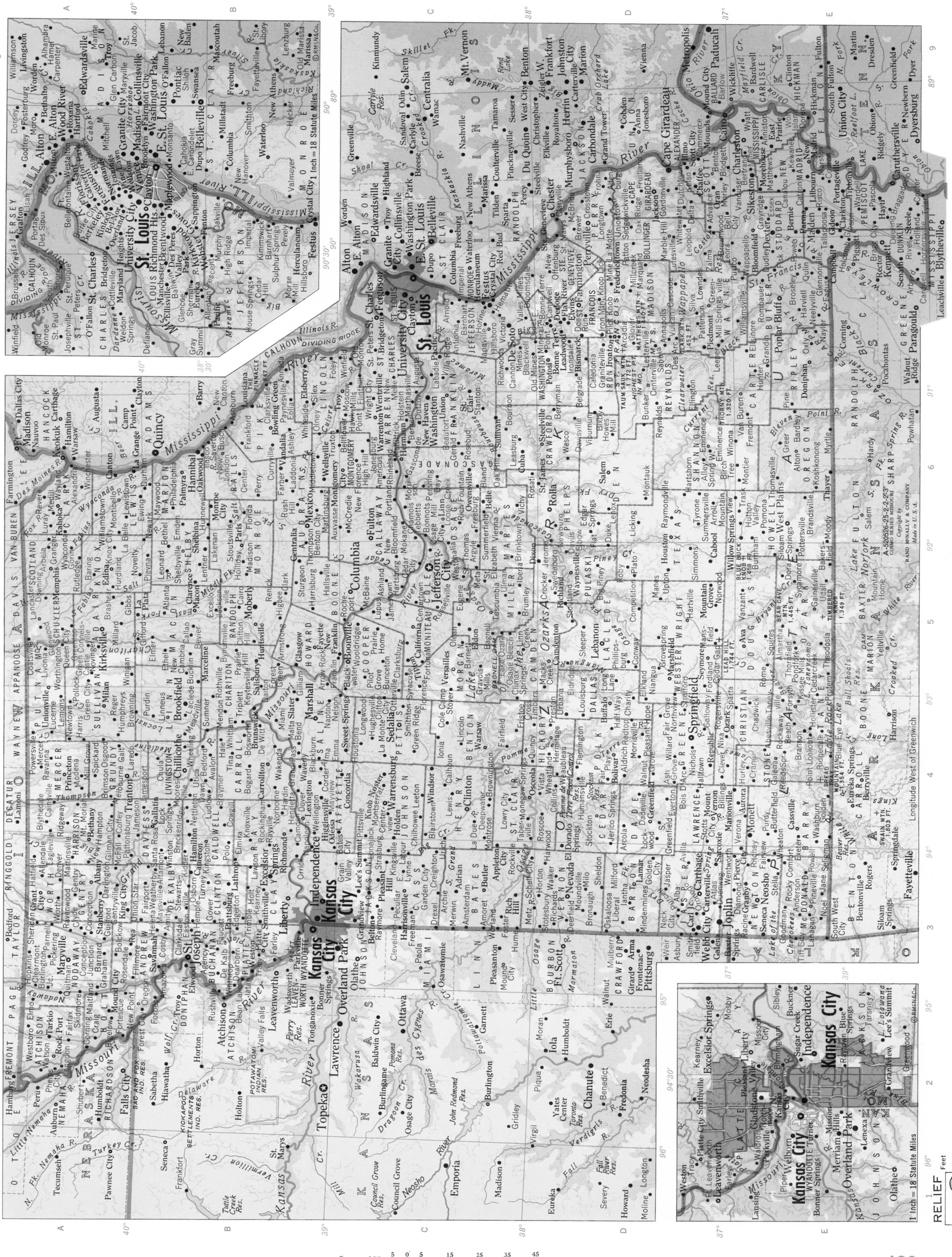

Lambert Conformal Conic Projection
SCALE 1:2,283,000 1 Inch = 36 Statute Miles

Statute Miles 5 0 5 15 25 35 45
Kilometers 5 0 5 15 25 35 45 55 65

1 Inch = 18 Statute Miles

RELIEF

Feet
5 000
2 000
1 000
500
100
Sea Level
500
5000
Below
Sea Level

NORTH DAKOTA

SOUTH DAKOTA

S A S K A T C H E W A N

A L B E R T A

B. C.

CANADA
U.S.

BOUNDARY PLATEAU

ROCKY MOUNTAINS

BITTERROOT RANGE

BEAVERHEAD RANGE

SALMON RIVER MOUNTAINS

ABSAROKA RANGE

BEARTOOTH RANGE

BIG HORN MOUNTAINS

BEAR LODGE MTS.

YELLOWSTONE NATIONAL PARK

GRAND TETON NAT. PARK

GLACIER NATIONAL PARK

WATERTON GLACIER INTERNATIONAL PEACE PARK

Great Falls
Helena
Butte
Billings
Missoula
Bozeman
Miles City
Glasgow
Havre
Kalispell
Lewistown
Livingston
Wolf Point
Glendive

190

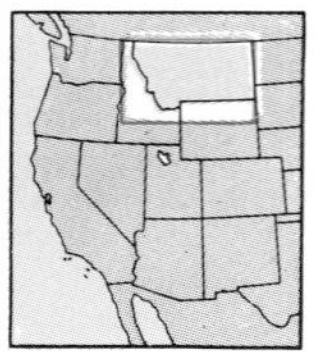

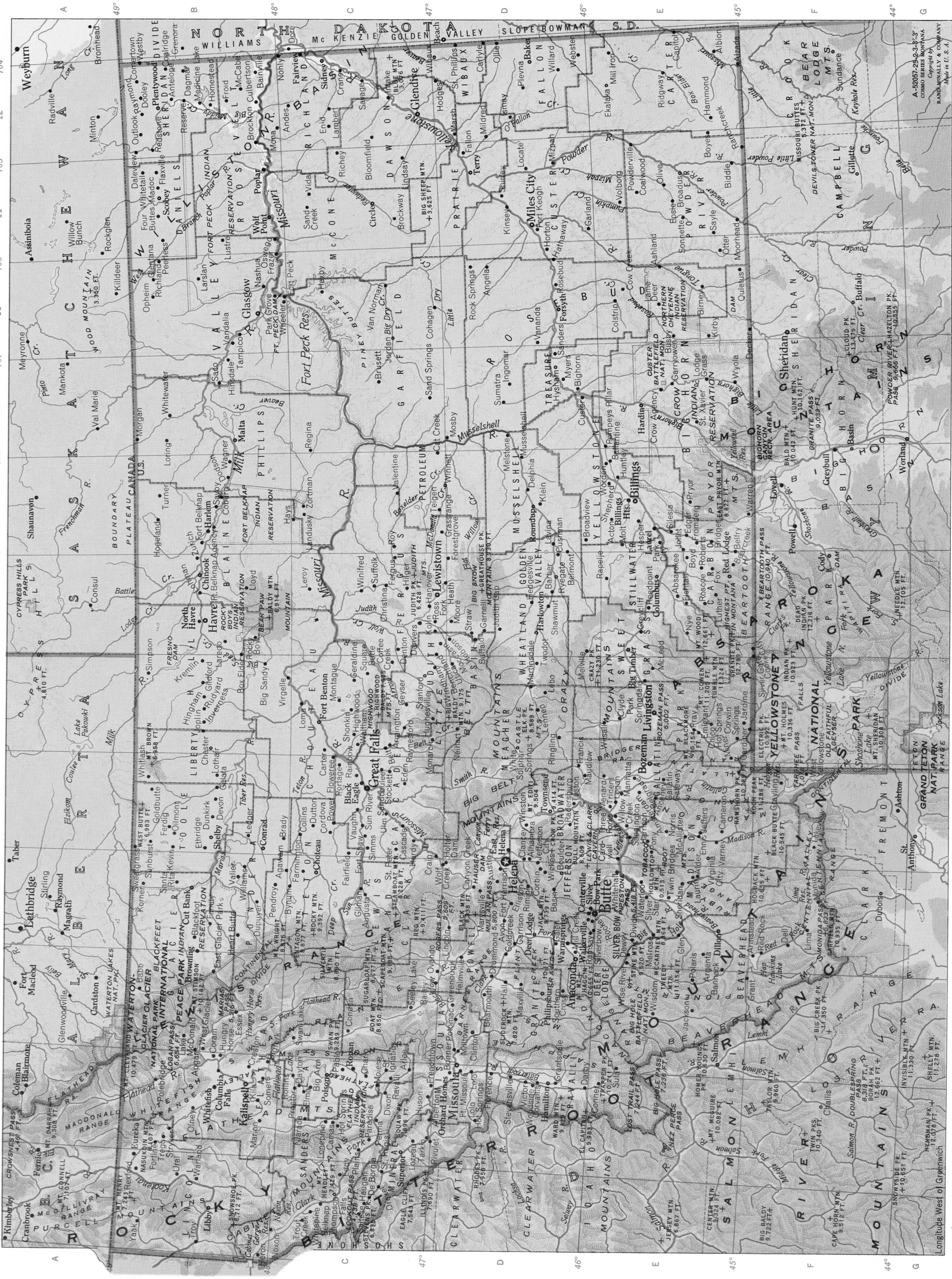

Statute Miles
10 0 10 20 30 40 50 60 70

Kilometers
10 0 10 30 50 70 90

Lambert Conformal Conic Projection
SCALE 1:2,999,000 1 Inch = 47.5 Statute Miles

A-52057-25-g-2-8-3
COSMO STATES MONTANA
Copyright by
RAND McNALLY & COMPANY
Made in U.S.A.

Longitude West of Greenwich

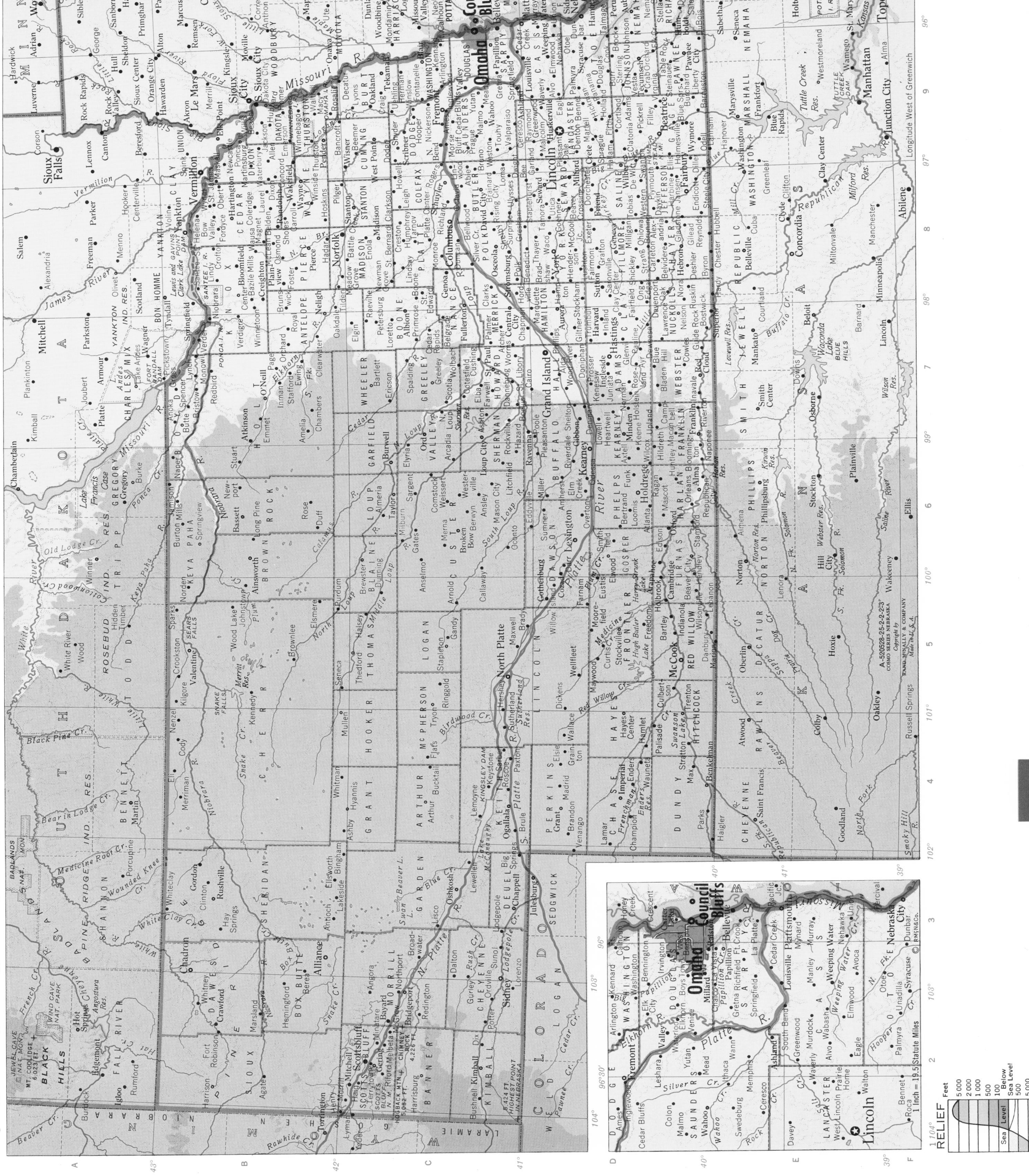

Lambert Conformal Conic Projection
SCALE 1:2,460,000 1 Inch = 39 Statute Miles

Statute Miles 5 0 5 10 20 30 40 50 60
Kilometers 5 0 5 15 35 55 75 95

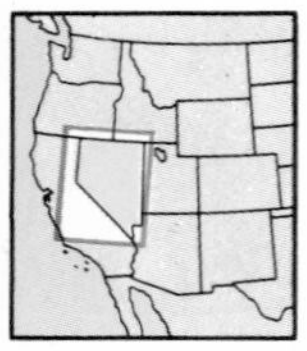

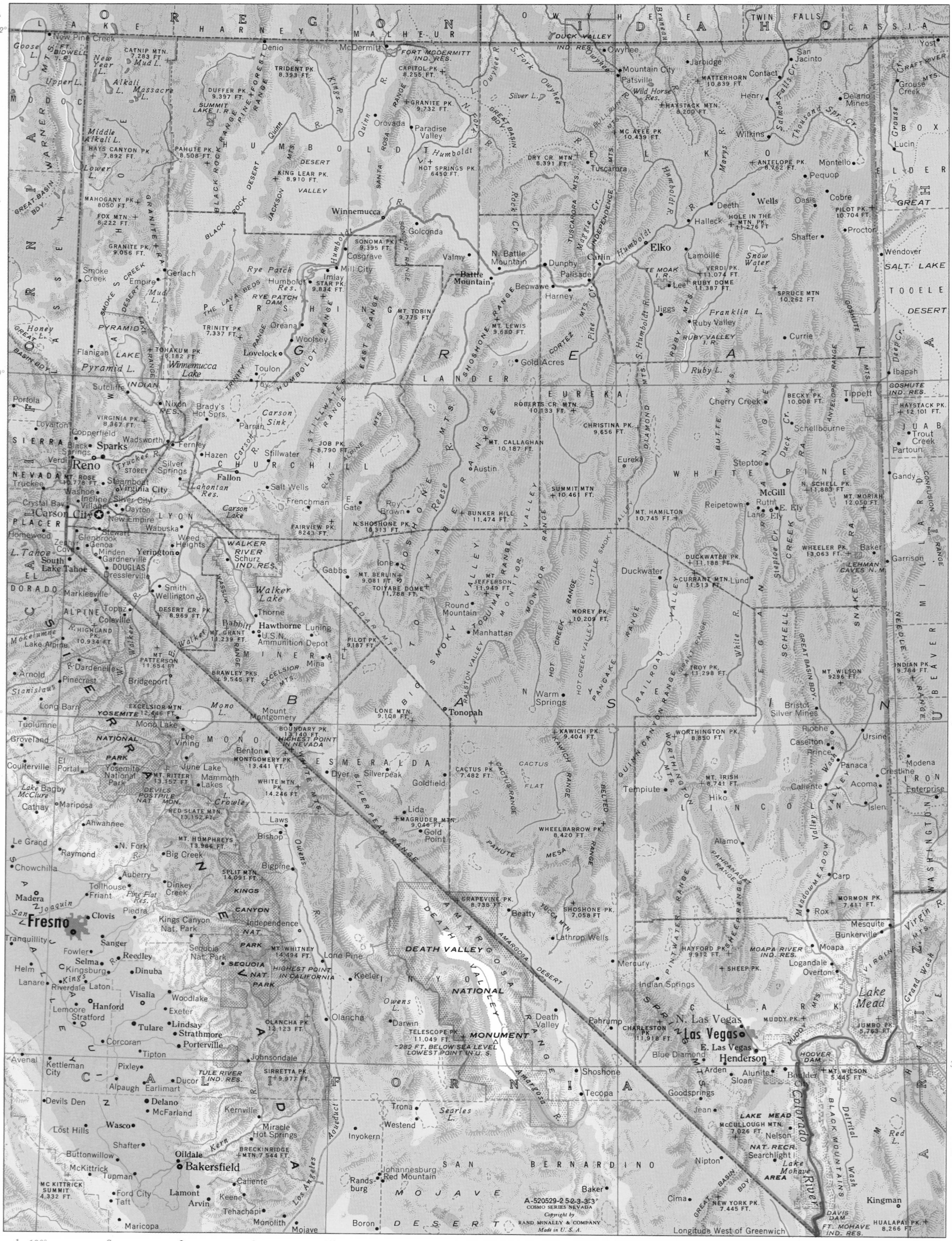

RELIEF

Feet: 5 000 · 2 000 · 1 000 · 500 · 100 · Sea Level · 100 Below Sea Level · 500 · 5 000

Statute Miles 5 0 5 10 20 30 40 50 60 70 80

Kilometers 5 0 10 20 40 60 80 100 120

Lambert Conformal Conic Projection
SCALE 1:2,630,000 1 Inch = 41.5 Statute Miles

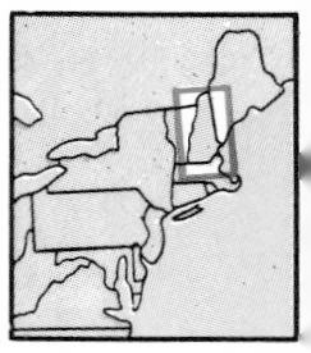

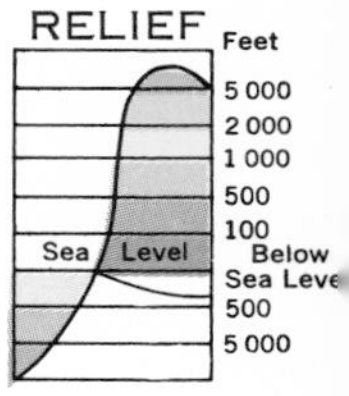

Lambert Conformal Conic Projection
SCALE 1:792,000 1 Inch = 12.75 Statute Miles

Statute Miles 5 0 5 10 20

Kilometers 5 0 5 10 15 20 25

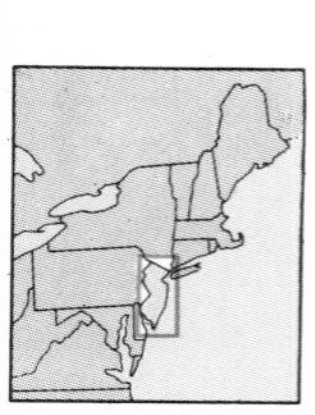

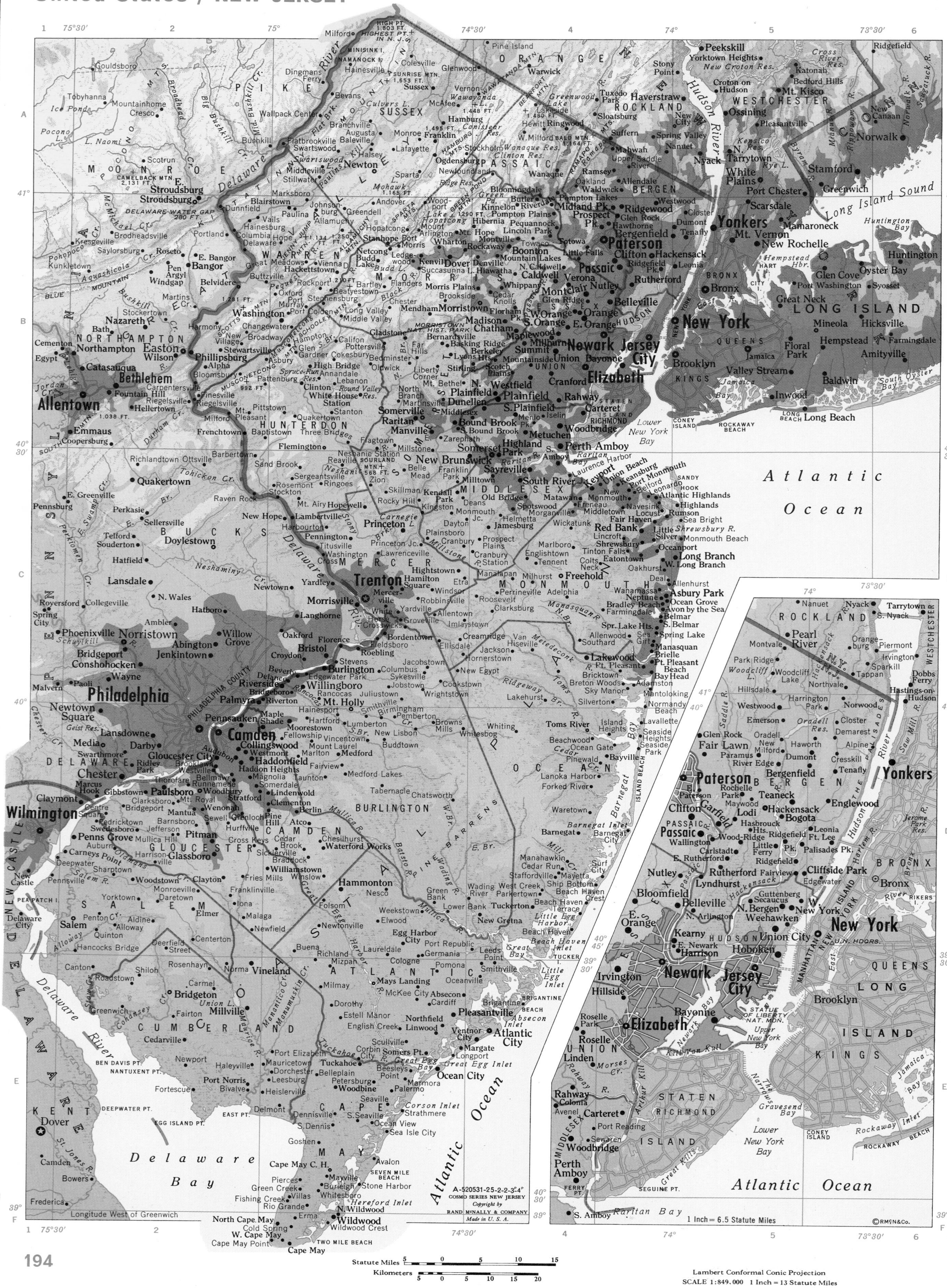
ORANGE
ROCKLAND
WESTCHESTER
PIKE
SUSSEX
PASSAIC
BERGEN
MONROE
NORTHAMPTON
WARREN
MORRIS
ESSEX
HUDSON
UNION
SOMERSET
HUNTERDON
BUCKS
MIDDLESEX
MERCER
MONMOUTH
BURLINGTON
OCEAN
CAMDEN
GLOUCESTER
SALEM
ATLANTIC
CUMBERLAND
CAPE MAY
DELAWARE
NEW CASTLE
KENT
QUEENS
KINGS
BRONX
RICHMOND
LONG ISLAND
STATEN ISLAND
New York
Newark
Jersey City
Paterson
Elizabeth
Trenton
Camden
Philadelphia
Wilmington
Atlantic City
Allentown
Bethlehem
Easton
Yonkers
New Brunswick
Perth Amboy
Asbury Park
Long Branch
Vineland
Millville
Bridgeton
Hammonton
Toms River
Lakewood
Princeton
Morristown
Phillipsburg
Cape May
Wildwood
Ocean City
Long Island Sound
Atlantic Ocean
Delaware Bay
Delaware River
Hudson River
Lower New York Bay
Raritan Bay
RELIEF
Feet
5 000
2 000
1 000
500
200
100
Sea Level
Below Sea Level
500
5 000
Longitude West of Greenwich
HIGH PT. 1,803 FT. HIGHEST PT. IN N. J.
1 Inch = 6.5 Statute Miles
Statute Miles 5 0 5 10 15
Kilometers 5 0 5 10 15 20
Lambert Conformal Conic Projection
SCALE 1:849,000 1 Inch = 13 Statute Miles
A-520531-25-2-2-3-4"
COSMO SERIES NEW JERSEY
Copyright by RAND McNALLY & COMPANY
Made in U. S. A.
©RM&Co.

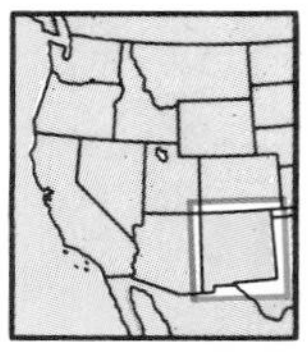

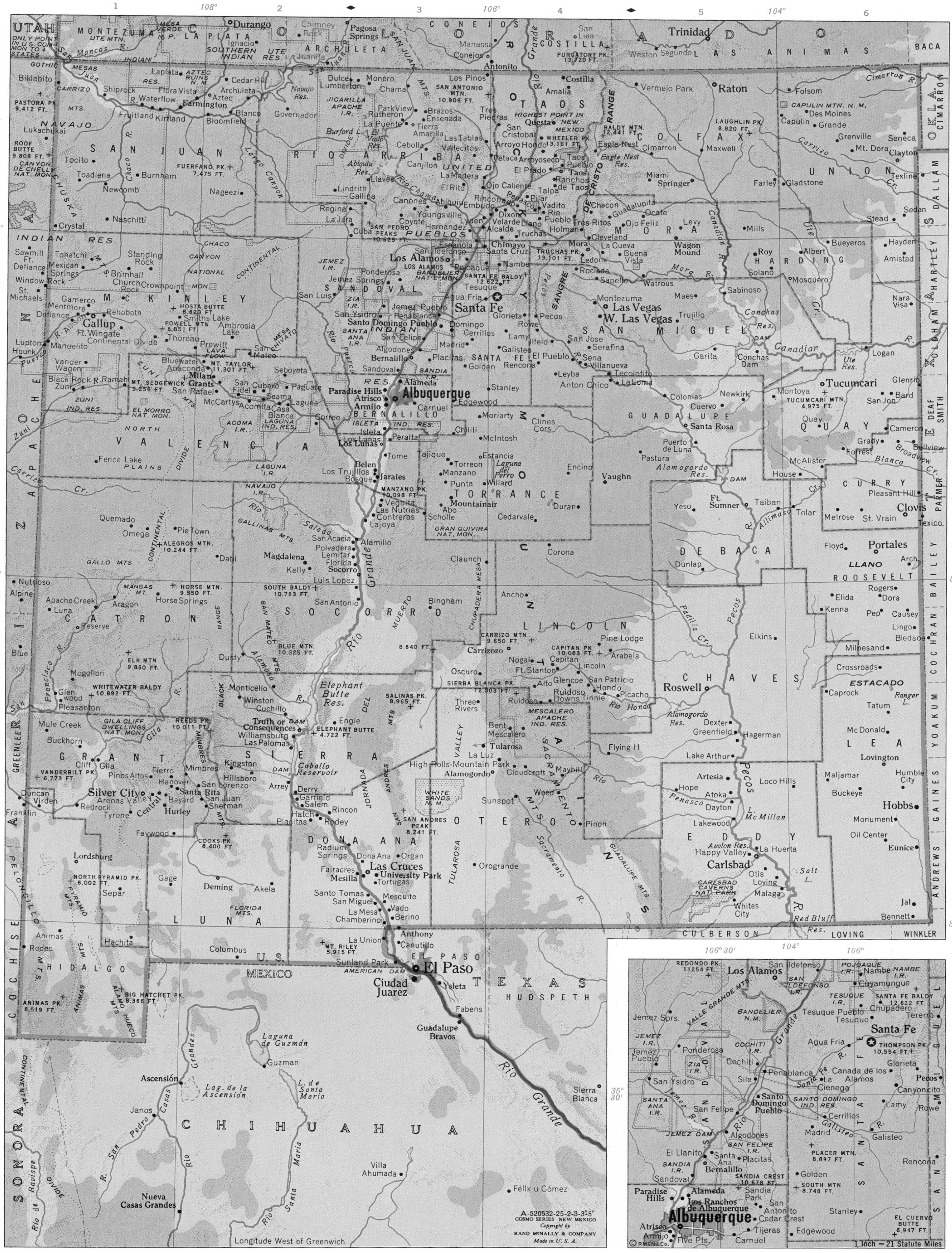

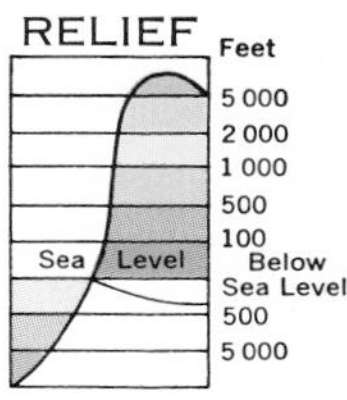

Lambert Conformal Conic Projection
SCALE 1:2,600,000 1 Inch = 41 Statute Miles

Statute Miles 10 0 10 20 30 40 50 60 70 80 90
Kilometers 10 0 10 20 40 60 80 100 120

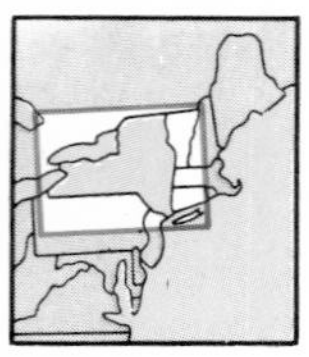

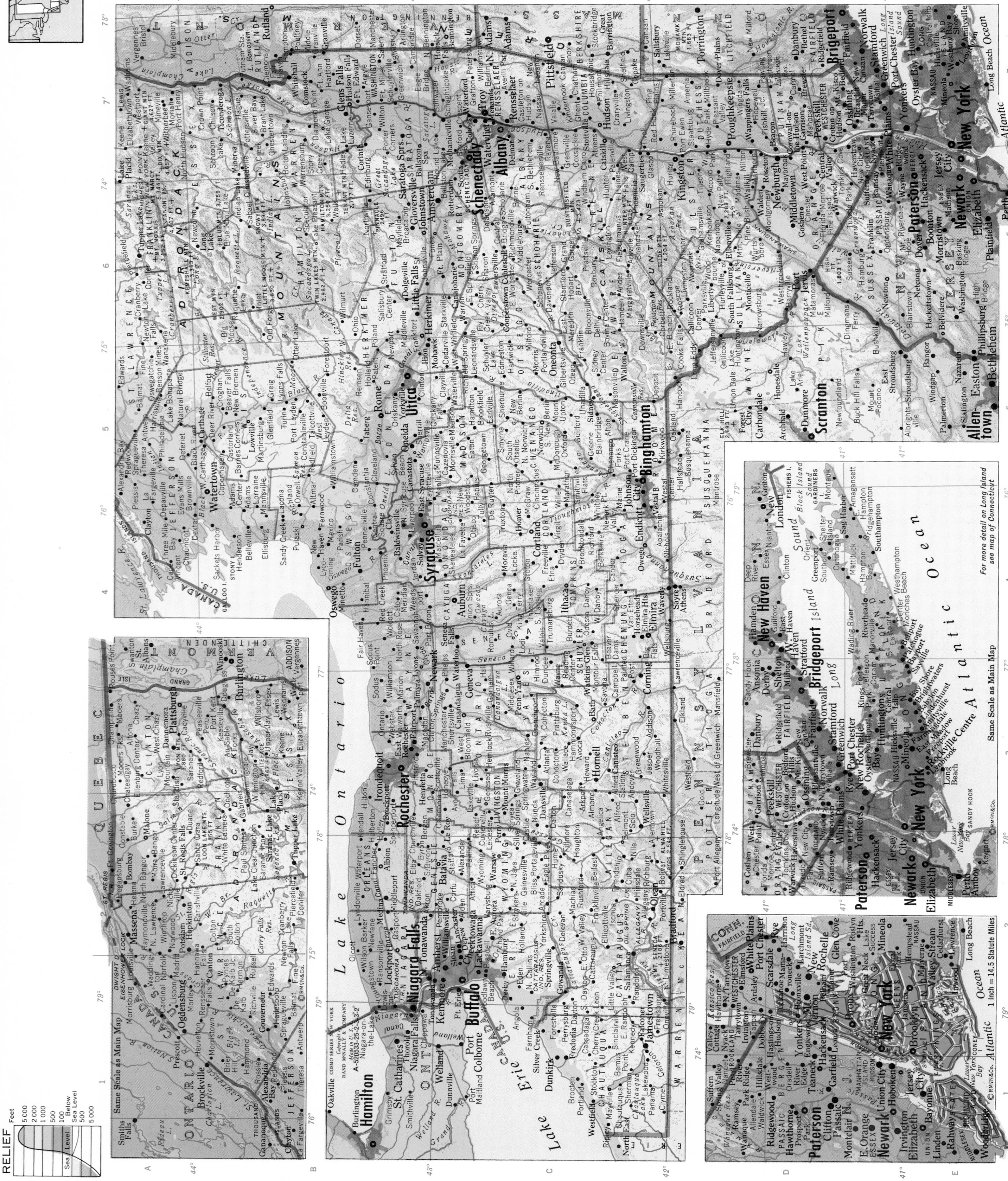

Statute Miles 5 0 5 10 20 30 40

Kilometers 5 0 5 15 25 35 45 55

Lambert Conformal Conic Projection

SCALE 1:1,862,000 1 Inch = 29 Statute Miles

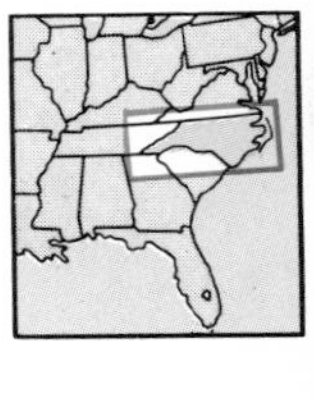

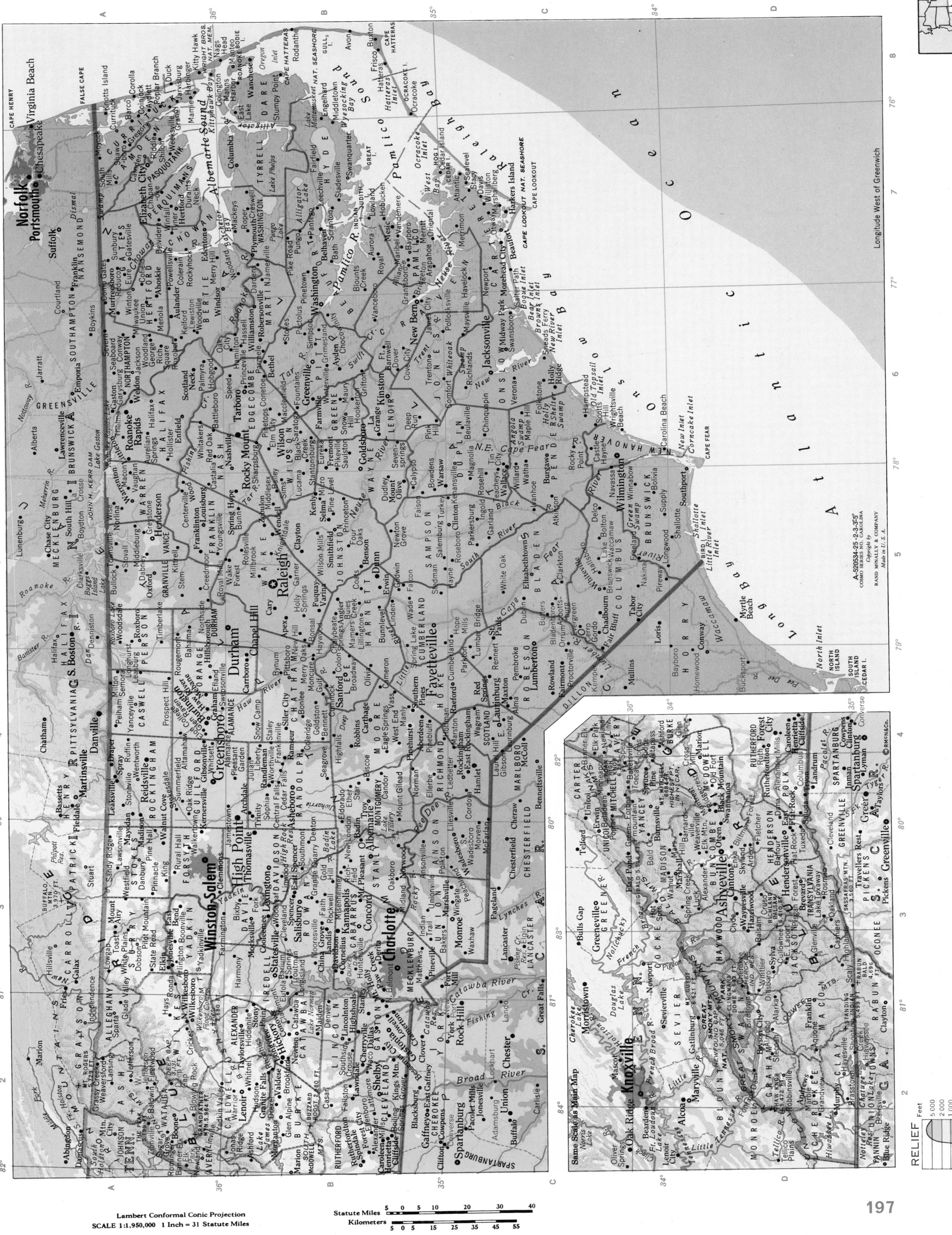

Lambert Conformal Conic Projection
SCALE 1:1,950,000 1 Inch = 31 Statute Miles

Statute Miles 5 0 5 10 20 30 40
Kilometers 5 0 5 15 25 35 45 55

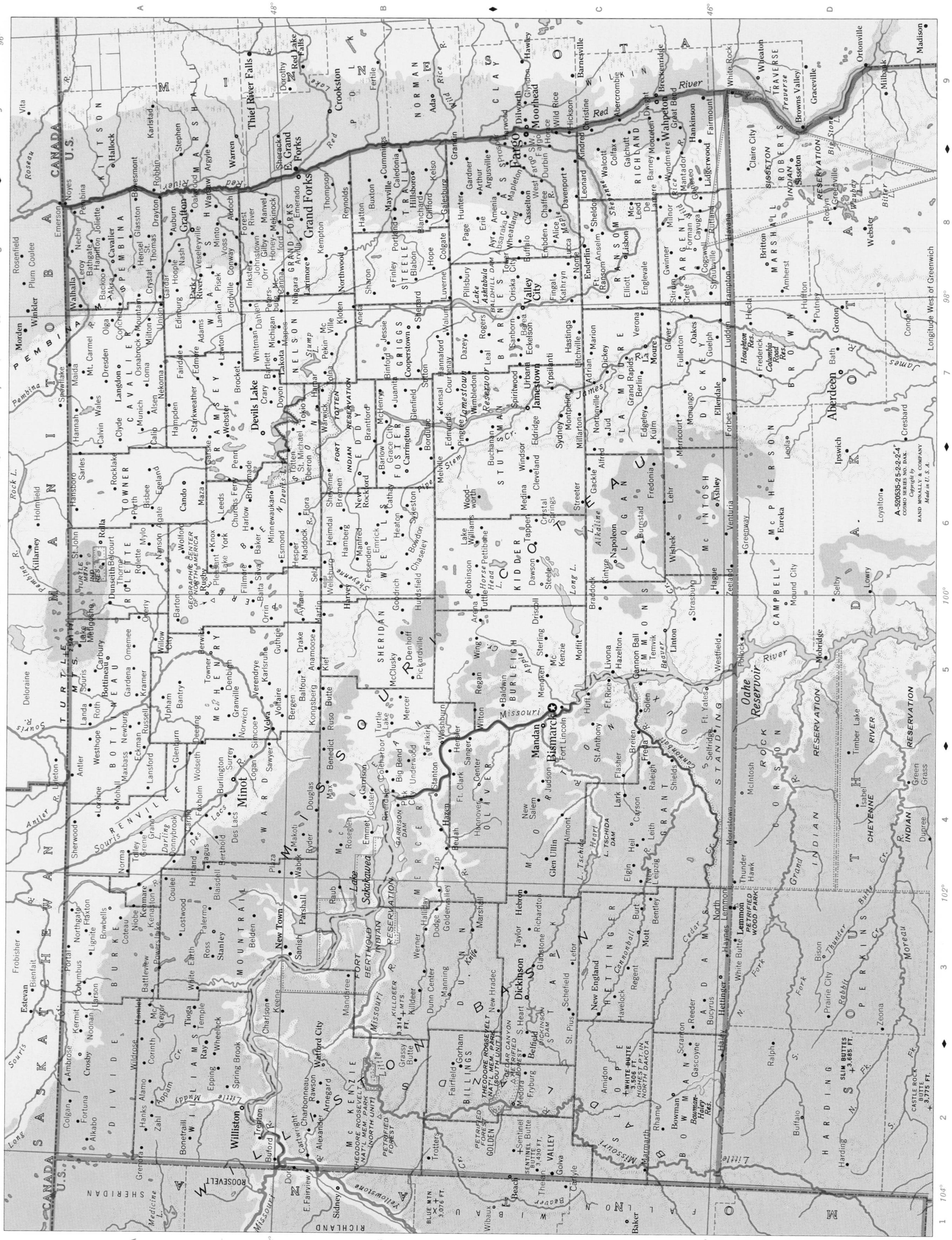

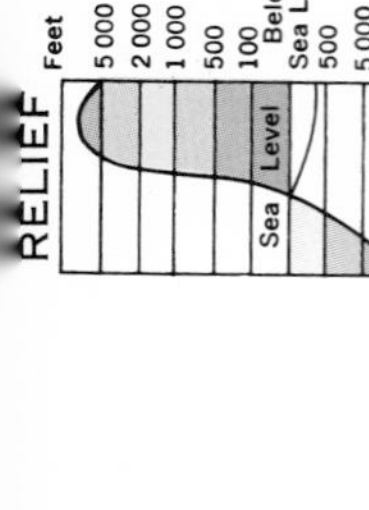

Statute Miles 5 0 5 10 20 30 40 50 60

Kilometers 5 0 5 15 25 35 45 55 65 75

Lambert Conformal Conic Projection
SCALE 1:2,091,000 1 Inch = 33 Statute Miles

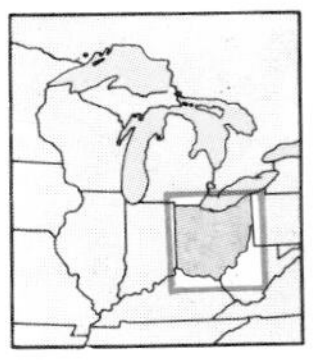

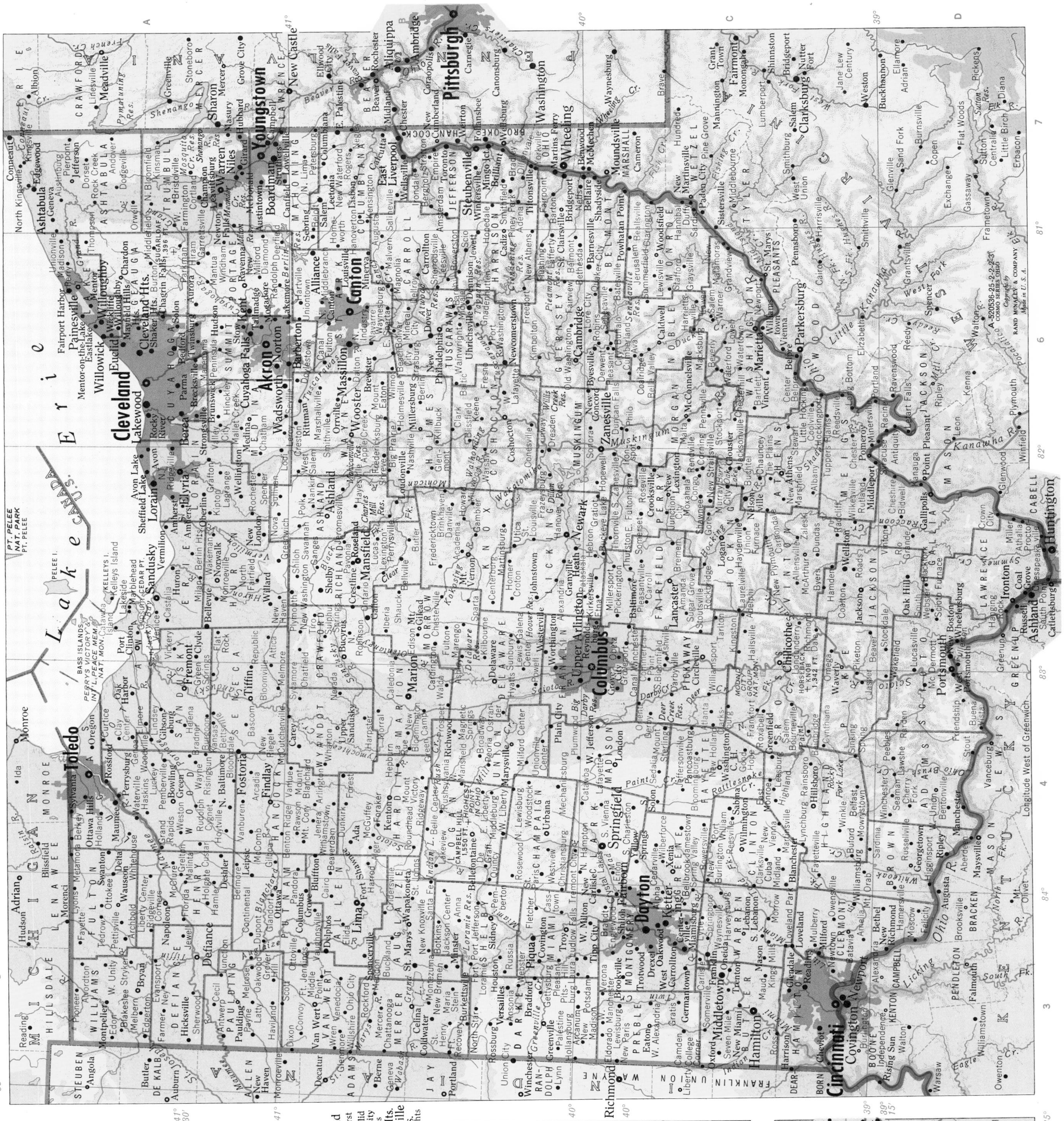

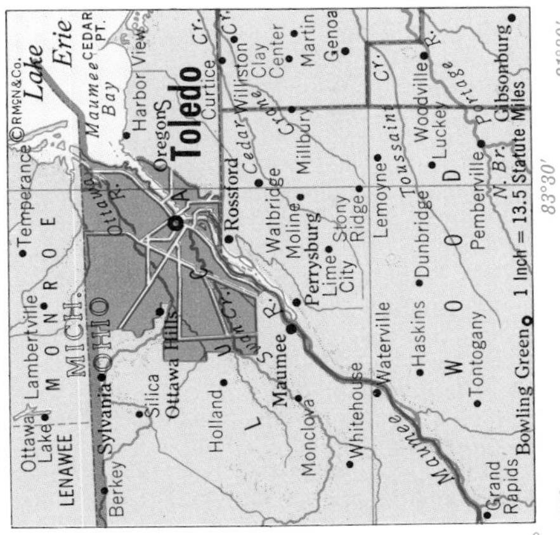

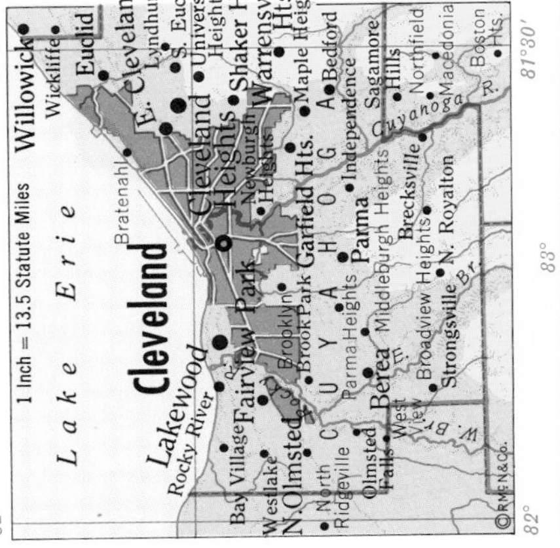

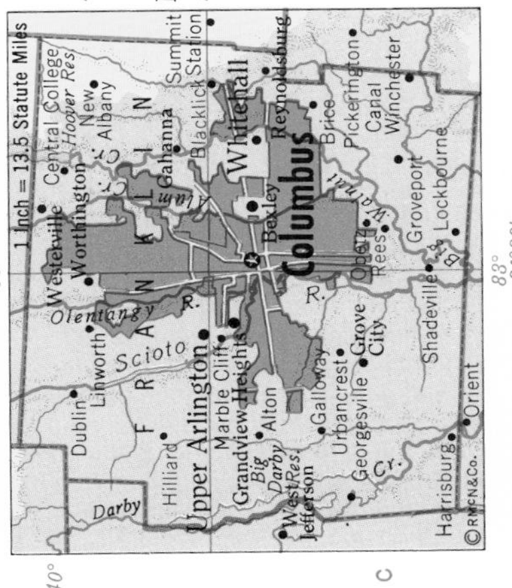

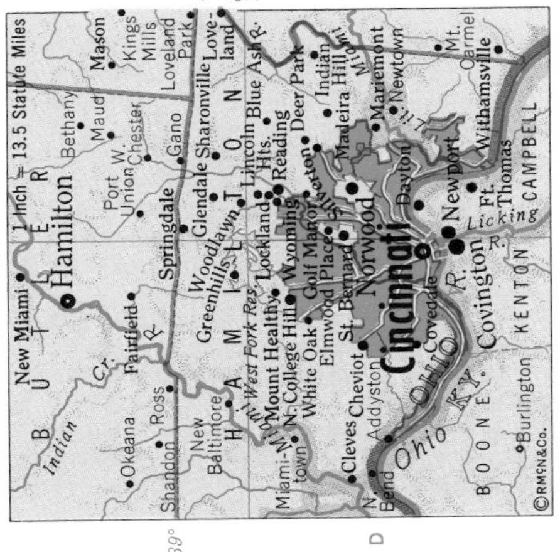

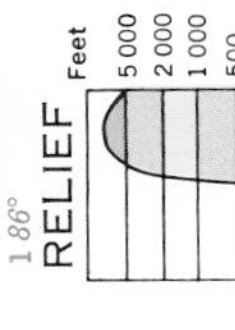

Lambert Conformal Conic Projection
SCALE 1:1,714,000 1 Inch = 27 Statute Miles

Statute Miles 5 0 5 10 20 30 40
Kilometers 5 0 5 15 25 35 45 55

RELIEF

Feet
5 000
2 000
1 000
500
Sea Level
500
5 000
Below Sea Level

RAND M^cNALLY & COMPANY
COSMO SERIES OKLAHOMA
Made in U. S. A.

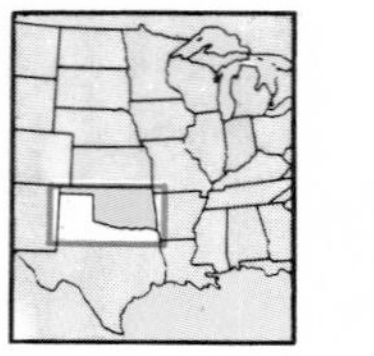

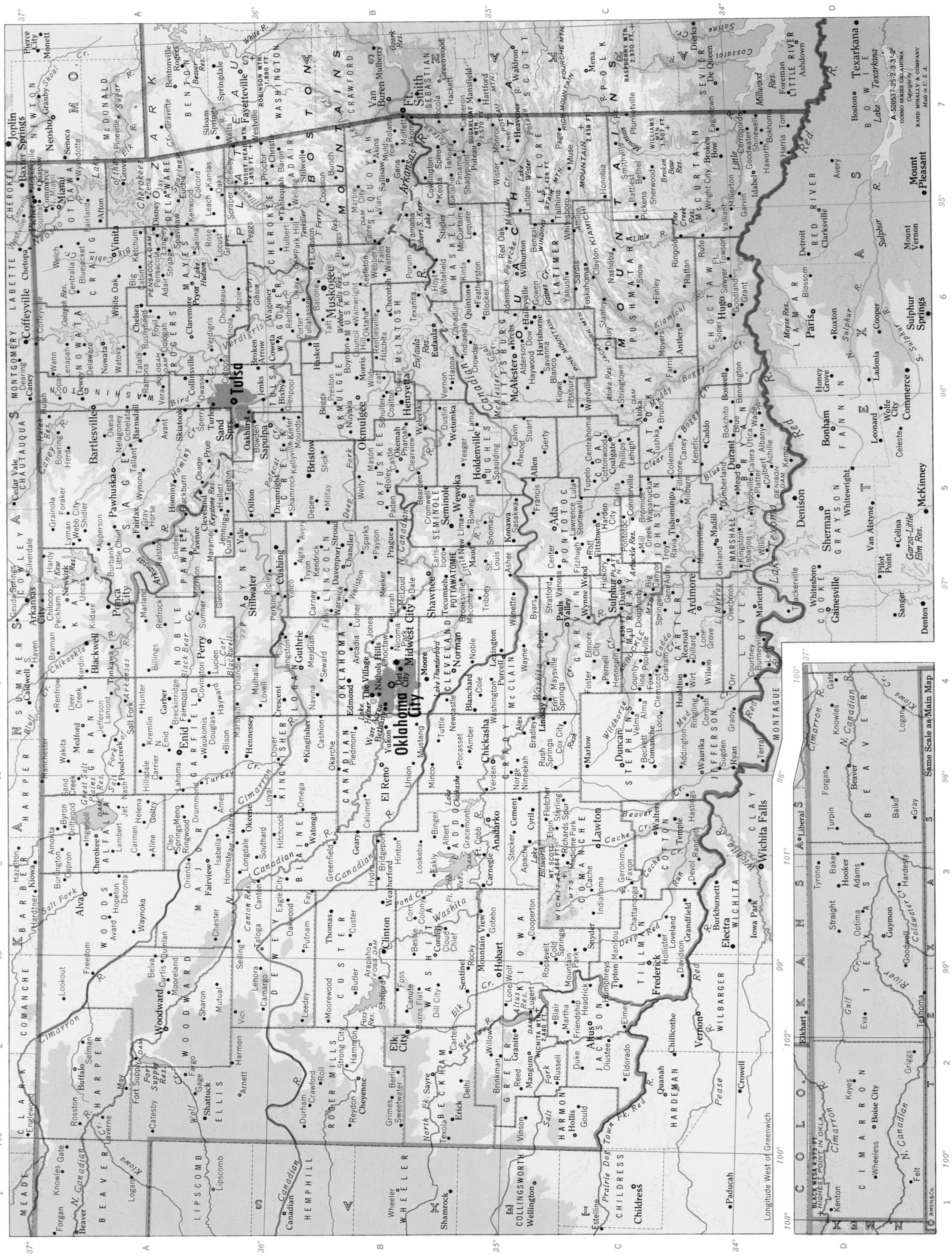

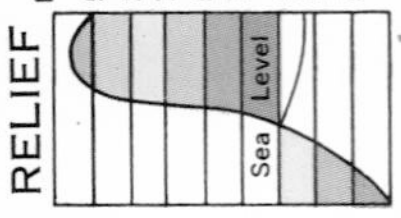

Statute Miles 5 0 5 10 20 30 40
Kilometers 5 0 5 15 25 35 45 55

Lambert Conformal Conic Projection
SCALE 1:1,957,000 1 Inch = 31 Statute Miles

R.M^cN.&Co.

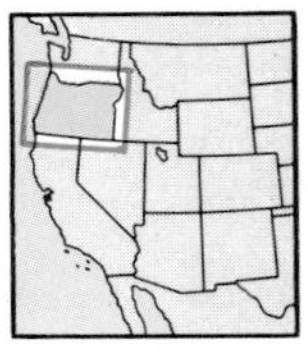

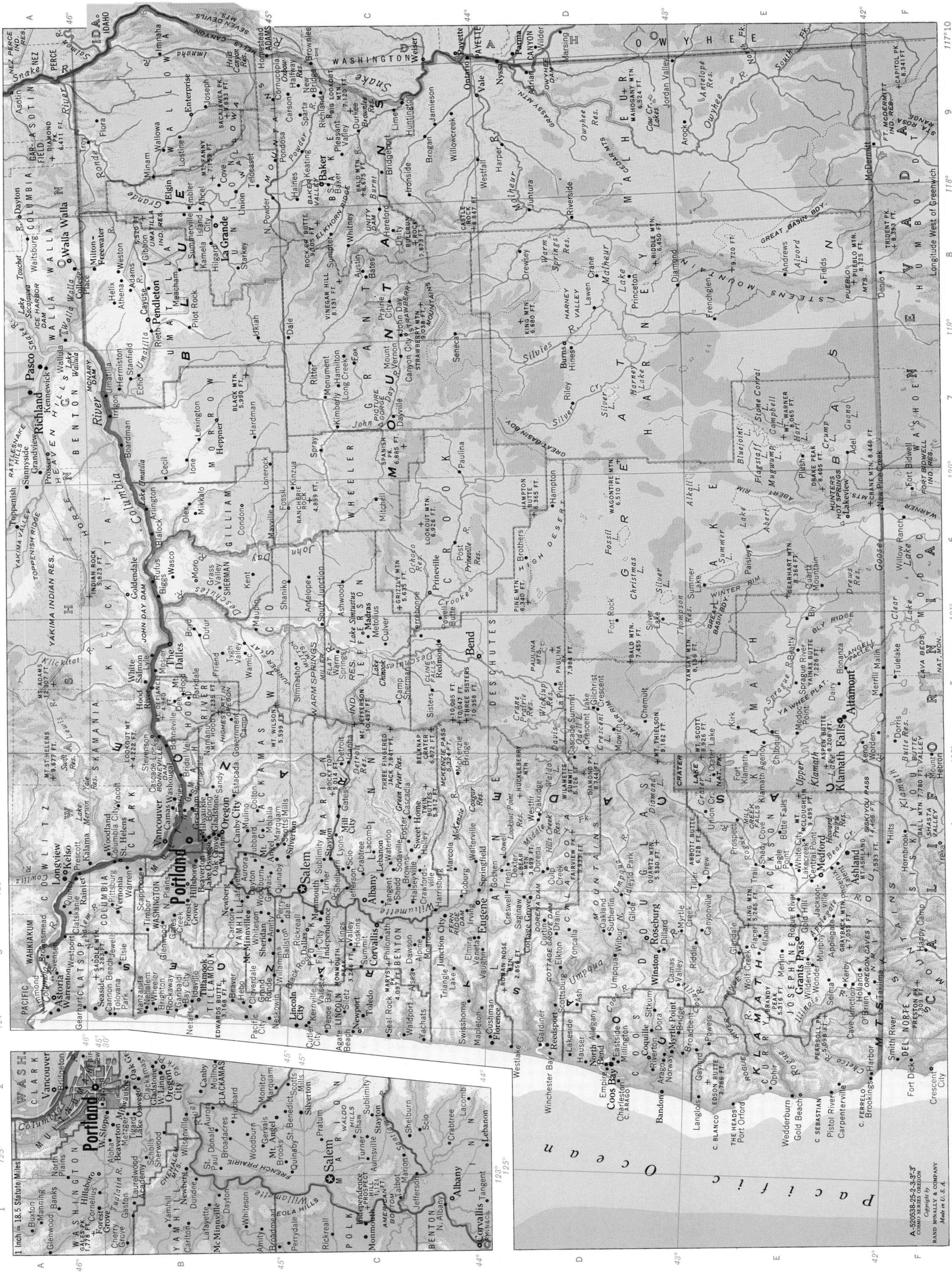

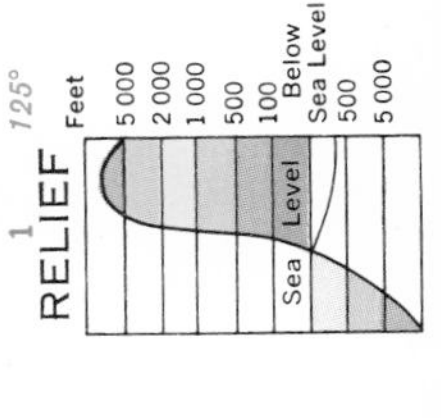

Lambert Conformal Conic Projection
SCALE 1:2,329,000 1 Inch = 37 Statute Miles

Statute Miles 5 0 5 10 20 30 40 50
Kilometers 5 0 5 15 25 35 45 55 65 75

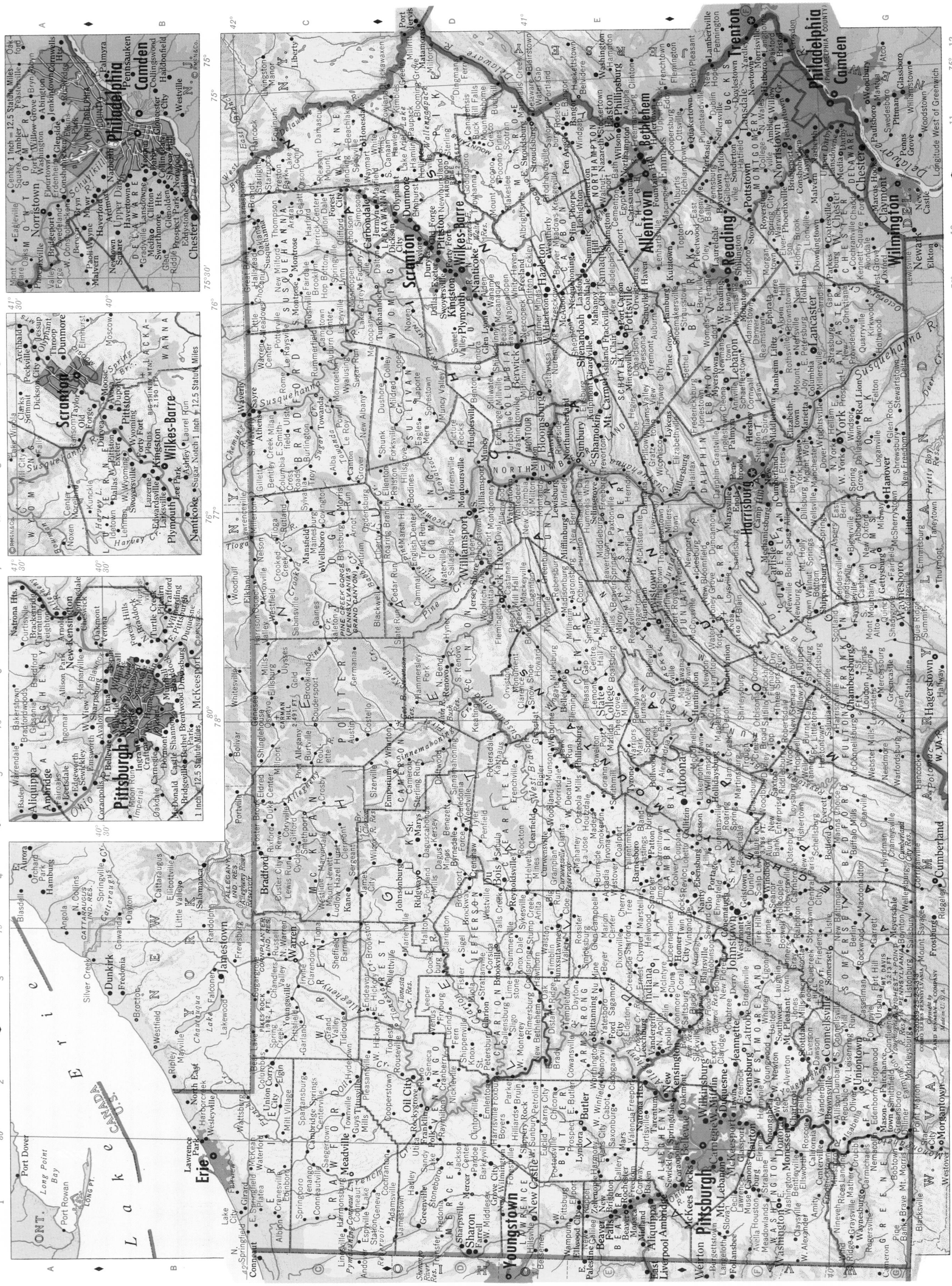

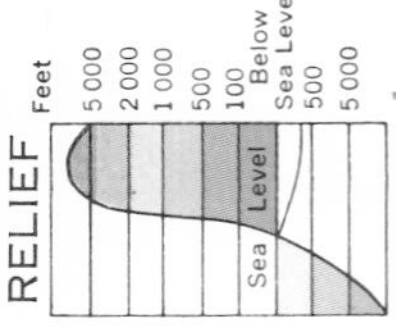

Statute Miles 5 0 5 10 20 30
Kilometers 5 0 5 15 25 35 45

Lambert Conformal Conic Projection
SCALE 1:1,593,000 1 Inch = 25 Statute Miles

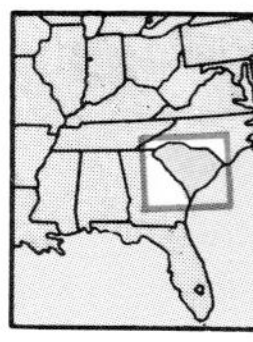

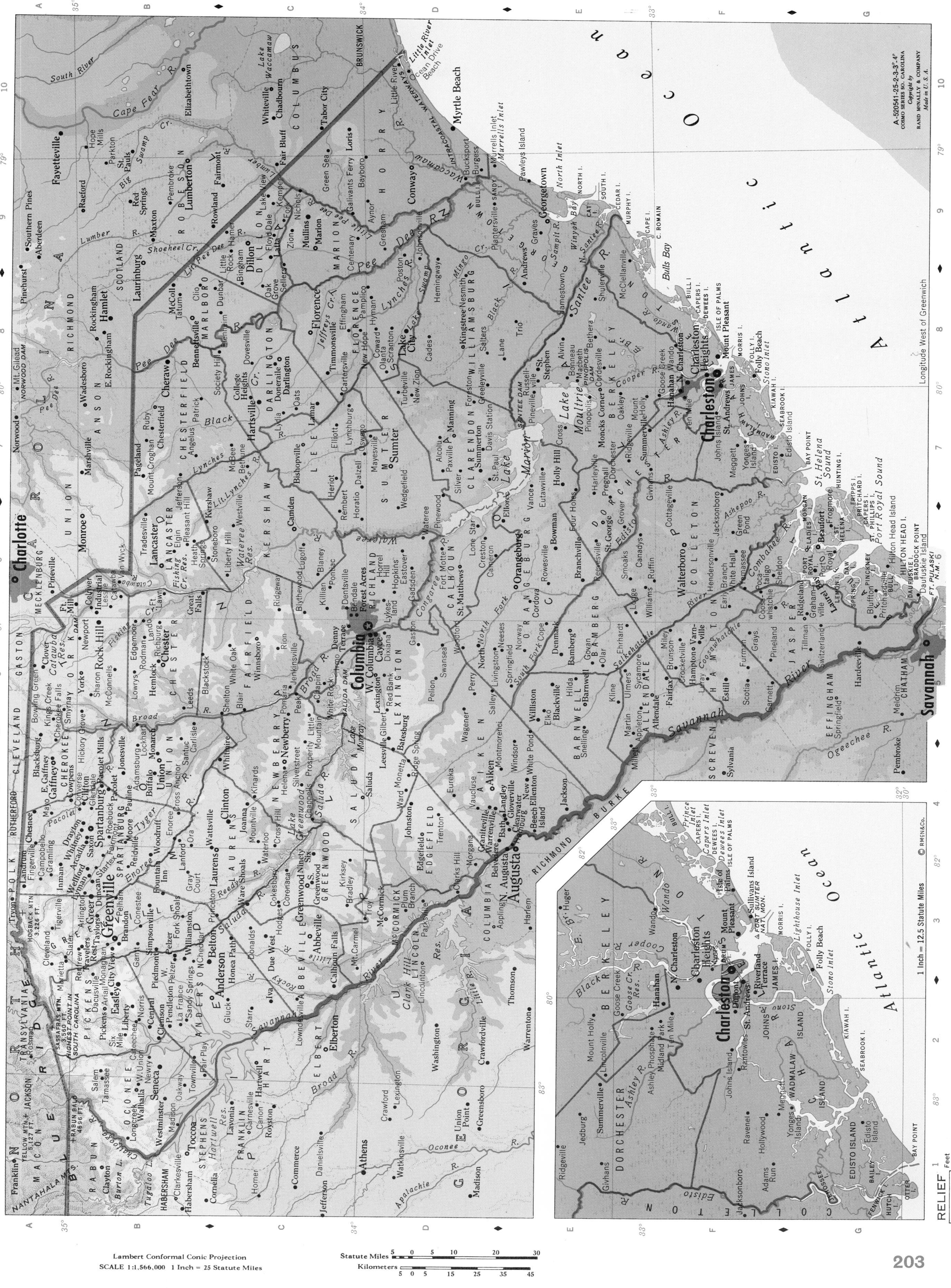

Lambert Conformal Conic Projection
SCALE 1:1,566,000 1 Inch = 25 Statute Miles

Statute Miles 5 0 5 10 20 30
Kilometers 5 0 5 15 25 35 45

RELIEF

Feet
5 000
2 000
1 000
500
100
Sea Level
500
5 000

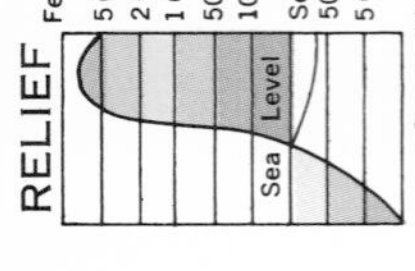

Statute Miles 5 0 5 10 20 30 40 50 60
Kilometers 5 0 5 15 25 35 45 55 65 75

Lambert Conformal Conic Projection
SCALE 1:2,091,000 1 Inch = 33 Statute Miles

A-520542-25-2-2-23
COMBO SERIES SO. DAK.
Copyright by
RAND M?NALLY & COMPANY
Made in U.S.A.

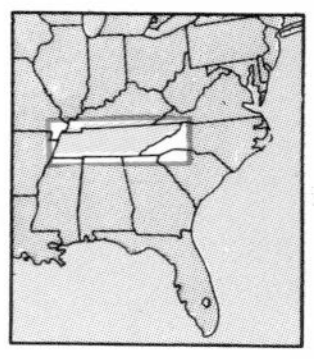

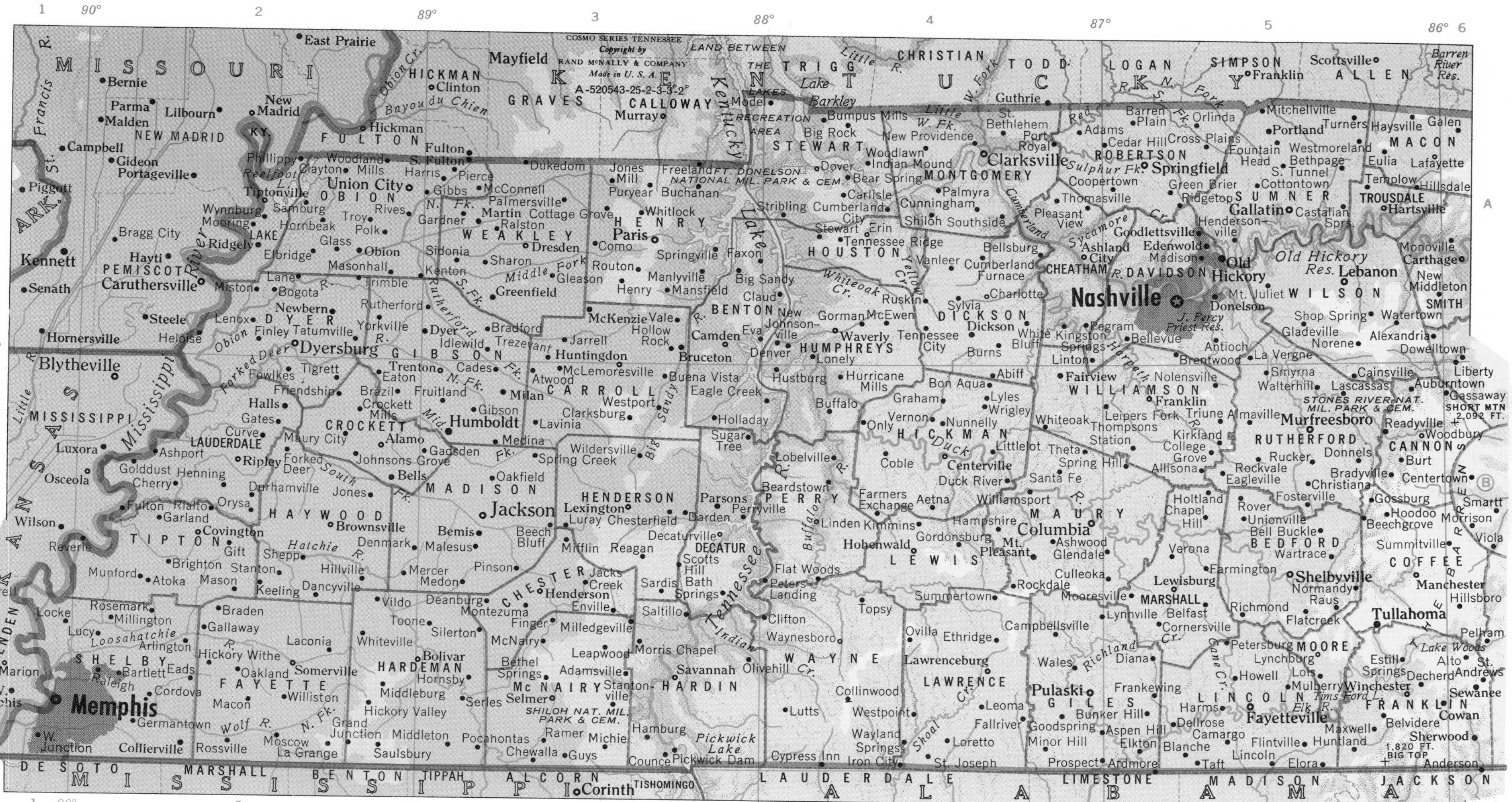

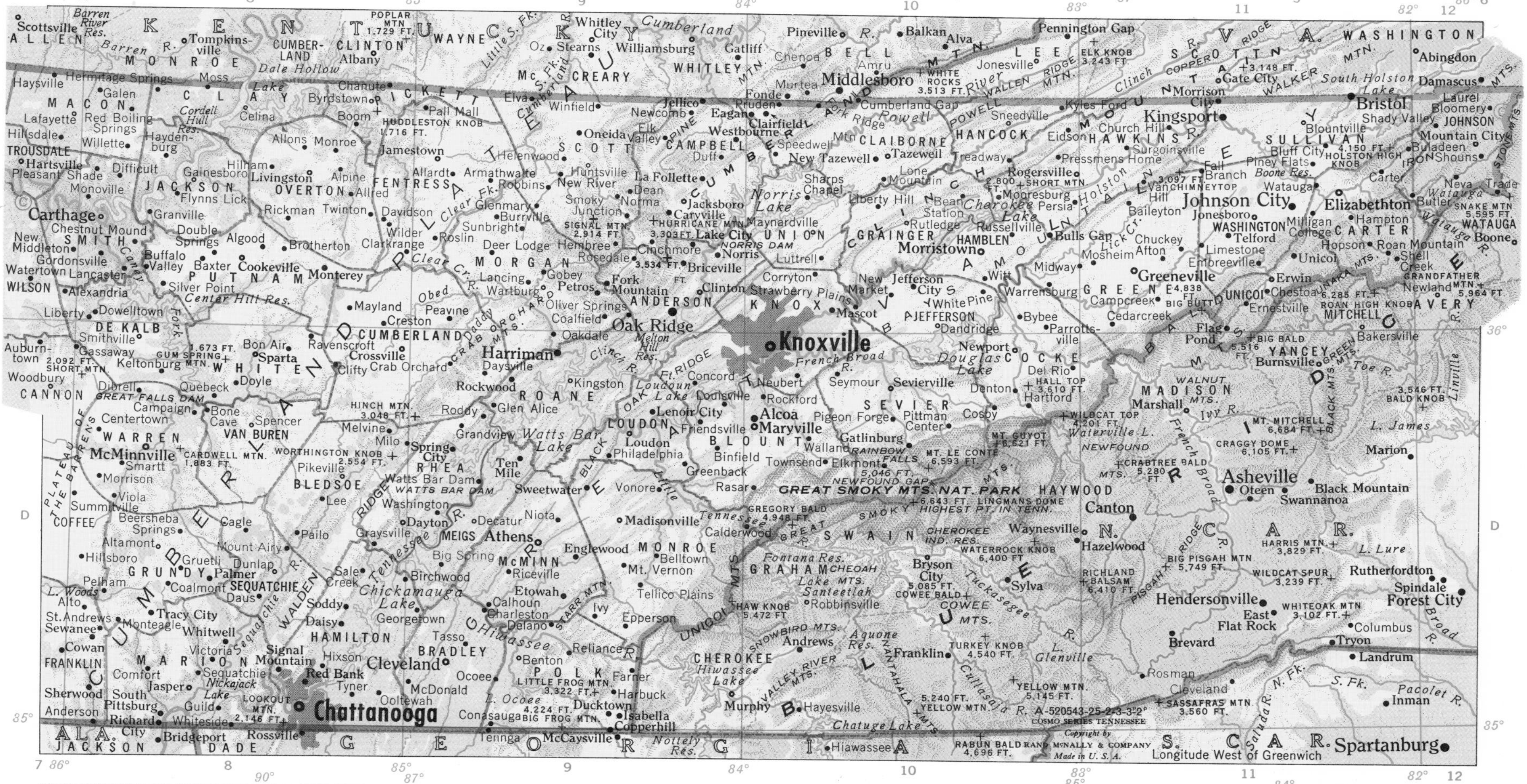

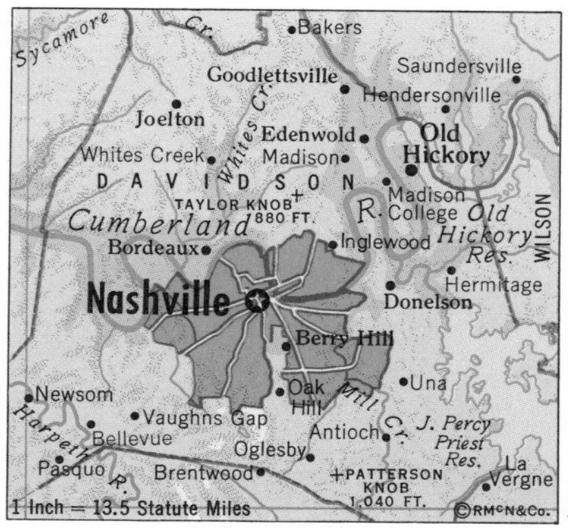

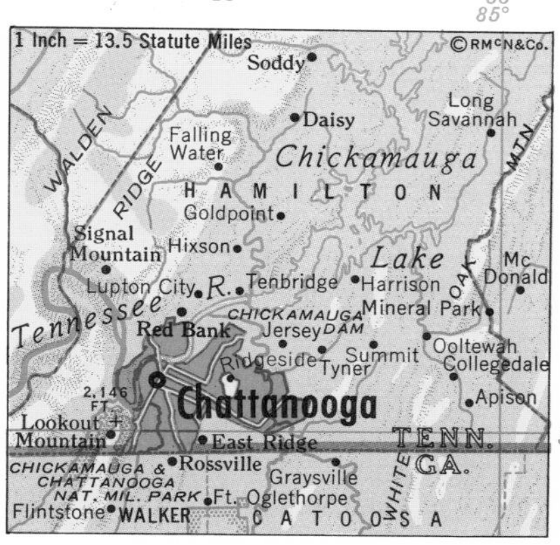

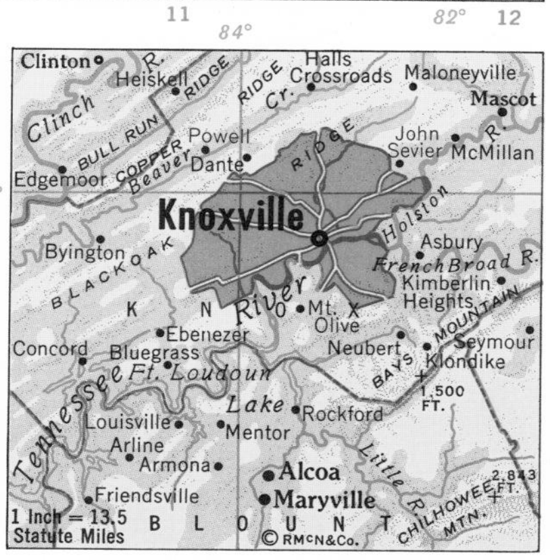

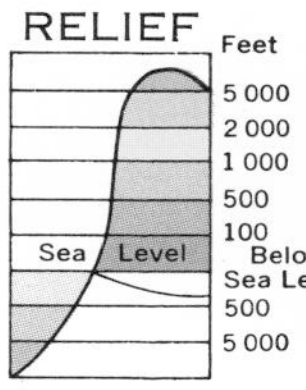

Lambert Conformal Conic Projection
SCALE 1:1,713,000 1 Inch = 27 Statute Miles

Statute Miles 5 0 5 10 20 30 40
Kilometers 5 0 5 15 25 35 45 55

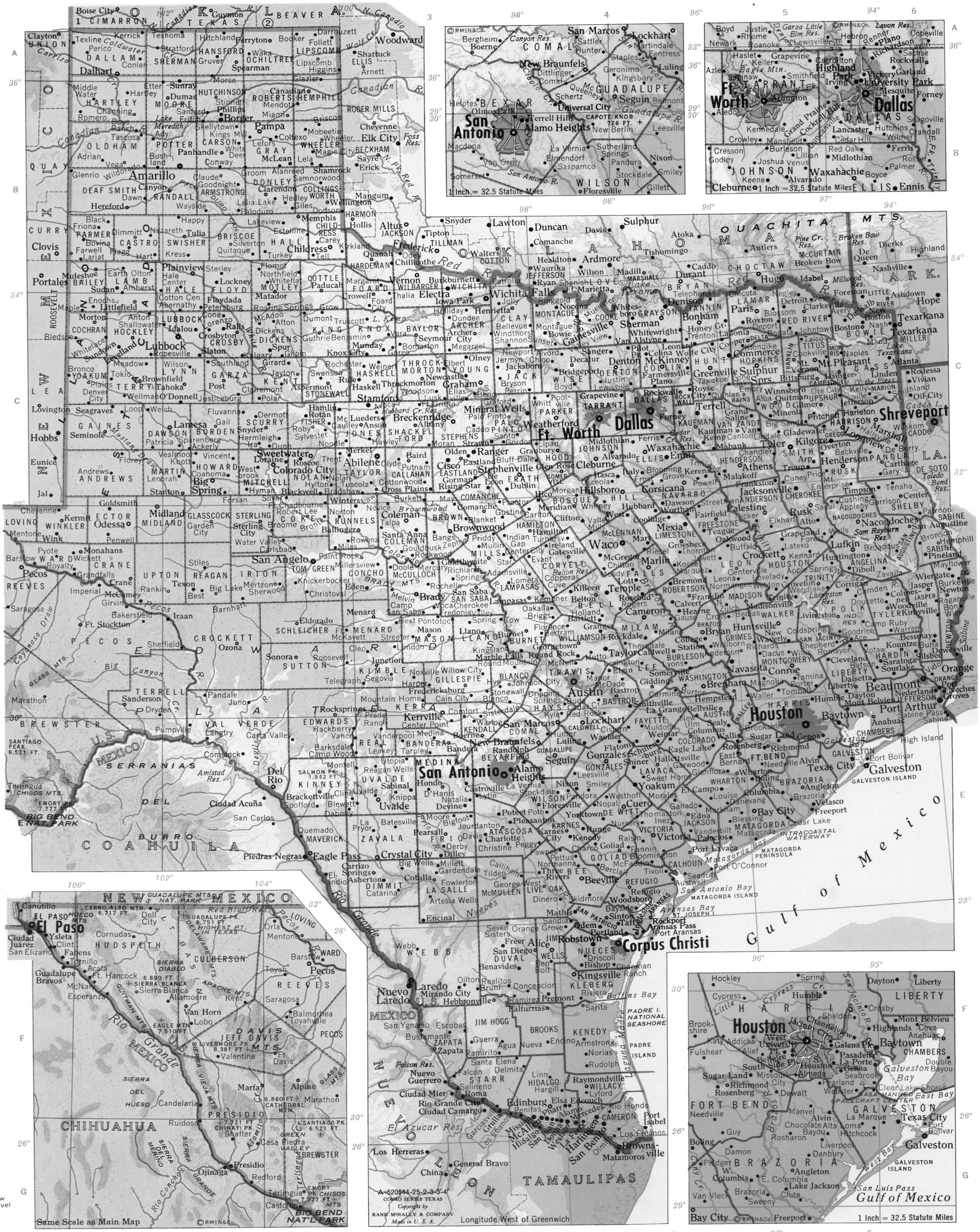

Statute Miles 10 0 10 20 30 40 50 60 70 80 90 100

Kilometers 10 0 10 20 40 60 80 100 120 140

Lambert Conformal Conic Projection
SCALE 1:4,096,000 1 Inch = 65 Statute Miles

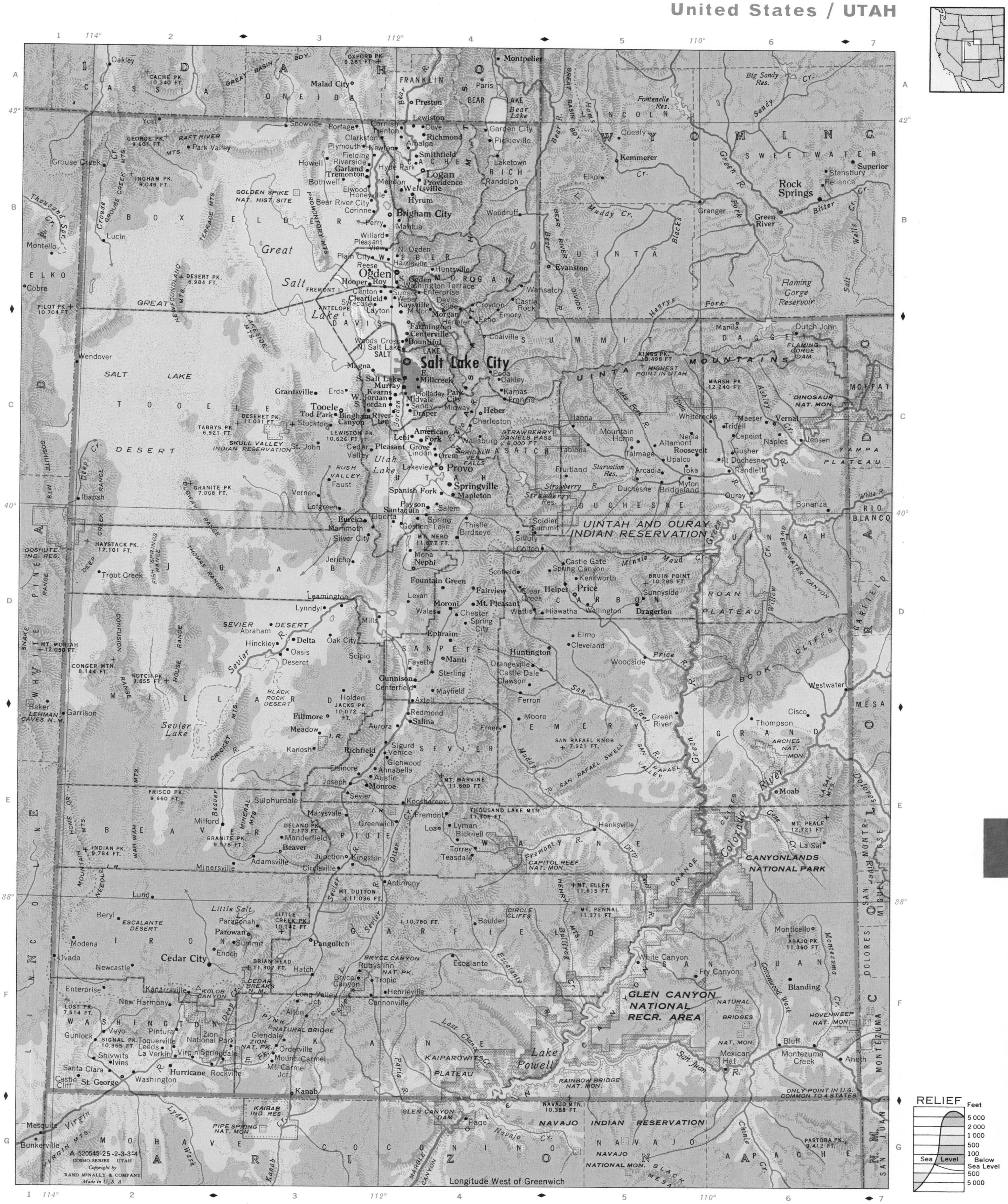

Lambert Conformal Conic Projection
SCALE 1:2,100,000 1 Inch = 33 Statute Miles

Statute Miles 5 0 5 10 20 30 40 50 60
Kilometers 5 0 10 20 40 60 80 100

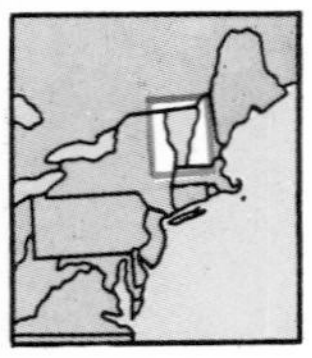

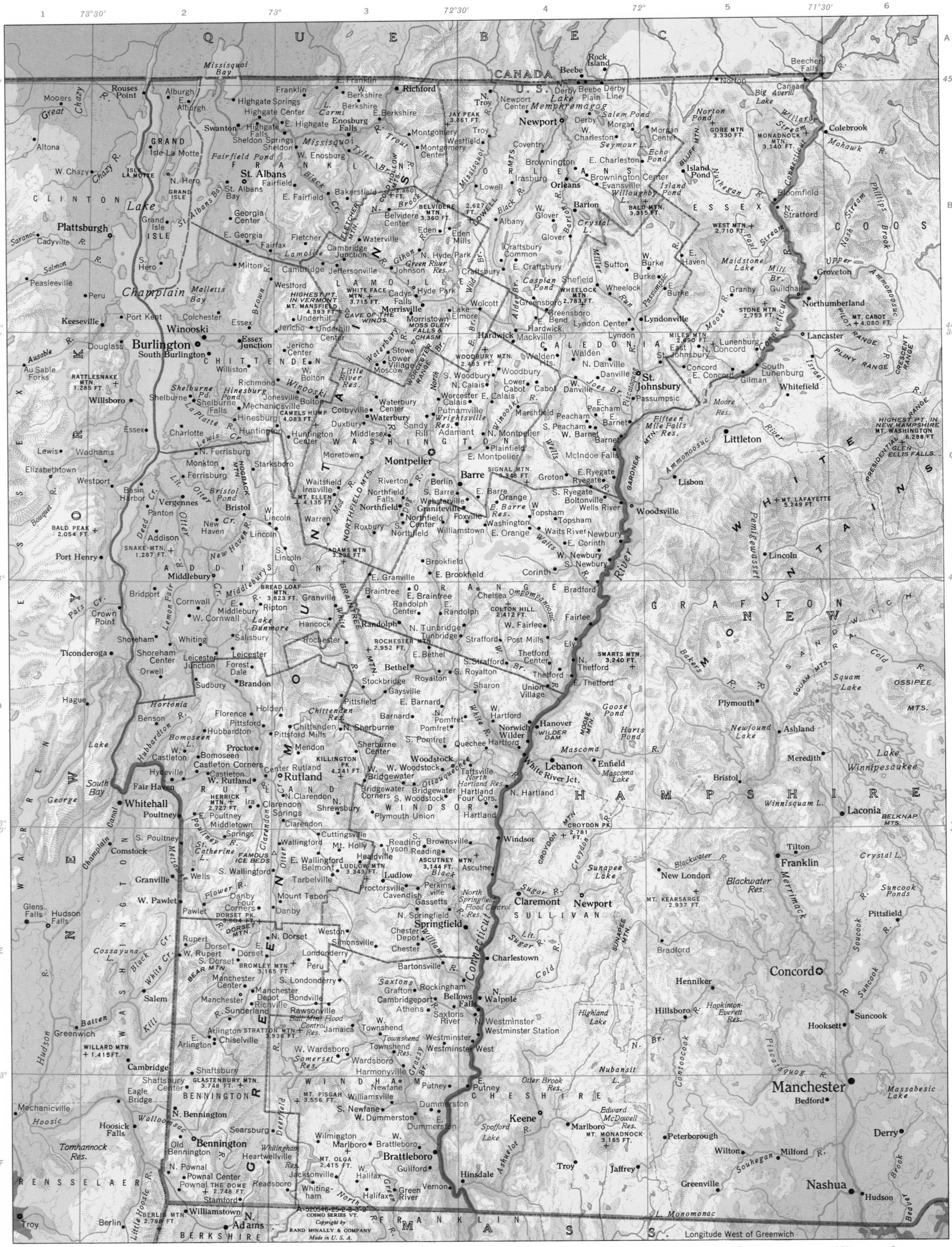

Statute Miles 5 0 5 20

Kilometers 5 0 5 10 15 20 25

Lambert Conformal Conic Projection

SCALE 1:903,000 1 Inch = 14.25 Statute Miles

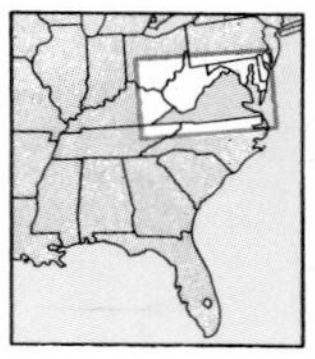

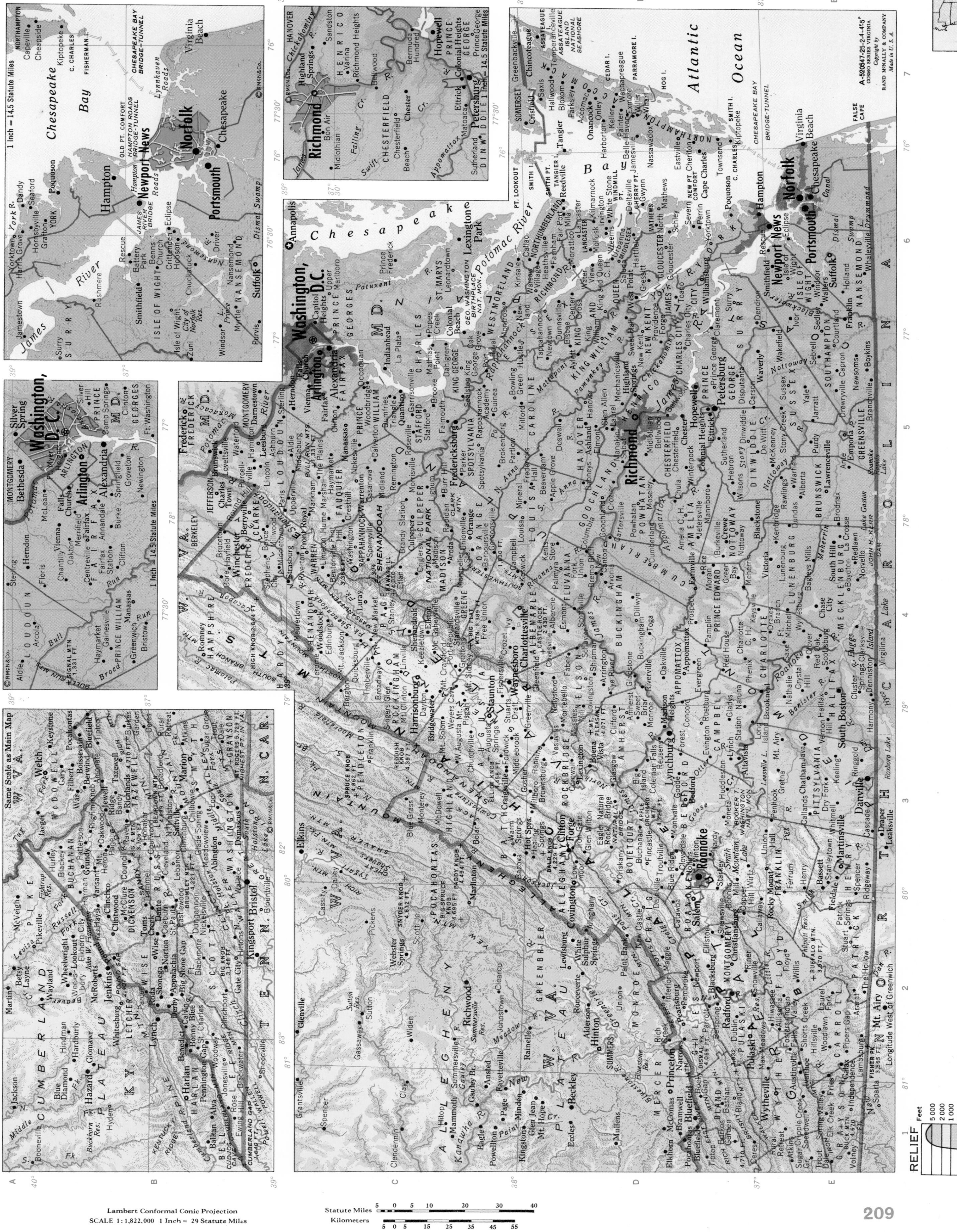

Lambert Conformal Conic Projection
SCALE 1 : 1,822,000 1 Inch = 29 Statute Miles

Statute Miles 5 0 5 10 20 30 40
Kilometers 5 0 5 15 25 35 45 55

RELIEF

Feet	
5 000	
2 000	
1 000	
500	
100	
Sea Level	
500	Below Sea Level
5 000	

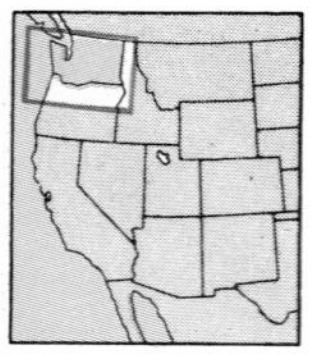

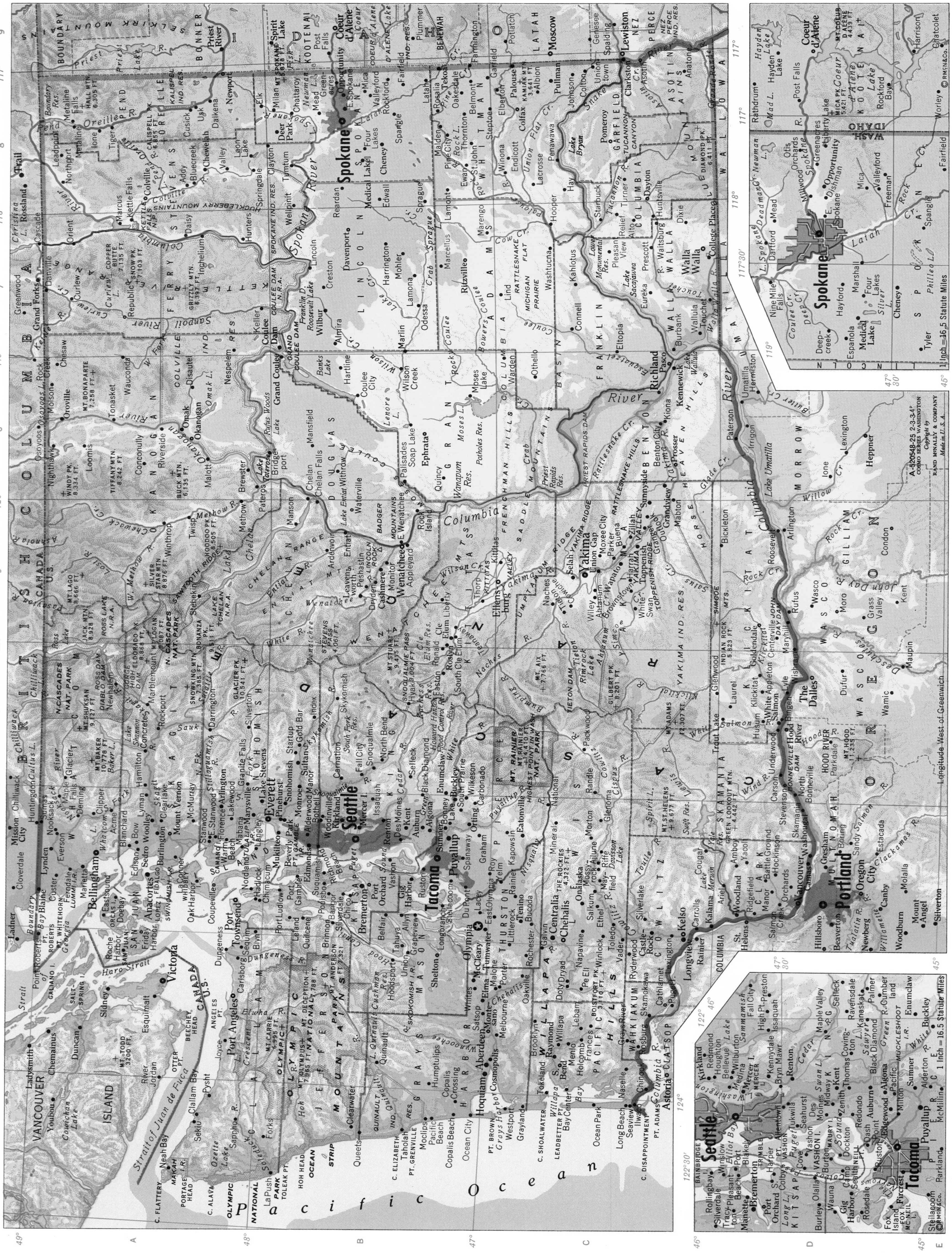

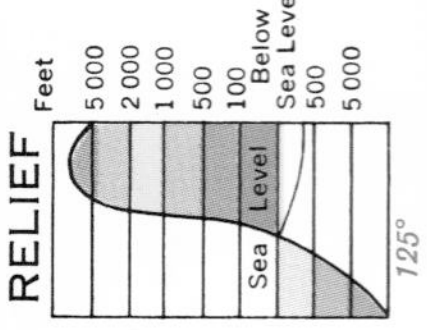

Statute Miles 5 0 5 10 20 30 40 50
Kilometers 5 0 5 15 25 35 45 55 65

Lambert Conformal Conic Projection
SCALE 1:2,068,000 Inch = 33 Statute Miles

Spokane
1 Inch = 16.5 Statute Miles

Seattle–Tacoma
1 inch = 16.5 Statute Miles

A-520548-25 2-3-3-4°
COSMO SERIES WASHINGTON
RAND M\=cNALLY & COMPANY
Made in U.S.A.

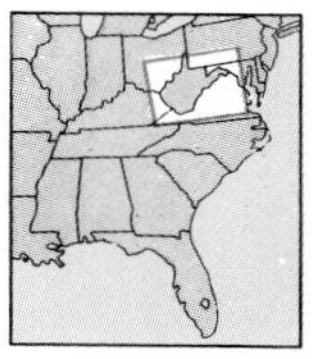

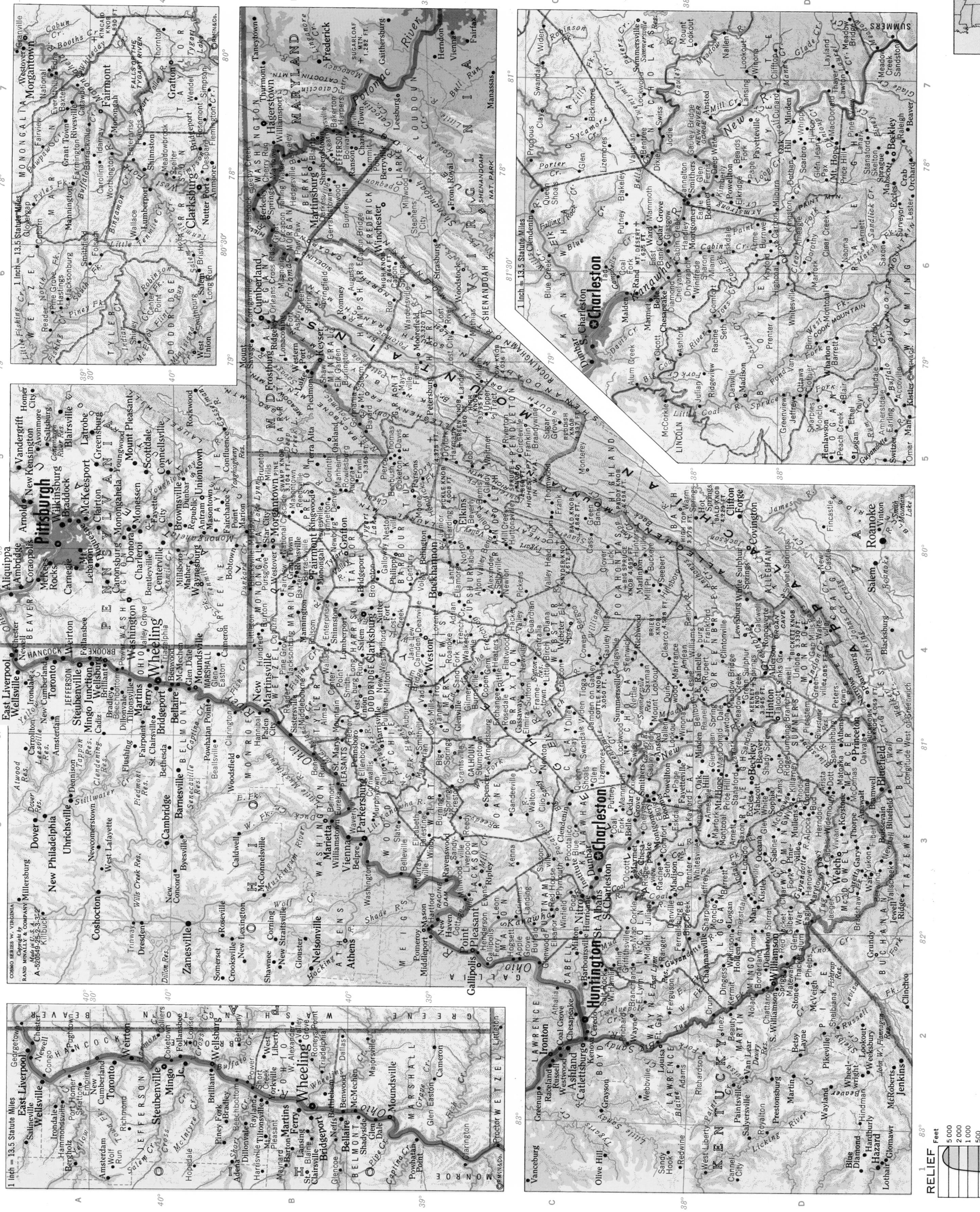

Lambert Conformal Conic Projection
SCALE 1:1,704,000 1 Inch = 27 Statute Miles

Statute Miles 5 0 5 10 20 30 40
Kilometers 5 0 5 15 25 35 45 55

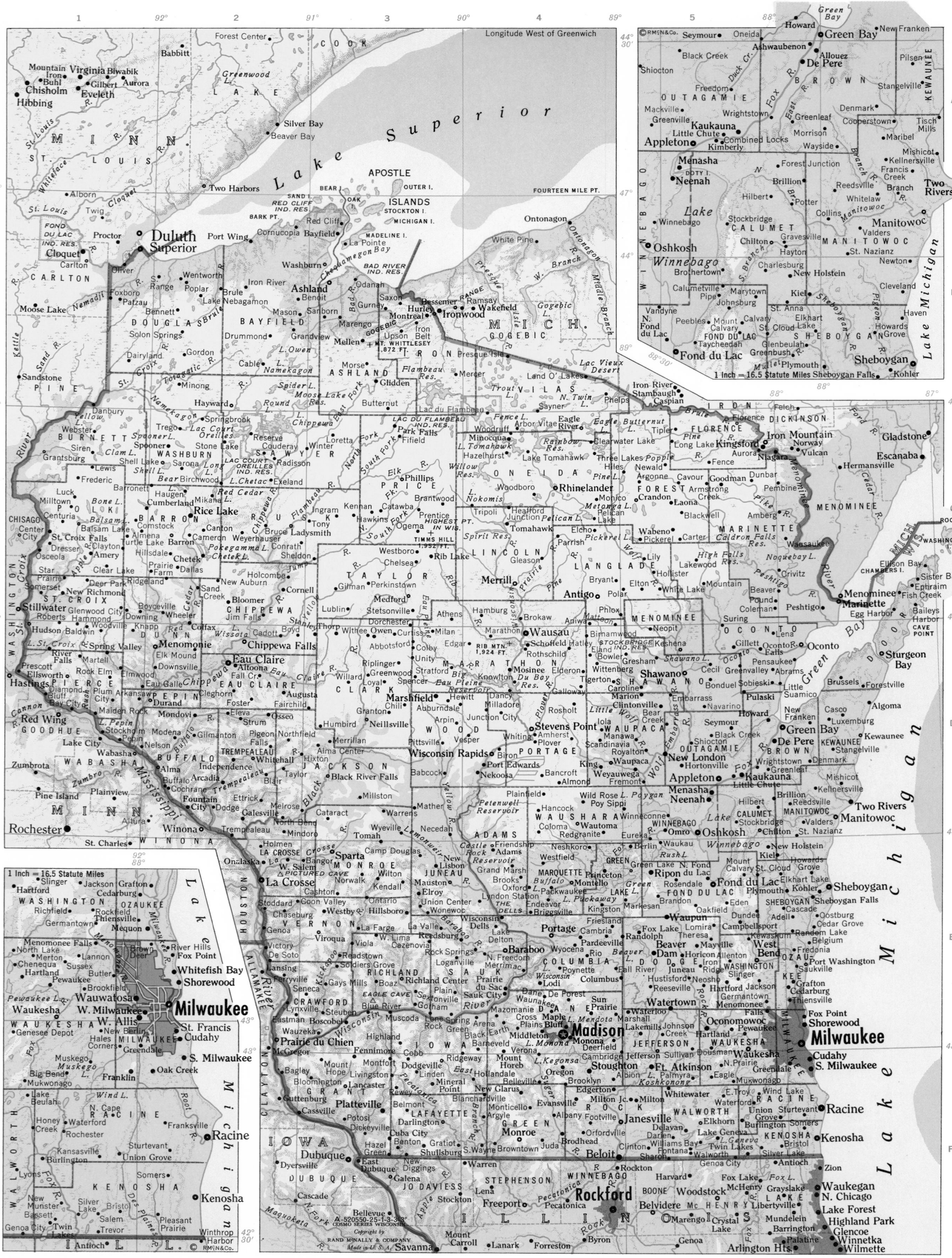

Statute Miles 5 0 5 10 20 30 40

Kilometers 5 0 5 15 25 35 45 55

Lambert Conformal Conic Projection
SCALE 1:2,088,000 1 Inch = 33 Statute Miles

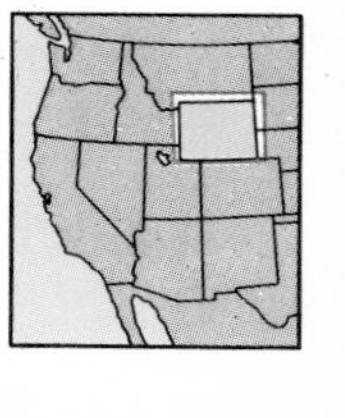

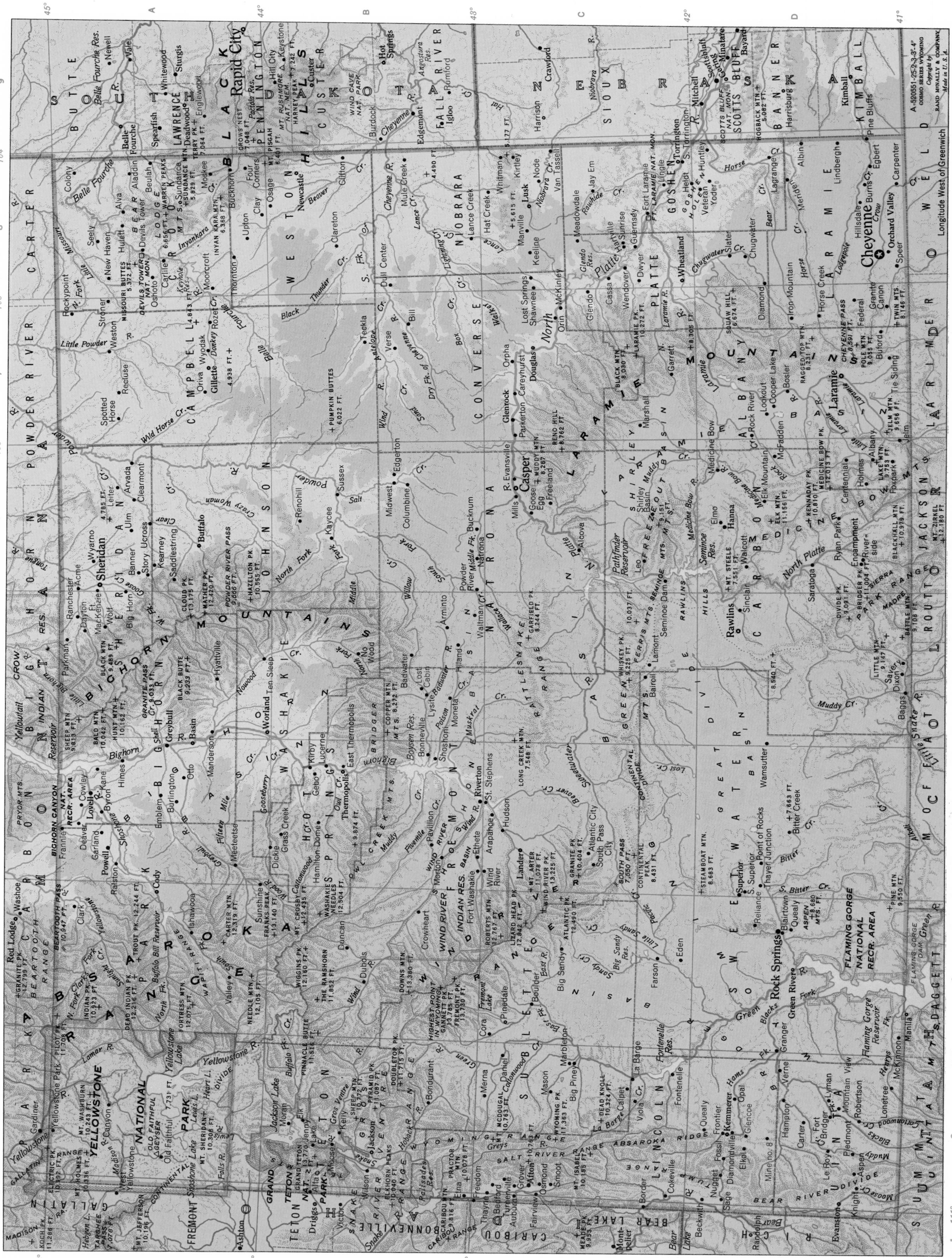

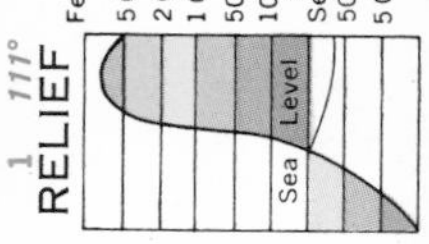

Lambert Conformal Conic Projection
SCALE 1:2,186,000 1 Inch = 34.5 Statute Miles

Statute Miles 5 0 5 10 20 30 40 50
Kilometers 5 0 5 15 25 35 45 55 65 75

MOON

This section tells about the moon, a ball of rock nearly 250,000 miles from the earth that has become man's new frontier.

You can use the maps, photographs, and diagrams in this section to trace the course of history-in-the-making on the earth's nearest neighbor in space. You can use the maps to locate the sites of new moon landings. The maps show many details of both the earth side of the moon (the side that always faces the earth), and the far side (the side that is hidden from the earth).

The photographs that follow the maps show you how the moon's landscape looks. The pages that follow the photographs carry tables that list important facts about the moon, define moon terms, and list the milestones that mark man's study of the moon. The final pages give information about man's historic first landing on the moon.

Man's knowledge of the moon results from a constant struggle during many generations to replace fantasy and guesswork with scientific facts. The maps in this section are examples of this effort. The first maps of the moon were merely crude outlines. Gradually, astronomers using more and more powerful telescopes and photographic instruments were able to fill in the details of the side of the moon we can see from the earth.

Soon after the dawn of the Space Age, in 1957, giant rockets hurled spacecraft to the moon. Some carried cameras that photographed nearly every square mile of the moon's surface and relayed the pictures back to the earth. Others carried instruments that sent back information about the surface crust of the moon. Spacecraft carrying men orbited the moon and came as close to it as ten miles. They looked at possible landing sites and tested equipment designed to achieve man's age-old ambition actually to set foot on the moon.

Then came the moment on July 20, 1969, when probably the most important footprints in history were made by the first men to step on the moon. These men opened the way for other moon landings and for possible exploration much farther out in space—to the earth's sister-planets of the solar system millions of miles away, and perhaps at some distant time to the stars beyond.

This article was critically reviewed by Harold F. Weaver, Professor of Astronomy and Director of Radio Astronomy Laboratory, University of California.

Opposite page: NASA photograph of the moon from *Apollo 8*.

MOON MAPS AND PHOTOGRAPHS

213c MAP OF THE EARTH SIDE OF THE MOON
213d MAP OF THE FAR SIDE OF THE MOON
213e-213h THE SURFACE OF THE MOON
213i, 213j FACTS ABOUT THE MOON
213k, 213l LANDING ON THE MOON

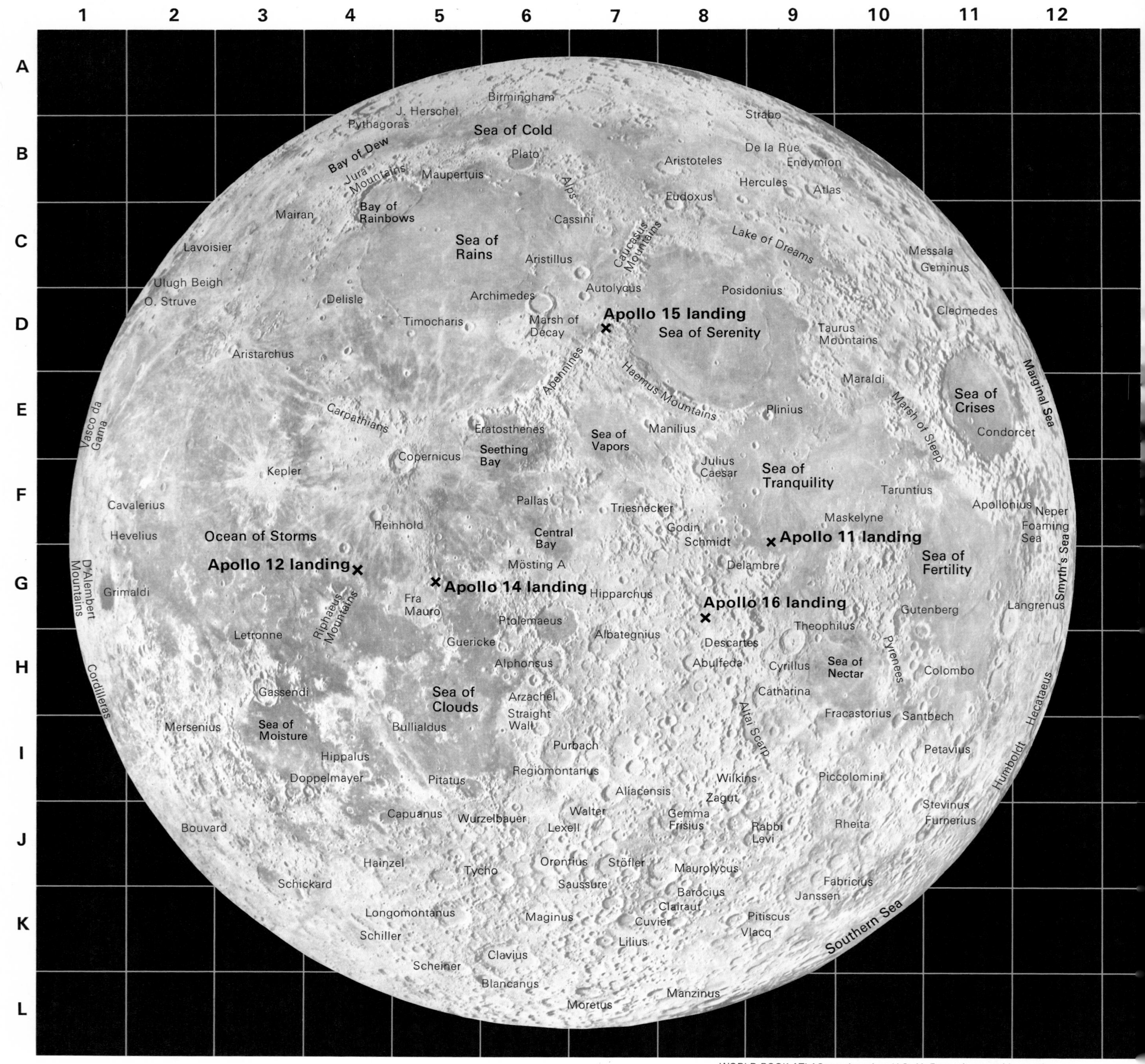

WORLD BOOK ATLAS map based on U.S. Air Force photographic mosaic.

MOON MAP INDEX

Abulfeda, crater H8
Albategnius, crater H7
Aliacensis, crater I7
Alphonsus, crater H6
Alps, mountain range B7
Altai Scarp, escarpment I9
Amundsen, crater L18
Anders, crater H13
Apennines, mountain range E6
Apollonius, crater F12
Archimedes, crater D6
Aristarchus, crater D3
Aristillus, crater C7
Aristoteles, crater B8
Arzachel, crater H6
Atlas, crater B9
Autolycus, crater C8
Barocius, crater J8
Bay of Dew, lowland B4
Bay of Rainbows, lowland C4
Belkovich, crater B16
Birmingham, crater A6
Blancanus, crater L6
Boltzmann, crater L19
Borman, crater H13
Boss, crater C14
Bouvard, crater J2
Brianchon, crater A20
Bullialdus, crater I5
Capuanus, crater J5
Carpathians, mountain range E4
Cassini, crater C7
Catharina, crater H9
Caucasus Mountains, mountains C7
Cavalerius, crater F1
Central Bay, lowland F6
Chebyshev, crater J22
Chernyshov, crater E20
Clairaut, crater K7
Clavius, crater K6
Cleomedes, crater D11
Colombo, crater H10
Condorcet, crater E12
Confucius, crater H22
Copernicus, crater E5
Cordilleras, mountain range H23
Cremona, crater A20
Cuvier, crater K7
Cyrillus, crater H9
D'Alembert Mountains, mountain range . . F24
Delambre, crater G8
De la Rue, crater B9
Delisle, crater D4
Descartes, region H8
Doppelmayer, crater I3
Eastern Sea, lowland H24
Edison, crater D14
Einstein, crater E24
Endymion, crater B9
Eratosthenes, crater E5
Eudoxus, crater B8
Fabricius, crater J9
Foaming Sea, lowland F12
Fracastorius, crater I9
Fra Mauro, crater G5
Furnerius, crater J10
Galois, crater H20
Gassendi, crater H3
Geminus, crater C10
Gemma Frisius, crater J8
Giordano Bruno, crater C14
Goddard, crater E13
Godin, crater F8
Grimaldi, crater G1
Guericke, crater H5
Gutenberg, crater G10
Haemus Mountains, mountains E7
Hainzel, crater J5
Hecataeus, crater H12
Hercules, crater B9
Hertz, crater E13
Hevelius, crater F1
Hippalus, crater I4
Hipparchus, crater G7
Humboldt, crater I11
Janssen, crater K9
Jeans, crater K15
J. Herschel, crater A5
Joliot-Curie, crater D13
Jules Verne, crater J16
Julius Caesar, crater F8
Jura Mountains, mountains B4
Kepler, crater F3
Kibalchich, crater F23
Kondratiuk, crater E21
Korolev, crater G20
Kovalevskaya, crater C22
Kurchatov, crater C16
Lake of Dreams, lowland C9
Langrenus, crater G11
Lavoisier, crater C2

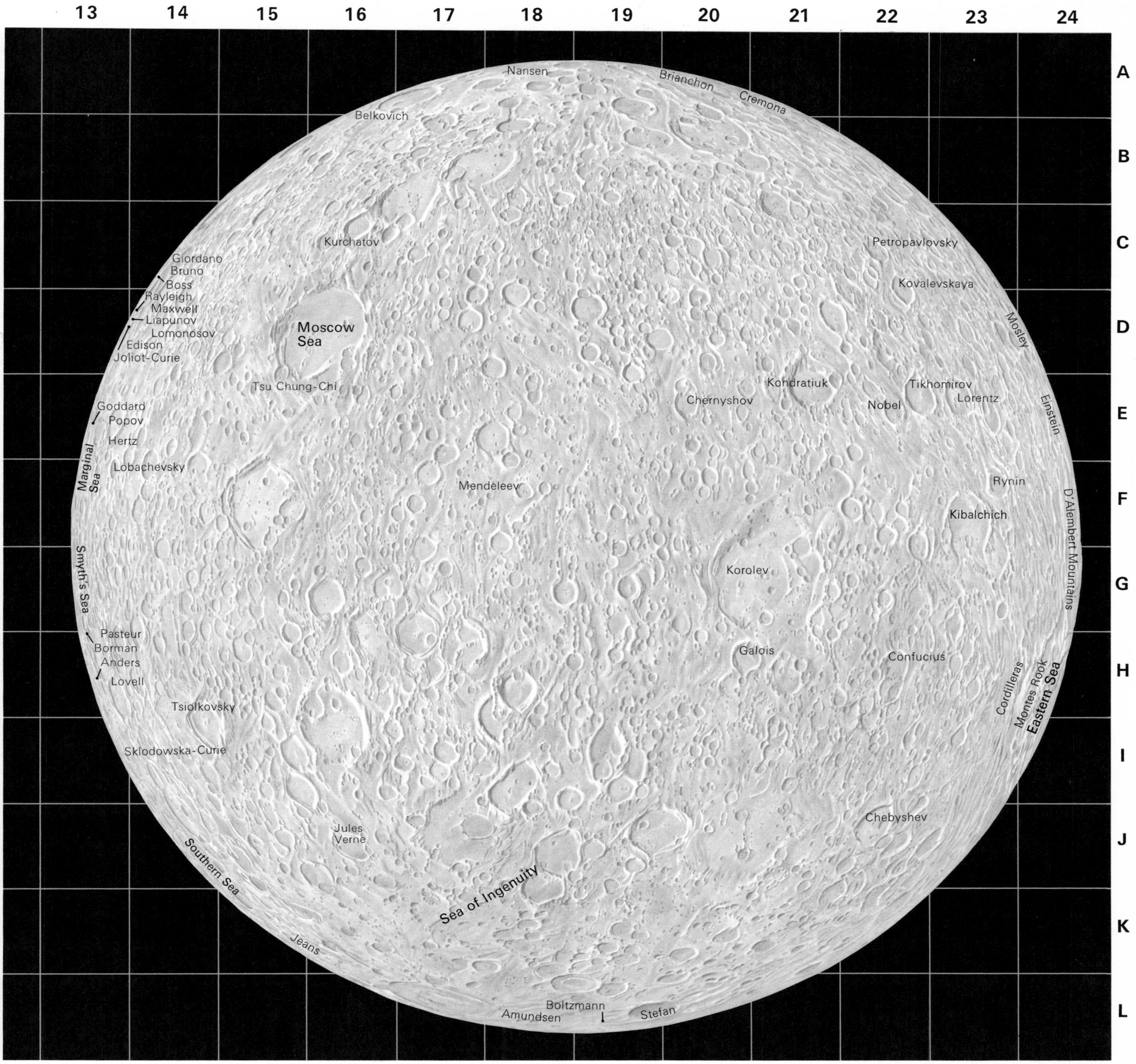

WORLD BOOK ATLAS map by Bernardo Guiliano. Adapted from the U.S. Air Force Lunar Chart.

Letronne, crater H3
Lexell, crater J6
Liapunov, crater D13
Lilius, crater K7
Lobachevsky, crater F13
Lomonosov, crater D14
Longomontanus, crater K5
Lorentz, crater E23
Lovell, crater H13
Maginus, crater K6
Mairan, crater C4
Manilius, crater E7
Manzinus, crater L7
Maraldi, crater E10
Marginal Sea, lowland F13
Marsh of Decay, lowland D6
Marsh of Sleep, lowland E10
Maskelyne, crater F9
Maupertuis, crater B5
Maurolycus, crater J8
Maxwell, crater D14
Mendeleev, crater F18
Mersenius, crater I2
Messala, crater C10
Montes Rook, mountain range H24
Moretus, crater L7
Moscow Sea, lowland D16
Mosley, crater D23
Mösting A, crater G6
Nansen, crater A18
Neper, crater F12
Nobel, crater E22
Ocean of Storms, lowland F2
Orontius, crater J6
O. Struve, crater D2
Pasteur, crater G13
Petavius, crater I11
Petropavlovsky, crater C22
Piccolomini, crater I9
Pitatus, crater I5
Pitiscus, crater K8
Plato, crater B6
Plinius, crater E9
Popov, crater E13
Posidonius, crater D9
Ptolemaeus, crater G6
Purbach, crater I6
Pyrenees,
mountain range H10
Pythagoras, crater B4
Rabbi Levi, crater J9
Rayleigh, crater D14
Regiomontanus, crater I6
Reinhold, crater F4
Rheita, crater J10
Riphaeus Mountains,
mountain range G4
Rynin, crater F23
Santbech, crater I10
Saussure, crater J6
Scheiner, crater K5
Schickard, crater J4
Schiller, crater K4
Schmidt, crater F8
Sea of Clouds, lowland H5
Sea of Cold, lowland B6
Sea of Crises, lowland E11
Sea of Fertility, lowland G11
Sea of Ingenuity, lowland K17
Sea of Moisture, lowland I3
Sea of Nectar, lowland H10
Sea of Rains, lowland C5
Sea of Serenity, lowland D8
Sea of Tranquility, lowland F9
Sea of Vapors, lowland E7
Seething Bay, lowland E6
Sklodowska-Curie, crater I14
Smyth's Sea, lowland G13
Southern Sea, lowland J14
Stefan, crater L19
Stevinus, crater I11
Stöfler, crater J7
Strabo, crater A9
Straight Wall, escarpment I6
Taruntius, crater F11
Taurus Mountains, mountains D9
Theophilus, crater G9
Tikhomirov, crater E22
Timocharis, crater D5
Triesnecker, crater F7
Tsiolkovsky, crater I14
Tsu Chung-Chi, crater E15
Tycho, crater J6
Ulugh Beigh, crater C2
Vasco da Gama, crater E1
Vlacq, crater K9
Walter, crater J7
Wilkins, crater I9
Wurzelbauer, crater J5
Zagut, crater I8

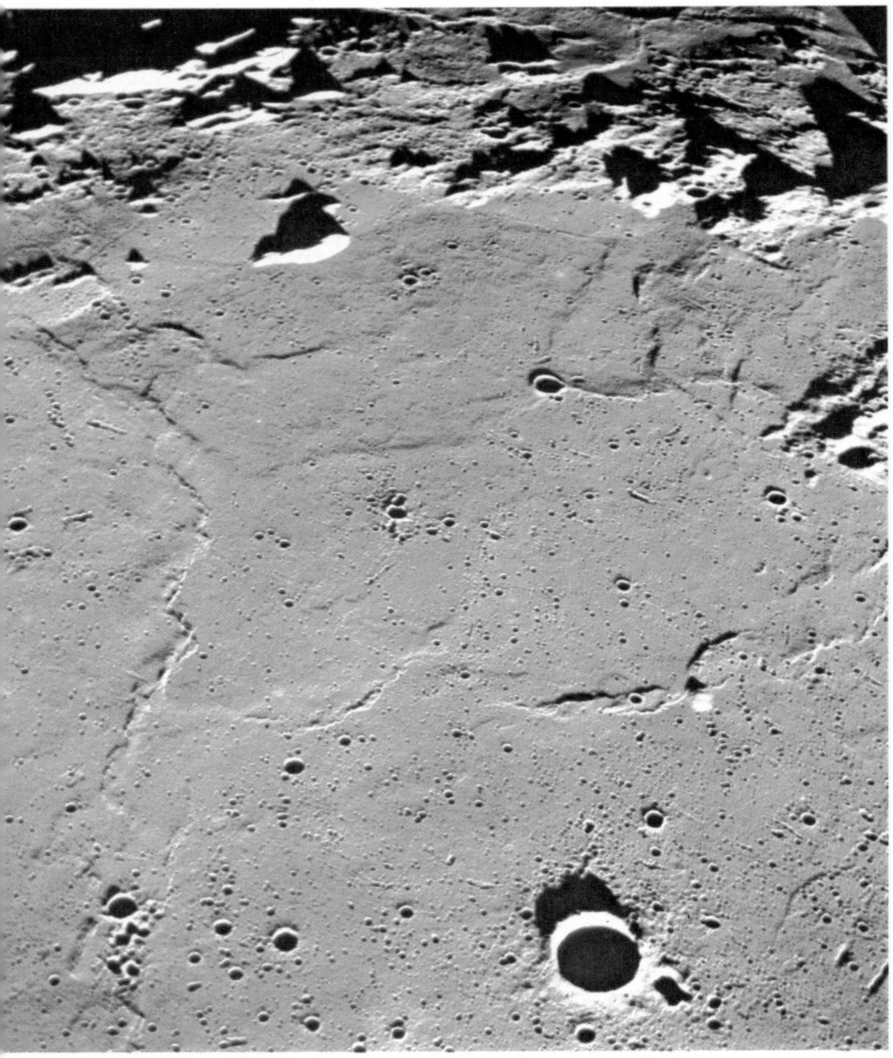

NASA photograph from *Apollo 10.*

Crater Bruce, in Central Bay, is about 3.7 miles in diameter.

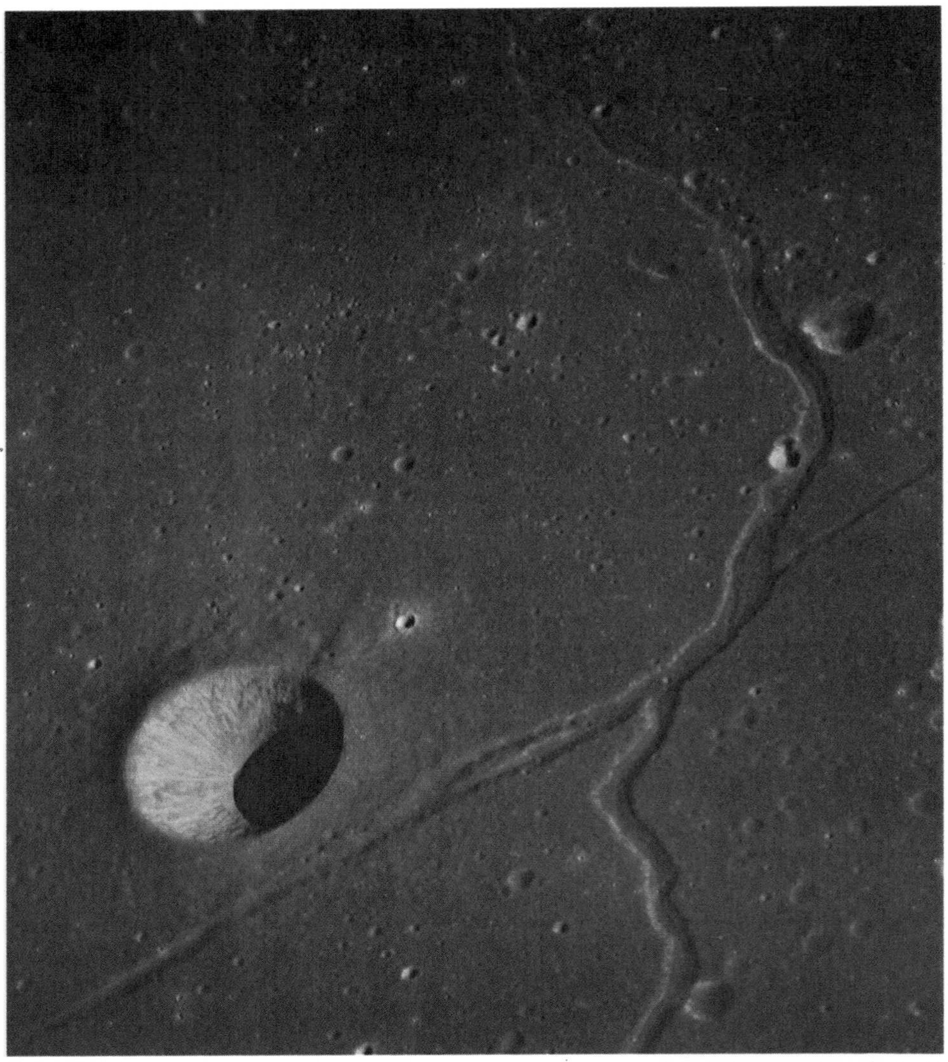

NASA photograph from *Apollo 10.*

Crater Maskelyne G and Diamond Back Rille. Maskelyne G has a diameter of about 4 miles.

Crater Firmicus, south of the Sea of Crises, is about 35 miles in diameter.

NASA photograph from *Apollo 10.*

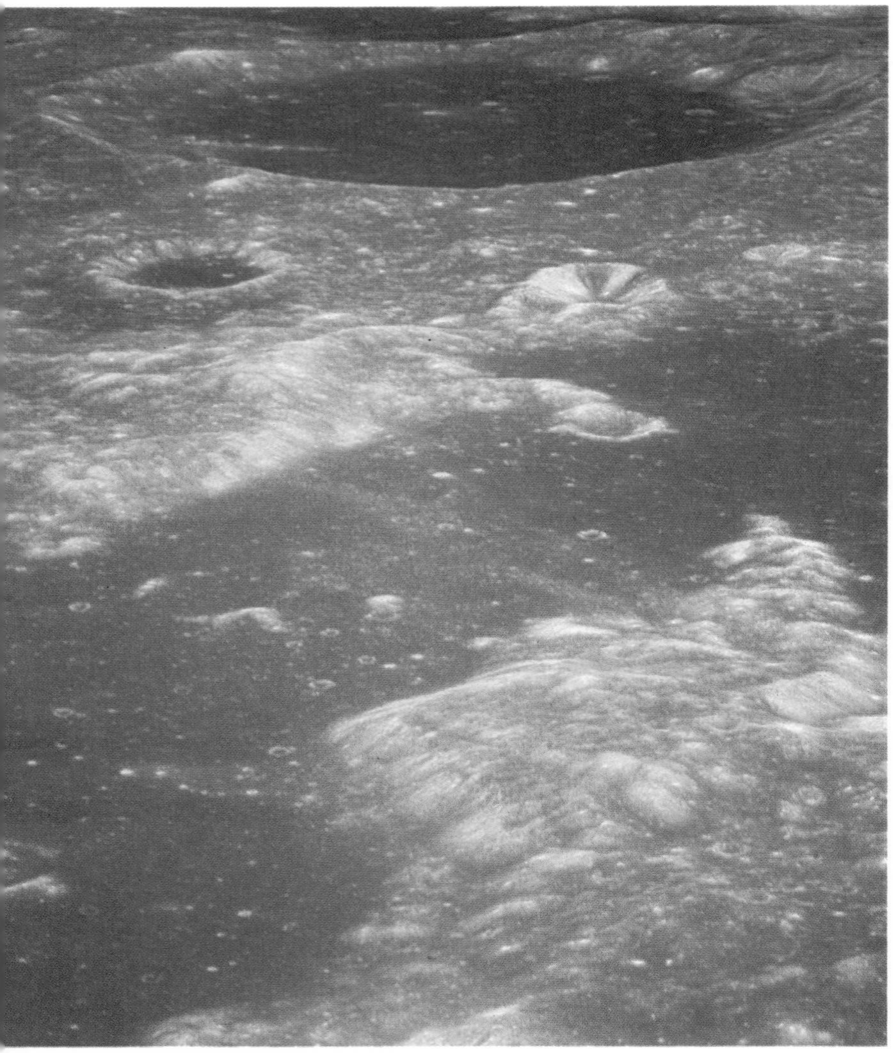

Small chain of craters on the far side of the moon.

NASA photograph from *Apollo 8.*

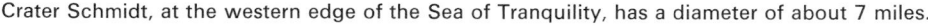

NASA photograph from *Apollo 10.*

Earthrise on the far side of the moon.

Crater Schmidt, at the western edge of the Sea of Tranquility, has a diameter of about 7 miles.

NASA photograph from *Apollo 10.*

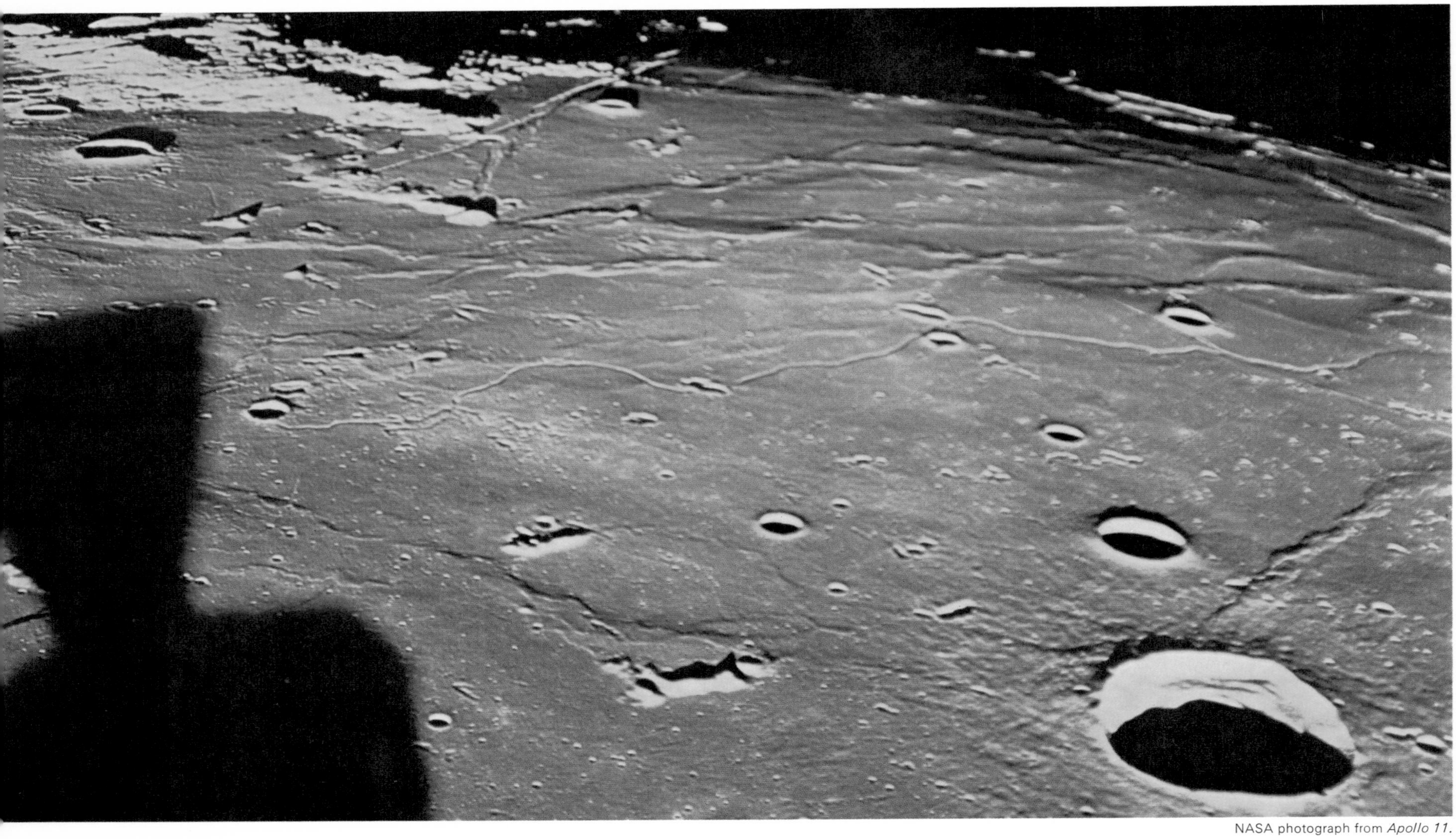

NASA photograph from *Apollo 11*.

View of landing site from lunar orbit; crater Maskelyne shows in foreground.

Scattered rocks and small craters near Eagle's landing site.

NASA photograph from *Apollo 11*.

NASA photograph from *Apollo 8*.
Crater Langrenus, about 85 miles across, lies on the east edge of the Sea of Fertility.

NASA photograph from *Apollo 11*.
Deep shadow shows on lunar crater and wall.

Far side of the moon has a rough surface.
NASA photograph from *Apollo 8*.

Crater Ritter, on the west edge of the Sea of Tranquility, is 18 miles across.
NASA photograph from *Apollo 10*.

Lick Observatory

FACTS ABOUT THE MOON

Diameter: 2,160 miles, about one-fourth that of the earth.

Circumference: 6,790 miles, compared to the earth's equatorial circumference of 24,900 miles.

Surface area: 14,650,000 square miles, compared to the earth's 196,940,000 square miles.

Distance from the earth: 252,711 miles at the farthest point in its orbit; 221,456 miles at the nearest point; mean distance—238,857.

Revolution period: The moon completes one revolution around the earth, from new moon to new moon, in 29 days, 12 hours, 44 minutes, 2.8 seconds.

Lengths of lunar day and night: Daylight and night each last about two weeks.

Surface temperature at the moon's equator: Ranges from about 260°F. in the lunar daytime to about −280°F. during lunar night.

Surface gravity: One-sixth that of earth

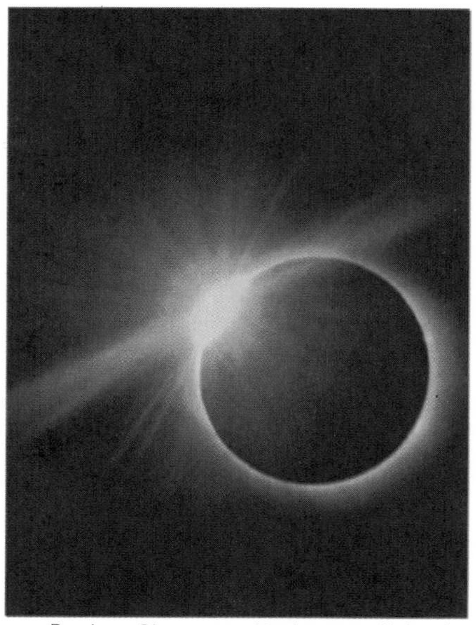

Dearborn Observatory, Northwestern University

Total solar eclipse came seconds after the photograph, *above,* was taken at Moose River, Ont., on Nov. 20, 1963.

The photographs, *below,* show how the earth and the moon compare in size.

NASA photographs

MOON TERMS

Apocynthion is the point farthest from the moon in the orbit of a lunar satellite.

Apogee is the point farthest from the earth in the orbit of the moon.

Crater is any cup-shaped depression on the moon's surface.

Crater pits are small crater formations on the moon. They vary in diameter from about 100 yards to several hundred yards.

Dome is a rounded elevation or bulge on the moon's surface that may be as much as 10 miles wide and from 50 to 200 feet in height.

Earthshine is reflected sunlight from the earth which slightly illuminates the dark portion of the moon.

Escape velocity is the speed an object must attain in order to free itself from the force of gravity exerted by a body of the solar system. The escape velocity on the moon is about 1½ miles per second, compared to about 7 miles per second on the earth.

Full moon is the phase of the moon that occurs when the moon is in the part of the sky just opposite from the sun, with its illuminated surface facing the earth, 14½ days after the new moon phase.

Gibbous moon is the phase between half and full moon.

Lunar eclipse occurs when the moon passes through the earth's shadow. At that time, the earth is directly between the moon and the sun.

Lunar rays are bright streaks that spread on the moon's surface from some craters. The rays are especially noticeable during full moon.

Mare (plural maria) is any one of the large, dark areas on the moon's surface. Once thought to be seas, they were named with the Latin word for sea. But they are plains, because the moon has no known water.

Metonic cycle is the period of 19 years between the times the phases of the moon occur on the same days of the month. The cycle is named for Meton, the Athenian scientist who was the first to observe the cycle, about 432 B.C.

Moonquake is the lunar equivalent of an earthquake.

Perigee is the point nearest to the earth in the orbit of the moon.

Pericynthion is the point closest to the moon in the orbit of a lunar satellite.

Perturbations are changes in the moon's orbit caused by the earth's gravitational influences, or by gravitational influences of other bodies in the solar system.

Phase of the moon is determined by the portion of the moon in its orbit as seen from the earth. Phases include the new moon, crescent, first quarter, gibbous, full, and last quarter.

Rill, or rille, is any one of the shallow, trenchlike depressions or cracks on the moon's surface.

Selenography is the science dealing with the description and mapping of the moon's surface; the lunar counterpart of geography.

Sidereal month (or period) is the time it takes the moon to complete its orbit around the earth with respect to a star. It is a period of 27 days, 7 hours, 43 minutes, 11.5 seconds.

Solar eclipse occurs when the moon passes directly between the sun and the earth, and the moon's shadow totally or partly hides the sun from view at certain locations on the earth.

Straight Wall is a 90-mile-long fault on the moon's surface. It is especially noticeable during the last quarter phase on the edge of the Sea of Clouds.

Synchronous rotation always keeps the same side of the moon facing the earth as the moon rotates on its axis and revolves around the earth in the same period.

Synodic month is the period from new moon to new moon. It lasts 29 days, 12 hours, 44 minutes, 2.8 seconds—the time it takes for the moon to complete all its phases.

Terminator is the dividing line on the moon's disk that marks the separation of the illuminated and dark portions of the surface.

Wane is the decrease in size of the visible disk of the moon during the interval between a full and a new moon.

Wax is the increase in size of the visible disk of the moon during the interval between a new and a full moon.

Wrinkle ridges are certain elevations, low and often branched, that can be seen in the lunar seas.

MILESTONES IN MAN'S STUDY OF THE MOON

c. 2200 B.C. The Mesopotamians kept records of lunar eclipses.

1000's B.C. The Chinese inscribed records of lunar eclipses on bone.

500's B.C. The Chaldeans predicted lunar eclipses, using records they had kept since the 700's B.C.

c. 459 B.C. Anaxagoras, a Greek philosopher, observed that the moon's light came from the sun, and suggested the cause of eclipses.

c. 432 B.C. Meton, an Athenian scientist, discovered that the phases of the moon occur on the same days of the month every 19 years. That period became known as the Metonic cycle.

c. 335 B.C. Aristotle, a Greek philosopher, used lunar eclipses to prove the ball-like shape of the earth.

c. 300 B.C. Babylonian astrologers devised lunar tables that predicted the lunar months.

c. 280 B.C. Aristarchus of Samos, a Greek astronomer, devised a method of measuring the distance of the moon from the earth.

c. 150 B.C. Hipparchus, a Greek astronomer, determined the difference between a sidereal and solar year, measured the period of the moon's revolution around the earth, discovered inequalities in the moon's motions, and measured the moon's distance from the earth.

c. 74 B.C. Posidonius, a Syrian philosopher and astronomer, explained the joint effect of the moon and the sun on the earth's tides.

A.D. c. 150 Ptolemy, an Egyptian astronomer, improved on many previous theories about the moon. Ptolemy's writings, called the *Almagest,* became the chief astronomical authority for 14 centuries.

c. 1500 Leonardo da Vinci, an Italian artist and scientist, correctly explained the light on the dimly seen disk of the crescent moon as light reflected from the earth, calling it "moon luster."

c. 1512 Copernicus, a Polish astronomer, founded present-day astronomy with his theory that the earth is a moving planet.

c. 1588-1598 Tycho Brahe, a Danish astronomer, made many accurate observations on which scientists later based theories about the motion of the moon and other bodies in the solar system.

c. 1600-1609 Johannes Kepler, a German astronomer and mathematician, explained the reddish color of the moon during a lunar eclipse as being caused by the earth's atmosphere refracting sunlight onto the moon's surface. He also discovered the oval shape of planetary and lunar orbits.

c. 1610 Galileo, an Italian astronomer and physicist, made the first practical use of the telescope to discover many new facts about the solar system. With telescopes that he perfected, Galileo was enabled to measure certain of the moon's craters and mountains.

1619 Father Christopher Scheiner, a German astronomer, made the first map of the moon showing features that are still identifiable.

c. 1620's Langrenus, a Belgian mathematician and mapmaker, made the second known map of the moon. It was printed in 1645.

c. 1645 Hevelius, of Danzig, charted over 250 lunar formations on a map. Scientists consider him a pioneer of lunar topography.

1651 Giovanni Battista Riccioli published a comprehensive astronomical book, *Almagestum novum,* in Bologna. It contained a map by Francesco Maria Grimaldi, with over 200 names of lunar features that are still used. The book was the first to state that there is no water on the moon.

1687 Sir Isaac Newton, an English scientist published his *Mathematical Principles of Natural Philosophy,* which included Newton's fundamental laws of motion and theory of gravitation. These helped explain the physical basis of the moon's motions and of tidal phenomena.

c. 1828 F. P. Gruithuisen, a Munich astronomer, suggested meteoric impact as the possible origin of certain craters on the moon.

1840 John William Draper, of the University of the City of New York, developed a successful *daguerreotype* (an early form of photograph) of the moon.

1850's William C. Bond and J. A. Whipple, of Harvard Observatory, made daguerreotypes and photographs of the moon that showed its principal features and many details.

1878 Julius Schmidt, a German astronomer, director of the Athens Observatory, published a map of the moon showing over 30,000 features.

1887 Theodor von Opplozer, a German astronomer and mathematician, published a list of computed eclipses of the moon covering 20 centuries—from about 1200 B.C. to A.D. 2163.

c. 1900 P. H. Puiseux and Maurice Loewy, French astronomers, prepared an atlas from plates made at the Paris Observatory with a 24-inch telescope. It included photographs of the moon which are considered the best made during the 1800's.

1920's Bernard Lyot, a French astronomer, studied polarized light reflected from the moon's surface, and concluded the surface must be covered with a layer of fine dust similar to volcanic ash.

1946 Radio waves were bounced from the moon's surface by the U.S. Army Signal Corps for the first radar contact with the moon.

1958 Spectrographic observations made by Nikolai Kozirev, Russian astronomer, at the Crimean Observatory, suggested that earlier sightings by astronomers might be gaseous emissions from the moon's crater, Alphonsus.

1959 On Sept. 12, *Luna 2* was launched by Russia and became the first spacecraft to strike the moon.
On Oct. 4, *Luna 3* was launched by Russia. It took the first photographs of the far side of the moon and radioed them to the earth.

1962 On April 23, *Ranger IV* was launched and became America's first spacecraft to strike the moon.

1966 On Jan. 31, Russia launched *Luna 9,* first spacecraft to make a soft landing on the moon. Pictures it sent to the earth showed that the moon's surface would bear weight.
On Mar. 31, Russia launched *Luna 10,* the first spacecraft to orbit the moon.

1967 On Sept. 8, America launched *Surveyor 5* which landed on the moon and sent information on lunar soil to the earth for analysis.

1968 On Dec. 21, America launched *Apollo 8* which made the first manned flight around the moon at Christmas, returning to the earth after 10 lunar orbits. It paved the way for landing on the moon.

1969 On July 20, *Apollo 11,* launched by America on July 16, landed on the moon near the western edge of the Sea of Tranquility. Neil A. Armstrong, mission commander, became the first man to set foot on the moon's surface.

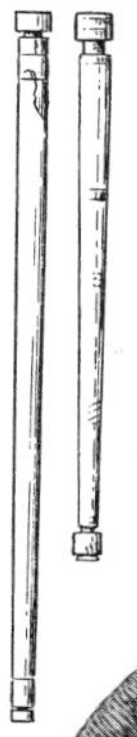

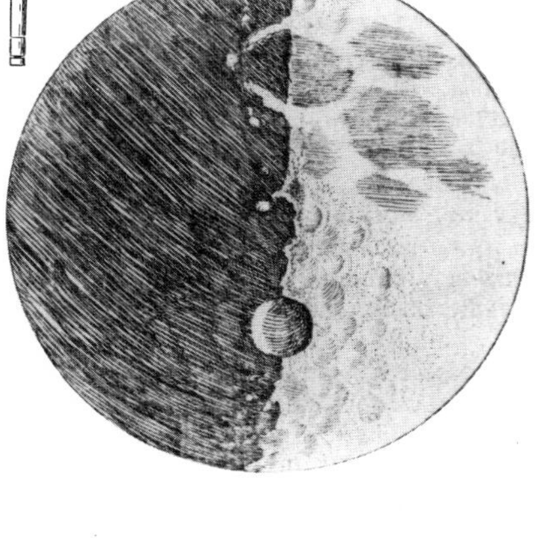

Galileo made one of the first maps of the moon, *below,* using small, hand telescopes he built, *left.*

Illustration by Galileo Galilei from *Sidereus Nuncius,* Venice, 1610. Courtesy University of Chicago Library

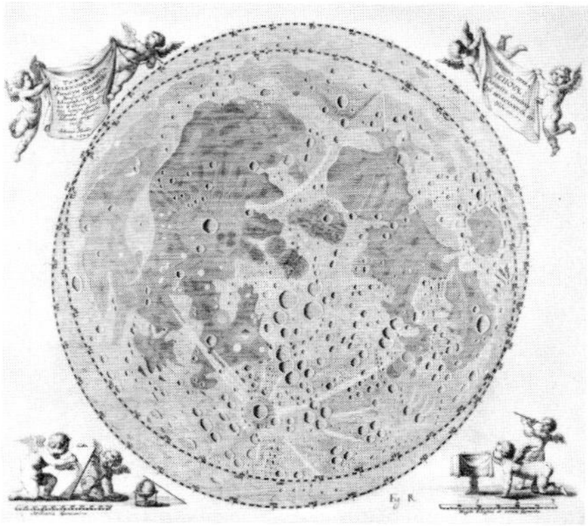

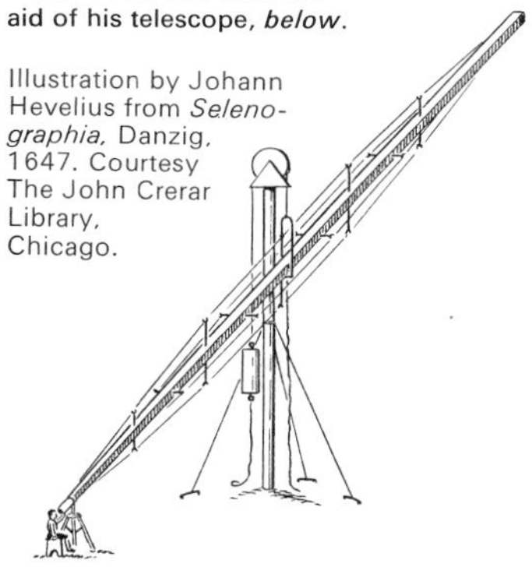

Hevelius charted over 250 lunar formations on a map he made about 1645, *left,* with the aid of his telescope, *below.*

Illustration by Johann Hevelius from *Selenographia,* Danzig, 1647. Courtesy The John Crerar Library, Chicago.

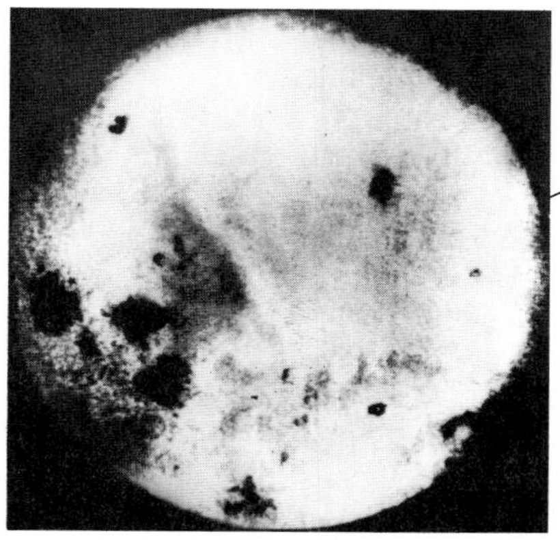

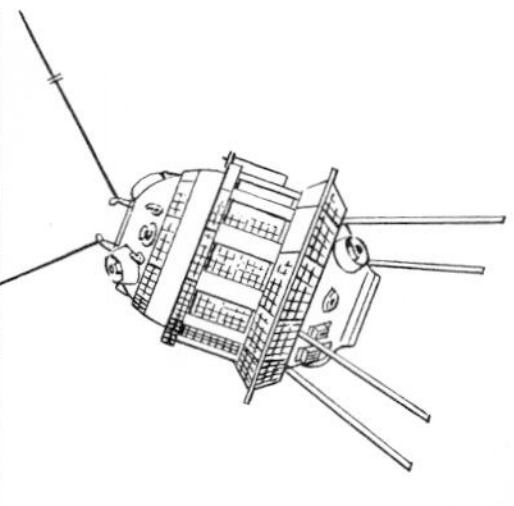

Russia's *Luna 3, above,* photographed the far side of the moon, *left,* in 1959.

Sovfoto

Early photograph of the moon, *right,* was taken in 1857 by William C. Bond at Harvard Observatory, *above.*

Courtesy Harvard College Observatory (William C. Bond, 1857)

A special camera, *above,* photographed one of the first footprints made by man on lunar soil, *right.*

NASA photograph

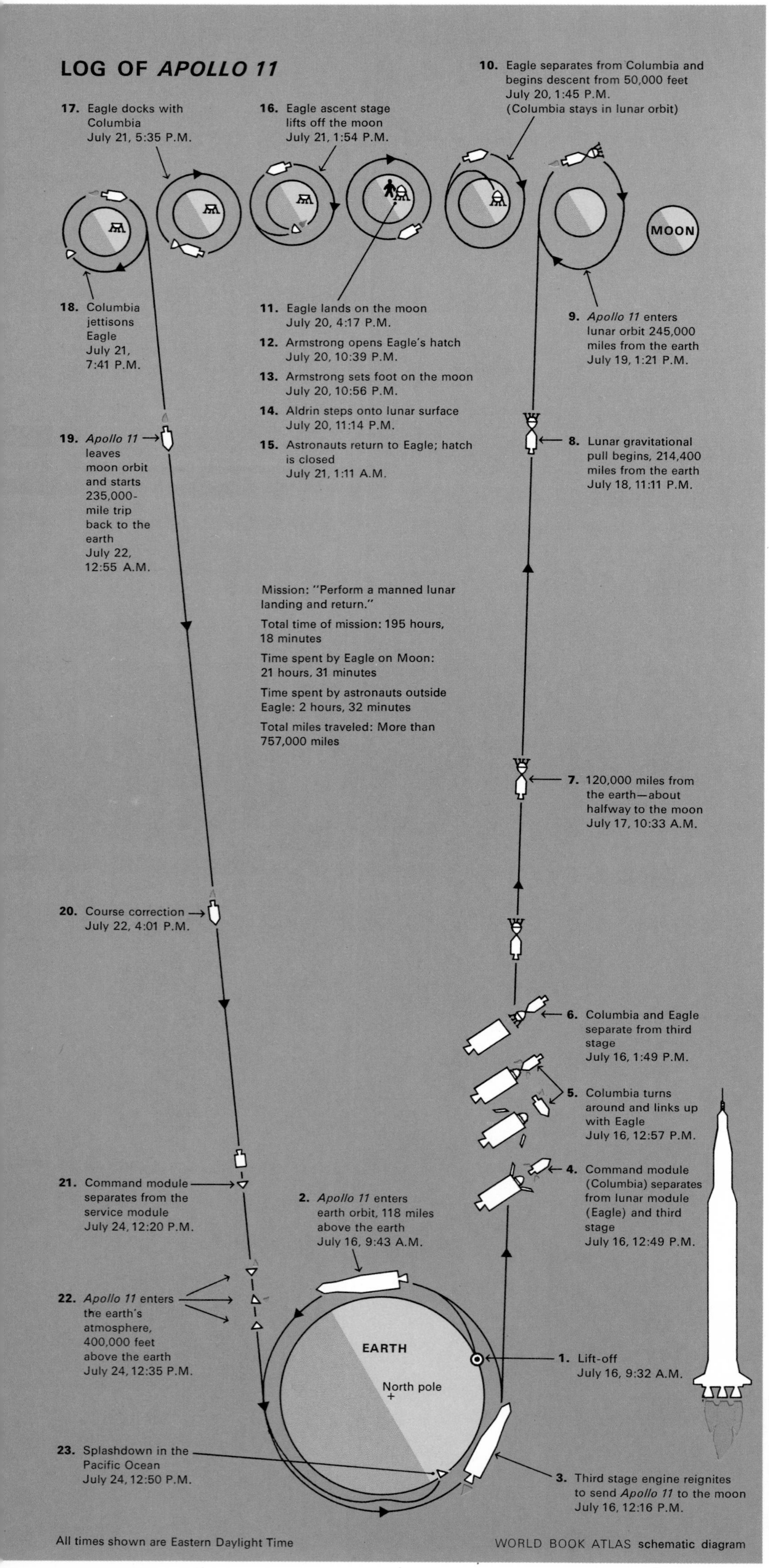
LOG OF *APOLLO 11*
17. Eagle docks with Columbia July 21, 5:35 P.M.
16. Eagle ascent stage lifts off the moon July 21, 1:54 P.M.
10. Eagle separates from Columbia and begins descent from 50,000 feet July 20, 1:45 P.M. (Columbia stays in lunar orbit)
MOON
18. Columbia jettisons Eagle July 21, 7:41 P.M.
11. Eagle lands on the moon July 20, 4:17 P.M.
12. Armstrong opens Eagle's hatch July 20, 10:39 P.M.
13. Armstrong sets foot on the moon July 20, 10:56 P.M.
14. Aldrin steps onto lunar surface July 20, 11:14 P.M.
15. Astronauts return to Eagle; hatch is closed July 21, 1:11 A.M.
9. *Apollo 11* enters lunar orbit 245,000 miles from the earth July 19, 1:21 P.M.
19. *Apollo 11* leaves moon orbit and starts 235,000-mile trip back to the earth July 22, 12:55 A.M.
8. Lunar gravitational pull begins, 214,400 miles from the earth July 18, 11:11 P.M.
Mission: "Perform a manned lunar landing and return."
Total time of mission: 195 hours, 18 minutes
Time spent by Eagle on Moon: 21 hours, 31 minutes
Time spent by astronauts outside Eagle: 2 hours, 32 minutes
Total miles traveled: More than 757,000 miles
7. 120,000 miles from the earth—about halfway to the moon July 17, 10:33 A.M.
20. Course correction July 22, 4:01 P.M.
6. Columbia and Eagle separate from third stage July 16, 1:49 P.M.
5. Columbia turns around and links up with Eagle July 16, 12:57 P.M.
4. Command module (Columbia) separates from lunar module (Eagle) and third stage July 16, 12:49 P.M.
21. Command module separates from the service module July 24, 12:20 P.M.
2. *Apollo 11* enters earth orbit, 118 miles above the earth July 16, 9:43 A.M.
22. *Apollo 11* enters the earth's atmosphere, 400,000 feet above the earth July 24, 12:35 P.M.
EARTH
North pole
1. Lift-off July 16, 9:32 A.M.
23. Splashdown in the Pacific Ocean July 24, 12:50 P.M.
3. Third stage engine reignites to send *Apollo 11* to the moon July 16, 12:16 P.M.
All times shown are Eastern Daylight Time
WORLD BOOK ATLAS schematic diagram

The diagram and photographs on these pages tell about the greatest adventure in the history of exploration—the first landing of men on the moon. You can use the diagram to follow the important stages in the mission of *Apollo 11.* Study the photographs for close-up glimpses of the mission's highlights. These "on-the-spot" pictures can help you form your own ideas about the most dramatic moments of the historic event.

The heroes of *Apollo 11* were Neil A. Armstrong, a civilian who was mission commander; U.S. Air Force Col. Edwin A. "Buzz" Aldrin, Jr., pilot of Eagle, the lunar module; and U.S. Air Force Lt. Col. Michael Collins, pilot of Columbia, the command module or mother ship.

Armstrong and Aldrin steered their four-legged craft to a smooth landing on the Sea of Tranquility at 4:17 P.M. (EDT) on July 20, 1969. Collins, orbiting the moon in Columbia, passed about 65 miles above them. The sun was just rising over the horizon of the moon when Armstrong reported to mission control at Houston: "Houston, Tranquility Base here. The Eagle has landed."

The words of Armstrong were heard by hundreds of millions who were watching and listening on television and radio. At 10:56 P.M. (EDT) Armstrong stepped onto the moon's surface, testing the crust with his left boot. He said: "That's one small step for a man, one giant leap for mankind." As he spoke, TV watchers saw the great event via a television camera attached to the side of Eagle. Then they saw the astronaut perform some of the carefully planned tasks of the mission. Perhaps the most important task was scooping up some of the powdery substance of the moon's surface and placing it in a container for delivery to scientists on the earth.

About 20 minutes after Armstrong stepped onto the moon, Aldrin joined him. Then they completed their scheduled tasks. These included gathering rock and soil samples, placing scientific instruments on the moon's surface, planting an American flag near Eagle, and uncovering a plaque on its side. The inscription on the plaque read: "Here men from the planet earth first set foot on the moon, July 1969 AD. We came in peace for all mankind."

President Richard M. Nixon talked with the men on the moon from the White House. He congratulated them and added: ". . . For one priceless moment in the whole history of man all the people on this earth are truly one—one in their pride in what you have done and one in our prayers that you will return safely to earth."

The safe return of the first men to land on the moon was achieved in a successful Pacific Ocean splashdown at 12:50 P.M. (EDT) on July 24, 1969.

Astronaut Armstrong rests inside Eagle after his historic walk on the moon.
NASA photograph from *Apollo 11*.

Astronaut Aldrin stands near Eagle and solar wind experiment.

NASA photograph from *Apollo 11*.

Astronaut Aldrin sets up seismic experiment package.

NASA photograph from *Apollo 11*.

Eagle approaches Columbia before linking up for homeward voyage.

NASA photograph from *Apollo 11*.

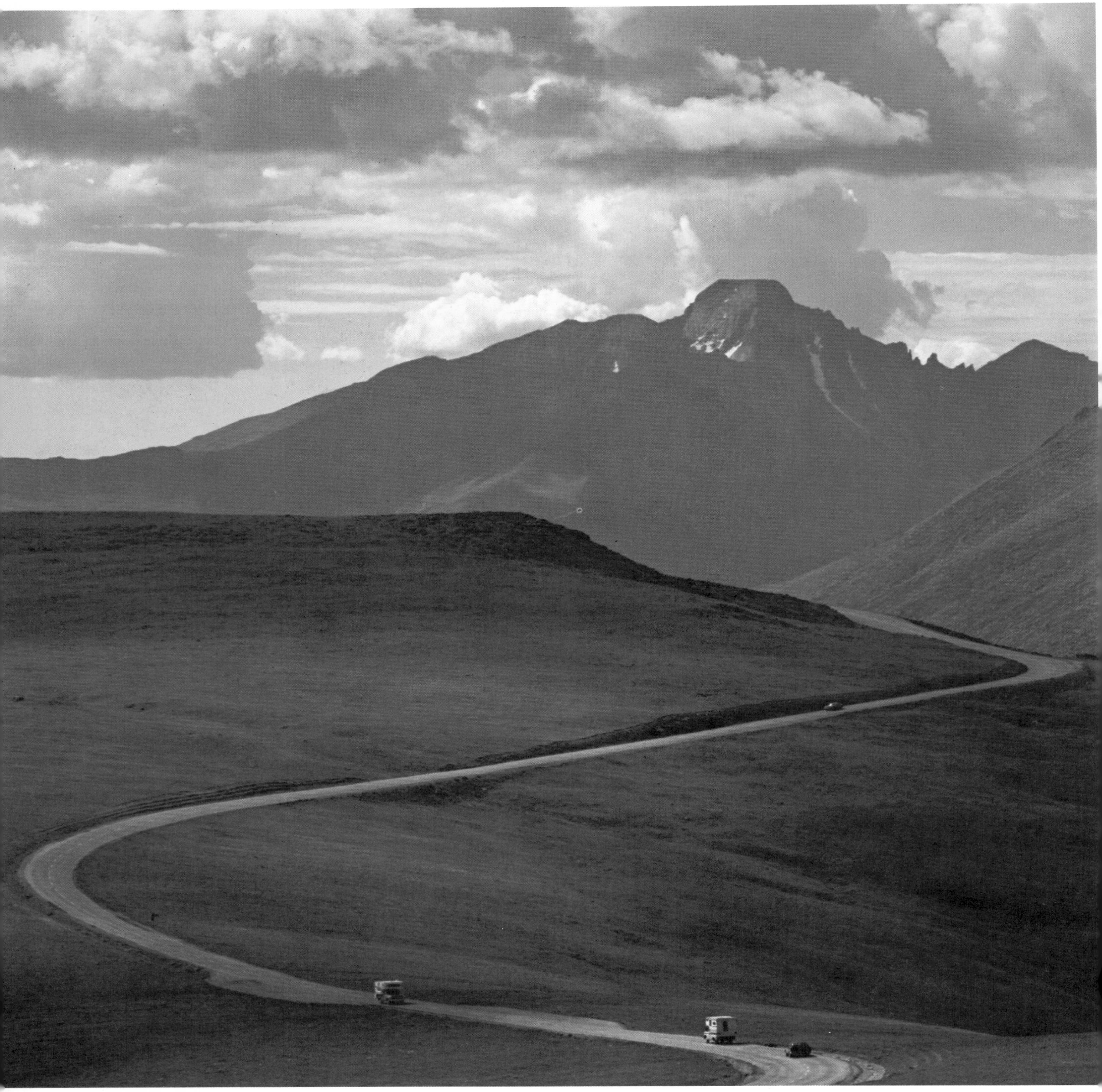

TRAVEL GUIDE

The Travel Guide of THE WORLD BOOK ATLAS helps readers plan interesting vacation trips by car in the United States, Canada, and Mexico. You may drive along the suggested routes or choose your own from the roads and highways shown on the maps. A map of major highways in North America and a table of distances between the major cities appear on pages 216 and 217. Using this map, you can locate the region in which you plan to travel. Detailed maps of four tourist regions are shown on pages 218 through 225. These maps show national parks, state and provincial parks, historic sites, famous buildings, natural landmarks, ski areas, and many other points of interest. An enlarged map of the New England States plus maps showing tourist routes in Alaska and Hawaii appear on pages 226 and 227.

Before you turn to the map of a specific tourist region, study the map at the right to determine the exact areas covered on each map. For example, if you are interested in travel through the Southwestern States, turn to the map on pages 220 and 221. Or, if you want information about routes in New England, see the map on pages 226 and 227.

The sample map below shows the symbols included on the travel maps in this section. At the bottom of this page is a list of the special abbreviations used on these maps.

TRAVEL GUIDE INDEX MAP

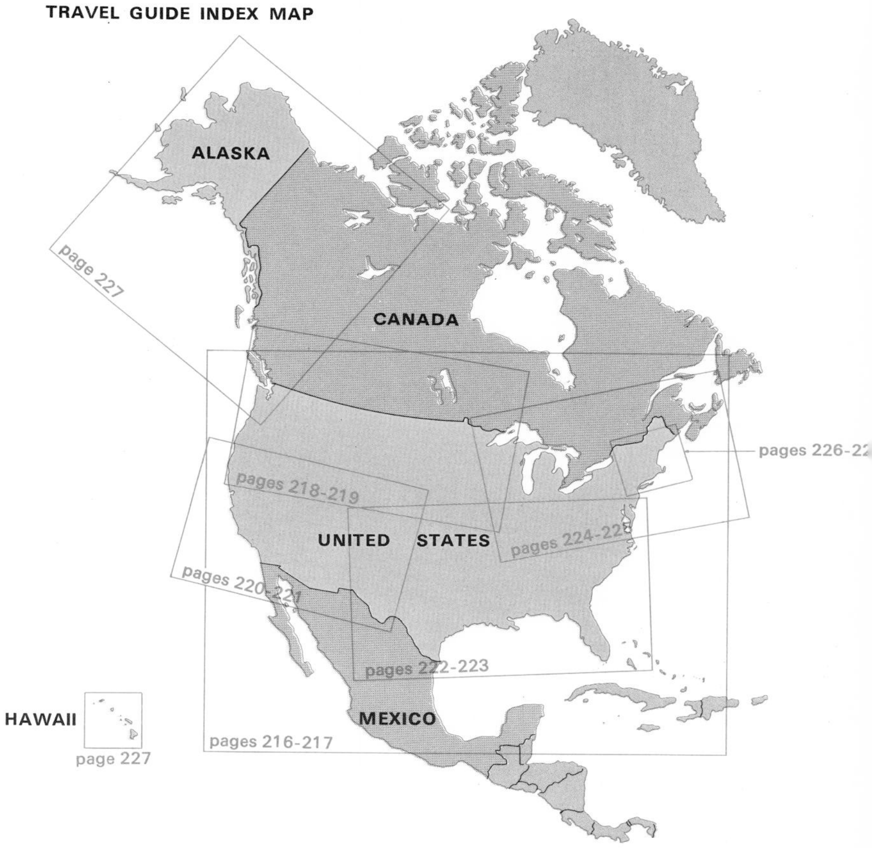

Map Symbols

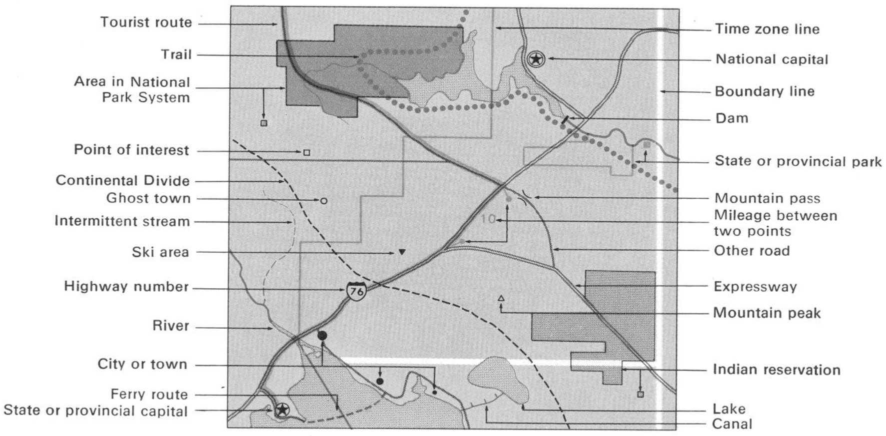

Map Abbreviations

N.B. . . . . National Battlefield
N.B.P. . . . . National Battlefield Park
N.B.S. . . . . National Battlefield Site
N.C. . . . . National Cemetery
N.H.P. . . . . National Historic Park
N.H.S. . . . . National Historic Site
N.L. . . . . National Lakeshore
N.M. . . . . National Monument
N.MEM. . . . . National Memorial
N.M.P. . . . . National Military Park
N.P. National Park
N.R.A. . . . . National Recreation Area
N.S. . . . . National Seashore

Opposite page: Longs Peak in Rocky Mountain National Park.—David Muench

TRAVEL GUIDE MAPS

	Atlanta, Georgia	Calgary, Alberta	Chicago, Illinois	Denver, Colorado	Houston, Texas	Kansas City, Missouri	Los Angeles, California	Mexico City, Mexico	Miami, Florida	Montreal, Quebec	New York, New York	San Francisco, California	Seattle, Washington	Washington, D.C.	Winnipeg, Manitoba
Acapulco, Mexico	2152	3298	2346	2097	1300	1941	2178	255	2556	3149	3014	2589	3324	2776	2727
Albuquerque, N. Mexico	1433	1432	1322	437	838	785	851	1405	1984	2183	2096	1146	1539	1887	1532
Anchorage, Alaska	4321	2198	3702	3334	4241	3607	3764	5060	4829	4244	4548	3353	2484	4403	2854
Atlanta, Georgia		2123	671	1436	852	842	2245	1897	663	1249	868	2579	2740	624	1541
Bangor, Maine	1329	2236	1190	2209	2104	1664	3245	3218	1856	386	459	3458	3081	697	1882
Billings, Montana	1839	559	1267	587	1638	909	1176	2411	2419	1869	2146	1179	809	1968	755
Birmingham, Alabama	155	2290	618	1301	701	707	2063	1746	803	1292	1023	2449	2605	779	1488
Bismarck, North Dakota	1422	811	866	688	1405	771	1656	2224	2218	1468	1651	1698	1210	1567	407
Boise, Idaho	2342	794	1832	906	1872	1500	932	2406	2963	3763	2704	635	505	2498	1409
Boston, Massachusetts	1090	2178	992	2016	1865	1400	3004	2979	1615	328	220	3265	3072	460	1758
Calgary, Alberta	2123		1654	1136	2153	1596	1641	3043	2804	2325	2478	1429	733	2355	829
Charleston, S. Carolina	299	2422	970	1735	1155	1141	2544	2196	612	1140	759	2878	2985	521	1840
Charleston, W. Virginia	496	2180	524	1391	1140	797	2375	2266	1059	832	543	2711	2600	382	1401
Charlotte, N. Carolina	237	2360	850	1673	1093	973	2482	2134	743	1006	625	2816	2781	387	1727
Cheyenne, Wyoming	1537	1035	1027	101	1162	695	1069	1925	2225	1818	1899	1226	1350	1715	994
Chicago, Illinois	671	1654		1062	1139	537	2115	2091	1352	804	824	2240	2076	701	877
Cleveland, Ohio	767	1985	331	1393	1372	744	2393	2471	1327	589	493	2571	2378	370	1201
Dallas, Texas	814	1912	923	820	241	518	1476	1168	1367	1776	1580	1790	2136	1446	1304
Denver, Colorado	1436	1136	1062		1061	594	1148	1804	2104	1866	1794	1324	1411	1696	1095
Des Moines, Iowa	962	1484	374	688	1042	254	1823	1940	1684	1178	1259	1866	1731	1075	700
Detroit, Michigan	774	1916	271	1333	1306	780	2415	2351	1437	533	670	2511	2347	547	1136
Edmonton, Alberta	2309	186	1690	1322	2229	1595	1827	3048	2817	2232	2536	1615	919	2391	842
Halifax, Nova Scotia	1849	3185	1710	2729	2624	2184	3765	3738	2376	860	979	3933	3555	1217	2356
Hanover, New Hampshire	1127	2526	960	2040	2019	1391	3040	3103	1654	201	259	3218	2896	497	1697
Houston, Texas	852	2153	1139	1061		788	1585	1045	1256	1839	1714	1950	2377	1476	1618
Indianapolis, Indiana	508	1848	194	1087	1042	493	2071	2149	1171	820	713	2407	2268	613	1062
Kansas City, Missouri	842	1596	537	594	788		1578	1686	1510	1313	1277	1914	1808	1102	859
Las Vegas, Nevada	2021	1336	1905	843	1426	1437	305	1852	2572	2709	2637	624	1198	2475	1688
Los Angeles, California	2245	1641	2115	1148	1585	1578		1923	2841	2948	2784	411	1280	2680	1993
Louisville, Kentucky	394	1962	308	1106	936	512	2190	1981	1057	934	738	2426	2320	604	1176
Memphis, Tennessee	382	2056	579	1054	560	460	1816	1605	1050	1310	1114	2214	2358	980	1319
Mexico City, Mexico	1897	3043	2091	1804	1045	1686	1923		2301	2884	2759	2334	3069	2521	2472
Miami, Florida	663	2804	1352	2104	1256	1510	2841	2301		1749	1395	3192	3421	1130	2222
Milwaukee, Wisconsin	761	1585	90	1152	1229	627	2205	2181	1442	894	914	2330	1984	791	780
Minneapolis, Minnesota	1090	1235	426	921	1291	503	2056	2189	1794	1188	1250	2099	1634	1127	451
Monterrey, Mexico	1345	2453	1501	1458	455	1096	1584	590	1711	2304	2169	1949	2685	1931	1882
Montreal, Quebec	1249	2325	804	1866	1839	1313	2948	2884	1749		381	3044	2695	619	1496
New Orleans, Louisiana	492	2458	981	1326	360	849	1945	1405	896	1650	1360	2296	2669	1116	1721
New York, New York	868	2478	824	1794	1714	1277	2784	2759	1395	381		3045	2852	238	1694
Norfolk, Virginia	593	2591	935	1802	1381	1208	2786	2472	1029	827	446	3122	3011	208	1812
Oklahoma City, Okla.	882	1770	856	674	446	356	1402	1373	1433	1632	1630	1697	2029	1421	1099
Omaha, Nebraska	1043	1395	498	564	911	201	1699	1838	1711	1302	1383	1742	1607	1199	658
Orlando, Florida	442	2565	1113	1865	1017	1271	2602	2062	239	1537	1156	2953	3182	915	1983
Ottawa, Ontario	1236	2207	733	1795	1768	1242	2877	2813	1823	118	489	2973	2577	693	1378
Philadelphia, Penna.	778	2493	766	1770	1624	1176	2726	2669	1278	471	90	3021	2828	148	1636
Phoenix, Arizona	1885	1631	1761	835	1180	1224	415	1563	2454	2622	2535	770	1487	2326	1928
Pittsburgh, Penna.	771	2124	470	1462	1439	868	2446	2524	1358	662	366	2713	2520	243	1343
Portland, Oregon	2765	782	2255	1329	2295	1923	1098	2829	3433	2818	2992	687	182	2921	1508
Quebec, Quebec	1415	2016	970	2032	2005	1479	3114	3050	2470	166	547	3210	2861	785	1662
Rapid City, S. Dakota	1592	890	929	420	1370	706	1423	2224	2216	1763	1815	1525	1075	1628	759
Regina, Saskatchewan	1758	475	1202	878	1741	1107	1639	2560	2329	1744	2048	1642	1014	1903	354
St. Louis, Missouri	562	1850	283	848	856	254	1832	1910	1346	1059	1057	2168	2062	848	1019
Salt Lake City, Utah	1970	890	1485	534	1480	1128	611	2081	2638	2276	2293	768	897	2173	1312
San Francisco, Calif.	2579	1429	2240	1324	1950	1914	411	2334	3192	3044	3045		869	2968	2018
Seattle, Washington	2740	733	2076	1411	2377	1808	1280	3069	3421	2695	2852	869		2777	1368
Syracuse, New York	1088	2268	658	1738	1717	1089	2737	2801	1594	244	260	2916	2763	464	1447
Thunder Bay, Ontario	1343	1273	672	1269	1639	851	2404	2537	2031	1052	1384	2447	1812	1343	444
Toronto, Ontario	972	2123	469	1531	1504	978	2613	2549	1631	335	513	2709	2514	561	1258
Vancouver, Br. Columbia	2780	657	2220	1555	2521	1862	1424	3055	3565	2982	2996	1013	144	2921	1486
Washington, D.C.	624	2355	701	1696	1476	1102	2680	2521	1130	619	238	2968	2777		1578
Winnipeg, Manitoba	1541	829	877	1095	1618	859	1993	2472	2222	1496	1694	2018	1368	1578	

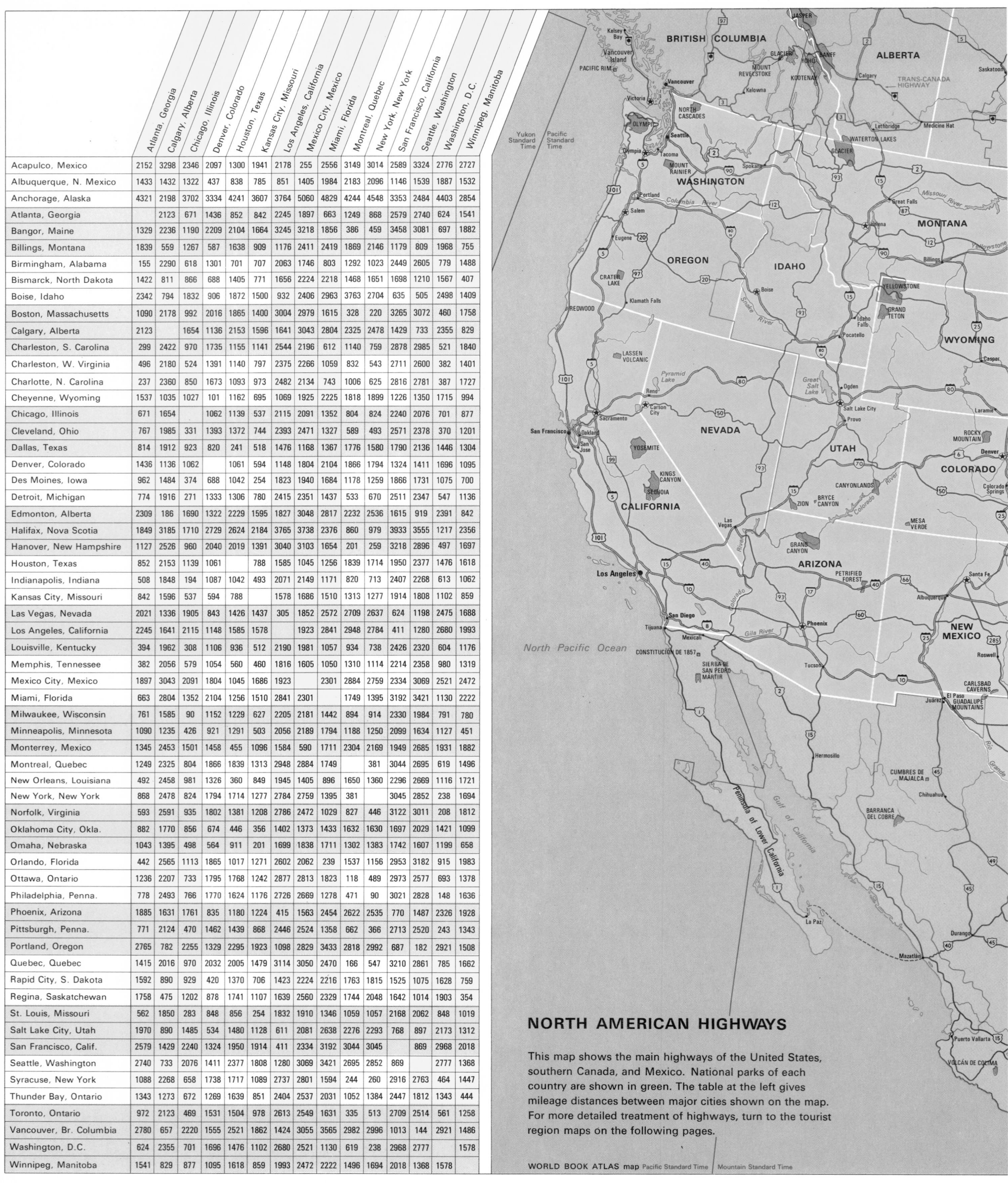

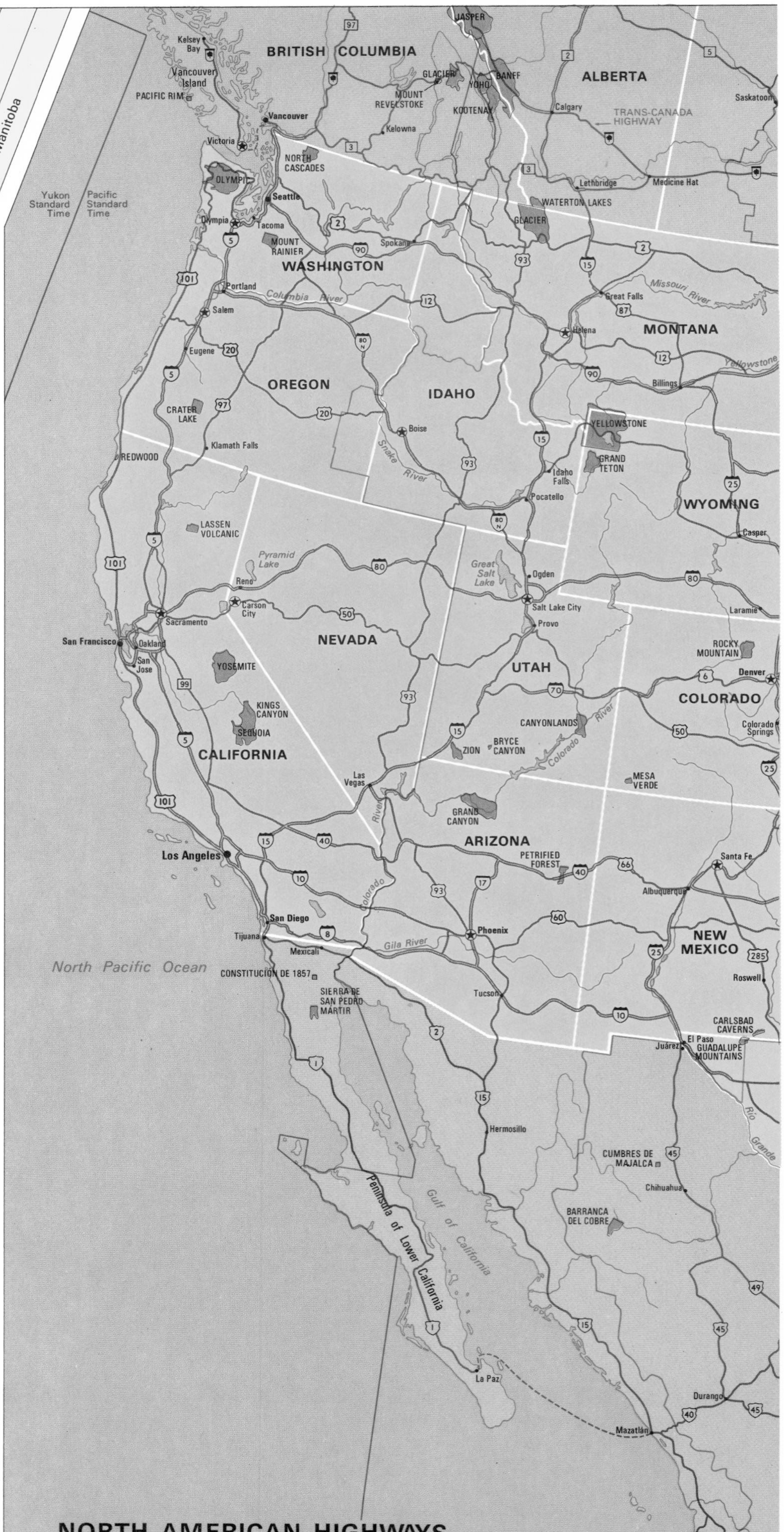

NORTH AMERICAN HIGHWAYS

This map shows the main highways of the United States, southern Canada, and Mexico. National parks of each country are shown in green. The table at the left gives mileage distances between major cities shown on the map. For more detailed treatment of highways, turn to the tourist region maps on the following pages.

WORLD BOOK ATLAS map Pacific Standard Time | Mountain Standard Time

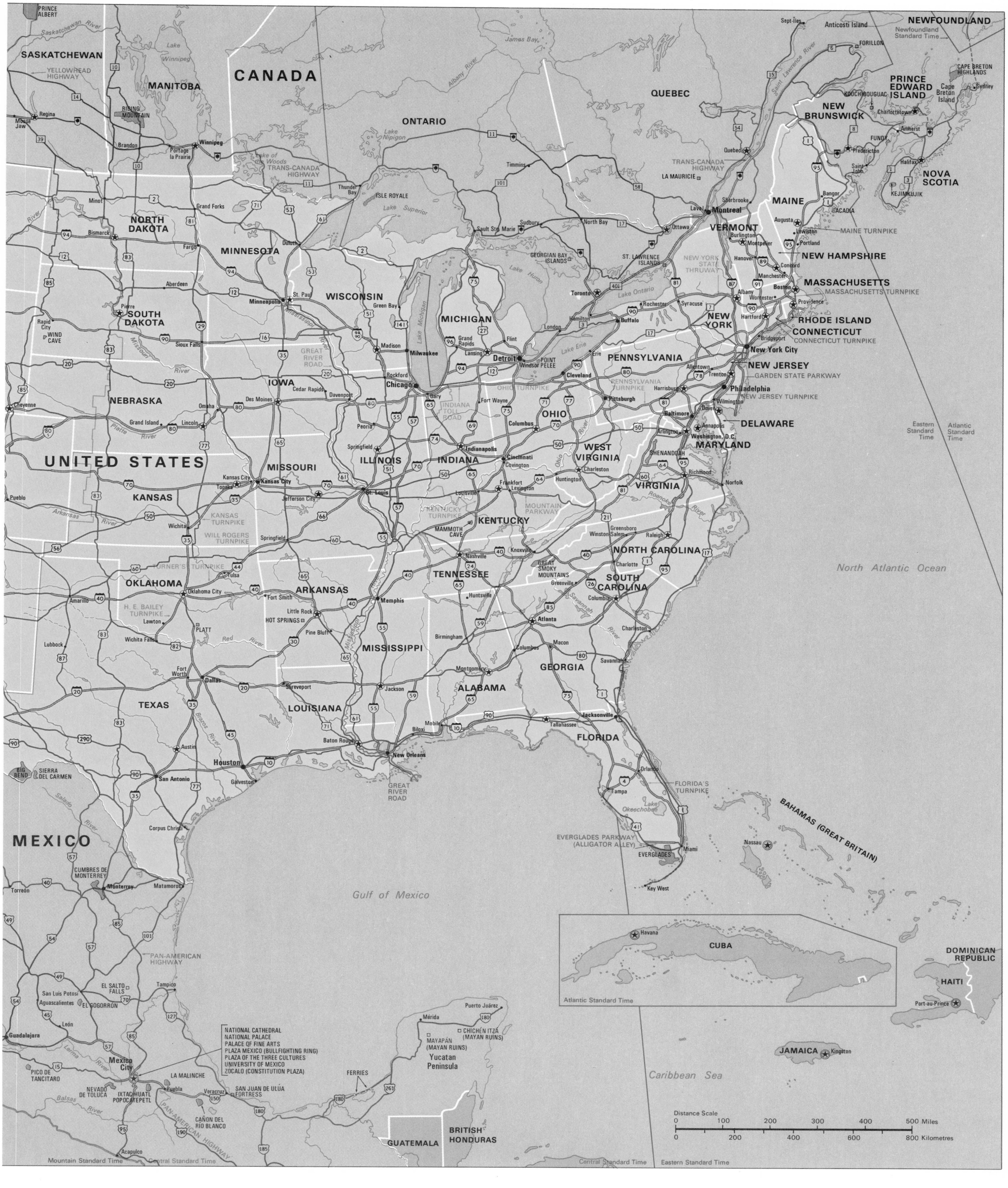
CANADA
UNITED STATES
MEXICO
SASKATCHEWAN
MANITOBA
ONTARIO
QUEBEC
NEWFOUNDLAND
Newfoundland Standard Time
PRINCE EDWARD ISLAND
NEW BRUNSWICK
NOVA SCOTIA
CAPE BRETON HIGHLANDS
TRANS-CANADA HIGHWAY
NORTH DAKOTA
SOUTH DAKOTA
NEBRASKA
KANSAS
OKLAHOMA
TEXAS
MINNESOTA
IOWA
MISSOURI
ARKANSAS
LOUISIANA
WISCONSIN
ILLINOIS
MICHIGAN
INDIANA
OHIO
KENTUCKY
TENNESSEE
MISSISSIPPI
ALABAMA
GEORGIA
FLORIDA
SOUTH CAROLINA
NORTH CAROLINA
VIRGINIA
WEST VIRGINIA
MARYLAND
DELAWARE
PENNSYLVANIA
NEW JERSEY
NEW YORK
CONNECTICUT
RHODE ISLAND
MASSACHUSETTS
VERMONT
NEW HAMPSHIRE
MAINE
MAINE TURNPIKE
MASSACHUSETTS TURNPIKE
CONNECTICUT TURNPIKE
GARDEN STATE PARKWAY
NEW JERSEY TURNPIKE
PENNSYLVANIA TURNPIKE
OHIO TURNPIKE
INDIANA TOLL ROAD
NEW YORK STATE THRUWAY
KANSAS TURNPIKE
WILL ROGERS TURNPIKE
TURNER'S TURNPIKE
H. E. BAILEY TURNPIKE
KENTUCKY TURNPIKE
MOUNTAIN PARKWAY
FLORIDA'S TURNPIKE
EVERGLADES PARKWAY (ALLIGATOR ALLEY)
GREAT RIVER ROAD
North Atlantic Ocean
Gulf of Mexico
Caribbean Sea
BAHAMAS (GREAT BRITAIN)
CUBA
JAMAICA
HAITI
DOMINICAN REPUBLIC
GUATEMALA
BRITISH HONDURAS
Yucatan Peninsula
PAN-AMERICAN HIGHWAY
NATIONAL CATHEDRAL
NATIONAL PALACE
PALACE OF FINE ARTS
PLAZA MEXICO (BULLFIGHTING RING)
PLAZA OF THE THREE CULTURES
UNIVERSITY OF MEXICO
ZOCALO (CONSTITUTION PLAZA)
Mountain Standard Time
Central Standard Time
Eastern Standard Time
Atlantic Standard Time
Distance Scale
0 100 200 300 400 500 Miles
0 200 400 600 800 Kilometres

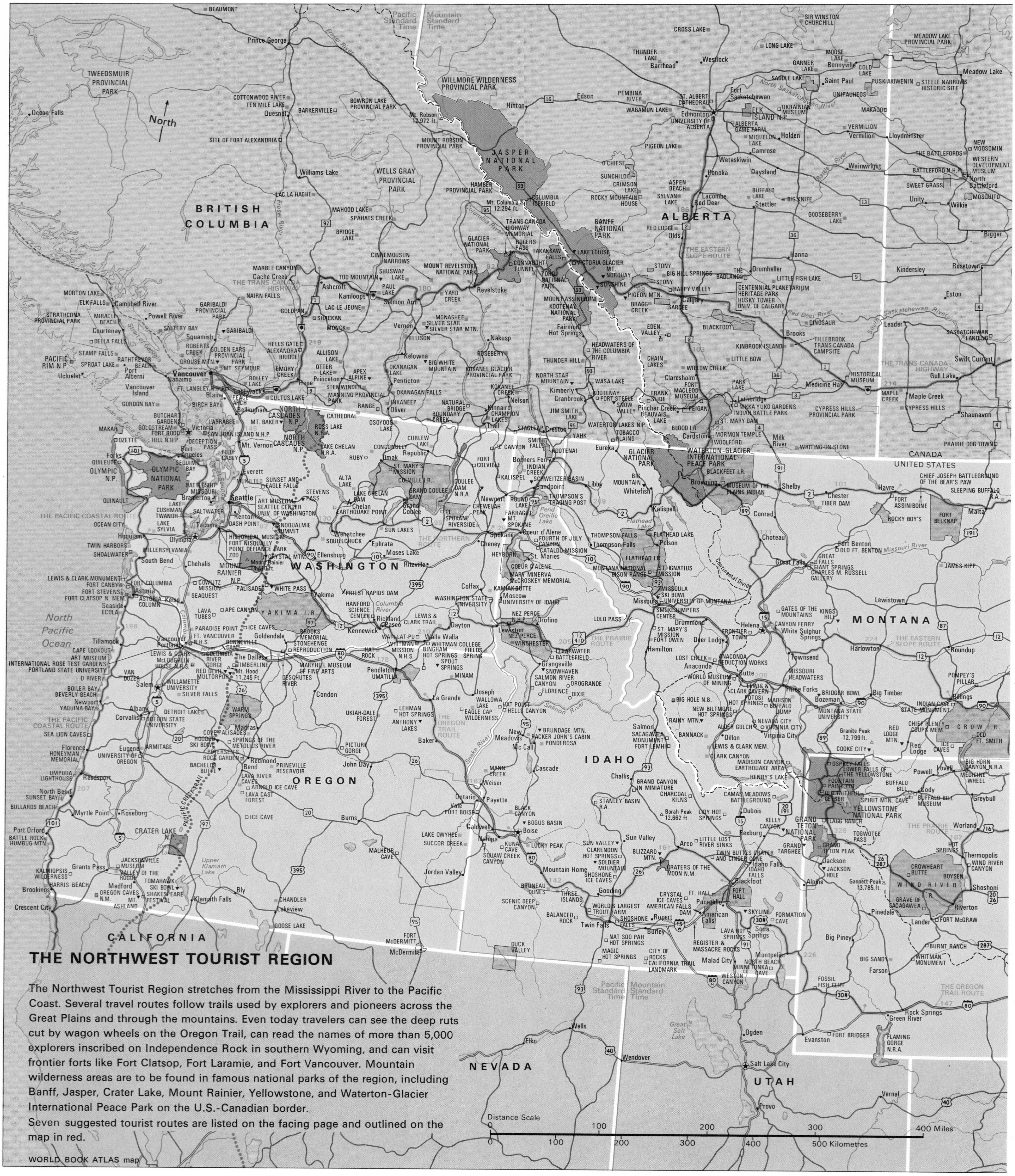

THE NORTHWEST TOURIST REGION

The Northwest Tourist Region stretches from the Mississippi River to the Pacific Coast. Several travel routes follow trails used by explorers and pioneers across the Great Plains and through the mountains. Even today travelers can see the deep ruts cut by wagon wheels on the Oregon Trail, can read the names of more than 5,000 explorers inscribed on Independence Rock in southern Wyoming, and can visit frontier forts like Fort Clatsop, Fort Laramie, and Fort Vancouver. Mountain wilderness areas are to be found in famous national parks of the region, including Banff, Jasper, Crater Lake, Mount Rainier, Yellowstone, and Waterton-Glacier International Peace Park on the U.S.-Canadian border.

Seven suggested tourist routes are listed on the facing page and outlined on the map in red.

WORLD BOOK ATLAS map

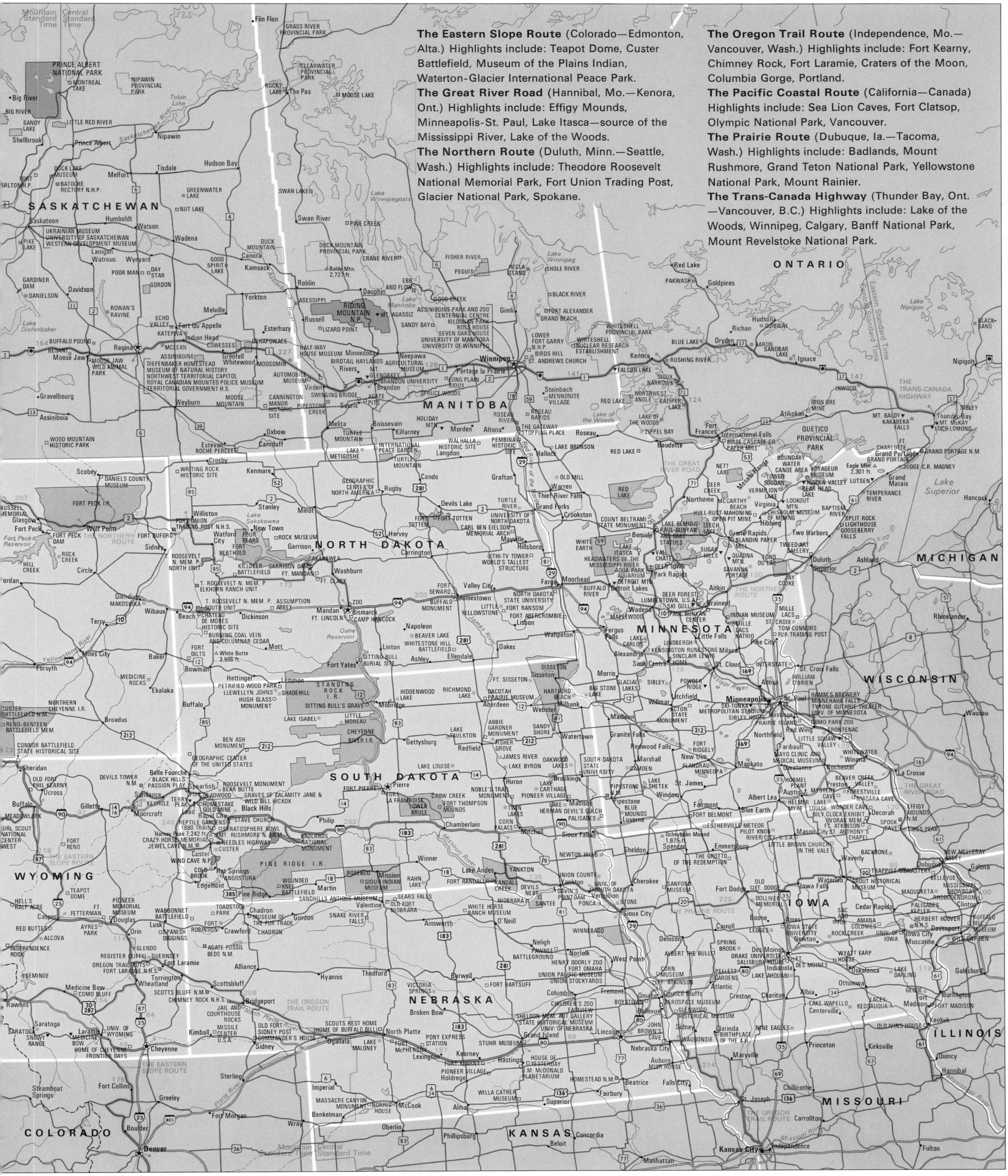

The Eastern Slope Route (Colorado—Edmonton, Alta.) Highlights include: Teapot Dome, Custer Battlefield, Museum of the Plains Indian, Waterton-Glacier International Peace Park.

The Great River Road (Hannibal, Mo.—Kenora, Ont.) Highlights include: Effigy Mounds, Minneapolis-St. Paul, Lake Itasca—source of the Mississippi River, Lake of the Woods.

The Northern Route (Duluth, Minn.—Seattle, Wash.) Highlights include: Theodore Roosevelt National Memorial Park, Fort Union Trading Post, Glacier National Park, Spokane.

The Oregon Trail Route (Independence, Mo.—Vancouver, Wash.) Highlights include: Fort Kearny, Chimney Rock, Fort Laramie, Craters of the Moon, Columbia Gorge, Portland.

The Pacific Coastal Route (California—Canada) Highlights include: Sea Lion Caves, Fort Clatsop, Olympic National Park, Vancouver.

The Prairie Route (Dubuque, Ia.—Tacoma, Wash.) Highlights include: Badlands, Mount Rushmore, Grand Teton National Park, Yellowstone National Park, Mount Rainier.

The Trans-Canada Highway (Thunder Bay, Ont.—Vancouver, B.C.) Highlights include: Lake of the Woods, Winnipeg, Calgary, Banff National Park, Mount Revelstoke National Park.

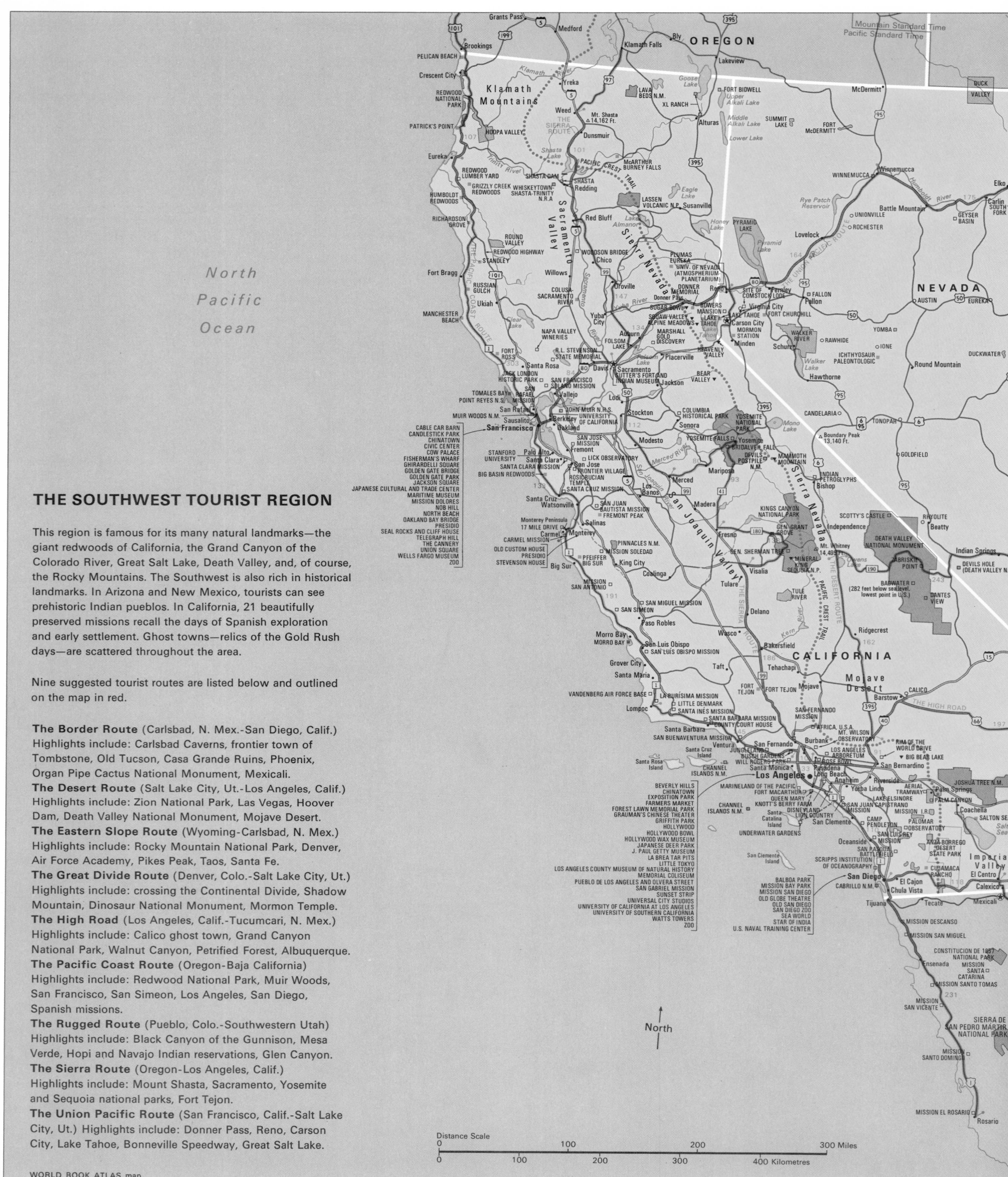

THE SOUTHWEST TOURIST REGION

This region is famous for its many natural landmarks—the giant redwoods of California, the Grand Canyon of the Colorado River, Great Salt Lake, Death Valley, and, of course, the Rocky Mountains. The Southwest is also rich in historical landmarks. In Arizona and New Mexico, tourists can see prehistoric Indian pueblos. In California, 21 beautifully preserved missions recall the days of Spanish exploration and early settlement. Ghost towns—relics of the Gold Rush days—are scattered throughout the area.

Nine suggested tourist routes are listed below and outlined on the map in red.

The Border Route (Carlsbad, N. Mex.-San Diego, Calif.) Highlights include: Carlsbad Caverns, frontier town of Tombstone, Old Tucson, Casa Grande Ruins, Phoenix, Organ Pipe Cactus National Monument, Mexicali.
The Desert Route (Salt Lake City, Ut.-Los Angeles, Calif.) Highlights include: Zion National Park, Las Vegas, Hoover Dam, Death Valley National Monument, Mojave Desert.
The Eastern Slope Route (Wyoming-Carlsbad, N. Mex.) Highlights include: Rocky Mountain National Park, Denver, Air Force Academy, Pikes Peak, Taos, Santa Fe.
The Great Divide Route (Denver, Colo.-Salt Lake City, Ut.) Highlights include: crossing the Continental Divide, Shadow Mountain, Dinosaur National Monument, Mormon Temple.
The High Road (Los Angeles, Calif.-Tucumcari, N. Mex.) Highlights include: Calico ghost town, Grand Canyon National Park, Walnut Canyon, Petrified Forest, Albuquerque.
The Pacific Coast Route (Oregon-Baja California) Highlights include: Redwood National Park, Muir Woods, San Francisco, San Simeon, Los Angeles, San Diego, Spanish missions.
The Rugged Route (Pueblo, Colo.-Southwestern Utah) Highlights include: Black Canyon of the Gunnison, Mesa Verde, Hopi and Navajo Indian reservations, Glen Canyon.
The Sierra Route (Oregon-Los Angeles, Calif.) Highlights include: Mount Shasta, Sacramento, Yosemite and Sequoia national parks, Fort Tejon.
The Union Pacific Route (San Francisco, Calif.-Salt Lake City, Ut.) Highlights include: Donner Pass, Reno, Carson City, Lake Tahoe, Bonneville Speedway, Great Salt Lake.

WORLD BOOK ATLAS map

IDAHO
WYOMING
NEBRASKA
UTAH
COLORADO
KANSAS
OKLAHOMA
ARIZONA
NEW MEXICO
TEXAS
BAJA CALIFORNIA
SONORA
CHIHUAHUA
COAHUILA
UNITED STATES
MEXICO
Gulf of California
Rocky Mountains
Continental Divide
Mountain Standard Time
Pacific Standard Time
Central Standard Time
Painted Desert
Gila Wilderness
THE GREAT DIVIDE ROUTE
THE RUGGED ROUTE
THE DESERT ROUTE
THE EASTERN SLOPE ROUTE
THE HIGH ROAD
THE BORDER ROUTE
American Falls
Twin Falls
Rupert
Soda Springs
Downey
Montpelier
Malad City
Big Piney
Farson
Kemmerer
Rock Springs
Green River
Rawlins
Laramie
Cheyenne
Fort Laramie
Torrington
Scottsbluff
Alliance
Hyannis
North Platte
Sidney
Evanston
Logan
LOGAN MORMON TEMPLE
GOLDEN SPIKE N.H.S.
HYRUM LAKE
Randolph
Brigham City
WILLARD BAY
Ogden
BEAR LAKE
Wells
BEEHIVE HOUSE
BRIGHAM YOUNG'S GRAVE
HANSEN PLANETARIUM
MORMON TEMPLE
AND TABERNACLE
PEACE GARDENS
PIONEER MONUMENT
UNIVERSITY OF UTAH
GREAT SALT LAKE
Great Salt Lake
JOHN M. BROWNING MUSEUM
Morgan
Bountiful
Salt Lake City
BONNEVILLE SPEEDWAY
Wendover
ROCKPORT LAKE
Kings Peak 13,498 Ft.
FLAMING GORGE N.R.A.
Flaming Gorge Reservoir
RUBY MOUNTAINS SCENIC AREA
RUBY VALLEY
OGDERS RANCH
BINGHAM CANYON COPPER PIT
Murray
Tooele
PARK CITY
ALTA
WASATCH MOUNTAIN
TIMPANOGOS CAVE N.M.
SKULL VALLEY
American Fork
UTAH LAKE
Utah Lake
Provo
BRIGHAM YOUNG UNIVERSITY
Spanish Fork City
UINTAH AND OURAY INDIAN RESERVATION
Duchesne
Vernal
NATURAL HISTORY STATE MUSEUM
DINOSAUR NATIONAL MONUMENT
GOSHUTE
Nephi
Mount Pleasant
Delta
YUBA LAKE
Ephraim
PALISADE LAKE
HAMILTON
Ely
RUTH
COPPER PIT
WARD CHARCOAL OVENS
LEHMAN CAVES N.M.
TERRITORIAL STATEHOUSE
Fillmore
KANOSH
Gunnison
Richfield
OLD COVE FORT
OLD FRISCO
BIG ROCK CANDY MOUNTAIN
MINERSVILLE LAKE
Beaver
PIUTE LAKE
CAPITOL REEF N.M.
BRISTOL
PIOCHE
EAGLE VALLEY RESERVOIR
CATHEDRAL GORGE
Panaca
Caliente
KERSHAW-RYAN
Panguitch
Cedar City
CEDAR BREAKS N.M.
BRYCE CANYON N.M.
BEAVER DAM
BRIGHAM YOUNG HOUSE
ZION NATIONAL PARK
SNOW CANYON
St. George
CORAL PINK SAND DUNES
INDIAN CLIFF DWELLINGS
PIPE SPRINGS N.M.
KAIBAB
Kanab
MOAPA RIVER
VALLEY OF FIRE
ELEPHANT ROCK
CONVENTION CENTER
THE STRIP
UNIVERSITY OF NEVADA
Las Vegas
Henderson
Boulder City
HOOVER DAM
LAKE MEAD NATIONAL RECREATION AREA
Lake Mead
UINTAH AND OURAY
Green River
GREEN RIVER
ARCHES N.M.
Moab
DEAD HORSE POINT
CANYONLANDS NATIONAL PARK
NEWSPAPER ROCK
Monticello
Blanding
NATURAL BRIDGES N.M.
HOVENWEEP N.M.
GLEN CANYON NATIONAL RECREATION AREA
GOOSENECKS
MONUMENT VALLEY
RAINBOW BRIDGE N.M.
FOUR CORNERS
MONUMENT VALLEY NAVAJO TRIBAL PARK
Page
GLEN CANYON DAM
NAVAJO N.M.
Kayenta
MARBLE CANYON N.M.
NAVAJO INDIAN RESERVATION
HOPI-NAVAJO INDIAN RESERVATION
GRAND CANYON N.M.
GRAND CANYON NATIONAL PARK
HAVASUPAI
Grand Canyon
YAVAPAI MUSEUM
TUSAYAN MUSEUM
Tuba City
HOPI VILLAGES
Polacca
HOPI INDIAN RESERVATION
CANYON DE CHELLY N.M.
Fort Defiance
HUBBELL TRADING POST N.H.S.
St. Michael
WINDOW ROCK
HUALAPAI
Lake Mohave
DAVIS DAM
GRAND CANYON CAVERNS
Kingman
Humphreys Peak 12,670 Ft.
WUPATKI N.M.
ARIZONA SNOW BOWL
SUNSET CRATER N.M.
WALNUT CANYON N.M.
Williams
LOWELL OBSERVATORY
MUSEUM OF NORTHERN ARIZONA
Flagstaff
METEOR CRATER
Winslow
PETRIFIED FOREST N.M.
Holbrook
MOHAVE
MITCHELL CAVERNS
Needles
OAK CREEK CANYON
JEROME STATE HISTORICAL PARK
JEROME
TUZIGOOT N.M.
YAVAPAI
Prescott
SMOKI MUSEUM
GRANITE DELLS
CAMP VERDE
MONTEZUMA CASTLE N.M.
Lake Havasu City
LONDON BRIDGE
LAKE HAVASU
TONTO NATURAL BRIDGE
Saint Johns
LYMAN LAKE
Show Low
BUCKSKIN MOUNTAIN
Parker
COLORADO RIVER INDIAN RESERVATION
Wickenburg
FORT APACHE INDIAN RESERVATION
SALT RIVER CANYON
BARTLETT DAM
Fort McDowell
ROOSEVELT DAM
T. Roosevelt Lake
TONTO N.M.
Blythe
DESERT BOTANICAL GARDENS
ENCANTO PARK
HEARD MUSEUM
PHOENIX ZOO
PIONEER VILLAGE
PUEBLO GRANDE MUSEUM
TALIESIN WEST
Phoenix
Scottsdale
ARIZONA STATE UNIVERSITY
Tempe
Chandler
APACHE TRAIL
Globe
SAN CARLOS INDIAN RESERVATION
San Carlos Reservoir
Superior
Florence
SOUTHWESTERN ARBORETUM
COOLIDGE DAM
GILA RIVER
GILA BEND
PAINTED ROCKS
MARICOPA
Casa Grande
CASA GRANDE RUINS N.M.
Gila Bend
PICACHO
IMPERIAL DAM
FORT YUMA
YUMA TERRITORIAL PRISON
Yuma
COCOPAH
San Luis
PINAL PIONEER PARKWAY
Safford
PICACHO PEAK
Ajo
PAPAGO INDIAN RESERVATION
SAGUARO N.M.
ARIZONA-SONORA DESERT MUSEUM
UNIVERSITY OF ARIZONA
Tucson
OLD TUCSON
SAGUARO N.M.
ORGAN PIPE CACTUS N.M.
KITT PEAK NATIONAL OBSERVATORY
SAN XAVIER
SAN XAVIER DEL BAC MISSION
COLOSSAL CAVE
Wilcox
CHIRICAHUA N.M.
FORT BOWIE N.M.
COCHISE STRONGHOLD
BIRD CAGE THEATER
BOOT HILL GRAVEYARD
COURT HOUSE
OK CORRAL
WELLS FARGO MUSEUM
WYATT EARP MUSEUM
Tombstone
TUBAC PRESIDIO
TUMACACORI N.M.
Sonoita
CORONADO N.M.
LAVENDER PIT
Douglas
Nogales
Agua Prieta
Lordsburg
SHAKESPEARE
Deming
ROCK HOUND
PANCHO VILLA
Craig
Meeker
STEAMBOAT LAKE
Steamboat Springs
SHADOW MOUNTAIN N.R.A.
ROCKY MOUNTAIN N.P.
HORSETOOTH RESERVOIR
Fort Collins
BOYD LAKE
Loveland
Greeley
JACKSON RESERVOIR
Sterling
Holyoke
Imperial
McCook
Fort Morgan
Akron
Wray
Platteville
FORT VASQUEZ
Boulder
UNIVERSITY OF COLORADO
BEECHER ISLAND BATTLEGROUND
Oberlin
St. Francis
GOLDEN GATE CANYON
WINTER PARK
LOVELAND BASIN
Central City
Golden
Denver
BUFFALO BILL'S GRAVE
ART MUSEUM
BOTANICAL GARDENS
CIVIC CENTER
COLORADO STATE MUSEUM
DENVER ZOO
GOVERNOR'S MANSION
MUSEUM OF NATURAL HISTORY
UNIVERSITY OF DENVER
U.S. MINT
BONNY RESERVOIR
Colby
Loveland Pass
Vail
MOUNT EVANS HIGHWAY
CHERRY CREEK
Littleton
RED ROCKS PARK
Castle Rock
ARAPAHOE BASIN
KEYSTONE
Burlington
Oakley
Rifle
SUNLIGHT
Glenwood Springs
BRECKENRIDGE
Leadville
ASPEN HIGHLAND
SNOWMASS
Aspen
VEGA RESERVOIR
DEXTER CABIN
HEALY HOUSE
ANTERO RESERVOIR
CAVE OF THE WINDS
AIR FORCE ACADEMY
GARDEN OF THE GODS
Colorado Springs
MANITOU INCLINE
SEVEN FALLS
Pikes Peak 14,110 Ft.
FLORISSANT FOSSIL BEDS N.M.
NORTH POLE (SANTA'S VILLAGE)
Mt. Elbert 14,431 Ft.
Cheyenne Wells
Scott City
HIGHLINE LAKE
Grand Junction
COLORADO N.M.
CRESTED BUTTE
Delta
BLACK CANYON OF THE GUNNISON N.M.
Gunnison
Salida
ROYAL GORGE
Canon City
Pueblo
EL PUEBLO MUSEUM
Garden City
Montrose
UTE INDIAN MUSEUM
CURECANTI N.R.A.
Uravan
Lamar
Las Animas
BENT'S OLD FORT N.H.S.
La Junta
Rocky Ford
THE EASTERN SLOPE ROUTE
Ouray
Silverton
GREAT SAND DUNES N.M.
Walsenburg
Springfield
DURANGO-SILVERTON NARROW GAUGE RAILROAD
Del Norte
Monte Vista
LATHROP
Alamosa
FORT GARLAND
Trinidad
BACA HOUSE AND PIONEER MUSEUM
Cortez
MESA VERDE N.P.
PAGOSA SPRINGS
PIKE'S STOCKADE
Durango
ECHO CANYON
Antonito
SOUTHERN UTE
YUCCA HOUSE N.M.
UTE MOUNTAIN
NAVAJO RESERVOIR
Raton
FOLSOM MAN STATE MONUMENT
CAPULIN MOUNTAIN N.M.
Boise City
Guymon
AZTEC RUINS N.M.
Shiprock
SHIPROCK PEAK
Farmington
NAVAJO LAKE
JICARILLA APACHE
RIO GRANDE GORGE
TAOS SKI VALLEY
Wheeler Peak 13,160 Ft.
Cimarron
PHILMONT SCOUT RANCH
Taos
PUEBLO DE TAOS
GORGE BRIDGE
CLAYTON LAKE
Clayton
Stratford
KIT CARSON STATE MONUMENT
GHOST RANCH MUSEUM
SAN ILDEFONSO PUEBLO
PUYE CLIFF DWELLINGS
SANTA CLARA
CHACO CANYON N.M.
LOS ALAMOS MUSEUM
Los Alamos
SAN JUAN
NAMBE
TESUQUE
FORT UNION N.M.
HYDE MEMORIAL
Mosquero
Dumas
Borger
Channing
JEMEZ STATE MONUMENT
BANDELIER N.M.
Santa Fe
SAN MIGUEL MISSION
PALACE OF THE GOVERNORS
STORRIE LAKE
PECOS N.M.
Las Vegas
CONCHAS LAKE
Conchas Reservoir
Logan
UTE LAKE
Vega
Amarillo
ZIA
JEMEZ
COCHITI
SANTO DOMINGO
GLORIETA BATTLE SITE
SAN FELIPE
Bernalillo
Albuquerque
CORONADO STATE MONUMENT
INDIAN ARTS MUSEUM
Gallup
BLUEWATER LAKE
LAGUNA
SANDIA PEAK
AERIAL TRAMWAY
OLD TOWN
UNIVERSITY OF NEW MEXICO
ISLETA PUEBLO
Tucumcari
Canyon
Grants
EL MORRO N.M.
ZUÑI
CANONCITO
ACOMA PUEBLO
ACOMA
ISLETA
ENCHANTED MESA
LAGUNA
Santa Rosa
Belen
ALAMOGORDO LAKE
Fort Sumner
GRAVE OF BILLY THE KID
Clovis
Plainview
Muleshoe
Vaughn
ABO STATE MONUMENT
GRAN QUIVIRA N.M.
ALAMO BAND NAVAJO
Portales
Socorro
Lubbock
Alpine
Luna
VALLEY OF FIRES
Carrizozo
LINCOLN STATE MONUMENT
Roswell
BOTTOMLESS LAKES
Brownfield
CORONADO TRAIL
MOGOLLON
GILA CLIFF DWELLINGS N.M.
Ruidoso
RUIDOSO DOWNS
MESCALERO APACHE
Elephant Butte Reservoir
Truth or Consequences
ELEPHANT BUTTE LAKE
Caballo Reservoir
CABALLO LAKE
HILLSBORO
Alamogordo
CLOUDCROFT
Artesia
Lovington
Seminole
Hobbs
Clifton
Silver City
WHITE SANDS N.M.
Lake McMillan
CITY OF ROCKS
Hatch
Andrews
Las Cruces
Carlsbad
Midland
SITTING BULL FALLS
Odessa
LA MESILLA
CARLSBAD CAVERNS N.P.
El Paso
Juárez
Pecos
Van Horn
Puerto Peñasco
San Felipe
El Socorro
Caborca
El Desemboque
Magdalena
MISSION MAGDALENA
Cananea
Janos
El Sueco
Buenaventura
CUMBRES DE MAJALCA NATIONAL PARK
Ojinaga
Presidio
Marfa
SIERRA DEL CARMEN NATIONAL PARK
Rio Grande
Colorado River
Gila River
Salt River
Verde River
Virgin River
San Pedro River
Santa Cruz River
Pecos River
South Platte River
Arkansas River
Powell Lake

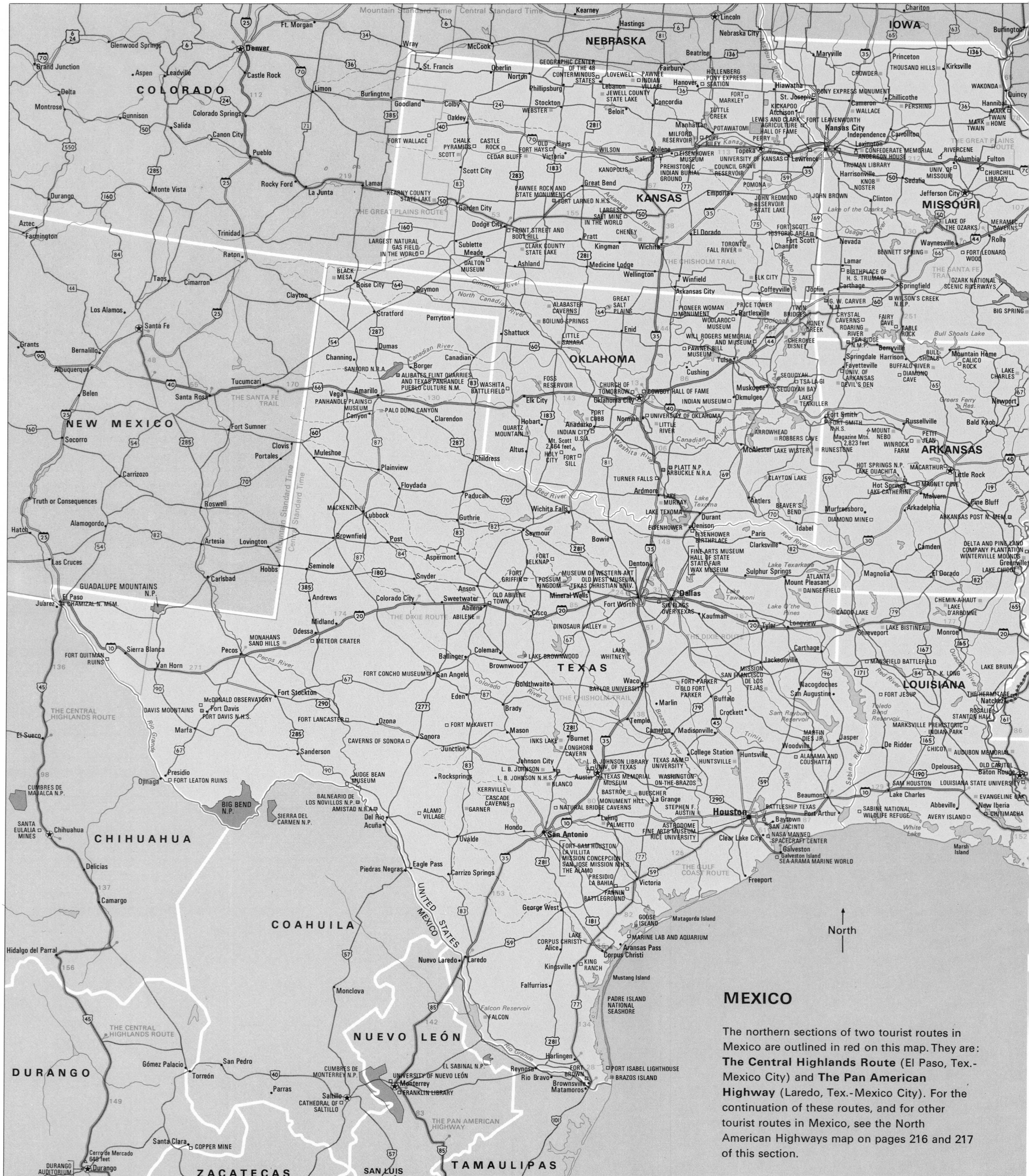

MEXICO

The northern sections of two tourist routes in Mexico are outlined in red on this map. They are: **The Central Highlands Route** (El Paso, Tex.-Mexico City) and **The Pan American Highway** (Laredo, Tex.-Mexico City). For the continuation of these routes, and for other tourist routes in Mexico, see the North American Highways map on pages 216 and 217 of this section.

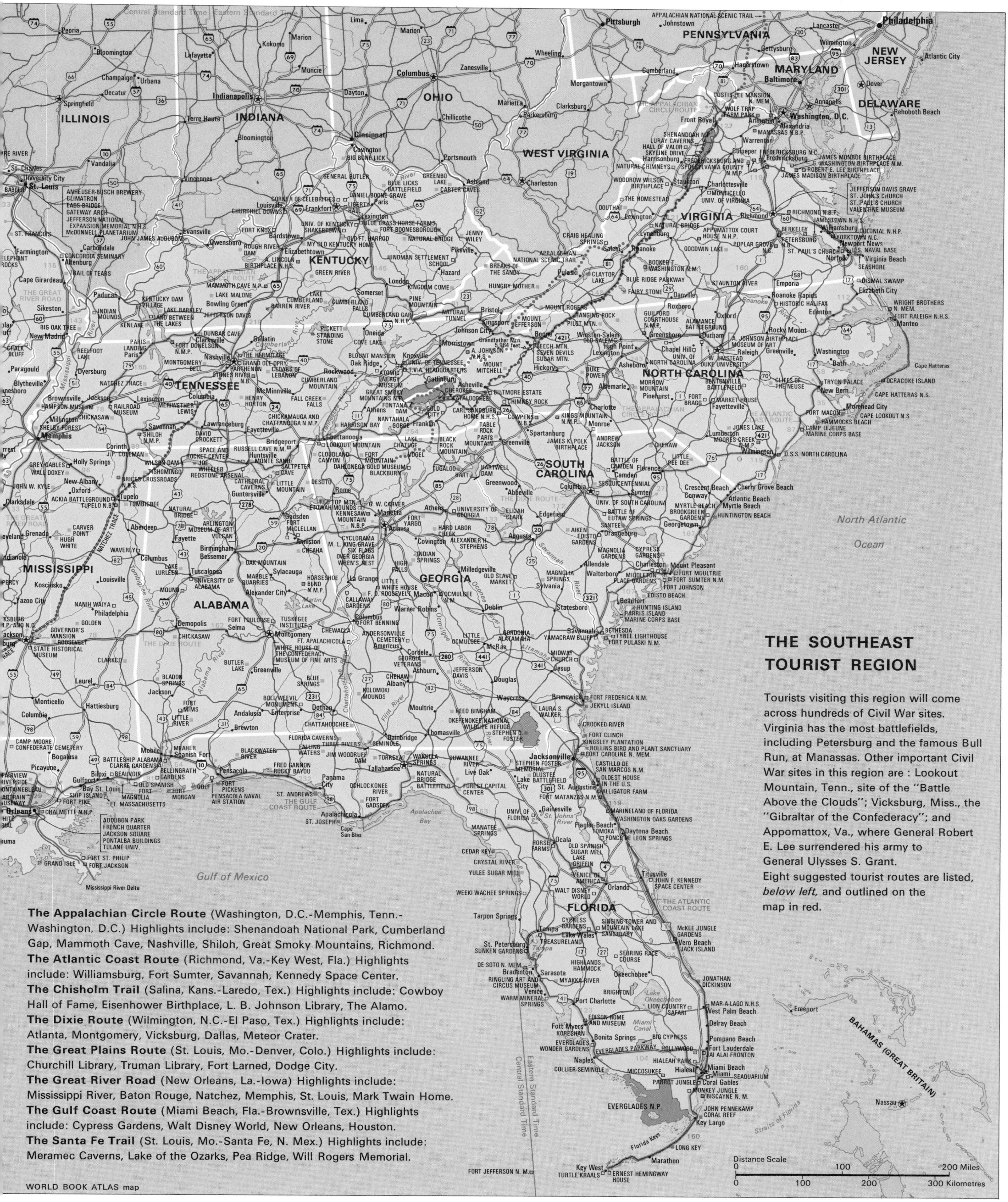

THE SOUTHEAST TOURIST REGION

Tourists visiting this region will come across hundreds of Civil War sites. Virginia has the most battlefields, including Petersburg and the famous Bull Run, at Manassas. Other important Civil War sites in this region are : Lookout Mountain, Tenn., site of the "Battle Above the Clouds"; Vicksburg, Miss., the "Gibraltar of the Confederacy"; and Appomattox, Va., where General Robert E. Lee surrendered his army to General Ulysses S. Grant.

Eight suggested tourist routes are listed, *below left*, and outlined on the map in red.

The Appalachian Circle Route (Washington, D.C.-Memphis, Tenn.-Washington, D.C.) Highlights include: Shenandoah National Park, Cumberland Gap, Mammoth Cave, Nashville, Shiloh, Great Smoky Mountains, Richmond.
The Atlantic Coast Route (Richmond, Va.-Key West, Fla.) Highlights include: Williamsburg, Fort Sumter, Savannah, Kennedy Space Center.
The Chisholm Trail (Salina, Kans.-Laredo, Tex.) Highlights include: Cowboy Hall of Fame, Eisenhower Birthplace, L. B. Johnson Library, The Alamo.
The Dixie Route (Wilmington, N.C.-El Paso, Tex.) Highlights include: Atlanta, Montgomery, Vicksburg, Dallas, Meteor Crater.
The Great Plains Route (St. Louis, Mo.-Denver, Colo.) Highlights include: Churchill Library, Truman Library, Fort Larned, Dodge City.
The Great River Road (New Orleans, La.-Iowa) Highlights include: Mississippi River, Baton Rouge, Natchez, Memphis, St. Louis, Mark Twain Home.
The Gulf Coast Route (Miami Beach, Fla.-Brownsville, Tex.) Highlights include: Cypress Gardens, Walt Disney World, New Orleans, Houston.
The Santa Fe Trail (St. Louis, Mo.-Santa Fe, N. Mex.) Highlights include: Meramec Caverns, Lake of the Ozarks, Pea Ridge, Will Rogers Memorial.

WORLD BOOK ATLAS map

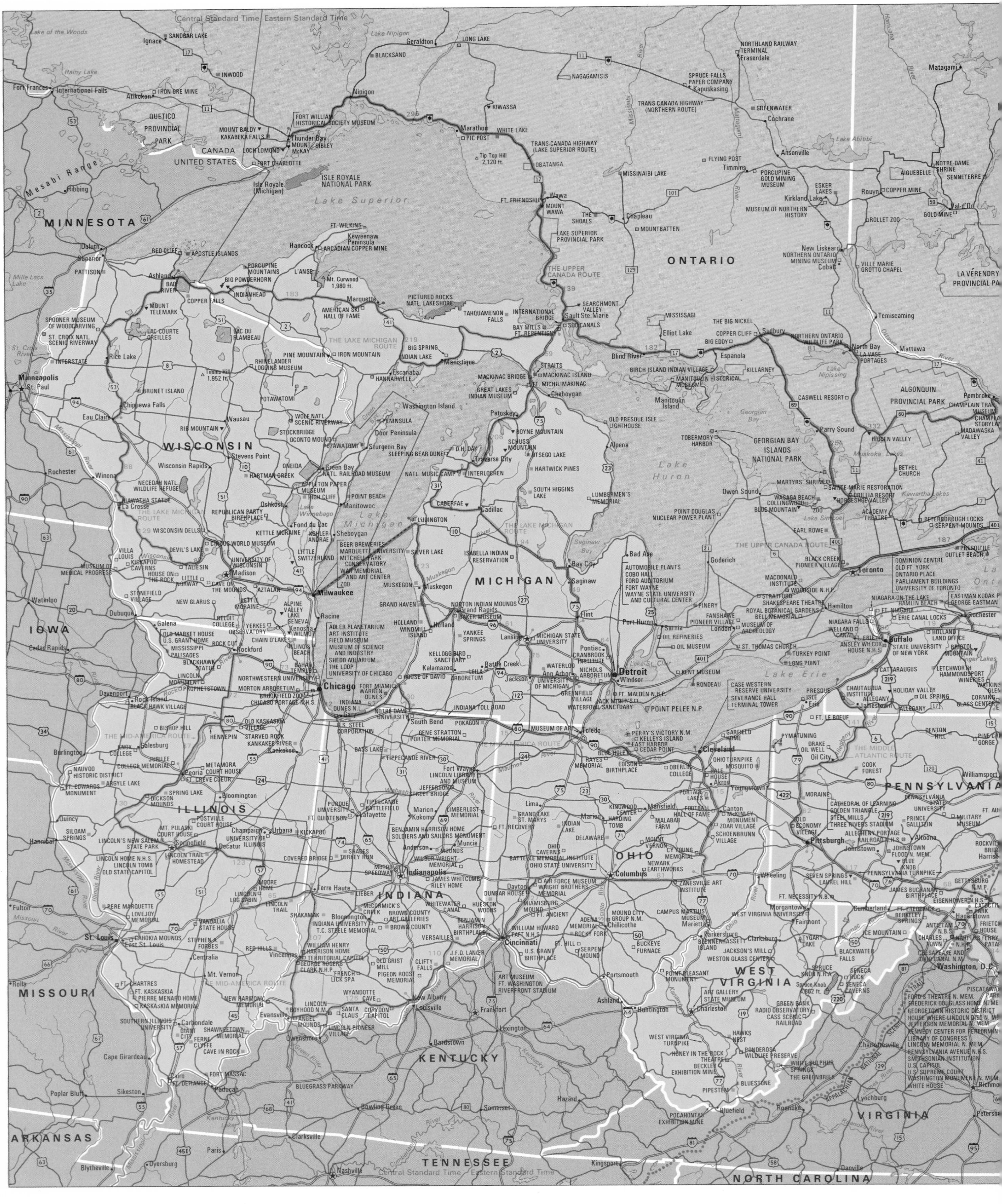
Central Standard Time
Eastern Standard Time
Lake of the Woods
Lake Nipigon
Lake Superior
Lake Michigan
Lake Huron
Lake Erie
Georgian Bay
CANADA
UNITED STATES
ONTARIO
MINNESOTA
WISCONSIN
MICHIGAN
IOWA
ILLINOIS
INDIANA
OHIO
PENNSYLVANIA
WEST VIRGINIA
VIRGINIA
KENTUCKY
TENNESSEE
NORTH CAROLINA
MISSOURI
ARKANSAS
QUETICO PROVINCIAL PARK
ISLE ROYALE NATIONAL PARK
ALGONQUIN PROVINCIAL PARK
GEORGIAN BAY ISLANDS NATIONAL PARK
TRANS-CANADA HIGHWAY (NORTHERN ROUTE)
TRANS-CANADA HIGHWAY (LAKE SUPERIOR ROUTE)
THE UPPER CANADA ROUTE
THE LAKE MICHIGAN ROUTE
THE MID-AMERICA ROUTE
THE MIDDLE ATLANTIC ROUTE
Thunder Bay
Sault Ste. Marie
Sudbury
Toronto
Minneapolis
St. Paul
Duluth
Milwaukee
Madison
Green Bay
Chicago
Detroit
Windsor
Lansing
Grand Rapids
Toledo
Cleveland
Buffalo
Pittsburgh
Columbus
Cincinnati
Indianapolis
Louisville
Springfield
St. Louis
Peoria
Fort Wayne
Akron
Nashville
Charleston
Washington, D.C.

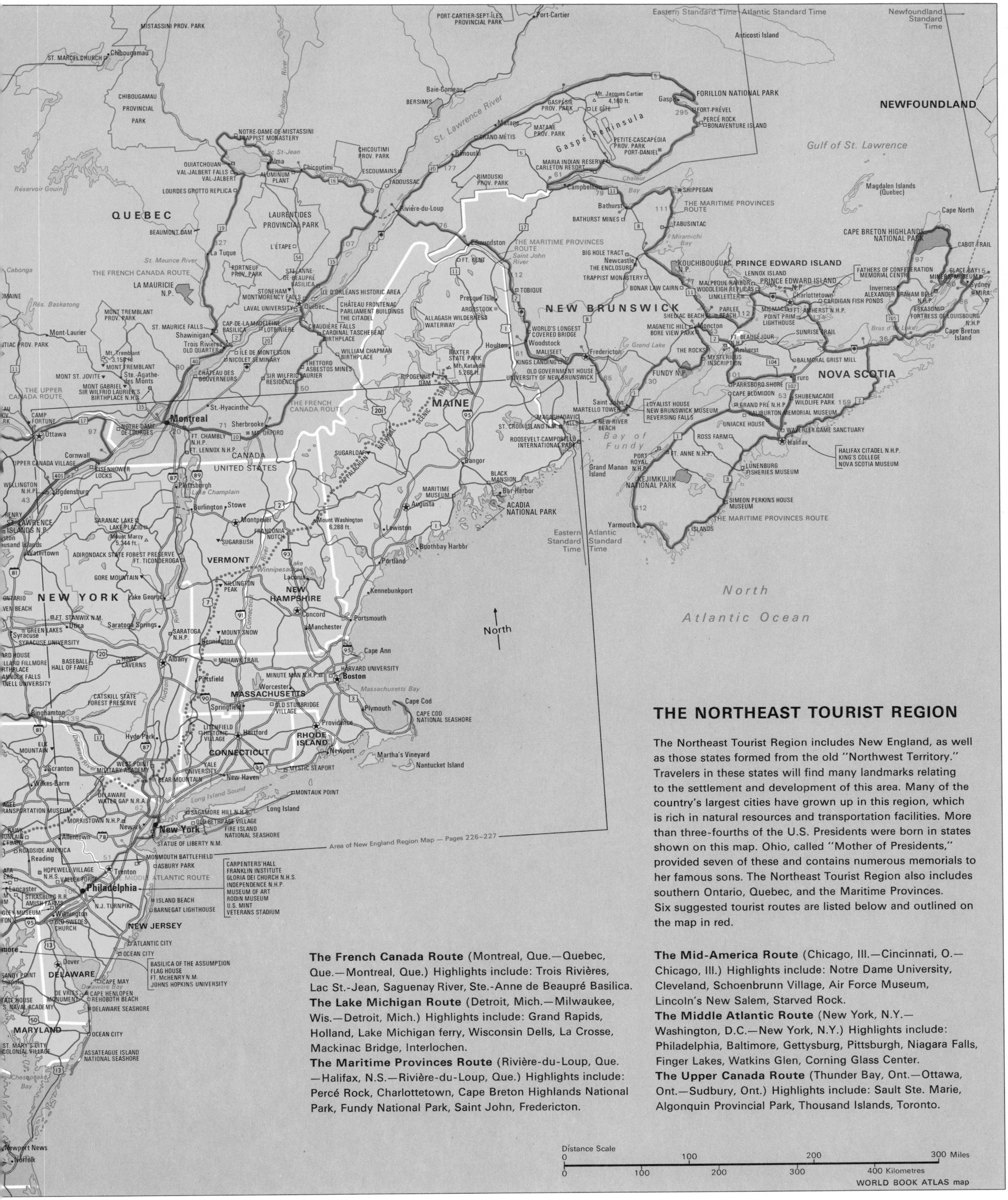

THE NORTHEAST TOURIST REGION

The Northeast Tourist Region includes New England, as well as those states formed from the old "Northwest Territory." Travelers in these states will find many landmarks relating to the settlement and development of this area. Many of the country's largest cities have grown up in this region, which is rich in natural resources and transportation facilities. More than three-fourths of the U.S. Presidents were born in states shown on this map. Ohio, called "Mother of Presidents," provided seven of these and contains numerous memorials to her famous sons. The Northeast Tourist Region also includes southern Ontario, Quebec, and the Maritime Provinces. Six suggested tourist routes are listed below and outlined on the map in red.

The French Canada Route (Montreal, Que.—Quebec, Que.—Montreal, Que.) Highlights include: Trois Rivières, Lac St.-Jean, Saguenay River, Ste.-Anne de Beaupré Basilica.
The Lake Michigan Route (Detroit, Mich.—Milwaukee, Wis.—Detroit, Mich.) Highlights include: Grand Rapids, Holland, Lake Michigan ferry, Wisconsin Dells, La Crosse, Mackinac Bridge, Interlochen.
The Maritime Provinces Route (Rivière-du-Loup, Que.—Halifax, N.S.—Rivière-du-Loup, Que.) Highlights include: Percé Rock, Charlottetown, Cape Breton Highlands National Park, Fundy National Park, Saint John, Fredericton.

The Mid-America Route (Chicago, Ill.—Cincinnati, O.—Chicago, Ill.) Highlights include: Notre Dame University, Cleveland, Schoenbrunn Village, Air Force Museum, Lincoln's New Salem, Starved Rock.
The Middle Atlantic Route (New York, N.Y.—Washington, D.C.—New York, N.Y.) Highlights include: Philadelphia, Baltimore, Gettysburg, Pittsburgh, Niagara Falls, Finger Lakes, Watkins Glen, Corning Glass Center.
The Upper Canada Route (Thunder Bay, Ont.—Ottawa, Ont.—Sudbury, Ont.) Highlights include: Sault Ste. Marie, Algonquin Provincial Park, Thousand Islands, Toronto.

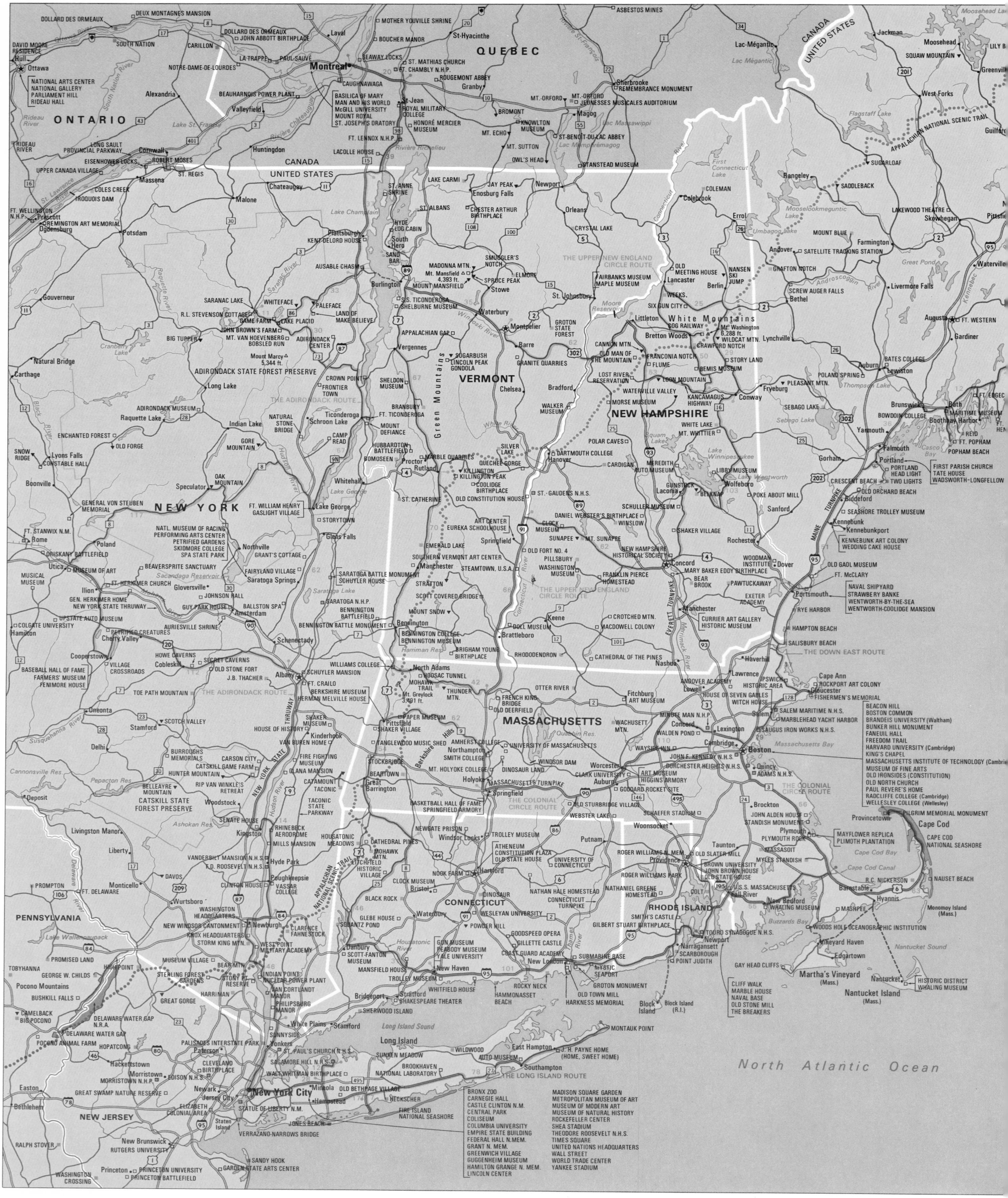
QUEBEC
ONTARIO
CANADA
UNITED STATES
NEW YORK
VERMONT
NEW HAMPSHIRE
MASSACHUSETTS
CONNECTICUT
RHODE ISLAND
PENNSYLVANIA
NEW JERSEY
North Atlantic Ocean
Ottawa
NATIONAL ARTS CENTER
NATIONAL GALLERY
PARLIAMENT HILL
RIDEAU HALL
Montreal
BASILICA OF MARY
MAN AND HIS WORLD
McGILL UNIVERSITY
MOUNT ROYAL
ST. JOSEPH'S ORATORY
DEUX MONTAGNES MANSION
DOLLARD DES ORMEAUX
DAVID MOORE RESIDENCE
Hull
SOUTH NATION
CARILLON
JOHN ABBOTT BIRTHPLACE
LA TRAPPE
PAUL SAUVÉ
NOTRE-DAME-DE-LOURDES
Laval
MOTHER YOUVILLE SHRINE
BOUCHER MANOR
St-Hyacinthe
SEAWAY LOCKS
ST. MATHIAS CHURCH
FT. CHAMBLY N.H.P.
ROUGEMONT ABBEY
Granby
CAUGHNAWAGA
BEAUHARNOIS POWER PLANT
Alexandria
Valleyfield
St-Jean
ROYAL MILITARY COLLEGE
HONORÉ MERCIER MUSEUM
FT. LENNOX N.H.P.
LACOLLE HOUSE
Huntingdon
Cornwall
LONG SAULT PROVINCIAL PARKWAY
EISENHOWER LOCKS
ROBERT MOSES
UPPER CANADA VILLAGE
Massena
ST. REGIS
COLES CREEK
IROQUOIS DAM
FT. WELLINGTON N.H.P.
Prescott
REMINGTON ART MEMORIAL
Ogdensburg
Potsdam
Malone
Chateaugay
ASBESTOS MINES
Sherbrooke
REMEMBRANCE MONUMENT
MT.-ORFORD
JEUNESSES MUSICALES AUDITORIUM
Magog
BROMONT
KNOWLTON MUSEUM
MT. ECHO
ST-BENOIT-DU-LAC ABBEY
MT. SUTTON
OWL'S HEAD
STANSTEAD MUSEUM
Lac-Mégantic
Jackman
Moosehead
SQUAW MOUNTAIN
Greenville
West Forks
APPALACHIAN NATIONAL SCENIC TRAIL
SUGARLOAF
Rangeley
SADDLEBACK
LAKEWOOD THEATRE
Skowhegan
Pittsfield
MOUNT BLUE
Farmington
Andover
SATELLITE TRACKING STATION
GRAFTON NOTCH
Livermore Falls
SCREW AUGER FALLS
Bethel
Waterville
Augusta
FT. WESTERN
Gardiner
Lewiston
Auburn
BATES COLLEGE
Lynchville
POLAND SPRING
PLEASANT MTN.
Fryeburg
Conway
Brunswick
BOWDOIN COLLEGE
Bath
MARITIME MUSEUM
Boothbay Harbor
Yarmouth
SEBAGO LAKE
Falmouth
Portland
PORTLAND HEAD LIGHT
TWO LIGHTS
FIRST PARISH CHURCH
TATE HOUSE
WADSWORTH-LONGFELLOW
FT. POPHAM
POPHAM BEACH
REID
FT. EDGECOMB
Gorham
CRESCENT BEACH
OLD ORCHARD BEACH
Biddeford
SEASHORE TROLLEY MUSEUM
Kennebunk
Kennebunkport
KENNEBUNK ART COLONY
WEDDING CAKE HOUSE
Sanford
Dover
OLD GAOL MUSEUM
FT. McCLARY
Portsmouth
NAVAL SHIPYARD
STRAWBERY BANKE
WENTWORTH-BY-THE-SEA
WENTWORTH-COOLIDGE MANSION
RYE HARBOR
HAMPTON BEACH
SALISBURY BEACH
THE DOWN EAST ROUTE
Haverhill
Lawrence
Ipswich
HISTORIC AREA
Cape Ann
ROCKPORT ART COLONY
Gloucester
FISHERMEN'S MEMORIAL
Salem
SALEM MARITIME N.H.S.
MARBLEHEAD YACHT HARBOR
SAUGUS IRON WORKS N.H.S.
BEACON HILL
BOSTON COMMON
BRANDEIS UNIVERSITY (Waltham)
BUNKER HILL MONUMENT
FANEUIL HALL
FREEDOM TRAIL
HARVARD UNIVERSITY (Cambridge)
KING'S CHAPEL
MASSACHUSETTS INSTITUTE OF TECHNOLOGY (Cambridge)
MUSEUM OF FINE ARTS
OLD IRONSIDES (CONSTITUTION)
OLD NORTH CHURCH
PAUL REVERE'S HOME
RADCLIFFE COLLEGE (Cambridge)
WELLESLEY COLLEGE (Wellesley)
Boston
Lexington
Cambridge
Concord
WALDEN POND
MINUTE MAN N.H.P.
WAYSIDE INN
JOHN F. KENNEDY N.H.S.
DORCHESTER HEIGHTS N.H.S.
Quincy
ADAMS N.H.S.
THE COLONIAL CIRCLE ROUTE
Brockton
JOHN ALDEN HOUSE
STANDISH MONUMENT
Plymouth
PLYMOUTH ROCK
MAYFLOWER REPLICA
PLIMOTH PLANTATION
Provincetown
PILGRIM MEMORIAL MONUMENT
Cape Cod
CAPE COD NATIONAL SEASHORE
Cape Cod Bay
Cape Cod Canal
MYLES STANDISH
MASSASOIT
Taunton
R.C. NICKERSON
NAUSET BEACH
Barnstable
Hyannis
Monomoy Island (Mass.)
MASHPEE
WOODS HOLE OCEANOGRAPHIC INSTITUTION
Vineyard Haven
Edgartown
Nantucket Sound
Martha's Vineyard (Mass.)
Nantucket
HISTORIC DISTRICT
WHALING MUSEUM
Nantucket Island (Mass.)
New Bedford
WHALING MUSEUM
Fall River
U.S.S. MASSACHUSETTS
Providence
ROGER WILLIAMS N. MEM.
OLD SLATER MILL
BROWN UNIVERSITY
JOHN BROWN HOUSE
OLD STATE HOUSE
ROGER WILLIAMS PARK
NATHANIEL GREENE HOMESTEAD
SMITH'S CASTLE
GILBERT STUART BIRTHPLACE
TOURO SYNAGOGUE N.H.S.
Newport
Narragansett
SCARBOROUGH
POINT JUDITH
GAY HEAD CLIFFS
CLIFF WALK
MARBLE HOUSE
NAVAL BASE
OLD STONE MILL
THE BREAKERS
Block Island
Block Island (R.I.)
Woonsocket
SCHAEFER STADIUM
WEBSTER LAKE
OLD STURBRIDGE VILLAGE
GODDARD ROCKET SITE
Worcester
CLARK UNIVERSITY
ART MUSEUM
HIGGINS ARMORY
Auburn
MASSACHUSETTS TURNPIKE
Springfield
BASKETBALL HALL OF FAME
SPRINGFIELD ARMORY
Holyoke
MT. HOLYOKE COLLEGE
DINOSAUR LAND
WINDSOR DAM
Northampton
SMITH COLLEGE
AMHERST COLLEGE
UNIVERSITY OF MASSACHUSETTS
Quabbin Res.
WACHUSETT MTN.
Fitchburg
ART MUSEUM
OTTER RIVER
FRENCH KING BRIDGE
OLD DEERFIELD
THUNDER MTN.
North Adams
HOOSAC TUNNEL
MOHAWK TRAIL
Mt. Greylock 3,491 ft.
Pittsfield
SHAKER VILLAGE
PAPER MUSEUM
BERKSHIRE MUSEUM
HERMAN MELVILLE HOUSE
TANGLEWOOD MUSIC SHED
STOCKBRIDGE
BEARTOWN
Great Barrington
Berkshire Hills
WILLIAMS COLLEGE
Lowell
ANDOVER ACADEMY
HOUSE OF SEVEN GABLES
WITCH HOUSE
Nashua
Manchester
CURRIER ART GALLERY
HISTORIC MUSEUM
EVERETT TURNPIKE
CATHEDRAL OF THE PINES
RHODODENDRON
Keene
CROTCHED MTN.
MACDOWELL COLONY
DOLL MUSEUM
Brattleboro
Concord
MARY BAKER EDDY BIRTHPLACE
BEAR BROOK
PAWTUCKAWAY
EXETER ACADEMY
Rochester
WOODMAN INSTITUTE
NEW HAMPSHIRE HISTORICAL SOCIETY
FRANKLIN PIERCE HOMESTEAD
WASHINGTON MUSEUM
PILLSBURY
OLD FORT NO. 4
SUNAPEE
MT. SUNAPEE
CLOCK MUSEUM
DANIEL WEBSTER'S BIRTHPLACE
WINSLOW
SHAKER VILLAGE
SCHULLER MUSEUM
ST.-GAUDENS N.H.S.
Laconia
GUNSTOCK
BELKNAP
MEREDITH AUTO MUSEUM
Wolfeboro
LIBBY MUSEUM
POKE ABOUT MILL
CARDIGAN
Hanover
DARTMOUTH COLLEGE
POLAR CAVES
WHITE LAKE
MT. WHITTIER
KANCAMAGUS HIGHWAY
LOON MOUNTAIN
WATERVILLE VALLEY
MORSE MUSEUM
LOST RIVER RESERVATION
BEMIS MUSEUM
FLUME
FRANCONIA NOTCH
OLD MAN OF THE MOUNTAIN
CANNON MTN.
Littleton
Bretton Woods
COG RAILWAY
White Mountains
Mt. Washington 6,288 ft.
WILDCAT MTN.
CRAWFORD NOTCH
STORY LAND
SIX GUN CITY
WEEKS
Lancaster
OLD MEETING HOUSE
Berlin
NANSEN SKI JUMP
Errol
Colebrook
COLEMAN
THE UPPER NEW ENGLAND CIRCLE ROUTE
FAIRBANKS MUSEUM
MAPLE MUSEUM
St. Johnsbury
GROTON STATE FOREST
Montpelier
Barre
GRANITE QUARRIES
Bradford
WALKER MUSEUM
Chelsea
CRYSTAL LAKE
Orleans
Newport
JAY PEAK
Enosburg Falls
CHESTER ARTHUR BIRTHPLACE
LAKE CARMI
ST. ALBANS
ST. ANNE SHRINE
HYDE LOG CABIN
South Hero
SAND BAR
Burlington
MADONNA MTN.
Mt. Mansfield 4,393 ft.
MOUNT MANSFIELD
SMUGGLER'S NOTCH
ELMORE
SPRUCE PEAK
Stowe
Waterbury
S.S. TICONDEROGA
SHELBURNE MUSEUM
APPALACHIAN GAP
Vergennes
SUGARBUSH
LINCOLN PEAK
GONDOLA
Green Mountains
SHELDON MUSEUM
BRANBURY
FT. TICONDEROGA
MOUNT DEFIANCE
HUBBARDTON BATTLEFIELD
BOMOSEEN
Proctor
Rutland
MARBLE QUARRIES
KILLINGTON
KILLINGTON PEAK
COOLIDGE BIRTHPLACE
QUECHEE GORGE
SILVER LAKE
OLD CONSTITUTION HOUSE
ST. CATHERINE
ART CENTER
EUREKA SCHOOLHOUSE
Springfield
EMERALD LAKE
SOUTHERN VERMONT ART CENTER
Manchester
STEAMTOWN, U.S.A.
STRATTON
SCOTT COVERED BRIDGE
MOUNT SNOW
Bennington
BENNINGTON COLLEGE
BENNINGTON MUSEUM
BRIGHAM YOUNG BIRTHPLACE
BENNINGTON BATTLEFIELD
BENNINGTON BATTLE MONUMENT
Lake Champlain
Plattsburgh
KENT-DELORD HOUSE
AUSABLE CHASM
WHITEFACE
PALEFACE
LAND OF MAKE BELIEVE
Lake Placid
SARANAC LAKE
R.L. STEVENSON COTTAGE
GAME FARM
JOHN BROWN'S FARM
MT. VAN HOEVENBERG BOBSLED RUN
ADIRONDACK CENTER
BIG TUPPER
Mount Marcy 5,344 ft.
ADIRONDACK STATE FOREST PRESERVE
CROWN POINT
FRONTIER TOWN
Long Lake
THE ADIRONDACK ROUTE
ADIRONDACK MUSEUM
Raquette Lake
Indian Lake
NATURAL STONE BRIDGE
Ticonderoga
Schroon Lake
CAMP READ
GORE MOUNTAIN
ENCHANTED FOREST
OLD FORGE
SNOW RIDGE
Lyons Falls
CONSTABLE HALL
Boonville
Speculator
OAK MOUNTAIN
Whitehall
Lake George
FT. WILLIAM HENRY
GASLIGHT VILLAGE
STORYTOWN
Glens Falls
GENERAL VON STEUBEN MEMORIAL
NATL. MUSEUM OF RACING
PERFORMING ARTS CENTER
PETRIFIED GARDENS
SKIDMORE COLLEGE
SPA STATE PARK
Northville
GRANT'S COTTAGE
FAIRYLAND VILLAGE
Saratoga Springs
SARATOGA BATTLE MONUMENT
SCHUYLER HOUSE
SARATOGA N.H.P.
BENNINGTON BATTLEFIELD
FT. STANWIX N.M.
Rome
Poland
ORISKANY BATTLEFIELD
Utica
MUSEUM OF ART
MUSICAL MUSEUM
Ilion
BEAVERSPRITE SANCTUARY
FT. HERKIMER CHURCH
Gloversville
GEN. HERKIMER HOME
NEW YORK STATE THRUWAY
JOHNSON HALL
GUY PARK HOUSE
BALLSTON SPA
Amsterdam
UPSTATE AUTO MUSEUM
PETRIFIED CREATURES
AURIESVILLE SHRINE
COLGATE UNIVERSITY
Hamilton
Cherry Valley
Schenectady
Cooperstown
BASEBALL HALL OF FAME
FARMERS' MUSEUM
FENIMORE HOUSE
VILLAGE CROSSROADS
HOWE CAVERNS
Cobleskill
SECRET CAVERNS
OLD STONE FORT
J.B. THACHER
Albany
FT. CRAILO
SCHUYLER MANSION
TOE PATH MOUNTAIN
Oneonta
SCOTCH VALLEY
Stamford
Delhi
SHAKER MUSEUM
HOUSE OF HISTORY
Kinderhook
VAN BUREN HOME
FIRE FIGHTING MUSEUM
OLANA MANSION
CATAMOUNT
TACONIC
TACONIC STATE PARKWAY
BURROUGHS MEMORIALS
CARSON CITY
CATSKILL GAME FARM
HUNTER MOUNTAIN
RIP VAN WINKLE'S RETREAT
BELLEAYRE MOUNTAIN
CATSKILL STATE FOREST PRESERVE
Woodstock
SENATE HOUSE
Kingston
RHINEBECK AERODROME
MILLS MANSION
VANDERBILT MANSION N.H.S.
F.D. ROOSEVELT N.H.S.
Hyde Park
Poughkeepsie
VASSAR COLLEGE
CLINTON HOUSE
Deposit
Livingston Manor
Liberty
DAVOS
Monticello
PROMPTON
FT. DELAWARE
Wurtsboro
WASHINGTON HEADQUARTERS
NEW WINDSOR CANTONMENT
Newburgh
KNOX HEADQUARTERS
STORM KING MTN.
WEST POINT MILITARY ACADEMY
CLARENCE FAHNESTOCK
APPALACHIAN NATIONAL SCENIC TRAIL
HOUSATONIC MEADOWS
CATHEDRAL PINES
MOHAWK MTN.
LITCHFIELD HISTORIC VILLAGE
CLOCK MUSEUM
Bristol
BLACK ROCK
GLEBE HOUSE
SQUANTZ POND
Danbury
SCOTT-FANTON MUSEUM
MANSFIELD HOUSE
Waterbury
NOOK FARM
Hartford
TROLLEY MUSEUM
NEWGATE PRISON
Windsor Locks
ATHENEUM
CONSTITUTION PLAZA
OLD STATE HOUSE
UNIVERSITY OF CONNECTICUT
DINOSAUR
NATHAN HALE HOMESTEAD
CONNECTICUT TURNPIKE
WESLEYAN UNIVERSITY
POWDER HILL
GOODSPEED OPERA
GILLETTE CASTLE
COAST GUARD ACADEMY
New London
SUBMARINE BASE
MYSTIC SEAPORT
GROTON MONUMENT
OLD TOWN MILL
HARKNESS MEMORIAL
ROCKY NECK
HAMMONASSET BEACH
WHITFIELD HOUSE
GUN MUSEUM
PEABODY MUSEUM
YALE UNIVERSITY
New Haven
TROLLEY MUSEUM
Stratford
SHAKESPEARE THEATER
Bridgeport
SHERWOOD ISLAND
Putnam
MUSEUM VILLAGE
BEAR MTN.
STERLING FOREST GARDENS
STONY PT. RESERVE
INDIAN POINT NUCLEAR POWER PLANT
HARRIMAN
VAN CORTLANDT MANOR
PHILIPSBURG MANOR
White Plains
Stamford
SUNNYSIDE
Yonkers
ST. PAUL'S CHURCH N.H.S.
SAGAMORE HILL N.H.S.
WALT WHITMAN BIRTHPLACE
OLD BETHPAGE VILLAGE
Mineola
Hempstead
HECKSCHER
FIRE ISLAND NATIONAL SEASHORE
JONES BEACH
Long Island Sound
Long Island
SUNKEN MEADOW
WILDWOOD
AUTO MUSEUM
East Hampton
J.H. PAYNE HOME (HOME, SWEET HOME)
MONTAUK POINT
BROOKHAVEN NATIONAL LABORATORY
Southampton
THE LONG ISLAND ROUTE
New York City
BRONX ZOO
CARNEGIE HALL
CASTLE CLINTON N.M.
CENTRAL PARK
COLISEUM
COLUMBIA UNIVERSITY
EMPIRE STATE BUILDING
FEDERAL HALL N.MEM.
GRANT N. MEM.
GREENWICH VILLAGE
GUGGENHEIM MUSEUM
HAMILTON GRANGE N. MEM.
LINCOLN CENTER
MADISON SQUARE GARDEN
METROPOLITAN MUSEUM OF ART
MUSEUM OF MODERN ART
MUSEUM OF NATURAL HISTORY
ROCKEFELLER CENTER
SHEA STADIUM
THEODORE ROOSEVELT N.H.S.
TIMES SQUARE
UNITED NATIONS HEADQUARTERS
WALL STREET
WORLD TRADE CENTER
YANKEE STADIUM
STATUE OF LIBERTY N.M.
Staten Island
VERRAZANO-NARROWS BRIDGE
Newark
Jersey City
ELIZABETH COLONIAL AREA
EDISON N.H.S.
Morristown
MORRISTOWN N.H.P.
GREAT SWAMP NATURE RESERVE
Hackettstown
Paterson
CLEVELAND BIRTHPLACE
PALISADES INTERSTATE PARK
HOPATCONG
POCONO ANIMAL FARM
DELAWARE WATER GAP
DELAWARE WATER GAP N.R.A.
CAMELBACK
BIG POCONO
BUSHKILL FALLS
Pocono Mountains
GEORGE W. CHILDS
TOBYHANNA
PROMISED LAND
HIGH POINT
GREAT GORGE
Lake Wallenpaupack
Easton
Bethlehem
New Brunswick
RUTGERS UNIVERSITY
RALPH STOVER
Princeton
PRINCETON UNIVERSITY
PRINCETON BATTLEFIELD
WASHINGTON CROSSING
SANDY HOOK
GARDEN STATE ARTS CENTER
Natural Bridge
Carthage
Gouverneur
Cranberry Lake
Lake St. Francis
Lake Memphremagog
Lake Massawippi
Lac Mégantic
Flagstaff Lake
Mooselookmeguntic Lake
Umbagog Lake
First Connecticut Lake
Moore Reservoir
Lake Winnipesaukee
Squam Lake
Sebago Lake
Casco Bay
Massachusetts Bay
Buzzards Bay
Ashokan Res.
Pepacton Res.
Cannonsville Res.
Sacandaga Reservoir
Saratoga Lake
Hudson River
Connecticut River
Delaware River
Susquehanna River
St. Lawrence River
Rivière Richelieu

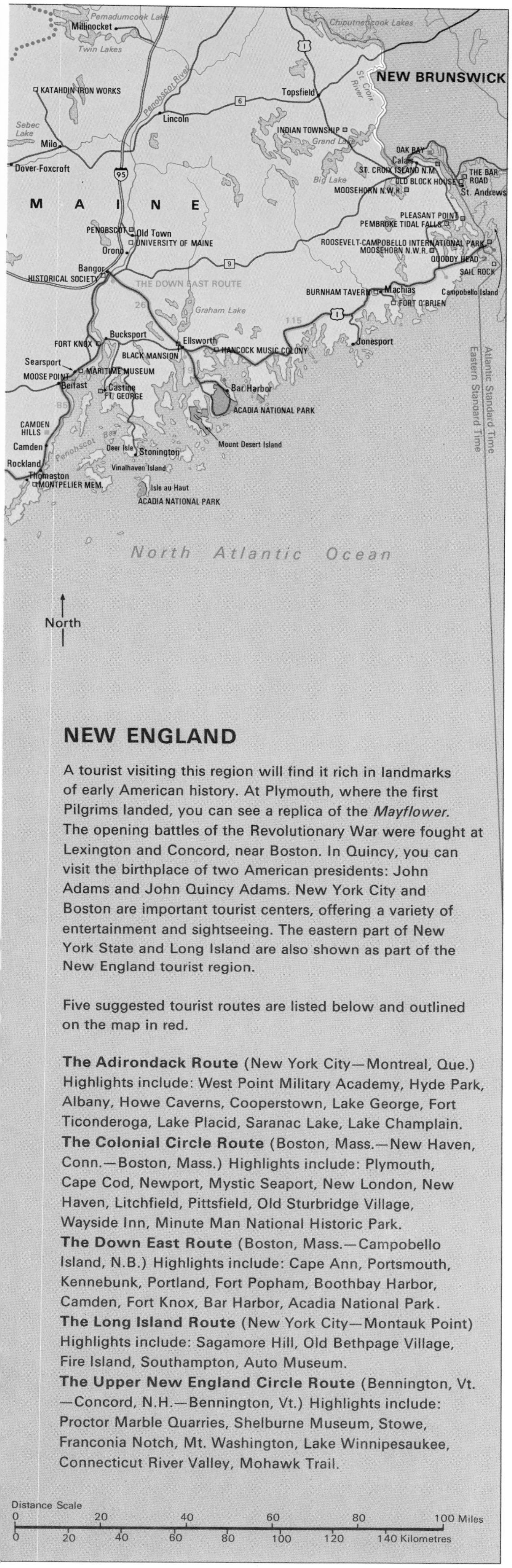

NEW ENGLAND

A tourist visiting this region will find it rich in landmarks of early American history. At Plymouth, where the first Pilgrims landed, you can see a replica of the *Mayflower*. The opening battles of the Revolutionary War were fought at Lexington and Concord, near Boston. In Quincy, you can visit the birthplace of two American presidents: John Adams and John Quincy Adams. New York City and Boston are important tourist centers, offering a variety of entertainment and sightseeing. The eastern part of New York State and Long Island are also shown as part of the New England tourist region.

Five suggested tourist routes are listed below and outlined on the map in red.

The Adirondack Route (New York City—Montreal, Que.) Highlights include: West Point Military Academy, Hyde Park, Albany, Howe Caverns, Cooperstown, Lake George, Fort Ticonderoga, Lake Placid, Saranac Lake, Lake Champlain.
The Colonial Circle Route (Boston, Mass.—New Haven, Conn.—Boston, Mass.) Highlights include: Plymouth, Cape Cod, Newport, Mystic Seaport, New London, New Haven, Litchfield, Pittsfield, Old Sturbridge Village, Wayside Inn, Minute Man National Historic Park.
The Down East Route (Boston, Mass.—Campobello Island, N.B.) Highlights include: Cape Ann, Portsmouth, Kennebunk, Portland, Fort Popham, Boothbay Harbor, Camden, Fort Knox, Bar Harbor, Acadia National Park.
The Long Island Route (New York City—Montauk Point) Highlights include: Sagamore Hill, Old Bethpage Village, Fire Island, Southampton, Auto Museum.
The Upper New England Circle Route (Bennington, Vt.—Concord, N.H.—Bennington, Vt.) Highlights include: Proctor Marble Quarries, Shelburne Museum, Stowe, Franconia Notch, Mt. Washington, Lake Winnipesaukee, Connecticut River Valley, Mohawk Trail.

Distance Scale
0 20 40 60 80 100 Miles
0 20 40 60 80 100 120 140 Kilometres

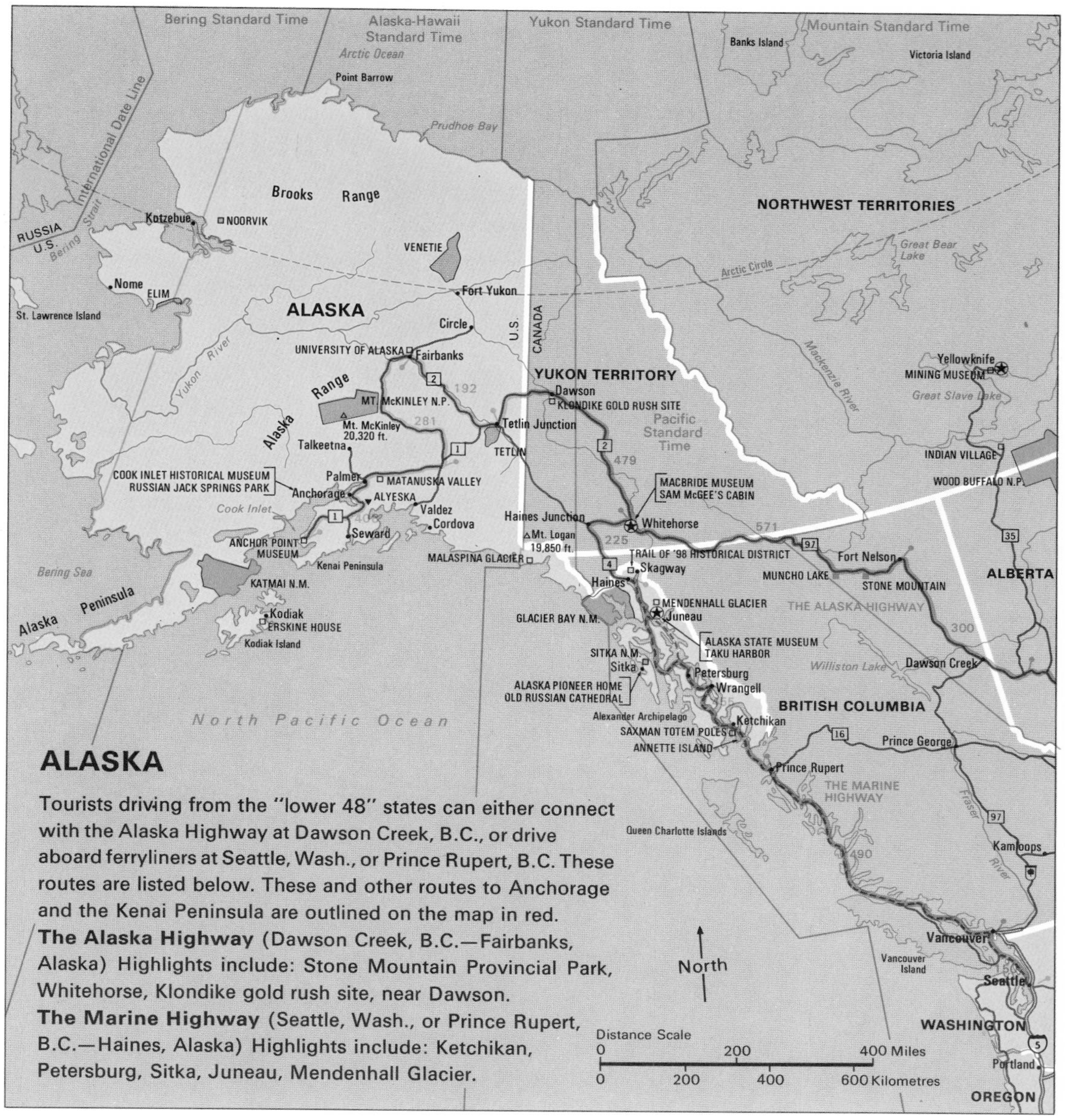

ALASKA

Tourists driving from the "lower 48" states can either connect with the Alaska Highway at Dawson Creek, B.C., or drive aboard ferryliners at Seattle, Wash., or Prince Rupert, B.C. These routes are listed below. These and other routes to Anchorage and the Kenai Peninsula are outlined on the map in red.
The Alaska Highway (Dawson Creek, B.C.—Fairbanks, Alaska) Highlights include: Stone Mountain Provincial Park, Whitehorse, Klondike gold rush site, near Dawson.
The Marine Highway (Seattle, Wash., or Prince Rupert, B.C.—Haines, Alaska) Highlights include: Ketchikan, Petersburg, Sitka, Juneau, Mendenhall Glacier.

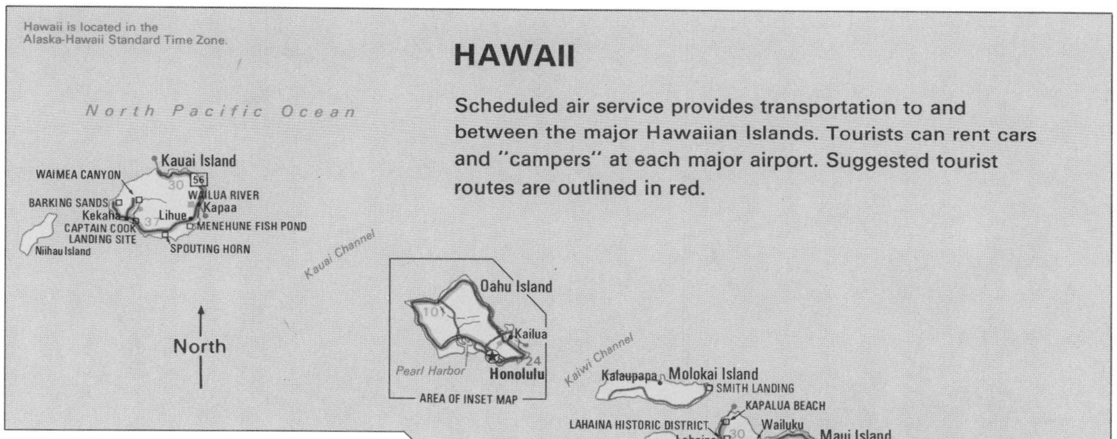

HAWAII

Scheduled air service provides transportation to and between the major Hawaiian Islands. Tourists can rent cars and "campers" at each major airport. Suggested tourist routes are outlined in red.

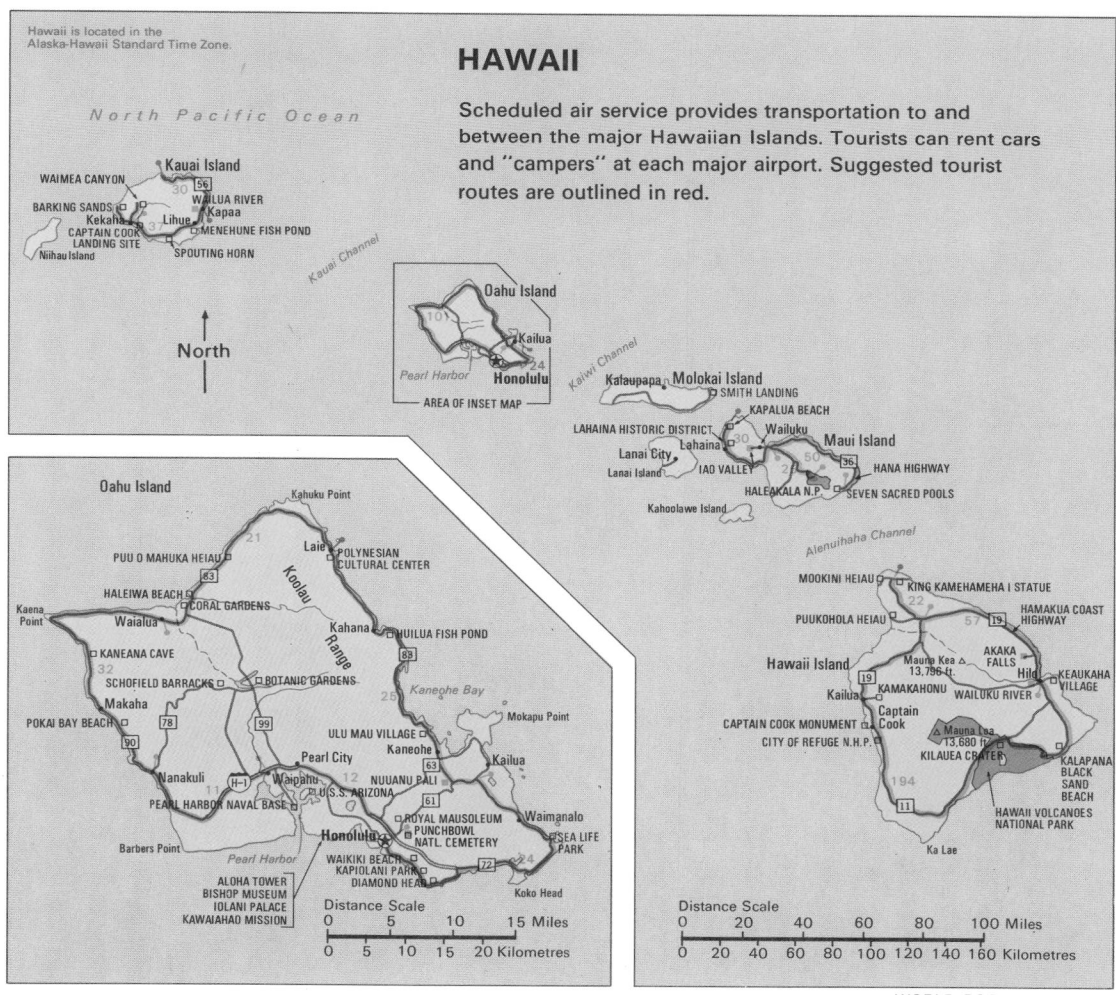

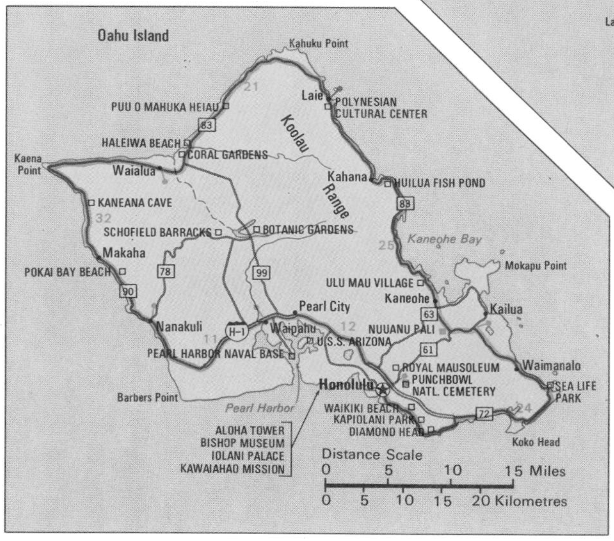

WORLD BOOK ATLAS maps

POPULATION
WITH PRONOUNCING GAZETTEER

In this section of THE WORLD BOOK ATLAS, you can look up the populations of thousands of places in the United States, Canada, and other countries. The populations are grouped into three up-to-date tables. The section on Major World Cities lists important cities outside the United States and Canada and gives the pronunciation of each. The table on Canada lists the populations for cities and towns reported in the census of Canada, province-by-province. The United States section lists populations, state-by-state, for places reported in the census of the United States. In the Canada and U.S. tables, you will also find state, province, and county populations. All three tables also list the major metropolitan area populations. You can find the populations of countries and other political divisions in the Political Facts and Figures table in the World section of the ATLAS.

LEARNING ABOUT POPULATION

These questions are designed to introduce you to the Population section. All of the questions can be answered by using the Major World Cities table in this section. Check your answers by turning to the last page of the ATLAS.

1. How would you rank these cities in order of population from largest to smallest—Madrid, Moscow, and Rome?
2. Tokyo proper has the largest population of any city in the world. About how many million persons live within the city limits of Tokyo—9 million, 10 million, or 14 million?
3. Buenos Aires has the largest metropolitan area population in Latin America. Is its population closer to 1 million, 3 million, or 7 million?
4. Calcutta and Osaka have about the same number of persons within their city limits. Is their population closer to 3 million, 5 million, or 7 million?
5. Moscow has the largest population of any Russian city. What is the second largest Russian city—Leningrad, Volgograd, or Odessa?
6. East Berlin and West Berlin cover almost the same area in square miles. Which city has the larger population?
7. Which African city has the most inhabitants—Casablanca, Johannesburg, or Cairo?
8. Melbourne and Sydney, the two largest cities in Australia, have more than 2 million persons each. What is the population of Canberra, the capital of Australia?
9. About the same number of persons live within the city limits of Paris and Delhi. Which city has the largest metropolitan area population?
10. Which Scandinavian capital has the largest population—Copenhagen, Oslo, or Stockholm?

Opposite page: Aerial photograph of Minneapolis-St. Paul, Minn.—Mark Hurd Aerial Surveys, Inc.

POPULATION TABLES

230-241 POPULATIONS AND PRONUNCIATIONS OF MAJOR WORLD CITIES

242-245 THE CENSUS OF CANADA

246-280 THE CENSUS OF THE UNITED STATES

MAJOR WORLD CITIES

This table includes more than 3,000 cities with populations over 40,000 plus the capital city of each independent country. United States and Canadian cities are listed in special census sections following this list of major world cities. For each of the cities with the largest metropolitan areas in the world, this table includes the population figure for the metropolitan area. This figure is identified by a star (★). In addition to listing the population figure for each city, the pronunciation is given by respelling each city name. For information on how to use this respelling system, turn to the *How to Get the Most Out of the World Book Atlas* section of the ATLAS. The respelling for each name was prepared for THE WORLD BOOK ATLAS by Clarence L. Barnhart, Editor in Chief of THE WORLD BOOK DICTIONARY and the THORNDIKE-BARNHART DICTIONARIES.

A

Aachen *(AH kun),* Germany, West...177,600

Aalst *(AHLST),* Belgium...45,760

Aba *(AH bah),* Nigeria...151,923

Abadan *(AH bah DAHN),* Iran...272,962

Abakan *(AH buh KAHN),* Soviet Union...90,000

Abeokuta *(AH bay OH koo tah),* Nigeria...217,201

Aberdeen *(AB ur DEEN),* Scotland...181,386

Abidjan *(AB ih JAHN),* Ivory Coast...500,000

Abū Zaby *(A boo ZAH bee)* United Arab Emirates...46,000

Acapulco *(AH kah POOL koh),* Mexico...174,378

Accra *(uh KRAH* or *ACK ruh),* Ghana...521,900

Achinsk *(AH chinsk),* Soviet Union...97,000

Acireale *(AH chee ray AH lay),* Italy...43,752

Adana *(AH dah nah),* Turkey...290,515

Adapazari *(AH dah PAH zah REE),* Turkey...85,579

Addis Ababa *(AD is AB uh buh),* Ethiopia...504,900

Ad Dīwānīyah *(ad DEE wah NEE yuh),* Iraq...60,486

Adelaide *(AD ul ayd),* Australia...809,466

Aden *(AH dun* or *AY dun),* Yemen (Aden)...150,000

Ado *(AH doh),* Nigeria...157,519

Ado-Ekiti *(AH doh AY kee tee),* Nigeria...182,673

Adoni *(uh DOH nee),* India...69,951

Adrianople *(AY dree uh NOH pul),* Turkey...46,264

Afragola *(AH frah GAW lah),* Italy...45,881

Agartala *(UG ur tuh LAH),* India...54,878

Agra *(AH gruh),* India...543,397

Agrigento *(AH gree JEN toh),* Italy...47,919

Aguascalientes *(AH gwahs kah LYEN-tays),* Mexico...181,277

Ahlen *(AH lun),* Germany, West...50,400

Ahmadabad *(AH mud ah BAHD),* India...1,347,999

Ahmadnagar (Ahmednagar) *(AH mud NUG ur),* India...127,728

Ahvāz *(ah WAHZ),* Iran...206,375

Aigáleos *(eh GAH lay os),* Greece...57,840

Aix-en-Provence *(AYKS* or *eks ahn praw VAHNS),* France...89,566

Aizuwakamatsu *(EYE zoo wah KAH mah tsoo),* Japan...104,065

Ajmer *(aj MEER),* India...253,160

Akashi *(ah KAH shee),* Japan...206,525

Akita *(ah KEE tah),* Japan...235,873

Akola *(uh KOH luh),* India...132,322

Aktyubinsk *(ahk TYOO binsk),* Soviet Union...150,000

Al 'Amārah *(al ah MAH ruh),* Iraq...64,674

Alapayevsk *(AH luh PAH yefsk),* Soviet Union...52,000

Albacete *(AHL bah THAY tay* or *AHL bah SAY tay),* Spain...84,074

Ålborg *(AWL bawrg),* Denmark...153,978

Alcamo *(AHL kah moh),* Italy...43,097

Alcoy *(ahl KOY),* Spain...60,889

Aldridge-Brownhills *(AWL drij BROWN hilz),* England...86,780

Aleksin *(ah LEK sin),* Soviet Union...61,000

Aleppo (Ḥalab) *(uh LEP oh) (huh LEB),* Syria...578,861

Alès *(ah LESS),* France...42,818

Alessandria *(AH les SAHN dree ah),* Italy...92,760

Alexandria (Al Iskandarīyah) *(AL ig ZAN dree uh) (al is KAHN-duh REE yuh),* Egypt...1,801,056

Al Fayyūm *(el fye YOOM),* Egypt...133,616

Algeciras *(AL juh SEER us),* Spain...76,746

Algiers (Alger) *(al JEERZ) (al ZHAY),* Algeria...903,530

Al Ḥillah *(al HIL uh),* Iraq...84,104

Al Ḥudaydah *(al hoh DAY duh),* Yemen (San 'ā')...75,000

Alicante *(AH lee KAHN tay),* Spain...162,944

Aligarh *(AL ih GAHR),* India...212,507

Alkmaar *(AHLK mahr),* Netherlands...51,542

Al Kūt *(al KOOT),* Iraq...41,822

Allahabad *(AL uh huh BAD),* India...475,098

Alleppey *(uh LEP ee),* India...153,122

Alma-Ata *(ahl MAH ah TAH),* Soviet Union...730,000

Al Maḥallah al Kubrá *(al muh HAL-uh al KOO bruh)* Egypt...225,232

Almalyk *(AHL muh LIK),* Soviet Union...81,000

Al Manṣūrah *(el man SOO ruh),* Egypt...191,459

Almelo *(AHL muh loh),* Netherlands...58,155

Almería *(AHL may REE uh),* Spain...105,413

Al'met'yevsk *(ahl MAY tyefsk),* Soviet Union...87,000

Al Minyā *(el MIN yuh),* Egypt...112,580

Almirante Brown *(AHL mee RAHN tay BROWN),* Argentina...136,924

Alor Setar *(AH lawr STAHR),* Malaysia...52,915

Altamura *(AHL tah MOO rah),* Italy...43,735

Altenburg *(AHL tun boork),* Germany, East...46,737

Altrincham *(AWL tring um),* England...41,030

Al Ubayyiḍ *(el oh BAYD),* Sudan...59,000

Alwar *(UL wur),* India...72,707

Amagasaki *(AH mah gah SAH kee),* Japan...553,696

Ambala *(um BAH luh),* India...76,204

Ambato *(ahm BAH toh),* Ecuador...57,864

Ambon (Amboina) *(am BOY nuh),* Indonesia...56,037

Amersfoort *(AH murs fohrt),* Netherlands...76,285

Amiens *(AH MYAN),* France...117,888

Amman *(AHM mahn),* Jordan...330,000

Amoy (Hsiamen) *(uh MOY) (SHYAH-MUN),* China...224,300

Amraoti (Amravati) *(um ROW tee),* India...160,086

Amritsar *(um RIT sur),* India...408,310

Amroha *(um ROH huh),* India...68,965

Amstelveen *(AHM stuhl vayn),* Netherlands...64,001

Amsterdam *(AM stur dam),* Netherlands...857,635

Anantapur *(uh NUN tuh poor),* India...52,280

Anápolis *(uh NAH poo lis),* Brazil...48,847

Anching *(AHN CHING),* China...105,300

Ancona *(ahng KOH nuh),* Italy...104,967

Anderlecht *(AHN dur lekt),* Belgium...100,738

Andizhan *(AHN dee ZHAHN),* Soviet Union...188,000

Andong *(AHN DAWNG),* Korea, South...76,434

Andorra *(an DAWR uh),* Andorra...5,465

Andria *(AHN dree uh),* Italy...70,831

Angarsk *(ahn GAHRSK),* Soviet Union...204,000

Angeles *(AN juh lus* or *AHN huh lays),* Philippines...75,900

Angers *(ahn ZHAY),* France...128,533

Angoulême *(AHN goo LEM),* France...47,822

Angren *(ahn GREN),* Soviet Union...76,000

Anjō *(ahn JO),* Japan...94,307

Ankara *(ANG kuh ruh),* Turkey...902,218

Annaba (Bône) *(AH nuh buh),* Algeria...152,006

An Najaf *(ahn NAH jahf),* Iraq...134,027

An Nāṣirīyah *(an NAH sih REE yuh),* Iraq...59,330

Annecy *(AHN SEE),* France...54,484

Anshan *(AHN SHAHN),* China...805,000

Antakya (Antioch) *(ahn TAHK yah) (AN tee ahk),* Turkey...57,584

Antalya *(ahn TAHL yah),* Turkey...71,632

Antequera *(AHN tay KAY rah),* Spain...42,327

Antofagasta *(AHN toh fah GAHS tah),* Chile...127,234

Antony *(AHN taw NEE),* France...56,638

Antratsit *(AHN trah TSEET),* Soviet Union...55,000

Antung, see Tantung

Antwerp (Antwerpen) *(ANT wurp), (AHNT VAIR pun),* Belgium...243,426

Anyang *(AHN YAHNG),* China...124,900

Anyang *(AHN YAHNG),* Korea, South...91,876

Anzhero-Sudzhensk *(ahn ZHAIR uh soo JENSK),* Soviet Union...106,000

Aomori *(ah OH moh ree),* Japan...240,063

Apeldoorn *(AH pul dohrn),* Netherlands...118,694

Apia *(AH pee uh),* Western Samoa...21,699

Aracaju *(AH ruh kuh ZHOO),* Brazil...150,000

Araçatuba *(AH ruh suh TOO buh),* Brazil...53,563

Arad *(ah RAHD),* Romania...139,072

Arāk *(ah RAHK),* Iran...71,925

Arao *(ah RAH oh),* Japan...55,452

Araraquara *(uh RAH ruh KWAH ruh),* Brazil...58,076

Archangel *(AHRK AYN jul),* Soviet Union...343,000

Ardabīl *(AHR duh BEEL),* Iran...83,596

Arequipa *(AH ray KEE pah),* Peru...87,400

Arezzo *(ah RET soh),* Italy...74,992

Argenteuil *(AHR zhahn TUH yuh),* France...90,480

Århus *(AWR HOOS),* Denmark...236,129

Arica *(ah REE kah),* Chile...63,967

Arles *(AHRL* or *AHRLZ),* France...45,774

Armavir *(AHR muh VEER),* Soviet Union...146,000

Armenia *(ahr MAY nyah),* Colombia...187,941

Arnhem *(AHRN hem),* Netherlands...135,090

Arrah *(AHR ruh),* India...76,766

Arras *(AR us* or *ah RAHS),* France...49,144

Artëm *(ahr TYAWM),* Soviet Union...61,000

Artëmovsk *(ahr TYAW mufsk),* Soviet Union...82,000

Aruppukkottai *(ah ROOP poo KOHT-tye),* India...50,200

Arzamas *(AHR zuh MAHS),* Soviet Union...67,000

Asahigawa *(ah sah HEE GAH wah),* Japan...288,492

Asansol *(AH sun SOHL),* India...120,587

Asbest *(ahz BEST),* Soviet Union...76,000

Aschaffenburg *(ah SHAHF un boork),* Germany, West...56,200

Ascoli Piceno *(AHS koh lee pee CHAY noh),* Italy...50,114

Ashibetsu *(ah shih BAY tsoo),* Japan...42,730

Ashikaga *(ah shee KAH gah),* Japan...156,004

Ashiya *(ah SHEE yah),* Japan...70,938

Ashkhabad *(AHSH kah BAHT),* Soviet Union...253,000

Ashton-under-Lyne *(ASH tun un-dur LINE),* England...48,280

Asmara *(az MAHR uh),* Ethiopia...131,800

Asnières *(ah NYAIR),* France...80,113

As Sulaymānīyah *(as SOO lie mah-NEE yuh),* Iraq...83,642

Asti *(AHS tee),* Italy...61,044

Astrakhan' *(AS truh KAN),* Soviet Union...411,000

Asunción *(AH soon SYAWN),* Paraguay...305,160

Aswan *(ahs WAHN),* Egypt...127,594

Asyut *(as YOOT),* Egypt...153,956

Atami *(ah TAH mee),* Japan...51,281

Athens (Athínai) *(ATH unz) (ah THEE neh),* Greece...627,564

Atsugi *(ah TSOO gee),* Japan...82,888

Aṭ Tā'if *(at TAH if),* Saudi Arabia...54,000

Atzcapotzalco *(AHTS kah poh-TSAHL koh),* Mexico...63,857

Aubervilliers *(OH bair vee LYAY),* France...73,695

Auckland *(AWK lund),* New Zealand...698,400

Augsburg *(OWKS boork* or *AWGZ burg),* Germany, West...214,400

Aulnay *(oh NAY),* France...61,521

Aurangabad *(ow RUNG guh BAHD),* India...87,579

Avellaneda *(AH vay yah NAY thah),* Argentina...329,626

Avellino *(AH vel LEE noh),* Italy...41,825

Avignon *(AH vee NYAWN),* France...86,096

Avilés *(AH vee LAYS),* Spain...76,318

Áyios Yeóryios, see Keratsinion

Ayr *(AIR),* Scotland...47,145

Azov *(uh ZAWF* or *AY zahf),* Soviet Union...59,000

Az Zaqāzīq *(ahz ZAH kah ZEEK),* Egypt...151,186

Az Zarqā' *(az ZAHR kah),* Jordan...96,080

B

Bacabal *(buh kuh BAHL),* Brazil...142,000

Bacău *(bah KUH oo),* Romania...95,576

Bacolod *(bah KOH lawd),* Philippines...142,000

Badajoz *(BAH thah HOHTH),* Spain...103,557

Badalona *(BAH thah LOH nah),* Spain...150,143

Bagé *(buh ZHEH),* Brazil...47,930

Baghdad *(BAG dad),* Iraq...1,657,424

Bāghlān *(BAHG lahn),* Afghanistan...92,432

Bago *(BAH goh),* Philippines...58,834

Baguio *(BAH gyoh),* Philippines...50,436

Bahāwalpur *(buh HAH wul POOR),* Pakistan...84,377

Bahía Blanca *(bah EE ah BLAHNG-kah),* Argentina...150,354

Bahraich *(bah RIKE),* India...56,033

Baia Mare *(BAH yah MAH ray),* Romania...79,542

Baku *(bah KOO),* Soviet Union ★1,261,000...847,000

Balakovo *(BAH luh KAW vuh),* Soviet Union...103,000

Balashikha *(BAH luh SHEE kuh),* Soviet Union...92,000

Balashov *(BAH luh SHAWF)*, Soviet Union . . . 83,000
Balikesir *(BAH lee keh SEER)*, Turkey . . . 69,256
Balikpapan *(BAH lik PAH pahn)*, Indonesia . . . 91,706
Balintawak (Escalante) *(bah lin TAH wahk) (ays kah LAHN tay)*, Philippines . . . 59,768
Balkhash *(bahl KAHSH)*, Soviet Union . . . 76,000
Ballarat *(BAL uh RAT)*, Australia . . . 58,434
Bally *(BAH lee)*, India . . . 125,238
Bamako *(BAH MAH KOH)*, Mali . . . 130,000
Bamberg *(BAM burg)*, Germany, West . . . 68,700
Bāmiān *(BAH mee AHN)*, Afghanistan . . . 43,949
Banaras (Varanasi) *(buh NAH rus)*, India . . . 553,173
Bandjarmasin *(BAHN jur MAH sin)*, Indonesia . . . 214,096
Bandung *(BAHN doong)*, Indonesia . . . 972,566
Bangalore *(BANG guh LOHR)*, India . . . 985,035
Bangkok (Krung Thep) *(BANG kahk) (KROONG TAYP)*, Thailand . . . 1,608,305
Bangui *(BAHNG gee)*, Central African Republic . . . 150,000
Banhā *(BEN hah)*, Egypt . . . 63,849
Banī Suwayf *(BEH nee soo WAYF)*, Egypt . . . 90,425
Banja Luka *(BAH nyah LOO kah)*, Yugoslavia . . . 58,000
Bankstown, Australia . . . 162,310
Bankura *(BAHNG koo ruh)*, India . . . 62,833
Ban Me Thuot *(BAHN meh TOO uht)*, Vietnam, South . . . 64,877
Bansalan *(BAHN sah LAHN)*, Philippines . . . 45,360
Banstead *(BAN sted)*, England . . . 42,100
Baraki Barak *(BUR uh kee BUR uk)*, Afghanistan . . . 45,505
Baranagar *(BUR uh NUG ur)*, India . . . 127,287
Baranovichi *(buh RAH nuh VEE-chee)*, Soviet Union . . . 102,000
Barbacena *(BAHR buh SAY nuh)*, Brazil . . . 41,931
Barcelona *(BAHR suh LOH nuh)*, Spain . . . 1,759,148
Barcelona *(BAHR suh LOH nuh)*, Venezuela . . . 51,902
Bareilly *(buh RAY lee)*, India . . . 294,892
Bari *(BAH ree)*, Italy . . . 329,832
Barisāl *(BUR ih SAHL)*, Bangladesh . . . 69,936
Barking *(BAHR king)*, England . . . 169,520
Barletta *(bahr LET uh)*, Italy . . . 68,035
Barnaul *(BAHR nuh OOL)*, Soviet Union . . . 439,000
Barnet *(BAHR net)*, England . . . 316,240
Barnsley *(BAHRNZ lee)*, England . . . 75,220
Baroda *(buh ROH duh)*, India . . . 348,179
Barquisimeto *(BAHR kee see MAY-toh)*, Venezuela . . . 262,711
Barrackpur (Barrackpore) *(BAR uk pohr)*, India . . . 63,778
Barra Mansa *(BAHR ruh MAHN suh)*, Brazil . . . 47,398
Barrancabermeja *(bahr RAHNG kah-behr MEH hah)*, Colombia . . . 59,625
Barranquilla *(BAHR rahng KEE yah)*, Colombia . . . 648,173
Barrow-in-Furness *(BAR oh in FUR-nes)*, England . . . 63,720
Barry *(BAR ee)*, Wales . . . 42,450
Barsi *(BAHR see)*, India . . . 50,389
Basel *(BAH zel)*, Switzerland . . . 212,100
Basilan *(bah SEE lahn)*, Philippines . . . 187,000
Basildon *(BAZ ul dun)*, England . . . 119,470
Basirhat *(buh SEER haht)*, India . . . 53,943
Basra *(BAS ruh* or *BUS ruh)*, Iraq . . . 310,950
Bassein *(buh SAYN)*, Burma . . . 77,905
Basseterre *(BAHS TAIR)*, St. Kitts-Nevis . . . 15,000
Bastia *(bah STEE ah)*, France . . . 49,375
Batala *(buh TAH luh)*, India . . . 51,300
Batangas *(bah TAHNG gahs)*, Philippines . . . 82,627
Bataysk *(buh TYSKE)*, Soviet Union . . . 85,000
Bath *(BATH)*, England . . . 84,870
Bathurst *(BATH urst)*, Gambia . . . 28,896
Batley *(BAT lee)*, England . . . 41,860
Batna *(BAT nuh)*, Algeria . . . 54,924
Batumi *(bah TOO mee)*, Soviet Union . . . 101,000
Bat Yam *(BAHT YAHM)*, Israel . . . 53,100
Bauru *(bow ROO)*, Brazil . . . 107,000
Bautzen *(BOWT sun)*, Germany, East . . . 43,670
Bayambang *(BAH yahm BAHNG)*, Philippines . . . 47,498
Baybay *(bie BIE)*, Philippines . . . 51,799
Bayreuth *(by ROYT)*, Germany, West . . . 63,400
Beau Bassin-Rose Hill *(BOH bah SAN ROHZ HIL)*, Mauritius . . . 65,920
Beawar *(bay AH wur)*, India . . . 53,931
Bebington *(BEB ing tun)*, England . . . 56,230
Bedford *(BED furd)*, England . . . 68,490
Beersheba *(beer SHEE buh)*, Israel . . . 65,200
Beeston & Stapleford *(BEE stun and STAY pul furd)*, England . . . 62,960
Begovat *(BYEH guh VAHT)*, Soviet Union . . . 58,000
Beirut (Beyrouth) *(bay ROOT)*, Lebanon . . . 700,000
Bejaïa *(beh JY uh)*, Algeria . . . 49,930
Békéscsaba *(BAY kaysh CHAW baw)*, Hungary . . . 55,408
Belaya Tserkov' *(BYEH luh yuh TSAIR kuf)*, Soviet Union . . . 109,000
Belém (Pará) *(buh LEM) (pah RAH)*, Brazil . . . 546,000
Belfast *(BEL fast)*, Northern Ireland . . . 390,700
Belford Roxo *(bel FAWR ROH shoo)*, Brazil . . . 43,621
Belfort *(bel FAWR)*, France . . . 53,214
Belgaum *(bel GOWM)*, India . . . 143,256
Belgorod *(BYEL guh rut)*, Soviet Union . . . 151,000
Belgrade (Beograd) *(BEL grayd) (beh AW grahd)* Yugoslavia . . . 697,000
Belize City *(buh LEEZ SIT ee)*, British Honduras . . . 41,444
Bellary *(beh LAH ree)*, India . . . 85,673
Bello *(BAY yoh)*, Colombia . . . 85,894
Belmopan *(BEL muh PAN)*, British Honduras . . . 2,000
Belo Horizonte *(BEH loh ree ZOHN-tee)*, Brazil . . . 1,092,000
Belogorsk *(BYEH luh GAWRSK)*, Soviet Union . . . 57,000
Beloretsk *(BYEH luh RETSK)*, Soviet Union . . . 67,000
Belovo *(BYEH luh vuh)*, Soviet Union . . . 108,000
Bel'tsy *(BYEL tsee)*, Soviet Union . . . 102,000
Bendery *(ben DEH ree)*, Soviet Union . . . 72,000
Bene Beraq *(buh NAY BRAHG)*, Israel . . . 60,400
Benevento *(BEN uh VEN toh)*, Italy . . . 55,381
Benfleet *(BEN fleet)*, England . . . 45,540
Bengasi (Banghāzī) *(ben GAH zee)*, Libya . . . 136,641
Benin City *(beh NEEN SIT ee)*, Nigeria . . . 100,694
Benoni *(buh NOH nee)*, South Africa . . . 149,563
Beppu *(BEP poo)*, Japan . . . 123,786
Berchem *(BEHR kum)*, Belgium . . . 49,605
Berdichev *(behr DYEE chef)*, Soviet Union . . . 71,000
Berdyansk *(behr DYAHNSK)*, Soviet Union . . . 100,000
Berezniki *(beh REZ nih KEE)*, Soviet Union . . . 145,000
Bergamo *(BAIR gah moh)*, Italy . . . 117,773
Bergen *(BUR gun)*, Norway . . . 115,738
Bergisch Gladbach *(BEHR gish GLAHT bahk)*, Germany, West . . . 50,100
Berhampore *(BUR um pohr)*, India . . . 62,317
Berhampur *(BUR um poor)*, India . . . 76,931
Berlin *(bur LIN)*, **East** Germany, East . . . 1,085,441
Berlin *(bur LIN)*, **West** Germany, West . . . 2,134,300
Bern *(BURN)*, Switzerland . . . 166,800
Bernburg *(BEHRN boork)*, Germany, East . . . 45,322
Besançon *(buh ZAHN SAWN)*, France . . . 113,220
Bexley *(BEKS lee)*, England . . . 215,470
Béziers *(bay ZYAY)*, France . . . 80,492
Bhadravati *(buh DRAH vuh tee)*, India . . . 65,776
Bhagalpur *(BAH gul poor)*, India . . . 162,419
Bhatinda *(buh TIN duh)*, India . . . 52,253
Bhatpara *(baht PAH ruh)*, India . . . 155,680
Bhaunagar (Bhavnagar) *(bow NUG ur)*, India . . . 195,980
Bhiwani *(bih VAH nee)*, India . . . 58,194
Bhopal *(boh PAHL)*, India . . . 237,966
Bhusaval (Bhusawal) *(boo SAH vul)*, India . . . 73,994
Białystok *(byah LIS tawk)*, Poland . . . 158,500
Bibai *(bee BYE)*, Japan . . . 47,369
Biel *(BEEL)*, Switzerland . . . 66,800
Bielefeld *(BEE luh felt)*, Germany, West . . . 169,300
Biella *(BYEL lah)*, Italy . . . 50,209
Bielsko-Biała *(BYEL skaw BYAH-lah)*, Poland . . . 87,100
Bien Hoa *(BYEN HOH ah)*, Vietnam, South . . . 87,135
Bihar *(bee HAHR)*, India . . . 78,581
Bijapur *(bee JAH poor)*, India . . . 78,854
Bikaner *(BIK uh NEER)*, India . . . 171,863
Bilaspur *(bee LAHS poor)*, India . . . 86,706
Bilbao *(bil BAH oh)*, Spain . . . 400,505
Bilbays *(BIL bays)*, Egypt . . . 58,070
Bindjai *(bin JY)*, Indonesia . . . 45,235
Birkenhead *(BUR kun hed)*, England . . . 142,480
Birmingham *(BUR ming um)*, England *2,425,020 . . . 1,074,940
Bisai *(bee SAH ee)*, Japan . . . 51,337
Bisceglie *(bee SHAY lyah)*, Italy . . . 41,451
Biskra *(BIS kruh)*, Algeria . . . 53,177
Bitola *(BEE taw lah)*, Yugoslavia . . . 55,000
Biysk *(BEESK)*, Soviet Union . . . 186,000
Bizerte *(BEE ZAIRT)*, Tunisia . . . 44,721
Blackburn *(BLAK burn)*, England . . . 100,370
Blackpool *(BLAK pool)*, England . . . 147,850
Blacktown *(BLACK town)*, Australia . . . 156,619
Blagoveshchensk *(BLAH guh VESH-chensk)*, Soviet Union . . . 128,000
Blantyre *(blan TIRE)*, Malawi . . . 109,795
Blida *(BLEE dah)*, Algeria . . . 85,683
Blitar *(BLEE tahr)*, Indonesia . . . 62,972
Bloemfontein *(BLOOM fawn TAYN)*, South Africa . . . 148,282
Blumenau *(BLOO muh NOW)*, Brazil . . . 46,591
Bobo Dioulasso *(BOH boh dyoo LAH-soh)*, Upper Volta . . . 45,000
Bobruysk *(bah BROO eesk)*, Soviet Union . . . 138,000
Bocholt *(BAWK awlt)*, Germany, West . . . 48,100
Bochum *(BOH koom)*, Germany, West . . . 346,900
Bōfu, see **Hōfu**
Bogor *(BOH gawr)*, Indonesia . . . 154,092
Bogotá *(BOH goh TAH)*, Colombia . . . 2,515,096
Boksburg *(BAHKS burg)*, South Africa . . . 104,171
Bologna *(boh LOH nyah)*, Italy . . . 482,438
Bolton *(BOHL tun)*, England . . . 153,700
Bolzano *(bohl TSAH noh)*, Italy . . . 88,799
Bombay *(bahm BAY)*, India . . . 4,902,651
Bondy *(bawn DEE)*, France . . . 51,652
Bonn *(BAHN* or *BAWN)*, Germany, West . . . 299,400
Bootle *(BOOT ul)*, England . . . 80,240
Bor *(BAWR)*, Soviet Union . . . 55,000
Borås *(boo ROHS)*, Sweden . . . 68,948
Bordeaux *(BAWR DOH)*, France . . . 266,662
Borgerhout *(BAWR gur howt)*, Belgium . . . 50,204
Borisoglebsk *(bah REE suh-GLEPSK)*, Soviet Union . . . 64,000
Borisov *(bah REE suf)*, Soviet Union . . . 84,000
Borovichi *(BAW ruh vee CHEE)*, Soviet Union . . . 55,000
Borūjerd *(BOH roo JAIRD)*, Iran . . . 71,486
Bottrop *(BAWT rawp)*, Germany, West . . . 108,200
Bouaké *(BWAH kay)*, Ivory Coast . . . 45,000
Boulogne-Billancourt *(boo LOHN bee yahn KOOR)*, France . . . 109,008
Boulogne-sur-Mer *(boo LOHN syoor MAIR)*, France . . . 49,276
Bourges *(BOORZH)*, France . . . 70,814
Bournemouth *(BAWRN muth)*, England . . . 151,460
Box Hill, Australia . . . 54,583
Bradford *(BRAD furd)*, England . . . 294,440
Brāhmanbāria *(BRAH mun BAHR yuh)*, Bangladesh . . . 44,784
Brăila *(bruh EE lah)*, Romania . . . 154,265
Brakpan *(BRAK pan)*, South Africa . . . 113,115
Brandenburg *(BRAN dun burg)*, Germany, East . . . 93,660
Brasília *(bruh ZEEL yuh)*, Brazil . . . 453,000
Brașov *(brah SHAWV)*, Romania . . . 185,259
Bratislava *(BRAH tih SLAH vah)*, Czechoslovakia . . . 283,539
Bratsk *(BRAHTSK)*, Soviet Union . . . 155,000
Braunschweig (Brunswick) *(BROWN-shvyk) (BRUNZ wick)*, Germany, West . . . 225,200
Brazzaville *(BRAZ uh vil* or *brah zah VEEL)*, Congo . . . 136,200
Breda *(bray DAH)*, Netherlands . . . 119,880
Bremen *(BRAY mun)*, Germany, West . . . 607,200
Bremerhaven *(BRAY mur HAH fun)*, Germany, West . . . 148,800
Brent *(BRENT)*, England . . . 284,460
Brentwood *(BRENT wood)*, England . . . 57,650
Brescia *(BRAY shah)*, Italy . . . 182,232
Brest *(BREST)*, France . . . 154,023
Brest *(BREST)*, Soviet Union . . . 122,000
Bridgetown *(BRIJ town)*, Barbados . . . 94,000
Brighton *(BRY tun)*, England . . . 164,680
Brindisi *(BRIN dih zee)*, Italy . . . 70,657
Brisbane *(BRIZ bun* or *BRIZ bayn)*, Australia . . . 816,987
Bristol *(BRIS tul)*, England . . . 427,780
Brive *(BREEV)*, France . . . 46,561
Brno *(BUR noh)*, Czechoslovakia . . . 335,918
Broach *(BROHCH)*, India . . . 73,639
Broadmeadows *(BRAWD MED ohz)*, Australia . . . 100,878
Bromley *(BRAHM lee)*, England . . . 304,230
Bruges (Brugge) *(BROOZH) (BRUG uh)*, Belgium . . . 52,424
Brunswick *(BRUNZ wik)*, Australia . . . 51,424
Brussels (Bruxelles) *(BRUS ulz) (bryoo SELL)*, Belgium . . . 170,086
Bryanka *(bree AHN kuh)*, Soviet Union . . . 71,000
Bryansk *(bree AHNSK)*, Soviet Union . . . 318,000
Bucaramanga *(BOO kah rah MAHNG-gah)*, Colombia . . . 318,267
Bucharest (București) *(BOO kuh-rest) (BOO koo RESHT)*, Romania . . . 1,488,328
Budapest *(BOO duh PEST)*, Hungary . . . 1,940,212
Budaun *(boo DOWN)*, India . . . 58,770
Buenaventura *(BWAY nah vain TOO-rah)*, Colombia . . . 70,079
Buenos Aires *(BWAY nohs I rays)*, Argentina *7,000,000 . . . 2,966,816
Buga *(BOO gah)*, Colombia . . . 65,535
Bugul'ma *(BOO gool MAH)*, Soviet Union . . . 72,000
Buguruslan *(BOO goo roos LAHN)*, Soviet Union . . . 49,000
Bujumbura *(boo jum BUR ruh)*, Burundi . . . 71,000
Bukhara *(boo KAH ruh)*, Soviet Union . . . 112,000
Bukittinggi *(BOO kit TING gee)*, Indonesia . . . 51,456
Bulan *(BOO lahn)*, Philippines . . . 46,520
Bulawayo *(BOO luh WAH yoh)*, Rhodesia . . . 226,000
Buraydah *(boo RYE duh)*, Saudi Arabia . . . 43,607
Burdwan *(bur DWAHN)*, India . . . 129,029
Burgas *(boor GAHS)*, Bulgaria . . . 106,127
Burgos *(BOOR gohs)*, Spain . . . 107,744
Burhanpur *(boor HAHN poor)*, India . . . 82,090
Burnley *(BURN lee)*, England . . . 76,880
Bursa *(boor SAH)*, Turkey . . . 212,518
Burton upon Trent *(BUR tun on TRENT)*, England . . . 50,850
Bury *(BEHR ee)*, England . . . 65,960
Busto Arsizio *(BOOS toh ahr SEE-tsyoh)*, Italy . . . 64,367
Butuan *(boo TOO ahn)*, Philippines . . . 82,485
Buzău *(boo ZUH oo)*, Romania . . . 73,288
Buzuluk *(BOO zoo LOOK)*, Soviet Union . . . 67,000
Bydgoszcz *(BID gawshch)*, Poland . . . 275,200
Bytom (Beuthen) *(BIH tawm) (BOY-ten)*, Poland . . . 186,700

C

Cabanatuan *(KAH bah nah TWAHN)*, Philippines . . . 69,580
Cabimas *(kah BEE mahs)*, Venezuela . . . 138,732
Cáceres *(KAH thay rays* or *KAH say rays)*, Spain . . . 56,274
Cadiz *(KAH thees)*, Philippines . . . 88,542
Cádiz *(kuh DIZ)*, Spain . . . 137,925
Caen *(KAHN)*, France . . . 110,262
Cagayan de Oro *(KAH gah YAHN day OH roh)*, Philippines . . . 68,274
Cagliari *(KAH lyah ree)*, Italy . . . 200,364
Cairo (Al Qāhirah) *(KY roh) (el KAH hih ruh)*, Egypt . . . 4,219,853
Calabar *(KAL uh bahr)*, Nigeria . . . 46,705
Calais *(kah LEH* or *KAL ay)*, France . . . 74,624
Calamba *(kah LAHM bah)*, Philippines . . . 57,715
Calbayog *(kahl BAH yohg)*, Philippines . . . 77,832

Calcutta *(kal KUT uh)*, India *4,764,979 . . . 3,072,196
Cali *(KAH lee)*, Colombia . . . 921,690
Calicut *(KAL ih kut)*, India . . . 306,114
Callao *(kah YAH oh)*, Peru . . . 321,700
Caloocan *(KAH loh OH kahn)*, Philippines . . . 174,500
Caltagirone *(KAHL tah jee ROH nay)*, Italy . . . 44,212
Caltanissetta *(KAHL tah nees-SAYT tah)*, Italy . . . 63,027
Camagüey *(KAH mah GWAY)*, Cuba . . . 178,600
Cambay *(kam BAY)*, India . . . 51,291
Camberwell *(KAM bur wel)*, Australia . . . 98,227
Cambridge *(KAYM brij)*, England . . . 100,470
Camden *(KAM dun)*, England . . . 231,680
Campeche *(kam PEE chee* or *kahm PAY chay)*, Mexico . . . 69,506
Campina Grande *(kum PEE nuh GRUN dee)*, Brazil . . . 152,000
Campinas *(kum PEE nus)*, Brazil . . . 242,000
Campo Grande *(KUM poo GRUN-dee)*, Brazil . . . 103,000
Campos *(KUM poos)*, Brazil . . . 372,000
Cam Ranh *(KAHM RAHN)*, Vietnam, South . . . 102,174
Can Tho *(KAHN TOH)*, Vietnam, South . . . 92,132
Canberra *(KAN BEAR uh* or *KAN bur-uh)*, Australia . . . 141,575
Cannes *(KAN)*, France . . . 67,152
Cannock *(KAN uk)*, England . . . 53,720
Canoas *(kuh NOH us)*, Brazil . . . 118,000
Canterbury *(KAN tur BEHR ee)*, Australia . . . 130,334
Canton (Kuangchou) *(kan TAHN) (GWAHNG JOH)*, China . . . 1,840,000
Cape Town, South Africa . . . 691,296
Caracas *(kah RAH kahs* or *kuh RACK-us)* Venezuela *1,958,977 . . . 786,710
Caratinga *(kahr uh TEENG guh)* Brazil . . . 119,000
Carcassonne *(kahr kah SAWN)*, France . . . 43,616
Cárdenas *(KAHR day nahs)*, Cuba . . . 67,400
Cardiff *(KAHR dif)*, Wales . . . 287,460
Carletonville *(CARL tun vil)*, South Africa . . . 40,641
Carlisle *(kahr LIL)*, England . . . 71,110
Carlton *(KAHRL tun)*, England . . . 42,220
Carpi *(KAHR pee)*, Italy . . . 45,208
Carrara *(kuh RAHR uh)*, Italy . . . 64,901
Cartagena *(KAHR tah HAY nah)*, Colombia . . . 322,530
Cartagena *(KAHR tah HAY nah)*, Spain . . . 147,353
Cartago *(kahr TAH goh)*, Colombia . . . 55,682
Caruaru *(KAHR wuh ROO)*, Brazil . . . 112,000
Casablanca *(CASS uh BLANK uh* or *CAHS uh BLAHNK uh)*, Morocco . . . 1,085,000
Caserta *(kah ZEHR tah)*, Italy . . . 50,381
Castellammare di Stabia *(kahs-TEL lahm MAH ray dee STAH byah)*, Italy . . . 64,618
Castellón de la Plana *(KAHS tay-LYOHN day lah PLAH nah)*, Spain . . . 87,206
Castries *(kass TREE* or *KAHS-treess)*, St. Lucia . . . 35,000
Castrop-Rauxel *(KAHS trawp ROWK sel)*, Germany, West . . . 83,400
Catania *(kuh TAIN yuh* or *kuh TAHN-yuh)*, Italy . . . 376,239
Catanzaro *(KAH tahn DZAH roh)*, Italy . . . 74,037
Caufield *(CAW feeld)*, Australia . . . 81,705
Cavite *(kah VEE tay)*, Philippines . . . 54,891
Caxias *(kuh SHEE ahs)* Brazil . . . 170,000
Caxias do Sul *(kuh SHEE us doo SOOL)*, Brazil . . . 106,000
Cebu *(say BOO)*, Philippines . . . 299,700
Celaya *(say LAH yah)*, Mexico . . . 79,977
Celle *(TSEL uh)*, Germany, West . . . 56,300
Cerignola *(CHAY ree NYAW lah)*, Italy . . . 49,287
Cesena *(chay ZEH nah)*, Italy . . . 79,704
České Budějovice *(CHES keh BOO-dyeh yaw vee tseh)*, Czechoslovakia . . . 78,037
Ceuta *(SEH oo tuh)*, Spanish Possessions in North Africa . . 82,000
Chalon *(shah LAWN)*, France . . . 50,589
Châlons-sur-Marne *(shah LAWN syoor MAHRN)*, France . . . 50,764
Chambéry *(shahm bay REE)*, France . . . 51,066
Champigny *(shahm pee NYEE)*, France . . . 70,419
Chanchiang (Fort Bayard) *(CHAHN JYAHNG) (fort BAY urd)*, China . . . 166,000
Chanda *(CHAHN duh)*, India . . . 51,484
Chandernagore *(CHUN dur nuh-GAWR)*, India . . . 67,105
Chandigarh *(CHUN dee GAHR)*, India . . . 89,321
Changchih *(CHAHNG CHUR)*, China . . . 97,800
Changchou *(CHAHNG JOH)*, China . . . 296,500
Changchou *(CHAHNG JOH)*, China . . . 81,200
Changchun *(CHAHNG CHOON)*, China . . . 975,000
Changhua *(CHAHNG HWAH)*, Taiwan . . . 119,944
Changsha *(CHAHNG SHAH)*, China . . . 703,000
Changshu *(CHAHNG SHOO)*, China . . . 101,400
Changsŏng *(CHAHNG SUNG)*, Korea, South . . . 103,312
Changte *(CHAHNG DUH)*, China . . . 94,800
Chaoan *(CHOW AHN)*, China . . . 101,300
Chapayevsk *(chah PAH yefsk)*, Soviet Union . . . 86,000
Chapra *(CHUP ruh)*, India . . . 75,580
Chardzhou *(chahr JOH)*, Soviet Union . . . 96,000
Chārikār *(CHAH rih KAHR)*, Afghanistan . . . 83,737
Charleroi *(SHAR luh RWAH)*, Belgium . . . 280,082
Charleville *(shahrl VEEL)*, France . . . 55,543
Châteauroux *(shah toh ROO)*, France . . . 49,138
Chatham *(CHAT um)*, England . . . 54,660
Chatsworth *(CHATS wurth)*, South Africa . . . 114,600
Cheadle and Gatley *(CHEE d'l and GAT lee)*, England . . . 56,040
Cheboksary *(CHEH buk SAH ree)*, Soviet Union . . . 216,000
Chechŏn *(CHEH CHUN)*, Korea, South . . . 50,423
Chefoo (Yentai) *(CHEE FOO) (YEN-TYE)*, China . . . 116,000
Cheju *(CHAY joo)*, Korea, South . . . 106,456
Chelmsford *(CHELMS furd)*, England . . . 56,090
Cheltenham *(CHELT num* or *CHEL ten um)*, England . . . 76,020
Chelyabinsk *(cheh LYAH binsk)*, Soviet Union . . . 874,000
Chemnitz (Karl-Marx-Stadt) *(KEM nits) (karl MARX shtaht)*, Germany, East . . . 299,312
Chenchiang (Chengchiang) *(JUN JYAHNG)*, China . . . 201,400
Chengchou *(JUNG JOH)*, China . . . 766,000
Chengte *(CHUNG DUH)*, China . . . 92,900
Chengtu *(CHUNG DOO)*, China . . . 1,107,000
Cheremkhovo *(CHEH rum KAW vuh)*, Soviet Union . . . 99,000
Cherepovets *(cheh REH puh vets)*, Soviet Union . . . 189,000
Cherkassy *(chair KAH see)*, Soviet Union . . . 159,000
Cherkessk *(chair KESK)*, Soviet Union . . . 67,000
Chernigov *(chair NEE guf)*, Soviet Union . . . 159,000
Chernogorsk *(CHAIR nuh GAWRSK)*, Soviet Union . . . 60,000
Chernovtsy *(chair NAWF tsee)*, Soviet Union . . . 187,000
Chertsey *(CHURT see)*, England . . . 44,630
Cheshunt *(CHESS unt)*, England . . . 43,780
Chester *(CHES tur)*, England . . . 60,620
Chesterfield *(CHES tur feeld)*, England . . . 70,850
Chiahsing *(JYAH SHING)*, China . . . 78,300
Chiai *(JEE EYE)*, Taiwan . . . 208,521
Chiamussu *(JYAH MOO SUH)*, China . . . 146,000
Chian *(JEE AHN)*, China . . . 52,800
Chiang Mai *(chee AHNG MY)*, Thailand . . . 65,736
Chiangmen (Kongmoon) *(JYAHNG MUN) (KAWNG MOON)*, China . . . 85,000
Chiba *(CHEE buh)*, Japan . . . 482,133
Chichibu *(CHEE chee boo)*, Japan . . . 60,867
Chichihaerh *(CHEE CHEE HAHR)*, China . . . 668,000
Chiclayo *(chee KLAH yoh)*, Peru . . . 134,100
Chieti *(KYAY tee)*, Italy . . . 47,792
Chigasaki *(chih GAH sah kee)*, Japan . . . 129,621
Chigwell *(CHIG wel)*, England . . . 56,350
Chihfeng *(CHUR FUNG)*, China . . . 49,000
Chihuahua *(chee WAH wah)*, Mexico . . . 257,027
Chillán *(chee YAHN)*, Chile . . . 81,262
Chilung *(JEE LOONG)*, Taiwan . . . 294,883
Chimbote *(cheem BOH tay)*, Peru . . . 59,990
Chimkent *(chim KENT)*, Soviet Union . . . 247,000
Chinchou *(JIN JOH)*, China . . . 352,200
Chingchiang *(CHING JYAHNG)*, China . . . 77,000
Chingola *(ching GOH luh)*, Zambia . . . 50,690
Chingshih *(JING SHUR)*, China . . . 50,000 to 100,000
Chingtechen *(JING DUH JUN)*, China . . . 92,000
Chinhae *(CHIN high)*, Korea, South . . . 91,947
Chinhuangtao *(CHIN WAHNG DOW)*, China . . . 186,800
Chining *(JEE NING)*, China . . . 86,200
Chiniot *(CHIN ee ut)*, Pakistan . . . 47,099
Chinju *(CHIN JOO)*, Korea, South . . . 104,202
Chinnampo (Nampo) *(CHIN nahm-POH) (NAHM poh)*, Korea, North . . . 165,000
Chioggia *(KYAWD jah)*, Italy . . . 47,151
Chirchik *(cheer CHEEK)*, Soviet Union . . . 108,000
Chistopol' *(CHEES tuh pul)*, Soviet Union . . . 60,000
Chita *(chee TAH)*, Soviet Union . . . 242,000
Chittagong *(CHIT uh gong)*, Bangladesh . . . 364,205
Chiuchiang *(JYOO JYAHNG)*, China . . . 64,600
Chōfu *(CHOH foo)*, Japan . . . 157,488
Chŏnan *(CHUN AHN)*, Korea, South . . . 78,316
Chŏngjin *(CHAWNG jin)*, Korea, North . . . 400,000
Chŏngju *(CHAWNG joo)*, Korea, South . . . 148,944
Chonju *(CHUN joo)*, Korea, South . . . 262,816
Chorzów *(KAW zhoof)*, Poland . . . 150,400
Chōshi *(CHOH shee)*, Japan . . . 90,415
Christchurch *(KRYST church)*, New Zealand . . . 275,968
Chüanchou *(CHYOO AHN JOH)*, China . . . 107,700
Chuchou *(CHOO JOH)*, China . . . 127,300
Chunchŏn *(CHOON chawn)*, Korea, South . . . 122,672
Chungju *(CHOONG joo)*, Korea, South . . . 87,727
Chungking (Chunching) *(JOONG CHING* or *choong KING)*, China . . . 2,121,000
Ch'ungmu *(CHOONG moo)*, Korea, South . . . 54,974
Chungshan *(JOONG SHAHN)*, China . . . 93,000
Chusovoy *(CHOO suh VOY)*, Soviet Union . . . 58,000
Ciego de Avila *(SYAY goh day AH vee la)*, Cuba . . . 54,700
Ciénaga *(SYAY nah gah)*, Colombia . . . 47,719
Cienfuegos *(syen FWAY gohs)*, Cuba . . . 91,800
Ciudad Bolívar *(syoo THAHTH boh-LEE vahr)*, Venezuela . . . 98,007
Ciudad Madero *(syoo THAHTH mah-THAY roh)*, Mexico . . . 90,830
Ciudad Obregón *(syoo THAHTH oh-bray GAWN)*, Mexico . . . 114,407
Ciudad Ojeda *(syoo THATH oh HAY thah)*, Venezuela . . . 79,571
Ciudad Victoria *(syoo THAHTH veek-TOH ryah)*, Mexico . . . 83,897
Clamart *(klah MAHR)*, France . . . 54,906
Clermont-Ferrand *(KLEHR MAWN FEH RAHN)*, France . . . 148,896
Clichy *(klee SHEE)*, France . . . 52,477
Cluj *(KLOOZH)*, Romania . . . 205,435
Clydebank *(KLYD BANK)*, Scotland . . . 50,211
Coatbridge *(KOHT brij)*, Scotland . . . 53,117
Coburg *(KOH burg)*, Australia . . . 65,428
Coburg *(KOH burg* or *KOH boork)*, Germany, West . . . 41,400
Cochabamba *(KOH chah BAM bah)*, Bolivia . . . 158,000
Coelho da Rocha *(KWAY lyoo duh RAW shuh)*, Brazil . . . 59,091
Coimbatore *(KOYM buh TOHR)*, India . . . 342,387
Colatina *(kaw luh TEE nuh)*, Brazil . . . 123,000
Colchester *(KOHL ches'tur* or *KOHL CHES tur)*, England . . . 72,630
Colima *(koh LEE mah)*, Mexico . . . 58,450
Colmar *(KOHL mahr)*, France . . . 59,550
Cologne (Köln) *(kuh LOHN) (KULN)*, Germany, West . . . 866,300
Colombes *(kaw LAWMB)*, France . . . 80,357
Colombo *(kuh LUM boh)*, Ceylon . . . 510,947
Colón *(koh LOHN)*, Panama . . . 67,641
Comilla *(kuh MILL uh)*, Bangladesh . . . 54,504
Como *(KOH moh)*, Italy . . . 81,983
Conakry *(KAHN uh kree)*, Guinea . . . 43,000
Concepción *(kohn sep SYOHN)*, Chile . . . 187,251
Concordia *(kawng KAWR thyah)*, Argentina . . . 56,654
Constanța *(kawn STAHN tsah)*, Romania . . . 176,234
Constantine *(KAHN stun teen)*, Algeria . . . 243,558
Copenhagen (København) *(KOH pun HAY gun) (KUH bun HOWN)*, Denmark *1,381,312 . . . 627,800
Corby *(KAWR bee)*, England . . . 48,150
Córdoba *(KAWR duh buh)*, Argentina . . . 589,153
Córdoba *(KAWR duh buh)*, Mexico . . . 78,495
Córdoba *(KAWR duh buh)*, Spain . . . 231,641
Cork *(KAWRK)*, Ireland . . . 122,146
Cornellá *(kawr nay YAH)*, Spain . . . 66,323
Coro *(KOH roh)*, Venezuela . . . 53,641
Coronel *(koh roh NEL)*, Chile . . . 46,257
Corrientes *(kawr RYEN tays)*, Argentina . . . 97,507
Cosenza *(koh ZEN tsah)*, Italy . . . 78,611
Cotonou *(KOH toh NOO)*, Dahomey . . . 119,400
Cottbus *(KAWT boos)*, Germany, East . . . 82,897
Courbevoie *(KOOR buh VWAH)*, France . . . 58,118
Coventry *(KAHV un tree)*, England . . . 335,410
Coyoacán *(KOH yoh ah KAHN)*, Mexico . . . 54,866
Craiova *(krah YOH vah)*, Romania . . . 179,363
Crawley *(KRAW lee)*, England . . . 63,310
Cremona *(kruh MOH nuh)*, Italy . . . 73,902
Crewe *(KROO)*, England . . . 52,220
Crotone *(kroh TOH nay)*, Italy . . . 43,256
Croydon *(KROY dun)*, England . . . 329,210
Cúcuta *(KOO koo tah)*, Colombia . . . 240,595
Cuddalore *(KUD uh lohr)*, India . . . 79,168
Cuenca *(KWENG kah)*, Ecuador . . . 65,058
Cuernavaca *(KWEHR nah VAH kah)*, Mexico . . . 134,117
Cuiabá *(KOO yuh BAH)*, Brazil . . . 43,112
Culiacán *(KOO lyah KAHN)*, Mexico . . . 167,956
Cumaná *(KOO mah NAH)*, Venezuela . . . 92,983
Cuneo *(KOO nay oh)*, Italy . . . 46,065
Curepipe *(KYOOR PEEP)*, Mauritius . . . 47,600
Curitiba *(KOO ree TEE buh)*, Brazil . . . 576,000
Cusco *(KOOS koh)*, Peru . . . 105,400
Cuttack *(kuh TACK)*, India . . . 174,048
Cuxhaven *(kooks HAH fun)*, Germany, West . . . 45,200
Częstochowa *(CHEN staw KAW vah)*, Poland . . . 184,500

D

Da Lat *(DAH LAHT)*, Vietnam, South . . . 89,656
Da Nang *(dah NAHNG)*, Vietnam, South . . . 427,834
Dąbrowa Górnicza *(dawm BRAW vah goor NEE chah)*, Poland . . . 60,100
Dacca *(DAK uh)*, Bangladesh . . . 556,712
Dagupan *(dah GOO pahn)*, Philippines . . . 63,191
Dairen-Port Arthur, see Port Arthur-Dairen
Dakar *(dah KAHR)*, Senegal . . . 581,000
Damanhūr *(DAH mahn HOOR)*, Egypt . . . 146,079
Damascus (Dimashq) *(duh MAS kus) (dih MAHSHK)*, Syria . . . 618,457
Damietta (Dumyāṭ) *(DAM ee ET uh) (doom YAHT)*, Egypt . . . 86,327
Danzig (Gdánsk) *(DAN sig) (guh DAHNSK)*, Poland . . . 364,000
Darbhanga *(dur BUNG guh)*, India . . . 114,543
Dar es Salaam *(DAHR ess suh LAHM)*, Tanzania . . . 190,200
Darlington *(DAHR ling tun)*, England . . . 84,830
Darmstadt *(DAHRM shtaht)*, Germany, West . . . 141,100
Dartford *(DAHRT furd)*, England . . . 46,510
Dasē *(DAH say)*, Ethiopia . . . 43,000
Daugavpils *(DOW gahf peels)*, Soviet Union . . . 101,000
Davangere *(DAH vung geh reh)*, India . . . 78,124
Davao *(DAH vow)*, Philippines . . . 269,300
Dayr az Zawr *(DIRE ahz ZOWR)*, Syria . . . 67,419
Debrecen *(DEH breh tsen)*, Hungary . . . 155,122
Děčín *(DYEH cheen)*, Czechoslovakia . . . 45,589
Dehiwala-Mount Lavinia *(DAY hih-WAH luh mount luh VIN ee uh)*, Ceylon . . . 111,013
Dehra Dun *(DAY ruh DOON)*, India . . . 133,574
Delft *(DELFT)*, Netherlands . . . 80,545
Delhi *(DEL ee)*, India *2,874,454 . . . 2,511,482
Delmenhorst *(DEL mun hawrst)*, Germany, West . . . 63,900
Den Helder *(dun HEL dur)*, Netherlands . . . 58,356
Denizli *(DEH niz LEE)*, Turkey . . . 61,820
Dera Ghāzi Khan *(DEHR uh GAH zee KAHN)*, Pakistan . . . 47,105
Dera Ismāil Khan *(DEHR uh is mah EEL KAHN)*, Pakistan . . . 46,140
Derbent *(dehr BENT)*, Soviet Union . . . 57,000

Derby *(DUR bee* or *DAHR bee)*, England 221,260
Dessau *(DESS ow)*, Germany, East 98,261
Detmold *(DET mohlt)*, Germany, West 64,500
Deurne *(DUR nuh)*, Belgium 74,119
Deventer *(DAY vun tur)*, Netherlands 62,777
Dewsbury *(DYOOZ bur ee)*, England 51,640
Dezfūl *(dez FOOL)*, Iran 84,499
Dhanbad *(DAHN bahd)*, India 46,756
Dharwar *(dahr WAHR)*, India 77,163
Dhulia *(DOO lee uh)*, India 98,893
Dibrugarh *(DIB roo gur)*, India 58,480
Dijon *(dee ZHAWN)*, France 145,357
Dimitrovgrad *(dih MEE trawv-graht)*, Bulgaria 41,787
Dindigul *(DIN dih gul)*, India 92,947
Dinslaken *(DINS LAH kun)*, Germany, West 54,500
Divinópolis *(DEE vee NAW poo lis)*, Brazil 41,544
Diyarbakir *(dee YAHR bah KEER)*, Turkey 102,624
Djakarta *(juh KAHR tuh)*, Indonesia 2,906,533
Djambi *(JAHM bee)*, Indonesia 113,080
Djibouti *(juh BOO tee)*, Afars and Issas 62,000
Dneprodzerzhinsk *(NEP roh dzehr-ZHINSK)*, Soviet Union 227,000
Dnepropetrovsk *(NEP roh puh-TRAWFSK)*, Soviet Union ... 863,000
Doha *(DOH huh)*, Qatar 45,000
Dolgoprudnyy *(DAWL guh PROOD nee)*, Soviet Union 53,000
Doncaster *(DONG kus tur)*, England 84,250
Donetsk *(dah NETSK)*, Soviet Union 879,000
Dordrecht *(DAWR drekt)*, Netherlands 88,461
Dortmund *(DAWRT moont)*, Germany, West 648,900
Douai *(doo AY)*, France 49,187
Douala *(doo AH luh)*, Cameroon 200,000
Drammen *(DRAHM un)*, Norway 49,250
Drancy *(drahn SEE)*, France 69,444
Dresden *(DREZ dun)*, Germany, East 501,508
Drogobych *(drah GAW bich)*, Soviet Union 56,000
Drushkovka *(droozh KAWF kah)*, Soviet Union 53,000
Dubayy *(doo BYE)*, United Arab Emirates 65,000
Dublin (Baile Átha Cliath) *(DUB-lin) (blah KLEE uh)*, Ireland .. 568,772
Dudley *(DUD lee)*, England 179,510
Duisburg *(DYOOS boork)*, Germany, West 457,900
Dún Laoghaire *(doon LAR ee)*, Ireland 51,772
Dunaújváros *(DOO nah OO ee VAH-rawsh)*, Hungary 44,200
Dundee *(dun DEE)*, Scotland 182,340
Dunedin *(dun EE din)*, New Zealand 111,059
Dunfermline *(dun FURM lin)*, Scotland 50,712
Duque de Caxias *(DOO kee dee kuh-SHEE us)*, Brazil 310,000
Durango *(doo RANG goh)*, Mexico 150,541
Durban *(DUR bun)*, South Africa 495,458
Düren *(DOO ruhn)*, Germany, West 54,900
Durrës *(DOOR us)*, Albania 47,870
Dushanbe *(DYOO shahn BEH)*, Soviet Union 374,000
Düsseldorf *(DYOOS ul dawrf)*, Germany, West 680,800
Dzerzhinsk *(dzehr ZHINSK)*, Soviet Union 221,000
Dzhambul *(jahm BOOL)*, Soviet Union 188,000
Dzhezkazgan *(JES kahz GAHN)*, Soviet Union 62,000

E

Ealing *(EE ling)*, England 298,720
East Kilbride *(EEST KIL bryd)*, Scotland 58,450
East London *(EEST LUN dun)*, South Africa 118,298
Eastbourne *(EEST bawrn* or *EEST-burn)*, England 68,200
Eastleigh *(EEST lee)*, England 44,150
Écija *(AY thee hah)*, Spain 52,562
Ede *(AY duh)*, Netherlands 68,772
Ede *(AY day)*, Nigeria 134,550
Edinburgh *(ED in BUR uh)*, Scotland 466,464
Eindhoven *(EYENT HOH vun)*, Netherlands 184,519
Eisenach *(I zuh nahk)*, Germany, East 50,906
El Asnam *(el ahs NAHM)*, Algeria 49,109
Elâzığ *(EH lah ZIG)*, Turkey 78,999
Elbląg (Elbing) *(EL blawnk) (EL-bing)*, Poland 86,000
Elche *(EL chay)*, Spain 105,623
Elektrostal' *(eh LEK truh STAHL)*, Soviet Union 123,000
El Ferrol del Caudillo *(el fehr ROHL del kow THEE lyoh)*, Spain 87,351
Ellesmere Port *(ELZ meer port)*, England 54,930
El Tigre *(el TEE gray)*, Venezuela 51,646
Eluru *(eh LOO roo)*, India 121,691
Emden *(EM dun)*, Germany, West 48,300
Emmen *(EM uhn)*, Netherlands 76,599
Enfield *(EN feeld)*, Australia 77,555
Enfield *(EN feeld)*, England 267,830
Engel's *(EN gels)*, Soviet Union 130,000
Enschede *(EN skuh DAY)*, Netherlands 135,677
Ensenada *(EN suh NAH duh)*, Mexico 77,687
Enugu *(eh NOO goo)*, Nigeria 138,457
Epsom [& Ewell] *(EP sum [and YOO ul])*, England 72,300
Erfurt *(EHR foort)*, Germany, East 195,994
Erlangen *(EHR LAHNG un)*, Germany, West 85,700
Ermelino Matarazzo *(EHR muh LEE noh MAH tuh RAH zoh)*, Brazil 52,969
Ernakulam *(ehr NAH koo lum)*, India 129,679
Erode *(eh ROHD)*, India 73,762
Erzincan *(EHR zin JAHN)*, Turkey 45,280
Erzurum *(EHR zuh ROOM)*, Turkey 106,301
Esbjerg *(ESS byehrg)*, Denmark 76,192
Esbo (Espoo) *(ESS boh) (ESS poh)*, Finland 93,041
Esher *(EE shur)*, England 63,120
Eskilstuna *(ESS kil STOO nuh)*, Sweden 62,428
Eskişehir *(ES kee sheh HEER)*, Turkey 174,451
Essen *(ESS un)*, Germany, West 704,800
Essendon *(ESS un dun)*, Australia 57,578
Esslingen *(ESS ling un)*, Germany, West 86,500
Esteban Echeverría *(es TAY bahn eh CHAY vay REE ah)*, Argentina 69,730
Etawah *(ee TAH wuh)*, India 69,681
Etterbeek *(ET ur bayk)*, Belgium 52,310
Exeter *(EK suh tur)*, England 93,010

F

Faenza *(fah EN zuh)*, Italy 51,085
Fairfield *(FAIR feeld)*, Australia 112,862
Faizābād *(FYE zuh bad)*, Afghanistan 57,756
Faizabad *(FYE zuh bad)*, India 83,717
Fano *(FAH noh)*, Italy 41,033
Fareham *(FAIR um)*, England 77,330
Faridabad *(fuh REED ah bahd)*, India 50,709
Farnborough *(FAHRN BUR uh)*, England 41,120
Farrukhabad *(fuh ROOK ah bahd)*, India 87,793
Feira de Santana *(FAY ruh dee sun TUH nuh)*, Brazil 133,000
Feodosiya *(fee uh DAW see yuh)*, Soviet Union 65,000
Fergana *(fur GAH nuh)*, Soviet Union 111,000
Ferrara *(fuh RAHR uh)*, Italy 156,038
Fez *(FEZ)*, Morocco 235,000
Firozabad *(fih ROHZ uh bad)*, India 98,611
Flensburg *(FLENSS boork)*, Germany, West 96,800
Florence (Firenze) *(FLAWR unss) (fee REN dzay)*, Italy 455,665
Florianópolis *(FLAWR ee uh NAHP-uh lis)*, Brazil 127,000
Foggia *(FAWD jah)*, Italy 122,716
Foligno *(faw LEE nyoh)*, Italy 48,069
Folkestone *(FOHK stun)*, England 44,040
Foochow (Fuchou) *(FOO chow* or *FOO JOH)*, China 616,000
Footscray *(FOOTS kray)*, Australia 57,710
Forest *(faw RAY)*, Belgium 55,188
Forlì *(fawr LEE)*, Italy 91,945
Fort Bayard, see Chanchiang.
Fort-de-France *(FAWR duh FRAHNS)*, Martinique 85,219
Fort-Lamy *(FAWR la MEE)*, Chad 100,000
Fortaleza *(FAWR tuh LAY zuh)*, Brazil 794,000
Foshan *(FUH SHAHN)*, China 122,500
Fouhsin *(FOO SHIN)*, China 188,600
Franca *(FRUNG kuh)*, Brazil 47,244
Frankfurt [am Main] *(FRAHNK furt [ahm MYN])*, Germany, West 660,400
Frankfurt [an der Oder] *(FRAHNK-furt [ahn dur OH dur])*, Germany, East 62,001
Frederiksberg *(FRED riks burg)*, Denmark 101,449
Freetown *(FREE town)*, Sierra Leone 148,000
Freiberg *(FRY behrk* or *FRY burg)*, Germany, East 50,272
Freiburg *(FRY boork* or *FRY burg)*, Germany, West 166,000
Freital *(FRY tahl)*, Germany, East 42,159
Frunze *(FROON zeh)*, Soviet Union 431,000
Fuchū *(foo CHOO)*, Japan 167,173
Fuji *(FOO jee)*, Japan 180,639
Fujieda *(FOO jee EH dah)*, Japan 78,750
Fujinomiya *(foo jee NOH mee yah)*, Japan 88,880
Fujisawa *(FOO jee SAH wuh)*, Japan 228,978
Fukuchiyama *(FOO koo chee YAH muh)*, Japan 57,174
Fukui *(foo KOO ee)*, Japan 200,509
Fukuoka *(FOO koo OH kuh)*, Japan 853,270
Fukushima *(FOO koo SHEE muh)*, Japan 227,451
Fukuyama *(FOO koo YAH muh)*, Japan 255,086
Fulda *(FOOL dah)*, Germany, West 44,300
Funabashi *(FOO nah BAH shee)*, Japan 325,426
Funchal *(foon SHAHL)*, Portugal (Madeira Is.) 43,301
Fürth *(FYOORT)*, Germany, West 94,300
Fushun *(FOO SHOON)*, China 985,000

G

Gaborone *(GAH beh ROH nuh)*, Botswana 18,000
Gabrovo *(GAH braw vaw)*, Bulgaria 57,758
Gadag *(GUD ug)*, India 76,614
Galați *(gah LAHTS)*, Romania 183,954
Galle *(GAHL)*, Ceylon 64,942
Gamagōri *(GAH mah GOH ree)*, Japan 82,868
Ganganagar *(GUNG gah NUG ur)*, India 63,854
Gangtok *(GAHNG tawk)*, Sikkim 6,848
Garden Reach *(GAHR dun REECH)*, India 144,456
Gatchina *(GAHT chih nuh)*, Soviet Union 63,000
Gateshead *(GAYTS hed)*, England 100,560
Gauhati *(gow HAH tee)*, India 136,864
Gävle *(YEV luh)*, Sweden 59,670
Gaya *(GUY uh)*, India 162,131
Gaza (Ghazzah) *(GAY zuh) (GAH zuh)*, Gaza Strip 144,000
Gaziantep *(GAH zee ahn TEP)*, Turkey 158,367
Gdynia *(guh DIN yah)*, Poland 179,200
Geelong *(juh LAWNG)*, Australia 115,047
Gela *(JEH lah)*, Italy 54,774
Gelsenkirchen *(GEL zun KIHR kun)*, Germany, West 348,600
General San Martín *(hay nay RAHL SAHN mahr TEEN)*, Argentina 279,213
General Sarmiento *(hay nay RAHL sahr MYEN toh)*, Argentina .. 167,160
Geneva (Genève) *(juh NEE vuh) (zhuh NEV)*, Switzerland ... 170,500
Genk *(GENGK)*, Belgium 55,806
Gennevilliers *(zhen vee YAH)*, France 46,074
Genoa (Genova) *(JEN oh uh) (JEH noh vah)*, Italy 842,732
Gentofte *(GEN TAWF tuh)*, Denmark 77,858
Georgetown *(JAWRJ town)*, Guyana 102,688
Georgetown (Pinang) *(JAWRJ town)*, Malaysia 234,930
Gera *(GAY rah)*, Germany, East 111,099
Germiston *(JUR mis tun)*, South Africa 210,298
Ghaziabad *(GAH zee ah BAHD)*, India 70,438
Ghent (Gent) *(GENT)*, Belgium 157,834
Gia Dinh *(ZHAH DIN)*, Vietnam, South 156,114
Giessen *(GEE sun)*, Germany, West 74,700
Gifu *(GEE foo)*, Japan 385,727
Gijón *(hee HOHN)*, Spain 152,784
Gillingham *(JIL ing um)*, England 88,370
Gingoog *(heen GOH awg)*, Philippines 52,677
Girardot *(HEE rahr DAWRT)*, Colombia 66,584
Giza (Al Jizah) *(GEE zuh) (el GEE zuh)*, Egypt 571,249
Gladbeck *(GLAHT bek)*, Germany, West 83,300
Glasgow *(GLASS koh)*, Scotland *1,755,328 945,034
Glazov *(GLAH zuf)*, Soviet Union 68,000
Gliwice (Gleiwitz) *(glee VEE-tseh) (GLY vits)*, Poland 166,600
Gloucester *(GLAHS tur)*, England 90,490
Gniezno *(guh NYEZ naw)*, Poland 50,000
Godhra *(GOH druh)*, India 52,167
Godoy Cruz *(goh THOY KROOS)*, Argentina 80,024
Goiânia *(goy UN uh)*, Brazil 317,000
Gold Coast *(GOLD kohst)*, Australia 68,974
Gomel' *(GAW mul)*, Soviet Union 272,000
Gómez Palacio *(GOH mes pah LAH-syoh)*, Mexico 79,650
Gondia *(GOHN dee uh)*, India 56,320
Göppingen *(GUP ing un)*, Germany, West 46,900
Gorakhpur *(GOH ruk poor)*, India 210,541
Gorgān *(gohr GAHN)*, Iran 51,181
Gorizia *(goh REET syah)*, Italy 42,187
Gorki (Gor'kiy) *(GAWR kee)*, Soviet Union 1,170,000
Görlitz *(GUR lits)*, Germany, East 87,308
Gorlovka *(GAWR luf kuh)*, Soviet Union 335,000
Gorontalo *(GAW rawn TAH loh)*, Indonesia 71,378
Gorzów Wielkopolski (Landsberg) *(GAW zhoof VYEL kaw PAWL skee) (LAHNTS behrk)*, Poland 70,300
Gosport *(GAHS port)*, England 75,680
Göteborg *(YUH tuh BAWR ih)*, Sweden 418,600
Gotha *(GOH thuh* or *GOH tuh)*, Germany, East 57,328
Göttingen *(GUT ing un)*, Germany, West 115,200
Gottwaldov (Zlín) *(GAWT vahl dawf) (ZLEEN)*, Czechoslovakia 65,216
Gouda *(GOW duh)*, Netherlands 46,262
Governador Valadares *(GOH vehr-nuh DOHR VAH luh DAH ris)*, Brazil 123,000
Granada *(gruh NAH duh)*, Spain 170,127
Gravesend *(GRAYV ZEND)*, England 55,160
Graz *(GRAHTS)*, Austria 250,300
Great Yarmouth *(grate YAHR muth)*, England 51,290
Greenock *(GREE nuk* or *GRIN uk* or *GREN uk)*, Scotland 71,069
Greenwich *(GRIN ij)*, England 229,700
Greifswald *(GRYFES vahlt)*, Germany, East 47,083
Grenoble *(gruh NOH bul)*, France 161,616
Grimsby *(GRIMZ bee)*, England 97,030
Grodno *(GRAWD naw)*, Soviet Union 132,000
Groningen *(GROH ning un)*, Netherlands 157,093
Grosseto *(grohs SAY toh)*, Italy 51,730
Groznyy *(GRAWZ nee)*, Soviet Union 341,000
Grudziadz *(GROO jawnts)*, Poland 74,700
Guadalajara *(GWAH thah lah HAH-rah)*, Mexico 1,193,601
Guantánamo *(gwahn TAH nah moh)*, Cuba 135,100
Guarapuava *(gwu ruh PWAH vah)*, Brazil 114,000
Guarulhos *(gwuh ROO lyoos)*, Brazil 115,000
Guatemala City *(GWAH tuh MAH luh SIT ee)*, Guatemala 577,120
Guayaquil *(GWAH yah KEEL)*, Ecuador 604,151
Gudiyatham *(GOO dih YAH tum)*, India 50,384
Guihulngan *(gee HOOL nuh GAHN)*, Philippines 92,993
Guildford *(GIL furd)*, England 55,520
Guinobatan *(GEE noh bah TAHN)*, Philippines 48,157
Gujrānwāla *(GOOJ run WAH luh)*, Pakistan 196,154
Gujrāt *(GOOJ raht)*, Pakistan 59,608
Gukovo *(GOO kuh vuh)*, Soviet Union 65,000
Gulbarga *(GOOL bur gah)*, India 97,069
Guntur *(goon TOOR)*, India 226,306
Gur'yev *(GOOR yif)*, Soviet Union 114,000
Gus'-Khrustal'nyy *(GOOS kroo STAHL nee)*, Soviet Union 65,000
Gütersloh *(GYOO turs loh)*, Germany, West 76,300
Gwalior *(GWAH lee awr)*, India 337,960
Győr *(DYUR)*, Hungary 87,105

H

Haarlem *(HAHR lum)*, Netherlands 173,133

Haarlemmermeer (*HAHR lum ur MAIR*), Netherlands 54,995
Hachinohe (*hah CHEE noh hay*), Japan 208,801
Hachiōji (*HAH chee OH jee*), Japan 253,527
Hackney (*HAK nee*), England 243,180
Haeju (*HIGH joo*), Korea, North 131,000
Hagen (*HAH gun*), Germany, West 203,000
Hagi (*HAH gee*), Japan 52,541
Hague, The ('s Gravenhage) (*thuh HAYG*) (*SKRAH vun HAH kuh*), Netherlands 576,160
Haifa (*HIGH fuh*), Israel 204,500
Haikou (*HIGH KOH*), China 135,300
Hailar (*HIGH LAHR*), China 43,200
Haiphong (*HIGH FONG*), Vietnam, North 182,496
Hakodate (*hah koh DAH tay*), Japan 241,663
Halberstadt (*HAHL bur shtaht*), Germany, East 46,774
Halesowen (*HAYLZ OH un*), England 51,180
Halifax (*HAL uh faks*), England 94,280
Halisahar (*HAH lih suh hur*), India 51,423
Halle (*HAHL uh*), Germany, East 257,300
Hälsingborg (*HEL sing bawr yuh*), Sweden 78,474
Haltemprice (*HAWLT um price*), England 51,150
Hama (Hamāh) (*hah MAH*), Syria 142,968
Hamadan (*HAM uh dan*), Iran 124,167
Hamamatsu (*hah MAH mah tsoo*), Japan 432,221
Hamburg (*HAM burg*), Germany, West 1,817,100
Hameln (*HAH muln*), Germany, West 47,100
Hamhŭng (*HAHM hoong*), Korea, North 525,000
Hamilton (*HAM ul tun*), New Zealand 80,812
Hamilton (*HAM ul tun*), Scotland 46,122
Hamm (*HAHM*), Germany, West 84,300
Hammersmith (*HAM ur smith*), England 197,590
Hanamaki (*HAH nah MAH kee*), Japan 63,753
Hanau (*HAH now*), Germany, West 55,700
Hanchung (*HAHN JOONG*), China 70,000
Handa (*HAHN dah*), Japan 80,663
Hangchow (Hangchou) (*HANG CHOW*), China 784,000
Hannover (*HAN OH ver*), Germany, West 517,800
Hanoi (*hah NOY* or *HAN oy*), Vietnam, North 414,620
Hantan (*HAHN DAHN*), China 90,000
Haokang (*HOW KAHNG*), China 90,000
Hapur (*HAH poor*), India 55,248
Harbin (Ha-erh-pin) (*HAHR bin*), China 1,552,000
Hardwar (*HUR dwahr*), India 58,513
Hargeisa (*hahr GAY suh*), Somalia 53,000
Haringey (*HAR ing gay*), England 245,270
Harlow (*HAHR loh*), England 74,110
Harrogate (*HAR uh gut* or *HAR oh-gayt*), England 62,200
Harrow (*HAR oh*), England 208,220
Hartlepool (*HAHRT lee pool*), England 98,760
Hastings (*HAY stingz*), England 69,110
Hathras (*HAH trus*), India 64,045
Hattingen (*HAH ting uhn*), Germany, West 60,500
Havana (La Habana) (*huh VAN uh*) (*lah ah BAH nah*), Cuba *1,700,300 1,008,500
Havant & Waterloo (*HAV unt and WAW tur LOO*), England 103,680
Havering (*HAYV ring*), England 252,290
Havířov (*HAH veer zhawf*), Czechoslovakia 81,317
Heerlen (*HAYR lun*), Netherlands 76,515
Heidelberg (*HY dul burg*), Australia 67,943
Heidelberg (*HY dul burg*), Germany, West 121,900
Heidenheim (*HIGH dun hime*), Germany, West 50,200
Heilbronn (*hile BRAWN*), Germany, West 99,400
Helmond (*HEL mawnt*), Netherlands 56,976
Helsinki (*HELL sing kee*), Finland 532,310
Hemel Hempstead (*HEM ul HEMP-sted*), England 65,300
Hengelo (*HENG uh loh*), Netherlands 68,348
Hengyang (*HUNG YAHNG*), China 235,000
Henzada (*HEN zuh DAH*), Burma 61,972
Herāt (*heh RAHT*), Afghanistan 65,735
Hereford (*HEHR uh furd*), England 47,140
Herford (*HEHR fawrt*), Germany, West 67,300
Hermosillo (*EHR moh SEE yoh*), Mexico 176,596
Herne (*HEHR nuh*), Germany, West 100,800
Herten (*HEHR tun*), Germany, West 52,400
Hidalgo del Parral (*ee THAHL goh del pahr RAHL*), Mexico 57,619
Higashi-murayama (*hee GAH shee moo RAH yah muh*), Japan . . 96,545
Higashi-ōsaka (*hee GAH shee-oh SAH kuh*), Japan 500,173
High Wycombe (*high WIK um*), England 56,980
Hikone (*hee KOH nay*), Japan 78,753
Hilden (*HIL dun*), Germany, West 50,000
Hildesheim (*HIL dus hime*), Germany, West 95,900
Hillingdon (*HIL ing dun*), England 236,990
Hilversum (*HIL vur sum*), Netherlands 101,685
Himeji (*hee MEH jee*), Japan 408,353
Himi (*HEE mee*), Japan 60,883
Hinckley (*HINGK lee*), England 44,530
Hino (*HEE noh*), Japan 98,557
Hirakata (*hee RAH kah tah*), Japan 217,369
Hiratsuka (*hee RAH tsoo kah*), Japan 163,671
Hirosaki (*hee ROH sah kee*), Japan 157,603
Hiroshima (*HE roh SHE muh*), Japan 541,998
Hissar (*hih SAHR*), India 60,222
Hita (*HEE tah*), Japan 64,866
Hitachi (*hee TAH chee*), Japan 193,210
Hobart (*HOH bahrt* or *HOH burt*), Australia 129,808
Hochuan (*HUH CHWAHN*), China . . . . 50,000 to 100,000
Hódmezővásárhely (*HOHD meh zuh-VAH shahr hay*), Hungary 52,797
Hof (*HOHF*), Germany, West 54,800
Hofei (*HUH FAY*), China 304,000
Hōfu (*HOH foo*), Japan 97,009
Hofuf (*hoo FOOF*), Saudi Arabia 51,837
Holguín (*ohl GEEN*), Cuba 100,500
Holon (*hoh LOHN*), Israel 69,900
Holroyd (*HAHL royd*), Australia 77,210
Homs (*HAWMS*), Syria 198,852
Hooghly-Chinsurah (*HOOG lee CHIN soo ruh*), India 83,104
Hoshiarpur (*HOH shee AHR poor*), India 50,739
Hospet (*HOHS pet*), India 53,242
Hospitalet (*AWS pee tah LET*), Spain 216,435
Hounslow (*HOWNZ loh*), England 205,580
Hove (*HOHV*), England 71,480
Howrah (*HOW ruh*), India 562,612
Hoyerswerda (*HOY urs VEHR dah*), Germany, East 58,663
Hradec Králové (*HRAH dets KRAH-law veh*), Czechoslovakia 69,587
Hsiangfan (*SHYAHNG FAHN*), China 73,300
Hsiangtan (*SHYAHNG TAHN*), China 183,600
Hsienyang (*SHYEN YAHNG*), China 70,000
Hsinchu (*SHIN CHOO*), Taiwan 178,366
Hsingtai (*SHING TIE*), China . . . . 50,000 to 100,000
Hsinhsiang (*SHIN SHYAHNG*), China 170,500
Hsining (*SHEE NING*), China 300,000
Hsinyang (*SHING YAHNG*), China . . . . 50,000 to 100,000
Hsuanhua (*shyoo AN HWAH*), China 114,100
Hsuchang (*SHYOO CHAHNG*), China 58,000
Huainan (*WHY NAHN*), China 268,900
Huancayo (*wahng KAH yoh*), Peru 64,153
Huangshih (*HWAHNG SHUR*), China 110,500
Hubli (*HOOB lee*), India 197,749
Huchou, see Wuhsing
Huddersfield (*HUD urz feeld*), England 130,990
Hue (*HWAY* or *hyoo AY*), Vietnam, South 209,217
Huelva (*WEL vuh*), Spain 94,897
Huhohaote (*HOO huh HOW duh*), China 314,000
Hull (Kingston upon Hull) (*HULL*) (*KING stun uh pon HULL*), England 294,720
Hunedoara (*HOO nay DWAH ruh*), Romania 77,989
Hurstville (*HURST vil*), Australia 67,070
Hürth (*HYOORT*), Germany, West 52,000
Hyderabad (*HY der uh BAD*), India 1,272,326
Hyderābād (*HY der uh BAD*), Pakistan 434,537

I

Iași (*YAHSH* or *YAH shee*), Romania 187,966
Ibadan (*ee BAH dun*), Nigeria 727,565
Ibagué (*EE bah GAY*), Colombia 206,022
Ibaraki (*EE bah RAH kee*), Japan 163,903
Ica (*EE kah*), Peru 49,097
Ichalkaranji (*EE chul KUR un-jee*), India 50,978
Ichang (*EE CHAHNG*), China . . . . 50,000 to 100,000
Ichihara (*ee CHEE hah ruh*), Japan 156,016
Ichikawa (*ee CHEE kah wah*), Japan 261,055
Ichinomiya (*ee chih NOH mee yah*), Japan 219,274
Ife (*EE fay*), Nigeria 150,818
Iida (*EE dah*), Japan 77,261
Iizuka (*EE zoo kah*), Japan 75,643
Ikeda (*ee KAY dah*), Japan 94,333
Ikerre (*EE keh reh*), Nigeria 107,216
Ilesha (*ee LESH uh*), Nigeria 192,302
Ilhéus (*ee LYEH oos*), Brazil 45,712
Iligan (*ee LEE gahn*), Philippines 58,433
Iloilo (*EE loh EE loh*), Philippines 180,900
Ilorin (*ee LAW rin*), Nigeria 241,849
Imabari (*ee MAH bah ree*), Japan 111,125
Imari (*ee MAH ree*), Japan 61,561
Imbābah (*im BAH buh*), Egypt 341,000
Imola (*EE moh lah*), Italy 51,289
Imphal (*IMP hul*), India 67,717
Inazawa (*ee NAH zah wuh*), Japan 78,180
Inchon (*IN chahn*), Korea, South 646,013
Indore (*in DOHR*), India 448,192
Ingolstadt (*ING gul shtaht*), Germany, West 72,000
Innsbruck (*INZ brook*), Austria 110,209
Inowrocław (*EE naw VRAW tslahf*), Poland 53,300
Inta (*in TAH*), Soviet Union 50,000
Invercargill (*IN vur KAHR gul*), New Zealand 50,681
Ipin (*EE PIN*), China 177,500
Ipoh (*EE poh*), Malaysia 125,776
Ipswich (*IPS wich*), Australia 61,514
Ipswich (*IPS wich*), England 121,700
Iquique (*ee KEE kay*), Chile 64,742
Iquitos (*ee KEE tohs*), Peru 57,777
Iráklion (Candia) (*ee RAK klee-awn*) (*KAN dee uh*), Greece . . 63,458
Irapuato (*EE rah PWAH toh*), Mexico 116,651
Irbid (*IHR bid*), Jordan 44,685
Irbīl (*ihr BEEL*), Iraq 90,956
Iri (*EE REE*), Korea, South 86,770
Iriga (*ee REE gah*), Philippines 75,439
Irkutsk (*ihr KOOTSK*), Soviet Union 451,000
Isahaya (*EE sah HAH yah*), Japan 65,261
Ise (*EE say*), Japan 103,576
Iserlohn (*EE zur LOHN*), Germany, West 57,800
Isesaki (Isezaki) (*ee SAY zah kee*), Japan 91,277
Isfahan (Eșfahān) (*ISS fuh han*) (*ES fah HAHN*), Iran 424,045
Ishimbay (*EE shim BYE*), Soviet Union 54,000
Ishinomaki (*ee SHEE noh mah kee*), Japan 106,681
Iskenderun (Alexandretta) (*is-KEN duh roon*) (*AL ig zan DRET-uh*), Turkey 69,259
Islāmābād (*is LAHM ah BAHD*), Pakistan 50,000
Islington (*IZ ling tun*), England 241,890
Ismailia (Al Ismā'īlīyah) (*IZ mah ee LEE uh*) (*el IZ mah ee LEE uh*), Egypt 144,163
Issy (*ee SEE*), France 50,442
Istanbul (*IS tahm BOOL*), Turkey *2,052,368 1,750,642
Itabuna (*EE tuh BOO nuh*), Brazil 54,268
Itagüí (*EE tah GWEE*), Colombia 60,318
Itami (*ee TAH mee*), Japan 153,763
Itō (*ee TOH*), Japan 63,003
Ivano-Frankovsk (*ee VAH nuh FRAHN kufsk*), Soviet Union 105,000
Ivanovo (*ee VAH nuh vuh*), Soviet Union 419,000
Ivry (*ee VREE*), France 60,455
Iwaki (*ee WAH kee*), Japan 327,164
Iwakuni (*ee WAH koo nee*), Japan 106,116
Iwamizawa (*ee WAH mee ZAH wah*), Japan 68,712
Iwo (*EE woh*), Nigeria 183,907
Ixelles (*eek SEL*), Belgium 92,860
Iyang (*EE YAHNG*), China . . . . 50,000 to 100,000
Izhevsk (*ee ZHEFSK*), Soviet Union 422,000
Izmail (*EEZ mah EEL*), Soviet Union 70,000
Izmir (Smyrna) (*iz MIHR*) (*SMUR-nuh*), Turkey 417,413
Izmit (Kocaeli) (*iz MIT*) (*KOH-jah eh LEE*), Turkey 90,061
Izumi (*ee ZOO mee*), Japan 95,987
Izumi-sano (*ee ZOO mee SAH noh*), Japan 77,000
Izumo (*ee ZOO moh*), Japan 69,078

J

Jabalpur (*JUB ul poor*), India 353,464
Jaboatão (*zhuh bwuh TOWN*), Brazil 110,000
Jaén (*hah AYN*), Spain 74,522
Jaffna (*JAHF nuh*), Ceylon 94,248
Jaipur (*JY poor*), India 474,574
Jalālābād (*juh LAL uh bad*), Afghanistan 44,952
Jalapa (*hah LAH pah*), Mexico 122,377
Jalgaon (*JAHL gown*), India 80,351
Jalna (*JAHL nuh*), India 67,158
Jalpaiguri (*JUL pie GOO ree*), India 48,738
Jamalpur (*juh MAHL poor*), India 57,039
Jammu (*JUM oo*), India 129,791
Jamnagar (*jahm NUG ur*), India 162,707
Jamshedpur (*JAHM shed POOR*), India 369,155
Janiuay (*HAH nee WYE*), Philippines 46,946
Jaunpur (*JOWN poor*), India 61,851
Jaworzno (*yah VAWZH naw*), Poland 62,000
Jelenia Góra (Hirschberg) (*yeh LEH nyah GOO rah*) (*HIHRSH behrk*), Poland 55,700
Jelgava (*YEL gah vah*), Soviet Union 55,000
Jena (*YAY nuh*), Germany, East 88,346
Jerez de la Frontera (*heh RETH day lah frohn TAY rah*), Spain 150,124
Jerusalem (*juh ROO suh lum*), Israel 262,000
Jessore (*jeh SOHR*), Bangladesh 46,366
Jhang Maghiāna (*JUNG MUG ee AH nuh*), Pakistan 94,971
Jhansi (*JAHN see*), India 161,674
Jhelum (*JAY lum*), Pakistan 52,585
João Pessoa (*ZHWOWN puh SOH-uh*), Brazil 182,000
Jodhpur (*JAHD pur*), India 252,652
Jogjakarta (*JAHK yuh KAHR tuh*), Indonesia 312,698
Johannesburg (*joh HAN is burg*), South Africa 654,682
Johor Baharu, see Johore Bahru
Johore Bahru (Johor Baharu) (*joh HOHR BAH roo*), Malaysia . . 74,909
Joinvile (*zhoyn VEE lee*), Brazil 44,255
Jönköping (*YUN CHUH ping*), Sweden 52,732
Juárez (*HWAH res*), Mexico 407,370
Juàzeiro do Norte (*zhwuh ZAY doo NAWR tee*), Brazil 53,421
Juddah (*JID uh*), Saudi Arabia 194,000
Juiz de Fora (*ZHWEEZ dee FAW-ruh*), Brazil 187,000
Jullundur (*JUL un dur*), India 256,611
Junagadh (*joo NAH gud*), India 74,298
Jundiaí (*ZHOON dyuh EE*), Brazil 119,000
Junín (*hoo NEEN*), Argentina 53,489
Jyväskylä (*YOO vas KOO la*), Finland 58,048

K

Kabankalan (*KAH bahng KAH lahn*), Philippines 59,341
Kabul (*KAH bool*), Afghanistan 449,000
Kadiyevka (*KAH dee yif kuh*), Soviet Union 137,000

Kadoma *(kah DOH mah)*, Japan . . . 141,041
Kaduna *(kuh DOO nuh)*, Nigeria . . . 173,849
Kaesŏng *(KAY song)*, Korea, North . . . 400,000
Kafr ash Shaykh *(KA fresh SHAYK)*, Egypt . . . 51,544
Kagoshima *(kah GOH shee muh)*, Japan . . . 403,340
Kaifeng *(KY FUNG)*, China . . . 299,100
Kaiserslautern *(KY zurs LOW-turn)*, Germany, West . . . 99,900
Kaizuka *(ky ZOO kuh)*, Japan . . . 73,366
Kakamigahara *(kah KAH mee GAH hah rah)*, Japan . . . 78,109
Kakinada *(KAHK uh NAH duh)*, India . . . 137,375
Kakogawa *(kah KOH gah wuh)*, Japan . . . 127,112
Kalāt-i-Ghilzai *(kuh LAHT ee gil ZYE)*, Afghanistan . . . 45,709
Kalgan (Changkiakou) *(kahl GAHN) (JAHNG JYAH KOH)*, China . . . 229,300
Kalinin *(kuh LEE nin)*, Soviet Union . . . 345,000
Kaliningrad (Königsberg) *(kuh LEE-nin grad) (KAY niks behrk)*, Soviet Union . . . 297,000
Kaliningrad *(kuh LEE nin grad)*, Soviet Union . . . 106,000
Kalisz *(KAH leesh)*, Poland . . . 79,300
Kallithéa *(KAH lee THEH ah)*, Greece . . . 54,720
Kaluga *(kah LOO guh)*, Soviet Union . . . 211,000
Kalyan *(KUL yahn)*, India . . . 73,482
Kamaishi *(kah MAH ee shee)*, Japan . . . 72,923
Kamakura *(kah mah KOO rah)*, Japan . . . 139,249
Kamarhati *(KAH mahr HAH tee)*, India . . . 155,900
Kamenets-Podol'skiy *(KAH muh nets puh DAWL skee)*, Soviet Union . . . 57,000
Kamensk-Shakhtinskiy *(KAH mensk SHAHK tin skee)*, Soviet Union . . . 68,000
Kamensk-Ural'skiy *(KAH mensk oo RAHL skee)*, Soviet Union . . 169,000
Kampala *(kahm PAH luh)*, Uganda . . . 46,735
Kamyshin *(kah MISH in)*, Soviet Union . . . 97,000
Kanazawa *(kah NAH zah wah)*, Japan . . . 361,379
Kanchipuram (Kancheepuram) *(kahn CHEE poor um)*, India . . . 92,714
Kanchou *(GAHN JOH)*, China . . . 98,600
Kanchrapara *(KAHNCH rah PAH ruh)*, India . . . 68,966
Kandahār *(KAN duh hahr)*, Afghanistan . . . 116,734
Kandy *(KAN dee)*, Ceylon . . . 67,768
Kangnŭng *(KAHNG noong)*, Korea, South . . . 64,720
Kano *(KAH noh)*, Nigeria . . . 342,610
Kanoya *(kah NOH yah)*, Japan . . . 66,995
Kanpur *(KAHN poor)*, India . . . 1,036,173
Kansk *(KAHNSK)*, Soviet Union . . . 95,000
Kanuma *(kah NOO mah)*, Japan . . . 77,746
Kaohsiung *(GOW SHYOONG)*, Taiwan . . . 663,388
Kaolack *(KOW lak)*, Senegal . . . 69,560
Kaposvár *(KAW pohsh vahr)*, Hungary . . . 54,027
Karabük *(KAH rah BYOOK)*, Turkey . . . 47,660
Karāchi *(kah RAH chee)*, Pakistan . . . 1,912,598
Karaganda *(KAH ruh gahn DAH)*, Soviet Union . . . 522,000
Karamai *(KAHR uh MYE)*, China . . . 43,000
Karatsu *(kah RAH tsoo)*, Japan . . . 74,233
Karbalā' *(KAHR buh luh)*, Iraq . . . 81,539
Kariya *(kah REE yah)*, Japan . . . 87,671
Karlsbad *(KAHRLZ bad)*, Czechoslovakia . . . 43,708
Karlsruhe *(KAHRLS ROO uh)*, Germany, West . . . 257,100
Karlstad *(KAHRL stahd)*, Sweden . . . 47,401
Karnal *(kur NAHL)*, India . . . 72,109
Karpinsk *(kahr PEENSK)*, Soviet Union . . . 41,000
Karur *(kuh ROOR)*, India . . . 50,564
Karviná *(KAHR vih nah)*, Czechoslovakia . . . 76,215
Kasaoka *(KAH sah OH kuh)*, Japan . . . 66,995
Kāshān *(kah SHAHN)*, Iran . . . 58,468
Kashgar (Koshih) *(KASH gahr) (KUH SHUR)*, China . . . 91,000
Kashiwa *(kah SHEE wah)*, Japan . . . 150,635
Kashiwazaki *(kah shih WAH zah-kee)*, Japan . . . 73,569
Kassel *(KAHS ul)*, Germany, West . . . 213,500
Kasugai *(kah SOO gye)*, Japan . . . 161,835
Kasūr *(kuh SOOR)*, Pakistan . . . 74,546
Katihar *(KUT ih hahr)*, India . . . 59,344
Katmandu *(KAT man DOO)*, Nepal . . . 122,507
Katowice *(KAH taw-VEE tseh)*, Poland . . . 292,300
Kaunas *(KOW nahs)*, Soviet Union . . . 306,000
Kavála *(kah VAH lah)*, Greece . . . 44,517
Kawachinagano (Kawachi) *(kah WAH chee)*, Japan . . . 50,338
Kawagoe *(kah WAH goh eh)*, Japan . . . 171,038
Kawaguchi *(kah WAH goo chee)*, Japan . . . 305,886
Kawanishi *(kah WAH nee shee)*, Japan . . . 87,127
Kawasaki *(kah wah SAH kee)*, Japan . . . 973,486
Kayseri *(KY seh REE)*, Turkey . . . 126,913
Kazan' *(kuh ZAN)*, Soviet Union . . . 869,000
Kazanlŭk *(KAH zahn LUCK)*, Bulgaria . . . 44,418
Kecskemét *(KECH keh mayt)*, Hungary . . . 77,484
Kediri *(kuh DEER ee)*, Indonesia . . . 158,918
Keighley *(KEETH lee)*, England . . . 55,650
Kemerovo *(KEH muh ruh vuh)*, Soviet Union . . . 385,000
Kempten *(KEMP tun)*, Germany, West . . . 44,600
Kenitra *(kih NEE truh)*, Morocco . . . 105,000
Kensington and Chelsea *(KEN zing tun and CHEL see)*, England . . . 201,720
Kentau *(ken TOW)*, Soviet Union . . . 55,000
Keratsinion (Áyios Yeóryios) *(KEH raht SEE nee awn) (AH yos YAWR yos)*, Greece . 61,673
Kerch' *(KEHRCH)*, Soviet Union . . . 128,000
Kerkrade *(KEHRK RAH duh)*, Netherlands . . . 50,206
Kermān *(kehr MAHN)*, Iran . . . 85,404
Kermanshah *(kehr MAHN SHAH)*, Iran . . . 187,930
Khabarovsk *(kah BAH rufsk)*, Soviet Union . . . 437,000
Khandwa *(KUND wah)*, India . . . 63,505
Khānewāl *(kah NAY vahl)*, Pakistan . . . 49,093
Khanh Hung *(KAHN HOONG)*, Vietnam, South . . . 59,015
Kharagpur *(KAH rug poor)*, India . . . 158,412
Kharkov *(KAHR kuf)*, Soviet Union . . . 1,223,000
Khartoum *(kahr TOOM)*, Sudan . . . 173,500
Khasavyurt *(KAH sahv YOORT)*, Soviet Union . . . 54,000
Khaskovo *(KAHS kaw vaw)*, Bulgaria . . . 57,682
Kherson *(kehr SAWN)*, Soviet Union . . . 261,000
Khimki *(KEEM kee)*, Soviet Union . . . 87,000
Khmel'nitskiy *(kuh mel NIT skee)*, Soviet Union . . . 113,000
Khorramābād *(KHOR um uh BAHD)*, Iran . . . 59,578
Khorramshahr *(KOHR um SHAHR)*, Iran . . . 88,536
Khulna *(KOOL nuh)*, Bangladesh . . . 127,970
Kidapawan *(KEE dah PAH wahn)*, Philippines . . . 61,675
Kidderminster *(KID ur MIN stur)*, England . . . 46,180
Kiel *(KEEL)*, Germany, West . . . 276,600
Kielce *(KYEL tseh)*, Poland . . . 117,800
Kiev *(KEE yuf)*, Soviet Union . . . 1,632,000
Kigali *(kee GAH lee)*, Rwanda . . . 4,273
Kilmarnock *(kil MAHR nuk)*, Scotland . . . 47,818
Kimberley *(KIM bur lee)*, South Africa . . . 103,789
Kimchaek (Sŏngjin) *(KIM chak) (SAWNG jin)*, Korea, North . 281,000
Kimch'on *(KIM chahn)*, Korea, South . . . 62,157
Kimry *(KEEM ree)*, Soviet Union . . . 53,000
Kineshma *(KEE nish muh)*, Soviet Union . . . 96,000
Kingston *(KING stun)*, Jamaica . . . 376,520
Kingston upon Thames *(KING stun up on TEMZ)*, England . . . 144,480
Kingstown *(KINGZ town)*, St. Vincent . . . 20,688
Kinshasa *(kin SHAH suh)*, Zaire . . . 507,868
Kirikkale *(kih RIK kah leh)*, Turkey . . . 58,881
Kirin (Chilin) *(KEE RIN) (JEE LIN)*, China . . . 568,000
Kirkcaldy *(kur KAWL dee)*, Scotland . . . 52,125
Kirkūk *(kihr KOOK)*, Iraq . . . 175,303
Kirov *(KEE ruf)*, Soviet Union . . . 332,000
Kirovabad *(KEE ruv ah BAHT)*, Soviet Union . . . 190,000
Kirovakan *(KEE ruv ah KAHN)*, Soviet Union . . . 107,000
Kirovograd *(KEE ruv uh GRAHT)*, Soviet Union . . . 189,000
Kirovsk *(KEE rufsk)*, Soviet Union . . . 50,000
Kirovsk *(KEE rufsk)*, Soviet Union . . . 46,000
Kiryū *(kihr YOO)*, Japan . . . 133,141
Kisangani *(KIH sahng GAH nee)*, Zaire . . . 149,887
Kiselëvsk *(KEE sih LEFSK)*, Soviet Union . . . 126,000
Kishinëv *(KISH ih nef)*, Soviet Union . . . 357,000
Kishiwada *(kee SHEE wah duh)*, Japan . . . 162,022
Kislovodsk *(KEES luh VAWTSK)*, Soviet Union . . . 90,000
Kitaibaraki *(kee tye BAH rah kee)*, Japan . . . 48,323
Kitakyūshū *(kee tah KYOO shoo)*, Japan . . . 1,042,321
Kitami *(kee TAH mee)*, Japan . . . 82,727
Kitwe *(KEE tway)*, Zambia . . . 123,200
Kizel *(kee ZEL)*, Soviet Union . . . 55,000
Kladno *(KLAHD naw)*, Czechoslovakia . . . 58,069
Klagenfurt *(KLAH gun foort)*, Austria . . . 69,218
Klang *(KLAHNG)*, Malaysia . . . 75,649
Klerksdorp *(KLEHRKS dawrp)*, South Africa . . . 199,516
Klin *(KLEEN)*, Soviet Union . . . 81,000
Klintsy *(kleen TSEE)*, Soviet Union . . . 58,000
Kobe *(KOH bee)*, Japan . . . 1,288,937
Koblenz *(KOH blents)*, Germany, West . . . 106,200
Kōchi *(KOH chee)*, Japan . . . 240,841
Kochiu *(GUH JYOO)*, China . . . 159,700
Kodaira *(koh DY rah)*, Japan . . . 137,373
Koerhchinyuichienchi *(KOH AHR CHIN YOO EE JYEN CHEE)*, China . . . 51,400
Kōfu *(KOH foo)*, Japan . . . 182,669
Koganei *(koh gah NAY)*, Japan . . . 94,448
Kohāt *(koh HAHT)*, Pakistan . . . 49,854
Kohtla-Järve *(KOHT lah YAR veh)*, Soviet Union . . . 68,000
Kokand *(koh KAND)*, Soviet Union . . . 133,000
Kokchetav *(KAWK cheh TAHF)*, Soviet Union . . . 81,000
Kokubunji *(koh koo BOON jee)*, Japan . . . 81,259
Kolar Gold Fields *(koh LAHR GOHLD feeldz)*, India . . . 167,610
Kolhapur *(KOH luh poor)*, India . . . 219,495
Kolomna *(kuh LAWM nuh)*, Soviet Union . . . 136,000
Kolwezi *(kohl WEH zee)*, Zaire . . . 54,446
Komaki *(koh MAH kee)*, Japan . . . 79,606
Komatsu *(koh MAH tsoo)*, Japan . . . 95,684
Kommunarsk *(KAH moo NAHRSK)*, Soviet Union . . . 123,000
Komsomol'sk *(KAHM suh MAWLSK)*, Soviet Union . . . 218,000
Kōnan *(KOH nan)*, Japan . . . 77,996
Kongmoon, see Chiangmen
Konotop *(KAH nuh TAWP)*, Soviet Union . . . 68,000
Konstantinovka *(KAHN stun TEE-nuf kuh)*, Soviet Union . . . 106,000
Konstanz *(KAWN stahnts)*, Germany, West . . . 61,200
Konya *(kawn YAH)*, Turkey . . . 157,801
Kopeysk *(kah PAYSK)*, Soviet Union . . . 156,000
Kōriyama *(KOH ree yah muh)*, Japan . . . 241,673
Korkino *(KAWR kee nuh)*, Soviet Union . . . 71,000
Kortrijk *(KAWRT rike)*, Belgium . . . 45,152
Koshigaya *(koh SHEE gah yuh)*, Japan . . . 139,368
Košice *(KAW shih tseh)*, Czechoslovakia . . . 145,027
Koszalin *(kaw SHAH leen)*, Poland . . . 60,600
Kostroma *(KAHS truh MAH)*, Soviet Union . . . 223,000
Kota *(KOH tuh)*, India . . . 155,330
Kota Kinabalu *(KOH tah KIN uh buh LOO)*, Mala. . . . 41,830
Kot-i-Ashru *(KOHT ee AHSH roo)*, Afghanistan . . . 49,896
Kotlas *(KAWT lus)*, Soviet Union . . . 56,000
Kottagudem *(KAHT uh GOO dem)*, India . . . 69,728
Kottayam *(KAHT uh yum)*, India . . . 52,685
Kotte *(KOHT tay)*, Ceylon . . . 54,455
Kovrov *(kahv RAWF)*, Soviet Union . . . 123,000
Kowloon *(KOW LOON)*, Hong Kong . . . 726,976
Kragujevac *(KRAH goo yeh vahts)*, Yugoslavia . . . 59,000
Kraków *(KRAH kow)*, Poland . . . 560,300
Kramatorsk *(KRAH muh TAWRSK)*, Soviet Union . . . 151,000
Krasnoarmeyskaya *(KRAHS nuh ahr-MAY skuh yuh)*, Soviet Union . . . 56,000
Krasnodar *(KRAHS nuh DAHR)*, Soviet Union . . . 465,000
Krasnodon *(KRAHS nuh DAWN)*, Soviet Union . . . 69,000
Krasnogorsk *(KRAHS nuh GAWRSK)*, Soviet Union . . . 63,000
Krasnokamsk *(KRAHS nuh KAHMSK)*, Soviet Union . . . 55,000
Krasnotur'insk *(KRAHS nuh too-REENSK)*, Soviet Union . . . 59,000
Krasnovodsk *(KRAHS nuh VAWTSK)*, Soviet Union . . . 48,000
Krasnoyarsk *(KRAHS nuh YAHRSK)*, Soviet Union . . . 648,000
Krasnyy Luch *(KRAHS nee LOOCH)*, Soviet Union . . . 103,000
Krefeld *(KRAY felt)*, Germany, West . . . 228,700
Kremenchug *(KREM in CHOOK)*, Soviet Union . . . 148,000
Krishnanagar (Krishnagar) *(KRISH nuh nuh gur)*, India . . . 70,440
Kristiansund *(KRIS tyahn SAHN or KRIS chuhn SAND)*, Norway . . 56,119
Krivoy Rog *(kree VOY RAWK)*, Soviet Union . . . 573,000
Kroonstad *(KROON staht)*, South Africa . . . 50,898
Kropotkin *(kruh PAWT kin)*, Soviet Union . . . 68,000
Krugersdorp *(KROO gurz dawrp)*, South Africa . . . 91,202
Kuala Lumpur *(KWAH luh LOOM-poor)*, Malaysia . . . 451,810
Kuching *(KOO ching)*, Malaysia . . . 50,579
Kudus *(KOO doos)*, Indonesia . . . 54,524
Kueilin *(GWAY LIN)*, China . . . 145,100
Kueiyang *(GWAY YAHNG)*, China . . . 504,000
Kuldja (Ining) *(KOOL jah) (EE NING)*, China . . . 108,200
Kulebaki *(KOO lih BAH kee)*, Soviet Union . . . 46,000
Kumagaya *(koo MAH gah yuh)*, Japan . . . 120,841
Kumamoto *(koo mah MOH toh)*, Japan . . . 440,020
Kumasi *(koo MAH see)*, Ghana . . . 249,200
Kumbakonam *(KOOM buh KOH num)*, India . . . 92,581
Kundūz *(koon DOOZ)*, Afghanistan . . . 73,645
Kungur *(koon GOOR)*, Soviet Union . . . 74,000
Kunming *(KOON MING)*, China . . . 880,000
Kunsan *(KOON SAHN)*, Korea, South . . . 112,453
Kuopio *(KWAW pyaw)*, Finland . . . 64,783
Kurashiki *(koo RAH shih kee)*, Japan . . . 339,799
Kure *(KOO ray)*, Japan . . . 235,193
Kurgan *(koor GAHN)*, Soviet Union . . . 244,000
Ku-ring-gai *(koo RING guy)*, Australia . . . 98,435
Kurnool *(kur NOOL)*, India . . . 126,522
Kursk *(KOORSK)*, Soviet Union . . . 284,000
Kurume *(koo ROO may)*, Japan . . . 194,178
Kushiro *(koo SHEE roh)*, Japan . . . 191,948
Kushva *(KOOSH vuh)*, Soviet Union . . . 47,000
Kustanay *(KOOS tuh NYE)*, Soviet Union . . . 123,000
Kütahya *(KYOO tah YAH)*, Turkey . . . 49,227
Kutaisi *(KOO tah EE see)*, Soviet Union . . . 161,000
Kuwait *(koo WITE or koo WAIT)*, Kuwait . . . 99,609
Kuwana *(koo WAH nah)*, Japan . . . 81,015
Kuybyshev *(KOO ee bih shuf)*, Soviet Union . . . 1,047,000
Kuznetsk *(kooz NETSK)*, Soviet Union . . . 84,000
Kwa Mashu *(KWAH MAH shoo)*, South Africa . . . 106,896
Kwangju *(KWAHNG joo)*, Korea, South . . . 502,753
Kyōmipo, see Songnim
Kyŏngju (Keishū) *(KYAWNG joo) (KAY shoo)*, Korea, South . . 92,093
Kyoto *(KYOH toh)*, Japan . . . 1,419,615
Kzyl-Orda *(kuh ZIL awr DAH)*, Soviet Union . . . 123,000

L

Labinsk *(LAH binsk)*, Soviet Union . . . 50,000
La Carlota *(lah kahr LOT tah)*, Philippines . . . 56,772
La Coruña *(lah koh ROON yah)*, Spain . . . 194,967
Lagos *(LAY gahs)*, Nigeria . . . 841,749
Lahore *(luh HOHR)*, Pakistan . . . 1,296,477
Lahti *(LAH tee)*, Finland . . . 89,349
La Laguna *(lah lah GOO nah)*, Spain (Canary Is.) . . . 71,067
La Línea *(lah LEE nay ah)*, Spain . . . 59,794
La Matanza *(lah mah TAHN sah)*, Argentina . . . 402,642
Lambeth *(LAM beth)*, England . . . 329,250
Lancaster *(LANG kus tur)*, England . . . 48,090
Lanchow (Lanchou) *(LAHN JOH)*, China . . . 699,000
Landshut *(LAHNTS hoot)*, Germany, West . . . 51,400
Lanús *(lah NOOS)*, Argentina . . . 381,561

Laoag *(lah WAHG)*, Philippines . . . 50,198

La Paz *(lah PAHS)*, Bolivia . . . 525,000

La Plata *(lah PLAH tah)*, Argentina . . . 330,310

Lappeenranta *(LAHP payn RAHN tah)*, Finland . . . 51,096

L'Aquila *(LAH kwee lah)*, Italy . . . 56,932

Lárisa *(LAH ree sah)*, Greece . . . 55,391

Lārkāna *(lahr KAH nuh)*, Pakistan . . . 48,008

La Rochelle *(lah raw SHEL)*, France . . . 73,347

La Serena *(lah say RAY nah)*, Chile . . . 50,251

Las Palmas de Gran Canaria *(lahs PAHL mahs day grahn kah NAHR yah)*, Spain (Canary Islands) . . . 263,328

La Spezia *(lah SPEH tsyah)*, Italy . . . 125,661

Latakia (Al Lādhiqīyah) *(LAT uh KEE uh) (ahl LAH thih KEE yuh)*, Syria . . . 85,993

Latina *(lah TEE nah)*, Italy . . . 49,331

Launceston *(LAWN sus tun)*, Australia . . . 62,181

Lausanne *(loh ZAN)*, Switzerland . . . 136,600

Leamington *(LEM ing tun)*, England . . . 44,970

Lecce *(LET chay)*, Italy . . . 75,297

Lecco *(LEK koh)*, Italy . . . 48,230

Leeds *(LEEDZ)*, England *1,730,290 . . . 506,080

Leeuwarden *(LAY wahr dun)*, Netherlands . . . 87,414

Legazpi *(lay GAHS pee)*, Philippines . . . 60,593

Leghorn (Livorno) *(LEG hawrn) (lee VOHR noh)*, Italy . . . 164,808

Legnano *(leh NYAH noh)*, Italy . . . 42,460

Legnica (Liegnitz) *(leg NEE tsah) (LEEG nits)*, Poland . . . 74,600

Le Havre *(luh AH vruh)*, France . . . 199,509

Leicester *(LES tur)*, England . . . 280,340

Leichhardt *(LIKE hahrt)*, Australia . . . 70,540

Leiden *(LY dun)*, Netherlands . . . 102,972

Leipzig *(LYPE sig)*, Germany, East . . . 584,365

Le Mans *(luh MAHN)*, France . . . 143,246

Leninabad *(LEN in ah BAHT)*, Soviet Union . . . 103,000

Leninakan *(LEN in ah KAHN)*, Soviet Union . . . 164,000

Leningrad *(LEN in grad)*, Soviet Union *3,950,000 . . . 3,513,000

Leninogorsk *(LEN in uh GAWRSK)*, Soviet Union . . . 72,000

Leninsk-Kuznetskiy *(LEN insk kooz NET skee)*, Soviet Union . . . 128,000

Lens *(LAHNS)*, France . . . 41,874

León *(lay OHN)*, Mexico . . . 364,990

León *(lay OHN)*, Nicaragua . . . 44,053

León *(lay OHN)*, Spain . . . 101,949

Lérida *(LAY ree thah)*, Spain . . . 82,319

Levallois-Perret *(luh VAL WAH peh REH)*, France . . . 58,941

Leverkusen *(LAY vur KOO zun)*, Germany, West . . . 111,600

Lewisham *(LOO ih shum)*, England . . . 281,140

Lhasa (Lasa) *(LAH suh)*, China . . . 70,000

Liaoyuan *(LYOW yoo AHN)*, China . . . 120,000

Liberec *(LEE beh rets)*, Czechoslovakia . . . 72,752

Libmanan *(leeb MAH nahn)*, Philippines . . . 52,512

Libreville *(LEE bruh VEEL)*, Gabon . . . 44,000

Liège *(LYEZH)*, Belgium . . . 155,420

Lienyunchiang *(LYEN YOON-JYAHNG)*, China . . . 207,600

Liepāja *(LYEH pah yah)*, Soviet Union . . . 93,000

Ligao *(lee GAH oh)*, Philippines . . . 53,376

Likasi *(lee KAH see)*, Zaire . . . 102,187

Lille *(LEEL)*, France . . . 190,546

Lima *(LEE mah)*, Peru . . . 2,415,700

Limeira *(lee MAY ruh)*, Brazil . . . 45,256

Limerick *(LIM ur ick)*, Ireland . . . 55,912

Limoges *(lee MOHZH)*, France . . . 132,935

Linares *(lee NAH rays)*, Spain . . . 61,935

Lincoln *(LING kun)*, England . . . 75,720

Lingayen *(LING gah YEN)*, Philippines . . . 45,321

Linhsia *(LIN SHAH)*, China . . . 50,000 to 100,000

Linköping *(LIN CHUH ping)*, Sweden . . . 70,752

Linz *(LINTS)*, Austria . . . 203,983

Lipa *(lee PAH)*, Philippines . . . 69,036

Lipetsk *(LEE pitsk)*, Soviet Union . . . 290,000

Lisbon (Lisboa) *(LIZ bun) (leezh BOH uh)*, Portugal . . . 822,000

Lisichansk *(li si CHAHNSK)*, Soviet Union . . . 117,000

Liuchou *(LYOO JOH)*, China . . . 158,800

Liverpool *(LIV ur pool)*, England *1,351,400 . . . 688,010

Ljubljana *(LYOO blyah nah)*, Yugoslavia . . . 182,000

Lobito *(loh BEE toh)*, Angola . . . 50,164

Łódź *(LOHDZ)*, Poland . . . 747,700

Logroño *(loh GROH nyoh)*, Spain . . . 79,050

Loho *(LOH HUH)*, China . . . 50,000 to 100,000

Lomas de Zamora *(LOH mahs day sah MOH rah)*, Argentina . . . 275,219

Lomé *(LAW MAY)*, Togo . . . 97,000

London *(LUN dun)*, England . . . 7,764,000

Londonderry *(LUN dun DEHR ee)*, Northern Ireland . . . 55,100

Londrina *(lohn DREE nuh)*, Brazil . . . 210,000

Longbenton *(lawng BEN tun)*, England . . . 48,650

Lorca *(LAWR kah)*, Spain . . . 62,896

Lorient *(lawr YAHN)*, France . . . 66,444

Los Teques *(lohs TAY kays)*, Venezuela . . . 47,140

Lota *(LOH tah)*, Chile . . . 60,125

Lourenço Marques *(loh REN soh-MAHR kuss)*, Mozambique . . . 78,530

Lower Hutt *(LOH ur HUT)*, New Zealand . . . 58,561

Lowestoft *(LOHS tawft* or *LOHS tuf)*, England . . . 49,850

Loyang *(LOH YAHNG)*, China . . . 171,200

Luanda *(loo AN duh)*, Angola . . . 224,540

Luang Prabang *(LWAHNG prah-BAHNG)*, Laos . . . 25,000

Luanshya *(loo AHN shyah)*, Zambia . . . 66,160

Lübeck *(LOO bek)*, Germany, West . . . 242,200

Lublin *(LOO bleen)*, Poland . . . 234,300

Lubumbashi *(LOO boom-BAH shee)*, Zaire . . . 233,145

Lucca *(LOOK kah)*, Italy . . . 88,428

Lucena *(loo SAY nah)*, Philippines . . . 49,264

Lucerne (Luzern) *(loo SURN) (loo-TSEHRN)*, Switzerland . . . 73,700

Luchou *(LOO JOH)*, China . . . 289,000

Lucknow *(LUK now)*, India . . . 690,902

Lüdenscheid *(LYOO dun shite)*, Germany, West . . . 80,100

Ludhiana *(LOO dee AH nuh)*, India . . . 301,184

Ludwigsburg *(LOOT viks boork)*, Germany, West . . . 79,500

Ludwigshafen *(LOOT viks HAH fun)*, Germany, West . . . 174,700

Lugo *(LOO goh)*, Spain . . . 70,043

Luluabourg *(loo LOO uh boor)*, Zaire . . . 140,897

Lund *(LUND)*, Sweden . . . 43,962

Lüneburg *(LYOO nuh boork)*, Germany, West . . . 59,900

Lünen *(LYOO nun)*, Germany, West . . . 72,200

Lusaka *(loo SAH kuh)*, Zambia . . . 151,400

Luton *(LOO tun)*, England . . . 155,390

Lutsk *(LOOTSK)*, Soviet Union . . . 94,000

Luxembourg *(LUCK sum burg)*, Luxembourg . . . 77,254

Lvov *(luh VAWF)*, Soviet Union . . . 553,000

Lyallpur *(LYE ul poor)*, Pakistan . . . 425,248

Lyon *(lee AWN)*, France *1,074,823 . . . 527,800

Lys'va *(LIS vuh)*, Soviet Union . . . 73,000

Lyubertsy *(LYOO ber tsee)*, Soviet Union . . . 139,000

M

Maastricht *(MAHS trikt)*, Netherlands . . . 94,986

Macao *(muh KOW)*, Macao . . . 161,252

Macclesfield *(MAK ulz feeld)*, England . . . 41,610

Maceió *(MAH say OH)*, Brazil . . . 214,000

Machida *(mah CHEE dah)*, Japan . . . 202,801

Madinat ash Sha'b *(mah DEE naht ahsh SHAHB)*, Yemen (Aden) . . . 1,000

Madiun *(MAH dee OON)*, Indonesia . . . 123,373

Madras *(muh DRAS)*, India . . . 1,927,431

Madrid *(muh DRID)*, Spain . . . 3,030,689

Madurai *(MAH doo RY)*, India . . . 464,729

Maebashi *(mah AY bah shee)*, Japan . . . 233,632

Magadan *(MAH guh DAHN)*, Soviet Union . . . 92,000

Magdeburg *(MAG duh boorg)*, Germany, East . . . 270,692

Magelang *(MAH geh LAHNG)*, Indonesia . . . 96,454

Magnitogorsk *(mag NEE tuh gawrsk)*, Soviet Union . . . 364,000

Maidenhead *(MAYD un hed)*, England . . . 44,980

Maidstone *(MAYD stohn* or *MAYD stun)*, England . . . 66,650

Maiduguri *(my DOO goo ree)*, Nigeria . . . 139,965

Maimāna *(MY mah NAH)*, Afghanistan . . . 50,990

Mainz *(MYNTS)*, Germany, West . . . 176,700

Maiquetía *(MY kay TEE ah)*, Venezuela . . . 102,154

Maisons-Alfort *(meh ZAWN ahl-FAWR)*, France . . . 53,149

Maizuru *(MY zoo roo)*, Japan . . . 95,895

Makasar *(muh KAS ur)*, Indonesia . . . 384,159

Makati *(MAH kah TEE)*, Philippines . . . 114,540

Makeyevka *(mah KAY yif kuh)*, Soviet Union . . . 393,000

Makhachkala *(mah KAHCH kah LAH)*, Soviet Union . . . 186,000

Malabon *(MAH lah BOHN)*, Philippines . . . 76,438

Malacca (Melaka) *(muh LACK uh)*, Malaysia . . . 69,848

Málaga *(MAL uh guh)*, Spain . . . 350,977

Malang *(muh LAHNG)*, Indonesia . . . 341,452

Malasiqui *(MAH lah SEE kee)*, Philippines . . . 50,730

Malatya *(MAH lah TYAH)*, Turkey . . . 105,207

Male *(MAH lay)*, Maldives . . . 11,202

Malegaon *(MAH luh GOWN)*, India . . . 163,455

Mallawi *(muh LAH wee)*, Egypt . . . 59,938

Malmö *(MAHL muh)*, Sweden . . . 245,803

Manado *(muh NAH doh)*, Indonesia . . . 129,912

Managua *(muh NAH gwuh)*, Nicaragua . . . 262,047

Manama *(mah NAH muh)*, Bahrain . . . 79,098

Manapla *(mah NAH plah)*, Philippines . . . 46,809

Manaus *(muh NOWS)*, Brazil . . . 242,000

Manchester *(MAN CHES tur* or *MAN chis tur)*, England *2,440,520 . . . 602,790

Mandalay *(MAN duh LAY)*, Burma . . . 195,348

Mandaluyong *(MAHN dah LOO yawng)*, Philippines . . . 71,619

Mangalore *(MANG guh lohr)*, India . . . 158,876

Manila *(muh NIL uh)*, Philippines . . . 1,356,000

Manisa *(MAH nee SAH)*, Turkey . . . 69,394

Manizales *(MAH nee SAH lays)*, Colombia . . . 286,908

Mannheim *(MAN hime)*, Germany, West . . . 330,900

Manresa *(mahn RAY sah)*, Spain . . . 62,670

Mansfield *(MANZ feeld)*, England . . . 55,850

Mantua (Mantova) *(MAN choo uh) (MAHN toh vah)*, Italy . . . 62,411

Manukau *(MAN oo kow)*, New Zealand . . . 104,024

Manzanillo *(MAHN sah NEE yoh)*, Cuba . . . 91,200

Mar del Plata *(MAHR del PLAH tah)*, Argentina . . . 211,365

Maracaibo *(MAR uh KY boh)*, Venezuela . . . 621,109

Maracay *(MAH rah KY)*, Venezuela . . . 178,811

Marāgheh *(mah rah GEH)*, Iran . . . 54,106

Maraş *(mah RAHSH)*, Turkey . . . 63,315

Marburg *(MAHR burg)*, Germany, West . . . 51,400

Mardān *(mahr DAHN)*, Pakistan . . . 77,932

Margate *(MAHR gate* or *MAHR gut)*, England . . . 49,210

Margelan *(MAHR geh LAHN)*, Soviet Union . . . 95,000

Marianao *(MAH ree ah NAH oh)*, Cuba . . . 454,700

Mariano Moreno *(mahr YAH noh moh RAY noh)*, Argentina . . . 59,338

Maribor *(MAH ree bawr)*, Yugoslavia . . . 94,000

Marília *(muh REEL yuh)*, Brazil . . . 103,000

Maringá *(mah ring GAH)*, Brazil . . . 147,000

Marion *(MAR ee un)*, Australia . . . 67,591

Marl *(MAHRL)*, Germany, West . . . 75,800

Marrakech *(muh RAH kesh)*, Morocco . . . 255,000

Marrickville *(MAR ik vil)*, Australia . . . 96,331

Marsala *(mahr SAH lah)*, Italy . . . 81,327

Marseille *(mahr SAY* or *mahr SAYLZ)*, France . . . 889,029

Marugame *(mah ROO gah may)*, Japan . . . 59,214

Mary *(mah REE)*, Soviet Union . . . 62,000

Masan *(mah sahn)*, Korea, South . . . 190,992

Maseru *(MAZ uh roo)*, Lesotho . . . 14,000

Masjed Soleymān *(mahs JED soh lay MAHN)*, Iran . . . 64,488

Massa *(MAHS sah)*, Italy . . . 56,988

Masulipatam *(MUS oo lih PUT um)*, India . . . 116,275

Matadi *(muh TAH dee)*, Zaire . . . 55,861

Matamoros *(MAT uh MOHR us)*, Mexico . . . 137,749

Matanzas *(mah TAHN sahs)*, Cuba . . . 84,100

Mataró *(MAH tah ROH)*, Spain . . . 68,465

Mathura *(MUT ur uh)*, India . . . 128,619

Matsubara *(mah tsoo BAH rah)*, Japan . . . 111,562

Matsudo *(mah TSOO doh)*, Japan . . . 253,591

Matsue *(mah TSOO ay)*, Japan . . . 118,005

Matsumoto *(mah tsoo MOH toh)*, Japan . . . 162,931

Matsuyama *(mah tsoo YAH mah)*, Japan . . . 322,902

Matsuzaka *(mah tsoo ZAH kah)*, Japan . . . 102,138

Mattancheri *(muh TAHN cheh ree)*, India . . . 83,896

Maturín *(MAH too REEN)*, Venezuela . . . 86,039

Mayagüez *(MAH yah GWAYS)*, Puerto Rico . . . 50,147

Maykop *(my KAWP)*, Soviet Union . . . 111,000

Mayuram *(mah YOO rum)*, India . . . 51,393

Mazatlán *(MAH sah TLAHN)*, Mexico . . . 119,553

Mbabane *(um bah BAHN)*, Swaziland . . . 13,800

Mecca (Makkah) *(MECK uh)*, Saudi Arabia . . . 185,000

Mechelen *(MEK uh lun)*, Belgium . . . 65,474

Medan *(may DAHN)*, Indonesia . . . 479,098

Medellín *(MAY thay YEEN* or *MAY duh LEEN)*, Colombia . 1,096,790

Medina (Al Madīnah) *(muh DEE nuh) (el muh DEE nuh)*, Saudi Arabia . . . 72,291

Meerut *(MEER ut)*, India . . . 227,108

Meissen *(MY sun)*, Germany, East . . . 45,571

Meknès *(mek NESS)*, Morocco . . . 185,000

Melaka, see Malacca

Melbourne *(MEL burn)*, Australia . . . 2,388,941

Melekess *(MEL uh KESS)*, Soviet Union . . . 81,000

Melilla *(may LEEL yah* or *may LEE yah)*, Spanish Possessions in North Africa . . 78,000

Melitopol' *(MEL ih TAW pul)*, Soviet Union . . . 137,000

Memel (Klaipėda) *(MAY mul) (KLY peh dah)*, Soviet Union . . . 140,000

Mendoza *(men DOH sah)*, Argentina . . . 109,122

Mérida *(MAY ree thah)*, Mexico . . . 212,097

Mérida *(MAY ree thah)*, Venezuela . . . 68,074

Merlo *(MAIR loh)*, Argentina . . . 100,146

Merseburg *(MEHR zuh boork)*, Germany, East . . . 55,986

Mersin *(mehr SEEN)*, Turkey . . . 87,267

Merthyr Tydfil *(MUR ther TID vil)*, Wales . . . 56,700

Merton *(MUR tun)*, England . . . 184,220

Meshed (Mashhad) *(muh SHED)*, Iran . . . 409,616

Mesquita *(mes KEE tuh)*, Brazil . . . 58,835

Messina *(muh SEE nuh)*, Italy . . . 258,118

Metz *(METS)*, France . . . 107,537

Meudon *(muh DAWN)*, France . . . 50,623

Mexicali *(MEK sih KAL ee)*, Mexico . . . 267,356

Mexico City *(MEK sih koh SIT ee)*, Mexico *8,589,631 . . . 2,902,969

Mezhdurechensk *(MYEZH doo RAY-chensk)*, Soviet Union . . . 82,000

Miass *(mee AHSS)*, Soviet Union . . . 132,000

Michurinsk *(mee CHOO rinsk)*, Soviet Union . . . 94,000

Midnapur *(MID nuh pohr)*, India . . . 59,532

Midsayap *(MID sah YAHP)*, Philippines . . . 46,169

Mieres *(MYAY rays)*, Spain . . . 69,044

Mihara *(mee HAH rah)*, Japan . . . 82,621

Mikasa *(mee KAH sah)*, Japan . . . 40,553

Milan (Milano) *(mih LAN) (mee LAH-noh)*, Italy . . . 1,666,300

Minden *(MIN dun)*, Germany, West . . . 51,500

Mineral'nyye Vody *(MEE nih RAHL nee-yih VAW dee)*, Soviet Union . . 55,000

Minsk *(MINSK)*, Soviet Union . . . 907,000

Miraj *(mih RAHJ)*, India . . . 53,345

Mīrpur Khās *(MEER poor KAHS)*, Pakistan . . . 60,861

Miryang *(MEER YAHNG)*, Korea, South . . . 41,689

Mirzapur *(MEER zuh poor)*, India . . . 108,691

Mishima *(MEE shih mah)*, Japan . . . 78,141

Miskolc *(MISH kohlts)*, Hungary . . . 172,952

Mitaka *(mee TAH kah),* Japan..................155,693
Mito *(MEE toh),* Japan..................173,789
Miyakonojō *(mee YAH koh noh JOH),* Japan..................114,802
Miyazaki *(mee yah ZAH kee),* Japan..................202,862
Modena *(MAW deh nah),* Italy..................147,501
Modjokerto *(MOH joh KEHR toh),* Indonesia..................51,732
Moers *(MURS),* Germany, West..................51,300
Mogadiscio *(MAHG uh DISH ee oh),* Somalia..................141,770
Mogi das Cruzes *(moo ZHEE dus KROO zees),* Brazil..................106,000
Mogilëv *(MOH gih lef* or *MAH gih LYAWF),* Soviet Union..................202,000
Mokpo *(MAWK poh),* Korea, South..................177,801
Molenbeek-St. Jean *(MOH lun bayk san ZHAHN),* Belgium..................66,309
Molfetta *(mahl FET uh),* Italy..................61,684
Mombasa *(mahm BAH suh),* Kenya..................179,575
Monaco *(MAHN uh koh),* Monaco..................1,774
Monchegorsk *(MAHN chih GAWRSK),* Soviet Union..................53,000
Mönchen-Gladbach *(MUN kun GLAHT-bahk),* Germany, West..................152,200
Monclova *(mawng KLOH vah),* Mexico..................78,134
Monghyr *(mahng GIHR),* India..................89,768
Monrovia *(mun ROH vee uh),* Liberia..................80,992
Montauban *(MAWN TOH BAHN),* France..................45,895
Montería *(MOHN tay REE ah),* Colombia..................158,202
Monterrey *(MAHN tuh RAY),* Mexico *1,213,479..................858,137
Montes Claros *(MOHN tees KLAH roos),* Brazil..................113,000
Montevideo *(MAHN tuh vuh DAY oh),* Uruguay..................1,202,890
Montgomery, see Sahiwal
Montluçon *(MAWN LYOO SAWN),* France..................57,871
Montpellier *(MAWN PEL YAY),* France..................161,910
Montreuil *(MAWN TRUH yuh),* France..................95,714
Montrouge *(mawn ROOZH),* France..................44,922
Monza *(MOHN tsah),* Italy..................84,445
Moorabbin *(moor AB in),* Australia..................109,548
Moradabad *(moh RAD uh bad),* India..................196,617
Moratuwa *(MOH ruh TOO wuh),* Ceylon..................77,632
Morelia *(moh RAYL yah),* Mexico..................161,040
Moriguchi *(moh REE goo chee),* Japan..................184,466
Morioka *(moh ree OH kah),* Japan..................196,036
Morley *(MAWR lee),* England..................43,960
Morón *(moh ROHN),* Argentina..................344,041
Morvi *(MOHR vee),* India..................50,192
Moscow (Moskva) *(MAHS kow* or *MAHS koh) (mus KVAH),* Soviet Union *7,061,000..6,942,000
Most *(MAWST),* Czechoslovakia..................54,875
Mostaganem *(maws TAH gah NEM),* Algeria..................63,297
Mostar *(MAW stahr),* Yugoslavia..................56,000
Mosul *(moh SOOL),* Iraq..................264,146
Motherwell [& Wishaw] *(MUTH ur wel [and WISH aw]),* Scotland..75,358
Moulmein *(mool MAYN),* Burma..................108,020
Mufulira *(MOO foo LEE rah),* Zambia..................69,310
Mühlhausen *(myool HOW zun),* Germany, East..................45,385
Mukachëvo *(moo KAH chih vuh),* Soviet Union..................57,000
Mukden (Shenyang) *(MOOK dun) (SHUN YAHNG),* China..2,411,000
Mukho *(MOO KOH),* Korea, South..................56,404
Mülheim *(MYOOL hime),* Germany, West..................191,000
Mulhouse *(myoo LOOZ),* France..................116,336
Multān *(mool TAHN),* Pakistan..................358,201
Munich (München) *(MYOO nik) (MYOON kun),* Germany, West..................1,326,300
Münster *(MYOON stur),* Germany, West..................204,600
Murcia *(MUR shuh* or *MOOR shuh),* Spain..................270,254
Murmansk *(moor MAHNSK),* Soviet Union..................309,000
Murom *(MOO rum),* Soviet Union..................99,000
Muroran *(moo roh RAHN),* Japan..................162,059
Musashino *(moo SAH shih noh),* Japan..................136,959
Muscat *(MUS kat),* Oman..................5,080
Mushin *(MOO shin),* Nigeria..................169,287
Mutanchiang *(MOO DAHN JYAHNG),* China..................151,400
Muzaffarnagar *(moo ZUF ur nug ur),* India..................87,622
Muzaffarpur *(moo ZUF ur poor),* India..................131,500
My Tho *(MEE TOH),* Vietnam, South..................109,967
Mymensingh *(MY mun SING),* Bangladesh..................53,256
Mysore *(my SOHR),* India..................259,907
Mytischi *(mih TEESH chee),* Soviet Union..................119,000

N

Nabadwip *(NUB ud WEEP),* India..................72,861
Nabua *(NAH bwah),* Philippines..................66,657
Nābulus *(NAH boo loos),* Jordan..................45,768
Nadiad *(NUH dee AHD),* India..................78,952
Naga *(NAH guh),* Philippines..................55,506
Nagano *(nah GAH noh),* Japan..................285,355
Nagaoka *(nah gah OH kuh),* Japan..................162,262
Nagapattinam *(NAY guh PUT in um),* India..................59,063
Nagasaki *(NAH guh SAH kee),* Japan..................421,114
Nagercoil *(NAH gur koyl),* India..................123,256
Nagoya *(nah GO yah),* Japan..................2,036,053
Nagpur *(NAHG poor),* India..................745,847
Naha *(NAH hah),* Japan..................276,380
Naihati *(ny HAH tee),* India..................58,457
Nairobi *(ny ROH bee),* Kenya..................266,794
Nakatsu *(nah KAH tsoo),* Japan..................57,461
Nakhodka *(nah KAWT kuh),* Soviet Union..................105,000
Nakhon Ratchasima *(nuh KAWN rah chuh SEE muh),* Thailand..42,218
Nal'chik *(NAHL chik),* Soviet Union..................146,000
Nam Dinh *(NAHM DIN),* Vietnam, North..................86,132
Namangan *(NAH mun GAHN),* Soviet Union..................175,000
Namwŏn *(NAHM WUN),* Korea, South..................43,998
Nanchang *(NAHN CHAHNG),* China..................508,000
Nanchung *(NAHN CHOONG),* China..................164,700
Nancy *(NAN see* or *NAHN SEE),* France..................123,428
Nander *(NAHN dur),* India..................81,087
Nanking (Nanching) *(NAN KING),* China..................1,419,000
Nanning *(NAHN NING),* China..................264,000
Nanterre *(nahn TEHR),* France..................90,332
Nantes *(NANTS* or *NAHNT),* France..................259,208
Nantung *(NAHN TOONG),* China..................260,400
Nanyang *(NAHN YAHNG),* China..........50,000 to 100,000
Naples (Napoli) *(NAY pulz) (NAH-poh lee),* Italy..................1,220,639
Nara *(NAH rah),* Japan..................208,266
Narashino *(NAH ruh SHEE noh),* Japan..................99,951
Nārāyanganj *(nah RAH yun gunj),* Bangladesh..................162,054
Nasik *(NAH sik),* India..................152,674
Nassau *(NAS aw),* Bahama Is...................80,907
Natal *(nuh TAHL),* Brazil..................228,000
Navotas *(nah VOH tahs),* Philippines..................49,262
Navsari *(nuv SAH ree),* India..................53,600
Nawābshāh *(nah WAHB shah),* Pakistan..................45,651
Ndola *(un DOH luh),* Zambia..................76,800
Néa Kokkiniá *(NAY uh kaw ki nee AH),* Greece..................83,266
Negombo *(nee GAHM boh),* Ceylon..................47,026
Neichiang *(NAY JYAHNG),* China..................190,200
Neiva *(NAY vah),* Colombia..................116,681
Nellore *(neh LOHR),* India..................122,799
Netanya *(nuh TAHN yuh),* Israel..................54,600
Netzahualcóyotl *(NETS ah wahl KOH yoh tuhl),* Mexico..................580,436
Neuilly-sur-Seine *(nuh YEE syoor SEN),* France..................70,995
Neumünster *(NOY MYOON stur),* Germany, West..................84,700
Neunkirchen *(NOYN KIHR kun),* Germany, West..................44,300
Neuss *(NOYSS),* Germany, West..................117,600
Neustadt *(NOY shtaht)* Germany, West..................51,100
Neves *(NAY vees),* Brazil..................85,741
Nevinnomyssk *(nyih VEE nuh MISK),* Soviet Union..................85,000
New Delhi *(new DEL ee),* India..................324,283
Newcastle *(NEW KASS ul),* Australia..................249,962
Newcastle upon Tyne *(NEW kass ul up on TYNE),* England..................244,880
Newcastle-under-Lyme *(NEW KASS-ul un dur LYME),* England..76,750
Newham *(NYOO um),* England..................255,130
Newport *(NEW pohrt),* Wales..................112,180
Newtownabbey *(NOO tuhn AB ee),* Northern Ireland..................50,880
Neyagawa *(nay YAH gah wah),* Japan..................206,961
Nezhin *(NEH zhin),* Soviet Union..................56,000
Nha Trang *(NYAH TRAHNG),* Vietnam, South..................103,184
Niamey *(nyah MAY),* Niger..................78,991
Nice *(NEES),* France..................322,442
Nichinan (Obi) *(NEE chee nahn) (OH bee),* Japan..................53,288
Nicosia *(NICK uh SEE uh),* Cyprus..................47,000
Niigata *(nee GAH tah),* Japan..................383,919
Niihama *(nee HAH mah),* Japan..................126,033
Nijmegen *(NY MAY gun),* Netherlands..................145,455
Nikolayev *(NEE kuh LAH yif),* Soviet Union..................331,000
Nikopol' *(nee KAW pul),* Soviet Union..................125,000
Nilópolis *(nee LAW poo lees),* Brazil..................123,000
Nîmes *(NEEM),* France..................123,292
Ningpo (Ninghsien) *(NING POH) (NING SHYEN),* China..................237,500
Niš *(NISH),* Yugoslavia..................98,000
Nishinomiya *(nee shee NOH mee yah),* Japan..................337,043
Nishio *(nee SHEE oh),* Japan..................75,193
Niterói *(NEE tuh ROY),* Brazil..................295,000
Nizamabad *(nih ZAHM ah bahd),* India..................79,093
Nizhniy Tagil *(NEEZH nee tah GEEL),* Soviet Union..................378,000
Nobeoka *(noh BAY oh kah),* Japan..................128,292
Nōgata *(noh GAH tah),* Japan..................55,615
Noginsk *(nuh GINSK),* Soviet Union..................104,000
Norderstedt *(NAWR duh shteht),* Germany, West..................54,700
Nordhausen *(NAWRT HOW zun),* Germany, East..................44,505
Nordhorn *(NAWRT hawrn),* Germany, West..................42,900
Noril'sk *(nuh RILSK),* Soviet Union..................136,000
Norrköping *(NAWR CHUH ping),* Sweden..................93,056
North Sydney *(north SID nee),* Australia..................52,290
Northampton *(nor THAMP tun),* England..................123,690
Northcote *(NORTH koht),* Australia..................59,162
Norwich *(NAHR ij* or *NAHR ich),* England..................118,940
Noshiro *(noh SHEE roh),* Japan..................55,615
Nottingham *(NAHT ing um),* England..................305,050
Nouakchott *(nwahk SHAWT),* Mauritania..................14,500
Nova Friburgo *(NAW vuh free BOOR goo),* Brazil..................49,901
Nova Iguaçu *(NAW vuh EE gwuh-SOO),* Brazil..................458,000
Novara *(noh VAH rah),* Italy..................87,704
Novgorod *(NAWV guh rut),* Soviet Union..................128,000
Novi Sad *(NAW vee SAHD),* Yugoslavia..................126,000
Novo Troitsk *(NAW vuh TRAW eetsk),* Soviet Union..................83,000
Novocherkassk *(NAW vuh chehr-KAHSK),* Soviet Union..................162,000
Novokuybyshevsk *(NAW vuh KOO ee-bih shufsk),* Soviet Union..................104,000
Novokuznetsk (Stalinsk) *(NAW-vuh kooz NETSK) (STAH linsk),* Soviet Union..................499,000
Novomoskovsk (Stalinogorsk) *(NAW vuh mus KAWFSK) (STAH lih-nuh GAWRSK),* Soviet Union..................134,000
Novomoskovsk *(NAW vuh mus KAWFSK),* Soviet Union..................61,000
Novorossiysk *(NAW vuh rah SEESK),* Soviet Union..................133,000
Novoshakhtinsk *(NAW vuh SHAHK-tinsk),* Soviet Union..................102,000
Novosibirsk *(NAW vuh see BEERSK),* Soviet Union..................1,161,000
Nowshera *(now SHEER uh),* Pakistan..................43,757
Nuevo Laredo *(NWAY voh lah-RAY doh),* Mexico..................148,867
Nukualofa *(NOO koo ah LOH fah),* Tonga..................15,545
Nukus *(noo KOOS),* Soviet Union..................74,000
Numazu *(noo MAH zoo),* Japan..................189,038
Nunawading *(NUN uh WAYD ing),* Australia..................90,686
Nuneaton *(nun EE tun),* England..................63,980
Nuremberg (Nürnberg) *(NYOOR um-burg) (NYOORN behrk),* Germany, West..................477,100
Nyíregyháza *(NYEE red yuh HAH zaw),* Hungary..................70,640

O

Oakleigh *(OHK lee),* Australia..................57,248
Oaxaca [de Juárez] *(wah HAH kah [day HWAH res]),* Mexico..................99,509
Oberhausen *(OH ber HOW zen),* Germany, West..................249,000
Obihiro *(oh BEE hee roh),* Japan..................131,568
Odawara *(oh DAH wah rah),* Japan..................156,654
Odense *(OH thun suh),* Denmark..................164,679
Odessa *(oh DES uh),* Soviet Union..................892,000
Offenbach *(AWF un bahk),* Germany, West..................118,800
Ōgaki *(OH gah kee),* Japan..................134,942
Ogbomosho *(AHG buh MOH shoh),* Nigeria..................370,963
Ōita *(OH ee tah),* Japan..................260,584
Okāra *(oh KAH ruh),* Pakistan..................68,299
Okaya *(oh KAH yah),* Japan..................60,350
Okayama *(oh kuh YAH muh),* Japan..................375,106
Okazaki *(oh kah ZAH kee),* Japan..................210,515
Oktyabr'skiy *(ahk TYAH bur skee),* Soviet Union..................77,000
Oldenburg *(OHL dun burg),* Germany, West..................131,400
Oldham *(OHL dum),* England..................109,100
Olinda *(oo LEEN duh),* Brazil..................116,000
Olomouc *(AW law mohts),* Czechoslovakia..................79,931
Olongapo *(oh LAWNG gah POH),* Philippines..................45,330
Olsztyn (Allenstein) *(AWL shtin) (AHL un shtine),* Poland..................89,700
Omdurman *(AHM dur MAN),* Sudan..................185,380
Ōme *(OH may),* Japan..................70,954
Ōmiya *(OH mee yah),* Japan..................268,777
Omsk *(AHMSK* or *AWMSK),* Soviet Union..................821,000
Ōmuta *(OH moo tah),* Japan..................175,143
Onitsha *(oh NICH uh),* Nigeria..................189,067
Onoda *(oh NOH dah),* Japan..................42,041
Onomichi *(oh NOH mee chee),* Japan..................101,363
Ootacamund *(OO tuh kuh mund),* India..................50,140
Opava *(AW pah vah),* Czechoslovakia..................50,194
Opole (Oppeln) *(aw PAW leh) (AWP uln),* Poland..................84,900
Oradea *(oh RAH dyah),* Romania..................139,902
Oran *(oh RAN* or *oh RAHN),* Algeria..................327,493
Ordzhonikidze *(AWR jahn ih KID zuh),* Soviet Union..................236,000
Örebro *(UR uh BROO),* Sweden..................79,889
Orekhovo-Zuyevo *(ah REH kuh vuh ZOO yih vuh),* Soviet Union..................120,000
Orël *(oh REL* or *ahr YAWL),* Soviet Union..................232,000
Orenburg *(OHR un burg),* Soviet Union..................345,000
Orense *(oh REN say),* Spain..................74,389
Orihuela *(OH ree WAY lah),* Spain..................44,830
Orizaba *(OHR uh ZAH buh),* Mexico..................92,517
Orléans *(AWR LAY AHN),* France..................95,828
Ormoc *(awr MAWK),* Philippines..................62,764
Orsha *(AWR shuh),* Soviet Union..................101,000
Orsk *(AWRSK),* Soviet Union..................225,000
Oruro *(oh ROO roh),* Bolivia..................91,000
Ōsaka *(oh SAH kuh),* Japan..................2,980,487
Osasco *(oo SAH skoo),* Brazil..................168,000
Osh *(AWSH),* Soviet Union..................120,000
Oshogbo *(oh SHAHG boh),* Nigeria..................242,336
Osijek *(AW see yek),* Yugoslavia..................84,000
Osinniki *(ah SEE nih kee),* Soviet Union..................62,000
Oslo *(AHS loh* or *AHZ loh),* Norway..................487,363
Osnabrück *(AHZ nuh brook),* Germany, West..................141,000
Osorno *(oh SOHR noh),* Chile..................73,627
Ostend *(ahs TEND),* Belgium..................57,359
Ostrava *(AW strah vah),* Czechoslovakia..................278,737
Ōta *(OH tah),* Japan..................98,257
Otaru *(oh TAH roo),* Japan..................191,856
Ōtsu *(OH tsoo),* Japan..................171,777
Ouagadougou *(WAH guh DOO goo),* Upper Volta..................59,126
Oujda *(OOJ duh),* Morocco..................130,000
Oulu *(OH loo),* Finland..................86,764
Oviedo *(oh VYAY thoh),* Spain..................142,769
Oxford *(AHKS furd),* England..................110,050
Oyama *(oh YAH mah),* Japan..................105,346
Oyo *(OH yoh),* Nigeria..................112,349

P

Pabianice *(PAH byah NEE tseh),* Poland..................60,800

Pābna (*PAHB nuh*), Bangladesh . . . 40,792
Pachuca [de Soto] (*pah CHOO kah [day SOH toh]*), Mexico . . . 83,892
Padang (*PAH dahng*), Indonesia . . . 143,699
Paderborn (*PAH dur BAWRN*), Germany, West . . . 68,700
Padua (Padova) (*PAD yoo uh*) (*PAH doh vah*), Italy . . . 205,057
Paisley (*PAYZ lee*), Scotland . . . 95,059
Pakanbaru (*PAH kahn BAH roo*), Indonesia . . . 70,821
Pakhoi, see Peihai
Palayamcottai (*PAH luh yum KAWT-eye*), India . . . 51,002
Palembang (*PAH lem BAHNG*), Indonesia . . . 474,971
Palencia (*puh LEN shuh*), Spain . . . 56,204
Palermo (*puh LUR moh*), Italy . . . 622,646
Palghat (*PAHL gaht*), India . . . 77,620
Palma de Mallorca (*PAHL mah day mah LYAWR kah*), Spain . . . 208,127
Palmerston North (*PAHM ur stun NORTH*), New Zealand . . . 51,893
Palmira (*pahl MEE rah*), Colombia . . . 106,502
Pamplona (*pahm PLOH nah*), Spain . . . 137,372
Panama City (*PAN uh maw SIT ee*), Panama . . . 418,013
Pančevo (*PAHN che vaw*), Yugoslavia . . . 52,000
Panevėžys (*PAH neh veh ZHEES*), Soviet Union . . . 73,000
Pangfou (*BUNG FOH*), China . . . 253,000
Pangkalpinang (*PAHNG kahl pee-NAHNG*), Indonesia . . . 60,283
Panihati (*PAH nih HAH tee*), India . . . 93,749
Panipat (*PAH nih put*), India . . . 67,026
Paochi (*BOW JEE*), China . . . 130,100
Paoting (*BOW DING*), China . . . 265,000
Paotou (*BOW TOH*), China . . . 149,400
Paramaribo (*PAR uh MAR uh boh*), Surinam . . . 135,000
Paraná (*PAH rah NAH*), Argentina . . . 124,898
Parangaba (*PAH rung GAH buh*), Brazil . . . 92,534
Parañaque (*PAH rah NYAH kay*), Philippines . . . 61,898
Pardubice (*PAHR doo bih tseh*), Czechoslovakia . . . 71,774
Parepare (*PAH ray PAH ray*), Indonesia . . . 67,992
Paris (*PAR is*), France *8,196,746 . . . 2,590,771
Parma (*PAHR muh*), Italy . . . 155,132
Parramatta (*PAR uh MAT uh*), Australia . . . 110,717
Pasay (*PAH sye*), Philippines . . . 157,800
Passo Fundo (*PAH soo FOON doo*), Brazil . . . 47,299
Pasto (*PAHS toh*), Colombia . . . 131,201
Pasuruan (*PAH soo roo AHN*), Indonesia . . . 63,408
Patan (*PAH tun*), India . . . 51,953
Patan (Lalitpur) (*PAH tun*) (*LUH lit poor*), Nepal . . . 48,577
Paterno (*PAH tehr NOH*), Italy . . . 42,935
Pathankot (*puh TAHN koht*), India . . . 54,810
Patiala (*PUT ee AH luh*), India . . . 142,568
Patna (*PUT nuh*), India . . . 414,506
Pátrai (Patras) (*PAH treh*) (*puh TRAS* or *PAT rus*), Greece . . . 95,364
Pau (*POH*), France . . . 74,005
Pavia (*pah VEE ah*), Italy . . . 74,962
Pavlodar (*PAHV luh DAHR*), Soviet Union . . . 187,000
Pavlograd (*PAHV luh GRAHT*), Soviet Union . . . 80,000
Pavlovo (*PAHV luh vuh*), Soviet Union . . . 63,000
Pavlovskiy Posad (*PAHV luf skee puh SAHT*), Soviet Union . . . 66,000
Paysandú (*PYE sahn DOO*), Uruguay . . . 51,645
Pazardzhik (*PAH zahr JIK*), Bulgaria . . . 55,410
Pécs (*PAYCH*), Hungary . . . 145,307
Pegu (*peh GOO*), Burma . . . 47,378
Peian (*BAY AHN*), China . . . 70,000
Peihai (*BAY HIGH*), China . . . 80,000
Pekalongan (*puh KAH LAWNG ahn*), Indonesia . . . 102,380
Peking (Peiching) (*PEE KING*), China . . . 4,010,000
Pelotas (*puh LOH tus*), Brazil . . . 201,000
Pematangsiantar (*puh MAH tahng-SYAHN tahr*), Indonesia . . . 114,870
Penchi (*BUN CHEE*), China . . . 449,000
Penrith (*PEN rith*), Australia . . . 60,242
Penza (*PEN zuh*), Soviet Union . . . 374,000
Pereira (*peh RAY rah*), Colombia . . . 235,468
Peristérion (*PEH ree STEH ree-awn*), Greece . . . 79,335
Perm' (*PEHRM*), Soviet Union . . . 850,000
Pernik (*PEHR nik*), Bulgaria . . . 75,844
Perpignan (*PEHR PEE NYAHN*), France . . . 102,191
Perth (*PURTH*), Australia . . . 639,622
Perth (*PURTH*), Scotland . . . 41,409
Perugia (*puh ROO juh*), Italy . . . 119,002
Pervomaysk (*PEHR vuh MYSK*), Soviet Union . . . 59,000
Pervomaysk (*PEHR vuh MYSK*), Soviet Union . . . 48,000
Pervoural'sk (*PEHR vuh oo RALSK*), Soviet Union . . . 117,000
Pesaro (*PAY zah roh*), Italy . . . 65,973
Pescara (*pess KAH rah*), Italy . . . 87,436
Peshāwar (*puh SHAH wur*), Pakistan . . . 218,691
Petah Tiqwa (*PEH tah TIK vuh*), Israel . . . 68,900
Peterborough (*PEE tur bur uh*), England . . . 66,460
Petropavlovsk (*PET ruh PAHV lufsk*), Soviet Union . . . 173,000
Petropavlovsk-Kamchatskiy (*PET ruh-PAHV lufsk kahm CHAHT skee*), Soviet Union . . . 154,000
Petrópolis (*puh TRAW poo lees*), Brazil . . . 191,000
Petrozavodsk (*PET ruh zah VAWTSK*), Soviet Union . . . 185,000
Pforzheim (*PFAWRTS hime*), Germany, West . . . 90,800
Phan Thiet (*FAHN TYET*), Vietnam, South . . . 80,122
Phnom Penh (*NAWM PEN*), Cambodia . . . 403,500
Piacenza (*pyah CHEN tsah*), Italy . . . 88,541
Piedras Negras (*PYAY thrahs NAY grahs*), Mexico . . . 44,992
Pietermaritzburg (*PEE ter MAR-its burg*), South Africa . . . 112,666
Pilibhit (*PEE lee BEET*), India . . . 57,527
Pinang, see Georgetown
Pinar del Río (*pee NAHR del REE-oh*), Cuba . . . 67,600
Pindaré-Mirim (*peen duh REH-mee REEM*), Brazil . . . 111,000
Pingliang (*PING LYAHNG*), China . . . 60,000
Pingtung (*PING DOONG*), Taiwan . . . 145,322
Pinsk (*PINSK*), Soviet Union . . . 62,000
Piotrków Trybunalski (*PYAW tur koof TRIH boo NAHL skee*), Poland . . . 58,300
Piracicaba (*PEE ruh see KAH buh*), Brazil . . . 132,000
Piraiévs (Piraeus) (*PEE reh EFS*) (*pie REE us*), Greece . . . 183,877
Pirmasens (*PIHR mah ZENSS*), Germany, West . . . 56,200
Pirna (*PIHR nah*), Germany, East . . . 42,562
Pisa (*PEE zuh*), Italy . . . 90,928
Pistoia (*pee STOH yah*), Italy . . . 84,561
Piteşti (*pee TESHT*), Romania . . . 80,854
Piura (*PYOO rah*), Peru . . . 106,400
Plauen (*PLOW un*), Germany, East . . . 81,907
Pleven (*PLEH ven*), Bulgaria . . . 79,234
Płock (*PLAWTSK*), Poland . . . 66,200
Ploieşti (*plaw YESHT*), Romania . . . 165,721
Plovdiv (*PLAWV diff*), Bulgaria . . . 222,737
Plymouth (*PLIM uth*), England . . . 246,290
Plymouth (*PLIM uth*), Montserrat . . . 1,911
Plzeň (*PUL zen ih*), Czechoslovakia . . . 148,032
Podol'sk (*pah DAWLSK*), Soviet Union . . . 169,000
Pohang (*POH hahng*), Korea, South . . . 79,451
Pohsien (*BAW SHYEN*), China . . . 50,000 to 100,000
Poitiers (*pwah TYAY*), France . . . 70,681
Polevskoy (*PAH lyif SKOY*), Soviet Union . . . 58,000
Pollachi (*puh LAH chee*), India . . . 54,369
Polotsk (*PAW lutsk*), Soviet Union . . . 64,000
Poltava (*pul TAH vuh*), Soviet Union . . . 220,000
Ponce (*PAWN say*), Puerto Rico . . . 128,233
Ponta Grossa (*POHN tuh GROH suh*), Brazil . . . 141,000
Pontevedra (*POHN tay VAY thrah*), Spain . . . 65,532
Pontianak (*PAHN tee AH nuk*), Indonesia . . . 150,220
Poole (*POOL*), England . . . 99,350
Poona (*POO nuh*), India . . . 806,351
Popayán (*POH pah YAHN*), Colombia . . . 97,714
Porbandar (*pohr BUN dur*), India . . . 75,081
Pori (*PAW ree*), Finland . . . 72,857
Port Arthur-Dairen (*PORT AHR thur-DYE REN*), China . . . 1,508,000
Port-au-Prince (*PORT oh PRINCE*), Haiti . . . 240,000
Port Elizabeth (*PORT ee LIZ uh-buth*), South Africa . . . 386,577
Port Harcourt (*PORT HAHR kurt* or *HAHR kohrt*), Nigeria . . . 208,237
Portici (*PAWR tee chee*), Italy . . . 50,373
Port Louis (*PORT LOO is*), Mauritius . . . 134,900
Porto (*POHR toh*), Portugal . . . 319,250
Pôrto Alegre (*POHR too uh LEH-gree*), Brazil . . . 889,000
Port-of-Spain (*PORT uv SPAYN*), Trinidad and Tobago . . . 93,954
Porto-Novo (*POHR tuh NOH voh*), Dahomey . . . 76,000
Port Said (Būr Sa'īd) (*port SIDE* or *PORT sah EED*) (*BOOR sah-EED*), Egypt . . . 282,977
Portsmouth (*PORTS muth*), England . . . 218,790
Port Sudan (*PORT soo DAN*), Sudan . . . 110,000
Port Talbot (*PORT TAWL but*), Wales . . . 51,310
Porz (*PAWRTS*), Germany, West . . . 78,100
Posadas (*poh SAH dahs*), Argentina . . . 70,691
Poshan (*BAW SHAN*), China . . . 806,000
Potchefstroom (*PAWCH uf stroom*), South Africa . . . 55,296
Potenza (*poh TEN tsah*), Italy . . . 46,721
Poti (*PAW tee*), Soviet Union . . . 46,000
Potosí (*POH toh SEE*), Bolivia . . . 64,000
Potsdam (*PAHTS dam*), Germany, East . . . 111,288
Poza Rica (*POH sah REE kah*), Mexico . . . 120,462
Poznań (*PAWZ nahn*), Poland . . . 455,500
Pozzuoli (*pawt SWAW lee*), Italy . . . 51,308
Prague (*PRAHG*), Czechoslovakia . . . 1,078,096
Prahran (*pruh RAN*), Australia . . . 56,493
Prato (*PRAH toh*), Italy . . . 118,219
Presidente Prudente (*PRAY zee-DAYN tee proo DAYN tee*), Brazil . . . 54,055
Preston (*PRES tun*), Australia . . . 91,668
Preston (*PRES tun*), England . . . 103,600
Pretoria (*pree TOHR ee uh*), South Africa . . . 543,950
Priluki (*pree LOO kee*), Soviet Union . . . 57,000
Probolinggo (*PROH buh LING goh*), Indonesia . . . 68,828
Proddatur (*PRAHD uh toor*), India . . . 50,616
Prokop'yevsk (*pruh KAWP yifsk*), Soviet Union . . . 275,000
Przemyśl (*PSHEH mish ul*), Poland . . . 52,400
Pskov (*PSKAWF*), Soviet Union . . . 127,000
Pudukkottai (*POO dook KOHT tie*), India . . . 50,488
Puebla (*PWEB luh* or *pyoo EB-luh*), Mexico . . . 401,603
Puente Alto (*PWEN tay AHL toh*), Chile . . . 73,810
Puerto Cabello (*PWEHR toh kah BAY yoh*), Venezuela . . . 66,253
Puerto la Cruz (*PWEHR toh lah KROOS*), Venezuela . . . 76,477
Puerto Montt (*PWEHR toh MOHNT*), Chile . . . 52,476
Puertollano (*PWEHR toh LYAH noh*), Spain . . . 56,030
Punta Arenas (*POON tah ah RAY-nahs*), Chile . . . 61,691
Punto Fijo (*POON toh FEE hoh*), Venezuela . . . 49,736
Puri (*POOR ee*), India . . . 60,815
Pusan (*POO sahn*), Korea, South . . . 1,880,710
Pyatigorsk (*PYAH tih GAWRSK*), Soviet Union . . . 93,000
Pyŏngyang (*PYAWNG yang*), Korea, North . . . 2,500,000

Q

Qala Āhangarān (*KUL uh AH hung guh RAHN*), Afghanistan . . . 55,965
Qal'a Nau (*KUL uh NOW*), Afghanistan . . . 69,970
Qazvin (*kahz VEEN*), Iran . . . 88,106
Qinā (*KIN uh*), Egypt . . . 68,536
Qom (*KOHM*), Iran . . . 134,292
Quan Long (*KWAHN LONG*), Vietnam, South . . . 59,331
Querétaro (*kay RAY tah roh*), Mexico . . . 112,993
Quetta (*KWET uh*), Pakistan . . . 106,633
Quezon City (*KAY sawn SIT ee*), Philippines . . . 482,400
Qui Nhon (*KWEE NYAWN*), Vietnam, South . . . 116,821
Quibdó (*keeb DOH*), Colombia . . . 58,402
Quilmes (*KEEL mayss*), Argentina . . . 318,144
Quilon (*KWEE lahn*), India . . . 91,018
Quimper (*kam PEHR*), France . . . 52,496
Quito (*KEE toh*), Ecuador . . . 409,967

R

Rabat (*ruh BAHT*), Morocco . . . 266,000
Rach Gia (*RAH ZHAH*), Vietnam, South . . . 66,745
Radom (*RAH dawm*), Poland . . . 152,500
Ragusa (*rah GOO zah*), Italy . . . 57,311
Rahīmyar Khān (*ruh HEE myahr KAHN*), Pakistan . . . 43,458
Raichur (*RYE choor*), India . . . 63,329
Raipur (*RYE poor*), India . . . 171,452
Rajah Buayan (*RAH juh BWAH yahn*), Philippines . . . 84,988
Rajahmundry (*RAH juh MUN dree*), India . . . 145,664
Rajapalaiyam (Rajapalayam) (*RAH juh PAH lye yum*), India . . . 71,203
Rajkot (*RAHJ koht*), India . . . 233,462
Rājshāhi (*rahj SHAH hee*), Bangladesh . . . 56,885
Ramat Gan (*rah MAHT GAHN*), Israel . . . 102,600
Ramenskoye (*RAH min skuh yuh*), Soviet Union . . . 61,000
Rampur (*RAHM poor*), India . . . 136,123
Rancagua (*rahng KAH gwah*), Chile . . . 66,288
Ranchi (*RAHN chee*), India . . . 132,277
Randers (*RAHN urs*), Denmark . . . 63,996
Randwick (*RAND wick*), Australia . . . 123,404
Rangoon (*rang GOON*), Burma . . . 821,800
Rasht (*RAHSHT*), Iran . . . 143,557
Ratlam (*rut LAHM*), India . . . 87,472
Raurkela (*ROOR kuh luh*), India . . . 90,287
Ravenna (*ruh VEN uh*), Italy . . . 120,929
Rāwalpindi (*RAH wul PIN dee*), Pakistan . . . 340,175
Reading (*RED ing*), England . . . 127,330
Recife (*ruh SEE fuh*), Brazil . . . 1,056,000
Recklinghausen (*REK ling HOW zun*), Germany, West . . . 125,500
Redbridge (*RED brij*), England . . . 246,090
Regensburg (*RAY gunz burg*), Germany, West . . . 128,100
Reggio di Calabria (*RAYD joh dee kah LAH bree ah*), Italy . . . 157,053
Reggio nell' Emilia (*RAYD joh nel lay MEEL yah*), Italy . . . 119,912
Reigate (*RYE gut*), England . . . 55,270
Reims (*REEMZ*), France . . . 152,967
Reinosa (*ray NO sah*), Mexico . . . 137,383
Remscheid (*REM shyte*), Germany, West . . . 137,400
Rennes (*REN*), France . . . 180,943
Resina (*reh ZEE nah*), Italy . . . 45,148
Resistencia (*RAY sees TEN syah*), Argentina . . . 84,036
Reşiţa (*RAY shee tsah*), Romania . . . 69,603
Reus (*REH oos*), Spain . . . 56,581
Reutlingen (*ROYT ling un*), Germany, West . . . 77,900
Revda (*REV duh*), Soviet Union . . . 59,000
Rey (*RAY*), Iran . . . 102,825
Reykjavík (*RAKE yuh VEEK*), Iceland . . . 81,026
Rezā'īyeh (*REE zah EE yuh*), Iran . . . 110,749
Rheine (*RYE nuh*), Germany, West . . . 51,200
Rheinhausen (*RINE HOW zun*), Germany, West . . . 71,700
Rheinkamp (*RINE kahmp*), Germany, West . . . 43,200
Rheydt (*RITE*), Germany, West . . . 100,600
Rhondda (*RAHN duh*), Wales . . . 95,590
Ribeirão Prêto (*REE bay ROWN PRAY too*), Brazil . . . 163,000
Richmond upon Thames (*RICH mund up on TEMZ*), England . . . 177,130
Riesa (*REE zah*), Germany, East . . . 49,746
Riga (Rīga) (*REE guh*), Soviet Union . . . 733,000
Rijeka (Fiume) (*ree YEH kah*) (*FYOO may*), Yugoslavia . . . 116,000
Rimini (*RIM uh nee*), Italy . . . 92,912
Rio Claro (*REE oo KLAH roo*), Brazil . . . 48,548
Río Cuarto (*REE oh KWAHR toh*), Argentina . . . 65,569
Rio de Janeiro (*REE oh duh juh NAY roh*), Brazil . . . 4,031,000
Rio Grande (*REE oo GRUN dee*), Brazil . . . 113,000
Riyadh (Ar Riyāḑ) (*ree YAHD*) (*ahr ree YATH*), Saudi Arabia . . . 225,000
Roanne (*raw AHN*), France . . . 53,373
Rochdale (*RAHCH dale*), England . . . 86,350
Rochester (*RAHCH us tur* or *RAHCH ESS tur*), England . . . 55,760

Rockdale (RAHK dale), Australia....83,995
Rockhampton (rahk HAMP tun), Australia....48,188
Rohtak (ROH tuk), India....88,193
Rome (Roma) (ROHM) (ROH mah), Italy....2,455,302
Roodepoort-Maraisburg (ROO duh-POORT muh RAYZ burg), South Africa....114,191
Rosario (roh SAHR ee oh), Argentina....671,852
Roseau (roh ZOH), Dominica....10,417
Rostock (RAHS tahk), Germany, East....198,396
Rostov-on-Don (rahs TAWF on DAHN), Soviet Union....789,000
Rotherham (RAHTH ur um), England....86,450
Rotterdam (RAHT ur dam), Netherlands....710,871
Roubaix (roo BAY), France....114,547
Rouen (roo AHN), France....120,471
Rourkela, see Raurkela
Roven'ki (rah vin KEE), Soviet Union....61,000
Rovigo (roh VEE goh), Italy....45,649
Rovno (RAWV nuh), Soviet Union....116,000
Roxas (ROH hahs), Philippines....49,326
Rubezhnoye (roo BYEZH nuh yuh), Soviet Union....58,000
Rubtsovsk (roop TSAWFSK), Soviet Union....145,000
Ruda Śląska (ROO dah SHLAWN-skah), Poland....140,300
Rudnyy (ROOD nee), Soviet Union....96,000
Rueil-Malmaison (RYOO AY MAHL MEH ZAWN), France....60,804
Rugby (RUG bee), England....57,190
Ruse (ROO seh), Bulgaria....128,384
Rüsselsheim (RYOOS uls hime), Germany, West....57,300
Rustavi (roos TAH vee), Soviet Union....98,000
Ryazan' (REE uh ZAHN), Soviet Union....351,000
Rybinsk (REE binsk), Soviet Union....218,000
Ryde (RIDE), Australia....88,622
Rzeszów (ZHEH shoof), Poland....77,300
Rzhev (ur ZHEF), Soviet Union....61,000

S

Saarbrücken (zahr BRYOOK un), Germany, West....130,800
Sabadell (SAH bah THEL), Spain....149,887
Safi (SAH fee), Morocco....100,000
Saga (SAH gah), Japan....143,454
Sagamihara (sah gah MEE hah rah), Japan....278,326
Sagar (SAH gur), India....85,491
Sagay (sah GYE), Philippines....71,335
Saharanpur (suh HAHR un poor), India....208,507
Sahiwal (sah HEE vahl), Pakistan....75,180
Saidpur (SIDE poor), Bangladesh....60,628
Saigon (sye GAHN), Vietnam, South....1,761,335
St. Albans (saynt AWL bunz), England....52,560
St.-Brieuc (SAN bree UH), France....50,281
St. Denis (SAN duh NEE), France....99,268
St. Denis (SAN duh NEE), Réunion....65,614
St. Étienne (SAN TAY TYEN), France....213,468
St. Gall (saynt GAWL), Switzerland....78,200
St. George's (saynt JAWR juz), Grenada....7,303
St. Gilles (SAN ZHEEL), Belgium....57,123
St. Helens (saynt HEL unz), England....120,470
St. John's (saynt JAHNZ), Antigua....21,595
St. Kilda (saynt KIL duh), Australia....60,742
St. Louis (SAN loo EE), Senegal....48,840
St.-Maur (SAN MAWR), France....77,251
St. Nazaire (SAN NAH ZEHR), France....63,289
St. Ouen (SAN TWAN), France....48,886
St. Quentin (saynt KWEN tun), France....64,196
Sakai (SAH kye), Japan....594,367
Sakaide (sah KYE day), Japan....64,147
Sakata (sah KAH tah), Japan....96,072
Salamanca (SAL uh MANG kuh), Spain....120,265
Salatiga (SAH luh TEE guh), Indonesia....58,135
Salavat (SAH luh VAHT), Soviet Union....114,000
Sale (SAYL), England....55,370
Salé (sah LAY), Morocco....89,000
Salem (SAY lum), India....278,791
Salerno (sah LAIR noh), Italy....123,589
Salford (SAWL furd), England....139,830
Salisbury (SAWLZ bur ee), Rhodesia....324,800
Salonika (Thessaloníki) (SAL uh NEE-kuh) (THEH sah law NEE kee), Greece....250,920
Salta (SAHL tah), Argentina....117,400
Saltillo (sahl TEE yoh), Mexico....161,114
Salto (SAHL toh), Uruguay....57,714
Salvador (SAL vuh dawr), Brazil....863,000
Salzburg (ZAHLTS boork), Austria....115,720
Salzgitter (ZAHLTS GIT ur), Germany, West....118,000
Sama (SAH mah), Spain....71,304
Samarinda (SAM uh RIN duh), Indonesia....69,715
Samarkand (SAM ur kand), Soviet Union....267,000
Sambhal (SUM bul), India....68,940
Samchŏnpo (SAHM chawn POH), Korea, South....54,495
Samsun (sahm SOON), Turkey....106,921
San Bernardo (SAN bur NAHR doh), Chile....62,510
San Carlos (sahn KAHR lohs), Philippines....148,900
San Carlos (sahn KAHR lohs), Philippines....73,900
San Cristóbal (SAHN krees TOH-bahl), Venezuela....141,773
San Fernando (SAHN fehr NAHN doh), Argentina....103,815
San Fernando (SAHN fehr NAHN doh), Spain....63,674
San Isidro (SAHN ee SEE throh), Argentina....196,188
San José (SAHN hoh SAY), Costa Rica....182,961
San Juan (sahn HWAHN), Argentina....106,564
San Juan (san HWAHN), Puerto Rico....452,749
San Juan del Monte (sahn HWAHN del MOHN tay), Philippines....56,861
San Luis Potosí (sahn LWEES POH-toh SEE), Mexico....230,039
San Marino (SAN muh REE noh), San Marino....4,057
San Martín, see General San Martín
San Miguel del Padrón (SAHN mee GEL del pah DROHN), Cuba....156,200
San Pablo (sahn PAH bloh), Philippines....70,680
San Pedro Sula (sahn PAY throh SOO lah), Honduras....58,632
San Remo (sahn RAY moh), Italy....55,209
San Salvador (san SAL vuh dawr), El Salvador....281,122
San Sebastián (sahn SAY bahs-TYAHN), Spain....161,944
San Severo (SAHN say VEH roh), Italy....48,443
San Vicente de Baracaldo (SAHN bee-SEN tay day BAH rah KAHL doh), Spain....113,253
Şan'ā' (sah NAH), Yemen (Şan'ā')....125,000
Sanandaj (seh nuhn DAHJ), Iran....54,578
Sancti Spíritus (SAHNGK tee SPEE-ree toos), Cuba....62,500
Sangju (SAHNG JOO), Korea, South....52,504
Sangli (SAHNG glee), India....73,838
Sanjō (SAHN joh), Japan....77,814
Sankt Pölten (zahnkt PUL tun), Austria....40,112
Sano (SAH noh), Japan....71,573
Santa Ana (SAHN tah AH nah), El Salvador....72,839
Santa Clara (SAHN tah KLAH rah), Cuba....137,700
Santa Coloma de Gramanet (SAHN tah koh LO mah day grah mah NET), Spain....91,162
Santa Cruz (SAHN tah KROOS), Bolivia....109,000
Santa Cruz de Tenerife (SAHN tah KROOS day TAY nay REE fay), Spain (Canary Is.)....180,666
Santa Fe (SAHN tah FAY), Argentina....259,560
Santa Isabel (SAHN tah EE sah-BEL), Equatorial Guinea....37,237
Santa Maria (SUN tuh muh REE uh), Brazil....137,000
Santa Marta (SAHN tah MAHR tah), Colombia....149,755
Santander (SAHN tahn DAIR), Spain....143,130
Santarém (SUN tuh RAYM), Brazil....107,000
Santiago (SAN tee AH goh or sahn TYAH goh), Chile...2,447,741
Santiago (SAN tee AH goh or sahn TYAH goh), Spain....67,675
Santiago de Cuba (sahn TYAH goh day KOO bah), Cuba....259,000
Santiago del Estero (sahn TYAH-goh del es TAY roh), Argentina....80,395
Santiago [de los Caballeros] (sahn TYAH goh [day lohs KAH-bah YAY rohs]), Dominican Republic....83,523
Santipur (SAHN tih poor), India....51,190
Santo André (SUN too un DREH), Brazil....278,000
Santo Domingo (SAHN toh doh MING-goh), Dominican Republic..367,053
Santo Domingo (SAHN toh doh MING-goh), Philippines....66,657
Santo Tomé de Guayana (SAHN toh toh MAY day gwah YAH nah), Venezuela....98,000
Santos (SAN tus), Brazil....300,000
São Bernardo (SOWN behr NAHR-doo), Brazil....61,645
São Caetano do Sul (SOWN kye TAH-noo doo SOOL), Brazil....129,000
São Carlos (sown KAHR loos), Brazil....50,010
São Gonçalo (SOWN gohn SAH loo), Brazil....316,000
São João de Meriti (sown ZHWOWN dee MAY ree TEE), Brazil....244,000
São José do Rio Prêto (SOWN zhoo-ZEH doo REE oo PRAY too), Brazil....66,476
São José dos Campos (SOWN zhoo-ZEH doos KUM poos), Brazil....55,349
São Leopoldo (SOWN lee oo PAWL-doo), Brazil....41,023
São Luís (SOWN loo EES), Brazil....213,000
São Paulo (SOWN POW loo), Brazil....5,383,000
São Vicente (SOWN vee SAYN tee), Brazil....73,578
Sapporo (sahp POH roh), Japan....1,010,123
Saragossa (Zaragoza) (SAR uh GAHS-uh) (SAH rah GOH sah), Spain....439,451
Sarajevo (sah RAH yeh vaw), Yugoslavia....227,000
Saran' (sah RAHN), Soviet Union....54,000
Saransk (sah RAHNSK), Soviet Union....190,000
Sarapul (sah RAH pool), Soviet Union....91,000
Saratov (suh RAH tuf), Soviet Union....758,000
Sarcelles (sahr SEL), France....51,674
Sargodha (sur GOH duh), Pakistan....129,291
Sariwŏn (SAH ree WUN), Korea, North....130,000
Sasebo (SAH seh boh), Japan....247,898
Sassari (SAHS sah ree), Italy....90,037
Satu Mare (SAH too MAH ray), Romania....81,235
Savona (sah VOH nah), Italy....72,115
Sawhāj (SOW HAHJ), Egypt....74,753
Scarborough (SKAHR bur uh), England....42,510
Schaerbeek (SKAHR bake), Belgium....122,389
Schiedam (skee DAHM), Netherlands....82,596
Schönebeck (SHUN uh bek), Germany, East....46,146
Schweinfurt (SHVINE foort), Germany, West....59,300
Schwerin (shvay REEN), Germany, East....96,949
Scunthorpe (SKUN thawrp), England....69,760
Seis de Septiembre, see Morón
Sekondi-Takoradi (SEK un DEE-TAH-kuh RAH dee), Ghana....110,800
Semarang (suh MAH rahng), Indonesia....503,153
Semipalatinsk (SEM ih puh LAH-tinsk), Soviet Union....236,000
Sendai (SEN dye), Japan....545,065
Seoul (Sŏul) (SOHL), Korea, South....5,536,377
Seraing (suh RAN), Belgium....41,178
Serampore (Serampur) (SEHR um poor), India....91,521
Seremban (suh REM bahn), Malaysia....52,091
Serov (SEH ruf), Soviet Union....100,000
Serpukhov (SEHR poo kuf), Soviet Union....124,000
Sesto San Giovanni (SES toh SAHN joh VAHN nee), Italy....71,384
Sétif (say TEEF), Algeria....87,581
Seto (SAY toh), Japan....92,681
Setúbal (suh TOO bul), Portugal....50,966
Sevastopol (suh VASS tuh pohl), Soviet Union....229,000
Severodonetsk (SAY vih ruh dah-NETSK), Soviet Union....90,000
Severodvinsk (SAY vih ruh-DVINSK), Soviet Union....145,000
Seville (Sevilla) (suh VIL) (say VEEL yah), Spain....622,145
Sfax (SFAHKS), Tunisia....65,645
Shadrinsk (SHAH drinsk), Soviet Union....73,000
Shahjahanpur (SHAH juh HAHN poor), India....117,703
Shakhtërsk (shahk TYAWRSK), Soviet Union....65,000
Shakhty (SHAHK tee), Soviet Union....205,000
Shanchung (SHAHN CHOONG), Taiwan....166,259
Shangchiu (SHAHNG JYOO), China....134,400
Shanghai (SHANG high), China....6,900,000
Shangjao (SHAHNG ROW), China....50,000 to 100,000
Shangshui (SHAHNG SHWAY), China....85,500
Shaohsing (SHOW SHING), China....130,600
Shaokuan (SHOW GWAHN), China....81,700
Shaoyang (SHOW YAHNG), China....117,700
Shashih (SHAH SEE), China....85,800
Shchëkino (SHCHAW kih nuh), Soviet Union....61,000
Shchëlkovo (SHCHAWL kuh vuh), Soviet Union....78,000
Sheffield (SHEF eeld), England....531,800
Shekūpura (shay KOO poor uh), Pakistan....41,635
's Hertogenbosch (SEHR toh gun-BAWS), Netherlands....80,425
Shibarghān (SHEE bur GAHN), Afghanistan....50,440
Shibata (shi BAH tah), Japan....74,459
Shibīn al Kawm (shih BEEN el KOHM), Egypt....66,290
Shihchiachuang (SHUR JYAH-JWAHNG), China....598,000
Shikārpur (shih KAHR poor), Pakistan....53,910
Shillong (shih LAWNG), India....72,438
Shimada (shi MAH dah), Japan....66,489
Shimizu (shih MEE zoo), Japan....234,966
Shimoga (shi MOH guh), India....63,764
Shimonoseki (SHEE moh noh SAY kee), Japan....258,425
Shiogama (shee OH gah mah), Japan....58,772
Shiraz (shee RAHZ), Iran....269,865
Shizuoka (shih ZOO oh kah), Japan....416,378
Shkodër (SHKOH dur), Albania....47,040
Sholapur (SHOH luh poor), India....375,900
Shostka (SHAWST kuh), Soviet Union....64,000
Shrewsbury (SHROOZ bur ee), England....53,760
Shubrā al Khayma (shoo BRAH el KAY muh), Egypt....104,139
Shumen (SHOO men), Bulgaria....59,362
Shuya (SHOO yuh), Soviet Union....69,000
Siālkot (see AHL koht), Pakistan....164,346
Sian (Hsian) (SHEE AHN), China....1,310,000
Siauliai (SHOW lye), Soviet Union....96,000
Sibiu (see BYOO), Romania....121,394
Sidi bel Abbès (SEE dee bel uh BESS), Algeria....86,581
Siegen (ZEE gun), Germany, West....58,000
Siemianowice Śląskie (sheh MYAH-naw VEE tseh SHLAWN skyeh), Poland....66,400
Siena (see EN uh), Italy....61,453
Sikar (SEE kur), India....50,636
Silay (see LYE), Philippines....60,324
Siliguri (sih LEE goo ree), India....65,471
Simferopol' (SIM fuh ROH pul), Soviet Union....250,000
Simla (SIM luh), India....42,597
Sincelejo (SEEN say LAY ho), Colombia....70,652
Singapore (SING guh pohr), Singapore....1,987,900
Sint-Niklaas (sint NIK lahs), Belgium....48,521
Sinŭiju (SHIN ee joo), Korea, North....500,000
Sirājganj (sih RAHJ gunj), Bangladesh....47,152
Sitapur (SEE tuh poor), India....53,884
Sivas (sih VAHS), Turkey....109,165
Skien (SHEE un or SHAY un), Norway....45,396
Skikda (SHIK duh), Algeria....60,535
Skopje (SKOH pyeh), Yugoslavia....228,000
Slavyansk (slah VYAHNSK), Soviet Union....124,000
Slavyansk-na-Kubani (SLAHV yahnsk nah koo BAH nyee), Soviet Union....52,000
Sliven (SLEE ven), Bulgaria....68,331
Slough (SLOU), England....92,070
Słupsk (Stolp) (SLOOPSK) (SHTAWLP), Poland....65,300
Smela (SMEH luh), Soviet Union....55,000
Smolensk (smoh LENSK), Soviet Union....211,000
Snezhnoye (snezh NAW yuh), Soviet Union....64,000
Soche (SWAH CHUH), China....80,000
Sochi (SAW chee), Soviet Union....224,000

Sofia (Sofiya) *(SOH fee uh) (SAW fee yah)*, Bulgaria....800,953
Sōka *(SO kah)*, Japan....123,269
Sokch'o *(SAWK cho)*, Korea, South....73,096
Sokol *(SAW kul)*, Soviet Union....50,000
Solihull *(SOH lih HUL)*, England....108,380
Solikamsk *(SAH lih KAHMSK)*, Soviet Union....89,000
Solingen *(ZOH ling un)*, Germany, West....175,900
Solna *(SAWL nah)*, Sweden....54,715
Songnim *(SAWNG NIM)*, Korea, North....96,000
Songt'an *(SAWNG TAHN)*, Korea, South....51,595
Soochow (Suchou) *(SOO CHOW* or *SOO JOH)*, China....633,000
Sopot *(SAW pawt)*, Poland....46,500
Sopron *(SHOH prohn)*, Hungary....44,950
Sorocaba *(SOH roo KAH buh)*, Brazil....137,000
Sosnowiec *(saw SNAW vyets)*, Poland....142,900
South Dum Dum *(south DUM dum)*, India....142,881
South Shields *(south SHEELDZ)*, England....107,210
South Suburban *(SOUTH suh BUR bun)*, India....237,592
Southampton *(sou THAMP tun)*, England....210,050
Southend-on-Sea *(SOUTH END on SEE)*, England....166,070
Southport *(SOUTH port)*, England....79,940
Southwark *(SUTH urk)*, England....293,120
Soweto *(soh WET oh)*, South Africa....592,571
Speyer *(SHPY ur)*, Germany, West....42,300
Split *(SPLIT)*, Yugoslavia....114,000
Springs *(SPRINGZ)*, South Africa....99,047
Srinagar *(sree NUG ur)*, India....325,284
Ssuping *(SUH PING)*, China....125,900
Stafford *(STAF urd)*, England....53,590
Staines *(STAYNZ)*, England....56,190
Stanley *(STAN lee)*, England....44,380
Stara Zagora *(STAH rah zah GAW-rah)*, Bulgaria....88,522
Stavanger *(stah VAHNG ur)*, Norway....81,741
Stavropol' *(STAHV ruh pul)*, Soviet Union....198,000
Sterlitamak *(STEHR lee tah MAHK)*, Soviet Union....185,000
Stettin (Szczecin) *(shteh TEEN) (SHCHEH cheen)*, Poland..331,700
Stevenage *(STEE vun ij)*, England....60,370
Stockholm *(STAHK home)*, Sweden....793,714
Stockport *(STAHK port)*, England....104,660
Stoke-on-Trent *(STOKE on TRENT)*, England....273,040
Stourbridge *(STOUR brij* or *STOOR brij)*, England....51,970
Stralsund *(SHTRAHL zoont)*, Germany, East....71,551
Strasbourg *(strahz BOOR* or *STRAS-burg)*, France....249,396
Stupino *(STOO pee nuh)*, Soviet Union....59,000
Stuttgart *(SHTOOT gahrt)*, Germany, West....628,400
Subotica *(SOO baw tee tsah)*, Yugoslavia....78,000
Suchan *(soo CHAHN)*, Soviet Union....50,000
Suchow (Hsuchow) *(SHYOO JOH)*, China....676,000
Sucre *(SOO kray)*, Bolivia....59,701
Suez (As Suways) *(soo EZ) (ess soo WAYSS)*, Egypt....260,422
Suita *(soo EE tah)*, Japan....259,619
Sukabumi *(soo kuh BOO mee)*, Indonesia....80,438
Sukhumi *(soo KOO mee)*, Soviet Union....102,000
Sukkur *(SOOK koor)*, Pakistan....103,216
Sumgait *(SOOM gah EET)*, Soviet Union....124,000
Sumy *(SOO mee)*, Soviet Union....159,000
Sunchŏn *(SOON chawn)*, Korea, South....90,910
Sunderland *(SUN dur lund)*, England....219,710
Sundsvall *(SOONTS vahl)*, Sweden....58,174
Sunshine *(SUN shine)*, Australia....76,521
Surabaja *(SOOR uh BAH yuh)*, Indonesia....1,007,945
Surakarta *(SOOR uh KAHR tuh)*, Indonesia....367,626
Surat *(SOOR ut* or *soo RAHT)*, India....355,171
Sūsah *(SOO suh)*, Tunisia....48,185
Sutton *(SUT'n)*, England....165,430
Sutton Coldfield *(SUT un KOHLD-feeld)*, England....82,040
Suva *(SOO vuh)*, Fiji....54,900
Suwŏn *(SOO wahn)*, Korea, South....170,518
Suzuka *(soo ZOO kah)*, Japan....121,185
Sverdlovsk *(svehrd LAWFSK)*, Soviet Union....1,026,000
Sverdlovsk *(svehrd LAWFSK)*, Soviet Union (Ukraine)....68,000
Svobodnyy *(svah BAWD nee)*, Soviet Union....63,000
Swansea *(SWAHN see)*, Wales....171,240
Swatow (Shantou) *(SWAH TOW) (SHAHN TOH)*, China....280,400
Świętochłowice *(SHVYEN taw klaw-VEE tseh)*, Poland....57,800
Swindon *(SWIN dun)*, England....97,840
Sydney *(SID nee)*, Australia....2,717,069
Syktyvkar *(SIK tif KAHR)*, Soviet Union....125,000
Syracuse (Siracusa) *(SIHR uh KYOOS) (SEE rah KOO zah)*, Italy....89,407
Syzran' *(SIZ run)*, Soviet Union....174,000
Szeged *(SEH ged)*, Hungary....118,490
Székesfehérvár *(SAY kesh FEH hayr-vahr)*, Hungary....72,490
Szolnok *(SAWL nawk)*, Hungary....61,418
Szombathely *(SOHM bawt hay)*, Hungary....64,745

T

Tabaco *(tah BAH koh)*, Philippines....46,416
Tabriz *(tuh BREEZ)*, Iran....403,413
Tachikawa *(tah CHEE kah wah)*, Japan....117,057
Tacloban *(tah KLOH bahn)*, Philippines....53,551
Taegu *(ty GOO)*, Korea, South....1,082,750
Taejŏn *(TAH jawn)*, Korea, South....414,598
Tagāb *(TAH gahb)*, Afghanistan....64,866
Taganrog *(TAH gahn RAWK)*, Soviet Union....254,000
Tagawa *(tah GAH wah)*, Japan....64,233
Taichou *(TIE JOH)*, China....159,800
Taichung *(TIE CHOONG)*, Taiwan....389,306
Tainan *(TIE NAHN)*, Taiwan....429,374
Taipei *(TIE PAY* or *TIE BAY)*, Taiwan....1,221,112
Taiping *(TIE PING)*, Malaysia....48,206
Taiyüan *(TIE yoo AHN)*, China....1,020,000
Ta'izz *(tah IZ)*, Yemen (San'ā')....60,000
Tajimi *(tah JEE mee)*, Japan....63,522
Tajrīsh *(tahj REESH)*, Iran....157,486
Takada *(tah KAH dah)*, Japan....75,053
Takamatsu *(tah kah MAH tsoo)*, Japan....274,367
Takaoka *(tah KAH oh kah)*, Japan....159,664
Takarazuka *(tah kah rah ZOO kah)*, Japan....127,179
Takasago *(tah kah SAH goh)*, Japan....68,900
Takasaki *(tah kah SAH kee)*, Japan....193,072
Takatsuki *(tah KAH tsoo kee)*, Japan....231,129
Takefu *(tah KAY foo)*, Japan....62,019
Talca *(TAHL kah)*, Chile....84,521
Talcahuano *(TAHL kah WAH noh)*, Chile....108,668
Taldy-Kurgan *(tahl DEE koor GAHN)*, Soviet Union....61,000
Tāliqān *(tah lee KAHN)*, Afghanistan....61,249
Talisay *(tah LEE sye)*, Philippines....46,308
Tallinn *(TAL un)*, Soviet Union....363,000
Tamano *(tah MAH noh)*, Japan....68,446
Tamatave *(TAH mah TAHV)*, Malagasy Republic....50,500
Tambov *(tahm BAWF)*, Soviet Union....229,000
Tampere *(TAHM peh reh)*, Finland....152,494
Tampico *(tahm PEE koh)*, Mexico....172,584
Tanabe *(tah NAH beh)*, Japan....63,368
Tananarive *(TAH NAH NAH REEV)*, Malagasy Republic....321,654
Tangier (Tanger) *(tan JEER) (tahn ZHAY)*, Morocco....110,000
Tangshan *(TAHNG SHAHN)*, China....800,000
Ṭanṭā *(TAHN tuh)*, Egypt....229,978
Tantung *(TAHN DOONG)*, China....360,000
Tapachula *(TAH pah CHOO lah)*, Mexico....60,620
Tarabulus (Tripoli) *(tah RAH blus) (TRIP uh lee)*, Lebanon....114,443
Taranto *(tuh RAN toh* or *TAH-rahn toh)*, Italy....197,716
Tarbes *(TAHRB)*, France....55,375
Tarlac *(TAHR lahk)*, Philippines....98,285
Tarnów *(TAHR noof)*, Poland....83,700
Tarragona *(TAR uh GOH nuh)*, Spain....69,921
Tarrasa *(tahr RAH sah)*, Spain....130,549
Tarsus *(TAHR sus)*, Turkey....57,035
Tartu *(TAHR too)*, Soviet Union....92,000
Tashauz *(TAH shah OOS)*, Soviet Union....63,000
Tashkent *(tash KENT)*, Soviet Union....1,385,000
Tatabánya *(TAW taw bahn yaw)*, Hungary....65,130
Tatung *(DAH TOONG)*, China....228,500
Taubaté *(TOW buh TEH)*, Brazil....64,863
Tavda *(tahv DAH)*, Soviet Union....49,000
Teesside *(TEEZ syd)*, England....392,500
Tegal *(teh GAHL)*, Indonesia....89,016
Tegucigalpa *(tuh GOO suh GAL puh)*, Honduras....170,535
Teheran (Tehrān) *(teh HRAHN)*, Iran....2,719,730
Tel Aviv-Yafo *(TEL uh VEEV YAH foh)*, Israel....392,100
Telukbetung *(tuh LOOK buh TOONG)*, Indonesia....133,901
Temir-Tau *(teh MEER TOW)*, Soviet Union....167,000
Temuco *(tay MOO koh)*, Chile....97,661
Tenali *(tay NAH lee)*, India....78,525
Teófilo Otoni *(tee AW fee loo oh TOH nee)*, Brazil....130,000
Tepic *(tay PEEK)*, Mexico....87,540
Teplice *(TEH plih tseh)*, Czechoslovakia....51,374
Teramo *(TEH rah moh)*, Italy....41,899
Teresina *(TAY ruh ZEE nuh)*, Brazil....198,000
Terni *(TEHR nee)*, Italy....95,072
Ternopol' *(tur NOH pul)*, Soviet Union....85,000
Tetouan *(tay TWAHN)*, Morocco....100,000
Thana *(TAH nuh)*, India....126,022
Thanjavur *(TUN juh VOOR)*, India....117,698
Thiès *(TYESS)*, Senegal....69,140
Thimbu *(TIM BOO)*, Bhutan....8,500
Thon Buri *(TAWN boo REE)*, Thailand....459,555
Thurrock *(THUR uk)*, England....123,230
Tienshui *(TYEN SHWAY)*, China....63,000
Tientsin (Tienching) *(TIN TSIN) (TYEN JING)*, China....3,220,000
Tiflis *(TIF lis)*, Soviet Union....889,000
Tigre *(TEE gray)*, Argentina....91,725
Tigri *(TEE gree)*, Afghanistan....66,714
Tijuana *(TEE uh WAHN uh)*, Mexico....227,306
Tikhoretsk *(TEE kuh RETSK)*, Soviet Union....60,000
Tilburg *(TIL burg)*, Netherlands....150,282
Timişoara *(tee mee SHWAH rah)*, Romania....195,470
Tiranë *(tee RAH nuh)*, Albania....156,950
Tiraspol' *(tee RAHS pul)*, Soviet Union....105,000
Tîrgu Mureş *(TEER goo MOO resh)*, Romania....103,790
Tiruchchirappalli (Tiruchirappalli) *(TIHR uh chuh RAHP uh lee)*, India....269,457
Tirunelveli *(TIHR uh NEL vuh lee)*, India....87,988
Tiruppur *(TIHR uh poor)*, India....79,773
Titagarh *(tih TAH gur)*, India....76,429
Tizi Ouzou *(tee ZEE oo ZOO)*, Algeria....48,888
Tjirebon *(CHIHR uh BAWN)*, Indonesia....158,299
Tlemcen *(tlem SEN)*, Algeria....71,186
Tobolsk *(tuh BAWLSK)*, Soviet Union....47,000
Tochigi *(TOH chee gee)*, Japan....78,345
Toki *(TOH kee)*, Japan....60,786
Tokorozawa *(toh koh ROH sah wah)*, Japan....136,611
Tokushima *(toh koo SHEE mah)*, Japan....223,451
Tokuyama *(toh koo YAH mah)*, Japan....98,520
Tokyo *(TOH kee oh)*, Japan...*11,408,071...8,840,942
Tolbukhin (Dobrich) *(tawl BOO kin) (DAW brich)*, Bulgaria....55,111
Toledo *(toh LAY thoh)*, Philippines....63,881
Toledo *(toh LEE doh)*, Spain....43,955
Toluca *(toh LOO kah)*, Mexico....114,079
Tolyatti *(tawl YAHT ee)*, Soviet Union....251,000
Tomakomai *(toh mah KOH my)*, Japan....269,276
Tomaszów Mazowiecki *(taw MAH-shoof MAH zaw VYETS kee)*, Poland....54,500
Tomsk *(TAHMSK* or *TAWMSK)*, Soviet Union....339,000
Tongduch'ŏn *(TAWNG DOO CHUN)*, Korea, South....60,245
Toowoomba *(too WOOM buh)*, Australia....57,543
Torbay *(TAWR BAY)*, England....100,680
Torez *(taw REZ)*, Soviet Union....93,000
Torre Annunziata *(TAWR ray ah-NOON tsee AH tah)*, Italy....58,400
Torre del Greco *(TAWR ray del GREH koh)*, Italy....77,576
Torreón *(TAWR ray OHN)*, Mexico....223,104
Tortosa *(tawr TOH sah)*, Spain....43,267
Toruń *(TAW roon)*, Poland...124,100
Tottori *(toht TOH ree)*, Japan....113,151
Toulon *(too LAHN)*, France....174,746
Toulouse *(too LOOZ)*, France....370,796
Tourcoing *(toor KWAN)*, France....98,755
Tours *(TOOR)*, France....128,120
Tower Hamlets *(TOW ur HAM lets)*, England....192,250
Townsville *(TOWNZ vil)*, Australia....68,442
Toyama *(toh YAH mah)*, Japan....269,276
Toyohashi *(toh yoh HAH shee)*, Japan....258,547
Toyokawa *(TOH yoh KAH wuh)*, Japan....85,860
Toyonaka *(toh YOH nah kah)*, Japan....368,498
Toyota *(toh YOH tah)*, Japan....125,203
Trabzon *(trahb ZAWN)*, Turkey....65,598
Trapani *(TRAH pah nee)*, Italy....77,139
Trento *(TREN toh)*, Italy....82,080
Tres de Febrero *(TRAYS day fay BRAY roh)*, Argentina....263,391
Treviso *(tray VEE zoh)*, Italy....75,017
Trichur *(trih CHOOR)*, India....73,038
Trier *(TREER)*, Germany, West....103,400
Trieste *(tree EST* or *tree ES-tay)*, Italy....276,046
Tripoli (Ṭarābulus) *(TRIP uh lee) (tah RAH blus)*, Libya....212,577
Trivandrum *(trih VAN drum)*, India....324,207
Troisdorf *(TROYS dawrf)*, Germany, West....50,300
Troitsk *(TRAW eetsk)*, Soviet Union....85,000
Trondheim *(TRAWN haym)*, Norway....126,190
Troyes *(TRWAH)*, France....74,898
Truc Giang *(TRUHK ZHAHNG)*, Vietnam, South....68,629
Trujillo *(troo HEE yoh)*, Peru....149,000
Tsangchou (Tsanghsien) *(TSAHNG JOH)*, China....50,000 to 100,000
Tselinograd (Akmolinsk) *(tseh-LEE nuh GRAHT) (ahk MAW linsk)*, Soviet Union....180,000
Tsinan (Chinan) *(JEE NAHN)*, China....862,000
Tsingtao (Chingtao) *(CHING DOW)*, China....1,121,000
Tsu *(TSOO)*, Japan....125,203
Tsuchiura *(tsoo CHEE oo rah)*, Japan....89,958
Tsuni *(DZOON YEE)*, China....97,500
Tsuruga *(tsoo ROO gah)*, Japan....56,445
Tsuruoka *(tsoo ROO aw kah)*, Japan....95,136
Tsuyama *(tsoo YAH mah)*, Japan....76,368
Tübingen *(TYOO bing un)*, Germany, West....56,000
Tucumán *(TOO koo MAHN)*, Argentina....271,546
Tuguegarao *(TOO gay gah RAH oh)*, Philippines....43,074
Tula *(TOO luh)*, Soviet Union....462,000
Tuluá *(too LWAH)*, Colombia....56,539
Tulun *(too LOON)*, Soviet Union....48,000
Tunbridge Wells *(TUN brij WELZ)*, England....43,930
Tunchi *(TOON CHEE)*, China....50,000 to 100,000
Tunghua *(TOONG HWAH)*, China....129,100
Tunis *(TYOO nis)*, Tunisia....662,000
Tunja *(TOON hah)*, Colombia....84,289
Turin (Torino) *(TYOOR in* or *tyoo RIN) (toh REE no)*, Italy....1,116,631
Turku *(TOOR koo)*, Finland....151,970
Tuticorin *(TOO tih kuh RIN)*, India....140,291
Tuxtla *(TOOS tlah)*, Mexico....66,851
Tuy Hoa *(TWEE HOH ah)*, Vietnam, South....62,212
Tuzla *(TOOZ lah)*, Yugoslavia....59,000
Tychy *(TEE kee)*, Poland....68,000
Tynemouth *(TINE mouth)*, England....72,790
Tyumen' *(tyoo MEN)*, Soviet Union....269,000
Tzukung *(DZUH GOONG)*, China....291,300
Tzupo, see Poshan

U

Ube *(OO bay)*, Japan . . . 152,935
Uberaba *(oo buh RAH buh)*, Brazil . . . 72,053
Uberlândia *(OO bur LUN dyuh)*, Brazil . . . 70,719
Uccle *(YOO kluh)*, Belgium . . . 75,915
Udaipur *(oo DYE poor)*, India . . . 124,768
Udine *(OO dee nay)*, Italy . . . 91,895
Ueda *(oo AY dah)*, Japan . . . 93,198
Ueno *(oo AY noh)*, Japan . . . 57,666
Ufa *(oo FAH)*, Soviet Union . . . 773,000
Ŭijŏngbu *(OO ee JAWNG boo)*, Korea, South . . . 94,518
Uitenhage *(YOO tun hayg* or *OY tun hah kuh)*, South Africa . . . 69,048
Uji *(OO jee)*, Japan . . . 103,497
Ujjain *(OO jine)*, India . . . 153,243
Ukhta *(ook TAH)*, Soviet Union . . . 63,000
Ulan Bator (Urga) *(OO lahn BAH tohr) (OOR guh)*, Mongolia . . . 195,300
Ulan-Ude *(oo LAHN oo DEH)*, Soviet Union . . . 254,000
Ulhasnagar *(OOL hus NUG ur)*, India . . . 124,797
Ulm *(OOLM)*, Germany, West . . . 92,500
Ulsan *(OOL SAHN)*, Korea, South . . . 159,340
Ul'yanovsk *(ool YAH nufsk)*, Soviet Union . . . 351,000
Uman' *(OO mun)*, Soviet Union . . . 63,000
Unna *(OO nah)*, Germany, West . . . 50,400
Uppsala *(UP SAH luh)*, Sweden . . . 84,272
Ural'sk *(oo RAHLSK)*, Soviet Union . . . 134,000
Urawa *(oo RAH wah)*, Japan . . . 269,397
Urfa *(oor FAH)*, Turkey . . . 72,873
Urgench *(oor GENCH)*, Soviet Union . . . 76,000
Uruapan *(oor RWAH pahn)*, Mexico . . . 82,667
Uruguaiana *(oo roo gwuh YUN uh)*, Brazil . . . 48,358
Urumchi *(oo ROOM chee)*, China . . . 275,000
Usol'ye-Sibirskoye *(oo SAWL yeh sih-BEER skuh yuh)*, Soviet Union . . . 87,000
Ussuriysk *(oo soo REESK)*, Soviet Union . . . 128,000
Ust'-Kamenogorsk *(OOST KAH mih nuh GAWRSK)*, Soviet Union . . . 230,000
Ústí nad Labem *(OOS tee nahd LAH-bem)*, Czechoslovakia . . . 72,299
Utrecht *(YOO trekt)*, Netherlands . . . 274,388
Utrera *(oo TRAY rah)*, Spain . . . 41,126
Utsunomiya *(oo tsoo NOH mee yah)*, Japan . . . 301,231
Uwajima *(oo WAH jih mah)*, Japan . . . 64,262
Uzhgorod *(OOZH guh rut)*, Soviet Union . . . 65,000
Uzlovaya *(oo zluh VAH yuh)*, Soviet Union . . . 62,000

V

Vaasa *(VAH sah)*, Finland . . . 49,583
Vaduz *(vah DOOTS)*, Liechtenstein . . . 3,957
Valdivia *(val DIV ee uh)*, Chile . . . 86,207
Valence *(va LAHNS)*, France . . . 62,358
Valencia *(vuh LEN shuh)*, Spain . . . 624,227
Valencia *(vuh LEN shuh)*, Venezuela . . . 210,222
Valenciennes *(vuh LEN see EN)*, France . . . 46,626
Valera *(vah LAY rah)*, Venezuela . . . 65,263
Valladolid *(VAL uh duh LID)*, Spain . . . 211,795
Valledupar *(VAH yay doo PAHR)*, Colombia . . . 128,655
Valletta *(vuh LET uh)*, Malta . . . 17,679
Valparai *(VAL puh RYE)*, India . . . 80,023
Valparaíso *(VAHL pah rah EE soh)*, Chile . . . 286,108
Varese *(vah RAY zay)*, Italy . . . 66,963
Varna *(VAHR nah)*, Bulgaria . . . 180,062
Västerås *(VES tur OHS)*, Sweden . . . 85,007
Velbert *(FEL burt)*, Germany, West . . . 57,000
Velikiye Luki *(veh LEE kee uh LOO kee)*, Soviet Union . . . 85,000
Vellore *(vuh LOHR)*, India . . . 118,631
Velsen *(VEL zuhn)*, Netherlands . . . 67,864
Venice (Venezia) *(VEN is) (veh NEH tsyah)*, Italy . . . 360,241
Venlo *(VEN loh)*, Netherlands . . . 61,675
Veracruz *(VAIR uh KROOZ* or *BAY rah KROOS)*, Mexico . . . 214,072
Veraval *(veh RAH vul)*, India . . . 46,637
Vercelli *(vehr CHEL lee)*, Italy . . . 50,907
Vereeniging *(vur AY nih ging)*, South Africa . . . 169,553
Verona *(vuh RO nuh)*, Italy . . . 230,907
Versailles *(vehr SY* or *vur-SAYLZ)*, France . . . 90,829
Viareggio *(vyah RAYD joh)*, Italy . . . 47,323
Vicente López *(vee SEN tay LOH pes)*, Argentina . . . 250,823
Vicenza *(vee CHEN tsah)*, Italy . . . 101,551
Vichuga *(VEE choo guh)*, Soviet Union . . . 53,000
Victoria *(vik TOHR ee uh)*, Hong Kong . . . 674,962
Vienna (Wien) *(vee EN uh) (VEEN)*, Austria . . . 1,640,106
Vientiane *(vyen TYAHN)*, Laos . . . 162,300
Viersen *(FEER zuhn)*, Germany, West . . . 84,000
Vigevano *(vee JEH vah noh)*, Italy . . . 57,069
Vigo *(VEE goh)*, Spain . . . 191,816
Vijayapuri *(vih JAH yuh POOR ee)*, India . . . 55,300
Vijayawada (Vijayavada) *(VEE jah yah VAH dah)*, India . . . 274,224
Villa de Guadalupe Hidalgo *(VEE yah day GWAH thah LOO pay ee THAHL goh)*, Mexico . . . 141,683
Villa Nueva *(VEE yah NWAY vah)*, Argentina . . . 85,718
Villahermosa *(VEE yah ehr MOH sah)*, Mexico . . . 99,565
Villavicencio *(VEE yah vee SEN syoh)*, Colombia . . . 75,425
Villejuif *(VEEL ZHWEEF)*, France . . . 51,120
Villeurbanne *(VEEL YOOR BAHN)*, France . . . 119,879
Vilnius *(VEEL nee oos)*, Soviet Union . . . 372,000
Viña del Mar *(VEE nyah del MAHR)*, Chile . . . 145,658
Vincennes *(vin SENZ)*, France . . . 49,143
Vinnitsa *(VIN it suh)*, Soviet Union . . . 211,000
Virudhunagar *(VIHR oo doo NUG ur)*, India . . . 54,827
Vishakhapatnam (Visakhapatnam) *(vih SAH kuh PUT num)*, India . . . 228,845
Vitarte *(vee TAHR tay)*, Peru . . . 62,971
Vitebsk *(VEE tepsk)*, Soviet Union . . . 231,000
Viterbo *(vee TEHR boh)*, Italy . . . 50,047
Vitória *(vee TAWR yuh)*, Brazil . . . 121,000
Vitoria *(vee TOHR yah)*, Spain . . . 123,921
Vitória da Conquista *(vee TAWR yuh duh kohng KEE stuh)*, Brazil . 46,778
Vitorino Freire *(vik tuh REE noh FRAY ree)*, Brazil . . . 104,000
Vitry-sur-Seine *(VEE TREE syoor SEN)*, France . . . 77,846
Vittoria *(veet TAW ree ah)*, Italy . . . 45,035
Vizianagram *(VIZ ee uh NUG rum)*, India . . . 76,808
Vlaardingen *(VLAHR ding un)*, Netherlands . . . 75,654
Vladimir *(VLAD ih mihr* or *vlah-DEE mihr)*, Soviet Union . . . 234,000
Vladivostok *(VLAH dih vahs TAWK)*, Soviet Union . . . 442,000
Vlorë *(VLOH ruh)*, Albania . . . 46,905
Volgograd (Stalingrad) *(VAWL guh-graht) (STAH lin grad)*, Soviet Union . . . 818,000
Vologda *(VAW lug duh)*, Soviet Union . . . 178,000
Vólos *(VAW laws)*, Greece . . . 49,221
Vol'sk *(VAWLSK)*, Soviet Union . . . 69,000
Volta Redonda *(VAWL tuh ree DOHN-duh)*, Brazil . . . 113,000
Volzhskiy *(VAWLSH skee)*, Soviet Union . . . 142,000
Vorkuta *(VAHR koo TAH)*, Soviet Union . . . 90,000
Voronezh *(vuh RAW nesh)*, Soviet Union . . . 660,000
Voroshilovgrad (Lugansk) *(vaw raw SHEE luhf GRAHT) (loo GAHNSK)*, Soviet Union . . . 382,000
Voskresensk *(vahs kreh SENSK)*, Soviet Union . . . 67,000
Votkinsk *(VAWT kinsk)*, Soviet Union . . . 74,000
Vung Tau *(VUNG TAH oo)*, Vietnam, South . . . 79,270
Vyborg *(VEE bawrg)*, Soviet Union . . . 65,000
Vyshniy Volochëk *(VISH nee VAH luh-CHAWK)*, Soviet Union . . . 74,000

W

Wad Madanī *(WAHD meh DAH nee)*, Sudan . . . 56,000
Wakayama *(wah kah YAH mah)*, Japan . . . 365,267
Wakefield *(WAYK feeld)*, England . . . 60,200
Wałbrzych (Waldenburg) *(VAHL-bzhik) (VAHL dun boork)*, Poland . . . 126,200
Wallasey *(WAHL uh see)*, England . . . 101,990
Wallsend *(WAWLZ END)*, England . . . 47,250
Walsall *(WAWL sawl* or *WAWL sul)*, England . . . 184,060
Waltham Forest *(WAWL thum FAWR-est)*, England . . . 236,900
Walton and Weybridge *(WAWL tun and WAY brij)*, England . . . 51,880
Wandsworth *(WAHNZ wurth)*, England . . . 321,720
Wanhsien *(WAHN SHYEN)*, China . . . 50,000 to 100,000
Wanne-Eickel *(VAHN uh I kul)*, Germany, West . . . 99,900
Warabi *(wah RAH bee)*, Japan . . . 77,225
Warangal *(WUR ung gul)*, India . . . 170,660
Warley *(WAWR lee)*, England . . . 168,970
Warrington *(WAWR ing tun)*, England . . . 71,830
Warsaw (Warszawa) *(WAWR saw) (vahr SHAH vah)*, Poland . . . 1,273,600
Watford *(WAHT furd)*, England . . . 76,730
Wattenscheid *(VAHT un shite)*, Germany, West . . . 80,500
Wattrelos *(vah truh LOH)*, France . . . 43,754
Waverley *(WAY vur lee)*, Australia . . . 68,192
Waverley *(WAY vur lee)*, Australia . . . 96,999
Weifang *(WAY FAHNG)*, China . . . 148,900
Weimar *(VYE mahr)*, Germany, East . . . 63,689
Weissenfels *(VISE un fels)*, Germany, East . . . 46,120
Welkom *(WEL kawm)*, South Africa . . . 66,217
Wellington *(WEL ing tun)*, New Zealand . . . 135,667
Welwyn Garden City *(WEL un GAHR-dun SIT ee)*, England . . . 41,150
Wenchow (Wenchou) *(WUN JOH)*, China . . . 201,600
West Bromwich *(WEST BRUM ij)*, England . . . 172,350
Westminster, City of *(WEST MIN stur)*, England . . . 243,960
Weston-super-Mare *(WES tun SOO-pur MAIR)*, England . . . 47,790
Weymouth & Melcombe Regis *(WAY-muth and MEL kum REE jis)*, England . . . 42,130
Widnes *(WID nus)*, England . . . 53,660
Wiesbaden *(VEES BAH dun)*, Germany, West . . . 260,600
Wigan *(WIG un)*, England . . . 79,410
Wilhelmshaven *(VIL helms HAH fun)*, Germany, West . . . 103,200
Willemstad *(VIL um staht)*, Netherlands Antilles . . . 43,547
Willoughby *(WILL uh bee)*, Australia . . . 53,758
Wilrijk *(VIL rike)*, Belgium . . . 41,388
Winterthur *(VIN tur toor)*, Switzerland . . . 91,000
Wismar *(VISS mahr)*, Germany, East . . . 56,057
Witten *(VIT un)*, Germany, West . . . 97,800
Wittenberg *(WIT un burg)*, Germany, East . . . 47,151
Włocławek *(vlaw TSLAH vek)*, Poland . . . 72,400
Woking *(WOH king)*, England (London) . . . 77,220
Wolfsburg *(VAWLFS boork)*, Germany, West . . . 89,400
Wollongong *(WOOL un gawng)*, Australia . . . 185,890
Wolverhampton *(WOOL vur HAMP tun)*, England . . . 264,840
Wŏnju *(WAHN joo)*, Korea, South . . . 111,972
Wonsan *(WUN sahn)*, Korea, North . . . 350,000
Woodville *(WOOD vil)*, Australia . . . 72,703
Worcester *(WOOS tur)*, England . . . 71,220
Worms *(VAWRMS)*, Germany, West . . . 78,000
Worthing *(WUR thing)*, England . . . 83,080
Wrocław (Breslau) *(VRAW tslahf) (BRES lou)*, Poland . . . 509,400
Wuchow (Wuchou) *(WOO JOH)*, China . . . 110,800
Wuhan *(WOO HAHN)*, China . . . 2,146,000
Wuhsi *(WOO SHEE)*, China . . . 613,000
Wuhsing *(WOO SHING)*, China . . . 63,000
Wuhu *(WOO HOO)*, China . . . 242,100
Wulanhaote, see Koerhchinyuichienchi
Wuppertal *(VOOP ur tahl)*, Germany, West . . . 414,700
Wutungchiao *(WOO TUNG CHYOU)*, China . . . 199,100
Würzburg *(WURTS burg)*, Germany, West . . . 120,300

Y

Yaan *(YAH AHN)*, China . . . 55,200
Yaizu *(YIE zoo)*, Japan . . . 82,737
Yakutsk *(yuh KOOTSK)*, Soviet Union . . . 108,000
Yalta *(YAHL tuh* or *YAWL tuh)*, Soviet Union . . . 62,000
Yamagata *(yah MAH gah tah)*, Japan . . . 204,127
Yamaguchi *(yah mah GOO chee)*, Japan . . . 101,041
Yamato *(yah MAH toh)*, Japan . . . 102,760
Yambol *(YAHM bawl)*, Bulgaria . . . 58,405
Yamunanagar *(yuh MOU nuh NUG ur)*, India . . . 51,700
Yangchou *(YAHNG JOH)*, China . . . 180,200
Yangchuan *(YAHNG CHYOO EN)*, China . . . 177,400
Yangi-Yul' *(YAHN gee YOOL)*, Soviet Union . . . 55,000
Yangmingshan *(YAHNG MING-SHAHN)*, Taiwan . . . 145,155
Yao *(YAH oh)*, Japan . . . 227,778
Yaoundé *(YAH OON DAY)*, Cameroon . . . 101,000
Yaroslavl' *(YAHR uh SLAH vul)*, Soviet Union . . . 517,000
Yatsushiro *(yaht SOO shih roh)*, Japan . . . 101,866
Yazd (Yezd) *(YAHZD) (YEZD)*, Iran . . . 93,241
Yegor'yevsk *(yih GAWR yifsk)*, Soviet Union . . . 67,000
Yelets *(yeh LETS)*, Soviet Union . . . 101,000
Yenakiyevo *(YEH nuh KEE yih vuh)*, Soviet Union . . . 92,000
Yencheng *(YEN CHUNG)*, China . . . 50,000
Yenchi *(YEN JEE)*, China . . . 70,000
Yerevan *(YEH reh VAHN)*, Soviet Union . . . 767,000
Yessentuki *(YEH sin too KEE)*, Soviet Union . . . 65,000
Yevpatoriya *(YEF pah TAW ree yuh)*, Soviet Union . . . 79,000
Yeysk *(YAYSK)*, Soviet Union . . . 64,000
Yinchuan *(YIN CHWAHN)*, China . . . 84,000
Yingkou *(YING KOH)*, China . . . 131,400
Yokkaichi *(yohk KYE chee)*, Japan . . . 229,234
Yokohama *(YOH kuh HAH muh)*, Japan . . . 2,328,264
Yokosuka *(yoh KOH soo kah)*, Japan . . . 347,576
Yonago *(yoh NAH goh)*, Japan . . . 109,096
Yonezawa *(yoh NAY zah wah)*, Japan . . . 69,871
York *(YAWRK)*, England . . . 108,600
Yoshkar-Ola *(yahsh KAHR ah LAH)*, Soviet Union . . . 166,000
Yŏsu *(YOH soo)*, Korea, South . . . 113,651
Yūbari *(YOO bah ree)*, Japan . . . 69,871
Yurga *(YOOR guh)*, Soviet Union . . . 62,000
Yutzu *(YOO TSUH)*, China . . . 60,000
Yuzhno-Sakhalinsk *(YOOZH nuh SAH-kuh LINSK)*, Soviet Union . . 106,000

Z

Zaandam *(zahn DAHM)*, Netherlands . . . 58,312
Zabrze (Hindenburg) *(ZAH bzheh) (HIN dun burg)*, Poland . . . 199,300
Zagorsk *(zah GAWRSK)*, Soviet Union . . . 92,000
Zagreb *(ZAH greb)*, Yugoslavia . . . 503,000
Zaḥlah (Zahle) *(ZAH luh)*, Lebanon . . . 53,121
Zamboanga *(SAHM boh AHNG gah)*, Philippines . . . 158,000
Zamora *(sah MOH rah* or *thah MOH-rah)*, Spain . . . 47,152
Zanjān *(zahn JAHN)*, Iran . . . 58,714
Zanzibar *(ZAN zuh bahr)*, Tanzania . . . 57,923
Zaporozh'ye *(ZAH puh RAWZH yuh)*, Soviet Union . . . 658,000
Zaria *(ZAHR ee uh)*, Nigeria . . . 192,706
Zeist *(ZYSTE)*, Netherlands . . . 55,950
Zeitz *(TSYTS)*, Germany, East . . . 46,736
Zelënodol'sk *(zuh LEH nuh DAWLSK)*, Soviet Union . . . 73,000
Zenica *(ZEH ni tsah)*, Yugoslavia . . . 54,000
Zhdanov *(ZHDAH nuf)*, Soviet Union . . . 417,000
Zhigulevsk *(zhih goo LYAWFSK)*, Soviet Union . . . 52,000
Zhitomir *(zhih TAW mihr)*, Soviet Union . . . 161,000
Zhukovka *(ZHOO kuf kuh)*, Soviet Union . . . 74,000
Zielona Góra (Grünberg) *(zheh LAW-nah GOO rah) (GRYOON behrk)*, Poland . . . 69,300
Žilina *(ZHIH lih nah)*, Czechoslovakia . . . 50,792
Zittau *(TSIT ow)*, Germany, East . . . 43,087
Zlatoust *(ZLAH tuh OOST)*, Soviet Union . . . 181,000
Zomba *(ZAHM buh)*, Malawi . . . 19,616
Zonguldak *(ZAWN gool DAHK)*, Turkey . . . 60,865
Zrenjanin *(ZREN yah nin)*, Yugoslavia . . . 59,000
Zurich *(ZOOR ik)*, Switzerland . . . 432,500
Zwickau *(TSVIK ow)*, Germany, East . . . 127,000
Zwolle *(ZWAWL uh)*, Netherlands . . . 73,253
Zyryanovsk *(zihr YAH nufsk)*, Soviet Union . . . 56,000

THE CENSUS OF CANADA

This table includes population figures for provinces, territories, counties, regional districts, and all incorporated places listed in the 1971 Census of Canada. The provinces and territories are arranged in alphabetical order, and each place is listed alphabetically under the province or territory in which it is located. Metropolitan area figures are also given for large cities in each province.

ALBERTA Total population: 1,627,874

METROPOLITAN AREAS

Calgary	403,319
Edmonton	495,702

PLACES

Acme	300
Airdrie	1,089
Alberta Beach	320
Alix	565
Alliance	230
Amisk	134
Andrew	466
Argentia Beach	2
Arrowwood	166
Athabasca	1,765
Barons	237
Barrhead	2,803
Bashaw	757
Bassano	861
Bawlf	182
Beaverlodge	1,157
Beiseker	414
Bellevue	1,242
Bentley	621
Berwyn	474
Big Valley	306
Bittern Lake	100
Black Diamond	945
Blackfalds	904
Blackie	168
Blairmore	2,037
Bon Accord	332
Bonnyville	2,587
Botha	99
Bow Island	1,159
Bowden	560
Boyle	460
Breton	352
Brooks	3,986
Bruderheim	350
Burdett	206
Calgary	403,319
Calmar	799
Camrose	8,673
Canmore	1,538
Carbon	343
Cardston	2,685
Carmangay	230
Caroline	339
Carstairs	884
Castor	1,166
Cayley	122
Cereal	220
Champion	335
Chauvin	349
Chinook	59
Chipman	181
Claresholm	2,935
Clive	247
Cluny	86
Clyde	233
Coaldale	2,798
Cochrane	1,046
Cold Lake	1,309
Coleman	1,534
Consort	659
Coronation	877
Coutts	407
Cowley	201
Craigmyle	72
Cremona	186
Crossfield	638
Crystal Springs	8
Czar	196
Daysland	593
Delburne	383
Delia	241
Derwent	203
Devon	1,468
Dewberry	160
Didsbury	1,821
Donalda	232
Donnelly	274
Drayton Valley	3,900
Drumheller	5,446
Duchess	228
Eaglesham	218
Eckville	660
Edberg	145
Edgerton	296
Edmonton	438,152
Edmonton Beach	148
Edson	3,818
Elk Point	729
Elnora	213
Empress	266
Entwistle	353
Evansburg	528
Fairview	2,109
Falher	918
Ferintosh	127
Foremost	568
Forestburg	669
Fort Assiniboine	173
Fort Macleod	2,715
Fort McMurray	6,847
Fort Saskatchewan	5,726
Fox Creek	1,281
Frank	224
Gadsby	47
Galahad	179
Ghost Lake	11
Gibbons	551
Girouxville	347
Gleichen	367
Glendon	354
Glenwood	200
Golden Days	19
Grand Centre	2,088
Grande Cache	2,525
Grande Prairie	13,079
Grandview	16
Granum	324
Grassy Lake	196
Grimshaw	1,714
Gull Lake	57
Hairy Hill	99
Halkirk	136
Hanna	2,545
Hardisty	594
Hay Lakes	211
Heisler	199
High Level	1,614
High Prairie	2,354
High River	2,676
Hill Spring	213
Hines Creek	438
Hinton	4,911
Holden	448
Hughenden	267
Hussar	170
Hythe	487
Innisfail	2,474
Innisfree	252
Irma	423
Irricana	139
Irvine	194
Island Lake	20
Killam	851
Kinuso	267
Kitscoty	320
Lac la Biche	1,791
Lacombe	3,436
Lakeview	8
Lamont	899
Lavoy	114
Leduc	4,000
Legal	563
Lethbridge	41,217
Linden	226
Lloydminster (Alta and Sask)	8,691
Lomond	165
Longview	189
Lougheed	217
Ma-Me-O Beach	89
Magrath	1,215
Manning	1,071
Mannville	646
Marwayne	351
Mayerthorpe	1,036
McLennan	1,090
Medicine Hat	26,518
Milk River	775
Millet	456
Milo	117
Minburn	106
Mirror	365
Morinville	1,475
Morrin	197
Mundare	511
Munson	54
Myrnam	403
Nakamun Park	3
Nampa	283
Nanton	991
New Norway	200
New Sarepta	202
Nobleford	401
Norglenwold	40
Okotoks	1,247
Olds	3,376
Onoway	496
Oyen	929
Paradise Valley	144
Peace River	5,039
Penhold	452
Picture Butte	1,008
Pincher Creek	3,227
Plamondon	189
Point Alison	10
Ponoka	4,414
Provost	1,489
Radway	170
Rainbow Lake	355
Raymond	2,156
Red Deer	27,674
Redcliff	2,255
Redwater	1,287
Rimbey	1,450
Rochon Sands	20
Rocky Mountain House	2,968
Rockyford	286
Rosalind	203
Rosemary	208
Ross Haven	21
Rumsey	95
Rycroft	461
Ryley	428
St. Albert	11,800
St. Paul	4,161
Sandy Beach	22
Sangudo	360
Seba Beach	165
Sedgewick	730
Sexsmith	559
Silver Beach	27
Silver Sands	2
Slave Lake	2,052
Smoky Lake	881
South View	19
Spirit River	1,091
Spruce Grove	3,029
Standard	267
Stavely	351
Stettler	4,168
Stirling	436
Stony Plain	1,770
Strathmore	1,148
Strome	226
Sundance Beach	5
Sundre	933
Sunset Point	26
Swan Hills	1,376
Sylvan Lake	1,597
Taber	4,765
Thorhild	509
Thorsby	595
Three Hills	1,354
Tilley	270
Tofield	924
Torrington	118
Trochu	739
Turner Valley	766
Two Hills	979
Val Quentin	41
Valleyview	1,708
Vauxhall	1,016
Vegreville	3,691
Vermilion	2,915
Veteran	267
Viking	1,178
Vilna	303
Vulcan	1,384
Wainwright	3,872
Wanham	268
Warburg	464
Warner	408
Warspite	110
Waskatenau	233
Wembley	348
West Cove	9
Westlock	3,246
Wetaskiwin	6,267
Whitecourt	3,202
Wildwood	386
Willingdon	325
Yellowstone	14
Youngstown	305

BRITISH COLUMBIA Total population: 2,184,621

METROPOLITAN AREAS

Vancouver	1,082,352
Victoria	195,800

REGIONAL DISTRICTS

Alberni-Clayoquot	31,747
Bulkley-Nechako	27,145
Capital	204,803
Cariboo	39,357
Central Fraser Valley	58,085
Central Kootenay	44,791
Central Okanagan	50,177
Columbia-Shuswap	30,641
Comox-Strathcona	47,345
Cowichan Valley	38,988
Dewdney-Alouette	40,096
East Kootenay	39,720
Fraser-Cheam	46,097
Fraser-Fort George	64,364
Greater Vancouver	1,028,334
Kitimat-Stikine	37,326
Kootenay Boundary	31,396
Mount Waddington	10,408
Nanaimo	48,006
North Okanagan	34,039
Ocean Falls	4,215
Okanagan-Similkameen	42,752
Peace River-Liard	43,996
Powell River	18,536
Skeena A	22,299
Squamish-Lillooet	13,081
Stikine	1,470
Sunshine Coast	9,655
Thompson-Nicola	75,752

PLACES

Abbotsford	706
Alert Bay	760
Armstrong	1,648
Ashcroft	1,916
Burns Lake	1,259
Cache Creek	1,013
Castlegar	3,072
Chase	1,212
Chetwynd	1,260
Chilliwack	9,135
Clinton	905
Comox	3,980
Courtenay	7,152
Cranbrook	12,000
Creston	3,204
Cumberland	1,718
Dawson Creek	11,885
Duncan	4,388
Enderby	1,158
Fernie	4,422
Fort Nelson	2,289
Fort St. James	1,483
Fort St. John	8,264
Fraser Lake	1,292
Fruitvale	1,379
Gibsons Landing	1,934
Golden	3,010
Grand Forks	3,173
Greenwood	868
Harrison Hot Springs	598
Hazelton	351
Hope	3,153
Invermere	1,065
Kamloops	26,168
Kaslo	755
Kelowna	19,412
Keremeos	605
Kimberley	7,641
Kinnaird	2,846
Ladysmith	3,664
Lake Cowichan	2,364
Langley	4,684
Lillooet	1,514
Lion's Bay	396
Logan Lake	3
Lumby	940
Lytton	494
Masset	975
McBride	658
Merritt	5,289
Midway	502
Montrose	1,137
Nakusp	1,163
Nanaimo	14,948
Nelson	9,400
New Denver	644
New Westminster	42,835
North Vancouver	31,847
Oliver	1,615
100 Mile House	1,120
Osoyoos	1,285
Parksville	2,169
Pemberton	157
Penticton	18,146
Port Alberni	20,063
Port Alice	1,507
Port Coquitlam	19,560
Port Edward	1,019
Port McNeil	934
Port Moody	10,778
Pouce Coupé	595
Prince George	33,101
Prince Rupert	15,747
Princeton	2,601
Qualicum Beach	1,245
Quesnel	6,252
Revelstoke	4,867
Rossland	3,896
Salmo	872
Sayward	465
Sechelt	590
Sidney	4,868
Silverton	246
Slocan	346
Smithers	3,864
South Fort George	1,282
Tahsis	1,351
Taylor	605
Telkwa	712
Tofino	461
Trail	11,149
Ucluelet	1,018
Valemount	693
Valleyview	3,787
Vancouver	426,256
Vanderhoof	1,653
Vernon	13,283
Victoria	61,761
Warfield	2,132
White Rock	10,349
Williams Lake	4,072
Zeballos	186

MANITOBA Total population: 988,247

METROPOLITAN AREA

Winnipeg	540,262

PLACES

Altona	2,122
Arborg	879
Beauséjour	2,236
Benito	479
Binscarth	469
Birtle	882
Boissevain	1,506
Bowsman	443
Brandon	31,150
Carberry	1,305
Carman	2,030
Cartwright	340
Crystal City	555
Dauphin	8,891
Deloraine	961
Dunnottar	222
East Kildonan	30,152
Elkhorn	569
Emerson	830
Erickson	531
Ethelbert	526
Flin Flon	9,344
Garson	301
Gilbert Plains	854
Gimli	2,041
Gladstone	933
Glenboro	698
Grandview	967
Great Falls	199
Gretna	522
Hamiota	822
Hartney	579
Killarney	2,074
Lac du Bonnet	952
MacGregor	744
Manitou	871
McCreary	545
Melita	1,132
Minitonas	610
Minnedosa	2,621
Morden	3,266
Morris	1,399
Napinka	135
Neepawa	3,215
Niverville	938
Norte Dame de Lourdes	613
Oak Lake	342
Pilot Mound	763
Plum Coulee	480
Portage la Prairie	12,950
Powerview	667
Rapid City	374
Rivers	1,175
Riverton	797
Roblin	1,753
Rossburn	638
Russell	1,526
St. Boniface	46,714
St. Claude	679
St. James-Assiniboia	71,431
St. Lazare	431
St. Pierre	846
St. Vital	32,963
Ste. Anne	1,062
Ste. Rose du Lac	818
Selkirk	9,331
Shoal Lake	833
Somerset	646
Souris	1,674
Steinbach	5,197
Stonewall	1,583
Swan River	3,522
Teulon	828
The Pas	6,062
Thompson	19,001
Transcona	22,490
Treherne	628
Tuxedo	3,258
Virden	2,823
Waskada	247
Wawanesa	478
West Kildonan	23,959
Winkler	2,983
Winnipeg	246,246
Winnipeg Beach	687
Winnipegosis	887

NEW BRUNSWICK Total population: 634,557

METROPOLITAN AREA

Saint John	106,744

COUNTIES

Albert	16,307
Carleton	24,428
Charlotte	24,551
Gloucester	74,752
Kent	24,901
Kings	33,285
Madawaska	34,976
Northumberland	51,561
Queens	12,486
Restigouche	41,289
St. John	92,162
Sunbury	21,268
Victoria	19,796
Westmorland	98,669
York	64,126

PLACES

Alma	425
Aroostook	550
Atholville	2,108
Baker Brook	561
Barker's Point	1,882
Bath	920
Bathurst	16,674
Belledune	784
Beresford	2,325
Bertrand	1,094
Blackville	915
Bridgedale	416
Bristol	771
Buctouche	1,964
Cambridge-Narrows	416
Campbellton	10,335
Canterbury	528
Cap-Pelé	2,081
Caraquet	3,441
Centreville	566
Charlo	1,621
Chartersville	320
Chatham	7,833
Chipman	1,977
Clair	704
Dalhousie	6,255
Dieppe	4,277
Doaktown	938
Dorchester	1,199
Douglastown	637

Drummond 637
East Riverside-Kingshurst 852
East Shediac 585
Edmundston 12,365
Eel River Crossing 1,075
Fairvale 2,050
Florenceville 584
Fredericton 24,254
Fredericton Junction 615
Gagetown 609
Gondola Point 850
Grand Falls 4,516
Grand Harbour 556
Grande Anse 545
Gunningsville 1,669
Hampton 1,748
Hartland 1,009
Harvey 383
Hillsborough 781
Jacquet River 866
Kedgwick 1,065
Lac Baker 360
Lamèque 933
Lewisville 3,710
Loggieville 877
Lower Caraquet 1,685
Marysville 3,872
McAdam 2,224
Meductic 172
Milltown 1,893
Millville 352
Minto 3,880
Moncton 47,891
Nackawic 1,324
Nashwaaksis 7,353
Neguac 1,498
Nelson Miramichi 1,580
Newcastle 6,460
Nigadoo 597
North Head 649
Norton 1,149
Oromocto 11,427
Pamdenec 422
Paquetville 479
Perth-Andover 2,108
Petit Rocher 1,624
Petitcodiac 1,569
Plaster Rock 1,331
Pointe Verte 524
Port Elgin 553
Quispamsis 2,215
Renforth 1,606
Rexton 755
Richibucto 1,850
Riverside-Albert 509
Riverview Heights 6,525
Rivière Verte 1,657
Rogersville 1,077
Rothesay 1,038
Sackville 3,180
St. André 315
St. Andrews 1,812
St. Anselme 1,150
St. Antoine 756
St. Basile 3,085
St. François de Madawaska 511
St. George 977
St. Hilaire 199
St. Jacques 1,072
Saint John 89,039
St. Joseph 687
St. Leonard 1,478
St. Louis de Kent 992
St. Martins 484
St. Quentin 2,093
St. Stephen 3,409
Ste. Anne de Madawaska 1,253
Salisbury 1,070
Seal Cove 613
Shediac 2,203
Shippegan 2,043
Silverwood 935
Stanley 388
Surrey 286
Sussex 3,942
Sussex Corner 700
Tide Head 797
Tracadie 2,222
Tracy 610
Westfield 461
Woodstock 4,846

NEWFOUNDLAND Total population: 522,104

METROPOLITAN AREA

St. John's 131,814

PLACES

Badger 1,187
Baie Verte 2,397
Bay de Verde 826
Bay Roberts 3,702
Belleoram 530
Bishop's Falls 4,133
Bonavista 4,215
Botwood 4,115
Brigus 746
Burgeo 2,226
Burin 2,586
Carbonear 4,732
Catalina 1,131
Change Islands 609
Channel-Port aux Basques 5,942
Clarenville 2,193
Clarke's Beach 877
Corner Brook 26,309
Cupids 691
Deer Lake 4,421
Dunville 1,742
Elliston 551
Englee 1,050
Fogo 1,155
Fortune 2,164
Freshwater 1,562
Gander 7,748
Gaultois 509
Glenwood 979
Glovertown 1,915
Grand Bank 3,476
Grand Falls 7,677
Greenspond 449
Happy Valley 4,937
Harbour Breton 2,196
Harbour Grace 2,771
Hare Bay 1,485
Holyrood 1,282
Jerseyside 1,061
Lamaline 553
Lawn 1,000
Lewisporte 3,175
Little Catalina 722
Lumsden 630
Main Brook 590
Marystown 4,960
Mount Pearl 7,211
Newtown 513
Norris Arm 1,191
Old Pelican 597
Pasadena 964
Placentia 2,211
Point Lemington 940
Port Union 578
Pouch Cove 1,483
Ramea 1,208
Robert's Arm 1,044
Roddickton 1,239
St. Alban's 1,941
St. Anthony 2,593
St. George's 2,082
St. John's 88,102
St. Lawrence 2,173
South Brook 802
South River 554
Spaniard's Bay 1,764
Springdale 3,224
Stephenville 7,770
Stephenville Crossing 2,129
Trepassey 1,443
Twillingate 1,437
Upper Island Cove 1,819
Wabana 5,421
Wesleyville 1,142
Whitbourne 1,235
Windsor 6,644
Winterton 794

NORTHWEST TERRITORIES Total population: 34,807

PLACES

Fort Smith 2,364
Hay River 2,406
Inuvik 2,669
Yellowknife 6,122

NOVA SCOTIA Total population: 788,960

METROPOLITAN AREA

Halifax 222,637

COUNTIES

Annapolis 21,841
Antigonish 16,814
Cape Breton 129,075
Colchester 37,735
Cumberland 35,160
Digby 20,349
Guysborough 12,864
Halifax 261,461
Hants 28,935
Inverness 20,375
Kings 44,975
Lunenburg 38,422
Pictou 46,104
Queens 12,950
Richmond 12,734
Shelburne 16,661
Victoria 7,823
Yarmouth 24,682

PLACES

Amherst 9,966
Annapolis Royal 758
Antigonish 5,489
Berwick 1,412
Bridgetown 1,039
Bridgewater 5,231
Canso 1,209
Clark's Harbour 1,082
Dartmouth 64,770
Digby 2,363
Dominion 2,879
Glace Bay 22,440
Halifax 122,035
Hantsport 1,447
Kentville 5,198
Liverpool 3,654
Lockeport 1,208
Louisburg 1,582
Lunenburg 3,215
Mahone Bay 1,333
Middleton 1,870
Mulgrave 1,196
New Glasgow 10,849
New Waterford 9,579
North Sydney 8,604
Oxford 1,473
Parrsboro 1,807
Pictou 4,250
Port Hawkesbury 3,372
Shelburne 2,689
Springhill 5,262
Stellarton 5,357
Stewiacke 1,040
Sydney 33,230
Sydney Mines 8,991
Trenton 3,331
Truro 13,047
Westville 3,898
Windsor 3,795
Wolfville 2,861
Yarmouth 8,516

ONTARIO Total population: 7,703,106

METROPOLITAN AREAS

Hamilton 498,523
Kitchener 226,846
London 286,011
Ottawa-Hull 602,510
St. Catharines-Niagara 303,429
Sudbury 155,424
Thunder Bay 112,093
Toronto 2,628,043
Windsor 258,643

COUNTIES, DISTRICTS, AND MUNICIPALITIES

Algoma 121,937
Brant 96,767
Bruce 47,385
Cochrane 95,836
Dufferin 21,200
Dundas 17,457
Durham 47,494
Elgin 66,608
Essex 306,399
Frontenac 101,692
Glengarry 18,480
Grenville 24,316
Grey 66,403
Haldimand 32,673
Haliburton 9,081
Halton 190,469
Hastings 99,393
Huron 52,951
Kenora 53,230
Kent 101,118
Lambton 114,314
Lanark 42,259
Leeds 50,093
Lennox & Addington 28,359
Manitoulin 10,931
Middlesex 282,014
Muskoka 31,938
Niagara 347,328
Nipissing 78,867
Norfolk 54,099
Northumberland 48,162
Ontario 196,257
Ottawa-Carleton 471,931
Oxford 80,349
Parry Sound 30,244
Peel 259,402
Perth 62,973
Peterborough 87,804
Prescott 27,832
Prince Edward 20,640
Rainy River 25,750
Renfrew 90,875
Russell 16,287
Simcoe 171,433
Stormont 61,302
Sudbury 198,079
Thunder Bay 145,390
Timiskaming 46,485
Toronto 2,086,017
Victoria 34,242
Waterloo 254,037
Wellington 108,581
Wentworth 401,883
York 166,060

PLACES

Acton 5,031
Ailsa Craig 608
Ajax 12,515
Alexandria 3,240
Alfred 1,230
Alliston 3,176
Almonte 3,696
Alvinston 702
Amherstburg 5,169
Arkona 469
Arnprior 6,016
Arthur 1,414
Athens 1,071
Aurora 13,614
Aylmer 4,755
Ayr 1,272
Bancroft 2,276
Barrie 27,676
Barrys Bay 1,432
Bath 810
Bayfield 503
Beachburg 549
Beachville 995
Beaverton 1,485
Beeton 1,061
Belle River 2,877
Belleville 35,128
Belmont 798
Blenheim 3,490
Blind River 3,450
Bloomfield 730
Blyth 814
Bobcaygeon 1,518
Bolton 2,984
Bonfield 694
Bothwell 810
Bowmanville 8,947
Bracebridge 6,903
Bradford 3,401
Braeside 522
Brampton 41,211
Brantford 64,421
Bridgeport 2,375
Brighton 2,956
Brockville 19,765
Bruce Mines 505
Brussels 908
Burk's Falls 891
Burlington 87,023
Cache Bay 727
Caledon East 910
Caledonia 3,183
Campbellford 3,522
Cannington 1,083
Capreol 3,470
Cardinal 1,865
Carleton Place 5,020
Casselman 1,337
Cayuga 1,084
Chalk River 1,094
Charlton 131
Chatham 35,317
Chatsworth 399
Chesley 1,693
Chesterville 1,252
Clifford 555
Clinton 3,154
Cobalt 2,197
Cobden 926
Cobourg 11,282
Cochrane 4,965
Colborne 1,588
Coldwater 759
Collingwood 9,775
Coniston 2,907
Cookstown 847
Copper Cliff 4,089
Cornwall 47,116
Courtright 590
Creemore 978
Deep River 5,671
Delhi 3,894
Deloro 255
Deseronto 1,863
Drayton 752
Dresden 2,369
Dryden 6,939
Dundalk 1,022
Dundas 17,208
Dunnville 5,576
Durham 2,448
Dutton 878
Eganville 1,395
Elmira 4,730
Elmvale 1,103
Elora 1,904
Embro 703
Englehart 1,721
Erie Beach 222
Erieau 509
Erin 1,446
Espanola 6,045
Essex 4,002
Exeter 3,354
Fenelon Falls 1,616
Fergus 5,433
Finch 397
Flesherton 524
Forest 2,355
Fort Erie 23,113
Fort Frances 9,947
Frankford 1,862
Galt 38,897
Gananoque 5,212
Georgetown 17,053
Geraldton 3,178
Glencoe 1,387
Goderich 6,813
Gore Bay 770
Grand Bend 696
Grand Valley 904
Gravenhurst 7,133
Grimsby 15,770
Guelph 60,087
Hagersville 2,292
Haileybury 5,280
Hamilton 309,173
Hanover 5,063
Harriston 1,785
Harrow 1,971
Hastings 938
Havelock 1,225
Hawkesbury 9,276
Hearst 3,501
Hensall 970
Hepworth 372
Hespeler 6,343
Highgate 424
Hilton Beach 165
Huntsville 9,784
Ingersoll 7,783
Iron Bridge 874
Iroquois 1,224
Iroquois Falls 7,271
Jarvis 965
Kapuskasing 12,834
Kearney 308
Keewatin 2,112
Kemptville 2,413
Kenora 10,952
Killaloe Station 810
Kincardine 3,239
Kingston 59,047
Kingsville 4,076
Kitchener 111,804
Lakefield 2,245
Lanark 861
Lancaster 617
Latchford 535
Leamington 10,435
Levack 2,948
Lincoln 14,274
Lindsay 12,746
Lion's Head 467
Listowel 4,677
Little Current 1,565
Lively 3,000
London 223,222
L'Orignal 1,405
Lucan 1,178
Lucknow 1,047
Madoc 1,353
Magnetawan 204
Markdale 1,236
Markham 36,684
Marmora 1,350
Massey 1,278
Mattawa 2,881
Maxville 846
Meaford 4,045
Merrickville 930
Midland 10,992
Mildmay 963
Millbrook 908
Milton 7,018
Milverton 1,193
Mississauga 156,070
Mitchell 2,545
Morrisburg 2,055
Mount Forest 3,037
Napanee 4,638
Neustadt 579
New Hamburg 3,008
New Liskeard 5,488
Newboro 296
Newburgh 620
Newbury 338
Newcastle 1,942
Newmarket 18,941
Niagara Falls 67,163
Niagara-on-the-Lake 12,552
North Bay 49,187
Norwich 1,806
Norwood 1,183
Oakville 61,483
Oil Springs 570
Omemee 777
Orangeville 8,074
Orillia 24,040
Oshawa 91,587
Ottawa 302,341
Owen Sound 18,469
Paisley 793
Palmerston 1,855
Paris 6,483
Parkhill 1,167
Parry Sound 5,842
Pelham 9,997
Pembroke 16,544
Penetanguishene 5,497
Perth 5,537
Petawawa 5,784
Peterborough 58,111
Petrolia 4,044
Pickering 2,537
Picton 4,875
Plantagenet 909
Point Edward 2,773
Port Burwell 700
Port Colborne 21,420
Port Credit 9,442
Port Dover 3,407
Port Elgin 2,855
Port Hope 8,872
Port McNicoll 1,450
Port Perry 2,977
Port Rowan 856
Port Stanley 1,725
Powassan 1,163
Prescott 5,165
Preston 16,723
Rainy River 1,196
Renfrew 9,173
Richmond 2,122
Richmond Hill 32,384
Ridgetown 2,836
Ripley 448
Rockcliffe Park 2,138
Rockland 3,649
Rodney 1,016
Rosseau 269
St. Catharines 109,722
St. Clair Beach 1,987
St. Isidore de Prescott 615
St. Marys 4,650
St. Thomas 25,545
Sarnia 57,644
Sault Ste. Marie 80,332
Seaforth 2,134
Shallow Lake 385
Shelburne 1,790
Simcoe 10,793
Sioux Lookout 2,530
Smiths Falls 9,585
Smooth Rock Falls 1,239
South River 1,052
Southampton 2,036
Springfield 522
Stayner 1,937
Stirling 1,500
Stittsville 1,994
Stoney Creek 8,380
Stratford 24,508
Strathroy 6,592
Streetsville 6,840
Sturgeon Falls 6,662
Sturgeon Point 36
Sudbury 90,535
Sundridge 723
Tara 643
Tavistock 1,490
Tecumseh 5,165
Teeswater 983
Thamesville 1,028
Thedford 719
Thessalon 1,879
Thornbury 1,220
Thornloe 138
Thorold 15,065
Thunder Bay 108,411
Tilbury 3,580
Tillsonburg 6,608
Timmins 28,542
Tiverton 567
Toronto 712,786
Tottenham 1,616
Trenton 14,589
Trout Creek 586
Tweed 1,738
Uxbridge 3,077
Vanier 22,477
Vankleek Hill 1,691
Vaughan 15,873
Victoria Harbour 1,243
Vienna 390
Walkerton 4,479

ONTARIO, Continued

Wallaceburg 10,550
Wardsville 388
Wasaga Beach 1,923
Waterdown 2,146
Waterford 2,403
Waterloo 36,677
Watford 1,400
Webbwood 585
Welland 44,397
Wellesley 816
Wellington 988
West Lorne 1,094
Westport 601
Wheatley 1,657
Whitby 25,324
Whitchurch-Stouffville 11,262
Wiarton 2,222
Winchester 1,575
Windsor 203,300
Wingham 2,913
Woodstock 26,173
Woodville 473
Wyoming 1,279
Zurich 767

PRINCE EDWARD ISLAND Total population: 111,641

COUNTIES

Kings 18,424
Prince 42,082
Queens 51,135

PLACES

Alberton 973
Borden 624
Bunburg 527
Cardigan 266
Central Bedegue 213
Charlottetown 19,133
Cornwall 657
Crapaud 246
Georgetown 767
Kensington 1,086
Kinkora 272
Miminegash 417
Miscouche 750
Montague 1,608
Morell 387
Mount Stewart 413
Murray Harbour 367
Murray River 478
North Rustico 767
O'Leary 795
Parkdale 2,313
St. Eleanors 1,621
St. Louis 166
St. Peters 370
Sherwood 3,807
Souris 1,393
Summerside 9,439
Tignish 1,060
Tyne Valley 150
Victoria 171
Wellington 347
Wilmot 737

QUEBEC Total population: 6,027,764

METROPOLITAN AREAS

Chicoutimi-Jonquière 133,703
Montréal 2,743,208
Québec 480,502

COUNTIES

Abitibi 112,244
Argenteuil 31,319
Arthabaska 51,524
Bagot 23,591
Beauce 63,960
Beauharnois 52,137
Bellechasse 23,517
Berthier 27,288
Bonaventure 41,701
Brome 15,311
Chambly 231,590
Champlain 113,150
Charlevoix:
Charlevoix-Est (Charlevoix East) 16,780
Charlevoix-Ouest (Charlevoix West) 13,650
Châteauguay 53,737
Chicoutimi 163,348
Compton 21,367
Deux-Montagnes (Two Mountains) 52,369
Dorchester 32,473
Drummond 64,144
Frontenac 27,293
Gaspé:
Gaspé-Est (Gaspé East) 41,727
Gaspé-Ouest (Gaspé West) 18,754
Îles-de-la-Madeleine (Magdalen Islands) 13,303
Hull:
Gatineau 55,729
Hull 109,946
Huntingdon 15,358
Iberville 20,400
Île-de-Montréal et Île-Jésus 2,187,153
Joliette 52,088
Kamouraska 26,264
Labelle 30,582
Lac-St. Jean (Lake St. John):
Lac-St. Jean-Est (Lake St. John East) 45,220
Lac-St. Jean-Ouest (Lake St. John West) 57,074
Laprairie 61,691
L'Assomption 62,198
Lévis 62,776
L'Islet 23,187
Lotbinière 27,373
Maskinongé 21,257
Matane:
Matane 30,261
Matapédia 26,856
Mégantic 58,020
Missisquoi 33,953
Montcalm 21,546
Montmagny 26,307
Montmorency:
Montmorency No. 1 20,401
Montmorency No. 2 (Île-d'Orléans) 5,435
Napierville 12,067
Nicolet 30,004
Papineau 31,793
Pontiac 19,570
Portneuf 51,540
Québec 423,162
Richelieu 47,093
Richmond 41,044
Rimouski 64,263
Rivière-du-Loup 39,488
Rouville 31,759
Saguenay 111,272
St. Hyacinthe 50,494
St. Jean 45,892
St. Maurice 108,366
Shefford 62,361
Sherbrooke 101,470
Soulanges 11,449
Stanstead 36,266
Témiscamingue (Timiskaming) 54,656
Témiscouata 23,189
Terrebonne 139,945
Vaudreuil 36,593
Verchères 35,273
Wolfe 16,197
Yamaska 15,206

PLACES

Abercorn 368
Acton Vale 4,564
Adamsville 495
Albanel 788
Alma 22,622
Amos 6,984
Amqui 3,797
Aucienne-Lorette 8,304
Andréville 446
Ange-Gardien 516
Angers 881
Angliers 404
Anjou 33,886
Annaville 464
Armagh 987
Arthabaska 4,479
Arvida 18,448
Asbestos 9,749
Aston-Jonction 324
Ayer's Cliff 873
Aylmer 7,198
Bagotville 6,041
Baie-Comeau 12,109
Baie-de-Shawinigan 847
Baie-d'Urfé 3,881
Baie-St.-Paul 4,163
Baie-Trinité 734
Baieville 507
Barkmere 52
Barraute 1,288
Barville 106
Beaconsfield 19,389
Beauceville 2,098
Beauceville-Est 2,192
Beauharnois 8,121
Beaulac 514
Beaulieu 659
Beauport 14,681
Beaupré 2,862
Bécancour 8,182
Bedford 2,786
Beebe Plain 1,236
Bélair 4,505
Belleterre 614
Beloeil 12,274
Bernierville 2,415
Berthierville 4,080
Bic 1,157
Bishopton 332
Black Lake 4,123
Blainville 9,630
Bois-des-Filion 4,061
Boucherville 19,997
Brome 292
Bromont 1,089
Bromptonville 2,771
Brossard 23,452
Brownsburg 3,481
Bryson 809
Buckingham 7,304
Cabano 3,063
Cadillac 1,102
Calumet 764
Campbell's Bay 1,186
Candiac 5,185
Cap-à-l'Aigle 679
Cap-aux-Meules 1,099
Cap-Chat 3,868
Cap-de-la-Madeleine 31,463
Carignan 3,340
Carillon 420
Causapscal 2,965
Chambly 11,469
Chambord 1,106
Champlain 632
Chandler 3,843
Chapais 2,914
Chapeau 537
Charlemagne 4,111
Charlesbourg 33,443
Charny 5,175
Château-Richer 3,111
Châteauguay 15,797
Châteauguay-Centre 17,942
Chénéville 718
Chesterville 324
Chibougamau 9,701
Chicoutimi 33,893
Chicoutimi-Nord 14,086
Chute-aux-Outardes 1,190
Clarenceville 339
Clermont 3,386
Coaticook 6,569
Compton 506
Contrecoeur 2,694
Cookshire 1,484
Côte-St.-Luc 24,375
Coteau-du-Lac 838
Coteau-Landing 846
Courville 6,222
Cowansville 11,920
Crabtree 1,706
Danville 2,566
Daveluyville 998
Deauville 761
Dégelis 3,046
De Grasse 102
Delson 2,941
Desbiens 1,813
Deschaillons 296
Deschaillons-sur St. Laurent 1,176
Deschambault 995
Deschênes 1,806
Deux-Montagnes 8,631
Disraëli 3,384
Dixville 549
Dolbeau 7,633
Dollard-des-Ormeaux 25,217
Donnacona 5,940
Dorion 6,209
Dorval 20,469
Douville 3,267
Drummondville 31,813
Drummondville Sud 8,989
Dunham 486
Duparquet 786
Durham-Sud 461
East Angus 4,715
East Broughton Station 1,127
East Farnham 360
Eastman 527
Estérel 94
Évain 605
Farnham 6,496
Ferme-Neuve 1,990
Forestville 1,606
Fort-Coulonge 1,784
Fortierville 516
Fossambault-sur-le-Lac 154
Francoeur 1,186
Frelighsburg 345
Gagnon 3,787
Gaspé 17,211
Gatineau 22,321
Giffard 13,135
Godbout 653
Gracefield 1,049
Granby 34,385
Grand Mère 17,137
Grandes-Bergeronnes 802
Greenfield Park 15,348
Grenville 1,495
Hampstead 7,033
Hatley 212
Hauterive 13,181
Hébertville-Station 1,163
Hemmingford 810
Henryville 666
Howick 575
Hudson 4,345
Hull 63,580
Huntingdon 3,087
Iberville 9,331
Île-Cadieux 45
Île-d'Entrée 247
Île-Dorval 7
Île-Perrot 4,021
Inverness 362
Joliette 20,127
Jonquière 28,430
Kamouraska 505
Kénogami 10,970
Kingsbury 229
Kingsey Falls 564
Kirkland 2,917
Labelle 1,492
Lac-à-la-Croix 572
Lac-au-Saumon 1,314
Lac-Bouchette 954
Lac-Brome 4,063
Lac-Carré 660
Lac-Delage 59
Lac-des-Ecorces 591
Lac-Etchemin 2,789
Lac-Mégantic 6,770
Lac-Poulin 2
Lac-St.-Joseph 7
Lac-Sergent 150
Lachine 44,423
Lachute 11,813
Lacolle 1,254
Laflèche 15,113
Lafontaine 2,980
La Guadeloupe 1,934
La Malbaie 4,036
Lambton 767
L'Annonciation 2,162
La Patrie 449
La Pérade 1,123
La Pocatière 4,256
La Prairie 8,309
La Providence 4,709
La Reine 450
La Salle 72,912
La Sarre 5,185
L'Assomption 4,915
La Station-du-Coteau 885
Laterrière 591
La Tuque 13,099
Laurentides 1,746
Laurier-Station 946
Laurierville 922
Lauzon 12,809
Laval 228,010
Lavaltrie 1,261
L'Avenir 364
Lawrenceville 551
Lebel-sur-Quévillon 2,936
Leclercville 396
Le Moyne 8,194
Lennoxville 3,859
L'Épiphanie 2,752
Léry 2,247
Les Becquets 496
Les Cèdres 436
Lévis 16,597
Linière 1,220
L'Isle-Verte 1,360
L'Islet 1,195
L'Islet-sur-Mer 772
Longueuil 97,590
Loretteville 11,644
Lorraine 3,145
Lorrainville 906
Lotbinière 537
Louiseville 4,042
Luceville 1,411
Lyster 879
Macamic 1,705
Magog 13,281
Malartic 5,347
Maniwaki 6,689
Manseau 756
Maple Grove 1,708
Marbleton 617
Marieville 4,563
Marsoui 600
Mascouche 8,812
Maskinongé 996
Masson 2,336
Massueville 632
Matagami 2,411
Matane 11,841
McMasterville 2,518
Melbourne 458
Melocheville 1,601
Mercier 4,011
Métis-sur-Mer 175
Mistassini 3,601
Mont-Gabriel 36
Mont-Joli 6,698
Mont-Laurier 8,240
Mont-Royal 21,561
Mont-St.-Hilaire 5,758
Mont-St.-Pierre 371
Montauban 246
Montebello 1,285
Montmagny 12,432
Montmorency 4,949
Montréal 1,214,352
Montréal-Est 5,076
Montréal-Nord 89,139
Montréal-Ouest 6,368
Murdochville 2,891
Napierville 1,987
Neuville 798
New Glasgow 128
New Richmond 3,957
Nicolet 4,714
Nominingue 699
Noranda 10,741
Norbertville 282
Normandin 1,823
North Hatley 728
Notre-Dame-des-Anges 790
Notre-Dame-des-Laurentides 5,080
Notre-Dame-d'Hebertville 1,506
Notre-Dame-du-Bon-Conseil 1,048
Notre-Dame-du-Lac 2,107
Omerville 1,102
Ormstown 1,517
Orsainville 12,520
Otterbourn Park 3,512
Outremont 28,552
Papineauville 1,384
Parent 452
Pascalis 39
Percé 5,617
Philipsburg 391
Pierrefonds 33,010
Pierreville 1,455
Pincourt 5,899
Plessisville 7,204
Pointe-au-Pic 1,231
Pointe-aux-Outardes 836
Pointe-aux-Trembles 35,567
Pointe-Calumet 2,214
Pointe-Claire 27,303
Pointe-des-Cascades 685
Pointe-du-Moulin 184
Pointe-Fortune 332
Pointe-Gatineau 15,640
Pointe-Lebel 756
Pont-Rouge 3,272
Port-Alfred 9,228
Port-Cartier 3,730
Portage-du-Fort 431
Portneuf 1,347
Prévost 296
Price 2,740
Princeville 3,829
Québec 186,088
Quyon 879
Rawdon 2,740
Repentigny 19,520
Richelieu 1,777
Richmond 4,317
Rigaud 2,138
Rimouski 26,887
Rimouski-Est 2,069
Ripon 588
Rivière-Beaudette 239
Rivière-du-Loup 12,760
Rivière-du-Moulin 4,393
Robertsonville 1,294
Roberval 8,330
Rock Island 1,094
Rosemère 6,710
Rougemont 853
Rouyn 17,821
Roxboro 7,633
Roxton Falls 1,139
Sacré-Coeur-de-Jésus 1,252
Saguenay 39
St.-Agapitville 1,493
St.-Alban 770
St.-Alexandre 404
St.-Alexis 460
St.-Ambroise 1,629
St.-André-du-Lac-St.-Jean 610
St.-André-Avellin 1,088
St.-André-Est 1,201
St.-Anselme 1,400
St.-Antoine 5,831
St.-Basile-le-Grand 4,402
St.-Basile-Sud 1,731
St.-Bernard 569
St.-Boniface-de-Shawinigan 2,581
St.-Bruno 1,276
St.-Bruno-de-Montarville 15,780
St.-Casimir 1,239
St.-Casimir-Est 472
St.-Césaire 2,279
St.-Charles 969
St.-Charles-des-Grondines 421
St.-Charles-sur-Richelieu 340
St.-Chrysostome 1,077
St.-Clet 249
St.-Coeur-de-Marie 1,218
St.-Cyrille 1,125
St.-Damase 1,106
St.-David-de-l'Auberivière 3,818
St.-Denis 899
St.-Dominique 1,722
St.-Elzéar 515
St.-Émile 2,645
St.-Éphrem-de-Tring 954
St.-Eustache 9,479
St.-Félicien 4,952
St.-Félix-de-Valois 1,455
St.-Flavien 645
St.-Francois-du-Lac 1,001
St.-Fulgence 999
St.-Gabriel 3,383
St.-Gédéon (Lac-St.Jean-Est Co.) 885
St.-Gédéon (Frontenac Co.) 1,174
St.-Georges (Champlain Co.) 2,061
St.-Georges (Beauce Co.) 7,554
St.-Georges-de-Cacouna 1,001
St.-Georges-de-Windsor 318
St.-Georges-Ouest 6,000
St.-Gérard 625
St.-Germain-de-Grantham 1,104
St.-Grégoire 655
St.-Grégoire-de-Greenlay 694
St.-Guillaume 834
St.-Henri 1,160
St.-Herménegilde 172
St.-Honoré 1,055
St.-Hubert 21,741
St.-Hugues 468
St.-Hyacinthe 24,562
St.-Isidore 736
St.-Jacques 1,975
St.-Jean 32,863
St.-Jean-Chrysostome 1,905
St.-Jean-de-Boischatel 1,685
St.-Jean-Vianney 184
St.-Jérôme (Terrebonne Co.) 26,524
St.-Jérôme (Lac-St. Jean-Est Co.) 1,910
St.-Joseph 4,945
St.-Joseph-de-Beauce 2,893
St.-Joseph-de-la-Rive 326
St.-Joseph-de-la-Rivière-Bleue 1,429
St.-Joseph-de-Sorel 3,290
St.-Jovite 3,132
St.-Lambert 18,616
St.-Laurent 62,955
St.-Leonard 52,040
St.-Leonard-d'Aston 995
St.-Liboire 667
St.-Luc 4,850
St.-Ludger 263
St.-Marc-des-Carrières 2,650
St.-Nicolas 1,975
St.-Noël 910
St.-Ours 838
St.-Pacôme 1,180
St.-Pamphile 3,542
St.-Pascal 2,513
St.-Patrice-de-Beaurivage 468
St.-Paulin 809
St.-Pie 1,709
St.-Pierre (Île-de-Montréal Co.) 6,801
St.-Pierre (Joliette Co.) 357
St.-Placide 288
St.-Polycarpe 530
St.-Prime 2,350
St.-Raphaël 1,216
St.-Raymond 4,036
St.-Rédempteur 1,652
St.-Rémi 2,282
St.-Romuald-d'Etchemin 8,394
St.-Sauveur-des-Monts 1,846
St.-Sébastien 418
St.-Siméon 1,186
St.-Stanislas 564
St.-Sylvère 210
St.-Sylvestre 466
St.-Théophile 469
St.-Timothée 1,613
St.-Tite 3,130
St.-Ubald 809
St.-Ulric 936
St.-Vallier 511
St.-Victor 1,017
St.-Wenceslas 408
St.-Zacharie 1,390
St.-Zotique 1,243
Ste.-Agathe 646
Ste.-Agathe-Sud 889
Ste.-Agathe-des-Monts 5,532
Ste.-Angèle-de-Mérici 688
Ste.-Anne-de-Beaupré 1,797
Ste.-Anne-de-Bellevue 4,976
Ste.-Anne-des-Monts 5,546
Ste.-Anne-du-Lac (Labelle Co.) 381
Ste.-Anne-du-Lac (Mégantic Co.) 2
Ste.-Clothilde-de-Horton 393
Ste.-Croix 1,545
Ste.-Félicité 816
Ste.-Foy 68,385
Ste.-Geneviève 2,847
Ste.-Hélène-de-Bagot 398
Ste.-Jeanne-d'Arc 936
Ste.-Madeleine 1,110
Ste.-Marie (Nicolet Co.) 181
Ste.-Marie (Beauce Co.) 4,307
Ste.-Marthe 198
Ste.-Monique 232
Ste.-Prudentienne 799
Ste.-Rosalie 2,210
Ste.-Scholastique 14,787
Ste.-Thècle 1,725
Ste.-Thérèse 17,175
Ste.-Thérèse-Ouest 7,278
Sault-au-Mouton 951
Sawyerville 864
Sayabec 1,789
Schefferville 3,271
Scotstown 917
Senneterre 4,303
Senneville 1,412
Sept-Îles 24,320
Shawbridge 969
Shawinigan 27,792
Shawinigan-Sud 11,470
Shawville 1,745
Sherbrooke 80,711
Sillery 13,932
Sorel 19,347
Stanstead Plain 1,192
Stukely-Sud 390
Sutton 1,684
Tadoussac 1,010
Temiscaming 2,428
Templeton 3,684
Terrebonne 9,212
Thetford Mines 22,003
Thurso 3,219
Tracy 11,842
Tring-Jonction 1,283
Trois-Pistoles 4,678
Trois-Rivières 55,869
Trois-Rivières-Ouest 8,057
Upton 818
Val-Barrette 521
Val-Brillant 690
Valcourt 2,411
Val-David 1,627
Val-d'Or 17,421
Val-St. Michel 2,050
Vallée-Jonction 1,295
Valleyfield (Salaberry-de-) 30,173
Vanier 9,717
Varennes 2,382
Vaudreuil 3,843

Vaudreuil-sur-le-Lac 285
Verchères 1,840
Verdun 74,718
Victoriaville 22,047
Ville-Marie 1,995
Villeneuve 4,062
Wakefield 325
Warden 384
Warwick 2,847
Waterloo 4,936
Waterville 1,476
Weedon-Centre 1,429
Westmount 23,606
Wickham 517
Windsor 6,023
Wottonville 683
Yamachiche 1,147
Yamaska 478
Yamaska-Est 320

SASKATCHEWAN Total population: 926,247

METROPOLITAN AREAS

Regina 140,734
Saskatoon 126,449

PLACES

Abbey 246
Aberdeen 288
Abernethy 253
Adanac 20
Admiral 77
Alameda 370
Alida 230
Allan 712
Alsask 819
Alvena 143
Aneroid 163
Antler 115
Arborfield 418
Archerwill 302
Arcola 539
Ardath 24
Ardill 26
Arelee 52
Arran 120
Asquith 355
Assiniboia 2,675
Atwater 60
Avonlea 391
Aylesbury 88
Aylsham 170
Balcarres 678
Balgonie 518
Bangor 69
Battleford 1,803
Beatty 97
Beechy 342
Belle Plaine 62
Bengough 650
Benson 83
Bethune 291
Bienfait 823
Big River 836
Biggar 2,607
Birch Hills 696
Birsay 123
Bjorkdale 223
Bladworth 125
Blaine Lake 671
Borden 187
Bounty 49
Bracken 64
Bradwell 100
Bredenbury 472
Briercrest 130
Broadview 959
Brock 205
Broderick 115
Brownlee 121
Bruno 728
B-Say-Tah 37
Buchanan 442
Buena Vista 28
Bulyea 109
Burstall 507
Cabri 737
Cadillac 217
Calder 186
Cando 193
Canora 2,603
Canwood 325
Carievale 229
Carlyle 1,101
Carlyle Lake Resort 13
Carmichael 21
Carnduff 1,075
Carragana 137
Carrot River 953
Central Butte 522
Ceylon 279
Chamberlain 161
Chaplin 368
Choiceland 456
Churchbridge 973
Climax 341
Coderre 161
Codette 175
Coleville 482
Colgate 59
Colonsay 526
Conquest 261
Consul 205
Coronach 379
Craik 503
Craven 126
Creelman 197
Creighton 1,857
Cudworth 799
Cupar 573
Cut Knife 560
Dafoe 46
Dalmeny 417
Davidson 1,043
Debden 340
Delisle 653
Denholm 71
Denzil 287
Dilke 130
Dinsmore 421
Disley 53
Dodsland 404
Dollard 92
Domremy 208
Drake 238
Drinkwater 118
Dubuc 153
Duck Lake 584
Duff 90
Dunblane 57
Dundurn 354
Duval 133
Dysart 243
Earl Grey 243
Eastend 784
Eatonia 610
Ebenezer 140
Edam 334
Edenwold 129
Elbow 361
Elfros 253
Elrose 573
Elstow 150
Endeavour 193
Englefeld 218
Ernfold 100
Esterhazy 2,896
Estevan 9,150
Eston 1,418
Etters Beach 2
Evesham 63
Eyebrow 181
Fairlight 127
Fenwood 112
Ferland 109
Fielding 38
Fife Lake 83
Fillmore 396
Findlater 96
Flaxcombe 99
Fleming 183
Foam Lake 1,331
Forget 118
Fort Qu'Appelle 1,606
Fosston 119
Fox Valley 489
Francis 159
Frobisher 245
Frontier 249
Gainsborough 375
Gerald 174
Girvin 86
Gladmar 131
Glaslyn 357
Glen Ewen 223
Glenavon 340
Glenside 94
Glentworth 126
Glidden 71
Golden Prairie 144
Goodeve 169
Goodsoil 219
Goodwater 71
Govan 354
Grandview Beach 2
Gravelbourg 1,428
Grayson 260
Grenfell 1,350
Guernsey 142
Gull Lake 1,156
Hafford 580
Hague 431
Halbrite 166
Handel 72
Hanley 390
Hardy 42
Harris 254
Hawarden 190
Hazenmore 127
Hazlet 198
Hepburn 305
Herbert 1,024
Herschel 89
Heward 79
Hodgeville 399
Holdfast 399
Horizon 23
Hubbard 119
Hudson Bay 1,971
Humboldt 3,881
Hyas 215
Imperial 486
Indian Head 1,810
Insinger 72
Invermay 412
Ituna 960
Jansen 241
Jasmin 30
Jedburgh 64
Kamsack 2,783
Kannata Valley 7
Katepwa Beach 44
Keeler 58
Kelfield 27
Kelliher 460
Kelvington 1,053
Kenaston 402
Kendal 90
Kennedy 264
Kerrobert 1,180
Khedive 91
Killaly 139
Kincaid 306
Kindersley 3,451
Kinistino 767
Kinley 74
Kipling 927
Kisbey 260
Krydor 136
Kyle 509
Lafleche 715
Laird 218
Lake Alma 173
Lake Lenore 392
Lampman 830
Lancer 199
Landis 297
Lang 183
Langenburg 1,236
Langham 535
Lanigan 1,430
La Ronge 906
Lashburn 494
Lawson 60
Leader 1,105
Leask 439
Lebret 278
Leipzig 87
Lemberg 409
Leney 26
Leoville 399
Leross 91
Leroy 435
Leslie 87
Lestock 452
Liberty 141
Limerick 178
Lintlaw 212
Lipton 401
Lloydminster (Sask. and Alta.) 8,691
Lockwood 60
Loon Lake 348
Loreburn 252
Love 133
Loverna 55
Lucky Lake 378
Lumsden 900
Luseland 728
Macklin 829
MacNutt 184
Macoun 172
Macrorie 120
Madison 58
Maidstone 691
Major 164
Makwa 126
Manitou Beach 118
Mankota 424
Manor 409
Mantario 48
Maple Creek 2,268
Marcelin 306
Marengo 133
Margo 225
Markinch 80
Marquis 131
Marsden 241
Marshall 195
Martensville 870
Maryfield 408
Maymont 167
Mazenod 73
McLean 178
McTaggart 58
Meacham 186
Meadow Lake 3,435
Meath Park 251
Medstead 172
Melfort 4,725
Melville 5,375
Mendham 163
Meota 233
Mervin 198
Metinota 11
Meyronne 142
Midale 647
Middle Lake 292
Milden 239
Milestone 483
Minton 215
Mistatim 165
Montmartre 510
Moose Jaw 31,854
Moosomin 2,407
Morse 455
Mortlach 310
Mossbank 460
Muenster 280
Naicam 711
Neilburg 298
Netherhill 67
Neudorf 469
Neville 154
Nipawin 4,057
Nokomis 533
Norquay 513
North Battleford 12,698
North Portal 189
Odessa 224
Ogema 457
Osage 55
Osler 182
Outlook 1,767
Oxbow 1,380
Paddockwood 230
Palmer 58
Pangman 242
Paradise Hill 344
Parkside 112
Paynton 204
Pelly 426
Pennant 215
Pense 270
Penzance 81
Perdue 411
Piapot 160
Pilger 109
Pilot Butte 403
Plato 66
Plenty 208
Plunkett 152
Ponteix 786
Porcupine Plain 830
Portreeve 58
Preeceville 1,118
Prelate 407
Primate 82
Prince Albert 28,464
Prud'homme 260
Punnichy 451
Qu'Appelle 451
Quill Lake 566
Quinton 195
Rabbit Lake 206
Radisson 416
Radville 1,024
Rama 188
Raymore 523
Redvers 846
Regina 139,469
Regina Beach 334
Rhein 295
Richard 39
Richmound 208
Ridgedale 169
Riverhurst 264
Robsart 52
Rocanville 891
Roche Percée 167
Rockglen 550
Rockhaven 53
Rose Valley 591
Rosetown 2,614
Rosthern 1,431
Rouleau 395
Ruddell 25
Rush Lake 162
Ruthilda 48
St. Benedict 193
St. Brieux 367
St. Gregor 125
St. Louis 387
St. Victor 85
St. Walburg 656
Saltcoats 509
Salvador 77
Saskatchewan Beach 9
Saskatoon 126,449
Sceptre 234
Scott 254
Sedley 268
Semans 331
Senlac 94
Shackleton 55
Shamrock 105
Shaunavon 2,244
Sheho 320
Shell Lake 255
Shellbrook 1,048
Silton 59
Simpson 239
Sintaluta 272
Smeaton 315
Smiley 124
Southey 548
Sovereign 91
Spalding 329
Speers 117
Spiritwood 719
Spring Valley 71
Springside 350
Springwater 99
Spruce Lake 106
Spy Hill 384
Star City 543
Stenen 225
Stewart Valley 138
Stockholm 357
Stornoway 37
Storthoaks 177
Stoughton 751
Stranraer 66
Strasbourg 759
Strongfield 110
Sturgis 617
Success 101
Summerberry 41
Swift Current 15,415
Tantallon 174
Tessier 40
Theodore 434
Tisdale 2,798
Togo 227
Tompkins 353
Torquay 377
Tramping Lake 241
Tribune 136
Tugaske 196
Turtleford 419
Tuxford 153
Unity 2,294
Val Marie 307
Valparaiso 50
Vanguard 315
Vanscoy 244
Vawn 119
Veregin 197
Vibank 275
Viceroy 152
Viscount 395
Vonda 258
Wadena 1,382
Wakaw 1,009
Wakaw Lake 3
Waldeck 242
Waldheim 606
Waldron 80
Wapella 518
Warman 781
Waseca 115
Watrous 1,541
Watson 840
Wawota 536
Webb 105
Weekes 183
Weirdale 108
Weldon 254
Welwyn 231
West Bend 41
Weyburn 8,815
White City 129
White Fox 354
Whitewood 1,098
Wilcox 189
Wilkie 1,642
Willow Bunch 482
Willowbrook 70
Windthorst 188
Wiseton 181
Wishart 269
Wolseley 975
Wood Mountain 86
Woodrow 73
Wroxton 92
Wynyard 1,932
Yarbo 160
Yellow Creek 163
Yellow Grass 500
Yorkton 13,430
Young 496
Zealandia 155
Zelma 51
Zenon Park 346

YUKON Total population: 18,388

PLACES

Dawson 762
Faro 863
Whitehorse 11,217

THE CENSUS OF THE UNITED STATES

This table includes final population figures for states, counties, and places listed in the 1970 Census of the United States. The states are arranged in alphabetical order and each place is listed alphabetically under the state in which it is located. The population figures for metropolitan areas (Standard Metropolitan Statistical Areas) are also given for each state.

ALABAMA Total population: 3,444,165

METROPOLITAN AREAS

- Birmingham 739,274
- Florence 117,743
- Gadsden 94,144
- Huntsville 228,239
- Mobile 376,690
- Montgomery 201,451
- Tuscaloosa 116,029

COUNTIES

- Autauga 24,460
- Baldwin 59,382
- Barbour 22,543
- Bibb 13,812
- Blount 26,853
- Bullock 11,824
- Butler 22,007
- Calhoun 103,092
- Chambers 36,356
- Cherokee 15,606
- Chilton 25,180
- Choctaw 16,589
- Clarke 26,724
- Clay 12,636
- Cleburne 10,996
- Coffee 34,872
- Colbert 49,632
- Conecuh 15,645
- Coosa 10,662
- Covington 34,079
- Crenshaw 13,188
- Cullman 52,445
- Dale 52,938
- Dallas 55,296
- De Kalb 41,981
- Elmore 33,661
- Escambia 34,912
- Etowah 94,144
- Fayette 16,252
- Franklin 23,933
- Geneva 21,924
- Greene 10,650
- Hale 15,888
- Henry 13,254
- Houston 56,574
- Jackson 39,202
- Jefferson 644,991
- Lamar 14,335
- Lauderdale 68,111
- Lawrence 27,281
- Lee 61,268
- Limestone 41,699
- Lowndes 12,897
- Macon 24,841
- Madison 186,540
- Marengo 23,819
- Marion 23,788
- Marshall 54,211
- Mobile 317,308
- Monroe 20,883
- Montgomery 167,790
- Morgan 77,306
- Perry 15,388
- Pickens 20,326
- Pike 25,038
- Randolph 18,331
- Russell 45,394
- St. Clair 27,956
- Shelby 38,037
- Sumter 16,974
- Talladega 65,280
- Tallapoosa 33,840
- Tuscaloosa 116,029
- Walker 56,246
- Washington 16,241
- Wilcox 16,303
- Winston 16,654

PLACES

- Abbeville 2,996
- Adamsville 2,412
- Addison 692
- Akron 535
- Alabaster 2,642
- Albertville 9,963
- Alexander City 12,358
- Aliceville 2,851
- Allgood 272
- Altoona 781
- Andalusia 10,092
- Anniston 31,533
- Anniston Northwest 6,609
- Arab 4,399
- Ardmore 761
- Ariton 643
- Arley 164
- Ashford 1,980
- Ashland 1,921
- Ashville 986
- Athens 14,360
- Atmore 8,293
- Attalla 7,510
- Auburn 22,767
- Autaugaville 870
- Avon 374
- Babbie 82
- Banks 170
- Bay Minette 6,727
- Bayou La Batre 2,664
- Bear Creek 336
- Beatrice 455
- Beaverton 265
- Benton 115
- Berry 679
- Bessemer 33,663
- Billingsley 110
- Birmingham 300,910
- Black 171
- Blountsville 1,254
- Blue Mountain 446
- Blue Springs 137
- Bluff Park 12,431
- Boaz 5,635
- Boligee 225
- Bon Air 214
- Branchville 225
- Brantley 1,066
- Brent 2,093
- Brewton 6,747
- Bridgeport 2,908
- Brighton 2,277
- Brilliant 726
- Brookside 990
- Brownville 501
- Brundidge 2,709
- Butler 2,064
- Calera 1,655
- Camden 1,742
- Camp Hill 1,554
- Carbon Hill 1,929
- Cardiff 127
- Carolina 192
- Carrollton 923
- Carrville 895
- Castleberry 666
- Cedar Bluff 956
- Center Point 15,675
- Centre 2,418
- Centreville 2,233
- Chatom 1,059
- Cherokee 1,484
- Chickasaw 8,447
- Childersburg 4,831
- Citronelle 1,935
- Clanton 5,868
- Clayton 1,626
- Cleveland 413
- Clio 1,065
- Cobb Town, see West End-Cobb Town
- Coffee Springs 329
- Coffeeville 441
- Collinsville 1,300
- Columbia 891
- Columbiana 2,248
- Cordova 2,750
- Cottonwood 1,149
- County Line 199
- Courtland 547
- Cowarts 350
- Craig 1,894
- Crossville 1,035
- Cuba 386
- Cullman 12,601
- Dadeville 2,847
- Daleville 5,182
- Daphne 2,382
- Daviston 247
- Dayton 115
- Decatur 38,044
- Demopolis 7,651
- Detroit 191
- Docena 1,140
- Dora 1,862
- Dothan 36,733
- Double Springs 957
- Dozier 304
- Dutton 423
- East Brewton 2,336
- Eclectic 1,184
- Edwardsville 146
- Elba 4,634
- Elberta 395
- Elkmont 394
- Enterprise 15,591
- Epes 293
- Ethelsville 98
- Eufaula 9,102
- Eunola 141
- Eutaw 2,805
- Eva 146
- Evergreen 3,924
- Excel 422
- Fairfax 2,772
- Fairfield 14,369
- Fairhope 5,720
- Fairview 313
- Falkville 946
- Faunsdale 227
- Fayette 4,568
- Five Points 247
- Flat Creek-Wegra-Praco 1,066
- Flint City 404
- Flomaton 1,584
- Florala 2,701
- Florence 34,031
- Foley 3,368
- Forestdale 6,091
- Fort Deposit 1,438
- Fort McClellan 5,334
- Fort Payne 8,435
- Fort Rucker 14,242
- Frisco City 1,286
- Fruithurst 229
- Fulton 628
- Fultondale 5,163
- Fyffe 311
- Gadsden 53,928
- Gainesville 255
- Gantts Quarry 63
- Garden City 745
- Gardendale 6,537
- Gaylesville 161
- Geiger 120
- Geneva 4,398
- Georgiana 2,148
- Geraldine 610
- Gilbertown 207
- Glen Allen 276
- Glencoe 2,901
- Glenwood 378
- Good Hope 840
- Goodwater 2,172
- Gordo 1,991
- Gordon 312
- Goshen 279
- Grant 382
- Graysville 3,182
- Greensboro 3,371
- Greenville 8,033
- Grimes 191
- Grove Hill 1,825
- Guin 2,220
- Gulf Shores 909
- Guntersville 6,491
- Gurley 647
- Gu-Win 231
- Hackleburg 726
- Haleburg 104
- Haleyville 4,190
- Hamilton 3,088
- Hammondville 221
- Hanceville 2,027
- Harpersville 639
- Hartford 2,648
- Hartselle 7,355
- Hayden 195
- Hayneville 473
- Headland 2,545
- Heath 229
- Heflin 2,872
- Helena 1,110
- Henagar 812
- Highland Lake 108
- Hillsboro 222
- Hobson City 1,124
- Hodges 207
- Hokes Bluff 2,133
- Holly Pond 325
- Hollywood 301
- Homewood 21,137
- Hoover 1,393
- Hueytown 8,673
- Huntsville 137,802
- Hurtsboro 937
- Irondale 3,166
- Jackson 5,957
- Jacksonville 7,715
- Jasper 10,798
- Jemison 1,423
- Kansas 227
- Kelly 325
- Kennedy 415
- Killen 683
- Kimberly 847
- Kinsey 219
- Kinston 540
- Lafayette 3,530
- Lakeview 83
- Lanett 6,908
- Langdale 2,235
- Leeds 6,991
- Leesburg 98
- Leighton 1,231
- Lester 70
- Level Plains 950
- Lexington 278
- Libertyville 141
- Lincoln 1,127
- Linden 2,697
- Lineville 1,984
- Lipscomb 3,225
- Lisman 628
- Little Shawmut 2,682
- Littleville 858
- Livingston 2,358
- Lockhart 698
- Louisville 785
- Lowndesboro 219
- Loxley 859
- Luverne 2,440
- Lynn 286
- Madison 3,086
- Madrid 238
- Malvern 227
- Maplesville 596
- Margaret 685
- Marion 4,289
- Maytown 667
- McKenzie 491
- Mentone 407
- Midfield 6,340
- Midland City 1,172
- Midway 558
- Mignon 1,726
- Millport 1,070
- Millry 911
- Mobile 190,026
- Monroeville 4,846
- Montevallo 3,719
- Montgomery 133,386
- Moody 504
- Mooresville 72
- Morris 519
- Moulton 2,470
- Moundville 996
- Mount Vernon 1,079
- Mountain Brook 19,509
- Mountainboro 311
- Mulga 582
- Muscle Shoals 6,907
- Myrtlewood 334
- Napier Field 572
- Nauvoo 265
- New Brockton 1,374
- New Hope 1,300
- New Site 378
- Newbern 286
- Newsome 38
- Newton 1,865
- Newville 465
- North Johns 241
- Northport 9,435
- Notasulga 833
- Oak Grove 482
- Oak Hill 86
- Oakman 853
- Odenville 533
- Ohatchee 445
- Oneonta 4,390
- Opelika 19,027
- Opp 6,493
- Orrville 362
- Owens Crossroads 767
- Oxford 4,361
- Ozark 13,555
- Paint Rock 226
- Parrish 1,742
- Pelham 931
- Pell City 5,602
- Petrey 122
- Phenix City 25,281
- Phil Campbell 1,230
- Pickensville 132
- Piedmont 5,063
- Pinckard 609
- Pine Apple 347
- Pine Hill 697
- Pisgah 519
- Pleasant Grove 5,090
- Pollard 86
- Praco, see Flat Creek-Wegra-Praco
- Prattville 13,116
- Prichard 41,578
- Ragland 1,239
- Rainbow City 3,107
- Rainsville 2,099
- Ranburne 371
- Red Bay 2,464
- Red Level 616
- Reece City 496
- Reform 1,893
- Repton 277
- River Falls 580
- River View 1,109
- Riverside 351
- Riverview 110
- Roanoke 5,251
- Robertsdale 2,078
- Rockford 603
- Rogersville 950
- Roosevelt 3,663
- Russellville 7,814
- Rutledge 353
- Samson 2,257
- Sanford 256
- Saraland 7,840
- Sardis 368
- Satsuma 2,035
- Scottsboro 9,324
- Section 702
- Selma 27,379
- Selmont-West Selmont 2,270
- Shawmut 2,181
- Sheffield 13,115
- Silas 345
- Siluria 678
- Silverhill 552
- Sipsey 608
- Slocomb 1,883
- Snead 347
- Somerville 185
- Southside 983
- Spanish Fort 2,364
- Springville 1,153
- Steele 798
- Stevenson 2,390
- Sulligent 1,762
- Sumiton 2,374
- Summerdale 550
- Sweet Water 265
- Sylacauga 12,255
- Sylvan Springs 344
- Sylvania 476
- Talladega 17,662
- Talladega Springs 143
- Tallassee 4,809
- Tarrant City 6,835
- Taylor 174
- Thomaston 824
- Thomasville 3,769
- Thorsby 944
- Town Creek 1,203
- Toxey 304
- Trafford 628
- Triana 228
- Trinity 881
- Troy 11,482
- Trussville 2,985
- Tuscaloosa 65,773
- Tuscumbia 8,828
- Tuskegee 11,028
- Union Grove 118
- Union Springs 4,324
- Uniontown 2,133
- Valley Head 470
- Vernon 2,190
- Vestavia Hills 8,311
- Vina 366
- Vincent 1,419
- Vinemont 480
- Vredenburgh 622
- Wadley 626
- Walnut Grove 224
- Warrior 2,621
- Waterloo 262
- Waverly 247
- Weaver 2,091
- Webb 354
- Wedowee 842
- Wegra, see Flat Creek-Wegra-Praco
- West Blocton 1,172
- West End-Cobb Town 5,515
- West Jefferson 233
- Weston 187
- Wetumpka 3,912
- Whites Chapel 334
- Wilsonville 659
- Wilton 573
- Winfield 3,292
- Woodland 177
- Woodville 322
- York 3,044

ALASKA Total population: 302,173

METROPOLITAN AREA

- Anchorage 126,333

CENSUS DIVISIONS

- Aleutian Islands 8,057
- Anchorage 124,542
- Angoon 503
- Barrow 2,663
- Bethel 7,579
- Bristol Bay Borough 1,147
- Bristol Bay 3,485
- Cordova-McCarthy 1,857
- Fairbanks 45,864
- Haines 1,504
- Juneau 13,556
- Kenai-Cook Inlet 14,250
- Ketchikan 10,041
- Kobuk 4,434
- Kodiak 9,409
- Kuskokwim 2,306
- Matanuska-Susitna 6,509
- Nome 5,749
- Outer Ketchikan 1,676
- Prince of Wales 2,106
- Seward 2,336
- Sitka 6,109
- Skagway-Yakutat 2,157
- Southeast Fairbanks 4,179
- Upper Yukon 1,684
- Valdez-Chitina-Whittier 3,098
- Wade Hampton 3,917
- Wrangell-Petersburg 4,913
- Yukon-Koyukuk 4,752

PLACES

- Adak Station 2,249
- Akhiok 115
- Akiachak 312
- Akiak 171
- Akolmiut 526
- Akutan 101
- Alakanuk 265
- Aleknagik 128
- Allakaket 174
- Ambler 169
- Anaktuvuk Pass 99
- Anchor Point 102
- Anchorage 48,081
- Anderson 362
- Angoon 400
- Aniak 205
- Annette 195
- Anvik 83
- Arctic Village 85
- Atka 88
- † Auke Bay 490
- Aurora-Johnston 1,464
- Barrow 2,104
- Basher 2
- Bay City 0
- Beaver 101
- Belkofski 59
- Bethel 2,416
- Big Lake 36
- Birchwood 1,219
- Brevig Mission 123
- Buckland 104
- Butte 448
- Campbell 40
- Cantwell 62
- Cape Lisburne 83
- Cape Pole 123
- Central 26
- Chalkyitsik 130
- Chefornak 146
- Chevak 387
- Chignik 83
- Chignik Lake 117
- Chistochina 33
- Chitina 38
- Chuathbaluk 94
- Chugiak 489
- Circle 54
- Clam Gulch 47
- Clarks Point 95
- Cold Bay 256
- College 3,434
- Cooper Landing 31
- Copper Center 206
- Cordova 1,164
- Craig 272
- Crooked Creek 59
- Deadhorse 163
- Deering 85
- Delta Junction 703
- Dillingham 914
- Diomede 84
- Donnelly 6
- Dot Lake 42
- † Douglas 1,243
- Eagle 36
- Eagle River 2,437
- Edna Bay 112
- Eek 186
- Egegik 148
- Eielson 6,149
- Eklutna 25
- Ekuk 51
- Ekwok 103
- Elfin Cove 49
- Elim 174
- Elmendorf 6,018
- Emanguk 439
- English Bay 58
- Ester 264
- Evansville 57
- Fairbanks 14,771
- False Pass 62
- Fire Lake 475
- Fort Greely 1,820
- Fort Richardson 10,751
- Fort Wainwright 9,097
- Fort Yukon 448
- † Fritz Cove 296
- Fritz Creek 27
- Gakona 88
- Galena 302
- Gambell 372
- Girdwood 144
- Glen Alps 18
- Glennallen 363
- Golovin 117
- Graehl 349
- Grayling 139
- Gulkana 53
- Gustavus 64
- Haines 463
- Halibut Cove 44
- Healy 79
- Herring Cove 114
- Holy Cross 199
- Homer 1,083
- Hoonah 748
- Hooper Bay 490
- Hope 51
- Houston 69
- Hughes 85
- Huslia 159
- Hydaburg 214
- Hyder 49
- Iguigig 36
- Iliamna 58
- Ivanof Bay 48
- Juneau 13,556
- Kachemak 76
- Kaguyak 59
- Kake 448
- Kakhonak 88
- Kaktovik 123
- Kalskag 122
- Kaltag 206
- Karluk 98
- Kasaan 30
- Kasilof 71
- Kenai 3,533

† Consolidated with Juneau in July, 1970.

Ketchikan 6,994
Kiana 278
King Cove 283
King Salmon 202
Kipnuk 325
Kivalina 188
Klawock 213
Klukwan 103
Kodiak 3,798
Kodiak Station 3,052
Koliganek 142
Kongiganak 190
Kotlik 228
Kotzebue 1,696
Koyuk 122
Koyukuk 124
Kwethluk 408
Kwigillingok 148
Kwinhagak 340
Larsen Bay 109
Lemeta 1,318
† Lemon Creek 1,042
† Lena Cove 300
Levelock 74
Lime Village 25
Long Island 7
Lower Kalskag 183
† Lower Mendenhall Valley 1,109
Manley Hot Springs 34
Manokotak 214
Marshall 175
McGrath 279
Meakerville 349
Mekoryuk 249
† Mendenhall Flats 164
Mentasta Lake 68
Metlakatla 1,050
Minto 168
Montana 33
Moose Pass 53
Mount Edgecumbe 835
Mountain Point 459
Mountain Village 419
Mud Bay 103
Mumtrak 218
Myers Chuck 37
Naknek 178
Napaiskak 188
Napakiak 259
Nelson Lagoon 43
Nenana 362
New Stuyahok 216
Newhalen 88
Newtok 114
Nightmute 127
Nikolai 112
Nikolski 57
Ninilchik 134
Noatak 293
Nome 2,488
Nondalton 184
Noorvik 462
† North Douglas 538
North Pole 265
Northway 40
Nulato 308
Old Harbor 290
Oscarville 41
Ouzinkie 160
Palmer 1,140
Pavlof Harbor 39
Pedro Bay 65
Pelican 133
Peninsula Point 175
Pennock Island 78
Perryville 94
Peters Creek 340
Petersburg 2,042
Pilot Point 68
Pilot Station 290
Pitkas Point 70
Platinum 55
Point Hope 386
Port Alexander 36
Port Chilkoot 220
Port Graham 107
Port Heiden 66
Port Higgins 189
Port Lions 227
Prudhoe Bay 49
Rampart 36
Red Devil 81
Ruby 145
Russian Mission 146
St. George 163
St. Marys 384
St. Michael 207
St. Paul 450
† Salmon Creek 302
Sand Lake 4,168
Sand Point 360
Savoonga 364
Saxman 135
Scammon Bay 166
Scow Bay 238
Selawik 429
Seldovia 437
Seward 1,587
Shageluk 167
Shaktolik 151
Sheldon Point 125
Shemya Station 1,131
Shishmaref 267
Shungnak 165
Shungnak Village 56
Sitka 3,370
Skagway 675
Sleetmute 109
Soldotna 1,202
South Bjerremark 402
South Naknek 154
Spenard 18,089
Squaw Harbor 65
Stebbins 231
Sterling 30
Stevens Village 74
Stony River 74
Summit 34
Suntrana 67
Sutton 76
Talkeetna 182
Tanacross 84
Tanana 120
Tanunak 274
Tatitlek 111
Teller 220
Tenakee Springs 86
Tetlin 114
Thorne Bay 443
Togiak 383
Tok 214
Toksook Bay 257
Tuluksak 195
Tuntutuliak 158
Twin Hills 67
Tyonek 232
Unalakleet 434
Unalaska 178
† Upper Mendenhall Valley 1,815
Usibelli 102
Usibelli Mine 65
Valdez 1,005
Venetie 112
Wainwright 315
Wales 131
Ward Cove 105
Wasilla 300
West Petersburg 36
White Mountain 87
Whittier 130
Wildwood Station 750
Willow 38
Woody Island 41
Wrangell 2,029
Yakutat 190

ARIZONA Total population: 1,772,482

METROPOLITAN AREAS

Phoenix 968,487
Tucson 351,667

COUNTIES

Apache 32,298
Cochise 61,910
Coconino 48,326
Gila 29,255
Graham 16,578
Greenlee 10,330
Maricopa 967,522
Mohave 25,857
Navajo 47,715
Pima 351,667
Pinal 67,916
Santa Cruz 13,966
Yavapai 36,733
Yuma 60,827

PLACES

Ajo 5,881
Apache Junction 2,390
Avondale 6,304
Bagdad 2,079
Benson 2,839
Bisbee 8,328
Buckeye 2,599
Bylas 1,125
Casa Grande 10,536
Cashion 2,705
Central Heights 2,289
Chandler 13,763
Clarkdale 892
Claypool 2,245
Clifton 5,087
Coolidge 4,651
Cottonwood 2,815
Douglas 12,462
Duncan 773
Eagar 1,279
El Mirage 3,258
Eloy 5,381
Flagstaff 26,117
Florence 2,173
Fort Huachuca 6,659
Fredonia 798
Gila Bend 1,795
Gilbert 1,971
Glendale 36,228
Globe 7,333
Goodyear 2,140
Grand Canyon 1,011
Hayden 1,283
Holbrook 4,759
Huachuca 1,233
Jerome 290
Kearny 2,829
Kingman 7,312
Litchfield Park 1,664
Luke 5,047
Mammoth 1,953
Mesa 62,853
Miami 3,394
Nogales 8,946
Page 1,439
Paradise Valley 7,155
Parker 1,948
Patagonia 630
Payson 1,490
Peoria 4,792
Phoenix 581,562
Pima 1,184
Plantsite 1,077
Prescott 13,030
Safford 5,333
St. Johns 1,320
San Carlos 2,542
San Manuel 4,332
Scottsdale 67,823
Sedona 2,022
Show Low 2,285
Sierra Vista 6,689
Snowflake 1,833
Somerton 2,225
South Tucson 6,220
Springerville 1,038
Stargo 1,194
Sun City 13,670
Superior 4,975
Surprise 2,427
Taylor Town 888
Tempe 62,907
Thatcher 2,320
Tolleson 3,881
Tombstone 1,241
Tucson 262,933
West Yuma 5,552
Wickenburg 2,698
Willcox 2,568
Williams (Coconino Co.) 2,386
Williams (Maricopa Co.) 3,443
Winkelman 974
Winslow 8,066
Youngtown 1,886
Yuma 29,007
Yuma Proving Ground 1,349
Yuma Station 3,460

ARKANSAS Total population: 1,923,295

METROPOLITAN AREAS

Fort Smith 160,421 (104,914 in Arkansas, 55,507 in Oklahoma)
Little Rock-North Little Rock 323,296
Pine Bluff 85,329
Texarkana 101,198 (67,813 in Texas, 33,385 in Arkansas)

COUNTIES

Arkansas 23,347
Ashley 24,976
Baxter 15,319
Benton 50,476
Boone 19,073
Bradley 12,778
Calhoun 5,573
Carroll 12,301
Chicot 18,164
Clark 21,537
Clay 18,771
Cleburne 10,349
Cleveland 6,605
Columbia 25,952
Conway 16,805
Craighead 52,068
Crawford 25,677
Crittenden 48,106
Cross 19,783
Dallas 10,022
Desha 18,761
Drew 15,157
Faulkner 31,572
Franklin 11,301
Fulton 7,699
Garland 54,131
Grant 9,711
Greene 24,765
Hempstead 19,308
Hot Spring 21,963
Howard 11,412
Independence 22,723
Izard 7,381
Jackson 20,452
Jefferson 85,329
Johnson 13,630
Lafayette 10,018
Lawrence 16,320
Lee 18,884
Lincoln 12,913
Little River 11,194
Logan 16,789
Lonoke 26,249
Madison 9,453
Marion 7,000
Miller 33,385
Mississippi 62,060
Monroe 15,657
Montgomery 5,821
Nevada 10,111
Newton 5,844
Ouachita 30,896
Perry 5,634
Phillips 40,046
Pike 8,711
Poinsett 26,822
Polk 13,297
Pope 28,607
Prairie 10,249
Pulaski 287,189
Randolph 12,645
St. Francis 30,799
Saline 36,107
Scott 8,207
Searcy 7,731
Sebastian 79,237
Sevier 11,272
Sharp 8,233
Stone 6,838
Union 45,428
Van Buren 8,275
Washington 77,370
White 39,253
Woodruff 11,566
Yell 14,208

PLACES

Adona 204
Alexander 297
Alicia 246
Allport 307
Alma 1,613
Almyra 220
Alpena 309
Altheimer 1,037
Altus 418
Amagon 136
Amity 614
Antoine 182
Arkadelphia 9,841
Arkansas City 615
Ash Flat 211
Ashdown 3,522
Athens 84
Atkins 2,015
Aubrey 351
Augusta 2,777
Austin 235
Avoca 173
Bald Knob 2,094
Banks 189
Barling 1,739
Bassett 265
Bates 109
Batesville 7,209
Bay 751
Bearden 1,272
Beaver 32
Beebe 2,805
Beedeville 144
Bellefonte 300
Belleville 379
Ben Lomond 155
Benton 16,499
Bentonville 5,508
Bergman 249
Berryville 2,271
Bethel Heights 284
Big Flat 189
Bigelow 258
Biggers 372
Birta 36
Black Oak 272
Black Rock 498
Blevins 265
Blue Eye 53
Blue Mountain 108
Bluff City 244
Blytheville 24,752
Bodcaw 158
Bonanza 342
Bono 428
Booneville 3,239
Bradford 826
Bradley 706
Branch 325
Brickeys 49
Brinkley 5,275
Brookland 465
Bryant 1,199
Buckner 392
Bull Shoals 430
Burdette 173
Cabot 2,903
Caldwell 292
Calico Rock 723
Calion 535
Camden 15,147
Cammack Village 1,165
Campbell Station 218
Caraway 952
Carlisle 2,048
Carthage 566
Casa 208
Cash 265
Caulksville 208
Cave City 807
Cave Springs 469
Center Hill 1,201
Center Point 144
Centerton 312
Charleston 1,497
Cherokee Village -Hidden Valley 1,300
Cherry Valley 556
Chester 82
Chidester 232
Clarendon 2,563
Clarksville 4,616
Cleveland 74
Clinton 1,029
Coal Hill 733
College City 645
Collins 26
Colt 301
Concord 163
Conway 15,510
Corning 2,705
Cotter 858
Cotton Plant 1,657
Cove 334
Coy 240
Crawfordsville 831
Crossett 6,191
Cushman 427
Daisy 100
Dalark 132
Damascus 255
Danville 1,362
Dardanelle 3,297
Datto 142
Decatur 847
Delaplaine 145
Delight 439
Dell 358
Denning 203
De Queen 3,863
Dermott 4,250
Des Arc 1,714
De Valls Bluff 622
De Witt 3,728
Diamond City 282
Diaz 283
Dierks 1,101
Dover 662
Dryden 21
Dumas 4,600
Dyer 486
Dyess 433
Earle 3,146
East Camden 589
Edmondson 412
Elaine 1,210
El Dorado 25,283
Elkins 418
Elm Springs 260
Emerson 393
Emmet 433
England 3,075
Enola 150
Eudora 3,687
Eureka Springs 1,670
Evening Shade 309
Everton 124
Farmington 908
Fayetteville 30,729
Fisher 361
Flippin 626
Fordyce 4,837
Foreman 1,173
Forrest City 12,521
Fort Smith 62,802
Fouke 506
Fountain Hill 266
Fourche 46
Franklin 117
Fredonia 340
Friendship 150
Fulton 323
Garfield 163
Garland 321
Gassville 434
Gateway 83
Gentry 1,022
Gilbert 45
Gillett 860
Gillham 200
Gilmore 461
Glenwood 1,212
Gosnell 1,386
Gould 1,683
Grady 688
Grannis 177
Gravette 1,154
Green Forest 1,354
Greenbrier 582
Greenland 650
Greenway 240
Greenwood 2,032
Greers Ferry 389
Griffithville 227
Grubbs 442
Guion 213
Gum Springs 269
Gurdon 2,075
Guy 179
Hackett 462
Halley 204
Hamburg 3,102
Hampton 1,252
Hardy 692
Harrell 269
Harrisburg 1,931
Harrison 7,239
Hartford 616
Hartman 400
Haskell 239
Hatfield 377
Havana 308
Hazen 1,605
Heber Springs 2,497
Hector 387
Helena 10,415
Hermitage 399
Hickory Ridge 410
Hidden Valley, see Cherokee Village-Hidden Valley
Higden 46
Higginson 343
Highfill 80
Hindsville 92
Holly Grove 840
Hope 8,810
Horatio 748
Horseshoe Bend 321
Hot Springs 35,631
Houston 200
Hoxie 2,265
Hughes 1,872
Humnoke 398
Humphrey 818
Hunter 131
Huntington 627
Huntsville 1,287
Huttig 822
Imboden 496
Jacksonport 306
Jacksonville 19,832
Jamestown 116
Jasper 394
Jerome 76
Johnson 274
Joiner 839
Jonesboro 27,050
Judsonia 1,667
Junction City 763
Keiser 688
Kelso 23
Kensett 1,444
Keo 226
Kibler 611
Kingsland 304
Knobel 375
Knoxville 202
Ladelle 35
Lake City 948
Lake Frances 31
Lake Village 3,310
Lamar 589
Lavaca 532
Leachville 1,582
Lead Hill 143
Leola 390
Lepanto 1,846
Leslie 563
Letona 191
Lewisville 1,653
Lincoln 1,023
Little Rock 132,483
Lockesburg 620
London 539
Lonoke 3,140
Lonsdale 104
Louann 245
Lowell 653
Luxora 1,566
Lynn 274
Madison 984
Magazine 677
Magness 139
Magnolia 11,303
Malvern 8,739
Mammoth Spring 1,072
Manila 1,961
Mansfield 981
Marianna 6,196
Marie 72
Marion 1,634
Marked Tree 3,208
Marmaduke 821
Marshall 1,397
Marvell 1,980
Mayflower 469
Maynard 224
McCaskill 58
McCrory 1,378
McDougal 328
McGehee 4,683
McNab 201
McNeil 684
McRae 643
Melbourne 1,043
Mena 4,530
Menifee 251
Midland 294
Mineral Springs 761
Minturn 97
Mitchellville 494
Monette 1,076
Monticello 5,085
Montrose 558
Moorefield 127
Moro 489
Morrilton 6,814
Mount Ida 819
Mount Pleasant 346
Mountain Home 3,936
Mountain View 1,866
Mountainburg 524
Mulberry 1,340
Murfreesboro 1,350
Nashville 4,016
Newark 849
Newport 7,725
Nimmons 135
Norfork 266
Norman 360
Norphlet 755
Norristown 170
North Crossett 2,891
North Little Rock 60,040
Norvell 440
Oak Grove 236
Oakhaven 83
Oden 141
Ogden 286
Oil Trough 524
O'Kean 244
Okolona 233
Ola 1,029
Omaha 160
Oppelo 147
Osceola 7,204
Oxford 271
Ozan 134
Ozark 2,592
Palestine 755
Pangburn 654
Paragould 10,639
Paraloma 60
Paris 3,646
Parkdale 459
Parkin 1,731
Patmos 77
Patterson 417
Pea Ridge 1,088
Peach Orchard 256
Perla 227
Perry 218
Perrytown 148
Perryville 815
Piggott 3,087
Pine Bluff 57,389
Plainview 677
Pleasant Plains 162
Plumerville 724
Pocahontas 4,544
Pollard 253
Portia 381
Portland 662
Pottsville 411
Powhatan 84
Poyen 265
Prairie Grove 1,582
Prattsville 299
Prescott 3,921
Princeton 41
Pyatt 137
Quitman 354
Ratcliff 184
Ravenden 219
Ravenden Springs 107

† Consolidated with Juneau in July, 1970.

ARKANSAS, Continued

Reader 143
Rector 1,990
Redfield 277
Reed 403
Rena 9
Reyno 356
Rison 1,214
Rockport 158
Roe 127
Rogers 11,050
Rondo 379
Rose Bud 157
Rudy 103
Russell 231
Russellville 11,750
St. Charles 201
St. Francis 297
St. Paul 145
Salem 1,277
Salesville 156
Saratoga 131
Scranton 222
Searcy 9,040
Sedgwick 168
Sheridan 2,480
Sherrill 208
Sherwood 2,754
Shirley 269
Sidney 109
Siloam Springs 6,009
Smackover 2,058
Smale 54
Smithville 59
Snow Lake 85
Southwest Little Rock 13,231
Sparkman 663
Springdale 16,783
Springtown 80
Stamps 2,427
Star City 2,032
Stephens 1,184
Strawberry 176
Strong 965
Stuttgart 10,477
Subiaco 375
Success 201
Sulphur Rock 224
Sulphur Springs 503
Summit 321
Swifton 703
Taylor 671
Texarkana 21,682
Thornton 331
Tillar 293
Tinsman 113
Tontitown 426
Traskwood 210
Trumann 5,938
Tuckerman 1,731
Tull 179
Tupelo 246
Turrell 783
Tyronza 510
Ulm 185
Umpire 105
Van Buren 8,373
Vandervoort 108
Victoria 198
Vilonia 423
Viola 360
Wabbaseka 644
Waldenburg 164
Waldo 1,658
Waldron 2,132
Walnut Ridge 3,800
Ward 619
Warren 6,433
Washington 290
Watson 371
Weiner 715
Weldon 133
West Fork 810
West Helena 11,007
West Memphis 25,892
West Point 184
Western Grove 179
Wheatley 507
Whelen Springs 126
Whitehall 1,300
Wickes 409
Widener 292
Williford 175
Wilmar 653
Wilmot 1,132
Wilson 1,009
Wilton 427
Winchester 234
Winslow 227
Winthrop 240
Woodberry 37
Wooster 307
Wynne 6,696
Yellville 860
Zinc 58

CALIFORNIA Total population: 19,953,134

METROPOLITAN AREAS

Anaheim-Santa Ana-Garden Grove 1,420,690
Bakersfield 329,271
Fresno 413,329
Los Angeles-Long Beach 7,036,887
Modesto 194,506
Oxnard-Simi Valley-Ventura 378,497
Riverside-San Bernardino-Ontario 1,140,609
Sacramento 803,610
Salinas-Seaside-Monterey 247,450
San Diego 1,357,854
San Francisco-Oakland 3,108,022
San Jose 1,066,421
Santa Barbara-Santa Maria-Lompoc 264,324
Santa Cruz 123,790
Santa Rosa 204,885
Stockton 289,564
Vallejo-Fairfield-Napa 250,955

COUNTIES

Alameda 1,073,184
Alpine 484
Amador 11,821
Butte 101,969
Calaveras 13,585
Colusa 12,430
Contra Costa 555,805
Del Norte 14,580
El Dorado 43,833
Fresno 413,329
Glenn 17,521
Humboldt 99,692
Imperial 74,492
Inyo 15,571
Kern 329,271
Kings 66,717
Lake 19,548
Lassen 16,796
Los Angeles 7,036,887
Madera 41,519
Marin 206,758
Mariposa 6,015
Mendocino 51,101
Merced 104,629
Modoc 7,469
Mono 4,016
Monterey 247,450
Napa 79,140
Nevada 26,346
Orange 1,420,690
Placer 77,632
Plumas 11,707
Riverside 459,074
Sacramento 634,190
San Benito 18,226
San Bernardino 681,535
San Diego 1,357,854
San Francisco 715,674
San Joaquin 289,564
San Luis Obispo 105,690
San Mateo 556,601
Santa Barbara 264,324
Santa Clara 1,066,421
Santa Cruz 123,790
Shasta 77,640
Sierra 2,365
Siskiyou 33,225
Solano 171,815
Sonoma 204,885
Stanislaus 194,506
Sutter 41,935
Tehama 29,517
Trinity 7,615
Tulare 188,322
Tuolumne 22,169
Ventura 378,497
Yolo 91,788
Yuba 44,736

PLACES

Adelanto 2,115
Alameda 70,968
Alamo-Danville 14,059
Albany 14,674
Alhambra 62,125
Alondra Park 12,193
Alpine 1,570
Alta Hill 1,185
Altadena 42,415
Alturas 2,799
Alum Rock 18,355
Amador 156
Anaheim 166,408
Anderson 5,492
Angels 1,710
Angwin 2,690
Antioch 28,060
Apple Valley 6,702
Aptos 8,704
Arbuckle 1,037
Arcadia 43,237
Arcata 8,985
Arden-Arcade 82,492
Armona 1,392
Arroyo Grande 7,454
Artesia 14,757
Arvin 5,199
Ashland 14,810
Atascadero 10,290
Atherton 8,085
Atwater 11,640
Auburn 6,570
August School Area 6,735
Avalon 1,520
Avenal 3,035
Avocado Heights 9,810
Azusa 25,217
Bakersfield 69,515
Baldwin Park 47,285
Banning 12,034
Barstow 17,442
Bayview-Pine Hills 2,340
Baywood-Los Osos 3,487
Beale East 7,029
Beale West 2,325
Beaumont 5,484
Bell 21,836
Bell Gardens 29,308
Bellflower 51,454
Belmont 23,667
Belvedere 2,599
Ben Lomond 2,793
Benicia 7,349
Berkeley 116,716
Bethel Island 1,398
Beverly Hills 33,416
Big Bear 5,268
Biggs 1,115
Bishop 3,498
Bloomington 11,957
Blue Lake 1,112
Blythe 7,047
Bonnyview 4,882
Boron 1,999
Boulder Creek 1,806
Bowman-Auburn North 2,089
Boyes Hot Springs 3,558
Bradbury 1,098
Brawley 13,746
Brea 18,447
Brentwood 2,649
Brisbane 3,003
Broderick-Bryte 12,782
Buellton 1,402
Buena Park 63,646
Burbank 88,871
Burlingame 27,320
Burney 2,190
Buttonwillow 1,193
Cabazon 598
Calexico 10,625
California City 1,309
Calipatria 1,824
Calistoga 1,882
Calwa 5,191
Camarillo 19,219
Camarillo Heights 5,892
Cambria 1,716
Cambrian Park 5,316
Camp Pendleton 32,861
Campbell 24,770
Capistrano Beach 4,149
Capitola 5,080
Cardiff-by-the-Sea 5,724
Carlsbad 14,944
Carmel-by-the-Sea 4,525
Carmel Valley 3,026
Carmichael 37,625
Carpinteria 6,982
Carson 71,150
Casitas Springs 1,113
Castle 1,903
Castro Valley 44,760
Castroville 3,235
Cathedral City 3,640
Cayucos 1,772
Central Valley 2,361
Ceres 6,029
Cerritos 15,856
Chemeketa Park-Redwood Estates 1,452
Cherry Valley 3,165
Cherryland 9,969
Chester 1,531
Chico 19,580
Chico North 6,656
Chico West 4,787
China Lake 11,105
Chino 20,411
Chowchilla 4,349
Chula Vista 67,901
Citrus Heights 21,760
Claremont 23,464
Clayton 1,385
Clearlake Highlands 2,836
Cloverdale 3,251
Clovis 13,856
Coachella 8,353
Coalinga 6,161
Colfax 798
Colma 537
Colton 20,016
Colusa 3,842
Commerce 10,536
Compton 78,611
Concord 85,164
Corcoran 5,249
Corning 3,573
Corona 27,519
Coronado 20,910
Corte Madera 8,464
Costa Mesa 72,660
Cotati 1,368
Cottonwood 1,288
Covina 30,380
Crescent City 2,586
Crescent North 3,053
Crest Forest 3,509
Cucamonga 5,796
Cudahy 16,998
Culver City 34,526
Cupertino 18,216
Cutler 2,503
Cutten 2,228
Cypress 31,569
Daly City 66,922
Dana Point 4,745
Danville, see Alamo-Danville
Davis 23,488
Del Aire 11,930
Delano 14,559
Delhi 2,063
Del Mar 3,956
Del Rey Oaks 1,823
Denair 1,128
Desert Hot Springs 2,738
Desert View Highlands 2,172
Diamond Bar 12,234
Dinuba 7,917
Dixon 4,432
Dominguez 5,980
Dorris 840
Dos Palos 2,496
Downey 88,445
Duarte 14,981
Dublin 13,641
Dunsmuir 2,214
Eagle Mountain 2,453
Earlimart 3,080
East Blythe 1,252
East Compton 5,853
East La Mirada 12,339
East Los Angeles 105,033
East Palo Alto 17,897
East Porterville 4,042
Easton 1,065
Edwards 10,331
El Cajon 52,273
El Centro 19,272
El Cerrito 25,190
El Encanto Heights 6,225
El Granada 1,473
Elk Grove 3,721
El Monte 69,852
El Paso de Robles 7,168
El Rio 6,173
El Segundo 15,620
Elsinore 3,530
El Toro 8,654
El Toro Station 6,970
El Verano 1,753
Emeryville 2,681
Empire 2,016
Encinitas 5,375
Enterprise 11,486
Escalon 2,366
Escondido 36,792
Esparto 1,088
Etna 667
Eureka 24,337
Exeter 4,475
Fair Oaks 11,256
Fairfax 7,661
Fairfield 44,146
Fallbrook 6,945
Farmersville 3,456
Felton 2,062
Ferndale 1,352
Fillmore 6,285
Firebaugh 2,517
Flintridge, see La Canada-Flintridge
Florence-Graham 42,895
Florin 9,646
Folsom 5,810
Fontana 20,673
Foothills, see Tustin-Foothills
Ford City 3,503
Fort Bragg 4,455
Fort Irwin 2,991
Fort Jones 515
Fortuna 4,203
Foster City 9,522
Fountain Valley 31,886
Fowler 2,239
Frazier Park 1,167
Freedom 5,563
Fremont 100,869
Fresno 165,972
Fullerton 85,987
Galt 3,200
Garden Acres 7,870
Garden Grove 121,371
Gardena 41,021
George 7,404
Gilroy 12,665
Glen Avon 5,759
Glendale 132,752
Glendora 31,349
Gonzales 2,575
Goshen 1,324
Graham, see Florence-Graham
Grand Terrace 5,901
Grass Valley 5,149
Greenacres 2,116
Greenfield 2,608
Greenville 1,073
Gridley 3,534
Grossmont-Mount Helix 8,723
Grover City 5,939
Guadalupe 3,145
Gustine 2,793
Hacienda Heights 35,969
Half Moon Bay 4,023
Hanford 15,179
Hanford Northwest 1,476
Hanford South 2,494
Harte, see Twain-Harte
Hawaiian Gardens 9,019
Hawthorne 53,304
Hayward 93,058
Healdsburg 5,438
Hemet 12,252
Hemet East 8,598
Hercules 252
Hermosa Beach 17,412
Hesperia 4,592
Hidden Hills 1,529
Highland 12,669
Hillsborough 8,753
Hollister 7,663
Holtville 3,496
Home Gardens 5,116
Homeland 1,187
Hughson 2,144
Huntington Beach 115,960
Huntington Park 33,744
Huron 1,525
Imperial 3,094
Imperial Beach 20,244
Indian Wells 760
Indio 14,459
Industry 714
Inglewood 89,985
Ione 2,369
Irwindale 784
Isla Vista 13,441
Isleton 909
Ivanhoe 1,595
Jackson 1,924
Joshua Tree 1,211
Kensington 5,823
Kerman 2,667
Keyes 1,875
King City 3,717
Kingsburg 3,843
La Canada-Flintridge 20,652
La Crescenta-Montrose 19,594
Ladera Heights 6,535
Lafayette 20,484
Laguna Beach 14,550
Laguna Hills 13,676
Laguna Niguel 4,644
La Habra 41,350
Lake Arrowhead 2,682
Lakeland Village 1,724
Lakeport 3,005
Lakeside 11,991
Lakewood 82,973
La Mesa 39,178
La Mirada 30,808
Lamont 7,007
Lancaster 32,570
La Palma 9,687
La Puente 31,092
Larkspur 10,487
La Selva Beach 1,171
Lathrop 2,137
Laton 1,071
La Verne 12,965
Lawndale 24,825
Lemon Grove 19,690
Lemoore 4,219
Lemoore Station 9,210
Lennox 16,121
Lenwood 3,834
Lincoln 3,176
Lincoln Village 6,112
Linda 7,731
Lindsay 5,206
Live Oak (Santa Cruz Co.) 6,443
Live Oak (Sutter Co.) 2,645
Livermore 37,703
Livingston 2,588
Lodi 28,691
Loma Linda 9,797
Lomita 19,784
Lompoc 25,284
Lompoc North 2,699
Lompoc Northwest 4,874
Lone Pine 1,241
Long Beach 358,633
Loomis 1,108
Los Alamitos 11,346
Los Altos 24,726
Los Altos Hills 6,865
Los Angeles 2,809,596
Los Banos 9,188
Los Gatos 23,735
Los Nietos, see West Whittier-Los Nietos
Los Osos, see Baywood-Los Osos
Loyalton 945
Lucerne 1,300
Lynwood 43,353
Madera 16,044
Manhattan Beach 35,352
Manteca 13,845
March 2,002
Maricopa 740
Marina 8,343
Martinez 16,506
Marysville 9,353
Mather 7,027
Maywood 16,996
McCloud 1,643
McFarland 4,177
Meiners Oaks-Mira Monte 7,025
Mendota 2,705
Menlo Park 26,906
Merced 22,670
Mill Valley 12,942
Millbrae 20,920
Milpitas 27,149
Mira Loma 8,482
Mira Monte, see Meiners Oaks-Mira Monte
Mission Viejo 11,933
Modesto 61,712
Mojave 2,573
Monrovia 30,015
Montague 890
Montara 1,459
Montclair 22,546
Monte Sereno 3,089
Montebello 42,807
Monterey 26,302
Monterey Park 49,166
Montrose, see La Crescenta-Montrose
Moorpark 3,380
Morada 2,936
Moraga 14,205
Morgan Hill 6,485
Morro Bay 7,109
Mount Helix, see Grossmont-Mount Helix
Mount Shasta 2,256
Mountain View 54,206
Mulberry 1,795
Muscoy 7,091
Napa 35,978
National City 43,184
Nebo Center 1,828
Needles 4,051
Nevada City 2,314
Newark 27,153
Newhall 9,651
Newman 2,505
Newport Beach 49,422
Nipomo 3,642
Norco 14,511
North Fair Oaks 9,740
North Highlands 31,854
North Island 6,002
Norwalk 91,827
Novato 31,006
Oak View 4,872
Oakdale 6,594
Oakland 361,561
Oakley 1,306
Oceano 2,564
Oceanside 40,494
Oildale 20,879
Ojai 5,591
Olivehurst 8,100
Ontario 64,118
Opal Cliffs 5,425
Orange 77,365
Orange Cove 3,392
Orangevale 16,493
Orcutt 8,500
Orinda 6,790
Orland 2,884
Orosi 2,757
Oroville 7,536
Otay-Castle Park 15,445
Oxnard 71,225
Pacific Grove 13,505
Pacifica 36,020
Pajaro 1,407
Palermo 1,966
Palm Desert 6,171
Palm Springs 20,936
Palmdale 8,511
Palmdale East 3,560
Palo Alto 56,181
Palos Verdes Estates 13,631
Palos Verdes Peninsula 38,918
Paradise 14,539
Paramount 34,734
Parkway-Sacramento South 28,574
Parlier 1,993
Pasadena 112,981
Pasatiempo 1,115
Patterson 3,147
Pendleton North 11,803
Pendleton South 13,692
Perris 4,228
Petaluma 24,870
Pico Rivera 54,170
Piedmont 10,917
Pine Hills, see Bayview-Pine Hills
Pinole 13,266
Pismo Beach 4,043
Pittsburg 20,651
Pixley 1,584
Placentia 21,948
Placerville 5,416
Planada 2,056
Pleasant Hill 24,610
Pleasanton 18,328
Plymouth 501
Point Arena 424
Point Mugu 3,351
Pomona 87,384
Poplar 1,239
Port Hueneme 14,295
Porterville 12,602
Porterville Northwest 2,517
Porterville West 6,200
Portola 1,625
Portola Valley 4,943
Poway 9,422
Project City 1,431
Quartz Hill 4,935
Quincy 3,343
Ramona 3,554
Rancho Cordova 30,451
Rancho Mirage 1,298
Rancho Rinconada 5,149
Rancho Santa Clarita 4,860
Red Bluff 7,676
Redding 16,659
Redlands 36,355
Redondo Beach 57,425
Redwood City 55,686
Redwood Estates, see Chemeketa Park-Redwood Estates
Reedley 8,131
Rialto 28,370
Richgrove 1,023
Richmond 79,043
Ridgecrest 7,629
Rio Dell 2,817
Rio Linda 7,524
Rio Vista 3,135
Ripon 2,679
Riverbank 3,949
Riverdale 1,722
Riverside 140,089
Rocklin 3,039
Rodeo 5,356
Rohnert Park 6,133
Rohnerville 2,781
Rolling Hills 2,050
Rolling Hills Estates 6,735
Rosamond 2,281
Roseland 5,105
Rosemead 40,972
Roseville 18,221
Ross 2,742
Rossmoor 12,922
Rowland Heights 16,881
Rubidoux 13,969
Ryans Slough 3,922
Sacramento 257,105
Sacramento South, see Parkway-Sacramento South
St. Helena 3,173
Salida 1,456
Salinas 58,896
San Andreas 1,564
San Anselmo 13,031
San Bernardino 104,783
San Bruno 36,254
San Carlos 25,924
San Clemente 17,063
San Diego 697,027
San Dimas 15,692
San Fernando 16,571
San Francisco 715,674
San Gabriel 29,336
San Jacinto 4,385
San Joaquin 1,506
San Jose 445,779
San Juan Bautista 1,164
San Juan Capistrano 3,781
San Leandro 68,698
San Lorenzo 24,633
San Luis Obispo 28,036
San Marcos 3,896
San Marino 14,177
San Martin 1,392
San Mateo 78,991
San Pablo 21,461
San Rafael 38,977
San Ramon Village 4,084
Sand City 212
Sanger 10,088
Santa Ana 156,876
Santa Ana Air Facility 2,106

Santa Barbara 70,215
Santa Clara 87,717
Santa Cruz 32,076
Santa Fe Springs 14,750
Santa Maria 32,749
Santa Maria South 7,129
Santa Monica 88,289
Santa Paula 18,001
Santa Rosa 50,006
Santee 21,107
Saratoga 27,110
Sausalito 6,158
Scotts Valley 3,621
Seal Beach 24,441
Searles Valley 3,828
Seaside 35,935
Sebastopol 3,993
Selma 7,459
Shafter 5,327
Sierra Madre 12,140
Signal Hill 5,582
Simi Valley 59,832
Solana Beach 5,023
Soledad 4,222
Solvang 2,004
Sonoma 4,112
Sonora 3,100
Soquel 5,795
South El Monte 13,443
South Gate 56,909
South Laguna 2,566
South Lake Tahoe 12,921
South Modesto 7,889
South Oroville 4,111
South Pasadena 22,979
South San Francisco 46,646
South San Gabriel 5,051
South San Jose Hills 12,386
South Taft 2,214
South Turlock 1,762
South Whittier 46,641
South Yuba City 5,352
Spring Valley 29,742
Stanford 8,691
Stanton 18,186
Stockton 109,963
Strathmore 1,221
Suisun City 2,917
Sun City 5,519
Sunnymead 6,708
Sunnyvale 95,408
Susanville 6,608
Sutter 1,488
Sutter Creek 1,508
Taft 4,285
Taft Heights 2,108
Tahoe City 1,394
Tehachapi 4,211
Tehama 317
Temple City 31,040
Terra Bella 1,037
Thermalito 4,217
Thousand Oaks 35,873
Tiburon 6,209
Torrance 134,584
Tracy 14,724
Trinidad 300
Truckee 1,392
Tulare 16,235
Tulare East 2,361
Tulare Northwest 1,950
Tulelake 857
Tuolumne 1,365
Turlock 13,992
Tustin 21,178
Tustin-Foothills 26,598
Twain-Harte 1,484
Twentynine Palms 5,667
Twentynine Palms Base 5,647
Twin Lakes 3,012
Ukiah 10,095
Union City 14,724
Upland 32,551
Vacaville 21,690
Valencia 4,243
Valinda 18,837
Vallejo 71,710
Vandenburg 13,193
Ventura (San
  Buenaventura) 57,964
Vernon 261
Victorville 10,845
View Park-
  Windsor Hills 12,268
Villa Park 2,723
Visalia 27,268
Vista 24,688
Walnut 5,992
Walnut Creek 39,844
Walnut Creek West 8,330
Walnut Park 8,925
Wasco 8,269
Waterford 2,243
Watsonville 14,569
Weaverville 1,489
Weed 2,983
West Athens 13,286
West Carson 15,501
West Compton 5,748
West Covina 68,034
West Hollywood 34,625
West Modesto 6,135
West Pittsburg 5,969
West Puente Valley 20,733
West Sacramento 12,002
West Whittier-
  Los Nietos 20,845
Westminster 59,874
Westmont 29,310
Westmorland 1,175
Westwood 1,862
Wheatland 1,280
Whittier 72,863
Williams 1,571
Willits 3,091
Willowbrook 28,705
Willows 4,085
Windsor 2,359
Windsor Hills, see View
  Park-Windsor Hills
Winters 2,419
Winton 3,393
Woodbridge 1,397
Woodlake 3,371
Woodland 20,677
Woodside 4,734
Woodville 1,031
Yermo 1,304
Yorba Linda 11,856
Yountville 2,332
Yreka City 5,394
Yuba City 13,986
Yucaipa 19,284
Yucca Valley 3,893

COLORADO Total population: 2,207,259

METROPOLITAN AREAS

Colorado Springs 235,972
Denver 1,227,529
Pueblo 118,238

COUNTIES

Adams 185,789
Alamosa 11,422
Arapahoe 162,142
Archuleta 2,733
Baca 5,674
Bent 6,493
Boulder 131,889
Chaffee 10,162
Cheyenne 2,396
Clear Creek 4,819
Conejos 7,846
Costilla 3,091
Crowley 3,086
Custer 1,120
Delta 15,286
Denver 514,678
Dolores 1,641
Douglas 8,407
Eagle 7,498
Elbert 3,903
El Paso 235,972
Fremont 21,942
Garfield 14,821
Gilpin 1,272
Grand 4,107
Gunnison 7,578
Hinsdale 202
Huerfano 6,590
Jackson 1,811
Jefferson 233,031
Kiowa 2,029
Kit Carson 7,530
Lake 8,282
La Plata 19,199
Larimer 89,900
Las Animas 15,744
Lincoln 4,836
Logan 18,852
Mesa 54,374
Mineral 786
Moffat 6,525
Montezuma 12,952
Montrose 18,366
Morgan 20,105
Otero 23,523
Ouray 1,546
Park 2,185
Phillips 4,131
Pitkin 6,185
Prowers 13,258
Pueblo 118,238
Rio Blanco 4,842
Rio Grande 10,494
Routt 6,592
Saguache 3,827
San Juan 831
San Miguel 1,949
Sedgwick 3,405
Summit 2,665
Teller 3,316
Washington 5,550
Weld 89,297
Yuma 8,544

PLACES

Aguilar 699
Akron 1,775
Alamosa 6,985
Alamosa East 1,040
Alma 73
Antonito 1,113
Applewood 8,214
Arriba 254
Arvada 46,814
Aspen 2,437
Ault 841
Aurora 74,974
Austin 1,163
Basalt 419
Bayfield 320
Bennett 613
Berthoud 1,446
Bethune 99
Black Hawk 217
Blanca 212
Blue River 8
Bonanza 10
Boone 448
Boulder 66,870
Bow Mar 945
Branson 70
Breckenridge 548
Brighton 8,309
Brookside 173
Broomfield 7,261
Brush 3,377
Buena Vista 1,962
Burlington 2,828
Calhan 465
Campo 206
Canon City 9,206
Carbondale 726
Castle Rock 1,531
Cedaredge 581
Center 1,470
Central City 228
Cheraw 129
Cherry Hills Village 4,605
Cheyenne Wells 982
Coal Creek 225
Cokedale 101
Collbran 225
Colorado Springs 135,060
Columbine Valley 481
Commerce City 17,407
Cortez 6,032
Craig 4,205
Crawford 171
Creede 653
Crested Butte 372
Crestone 34
Cripple Creek 425
Crook 199
Crowley 216
Dacono 360
De Beque 155
Deer Trail 374
Del Norte 1,569
Delta 3,694
Denver 514,678
Derby 10,206
Dillon 182
Dinosaur 247
Dolores 820
Dove Creek 619
Durango 10,333
Eads 795
Eagle 790
East Canon 1,805
Eaton 1,389
Eckley 193
Edgewater 4,866
Elizabeth 493
Empire 249
Englewood 33,695
Erie 1,090
Estes Park 1,616
Evans 2,570
Evergreen 2,321
Fairplay 419
Federal Heights 1,502
Firestone 570
Flagler 615
Fleming 349
Florence 2,846
Fort Carson 19,399
Fort Collins 43,337
Fort Collins West 1,693
Fort Lupton 2,489
Fort Morgan 7,594
Fountain 3,515
Fowler 1,241
Fraser 221
Frederick 696
Freshwater 24
Frisco 471
Fruita 1,822
Garden City 142
Genoa 161
Georgetown 542
Gilcrest 382
Glendale 765
Glenwood Springs 4,106
Golden 9,817
Granada 551
Granby 554
Grand Junction 20,170
Grand Lake 189
Grand Valley 270
Greeley 38,902
Green Mountain Falls 359
Greenwood Village 3,095
Grover 121
Gunnison 4,613
Gypsum 420
Hartman 129
Haswell 135
Haxtun 899
Hayden 763
Hillrose 121
Holly 993
Holyoke 1,640
Hooper 80
Hot Sulphur Springs 220
Hotchkiss 507
Hudson 518
Hugo 759
Idaho Springs 2,003
Ignacio 613
Iliff 193
Ironton 0
Jamestown 185
Johnstown 1,191
Julesburg 1,578
Keenesburg 427
Keota 6
Kersey 474
Kiowa 235
Kit Carson 220
Kremmling 764
Lafayette 3,498
La Jara 768
La Junta 7,938
Lake City 91
Lakeside 17
Lakewood 92,787
Lamar 7,797
La Salle 1,227
Las Animas 3,148
La Veta 589
Leadville 4,314
Leadville North 1,717
Limon 1,814
Lincoln Park 2,984
Littleton 26,466
Littleton Southeast 22,899
Log Lane Village 329
Longmont 23,209
Louisville 2,409
Loveland 16,220
Lyons 958
Manassa 814
Mancos 709
Manitou Springs 4,278
Manzanola 451
Mead 195
Meeker 1,597
Merino 260
Milliken 702
Minturn 706
Moffat 98
Monte Vista 3,909
Montezuma 6
Montrose 6,496
Monument 393
Morrison 439
Mountain View 706
Naturita 820
Nederland 492
New Castle 499
North Glenn 27,937
North La Junta 1,249
Norwood 408
Nucla 949
Nunn 269
Oak Creek 492
Olathe 756
Olney Springs 264
Ophir 6
Orchard Mesa 5,824
Ordway 1,017
Otis 521
Ouray 741
Ovid 463
Pagosa Springs 1,360
Palisade 874
Palmer Lake 947
Paoli 52
Paonia 1,161
Peetz 186
Pierce 452
Pitkin 44
Platteville 683
Poncha Springs 198
Portland 24
Pritchett 170
Prospect Heights 38
Pueblo 97,453
Ramah 101
Rangely 1,591
Raymer 68
Red Cliff 621
Rico 275
Ridgway 262
Rifle 2,150
Rockvale 359
Rocky Ford 4,859
Romeo 352
Rosedale 66
Rye 207
Saguache 642
Salida 4,355
San Luis 781
Sanford 638
Sawpit 26
Security-Widefield 15,297
Sedgwick 208
Seibert 192
Severance 59
Sheridan 4,787
Sheridan Lake 86
Sherrelwood 18,868
Silt 434
Silver Cliff 126
Silver Plume 164
Silverthorne 400
Silverton 797
Simla 460
Springfield 1,660
Starkville 166
Steamboat Springs 2,340
Sterling 10,636
Stratton 790
Stratton Meadows 6,223
Sugar City 307
Superior 171
Swink 381
Telluride 553
Thornton 13,326
Timnath 177
Trinidad 9,901
Two Buttes 138
Vail 484
Victor 258
Vilas 83
Vona 114
Walden 907
Walsenburg 4,329
Walsh 989
Ward 32
Welby 6,875
Wellington 691
Westcliffe 243
Westminster 19,432
Westminster East 7,576
Wheat Ridge 29,795
Widefield, see
  Security-Widefield
Wiley 357
Williamsburg 75
Windsor 1,564
Woodland Park 1,022
Wray 1,953
Yampa 286
Yuma 2,259

CONNECTICUT Total population: 3,032,217

METROPOLITAN AREAS

Bridgeport 389,153
Bristol 65,808
Danbury 78,405
Hartford 663,891
Meriden 55,959
New Britain 145,269
New Haven 355,538
Norwalk 120,099
Norwich-Groton-
  New London 208,718
Stamford 206,419
Waterbury 208,956

COUNTIES

Fairfield 792,814
Hartford 816,737
Litchfield 144,091
Middlesex 115,018
New Haven 744,948
New London 230,654
Tolland 103,440
Windham 84,515

TOWNS AND PLACES

Andover 2,099▲
Ansonia 21,160▲▲
Ashford 2,156▲
Avon 8,352▲
Bantam 881
Barkhamsted 2,066▲
Beacon Falls 3,546▲
Berlin 14,149▲
Bethany 3,857▲
Bethel 10,945▲
Bethlehem 1,923▲
Bloomfield 18,301▲
Bolton 3,691▲
Bozrah 2,036▲
Branford 2,080
Branford 20,444▲
Bridgeport 156,542▲▲
Bridgewater 1,277▲
Bristol 55,487▲▲
Broad Brook 1,548
Brookfield 9,688▲
Brooklyn 4,965▲
Burlington 4,070▲
Canaan 1,083
Canaan 931▲
Canterbury 2,673▲
Canton 6,868▲
Chaplin 1,621▲
Cheshire 19,051▲
Chester 1,569
Chester 2,982▲
Clinton 5,957
Clinton 10,267▲
Colchester 3,529
Colchester 6,603▲
Colebrook 1,020▲
Collinsville 2,897
Columbia 3,129▲
Conning Towers-
  Nautilus Park 9,791
Cornwall 1,177▲
Coventry 8,140▲
Cromwell 7,400▲
Danbury 50,781▲▲
Danielson 4,580
Darien 20,411▲
Deep River 2,333
Deep River 3,690▲
Derby 12,599▲▲
Durham 4,489▲
East Brooklyn 1,377
East Granby 3,532▲
East Haddam 4,676▲
East Hampton 1,982
East Hampton 7,078▲
East Hartford 57,583▲
East Haven 25,120▲
East Lyme 11,399▲
East Windsor 8,513▲
Eastford 922▲
Easton 4,885▲
Ellington 7,707▲
Enfield 46,189▲
Essex 2,473
Essex 4,911▲
Fairfield 56,487▲
Farmington 14,390▲
Fenwick 45
Franklin 1,356▲
Georgetown 1,101
Glastonbury 20,651▲
Goshen 1,351▲
Granby 6,150▲
Greenwich 59,755▲
Griswold 7,763▲
Groton 8,933
Groton 38,244▲
Guilford 3,632
Guilford 12,033▲
Haddam 4,934▲
Hamden 49,357▲
Hampton 1,129▲
Hartford 158,017▲▲
Hartland 1,303▲
Harwinton 4,318▲
Hebron 3,815▲
Jewett City 3,372
Kent 1,990▲
Killingly 13,573▲
Killingworth 2,435▲
Lake Pocotopaug 1,515
Lebanon 3,804▲
Ledyard 14,837▲
Lisbon 2,808▲
Litchfield 1,559
Litchfield 7,399▲
Lyme 1,484▲
Madison 4,310
Madison 9,768▲
Manchester 47,994▲
Mansfield 19,994▲
Marlborough 2,991▲
Meriden 55,959▲▲
Middlebury 5,542▲
Middlefield 4,132▲
Middletown 36,924▲▲
Milford 50,858▲▲
Monroe 12,047▲
Montville 1,688
Montville 15,662▲
Moodus 1,352
Moosup 3,376
Morningside Park 3,458
Morris 1,609▲
Mystic 2,568
Naugatuck 23,034▲▲
Nautilus Park, see Conning
  Towers-Nautilus Park
New Britain 83,441▲▲
New Canaan 17,455▲
New Fairfield 6,991▲
New Hartford 1,076
New Hartford 3,970▲
New Haven 137,707▲▲
New London 31,630▲▲
New Milford 4,606
New Milford 14,601▲
Newington 26,037
Newtown 1,963
Newtown 16,942▲
Niantic 3,422
Noank 1,371
Norfolk 2,073▲
North Branford 10,778▲
North Canaan 3,045▲
North Grosvenor Dale 2,156
North Haven 22,194▲
North Stonington 3,748▲
Norwalk 79,113▲▲
Norwich 41,739▲▲
Old Lyme 4,964▲
Old Saybrook 2,281
Old Saybrook 8,468▲
Orange 13,524▲
Oxford 4,480▲
Pawcatuck 5,255
Plainfield 2,923
Plainfield 11,957▲
Plainville 16,733▲
Pleasure Beach 1,394
Plymouth 10,321▲
Pomfret 2,529▲
Poquonock Bridge 3,165
Portland 8,812▲
Preston 3,593▲
Prospect 6,543▲
Putnam 6,918
Putnam 8,598▲
Quaker Hill 2,068
Redding 5,590▲
Ridgefield 5,878
Ridgefield 18,188▲
Rocky Hill 11,103▲
Roxbury 1,238▲
Salem 1,453▲
Salisbury 3,573▲
Scotland 1,022▲
Seymour 12,776▲
Sharon 2,491▲
Shelton 27,165▲▲
Sherman 1,459▲
Simsbury 4,994
Simsbury 17,475▲
Somers 1,274
Somers 6,893▲
South Coventry 3,735
South Windsor 15,553▲
Southbury 7,852▲
Southington 30,946▲
Sprague 2,912▲
Stafford 8,680▲
Stafford Springs 3,339
Stamford 108,798▲▲
Sterling 1,853▲
Stonington 1,413
Stonington 15,940▲
Storrs 10,691
Stratford 49,775▲
Suffield 8,634▲
Tariffville 1,337
Thomaston 6,233▲
Thompson 7,580▲
Tolland 7,857▲
Torrington 31,952▲▲
Trumbull 31,394▲
Uncasville 1,750
Union 443▲
Vernon 27,237▲
Voluntown 1,452▲
Wallingford 35,714▲
Warren 827▲
Washington 3,121▲
Waterbury 108,033▲▲
Waterford 17,227▲
Watertown 18,610▲
Weatogue 2,396
West Hartford 68,031▲
West Haven 52,851▲▲
West Mystic 3,415
West Simsbury 1,419
Westbrook 1,509
Westbrook 3,820▲
Weston 7,417▲
Westport 27,414▲
Wethersfield 26,662▲
Willimantic 14,402
Willington 3,755▲
Wilton 13,572▲
Winchester 11,106▲
Windham 19,626▲
Windsor 22,502▲
Windsor Locks 15,080▲
Winsted 8,954
Wolcott 12,495▲
Woodbridge 7,673▲
Woodbury 1,342
Woodbury 5,869▲
Woodstock 4,311▲

▲ Population of entire town (township).
▲▲ City and town (township) with the same name and population.

DELAWARE Total population: 548,104

METROPOLITAN AREA

Wilmington 499,493 (385,856 in Delaware, 60,346 in New Jersey, 53,291 in Maryland)

COUNTIES

Kent 81,892
New Castle 385,856
Sussex 80,356

PLACES

Arden 555
Bellefonte 1,442
Bethany Beach 189
Bethel 219
Blades 632
Bowers 268
Bridgeville 1,317
Brookside Park 7,856
Camden 1,241
Chelsea, see Wilmington Manor-Chelsea-Leedom
Cheswold 286
Claymont 6,584
Clayton 1,015
Dagsboro 375
Delaware City 2,024
Delmar 943
Dover 17,488
Dover Base 8,106
Dupont Manor 1,256
Ellendale 399
Elsmere 8,415
Farmington 109
Felton 495
Fenwick Island 56
Frankford 635
Frederica 878
Georgetown 1,844
Greenwood 654
Harrington 2,407
Hartly 180
Highland Acres 1,471
Houston 317
Kent Acres-South Dover Manor 1,573
Kenton 205
Laurel 2,408
Leedom, see Wilmington Manor-Chelsea-Leedom
Leipsic 247
Lewes 2,563
Little Creek 215
Magnolia 319
Middletown 2,644
Milford 5,314
Millsboro 1,073
Millville 224
Milton 1,490
New Castle 4,814
Newark 21,078
Newport 1,366
Ocean View 411
Odessa 547
Rehoboth Beach 1,614
Rodney Village 2,127
Seaford 5,537
Selbyville 1,099
Slaughter Beach 84
Smyrna 4,243
South Dover Manor, see Kent Acres-South Dover Manor
Townsend 505
Viola 154
Wilmington 80,386
Wilmington Manor-Chelsea-Leedom 10,134
Woodside 223
Wyoming 1,062

DISTRICT OF COLUMBIA Total population: 756,510

METROPOLITAN AREA

Washington 2,861,123 (1,183,376 in Maryland, 921,237 in Virginia, 756,510 in District of Columbia)

CITY

Washington 756,510

FLORIDA Total population: 6,789,443

METROPOLITAN AREAS

Daytona Beach 169,487
Fort Lauderdale-Hollywood 620,100
Fort Myers 105,216
Gainesville 104,764
Jacksonville 528,865
Lakeland-Winter Haven 227,697
Melbourne-Titusville-Cocoa 230,006
Miami 1,267,792
Orlando 428,003
Pensacola 243,075
Sarasota 120,413
Tallahassee 103,047
Tampa-St. Petersburg 1,012,594
West Palm Beach 348,753

COUNTIES

Alachua 104,764
Baker 9,242
Bay 75,283
Bradford 14,625
Brevard 230,006
Broward 620,100
Calhoun 7,624
Charlotte 27,559
Citrus 19,196
Clay 32,059
Collier 38,040
Columbia 25,250
Dade 1,267,792
De Soto 13,060
Dixie 5,480
Duval 528,865
Escambia 205,334
Flagler 4,454
Franklin 7,065
Gadsden 39,184
Gilchrist 3,551
Glades 3,669
Gulf 10,096
Hamilton 7,787
Hardee 14,889
Hendry 11,859
Hernando 17,004
Highlands 29,507
Hillsborough 490,265
Holmes 10,720
Indian River 35,992
Jackson 34,434
Jefferson 8,778
Lafayette 2,892
Lake 69,305
Lee 105,216
Leon 103,047
Levy 12,756
Liberty 3,379
Madison 13,481
Manatee 97,115
Marion 69,030
Martin 28,035
Monroe 52,586
Nassau 20,626
Okaloosa 88,187
Okeechobee 11,233
Orange 344,311
Osceola 25,267
Palm Beach 348,753
Pasco 75,955
Pinellas 522,329
Polk 227,697
Putnam 36,424
St. Johns 31,035
St. Lucie 50,836
Santa Rosa 37,741
Sarasota 120,413
Seminole 83,692
Sumter 14,839
Suwannee 15,559
Taylor 13,641
Union 8,112
Volusia 169,487
Wakulla 6,308
Walton 16,087
Washington 11,453

PLACES

Alachua 2,252
Alford 402
Altamonte Springs 4,391
Altha 423
Anna Maria 1,137
Apalachicola 3,102
Apollo Beach 1,042
Apopka 4,045
Arcadia 5,658
Archer 898
Astatula 388
Atlantis 425
Auburndale 5,386
Avon Park 6,712
Azalea Park 7,367
Bal Harbour 2,038
Bartow 12,891
Bay Harbor Islands 4,619
Bay Lake 24
Bayshore Gardens 9,255
Bayview 696
Beacon Squier 2,927
Bell 227
Belle Glade 15,949
Belle Glade Camp 1,892
Belle Isle 2,705
Belleair 2,962
Belleair Beach 952
Belleair Bluffs 1,910
Belleair Shores 124
Belleview 916
Beverly Beach 21
Biscayne Park 2,717
Bithlo 684
Blountstown 2,384
Boca Chica 2,817
Boca Raton 28,506
Bonifay 2,068
Bonita Springs 1,932
Boulogne 77
Bowling Green 1,357
Boynton Beach 18,115
Bradenton 21,040
Bradenton Beach 1,370
Bradley Junction 1,276
Brandon 12,749
Branford 820
Briny Breezes 481
Bristol 626
Broadview Park-Rock Hill 6,049
Bronson 698
Brooker 340
Brooksville 4,060
Browardale 17,444
Browns Village 23,442
Buena Vista 3,407
Bunche Park 5,773
Bunnell 1,687
Bushnell 700
Callahan 772
Callaway 3,240
Campbellton 304
Cantonment 3,241
Cape Canaveral 4,258
Cape Coral 10,193
Carol City 27,361
Carrabelle 1,044
Carver Ranch Estates 5,515
Caryville 724
Casselberry 9,438
Cedar Grove 689
Cedar Hammock-Bradenton South 10,820
Cedar Key 714
Center Hill 371
Century 2,679
Chattahoochee 7,944
Chiefland 1,965
Chipley 3,347
Cinco Bayou 362
Clearwater 52,074
Clermont 3,661
Clewiston 3,896
Cloud Lake 136
Cocoa 16,110
Cocoa Beach 9,952
Cocoa West 5,779
Coconut Creek 1,359
Coleman 614
Collier Manor-Cresthaven 7,202
Colonial Hills 2,193
Combee Settlement 4,963
Conway 8,642
Cooper City 2,535
Coral Cove 1,520
Coral Gables 42,494
Coral Springs 1,489
Cottondale 765
Country Estates 1,950
Crescent City 1,734
Crestview 7,952
Cross City 2,268
Crystal River 1,696
Cutler Ridge 17,441
Cypress 266
Cypress Gardens 3,757
Cypress Quarters 1,310
Dade City 4,241
Dade City East 1,163
Dade City North 1,837
Dania 9,013
Davenport 1,303
Davie 4,977
Daytona Beach 45,327
Daytona Beach Shores 768
De Bary 3,154
Deerfield Beach 16,662
De Funiak Springs 4,966
De Land 11,641
De Leon Springs 1,134
Delray Beach 19,366
Deltona 4,868
Destin 1,536
Dover 2,094
Dundee 1,660
Dunedin 17,639
Dunnellon 1,146
Eagle Lake 1,373
East Auburndale 2,621
East Lake-Orient Park 5,697
East Naples 6,152
East Palatka 1,446
East Winter Haven 1,148
Eastpoint 1,188
Eatonville 2,024
Ebro 125
Edgewater 3,348
Edgewater Gulf Beach 84
Edgewood 392
Eglin 7,769
Egypt Lake 7,556
Ellenton 1,421
Eloise 1,504
El Portal 2,068
El Ranchero Vill-Golf Lake Estates 1,859
Englewood 5,108
Esto 210
Eustis 6,722
Everglades 462
Fellsmere 813
Fern Crest Village 1,009
Fernandina Beach 6,955
Five Points 1,214
Flagler Beach 1,042
Florida City 5,133
Florida Ridge 1,338
Forest Hills 1,215
Fort Lauderdale 139,590
Fort Meade 4,374
Fort Myers 27,351
Fort Myers Beach 4,305
Fort Myers Southeast 3,150
Fort Myers Southwest 5,086
Fort Myers Villas-Pine Manor 3,408
Fort Pierce 29,721
Fort Pierce Northwest 3,269
Fort Walton Beach 19,994
Fort White 365
Frostproof 2,814
Fruitland Park 1,359
Fruitville 1,531
Gainesville 64,510
Gifford 5,772
Glen Ridge 216
Glen St. Mary 357
Golden Beach 849
Golf 50
Golfview 201
Goulds 6,690
Graceville 2,560
Grand Ridge 512
Green Cove Springs 3,857
Greenacres City 1,731
Greensboro 716
Greenville 1,141
Greenwood 1,130
Gretna 883
Grove City 1,252
Groveland 1,928
Gulf Breeze 4,190
Gulf Gate Estates 5,874
Gulf Harbors 1,177
Gulf Stream 408
Gulfport 9,730
Hacienda Village 15
Haines City 8,956
Hallandale 23,849
Hampton 386
Harlem 2,006
Hastings 320
Havana 2,022
Haverhill 1,034
Hawthorn 1,126
Hernando 524
Hialeah 102,452
Hialeah Gardens 492
High Springs 2,787
Highland Beach 40
Highland City 1,020
Highland Park 88
Hiland Park 3,691
Hillcrest Heights 154
Hilliard 1,205
Hillsboro Beach 713
Hobe Sound 2,029
Holden Heights 6,206
Holiday Gardens 2,132
Holiday Hills 1,657
Holly Hill 8,191
Hollywood 106,873
Hollywood Ridge Farms 302
Holmes Beach 2,699
Homestead 13,674
Homestead Base 8,257
Horseshoe Beach 124
Howey-in-the-Hills 466
Hudson 2,278
Hurlburt 2,155
Hypoluxo 336
Immokalee 3,764
Indialantic 2,685
Indian Creek 82
Indian Harbour Beach 5,371
Indian River Shores 76
Indian Rocks Beach 2,666
Indian Rocks Beach South Shore 791
Indiantown 2,283
Inglis 449
Interlachen 478
Inverness 2,299
Islamorada 1,251
Islandia 8
Jacksonville 528,865
Jan Phyl Village 1,340
Jasmine Estates 2,967
Jasper 2,221
Jay Town 646
Jennings 582
June Park 3,090
Juno Beach 747
Jupiter 3,136
Jupiter Inlet Beach Colony 396
Jupiter Island 295
Kendall 35,497
Kenneth City 3,862
Kensington Park 3,138
Key Colony Beach 371
Key Largo 2,866
Key West 29,312
Keystone Heights 800
Kissimmee 7,119
La Belle 1,823
Lacoochee 1,380
La Crosse 365
Lady Lake 382
Lake Alfred 2,847
Lake Buena Vista 12
Lake Butler 1,598
Lake Carroll 5,577
Lake City 10,575
Lake Clarke Shores 2,328
Lake Forest 5,216
Lake Hamilton 836
Lake Helen 1,303
Lake Holloway 6,227
Lake Magdalene 9,266
Lake Park 6,993
Lake Placid 656
Lake Ship Heights 1,114
Lake Wales 8,240
Lake Worth 23,714
Lakeland 41,550
Lantana 7,126
Largo 22,031
Lauderdale-by-the-Sea 2,879
Lauderdale Lakes 10,577
Lauderhill 8,465
Laurel Hill 418
Lawtey 636
Layton 100
Lazy Lake 48
Lee 240
Leesburg 11,869
Lehigh Acres 4,394
Leto 8,458
Lighthouse Point 9,071
Live Oak 6,830
Lockhart 5,809
Long Beach Resort 167
Longboat Key 2,850
Longwood 3,203
Lynn Haven 4,044
Macclenny 2,733
Madeira Beach 4,342
Madison 3,737
Maitland 7,157
Malabar 634
Malone 667
Manalapan 205
Mangonia Park 827
Marathon 4,397
Margate 8,867
Marianna 6,741
Marineland 13
Mary Esther 3,192
Mascotte 966
Mayo 793
McIntosh 287
Medley 351
Melbourne 40,236
Melbourne Beach 2,262
Melbourne Village 597
Melrose Park 6,111
Memphis 3,207
Merritt Island 29,233
Mexico Beach 588
Miami 334,859
Miami Beach 87,072
Miami Shores 9,425
Miami Springs 13,279
Micanopy 759
Midway-Canaan 2,060
Milton 5,360
Mims 8,309
Minneola 878
Miramar 23,973
Monticello 2,473
Montverde 308
Moore Haven 974
Mount Dora 4,543
Mulberry 2,701
Myrtle Grove 16,186
Naples 12,042
Naples Park 1,522
New Port Richey 6,098
New Port Richey East-Richey Lakes 2,758
New Smyrna Beach 10,580
Newberry 1,247
Niceville 4,024
Nokomis-Laurel 3,238
North Andrews Terrace 7,082
North Bay 4,831
North Fort Myers 8,798
North Lauderdale 1,213
North Miami 34,767
North Miami Beach 30,833
North Naples 3,201
North Orlando 1,161
North Palm Beach 9,035
North Port Charlotte 2,244
North Redington Beach 768
North Winter Haven 1,659
Norwood 14,973
Oak Hill 747
Oakland 672
Oakland Park 16,261
Ocala 22,583
Ocean Breeze 714
Ocean City 5,267
Ocean Ridge 1,074
Ocoee 3,937
Okeechobee 3,715
Oldsmar 1,538
Ona 236
Oneco 3,246
Opa-locka 11,902
Orange City 1,777
Orange Park 7,619
Orchid 8
Orlando 99,006
Ormond Beach 14,063
Ormond-by-the-Sea 6,002
Osprey 1,115
Oviedo 1,870
Oxford 490
Pace 1,776
Pahokee 5,663
Painters Hill 14
Palatka 9,444
Palm Bay 7,199
Palm Beach 9,086
Palm Beach Gardens 6,102
Palm Beach Shores 1,214
Palm River-Clair Mel 8,536
Palm Shores 202
Palm Springs 4,340
Palma Sola 1,745
Palmetto 7,422
Panama City 32,096
Panama City Beach 67
Parker 4,212
Parkland 165
Patrick North 1,652
Patrick South 1,583
Paxton 243
Pembroke Park 2,949
Pembroke Pines 15,520
Penney Farms 561
Pennsuco 74
Pensacola 59,507
Perrine 10,257
Perry 7,701
Pierson 654
Pine Craft 1,208
Pine Hills 13,882
Pine Manor, see Fort Myers Villas-Pine Manor
Pine Shores 1,115
Pinellas Park 22,287
Plant City 15,451
Plantation 23,523
Polk City 151
Pomona Park 578
Pompano Beach 38,544
Pompano Beach Highlands 5,014
Ponce de Leon 288
Ponce Inlet 328
Port Charlotte 10,769
Port Orange 3,781
Port Richey 1,259
Port St. Joe 4,401
Port St. Lucie 330
Progress Village 2,573
Punta Gorda 3,879
Quincy 8,334
Reddick 305
Redington Beach 1,583
Redington Shores 1,733
Richey Lakes, see New Port Richey East-Richey Lakes
Richmond Heights 6,663
Ridge Wood Heights 2,528
Riverland Village-Lauderdale Isles 5,512
Riverview 2,225
Riviera Beach 21,401
Rock Hill, see Broadview Park-Rock Hill
Rockledge 10,523
Royal Palm Beach 475
Ruskin 2,414
Safety Harbor 3,103
St. Augustine 12,352
St. Augustine Beach 632
St. Cloud 5,041
St. Leo 1,145
St. Lucie 428
St. Marks 366
St. Petersburg 216,232
St. Petersburg Beach 8,024
Salerno 1,161
Samoset 4,070
San Antonio 473
Sanford 17,393
Sarasota 40,237
Sarasota North 1,737
Sarasota South 3,730
Sarasota Southeast 6,885
Sarasota Springs 4,405
Satellite Beach 6,558
Sea Ranch Lakes 660
Sebastian 825
Sebring 7,223
Sewalls Point 298
Shalimar 578
Siesta Key 4,460
Sneads 1,550
Solana 1,286
Sopchoppy 460
South Apopka 2,293
South Bay 2,958
South Daytona 4,979
South Flomaton 329
South Gate Ridge 2,043
South Miami 11,780
South Miami Heights 10,395
South Palm Beach 188
South Pasadena 2,063
South Patrick Shores 10,313
South Peninsula 3,302
Southport 1,560
Springfield 5,949
Starke 4,848
Stuart 4,820
Sun City Center 2,143
Sunrise Golf Village 7,403
Surfside 3,614
Suwannee River 115
Sweetwater 3,357
Sweetwater Creek 19,453
Taft 1,183
Tahitian Gardens 1,286
Tallahassee 72,586
Tamarac 5,078
Tampa 277,767

Tarpon Springs 7,118
Tavares 3,261
Temple Terrace 7,347
Tequesta 2,642
Tice 7,254
Titusville 30,515
Trailer Estates 1,759
Treasure Island 6,120
Trenton 1,074
Tri Par Estates 1,080
Tyndall 4,248
Umatilla 1,600
Union Park 3,166
University 10,039
University Park 1,032
Valparaiso 6,504
Venice 6,648
Venice South 4,680
Vernon 691
Vero Beach 11,908
Vero Beach South 7,330
Virginia Gardens 2,524
Wahneta 2,733
Waldo 800
Ward Ridge 8
Warrington 15,848
Watertown 3,624
Wauchula 3,007
Wausau 288
Waverly 1,172
Webster 739
Weeki Wachee 76
Welaka 496
West Auburndale 2,148
West Bradenton 6,162
West Eau Gallie 2,705
West End 5,289
West Melbourne 3,050
West Miami 5,494
West Palm Beach 57,375
West Panama City Beach 1,052
West Pensacola 20,924
West Winter Haven 7,716
Westwood Lakes 12,811
Wewahitchka 1,733
White Springs 767
Whitfield Estates 1,362
Whiting Field 3,439
Wildwood 2,082
Williston 1,939
Wilton Manors 10,948
Windermere 894
Winston 4,505
Winter Garden 5,153
Winter Haven 16,136
Winter Park 21,895
Worthington Springs 214
Yankeetown 490
Zephyrhills 3,369
Zolfo Springs 1,117

GEORGIA Total population: 4,589,575

METROPOLITAN AREAS

Albany 89,639
Atlanta 1,390,164
Augusta 253,460
(162,437 in Georgia, 91,023 in South Carolina)
Columbus 238,584
(193,190 in Georgia, 45,394 in Alabama)
Macon 206,342
Savannah 187,816

COUNTIES

Appling 12,726
Atkinson 5,879
Bacon 8,233
Baker 3,875
Baldwin 34,240
Banks 6,833
Barrow 16,859
Bartow 32,663
Ben Hill 13,171
Berrien 11,556
Bibb 143,418
Bleckley 10,291
Brantley 5,940
Brooks 13,743
Bryan 6,539
Bulloch 31,585
Burke 18,255
Butts 10,560
Calhoun 6,606
Camden 11,334
Candler 6,412
Carroll 45,404
Catoosa 28,271
Charlton 5,680
Chatham 187,816
Chattahoochee 25,813
Chattooga 20,541
Cherokee 31,059
Clarke 65,177
Clay 3,636
Clayton 98,043
Clinch 6,405
Cobb 196,793
Coffee 22,828
Colquitt 32,298
Columbia 22,327
Cook 12,129
Coweta 32,310
Crawford 5,748
Crisp 18,087
Dade 9,910
Dawson 3,639
Decatur 22,310
De Kalb 415,387
Dodge 15,658
Dooly 10,404
Dougherty 89,639
Douglas 28,659
Early 12,682
Echols 1,924
Effingham 13,632
Elbert 17,262
Emanuel 18,357
Evans 7,290
Fannin 13,357
Fayette 11,364
Floyd 73,742
Forsyth 16,928
Franklin 12,784
Fulton 607,592
Gilmer 8,956
Glascock 2,280
Glynn 50,528
Gordon 23,570
Grady 17,826
Greene 10,212
Gwinnett 72,349
Habersham 20,691
Hall 59,405
Hancock 9,019
Haralson 15,927
Harris 11,520
Hart 15,814
Heard 5,354
Henry 23,724
Houston 62,924
Irwin 8,036
Jackson 21,093
Jasper 5,760
Jeff Davis 9,425
Jefferson 17,174
Jenkins 8,332
Johnson 7,727
Jones 12,218
Lamar 10,688
Lanier 5,031
Laurens 32,738
Lee 7,044
Liberty 17,569
Lincoln 5,895
Long 3,746
Lowndes 55,112
Lumpkin 8,728
Macon 12,933
Madison 13,517
Marion 5,099
McDuffie 15,276
McIntosh 7,371
Meriwether 19,461
Miller 6,424
Mitchell 18,956
Monroe 10,991
Montgomery 6,099
Morgan 9,904
Murray 12,986
Muscogee 167,377
Newton 26,282
Oconee 7,915
Oglethorpe 7,598
Paulding 17,520
Peach 15,990
Pickens 9,620
Pierce 9,281
Pike 7,316
Polk 29,656
Pulaski 8,066
Putnam 8,394
Quitman 2,180
Rabun 8,327
Randolph 8,734
Richmond 162,437
Rockdale 18,152
Schley 3,097
Screven 12,591
Seminole 7,059
Spalding 39,514
Stephens 20,331
Stewart 6,511
Sumter 26,931
Talbot 6,625
Taliaferro 2,423
Tattnall 16,557
Taylor 7,865
Telfair 11,394
Terrell 11,416
Thomas 34,562
Tift 27,288
Toombs 19,151
Towns 4,565
Treutlen 5,647
Troup 44,466
Turner 8,790
Twiggs 8,222
Union 6,811
Upson 23,505
Walker 50,691
Walton 23,404
Ware 33,525
Warren 6,669
Washington 17,480
Wayne 17,858
Webster 2,362
Wheeler 4,596
White 7,742
Whitfield 55,108
Wilcox 6,998
Wilkes 10,184
Wilkinson 9,393
Worth 14,770

PLACES

Abbeville 781
Acworth 3,929
Adairsville 1,676
Adel 4,972
Adrian 705
Ailey 487
Alamo 833
Alapaha 633
Albany 72,623
Aldora 322
Allenhurst 230
Allentown 295
Alma 3,756
Alpharetta 2,455
Alston 104
Alto 372
Alto Park-Garden Lakes 2,963
Alvaton 114
Ambrose 253
Americus 16,091
Andersonville 274
Arabi 305
Arcade 229
Argyle 206
Arlington 1,698
Arnoldsville 181
Ashburn 4,209
Athens 44,342
Atlanta 497,421
Attapulgus 513
Auburn 361
Augusta 59,864
Austell 2,632
Avalon 204
Avera 217
Avondale Estates 1,735
Baconton 710
Bainbridge 10,887
Baldwin 772
Ball Ground 617
Barnesville 4,935
Bartow 333
Barwick 432
Baxley 3,503
Bellville 234
Berkeley Lake 219
Berlin 422
Bethlehem 304
Between 94
Bibb City 812
Bishop 235
Blackshear 2,624
Blairsville 491
Blakely 5,267
Bloomingdale 1,588
Blue Ridge 1,602
Bluffton 105
Blythe 333
Bogart 667
Boston 1,443
Bostwick 289
Bowdon 1,753
Bowersville 301
Bowman 724
Boykin 90
Braselton 386
Braswell 30
Bremen 3,484
Brinson 231
Bronwood 500
Brooklet 683
Brooks 172
Broxton 957
Brunswick 19,585
Buchanan 800
Buckhead 177
Buena Vista 1,486
Buford 4,640
Butler 1,589
Byromville 419
Byron 1,368
Cadwell 354
Cairo 8,061
Calhoun 4,748
Camak 224
Camilla 4,987
Campton 93
Canon 709
Canton 3,654
Carl 234
Carlton 294
Carnesville 510
Carrollton 13,520
Cartersville 9,929
Cave Springs 1,305
Cecil 265
Cedartown 9,253
Center 213
Centerville 1,725
Centralhatchee 186
Chalybeate Springs 266
Chamblee 9,127
Charles 61
Chatsworth 2,706
Chauncey 308
Chester 409
Chickamauga 1,842
Clarkesville 1,294
Clarkston 3,127
Claxton 2,669
Clayton 1,569
Clermont 290
Cleveland 1,353
Climax 275
Cobb 125
Cobbtown 321
Cochran 5,161
Cohutta 393
Colbert 532
Coleman 168
Colemans Lake 17
College Park 18,203
Collins 574
Colquitt 2,026
Columbus 167,377
Comer 828
Commerce 3,702
Concord 312
Conyers 4,890
Coolidge 717
Cordele 10,733
Corinth 107
Cornelia 3,014
Cotton 102
Covington 10,267
Crawford 624
Crawfordville 735
Crosland 158
Culloden 272
Cumming 2,031
Cusseta 1,251
Cuthbert 3,972
Dacula 782
Dahlonega 2,658
Daisy 150
Dallas 2,133
Dalton 18,872
Damascus 272
Danielsville 378
Danville 515
Darien 1,826
Dasher 452
Davisboro 476
Dawson 5,383
Dawsonville 288
Dearing 555
Decatur 21,943
Deenwood 3,015
Deepstep 107
Demorest 1,070
Denton 244
Desoto 321
Dexter 438
Dickey 47
Dillard 186
Dock Junction 6,009
Doerun 1,157
Donalsonville 2,907
Doraville 9,157
Douglas 10,195
Douglasville 5,472
Dublin 15,143
Ducktown 66
Dudley 423
Duluth 1,810
Du Pont 252
Durand 192
East Dublin 1,986
East Ellijay 488
East Griffin 1,479
East Juliette 163
East Newnan 1,634
East Point 39,315
Eastman 5,416
Eastville 135
Eatonton 4,125
Edge Hill 46
Edison 1,210
Elberton 6,438
Ellaville 1,391
Ellenton 337
Ellijay 1,326
Emerson 813
Enigma 505
Ephesus 212
Eton 286
Experiment 2,256
Fairburn 3,143
Fairmount 623
Farmington 121
Farrar 87
Fayetteville 2,160
Fitzgerald 8,187
Flemington 265
Flovilla 289
Flowery Branch 779
Folkston 2,112
Forest Park 19,994
Forsyth 3,736
Fort Benning 27,495
Fort Gaines 1,255
Fort Gordon 15,589
Fort Oglethorpe 3,869
Fort Stewart 4,467
Fort Valley 9,251
Franklin 749
Franklin Springs 501
Funston 293
Gainesville 15,459
Gainesville Cotton Mills 2,060
Garden City 5,790
Garfield 214
Gay 200
Geneva 250
Georgetown 860
Gibson 701
Gillsville 100
Girard 241
Glennville 2,965
Glenwood 670
Glynco 2,558
Good Hope 202
Gordon 2,553
Grantville 1,128
Gratis 56
Gray 2,014
Grayson 366
Graysville 80
Greensboro 2,583
Greenville 1,085
Griffin 22,734
Grovetown 3,169
Guyton 742
Hagan 572
Hahira 1,326
Hamilton 357
Hampton 1,551
Hapeville 9,567
Haralson 162
Harlem 1,540
Harrison 329
Hartwell 4,865
Hawkinsville 4,077
Hazlehurst 4,065
Helen 252
Helena 1,230
Hephzibah 987
Hiawassee 415
Higgston 175
Hilltonia 294
Hinesville 4,115
Hiram 441
Hoboken 424
Hogansville 3,075
Holly Springs 575
Homeland 595
Homer 365
Homerville 3,025
Hoschton 509
Howell 99
Hull 222
Ideal 543
Ila 202
Iron City 351
Irwinton 757
Ivey 245
Jackson 3,778
Jacksonville 227
Jakin 172
Jasper 1,202
Jefferson 1,647
Jeffersonville 1,302
Jenkinsburg 382
Jersey 180
Jesup 9,091
Jonesboro 4,105
Junction City 269
Kennesaw 3,548
Kingsland 1,831
Kingston 714
Kite 336
La Fayette 6,044
La Grange 23,301
Lake City 2,306
Lake Park 361
Lakeland 2,569
Lavonia 2,044
Lawrenceville 5,115
Leary 907
Leesburg 996
Lenox 860
Leslie 562
Lexington 322
Lilburn 1,668
Lilly 155
Lincoln Park 1,852
Lincolnton 1,442
Lindale 2,768
Linwood 588
Lithonia 2,270
Locust Grove 642
Loganville 1,318
Lone Oak 129
Lookout Mountain 1,538
Louisville 2,691
Lovett 50
Ludowici 1,419
Lula 736
Lumber City 1,377
Lumpkin 1,431
Luthersville 400
Lyerly 426
Lyons 3,739
Macon 122,423
Madison 2,890
Manassas 144
Manchester 4,779
Mansfield 340
Marietta 27,216
Marine Corps Center 1,819
Marshallville 1,376
Martin 201
Matthews 94
Maxeys 229
Maysville 553
McCaysville 1,871
McDonough 2,675
McIntyre 471
McRae 3,151
Meansville 313
Meigs 1,226
Menlo 593
Merrillville 120
Metcalf 213
Metter 2,912
Middleton 106
Midville 665
Midway 167
Midway-Hardwick 14,047
Milan 1,084
Milledgeville 11,601
Millen 3,713
Milner 270
Milstead 1,157
Mineral Bluff 119
Minter 174
Mitchell 187
Modoc 23
Molena 389
Monroe 8,071
Montezuma 4,125
Monticello 2,132
Montrose 199
Moody 1,424
Moreland 363
Morgan 280
Morganton 205
Morrow 3,708
Morven 449
Moultrie 14,400
Mount Airy 463
Mount Vernon 1,579
Mount Zion 264
Mountain City 594
Mountain Park 268
Mountain View 2,330
Mountville 218
Nahunta 974
Nashville 4,323
Naylor 244
Nelson 613
Newborn 294
Newington 402
Newnan 11,205
Newton 624
Nicholls 1,150
Nicholson 397
Norcross 2,755
Norman Park 912
Normantown 71
North High Shoals 165
Norwood 272
Nunez 117
Oak Park 226
Oakfield 171
Oakman 178
Oakwood 250
Ochlocknee 611
Ocilla 3,185
Oconee 262
Odessadale 70
Odum 379
Oglethorpe 1,286
Ohoopee 64
Oliver 217
Omaha 188
Omega 831
Oxford 1,373
Palmetto 2,045
Parrott 222
Patterson 788
Pavo 775
Payne 236
Peachtree City 793
Pearson 1,700
Pelham 4,539
Pembroke 1,361
Pendergrass 267
Penfield 112
Perry 7,771
Phillipsburg 2,335
Pine Lake 866
Pine Mountain 862
Pine Park 330
Pinehurst 405
Pineora 266
Pineview 528
Pitts 345
Plainfield 77
Plains 683
Plainville 192
Pocotalago 99
Pooler 1,517
Port Wentworth 3,905
Portal 643
Porterdale 1,773
Poulan 766
Powder Springs 2,559
Preston 226
Primrose 28
Pulaski 230
Quitman 4,818
Raleigh 77
Ranger 140
Ray City 617
Rayle 110
Rebecca 266
Reidsville 1,806
Remerton 523
Reno 54
Rentz 392
Rest Haven 188
Reynolds 1,253
Rhine 471
Riceboro 252
Richland 1,823
Richmond Hill 826
Riddleville 143
Rincon 1,854
Ringgold 1,381
Riverdale 2,521
Riverside (Colquitt Co.) 114
Riverside (Floyd Co.) 1,159
Roberta 746
Rochelle 1,380
Rockmart 3,857
Rocky Ford 252
Rocky Mount 53
Rome 30,759
Roopville 221
Rossville 3,957
Roswell 5,430
Royston 2,428
Ruckersville 82
Russell 378
Rutledge 628
St. Marks 25
St. Marys 3,408
St. Simons 5,346
Sale City 323
Sandersville 5,546
Santa Claus 118
Sardis 643
Sasser 339
Savannah 118,349
Savannah Beach 1,786
Scotland 261
Scott 215
Screven 936
Senoia 910
Shady Dale 190
Shannon 1,563
Sharon 160
Sharpsburg 161
Shellman 1,166
Shiloh 298
Siloam 319
Smithonia 20
Smithville 713
Smyrna 19,157
Snellville 1,990
Social Circle 1,961
Soperton 2,596
Sparks 1,337
Sparta 2,172
Spring Place 241
Springfield 1,001
Stapleton 390
Statesboro 14,616
Statham 817
Stillmore 522
Stockbridge 1,561
Stone Mountain 1,899
Sugar Hill 1,745
Sugar Valley 143
Summertown 159
Summerville 5,043
Sumner 207
Sunnyside 209
Surrency 352
Suwanee 615
Swainsboro 7,325
Sycamore 547
Sylvania 3,199
Sylvester 4,226
Talbotton 1,045
Talking Rock 76
Tallapoosa 2,896
Tallulah Falls 255
Talmo 163
Tarrytown 188

GEORGIA, Continued

Taylorsville 253
Tazewell 120
Temple 864
Tennille 1,753
The Rock 136
Thomaston 10,024
Thomasville 18,155
Thomson 6,503
Thunderbolt 2,750
Tifton 12,179
Tiger 312
Tignall 756
Toccoa 6,971
Toomsboro 682
Towns 71
Trenton 1,523
Trion 1,965
Tunnel Hill 1,146
Turin 242
Twin City 1,119
Ty Ty 447
Tyrone 131
Unadilla 1,457
Union City 3,031
Union Point 1,624
Unionville 1,646
Uvalda 663
Valdosta 32,303
Vanna 149
Varnell 314
Vernonburg 136
Vidalia 9,507
Vidette 131
Vienna 2,341
Villa Rica 3,922
Waco 431
Wadley 1,989
Waleska 487
Walnut Grove 175
Warm Springs 523
Warner Robins 33,491
Warrenton 2,073
Warwick 466
Washington 4,094
Watkinsville 986
Waverly Hall 671
Waycross 18,996
Waynesboro 5,530
Wesley 49
West Point 4,232
Weston 73
Whigham 381
White 462
White Plains 236
White Sulphur Springs 38
Whitesburg 720
Willacoochee 1,120
Williamson 284
Wilmington Island 3,284
Winder 6,605
Windsor Forest 7,288
Winterville 551
Woodbine 1,002
Woodbury 1,422
Woodland 689
Woodstock 870
Woodville 379
Woolsey 91
Wrens 2,204
Wrightsville 2,106
Yatesville 423
Young Harris 544
Zebulon 776

HAWAII Total population: 769,913

METROPOLITAN AREA

Honolulu 630,528

COUNTIES

Hawaii 63,468
Honolulu 630,528
Kauai 29,761
Maui 46,156

PLACES

Aiea 12,560
Anahola 638
Barbers Point Housing 3,187
Captain Cook 1,263
Eleele 758
Ewa 2,906
Ewa Beach 7,765
Foster Village 3,755
Haiku 464
Hakalau 742
Halawa Heights 5,809
Haleiwa 2,626
Haliimaile 638
Hana 459
Hanalei 153
Hanamaulu 2,461
Hanapepe 1,388
Hauula 2,048
Hawi 797
Hickam Housing 7,352
Hilo 26,353
Honokaa 1,555
Honokahua 431
Honolulu 324,871
Honomu 737
Iroquois Point 4,572
Kaaawa 848
Kahaluu 1,657
Kahuku 917
Kahului 8,280
Kailua (Hawaii Co.) 365
Kailua (Honolulu Co.) 33,783
Kalaheo 1,514
Kaneohe 29,903
Kapaa 3,794
Kapaau 237
Kaumakani 1,014
Kaunakakai 1,070
Keaau 951
Kealakekua 740
Kekaha 2,404
Kilauea 671
Koloa 1,368
Kualapuu 441
Kukuihaele 310
Lahaina 3,718
Laie 3,009
Lanai City 2,122
Laupahoehoe 452
Lihue 3,124
Lower Paia 1,105
Maili 4,397
Makaha 4,644
Makakilo City 3,499
Makapala 201
Makawao 1,066
Mauna Loa 872
Maunawili 5,303
Mililani Town 2,035
Mokapu 7,860
Mountain View 419
Naalehu 1,014
Nanakuli 6,506
Ookala 486
Paauilo 710
Pacific Palisades 7,846
Pahala 1,507
Pahoa 924
Paia 541
Papaaloa 319
Papaikou 1,888
Pauwela 355
Pearl City 19,552
Poipu 466
Puhi 772
Pukalani 1,629
Puunene 1,132
Schofield Barracks 13,516
Wahiawa 17,598
Waialua 4,047
Waianae 3,302
Waihee 346
Waikapu 598
Wailua 1,379
Wailuku 7,979
Waimalu 2,982
Waimanalo 2,081
Waimanalo Beach 3,045
Waimea (Hawaii Co.) 756
Waimea (Kauai Co.) 1,569
Waipahu 24,150
Waipio Acres 2,146
Whitmore Village 2,015

IDAHO Total population: 713,008

METROPOLITAN AREA

Boise 112,230

COUNTIES

Ada 112,230
Adams 2,877
Bannock 52,200
Bear Lake 5,801
Benewah 6,230
Bingham 29,167
Blaine 5,749
Boise 1,763
Bonner 15,560
Bonneville 52,457
Boundary 5,484
Butte 2,925
Camas 728
Canyon 61,288
Caribou 6,534
Cassia 17,017
Clark 741
Clearwater 10,871
Custer 2,967
Elmore 17,479
Franklin 7,373
Fremont 8,710
Gem 9,387
Gooding 8,645
Idaho 12,891
Jefferson 11,740
Jerome 10,253
Kootenai 35,332
Latah 24,891
Lemhi 5,566
Lewis 3,867
Lincoln 3,057
Madison 13,452
Minidoka 15,731
Nez Perce 30,376
Oneida 2,864
Owyhee 6,422
Payette 12,401
Power 4,864
Shoshone 19,718
Teton 2,351
Twin Falls 41,807
Valley 3,609
Washington 7,633

PLACES

Aberdeen 1,542
Acequia 107
Albion 229
American Falls 2,769
Ammon 2,545
Arco 1,244
Arimo 252
Ashton 1,187
Athol 190
Atomic City 24
Bancroft 366
Basalt 349
Bellevue 537
Blackfoot 8,716
Bliss 114
Bloomington 186
Boise City 74,990
Bonners Ferry 1,909
Bovill 343
Buhl 2,975
Burley 8,279
Butte City 42
Caldwell 14,219
Cambridge 383
Cascade 833
Castleford 174
Challis 784
Chatcolet 95
Chubbuck 2,924
Clarks Fork 367
Clayton 36
Clifton 137
Coeur d'Alene 16,228
Cottonwood 867
Council 899
Craigmont 554
Crouch 71
Culdesac 211
Dalton Gardens 1,559
Dayton 198
Deary 411
Declo 251
Dietrich 84
Donnelly 114
Downey 586
Driggs 727
Drummond 13
Dubois 400
East Hope 175
Eden 343
Elk River 383
Emmett 3,945
Fairfield 336
Ferdinand 157
Fernan Lake 179
Filer 1,173
Firth 362
Franklin 402
Fruitland 1,576
Garden City 2,368
Genesee 619
Georgetown 421
Glenns Ferry 1,386
Gooding 2,599
Grace 826
Grangeville 3,636
Hagerman 436
Hailey 1,425
Hamer 81
Hansen 415
Harrison 249
Hauser 349
Hayden 1,285
Hayden Lake 260
Hazelton 396
Heise 84
Heyburn 1,637
Hollister 57
Homedale 1,411
Hope 63
Horseshoe Bend 511
Huetter 49
Idaho City 164
Idaho Falls 35,776
Inkom 522
Iona 890
Irwin 228
Island Park 136
Jerome 4,183
Juliaetta 423
Kamiah 1,307
Kellogg 3,811
Kendrick 426
Ketchum 1,454
Kimberly 1,557
Kooskia 809
Kootenai 168
Kuna 593
Lapwai 400
Lava Hot Springs 516
Leadore 111
Lewiston 26,068
Lewisville 468
Lost River 0
Mackay 539
Malad City 1,848
Malta 196
Marsing 610
McCall 1,758
McCammon 623
Melba 197
Menan 545
Meridian 2,616
Middleton 739
Midvale 176
Minidoka 131
Montpelier 2,604
Moore 156
Moscow 14,146
Mountain Home 6,451
Mountain Home Base 6,038
Moyie Springs 203
Mud Lake 194
Mullan 1,279
Murtaugh 124
Nampa 20,768
New Meadows 605
New Plymouth 986
Newdale 267
Nezperce 555
Notus 304
Oakley 656
Oldtown 161
Onaway 166
Orofino 3,883
Osburn 2,248
Oxford 75
Paris 615
Parker 266
Parma 1,228
Patterson 4
Paul 911
Payette 4,521
Pearl 8
Peck 238
Pierce 1,218
Pinehurst 1,934
Placerville 14
Plummer 443
Pocatello 40,036
Ponderay 275
Post Falls 2,371
Potlatch 871
Preston 3,310
Priest River 1,493
Rathdrum 741
Reubens 81
Rexburg 8,272
Richfield 290
Rigby 2,293
Riggins 533
Ririe 575
Roberts 393
Rockland 209
Rupert 4,563
St. Anthony 2,877
St. Charles 200
St. Maries 2,571
Salmon 2,910
Sandpoint 4,144
Shelley 2,614
Shoshone 1,233
Smelterville 967
Soda Springs 2,977
Spencer 45
Spirit Lake 622
Stanley 47
State Line 22
Stites 263
Sugar City 617
Sun Valley 180
Swan Valley 235
Tensed 151
Teton 390
Tetonia 176
Troy 541
Twin Falls 21,914
Ucon 664
Victor 241
Wallace 2,206
Wardner 492
Warm River 10
Weippe 713
Weiser 4,108
Wendell 1,122
Weston 230
White Bird 185
Wilder 564
Winchester 274
Worley 235

ILLINOIS Total population: 11,113,976

METROPOLITAN AREAS

Bloomington-Normal 104,389
Champaign-Urbana 163,281
Chicago 6,978,733
Davenport-Rock Island-Moline 362,638 (219,951 in Illinois, 142,687 in Iowa)
Decatur 125,010
Peoria 341,979
Rockford 272,063
Springfield 161,335

COUNTIES

Adams 70,861
Alexander 12,015
Bond 14,012
Boone 25,440
Brown 5,586
Bureau 38,541
Calhoun 5,675
Carroll 19,276
Cass 14,219
Champaign 163,281
Christian 35,948
Clark 16,216
Clay 14,735
Clinton 28,315
Coles 47,815
Cook 5,493,529
Crawford 19,824
Cumberland 9,772
De Kalb 71,654
De Witt 16,975
Douglas 18,997
Du Page 492,181
Edgar 21,591
Edwards 7,090
Effingham 24,608
Fayette 20,752
Ford 16,382
Franklin 38,329
Fulton 41,900
Gallatin 7,418
Greene 17,014
Grundy 26,535
Hamilton 8,665
Hancock 23,664
Hardin 4,914
Henderson 8,451
Henry 53,217
Iroquois 33,532
Jackson 55,008
Jasper 10,741
Jefferson 31,848
Jersey 18,492
Jo Daviess 21,766
Johnson 7,550
Kane 251,005
Kankakee 97,250
Kendall 26,374
Knox 60,939
Lake 382,638
La Salle 111,409
Lawrence 17,522
Lee 37,947
Livingston 40,690
Logan 33,538
Macon 125,010
Macoupin 44,557
Madison 250,934
Marion 38,986
Marshall 13,302
Mason 16,180
Massac 13,889
McDonough 36,653
McHenry 111,555
McLean 104,389
Menard 9,685
Mercer 17,294
Monroe 18,831
Montgomery 30,260
Morgan 36,174
Moultrie 13,263
Ogle 42,867
Peoria 195,318
Perry 19,757
Piatt 15,509
Pike 19,185
Pope 3,857
Pulaski 8,741
Putnam 5,007
Randolph 31,379
Richland 16,829
Rock Island 166,734
St. Clair 285,199
Saline 25,721
Sangamon 161,335
Schuyler 8,135
Scott 6,096
Shelby 22,589
Stark 7,510
Stephenson 48,861
Tazewell 118,649
Union 16,071
Vermilion 97,047
Wabash 12,841
Warren 21,595
Washington 13,780
Wayne 17,004
White 17,312
Whiteside 62,877
Will 247,825
Williamson 49,021
Winnebago 246,623
Woodford 28,012

PLACES

Abingdon 3,936
Addieville 274
Addison 24,482
Adeline 156
Albany 942
Albers 656
Albion 1,791
Aledo 3,325
Alexis 946
Algonquin 3,515
Alhambra 594
Allendale 425
Allenville 185
Allerton 327
Alma 369
Alorton 3,573
Alpha 771
Alsey 242
Alsip 11,141
Altamont 1,929
Alto Pass 304
Alton 39,700
Altona 542
Alvan 318
Amboy 2,184
Anchor 200
Andalusia 950
Andover 420
Anna 4,766
Annawan 787
Antioch 3,189
Apple River 482
Arbury Hills 1,291
Arcola 2,276
Arenzville 403
Argenta 1,034
Arlington 250
Arlington Heights 64,884
Armington 368
Aroma Park 896
Aroma Park Northwest 2,010
Arrowsmith 305
Arthur 2,214
Ashkum 590
Ashland 1,128
Ashley 655
Ashmore 428
Ashton 1,112
Assumption 1,487
Astoria 1,281
Athens 1,158
Atkinson 1,053
Atlanta 1,640
Atwood 1,264
Auburn 2,594
Augusta 824
Aurora 74,182
Ava 728
Aviston 828
Avon 1,013
Baldwin 467
Banner 235
Bannockburn 1,359
Bardolph 331
Barrington 8,674
Barrington Hills 2,712
Barry 1,444
Bartelso 439
Bartlett 3,501
Bartonville 7,221
Basco 193
Batavia 8,994
Batchtown 217
Bath 422
Bay View Gardens 472
Baylis 307
Beardstown 6,222
Beaverville 442
Beckemeyer 1,069
Bedford Park 583
Beecher 1,770
Beecher City 466
Belgium 578
Belknap 193
Belle Prairie City 52
Belle Rive 279
Belleville 41,699
Bellevue 1,189
Bellflower 400
Bellmont 292
Bellwood 22,096
Belvidere 14,061
Bement 1,638
Benld 1,736
Bensenville 12,956
Benson 490
Bently 94
Benton 6,833
Berkeley 6,152
Berlin 175
Berwyn 52,502
Bethalto 7,074
Bethany 1,235
Biggsville 391
Bingham 84
Birds 215
Bishop Hill 191
Blandinsville 922
Bloomingdale 2,974
Bloomington 39,992
Blue Island 22,958
Blue Mound 1,181
Bluffs 866
Bluford 465
Bolingbrook 7,643
Bone Gap 308
Bonfield 241
Bonnie 314
Bourbonnais 5,909
Bowen 489
Braceville 668
Bradford 885
Bradley 9,881
Braidwood 2,323
Breese 2,885
Bridge View 12,522
Bridgeport 2,262
Brighton 1,889
Brimfield 729
Broadlands 315
Broadview 9,623
Broadwell 159
Brocton 349
Brookfield 20,284
Brooklyn 1,702
Brookport 1,046
Broughton 235
Browning 276
Browns 198
Brownstown 689
Brussels 191
Bryant 326
Buckingham 198
Buckley 680
Buckner 489
Buda 675
Buffalo 462
Buffalo Grove 11,799
Bulpitt 275
Buncombe 187
Bunker Hill 1,465
Burbank 29,900
Bureau Junction 466
Burlington 456
Burnham 3,634

Burnt Prairie 140
Burr Ridge 1,637
Bush 357
Bushnell 3,703
Butler 233
Byron 1,749
Cabery 287
Cahokia 20,649
Cairo 6,277
Calhoun 238
Calumet City 33,107
Calumet Park 10,069
Camargo 241
Cambria 798
Cambridge 2,095
Camden 121
Camp Point 1,143
Campbell Hill 300
Campus 217
Canton 14,217
Cantrall 138
Capron 654
Carbon Cliff 1,369
Carbon Hill 317
Carbondale 22,816
Carlinville 5,675
Carlock 373
Carlyle 3,139
Carmi 6,033
Carol Stream 4,434
Carpentersville 24,059
Carrier Mills 2,013
Carrollton 2,866
Carterville 3,061
Carthage 3,350
Cary 4,358
Casey 2,994
Caseyville 3,411
Catlin 2,093
Cave in Rock 503
Cedar Point 304
Cedarville 578
Central City (Marion Co.) 1,377
Central City (Grundy Co.) 56
Centralia 15,217
Centreville 11,378
Cerro Gordo 1,368
Chadwick 605
Champaign 56,532
Chandlerville 762
Channahon 1,505
Chapin 552
Charleston 16,421
Chatham 2,788
Chatsworth 1,255
Chebanse 1,185
Chenoa 1,860
Cherry 551
Cherry Valley 952
Chester 5,310
Chesterfield 262
Chicago 3,369,359
Chicago Heights 40,900
Chicago Ridge 9,187
Chillicothe 6,052
Chrisman 1,285
Christopher 2,910
Cicero 67,058
Cisco 358
Cisne 615
Cissna Park 773
Claremont 269
Clarendon Hills 6,750
Clay City 1,049
Clayton 727
Clear Lake 228
Cleveland 267
Clifton 1,339
Clinton 7,570
Coal City 3,040
Coal Valley 3,088
Coalton 304
Coatsburg 188
Cobden 1,114
Coffeen 641
Colchester 1,747
Coleta 208
Colfax 935
Collinsville 18,015
Colona 1,293
Colp 271
Columbia 4,188
Columbus 131
Compton 399
Concord 207
Congerville 266
Cooksville 241
Cordova 589
Cornell 532
Cortland 541
Cottage Hills 1,261
Coulterville 1,186
Country Club Hills 6,920
Countryside 2,864
Cowden 537
Crainville 549
Creal Springs 830
Crescent 597
Crest Hill 7,460
Creston 595
Crestwood 5,770
Crete 4,656
Creve Coeur 6,440
Crossville 860
Crystal Lake 14,541
Cuba 1,581
Cullom 572
Cutler 508
Cypress 261
Dahlgren 487
Dakota 440
Dallas City 1,284
Dalton City 427
Dalzell 579
Dana 173
Danforth 404
Danvers 854
Danville 42,570
Darien 7,789
Davis 525
Dawson 427
Decatur 90,397
Deer Creek 647

Deer Grove 66
Deer Park 834
Deerfield 18,876
De Kalb 32,949
Deland 418
Delavan 1,844
Depue 1,919
De Soto 966
Des Plaines 57,239
Detroit 124
Dewey Park, see Dunlap Lake-Dewey Park
De Witt 199
Diamond 452
Diamond Lake 1,343
Dieterich 532
Divernon 1,010
Dix 167
Dixmoor 4,735
Dixon 18,147
Dolton 25,937
Dongola 825
Donnellson 311
Donovan 343
Dorchester 170
Dover 176
Dowell 423
Downers Grove 32,751
Downs 651
Du Bois 234
Dunfermline 282
Dunlap 656
Dunlap Lake-Dewey Park 2,029
Dupo 2,842
Du Quoin 6,691
Durand 972
Dwight 3,841
Eagerville 116
Earlville 1,410
East Alton 7,309
East Brooklyn 72
East Carondelet 542
East Chicago Heights 5,000
East Dubuque 2,408
East Dundee 2,920
East Galesburg 706
East Gillespie 187
East Hazelcrest 1,885
East Moline 20,832
East Peoria 18,455
East St. Louis 69,996
Easton 386
Eddyville 127
Edgewood 495
Edinburg 1,153
Edwardsville 11,070
Effingham 9,458
Eileen 371
Elburn 1,122
El Dara 82
Eldorado 3,876
Eldred 292
Elgin 55,691
Elizabeth 707
Elizabethtown 436
Elk Grove Village 21,907
Elk Hart City 435
Elkville 850
Elliott 365
Ellis Grove 277
Ellisville 137
Ellsworth 259
Elmhurst 48,887
Elmwood 2,014
Elmwood Park 26,160
El Paso 2,291
Elsah 928
Elvaston 238
Elwood 794
Emden 552
Emington 101
Energy 812
Enfield 764
Equality 732
Erie 1,566
Essex 364
Eureka 3,028
Evanston 79,808
Evansville 838
Evergreen Park 25,921
Ewing 220
Exeter 76
Fairbury 3,359
Fairfield 5,897
Fairmont 1,521
Fairmont City 2,769
Fairmount 785
Fairview 601
Fairview Heights 8,625
Farina 634
Farmer City 2,217
Farmersville 495
Farmington 2,959
Fayetteville 379
Ferris 200
Fidelity 132
Fieldon 257
Fillmore 397
Findlay 809
Fisher 1,525
Fithian 562
Flanagan 878
Flat Rock 504
Flora 5,283
Florence 65
Flossmoor 7,846
Foosland 172
Forest City 301
Forest Homes 1,998
Forest Park 15,472
Forest View 927
Forrest 1,219
Forreston 1,227
Forsyth 585
Fox Lake 4,511
Fox Lake Hills 1,869
Fox River 1,067
Fox River Grove 2,245
Fox River Valley Gardens 428
Frankfort 2,325
Franklin 565
Franklin Grove 968
Franklin Park 20,348

Freeburg 2,495
Freemanspur 363
Freeport 27,736
Fulton 3,630
Fults 101
Gages Lake-Wildwood 5,337
Galatia 792
Galena 3,930
Galesburg 36,290
Galva 3,061
Gardner 1,212
Garrett 224
Gays 269
Geff 294
Geneseo 5,840
Geneva 9,115
Genoa 3,003
Georgetown 3,984
German Valley 206
Germantown 1,108
Germantown Hills 278
Gibson City 3,454
Gifford 814
Gilberts 336
Gillespie 3,457
Gilman 1,786
Girard 1,881
Gladstone 344
Glasford 1,066
Glasgow 148
Glen Carbon 1,897
Glen Ellyn 21,909
Glencoe 10,675
Glendale Heights 11,406
Glenview 24,880
Glenwood 7,416
Godfrey 1,225
Godley 242
Golconda 922
Golden 571
Golden Gate 99
Golf 474
Good Hope 477
Goodfield 329
Goreville 1,109
Gorham 361
Grafton 1,018
Grand Ridge 698
Grand Tower 664
Grandview 2,242
Granite City 40,440
Grant Park 914
Grantfork 162
Granville 1,232
Grayslake 4,907
Grayville 2,035
Green Oaks 659
Green Rock 2,744
Green Valley 617
Greenfield 1,179
Greenup 1,618
Greenview 740
Greenville 4,631
Gridley 1,007
Griggsville 1,245
Gulf Port 220
Gurnee 2,738
Hainesville 142
Hamburg 162
Hamel 454
Hamilton 2,764
Hamletsburg 79
Hammond 502
Hampshire 1,611
Hampton 1,612
Hanaford 289
Hanna City 1,282
Hanover 1,243
Hanover Park 11,916
Hardin 1,035
Harmon 205
Harrisburg 9,535
Hartford 2,243
Hartsburg 363
Harvard 5,177
Harvel 275
Harvey 34,636
Harwood Heights 9,060
Havana 4,376
Hawthorn Woods 939
Hazel Crest 10,329
Hebron 781
Hecker 380
Hegeler-Home Gardens 1,595
Henderson 210
Hennepin 535
Henning 253
Henry 2,610
Herrick 537
Herrin 9,623
Herscher 988
Hettick 258
Heyworth 1,441
Hickory Hills 13,176
Hidalgo 171
Highland 5,981
Highland Park 32,263
Highwood 4,973
Hillcrest 630
Hillery-Batestown 2,179
Hillsboro 4,267
Hillsdale 539
Hillside 8,888
Hillview 322
Hinckley 1,053
Hindsboro 418
Hinsdale 15,918
Hodgkins 2,270
Hoffman 346
Hoffman Estates 22,238
Hollowayville 94
Homer 1,354
Hometown 6,729
Homewood 18,871
Hoopeston 6,461
Hooppole 227
Hopedale 923
Hoyleton 457
Hudson 802
Huey 205
Hull 585
Humboldt 366
Hume 496

Huntley 1,432
Hurst 934
Hutsonville 544
Illiopolis 1,122
Ina 333
Indian Creek 270
Indian Head Park 473
Indianola 374
Industry 558
Ingleside 1,621
Inverness 1,674
Iola 163
Ipava 608
Iroquois 226
Irving 599
Irvington 489
Irwin 87
Island Lake 1,973
Itasca 4,638
Iuka 343
Ivesdale 357
Jacksonville 20,553
Jeiseyville 182
Jerome 1,673
Jerseyville 7,446
Jewett 211
Johnsonville 72
Johnston City 3,928
Joliet 78,887
Jonesboro 1,676
Joppa 531
Joy 513
Junction 199
Junction City 305
Justice 9,473
Kampsville 439
Kane 432
Kangley 290
Kankakee 30,944
Kansas 779
Kappa 131
Karnak 641
Kaskaskia 79
Keenes 97
Keensburg 242
Keithsburg 836
Kell 173
Kempton 263
Ken Rock 5,945
Kenilworth 2,980
Kenney 367
Kewanee 15,762
Keyesport 352
Kilbourne 441
Kildeer 643
Kincaid 1,424
Kinderhook 281
Kingston 481
Kingston Mines 380
Kinmundy 759
Kinsman 153
Kirkland 1,138
Kirkwood 817
Knoxville 2,930
Lacon 2,147
Ladd 1,328
La Fayette 268
La Grange 17,814
La Grange Highlands 6,842
La Grange Park 15,459
La Harpe 1,240
Lake Barrington 347
Lake Bluff 5,008
Lake Catherine 1,219
Lake Forest 15,642
Lake in the Hills 3,240
Lake Villa 1,090
Lake Zurich 4,082
Lakemoor 797
Lakewood 782
La Moille 669
Lanark 1,495
Lansing 25,805
La Prairie 85
La Rose 165
La Salle 10,736
Latham 361
Lawrenceville 5,863
Leaf River 633
Lebanon 3,564
Lee 252
Leland 743
Leland Grove 1,624
Lemont 5,080
Lena 1,722
Lenzburg 437
Leonore 196
Lerna 288
Leroy 2,435
Lewistown 2,706
Lexington 1,615
Liberty 369
Libertyville 11,684
Lima 125
Lincoln 17,582
Lincolnshire 2,531
Lincolnwood 12,929
Lindenhurst 3,141
Lisbon 261
Lisle 5,329
Litchfield 7,190
Little York 297
Littleton 208
Liverpool 218
Livingston 916
Loami 537
Lockport 9,985
Loda 525
Lomax 565
Lombard 36,194
London Mills 610
Long Grove 1,196
Long Point 310
Long View 224
Loraine 372
Lostant 465
Louisville 1,020
Loves Park 12,390
Lovington 1,303
Ludlow 531
Lyndon 673
Lynnville 125
Lynwood 1,042

Lyons 11,124
Macedonia 86
Mackinaw 1,293
Macomb 19,643
Macon 1,249
Madison 7,042
Maeystown 109
Magnolia 328
Mahomet 1,296
Makanda 176
Malden 262
Malta 961
Manchester 335
Manhattan 1,530
Manito 1,334
Manlius 402
Mansfield 870
Manteno 2,864
Maple Park 660
Mapleton 281
Maquon 374
Marengo 4,235
Marietta 169
Marine 882
Marion 11,724
Marissa 2,004
Mark 379
Markham 15,987
Maroa 1,467
Marquette Heights 2,758
Marseilles 4,320
Marshall 3,468
Martinsville 1,374
Martinton 278
Maryville 1,067
Mascoutah 5,045
Mason 415
Mason City 2,611
Mathersville 699
Matteson 4,741
Mattoon 19,681
Maunie 275
Maywood 29,019
Mazon 727
McCook 333
McCullom Lake 873
McHenry 6,772
McLean 820
McLeansboro 2,630
McNabb 246
Meadowbrook 1,295
Mechanicsburg 490
Media 180
Medora 505
Melrose Park 22,716
Melvin 492
Mendon 883
Mendota 6,902
Menominee 217
Meredosia 1,178
Merrionette Park 2,303
Metamora 2,176
Metcalf 269
Metropolis 6,940
Mettawa 285
Meyers Bay 1,055
Middletown 626
Midlothian 15,939
Milan 4,873
Milford 1,656
Mill Creek 78
Mill Shoals 292
Milledgeville 1,130
Millington 338
Millstadt 2,168
Milton 337
Mineral 286
Minier 986
Minonk 2,267
Minooka 768
Modesto 221
Mokena 1,643
Moline 46,237
Momence 2,836
Monee 940
Monmouth 11,022
Montgomery 3,278
Monticello 4,130
Montrose 312
Morris 8,194
Morrison 4,387
Morrisonville 1,178
Morristown 669
Morton 10,419
Morton Grove 26,369
Mound City 1,177
Mound Station 203
Mounds 1,718
Mount Auburn 520
Mount Carmel 8,096
Mount Carroll 2,143
Mount Clare 298
Mount Erie 149
Mount Morris 3,173
Mount Olive 2,288
Mount Prospect 34,995
Mount Pulaski 1,677
Mount Sterling 2,182
Mount Vernon 16,382
Mount Zion 2,343
Moweaqua 1,687
Muddy 109
Mulberry Grove 697
Muncie 232
Mundelein 16,128
Murphysboro 10,013
Murrayville 595
Naperville 23,885
Naplate 686
Naples 100
Nashville 3,027
Nason 186
National City 124
Nauvoo 1,047
Nebo 454
Nelson 263
Neoga 1,270
Neponset 507
New Athens 2,000
New Baden 1,953
New Bedford 152
New Berlin 754
New Boston 706

New Burnside 249
New Canton 486
New Douglas 378
New Grand Chain 215
New Haven 606
New Holland 321
New Lenox 2,855
New Minden 188
New Salem 165
Newark 590
Newman 1,018
Newton 3,024
Niantic 705
Niles 31,432
Nilwood 245
Noble 719
Nokomis 2,532
Nora 175
Normal 26,396
Norridge 17,020
Norris 359
Norris City 1,319
North Aurora 4,833
North Barrington 1,411
North Chicago 47,275
North City 356
North Henderson 246
North Park 15,679
North Pekin 1,886
North Riverside 8,097
North Utica 974
Northbrook 27,297
Northfield 5,010
Northlake 14,212
Norwood 632
Oak Brook 4,164
Oak Forest 17,870
Oak Grove 618
Oak Lawn 60,305
Oak Park 62,511
Oakbrook Terrace 1,126
Oakford 272
Oakland 1,012
Oakwood 1,367
Oakwood Heights 3,229
Oakwood Hills 476
Oblong 1,860
Oconee 218
Odell 1,076
Odin 1,263
O'Fallon 7,268
Ogden 703
Oglesby 4,175
Ohio 506
Ohlman 193
Okawville 992
Old Marissa 206
Old Mill Creek 164
Old Ripley 127
Old Shawneetown 342
Olmsted 453
Olney 8,974
Olympia Fields 3,478
Omaha 304
Onarga 1,436
Oneida 728
Oquawka 1,352
Orangeville 538
Oreana 1,092
Oregon 3,539
Orient 502
Orion 1,801
Orland Park 6,391
Oswego 1,862
Ottawa 18,716
Otterville 142
Owaneco 278
Palatine 25,904
Palestine 1,640
Palmer 244
Palmyra 776
Palos Heights 9,915
Palos Hills 6,629
Palos Park 3,297
Pana 6,326
Panama 423
Panola 30
Papineau 219
Paris 9,971
Park City 2,855
Park Forest 30,638
Park Forest South 1,748
Park Ridge 42,614
Parkersburg 262
Patoka 562
Paw Paw 846
Pawnee 1,936
Paxton 4,373
Payson 589
Pearl 323
Pearl City 535
Pecatonica 1,781
Pekin 31,375
Peoria 126,963
Peoria Heights 7,943
Peotone 2,345
Percy 967
Perry 451
Peru 11,772
Pesotum 536
Petersburg 2,632
Petite Lake 1,275
Phillipstown 55
Philo 1,022
Phoenix 3,596
Pierron 467
Pinckneyville 3,377
Pingree Grove 174
Piper City 817
Pittsburg 509
Pittsfield 4,244
Plainfield 2,928
Plainville 289
Plano 4,664
Pleasant Hill 1,064
Pleasant Plains 644
Plymouth 740
Pocahontas 764
Polo 2,542
Pontiac 10,595
Pontoon Beach 2,448
Pontoosuc 226
Poplar Grove 607

ILLINOIS, Continued

Port Byron 1,222
Posen 5,498
Potomac 909
Prairie City 630
Prairie du Rocher 658
Princeton 6,959
Princeville 1,455
Prophetstown 1,915
Prospect Heights 13,333
Pulaski 471
Quincy 45,288
Quincy Southeast 1,419
Radom 172
Raleigh 215
Ramsey 830
Rankin 727
Ransom 440
Rantoul 25,562
Rapids City 656
Raritan 206
Raymond 890
Red Bud 2,559
Reddick 247
Redmon 251
Reynolds 610
Richmond 1,153
Richton Park 2,558
Richview 306
Ridge Farm 1,015
Ridgway 1,160
Ridott 244
Rio 186
Ripley 159
River Forest 13,402
River Grove 11,465
Riverdale 15,806
Riverside 10,432
Riverton 2,090
Riverwoods 1,571
Roanoke 2,040
Robbins 9,641
Roberts 506
Robinson 7,178
Rochelle 8,594
Rochester 1,667
Rock City 251
Rock Falls 10,287
Rock Island 50,166
Rockbridge 256
Rockdale 2,085
Rockford 147,370
Rockton 2,099
Rockwood 59
Rolling Meadows 19,178
Rome 1,919
Romeoville 12,674
Roodhouse 2,357
Roscoe 1,070
Rose Hill 103
Roselle 6,207
Rosemont 4,360
Roseville 1,111
Rosewood 3,391
Rosiclare 1,421
Rossville 1,420
Round Lake 1,531
Round Lake Beach 5,717
Round Lake Heights 1,144
Round Lake Park 3,148
Roxana 1,882
Royal 197
Royalton 1,166
Ruma 154
Rushville 3,300
Russellville 174
Rutland 437
Sadorus 454
Sailor Springs 137
St. Anne 1,271
St. Augustine 204
St. Charles (Kane Co.) 12,928
St. Charles (Du Page Co.) 0
St. David 773
St. Elmo 1,676
St. Francisville 997
St. Jacob 659
St. Johns 220
St. Joseph 1,554
St. Libory 448
St. Peter 380
Ste. Marie 335
Salem 6,187
San Jose 681
Sandoval 1,332
Sandwich 5,056
Sauget 220
Sauk 7,479
Saunemin 415
Savanna 4,942
Savoy 592
Sawyerville 315
Saybrook 814
Scales Mound 382
Schaumburg 18,730
Schiller Park 12,712
Schram City 657
Sciota 101
Scott 7,871
Scottville 196
Seaton 251
Seatonville 318
Secor 508
Seneca 1,781
Sesser 2,125
Shabbona 730
Shannon 848
Shaw 1,329
Shawneetown 1,742
Sheffield 1,038
Shelbyville 4,597
Sheldon 1,455
Sheridan 724
Sherman 327
Sherrard 808
Shiloh 945
Shipman 482
Shorewood 1,749
Shumway 235
Sibley 381
Sidell 645
Sidney 915
Sigel 337
Silvis 5,907
Simpson 82
Sims 317
Skokie 68,627
Sleepy Hollow 1,729
Smithboro 203
Smithfield 318
Smithton 847
Somonauk 1,112
Sorento 625
South Barrington 348
South Beloit 3,804
South Chicago Heights 4,923
South Elgin 4,289
South Holland 23,931
South Jacksonville 2,950
South Pekin 955
South Roxana 2,241
South Streator 1,869
South Wilmington 725
Southern View 1,504
Sparland 585
Sparta 4,307
Spaulding 220
Spillertown 305
Spring Bay 427
Spring Grove 348
Spring Valley 5,605
Springerton 228
Springfield 91,753
Standard 282
Standard City 139
Stanford 657
Staunton 4,396
Steeleville 1,957
Steger 8,104
Sterling 16,113
Sterling West 2,171
Steward 308
Stewardson 729
Stickney 6,601
Stillman Valley 871
Stockton 1,930
Stone Park 4,429
Stonefort 325
Stonington 1,096
Stoy 199
Strasburg 456
Strawn 144
Streamwood 18,176
Streator 15,600
Streator East 1,660
Streator West 2,077
Stronghurst 836
Sublette 361
Sugar Grove 1,230
Sullivan 4,112
Summerfield 443
Summit 11,569
Sumner 1,201
Sunnyside 367
Swansea 5,432
Sycamore 7,843
Symerton 155
Table Grove 469
Tallula 643
Tamaroa 799
Tamms 645
Tampico 838
Taylor Springs 620
Taylorville 10,927
Tennessee 179
Teutopolis 1,249
Thawville 271
Thayer 616
Thebes 442
Third Lake 199
Thomasboro 806
Thompsonville 449
Thomson 617
Thornton 3,714
Tilden 909
Tilton 2,544
Time 39
Tinley Park 12,382
Tiskilwa 973
Toledo 1,068
Tolono 2,027
Toluca 1,319
Tonica 821
Topeka 74
Toulon 1,207
Tovey 443
Towanda 578
Tower Hill 683
Tower Lakes 932
Tremont 1,942
Trenton 2,328
Troy 2,144
Troy Grove 281
Tuscola 3,917
Ullin 546
Union 579
Union Hill 156
Urbain 49
Urbana 32,800
Ursa 423
Valier 628
Valley City 66
Valley View 1,723
Valmeyer 733
Vandalia 5,160
Varna 417
Venedy 155
Venetian Village 2,554
Venice 4,680
Vergennes 323
Vermilion 333
Vermont 947
Vernon 203
Vernon Hills 1,056
Verona 220
Versailles 429
Victoria 441
Vienna 1,325
Villa Grove 2,605
Villa Hills 1,585
Villa Park 25,891
Viola 946
Virden 3,504
Virginia 1,814
Wadsworth 756
Waggoner 257
Walnut 1,295
Walnut Hill 149
Walshville 100
Waltonville 381
Wamac 1,347
Wapella 572
Warren 1,523
Warrensburg 738
Warrenville 3,268
Warsaw 1,758
Washburn 1,173
Washington 6,790
Washington Park 9,524
Wataga 570
Waterloo 4,546
Waterman 990
Watseka 5,294
Watson 276
Wauconda 5,460
Waukegan 65,269
Waverly 1,442
Wayne 572
Wayne City 985
Waynesville 522
Weldon 553
Wellington 410
Wenona 1,080
Wenonah 92
West Brooklyn 225
West Chicago 10,111
West City 637
West Dundee 3,295
West End 7,554
West Frankfort 8,854
West Peoria 6,873
West Point 237
West Salem 979
Westchester 20,033
Western Springs 12,147
Westfield 678
Westhaven 470
Westmont 8,920
Westville 3,655
Wheaton 31,138
Wheeler 173
Wheeling 14,746
White City 196
White Hall 2,979
Whiteash 181
Wildwood, see Gages Lake-Wildwood
Williamsfield 552
Williamson 324
Williamsville 923
Willisville 659
Willow Hill 296
Willow Springs 3,318
Willowbrook 1,169
Wilmette 32,134
Wilmington (Will Co.) 4,335
Wilmington (Greene Co.) 141
Wilsonville 691
Winchester 1,788
Windsor (Shelby Co.) 1,126
Windsor (Mercer Co.) 723
Winfield 4,285
Winnebago 1,285
Winnetka 13,998
Winslow 330
Winthrop Harbor 4,794
Witt 1,040
Wonder Lake 4,806
Wood Dale 8,831
Wood River 13,186
Woodhull 898
Woodland 350
Woodlawn 308
Woodridge 11,028
Woodson 384
Woodstock 10,226
Worden 1,091
Worth 11,999
Wyanet 1,005
Wyoming 1,563
Xenia 464
Yale 108
Yates City 840
Yorkville 2,049
Zeigler 1,940
Zion 17,268

INDIANA Total population: 5,193,669

METROPOLITAN AREAS

Anderson 138,451
Evansville 232,775
(196,744 in Indiana, 36,031 in Kentucky)
Fort Wayne 280,455
Gary-Hammond-East Chicago 633,367
Indianapolis 1,109,882
Lafayette-West Lafayette 109,378
Muncie 129,219
South Bend 280,031
Terre Haute 175,143

COUNTIES

Adams 26,871
Allen 280,455
Bartholomew 57,022
Benton 11,262
Blackford 15,888
Boone 30,870
Brown 9,057
Carroll 17,734
Cass 40,456
Clark 75,876
Clay 23,933
Clinton 30,547
Crawford 8,033
Daviess 26,602
Dearborn 29,430
Decatur 22,738
De Kalb 30,837
Delaware 129,219
Dubois 30,934
Elkhart 126,529
Fayette 26,216
Floyd 55,622
Fountain 18,257
Franklin 16,943
Fulton 16,984
Gibson 30,444
Grant 83,955
Greene 26,894
Hamilton 54,532
Hancock 35,096
Harrison 20,423
Hendricks 53,974
Henry 52,603
Howard 83,198
Huntington 34,970
Jackson 33,187
Jasper 20,429
Jay 23,575
Jefferson 27,006
Jennings 19,454
Johnson 61,138
Knox 41,546
Kosciusko 48,127
Lagrange 20,890
Lake 546,253
La Porte 105,342
Lawrence 38,038
Madison 138,451
Marion 792,299
Marshall 34,986
Martin 10,969
Miami 39,246
Monroe 84,849
Montgomery 33,930
Morgan 44,176
Newton 11,606
Noble 31,382
Ohio 4,289
Orange 16,968
Owen 12,163
Parke 14,600
Perry 19,075
Pike 12,281
Porter 87,114
Posey 21,740
Pulaski 12,534
Putnam 26,932
Randolph 28,915
Ripley 21,138
Rush 20,352
St. Joseph 245,045
Scott 17,144
Shelby 37,797
Spencer 17,134
Starke 19,280
Steuben 20,159
Sullivan 19,889
Switzerland 6,306
Tippecanoe 109,378
Tipton 16,650
Union 6,582
Vanderburgh 168,772
Vermillion 16,793
Vigo 114,528
Wabash 35,553
Warren 8,705
Warrick 27,972
Washington 19,278
Wayne 79,109
Wells 23,821
White 20,995
Whitley 23,395

PLACES

Advance 561
Akron 1,019
Alamo 145
Albany 2,293
Albion 1,498
Alexandria 5,097
Alfordsville 105
Alton 56
Altona 269
Ambia 300
Amboy 473
Amo 422
Anderson 70,787
Andrews 1,207
Angola 5,117
Arcadia 1,338
Argos 1,393
Ashley 721
Atlanta 620
Attica 4,262
Auburn 7,337
Aurora 4,293
Austin 4,902
Avilla 881
Bainbridge 703
Bargersville 873
Batesville 3,799
Battle Ground 818
Bedford 13,087
Beech Grove 13,468
Berne 2,988
Bethany 121
Beverly Shores 946
Bicknell 3,717
Birdseye 404
Black Oak 9,624
Bloomfield 2,565
Bloomingdale 391
Bloomington 42,890
Blountsville 220
Bluffton 8,297
Boonville 5,736
Boston 210
Boswell 998
Bourbon 1,606
Brazil 8,163
Bremen 3,487
Bristol 1,100
Broadview 2,362
Brook 919
Brooklyn 911
Brooksburg 104
Brookston 1,232
Brookville 2,864
Brownsburg 5,186
Brownstown 2,376
Bruceville 627
Bryant 320
Bunker Hill 956
Burket 210
Burlington 685
Burnettsville 510
Burns Harbor 1,284
Butler 2,394
Cadiz 200
Cambridge City 2,481
Camden 577
Campbellsburg 678
Cannelburg 149
Cannelton 2,280
Carbon 344
Carlisle 714
Carmel 6,568
Carthage 946
Cayuga 1,090
Cedar Grove 248
Cedar Lake 7,589
Center Point 275
Centerville 2,380
Chain-O-Lakes, see Lydick-Chain-O-Lakes
Chalmers 544
Chandler 2,032
Charlestown 5,890
Chesterfield 3,001
Chesterton 6,177
Chrisney 550
Churubusco 1,528
Cicero 1,378
Clarks Hill 741
Clarksville 13,806
Clay City 900
Claypool 468
Clayton 736
Clear Lake 271
Clifford 275
Clinton 5,340
Cloverdale 870
Coatesville 453
Colfax 633
Columbia City 4,911
Columbus 27,141
Connersville 17,604
Converse 1,163
Corunna 359
Corydon 2,719
Country Club Heights 118
Covington 2,641
Crandall 188
Crane 339
Crawfordsville 13,842
Cromwell 475
Crothersville 1,663
Crown Point 10,931
Culver 1,783
Cumberland 479
Cynthiana 793
Dale 1,113
Daleville 1,730
Dana 720
Danville 3,771
Darlington 802
Decatur 8,445
Decker 268
Delphi 2,582
De Motte 1,697
Denver 566
Dillsboro 840
Dublin 1,021
Dugger 1,150
Dune Acres 301
Dunkirk 3,465
Dunreith 200
Dupont 357
Dyer 4,906
Earl Park 478
East Chicago 46,982
East Gary 9,858
East Germantown 447
Eaton 1,594
Economy 285
Edgewood 2,326
Edinburg 4,906
Edwardsport 482
Elberfeld 834
Elizabeth 195
Elizabethtown 519
Elkhart 43,152
Ellettsville 1,627
Elnora 873
Elwood 11,196
Englewood 1,219
English 664
Etna Green 516
Evansville 138,764
Fairmount 3,427
Fairview Park 1,067
Farmersburg 962
Farmland 1,262
Ferdinand 1,432
Fishers 628
Flora 1,877
Fort Branch 2,535
Fort Wayne 177,671
Fortville 2,460
Fountain City 852
Fowler 2,643
Fowlerton 337
Francesville 1,015
Francisco 621
Frankfort 14,956
Franklin 11,477
Frankton 1,796
Fredericksburg 207
Fremont 1,043
French Lick 2,059
Fulton 372
Galveston 1,284
Garrett 4,715
Gary 175,415
Gas City 5,742
Gaston 928
Geneva 1,100
Gentryville 281
Georgetown 1,273
Gimco City 6
Glenwood 452
Goodland 1,176
Goshen 17,171
Gosport 692
Grabill 570
Grandview 696
Greencastle 8,852
Greendale 3,783
Greenfield 9,986
Greensboro 225
Greensburg 8,620
Greensfork 444
Greentown 1,870
Greenville 611
Greenwood 11,408
Griffin 178
Griffith 18,168
Grissom 4,963
Hagerstown 2,059
Hamilton 537
Hamlet 761
Hammond 107,790
Hanover 3,018
Hardinsburg 263
Hartford City 8,207
Hartsville 434
Haubstadt 1,171
Hazleton 416
Hebron 1,624
Highland 24,947
Hillsboro 505
Hobart 21,485
Holland 662
Hope 1,603
Hudson 464
Hudson Lake 1,134
Huntertown 775
Huntingburg 4,794
Huntington 16,217
Hymera 907
Indian Village 86
Indianapolis 744,624
Ingalls 888
Jamestown 938
Jasonville 2,335
Jasper 8,641
Jeffersonville 20,008
Jonesboro 2,466
Jonesville 202
Judson 35
Kempton 469
Kendallville 6,838
Kennard 518
Kentland 1,864
Kewanna 614
Kingman 530
Kingsbury 314
Kingsford Heights 1,200
Kirklin 736
Knightstown 2,456
Knightsville 788
Knox 3,519
Kokomo 44,042
Kouts 1,388
Laconia 64
La Crosse 696
Ladoga 1,099
Lafayette 44,955
La Fontaine 793
Lagrange 2,053
Lagro 552
Lakeville 712
Lanesville 586
La Paz 604
Lapel 1,725
La Porte 22,140
Larwill 324
Laurel 753
Lawrence 16,646
Lawrenceburg 4,636
Leavenworth 330
Lebanon 9,766
Leesburg 561
Lewisville 530
Liberty 1,831
Ligonier 3,034
Linden 713
Linton 5,450
Little York 191
Livonia 120
Lizton 397
Logansport 19,255
Long Beach 2,740
Loogootee 2,953
Losantville 212
Lottaville, see Merrillville-Lottaville-Rexville
Lowell 3,839
Lydick-Chain-O-Lakes 1,341
Lynn 1,360
Lynnville 556
Lyons 702
Mackey 121
Macy 273
Madison 13,081
Marengo 767
Marion 39,607
Markle 963
Markleville 457
Marshall 365
Martinsville 9,723
Matthews 728
Mauckport 119
Medaryville 732
Medora 788

Mellott....325
Mentone....830
Merom....305
Merrillville-Lottaville-Rexville....15,918
Michiana Shores....449
Michigan City....39,369
Michigantown....457
Middlebury....1,055
Middletown....2,046
Milan....1,260
Milford (Kosciusko Co.)....1,264
Milford (Decatur Co.)....187
Millersburg....618
Millhousen....252
Milltown....829
Milton....694
Mishawaka....35,517
Mitchell....4,092
Modoc....275
Monon....1,548
Monroe....622
Monroe City....603
Monroeville....1,353
Monterey....268
Montezuma....1,192
Mongomery....411
Monticello....4,869
Montpelier....2,093
Mooreland....495
Moores Hill....616
Mooresville....5,800
Morgantown....1,134
Morocco....1,285
Morristown....838
Mount Auburn....157
Mount Ayr....194
Mount Carmel....128
Mount Etna....164
Mount Summit....395
Mount Vernon....6,770
Mulberry....1,075
Muncie....69,080
Munster....16,514
Napoleon....282
Nappanee....4,159
Nashville....527
New Albany....38,402
New Amsterdam....32
New Carlisle....1,434
New Castle....21,215
New Chicago....2,231
New Harmony....971
New Haven....5,728
New Market....640
New Middletown....133
New Palestine....863
New Paris....1,080
New Pekin....912
New Providence....337
New Richmond....381
New Ross....318
New Whiteland....4,200
Newberry....295
Newburgh....2,302
Newpoint....381
Newport....708
Newtown....286
Noblesville....7,548
North Grove....107
North Judson....1,738
North Liberty....1,259
North Manchester....5,791
North Salem....601
North Vernon....4,582
North Webster....456
Oakland City....3,289
Oaktown....726
Odon....1,433
Ogden Dunes....1,361
Oldenburg....758
Onward....111
Oolitic....1,155
Orestes....519
Orland....457
Orleans....1,834
Osceola....1,572
Osgood....1,346
Ossian....1,538
Otterbein....899
Owensville....1,056
Oxford....1,098
Palmyra....483
Paoli....3,281
Paragon....538
Parker City....1,179
Patoka....529
Patriot....216
Pendleton....2,243
Pennville....798
Perrysville....510
Peru....14,139
Petersburg....2,697
Pierceton....1,175
Pine Lake....1,954
Pine Village....291
Pittsboro....867
Plainfield....8,211
Plainville....538
Plymouth....7,661
Poneto....286
Portage....19,127
Porter....3,058
Portland....7,115
Poseyville....1,035
Pottawattamie Park....374
Princes Lakes....597
Princeton....7,431
Redkey....1,667
Remington....1,127
Rensselaer....4,688
Rexville, see Merrillville-Lottaville-Rexville
Reynolds....641
Richmond....43,999
Ridgeville....924
Riley....257
Rising Sun....2,305
River Forest....27
Roachdale....1,004
Roann....509
Roanoke....858
Rochester....4,631
Rockport....2,565
Rockville....2,820
Rome City....1,354
Rosedale....817
Roseland....895
Rossville....830
Royal Center....987
Rushville....6,686
Russellville....390
Russiaville....844
St. Joe....564
St. John....1,757
St. Leon....435
St. Paul....785
Salamonia....162
Salem....5,041
Saltillo....134
Sandborn....528
Santa Claus....63
Saratoga....406
Schererville....3,663
Schneider....426
Scottsburg....4,791
Seelyville....1,195
Sellersburg....3,177
Selma....890
Seymour....13,352
Sharpsville....672
Shelburn....1,281
Shelbyville....15,094
Sheridan....2,137
Shipshewana....448
Shirley....958
Shoals....1,039
Sidney....179
Silver Lake....588
Smith Valley....1,679
Somerville....313
South Bend....125,580
South Whitley....1,362
Southport....2,505
Speedway....15,056
Spencer....2,423
Spiceland....957
Spring Grove....437
Spring Lake Park....263
Springport....236
Spurgeon....285
State Line City....176
Staunton....582
Stilesville....352
Stinesville....291
Straughn....329
Sullivan....4,683
Sulphur Springs....387
Summitville....1,104
Sunman....707
Swayzee....1,073
Sweetser....1,076
Switz City....301
Syracuse....1,546
Tell City....7,933
Tennyson....335
Terre Haute....70,286
Thorntown....1,399
Tipton....5,176
Topeka....677
Town of Pines....1,007
Trafalgar....457
Trail Creek....2,697
Tri Lakes....1,193
Troy....575
Ulen....138
Union City....3,995
Uniondale....349
Universal....462
Upland....3,202
Valparaiso....20,020
Van Buren....1,057
Veedersburg....1,837
Vera Cruz....140
Vernon....440
Versailles....1,020
Vevay....1,463
Vincennes....19,867
Wabash....13,379
Wakarusa....1,160
Walkerton....2,006
Wallace....136
Walton....1,054
Wanatah....773
Warren....1,229
Warsaw....7,506
Washington....11,358
Waterloo....1,876
Waveland....557
Waynetown....993
West Baden Springs....930
West College Corner....709
West Glen Park....6,602
West Harrison....395
West Lafayette....19,157
West Lebanon....899
West Terre Haute....2,704
Westfield....1,837
Westport....1,170
Westville....2,614
Wheatfield....713
Wheatland....562
Whiteland....1,492
Whitestown....569
Whitewater....111
Whiting....7,247
Wilkinson....480
Williamsport....1,661
Winamac....2,341
Winchester....5,493
Windfall City....946
Wingate....437
Winona Lake....2,811
Winslow....1,030
Wolcott....894
Wolcottville....915
Woodburn....688
Woodlawn Heights....51
Worthington....1,691
Yeoman....145
Yorktown....1,673
Zionsville....1,857

IOWA Total population: 2,825,041

METROPOLITAN AREAS

Cedar Rapids....163,213
Davenport-Rock Island-Moline....362,638 (219,951 in Illinois, 142,687 in Iowa)
Des Moines....286,101
Dubuque....90,609
Sioux City....116,189 (103,052 in Iowa, 13,137 in Nebraska)
Waterloo....132,916

COUNTIES

Adair....9,487
Adams....6,322
Allamakee....14,968
Appanoose....15,007
Audubon....9,595
Benton....22,885
Black Hawk....132,916
Boone....26,470
Bremer....22,737
Buchanan....21,762
Buena Vista....20,693
Butler....16,953
Calhoun....14,287
Carroll....22,912
Cass....17,007
Cedar....17,655
Cerro Gordo....49,223
Cherokee....17,269
Chickasaw....14,969
Clarke....7,581
Clay....18,464
Clayton....20,606
Clinton....56,749
Crawford....19,198
Dallas....26,085
Davis....8,207
Decatur....9,737
Delaware....18,770
Des Moines....46,982
Dickinson....12,565
Dubuque....90,609
Emmet....14,009
Fayette....26,898
Floyd....19,860
Franklin....13,255
Fremont....9,282
Greene....12,716
Grundy....14,119
Guthrie....12,243
Hamilton....18,383
Hancock....13,492
Hardin....22,248
Harrison....16,240
Henry....18,114
Howard....11,442
Humboldt....12,519
Ida....9,283
Iowa....15,419
Jackson....20,839
Jasper....35,425
Jefferson....15,774
Johnson....72,127
Jones....19,868
Keokuk....13,943
Kossuth....22,937
Lee....42,996
Linn....163,213
Louisa....10,682
Lucas....10,163
Lyon....13,340
Madison....11,558
Mahaska....22,177
Marion....26,352
Marshall....41,076
Mills....11,832
Mitchell....13,108
Monona....12,069
Monroe....9,357
Montgomery....12,781
Muscatine....37,181
O'Brien....17,522
Osceola....8,555
Page....18,537
Palo Alto....13,289
Plymouth....24,322
Pocahontas....12,757
Polk....286,130
Pottawattamie....86,991
Poweshiek....18,803
Ringgold....6,373
Sac....15,573
Scott....142,687
Shelby....15,528
Sioux....27,996
Story....62,783
Tama....20,147
Taylor....8,790
Union....13,557
Van Buren....8,643
Wapello....42,149
Warren....27,432
Washington....18,967
Wayne....8,405
Webster....48,391
Winnebago....12,990
Winneshiek....21,758
Woodbury....103,052
Worth....8,968
Wright....17,294

PLACES

Ackley....1,794
Ackworth....111
Adair....750
Adel....2,419
Afton....823
Agency....610
Ainsworth....455
Akron....1,324
Albert City....683
Albia....4,151
Albion....772
Alburnett....418
Alden....876
Alexander....249
Algona....6,032
Allerton....643
Allison....1,071
Alta....1,717
Alta Vista....283
Alton....1,018
Altoona....2,883
Alvord....204
Ames....39,505
Anamosa....4,389
Andover....90
Andrew....335
Anita....1,101
Ankeny....9,151
Anthon....711
Aplington....936
Arcadia....414
Archer....134
Aredale....126
Arion....199
Arispe....93
Arlington....481
Armstrong....1,061
Arnolds Park....970
Arthur....273
Asbury....410
Ashton....483
Aspinwall....81
Atalissa....244
Athelstan....65
Atkins....581
Atlantic....7,306
Auburn....329
Audubon....2,907
Aurelia....1,065
Aurora....229
Avoca....1,535
Ayrshire....243
Badger....465
Bagley....365
Baldwin....172
Balltown....79
Bancroft....1,103
Bankston....28
Barnes City....238
Barnum....147
Bassett....152
Batavia....525
Battle Creek....837
Baxter....788
Bayard....628
Beacon....338
Beaconsfield....48
Beaman....222
Beaver....113
Bedford....1,733
Belle Plaine....2,810
Bellevue....2,336
Belmond....2,358
Bennett....385
Benton....46
Berkley....56
Bernard....148
Bertram....177
Bettendorf....22,126
Bevington....54
Birmingham....452
Blairsburg....287
Blairstown....612
Blakesburg....403
Blanchard....139
Blencoe....255
Blockton....273
Bloomfield....2,718
Blue Grass....1,032
Bode....372
Bonaparte....517
Bondurant....462
Boone....12,468
Bouton....160
Boxholm....242
Boyden....670
Braddyville....207
Bradgate....130
Brandon....432
Brayton....151
Breda....518
Bridgewater....188
Brighton....632
Bristow....230
Britt....2,069
Bronson....193
Brooklyn....1,410
Brunsville....125
Buck Grove....41
Buckeye....143
Buffalo....1,513
Buffalo Center....1,118
Burlington....32,366
Burt....608
Bussey....498
Calamus....396
Callender....421
Calmar....1,008
Calumet....219
Camanche....3,470
Cambridge....661
Cantril....258
Carbon....135
Carlisle....2,246
Carpenter....122
Carroll....8,716
Carson....756
Carter Lake....3,268
Cascade....1,744
Casey....561
Castalia....210
Castana....211
Cedar Falls....29,597
Cedar Rapids....110,642
Center Junction....172
Center Point....1,456
Centerville....6,531
Central City....1,116
Centralia....105
Chariton....5,009
Charles City....9,268
Charlotte....444
Charter Oak....715
Chatsworth....90
Chelsea....381
Cherokee....7,272
Chester....185
Chillicothe....126
Churdan....598
Cincinnati....570
Clare....249
Clarence....915
Clarinda....5,420
Clarion....2,972
Clarksville....1,360
Clayton....113
Clear Lake City....6,430
Clearfield....430
Cleghorn....274
Clemons....178
Clermont....582
Clinton....34,719
Clio....113
Clive....3,005
Clutier....275
Coburg....36
Coggon....656
Coin....294
Colesburg....379
Colfax....2,293
College Springs....295
Collins....404
Colo....606
Columbus City....312
Columbus Junction....1,205
Colwell....100
Conesville....295
Conrad....932
Conway....91
Coon Rapids....1,381
Coppock....58
Coralville....6,130
Corning....2,095
Correctionville....870
Corwith....438
Corydon....1,745
Cotter....55
Coulter....262
Council Bluffs....60,348
Craig....98
Crawfordsville....288
Crescent....284
Cresco....3,927
Creston....8,234
Cromwell....168
Crystal Lake....276
Cumberland....385
Cumming....189
Curlew....95
Cushing....204
Cylinder....133
Dakota City....746
Dallas....438
Dallas Center....1,128
Dana....118
Danbury....527
Danville....948
Davenport....98,469
Davis City....301
Dawson....232
Dayton....909
Decatur City....198
Decorah....7,458
Dedham....325
Deep River....323
Defiance....392
Delaware....153
Delhi....527
Delmar....599
Deloit....279
Delphos....35
Delta....475
Denison....6,300
Denver....1,169
Derby....161
Des Moines....201,404
De Soto....369
De Witt....3,647
Dexter....652
Diagonal....327
Dickens....240
Dike....794
Dixon....276
Dolliver....95
Donahue....216
Donnan....18
Donnellson....798
Doon....437
Dougherty....133
Dow City....571
Dows....777
Drakesville....163
Dubuque....62,309
Dumont....724
Duncombe....418
Dundee....166
Dunkerton....563
Dunlap....1,292
Durango....55
Durant....1,472
Dyersville....3,437
Dysart....1,251
Eagle Grove....4,489
Earlham....974
Earling....573
Earlville....751
Early....727
East Peru....184
Eddyville....945
Edgewood....786
Elberon....203
Eldon....1,319
Eldora....3,223
Eldridge....1,535
Elgin....613
Elk Horn....667
Elk Run Heights....1,175
Elkader....1,592
Elkhart....269
Elkport....87
Elliott....423
Ellston....76
Ellsworth....443
Elma....601
Ely....275
Emerson....484
Emmetsburg....4,150
Epworth....1,132
Essex....770
Estherville....8,108
Evansdale....5,038
Everly....699
Exira....966
Exline....224
Fairbank....810
Fairfax....635
Fairfield....8,715
Farley....1,096
Farmersburg....232
Farmington....800
Farnhamville....393
Farragut....521
Fayette....1,947
Fenton....403
Ferguson....203
Fertile....394
Floris....145
Floyd....380
Fonda....980
Fontanelle....752
Forest City....3,841
Fort Atkinson....339
Fort Dodge....31,263
Fort Madison....13,996
Fostoria....219
Franklin....111
Fraser....143
Fredericksburg....912
Frederika....190
Fredonia....168
Fremont....480
Galt....50
Galva....412
Garber....148
Garden Grove....285
Garnavillo....634
Garner....2,257
Garrison....383
Garwin....563
Geneva....201
George....1,194
Gibson....80
Gilbert....521
Gilbertville....655
Gilman....513
Gilmore City....766
Gladbrook....961
Glenwood....4,421
Glidden....964
Goldfield....722
Goodell....218
Goose Lake....218
Gowrie....1,225
Graettinger....907
Graf....70
Grafton....254
Grand Junction....967
Grand Mound....627
Grand River....211
Grandview....357
Granger....661
Grant....152
Granville....383
Gravity....286
Gray....145
Greeley....323
Green Island....112
Greene....1,363
Greenfield....2,212
Greenville....117
Grimes....834
Grinnell....8,402
Griswold....1,181
Grundy Center....2,712
Gruver....135
Guernsey....94
Guthrie Center....1,834
Guttenberg....2,177
Halbur....235
Hamburg....1,649
Hamilton....186
Hampton....4,376
Hancock....228
Hanlontown....182
Hansell....124
Harcourt....305
Hardy....73
Harlan....5,049
Harper....173
Harpers Ferry....227
Harris....195
Hartford....582
Hartley....1,694
Hartwick....101
Harvey....217
Hastings....229
Havelock....248
Haverill....160
Hawarden....2,789
Hawkeye....529
Hayesville....93
Hazleton....626
Hedrick....790
Henderson....211
Hepburn....38
Hiawatha....2,416
Hills....507
Hillsboro....252
Hinton....488
Holland....258
Holstein....1,445
Holy Cross....290

IOWA, Continued

Hopkinton 800
Hornick 250
Hospers 646
Houghton 119
Hubbard 846
Hudson 1,535
Hull 1,523
Humboldt 4,665
Humeston 673
Hurstville 88
Huxley 937
Ida Grove 2,261
Imogene 192
Independence 5,910
Indianola 8,852
Inwood 644
Ionia 270
Iowa City 46,850
Iowa Falls 6,454
Ireton 582
Irwin 446
Jackson Junction 106
Jamaica 271
Janesville 741
Jefferson 4,735
Jesup 1,662
Jewell 1,152
Johnston 222
Joice 201
Jolley 112
Kalona 1,488
Kamrar 243
Kanawha 822
Kellerton 299
Kelley 235
Kellogg 607
Kensett 345
Kent 86
Keokuk 14,631
Keosauqua 1,018
Keota 1,112
Keswick 257
Keystone 549
Kimballton 343
Kingsley 1,097
Kinross 98
Kirkman 72
Kirkville 222
Kiron 275
Klemme 554
Knierim 131
Knoxville 7,755
Lacona 424
Ladora 321
Lake City 1,910
Lake Mills 2,124
Lake Park 918
Lake View 1,249
Lakeside 353
Lakota 385
Lambs Grove 239
Lamoni 2,540
Lamont 498
La Motte 326
Lanesboro 203
Lansing 1,218
La Porte City 2,256
Larchwood 611
Larrabee 167
Latimer 393
Laurel 245
Laurens 1,756
Lawler 513
Lawton 406
Le Claire 2,520
Ledyard 240
Le Grand 565
Lehigh 739
Leighton 140
Leland 223
Le Mars 8,159
Lenox 1,215
Leon 2,142
Le Roy 43
Lester 238
Letts 434
Lewis 526
Libertyville 329
Lidderdale 173
Lime Springs 497
Lincoln 184
Linden 278
Lineville 385
Linn Grove 240
Lisbon 1,329
Liscomb 328
Little Rock 531
Little Sioux 239
Littleport 97
Livermore 510
Lockridge 232
Logan 1,526
Lohrville 553
Lone Rock 166
Lone Tree 834
Long Grove 269
Lorimor 346
Lost Nation 547
Lovilia 640
Low Moor 347
Lowden 667
Luana 225
Lucas 247
Luther 189
Luverne 380
Luxemburg 185
Luzerne 134
Lynnville 381
Lytton 378
Macedonia 330
Macksburg 142
Madrid 2,448
Magnolia 206
Malcom 388
Mallard 384
Maloy 45
Malvern 1,158
Manchester 4,641
Manilla 943
Manly 1,294
Manning 1,656
Manson 1,993
Mapleton 1,647
Maquoketa 5,677
Marathon 447
Marble Rock 461
Marcus 1,272
Marengo 2,235
Marion 18,028
Marne 187
Marquette 509
Marshalltown 26,219
Martelle 341
Martensdale 306
Martinsburg 140
Marysville 91
Mason City 30,379
Masonville 147
Massena 433
Matlock 89
Maurice 266
Maxwell 758
Maynard 503
Maysville 170
McCallsburg 307
McCausland 226
McClelland 146
McGregor 990
McIntire 234
Mechanicsville 989
Mediapolis 1,242
Melbourne 661
Melcher 913
Melrose 192
Melvin 325
Menlo 391
Meriden 167
Merrill 790
Meservey 354
Middletown 443
Miles 409
Milford 1,668
Millersburg 187
Millerton 82
Millville 27
Milo 561
Milton 567
Minburn 378
Minden 433
Mingo 260
Missouri Valley 3,519
Mitchell 233
Mitchellville 1,341
Modale 297
Mondamin 420
Moneta 41
Monmouth 257
Monona 1,395
Monroe 1,389
Montezuma 1,353
Monticello 3,509
Montour 334
Montrose 735
Moorhead 271
Moorland 269
Moravia 699
Morley 123
Morning Sun 906
Morrison 136
Moulton 763
Mount Auburn 200
Mount Ayr 1,762
Mount Pleasant 7,007
Mount Sterling 87
Mount Union 173
Mount Vernon 3,018
Moville 1,198
Murray 620
Muscatine 22,405
Mystic 696
Nashua 1,712
Nemaha 117
Neola 968
Nevada 4,952
New Albin 644
New Hampton 3,621
New Hartford 690
New Liberty 141
New London 1,900
New Market 501
New Providence 208
New Sharon 944
New Vienna 392
New Virginia 452
Newell 877
Newhall 701
Newton 15,619
Nichols 396
Nodaway 176
Nora Springs 1,337
North Buena Vista 118
North English 965
North Liberty 1,055
North Washington 134
Northboro 115
Northwood 1,950
Norwalk 1,745
Norway 554
Numa 165
Oakland 1,603
Oakville 369
Ocheyedan 545
Odebolt 1,323
Oelwein 7,735
Ogden 1,661
Okoboji 361
Old Town 24
Olds 206
Olin 710
Ollie 268
Onawa 3,154
Oneida 55
Onslow 253
Orange City 3,572
Orchard 115
Orient 324
Orleans 396
Osage 3,815
Osceola 3,124
Oskaloosa 11,224
Ossian 847
Osterdock 59
Otho 581
Oto 203
Ottosen 93
Ottumwa 29,610
Owasa 69
Oxford 666
Oxford Junction 666
Oyens 145
Pacific Junction 505
Packwood 157
Palmer 264
Palo 430
Panama 221
Panora 982
Panorama Park 219
Parkersburg 1,631
Parnell 175
Paton 329
Patterson 120
Paullina 1,257
Pella City 6,668
Peosta 57
Perry 6,906
Persia 316
Peterson 469
Pierson 421
Pilot Mound 214
Pioneer 56
Pisgah 286
Plain View 23
Plainfield 446
Plano 109
Pleasant Hill 1,535
Pleasant Plain 121
Pleasanton 62
Pleasantville 1,297
Plover 129
Plymouth 461
Pocahontas 2,338
Polk City 715
Pomeroy 765
Popejoy 147
Portsmouth 239
Postville 1,546
Prairie City 1,141
Prairieburg 182
Prescott 305
Preston 950
Primghar 995
Princeton 633
Promise City 148
Protivin 333
Pulaski 255
Quasqueton 464
Quimby 395
Radcliffe 548
Rake 324
Ralston 129
Randalia 81
Randall 179
Randolph 214
Rathbun 113
Raymond 582
Readlyn 616
Reasnor 284
Red Oak 6,210
Redding 111
Redfield 921
Reinbeck 1,711
Rembrandt 250
Remsen 1,367
Renwick 429
Rhodes 347
Riceville 877
Richland 595
Rickardsville 193
Ricketts 141
Ridgeway 218
Ridotto 0
Rinard 88
Ringsted 509
Rippey 270
Riverdale 684
Riverside 758
Riverton 331
Robins 663
Rock Falls 150
Rock Rapids 2,632
Rock Valley 2,205
Rockford 902
Rockwell 923
Rockwell City 2,396
Rodman 104
Rodney 66
Roland 803
Rolfe 767
Rome 135
Rose Hill 192
Rossie 91
Rowan 231
Rowley 241
Royal 469
Rudd 429
Runnells 354
Russell 591
Ruthven 708
Rutland 215
Ryan 343
Sabula 845
Sac City 3,268
Sageville 338
St. Ansgar 994
St. Anthony 156
St. Charles 443
St. Donatus 164
St. Lucas 194
St. Marys 105
St. Olaf 140
St. Paul 129
Salem 458
Salix 387
Sanborn 1,465
Sandyville 89
Scarville 81
Schaller 835
Schleswig 875
Scranton 751
Searsboro 140
Sergeant Bluff 1,153
Seymour 931
Shambaugh 178
Shannon City 100
Sharpsburg 106
Sheffield 1,070
Shelby 537
Sheldahl 285
Sheldon 4,535
Shell Rock 1,159
Shellsburg 740
Shenandoah 5,968
Sherrill 190
Shueyville 154
Sibley 2,749
Sidney 1,061
Sigourney 2,319
Silver City 272
Sioux Center 3,450
Sioux City 85,925
Sioux Rapids 813
Slater 1,094
Sloan 799
Smithland 293
Soldier 242
Solon 837
Somers 197
South English 218
Spencer 10,278
Spillville 361
Spirit Lake 3,014
Spragueville 112
Spring Hill 131
Springbrook 196
Springville 970
Stacyville 598
Stanhope 482
Stanley 151
Stanton 574
Stanwood 642
State Center 1,232
Steamboat Rock 394
Stockport 334
Stockton 222
Storm Lake 8,591
Story City 2,104
Stout 196
Stratford 710
Strawberry Point 1,281
Struble 59
Stuart 1,354
Sully 685
Sumner 2,174
Superior 139
Sutherland 875
Swaledale 222
Swan 56
Swea City 774
Swisher 417
Tabor 957
Tama 3,000
Templeton 312
Tennant 93
Terril 397
Thayer 100
Thompson 600
Thor 212
Thornburg 98
Thornton 410
Thurman 230
Tiffin 299
Tingley 244
Tipton 2,877
Titonka 599
Toledo 2,361
Toronto 145
Traer 1,682
Treynor 472
Tripoli 1,345
Truesdale 132
Truro 359
Turin 115
Udell 71
Underwood 424
Union 484
Unionville 161
University Heights 1,265
University Park 534
Urbana 552
Urbandale 14,434
Ute 512
Vail 486
Valeria 96
Van Horne 613
Van Meter 464
Van Wert 244
Varina 140
Ventura 543
Victor 949
Villisca 1,402
Vincent 204
Vining 71
Vinton 4,845
Volga City 305
Wadena 237
Wahpeton 149
Walcott 989
Walford 286
Walker 622
Wall Lake 936
Wallingford 245
Walnut 870
Wapello 1,873
Washburn 1,408
Washington 6,317
Washta 319
Waterloo 75,533
Waterville 158
Waucoma 357
Waukee 1,577
Waukon 3,883
Waverly 7,205
Wayland 702
Webb 234
Webster 130
Webster City 8,488
Weldon 155
Wellman 977
Wellsburg 754
Welton 104
Wesley 548
West Bend 865
West Branch 1,322
West Burlington 3,139
West Chester 199
West Des Moines 16,441
West Liberty 2,296
West Okoboji 210
West Point 1,045
West Union 2,624
Westfield 148
Westgate 204
Westphalia 121
Westside 389
What Cheer 868
Wheatland 832
Whiting 590
Whittemore 658
Whitten 194
Willey 72
Williams 456
Williamsburg 1,544
Williamson 216
Wilton 1,873
Windsor Heights 6,303
Winfield 897
Winterset 3,654
Winthrop 750
Wiota 171
Woden 265
Woodbine 1,349
Woodburn 186
Woodward 1,010
Woolstock 222
Worthington 365
Wyoming 746
Yale 301
Yetter 47
Yorktown 105
Zearing 535
Zwingle 96

KANSAS Total population: 2,249,071

METROPOLITAN AREAS

Kansas City 1,256,327 (406,918 in Kansas, 849,409 in Missouri)
Topeka 155,322
Wichita 389,352

COUNTIES

Allen 15,043
Anderson 8,501
Atchison 19,165
Barber 7,016
Barton 30,663
Bourbon 15,215
Brown 11,685
Butler 38,658
Chase 3,408
Chautauqua 4,642
Cherokee 21,549
Cheyenne 4,256
Clark 2,896
Clay 9,890
Cloud 13,466
Coffey 7,397
Comanche 2,702
Cowley 35,012
Crawford 37,850
Decatur 4,988
Dickinson 19,993
Doniphan 9,107
Douglas 57,932
Edwards 4,581
Elk 3,858
Ellis 24,730
Ellsworth 6,146
Finney 19,029
Ford 22,587
Franklin 20,007
Geary 28,111
Gove 3,940
Graham 4,751
Grant 5,961
Gray 4,516
Greeley 1,819
Greenwood 9,141
Hamilton 2,747
Harper 7,871
Harvey 27,236
Haskell 3,672
Hodgeman 2,662
Jackson 10,342
Jefferson 11,945
Jewell 6,099
Johnson 220,073
Kearny 3,047
Kingman 8,886
Kiowa 4,088
Labette 25,775
Lane 2,707
Leavenworth 53,340
Lincoln 4,582
Linn 7,770
Logan 3,814
Lyon 32,071
Marion 13,935
Marshall 13,139
McPherson 24,778
Meade 4,912
Miami 19,254
Mitchell 8,010
Montgomery 39,949
Morris 6,432
Morton 3,576
Nemaha 11,825
Neosho 18,812
Ness 4,791
Norton 7,279
Osage 13,352
Osborne 6,416
Ottawa 6,183
Pawnee 8,484
Phillips 7,888
Pottawatomie 11,755
Pratt 10,056
Rawlins 4,393
Reno 60,765
Republic 8,498
Rice 12,320
Riley 56,788
Rooks 7,628
Rush 5,117
Russell 9,428
Saline 46,592
Scott 5,606
Sedgwick 350,694
Seward 15,744
Shawnee 155,322
Sheridan 3,859
Sherman 7,792
Smith 6,757
Stafford 5,943
Stanton 2,287
Stevens 4,198
Sumner 23,553
Thomas 7,501
Trego 4,436
Wabaunsee 6,397
Wallace 2,215
Washington 9,249
Wichita 3,274
Wilson 11,317
Woodson 4,789
Wyandotte 186,845

PLACES

Abbyville 143
Abilene 6,661
Admire 144
Agenda 107
Agra 294
Albert 235
Alden 238
Alexander 129
Allen 175
Alma 905
Almena 489
Alta Vista 402
Altamont 845
Alton 214
Altoona 475
Americus 441
Andale 500
Andover 1,880
Anthony 2,653
Arcadia 388
Argonia 591
Arkansas City 13,216
Arlington 503
Arma 1,348
Ashland 1,244
Assaria 303
Atchison 12,565
Athol 108
Atlanta 216
Attica 639
Atwood 1,658
Auburn 261
Augusta 5,977
Aurora 120
Axtell 456
Baldwin City 2,520
Barnard 190
Barnes 209
Bartlett 138
Basehor 724
Bassett 62
Baxter Springs 4,489
Bazine 386
Beattie 288
Belle Plaine 1,553
Belleville 3,063
Beloit 4,121
Belpre 191
Belvue 161
Benedict 91
Bennington 561
Bentley 260
Benton 517
Bern 191
Beverly 193
Bird City 671
Bison 285
Blue Mound 308
Blue Rapids 1,148
Bluff City 109
Bogue 257
Bonner Springs 3,662
Brewster 320
Bronson 397
Brookville 238
Brownell 98
Bucklin 771
Buffalo 321
Buhler 1,019
Bunker Hill 181
Burden 503
Burdett 285
Burlingame 999
Burlington 2,099
Burns 268
Burr Oak 426
Burrton 808
Bushong 39
Bushton 397
Byers 46
Caldwell 1,540
Cambridge 110
Camp Forsyth 3,290
Camp Funston 4,147
Camp Whiteside, see Fort Riley-Camp Whiteside
Caney 2,192
Canton 893
Carbondale 1,041
Carlton 40
Cassoday 123
Cawker City 726

Cedar 46
Cedar Point 73
Cedar Vale 665
Centralia 511
Chanute 10,341
Chapman 1,132
Chase 800
Chautauqua 137
Cheney 1,160
Cherokee 790
Cherryvale 2,609
Chetopa 1,596
Cimarron 1,373
Circleville 178
Claflin 887
Clay Center 4,963
Clayton 127
Clearwater 1,435
Clifton 718
Climax 64
Clyde 946
Coats 152
Coffeyville 15,116
Colby 4,658
Coldwater 1,016
Collyer 182
Colony 382
Columbus 3,356
Colwich 879
Concordia 7,221
Conway Springs 1,153
Coolidge 102
Copeland 267
Corning 162
Cottonwood Falls 987
Council Grove 2,403
Countryside 403
Courtland 403
Coyville 93
Cuba 290
Cullison 117
Culver 148
Cunningham 483
Damar 245
Danville 80
Dearing 338
Deerfield 474
Delia 168
Delphos 599
Denison 248
Denton 162
Derby 7,947
De Soto 1,839
Dexter 286
Dighton 1,540
Dodge City 14,127
Dorrance 234
Douglass 1,126
Downs 1,268
Dresden 103
Dunlap 102
Durham 143
Dwight 322
Earlton 102
East Forbes 0
Eastborough 1,141
Easton 435
Edgerton 513
Edmond 90
Edna 418
Edwardsville 619
Effingham 605
Elbing 128
El Dorado 12,308
Elgin 115
Elk City 432
Elk Falls 124
Elkhart 2,089
Ellinwood 2,416
Ellis 2,137
Ellsworth 2,080
Elmdale 102
Elsmore 116
Elwood 1,283
Emmett 156
Emporia 23,327
Englewood 158
Ensign 237
Enterprise 868
Erie 1,414
Esbon 206
Eskridge 589
Eudora 2,071
Eureka 3,576
Everest 304
Fairview 283
Fairway 5,133
Fall River 191
Florence 716
Fontana 160
Ford 246
Formoso 180
Fort Leavenworth 8,060
Fort Riley-Camp Whiteside 2,310
Fort Scott 8,967
Fowler 588
Frankfort 960
Frederick 39
Fredonia 3,080
Freeport 21
Frontenac 2,223
Fulton 213
Galatia 78
Galena 3,712
Galesburg 146
Galva 522
Garden City 14,790
Garden Plain 678
Gardner 1,839
Garfield 261
Garnett 3,169
Gas 438
Gaylord 211
Gem 80
Geneseo 453
Geuda Springs 223
Girard 2,591
Glade 180
Glasco 767
Glen Elder 422
Goddard 955
Goessel 386
Goff 207
Goodland 5,510
Gorham 379
Gove City 172
Grainfield 374
Grandview Plaza 734
Great Bend 16,133
Greeley 368
Green 163
Greenleaf 448
Greensburg 1,907
Grenola 290
Gridley 328
Grinnell 449
Gypsum 391
Haddam 289
Halstead 1,716
Hamilton 349
Hamlin 95
Hanover 793
Hanston 282
Hardtner 300
Harper 1,665
Harris 41
Hartford 478
Harveyville 279
Havana 144
Haven 1,146
Havensville 163
Haviland 705
Hays 15,396
Haysville 6,483
Hazelton 176
Hepler 152
Herington 3,165
Herndon 268
Hesston 1,926
Hiawatha 3,365
Highland 899
Hill City 2,071
Hillsboro 2,730
Hoisington 3,710
Holcomb 272
Hollenberg 47
Holmdel Gardens 1,960
Holton 3,063
Holyrood 593
Hope 438
Horace 137
Horton 2,177
Howard 918
Hoxie 1,419
Hoyt 420
Hudson 181
Hugoton 2,739
Humboldt 2,249
Hunnewell 77
Hunter 150
Huron 106
Hutchinson 36,885
Independence 10,347
Ingalls 235
Inman 836
Iola 6,493
Isabel 147
Iuka 210
Jamestown 470
Jennings 224
Jetmore 936
Jewell 569
Johnson City 1,038
Junction City 19,018
Kanopolis 626
Kanorado 278
Kansas City 168,213
Kechi 229
Kensington 653
Kincaid 189
Kingman 3,622
Kinsley 2,212
Kiowa 1,414
Kirwin 293
Kismet 294
Labette 105
La Crosse 1,583
La Cygne 989
La Harpe 509
Lakin 1,570
Lancaster 279
Lane 254
Langdon 93
Lansing 3,797
Larned 4,567
Latham 156
Latimer 29
Lawrence 45,698
Leavenworth 25,147
Leawood 10,349
Lebanon 517
Lebo 589
Lecompton 434
Lehigh 168
Lenexa 5,242
Lenora 439
Leon 510
Leona 72
Leonardville 412
Leoti 1,916
Le Roy 551
Lewis 525
Liberal 13,789
Liberty 185
Liebenthal 169
Lincoln Center 1,582
Lincolnville 218
Lindsborg 2,764
Linn 388
Linwood 323
Little River 493
Logan 760
Lone Elm 66
Long Island 195
Longford 99
Longton 304
Lorraine 153
Lost Springs 103
Louisburg 1,033
Louisville 204
Lucas 524
Luray 303
Lyndon 958
Lyons 4,355
Macksville 484
Madison 1,061
Mahaska 122
Maize 785
Manchester 92
Manhattan 27,575
Mankato 1,287
Manter 219
Maple Hill 327
Mapleton 112
Marion 2,052
Marquette 578
Marysville 3,588
Matfield Green 77
Mayetta 246
Mayfield 110
McCracken 333
McCune 487
McDonald 269
McFarland 209
McLouth 623
McPherson 10,851
Meade 1,899
Medicine Lodge 2,545
Melvern 455
Menlo 48
Meriden 472
Merriam 10,851
Milan 162
Mildred 42
Milford 296
Miltonvale 718
Minneapolis 1,971
Minneola 630
Mission 8,376
Mission Hills 4,177
Mission Woods 242
Moline 555
Montezuma 606
Moran 550
Morganville 257
Morland 300
Morrill 308
Morrowville 201
Moscow 228
Mound City 714
Mound Valley 467
Moundridge 1,271
Mount Hope 665
Mulberry 622
Mullinville 376
Mulvane 3,185
Munden 123
Muscotah 206
Narka 130
Nashville 107
Natoma 603
Neodesha 3,295
Neosho Falls 184
Neosho Rapids 234
Ness City 1,756
Netawaka 192
New Albany 59
New Cambria 160
Newton 15,439
Nickerson 1,187
Niotaze 83
Norcatur 284
North Fort Riley 12,469
North Newton 963
Norton 3,627
Nortonville 727
Norwich 414
Oak Hill 41
Oakley 2,327
Oberlin 2,291
Offerle 212
Ogden 1,491
Oketo 133
Olathe 17,917
Olivet 64
Olmitz 161
Olpe 453
Olsburg 151
Onaga 761
Oneida 112
Osage City 2,600
Osawatomie 4,294
Osborne 1,980
Oskaloosa 955
Oswego 2,200
Otis 387
Ottawa 11,036
Overbrook 748
Overland Park 79,034
Oxford 1,113
Ozawkie 137
Palco 398
Palmer 166
Paola 4,622
Paradise 145
Park 178
Park City 2,529
Parker 255
Parkerville 25
Parsons 13,015
Partridge 302
Pawnee Rock 442
Paxico 216
Peabody 1,368
Penalosa 32
Perry 664
Peru 289
Phillipsburg 3,241
Pittsburg 20,171
Plainville 2,627
Pleasanton 1,216
Plevna 124
Pomona 541
Portis 178
Potwin 497
Powhattan 111
Prairie View 201
Prairie Village 28,138
Pratt 6,736
Prescott 222
Preston 239
Pretty Prairie 561
Princeton 159
Protection 673
Quenemo 429
Quinter 930
Radium 55
Ramona 121
Randall 195
Randolph 106
Ransom 416
Rantoul 163
Raymond 133
Reading 247
Redfield 138
Republic 243
Reserve 117
Rexford 231
Richfield 82
Richmond 464
Riley 668
Robinson 278
Roeland Park 9,974
Rolla 400
Rose Hill 387
Roseland 113
Rossville 934
Rozel 236
Rush Center 237
Russell 5,371
Russell Springs 83
Sabetha 2,376
St. Francis 1,725
St. George 241
St. John 1,477
St. Marys 1,434
St. Paul 804
Salina 37,714
Satanta 1,161
Savonburg 109
Sawyer 164
Scammon 457
Scandia 567
Schoenchen 182
Scott City 4,001
Scottsville 46
Scranton 575
Sedan 1,555
Sedgwick 1,083
Selden 271
Seneca 2,182
Severance 128
Severy 384
Seward 66
Sharon 265
Sharon Springs 1,012
Shawnee 20,482
Silver Lake 811
Simpson 131
Smith Center 2,389
Smolan 175
Soldier 173
Solomon 973
South Haven 413
South Hutchinson 1,879
Spearville 738
Speed 58
Spivey 78
Spring Hill 1,186
Stafford 1,414
Stark 124
Sterling 2,312
Stockton 1,818
Strong City 545
Sublette 1,208
Summerfield 254
Sun City 119
Sunflower 1,744
Susank 59
Sylvan Grove 403
Sylvia 390
Syracuse 1,720
Tampa 154
Tescott 393
Thayer 430
Timken 123
Tipton 315
Tonganoxie 1,717
Topeka 125,011
Toronto 431
Towanda 1,190
Treece 225
Tribune 1,013
Troy 1,047
Turon 430
Tyro 206
Udall 668
Ulysses 3,779
Uniontown 286
Utica 297
Valley Center 2,551
Valley Falls 1,169
Vermillion 191
Victoria 1,246
Vining 84
Viola 193
Virgil 179
Wa Keeney 2,334
Wakefield 583
Waldo 123
Waldron 24
Wallace 112
Walnut 330
Walton 211
Wamego 2,507
Washington 1,584
Waterville 632
Wathena 1,150
Waverly 510
Webber 49
Weir 740
Wellington 8,072
Wellsford 9
Wellsville 1,183
West Mineral 232
West Plains 857
Westmoreland 485
Westphalia 185
Westwood 2,329
Westwood Hills 414
Wetmore 392
Wheaton 106
White City 458
White Cloud 210
Whitewater 520
Whiting 256
Wichita 276,554
Willard 124
Williamsburg 286
Willis 82
Willowbrook 100
Wilmore 96
Wilsey 169
Wilson 870
Winchester 492
Windom 183
Winfield 11,405
Winona 293
Woodbine 170
Woodston 211
Yates Center 1,967
Zenda 142
Zurich 189

KENTUCKY Total population: 3,219,311

METROPOLITAN AREAS

Huntington-Ashland 253,743
(144,499 in West Virginia, 56,868 in Ohio, 52,376 in Kentucky)
Lexington 174,323
Louisville 826,553
(695,055 in Kentucky, 131,498 in Indiana)
Owensboro 79,486

COUNTIES

Adair 13,037
Allen 12,598
Anderson 9,358
Ballard 8,276
Barren 28,677
Bath 9,235
Bell 31,087
Boone 32,812
Bourbon 18,476
Boyd 52,376
Boyle 21,090
Bracken 7,227
Breathitt 14,221
Breckinridge 14,789
Bullitt 26,090
Butler 9,723
Caldwell 13,179
Calloway 27,692
Campbell 88,501
Carlisle 5,354
Carroll 8,523
Carter 19,850
Casey 12,930
Christian 56,224
Clark 24,090
Clay 18,481
Clinton 8,174
Crittenden 8,493
Cumberland 6,850
Daviess 79,486
Edmonson 8,751
Elliott 5,933
Estill 12,752
Fayette 174,323
Fleming 11,366
Floyd 35,889
Franklin 34,481
Fulton 10,183
Gallatin 4,134
Garrard 9,457
Grant 9,999
Graves 30,939
Grayson 16,445
Green 10,350
Greenup 33,192
Hancock 7,080
Hardin 78,421
Harlan 37,370
Harrison 14,158
Hart 13,980
Henderson 36,031
Henry 10,910
Hickman 6,264
Hopkins 38,167
Jackson 10,005
Jefferson 695,055
Jessamine 17,430
Johnson 17,539
Kenton 129,440
Knott 14,698
Knox 23,689
Larue 10,672
Laurel 27,386
Lawrence 10,726
Lee 6,587
Leslie 11,623
Letcher 23,165
Lewis 12,355
Lincoln 16,663
Livingston 7,596
Logan 21,793
Lyon 5,562
Madison 42,730
Magoffin 10,443
Marion 16,714
Marshall 20,381
Martin 9,377
Mason 17,273
McCracken 58,281
McCreary 12,548
McLean 9,062
Meade 18,796
Menifee 4,050
Mercer 15,960
Metcalfe 8,177
Monroe 11,642
Montgomery 15,364
Morgan 10,019
Muhlenberg 27,537
Nelson 23,477
Nicholas 6,508
Ohio 18,790
Oldham 14,687
Owen 7,470
Owsley 5,023
Pendleton 9,949
Perry 25,714
Pike 61,059
Powell 7,704
Pulaski 35,234
Robertson 2,163
Rockcastle 12,305
Rowan 17,010
Russell 10,542
Scott 17,948
Shelby 18,999
Simpson 13,054
Spencer 5,488
Taylor 17,138
Todd 10,823
Trigg 8,620
Trimble 5,349
Union 15,882
Warren 57,432
Washington 10,728
Wayne 14,268
Webster 13,282
Whitley 24,145
Wolfe 5,669
Woodford 14,434

PLACES

Adairville 973
Albany 1,891
Alexandria 3,844
Allen City 724
Allensville 266
Anchorage 1,477
Arlington 549
Ashland 29,245
Auburn 1,160
Audubon Park 1,862
Augusta 1,434
Barbourmeade 884
Barbourville 3,549
Bardstown 5,816
Bardwell 1,049
Barlow 746
Beattyville 923
Beaver Dam 2,622
Bedford 780
Beech Grove 233
Beechwood Village 1,788
Bellefonte 966
Bellemeade 576
Bellevue 8,847
Bellewood 410
Benham 1,000
Benton 3,652
Berea 6,956
Berry 266
Blandville 116
Bloomfield 1,072
Blue Ridge Manor 601
Bonnieville 328
Booneville 126
Bowling Green 36,253
Bradfordsville 338
Brandenburg 1,637
Bremen 299
Briarwood 327
Broad Fields 534
Brodhead 769
Bromley 1,069
Brooksville 609
Brownsboro 494
Brownsboro Farm 823
Brownsville 542
Buechel 5,359
Buffalo 142
Burgin 1,002
Burkesville 1,717
Burnside 586
Burton 145
Butler 558
Cadiz 1,987
Calhoun 901
California 90
Calvert City 2,104
Cambridge 251
Campbellsburg 479
Campbellsville 7,598
Campton 419
Caneyville 530
Carlisle 1,579
Carrollton 3,884
Carrsville 110
Carter 94
Catlettsburg 3,420
Cave City 1,818
Cedarville 140
Centertown 323
Centerville 209
Central City 3,455
Cerulean Springs 253
Cherrywood 481
Clarkson 660
Clay 1,426
Clay City 983
Clinton 1,618
Cloverport 1,388
Coal Run 234
Cold Spring 5,348
Columbia 3,234
Columbus 371
Concord 108
Corbin 7,317
Corinth 236
Corydon 880
Covington 52,535
Crab Orchard 861
Crescent Park 598
Crescent Springs 1,662

KENTUCKY, Continued

Crestview 657
Crestview Hills 1,114
Crittenden 359
Crofton 631
Cumberland 3,317
Cynthiana 6,356
Danville 11,542
Dawson Springs 2,830
Dayton 8,691
Devondale 1,071
Dexter 238
Dixon 572
Dover 277
Drakesboro 907
Druid Hills 416
Dry Ridge 1,100
Dycusburg 89
Earlington 2,321
Eddyville 1,981
Edgewood 4,139
Edmonton 958
Ekron 190
Elizabethtown 11,748
Elkhorn City 1,081
Elkton 1,612
Elsmere 5,161
Eminence 2,225
Erlanger 12,676
Eubank 230
Evarts 1,182
Fairfield 163
Fairmeade 317
Fairview 235
Falmouth 2,593
Ferguson 507
Flatwoods 7,380
Fleming 473
Flemingsburg 2,483
Florence 11,457
Fordsville 489
Forest Hills 469
Fort Campbell North 13,616
Fort Knox 37,608
Fort Mitchell 6,982
Fort Thomas 16,338
Fort Wright-Lookout Heights 4,819
Foster 91
Fountain Run 128
Frankfort 21,356
Franklin 6,553
Fredonia 450
Frenchburg 467
Fulton 3,250
Gamaliel 431
Georgetown 8,629
Germantown 332
Ghent 385
Gilbertsville 241
Glasgow 11,301
Grand Rivers 438
Gratz 105
Graymoor 1,419
Grayson 2,184
Greensburg 1,990
Greenup 1,284
Greenville 3,875
Guthrie 1,200
Hanson 378
Hardin 522
Hardinsburg 1,547
Harlan 3,318
Harrodsburg 6,741
Hartford 1,868
Hawesville 1,262
Hazard 5,459
Hazel 424
Henderson 22,976
Hickman 3,048
Hickory Grove 173
Highland Heights 460
Hindman 808
Hiseville 152
Hodgenville 2,562
Hollyvilla 907
Hopeful Heights 473
Hopkinsville 21,250
Horse Cave 2,068
Houston Acres 684
Hurstbourne Acres 289
Hustonville 413
Hyden 482
Independence 1,784
Indian Hills 600
Indian Hills Cherokee Section 282
Inez 469
Irvine 2,918
Irvington 1,300
Island 410
Jackson 1,887
Jamestown 1,027
Jeffersontown 9,701
Jenkins 2,552
Junction City 1,046
Keeneland 587
Kenton Vale 178
Kevil 274
Kingsley 504
Kuttawa 453
La Center 1,044
Lackey 294
Lafayette 158
La Grange 1,713
Lake Louisvilla 430
Lakeside Park 2,511
Lakeview 478
Lancaster 3,230
Latonia Lakes 428
Lawrenceburg 3,579
Lebanon 5,528
Lebanon Junction 1,571
Leitchfield 2,983
Lewisburg 651
Lewisport 1,595
Lexington 108,137
Liberty 1,765
Lincolnshire 222
Livermore 1,594
Livingston 338
Lockport 105
London 4,337
Lone Oak 3,759
Lookout Heights, see Fort Wright-Lookout Heights
Loretto 985
Louisa 1,781
Louisville 361,472
Loyall 1,212
Ludlow 5,815
Lyndon 460
Lynnview 1,165
Madisonville 15,332
Manchester 1,664
Marion 3,008
Martin 786
Mary Hill Estates 211
Mayfield 10,724
Maysville 7,411
McHenry 420
McKee 255
McRoberts 1,037
Meadow Vale 1,231
Meadowview Estates 139
Middlesborough 11,844
Midway 1,278
Millersburg 788
Milton 756
Minor Lane Heights 2,217
Mockingbird Valley 255
Monterey 205
Monticello 3,618
Moorland 705
Morehead 7,191
Morganfield 3,563
Morgantown 1,394
Mortons Gap 1,169
Mount Olivet 442
Mount Sterling 5,083
Mount Vernon 1,639
Mount Washington 2,020
Muldraugh 1,773
Munfordville 1,233
Murray 13,537
Nebo 274
Neon 705
New Castle 755
New Haven 977
Newport 25,998
Nicholasville 5,829
Norbourne Estates 467
North Middletown 433
Northfield 192
Nortonville 699
Oakland 144
Okolona 17,643
Olive Hill 1,197
Owensboro 50,329
Owenton 1,280
Owingsville 1,381
Paducah 31,627
Paintsville 3,868
Paris 7,823
Park City 567
Park Hills 3,999
Parkway Village 829
Pembroke 634
Perryville 730
Petersburg 430
Pewee Valley 950
Phelps 770
Pikeville 4,576
Pineville 2,817
Plantation 895
Pleasant Valley 257
Pleasure Ridge Park 28,566
Pleasureville 747
Plum Springs 185
Plymouth Village 230
Powderly 631
Prestonburg 3,422
Prestonville 252
Princeton 6,292
Providence 4,270
Raceland 1,857
Radcliff 7,881
Ravenna 784
Richlawn 578
Richmond 16,861
Ridgeview Heights 189
Rochester 252
Rockport 377
Rolling Fields 737
Rolling Hills 1,313
Rosewood 69
Royville 54
Russell 1,982
Russell Springs 1,641
Russellville 6,456
Sacramento 437
Sadieville 272
St. Charles 373
St. Matthews 13,152
St. Regis Park 1,527
Salt Lick 441
Salyersville 1,196
Sanders 268
Sandy Hook 192
Sardis 183
Science Hill 470
Scottsville 3,584
Sebree 1,092
Seco 88
Sedalia 185
Seneca Gardens 822
Sharpsburg 307
Shelbyville 4,182
Shepherdsville 2,769
Shively 19,223
Silver Grove 1,365
Simpsonville 628
Slaughtersville 276
Smithfield 185
Smithland 514
Smiths Grove 756
Somerset 10,436
Sonora 390
South Carrollton 218
South Park View 287
South Shore 676
Southgate 3,212
Sparta 213
Springfield 2,961
Springlee 583
Stamping Ground 411
Stanford 2,474
Stanton 2,037
Strathmoor Gardens 337
Strathmoor Manor 464
Strathmoor Village 540
Sturgis 2,210
Taylor Mill 3,253
Taylorsville 897
Tompkinsville 2,207
Trenton 496
Uniontown 1,255
Upton 552
Valley Station 24,471
Vanceburg 1,773
Van Lear 1,033
Versailles 5,679
Vicco 377
Villa Hills 1,647
Vine Grove 2,987
Wallins Creek 369
Walton 1,801
Warfield 236
Warsaw 1,232
Washington 439
Water Valley 285
Waverly 335
Wayland 384
Wellington 727
West Buechel 1,581
West Liberty 1,387
West Point 1,741
Westwood 777
Wheatcroft 229
Wheelwright 793
White Plains 729
Whitesburg 1,137
Whitesville 752
Whitley City 1,060
Wickliffe 1,211
Wilders 823
Wildwood 412
Williamsburg 3,687
Williamstown 2,063
Wilmore 3,466
Winchester 13,402
Windy Hills 1,692
Wingo 593
Winston Park 578
Woodburn 351
Woodbury 139
Woodland Hills 1,233
Woodlawn (Campbell Co.) 525
Woodlawn (McCracken Co.) 1,639
Woodlawn Park 1,237
Worthington 1,364
Worthville 258
Yorktown 174

LOUISIANA Total population: 3,643,180

METROPOLITAN AREAS

Alexandria 118,078
Baton Rouge 285,167
Lafayette 111,745
Lake Charles 145,415
Monroe 115,387
New Orleans 1,046,470
Shreveport 293,887

PARISHES

Acadia 52,109
Allen 20,794
Ascension 37,086
Assumption 19,654
Avoyelles 37,751
Beauregard 22,888
Bienville 16,024
Bossier 63,703
Caddo 230,184
Calcasieu 145,415
Caldwell 9,354
Cameron 8,194
Catahoula 11,769
Claiborne 17,024
Concordia 22,578
De Soto 22,764
East Baton Rouge 285,167
East Carroll 12,884
East Feliciana 17,657
Evangeline 31,932
Franklin 23,946
Grant 13,671
Iberia 57,397
Iberville 30,746
Jackson 15,963
Jefferson 338,229
Jefferson Davis 29,554
Lafayette 111,745
Lafourche 68,941
La Salle 13,295
Lincoln 33,800
Livingston 36,511
Madison 15,065
Morehouse 32,463
Natchitoches 35,219
Orleans 593,471
Ouachita 115,387
Plaquemines 25,225
Pointe Coupee 22,002
Rapides 118,078
Red River 9,226
Richland 21,774
Sabine 18,638
St. Bernard 51,185
St. Charles 29,550
St. Helena 9,937
St. James 19,733
St. John the Baptist 23,813
St. Landry 80,364
St. Martin 32,453
St. Mary 60,752
St. Tammany 63,585
Tangipahoa 65,875
Tensas 9,732
Terrebonne 76,049
Union 18,447
Vermilion 43,071
Vernon 53,794
Washington 41,987
Webster 39,939
West Baton Rouge 16,864
West Carroll 13,028
West Feliciana 11,376
Winn 16,369

PLACES

Abbeville 10,996
Abita Springs 839
Addis 724
Albany 700
Alexandria 41,557
Alexandria Southwest 3,151
Allemands 2,318
Amelia 2,292
Amite City 3,593
Anandale 1,779
Angie 317
Arcadia 2,970
Arnaudville 1,673
Ashland 211
Athens 387
Baker 8,281
Baldwin 2,117
Basile 1,779
Baskin 177
Bastrop 14,713
Baton Rouge 165,963
Bayou Cane 9,077
Bayou Vista 5,121
Belcher 482
Benton 1,493
Bernice 1,794
Berwick 4,168
Bienville 287
Blanchard 806
Bogalusa 18,412
Bonita 533
Bossier City 41,595
Boyce 1,240
Breaux Bridge 4,942
Broussard 1,707
Brusly 1,282
Bryceland 65
Bunkie 5,395
Buras-Triumph 4,113
Calvin 286
Campti 1,078
Cankton 260
Carencro 2,302
Castor 183
Chatham 827
Cheneyville 1,082
Choudrant 555
Church Point 3,865
Clarence 448
Clarks 889
Clayton 1,103
Clinton 1,884
Colfax 1,892
Collinston 397
Columbia 1,000
Converse 375
Cooper Road 9,034
Corbin 189
Cotton Valley 1,261
Cottonport 1,924
Coushatta 1,492
Covington 7,170
Crowley 16,104
Cullen 1,956
Delcambre 1,975
Delhi 2,887
Delta 153
Denham Springs 6,752
De Quincy 3,448
De Ridder 8,030
Dixie Inn 456
Dodson 457
Donaldsonville 7,367
Doyline 716
Dry Prong 352
Dubach 1,096
Dubberly 212
Duson 1,199
East Hodge 363
Edgefield 201
Elizabeth 504
Elton 1,598
England 3,715
Epps 448
Erath 2,024
Eros 164
Estherwood 661
Eunice 11,390
Evergreen 307
Farmerville 3,416
Fenton 404
Ferriday 5,239
Florien 639
Folsom 249
Fordoche 488
Forest 221
Forest Hill 370
Franklin 9,325
Franklinton 3,562
Garyville 2,474
Georgetown 306
Gibsland 1,380
Gilbert 746
Gilliam 211
Glenmora 1,651
Golden Meadow 2,681
Goldonna 337
Gonzales 4,512
Grambling 4,407
Gramercy 2,567
Grand Cane 284
Grand Coteau 1,301
Grand Isle 2,236
Grayson 516
Greensburg 652
Greenwood 212
Gretna 24,875
Grosse Tete 710
Gueydan 1,984
Hahnville 2,362
Hall Summit 190
Hammond 12,487
Hammond East 1,342
Harahan 13,037
Harrisonburg 626
Harvey 6,347
Haughton 885
Haynesville 3,055
Heflin 314
Hessmer 454
Hodge 818
Hollywood 1,794
Homer 4,483
Hornbeck 525
Hosston 428
Houma 30,922
Ida 370
Independence 1,770
Iota 1,271
Iowa 1,944
Jackson 4,697
Jamestown 153
Jeanerette 6,322
Jefferson Heights 16,489
Jena 2,431
Jennings 11,783
Jonesboro 5,072
Jonesville 2,761
Junction City 733
Kaplan 5,540
Keatchie 328
Kenner 29,858
Kentwood 2,736
Kilbourne 370
Kinder 2,307
Krotz Springs 1,435
Lafayette 68,908
Lafayette Southwest 5,498
Lafitte 1,223
Lake Arthur 3,551
Lake Charles 77,998
Lake Providence 6,183
Laplace 5,953
Larose 4,267
Lecompte 1,518
Leesville 8,928
Leonville 512
Lillie 160
Lisbon 151
Little Farms 15,713
Livingston 1,398
Livonia 611
Lockport 2,398
Logansport 1,330
Longstreet 182
Loreauville 728
Luling 3,255
Lutcher 3,911
Madisonville 801
Mamou 3,275
Mandeville 2,571
Mangham 544
Mansfield 6,432
Mansura 1,699
Many 3,112
Maringouin 1,365
Marion 796
Marksville 4,519
Marrero 29,015
Maurice 476
McNary 220
Melville 2,076
Mer Rouge 819
Mermentau 756
Merryville 1,286
Metairie 136,477
Minden 13,996
Monroe 56,374
Montgomery 923
Montpelier 211
Mooringsport 830
Moreauville 807
Morgan City 16,586
Morganza 836
Morse 759
Mound 78
Mount Lebanon 102
Napoleonville 1,008
Natchitoches 15,974
New Iberia 30,147
New Orleans 593,471
New Roads 3,945
New Sarpy 1,643
Newellton 1,403
Newllano 1,800
Noble 209
Norco 4,773
North Fort Polk 7,955
North Hodge 640
Norwood 348
Oak Grove 1,980
Oak Ridge 276
Oakdale 7,301
Oberlin 1,857
Oil City 907
Olla 1,387
Opelousas 20,387
Palmetto 312
Parks 491
Patterson 4,409
Pearl River 1,361
Pine Prairie 515
Pineville 8,951
Pioneer 188
Plain Dealing 1,300
Plaquemine 7,739
Plaquemine Southwest 1,224
Plaucheville 224
Pleasant Hill 826
Pollock 341
Ponchatoula 4,545
Port Allen 5,728
Port Barre 2,133
Port Sulphur 3,022
Port Vincent 387
Powhatan 277
Provencal 530
Quitman 169
Raceland 4,880
Rayne 9,510
Rayville 3,962
Reeves 214
Reserve 6,381
Ridgecrest 1,076
Ringgold 1,731
Robeline 274
Rodessa 273
Rosedale 621
Roseland 1,273
Rosepine 587
Ruston 17,365
St. Francisville 1,603
St. Joseph 1,864
St. Martinville 7,153
St. Rose 2,106
Saline 307
Samtown 4,210
Sarepta 882
Scotlandville 22,557
Scott 1,334
Seymourville 2,506
Shongaloo 173
Shreveport 182,064
Sibley 869
Sicily Island 630
Sikes 237
Simmesport 2,027
Simpson 491
Simsboro 412
Slaughter 580
Slidell 16,101
Sorrento 1,182
South Fort Polk 15,600
South Mansfield 439
Spearsville 197
Springfield 423
Springhill 6,496
Stanley 145
Sterlington 1,118
Sulphur 15,247
Sun 288
Sunset 1,675
Tallulah 9,643
Tangipahoa 469
Terry Town 13,832
Thibodaux 15,028
Tickfaw 370
Tullos 600
Turkey Creek 280
Urania 874
Vacherie 2,145
Varnado 320
Vidalia 5,538
Ville Platte 9,692
Vinton 3,454
Vivian 4,046
Walker 1,363
Wardville 1,087
Washington 1,473
Waterproof 1,438
Welsh 3,203
West Monroe 14,868
Westlake 4,082
Westwego 11,402
White Castle 2,206
Wilson 606
Winnfield 7,142
Winnsboro 5,349
Wisner 1,339
Woodworth 409
Youngsville 1,002
Zachary 4,964
Zwolle 2,169

MAINE Total population: 993,663

METROPOLITAN AREAS

Lewiston-Auburn 72,474
Portland 141,625

COUNTIES

Androscoggin 91,279
Aroostook 94,078
Cumberland 192,528
Franklin 22,444
Hancock 34,590
Kennebec 95,306
Knox 29,013
Lincoln 20,537
Oxford 43,457
Penobscot 125,393
Piscataquis 16,285
Sagadahoc 23,452
Somerset 40,597
Waldo 23,328
Washington 29,859
York 111,576

TOWNS AND PLACES

Abbot 453▲
Acton 697▲
Addison 773▲
Albion 1,056▲
Alexander 169▲
Alfred 1,211▲
Alna 315▲
Alton 340▲
Amherst 148▲
Amity 156▲
Andover 791▲
Anson 2,168▲
Appleton 628▲
Arrowsic 188▲
Arundel 1,322▲
Ashland 1,761▲
Athens 592▲
Atkinson 213▲
Auburn 24,151
Augusta 21,945
Aurora 72▲
Avon 495▲
Baileyville 2,167▲
Baldwin 878▲
Bancroft 53▲
Bangor 33,168
Bar Harbor 2,392
Bar Harbor 3,716▲
Bath 9,679
Beals 663▲
Beddington 32▲
Belfast 5,957
Belgrade 1,302▲
Belmont 349▲
Benedicta 177▲
Benton 1,729▲
Berwick 1,765
Berwick 3,136▲
Bethel 2,220▲
Biddeford 19,983
Bingham 1,184
Bingham 1,254▲
Blaine 903▲
Bluehill 1,367▲
Boothbay 1,814▲
Boothbay Harbor 2,320▲
Bowdoin 858▲
Bowdoinham 1,294▲
Bowerbank 29▲
Bradford 569▲
Bradley 1,010▲
Bremen 454▲
Brewer 9,300
Bridgewater 895▲
Bridgton 1,779
Bridgton 2,967▲
Bristol 1,721▲
Brooklin 598▲
Brooks 751▲
Brooksville 673▲
Brownfield 478▲
Brownville 1,490▲
Brunswick 10,867
Brunswick 16,195▲
Brunswick Station 1,679
Buckfield 929▲
Bucksport 2,456
Bucksport 3,756▲
Burlington 266▲
Burnham 802▲
Buxton 3,135▲
Byron 132▲
Calais 4,044▲
Cambridge 281▲
Camden 3,492
Camden 4,115▲
Canaan 904▲
Canton 742▲
Cape Elizabeth 7,873▲
Caribou 10,419
Carmel 1,301▲
Carthage 354▲
Casco 1,256▲
Castine 1,080▲
Castle Hill 519▲
Centerville 19▲
Chapman 328▲
Charleston 909▲
Charlotte 199▲
Chelsea 2,095▲
Cherryfield 771▲
Chester 255▲
Chesterville 643▲
China 1,850▲
Chisholm 1,530
Clifton 233▲
Clinton 1,124
Clinton 1,971▲
Columbia 162▲
Columbia Falls 367▲
Cooper 88▲
Corinna 1,700▲
Corinth 1,212▲
Cornish 839▲
Cornville 623▲
Cranberry Isles 186▲
Crawford 74▲
Crystal 281▲
Cumberland 4,096▲
Cushing 522▲
Cutler 588▲
Damariscotta-Newcastle 1,188
Damariscotta 1,264▲
Danforth 794▲
Dayton 546▲
Deblois 20▲
Dedham 522▲
Deer Isle 1,211▲
Denmark 397▲
Dennysville 278▲
Detroit 663▲
Dexter 2,732
Dexter 3,725▲
Dixfield 1,535
Dixfield 2,188▲
Dixmont 559▲
Dover-Foxcroft 3,102
Dover-Foxcroft 4,178▲
Dresden 787▲
Durham 1,264▲
Dyer Brook 165▲
Eagle Lake 908▲
East Machias 1,057▲
East Millinocket 2,564
East Millinocket 2,567▲
Eastbrook 188▲
Easton 1,305▲
Eastport 1,989
Eddington 1,358▲
Edgecomb 549▲
Edinburg 67▲
Eliot 3,497▲
Ellsworth 4,603
Embden 418▲
Enfield 1,148▲
Etna 526▲
Eustis 595▲
Exeter 663▲
Fairfield 3,694
Fairfield 5,684▲
Falmouth 6,291▲
Falmouth Foreside 1,621
Farmingdale 1,832
Farmingdale 2,423▲
Farmington 3,096
Farmington 5,657▲
Fayette 447▲
Fort Fairfield 2,322
Fort Fairfield 4,859▲
Fort Kent 2,876
Fort Kent 4,575▲
Frankfort 620▲
Franklin 708▲
Freedom 373▲
Freeport 1,822
Freeport 4,781▲
Frenchville 1,375▲
Friendship 834▲
Fryeburg 1,075
Fryeburg 2,208▲
Gardiner 6,685
Garland 596▲
Georgetown 464▲
Gilead 153▲
Glenburn 1,196▲
Gorham 3,337
Gorham 7,839▲
Gouldsboro 1,310▲
Grand Isle 797▲
Gray 2,939▲
Greenbush 591▲
Greene 1,772▲
Greenfield 117▲
Greenville 1,714
Greenville 1,894▲
Greenwood 610▲
Guilford 1,216
Guilford 1,694▲
Hallowell 2,814
Hampden 2,207
Hampden 4,693▲
Hancock 1,070▲
Hanover 275▲
Harmony 650▲
Harpswell 2,552▲
Harrington 553▲
Harrison 1,045▲
Hartford 312▲
Hartland 1,414▲
Haynesville 157▲
Hebron 532▲
Hermon 2,376▲
Hersey 81▲
Hiram 686▲
Hodgdon 933▲
Holden 1,841▲
Hollis 1,560▲
Hope 500▲
Houlton 6,760
Houlton 8,111▲
Howland 1,418
Howland 1,468▲
Hudson 482▲
Industry 347▲
Island Falls 913▲
Isle au Haut 45▲
Islesborough 421▲
Jackman 848▲
Jackson 217▲
Jay 3,954▲
Jefferson 1,242▲
Jonesboro 448▲
Jonesport 1,073
Jonesport 1,326▲
Kenduskeag 733▲
Kennebunk 2,764
Kennebunk 5,646▲
Kennebunkport 1,097
Kennebunkport 2,160▲
Kingfield 877▲
Kittery 7,363
Kittery 11,028▲
Kittery Point 1,172
Knox 443▲
Lagrange 393▲
Lamoine 615▲
Lebanon 1,983▲
Lee 599▲
Leeds 1,031▲
Levant 802▲
Lewiston 41,779
Liberty 515▲
Limerick 963▲
Limestone 1,572
Limestone 10,360▲
Limington 1,066▲
Lincoln 3,482
Lincoln 4,759▲
Lincolnville 955▲
Linneus 608▲
Lisbon 1,475
Lisbon 6,544▲
Lisbon Falls 3,257
Litchfield 1,222▲
Little Falls-South Windham 1,453
Littleton 958▲
Livermore 1,610▲
Livermore Falls 2,378
Livermore Falls 3,450▲
Loring 7,881
Lovell 607▲
Lowell 154▲
Lubec 1,949▲
Ludlow 259▲
Lyman 864▲
Machias 1,368
Machias 2,441▲
Machiasport 887▲
Madawaska 4,452
Madawaska 5,585▲
Madison 2,920
Madison 4,278▲
Madrid 107▲
Manchester 1,331▲
Mapleton 1,598▲
Mariaville 108▲
Mars Hill 1,875▲
Mars Hill-Blaine 1,854
Marshfield 227▲
Masardis 317▲
Mattawamkeag 988▲
Maxfield 24▲
Mechanic Falls 1,872
Mechanic Falls 2,193▲
Meddybemps 76▲
Medford 146▲
Medway 1,491▲
Mercer 313▲
Merrill 271▲
Mexico 3,325
Mexico 4,309▲
Milbridge 1,154▲
Milford 1,519
Milford 1,828▲
Millinocket 7,558
Millinocket 7,742▲
Milo 1,514
Milo 2,572▲
Minot 919▲
Monmouth 2,062▲
Monroe 478▲
Monson 669▲
Monticello 1,072▲
Montville 430▲
Moose River 255▲
Morrill 410▲
Moscow 586▲
Mount Desert 1,659▲
Mount Vernon 680▲
Naples 956▲
New Gloucester 2,811▲
New Limerick 427▲
New Portland 559▲
New Sharon 725▲
New Sweden 639▲
New Vineyard 444▲
Newburgh 835▲
Newcastle 1,076▲
Newfield 458▲
Newport 1,588
Newport 2,260▲
Newry 208▲
Nobleborough 850▲
Norridgewock 1,067
Norridgewock 1,964▲
North Berwick 1,449
North Berwick 2,224▲
North Haven 399▲
North Yarmouth 1,383▲
Northfield 57▲
Northport 744▲
Norway 2,430
Norway 3,595▲
Oakfield 836▲
Oakland 2,261
Oakland 3,535▲
Old Orchard Beach 5,273
Old Orchard Beach 5,404▲
Old Town 9,057
Orient 83▲
Orland 1,307▲
Orono 9,146
Orono 9,989▲
Orrington 2,702▲
Otis 123▲
Otisfield 589▲
Owls Head 1,281▲
Oxford 1,892▲
Palermo 645▲
Palmyra 1,104▲
Paris 3,739▲
Parkman 457▲
Parsonfield 971▲
Passadumkeag 326▲
Patten 1,068
Patten 1,266▲
Pembroke 700▲
Penobscot 786▲
Perham 436▲
Perry 878▲
Peru 1,345▲
Phillips 979▲
Phippsburg 1,229▲
Pittsfield 3,398
Pittsfield 4,274▲
Pittston 1,617▲
Plymouth 542▲
Poland 2,015▲
Portage Lake 477▲
Porter 1,115▲
Portland 65,116
Pownal 800▲
Presque Isle 11,452
Princeton 956▲
Prospect 358▲
Randolph 1,548
Randolph 1,741▲
Rangeley 941▲
Raymond 1,328▲
Readfield 1,258▲
Richmond 1,449
Richmond 2,168▲
Ripley 297▲
Robbinston 396▲
Rockland 8,505
Rockport 2,067▲
Rome 362▲
Roque Bluffs 153▲
Roxbury 271▲
Rumford 6,198
Rumford 9,363▲
Saco 11,678
St. Agatha 868▲
St. Albans 1,041▲
St. George 1,639▲
Sanford 10,457
Sanford 15,812▲
Sangerville 1,107▲
Scarborough 7,845▲
Searsmont 624▲
Searsport 1,110
Searsport 1,951▲
Sebago 708▲
Sebec 325▲
Sedgwick 578▲
Shapleigh 559▲
Sherman 949▲
Shirley 174▲
Sidney 1,319▲
Skowhegan 6,571
Skowhegan 7,601▲
Smithfield 527▲
Smyrna 318▲
Solon 712▲
Sorrento 199▲
South Berwick 1,863
South Berwick 3,488▲
South Bristol 664▲
South Eliot 1,635
South Paris 2,315
South Portland 23,267
South Thomaston 831▲
Southport 473▲
South Windham, see Little Falls-South Windham
Southwest Harbor 1,657▲
Springfield 336▲
Springvale 2,914
Stacyville 547▲
Standish 3,122▲
Starks 323▲
Stetson 395▲
Steuben 697▲
Stockholm 388▲
Stockton Springs 1,142▲
Stoneham 160▲
Stonington 1,291▲
Stow 109▲
Strong 1,132▲
Sullivan 824▲
Sumner 525▲
Surry 623▲
Swans Island 323▲
Swanville 487▲
Sweden 110▲
Talmadge 25▲
Temple 367▲
Thomaston 2,160
Thomaston 2,646▲
Thorndike 439▲
Topsham 2,700
Topsham 5,022▲
Tremont 1,003▲
Trenton 392▲
Troy 543▲
Turner 2,246▲
Union 1,189▲
Unity 1,280▲
Upton 54▲
Van Buren 3,429
Van Buren 3,971▲
Vanceboro 263▲
Vassalborough 2,618▲
Veazie 1,174
Veazie 1,556▲
Verona 437▲
Vienna 205▲
Vinalhaven 1,135▲
Wade 255▲
Waite 70▲
Waldo 431▲
Waldoboro 3,146▲
Wales 624▲
Waltham 167▲
Warren 1,864▲
Washburn 1,098
Washburn 1,914▲
Washington 723▲
Waterboro 1,208▲
Waterford 760▲
Waterville 18,192
Wayne 577▲
Webster 1,681▲
Weld 360▲
Wellington 232▲
Wells 4,448▲
Wesley 110▲
West Bath 836▲
West Gardiner 1,435▲
West Paris 1,171▲
Westbrook 14,444
Westfield 517▲
Weston 162▲
Westport Island 228▲
Whitefield 1,131▲
Whiting 269▲
Whitneyville 155▲
Willimantic 126▲
Wilton 2,225
Wilton 3,802▲
Windham 6,593▲
Windsor 1,097▲
Winn 516▲
Winslow 5,389
Winslow 7,299▲
Winter Harbor 1,028▲
Winterport 1,963▲
Winthrop 2,571
Winthrop 4,335▲
Wiscasset 2,244▲
Woodland (Washington Co.) 1,534
Woodland (Aroostook Co.) 1,218▲
Woodstock 1,005▲
Woodville 62▲
Woolwich 1,710▲
Yarmouth 2,421
Yarmouth 4,854▲
York 2,912
York 5,690▲

MARYLAND Total population: 3,922,399

METROPOLITAN AREA

Baltimore 2,070,670

COUNTIES

Allegany 84,044
Anne Arundel 297,539
Baltimore 621,077
Baltimore (Independent City) 905,759
Calvert 20,682
Caroline 19,781
Carroll 69,006
Cecil 53,291
Charles 47,678
Dorchester 29,405
Frederick 84,927
Garrett 21,476
Harford 115,378
Howard 61,911
Kent 16,146
Montgomery 522,809
Prince Georges 660,567
Queen Annes 18,422
St. Marys 47,388
Somerset 18,924
Talbot 23,682
Washington 103,829
Wicomico 54,236
Worcester 24,442

PLACES

Aberdeen 12,375
Aberdeen Proving Ground 7,403
Accident 237
Allview 2,314
Andrews 6,418
Annapolis 29,592
Arbutus 22,745
Aspen Hill 16,799
Avenel-Hillandale 19,520
Bainbridge Center 5,257
Baltimore 905,759
Baltimore Highlands, see Lansdowne-Baltimore Highlands
Barclay 187
Barnesville 162
Barton 723
Bel Air 6,307
Bel Air North 2,771
Bel Air South 3,360
Beltsville 8,912
Berlin 1,942
Berwyn Heights 3,934
Bethesda 71,621
Betterton 327
Birchwood City 9,558
Bladensburg 7,488
Boonsboro 1,410
Bowie 35,028
Bowling Green, see Potomac Park-Bowling Green
Brentwood 3,426
Brookeville 136
Brooklyn 13,896
Brookview 95
Brunswick 3,566
Burkittsville 221
Calverton 6,543
Cambridge 11,595
Camp Springs 22,776
Capitol Heights 2,852
Carmody Hills-Pepper Mill Village 6,245
Catonsville 54,812
Cecilton 581
Cedar Heights, see Chapel Oaks-Cedar Heights
Centreville 1,853
Chapel Oaks-Cedar Heights 6,049
Charlestown 721
Chesapeake Beach 934
Chesapeake City 1,031
Chestertown 3,476
Cheverly 6,696
Chevy Chase 16,424
Chevy Chase Section Four 2,266
Chevy Chase (Village) 2,265
Chillum 35,656
Church Creek 130
Church Hill 247
Clear Spring 499
Colesville 9,455
College Park 26,156
Colmar Manor 1,715
Columbia 8,815
Coral Hills 7,105
Cottage City 993
Cresaptown 1,731
Crisfield 3,078
Crofton 4,478
Cumberland 29,724
Damascus 2,638
Deale 1,059
Deer Park 310
Defense Heights 6,775
Delmar 1,191
Denton 1,561
District Heights 8,424
Dundalk 85,377
Eagle Harbor 200
East New Market 251
East Pines, see Riverdale Heights-East Pines
Easton 6,809
Edgemere 10,352
Edgewood 8,551
Edmonston 1,441
Eldersburg-Flohrville 1,739
Eldorado 99
Elkton 5,362
Ellicott City 9,506
Emmitsburg 1,532
Essex 38,193
Fairmount Heights 1,972
Federalsburg 1,917
Ferndale 9,929
Flohrville, see Eldersburg-Flohrville
Forest Heights 3,600
Forestville 16,152
Fort Meade 16,699
Fort Ritchie 2,126
Fountain Head 2,029
Frederick 23,641
Friendsville 566
Frostburg 7,327
Fruitland 2,315
Funkstown 1,051
Gaithersburg 8,344
Galena 361
Galestown 123
Garrett Park 1,258
Glen Burnie 38,608
Glen Echo 297
Glenarden 4,502
Goldsboro 231
Good Luck 10,584
Grantsville 517
Grasonville 1,182
Greenbelt 18,199
Greensboro 1,173
Hagerstown 35,862
Halfway 6,106
Halpine 5,912
Hampstead 961
Hancock 1,832
Havre de Grace 9,791
Hebron 705
Henderson 135
Highland Beach 6
Hillandale, see Avenel-Hillandale
Hillcrest Heights 24,037
Hillsboro 177
Hurlock 1,056
Hyattsville 14,998
Indian Head 1,350
Indian Head Plant 1,449
Joppatowne 9,092
Keedysville 431
Kemp Mill 10,037
Kensington 2,322
Kentland 9,649
Kitzmillerville 443
Landover 5,597
Landover Hills 2,691
Langley Park 11,564
Lanham-Seabrook 13,244
Lansdowne-Baltimore Highlands 16,976
La Plata 1,561
Laurel 10,525
La Vale-Narrows Park 3,971
Laytonsville 293
Leonardtown 1,406
Lexington Park-Patuxent River 9,136
Linthicum 9,830
Loch Lynn Heights 507
Lonaconing 1,572
Londontowne 3,864
Luke 424
Lutherville-Timonium 24,055
Manchester 1,466
Mardela Springs 356
Marydel 176
Maryland City 7,102
Maugansville 1,069
Mayo 2,154
Middle River 19,935
Middletown 1,262
Midland 665
Millington 474
Montrose 6,140
Morningside 1,665
Mount Airy 1,825
Mount Rainier 8,180
Mount Savage 1,413
Mountain Lake Park 1,263
Myersville 450
Narrows Park, see La Vale-Narrows Park
New Carrollton 13,395
New Market 339
New Windsor 788
North Beach 761
North Brentwood 758
North East 1,818
North Potomac 12,546
North Takoma Park 7,373
Oakland (Carroll Co.) 1,256
Oakland (Garrett Co.) 1,786
Ocean City 1,493
Odenton 5,989
Olney 2,138
Overlea 13,086
Owings Mills 7,360
Oxford 750
Oxon Hill 11,974
Palmer Park 8,172
Parkville 33,897
Patuxent River, see Lexington Park-Patuxent River
Pepper Mill Village, see Carmody Hills-Pepper Mill Village
Perry Hall 5,446
Perryville 2,091
Pikesville 25,395

▲ Population of entire town (township).

MARYLAND, Continued

Pittsville 477
Pleasant Hills 1,754
Pocomoke City 3,573
Poolesville 349
Port Deposit 906
Potomac Heights 1,983
Potomac Park-Bowling Green 2,253
Potomac Valley 5,094
Preston 509
Princess Anne 975
Pumphrey 6,370
Queen Anne 292
Queenstown 387
Randallstown 33,683
Randolph 13,233
Reisterstown 14,037
Ridgely 822
Rising Sun 956
Riverdale 5,724
Riverdale Heights-East Pines 8,941
Riviera Beach 7,464
Rock Hall 1,125
Rockville 41,564
Rosedale 19,417
Rosemont 250
St. Michaels 1,456
Salisbury 15,252
Savage 2,116
Seabrook, see Lanham-Seabrook
Seat Pleasant 7,217
Secretary 352
Selby-on-the-Bay 2,450
Severna Park 16,358
Shady Side 1,562
Sharpsburg 833
Sharptown 660
Silver Hill, see Suitland-Silver Hill
Silver Spring 77,496
Smithsburg 671
Snow Hill 2,201
Somerset 1,303
South Gate 9,356
South Kensington 10,289
South Laurel 13,345
Sudlersville 417
Suitland-Silver Hill 30,355
Sykesville 1,399
Takoma Park 18,455
Taneytown 1,731
Templeville 102
Thurmont 2,359
Timonium, see Lutherville-Timonium
Towson 77,809
Trappe 426
Union Bridge 904
University Park 2,926
Upper Marlboro 646
Vienna 358
Waldorf 7,368
Walker Mill 6,322
Walkersville 1,269
Washington Grove 688
West Laurel 4,478
Westernport 3,106
Westminster 7,207
Westminster South 2,242
Wheaton 66,247
White Oak 19,769
Willards 494
Williamsport 2,270
Woodlawn-Woodmoor 28,811
Woodmoor, see Woodlawn-Woodmoor
Woodsboro 439

MASSACHUSETTS Total population: 5,689,170

METROPOLITAN AREAS

Boston 2,753,700
Brockton 189,820
Fall River 149,976
Fitchburg-Leominster 97,164
Lawrence-Haverhill 232,415 (205,641 in Massachusetts, 26,774 in New Hampshire)
Lowell 212,860
New Bedford 152,642
Pittsfield 79,727
Springfield-Chicopee-Holyoke 529,922
Worcester 344,320

COUNTIES

Barnstable 96,656
Berkshire 149,402
Bristol 444,301
Dukes 6,117
Essex 637,887
Franklin 59,210
Hampden 459,050
Hampshire 123,981
Middlesex 1,398,355
Nantucket 3,774
Norfolk 604,854
Plymouth 333,314
Suffolk 735,190
Worcester 637,079

TOWNS AND PLACES

Abington 12,334▲
Acton 14,770▲
Acushnet 7,767▲
Adams 11,256
Adams 11,772▲
Agawam 21,717▲
Alford 302▲
Amesbury 10,088
Amesbury 11,388▲
Amherst 17,926
Amherst 26,331▲
Andover 23,695▲
Arlington 53,524▲
Ashburnham 1,013
Ashburnham 3,484▲
Ashby 2,274▲
Ashfield 1,274▲
Ashland 8,882▲
Athol 9,723
Athol 11,185▲
Attleboro 32,907
Auburn 15,347▲
Avon 5,295▲
Ayer 3,292
Ayer 8,283▲
Baldwinsville 1,739
Barnstable 1,202
Barnstable 19,842▲
Barre 1,098
Barre 3,825▲
Becket 929▲
Bedford 13,513▲
Belchertown 2,636
Belchertown 5,936▲
Bellingham 4,228
Bellingham 13,967▲
Belmont 28,285▲
Berkley 2,027▲
Berlin 2,099▲
Bernardston 1,659▲
Beverly 38,348
Billerica 31,648▲
Blackstone 6,566▲
Blandford 863▲
Bolton 1,905▲
Bondsville 1,657
Boston 641,071
Bourne 1,992
Bourne 12,636▲
Boxborough 1,451▲
Boxford 2,026
Boxford 4,032▲
Boylston 2,774▲
Braintree 35,050▲
Brewster 1,790▲
Bridgewater 4,032
Bridgewater 11,829▲
Brimfield 1,907▲
Brockton 89,040
Brookfield 1,197
Brookfield 2,063▲
Brookline 58,689▲
Buckland 1,892▲
Burlington 21,980▲
Buzzards Bay 2,422
Cambridge 100,361
Canton 17,100▲
Carlisle 2,871▲
Carver 2,420▲
Centerville 2,876
Charlemont 897▲
Charlton 4,654▲
Chatham 1,652
Chatham 4,554▲
Chelmsford 31,432▲
Chelsea 30,625
Cheshire 1,021
Cheshire 3,006▲
Chester 1,025▲
Chesterfield 704▲
Chicopee 66,676
Chilmark 340▲
Clarksburg 1,987▲
Clicquot, see Millis-Clicquot
Clinton 13,383▲
Cohasset 6,954▲
Colrain 1,420▲
Concord 16,148▲
Conway 998▲
Cordaville 1,457
Cummington 562▲
Dalton 7,505▲
Danvers 26,151▲
Dartmouth 18,800▲
Dedham 26,938▲
Deerfield 3,850▲
Dennis 6,454▲
Dennis Port 1,410
Dighton 4,667▲
Douglas 2,947▲
Dover 1,881
Dover 4,529▲
Dracut 18,214▲
Dudley 8,087▲
Dunstable 1,292▲
Duxbury 2,477
Duxbury 7,636▲
East Bridgewater 8,347▲
East Brookfield 1,392
East Brookfield 1,800▲
East Douglas 1,763
East Falmouth 2,971
East Longmeadow 13,029▲
Eastham 2,043▲
Easthampton 13,012▲
Easton 12,157▲
Edgartown 1,006
Edgartown 1,481▲
Egremont 1,138▲
Erving 1,260▲
Essex 1,626
Essex 2,670▲
Everett 42,485
Fairhaven 16,332▲
Fall River 96,898
Falmouth 5,806
Falmouth 15,942▲
Fisherville 1,958
Fiskdale 1,612
Fitchburg 43,343
Florida 672▲
Fort Devens 12,951
Foxborough 4,090
Foxborough 14,218▲
Framingham 64,048▲
Franklin 8,863
Franklin 17,830▲
Freetown 4,270▲
Gardner 19,748
Gay Head 118▲
Georgetown 5,290▲
Gilbertville 1,247
Gill 1,100▲
Gloucester 27,941
Goshen 483▲
Gosnold 83▲
Grafton 11,659▲
Granby 1,354
Granby 5,473▲
Granville 1,008▲
Great Barrington 3,203
Great Barrington 7,537▲
Greenfield 14,642
Greenfield 18,116▲
Groton 1,314
Groton 5,109▲
Groveland 5,382▲
Hadley 3,750▲
Halifax 3,537▲
Hamilton 6,373▲
Hampden 4,572▲
Hancock 675▲
Hanover 10,107▲
Hanson 7,148▲
Hardwick 2,379▲
Harvard 12,536▲
Harwich 3,842
Harwich 5,892▲
Hatfield 1,380
Hatfield 2,825▲
Haverhill 46,120
Hawley 224▲
Heath 383▲
Hingham 18,845▲
Hinsdale 1,588▲
Holbrook 11,775▲
Holden 12,564▲
Holland 931▲
Holliston 12,069▲
Holyoke 50,112
Hopedale 3,089
Hopedale 4,292▲
Hopkinton 1,956
Hopkinton 5,981▲
Housatonic 1,344
Hubbardston 1,437▲
Hudson 14,283
Hudson 16,084▲
Hull 9,961▲
Huntington 1,593▲
Hyannis 6,847
Ipswich 5,022
Ipswich 10,750▲
Kingston 3,772
Kingston 5,999▲
Lakeville 1,432
Lakeville 4,376▲
Lancaster 6,095▲
Lanesborough 2,972▲
Lawrence 66,915
Lee 3,389
Lee 6,426▲
Leicester 3,173
Leicester 9,140▲
Lenox 2,208
Lenox 5,804▲
Leominster 32,939
Leverett 1,005▲
Lexington 31,886▲
Leyden 376▲
Lincoln 7,567▲
Littleton 6,380▲
Littleton Common 2,764
Longmeadow 15,630▲
Lowell 94,239
Ludlow 17,580▲
Lunenburg 7,419▲
Lynn 90,294
Lynnfield 10,826▲
Malden 56,127
Manchester 5,151▲
Mansfield 4,778
Mansfield 9,939▲
Marblehead 21,295▲
Marion 1,262
Marion 3,466▲
Marlborough 27,936
Marshfield 2,562
Marshfield 15,223▲
Marshfield Hills 1,646
Mashpee 1,288▲
Mattapoisett 2,188
Mattapoisett 4,500▲
Maynard 9,710▲
Medfield 9,821▲
Medford 64,397
Medway 3,716
Medway 7,938▲
Melrose 33,180
Mendon 2,524▲
Merino Village 3,470
Merrimac 4,245▲
Methuen 35,456▲
Middleborough 6,259
Middleborough 13,607▲
Middlefield 288▲
Middleton 4,044▲
Milford 13,740
Milford 19,352▲
Millbury 11,987▲
Millers Falls 1,186
Millis 5,686▲
Millis-Clicquot 3,217
Millville 1,197
Millville 1,764▲
Milton 27,190▲
Monroe 216▲
Monson 2,310
Monson 7,355▲
Montague 8,451▲
Monterey 600▲
Montgomery 446▲
Mount Washington 52▲
Nahant 4,119▲
Nantucket 2,461
Nantucket 3,774▲
Natick 31,057▲
Needham 29,748▲
New Ashford 183▲
New Bedford 101,777
New Braintree 631▲
New Marlborough 1,031▲
New Salem 474▲
Newbury 3,804▲
Newburyport 15,807
Newton 91,263
Norfolk 4,656▲
North Adams 19,195
North Amherst 2,854
North Andover 16,284▲
North Attleborough 18,665▲
North Brookfield 2,677
North Brookfield 3,967▲
North Dighton 1,264
North Oxford 1,550
North Pembroke 2,881
North Plymouth 3,434
North Reading 11,264▲
North Scituate 5,507
North Uxbridge 1,960
Northampton 29,664
Northborough 9,218▲
Northbridge 3,321
Northbridge 11,795▲
Northfield 1,191
Northfield 2,631▲
Norton 2,073
Norton 9,487▲
Norwell 7,796▲
Norwood 30,815▲
Oak Bluffs 1,385▲
Oakham 730▲
Onset 1,771
Orange 3,847
Orange 6,104▲
Orleans 3,055▲
Osterville 1,286
Otis 5,596
Otis 820▲
Oxford 6,109
Oxford 10,345▲
Palmer 3,649
Palmer 11,680▲
Paxton 3,731▲
Peabody 48,080
Pelham 937▲
Pembroke 11,193▲
Pepperell 1,076
Pepperell 5,887▲
Peru 256▲
Petersham 1,014▲
Phillipston 872▲
Pigeon Cove 1,466
Pinehurst 5,681
Pittsfield 57,020
Plainfield 287▲
Plainville 4,953▲
Plymouth 6,940
Plymouth 18,606▲
Plympton 1,224▲
Princeton 1,681▲
Provincetown 2,836
Provincetown 2,911▲
Quincy 87,966
Randolph 27,035▲
Raynham 2,526
Raynham 6,705▲
Reading 22,539▲
Rehoboth 6,512▲
Revere 43,159
Richmond 1,461▲
Rochdale 1,320
Rochester 1,770▲
Rockland 15,674▲
Rockport 4,166
Rockport 5,636▲
Rowe 277▲
Rowley 1,325
Rowley 3,040▲
Royalston 809▲
Russell 1,382▲
Rutland 1,751
Rutland 3,198▲
Sagamore 1,007
Salem 40,556
Salisbury 2,439
Salisbury 4,179▲
Sand Hills, see Shore Acres-Sand Hills
Sandisfield 547▲
Sandwich 1,305
Sandwich 5,239▲
Saugus 25,110▲
Savoy 322▲
Scituate 3,738
Scituate 16,973▲
Seekonk 11,116▲
Sharon 12,367▲
Sheffield 2,374▲
Shelburne 1,836▲
Shelburne Falls 2,183
Sherborn 3,309▲
Shirley 1,718
Shirley 4,909▲
Shore Acres-Sand Hills 2,949
Shrewsbury 19,196▲
Shutesbury 489▲
Somerset 18,088▲
Somerville 88,779
South Ashburnham 1,181
South Deerfield 1,628
South Duxbury 2,075
South Hadley 17,033▲
South Lancaster 2,679
South Yarmouth 5,380
Southampton 3,069▲
Southborough 5,798▲
Southbridge 14,261
Southbridge 17,057▲
Southwick 1,263
Southwick 6,330▲
Spencer 5,895
Spencer 8,779▲
Springfield 163,905
Sterling 4,247▲
Stockbridge 1,147
Stockbridge 2,312▲
Stoneham 20,725▲
Stoughton 23,459▲
Stow 3,984▲
Sturbridge 4,878▲
Sudbury 13,506▲
Sunderland 2,236▲
Sutton 4,590▲
Swampscott 13,578▲
Swansea 12,640▲
Taunton 43,756
Templeton 5,863▲
Tewksbury 22,755▲
Three Rivers 3,366
Tisbury 2,257▲
Tolland 172▲
Topsfield 5,225▲
Townsend 1,329
Townsend 4,281▲
Truro 1,234▲
Turners Falls 5,168
Tyngsborough 4,204▲
Tyringham 234▲
Upton 3,484▲
Upton-West Upton 2,131
Uxbridge 3,380
Uxbridge 8,253▲
Vineyard Haven 1,599
Wakefield 25,402▲
Wales 852▲
Walpole 18,149▲
Waltham 61,582
Ware 6,509
Ware 8,187▲
Wareham 11,492▲
Wareham-Wareham Center 2,024
Warren 1,688
Warren 3,633▲
Warwick 492▲
Washington 406▲
Watertown 39,307▲
Wayland 1,752
Wayland 13,461▲
Webster 12,432
Webster 14,917▲
Wellesley 28,051▲
Wellfleet 1,743▲
Wendell 405▲
Wenham 3,849▲
West Boylston 6,369▲
West Bridgewater 1,920
West Bridgewater 7,152▲
West Brookfield 1,536
West Brookfield 2,653▲
West Dennis 1,896
West Medway 2,269
West Newbury 2,254▲
West Springfield 28,461▲
West Stockbridge 1,354▲
West Tisbury 453▲
West Warren 1,237
West Yarmouth 3,699
Westborough 4,474
Westborough 12,594▲
Westfield 31,433
Westford 10,368▲
Westhampton 793▲
Westminster 4,273▲
Weston 10,870▲
Westport 9,791▲
Westwood 12,750▲
Weymouth 54,610▲
Whately 1,145▲
Whitinsville 5,210
Whitman 13,059▲
Wilbraham 3,540
Wilbraham 11,984▲
Williamsburg 2,342▲
Williamstown 4,285
Williamstown 8,454▲
Wilmington 17,102▲
Winchendon 3,997
Winchendon 6,635▲
Winchester 22,269▲
Windsor 468▲
Winthrop 20,335▲
Woburn 37,406
Worcester 176,572
Worthington 712▲
Wrentham 1,723
Wrentham 7,315▲
Yarmouth 12,033▲

MICHIGAN Total population: 8,875,083

METROPOLITAN AREAS

Ann Arbor 234,103
Battle Creek 141,963
Bay City 117,339
Detroit 4,203,548
Flint 497,950
Grand Rapids 539,225
Jackson 143,274
Kalamazoo 201,550
Lansing-East Lansing 378,423
Muskegon-Muskegon Heights 157,426
Saginaw 219,743

COUNTIES

Alcona 7,113
Alger 8,568
Allegan 66,575
Alpena 30,708
Antrim 12,612
Arenac 11,149
Baraga 7,789
Barry 38,166
Bay 117,339
Benzie 8,593
Berrien 163,940
Branch 37,906
Calhoun 141,963
Cass 43,312
Charlevoix 16,541
Cheboygan 16,573
Chippewa 32,412
Clare 16,695
Clinton 48,492
Crawford 6,482
Delta 35,924
Dickinson 23,753
Eaton 68,892
Emmet 18,331
Genesee 445,589
Gladwin 13,471
Gogebic 20,676
Grand Traverse 39,175
Gratiot 39,246
Hillsdale 37,171
Houghton 34,652
Huron 34,083
Ingham 261,039
Ionia 45,848
Iosco 24,905
Iron 13,813
Isabella 44,594
Jackson 143,274
Kalamazoo 201,550
Kalkaska 5,272
Kent 411,044
Keweenaw 2,264
Lake 5,661
Lapeer 52,361
Leelanau 10,872
Lenawee 81,951
Livingston 58,967
Luce 6,789
Mackinac 9,660
Macomb 625,309
Manistee 20,094
Marquette 64,686
Mason 22,612
Mecosta 27,992
Menominee 24,587
Midland 63,769
Missaukee 7,126
Monroe 118,479
Montcalm 39,660
Montmorency 5,247
Muskegon 157,426
Newaygo 27,992
Oakland 907,871
Oceana 17,984
Ogemaw 11,903
Ontonagon 10,548
Osceola 14,838
Oscoda 4,726
Otsego 10,422
Ottawa 128,181
Presque Isle 12,836
Roscommon 9,892
Saginaw 219,743
St. Clair 120,175
St. Joseph 47,392
Sanilac 35,181
Schoolcraft 8,226
Shiawassee 63,075
Tuscola 48,603
Van Buren 56,173
Washtenaw 234,103
Wayne 2,670,368
Wexford 19,717

PLACES

Addison 595
Adrian 20,382
Ahmeek 238
Akron 525
Alanson 362
Albion 12,112
Algonac 3,684
Allegan 4,516
Allen 385
Allen Park 40,747
Alma 9,790
Almont 1,634
Alpena 13,805
Alpha 282
Anchor Bay Gardens 2,272
Ann Arbor 99,797
Applegate 301
Armada 1,352
Ashley 521
Athens 996
Auburn 1,919
Au Gres 564
Augusta 1,025
Bad Axe 2,999
Baldwin 612
Bancroft 724
Bangor 2,050
Baraga 1,116
Baroda 439
Barryton 368
Battle Creek 38,931
Bay City 49,449
Bayport Park-Lakeside 2,101
Bear Lake 376
Beaverton 954

▲ Population of entire town (township).

Beechwood 2,714
Belding 5,121
Bellaire 897
Belleville 2,406
Bellevue 1,297
Benton Central 8,067
Benton Harbor 16,481
Benton South 4,496
Benzonia 412
Berkley 21,879
Berrien Springs 1,951
Bessemer 2,805
Beulah 461
Beverly Hills 13,598
Big Rapids 11,995
Bingham Farms 566
Birch Run 932
Birmingham 26,170
Blissfield 2,753
Bloomfield Hills 3,672
Bloomingdale 496
Boyne City 2,969
Boyne Falls 347
Breckenridge 1,257
Breedsville 209
Bridgman 1,621
Brighton 2,457
Britton 697
Bronson 2,390
Brooklyn 1,112
Brown City 1,142
Brownlee Park 2,985
Buchanan 4,645
Buckley 244
Bunny Run 1,391
Burlington 314
Burr Oak 873
Byron 655
Cadillac 9,990
Caledonia 716
Calumet 1,007
Camden 405
Capac 1,279
Capehart, see Selfridge-Capehart
Carleton 1,503
Caro 3,701
Carrollton 7,300
Carson City 1,217
Carsonville 621
Caseville 607
Casnovia 403
Caspian 1,165
Cass City 1,974
Cassopolis 2,108
Cedar Springs 1,807
Cement City 531
Center Line 10,379
Central Lake 741
Centreville 1,044
Charlevoix 3,519
Charlotte 8,244
Chatham 246
Cheboygan 5,553
Chelsea 3,858
Chesaning 2,876
Clair Haven 2,177
Clair Haven West 1,367
Clare 2,639
Clarkston 1,034
Clarksville 346
Clawson 17,617
Clayton 505
Clifford 472
Climax 594
Clinton 1,677
Clio 2,357
Coldwater 9,155
Coleman 1,295
Coloma 1,814
Colon 1,172
Columbiaville 935
Comstock 5,003
Comstock Park 5,766
Concord 983
Constantine 1,733
Coopersville 2,129
Copemish 237
Copper City 252
Corunna 2,829
Croswell 1,954
Crystal Falls 2,000
Custer 320
Cutlerville 6,267
Daggett 366
Dansville 486
Davison 5,259
Dearborn 104,199
Dearborn Heights 80,069
Decatur 1,764
Deckerville 817
Deerfield 834
De Tour 494
Detroit 1,513,601
Detroit Beach 2,053
Devils Lake, see Manitou Beach-Devils Lake
De Witt 1,829
Dexter 1,729
Dimondale 970
Douglas 813
Dowagiac 6,583
Drayton Plains 16,462
Dryden 654
Dundee 2,472
Durand 3,678
Eagle 175
East Detroit 45,920
East Grand Rapids 12,565
East Jordan 2,041
East Kingsford 1,155
East Lake 512
East Lansing 47,540
East Tawas 2,372
Eastwood 9,682
Eaton Rapids 4,494
Eau Claire 527
Ecorse 17,515
Edmore 1,149
Edwardsburg 1,107
Elberta 542
Elk Rapids 1,249
Elkton 973
Ellsworth 362
Elsie 988
Emmett 297
Empire 409
Escanaba 15,368
Essexville 4,990
Estral Beach 419
Evart 1,707
Fair Plain 3,680
Fairgrove 629
Farmington 10,329
Farwell 777
Fennville 811
Fenton 8,284
Ferndale 30,850
Ferrysburg 2,196
Fife Lake 274
Flat Rock 5,643
Flint 193,317
Flower Hills, see Shorewood Hills-Flower Hills
Flushing 7,190
Forestville 110
Fountain 156
Fowler 1,020
Fowlerville 1,978
Frankenmuth 2,834
Frankfort 1,660
Franklin 3,344
Fraser 11,868
Freeland 1,303
Freeport 501
Freesoil 186
Fremont 3,465
Fruitport 1,409
Gaastra 479
Gagetown 408
Gaines 408
Galesburg 1,355
Galien 691
Garden 336
Garden City 41,864
Gaylord 3,012
Gibraltar 3,842
Gladstone 5,237
Gladwin 2,071
Gobles 801
Goodrich 774
Grand Beach 165
Grand Blanc 5,132
Grand Haven 11,844
Grand Ledge 6,032
Grand Rapids 197,649
Grandville 10,764
Grant 772
Grass Lake 1,061
Grayling 2,143
Greenville 7,493
Grosse Ile 8,306
Grosse Pointe 6,637
Grosse Pointe Farms 11,701
Grosse Pointe Park 15,641
Grosse Pointe Shores 3,042
Grosse Pointe Woods 21,878
Gwinn 1,054
Hamtramck 27,245
Hancock 4,820
Hanover 513
Harbor Beach 2,134
Harbor Springs 1,662
Harper Woods 20,186
Harrietta 132
Harrison 1,460
Harrisville 541
Hart 2,139
Hartford 2,508
Hastings 6,501
Hazel Park 23,784
Hersey 276
Hesperia 877
Highland Park 35,444
Hillman 366
Hillsdale 7,728
Holland 26,337
Holly 4,355
Holt 6,980
Homer 1,617
Honor 282
Hopkins 566
Houghton 6,067
Houghton Lake Heights 1,252
Howard City 1,060
Howell 5,224
Hubbardston 403
Hubbell 1,251
Hudson 2,618
Hudsonville 3,523
Huntington Woods 8,536
Imlay City 1,980
Inkster 38,595
Ionia 6,361
Iron Mountain 8,702
Iron River 2,684
Ironwood 8,711
Ishpeming 8,245
Ithaca 2,749
Jackson 45,484
Jenison 11,266
Jonesville 2,081
Kalamazoo 85,555
Kaleva 377
Kalkaska 1,475
Keego Harbor 3,092
Kent City 686
Kentwood 20,310
Kincheloe 6,331
Kinde 618
Kingsford 5,276
Kingsley 632
Kingston 464
K. I. Sawyer 8,224
Laingsburg 1,159
Lake Angelus 573
Lake Ann 172
Lake City 704
Lake Linden 1,214
Lake Michigan Beach 1,201
Lake Odessa 1,924
Lake Orion 2,921
Lake Orion Heights 2,552
Lakeside, see Bayport Park-Lakeside
Lakeview (Calhoun Co.) 11,391
Lakeview (Montcalm Co.) 1,118
Lakewood Club 590
Lambertville 5,721
L'Anse 2,538
Lansing 131,546
Lapeer 6,314
Lapeer Heights 7,130
Lathrup Village 4,676
Laurium 2,868
Lawrence 790
Lawton 1,358
Leonard 378
Le Roy 248
Leslie 1,894
Level Park-Oak Park 3,080
Lexington 834
Lincoln 371
Lincoln Park 52,984
Linden 1,546
Litchfield 1,167
Livonia 110,109
Lowell 3,068
Ludington 9,021
Luna Pier 1,418
Luther 320
Lyons 758
Mackinac Island 517
Mackinaw City 810
Madison Heights 38,599
Mancelona 1,255
Manchester 1,650
Manistee 7,723
Manistique 4,324
Manitou Beach-Devils Lake 1,892
Manton 1,107
Maple Rapids 683
Marcellus 1,139
Marine City 4,567
Marion 891
Marlette 1,706
Marquette 21,967
Marshall 7,253
Martin 502
Marysville 5,610
Mason 5,468
Mattawan 1,569
Maybee 485
Mayville 872
McBain 520
McBride 272
Mecosta 396
Melvin 202
Melvindale 13,862
Memphis 1,121
Mendon 949
Menominee 10,748
Merrill 961
Mesick 376
Metamora 468
Michiana 233
Middleville 1,865
Midland 35,176
Milan 4,533
Milford 4,699
Millersburg 200
Millington 1,099
Minden City 327
Mineral Hills 234
Monroe 23,894
Montague 2,396
Montgomery 404
Montrose 1,789
Morenci 2,132
Morley 481
Morrice 734
Mount Clemens 20,476
Mount Morris 3,778
Mount Pleasant 20,524
Muir 617
Mulliken 454
Munising 3,677
Muskegon 44,631
Muskegon Heights 17,304
Nashville 1,558
Negaunee 5,248
New Baltimore 4,132
New Buffalo 2,784
New Era 466
New Haven 1,855
New Lothrop 596
Newaygo 1,381
Newberry 2,334
Niles 12,988
North Adams 574
North Branch 932
North Muskegon 4,243
Northport 594
Northville 5,400
Norton Shores 22,271
Norway 3,033
Novi 9,668
Oak Park (Oakland Co.) 36,762
Oak Park (Calhoun Co.), see Level Park-Oak Park
Oakley 418
Okemos 7,770
Olivet 1,629
Omer 366
Onaway 1,262
Onekama 638
Onsted 555
Ontonagon 2,432
Orchard Lake Village 1,487
Ortonville 983
Oscoda-Au Sable 3,475
Otisville 724
Otsego 3,957
Otter Lake 551
Ovid 1,650
Owendale 312
Owosso 17,179
Oxford 2,536
Parchment 2,027
Parma 880
Patterson Gardens 2,169
Paw Paw 3,160
Paw Paw Lake 3,726
Pearl Beach 1,744
Peck 580
Pellston 469
Pentwater 993
Perrinton 489
Perry 1,531
Petersburg 1,227
Petoskey 6,342
Pewamo 498
Pierson 193
Pigeon 1,174
Pinckney 921
Pinconning 1,320
Plainwell 3,195
Pleasant Ridge 3,989
Plymouth 11,758
Pontiac 85,279
Port Austin 883
Port Hope 377
Port Huron 35,794
Port Sanilac 493
Portage 33,590
Portland 3,817
Posen 339
Potterville 1,280
Powers 560
Prescott 306
Quakertown 837
Quakertown North 7,101
Quincy 1,540
Ramsay 1,068
Ravenna 1,048
Reading 1,125
Reed City 2,286
Reese 1,050
Richland 728
Richmond 3,234
River Rouge 15,947
Riverview 11,342
Rochester 7,054
Rockford 2,428
Rockwood 3,225
Rogers City 4,275
Romeo 4,012
Roosevelt Park 4,176
Roscommon 810
Rose City 530
Rosebush 439
Roseville 60,529
Rothbury 394
Royal Oak 86,238
Saginaw 91,849
St. Charles 2,046
St. Clair 4,770
St. Clair Shores 88,093
St. Ignace 2,892
St. Johns 6,672
St. Joseph 11,042
St. Louis 4,101
Saline 4,811
Sand Lake 380
Sandusky 2,071
Sanford 818
Saranac 1,223
Saugatuck 1,022
Sault Ste. Marie 15,136
Schoolcraft 1,277
Scottville 1,202
Sebewaing 2,053
Selfridge Air Force Base 1,614
Selfridge-Capehart 1,694
Seven Harbors, see White Lake-Seven Harbors
Shelby 1,703
Shepherd 1,416
Sheridan 653
Sherwood 400
Shoreham 666
Shorewood Hills-Flower Hills 1,629
South Haven 6,471
South Lyon 2,675
South Monroe 3,012
South Range 898
South Rockwood 1,477
Southfield 69,285
Southgate 33,909
Sparlingville 1,845
Sparta 3,094
Spring Arbor 1,832
Spring Lake 3,034
Springfield 3,994
Springfield Place 4,831
Springport 723
Stambaugh 1,458
Standish 1,184
Stanton 1,089
Stanwood 241
Stephenson 800
Sterling 507
Sterling Heights 61,365
Stevensville 1,107
Stockbridge 1,190
Stony Point 1,370
Sturgis 9,295
Sunfield 497
Sunrise Heights 1,626
Suttons Bay 522
Swartz Creek 4,928
Sylvan Lake 2,219
Tawas City 1,666
Taylor 70,020
Tecumseh 7,120
Tekonsha 739
Thompsonville 312
Three Oaks 1,750
Three Rivers 7,355
Traverse City 18,048
Trenton 24,127
Troy 39,419
Turner 182
Tustin 230
Twining 198
Ubly 899
Union City 1,740
Unionville 647
Utica 3,504
Vandalia 427
Vanderbilt 522
Vassar 2,802
Vermontville 857
Vernon 818
Verona Park 2,107
Vicksburg 2,139
Wakefield 2,757
Waldron 564
Walker 11,492
Walkerville 319
Walled Lake 3,759
Warren 179,260
Washington 1,563
Watervliet 2,059
Wayland 2,054
Wayne 21,054
Webberville 1,251
Wells 1,085
West Branch 1,912
Westland 86,749
Westphalia 806
Westwood 9,143
White Cloud 1,044
White Lake-Seven Harbors 4,504
White Pigeon 1,455
White Pine 1,218
Whitehall 3,017
Whitmore Lake 2,763
Whittemore 460
Williamston 2,600
Wixom 2,010
Wolf Lake 2,258
Wolverine 303
Wolverine Lake 4,301
Wood Creek Farms 1,090
Woodhaven 3,566
Woodland 473
Woodland Beach 2,249
Wurtsmith 6,932
Wyandotte 41,061
Wyoming 56,560
Yale 1,505
Ypsilanti 29,538
Zeeland 4,734
Zilwaukee 2,072

MINNESOTA Total population: 3,805,069

METROPOLITAN AREAS

Duluth-Superior 265,350 (220,693 in Minnesota, 44,657 in Wisconsin)
Fargo-Moorhead 120,261 (73,653 in North Dakota, 46,608 in Minnesota)
Minneapolis-St. Paul 1,813,781
Rochester 84,104

COUNTIES

Aitkin 11,403
Anoka 154,595
Becker 24,372
Beltrami 26,373
Benton 20,841
Big Stone 7,941
Blue Earth 52,322
Brown 28,887
Carlton 28,072
Carver 28,331
Cass 17,323
Chippewa 15,109
Chisago 17,492
Clay 46,608
Clearwater 8,013
Cook 3,423
Cottonwood 14,887
Crow Wing 34,826
Dakota 139,808
Dodge 13,037
Douglas 22,910
Faribault 20,896
Fillmore 21,916
Freeborn 38,064
Goodhue 34,763
Grant 7,462
Hennepin 960,080
Houston 17,556
Hubbard 10,583
Isanti 16,560
Itasca 35,530
Jackson 14,352
Kanabec 9,775
Kandiyohi 30,548
Kittson 6,853
Koochiching 17,131
Lac Qui Parle 11,164
Lake 13,351
Lake of the Woods 3,987
Le Sueur 21,332
Lincoln 8,143
Lyon 24,273
Mahnomen 5,638
Marshall 13,060
Martin 24,316
McLeod 27,662
Meeker 18,349
Mille Lacs 15,703
Morrison 26,949
Mower 43,783
Murray 12,508
Nicollet 24,518
Nobles 23,208
Norman 10,008
Olmsted 84,104
Otter Tail 46,097
Pennington 13,266
Pine 16,821
Pipestone 12,791
Polk 34,435
Pope 11,107
Ramsey 476,350
Red Lake 5,388
Redwood 20,024
Renville 21,139
Rice 41,582
Rock 11,346
Roseau 11,569
St. Louis 220,693
Scott 32,423
Sherburne 18,344
Sibley 15,845
Stearns 95,400
Steele 26,931
Stevens 11,218
Swift 13,177
Todd 22,114
Traverse 6,254
Wabasha 17,224
Wadena 12,412
Waseca 16,663
Washington 82,948
Watonwan 13,298
Wilkin 9,389
Winona 44,409
Wright 38,933
Yellow Medicine 14,523

PLACES

Ada 2,076
Adams 771
Adrian 1,350
Afton 248
Aitkin 1,553
Akeley 468
Albany 1,599
Albert Lea 19,418
Alberta 140
Albertville 451
Alden 713
Aldrich 85
Alexandria 6,973
Alpha 179
Altura 334
Alvarado 302
Amboy 571
Annandale 1,234
Anoka 13,489
Apple Valley 8,502
Appleton 1,789
Arco 121
Arden Hills 4,975
Argyle 739
Arlington 1,823
Ashby 415
Askov 287
Atwater 956
Audubon 297
Aurora 2,531
Austin 25,074
Avoca 203
Avon 725
Babbitt 3,076
Backus 257
Badger 327
Bagley 1,314
Balaton 649
Barnesville 1,782
Barnum 382
Barrett 342
Barry 52
Battle Lake 772
Baudette 1,547
Baxter 1,556
Bayport 2,987
Beardsley 366
Beaver Bay 362
Beaver Creek 235
Becker 365
Bejou 157
Belgrade 713
Belle Plaine 2,328
Bellechester 199
Bellingham 263
Beltrami 171
Belview 429
Bemidji 11,490
Bena 169
Benson 3,484
Bertha 512
Bethel 311
Big Falls 534
Big Lake 1,015
Bigelow 262
Bigfork 399
Bingham Lake 214
Birchwood 926
Bird Island 1,309
Biscay 105
Biwabik 1,483
Blackduck 595
Blaine 20,625
Blomkest 172
Blooming Prairie 1,804
Bloomington 81,970
Blue Earth 3,965
Bluffton 195
Bock 105
Borup 128
Bovey 858
Bowlus 268
Boy River 44
Boyd 311
Braham 744
Brainerd 11,667
Branch 880
Brandon 414
Breckenridge 4,200
Brewster 563
Bricelyn 470
Brook Park 113
Brooklyn Center 35,173
Brooklyn Park 26,230
Brooks 163
Brookston 137
Brooten 615
Browerville 665
Browns Valley 906
Brownsdale 625

MINNESOTA, Continued

Brownsville 417
Brownton 688
Bruno 130
Buckman 158
Buffalo 3,275
Buffalo Lake 758
Buhl 1,303
Burnsville 19,940
Burtrum 135
Butterfield 619
Byron 1,419
Caledonia 2,619
Callaway 233
Calumet 460
Cambridge 2,720
Campbell 339
Canby 2,147
Cannon Falls 2,072
Canton 391
Carlos 278
Carlton 884
Carver 669
Cass Lake 1,317
Cedar Mills 81
Center City 324
Centerville 534
Ceylon 487
Champlin 2,275
Chandler 319
Chanhassen 4,879
Chaska 4,352
Chatfield 1,885
Chickamaw Beach 87
Chisago City 1,068
Chisholm 5,913
Chokio 455
Circle Pines 3,918
Clara City 1,491
Claremont 520
Clarissa 599
Clarkfield 1,084
Clarks Grove 480
Clear Lake 280
Clearbrook 599
Clearwater 282
Clements 252
Cleveland 492
Climax 255
Clinton 608
Clitherall 131
Clontarf 147
Cloquet 8,699
Coates 212
Cobden 113
Cohasset 536
Cokato 1,735
Cold Spring 2,006
Coleraine 1,086
Cologne 518
Columbia Heights 23,837
Comfrey 525
Comstock 135
Conger 167
Cook 687
Cooley 33
Coon Rapids 30,505
Corcoran 1,656
Correll 95
Cosmos 570
Cottage Grove 13,419
Cottonwood 794
Courtland 300
Cromwell 181
Crookston 8,312
Crosby 2,241
Cross Lake 358
Crystal 30,925
Currie 368
Cuyuna 82
Cyrus 289
Dakota 369
Dalton 221
Danube 497
Danvers 136
Darfur 179
Darwin 231
Dassel 1,058
Dawson 1,699
Dayton 517
Deephaven 3,853
Deer Creek 287
Deer River 815
Deerwood 448
De Graff 195
Delano 1,851
Delavan 281
Delhi 154
Dellwood 524
Denham 56
Dennison 162
Dent 156
Detroit Lakes 5,797
Dexter 252
Dilworth 2,321
Dodge Center 1,603
Donaldson 69
Donnelly 252
Doran 101
Dover 321
Dovray 104
Duluth 100,578
Dumont 204
Dundas 460
Dundee 138
Dunnell 237
Eagle Bend 557
Eagle Lake 839
East Bethel 2,586
East Grand Forks 7,607
East Gull Lake 440
Easton 352
Echo 356
Eden Prairie 6,938
Eden Valley 776
Edgerton 1,119
Edina 44,046
Effie 165
Eitzen 208
Elba 158
Elbow Lake 1,484
Elgin 580
Elizabeth 188
Elk River 2,252
Elko 115
Elkton 134
Ellendale 569
Ellsworth 588
Elmdale 116
Elmore 910
Elrosa 203
Ely 4,904
Elysian 445
Emily 386
Emmons 412
Erhard 148
Erskine 571
Evan 126
Evansville 553
Eveleth 4,721
Excelsior 2,563
Eyota 639
Fairfax 1,432
Fairmont 10,751
Falcon Heights 5,641
Faribault 16,595
Farmington 3,104
Farwell 102
Federal Dam 147
Felton 232
Fergus Falls 12,443
Fertile 955
Fifty Lakes 143
Finlayson 192
Fisher 383
Flensburg 259
Floodwood 650
Florence 58
Foley 1,271
Forada 158
Forest Lake 3,207
Foreston 273
Fort Ripley 54
Fosston 1,684
Fountain 347
Foxhome 185
Franklin (Renville Co.) 557
Franklin (St. Louis Co.) 41
Fraser 48
Frazee 1,015
Freeborn 296
Freeport 593
Fridley 29,233
Frost 290
Fulda 1,226
Funkley 19
Garfield 198
Garrison 125
Garvin 201
Gary 265
Gaylord 1,720
Gem Lake 216
Geneva 358
Genola 97
Georgetown 141
Ghent 301
Gibbon 877
Gilbert 2,287
Gilman 111
Glencoe 4,217
Glenville 740
Glenwood 2,584
Glyndon 674
Golden Valley 24,246
Gonvick 344
Good Thunder 489
Goodhue 539
Goodridge 144
Goodview 1,829
Graceville 735
Granada 381
Grand Marais 1,301
Grand Meadow 869
Grand Rapids 7,247
Granite Falls 3,225
Grasston 132
Green Isle 363
Greenbush 787
Greenfield 977
Greenwald 244
Greenwood 587
Grey Eagle 325
Grove City 502
Grygla 211
Gully 96
Hackensack 220
Hadley 119
Hallock 1,477
Halma 96
Halstad 598
Hamburg 405
Hammond 179
Hampton 369
Hancock 806
Hanley Falls 265
Hanover 365
Hanska 442
Harding 119
Hardwick 274
Harmony 1,130
Harris 559
Hartland 331
Hastings 12,195
Hatfield 96
Hawley 1,371
Hayfield 939
Hayward 261
Hazel Run 115
Hector 1,178
Heidelberg 72
Henderson 730
Hendricks 712
Hendrum 311
Henning 850
Henriette 56
Herman 619
Heron Lake 777
Hewitt 198
Hibbing 16,104
Hill City 357
Hillman 49
Hills 571
Hilltop 1,015
Hinckley 885
Hitterdal 201
Hoffman 627
Hokah 697
Holdingford 551
Holland 263
Hollandale 287
Holloway 146
Holt 97
Hopkins 13,428
Houston 1,090
Howard Lake 1,162
Hoyt Lakes 3,634
Hugo 751
Humboldt 112
Hutchinson 8,031
Ihlen 132
Independence 1,993
International Falls 6,439
Inver Grove Heights 12,148
Iona 260
Iron Junction 150
Ironton 562
Isanti 679
Island View 44
Isle 551
Ivanhoe 738
Jackson 3,550
Janesville 1,557
Jasper 754
Jeffers 436
Jenkins 148
Johnson 53
Jordan 1,836
Kandiyohi 295
Karlstad 727
Kasota 732
Kasson 1,883
Keewatin 1,382
Kelliher 289
Kellogg 403
Kennedy 424
Kenneth 89
Kensington 308
Kent 139
Kenyon 1,575
Kerkhoven 641
Kerrick 114
Kettle River 173
Kiester 681
Kilkenny 182
Kimball Prairie 567
Kinbrae 37
Kingston 115
Kinney 325
La Crescent 3,296
Lafayette 498
Lake Benton 759
Lake Bronson 325
Lake City 3,594
Lake Crystal 1,807
Lake Elmo 4,032
Lake Henry 92
Lake Lillian 316
Lake Park 658
Lake St. Croix Beach 1,111
Lake Shore 410
Lake Wilson 378
Lakefield 1,820
Lakeland 962
Lakeland Shores 72
Lakeville 7,556
Lamberton 962
Lancaster 382
Landfall 671
Lanesboro 850
Laporte 154
La Prairie 413
La Salle 132
Lastrup 161
Lauderdale 2,571
Le Center 1,890
Lengby 140
Leonard 54
Leonidas 157
Le Roy 870
Lester Prairie 1,162
Le Sueur 3,745
Lewiston 1,000
Lewisville 291
Lexington 2,140
Lilydale 664
Lindstrom 1,260
Lino Lakes 3,692
Lismore 323
Litchfield 5,262
Little Canada 3,481
Little Falls 7,467
Littlefork 824
Long Beach 219
Long Lake 1,506
Long Prairie 2,416
Longville 171
Lonsdale 622
Loretto 340
Louisburg 75
Lowry 257
Lucan 254
Luverne 4,703
Lyle 522
Lynd 267
Mabel 888
Madelia 2,316
Madison 2,242
Madison Lake 587
Magnolia 233
Mahnomen 1,313
Mahtomedi 2,640
Manchester 89
Manhattan Beach 46
Mankato 30,895
Mantorville 479
Maple Grove 6,275
Maple Lake 1,124
Maple Plain 1,169
Mapleton 1,307
Mapleview 328
Maplewood 25,222
Marble 682
Marietta 264
Marine-on-St. Croix 513
Marshall 9,886
Mayer 325
Maynard 455
Mazeppa 498
McGrath 70
McGregor 331
McIntosh 753
McKinley 317
Meadowlands 128
Medford 690
Medicine Lake 446
Medina 2,396
Meire Grove 171
Melrose 2,273
Menahga 835
Mendota 327
Mendota Heights 6,165
Mentor 236
Middle River 369
Miesville 192
Milaca 1,940
Milan 427
Millerville 109
Millville 139
Milroy 247
Miltona 172
Minneapolis 434,400
Minneiska 80
Minneota 1,320
Minnesota City 301
Minnesota Lake 738
Minnetonka 35,737
Minnetonka Beach 586
Minnetrista 2,878
Mizpah 118
Montevideo 5,661
Montgomery 2,281
Monticello 1,636
Montrose 379
Moorhead 29,687
Moose Lake 1,400
Mora 2,582
Morgan 972
Morris 5,366
Morristown 659
Morton 591
Motley 351
Mound 7,572
Mounds View 10,641
Mountain Iron 1,698
Mountain Lake 1,986
Murdock 358
Myrtle 83
Nashua 114
Nashwauk 1,341
Nassau 126
Nelson 175
Nerstrand 231
Nevis 308
New Auburn 274
New Brighton 19,507
New Germany 303
New Hope 23,180
New London 736
New Market 215
New Munich 307
New Prague 2,680
New Richland 1,113
New Trier 153
New Ulm 13,051
New York Mills 791
Newfolden 390
Newport 2,922
Nicollet 618
Nielsville 156
Nimrod 64
Nisswa 1,011
Norcross 137
North Branch 1,106
North Cross Lake 362
North Mankato 7,347
North Oaks 2,002
North Redwood 155
North St. Paul 11,950
Northfield 10,235
Northome 351
Northrop 188
Norwood 1,058
Oak Park Heights 1,238
Oakdale 7,304
Odessa 194
Odin 166
Ogema 236
Ogilvie 384
Okabena 237
Oklee 536
Olivia 2,553
Onamia 670
Ormsby 199
Orono 6,787
Oronoco 564
Orr 315
Ortonville 2,665
Osakis 1,306
Oslo 417
Osseo 2,908
Ostrander 216
Otter Tail 180
Owatonna 15,341
Palisade 149
Park Rapids 2,772
Parkers Prairie 882
Paynesville 1,920
Pease 187
Pelican Lakes 233
Pelican Rapids 1,835
Pemberton 128
Pennock 255
Pequot Lakes 499
Perham 1,933
Perley 149
Peterson 269
Pierz 893
Pillager 374
Pine City 2,143
Pine Island 1,640
Pine River 803
Pine Springs 204
Pipestone 5,328
Plainview 2,093
Plato 303
Pleasant Lake 65
Plummer 285
Plymouth 18,077
Porter 207
Preston 1,413
Princeton 2,531
Prinsburg 448
Prior Lake 1,114
Proctor 3,123
Quamba 114
Racine 197
Randall 536
Randolph 350
Ranier 255
Raymond 589
Red Lake Falls 1,740
Red Wing 10,441
Redwood Falls 4,774
Regal 44
Remer 403
Renville 1,252
Revere 166
Rice 366
Richfield 47,231
Richmond 866
Richville 102
Riverton 103
Robbinsdale 16,845
Rochester 53,766
Rockford 730
Rockville 302
Rogers 544
Rollingstone 450
Ronneby 59
Roosevelt 104
Roscoe 195
Rose Creek 390
Roseau 2,552
Rosemount 1,337
Roseville 34,518
Rothsay 448
Round Lake 506
Royalton 534
Rush City 1,130
Rushford (City) 1,318
Rushford (Village) 601
Rushmore 394
Russell 398
Ruthton 405
Rutledge 123
Sabin 333
Sacred Heart 707
St. Anthony (Stearns Co.) 66
St. Anthony (Hennepin and Ramsey counties) 9,239
St. Bonifacius 685
St. Charles 1,942
St. Clair 488
St. Cloud 39,691
St. Francis 897
St. Hilaire 337
St. James 4,027
St. Joseph 1,786
St. Leo 153
St. Louis Park 48,922
St. Martin 188
St. Marys Point 319
St. Michael 1,021
St. Paul 309,828
St. Paul Park 5,587
St. Peter 8,339
St. Rosa 93
St. Stephens 331
St. Vincent 177
Sanborn 505
Sandstone 1,641
Sargeant 85
Sartell 1,323
Sauk Centre 3,750
Sauk Rapids 5,051
Savage 3,611
Scanlon 1,132
Seaforth 132
Sebeka 668
Sedan 55
Shafer 149
Shakopee 6,876
Shelly 260
Sherburn 1,190
Shevlin 185
Shoreview 10,995
Shorewood 4,223
Silver Bay 3,504
Silver Lake 694
Skyline 400
Slayton 2,351
Sleepy Eye 3,461
Sobieski 189
Solway 96
South Haven 238
South International Falls 2,116
South St. Paul 25,016
Spicer 586
Spring Grove 1,290
Spring Hill 90
Spring Lake Park 6,417
Spring Park 1,087
Spring Valley 2,572
Springfield 2,530
Squaw Lake 113
Stacy 278
Staples 2,657
Starbuck 1,138
Steen 191
Stephen 904
Stewart 666
Stewartville 2,802
Stillwater 10,191
Stockton 346
Storden 364
Strandquist 138
Strathcona 31
Sturgeon Lake 167
Sunburg 144
Sunfish Lake 269
Swanville 300
Taconite 352
Tamarack 100
Taopi 59
Taunton 195
Taylors Falls 587
Tenney 24
Tenstrike 138
Thief River Falls 8,618
Thomson 159
Tintah 167
Tonka Bay 1,397
Tower 699
Tracy 2,516
Trail 99
Trimont 835
Trommald 82
Trosky 109
Truman 1,137
Turtle River 50
Twin Lakes 230
Twin Valley 868
Two Harbors 4,437
Tyler 1,069
Ulen 486
Underwood 278
Upsala 312
Urbank 125
Utica 240
Vadnais Heights 3,391
Vergas 281
Vermillion 359
Verndale 570
Vernon Center 347
Vesta 330
Victoria 850
Viking 118
Villard 221
Vining 121
Virginia 12,450
Wabasha 2,371
Wabasso 738
Waconia 2,445
Wadena 4,640
Wahkon 208
Waite Park 2,824
Waldorf 285
Walker 1,073
Walnut Grove 756
Walters 152
Waltham 189
Wanamingo 574
Wanda 124
Warba 148
Warren 1,999
Warroad 1,086
Waseca 6,789
Watertown 1,390
Waterville 1,539
Watkins 785
Watson 228
Waubun 345
Waverly 573
Wayzata 3,700
Welcome 694
Wells 2,791
Wendell 247
West Concord 718
West St. Paul 18,799
West Union 71
Westbrook 990
Westport 65
Whalan 114
Wheaton 2,029
White Bear Lake 23,313
Wilder 132
Willernie 697
Williams 220
Willmar 12,869
Willow River 331
Wilmont 390
Wilton 119
Windom 3,952
Winger 228
Winnebago 1,791
Winona 26,438
Winsted 1,266
Winthrop 1,391
Winton 193
Wolf Lake 58
Wolverton 171
Wood Lake 418
Woodbury 6,184
Woodland 544
Woodstock 217
Worthington 9,916
Wrenshall 147
Wright 132
Wykoff 450
Wyoming 695
Young America 611
Zemple 71
Zimmerman 495
Zumbro Falls 203
Zumbrota 1,929

MISSISSIPPI Total population: 2,216,912

METROPOLITAN AREAS

Biloxi-Gulfport 134,582
Jackson 258,906

COUNTIES

Adams 37,293
Alcorn 27,179
Amite 13,763
Attala 19,570
Benton 7,505
Bolivar 49,409
Calhoun 14,623
Carroll 9,397
Chickasaw 16,805
Choctaw 8,440
Claiborne 10,086
Clarke 15,049

Clay	18,840
Coahoma	40,447
Copiah	24,749
Covington	14,002
De Soto	35,885
Forrest	57,849
Franklin	8,011
George	12,459
Greene	8,545
Grenada	19,854
Hancock	17,387
Harrison	134,582
Hinds	214,973
Holmes	23,120
Humphreys	14,601
Issaquena	2,737
Itawamba	16,847
Jackson	87,975
Jasper	15,994
Jefferson	9,295
Jefferson Davis	12,936
Jones	56,357
Kemper	10,233
Lafayette	24,181
Lamar	15,209
Lauderdale	67,087
Lawrence	11,137
Leake	17,085
Lee	46,148
Leflore	42,111
Lincoln	26,198
Lowndes	49,700
Madison	29,737
Marion	22,871
Marshall	24,027
Monroe	34,043
Montgomery	12,918
Neshoba	20,802
Newton	18,983
Noxubee	14,288
Oktibbeha	28,752
Panola	26,829
Pearl River	27,802
Perry	9,065
Pike	31,756
Pontotoc	17,363
Prentiss	20,133
Quitman	15,888
Rankin	43,933
Scott	21,369
Sharkey	8,937
Simpson	19,947
Smith	13,561
Stone	8,101
Sunflower	37,047
Tallahatchie	19,338
Tate	18,544
Tippah	15,852
Tishomingo	14,940
Tunica	11,854
Union	19,096
Walthall	12,500
Warren	44,981
Washington	70,581
Wayne	16,650
Webster	10,047
Wilkinson	11,099
Winston	18,406
Yalobusha	11,915
Yazoo	27,304

PLACES

Aberdeen	6,157
Ackerman	1,502
Alligator	280
Amory	7,236
Anguilla	612
Arcola	517
Artesia	444
Ashland	348
Baldwyn	2,366
Bassfield	354
Batesville	3,796
Bay St. Louis	6,752
Bay Springs	1,801
Beaumont	1,061
Beauregard	199
Belmont	968
Belzoni	3,146
Benoit	473
Bentonia	544
Beulah	443
Big Creek	148
Biloxi	48,486
Blue Mountain	677
Blue Springs	125
Bolton	787
Booneville	5,895
Boyle	861
Brandon	2,685
Braxton	180
Brookhaven	10,700
Brooksville	978
Bruce	2,033
Bude	1,146
Burnsville	435
Byhalia	702
Caledonia	245
Calhoun City	1,847
Canton	10,503
Carrollton	295
Carthage	3,031
Cary	517
Centreville	1,819
Charleston	2,821
Chunky	280
Clarksdale	21,673
Cleveland	13,327
Clinton	7,246
Coffeeville	1,024
Coldwater	1,450
Collins	1,934
Columbia	7,587
Columbus	25,795
Columbus Base	4,074
Como	1,003
Corinth	11,581
Courtland	316
Crawford	391
Crenshaw	1,271
Crosby	491
Crowder	815
Cruger	415
Crystal Springs	4,180
Decatur	1,311
De Kalb	1,072
Derma	660
D'Iberville	7,288
D'Lo	485
Doddsville	276
Drew	2,574
Duck Hill	809
Duncan	599
Durant	2,752
Ecru	417
Eden	152
Edwards	1,236
Ellisville	4,643
Enid	80
Enterprise	458
Escatawpa	1,579
Ethel	560
Eupora	1,792
Fayette	1,725
Flora	987
Florence	404
Flowood	352
Forest	4,085
French Camp	174
Friars Point	1,177
Fulton	2,899
Gallman	75
Gattman	175
Gautier	2,087
Georgetown	339
Glendora	201
Gloster	1,401
Golden	115
Goodman	1,194
Greenville	39,648
Greenville North	2,154
Greenwood	22,400
Grenada	9,944
Gulfport	40,791
Gunnison	545
Guntown	304
Hattiesburg	38,277
Hattiesburg South	2,491
Hazlehurst	4,577
Heidelberg	1,112
Hernando	2,499
Hickory	570
Hickory Flat	354
Hollandale	3,260
Holly Springs	5,728
Houlka	646
Houston	2,720
Indianola	8,947
Inverness	1,119
Isola	458
Itta Bena	2,489
Iuka	2,389
Jackson	153,968
Jonestown	1,110
Kilmichael	543
Kosciusko	7,266
Kossuth	227
Lake	441
Lambert	1,511
Laurel	24,145
Leakesville	1,090
Learned	116
Leland	6,000
Lena	233
Lexington	2,756
Liberty	612
Long Beach	6,170
Louin	382
Louise	444
Louisville	6,626
Lucedale	2,083
Lula	445
Lumberton	2,084
Lyon	383
Maben	862
Macon	2,612
Madison	853
Magee	2,973
Magnolia	1,913
Mantee	142
Marks	2,609
Mathiston	570
McComb	11,969
McComb South	1,085
McCool	225
McLain	632
Meadville	594
Mendenhall	2,402
Meridian	45,083
Meridian Station	2,465
Merigold	772
Mize	372
Monticello	1,790
Montrose	160
Moorhead	2,284
Morgan City	207
Morgantown	2,008
Morton	2,672
Moss Point	19,321
Mound Bayou	2,134
Mount Olive	923
Myrtle	308
Natchez	19,704
Nettleton	1,591
New Albany	6,426
New Augusta	511
Newhebron	456
Newton	3,556
North Carrollton	611
Noxapater	554
Oakland	493
Oakvale	166
Ocean Springs	9,580
Okolona	3,002
Olive Branch	1,513
Osyka	628
Oxford	13,846
Pace	629
Pachuta	271
Paden	97
Pascagoula	27,264
Pass Christian	2,979
Pearl	9,623
Pelahatchie	1,306
Petal	6,986
Philadelphia	6,274
Picayune	10,467
Pickens	1,012
Pinola	102
Pittsboro	188
Plantersville	910
Pontotoc	3,453
Pope	210
Poplarville	2,312
Port Gibson	2,589
Potts Camp	459
Prairie	82
Prentiss	1,789
Puckett	333
Purvis	1,860
Quitman	2,702
Raleigh	1,018
Randolph	205
Raymond	1,620
Richton	1,110
Ridgeland	1,650
Rienzi	363
Ripley	3,482
Rolling Fork	2,034
Rome	171
Rosedale	2,599
Roxie	662
Ruleville	2,351
Sallis	213
Saltillo	836
Sandersville	694
Sardis	2,391
Satartia	85
Schlater	398
Scooba	626
Sebastopol	268
Seminary	269
Senatobia	4,247
Shannon	575
Shaw	2,513
Shelby	2,645
Sherman	468
Shubuta	602
Shuqualak	591
Sidon	348
Silver City	370
Silver Creek	257
Slate Springs	105
Sledge	516
Smithville	552
Southaven	8,931
Starkville	11,369
State College	4,595
State Line	598
Stonewall	1,161
Sturgis	321
Summit	1,640
Sumner	533
Sumrall	955
Sunflower	983
Sylvarena	115
Taylor	92
Taylorsville	1,299
Tchula	1,729
Terry	546
Tillatoba	102
Tishomingo	410
Toccopola	175
Tunica	1,685
Tunica North	1,325
Tupelo	20,471
Tutwiler	1,103
Tylertown	1,736
Union	1,856
Utica	1,019
Vaiden	716
Vardaman	777
Verona	1,877
Vicksburg	25,478
Walnut	458
Walnut Grove	398
Walthall	161
Water Valley	3,285
Waveland	3,108
Waynesboro	4,368
Weathersby	85
Webb	751
Weir	573
Wesson	1,253
West	305
West Gulfport	6,996
West Point	8,714
Wiggins	2,995
Winona	5,521
Winstonville	536
Woodland	130
Woodville	1,734
Yazoo City	10,796

MISSOURI Total population: 4,677,399

METROPOLITAN AREAS

Columbia	80,911
Kansas City (849,409 in Missouri, 406,918 in Kansas)	1,256,327
St. Joseph	86,915
St. Louis (1,827,681 in Missouri, 536,133 in Illinois)	2,363,814
Springfield	152,929

COUNTIES

Adair	22,472
Andrew	11,913
Atchison	9,240
Audrain	25,362
Barry	19,597
Barton	10,431
Bates	15,468
Benton	9,695
Bollinger	8,820
Boone	80,911
Buchanan	86,915
Butler	33,529
Caldwell	8,351
Callaway	25,991
Camden	13,315
Cape Girardeau	49,350
Carroll	12,565
Carter	3,878
Cass	39,448
Cedar	9,424
Chariton	11,084
Christian	15,124
Clark	8,260
Clay	123,702
Clinton	12,462
Cole	46,228
Cooper	14,732
Crawford	14,828
Dade	6,850
Dallas	10,054
Daviess	8,420
De Kalb	7,305
Dent	11,457
Douglas	9,268
Dunklin	33,742
Franklin	55,127
Gasconade	11,878
Gentry	8,060
Greene	152,929
Grundy	11,819
Harrison	10,257
Henry	18,451
Hickory	4,481
Holt	6,654
Howard	10,561
Howell	23,521
Iron	9,529
Jackson	654,178
Jasper	79,852
Jefferson	105,647
Johnson	34,172
Knox	5,692
Laclede	19,944
Lafayette	26,626
Lawrence	24,585
Lewis	10,993
Lincoln	18,041
Linn	15,125
Livingston	15,368
Macon	15,432
Madison	8,641
Maries	6,851
Marion	28,121
McDonald	12,357
Mercer	4,910
Miller	15,026
Mississippi	16,647
Moniteau	10,742
Monroe	9,542
Montgomery	11,000
Morgan	10,068
New Madrid	23,420
Newton	32,981
Nodaway	22,467
Oregon	9,180
Osage	10,994
Ozark	6,226
Pemiscot	26,373
Perry	14,393
Pettis	34,137
Phelps	29,567
Pike	16,928
Platte	32,081
Polk	15,415
Pulaski	53,967
Putnam	5,916
Ralls	7,764
Randolph	22,434
Ray	17,599
Reynolds	6,106
Ripley	9,803
St. Charles	92,986
St. Clair	7,667
St. Francois	36,875
St. Louis	951,685
St. Louis (Independent City)	622,236
Ste. Genevieve	12,867
Saline	24,837
Schuyler	4,665
Scotland	5,499
Scott	33,250
Shannon	7,196
Shelby	7,906
Stoddard	25,771
Stone	9,921
Sullivan	7,572
Taney	13,023
Texas	18,320
Vernon	19,065
Warren	9,699
Washington	15,086
Wayne	8,546
Webster	15,562
Worth	3,359
Wright	13,667

PLACES

Adrian	1,259
Advance	903
Affton	24,898
Agency	141
Airport Drive	300
Alba	365
Albany	1,804
Aldrich	66
Alexandria	453
Allendale	104
Alma	380
Altamont	225
Altenburg	277
Alton	715
Amazonia	326
Amity	86
Amoret	219
Amsterdam	120
Anderson	1,065
Annada	109
Annapolis	330
Anniston	515
Appleton	77
Appleton City	1,058
Arbela	70
Arbor Terrace	1,440
Arbyrd	575
Arcadia	627
Archie	525
Argyle	262
Arkoe	49
Armstrong	354
Arrow Rock	81
Asbury	201
Ash Grove	934
Ashburn	119
Ashland	769
Atlanta	377
Augusta	259
Aullville	108
Aurora	5,359
Auxvasse	808
Ava	2,504
Avilla	119
Avondale	512
Bagnell	60
Baker	72
Bakersfield	210
Ballwin	10,656
Baring	206
Barnard	206
Barnett	167
Bates City	229
Belgique	18
Bell City	424
Bella Villa	1,018
Belle	1,133
Bellefontaine Neighbors	14,084
Bellerive	437
Bellflower	360
Bel-Nor	2,085
Bel-Ridge	5,561
Belton	12,179
Benton	640
Benton City	121
Berdell Hills	449
Berger	226
Berkeley	19,743
Bernie	1,641
Bertrand	604
Bethany	2,914
Bethel	143
Beverly Hills	846
Bevier	806
Bigelow	84
Billings	760
Birch Tree	573
Birmingham	266
Bismarck	1,387
Blackburn	294
Blackwater	249
Blairstown	161
Bland	621
Blodgett	220
Bloomfield	1,584
Bloomsdale	411
Blue Eye	91
Blue Springs	6,779
Blue Summit	1,283
Blythedale	213
Bogard	294
Bolckow	225
Bolivar	4,769
Bonne Terre	3,622
Boonville	7,514
Bosworth	386
Bourbon	955
Bowers Mill	13
Bowling Green	2,936
Bradleyville	92
Bragg City	210
Brandsville	145
Branson	2,175
Brashear	316
Brasher	80
Braymer	919
Breckenridge	598
Breckenridge Hills	7,011
Brentwood	11,248
Bridgeton	19,992
Bridgeton Terrace	332
Brimson	103
Bronaugh	203
Brookfield	5,491
Brooklyn Heights	128
Browning	412
Brownington	95
Brumley	87
Brunswick	1,370
Bucklin	654
Buckner	1,695
Buell	69
Buffalo	1,915
Bunceton	437
Bunker	447
Burgess	69
Burlington Junction	634
Butler	3,984
Butterfield	125
Cabool	1,848
Cainsville	454
Cairo	248
Caledonia	113
Calhoun	360
California	3,105
Callao	373
Calverton Park	2,025
Camden	286
Camden Point	227
Camdenton	1,636
Cameron	3,960
Campbell	1,979
Canalou	358
Canton	2,680
Cape Girardeau	31,282
Cardwell	859
Carl Junction	1,661
Carrollton	4,847
Carterville	1,716
Carthage	11,035
Caruthersville	7,350
Cassville	1,910
Catron	122
Cedar City	454
Center	588
Centertown	277
Centerview	234
Centerville	209
Centralia	3,618
Chaffee	2,793
Chamois	615
Champ	19
Charlack	1,872
Charleston	5,131
Cherryville	47
Chilhowee	297
Chillicothe	9,519
Chula	244
Clarence	1,050
Clark	271
Clarksburg	343
Clarksdale	248
Clarkson Valley	157
Clarksville	668
Clarkton	1,177
Claycomo	1,841
Clayton	16,222
Clearmont	226
Cleveland	256
Clever	430
Cliff Village	39
Clifton Hill	174
Climax Springs	104
Clinton	7,504
Clyde	158
Cobalt City	238
Coffey	157
Cole Camp	1,038
Collins	150
Columbia	58,804
Commerce	234
Conception Junction	237
Concord	21,217
Concordia	1,854
Conway	547
Cool Valley	2,059
Cooter	414
Corder	476
Corning	134
Cosby	130
Country Club Hills	1,644
Country Club Village	943
Country Life Acres	60
Cowgill	232
Craig	369
Crane	1,003
Creighton	294
Crestwood	15,123
Creve Coeur	8,967
Crocker	814
Cross Timbers	204
Crosstown	66
Crowder	89
Crystal City	3,898
Crystal Lake Park	356
Cuba	2,070
Curryville	337
Dadeville	149
Dalton	135
Darlington	164
Dearborn	543
Deepwater	565
Deering	138
De Kalb	287
Dellwood	7,137
Delta	462
Dennis Acres	64
Denton	89
Denver	104
Des Arc	222
Desloge	2,818
De Soto	5,984
Des Peres	5,333
Dewitt	135
Dexter	6,024
Diamond	608
Diehlstadt	155
Diggins	140
Dillard	36
Dixon	1,387
Doniphan	1,850
Doolittle	509
Dover	133
Downing	406
Drexel	723
Dudley	248
Duenweg	656
Dunlap	47
Duquesne	738
Eagleville	388
East Lynne	255
East Prairie	3,275
Easton	183
Edgerton	477
Edina	1,574
Edmundson	2,298
Eldon	3,520
Eldorado Springs	3,300
Ellington	1,094
Ellisville	4,681
Ellsinore	342
Elmer	193
Elmira	124
Elmo	199
Elsberry	1,398
Elvins	1,660
Eminence	520
Emma	224
Eolia	321
Essex	493
Esther	1,040
Ethel	162
Eugene	163
Eureka	2,384
Everton	264

MISSOURI, Continued

Ewing 330
Excelsior Springs 9,411
Exeter 434
Fair Grove 431
Fair Play 328
Fairfax 835
Fairview 263
Fairview Acres 43
Farber 470
Farley 174
Farmington 6,590
Fayette 3,520
Fenton 2,275
Ferguson 28,759
Ferrelview 140
Festus 7,530
Fidelity 191
Fillmore 251
Fisk 503
Flat River 4,550
Fleming 152
Flemington 126
Flordell Hills 989
Florissant 65,908
Foley 224
Ford City 42
Fordland 399
Forest City 365
Forsyth 803
Fort Leonard Wood 33,799
Fortescue 63
Foster 178
Frankford 472
Franklin 252
Fredericktown 3,799
Freeburg 577
Freeman 417
Freistatt 115
Fremont 107
Frohna 225
Frontenac 3,920
Fulton 12,248
Gainesville 627
Galena 391
Gallatin 1,833
Galt 261
Garden City 633
Gasconade 235
Gentry 143
Gerald 762
Gerster 42
Gibbs 112
Gibson 75
Gideon 1,112
Gilliam 248
Gilman 376
Gladstone 23,422
Glasgow 1,336
Glen Echo Park 268
Glenaire 505
Glenallen 134
Glendale 6,891
Glenwood 184
Gobler 73
Golden City 810
Goodfellow Terrace 744
Goodman 565
Gordonville 125
Gower 758
Graham 213
Grain Valley 709
Granby 1,678
Grand Pass 72
Grandin 243
Grandview 17,456
Granger 105
Grant City 1,095
Grantwood 994
Gravois Mills 34
Grayson 62
Green City 632
Green Ridge 403
Greencastle 235
Greendale 972
Greenfield 1,172
Greentop 351
Greenville 328
Greenwood 925
Guilford 105
Gunn City 71
Hale 461
Hallsville 790
Halltown 106
Hamilton 1,645
Hanley Hills 2,726
Hannibal 18,698
Hardin 683
Harris 174
Harrisburg 150
Harrisonville 5,052
Hartsburg 120
Hartville 524
Harviell 160
Harwood 91
Hawk Point 354
Hayti 3,841
Haywood City 420
Hazelwood 14,082
Henley 64
Henrietta 466
Herculaneum 1,885
Hermann 2,658
Hermitage 284
Higbee 641
Higginsville 4,318
High Hill 192
Highley Heights 119
Hillhouse Addition 110
Hillsboro 831
Hillsdale 2,599
Hoberg 64
Holcomb 593
Holden 2,089
Holland 329
Holliday 167
Hollister 906
Hollywood 86
Holt 319
Homestown 273
Hopkins 656
Hornersville 693
Houston 2,178
Houston Lake 338
Houstonia 312
Howardville 500
Hughesville 92
Humansville 825
Hume 350
Humphreys 140
Hunnewell 304
Hunter 129
Huntleigh 714
Huntsville 1,442
Hurdland 225
Hurley 148
Hurricane Deck 169
Iberia 741
Illmo 1,232
Independence 111,630
Ionia 151
Iron Gates 367
Irondale 319
Ironton 1,452
Jackson 5,896
Jacksonville 142
Jameson 172
Jamesport 614
Jamestown 243
Jasper 796
Jefferson City 32,407
Jennings 19,379
Jerico Springs 188
Jonesburg 479
Joplin 39,256
Junction City 166
Kahoka 2,207
Kansas City 507,330
Kearney 984
Kelso 401
Kennett 10,090
Keytesville 730
Kidder 231
Kimmswick 268
King City 1,023
Kingdom City 53
Kingston 291
Kingsville 284
Kinloch 5,629
Kirksville 15,560
Kirkwood 31,769
Knob Noster 2,264
Knox City 284
Koshkonong 216
La Belle 848
Laclede 430
Laddonia 745
La Due 10,594
La Grange 1,237
Lake Lotawana 1,786
Lake Ozark 507
Lake Tapawingo 867
Lake Waukomis 1,105
Lake Winnebago 432
Lakeshire 1,186
Lakeside 124
Lamar 3,760
Lamar Heights 96
Lambert 39
La Monte 814
Lanagan 374
Lancaster 821
La Plata 1,377
Laredo 383
Larussell 97
Latham 89
Lathrop 1,268
La Tour 83
Laurie 106
Lawson 1,034
Leadington 299
Leadwood 1,397
Leasburg 218
Leawood 174
Lebanon 8,616
Lee's Summit 16,230
Leeton 425
Lemay 40,516
Leonard 107
Leslie 81
Levasy 283
Lewistown 615
Lexington 5,388
Liberal 644
Liberty 13,704
Licking 1,002
Lilbourn 1,152
Lincoln 574
Linn 1,289
Linn Creek 268
Linneus 400
Lithium 56
Livonia 119
Lock Springs 85
Lockwood 887
Lohman 109
Lone Jack 199
Longtown 113
Louisburg 152
Louisiana 4,533
Lowry City 520
Lucerne 126
Ludlow 175
Lupus 68
Luray 149
Lutesville 626
Mackenzie 224
Macks Creek 106
Macon 5,301
Madison 540
Maitland 319
Malden 5,374
Malta Bend 342
Manchester 5,031
Mansfield 1,056
Maplewood 12,785
Marble Hill 589
Marceline 2,622
Margona Village 321
Marionville 1,496
Marlborough 1,459
Marquand 400
Marshall 12,051
Marshfield 2,961
Marston 666
Marthasville 415
Martinsburg 318
Mary Ridge 602
Maryland Heights 8,805
Maryville 9,970
Matthews 538
Maysville 1,045
Mayview 330
McFall 203
McKittrick 101
Meadville 409
Memphis 2,081
Mendon 289
Menfro 37
Mercer 364
Merwin 64
Meta 387
Metz 120
Mexico 11,807
Miami 205
Middle Grove 55
Middletown 235
Midway 234
Milan 1,794
Mill Spring 207
Miller 676
Milo 80
Mindenmines 279
Miner 640
Mineral Point 369
Missouri City 375
Moberly 12,988
Modena 61
Mokane 398
Moline Acres 3,722
Monett 5,937
Monroe City 2,456
Montevallo 54
Montgomery City 2,187
Monticello 157
Montrose 531
Mooresville 131
Morehouse 1,332
Morley 528
Morrison 234
Morrisville 256
Mosby 337
Moscow Mills 399
Mound City 1,202
Moundville 149
Mount Leonard 139
Mount Moriah 165
Mount Vernon 2,600
Mountain Grove 3,377
Mountain View 1,320
Napoleon 263
Naylor 586
Neck City 114
Neelyville 231
Nelson 230
Neosho 7,517
Nevada 9,736
New Bloomfield 427
New Cambria 260
New Florence 635
New Franklin 1,122
New Hamburg 185
New Hampton 327
New Haven 1,474
New London 967
New Madrid 2,719
Newark 114
Newburg 806
Newtonia 208
Newtown 211
Niangua 309
Nixa 1,636
Noel 924
Norborne 950
Normandy 6,183
North Kansas City 5,183
North Lilbourn 334
Northmoor 562
Northwoods 4,611
Northwye 138
Norwood 294
Norwood Court 122
Novelty 156
Novinger 547
Oak Grove (Jackson Co.) 2,025
Oak Grove (Franklin Co.) 340
Oak Ridge 181
Oakland 1,609
Oakland Park 156
Oaks 162
Oakview 541
Oakwood 163
Oakwood Manor 170
Oakwood Park 295
Odessa 2,839
O'Fallon 7,018
Old Monroe 330
Olean 151
Olivette 9,238
Olympia Village 399
Oran 1,226
Oregon 789
Oronogo 492
Orrick 883
Osage Beach 1,091
Osborn 338
Osceola 874
Osgood 108
Otterville 440
Overland 24,949
Owensville 2,416
Ozark 2,384
Pacific 3,247
Pagedale 5,083
Palmyra 3,188
Paris 1,442
Parkdale 836
Parkville 1,253
Parkway 233
Parma 1,051
Parnell 232
Pasadena Hills 1,337
Pasadena Park 760
Pascola 180
Passaic 56
Pattonsburg 540
Peach Orchard 64
Peculiar 705
Peerless Park 51
Perkins 130
Perry 839
Perryville 5,149
Pevely 517
Phelps City 76
Phillipsburg 173
Pickering 245
Piedmont 1,906
Pierce City 1,097
Pilot Grove 701
Pilot Knob 582
Pine Lawn 5,773
Pineville 444
Piney Park 106
Platte City 2,022
Platte Woods 484
Plattsburg 1,832
Pleasant Hill 3,396
Pleasant Hope 265
Pleasant Valley 1,535
Pocahontas 127
Polo 438
Poplar Bluff 16,653
Portage Des Sioux 509
Portageville 3,117
Potosi 2,761
Powersville 125
Prairie Hill 69
Prairie Home 231
Prathersville 153
Preston 132
Princeton 1,328
Protem 22
Purcell 325
Purdin 236
Purdy 588
Puxico 759
Queen City 588
Quitman 95
Qulin 496
Randolph 106
Ravenwood 336
Raymondville 284
Raymore 587
Raytown 33,306
Rayville 202
Rea 54
Redings Mill 179
Reeds 122
Reeds Spring 286
Reger 75
Renick 188
Rensselaer 58
Republic 2,411
Revere 184
Rhineland 190
Rich Hill 1,661
Richards 105
Richland 1,783
Richmond 4,948
Richmond Heights 13,802
Ridgeway 469
Risco 412
Ritchey 101
Rivermines 402
Riverside 2,123
Riverview 3,741
Rives 120
Roanoke 34
Rocheport 307
Rock Hill 6,815
Rockaway Beach 195
Rockport 1,575
Rockville 203
Rocky Comfort 141
Rogersville 574
Rolla 13,245
Roscoe 137
Rosebud 305
Rosendale 245
Rothville 131
Rush Hill 151
Rushville 300
Russellville 557
Rutledge 139
Saginaw 224
St. Ann 18,215
St. Charles 31,834
St. Clair 2,978
St. Elizabeth 287
St. George 2,033
St. James 2,929
St. John 8,960
St. Joseph 72,691
St. Jude Acres 246
St. Louis 622,236
St. Marys 645
St. Peters 486
St. Robert 1,465
Ste. Genevieve 4,468
Salem 4,363
Salisbury 1,960
Sandy Hook 29
Sappington 10,603
Sarcoxie 1,175
Savannah 3,324
Schell City 367
Schuermann Heights 290
Scott City 2,464
Sedalia 22,847
Sedgewickville 92
Seligman 424
Senath 1,484
Seneca 1,577
Seymour 1,208
Shawneetown 40
Shelbina 2,060
Shelbyville 601
Sheldon 498
Sheridan 251
Shoal Creek Drive 329
Shrewsbury 5,896
Sibley 279
Sikeston 14,699
Silex 306
Silver Creek 410
Skidmore 440
Slater 2,576
Smithton 402
Smithville 1,785
South Gifford 64
South Gorin 220
South Greenfield 144
South Lineville 52
South West City 453
Spanish Lake 15,647
Sparta 380
Spickardsville 408
Spring Valley 60
Springfield 120,096
Stanberry 1,479
Stark City 122
Steele 2,107
Steelville 1,392
Stella 197
Stewartsville 634
Stockton 1,063
Stotesbury 35
Stotts City 203
Stoutland 205
Stoutsville 61
Stover 849
Strafford 491
Strasburg 181
Sturgeon 787
Sugar Creek 4,755
Sullivan 5,111
Summersville 435
Sumner 178
Sunnyvale 311
Sunrise Beach 126
Sunset Hills 4,126
Sweet Springs 1,716
Sycamore Hills 821
Syracuse 199
Taneyville 157
Tarkio 2,517
Tarrants 45
Tarsney Lakes 401
Thayer 1,609
Theodosia 132
Times Beach 1,265
Tina 167
Tindall 92
Tipton 1,914
Town and Country 2,645
Tracy 252
Trenton 6,063
Trimble 206
Triplett 191
Troy 2,538
Truesdale 262
Turney 142
Tuscumbia 256
Twin Oaks 41
Union 5,183
Union Star 417
Unionville 2,075
Unity 242
University City 46,309
Uplands Park 695
Urbana 369
Urich 433
Valley Park 3,662
Van Buren 714
Vandalia 3,160
Vandiver 102
Vanduser 306
Velda Village 2,112
Velda Village Hills 1,179
Verona 515
Versailles 2,244
Vibbard 89
Viburnum 520
Vienna 505
Vinita Park 3,657
Vinita Terrace 279
Vista 44
Waco 108
Wakenda 116
Walker 227
Walnut Grove 442
Wardell 275
Wardsville 460
Warrensburg 13,125
Warrenton 2,057
Warsaw 1,423
Warson Woods 2,544
Washburn 257
Washington 8,499
Watson 164
Waverly 827
Wayland 467
Waynesville 3,375
Weatherby 91
Weatherby Lake 832
Weaubleau 343
Webb City 6,923
Webster Groves 27,455
Wellington 720
Wellston 7,050
Wellsville 1,565
Wentworth 132
Wentzville 3,223
West Line 114
West Plains 6,893
Westboro 234
Weston 1,267
Westphalia 332
Westwood 311
Wheatland 317
Wheaton 360
Wheeling 268
White Oak 54
Whiteman 5,040
Whiteside 125
Whitewater 135
Wilbur Park 692
Willard 1,018
Williamsville 398
Willow Springs 2,045
Wilson City 295
Winchester 2,329
Windsor 2,734
Winfield 620
Winona 973
Winston 189
Woods Heights 362
Woodson Terrace 5,880
Wooldridge 97
Worth 113
Wright City 943
Wyaconda 356
Wyatt 562
Zalma 118

MONTANA Total population: 694,409

METROPOLITAN AREAS

Billings 87,367
Great Falls 81,804

COUNTIES

Beaverhead 8,187
Big Horn 10,057
Blaine 6,727
Broadwater 2,526
Carbon 7,080
Carter 1,956
Cascade 81,804
Chouteau 6,473
Custer 12,174
Daniels 3,083
Dawson 11,269
Deer Lodge 15,652
Fallon 4,050
Fergus 12,611
Flathead 39,460
Gallatin 32,505
Garfield 1,796
Glacier 10,783
Golden Valley 931
Granite 2,737
Hill 17,358
Jefferson 5,238
Judith Basin 2,667
Lake 14,445
Lewis and Clark 33,281
Liberty 2,359
Lincoln 18,063
Madison 5,014
McCone 2,875
Meagher 2,122
Mineral 2,958
Missoula 58,263
Musselshell 3,734
Park 11,197
Petroleum 675
Phillips 5,386
Pondera 6,611
Powder River 2,862
Powell 6,660
Prairie 1,752
Ravalli 14,409
Richland 9,837
Roosevelt 10,365
Rosebud 6,032
Sanders 7,093
Sheridan 5,779
Silver Bow 41,981
Stillwater 4,632
Sweet Grass 2,980
Teton 6,116
Toole 5,839
Treasure 1,069
Valley 11,471
Wheatland 2,529
Wibaux 1,465
Yellowstone 87,367
Yellowstone National Park 64

PLACES

Alberton 363
Anaconda 9,771
Bainville 217
Baker 2,584
Bearcreek 31
Belgrade 1,307
Belt 656
Big Sandy 827
Big Timber 1,592
Billings 61,581
Boulder 1,342
Bozeman 18,670
Bridger 717
Broadus 799
Broadview 123
Brockton 401
Browning 1,700
Butte 23,368
Cascade 714
Centerville-Dublin Gulch 2,284
Chester 936
Chinook 1,813
Choteau 1,586
Circle 964
Clyde Park 244
Columbia Falls 2,652
Columbus 1,173
Conrad 2,770
Culbertson 821
Cut Bank 4,004

Darby 538
Deer Lodge 4,306
Denton 398
Dillon 4,548
Dodson 196
Drummond 494
Dublin Gulch, see Centerville-Dublin Gulch
Dutton 415
East Butte, see McQueen-East Butte
East Helena 1,651
Ekalaka 663
Ennis 501
Eureka 1,195
Fairfield 638
Fairview 956
Flaxville 185
Floral Park 5,113
Forsyth 1,873
Fort Benton 1,863
Froid 330
Fromberg 364
Geraldine 370
Glasgow 4,700
Glendive 6,305
Glass Range 181
Great Falls 60,091
Hamilton 2,499
Hardin 2,733
Harlem 1,094
Harlowton 1,375
Havre 10,558
Havre North 1,073
Helena 22,730
Hingham 262
Hobson 192
Hot Springs 664
Hysham 373
Ismay 40
Joliet 412
Jordan 529
Judith Gap 160
Kalispell 10,526
Kevin 250
Laurel 4,454
Lavina 169
Lewistown 6,437
Libby 3,286
Lima 351
Livingston 6,883
Lodge Grass 806
Malmstrom 8,374
Malta 2,195
Manhattan 816
McQueen-East Butte 1,084
Medicine Lake 393
Melstone 227
Miles City 9,023
Missoula 29,497
Missoula South 4,886
Missoula West 9,148
Moore 219
Nashua 513
Neihart 109
Opheim 306
Outlook 153
Philipsburg 1,128
Plains 1,046
Plentywood 2,381
Plevna 189
Polson 2,464
Poplar 1,389
Rattlesnake 1,492
Red Lodge 1,844
Rexford 243
Richey 389
Ronan 1,347
Roundup 2,116
Ryegate 261
Saco 356
St. Ignatius 925
Scobey 1,486
Shelby 3,111
Sheridan 636
Sidney 4,543
Silver Bow Park 5,524
Stanford 505
Stevensville 829
Sunburst 604
Superior 993
Terry 870
Thompson Falls 1,356
Three Forks 1,188
Townsend 1,371
Troy 1,046
Twin Bridges 613
Valier 651
Virginia City 149
Walkerville 1,097
West Yellowstone 756
Westby 287
White Sulphur Springs 1,200
Whitefish 3,349
Whitehall 1,035
Wibaux 644
Winifred 190
Winnett 271
Wolf Point 3,095

NEBRASKA Total population: 1,483,791

METROPOLITAN AREAS

Lincoln 167,972
Omaha 541,453
(454,462 in Nebraska, 86,991 in Iowa)

COUNTIES

Adams 30,553
Antelope 9,047
Arthur 606
Banner 1,034
Blaine 847
Boone 8,190
Box Butte 10,094
Boyd 3,752
Brown 4,021
Buffalo 31,222
Burt 9,247
Butler 9,461
Cass 18,076
Cedar 12,192
Chase 4,129
Cherry 6,846
Cheyenne 10,778
Clay 8,266
Colfax 9,498
Cuming 12,034
Custer 14,092
Dakota 13,137
Dawes 9,693
Dawson 19,467
Deuel 2,717
Dixon 7,453
Dodge 34,782
Douglas 389,455
Dundy 2,926
Fillmore 8,137
Franklin 4,566
Frontier 3,982
Furnas 6,897
Gage 25,719
Garden 2,929
Garfield 2,411
Gosper 2,178
Grant 1,019
Greeley 4,000
Hall 42,851
Hamilton 8,867
Harlan 4,357
Hayes 1,530
Hitchcock 4,051
Holt 12,933
Hooker 939
Howard 6,807
Jefferson 10,436
Johnson 5,743
Kearney 6,707
Keith 8,487
Keya Paha 1,340
Kimball 6,009
Knox 11,723
Lancaster 167,972
Lincoln 29,538
Logan 991
Loup 854
Madison 27,402
McPherson 623
Merrick 8,751
Morrill 5,813
Nance 5,142
Nemaha 8,976
Nuckolls 7,404
Otoe 15,576
Pawnee 4,473
Perkins 3,423
Phelps 9,553
Pierce 8,493
Platte 26,508
Polk 6,468
Red Willow 12,191
Richardson 12,277
Rock 2,231
Saline 12,809
Sarpy 63,696
Saunders 17,018
Scotts Bluff 36,432
Seward 14,460
Sheridan 7,285
Sherman 4,725
Sioux 2,034
Stanton 5,758
Thayer 7,779
Thomas 954
Thurston 6,942
Valley 5,783
Washington 13,310
Wayne 10,400
Webster 6,477
Wheeler 1,054
York 13,685

PLACES

Abie 78
Adams 463
Ainsworth 2,073
Albion 2,074
Alda 456
Alexandria 225
Allen 309
Alliance 6,862
Alma 1,299
Alvo 151
Amherst 259
Angus 17
Anoka 25
Anselmo 180
Ansley 631
Arapahoe 1,147
Arcadia 418
Arlington 910
Arnold 752
Arthur 175
Ashland 2,176
Ashton 277
Atkinson 1,406
Atlanta 101
Auburn 3,650
Aurora 3,180
Avoca 229
Axtell 500
Ayr 140
Bancroft 545
Barada 58
Barneston 149
Bartlett 193
Bartley 283
Bassett 983
Battle Creek 1,158
Bayard 1,338
Bazile Mills 44
Beatrice 12,389
Beaver City 802
Beaver Crossing 400
Bee 156
Beemer 699
Belden 162
Belgrade 210
Bellevue 19,449
Bellwood 361
Belvidere 162
Benedict 209
Benkelman 1,349
Bennet 489
Bennington 683
Bertrand 662
Berwyn 110
Big Springs 472
Bladen 293
Blair 6,106
Bloomfield 1,287
Bloomington 165
Blue Hill 1,201
Blue Springs 494
Boys Town 989
Bradshaw 347
Brady 311
Brainard 309
Brewster 54
Bridgeport 1,490
Bristow 127
Broadwater 141
Brock 192
Broken Bow 3,734
Brownville 174
Brule 423
Bruning 315
Bruno 142
Brunswick 229
Burchard 131
Burr 108
Burton 23
Burwell 1,341
Bushnell 211
Butte 575
Byron 171
Cairo 686
Callaway 523
Cambridge 1,145
Campbell 447
Carleton 163
Carroll 235
Cedar Bluffs 616
Cedar Rapids 449
Center 111
Central City 2,803
Ceresco 474
Chadron 5,853
Chambers 321
Chapman 371
Chappell 1,204
Chester 459
Clarks 480
Clarkson 805
Clatonia 224
Clay Center 952
Clearwater 398
Clinton 55
Cody 246
Coleridge 608
Colon 109
Columbus 15,471
Comstock 144
Concord 180
Cook 328
Cordova 141
Cornlea 54
Cortland 326
Cotesfield 76
Cowles 57
Cozad 4,219
Crab Orchard 96
Craig 295
Crawford 1,291
Creighton 1,461
Creston 171
Crete 4,444
Crofton 677
Crookston 86
Culbertson 801
Curtis 1,166
Cushing 43
Dakota City 1,057
Dalton 354
Danbury 174
Dannebrog 384
Darr 15
Davenport 427
Davey 163
David City 2,380
Dawson 251
Daykin 192
Decatur 679
Denton 151
Deshler 937
Deweese 86
De Witt 651
Dickens 22
Diller 287
Dix 342
Dixon 128
Dodge 704
Doniphan 542
Dorchester 492
Douglas 175
Dubois 185
Dunbar 252
Duncan 298
Dunning 162
Dwight 224
Eagle 441
Eddyville 128
Edgar 707
Edison 199
Elba 211
Elgin 917
Elk Creek 151
Elkhorn 1,184
Elm Creek 798
Elmwood 548
Elsie 125
Elwood 601
Elyria 55
Emerson 850
Emmet 70
Endicott 167
Ericson 102
Eustis 400
Ewing 552
Exeter 759
Fairbury 5,265
Fairfield 487
Fairmont 761
Falls City 5,444
Farnam 259
Farwell 172
Filley 138
Firth 328
Fordyce 146
Fort Calhoun 642
Foster 79
Franklin 1,193
Fremont 22,962
Friend 1,126
Fullerton 1,444
Funk 143
Gandy 50
Garland 244
Garrison 60
Geneva 2,275
Genoa 1,174
Gering 5,639
Gibbon 1,388
Gilead 60
Giltner 408
Glenville 332
Goehner 113
Gordon 2,106
Gothenburg 3,154
Grafton 128
Grainton 20
Grand Island 31,269
Grant 1,099
Greeley Center 580
Greenwood 506
Gresham 248
Gretna 1,557
Gross 8
Guide Rock 318
Gurley 233
Hadar 172
Haigler 237
Hallam 280
Halsey 131
Hamlet 64
Hampton 387
Harbine 44
Hardy 250
Harrison 377
Hartington 1,581
Harvard 1,230
Hastings 23,580
Hay Springs 682
Hayes Center 237
Hazard 72
Heartwell 104
Hebron 1,667
Hemingford 734
Henderson 901
Hendley 58
Henry 147
Herman 323
Hershey 526
Hickman 415
Hildreth 352
Holbrook 307
Holdrege 5,635
Holstein 231
Homer 457
Hooper 895
Hordville 147
Hoskins 271
Howard City 182
Howells 682
Hubbard 151
Hubbell 83
Humboldt 1,194
Humphrey 862
Huntley 67
Hyannis 345
Imperial 1,589
Indianola 672
Inglewood 275
Inman 160
Ithaca 121
Jackson 232
Jansen 191
Johnson 350
Johnstown 82
Julian 80
Juniata 480
Kearney 19,181
Kenesaw 728
Kennard 336
Kilgore 110
Kimball 3,680
Lamar 30
Laurel 1,009
La Vista 4,807
Lawrence 343
Lebanon 118
Leigh 501
Leshara 102
Lewellen 376
Lewiston 88
Lexington 5,618
Liberty 118
Lincoln 149,518
Lindsay 291
Linwood 108
Litchfield 248
Lodgepole 407
Long Pine 363
Loomis 323
Lorton Village 47
Louisville 1,036
Loup City 1,456
Lushton 34
Lyman 561
Lynch 375
Lyons 1,177
Madison 1,595
Madrid 234
Magnet 88
Malcolm 132
Malmo 131
Manley 150
Marquette 239
Marsland 17
Martinsburg 73
Maskell 43
Mason City 196
Maxwell 282
Maywood 309
McCook 8,285
McCool Junction 289
McGrew 79
McLean 67
Mead 488
Meadow Grove 372
Melbeta 124
Memphis 71
Merna 322
Merriman 172
Milford 1,846
Millard 7,460
Miller 130
Milligan 319
Minatare 939
Minden 2,669
Mitchell 1,842
Monowi 16
Monroe 259
Moorefield 56
Morrill 937
Morse Bluff 162
Mullen 667
Murdock 262
Murray 286
Naper 159
Naponee 187
Nebraska City 7,441
Nehawka 298
Neligh 1,764
Nelson 746
Nemaha 207
Nenzel 27
Newcastle 347
Newman Grove 863
Newport 141
Nickerson 214
Niobrara 602
Nora 43
Norfolk 16,607
Norman 52
North Bend 1,350
North Loup 441
North Platte 19,447
Oak 100
Oakdale 322
Oakland 1,355
Obert 36
Oconto 155
Octavia 97
Odell 349
Offutt East 5,195
Offutt West 8,445
Ogallala 4,976
Ohiowa 156
Omaha 347,328
O'Neill 3,753
Ong 129
Orchard 467
Ord 2,439
Orleans 592
Osceola 923
Oshkosh 1,067
Osmond 883
Otoe 204
Overton 506
Oxford 1,116
Page 177
Palisade 372
Palmer 391
Palmyra 386
Panama 153
Papillion 5,606
Parkview 1,089
Pawnee City 1,267
Paxton 503
Pender 1,229
Peru 1,380
Petersburg 370
Phillips 341
Pickrell 118
Pierce 1,360
Pilger 470
Plainview 1,494
Platte Center 384
Plattsmouth 6,371
Pleasant Dale 258
Pleasanton 261
Plymouth 424
Polk 413
Ponca 984
Poole 19
Potter 356
Prague 291
Preston 64
Primrose 88
Prosser 70
Ragan 60
Ralston 4,265
Randolph 1,130
Ravenna 1,356
Raymond 187
Red Cloud 2,195
Republican City 179
Reynolds 115
Richland 123
Rising City 344
Riverdale 155
Riverton 220
Roca 118
Rockville 114
Rogers 95
Rosalie 204
Roseland 212
Royal 86
Rulo 299
Rushville 1,137
Ruskin 229
St. Edward 853
St. Helena 102
St. Paul 2,026
Salem 214
Sargent 789
Saronville 74
Schuyler 3,597
Scotia 354
Scottsbluff 14,507
Scribner 1,031
Seneca 111
Seward 5,294
Shelby 647
Shelton 1,028
Shickley 385
Sholes 22
Shubert 240
Sidney 6,403
Silver Creek 483
Smithfield 58
Snyder 383
South Bend 86
South Sioux City 7,920
Spalding 676
Spencer 606
Sprague 119
Springfield 795
Springview 260
Stamford 207
Stanton 1,363
Staplehurst 227
Stapleton 311
Steele City 176
Steinauer 118
Stella 282
Sterling 476
Stockham 65
Stockville 61
Strang 47
Stratton 481
Stromsburg 1,215
Stuart 561
Sumner 184
Superior 2,779
Surprise 77
Sutherland 840
Sutton 1,361
Swanton 160
Syracuse 1,562
Table Rock 429
Talmage 285
Tamora 93
Tarnov 63
Taylor 240
Tecumseh 2,058
Tekamah 1,848
Terrytown 747
Thayer 78
Thedford 303
Thurston 117
Tilden 947
Tobias 124
Trenton 770
Trumbull 220
Uehling 249
Ulysses 312
Unadilla 271
Union 275
Upland 205
Utica 602
Valentine 2,662
Valley 1,595
Valparaiso 415
Venango 218
Verdel 74
Verdigre 570
Verdon 265
Virginia 83
Waco 214
Wahoo 3,835
Wakefield 1,160
Wallace 241
Walthill 897
Washington 76
Waterbury 81
Waterloo 455
Wauneta 738
Wausa 720
Waverly 1,152
Wayne 5,379
Weeping Water 1,143
Wellfleet 51
West Point 3,385
Western 344
Weston 285
Whitney 82
Wilber 1,483
Wilcox 280
Wilsonville 266
Winnebago 675
Winnetoon 84
Winside 453
Winslow 145
Wisner 1,315
Wolbach 366
Wood Lake 117
Wood River 1,061
Wymore 1,790
Wynot 226
York 6,778
Yutan 507

NEVADA Total population: 488,738

METROPOLITAN AREAS

Las Vegas....................273,288
Reno.........................121,068

COUNTIES

Carson City (Independent City)....................15,468
Churchill....................10,513
Clark........................273,288
Douglas......................6,882
Elko.........................13,958
Esmeralda....................629
Eureka.......................948
Humboldt.....................6,375
Lander.......................2,666
Lincoln......................2,557
Lyon.........................8,221
Mineral......................7,051
Nye..........................5,599
Pershing.....................2,670
Storey.......................695
Washoe.......................121,068
White Pine...................10,150

PLACES

Babbitt......................1,579
Battle Mountain..............1,856
Boulder City.................5,223
Caliente.....................916
Carlin.......................1,313
Carson City..................15,468
East Ely.....................1,992
East Las Vegas...............6,501
Elko.........................7,621
Ely..........................4,176
Fallon.......................2,959
Fallon Station...............1,045
Gabbs........................874
Gardnerville-Minden..........1,320
Hawthorne....................3,539
Henderson....................16,395
Las Vegas....................125,787
Lovelock.....................1,571
McGill.......................2,164
Minden, see Gardnerville-Minden
Nellis.......................6,449
North Las Vegas..............36,216
Paradise.....................24,477
Reno.........................72,863
Sparks.......................24,187
Sunrise Manor................10,886
Sun Valley...................2,414
Tonopah......................1,716
Vegas Creek..................8,970
Wells........................1,081
Winchester...................13,981
Winnemucca...................3,587
Yerington....................2,010

NEW HAMPSHIRE Total population: 737,681

METROPOLITAN AREAS

Manchester...................108,461
Nashua.......................66,458

COUNTIES

Belknap......................32,367
Carroll......................18,548
Cheshire.....................52,364
Coos.........................34,291
Grafton......................54,914
Hillsborough.................223,941
Merrimack....................80,925
Rockingham...................138,951
Strafford....................70,431
Sullivan.....................30,949

TOWNS AND PLACES

Acworth......................459▲
Albany.......................259▲
Alexandria...................466▲
Allenstown...................2,732▲
Alstead......................1,185▲
Alton........................1,647▲
Amherst......................4,605▲
Andover......................1,138▲
Antrim.......................2,122▲
Ashland......................1,391
Ashland......................1,599▲
Atkinson.....................2,291▲
Auburn.......................2,035▲
Barnstead....................1,119▲
Barrington...................1,865▲
Bartlett.....................1,098▲
Bath.........................607▲
Bedford......................5,859▲
Belmont......................2,493▲
Bennington...................639▲
Benton.......................194▲
Berlin.......................15,256
Bethlehem....................1,142▲
Boscawen.....................3,162▲
Bow..........................2,479▲
Bradford.....................679▲
Brentwood....................1,468▲
Bridgewater..................398▲
Bristol......................1,080
Bristol......................1,670▲
Brookfield...................198▲
Brookline....................1,167▲
Campton......................1,171▲
Canaan.......................1,923▲
Candia.......................1,997▲
Canterbury...................895▲
Carroll......................310▲
Center Harbor................540▲
Charlestown..................1,285
Charlestown..................3,274▲
Chatham......................134▲
Chester......................1,382▲
Chesterfield.................1,817▲
Chichester...................1,083▲
Claremont....................14,221
Clarksville..................166▲
Colebrook....................1,070
Colebrook....................2,094▲
Columbia.....................467▲
Concord......................30,022
Conway.......................1,489
Conway.......................4,865▲
Cornish......................1,268▲
Croydon......................396▲
Dalton.......................425▲
Danbury......................489▲
Danville.....................924▲
Deerfield....................1,178▲
Deering......................578▲
Derry........................6,090
Derry........................11,712▲
Dorchester...................141▲
Dover........................20,850
Dublin.......................837▲
Dummer.......................225▲
Dunbarton....................825▲
Durham.......................7,221
Durham.......................8,869▲
East Kingston................838▲
Easton.......................92▲
Eaton........................221▲
Effingham....................360▲
Ellsworth....................13▲
Enfield......................1,408
Enfield......................2,345▲
Epping.......................1,097
Epping.......................2,356▲
Epsom........................1,469▲
Errol........................199▲
Exeter.......................6,439
Exeter.......................8,892▲
Farmington...................2,884
Farmington...................3,588▲
Fitzwilliam..................1,362▲
Francestown..................525▲
Franconia....................655▲
Franklin.....................7,292
Freedom......................387▲
Fremont......................993▲
Gilford......................3,219▲
Gilmanton....................1,010▲
Gilsum.......................570▲
Goffstown....................2,272
Goffstown....................9,284▲
Gorham.......................2,020
Gorham.......................2,998▲
Goshen.......................395▲
Grafton......................370▲
Grantham.....................366▲
Greenfield...................1,058▲
Greenland....................1,784▲
Greenville...................1,332
Greenville...................1,587▲
Groton.......................120▲
Groveton.....................1,597
Hampstead....................2,401▲
Hampton......................5,407
Hampton......................8,011▲
Hampton Falls................1,254▲
Hancock......................909▲
Hanover......................6,147
Hanover......................8,494▲
Harrisville..................584▲
Haverhill....................3,090▲
Hebron.......................234▲
Henniker.....................2,348▲
Hill.........................450▲
Hillsborough.................1,784
Hillsborough.................2,775▲
Hinsdale.....................1,059
Hinsdale.....................3,276▲
Holderness...................1,048▲
Hollis.......................2,616▲
Hooksett.....................1,303
Hooksett.....................5,564▲
Hopkinton....................3,007▲
Hudson.......................10,638▲
Jackson......................404▲
Jaffrey......................1,922
Jaffrey......................3,353▲
Jefferson....................714▲
Keene........................20,467
Kensington...................1,044▲
Kingston.....................2,882▲
Laconia......................14,888
Lancaster....................2,120
Lancaster....................3,166▲
Landaff......................292▲
Langdon......................337▲
Lebanon......................9,725
Lee..........................1,481▲
Lempster.....................360▲
Lincoln......................1,341▲
Lisbon.......................1,247
Lisbon.......................1,480▲
Litchfield...................1,420▲
Littleton....................4,180
Littleton....................5,290▲
Londonderry..................5,346▲
Loudon.......................1,707▲
Lyman........................213▲
Lyme.........................1,112▲
Lyndeborough.................789▲
Madbury......................704▲
Madison......................572▲
Manchester...................87,754
Marlborough..................1,231
Marlborough..................1,671▲
Marlow.......................390▲
Mason........................518▲
Meredith.....................1,017
Meredith.....................2,904▲
Merrimack....................8,595▲
Middleton....................430▲
Milan........................713▲
Milford......................4,997
Milford......................6,622▲
Milton.......................1,859▲
Monroe.......................385▲
Mont Vernon..................906▲
Moultonborough...............1,310▲
Nashua.......................55,820
Nelson.......................304▲
New Boston...................1,390▲
New Castle...................975▲
New Durham...................583▲
New Hampton.................946▲
New Ipswich..................1,803▲
New London...................1,347
New London...................2,236▲
Newbury......................509▲
Newfields....................843▲
Newington....................798▲
Newmarket....................2,645
Newmarket....................3,361▲
Newport......................3,296
Newport......................5,899▲
Newton.......................1,920▲
North Conway.................1,723
North Hampton................3,259▲
Northfield...................2,193▲
Northumberland...............2,493▲
Northwood....................1,526▲
Nottingham...................952▲
Orange.......................103▲
Orford.......................793▲
Ossipee......................1,647▲
Pelham.......................5,408▲
Pembroke.....................4,261▲
Peterborough.................2,078
Peterborough.................3,807▲
Piermont.....................462▲
Pittsburg....................726▲
Pittsfield...................1,662
Pittsfield...................2,517▲
Plainfield...................1,323▲
Plaistow.....................4,712▲
Plymouth.....................3,109
Plymouth.....................4,225▲
Portsmouth...................25,717▲
Randolph.....................169▲
Raymond......................3,003▲
Richmond.....................287▲
Rindge.......................2,175▲
Rochester....................17,938
Rollinsford..................2,273▲
Roxbury......................161▲
Rumney.......................870▲
Rye..........................4,083▲
Salem........................20,142▲
Salisbury....................589▲
Sanbornton...................1,022▲
Sandown......................741▲
Sandwich.....................666▲
Seabrook.....................3,053▲
Sharon.......................136▲
Shelburne....................199▲
Somersworth..................9,026
South Hampton................558▲
Springfield..................310▲
Stark........................343▲
Stewartstown.................1,008▲
Stoddard.....................242▲
Strafford....................965▲
Stratford....................980▲
Stratham.....................1,512▲
Sugar Hill...................336▲
Sullivan.....................376▲
Sunapee......................1,384▲
Suncook......................4,280
Surry........................507▲
Sutton.......................642▲
Swanzey......................4,254▲
Tamworth.....................1,054▲
Temple.......................441▲
Thornton.....................594▲
Tilton.......................2,579▲
Tilton-Northfield Compact....2,420
Troy.........................1,123
Troy.........................1,713▲
Tuftonboro...................910▲
Unity........................709▲
Wakefield....................1,420▲
Walpole......................2,966▲
Warner.......................1,441▲
Warren.......................539▲
Washington...................248▲
Waterville Valley............109▲
Weare........................1,851▲
Webster......................680▲
Wentworth....................376▲
Westmoreland.................998▲
Whitefield...................1,093
Whitefield...................1,538▲
Wilmot.......................516▲
Wilton.......................1,161
Wilton.......................2,276▲
Winchester...................2,869▲
Windham......................3,008▲
Windsor......................43▲
Wolfeboro....................1,718
Wolfeboro....................3,036▲
Woodstock....................897▲
Woodsville...................1,336

NEW JERSEY Total population: 7,168,164

METROPOLITAN AREAS

Atlantic City................175,043
Jersey City..................609,266
Long Branch-Asbury Park......461,849
New Brunswick-Perth Amboy-Sayreville....583,813
Newark.......................1,858,869
Paterson-Clifton-Passaic.....1,357,930
Trenton......................303,968
Vineland-Millville-Bridgeton.....121,374

COUNTIES

Atlantic.....................175,043
Bergen.......................897,148
Burlington...................323,132
Camden.......................456,291
Cape May.....................59,554
Cumberland...................121,374
Essex........................932,299
Gloucester...................172,681
Hudson.......................609,266
Hunterdon....................69,718
Mercer.......................303,968
Middlesex....................583,813
Monmouth.....................461,849
Morris.......................383,454
Ocean........................208,470
Passaic......................460,782
Salem........................60,346
Somerset.....................198,372
Sussex.......................77,528
Union........................543,116
Warren.......................73,960

PLACES

Absecon......................6,094
Allendale....................6,240
Allenhurst...................1,012
Allentown....................1,603
Alpha........................2,829
Alpine.......................1,344
Andover......................813
Asbury Park..................16,533
Atlantic City................47,859
Atlantic Highlands...........5,102
Audubon......................10,802
Audubon Park.................1,492
Avalon.......................1,283
Avon-by-the-Sea..............2,163
Barnegat Light...............554
Barrington...................8,409
Bay Head.....................1,083
Bayonne......................72,743
Beach Haven..................1,488
Beachwood....................4,390
Belleville...................34,772
Bellmawr.....................15,618
Belmar.......................5,782
Belvidere....................2,722
Bergenfield..................29,000
Berlin.......................4,997
Bernardsville................6,652
Beverly......................3,105
Bloomfield...................52,029
Bloomingdale.................7,797
Bloomsbury...................879
Bogota.......................8,960
Boonton......................9,261
Bordentown...................4,490
Bound Brook..................10,450
Bradley Beach................4,163
Branchville..................911
Bridgeton....................20,435
Brielle......................3,594
Brigantine...................6,741
Brooklawn....................2,870
Browns Mills.................7,144
Budd Lake....................3,168
Buena........................3,283
Burlington...................11,991
Butler.......................7,051
Caldwell.....................8,719
Califon......................970
Camden.......................102,551
Candlewood...................5,629
Cape May.....................4,392
Cape May Court House.........2,062
Cape May Point...............204
Carlstadt....................6,724
Carteret.....................23,137
Chatham......................9,566
Chesilhurst..................801
Chester......................1,299
Clayton......................5,193
Clementon....................4,492
Cliffside Park...............18,891
Cliffwood-Cliffwood Beach....7,056
Clifton......................82,437
Clinton......................1,742
Closter......................8,604
Collingswood.................17,422
Corbin City..................258
Cranbury.....................1,253
Cresskill....................8,298
Deal.........................2,401
Demarest.....................5,133
Dover........................15,039
Dumont.......................20,155
Dunellen.....................7,072
East Newark..................1,922
East Orange..................75,471
East Paterson................20,511
East Rutherford..............8,536
Eatontown....................14,619
Edgewater....................4,987
Egg Harbor City..............4,304
Elizabeth....................112,654
Elmer........................1,592
Emerson......................8,428
Englewood....................24,985
Englewood Cliffs.............5,938
Englishtown..................1,048
Esponong.....................1,941
Essex Fells..................2,541
Estell Manor.................539
Fair Haven...................6,142
Fair Lawn....................37,975
Fairfield....................6,731
Fairview.....................10,698
Fanwood......................8,920
Far Hills....................780
Farmingdale..................1,148
Fieldsboro...................615
Flemington...................3,917
Florence-Roebling............7,551
Florham Park.................8,094
Folsom.......................1,767
Forked River.................1,422
Fort Dix.....................26,290
Fort Lee.....................30,631
Franklin.....................4,236
Franklin Lakes...............7,550
Freehold.....................10,545
Frenchtown...................1,459
Garfield.....................30,797
Garwood......................5,260
Gibbsboro....................2,634
Gilford Park.................4,007
Gladstone, see Peapack-Gladstone
Glassboro....................12,938
Glen Gardner.................874
Glen Ridge...................8,518
Glen Rock....................13,011
Gloucester City..............14,707
Guttenberg...................5,754
Hackensack...................36,008
Hackettstown.................9,472
Haddon Heights...............9,365
Haddonfield..................13,118
Haledon......................6,767
Hamburg......................1,820
Hammonton....................11,464
Hampton......................1,386
Harrington Park..............4,841
Harrison.....................11,811
Harvey Cedars................314
Hasbrouck Heights............13,651
Haworth......................3,760
Hawthorne....................19,173
Helmetta.....................955
High Bridge..................2,606
Highland Park................14,385
Highlands....................3,916
Hightstown...................5,431
Hillsdale....................11,768
Hi-Nella.....................1,195
Hoboken......................45,380
Hohokus......................4,348
Hopatcong....................9,052
Hopewell.....................2,271
Interlaken...................1,182
Irvington....................59,743
Island Heights...............1,397
Jamesburg....................4,584
Jersey City..................260,545
Keansburg....................9,720
Kearny.......................37,585
Kendall Park.................7,412
Kenilworth...................9,165
Keyport......................7,205
Kinnelon.....................7,600
Lake Hiawatha................11,389
Lake Mohawk..................6,262
Lake Parsippany..............7,488
Lake Telemark................1,086
Lakehurst....................2,641
Lakewood.....................17,874
Lambertville.................4,359
Laurel Springs...............2,566
Laurence Harbor..............6,715
Lavallette...................1,509
Lawnside.....................2,757
Lebanon......................885
Leonia.......................8,847
Lincoln Park.................9,034
Linden.......................41,409
Lindenwold...................12,199
Linwood......................6,159
Little Ferry.................9,042
Little Silver................6,010
Loch Arbour..................395
Lodi.........................25,213
Long Branch..................31,774
Long Valley..................1,645
Longport.....................1,225
Madison......................16,710
Magnolia.....................5,893
Manahawkin...................1,278
Manasquan....................4,971
Montoloking..................319
Manville.....................13,029
Margate City.................10,576
Marlton......................10,180
Matawan......................9,136
Mays Landing.................1,272
Maywood......................11,087
McGuire......................10,933
Medford......................1,448
Medford Lakes................4,792
Mendham......................3,729
Mercerville-Hamilton Square....24,465
Merchantville................4,425
Metuchen.....................16,031
Middlesex....................15,038
Midland Park.................8,159
Milford......................1,230
Millstone....................630
Milltown.....................6,470
Millville....................21,366
Monmouth Beach...............2,042
Montclair....................44,043
Montvale.....................7,327
Moonachie....................2,951
Moorestown-Lenola............14,179
Morris Plains................5,540
Morristown...................17,662
Mount Arlington..............3,590
Mount Ephraim................5,625
Mount Freedom................1,621
Mountain Lakes...............4,739
Mountainside.................7,520
National Park................3,730
Neptune City.................5,502
Netcong......................2,858
New Brunswick................41,885
New Egypt....................1,769
New Milford..................19,149
New Providence...............13,796
New Shrewsbury...............8,395
Newark.......................382,288
Newfield.....................1,487
Newton.......................7,297
North Arlington..............18,096
North Caldwell...............6,425
North Cape May...............3,812
North Haledon................7,614
North Plainfield.............21,796
North Wildwood...............3,914
Northfield...................8,875
Northvale....................5,177
Norwood......................4,398
Nutley.......................31,913
Oakhurst.....................5,558
Oakland......................14,420
Oaklyn.......................4,626
Ocean City...................10,575
Ocean Gate...................1,081
Oceanport....................7,503
Ogdensburg...................2,222
Old Bridge...................25,176
Old Tappan...................3,917
Oradell......................8,903
Orange.......................32,566
Oxford.......................1,411
Palisades Park...............13,351
Palmyra......................6,969
Paramus......................28,381
Park Ridge...................8,709
Passaic......................55,124
Paterson.....................144,824
Paulsboro....................8,084
Peapack-Gladstone............1,924
Pemberton....................1,344
Pennington...................2,151
Penns Grove..................5,727
Pennsville...................11,014
Perth Amboy..................38,798
Phillipsburg.................17,849
Pine Beach...................1,395
Pine Hill....................5,132
Pine Valley..................23
Pitman.......................10,257
Plainfield...................46,862
Pleasantville................13,778
Point Pleasant...............15,968
Point Pleasant Beach.........4,882
Pompton Lakes................11,397
Port Norris..................1,955
Port Republic................586
Princeton....................12,311
Princeton North..............5,488
Prospect Park................5,176
Rahway.......................29,114
Ramblewood...................5,556
Ramsey.......................12,571
Raritan......................6,691
Red Bank.....................12,847
Ridgefield...................11,308
Ridgefield Park..............13,990
Ridgewood....................27,547
Ringwood.....................10,393
Rio Grande...................1,203
River Edge...................12,850
Riverdale....................2,729
Riverton.....................3,412
Rockaway.....................6,383
Rockleigh....................308
Rocky Hill...................917
Roebling, see Florence-Roebling
Roosevelt....................814
Roseland.....................4,453
Roselle......................22,585
Roselle Park.................14,277
Rumson.......................7,421
Runnemede....................10,475
Rutherford...................20,802
Saddle River.................2,437
Salem........................7,648
Sayreville...................32,508
Sea Bright...................1,339
Sea Girt.....................2,207
Sea Isle City................1,712
Seabrook Farms...............1,569
Seaside Heights..............1,248
Seaside Park.................1,432
Secaucus.....................13,228
Shiloh.......................573
Ship Bottom..................1,079
Shore Hills..................3,064
Shrewsbury...................3,315
Somerdale....................6,510
Somers Point.................7,919
Somerville...................13,652
South Amboy..................9,338
South Belmar.................1,490
South Bound Brook............4,525
South Orange.................16,971
South Plainfield.............21,142
South River..................15,428
South Toms River.............3,981
Spotswood....................7,891
Spring Lake..................3,896
Spring Lake Heights..........4,602
Stanhope.....................3,040
Stockton.....................619
Stone Harbor.................1,089
Stratford....................9,801
Strathmore...................7,674
Summit.......................23,620
Surf City....................1,129
Sussex.......................2,038
Swedesboro...................2,287
Tavistock....................12

▲ Population of entire town (township).

Tenafly 14,827
Teterboro 19
Toms River 7,303
Totowa 11,580
Trenton 104,638
Tuckerton 1,926
Union Beach 6,472
Union City 58,537
Upper Greenwood Lake 1,505
Upper Saddle River 7,949
Ventnor City 10,385
Verona 15,067
Victory Gardens 1,027
Villas 3,155
Vineland 47,399
Waldwick 12,313
Wallington 10,284
Wanaque 8,636
Washington 5,943
Watchung 4,750
Wenonah 2,364
West Caldwell 11,887
West Cape May 1,005
West Long Branch 6,845
West New York 40,627
West Orange 43,715
West Paterson 11,692
West Wildwood 235
Westfield 33,720
Westville 5,170
Westwood 11,105
Wharton 5,535
White Horse-Yardville 18,680
White House Station 1,019
White Meadow Lake 8,499
Wildwood 4,110
Wildwood Crest 3,483
Williamstown 4,075
Wood-Lynne 3,101
Wood-Ridge 8,311
Woodbine 2,625
Woodbury 12,408
Woodbury Heights 3,621
Woodcliff Lake 5,506
Woodstown 3,137
Wrightstown 2,719
Yardville, see White Horse-Yardville

NEW MEXICO Total population: 1,016,000

METROPOLITAN AREA

Albuquerque 315,774

COUNTIES

Bernalillo 315,774
Catron 2,198
Chaves 43,335
Colfax 12,170
Curry 39,517
De Baca 2,547
Dona Ana 69,773
Eddy 41,119
Grant 22,030
Guadalupe 4,969
Harding 1,348
Hidalgo 4,734
Lea 49,554
Lincoln 7,560
Los Alamos 15,198
Luna 11,706
McKinley 43,208
Mora 4,673
Otero 41,097
Quay 10,903
Rio Arriba 25,170
Roosevelt 16,479
San Juan 52,517
San Miguel 21,951
Sandoval 17,492
Santa Fe 53,756
Sierra 7,189
Socorro 9,763
Taos 17,516
Torrance 5,290
Union 4,925
Valencia 40,539

PLACES

Alamogordo 23,035
Albuquerque 243,751
Anthony 1,728
Artesia 10,315
Aztec 3,354
Bayard 2,908
Belen 4,823
Bernalillo 2,016
Bloomfield 1,574
Cannon 5,461
Capitan 439
Carlsbad 21,297
Carrizozo 1,123
Causey 150
Central 1,864
Chama 899
Cimarron 927
Clayton 2,931
Cloudcroft 525
Clovis 28,495
Columbus 241
Corona 262
Deming 8,343
Des Moines 204
Dexter 746
Dora 196
Elida 233
Encino 250
Espanola 4,528
Estancia 721
Eunice 2,641
Farmington 21,979
Floyd 248
Folsom 75
Fort Sumner 1,615
Gallup 14,596
Grady 104
Grants 8,768
Grenville 21
Hagerman 953
Hatch 867
Hobbs 26,025
Holloman 8,001
Hope 90
House 119
Hurley 1,796
Isleta Pueblo 1,080
Jal 2,602
Jemez Pueblo 1,197
Jemez Springs 356
Lake Arthur 306
La Mesilla 1,713
Las Cruces 37,857
Las Vegas (city) 7,528
Las Vegas (town) 6,307
Logan 386
Lordsburg 3,429
Los Alamos 11,310
Los Lunas 973
Los Ranchos de Albuquerque 1,900
Loving 1,192
Lovington 8,915
Magdalena 652
Maxwell 393
Meadow Vista 1,402
Melrose 636
Milan 2,185
Moriarty 758
Mosquero 244
Mountainair 1,022
North Valley 10,366
Pecos 598
Portales 10,554
Questa 1,095
Raton 6,962
Roswell 33,908
Roy 476
Ruidoso 2,216
Ruidoso Downs 702
San Felipe Pueblo 1,187
San Jon 308
Sandia 6,867
Santa Fe 41,167
Santa Rosa 2,485
Santo Domingo Pueblo 1,662
Silver City 7,751
Socorro 4,687
South Valley 29,389
Springer 1,574
Taos 2,475
Taos Pueblo 1,030
Tatum 982
Texico 772
Tortugas, see University Park-Tortugas
Truth or Consequences 4,656
Tucumcari 7,189
Tularosa 2,851
University Park-Tortugas 4,165
Vaughn 867
Virden 151
Wagon Mound 630
White Rock 3,861
White Sands 4,167
Willard 209
Williamsburg 367
Zuni Pueblo 3,958

NEW YORK Total population: 18,241,266

METROPOLITAN AREAS

Albany-Schenectady-Troy 722,094
Binghamton 302,672
(268,328 in New York, 34,344 in Pennsylvania)
Buffalo 1,349,211
Elmira 101,537
New York 11,566,740
Poughkeepsie 222,295
Rochester 882,667
Syracuse 636,596
Utica-Rome 340,670

COUNTIES

Albany 286,742
Allegany 46,458
Bronx 1,471,701
Broome 221,815
Cattaraugus 81,666
Cayuga 77,439
Chautauqua 147,305
Chemung 101,537
Chenango 46,368
Clinton 72,934
Columbia 51,519
Cortland 45,894
Delaware 44,718
Dutchess 222,295
Erie 1,113,491
Essex 34,631
Franklin 43,931
Fulton 52,637
Genesee 58,722
Greene 33,136
Hamilton 4,714
Herkimer 67,633
Jefferson 88,508
Kings 2,602,012
Lewis 23,644
Livingston 54,041
Madison 62,864
Monroe 711,917
Montgomery 55,883
Nassau 1,428,838
New York 1,539,233
Niagara 235,720
Oneida 273,037
Onondaga 472,835
Ontario 78,849
Orange 221,657
Orleans 37,305
Oswego 100,897
Otsego 56,181
Putnam 56,696
Queens 1,987,174
Rensselaer 152,510
Richmond 295,443
Rockland 229,903
St. Lawrence 111,991
Saratoga 121,764
Schenectady 161,078
Schoharie 24,750
Schuyler 16,737
Seneca 35,083
Steuben 99,546
Suffolk 1,127,030
Sullivan 52,580
Tioga 46,513
Tompkins 77,064
Ulster 141,241
Warren 49,402
Washington 52,725
Wayne 79,404
Westchester 894,406
Wyoming 37,688
Yates 19,831

PLACES

Adams 1,951
Addison 2,104
Afton 1,064
Akron 2,863
Albany 115,781
Albertson 6,825
Albion 5,122
Alden 2,651
Alexander 474
Alexandria Bay 1,440
Alfred 3,804
Allegany 2,050
Almond 658
Altamont 1,561
Altmar 448
Amenia 1,157
Ames 198
Amityville 9,794
Amsterdam 25,524
Andes 353
Andover 1,214
Angelica 948
Angola 2,676
Angola on the Lake 1,573
Antwerp 872
Apalachin 1,233
Arcade 1,972
Ardsley 4,470
Argyle 392
Arkport 984
Arlington 11,203
Asharoken 540
Athens 1,718
Atlantic Beach 1,640
Attica 2,911
Auburn 34,599
Aurora 1,072
Averill Park 1,471
Avoca 1,153
Avon 3,260
Babylon 12,897
Bainbridge 1,674
Baldwin 34,525
Baldwinsville 6,298
Ballston Spa 4,968
Balmville 3,214
Barker 567
Batavia 17,338
Bath 6,053
Baxter Estates 1,026
Bay Shore 11,119
Bayport 8,232
Bayville 6,147
Beacon 13,255
Belle Terre 678
Bellerose 1,136
Bellmore 18,431
Bellport 3,046
Belmont 1,102
Bemus Point 487
Bergen 1,018
Bethpage 18,555
Big Flats 2,509
Billington Heights 1,278
Binghamton 64,123
Black River 1,307
Blasdell 3,910
Blauvelt 5,426
Bloomingburg 323
Bloomingdale 536
Bohemia 8,926
Bolivar 1,379
Boonville 2,488
Boysen Bay 1,191
Brentwood 28,327
Brewerton 1,985
Brewster 1,638
Brewster Heights 1,265
Brewster Hills 1,745
Briarcliff Manor 6,521
Bridgewater 601
Brightwaters 3,808
Brinckerhoff 2,094
Broadalbin 1,452
Brockport 7,878
Brocton 1,370
Bronxville 6,674
Brookville 3,212
Brownville 1,187
Brushton 547
Buchanan 2,110
Buffalo 462,768
Burdett 454
Burke 237
Caledonia 2,327
Cambridge 1,769
Camden 2,936
Camillus 1,534
Canajoharie 2,686
Canandaigua 10,488
Canaseraga 750
Canastota 5,033
Candor 939
Canisteo 2,772
Canton 6,398
Cape Vincent 820
Carle Place 6,326
Carmel 3,395
Carthage 3,889
Cassadaga 905
Castile 1,330
Castleton-on-Hudson 1,730
Castorland 327
Cato 601
Catskill 5,317
Cattaraugus 1,200
Cayuga 693
Cayuga Heights 3,130
Cazenovia 3,031
Cedarhurst 6,941
Celoron 1,456
Center Moriches 3,802
Centereach 9,427
Central Islip 36,391
Central Square 1,298
Centre Island 374
Champlain 1,426
Champlain Park 1,207
Chateaugay 976
Chatham 2,239
Chaumont 567
Chenango Bridge, see Nimmonsburg-Chenango Bridge
Cherry Creek 658
Cherry Valley 661
Chester 1,627
Chittenango 3,605
Churchville 1,065
Clarence 2,014
Clarence Center 1,332
Clark Mills 1,206
Clayton 1,970
Clayville 535
Cleveland 821
Clifton Knolls 5,771
Clifton Springs 2,058
Clinton 2,271
Clyde 2,828
Cobleskill 4,368
Cohocton 897
Cohoes 18,653
Cold Brook 413
Cold Spring 2,083
Cold Spring Harbor 5,450
Colden Hill 1,688
Colonie 8,701
Commack 24,138
Congers 5,928
Constableville 347
Cooperstown 2,403
Copenhagen 734
Copiague 19,632
Corfu 722
Corinth 3,267
Corning 15,792
Cornwall 3,131
Cortland 19,621
Country Knolls 2,082
Cove Neck 344
Coxsackie 2,399
Croghan 765
Croton-on-Hudson 7,523
Cuba 1,735
Dannemora 3,735
Dansville 5,436
Deer Park 32,274
Deferiet 347
Delanson 508
Delevan 994
Delhi 3,017
Depew 22,158
Deposit 2,061
Dering Harbor 24
De Ruyter 643
De Witt 10,032
Dexter 1,061
Dix Hills 10,050
Dobbs Ferry 10,353
Dolgeville 2,872
Dresden 450
Dryden 1,490
Dundee 1,539
Dunkirk 16,855
Earlville 1,050
East Aurora 7,033
East Bloomfield 643
East Cayuga Heights 2,611
East Glenville 5,898
East Half Hollow Hills 9,691
East Hampton 1,753
East Herkimer 1,135
East Hills 8,624
East Islip 6,861
East Massapequa 15,926
East Meadow 46,290
East Middletown 2,640
East Moriches 1,702
East Neck 5,221
East Northport 12,392
East Patchogue 8,092
East Quogue 1,143
East Randolph 636
East Rochester 8,347
East Rockaway 10,323
East Syracuse 4,333
East Vestal 10,472
East Williston 2,808
Eastchester 23,750
Eastport 1,308
Eden 2,962
Edwards 576
Elba 752
Elbridge 1,040
Elizabethtown 607
Ellenville 4,482
Ellicottville 955
Ellisburg 337
Elma 2,784
Elmira 39,945
Elmira Heights 4,906
Elmira Heights North 2,906
Elmont 29,363
Elmsford 3,911
Elwood 15,031
Endicott 16,556
Endwell 15,999
Esperance 408
Evans Mills 714
Fabius 374
Fair Haven 859
Fairmount 15,317
Fairport 6,474
Fairview 8,517
Falconer 2,983
Farmingdale 9,297
Farnham 546
Fayetteville 4,996
Fernwood 3,659
Fillmore 537
Firthcliffe 4,025
Fishkill 913
Flanders 1,905
Fleischmanns 434
Floral Park 18,466
Florida 1,674
Flower Hill 4,486
Fonda 1,120
Forestville 908
Fort Ann 562
Fort Covington 983
Fort Edward 3,733
Fort Johnson 711
Fort Plain 2,809
Fort Salonga 1,604
Frankfort 3,305
Franklin 552
Franklin Square 32,156
Franklinville 1,948
Fredonia 10,326
Freeport 40,374
Freetown 1,543
Freeville 664
Frewsburg 1,772
Friendship 1,285
Fulton 14,003
Fultonville 812
Gainesville 385
Galway 270
Gang Mills 1,258
Garden City 25,373
Garden City Park 7,488
Gardnertown 4,614
Geneseo 5,714
Geneva 16,793
Gilbertsville 552
Glasco 1,169
Glen Cove 25,770
Glen Park 587
Glenham 2,720
Glens Falls 17,222
Gloversville 19,677
Golden's Bridge 1,101
Goshen 4,342
Gouverneur 4,574
Gowanda 3,110
Grand View-on-Hudson 325
Granville 2,784
Great Neck 10,731
Great Neck Estates 3,131
Great Neck Plaza 5,921
Green Island 3,297
Greene 1,874
Greenlawn 8,493
Greenport 2,481
Greenwich 2,092
Greenwood Lake 2,262
Groton 2,112
Hagaman 1,410
Half Hollow Hills 12,081
Halfmoon Junction 1,915
Hamburg 10,215
Hamilton 3,636
Hammond 273
Hammondsport 1,066
Hampton Bays 1,862
Hancock 1,688
Hannibal 686
Harriman 955
Harrisville 836
Hartsdale 12,226
Hastings-on-Hudson 9,479
Hauppauge 13,957
Haverstraw 8,198
Haviland 3,447
Head of the Harbor 943
Hempstead 39,411
Herkimer 8,960
Hermon 521
Herricks 9,112
Herrings 137
Heuvelton 770
Hewlett 6,796
Hewlett Bay Park 586
Hewlett Harbor 1,545
Hewlett Neck 529
Hicksville 49,820
Highland 2,184
Highland Falls 4,638
Hillburn 1,058
Hillcrest 5,357
Hillis 2,750
Hilton 2,440
Hobart 531
Holbrook-Holtsville 12,103
Holcomb 778
Holland Patent 556
Holley 1,868
Homer 4,143
Honeoye Falls 2,248
Hoosick Falls 3,897
Hopewell Junction 2,055
Hornell 12,144
Horseheads 7,989
Houghton 1,620
Hudson 8,940
Hudson Falls 7,917
Hunter 238
Huntington 12,601
Huntington Bay 1,789
Huntington Station 28,817
Hurley 4,081
Hyde Park 2,805
Ilion 9,808
Interlaken 733
Inwood 8,433
Irvington 5,878
Island Park 5,396
Islip 7,692
Ithaca 26,226
Jamestown 39,795
Jamestown West 2,491
Jefferson Valley-Yorktown 9,008
Jeffersonville 421
Jericho 14,010
Johnson City 18,025
Johnstown 10,045
Jordan 1,493
Keeseville 2,122
Kenmore 20,980
Kensington 1,582
Kerhonkson 1,243
Kinderhook 1,233
Kings Park 5,555
Kings Point 5,614
Kingston 25,544
Lackawanna 28,657
Lacona 556
Lake 1,352
Lake Carmel 4,796
Lake Erie Beach 3,467
Lake George 1,046
Lake Grove 8,133
Lake Katrine 1,092
Lake Placid 2,731
Lake Success 3,254
Lakeview 5,471
Lakewood 3,864
Lancaster 13,365
Larchmont 7,203
Latham 9,661
Lattingtown 1,773
Laurel Hollow 1,401
Laurens 320
Lawrence 6,566
Leicester 368
Le Roy 5,118
Levittown 65,440
Lewiston 3,292
Liberty 4,293
Lima 1,686
Limestone 535
Lincoln Park 2,851
Lindenhurst 28,359
Lisle 336
Little Falls 7,629
Little Valley 1,340
Liverpool 3,307
Livingston Manor 1,522
Livonia 1,278
Lloyd Harbor 3,371
Lockport 25,399
Locust Grove 11,626
Lodi 353
Long Beach 33,127
Lorenz Park 1,995
Loudonville 9,299
Lowville 3,671
Lynbrook 23,776
Lyndonville 888
Lyons 4,496
Lyons Falls 852
Macedon 1,168
Madison 386
Mahopac 5,265
Malone 8,048
Malverne 10,036
Mamaroneck 18,909
Manchester 1,305
Manhasset 8,541
Manlius 4,295
Mannsville 494
Manorhaven 5,488
Marathon 1,053
Marcellus 2,017
Margaretville 816
Marlboro 1,580
Massapequa 26,821
Massapequa Park 22,112
Massena 14,042
Mastic Beach 4,870
Matinecock 841
Mattituck 1,995
Mattydale 8,292
Maybrook 1,536
Mayfield 981
Mayville 1,567
McGraw 1,319
Mechanicville 6,247
Medina 6,415
Melrose Park 2,189
Melville 6,641
Menands 3,449

NEW YORK, Continued

Meridian ... 369
Merrick ... 25,904
Merriewold Lake ... 2,564
Mexico ... 1,555
Middleburg ... 1,410
Middlehope ... 2,327
Middleport ... 2,132
Middletown ... 22,607
Middleville ... 725
Milford ... 527
Mill Neck ... 982
Millbrook ... 1,735
Millerton ... 1,042
Millport ... 480
Milton ... 1,861
Mineola ... 21,845
Mineville-Witherbee ... 1,967
Minoa ... 2,245
Mohawk ... 3,301
Monroe ... 4,439
Monsey ... 8,797
Montgomery ... 1,533
Monticello ... 5,991
Montour Falls ... 1,534
Mooers ... 536
Moravia ... 1,642
Morris ... 675
Morrisonville ... 1,276
Morristown ... 532
Morrisville ... 2,296
Mount Kisco ... 8,172
Mount Morris ... 3,417
Mount Vernon ... 72,778
Munnsville ... 435
Munsey Park ... 2,980
Munsons Corners ... 2,076
Muttontown ... 2,081
Myers Corner ... 2,826
Nanuet ... 10,447
Naples ... 1,324
Nassau ... 1,466
Nelliston ... 716
Nelsonville ... 583
Nesconset ... 10,048
New Berlin ... 1,369
New Cassel ... 8,721
New City ... 27,344
New Hackensack ... 1,111
New Hamburg ... 1,064
New Hartford ... 2,433
New Hyde Park ... 10,116
New Paltz ... 6,058
New Rochelle ... 75,385
New Square ... 1,156
New Windsor ... 8,803
New York City ... 7,895,563
New York Mills ... 3,805
Newark ... 11,644
Newark Valley ... 1,286
Newburgh ... 26,219
Newfane ... 2,588
Newport ... 908
Niagara Falls ... 85,615
Nichols ... 638
Nimmonsburg-Chenango Bridge ... 5,059
Niskayuna ... 6,186
Nissequogue ... 1,120
Norfolk ... 1,379
North Amityville ... 11,936
North Babylon ... 39,526
North Ballston Spa ... 1,296
North Bellmore ... 22,893
North Bellport ... 5,903
North Boston ... 1,635
North Chili ... 3,163
North Collins ... 1,675
North Great River ... 12,080
North Haven ... 694
North Hills ... 295
North Hornell ... 919
North Lindenhurst ... 11,117
North Massapequa ... 23,123
North Merrick ... 13,650
North New Hyde Park ... 18,154
North Patchogue ... 5,232
North Pelham ... 5,184
North Syracuse ... 8,687
North Tarrytown ... 8,334
North Tonawanda ... 36,012
North Valley Stream ... 14,881
North Wantagh ... 15,053
Northport ... 7,494
Northville ... 1,192
Norwich ... 8,843
Norwood ... 2,098
Nunda ... 1,254
Nyack ... 6,659
Oakdale ... 7,334
Oakfield ... 1,964
Ocean Beach ... 109
Oceanside ... 35,372
Odessa ... 606
Ogdensburg ... 14,554
Olcott ... 1,592
Old Bethpage ... 7,084
Old Brookville ... 1,785
Old Field ... 812
Old Westbury ... 2,667
Olean ... 19,169
Oneida ... 11,658
Oneida Castle ... 788
Oneonta ... 16,030
Oniad Lake ... 1,587
Orange Lake ... 4,348
Orchard Park ... 3,732
Oriskany ... 1,627
Oriskany Falls ... 927
Ossining ... 21,659
Oswego ... 20,913
Otego ... 956
Otisville ... 933
Ovid ... 779
Owego ... 5,152
Oxford ... 1,944
Oyster Bay Cove ... 1,320
Painted Post ... 2,496
Palatine Bridge ... 601
Palmyra ... 3,776
Panama ... 489
Parish ... 634
Patchogue ... 11,582
Pawling ... 1,914
Pearl River ... 17,146
Peekskill ... 19,283
Pelham ... 2,076
Pelham Manor ... 6,673
Penn Yan ... 5,293
Perry ... 4,538
Perrysburg ... 433
Peru ... 1,261
Phelps ... 1,989
Philadelphia ... 858
Philmont ... 1,674
Phoenix ... 2,617
Piermont ... 2,386
Pike ... 373
Pine Bush ... 1,183
Pine Hill ... 247
Pine Neck-West Tiana ... 1,326
Pittsford ... 1,755
Plainedge ... 10,759
Plainview ... 31,695
Plandome ... 1,593
Plandome Heights ... 1,032
Plandome Manor ... 835
Plattsburgh ... 18,715
Plattsburgh Air Force Base ... 7,078
Pleasant Valley ... 1,372
Pleasantville ... 7,110
Poland ... 629
Pomona ... 1,792
Ponquogue ... 1,474
Poquott ... 427
Port Byron ... 1,330
Port Chester ... 25,803
Port Dickinson ... 2,132
Port Ewen ... 2,882
Port Henry ... 1,532
Port Jefferson ... 5,515
Port Jefferson Station ... 7,403
Port Jervis ... 8,852
Port Leyden ... 862
Port Washington ... 15,923
Port Washington North ... 2,883
Portville ... 1,304
Potsdam ... 9,985
Poughkeepsie ... 32,029
Prattsburg ... 765
Prospect ... 392
Pulaski ... 2,480
Putnam Lake ... 1,425
Quogue ... 865
Randolph ... 1,498
Ransomville ... 1,034
Ravena ... 2,797
Red Creek ... 626
Red Hook ... 1,680
Red Oaks Mill ... 3,919
Remsen ... 602
Rensselaer ... 10,136
Rensselaer Falls ... 332
Rhinebeck ... 2,336
Richburg ... 482
Richfield Springs ... 1,540
Richmondville ... 826
Richville ... 334
Ripley ... 1,173
Riverhead ... 7,585
Riverside ... 911
Rochdale ... 1,819
Rochester ... 296,233
Rockville Centre ... 27,444
Roessleville ... 5,476
Rolling Acres ... 1,152
Rome ... 50,148
Ronkonkoma ... 7,284
Roosevelt ... 15,008
Rosendale ... 1,220
Roslyn ... 2,607
Roslyn Estates ... 1,420
Roslyn Harbor ... 977
Roslyn Heights ... 7,242
Rotterdam ... 25,214
Round Lake ... 886
Rouses Point ... 2,250
Rushville ... 568
Russell Gardens ... 1,174
Rye ... 15,869
Sackets Harbor ... 1,202
Saddle Rock ... 895
Sag Harbor ... 2,363
St. James ... 10,500
St. Johnsville ... 2,089
Salamanca ... 7,877
Salem ... 1,025
Saltaire ... 37
San Remo ... 8,302
Sand Ridge ... 1,109
Sands Point ... 2,916
Sandy Beach ... 1,691
Sandy Creek ... 731
Saranac Lake ... 6,086
Saratoga Springs ... 18,845
Saugerties ... 4,190
Saugerties South ... 3,159
Savannah ... 636
Savona ... 933
Sayville ... 11,680
Scarsdale ... 19,229
Schaghticoke ... 860
Schenectady ... 77,958
Schenevus ... 540
Schoharie ... 1,125
Schuylerville ... 1,402
Scotchtown ... 2,119
Scotia ... 8,224
Scottsville ... 1,967
Sea Cliff ... 5,890
Seaford ... 17,379
Selden ... 11,613
Seneca Falls ... 7,794
Setauket-South Setauket ... 6,857
Sharon Springs ... 421
Sherburne ... 1,613
Sherman ... 769
Sherrill ... 2,986
Shirley ... 6,280
Shoreham ... 524
Shortsville ... 1,516
Sidney ... 4,789
Silver Creek ... 3,182
Silver Springs ... 823
Sinclairville ... 772
Skaneateles ... 3,055
Slabtown ... 2,753
Sloan ... 5,216
Sloatsburg ... 3,134
Smyrna ... 247
Sodus ... 1,813
Sodus Point ... 1,172
Solvay ... 8,280
South Corning ... 1,414
South Dayton ... 688
South Fallsburg ... 1,590
South Farmingdale ... 20,464
South Floral Park ... 1,032
South Glens Falls ... 4,013
South Holbrook ... 6,700
South Hudson Falls ... 2,097
South Huntington ... 9,115
South Lockport ... 1,341
South Nyack ... 3,435
South Setauket, see Setauket-South Setauket
South Stony Brook ... 15,329
South Valley Stream ... 6,595
South Westbury ... 10,978
Southampton ... 4,904
Southold ... 2,030
Southport ... 8,685
Spackenkill ... 2,725
Speculator ... 390
Spencer ... 854
Spencerport ... 2,929
Spring Valley ... 18,112
Springville ... 4,350
Sproutville ... 1,871
Stamford ... 1,286
Stewart ... 1,230
Stewart Manor ... 2,183
Stillwater ... 1,428
Stony Brook ... 6,391
Stony Point ... 8,270
Stottville ... 1,106
Suffern ... 8,273
Syosset ... 10,084
Syracuse ... 197,297
Tannersville ... 650
Tappan ... 7,424
Tarrytown ... 11,115
Theresa ... 985
Thomaston ... 2,486
Thornwood ... 6,874
Ticonderoga ... 3,268
Tillson ... 1,256
Tivoli ... 739
Tonawanda ... 21,898
Town Line ... 2,434
Trenton ... 423
Tribes Hill ... 1,184
Troy ... 62,918
Trumansburg ... 1,803
Tuckahoe ... 6,236
Tully ... 899
Tupper Lake ... 4,854
Turin ... 293
Tuxedo Park ... 861
Twin Orchards, see Vestal-Twin Orchards
Unadilla ... 1,489
Union Springs ... 1,183
Uniondale ... 22,077
Unionville ... 576
Upper Brookville ... 1,182
Upper Nyack ... 2,096
Utica ... 91,611
Valatie ... 1,288
Valley Cottage ... 6,007
Valley Falls ... 681
Valley Stream ... 40,413
Van Etten ... 522
Van Keurens ... 3,292
Vernon ... 1,108
Vernon Valley ... 7,925
Vestal-Twin Orchards ... 8,303
Victor ... 2,187
Victory ... 718
Village of the Branch ... 1,675
Viola ... 5,136
Voorheesville ... 2,826
Waddington ... 955
Walden ... 5,277
Wallkill ... 1,849
Walton ... 3,744
Wampsville ... 586
Wantagh ... 21,873
Wappingers Falls ... 5,607
Wappingers Falls East ... 2,017
Wappingers Lake ... 1,958
Warrensburg ... 2,743
Warsaw ... 3,619
Warwick ... 3,604
Washington Heights ... 1,204
Washingtonville ... 1,887
Waterford ... 2,879
Waterloo ... 5,418
Watertown ... 30,787
Waterville ... 1,808
Watervliet ... 12,404
Watkins Glen ... 2,716
Waverly ... 5,261
Wayland ... 2,022
Webster ... 5,037
Weedsport ... 1,900
Wellsburg ... 779
Wellsville ... 5,815
West Amityville ... 6,424
West Babylon ... 12,893
West Carthage ... 2,047
West Elmira ... 5,901
West End ... 1,692
West Glens Falls ... 3,363
West Haverstraw ... 8,558
West Hempstead ... 20,375
West Islip ... 17,374
West Nyack ... 5,510
West Sand Lake ... 1,875
West Sayville ... 7,386
West Tiana, see Pine Neck-West Tiana
West Winfield ... 1,018
Westbury ... 15,362
Westfield ... 3,651
Westhampton ... 1,156
Westhampton Beach ... 1,926
Westmere ... 6,364
Westport ... 673
Westvale ... 7,253
White Plains ... 50,346
Whitehall ... 3,764
Whitesboro ... 4,805
Whitney Point ... 1,058
Williamson ... 1,991
Williamsville ... 6,835
Williston Park ... 9,154
Wilson ... 1,284
Windsor ... 1,098
Witherbee, see Mineville-Witherbee
Wolcott ... 1,617
Woodbourne ... 1,155
Woodhull ... 313
Woodmere ... 19,831
Woodridge ... 1,071
Woodsburgh ... 817
Woodstock ... 1,073
Wurtsboro ... 732
Wyandanch ... 15,716
Wyoming ... 514
Yaphank ... 5,460
Yonkers ... 204,297
Yorktown, see Jefferson Valley-Yorktown
Yorktown Heights ... 6,805
Yorkville ... 3,425
Youngstown ... 2,169

NORTH CAROLINA Total population: 5,082,059

METROPOLITAN AREAS

Asheville ... 145,056
Charlotte ... 409,370
Durham ... 190,388
Fayetteville ... 212,042
Greensboro-Winston-Salem-High Point ... 603,895
Raleigh ... 228,453
Wilmington ... 107,219

COUNTIES

Alamance ... 96,362
Alexander ... 19,466
Alleghany ... 8,134
Anson ... 23,488
Ashe ... 19,571
Avery ... 12,655
Beaufort ... 35,980
Bertie ... 20,528
Bladen ... 26,477
Brunswick ... 24,223
Buncombe ... 145,056
Burke ... 60,364
Cabarrus ... 74,629
Caldwell ... 56,699
Camden ... 5,453
Carteret ... 31,603
Caswell ... 19,055
Catawba ... 90,873
Chatham ... 29,554
Cherokee ... 16,330
Chowan ... 10,764
Clay ... 5,180
Cleveland ... 72,556
Columbus ... 46,937
Craven ... 62,554
Cumberland ... 212,042
Currituck ... 6,976
Dare ... 6,995
Davidson ... 95,627
Davie ... 18,855
Duplin ... 38,015
Durham ... 132,681
Edgecombe ... 52,341
Forsyth ... 214,348
Franklin ... 26,820
Gaston ... 148,415
Gates ... 8,524
Graham ... 6,562
Granville ... 32,762
Greene ... 14,967
Guilford ... 288,590
Halifax ... 53,884
Harnett ... 49,667
Haywood ... 41,710
Henderson ... 42,804
Hertford ... 23,529
Hoke ... 16,436
Hyde ... 5,571
Iredell ... 72,197
Jackson ... 21,593
Johnston ... 61,737
Jones ... 9,779
Lee ... 30,467
Lenoir ... 55,204
Lincoln ... 32,682
Macon ... 15,788
Madison ... 16,003
Martin ... 24,730
McDowell ... 30,648
Mecklenburg ... 354,656
Mitchell ... 13,447
Montgomery ... 19,267
Moore ... 39,048
Nash ... 59,122
New Hanover ... 82,996
Northampton ... 24,009
Onslow ... 103,126
Orange ... 57,707
Pamlico ... 9,467
Pasquotank ... 26,824
Pender ... 18,149
Perquimans ... 8,351
Person ... 25,914
Pitt ... 73,900
Polk ... 11,735
Randolph ... 76,358
Richmond ... 39,889
Robeson ... 84,842
Rockingham ... 72,402
Rowan ... 90,035
Rutherford ... 47,337
Sampson ... 44,954
Scotland ... 26,929
Stanly ... 42,822
Stokes ... 23,782
Surry ... 51,415
Swain ... 7,861
Transylvania ... 19,713
Tyrrell ... 3,806
Union ... 54,714
Vance ... 32,691
Wake ... 228,453
Warren ... 15,810
Washington ... 14,038
Watauga ... 23,404
Wayne ... 85,408
Wilkes ... 49,524
Wilson ... 57,486
Yadkin ... 24,599
Yancey ... 12,629

PLACES

Aberdeen ... 1,592
Acme ... 459
Advance ... 206
Ahoskie ... 5,105
Albemarle ... 11,126
Alexander Mills ... 988
Alliance ... 577
Andrews ... 1,384
Angier ... 1,431
Ansonville ... 694
Apex ... 2,192
Arapahoe ... 212
Archdale ... 6,103
Arlington ... 711
Asheboro ... 10,797
Asheboro South ... 1,998
Asheboro West ... 1,158
Asheville ... 57,681
Askewville ... 247
Atkinson ... 325
Atlantic Beach ... 300
Aulander ... 947
Aurora ... 620
Autryville ... 213
Avondale, see Henrietta-Avondale
Ayden ... 3,450
Badin ... 1,626
Bailey ... 724
Bakersville ... 409
Balfour-Druid Hills ... 2,014
Balfours ... 4,836
Banner Elk ... 754
Bannertown ... 1,138
Barker Heights ... 2,933
Bath ... 231
Battleboro ... 688
Bayboro ... 665
Beargrass ... 99
Beaufort ... 3,368
Belhaven ... 2,259
Belmont ... 4,814
Belmont South ... 2,278
Belmont-South Rosemary ... 2,260
Benson ... 2,267
Bessemer City ... 5,217
Bethel ... 1,514
Beulaville ... 1,156
Biltmore Forest ... 1,298
Biscoe ... 1,244
Black Creek ... 449
Black Mountain ... 3,204
Bladenboro ... 783
Bladenboro North ... 1,705
Blowing Rock ... 801
Boger City ... 2,203
Boiling Spring Lakes ... 245
Boiling Springs ... 2,284
Bolivia ... 185
Bolton ... 534
Boone ... 8,754
Boonville ... 687
Bostic ... 289
Brevard ... 5,243
Bridgeton ... 520
Broadway ... 694
Brookford ... 590
Brunswick ... 206
Bryson City ... 1,290
Buies Creek ... 2,024
Bunlevel ... 200
Bunn ... 284
Burgaw ... 1,744
Burlington ... 35,930
Burnsville ... 1,348
Butner ... 3,538
Calypso ... 462
Cameron ... 204
Camp Lejeune Central ... 34,549
Candor ... 561
Canton ... 5,158
Cape Carteret ... 616
Carolina Beach ... 1,663
Carrboro ... 3,472
Carthage ... 1,034
Cary ... 7,430
Cashiers ... 230
Castalia ... 265
Catawba ... 565
Centerville ... 123
Cerro Gordo ... 184
Chadbourn ... 2,213
Chadwick Acres ... 12
Chapel Hill ... 25,537
Charlotte ... 241,178
Cherry Point ... 12,029
Cherryville ... 5,258
China Grove ... 1,788
Chocowinity ... 566
Claremont ... 788
Clarkton ... 662
Clayton ... 3,103
Cleveland ... 614
Clinchfield, see East Marion-Clinchfield
Clinton ... 7,157
Clyde ... 900
Coats ... 1,051
Colerain ... 373
Columbia ... 902
Columbus ... 731
Como ... 211
Concord ... 18,464
Concord North ... 2,350
Conetoe ... 160
Conover ... 3,355
Conway ... 694
Cooleemee ... 1,115
Cornelius ... 1,296
Council ... 38
Cove City ... 485
Cramerton ... 2,142
Creedmoor ... 1,405
Creswell ... 633
Crossnore ... 264
Culberson ... 83
Dallas ... 4,059
Danbury ... 152
Daniels-Rhyne ... 2,273
Davidson ... 2,931
Dellview ... 11
Denton ... 1,017
Dillsboro ... 215
Dobson ... 933
Dover ... 585
Drexel ... 1,431
Druid Hills, see Balfour-Druid Hills
Dublin ... 283
Dudley ... 199
Dundarrach ... 53
Dunn ... 8,302
Durham ... 95,438
East Bend ... 485
East Flat Rock ... 2,627
East Laurinburg ... 487
East Marion-Clinchfield ... 3,015
East Rockingham ... 2,858
East Spencer ... 2,217
Edenton ... 4,766
Eden ... 15,871
Edward ... 115
Elizabeth City ... 14,069
Elizabethtown ... 1,418
Elk Park ... 503
Elkin ... 2,899
Ellenboro ... 465
Ellerbe ... 913
Elm City ... 1,201
Elon College ... 2,150
Emerald Isle ... 122
Enfield ... 3,272
Erwin ... 2,852
Eureka ... 263
Everetts ... 198
Fair Bluff ... 1,039
Fairmont ... 2,827
Faison ... 598
Faith ... 506
Falcon ... 357
Falkland ... 130
Farmville ... 4,424
Fayetteville ... 53,510
Flat Rock ... 1,688
Forest City ... 7,179
Fort Bragg ... 46,995
Fountain ... 434
Four Oaks ... 1,057
Franklin ... 2,336
Franklinton ... 1,459
Franklinville ... 794
Fremont ... 1,596
Fuquay-Varina ... 3,576
Garland ... 656
Garner ... 4,923
Garysburg ... 231
Gaston ... 1,105
Gastonia ... 47,142
Gastonia East ... 2,370
Gastonia North ... 1,316
Gastonia South ... 3,718
Gatesville ... 338
Gibson ... 502
Gibsonville ... 2,019
Gieger, see New River-Gieger
Glen Alpine ... 797
Glen Raven ... 2,848
Godwin ... 129
Gold Point ... 108
Goldsboro ... 26,810
Goldston ... 364
Graham ... 8,172
Granite Falls ... 2,388
Granite Quarry ... 1,344
Greensboro ... 144,076
Greenville ... 29,063
Grifton ... 1,860
Grimesland ... 394
Grover ... 555
Guilford College ... 61
Halifax ... 335
Hamilton ... 579
Hamlet ... 4,627
Harkers Island ... 1,633
Harmony ... 377
Harrells ... 249
Harrellsville ... 165
Hassell ... 160
Havelock ... 5,283

Haw River 1,542
Hayesville 428
Hazelwood 2,057
Henderson 13,896
Henderson North 1,997
Henderson South 1,843
Hendersonville 6,443
Hendersonville West 1,558
Henrietta-Avondale 1,307
Hertford 2,023
Hickory 20,569
Hickory East 4,181
Hickory North 2,325
High Point 63,259
Highlands 583
Hildebran 481
Hillsboro 1,444
Hobgood 530
Hoffman 434
Holden Beach 136
Holly Ridge 415
Holly Springs 697
Hookerton 441
Hope Mills 1,866
Hot Springs 653
Hudson 2,820
Huntersville 1,538
Indian Trail 405
Jackson 762
Jacksonville 16,289
James City 2,577
Jamestown 1,297
Jamesville 533
Jefferson 943
Johnson, see Seymour-Johnson
Jonesville 1,659
Jupiter 208
Kannapolis 36,293
Kelford 295
Kenansville 762
Kenly 1,370
Kernersville 4,815
Kill Devil Hills 357
King 1,033
Kings Mountain 8,465
Kinston 23,020
Kittrell 427
Knightdale 815
Kure Beach 394
La Grange 2,679
Lake Lure 456
Lake Waccamaw 924
Landis 2,297
Landis Northeast 1,353
Lansing 283
Lasker 114
Lattimore 257
Laurel Hill 1,215
Laurel Park 581
Laurinburg 8,859
Laurinburg West 1,156
Lawndale 544
Lenoir 14,705
Lewiston 327
Lexington 17,205
Liberty 2,167
Lilesville 641
Lillington 1,155
Lincolnton 5,293
Linden 205
Littleton 903
Long Beach 493
Longhurst 1,485
Longview 3,360
Longwood Park 1,284
Louisburg 2,941
Love Valley 40
Lowell 3,307
Lucama 610
Lumber Bridge 117
Lumberton 16,961
MacClesfield 536
Macon 179
Madison 2,018
Magnolia 614
Maiden 2,416
Manteo 547
Margaretsville 95
Marietta 70
Marion 3,335
Mars Hill 1,623
Marshall 982
Marshville 1,405
Matthews 783
Maury 421
Maxton 1,885
Mayodan 2,875
Maysville 912
McAdenville 950
McDonald 80
McFarlan 140
Mebane 2,433
Micro 300
Middleburg 149
Middlesex 729
Milton 235
Milwaukee 376
Mocksville 2,529
Monroe 11,282
Montreat 581
Mooresville 8,808
Morehead City 5,233
Morganton 13,625
Morgantown 3,547
Morrisville 209
Mortimer 27
Morven 562
Mount Airy 7,325
Mount Gilead 1,286
Mount Holly 5,107
Mount Olive 4,914
Mount Pleasant 1,174
Murfreesboro 3,508
Murphy 2,082
Nags Head 414
Nashville 1,670
New Bern 14,660
New London 285
New River-Gieger 8,699
Newland 524
Newport 1,735
Newton 7,857
Newton Grove 546
Norlina 969
North Belmont 10,678
North Wilkesboro 3,357
Norwood 1,896
Oak City 559
Oakboro 568
Ocean Isle Beach 78
Old Fort 676
Oriental 445
Orrum 162
Oxford 7,178
Palmyra 27
Pantego 218
Parkersburg 56
Parkton 550
Parkwood 2,267
Parmele 373
Patterson 344
Peachland 556
Pembroke 1,982
Phillipsville 1,239
Pikeville 580
Pilot Mountain 1,309
Pine Level 983
Pinebluff 570
Pinehurst 1,056
Pinetops 1,379
Pinetown 278
Pineville 1,948
Pink Hill 522
Pittsboro 1,447
Plymouth 4,774
Polkton 845
Pollocksville 456
Powellsville 247
Princeton 1,044
Princeville 654
Proctorville 157
Raeford 3,180
Raleigh 123,793
Ramseur 1,328
Randleman 2,312
Ranlo 2,092
Red Oak 359
Red Springs 3,383
Reidsville 13,636
Rhodhiss 784
Rhyne, see Daniels-Rhyne
Rich Square 1,254
Richfield 306
Richlands 935
Roanoke Rapids 13,508
Robbins 1,059
Robbinsville 777
Robersonville 1,910
Rockingham 5,852
Rockwell 999
Rocky Mount 34,284
Rolesville 529
Ronda 465
Roper 649
Rose Hill 1,448
Roseboro 1,235
Rosman 407
Rowan Mill 1,184
Rowland 1,358
Roxboro 5,370
Roxobel 347
Royal Pines 2,041
Rural Hall 2,338
Ruth 360
Rutherfordton 3,245
St. Pauls 2,011
Salemburg 669
Salisbury 22,515
Saluda 546
Sanford 11,716
Saratoga 391
Scotland Neck 2,869
Seaboard 611
Seagrove 354
Selma 4,356
Seven Springs 188
Severn 356
Seymour-Johnson 8,172
Shallotte 597
Sharpsburg 789
Shelby 16,328
Siler City 4,689
Sims 205
Skyland 2,177
Smithfield 6,677
Smithtown 196
Snow Hill 1,359
South Belmont 2,125
South Creek 73
South Goldsboro 2,094
South Rosemary, see Belmont-South Rosemary
South Salisbury 2,199
South Wadesboro 109
South Weldon 1,630
Southern Pines 5,937
Southport 2,220
Sparta 1,304
Speed 142
Spencer 3,075
Spencer Mountain 300
Spindale 3,848
Spring Hope 1,334
Spring Lake 3,968
Spruce Pine 2,333
Staley 239
Stanfield 458
Stanley 2,336
Stanleyville 2,362
Stantonsburg 869
Star 892
Statesville 19,996
Stedman 505
Stem 242
Stoneville 1,030
Stonewall 335
Stony Point 1,001
Stovall 405
Sunset Beach 108
Surf City 166
Swan Station 196
Swannanoa 1,966
Swansboro 1,207
Sylva 1,561
Tabor City 2,400
Tarboro 9,425
Tarheel 87
Taylorsville 1,231
Teacheys 219
Thomasville 15,230
Toast 2,635
Todd 98
Topsail Beach 41
Trent Woods 719
Trenton 539
Troutman 797
Troy 2,429
Tryon 1,951
Turkey 329
Valdese 3,182
Vanceboro 758
Vandemere 379
Varina, see Fuquay-Varina
Vass 885
Waco 245
Wade 315
Wadesboro 3,977
Wagram 718
Wake Forest 3,148
Walkertown 1,652
Wallace 2,905
Walnut Cove 1,213
Walstonburg 176
Warrensville 224
Warrenton 1,035
Warsaw 2,701
Washington 8,961
Washington Park 517
Watha 181
Waxhaw 1,248
Waynesville 6,488
Weaverville 1,280
Webster 181
Weldon 2,304
Wendell 1,929
West Burlington 1,471
West Concord 5,347
West Hillsborough 1,696
West Jefferson 889
West Marion 3,034
West Statesville 1,905
Whispering Pines 362
Whitakers 926
White Lake 232
Whiteville 4,195
Wilkesboro 1,974
Williamston 6,570
Wilmington 46,169
Wilson 29,347
Wilson Mills 283
Windsor 2,199
Winfall 581
Wingate 2,569
Winston-Salem 134,676
Winterville 1,437
Winton 917
Woodland 744
Woodville 253
Wrightsville Beach 1,701
Yadkinville 2,232
Yanceyville 1,274
Yaupon Beach 334
Youngsville 555
Zebulon 1,839

NORTH DAKOTA Total population: 617,761

METROPOLITAN AREA

Fargo-Moorhead 120,238 (73,653 in North Dakota, 46,585 in Minnesota)

COUNTIES

Adams 3,832
Barnes 14,669
Benson 8,245
Billings 1,198
Bottineau 9,496
Bowman 3,901
Burke 4,739
Burleigh 40,714
Cass 73,653
Cavalier 8,213
Dickey 6,976
Divide 4,564
Dunn 4,895
Eddy 4,103
Emmons 7,200
Foster 4,832
Golden Valley 2,611
Grand Forks 61,102
Grant 5,009
Griggs 4,184
Hettinger 5,075
Kidder 4,362
La Moure 7,117
Logan 4,245
McHenry 8,977
McIntosh 5,545
McKenzie 6,127
McLean 11,251
Mercer 6,175
Morton 20,310
Mountrail 8,437
Nelson 5,776
Oliver 2,322
Pembina 10,728
Pierce 6,323
Ramsey 12,915
Ransom 7,102
Renville 3,828
Richland 18,089
Rolette 11,549
Sargent 5,937
Sheridan 3,232
Sioux 3,632
Slope 1,484
Stark 19,613
Steele 3,749
Stutsman 23,550
Towner 4,645
Traill 9,571
Walsh 16,251
Ward 58,560
Wells 7,847
Williams 19,301

PLACES

Abercrombie 262
Adams 284
Alamo 124
Alexander 208
Alice 83
Almont 109
Alsen 201
Ambrose 109
Amenia 80
Amidon 54
Anamoose 401
Aneta 376
Antler 135
Ardoch 70
Argusville 118
Arnegard 141
Arthur 412
Ashley 1,236
Ayr 48
Balfour 93
Balta 133
Bantry 40
Barney 81
Bartlett 19
Barton 34
Bathgate 133
Beach 1,408
Belfield 1,130
Benedict 72
Bergen 24
Berlin 76
Berthold 398
Berwick 33
Beulah 1,344
Binford 242
Bisbee 305
Bismarck 34,703
Bottineau 2,760
Bowbells 584
Bowdon 229
Bowman 1,762
Braddock 106
Brinsmade 36
Brocket 95
Bucyrus 42
Buffalo 241
Burlington 247
Butte 193
Buxton 235
Calio 75
Calvin 78
Cando 1,512
Canton 81
Carpio 215
Carrington 2,491
Carson 466
Casselton 1,485
Cathay 110
Cavalier 1,381
Cayuga 116
Center 619
Churchs Ferry 139
Cleveland 128
Clifford 84
Cogswell 203
Coleharbor 78
Colfax 70
Columbus 465
Conway 57
Cooperstown 1,485
Courtenay 125
Crary 150
Crosby 1,545
Crystal 272
Davenport 147
Dawson 131
Dazey 128
Deering 75
Des Lacs 197
Devils Lake 7,078
Dickey 118
Dickinson 12,405
Dodge 121
Donnybrook 163
Douglas 144
Drake 636
Drayton 1,095
Dunn Center 107
Dunseith 811
Dwight 93
Eckman 9
Edgeley 888
Edinburg 315
Edmore 398
Egeland 96
Elgin 839
Ellendale 1,517
Elliott 50
Emerado 515
Enderlin 1,343
Epping 140
Esmond 416
Fairdale 102
Fairmount 412
Fargo 53,365
Fessenden 815
Fingal 166
Finley 809
Flasher 467
Flaxton 286
Forbes 88
Fordville 361
Forest River 169
Forman 596
Fort Yates 1,153
Fortuna 216
Fredonia 100
Fullerton 110
Gackle 470
Galesburg 134
Gardena 84
Gardner 96
Garrison 1,614
Gascoyne 34
Gilby 268
Gladstone 222
Glen Ullin 1,070
Glenburn 381
Glenfield 127
Golden Valley 235
Golva 104
Goodrich 300
Grafton 5,946
Grand Forks 39,008
Grand Forks Base 10,474
Grandin 187
Grano 4
Granville 282
Great Bend 86
Grenora 401
Gwinner 623
Hague 146
Halliday 413
Hamberg 51
Hamilton 110
Hampden 114
Hankinson 1,125
Hanks 13
Hannaford 244
Hannah 145
Hansboro 49
Harvey 2,361
Hatton 808
Havana 156
Haynes 53
Hazelton 374
Hazen 1,240
Hebron 1,103
Hettinger 1,655
Hillsboro 1,309
Hoople 330
Hope 364
Horace 276
Hunter 362
Hurdsfield 139
Inkster 198
Jamestown 15,385
Jud 110
Karlsruhe 172
Kathryn 109
Kenmare 1,515
Kensal 263
Kief 46
Killdeer 615
Kindred 495
Knox 104
Kramer 125
Kulm 625
Lakota 964
La Moure 951
Landa 61
Langdon 2,182
Lankin 221
Lansford 296
Larimore 1,469
Larson 35
Lawton 123
Leal 41
Leeds 626
Lehr 287
Leith 92
Leonard 221
Lidgerwood 1,000
Lignite 354
Linton 1,695
Lisbon 2,090
Litchville 294
Loma 6
Loraine 33
Ludden 44
Luverne 84
Maddock 708
Makoti 159
Mandan 11,093
Mantador 95
Manvel 265
Mapleton 219
Marion 215
Marmarth 247
Martin 120
Max 301
Maxbass 174
Mayville 2,554
Maza 20
McClusky 664
McHenry 152
McVille 583
Medina 488
Medora 129
Mercer 132
Merricourt 22
Michigan City 447
Milnor 645
Milton 198
Minnewaukan 496
Minot 32,290
Minot Base 12,077
Minto 636
Mohall 950
Monango 112
Montpelier 116
Mooreton 158
Mott 1,368
Mountain 146
Munich 249
Mylo 51
Napoleon 1,036
Neche 451
Nekoma 84
New England 906
New Leipzig 354
New Rockford 1,969
New Salem 943
New Town 1,428
Newburg 125
Niagara 115
Nome 103
Noonan 403
Northwood 1,189
Oakes 1,742
Oberon 151
Omemee 5
Oriska 128
Osnabrock 255
Overly 28
Page 367
Palermo 146
Park River 1,680
Parshall 1,246
Pekin 120
Pembina 741
Perth 44
Petersburg 266
Pettibone 173
Pick City 119
Pillsbury 50
Pingree 76
Pisek 154
Plaza 291
Portal 251
Portland 534
Powers Lake 523
Rawson 10
Ray 776
Reeder 306
Regan 74
Regent 344
Reynolds 236
Rhame 206
Richardton 799
Robinson 125
Rock Lake 270
Rogers 96
Rolette 579
Rolla 1,458
Ross 125
Rugby 2,889
Ruso 15
Russell 14
Rutland 225
Ryder 211
St. John 367
St. Thomas 508
Sanborn 255
Sanish 25
Sarles 148
Sawyer 373
Scranton 360
Selfridge 346
Sentinel Butte 125
Sharon 201
Sheldon 192
Sherwood 369
Sheyenne 362
Sibley 20
Solen 180
Souris 151
South Heart 132
Spring Brook 27
Stanley 1,581
Stanton 517
Starkweather 193
Steele 696
Strasburg 642
Streeter 324
Surrey 361
Sykeston 232
Tagus 14
Tappen 294
Taylor 162
Thompson 291
Tioga 1,667
Tolley 163
Tolna 247
Tower City 289
Towner 870
Turtle Lake 712
Tuttle 216
Underwood 781
Upham 272
Valley City 7,843
Velva 1,241
Venturia 77
Verona 140
Voltaire 54
Wahpeton 7,076
Wales 116
Walhalla 1,471
Warwick 168
Washburn 804
Watford City 1,768
Werner 21
West Fargo 5,161
West Fargo Industrial Park 104
Westhope 705
Wheelock 21
White Earth 128
Wildrose 235
Williston 11,280
Willow City 403
Wilton 695
Wimbledon 337
Wing 223
Wishek 1,275
Wolford 81
Woodworth 139
Wyndmere 516
York 102
Zap 271
Zeeland 313

OHIO Total population: 10,652,017

METROPOLITAN AREAS

Akron	679,239
Canton	372,210
Cincinnati (1,104,668 in Ohio, 250,813 in Kentucky, 29,430 in Indiana)	1,384,911
Cleveland	2,064,194
Columbus	916,228
Dayton	850,266
Hamilton-Middletown	226,207
Lima	171,472
Lorain-Elyria	256,843
Mansfield	129,997
Springfield	157,115
Steubenville-Weirton (96,193 in Ohio, 69,434 in West Virginia)	165,627
Toledo (574,092 in Ohio, 118,479 in Michigan)	692,571
Youngstown-Warren	536,003

COUNTIES

Adams	18,957
Allen	111,144
Ashland	43,303
Ashtabula	98,237
Athens	54,889
Auglaize	38,602
Belmont	80,917
Brown	26,635
Butler	226,207
Carroll	21,579
Champaign	30,491
Clark	157,115
Clermont	95,725
Clinton	31,464
Columbiana	108,310
Coshocton	33,486
Crawford	50,364
Cuyahoga	1,721,300
Darke	49,141
Defiance	36,949
Delaware	42,908
Erie	75,909
Fairfield	73,301
Fayette	25,461
Franklin	833,249
Fulton	33,071
Gallia	25,239
Geauga	62,977
Greene	125,057
Guernsey	37,665
Hamilton	924,018
Hancock	61,217
Hardin	30,813
Harrison	17,013
Henry	27,058
Highland	28,996
Hocking	20,322
Holmes	23,024
Huron	49,587
Jackson	27,174
Jefferson	96,193
Knox	41,795
Lake	197,200
Lawrence	56,868
Licking	107,799
Logan	35,072
Lorain	256,843
Lucas	484,370
Madison	28,318
Mahoning	303,424
Marion	64,724
Medina	82,717
Meigs	19,799
Mercer	35,265
Miami	84,342
Monroe	15,739
Montgomery	606,148
Morgan	12,375
Morrow	21,348
Muskingum	77,826
Noble	10,428
Ottawa	37,099
Paulding	19,329
Perry	27,434
Pickaway	40,071
Pike	19,114
Portage	125,868
Preble	34,719
Putnam	31,134
Richland	129,997
Ross	61,211
Sandusky	60,983
Scioto	76,951
Seneca	60,696
Shelby	37,748
Stark	372,210
Summit	553,371
Trumbull	232,579
Tuscarawas	77,211
Union	23,786
Van Wert	29,194
Vinton	9,420
Warren	84,925
Washington	57,160
Wayne	87,123
Williams	33,669
Wood	89,722
Wyandot	21,826

PLACES

Aberdeen	1,165
Academia, see North Mount Vernon-Academia	
Ada	5,309
Adamsville	174
Addyston	1,336
Adelphi	455
Adena	1,134
Akron	275,425
Albany	899
Alexandria	588
Alger	1,071
Alliance	26,547
Alvordton	351
Amanda	788
Amberley	5,574
Amelia	820
Amesville	295
Amherst	9,902
Amsterdam	882
Andover	1,179
Anna	792
Ansonia	1,044
Antioch	112
Antwerp	1,735
Apple Creek	784
Aquilla	389
Arcadia	689
Arcanum	1,993
Archbold	3,047
Arlington	1,066
Arlington Heights	1,476
Ashland	19,872
Ashley	1,034
Ashtabula	24,313
Ashville	1,772
Athalia	287
Athens	23,310
Attica	1,005
Aurora	6,549
Austintown	29,393
Avon	7,214
Avon Lake	12,261
Avondale	5,195
Bailey Lakes	394
Bainbridge	1,057
Bairdstown	138
Ballville	1,652
Baltic	571
Baltimore	2,418
Barberton	33,052
Barnesville	4,292
Barnhill	339
Batavia	1,894
Batesville	148
Bay View	798
Bay Village	18,163
Beach City	1,133
Beachwood	9,631
Beallsville	452
Beaver	317
Beaverdam	525
Bedford	17,552
Bedford Heights	13,063
Bellaire	9,655
Bellbrook	1,268
Belle Center	985
Belle Valley	393
Bellefontaine	11,255
Bellevue	8,604
Bellville	1,685
Belmont	666
Belmore	319
Beloit	921
Belpre	7,189
Bentleyville	338
Benton Ridge	329
Berea	22,396
Bergholz	914
Berkey	294
Berlin Heights	828
Bethel	2,214
Bethesda	1,157
Bettsville	833
Beverly	1,396
Bexley	14,888
Blacklick Estates	8,351
Blakeslee	163
Blanchester	3,080
Bloomdale	727
Bloomingburg	895
Bloomingdale	289
Bloomville	884
Blue Ash	8,324
Bluffton	2,935
Boardman	30,852
Bolivar	1,084
Boston Heights	846
Botkins	1,057
Bowerston	479
Bowersville	358
Bowling Green	21,760
Bradford	2,163
Bradner	1,140
Brady Lake	450
Bratenahl	1,613
Brecksville	9,137
Bremen	1,413
Brewster	2,020
Briarwood Beach	508
Brice	228
Bridgeport	3,001
Bridgetown	13,352
Brilliant	2,178
Broadview Heights	11,463
Brook Park	30,774
Brooklyn	13,142
Brooklyn Heights	1,527
Brookside	939
Brookville	4,403
Broughton	155
Brunswick	15,852
Bryan	7,008
Buchtel	592
Buckeye Lake	2,961
Buckland	281
Bucyrus	13,111
Burbank	354
Burgoon	221
Burkettsville	279
Burton	1,214
Butler	1,052
Butlerville	204
Byesville	2,097
Cadiz	3,060
Cairo	587
Caldwell	2,082
Caledonia	792
Cambridge	13,656
Camden	1,507
Campbell	12,577
Canal Fulton	2,367
Canal Winchester	2,412
Canfield	4,997
Canton	110,053
Cardington	1,730
Carey	3,523
Carlisle	3,821
Carroll	614
Carrollton	2,817
Casstown	380
Castalia	1,045
Castine	150
Catawba	323
Cecil	295
Cedarville	2,342
Celina	7,779
Centerburg	1,038
Centerville	10,333
Centreville	114
Chagrin Falls	4,848
Chambersburg	156
Chardon	3,991
Chatfield	291
Chauncey	1,117
Cherry Fork	176
Chesapeake	1,364
Cheshire	315
Chesterhill	361
Chesterville	264
Cheviot	11,135
Chickasaw	326
Chillicothe	24,842
Chillicothe West	1,122
Chilo	174
Chippewa-on-the-Lake	341
Christiansburg	724
Churchill	7,457
Cincinnati	452,524
Circleville	11,687
Clarington	338
Clarksburg	457
Clarksville	574
Clay Center	370
Clayton	773
Cleveland	750,903
Cleveland Heights	60,767
Cleves	2,044
Clifton	216
Clinton	1,335
Cloverdale	253
Clyde	5,503
Coal Grove	2,759
Coalton	550
Coldwater	3,533
College Corner	408
Columbiana	4,959
Columbus	539,677
Columbus Grove	2,290
Commercial Point	320
Conesville	448
Congress	205
Conneaut	14,552
Continental	1,185
Convoy	991
Coolville	672
Corning	838
Cortland	2,525
Corwin	346
Coshocton	13,747
Covedale	6,639
Covington	2,575
Craig Beach	1,451
Crestline	5,947
Creston	1,632
Cridersville	1,103
Crooksville	2,828
Crown City	371
Crystal Lakes	5,851
Cumberland	463
Custar	277
Cuyahoga Falls	49,678
Cuyahoga Heights	866
Cygnet	629
Dalton	1,177
Danville	1,025
Darbydale	743
Darbyville	229
Dayton	243,601
Deer Park	7,415
Deersville	91
Defiance	16,281
De Graff	1,117
Delaware	15,008
Dellroy	363
Delphos	7,608
Delta	2,544
Dennison	3,506
Deshler	1,938
Devola	1,989
Dexter City	178
Dillonvale	1,095
Donnelsville	278
Dover	11,516
Doylestown	2,373
Dresden	1,516
Dublin	681
Dunkirk	1,036
Dupont	302
East Alliance	1,175
East Canton	1,631
East Cleveland	39,600
East Liverpool	20,020
East Liverpool North	6,223
East Palestine	5,604
East Sparta	959
Eastlake	19,690
Eaton	6,020
Eaton Estates	2,076
Edgerton	2,126
Edgewood	2,437
Edison	569
Edon	803
Eldorado	483
Elgin	89
Elida	1,211
Elmore	1,316
Elmwood Place	3,525
Elyria	53,427
Empire	491
Englewood	7,885
Enon	1,929
Euclid	71,552
Evendale	1,967
Fairborn	32,267
Fairfax	2,705
Fairfield	14,680
Fairlawn	6,102
Fairport	3,665
Fairview	110
Fairview Park	21,681
Farmersville	865
Fayette	1,175
Fayetteville	415
Felicity	786
Findlay	35,800
Fletcher	539
Florida	285
Flushing	1,207
Forest	1,535
Forest Park	15,139
Fort Jennings	533
Fort Loramie	744
Fort McKinley	11,536
Fort Recovery	1,348
Fort Shawnee	3,436
Fostoria	16,037
Frankfort	948
Franklin	10,075
Frazeysburg	941
Fredericksburg	601
Fredericktown	1,935
Freeport	490
Fremont	18,490
Fulton	377
Fultonham	228
Gahanna	12,400
Galena	361
Galion	13,123
Gallipolis	7,490
Gambier	1,571
Gann	172
Garfield Heights	41,417
Garrettsville	1,718
Gates Mills	2,378
Geneva	6,449
Geneva-on-the-Lake	877
Genoa	2,139
Georgetown	2,949
Germantown	4,088
Gettysburg	526
Gibsonburg	2,585
Gilboa	212
Girard	14,119
Glandorf	732
Glendale	2,690
Glenford	177
Glenmont	266
Glenwillow	526
Gloria Glens Park	332
Glouster	2,121
Gnadenhutten	1,466
Golf Manor	5,170
Gordon	232
Goshen	1,174
Grafton	1,771
Grand Rapids	976
Grand River	613
Grandview Heights	8,460
Granville	3,963
Gratiot	232
Gratis	621
Graysville	97
Green Camp	537
Green Springs	1,279
Greenfield	4,780
Greenhills	6,092
Greenville	12,380
Greenwich	1,473
Grove City	13,911
Groveport	2,490
Grover Hill	536
Hamden	953
Hamersville	567
Hamilton	67,865
Hamler	681
Hanging Rock	278
Hanover	626
Hanoverton	483
Harbor View	238
Harpster	291
Harrisburg	556
Harrison	4,408
Harrisville	345
Harrod	533
Hartford	455
Hartville	1,752
Harveysburg	486
Haskins	549
Haviland	231
Hayesville	506
Heath	6,768
Hebron	1,699
Helena	298
Hemlock	199
Hicksville	3,461
Higginsport	383
Highland	243
Highland Heights	5,926
Hilliard	8,369
Hills and Dales	280
Hillsboro	5,584
Hiram	1,484
Holgate	1,541
Holland	1,108
Hollansburg	364
Holloway	488
Holmesville	412
Hopedale	916
Hoytville	403
Hubbard	8,583
Huber Heights	18,943
Hudson	3,933
Hunting Valley	797
Huntsville	475
Huron	6,896
Independence	7,034
Indian Hill	5,651
Irondale	602
Ironton	15,030
Ithaca	161
Jackson	6,843
Jackson Center	1,119
Jacksonburgh	92
Jacksonville	545
Jamestown	1,790
Jefferson (Ashtabula Co.)	2,472
Jefferson (Madison Co.)	3,664
Jeffersonville	1,031
Jenera	282
Jeromesville	559
Jerry City	470
Jerusalem	205
Jewett	901
Johnstown	3,208
Junction City	732
Kalida	900
Kelleys Island	175
Kent	28,183
Kenton	8,315
Kenwood	15,789
Kettering	69,599
Kettlersville	252
Killbuck	893
Kimbolton	247
Kingston	1,157
Kingsville	1,129
Kipton	353
Kirby	178
Kirkersville	578
Kirtland	5,530
Kirtland Hills	452
Knollwood	5,513
Lafayette	486
Lagrange	1,074
Lakeline	223
Lakemore	2,708
Lakeview	1,026
Lakewood	70,173
Lancaster	32,911
La Rue	867
Latty	269
Laura	464
Laurelville	624
Lawrenceville	687
Lebanon	7,934
Leesburg	984
Leesville	221
Leetonia	2,342
Leipsic	2,072
Leroy	715
Lewisburg	1,553
Lewisville	294
Lexington	2,972
Liberty Center	1,007
Lima	53,734
Limaville	303
Lincoln Heights	6,099
Lincoln Village	11,215
Lindsey	652
Linndale	145
Lisbon	3,521
Lithopolis	705
Lockbourne	420
Lockbourne Air Force Base	5,623
Lockington	242
Lockland	5,288
Lodi	2,399
Logan	6,269
London	6,481
Lorain	78,185
Lore City	401
Loudonville	2,865
Louisville	6,298
Loveland	7,144
Lowell	852
Lowellville	1,836
Lower Salem	106
Lucas	771
Luckey	996
Ludlow Falls	292
Lynchburg	1,186
Lyndhurst	19,749
Lyons	630
Macedonia	6,375
Macksburg	266
Madeira	6,713
Madison	1,678
Madison North	6,882
Magnetic Springs	349
Magnolia	1,064
Maineville	333
Malinta	391
Malta	1,017
Malvern	1,256
Manchester	2,195
Mansfield	55,047
Mantua	1,199
Maple Heights	34,093
Marble Cliff	676
Marblehead	726
Marengo	330
Mariemont	4,540
Marietta	16,861
Marion	38,646
Marion East	1,079
Marseilles	155
Marshallville	693
Martins Ferry	10,757
Martinsburg	234
Martinsville	500
Marysville	5,744
Mason	5,677
Massillon	32,539
Masury	2,060
Maumee	15,937
Mayfield	3,548
Mayfield Heights	22,139
McArthur	1,543
McClure	699
McComb	1,329
McConnelsville	2,107
McDonald	3,177
McGuffey	704
Mechanicsburg	1,686
Medina	10,913
Melrose	302
Mendon	672
Mentor	36,912
Mentor-on-the-Lake	6,517
Metamora	594
Meyers Lake	173
Miamisburg	14,797
Middleburg Heights	12,367
Middlefield	1,726
Middlepoint	543
Middleport	2,784
Middletown	48,767
Midland	388
Midvale	636
Midway	318
Mifflin	215
Milan	1,405
Milford	4,828
Milford Center	753
Millbury	771
Milledgeville	207
Miller City	206
Millersburg	2,979
Millersport	777
Millville	697
Milton Center	244
Miltonsburg	68
Mineral City	860
Minerva	4,359
Minerva Park	1,402
Mingo Junction	5,278
Minster	2,405
Mogadore	3,858
Monroe	3,492
Monroeville	1,455
Montezuma	260
Montgomery	5,683
Montpelier	4,184
Moraine	4,898
Moreland Hills	3,000
Morral	452
Morristown	385
Morrow	1,486
Moscow	348
Mount Blanchard	473
Mount Cory	302
Mount Eaton	242
Mount Gilead	2,971
Mount Healthy	7,446
Mount Orab	1,306
Mount Pleasant	635
Mount Sterling	1,536
Mount Vernon	13,373
Mount Victory	633
Mowrystown	465
Munroe Falls	3,794
Murray City	562
Mutual	177
Napoleon	7,791
Nashville	221
Navarre	1,607
Nellie	140
Nelsonville	4,812
Nevada	917
Neville	179
New Albany	513
New Alexandria	425
New Athens	450
New Bavaria	149
New Bloomington	343
New Boston	3,325
New Bremen	2,185
New Carlisle	6,112
New Concord	2,318
New Holland	796
New Knoxville	852
New Lebanon	4,248
New Lexington	4,921
New London	2,336
New Madison	959
New Matamoras	940
New Miami	3,273
New Middletown	1,664
New Paris	1,692
New Philadelphia	15,184
New Richmond	2,650
New Riegel	340
New Rome	104
New Straitsville	947
New Vienna	849
New Washington	1,251
New Waterford	735
New Weston	174
Newark	41,836
Newburgh Heights	3,396
Newcomerstown	4,155
Newton Falls	5,378
Newtonsville	385
Newtown	2,047
Ney	378
Niles	21,581
North Baltimore	3,143
North Bend	638
North Canton	15,228
North College Hill	12,363
North Fairfield	540
North Hampton	489
North Kingsville	2,458
North Lewisburg	840
North Mount Vernon-Academia	1,447
North Olmsted	34,861
North Perry	851
North Randall	1,212
North Ridgeville	13,152
North Robinson	277
North Royalton	12,807
North Star	296
North Zanesville	3,399
Northfield	1,089
Northridge (Clark Co.)	12
Northridge (Montgomery Co.)	10,084
Northwood	4,222
Norton	12,308
Norwalk	13,386
Norwich	163
Norwood	30,420
Oak Harbor	2,807
Oak Hill	1,642
Oakwood (Montgomery Co.)	10,095
Oakwood (Cuyahoga Co.)	3,127
Oakwood (Paulding Co.)	804
Oberlin	8,761
Obetz	2,248
Octa	96
Ohio City	816
Old Washington	346
Olmsted Falls	2,504
Ontario	4,345

Orange 2,112
Orangeville 268
Oregon 16,563
Orient 313
Orrville 7,408
Orwell 965
Osgood 289
Ostrander 399
Ottawa 3,622
Ottawa Hills 4,270
Ottoville 914
Otway 177
Overlook-Page Manor 19,596
Owensville 707
Oxford 15,868
Page Manor, see Overlook-Page Manor
Painesville 16,536
Painesville Southwest 5,461
Palestine 246
Pandora 857
Parma 100,216
Parma Heights 27,192
Parral 271
Pataskala 1,831
Patterson 201
Paulding 2,983
Payne 1,351
Peebles 1,629
Pemberville 1,301
Peninsula 692
Pepper Pike 5,933
Perry 917
Perrysburg 7,693
Perrysville 752
Phillipsburg 831
Philo 846
Pickerington 696
Piketon 1,347
Pioneer 968
Piqua 20,741
Pitsburg 462
Plain City 2,254
Plainfield 183
Pleasant City 494
Pleasant Hill 1,025
Pleasant Plain 223
Pleasantville 754
Plymouth 1,993
Poland 3,097
Polk 435
Pomeroy 2,672
Port Clinton 7,202
Port Jefferson 416
Port Washington 550
Port William 323
Portage 494
Portsmouth 27,633
Potsdam 311
Powell 374
Powhatan Point 2,167
Proctorville 881
Prospect 1,031
Put-in-Bay 135
Quaker City 510
Quincy 686
Racine 583
Rarden 232
Ravenna 11,780
Rawson 466
Rayland 617
Reading 14,303
Reminderville 215
Rendville 82
Reno Beach 1,049
Republic 705
Reynoldsburg 13,921
Richfield 3,228
Richmond 777
Richmond Heights 9,220
Richwood 2,072
Ridgeway 379
Rio Grande 814
Ripley 2,745
Rising Sun 730
Rittman 6,308
Riverlea 558
Riverside 447
Rochester 210
Rock Creek 731
Rockford 1,207
Rocky Ridge 385
Rocky River 22,958
Rogers 310
Rome 90
Rosemount 1,786
Roseville 1,767
Ross 1,661
Rossburg 275
Rossford 5,302
Roswell 317
Rushsylvania 526
Rushville 289
Russells Point 1,104
Russellville 399
Russia 420
Rutland 663
Sabina 2,160
St. Bernard 6,080
St. Clairsville 4,754
St. Henry 1,276
St. Louisville 385
St. Martin 148
St. Marys 7,699
St. Paris 1,646
Salem 14,186
Salesville 154
Salineville 1,686
Sandusky 32,674
Sandusky South 8,501
Sarahsville 181
Sardinia 824
Savannah 361
Scio 1,002
Scott 329
Seaman 866
Sebring 4,954
Senecaville 497
Seven Hills 12,700
Seven Mile 699
Seville 1,402
Shadyside 5,070
Shaker Heights 36,306
Sharon West 3,120
Sharonville 10,985
Shawnee 914
Shawnee Hills 428
Sheffield 1,730
Sheffield Lake 8,734
Shelby 9,847
Sherrodsville 400
Sherwood 784
Shiloh (Montgomery Co.) 11,368
Shiloh (Richland Co.) 817
Shreve 1,635
Sidney 16,332
Silver Lake 3,637
Silverton 6,588
Sinking Spring 178
Smithfield 1,245
Smithville 1,278
Solon 11,519
Somerset 1,417
Somerville 388
South Amherst 2,913
South Bloomfield 610
South Charleston 1,500
South Euclid 29,579
South Lebanon 3,014
South Mount Vernon 1,044
South Point 2,243
South Russell 2,673
South Salem 209
South Solon 415
South Webster 825
South Zanesville 1,436
Sparta 213
Spencer 758
Spencerville 2,241
Spring Valley 667
Springboro 2,799
Springdale 8,127
Springfield 81,926
Stafford 120
Steubenville 30,771
Stockport 471
Stone Creek 171
Stony Prairie 1,913
Stoutsville 573
Stow 19,847
Strasburg 1,874
Stratton 386
Streetsboro 7,966
Strongsville 15,182
Struthers 15,343
Stryker 1,296
Sugar Bush Knolls 119
Sugar Grove 469
Sugarcreek 1,771
Summerfield 306
Summitville 143
Sunbury 2,512
Swanton 2,927
Sycamore 1,096
Sylvania 12,031
Syracuse 684
Tallmadge 15,274
Tarlton 412
Terrace Park 2,266
The Plains 1,568
Thornville 679
Thurston 428
Tiffin 21,596
Tiltonsville 2,123
Timberlake 964
Tipp City 5,090
Tiro 310
Toledo 383,818
Tontogany 395
Toronto 7,705
Tremont City 426
Trenton 5,278
Trimble 542
Trotwood 6,997
Troy 17,186
Tuscarawas 830
Twinsburg 6,432
Uhrichsville 5,731
Union 3,654
Union City 1,808
Unionville Center 255
Uniopolis 291
University Heights 17,055
Upper Arlington 38,630
Upper Sandusky 5,645
Urbana 11,237
Urbancrest 754
Utica 1,977
Valley View (Cuyahoga Co.) 1,422
Valley View (Franklin Co.) 909
Van Buren 319
Van Wert 11,320
Vandalia 10,796
Vanlue 539
Venedocia 202
Vermilion 9,872
Verona 593
Versailles 2,441
Vienna 545
Vinton 352
Wadsworth 13,142
Waite Hill 514
Wakeman 822
Walbridge 3,208
Waldo 428
Walton Hills 2,508
Wapakoneta 7,324
Warren 63,494
Warrensville Heights 18,925
Warsaw 725
Washington 12,495
Washingtonville 747
Waterville 2,940
Wauseon 4,932
Waverly 4,858
Wayne 921
Waynesburg 1,337
Waynesfield 704
Waynesville 1,638
Wellington 4,137
Wellston 5,410
Wellsville 5,891
West Alexandria 1,553
West Carrollton 10,748
West Elkton 291
West Farmington 650
West Lafayette 1,719
West Leipsic 378
West Liberty 1,580
West Manchester 469
West Mansfield 753
West Millgrove 215
West Milton 3,696
West Portsmouth 3,396
West Rushville 189
West Salem 1,058
West Union 1,951
West Unity 1,589
West View 2,523
Westerville 12,530
Westlake 15,689
Weston 1,269
Wharton 422
Wheelersburg 3,709
Whitehall 25,263
Whitehouse 1,542
Wickliffe 21,354
Wilkesville 181
Willard 5,510
Williamsburg 2,054
Williamsport 857
Willoughby 18,634
Willoughby Hills 5,247
Willowick 21,237
Willshire 623
Wilmington 10,051
Wilmot 378
Wilson 133
Winchester 760
Windham 3,360
Wintersville 4,921
Woodlawn 3,251
Woodmere 976
Woodsfield 3,239
Woodstock 281
Woodville 1,834
Woodworth 1,054
Wooster 18,703
Worthington 15,326
Wren 282
Wright-Patterson 10,151
Wyoming 9,089
Xenia 25,373
Yankee Lake 43
Yellow Springs 4,624
Yorkshire 151
Yorkville 1,656
Youngstown 139,788
Zaleski 304
Zanesfield 272
Zanesville 33,045
Zoar 228

OKLAHOMA Total population: 2,559,253

METROPOLITAN AREAS

Lawton 108,144
Oklahoma City 640,889
Tulsa 475,991

COUNTIES

Adair 15,141
Alfalfa 7,224
Atoka 10,972
Beaver 6,282
Beckham 15,754
Blaine 11,794
Bryan 25,552
Caddo 28,931
Canadian 32,245
Carter 37,349
Cherokee 23,174
Choctaw 15,141
Cimarron 4,145
Cleveland 81,839
Coal 5,525
Comanche 108,144
Cotton 6,832
Craig 14,722
Creek 45,532
Custer 22,665
Delaware 17,767
Dewey 5,656
Ellis 5,129
Garfield 55,365
Garvin 24,874
Grady 29,354
Grant 7,117
Greer 7,979
Harmon 5,136
Harper 5,151
Haskell 9,578
Hughes 13,228
Jackson 30,902
Jefferson 7,125
Johnston 7,870
Kay 48,791
Kingfisher 12,857
Kiowa 12,532
Latimer 8,601
Le Flore 32,137
Lincoln 19,482
Logan 19,645
Love 5,637
Major 7,529
Marshall 7,682
Mayes 23,302
McClain 14,157
McCurtain 28,642
McIntosh 12,472
Murray 10,669
Muskogee 59,542
Noble 10,043
Nowata 9,773
Okfuskee 10,683
Oklahoma 526,805
Okmulgee 35,358
Osage 29,750
Ottawa 29,800
Pawnee 11,338
Payne 50,654
Pittsburg 37,521
Pontotoc 27,867
Pottawatomie 43,134
Pushmataha 9,385
Roger Mills 4,452
Rogers 28,425
Seminole 25,144
Sequoyah 23,370
Stephens 35,902
Texas 16,352
Tillman 12,901
Tulsa 401,663
Wagoner 22,163
Washington 42,277
Washita 12,141
Woods 11,920
Woodward 15,537

PLACES

Achille 382
Ada 14,859
Adair 459
Addington 123
Afton 1,022
Agra 335
Albion 186
Alderson 215
Alex 492
Aline 260
Allen 974
Altus 23,302
Alva 7,440
Ames 227
Amorita 63
Anadarko 6,682
Antlers 2,685
Apache 1,421
Arapaho 531
Ardmore 20,881
Arkoma 2,098
Arnett 711
Asher 437
Ashland 73
Atoka 3,346
Avant 439
Avard 59
Barnsdall 1,579
Bartlesville 29,683
Beaver 1,853
Beggs 1,107
Bennington 288
Bernice 189
Bessie 210
Bethany 21,785
Bethel Acres 1,083
Big Cabin 198
Billings 618
Binger 730
Bixby 3,973
Blackburn 88
Blackwell 8,645
Blair 1,114
Blanchard 1,580
Bluejacket 234
Boise City 1,993
Bokchito 607
Bokoshe 588
Boley 514
Boswell 755
Boynton 522
Bradley 247
Braggs 325
Braman 295
Breckenridge 70
Bridgeport 142
Brinkman 7
Bristow 4,653
Broken Arrow 11,787
Broken Bow 2,980
Bromide 231
Bryant 86
Buffalo 1,579
Burbank 188
Burlington 165
Burns Flat 988
Butler 315
Byars 247
Byron 72
Cache 1,106
Caddo 886
Calera 1,063
Calumet 386
Calvin 359
Camargo 236
Cameron 311
Canadian 304
Caney 200
Canton 844
Canute 420
Capron 80
Carmen 519
Carnegie 1,723
Carney 396
Carter 311
Cashion 329
Castle 212
Catoosa 970
Cement 892
Centrahoma 155
Centralia 43
Chandler 2,529
Chattanooga 302
Checotah 3,074
Chelsea 1,622
Cherokee 2,119
Cheyenne 892
Chickasha 14,194
Choctaw 4,750
Chouteau 1,046
Claremore 9,084
Clayton 718
Cleo Springs 344
Cleveland 2,573
Clinton 8,513
Coalgate 1,859
Colbert 814
Colcord 438
Collinsville 3,009
Comanche 1,862
Commerce 2,593
Cooperton 55
Copan 558
Corn 409
Cornish 90
Council Hill 135
Covington 605
Coweta 2,457
Cowlington 751
Coyle 303
Crescent 1,568
Cromwell 287
Crowder 339
Cushing 7,529
Custer City 486
Cyril 1,302
Dacoma 226
Davenport 831
Davidson 515
Davis 2,223
Deer Creek 203
Del City 27,133
Delaware 534
Depew 739
Devol 129
Dewar 933
Dewey 3,958
Dibble 184
Dickson 798
Dill City 578
Disney 303
Dougherty 211
Douglas 79
Driftwood 27
Drummond 326
Drumright 2,931
Duke 486
Duncan 19,718
Durant 11,118
Dustin 502
Eakly 228
Earlsboro 248
Edmond 16,633
Eldorado 737
Elgin 840
Elk City 7,323
Elmer 138
Elmore City 653
El Reno 14,510
Empire 23
Enid 44,008
Erick 1,285
Eufaula 2,355
Fair Oaks 23
Fairfax 1,889
Fairland 814
Fairmont 154
Fairview 2,894
Fallis 39
Fanshaw 199
Fargo 262
Faxon 121
Fletcher 950
Foraker 52
Forest Park 835
Forgan 496
Fort Cobb 722
Fort Gibson 1,418
Fort Sill 21,217
Fort Supply 550
Fort Towson 430
Foss 150
Foyil 164
Francis 283
Frederick 6,132
Freedom 292
Gage 536
Gans 238
Garber 1,011
Garvin 117
Gate 151
Geary 1,380
Gene Autry 120
Geronimo 587
Gerty 139
Glencoe 421
Glenpool 770
Goldsby 298
Goltry 287
Goodwell 1,467
Gore 478
Gotebo 376
Gould 368
Gracemont 424
Grainola 66
Grand Lake Towne 23
Grandfield 1,524
Granite 1,808
Grant 273
Grayson 142
Greenfield 143
Grove 2,000
Guthrie 9,575
Guymon 7,674
Haileyville 928
Hall Park 163
Hallett 125
Hammon 677
Hanna 181
Hardesty 223
Hardy 5
Harrah 1,931
Hartshorne 2,121
Haskell 2,063
Hastings 184
Haworth 293
Headrick 139
Healdton 2,324
Heavener 2,566
Helena 769
Hendrix 117
Hennessey 2,181
Henryetta 6,430
Hickory 62
Hillsdale 77
Hinton 889
Hitchcock 160
Hitchita 160
Hobart 4,638
Hoffman 262
Holdenville 5,181
Hollis 3,150
Hollister 105
Hominy 2,274
Hooker 1,615
Howe 403
Hugo 6,585
Hulbert 505
Hunter 274
Hydro 805
Idabel 5,946
Indiahoma 434
Indianola 205
Ingersoll 17
Inola 948
Jay 1,594
Jefferson 128
Jenks 1,997
Jennings 338
Jet 317
Jones 1,666
Kansas 317
Kaw City 283
Kellyville 685
Kemp 153
Kendrick 126
Kenefick 153
Keota 685
Ketchum 238
Keyes 569
Kiefer 803
Kildare 79
Kingfisher 4,042
Kingston 710
Kinta 247
Kiowa 754
Knowles 52
Konawa 1,719
Krebs 1,515
Kremlin 200
Lahoma 299
Lake Aluma 124
Lamar 153
Lambert 16
Lamont 478
Langley 481
Langston 486
Laverne 1,373
Lawton 74,470
Leedey 465
Le Flore 175
Lehigh 296
Lenapah 325
Leon 112
Lexington 1,516
Lima 238
Lindsay 3,705
Little City 80
Loco 193
Locust Grove 1,090
Lone Grove 1,240
Lone Wolf 584
Longdale 331
Lookeba 165
Lotsee 16
Loveland 36
Lovell 28
Loyal 107
Luther 836
Macomb 41
Madill 2,875
Manchester 165
Mangum 4,066
Manitou 308
Mannford 892
Mannsville 364
Maramec 128
Marble City 299
Marietta 2,013
Marland 236
Marlow 3,995
Marshall 420
Martha 268
Maud 1,143
May 91
Maysville 1,380
McAlester 18,802
McBride 44
McCurtain 575
McLoud 2,159
Medford 1,304
Meeker 683
Meno 119
Meridian 104
Miami 13,880
Midwest City 48,114
Milburn 275
Mill Creek 234
Minco 1,129
Moffett 312
Moore 18,761
Mooreland 1,196
Morris 1,119
Morrison 421
Mounds 766
Mountain Park 458
Mountain View 1,110
Muldrow 1,680
Mulhall 250
Muskogee 37,331
Mustang 2,637
Mutual 94
Nardin 135
Nash 294
New Alluwe 116
New Castle 1,271
New Cordell 3,261
New Prue 202
New Tulsa 17
New Woodville 118
Newkirk 2,173
Nichols Hills 4,478
Nicoma Park 2,560
Noble 2,241
Norman 52,117
North Enid 730
North Miami 503
Nowata 3,679
Oakland 317
Oaks 219
Oakwood 129
Ochelata 330
Oilton 1,087
Okarche 826

OKLAHOMA, Continued

Okay 419
Okeene 1,421
Okemah 2,913
Oklahoma City 366,481
Okmulgee 15,180
Oktaha 193
Olustee 819
Oolagah 458
Optima 103
Orlando 202
Osage 170
Owasso 3,491
Paden 442
Panama 1,121
Paoli 480
Pauls Valley 5,769
Pawhuska 4,238
Pawnee 2,443
Peggs 82
Pensacola 56
Peoria 179
Perkins 1,029
Perry 5,341
Phillips 106
Picher 2,363
Piedmont 269
Pittsburg 282
Pocola 1,840
Ponca City 25,940
Pond Creek 903
Porter 624
Porum 658
Poteau 5,500
Prague 1,802
Pryor 7,057
Purcell 4,076
Putnam 84
Quapaw 967
Quay 41
Quinlan 81
Quinton 1,262
Ralston 443
Ramona 600
Randlett 384
Ratliff City 250
Ravia 373
Red Bird 230
Red Oak 609
Red Rock 233
Renfrow 39
Rentiesville 96
Reydon 215
Ringling 1,206
Ringwood 241
Ripley 307
Rocky 260
Roff 632
Roland 827
Roosevelt 353
Rosedale 98
Rosston 56
Rush Springs 1,381
Ryan 1,011
St. Louis 207
Salina 1,024
Sallisaw 4,888
Sand Springs 11,519
Sapulpa 15,159
Sasakwa 321
Savanna 948
Sayre 2,712
Scullin 9
Seiling 1,033
Seminole 7,878
Sentinel 984
Shamrock 204
Sharon 155
Shattuck 1,546
Shawnee 25,075
Shidler 717
Skedee 117
Skiatook 2,930
Slick 171
Smith Village 93
Smithville 144
Snyder 1,671
Soper 322
South Coffeyville 646
Sparks 183
Spavinaw 470
Spencer 3,603
Sperry 1,123
Spiro 2,057
Springer 256
Springlake Park 14
Sterling 675
Stidham 53
Stigler 2,347
Stillwater 31,126
Stilwell 2,134
Stonewall 653
Strang 164
Stratford 1,278
Stringtown 397
Strong City 40
Stroud 2,502
Stuart 294
Sugden 54
Sulphur 5,158
Sumner 16
Swink 88
Taft 525
Tahlequah 9,254
Talala 163
Talihina 1,227
Taloga 363
Tamaha 83
Tecumseh 4,451
Temple 1,354
Terlton 111
Terral 636
Texhoma 921
Texola 144
Thackerville 257
The Village 13,695
Thomas 1,336
Tipton 1,206
Tishomingo 2,663
Tonkawa 3,337
Tryon 301
Tullahassee 183
Tulsa 331,638
Tupelo 485
Tuttle 1,640
Tyrone 588
Uncas 53
Union City 306
Valley Brook 2,869
Valliant 840
Velma 611
Vera 215
Verden 439
Vian 1,131
Vici 694
Vinita 5,847
Wagoner 4,959
Wainwright 135
Wakita 426
Walters 2,611
Wanette 303
Wann 135
Wapanucka 425
Warner 1,217
Warr Acres 9,887
Warwick 146
Washington 322
Washunga 25
Watonga 3,696
Watts 326
Waukomis 241
Waurika 1,833
Wayne 618
Waynoka 1,444
Weatherford 7,959
Webb City 186
Webbers Falls 485
Welch 651
Weleetka 1,199
Wellston 789
West Siloam Springs 210
Westville 934
Wetumka 1,687
Wewoka 5,284
Wilburton 2,280
Willow 188
Wilson 1,569
Wister 927
Woodlawn Park 220
Woodward 8,710
Wright City 1,068
Wyandotte 297
Wynnewood 2,374
Wynona 547
Yale 1,239
Yeager 107
Yukon 8,411

OREGON Total population: 2,091,385

METROPOLITAN AREAS

Eugene-Springfield 213,358
Portland 1,009,129
(880,675 in Oregon, 128,454 in Washington)
Salem 186,658

COUNTIES

Baker 14,919
Benton 53,776
Clackamas 166,088
Clatsop 28,473
Columbia 28,790
Coos 56,515
Crook 9,985
Curry 13,006
Deschutes 30,442
Douglas 71,743
Gilliam 2,342
Grant 6,996
Harney 7,215
Hood River 13,187
Jackson 94,533
Jefferson 8,548
Josephine 35,746
Klamath 50,021
Lake 6,343
Lane 213,358
Lincoln 25,755
Linn 71,914
Malheur 23,169
Marion 151,309
Morrow 4,465
Multnomah 556,667
Polk 35,349
Sherman 2,139
Tillamook 17,930
Umatilla 44,923
Union 19,377
Wallowa 6,247
Wasco 20,133
Washington 157,920
Wheeler 1,849
Yamhill 40,213

PLACES

Adams 219
Albany 18,181
Altamont 15,746
Amity 708
Antelope 51
Arlington 375
Ashland 12,342
Astoria 10,244
Athena 872
Aumsville 590
Aurora 306
Baker 9,354
Bandon 1,832
Banks 430
Barlow 105
Barview 1,388
Bay City 898
Beaverton 18,577
Bend 13,710
Boardman 192
Bonanza 230
Brookings 2,720
Brownsville 1,034
Bunker Hill 1,549
Burns 3,293
Butte Falls 358
Canby 3,813
Cannon Beach 779
Canyon City 600
Canyonville 940
Carlton 1,126
Cascade Locks 574
Cave Junction 415
Central Point 4,004
Central Point West 1,988
Chenoweth 2,329
Chiloquin 826
City of the Dalles 10,423
Clatskanie 1,286
Coburg 665
Columbia City 537
Condon 973
Coos Bay 13,466
Coquille 4,437
Cornelius 1,903
Corvallis 35,153
Cottage Grove 6,004
Cove 363
Creswell 1,199
Culver 407
Dallas 6,361
Dayton 949
Dayville 197
Detroit 328
Donald 231
Drain 1,204
Drewsey 22
Dufur 493
Dundee 588
Dunes 976
Durham 410
Eagle Point 1,241
Eastside 1,331
Echo 479
Elgin 1,375
Elkton 176
Enterprise 1,680
Estacada 1,164
Eugene 76,346
Fairview 1,045
Falcon Heights 1,389
Falls City 745
Florence 2,246
Forest Grove 8,275
Fossil 511
Four Corners 6,199
Freewater, see Milton-Freewater
Fruitdale 2,655
Garibaldi 1,083
Gaston 429
Gates 250
Gearhart 829
Gervais 746
Gladstone 6,237
Glendale 709
Gold Beach 1,554
Gold Hill 603
Granite 4
Grants Pass 12,455
Grants Pass Southwest 3,431
Grass Valley 153
Green 1,612
Gresham 9,875
Haines 212
Halfway 317
Halsey 467
Hammond 500
Happy Valley 1,392
Hardman 19
Harrisburg 1,311
Hayesville 5,518
Helix 152
Heppner 1,429
Hermiston 4,893
Hillsboro 14,675
Hines 1,407
Hood River 3,991
Hubbard 975
Huntington 507
Idanha 382
Imbler 139
Independence 2,594
Ione 355
Irrigon 261
Island City 202
Jacksonville 1,611
Jefferson 936
John Day 1,566
Jordan Valley 196
Joseph 839
Junction City 2,373
Juntura 56
Keizer 11,405
King 1,427
Klamath Falls 15,775
Lafayette 786
La Grande 9,645
Lake Oswego 14,573
Lakeview 2,705
Lebanon 6,636
Lebanon South 2,229
Lexington 230
Lincoln City 4,198
Lonerock 12
Long Creek 196
Lostine 196
Lowell 567
Lyons 645
Madras 1,689
Malin 486
Manzanita 261
Maupin 428
May Park 1,466
Maywood Park 1,230
McMinnville 10,125
McNulty 1,017
Medford 28,454
Medford West 3,919
Merrill 722
Metolius 270
Mill City 1,451
Milton-Freewater 4,105
Milwaukie 16,379
Mitchell 196
Molalla 2,005
Monmouth 5,237
Monroe 443
Monument 161
Moro 290
Mosier 217
Mount Angel 1,973
Mount Vernon 423
Myrtle Creek 2,733
Myrtle Creek South 1,039
Myrtle Point 2,511
Nehalem 241
Newberg 6,507
Newport 5,188
North Bend 8,553
North Powder 304
Nyssa 2,620
Oakland 1,010
Oakridge 3,422
Ontario 6,523
Oregon City 9,176
Paisley 260
Pendleton 13,197
Philomath 1,688
Phoenix 1,287
Pilot Rock 1,612
Port Orford 1,037
Portland 382,619
Powers 842
Prairie City 867
Prescott 105
Prineville 4,101
Rainier 1,731
Redmond 3,721
Reedsport 4,039
Richland 133
Riddle 1,042
Rockaway 665
Rogue River 841
Roseburg 14,461
Rufus 317
St. Helens 6,212
St. Paul 347
Salem 68,296
Sandy 1,544
Scappoose 1,859
Scio 447
Scotts Mills 208
Seaside 4,402
Shaniko 58
Sheridan 1,881
Sherwood 1,396
Siletz 596
Silverton 4,301
Sisters 516
Sodaville 125
South Medford 3,497
Spray 161
Springfield 27,047
Stanfield 891
Stayton 3,170
Sublimity 634
Summerville 76
Sumpter 120
Sutherlin 3,070
Sweet Home 3,799
Talent 1,389
Tigard 5,302
Tillamook 3,968
Toledo 2,818
Troutdale 575
Tualatin 750
Turner 846
Umatilla 679
Union 1,531
Vale 1,448
Veneta 1,377
Vernonia 1,643
Waldport 700
Wallowa 811
Warrenton 1,825
Wasco 412
Waterloo 186
West Linn 7,091
Westfall 0
Weston 660
Wheeler 262
Willamina 1,193
Winston 2,468
Wood Village 1,533
Woodburn 7,495
Yachats 441
Yamhill 516
Yoncalla 675

PENNSYLVANIA Total population: 11,793,909

METROPOLITAN AREAS

Allentown-Bethlehem-Easton 543,642
(469,672 in Pennsylvania, 73,960 in New Jersey)
Altoona 135,356
Erie 263,654
Harrisburg 410,505
Johnstown 262,822
Lancaster 320,079
Philadelphia 4,820,915
(3,868,811 in Pennsylvania, 952,104 in New Jersey)
Pittsburgh 2,401,362
Reading 296,382
Scranton 234,107
Wilkes-Barre-Hazleton 342,301
Williamsport 113,296
York 329,540

COUNTIES

Adams 56,937
Allegheny 1,605,133
Armstrong 75,590
Beaver 208,418
Bedford 42,353
Berks 296,382
Blair 135,356
Bradford 57,962
Bucks 415,056
Butler 127,941
Cambria 186,785
Cameron 7,096
Carbon 50,573
Centre 99,267
Chester 278,311
Clarion 38,414
Clearfield 74,619
Clinton 37,721
Columbia 55,114
Crawford 81,342
Cumberland 158,177
Dauphin 223,713
Delaware 601,425
Elk 37,770
Erie 263,654
Fayette 154,667
Forest 4,926
Franklin 100,833
Fulton 10,776
Greene 36,090
Huntingdon 39,108
Indiana 79,451
Jefferson 43,695
Juniata 16,712
Lackawanna 234,107
Lancaster 320,079
Lawrence 107,374
Lebanon 99,665
Lehigh 255,304
Luzerne 342,301
Lycoming 113,296
McKean 51,915
Mercer 127,225
Mifflin 45,268
Monroe 45,422
Montgomery 623,921
Montour 16,508
Northampton 214,368
Northumberland 99,190
Perry 28,615
Philadelphia 1,950,098
Pike 11,818
Potter 16,395
Schuylkill 160,089
Snyder 29,269
Somerset 76,037
Sullivan 5,961
Susquehanna 34,344
Tioga 39,691
Union 28,603
Venango 62,353
Warren 47,682
Washington 210,876
Wayne 29,581
Westmoreland 376,935
Wyoming 19,082
York 272,603

PLACES

Abbottstown 552
Abington 8,594
Adamsburg 251
Adamstown 1,202
Addison 370
Akron 3,149
Alba 184
Albion 1,768
Alburtis 1,142
Aldan 5,001
Alexandria 495
Aliquippa 22,277
Allenport 762
Allentown 109,527
Allison 1,040
Almedia 1,157
Altoona 63,115
Ambler 7,800
Ambridge 11,324
Annville 4,704
Apollo 2,308
Applewold 515
Archbald 6,118
Ardmore 5,801
Ardsley, see North Hills-Ardsley
Arendtsville 589
Arlington Heights-Pocono Park 1,777
Armagh 165
Arnold 8,174
Arnold City, see Fairhope-Arnold City
Arona 453
Ashland 4,737
Ashley 4,095
Ashville 409
Aspinwall 3,541
Atglen 740
Athens 4,173
Atlas 1,527
Atwood 123
Auburn 895
Austin 626
Avalon 7,010
Avella 1,109
Avis 1,749
Avoca 3,543
Avon 1,271
Avondale 1,025
Avonmore 1,267
Baden 5,536
Bala Cynwyd 6,483
Baldwin 26,729
Bally 1,197
Bangor 5,425
Barkeyville 218
Barnesboro 2,708
Bath 1,829
Beallsville 434
Bear Lake 281
Beaver 6,100
Beaver Falls 14,375
Beaver Meadows 1,274
Beaverdale-Lloydell 1,579
Beavertown 783
Bechtelsville 728
Bedford 3,302
Beech Creek 639
Bell Acres 1,264
Belle Vernon 1,496
Bellefonte 6,828
Belleville 1,817
Bellevue 11,586
Bellwood 2,395
Ben Avon 2,713
Ben Avon Heights 443
Bendersville 528
Benson 297
Bentleyville 2,714
Benton 1,027
Berlin 1,766
Bernville 848
Berrysburg 443
Berwick 12,274
Bessemer 1,427
Bethany 267
Bethel Park 34,791
Bethlehem 72,686
Big Beaver 2,739
Big Run 826
Biglerville 977
Birdsboro 3,196
Birmingham 115
Black Lick 1,074
Blain 287
Blairsville 4,411
Blakely 6,391
Blandon 1,113
Blawnox 1,907
Bloomfield 1,032
Blooming Valley 358
Bloomsburg 11,652
Blossburg 1,753
Bobtown 1,055
Boiling Springs 1,521
Bolivar 668
Bonneauville 819
Boswell 1,529
Bowmanstown 864
Boyertown 4,428
Brackenridge 4,796
Braddock 8,795
Braddock Hills 2,459
Bradford 12,672
Bradford Woods 970
Brandywine Village 11,411
Brentwood 13,732
Briar Creek 456
Bridgeport 5,630
Bridgeville 6,717
Bridgewater 966
Brisbin 364
Bristol 12,085
Broad Top City 283
Brockway 2,529
Brookhaven 7,370
Brookville 4,314
Brownstown 1,035
Brownsville 4,856
Bruin 673
Bryn Athyn 970
Bryn Mawr 5,737
Buffington, see New Salem-Buffington
Burgettstown 2,118
Burlington 148
Burnham 2,607
Burnside 316
Butler 18,691
California 6,635
Callensburg 249
Callery 416
Calumet-Norvelt 2,588
Cambridge Springs 1,998
Camp Hill 9,931
Campbelltown 1,355
Canonsburg 11,439
Canton 2,037
Carbondale 12,808
Carlisle 18,079
Carlisle Barracks 4,358
Carmichaels 608
Carnegie 10,864
Carnot-Moon 13,093
Carrolltown 1,507
Cassandra 250
Casselman 114
Cassville 205
Castle Shannon 11,899
Catasauqua 5,702
Catawissa 1,701
Cedar Heights 6,303
Cedarbrook-Melrose Park 9,980
Centerport 227
Centerville (Crawford Co.) 246
Centerville (Washington Co.) 4,175
Central City 1,547
Centralia 1,165
Centre Hall 1,282
Chalfant 1,370
Chalfont 2,366
Chambersburg 17,315
Chapman 191
Charleroi 6,723
Chatwood 7,168
Cherry Tree 485
Cherry Valley 73
Chest Springs 178
Chester 56,331
Chester Heights 749

Chester Hill 868
Cheswick 2,580
Chevy Chase Heights 1,185
Chicora 1,166
Christiana 1,132
Churchill 4,690
Clairton 15,051
Clarendon 735
Clarion 6,095
Clark 467
Clarks Green 1,674
Clarks Summit 5,376
Clarksville 269
Claysburg 1,516
Claysville 951
Clearfield 8,176
Cleona 2,040
Clifton Heights 8,348
Clintonville 321
Clymer 2,054
Coal Center 317
Coaldale (Bedford Co.) 174
Coaldale (Schuylkill Co.) 3,023
Coalmont 129
Coalport 796
Coatesville 12,331
Cochranton 1,229
Cokeburg 845
Collegeville 3,191
Collingdale 10,605
Columbia 11,237
Colver 1,175
Colwyn 3,169
Confluence 954
Conneaut Lake 745
Conneautville 1,032
Connellsville 11,643
Connoquenessing 553
Conshohocken 10,195
Conway 2,822
Conyngham 1,850
Coopersburg 2,326
Cooperstown 478
Coplay 3,642
Coraopolis 8,435
Cornwall 2,111
Corry 7,435
Corsica 374
Coudersport 2,831
Courtdale 1,027
Crabtree 1,021
Crafton 8,233
Cranesville 705
Creekside 425
Cresson 2,446
Cressona 1,814
Cross Roads 163
Curtisville 1,337
Curwensville 3,189
Daisytown 371
Dale 2,274
Dallas 2,913
Dallastown 3,560
Dalton 1,282
Danville 6,176
Darby 13,729
Darlington 344
Dauphin 998
Dawson 676
Dayton 715
Deemston 711
Deer Lake 347
Delaware Water Gap 533
Delmont 1,934
Delta 778
Denver 2,248
Derry 3,338
Dickson City 7,698
Dillsburg 1,441
Donegal 255
Donora 8,825
Dormont 12,856
Dover 1,168
Downingtown 7,437
Doylestown 8,270
Dravosburg 2,916
Drifton, see Woodside-Drifton
Driftwood 184
Dublin 657
Du Bois 10,112
Duboistown 1,468
Dudley 232
Dunbar 1,499
Duncannon 1,739
Duncansville 1,427
Dunlevy 405
Dunmore 17,300
Dupont 3,431
Duquesne 11,410
Duryea 5,264
Dushore 718
Eagles Mere 157
East Bangor 905
East Berlin 1,086
East Berwick 2,090
East Brady 1,218
East Butler 919
East Conemaugh 2,710
East Faxon 4,175
East Greenville 2,003
East Lansdowne 3,186
East McKeesport 3,233
East Petersburg 3,407
East Pittsburgh 3,006
East Prospect 547
East Rochester 920
East Side 152
East Springfield 593
East Stroudsburg 7,894
East Uniontown 2,333
East Vandergrift 1,167
East Washington 2,198
Eastlawn Gardens 1,613
Easton 30,256
Eastvale 421
Eau Claire 428
Ebensburg 4,318
Economy 7,176
Eddystone 2,706
Edgewood (Allegheny Co.) 5,138
Edgewood (Northumberland Co.) 3,186
Edgeworth 2,200
Edinboro 4,871
Edwardsville 5,633
Ehrenfeld 397
Elco 459
Elderton 428
Eldora, see Fisher-Eldora
Eldred 1,092
Elgin 173
Elizabeth 2,273
Elizabethtown 8,072
Elizabethville 1,629
Elkland 1,942
Ellport 1,350
Ellsworth 1,268
Ellwood City 10,857
Elverson 509
Elysburg 1,337
Emlenton 854
Emmaus 11,511
Emporium 3,074
Emsworth 3,345
Enlow, see Imperial-Enlow
Enon Valley 427
Ephrata 9,662
Erie 129,231
Espy 1,652
Etna 5,819
Evans City 2,144
Everett 2,243
Everson 1,143
Exeter 4,670
Export 1,402
Factoryville 922
Fairchance 1,906
Fairdale 1,621
Fairfield 547
Fairhope-Arnold City 3,239
Fairview (Butler Co.) 235
Fairview (Erie Co.) 1,707
Fairview-Ferndale 3,723
Falls Creek 1,255
Fallston 571
Farrell 11,022
Fawn Grove 485
Faxon 1,946
Fayette City 968
Fayetteville 2,449
Fellsburg 1,092
Felton 425
Ferndale (Cambria Co.) 2,482
Ferndale (Northumberland Co.), see Fairview-Ferndale
Finleyville 379
Fisher-Eldora 3,101
Fleetwood 3,064
Flemington 1,519
Flourtown 9,149
Folcroft 9,610
Ford City 4,749
Ford Cliff 526
Forest City 2,322
Forest Hills 9,561
Forksville 158
Forty Fort 6,114
Fountain Hill 5,384
Fox Chapel 4,684
Foxburg 353
Frackville 5,445
Frankfort Springs 144
Franklin (Cambria Co.) 864
Franklin (Venango Co.) 8,629
Franklin Park 5,310
Franklintown 279
Fredericksburg 1,073
Fredericktown 1,067
Fredonia 731
Freeburg 636
Freedom 2,643
Freeland 4,784
Freemansburg 1,681
Freeport 2,375
Friendsville 77
Fullerton 7,908
Galeton 1,552
Gallitzin 2,496
Gap 1,022
Garden View 2,662
Garrett 616
Geistown 3,633
General Wayne 5,368
Georgetown 234
Gettysburg 7,275
Gilberton 1,293
Girard 2,613
Girardville 2,450
Glasgow 112
Glassport 7,450
Glen Campbell 408
Glen Hope 163
Glen Lyon 3,408
Glen Rock 1,600
Glendon 637
Glenfield 406
Glenolden 8,697
Glenside 17,353
Goldsboro 576
Gordon 856
Grampian 511
Gratz 675
Great Bend 826
Green Tree 6,441
Greencastle 3,293
Greenlane 543
Greensboro 439
Greensburg 15,870
Greenville 8,704
Grove City 8,312
Halifax 907
Hallam 1,825
Hallstead 1,447
Hamburg 3,909
Hanover 15,623
Harleysville 1,448
Harmony 1,207
Harrisburg 68,061
Harrisville 944
Hartleton 223
Harveys Lake 1,693
Hastings 1,791
Hatboro 8,880
Hatboro West 13,542
Hatfield (Montgomery Co.) 2,385
Hatfield (Fayette Co.), see Leith-Hatfield
Hawley 1,331
Hawthorne 552
Haysville 154
Hayti 1,559
Hazleton 30,426
Heidelberg 2,034
Hellertown 6,613
Herndon 507
Hershey 7,407
Highfield 2,994
Highland Park (Mifflin Co.) 1,704
Highland Park (Northampton Co.) 5,500
Highspire 2,947
Hillcrest 3,897
Hiller 1,688
Hollidaysburg 6,262
Homeacre-Lyndora 8,415
Homer City 2,465
Homestead 6,309
Hometown 1,013
Homewood 212
Honesdale 5,224
Honey Brook 1,115
Hookstown 246
Hooversville 962
Hop Bottom 430
Hopewell 290
Hopwood 2,190
Houston 1,812
Houtzdale 1,193
Howard 751
Hughestown 1,407
Hughesville 2,249
Hulmeville 908
Hummelstown 4,723
Hunker 375
Huntingdon 6,987
Hyde 1,264
Hyde Park 729
Hydetown 725
Hyndman 1,151
Imperial-Enlow 2,385
Indian Lake 129
Indiana 16,100
Industry 2,442
Ingram 4,902
Irvona 714
Irwin 4,059
Ivyland 600
Jackson Center 691
Jacksonville 141
Jacobus 1,360
Jamestown 937
Jeannette 15,209
Jeddo 177
Jefferson (Allegheny Co.) 8,512
Jefferson (Greene Co.) 366
Jefferson (York Co.) 540
Jefferson-Trooper 13,022
Jenkintown 5,990
Jennerstown 621
Jermyn 2,435
Jerome 1,158
Jersey Shore 5,322
Jessup 4,948
Jim Thorpe 5,456
Johnsonburg 4,304
Johnstown 42,476
Jonestown 954
Juniata Terrace 733
Kane 5,001
Karns City 379
Kenhorst 3,482
Kenilworth 1,598
Kennett Square 4,876
Kingston 18,325
Kistler 369
Kittanning 6,231
Kittanning Heights 1,347
Knox 1,306
Knoxville 698
Koppel 1,312
Kulpmont 4,026
Kutztown 4,166
Laceyville 452
Lafayette Hills-Plymouth Meeting 8,263
Laflin 399
Lake City 2,117
Lancaster 57,690
Landingville 175
Landisburg 269
Lanesboro 550
Langhorne 1,889
Langhorne Manor 1,505
Lansdale 18,451
Lansdowne 14,090
Lansford 5,168
Laporte 207
Larksville 3,937
Latrobe 11,749
Laurel Run 327
Laureldale 4,519
Lawrenceville 605
Lawson Heights 3,844
Lebanon 28,572
Lebanon South 3,457
Leechburg 2,999
Leesport 1,158
Leetsdale 1,862
Lehighton 6,095
Leith-Hatfield 2,668
Lemont 2,547
Lemoyne 4,625
Lenape Heights 1,233
Lenhartsville 220
Le Raysville 346
Lewis Run 756
Lewisberry 490
Lewisburg 6,376
Lewistown 11,098
Liberty (Allegheny Co.) 3,594
Liberty (Tioga Co.) 235
Ligonier 2,258
Lilly 1,429
Lincoln 1,885
Linesville 1,265
Linntown-West Lawn 1,851
Lititz 7,072
Little Meadows 337
Littlestown 3,026
Liverpool 847
Lloydell, see Beaverdale-Lloydell
Lock Haven 11,427
Loganton 436
Loganville 921
Long Branch 582
Lorain 972
Loretto 1,661
Lower Burrell 13,654
Loyalhanna, see McChesneytown-Loyalhanna
Lucerne Mines 1,380
Lumber City 57
Luzerne 4,504
Lykens 2,506
Lyndora, see Homeacre-Lyndora
Lynnwood-Pricedale 3,191
Lyons 589
Macungie 1,414
Madison 436
Mahaffey 482
Mahanoy City 7,257
Malvern 2,583
Manchester 2,391
Manheim 5,434
Manns Choice 334
Manor 2,276
Manorville 445
Mansfield 4,114
Mapleton 661
Marcus Hook 3,041
Marianna 875
Marietta 2,838
Marion Center 446
Marion Heights 958
Marklesburg 232
Markleysburg 367
Mars 1,488
Marshallton 1,846
Martinsburg 2,088
Marysville 2,328
Masontown 4,226
Matamoras 2,244
Mayfield 2,176
McAdoo 3,326
McChesneytown-Loyalhanna 4,283
McClure 1,094
McConnellsburg 1,228
McDonald 2,879
McEwensville 247
McGovern, see Meadowlands-McGovern
McKees Rocks 11,901
McKeesport 37,977
McSherrystown 2,773
McVeytown 486
Meadowlands-McGovern 3,609
Meadville 16,573
Mechanicsburg 9,385
Mechanicsville (Montour Co.) 2,046
Mechanicsville (Schuylkill Co.) 663
Media 6,444
Melrose Park, see Cedarbrook-Melrose Park
Mercer 2,773
Mercersburg 1,727
Meridian 2,234
Merion 5,686
Merrittstown, see Republic-Merrittstown
Meshoppen 482
Meyersdale 2,648
Middleboro 462
Middleburg 1,369
Middleport 609
Middletown 9,080
Midland 5,271
Midway (Adams Co.) 1,636
Midway (Washington Co.) 1,188
Mifflin 640
Mifflinburg 2,607
Mifflintown 822
Mifflinville 1,074
Milesburg 1,196
Milford 1,190
Mill Creek 421
Mill Hall 1,838
Mill Village 372
Millbourne 637
Millersburg 3,074
Millerstown 612
Millersville 6,396
Millheim 871
Millvale 5,815
Millville 896
Milroy 1,575
Milton 7,723
Minersville 6,012
Modena 867
Mohnton 2,153
Monaca 7,486
Monessen 15,216
Monongahela 7,113
Monroe 627
Monroeville 29,011
Mont Alto 1,532
Mont Clare 1,274
Montgomery 1,902
Montoursville 5,985
Montrose 2,058
Moon, see Carnot-Moon
Moosic 4,273
Morrisville (Bucks Co.) 11,309
Morrisville (Greene Co.) 1,232
Morton 2,602
Moscow 1,430
Mount Carbon 184
Mount Carmel 9,317
Mount Gretna 153
Mount Holly Springs 2,009
Mount Jewett 1,060
Mount Joy 5,041
Mount Oliver 5,487
Mount Penn 3,465
Mount Pleasant 5,895
Mount Pocono 1,019
Mount Union 3,662
Mount Wolf 1,811
Mountville 1,454
Muncy 2,872
Munhall 16,574
Muse 1,358
Myerstown 3,645
Nanticoke 14,632
Nanty-Glo 4,298
Narberth 5,151
Nazareth 5,815
Nemacolin 1,273
Nescopeck 1,897
Nesquehoning 3,338
New Albany 382
New Alexandria 690
New Baltimore 214
New Beaver 1,426
New Berlin 821
New Berlinville 1,145
New Bethlehem 1,406
New Brighton 7,637
New Britain 2,428
New Buffalo 150
New Castle 38,559
New Castle Northwest 1,974
New Centerville 253
New Columbus 149
New Cumberland 9,803
New Eagle 2,497
New Florence 929
New Freedom 1,495
New Galilee 624
New Holland 3,971
New Hope 978
New Kensington 20,312
New Lebanon 211
New Milford 1,143
New Oxford 1,495
New Paris 204
New Philadelphia 1,528
New Ringgold 314
New Salem 384
New Salem-Buffington 1,337
New Stanton 1,793
New Washington 58
New Wilmington 2,721
Newburg (Clearfield Co.) 151
Newburg (Cumberland Co.) 320
Newell 650
Newmanstown 1,532
Newport 1,747
Newry 444
Newton Hamilton 280
Newtown 2,216
Newville 1,631
Nicholson 877
Norristown 38,169
North Apollo 1,618
North Ardmore 5,856
North Belle Vernon 2,916
North Braddock 10,838
North Catasauqua 2,941
North Charleroi 1,964
North Connellsville 1,226
North East 3,846
North Hills-Ardsley 13,173
North Irwin 1,306
North Vandergrift 1,784
North Wales 3,911
North Warren 1,360
North York 2,032
Northampton 8,389
Northumberland 4,102
Norvelt, see Calumet-Norvelt
Norwood 7,229
Nuangola 464
Oak Lane 6,192
Oakdale 2,136
Oakland (Lawrence Co.) 2,135
Oakland (Susquehanna Co.) 817
Oakmont 7,550
Oakwood 3,094
Ogontz 5,463
Ohiopyle 140
Ohioville 3,918
Oil City 15,033
Oklahoma 1,084
Old Forge 9,522
Oliver 3,091
Olyphant 5,422
Orangeville 431
Orbisonia 554
Orchard Hills 1,300
Oreland 9,114
Orrstown 262
Orwigsburg 2,661
Osborne 579
Osceola 1,671
Oswayo 195
Oxford 3,658
Paint 1,233
Palmdale 1,724
Palmerton 5,620
Palmyra 7,615
Palo Alto 1,428
Paoli 5,835
Parker City 843
Parkesburg 2,701
Parkside 2,343
Parkville 5,120
Parryville 528
Patterson Heights 777
Patton 2,762
Paxtang 2,160
Pen Argyl 3,668
Penbrook 3,379
Pencoyd 6,650
Penn 735
Penn Square-Plymouth Valley 20,238
Penn Wynne 6,038
Penndel 2,248
Pennsburg 2,260
Pennville 1,100
Perkasie 5,451
Perryopolis 2,043
Petersburg 555
Petrolia 432
Philadelphia 1,950,098
Philipsburg 3,700
Phoenixville 14,823
Picture Rocks 570
Pillow 332
Pine Grove 2,197
Pitcairn 4,741
Pittsburgh 520,117
Pittston 11,113
Plains 6,606
Platea 354
Pleasant Gap 1,773
Pleasant Hill 1,071
Pleasant Hills 10,409
Pleasantville (Bedford Co.) 303
Pleasantville (Venango Co.) 1,005
Plum 21,922
Plumville 429
Plymouth 9,536
Plymouth Meeting, see Lafayette Hills-Plymouth Meeting
Plymouth Valley, see Penn Square-Plymouth Valley
Plymptonville 1,040
Pocono Park, see Arlington Heights-Pocono Park
Point Marion 1,750
Polk 3,673
Port Allegany 2,703
Port Carbon 2,717
Port Clinton 363
Port Matilda 680
Port Royal 829
Port Vue 5,862
Portage 4,151
Portersville 292
Portland 612
Pottstown 25,355
Pottsville 19,715
Pricedale, see Lynwood-Pricedale
Primrose 1,227
Pringle 1,155
Prompton 224
Prospect 973
Prospect Park 7,250
Punxsutawney 7,792
Quakertown 7,276
Quarryville 1,571
Railroad 308
Rainsburg 179
Ramey 542
Rankin 3,704
Reading 87,643
Reamstown 1,050
Red Hill 1,201
Red Lion 5,645
Renovo 2,620
Republic-Merrittstown 2,194
Reynoldsville 2,771
Rices Landing 473
Richland 1,444
Richlandtown 856
Ridgway 6,022
Ridley Park 9,025
Riegelsville 1,050
Rimersburg 1,146
Ringtown 880
Riverside 1,905
Roaring Spring 2,811
Robesonia 1,685
Rochester 4,819
Rockhill 480
Rockledge 2,564
Rockwood 1,051
Rome 338
Roscoe 1,176
Rose Valley 1,349
Roseto 1,538
Roseville 178
Roslyn 18,317
Rosslyn Farms 608
Rothsville 1,318
Rouseville 877
Rouzerville 1,419
Royalton 1,040
Royersford 4,235
Rural Valley 962
Russellton 1,597
Rutledge 1,167
Rydal 5,083
Saegertown 1,348
St. Clair 4,576
St. Clairsville 96
St. Lawrence 1,256
St. Marys 7,470
St. Michael 1,248
St. Petersburg 416
Salisbury 895
Salladasburg 239
Saltillo 341
Saltsburg 1,037
Sandy 2,000
Sandy Lake 772
Sankertown 881
Saxonburg 1,191
Saxton 858
Sayre 7,473
Scalp Level 1,353
Schaefferstown 1,027
Schellsburg 271
Schuylkill Haven 6,125
Schwenksville 809
Scottdale 5,818
Scranton 103,564
Selinsgrove 5,116
Sellersville 2,829
Seven Springs 37
Seven Valleys 688
Seward 746
Sewickley 5,660
Sewickley Heights 797
Sewickley Hills 270
Shade Gap 186
Shamokin 11,719
Shamokin Dam 1,562
Shanksville 275
Sharon 22,653
Sharon Hill 7,464
Sharon North 1,328
Sharpsburg 5,453
Sharpsville 6,126
Sheakleyville 141
Sheffield 1,564
Shelocta 121
Shenandoah 8,287
Shenandoah Heights 1,471
Shickshinny 1,685
Shillington 6,249
Shinglehouse 1,320
Shippensburg 6,536
Shippenville 602
Shippingport 328

PENNSYLVANIA, Continued

Shiremanstown 1,773
Shirleysburg 238
Shoemakersville 1,427
Shrewsbury 1,716
Silverdale 545
Sinking Spring 2,862
Skyline View 1,996
Slatington 4,687
Slickville 1,066
Sligo 825
Slippery Rock 4,949
Smethport 1,883
Smicksburg 79
Smithfield 969
Smithfield Center 1,061
Smithton 552
Snow Shoe 874
Snydertown 267
Somerset 6,269
Souderton 6,366
South Bethlehem 500
South Coatesville 1,583
South Connellsville 2,385
South Fork 1,661
South Greensburg 3,288
South Heights 799
South New Castle 940
South Philipsburg 472
South Pottstown 2,734
South Renovo 662
South Uniontown 3,546
South Waverly 1,307
South Williamsport 7,153
Southmont 2,653
Southwest Greensburg 3,186
Spangler 3,109
Spartansburg 464
Speers 1,408
Spring City 3,578
Spring Grove 1,669
Spring Hill 1,323
Springboro 584
Springdale 5,202
Starrucca 292
State College 33,778
Steelton 8,556
Stewartstown 1,157
Stillwater 208
Stockdale 720
Stockertown 753
Stoneboro 1,129
Stowe 3,596
Stoystown 446
Strabane 2,309
Strasburg 1,897
Strattanville 559
Strausstown 401
Stroudsburg 5,451
Sugar Creek 5,944
Sugar Grove 701
Sugar Notch 1,333
Summerhill 726
Summerville 859
Summit Hill 3,811
Sunbury 13,025
Susquehanna Depot 2,319
Suterville 830
Swarthmore 6,156
Swissvale 13,819
Swoyersville 6,786
Sykesville 1,311
Sylvania 241
Tamaqua 9,246
Tarentum 7,379
Tatamy 891
Taylor 6,977
Telford 3,409
Temple 1,667
Terre Hill 1,129
Thompson 307
Thompsontown 677
Thornburg 617
Thorndale 1,606
Three Springs 495
Throop 4,307
Tidioute 939
Timblin 218
Tioga 624
Tionesta 711
Titusville 7,331
Topton 1,744
Toughkenamon 1,233
Towanda 4,224
Tower City 1,774
Townville 349
Trafford 4,383
Trainer 2,336
Trappe 1,676
Tremont 1,833
Tresckow 1,146
Trevorton 2,196
Trooper, see Jefferson-Trooper
Troutville 190
Troy 1,315
Trumbauersville 831
Tullytown 2,194
Tunkhannock 2,251
Tunnelhill 508
Turbotville 627
Turtle Creek 8,308
Twilight 272
Tyrone 7,072
Ulysses 590
Union City 3,631
Uniondale 279
Uniontown 16,282
Unionville 375
Upland 3,930
Ursina 284
Utica 281
Valencia 351
Valley View 1,585
Vanderbilt 755
Vandergrift 7,873
Vandling 633
Venango 275
Verona 3,737
Versailles 2,754
Vintondale 812
Volant 226
Wall 1,265
Wallaceton 377
Walnutport 1,942
Wampum 1,189
Warren 12,998
Warrior Run 816
Washington (Lancaster Co.) 425
Washington (Washington Co.) 19,827
Washington North 2,855
Washington West 3,297
Washingtonville 174
Waterford 1,468
Watsontown 2,514
Wattsburg 453
Waymart 1,122
Wayne Heights 1,005
Waynesboro 10,011
Waynesburg 5,152
Weatherly 2,554
Weissport 561
Weissport East 2,027
Wellersburg 266
Wellsboro 4,003
Wellsville 346
Wernersville 1,761
Wesleyville 3,920
West Alexander 402
West Brownsville 1,426
West Chester 19,301
West Conshohocken 2,194
West Derry 1,497
West Easton 1,123
West Elizabeth 848
West Fairview 1,388
West Grove 1,870
West Hazleton 6,059
West Homestead 3,789
West Kittanning 956
West Lawn (Berks Co.) 1,973
West Lawn (Union Co.), see Linntown-West Lawn
West Leechburg 1,422
West Liberty 224
West Mayfield 2,152
West Middlesex 1,293
West Middletown 195
West Mifflin 28,070
West Newton 3,648
West Pittston 7,074
West Reading 4,578
West Sunbury 683
West View 8,312
West Wyoming 3,659
West York 5,314
Westfield 1,273
Westmont 6,673
Westover 501
Wheatland 1,421
Whitaker 1,797
White Haven 2,134
White Oak 9,304
Whitehall 16,551
Wiconisco Center 1,236
Wilkes-Barre 58,856
Wilkinsburg 26,780
Williamsburg 1,704
Williamsport 37,918
Williamstown 1,919
Willow Grove 16,494
Wilmerding 3,218
Wilmore 386
Wilson 8,482
Wind Gap 2,270
Windber 6,332
Windsor 1,298
Winterstown 424
Wolfdale 1,202
Womelsdorf 1,551
Woodbury 298
Woodcock 108
Woodland Heights 1,329
Woodside-Drifton 1,295
Wormleysburg 3,192
Worthington 816
Worthville 100
Wrightsville 2,668
Wyalusing 723
Wyoming 4,195
Wyomissing 7,136
Wyomissing Hills 1,744
Yardley 2,616
Yatesville 407
Yeadon 12,136
Yeagertown 1,363
Yoe 790
York 50,335
York Haven 671
York Springs 467
Yorkana 262
Youngstown 478
Youngsville 2,158
Youngwood 3,057
Zelienople 3,602

RHODE ISLAND Total population: 949,723

METROPOLITAN AREA

Providence-Warwick-Pawtucket 914,110 (792,515 in Rhode Island, 121,595 in Massachusetts)

COUNTIES

Bristol 45,937
Kent 142,382
Newport 94,228
Providence 581,470
Washington 85,706

TOWNS AND PLACES

Ashaway 1,559
Barrington 17,554▲
Bradford 1,333
Bristol 17,860▲
Burrillville 10,087▲
Central Falls 18,716
Charlestown 2,863▲
Coventry 22,947▲
Cranston 74,287
Cumberland 26,605▲
East Greenwich 9,577▲
East Providence 48,207
Exeter 3,245▲
Foster 2,626▲
Glocester 5,160▲
Harrisville 1,053
Hope Valley 1,326
Hopkinton 5,392▲
Jamestown 2,911▲
Jamestown 2,114
Johnston 22,037▲
Kingston 5,601
Lincoln 16,182▲
Little Compton 2,385▲
Middletown 29,290▲
Narragansett 7,138▲
Narragansett Pier 2,686
New Shoreham 489▲
Newport 34,562
Newport East 10,285
North Kingstown 29,793▲
North Providence 24,337▲
North Smithfield 9,349▲
Pascoag 3,132
Pawtucket 76,984
Peacedale, see Wakefield-Peacedale
Portsmouth 12,521▲
Providence 179,116
Richmond 2,625▲
Scituate 7,489▲
Smithfield 13,468▲
South Kingstown 16,913▲
The Anchorage 3,441
Tiverton 12,559▲
Wakefield-Peacedale 6,331
Warren 10,523▲
Warwick 83,694
West Greenwich 1,841▲
West Warwick 24,323▲
Westerly 17,248▲
Westerly 13,654
Woonsocket 46,820

SOUTH CAROLINA Total population: 2,590,516

METROPOLITAN AREAS

Charleston 303,849
Columbia 322,880
Greenville 299,730
Spartanburg 173,724

COUNTIES

Abbeville 21,112
Aiken 91,023
Allendale 9,783
Anderson 105,474
Bamberg 15,950
Barnwell 17,176
Beaufort 51,136
Berkeley 56,199
Calhoun 10,780
Charleston 247,650
Cherokee 36,791
Chester 29,811
Chesterfield 33,667
Clarendon 25,604
Colleton 27,622
Darlington 53,442
Dillon 28,838
Dorchester 32,276
Edgefield 15,692
Fairfield 19,999
Florence 89,636
Georgetown 33,500
Greenville 240,774
Greenwood 49,686
Hampton 15,878
Horry 69,992
Jasper 11,885
Kershaw 34,727
Lancaster 43,328
Laurens 49,713
Lee 18,323
Lexington 89,012
Marion 30,270
Marlboro 27,151
McCormick 7,955
Newberry 29,273
Oconee 40,728
Orangeburg 69,789
Pickens 58,956
Richland 233,868
Saluda 14,528
Spartanburg 173,724
Sumter 79,425
Union 29,230
Williamsburg 34,243
York 85,216

PLACES

Abbeville 5,515
Aiken 13,436
Aiken West 2,689
Allendale 3,620
Anderson 27,556
Andrews 2,879
Aragon Mills, see Baldwin-Aragon Mills
Arcadia 1,887
Arcadia Lakes 741
Ardincaple 726
Arial 1,150
Arkwright 2,059
Atlantic Beach 215
Avondale-Moorland 5,236
Aynor 536
Baldwin-Aragon Mills 1,042
Bamberg 3,406
Barnwell 4,439
Batesburg 4,036
Bath 1,576
Beaufort 9,434
Beaufort Station 2,295
Belton 5,257
Bennettsville 7,468
Bennettsville Southwest 1,726
Berea 7,186
Bethune 506
Bishopville 3,404
Blacksburg 1,977
Blackville 2,395
Blenheim 236
Bluffton 529
Bonneau 365
Bowman 1,095
Boyden Arbor 416
Branchville 1,011
Brunson 559
Buffalo 1,461
Burnettown 434
Calhoun Falls 2,234
Camden 8,532
Cameron 476
Campobello 530
Capehart 4,490
Carlisle 670
Cayce 9,967
Central 1,550
Central Pacolet 483
Chapin 342
Chappells 74
Charleston 66,945
Charleston Base 6,238
Charleston Yard 13,565
Cheraw 5,627
Chesnee 1,069
Chester 7,045
Chesterfield 1,667
City View 2,497
Clemson 5,578
Clinton 8,138
Clio 936
Clover 3,506
Columbia 113,542
Conway 8,151
Cope 202
Cordova 205
Cottageville 497
Coward 466
Cowpens 2,109
Cross Hill 579
Darlington 6,990
Denmark 3,571
Dillon 6,735
Donalds 392
Doneraile 1,417
Due West 1,380
Duncan 1,266
Easley 11,175
East Gaffney 3,750
Eastover 817
Edgefield 2,750
Ehrhardt 478
Elgin 374
Elko 202
Elloree 940
Estill 1,954
Eureka 1,524
Eutawville 386
Fairfax 1,937
Florence 25,997
Folly Beach 1,157
Forest Acres 6,808
Forest Lake 39
Fort Lawn 510
Fort Mill 4,505
Fountain Inn 3,391
Furman 239
Gaffney 13,253
Gantt 11,386
Georgetown 10,449
Gilbert 186
Gloverville 1,682
Goose Creek 3,656
Govan 136
Graniteville 1,127
Gray Court 859
Great Falls 2,727
Greeleyville 542
Greenville 61,436
Greenwood 21,069
Greer 10,642
Hampton (Greenville Co.), see Wade-Hampton
Hampton (Hampton Co.) 2,845
Hanahan 8,376
Hardeeville 853
Harleyville 704
Hartsville 8,017
Heath Springs 955
Hemingway 1,026
Hickory Grove 377
Hilda 331
Hodges 214
Holly Hill 1,178
Hollywood 339
Honea Path 3,707
Inman 1,661
Inman Mills 1,811
Irmo 517
Irwin 1,424
Isle of Palms 2,657
Iva 1,114
Jackson 1,928
Jamestown 190
Jefferson 709
Joanna 1,631
Johnsonville 1,267
Johnston 2,552
Jonesville 1,447
Kershaw 1,818
Kingstree 3,381
Kline 305
Lake City 6,247
Lakeview 949
Lamar 1,250
Lancaster 9,186
Lancaster Mills 2,558
Landrum 1,859
Lane 517
Latta 1,764
Laurens 10,298
Leesville 1,907
Lexington 969
Liberty 2,860
Lincolnville 504
Little Mountain 240
Livingston 165
Lockhart 103
Lodge 168
Loris 1,741
Lowndesville 219
Lowrys 260
Luray 72
Lyman 1,159
Lynchburg 546
Madison 1,337
Manning 4,025
Marietta, see Slater-Marietta
Marion 7,435
Mauldin 3,797
Mayesville 757
McBee 592
McClellanville 304
McColl 2,524
McConnells 213
McCormick 1,864
Meggett 180
Monarch Mills 1,726
Moncks Corner 2,314
Moorland, see Avondale-Moorland
Mount Carmel 138
Mount Croghan 123
Mount Pleasant 6,691
Mullins 6,006
Myrtle Beach 9,035
Myrtle Beach Base 3,864
Neeses 388
New Ellenton 2,546
Newberry 9,218
Nichols 549
Ninety-Six 2,166
Norris 757
North 1,076
North Augusta 12,883
North Hartsville 1,485
North Myrtle Beach 1,957
Norway 579
Olanta 640
Olar 423
Orangeburg 13,252
Pacolet 1,418
Pacolet Mills 1,504
Pacolet Park 162
Pageland 2,122
Pamplico 1,068
Parksville 164
Parris Island 8,868
Patrick 421
Paxville 261
Peak 87
Pelion 216
Pelzer 130
Pelzer North 1,202
Pendleton 2,615
Perry 209
Pickens 2,954
Piedmont 2,242
Pinehurst-Sheppard Park 1,711
Pineridge 633
Pinewood 687
Plum Branch 108
Pomaria 264
Port Royal 2,865
Prosperity 762
Quinby 788
Ravenel 931
Red River 222
Reevesville 247
Reidville 460
Richburg 304
Ridge Spring 644
Ridgeland 1,165
Ridgeville 563
Ridgeway 437
Rock Hill 33,846
Rowesville 392
Ruby 306
St. Andrews 9,202
St. George 1,806
St. Matthews 2,403
St. Stephens 1,506
Salem 301
Salley 450
Saluda 2,442
Santee 137
Saxon 4,807
Scotia 64
Scranton 732
Sellers 561
Seneca 6,382
Shannontown 7,491
Sharon 268
Shaw 5,819
Sheppard Park, see Pinehurst-Sheppard Park
Silverstreet 156
Simpsonville 3,308
Six Mile 361
Slater-Marietta 1,764
Smoaks 155
Smyrna 85
Society Hill 806
South Congaree 1,434
Southern Shops 2,864
Spartanburg 44,546
Springdale (Lancaster Co.) 3,193
Springdale (Lexington Co.) 2,638
Springfield 724
Starr 190
Startex 1,203
Stuckey 193
Sullivans Island 1,426
Summerton 1,305
Summerville 3,839
Summit 130
Sumter 24,555
Surfside Beach 1,329
Swansea 691
Sycamore 229
Tatum 115
Taylors 6,831
Timmonsville 2,246
Travelers Rest 2,241
Trenton 362
Troy 207
Turbeville 442
Ulmers 109
Union 10,775
Utica 1,218
Vance 54
Varnville 1,555
Wade-Hampton 17,152
Wagener 723
Walhalla 3,662
Walterboro 6,257
Wards 150
Ware Shoals 2,480
Warrenville 1,059
Waterloo 112
Watts Mills 1,181
Wellford 1,298
West Columbia 7,838
West Pelzer 861
West Union 388
Westminster 2,521
Westview 1,105
Whitmire 2,226
Whitney 2,891
Willams 201
Williamston 3,991
Williston 2,594
Windy Hill 1,671
Winnsboro 3,411
Winnsboro Mills 2,312
Woodford 195
Woodruff 4,576
Woodside 227
Woodville 140
Yemassee 745
York 5,081

SOUTH DAKOTA Total population: 666,257

METROPOLITAN AREA

Sioux Falls 95,209

COUNTIES

Aurora 4,183
Beadle 20,877
Bennett 3,088
Bon Homme 8,577
Brookings 22,158
Brown 36,920
Brule 5,870
Buffalo 1,739
Butte 7,825
Campbell 2,866
Charles Mix 9,994
Clark 5,515
Clay 12,923
Codington 19,140
Corson 4,994
Custer 4,698
Davison 17,319
Day 8,713
Deuel 5,686
Dewey 5,170
Douglas 4,569
Edmunds 5,548
Fall River 7,505
Faulk 3,893
Grant 9,005
Gregory 6,710
Haakon 2,802
Hamlin 5,172
Hand 5,883
Hanson 3,781
Harding 1,855
Hughes 11,632
Hutchinson 10,379
Hyde 2,515
Jackson 1,531
Jerauld 3,310
Jones 1,882
Kingsbury 7,657
Lake 11,456
Lawrence 17,453
Lincoln 11,761
Lyman 4,060

▲ Population of entire town (township)

Marshall.....5,965
McCook.....7,246
McPherson.....5,022
Meade.....16,618
Mellette.....2,420
Miner.....4,454
Minnehaha.....95,209
Moody.....7,622
Pennington.....59,349
Perkins.....4,769
Potter.....4,449
Roberts.....11,678
Sanborn.....3,697
Shannon.....8,198
Spink.....10,595
Stanley.....2,457
Sully.....2,362
Todd.....6,606
Tripp.....8,171
Turner.....9,872
Union.....9,643
Walworth.....7,842
Washabaugh.....1,389
Yankton.....19,039
Ziebach.....2,221

PLACES

Aberdeen.....26,476
Agar.....156
Akaska.....46
Albee.....26
Alcester.....627
Alexandria.....598
Alpena.....307
Altamont.....54
Andover.....138
Ardmore.....14
Arlington.....954
Armour.....925
Artas.....73
Artesian.....277
Ashton.....137
Astoria.....153
Aurora.....237
Avon.....610
Badger.....122
Baltic.....364
Bancroft.....48
Belle Fourche.....4,236
Belvidere.....96
Beresford.....1,655
Big Stone City.....631
Bison.....406
Blunt.....445
Bonesteel.....354
Bowdle.....667
Box Elder.....607
Bradley.....157
Brandon.....1,431
Brandt.....132
Brentford.....94
Bridgewater.....633
Bristol.....470
Britton.....1,465
Broadland.....45
Brookings.....13,717
Bruce.....217
Bryant.....502
Buffalo.....393
Buffalo Gap.....155
Burke.....892
Bushnell.....65
Butler.....38
Camp Crook.....150
Canistota.....636
Canova.....204
Canton.....2,665
Carter.....17
Carthage.....362
Castlewood.....523
Cavour.....134
Centerville.....910
Central City.....188
Chamberlain.....2,626
Chancellor.....220
Chelsea.....45
Claire City.....100
Claremont.....214
Clark.....1,356
Clear Lake.....1,157
Colman.....456
Colome.....375
Colton.....601
Columbia.....240
Conde.....279
Corona.....133
Corsica.....615
Cottonwood.....16
Cresbard.....224
Custer.....1,597
Dallas.....233
Dante.....88
Davis.....101
Deadwood.....2,409
Dell Rapids.....1,991
Delmont.....260
De Smet.....1,336
Dimock.....167
Doland.....430
Dolton.....60
Draper.....200
Dupree.....523
Eagle Butte.....530
Eden.....132
Egan.....281
Elk Point.....1,372
Elkton.....541
Ellsworth.....5,805
Emery.....452
Erwin.....106
Esmond.....19
Estelline.....276
Ethan.....309
Eureka.....1,547
Fairburn.....50
Fairfax.....199
Fairview.....72
Faith.....576
Farmer.....58
Faulkton.....955
Flandreau.....2,027
Florence.....175
Fort Pierre.....1,448
Frankfort.....192
Frederick.....359
Freeman.....1,357
Fruitdale.....74
Fulton.....101
Garden City.....126
Garretson.....847
Gary.....366
Gayville.....269
Geddes.....308
Gettysburg.....1,915
Glenham.....178
Goodwin.....114
Gregory.....1,756
Grenville.....154
Groton.....1,021
Harrisburg.....338
Harrold.....184
Hartford.....800
Hayti.....393
Hazel.....101
Hecla.....407
Henry.....182
Hermosa.....150
Herreid.....672
Herrick.....126
Hetland.....81
Highmore.....1,173
Hill City.....389
Hillsview.....19
Hitchcock.....150
Hosmer.....437
Hot Springs.....4,434
Hoven.....671
Howard.....1,175
Hudson.....366
Humboldt.....411
Hurley.....399
Huron.....14,299
Interior.....81
Ipswich.....1,187
Irene.....461
Iroquois.....375
Isabel.....394
Java.....305
Jefferson.....474
Kadoka.....815
Kennebec.....372
Kimball.....825
Kranzburg.....143
Labolt.....90
Lake Andes.....948
Lake City.....44
Lake Norden.....393
Lake Preston.....812
Lane.....94
Langford.....328
Lead.....5,420
Lebanon.....182
Lemmon.....1,997
Lennox.....1,487
Leola.....787
Lesterville.....181
Letcher.....201
Lily.....62
Long Lake.....128
Lowry.....35
Loyalton.....10
Madison.....6,315
Marion.....844
Martin.....1,248
Marvin.....65
McIntosh.....563
McLaughlin.....863
Mellette.....199
Menno.....796
Midland.....270
Milbank.....3,727
Miller.....2,148
Mission.....739
Mission Hill.....161
Mitchell.....13,425
Mobridge.....4,545
Monroe.....134
Montrose.....377
Morristown.....144
Mound City.....164
Mount Vernon.....398
Murdo.....865
Naples.....38
New Effington.....258
New Underwood.....416
New Witten.....102
Newell.....664
Nisland.....157
North Eagle Butte.....1,351
North Sioux City.....860
Northville.....119
Nunda.....85
Oacoma.....215
Oelrichs.....94
Oldham.....244
Olivet.....103
Onaka.....69
Onida.....785
Orient.....131
Ortley.....111
Parker.....1,005
Parkston.....1,611
Peever.....202
Philip.....983
Pierpont.....241
Pierre.....9,699
Pine Ridge.....2,768
Plankinton.....613
Platte.....1,351
Pollock.....341
Presho.....922
Pringle.....86
Pukwana.....208
Quinn.....105
Ramona.....227
Rapid City.....43,836
Ravinia.....109
Raymond.....114
Redfield.....2,943
Ree Heights.....183
Reliance.....204
Revillo.....142
Rockham.....60
Roscoe.....398
Rosholt.....456
Roslyn.....250
Roswell.....32
St. Francis.....300
St. Lawrence.....249
Salem.....1,391
Scotland.....984
Selby.....957
Seneca.....118
Sherman.....82
Sinai.....147
Sioux Falls.....72,488
Sisseton.....3,094
South Shore.....199
Spearfish.....4,661
Spencer.....385
Springfield.....1,566
Stickney.....421
Stockholm.....116
Strandburg.....98
Stratford.....106
Sturgis.....4,536
Summit.....332
Tabor.....388
Tea.....302
Timber Lake.....625
Tolstoy.....99
Toronto.....216
Trent.....177
Tripp.....851
Tulare.....211
Turton.....121
Twin Brooks.....122
Tyndall.....1,245
Utica.....89
Valley Springs.....566
Veblen.....377
Verdon.....18
Vermillion.....9,128
Viborg.....662
Vienna.....119
Vilas.....33
Villa Ranchaero.....3,171
Virgil.....43
Volga.....982
Volin.....157
Wagner.....1,655
Wakonda.....290
Wall.....786
Wallace.....95
Ward.....57
Wasta.....127
Watertown.....13,388
Waubay.....696
Webster.....2,252
Wentworth.....196
Wessington.....380
Wessington Springs.....1,300
Wetonka.....31
White.....418
White Lake.....395
White River.....617
White Rock.....35
Whitewood.....689
Willow Lake.....353
Wilmot.....518
Winfred.....110
Winner.....3,789
Wolsey.....436
Wood.....132
Woonsocket.....852
Worthing.....294
Yale.....148
Yankton.....11,919

TENNESSEE Total population: 3,924,164

METROPOLITAN AREAS

Chattanooga.....304,927 (254,236 in Tennessee, 50,691 in Georgia)
Knoxville.....400,337
Memphis.....770,217 (722,111 in Tennessee, 48,106 in Arkansas)
Nashville.....541,160

COUNTIES

Anderson.....60,300
Bedford.....25,039
Benton.....12,126
Bledsoe.....7,643
Blount.....63,744
Bradley.....50,686
Campbell.....26,045
Cannon.....8,467
Carroll.....25,741
Carter.....43,259
Cheatham.....13,199
Chester.....9,927
Claiborne.....19,420
Clay.....6,624
Cocke.....25,283
Coffee.....32,572
Crockett.....14,402
Cumberland.....20,733
Davidson.....448,003
Decatur.....9,457
De Kalb.....11,151
Dickson.....21,977
Dyer.....30,427
Fayette.....22,692
Fentress.....12,593
Franklin.....27,289
Gibson.....47,871
Giles.....22,138
Grainger.....13,948
Greene.....47,630
Grundy.....10,631
Hamblen.....38,696
Hamilton.....254,236
Hancock.....6,719
Hardeman.....22,435
Hardin.....18,212
Hawkins.....33,757
Haywood.....19,596
Henderson.....17,360
Henry.....23,749
Hickman.....12,096
Houston.....5,853
Humphreys.....13,560
Jackson.....8,141
Jefferson.....24,940
Johnson.....11,569
Knox.....276,293
Lake.....8,091
Lauderdale.....20,271
Lawrence.....29,097
Lewis.....6,761
Lincoln.....24,318
Loudon.....24,266
Macon.....12,315
Madison.....65,774
Marion.....20,577
Marshall.....17,319
Maury.....44,028
McMinn.....35,462
McNairy.....18,369
Meigs.....5,219
Monroe.....23,475
Montgomery.....62,721
Moore.....3,568
Morgan.....13,619
Obion.....29,936
Overton.....14,866
Perry.....5,238
Pickett.....3,774
Polk.....11,669
Putnam.....35,487
Rhea.....17,202
Roane.....38,881
Robertson.....29,102
Rutherford.....59,428
Scott.....14,762
Sequatchie.....6,331
Sevier.....28,241
Shelby.....722,111
Smith.....12,509
Stewart.....7,319
Sullivan.....127,329
Sumner.....56,284
Tipton.....28,001
Trousdale.....5,155
Unicoi.....15,254
Union.....9,072
Van Buren.....3,758
Warren.....26,972
Washington.....73,924
Wayne.....12,365
Weakley.....28,827
White.....16,355
Williamson.....34,423
Wilson.....36,999

PLACES

Adair.....51
Adams.....458
Adamsville.....1,344
Alamo.....2,499
Alcoa.....7,739
Alexandria.....680
Algood.....1,808
Allardt.....610
Altamont.....546
Ardmore.....601
Arlington.....1,349
Ashland City.....2,027
Athens.....11,790
Atoka.....446
Atwood.....937
Auburntown.....213
Baileyton.....258
Banner Hill.....2,517
Bartlett.....1,150
Baxter.....1,229
Beersheba Springs.....560
Bell Buckle.....393
Bells.....1,474
Bemis.....1,883
Benton.....749
Berry's Chapel.....1,345
Bethel Springs.....781
Big Sandy.....539
Bloomingdale.....3,120
Bluff City.....985
Bolivar.....6,674
Bradford.....968
Braemar-Hampton.....1,100
Brentwood.....4,099
Brighton.....952
Bristol.....20,064
Brownsville.....7,011
Bruceton.....1,450
Bulls Gap.....774
Burlison.....397
Burns.....456
Byrdstown.....582
Calhoun.....624
Camden.....3,052
Carthage.....2,491
Caryville.....648
Cedar Hill.....355
Celina.....1,370
Centertown.....181
Centerville.....2,592
Chapel Hill.....752
Charleston.....792
Charlotte.....610
Chattanooga.....119,082
Church Hill.....2,822
Clarksburg.....349
Clarksville.....31,719
Cleveland.....20,651
Clifton City.....737
Clinton.....4,794
Coalmont.....518
Collegedale.....3,031
Collierville.....3,651
Collinwood.....922
Colonial Heights.....3,027
Columbia.....21,471
Cookeville.....14,270
Copperhill.....563
Cornersville.....655
Cottage Grove.....119
Covington.....5,801
Cowan.....1,772
Crossville.....5,381
Cumberland City.....416
Cumberland Gap.....231
Dandridge.....1,270
Davidson, see Nashville-Davidson
Dayton.....4,361
Decatur.....698
Decaturville.....958
Decherd.....2,148
Denmark.....61
Dickson.....5,665
Dover.....1,179
Dowelltown.....329
Doyle.....472
Dresden.....1,939
Ducktown.....562
Dunlap.....1,672
Dyer.....2,501
Dyersburg.....14,523
Eagleton Village.....5,345
Eagleville.....437
East Cleveland.....1,870
East Ridge.....21,799
Eastview.....423
Elizabethton.....12,269
Elkton.....341
Embreeville Junction.....1,293
Englewood.....1,878
Enville.....228
Erin.....1,165
Erwin.....4,715
Estill Springs.....919
Etowah.....3,736
Fairview.....1,630
Fayetteville.....7,030
Fort Campbell South.....9,279
Franklin.....9,497
Friendship.....441
Friendsville.....575
Gadsden.....523
Gainesboro.....1,101
Gallatin.....13,271
Gallaway.....304
Garland.....292
Gates.....523
Gatlinburg.....2,329
Germantown.....3,474
Gibson.....302
Gilt Edge.....406
Gleason.....1,314
Gordonsville.....601
Grand Junction.....427
Graysville.....951
Greater Hendersonville.....11,996
Greenback.....318
Greenbrier.....2,279
Greeneville.....13,722
Greenfield.....2,050
Halls.....2,323
Harriman.....8,734
Hartsville.....2,243
Henderson.....3,581
Hendersonville.....262
Henning.....605
Henry.....302
Hickory Valley.....180
Hixson.....6,188
Hohenwald.....3,385
Hollow Rock.....722
Hornbeak.....418
Hornsby.....212
Humboldt.....10,066
Huntingdon.....3,661
Huntland.....849
Huntsville.....337
Iron City.....504
Jacksboro.....689
Jackson.....39,996
Jamestown.....1,899
Jasper.....1,931
Jefferson City.....5,124
Jellico.....2,235
Johnson City.....33,770
Johnson City Southeast.....1,509
Jonesboro.....1,510
Karns.....1,105
Kenton.....1,439
Kimball.....807
Kingsport.....31,938
Kingsport North.....13,118
Kingston.....4,142
Kingston Springs.....312
Knoxville.....174,587
Lafayette.....2,583
La Follette.....6,902
La Grange.....213
Lake City.....1,923
Lake Hills-Murray Hills.....7,806
La Vergne.....2,825
Lawrenceburg.....8,889
Lebanon.....12,492
Lenoir City.....5,324
Lewisburg.....7,207
Lexington.....5,024
Liberty.....332
Linden.....1,062
Livingston.....3,050
Lobelville.....773
Long Island.....1,352
Lookout Mountain.....1,741
Loretto.....1,375
Loudon.....3,728
Luttrell.....819
Lynchburg.....538
Lynnville.....327
Madisonville.....2,614
Manchester.....6,208
Martin.....7,781
Maryville.....13,808
Mason.....443
Maury City.....813
Maynardville.....702
McEwen.....1,237
McKenzie.....4,873
McLemoresville.....328
McMinnville.....10,662
Medina.....755
Medon.....136
Memphis.....623,530
Michie.....377
Middleton.....654
Milan.....7,313
Milledgeville.....349
Millington.....21,177
Minor Hill.....315
Mitchellville.....177
Monteagle.....934
Monterey.....2,351
Morrison.....379
Morrison City.....2,178
Morristown.....20,318
Moscow.....448
Mount Carmel.....2,821
Mount Pleasant.....3,530
Mountain City.....1,883
Munford.....1,281
Murfreesboro.....26,360
Murray Hills, see Lake Hills-Murray Hills
Nashville-Davidson.....447,877
New Johnsonville.....970
New Tazewell.....1,192
Newbern.....2,124
Newport.....7,328
Niota.....629
Normandy.....122
Norris.....1,359
Oak Ridge.....28,319
Oakdale.....376
Oakland.....353
Obion.....1,010
Oliver Springs.....3,405
Oneida.....2,602
Orebank.....1,111
Orlinda.....347
Orme.....122
Palmer.....898
Paris.....9,892
Parrottsville.....115
Parsons.....2,167
Petersburg.....463
Philadelphia.....554
Pigeon Forge.....1,361
Pikeville.....1,454
Pleasant Hill.....293
Portland.....2,872
Pulaski.....6,989
Puryear.....458
Ramer.....347
Red Bank.....12,715
Red Boiling Springs.....726
Rheatown.....156
Richard City.....132
Ridgely.....1,657
Ridgeside.....458
Ridgetop.....810
Ripley.....4,794
Rives.....385
Rockwood.....5,259
Rogersville.....4,076
Rossville.....410
Rutherford.....1,385
Rutledge.....863
St. Joseph.....637
Saltillo.....423
Samburg.....463
Sardis.....350
Saulsbury.....156
Savannah.....5,576
Scotts Hill.....638
Selmer.....3,495
Sevierville.....2,661
Sewanee.....1,886
Sharon.....1,188
Shelbyville.....12,262
Signal Mountain.....4,839
Silerton.....88
Slayden.....95
Smithville.....2,997
Smyrna.....5,698
Sneedville.....874
Soddy-Daisy.....7,569
Somerville.....1,816
South Carthage.....859
South Cleveland.....5,070
South Clinton.....1,484
South Fulton.....3,122
South Pittsburg.....3,613
Sparta.....4,930
Spencer.....1,179
Spring City.....1,756
Spring Hill.....685
Springfield.....9,720
Stanton.....372
Stantonville.....296
Surgoinsville.....1,285
Sweetwater.....4,340
Tazewell.....1,860
Tellico Plains.....773
Tennessee Ridge.....664
Tiptonville.....2,424
Toone.....200
Townsend.....267
Tracy City.....1,388
Trenton.....4,226
Trezevant.....877
Trimble.....675
Troy.....826
Tullahoma.....15,311
Tusculum.....1,157
Union City.....11,925
Vanleer.....320
Viola.....193
Vonore.....524
Wartburg.....541
Wartrace.....616
Watauga.....314
Watertown.....1,061
Waverly.....3,794
Waynesboro.....1,983
Westmoreland.....1,423
White Bluff.....1,163
White Pine.....1,532
Whiteville.....992
Whitwell.....1,669
Winchester.....5,256
Woodbury.....1,725
Woodland Mills.....396
Yorkville.....243

TEXAS Total population: 11,196,730

METROPOLITAN AREAS

Abilene	113,959
Amarillo	144,396
Austin	295,516
Beaumont-Port Arthur-Orange	317,572
Brownsville-Harlingen-San Benito	140,368
Bryan-College Station	57,978
Corpus Christi	284,832
Dallas	1,555,950
El Paso	359,291
Fort Worth	762,086
Galveston-Texas City	169,812
Houston	1,985,031
Killeen-Temple	159,794
Laredo	72,859
Lubbock	179,295
McAllen-Pharr-Edinburg	181,535
Midland	65,433
Odessa	91,805
San Angelo	71,047
San Antonio	864,014
Sherman-Denison	83,225
Texarkana (67,813 in Texas, 33,385 in Arkansas)	101,198
Tyler	97,096
Waco	147,553
Wichita Falls	126,322

COUNTIES

Anderson	27,789
Andrews	10,372
Angelina	49,349
Aransas	8,902
Archer	5,759
Armstrong	1,895
Atascosa	18,696
Austin	13,831
Bailey	8,487
Bandera	4,747
Bastrop	17,297
Baylor	5,221
Bee	22,737
Bell	124,483
Bexar	830,460
Blanco	3,567
Borden	888
Bosque	10,966
Bowie	67,813
Brazoria	108,312
Brazos	57,978
Brewster	7,780
Briscoe	2,794
Brooks	8,005
Brown	25,877
Burleson	9,999
Burnet	11,420
Caldwell	21,178
Calhoun	17,831
Callahan	8,205
Cameron	140,368
Camp	8,005
Carson	6,358
Cass	24,133
Castro	10,394
Chambers	12,187
Cherokee	32,008
Childress	6,605
Clay	8,079
Cochran	5,326
Coke	3,087
Coleman	10,288
Collin	66,920
Collingsworth	4,755
Colorado	17,638
Comal	24,165
Comanche	11,898
Concho	2,937
Cooke	23,471
Coryell	35,311
Cottle	3,204
Crane	4,172
Crockett	3,885
Crosby	9,085
Culberson	3,429
Dallam	6,012
Dallas	1,327,321
Dawson	16,604
Deaf Smith	18,999
Delta	4,927
Denton	75,633
De Witt	18,660
Dickens	3,737
Dimmit	9,039
Donley	3,641
Duval	11,722
Eastland	18,092
Ector	91,805
Edwards	2,107
Ellis	46,638
El Paso	359,291
Erath	18,141
Falls	17,300
Fannin	22,705
Fayette	17,650
Fisher	6,344
Floyd	11,044
Foard	2,211
Fort Bend	52,314
Franklin	5,291
Freestone	11,116
Frio	11,159
Gaines	11,593
Galveston	169,812
Garza	5,289
Gillespie	10,553
Glasscock	1,155
Goliad	4,869
Gonzales	16,375
Gray	26,949
Grayson	83,225
Gregg	75,929
Grimes	11,855
Guadalupe	33,554
Hale	34,137
Hall	6,015
Hamilton	7,198
Hansford	6,351
Hardeman	6,795
Hardin	29,996
Harris	1,741,912
Harrison	44,841
Hartley	2,782
Haskell	8,512
Hays	27,642
Hemphill	3,084
Henderson	26,466
Hidalgo	181,535
Hill	22,596
Hockley	20,396
Hood	6,368
Hopkins	20,710
Houston	17,855
Howard	37,796
Hudspeth	2,392
Hunt	47,948
Hutchinson	24,443
Irion	1,070
Jack	6,711
Jackson	12,975
Jasper	24,692
Jeff Davis	1,527
Jefferson	246,402
Jim Hogg	4,654
Jim Wells	33,032
Johnson	45,769
Jones	16,106
Karnes	13,462
Kaufman	32,392
Kendall	6,964
Kenedy	678
Kent	1,434
Kerr	19,454
Kimble	3,904
King	464
Kinney	2,006
Kleberg	33,166
Knox	5,972
Lamar	36,062
Lamb	17,770
Lampasas	9,323
La Salle	5,014
Lavaca	17,903
Lee	8,048
Leon	8,738
Liberty	33,014
Limestone	18,100
Lipscomb	3,486
Live Oak	6,697
Llano	6,979
Loving	164
Lubbock	179,295
Lynn	9,107
Madison	7,693
Marion	8,517
Martin	4,774
Mason	3,356
Matagorda	27,913
Maverick	18,093
McCulloch	8,571
McLennan	147,553
McMullen	1,095
Medina	20,249
Menard	2,646
Midland	65,433
Milam	20,028
Mills	4,212
Mitchell	9,073
Montague	15,326
Montgomery	49,479
Moore	14,060
Morris	12,310
Motley	2,178
Nacogdoches	36,362
Navarro	31,150
Newton	11,657
Nolan	16,220
Nueces	237,544
Ochiltree	9,704
Oldham	2,258
Orange	71,170
Palo Pinto	28,962
Panola	15,894
Parker	33,888
Parmer	10,509
Pecos	13,748
Polk	14,457
Potter	90,511
Presidio	4,842
Rains	3,752
Randall	53,885
Reagan	3,239
Real	2,013
Red River	14,298
Reeves	16,526
Refugio	9,494
Roberts	967
Robertson	14,389
Rockwall	7,046
Runnels	12,108
Rusk	34,102
Sabine	7,187
San Augustine	7,858
San Jacinto	6,702
San Patricio	47,288
San Saba	5,540
Schleicher	2,277
Scurry	15,760
Shackelford	3,323
Shelby	19,672
Sherman	3,657
Smith	97,096
Somervell	2,793
Starr	17,707
Stephens	8,414
Sterling	1,056
Stonewall	2,397
Sutton	3,175
Swisher	10,373
Tarrant	716,317
Taylor	97,853
Terrell	1,940
Terry	14,118
Throckmorton	2,205
Titus	16,702
Tom Green	71,047
Travis	295,516
Trinity	7,628
Tyler	12,417
Upshur	20,976
Upton	4,697
Uvalde	17,348
Val Verde	27,471
Van Zandt	22,155
Victoria	53,766
Walker	27,680
Waller	14,285
Ward	13,019
Washington	18,842
Webb	72,859
Wharton	36,729
Wheeler	6,434
Wichita	120,563
Wilbarger	15,355
Willacy	15,570
Williamson	37,305
Wilson	13,041
Winkler	9,640
Wise	19,687
Wood	18,589
Yoakum	7,344
Young	15,400
Zapata	4,352
Zavala	11,370

PLACES

Abbott	375
Abernathy	2,625
Abilene	89,653
Ackerly	348
Addison	595
Adrian	228
Agua Dulce	742
Alamo	4,291
Alamo Heights	6,933
Alba	555
Albany	1,978
Aledo	620
Alice	20,121
Alice Southwest	1,908
Allen	1,940
Alpine	5,971
Alta Loma	1,536
Alto	1,045
Alvarado	2,129
Alvin	10,671
Alvord	791
Amarillo	127,010
Amherst	825
Anahuac	1,881
Andrews	8,625
Angleton	9,770
Angleton South	1,017
Anna	736
Annona	373
Anson	2,615
Anthony	2,154
Anton	1,034
Appleby	280
Aransas Pass	5,813
Archer City	1,722
Argyle	443
Arlington	89,723
Arp	816
Asherton	1,645
Aspermont	1,198
Athens	9,582
Atlanta	5,007
Aubrey	731
Austin	251,808
Austwell	284
Avery	491
Avinger	642
Azle	4,493
Bailey	197
Baileys Prairie	228
Baird	1,538
Balch Springs	10,464
Balcones Heights	2,504
Ballinger	4,203
Balmorhea	655
Bandera	891
Bangs	1,214
Bardwell	277
Barrett	2,750
Barry	149
Barstow	614
Bartlett	1,622
Bastrop	3,112
Bay City	11,733
Baytown	43,980
Bayview	312
Beaumont	117,548
Beckville	582
Bedford	10,049
Beeville	13,506
Bellaire	19,009
Bellevue	323
Bellmead	7,698
Bells	778
Bellville	2,371
Belton	8,696
Benavides	2,112
Benbrook	8,169
Benjamin	308
Bessmay-Buna	1,649
Beverly Hills	2,289
Bevil Oaks	663
Big Lake	2,489
Big Sandy	1,022
Big Spring	28,735
Big Wells	711
Biggs	4,226
Bishop	3,466
Blackwell	279
Blanco	1,022
Blanket	346
Bloomburg	231
Blooming Grove	740
Bloomington	1,676
Blossom	816
Blue Mound	1,283
Blue Ridge	384
Blum	382
Boerne	2,432
Bogata	1,287
Bonham	7,698
Booker	904
Borger	14,195
Bovina	1,428
Bowie	5,185
Boyd	695
Brackettville	1,539
Brady	5,557
Brandon	80
Brazoria	1,681
Breckenridge	5,944
Bremond	822
Brenham	8,922
Bridge City	8,164
Bridgeport	3,614
Bronte	925
Brookshire	1,683
Brookside	1,507
Brownfield	9,647
Brownsboro	474
Brownsville	52,522
Brownwood	17,368
Bryan	33,719
Bryson	455
Buckingham	41
Buda	498
Buffalo	1,242
Buffalo Gap	320
Bullard	573
Bunavista	1,402
Bunker Hill Village	3,977
Burkburnett	9,230
Burke	188
Burleson	7,713
Burnet	2,864
Byers	553
Cactus	644
Caddo Mills	935
Caldwell	2,308
Calvert	2,072
Cameron	5,546
Camp Wood	660
Campbellton	279
Canadian	2,292
Canton	2,283
Canutillo	1,588
Canyon	8,333
Carbon	264
Carrizo Springs	5,374
Carrollton	13,855
Carthage	5,392
Castle Hills	5,311
Castroville	1,893
Cedar Hill	2,610
Celeste	736
Celina	1,272
Center	4,989
Centerville	831
Chandler	765
Channing	336
Charlotte	1,329
Chase	1,221
Chester	260
Chico	723
Childress	5,408
Chillicothe	1,116
China Grove	329
Christine	289
Cibolo	440
Cisco	4,160
Clarendon	1,974
Clarksville	3,346
Clarksville City	398
Claude	992
Clear Lake Shores	865
Cleburne	16,015
Cleveland	5,627
Clifton	2,578
Clute City	6,023
Clyde	1,635
Coahoma	1,158
Cockrell Hill	3,515
Coleman	5,608
College Station	17,676
Colleyville	3,368
Collinsville	768
Colorado City	5,227
Columbus	3,342
Comanche	3,933
Combes	689
Commerce	9,534
Como	474
Conroe	11,969
Converse	1,383
Cool	21
Coolidge	786
Cooper	2,258
Coppell	1,728
Copperas Cove	10,818
Corinth	461
Corpus Christi	204,525
Corrigan	1,304
Corsicana	19,972
Cotulla	3,415
Cove City	1,578
Crandall	774
Crane	3,427
Crawford	477
Crockett	6,616
Crosby	1,118
Crosbyton	2,251
Cross Plains	1,192
Crowell	1,399
Crowley	2,662
Crystal City	8,104
Cuero	6,956
Cumby	628
Cushing	396
Cut and Shoot	451
Daingerfield	2,630
Daisetta	1,084
Dalhart	5,705
Dallas	844,401
Dalworthington Gardens	757
Danbury	807
Darrouzett	396
Dawson	848
Dayton	3,804
Decatur	3,240
Deer Park	12,773
De Kalb	2,197
De Leon	2,170
Dell City	383
Del Rio	21,330
Denison	24,923
Denton	39,874
Denver City	4,133
Deport	761
De Soto	6,617
Detroit	668
Devine	3,311
Diboll	3,557
Dickens	295
Dickinson	10,776
Dilley	2,362
Dimmitt	4,327
Dodd City	302
Dodson	239
Donna	7,365
Douglassville	282
Driscoll	626
Dublin	2,810
Dumas	9,771
Duncanville	14,105
Eagle Lake	3,587
Eagle Pass	15,364
Early	1,097
Earth	1,152
East Bernard	1,159
East Tawakoni	278
Eastland	3,178
Easton	297
Ector	549
Edcouch	2,656
Eden	1,291
Edgecliff	1,143
Edgewood	1,176
Edinburg	17,163
Edmonson	99
Edna	5,332
Edom	201
El Campo	9,332
El Campo South	1,111
Eldorado	1,446
Electra	3,895
Elgin	3,832
Elkhart	997
El Lago	2,298
Elmendorf	400
El Paso	322,261
Elsa	4,400
Emhouse	158
Emory	693
Enloe	113
Ennis	11,046
Estelline	301
Euless	19,316
Eustace	491
Everman	4,570
Fabens	3,241
Fairfield	2,074
Fairview	463
Falfurrias	6,355
Falls City	442
Farmers Branch	27,492
Farmersville	2,311
Farwell	1,185
Fate	329
Fayetteville	400
Ferris	2,180
Flatonia	1,108
Florence	672
Floresville	3,707
Flower Mound	1,685
Floydada	4,109
Follett	522
Forest Hill	8,236
Forney	1,745
Forsan	237
Fort Bliss	13,288
Fort Hood	32,597
Fort Sam Houston	10,553
Fort Stockton	8,283
Fort Wolters	3,743
Fort Worth	393,476
Franklin	1,063
Frankston	1,056
Fredericksburg	5,326
Freeport	11,997
Freer	2,804
Friendswood	5,675
Friona	3,111
Frisco	1,845
Fritch	1,778
Frost	548
Fruitvale	206
Fulton	1,101
Gainesville	13,830
Galena Park	10,479
Galveston	61,809
Ganado	1,640
Garland	81,437
Garrett	225
Garrison	1,082
Gary City	202
Gatesville	4,683
George West	2,022
Georgetown	6,395
Giddings	2,783
Gilmer	4,196
Gladewater	5,574
Glen Rose	1,554
Glenn Heights	240
Godley	533
Goldsmith	387
Goldthwaite	1,693
Goliad	1,709
Gonzales	5,854
Gordon	457
Goree	538
Gorman	1,236
Graford	613
Graham	7,477
Granbury	2,473
Grand Prairie	50,904
Grand Saline	2,257
Grandfalls	622
Grandview	935
Granger	1,256
Granite Shoals	342
Grapeland	1,211
Grapevine	7,023
Greenville	22,043
Gregory	2,246
Grey Forest	385
Griffing Park	2,075
Groesbeck	2,396
Groom	808
Groves	18,067
Groveton	1,219
Gruver	1,265
Gun Barrel	303
Gunter	647
Gustine	357
Hale Center	1,964
Hallettsville	2,712
Hallsville	1,038
Haltom City	28,127
Hamilton	2,760
Hamlin	3,325
Happy	672
Harker Heights	4,216
Harlingen	33,503
Hart	905
Harwood	112
Haskell	3,655
Haslet	276
Hawkins	977
Hearne	4,982
Heath	449
Hebbronville	4,079
Hedley	439
Hedwig Village	3,255
Hemphill	1,005
Hempstead	1,891
Henderson	10,187
Henrietta	2,897
Hereford	13,414
Hewitt	569
Hickory Creek	218
Hico	975
Hidalgo	1,289
Higgins	582
Highland	516
Highland Park	10,133
Highlands	3,462
Hill Country Village	636
Hillcrest	650
Hillsboro	7,224
Hilshire Village	627
Hitchcock	5,565
Holland	723
Holliday	1,048
Hollywood Park	2,299
Hondo	5,487
Honey Grove	1,853
Hooks	2,545
Houston	1,232,802
Howe	1,359
Hubbard	1,572
Hughes Springs	1,701
Humble	3,278
Hunters Creek Village	3,959
Huntington	1,192
Huntsville	17,610
Hurst	27,215
Hutchins	1,755
Hutto	545
Huxley	23
Idalou	1,729
Impact	61
Ingleside	3,763
Iowa Park	5,796
Iraan	996
Iredell	316
Irving	97,260
Italy	1,309
Itasca	1,483
Jacinto City	9,563
Jacksboro	3,554
Jacksonville	9,734
Jasper	6,251
Jayton	703
Jefferson	2,866
Jersey Village	765
Jewett	447
Joaquin	819
Johnson City	767
Jones Creek	1,268
Josephine	296
Joshua	924
Jourdanton	1,841
Junction	2,654
Justin	741
Karnes City	2,926
Katy	2,923
Kaufman	4,012
Keene	2,440
Keller	1,474
Kemah	1,144
Kemp	999
Kenedy	4,156
Kennedale	3,076
Kerens	1,446
Kermit	7,884
Kerrville	12,672
Kilgore	9,495
Killeen	35,507
Kingsville	28,915
Kingsville Station	1,127
Kirby	2,558
Kirbyville	1,869
Kirvin	65
Kleberg	4,768
Knox City	1,536
Kosse	471
Kountze	2,173
Kress	578
Krum	454
Kyle	1,629
Lackland	19,141
La Coste	768
Lacy-Lakeview	2,558
Ladonia	757
La Feria	2,642
La Grange	3,092
La Grulla	1,194
Laguna Vista	287
La Isla	29
La Joya	1,217
Lake Barbara	605
Lake Dallas	1,431
Lake Jackson	13,376

Lake Worth Village 4,958
Lakeport 411
Lakeside (Archer Co.) 187
Lakeside (Tarrant Co.) 988
Lakeview (Hall Co.) 214
Lakeview (Jefferson Co.) 3,567
La Marque 16,131
Lamesa 11,559
Lampasas 5,922
Lancaster 10,522
La Porte 7,149
Laredo 69,024
Laughlin 3,458
La Vernia 265
La Villa 1,255
La Ward 247
Lawn 344
Lawrence 98
League City 10,818
Leakey 393
Leary 352
Lefors 816
Leon Valley 1,960
Leona 96
Leonard 1,423
Levelland 11,445
Lewisville 9,264
Lexington 719
Liberty 5,591
Lindale 1,631
Linden 2,264
Lindsay 435
Lipan 333
Little Elm 363
Littlefield 6,738
Live Oak 2,779
Liverpool 319
Livingston 3,965
Llano 2,608
Lockhart 6,489
Lockney 2,094
Lomax 894
Lometa 633
Lone Oak 518
Lone Star 1,760
Longview 45,547
Loraine 700
Lorena 406
Lorenzo 1,206
Los Fresnos 1,297
Lott 799
Lovelady 388
Lubbock 149,101
Lucas 540
Lueders 511
Lufkin 23,049
Luling 4,719
Lyford 1,425
Lytle 1,271
Mabank 1,239
Madisonville 2,881
Malakoff 2,045
Malone 305
Manor 940
Mansfield 3,658
Manvel 106
Marble Falls 2,209
Marfa 2,682
Marion 655
Marlin 6,351
Marquez 185
Marshall 22,937
Mart 2,183
Mason 1,806
Matador 1,091
Mathis 5,351
Maud 1,107
Maypearl 462
McAllen 37,636
McCamey 2,647
McGregor 4,365
McKinney 15,193
McLean 1,183
McNair 2,039
Meadow 491
Megargel 373
Melvin 290
Memphis 3,227
Menard 1,740
Mercedes 9,355
Meridian 1,162
Merkel 2,163
Mertens 109
Mertzon 513
Mesa 50
Mesquite 55,131
Mexia 5,943
Miami 611
Midland 59,463
Midlothian 2,322
Miles 631
Milford 664
Mineola 3,926
Mineral Wells 18,411
Mingus 273
Mission 13,043
Missouri City 4,136
Monahans 8,333
Mont Belvieu 1,144
Montague Village 1,265
Montgomery 216
Moody 1,286
Moran 335
Morgan 415
Morgans Point 593
Morton 2,738
Moulton 968
Mount Calm 363
Mount Enterprise 425
Mount Pleasant 9,459
Mount Vernon 1,806
Muenster 1,411
Muleshoe 4,525
Mullin 203
Munday 1,726
Murchison 432
Murphy 261
Nacogdoches 22,544
Naples 1,726
Nash 1,961
Natalia 1,296
Navasota 5,111
Nederland 16,810
Needville 1,024
Nesbitt 60
New Boston 4,034
New Braunfels 17,859
New Home 252
New London 899
New Summerfield 344
New Waverly 496
Newark 407
Newcastle 624
Newton 1,529
Nixon 1,925
Nocona 2,871
Nolanville 902
Nordheim 369
Normangee 657
North Cleveland 404
North Richland Hills 16,514
North San Pedro 2,229
Northcrest 1,669
Northlake 20
Novice 191
O'Brien 258
O'Donnell 1,148
Oakwood 547
Odem 2,130
Odessa 78,380
Oglesby 440
Olmos Park 2,250
Olney 3,624
Olton 1,782
Omaha 898
Orange 24,457
Orange Grove 1,075
Ore 830
Overton 2,084
Ovilla 339
Ozona 2,864
Paducah 2,052
Paint Rock 193
Palacios 3,642
Palestine 14,525
Palmer 601
Palmhurst 120
Pampa 21,726
Panhandle 2,141
Pantego 1,812
Paris 23,441
Pasadena 89,277
Patton 667
Peacock 131
Pear Ridge 3,697
Pearland 6,444
Pearsall 5,545
Pecan Gap 270
Pecos 12,682
Penelope 212
Perrin 1,709
Perryton 7,810
Petersburg 1,300
Petrolia 584
Pflugerville 549
Pharr 15,829
Phillips 2,515
Pilot Point 1,663
Pine Forest 512
Pinehurst 2,198
Pineland 1,127
Piney Point Village 2,548
Pittsburg 3,844
Plains 1,087
Plainview 19,096
Plano 17,872
Pleasant Valley 323
Pleasanton 5,407
Point 419
Point Comfort 1,446
Ponder 208
Port Aransas 1,218
Port Arthur 57,371
Port Isabel 3,067
Port Lavaca 10,491
Port Neches 10,894
Portland 7,302
Post 3,854
Poteet 3,013
Poth 1,296
Pottsboro 748
Powell 121
Prairie View 3,589
Premont 3,282
Primera 902
Princeton 1,105
Prosper 501
Purdon 133
Putnam 134
Pyote 155
Quanah 3,948
Queen City 1,227
Quinlan 844
Quitaque 601
Quitman 1,494
Ralls 1,962
Randolph 5,329
Ranger 3,094
Rankin 1,105
Ravenna 186
Raymondville 7,987
Red Oak 767
Reese 2,545
Refugio 4,340
Reklaw 171
Renner 339
Reno (Lamar Co.) 487
Reno (Parker Co.) 688
Retreat 263
Rhome 393
Rice 284
Richardson 48,582
Richland 309
Richland Hills 8,865
Richland Springs 425
Richmond 5,777
Richwood 1,452
Rio Grande City 5,676
Rio Hondo 1,167
Rio Vista 370
Rising Star 1,009
River Oaks 8,193
Roanoke 817
Roaring Springs 308
Robert Lee 1,119
Robinson 3,807
Robstown 11,217
Roby 784
Rochester 529
Rockdale 4,655
Rockport 3,879
Rocksprings 1,221
Rockwall 3,121
Rogers 1,030
Rollingwood 780
Roma-Los Saenz 2,154
Ropesville 483
Roscoe 1,580
Rose Hill Acres 431
Rosebud 1,597
Rosenberg 12,098
Rotan 2,404
Round Rock 2,811
Round Top 94
Rowlett 2,579
Royse City 1,535
Rule 1,024
Runge 1,147
Rusk 4,914
Sabinal 1,554
Sachse 777
Sadler 309
Saginaw 2,382
St. Hedwig 690
St. Jo 1,054
San Angelo 63,884
San Antonio 654,153
San Augustine 2,539
San Benito 15,176
San Diego 4,490
San Felipe 422
San Juan 5,070
San Marcos 18,860
San Perlita 352
San Saba 2,555
Sanderson 1,229
Sanford 181
Sanger 1,603
Sansom Park Village 4,771
Santa Anna 1,310
Santa Rosa 1,466
Savoy 756
Schertz 4,061
Schulenburg 2,294
Scottsville 259
Seabrook 3,811
Seadrift 1,092
Seagoville 4,390
Seagraves 2,440
Sealy 2,685
Seguin 15,934
Selma 207
Seminole 5,007
Seymour 3,469
Shady Shores 543
Shallowater 1,339
Shamrock 2,644
Shavano Park 881
Sheldon 1,665
Shepherd 928
Sherman 29,061
Shiner 2,102
Shoreacres 1,872
Silsbee 7,271
Silverton 1,026
Sinton 5,563
Skellytown 716
Slaton 6,583
Smiley 440
Smithville 2,959
Smyer 265
Snyder 11,171
Somerville 1,250
Sonoma 678
Sonora 2,149
Sour Lake 1,694
South Houston 11,527
South San Pedro 3,065
South Side Place 1,466
Southlake 2,031
Southland 168
Southmayd 222
Spearman 3,435
Splendora 194
Spofford 69
Spring Valley 3,170
Springlake 209
Springtown 1,194
Spur 1,747
Stafford 2,906
Stamford 4,558
Stanton 2,117
Stephenville 9,277
Sterling City 780
Stinnett 2,014
Stockdale 1,132
Stratford 2,139
Strawn 786
Streetman 286
Sudan 976
Sugar Land 3,318
Sulphur Springs 10,642
Sundown 1,129
Sunnyvale 995
Sunray 1,854
Sunrise 1,213
Sunset Valley 292
Sweeny 3,191
Sweetwater 12,020
Taft 3,274
Taft Southwest 2,026
Tahoka 2,956
Talco 837
Talpa 121
Tatum 684
Taylor 9,616
Taylor Lake Village 1,004
Teague 2,867
Tehuacana 285
Temple 33,431
Tenaha 1,094
Terrell 14,182
Terrell Hills 5,225
Texarkana 30,497
Texas City 38,908
Texhoma 356
Texline 387
Thorndale 1,031
Thornton 433
Thrall 619
Three Rivers 1,761
Throckmorton 1,105
Timpson 1,254
Tioga 456
Tolar 312
Tom Bean 540
Tomball 2,734
Tool 121
Toyah 245
Trent 333
Trenton 599
Trinidad 1,079
Trinity 2,512
Troup 1,668
Troy 542
Tulia 5,294
Turkey 680
Tuscola 497
Tye 857
Tyler 57,770
Uncertain 202
Universal City 7,613
University Park 23,498
Uvalde 10,764
Valentine 213
Valley Mills 1,022
Van 1,593
Van Alstyne 1,981
Van Horn 2,889
Van Vleck 1,051
Vega 839
Venus 414
Vernon 11,454
Victoria 41,349
Vidor 9,738
Waco 95,326
Waelder 1,138
Wake Village 2,408
Waller 1,123
Wallis 1,028
Walnut Springs 495
Warren City 150
Waskom 1,460
Watauga 3,778
Waxahachie 13,452
Weatherford 11,750
Webster 2,231
Weimar 2,104
Weinert 255
Wellington 2,884
Wells 671
Weslaco 15,313
West 2,406
West Columbia 3,335
West Lake Hills 1,488
West Mountain 194
West Orange 4,820
West Tawakoni 465
West University Place 13,317
Westbrook 298
Westlake 128
Westminster 257
Westover Hills 374
Westworth 4,578
Wharton 7,881
Wheeler 1,116
White Deer 1,092
White Oak 2,300
White Settlement 13,449
Whiteface 394
Whitehouse 1,245
Whitesboro 2,927
Whitewright 1,742
Whitney 1,371
Wichita Falls 96,265
Wickett 598
Willis 1,577
Willow Park 230
Wills Point 2,636
Wilmer 1,922
Wilson 433
Windcrest 3,371
Windom 247
Windthorst 377
Winfield 268
Wink 1,023
Winnie 1,543
Winnsboro 3,064
Winona 155
Winters 2,907
Wolfe City 1,433
Wolfforth 1,090
Woodbranch 378
Woodland Hills 366
Woodsboro 1,839
Woodson 340
Woodville 2,662
Woodway 4,819
Wortham 1,036
Wylie 2,675
Yantis 223
Yoakum 5,755
Yorktown 2,411
Zapata 2,102

UTAH Total population: 1,059,273

METROPOLITAN AREAS

Ogden 126,278
Provo-Orem 137,776
Salt Lake City 557,635

COUNTIES

Beaver 3,800
Box Elder 28,129
Cache 42,331
Carbon 15,647
Daggett 666
Davis 99,028
Duchesne 7,299
Emery 5,137
Garfield 3,157
Grand 6,688
Iron 12,177
Juab 4,574
Kane 2,421
Millard 6,988
Morgan 3,983
Piute 1,164
Rich 1,615
Salt Lake 458,607
San Juan 9,606
Sanpete 10,976
Sevier 10,103
Summit 5,879
Tooele 21,545
Uintah 12,684
Utah 137,776
Wasatch 5,863
Washington 13,669
Wayne 1,483
Weber 126,278

PLACES

Alpine 1,047
Altamont 129
Alton 62
Amalga 207
American Fork 7,713
Annabella 221
Antimony 113
Aurora 493
Bear River 445
Beaver 1,453
Bicknell 264
Bingham Canyon 31
Blanding 2,250
Boulder 93
Bountiful 27,853
Brigham City 14,007
Cannonville 113
Castle Dale 541
Castle Gate 205
Cedar City 8,946
Cedar Fort 188
Centerfield 419
Centerville 3,268
Central 32
Charleston 196
Circleville 443
Clarkston 420
Clearfield 13,316
Cleveland 244
Clinton 1,768
Coalville 864
Corinne 471
Cornish 173
Cottonwood 8,431
Delta 1,610
Deweyville 248
Dragerton 1,614
Duchesne 1,094
Dugway 2,357
East Layton 763
East Millcreek 26,579
Elmo 141
Elsinore 357
Elwood 294
Emery 216
Enoch 120
Enterprise 844
Ephraim 2,127
Escalante 638
Eureka 753
Fairview 696
Farmington 2,526
Fayette 93
Ferron 663
Fielding 254
Fillmore 1,411
Fountain Green 467
Francis 268
Fruit Heights 800
Garden City 134
Garland 1,187
Genola 424
Glendale 200
Glenwood 212
Goshen 459
Granger-Hunter 9,029
Granite Park 9,573
Grantsville 2,931
Green River 1,033
Gunnison 1,073
Harrisville 603
Hatch 139
Heber 3,245
Helper 1,964
Henefer 446
Henrieville 145
Hiawatha 166
Hilldale 480
Hinckley 400
Holden 351
Holladay 23,014
Honeyville 640
Howell 146
Hunter, see Granger-Hunter
Huntington 857
Huntsville 553
Hurricane 1,408
Hyde Park 1,025
Hyrum 2,340
Ivins 137
Joseph 125
Junction 135
Kamas 806
Kanab 1,381
Kanarraville 204
Kanosh 319
Kaysville 6,192
Kearns 17,071
Kingston 114
Koosharem 141
Laketown 208
La Verkin 463
Layton 13,603
Leamington 112
Leeds 151
Lehi 4,659
Levan 376
Lewiston 1,244
Lindon 1,644
Loa 324
Logan 22,333
Lynndyl 111
Maeser 1,248
Magna 5,509
Manila 226
Manti 1,803
Mantua 413
Mapleton 1,980
Marysvale 289
Mayfield 267
Meadow 238
Mendon 345
Midvale 7,840
Midway 804
Milford 1,304
Millville 441
Minersville 448
Moab 4,793
Mona 309
Monroe 918
Monticello 1,431
Morgan City 1,586
Moroni 894
Mount Olympus 5,909
Mount Pleasant 1,516
Murray 21,206
Myton 322
Nephi 2,699
New Harmony 78
Newton 444
Nibley 367
North Logan 1,405
North Ogden 5,257
North Salt Lake 2,143
Oak City 278
Oakley 265
Ogden 69,478
Onaqui 541
Ophir 76
Orangeville 511
Orderville 399
Orem 25,729
Panguitch 1,318
Paradise 399
Paragonah 275
Park City 1,193
Parowan 1,423
Payson 4,501
Perry 909
Pickleville 106
Plain City 1,543
Pleasant Grove 5,327
Pleasant View 2,028
Plymouth 203
Portage 144
Price 6,218
Providence 1,608
Provo 53,131
Randolph 500
Redmond 409
Richfield 4,471
Richmond 1,000
River Heights 1,008
Riverdale 3,704
Riverton 2,820
Roosevelt 2,005
Roy 14,356
St. George 7,097
Salem 1,081
Salina 1,494
Salt Lake City 175,885
Sandy City 6,438
Santa Clara 271
Santaquin 1,236
Scipio 264
Scofield 71
Sigurd 291
Smithfield 3,342
Snowville 174
Soldier Summit 13
South Jordan 2,942
South Ogden 9,991
South Salt Lake 7,810
South Weber 1,073
Spanish Fork 7,284
Spring City 456
Springdale 172
Springville 8,790
Sterling 144
Stockton 469
Sunnyside 485
Sunset 6,268
Syracuse 1,843
Tabiona 125
Tooele 12,539
Toquerville 185
Torrey 84
Tremonton 2,794
Trenton 390
Tropic 329
Uintah 400
Vernal 3,908
Virgin 119
Wales 89
Wallsburg 211
Washington 750
Washington Terrace 7,241
Wellington 922
Wellsville 1,267
Wendover 781
West Bountiful 1,246
West Jordan 4,221
West Point 1,020
White City 6,402
Willard 1,045
Woodruff 173
Woods Cross 3,124
Yost 51

VERMONT Total population: 444,732

COUNTIES

Addison 24,266
Bennington 29,282
Caledonia 22,789
Chittenden 99,131
Essex 5,416
Franklin 31,282
Grand Isle 3,574
Lamoille 13,309
Orange 17,676
Orleans 20,153
Rutland 52,637
Washington 47,659
Windham 33,476
Windsor 44,082

TOWNS AND PLACES

Addison 717▲
Albany 528▲
Albany 175
Alburg 1,271▲
Alburg 520
Andover 239▲
Arlington 1,212
Arlington 1,934▲
Athens 159▲
Bakersfield 635▲
Baltimore 170▲
Barnard 569▲
Barnet 1,342▲
Barre 10,209
Barre 6,509▲
Barton 2,874▲
Barton 1,051
Bellows Falls 3,505
Belvidere 189▲
Bennington 14,586▲
Bennington 7,950
Benson 583▲
Berkshire 931▲
Berlin 2,050▲
Bethel 1,347▲
Bloomfield 196▲
Bolton 427▲
Bradford 1,627▲
Bradford 709
Braintree 751▲
Brandon 1,720
Brandon 3,697▲
Brattleboro 9,055
Brattleboro 12,239▲
Bridgewater 783▲
Bridport 809▲
Brighton 1,365▲
Bristol 2,744▲
Bristol 1,737
Brookfield 606▲
Brookline 180▲
Brownington 522▲
Brunswick 45▲
Burke 1,053▲
Burlington 38,633
Cabot 663▲
Cabot 253
Calais 749▲
Cambridge 1,528▲
Cambridge 235
Canaan 949▲
Castleton 2,837▲
Cavendish 1,264▲
Charleston 654▲
Charlotte 1,802▲
Chelsea 983▲
Chester 2,371▲
Chittenden 646▲
Clarendon 1,537▲
Colchester 8,776▲
Concord 896▲
Concord 353
Corinth 683▲
Cornwall 900▲
Coventry 492▲
Craftsbury 632▲
Danby 910▲
Danville 1,405▲
Derby 3,252▲
Derby Center 547
Derby Line 834
Dorset 1,293▲
Dover 555▲
Dummerston 1,295▲
Duxbury 621▲
East Haven 197▲
East Montpelier 1,597▲
Eden 513▲
Elmore 292▲
Enosburg 1,918▲
Enosburg Falls 1,266
Essex 10,951▲
Essex Junction 6,511
Fair Haven 2,287
Fair Haven 2,777▲
Fairfax 1,366▲
Fairfield 1,285▲
Fairlee 604▲
Fayston 292▲
Ferrisburg 1,875▲
Fletcher 456▲
Franklin 821▲
Georgia 1,711▲
Glover 649▲
Glover 244
Goshen 120▲
Grafton 465▲
Granby 52▲
Grand Isle 809▲
Granville 255▲
Greensboro 593▲
Groton 666▲
Groton 438
Guildhall 169▲
Guilford 1,108▲
Halifax 295▲
Hancock 283▲
Hardwick 2,466▲
Hardwick 1,503
Hartford 6,477▲
Hartland 1,806▲
Highgate 1,936▲
Hinesburg 1,775▲
Holland 383▲
Hubbardton 228▲
Huntington 748▲
Hyde Park 1,347▲
Hyde Park 418
Ira 284▲
Irasburg 775▲
Island Pond 1,123
Isle La Motte 262▲
Jacksonville 251
Jamaica 590▲
Jay 182▲
Jeffersonville 382
Jericho 2,343▲
Johnson 1,927▲
Johnson 1,296
Kirby 224▲
Landgrove 104▲
Leicester 583▲
Lemington 120▲
Lincoln 599▲
Londonderry 1,037▲
Lowell 515▲
Ludlow 2,463▲
Ludlow 1,508
Lunenburg 1,061▲
Lyndon 3,705▲
Lyndon Center 246
Lyndonville 1,415
Maidstone 94▲
Manchester 2,919▲
Manchester 435
Manchester Depot 1,560
Marlboro 592▲
Marshfield 1,033▲
Marshfield 322
Mendon 743▲
Middlebury 6,532▲
Middlesex 857▲
Middletown Springs 426▲
Milton 4,495▲
Milton 1,164
Monkton 765▲
Montgomery 651▲
Montpelier 8,609
Moretown 904▲
Morgan 286▲
Morristown 4,052▲
Morrisville 2,116
Mount Holly 687▲
Mount Tabor 184▲
New Haven 1,039▲
Newark 144▲
Newbury 1,440▲
Newfane 900▲
Newfane 183
Newport 4,664
Newport 1,125▲
North Bennington 984
North Hero 364▲
North Troy 774
North Westminster 348
Northfield 4,870▲
Northfield 2,139
Norton 207▲
Norwich 1,966▲
Old Bennington 268
Orange 540▲
Orleans 1,138
Orwell 851▲
Panton 416▲
Pawlet 1,184▲
Peacham 446▲
Perkinsville 188
Peru 243▲
Pittsfield 249▲
Pittsford 2,306▲
Pittsford 682
Plainfield 1,399▲
Plainfield 949
Plymouth 283▲
Pomfret 620▲
Poultney 3,217▲
Poultney 1,914
Pownal 2,441▲
Proctor 2,095▲
Proctorsville 512
Putney 1,727▲
Randolph 3,882▲
Randolph 2,115
Reading 564▲
Readsboro 638▲
Readsboro 469
Richford 2,116▲
Richford 1,527
Richmond 2,249▲
Richmond 935
Ripton 187▲
Rochester 884▲
Rockingham 5,501▲
Roxbury 354▲
Royalton 1,399▲
Rupert 582▲
Rutland 19,293
Rutland 2,248▲
Ryegate 830▲
St. Albans 8,082
St. Albans 3,270▲
St. George 477▲
St. Johnsbury 8,409▲
Salisbury 649▲
Sandgate 127▲
Saxtons River 581
Searsburg 84▲
Shaftsbury 2,411▲
Sharon 541▲
Sheffield 307▲
Shelburne 3,728▲
Shelburne Road Section 2,591
Sheldon 1,481▲
Sherburne 558▲
Shoreham 790▲
Shrewsbury 570▲
South Burlington 10,032▲
South Hero 868▲
Springfield 5,632
Springfield 10,063▲
Stamford 752▲
Stannard 88▲
Starksboro 668▲
Stockbridge 389▲
Stowe 2,388▲
Stowe 435
Strafford 536▲
Stratton 104▲
Sudbury 253▲
Sunderland 601▲
Sutton 438▲
Swanton 4,622▲
Swanton 2,630
Thetford 1,422▲
Tinmouth 268▲
Topsham 686▲
Townshend 668▲
Townshend 159
Troy 1,457▲
Tunbridge 791▲
Underhill 1,198▲
Vergennes 2,242
Vernon 1,024▲
Vershire 299▲
Victory 42▲
Waitsfield 837▲
Walden 442▲
Wallingford 1,676▲
Waltham 265▲
Wardsboro 391▲
Warren 588▲
Washington 667▲
Waterbury 4,614▲
Waterbury 2,840
Waterford 586▲
Waterville 397▲
Weathersfield 2,040▲
Wells 560▲
Wells River 419
West Burke 358
West Fairlee 337▲
West Glover 55
West Haven 240▲
West Rutland 1,875
West Rutland 2,381▲
West Windsor 571▲
Westfield 375▲
Westford 991▲
Westminster 1,875▲
Westminster 446
Westmore 195▲
Weston 507▲
Weybridge 618▲
Wheelock 238▲
White River Junction 2,379
Whiting 359▲
Whitingham 1,011▲
Wilder 1,328
Williamstown 1,822▲
Williston 3,187▲
Williston Road Section 5,376
Wilmington 1,586▲
Wilmington 632
Windham 174▲
Windsor 4,158▲
Winhall 281▲
Winooski 7,309
Wolcott 676▲
Woodbury 399▲
Woodford 286▲
Woodstock 2,608▲
Woodstock 1,154
Worcester 505▲

VIRGINIA Total population: 4,648,494

METROPOLITAN AREAS

Lynchburg 123,474
Newport News-Hampton 292,159
Norfolk-Virginia Beach-Portsmouth 680,600
Petersburg-Colonial Heights-Hopewell 128,809
Richmond 518,319
Roanoke 181,436

COUNTIES

Accomack 29,004
Albemarle 37,780
Alleghany 12,461
Amelia 7,592
Amherst 26,072
Appomattox 9,784
Arlington 174,284
Augusta 44,220
Bath 5,192
Bedford 26,728
Bland 5,423
Botetourt 18,193
Brunswick 16,172
Buchanan 32,071
Buckingham 10,597
Campbell 43,319
Caroline 13,925
Carroll 23,092
Charles City 6,158
Charlotte 12,366
Chesterfield 77,046
Clarke 8,102
Craig 3,524
Culpeper 18,218
Cumberland 6,179
Dickenson 16,077
Dinwiddie 25,046
Essex 7,099
Fairfax 455,021
Fauquier 26,375
Floyd 9,775
Fluvanna 7,621
Franklin 28,163
Frederick 28,893
Giles 16,741
Gloucester 14,059
Goochland 10,069
Grayson 15,439
Greene 5,248
Greensville 9,604
Halifax 30,076
Hanover 37,479
Henrico 154,364
Henry 50,901
Highland 2,529
Isle of Wight 18,285
James City 17,853
King and Queen 5,491
King George 8,039
King William 7,497
Lancaster 9,126
Lee 20,321
Loudoun 37,150
Louisa 14,004
Lunenberg 11,687
Madison 8,638
Mathews 7,168
Mecklenburg 29,426
Middlesex 6,295
Montgomery 47,157
Nansemond 35,166
Nelson 11,702
New Kent 5,300
Northampton 14,442
Northumberland 9,239
Nottoway 14,260
Orange 13,792
Page 16,581
Patrick 15,282
Pittsylvania 58,789
Powhatan 7,696
Prince Edward 14,379
Prince George 29,092
Prince William 111,102
Pulaski 29,564
Rappahannock 5,199
Richmond 6,504
Roanoke 67,339
Rockbridge 16,637
Rockingham 47,890
Russell 24,533
Scott 24,376
Shenandoah 22,852
Smyth 31,349
Southampton 18,582
Spotsylvania 16,424
Stafford 24,587
Surry 5,882
Sussex 11,464
Tazewell 39,816
Warren 15,301
Washington 40,835
Westmoreland 12,142
Wise 35,947
Wythe 22,139
York 33,203

INDEPENDENT CITIES

Alexandria 110,938
Bedford 6,011
Bristol 14,857
Buena Vista 6,425
Charlottesville 38,880
Chesapeake 89,580
Clifton Forge 5,501
Colonial Heights 15,097
Covington 10,060
Danville 46,391
Emporia 5,300
Fairfax 21,970
Falls Church 10,772
Franklin 6,880
Fredericksburg 14,450
Galax 6,278
Hampton 120,779
Harrisonburg 14,605
Hopewell 23,471
Lexington 7,597
Lynchburg 54,083
Martinsville 19,653
Newport News 138,177
Norfolk 307,951
Norton 4,001
Petersburg 36,103
Portsmouth 110,963
Radford 11,596
Richmond 249,430
Roanoke 92,115
Salem 21,982
South Boston 6,889
Staunton 24,504
Suffolk 9,858
Virginia Beach 172,106
Waynesboro 16,707
Williamsburg 9,069
Winchester 14,643

PLACES

Abingdon 4,376
Accomac 373
Alberta 466
Alexandria 110,938
Altavista 2,708
Amherst 1,108
Annandale 27,405
Appalachia 2,161
Appomattox 1,400
Arlington 174,284
Ashland 2,934
Bailey's Crossroads 7,295
Bassett 3,058
Bedford 6,011
Belle Haven 504
Belleview 8,299
Berryville 1,569
Big Stone Gap 4,153
Blacksburg 9,384
Blackstone 3,412
Bloxom 391
Bluefield 5,286
Bon Air 10,771
Boones Mill 363
Bowling Green 528
Boyce 378
Boydton 541
Boykins 742
Branchville 189
Bridgewater 2,828
Bristol 14,857
Broadway 887
Brodnax 569
Brookneal 1,037
Buchanan 1,326
Buena Vista 6,425
Burkeville 703
Camp Barrett 1,076
Cape Charles 1,689
Capron 314
Cedar Bluff 1,050
Charlotte Courthouse 539
Charlottesville 38,880
Chase City 2,909
Chatham 1,801
Cheriton 655
Chesapeake 89,580
Chester 5,556
Chilhowie 1,317
Chincoteague 1,867
Christiansburg 7,857
Claremont 383
Clarksville 1,641
Cleveland 357
Clifton 178
Clifton Forge 5,501
Clinchport 286
Clintwood 1,320
Clover 227
Coeburn 2,362
Collinsville 6,015
Colonial Beach 2,058
Colonial Heights 15,097
Columbia 125
Courtland 899
Covington 10,060
Craigsville 988
Crewe 1,797
Crozet 1,433
Culpeper 6,056
Dale City 13,857
Damascus 1,230
Dante 1,153
Danville 46,391
Dayton 978
Dendron 336
Dillwyn 497
Drakes Branch 702
Draper 276
Dublin 1,653
Duffield 63
Dumfries 1,890
Dungannon 282
Eastville 203
Edinburg 766
Elkton 1,511
Emporia 5,300
Exmore 1,421
Fairfax 21,970
Fairlawn 1,767
Falls Church 10,772
Falmouth 2,139
Farmville 4,331
Fieldale 1,337
Fincastle 397
Floyd 474
Fort Belvoir 14,591
Fort Hunt 10,415
Fort Lee 12,435
Franklin 6,880
Fredericksburg 14,450
Fries 885
Front Royal 8,211
Galax 6,278
Gate City 1,914
Glade Spring 1,615
Glasgow 1,304
Glen Lyn 191
Glenwood 1,295
Gordonsville 1,253
Goshen 121
Gretna 986
Grottoes 1,166
Groveton 11,750
Grundy 2,054
Halifax 899
Hallwood 254
Hamilton 502
Hampton 120,779
Harrisonburg 14,605
Haymarket 288
Haysi 428
Herndon 4,301
Highland Springs 7,345
Hillsboro 135
Hillsville 1,149
Holland 400
Honaker 911
Hopewell 23,471
Huntington 5,559
Hurt 1,434
Independence 673
Iron Gate 692
Irvington 504
Ivor 444
Jarratt 591
Jefferson 25,432
Jericho 2,438
Jonesville 700
Keller 235
Kenbridge 1,223
Keyesville 818
Kilmarnock 841
La Crosse 674
Lake Barcroft 11,605
Lakeside 11,137
Lawrenceville 1,636
Lebanon 2,272
Leesburg 4,821
Lexington 7,597
Lincolnia 10,761
Lloyd Place 2,367
Long Branch 21,634
Louisa 633
Lovettsville 185
Luray 3,612
Lyman Park-Thomason Park 3,765
Lynchburg 54,083
Madison 299
Manassas 9,164
Manassas Park 6,844
Mantua 6,911
Marion 8,158
Martinsville 19,653
Marumsco, see Woodbridge-Marumsco
Matoaca 829
McKenny 489
McLean 17,698
Mechanicsville 5,189
Melfa 459
Middleburg 833
Middletown 507
Mineral 397
Monterey 223
Montross 419
Mount Crawford 276
Mount Jackson 681
Narrows 2,421
Nassawadox 591
New Market 718
Newcastle 225
Newport News 138,177
Newsoms 389
Nickelsville 338
Norfolk 307,951
North Pulaski 1,315
North Springfield 8,631
Norton 4,172
Occoquan 975
Onancock 1,614
Onley 464
Orange 2,768
Painter 363
Pamplin City 394
Parksley 903
Pearisburg 2,169
Pembroke 1,095
Pennington Gap 1,886
Petersburg 36,103
Phenix 260
Pleasant Hill 2,277
Pocahontas 891
Poquoson 5,441
Port Royal 199
Portsmouth 110,963
Pound 995
Pulaski 10,279
Purcellville 1,775
Quantico 719
Quantico Station 6,213
Radford 11,596
Raven 1,819
Remington 321
Reston 5,723
Rich Creek 729
Richlands 4,843
Richmond 249,430
Ridgeway 624
Roanoke 92,115
Rocky Mount 4,002
Rose Hill 14,492
Round Hill 581
Rural Retreat 872
St. Charles 368
St. Paul 948
Salem 21,982
Saltville 2,527
Saratoga Place 1,245
Saxis 451
Scottsburg 157
Scottsville 290
Seven Corners 5,590
Shenandoah 1,714
Smithfield 2,713
South Boston 6,889
South Hill 3,858
Springfield 11,613
Stanardsville 296
Stanley 1,208
Staunton 24,504
Stephens City 802
Sterling Park 8,321
Stony Creek 430
Strasburg 2,431
Stuart 947
Suffolk 9,858
Surry 269
Tangier 814
Tappahannock 1,111
Tazewell 4,168
The Plains 418
Timberville 959
Toms Brook 258
Triangle 3,021
Troutdale 209
Troutville 522
Urbanna 475
Victoria 1,408
Vienna 17,146
Vint Hill Farms Station 1,018
Vinton 6,347
Virgilina 249
Virginia Beach 172,106
Wachapreague 399
Wakefield 942
Warrenton 4,027
Warsaw 511
Washington 189
Waverly 1,717
Waynesboro 16,707

▲ Population of entire town (township)

Weber City 1,676
West Point 2,600
West Springfield 14,143
Whaleyville 332
White Stone 381
Williamsburg 9,069
Winchester 14,643
Windsor 685
Wise 2,891
Woodbridge-Marumsco 25,412
Woodstock 2,338
Wytheville 6,069
Yorkshire 4,649

WASHINGTON Total population: 3,409,169

METROPOLITAN AREAS

Richland-Kennewick 93,356
Seattle-Everett 1,421,869
Spokane 287,487
Tacoma 412,344
Yakima 144,971

COUNTIES

Adams 12,014
Asotin 13,799
Benton 67,540
Chelan 41,355
Clallam 34,770
Clark 128,454
Columbia 4,439
Cowlitz 68,616
Douglas 16,787
Ferry 3,655
Franklin 25,816
Garfield 2,911
Grant 41,881
Grays Harbor 59,553
Island 27,011
Jefferson 10,661
King 1,156,633
Kitsap 101,732
Kittitas 25,039
Klickitat 12,138
Lewis 45,467
Lincoln 9,572
Mason 20,918
Okanogan 25,867
Pacific 15,796
Pend Oreille 6,025
Pierce 412,344
San Juan 3,856
Skagit 52,381
Skamania 5,845
Snohomish 265,236
Spokane 287,487
Stevens 17,405
Thurston 76,894
Wahkiakum 3,592
Walla Walla 42,176
Whatcom 81,983
Whitman 37,900
Yakima 144,971

PLACES

Aberdeen 18,489
Airway Heights 744
Albion 687
Algona 1,276
Almira 376
Anacortes 7,701
Arlington 2,261
Asotin 637
Auburn 21,817
Ault Field 1,478
Battle Ground 1,438
Beacon Hill 1,263
Beaux Arts Village 475
Bellevue 61,102
Bellingham 39,375
Benton City 1,070
Bingen 671
Black Diamond 1,160
Blaine 1,955
Bonney Lake 2,700
Bothell 4,883
Bremerton 35,307
Brewster 1,059
Bridgeport 952
Brier 3,093
Buckley 3,446
Bucoda 421
Burlington 3,138
Camas 5,790
Carbonado 394
Carnation 530
Cashmere 1,976
Castle Rock 1,647
Cathlamet 647
Central Park 2,720
Centralia 10,054
Chehalis 5,727
Chelan 2,684
Cheney 6,358
Chewelah 1,365
Clarkston 6,312
Cle Elum 1,725
Clyde Hill 2,987
Colfax 2,664
College Place 4,510
Colton 279
Columbia Heights 1,572
Colville 3,742
Conconully 122
Concrete 573
Connell 1,161
Cosmopolis 1,599
Coulee City 558
Coulee Dam 1,425
Coupeville 678
Creston 325
Cusick 257
Darrington 1,094
Davenport 1,363
Dayton 2,596
Deer Park 1,295
Des Moines 4,099
Dishman 9,079
Dupont 384
Duvall 607
East Wenatchee 913
East Wenatchee Bench 2,446
Eatonville 852
Edmonds 23,998
Electric City 651
Ellensburg 13,568
Elma 2,227
Elmer City 324
Endicott 333
Enetai 2,878
Entiat 355
Enumclaw 4,703
Ephrata 5,255
Erlands Point 1,017
Everett 53,622
Everson 633
Fairchild 6,754
Fairfield 469
Fairview 2,111
Farmington 140
Ferndale 2,164
Fife 1,458
Fircrest 5,651
Fords Prairie 2,250
Forks 1,682
Fort Lewis 38,054
Friday Harbor 803
Fruitvale 3,275
Garfield 610
Garrett 1,586
Geiger Heights 1,424
George 273
Gig Harbor 1,657
Gold Bar 504
Goldendale 2,484
Grand Coulee 1,302
Grandview 3,605
Granger 1,567
Granite Falls 813
Green Acres 2,324
Hamilton 196
Harrah 305
Harrington 489
Hartline 189
Hatton 60
Highland, see West Clarkston-Highland
Hoquiam 10,466
Hunts Point 578
Ilwaco 506
Index 169
Ione 529
Issaquah 4,313
Kahlotus 308
Kalama 1,106
Kelso 10,296
Kennewick 15,212
Kent 16,275
Kettle Falls 893
Kirkland 15,249
Kittitas 637
Krupp 52
La Center 300
Lacey 9,696
La Conner 639
La Crosse 426
Lake Forest Park 2,530
Lake Stevens 1,283
Lakes District 48,195
Lamont 88
Langley 547
Latah 169
Leavenworth 1,322
Lind 622
Long Beach 968
Longview 28,373
Lyman 324
Lynden 2,808
Lynnwood 16,919
Mabton 926
Malden 219
Mansfield 273
Marcus 142
Marysville 4,343
Mattawa 180
McChord 6,515
McCleary 1,265
Mead 1,099
Medical Lake 3,529
Medina 3,455
Mercer Island (city) 19,047
Mercer Island (town) 772
Mesa 274
Metaline 197
Metaline Falls 307
Millwood 1,770
Milton 2,607
Monroe 2,687
Montesano 2,847
Morton 1,134
Moses Lake 10,310
Moses Lake North 2,672
Mossyrock 409
Mount Vernon 8,804
Mountlake Terrace 16,600
Moxee City 600
Mukilteo 1,369
Naches 666
Napavine 377
Navy Yard City 2,827
Nespelem 323
Newport 1,418
Nooksack 322
Normandy Park 4,202
North Bend 1,625
North Bonneville 459
Northport 423
Oak Harbor 9,167
Oakesdale 447
Oakville 460
Odessa 1,074
Okanogan 2,015
Olympia 23,111
Omak 4,164
Opportunity 16,604
Oroville 1,555
Orting 1,643
Othello 4,122
Pacific 1,831
Palouse 948
Parkland 21,012
Pasco 13,920
Pasco West 3,809
Pateros 472
Pe Ell 582
Pomeroy 1,823
Port Angeles 16,367
Port Angeles East 1,523
Port Orchard 3,904
Port Townsend 5,241
Poulsbo 1,856
Prescott 242
Prosser 2,954
Pullman 20,509
Puyallup 14,742
Quincy 3,237
Rainier 382
Raymond 3,126
Reardan 389
Redmond 11,031
Renton 26,229
Republic 862
Richland 26,290
Ridgefield 1,004
Ritzville 1,876
Riverside 228
Rock Island 191
Rockford 327
Rocky Point 1,733
Rosalia 569
Roslyn 1,031
Roy 381
Royal City 477
Ruston 668
St. John 575
Seattle 530,831
Sedro-Woolley 4,598
Selah 3,070
Sequim 1,549
Shelton 6,515
Shoultes 4,754
Skykomish 283
Snohomish 5,174
Snoqualmie 1,260
Soap Lake 1,064
South Bend 1,795
South Broadway 3,298
South Cle Elum 374
South Prairie 206
Spanaway 5,768
Spangle 179
Spokane 170,516
Sprague 550
Springdale 215
Stanwood 1,347
Starbuck 216
Steilacoom 2,850
Stevenson 916
Sultan 1,119
Sumas 689
Sumner 4,325
Sunnyside 6,751
Tacoma 154,581
Tekoa 808
Tenino 962
Terrace Heights 1,033
Thompson Place-Tanglewilde 3,423
Tieton 415
Toledo 654
Tonasket 951
Toppenish 5,744
Town and Country 6,484
Tracyton 1,413
Tukwila 3,496
Tumwater 5,373
Twisp 756
Union Gap 2,040
Uniontown 310
University Place 13,230
Vader 387
Vancouver 41,859
Waitsburg 953
Walla Walla 23,619
Walla Walla East 2,840
Wapato 2,841
Warden 1,254
Washougal 3,388
Washtucna 316
Waterville 919
Waverly 48
Wenatchee 16,912
West Clarkston-Highland 3,797
West Richland 1,107
West Wenatchee 2,134
Westlake 258
Westport 1,364
White Salmon 1,585
Wilbur 1,074
Wilkeson 317
Wilson Creek 184
Winlock 890
Winslow 1,461
Winthrop 371
Woodland 1,622
Woodway 879
Woolley, see Sedro-Woolley
Yacolt 488
Yakima 45,588
Yarrow Point 1,103
Yelm 628
Zillah 1,138

WEST VIRGINIA Total population: 1,744,237

METROPOLITAN AREAS

Charleston 229,515
Huntington-Ashland 253,743
(144,499 in West Virginia, 56,868 in Ohio, 52,376 in Kentucky)
Parkersburg-Marietta 143,978
(86,818 in W. Va.; 57,160 in O.)
Steubenville-Weirton 165,627
(96,193 in Ohio, 69,434 in West Virginia)
Wheeling 182,712
(101,795 in West Virginia, 80,917 in Ohio)

COUNTIES

Barbour 14,030
Berkeley 36,356
Boone 25,118
Braxton 12,666
Brooke 29,685
Cabell 106,918
Calhoun 7,046
Clay 9,330
Doddridge 6,389
Fayette 49,332
Gilmer 7,782
Grant 8,607
Greenbrier 32,090
Hampshire 11,710
Hancock 39,749
Hardy 8,855
Harrison 73,028
Jackson 20,903
Jefferson 21,280
Kanawha 229,515
Lewis 17,847
Lincoln 18,912
Logan 46,269
Marion 61,356
Marshall 37,598
Mason 24,306
McDowell 50,666
Mercer 63,206
Mineral 23,109
Mingo 32,780
Monongalia 63,714
Monroe 11,272
Morgan 8,547
Nicholas 22,552
Ohio 64,197
Pendleton 7,031
Pleasants 7,274
Pocahontas 8,870
Preston 25,455
Putnam 27,625
Raleigh 70,080
Randolph 24,596
Ritchie 10,145
Roane 14,111
Summers 13,213
Taylor 13,878
Tucker 7,447
Tyler 9,929
Upshur 19,092
Wayne 37,581
Webster 9,809
Wetzel 20,314
Wirt 4,154
Wood 86,818
Wyoming 30,095

PLACES

Addison 1,038
Albright 319
Alderson 1,278
Amherstdale-Robinette 1,602
Anawalt 801
Anmoore 944
Ansted 1,511
Athens 967
Auburn 115
Bancroft 446
Barbourville 2,279
Barrackville 1,596
Bath 944
Bayard 475
Beckley 19,884
Beech Bottom 544
Belington 1,567
Belle 1,786
Belmont 802
Benwood 2,737
Bethany 602
Bethlehem 2,461
Beverly 470
Blacksville 264
Bluefield 15,921
Bolivar 943
Boomer 1,261
Bradshaw 1,048
Bramwell 1,125
Brandonville 82
Bridgeport 4,777
Bruceton Mills 209
Buckhannon 7,261
Buffalo 831
Burnsville 591
Cairo 412
Camden-on-Gauley 243
Cameron 1,537
Capon Bridge 211
Cass 173
Cedar Grove 1,275
Ceredo 1,583
Chapmanville 1,175
Charles Town 3,023
Charleston 71,505
Chattaroy 1,145
Chesapeake 2,428
Chester 3,614
Clarksburg 24,864
Clay 479
Clearview 512
Clendenin 1,438
Coal City 1,089
Colored Hill 1,031
Corrinne 1,090
Cowen 467
Crab Orchard 1,758
Culloden 1,033
Danville 580
Davis 868
Davy 993
Delbarton 903
Despard 1,400
Dunbar 9,151
Durbin 347
East Bank 1,025
East View 1,618
Eccles 1,105
Eleanor 1,035
Elizabeth 821
Elk Garden 291
Elkins 8,287
Elkview 1,486
Ellenboro 267
Fairmont 26,093
Fairview 640
Falling Springs 255
Farmington 595
Fayetteville 1,712
Flatwoods 220
Flemington 458
Follansbee 3,883
Fort Gay 792
Franklin 695
Friendly 190
Gassaway 1,253
Gilbert 778
Glasgow 904
Glen Hedrick 1,711
Glen Jean-Hilltop 1,510
Glendale 2,150
Glenville 2,183
Grafton 6,433
Graham Heights 1,008
Grant Town 946
Grantsville 795
Granville 1,027
Hambleton 328
Hamlin 1,024
Harman 142
Harpers Ferry 423
Harrisville 1,464
Hartford City 527
Hedgesville 274
Henderson 496
Hendricks 317
Hillsboro 267
Hilltop, see Glen Jean-Hilltop
Hinton 4,503
Holden 2,325
Hundred 475
Huntington 74,315
Hurricane 3,491
Huttonsville 167
Iaeger 822
Jane Lew 397
Junior 513
Kenova 4,860
Kermit 716
Keyser 6,586
Keystone 1,008
Kimball 962
Kingwood 2,550
Layopolis 252
Leon 192
Lester 507
Lewisburg 2,407
Lilly Grove 1,655
Littleton 333
Logan 3,311
Lost Creek 571
Lumberport 957
Mabscott 1,254
MacArthur 1,614
Madison 2,342
Mallory 1,240
Man 1,201
Mannington 2,747
Marlinton 1,286
Marmet 2,339
Martinsburg 14,626
Mason 1,319
Masontown 868
Matewan 651
Matoaka 608
McMechen 2,808
Meadow Bridge 429
Middlebourne 814
Mill Creek 800
Milton 1,597
Mitchell Heights 524
Monongah 1,194
Montgomery 2,525
Montrose 115
Moorefield 2,124
Morgantown 29,431
Moundsville 13,560
Mount Gay 3,843
Mount Hope 1,829
Mullens 2,967
New Cumberland 1,865
New Haven 1,538
New Martinsville 6,528
Newburg 457
Newell 2,300
Nitro 8,019
Northfork 737
Nutter Fort 2,379
Oak Hill 4,738
Oakvale 292
Oceana 1,580
Osage 322
Paden City 3,674
Parkersburg 44,208
Parsons 1,784
Paw Paw 706
Pax 288
Pennsboro 1,614
Petersburg 2,177
Peterstown 563
Philippi 3,002
Piedmont 1,763
Pine Grove 630
Pineville 1,187
Poca 772
Point Pleasant 6,122
Pratt 671
Princeton 7,253
Pullman 157
Quinwood 370
Rainelle 1,826
Ranson 2,189
Ravenswood 4,240
Reedsville 379
Reedy 351
Rhodell 500
Richwood 3,717
Ridgeley 1,112
Ripley 3,244
Rivesville 1,108
Roderfield 1,161
Romney 2,364
Ronceverte 1,981
Rowlesburg 829
Rupert 1,027
St. Albans 14,356
St. Marys 2,348
Salem 2,597
Sand Fork 252
Shepherdstown 1,688
Shinnston 2,576
Sistersville 2,246
Smithers 2,020
Smithfield 294
Sophia 1,303
South Charleston 16,333
Spencer City 2,271
Star City 1,312
Stonewood 1,950
Summersville 2,429
Sutton 1,031
Sylvester 245
Terra Alta 1,474
Thomas 713
Thurmond 86
Triadelphia 547
Tunnelton 369
Union 566
Valley Grove 509
Vienna 11,549
War 2,004
Wardensville 288
Wayne 1,385
Weirton 27,131
Welch 4,149
Wellsburg 4,600
West Hamlin 715
West Logan 685
West Milford 356
West Union 1,141
Weston 7,323
Westover 5,086
Wheeling 48,188
White Sulphur Springs 2,869
Whitesville 781
Whitmer 411
Williamson 5,831
Williamstown 2,743
Winfield 328
Womelsdorf 234
Worthington 288

WISCONSIN Total population: 4,417,933

METROPOLITAN AREAS

Appleton-Oshkosh 276,893
Duluth-Superior 265,350
(220,693 in Minnesota, 44,657 in Wisconsin)
Green Bay 158,244
Kenosha 117,917
La Crosse 80,468
Madison 290,272
Milwaukee 1,403,887
Racine 170,838

COUNTIES

Adams 9,234
Ashland 16,743
Barron 33,955
Bayfield 11,683
Brown 158,244
Buffalo 13,743
Burnett 9,276
Calumet 27,604
Chippewa 47,717
Clark 30,361
Columbia 40,150
Crawford 15,252
Dane 290,272
Dodge 69,004
Door 20,106
Douglas 44,657
Dunn 29,154
Eau Claire 67,219
Florence 3,298
Fond du Lac 84,567
Forest 7,691
Grant 48,398

WISCONSIN, Continued

Green 26,714
Green Lake 16,878
Iowa 19,306
Iron 6,533
Jackson 15,325
Jefferson 60,060
Juneau 18,455
Kenosha 117,917
Kewaunee 18,961
La Crosse 80,468
Lafayette 17,456
Langlade 19,220
Lincoln 23,499
Manitowoc 82,294
Marathon 97,457
Marinette 35,810
Marquette 8,865
Menominee 2,607
Milwaukee 1,054,063
Monroe 31,610
Oconto 25,553
Oneida 24,427
Outagamie 119,356
Ozaukee 54,421
Pepin 7,319
Pierce 26,652
Polk 26,666
Portage 47,541
Price 14,520
Racine 170,838
Richland 17,079
Rock 131,970
Rusk 14,238
St. Croix 34,354
Sauk 39,057
Sawyer 9,670
Shawano 32,650
Sheboygan 96,660
Taylor 16,958
Trempealeau 23,344
Vernon 24,557
Vilas 10,958
Walworth 63,444
Washburn 10,601
Washington 63,839
Waukesha 231,365
Waupaca 37,780
Waushara 14,795
Winnebago 129,931
Wood 65,362

PLACES

Abbotsford 1,375
Adams 1,440
Adell 380
Albany 875
Algoma 4,023
Allouez 13,753
Alma 956
Alma Center 495
Almena 423
Almond 440
Altoona 2,842
Amery 2,126
Amherst 585
Amherst Junction 141
Aniwa 233
Antigo 9,005
Appleton 57,143
Arcadia 2,159
Arena 377
Argyle 673
Arlington 379
Ashland 9,615
Ashwaubenon 9,323
Athens 856
Auburndale 468
Augusta 1,242
Avoca 421
Bagley 271
Baldwin 1,399
Balsam Lake 648
Bangor 974
Baraboo 7,931
Barneveld 528
Barron 2,337
Bay City 317
Bayfield 874
Bayside 4,461
Bear Creek 520
Beaver Dam 14,265
Belgium 809
Bell Center 110
Belleville 1,063
Belmont 688
Beloit 35,729
Beloit West 1,903
Benton 873
Berlin 5,338
Big Bend 1,148
Big Falls 112
Birchwood 394
Birnamwood 632
Biron 771
Black Creek 921
Black Earth 1,114
Black River Falls 3,273
Blair 1,036
Blanchardville 671
Bloomer 3,143
Bloomington 719
Blue Mounds 261
Blue River 369
Boaz 126
Bohners Lake 1,417
Bonduel 995
Boscobel 2,510
Bowler 272
Boyceville 725
Boyd 574
Brandon 872
Brillion 2,588
Brodhead 2,515
Brokaw 312
Brookfield 32,140
Brooklyn 565
Brown Deer 12,622
Browns Lake 1,669
Brownsville 374
Browntown 253
Bruce 799
Buffalo 671
Burlington 7,479
Butler 2,261
Butternut 453
Cable 281
Cadott 977
Cambria 631
Cambridge 689
Cameron 893
Camp Douglas 547
Camp Lake 1,898
Campbellsport 1,681
Cascade 603
Casco 481
Cashton 824
Cassville 1,343
Catawba 215
Cazenovia 335
Cecil 369
Cedar Grove 1,276
Cedarburg 7,697
Centuria 632
Chaseburg 224
Chenequa 642
Chenequa North 1,106
Chetek 1,630
Chilton 3,030
Chippewa Falls 12,351
Clayton 306
Clear Lake 721
Cleveland 761
Clinton 1,333
Clintonville 4,600
Clyman 328
Cobb 410
Cochrane 506
Colby 1,178
Coleman 683
Colfax 1,026
Coloma 336
Columbus 3,789
Combined Locks 2,734
Como 1,132
Conrath 114
Coon Valley 596
Cornell 1,616
Cottage Grove 478
Couderay 123
Crandon 1,582
Cross Plains 1,478
Cuba City 1,993
Cudahy 22,078
Cumberland 1,839
Curtiss 135
Dallas 359
Dane 486
Darien 839
Darlington 2,351
Deer Park 217
Deerfield 1,067
De Forest 1,911
Delafield 3,182
Delavan 5,526
Delavan Lake 2,124
Denmark 1,364
De Pere 13,309
De Soto 295
Dickeyville 1,057
Dodgeville 3,255
Dorchester 491
Dousman 451
Downing 215
Doylestown 265
Dresser 533
Durand 2,103
Eagle River 1,326
Eagle 745
East Troy 1,711
Eastman 319
Eau Claire 44,619
Eau Claire Southeast 2,316
Eden 376
Edgar 928
Edgerton 4,118
Egg Harbor 184
Eland 229
Elderon 185
Eleva 574
Elk Mound 471
Elkhart Lake 787
Elkhorn 3,992
Ellsworth 1,983
Elm Grove 7,201
Elmwood 737
Elmwood Park 456
Elroy 1,513
Embarrass 472
Endeavor 328
Ephraim 236
Ettrick 463
Evansville 2,992
Exeland 189
Fairchild 562
Fairwater 373
Fall Creek 825
Fall River 633
Fennimore 1,861
Fenwood 147
Ferryville 183
Fond du Lac 35,515
Fontana on Geneva Lake 1,464
Footville 698
Forestville 349
Fort Atkinson 9,164
Fountain City 1,017
Fox Lake 1,242
Fox Point 7,937
Francis Creek 492
Franklin 12,247
Frederic 908
Fredonia 1,045
Fremont 598
Friendship 641
Friesland 301
Galesville 1,162
Gays Mills 623
Genoa 305
Genoa City 1,085
Germantown 6,974
Gillett 1,288
Gilman 328
Glen Flora 69
Glenbeulah 496
Glendale 13,436
Glenwood City 822
Grafton 5,998
Granton 288
Grantsburg 930
Gratiot 249
Green Bay 87,809
Green Lake 1,109
Greendale 15,089
Greenfield 24,424
Greenwood 1,036
Gresham 448
Hales Corners 7,771
Hallie 1,223
Hammond 768
Hancock 404
Hartford 6,499
Hartland 2,763
Hatley 315
Haugen 246
Hawkins 385
Hayward 1,457
Hazel Green 982
Highland 785
Hilbert 896
Hillsboro 1,231
Hixton 300
Hollandale 256
Holmen 1,081
Horicon 3,356
Hortonville 1,524
Howard 4,911
Howards Grove-Millersville 998
Hudson 5,049
Hurley 2,418
Hustisford 789
Hustler 190
Hutchins 409
Independence 1,036
Ingram 109
Iola 900
Iron Ridge 480
Ironton 195
Jackson 561
Janesville 46,426
Jefferson 5,429
Johnson Creek 790
Junction City 396
Juneau 2,043
Kaukauna 11,292
Kekoskee 233
Kendall 468
Kennan 167
Kenosha 78,805
Kewaskum 1,926
Kewaunee 2,901
Kiel 2,848
Kimberly 6,131
Kingston 343
Knapp 369
Kohler 1,738
Lac La Belle 227
La Crosse 51,153
Ladysmith 3,674
La Farge 748
Lake Butte des Morts 1,111
Lake Delton 1,059
Lake Geneva 4,890
Lake Mills 3,556
Lake Nebagamon 523
Lake Wazeecha 1,285
Lake Wissota 1,419
Lancaster 3,756
Lannon 1,056
La Valle 411
Lena 569
Lime Ridge 203
Linden 408
Little Chute 5,365
Livingston 503
Lodi 1,831
Loganville 199
Lohrville 195
Lomira 1,084
Lone Rock 506
Lowell 322
Loyal 1,126
Lublin 143
Luck 848
Luxemburg 853
Lyndon Station 533
Lynxville 149
Madison 173,258
Maiden Rock 172
Manawa 1,105
Manitowoc 33,430
Maple Bluff 1,974
Marathon City 1,214
Maribel 316
Marinette 12,696
Marion 1,218
Markesan 1,378
Marquette 161
Marshall 1,043
Marshfield 15,619
Mason 119
Mattoon 377
Mauston 3,466
Mayville 4,139
Mazomanie 1,217
McFarland 2,386
Medford 3,454
Mellen 1,168
Melrose 505
Melvina 116
Menasha 14,905
Menomonee Falls 31,697
Menomonie 11,275
Mequon 12,110
Merrill 9,502
Merrillan 612
Merrimac 376
Merton 646
Middleton 8,286
Milladore 229
Millersville, see Howards Grove-Millersville
Milltown 634
Milton 3,699
Milwaukee 717,099
Mineral Point 2,305
Minong 420
Mishicot 938
Mondovi 2,338
Monona 10,420
Monroe 8,654
Montello 1,082
Montfort 518
Monticello 870
Montreal 877
Mosinee 2,395
Mount Calvary 942
Mount Hope 176
Mount Horeb 2,402
Mount Sterling 181
Mukwonago 2,367
Muscoda 1,099
Muskego 11,573
Nashotah 410
Necedah 740
Neenah 22,892
Neillsville 2,750
Nekoosa 2,409
Nelsonville 152
Neopit 1,122
Neosho 400
Neshkoro 385
New Auburn 368
New Berlin 26,937
New Glarus 1,454
New Holstein 3,012
New Lisbon 1,361
New London 5,801
New Richmond 3,707
Niagara 2,347
Nichols 207
North Bay 263
North Fond du Lac 3,286
North Freedom 596
North Hudson 1,547
North Prairie 669
Norwalk 432
Oak Creek 13,901
Oakfield 918
Oconomowoc 8,741
Oconomowoc Lake 599
Oconomowoc Lake South 1,473
Oconto 4,667
Oconto Falls 2,517
Ogdensburg 206
Okauchee Lake 3,134
Oliver 210
Omro 2,341
Onalaska 4,909
Ontario 392
Oostburg 1,309
Oregon 2,553
Orfordville 888
Osceola 1,152
Oshkosh 53,221
Osseo 1,356
Owen 1,031
Oxford 453
Paddock Lake 1,470
Palmyra 1,341
Pardeeville 1,507
Park Falls 2,953
Park Ridge 817
Patch Grove 187
Pell Lake 1,284
Pepin 747
Perry Go Place 5,912
Peshtigo 2,836
Pewaukee 3,271
Pewaukee West 3,401
Phillips 1,511
Pigeon Falls 198
Pittsville 708
Plain 688
Plainfield 642
Platteville 9,599
Plum City 451
Plymouth 5,810
Poplar 455
Port Edwards 2,126
Port Washington 8,752
Portage 7,821
Potosi 713
Pound 284
Poynette 1,118
Prairie du Chien 5,540
Prairie du Sac 1,902
Prairie Farm 426
Prentice 519
Prescott 2,331
Princeton 1,446
Pulaski 1,717
Racine 95,162
Radisson 206
Randolph 1,582
Random Lake 1,068
Readstown 395
Redgranite 645
Reedsburg 4,585
Reedsville 994
Reeseville 566
Rewey 232
Rhinelander 8,218
Rib Lake 782
Rice Lake 7,278
Richland Center 5,086
Ridgeland 266
Ridgeway 463
Rio 792
Ripon 7,053
River Falls 7,238
River Hills 1,561
Roberts 484
Rochester 436
Rock Springs 432
Rockdale 172
Rockland 278
Rosendale 464
Rosholt 466
Rothschild 3,141
Rudolph 349
St. Cloud 550
St. Croix Falls 1,425
St. Francis 10,489
St. Nazianz 718
Sauk City 2,385
Saukville 1,389
Scandinavia 268
Schofield 2,577
Seymour 2,194
Sharon 1,216
Shawano 6,488
Sheboygan 48,484
Sheboygan Falls 4,771
Sheboygan South 1,920
Sheboygan West 1,361
Sheldon 218
Shell Lake 928
Sherwood 350
Shiocton 830
Shorewood 15,576
Shorewood Hills 2,206
Shullsburg 1,376
Silver Lake 1,210
Siren 639
Sister Bay 483
Slinger 1,022
Soldiers Grove 514
Solon Springs 598
Somerset 778
South Milwaukee 23,297
South Wayne 436
Sparta 6,258
Spencer 1,181
Spooner 2,444
Spring Green 1,199
Spring Valley 995
Stanley 2,049
Star Prairie 362
Stetsonville 305
Steuben 179
Stevens Point 23,479
Stockbridge 582
Stockholm 99
Stoddard 750
Stoughton 6,081
Stratford 1,239
Strum 738
Sturgeon Bay 6,776
Sturtevant 3,376
Sullivan 467
Sun Prairie 9,935
Superior (city) 32,237
Superior (village) 476
Suring 499
Sussex 2,758
Taylor 322
Tennyson 402
Theresa 611
Thiensville 3,182
Thorp 1,469
Tigerton 742
Tomah 5,647
Tomahawk 3,419
Tony 144
Trempealeau 743
Turtle Lake 637
Twin Lakes 2,276
Two Rivers 13,553
Union Center 205
Union Grove 2,703
Unity 363
Valders 821
Verona 2,334
Vesper 355
Viola 659
Viroqua 3,739
Waldo 408
Wales 691
Walworth 1,637
Washburn 1,957
Waterford 1,922
Waterloo 2,253
Watertown 15,683
Waukesha 40,258
Waunakee 2,181
Waupaca 4,342
Waupun 7,946
Wausau 32,806
Wausau West 6,399
Wausaukee 557
Wautoma 1,624
Wauwatosa 58,676
Wauzeka 437
Webster 502
West Allis 71,723
West Baraboo 563
West Bend 16,555
West Milwaukee 4,405
West Salem 2,180
Westby 1,568
Westfield 884
Weston 3,375
Weyauwega 1,377
Weyerhauser 285
Wheeler 212
White Lake 309
Whitefish Bay 17,394
Whitehall 1,486
Whitelaw 557
Whitewater 12,038
Whiting 1,782
Wild Rose 585
Williams Bay 1,554
Wilson 130
Wilton 516
Wind Point 1,251
Winneconne 1,608
Wisconsin Dells 2,401
Wisconsin Rapids 18,587
Withee 480
Wittenberg 895
Wonewoc 835
Woodman 102
Woodville 522
Wrightstown 1,020
Wyeville 203
Wyocena 809
Yuba 79

WYOMING Total population: 332,416

COUNTIES

Albany 26,431
Big Horn 10,202
Campbell 12,957
Carbon 13,354
Converse 5,938
Crook 4,535
Fremont 28,352
Goshen 10,885
Hot Springs 4,952
Johnson 5,587
Laramie 56,360
Lincoln 8,640
Natrona 51,264
Niobrara 2,924
Park 17,752
Platte 6,486
Sheridan 17,852
Sublette 3,755
Sweetwater 18,391
Teton 4,823
Uinta 7,100
Washakie 7,569
Weston 6,307

PLACES

Afton 1,290
Albin 118
Baggs 146
Basin 1,145
Big Piney 570
Buffalo 3,394
Burns 185
Byron 397
Casper 39,361
Cheyenne 40,914
Chugwater 187
Clearmont 141
Cody 5,161
Cokeville 440
Cowley 366
Dayton 396
Deaver 112
Diamondville 485
Dixon 72
Douglas 2,677
Dubois 898
East Thermopolis 316
Edgerton 350
Elk Mountain 127
Elmo 53
Encampment 321
Evanston 4,462
Evansville 832
Fort Laramie 197
Fox Farm 1,329
Frannie 139
Gillette 7,194
Glendo 210
Glenrock 1,515
Granger 137
Green River 4,196
Greybull 1,953
Guernsey 793
Hanna 460
Hartville 246
Hudson 381
Hulett 318
Jackson 2,101
Kaycee 272
Kemmerer 2,292
Kirby 75
La Grange 189
Lander 7,125
Laramie 23,143
Lingle 446
Lost Cabin 25
Lost Springs 7
Lovell 2,371
Lusk 1,495
Lyman 643
Manderson 117
Manville 92
Marbleton 223
Medicine Bow 455
Meeteetse 459
Mills 1,724
Moorcroft 981
Mountain View 1,641
Newcastle 3,432
Opal 34
Orchard Valley 1,015
Paradise Valley 1,764
Pavillion 181
Pine Bluffs 937
Pinedale 948
Powell 4,807
Ranchester 208
Rawlins 7,855
Riverside 46
Riverton 7,995
Rock River 344
Rock Springs 11,657
Saratoga 1,181
Sheridan 10,856
Shoshoni 562
Sinclair 445
South Superior 197
Sundance 1,056
Ten Sleep 320
Thayne 195
Thermopolis 3,063
Torrington 4,237
Upton 987
Van Tassell 21
Wamsutter 139
Warren 4,527
Wheatland 2,498
Worland 5,055
Yoder 101

INDEX

The index lists in alphabetical order 80,000 cities, towns, and other geographic features that appear on the reference maps of The World Book Atlas. Each name in the index is followed by the map index key and the number of the page on which the name appears. Each entry in the index also includes the state, province, country, or continent in which the geographic or political feature is located. Many entries also include a descriptive term. A typical entry reads:

Adams, mtn., Mass........A2 **185** ← Map page
(A2 ← Map index key)

To learn how to use map index keys turn to the How to Get the Most Out of the Atlas section, pages XII and XIII.

Some places appear on both a large map and on a smaller inset map. In these cases, more than one index key may be given for a single page:

Aguililla, Mex........D4, n12 **129**
(D4 ← Large map index key; n12 ← Inset map index key)

For ease of use, different styles of type are used to distinguish the different classes of political names, physical features, and points of interest.

Countries and major political units appear in CAPITAL letters:

ALGERIA, country, Afr....D4 **102**

All other political units and place names appear in capital and lower case letters:

Alameda, N. Mex......B3, G5 **195**

Cities, towns, counties, states, and provinces that are included in one of the population tables on pages 230 to 280 appear in **bold face** type:

Anyang, China...........D7 **91**

Physical features and points of interest appear in *italic* type:

Ashepoo, riv., S. C.........F6 **203**

Some names are included in the index that were omitted from the maps because of lack of space. These entries may be identified by an asterisk (*) and reference is given to the approximate location of the place.

Ashibetsu, Jap..........*E11 **93**

Some long names may appear on the map in a shortened form, with the full name given in the index. The part of the name not on the map appears in brackets in the index:

Argenton [-sur-Creuse].

INDEX

A

Aachen, Ger....C3 60
Aalen, Ger....E5 61
Aalsmeer, Neth....B4 59
Aalst, Bel....D4 59
Aalten, Neth....C6 59
Äänekoski, Fin....F11 63
Aaqraba, Syr....A8 84
Aarau, Switz....B4 66
Aare, riv., Switz....B3 66
Aargau, canton, Switz....B4 66
Aaronsburg, Pa....E7 202
Aarschot, Bel....D4 59
Aba, Zaire....A5 106
Aba, Nig....E6 103
Abacaxis, riv., Braz....C3 139
Abadan, Iran....F4 86
Abādeh, Iran....F6 86
Abadla, Alg....C4 102
Abaeté, Braz....E1 138
Abaetetuba, Braz....C5 139
Abaí, Par....E4 135
Abajo, peak, Utah....F6 207
Abakan, Sov. Un....D12 71
Abala, Con....F3 104
Abancay, Peru....D3 134
Abanda, Ala....B4 166
Abanilla, Sp....C5 65
Abano-Terme, It....D7 66
Abâr el Brins, Eg....D2 84
Abarqu, Iran....F6 86
'Abasān, Gaza Strip....C6 84
Abashiri, Jap....D12 93
Abau, Pap....m12 111
Abba, Ga....E3 175
'Abbasiya, Sud....C3 105
Abbaye, pt., Mich....B2 186
Abbeville, Ala....D4 166
Abbeville, Fr....B4 58
Abbeville, Ga....E3 175
Abbeville, La....E3 183
Abbeville, Miss....A4 188
Abbeville, S.C....C3 203
Abbeville, co., S.C....C3 203
Abbey, Sask., Can....G1 155
Abbey, head, Scot....F5 57
Abbiategrasso, It....B2 67
Abbot Village, Maine....C3 184
Abbotsford, B.C., Can....A10 149
Abbotsford, Wis....D3 212
Abbott, Ark....B1 169
Abbott, Tex....*D4 206
Abbottsburg, N.C....C5 197
Abbottstown, Pa....G8 202
Abbyville, Kans....B3, E5 181
'Abd al Kūrī, isl., Yemen (Aden)....C7 105
Abe, lake, Afars & Is., Eth....C5 105
Abéché, Chad....C4 104
Abee, Alta., Can....B4 148
Abejorral, Col....B2 133
Abengourou, I.C....E4 103
Åbenrå, Den....C3 62
Åbenrå, co., Den....D3 62
Åbenrå, fjord, Den....C3 62
Abeokuta, Nig....E5 103
Aberayron, Wales....B3 56
Aberchirder, Scot....C6 57
Abercorn, Que., Can....D5 154
Abercrombie, N. Dak....C9 198
Aberdare, Wales....C4 56
Aberdaron, Wales....B3 56
Aberdeen, Sask., Can....E2 155
Aberdeen, Idaho....G6 177
Aberdeen, Ky....C3 182
Aberdeen, Md....A5 173
Aberdeen, Miss....B5 188
Aberdeen, N.C....B4 197
Aberdeen, Ohio....D4 199
Aberdeen, Scot....C6 57
Aberdeen, S. Afr....D3 107
Aberdeen, S. Dak....B7 204
Aberdeen, Wash....C2 210
Aberdeen, co., Scot....C5 57
Aberdeen, lake, N. W. Ter., Can....D13 142
Aberdovey, Wales....B3 56
Aberfeldy, Scot....D5 57
Aberfoyle, Scot....D4 57
Abergavenny, Wales....C4 56
Abernant, Ala....B2 166
Abernathy, Tex....C2 206
Abernethy, Sask., Can....G4 155
Abert, lake, Oreg....E6 201
Abertillery, Wales....C4 56
Aberystwyth, Wales....B3 56
Abesville, Mo....E4 189
Abhā, Sau. Ar....B5 105
Abidjan, I.C....E4 103
Abie, Nebr....C9 191
Abiff, Tenn....B4 205
Abilene, Kans....D6 181
Abilene, Tex....C3 206
Abingdon, Eng....C6 56
Abingdon, Ill....C3 178
Abingdon, Iowa....C5 180
Abingdon, Md....B5 173
Abingdon, Va....B3 209
Abington, Conn....B8 172
Abington, Mass....B6, E3 185
Abington, Pa....A11 202
Abiquiu, res., N. Mex....A3 195
Abisko, Swe....C8 63
Abita Springs, La....A7, D5 183
Abitibi, co., Que., Can....*B2 154
Abitibi, lake, Ont., Que., Can....E9 **153**, B1 154
Abitibi, riv., Ont., Can....E9 153
Ablingi, isl., Bis. Arch.... 115
Ablon, Fr....h10 58
Abloviak, fjord, Que., Can..f8 152
Åbo, see Turku, Fin.
Aboisso, I.C....E4 103
Abomey, Dah....E5 103
Abong Abeng, mtn., Indon..J2 89
Abony, Hung....B5 68
Aboriginal, reserve, Austl..D4 110
Abou Deïa, Chad....C3 104
Abou Kémal, Syr....E13 **85**, C8 101
Aboyne, Scot....C6 57
Abraham, Utah....D3 207
Abraham Lincoln Birthplace, nat. historical park, Ky...C4 182
Abrams, Wis....D5 212
Abrantes, Port....C1 65
Abrego, Col....B3 133
Abruzzi and Molise, reg., It....C4 67
Absaraka, N. Dak....C8 198
Absaroka, range, Wyo....A3 213
Absaroka, ridge, Wyo....C2 213
Absarokee, Mont....E7 190
Absecon, N.J....E3 194
Absecon, inlet, N.J....E4 194
Abu 'Ali, isl., Sau. Ar....H4 86
Abū Dīs, Jordan....h12 84
Abū Ḩadrīyah, Sau. Ar....H4 86
Abu Hamed, Sud....B3 105
Abū Ḩammād al Maḩaţţah, Eg....D3 84
Abū Ḩummuş, Eg....C2 84
Abū Kabīr, Eg....D3 84
Abu Kershola, Sud....C3 105
Abu Musa, isl., Sau. Ar....I7 86
Abū Qīr, Eg....C2 84
Abū Qīr, bay, Eg....C2 84
Abū Qurqāş, Eg....I8 85
Abu Shagara, cape, Sud....A4 105
Abū Sunbul, ruins, Eg....I8 85
Abu Tabari (Well), Sud....B2 105
Abu 'Uruq (Well), Sud....B3 105
Abū Ẓaby, U.A.E....G8 77
Abū Zanīmah, Eg....D6 101
Abuja, Nig....E6 103
Abūksāh, Eg....E2 84
Abumombazi, Zaire....A3 106
Abunã, riv., Bol., Braz....C4 134
Åby, Swe....u34 63
Abyei, Sud....D2 105
Abyssinia.... 99
see also Ethiopia
Academia, Ohio....B5 199
Academy, S. Dak....D6 204
Acadia, par., La....D3 183
Acadia, nat. park, Maine....D4 184
Acadia Valley, Alta., Can..D5 148
Acajutla, Sal....D3 130
Acala, Tex....F1 206
Acámbaro, Mex....C4, m13 129
Acaponeta, Mex....C3 129
Acapulco, Mex....D5 129
Acaraí, mts., Braz....B3 139
Acaraú, Braz....B2 138
Acaray, riv., Par....E4 135
Acari, Braz....h5 138
Acarí, Peru....E3 134
Acarigua, Ven....B4 133
Acatlán, Mex....D5, n14 129
Acayucan, Mex....D6 129
Accident, Md....D1 173
Accomac, Va....D7 209
Accomack, co., Va....D7 209
Accord, Mass....D3 185
Accord, N.Y....D6 196
Accord, pond, Mass....D3 185
Accoville, W. Va....D3, D5 211
Accra, Ghana....E5 103
Accrington, Eng....A5 56
Ace, Tex....D5 206
Aceguá, Ur....E2 137
Acequia, Idaho....G5 177
Achacachi, Bol....C2 135
Achaea: c. 450 B.C.... 42
c. 50 B.C.... 44
Achao, Chile....C2 136
Achar, Ur....E1 137
Acharacle, Scot....D3 57
Achard, pt., San Cristobal I.. 115
Achen, lake, Aus....B7 66
Acheng, China....D3 93
Achenkirch, Aus....B7 66
Achern, Ger....E3 61
Achicourt, Fr....D2 59
Achill, isl., Ire....D1 55
Achill Sound, Ire....D2 55
Achille, Okla....D5 200
Achinsk, Sov. Un....D12 71
Achiras, Arg....A4 136
Achourat (Well), Mali....B4 103
Acıpayam, Tur....D7 69
Acireale, It....F5 67
Ackerly, Tex....C2 206
Ackerman, Miss....B4 188
Ackia Battleground, nat. mon., Miss....A5 188
Ackley, Iowa....B4 180
Acklins, isl., Ba. Is....D6 131
Ackworth, Iowa....*C4 180
Acmar, Ala....B3 166
Acme, Alta., Can....D4 148
Acme, La....C4 183
Acme, Mich....D5 186
Acme, Wash....A3 210
Acme, W. Va....D6 211
Acme, Wyo....A6 213
Acobamba, Peru....D3 134
Acoma, Nev....F7 192
Acoma, Indian res., N. Mex....C2 195
Acomayo, Peru....D3 134
Acomita, N. Mex....B2 195
Aconcagua, prov., Chile...A2 136
Aconcagua, peak, Arg....A3 136
Acopiara, Braz....C3 138
Acosta, Pa....F3 202
Acoyapa, Nic....E5 130
Acqui, It....B2 67
Acre, state, Braz....C3 134
Acre, bay, Isr....B7 84
Acre, riv., Braz....D4 134
Acree, Ga....E2 175
Acton, Calif....E4 170
Acton, Ont., Can....D4 153
Acton, Eng....*k11 55
Acton, Ind....E6, I8 179
Acton, Maine....E2 184
Acton, Mass....B5, C1 185
Acton, Mont....E8 190
Acton Vale, Que., Can....D5 154
Actopan, Mex....m14 129
Açu, Braz....C3 138
Açuruá, plat., Braz....D2 138
Acushnet, Mass....C6 185
Acworth, Ga....B2 175
Acworth, N.H....D2 193
Ada Ghana....E5 103
Ada, Kans....C6 181
Ada, Minn....C2 187
Ada, Ohio....B4 199
Ada, Okinawa.... 114
Ada, Okla....C5 200
Ada, Yugo....C5 68
Ada, co., Idaho....F2 177
Ada, mtn., Alsk....m22 167
Adair, Ill....C3 178
Adair, Iowa....C3 180
Adair, Okla....A6 200
Adair, co., Iowa....C3 180
Adair, co., Ky....C4 182
Adair, co., Mo....A5 189
Adair, co., Okla....B7 200
Adairsville, Ga....B2 175
Adairville, Ky....D3 182
Adak, isl., Alsk....E4 167
Adam, isl., Md....D5 173
Adam, port, Maramasike I.... 115
Adamana, Ariz....C6 168
Adamant, Vt....C3 208
Adamantina, Braz....C2 137
Adamello, peak, It....E5 60
Adamitullo, Eth....D4 105
Adams, Ind....F6 179
Adams, Ky....B7 182
Adams, Mass....A1 185
Adams, Minn....G6 187
Adams, Miss....C3 188
Adams, Nebr....D9 191
Adams, N.Y....B4 196
Adams, N. Dak....A7 198
Adams, Okla....D3 200
Adams, Oreg....B8 201
Adams, Tenn....A4 205
Adams, Wis....E4 212
Adams, co., Colo....B6 171
Adams, co., Idaho....E2 177
Adams, co., Ill....D2 178
Adams, co., Ind....C8 179
Adams, co., Iowa....C3 180
Adams, co., Miss....D2 188
Adams, co., Nebr....D7 191
Adams, co., N. Dak....C3 198

INDEX KEY Each place listed in **Bold-faced Type** has its population listed in the Population tables, pages 230 to 280.
Each country, shown in CAPITAL LETTERS, has its population listed in the World Political Information Table, pages 6 to 10.
* Does not appear on map; key shows general location.

Adams, co., Ohio........D4 **199**
Adams, co., Pa..........G7 **202**
Adams, co., Wash........B7 **210**
Adams, co., Wis.........D4 **212**
Adams, lake, B.C., Can.....D8 **149**
Adams, mtn., Mass........A2 **185**
Adams, mtn., N.H..........B4 **193**
Adams, mtn., Vt...........C3 **208**
Adams, mtn., Wash........C4 **210**
Adams, pt., Mich...........C7 **186**
Adams Bridge, shoals,
India........................G6 **87**
Adams Center, N.Y.......B5 **196**
Adams Run, S.C...........F1 **203**
Adamsburg, S.C...........B4 **203**
Adamson, Okla............C6 **200**
Adamston, N.J.............C4 **194**
Adamstown, Md...........B3 **173**
Adamstown, Pa...........F9 **202**
Adamsville, Ala...........E4 **166**
Adamsville, Que., Can....D5 **154**
Adamsville, Ga.............B5 **175**
Adamsville, Pa..............C1 **202**
Adamsville, R.I............C12 **172**
Adamsville, Tenn..........B3 **205**
Adamsville, Tex.............D3 **206**
Adamsville, Utah...........E3 **207**
Adana, Tur...............D10 **85**
Adanac, Sask., Can........E1 **155**
Adapazari, Tur............B8 **85**
Adarama, Sud..............B3 **105**
Adare, cape, Ant...........B30 **120**
Adavale, Aust...............B5 **112**
Adaza, Iowa.................B3 **180**
Adda, riv., It...............B2 **67**
Aḏ Ḏab'ah, Eg..............C5 **101**
Ad Dammān, Sau. Ar....*H4 **86**
Addicks, Tex................F4 **206**
Addielee, Okla..............B7 **200**
Addieville, Ill..............E4 **178**
Ad Dilinjāt, Eg..............D2 **84**
Addington, Okla...........C4 **200**
Addis, La...................D4 **183**
Addis Ababa, Eth.........D4 **105**
Addison, Ala..............A2 **166**
Addison, Ill.................F2 **178**
Addison, Maine...........D5 **184**
Addison, Mich...........*F6 **186**
Addison, N.Y..............C3 **196**
Addison, Vt................C2 **208**
Addison, co., Vt...........C2 **208**
Ad Dīwān, Eg...............E6 **101**
Ad Dīwānīyah,
Iraq............F15 **85,** F2 **86**
Addy, Wash..................A8 **210**
Addyston, Ohio............D2 **199**
Adel, Ga....................E3 **175**
Adel, Iowa..................C3 **180**
Adel, Oreg...................E7 **201**
Adelaide, Austl...F6 **111,** G2 **112**
Adelaide, isl., Ant..........C6 **120**
Adelanto, Calif............E5 **170**
Adelie, coast, Ant.........C27 **120**
Adeline, Ill...............*A4 **178**
Adell, Wis...................E6 **212**
Adelphi, Iowa...............A7 **180**
Adelphi, Ohio..............C5 **199**
Adelphia, N.J...............C4 **194**
Adelup, pt., Guam............ **114**
Aden, Yemen (Aden).....C6 **105**
Adena, Ohio...............B7 **199**
Adenau, Ger.................C1 **61**
Adgateville, Ga.............C3 **175**
Adger, Ala.............B2, E4 **166**
Adige, riv., It...............B3 **67**
Adigrāt, Eth.................C4 **105**
Adilabad, India.............H7 **88**
Adin, Calif...................B3 **170**
Adindān, Eg.................E6 **101**
Adirondack, mts., N.Y......A6 **196**
Adıyaman, Tur............C12 **85**
Adjud, Rom..................B8 **68**
Adjuntas, P.R...............C4 **132**
Adjuntas, mun., P.R.......C3 **132**
Adl Ugri, Eth................C4 **105**
Adlavik, is., Newf., Can...g10 **152**
Admaston, Ont., Can......B8 **153**
Admiral, Sask., Can.......H1 **155**
Admirals Beach, Newf.,
Can...........................E5 **152**
Admiralty, isl., Alsk.......m22 **167**
Admiralty, is., N. Gui......G8 **113**
Admire, Kans..............D7 **181**
Ado, Nig.....................E5 **103**
Ado-Ekiti, Nig.............E6 **103**
Adobe Creek, res., Colo....C7 **171**
Adok, Sud....................D3 **105**
Adola, Eth....................D4 **105**
Adolfo Alsina, Arg..........B4 **136**
Adolphus, Ky.................D3 **182**
Adona, Ark..................B3 **169**
Adoni, India...............*E6 **87**
Adony, Hung..................B4 **68**
Adorf, Ger....................C7 **61**
Adra, Sp.......................D4 **65**
Adrano, It....................F5 **67**
Adrar, Alg....................D4 **102**
Adrar, sand dunes, Maur...B2 **103**
Adrar des Iforas, reg.,
Alg., Mali.................B5 **103**
Adrar Nahalet, Alg.........E5 **102**
Adré, Chad...................C4 **104**
Adrī, Libya...................D2 **101**
Adria, It.......................B4 **67**
Adrian, Ga..................D4 **175**
Adrian, Mich...............G6 **186**
Adrian, Minn...............G3 **187**
Adrian, Mo..................C3 **189**
Adrian, N. Dak..............C7 **198**
Adrian, Oreg.................D9 **201**
Adrian, Tex..................B1 **206**
Adrian, W. Va................C4 **211**
Adrianople, Tur............B6 **69**
Adriatic, sea, Eur...........E8 **66**
Aduwā, Eth...................C4 **105**
Advance, Ind................D4 **179**
Advance, Mo.................D8 **189**
Advocate Harbour, N.S.,
Can..........................D5 **151**
Ady, Tex.......................B2 **206**
Adzopé, I.C...................E4 **103**
Aebelö, isl., Den............C4 **62**
Aegean, sea, Grc............C5 **69**
Aegina, see Aíyina, isl., Grc.
Aerö, isl., Den...............D4 **62**
Aerösköbing, Den..........D4 **62**
Aetna, Alta., Can...........E4 **148**
Aetna, Kans..................E5 **181**
Aetna, Tenn..................B4 **205**
Aetolian League............ **43**
AFARS & ISSAS, Fr. dep.,
Afr...................C5 **105, 99**
Afghan empire: c. 1775..... **82**
AFGHANISTAN, country,
Asia........................E12 **86**
Afgoi, Som....................E6 **105**
Aflou, Alg.....................C5 **102**
Afmadu, Som.................E5 **105**
Afognak, isl., Alsk..........D9 **167**
Afono, bay, Am. Sam......... **114**
Afonso Cláudio, Braz......F2 **138**
Afragola, It..............*D5 **67**
Africa, cont.................... **97**
partition of................... **99**
Africa, diocese of............ **46**
Africa, Roman prov.......... **44**
Afton, Iowa..................C3 **180**
Afton, Mich...................C6 **186**
Afton, Minn..................E8 **187**
Afton, N.Y....................C5 **196**
Afton, Okla...................A7 **200**
Afton, Tenn..................C11 **205**
Afton, Tex......................C2 **206**
Afton, Wyo...................C2 **213**
Aftout, sand dunes, Alg....D4 **102**
Afula, Isr......................B7 **84**
Afyonkarahisar, Tur.......C8 **85**
Agadem, Niger..............C7 **103**
Agadès, Niger...............C6 **103**
Agadir, Mor...................C3 **102**
Agalak (Well), Niger.......C6 **103**
Agalta, mts., Hond..........C5 **130**
Agamiaure, mts., Braz......B4 **139**
Agana, Guam...........**114, 115**
Agana, bay, Guam............ **114**
Agar, India....................F6 **88**
Agar, S. Dak.................C5 **204**
Agartala, India..............D9 **87**
Agassiz, B.C., Can...A11, E7 **149**
Agassiz, cape, Ant..........C6 **120**
Agat, bay, Guam.............. **114**
Agata, isl., Fiji................ **114**
Agate, Colo...................B7 **171**
Agate, Nebr...................B2 **191**
Agate, N. Dak.................A6 **198**
Agate Beach, Oreg..........C3 **201**
Agattu, isl., Alsk.............E2 **167**
Agawam, Mass..............B2 **185**
Agawam, Mont...............B4 **190**
Agayman, Sov. Un.........H10 **72**
Agbor, Nig.....................E6 **103**
Agboville, I.C.................E4 **103**
Agdam, Sov. Un..............B3 **86**
Agde, Fr.........................F5 **58**
Agedábia, see Ajdábiyah,
Libya.
Agematsu, Jap...............n16 **93**
Agen, Fr.........................E4 **58**
Agency, Iowa.................D5 **180**
Agency, Mo...................B3 **189**
Agenda, Kans................C6 **181**
Ageri, lake, Switz.............B4 **66**
Agersö, isl., Den..............C5 **62**
Agfayan, bay, Guam.......... **114**
Āghā Jārī, Iran................F4 **86**
Aghéila, see Al Uqaylah,
Libya.
A Ghlo, mtn., Scot...........D5 **57**
Agincourt, Ont., Can........E7 **153**
Agingan, pt., Saipan......... **114**
Agira, It.........................F5 **67**
Agnes, lake, Ont., Can......B7 **187**
Agno, Phil.....................n12 **90**
Agnone, It......................D5 **67**
Agnos, Ark.....................A4 **169**
Agogna, riv., It...............D4 **66**
Agordat, Eth...................B4 **105**
Agordo, It.......................C8 **66**
Agra, India.........C6 **87,** D6 **88**
Agra, Kans....................C4 **181**
Agra, Okla.....................B5 **200**
Agrado, Col....................C2 **133**
Agria, pt., Phil...............o13 **90**
Agricola, Kans................D8 **181**
Agricola, Miss.................E5 **188**
Agrícola Oriental, Mex...*D5 **129**
Agrigan, see Agrihan, isl.,
Mariana Is.
Agrigento, It.................F4 **67**
Agrihan (Agrigan), isl.,
Mariana Is.................... **115**
Agrínion, Grc..................C3 **69**
Agropoli, It.....................D5 **67**
Agua Caliente, Ariz..........E2 **168**
Agua Dulce, mts., Ariz.....E2 **168**
Agua Fria, N. Mex...........B1 **195**
Agua Fria, riv., Ariz....D3, G1 **168**
Agua Nueva, Tex.............F3 **206**
Água Preta, Braz..............k6 **138**
Agua Prieta, Mex.............A3 **129**
Aguacate, Cuba..............k12 **131**
Aguacate, P.R.................B2 **132**
Aguada, P.R....................B2 **132**
Aguada, mun., P.R...........B2 **132**
Aguadas, Col...................B2 **133**
Aguadilla, P.R.................B2 **132**
Aguadilla, mun., P.R........B2 **132**
Aguadilla, bay, P.R..........B2 **132**
Aguadulce, Pan...............F7 **130**
Aguaí, Braz....................m8 **137**
Aguán, riv., Hond............C4 **130**
Aguanish, Que., Can.........h9 **152**
Aguapeí, riv., Braz..........C2 **137**
Aguapey, riv., Arg............E4 **135**
Aguaray, Arg...................D3 **135**
Aguas Buenas, P.R...........B6 **132**
Aguas Buenas, mun., P.R..B6 **132**
Aguascalientes,
Mex................C4, m12 **129**
Aguascalientes, state,
Mex................C4, k12 **129**
Agudos, Braz...................C3 **137**
Agueda, Port...................B1 **65**
Agueda, riv., Sp..............B2 **65**
Agueloc, Mali..................C5 **103**
Aguelt Nemadi (Well),
Maur.........................C2 **103**
Aguéraktem (Well), Mali...B3 **103**
Aguijan (Agiguan), isl.,
Mariana Is.................... **115**
Aguila, Ariz....................D2 **168**
Aguila, pt., P.R...............D2 **132**
Aguilar, Colo.................D6 **171**
Aguilar, Sp......................D3 **65**
Aguilas, Sp......................D5 **65**
Aguililla, Mex..........D4, n12 **129**
Agujita, Mex....................B4 **129**
Agulhas, cape, S. Afr........D3 **107**
Aḥaggar, mts., Alg...........E6 **102**
Ahar, Iran.......................B3 **86**
Ahaus, Ger......................A2 **61**
Ahiri, India.....................H8 **88**
Ahklun, mts., Alsk...........D7 **167**
Ahlen, Ger......................B2 **61**
Ahlhorn, Ger....................F2 **62**
Ahmadabad,
India............D5 **87,** F4 **88**
Ahmadpur, Pak...............C5 **87**
Ahmar, mts., Eth.............D5 **105**
Ahmar, sand dunes, Alg.,
Mali...........................D4 **102**
Ahmednagar, India.........E5 **87**
Ahmeek, Mich.............*A2 **186**
Ahmic, lake, Ont., Can......B5 **153**
Aho, Jap........................o15 **93**
Ahoskie, N.C..................A7 **197**
Ahousat, B.C., Can...........E4 **149**
Ahrdorf, Ger....................C1 **61**
Ahrensbök, Ger...............D4 **62**
Ahrweiler, Ger.................C2 **61**
Ahsahka, Idaho...............C2 **177**
Ahtanum, Wash...............C5 **210**
Ahtanum, creek, Wash.....C5 **210**
Ahuacatlán, Mex.............m11 **129**
Ahuachapán, Sal.............D3 **130**
Ahualulco de Mercado,
Mex..........................m12 **129**
Ahukini, Haw..................B2 **176**
Åhus, Swe.......................C8 **62**
Ahvāz (Nāsiri), Iran.........F4 **86**
Ahvenanmaa, is., Fin.......G8 **63**
Ahwahnee, Calif..............D4 **170**
Aibonito, P.R...................C5 **132**
Aibonito, mun., P.R.........C5 **132**
Aichach, Ger...................E6 **61**
Aiea, Haw...............B4, g10 **176**

INDEX KEY Each place listed in **Bold-faced Type** has its population listed in the Population tables, pages 230 to 280.
Each country, shown in CAPITAL LETTERS, has its population listed in the World Political Information Table, pages 6 to 10.
* Does not appear on map; key shows general location.

Aigáleos, Grc. h11 **69**
Aigaleos, mts., Grc. h11 **69**
Aigen, Aus. D6 **60**
Aiguá, Ur. E2 **137**
Aigues-Mortes, Fr. F6 **58**
Aiguilles, Fr. E2 **66**
Aigun, China A10 **91**
Aihsien, China C8 **89**
Aija, Peru C2 **134**
Aikawa, Jap. G9 **93**
Aiken, S.C. D4 **203**
Aiken, co., S.C. D4 **203**
Aiken South, S.C. *D4 **203**
Aiken West, S.C. *D4 **203**
Aikin, Md. A5 **173**
Ailey, Ga. D4 **175**
Ailinginae, atoll, Marshall Is. **115**
Ailinglapalap, atoll, Marshall Is. **115**
Ailsa Craig, Ont., Can. D3 **153**
Ailuk, atoll, Marshall Is. **115**
Aima, lake, Braz. D5 **133**
Aimorés, Braz. E2 **138**
Aimwell, Ala. C2 **166**
Ain, dept., Fr. C1 **66**
Ain, riv., Fr. C1 **66**
Aïn Beïda, Alg. B6 **102**
Aïn Ben Tili, Maur. A3 **103**
Aïn el Bagha, Eg. E5 **84**
Aïn Oadeis, Eg. D6 **84**
Aïn-Oussera, Alg. G8 **64**
Aïn-Sefra, Alg. C4 **102**
Aïn Sudr, Eg. E5 **84**
Aïn Témouchent, Alg. B4 **102**
Ainabo, Som. D6 **105**
Ainos, mtn., Grc. C3 **69**
Ainslie, lake, N.S., Can. C8 **151**
Ainsworth, Iowa C6 **180**
Ainsworth, Nebr. B6 **191**
Aïoun el Atrous, Maur. C3 **103**
Aipe, Col. C2 **133**
Aiquile, Bol. C2 **135**
Air (Azbine), reg., Niger C6 **103**
Air Line, Ga. B3 **175**
Airabu, isl., Indon. K7 **89**
Airai, Palau Is. **114**
Airaines, Fr. E9 **56**
Aird, isl., Ont., Can. B8 **186**
Airdrie, Alta., Can. D3 **148**
Airdrie, Scot. E5 **57**
Aire, Fr. F3 **58**
Aire, riv., Eng. A6 **56**
Aire, riv., Fr. E5 **59**
Aire-sur-la-Lys, Fr. D2 **59**
Airolo, Switz. C4 **66**
Airport Drive, Mo. *D3 **189**
Airukiijl, isl., Bikini **114**
Aisch, riv., Ger. D5 **61**
Aisega, New Britain I. **115**
Aisén, prov., Chile D2 **136**
Aisne, dept., Fr. E3 **59**
Aisne, riv., Fr. C6 **58**
Aissa, mtn., Alg. C4 **102**
Aitape, N. Gui. h11 **111**
Aitkin, Minn. D5 **187**
Aitkin, co., Minn. D5 **187**
Aitolikón, Grc. C3 **69**
Aiud, Rom. B6 **68**
Aiuruoca, Braz. g5 **137**
Aiwa, isl., Fiji **114**
Aix, mtn., Wash. C4 **210**
Aix [-en-Provence], Fr. F6 **58**
Aix-les-Bains, Fr. D1 **66**
Aiyáleo, Grc. *C4 **69**
Aiyina, Grc. D4 **69**
Aiyina (Aegina), isl., Grc. D4 **69**
Aiyion, Grc. C4 **69**
Aiyon, Palau Is. **114**
Ajaccio, Fr. D2 **67**
Ajaccio, gulf, Fr. D2 **67**
Ajana, Austl. E1 **111**
Ajanta, India G5 **88**
Ajax, Ont., Can. D5 **153**
Ajayan, bay, Guam **114**
Ajdábiyah (Agedábia), Libya C4 **101**
Ajigasawa, Jap. F10 **93**
'Ajlūn, Jordan B7 **84**
Ajlune, Wash. C3 **210**
Ajmer, India C5 **87**, D5 **88**
Ajo, Ariz. E3 **168**
Ajoe, is., Indon. E8 **90**
Ajuana, riv., Braz. D4 **133**
Ajut, isl., New Britain I. **115**
Akabira, Jap. *E11 **93**
Akaishi-Sammyaku, mts., Jap. n17 **93**
Akalkot, India I6 **88**
Akaroa, N.Z. O14 **112**
Akashi, Jap. I7 **93**
Akaska, S. Dak. B5 **204**
Akçaabat, Tur. B12 **85**
Akçadağ, Tur. C11 **85**
Akchar, sand dunes, Maur. B2 **103**
Akdağmadeni, Tur. C10 **85**
Akechi, Jap. n16 **93**
Akela, N. Mex. E2 **195**
Akeley, Minn. C4 **187**
Aken, Ger. B7 **61**
Akers, La. B7, D5 **183**
Akesum, Eth. C4 **105**
Aketi, Zaire A3 **106**
Akhaltsikhe, Sov. Un. B14 **85**
Akharnai, Grc. g11 **69**
Akhḍar, mts., Libya C4 **101**
Akhelóös, riv., Grc. C3 **69**
Akhiok, Alsk. D9 **167**
Akhisar, Tur. C6 **85**
Akhmīm, Eg. D6 **101**
Akhtopol, Bul. D8 **68**
Akhtyrka, Sov. Un. F10 **72**
Aki, Jap. J6 **93**
Akiachak, Alsk. C7 **167**
Akiak, Alsk. C7 **167**
Akimiski, isl., N.W. Ter., Can. F16 **143**
Akins, Okla. B7 **200**
Akirkeby, Den. A3 **70**
Akita, Jap. G10 **93**
Akjoujt, Maur. C2 **103**
Akkeshi, Jap. E12 **93**
'Akko, Isr. B7 **84**
Akmolinsk, see Tselinograd, Sov. Un.
Ako, Bougainville I. **115**
Akobo, Sud. D3 **105**
Akobo, riv., Eth., Sud. D3 **105**
Akola, India D6 **87**
Akonolinga, Cam. E2 **104**
Akpatok, isl., N.W. Ter., Can. D19 **143**
Akra, India D8 **87**
Akra, N. Dak. A8 **198**
Akranes, Ice. n21 **63**
Akritas, cape, Grc. D3 **69**
Akritis, isl., Grc. D6 **69**
Akron, Ala. C2 **166**
Akron, Colo. A7 **171**
Akron, Ind. B5 **179**
Akron, Iowa B1 **180**
Akron, Mich. E7 **186**
Akron, N.Y. B2 **196**
Akron, Ohio A6 **199**
Akron, Pa. F9 **202**
Aksaray, Tur. C10 **85**
Akşehir, Tur. C8 **85**
Akşehir, lake, Tur. C8 **85**
Akseki, Tur. D8 **85**
Aksenovo-Zilovskoye, Sov. Un. D14 **71**
Akshimrau, Sov. Un. E4 **73**
Aksu, China E11 **71**
Aktogay, Sov. Un. D9 **73**
Aktumsyk, Sov. Un. D5 **73**
Aktyubinsk, Sov. Un. C5 **73**
Akure, Nig. E6 **103**
Akureyri, Ice. n23 **63**
Akuseki, isl., Jap. L4 **93**
Akutan, Alsk. E6 **167**
Ala Shan, mts., China D6 **91**
Alabama, state, U.S. **166**
in 1819 **163**
in 1861 **164**
Alabama, riv., Ala. D2 **166**
Alabama Port, Ala. E1 **166**
Alabaster, Ala. B3 **166**
Alabaster, Mich. D7 **186**
Alabat, isl., Phil. o14 **90**
Al Abyār, Libya F3 **85**
Alachua, Fla. C4 **174**
Alachua, co., Fla. C4 **174**
Aladdin,Wyo. A8 **213**
Alagna, It. D3 **66**
Alagoa Grande, Braz. C3, h6 **138**
Alagoas, state, Braz. C3, k5 **138**
Alagoinhas, Braz. D3 **138**
Alagón, Sp. B5 **65**
Al-Ahmadi, Kuw. G4 **86**
Al 'Ajamīyīn, Eg. E2 **84**
Alajuela, C.R. E5 **130**
Alakanuk, Alsk. C7 **167**
Alakol, lake, Sov. Un. D10 **73**
Alalakeiki, chan., Haw. C5 **176**
Al 'Alamayn (El Alamein), Eg. C5 **101**
Alalān, Iran C4 **86**
Alamagan, isl., Mariana Is. **115**
Alamance, N.C. B4 **197**
Alamance, co., N.C. B4 **197**
Al 'Amārah, Iraq F3 **86**
Alameda, Calif. B5 **170**
Alameda, Sask., Can. H4 **155**
Alameda, N. Mex. B3, G5 **195**
Alameda, co., Calif. D3 **170**
Al 'Āmirīyah, Eg. G7 **85**
Alaminos, Phil. n12 **90**
Alamito, creek, Tex. F2 **206**
Alamo, Calif. *B6 **170**
Alamo, Ga. D4 **175**
Alamo, Ind. E3 **179**
Alamo, Mex. m15 **129**
Alamo, Nev. F6 **192**
Alamo, N. Dak. A2 **198**
Alamo, Tenn. B2 **205**
Alamo, Tex. F3 **206**
Alamo Heights, Tex. B4, E3 **206**
Alamo, res., Ariz. C2 **168**
Alamo Hueco, mts., N. Mex. F1 **195**
Alamogordo, N. Mex. E4 **195**
Alamogordo, res., N. Mex. C5 **195**
Alamos, Mex. B3 **129**
Alamosa, Colo. D5 **171**
Alamosa, co., Colo. D5 **171**
Alamosa, creek, Colo. D4 **171**
Alamosa, riv., N. Mex. D2 **195**
Alanreed, Tex. B2 **206**
Alanson, Mich. C6 **186**
Alantika, mts., Cam. D2 **104**
Alanya, Tur. D9 **85**
Alaotra, lake, Malag. g9 **107**
Alapaha, Ga. E3 **175**
Alapaha, riv., Ga. E3 **175**
Al 'Aqabah, Jordan E7 **84**
Alaqua, Fla. G3 **174**
Alardyce, hbr., Santa Isabel I. **115**
Al 'Arīsh, Eg. C6 **101**
Alarka, N.C. D3 **197**
Alaşehir, Tur. C7 **85**
Al Ashkharah, Oman D2 **87**
Alaska, state, U.S. **167**
Alaska, gulf, Alsk. D10 **167**
Alaska, pen., Alsk. D8 **167**
Alaska, range, Alsk. C9 **167**
Alassio, It. C2 **67**
Alatyr, Sov. Un. C3 **73**
Alau, isl., Haw. C6 **176**
Alausí, Ec. B2 **134**
Alava, cape, Wash. A1 **210**
Alaverdi, Sov. Un. B15 **85**
Al 'Aynā, Jordan D7 **84**
Al 'Ayzarīyah (Bethany), Jordan h12 **84**
Al 'Azair, Iraq F3 **86**
Alba, It. B2 **67**
Alba, Mich. D6 **186**
Alba, Mo. D3 **189**
Alba, Pa. C8 **202**
Alba, Tex. C5 **206**
Alba de Tormes, Sp. B3 **65**
Alba Iulia, Rom. B6 **68**
Albacete, Sp. C5 **65**
Ålbaek, Den. A4 **62**
Ålbaek, bay, Den. A4 **62**
Al Bājhūr, Eg. D3 **84**
Albalate [del Arzobispo], Sp. B5 **65**
Al Ballāḥ, Eg. D4 **84**
Albanel, lake, Que., Can. F18 **143**
ALBANIA, country, Eur. B3 **69**
c. 1360 **48**
in 1922–40 **53**
in 1950 **54**
Albano, lake, It. h9 **67**
Albano Laziale, It. D4, h9 **67**
Albany, Austl. F2 **111**
Albany, Calif. *D2 **170**
Albany, P.E.I., Can. C6 **151**
Albany, Ga. E2 **175**
Albany, Ill. B3 **178**
Albany, Ind. D7 **179**
Albany, Ky. D4 **182**
Albany, La. A6 **183**
Albany, Minn. E4 **187**
Albany, Mo. A3 **189**
Albany, N.Y. C7 **196**
Albany, Ohio C5 **199**
Albany, Okla. D5 **200**
Albany, Oreg. C1, C3 **201**
Albany, Tex. C3 **206**
Albany, Vt. B4 **208**
Albany, Wis. F4 **212**
Albany, Wyo. D6 **213**
Albany, co., N.Y. C7 **196**
Albany, co., Wyo. D7 **213**
Albany, riv., Ont., Can. E9 **153**
Al Barkāt, Libya E2 **101**
Al Baṭānūn, Eg. D2 **84**
Al Bawīṭī, Eg. D5 **101**
Al Bayḍā, Libya C4 **101**
Albee, S. Dak. B9 **204**
Albemarle, N.C. B3 **197**
Albemarle, co., Va. D4 **209**
Albemarle, see Isabela, isl., Ec.
Albemarle, sound, N.C. A7 **197**
Albenga, It. B2 **67**
Alberche, riv., Sp. B3 **65**
Alberene, Va. D4 **209**
Ålberga, Swe. u34 **63**
Albergaria-a-Velha, Port. B1 **65**
Alberni, B.C., Can. E5 **149**
Albers, Ill. *E4 **178**
Albersdorf, Ger. D3 **62**
Albert, N.B., Can. D5 **151**
Albert, Fr. B5 **58**
Albert, Kans. D5 **181**
Albert, N. Mex. B6 **195**
Albert, Okla. B3 **200**
Albert, co., N.B., Can. D5 **151**
Albert, lake, Ug. A5 **106**
Albert Canyon, B.C., Can. D9 **149**
Albert City, Iowa B3 **180**
Albert Lea, Minn. G5 **187**
Albert Markham, mtn., Ant. A28 **120**
Albert Nile, riv., Ug. A5 **106**
Alberta, Ala. C2 **166**
Alberta, Minn. E2 **187**
Alberta, Va. E5 **209**
Alberta, prov., Can. **148**
Alberta, mtn., Alta., Can. C2 **148**
Alberton, P.E.I., Can. C5 **151**
Alberton, Mont. C2 **190**
Albertville, Ala. A3 **166**
Albertville, Sask., Can. D3 **155**
Albertville, Fr. E7 **58**
Albertville, Minn. E5 **187**
Albi, Fr. F5 **58**
Albia, Iowa C5 **180**
Albin, Miss. B3 **188**
Albin, Wyo. D8 **213**
Albina, Sur. A4 **139**
Albion, Calif. C2 **170**
Albion, Idaho G5 **177**
Albion, Ill. E5 **178**
Albion, Ind. B7 **179**
Albion, Iowa B5 **180**
Albion, Maine D3 **184**
Albion, Mich. F6 **186**
Albion, Mont. E12 **190**
Albion, Nebr. C7 **191**
Albion, N.Y. B2 **196**
Albion, Okla. C6 **200**
Albion, Pa. C1 **202**
Albion, R.I. B11 **172**
Albion, Wash. C8 **210**
Albion, Wis. F4 **212**
Al Bīrah, Jordan h11 **84**
Alboran, isl., Sp. E4 **65**
Ålborg, Den. A3 **62**
Ålborg, co., Den. B3 **62**
Ålborg, bay, Den. B4 **62**
Alborn, Minn. D6 **187**
Albox, Sp. D4 **65**
Albreda, B.C., Can. C8 **149**
Albright, W. Va. *B5 **211**
Albrightsville, Pa. D10 **202**
Al Bu'ayrāt, Libya I14 **64**, C3 **101**
Albufeira, Port. D1 **65**
Albuñol, Sp. D4 **65**
Albuquerque, N. Mex. B3, G5 **195**
Alburg, Vt. B2 **208**
Alburnett, Iowa B6 **180**
Alburquerque, Sp. C2 **65**
Alburtis, Pa. E10 **202**
Albury, Austl. H6 **112**
Al Busaiya, Iraq F3 **86**
Al Buşayli, Eg. C2 **84**
Alca, Peru E3 **134**
Alcabideche, Port. f9 **65**
Alcácer do Sal, Port. C1 **65**
Alcalá de Chisvert, Sp. B6 **65**
Alcalá [de Guadaira], Sp. D3 **65**
Alcalá de Henares, Sp. B4, p18 **65**
Alaclá de los Gazules, Sp. D3 **65**
Alcalá la Real, Sp. D4 **65**
Alcalde, N. Mex. A3 **195**
Alcamo, It. F4 **67**
Alcanadre, riv., Sp. B5 **65**
Alcanar, Sp. B6 **65**
Alcañiz, Sp. B5 **65**
Alcântara, Braz. B2 **138**
Alcantarilla, Sp. D5 **65**
Alcaraz, Sp. C4 **65**
Alcaudete, Sp. D3 **65**
Alcázar de San Juan, Sp. C4 **65**
Alcazarquivir, Mor. B3 **102**
Alcester, S. Dak. D9 **204**
Alcira, Sp. C5 **65**
Alco, Ark. B3 **169**
Alco, La. C2 **183**
Alcoa, Tenn. D10, E11 **205**
Alcobendas, Sp. o17 **65**
Alcochete, Port. f10 **65**
Alcolu, S.C. D7 **203**
Alcomdale, Alta., Can. C4 **148**
Alcona, co., Mich. D7 **186**
Alcora, Sp. B5 **65**
Alcorcón, Sp. p17 **65**
Alcorisa, Sp. B5 **65**
Alcorn, Ky. C5 **182**
Alcorn, Miss. D2 **188**
Alcorn, co., Miss. A5 **188**
Alcova, Wyo. C6 **213**
Alcoy, Sp. C5 **65**
Alda, Nebr. D7 **191**
Aldama, Mex. B3 **129**
Aldan, Pa. *G11 **202**
Aldan, Sov. Un. D15 **71**
Aldan, plat., Sov. Un. D15 **71**
Aldan, riv., Sov. Un. C16 **71**
Aldeburgh, Eng. B9 **56**
Aldecoa, Cuba h11 **131**
Alden, Ill. A5 **178**
Alden, Iowa B4 **180**
Alden, Kans. D5 **181**
Alden, Mich. D5 **186**
Alden, Minn. G5 **187**
Alden, N.Y. C2 **196**
Alden, Pa. D9 **202**
Alden Bridge, La. B2 **183**
Alder, Mont. E4 **190**
Alder, brook, Vt. B4 **208**
Alder, mtn., Scot. D4 **56**
Alderney, isl., Guernsey F5 **55**
Aldershot, Eng. C7 **56**
Alderson, Okla. C6 **200**
Alderson, W. Va. D4 **211**
Aldersyde, Alta., Can. D4 **148**
Alderwood Manor, Wash. B3 **210**
Aldie, Va. A4, C5 **209**
Aldin, pt., Fiji **114**
Aldine, N.J. D2 **194**
Aldora, Ga. C2 **175**
Aldrich, Ala. B3 **166**
Aldrich, Minn. D4 **187**
Aldrich, Mo. D4 **189**
Aldridge, Eng. *B6 **56**
Ale, riv., Scot. E6 **57**
Aledo, Ill. B3 **178**
Aledo, Tex. B5 **206**
Aleg, Maur. C2 **103**
Alegre, Braz. C4 **137**
Alegrete, Braz. D1 **137**
Alegros, mtn., N. Mex. C1 **195**
Aleknagik, Alsk. D8 **167**
Aleksander, wadi, Isr. f10 **84**
Aleksandriya, Sov. Un. G9 **72**
Aleksandrov, Sov. Un. C12 **72**
Aleksandrov-Gay, Sov. Un. C3 **73**
Aleksandrovsk [-Sakhalinskiy], Sov. Un. D17 **71**
Aleksandrovskoye, Sov. Un. A9 **73**
Aleksandrów, Pol. B5 **70**
Aleksandrów, Pol. C5 **70**
Aleksin, Sov. Un. D11 **72**
Aleksinac, Yugo. D5 **68**
Alelai, pt., W. Sam. **114**
Alemania, Arg. E2 **135**
Alençon, Fr. C4 **58**
Alenquer, Braz. C4 **139**
Alenquer, Port. C1 **65**
Alentejo, reg., Port. C2 **65**
Alepokhóri, Grc. g10 **69**
Aleppo (Ḥalab), Syr. D11 **85**
Aleria, Fr. C2 **67**
Alert, Ind. F6 **179**
Alert Bay, B.C., Can. D4 **149**
Alès, Fr. E6 **58**
Alessandria, It. B2 **67**
Ålestrup, Den. B3 **62**
Ålesund, Nor. F2 **63**
Alet, Fr. F5 **58**
Aleutian, is., Alsk. E3 **167**
Aleutian, range, Alsk. D9 **167**
Alex, Okla. C4 **200**
Alexander, Ark. C3, D5 **169**
Alexander, Man., Can. E1 **150**
Alexander, Ga. C5 **175**
Alexander, Ill. D3 **178**
Alexander, Iowa B4 **180**
Alexander, Kans. D4 **181**
Alexander, Maine C5 **184**
Alexander, N.Y. C2 **196**
Alexander, N.C. D3 **197**
Alexander, N.Dak. B2 **198**
Alexander, W. Va. C4 **211**
Alexander, co., Ill. F4 **178**
Alexander, co., N.C. B2 **197**
Alexander, arch., Alsk. D12 **167**
Alexander, cape, Choiseul I. **115**
Alexander, isl., Ant. B5 **120**
Alexander, lake, Minn. D4 **187**
Alexander Bay, S. Afr. C2 **107**
Alexander City, Ala. C4 **166**
Alexander Mills, N.C. B2, D4 **197**
Alexander's empire **43**
Alexandra, N.Z. P12 **112**
Alexandra, isl., Sov. Un. A10 **118**
Alexandretta, see İskenderun, Tur.
Alexandretta, gulf, Tur. D10 **85**
Alexandria, Ala. B4 **166**
Alexandria, B.C., Can. C6 **149**
Alexandria, Ont., Can. B10 **153**
Alexandria (Al Iskandarīyah), Eg. C5 **101**
Alexandria, Ind. D6 **179**
Alexandria, Ky. A7, B5 **182**
Alexandria, La. C3 **183**
Alexandria, Minn. E3 **187**
Alexandria, Mo. A6 **189**
Alexandria, Nebr. D8 **191**
Alexandria, N.H. C3 **193**
Alexandria, Ohio B5 **199**
Alexandria, Pa. E5 **202**
Alexandria, Rom. D7 **68**
Alexandria, S. Afr. *C4 **107**
Alexandria, S. Dak. D8 **204**
Alexandria, Tenn. C7 **205**
Alexandria (Independent City), Va. B5, C5 **209**
Alexandria Bay, N.Y. A5, B1 **196**
Alexandria Southwest, La. *C3 **183**
Alexandrina, lake, Austl. G2 **112**
Alexandroúpolis, Grc. B5 **69**
Alexis, Ill. B3 **178**
Alexis, riv., Newf., Can. B3 **152**
Alexis Creek, B.C., Can. C6 **149**
Aleysk, Sov. Un. C10 **73**
Alfalfa, co., Okla. A3 **200**
Al Fandaqūmīyah, Jordan B7, f11 **84**
Al Farāfirah, Eg. D5 **101**
Alfaro, Sp. A5 **65**
Alfatar, Bul. D8 **68**
Al Fayyūm, Eg. E2 **84**
Alfeld, Ger. B4 **61**
Alfenas, Braz. C3, k9 **137**
Alfiós (Alpheus), riv., Grc. D3 **69**
Alfonsine, It. E8 **66**
Alford, Eng. A8 **56**
Alford, Fla. B1, G3 **174**
Alford, Ind. H3 **179**
Alford, Mass. B1 **185**
Alford, Scot. C6 **57**
Alfordsville, Ind. G4 **179**
Alfortville, Fr. g10 **58**
Alfred, Ont., Can. B10 **153**
Alfred, Maine E2 **184**
Alfred, N.Y. C3 **196**
Alfred, N. Dak. C7 **198**
Alfred Mills, Maine E2 **184**
Alfred Station, N.Y. C3 **196**
Al Fuqahā, Libya D3 **101**
Algā, Eth. D4 **105**
Algarrobal, Chile E1 **135**
Algarrobo, Chile E1 **135**
Algarrobo del Aguilla, Arg. B3 **136**
Algarve, reg., Port. D1 **65**
Algeciras, Sp. D3 **65**
Algemesí, Sp. C5 **65**
Alger, see Algiers, Alg.
Alger, Mich. D6 **186**
Alger, Ohio B4 **199**
Alger, co., Mich. B4 **186**
ALGERIA, country, Afr. D4 **102**
in 1830 **99**
Algete, Sp. o18 **65**
Al Ghayatah, Eg. D2 **84**
Alghero, It. D2 **67**
Al Ghurdaqah, Eg. D6 **101**
Algiers (Alger), Alg. F8 **64**, B5 **102**
Algoa, bay, S. Afr. D4 **107**
Algodones, N. Mex. B3, G5 **195**
Algoma, Miss. A4 **188**
Algoma, Wis. D6 **212**
Algoma, co., Ont., Can. A2 **153**
Algoma Mills, Ont., Can. A2 **153**
Algona, Iowa A3 **180**
Algona, Wash. B3, D2 **210**
Algonac, Mich. F8 **186**
Algonquin, Ont., Can. C9 **153**
Algonquin, Ill. A5, E2 **178**
Algonquin, prov. park, Ont., Can. B6 **153**
Algonquin Park, Ont., Can. B6 **153**
Algood, Tenn. C8 **205**
Algorta, Ur. E1 **137**
Al Ḥāfir (Oasis), Sau. Ar. H13 **85**
Alhama, Sp. D4 **65**
Alhama, Sp. D5 **65**
Alhambra, Calif. F2 **170**
Alhambra, Ill. E4 **178**
Alhambra, Mont. D5 **190**
Al Ḥāmūl, Eg. C3 **84**
Alhaurín el Grande, Sp. D3 **65**
Al Ḥawṣah (Oasis), Jordan H11 **85**
Al Ḥayy, Eg. E3 **84**
Al Ḥayyānīyah (Oasis), Sau. Ar. H14 **85**
Al Ḥillah, Iraq F15 **85**, E2 **86**
Al Ḥinnāh, Sau. Ar. H4 **86**
Alhos Vedros, Port. f9 **65**
Al Ḥudaydah, Yemen (Ṣan'ā') C5 **105**
Al Ḥumaymah, Jordan E7 **84**
Al Ḥuṣn, Jordan B7 **84**
'Ali Gharbi, Iraq E3 **86**
Ali-Sabieh, Afars & Is. C5 **105**
Aliákmon, riv., Grc. B3 **69**
Alibag, India H4 **88**
Alicahue, Chile A2 **136**
Alicante, Sp. C5 **65**
Alicante, gulf, Sp. C5 **65**
Alice, Ont., Can. B7 **153**
Alice, N. Dak. C8 **198**
Alice, Tex. F3 **206**
Alice, lake, Minn. C7 **187**
Alice Southwest, Tex. *F3 **206**
Alice Springs, Austl. D5 **111**
Alicel, Oreg. B9 **201**
Aliceville, Ala. B1 **166**
Aliceville, Kans. D8 **181**
Alicia, Ark. B4 **169**
Alicudi, isl., It. E5 **67**
Alida, Sask., Can. H5 **155**
Alief, Tex. F4 **206**
Aligarh, India C6 **87**
Alīgūdarz, Iran E4 **86**
Alim, isl., Bis. Arch. **115**
Alindao, Cen. Afr. Rep. E4 **104**
Aline, Ga. D4 **175**
Aline, Okla. A3 **200**
Alingsås, Swe. I5 **63**
Alipur Duar, India D12 **88**
Aliquippa, Pa. A5, E1 **202**
Alisal, Calif. C6 **170**
Al Iskandarīyah, see Alexandria, Eg.
Al Ismā'īlīyah, see Ismailia, Eg.
Alistráti, Grc. B5 **69**
Aliwal North, S. Afr. D4 **107**
Alix, Ark. B2 **169**
Alix, Alta., Can. C4 **148**
Al Jaghbūb, Libya D4 **101**
Al Jāniyah, Jordan h11 **84**
Al Jawf, Sau. Ar. D7 **101**
Al Jawsh, Libya C2 **101**
Aljezur, Port. D1 **65**
Al Jizah, see Giza, Eg.
Aljustrel, Port. D1 **65**
Alkabo, N. Dak. A2 **198**
Al Kadhimain, Iraq F15 **85**
Alkali, lake, Nev. B2 **192**
Alkali, lake, Oreg. E6 **201**
Alkaline, lake, N. Dak. C6 **198**
Al Karak, Jordan C7 **84**
Al Kawm aṭ Ṭawīl, Eg. C3 **84**
Al Khābūrah, Oman D2 **87**
Al Khalīl (Hebron), Jordan C7 **84**
Al Khalūf, Oman D2 **87**
Al Khārijah, Eg. D6 **101**
Al Khasab, Oman H8 **86**
Al Khaṭaṭibah, Eg. D2 **84**
Al Khums, Libya C2 **101**
Al Khurmah, Sau. Ar. A5 **105**
Alkionídhes, gulf, Grc. g10 **69**
Alkionídhes, is., Grc. g9 **69**
Alkmaar, Neth. B4 **59**
Al Kubr, isl., Kuw. G4 **86**
Al Kūbrī, Eg. D4 **84**
Al Kufrah, oasis, Libya, Eg. E4 **101**
Al Kuh, cape, Iran I8 **86**
Al Kuntillah, Eg. E6 **84**
Al Kūt, Iraq E3 **86**
Al Lādhiqīyah, see Latakia Syr.
Allagash, Maine A3 **184**
Allagash, lake, Maine B3 **184**
Allagash, riv., Maine B3 **184**
Allahabad, India C7 **87**, E8 **88**
Allakaket, Alsk. B9 **167**
Allamakee, co., Iowa A6 **180**
Allamoore, Tex. F2 **206**
Allamuchy, mtn., N.J. B3 **194**
Allan, Sask., Can. F2 **155**
Allanmyo, Bur. E10 **87**
Allâqui, wadi, Eg. E6 **101**
Allardt, Tenn. C9 **205**
Allariz, Sp. A2 **65**
Allaykha, Sov. Un. B36 **118**
Alleene, Ark. D1 **169**
Allegan, Mich. F5 **186**
Allegan, co., Mich. F4 **186**
Allegany, N.Y. C2 **196**
Allegany, Oreg. D2 **201**
Allegany, co., Md. A1 **173**
Allegany, co., N.Y. C2 **196**
Allegany, Indian res., N.Y. C2 **196**
Alleghany, Calif. C3 **170**
Alleghany, Va. D2 **209**
Alleghany, co., N.C. A2 **197**
Alleghany, co., Va. D3 **209**
Allegheny, co., Pa. E2 **202**
Allegheny, mts., U.S. C11 **159**
Allegheny, plat., Pa., W. Va. C3 **211**
Allegheny, riv., N.Y., Pa. E2 **202**
Allegheny River, res., N.Y., Pa. B4 **202**
Alleman, Iowa A7 **180**
Allen, Ala. D2 **166**
Allen, Kans. D7 **181**
Allen, Ky. C7 **182**
Allen, Md. D6 **173**
Allen, Mich. *G6 **186**
Allen, Nebr. B9 **191**
Allen, Okla. C5 **200**
Allen, Pa. F7 **202**
Allen, S. Dak. D4 **204**
Allen, co., Ind. B7 **179**
Allen, co., Kans. E8 **181**
Allen, co., Ky. D3 **182**
Allen, co., Ohio B3 **199**
Allen, par., La. D3 **183**
Allen, lake, Ire. C2 **55**
Allen, mtn., Alsk. C11 **167**

INDEX KEY Each place listed in **Bold-faced Type** has its population listed in the Population tables, pages 230 to 280.
Each country, shown in CAPITAL LETTERS, has its population listed in the World Political Information Table, pages 6 to 10.
* Does not appear on map; key shows general location.

Allen, mtn., N.Z. Q11 112
Allen Park, Mich. A7 186
Allendale, Ill. E6 178
Allendale, Mo. A3 189
Allendale, N.J. A4 194
Allendale, S.C. E5 203
Allendale, co., S.C. E5 203
Allende, Mex. B4 129
Allenford, Ont., Can. C3 153
Allenhurst, Fla. D6 174
Allenhurst, Ga. E5 175
Allenhurst, N.J. C4 194
Allenport, Pa. *F2 202
Allens Mills, Maine D2 184
Allenspark, Colo. A5 171
Allenstown, N.H. D4 193
Allensville, Ky. D2 182
Allensville, Ohio C5 199
Allensville, Pa. E6 202
Allenton, Ala. D2 166
Allenton, Mo. B7 189
Allenton, Wis. E5 212
Allentown, Ga. D3 175
Allentown, N.J. C3 194
Allentown, N.Y. C2 196
Allentown, Pa. E11 202
Allentown, Wash. D1 210
Allenville, Ill. D5 178
Allenville, Mich. C6 186
Allenwood, N.J. C4 194
Allenwood, Pa. D8 202
Alleppey, India G6 87
Aller, Sp. A3 65
Aller, riv., Ger. A6 61
Allerton, Ill. D6 178
Allerton, Iowa D4 180
Allerton, pt., Mass. B6 185
Alley, Mo. D6 189
Alley Spring, Mo. D6 189
Allgood, Ala. B3 166
Alliance, Alta., Can. C5 148
Alliance, Nebr. B3 191
Alliance, N.C. B7 197
Alliance, Ohio B6 199
Alliance Cut, pass, N. Cal. 115
Allier, riv., Fr. D5 58
Al Līfīyah (Oasis), Sau. Ar. G14 85
Alligator, Miss. A3 188
Alligator, lake, Maine D4 184
Alligator, lake, N.C. B7 197
Alligator, riv., N.C. B7 197
Allimaso, creek, N. Mex. C5 195
Allingåbro, Den. B4 62
Allinge, Den. C8 62
Allison, Colo. D3 171
Allison, Iowa B5 180
Allison, N. Mex. B1 195
Allison, Pa. G2 202
Allison Harbour, B.C., Can. D4 149
Allison Park, Pa. A6 202
Allisona, Tenn. B5 205
Allisonia, Va. E2 209
Alliston, Ont., Can. C5 153
Al Līth, Sau. Ar. A5 105
Alloa, Scot. D5 57
Allons, Tenn. C8 205
Allouez, Mich. A2 186
Allouez, Wis. A6 212
Alloway, N.J. D2 194
Alloway, creek, N.J. D2 194
Allred, Tenn. C8 205
Allsboro, Ala. A1 166
Al Luḩayyah, Yemen B5 105
Allumette, lake, Ont., Can. B7 153
Allyn, Wash. B3 210
Allyns Point, Conn. D8 172
Alma, Ark. B1 169
Alma, N.B., Can. D5 151
Alma, Ont., Can. D4 153
Alma, Que., Can. A6 154
Alma, Colo. B4 171
Alma, Ga. E4 175
Alma, Ill. E5 178
Alma, Kans. C7 181
Alma, Mich. E6 186
Alma, Mo. B4 189
Alma, Nebr. D6 191
Alma, N.C. C4 197
Alma, Okla. C4 200
Alma, W. Va. B4 211
Alma, Wis. D2 212
Alma, hill, N.Y. C2 196
Alma-Ata, Sov. Un. E9 73
Alma Center, Wis. D3 212
Al Ma'ādī, Eg. E3 84
Almada, Port. C1, f9 65
Almadén, Sp. C3 65
Al Madīnah, see Medina, Sau. Ar.
Al Mafraq, Jordan F11 85
Almagro, Sp. C4 65
Al Maḩallah al Kubrá, Eg. D3 84
Al Maḩmūdīyah, Eg. C2 84
Al Maḩsamah, Eg. D4 84
Al Maḩṭab, Sau. Ar. H11 85
Al Makīlī, Libya F4 85
Almalyk, Sov. Un. *E9 71
Almanor, lake, Calif. B3 170
Almansa, Sp. C5 65
Al Manṣūrah, Eg. C3 84, C6 101
Al Manzilah, Eg. C3 84
Almanzora, riv., Sp. D4 65
Almargem [do Bispo], Port. f9 65
Al Marj (Barce), Libya F3 85
Almartha, Mo. E5 189
Al Maṭarīyah, Eg. C4 84
Almaville, Tenn. B5 205
Almazán, Sp. B4 65
Al Mazār, Jordan C7 84
Almeirim, Braz. C4 139
Almeirim, Port. C1 65
Almelo, Neth. B6 59
Almelund, Minn. E6 187
Almena, Kans. C4 181
Almena, Wis. C1 212
Almendares, Cuba h11 131
Almendralejo, Sp. C2 65
Almeria, Nebr. C6 191
Almería, Sp. D4 65
Almería, gulf, Sp. D4 65
Almería, riv., Sp. D4 65
Al'met'yevsk, Sov. Un. C4 73
Älmhult, Swe. B8 62
Al Minya, Eg. D6 101
Almira, Wash. B7 210
Almirante, Pan. F6 130
Almirante Brown, Arg. g7 136
Almirós, Grc. C4 69
Al Mish'ab, cape, Sau. Ar. G4 86
Almo, Idaho G5 177
Almo, Ky. B3 182
Almodôvar, Port. D1 65
Almodóvar, Sp. C3 65
Almogía, Sp. D3 65
Almon, Ga. C3 175
Almonaster, Sp. D2 65
Almond, Ala. B4 166
Almond, N.Y. C3 196
Almond, N.C. D2 197
Almond, Wis. D4 212
Almond, riv., Scot. D5 57
Almont, Colo. C4 171
Almont, Mich. F7 186
Almont, N. Dak. C4 198
Almonte, Ont., Can. B8 153
Almonte, Sp. D2 65
Almonte, riv., Sp. C3 65
Almora, India C6 88
Almora, Minn. D3 187
Almoradí, Sp. C5 65
Almoravides, dominions of 47
Al Mubarraz, Sau. Ar. *G7 77
Al Mughayyir, Jordan g12 84
Al Mukallā, Yemen (Aden) C6 105
Al Mukhā, Yemen (Ṣan'ā') C5 105
Almuñécar, Sp. D4 65
Al Muwayliḩ, Sau. Ar. I10 85
Almyra, Ark. C4 169
Aln, riv., Eng. E11 57
Alna, Maine *D3 184
Alness, Scot. C4 57
Alnwick, Eng. C6 55
Aloha, Oreg. B2 201
Along, bay, Viet. B7 89
Alonsa, Man., Can. D2 150
Alor, isl., Indon. G6 90
Alor Setar, Mala. I4 89
Álora, Sp. D3 65
Alorton (Fireworks), Ill. *E3 178
Alosno, Sp. D2 65
Alpachiri, Arg. B4 136
Alpaugh, Calif. E4 170
Alpbach, Aus. E5 60
Alpena, Ark. A2 169
Alpena, Mich. C7 186
Alpena, S. Dak. C7 204
Alpena, co., Mich. D7 186
Alpes-de-Haute, dept., Fr. E2 66
Alpha, Ill. B3 178
Alpha, Iowa B5 180
Alpha, Ky. D4 182
Alpha, Mich. B2 186
Alpha, Minn. G4 187
Alpha, N.J. B2 194
Alpha, Ohio C3 199
Alpharetta, Ga. B2 175
Alphen aan den Rijn, Neth. B4 59
Alpiarça, Port. C1 65
Alpine, Ala. B3 166
Alpine, Ariz. D6 168
Alpine, Ark. C2 169
Alpine, Calif. *F5 170
Alpine, Idaho F7 177
Alpine, N.J. D5 194
Alpine, Oreg. C3 201
Alpine, Tenn. C8 205
Alpine, Tex. F2 206
Alpine, co., Calif. C4 170
Alpoca, W. Va. D3 211
Alps, mts., Eur. F9 40
Al Qaddāḩīyah, Libya I14 64
Al Qāhirah, see Cairo, Eg.
Al Qanāyāt, Eg. D3 84
Al Qanṭarah, Eg. D4 84
Al Qaryah ash Sharqīyah, Libya C2 101
Al Qaşabāt, Libya C2 101
Al Qaşr, Eg. D5 101
Al Qaţīf, Sau. Ar. H5 86
Al Qaţrānah, Jordan G11 85
Al Qaţrūn, Libya E2 101
Al Qayrawān, Tun. B6 102
Al Qulaiyaba (Oasis), Sau. Ar. H14 85
Al Qunaytirah, Syr. F10 85
Al Qurna, Iraq F3 86
Al Quşaymah, Eg. D6 84
Al Quşayr, Eg. D6 101
Alright, isl., Que., Can. B8 151
Alrö, Den. C4 62
Als, Den. B4 62
Alsace, former prov., Fr. C7 58
in 1871 51
in 1922–40 53
Alsask, Sask., Can. F1 155
Alsasua, Sp. A4 65
Alsdorf, Ger. D6 59
Alsea, Oreg. C3 201
Alsek, riv., Alsk., Yukon, Can. D12 167
Alsen, N. Dak. A7 198
Alsenbrück-Langmeil, Ger. D2 61
Alsey, Ill. D3 178
Alsfeld, Ger. C4 61
Alsike, Swe. t35 63
Alsip, Ill. *F3 178
Alsium, see Palo, It.
Alstead, N.H. D2 193
Alstead, riv., Sask., Can. B2 155
Alstead Center, N.H. D2 193
Alston, Eng. F6 57
Alston, Ga. D4 175
Alta, Iowa B2 180
Alta, Wyo. B2 213
Alta Gracia, Arg. A4 136
Alta Hill, Calif. *C3 170
Alta Loma, Tex. G5 206
Alta Vista, Iowa A5 180
Alta Vista, Kans. D7 181
Altadena, Calif. *F2 170
Altaelv, riv., Nor. C10 63
Altagracia, Ven. A3 133
Altagracia de Orituco, Ven. B4 133
Al Tahoe, Calif. C4 170
Altai, mts., Asia B2 91
Altamaha, riv., Ga. E4 175
Altamaha, sound, Ga. E5 175
Altamahaw, N.C. A4 197
Altamira, Braz. C4 139
Altamira, Chile E2 135
Altamirano, Arg. g7 136
Altamont, Calif. B6 170
Altamont, Man., Can. E2 150
Altamont, Ill. D5 178
Altamont, Kans. E8 181
Altamont, Mo. B3 189
Altamont, N.Y. C6 196
Altamont, Oreg. E5 201
Altamont, S. Dak. C9 204
Altamont, Tenn. D8 205
Altamont, Utah C5 207
Altamonte Springs, Fla. D5 174
Altamura, It. D6 67
Altamura, isl., Mex. C3 129
Altapass, N.C. C4 197
Altar, Mex. A2 129
Altario, Alta., Can. D5 148
Altavista, Va. D3 209
Altdorf, Ger. D6 61
Altdorf, Switz. C4 66
Alte Mellum, isl., Ger. E2 62
Altefähr, Ger. D7 62
Altenberg, Ger. C8 61
Altenbruch, Ger. E2 62
Altenburg, Ger. C7 61
Altenburg, Mo. D8 189
Altenkirchen, Ger. C2 61
Altenkirchen, Ger. D7 62
Altenmarkt, Ger. A8 66
Altentreptow, Ger. E7 62
Alter do Chão, Port. C2 65
Altha, Fla. B1 174
Altheim, Aus. A9 66
Altheimer, Ark. C4 169
Altinho, Braz. C3, k6 138
Altkirch, Fr. B3 66
Altman, Ga. D5 175
Altmar, N.Y. B4 196
Altmühl, riv., Ger. E6 61
Altnaharra, Scot. B4 57
Alto, Ga. B3 175
Alto, La. B4 183
Alto, Mich. F5 186
Alto, N. Mex. D4 195
Alto, Tenn. B6 205
Alto, Tex. D5 206
Alto Araguaia, Braz. B2 137
Alto Cedro, Cuba E6 131
Alto Longá, Braz. C2 138
Alto Molocuè, Moz. A6 107
Alto Pass, Ill. F4 178
Alto Park, Ga. *B1 175
Alto Ritacuba, mtn., Col. B3 133
Alto Trombetas, riv., Braz. B3 139
Altomünster, Ger. A7 66
Alton, Ala. B3, E5 166
Alton, Ont., Can. D4 153
Alton, Eng. C7 56
Alton, Ill. E3 178
Alton, Iowa B1 180
Alton, Kans. C5 181
Alton, La. B8 183
Alton, Mo. E6 189
Alton, N.H. D4 193
Alton, Ohio C2 199
Alton, R.I. D10 172
Alton, Utah F3 207
Alton, W. Va. C4 211
Alton Bay, N.H. D4 193
Alton North, Ill. *E3 178
Alton North East, Ill. *E3 178
Altona, Man., Can. E3 150
Altona, Ger. E3 62
Altona, Ill. B3 178
Altona, Ind. B7 179
Altona, Mich. E5 186
Altona, N.Y. A7 196
Altoona, Ala. A3 166
Altoona, Fla. D5 174
Altoona, Iowa A7, C4 180
Altoona, Kans. E8 181
Altoona, Pa. E5 202
Altoona, Wis. D2 212
Altötting, Ger. A8 66
Altrincham, Eng. A5 56
Altro, Ky. C6 182
Altstätten, Switz. B5 66
Altun Köprü, Iraq E15 85
Altura, Minn. F7 187
Alturas, Calif. B3 170
Altus, Ark. B2 169
Altus, Okla. C2 200
Altus, res. and dam, Okla. C2 200
Altyn Tagh, mts., China D2 91
Al Ubayyiḑ, Sud. C3 105
Al 'Ujaylāt, Libya H13 64
Alula, Som. C7 105
Alum, creek, Ohio C2 199
Alum Bank (Pleasantville), Pa. F4 202
Alum Bridge, W. Va. B4 211
Alum Creek, W. Va. C5 211
Alum Rock, Calif. *D3 170
Aluminé, Arg. B2 136
Alunite, Nev. H7 192
Alupka, Sov. Un. I10 72
Al 'Uqaylah (Aghéila), Libya C3 101
Al 'Uqayr, Sau. Ar. I5 86
Al Uqşur (Luxor), Eg. D6 101
Al Uthaylah, Libya C4 101
Alva, Fla. F5 174
Alva, Ky. D6 182
Alva, Okla. A3 200
Alva, Wyo. A8 213
Alvarado, Mex. D5 129
Alvarado, Minn. B2 187
Alvarado, Tex. B5, C4 206
Alvaton, Ga. C2 175
Alvdalen, Swe. G6 63
Alvear, Arg. E4 135
Alvena, Sask., Can. E2 155
Alverca [do Ribatejo], Port. f9 65
Alverton, Pa. F2 202
Alvesta, Swe. B8 62
Alvin, Ill. C6 178
Alvin, S.C. E8 203
Alvin, Tex. E5, F5 206
Alvin R. Bush, res., Pa. D6 202
Alvinston, Ont., Can. E3 153
Alviso, Calif. *D2 170
Alvo, Nebr. D9, E2 191
Alvord, Iowa A1 180
Alvord, Tex. C4 206
Alvord, lake, Oreg. E8 201
Alvordton, Ohio A3 199
Älvsborg, co., Swe. A6 62
Älvsjö, Swe. t36 63
Alvwood, Minn. C4 187
Al Wajh, Sau. Ar. D7 101
Alwar, India C6 87
Al Wāsiţah, Eg. E3 84
Aly, Ark. C2 169
Alyaty-Pristan, Sov. Un. F3 73
Alyth, Scot. D5 57
Alytus, Sov. Un. A8 70
Alz, riv., Ger. D6 60
Alzada, Mont. E12 190
Alzey, Ger. D3 61
Ama, La. C7 183
Amadeus, lake, Austl. D5 110
Amadi, Sud. D3 105
Amado, Ariz. F4 168
Amador, Calif. *C3 170
Amador, co., Calif. C3 170
Amagansett, N.Y. D4 196
Amagasaki, Jap. o14 93
Amager, isl., Den. C6 62
Amagon, Ark. B4 169
Amahai, Indon. F7 90
Amakusa, sea, Jap. J4 93
Åmål, Swe. H5 63
Amalfi, It. D5 67
Amalga, Utah B4 207
Amalia, N. Mex. A4 195
Amaliás, Grc. D3 69
Amalner, India G5 88
Amamio, isl., Ryūkyū Is. F10 91
Amana, Iowa C6 180
Amanã, lake, Braz. D5 133
Amanda, Ohio C5 199
Amangeldy, Sov. Un. C7 73
Amantea, It. E6 67
Amantes, pt., Guam 114
Amapá, Braz. B4 139
Amapá, ter., Braz. B4 139
'Amara, Iraq F3 86
Amaraji, Braz. k6 138
Amarante, Braz. C2 138
Amaranth, Man., Can. D2 150
Amargosa, Braz. D3 138
Amargosa, range, Calif. D5 170
Amargosa, riv., Calif. E5 170
Amarillo, Tex. B2 206
Amaro, mtn., It. C5 67
Amaroúsion, Grc. g11 69
Amasa, Mich. B2 186
Amasra, Tur. B9 85
Amasya, Tur. B10 85
Amazon, Sask., Can. F3 155
Amazon, see Solimões, riv., Braz., Peru
Amazon, see Amazonas, riv., S.A.
Amazonas, dept., Peru B2 134
Amazonas, comisaría, Col. D3 133
Amazonas, state, Braz. C3 134
Amazonas, ter., Ven. C4 133
Amazonas (Amazon), riv., S.A. D5 124, C3 139
Amazonia, Mo. B3 189
Ambala, India B6 88
Ambala Cantonment, India *B6 88
Ambalavao, Malag. h9 107
Ambam, Cam. E2 104
Ambanja, Malag. f9 107
Ambarchik, Sov. Un. C19 71
Ambato, Ec. B2 134
Ambato-Boeni, Malag. g9 107
Ambatosorata, Malag. g9 107
Amber, Okla. B4 200
Amberg, Ger. D6 61
Amberg, Wis. C6 212
Ambérieu [-en-Bugey], Fr. E6 58
Amberley, Ohio *D2 199
Amberson, Pa. F6 202
Ambia, Ind. D3 179
Ambikapur, India F9 88
Ambilobe, Malag. f9 107
Amble, Eng. E7 57
Ambler, Pa. A11, F11 202
Ambo, Eth. D4 105
Ambo, chan., Kwajalein 114
Ambo, Peru D2 134
Amboear, Indon. F8 90
Amboina, Indon. F7 90
Amboina, isl., Indon. F7 90
Amboise, Fr. D4 58
Ambositra, Malag. h9 107
Ambovombe, Malag. i9 107
Amboy, Calif. E6 170
Amboy, Ga. E3 175
Amboy, Ill. B4 178
Amboy, Ind. C6 179
Amboy, Minn. G4 187
Amboy, Wash. D3 210
Ambridge, Pa. A5, E1 202
Ambrin, isl., New Hebr. 115
Ambriz, Ang. C1 106
Ambrizete, Ang. C1 106
Ambrose, Ga. E3 175
Ambrose, N. Dak. A2 198
Ambrosia Lake, N. Mex. B2 195
Amchitka, isl., Alsk. E3 167
Amchitka, pass, Alsk. E4 167
Am Dam, Chad C4 104
Amderma, Sov. Un. C9 71
Ameagle, W. Va. D3, D6 211
Ameca, Mex. C4, m11 129
Amecameca, Mex. n14 129
Amechtil, sand dunes, Maur. C2 103
Ameland, isl., Neth. A5 59
Amelia, La. C5, E4 183
Amelia, Nebr. B7 191
Amelia, Ohio C3 199
Amelia City, Fla. A7 174
Amelia, co., Va. D4 209
Amelia, isl., Fla. A7 174
Amelia Court House, Va. D5 209
Amelinghausen, Ger. E4 62
Amendolara, It. E6 67
Amenia, N.Y. D7 196
Amenia, N. Dak. B8 198
American, highland, Ant. B21 120
American, riv., Calif. C3 170
American Bottom, val., Oreg. C1 201
American Falls, Idaho G6 177
American Falls, dam, Idaho G6 177
American Fork, Utah C4 207
AMERICAN SAMOA, U.S. dep., Oceania 114
Americus, Ga. D2 175
Americus, Kans. D7 181
Americus, Mo. C6 189
Amersfoort, Neth. B5 59
Amery, Man., Can. A4 150
Amery, Wis. C1 212
Amery, ice shelf, Ant. B20 120
Ames, Iowa B4 180
Ames, Kans. C6 181
Ames, Nebr. C9, D2 191
Ames, Okla. A3 200
Amesbury, Mass. A6 185
Ámfissa, Grc. C4 69
Amga, Sov. Un. C16 71
Amgu, Sov. Un. D8 93
Amgun, riv., Sov. Un. D16 71
Amhar, plat., Eth. D4 105
Amherst, N.S., Can. D5 151
Amherst, Colo. A8 171
Amherst, Maine D4 184
Amherst, Mass. B2 185
Amherst, Nebr. D6 191
Amherst, N.H. E3 193
Amherst, N.Y. C2 196
Amherst, Ohio A5 199
Amherst, S. Dak. B8 204
Amherst, Tex. B1 206
Amherst, Va. D3 209
Amherst, Wis. D4 212
Amherst, co., Va. D3 209
Amherst, isl., Que., Can. B7 151
Amherstburg, Ont., Can. E1 153
Amherstdale, W. Va. D3, D5 211
Amiata, mtn., It. C3 67
Amidon, N. Dak. C2 198
Amiens, Fr. C5 58
Aminuis, S.W. Afr. B2 107
'Amir, cape, Libya A2 101
Amiret, Minn. F3 187
Amisk, Alta., Can. C5 148
Amisk, lake, Sask., Can C4 155
Amistad, N. Mex. B6 195
Amistad, res., Mex., Tex. E2 206
Amite, La. D5 183
Amite, co., Miss. D3 188
Amite, riv., La. D5 183
Amity, Ark. C2 169
Amity, Mo. B3 189
Amity, Oreg. B1, B3 201
Amity, Pa. F1 202
Amityville, N.Y. E3, E7 196
Amizmiz, Mor. I2 64
Amkyokyung, China C11 88
Amlekhganj, Nep. D10 88
Amlwch, Wales A3 56
Amman, Jordon G10 85
Ammanford, Wales C3 56
Ammeloe, Ger. A1 61
Ammendorf, Ger. B7 61
Ammer, lake, Ger. B7 66
Ammon, Idaho F7 177
Ammonoosuc, riv., N.H. B3 193
Amne Machin, mts., China D4 91
Amo, Ind. E4 179
Āmol, Iran C6 86
Amoret, Mo. C3 189
Amorgós, isl., Grc. D5 69
Amorita, Okla. A3 200
Amory, Miss. B5 188
Amos, Que., Can. E10 153
Amoy, China G8 91
Ampanihy, Malag. h8 107
Amparo, Braz. C3, m8 137
Amper, riv., Ger. E6 61
Ampezzo, It. C8 66
Amposta, Sp. B6 65
Amqui, Que., Can. *B3 154
'Amrān, Yemen (Ṣan'ā') B5 105
Amravati, India G6 88
Amreli, India G3 88
Amritsar, India B5 88
Amroha, India C7 88
Amrum, isl., Ger. D2 62
Amstelveen, Neth. B4 59
Amsterdam, Ga. F2 175
Amsterdam, Mo. C3 189
Amsterdam, Mont. E5 190
Amsterdam, Neth. B4 59
Amsterdam, N.Y. C6 196
Amsterdam, Ohio B7 199
Amstetten, Aus. D7 60
Amston, Conn. C7 172
Am Timan, Chad C4 104
Amu Darya (Oxus), riv., Afg., Sov. Un. C13 86
Amukta, pass, Alsk. E5 167
Amundsen, bay, Ant. C17 120
Amundsen, glacier, Ant. A32 120
Amundsen, gulf, N.W. Ter., Can. B8 142
Amundsen, sea, Ant. B1 120
Amur, riv., Sov. Un. E16 71
Amvrakia, gulf, Grc. C3 69
Amwaco, Idaho E8 210
'Ana, Iraq E13 85
Ana Maria, gulf, Cuba E4 131
Anabar, riv., Sov. Un. B14 71
Anabtā, Jordan f11 84
Anacoco, La. C2 183
Anacoco, bayou, La. C2 185
Anaconda, Mont. D4 190
Anaconda, N. Mex. B2 195
Anaconda, range, Mont. E3 190
Anacortes, Wash. A3 210
Anacostia, riv., Md. C1 173
Anadarko, Okla. B3 200
Anadia, Braz. C3, k5 138
Anadyr, Sov. Un. C20 71
Anadyr, gulf, Sov. Un. C21 71
Anadyr, range, Sov. Un. C20 71
Anadyr, riv., Sov. Un. C20 71
Anae, isl., Guam 114
Anáfi (Anaphe), isl., Grc. D5 69
Anagance, N.B., Can. D4 151
Anaheim, Calif. F3, F5 170
Anahia Bay, Man., Can. D2 150
Anahim Lake, B.C., Can. C5 149
Anahola, Haw. A2 176
Anahuac, Tex. E5, F5 206
Anajás, Braz. C5 139
Anakapalle, India I9 88
Anakie, Austl. A6 112
Anaklia, Sov. Un. A13 85
Analalava, Malag. f9 107
Anambas, is., Indon. E3 90
Anamoose, N. Dak. B5 198
Anamosa, Iowa B6 180
Anamur, Tur. D9 85
Anamur, cape, Tur. D9 85
Anandale, La. *D4 183
Anandpur, India F10 88
Anantapur, India F6 87
Anantnag, India B6 87
Ananyev, Sov. Un. H7 72
Anao, pt., Guam 114
Anapa, Sov. Un. I11 72
Anápolis, Braz. E1 138
Anapú, riv., Braz. C4 139
Anār, Iran F7 86
Anārak, Iran E6 86
Anardara, Afg. E10 86
Añasco, P.R. B2 132
Añasco, mun., P.R. B2 132
Anastasia, isl., Fla. C5 174
'Anātā, Jordan h12 84
Anatahan (Anatajan) isl., Mariana Is. 115
Anatone, Wash. C8 210
Añatuya, Arg. E3 135
Anauá, riv., Braz. C5 133
Anawalt, W. Va. D3 211
Ancash, dept., Peru C2 134
Ancenis, Fr. D3 58
Anchi, China F8 91
Anchieta, Braz. F2 138
Anching, China I7 92
Ancho, N. Mex. C5 195
Anchor, Ill. *C5 178
Anchor Bay Gardens, Mich. *F8 186
Anchor Point, Alsk. h16, D9 167
Anchorage, Alsk. C10, g17 167
Anchorage, Ky. A4 182
Ancienne-Lorette, Que., Can. C6, C8 154
Anclote, keys, Fla. D4 174
Anco, Ky. C6 182
Ancon, C.Z. m11 130
Ancón, Peru D2 134
Ancona, It. C4 67
Ancud, Chile C2 136
Ancud, gulf, Chile C2 136
Andacollo, Arg. B2 136
Andahuaylas, Peru D3 134
Andale, Kans. B4, E6 181
Andalgalá, Arg. E2 135
Andalsnes, Nor. F2 63
Andalusia, Ala. D3 166
Andalusia, Ill. B3 178
Andalusia, reg., Sp. D3 65
Andaman, is., India F9 87
Andaman, sea, Asia F10 87
Andamarca, Bol. C2 135
Andamarca, Peru D3 134
Andapa, Malag. f9 107

INDEX KEY Each place listed in **Bold-faced Type** has its population listed in the Population tables, pages 230 to 280.
Each country, shown in CAPITAL LETTERS, has its population listed in the World Political Information Tables, pages 6 to 10.
* Does not appear on map; key shows general location.

Andavaka, cape, Malag i9 107
Andebu, Nor p28 63
Andenne, Bel D5 59
Anderlecht, Bel D4 59
Andermatt, Switz C4 66
Andernach, Ger C2 61
Anderslöv, Swe C7 62
Anderson, Ala A2 166
Anderson, Arg g6 136
Anderson, Calif B2 170
Anderson, Ind D6 179
Anderson, Mo E3 189
Anderson, S.C B2 203
Anderson, Tenn B6 205
Anderson, Tex D5 206
Anderson, co., Kans D8 181
Anderson, co., Ky C4 182
Anderson, co., S.C B2 203
Anderson, co., Tenn C9 205
Anderson, co. Tex D5 206
Anderson, mtn., Wash B2 210
Anderson, riv., N.W. Ter., Can C7 142
Anderson, riv., Ind H4 179
Anderson Dam, Idaho F3 177
Anderson East Side, Ind *D6 179
Anderson Ranch, res., Idaho F3 177
Andersonville, Ga D2 175
Andersonville, Ind F7 179
Andes, Col B2 133
Andes, Mont C12 190
Andes, N.Y C6 196
Andes, lake, S. Dak D7 204
Andes, mts., S.A D3, H3 124
Andhra Pradesh, state, India E6 87
Andidanob, mtn., Sud A4 105
Andikithira, isl., Grc E4 69
Andilamena, Malag g9 107
Andīmeshk, Iran E4 86
Anding, Miss C3 188
Andizhan, Sov. Un E8 73
Andkhui, Afg C12 86
Andoas, Peru B2 134
Andong, Kor H4 93
Andorra, And A6 65
ANDORRA, country, Eur A6 65
Andover, N.B., Can C2 151
Andover, Conn C7 172
Andover, Eng C6 56
Andover, Ill B3 178
Andover, Iowa *C7 180
Andover, Kans B6 181
Andover, Maine D2 184
Andover, Mass A5 185
Andover, N.H D3 193
Andover, N.J B3 194
Andover, N.Y C3 196
Andover, Ohio A7 199
Andover, S. Dak B8 204
Andover, Vt *E3 208
Andöy, isl., Nor C6 63
Andrade, Haw D6 176
Andraitx, Sp C7 65
Andreanof, is., Alsk E4 167
Andreas, cape, Cyp E10 85
Andrelandia, Braz g5 137
Andrew, Alta., Can C4 148
Andrew, Iowa B7 180
Andrew, co., Mo B3 189
Andrew, isl., N.S., Can D9 151
Andrew Jackson, mtn., Ant B6 120
Andrews, Ind C6 179
Andrews, Md D5 173
Andrews, N.C D2 197
Andrews, Oreg E8 201
Andrews, S.C E8 203
Andrews, Tex C1 206
Andrews, co., Tex C1 206
Andreyevka, Sov. Un G11 72
Andria, It D6 67
Androka, Malag h8 107
Ándros, Grc D5 69
Andros, isl., Ba. Is C4 131
Ándros, isl., Grc D5 69
Androscoggin, co., Maine D2 184
Androscoggin, lake, Maine D2 184
Androscoggin, riv., Maine, N.H D2 184, A4 193
Andrychow, Pol h10 70
Andsfjord, fiord, Nor C7 63
Andújar, Sp C3 65
Anéfis, Mali C5 103
Anegada, bay, Arg C4 136
Anegada, isl., Vir. Is m14 131
Anegada, passage, N.A m15 131
Anegam, Ariz E3 168
Aneityum, isl., New Hebr 115
Anerley, Sask., Can F2 155
Aneroid, Sask., Can H2 155
Aneta, N. Dak B8 198
Aneth, Utah F6 207
Aneto, mtn., Sp A6 65
Angadanan, Phil n13 90
Angamos, pt., Chile D1 135
Angangchi, China B9 91
Angara, riv., Sov. Un D13 71
Angarsk, Sov. Un A5 91
Angaur, isl., Palau Is 114
Angel, falls, Ven B5 133
Angel de la Guarda, isl., Mex B2 129
Angela, Mont D10 190
Angeles, Phil o13 90
Angeles, P.R B3 132
Angeles, pt., Wash A2 210
Ängelholm, Swe I5 63
Angelica, N.Y C2 196
Angelina, co., Tex D5 206
Angels Camp, Calif C3 170
Angelus, Kans C3 181
Angelus, S.C B7 203
Ångermanälven, riv., Swe F7 63
Angermünde, Ger B7 60
Angers, Que., Can D2 154
Angers, Fr D3 58
Angicos, Braz C3 138
Angie, La D6 183
Angier, N.C B5 197
Angikuni, lake, N.W. Ter., Can D13 142
Angkor, ruins, Camb F5 89
Angle Inlet, Minn A3 187
Anglem, mtn., N.Z Q11 112
Anglesey, co., Wales A3 56
Anglesey, is., Wales D4 55
Anglet, Fr F3 58
Angleton, Tex E5, G5 206
Anglia, Sask., Can F1 155
Angliers, Que., Can G17 145
Angling, riv., Man., Can A5 150
Anglo-Egyptian Sudan, see Sudan, country, Afr.
Angmagssalik, Grnld C18 118
Ango, Zaire A4 106
Angoche, isl., Moz A6 107
Angohrān, Iran H8 86
Angol, Chile B2 136
Angola, Ind A8 179
Angola, N.Y C1 196
ANGOLA, Port. dep., Afr D2 106
Angola, swamp, N.C C6 197
Angoon, Alsk D13, m22 167
Angora, Nebr C2 191
Angostura, res., S. Dak D2 204
Angoulême, Fr E4 58
Angra do Heroismo, Port. (Azores) g9 102
Angra dos Reis, Braz C4, h5 137
Angren, Sov. Un E7 73
Anguilla, Miss C3 188
ANGUILLA, Br. dep., N.A m15 131
Anguillara, It g8 67
Anguille, cape, Newf., Can E2 152
Anguille, mts., Newf., Can E2 152
Angumu, Zaire B4 106
Angus, Ont., Can C5 153
Angus, Iowa C3 180
Angus, Minn B2 187
Angus, co., Scot D5 57
Angusville, Man., Can D1 150
Angwin, Calif A5 170
Anhalt: c. 1870 51
Anhembí, Braz m7 137
Anholt, isl., Den B5 62
Anholt By, Den B5 62
Anhsi, China C4 91
Anhua, China J4 92
Anhwei, prov., China E8 91
Ani, New Britain I 115
Aniak, Alsk C8 167
Aniene, riv., It h9 67
Animas, N. Mex F1 195
Animas, mts., N. Mex F1 195
Animas, peak, N. Mex F1 195
Anina, Rom C5 68
Anita, Iowa C3 180
Anita, Pa D4 202
Aniva (Rutaka), Sov. Un C11 93
Aniva, bay, Sov. Un C11 93
Aniva, cape, Sov. Un C11 93
Aniwa, Wis C4 212
Aniwa, isl., New Hebr 115
Anizy-le-Château, Fr E3 59
Anjar, India F3 88
Anjean, W. Va C4 211
Anjō, Jap o16 93
Anjou, former prov., Fr D3 58
Anjouan, isl., Comoro Is f8 107
Anju, Kor G2 93
Anjum, Neth A6 59
Ankang, China H3 92
Anka, Nig D6 103
Ankara, Tur C9 85
Ankaratra, mts., Malag g9 107
Ankavandra, Malag g9 107
Ankazoabo, Malag h8 107
Ankeny, Iowa A7, C4 180
An Khe, Viet F8 89
Anklam, Ger B6 60
Ankobar, Eth D4 105
Ankona, Fla E6 174
Ankoro, Zaire C4 106
Ankuang, China D1 93
An Loc, Viet G7 89
Anlu, China I5 92
Anlung, China F6 91
Anmoore, W. Va B7 211
Ann, cape, Ant B18 120
Ann, cape, Mass A6 185
Ann Arbor, Mich A6, F7 186
Anna, Ill F4 178
Anna, Ohio B3 199
Anna, Sov. Un F13 72
Anna, Tex *C4 206
Anna Maria, Fla F1 174
Anna Maria, key, Fla F1 174
Annaba, Alg F10 64, B6 102
Annabella, Utah E3 207
Annaberg-Buchholz, Ger C8 61
Annaburg, Ger B8 61
Annada, Mo B7 189
An Nafud, des, Sau. Ar H13 85
An Najaf, Iraq G15 85
An Nakhl, Eg E5 84
Annam, reg., Viet D7 89
c. 750 80
c. 1294 81
c. 1775 82
Annan, Scot F5 57
Annan, riv., Scot E5 57
Annandale, Minn E4 187
Annandale, N.J B3 194
Annandale, Va B5 209
Annapolis, Ill D6 178
Annapolis, Ind E3 179
Annapolis, Md C5 173
Annapolis, Mo D7 189
Annapolis, Wash D1 210
Annapolis, co., N.S., Can E4 151
Annapolis, riv., N.S., Can E4 151
Annapolis Junction, Md B4 173
Annapolis Royal, N.S., Can E4 151
Annapurna 1, peak, Nep C9 88
An Nārt, mtn., Libya E4 101
An Nāşirīyah, Iraq F3 86
Annawan, Ill B4 178
An Nawfalīyah, Libya C3 101
An Nazlah, Gaza Strip C6 84
Anne Arundel, co., Md B4 173
Annecy, Fr E7 58
Annemasse, Fr D7 58
Annette, Alsk n24 167
An Nhon, Viet F8 89
Annieopsquotch, mts., Newf., Can D3 152
Anniston, Ala B4 166
Anniston, Mo E8 189
Annobón, isl., Afr F1 104
Annonay, Fr E6 58
Annotto Bay, Jam F5 131
Annsjon, lake, Swe u33 63
Annursnack, hill, Mass C1 185
Annville, Ky C6 182
Annville, Pa F8 202
Ano Nuevo, pt., Calif C5 170
Áno Theológos, Grc B5 69
Áno Viánnos, Grc E5 69
Anoka, Minn E5, E6 187
Anoka, Nebr B7 191
Anoka, co., Minn E5 187
Anona, Fla E1 174
Anou Mellène (Well), Mali C5 103
Anóyia, Grc E5 69
Anpei, China D3 92
Anping, China E6 92
Anping, China E4 92
Ansbach, Ger D5 61
Anse d'Hainault, Hai F6 131
Anselm, N. Dak C8 198
Anselmo, Nebr C6 191
Anserma, Col B2 133
Anshan, China C9 91, D10 92
Anshun, China F6 91
Ansley, Ala D3 166
Ansley, La B3 183
Ansley, Miss E4 188
Ansley, Nebr C6 191
Anson, Maine D3 184
Anson, Tex C3 206
Anson, co., N.C B3 197
Ansŏng, Kor H2 93
Ansongo, Mali C5 103
Ansonia, Conn D4 172
Ansonia, Ohio B3 199
Ansonville, Ont., Can E9 153
Ansonville, N.C B3 197
Ansted, W. Va C3, D7 211
Anstruther, Scot D6 57
Anta, China C2 93
Anta, Peru D3 134
Antabamba, Peru D3 134
Antakya (Antioch), Tur D11 85
Antalaha, Malag f10 107
Antalāt, Libya C4 101
Antalya, Tur D8 85
Antalya, gulf, Tur D8 85
Antarctica, cont 120
Antarctic, pen., Ant B6 120
Ante, Va E5 209
Antelope, Sask., Can G1 155
Antelope, Kan D7 181
Antelope, Mont B12 190
Antelope, Oreg C6 201
Antelope, co., Nebr B7 191
Antelope, creek, Wyo B7 213
Antelope, isl., Utah B3 207
Antelope, lake, Sask., Can G1 155
Antelope, peak, Nev B7 192
Antelope, range, Nev D7 192
Antelope, res., Oreg E9 201
Antelope Mine, Rh B4 107
Antequera, Sp D3 65
Antero, peak, Colo C4 171
Antes Fort, Pa D7 202
Anthon, Iowa B2 180
Anthony, Ark D2 169
Anthony, Fla C4 174
Anthony, Kans E5 181
Anthony, N. Mex E3 195
Anthony, R.I C10 172
Anthony, Tex *E1 206
Anthonys, creek, W. Va D4 211
Anti-Atlas, mts., Mor C3 102
Antibes, Fr F7 58
Anticosti, isl., Que., Can B3 154
Antietam, nat. battlefield site, Md B2 173
Antigo, Wis C4 212
Antigonid Kingdom 43
Antigonish, N.S., Can D7 151
Antigonish, co., N.S., Can D8 151
ANTIGUA, Br. dep., N.A n16 131
Antigua, isl., N.A n16 131
Antigua Guatemala, Guat C2 130
Antilla, Cuba E6 131
Antimony, Utah E4 207
Antioch, Calif B6 170
Antioch, Ill A5, D2 178
Antioch, Ind D4 179
Antioch, Nebr B3 191
Antioch, Tenn A5, E9 205
Antioch, see Antakya, Tur.
Antionia, Mo C7 189
Antioquia, Col B2 133
Antioquia, dept., Col B2 133
Antiquity, Ohio D6 199
Antler, Sask., Can H5 155
Antler, N. Dak A4 198
Antler, riv., Man., Can E1 150
Antler, riv., Sask., Can H5 155
Antlers, Okla C6 200
Antofagasta, Chile D1 135
Antofagasta, prov., Chile D2 135
Antofagasta de la Sierra, Arg E2 135
Antofalla, vol., Arg E2 135
Antoine, Ark C2 169
Anton, Colo B7 171
Anton, Tex C1 206
Anton Chico, N. Mex B4 195
Antongil, bay, Malag g9 107
Antonina, Braz D3 137
Antonino, Kans D4 181
Antonio de Biedma, Arg D3 136
Antônio Dias, Braz E2 138
António Enes, Moz A6 107
Antonito, Colo D4 171
Antony, Fr g10 58
Antratsit, Sov. Un q22 72
Antrim, Mich D5 186
Antrim, N.H D3 193
Antrim, Pa C7 202
Antrim, co., Mich C5 186
Antrim, mts., N. Ire C3 55
Antsalova, Malag g8 107
Antsirabe, Malag g9 107
Antsirane, see Diégo-Suarez, Malag.
Antung, China C9 91, F2 93
Antwerp (Antwerpen), Bel C4 59
Antwerp, N.Y A5, B1 196
Antwerp, Ohio A3 199
Antwerpen, see Antwerp, Bel.
Antwerpen, prov., Bel C4 59
Anua, Am. Sam 114
An Uaimh, Ire D3 55
Anuradhapura, Cey G7 87
Anvers, isl., Ant C6 120
Anvik, Alsk C7 167
Anyang, China D7 91
Anyang, Kor H3 93
Anyi, China E7 91
Anykščiai, Sov. Un A8 70
Anzá, Col B2 133
Anzhero-Sudzhensk, Sov. Un B11 73
Anzin, Fr D3 58
Anzio, It D4, k9 67
Anzoátegui, state, Ven B5 133
Aoba, isl., New Hebr 115
Aojidong, Kor E5 93
Aomoen, isl., Bikini 114
Aomon, isl., Eniwetok 114
Aomori, Jap F10 93
Aore, isl., New Hebr 115
Aosta, It B1 67
Aouk, riv., Cen. Afr. Rep D4 104
Aoulef, Alg D5 102
Apa, riv., Par D4 135
Apache, Okla C3 200
Apache, co., Ariz B6 168
Apache, mts., Tex F2 206
Apache, peak, Ariz F5 168
Apache Creek, N. Mex D1 195
Apache Junction, Ariz G3 168
Apaiang, isl., Gilbert Is 115
Apalachee, Ga C3 175
Apalachee, bay, Fla B2 174
Apalachicola, Fla C2 174
Apalachicola, bay, Fla C2 174
Apalachicola, riv., Fla B1 174
Apalachin, N.Y G4 196
Apamama, isl., Gilbert Is 115
Apan, Mex n14 129
Apaporis, riv., Col C3 133
Aparri, Phil B6 90
Apatin, Yugo C4 68
Apatity, Sov. Un D15 63
Apatzingán, Mex n12 129
Apeldoorn, Neth B5 59
Apennine, tunnel, It B3 67
Apennines, mts., It C4 67
Apex, N.C B5 197
Apgar, Mont B3 190
Api, peak, Nep C8 88
Apia, W. Sam 114
Apia, hbr., W. Sam 114
Apiacás, mts., Braz E3 139
Apiaí, Braz C3 137
Apíranthos, Grc D5 69
Apishapa, riv., Colo D6 171
Apison, Tenn E10 205
Apizaco, Mex n14 129
Aplao, Peru E3 134
Aplin, Ark C3 169
Aplington, Iowa B5 180
Apo, vol., Phil D7 90
Apodi, Braz C3 138
Apohaqui, N.B., Can D4 151
Apolda, Ger B6 61
Apolima, isl., W. Sam 114
Apolima, strait, W. Sam 114
Apollo, Pa E2 202
Apopka, Fla D5 174
Aporé, riv., Braz B2 137
Apostle, is., Wis A3 212
Apóstoles, Arg E4 135
Appalachia, Va B2 209
Appalachian, mts., U.S C11 159
Appam, N. Dak A2 198
Appanoose, co., Iowa D5 180
Appenzell, Switz B5 66
Appenzell, canton, Switz B5 66
Apperson, Okla A5 200
Appingedam, Neth A6 59
Apple, creek, N. Dak C5 198
Apple, riv., Ill F3 212
Apple, riv., Wis C1 212
Apple Creek, Ohio B6 199
Apple Grove, Va D5 209
Apple Grove, W. Va C2 211
Apple Hill, Ont., Can B10 153
Apple Orchard, mtn., Va D3 209
Apple River, N.S., Can D5 151
Apple River, Ill A3 178
Apple Springs, Tex D5 206
Apple Valley, Calif E5 170
Appleby, Eng F6 57
Appleby, Tex D5 206
Applecross, Scot C3 57
Applegate, Oreg E3 201
Applegate, Mich E8 186
Applegate, riv., Oreg E3 201
Appleton, Ark B3 169
Appleton, Maine D3 184
Appleton, Minn E2 187
Appleton, S.C E5 203
Appleton, Wash D4 210
Appleton, Wis A5, D5 212
Appleton City, Mo C3 189
Applewold, Pa *E2 202
Appleyard, Wash B5 210
Appling, Ga C4 175
Appling, co., Ga E4 175
Appomattox, Va D4 209
Appomattox, co., Va D4 209
Appomattox, riv., Va D4 209
Approuague, Fr. Gu B4 139
Apra, hbr., Guam 114
Aprelsk, Sov. Un D14 71
Aprilia, It D4, h9 67
Apsley, Ont., Can C6 153
Apt, Fr F6 58
Aptos, Calif C6 170
Apuaí, riv., Braz D5 133
Apulia, reg., It D6 67
Apulyont, lake, Tur B7 69
Apure, state, Ven B4 133
Apure, riv., Ven B4 133
Apurímac, dept., Peru D3 134
Apurímac, riv., Peru D3 134
'Aqaba, gulf, Afr., Asia H10 85
'Aqiq, Sud B4 105
Aqir, Isr h10 84
Aq Kupruk, Afg C13 86
'Aqrabah, Jordan B7, g12 84
Aquarius, mts., Ariz C2 168
Aquasco, Md C4 173
Aquashicola, creek, Pa B2 194
Aquebogue, N.Y F6 172
Aquidauana, Braz C1 137
Aquidneck, isl., R.I C11 172
Aquileia, It D9 66
Aquiles Serdán, Mex B3 129
Aquin, Hai F7 131
Aquitaine: c. 814 47
c. 1360 48
Aquone, N.C D2 197
Arab, Ala A3 166
Arabela, N. Mex D4 195
Arabi, Ga E3 175
Arabi, La C8 183
Arabia: c. 500 B.C 78
see also Saudi Arabia
Arabian, des., Eg E3 84
Arabian, sea, Asia H9 76
Arabs, gulf, Eg G7 85
Araby, Ariz E1 168
Aracaju, Braz E7 138
Aracati, Braz B3 138
Araçatuba, Braz C2 137
Aracena, Sp D2 65
Arachosia: c. 500 B.C 78
Aracruz, Braz E2 138
Araçuaí, Braz E2 138
Arad, Rom B5 68
Araduey, riv., Sp B3 65
Arafura, sea, Indon G8 90
Arago, Oreg D2 201
Arago, cape, Oreg D2 201
Aragon, Ga B1 175
Aragon, N. Mex D1 195
Aragon, reg., Sp B5 65
c. 1140 47
c. 1360 48
Aragón, riv., Sp A5 65
Aragua, state, Ven A4 133
Araguaia, riv., Braz D6 124
Aragua de Barcelona, Ven B5 133
Araguao, riv. mouth, Ven B5 133
Araguari, Braz E1 138
Araguarí, riv., Braz B4 139
Arai, Jap o16 93
Arāk (Sultanabad), Iran D4 86
Arakabesan, isl., Palau Is 114
Arakan, range, Bur E9 87
Árakhthos, riv., Grc C3 69
Aral, sea, Sov. Un D5 73
Aral Karkum, des., Sov. Un D6 73
Aralsk, Sov. Un D6 73
Aramac, Austl D8 111
Aran, isl., Ire C2 55
Aran, is., Ire D2 55
Aranda de Duero, Sp B4 65
Arandas, Mex m12 129
Aranjuez, Sp B4 65
Aransas, co., Tex E4 206
Aransas, bay, Tex E4 206
Aransas Pass, Tex F4 206
Aranyaprathet, Thai F5 89
Arao, Jap J5 93
Araouane, Mali C4 103
Arapaho, Okla B3 200
Arapahoe, Colo C8 171
Arapahoe, Nebr D6 191
Arapahoe, N.C B7 197
Arapahoe, Wyo C4 213
Arapahoe, co., Colo B6 171
Arapey, Ur E1 137
Arapey Grande, riv., Ur E1 137
Arapkir, Tur C12 85
Ar'ar, wadi, Sau. Ar G13 85
Araranguá, Braz D3 137
Araraquara, Braz C3, k7 137
Araras, Braz C3, m8 137
Araras, mts., Braz B2 137
Ararat, Ala D1 166
Ararat, Austl H4 112
Ararat, Pa C10 202
Ararat, Va E2 209
Ararat, mtn., Tur C15 85
Arareh, Indon F9 90
Araripe, mts., Braz C3 138
Araruna, Braz h6 138
Aras, riv., Asia B3 86
Aratane (Well), Maur C3 103
Arauca, Col B3 133
Arauca, intendencia, Col B3 133
Arauca, riv., Ven B4 133
Arauco, Chile B2 136
Arauco, prov., Chile B2 136
Aravalli, range, India D5 87
Arawe, New Britain I 115
Araxá, Braz E1 138
Arayat, Phil o13 90
Arba Jahan, Ken A6 106
Arbela, Mo A5 189
Arboga, Swe t33 63
Arbois, Fr D6 58
Arboles, Colo D3 171
Arbon, Idaho G6 177
Arbon, Switz B5 66
Arbor Terrace, Mo *C7 189
Arbor Vitae, Wis C4 212
Arborea, It E2 67
Arborfield, Sask., Can D4 155
Arborg, Man., Can D3 150
Arbroath, Scot D6 57
Arbuckle, Calif C2 170
Arbuckle, lake, Fla E5 174
Arbuckle, mts., Okla C4 200
Arbuckle, res., Okla C5 200
Arbyrd, Mo E7 189
Arcachon, Fr E3 58
Arcade, Ga B3 175
Arcade, N.Y C2 196
Arcadia, Calif F2 170
Arcadia, N.S., Can F3 151
Arcadia, Fla E5 174
Arcadia, Ind D5 179
Arcadia, Iowa B2 180
Arcadia, Kans E9 181
Arcadia, La B3 183
Arcadia, Mich D4 186
Arcadia, Mo D7 189
Arcadia, Nebr C6 191
Arcadia, Ohio A4 199
Arcadia, Okla B4 200
Arcadia, Pa E4 202
Arcadia, R.I C10 172
Arcadia, S.C B4 203
Arcadia, Utah C5 207
Arcadia, Wis D2 212
Arcanum, Ohio C3 199
Arcata, Calif B1 170
Arcelia, Mex n13 129
Arch, N. Mex C6 195
Archambault, lake, Que., Can C3 154
Archangel, Sov. Un E19 63, C7 71
Archbald, Pa A9 202
Archbold, Ohio A3 199
Archdale, N.C B4 197
Archer, Fla C4 174
Archer, Iowa A2 180
Archer, Nebr C7 191
Archer, co., Tex C3 206
Archer, City, Tex C3 206
Archers Post, Ken A6 106
Archerwill, Sask., Can E4 155
Arches, nat. mon., Utah E6 207
Archidona, Sp D3 65
Archie, Mo C3 189
Archive, Sask., Can G3 155
Archuleta, N. Mex A2 195
Archuleta, co., Colo D3 171
Archway, cape, New Britain I 115
Arcila, Mor G4 64
Arcis-sur-Aube, Fr C6 58
Arco, Ga E5 175
Arco, Idaho F5 177
Arco, Minn F2 187
Arcola, Sask., Can H4 155
Arcola, Ill D5 178
Arcola, Ind B7 179
Arcola, Miss B3 188
Arcola, Mo D4 189
Arcola, Va A4 209
Arcos de la Frontera, Sp D3 65
Arcoverde, Braz C3, k5 138
Arctic, Alsk B10 167
Arctic, ocean B33 118
Arctic Bay, N.W. Ter., Can B15 144
Arctic Village, Alsk B10 167
Arcueil, Fr g10 58
Arda, riv., Bul E7 68
Ardabīl, Iran B4 86
Ardahan, Tur B14 85
Ardakān, Iran F6 86
Ardath, Sask., Can F2 155
Ardatov, Sov. Un D16 72
Ardbeg, Ont., Can B4 153
Ardea, It h9 67
Ardee, Ire D3 55
Arden, Ark D1 169
Arden, Man., Can D2 150
Arden, Ont., Can C8 153
Arden (Ardentown) Del A7 173
Arden, Den B3 62
Arden, Nev G6 192
Arden, N.C D3 197
Arden Hills, Minn *E7 187
Ardennes, dept., Fr E4 59
Ardennes, mts., Bel E5 59
Ardenno, It C5 66
Ardenvoir, Wash B5 210
Ardestān, Iran E6 86
Ardila, riv., Port C2 65
Ardill, Sask., Can H3 155
Ardino, Bul E7 68
Ardley, Alta., Can C4 148
Ardmore, Ala A3 166

INDEX KEY Each place listed in **Bold-faced Type** has its population listed in the Population tables, pages 230 to 280.
Each country, shown in CAPITAL LETTERS, has its population listed in the World Political Information Table, pages 6 to 10.
* Does not appear on map; key shows general location.

Ardmore, Alta., Can...B5 148
Ardmore, Md...C4 173
Ardmore, Okla...C4 200
Ardmore, Pa...B11 202
Ardmore, S. Dak...D2 204
Ardmore, Tenn...B5 205
Ardoch, N. Dak...A8 198
Ardpatrick, pt. Scot...E3 57
Ardres, Fr...D9 56
Ardrossan, Austl...G1 112
Ardrossan, Alta., Can...C4 148
Ardrossan, Scot...E4 57
Ardsley, N.Y...*D7 196
Ardvasar, Scot...C3 57
Arebeb (Well), Mali...B5 103
Arecibo, P.R...B4 132
Arecibo, mun., P.R...B4 132
Aredale, Iowa...B4 180
Areia, Braz...h6 138
Areia Branca, Braz...B3 138
Arelee, Sask., Can...E2 155
Arena, N. Dak...B5 198
Arena, Wis...E4 212
Arena, pt., Calif...C2 170
Arena, pt., Mex...C3 129
Arenac, co., Mich...D7 186
Arenal, P.R...D5 132
Arenas de San Pedro, Sp. B3 65
Arenas Valley, N. Mex...E1 195
Arendal, Nor...H3 63
Arendonk, Bel...C5 59
Arendsee, Ger...F5 62
Arendtsville, Pa...G7 202
Arenillas, Ec...B1 134
Arenzville, Ill...D3 178
Areópolis, Grc...D4 69
Arequipa, Peru...E3 134
Arequipa, dept., Peru...E3 134
Arezzo, It...C3 67
Arga, riv., Sp...A5 65
Argalastí, Grc...C4 69
Arganda, Sp...p18 65
Argelès-Gazost, Fr...F3 58
Argenta, Ill...D5 178
Argenta, It...B3 67
Argenta, Mont...E4 190
Argentan, Fr...C4 58
Argentat, Fr...E4 58
Argenteuil, Fr...C5, g10 58
Argenteuil, co., Que., Can...D3 154
Argentia, Newf., Can...E4 152
Argentia Beach, Alta., Can...*C3 148
ARGENTINA, country, S.A...E2 135, 127
Argentino, lake, Arg...E2 136
Argenton [-sur-Creuse], Fr...D4 58
Argesul, riv., Rom...C7 68
Arghandab, res., Afg...F12 86
Argo, Ala...B3 166
Argo, Ill...F2 178
Argo, Sud...B3 105
Argolis, gulf, Grc...D4 69
Argonia, Kans...E6 181
Argonne, S. Dak...C8 204
Argonne, Wis...C5 212
Argonne, forest, Fr...E4 59
Argonne, plat., Fr...C6 58
Argos, Grc...D4 69
Argos, Ind...B5 179
Árgos Orestikón, Grc...B3 69
Argostólion, Grc...C3 69
Argun, riv., Sov. Un...D14 71
Argungu, Nig...D5 103
Argusville, N. Dak...B9 198
Argyle, N.S., Can...F4 151
Argyle, Fla...G3 174
Argyle, Ga...E4 175
Argyle, Iowa...D6 180
Argyle, Mich...E8 186
Argyle, Minn...B2 187
Argyle, Mo...C5 189
Argyle, N.Y...B7 196
Argyle, Wis...F4 212
Argyle Downs, Austl...C4 111
Argyll, co., Scot...D3 57
Arhno, atoll, Marshall Is... 115
Århus, Den...B4 62
Århus, co., Den...B4 62
Århus, bay, Den...B4 62
Aria: c. 500 B.C.... 78
Ariail, S.C...B2 203
Ariake, bay, Jap...K5 93
Ariano Irpino, It...D5 67
Ariano nel Polesine, It...E8 66
Arica, Chile...C1 135
Arichat, N.S., Can...D8 151
Ariège, riv., Fr...F4 58
Ariel, Wash...D3 210
Arieşul, riv., Rom...B6 68
Arīḥā (Jericho), Jordan...C7, h12 84
Arikaree, riv., Colo...B8 171
Arimo, Idaho...G6 177
Aringay, Phil...n13 90
Arinos, riv., Braz...E3 139
Ario de Rosales, Mex...D4, n13 129
Arion, Iowa...C2 180
Aripeka, Fla...D4 174
Aripine, Ariz...C5 168
Aripuanã, riv., Braz...D2 139
Arisaig, Scot...D3 57
Arisaig, sound, Scot...D2 57
Arispe, Iowa...D3 180
Arista, W. Va...D3 211
Aristazabal, isl., B.C., Can...C3 149
Ariton, Ala...D4 166
Arivaca, Ariz...F4 168
Arivonimamo, Malag...g9 107
Arizaro, salt flat, Arg...D2 135
Arizola, Ariz...E4 168
Arizona, Arg...B3 136
Arizona, state, U.S.... 168
Arizpe, Mex...A2 129
Arjay, Ky...D6 182
Arjeplog, Swe...D7 63
Arjona, Col...A2 133
Arjona, Sp...D3 65
Arkabutla, Miss...A3 188
Arkabutla, res., Miss...A4 188
Arkadelphia, Ala...B3 166
Arkadelphia, Ark...C2 169
Arkaig, lake, Scot...D3 57
Arkansas, state, U.S.... 169
Arkansas, co., Ark...C4 169
Arkansas, riv., U.S...C9 159
Arkansas City, Ark...D4 169
Arkansas City, Kans...E6 181
Arkansas Post, Ark...C4 169
Arkansaw, Wis...D1 212
Arkhangelskoye, Sov. Un...F13 72
Arkhara, Sov. Un...B5 93
Arkinda, Ark...D1 169
Arklow, Ire...D3 55
Arkoma, Okla...B7 200
Arkona, Ont., Can...D3 153
Arkonam, India...F6 87
Arkport, N.Y...C3 196
Arkville, N.Y...C6 196
Arkwright, Ga...D3 175
Arkwright, R.I...C10 172
Arkwright, S.C...*B4 203
Arlanza, riv., Sp...A4 65
Arlanzón, riv., Sp...A4 65
Arlberg, tunnel, Aus...E5 60
Arlee, Mont...C2 190
Arles, Fr...F6 58
Arley, Ala...A2 166
Arline, Tenn...E11 205
Arlington, Ariz...D3 168
Arlington, Colo...C7 171
Arlington, Fla...B5, B6 174
Arlington, Ga...E2 175
Arlington, Ill...B4 178
Arlington, Ind...E6 179
Arlington, Iowa...B6 180
Arlington, Kans...B3, E5 181
Arlington, Ky...B2 182
Arlington, Mass...C2 185
Arlington, Minn...F4 187
Arlington, Nebr...C9, D2 191
Arlington, N.Y...*D7 196
Arlington, N.C...A3 197
Arlington, Ohio...B4 199
Arlington, Oreg...B6 201
Arlington, S.C...B3 203
Arlington, S. Dak...C8 204
Arlington, Tenn...B2 205
Arlington, Tex...B5 206
Arlington, Vt...E2 208
Arlington, Va...B5, C5 209
Arlington, Wash...A3 210
Arlington, co., Va...B5 209
Arlington Beach, S. Dak...C8 204
Arlington Heights, Ill...A5, E2 178
Arlington Heights, Ohio...*C3 199
Arlon, Bel...E5 59
Arltunga, Austl...D5 111
Arly, riv., Fr...D2 66
Arm, Miss...D3 188
Arma, Kans...E9 181
Armada, Mich...F8 186
Armagh, Que., Can...C7 154
Armagh, N. Ire...C3 55
Armagh, Pa...F3 202
Armathwaite, Tenn...C9 205
Armavir, Sov. Un...I13 72
Armenia, Col...C2 133
Armenia (S.S.R.) rep., Sov. Un...E7 71
in 1st cent. B.C.... 44
c. 500 B.C.... 78
in 114–117 A.D.... 45
c. 1140... 47
c. 1360... 48
in 1922–40... 93
Armentières, Fr...B5 58
Armeria, riv., Mex...n12 129
Armero, Col...C3 133
Armidale, Austl...E8 112
Armijo, N. Mex...B3, G5 195
Armington, Ill...C4 178
Armington, Mont...C6 190
Arminto, Wyo...B5 213
Armit, lake, Man., Can...C1 150
Armley, Sask., Can...D3 155
Armona, Calif...*D4 170
Armorel, Ark...B6 169
Armour, S. Dak...D7 204
Armstead, Ala...B3 166
Armstead, Mont...F4 190
Armstrong, B.C., Can...D8 149
Armstrong, Fla...C5 174
Armstrong, Ill...C6 178
Armstrong, Iowa...A3 180
Armstrong, Mo...B5 189
Armstrong, Tex...F4 206
Armstrong, co., Pa...E3 202
Armstrong, co., Tex...B2 206
Armstrong, creek, W. Va...D6 211
Armstrong Creek, Wis...C5 212
Armuchee, Ga...B1 175
Armyansk, Sov. Un...H9 72
Arnaud, Man., Can...E3 150
Arnaudville, La...D4 183
Arnavon, is., Sol. Is... 115
Arneburg, Ger...F5 62
Arnedo, Sp...A4 65
Arnegard, N. Dak...B2 198
Arneiroz, Braz...C2 138
Arnett, Okla...A2 200
Arnett, W. Va...D3, D6 211
Arnhem, Neth...C5 59
Arnhem, cape, Austl...B6 110
Arnhem Land, reg., Austl...B5 110
Árnissa, Grc...B3 69
Arno, riv., It...C3 67
Arnold, Calif...C3 170
Arnold, Kans...D3 181
Arnold, Mich...B3 186
Arnold, Minn...D6 187
Arnold, Mo...C7 189
Arnold, Nebr...C5 191
Arnold, Pa...A7 202
Arnold Mills, R.I...B11 172
Arnolds Park, Iowa...A2 180
Arnoldsburg, W. Va...C3 211
Arnoldsville, Ga...C3 175
Arnot, Pa...C7 202
Arnouville [-lès-Gonesse], Fr...g10 58
Arnöy, isl., Nor...B9 63
Arnprior, Ont., Can...B8 153
Arnsberg, Ger...B3 61
Arnstadt, Ger...C5 61
Arnstein, Ont., Can...B5 153
Arntz, Ariz...C5 168
Årö, isl., Den...C3 62
Aroa, Ven...A4 133
Aroab, S. W. Afr...C2 107
Arock, Oreg...E9 201
Aroda, Va...C4 209
Arolsen, Ger...B4 61
Aroma, Sud...B4 105
Aroma Park, Ill...B6 178
Aromas, Calif...C6 170
Aroostook, co., Maine...B4 184
Aroostook, riv., Maine...B4 184
Aroostook Junction, N.B., Can...C2 151
Åros, Nor...p28 63
Arosa, Switz...C5 66
Arp, Tex...C5 206
Arpajon, Fr...F2 59
Arpin, Wis...D3 212
Arques, Fr...D2 59
Arques-la-Bataille, Fr...E9 56
Arrābah, Jordan...B7 84
Arrah, India...C7 87
Arraias, Braz...D1 138
Arraiján, Pan...m11 130
Arraiolos, Port...C2 65
Ar Ramādī, Iraq...F14 85
Ar Ramthā, Jordan...B8 84
Arran, Sask., Can...F5 155
Arran, Fla...B2 174
Arran, isl., Scot...E3 57
Ar Raqqah, Syr...E12 85
Arras, Fr...B5 58
Ar Rawḍah, Eg...H8 85
Arrecife, Sp. (Can. Is.)...D2 102
Arrecifes, Arg...g6 136
Arrecifes, riv., Arg...g7 136
Arrey, N. Mex...E2 195
Arriaga, Mex...m13 129
Arriba, Colo...B7 171
Arriikan, isl., Bikini Is... 114
Arrington, Kans...A7, C8 181
Arrington, Va...D4 209
Ar Riyāḍ, see Riyadh, Sau. Ar.
Arrochar, Scot...D4 57
Arroio Grande, Braz...E2 137
Arroll, Mo...D6 189
Arrone, riv., It...h8 67
Arrow, lake, Ont., Can...A7 187
Arrow, riv., Ont., Can...A7 187
Arrow, riv., Mont...C6 190
Arrow Rock, Mo...B5 189
Arrowhead, B.C., Can...D9 149
Arrowsic, Maine...*E3 184
Arrowsmith, Ill...C5 178
Arrowwood, Alta., Can...D4 148
Arroyo, P.R...D6 132
Arroyo, mun., P.R...D6 132
Arroyo Arenas, Cuba...k11 131
Arroyo de la Luz, Sp...C2 65
Arroyo Grande, Calif...E3 170
Arroyo Grande, Ur...f8 136
Arroyo Hondo, N. Mex...A4 195
Arroyo Naranjo, Cuba...k12 131
Arroyoseco, N. Mex...A4 195
Års, Den...B3 62
Arsacides, cape, Malaita I... 115
Arsenyev, Sov. Un...D6 93
Årstad, Swe...B6 62
Art, isl., N. Cal... 115
Árta, Grc...C3 69
Artaiyan (Oasis), Sau. Ar...H13 85
Artas, S. Dak...B6 204
Artashat, Sov. Un...B2 86
Artëm, Sov. Un...E16 71
Artemisa, Cuba...D2 131
Artëmovsk, Sov. Un...G10, q21 72
Artemovskiy, Sov. Un...B6 73
Artemus, Ky...D6 182
Artena, It...h9 67
Arter, mtn., Wyo...C4 213
Artern, Ger...B6 61
Artesia, Bots...B4 107
Artesia, Calif...*F4 170
Artesia, Colo...*A1 171
Artesia, Miss...B5 188
Artesia, N. Mex...E5 195
Artesian, S. Dak...C8 204
Artesia Wells, Tex...E3 206
Arth, Switz...B4 66
Arthabaska, Que., Can...C6 154
Arthabaska, co., Que., Can...C5 154
Arthur, Ont., Can...D4 153
Arthur, Ill...D5 178
Arthur, Ind...H3 179
Arthur, Iowa...B2 180
Arthur, Nebr...C4 191
Arthur, N. Dak...B8 198
Arthur, co., Nebr...C4 191
Arthur, kill, N.J...E4 194
Arthur, lake, La...D3 183
Arthur's Town, Ba. Is...C6 131
Artigas, Ur...E1 137
Artland, Sask., Can...E1 155
Artois, former prov., Fr...B5 58
Artois, hills, Fr...D2 59
Artvin, Tur...B13 85
Aru, Zaire...A5 106
Aru, is., Indon...G8 90
Aru, pt., Ponape... 114
Arua, Ug...A5 106
Aruanã, Braz...A2 137
Aruba, isl., Neth. Antilles...A4 133
Arucas, Sp. (Can. Is.)...m14 65
Arun, riv., Eng...D7 56
Arundel, Que., Can...D3 154
Arundel, Eng...D7 56
Arundel, Maine...*E2 184
Arunta, des., Austl...D6 110
Aruppukkottai, India...*G6 87
Arusha, Tan...B6 106
Arusi, reg., Eth...D4 105
Aruwimi, riv., Zaire...A4 106
Arvada, Colo...B5 171
Arvada, Wyo...A6 213
Arve, riv., Fr...D2 66
Arvida, Que., Can...A6 154
Arvidsjaur, Swe...E8 63
Arvika, Swe...H5 63
Arvilla, N. Dak...B8 198
Arvin, Calif...E4 170
Arvonia, Va...D4 209
Arys, Sov. Un...E7 73
Arzamas, Sov. Un...B2 73
Arzew, Alg...G6 64
Arzgir, Sov. Un...I15 72
Arzúa, Sp...A1 65
Aš, Czech...C2 70
Ås, Swe...A6 62
Aså, Den...A4 62
Asab, S. W. Afr...C2 107
Asahigawa, Jap...E11 93
Asalā, Eth...D4 105
Asan, Guam... 114
Asan, pt., Guam... 114
Asansol, India...D8 87
Asbach, Ger...C2 61
Asberrys, Va...B3 209
Asbest, Sov. Un...B6 73
Asbestos, Que., Can...D6 154
Asbury, Mo...D3 189
Asbury, N.J...B2 194
Asbury, Tenn...E11 205
Asbury Park, N.J...C4 194
Ascensión, Mex...A3 129
Ascension, par., La...D5 183
Ascension, isl., Atl. O...G4 96
Ascension Isl. Br. dep., Atl. O...G4 97
Aschaffenburg, Ger...D4 61
Aschersleben, Ger...B6 61
Ascoli Piceno, It...C4 67
Ascope, Peru...C2 134
Ascot Corner, Que., Can...D6 154
Ascotan, Chile...D2 135
Ascutney, Vt...E4 208
Ascutney, mtn., Vt...E4 208
Åsele, Swe...E7 63
Asenovgrad, Bul...E7 68
Ash, Oreg...D3 201
Ash Flat, Ark...A4 169
Ash Fork, Ariz...B3 168
Ash Grove, Mo...D4 189
Ash Lake, Minn...B6 187
Ash Shabicha, Iraq...G14 85
Ash Shallāl, Eg...E6 101
Ash Shariqah, U.A.E...I7 86
Ash Shaṭṭ, Eg...E4 84
Ash Shawāshinah, Eg...E2 84
Ash Shawbak, Jordan...D7 84
Ash Shuwayrif, Libya...D2 101
Asha, Sov. Un...B5 73
Ashanti, reg., Ghana...E4 103
Asharoken, N.Y...F3 172
Ashaway, R.I...D9 172
Ashbourne, Eng...A4 56
Ashburn, Ga...E3 175
Ashburn, Mo...B6 189
Ashburn, Va...B5 209
Ashburnham, Mass...A4 185
Ashburton, Eng...D4 56
Ashburton, N.Z...o13 112
Ashburton, riv., Austl...D2 110
Ashby, Ala...B3 166
Ashby, Mass...A4 185
Ashby, Minn...D3 187
Ashby, Nebr...B4 191
Ashbyburg, Ky...C2 182
Ashcroft, B.C., Can...D7 149
Ashdod, Isr...C6, h9 84
Ashdot Ya'aqov, Isr...B7 84
Ashdown, Ark...D1 169
Ashe, co., N.C...A2 197
Asheboro, N.C...B4 197
Asheboro South, N.C...*B4 197
Asheboro West, N.C...*B4 197
Ashepoo, riv., S.C...F6 203
Asher, Ariz...E1 168
Asher, Okla...C5 200
Ashern, Man., Can...D2 150
Asherton, Tex...E3 206
Asherville, Kans...C6 181
Asheville, N.C...D3 197
Ashfield, Mass...A2 185
Ashford, Ala...D4 166
Ashford, Conn...B8 172
Ashford, Eng...C8 56
Ashford, N.C...B2, C4 197
Ashford, W. Va...C6 211
Ashibetsu, Jap...*E11 93
Ashikaga, Jap...H9, m18 93
Ashington, Eng...E7 57
Ashio, Jap...H9 93
Ashiya, Jap...*I7 93
Ashkhabad, Sov. Un...F8 71
Ashkum, Ill...C6 178
Ashland, Ala...B4 166
Ashland, Ill...D3 178
Ashland, Kans...E4 181
Ashland, Ky...B7 182
Ashland, La...B2 183
Ashland, Maine...B4 184
Ashland, Mass...D1 185
Ashland, Miss...A4 188
Ashland, Mo...C5 189
Ashland, Mont...E10 190
Ashland, Nebr...C9, E2 191
Ashland, N.H...C3 193
Ashland, Ohio...B5 199
Ashland, Oreg...E4 201
Ashland, Pa...E9 202
Ashland, Va...D5 209
Ashland, Wis...B3 212
Ashland, co., Ohio...B5 199
Ashland, co., Wis...B3 212
Ashland, mtn., Oreg...E4 201
Ashland, res., Mass...D1 185
Ashland City, Tenn...A4 205
Ashley, Ill...E4 178
Ashley, Ind...A7 179
Ashley, Mich...E6 186
Ashley, Mo...B6 189
Ashley, N. Dak...C6 198
Ashley, Ohio...B5 199
Ashley, Pa...B8 202
Ashley, co., Ark...D4 169
Ashley, creek, Utah...C6 207
Ashley, riv., S.C...F7 203
Ashley Falls, Mass...B1 185
Ashmont, Alta., Can...B5 148
Ashmore, Ill...D5 178
Ashmūn, Eg...D2 84
Ashnola, riv., Can., U.S...A5 210
Ashokan, N.Y...D6 196
Ashokan, res., N.Y...D6 196
Ashport, Tenn...B2 205
Ashtabula, Ohio...A7 199
Ashtabula, co., Ohio...A7 199
Ashtabula, lake, N. Dak...B7 198
Ashton, Ont., Can...B8 153
Ashton, Idaho...E7 177
Ashton, Ill...B4 178
Ashton, Iowa...A2 180
Ashton, Md...B3 173
Ashton, Mich...E5 186
Ashton, Nebr...C7 191
Ashton, R.I...B11 172
Ashton, S. Dak...B7 204
Ashton-under-Lyne, Eng...*A5 56
Ashuanipi, lake, Newf., Can...h8 152
Ashuelot, N.H...E2 193
Ashuelot, riv., N.H...E2 193
Ashville, Ala...B3 166
Ashville, Man., Can...D1 150
Ashville, Ohio...C5 199
Ashwaubenon, Wis...A6 212
Ashwood, Oreg...C6 201
Ashwood, Tenn...B4 205
Asia, cont.... 77
c. 750 A.D.... 80
c. 1294... 81
c. 1775... 82
after World War II... 83
Asia, diocese of... 46
Asia, Roman prov. of:
c. 50 B.C.... 44
c. 120 A.D.... 45
Asiago, It...D7 66
Asifabad, India...H7 88
Asiga, pt., Guam... 114
Asiga, pt., Tinian... 114
Asinara, gulf, It...D2 67
Asinara, isl., It...D2 67
Asino, Sov. Un...B11 73
Asir, reg., Sau. Ar...B5 105
'Asīrah ash Shamālīyah, Jordan...g12 84
Asker, Nor...p28 63
Askersund, Swe...H6 63
Askew, Miss...A3 188
Askim, Nor...p29 63
Askim, Swe...A5 62
Askö, isl., Swe...u35 63
Askov, Minn...D6 187
Asmar, Afg...D15 86
Asmara, Eth...B4 105
Asnaes, Den...C5 62
Asnebumskit, hill, Mass...B4 185
Åsnen, lake, Swe...B8 62
Asnières [-sur-Seine], Fr...g10 58
Asomante, P.R...B4 132
Asopós, riv., Grc...g11 69
Asosā, Eth...C3 105
Asotin, Wash...C8 210
Asotin, co., Wash...C8 210
Asotin, creek, Wash...C8 210
Aspe, Sp...C5 65
Aspen, Colo...B4 171
Aspen, butte, Oreg...E4 201
Aspen, mts., Wyo...D3 213
Aspen Hill, Tenn...B5 205
Asperg, Ger...E4 61
Aspermont, Tex...C2 206
Aspers, Pa...G7 202
Aspinwall, Iowa...C2 180
Aspinwall, Pa...*A6 202
Aspiring, mtn., N.Z...p12 112
Aspres [-sur-Buëch], Fr...E1 66
Asprópirgos, Grc...g11 69
Aspy, bay, N.S., Can...C9 151
Asquith, Sask., Can...E2 155
Assab, Eth...C5 105
Assabet, riv., Mass...D1 185
Aş Şaff, Eg...E3 84
Aş Şāfīyah, Jordan...C7 84
Assaikwatamo, riv., Man., Can...A3 150
Aş Şaliḥīyah, Eg...D4 84
Aş Şallūm, Eg...C4 101
As Salman, Iraq...G15 85
As Salṭ, Jordan...F10 85
As Salwá, Sau. Ar...I5 86
Assam, state, India...C9 87
Assaria, Kans...D6 181
Assateague, isl., Va...D7 209
Assateague Island, nat. seashore, Md., Va...D7 173, 209
Assawoman, bay, Md...D7 173
Assawompset, pond, Mass...C6 185
Assen, Neth...B6 59
Assens, Den...B4 62
Assens, co., Den...C3 62
As Sinbillāwayn, Eg...D3 84
Assiniboia, Sask., Can...H3 155
Assiniboine, riv., Man., Sask., Can...E4 155
Assinie, I.C...E4 103
Assinika, riv., Man., Can...C4 150
Assinippi, Mass...D4 185
Assis, Braz...C2 137
Assisi, It...C4 67
Assonet, Mass...C5 185
Assonguson, see Asuncion, isl., Mariana Is.
Aş Şūfīyah, Eg...D3 84
As Sulaymānīyah, Iraq...E15 85
As Sulṭān, Libya...C3 101
Assumption, Ill...D4 178
Assumption, par., La...E4 183
As Suwaydā', Syr...F11 85
As Suways, see Suez, Eg.
Assyria: in 7th cent. B.C.... 42
c. 500 B.C.... 78
in Alexander's empire... 43
in 115–117 A.D.... 45
Astakós, Grc...C3 69
Āstārā, Iran...B4 86
Astatula, Fla...*D5 174
Asten, Neth...C5 59
Asterābād, see Gorgān, Iran
Asti, It...B2 67
Astipalaia, isl., Grc...D6 69
Astola, isl., Pak...I11 86
Aston, Pa...*G11 202
Aston, cape, N.W. Ter., Can...B19 143
Aston Junction, Que., Can...C5 154
Astor, Fla...C5 174
Astorga, Sp...A2 65
Astoria, Ill...C3 178
Astoria, Oreg...A3 201
Astoria, S. Dak...C9 204
Astorville, Ont., Can...A5 153
Astrakhan', Sov. Un...D3 73
Astrolabe, cape, Malaita I... 115
Astrolabe, reefs, Loyalty Is... 115
Astura, riv., It...h9 67
Asturias, reg., Sp...A2 65
Asuisui, cape, W. Sam... 114
Asuke, Jap...n16 93
Asunción, Par...E4 135
Asuncion (Assonguson), isl., Mariana Is... 115
Asunción Mita, Guat...C3 130
Asunden, lake, Swe...A7 62
Aswan, Eg...E6 101
Aswān High, dam, Eg...E6 101
Asyut, Eg...D6 101
As Zaqāzīq, Eg...D6 101
Ata, cove, Malaita I... 115
Atacama, prov., Chile...E1 135
Atacama, des., Chile...D2 135
Atakpamé, Togo...E5 103
Atalaia, Braz...k6 138
Atalándi, Grc...C4 69
Ataliklikun, bay, New Britain I... 115
Atalissa, Iowa...C6 180
Atami, Jap...n18 93
Atantano, Guam... 114
Atar, Maur...B2 103
Aṭārūt, Jordan...h11 84
Atascadero, Calif...E3 170
Atascosa, co., Tex...E3 206
Atasuskiy, Sov. Un...D8 73
Atatyn Hiid, Mong...A3 92
Ataúro, isl., Port. Timor...G7 90
Atbara, Sud...B3 105
Atbara, riv., Sud...B4 105
Atbasar, Sov. Un...C7 73
Atchafalaya, La...D4 183
Atchafalaya, bay, La...E4 183
Atchafalaya, riv., La...D4 183
Atchison, Kans...A8, C8 181
Atchison, co., Kans...C8 181
Atchison, co., Mo...A2 189
Atchugau, mtn., Saipan... 114
Atco, Ga...B2 175
Atco, N.J...D3 194
Atenango, riv., Mex...n14 129
Ath, Bel...D3 59
Ath Thamad, Eg...D6 101
Atha Road, Ont., Can...E7 153
Athabasca, Alta., Can...B4 148
Athabasca, lake, Alta. and Sask., Can...A1 155
Athabasca, riv., Alta., Can...B4 148
Athalia, Ohio...D5 199
Athalmer, B.C., Can...D9 149
Athapapuskow, lake, Man., Can...B1 150
Athelstan, Que., Can...D3 154
Athelstan, Iowa...D3 180
Athena, Oreg...B8 201
Athenian empire: c. 450 B.C.... 42
Athens, Ala...A3 166
Athens, Ark...C2 169
Athens, Ont., Can...C9 153
Athens, Ga...C3 175
Athens (Athínai), Grc...C4, h11 69

Athens, Ill. D4 178
Athens, Ind. B5 179
Athens, Ky. C5 182
Athens, La. B2 183
Athens, Maine D3 184
Athens, Mich. F5 186
Athens, N.Y. C7 196
Athens, Ohio C5 199
Athens, Pa. C8 202
Athens, Tenn. D9 205
Athens, Tex. C5 206
Athens, Vt. E3 208
Athens, W. Va. D3 211
Athens, Wis. C3 212
Athens, co., Ohio C5 199
Athensville, Ill. D3 178
Atherley, Ont., Can. C5 153
Atherton, Calif. *B5 170
Athertonville, Ky. C4 182
Athínai, see Athens, Grc.
Athis-Mons, Fr. h10 58
Athlone, Ire. D3 55
Athok, Bur. E10 87
Athol, Idaho B2 177
Athol, Kans. C5 181
Athol, Mass. A3 185
Athol, S. Dak. C7 204
Atholville, N.B., Can. *B3 151
Athos, mtn., Grc. B5 69
Athy, Ire. D3 55
Atibaia, Braz. m8 137
Atico, Peru E3 134
Atikameg, Alta., Can. B3 148
Atikameg, lake, Man., Can. B1 150
Atikokan, Ont., Can. E8 153
Atikonak, lake, Newf., Can. h8 152
Atikonipi, lake, Que., Can. C2 152
Atimonan, Phil. p13 90
Atiquizaya, Sal. D3 130
Atizapán de Zaragoza, Mex. g9 129
Atka, Alsk. E5 167
Atka, isl., Alsk. E5 167
Atkarsk, Sov. Un. F15 72
Atkins, Ark. B3 169
Atkins, Iowa B6 180
Atkins, Va. B3, E1 209
Atkinson, Ga. E5 175
Atkinson, Ill. B3 178
Atkinson, Maine *C3 184
Atkinson, Nebr. B7 191
Atkinson, N.C. C5 197
Atkinson, co., Ga. E4 175
Atkinson, lake, Man., Can. A4 150
Atkinson Depot, N.H. E4 193
Atlanta, Ark. D2 169
Atlanta, Ga. B5, C2 175
Atlanta, Idaho F3 177
Atlanta, Ill. C4 178
Atlanta, Ind. D5 179
Atlanta, Kans. E7 181
Atlanta, La. C3 183
Atlanta, Mich. C6 186
Atlanta, Mo. B5 189
Atlanta, Nebr. D6 191
Atlanta, N.Y. C3 196
Atlanta, Ohio C4 199
Atlanta, Tex. C5 206
Atlantic, Iowa C2 180
Atlantic, N.C. C7 197
Atlantic, co., N.J. E3 194
Atlantic, ocean B2 96, B5 124
Atlantic, peak, Wyo. C3 213
Atlantic Beach, Fla. B6 174
Atlantic Beach, N.Y. *E3 196
Atlantic City, N.J. E4 194
Atlantic City, Wyo. C4 213
Atlantic Highlands, N.J. C4 194
Atlantic Mine, Mich. A2 186
Atlántico, dept., Col. A2 133
Atlas, Pa. *E9 202
Atlas, mts., Afr. C5 96
Atlee, Alta., Can. D5 148
Atlin, B.C., Can. D2 149
Atlin, lake, B.C., Can. E6 142
Atlit, Isr. B6 84
Atlixco, Mex. n14 129
Atmore, Ala. D2 166
Atna, peak, B.C., Can. C3 149
Atna, ra., B.C., Can. B4 149
Atocha, Bol. D2 135
Atoka, N. Mex. E5 195
Atoka, Okla. C5 200
Atoka, Tenn. B2 205
Atoka, co., Okla. C5 200
Atoka, res., Okla. C5 200
Atomic City, Idaho F6 177
Atotonilco el Alto, Mex. m12 129
Atoyac, Mex. m12 129
Atoyac, riv., Mex. n14 129
Atrato, riv., Col. B2 133
Atrek, riv., Iran C8 86
Atrisco, N. Mex. B3, G5 195
Atsion, N.J. D3 194
Atsugi, Jap. n18 93
Atsukeshi, bay, Jap. E12 93
Atsuma, Jap. E10 93
Atsumi, bay, Jap. o16 93
At Tabbīn, Eg. E3 84
At Ţafīlah, Jordan D7 84
Aţ Ţā'if, Sau. Ar. A5 105
Attala, co., Miss. B4 188
Attalla, Ala. A3 166
Aţ Ţallāb, Libya E4 101
At Tamīmī, Libya C4 101
Attapulgus, Ga. F2 175
'Aţţārah, Jordan g11 84
Attavyros, mtn., Grc. D6 69
Attawapiskat, Ont., Can. E9 153
Attawapiskat, riv., Ont., Can. D9 153
Attawaugan, Conn. B9 172
Aţ Ţayyibah, Jordan C7, h12 84
Attean, pond, Maine C2 184
Attica, Ind. D3 179
Attica, Kans. E5 181
Attica, Mich. E7 186
Attica, N.Y. C2 196
Attica, Ohio A5 199
Attica, reg., Grc. g11 69
Attigny, Fr. E4 59
Attikamagen, lake, Newf., Can. g8 152
Aţ Ţīnah, Eg. C4 84
Attleboro, Mass. C5 185
Attleborough, Eng. B9 56
Attopeu, Laos E7 89
Attow, mtn., Scot. C3 57
Attu, isl., Alsk. E2 167
Aţ Ţūr, Eg. D6 101
Atuel, riv., Arg. B3 136
Atuu, Am. Sam. 114
Åtvidaberg, Swe. H6 63
Atwater, Calif. D3 170
Atwater, Sask., Can. G4 155
Atwater, Minn. E4 187
Atwood, Ont., Can. D3 153
Atwood, Colo. A7 171
Atwood, Ill. D5 178
Atwood Ind. B6 179
Atwood, Kans. C2 181
Atwood, Okla. C5 200
Atwood, Tenn. B3 205
Atwood, res., Ohio B6 199
Atzcapotzalco, Mex. h9, n14 129
Aua, Am. Sam. 114
Auasc, Eth. D5 105
Auau, chan., Haw. C5 176
Auaz, mts., S.W. Afr. B2 107
Aubagne, Fr. F6 58
Aube, dept., Fr. F4 59
Aube, riv., Fr. F4 59
Aubenas, Fr. E6 58
Auberry, Calif. D4 170
Aubervilliers, Fr. g10 58
Aubière, Fr. E5 58
Aubigny-sur-Nère, Fr. D5 58
Aubin, Fr. E5 58
Aubrey, Ark. C5 169
Aubrey, Que., Can. D4 154
Auburn, Ala. C4 166
Auburn, Calif. C3 170
Auburn, Ont., Can. D3 153
Auburn, Ga. B3 175
Auburn, Ill. D4 178
Auburn, Ind. B7 179
Auburn, Iowa B3 180
Auburn, Kans. D8 181
Auburn, Ky. D3 182
Auburn, Maine D2, D5 184
Auburn, Mass. B4 185
Auburn, Mich. E6 186
Auburn, Miss. D3 188
Auburn, Nebr. D10 191
Auburn, N.H. D4 193
Auburn, N.J. D2 194
Auburn, N.Y. C4 196
Auburn, N. Dak. A8 198
Auburn, Pa. E9 202
Auburn, Wash. B3, D2 214
Auburn, W. Va. B4 211
Auburn, Wyo. C1 213
Auburn Center, Pa. C9 202
Auburn Heights, Mich. F7 186
Auburndale, Fla. D5 174
Auburndale, Wis. D3 212
Auburntown, Tenn. B5 205
Aubusson, Fr. E5 58
Auch, Fr. F4 58
Auchel, Fr. D2 59
Auchterarder, Scot. D5 57
Aucilla, Fla. B3 174
Aucilla, riv., Fla. B3 174
Auckland, N.Z. L15 112
Auckland, isl., Pac. O. D29 120
Aude, riv., Fr. F5 58
Audègle, Som. E5 105
Audet, Que., Can. D7 154
Audierne, Fr. C1 58
Audincourt, Fr. D7 58
Audrain, co., Mo. B6 189
Audubon, Iowa C3 180
Audubon, Minn. D3 187
Audubon, N.J. D2 194
Audubon, co., Iowa C3 180
Audubon Park, Ky. *B4 182
Audubon Park, N.J. *D2 194
Audun-le-Roman, Fr. E5 59
Aue, Ger. C7 61
Auerbach, Ger. C7 61
Au Fer, pt., La. E4 183
Augathella, Austl. B6 112
Augerville, Conn. D5 172
Auglaize, co., Ohio B3 199
Auglaize, riv., Ohio A3 199
Au Gres, Mich. D7 186
Augsburg, Ger. E5 61
Augusta, Austl. F2 111
Augusta, Ark. B4 169
Augusta, Ga. C5 175
Augusta, Ill. C3 178
Augusta, Ind. H3 179
Augusta, Ind. H7 179
Augusta, It. F5 67
Augusta, Kans. B6, E7 181
Augusta, Ky. B6 182
Augusta, Maine D3 184
Augusta, Mich. F5 186
Augusta, Mo. C7 189
Augusta, Mont. C4 190
Augusta, N.J. A3 194
Augusta, Ohio B6 199
Augusta, Wis. D2 212
Augusta, W. Va. B6 211
Augusta, co., Va. C3 209
Augusta Springs, Va. C3 209
Augustenborg, Den. D3 62
Augustów, Pol. B7 70
Auja, see Yarkon, riv., Isr.
Auke Bay, Alsk. k22 167
Aulander, N.C. A6 197
Aulendorf, Ger. B5 66
Aulnay, Fr. g10 58
Aulnay-sous-Bois, Fr. g11 58
Aulne, riv., Fr. C1 58
Aulneau, pen., Ont., Can. E4 150
Aulnoye [-Aymeries], Fr. D3 59
Ault, Colo. A6 171
Aumale, Fr. E9 56
Aumsville, Oreg. C2 201
Auneuil, Fr. E2 59
Auning, Den. B4 62
Auno, Nig. D7 103
Aunuu, isl., Am. Sam. 114
Aur, atoll, Marshall Is. 115
Aur, isl., Mala. K6 89
Aura, Mich. B2 186
Auraiya, India D7 88
Aurangabad, India G5 88
Auray, Fr. D2 58
Aurelia, Iowa B2 180
Aurelian Springs, N.C. A6 197
Aurich, Ger. B3 60
Aurillac, Fr. E5 58
Aurora, Ont., Can. D5 153
Aurora, Colo. B6 171
Aurora, Guy. A3 139
Aurora, Ill. B5, F1 178
Aurora, Ind. F8 179
Aurora, Iowa B6 180
Aurora, Kans. C6 181
Aurora, Maine D4 184
Aurora, Minn. C6 187
Aurora, Mo. E4 189
Aurora, Nebr. D7 191
Aurora, N.Y. C4 196
Aurora, N.C. B7 197
Aurora, Ohio A6 199
Aurora, Oreg. B2, B4 201
Aurora, S. Dak. C9 204
Aurora, Utah E4 207
Aurora, W. Va. B5 211
Aurora, Wis. C5 212
Aurora, co., S. Dak. D7 204
Aurora, isl., New Hebr. 115
Aurora Center, S. Dak. D7 204
Aurskog, Nor. p29 63
Aus, S. W. Afr. C2 107
Au Sable, pt., Mich. B4 186
Au Sable, pt., Mich. D7 186
Au Sable, riv., Mich. D6 186
Ausable, riv., N.Y. B3 196
Au Sable Forks, N.Y. B3 196
Aussa, riv., It. D9 66
Austell, Ga. B4 175
Austin, Ark. C4 169
Austin, Man., Can. E2 150
Austin, Ind. G6 179
Austin, Ky. D3 182
Austin, Minn. G6 187
Austin, Mont. D4 190
Austin, Nev. D4 192
Austin, Oreg. C8 201
Austin, Pa. C5 202
Austin, Tex. D4 206
Austin, Utah E3 207
Austin, co., Tex. E4 206
Austin, lake, Austl. E2 110
Austin Lake, Mich. *F5 186
Austinburg, Ohio A7 199
Austintown, Ohio A7 199
Austinville, Iowa B5 180
Austinville, Va. E2 209
AUSTRALIA, country, Oceania 111
Australian Alps, mts., Austl. G8 110
Australian Capital Territory, Austl. G7 112
AUSTRIA, country, Eur. E6 60
c. 1721 49
in 1810 50
in 1815 50
in 1938 53
in 1950 54
see also Austria-Hungary
Austria-Hungary: in 1914 52
Austrian Netherlands 49
Austwell, Tex. E4 206
Autauga, co., Ala. C3 166
Autaugaville, Ala. C3 166
Authie, riv., Fr. D2 59
Autlán de Navarro, Mex. D4, n11 129
Au Train, Mich. B4 186
Autun, Fr. D6 58
Auvergne, Ark. B4 169
Auvergne, mts., Fr. E5 58
Auvergne, former prov., Fr. E5 58
Auvers [-sur-Oise], Fr. E2 59
Aux Barques, pt., Mich. D8 186
Aux Chene, riv., La. C8 183
Aux Pins, pt., Ont., Can. E3 153
Auxerre, Fr. D5 58
Auxier, Ky. C7 182
Auxi-le-Château, Fr. D10 56
Auxonne, Fr. D6 58
Auxvasse, Mo. C6 189
Ava, Ill. F4 178
Ava, Mo. E5 189
Ava, Ohio C6 199
Avakubi, Zaire A4 106
Avallon, Fr. D5 58
Avalon, Calif. F4 170
Avalon, Ga. B3 175
Avalon, Mo. B4 189
Avalon, N.J. E3 194
Avalon, Pa. A5 202
Avalon, pen., Newf., Can. E5 152
Avalon, res., N. Mex. E5 195
Avanos, Tur. C10 85
Avant, Okla. A5 200
Avard, Okla. A3 200
Avaré, Braz. C3 137
Āvāz, Iran E10 86
Aveiro, Port. B1 65
Avella, Pa. F1 202
Avellaneda, Arg. A5, g7 136
Avellino, It. D5 67
Avenal, Calif. E3 170
Avenel, N.J. E4 194
Avening, Ont., Can. C4 153
Avenwedde, Ger. B3 61
Avera, Ga. C4 175
Averill, Minn. D2 187
Averill Park, N.Y. C7 196
Aversa, It. D5 67
Avery, Idaho B3 177
Avery, Iowa C5 180
Avery, Okla. B5 200
Avery, Tex. C5 206
Avery, co., N.C. A2 197
Avery Island, La. E4 183
Aves, is., Ven. A4 133
Avesnes [-sur-Helpe], Fr. D3 59
Avesta, Swe. G7 63
Avezzano, It. C4 67
Aviá Teraí, Arg. E3 135
Aviemore, Scot. C5 57
Avigliano, It. D5 67
Avignon, Fr. F6 58
Ávila, Sp. B3 65
Avila Beach, Calif. E3 170
Avilés, Sp. A3 65
Avilla, Ind. B7 179
Avilla, Mo. D3 189
Avinger, Tex. *C5 206
Avis, Pa. D7 202
Avisio, riv., It. C7 66
Aviston, Ill. *E4 178
Avize, Fr. F4 59
Avlón, Grc. g11 69
Avlum, Den. B2 62
Avoca, Ala. A2 166
Avoca, Ark. A1 169
Avoca, Ind. G4 179
Avoca, Iowa C2 180
Avoca, Mich. E8 186
Avoca, Minn. G3 187
Avoca, Nebr. E3 191
Avoca, N.Y. C3 196
Avoca, Pa. B9 202
Avoca, Tex. C3 206
Avola, B.C., Can. D8 149
Avola, It. F5 67
Avon, Ala. *D4 166
Avon, Ont., Can. E4 153
Avon, Colo. B4 171
Avon, Conn. B5 172
Avon, Ill. C3 178
Avon, Iowa A7 180
Avon, Maine *D2 184
Avon, Mass. B5, E3 185
Avon, Minn. E4 187
Avon, Miss. B2 188
Avon, Mont. D4 190
Avon, N.Y. C3 196
Avon, N.C. B8 197
Avon, Ohio A5 199
Avon, Pa. *F9 202
Avon, S. Dak. E7 204
Avon, riv., Eng. E6 55, D6 56
Avon, riv., Eng. D6 55, B5 56
Avon, riv., Eng. C5 56
Avon, riv., Scot. C5 57
Avon by the Sea, N.J. C4 194
Avon Lake, Ohio A5 199
Avon Park, Fla. E5 174
Avondale, Ariz. G1 168
Avondale, Colo. C6 171
Avondale, Mo. B3 189
Avondale, Pa. G10 202
Avondale, R.I. D9 172
Avondale Estates, Ga. B5 175
Avonlea, Sask., Can. G3 155
Avonmore, Pa. E3 202
Avoyelles, par., La. C3 183
Avranches, Fr. C3 58
Awa, isl., Jap. G9 93
Awaji, isl., Jap. I7 93
Awaleng, is., Bis. Arch. 115
'Awarta, Jordan B7 84
Awāsh, riv., Eth. C5 105
Awashi, Okinawa 114
Awbārī, Libya D2 101
Awe, lake, Scot. D3 57
Aweil, Sud. D2 105
Awjilah, Libya D4 101
Ax-les-Thermes, Fr. F4 58
Axel, Neth. C3 59
Axel Heiberg, isl., N.W. Ter., Can. B24 118
Axial, Colo. A3 171
Axial, basin, Colo. A2 171
Axim, Ghana F4 103
Axiós (Vardar), riv., Grc. B4 69
Axis, Ala. E1 166
Axson, Ga. E4 175
Axtell, Kans. C7 181
Axtell, Nebr. D6 191
Axtell, Utah D4 207
Ay, Fr. C5 58
Ay, riv., Sov. Un. B5 73
Ayabaca, Peru B2 134
Ayabe, Jap. n14 93
Ayacucho, Arg. B5 136
Ayacucho, Peru D3 134
Ayacucho, dept., Peru D3 134
Ayaguz, Sov. Un. D10 73
Ayamonte, Sp. D2 65
Ayan, Sov. Un. D16 71
Ayapel, Col. B2 133
Ayapel, mts., Col. B3 133
Ayaş, Tur. B9 85
Ayaviri, Peru D3 134
Aycliffe, Eng. F7 57
Aydar, riv., Sov. Un. G12 72
Ayden, N.C. B6 197
Aydìn, Tur. D6 85
Aydlett, N.C. A8 197
Ayer, Mass. A4, C1 185
Ayers Cliff, Que., Can. D5 154
Ayia, Grc. C4 69
Ayia Paraskeví, Grc. C6 69
Ayiássos, Grc. C6 69
Áyios Dhimítrios, Grc. g11 69
Ayios Nikólaos, Grc. E5 69
Aylen, lake, Ont., Can. B7 153
Aylesbury, Sask., Can. G3 155
Aylesbury, Eng. C7 56
Aylesford, N.S., Can. D5 151
Aylett, Va. D5 209
Aylmer, N. Dak. B5 198
Aylmer, lake, N.W. Ter., Can. D11 142
Aylmer, mtn., Alta., Can. D3 148
Aylmer East, Que., Can. D2 154
Aylmer West, Ont., Can. E4 153
Aylsham, Sask., Can. D4 155
Ayn Sīdī Muḩammad (Oasis), Libya H3 85
'Ayn Yabrūd, Jordan h11 84
Aynor, S.C. D9 203
Ayon, isl., Sov. Un. C19 71
Ayora, Sp. C5 65
Ayr, Nebr. D7 191
Ayr, N. Dak. B8 198
Ayr, Scot. E4 57
Ayr, co., Scot. E4 57
Ayr, riv., Scot. E4 57
Ayrshire, Ind. H3 179
Ayrshire, Iowa A3 180
Ayshā, Eth. C5 105
Ayton, Ont., Can. C4 153
Aytos, Bul. D8 68
Ayutla, Guat. C1 130
Ayutla [de los Libres], Mex. D5 129
Ayutthaya, Thai. C2 89
Ayvacık, Tur. C6 85
Ayvalık, Tur. C6 85
Azalia, Ind. F6 179
Azama, Okinawa 114
Azamgarh, India D9 88
Azángaro, Peru D3 134
Azaouak Assakari, wadi, Mali C5 103
Azaouad, sand dunes, Mali C4 103
Azare, Nig. D7 103
Azbine, see Air, reg., Niger
Azemmour, Mor. C3 102
Azerbaidzhan, (S.S.R.), rep., Sov. Un. E7 71
Azerbaijan: c. 1294 81
in 1914 52
in 1922–40 53
Azilal, Mor. I3 64
Azilek (Well), Niger C6 103
Aziscoos, lake, Maine C1 184
Azle, Tex. B5 206
Azogues, Ec. B2 134
Azor, Isr. g10 84
Azores, is., Atl. O. h8 102
Azores Islands, reg., Atl. O. h8 102
Azov, Sov. Un. H12 72
Azov, sea, Sov. Un. H11 72
Azrou, Mor. C3 102
Aztec, Ariz. E2 168
Aztec, N. Mex. A2 195
Aztec, peak, Ariz. D5 168
Aztec Ruins, nat. mon., N. Mex. A1 195
Azua, Dom. Rep. F8 131
Azuaga, Sp. C3 65
Azuay, prov., Ec. B2 134
Azuero, pen., Pan. G7 130
Azul, Arg. B5 136
Azul, range, Peru C2 134
Azurdui, Bol. C3 135
Azusa, Calif. F3 170
Aẓ Ẓahiriyah, Jordan C6 84
Aẓ Ẓahrān (Dhahran), Sau. Ar. H5 86
Az Zarqā', Jordan B8 84
Az Zāwiyah, Jordan g11 84
Az Zāwiyah, Libya C2 101
Azzāz, cape, Libya C5 101
Azzel Matti, lake, Alg. D5 101
Az Zubair, Iraq F3 86
'Azzūn, Jordan g11 84

B

Baal, Ger. C6 59
Baalbek, Leb. E11 85
Baarle-Hertog, Bel. C4 59
Bab el Mandeb, strait, Afr. C5 105
Baba, cape, Tur. C6 69
Babadag, Rom. C9 68
Babaeski, Tur. B6 69
Babahoyo, Ec. B2 134
Babana, Nig. D5 103
Babanusa, Sud. C2 105
Babati, Tan. B6 106
Babayevo, Sov. Un. B11 72
Babb, Mont. B3 190
Babb, creek, Pa. C7 202
Babbie, Ala. D3 166
Babbitt, Nev. E3 192
Babbitt, Minn. C7 187
Babcock, Wis. D3 212
Babelthuap, isl., Palau Is. 114
Babenhausen, Ger. A6 66
Babi, is., Indon. K2 89
Babine, lake, B.C., Can. B4 149
Babine, ra., B.C., Can. B4 149
Babine, riv., B.C., Can. B4 149
Babo, Indon. F8 90
Bābol, Iran C6 86
Baboquivari, mts., Ariz. F4 168
Baboquivari, peak, Ariz. F4 168
Baboua, Cen. Afr. Rep. D2 104
Babson Park, Fla. E5 174
Babuna, mts., Yugo. E5 68
Babuskin, Sov. Un. A6 91
Babuyan, is., Phil. B6 90
Babyak, Bul. E6 68
Babylon, N.Y. E3 196
Babylonia: in 7th cent. B.C. 42
in Alexander's empire 44
Bac Kan, Viet. A6 89
Bac Ninh, Viet. B7 89
Bac Quang, Viet. A6 89
Baca, co., Colo. D8 171
Bacabal, Braz. B2 138
Bacalar, Mex. D7 129
Bacău, Rom. B8 68
Baccalieu, isl., Newf., Can. D5 152
Baccarat, Fr. C7 58
Baccaro, pt., N.S., Can. F4 151
Bacerac, Mex. A3 129
Bach, Mich. E7 186
Bacharach, Ger. C2 61
Bachau, India F3 88
Back, Scot. B2 57
Back, river, N.W. Ter., Can. C12 142
Back Creek, Va. B4 209
Bačka Palanka, Yugo. C4 68
Bačka Topola, Yugo. C4 68
Backbone, mtn., Md. D1 173
Backnang, Ger. E4 61
Backoo, N. Dak. A8 198
Backus, Minn. D4 187
Backway, bay, Newf., Can. A2 152
Bacliff, Tex. *E5 206
Bacnotan, Phil. n13 90
Bacobi, Ariz. B5 168
Bacolod, Phil. C6 90
Bacon, co., Ga. E4 175
Bacone, Okla. B6 200
Baconton, Ga. E2 175
Bacoor, Phil. o13 90
Bacova, Va. C3 209
Bacqueville-en-Caux, Fr. E8 56
Bácsalmás, Hung. B4 68
Bactria: c. 500 B.C. 78
c. 325 B.C. 43
c. 225 B.C. 43
c. 100 B.C. 79
Bácum, Mex. B2 129
Bad, riv., S. Dak. C5 204
Bad, riv., Wis. B3 212
Bad Aibling, Ger. B8 66
Bad Axe, Mich. E8 186
Bad Berneck, Ger. C6 61
Bad Bramstedt, Ger. E3 62
Bad Doberan, Ger. A5 60
Bad Freienwalde, Ger. B7 60
Bad Friedrichshall, Ger. D4 61
Bad Hersfeld, Ger. C4 60
Bad Homburg, Ger. C3 61
Bad Ischl, Aus. E6 60
Bad Kissingen, Ger. C5 61
Bad Kreuznach, Ger. D2 61
Bad Lauterberg, Ger. B5 61
Bad Liebenwerda, Ger. B8 61
Bad Lippspringe, Ger. B3 61
Bad Mergentheim, Ger. D4 61
Bad Muskau, Ger. B9 61
Bad Nauheim, Ger. C3 61
Bad Neustadt, Ger. C5 61
Bad Oeynhausen, Ger. A3 61
Bad Oldesloe, Ger. B5 60
Bad Orb, Ger. C4 61
Bad Pyrmont, Ger. B4 61
Bad Reichenhall, Ger. E6 60
Bad River, Indian res., Wis. B3 212
Bad Salzuflen, Ger. A3 61
Bad Salzungen, Ger. C5 61
Bad Schandau, Ger. C9 61
Bad Segeberg, Ger. E4 62
Bad Sülze, Ger. D6 62
Bad Tennstedt, Ger. B5 61
Bad Tölz, Ger. E5 60
Bad Wildungen, Ger. B4 61
Bad Wörishofen, Ger. B6 66
Bad Zwischenahn, Ger. A8 59
Badajoz, Sp. C2 65
Badalona, Sp. B7 65
Baddeck, N.S., Can. C9 151
Baden, Aus. D8 60
Baden, Ont., Can. D4 153
Baden, Pa. A5, E1 202
Baden, Switz. B4 66
Baden, reg., Ger. D4 60
in 1815 50
in 1871 51
Baden-Baden, Ger. E3 61
Baden-Württemberg, state, Ger. D4 61
Badgastein, Aus. B9 66
Badger, Man., Can. E4 150
Badger, Newf., Can. D3 152
Badger, Iowa B3 180
Badger, Minn. B2 187
Badger, S. Dak. C8 204
Badger, creek, Colo. B7 171
Badger, mts., Wash. B5 210
Badi, Iraq E13 85
Badia Polesine, It. D7 66
Badin, N.C. B3 197
Badin, Pak. E2 88
Badin, lake, N.C. B3 197
Badlands, reg., N. Dak. C2 198
Badlands, nat. mon., S. Dak. D3 204
Badon, Viet. D7 89
Badoumbé, Mali D2 103
Badra, Iraq E2 86

INDEX KEY Each place listed in **Bold-faced Type** has its population listed in the Population tables, pages 230 to 280.
Each country, shown in CAPITAL LETTERS, has its population listed in the World Political Information Table, pages 6 to 10.
* Does not appear on map; key shows general location.

Baduein, Eth. D5 105
Badulla, Cey. G7 87
Badwater, Wyo. B5 213
Badwater, riv., Wyo. B5 213
Baena, Sp. D3 65
Baependi, Braz. C4 137
Baeza, Ec. B2 134
Baeza, Sp. D4 65
Bafang, Cam. D2 104
Bafata, Port. Gui. D2 103
Baffin, bay, N.W. Ter., Can. B18 143
Baffin, isl., N.W. Ter., Can. C18 143
Baffins, bay, Tex. F4 206
Baffling, pt., Efate I. 115
Bafia, Cam. E2 104
Bafoulabé, Mali D2 103
Bāfq, Iran F7 86
Bafra, Tur. B10 85
Bafra, cape, Tur. B11 85
Bāft, Iran G8 86
Bafwasende, Zaire A4 106
Baga, isl., Sol. Is. 115
Bagabag, Phil. n13 90
Bagaces, C.R. E5 130
Bagamoyo, Tan. C6 106
Bagan Siapiapi, Indon. K4 89, E2 90
Bagana, Nig. E6 103
Bagata, Zaire B2 106
Bagby, Calif. D3 170
Bagdad, Ariz. C2 168
Bagdad, Fla. G2 174
Bagdad, Ky. B4 182
Bagé, Braz. E2 137
Bagēmder, reg., Eth. C4 105
Bagenkop, Den. D4 62
Bagerhat, Bngl. F12 88
Baggs, Wyo. D5 213
Baghdad, Iraq E2 86
Baghdad, caliphate of 81
Bagheria, It. E4 67
Baghlān, Afg. C14 86
Bagh nam Faoileann, riv., Scot. C2 57
Bagley, Iowa C3 180
Bagley, Minn. C3 187
Bagley, Wis. F2 212
Bagleys Mills, Va. E4 209
Bagnacavallo, It. E7 66
Bagnara [Calabra], It. E5 67
Bagnell, Mo. C5 189
Bagnell, dam, Mo. C5 189
Bagnères-de-Bigorre, Fr. F4 58
Bagnères-de-Luchon, Fr. F4 58
Bagnolet, Fr. g10 58
Bagnols [-sur-Cèze], Fr. E6 58
Bågö, isl., Den. C3 62
Bago, Phil. *C6 90
Bagoe, riv., Mali D3 103
Bagolino, It. D6 66
Bagot, co., Que., Can. D5 154
Bagotville, Que., Can. A7 154
Bagrash Köl, lake, China C2 91
Bagrationovsk, Sov. Un. A6 70
Baguezane, mtn., Niger C6 103
Baguio, Phil. B6, n13 90
Bahado (Oasis), Som. D6 105
Bahama, N.C. A5 197
BAHAMA ISLANDS, Br. dep., N.A. C6 131
Bahawalnagar, Pak. C4 88
Bahāwalpur, Pak. C5 87
Bāherdār-Giyorgis, Eth. C4 105
Bahia, state, Braz. D2 138
Bahía, is., Hond. B4 130
Bahía Blanca, Arg. B4 136
Bahía de Caráquez, Ec. B1 134
Bahía Negra, Par. D4 135
Bahr el Abyad (White Nile), riv., Sud. C3 105
Bahr el Arab, riv., Sud. D2 105
Bahr el Azraq (Blue Nile), riv., Sud. C3 105
Bahr el Ghazal, reg., Sud. D2 105
Bahr el Ghazal, riv., Sud. D2 105
Bahr el Jèbel (Mountain Nile), riv., Sud. D3 105
Bahraich, India D8 88
BAHRAIN (Bahrein), country, Asia H5 86
Bahrāmābād, Iran F8 86
Bahrgan, cape, Iran G4 86
Bahriyah, oasis, Eg. D5 101
Bāhū Kalāt, Iran I10 86
Baia, New Britain I. 115
Baía dos Tigres, Ang. E1 106
Baia Mare, Rom. B6 68
Baião, Braz. C5 139
Baïbokoum, Chad D3 104
Baidarik, riv., Mong. B4 91
Baie-Comeau, Que., Can. *G19 145
Baie de Wasai, Mich. B6 186
Baie-d'Urfé, Que., Can. D8 154
Baie-Johan-Beetz, Que., Can. h9 152
Baie-St. Paul, Que., Can. B7 154
Baie-Ste. Catherine, Que., Can. A8 154
Baie Verte, N.B., Can. C5 151
Baie Verte, Newf., Can. D3 152
Baiersbronn, Ger. E3 61
Baile Átha Cliath, see Dublin, Ire.
Bailén, Sp. C4 65
Băileşti, Rom. C6 68
Bailey, Colo. B5 171
Bailey, N.C. B5 197
Bailey, co., Tex. B1 206
Bailey, brook, Maine B2 184
Bailey, isl., S.C. G1 203
Bailey Island, Maine E5 184
Baileys Harbor, Wis. C6 212
Baileyton, Ala. A3 166
Baileyton, Tenn. C11 205
Baileyville, Ill. A4 178
Baileyville, Kans. C7 181
Baileyville, Maine *C5 184
Bain-de-Bretagne, Fr. D3 58
Bainbridge, Ga. F2 175
Bainbridge, Ind. E4 179
Bainbridge, N.Y. C5 196
Bainbridge, Ohio C4 199
Bainbridge, is., Wash. D1 210
Bains, La. D4 183
Bainville, Mont. B12 190
Baio, New Ire. I. 115
Baird, Miss. B3 188
Baird, Tex. C3 206
Baird, inlet, Alsk. C7 167
Baird, mts., Alsk. B7 167
Bairdford, Pa. A6 202
Bairiki, isl., Tarawa 114
Bairnsdale, Austl. H6 112
Bairoil, Wyo. C5 213
Bait, range, B.C., Can. B4 149
Baixa Verde, Braz. g6 138
Baixo Longa, Ang. E2 106
Baja, Hung. B4 68
Baja California, state, Mex. A1 129
Baja California Sur, ter., Mex. B2 129
Bajadero, P.R. B4 132
Bajah, Tun. B6 102
Bajmok, Yugo. C4 68
Bakala, Cen. Afr. Rep. D4 104
Bakar, Yugo. C2 68
Bakel, Sen. D2 103
Baker, Calif. E5 170
Baker, Fla. G2 174
Baker, Idaho D5 177
Baker, La. D4 183
Baker, Minn. D2 187
Baker, Mont. D12 190
Baker, Nev. E7 192
Baker, N. Dak. A6 198
Baker, Okla. D3 200
Baker, Oreg. C9 201
Baker, co., Fla. B4 174
Baker, co., Ga. E2 175
Baker, co., Oreg. C9 201
Baker, butte, Ariz. C4 168
Baker, isl., Oceania F11 113
Baker, lake, N.W. Ter., Can. D13 142
Baker, lake, Maine B3 184
Baker, lake, Wash. A4 210
Baker, mtn., Maine C3 184
Baker, mtn., Wash. A4 210
Baker, valley, Oreg. C9 201
Baker Brook, N.B., Can. *B1 151
Baker Lake, N.W. Ter., Can. D13 144
Bakerhill, Ala. D4 166
Bakers, N.C. B3 197
Bakers, Tenn. E9 205
Bakers, bayou, Ark. D6 169
Bakers, isl., Mass. C4 185
Bakers, riv., N.H. C3 193
Bakers Mill, Fla. B4 174
Bakersfield, Calif. E4 170
Bakersfield, Mo. E5 189
Bakersfield, Tex. D1 206
Bakersfield, Vt. B3 208
Bakerstown, Pa. A6 202
Bakersville, Conn. B4 172
Bakersville, N.C. C4 197
Bakerton, see Elmora, Pa.
Bakerton, W. Va. B7 211
Bakhchisaray, Sov. Un. I9 72
Bakhmut, riv., Sov. Un. q21 72
Bakir, riv., Tur. C6 69
Bāko, Eth. D4 105
Bako, I.C. E3 103
Bakony Forest, mts., Hung. B3 68
Bakouma, Cen. Afr. Rep. D4 104
Bakoy, riv., Mali D3 103
Baku, Zaire A5 106
Baku, Sov. Un. E3 73
Bakundi, Nig. E7 103
Bakungan, Indon. K2 89
Bal Harbour, Fla. *G6 174
Bala, Ont., Can. C5 153
Bala, Kans. C7 181
Bâlâ, Tur. C9 85
Bala, mts., Bol. B2 135
Bala Murghab, Afg. D11 86
Balabac, isl., Phil. D5 90
Balabac, strait, Phil. D5 90
Balabio, isl., N. Cal. 115
Balad, Som. E6 105
Balaghat, India G8 88
Balaguer, Sp. B6 65
Bal'ah, Jordan f11 84
Balaka, Malawi D6 106
Balaklava, Austl. G2 112
Balakleya, Sov. Un. G11 72
Balakovo, Sov. Un. C3 73
Balallan, Scot. B2 57
Balancán, Mex. D6 129
Balanda, Sov. Un. F15 72
Balanga, Phil. C6, o13 90
Balangir, India G9 88
Balaoan, Phil. n13 90
Balashikha, Sov. Un. D11 72
Balashov, Sov. Un. C2 73
Balasore, India G11 88
Balassagyarmat, Hung. A4 68
Balāt, Eg. D5 101
Balaton, Minn. F3 187
Balaton, lake, Hung. B3 68
Balayan, Phil. p13 90
Balayan, bay, Phil. p13 90
Balboa, C.Z. m11 130
Balboa Heights, C.Z. m11 130
Balcarce, Arg. B5 136
Balcarres, Sask., Can. G4 151
Balch, Ark. B4 169
Balch Springs, Tex. *C4 206
Balchen, glacier, Ant. B34 120
Balchik, Bul. D9 68
Balclutha, N.Z. Q12 112
Balcones Heights, Tex. *E3 206
Bald, hill, R.I. C10 172
Bald, mtn., Colo. A5 171
Bald, mtn., Conn. B7 172
Bald, mtn., N.J. A4 194
Bald, mtn., Oreg. C9 201
Bald, mtn., Oreg. D5 201
Bald, mtn., Vt. B5 208
Bald, mtn. Wyo. A5 213
Bald, mts., N.C. C3 197
Bald, mts., Tenn. C11 205
Bald, peak, N.B., Can. A5 184
Bald Creek, N. C. C3 197
Bald Eagle, Minn. E7 187
Bald Eagle, lake, Minn. C7 187
Bald Eagle, lake, Minn. E7 187
Bald Knob, Ark. B4 169
Bald Knob, mtn., Va. D3 209
Bald Knob, mtn., W. Va. C5 211
Baldhill, dam, N. Dak. C7 198
Baldock, lake, Man., Can. A3 150
Baldur, Man., Can. E2 150
Baldwin, Fla. B5 174
Baldwin, Ga. B3 175
Baldwin, Ill. E4 178
Baldwin, Iowa B7 180
Baldwin, La. E4 183
Baldwin, Md. B5 173
Baldwin, Mich. E5 186
Baldwin, N.Y. G2 172
Baldwin, N.C. A2 197
Baldwin, N. Dak. B5 198
Baldwin, Pa. *F1 202
Baldwin, Wis. D1 212
Baldwin, co., Ala. E2 166
Baldwin, co., Ga. C3 175
Baldwin, pen., Alsk. B7 167
Baldwin City, Kans. D8 181
Baldwin Heights, Ind. H2 179
Baldwin Park, Calif. *E5 170
Baldwinsville, N.Y. B4 196
Baldwinton, Sask., Can. E1 155
Baldwinville, Mass. A3 185
Baldwyn, Miss. A5 188
Baldy, mtn., B.C., Can. D7 149
Baldy, mtn., Man., Can. D1 150
Baldy, mtn., Mont. B7 190
Baldy, mtn., N. Mex. A4 195
Baldy, peak, Ariz. D6 168
Balearic, is., Sp. C6 65
Baler, Phil. o13 90
Baleshare, isl., Scot. C1 57
Balesin, isl., Phil. o13 90
Baleville, N.J. A3 194
Balfour, N.C. D3 197
Balfour, N. Dak. B5 198
Balfour, chan., Sol. Is. 115
Balgonie, Sask., Can. G3 155
Bali, India E4 88
Bali, isl., Indon. G5 90
Balikesir, Tur. C6 69
Balikpapan, Indon. F5 90
Balingen, Ger. A4 66
Balintang, chan., Phil. B6 90
Balintawak, Phil. C6 90
Baliuag, Phil. o13 90
Balje, Ger. B4 60
Baljennie, Sask., Can. E2 155
Balkan, Ky. D6 182
Balkan, mts., Bul. D7 68
Balkh, Afg. C13 86
Balkhash, Sov. Un. D8 73
Balkhash, lake, Sov. Un. D9 73
Balki, Sov. Un. H10 72
Balko, Okla. D3 200
Ball Club, Minn. C5 187
Ball Ground, Ga. B2 175
Ballachulish, Scot. D3 57
Ballaja, P.R. C2 132
Ballantine, Mont. E8 190
Ballantrae, Scot. E4 57
Ballarat, Austl. H4 112
Ballard, co., Ky. A2 182
Ballard Vale, Mass. A5, C2 185
Ballater, Scot. C5 57
Ballclub, lake, Minn. C5 187
Ballé, Mali C3 103
Ballenas, bay, Mex. B2 129
Ballenstedt, Ger. B6 61
Ballerup, Den. C6 62
Balli, cape, New Britain I. 115
Ballia, India E10 88
Balliguda, India G9 88
Ballina, Austl. D9 112
Ballina, Ire. C2 55
Ballinasloe, Ire. D2 55
Ballinger, Tex. D3 206
Ballinluig, Scot. D5 57
Ballouville, Conn. B9 172
Ballston, Oreg. B3 201
Ballston Lake, N.Y. C7 196
Ballston Spa, N.Y. B7 196
Ballville, Ohio *A4 199
Ballwin, Mo. B7 189
Bally, India *F12 88
Bally, Pa. F10 202
Ballycastle, N. Ire. C3 55
Ballymena, N. Ire. C3 55
Ballyshannon, Ire. C2 55
Balm, Fla. E4 174
Balmat, N.Y. A5, B1 196
Balmazújváros, Hung. B5 68
Balmoral, Man., Can. D3 150
Balmoral Castle, Scot. C5 57
Balmorhea, Tex. F2 206
Balmville, N.Y. *D6 196
Baloda Bazar, India G9 88
Balonne, riv., Austl. C7 112
Balotra, India E4 88
Balovale, Zambia D3 106
Balrampur, India D9 88
Balranald, Austl. G4 112
Bals, Rom. C7 68
Balsam, N.C. D3 197
Balsam, lake, Ont., Can. C6 153
Balsam, lake, Wis. C1 212
Balsam Lake, Wis. C1 212
Balsas, Braz. C1 138
Balsas, riv., Braz. C1 138
Balsas, riv., Braz. D1 138
Balsas, riv., Mex. D4 129
Balta, N. Dak. A5 198
Balta, Sov. Un. H7 72
Baltic, Conn. C8 172
Baltic, Ohio B6 199
Baltic, S. Dak. D9 204
Baltic, sea, Eur. I8 63
Balţīm, Eg., U.A.R. C3 84
Baltimore, Ont., Can. C6 153
Baltimore (Independent City), Md. B4, C2 173
Baltimore Highlands, Md. C2 173
Baltimore, Ohio C5 199
Baltimore, co., Md. B4 173
Baltiysk, Sov. Un. A5 70
Baltra, isl., Ec. g5 134
Baltrum, Ger. A7 59
Baltrum, isl., Ger. A7 59
Baluan, isl., Bis. Arch. 115
Baluchistan, reg., Pak. C3 87
Balya, Tur. C6 69
Balzac, Alta., Can. D3 148
Balzar, Ec. B2 134
Bam, Iran G9 86
Bam, lake, China B9 87
Bama, Nig. D7 103
Bamako, Mali D3 103
Bamba, Mali C4 103
Bambang, Phil. n13 90
Bambari, Cen. Afr. Rep. D4 104
Bambatana, Choiseul I. 115
Bamberg, Ger. D5 61
Bamberg, S.C. E5 203
Bamberg, co., S.C. E5 203
Bambesa, Zaire A4 106
Bambuí, Braz. F1 138
Bamburgh, Eng. E7 57
Bambuto, mts., Nig., Cam. E6 103
Bamenda [Mankou], Cam. E7 103
Bāmiān, Afg. D13 86, A4 87
Bampūr, Iran H10 86
Bampur, riv., Iran H9 86
Ban Bangsaphan Yai, Thai. G3 89
Ban Hat Yai, see Hadyai, Thai.
Ban Houei Sai, Laos B4 89
Ban Me Thuot, Viet. F8 89
Baña Buey, Cuba k11 131
Banalia, Zaire A4 106
Banamba, Mali D3 103
Banana, Zaire C1 106
Bananal, Braz. h5 137
Bananal, isl., Braz. E4 139
Bananeiras, Braz. C3, h6 138
Banaras (Varanasi), India C7 87, E9 88
Banās, cape, Eg. E7 101
Banas, riv., India E4 88
Banat, reg., Rom., Yugo. C5 68
in 1721 49
Banban, reef, Bis. Arch. 115
Banbridge, N. Ire. C3 55
Banbury, Eng. B6 56
Banchory, Scot. C6 57
Banco, Col. B3 133
Bancroft, Ont., Can. B7 153
Bancroft, Idaho G7 177
Bancroft, Iowa A3 180
Bancroft, La. D2 183
Bancroft, Maine C4 184
Bancroft, Mich. F6 186
Bancroft, Nebr. B9 191
Bancroft, S. Dak. C8 204
Bancroft, Wis. D4 212
Banda, India E8 88
Banda, is., Indon. F7 90
Banda, sea, Indon. G7 90
Banda Atjeh, Indon. k11 90
Bandama, riv., I.C. E3 103
Bandana, Ky. A2 182
Bandar, Afg. D12 86
Bandar 'Abbās, Iran H8 86
Bandar Baharu, Mala. J4 89
Bandar Maharani, Mala. K5 89
Bandar Penggaram, Mala. L5 89
Bandar Seri Begawan, Bru. E4 90
Bandar-e Chīrū, Iran H6 86
Bandar-e Deylam, Iran F5 86
Bandar-e Pahlavī, Iran C4 86
Bandar-e Rīg, Iran G5 86
Bandar-e Shāh, Iran C7 86
Bandar-e Shāhpūr, Iran F4 86
Bande, Sp. A2 65
Banded, peak, Colo. D4 171
Bandeira, peak, Braz. F2 138
Bandelier, nat. mon., N.Mex. B3 195
Bandera, Arg. E3 135
Bandera, Tex. E3 206
Bandera, co., Tex. E3 206
Banderas, bay, Mex. m11 129
Bandholm, Den. D5 62
Bandiagara, Mali D4 103
Bandikui, India D6 88
Bandirma, Tur. B6 69
Bandjarmasin, Indon. F4 90
Bandon, Oreg. D2 201
Bandundu, Zaire B2 106
Bandung, Indon. G3 90
Bandy, Va. B3 209
Banes, Cuba E6 131
Banff, Alta., Can. D3 148
Banff, Scot. C6 57
Banff, co., Scot. C5 57
Banff, nat. park, Alta., Can. D2 148
Banfora, Upper Volta D4 103
Bangalore, India F6 87
Bangassou, Cen. Afr. Rep. E4 104
Banggai, Indon. F6 90
Banghāzī, see Bengasi, Libya
Bangka, isl., Indon. F3 90
Bangkalan, Indon. G4 90
Bangkok (Krung Thep), Thai. F4 89
BANGLADESH, country, Asia D8 87
Bangor, Ala. B3 166
Bangor, Sask., Can. G4 155
Bangor, Maine D4 184
Bangor, Mich. F4 186
Bangor, N.Y. A2 196
Bangor, N. Ire. C4 55
Bangor, Pa. E11 202
Bangor, Wales A3 56
Bangor, Wis. E3 212
Bangs, Tex. D3 206
Bangs, mtn., Ariz. A2 168
Bangu, Zaire C3 106
Bangued, Phil. B6 90
Banguey, isl., Mala. D5 90
Bangui, Cen. Afr. Rep. E3 104
Bangweulu, lake, Zambia D4 106
Banhā, Eg. D3 84
Baní, Dom. Rep. F8 131
Bani, Phil. n12 90
Banī Na'īm, Jordan C7 84
Banī Suhaylah, Gaza Strip C6 84
Bani Suwayf, Eg. D6 101
Baniara, Pap. k12 111
Baniata, pt., Rendova I. 115
Baniloudi, Niger C5 103
Banister, riv., Va. E4 209
Bāniyās, Syr. E10 85
Baniyas, Syr. A7 84
Banja Luka, Yugo. C3 68
Banjuwangi, Indon. G4 90
Bankasse, Mali D4 103
Bankfoot, Scot. D5 57
Bankhead, Ala. B2 166
Bankhead, lake, Ala. B2 166
Banks, Ala. D4 166
Banks, Ark. D3 169
Banks, Idaho E2 177
Banks, Miss. A3 188
Banks, Oreg. A1 201
Banks, co., Ga. B3 175
Banks, bay, Ec. g5 134
Banks, isl., Austl. B7 110
Banks, isl., B.C., Can. C2 149
Banks, isl., N.W. Ter., Can. B8 142
Banks, is., New Hebr. 115
Banks, lake, Ga. F3 175
Banks, pen., N.Z. O14 112
Banksian, riv., Man., Can. C4 150
Bankston, Ala. B2 166
Bankstown, Austl. *F9 111
Bankura, India F11 88
Bannack, Mont. E3 190
Banner, Miss. A4 188
Banner, Wyo. A6 213
Banner, co., Nebr. C2 191
Banner Elk, N.C. A2, C4 197
Banner Hill, Tenn. *C11 205
Bannerman, Man., Can. E2 150
Bannertown, N.C. *A3 197
Banning, Calif. F5 170
Banning, Ga. C2 175
Bannock, co., Idaho G6 177
Bannockburn, Ont., Can. C7 153
Bannockburn, Ill. *A6 178
Bannu, Pak. B5 87
Bañolas, Sp. A7 65
Baños, Ec. B2 134
Bansalan, Phil. D7 90
Banská Bystrica, Czech. D5 70
Banská Stiavnica, Czech. D5 70
Bansko, Bul. E6 68
Banstead, Eng. C7 56
Banswara, India F5 88
Bantam, Conn. C4 172
Bantam, lake, Conn. C4 172
Bantam, riv., Conn. B4 172
Bantry, Ire. E2 55
Bantry, N. Dak. A5 198
Bantry, bay, Ire. E2 55
Banyak, is., Indon. K2 89
Banyo, Cam. D2 104
Banzare, coast, Ant. C25 120
Banzyville, Zaire A3 106
Baoulé, riv., Mali D3 103
Bapaume, Fr. D2 59
Bapchule, Ariz. D4, H2 168
Baptiste, Ont., Can. B7 153
Baptistown, N.J. B2 194
Ba'quba, Iraq F15 85
Baquedano, Chile D2 135
Bar, Sov. Un. G6 72
Bar, Yugo. D4 68
Bar Harbor, Maine D4 184
Bar-le-Duc, Fr. C6 58
Bar Mills, Maine E2 184
Bar-sur-Aube, Fr. C6 58
Bar [-sur-Seine], Fr. C6 58
Bara, Sud. C3 105
Barabil, India F10 88
Barabinsk, Sov. Un. B9 73
Baraboo, Wis. E4 212
Baraboo, riv., Wis. E3 212
Barachois Pond, prov. park, Newf., Can. D2 152
Baracoa, Cuba E6 131
Barada, Nebr. D10 191
Baradères, Hai. F7 131
Baradero, Arg. f7 136
Baraga, Mich. B2 186
Baraga, co., Mich. B2 186
Barahona, Dom. Rep. F8 131
Barajas de Madrid, Sp. p17 65
Barak Khel, Afg. E13 86
Barakī Barak, Afg. E14 86
Barakot, India G10 88
Baramula, India B5 87
Baran, India E6 88
Baranagar, India *F12 88
Baranof, Alsk. m22 167
Baranof, isl., Alsk. m22 167
Baranovichi, Sov. Un. E5 72
Barataria, La. C7, E5 183
Barataria, bay, La. E6 183
Barataria, bayou, La. C7 183
Baraunī, India *C8 87
Baraya, Col. C2 133
Barbacena, Braz. C4, g6 137
Barbacoas, Col. C2 133
Barbado, riv., Braz. C3 135
BARBADOS, country, N.A. p17 131
Barbalha, Braz. C3 138
Barbarian invasions 46
Barbarossa, crusade of 47
Barbastro, Sp. A6 65
Barbate, Sp. D3 65
Barbeau, Mich. B6 186
Barber, Idaho F2 177
Barber, Mont. D7 190
Barber, co., Kans. E5 181
Barberton, Ohio A6 199
Barberton, S. Afr. C5 107
Barbertown, N.J. C2 194
Barberville, Fla. C5 174
Barbezieux, Fr. E3 58
Barbour, co., Ala. D4 166
Barbour, co., W. Va. B4 211
Barboursville, Va. C4 209
Barboursville, W. Va. C2 211
Barbourville, Ky. D6 182
Barbuda, isl., Antigua n16 131
Barby, Ger. B6 61
Barca de Alva, Port. B2 65
Barcaldine, Austl. A5 112
Barcarena, Port. F9 65
Barcarrota, Sp. C2 65
Barcellona [Pozzo di Gotto], It. E5 67
Barcelona, Sp. B7 65
Barcelona, Ven. A5 133
Barceloneta, P.R. B4 132
Barceloneta, mun., P.R. B4 132
Barcelonnette, Fr. E7 58
Barcelos, Braz. D5 133
Barcelos, Port. B1 65
Barclay, Kans. D8 181
Barclay, Md. B6 173
Barco, N.C. A8 197
Barcoo, riv., Austl. B4 112
Barcroft, lake, Md. C1 173
Bard, N. Mex. B6 195
Bardejov, Czech. D6 70
Bardera, Som. E5 105
Bardi, It. E5 66
Bardīyah, Libya C5 101
Bardley, Mo. E6 189
Bardolph, Ill. C3 178
Bardonecchia, It. D2 66
Bardsey, isl., Wales B3 56
Bardstown, Ky. C4 182
Bardstown Junction, Ky. C4 182
Bardswell, is., B.C., Can. C3 149
Bardwell, Ky. B2 182
Bare Hill, pond, Mass. C1 185
Bareilly, India C7 88
Barenburg, Ger. F2 62
Barentin, Fr. C4 58
Barents, isl., Nor. B12 118
Barents, sea, Sov. Un. B5 71
Barentu, Eth. B4 105
Barfleur, pt., Fr. C3 58
Bargal, Som. C7 105
Bargarh, India G9 88
Barge, canal, N.Y. B2 196
Bargersville, Ind. E5 179
Barguzin, Sov. Un. D13 71
Bari, It. D6 67
Barika, Alg. B6 102
Barinas, P.R. C3 132
Barinas, Ven. B3 133
Barinas, state, Ven. B3 133
Baring, Maine C5 184
Baring, Mo. A5 189
Baripada, India G11 88
Barirí, Braz. C3, m7 137
Bārīs, Eg. E6 101
Barisāl, Bngl. F13 88
Barisan, mts., Indon. F2 90
Barium Springs, N.C. B3 197
Bark, lake, Ont., Can. B7 153
Bark, pt., Wis. B2 212
Bark River, Mich. C3 186
Barker, N.Y. B2 196
Barker Heights, N.C. *D3 197
Barker's Point, N.B., Can. *D3 151
Barkerville, B.C., Can. C7 149
Barkeryd, Swe. A8 62
Barkeyville, Pa. D2 202
Barkhamsted, Conn. B5 172
Barkhamsted, res., Conn. B5 172
Barking, Eng. *k13 55
Barkley, dam, Ky. C1 182
Barkley, lake, Ky., Tenn. B3 182, A4 205
Barkly East, S. Afr. D4 107
Barköl (Chensi), China C3 91
Barksdale, Tex. E2 206
Barlad, Rom. B8 68
Barlee, lake, Austl. E2 110
Barletta, It. D6 67
Barling, Ark. B1 169
Barlow, Ky. A1 182
Barlow, N. Dak. B6 198
Barlow Bend, Ala. D2 166
Barmer, India E3 88
Barmouth, Wales B3 56
Barnaby River, N.B., Can. C4 151
Barnard, Kans. C5 181
Barnard, Mo. A3 189
Barnard, S. Dak. B7 204
Barnard, Vt. D3 208
Barnard Castle, Eng. F7 57

INDEX KEY Each place listed in **Bold-faced Type** has its population listed in the Population tables, pages 230 to 280.
Each country, shown in CAPITAL LETTERS, has its population listed in the World Political Information Table, pages 6 to 10.
* Does not appear on map; key shows general location.

Barnardsville, N.C. ... D3 197
Barnasht, Eg ... E3 84
Barnaul, Sov. Un ... C10 73
Barnegat, N.J ... D4 194
Barnegat, bay, N.J ... D4 194
Barnegat City, N.J ... D4 194
Barnes, Kans ... C7 181
Barnes, Miss ... C4 188
Barnes, Oreg ... *D3 201
Barnes, Pa ... C3 202
Barnes, co., N. Dak ... B7 198
Barnes, sound, Fla ... G6 174
Barnes City, Iowa ... C5 180
Barnes Corners, N.Y ... B5 196
Barnesboro, Pa ... E4 202
Barnesdale, Ont., Can ... B5 153
Barneston, Nebr ... D9 191
Barnesville, Ga ... C2 175
Barnesville, Md ... B3 173
Barnesville, Minn ... D2 187
Barnesville, Ohio ... C6 199
Barnet, Eng ... k12 57
Barnet, Vt ... C4 208
Barnett, Miss ... D5 188
Barnett, Mo ... C5 189
Barneveld, Neth ... B5 59
Barneveld, Wis ... E4 212
Barneville-sur-Mer, Fr ... C3 58
Barney, Ga ... E3 175
Barney, N. Dak ... C8 198
Barnhart, Mo ... B8, C7 189
Barnsboro, N.J ... D2 194
Barnsdall, Okla ... A5 200
Barnsley, Eng ... A6 56
Barnstable, Mass ... C7 185
Barnstable, co., Mass ... C7 185
Barnstaple, Eng ... C3 56
Barnstaple, bay, Eng ... C3 56
Barnstead, N.H ... D4 193
Barnston, Que., Can ... D6 154
Barnum, Iowa ... B3 180
Barnum, Minn ... D6 187
Barnwell, Alta., Can ... E4 148
Barnwell, S.C ... E5 203
Barnwell, co., S.C ... E5 203
Baro, Nig ... E6 103
Baro, riv., Eth ... D3 105
Baroda, India ... F4 88
Barola, isl., Sol. Is ... 115
Baron, Okla ... B7 200
Barons, Alta., Can ... E4 148
Barotse, prov., Zambia ... E3 106
Barqah, see Cyrenaica, prov., Libya
Barquisimeto, Ven ... A4 133
Barr, Colo ... B6 171
Barr, Fr ... C7 58
Barr, Miss ... A4 188
Barra, Braz ... D2 138
Barra, Braz ... h5 138
Barra, isl., Scot ... D1 57
Barra do Corda, Braz ... C1 138
Barra do Piraí, Braz ... C4, h6 137
Barra Mansa, Braz ... C4, h5 137
Barraba, Austl ... E8 112
Barrackpore, India ... F12 88
Barrackville, W. Va ... A7, B4 211
Barranca, Peru ... B2 134
Barrancabermeja, Col ... B3 133
Barrancas, Ven ... B5 133
Barranquilla, Col ... A3 133
Barranquitas, P.R ... C5 132
Barranquitas, mun., P.R ... C5 132
Barraza, Chile ... A2 136
Barre, Que., Can ... C7 154
Barre, Mass ... B3 185
Barre, Vt ... C4 208
Barre, lake, La ... E5 183
Barre des Écrins, mtn., Fr ... E7 58
Barre Falls, res., Mass ... B4 185
Barre Plains, Mass ... B3 185
Barreiras, Braz ... D1 138
Barreirinhas, Braz ... B2 138
Barreiro, Braz ... h5 137
Barreiro, Port ... C1, f9 65
Barreiros, Braz ... C3, k6 138
Barrellville, Md ... D2 173
Barren, co., Ky ... D4 182
Barren, isl., Alsk ... h15 167
Barren, is., Malag ... g8 107
Barren, isl., Md ... D5 173
Barren Plain, Tenn ... A5 205
Barren River, res., Ky ... D3 182
Barrens, plat., Tenn ... B6 205
Barretos, Braz ... F1 138
Barrett, Minn ... E3 187
Barrett, Tex ... *F5 206
Barrett, W. Va ... D3, D6 211
Barretts, Ga ... F3 175
Barretts, hill, Mass ... C1 185
Barrhead, Alta., Can ... B3 148
Barrhead, Scot ... E4 57
Barrhill, Scot ... E4 57
Barrie, Ont., Can ... C5 153
Barrie, isl., Ont., Can ... B2 153
Barrière, B.C., Can ... D7 149
Barrigada, Guam ... 114
Barrigada, hill, Guam ... 114
Barrington, N.S., Can ... F4 151
Barrington, Ill ... A5, E2 178
Barrington, N.H ... D4 193
Barrington, N.J ... *D2 194
Barrington, R.I ... C11 172
Barrington, lake, Man., Can ... A1 150
Barrington Hills, Ill ... *A5 178
Barrington Passage, N.S., Can ... F4 151
Barrington Tops, mtn., Austl ... F8 112
Barrio Azul, Cuba ... k11 131
Barron, Wis ... C2 212
Barron, co., Wis ... C2 212
Barronett, Wis ... C2 212
Barrow, Alsk ... A8 167
Barrow, Arg ... B4 136
Barrow, co., Ga ... B3 175
Barrow, isl., Austl ... D2 110
Barrow, pt., Alsk ... A8 167
Barrow, riv., Ire ... D3 55
Barrow Creek, Austl ... D5 111
Barrow-in-Furness, Eng ... C5 55
Barrows, Man., Can ... C1 150
Barruelo de Santullán, Sp ... A3 65
Barry, Ill ... D2 178
Barry, Wales ... C4 56
Barry, co., Mich ... F5 186
Barry, co., Mo ... E4 189
Barrys Bay, Ont., Can ... B7 153
Barryton, Mich ... E5 186
Barryville, N.Y ... D6 196
Barsi, India ... H5 88
Barsinghausen, Ger ... A4 61
Barsö, isl., Den ... C3 62
Barstow, Calif ... E5 170
Barstow, Tex ... D1, F2 206
Bartelso, Ill ... E4 178
Barth, Fla ... G2 174
Barth, Ger ... A6 60
Bartholomew, co., Ind ... F6 179
Bartholomew, bayou, Ark ... C4 169
Bartica, Guy ... A3 139
Bartin, Tur ... B9 85
Bartlesville, Okla ... A6 200
Bartlett, Ill ... E2 178
Bartlett, Kans ... E8 181
Bartlett, Nebr ... C7 191
Bartlett, N.H ... B4 193
Bartlett, N. Dak ... A7 198
Bartlett, Ohio ... C6 199
Bartlett, Tenn ... B2, E8 205
Bartlett, Tex ... D4 206
Bartlett, res., Ariz ... D4, F3 168
Bartletts Ferry, dam, Ala., Ga ... C4 166, D1 175
Bartletts Harbour, Newf., Can ... C3 152
Bartley, Nebr ... D5 191
Bartley, N.J ... B3 194
Bartolomeu Dias, Moz ... B6 107
Barton, Ala ... A2 166
Barton, Ark ... C5 169
Barton, Md ... D1 173
Barton, N. Dak ... A5 198
Barton, Ohio ... B7 199
Barton, Vt ... B4 208
Barton, Wis ... *E5 212
Barton, co., Kans ... D5 181
Barton, co., Mo ... D3 189
Barton, riv., Vt ... B4 208
Barton-on-Humber, Eng ... A7 56
Bartonsville, Vt ... E3 208
Bartonville, Ill ... C4 178
Bartoszyce, Pol ... A6 70
Bartow, Fla ... E5 174
Bartow, Ga ... D4 175
Bartow, co., Ga ... B2 175
Baruth, Ger ... A8 61
Barvas, Scot ... B2 57
Barvenkovo, Sov. Un ... G11 72
Barwani, India ... F5 88
Barwice, Pol ... F8 62
Barwick, Ga ... F3 175
Barwick, Ky ... C6 182
Barwon, riv., Austl ... D7 112
Barybino, Sov. Un ... n17 72
Barycz, riv., Pol ... C4 70
Bārz Shovār, Iran ... F5 86
Bas-Rhin, dept., Fr ... F7 59, A3 66
Basāki, Iran ... F5 86
Basalt, Colo ... B3 171
Basalt, Idaho ... F6 177
Basankusu, Zaire ... A2 106
Basantpur, India ... D11 88
Basbulak, Sov. Un ... E6 73
Basco, Ill ... C2 178
Bascom, Fla ... B1 174
Bascom, Ohio ... A4 199
Basehor, Kans ... B8 181
Basekpio, Zaire ... A3 106
Basel, Switz ... B3 66
Basel-Land, sub canton, Switz ... B3 66
Bashagird, range, Iran ... H9 86
Bashaw, Alta., Can ... C4 148
Bashi, Ala ... D2 166
Basiad, bay, Phil ... o14 90
Basic, Miss ... C5 188
Basilan, Phil ... D6 90
Basilan, isl., Phil ... D6 90
Basildon, Eng ... C8 56
Basile, La ... D3 183
Basilicata, reg., It ... D5 67
Basilio, Braz ... E2 137
Basim, India ... G6 88
Basin, Mont ... D4 190
Basin, Wyo ... A4 213
Basin, lake, Sask., Can ... E3 155
Basin Harbor, Vt ... C2 208
Basinger, Fla ... E5 174
Basingstoke, Eng ... C6 56
Basirhat, India ... *D8 87
Baška, Yugo ... C2 68
Baskahegan, lake, Maine ... C5 184
Baskett, Ky ... C2 182
Baskin, Fla ... E1 174
Baskin, La ... B4 183
Basking Ridge, N.J ... B3 194
Basoko, Zaire ... A3 106
Basongo, Zaire ... B3 106
Basque Provinces, reg., Sp ... A4 65
Basra, Iraq ... F3 86
Bass, is., Ohio ... A4 199
Bass, lake, Ind ... B4 179
Bass, strait, Austl ... I5 112
Bass River, N.S., Can ... D6 151
Bassac, Laos ... E6 89
Bassano, Alta., Can ... D4 148
Bassano del Grappa, It ... B3 67
Basse-Terre, Guad ... o16 131
Bassein, Bur ... E9 87
Basseterre, St. Kitts-Nevis ... n15 131
Bassett, Iowa ... A5 180
Bassett, Kans ... E8 181
Bassett, Nebr ... B6 191
Bassett, Va ... E3 209
Bassett, creek, Ala ... D2 166
Bassett, peak, Ariz ... E5 168
Bassfield, Miss ... D4 188
Bassikounou, Maur ... C3 103
Bassum, Ger ... F2 62
Basswood, Man., Can ... D1 150
Basswood, lake, Ont., Can ... B7 187
Båstads, Swe ... B6 62
Bastak, Iran ... H7 86
Bastelica, Fr ... D2 67
Basti, India ... D9 88
Bastia, Fr ... C2 67
Bastian, Va ... D1 209
Bastogne, Bel ... D5 59
Bastrop, La ... B4 183
Bastrop, Tex ... D4 206
Bastrop, co., Tex ... D4 206
Bastuträsk, Swe ... E9 63
Basyūn, Eg ... D2 84
Bat Yam, Isr ... g9 84
Bata, Equat. Gui ... E1 104
Bataan, Phil ... p13 90
Batabanó, Cuba ... D2 131
Batala, India ... B5 88
Batam, isl., Indon ... L5 89
Batan, is., Phil ... A6 90
Batangafo, Cen. Afr. Rep ... D3 104
Batangas, Phil ... C6, p13 90
Bataques, Mex ... F6 170
Bátaszék, Hung ... B4 68
Batatais, Braz ... F1 138
Batavia, Arg ... A3 136
Batavia, Ark ... A2 169
Batavia, Ill ... B5, F2 178
Batavia, see Djakarta, Indon.
Batavia, Iowa ... D5 180
Batavia, N.Y ... C2 196
Batavia, Ohio ... C3 199
Bataysk, Sov. Un ... H12 72
Batchelor, bay, N.C ... B7 197
Batchtown, Ill ... D3 178
Bateman, Sask., Can ... G2 155
Bates, Ark ... C1 169
Bates, Oreg ... C8 201
Bates, co., Mo ... C3 189
Bates City, Mo ... B3 189
Batesburg, S.C ... D4 203
Batesland, S. Dak ... D3 204
Batesville, Ala ... C4 166
Batesville, Ark ... B4 169
Batesville, Ind ... F7 179
Batesville, Miss ... A4 188
Batesville, Ohio ... C6 199
Batesville, Tex ... E3 206
Bath, N.B., Can ... C2 151
Bath, Ont., Can ... C8 153
Bath, Eng ... C5 56
Bath, Ill ... C3 178
Bath, Ind ... E8 179
Bath, Maine ... E3, E6 184
Bath, Mich ... F6 186
Bath, N.H ... B3 193
Bath, N.Y ... C3 196
Bath, N.C ... B7 197
Bath, Pa ... E11 202
Bath, S.C ... D4 203
Bath, S. Dak ... B7 204
Bath, co., Ky ... B6 182
Bath, co., Va ... C3 209
Bath Springs, Tenn ... B3 205
Batha de Laïri, riv., Chad ... C3 104
Bathgate, N. Dak ... A8 198
Bathgate, Scot ... E5 57
Bathsheba, Barb ... p17 131
Bathurst, Austl ... F7 112
Bathurst, N.B., Can ... B4 151
Bathurst, Gam ... D1 103
Bathurst, cape, N.W. Ter., Can ... B7 142
Bathurst, inlet, N.W. Ter., Can ... C11 142
Bathurst, isl., Austl ... B4 110
Bathurst, isl., N.W. Ter., Can ... A12 142
Bathurst Inlet, N.W. Ter., Can ... C11 144
Batié, Upper Volta ... E4 103
Batiscan, Que., Can ... C5 154
Batiscan, riv., Que., Can ... B5 154
Batkanu, S.L ... E2 103
Batley, Eng ... A6 56
Batna, Alg ... B6 102
Batoche, Sask., Can ... E2 155
Baton Rouge, La ... B5, D4 183
Batouri, Cam ... E2 104
Batovi, riv., Braz ... E4 139
Batroun, Leb ... E10 85
Batson, Tex ... D5 206
Batsto, riv., N.J ... D3 194
Battambang, Camb ... F5 89
Battery Park, Va ... B6 209
Batticaloa, Cey ... G7 87
Battiest, Okla ... C7 200
Battīr, Isr ... k11 84
Battle, creek, Sask., Can ... H1 155
Battle, creek, Mont ... A7 190
Battle, mtn., Wyo ... D5 213
Battle, riv., Alta., Can ... C5 148
Battle, riv., Sask., Can ... E1 155
Battle, riv., Minn ... C4 187
Battle Creek, Sask., Can ... H1 155
Battle Creek, Iowa ... B2 180
Battle Creek, Mich ... F5 186
Battle Creek, Nebr ... C8 191
Battle Ground, Ind ... C4 179
Battle Ground, Wash ... D3 210
Battle Harbour, Newf., Can ... B4, h11 152
Battle Lake, Minn ... D3 187
Battle Mountain, Nev ... C5 192
Battleboro, N.C ... A6 197
Battleford, Sask., Can ... E1 155
Battlement, mesa, Colo ... B2 171
Battles, Miss ... D5 188
Battleview, N. Dak ... A3 198
Battonya, Hung ... B5 68
Battrum, Sask., Can ... G1 155
Batu (Kipchak) empire ... 81
Batu, is., Indon ... F1 90
Batu, mtn., Eth ... D4 105
Batuc, Mex ... B3 129
Batumi, Sov. Un ... E7 71
Baturadja, Indon ... F2 90
Baturino, Sov. Un ... B11 73
Baturité, Braz ... B3 138
Bat Yam, Isr ... g9 84
Bauan, Phil ... p13 90
Bauang, Phil ... B6, n13 90
Baubau, Indon ... G6 90
Bauchi, Nig ... D6 103
Baudette, Minn ... B4 187
Baudissin, isl., Bis. Arch ... 115
Baugé, Fr ... D3 58
Bauld, cape, Newf., Can ... C4 152
Baume-les-Dames, Fr ... B2 66
Baunei, It ... D2 67
Baures, Bol ... B3 135
Bauru, Braz ... C3 137
Bautzen, Ger ... B9 61
Bauxite, Ark ... C3, E5 169
Bavaria, Kans ... D6 181
Bavaria, reg., Ger ... D5 60
c. 814 ... 47
c. 1360 ... 48
in 1721 ... 49
in 1815 ... 50
in 1871 ... 51
in 1922–40 ... 53
Bavarian Alps, mts., Aus., Ger ... B7 66
Bavay, Fr ... D3 59
Båven, lake, Swe ... t34 63
Bavispe, Mex ... A3 129
Bawean, isl., Indon ... G4 90
Bawku, Ghana ... D4 103
Bawlf, Alta., Can ... C4 148
Baxley, Ga ... E4 175
Baxter, Colo ... C6 171
Baxter, Iowa ... C4 180
Baxter, Minn ... D4 187
Baxter, Tenn ... C8 205
Baxter, W. Va ... A7, B4 211
Baxter, co., Ark ... A3 169
Baxter Estates, N.Y ... *D2 196
Baxter Springs, Kans ... E9 181
Baxterville, Colo ... D4 171
Baxterville, Miss ... D4 188
Bay, Ark ... B5 169
Bay, Mo ... C6 189
Bay, co., Fla ... G3 174
Bay, co., Mich ... E6 186
Bay, pt., S.C ... G7 203
Bay, Laguna de, lake, Phil ... o13 90
Bay Bulls, Newf., Can ... E5 152
Bay Center, Wash ... C2 210
Bay City, Mich ... E7 186
Bay City, Oreg ... B3 201
Bay City, Tex ... E5, G4 206
Bay City, Wis ... D1 212
Bay de Verde, Newf., Can ... D5 152
Bay Harbour Islands, Fla ... *F3 174
Bay Head, N.J ... C4 194
Bay l'Argent, Newf., Can ... E4 152
Bay Mills, Indian res., Mich ... B6 186
Bay Minette, Ala ... E2 166
Bay of Islands, bay, Newf., Can ... D2 152
Bay of Wales, bay, Ant ... B32 120
Bay Port, Mich ... E7 186
Bay Ridge, Md ... C5 173
Bay Roberts, Newf., Can ... E5 152
Bay St. Louis, Miss ... E2, E4 188
Bay Shore, N.Y ... E3, E7 196
Bay Springs, Miss ... D4 188
Bay Trail, Sask., Can ... E3 155
Bay View, Ala ... E4 166
Bay View, Mich ... C6 186
Bay View, Ohio ... *A5 199
Bay Village, Ark ... B5 169
Bay Village, Ohio ... B1 199
Baya Dzur-Gunen, Mong ... B5 91
Bayambang, Phil ... o13 90
Bayamo, Cuba ... E5 131
Bayamón, P.R ... B6 132
Bayamón, mun., P.R ... B6 132
Bayamón, riv., P.R ... B6 132
Bayan-Aul, Sov. Un ... C9 73
Bayaney, P.R ... B3 132
Bayanga, Cen. Afr. Rep ... E3 104
Bayanovka, Sov. Un ... C8 71
Bayard, Fla ... B5, C6 174
Bayard, Iowa ... C3 180
Bayard, Nebr ... C2 191
Bayard, N. Mex ... E1 195
Bayard, W. Va ... B5 211
Baybay, Phil ... *C6 90
Bayble, Scot ... B2 57
Bayboro, N.C ... B7 197
Bayboro, S.C ... D9 203
Bayburt, Tur ... B13 85
Baydaratskaya, bay, Sov. Un ... B8 118
Bayern, state, Ger ... D6 61, A7 66
Bayeux, Fr ... C3 58
Bayfield, Ont., Can ... D3 153
Bayfield, Colo ... D3 171
Bayfield, Wis ... B3 212
Bayfield, co., Wis ... B2 212
Bayındır, Tur ... C6 69
Baykal, lake, Sov. Un ... D13 71
Baykal, mts., Sov. Un ... D13 71
Baykonur, Sov. Un ... D7 73
Baylis, Ill ... D3 178
Baylor, co., Tex ... C3 206
Baymak, Sov. Un ... C5 73
Bayombong, Phil ... n13 90
Bayonne, Fr ... F3 58
Bayonne, N.J ... B4, E5 194
Bayou Bodcau, res., La ... B2 183
Bayou Cane, La ... *E5 183
Bayou Current, La ... D4 183
Bayou George, Fla ... G3 174
Bayou Goula, La ... B5, D4 183
Bayou LaBatre, Ala ... E1 166
Bayou Meto, Ark ... C4 169
Bayóvar, Peru ... C1 134
Bayport, N.S., Can ... E5 151
Bayport, Minn ... E6, E8 187
Bayport, N.Y ... E3 196
Bayram-Ali, Sov. Un ... C11 86
Bayramiç, Tur ... C6 69
Bayreuth, Ger ... D6 61
Bayrischzell, Ger ... B8 66
Bays, lake, Ont., Can ... B5 153
Bays, mtn., Tenn ... C10 205
Bayshore, Mich ... C5 186
Bayshore Gardens, Fla ... *E4 174
Bayside, Maine ... D4 184
Bayside, Tex ... E4 206
Bayside, Wis ... *E6 212
Baysun, Sov. Un ... B13 86
Bayt Dajan, Jordan ... g12 84
Bayt Jālā, Jordan ... C7, k11 84
Bayt Laḥm (Bethlehem), Jordan ... C7, k11 84
Baytillū, Jordan ... h11 84
Baytown, Tex ... E5, F5 206
Bayview, Idaho ... B2 177
Bayville, N.J ... D4 194
Bayville, N.Y ... F2 172
Baza, Sp ... D4 65
Bazaar, Kans ... D7 181
Bazaruto, isl., Moz ... B6 107
Bazemore, Ala ... B2 166
Bazile Mills, Nebr ... B8 191
Bazine, Kans ... D4 181
Bazman Kuh, mtn., Iran ... G10 86
Baztán, Sp ... A5 65
Beach, Ga ... E4 175
Beach, N. Dak ... C1 198
Beach, Va ... B7 209
Beach, pond, Conn., R.I ... C9 172
Beach City, Ohio ... B6 199
Beach Haven, N.J ... D4 194
Beach Haven, Pa ... D9 202
Beach Haven, inlet, N.J ... D4 194
Beach Haven Crest, N.J ... D4 194
Beach Haven Terrace, N.J. D4 194
Beachburg, Ont., Can ... B8 153
Beachlake, Pa ... C11 202
Beachport, Austl ... G7 111
Beachville, Ont., Can ... D4 153
Beachville, Md ... D5 173
Beachwood, N.J ... D4 194
Beachwood, Ohio ... *A6 199
Beachy, head, Eng ... D8 56
Beacon, Iowa ... C5 180
Beacon, N.Y ... D7 196
Beacon Falls, Conn ... D4 172
Beacon Hill, Fla ... C1, H3 174
Beacon Hill, Wash ... *C3 210
Beaconsfield, Que., Can ... D8 154
Beaconsfield, Iowa ... D3 180
Beadle, Sask., Can ... F1 155
Beadle, co., S. Dak ... C7 204
Beagle, Kans ... D9 181
Beal City, Mich ... E6 186
Bealanana, Malag ... f9 107
Beale, cape, B.C., Can ... E5 149
Beallsville, Ohio ... C6 199
Beals, Ky ... C2 182
Beals, Maine ... D5 184
Beamsville, Ont., Can ... D5 153
Bean City, Fla ... F6 174
Bean Hill, Conn ... C8 172
Bean Lake, Mo ... B3 189
Bean Station, Tenn ... C10 205
Bear, Del ... A6 173
Bear, Idaho ... D2 177
Bear, cave, Mich ... G4 186
Bear, creek, Ala., Miss ... A1 166, A6 188
Bear, creek, Colo ... D8 171
Bear, creek, Kans ... E2 181
Bear, creek, Oreg ... E4 201
Bear, creek, Wyo ... D8 213
Bear, inlet, N.C ... C6 197
Bear, isl., Man., Can ... B3 150
Bear, isl., Wis ... A3 212
Bear, lake, Alta., Can ... B1 148
Bear, lake, B.C., Can ... A4 149
Bear, lake, Man., Can ... B4 150
Bear, lake, Idaho, Utah ... G7 177, A4 207
Bear, lake, Wis ... C2 212
Bear, mtn., Ark ... C5 169
Bear, mtn., Ky ... C5 182
Bear, mtn., Mass ... A3 185
Bear, mtn., Oreg ... D4 201
Bear, mtn., Vt ... E2 208
Bear, riv., Utah, Wyo ... A5 207, D1 213
Bear, swamp, Mass ... E3 185
Bear Cave, mtn., Mo ... E5 189
Bear Creek, Ala ... A2 166
Bear Creek, S. Dak ... C4 204
Bear Creek, Wis ... D5 212
Bear Lake, Mich ... D4 186
Bear Lake, Pa ... C3 202
Bear Lake, co., Idaho ... G7 177
Bear Lodge, mts., Wyo ... A8 213
Bear Paw, mtn., Mont ... B7 190
Bear Pond, mts., Md ... A2 173
Bear River, N.S., Can ... E4 151
Bear River, divide, Wyo ... D2 213
Bear River City, Utah ... B3 207
Bear Spring, Tenn ... A4 205
Bear Town (McComb South), Miss ... D3 188
Bearcreek, Mont ... E7 190
Bearden, Ark ... D3 169
Bearden, Okla ... B5 200
Beardmore, glacier, Ant ... A30 120
Beards Fork, W. Va ... D7 211
Beardsley, Kans ... C2 181
Beardsley, Minn ... E2 187
Beardstown, Ill ... C3 178
Beardstown, Tenn ... B4 205
Bearfort, mtn., N.J ... A4 194
Bearmouth, Mont ... D3 190
Béarn, former prov., Fr ... F3 58
Beartooth, pass, Wyo ... A3 213
Beartooth, range, Mont., Wyo ... E7 190
Beartown, mtn., Va ... B3 209
Beas de Segura, Sp ... C4 65
Beason, Ill ... C4 178
Beata, cape, Dom. Rep ... G8 131
Beaton, B.C., Can ... D9 149
Beatrice, Ala ... D2 166
Beatrice, Nebr ... D9 191
Beatrice, Rh ... A5 107
Beattie, Kans ... C7 181
Beatton, riv., B.C., Can ... A7 149
Beatty, Sask., Can ... E3 155
Beatty, Miss ... B4 188
Beatty, Nev ... G5 192
Beattyville, Ky ... C6 182
Beatyestown, N.J ... B3 194
Beau, lake, Maine ... A3 184
Beaucaire, Fr ... F6 58
Beauce, co., Que., Can ... C7 154
Beauceville, Que., Can ... *C7 154
Beauceville-Est, Que., Can ... C7 154
Beaucoup, creek, La ... B3 183
Beaucourt, Fr ... D7 58
Beaufort, Mala ... D5 90
Beaufort, Mo ... C6 189
Beaufort, N.C ... C7 197
Beaufort, S.C ... G6 203
Beaufort, co., N.C ... B6 197
Beaufort, co., S.C ... G6 203
Beaufort, sea, N.A ... B5 142
Beaufort West, S. Afr ... D3 107
Beaugency, Fr ... D4 58
Beauharnois, Que., Can ... D4, D8 154
Beauharnois, co., Que., Can ... D3 154
Beaulieu, Minn ... C3 187
Beauly, Scot ... C4 57
Beauly, firth, Scot ... C4 57
Beauly, riv., Scot ... C4 57
Beaumaris, Wales ... A3 56
Beaumaris, bay, Wales ... A4 56
Beaumont, Bel ... D4 59
Beaumont, Calif ... F4 170
Beaumont, Newf., Can ... D4 152
Beaumont, Que., Can ... C6 154
Beaumont, Fr ... F4 58
Beaumont, Kans ... E7 181
Beaumont, Miss ... D5 188
Beaumont, Tex ... D5 206
Beaumont Place, Tex ... *E5 206
Beaumont [-sur-Oise], Fr ... E2 59
Beaune, Fr ... D6 58
Beauport, Que., Can ... C9 154
Beaupré, Que., Can ... B7 154
Beaupre, is., Loyalty Is ... 115
Beauraing, Bel ... D4 59
Beauregard, Miss ... D3 188
Beauregard, par., La ... D2 183
Beaurivage, Que., Can ... C6 154
Beausejour, Man., Can ... D3 150
Beauty, Ky ... C7 182
Beauvais, Fr ... C5 58
Beauval, Sask., Can ... B2 155
Beauval, Fr ... D2 59
Beauvallon, Alta., Can ... C5 148
Beaver, Alsk ... B10 167
Beaver, Ark ... *A2 169
Beaver, Kans ... D5 181
Beaver, Ohio ... C5 199
Beaver, Okla ... A1, D4 200
Beaver, Oreg ... B3 201
Beaver, Pa ... E1 202
Beaver, Utah ... E3 207
Beaver (Glen Hedrick), W. Va ... D3, D7 211
Beaver, Wis ... C5 212
Beaver, co., Okla ... A1 200
Beaver, co., Pa ... E1 202
Beaver, co., Utah ... E2 207
Beaver, brook, N.H ... E4 193
Beaver, creek, Sask., Can ... F2 155
Beaver, creek, Iowa ... A7 180
Beaver, creek, Kans ... C2 181
Beaver, creek, Kans., Nebr ... C5 181, D5 191
Beaver, creek, Ky ... C7 182
Beaver, creek, Md ... A2 173
Beaver, creek, Mo ... E5 189
Beaver, creek, Mont ... B9 190
Beaver, creek, Mont ... C12 190
Beaver, creek, N. Dak ... C5 198
Beaver, creek, Okla ... C3 200
Beaver, creek, Tenn ... E11 205
Beaver, creek, Wyo ... B8 213
Beaver, creek, Wyo ... C4 213
Beaver, isl., Mich ... C5 186
Beaver, lake, Nebr ... C3 191
Beaver, lake, Wis ... E5 212
Beaver, res., Ark ... A2 169
Beaver, riv., N.Y ... B5 196
Beaver, riv., Utah ... E2 207
Beaver Bank, N.S., Can ... E6 151

INDEX KEY Each place listed in **Bold-faced Type** has its population listed in the Population tables, pages 230 to 280.
Each country, shown in CAPITAL LETTERS, has its population listed in the World Political Information Tables, pages 6 to 10.
* Does not appear on map; key shows general location.

Beaver Bay, Minn. C7 187
Beaver City, Nebr. D6 191
Beaver Creek, Minn. G2 187
Beaver Creek, mtn., Ala. B3 166
Beaver Crossing, Nebr. D8 191
Beaver Dam, Ariz. A2 168
Beaver Dam, Ind. B5 179
Beaver Dam, Ky. C3 182
Beaver Dam, Wis. E5 212
Beaver Dams, N.Y. C4 196
Beaver Falls, N.Y. B5 196
Beaver Falls, Pa. E1 202
Beaver Meadows, Pa. E10 202
Beaver Point, Colo. A5 171
Beaver Run, res., Pa. E2 202
Beaver Springs, Pa. E7 202
Beaverdale, Pa. F4 202
Beaverdam, Ohio B4 199
Beaverdam, Va. D5 209
Beaverdell, B.C., Can. E8 149
Beaverfoot, riv., B.C., Can. D2 148
Beaverhead, co., Mont. E3 190
Beaverhead, mts., Mont. E3 190
Beaverhead, riv., Mont. E4 190
Beaverhill, lake, Alta., Can. C4 148
Beaverhill, lake, Man., Can. B4 150
Beaverlick, Ky. A7 182
Beaverlodge, Atla., Can. B1 148
Beavertail, pt., R.I. D11 172
Beaverton, Ala. B1 166
Beaverton, Ont., Can. C5 153
Beaverton, Mich. E6 186
Beaverton, Oreg. B2, B4 201
Beavertown, Pa. E7 202
Beaverville, Ill. C6 178
Beawar, India D5 88
Beazley, Arg. A3 136
Bebedouro, Braz. C3 137
Bebington, Eng. *A5 56
Bebra, Ger. C4 61
Bécancour, Que., Can. C5 154
Beccles, Eng. B9 56
Bečej, Yugo. C5 68
Becerreá, Sp. A2 65
Becharof, lake, Alsk. D8 167
Bechyně, Czech. D9 61
Beckemeyer, Ill. E4 178
Beckenham, Eng. *C7 56
Becker, Minn. E5 187
Becker, Miss. B5 188
Becker, co., Minn. D3 187
Becket, Mass. B1 185
Beckett, Okla. C4 200
Beckham, co., Okla. B2 200
Beckley, W. Va. D3, D7 211
Beckleys, Conn. C6 172
Beckum, Ger. B3 61
Beckville, Tex. C5 206
Beckwith, Wyo. D2 213
Beckwith, creek, La. D2 183
Becky, peak, Nev. D7 192
Bedale, Eng. F7 57
Bédarieux, Fr. F5 58
Bedburg, Ger. C1 61
Beddington, Maine D4 184
Bederkesa, Ger. E2 62
Bedford, N.S., Can. E6 151
Bedford, Que., Can. D5 154
Bedford, Eng. B7 56
Bedford, Ind. G5 179
Bedford, Iowa D3 180
Bedford, Ky. B4 182
Bedford, Mass. B5, C2 185
Bedford, Mich. F5 186
Bedford, Mo. B4 189
Bedford, N.H. E3 193
Bedford, N.Y. D7 196
Bedford, Ohio A6, B2 199
Bedford, Pa. F4 202
Bedford, Tex. *C4 206
Bedford (Independent City), Va. D3 209
Bedford, Wyo. C2 213
Bedford, co., Eng. B7 56
Bedford, co., Pa. G4 202
Bedford, co., Tenn. B5 205
Bedford, co., Va. D3 209
Bedford Heights, Ohio *A6 199
Bedford Hills, N.Y. D3 196
Bedford Park, Ill. *B6 178
Bedias, Tex. D5 206
Bédja, Tun. B6 102
Bedlington, Eng. C6 55
Bedminster, N.J. B3 194
Bedourie, Austl. B2 112
Bedrock, Colo. C2 171
Będzin, Pol. g10 70
Bee, Nebr. C8 191
Bee, co., Tex. E4 206
Bee Branch, Ark. B3 169
Bee Ridge, Fla. E4, F2 174
Beebe, Ark. B4 169
Beebe Plain, Vt. A4 208
Beebe River, N.H. C3 193
Beech, fork, Ky. C4 182
Beech Bluff, Tenn. B3 205
Beech Creek, Ky. C2 182
Beech Creek, Pa. D6 202
Beech Grove, Ark. A5 169
Beech Grove, Ind. E5, H8 179
Beech Grove, Ky. C2 182
Beech Island, S.C. E4 203
Beechbottom, W. Va. A4, B2 211
Beecher, Ill. B6 178
Beecher City, Ill. D5 178
Beecher Falls, Vt. A5 208
Beechey, head, B.C., Can. B9 149
Beechgrove, Tenn. B5 205
Beechwood, Mass. D4 185
Beechwood, Mich. *F4 186
Beechwood Village, Ky. *A4 182
Beechy, Sask., Can. G2 155
Beechy, cape, New Britain I. 115
Beecroft, head, Austl. G8 112
Beedeville, Ark. B4 169
Beef, isl., Vir. Is. f16 132
Beek, Neth. D5 59
Beeler, Kans. D3 181
Beelitz, Ger. A7 61
Beemer, Nebr. C9 191
Beer Tuvya, Isr. k10 84
Beersheba, Isr. C6 84
Beersheba Springs, Tenn. D8 205
Beersville, N.B., Can. C4 151
Beeskow, Ger. A9 61
Beesleys Point, N.J. E3 194
Beeston & Stapleford, Eng. *B6 56
Beeton, Ont., Can. C5 153
Beetzendorf, Ger. F5 62
Beeville, Tex. E4 206
Befale, Zaire A3 106
Bega, Austl. H7 112
Begat, cape, N. Cal. 115
Beggs, Okla. B5 200
Bègles, Fr. E3 58
Begovat, Sov. Un. F9 71
Béhague, pt., Fr. Gu. B4 139
Behbehān, Iran F5 86
Behm, canal, Alsk. n24 167
Beilngries, Ger. D6 61
Beilul, Eth. C5 105
Beira, Moz. A5 107
Beira, reg., Port. B2 65
Beirne, Ark. D2 169
Beirut (Beyrouth), Leb. F10 85
Beiseker, Alta., Can. D4 148
Beit Guvrin, Isr. C6 84
Beit Lid, Isr. f10 84
Beit-Shan, Isr. B7 84
Beitbridge, Rh. B5 107
Beith, Scot. E4 57
Beiuş, Rom. B6 68
Beja, Port. C2 65
Bejaia, Alg. B6 102
Béjar, Sp. B3 65
Bejestan, Iran D9 86
Bejou, Minn. C3 187
Bejuco, Pan. F8 130
Bekdash, Sov. Un. E4 73
Békés, Hung. B5 68
Békéscsaba, Hung. B5 68
Bekily, Malag. h9 107
Bel Air, Md. A5 173
Bel Alton, Md. D4 173
Bel-Nor, Mo. A8 189
Bel-Ridge, Mo. *C7 189
Bela, India E8 88
Bela, Pak. C4 87
Bela Crkva, Yugo. C5 68
Bela Vista, Braz. C1 137
Bela Vista, Moz. C5 107
Belaga, Mala. E4 90
Belalcázar, Sp. C3 65
Belanger, riv., Man., Can. C3 150
Belanger, riv., Sask., Can. A2 155
Belas, Port. f9 65
Belawan, Indon. E1, m11 90
Belaya, riv., Sov. Un. C5 73
Belaya Glina, Sov. Un. H13 72
Belaya Tserkov', Sov. Un. G8 72
Belcamp, Md. B5 173
Belcher, Ky. C7 182
Belcher, La. B2 183
Belcher, is., N.W. Ter., Can. E17 143
Belchertown, Mass. B3 185
Belchirag, Afg. D12 86
Belcourt, N. Dak. A6 198
Belden, Miss. A5 188
Belden, Nebr. B8 191
Belden, N. Dak. A3 198
Belding, Mich. E5 186
Belecke, Ger. B3 61
Belém (Pará), Braz. B1 138
Belém, Port. f9 65
Belén, Arg. E2 135
Belen, Miss. A3 188
Belen, N. Mex. C3 195
Belén, Par. D4 135
Belep. is., N. Cal. 115
Belet Uin, Som. E6 105
Belev, Sov. Un. E11 72
Belfair, Wash. B3 210
Belfast, P.E.I., Can. C7 151
Belfast, Maine D3 184
Belfast, N.Y. C2 196
Belfast, N. Ire. C4 55
Belfast, Ohio C4 199
Belfast, Tenn. B5 205
Belfield, N. Dak. C2 198
Bēlfodiya, Eth. C3 105
Belford, Eng. E7 57
Belford, N.J. C4 194
Belford Roxo, Braz. C4 137
Belfort, Fr. D7 58
Belfort, N.Y. B5 196
Belfort, dept., Fr. B2 66
Belfry, Ky. C7 182
Belfry, Mont. E8 190
Belgaum, India E5 87
Belgian Congo, see Zaire, country, Afr.
Belgica, mts., Ant. B16 120
Belgium, Ill. C6 178
Belgium, Wis. E6 212
BELGIUM, country, Eur. D4 59
after World War II 54
Belgorod, Sov. Un. F11 72
Belgorod-Dnestrovskiy, Sov. Un. H8 72
Belgrade, Maine D3 184
Belgrade, Minn. E3 187
Belgrade, Mo. D7 189
Belgrade, Mont. E5 190
Belgrade, Nebr. C7 191
Belgrade (Beograd), Yugo. C5 68
Belgrade Lakes, Maine D3 184
Belgreen, Ala. A2 166
Belhaven, N.C. B7 197
Beli Lom, riv., Bul. D8 68
Belik, New Ire. I. 115
Belington, W. Va. B5 211
Belingwe, Rh. B4 107
Belitung, isl., Indon. F3 90
Belize, riv., Br. Hond., Guat. B3 130
Belk, Ala. B2 166
Belkino, Sov. Un. B11 93
Belknap, Ill. F5 178
Belknap, Iowa D5 180
Belknap, Mont. C1 190
Belknap, co., N.H. C3 193
Belknap, crater, Oreg. C5 201
Belknap, mtn., N.H. C4 193
Belkofski, Alsk. D7 167
Bell, Calif. F2 170
Bell, Fla. C4 174
Bell, co., Ky. D6 182
Bell, co., Tex. D4 206
Bell, isl., Newf., Can. C4 152
Bell, isl., Newf., Can. E5 152
Bell Buckle, Tenn. B5 205
Bell City, La. D3 183
Bell City, Mo. D8 189
Bell Gardens, Calif. *E4 170
Bell Irving, riv., B.C., Can. A3 149
Bell Island, see Wabana, Newf., Can.
Bell Ville, Arg. A4 136
Bella Bella, B.C., Can. C3 149
Bella Coola, B.C., Can. C4 149
Bella Coola, riv., B.C., Can. C4 149
Bella Unión, Ur. E1 137
Bella Villa, Mo. *C7 189
Bella Vista, Arg. E2 135
Bella Vista, Arg. E4 135
Bella Vista, Ark. A1 169
Bella Vista, Par. D4 135
Bellac, Fr. D4 58
Bellagio, It. D6 66
Bellaire, Kans. C5 181
Bellaire, Mich. D5 186
Bellaire, Ohio C7 199
Bellaire, Tex. F5 206
Bellamy, Ala. C1 166
Bellary, India E6 87
Bellbrook, Ohio C3 199
Bellburn, W. Va. C4 211
Belle, Mo. C6 189
Belle, W. Va. C3, C6 211
Belle, bay, Newf., Can. E4 152
Belle, isl., Newf., Can. C4 152
Belle, isl., Fr. D2 58
Belle, riv., La. C5 183
Belle, riv., Mich. E2 153
Belle Center, Ohio B4 199
Belle Chasse, La. C7, E6 183
Belle Fourche, S. Dak. C2 204
Belle Fourche, res., S. Dak. C2 204
Belle Fourche, riv., S. Dak., Wyo. C2 204, A7 213
Belle Glade, Fla. F6 174
Belle Haven, Va. D7 209
Belle Isle, Fla. D5 174
Belle Isle, strait, Newf., Can. C3 152
Belle Mead, N.J. C3 194
Belle Meade, Tenn. *A5 205
Belle Mina, Ala. A3 166
Belle Plaine, Sask., Can. G3 155
Belle Plaine, Iowa C5 180
Belle Plaine, Kans. E6 181
Belle Plaine, Minn. F5 187
Belle Rive, Ill. E5 178
Belle River, Ont., Can. E2 153
Belle Rose, La. B5, D4 183
Belle Valley, Ohio C6 199
Belle Vernon, Pa. F2 202
Belleair, Fla. E1 174
Belleair Beach, Fla. *E4 174
Bellechasse, co., Que., Can. C7 154
Belledune, N.B., Can. B4 151
Bellefont, Kans. E4 181
Bellefontaine, Miss. B4 188
Bellefontaine, Ohio B4 199
Bellefontaine Neighbors, Mo. *A8 189
Bellefonte, Ark. A2 169
Bellefonte, Del. A7 173
Bellefonte, Pa. E6 202
Bellegarde-sur-Valserine, Fr. C1 66
Belleisle Creek, N.B., Can. D4 151
Bellemeade, Ky. *B4 182
Belleoram, Newf., Can. E4 152
Belleplain, N.J. E3 194
Bellerive, Que., Can. E8 154
Bellerose, N.Y. *E3 196
Belleterre, Que., Can. *B2 154
Belleview, Fla. C4 174
Belleville, Ark. B2 169
Belleville, N.S., Can. F4 151
Belleville, Ont., Can. C7 153
Belleville, Ill. E4 178
Belleville, Kans. C6 181
Belleville, Mich. F7 186
Belleville, N.J. B4, D5 194
Belleville, N.Y. B4 196
Belleville, Pa. E6 202
Belleville, R.I. C11 172
Belleville, W. Va. B3 211
Belleville, Wis. F4 212
Belleville North, Mich. *A7 186
Belleville [-sur-Saône], Fr. D6 58
Bellevue, Alta., Can. E3 148
Bellevue, Idaho F4 177
Bellevue, Ill. *C4 178
Bellevue, Iowa B7 180
Bellevue, Ky. A7 182
Bellevue, Md. C5 173
Bellevue, Mich. F5 186
Bellevue, Nebr. C10, E3 191
Bellevue, Ohio A5 199
Bellevue, Pa. B5, F1 202
Bellevue, Tenn. A5, E9 205
Bellevue, Tex. C3 206
Bellevue, Wash. D2 210
Bellewood, Ky. *B4 182
Belley, Fr. E6 58
Bellflower, Calif. *F2 170
Bellflower, Ill. C5 178
Bellflower, Mo. C6 189
Bellglade Camp, Fla. *F6 176
Bellingham, Eng. E6 57
Bellingham, Mass. B5, E1 185
Bellingham, Minn. E2 187
Bellingham, Wash. A3 210
Bellingshausen, sea, Ant. C4 120
Bellinzona, Switz. C5 66
Bellis, Atla., Can. B4 148
Bellivela, Lib. E3 103
Bellmawr, N.J. D2 194
Bellmead, Tex. *D4 206
Bellmont, Ill. E6 178
Bellmore, Ind. E3 179
Bellmore, N.Y. G2 172
Bello, Col. B2 133
Bello, Cuba h11 131
Bellona, isl., Sol. Is. 115
Bellows Falls, Vt. E4 208
Belloy, Alta., Can. B1 148
Bellport, N.Y. F5 172
Bells, Tenn. B2 205
Bells, creek, W. Va. C6 211
Bells Corners, Ont., Can. A9 153
Bellsburg, Tenn. A4 205
Belltown, Del. C7 173
Belltown, Tenn. D9 205
Belluno, It. A4 67
Bellville, Ga. D5 175
Bellville, Ohio B5 199
Bellville, Tex. E4 206
Bellvue, Colo. A5 171
Bellwood, Ala. D4 166
Bellwood, Ill. F2 178
Bellwood, Nebr. C8 191
Bellwood, Pa. E5 202
Belmar, N.J. C4 194
Bélmez, Sp. C3 65
Belmond, Iowa B4 180
Belmont, Calif. B5 170
Belmont, Man., Can. E2 150
Belmont, N.S., Can. D6 151
Belmont, Ont., Can. E3 153
Belmont, Kans. E6 181
Belmont, La. C2 183
Belmont, Mass. C2 185
Belmont, Miss. A5 188
Belmont, Mont. D7 190
Belmont, N.H. D4 193
Belmont, N.Y. C2 196
Belmont, N.C. B2 197
Belmont, Ohio B6 199
Belmont, Tex. B4 206
Belmont, Vt. E3 208
Belmont, Wash. B8 210
Belmont, W. Va. B3 211
Belmont, Wis. F3 212
Belmont, co., Ohio C6 199
Belmonte, Braz. E3 138
Belmopan, Br. Hond. B3 130
Belmore, Ohio A4 199
Belo, Malag. g8 107
Belo Horizonte, Braz. E2 138
Beloeil, Que., Can. D4 154
Belogorsk, Sov. Un. D15 71
Beloit, Iowa A1 180
Beloit, Kans. C5 181
Beloit, Ohio B7 199
Beloit, Wis. F4 212
Beloit West, Wis. *F4 212
Belokany, Sov. Un. B16 85
Belomorsk, Sov. Un. C14 41
Belopolye, Sov. Un. F10 72
Beloretsk, Sov. Un. C5 73
Belot, Cuba h12 131
Belovo, Sov. Un. *D11 71
Beloye, lake, Sov. Un. A11 72
Belozersk, Sov. Un. B11 72
Belper, Eng. A6 56
Belpre, Kans. E4 181
Belpre, Ohio C6 199
Belspring, Va. D2 209
Belt, Mont. C6 190
Belt, creek, Mont. C6 190
Belted, range, Nev. F5 192
Belterra, Braz. C4 139
Belton, Mo. C3 189
Belton, S.C. B3 203
Belton, Tex. D4 206
Belton, res., Tex. D4 206
Beltrami, Minn. C2 187
Beltrami, co., Minn. B3 187
Beltsville, Md. B4 173
Bel'tsy, Sov. Un. H6 72
Belua, Bougainville I. 115
Belukha, mtn., Sov. Un. E11 71
Beluran, Mala. D5 90
Belva, Okla. A2 200
Belvedere, Calif. *D2 170
Belvedere, S.C. D4 203
Belvedere Marittimo, It. E5 67
Belvidere, Ill. A5 178
Belvidere, Kans. E4 181
Belvidere, Nebr. D8 191
Belvidere, N.J. B2 194
Belvidere, N.C. A7 197
Belvidere, S. Dak. D4 204
Belvidere, Tenn. B5 205
Belvidere, mtn., Vt. B3 208
Belvidere Center, Vt. B3 208
Belview, Minn. F3 187
Belvue, Kans. C7 181
Belwood, Ont., Can. D4 153
Belyando, riv., Austl. D8 110
Belyy, Sov. Un. D9 72
Belyy, isl., Sov. Un. B9 71
Belzig, Ger. A7 61
Belzoni, Miss. B3 188
Bembezar, riv., Sp. D3 65
Bement, Ill. D5 178
Bemidji, Minn. C4 187
Bemis, S. Dak. C9 204
Bemis, Tenn. B3 205
Bemis, W. Va. C5 211
Bemiss, Ga. F3 175
Bemus Point, N.Y. C1 196
Ben Avon, Pa. *E1 202
Ben Bolt, Tex. F3 206
Ben Cat, Viet. G7 89
Ben Davis, Ind. H7 179
Ben Davis, pt., N.J. E2 194
Ben Gardane, Tun. C7 102
Ben Goi, bay, Viet. F8 89
Ben Hill, Ga. B5 175
Ben Hill, co., Ga. E3 175
Ben Lomond, Ark. D1 169
Ben Lomond, Calif. C5 170
Bena, Minn. C4 187
Bena Dibele, Zaire B3 106
Benabarre, Sp. A6 65
Benadir, reg., Som. E5 105
Benalla, Austl. H5 112
Benalto, Alta., Can. C3 148
Benanee, Austl. G4 112
Beňatky nad Jizerou, Czech. n18 70
Benavente, Sp. A3 65
Benavides, Tex. F3 206
Benbecula, isl., Scot. C1 57
Benbrook, Tex. *C4 206
Benbush, W. Va. B5 211
Benchland, Mont. C7 190
Bend, Oreg. C5 201
Bendale, S.C. C6 203
Bendeleben, mtn., Alsk. B7 167
Bender Beila, Som. D7 105
Bendersville, Pa. G7 202
Bendery, Sov. Un. H7 72
Bendigo, Austl. H5 112
Bendorf, Ger. C2 61
Bene Beraq, Isr. g10 84
Benedict, Kans. E8 181
Benedict, Md. C4 173
Benedict, Nebr. C8 191
Benedict, N. Dak. B4 198
Benedict, Va. B2 209
Benedicta, Maine C4 184
Benenitra, Malag. h9 107
Beneraird, mtn., Scot. E4 57
Benešov, Czech. D3, o18 70
Bénestroff, Fr. F6 59
Benevento, It. D5 67
Benevolence, Ga. E2 175
Benewah, co., Idaho B2 177
Benezett, Pa. D5 202
Benfeld, Fr. A3 66
Benfleet, Eng. C8 56
Bengal, Okla. C6 200
Bengal, reg., Bngl., India D8 87
Bengal, bay, India F8 87
Bengasi (Banghāzi), Libya C4 101
Bengkalis, Indon. E2 90
Bengkulu, Indon. F2 90
Bengough, Sask., Can. H3 155
Benguela, Ang. D1 106
Benguela, dist., Ang. D1 106
Benguerir, Mor. H3 64
Benham, Ky. D7 182
Beni, Zaire A4 106
Beni, Nig. D7 103
Beni, dept., Bol. B2 135
Beni, riv., Bol. B2 135
Beni Abbes, Alg. C4 102
Beni Ounif, Alg. C4 102
Beni Saf, Alg. B4 102
Benicarló, Sp. B6 65
Benicia, Calif. B5 170
Benicito, riv., Bol. B3 135
Benin City, Nig. E6 103
Benisa, Sp. C6 65
Benito, Man., Can. D1 150
Benjamin, Tex. C3 206
Benjamin Constant, Braz. B3 134
Benjes, Tenn. E8 205
Benkelman, Nebr. D4 191
Benkovac, Yugo. C2 68
Benld, Ill. D4 178
Bennane, head, Scot. E3 57
Benndale, Miss. E5 188
Bennet, Nebr. D9, F2 191
Bennett, B.C., Can. E6 144
Bennett, Colo. B6 171
Bennett, Iowa C7 180
Bennett, N. Mex. E6 195
Bennett, N.C. B4 197
Bennett, Wis. B2 212
Bennett, co., S. Dak. D4 204
Bennett, creek, Md. B3 173
Bennett, isl., Sov. Un. B18 71
Bennett, lake, Man., Can. C3 150
Bennetts, Ind. C5 179
Bennettsville, S.C. B8 203
Bennetsville Southwest, S.C. *B8 203
Bennington, Idaho G7 177
Bennington, Kans. C6 181
Bennington, Nebr. D3 191
Bennington, N.H. D3 193
Bennington, Okla. C5 200
Bennington, Vt. F2 208
Bennington, co., Vt. F2 208
Benns Church, Va. B6 209
Benq e Viejo, Br Hond. B3 130
Bennt Jbail, Leb. A7 84
Benoit, Miss. B2 188
Benoit, Wis. B2 212
Benoni, S. Afr. *C4 107
Benoud, Alg. C5 102
Bénoué, riv., Cam. D2 104
Benq e Viejo, Br Hond. B2 130
Bens, pt., N.Y. E8 172
Bens Run, W. Va. B3 211
Bensané, Guinea D2 103
Bensberg, Ger. C2 61
Bensenville, Ill. B6, E2 178
Bensheim, Ger. D3 61
Benson, Ariz. F5 168
Benson, Sask., Can. H4 155
Benson, Ill. C4 178
Benson, La. C2 183
Benson, Md. A5 173
Benson, Minn. E3 187
Benson, N.C. B5 197
Benson, Pa. *F4 202
Benson, Vt. D2 208
Benson, co., N. Dak. A6 198
Benson Mines, N.Y. A6 196
Bent, N. Mex. D4 195
Bent, co., Colo. D7 171
Bentheim, Ger. A2 61
Bentiu, Sud. D2 105
Bentley, Alta., Can. C3 148
Bentley, Iowa C2 180
Bentley, Kans. B5, E6 181
Bentley, La. C3 183
Bentley, Mich. E6 186
Bentley, N. Dak. C3 198
Bentley Creek, Pa. C8 202
Bentley Springs, Md. A4 173
Bentleyville, Pa. F1 202
Benton, Ark. C3, E5 169
Benton, Calif. D4 170
Benton, N.B., Can. D2 151
Benton, Ill. E5 178
Benton, Ind. A6 179
Benton, Iowa D3 180
Benton, Kans. B6, E6 181
Benton, Ky. B2 183
Benton, La. B2 183
Benton, Maine D3 184
Benton, Miss. C3 188
Benton, Mo. D8 189
Benton, N.H. B3 193
Benton, Pa. D9 202
Benton, Tenn. D9 205
Benton, Tex. *E3 206
Benton, Wis. F3 212
Benton, co., Ark. A1 169
Benton, co., Ind. C3 179
Benton, co., Iowa B5 180
Benton, co., Minn. E4 187
Benton, co., Miss. A4 188
Benton, co., Mo. C4 189
Benton, co., Oreg. C3 201
Benton, co., Tenn. A3 205
Benton, co., Wash. C6 210
Benton City, Mo. B6 189
Benton City, Wash. C6 210
Benton Harbor, Mich. F4 186
Benton Heights, Mich. *F4 186
Benton Ridge, Ohio A4 199
Benton Station, Alta., Can. D5 148
Bentonia, Miss. C3 188
Bentonville, Ark. A1 169
Bentonville, Ohio D4 199
Bentonville, Va. C4 209
Bentree, W. Va. C7 211
Benue, riv., Nig. E6 103
Benwood, W. Va. A4, B2 211
Benzie, co., Mich. D4 186
Benzonia, Mich. D4 186
Beo, Indon. E7 90
Beograd, see Belgrade, Yugo.
Béoumi, I.C. E3 103
Beowawe, Nev. C5 192
Beppu, Jap. J5 93
Berach, riv., India E5 88
Berando, Guadalcanal I. 115
Berat, Alb. B2 69
Berber, Sud. B3 105
Berbera, Som. C6 105
Berbérati, Cen. Afr. Rep. E3 104
Berberia, isl., P.R. D5 132
Berbice, riv., Guy. A3 139
Berceto, It. E6 66
Berchem, Eng. C4 59
Berchogur, Sov. Un. D5 73
Berchtesgaden, Ger. E6 60
Berck-sur-Mer, Fr. B4 58
Berclair, Miss. B3 188
Berclair, Tex. E4 206
Berdichev, Sov. Un. G7 72
Berdyansk, Sov. Un. H11 72
Berea, Ky. C5 182
Berea, Nebr. B3 191
Berea, N. Dak. C7 198
Berea, Ohio A6 199
Berebere, Indon. E7 90
Beregovo, Sov. Un. G4 72
Bereku, Tan. B6 106
Berenice, ruins, Eg. E7 101
Berens, isl., Man., Can. C3 150
Berens River, Man., Can. C3, D5 150
Beresford, Man., Can. E1 150
Beresford, N.B., Can. *B4 151
Beresford, S. Dak. D9 204
Berettyóújfalu, Hung. B5 68
Berezhany, Sov. Un. G5 72
Berezina, riv., Sov. Un. E7 72
Berezna, Sov. Un. F8 72
Berezniki, Sov. Un. B5 73
Berezovo, Sov. Un. C9 71
Berg: in 1812 51
Berg, Nor. q27 63
Berga, Sp. A6 65
Berga, Swe. B8 62
Bergama, Tur. C6 69
Bergamasque Alps, mts., It. C5 66
Bergamo, It. B2 67
Bergedorf, Ger. B5 60
Bergen, see Mons, Bel.
Bergen, Ger. A6 60
Bergen [bei Celle], Ger. F3 62
Bergen, N.Y. B3 196

INDEX KEY Each place listed in **Bold-faced Type** has its population listed in the Population tables, pages 230 to 280. Each country, shown in CAPITAL LETTERS, has its population listed in the World Political Information Table, pages 6 to 10. * Does not appear on map; key shows general location.

Bergen, N. Dak. A5 198
Bergen, Nor. G1 63
Bergen, co., N.J. B4 194
Bergen aan Zee, Neth. B4 59
Bergen op Zoom, Neth. C4 59
Bergenfield, N.J. B5, D5 194
Berger, Mo. C6 189
Bergerac, Fr. E4 58
Bergheim, Tex. A3 206
Bergholz, Ohio B7 199
Bergisch Gladbach, Ger. C2 61
Bergland, Ont., Can. B4 187
Bergland, Mich. A5 186
Bergman, Ark. A2 169
Bergoo, W. Va. C4 211
Bergton, Va. C4 209
Berguent, Mor. C4 102
Bergzabern, Ger. D3 61
Berhampore, India E12 88
Berhampur, India H10 88
Bering, sea, Alsk. D3 167
Bering, strait, Alsk. C5 167
Berino, N. Mex. E3 195
Berislav, Sov. Un. H9 72
Berja, Sp. D4 65
Berkeley, Calif. B5, D2 170
Berkeley, Ont., Can. C4 153
Berkeley, Ill. *F2 178
Berkeley, Ky. B2 182
Berkeley, Mo. A8 189
Berkeley, R.I. B11 172
Berkeley, W. Va. B7 211
Berkeley, co., S.C. E8 203
Berkeley, co., W. Va. B6 211
Berkeley, cape, Ec. g5 134
Berkeley Heights, N.J. B4 194
Berkeley Springs (Bath), W. Va. B6 211
Berkey, Ohio A1, A4 199
Berkley, Iowa C3 180
Berkley, Mass. C5 185
Berkley, Mich. A7, F7 186
Berkner, isl., Ant. B7 120
Berkovitsa, Bul. D6 68
Berks, co., Eng. C6 56
Berks, co., Pa. F9 202
Berkshire, Mass. A1 185
Berkshire, N.Y. C4 196
Berkshire, Vt. B3 208
Berkshire, co., Mass. B1 185
Berkshire, hills, Mass. B1 185
Berland, riv., Alta., Can. C1 148
Berleburg, Ger. B3 61
Berlengas, is., Port. C1 65
Berlin, Conn. C6 172
Berlin, Ga. E3 175
Berlin, Ger. B6 60
Berlin, East, Ger. *B6 60
Berlin, West, Ger. *B6 60
Berlin, Md. D7 173
Berlin, Mass. B4 185
Berlin, N.H. *B4 193
Berlin, N.J. D3 194
Berlin, N.Y. C7 196
Berlin, N. Dak. C7 198
Berlin, Ohio B6 199
Berlin, Okla. B2 200
Berlin, Pa. G4 202
Berlin, Vt. C3 208
Berlin, Wis. E5 212
Berlin, mtn., Mass. A1 185
Berlin, mtn., Nev. E4 192
Berlin, res., Ohio A6 199
Berlin Heights, Ohio A5 199
Bermejo, riv., Arg. E4 135
Bermeo, Sp. A4 65
BERMUDA, Br. dep., N.A D15 159
Bermuda Hundred, Va. C7 209
Bern, Kans. C8 181
Bern, Switz. C3 66
Bern, canton, Switz. B3 66
Bernadin, cape, Lifou I. 115
Bernalillo, N. Mex. B3, G5 195
Bernalillo, co., N. Mex. C3 195
Bernard, Iowa B7 180
Bernard, Maine D4 184
Bernard, is., Truk. 114
Bernard, lake, Ont., Can. B5 153
Bernardston, Mass. A2 185
Bernardsville, N.J. B3 194
Bernasconi, Arg. B4 136
Bernau, Ger. B6 60
Bernau, Ger. B8 66
Bernay, Fr. C4 58
Bernburg, Ger. B6 61
Berndorf, Aus. E8 60
Berne, Ind. C8 179
Berne, N.Y. C6 196
Berneray, isl., Scot. C1 57
Bernese Alps, mts., Switz. C3 66
Bernice, La. B3 183
Bernice, Okla. *A7 200
Bernie, Mo. E8 189
Bernina, mtn., Switz. C5 66
Bernina, pass, Switz. C6 66
Bernstadt, Ky. C5 182
Bernville, Pa. F9 202
Beroroha, Malag. h9 107
Beroun, Czech. D3, o17 70
Beroun, Minn. E6 187
Berounka, riv., Czech. o17 70
Berre, Fr. F6 58
Berrechid, Mor. C3 102
Berrien, co., Ga. E3 175
Berrien, co., Mich. G4 186
Berrien Springs, Mich. F4 186
Berry, Ala. B2 166
Berry, Ky. B5 182
Berry, former prov., Fr. D4 58
Berry Hill, Tenn. E9 205
Berry Mills, Maine D2 184
Berrydale, Fla. G2 174
Berryessa, lake, Calif. A5 170
Berryessa Lake, res., Calif. C2 170
Berryman, Mo. D6 189
Berryton, Ga. B1 175
Berryville, Ark. A2 169
Berryville, Va. B5 209
Bersenbrück, Ger. B7 59
Bershad, Sov. Un. G7 72
Bertha, Minn. D3 187
Berthier, co., Que., Can. C4 154
Berthierville, Que., Can. C4 154
Berthold, N. Dak. A4 198
Berthoud, Colo. A5 171
Berthoud, pass, Colo. B5 171
Bertie, N.C. *B7 197
Bertie, co., N.C. A6 197
Bertram, Tex. D3 206
Bertrand, Mo. E8 189
Bertrand, Nebr. D6 191
Bertrand, N.B., Can. *B5 151
Bertrandville, La. C7, E5 183
Bertrix, Bel. E5 59
Berwick, N.S., Can. D5 151
Berwick, Ill. C3 178
Berwick, Iowa A7 180
Berwick, La. C5, E4 183
Berwick, Maine E2 184
Berwick, N. Dak. A5 198
Berwick, Pa. D9 202
Berwick, co., Scot. E6 57
Berwick-on-Tweed, Eng. C6 55
Berwind, W. Va. D3 211
Berwyn, Alta., Can. A2 148
Berwyn, Ill. F2 178
Berwyn, Nebr. C6 191
Berwyn, Pa. A10 202
Berwyn Heights, Md. *C4 173
Beryl, Utah F2 207
Besa, Indon. E7 90
Besalampy, Malag. g8 107
Besançon, Fr. D7 58, B2 66
Beskides, mts., Czech., Pol. D5 70
Besnard, lake, Sask., Can. B3 155
Besni, Tur. D11 85
Bessarabia: in 1940 53
in 1950 54
Bessèges, Fr. E6 58
Bessemer, Ala. B3, E4 166
Bessemer, Mich. A5 186
Bessemer, Pa. E1 202
Bessemer City, N.C. B2 197
Bessie, Okla. B3 200
Bessmay, Tex. D6 206
Best, Tex. D2 206
Bestobe, Sov. Un. C8 73
Betafo, Malag. g9 107
Betanzos, Sp. A1 65
Bétaré Oya, Cam. D2 104
Bethalto, Ill. E3 178
Bethanie, S.W. Afr. E2 106
Bethany, Ont., Can. C6 153
Bethany, Conn. D5 172
Bethany, Ill. D5 178
Bethany, see Al 'Ayzarīyah, Jordan
Bethany, La. B1 183
Bethany, Mo. A3 189
Bethany, Ohio C2 199
Bethany, Okla. B4 200
Bethany, W. Va. B2 211
Bethany Beach, Del. C7 173
Bethel, Alsk. C7 167
Bethel, Conn. D3 172
Bethel, Del. C6 173
Bethel, Ky. B6 182
Bethel, Maine D2 184
Bethel, Minn. E5 187
Bethel, Mo. B5 189
Bethel, N.C. B6 197
Bethel, Ohio D3 199
Bethel, Okla. C7 200
Bethel (Bethel Park), Pa. *F1 202
Bethel, Pa. F9 202
Bethel, Vt. D3 208
Bethel Springs, Tenn. B3 205
Bethera, S.C. E8 203
Bethesda, Ark. B4 169
Bethesda, Md. C1, C3 173
Bethesda, Ohio B6 199
Bethesda, Wales A3 56
Bethlehem, Conn. C4 172
Bethlehem, Ga. C3 175
Bethlehem, Ind. G7 179
Bethlehem, see Bayt Laḥm, Jordan
Bethlehem, Md. C6 173
Bethlehem, N.H. B3 193
Bethlehem, Pa. E11 202
Bethlehem, S. Afr. C4 107
Bethlehem, W. Va. B2 211
Bethpage, N.Y. G3 172
Bethpage, Tenn. A5 205
Bethulie, S. Afr. D4 107
Bethune, Sask., Can. G3 155
Bethune, Colo. B8 171
Béthune, Fr. D2 59
Bethune, S.C. C7 203
Betioky, Malag. h8 107
Betoota, Austl. B3 112
Betpak-Dala, Sov. Un. D8 73
Betpak-Dala (Golodnaya Steppe), steppe, Sov. Un. D7 73
Betroka, Malag. h9 107
Betsiamites, Que., Can. B3 154
Betsie, pt., Mich. D4 186
Betsy Layne, Ky. C7 182
Bette, peak, Libya E3 101
Bettendorf, Iowa C7, D7 180
Betteravia, Calif. E3 170
Betterton, Md. B5 173
Bettiah, India D10 88
Bettles Field, Alsk. B9 167
Bettsville, Ohio A4 199
Bettyhill, Scot. B4 57
Betul, India G6 88
Betwa, riv., India E7 88
Betzdorf, Ger. C2 61
Beuel, Ger. C2 61
Beulah, Ala. C4 166
Beulah, Man., Can. D1 150
Beulah, Colo. C6 171
Beulah, Mich. D4 186
Beulah, Miss. B3 188
Beulah, N. Dak. B4 198
Beulah, Wyo. A8 213
Beulah, lake, Miss. B2 188
Beulaville, N.C. C6 197
Bevans, N.J. A3 194
Beverley, Sask., Can. G1 155
Beverley, Eng. D6 55
Beverly, Kans. C6 181
Beverly, Ky. D6 182
Beverly, Mass. A6, C3 185
Beverly, N.J. C3 194
Beverly, Ohio C6 199
Beverly, W. Va. C5 211
Beverly, head, Newf., Can. D2 152
Beverly Farms, Mass. C4 185
Beverly Hills, Calif. F2 170
Beverly Hills, Mich. *F7 186
Beverly Hills, Mo. *C7 189
Beverly Park, Wash. B3 210
Beverly Park South, Wash. *B3 210
Beverly Shores, Ind. A4 179
Beverstedt, Ger. E2 62
Beverwijk, Neth. B4 59
Bevier, Mo. B5 189
Bewdley, Ont., Can. C6 153
Bexar, Ala. A1 166
Bexar, co., Tex. E3 206
Bexhill-on-Sea, Eng. D8 56
Bexley, Eng. *C8 56
Bexley, Miss. E5 188
Bexley, Ohio C2 199
Beyer, Pa. E3 202
Beykoz, Tur. B7 69
Beyla, Guinea E3 103
Beypazari, Tur. B8 85
Beyram, Iran H6 86
Beyrouth, see Beirut, Leb.
Beyşehir, Tur. D8 85
Beyşehir, lake, Tur. D8 85
Bezau, Aus. B5 66
Bezerros, Braz. C3, k6 138
Bezhetsk, Sov. Un. C11 72
Bezhitsa, Sov. Un. E10 72
Béziers, Fr. F5 58
Bezmer, Bul. D8 68
Bezons, Fr. g9 58
Bezwada, see Vijayavada, India
Bhadra, India C5 88
Bhadrachalam, India I8 88
Bhadrakh, India G11 88
Bhadravati, India *F6 87
Bhag, Pak. C4 87
Bhagalpur, India C8 87, E11 88
Bhakkar, Pak. B5 87
Bhamo, Bur. D10 87
Bhandara, India G7 88
Bharatpur, India D6 88
Bharatpur, India F8 88
Bhatinda, India B5 88
Bhatpara, India D8 87, F12 88
Bhavnagar, India D5 87, G4 88
Bhawani-Patna, India H9 88
Bheigeir, mtn., Scot. E2 57
Bhilainagar, India *D7 87
Bhilsa, India F6 88
Bhima, riv., India E6 87
Bhind, India D7 88
Bhiwani, India C6 88
Bhola, Bngl. F13 88
Bhopal, India D6 87, F6 88
Bhopalpatnam, India H8 88
Bhor, India H4 88
Bhreac, mtn., Scot. D3 57
Bhubaneswar, India D8 87
Bhuj, India F2 88
Bhusawal, India G5 88
BHUTAN, country, Asia C9 87
Biābānak, Iran E7 86
Biaboye, Zaire A4 106
Biafra, bight, Afr. E1 104
Biak, is., Indon. F9 90
Biala, Eg. C3 84
Biała, riv., Pol. h10 70
Biała Podlaska, Pol. B7 70
Biała Przemsza, riv., Pol. g11 70
Białogard, Pol. A4 70
Białowieza, Pol. B7 70
Białystok, Pol. B7 70
Bianco, It. E6 67
Biang, Indon. E7 90
Biarritz, Fr. F3 58
Biasca, Switz. C4 66
Bibā, Eg. D6 101
Bibai, Jap. E10 93
Bibb, co., Ala. C2 166
Bibb, co., Ga. D3 175
Bibb City, Ga. D2 175
Biberach, Ger. D4 60
Bibi, N. Gui. k12 111
Bible Grove, Ill. E5 178
Bic, Que., Can. A9 154
Bic, isl., Que., Can. A9 154
Bicester, Eng. C6 56
Biche, lake, Atla., Can. B4 148
Bichl, Ger. B7 66
Bickerton, cape, Ant. C26 120
Bickett Knob, mtn., W. Va. D4 211
Bickle Knob, mtn., W. Va. C5 211
Bickleton, Wash. D5 210
Bickmore, W. Va. C7 211
Bicknell, Ind. G3 179
Bicknell, Utah E4 207
Bicske, Hung. B4 68
Bida, Nig. E6 103
Bidar, India I6 88
Biddeford, Maine E2, E4 184
Biddiyā, Jordan g11 84
Biddle, Mont. E11 190
Bidean Nam Bian, mtn., Scot. D3 57
Bideford, Eng. C3 56
Bideford, bay, Eng. C3 56
Bidon Cinq, Alg. E5 102
Bidwell, Ohio D5 199
Bidwell, mtn., Oreg. A3 170
Bie-Cuando Cubango, dist., Ang. D2 106
Bieber, Calif. B3 170
Biebrza, riv., Pol. B7 70
Biedenkopf, Ger. C3 61
Biel, Switz. B3 66
Biel (Bienne), lake, Switz. B3 66
Bielawa, Pol. C4 70
Bield, Man., Can. D1 150
Bielefeld, Ger. A3 61
Biella, It. B2 67
Bielsk Podlaski, Pol. B7 70
Bielsko-Biała, Pol. D5, h10 70
Bien Hoa, Viet. G7 89
Bienfait, Sask., Can. H4 155
Bienne, see Biel, lake, Switz.
Bienville, La. B3 183
Bienville, par., La. B2 183
Bienville, lake, Que., Can. A2 154
Bierawka, riv., Pol. g9 70
Bieruń Nowy, Pol. g10 70
Bieruń Stary, Pol. g10 70
Biese, riv., Ger. F5 62
Bietigheim, Ger. E4 61
Bièvre, riv., Fr. g9 58
Bièvres, Fr. g9 58
Biferno, riv., It. D5 67
Big, bayou, Ark. D4 169
Big, creek, Ark. C5 169
Big, creek, B.C., Can. D6 149
Big, creek, Ind. G7 179
Big, creek, Ind. H2 179
Big, creek, Kans. D4 181
Big, creek, La. B4 183
Big, creek, Mo. A3 189
Big, creek, Mo. C3 189
Big, creek, Tenn. B8 205
Big, isl., N.W. Ter., Can. D18 143
Big, lake, Maine C5 184
Big, ridge, Ala. A4 166
Big, riv., Sask., Can. D2 155
Big, riv., Mo. C7 189
Big A, mtn., Va. B3 209
Big Arm, Mont. C2 190
Big Averill, lake, Vt. B5 208
Big Bald, mtn., N.B., Can. B3 151
Big Bald, mtn., Ga. B2 175
Big Bald, mtn., N.C. C3 197
Big Bald, mtn., Tenn. D11 205
Big Baldy, mtn., Idaho E3 177
Big Baldy, mtn., Mont. D6 190
Big Bay, Mich. B3 186
Big Bay de Noc, bay, Mich. C4 186
Big Bear City, Calif. E5 170
Big Bear Lake, Calif. *E5 170
Big Beaver, Sask., Can. H3 155
Big Beaver, Pa. *E1 202
Big Belt, mts., Mont. D5 190
Big Bend, Calif. B3 170
Big Bend, N. Dak. B4 198
Big Bend, Wis. F1 212
Big Bend, dam, S. Dak. C6 204
Big Bend, nat. park, Tex. E1 206
Big Birch, lake, Minn. E4 187
Big Black, riv., Miss. C3 188
Big Blue, riv., Nebr. D9 191
Big Bow, Kans. E2 181
Big Bushkill, creek, Pa. A2 194
Big Butt, mtn., Tenn. C11 205
Big Cabin, Okla. A6 200
Big Cabin, creek, Okla. A6 200
Big Cane, La. D4 183
Big Canyon, Okla. C4 200
Big Canyon, creek, Tex. D1 206
Big Clifty, Ky. C3 182
Big Coal, riv., W. Va. C3, C5 211
Big Corney, creek, Ark., La. D3 169
Big Cow, creek, Kans. D5 181
Big Creek, Calif. D4 170
Big Creek, B.C., Can. D6 149
Big Creek, Idaho D3 177
Big Creek, Ky. C6 182
Big Creek, W. Va. C2 211
Big Creek, lake, Ala. E1 166
Big Creek, peak, Idaho E5 177
Big Cypress, Indian res., Fla. F5 174
Big Cypress, swamp, Fla. F5 174
Big Darby, res., Ohio C1 199
Big Delta, Alsk. C10 167
Big Dry, creek, Mont. C10 190
Big Duke, dam, N.C. B3 197
Big Eau Pleine, res., Wis. D3 212
Big Elk, creek, Md., Pa. A6 173
Big Escambia, creek, Ala., Fla. D6 166
Big Falls, Minn. B5 187
Big Flat, mtn., Va. C4 209
Big Flats, N.Y. C4 196
Big Fork, riv., Minn. B5 187
Big Frog, mtn., Tenn. D9 205
Big Grass, isl., Fla. C3 174
Big Gully, creek, Sask., Can. D1 155
Big Hatchet, peak, N. Mex. F1 195
Big Hickory, pass, Fla. F5 174
Big Hole, riv., Mont. E4 190
Big Hole Battlefield, nat. mon., Mont. E3 190
Big Horn, Wyo. A5 213
Big Horn, co., Mont. E9 190
Big Horn, co., Wyo. A4 213
Big Horn, basin, Wyo. A4 213
Big Horn, mts., Ariz. D2 168
Big Island, Va. D3 209
Big Kandiyohi, lake, Minn. F4 187
Big Kennesaw, mtn., Ga. A4, C2 175
Big Knob, mtn., Pa. F6 202
Big Knob, mtn., Va. B2 209
Big Lake, Minn. E5 187
Big Lake, Tex. D2 206
Big Lookout, mtn., Oreg. C9 201
Big Lost, riv., Idaho F5 177
Big Marine, lake, Minn. E7 187
Big Maumelle Lake, res., Ark. C3 169
Big Monon, creek, Ind. C4 179
Big Moose, N.Y. B6 196
Big Muddy, creek, Mont. B12 190
Big Muddy, lake, Sask., Can. H3 155
Big Muddy, riv., Ill. F4 178
Big Payette, lake, Idaho E2 177
Big Pine, Calif. D4 170
Big Pine, mtn., Calif. E4 170
Big Piney, Mo. D5 189
Big Piney, Wyo. C2 213
Big Pipe, creek, Md. A3 173
Big Prairie, Ohio B5 199
Big Raccoon, creek, Ind. E4 179
Big Rapids, Mich. E5 186
Big River, Sask., Can. D2 155
Big Rock, Ill. B5 178
Big Rock, Tenn. A4 205
Big Rock, mtn., Ark. D6 169
Big Run, Pa. E4 202
Big Sable, pt., Mich. D4 186
Big Sand, creek, Mont. B6 190
Big Sandy, Mont. B6 190
Big Sandy, Tenn. A3 205
Big Sandy, Tex. C5 206
Big Sandy, Wyo. C3 213
Big Sandy, creek, Colo. C8 171
Big Sandy, creek, W. Va. C3 211
Big Sandy, lake, Sask., Can. C3 155
Big Sandy, res., Wyo. C3 213
Big Sandy, riv., Ariz. C2 168
Big Sandy, riv., Ky., W. Va. B7 182
Big Sandy, riv., Tenn. B3 205
Big Satilla, creek, Ga. E4 175
Big Savage, mtn., Md. D2 173
Big Sheep, mtn., Mont. C11 190
Big Shiney, mtn., Pa. B9 202
Big Sioux, riv., Iowa, S. Dak. B1 180, E9 204
Big Slough, creek, Kans. B5 181
Big Smoky, valley, Nev. E4 192
Big Snow, mtn., Mont. D7 190
Big Soldier, creek, Kans. C8 181
Big Southern, butte, Idaho F5 177
Big Spencer, mtn., Maine C4 184
Big Spring, Ky. C3 182
Big Spring, Md. A2 173
Big Spring, Tenn. D9 205
Big Spring, Tex. C2 206
Big Springs, Kans. B7 181
Big Springs, Nebr. C3 191
Big Springs, W. Va. C3 211
Big Spruce Knob, mtn., W. Va. C4 211
Big Squaw, mtn., Maine C3 184
Big Stone, co., Minn. E2 187
Big Stone, lake, Minn. E2 187
Big Stone, lake, S. Dak. B9 204
Big Stone City, S. Dak. B9 204
Big Stone Gap, Va. B2 209
Big Sunflower, riv., Miss. B3 188
Big Sur, Calif. D3 170
Big Thompson, riv., Colo. A5 171
Big Timber, Mont. E7 190
Big Top, mtn., Tenn. B5 205
Big Valley, Alta., Can. C4 148
Big Walnut, creek, Ohio C2 199
Big Wells, Tex. E3 206
Big Wills, creek, Ala. A3 166
Big Wills, valley, Ala. A3 166
Big Wood, riv., Idaho F4 177
Biga, Tur. B6 69
Bigbee, Miss. A5 188
Bigbee Valley, Miss. B5 188
Bigbone, Ky. A6 182
Bigej, isl., Kwajalein 114
Bigelow, Ark. B3 169
Bigelow, Minn. G3 187
Bigelow, Mo. A2 189
Bigelow, mtn., Maine C2 184
Bigflat, Ark. A3 169
Bigfoot, Tex. E3 206
Bigfork, Minn. C5 187
Bigfork, Mont. B2 190
Biggar, Sask., Can. E1 155
Biggar, Scot. E5 57
Biggerann, isl., Kwajalein 114
Biggers, Ark. A5 169
Biggersville, Miss. A5 188
Biggleswade, Eng. B7 56
Biggs, Calif. C3 170
Biggs, Oreg. B6 201
Biggsville, Ill. C3 178
Bighorn, Mont. D9 190
Bighorn, mts., Wyo. A5 213
Bighorn, riv., Mont., Wyo. A4 213
Bighorn Canyon, nat. recreation area, Mont., Wyo. A4 213
Bigi, isl., Kwajalein 114
Bigler, Pa. E5 202
Biglerville, Pa. G7 202
Bignona, Sen. D1 103
Bigonville, Lux. E5 59
Bigou, Calif. C4 170
Bigpoint, Miss. E5 188
Bigpool, Md. A1 173
Bigsby, isl., Ont., Can. A4 187
Bigstick, lake, Sask., Can. G1 155
Bigstone, lake, Man., Can. C4 150
Bigstone, lake, Sask., Can. C4 155
Bigstone, riv., Man., Can. B4 150
Biguaçu, Braz. D3 137
Bigwood, Ont., Can. A4 153
Bihać, Yugo. C2 68
Bihar, India E10 88
Bihar, state, India D8 87
Bihor, mtn., Rom. B6 68
Biiziri, isl., Eniwetok 114
Bijagós, is., Port. Gui. D1 103
Bijapur, India I5 88
Bijār, Iran D3 86
Bijeljina, Yugo. C4 68
Bijelo Polje, Yugo. D4 68
Bijnor, India C7 88
Bijou, creek, Colo. B6 171
Bijou Hills, S. Dak. D6 204
Bikampur, India D4 88
Bikaner, India C5 87, D4 88
Bikar, atoll, Marshall Is. 115
Bikeman, isl., Tarawa Is. 114
Bikin, Sov. Un. C7 93
Bikin, riv., Sov. Un. C7 93
Bikini, isl., Bikini I. 114
Bikini, is., Marshall Is. 114, 115
Bikita, Rh. B5 107
Biklabito, N. Mex. A1 195
Bikolia, isl., Sol. Is. 115
Bilaspur, India F9 88
Bilauktaung, range, Thai. F3 89
Bilbao, Sp. A4 65
Bilbays, Eg. D3 84
Bíldudalur, Ice. n21 63
Bileća, Yugo. D4 68
Bilecik, Tur. B7 85
Biłgoraj, Pol. C7 70
Bili, Zaire A4 106
Bilin, Bur. E10 87
Bilina, Czech. C8 61
Bill, Wyo. B7 213
Bill Williams, mtn., Ariz. B3 168
Billerica, Mass. A5, C2 185
Billet, Ill. E6 178
Billings, Mo. D4 189
Billings, Mont. E8 190
Billings, Okla. A4 200
Billings, co., N. Dak. B2 198
Billings Heights, Mont. E8 190
Billingsley, Ala. C3 166
Bilma, Niger C7 103
Biloela, Austl. B8 112
Biloxi, Miss. E2, E5 188
Biloxi, bay, Miss. E5 188
Biloxi, riv., Miss. E4 188
Bilqas Qism Awwal, Eg. C3 84
Biltine, Chad C4 104
Biltmore Forest, N.C. D3 197
Bilzen, Bel. D5 59
Bim, W. Va. D6 211
Bimberi, peak, Austl. G7 112
Bimini, is., Ba. Is. C4 131
Binalonan, Phil. n13 90
Biñan, Phil. o13 90
Bindjai, Indon. *K3 89
Bindle, Austl. C7 112
Bindloss, Alta., Can. D5 148
Bindura, Rh. A5 107
Binfield, Tenn. D9 205
Binford, N. Dak. B7 198
Binga, Zaire A3 106
Bingamon, creek, W. Va. A6 211
Bingen, Ger. D2 61
Bingen, Wash. D4 210
Binger, Okla. B3 200
Bingham, Ill. D4 178
Bingham, Maine C3 184
Bingham, Nebr. B3 191
Bingham, N. Mex. D3 195
Bingham, S.C. C8 203
Bingham, co., Idaho F6 177
Bingham Canyon, Utah C3 207
Bingham Lake, Minn. G3 187
Binghamton, N.Y. C5 196
Bingley, Eng. G7 57
Bingöl (Çapakçur), Tur. C13 85
Binnaway, Austl. E7 112
Binscarth Man., Can. D1 150
Bintan, is., Indon. L6 89
Bintang, mtn., Mala. J4 89
Bintuhan, Indon. F2 90
Bintulu, Mala. E4 90
Binyamina, Isr. B6 84
Bio-Bio, prov., Chile B2 136
Bío Bío, riv., Chile B2 136
Bippus, Ind. C6 179
Bir, India H5 88
Bi'r Abu Hadd (Well), Eg. E6 101
Bir Abu Reida (Oasis), Eg. D4 84
Bi'r Al 'Abd, Eg. C5 84
Bi'r Al 'Ajramīyah (Oasis), Eg. E3 84
Bi'r al 'Aṭash (Well), Libya D4 101
Bi'r al Ghaylānīyah (Well), Libya D2 101
Bi'r al Ghuzayl (Well), Libya D2 101
Bi'r al Ḥadīrah (Oasis), Eg. D6 84
Bi'r al Ḥaysī, Eg. E6 84
Bi'r Al Hukayyim, Libya G4 85
Bi'r al Jidy (Oasis), Eg. D5 84
Bi'r al Jilbānah (Oasis), Eg. D4 84
Bi'r al Jufayr (Oasis), Eg. D4 84
Bi'r al Lahtān (Oasis), Eg. D5 84
Bi'r al Mazār, Eg. C5 84
Bi'r Al 'Uzaym, Libya G4 85
Bi'r an Nuṣf (Well), Eg. C5 101

INDEX KEY Each place listed in **Bold-faced Type** has its population listed in the Population tables, pages 230 to 280.
Each country, shown in CAPITAL LETTERS, has its population listed in the World Political Information Table, pages 6 to 10.
* Does not appear on map; key shows general location.

Bi'r ar Rummānah, Eg. G9 85
Bi'r ash Shaqqah, Libya G5 85
Bi'r Bayzaḩ (Well), Eg. D6 101
Bi'r bū Jarrāran (Well), Libya D2 101
Bir el Ksaib (Well), Mali B3 103
Bi'r Fajr (Oasis), Sau. Ar. H11 85
Bi'r Ghētta (Oasis), Eg. E5 84
Bi'r Ḩasanah (Oasis), Eg. D5 84
Bi'r Hooker (Oasis), Eg. D2 84
Bi'r Jumayl (Oasis), Eg. D5 84
Bi'r Māliḩah (Oasis), Eg. E5 84
Bi'r Misāḩah (Well), Eg. E5 101
Bir-Moghrein, Maur. A2 103
Bi'r Murākh (Oasis), Eg. E6 84
Bi'r Murr (Well), Eg. E6 101
Bi'r Rawḑ Sālim (Oasis), Eg. D5 84
Bir Sejri (Oasis), Syr. F12 85
Bir Tarfawi (Well), Sud. A3 105
Bi'r Umm Ḩuşayrah (Oasis), Eg. D6 84
Bir Zreigat (Well), Maur. B3 103
Bira, Sov. Un. B6 93
Birakan, Sov. Un. B5 93
Birao, Cen Afr. Rep. C4 104
Birch, isl., Man., Can. C2 150
Birch, lake, Sask., Can. D1 155
Birch, lake, Minn. C6 187
Birch, riv., W. Va. C4 211
Birch Hills, Sask., Can. E3 155
Birch Island, B.C., Can. D8 149
Birch River, Man., Can. C1 150
Birch Rock, hill, Pa. F3 202
Birch Run, Mich. E7 186
Birch Tree, Mo. E6 189
Birchwood, Minn. *E5 187
Birchwood, Tenn. D9 205
Birchwood, Wis. C2 212
Bird, creek, Okla. A6 200
Bird, isl., N.C. D5 197
Bird City, Kans. C2 181
Bird Island, Minn. F4 187
Birds, Ill. E6 178
Birds Creek, Ont., Can. B7 153
Birdsboro, Pa. F10 202
Birdseye, Ind. H4 179
Birdseye, Utah D4 207
Birdsville, Austl. B2 112
Birdsville, Ky. A3 182
Birdtail, creek, Man., Can. D1 150
Birdtown, N.C. D3 197
Birdum, Austl. C5 111
Birdwood, creek, Nebr. C4 191
Birecik, Tur. D11 85
Birganj, Nepal D10 88
Birimbāl, Eg. C2 84
Birjand, Iran E9 86
Birkat as Sab', Eg. D3 84
Birkat Qārūn, lake, Eg. E2 84
Birkenfeld, Ger. D2 61
Birkenhead, Eng. A4 56
Birmingham, Ala. B3, E4 166
Birmingham, Sask., Can. G4 155
Birmingham, Eng. B6 56
Birmingham, Iowa D6 180
Birmingham, Kans. A6 181
Birmingham, Mich. A7, F7 186
Birmingham, Mo. E2 189
Birmingham, N.J. D3 194
Birnamwood, Wis. D4 212
Birney, Mont. E10 190
Birni-Nkoni, Niger D6 103
Birnie, Man., Can. D2 150
Birnin Kebbi, Nig. D5 103
Birobidzhan, Sov. Un. E16 71
Biron, Wis. D4 212
Birr, Ire. D3 55
Birsay, Sask., Can. F2 155
Birta, Ark. *C2 169
Birtle, Man., Can. D1 150
Biryulevo, Sov. Un. n17 72
Bisai, Jap. *I8 93
Bisbee, Ariz. F6 168
Bisbee, N. Dak. A6 198
Biscay, bay, Fr., Sp. E2 58
Biscayne, bay, Fla. G6 174
Biscayne, key, Fla. F3 174
Biscayne Park, Fla. F3 174
Bisceglie, It. D6 67
Bischheim, Fr. F7 59
Bischofshofen, Aus. B9 66
Bischofswerda, Ger. B9 61
Bischwiller, Fr. F7 59
Biscoe, N.C. B4 197
Biscoe, Va. D5 209
Biscoe, is., Ant. C6 120
Biševo, isl., Yugo. D2 68
Bishnupur, India F11 88
Bishop, Calif. D4 170
Bishop, Ga. C3 175
Bishop, Md. D7 173
Bishop, Tex. F4 206
Bishop Auckland, Eng. F7 57
Bishopric, Sask., Can. H3 155
Bishop's Castle, Eng. B5 56
Bishop's Falls, Newf., Can. D4 152
Bishops Head, Md. D5 173
Bishops Mills, Ont., Can. C9 153
Bishop's Stortford, Eng. C8 56
Bishopton, Que., Can. D6 154
Bishopville, Md. D7 173
Bishopville, S.C. C7 203
Biskra, Alg. C6 102
Bismarck, Ark. D5 169
Bismarck, Ill. C6 178
Bismarck, Mo. D7 189
Bismarck, N. Dak. C5 198
Bismarck, arch., N. Gui. h12 110, G8 113
Bismarck, cape, Grnld. B16 118
Bismarck, range, N. Gui. k11 110
Bismark, Ger. F5 62
Bismark's empire 51
Bison, Kans. D4 181
Bison, Okla. A4 200
Bison, S. Dak. B3 204
Bison, lake, Alta., Can. A2 148
Bison, peak, Colo. B5 171
Bissamcuttack, India H9 88
Bissau, Port. Gui. D1 103
Bissett, Man., Can. D4 150
Bistineau, lake, La. B2 183
Bistrița, Rom. B7 68
Bistrița, riv., Rom. B7 68
Bitam, Gabon E2 104
Bitburg, Ger. E6 59
Bitche, Fr. E7 59
Bitely, Mich. E5 186
Bithlo, Fla. *D5 174
Bithynia: c. 450 B.C. 42
in 1st cent. B.C. 44
c. 120 A.D. 45
Bititu, isl., Tarawa Is. 114
Bitjoli, Indon. E7 90
Bitlis, Tur. C14 85
Bitola, Yugo. E5 68
Bitonto, It. D6 67
Bitter, creek, Wyo. D4 213
Bitter, lake, Sask., Can. G1 155
Bitter, lake, S. Dak. B8 204
Bitter Creek, Wyo. D4 213
Bitterfeld, Ger. B7 61
Bitterfontein, S. Afr. D2 107
Bittern, lake, Sask., Can. D3 155
Bittern Lake, Alta., Can. C4 148
Bitterroot, range, U.S. A4 158
Bitterroot, riv., Mont. D2 190
Bittinger, Md. D1 173
Bityug, riv., Sov. Un. F13 72
Biu, Nig. D7 103
Bivalve, Md. D6 173
Bivalve, N.J. E2 194
Biwa, lake, Jap. n15 93
Biwabik, Minn. C6 187
Bixby, Okla. B6 200
Bixby, Minn. G5 187
Bixby, Mo. D6 189
Bixby, N.C. B3 197
Biysk, Sov. Un. C11 73
Bizerte, Tun. B6 102
Bizuta, Mong. B8 91
Bjelovar, Yugo. C3 68
Bjerringbro, Den. B3 62
Bjorkdale, Sask., Can. *E4 155
Björlanda, Swe. A5 62
Bjornefjord, fjord, Nor. G1 63
Blabon, N. Dak. B8 198
Black, Ala. D4 166
Black, Tex. B1 206
Black, bayou, La. E5 183
Black, butte, Mont. F5 190
Black, butte, Wyo. A5 213
Black, canyon, Colo. C3 171
Black, creek, Miss. E4 188
Black, creek, S.C. B7 203
Black, creek, Vt. B3 208
Black, head, Newf., Can. E5 152
Black, hills, S. Dak., Wyo. C2 204, A9 213
Black, isl., Man., Can. D3 150
Black, lake, Sask., Can. E11 142
Black, lake, Mich. C6 186
Black, lake, N.Y. B1 196
Black, mesa, Ariz. A5 168
Black, mesa, Okla. D1 200
Black, mtn., Ariz. E4 168
Black, mtn., Colo. A5 171
Black, mtn., Idaho C3, C6 177
Black, mtn., Ky. D7 182
Black, mtn., Mont. D4 190
Black, mtn., Oreg. B7 201
Black, mtn., Wyo. A5 213
Black, mtn., Wyo. C7 213
Black, mts., Ariz. B1 168
Black, mts., Wales C4 56
Black, peak, Ariz. C1 168
Black, pond, Maine B3 184
Black, range, N. Mex. D2 195
Black, riv., Ariz. D5 168
Black, riv., Ark. B4 169
Black, riv., Man., Can. D4 150
Black, riv., La. C4 183
Black, riv., Maine B3 184
Black., riv., Mich C6 186
Black, riv., Mich. E8 186
Black, riv., Mo. D7 189
Black, riv., N.J. B3 194
Black, riv., N.Y. B5 196
Black, riv., N.C. C5 197
Black, riv., S.C. D8 203
Black, riv., S.C. E2 203
Black, riv., Vt. B4 208
Black, riv., Vt. E3 208
Black, riv., Viet. B5 89
Black, riv., Wis. D3 212
Black, sea, Eur. G14 40
Black Bear, bay, Newf., Can. B4 152
Black Bear, creek, Okla. A4 200
Black Bear Island, lake, Sask., Can. B3 155
Black Canyon City, Ariz. C3 168
Black Canyon of the Gunnison, nat. mon., Colo. C3 171
Black Creek, N.C. B6 197
Black Creek, Wis. A5, D5 212
Black Diamond, Alta., Can. D3 148
Black Diamond, Wash. B4, D2 210
Black Dome, mtn., B.C., Can. C4 149
Black Down, hills, Eng. D4 56
Black Eagle, Mont. C5 190
Black Earth, Wis. E4 212
Black Forest, Colo. C6 171
Black Forest, mts., Ger. E3 61
Black Fork, Ark. C1 169
Black Hawk, Ont., Can. B5 187
Black Hawk, Colo. *B5 171
Black Hawk, Miss. B3 188
Black Hawk, S. Dak. C2 204
Black Hawk, co., Iowa B5 180
Black Jack, mtn., Ga. A5 175
Black Lake, Que., Can. C6 154
Black Lake, bayou, La. B2 183
Black Lick, Pa. F3 202
Black Mountain, N.C. D4 197
Black Oak, Ark. B5 169
Black Oak, Ind. A3 179
Black Pine, peak, Idaho G5 177
Black Point, Calif. B5 170
Black River, Jam. F5 131
Black River, N.Y. A5 196
Black River Falls, Wis. D3 212
Black Rock, Ark. A4 169
Black Rock, N. Mex. B1 195
Black Rock, des., Nev. C3 192
Black Rock, des., Utah D3 207
Black Rock, range, Nev. B3 192
Black Springs, Ark. C2 169
Black Springs, Nev. D2 192
Black Squirrel, creek, Colo. C6 171
Black Thunder, creek, Wyo. B7 213
Black Volta, riv., Ghana E4 103
Black Walnut, pt., Md. C5 173
Black Warrior, riv., Ala. C2 166
Blackall, Austl. B5 112
Blackbeard, isl., Ga. E5 175
Blackburn, Eng. A5 56
Blackburn, Mo. B4 189
Blackburn, Okla. A5 200
Blackburn, mtn., Alsk. C11 167
Blackduck, Minn. C4 187
Blackey, Va. B3 209
Blackfalds, Alta., Can. C4 148
Blackfeet, Indian res., Mont. B4 190
Blackfoot, Alta., Can. C5 148
Blackfoot, Idaho F6 177
Blackfoot, Mont. B4 190
Blackfoot, mts., Idaho F7 177
Blackfoot, res., Idaho G7 177
Blackfoot, riv., Mont. D3 190
Blackford, Ky. C2 182
Blackford, co., Ind. D7 179
Blackfork, Ohio D5 199
Blackhall, mtn., Wyo. E6 213
Blackhead, bay, Newf., Can. D5 152
Blackie, Alta., Can. D4 148
Blackjack, Mo. A8 189
Blacklick, Ohio C2 199
Blackman, Fla. G2 174
Blackmore, mtn., Mont. E6 190
Blackoak, ridge, Tenn. D9, E11 205
Blackpool, Eng. A4 56
Blackriver, Mich. D7 186
Blacks, fork, Utah B5 207
Blacks, fork, Wyo. D3 213
Blacks Harbour, N.B., Can. D3 151
Blacksburg, S.C. A4 203
Blacksburg, Va. D2 209
Blackshear, Ga. E4 175
Blacksod, bay, Ire. C1 55
Blackstock, Ont., Can. C6 153
Blackstock, S.C. B5 203
Blackstone, Mass. B4 185
Blackstone, Va. D5 209
Blackstone, riv., Alta., Can. C2 148
Blacksville, W.Va. B4 211
Blackton, Ark. C4 169
Blacktown, Austl. *F9 111
Blackville, N.B., Can. C4 151
Blackville, S.C. E5 203
Blackwater, Mo. C5 189
Blackwater, Va. B2 209
Blackwater, res., N.H. D3 193
Blackwater, res., Scot. D4 57
Blackwater, riv., Eng. C8 56
Blackwater, riv., Fla. G2 174
Blackwater, riv., Md. D5 173
Blackwater, riv., N.H. D3 193
Blackwater, riv., Va. E6 209
Blackwell, Ark. B3 169
Blackwell, Mo. C7 189
Blackwell, Okla. A4 200
Blackwell, Pa. C7 202
Blackwell, Tex. C2 206
Blackwell, Wis. C5 212
Bladen, Nebr. D7 191
Bladen, co., N.C. C5 197
Bladenboro, N.C. C5 197
Bladensburg, Md. C2 173
Blades, Del. C6 173
Bladon Springs, Ala. D1 166
Bladworth, Sask., Can. F2 155
Blagodarnoye, Sov. Un. D2 73
Blagoevgrad (Gorna-Dzhumaya), Bul. D6 68
Blagoveshchensk, Sov. Un. D15 71
Blain, Fr. D3 58
Blain, Pa. F7 202
Blaine, Kans. C7 181
Blaine, Maine B5 184
Blaine, Minn. E7 187
Blaine, Miss. B3 188
Blaine, Wash. A3 210
Blaine, co., Idaho F4 177
Blaine, co., Mont. B7 190
Blaine, co., Nebr. C6 191
Blaine, co., Okla. B3 200
Blaine Lake, Sask., Can. E2 155
Blainville, Que., Can. *D4 154
Blair, Kans. C8 181
Blair, Nebr. C9 191
Blair, N.H. C3 193
Blair, Okla. C2 200
Blair, S.C. C5 203
Blair, W. Va. D5 211
Blair, Wis. D2 212
Blair, co., Pa. E5 202
Blair-Atholl, Scot. D5 57
Blairgowrie [& Rattray], Scot. D5 57
Blairmore, Alta., Can. E3 148
Blairsburg, Iowa B4 180
Blairsden, Calif. C3 170
Blairstown, Iowa C5 180
Blairstown, Mo. C4 189
Blairstown, N.J. B3 194
Blairsville, Ga. B3 175
Blairsville, Pa. F3 202
Blairton, W. Va. B7 211
Blairtown, Wyo. D3 213
Blaisdell, N. Dak. A3 198
Blaj, Rom. B6 68
Blakeley, Minn. F5 187
Blakeley, W. Va. C6 211
Blakely, Ark. C6 169
Blakely, Ga. E2 175
Blakeman, Kans. C2 181
Blakes, pt., Mich. A2 186
Blakesburg, Iowa D5 180
Blakeslee, Ohio A3 199
Blakeslee, Pa. D10 202
Blalock, Oreg. B6 201
Blâmont, Fr. F6 59
Blanc, cape, Maur. B1 103
Blanc, cape, Tun. F11 64
Blanc, mtn., Fr. E7 59
Blanc Sablon, Que., Can. C3, h10 152
Blanca, Colo. D5 171
Blanca, bay, Arg. B4 136
Blanca, cape, Oreg. E2 201
Blanca, peak, Colo. D5 171
Blanca, pt., Mex. B2 129
Blanca, range, Peru C2 134
Blanchard, Idaho A2 177
Blanchard, Iowa D2 180
Blanchard, La. B2 183
Blanchard, Maine C3 184
Blanchard, Mich. E5 186
Blanchard, N. Dak. B8 198
Blanchard, Okla. B4 200
Blanchard, Pa. D6 202
Blanchard, Wash. A3 210
Blanchard, riv., Ohio A3 199
Blanchardville, Wis. F4 212
Blanche, Que., Can. D2 154
Blanche, Tenn. B5 205
Blanche, chan., Sol. Is. 115
Blanche, lake, Austl. D2 112
Blanchester, Ohio C4 199
Blanco, N. Mex. A2 195
Blanco, Okla. C6 200
Blanco, Tex. D3 206
Blanco, co., Tex. D3 206
Blanco, cape, C.R. F5 130
Blanco, cape, Oreg. E2 201
Blanco, creek, N. Mex. C6 195
Blanco, riv., Arg. E2 135
Blanco, riv., Bol. B3 135
Blanco, riv., Mex. n15 129
Blanco, riv., P.R. C6 132
Bland, Mo. C6 189
Bland, Va. D1 209
Bland, co., Va. D1 209
Blandburg, Pa. E5 202
Blandford [Forum], Eng. D5 56
Blandford, Mass. B2 185
Blanding, Utah F6 207
Blandinsville, Ill. C3 178
Blandville, Ky. A2 182
Blaney, S.C. C6 203
Blanford, Ind. E2 179
Blangy-sur-Bresle, Fr. E9 56
Blankenberge, Bel. C3 59
Blankenburg, Ger. B5 61
Blankenfelde, Ger. A8 61
Blankenheim, Ger. C1 61
Blanket, Tex. D3 206
Blantyre [-Limbe], Malawi E6 106
Blasdell, N.Y. C2 196
Blatna, Czech. D2 61
Blato, Yugo. D3 68
Blaubeuren, Ger. A4 61
Blawnox, Pa. B6 202
Blaye, Fr. E3 58
Błażowa, Pol. D7 70
Bleckede, Ger. E4 62
Bleckley, co., Ga. D3 175
Bled-Grad, Yugo. B2 68
Błędów, Pol. g10 70
Bledsoe, Tex. C1 206
Bledsoe, co., Tenn. D8 205
Bleecker, Ala. C4 166
Bleicherode, Ger. B5 61
Blekinge, co., Swe. B8 62
Blencoe, Iowa C1 180
Blende, Colo. C6 171
Blendecques, Fr. D10 56
Blenheim, Ont., Can. E2 153
Blenheim, N.Z. N14 112
Blenheim, S.C. C8 203
Blessing, Tex. E4 206
Blevins, Ark. D2 169
Blewett, Tex. E2 206
Blida, Alg. B5 102
Blija, Neth. A5 59
Blind, riv., La. B6 183
Blind River, Ont., Can. A2 153
Bliss, Idaho G4 177
Bliss, N.Y. C2 196
Blissfield, Mich. G7 186
Blita, Togo E5 103
Blitar, Indon. *G4 90
Blitzen, Oreg. E7 201
Blocher, Ind. G6 179
Block, isl., R.I. E10 172
Block Island, R.I. E10 172
Block Island, sound, R.I. E9 172
Blocker, Okla. B6 200
Blockton, Iowa D3 180
Blodgett, Mo. D8 189
Blodgett Landing, N.H. D2 193
Bloedel, B.C., Can. D5 149
Bloemfontein, S. Afr. C4 107
Blois, Fr. D4 58
Blokhus, Den. A3 62
Blomberg, Ger. B4 61
Blomkest, Minn. *F3 187
Blönduós, Ice. n22 63
Błonie, Pol. m13 70
Blood, mtn., Ga. B3 175
Bloodroot, mtn., Vt. D3 208
Bloodsworth, isl., Md. D5 173
Bloodvein, riv., Man., Can. D3 150
Bloom, Kans. E4 181
Bloomdale, Ohio A4 199
Bloomer, Wis. C2 212
Bloomfield, Calif. B4 170
Bloomfield, Ont., Can. D7 153
Bloomfield, Conn. B6 172
Bloomfield, Ind. F4 179
Bloomfield, Iowa D5 180
Bloomfield, Ky. C4 182
Bloomfield, Mo. E8 189
Bloomfield, Mont. C12 190
Bloomfield, Nebr. B8 191
Bloomfield, N.J. D4 194
Bloomfield, N. Mex. A2 195
Bloomfield, Vt. B5 208
Bloomfield Hills, Mich. A7 186
Bloomfield Station, N.B., Can. D4 151
Blooming Grove, Pa. D11 202
Blooming Grove, Tex. C4 206
Blooming Prairie, Minn. G5 187
Bloomingburg, Ohio C4 199
Bloomingdale, Ga. D5 175
Bloomingdale, Ill. E2 178
Bloomingdale, Ind. E3 179
Bloomingdale, Mich. F5 186
Bloomingdale, N.J. A4 194
Bloomingdale, N.Y. B3 196
Bloomingdale, Ohio *B7 199
Bloomington, Idaho *G7 177
Bloomington, Ill. C4 178
Bloomington, Ind. F4 179
Bloomington, Md. D1 173
Bloomington, Minn. F7 187
Bloomington, Nebr. D6 191
Bloomington, Tex. E4 206
Bloomington, Wis. F3 212
Bloomsburg, Pa. E9 202
Bloomsbury, N.J. B2 194
Bloomsdale, Mo. C7 189
Bloomville, N.Y. C6 196
Bloomville, Ohio A4 199
Blossburg, Ala. E4 166
Blossburg, Pa. C7 202
Blosseville, coast, Grnld. C17 118
Blossom, Tex. C5 206
Blount, co., Ala. B3 166
Blount, co., Tenn. D10 205
Blount Springs, Ala. B3 166
Blounts Creek, N.C. B7 197
Blountstown, Fla. B1 174
Blountsville, Ala. A3 166
Blountsville, Ind. *D7 179
Blountville, Tenn. C11 205
Blovice, Czech. D8 61
Blowing Rock, N.C. A2 197
Bloxom, Va. D7 209
Blucher, Sask., Can. F2 155
Bludenz, Aus. E4 60
Blue, Ariz. D6 168
Blue, Okla. C5 200
Blue, bayou, La. E5 183
Blue, creek, Nebr. C3 191
Blue, creek, W. Va. C6 211
Blue, lake, Minn. A6 187
Blue, mound, Kans. C4 181
Blue, mtn., Ark. C1 169
Blue, mtn., N.B., Can. B3 151
Blue, mtn., Newf., Can. C3 152
Blue, mtn., Maine D2 184
Blue, mtn., Mont. C12 190
Blue, mtn., N.H. A4 193
Blue, mtn., N. Mex. D2 195
Blue, mtn., N.Y. B6 196
Blue, mtn., Pa. B1 194, F6 202
Blue, mts., Austl. F8 110
Blue, mts., Oreg. B8 201
Blue, mts., Tex. D3 206
Blue, mts., Wash. C8 210
Blue, pt., N.Y. G4 172
Blue, riv., Ind. E6 179
Blue, riv., Ind. H5 179
Blue, riv., Mo. E2 189
Blue, riv., Okla. C5 200
Blue Ash, Ohio D2 199
Blue Buck, pt., La. D2 183
Blue Buck Knob, mtn., Mo. E5 189
Blue Creek, W. Va. C3, C6 211
Blue Diamond, Nev. G6 192
Blue Earth, Minn. G4 187
Blue Earth, co., Minn. F4 187
Blue Earth, riv., Iowa, Minn. A3 180
Blue Eye, Ark. *A2 169
Blue Eye, Mo. E4 189
Blue Grass, Iowa C7 180
Blue Grass, Va. C3 209
Blue Hill, Maine D4 184
Blue Hill, Nebr. D7 191
Blue Hill Falls, Maine D4 184
Blue Hills, range, N.H. D4 193
Blue Hills of Coteau, hills, Newf., Can. E2 152
Blue Island, Ill. B6, F3 178
Blue Knob, mtn., Pa. F4 202
Blue Lake, Calif. B2 170
Blue Mesa, res., Colo. C3 171
Blue Mound, Ill. D4 178
Blue Mound, Kans. D8 181
Blue Mound, Tex. *B5 206
Blue Mountain, Ala. B4 166
Blue Mountain, Ark. B2 169
Blue Mountain, Colo. A2 171
Blue Mountain, Miss. A4 188
Blue Mountain, res., Ark. B2 169
Blue Mountain Lake, N.Y. B6 196
Blue Mud, bay, Austl. B6 110
Blue Nile, reg., Sud. C3 105
Blue Nile, see Bahr el Azraq, riv., Sud.
Blue Point, Maine E5 184
Blue Point, N.Y. G4 172
Blue Rapids, Kans. C7 181
Blue Ridge, Alta., Can. B3 148
Blue Ridge, Ga. B2 175
Blue Ridge, Ind. E6 179
Blue Ridge, Va. D3 209
Blue Ridge, lake, Ga. B2 175
Blue Ridge, mts., U.S. C11 159
Blue Ridge Summit, Pa. G7 202
Blue River, B.C., Can. C8 149
Blue River, Wis. E3 212
Blue Springs, Ala. D4 166
Blue Springs, Mo. E2 189
Blue Springs, Miss. A5 188
Blue Springs, Nebr. D9 191
Blueberry, creek, B.C., Can. D2 148
Blueberry, riv., B.C., Can. A7 149
Bluecreek, Wash. A8 210
Bluefield, Va. B3 209
Bluefield, W. Va. D3 211
Bluefields, Nic. D6 130
Bluegrass, Tenn. E11 205
Bluehole, Ky. C6 182
Bluejacket, Okla. A6 200
Bluejoint, lake, Oreg. E7 201
Bluesky, Alta., Can. A1 148
Bluestone, res., Va., W. Va. D2 209, D4 211
Bluestone, riv., W. Va. D3 211
Bluevale, Ont., Can. D3 153
Bluewater, N. Mex. B2 195
Bluff, Ill. E4 178
Bluff, N.Z. Q12 112
Bluff, Utah F6 207
Bluff, creek, Kans. E4 181
Bluff, creek, Kans. E6 181
Bluff, creek, Okla. A4 200
Bluff, head, Malaita I. 115
Bluff, mtn., Vt. B5 208
Bluff City, Ark. D2 169
Bluff City, Kans. E6 181
Bluff City, Ky. C2 182
Bluff City, Tenn. C11 205
Bluff Creek, res., Okla. B4 200
Bluff Dale, Tex. C3 206
Bluffs, Ill. D3 178
Bluffton, Ark. C2 169
Bluffton, Ga. E2 175
Bluffton, Ind. C7 179
Bluffton, Minn. D3 187
Bluffton, Ohio B4 199
Bluffton, S.C. G6 203
Bluford, Ill. E5 178
Blumenau, Braz. D3 137
Blumengard Colony, S. Dak. B6 204
Blumenhof, Sask., Can. G2 155
Blunt, S. Dak. C6 204
Bly, Calif. *F5 170
Bly, Oreg. E5 201
Bly, ridge, Oreg. E5 201
Blying, sound, Alsk. h17 167
Blyn, Wash. A3 210
Blyth, Ont., Can. D3 153
Blyth, Eng. C6 55
Blyth, riv., Eng. E7 57
Blythe, Calif. F6 170
Blythe, Ga. C4 175
Blythedale, Mo. A4 189
Blytheville, Ark. B6 169
Blythewood, S.C. C6 203
Bo, S.L. E2 103
Boa Vista, Braz. C5 133
Boac, Phil. C6 90
Boaco, Nic. D5 130
Boakview, Ont., Can. B4 153
Boalsburg, Pa. E6 202
Boang, isl., Bis. Arch. 115
Board Camp, Ark. C1 169
Boardman, Ohio A7 199
Boardman, Oreg. B7 201
Boardmans Bridge, Conn. C3 172
Boaz, Ala. A3 166
Boaz, Wis. E3 212
Bobbili, India H9 88
Bobbio, It. E5 66
Bobcaygeon, Ont., Can. C6 153
Bobigny, Fr. g10 58
Böblingen, Ger. E4 61
Bobo, Miss. A3 188
Bobo-Dioulasso, Upper Volta D4 103
Bobov Dol, Bul. D6 68
Bóbr, riv., Pol. C3 70
Bobrawa, riv., Ger. B10 61
Bobrinets, Sov. Un. G9 72
Bobrka, Sov. Un. G5 72
Bobruysk, Sov. Un. E7 72
Bobtown, Pa. G2 202
Bobures, Ven. B3 133
Boca Chica, is., Fla. H5 174
Boca Chica Central, P.R. D4 132
Boca Ciega, bay, Fla. E1 174
Bôca do Acre, Braz. C4 134
Boca Grande, Fla. F4 174
Boca Raton, Fla. F6 174

INDEX KEY Each place listed in **Bold-faced Type** has its population listed in the Population tables, pages 230 to 280. Each country, shown in CAPITAL LETTERS, has its population listed in the World Political Information Table, pages 6 to 10.
* Does not appear on map; key shows general location.

Bocaiúva, Braz. E2 138
Bocaranga, Cen. Afr. Rep. D3 104
Bocas del Toro, Pan. F6 130
Bocay, Nic. C5 130
Boccea (Buxus), It. h8 67
Bochnia, Pol. D6 70
Bocholt, Ger. B1 61
Bochov, Czech. C8 61
Bochum, Ger. B2 61
Bock, Minn. E5 187
Bockhorn, Ger. E2 62
Bockum-Hövel, Ger. B2 61
Boda, Cen. Afr. Rep. E3 104
Bodafors, Swe. A8 62
Bodaybo, Sov. Un. D14 71
Bodcau, creek, Ark. D2 169
Bodcaw, Ark. D2 169
Boddam, Scot. C7 57
Bode, Iowa B3 180
Bode, riv., Ger. B6 61
Bodega, head, Calif. C2 170
Bodele, reg., Afr. B3 104
Boden, Ill. B3 178
Boden, Swe. E9 63
Bodensee (Constance), lake, Ger., Switz. B5 66
Boderg, lake, Ire. D3 55
Bodhia, mtn., Eg. E5 84
Bodie, isl., N.C. B8 197
Bodine, mtn., B.C., Can. B5 149
Bodines, Pa. D8 202
Bodkin, pt., Md. B5 173
Bodmin, Eng. D3 56
Bodmin, moor, Eng. D3 56
Bodo, Alta., Can. C5 148
Bodo, Nor. D6 63
Bodrog, riv., Hung. A5 68
Bodrum (Halicarnassus), Tur. D6 85
Bódva, riv., Hung. A5 68
Boelus (Howard City), Nebr. C7 191
Boende, Zaire B3 106
Boerne, Tex. A3, E3 206
Boeuf, bayou, La. C3 183
Boeuf, lake, La. E5 183
Boeuf, riv., Ark., La. D4 **169**, B4 183
Boffa, Guinea D2 103
Bofu, Jap. I5 93
Bog Brook, res., N.Y. D2 172
Bogale, Bur. E10 87
Bogallua, isl., Eniwetok 114
Bogalusa, La. D6 183
Bogan, isl., Eniwetok 114
Bogan, riv., Austl. E6 112
Bogandé, Upper Volta D4 103
Bogard, Mo. B4 189
Bogart, Ga. C3 175
Bogata, Tex. C5 206
Bogatynia, Pol. C9 61
Bogbonga, Zaire A2 106
Bogen, Ger. E7 61
Bogenfels, S.W. Afr. C2 107
Bogense, Den. C4 62
Boger City, N.C. *B2 197
Boggerik, isl., Kwajalein 114
Boggs, cape, Ant. B6 120
Boghari, Alg. B5 102
Boghé, Maur. C2 103
Bognor Regis, Eng. D7 56
Bogodukhov, Sov. Un. F10 72
Bogon, isl., Eniwetok 114
Bogor, Indon. G3 90
Bogoroditsk, Sov. Un. E12 72
Bogorodsk, Sov. Un. C14 72
Bogotá, Col. C3 133
Bogota, N.J. D5 194
Bogota, Tenn. A2 205
Bogra, Bngl. E12 88
Bogue, Kans. C4 181
Bogue Chitto, Miss. D3 188
Bogue Chitto, riv., La., Miss. D5 **183**, D3 188
Bogue Phalia, riv., Miss. B3 188
Boguslav, Sov. Un. G8 72
Bohain-en-Vermandois, Fr. E3 59
Boharm, Sask., Can. G3 155
Bohemia, La. E6 183
Bohemia (Čechy), reg., Czech. D3 70
c. 1360 48
in 1721 49
in 1815 50
in 1914 52
Bohemian Forest, mts., Ger. D7 61
Bohemian-Moravian, highlands, Czech. D3 70
Bohemond, crusade of 47
Böhme, riv., Ger. F3 62
Bohmte, Ger. A3 61
Bohol, isl., Phil. D6 90
Bohotleh, Som. D6 105
Boice, Miss. D5 188
Boiestown, N.B., Can. C3 151
Boiling Springs, N.C. B2 197
Boiling Springs, Pa. F7 202
Bois, lake, N.W. Ter., Can. C8 142
Bois Blanc, isl., Mich. C6 186
Bois-Colombes, Fr. g10 58
Bois D'Arc, Mo. D4 189
Bois de Sioux, riv., Minn. E2 187
Bois-des-Filion, Que., Can. D8 154
Bois Fort, Minn. B5 187
Boischatel, Que., Can. C6, C9 154
Boisdale, N.S., Can. C9 151
Boisdale, inlet, Scot. C1 57
Boise, Idaho F2 177
Boise, co., Idaho F3 177
Boise, riv., Idaho F3 177
Boise City, Okla. D2 200
Boissevain, Man., Can. E1 150
Boissevain, Va. B3 209
Boistfort, peak, Wash. C2 210
Boizenburg, Ger. E4 62
Bojador, cape, Sp. Sahara D1 102
Bojnūrd, Iran C8 86
Bokanda, I.C. E4 103
Bokchito, Okla. C5 200
Boké, Guinea D2 103
Bokeelia, Fla. F4 174
Bokhara, emirate of: c. 1775 82
Bokhoma, Okla. D7 200
Boko, Zaire C2 106
Bokobyaadaa, isl., Bikini I. 114
Bokoro, Chad C3 104
Bokororyuru, isl., Bikini I. 114
Bokoshe, Okla. B7 200
Bokovo-Antratsit, Sov. Un. *G12 72
Boksburg, S. Afr. *C4 107
Bokungu, Zaire B3 106
Bol, Chad C2 104
Bolafa, Zaire A3 106
Boland, riv., Ont., Can. B8 186
Bolanos, mtn., Guam 114
Bolaños, riv., Mex. m12 129
Bolar, Va. C3 209
Bolbec, Fr. C4 58
Bolckow, Mo. A3 189
Bolding, Ark. D3 169
Bole, Ghana E4 103
Boleko, Zaire B2 106
Boles, Ark. C1 169
Bolesławiec, Pol. C3 70
Boley, Okla. B5 200
Bolgrad, Sov. Un. I7 72
Boli, see Bolu, Tur.
Bolia, Zaire B2 106
Boligee, Ala. C1 166
Bolinao, Phil. n12 90
Bolinao, cape, Phil. n12 90
Boling, Tex. E5, G4 206
Bolinger, Ala. D1 166
Bolívar, Arg. B4 136
Bolívar, Col. B2 133
Bolivar, Mo. D4 189
Bolivar, N.Y. C2 196
Bolivar, Ohio B6 199
Bolivar, Pa. F3 202
Bolívar, Peru C2 134
Bolivar, Tenn. B3 205
Bolivar, W. Va. B7 211
Bolivar, co., Miss. B3 188
Bolívar, dept., Col. B3 133
Bolívar, prov., Ec. B2 134
Bolívar, state, Ven. B4 133
Bolivar, lake, Miss. B2 188
Bolívar, Pico, peak, Ven. B3 133
Bolivia, N.C. C5 197
BOLIVIA, country, S.A. C2 135
in 1825-1907 127
Bolkhov, Sov. Un. E11 72
Bollebygd, Swe. A6 62
Bolling, Ala. D3 166
Bollinger, co., Mo. D7 189
Bollnäs, Swe. G7 63
Bollullos, Sp. D2 65
Bolmen, lake, Swe. B7 62
Bolnisi, Sov. Un. B15 85
Bolobo, Zaire B2 106
Bologna, It. E7 **66**, B3 67
Bologoye, Sov. Un. C10 72
Bolomba, Zaire A2 106
Bolon, lake, Sov. Un. B8 93
Bolonda, Guadalcanal I. 115
Bolotnoye, Sov. Un. B10 73
Bolovens, plat., Laos E7 89
Bolsena, lake, It. C3 67
Bolshaya Boktybay, mtn., Sov. Un. D5 73
Bolshaya Irgiz, riv., Sov. Un. C3 73
Bolshaya Lepetikha, Sov. Un. H9 72
Bolshaya Uzen, riv., Sov. Un. D3 73
Bolshaya Viska, Sov. Un. G8 72
Bolshaya Yugan, riv., Sov. Un. B8 73
Bolshoy Tokmak, Sov. Un. H10 72
Bolshoya Hamenka, riv., Sov. Un. q22 72
Bolsward, Neth. A5 59
Bolton, Ont., Can. D5 153
Bolton, Eng. A5 56
Bolton, Mass. B4, C1 185
Bolton, Miss. C3 188
Bolton, N.C. C5 197
Bolton, Vt. C3 208
Bolton, lake, Man., Can. B4 150
Bolton, riv., Man., Can. B4 150
Bolton Center, Conn. B7 172
Bolton Landing, N.Y. B7 196
Boltonville, Vt. C4 208
Bolu, Tur. B8 85
Bolvadin, Tur. C8 85
Bolzano, It. A3 67
Bom Conselho, Braz. C3, k5 138
Bom Despacho, Braz. E1 138
Bom Jardim, Braz. g5 137
Bom Jardim, Braz. h6 138
Bom Jesus, Braz. C2 138
Bom Jesus da Lapa, Braz. D2 138
Boma, Zaire C1 106
Bomarton, Tex. C3 206
Bombala, Austl. H7 112
Bombay, India E5 **87**, H4 88
Bombay, N.Y. A2 196
Bombay Hook, isl., Del. B7 173
Bombetoka, bay, Malag. g9 107
Bomboma, Zaire A2 106
Bomokandi, riv., Zaire A4 106
Bomongo, Zaire A2 106
Bomoseen, Vt. D2 208
Bomoseen, lake, Vt. D2 208
Bomu, riv., Cen. Afr. Rep., Zaire A3 106
Bon, cape, Tun. B7 102
Bon Accord, Alta., Can. C4 148
Bon Air, Ala. B3 166
Bon Air, Tenn. D8 205
Bon Air, Va. G7 209
Bon Aqua, Tenn. B4 205
Bon Ecno, prov. park, Ont., Can. C7 153
Bon Homme, co., S. Dak. D8 204
Bon Homme Colony, S. Dak. E8 204
Bon Secour, Ala. E2 166
Bon Wier, Tex. D6 206
Bonaigarh, India G10 88
Bonaire, Ga. D3 175
Bonaire, isl., Neth. Antilles A4 133
Bonanza, Ark. B1 169
Bonanza, Colo. C4 171
Bonanza, Oreg. E5 201
Bonanza, Utah C6 207
Bonanza, peak, Wash. A5 210
Bonaparte, Iowa D6 180
Bonaparte, lake, B.C., Can. D7 149
Bonaparte, mtn., Wash. A6 210
Bonaparte, riv., B.C., Can. D7 149
Boñar, Sp. A3 65
Bonar Bridge, Scot. C4 57
Bonarlaw, Ont., Can. C7 153
Bonasila Dome, mtn., Alsk. C7 167
Bonaventure, co., Que., Can. A3 151
Bonavista, Newf., Can. D5 152
Bonavista, bay, Newf., Can. D5 152
Bonavista, cape, Newf., Can. D5 152
Bond, Colo. B4 171
Bond, Ky. C5 182
Bond, Miss. E4 188
Bond, co., Ill. E4 178
Bond, reef, N. Cal. 115
Bondeno, It. E7 66
Bondo, Zaire A3 106
Bondoukou, I.C. E4 103
Bondsville, Mass. B3 185
Bonduel, Wis. D5 212
Bondurant, Iowa A7, C4 180
Bondurant, Wyo. B2 213
Bondville, Vt. E3 208
Bondy, Fr. g10 58
Bone, gulf, Indon. F6 90
Bone, lake, Wis. C1 212
Bone Cave, Tenn. D8 205
Bone Gap, Ill. E6 178
Bonesteel, S. Dak. D7 204
Bonetraill, N. Dak. A2 198
Bonfield, Ont., Can. A5 153
Bonfouca, La. B8 183
Bong, Efate I. 115
Bongā, Eth. D4 105
Bongandanga, Zaire A3 106
Bongor, Chad C3 104
Bonham, Tex. C4 206
Bonidee, bayou, La. B4 183
Bonifacio, Fr. D2 67
Bonifacio, strait, It. D2 67
Bonifay, Fla. G3 174
Bonilla, S. Dak. C7 204
BONIN ISLANDS, Jap. E8 113
Bonita, Ariz. E6 168
Bonita, La. B4 183
Bonita, Miss. C5 188
Bonita Springs, Fla. F5 174
Bonito, Braz. k6 138
Bonlee, N.C. B4 197
Bonn, Ger. C2 61
Bonne, bay, Newf., Can. D2 152
Bonne Terre, Mo. D7 189
Bonneau, S.C. E8 203
Bonner, Mont. D3 190
Bonner, co., Idaho A2 177
Bonner Springs, Kans. B8, C9 181
Bonnerdale, Ark. C2 169
Bonners Ferry, Idaho A2 177
Bönnerup Strand, Den. B4 62
Bonnet, lake, Man., Can. D4 150
Bonnet Carre, spillway and floodway, La. B7 183
Bonnétable, Fr. C4 58
Bonneville, Fr. C2 66
Bonneville, Oreg. B5 201
Bonneville, Wyo. B4 213
Bonneville, co., Idaho F7 177
Bonneville, dam, Oreg., Wash. B4 **201**, D4 210
Bonneville, peak, Idaho G6 177
Bonney Lake, Wash. B3 210
Bonnie, Ill. E5 178
Bonnie Doone, N.C. *B5 197
Bonnieville, Ky. C4 182
Bonnots Mill, Mo. C6 189
Bonny, Nig. F6 103
Bonny, res., Colo. B8 171
Bonny Blue, Va. B2 209
Bonnyville, Calif. *B2 170
Bonnyville, Alta., Can. B5 148
Bono, Ark. B5 169
Bonorva, It. D2 67
Bonsal, N.C. B5 197
Bonsecours, Que., Can. D5 154
Bonsucesso, Braz. m7 137
Bontang, Indon. E5 90
Bonthain, Indon. G5 90
Bonthe, S.L. E2 103
Book, cliffs, Colo., Utah B1 171
Booker, Tex. A2 206
Booker T. Washington, nat. mon., Va. D3 209
Booligal, Austl. F5 112
Boom, Tenn. C8 205
Boomer, W. Va. C3, D6 211
Boon, Mich. D5 186
Boone, Colo. C6 171
Boone, Iowa B4 180
Boone, Nebr. C8 191
Boone, N.C. A2 197
Boone, co., Ark. A2 169
Boone, co., Ill. A5 178
Boone, co., Ind. D4 179
Boone, co., Iowa C3 180
Boone, co., Ky. B5 182
Boone, co., Mo. B5 189
Boone, co., Nebr. C7 191
Boone, co., W. Va. C3 211
Boone, res., Tenn. C11 205
Boone, riv., Iowa B4 180
Boone Grove, Ind. B3 179
Boones Mill, Va. D3 209
Booneville, Ark. B2 169
Booneville, Ky. C6 182
Booneville, Miss. A5 188
Boons, pond, Mass. C1 185
Boonsboro, Md. A2 173
Boonton, N.J. B4 194
Boonville, Calif. C2 170
Boonville, Ind. H3 179
Boonville, Mo. C5 189
Boonville, N.Y. B5 196
Boonville, N.C. A3 197
Boot, Eng. F5 57
Booth, Ala. C3 166
Boothbay, Maine E3 184
Boothbay Harbor, Maine E3 184
Boothby, cape, Ant. C18 120
Boothia, gulf, N.W. Ter., Can. C15 142
Boothia, pen., N.W. Ter., Can. B14 142
Booths, creek, W. Va. A7 211
Boothville, La. E6 183
Bootle, Eng. A4 56
Booué, Gabon E2 104
Boporo, Lib. E2 103
Boppard, Ger. C2 61
Boque, inlet, N.C. C6 197
Boquerón, P.R. C2 132
Boqueron, dept., Par. D3 135
Boqueron, pass, Peru C2 134
Boqueron, riv., Pan. k11 130
Boquete, Pan. F6 130
Bor, Sov. Un. C15 **72**, B2 73
Bor, Sud. D3 105
Bor, Yugo. C6 68
Bor Nor, lake, China B8 91
Borah, peak, Idaho E5 177
Borama, Som. C5 105
Borås, Swe. A6 **62**, I5 63
Borāzjān, Iran G5 86
Borba, Braz. C3 139
Borborema, plat., Braz. h5 138
Borculo, Neth. B6 59
Bordeaux, Fr. E3 58
Bordeaux, Tenn. E9 205
Borden, Sask., Can. E2 155
Borden (New Providence), Ind. H6 179
Borden, co., Tex. C2 206
Borden, isl., N.W. Ter., Can. B26 118
Borden Springs, Ala. B4 166
Bordentown, N.J. C3 194
Border, Wyo. C2 213
Borderland, W. Va. D2 211
Bordertown, Austl. H3 112
Bordighera, It. C1 67
Bordj Amquid, Alg. D6 102
Bordj Flamand, Alg. D5 102
Bordj Fouchet, Alg. D3 102
Bordj Ouallen, Alg. E5 102
Bordj Viollette, Alg. D4 102
Bordley, Ky. C2 182
Bordulac, N. Dak. B7 198
Bordzon, Mong. C1 92
Boré, Mali C4 103
Boren, lake, Swe. u33 63
Borensberg, Swe. u33 63
Borgå, Fin. G11 63
Borgan, bay, New Britain I. 115
Börger, Ger. B7 59
Borger, Neth. B6 59
Borger, Tex. B2 206
Borgerhout, Bel. *C4 59
Borgholm, Swe. I7 63
Borghorst, Ger. A2 61
Borgne, lake, La. D6 183
Borgo Piave, It. k9 67
Borgo Val di Taro, It. B2 67
Borgo Valsugana, It. C7 66
Borgomanero, It. B2 67
Borikhane, Laos C5 89
Borinquen, P.R. B2 132
Borislav, Sov. Un. G4 72
Borisoglebsk, Sov. Un. C2 73
Borisov, Sov. Un. D7 72
Borispol, Sov. Un. F8 72
Borja, Sp. B5 65
Borjas Blancas, Sp. B6 65
Borken, Ger. B1 61
Borken, Ger. B4 61
Börkop, Den. C3 62
Borkou, reg., Chad B3 104
Borkum, Ger. A6 59
Borkum, isl., Ger. B3 60
Borlänge, Swe. G6 63
Bormes, Fr. F7 58
Bormida, riv., It. E4 66
Bormio, It. C6 66
Borna, Ger. B7 61
Borne, Neth. B6 59
Borneo, North, see North Borneo, reg., Mala.
Borneo (Kalimantan), isl., Asia E4 90
Bornheim, Ger. C2 61
Bornholm, co., Den. C8 62
Bornholm, isl., Den. C8 62
Bornos, Sp. D3 65
Boromlya, Sov. Un. F10 72
Boromo, Upper Volta D4 103
Boron, Calif. E5 170
Borovan, Bul. D6 68
Borovichi, Sov. Un. B9 72
Borovskoye, Sov. Un. q21 72
Borrby, Swe. C8 62
Borre, Den. D6 62
Borrego Springs, Calif. F5 170
Borroloola, Austl. C6 111
Bort-les-Orgues, Fr. E5 58
Boruca, C.R. F6 130
Borūjerd, Iran E4 86
Borup, Minn. C2 187
Borzna, Sov. Un. F9 72
Borzonasca, It. E5 66
Bosa, It. D2 67
Bosanska Dubica, Yugo. C3 68
Bosanska Gradiska, Yugo. C3 68
Bosanska Kostajnica, Yugo. C3 68
Bosanski Novi, Yugo. C3 68
Bosanski Petrovac, Yugo. C3 68
Bosanski Šamac, Yugo. C4 68
Bosaso, Som. C6 105
Boscawen, N.H. D3 193
Bosco, La. B3 183
Boscobel, Wis. E3 212
Bosdagan, Tur. D7 69
Boshrūyeh, Iran E8 86
Boskovice, Czech. D4 70
Bosler, Wyo. D7 213
Bosna, riv., Yugo. C3 68
Bosnek, Indon. F9 90
Bosnia, reg., Yugo. C3 68
c. 1360 48
in 1721 49
in 1914 52
Bosobolo, Zaire A2 106
Bosporus, strait, Tur. B7 85
Bosque, N. Mex. C3 195
Bosque, co., Tex. D4 206
Bossangoa, Cen. Afr. Rep. D3 104
Bossembélé, Cen. Afr. Rep. D3 104
Bossier, par., La. B2 183
Bossier City, La. B2 183
Bosso, Niger D7 103
Boston, Eng. B7 56
Boston, Ga. F3 175
Boston, Ind. E8 179
Boston, Mass. B5, D3 185
Boston, Tex. C5 206
Boston, bay, Mass. B6 185
Boston, mts., Ark. B2 169
Boston, mts., Okla. B7 200
Boston Bar, B.C., Can. E7 149
Boston Heights, Ohio B2 199
Bostonnais, riv., Que., Can. B5 154
Bostwick, Fla. C5 174
Bostwick, Ga. C3 175
Bostwick, Nebr. D7 191
Boswarlos, Newf., Can. D2 152
Boswell, Ark. A3 169
Boswell, B.C., Can. E9 149
Boswell, Ind. C3 179
Boswell, Okla. C6 200
Boswell, Pa. F3 202
Bosworth, Mo. B4 189
Botetourt, co., Va. D3 209
Botev, peak, Bul. D7 68
Botevgrad, Bul. D6 68
Botha, Alta., Can. C4 148
Bothell, Wash. B3 210
Bothnia, gulf, Eur. F9 63
Bothwell, Ont., Can. E3 153
Bothwell, P.E.I., Can. C7 151
Bothwell, Utah B3 207
Botiala, Som. C6 105
Botijas, P.R. C5 132
Botkinburg, Ark. B3 169
Botkins, Ohio B3 199
Botkyrka, Swe. t35 63
Botolan, Phil. o13 90
Botoşani, Rom. B8 68
Botrange, mtn., Bel. D6 59
Botsford, Conn. D3 172
BOTSWANA, country., Afr. B3 **107**, 99
Bottineau, N. Dak. A5 198
Bottineau, co., N. Dak. A4 198
Bottrop, Ger. B1 61
Botucatú, Braz. C3, m7 137
Botwood, Newf., Can. D4 152
Bou Arfa, Mor. C4 102
Bou Djébena (Well), Mali C4 103
Bou Saada, Alg. B5 102
Bouaflé, I.C. E3 103
Bouaké, I.C. E3 103
Bouar, Cen. Afr. Rep. D3 104
Boucau, Fr. F3 58
Boucher, lake, Que., Can. C2 152
Boucherville, Que., Can. D4, D9 154
Bouchette, Que., Can. C2 154
Boudenib, Mor. C4 102
Boudreaux, lake, La. E5 183
Bougainville, isl., Sol. Is. 115
Bougainville, strait, New Hebr. 115
Bougainville, strait, Sol. Is. 115
Bougaroun, cape, Alg. F10 64
Bougival, Fr. g9 58
Bougouni, Mali D3 103
Bouillon, Bel. E5 59
Boulder, Austl. F3 111
Boulder, Colo. A5 171
Boulder, Mont. D4 190
Boulder, Utah F4 207
Boulder, Wyo. C3 213
Boulder, co., Colo. A5 171
Boulder City, Nev. H7 192
Boulder Creek, Calif. C5 170
Boulevard, Calif. F5 170
Boulevard Heights, Md. C2 173
Boulloum (Well), Niger C7 103
Boulogne-Billancourt, Fr. C5, g9 58
Boulogne-sur-Mer, Fr. B4 58
Boulsa, Upper Volta D4 103
Boumalne, Mor. C3 102
Bouna, I.C. E4 103
Bound Brook, N.J. B3 194
Boundary, Alsk. C11 167
Boundary, co., Idaho A2 177
Boundary, peak, Nev. F3 192
Boundary, range, B.C., Can. A2 149
Boundary, ranges, Alsk., B.C., Can. k22 167
Boundary, res., B.C., Can., Wash. A8 210
Boundary Bald, mtn., Maine C2 184
Boundiali, I.C. E3 103
Bountiful, Utah C4 207
Bounty, Sask., Can. F2 155
Bounty, is., Pac. O. J11 113
Bour-Khaya, bay, Sov. Un. B2 118
Bourbeuse, riv., Mo. C6 189
Bourbon, Ind. B5 179
Bourbon, Mo. C6 189
Bourbon, co., Kans. E9 181
Bourbon, co., Ky. B5 182
Bourbonnais, Ill. B6 178
Bourbonnais, former prov., Fr. D5 58
Bourbonne-les-Bains, Fr. B1 66
Bourem, Mali C4 103
Bourg, La. E5 183
Bourg-Bruche, Fr. A3 66
Bourg-de-Péage, Fr. E6 58
Bourg [-en-Bresse], Fr. D6 58
Bourg-la-Reine, Fr. g10 58
Bourg-St. Andéol, Fr. E6 58
Bourg-St. Maurice, Fr. D2 66
Bourges, Fr. D5 58
Bourget, Ont., Can. B9 153
Bourget, lake, Fr. D1 66
Bourgoin, Fr. E6 58
Bourjeïmat (Well), Maur. C2 103
Bourke, Austl. E5 112
Bourlamaque, Que., Can. *E9 153
Bourne, Eng. B7 56
Bourne, Mass. C6 185
Bournemouth, Eng. D6 56
Bourneville, Ohio C4 199
Bouse, Ariz. D2 168
Bousso, Chad C3 104
Boutaiha, Syr. B7 84
Boutilimit, Maur. C2 103
Bouton, Iowa *C3 180
Boutte, La. C6 183
Bouvet, isl., Atl. O. D13 120
Bovey, Minn. C5 187
Bovill, Idaho C2 177
Bovina, Miss. C3 188
Bovina, Tex. B1 206
Bovina Center, N.Y. C6 196
Bow, N.H. D3 193
Bow, Wash. A3 210
Bow, riv., Alta., Can. D4 148
Bow Island, Alta., Can. E5 148
Bow Mar, Colo. *B5 171
Bow Valley, Nebr. B8 191
Bowbells, N. Dak. A3 198
Bowden, Alta., Can. D3 148
Bowden, Okla. A5 200
Bowdens, N.C. B5 197
Bowdle S. Dak. B6 204
Bowdoin, Maine D6 184
Bowdoinham, Maine D3, D6 184
Bowdon, Ga. C1 175
Bowdon, N. Dak. B6 198
Bowen, Austl. C8 111
Bowen, Ill. C2 178
Bowen, cape, N.W. Ter., Can. B18 143
Bowens Mill, Ga. E3 175
Bowers, Del. B7 173
Bowers, coulee, Wash. B7 210
Bowerston, Ohio B6 199
Bowersville, Ga. B3 175
Bowersville, Ohio C4 199
Bowesmont, N. Dak. A8 198
Bowie, Ariz. E6 168
Bowie, Colo. C3 171
Bowie, Md. B4 173
Bowie, Tex. C4 206
Bowie, co., Tex. C5 206
Bowie, creek, Miss. D4 188
Bowlegs, Okla. B5 200
Bowler, Wis. D5 212
Bowling Green, Fla. E5 174
Bowling Green, Ind. F3 179
Bowling Green, Ky. D3 182
Bowling Green, Mo. B6 189
Bowling Green, Ohio A2, A4 199
Bowling Green, S.C. A5 203
Bowling Green, Va. C5 209
Bowlus, Minn. E4 187
Bowman, Ga. B3 175
Bowman, N. Dak. C2 198
Bowman, S.C. E6 203
Bowman, co., N. Dak. C2 198
Bowman, creek, Pa. A7 202
Bowman, mtn., B.C., Can. D7 149
Bowman-Haley, res., N. Dak. C2 198
Bowmanstown, Pa. *E10 202
Bowmanville, Ont., Can. D6 153
Bowmont, Idaho F2 177
Bowmore, Scot. E2 57
Bowokan, is., Indon. F6 90
Bowring, Okla. A5 200
Bowringpet, India F6 87
Bowser, lake, B.C., Can. A3 149
Bowsman, Man., Can. C1 150
Bowstring, lake, Minn. C5 187
Bowstring, riv., Minn. C5 187
Box, creek, Wyo. B7 213
Box Butte, co., Nebr. B2 191
Box Butte, creek, Nebr. B3 191
Box Elder, Mont. B6 190
Box Elder, S. Dak. C2 204
Box Elder, co., Utah B2 207
Box Elder, creek, Mont. E12 190

INDEX KEY Each place listed in **Bold-faced Type** has its population listed in the Population tables, pages 230 to 280.
Each country, shown in CAPITAL LETTERS, has its population listed in the World Political Information Table, pages 6 to 10.
* Does not appear on map; key shows general location.

Box Hill, Austl. *H5 112
Boxboro, Mass. A5, C1 185
Boxelder, creek, Colo. A6 171
Boxelder, creek, Mont. C8 190
Boxford, Mass. A6 185
Boxholm, Iowa B3 180
Boxmeer, Neth. C5 59
Boxtel, Neth. C5 59
Boy River, Minn. C4 187
Boyacá, dept., Col. B3 133
Boyce, La. C3 183
Boyce, Tex. B5 206
Boyce, Va. B4 209
Boyceville, Wis. C1 212
Boyd, Fla. B3 174
Boyd, Minn. F3 187
Boyd, Mont. E7 190
Boyd, Oreg. B5 201
Boyd, Tex. A5, C4 206
Boyd, Wis. D2 212
Boyd, co., Ky. B7 182
Boyd, co., Nebr. B7 191
Boyd, lake, Maine C4 184
Boydell, Ark. D4 169
Boyden, Iowa A2 180
Boyds, Md. B3 173
Boyds Cove, Newf., Can. D4 152
Boydsville, Ark. A5 169
Boydton, Va. E4 209
Boyer, riv., Iowa C2 180
Boyer Knob, mtn., Md. D3 173
Boyera, Zaire B2 106
Boyero, Colo. C7 171
Boyers, Pa. D2 202
Boyertown, Pa. F10 202
Boyes, Mont. E11 190
Boyes Hot Springs, Calif. B5 170
Boykin, Ga. E2 175
Boykins, Va. E5 209
Boyle, Alta., Can. B4 148
Boyle, Ire. C2 55
Boyle, Miss. B3 188
Boyle, co., Ky. C5 182
Boylston, Ala. C3 166
Boylston, N.S., Can. D8 151
Boylston Center (Boylston), Mass. B4 185
Boyne City, Mich. C5 186
Boyne Falls, Mich. C6 186
Boynton, Okla. B6 200
Boynton, Pa. G3 202
Boynton Beach, Fla. F6 174
Boys Ranch, Tex. B1 206
Boys Town, Nebr. D3 191
Boysen, res., Wyo. B4 213
Boz, cape, Tur. B7 69
Bozcaada, Tur. C6 69
Bozcaada (Tenedos), isl., Tur. C6 69
Bozeman, Mont. E5 190
Bozeman, pass, Mont. E6 190
Bozman, Md. C5 173
Bozoum, Cen. Afr. Rep. D3 104
Bozovici, Rom. C5 68
Bozrah, Conn. *C8 172
Bozüyük, Tur. C8 85
Bra, It. B1 67
Brabant, isl., Ant. C6 120
Brabant, lake, Sask., Can. A4 155
Brabant, prov., Bel. D4 59
Brabrand, Den. B4 62
Brač, isl., Yugo. D3 68
Bracadale, Scot. C2 57
Bracadale, bay, Scot. C2 57
Bracciano, It. g8 67
Bracciano, lake, It. C4 67
Bracebridge, Ont., Can. B5 153
Braceville, Ill. B5 178
Brach, Libya D2 101
Bracken, Sask., Can. H1 155
Bracken, co., Ky. B5 182
Brackenridge, Pa. A7 202
Brackettville, Tex. E2 206
Brackley, Eng. B6 56
Brackwede, Ger. B3 61
Brad, Rom. B6 68
Bradano, riv., It. D6 67
Braddock, N.J. D3 194
Braddock, N. Dak. C5 198
Braddock, Pa. B6 202
Braddock Heights, Md. B2 173
Braddock Hills, Pa. *F1 202
Braddyville, Iowa D2 180
Braden, Tenn. B2 205
Bradenton, Fla. E4, F2 174
Bradenton Beach, Fla. *E4 174
Bradenton South, Fla. *E4 174
Bradenville, Pa. F3 202
Bradford, Ark. B4 169
Bradford, Ont., Can. C5 153
Bradford, Eng. A6 56
Bradford, Ill. B4 178
Bradford, Iowa B4 180
Bradford, Maine C4 184
Bradford, N.H. D3 193
Bradford, Ohio B3 199
Bradford, Pa. C4 202
Bradford, R.I. D9 172
Bradford, Tenn. A3 205
Bradford Vt. D4 208
Bradford co., Fla. C4 174
Bradford, co., Pa. C8 202
Bradford, mtn., Conn. B3 172
Bradford Center, Maine C4 184
Bradfordsville, Ky. C4 182
Bradfordwoods, Pa. A5 202
Bradgate, Iowa B3 180
Bradley, Ala. D3 166
Bradley, Ark. D2 169
Bradley, Calif. E3 170
Bradley, Fla. E5 174
Bradley, Ill. B6 178
Bradley, Maine D4 184
Bradley, Ohio B7 199
Bradley, Okla. C4 200
Bradley, S.C. C3 203
Bradley, S. Dak. B8 204
Bradley, co., Ark. D3 169
Bradley, co., Tenn. D9 205
Bradley Beach, N.J. C4 194
Bradleyton, Ala. D3 166
Bradner, Ohio A4 199
Bradore, bay, Newf., Can. C3 152
Bradore, hills, Newf., Can. C3 152
Bradshaw, Ind. E2 179
Bradshaw, Nebr. D8 191
Bradshaw, Tex. C3 206
Bradshaw, W. Va. D3 211
Bradshaw, mts., Ariz. C3 168
Bradstreet, Mass. B2 185
Bradwardine, Man., Can. E1 150
Bradwell, Sask., Can. F2 155
Brady, Mont. B5 190
Brady, Nebr. C5 191
Brady, Tex. D3 206
Brady, mts., Tex. D3 206
Brady's Hot Springs, Nev. D3 192
Bradyville, Tenn. B5 205
Braedstrup, Den. C3 62
Braemar, Scot. D5 57
Braeside, Ont., Can. B8 153
Braga, Port. B1 65
Bragado, Arg. B4, g6 136
Bragança, Braz. B1 138
Bragança, Port. B2 65
Bragança Paulista, Braz. C3, m8 137
Bragg City, Mo. E8 189
Braggadocio, Mo. E8 189
Braggs, Okla. B6 200
Braham, Minn. E5 187
Brāhmanbāria, Bngl. D9 87
Brahmani, riv., India G10 88
Brahmaputra, riv., Asia C9 87
Brahmaputra, see Tsangpo, riv., China
Brahme, riv., Ger. D3 62
Braidwood, Ill. B5 178
Brăila, Rom. C8 68
Brainard, Nebr. C9 191
Braine-le-Comte, Bel. D4 59
Brainerd, Kans. B6 181
Brainerd, Minn. D4 187
Braintree, Mass. B5, D3 185
Braintree, Vt. D3 208
Braintree, mtn., Vt. D3 208
Braithwaite, La. C7 183
Brake, Ger. E2 62
Brakel, Ger. B4 61
Brakpan, S. Afr. C4 107
Bralorne, B.C., Can. D6 149
Braman, Okla. A4 200
Bramhapuri, India G7 88
Bramminge, Den. C2 62
Brampton, Ont., Can. D5, E6 153
Brampton, Eng. F6 57
Brampton, N. Dak. D8 198
Bramsche, Ger. B7 59
Bramwell, W. Va. D3 211
Branaman, Ariz. D5 168
Branch, Ark. B2 169
Branch, Newf., Can. E5 152
Branch, La. D3 183
Branch, Miss. C4 188
Branch, Wis. B6 212
Branch, co., Mich. G5 186
Branch, pond, Maine D4 184
Branch, riv., Wis. A6 212
Branchland, W. Va. C2 211
Branchport, N.Y. C3 196
Branchville, Ala. B3 166
Branchville, Conn. D3 172
Branchville, N.J. A3 194
Branchville, S.C. E6 203
Branchville, Va. E5 209
Branco, riv., Braz. C5 133
Branco, riv., Braz. E2 139
Brandberg, mtn., S.W. Afr. B1 107
Brande, Den. C3 62
Brandenburg, Ger. A7 61
Brandenburg, Ky. B3 182
Brandenburg, former state, Ger. A7 61
Brandenburg, reg., Ger. B6 60
c. 1360 48
in 1721 49
in 1867 51
Brandon, Man., Can. E2 150
Brandon, Colo. C8 171
Brandon, Fla. E4 174
Brandon, Iowa B6 180
Brandon, Minn. E3 187
Brandon, Miss. C4 188
Brandon, Nebr. D4 191
Brandon, S.C. B3 203
Brandon, S. Dak. D9 204
Brandon, Vt. D2 208
Brandon, Wis. E5 212
Brandon, hill, Ire. D1 55
Brandsville, Mo. E6 189
Brandt, Ohio C3 199
Brandt, Pa. C10 202
Brandt, S. Dak. C9 204
Brandvlei, S. Afr. D3 107
Brandy, peak, Oreg. E3 201
Brandy Station, Va. C5 209
Brandýs nad Labem, Czech. n18 70
Brandywine, Md. C4 173
Brandywine, W. Va. C5 211
Brandywine, creek, Del. A6 173
Braniewo, Pol. A5 70
Bransfield, strait, Ant. C6 120
Brańsk, Pol. B7 70
Branson, Colo. D7 171
Branson, Mo. E4 189
Brant, Alta., Can. D4 148
Brant, co., Ont., Can. D4 153
Brant Lake, N.Y. B7 196
Brant Rock, Mass. B6 185
Brantford, Ont., Can. D4 153
Brantford, N. Dak. B7 198
Brantley, Ala. D3 166
Brantley, co., Ga. E4 175
Brantwood, Wis. C3 212
Bras-d'Apic, Que., Can. C7 154
Bras d'Or, lake, N.S., Can. D9 151
Brasfield, Ark. C4 169
Brashear, Mo. A5 189
Brasiléia, Braz. D4 134
Brasília, Braz. B3 137, E1 138
Brasília, Braz. E2 138
Braşov, Rom. C7 68
Brass, Nig. F6 103
Brass, is., Vir. Is. f15 132
Brasstown, N.C. D2 197
Brasstown Bald, mtn., Ga. B3 175
Brassua, lake, Maine C3 184
Bratenahl, Ohio B2 199
Bratislava, Czech. D4 70
Bratsk, Sov. Un. *D13 71
Bratslav, Sov. Un. G7 72
Bratt, Fla. G1 174
Brattleboro, Vt. F3 208
Braunau [am Inn], Aus. D6 60
Braunfels, Ger. C3 61
Braunschweig (Brunswick), Ger. A5 61
Brava, Som. E5 105
Brave, Pa. G1 202
Bråviken, lake, Swe. u34 63
Bravo, riv., Chile D2 136
Brawley, Calif. F6 170
Braxton, Miss. C4 188
Braxton, co., W. Va. C4 211
Bray, Ire. D3 55
Braymer, Mo. B4 189
Brayton, Iowa C3 180
Brazeau, mtn., Alta., Can. C2 148
Brazeau, riv., Alta., Can. C2 148
Brazil, Ind. E3 179
Brazil, Iowa D5 180
Brazil, Tenn. B2 205
BRAZIL, country, S.A. C3 137, C2 138
Brazil Lake, N.S., Can. F4 151
Brazilton, Kans. E9 181
Brazoria, Tex. E5, G4 206
Brazoria, co., Tex. E5 206
Brazos, N. Mex. A3 195
Brazos, co., Tex. D4 206
Brazos, peak, N. Mex. A3 195
Brazos, riv., Tex. D4 206
Brazzaville, Con. F3 104
Brčko, Yugo. C4 68
Brda, riv., Pol. B4 70
Brea, Calif. F3 170
Brea, pt., P.R. D3 132
Bread Loaf, mtn., Vt. D3 208
Bread Tray, mtn., Mo. E5 189
Breaden, lake, Austl. E4 110
Breakenridge, mtn., B.C., Can. E7 149
Breaker, pt., Am. Sam. 114
Breakeyville, Que., Can. C9 154
Breathitt, co., Ky. C6 182
Breaux Bridge, La. D4 183
Brechin, Ont., Can. C5 153
Brechin, Scot. D6 57
Breckenridge, Colo. B4 171
Breckenridge, Mich. E6 186
Breckenridge, Minn. D2 187
Breckenridge, Mo. B4 189
Breckenridge, Tex. C3 206
Breckenridge Hills, Mo. *A8 189
Breckenridge Station, Que., Can. A9 153
Breckinridge, Okla. A4 200
Breckinridge, co., Ky. C3 182
Brecknock, co., Wales C4 56
Brecksville, Ohio A6, B2 199
Břeclav, Czech. D4 70
Brecon, Wales C4 56
Brecon Beacons, mts., Wales C4 56
Breda, Iowa B3 180
Breda, Neth. C4 59
Bredaryd, Swe. B7 62
Bredasdorp, S. Afr. D3 107
Bredenbury, Sask., Can. G4 155
Bredstedt, Ger. D2 62
Bree, Bel. C5 59
Breese, Ill. E4 178
Bregalnica, riv., Yugo. E6 68
Bregenz, Aus. E4 60
Bregovo, Bul. C6 68
Breien, N. Dak. C5 198
Breil [sur Roya], Fr. F7 58
Breisach, Ger. A3 66
Brejo, Braz. B2 138
Bremen, Ala. B2 166
Bremen, Ga. C1 175
Bremen, Ger. B4 60, E2 62
Bremen, Ind. B5 179
Bremen, Ky. C2 182
Bremen, N. Dak. B6 198
Bremen, Ohio C5 199
Bremen, state, Ger. E2 62
Bremer, co., Iowa B5 180
Bremerhaven, Ger. B4 60, E2 62
Bremerton, Wash. B3, D1 210
Bremervörde, Ger. E3 62
Bremo Bluff, Va. D4 209
Bremond, Tex. D4 206
Brendon, hills, Eng. C4 56
Brenham, Tex. D4 206
Brenish, Scot. B1 57
Brenner, pass, Aus., It. E5 60, C7 66
Brent, Ala. C2 166
Brent, Ont., Can. A6 153
Brent, Eng. C7 56
Brent, Fla. G2 174
Brenta, riv., It. D7 66
Brentford, S. Dak. B7 204
Brentford & Chiswick, Eng. *m11 55
Brenton, pt., R.I. D11 172
Brentwood, Calif. B6 170
Brentwood, Eng. *C8 56
Brentwood, Md. C1 173
Brentwood, Mo. B8 189
Brentwood, N.H. E4 193
Brentwood, N.Y. F4 172
Brentwood, Pa. B6 202
Brentwood, Tenn. A5, E9 205
Brescia, It. D6 66, B3 67
Breskens, Neth. C3 59
Breslau, see Wrocław, Pol.
Bressanone, It. A3 67
Bressuire, Fr. D3 58
Brest, Fr. C1 58
Brest, Sov. Un. E4 72
Breteuil, Fr. E2 59
Bretigny [-sur-Orge], Fr. F2 59
Breton, Alta., Can. C3 148
Breton, isl., La. E6 183
Breton, sound, La. E6 183
Breton, strait, Fr. D3 58
Breton Woods, N.J. C4 194
Bretton Woods, N.H. B4 193
Breuil, It. D3 66
Brevard, N.C. D3 197
Brevard, co., Fla. D6 174
Breves, Braz. C4 139
Brevik, Nor. p27 63
Břevnov, Czech. n17 70
Brevoort, lake, Mich. B6 186
Brewarrina, Austl. E6 112
Brewer, Maine D4 184
Brewer, Mo. D8 189
Brewers, Hond. C5 130
Brewster, Kans. C2 181
Brewster, Mass. C7 185
Brewster, Minn. G3 187
Brewster, Nebr. C6 191
Brewster, N.Y. D3, D7 196
Brewster, Ohio B6 199
Brewster, Wash. A6 210
Brewster, co., Tex. E1 206
Brewster, is., Mass. D3 185
Brewton, Ala. D2 166
Brewton, Ga. D4 175
Brežice, Yugo. C2 68
Březnice, Czech. D8 61
Breznik, Bul. D6 68
Brezno [nad Hronom], Czech. D5 70
Bria, Cen. Afr. Rep. D4 104
Brian Boru, peak, B.C., Can. B4 149
Brian Head, mtn., Utah F3 207
Briançon, Fr. E7 58
Briarcliff Manor, N.Y. D7 196
Briare, Fr. D5 58
Brice, Ohio C2 199
Bricelyn, Minn. G5 187
Briceville, Tenn. C9 205
Brickaville, Malag. g9 107
Brickeys, Ark. C5 169
Bricktown, N.J. C4 194
Brickyard, Ala. C4 166
Bridal Veil, Oreg. B4 201
Bridal Veil, falls, Utah C4 207
Brideport, Mich. E7 186
Bridesville, B.C., Can. E8 149
Bridge, Oreg. D3 201
Bridge City, Tex. *D6 206
Bridge Lake, B.C., Can. D7 149
Bridgeboro, Ga. E3 175
Bridgeboro, N.J. C3 194
Bridgedale, N.B., Can. *C5 151
Bridgeford, Sask., Can. G2 155
Bridgehampton, N.Y. D4 196
Bridgeland, Utah C5 207
Bridgend, Wales C4 56
Bridgeport, Ala. A4 166
Bridgeport, Calif. C4 170
Bridgeport, Ont., Can. *D4 153
Bridgeport, Conn. E4 172
Bridgeport, Ill. E6 178
Bridgeport, Ind. H7 179
Bridgeport, Mich. E7 186
Bridgeport, Nebr. C2 191
Bridgeport, N.J. D2 194
Bridgeport, Ohio B7 199
Bridgeport, Okla. B3 200
Bridgeport, Oreg. C9 201
Bridgeport, Pa. A10, F11 202
Bridgeport, Tex. C4 206
Bridgeport, Wash. A6 210
Bridgeport, W. Va. B4, B7 211
Bridger, Mont. E8 190
Bridger, S. Dak. C4 204
Bridger, basin, Wyo. D3 213
Bridger, mts., Wyo. B4 213
Bridger, peak, Wyo. D5 213
Bridger, range, Mont. E6 190
Bridgeton, Ind. E3 179
Bridgeton, Mo. A8, C7 189
Bridgeton, N.J. E2 194
Bridgeton, N.C. B6 197
Bridgeton, Oreg. A2 201
Bridgeton Terrace, Mo. *C7 189
Bridgetown, Barb. p17 131
Bridgetown, N.S., Can. E4 151
Bridgeville, N.S., Can. D7 151
Bridgeville, Del. C6 173
Bridgeville, Pa. B5 202
Bridgewater, Austl. o15 111
Bridgewater, N.S., Can. E5 151
Bridgewater, Conn. C3 172
Bridgewater, Iowa C3 180
Bridgewater, Maine B5 184
Bridgewater, Mass. C6 185
Bridgewater, N.H. C3 193
Bridgewater, S. Dak. D8 204
Bridgewater, Vt. D3 208
Bridgewater, Va. C4 209
Bridgewater Corners, Vt. D3 208
Bridgman, Mich. G4 186
Bridgnorth, Eng. B5 56
Bridgton, Maine D2 184
Bridgwater, Eng. C5 56
Bridgwater, bay, Eng. C4 56
Bridlington, Eng. C6 55
Bridport, Eng. D5 56
Bridport, Vt. D2 208
Brielle, N.J. C4 194
Brienz, lake, Switz. C3 66
Brier, creek, Ga. C5 175
Brier Hill, N.Y. B1 196
Briercrest, Sask., Can. G3 155
Briereville, Alta., Can. B5 148
Brierfield, Ala. B3 166
Brierley Hill, Eng. *B6 56
Brierly Knob, mtn., W. Va. C4 211
Brig Bay, Newf., Can. C3 152
Brig Harbour, isl., Newf., Can. A3 152
Brigantine, N.J. E4 194
Brigantine, beach, N.J. E4 194
Brigden, Ont., Can. E2 153
Brigg, Eng. A7 56
Briggs, Tex. D4 206
Briggsdale, Colo. A6 171
Briggsville, Ark. C2 169
Briggsville, Mass. A1 185
Briggsville, Wis. E4 212
Brigham City, Utah B3 207
Bright, Ont., Can. D4 153
Bright, lake, Ont., Can. B7 186
Brighton, Ala. B3, E4 166
Brighton, Ont., Can. C7 153
Brighton, Colo. B6 171
Brighton, Eng. D7 56
Brighton, Ill. D3 178
Brighton, Iowa C6 180
Brighton, Maine C3 184
Brighton, Mich. F7 186
Brighton, Oreg. B3 201
Brighton, Tenn. B2 205
Brighton, Indian res., Fla. E5 174
Brightsand, lake, Sask., Can. D1 155
Brightshade, Ky. C6 182
Brightwaters, N.Y. E3 196
Brigie, hill, Scot. F3 57
Brignoles, Fr. F7 58
Brigus, Newf., Can. E5 152
Brihuega, Sp. B4 65
Brijnagar, India E6 88
Brilhante, riv., Braz. C2 137
Brilliant, Ala. A2 166
Brilliant, B.C., Can. E9 149
Brilliant, Ohio B7 199
Brillion, Wis. A6, D5 212
Brilon, Ger. B3 61
Brimfield, Ill. C4 178
Brimfield, Mass. *B3 185
Brimhall, N. Mex. B1 195
Brimley, Mich. B6 186
Brimson, Minn. C7 187
Brimson, Mo. A4 189
Brindisi, It. D6 67
Bringhurst, Ind. C4 179
Brinje, Yugo. C2 68
Brinkhaven (Gann), Ohio B5 199
Brinkley, Ark. C4 169
Brinkman, Okla. B2 200
Brinkworth, Austl. F2 112
Brinnon, Wash. B3 210
Brinsmade, N. Dak. A6 198
Brinson, Ga. F2 175
Brion, isl., Que., Can. B8 151
Brioude, Fr. E5 58
Brisbane, Austl. C9 112
Briscoe, Tex. B2 206
Briscoe, co., Tex. B2 206
Bristol, N.B., Can. C2 151
Bristol, Colo. C8 171
Bristol, Conn. C5 172
Bristol, Eng. C5 56
Bristol, Fla. B2 174
Bristol, Ill. B5 178
Bristol, Ind. A6 179
Bristol, La. D3 183
Bristol, Maine *E3 184
Bristol, Md. C4 173
Bristol, N.H. C3 193
Bristol, Pa. F12 202
Bristol, R.I. C12 172
Bristol, S. Dak. B8 204
Bristol, Tenn. C11 205
Bristol, Vt. C2 208
Bristol (Independent City), Va. B2 209
Bristol, W. Va. B6 211
Bristol, Wis. F1, F5 212
Bristol, co., Mass. C5 185
Bristol, co., R.I. C11 172
Bristol, bay, Alsk. D7 167
Bristol, chan., Eng. C4 56
Bristol, pond, Vt. C2 208
Bristol Ferry, R.I. C12 172
Bristol Silver Mines Nev. E7 192
Bristolville, Ohio A7 199
Bristow, Ind. H4 179
Bristow, Iowa B5 180
Bristow, Nebr. B7 191
Bristow, Okla. B5 200
Bristow, Va. B4 209
Britain: c. 400 A.D. 46
Britannia 44
c. 120 A.D. 45
Britannia Bay, Ont., Can. A9 153
Britannia Beach, B.C., Can. E6 149
British, mts., Yukon, Can. B11 167
British Central Africa 99
British Columbia, prov., Can. 149
BRITISH HONDURAS, dep., N.A. B3 130
British North America: after Seven Years' War 162
British North Borneo, see North Borneo, reg., Mala.
British Somaliland 99
see also Somalia
British South Africa Co. 99
British Virgin Islands, see Virgin Islands British dep., N.A.
Britstown, S. Afr. D3 107
Britt, Ont., Can. B4 153
Britt, Iowa A4 180
Britt, Minn. C6 187
Brittany (Bretagne), former prov., Fr. C2 58
c. 814 47
Britton, Mich. G7 186
Britton, S. Dak. B8 204
Brive, [-la-Gaillarde], Fr. E4 58
Briviesca, Sp. A4 65
Brixham, Eng. D4 56
Brno, Czech. D4 70
Broach, India G4 88
Broad, bay, Scot. B2 57
Broad, riv., Ga. B4 175
Broad, riv., S.C. C5 203
Broad, run, Va. B4 209
Broad Brook, Conn. B6 172
Broad Law, mtn., Scot. E5 57
Broad Top, Pa. F5 202
Broadacres, Sask., Can. E1 155
Broadacres, Oreg. B2 201
Broadalbin, N.Y. B6 196
Broadback, riv., Que., Can. F17 143
Broadbent, Oreg. D2 201
Broaddus, Tex. D5 206
Broadford, Scot. C3 57
Broadford, Va. B3 209
Broadhead, creek, Pa. A2 194
Broadkill, riv., Del. C7 173
Broadkill Beach, Del. C7 173
Broadland, S. Dak. C7 204
Broadlands, Ill. D5 178
Broadmead, Oreg. B1 201
Broadmeadows, Austl. *H5 112
Broadmoor, Colo. C6 171
Broadus, Mont. E11 190
Broadview, Sask., Can. G4 155
Broadview, Ill. *F2 178
Broadview, Ind. *F4 179
Broadview, Mont. D8 190
Broadview, N. Mex. C6 195
Broadview Heights, Ohio B2 199
Broadwater, Nebr. C3 191
Broadwater, co., Mont. D5 190
Broadway, N.J. B2 194
Broadway, N.C. B4 197
Broadway, Ohio B4 199
Broadway, Va. C4 209
Broager, Den. D3 62
Brochet, Man., Can. C4 150
Brock, Sask., Can. *F2 155
Brock, Nebr. D10 191
Brocken, mtn., Ger. B5 61
Brocket, Alta., Can. E4 148
Brocket, N. Dak. A7 198
Brockport, N.Y. B3 196
Brockport, Pa. D4 202
Brockton, Mass. B5, E3 185
Brockton, Mont. B12 190
Brockton, res., Mass. E3 185
Brockville, Ont., Can. C9 153
Brockway, Mont. C11 190
Brockway, Pa. D4 202
Brockwell, Ark. A4 169
Brocton, Ill. D6 178
Brocton, N.Y. C1 196
Brod, Yugo. C4 68
Broderick, Calif. A6 170
Broderick, Sask., Can. F2 155
Brodeur, pen., N.W. Ter., Can. B15 142
Brodhead, Ky. C5 182
Brodhead, Wis. F4 212
Brodheadsville, Pa. E11 202
Brodick, Scot. E3 57
Brodnax, Va. E4 209
Brodnica, Pol. B5 70
Brody, Sov. Un. F5 72
Brogan, Oreg. C9 201
Brokaw, Wis. C4 212
Broken Arrow, Okla. A6 200
Broken Bow, Nebr. C6 191
Broken Bow, Okla. C7 200
Broken Bow, res., Okla. C7 200
Broken Hill, Austl. E3 112
Brokenburg, Va. C5 209
Brome, Ger. F4 62
Brome, co., Que., Can. D5 154
Brome, lake, Que., Can. D5 154
Bromhead, Sask., Can. H4 155
Bromide, Okla. C5 200
Bromley, Eng. m13 55
Bromley, Ky. *A5 182
Bromley, mtn., Vt. E3 208
Bromptonville, Que., Can. D6 154
Bromsgrove, Eng. B5 56
Bromyard, Eng. B5 56
Bronaugh, Mo. D3 189
Bronco, Tex. C1 206
Brønderslev, Den. A3 62
Brong-Ahafo, reg., Ghana E4 103
Bronnitsy, Sov. Un. n18 72
Brønnøysund, Nor. E5 63
Bronson, Fla. C4 174
Bronson, Iowa B1 180
Bronson, Kans. E8 181

INDEX KEY Each place listed in **Bold-faced Type** has its population listed in the Population tables, pages 230 to 280.
Each country, shown in CAPITAL LETTERS, has its population listed in the World Political Information Table, pages 6 to 10.
* Does not appear on map; key shows general location.

Bronson, Mich. G5 186
Bronson, Tex. D5 206
Bronte, Tex. D2 206
Bronwood, Ga. E2 175
Bronx, borough and co., N.Y. D2 196
Bronxville, N.Y. D2 196
Brook, Ind. C3 179
Brook Park, Minn. E5 187
Brook Park, Ohio B2 199
Brooke, Va. C5 209
Brooke, co., W. Va. A4 211
Brooker, Fla. C4 174
Brookeville, Md. B3 173
Brookfield, N.S., Can. D6 151
Brookfield, Conn. D3 172
Brookfield, Ga. E3 175
Brookfield, Ill. F2 178
Brookfield, Mass. B3 185
Brookfield, Mo. B4 189
Brookfield, N.H. C4 193
Brookfield, N.Y. C5 196
Brookfield, Vt. C3 208
Brookfield, Wis. E1 212
Brookfield Center, Conn. D3 172
Brookfield Mines, N.S., Can. E5 151
Brookford, N.C. B2 197
Brookhaven, Miss. D3 188
Brookhaven, N.Y. F5 172
Brookhaven, Pa. *G11 202
Brooking, Sask., Can. H3 155
Brookings, Oreg. E2 201
Brookings, S. Dak. C9 204
Brookings, co., S. Dak. C9 204
Brookland, Ark. B5 169
Brookland, Pa. C6 202
Brooklands, Man., Can. *E3 150
Brooklandville, Md. C2 173
Brooklawn, N.J. D2 194
Brooklet, Ga. D5 175
Brooklin, Ont., Can. D6 153
Brooklin, Maine D4 184
Brookline, Mass. B5, D2 185
Brookline, N.H. E3 193
Brooklyn, Ala. D3 166
Brooklyn, N.S., Can. E5 151
Brooklyn, Conn. *B9 172
Brooklyn, Ga. D2 175
Brooklyn (Lovejoy), Ill. B8 189
Brooklyn, Ill. C3 178
Brooklyn, Ind. E5 179
Brooklyn, Iowa C5 180
Brooklyn, Mich. F6 186
Brooklyn, Miss. D4 188
Brooklyn, Ohio B2 199
Brooklyn, Pa. C10 202
Brooklyn, Wash. C2 210
Brooklyn, Wis. F4 212
Brooklyn, borough (Kings co.), N.Y. E1 196
Brooklyn Center, Minn. E6 187
Brooklyn Heights, Ohio *A6 199
Brooklyn Park, Md. C2 173
Brooklyn Park, Minn. *E6 187
Brookmere, B.C., Can. E7 149
Brookneal, Va. D4 209
Brookport, Ill. F5 178
Brooks, Ala. D3 166
Brooks, Alta., Can. D5 148
Brooks, Iowa D3 180
Brooks, Ky. A4 182
Brooks, Maine D3 184
Brooks, Minn. C3 187
Brooks, Oreg. B2 201
Brooks, Wis. E4 212
Brooks, co., Ga. F3 175
Brooks, co., Tex. F3 206
Brooks, pen., B.C., Can. D4 149
Brooks, range, Alsk. B8 167
Brooksburg, Ind. G7 179
Brooksby, Sask., Can. E3 155
Brookshire, Tex. E5, F4 206
Brookside, Ala. E4 166
Brookside, Colo. C5 171
Brookside, Del. A6 173
Brookside, N.J. B3 194
Brookside, Ohio *B7 199
Brookside, Tex. *E5 206
Brookston, Ind. C4 179
Brookston, Minn. D6 187
Brookston, Pa. C4 202
Brooksville, Fla. D4 174
Brooksville, Ky. B5 182
Brooksville, Okla. B5 200
Brooksville, Maine D4 184
Brooksville, Miss. B5 188
Brookton, Maine C5 184
Brooktondale, N.Y. C4 196
Brookvale, Colo. B5 171
Brookview, Md. C6 173
Brookville, Ill. A4 178
Brookville, Ind. F7 179
Brookville, Kans. D6 181
Brookville, Mass. E3 185
Brookville, N.Y. *F2 172
Brookville, Ohio C3 199
Brookville, Pa. D3 202
Brookwood, Ala. B2 166
Broom, inlet, Scot. C3 57
Broome, Austl. C3 111
Broome, Tex. D2 206
Broome, co., N.Y. C5 196
Broomes Island, Md. D4 173
Broomfield Heights, Colo. *B5 171
Brooten, Minn. E3 187
Brora, Scot. B5 57
Brora, riv., Scot. B4 57
Brösarp, Swe. C6 62
Broseley, Mo. E7 189
Brossard, Que., Can. D9 154
Brotas de Macaúbas, Braz. D2 138
Brothers, Oreg. D6 201
Brothers, is., Thai. I3 89
Brotherton, Tenn. C8 205
Brothertown, Wis. B5 212
Brough, Eng. F6 57
Brough, head, Scot. A5 57
Brough Ness, cape, Scot. B6 57
Broughton, Ill. F5 178
Broughton, Kans. C6 181
Broughton Station, Que., Can. C6 154
Broussard, La. D4 183
Brovst, Den. A3 62
Broward, co., Fla. F6 174
Browerville, Minn. D4 187
Brown, co., Ill. D3 178
Brown, co., Ind. F5 179
Brown, co., Kans. C8 181
Brown, co., Minn. F4 187
Brown, co., Nebr. B6 191
Brown, co., Ohio D4 199
Brown, co., S. Dak. B7 204
Brown, co., Tex. D3 206
Brown, co., Wis. D6 212
Brown, cape, N.W. Ter., Can. C16 143
Brown, mtn., Mont. B5 190
Brown, pt., Wash. C1 210
Brown, riv., Vt. B2 208
Brown City, Mich. E8 186
Brown Deer, Wis. E2 212
Brown or Roan, cliffs, Colo., Utah D6 207
Brownell, Kans. D4 181
Brownfield, Ill. F5 178
Brownfield, Maine E2 184
Brownfield, Tex. C1 206
Browning, Sask., Can. H4 155
Browning, Ill. C3 178
Browning, Mo. A4 189
Browning, Mont. B3 190
Browning, entrance, B.C., Can. C2 149
Brownington, Mo. C4 189
Brownington, Vt. B4 208
Brownington Center, Vt. B4 208
Brownlee, Sask., Can. G2 155
Brownlee, Nebr. B5 191
Brownlee, Oreg. C10 201
Brownlee, res., Idaho, Oreg. E1 177
Browns, Ill. E6 178
Browns, Mont. B5 190
Browns, inlet, N.C. C6 197
Browns, peak, Ariz. D4 168
Browns Mills, N.J. D3 194
Browns Valley, Ind. E4 179
Browns Valley, Minn. E2 187
Brownsboro, Ky. A4 182
Brownsboro, Tex. *C5 206
Brownsburg, Que., Can. D3 154
Brownsburg, Ind. E5 179
Brownsburg, Va. D3 209
Brownsdale, Minn. G6 187
Brownsmead, Oreg. A3 201
Brownstown, Ill. E5 178
Brownstown, Ind. G5 179
Brownstown, Pa. *F4 202
Brownstown, Pa. F9 202
Brownstown, Wash. C5 210
Brownsville, Ind. E7 179
Brownsville, Ky. C3 182
Brownsville, Minn. G7 187
Brownsville, Oreg. C4 201
Brownsville, Pa. F2 202
Brownsville, Tenn. B2 205
Brownsville, Tex. G4 206
Brownsville, Vt. E4 208
Brownton, Minn. F4 187
Brownton, W. Va. B4 211
Browntown, Wis. F4 212
Brownvale, Alta., Can. A2 148
Brownville, Ala. B2 166
Brownville, Maine C3 184
Brownville, Nebr. D10 191
Brownville, N.Y. A5 196
Brownville Junction, Maine C3 184
Brownwood, Mo. D8 189
Brownwood, Tex. D3 206
Brownwood, Tex. *D6 206
Brownwood, lake, Tex. D3 206
Broxton, Ga. E4 175
Broye, riv., Switz. C2 66
Brozas, Sp. C2 65
Bruay-en-Artois, Fr. D2 59
Bruce, Alta., Can. C4 148
Bruce, Fla. G3 174
Bruce, Miss. B4 188
Bruce, S. Dak. C9 204
Bruce, Wis. C2 212
Bruce, co., Ont., Can. C3 153
Bruce, mtn., Austl. D2 110
Bruce, pen., Ont., Can. B3 153
Bruce Crossing, Mich. A6 186
Brucefield, Ont., Can. D3 153
Bruceton, Tenn. A3 205
Bruceton Mills, W. Va. B5 211
Brucetown, Va. B4 209
Bruceville, Ind. G3 179
Bruchsal, Ger. D3 61
Bruck, Aus. E7 60
Brück, Ger. A7 61
Bruck [-Fusch] (Bruck an der Grossglocknerstrasse), Aus. B8 66
Brückenau, Ger. C4 61
Bruederheim, Alta., Can. C4 148
Bruels, pt., Calif. C2 170
Bruges (Brugge), Bel. C3 59
Brugge, see Bruges, Bel.
Brühl, Ger. C1 61
Bruin, Pa. D2 202
Bruin Point, mtn., Utah D5 207
Brule, Nebr. C4 191
Brule, Wis. B2 212
Brule, co., S. Dak. D6 204
Brule, riv., Mich. C2 186
Brule, riv., Wis. B2 212
Brule Lake Station, Ont., Can. B6 153
Brumath, Fr. C7 58
Brumley, Mo. C5 189
Brumley, mtn., Va. B2 209
Brundidge, Ala. D4 166
Bruneau, Idaho G3 177
Bruneau, riv., Idaho, Nev. B6 192, G3 177
BRUNEI, Br. dep., Asia E4 90
Brunete, Sp. p16 65
Brunette, isl., Newf., Can. E4 152
Brunette Downs, Austl. C6 111
Bruni, Tex. F3 206
Brunico, It. C7 66
Bruning, Nebr. D8 191
Brunkild, Man., Can. E3 150
Bruno, Sask., Can. E3 155
Bruno, Minn. D6 187
Bruno, Nebr. C9 191
Bruno, Okla. C5 200
Brunsbüttelkoog, Ger. E3 62
Brunson, S.C. F5 203
Brunsville, Iowa B1 180
Brunswick, Austl. *H5 112
Brunswick, Ga. E5 175
Brunswick, see Braunschweig, Ger.
Brunswick, Ind. B2 179
Brunswick, Maine E3, E5 184
Brunswick, Md. B2 173
Brunswick, Mo. B4 189
Brunswick, Nebr. B8 191
Brunswick, N.C. C5 197
Brunswick, Ohio A6 199
Brunswick, co., N.C. C5 197
Brunswick, co., Va. E5 209
Brunswick, pen., Chile h11 136
Brusett, Mont. C9 190
Brush, Colo. A7 171
Brushton, N.Y. *A2 196
Brushy, mts., Va. D1 209
Brushy, mts., N.C. A2 197
Brusly, La. B5, D4 183
Brusque, Braz. D3 137
Brussels (Bruxelles), Bel. D4 59
Brussels, Ont., Can. D3 153
Brussels, Ill. E3 178
Brussels, Wis. D6 212
Bruton, Eng. C5 56
Bruxelles: see Brussels, Bel.
Bruyeres-en-Vosges, Fr. A2 66
Bryan, Ohio A3 199
Bryan, Tex. D4 206
Bryan, co., Ga. D5 175
Bryan, co., Okla. D5 200
Bryan, lake, Wash. C8 210
Bryanka, Sov. Un. D12 71
Bryans Road, Md. C3 173
Bryansk, Sov. Un. E10 72
Bryant, Ark. C3, D5 169
Bryant, Sask., Can. H4 155
Bryant, Fla. F6 174
Bryant. Ill. C3 178
Bryant, Ind. C8 179
Bryant, S. Dak. C8 204
Bryant, Wis. C4 212
Bryant, creek, Mo. E5 189
Bryant, mtn., Mass. B2 185
Bryant Pond, Maine D2 184
Bryantown, Md. C4 173
Bryantsville, Ky. C5 182
Bryantville, Mass. B6 185
Bryce Canyon, Utah F3 207
Bryce Canyon, nat. park, Utah F3 207
Bryceland, La. B3 183
Bryceville, Fla. B5 174
Bryn Athyn, Pa. A12 202
Bryn Mawr, Pa. A11 202
Bryn Mawr, Wash. D2 210
Brynica, riv., Pol. g9 70
Bryson, Tex. C3 206
Bryson City, N.C. D2 197
Brzeg, Pol. C4 70
Brzesko, Pol. D6 70
Brzezinka, Pol. g10 70
Brzeziny, Pol. C5 70
Brzozów, Pol. D7 70
B-Say-Tah, Sask., Can. G4 155
Bū Nujaym, Libya C3 101
Bubiyan, isl., Kuw. G4 86
Bucaramanga, Col. B3 133
Buccaneer, arch., Austl. C3 110
Buchan Ness, cape, Scot. C7 57
Buchanan, Sask., Can. F4 155
Buchanan, Ga. C1 175
Buchanan, Lib. E2 103
Buchanan, Mich. G4 186
Buchanan, N.Y. *D7 196
Buchanan, N. Dak. B7 198
Buchanan, Tenn. A3 205
Buchanan, Va. D3 209
Buchanan, co., Iowa B6 180
Buchanan, co., Mo. B3 189
Buchanan, co., Va. B3 209
Buchans, Newf., Can. D3 152
Buchardo, Arg. A4 136
Bucharest (Bucureşti), Rom. C8 68
Buchen, Ger. D4 61
Buchholz, Ger. E3 62
Buchloe, Ger. D5 60
Buchon, pt., Calif. E3 170
Buchs, Switz. B5 66
Buchtel, Ohio C5 199
Buck, creek, Ky. C5 182
Buck, isl., Vir. Is. h17 132
Buck, mtn., Va. E1 209
Buck, mtn., Wash. A6 210
Buck Creek, Ind. D4 179
Buck Hill Falls, Pa. D11 202
Buckatunna, Miss. D5 188
Bückeburg, Ger. A4 61
Buckeye, Ariz. D3, G1 168
Buckeye, Iowa B4 180
Buckeye, N. Mex. E6 195
Buckeye, W. Va. C4 211
Buckeye Lake, Ohio C5 199
Buckeystown, Md. B3 173
Buckfield, Maine D2 184
Buckhannon, W. Va. C4 211
Buckhaven [& Methil], Scot. D5 57
Buckhead, Ga. C3 175
Buckhorn, Ariz. D4, G3 168
Buckhorn, N. Mex. D1 195
Buckhorn, Wyo. A8 213
Buckhorn, res., Ky. C6 182
Buckhorn Knob, mtn., W. Va. D4 211
Buckie, Scot. C6 57
Buckingham, Que., Can. D2 154
Buckingham, Colo. A7 171
Buckingham, Va. D4 209
Buckingham, co., Eng. C7 56
Buckingham, co., Va. D4 209
Buckland (Elephant Point), Alsk. B7 167
Buckland, Que., Can. C7 154
Buckland, Conn. B6 172
Buckland, Mass. A2 185
Buckland, Ohio B3 199
Buckley, Ill. C5 178
Buckley, Mich. D5 186
Buckley, Wash. B3 210
Bucklin, Kans. E4 181
Bucklin, Mo. B5 189
Buckman, Minn. E4 187
Buckner, Ark. D2 169
Buckner, Ill. F4 178
Buckner, Ky. A4 182
Buckner, Mo. E3 189
Buckner, creek, Kans. E3 181
Bucknum, Wyo. B6 213
Bucks, Ala. E1 166
Bucks, co., Pa. F11 202
Bucks Harbor, Maine D5 184
Buckskin, Ind. H3 179
Buckskin, mts., Ariz. C2 168
Bucksport, Maine D4 184
Bucksport, S.C. D9 203
Bucktail, Nebr. C4 191
Buckville, Ark. C2 169
Buco Zau, Ang. B1 106
Bucoda, Wash. C3 210
Bucovina, reg., Rom., Sov. Un. B7 68
Bucovina: *see also* Bukovina
Buctouche, N.B., Can. C5 151
Bucureşti, see Bucharest, Rom.
Bucyrus, Kans. D9 181
Bucyrus, N. Dak. C3 198
Bucyrus, Ohio B5 199
Bud, W. Va. D3 211
Buda, Ill. B4 178
Buda, Tex. D4 206
Buda, Port. Gui. D1 103
Budapest, Hung. B4 68
Budaun, India C7 88
Budd, coast, Ant. C24 120
Budd, lake, N.J. B3 194
Budd Lake, N.J. B3 194
Buddon Ness, cape, Scot. D6 57
Buddtown, N.J. D3 194
Bude, Eng. D3 56
Bude, Miss. D3 188
Bude, bay, Eng. D3 56
Büdingen, Ger. C4 61
Budjala, Zaire A2 106
Budňany, Czech. o17 70
Budrio, It. B3 67
Budyně, Czech. n17 70
Buechel, Ky. A4, B4 182
Buena, N.J. D3 194
Buena, Wash. C5 210
Buena Park, Calif. *F3 170
Buena Vista, Ala. D2 166
Buena Vista, Bol. C3 135
Buena Vista, Colo. C4 171
Buena Vista, Ga. D2 175
Buena Vista, Miss. B5 188
Buena Vista, N. Mex. B4 195
Buena Vista, Ohio D4 199
Buena Vista, Sask., Can. *G3 155
Buena Vista, Tenn. B3 205
Buena Vista (Independent City), Va. D3 209
Buena Vista, co., Iowa B2 180
Buenaventura, Col. C2 133
Buenaventura, Mex. B3 129
Buenos Aires, Arg. A5, g7 136
Buenos Aires, C.R. F6 130
Buenos Aires, prov., Arg. B4, B5 136
Buenos Aires, lake, Arg. D2 136
Bueyeros, N. Mex. B6 195
Buffalo, Ala. C4 166
Buffalo, Alta., Can. D5 148
Buffalo, Ill. D4 178
Buffalo, Ind. C4 179
Buffalo, Iowa C7, D7 180
Buffalo, Kans. E8 181
Buffalo, Ky. *C4 182
Buffalo, Minn. E5 187
Buffalo, Mo. D4 189
Buffalo, Mont. D7 190
Buffalo, N.Y. C2 196
Buffalo, N. Dak. C8 198
Buffalo, Ohio C6 199
Buffalo, Okla. A2 200
Buffalo, S.C. B4 203
Buffalo, S. Dak. B2 204
Buffalo, Tenn. B4 205
Buffalo, Tex. D4 206
Buffalo, W. Va. C3 211
Buffalo, Wis. D2 212
Buffalo, Wyo. A6 213
Buffalo, co., Nebr. D6 191
Buffalo, co., S. Dak. C6 204
Buffalo, co., Wis. D2 212
Buffalo, creek, Kans. C5 181
Buffalo, creek, W. Va. A6 211
Buffalo, creek, W. Va. D5 211
Buffalo, lake, Alta., Can. C4 148
Buffalo, lake, N.W. Ter., Can. D10 142
Buffalo, lake, Wis. E4 212
Buffalo, mtn., Va. E2 209
Buffalo, riv., Ark. B3 169
Buffalo, riv., Minn. D2 187
Buffalo, riv., Tenn. B4 205
Buffalo, riv., Wis. D2 212
Buffalo Bill, res., Wyo. A3 213
Buffalo Center, Iowa A4 180
Buffalo Creek, Colo. B5 171
Buffalo Fork, creek, Wyo. B2 213
Buffalo Gap, Sask., Can. H3 155
Buffalo Gap, S. Dak. D2 204
Buffalo Grove, Ill. *A6 178
Buffalo Lake, Minn. F4 187
Buffalo Mills, Pa. G4 202
Buffalo Narrows, Sask., Can. B1 155
Buffalo Valley, Tenn. C8 205
Buffumville, res., Mass. B4 185
Buford, Colo. B3 171
Buford, Ga. B2 175
Buford, N. Dak. A2 198
Buford, Ohio C4 199
Buford, Wyo. D7 213
Bug, riv., Pol., Sov. Un. B6 70, F5 72
Buga, Col. C2 133
Bugach, Sov. Un. G5 72
Buganda, reg., Ug. A5 106
Bugene, Tan. B5 106
Buggs Island, lake, N.C., Va. A5 197, E4 209
Bugojno, Yugo. C3 68
Bugul'ma, Sov. Un. C4 73
Bugumal, New Ire. I. 115
Buguruslan, Sov. Un. C4 73
Buhl, Ala. B2 166
Bühl, Ger. D7 58
Bühl, Ger. E3 61
Buhl, Idaho G4 177
Buhl, Minn. C6 187
Buhler, Kans. A4, D6 181
Bühlertal, Ger. E3 61
Buhuşi, Rom. B8 68
Buie, inlet, Scot. D3 57
Buies Creek, N.C. B5 197
Builth Wells, Wales B4 56
Buitenpost, Neth. A6 59
Bujalance, Sp. D3 65
Bujumbura, Burundi B4 106
Buka, isl., Sol. Is. 115
Buka, passage, Sol. Is. 115
Bukama, Con. K. C4 106
Bukavu, Con. K. B4 106
Bukene, Tan. B5 106
Bukhara, Sov. Un. F9 71
Bukittinggi, Indon. *F4 90
Bukoba, Tan. B5 106
Bukovina (Bucovina): in 1940. 53
in 1950 54
Bukuru, Nig. E6 103
Bula, Zaire A4 106
Bula, Indon. F8 90
Buladean, N.C. C4 197
Buladeen, Tenn. C12 205
Bulan, Ky. C6 182
Bulan, Phil. C6 90
Bulawayo, Rh. B4 107
Bulfontein, S. Afr. C4 107
BULGARIA, country, Eur. D7 68
c. 1140 47
c. 1294 81
c. 1360 48
c. 1940 53
in 1950 54
Bulgroo, Austl. B4 112
Bulhar, Som. C5 105
Bulkley, riv., B.C., Can. B4 149
Bull, creek, S. Dak. B2 204
Bull, isl., S.C. F4, F8 203
Bull, mtn., Mont. D4 190
Bull Run, mts., Nev. B5 192
Bull Run, mts., Va. C5 209
Bull Run, ridge, Tenn. E11 205
Bull Shoals, Ark. *A3 169
Bull Shoals, res., Ark., Mo. A3 169
Bullange, Bel. D6 59
Bullaque, riv., Sp. C3 65
Bullard, Ga. D3 175
Bullas, Sp. C5 65
Bullay, Ger. C2 61
Bulle, Switz. C3 66
Bullfrog, creek, Utah F5 207
Bullhead, S. Dak. B4 204
Bullhead City, Ariz. B1 168
Bullitt, co., Ky. C4 182
Bullittsville, Ky. A6 182
Bulloch, co., Ga. D5 175
Bullock, N.C. A5 197
Bullock, co., Ala. C4 166
Bulloo, riv., Austl. C5 112
Bullrun Rock, mtn., Oreg. C8 201
Bulls, bay, S.C. F8 203
Bulls Gap, Tenn. C10 205
Bulnes, Chile B2 136
Bulo Burti, Som. E6 105
Buloir, is., Alsk. E3 167
Bulsar, India G4 88
Buluan, Phil. D6 90
Bulun, Sov. Un. B15 71
Bulun Tokhoi (Puluntohai), China B2 91
Bulungu, Zaire B2 106
Bulupari, N. Cal. 115
Bulwark, Alta., Can. C5 148
Bulyea, Sask., Can. G3 155
Bumba, Zaire A3 106
Bumble Bee, Ariz. C3 168
Bumpus Mills, Tenn. A4 205
Buna, Pap. k12 111
Buna, Tex. D6 206
Bunbury, Austl. F2 111
Bunbury, P.E.I., Can. *C6 151
Bunceton, Mo. C5 189
Bunch, Okla. B7 200
Buncombe, Ill. F5 178
Buncombe, co., N.C. D3 197
Bundaberg, Austl. B9 112
Bünde, Ger. A3 61
Bundi, India E5 88
Bundick, creek, La. D2 183
Bunessan, Scot. D2 57
Bungay, Eng. B9 56
Bungo, strait, Jap. J6 93
Bunia, Zaire A5 106
Bunker, Mo. D6 189
Bunker Hill, Ill. D4 178
Bunker Hill, Ind. C5 179
Bunker Hill, Kans. D5 181
Bunker Hill, Oreg. *D2 201
Bunker Hill, Tenn. B5 205
Bunker Hill, Tex. *E5 206
Bunker Hill, W. Va. B6 211
Bunker Hill, peak, Nev. D4 192
Bunkerville, Nev. G7 192
Bunkeya, Zaire D4 106
Bunkie, La. D3 183
Bunn, Ark. C3 169
Bunn, N.C. B5 197
Bunnell, Fla. C5 174
Bunnlevel, N.C. B5 197
Bunny Run, Mich. *F7 186
Buo Ha, Viet. A6 89
Bupto, China B10 88
Bur Acaba, Som. E5 105
Bur Gavo, Som. F5 105
Būr Sa'īd, see Port Said, Eg.
Būr Tawfiq, Eg. E4 84
Bura, Ken. B7 106
Burail, N. Cal. 115
Burail, bay, N. Cal. 115
Buraku, is., Sol. Is. 115
Buram, Sud. C2 105
Buran, Som. C6 105
Burao, Som. D6 105
Buras, La. E6 183
Buraydah, Sau. Ar. *G7 77
Burayk, Libya D2 101
Burbank, Calif. E4, F2 170
Burbank, Ill. *B6 178
Burbank, Okla. A5 200
Burbank, S. Dak. E9 204
Burbank, Wash. C7 210
Burchard, Nebr. D9 191
Burden, Kans. E7 181
Burdett, Alta., Can. E5 148
Burdett, Kans. D4 181
Burdett, N.Y. C4 196
Burdette, Ark. B6 169
Burdick, Kans. D7 181
Burditt, lake, Ont., Can. B5 187
Burdock, S. Dak. D2 204
Burdur, Tur. D8 69
Burdwan, India F11 88
Bureau, Ill. B4 178
Bureau, co., Ill. B4 178
Bureinsky, range, Sov. Un. B6 93
Büren, Ger. B3 61
Bureya, Sov. Un. B4 93
Bureya, riv., Sov. Un. A5 93
Burford, Ont., Can. D4 153
Burford, lake, N. Mex. A3 195
Burg, Ger. A6 61
Burg [auf Fehmarn], Ger. D5 62
Burgas, Bul. D8 68
Burgas, gulf, Bul. D8 68
Burgaw, N.C. C6 197
Burgdorf, Ger. F3 62
Burgdorf, Switz. B3 66
Burgeo, Newf., Can. E3 152
Burgesdorp, S. Afr. D4 107
Burgess, S.C. D9 203
Burgess Hill, Eng. D7 56
Burgettstown, Pa. F1 202
Burghausen, Ger. A8 66
Burghead, Scot. C5 57
Burgin, Ky. C5 182
Burglengenfeld, Ger. D7 61
Burgoon, Ohio A4 199
Burgos, Phil. n12 90
Burgos, Sp. A4 65
Burgreuland, Bel. D6 59
Burgstädt, Ger. C7 61
Burgsteinfurt, Ger. A2 61
Burgsvik, Swe. I8 63
Burgundy (Bourgogne), former prov., Fr. D6 58
c. 814 47
c. 1360 48
Burhanpur, India G6 88
Burhave, Ger. E2 62
Burí, Braz. m7 137
Burin, Newf., Can. E4 152
Būrīn, Jordan g12 84
Burin, pen., Newf., Can. E4 152
Buriram, Thai. E5 89
Burj al 'Arab, Eg. G7 85
Burk, chan., B.C., Can. C4 149
Burkburnett, Tex. B3 206
Burke, Idaho B3 177
Burke, N.Y. A3 196
Burke, S. Dak. D6 204
Burke, Va. B4 209
Burke, co, Ga. C4 175
Burke, co., N.C. B2 197
Burke, co, N. Dak. A3 198
Burke City, Mo. A8 189
Burkes Garden, Va. B3, D1 209
Burkesville, Ky. D4 182
Burket, Ind. B6 179
Burketon Station, Ont., Can. C6 153
Burketown, Austl. *C6 111
Burkett, Tex. C3 206

INDEX KEY Each place listed in **Bold-faced Type** has its population listed in the Population tables, pages 230 to 280.
Each country, shown in CAPITAL LETTERS, has its population listed in the World Political Information Table, pages 6 to 10.
* Does not appear on map; key shows general location.

Burkettsville, Ohio..........B3 199
Burkeville, Tex..........D6 206
Burkeville, Va..........D4 209
Burkley, lake, Ky..........F5 178
Burks Falls, Ont., Can..........B5 153
Burkville, Ala..........C3 166
Burkville, Mass..........A2 185
Burleigh, N.J..........E3 194
Burleigh co., N. Dak..........C5 198
Burleson, Tex..........B5 206
Burleson, co., Tex..........D4 206
Burley, Idaho..........G5 177
Burley, Wash..........D1 210
Burli-Tyube, Sov. Un..........D9 73
Burlingame, Calif..........B5 170
Burlingame, Kans..........D8 181
Burlington, Newf., Can..........D3 152
Burlington, Ont., Can..........D5 153
Burlington, Colo..........B8 171
Burlington, Conn..........B5 172
Burlington, Ill..........A5 178
Burlington, Ind..........D5 179
Burlington, Iowa..........D6 180
Burlington, Kans..........D8 181
Burlington, Ky..........A5, A6 182
Burlington, Maine..........C4 184
Burlington, Mass..........C2 185
Burlington, N.J..........C3 194
Burlington, N.C..........A4 197
Burlington, N. Dak..........A4 198
Burlington, Okla..........A3 200
Burlington, Pa..........C8 202
Burlington, Vt..........C2 208
Burlington, Wash..........A3 210
Burlington, W. Va..........B6 211
Burlington, Wis..........F1, F5 212
Burlington, Wyo..........A4 213
Burlington, co., N.J..........D3 194
Burlington Junction, Mo..........A2 189
BURMA, country, Asia..........D10 87
c. 1950.......... 83
Burmis, Alta., Can..........E3 148
Burnaby,Wash..........A10 149
Burnaby, isl., B.C., Can..........C2 149
Burnet, Tex..........D3 206
Burnet, co., Tex..........D3 206
Burnett, Ind..........E3 179
Burnett, co., Wis..........C1 212
Burnett, riv., Austl..........B8 112
Burnettsville, Ind..........C4 179
Burney, Calif..........B3 170
Burney, Ind..........F6 179
Burneyville, Okla..........D4 200
Burnham, Ill..........*F3 178
Burnham, Maine..........D3 184
Burnham, Mo..........E6 189
Burnham, N. Mex..........A1 195
Burnham, Pa..........E6 202
Burnham-on-Sea, Eng..........C5 56
Burnie, Austl..........o15 111
Burning Springs, Ky..........C6 182
Burning Springs, W. Va..........C3 211
Burnley, Eng..........A5 56
Burns, Austl..........F3 112
Burns, Colo..........B4 171
Burns, Kans..........A6, D7 181
Burns, Miss..........C4 188
Burns, Oreg..........D7 201
Burns, Tenn..........A4 205
Burns, Wyo..........D8 213
Burns City, Ind..........G4 179
Burns Flat, Okla..........B2 200
Burns Lake, B.C., Can..........B5 149
Burnside, Ill..........C2 178
Burnside, Ky..........D5 182
Burnside, La..........B5 183
Burnside, Miss..........C4 188
Burnside, Pa..........E4 202
Burnstad, N. Dak..........C6 198
Burnsville, Ala..........C3 166
Burnsville, N.B., Can..........B4 151
Burnsville, Miss..........A5 188
Burnsville, N.C..........C4 197
Burnsville, W. Va..........C4 211
Burnt, riv., Alta., Can..........B1 148
Burnt, riv., Oreg..........C9 201
Burnt Cabins, Pa..........F6 202
Burnt Corn, Ala..........D2 166
Burnt Prairie (Liberty), Ill..........E5 178
Burnt River, Ont., Can..........C6 153
Burntisland, Scot..........D5 57
Burntroot, lake, Ont., Can..........B6 153
Burntside, lake, Minn..........C6 187
Burntwood, lake, Man., Can..........B1 150
Burntwood, riv., Man., Can..........B2 150
Burnwell, Ala..........E4 166
Burnwell, W. Va..........D6 211
Burqā, Jordan..........B7, f11 84
Burr, Minn..........F2 187
Burr, Nebr..........D9 191
Burr Hill, Va..........C5 209
Burr Oak, Iowa..........A6 180
Burr Oak, Kans..........C5 181
Burr Oak, Mich..........G5 186
Burr Oak Lake, res., Ohio..........C5 199
Burra, Austl..........F2 112
Burray, isl., Scot..........B6 57
Burriana, Sp..........C5 65
Burrillville, R.I..........*B10 172
Burro, mts., Mex..........E1 206
Burroughs, Ga..........E5 175
Burrow, head, Scot..........F4 57
Burrows, Ind..........C4 179
Burrton, Kans..........A4, D6 181
Burruyacú, Arg..........E3 135
Burrville, Tenn..........C9 205
Burrwood, La..........F6 183
Burry Port, Wales..........C3 56
Bursa, Tur..........B7 69
Burstall, Sask., Can..........G1 155
Burt, Iowa..........A3 180
Burt, N. Dak..........C3 198
Burt, Tenn..........B5 205
Burt, co., Nebr..........C9 191
Burt, lake, Mich..........C6 186
Burton, Calif..........*D4 170
Burton, Ill..........D2 178
Burton, Ky..........*C7 182
Burton, Nebr..........B6 191
Burton, Ohio..........A6 199
Burton, Tex..........D4 206
Burton, Wash..........D1 210
Burton, W. Va..........B4 211
Burton, lake, Ga..........B3 175
Burton on Trent, Eng..........B6 56
Burträsk, Swe..........E9 63
Burtrum, Minn..........E4 187
Burtts Corner, N.B., Can..........C3 151
Burṭus, Eg..........D3 84
Burtville, Pa..........C5 202
Buru, isl., Indon..........F7 90
Burullus, lake, Eg..........C2 84
Burūn, cape, Eg..........C5 84
BURUNDI, country, Afr..........B4 106
Burwash, Ont., Can..........A4 153
Burwell, Nebr..........C6 191
Bury, Que., Can..........D6 154
Bury, Eng..........A5 56
Bury St. Edmunds, Eng..........B8 56
Burynshik, Sov. Un..........D4 73
Busby, Alta., Can..........C4 148
Busby, Mont..........E10 190
Busch, Mo..........B6 189
Büschfeld, Ger..........D1 61
Bush, Ill..........*F4 178
Bush, Ky..........C6 182
Bush, Miss..........D4 188
Bush, riv., Md..........B5 173
Bush City, Kans..........D8 181
Būshehr, Iran..........G5 86
Bushenyi, Ug..........B5 106
Bushimaie, riv., Zaire..........C3 106
Bushkill, Pa..........D11 202
Bushkill, creek, Pa..........B2 194
Bushland, Tex..........B1 206
Bushnell, Fla..........D4 174
Bushnell, Ill..........C3 178
Bushnell, Nebr..........C2 191
Bushnell, S. Dak..........C9 204
Bushong, Kans..........D7 181
Bushton, Kans..........D5 181
Bushy Head, mtn., Okla..........A7 200
Businga, Zaire..........A3 106
Busk, Sov. Un..........G5 72
Busko, Pol..........C6 70
Buşrá ash Shām, Syr..........F11 85
Bussa, Nig..........D5 103
Busselton, Austl..........F2 111
Busseto, It..........E6 66
Bussey, Iowa..........C5 180
Bussum, Neth..........B5 59
Bustamante, Tex..........F3 206
Busto Arsizio, It..........B2 67
Büsum, Ger..........D2 62
Buta, Zaire..........A3 106
Buta Ranquil, Arg..........B3 136
Bute, co., Scot..........E3 57
Bute, inlet, B.C., Can..........D5 149
Bute, isl., Scot..........E3 57
Butedale, B.C., Can..........C3 149
Buthier, riv., It..........D3 66
Butkhak, Afg..........D14 86
Butler, Ala..........C1 166
Butler, Ga..........D2 175
Butler, Ill..........D4 178
Butler, Ind..........B8 179
Butler, Ky..........B5, B7 182
Butler, Mo..........C3 189
Butler, N.J..........B4 194
Butler, Ohio..........B5 199
Butler, Okla..........B2 200
Butler, Pa..........E2 202
Butler, S. Dak..........B8 204
Butler, Tenn..........C12 205
Butler, Wis..........E1 212
Butler, co., Ala..........D3 166
Butler, co., Iowa..........B5 180
Butler, co., Kans..........E7 181
Butler, co., Ky..........C3 182
Butler, co., Mo..........E7 189
Butler, co., Nebr..........C8 191
Butler, co., Ohio..........C3 199
Butler, co., Pa..........E2 202
Butler, lake, Fla..........E2 174
Butlerville, Ind..........F6 179
Butovo, Sov. Un..........n17 72
Butt of Lewis, cape, Scot..........B2 57
Buttahatchie, riv., Ala..........B1 166
Buttahatchie, riv., Miss..........B5 188
Butte, Mont..........D4 190
Butte, Nebr..........B7 191
Butte, N. Dak..........B5 198
Butte, co., Calif..........C3 170
Butte, co., Idaho..........F5 177
Butte, co., S. Dak..........C2 204
Butte, mts., Nev..........D6 192
Butte City, Idaho..........F5 177
Butte Falls, Oreg..........E4 201
Butterfield, Ark..........D6 169
Butterfield, Minn..........G4 187
Butterfield Mo..........E4 189
Butternut, Wis..........B3 212
Butternut, lake, Wis..........C5 212
Butternut Ridge, N.B., Can..........D4 151
Butters, N.C..........C5 197
Butterworth, Mala..........J4 89
Butterworth, S. Afr..........D4 107
Buttonwillow, Calif..........E4 170
Butts, co., Ga..........C3 175
Buttzville, N.J..........B2 194
Butuan, Phil..........D7 90
Butung, isl., Indon..........F6 90
Buturlinovka, Sov. Un..........C2 73
Butzbach, Ger..........C3 61
Bützow, Ger..........B5 60
Buxtehude, Ger..........B4 60
Buxton, Eng..........A6 56
Buxton, Guy..........A3 139
Buxton, N.C..........B8 197
Buxton, N. Dak..........B8 198
Buxton, Oreg..........A1 201
Buxton, mtn., B.C., Can..........D3 149
Buy, Sov. Un..........B2 73
Buyck, Minn..........B6 187
Buynaksk, Sov. Un..........E3 73
Büyük Menderes (Maeander), riv., Tur..........D7 69
Büyükliman, see Vakfikebir, Tur.
Buzachi, pen., Sov. Un..........E4 73
Buzancy, Fr..........E4 59
Buzău, Rom..........C8 68
Buzău, riv., Rom..........C8 68
Buzaymah, Libya..........E4 101
Buzet, Yugo..........C1 68
Buzuluk, Sov. Un..........C4 73
Buzzard Roost, mtn., N.C..........B2 197
Buzzards, bay, Mass..........C6 185
Buzzards Bay, Mass..........C6 185
Byala, Bul..........D7 68
Byala Slatina, Bul..........D6 68
Byam Martin, isl., N.W. Ter., Can..........A12 142
Byars, Okla..........C4 200
Bybee, Tenn..........C10 205
Bydgoszcz, Pol..........B5 70
Byelorussia (S.S.R.) (White Russia), rep., Sov. Un..........E5 72
Byemoor, Alta., Can..........D4 148
Byers, Colo..........B6 171
Byers, Kans..........E5 181
Byers, Ohio..........C5 199
Byesville, Ohio..........C6 199
Byfield, Mass..........A6 185
Bygland, Nor..........H2 63
Byhalia, Miss..........A4 188
Byington, Tenn..........E11 205
Bykovo, Sov. Un..........G15 72
Bykovo, Sov. Un..........n18 72
Bylas, Ariz..........D5 168
Bylot, isl., N.W. Ter., Can..........B17 143
Byng Inlet, Ont., Can..........B4 153
Bynum, Mont..........C4 190
Bynum, N.C..........B4 197
Bynumville, Mo..........B5 189
Byram, Miss..........C3 188
Byram, riv., Conn..........A5 194
Byrdstown, Tenn..........C8 205
Byrnedale, Pa..........D4 202
Byrock, Austl..........E6 112
Byromville, Ga..........D3 175
Byron, Calif..........B6 170
Byron, Ga..........D3 175
Byron, Ill..........A4 178
Byron, Maine..........D2 184
Byron, Minn..........F6 187
Byron, Nebr..........D8 191
Byron, Okla..........A3 200
Byron, Wyo..........A4 213
Byron, cape, Austl..........D9 112
Byrum, Den..........A5 62
Byšice, Czech..........n18 70
Bystrá, riv., Czech..........o18 70
Bystrzyca, Pol..........C4 70
Bytom, Pol..........C5, g9 70
Bytosh, Sov. Un..........E10 72
Bytów, Pol..........A4 70
Byzantine empire: c. 1140.......... 47
c. 1360.......... 48

C

C.J. Strike, res., Idaho..........G3 177
Ca, riv., Viet..........C6 89
Caacupé, Par..........E4 135
Caamaño, sound, B.C., Can..........C3 149
Caapucú, Par..........E4 135
Caazapá, Par..........E4 135
Cabaceiras, Braz..........h5 138
Cabalete, isl., Phil..........o13 90
Caballo, pt., P.R..........g12 132
Caballo, res., N. Mex..........E2 195
Cabana, Peru..........C2 134
Cabanatuan, Phil..........o13 90
Cabano, Que., Can..........B9 154
Cabarrus, co., N. C..........B3 197
Cabarruyan, isl., Phil..........n12 90
Cabazon, Calif..........*F5 170
Cabbage, swamp, Fla..........C6 174
Cabedelo, Braz..........C4, h6 138
Cabell, co., W. Va..........C2 211
Cabery, Ill..........C5 178
Cabeza del Buey, Sp..........C3 65
Cabezas, Bol..........C3 135
Cabimas, Ven..........A3 133
Cabin, creek, W. Va..........D6 211
Cabin Creek, W. Va..........C6 211
Cabin John, Md..........C1, C3 173
Cabinda, Ang..........C1 106
Cabinda, reg., Ang..........C1 106
Cabinet, Idaho..........A2 177
Cabinet, mts., Mont..........B1 190
Cabinet Gorge, res., Mont..........B1 190
Cable, Wis..........B2 212
Cabo, Braz..........k6 138
Cabo Blanco, Arg..........D3 136
Cabo Delgado, prov., Moz..........D6 106
Cabo Frio, Braz..........C4 137
Cabo Gracias a Dios, Nic..........C6 130
Cabo Raso, Arg..........C3 136
Cabo Rojo, P.R..........C2 132
Cabo Rojo, mun., P.R..........C2 132
Cabonga, res., Que., Can..........G17 143
Cabool, Mo..........D5 189
Caboolture, Austl..........C9 112
Caborca, Mex..........A2 129
Cabot, Ark..........C3 169
Cabot, Pa..........E2 202
Cabot, Vt..........C4 208
Cabot, head, Ont., Can..........B3 153
Cabot, mtn., N.H..........B6 208
Cabot, strait, Newf., Can..........E2 152
Cabra, Sp..........D3 65
Cabras, isl., Guam.......... 114
Cabras, isl., P.R..........C8 132
Cabrera, isl., Sp..........C7 65
Cabri, Sask., Can..........G1 155
Cabri, lake, Sask., Can..........F1 155
Cabriel, riv., Sp..........C5 65
Cabrillo, nat. mon., Calif..........E2 170
Cabrobó, Braz..........C3 138
Cabullón, pt., P.R..........D4 132
Čacak, Yugo..........D5 68
Caçapava, Braz..........C3 137
Cacapava do Sul, Braz..........E2 137
Cacequi, Braz..........D2 137
Cáceres, Braz..........C4 135
Cáceres, Col..........B2 133
Cáceres, Sp..........C2 65
Cachan, Fr..........g10 58
Cache, Ill..........F4 178
Cache, Okla..........C3 200
Cache, co., Utah..........B4 207
Cache, creek, Okla..........C3 200
Cache, mtn., Alsk..........B10 167
Cache, peak, Idaho..........G5 177
Cache, riv., Ark..........B4 169
Cache, riv., Ill..........F4 178
Cache Bay, Ont., Can..........A5 153
Cache Creek, B.C., Can..........*D7 149
Cache la Poudre, riv., Colo..........A5 171
Cachi, Arg..........E2 135
Cachi, mts., Arg..........D2 135
Cachimbo, mts., Braz..........D4 139
Cachinal, Chile..........D2 135
Cachoeira, Braz..........D3 138
Cachoeira do Sul, Braz..........E2 137
Cachoeiro do Itapemirim, Braz..........C4 137
Cacique, Pan..........h11 130
Cacola, Ang..........D2 106
Caconda, Ang..........D2 106
Cacouna, Que., Can..........B8 154
Cactus, Ariz..........D3, G2 168
Cactus, flat, Nev..........F5 192
Cactus, peak, Nev..........F5 192
Cactus, range, Nev..........F5 192
Cactus Lake, Sask., Can..........E1 155
Caddo, Okla..........C5 200
Caddo, Tex..........C3 206
Caddo, co., Okla..........B3 200
Caddo, par., La..........B2 183
Caddo, creek, Okla..........C4 200
Caddo, lake, La., Tex..........B1 183
Caddo, mts., Ark..........C2 169
Caddo, riv., Ark..........C2 169
Caddo Gap, Ark..........C2 169
Caddo Mills, Tex..........*C4 206
Caddoa, Colo..........C8 171
Cade, La..........D4 183
Cadena, mtn., P.R..........B2 132
Cades, S.C..........D8 203
Cades, Tenn..........B3 205
Cadig, mtn., Phil..........o14 90
Cadillac, Que., Can..........*B2 154
Cadillac, Sask., Can..........H2 155
Cadillac, Fr..........E3 58
Cadillac, Mich..........D5 186
Cadillac, mtn., Maine..........D4 184
Cadiz, Calif..........E6 170
Cadiz, Ind..........*E7 179
Cadiz, Ky..........D2 182
Cadiz, Ohio..........B6 199
Cadiz, Phil..........C6 90
Cádiz, Sp..........D2 65
Cádiz, gulf, Sp..........D2 65
Cadogan, Alta., Can..........C5 148
Cadogan, Pa..........E2 202
Cadomin, Alta., Can..........C2 148
Cadott, Wis..........D2 212
Cadotte, riv., Alta., Can..........A2 148
Cadron, creek, Ark..........B3 169
Cadwell, Ga..........D3 175
Cadys Falls, Vt..........B3 208
Cadyville, N.Y..........A3 196
Caen, Fr..........C3 58
Caernarvon, Wales..........A3 56
Caernarvon, co., Wales..........A3 56
Caernarvon, bay, Wales..........A3 56
Caerphilly, Wales..........C4 56
Caetité, Braz..........D2 138
Cafayate, Arg..........E2 135
Cagayan, Phil..........D6 90
Cagayan, is., Phil..........D6 90
Cagayan, riv., Phil..........B6, n13 90
Cagayan Sulu, isl., Phil..........D5 90
Cagle, Tenn..........D8 205
Cagli, It..........C4 67
Cagliari, It..........E2 67
Cagliari, gulf, It..........E2 67
Cagnes-sur-Mer, Fr..........F7 58
Caguán, riv., Col..........C3 133
Caguas, P.R..........C6 132
Caguas, mun., P.R..........C6 132
Cahaba, riv., Ala..........C2 166
Cahaba, valley, Ala..........E5 166
Cahokia, Ill..........B8 189
Cahokia, creek, Ill..........A8 189
Cahone, Colo..........D2 171
Cahors, Fr..........E4 58
Cahuinari, riv., Col..........D3 133
Caí, Braz..........E2 137
Caiapó, mts., Braz..........B2 137
Caiapônia, Braz..........B2 137
Caibarién, Cuba..........D4 131
Caicara, Ven..........B4 133
Caicedonia, Col..........C2 133
Caicó, Braz..........C3 138
Caicos, is., Turks & Caicos Is..........E7 131
Caicos, passage, Ba. Is..........E7 131
Caigo o no Caigo, pt., P.R..........e10 132
Cailloma, Peru..........E3 134
Caillou, bay, La..........E5 183
Caillou, lake, La..........E5 183
Caiman, pt., Phil..........o12 90
Caimanera, Cuba..........F6 131
Caimito, riv., Pan..........m11 130
Cain City, Tex..........D3 206
Cains, riv., N.B., Can..........C4 151
Cains Store, Ky..........C5 182
Cainsville, Mo..........A4 189
Cainsville, Tenn..........B5 205
Caintown, Ont., Can..........C9 153
Cairn Table, mtn., Scot..........E5 57
Cairnbrook, Pa..........F4 202
Cairngorm, mts., Scot..........C5 57
Cairns, Austl..........C8 111
Cairnsmore, mtn., Scot..........E4 57
Cairo (Al Qāhirah), Eg..........D3 84, D6 101
Cairo, Ga..........F2 175
Cairo, Ill..........F4 178
Cairo, Kans..........E5 181
Cairo, Mo..........B5 189
Cairo, Nebr..........C7 191
Cairo, N.Y..........C7 196
Cairo, Ohio..........B3 199
Cairo, W. Va..........B3 211
Caithness, co., Scot..........B5 57
Caiundo, Ang..........E2 106
Cajabamba, Peru..........C2 134
Cajacay, Peru..........D2 134
Cajamarca, Peru..........C2 134
Cajamarca, dept., Peru..........C2 134
Cajatambo, Peru..........D2 134
Cajàzeiras, Braz..........C3 138
Čajniče, Yugo..........D4 68
Čakovec, Yugo..........B3 68
Cakovice, Czech..........n18 70
Calabar, Nig..........F6 103
Calabogie, Ont., Can..........B8 153
Calabogie, lake, Ont., Can..........B8 153
Calabozo, Ven..........B4 133
Calabria, reg., It..........E6 67
Calafat, Rom..........D6 68
Calahorra, Sp..........A4 65
Calais, Fr..........B4 58
Calais, Maine..........C5 184
Calais, Vt..........C4 208
Calalaste, mts., Arg..........E2 135
Calama, Chile..........D2 135
Calamar, Col..........A3 133
Calamba, Phil..........o13 90
Calamian Group, is., Phil..........C6 90
Calamocha, Sp..........B5 65
Calamus, Iowa..........C7 180
Calamus, riv., Nebr..........B6 191
Calañas, Sp..........D2 65
Calanda, Sp..........B5 65
Calanscio, des., Libya..........D4 101
Calanscio, sand sea, Libya..........D4 101
Calapan, Phil..........C6 90
Calapooya, mts., Oreg..........D3 201
Călărăiş, Rom..........C8 68
Calarcá, Col..........C2 133
Calasparra, Sp..........C5 65
Calatayud, Sp..........B5 65
Calau, Ger..........B8 61
Calauag, Phil..........p14 90
Calaveras, co., Calif..........C3 170
Calbayog, Phil..........C7 91
Calbe, Ger..........B6 61
Calbuco, Chile..........C2 136
Calca, Peru..........D3 134
Calcasieu, par., La..........D2 183
Calcasieu, lake, La..........E2 183
Calcasieu, pass, La..........E2 183
Calcasieu, riv., La..........D2 183
Calceta, Ec..........B1 134
Calcha, Bol..........D2 135
Calchaqui, riv., Arg..........E2 135
Calcutta, India..........D8 87, F12 88
Calcutta, Ohio..........B7 199
Caldaro, It..........C7 66
Caldas, dept., Col..........B2 133
Caldas da Rainha, Port..........C1 65
Calder, Sask., Can..........F5 155
Calder, Idaho..........B2 177
Calder, lake, Scot..........B5 57
Caldera, Chile..........E1 135
Calderwood, Tenn..........D10 205
Caldew, riv., Eng..........F5 57
Caldron Falls, res., Wis..........C5 212
Caldwell, Idaho..........F2 177
Caldwell, Kans..........E6 181
Caldwell, N.J..........B4 194
Caldwell, Ohio..........C6 199
Caldwell, Tex..........D4 206
Caldwell, W. Va..........D4 211
Caldwell, co., Ky..........C2 182
Caldwell, co., Mo..........B3 189
Caldwell, co., N.C..........B2 197
Caldwell, co., Tex..........E4 206
Caldwell, par., La..........B3 183
Cale, Ark..........D2 169
Caledonia, N.S., Can..........E4 151
Caledonia, Ont., Can..........D5 153
Caledonia, Ill..........A5 178
Caledonia, Mich..........F5 186
Caledonia, Minn..........G7 187
Caledonia, Miss..........B5 188
Caledonia, Mo..........D7 189
Caledonia, N.Y..........C3 196
Caledonia, N. Dak..........B9 198
Caledonia, Ohio..........B5 199
Caledonia, Pa..........D5 202
Caledonia, co., Vt..........C4 208
Caledonian, canal, Scot..........C4 57
Calella, Sp..........B7 65
Calenzana, Fr..........C2 67
Calera, Ala..........B3 166
Calera, Okla..........D5 200
Caleta Buena, Chile..........C2 135
Caleta Olivia, Arg..........D3 136
Calexico, Calif..........F6 170
Calf of Man, isl., I. of Man..........C4 55
Calgary, Alta., Can..........D3 148
Calha, pt., Port..........F9 65
Calhan, Colo..........B6 171
Calheta, Port. (Madeira Is.)..........h11 65
Calhoun, Ala..........C3 166
Calhoun, N.B., Can..........C5 151
Calhoun, Ga..........B2 175
Calhoun, Ill..........E5 178
Calhoun, Ky..........C2 182
Calhoun, La..........B3 183
Calhoun, Mo..........C4 189
Calhoun, Tenn..........D9 205
Calhoun, co., Ala..........B4 166
Calhoun, co., Ark..........D3 169
Calhoun, co., Fla..........B1 174
Calhoun, co., Ga..........E2 175
Calhoun, co., Ill..........D3 178
Calhoun, co., Iowa..........B3 180
Calhoun, co., Mich..........F5 186
Calhoun, co., Miss..........B4 188
Calhoun, co., S.C..........D6 203
Calhoun, co., Tex..........E4 206
Calhoun, co., W. Va..........C3 211
Calhoun City, Miss..........B4 188
Calhoun Falls, S.C..........C3 203
Cali, Col..........C2 133
Calico Rock, Ark..........A3 169
Calicut, India..........F6 87
Caliente, Calif..........E4 170
Caliente, Nev..........F7 192
Califon, N.J..........B3 194
California, Iowa..........C2 180
California, Ky..........A7 182
California, Mo..........C5 189
California, Pa..........F2 202
California, state, U.S.......... 170
in 1850.......... 163
California, gulf, Mex..........B2 129
California Junction, Iowa..........C2 180
Caliman, mts., Rom..........B7 68
Calingasta, Arg..........A3 136
Calio, N. Dak..........A7 198
Calion, Ark..........D3 169
Calipatria, Calif..........F6 170
Calistoga, Calif..........A5, C2 170
Calispell, peak, Wash..........A8 210
Callabonna, lake, Austl..........D3 112
Callabonna, riv., Austl..........D3 112
Callafo, Eth..........D5 105
Callaghan, mtn., Nev..........D5 192
Callahan, Fla..........B5, B6 174
Callahan, co., Tex..........C3 206
Callander, Ont., Can..........A5 153
Callander, Scot..........D4 57
Callands, Va..........E3 209
Callao, Mo..........B5 189
Callao, Peru..........D2 134
Callao, Va..........D6 209
Callaway, Md..........D4 173
Callaway, Minn..........D3 187
Callaway, Nebr..........C6 191
Callaway, Va..........D2 209
Callaway, co., Mo..........C6 189
Callender, Iowa..........B3 180
Callensburg, Pa..........D2 202
Callery, Pa..........E1 202
Callicoon, N.Y..........D5 196
Callicoon Center, N.Y..........D6 196
Calliham, Tex..........E3 206
Calling, lake, Alta., Can..........B4 148
Calling Lake, Alta., Can..........B4 148
Calloway, co., Ky..........B3 182
Calmar, Alta., Can..........C4 148
Calmar, Iowa..........A6 180
Calne, Eng..........C5 56
Caloocan, Phil..........o13 90
Caloosahatchee, riv., Fla..........F5 174
Calpella, Calif..........C2 170
Calpet, Wyo..........C2 213
Caltagirone, It..........F5 67
Caltanissetta, It..........F5 67
Caluire [-et-Cuire], Fr..........E6 58
Calulo, Ang..........D1 106
Calumet, Ala..........B2 166
Calumet, Que., Can..........D3 154
Calumet, Iowa..........B2 180
Calumet, Mich..........A2 186
Calumet, Minn..........C5 187
Calumet, Okla..........B3 200
Calumet, Pa..........*F3 202
Calumet, co., Wis..........D5 212
Calumet, lake, Ill..........F3 178
Calumet City, Ill..........B6, F3 178
Calumet Park, Ill..........*B6 178
Calumet Sag, chan., Ill..........F2 178
Calumetville, Wis..........B5 212
Calva, Ariz..........D5 168
Calvario, Cuba..........k12 131
Calvary, Ga..........F2 175
Calvary, Wis..........B5 212
Calvert, Ala..........D1 166
Calvert, Tex..........D4 206
Calvert, co., Md..........C4 173
Calvert, isl., B.C., Can..........D3 149
Calvert City, Ky..........A3 182
Calverton, Va..........C5 209
Calverton Park, Mo..........A8 189
Calvi, Fr..........C2 67
Calvillo, Mex..........m12 129
Calvin, La..........C3 183
Calvin, N. Dak..........A7 198
Calvin, Okla..........C5 200
Calvin, Va..........B2 209
Calvinia, S. Afr..........D2 107
Calvörde, Ger..........A6 61
Calw, Ger..........E3 61
Calypso, N.C..........B5 197
Calzada de Calatrava, Sp..........C4 65
Cam, riv., Eng..........B8 56
Cam Ranh, Viet..........G8 89
Camabatela, Ang..........C2 106
Camacho, Mex..........C4 129
Camagüey, Cuba..........E5 131
Camagüey, prov., Cuba..........E5 131

Camak, Ga. C4 175
Camamu, Braz. D3 138
Camaná, Peru E3 134
Camanche, Iowa C7 180
Camano, isl., Wash. A3 210
Camaquã, Braz. E2 137
Camargo, Bol. D2 135
Camargo, Ill. D5 178
Camargo, see Ciudad Camargo, Mex.
Camargo, Okla. A2 200
Camargo, Tenn. B5 205
Camarillo, Calif. *E4 170
Camarillo Heights, Calif. *E4 170
Camarón, cape, Hond. C5 130
Camarones, Arg. C3 136
Camas, Idaho E6 177
Camas, Mont. C2 190
Camas, Wash. D3 210
Camas, co., Idaho F4 177
Camas Valley, Oreg. D3 201
Camataquí, Bol. D2 135
Cambalache Central, P.R. B4 132
Cambay, India F4 88
Cambay, gulf, India G4 88
Camberwell, Austl. *G8 111
CAMBODIA, country, Asia F5 89
c. 1775 82
after World War II 83
Camborne [-Redruth], Eng. D2 56
Cambra, Pa. D9 202
Cambrai, Fr. B5 58
Cambria, Calif. E3 170
Cambria, Ill. *F4 178
Cambria, Iowa D4 180
Cambria, Mich. G6 186
Cambria, Wis. E4 212
Cambria, co., Pa. E4 202
Cambrian, mts., Wales B4 56
Cambridge, Eng. B8 56
Cambridge, Idaho E2 177
Cambridge, Ill. B3 178
Cambridge, Iowa A7, C4 180
Cambridge, Kans. E7 181
Cambridge, Ky. *B4 182
Cambridge, Maine C3 184
Cambridge, Md. C5 173
Cambridge, Mass. B5, D3 185
Cambridge, Minn. E5 187
Cambridge, Nebr. D5 191
Cambridge, N.Y. B7 196
Cambridge, Ohio B6 199
Cambridge, Vt. B3 208
Cambridge, Wis. F4 212
Cambridge, co., Eng. B8 56
Cambrige, res., Mass. C2 185
Cambridge Bay, N.W. Ter., Can. C12 144
Cambridge City, Ind. E7 179
Cambridge Junction, Vt. B3 208
Cambridge-Narrows, N.B., Can. *D3 151
Cambridge Springs, Pa. C1 202
Cambridgeport, Vt. E3 208
Cambuí, Braz. m8 137
Camby, Ind. E5, I7 179
Camden, Ala. D2 166
Camden, Ark. D3 169
Camden, Del. B6 173
Camden, Eng. C7 56
Camden, Ill. C3 178
Camden, Ind. C4 179
Camden, Maine D3 184
Camden, Mich. G6 186
Camden, Miss. C4 188
Camden, Mo. B3 189
Camden, N.J. D2 194
Camden, N.Y. B5 196
Camden, N.C. A7 197
Camden, Ohio C3 199
Camden, S.C. C6 203
Camden, Tenn. A3 205
Camden, Tex. D5 206
Camden, W. Va. B4 211
Camden, co., Ga. F5 175
Camden, co., Mo. C5 189
Camden, co., N.J. D3 194
Camden, co., N.C. A7 197
Camden on Gauley, W. Va. C4 211
Camdenton, Mo. D5 189
Camelback, mtn., Ariz. G2 168
Camelback, mtn., Pa. A2 194
Camels Hump, mtn., Vt. C3 208
Cameo, Colo. B2 171
Camerino, It. C4 67
Cameron, Ariz. B4 168
Cameron, Ill. C3 178
Cameron, La. E2 183
Cameron, Mo. B3 189
Cameron, Mont. E5 190
Cameron, N. Mex. C6 195
Cameron, N.C. B4 197
Cameron, Okla. B7 200
Cameron, Pa. D5 202
Cameron, S.C. D6 203
Cameron, Tex. D4 206
Cameron, W. Va. B4, C2 211
Cameron, Wis. C2 212
Cameron, co., Pa. D5 202
Cameron, co., Tex. F4 206
Cameron, par., La. E2 183
Cameron, hills, N.W. Ter., Can. D9 142
CAMEROON, country, Afr. D2 104
Cameroon, mtn., Cam. F6 103
Cameroons, French, see Cameroon, country, Afr.
Câmetá, Braz. C5 139
Camiling, Phil. o13 90
Camilla, Ga. E2 175
Camillus, N.Y. *B4 196
Caminha, Port. B1 65
Camino, Calif. C3 170
Camlachie, Ont., Can. D2 153
Cammack Village, Ark. C3, D5 169
Cammal, Pa. D7 202
Cammin, see Kamień Pomorski, Pol.
Camocim, Braz. B2 138
Camooweal, Austl. C6 111
Camp, co., Tex. C5 206
Camp Crook, S. Dak. B2 204
Camp Douglas, Wis. E3 212
Camp Hill, Ala. C4 166
Camp Hill, Pa. F8 202
Camp Howard Ridge, mtn., Idaho D2 177
Camp Pendleton, Calif. *F5 170
Camp Point, Ill. C2 178
Camp Ruby, Tex. D5 206
Camp San Saba, Tex. D3 206
Camp Sealth, Wash. D1 210
Camp Sherman, Oreg. C5 201
Camp Springs, Md. C2 173
Camp Verde, Ariz. C4 168
Camp Wood, Ariz. C3 168
Camp Wood, Tex. E2 206
Campagna di Roma, reg., It. h9 67
Campaign, Tenn. D8 205
Campana, Arg. g7 136
Campana, isl., Chile D1 136
Campanario, Sp. C3 65
Campania, reg., It. D5 67
Campania, isl., B.C., Can. C3 149
Campanquiz, mts., Peru B2 134
Campbell, Ala. D2 166
Campbell, Calif. C6 170
Campbell, Fla. D5 174
Campbell, Minn. D2 187
Campbell, Mo. E7 189
Campbell, Nebr. D7 191
Campbell, N.Y. C3 196
Campbell, Ohio A7 199
Campbell, Va. C4 209
Campbell, co., Ky. B5 182
Campbell, co., S. Dak. B5 204
Campbell, co., Tenn. C9 205
Campbell, co., Va. D3 209
Campbell, co., Wyo. A7 213
Campbell, cape, N.Z. N15 112
Campbell, hill, Ohio B4 199
Campbell, isl., B.C., Can. C3 149
Campbell, isl., Pac. O. D29 120
Campbell, lake, Oreg. E7 201
Campbell, mtn., Yukon, Can. D5 142
Campbell Hill, Ill. F4 178
Campbell Island, B.C., Can. C3 149
Campbell River, B.C., Can. D5 149
Campbell Station, Ark. *B4 169
Campbellford, Ont., Can. C7 153
Campbellpur, Pak. B5 87
Campbells, creek, W. Va. C6 211
Campbells Bay, Que., Can. B8 153
Campbellsburg, Ind. G5 179
Campbellsburg, Ky. B4 182
Campbellsport, Wis. E5 212
Campbellsville, Ky. C4 182
Campbellsville, Tenn. B4 205
Campbellton, N.B., Can. A3 151
Campbellton, Newf., Can. D4 152
Campbellton, Fla. B1, G3 174
Campbellton, Tex. *E3 206
Campbelltown, Pa. *F9 202
Campbeltown, Scot. E3 57
Campcreek, Tenn. C11 205
Campeche, Mex. D6 129
Campeche, state, Mex. D6 129
Campeche, gulf, Mex. C6 129
Campechuela, Cuba E5 131
Camperdown, Austl. I4 112
Campgrove, Ill. B4 178
Campiglia Marittima, It. C3 67
Câmpina, Rom. C7 68
Campina Grande, Braz. C3, h6 138
Campinas, Braz. C3, m8 137
Campion, Colo. A5 171
Campione d'Italia, It. D4 66
Campo, Calif. F5 170
Campo, Cam. E1 104
Campo, Colo. D8 171
Campo Belo, Braz. F1 138
Campo de Criptana, Sp. C4 65
Campo Gallo, Arg. E3 135
Campo Grande, Braz. C2 137
Campo Maior, Braz. B2 138
Campo Maior, Port. C2 65
Campo Real, Sp. p18 65
Campo Tures, It. C7 66
Campoalegre, Col. C2 133
Campobasso, It. D5 67
Campobello, S.C. A3 203
Campobello, isl., N.B., Can. E3 151
Campos, Braz. C4 137
Campos Novos, Braz. D2 137
Campos Sales, Braz. C2 138
Camposampiero, It. D7 66
Campti, La. C2 183
Campton, Fla. G2 174
Campton, Ga. C3 175
Campton, Ky. C6 182
Campton, N.H. C3 193
Camptown, Pa. C9 202
Câmpulung, Rom. C7 68
Câmpulung Moldovenesc, Rom. B7 68
Campus, Ill. B5 178
Campville, Fla. C4 174
Camrose, Alta., Can. C4 148
Camuy, P.R. B3 132
Camuy, mun., P.R. B3 132
Camuy, riv., P.R. B3 132
Can Tho, Viet. G6 89
Caña Gorda, is., P.R. D3 132
Canaan, Conn. A3 172
Canaan, Ind. G7 179
Canaan, Maine D3 184
Canaan, Miss. A4 188
Canaan, N.H. C2 193
Canaan, N.Y. C7 196
Canaan, Vt. A5 208
Canaan, riv., N.B., Can. C4 151
Canaan Center, N.H. C2 193
Canaan Station, N.B., Can. C4 151
Canaan Street, N.H. C2 193
CANADA, country, N.A. 144
in 1792-1840 146
dominion of 147
Canada, bay, Newf., Can. C3 152
Cañada de Gómez, Arg. A4 136
Cañada de los Alamos, N. Mex. F6 195
Canada Falls Deadwater, lake, Maine C2 184
Canadensis, Pa. D11 202
Canadian, Okla. B6 200
Canadian, Tex. B2 206
Canadian, co., Okla. B3 200
Canadian, riv., U.S. C7 158
Cañadon León, Arg. D2 136
Canadys, S.C. E6 203
Canairiktok, riv., Newf., Can. g9 152
Canajoharie, N.Y. C6 196
Çanakkale, Tur. B6 69
Canal [Township], Pa. D2 202
Canal, riv., Ven. A4 134
Canal Fulton, Ohio B6 199
Canal Point, Fla. F6 174
Canal Winchester, Ohio C2, C5 199
CANAL ZONE, U.S. dep., N.A. k11 130
Canale, It. E3 66
Canalou, Mo. E8 189
Canandaigua, N.Y. C3 196
Canandaigua, lake, N.Y. C3 196
Cananea, Mex. A2 129
Cananéia, Braz. D3 137
Cañar, Ec. B2 134
Cañar, prov., Ec. B2 134
Canary, is., Afr. m14 65
Canary Islands, Sp. overseas prov., Afr. D1 102
Cañas, C.R. E5 130
Canaseraga, N.Y. C3 196
Canastota, N.Y. B5 196
Canavieiras, Braz. E3 138
Cañazas, Pan. F7 130
Canazei, It. C7 66
Canbelego, Austl. E6 112
Canberra, Austl. G8 111, G7 112
Canby, Calif. B3 170
Canby, Minn. F2 187
Canby, Oreg. B2, B4 201
Cancale, Fr. C3 58
Canche, riv., Fr. D1 59
Cancienne, La. C5 183
Cándala, Som. C6 105
Candelaria, Cuba D2 131
Candelaria, Phil. o12 90
Candelaria, Tex. F2 206
Candeleda, Sp. B3 65
Candelero, pt., P.R. C7 132
Candia, see Iráklion, Grc.
Candia, N.H. D4 193
Candia Village, N.H. D4 193
Candle, Alsk. B7 167
Candle, lake, Sask., Can. D3 155
Candler, Fla. C5 174
Candler, co., Ga. D4 175
Candlewood, lake, Conn. C3 172
Cando, Sask., Can. E1 155
Cando, N. Dak. A6 198
Candor, N.Y. C4 196
Candor, N.C. B3 197
Cane, creek, Tenn. B5 205
Cane, creek, Utah E6 207
Cane, riv., La. C2 183
Cane Valley, Ky. C4 182
Caneel, bay, Vir. Is. f15 132
Canela, Braz. D2 137
Canelones, Ur. E1 137
Cañete, Chile B2 136
Cañete, Peru D2 134
Caney, Kans. E8 181
Caney, Ky. C6 182
Caney, Okla. C5 200
Caney, fork, Tenn. C8 205
Caney, riv., Okla. A5 200
Caneyville, Ky. C3 182
Canfield, Ark. D2 169
Canfield, Ohio A7 199
Cangallo, Peru D3 134
Cangamba, Ang. D3 106
Cangas, Sp. A1 65
Cangas de Narcea, Sp. A2 65
Cangas de Onís, Sp. A3 65
Canguaretama, Braz. C3, h6 138
Caniapiscau, lake, Que., Can. F19 143
Caniapiscau, riv., Que., Can. A2 154
Canguçu, Braz. E2 137
Canhotinho, Braz. k5 138
Caniçado, Moz. B5 107
Canicanian, Phil. o13 90
Canicattì, It. F4 67
Caniles, Sp. D4 65
Canim Lake, B.C., Can. D7 149
Canindé, Braz. B3 138
Canistear, res., N.J. A4 194
Canisteo, N.Y. C3 196
Canisteo, riv., N.Y. C3 196
Canistota, S. Dak. D8 204
Canjilon, N. Mex. A3 195
Çankiri, Tur. B9 85
Canmer, Ky. C4 182
Canmore, Alta., Can. D3 148
Canna, isl., Scot. C2 57
Canna, sound, Scot. D2 57
Cannanore, India *F6 87
Cannel City, Ky. C6 182
Cannelburg, Ind. G4 179
Cannelton, Ind. I4 179
Cannelton, W. Va. C6 211
Cannes, Fr. F7 58
Cannes, bayou, La. D3 183
Canneto sull'Oglio, It. D6 66
Cannich, Scot. C4 57
Canning, N.S., Can. D5 151
Canning, S. Dak. C6 204
Cannington, Ont., Can. C5 153
Cannock, Eng. B5 56
Cannon, Del. C6 173
Cannon, co., Tenn. B5 205
Cannon, riv., Minn. F6 187
Cannon Ball, N. Dak. C5 198
Cannon Beach, Oreg. B3 201
Cannon Falls, Minn. F6 187
Cannon Mines, Mo. C7 189
Cannonball, riv., N. Dak. C4 198
Cannondale, Conn. E3 172
Cannonsburg, Ky. B7 182
Cannonsburg, Miss. D2 188
Cannonsville, res., N.Y. C5 196
Cannonville, Utah F3 207
Cano, Cuba k11 131
Canoas, Braz. *E2 137
Canobie Lake, N.H. E4 193
Canoe, Ala. D2 166
Canoe, B.C., Can. D8 149
Canoe Lake, Ont., Can. B6 153
Canoinhas, Braz. D2 137
Canon, Ga. B3 175
Canon City, Colo. C5 171
Canonchet, R.I. D10 172
Canones, N. Mex. A3 195
Canonsburg, Pa. F1 202
Canoochee, riv., Ga. D5 175
Canora, Sask., Can. F4 155
Canosa, It. D6 67
Canova, S. Dak. D8 204
Canóvanas Central, P.R. B7 132
Canso, N.S., Can. D8 151
Canso, cape, N.S., Can. G20 143
Cantabrian, mts., Sp. A3 65
Cantanhede, Port. B1 65
Cantaura, Ven. B5 133
Canterbury, Austl. B3 112
Canterbury, Conn. C9 172
Canterbury, Eng. C9 56
Canterbury, N.B., Can. *D2 151
Canterbury, N.H. D3 193
Canterbury, bight, N.Z. P13 112
Canterbury Station, N.B., Can. D2 151
Cantley, Que., Can. D2 154
Canton, China G7 91
Canton, Conn. B5 172
Canton, Ga. B2 175
Canton, Ill. C3 178
Canton, Kans. D6 181
Canton, Ky. D2 182
Canton, Maine D2 184
Canton, Mass. B5, D2 185
Canton, Minn. G7 187
Canton, Miss. C3 188
Canton, Mo. A6 189
Canton, N.J. E2 194
Canton, N.Y. B2 196
Canton, N.C. D3 197
Canton, Ohio B6 199
Canton, Okla. A3 200
Canton Pa. C8 202
Canton, S. Dak. D9 204
Canton, Tex. C5 206
Canton, Wis. C2 212
Canton, res., Okla. A3 200
Canton Center, Conn. B5 172
Cantonment, Fla. G2 174
Cantril, Iowa D5 180
Cantuar, Sask., Can. G1 155
Cantwell, Alsk. C10 167
Cantwell, Mo. D7 189
Cañuelas, Arg. B5, g7 136
Canutama, Braz. D2 139
Canute, Okla. B2 200
Canutillo, Tex. E1 206
Canwood, Sask., Can. D2 155
Cany-Barville, Fr. E8 56
Canyon, N. Mex. F5 195
Canyon, Tex. B2 206
Canyon, Wyo. A2 213
Canyon, co., Idaho F2 177
Canyon, res., Tex. A4 206
Canyon City, Ore. C8 201
Canyon Creek, Mont. D4 190
Canyon De Chelly, nat. mon., Ariz. A6 168
Canyon Ferry, res., Mont. D5 190
Canyoncito, N. Mex. F6 195
Canyonlands, nat. park, Utah E6 207
Canyonville, Oreg. E3 201
Cao Bang, Viet. A7 89
Caorle, It. D8 66
Cap-à-l'Aigle, Que., Can. B7 154
Cap-Chat, Que., Can. G19 145
Cap de la Madeleine, Que., Can. C5 154
Cap-Haïtien, Hai. E7 131
Cap-Pelé, N.B., Can. *C5 151
Cap Rouge, Que., Can. C9 154
Cap-St. Ignace, Que., Can. B7 154
Cap-Santé, Que., Can. C6 154
Capa, P.R. B2 132
Capa, S. Dak. C5 204
Capac, Mich. F8 186
Çapakçur, see Bingöl, Tur.
Capalonga, Phil. o14 90
Capanaparo, riv., Ven. B4 133
Capanema, Braz. B1 138
Capão Bonito, Braz. C3, m7 137
Caparica, Port. f9 65
Capasin, Sask., Can. D2 155
Capatárida, Ven. A3 133
Capbreton, Fr. F3 58
Capdenac-Gare, Fr. E5 58
Capdevila, Cuba k11 131
Cape, isl., S.C. E9 203
Cape Breton, co., N.S., Can. D9 151
Cape Breton, isl., N.S., Can. G20 143
Cape Breton Highlands, nat. park, N.S., Can. G20 145, C9 151
Cape Broyle, Newf., Can. E5 152
Cape Canaveral, Fla. D6 174
Cape Charles, Newf., Can. B4 152
Cape Charles, Va. D6 209
Cape Coast, Ghana E4 103
Cape Cod, bay, Mass. C7 185
Cape Cod, canal, Mass. C6 185
Cape Cod, nat. seashore, Mass. C7 185
Cape Colony: in late 19th cent. 99
Cape Elizabeth (The Cape), Maine E2, E5 184
Cape Fear, riv., N.C. C5 197
Cape Girardeau, Mo. D8 189
Cape Girardeau, co., Mo. D8 189
Cape Hatteras, nat. seashore recreational area, N.C. B8 197
Cape Horn, mtn., Idaho E3 177
Cape La Hune, Newf., Can. E3 152
Cape Lookout, nat. seashore, N.C. C7 197
Cape May, N.J. F3 194
Cape May, co., N.J. E3 194
Cape May Court House, N.J. E3 194
Cape May Point, N.J. F3 194
Cape Neddick, Maine E2 184
Cape of Good Hope, prov., S. Afr. D3 107
Cape Porpoise, Maine E2 184
Cape Ray, Newf., Can. E2 152
Cape Tormentine, N.B., Can. C6 151
Cape Town, S. Afr. D2 107
CAPE VERDE ISLANDS, Port. dep., Afr. E3 97
Cape Verde, is., Atl. O. E3 96
Cape Vincent, N.Y. A4 196
Cape York, pen., Austl. B7 110
Capelinha, Braz. E2 138
Capella, is., Vir. Is. f15 132
Capels, W. Va. D3 211
Caper's, is., S.C. F8 203
Capers, is., S.C. G6 203
Capesterre, Guad. n16 131
Capeto, Chile D2 135
Capeville, Va. A7 209
Capilla del Monte, Arg. A4 136
Capilla del Señor, Arg. g7 136
Capinota, Bol. C2 135
Capistrano Beach, Calif. *F5 170
Capitan, N. Mex. D4 195
Capitán Bado, Par. D4 135
Capitol, Mont. E12 190
Capitol, peak, Nev. B4 192
Capitol Heights, Md. C2, C4 173
Capitol Reef, nat. mon., Utah E4 207
Capitola, Calif. *D3 170
Capitola, Fla. B2 174
Capivarí, Braz. m8 137
Capleville, Tenn. E8 205
Capon Bridge, W. Va. B6 211
Capon Springs, W. Va. B6 211
Capote Knob, mtn., Tex. B4 206
Cappadocia: in Roman empire 45
c. 500 B.C. 78
Capps, Ala. D4 166
Capraia, isl., It. C2 67
Caprara, pt., It. D2 67
Capreol, Ont., Can. E9 153
Caprera, isl., It. D2 67
Capri, isl., It. D5 67
Capricorn, is., Austl. A9 112
Caprock, N. Mex. D6 195
Capron, Ill. A5 178
Capron, Okla. A3 200
Capron, Va. E5 209
Capshaw, Ala. A3 166
Captain Cook, Haw. D6 176
Captiva, Fla. F4 174
Captiva, isl., Fla. F4 174
Capua, It. D5 67
Capulin, Colo. D4 171
Capulin, N. Mex. A6 195
Capulin Mountain, nat. mon., N. Mex. A6 195
Caputa, S. Dak. D3 204
Caquetá, intendencia, Col. C3 133
Caquetá, riv., Col. D3 133
Car Nicobar, isl., India G9 87
Carabaña, Sp. p18 65
Carabanchel Bajo, Sp. p17 65
Carabobo, state, Ven. A4 133
Caracal, Rom. C7 68
Caracas, Ven. A4 133
Carajás, mts., Braz. D4 139
Carangola, Braz. F2 138
Caransebeș, Rom. C6 68
Carapari, Bol. D3 135
Carapeguá, Par. E4 135
Caraquet, N.B., Can. B5 151
Caratinga, Braz. E2 138
Caratunk, Maine C3 184
Caraúbas, Braz. C3 138
Caraúbas, Braz. h5 138
Caravaca, Sp. C5 65
Caravelas, Braz. E3 138
Caravelí, Peru E3 134
Caraway, Ark. B5 169
Caraz, Peru C2 134
Caràzinho, Braz. D2 137
Carballino, Sp. A1 65
Carballo, Sp. A1 65
Carberry, Man., Can. E2 150
Carbó, Mex. B2 129
Carbon, Alta., Can. D4 148
Carbon, Ind. E3 179
Carbon, Iowa C3 180
Carbon, Tex. *C3 206
Carbon, W. Va. D6 211
Carbon, co., Mont. E7 190
Carbon, co., Pa. E10 202
Carbon, co., Utah D5 207
Carbon, co., Wyo. E5 213
Carbon Cliff, Ill. *B3 178
Carbon Hill, Ala. B2 166
Carbonado, Wash. B3 210
Carbonara, cape, It. E2 67
Carbondale, Alta., Can. C4 148
Carbondale, Colo. B3 171
Carbondale, Ill. F4 178
Carbondale, Kans. D8 181
Carbondale, Ohio C3 199
Carbondale, Pa. C10 202
Carbonear, Newf., Can. E5 152
Carbonia, It. E2 67
Carbury, N. Dak. A5 198
Carcagente, Sp. C5 65
Carcans, lagoon, Fr. E3 58
Carcassonne, Fr. F5 58
Carchi, prov., Ec. A2 134
Carcross, Yukon, Can. D6 144
Çardak, Tur. D7 69
Cardale, Man., Can. D1 150
Cárdenas, Cuba D3 131
Cárdenas, Mex. m14 129
Cárdenas, Mex. D6 129
Carderview, Tenn. C12 205
Cardiel, lake, Arg. D2 136
Cardiff, Ala. E4 166
Cardiff, Colo. B3 171
Cardiff, Md. A5 173
Cardiff, N.J. E3 194
Cardiff, Wales C4 56
Cardiff-by-the-Sea, Calif. *F5 170
Cardigan, P.E.I., Can. C7 151
Cardigan, Wales B3 56
Cardigan, co., Wales B3 56
Cardigan, bay, P.E.I., Can. C7 151
Cardigan, bay, Wales B3 56
Cardigan, mtn., N.H. C3 193
Cardinal, Man., Can. E2 150
Cardinal, Ont., Can. C9 153
Cardinal, lake, Alta., Can. A2 148
Cardington, Ohio B5 199
Cardona, Ur. E1 137
Cardross, Sask., Can. H3 155
Cardston, Alta., Can. E4 148
Cardville, Maine C4 184
Cardwell, Mo. E7 189
Cardwell, Mont. E5 190
Cardwell, mtn., Tenn. D8 205
Carega, mtn., It. D7 66
Carei, Rom. B6 68
Carencro, La. D3 183
Carenero, Ven. A4 133
Carentan, Fr. C3 58
Caretta, W. Va. D3 211
Carey, Idaho F5 177
Carey, Ohio B4 199
Carey, Tex. B2 206
Careyhurst, Wyo. C7 213
Careysburg, Lib. E2 103
Careywood, Idaho A2 177
Carhaix, Fr. C2 58
Carhuaz, Peru C2 134
Caria: c. 450 B.C. 42
Cariamanga, Ec. B2 134
Cariati, It. E6 67
Caribana, pt., Col. B2 133
Caribbean, sea, N.A. B3 124
Caribe Central, P.R. D5 132
Caribes, is., P.R. D6 132
Cariboo, mts., B.C., Can. F8 142
Caribou, Maine B4 184
Caribou, co., Idaho G7 177
Caribou, isl., N.S., Can. D7 151
Caribou, lake, Maine C3 184
Caribou, mtn., Idaho F7 177
Caribou, mtn., Maine C2 184
Caribou, mts., Alta., Can. E9 142
Caribou, range, Idaho F7 177
Carichic, Mex. B3 129
Carievale, Sask., Can. H5 155
Carignan, Fr. E5 59
Carinhanha, Braz. D2 138
Carini, It. E4 67
Carinish, Scot. C1 57
Carinthia, reg., Aus. E6 60
Caripe, Ven. A5 133
Caripito, Ven. A5 133
Cariris Velhos, mts., Braz. h5 138
Cariús, Braz. C3 138
Carl Blackwell, lake, Okla. A4 200
Carl Junction, Mo. D3 189
Carlanna, Alsk. n24 167
Carleton, Mich. F7 186
Carleton, Nebr. D8 191
Carleton, co., Ont., Can. B9 153
Carleton, co., N.B., Can. C2 151
Carleton, mtn., N.B., Can. B3 151
Carleton Place, Ont., Can. B8 153
Carletonville, S. Afr. *C4 107
Carlile, Wyo. A8 213
Carlin, Nev. C5 192
Carlinville, Ill. D4 178
Carlisle, Ark. C4 169
Carlisle, Eng. C5 55
Carlisle, Ind. G3 179
Carlisle, Iowa A7, C4 180
Carlisle, Ky. B5 182

INDEX KEY Each place listed in **Bold-faced Type** has its population listed in the Population tables, pages 230 to 280.
Each country, shown in CAPITAL LETTERS, has its population listed in the World Political Information Table, pages 6 to 10.
* Does not appear on map; key shows general location.

Carlisle, Mass. *A5 185
Carlisle, Ohio C3 199
Carlisle, Pa. F7 202
Carlisle, S.C. B5 203
Carlisle, Tenn. A4 205
Carlisle, Tex. D5 206
Carlisle, co., Ky. B2 182
Carlock, Ill. C4 178
Carloforte, It. E2 67
Carlos, Md. D2 173
Carlos, Minn. E3 187
Carlos Casares, Arg. B4 136
Carlos Chagas, Braz. E2 138
Carlos Tejedor, Arg. B4 136
Carloway, Scot. B2 57
Carlowville, Ala. C2 166
Carlsbad, Calif. F5 170
Carlsbad, N. Mex. E5 195
Carlsbad, Tex. D2 206
Carlsbad Caverns, nat. park, N. Mex. E5 195
Carlsbad Springs, Ont., Can. A10 153
Carlsborg, Wash. A2 210
Carlstadt, N.J. D5 194
Carlton, Ala. D2 166
Carlton, Sask., Can. E2 155
Carlton, Eng. B6 56
Carlton, Ga. B3 175
Carlton, Kans. D6 181
Carlton, Minn. D6 187
Carlton, Oreg. B1, B3 201
Carlton, Tex. D3 206
Carlton, co., Minn. D6 187
Carluke, Scot. E5 57
Carlyle, Sask., Can. H4 155
Carlyle, Ill. E4 178
Carlyle, Mont. D12 190
Carlyle, res., Ill. E4 178
Carmacks, Yukon, Can. D5 144
Carmagnola, It. B1 67
Carman, Man., Can. E2 150
Carman, hill, Pa. C6 202
Carmangay, Alta., Can. D4 148
Carmania: c. 500 B.C. 78
Carmans, riv., N.Y. F5 172
Carmanville, Newf., Can. D4 152
Carmarthen, Wales C3 56
Carmarthen, co., Wales C3 56
Carmarthen, bay, Wales C3 56
Carmaux, Fr. E5 58
Carmel, Calif. C6, D3 170
Carmel, Sask., Can. E3 155
Carmel, Ind. E5 179
Carmel, Maine D3 184
Carmel, N.J. E2 194
Carmel, N.Y. D7 196
Carmel, mtn., Isr. B7 84
Carmel, pt., Calif. C6 170
Carmel Valley, Calif. *D3 170
Carmel Woods, Calif. *D3 170
Carmelo, Ur. E1 137
Carmen, Ariz. F4 168
Carmen, Idaho D5 177
Carmen, Okla. A3 200
Carmen, isl., Mex. B2 129
Carmen Alto, Chile D2 135
Carmen de Areco, Arg. A5, g7 136
Carmen de Patagones, Arg. C4 136
Carmen del Paraná, Par. E4 135
Carmen-Sylva, Rom. C9 68
Carmi, Ill. E5 178
Carmi, lake, Vt. B3 208
Carmichael, Calif. A6 170
Carmichael, Sask., Can. G1 155
Carmichaels, Pa. G2 202
Carmine, Tex. D4 206
Carmona, Sp. D3 65
Carmyllie, Scot. D6 57
Carnarvon, Austl. D1 111
Carnarvon, Iowa B2 180
Carnarvon, S. Afr. D3 107
Carnation, Wash. B4 210
Carnaxide, Port. f9 65
Carnduff, Sask., Can. H5 155
Carnegie, Ga. E2 175
Carnegie, Okla. B3 200
Carnegie, Pa. B5, F1 202
Carnegie, lake, N.J. C3 194
Carneiro, Kans. D5 181
Carnes, Miss. D4 188
Carnesville, Ga. B3 175
Carney, Mich. C3 186
Carney, Okla. B4 200
Carneys Point, N.J. D2 194
Carnforth, Eng. F6 57
Carnic Alps, mts., Aus. E6 60
Carniola: c. 1860 51
Carn Mairg, mtn., Scot. C4 57
Carn Mor, mtn., Scot. C5 57
Carnot, Cen. Afr. Rep. D3 104
Carnoustie, Scot. D6 57
Carnuel, N. Mex. B3, G5 195
Carnwath, Scot. E5 57
Caro, Mich. E7 186
Carol City, Fla. E3 174
Carol Stream, Ill. *B5 178
Caroleen, N.C. B2 197
Carolina, Braz. C1 138
Carolina, P.R. B7 132
Carolina, mun., P.R. B7 132
Carolina, R.I. D10 172
Carolina, S. Afr. C5 107
Carolina, W. Va. A7 211
Carolina Beach, N.C. C6 197
Caroline, Wis. D5 212
Caroline, co., Md. C6 173
Caroline, co., Va. D5 209
Caroline, atoll, Pac. O. G13 113
Caroline, is., Pac. O. F8 113
Caron, Sask., Can. G3 155
Caron Brook, N.B., Can. A4 184
Carona, Kans. E9 181
Caroní, riv., Ven. C5 133
Carora, Ven. A3 133
Carouge, Switz. C2 66
Carp, Ont., Can. A8, B8 153
Carp, Nev. F7 192
Carp, lake, B.C., Can. B6 149
Carpathians, mts., Czech., Pol., Rom. B7 68, D5 70
Carpentaria, gulf, Austl. B6 110
Carpenter, Ill. A9 189
Carpenter, Iowa A4 180
Carpenter, Miss. C3 188
Carpenter, S. Dak. C8 204
Carpenter, Wyo. D8 213
Carpenter, dam, Ark. D6 169
Carpentersville, Ill. E2 178
Carpentersville, N.J. B2 194
Carpenterville, Oreg. E2 201
Carpentras, Fr. E6 58
Carpi, It. B3 67
Carpinteria, Calif. E4 170
Carpio, N. Dak. A4 198
Carr, Colo. A6 171
Carr, mtn., N.H. C3 197
Carr Bridge, Scot. C5 57
Carrabassett, Maine C2 184
Carrabelle, Fla. C2 174
Carradale, Scot. E3 57
Carragana, Sask., Can. F4 155
Carrantuo, hill, Ire. D2 55
Carranza, cape, Chile B2 136
Carrara, It. B3 67
Carrboro, N.C. B3 197
Carrick, Ire. D3 55
Carrie, mtn., Wash. B2 210
Carrier, Que., Can. C9 154
Carrier, Okla. A3 200
Carriere, Miss. E4 188
Carriers Mills, Ill. F5 178
Carrigain, mtn., N.H. B4 193
Carrigan, peak, Ariz. C2 168
Carrington, N. Dak. B6 198
Carrión, riv., Sp. A3 65
Carrión de los Condes, Sp. A3 65
Carrizal Bajo, Chile E1 135
Carrizo, creek, Ariz., N. Mex. C6 168
Carrizo, creek, N. Mex., Tex. A6 195
Carrizo, mtn., N. Mex. D4 195
Carrizo, mts., Ariz., N. Mex. A6 168
Carrizo Springs, Tex. E3 206
Carrizozo, N. Mex. D4 195
Carroll, Man., Can. E1 150
Carroll, Iowa B3 180
Carroll, Maine C4 184
Carroll, Nebr. B8 191
Carroll, N.H. B3 193
Carroll, Ohio C5 199
Carroll, co., Ark. A2 169
Carroll, co., Ga. C1 175
Carroll, co., Ill. A4 178
Carroll, co., Ind. C4 179
Carroll, co., Iowa B3 180
Carroll, co., Ky. B4 182
Carroll, co., Md. A3 173
Carroll, co., Miss. B3 188
Carroll, co., Mo. B4 189
Carroll, co., N.H. C4 193
Carroll, co., Ohio B6 199
Carroll, co., Tenn. B3 205
Carroll, co., Va. E2 209
Carrolls, Wash. C3 210
Carrollton, Ala. B1 166
Carrollton, Ga. C1 175
Carrollton, Ill. D3 178
Carrollton, Ky. B4 182
Carrollton (P.O.), Md. A4 173
Carrollton, Md. *C4 173
Carrollton, Mich. E7 186
Carrollton, Miss. B4 188
Carrollton, Mo. B4 189
Carrollton, Ohio B6 199
Carrollton, Tex. B5 206
Carrolltown, Pa. E4 202
Carron, inlet, Scot. B4 55
Carron, riv., Scot. C3 57
Carrot, riv., Man., Sask., Can. C1 150, D4 155
Carrot River, Sask., Can. D4 155
Carrsville, Ky. A3 182
Carruthers, Sask., Can. E1 155
Carrville, Ala. C4 166
Carry Falls, res., N.Y. B2 196
Carrying Place, Ont., Can. C7 153
Çarşamba, Tur. B11 85
Carseland, Alta., Can. D4 148
Carshalton, Eng. *m12 55
Carson (N. Wilmington), Calif. *F2 170
Carson, Iowa C2 180
Carson, Maine B4 184
Carson, Miss. D4 188
Carson, N. Dak. C4 198
Carson, Oreg. C9 201
Carson, Va. D5 209
Carson, Wash. D4 210
Carson, co., Tex. B2 206
Carson, lake, Nev. D3 192
Carson, riv., Nev. D3 192
Carson, sink, Nev. D3 192
Carson City, Mich. E6 186
Carson City, Nev. D2 192
Carsonville, Mich. E8 186
Carstairs, Alta., Can. D3 148
Carta Valley, Tex. E2 206
Cartagena, Chile A2 136
Cartagena, Col. A2 133
Cartagena, Sp. D5 65
Cartagena, lake, P.R. C2 132
Cartago, Col. C2 133
Cartago, C.R. F6 130
Cartaxo, Port. C1 65
Cartaya, Sp. D2 65
Carter, Ky. B6 182
Carter, Mont. C6 190
Carter, Okla. B2 200
Carter, S. Dak. D5 204
Carter, Tenn. C11 205
Carter, Wis. C5 212
Carter, Wyo. D2 213
Carter, co., Ky. B6 182
Carter, co., Mo. E7 189
Carter, co., Mont. E12 190
Carter, co., Okla. C4 200
Carter, co., Tenn. C11 205
Carter, mtn., Wyo. A3 213
Carter Dome, mtn., N.H. B4 193
Carter Lake, Iowa C2 180
Carteret (Roosevelt), N.J. B4, E4 194
Carteret, co., N.C. C7 197
Carters, Ga. B2 175
Carters, lake, Ga. B2 175
Cartersburg, Ind. E5 179
Cartersville, Ga. B2 175
Cartersville, S.C. C7 203
Cartersville, Va. D4 209
Cartertown, Ky. D3 182
Carterville, Ill. F4 178
Carterville, Mo. D3 189
Carthage, Ark. C3 169
Carthage, Ill. C2 178
Carthage, Ind. E6 179
Carthage, Miss. C4 188
Carthage, Mo. D3 189
Carthage, N.Y. B5 196
Carthage, N.C. B4 197
Carthage, S. Dak. C8 204
Carthage, Tenn. C8 205
Carthage, Tex. C5 206
Carthage, ruins, Tun. B2 101
Cartwright, Man., Can. E2 150
Cartwright, Newf., Can. B3, h10 152
Cartwright, N. Dak. B2 198
Caruaru, Braz. C3, k6 138
Carúpano, Ven. A5 133
Caruthersville, Mo. E8 189
Carver, Mass. C6 185
Carver, Minn. *F5 187
Carver, co., Minn. F5 187
Carville, La. B5 183
Carvin, Fr. D2 59
Cary, Ga. D3 175
Cary, Ill. A5, E2 178
Cary, Miss. C3 188
Cary, N.C. B5 197
Caryville, Fla. G3 174
Caryville, Mass. E1 185
Caryville, Tenn. C9 205
Casa Ark. B2 169
Casa Blanca, Cuba h12 131
Casa Blanca, N. Mex. B2 195
Casa Branca, Braz. C3, k8 137
Casa de Piedra, P.R. B3 132
Casa Grande, Ariz. E4 168
Casa Grande, nat. mon., Ariz. E4 168
Casa Piedra, Tex. F2 206
Casablanca, Mor. H3 64, C3 102
Casale Monferrato, It. B2 67
Casalmaggiore, It. B3 67
Casanova, Va. C5 209
Casape, It. h9 67
Casar, N.C. B2 197
Casarano, It. D7 67
Casas Grandes, riv., Mex. G2 195
Cascade, B.C., Can. E8 149
Cascade, Colo. C6 171
Cascade, Idaho E2 177
Cascade, Iowa B6 180
Cascade, Mo. D7 189
Cascade, Mont. C5 190
Cascade, N.H. B4 193
Cascade, Va. E3 209
Cascade, W. Va. B5 211
Cascade, Wis. E5 212
Cascade, co., Mont. C5 190
Cascade, range, B.C., Can. E7 149
Cascade, range, U.S. B3 158
Cascade Locks, Oreg. B5 201
Cascade Summit, Oreg. D4 201
Cascadia, Oreg. C4 201
Cascais, Port. C1, f9 65
Cascavel, Braz. B3 138
Cascilla, Miss. B3 188
Casco, Maine D2 184
Casco, Wis. D6 212
Casco, bay, Maine E3 184
Caselton, Nev. F7 192
Caserta, It. D5 67
Caseville, Mich. E7 186
Casey, Ill. D6 178
Casey, Iowa C3 180
Casey, co., Ky. C5 182
Casey, bay, Ant. C17 120
Casey, key, Fla. E4 174
Casey, mtn., Idaho A2 177
Caseyville, Ill. *E3 178
Cash, Ark. B5 169
Cashel, Ire. D3 55
Cashiers, N.C. D3 197
Cashion, Ariz. D3 168
Cashion, Okla. B4 200
Cashmere, Wash. B5 210
Cashton, Wis. E3 212
Cashtown, Pa. G7 202
Casiguran, Phil. n14 90
Casilda, Arg. A4 136
Casilda, Cuba E4 131
Casino, Austl. D9 112
Casiquiare, riv., Ven. C4 133
Casky, Ky. D2 182
Čáslav, Czech. D3 70
Casma, Peru C2 134
Casmalia, Calif. E3 170
Casnovia, Mich. *E5 186
Caspar, Calif. C2 170
Caspe, Sp. B5 65
Casper, Wyo. C6 213
Caspian, Mich. B2 186
Caspian, depression, Sov. Un. D4 73
Caspian, pond, Vt. B4 208
Caspian, sea, Iran, Sov. Un. E7 71
Caspiana, La. B2 183
Cass, Ind. F3 179
Cass, W. Va. C5 211
Cass, co., Ill. D3 178
Cass, co., Ind. C5 179
Cass, co., Iowa C3 180
Cass, co., Mich. G4 186
Cass, co., Minn. D4 187
Cass, co., Mo. C3 189
Cass, co., Nebr. D9 191
Cass, co., N. Dak. C8 198
Cass, co., Tex. C5 206
Cass, lake, Minn. C4 187
Cass, riv., Mich. E7 186
Cass City, Mich. E7 186
Cass Lake, Minn. C4 187
Cassá, Sp. B7 65
Cassa, Wyo. C8 213
Cassadaga, N.Y. C1 196
Cassandra, Pa. *F4 202
Cassandra, see Kassandra, gulf, Grc.
Cassel, Fr. D2 59
Cassel, see Kassel, Ger.
Casselberry, Fla. *D5 174
Casselman, Ont., Can. B9 153
Casselman, Pa. G3 202
Casselman, riv., Md. D1 173
Casselton, N. Dak. C8 198
Cassia, Fla. D5 174
Cassia, co., Idaho G5 177
Cassidy, B.C., Can. A9 149
Cassino, It. D4 67
Cassiporé, riv., Braz. B4 139
Cassoday, Kans. D7 181
Cassopolis, Mich. G4 186
Casstown, Ohio B3 199
Cassville, Ga. B2 175
Cassville, Mo. E4 189
Cassville, Wis. F3 212
Castalia, Iowa A6 180
Castalia, N.C. A5 197
Castalia, Ohio A5 199
Castalian Springs, Tenn. A5 205
Castana, Iowa B2 180
Castanea, Pa. D7 202
Castanheira de Pêra, Port. B1 65
Castaños, Mex. B4 129
Castel di Guido, It. h8 67
Castel Gandolfo, It. h9 67
Castel Giuliano, It. g8 67
Castel Madama, It. h9 67
Castel San Pietro dell'Emilia, It. E7 66
Castelfranco Emilia, It. E7 66
Castelfranco Veneto, It. D7 66
Casteljaloux, Fr. E4 58
Castella, Calif. B2 170
Castellammare di Stabia, It. *D5 67
Castellamonte, It. D3 66
Castelli, Arg. B5 136
Castelli, Arg. E3 135
Castellón de la Plana, Sp. C5 65
Castelnaudary, Fr. F5 58
Castelo, Braz. F2 138
Castelo Branco, Port. C2 65
Castelo de Vide, Port. C2 65
Castelsarrasin, Fr. E4 58
Castelvetrano, It. F4 67
Casterton, Austl. H3 112
Castile: c. 1140 47
c. 1360 48
Castile, N.Y. C2 196
Castilla, Peru C1 134
Castillo de la Punta, fort, Cuba h12 131
Castillo de San Marcos, nat. mon., Fla. C5 174
Castillo del Morro, fort, Cuba h12 131
Castillos, Ur. E2 137
Castine, Maine D4 184
Castle, Okla. B5 200
Castle, mtn., Yukon, Can. D6 144
Castle, mts., Mont. D6 190
Castle, peak, Colo. B4 171
Castle, peak, Idaho E4 177
Castle, rock, Oreg. C8 201
Castle Butte, Ariz. B5 168
Castle Cliff, Utah F2 207
Castle Dale, Utah D4 207
Castle Dome, peak, Ariz. E1 168
Castle Douglas, Scot. F5 57
Castle Gate, Utah D5 207
Castle Hayne, N.C. C6 197
Castle Hill, Iowa *B5 180
Castle Hill, Maine *B4 184
Castle Hills, Tex. *E3 206
Castle Hot Springs, Ariz. D3 168
Castle Rock, Colo. B6 171
Castle Rock, Minn. F5 187
Castle Rock, S. Dak. C2 204
Castle Rock, Utah B4 207
Castle Rock, Wash. C3 210
Castle Rock, butte, S. Dak. C2 204
Castle Rock, mtn., Va. D4 209
Castle Rock, res., Wis. E4 212
Castle Shannon, Pa. B5 202
Castlebar, Ire. D2 55
Castlebay, Scot. D1 57
Castleberry, Ala. D2 166
Castledome, mts., Ariz. D1 168
Castleford, Idaho G4 177
Castlegar, B.C., Can. E9 149
Castlemaine, Austl. H5 112
Castleton, Ont., Can. C7 153
Castleton, Ill. B4 178
Castleton, Ind. H8 179
Castleton, Kans. B4 181
Castleton, Vt. D2 208
Castleton Corners, Vt. D2 208
Castleton on Hudson, N.Y. C7 196
Castletown, I. of Man F4 57
Castletown, Scot. B5 57
Castlewood, S. Dak. C8 204
Castlewood, Va. B2 209
Castolon, Tex. G2 206
Castor, Alta., Can. C5 148
Castor, La. B2 183
Castor, riv., Mo. D7 189
Castorland, N.Y. B5 196
Castres, Fr. F5 58
Castries, St. Lucia o16 131
Castro, Braz. C3 137
Castro, Chile C2 136
Castro, Sp. D3 65
Castro, co., Tex. B1 206
Castro Alves, Braz. D3 138
Castro Daire, Port. B2 65
Castro Marim, Port. D2 65
Castro Urdiales, Sp. A4 65
Castro Valley, Calif. B5 170
Castro Verde, Port. D1 65
Castrop-Rauxel, Ger. *B2 61
Castropol, Sp. A2 65
Castrovillari, It. E6 67
Castroville (Del Monte Junction), Calif. C6, D3 170
Castroville, Tex. E3 206
Castrovirreyna, Peru D2 134
Castuera, Sp. C3 65
Caswell, Maine *B5 184
Caswell, co., N.C. A4 197
Cat, isl., Ba. Is. C6 131
Cat, isl., Miss. E4 188
Cat, isl., S.C. E9 203
Cat Creek, Mont. C8 190
Cat Law, mtn., Scot. D5 57
Catacamas, Hond. C5 130
Catacaos, Peru C1 134
Catacocha, Ec. B2 134
Catacombs, tombs, It. h9 67
Cataguases, Braz. C4, g6 137
Catahoula, par., La. C4 183
Catahoula, lake, La. C3 183
Catalão, Braz. E1 138
Çatalca, Tur. B7 69
Catalina, Newf., Can. D5 152
Catalina, pt., Guam 114
Catalonia, reg., Sp. B6 65
Catamarca, Arg. E2 135
Catamarca, prov., Arg. E2 135
Catanauan, Phil. p14 90
Catanduanes, isl., Phil. C6 90
Catanduva, Braz. C3 137
Catania, It. F5 67
Catania, gulf, It. F5 67
Cataño, P.R. B6 132
Cataño, mun., P.R. B6 132
Catanzaro, It. E6 67
Cataouatche, lake, La. C7 183
Cataract, Ind. F4 179
Cataract, Wis. D3 212
Cataract, lake, Ind. E4 179
Catarina, Tex. E3 206
Catarroja, Sp. C5 65
Catasauqua, Pa. E11 202
Cataula, Ga. D2 175
Cataumet, Mass. C6 185
Catawba, N.C. B2 197
Catawba, Ohio C4 199
Catawba, S.C. B6 203
Catawba, Va. D2 209
Catawba, W. Va. A7 211
Catawba, Wis. C3 212
Catawba, co., N.C. B2 197
Catawba, res., S.C., N.C. A5 203
Catawba, riv., S.C. B6 203
Catawba Island, Ohio A5 199
Catawissa, Pa. E9 202
Catbalogan, Phil. C6 90
Cateechee, S.C. B2 203
Cater, Sask., Can. D1 155
Cates, Ind. E3 179
Catesby, Okla. A2 200
Catete, Ang. C1 106
Cathance, lake, Maine D5 184
Catharine, Kans. D4 181
Cathay, Calif. D3 170
Cathay, N. Dak. B6 198
Cathedral, bluffs, Colo. B2 171
Cathedral, mtn., Tex. F2 206
Cathedral City, Calif. F5 170
Catherine, Ala. C2 166
Catherine, lake, Ark. C3 169
Cathlamet, Wash. C2 210
Catlettsburg, Ky. B7 182
Catlin, Ill. C6 178
Catlin, Ind. E3 179
Catnip, mtn., Nev. B2 192
Cato, Ark. C3 169
Cato, N.Y. B4 196
Catoche, cape, Mex. C7 129
Catoctin, creek, Md., Va. B2 173
Catoctin, mtn., Md., Va. B2 173
Catoctin Furnace, Md. A3 173
Catonsville, Md. B4, C2 173
Catoosa, Okla. A6 200
Catoosa, co., Ga. B1 175
Catriló, Arg. B4 136
Catrimani, riv., Braz. C5 133
Catron, Mo. E8 189
Catron, co., N. Mex. D1 195
Catskill, N.Y. C7 196
Catskill, mts., N.Y. C6 196
Catt, mtn., B.C., Can. B3 149
Cattaraugus, N.Y. C2 196
Cattaraugus, co., N.Y. C2 196
Cattaraugus, creek, N.Y. C2 196
Cattaraugus, Indian res., N.Y. C2 196
Cattolica, It. C4 67
Catuá, riv., Braz. C2 139
Catumbela, riv., Ang. D1 106
Cauca, dept., Col. C2 133
Cauca, riv., Col. B2 133
Cauca, val., Col. C2 133
Caucasia, Col. B2 133
Caucasus, mts., Sov. Un. E2 73
Caucomgomac, lake, Maine B3 184
Caudebec-les-Elbeuf, Fr. C4 58
Caudéran, Fr. E3 58
Caudete, Sp. C5 65
Caudry, Fr. B5 58
Caufield, Austl. *I5 112
Caughnawaga, Que., Can. D4, D9 154
Caúngula, Ang. C2 106
Cauquenes, Chile B2 136
Caura, riv., Ven. B5 133
Causapscal, Que., Can. *B3 154
Causey, N. Mex. D6 195
Caussade, Fr. E4 58
Cauthron, Ark. C1 169
Cautín, prov., Chile B2 136
Caution, cape, B.C., Can. D3 149
Cauvery, riv., India F6 87
Caux, Fr. Gu. B4 139
Cavado, riv., Port. B1 65
Cavaillon, Fr. F6 58
Cavalier, N. Dak. A8 198
Cavalier, co., N. Dak. A7 198
Cavalla, riv., I.C. E3 103
Cavallo, mtn., It. C8 66
Cavan, Ire. C3 55
Cavarzere, It. B4 67
Cave, It. h9 67
Cave, pt., Wis. D6 212
Cave City, Ark. B4 169
Cave City, Ky. C4 182
Cave Creek, res., Ariz. F2 168
Cave in Rock, Ill. F5 178
Cave Junction, Oreg. E3 201
Cave of the Winds, cave, Vt. B3 208
Cave Spring, Ga. B1 175
Cave Springs, Ark. A1 169
Cave Springs, cave, Ga. B1 175
Cavecreek, Ariz. D4, F2 168
Cavell, Sask., Can. E1 155
Cavendish, Alta., Can. D5 148
Cavendish, Vt. E3 208
Cavetown, Md. A2 173
Cavite, Phil. o13 90
Cavour, S. Dak. C7 204
Cavour, Wis. C5 212
Cawdor, Scot. C5 57
Cawker City, Kans. C5 181
Cawnpore, see Kanpur, India
Cawood, Ky. D6 182
Caxias, Braz. B2 138
Caxias do Sul, Braz. D2 137
Caxito, Ang. C1 106
Cayambe, Ec. A2 134
Cayce, Ky. B2 182
Cayce, S.C. D5 203
Cayenne, Fr. Gu. B4 139
Cayeux-sur-Mer, Fr. D9 56
Cayey, P.R. C6 132
Cayey, mun., P.R. C6 132
Cayey Central, P.R. C6 132
Cayley, Alta., Can. D4 148
Cayman Brac, isl., Cayman Is. F4 131
CAYMAN ISLANDS, Br. dep., N.A. F3 131
Cayo, Br. Hond. B3 130
Cayo, isl., Cuba D4 131
Cayo Largo, isl., Cuba E3 131
Cayuga, Ont., Can. E5 153
Cayuga, Ind. E3 179
Cayuga, Miss. C3 188
Cayuga, N.Y. *C4 196
Cayuga, N. Dak. C8 198
Cayuga, co., N.Y. C4 196
Cayuga, lake, N.Y. C4 196
Cayuga Heights, N.Y. *C4 196
Cayuse, Oreg. B8 201
Cazalla de la Sierra, Sp. D3 65
Cazaux, lagoon, Fr. E3 58
Cazenovia, N.Y. C5 196
Cazenovia, Wis. E3 212
Čazma, riv., Yugo. C3 68
Cazombo, Ang. D3 106
Cazorla, Sp. D4 65
Céa, riv., Sp. A3 65
Ceará, state, Braz. C3 138
Ceará Mirim, Braz. C3, g6 138
Ceará Mirim, riv., Braz. g6 138
Cebolla, N. Mex. A3 195
Cebollar, Arg. E2 135
Cebollati, riv., Ur. E2 137
Cebreros, Sp. B3 65
Cebu, Phil. C6 90
Cebu, isl., Phil. D6 90
Cecil, Ala. C4 166
Cecil, Ga. E3 175
Cecil, Ohio A3 199
Cecil, Oreg. B7 201
Cecil, Pa. F1 202
Cecil, Wis. D5 212
Cecil, co., Md. A6 173
Cecilia, Ky. C4 182
Cecilton, Md. B6 173
Cecina, It. C3 67
Cedar, Kans. C5 181
Cedar, Mich. D5 186
Cedar, Minn. E5 187
Cedar, co., Iowa C6 180
Cedar, co., Mo. D4 189
Cedar, co., Nebr. B8 191
Cedar, creek, Colo. A7 171

INDEX KEY Each place listed in **Bold-faced Type** has its population listed in the Population tables, pages 230 to 280. Each country, shown in CAPITAL LETTERS, has its population listed in the World Political Information Table, pages 6 to 10.
* Does not appear on map; key shows general location.

Cedar, creek, Ind. B7 179
Cedar, creek, Iowa D6 180
Cedar, creek, Mo C5 189
Cedar, creek, N.J D4 194
Cedar, creek, N. Dak C3 198
Cedar, creek, Ohio A2 199
Cedar, isl., N.C C7 197
Cedar, isl., S.C E9 203
Cedar, isl., Va D7 209
Cedar, keys, Fla C3 174
Cedar, lake, Man., Can C1 150
Cedar, lake, Ont., Can A6 153
Cedar, mtn., Calif B3 170
Cedar, mts., Nev E4 192
Cedar, mts., Oreg D9 201
Cedar, pt., Md D5 173
Cedar, pt., Ohio A5 199
Cedar, riv., Iowa, Minn C6 180
Cedar, riv., Nebr C7 191
Cedar, riv., Wash B4 210
Cedar, riv., Wis C2 212
Cedar, swamp, Mass C3 185
Cedar Bluff, Ala A4 166
Cedar Bluff, Ky C2 182
Cedar Bluff, Va *A3 209
Cedar Bluff, res., Kans D4 181
Cedar Bluffs, Kans C3 181
Cedar Bluffs, Nebr C9, D2 191
Cedar Breaks, nat. mon., Utah F3 207
Cedar Brook, N.J D3 194
Cedar Butte, S Dak D4 204
Cedar Canyon, petrified forest, N. Dak C2 198
Cedar City, Mo C5 189
Cedar City, Utah F2 207
Cedar Creek, Ariz D5 168
Cedar Creek, Nebr C9, E3 191
Cedar Creek, Tex D4 206
Cedar Creek, res., Tex C4 206
Cedarcreek, Tenn C11 205
Cedar Crest, N. Mex G5 195
Cedar Falls, Iowa B5 180
Cedar Falls, N.C B4 197
Cedar Gap, Mo D5 189
Cedar Grove, Fla *G3 174
Cedar Grove, Ind F8 179
Cedar Grove, N.J *B4 194
Cedar Grove, W. Va C3, C6 211
Cedar Grove, Wis E6 212
Cedar Hammock, Fla *E4 174
Cedar Hill, Mo B7 189
Cedar Hill, N. Mex A2 195
Cedar Hill, Tenn A5 205
Cedar Hill, Tex B5 206
Cedar Island (Roe), N.C C7 197
Cedar Key, Fla C3 174
Cedar Knolls, N.J B4 194
Cedar Lake, Ala A3 166
Cedar Lake, Ind B3 179
Cedar Lake, Tex E5 206
Cedar Mills, Minn F4 187
Cedar Point, Ill B4 178
Cedar Point, Kans D7 181
Cedar Rapids, Iowa C6 180
Cedar Rapids, Nebr C7 191
Cedar Ridge, Ariz A4 168
Cedar River, Mich C3 186
Cedar Run, N.J D4 194
Cedar Run, Pa C7 202
Cedar Springs, Ont., Can E2 153
Cedar Springs, Ga E1 175
Cedar Springs, Mich E5 186
Cedar Vale, Kans E7 181
Cedar Valley, Utah C3 207
Cedarbluff, Miss B5 188
Cedarburg, Wis E1, E6 212
Cedarcreek, Mo E5 189
Cedaredge, Colo C3 171
Cedarhurst, N.Y E2 196
Cedars, Que., Can D8 154
Cedartown, Ga B1 175
Cedarvale, B.C., Can B3 149
Cedarvale, N. Mex C4 195
Cedarville, Ark B1 169
Cedarville, Calif B1 170
Cedarville, Ill A4 178
Cedarville, Ind B7 179
Cedarville, Mich B6 186
Cedarville, N.J E2 194
Cedarville, N.Y C5 196
Cedarville, Ohio C4 199
Cedarwood, Colo D6 171
Cedarwood Park, N.J *C4 194
Cedoux, Sask., Can H4 155
Cedros, Hond C4 130
Cedros, isl., Mex B1 129
Ceduna, Austl F5 111
Cedynia, Pol F8 62
Ceepeecee, B.C., Can E4 149
Cefalù, It E5 67
Cega, riv., Sp B3 65
Cegléd, Hung B4 67
Ceglie Messapico, It D6 67
Cehegín, Sp C5 65
Ceiba, P.R B8, f12 132
Ceiba, mun., P.R B8, f12 132
Cela, Ang D2 106
Celákovice, Czech n18 70
Celanese Village, Ga *B1 175
Celaya, Mex m13 129
Celebes, isl., Indon F6 90
Celebes, sea, Indon E6 90
Celendín, Peru C2 134
Celeste, Tex *C4 206
Celica, Ec B2 134
Celina, Ohio B3 199
Celina, Tenn C8 205
Celina, Tex C4 206
Celje, Yugo B2 68
Celle, Ger B5 60
Cellina, riv., It C8 66
Celoron, N.Y C1 196
Celriver, S.C B6 203
Cement, Okla C3 200
Cement City, Mich F6 186
Cementon, Pa E10 202
Çemişkezek, Tur C12 85
Cemmaes, head, Wales B3 56
Cencia, Eth D4 105
Cenon, Fr E3 58
Centenary, S.C C9 203
Centennial, Wyo D6 213
Centennial, range, Idaho, Mont E7 177, F4 190
Centennial, val., Mont F4 190
Center, Colo D4 171
Center, Ga B3 175
Center, Ind D5 179
Center, Ky C4 182
Center, Miss C4 188
Center, Mo B6 189
Center, Nebr B8 191
Center, N. Dak B4 198
Center, Okla C5 200
Center, S. Dak D8 204
Center, Tex D5 206
Center, mtn., Idaho D3 177
Center Barnstead, N.H D4 193
Center Belpre, Ohio C6 199
Center City, Minn E6 187
Center City, Tex D3 206
Center Conway, N.H C4 193
Center Cross, Va D6 209
Center Effingham, N.H C4 193
Center Harbor, N.H C4 193
Center Hill, Ark B4 169
Center Hill, Fla D5 174
Center Hill, res., Tenn C8 205
Center Junction, Iowa B6 180
Center Line, Mich *F7 186
Center Lovell, Maine D2 184
Center Montville, Maine D3 184
Center Moreland, Pa A8 202
Center Moriches, N.Y D4 196
Center Ossipee, N.H C4 193
Center Point, Ala E5 166
Center Point, Ark C2 169
Center Point, Iowa B6 180
Center Point, S. Dak D8 204
Center Point, Tex E3 206
Center Point, W. Va A6, B4 211
Center Ridge, Ark B3 169
Center Rutland, Vt D2 208
Center Sandwich, N.H C4 193
Center Square, Pa A11 202
Center Stafford, N.H D4 193
Center Star, Ala A2 166
Center Tuftonboro, N.H C4 193
Centerbrook, Conn D7 172
Centerburg, Ohio B5 199
Centereach, N.Y *E3 196
Centerfield, Utah D4 207
Centerpoint, Ind F3 179
Centerport, N.Y *D3 196
Centerport, Pa *F9 202
Centerton, Ark A1 169
Centerton, Ind E5 179
Centerton, N.J D2 194
Centertown, Ky C3 182
Centertown, Mo C5 189
Centertown, Tenn D8 205
Centerview, Mo C4 189
Centerville, Ariz C3 168
Centerville, Ark B2 169
Centerville, Conn D5 172
Centerville, Ga B6 175
Centerville, Ind E8 179
Centerville, Iowa D5 180
Centerville, Kans D8 181
Centerville, La E4 183
Centerville, Maine D5 184
Centerville, Minn E7 187
Centerville, Mo D7 189
Centerville, Mont D4 190
Centerville, N.C A5 197
Centerville, N.Y F6 172
Centerville, Ohio C3 199
Centerville, Pa C2 202
Centerville, Pa F2 202
Centerville, S. Dak D9 204
Centerville, Tenn B4 205
Centerville, Tex D5 206
Centerville, Utah C4 207
Centerville, Wash D5 210
Cento, It E7 66
Centrahoma, Okla C5 200
Central, Ala C3 166
Central, Ariz E6 168
Central, N. Mex E1 195
Central, S.C B2 203
Central, Utah *F2 207
Central, dist., Alsk C9 167
Central, prov., Malawi D5 106
Central, prov., Zambia E4 106
Central, reg., Ghana E4 103
Central, reg., Ken B6 106
Central, reg., Tan C6 106
Central, plat., Tan C5 106
Central, range, Dom. Rep F8 131
CENTRAL AFRICAN REPUBLIC, country, Afr D3 104
Central Aguirre, P.R D6 132
Central America, reg., N.A 130
in 1800's 127
Central Barren, Ind H5 179
Central Bedeque, P.E.I., Can *C6 151
Central Bridge, N.Y C6 196
Central Butte, Sask., Can G2 155
Central City, Colo B5 171
Central City, Ill *B5 178
Central City, Ill E4 178
Central City, Iowa B6 180
Central City, Ky C2 182
Central City, Nebr C8 191
Central City, Pa F4 202
Central City, S. Dak C2 204
Central College, Ohio B2 199
Central Falls, N.C B4 197
Central Falls, R.I B11 172
Central Heights, Ariz D5 168
Central Heights, Iowa A4 180
Central Islip, N.Y D3, E7 196
Central Java, see Java, isl., Indon.
Central Lake, Mich C5 186
Central Makran, range, Iran, Pak C3 87
Central Pacolet, S.C *B4 203
Central Park, Ill *C6 178
Central Park, Wash *C2 210
Central Point, Oreg E4 201
Central Provinces, see Madhya Pradesh, state, India
Central Siberian, uplands, Sov. Un C13 71
Central Square, N.Y B4 196
Central Sumatra, see Sumatra, Isl., Indon.
Central Valley, Calif B2 170
Central Valley, N.Y D2, D6 196
Central Village, Conn C9 172
Central Village, Mass C5 185
Centralhatchee, Ga C1 175
Centralia, Ont., Can D3 153
Centralia, Ill E4 178
Centralia, Iowa *B7 180
Centralia, Kans C7 181
Centralia, Mo B5 189
Centralia, Okla A6 200
Centralia, Pa *E9 202
Centralia, Wash C3 210
Centralia, W. Va C4 211
Centre, Ala A4 166
Centre, co., Pa E6 202
Centre, peak, B.C., Can B4 149
Centre Hall, Pa E6 202
Centre Island, N.Y *D3 196
Centre Square, N.J D2 194
Centreville, Ala C2 166
Centreville, N.B., Can C2 151
Centreville, N.S., Can E3 151
Centreville, Ill *E3 178
Centreville, Md B5 173
Centreville, Mich G5 186
Centreville, Miss D2 188
Centreville, Va B4 209
Centro Comunal Nogueras, P.R C6 132
Centro Puntas, P.R B1 132
Centropolis, Kans D8 181
Centuria, Wis C1 212
Century, Fla G2 174
Century, W. Va B4 211
Ceram, isl., Indon F7 90
Čerčany, Czech o18 70
Cereal, Atla., Can D5 148
Cereales, Arg B4 136
Ceredo, W. Va C2 211
Ceres, Calif D3 170
Ceres, It D3 66
Ceres, N.Y C2 196
Ceres, Va B3, D1 209
Ceres Northwest, Calif *D3 170
Ceresco, Nebr C9, E2 191
Céret, Fr F5 58
Ceretè, Col B2 133
Cerignola, It D5 67
Cerillos, P.R C2 132
Cerknica, Yugo C2 68
Cernavodă, Rom C9 68
Cernay, Fr D7 58
Cerralvo, Mex B5 129
Cerralvo, isl., Mex C3 129
Cerrillos, N. Mex B3, G6 195
Cerritos, Mex C4 129
Cerro Alto, mtn., Tex E1 206
Cerro Azul, Peru D2 134
Cerro Bolívar, Ven B5 133
Cerro Colorado, Ur E1 137
Cerro de Pasco, Peru D2 134
Cerro Gordo, Ill D5 178
Cerro Gordo, N.C C5 197
Cerro Gordo, co., Iowa A4 180
Cerro Negro, Chile D2 135
Cerrode de Punta, peak, P.R C4 132
Cerrogordo, Okla D7 200
Cerulean, Ky D2 182
Cervantes, Phil B6 90
Cervantes, Sp A2 65
Cervera del Río Alhama, Sp A5 65
Cerveteri, It h8 67
Cervignano del Friuli, It D9 66
Cervione, Fr C2 67
Cesena, It B4 67
Cesenatico, It B4 67
Česka Kamenice, Czech C9 61
Česká Lípa, Czech C3 70
Česká Třebová, Czech D4 70
České Budějovice, Czech D3 70
Český Brod, Czech n18 70
Český Krumlov, Czech D3 70
Çeşme, Tur C6 69
Cess, riv., Lib E3 103
Cessford, Alta., Can D5 148
Cessnock, Austl F8 112
Cetina, riv., Yugo D3 68
Cetinje, Yugo D4 68
Cetraro, It E5 67
Cetti, bay, Guam 114
Ceuta, Sp. dep., Afr G4 64
Cévennes, mts., Fr E5 58
Cevio, Switz C4 66
Ceyhan, riv., Tur D11 85
Ceylon, Ont., Can C4 153
Ceylon, Sask., Can H3 155
Ceylon, Minn G4 187
CEYLON, country, Asia G7 87
c. 250 B.C. 79
c. 400 A.D. 79
in 1660-1798 82
c. 1950 83
Chabařovice, Czech C2 61
Chacabuco, Arg A4, g6 136
Chacahoula, La C5, E5 183
Chacao, Ven *A4 133
Chachapoyas, Peru C2 134
Chachoengsao, Thai F4 89
Chachran, Pak C3 88
Chachro, Pak E3 88
Chaco, prov., Arg E3 135
Chaco, riv., N. Mex A1 195
Chaco Canyon, nat. mon., N. Mex B2 195
Chacon, N. Mex A4 195
CHAD, country, Afr B3 104
Chad, lake, Chad C2 104
Chadbourn, N.C C5 197
Chadds Ford, Pa G10 202
Chadiza, Zambia D5 106
Chadron, Nebr B3 191
Chadwick, Ill A4 178
Chadwick, Mo E4 189
Chaerhsen, China A9 92
Chaffee, Mo D8 189
Chaffee, N. Dak C8 198
Chaffee, co., Colo C4 171
Chagodoshcha, riv., Sov. Un B10 72
Chagny, Fr D6 58
Chagres, riv., Pan k12 130
Chagrin Falls, Ohio A6 199
Chagyl, Sov. Un E5 73
Chāh Bahār, Iran I10 86
Chahal, Guat C3 130
Chahar Burjak, Afg F11 86
Chahba, Syr F11 85
Chaibasa, India D8 87
Chainat, Thai E4 89
Chaires, Fla B2 174
Chakai, Pak A5 87
Chake Chake, Tan C6 106
Chakradharpur, India D8 87
Chakwal, Pak B5 87
Chala, Peru E3 134
Chalatenango, Sal C3 130
Chalchuapa, Sal D3 130
Chalco, Nebr E3 191
Chalender, Ariz B3 168
Chalfant, Pa *F2 202
Chalfont, Pa *F11 202
Chalhuanca, Peru D3 134
Chaling, China K5 92
Chalk River, Ont., Can A7 153
Chalke, see Khalkí, isl., Grc.
Chalkyitsik, Alsk B11 167
Challans, Fr D3 58
Challapata, Bol C2 135
Challis, Idaho E4 177
Chalmers, Ind C4 179
Chalmette, La C7, E6 183
Chalmette, nat. hist. park and cem., La C7 183
Chalon-sur-Saône, Fr D6 58
Châlons-sur-Marne, Fr C6 58
Chalus, Iran C5 86
Chalybeate, Miss A5 188
Chalybeate Springs, N.C B5 197
Cham, Ger D7 61
Cham, pt., Okinawa 114
Chama, Colo D5 171
Chama, N. Mex A3 195
Chamaicó, Arg B4 136
Chamalières, Fr E5 58
Chaman, Pak B4 87
Chamba, Tan D6 106
Chamberino, N. Mex E3 195
Chamberlain, Sask., Can G3 155
Chamberlain, S. Dak D6 204
Chamberlain, lake, Maine B3 184
Chamberlin, mtn., Alsk B10 167
Chambers, Ariz B6 168
Chambers, Nebr B7 191
Chambers, co., Ala C4 166
Chambers, co., Tex E5 206
Chambers, isl., Wis C6 212
Chambersburg, Pa G6 202
Chambéry, Fr E6 58
Chambezi, riv., Zambia D5 106
Chamblee, Ga A5 175
Chambly, Que., Can D4 154
Chambly, Fr E2 59
Chambly, co., Que., Can D4 154
Chambord, Que., Can A5 154
Chamcook, N.B., Can D2 151
Chamdo (Changtu), China E4 91
Chamical, Arg F2 135
Chamois, Mo C6 189
Chamonix-Mont-Blanc, Fr D2 66
Champ, Md D6 173
Champ, Mo *C7 189
Champagne, Yukon, Can D5 144
Champagne, former prov., Fr C5 58
Champagnole, Fr D6 58
Champaign, Ill C5 178
Champaign, co., Ill C5 178
Champaign, co., Ohio B4 199
Champdore, lake, Que., Can g8 152
Champerico, Guat C2 130
Champigneulles, Fr F6 59
Champigny-sur-Marne, Fr g11 58
Champion, Alta., Can D4 148
Champion, Mich B3 186
Champion, Nebr D4 191
Champion, Ohio A7 199
Champlain, Que., Can C5 154
Champlain, N.Y A3 196
Champlain, co., Que., Can B4 154
Champlain, lake, N.Y., Vt., Que., Can B2 208, E4 154
Champlin, Minn E6 187
Champlitte, Fr D6 58
Champneys West, Newf., Can D5 152
Champotón, Mex D6 129
Champua, India F10 88
Chana, Ill B4 178
Chañaral, Chile E1 135
Chanārān, Iran C9 86
Chañarcillo, Chile E1 135
Chança, riv., Port D2 65
Chancay, Peru D2 134
Chance, Ala D2 166
Chance, Md D6 173
Chancellor, Ala D4 166
Chancellor, S. Dak D8 204
Chanchelulla, peak, Calif B2 170
Chanchiang, see Fort Bayard, China
Chanco, Chile B2 136
Chanda, India E6 87
Chandalar, riv., Alsk B10 167
Chandausi, India C7 88
Chandeleur, is., La E7 183
Chandeleur, sound, La E6 183
Chandernagore, India *F12 88
Chandigarh, India B6 87, B6 88
Chandler, Ariz D4, G2 168
Chandler, Que., Can B3 154
Chandler, Ind H3 179
Chandler, Minn G3 187
Chandler, Okla B5 200
Chandler, Tex C5 206
Chandler Heights, Ariz G3 168
Chandlers, brook, N.H A4 193
Chandlers Valley, Pa C3 202
Chandlerville, Ill C3 178
Chandos, lake, Ont., Can C6 153
Chandpur, Bngl D9 87
Chandrakona, India F11 88
Chaneliak, Alsk C7 167
Chaneysville, Pa G5 202
Chānf, Iran H10 86
Chang, riv., China C11 87
Changchih, China F5 92
Changchiu, China F7 92
Changchou, China E8 91
Changchun, China C10 91, E2 93
Change Islands, Newf., Can D4 152
Changewater, N.J B3 194
Changhsing, China I8 92
Changhua, China I8 92
Changhua, Taiwan *G9 91
Changjin, Kor F3 93
Changkiakou, see Kalgan, China
Changli, China E8 92
Changling, China D1 93
Changpai (Paektu-san), mts., China E3 93
Changpei, China C7 91
Changping, China D7 92
Changsha, China F7 91, J5 92
Changshu, China *E9 91
Changsŏng, Kor F2 93
Changsŏng, Kor H4 93
Changte, China F7 91
Changting, China F8 91
Changtu, see Chamdo, China
Changtze, China D6 91
Changwu, China C10 92
Changwu, China D6 91
Changyeh, China D5 91
Changyŏn, Kor G2 93
Chanhassen, Minn F5 187
Channahon, Ill B5 178
Channel, is., Eur F5 55
Channel Islands, nat. mon., Calif F4 170
Channel Lake, Ill *D2 178
Channel-Port aux Basques, Newf., Can E2 152
Channelview, Tex F5 206
Channing, Mich B2 186
Channing, Tex B1 206
Chantada, Sp A2 65
Chanthaburi, Thai F5 89
Chantilly, Fr C5 58
Chantilly, Va B4 209
Chantrey, inlet, N.W. Ter., Can C13 142
Chanute, Kans E8 181
Chanute, Tenn C8 205
Chany, lake, Sov. Un C9 73
Chanyü, China B10 92
Chao, lake, China I7 92
Chao Phraya (Menam), riv., Thai E4 89
Chaoan (Chaochow), China G8 91
Chaoan, China G8 91
Chaochou, China D2 93
Chaotung, China C3 93
Chaotung, China F5 91
Chaoyang, China C9 91
Chapada, mts., Braz B1 137
Chapadinha, Braz B2 138
Chapala, lake, Mex m12 129
Chapanoke, N.C A7 197
Chaparral, Col C2 133
Chapayevsk, Sov. Un C3 73
Chapel Hill, N.C B4 197
Chapel Hill, Tenn B5 205
Chapelhill, Ky D3 182
Chapin, Ill D3 178
Chapin, Iowa B4 180
Chapin, S.C C5 203
Chapleau, Ont., Can E9 153
Chaplin, Sask., Can G2 155
Chaplin, Conn B8 172
Chaplin, Ky C4 182
Chaplin, lake, Sask., Can G2 155
Chaplin, riv., Ky C4 182
Chaplygin, Sov. Un E12 72
Chapman, Ala D3 166
Chapman, Kans D6 181
Chapman, Maine B4 184
Chapman, Nebr C7 191
Chapman, Pa *E10 202
Chapman, cape, N.W. Ter., Can C15 142
Chapman, lake Ind B6 179
Chapman Camp, B.C., Can E9 149
Chapman Ranch, Tex F4 206
Chapmanville, W. Va D2 211
Chappaquiddick, isl., Mass D7 185
Chappell, Nebr C3 191
Chappells, S.C C4 203
Chapra, India C7 87, E10 88
Chaptico, creek, Md D4 173
Chaqui, Bol C2 135
Char (Well), Maur B2 103
Charadai, Arg E4 135
Charagua, Bol C3 135
Charalá, Col B3 133
Charaña, Bol C2 135
Charbonneau, N. Dak B2 198
Charcas, Mex C4 129
Charco, Tex E4 206
Charco Hondo, P.R B4 132
Charcot, isl., Ant B5 120
Chard, Eng D5 56
Chardon, Ohio A6 199
Chardzhou, Sov. Un F9 71
Charente, riv., Fr E3 58
Charenton, La E4 183
Charenton-le-Pont, Fr g10 58
Charette, Que., Can C5 154
Chari, riv., Chad C3 104
Chārikār, Afg D14 86
Charing, Ga D2 175
Chariton, Iowa C4 180
Chariton, co., Mo B4 189
Chariton, riv., Iowa, Mo A5 189
Charity, Guy A3 139
Charity, Mo D4 189
Charkhlik, China D2 91
Charlack, Mo *A8 189
Charlemagne, Que., Can D4, D9 154
Charlemagne's empire 47
Charlemont, Mass A2 185
Charleroi, Bel D4 59
Charleroi, Pa F2 202
Charles, co., Md C3 173
Charles, cape, Va D6 209
Charles, mound, Ill A3 178
Charles, riv., Mass B5 185
Charles City, Iowa A5 180
Charles City, Va D5 209
Charles City, co., Va D5 209
Charles Mill, res., Ohio B5 199
Charles Mix, co., S. Dak D7 204
Charles Town, W. Va B7 211
Charlesbourg, Que., Can C9 154
Charlesburg, Wis B5 212
Charleston, Ark B1 169
Charleston, Ill D5 178
Charleston, Maine C3 184
Charleston, Miss A3 188
Charleston, Mo E8 189
Charleston, Oreg D2 201
Charleston, S.C F3, F8 203
Charleston, Tenn D9 205
Charleston, Utah C4 207
Charleston, Vt *B4 208
Charleston, W. Va C3, C6 211
Charleston, co., S.C F8 203
Charleston, peak, Nev G6 192
Charleston Heights, S.C F2, F8 203
Charlestown, Br. W.I n15 131
Charlestown, Ind H6 179
Charlestown, Md A6 173
Charlestown, N.H D2 193
Charlestown, R.I D10 172
Charlestown, St. Kitts-Nevis n15 131
Charlesville, Zaire C3 106
Charleville, Austl C6 112
Charleville, Fr C6 58
Charlevoix, Mich C5 186
Charlevoix, co., Mich C5 186
Charlevoix, lake, Mich C5 186
Charlevoix Est, co., Que., Can B7 154
Charlevoix Ouest, co., Que., Can B6 154
Charlie Lake, B.C., Can A7 149
Charlieu, Fr D6 58
Charlo, Mont C2 190
Charlo Station, N.B., Can B3 151
Charlotte, Iowa C7 180
Charlotte, Maine C5 184
Charlotte, Mich F6 186
Charlotte, N.C B3 197
Charlotte, Tenn A4 205
Charlotte, Tex E3 206
Charlotte, Vt C2 208
Charlotte, co., N.B., Can D3 151
Charlotte, co., Fla F4 174
Charlotte, co., Va D4 209
Charlotte, harbor, Fla F4 174
Charlotte, lake, B.C., Can C5 149
Charlotte Amalie, Vir. Is m14 131, f15 132
Charlotte Court House, Va D4 209
Charlotte Hall, Md D4 173
Charlotte Harbor, Fla F4 174
Charlotte Waters, Austl E5 111
Charlottenburg, Ger A8 61
Charlottenburg, Sur A4 139
Charlottesville, Ind E6 179
Charlottesville (Independent City), Va C4 209
Charlottetown, P.E.I., Can C6 151
Charlson, N. Dak A3 198

INDEX KEY Each place listed in **Bold-faced Type** has its population listed in the Population tables, pages 230 to 280.
Each country, shown in CAPITAL LETTERS, has its population listed in the World Political Information Table, pages 6 to 10.
* Does not appear on map; key shows general location.

Charlton, co., Ga. F4 175
Charlton City, Mass. B4 185
Charlton Depot, Mass. B4 185
Charmes, Fr. C7 58
Charny, Que., Can. C6, C9 154
Charouïn, Alg. D4 102
Charron, lake, Man., Can. C4 150
Charskiy, Sov. Un. D10 73
Charter Oak, Iowa B2 180
Charters Towers, Austl. D8 111
Chartersville, N.B., Can. *C5 151
Chartierville, Que., Can. D6 154
Chartley, Mass. C5 185
Chartrand, Ont., Can. A10 153
Chartres, Fr. C4 58
Chascomús, Arg. B5 136
Chase, B.C., Can. D8 149
Chase, Kans. D5 181
Chase, Mich. E5 186
Chase, co., Kans. D7 181
Chase, co., Nebr. D4 191
Chase, mtn., Maine B4 184
Chase City, Va. E4 209
Chaseburg, Wis. E2 212
Chaseley, N. Dak. B6 198
Chasicó, Arg. C3 136
Chaska, Minn. F5 187
Chasŏng, Kor. F3 93
Chasov Yar, Sov. Un. q20 72
Chassahowitzka, bay, Fla. D4 174
Chasseral, mtn., Switz. B3 66
Chastang, Ala. D1 166
Chataignier, La. D3 183
Chatanika, Alsk. B10 167
Chatawa, Miss. D3 188
Chatcolet, Idaho B2 177
Château-du-Loir, Fr. D4 58
Château-Gontier, Fr. D3 58
Château-Renault, Fr. D4 58
Château-Richer, Que., Can. *C6 154
Château-Salins, Fr. F6 59
Château-Thierry, Fr. C5 58
Chateaubriand, bay, Loyalty Is. 115
Châteaubriant, Fr. D3 58
Châteaudun, Fr. C4 58
Chateaugay, N.Y. A3 196
Châteauguay, Que., Can. D4, D8 154
Châteauguay, co., Que., Can. D4 154
Châteauguay Heights, Que., Can. D8 154
Châteauneuf [-sur-Loire], Fr. D5 58
Châteauroux, Fr. D4 58
Châtellerault, Fr. D4 58
Chatfield, Ark. B5 169
Chatfield, Man., Can. D3 150
Chatfield, Minn. G6 187
Chatfield, Ohio B5 199
Chatham, Alsk. D13, m22 167
Chatham, N.B., Can. B4 151
Chatham, Ont., Can. E2 153
Chatham, Eng. C8 56
Chatham, Ill. D4 178
Chatham, La. B3 183
Chatham, Mass. C8 185
Chatham, Mich. B4 186
Chatham, Miss. B2 188
Chatham, N.H. B4 193
Chatham, N.J. B4 194
Chatham, N.Y. C7 196
Chatham, Ohio A5 199
Chatham, Va. E3 209
Chatham, co., Ga. E5 175
Chatham, co., N.C. B4 197
Chatham, see San Cristóbal, isl., Ec.
Chatham, is., Pac. O. I11 113
Chatham, sound, B.C., Can. B2 149
Chatham, strait, Alsk. m22 167
Chatham Head, N.B., Can. C4 151
Chatillon, It. D3 66
Châtillon-sur-Seine, Fr. D6 58
Chatkal, range, Sov. Un. E8 73
Chatom, Ala. D1 166
Chatrapur, India H10 88
Chatsworth, Ont., Can. C4 153
Chatsworth, Ga. B2 175
Chatsworth, Ill. C5 178
Chatsworth, Iowa B1 180
Chatsworth, N.J. D3 194
Chatsworth, S. Afr. *C5 107
Chattahoochee, Fla. B2 174
Chattahoochee, co., Ga. D2 175
Chattahoochee, riv., U.S. D10 159
Chattanooga, Ohio B3 199
Chattanooga, Okla. C3 200
Chattanooga, Tenn. D8, E10 205
Chattaroy, Wash. B8 210
Chattaroy, W. Va. D2 211
Chatteris, Eng. B8 56
Chattooga, co., Ga. B1 175
Chattooga, riv., S.C. B1 203
Chatuge, lake, N.C. D2 197
Chatwood, Pa. *G10 202
Chau Phu, Viet. G6 89
Chaudrant, bayou, La. B3 183
Chauk, Bur. D9 87
Chaumont, Fr. C6 58
Chaumont, N.Y. A4 196
Chauncey, Ga. D3 175
Chauncey, Ohio C5 199
Chauncey, pond, Mass. D1 185
Chauny, Fr. C5 58
Chautauqua, Kans. E7 181
Chautauqua, N.Y. C1 196
Chautauqua, co., Kans. E7 181
Chautauqua, co., N.Y. C1 196
Chauvigny, Fr. D4 58
Chauvin, Alta., Can. C5 148
Chauvin, La. E5 183
Chavanga, Sov. Un. D17 63
Chaves, Braz. C5 139
Chaves, Port. B2 65
Chaves, co., N. Mex. D5 195
Chavies, Ky. C6 182
Chavinda, Mex. m12 129
Chavuma, Zambia D3 106
Chazelles [-sur-Lyon], Fr. E6 58
Chazy, N.Y. A3 196
Cheadle, Alta., Can. D4 148
Cheadle & Gatley, Eng. A5 56
Cheaha, mtn., Ala. B4 166
Cheapside, Va. A7 209
Cheat, mtn., W. Va. C5 211
Cheat, riv., W. Va. B5 211
Cheatham, co., Tenn. A4 205
Cheb, Czech. C2 70
Chebacco, lake, Mass. C4 185
Chebanse, Ill. C6 178
Chebeague Island, Maine E2, E5 184
Cheboksary, Sov. Un. B3 73
Cheboygan, Mich. C6 186
Cheboygan, co., Mich. C6 186
Chech, sand dunes, Alg., Mali E4 102
Checheng, China G6 92
Chechŏn, Kor. H4 93
Checotah, Okla. B6 200
Chedabucto, bay, N.S., Can. D8 151
Cheddar, Eng. C5 56
Cheddar, S.C. B3 203
Cheduba, isl., Bur. E9 87
Cheecham, hills, Alta., Can. B4 148
Cheektowaga (Cheektowaga-Northwest), N.Y. C2 196
Cheektowaga-Southwest N.Y. *C2 196
Cheepie, Austl. C5 112
Cheesman, lake, Colo. B5 171
Chefoo, China F9 92
Chefuncte, riv., La. D5 183
Chehalem, mts., Oreg. B1 201
Chehalis, Wash. C3 210
Chehalis, riv., Wash. C2 210
Cheïkh Meskîne, Syr. B8 84
Cheïkh Saad, Syr. B7 84
Cheju, Kor. J3 93
Cheju, isl., Kor. J3 93
Chekhov, Sov. Un. C11 93
Chekiang, prov., China F8 91
Chekunda, Sov. Un. A6 93
Chela, mts., Ang. E1 106
Chelan, Sask., Can. E4 155
Chelan, Wash. B6 210
Chelan, co., Wash. B5 210
Chelan, lake, Wash. A5 210
Chelan, range, Wash. A5 210
Chelan Falls, Wash. B6 210
Cheleiros, Port. f9 65
Cheleken, Sov. Un. B6 86
Cheleken, isl., Sov. Un. B6 86
Chelforó, Arg. B3 136
Cheli, China G5 91
Chelia, mtn., Alg. B6 102
Cheliff, riv., Alg. B5 102
Chelkar, Sov. Un. D5 73
Chelkar, lake, Sov. Un. C4 73
Chelkar-Tengiz, lake, Sov. Un. D6 73
Chellala, Alg. G8 64
Chelles, Fr. F2 59
Chełm [Lubelski], Pol. C7 70
Chełmno, Pol. B5 70
Chelmsford, Ont., Can. *E9 153
Chelmsford, Eng. C8 56
Chelmsford, Mass. A5, C2 185
Chełmża, Pol. B5 70
Chelsea, Que., Can. D2 154
Chelsea, Iowa C5 180
Chelsea, Maine D3 184
Chelsea, Mass. B5, D3 185
Chelsea, Mich. F6 186
Chelsea, Okla. A6 200
Chelsea, S. Dak. B7 204
Chelsea, Vt. D4 208
Chelsea, Wis. C3 212
Cheltenham, Eng. C5 56
Cheltenham Md. C4 173
Cheltenham, Pa. *F11 202
Chelva, Sp. C5 65
Chelyabinsk, Sov. Un. B6 73
Chelyan, W. Va. C3, C6 211
Chelyuskin, cape, Sov. Un. B13 71
Chemainus, B.C., Can. B9, E6 149
Chemehuevi, Indian res., Calif. E6 170
Chemillé, Fr. D3 58
Chemnitz (Karl-Marx-Stadt), Ger. C7 61
Chemquassabamticook, lake, Maine B3 184
Chemult, Oreg. D5 201
Chemung, Ill. A5 178
Chemung, co., N.Y. C4 196
Chen, mtn., Sov. Un. C17 71
Chenab, riv., Pak. B5 87
Chenachane (Oasis), Alg. D4 102
Chenan, China H3 92
Chenango, co., N.Y. C5 196
Chenango, riv., N.Y. C5 196
Chenango Forks, N.Y. C5 196
Chenchi, China K4 92
Chene, bayou, La. C5 183
Chenega, Alsk. C10 167
Chenequa, Wis. E1 212
Chénéville, Que., Can. D2 154
Cheney, Kans. B4, E6 181
Cheney, Wash. B8, D7 210
Cheney, res., Kans. B4, E6 181
Cheneyville, La. C3 183
Cheng, China J9 92
Chengan, China J2 92
Chengane, riv., Moz. B5 107
Chengchan Tow, pt., China D9 91
Chengchiang, China E8 91
Chengchou, China G5 92
Chenghai, China G8 91
Chenghsien, see Chengchow, China
Chenghwa, see Sharasume, China
Chengkou, China I3 92
Chengku, China H2 92
Chengte (Jehol), China C8 91
Chengtu, China E5 91
Chengyangkuan, China H6 92
Chenhsien, China F7 91
Chenkang, China G4 91
Chennan, China F5 91
Chenoa, Ill. C5 178
Chenpa, China H2 92
Chenping, China I3 92
Chensi, see Barköl, China
Chentung, China B10 92
Chenyüan, China K3 92
Cheo Reo, Viet. F8 89
Chepachet, R.I. B10 172
Chepén, Peru C2 134
Chepes, Arg. A3 136
Chepo, Pan. F8 130
Chepstow, Wales C5 56
Chequamegon, bay, Wis. B3 212
Cher, riv., Fr. D4 58
Cheran, India E13 88
Cheraw, Colo. C7 171
Cheraw, Miss. D4 188
Cheraw, S.C. B8 203
Cherbourg, Fr. C3 58
Cherchel, Alg. B5 102
Cherchen, China A8 87
Cherdyn, Sov. Un. A5 73
Cheremkhovo, Sov. Un. D13 71
Cheren, Eth. B4 105
Cherepanovo, Sov. Un. C10 73
Cherepovets, Sov. Un. B1 73
Cherhill, Alta., Can. C3 148
Cheriton, Va. D7 209
Cherkassy, Sov. Un. G9 72
Cherkessk, Sov. Un. *E1 73
Cherlakskiy, Sov. Un. C8 73
Chernigov, Sov. Un. F8 72
Chernigovka, Sov. Un. H11 72
Chernobay, Sov. Un. G9 72
Chernobyl, Sov. Un. F8 72
Chernofski, Alsk. E6 167
Chernogorsk, Sov. Un. *D12 71
Chernomorskoye, Sov. Un. I9 72
Chernovtsy, Sov. Un. A7 68, G5 72
Chernoye, Sov. Un. r32 63
Chernyakhovsk (Insterburg), Sov. Un. D3 72
Cherokee, Ala. A2 166
Cherokee, Iowa B2 180
Cherokee, Kans. E9 181
Cherokee, N.C. D3 197
Cherokee, Okla. A3 200
Cherokee, Tex. D3 206
Cherokee, co., Ala. A4 166
Cherokee, co., Ga. B2 175
Cherokee, co., Iowa B2 180
Cherokee, co., Kans. E9 181
Cherokee, co., N.C. D2 197
Cherokee, co., Okla. B6 200
Cherokee, co., S.C. A4 203
Cherokee, co., Tex. D5 206
Cherokee, Indian res., N.C. D3 197
Cherokee, lake, Okla. A7 200
Cherokee, lake, Tenn. C10 205
Cherokee Falls, S.C. A4 203
Cherokee Sound, Ba. Is. B5 131
Cherquenco, Chile B2 136
Cherrapunji, India C9 87
Cherry, Conn. B5 172
Cherry, Ill. B4 178
Cherry, Tenn. B2 205
Cherry, co., Nebr. B4 191
Cherry, creek, Colo. B6 171
Cherry, creek, S. Dak. C3 204
Cherry, pt., Va. D6 209
Cherry Creek, Nev. D7 192
Cherry Creek, N.Y. C1 196
Cherry Creek, S. Dak. C4 204
Cherry Fork, Ohio D4 199
Cherry Grove, Oreg. B1 201
Cherry Hill, Ark. C1 169
Cherry Hill, Md. A6 173
Cherry Hill, pt., N.Y. E8 172
Cherry Hills Village, Colo. *B6 171
Cherry Run, W. Va. B6 211
Cherry Tree, Pa. E4 202
Cherry Valley, Ark. B5 169
Cherry Valley, Ont., Can. D7 153
Cherry Valley, Ill. A5 178
Cherry Valley, N.Y. C6 196
Cherryfield, Maine D5 184
Cherrygrove, Minn. G6 187
Cherryvale, Kans. E8 181
Cherryville, N.C. B2 197
Cherskiy, mts., Sov. Un. C17 71
Chertsey, Eng. C7 56
Chesaning, Mich. E6 186
Chesapeake, Ohio D5 199
Chesapeake (Independent City), Va. B7, E6 209
Chesapeake, W. Va. C3, C6 211
Chesapeake, bay, U.S. C12 159
Chesapeake Bay, bridge and tunnel, Va. B7, E7 209
Chesapeake Beach, Md. C4 173
Chesapeake City, Md. A6 173
Chesapeake and Delaware, canal, Del. A6 173
Chesaw, Wash. A6 210
Chesham, N.H. E2 193
Cheshire, Conn. D5 172
Cheshire, Mass. A1 185
Cheshire, Ohio D5 199
Cheshire, co., Eng. A5 56
Cheshire, co., N.H. E2 193
Cheshire, res., Mass. A1 185
Cheshskaya, bay, Sov. Un. B17 40
Cheshunt, Eng. k12 55
Chesilhurst, N.J. D3 194
Chesley, Ont., Can. C3 153
Chesnee, S.C. A4 203
Chester, Ark. B1 169
Chester, Calif. B3 170
Chester, N.S., Can. E5 151
Chester, Conn. *D7 172
Chester, Eng. A5 56
Chester, Fla. A6, B5 174
Chester, Ga. D3 175
Chester, Idaho F7 177
Chester, Ill. F4 178
Chester, Iowa A5 180
Chester, Md. C5 173
Chester, Mass. B2 185
Chester, Mont. B6 190
Chester, Nebr. D8 191
Chester, N.H. E4 193
Chester, N.J. B3 194
Chester, N.Y. D2, D6 196
Chester, Ohio C6 199
Chester, Okla. A3 200
Chester, Pa. B10, G11 202
Chester, S.C. B5 203
Chester, S. Dak. D9 204
Chester, Utah D4 207
Chester, Vt. E3 208
Chester, Va. C7, D5 209
Chester, W. Va. A2, A4 211
Chester, co., Pa. G10 202
Chester, co., S.C. B5 203
Chester, co., Tenn. B3 205
Chester, creek, Pa. D1 194
Chester, riv., Md. B5 173
Chester Basin, N.S., Can. E5 151
Chester Depot, Vt. E3 208
Chester Heights, Pa. *G11 202
Chester Hill, Pa. *E5 202
Chesterfield, Conn. D8 172
Chesterfield, Eng. A6 56
Chesterfield, Ill. D3 178
Chesterfield, Ind. D6 179
Chesterfield, Mass. B2 185
Chesterfield, N.H. E2 193
Chesterfield, S.C. B7 203
Chesterfield, Tenn. B3 205
Chesterfield, Va. C7, D5 209
Chesterfield, co., S.C. B7 203
Chesterfield, co., Va. D5 209
Chesterfield, inlet, N.W. Ter., Can. D14 142
Chesterfield, is., Pac. O. H9 113
Chesterfield Inlet, N.W. Ter., Can. D14 144
Chesterhill, Ohio C6 199
Chesterton, Ind. A3 179
Chestertown, Md. B5 173
Chestertown, N.Y. B7 196
Chesterville, Ont., Can. B9 153
Chesterville, Maine *D2 184
Chesterville, Miss. A5 188
Chesterville, Ohio B5 199
Chestnut, Ill. C4 178
Chestnut Hill, Conn. C7 172
Chestnut Mound, Tenn. C8 205
Chestoa, Tenn. C11 205
Chesuncook, lake, Maine C3 184
Cheswick, Pa. A6 202
Cheswold, Del. B6 173
Chetac, lake, Wis. C2 212
Chetco, riv., Oreg. E2 201
Chetek, Wis. C2 212
Chetek, lake, Wis. C2 212
Cheticamp, N.S., Can. C8 151
Chetopa, Kans. E8 181
Chetumal, bay, Mex. D7 129
Chevalon, creek, Ariz. C5 168
Cheverie, N.S., Can. D5 151
Cheverly, Md. *C1 173
Cheviot, Sask., Can. E2 155
Cheviot, N.Z. O14 112
Cheviot, Ohio C3, D2 199
Cheviot, hills, Scot., Eng. E6 57
Chevreuil, bayou, La. C6 183
Chevreuil, pt., La. E4 183
Chevy Chase, Md. C1, C3 173
Chevy Chase Heights, Pa. *E3 202
Chevy Chase Section Four, Md. *C3 173
Chewack, creek, Wash. A5 210
Chewalla, Tenn. B3 205
Chewelah, Wash. A8 210
Chewey, Okla. A7 200
Chewsville, Md. A2 173
Cheyenne, Okla. B2 200
Cheyenne, Tex. D1 206
Cheyenne, Wyo. D8 213
Cheyenne, co., Colo. C8 171
Cheyenne, co., Kans. C2 181
Cheyenne, co., Nebr. C2 191
Cheyenne, pass, Wyo. D7 213
Cheyenne, riv., S. Dak., Wyo. C4 204
Cheyenne Agency, S. Dak. B5 204
Cheyenne River, Indian res., S. Dak. B4 204
Cheyenne Wells, Colo. C8 171
Chhatarpur, India E7 88
Chhindwara, India F7 88
Chi, China G6 92
Chia, China E4 92
Chiahsing, China I9 92
Chiai, Taiwan *G9 91
Chialing, riv., China I2 92
Chiamboni (Dicks Head), cape, Ken. B7 106
Chiamussu, China B11 91
Chian, China F3 93
Chian, China K6 92
Chiang Kham, Thai. C4 89
Chiang Khong, Thai. B4 89
Chiang Mai, Thai. C3 89
Chiang Rai, Thai. C3 89
Chiangling, China I5 92
Chiangmen, see Kongmoon, China
Chiangyin, China I9 92
Chiangyu, China E5 91
Chiaochia, China F5 91
Chiaoho, China E3 93
Chiaotso, China D7 91, G5 92
Chiapa de Corzo, Mex. D6 129
Chiapas, state, Mex. D6 129
Chiari, It. B2 67
Chiashan, China H8 92
Chiatura, Sov. Un. A14 85
Chiautla de Tapia, Mex. n14 129
Chiavari, It. B2 67
Chiavenna, It. C5 66
Chiawuli Tak, Ariz. F4 168
Chiayü, China J5 92
Chiba, Jap. I10, n19 93
Chibana, Okinawa 114
Chiblow, lake, Ont., Can. A1 153
Chibougamau, Que., Can. B2 154
Chibuto, Moz. B5 107
Chicago, Ill. B6, F3 178
Chicago Heights, Ill. B6, F3 178
Chicago Ridge, Ill. *F3 178
Chicago Sanitary and Ship, canal, Ill. F2 178
Chicamacomico, creek, Md. D6 173
Chicapa, riv., Ang. C3 106
Chichagof, hbr., Alsk. E2 167
Chichagof, isl., Alsk. m22 167
Chichaoua, Mor. C3 102
Chichen Itzá, ruins, Mex. C7 129
Chichester, Eng. D7 56
Chichester, N.H. D4 193
Chichiang, China J2 92
Chichibu, Jap. m18 93
Chichihaerh, China B9 91
Chichun, China I6 92
Chickahominy, riv., Va. D5 209
Chickaloon, Alsk. C10, g17 167
Chickamauga, Ga. B1 175
Chickamauga, dam, Tenn. E10 205
Chickamauga, lake, Tenn. D8 205
Chickasaw, Ala. E1 166
Chickasaw, co., Iowa A5 180
Chickasaw, co., Miss. B5 188
Chickasawhay, riv., Miss. D5 188
Chickasha, Okla. B4 200
Chickasha, lake, Okla. B3 200
Chicken, Alsk. C11 167
Chiclana, Sp. D2 65
Chiclayo, Peru C2 134
Chico, riv., Arg. C3 136
Chico, Calif. C3 170
Chico Hot Springs, Mont. E6 190
Chico, Tex. C4 206
Chico, Wash. B3 210
Chico Vecino, Calif. *C3 170
Chicoa, Moz. A5 107
Chicomo, Moz. B5 107
Chicontepec, Mex. m14 129
Chicopee, Ga. B3 175
Chicopee, Kans. E9 181
Chicopee, Mass. B2 185
Chicora, Miss. D5 188
Chicora (Millerstown), Pa. E2 202
Chicot, Ark. D4 169
Chicot, co., Ark. D4 169
Chicot, isl., La. E6 183
Chicot, lake, Ark. D4 169
Chicot, pt., La. E6 183
Chicota, Tex. C5 206
Chicoutimi, Que., Can. A6, B2 154
Chicoutimi, co., Que., Can. A6 154
Chicoutimi, riv., Que., Can. A6 154
Chicoutimi-Nord, Que., Can. A6 154
Chidester, Ark. D2 169
Chidley, cape, Newf., Can. f8 152
Chieerete, isl., Bikini 114
Chiefland, Fla. C4 174
Chiefs, pt., Ont., Can. C3 153
Chiehhsiu, China F4 92
Chiehyang, China G8 91
Chiem, lake, Ger. E6 60
Chien, China G3 92
Chienan, China D8 92
Chienchang, China F2 93
Chienchiang, China J3 92
Chienli, China J5 92
Chienning, China K7 92
Chienou, China K8 92
Chienping, China D8 92
Chienshan, China I7 92
Chienshih, China I3 92
Chienshui, China G5 91
Chientang, riv., China J8 92
Chiente, China J8 92
Chienyang, China F8 91
Chierhkalang, China C10 92
Chieri, It. B1 67
Chiers, riv., Fr. E5 59
Chiese, riv., It. D6 66
Chieti, It. C5 67
Chigasaki, Jap. *I9 93
Chigirin, Sov. Un. G9 72
Chignahuapan, Mex. n14 129
Chignecto, bay, N.S., Can. D5 151
Chignik, Alsk. D8 167
Chigubo, Moz. B5 107
Chigwell, Eng. k13 55
Chihchiang, China F6 91
Chihchiang, China I4 92
Chihfeng, China C8 92
Chihli (Pohai), gulf, China D8 91
Chihsi, China B11 91
Chihtan, China D6 91
Chihuahua, Mex. B3 129
Chihuahua, state, Mex. B3 129
Chii-San, peak, Kor. I3 93
Chiili, Sov. Un. E7 73
Chikan, China A9 91
Chikaskia, riv., Kans., Okla. A4 200
Chiko, China B4 93
Chikura, Jap. o18 93
Chikwolnepy, stream, N.H. A4 193
Chilapa, Mex. D5, o14 129
Chilca, Peru D2 134
Chilcat, pass, B.C., Can. E5 142
Chilcotin, riv., B.C., Can. C6 149
Childersburg, Ala. B3 166
Childress, Tex. B2 206
Childress, co., Tex. B2 206
CHILE, country, S.A. E1 135, C2 136
Chilecito, Arg. E2 135
Chilete, Peru C2 134
Chilhowee, Mo. C4 189
Chilhowee, Tenn. D9 205
Chilhowee, mtn., Tenn. E12 205
Chilhowie, Va. B3 209
Chili, Ind. C5 179
Chili, Wis. D3 212
Chilibre, Pan. k11 130
Chilili, N. Mex. C3 195
Chilin, see Kirin, China
Chilka, lake, India H10 88
Chilko, lake, B.C., Can. D5 149
Chilko, riv., B.C., Can. D6 149
Chillán, Chile B2 136
Chillicothe, Ill. C4 178
Chillicothe, Iowa C5 180
Chillicothe, Mo. B4 189
Chillicothe, Ohio C5 199
Chillicothe, Tex. B3 206
Chilliwack, B.C., Can. B11, E7 149
Chilliwack, lake, B.C., Can. A4 210
Chilliwack, riv., B.C., Can. A4 210
Chilmark, Mass. D6 185
Chilocco, Okla. A4 200
Chiloé, prov., Chile C2 136
Chiloé, isl., Chile C2 136
Chiloquin, Oreg. E5 201
Chilpancingo [de los Bravos], Mex. D5, o14 129
Chilson, N.Y. B7 196
Chilton, Ky. C5 182
Chilton, Tex. D4 206
Chilton, Wis. B5, D5 212
Chilton, co., Ala. C3 166
Chilumba, Malawi D5 106
Chilung (Keelung), Taiwan F9 91
Chilwa, lake, Malawi, Moz. E6 106
Chimacum, Wash. A3 210
Chimalhuacán, Mex. h10 129
Chimaltenango, Guat. C2 130
Chimán, Pan. F8 130
Chimay, Bel. D4 59
Chimayo, N. Mex. A4 195
Chimbay, Sov. Un. E5 73
Chimborazo, prov., Ec. B2 134
Chimborazo, vol., Ec. B2 134
Chimbote, Peru C2 134
Chimen, China J7 92
Chimkent, Sov. Un. E7 73
Chimney Rock, Colo. D3 171
Chimney Rock, mtn., Ky. D5 182
Chimney Rock, mtn., Nebr. C2 191
Chimneytop, mtn., Tenn. C11 205
Chimo, China F9 92
Chin, Alta., Can. E4 148
Chin, China F5 92
Chin, cape, Ont., Can. B3 153
Chin, riv., China G5 92
China, Maine D3 184
China, Mex. B5 129
CHINA, country, Asia E5 91
c. 500 B.C. 79
c. 100 B.C. 79
c. 750 A.D. 80
c. 1294 81
after World War II 83
China, lake, Maine D3 184
China Grove, Ala. C4 166
China Grove, N.C. B3 197
Chinaja, Guat. B2 130
Chinan, see Tsinan, China
Chinandega, Nic. D4 130
Chinati, peak, Tex. F2 206
Chincha Alta, Peru D2 134
Chincheng, China G5 92
Chincheros, Peru D3 134
Chinchilla, Austl. C8 112
Chinchilla, Sp. C5 65
Chinchou, China D9 92
Chincoteague, Va. D7 209
Chincoteague, bay, Md., Va. D7 173
Chinde, Moz. A6 107
Chindo, Kor. I3 93
Chindwin, riv., Bur. C10 87
Ching, China I8 92
Ching, China K3 92
Ching, riv., China G3 92
Chingcheng, China C3 93
Chingchiang, China J6 92
Chingchien, China F4 92
Chingchuan, China G2 92
Chinghai, China D5 91
Chinghsing, China A10 92
Chingliu, China F8 91
Chingmen, China I5 92
Chingning, China G1 92
Chingola, Zambia D4 106
Chingpeng, China C7 92
Chingpien, China F3 92
Chingpu, China I9 92

Chingshan, China......I5 92
Chingshih, China......F7 91
Chingtai, China......D5 92
Chingtao, see Tsingtao, China
Chingte, China......I8 92
Chingtechen, China......F8 91
Chingtzukuan, China......H4 92
Chinguar, Ang......D2 106
Chinguetti, Maur......B2 103
Chingyang, China......D6 91
Chingyüan, China......E2 93
Chingyün, China......F7 92
Chinhàe, Kor......I4 93
Chinhsi, China......D9 92
Chinhsien, China......E9 92
Chinhua, China......J8 92
Chinhuangtao, China......D8 91
Chining, China......C7 91
Chining, China......G7 92
Chiniot, Pak......B5 87
Chinipas, Mex......B3 129
Chinit, riv., Camb......F6 89
Chinju, Kor......I4 93
Chinko, riv., Cen. Afr. Rep...D4 104
Chinle, Ariz......A6 168
Chinle, creek, Ariz......A6 168
Chinle, val., Ariz......A6 168
Chinnampo (Nampo), Kor. G2 93
Chinniuchen, China......I6 92
Chinnur, India......H7 88
Chino, Calif......E5, F3 170
Chino Valley, Ariz......C3 168
Chinon, Fr......D4 58
Chinook, Alta., Can......D5 148
Chinook, Mont......B7 190
Chinook, Wash......C2 210
Chinook, lake, Oreg......C5 201
Chinquapin, N.C......C6 197
Chinsali, Zambia......D5 106
Chinsha, riv., China......F4 91
Chinshanchen, China......A10 91
Chinta, China......C4 91
Chinteche, Malawi......D5 106
Chinú, Col......B2 133
Chinyang, China......G5 92
Chinyün, China......J9 92
Chiôco, Moz......A5 107
Chioggia, It......B4 67
Chios, see Khíos, isl., Grc.
Chip, lake, Alta., Can......C3 148
Chipata, Zambia......D5 106
Chipewyan, riv., Alta., Can. A4 148
Chipinga, Rh......B5 107
Chipita Park, Colo......C5 171
Chipley, Fla......G3 174
Chipman, N.B., Can......C4 151
Chippawa, Ont., Can......D5 153
Chippenham, Eng......C5 56
Chippewa, co., Mich......B6 186
Chippewa, co., Minn......E3 187
Chippewa, co., Wis......C2 212
Chippewa, lake, Wis......C2 212
Chippewa, riv., Minn......E3 187
Chippewa, riv., Wis......D2 212
Chippewa Falls, Wis......D2 212
Chippewa Lake, Mich......E5 186
Chiputneticook, lakes, Maine......C5 184
Chiquimula, Guat......C3 130
Chiquimulilla, Guat......C2 130
Chiquinquirá, Col......B3 133
Chiquita, lake, Arg......A4 136
Chira, riv., Ec., Peru......B1 134
Chiradzulu, Malawi......E6 106
Chiras, Afg......D12 86
Chirchik, Sov. Un......E7 73
Chiricahua, nat. mon., Ariz...F6 168
Chiricahua, peak, Ariz......F6 168
Chirikof, isl., Alsk......D8 167
Chiriquí, gulf, Pan......G7 130
Chiriquí Grande, Pan......F6 130
Chirmiri, India......F9 88
Chiromo, Malawi......E6 106
Chirpan, Bul......D7 68
Chirripó Grande, mtn., C.R...F6 130
Chirundu, Rh......E4 107
Chisago, co., Minn......E6 187
Chisago City, Minn......E6 187
Chisamba, Zambia......D4 106
Chisana, Alsk......C11 167
Chiselville, Vt......E2 208
Chisholm, Maine......D2 184
Chisholm, Minn......C6 187
Chisholm Mills, Alta., Can. B3 148
Chishui, China......I6 92
Chisimaio (Kismayu), Som......F5 105
Chisineu-Cris, Rom......B5 68
Chislehurst & Sidcup, Eng......*m13 55
Chisos, mts., Tex......E1 206
Chistochina, Alsk....C11, f19 167
Chistopol, Sov. Un......B4 73
Chita, Sov. Un......D14 71
Chitai (Kuchêng), China....C2 91
Chitaldroog, India......F6 87
Chitek, Sask., Can......D2 155
Chitek, lake, Man., Can......C2 150
Chitembo, Ang......D2 106
Chitina, Alsk......C11, g19 167
Chitipa, Malawi......C5 106
Chitral, Pak......A5 87
Chitré, Pan......G7 130
Chittagong, Bngl......D9 87
Chittenango, N.Y......B5 196
Chittenden, Vt......D3 208
Chittenden, co., Vt......C2 208
Chittenden, res., Vt......D3 208
Chittoor, India......F6 87
Chiuchiang, China......F8 91
Chiuchiu, China......D2 135
Chiuchuan, China......D4 91
Chiumbe, riv., Ang......C3 106
Chiume, Ang......E3 106
Chiupu, China......I7 92
Chiusi, It......C3 67
Chivasso, It......B1 67
Chivato, mesa, N. Mex......B2 195
Chivay, Peru......E3 134
Chivilcoy, Arg......A4, g6 136
Chivington, Colo......C8 171
Chiyang, China......F7 91
Chizhapka, riv., Sov. Un......B9 73
Chloride, Ariz......B1 168
Chmielnik, Pol......C6 70
Cho, China......E7 92
Choapa, riv., Chile......A2 136
Choapan, Mex......D5 129
Chobe, riv., Bech., S.W. Afr. A3 107
Choccolocco, Ala......B4 166
Choccolocco, creek, Ala......B4 166
Chochiwon, Kor......H3 93
Choco, dept., Col......C2 133
Chocó, bay, Col......C2 133
Chocó, range, Col......B2 133
Chocolate, mts., Ariz......D1 168
Chocolate Bayou, Tex......G5 206
Chocontá, Col......B3 133
Coconut [Township], Pa......C10 202
Chocorua, N.H......C4 193
Chocorua, mtn., N.H......C4 193
Chocowinity, N.C......B6 197
Choctaw, Ala......C1 166
Choctaw, Okla......B4 200
Choctaw, co., Ala......C1 166
Choctaw, co., Miss......B4 188
Choctaw, co., Okla......C6 200
Choctaw, Indian res., Miss......C4 188
Choctaw Bluff, Ala......D2 166
Choctawhatchee, bay, Fla...G2 174
Choctawhatchee, riv., Ala., Fla......D4 166
Chodžiež, Pol......B4 70
Choele Choel, Arg......B3 136
Chōfu, Jap......*I10 93
Choibalsan, Mong......B7 91
Choiceland, Sask., Can......D3 155
Choiseul, isl., Sol. Is...... 115
Choisy-le-Roi, Fr......g10 58
Choix, Mex......B3 129
Chojna, Pol......B3 70
Chojnice, Pol......B4 70
Chojnów, Pol......C3 70
Chokai-San, peak, Jap......G10 93
Choke, mts., Eth......C4 105
Chokio, Minn......E2 187
Chokoloskee, Fla......G5 174
Cholame, Calif......E3 170
Cholet, Fr......D3 58
Cholo, Malawi......E6 106
Cholo, riv., China......B9 91
Choluteca, Hond......D4 130
Choluteca, riv., Hond......D4 130
Choma, Zambia......E4 106
Chomo Lhari, peak, Bhu...D12 88
Chomutov, Czech......C2 70
Chon Buri, Thai......F4 89
Chŏnan, Kor......H3 93
Chone, Ec......B1 134
Chŏngjin, Kor......F4 93
Chŏngju, Kor......H3 93
Chongsŏng, Kor......E4 93
Chŏnju, Kor......I3 93
Chonos, arch., Chile......C2 136
Chonzie, mtn., Scot......D5 57
Chopin, riv., Braz......D2 137
Choptank, Md......C6 173
Choptank, riv., Md......C6 173
Chorasmia: c. 500 B.C...... 78
Chorrera, Cuba......k12 131
Chorrillos, Peru......D2 134
Chortkov, Sov. Un......G5 72
Chŏrwŏn, Kor......G3 93
Chorzów, Pol......C5, g9 70
Chos Malal, Arg......B2 136
Chosan, Kor......F2 93
Chosen, see Korea, Asia
Chosen, Fla......F6 174
Chōshi, Jap......I10, n19 93
Chosica, Peru......D2 134
Choszczno, Pol......B3 70
Chota, Peru......C2 134
Choteau, Mont......C4 190
Chotĕtov, Czech......n18 70
Choudrant, La......B3 183
Choushan, is., China......I10 92
Chouteau, Okla......A6 200
Chouteau, co., Mont......C6 190
Choutsun, China......F7 92
Chowan, co., N.C......A7 197
Chowan, riv., N.C......A7 197
Chowchilla, Calif......D3 170
Choyren, Mong......B6 91
Chrisman, Ill......D6 178
Chrisney, Ind......H3 179
Christchurch, Eng......D6 56
Christchurch, N.Z......O14 112
Christian, co., Ill......D4 178
Christian, co., Ky......D2 182
Christian, co., Mo......E4 189
Christian, isl., Ont., Can......C4 153
Christian, sound, Alsk......m22 167
Christiana, Del......A6 173
Christiana, Pa......G9 202
Christiana, S. Afr......C4 107
Christiana, Tenn......B5 205
Christiansburg, Ohio......B3 199
Christiansburg, Va......D2 209
Christiansfeld, Den......C3 62
Christiansted, Vir. Is......n14 131
Christie, mtn., N.W. Ter., Can......D7 142
Christina, Mont......C7 190
Christina, lake, Alta., Can..B5 148
Christina, lake, B.C., Can..A7 210
Christina, lake, Minn......D3 187
Christina, peak, Nev......D6 192
Christina, riv., Alta., Can...A5 148
Christine, N. Dak......C9 198
Christine, Tex......E3 206
Christmas, Ariz......E5 168
Christmas, Fla......D5 174
Christmas, isl., Oceania...F12 113
Christmas, lake, Oreg......D6 201
CHRISTMAS ISLAND, Austl. dep., Oceania......G5 113
Christopher, Ill......F4 178
Christopol, Sov. Un......B4 73
Christoval, Tex......D2 206
Chromo, Colo......D4 171
Chrudim, Czech......D3 70
Chrysler, Ala......D2 166
Chrzanów, Pol......g10 70
Chu, China......E6 91
Chu, China......H8 92
Chu, Sov. Un......E8 73
Chu Chua, B.C., Can......D7 149
Chualar, Calif......C6 170
Chüan, China......F7 91
Chüanchou, China......G8 91
Chuangho, China......E10 92
Chubbuck, Idaho......G6 177
Chubut, prov., Arg......C3 136
Chucheng, China......F8 92
Chuchi, China......J9 92
Chuchou, China......K5 92
Chuckatuck, Va......B6 209
Chuckey, Tenn......C11 205
Chudovo, Sov. Un......B8 72
Chuehshan, China......H6 92
Chugach, is., Alsk......h16 167
Chugach, mts., Alsk......g17 167
Chugiak, Alsk......C10, g17 167
Chuguchak, China......B1 91
Chuguyev, Sov. Un......G11 72
Chugwater, Wyo......D8 213
Chugwater, creek, Wyo......D8 213
Chuho, China......D4 93
Chühsien, China......J8 92
Chühsien, China......G8 92
Chui Chuischu, Ariz......E4 168
Chuius, mtn., B.C., Can......B5 149
Chukai, Mala......J5 89
Chukudu Kraal, Bots......B3 107
Chukut Kuk, Ariz......F3 168
Chula, Ga......E3 175
Chula, Mo......B4 189
Chula, Va......D5 209
Chula Vista, Calif......E2, F5 170
Chulahoma, Miss......A4 188
Chülu, China......F6 92
Chulucanas, Peru......C1 134
Chulumani, Bol......C2 135
Chulym, Sov. Un......B10 73
Chulym, riv., Sov. Un......B11 73
Chumar, India......A7 88
Chumatien, China .E7 91, H6 92
Chumbicha, Arg......E2 135
Chumikan, Sov. Un......D16 71
Chumphon, Thai......G3 89
Chumysh, riv., Sov. Un...C10 73
Chunchŏn, Kor......H3 93
Chunchula, Ala......E1 166
Chungan, China......K7 92
Chungchou, China......E6 91
Chunghsiang, China......I5 92
Chungju, Kor......H3 93
Chungking, China......J2 92
Ch'ungmu, Kor......E10 91
Chungtien, China......F4 91
Chungwei, China......D6 91
Chunky, Miss......C5 188
Chunya, Tan......C5 106
Chupaca, Peru......D2 134
Chupadera, mesa, N. Mex...D3 195
Chupadero, N. Mex......F6 195
Chuquibamba, Peru......E3 134
Chuquicamata, Chile......D2 135
Chuquisaca, dept., Bol......D3 135
Chur, Switz......C5 66
Church, mtn., B.C., Can...B11 149
Church, states of the: in 9th cent...... 47
see also Papal states
Church Creek, Md......C5 173
Church Hill, Md......B6 173
Church Hill, Miss......D2 188
Church Hill, Tenn......C11 205
Church Point, La......D3 183
Church Point, N.S., Can......E3 151
Church Rock, N. Mex......B1 195
Church Stretton, Eng......B5 56
Churchbridge, Sask., Can......G5 155
Churchill, Man., Can......C5 150
Churchill, Pa......*F2 202
Churchill, co., Nev......D3 192
Churchill, cape, Man., Can......C5 150
Churchill, falls, Newf., Can..h8 152
Churchill, lake, Sask., Can..B1 155
Churchill, lake, Maine......B3 184
Churchill, mtn., B.C., Can..E6 149
Churchill, riv., Man., Sask., Can......E11 142
Churchill, riv., Newf., Can...h9 152
Churchs Ferry, N. Dak......A6 198
Churchton, Md......C4 173
Churchville, Md......A5 173
Churchville, N.Y......B3 196
Churchville, Va......C3 209
Churdan, Iowa......B3 180
Churu, India......C5 88
Churubusco, Ind......B7 179
Churubusco, N.Y......A3 196
Churuguara, Ven......A4 133
Churumuco, Mex......n13 129
Chushan, China......E7 91
Chushul, India......B6 87
Chuska, mts., N. Mex......A1 195
Chusovoy, Sov. Un......B5 73
Chute-Shipshaw, Que., Can......A6 154
Chybie, Pol......h9 70
Ciales, P.R......B5 132
Ciales, mun., P.R......B4 132
Ciano d'Enza, It......E6 66
Cibolo, creek, Tex......B4 206
Ciçekdağ, Tur......C10 85
Cicero, Ill......B6, F3 178
Cicero, Ind......D5 179
Cícero Dantas, Braz......D3 138
Cide, Tur......B9 85
Cidra, P.R......C6 132
Cidra, mun., P.R......C6 132
Ciechanów, Pol......B6 70
Ciego de Avila, Cuba......E4 131
Ciempozuelos, Sp......B4 65
Ciénaga, Col......A3 133
Ciénaga de Oro, Col......B2 133
Cienfuegos, Cuba......D3 131
Cieszyn, Pol......D5 70
Cieza, Sp......C5 65
Ciężkowice, Pol......g10 70
Cihanbeyli, Tur......C9 85
Cihuatlán, Mex......n11 129
Cilicia: in 612-550 B.C...... 42
c. 500 B.C...... 78
in 1st cent. B.C...... 44
c. 120 A.D...... 45
Cima, Calif......E6 170
Cimarron, Colo......C3 171
Cimarron, Kans......E3 181
Cimarron, N. Mex......A5 195
Cimarron, co., Okla......D2 200
Cimarron, riv., U.S......C8 158
Cinchmore, Tenn......C9 205
Cincinnati, Iowa......D5 180
Cincinnati, Ohio......C3, D2 199
Cincinnatus, N.Y......C5 196
Cinco Bayou, Fla......*G2 174
Çine, Tur......D7 69
Cinto, mtn., Fr......C2 67
Cipolletti, Arg......B3 136
Circle, Alsk......B11 167
Circle, Mont......C11 190
Circle, cliffs, Utah......F4 207
Circle Pines, Minn......*E5 187
Circle Springs, Alsk......B11 167
Circleville, Kans......C8 181
Circleville, Ohio......C5 199
Circleville, Utah......E3 207
Circleville, W. Va......C5 211
Cirencester, Eng......C6 56
Cirque, mtn., Newf., Can......f9 152
Cirrik, Alb......E4 68
Cisco, Ill......D5 178
Cisco, Ky......C6 182
Cisco, Tex......C3 206
Cisco, Utah......E6 207
Cisne, Ill......E5 178
Cisneros, Col......B2 133
Ciso, Ga......B2 175
Cispus, riv., Wash......C4 210
Cissna Park, Ill......C6 178
Cistern, Tex......E4 206
Cisterna di Latina, It......h9 67
Cistierna, Sp......A3 65
Citra, Fla......C4 174
Citronelle, Ala......D1 166
Citrus, co., Fla......D4 174
Città di Castello, It......C4 67
Cittadella, It......B3 67
City, isl., N.Y......B5 194
City Mills, Mass......E2 185
City of Norfolk, res., Va...B6 209
City Park, Ill......*D4 178
City Point, Fla......D6 174
City View, S.C......B3 203
Ciucul, mts., Rom......B7 68
Ciudad Acuña, Mex......E2 206
Ciudad Altamirano, Mex..n13 129
Ciudad Bolívar, Ven......B5 133
Ciudad Bolivia, Ven......B3 133
Ciudad Camargo, Mex......B3 129
Ciudad Camargo, Mex......F3 206
Ciudad Chetumal, Mex......D7 129
Ciudad de las Casas, Mex......D6 129
Ciudad de Valles, Mex......C5, m14 129
Ciudad del Carmem, Mex......D6 129
Ciudad del Maíz, Mex......C5 129
Ciudad Dr. Hernández Alvarez, Mex......m13 129
Ciudad García [Salinas], Mex......C4 129
Ciudad Guzmán, Mex......D4, n12 129
Ciudad Hidalgo, Mex......n13 129
Ciudad Juarez, Mex......F3 195
Ciudad Lerdo, Mex......B4 129
Ciudad Madero, Mex......C5 129
Ciudad Mante, Mex......C5 129
Ciudad Melchor, Mex......B4 129
Ciudad Mier, Mex......F3 206
Ciudad Obregón, Mex......B3 129
Ciudad Ojeda, Ven......A3 133
Ciudad Real, Sp......C4 65
Ciudad Rodrigo, Sp......B2 65
Ciudad Serdán, Mex......n15 129
Ciudad Victoria, Mex......C5 129
Ciudadela, Sp......B7 65
Cividale del Friuli, It......A4 67
Civil War, American, campaigns of...... 164
Civitanova Marche, It......C4 67
Civitavecchia, It......C3 67
Civray, Fr......D4 58
Çivril, Tur......C7 69
Cizre, Tur......D14 85
Clachan, Scot......C1 57
Clackamas, Oreg......B2 201
Clackamas, co., Oreg......B4 201
Clackmannan, co., Scot......D5 57
Clacton-on-Sea, Eng......C9 56
Claflin, Kans......D5 181
Claiborne, Ala......D2 166
Claiborne, Md......C5 173
Claiborne, co., Miss......D3 188
Claiborne, co., Tenn......C10 205
Claiborne, par., La......B2 183
Clair, N.B., Can......B1 151
Clair, Sask., Can......E3 155
Clair Engle, lake, Calif......B2 170
Claire, lake, Alta., Can......D1 148
Claire, riv., Viet......B6 89
Claire City, S. Dak......B8 204
Clair Haven, Mich......*F8 186
Clairemont, Tex......C2 206
Clairfield, Tenn......C10 205
Clairmont, Alta., Can......B1 148
Clairmont Springs, Ala......B4 166
Clairton, Pa......F2 202
Clallam, co., Wash......A1 210
Clallam Bay, Wash......A1 210
Clam, lake, Wis......C1 212
Clamart, Fr......g10 58
Clamecy, Fr......D5 58
Clan Alpine, mts., Nev......D3 192
Clancey, Mont......D5 190
Clandeboye, Ont., Can......D3 153
Clandonald, Alta., Can......C5 148
Clanton, Ala......C3 166
Clanwilliam, Man., Can......D2 150
Clanwilliam, S. Afr......D2 107
Clapperton, isl., Ont., Can..A2 153
Clara, Miss......D5 188
Clara City, Minn......F3 187
Clare, Austl......F2 112
Clare, Ind......D6 179
Clare, Iowa......B3 180
Clare, Mich......E6 186
Clare, co., Mich......E6 186
Clare, isl., Ire......D1 55
Claremont, Calif......F3 170
Claremont, Minn......F6 187
Claremont, N.H......D2 193
Claremont, N.C......B2 197
Claremont, S. Dak......B8 204
Claremont, Va......D6 209
Claremont, mtn., Calif......C3 170
Claremore, Okla......A6 200
Claremorris, Ire......D2 55
Clarence, Iowa......C6 180
Clarence, La......C2 183
Clarence, Mo......B5 189
Clarence, N.Y......*C2 196
Clarence, Pa......D6 202
Clarence, strait, Austl......B4 110
Clarence Town, Ba. Is......D6 131
Clarenceville, Que., Can......D4 154
Clarendon, Ark......C4 169
Clarendon, Pa......C3 202
Clarendon, Tex......B2 206
Clarendon, Vt......D3 208
Clarendon, co., S.C......D7 203
Clarendon, riv., Vt......E2 208
Clarendon Hills, Ill......F2 178
Clarendon Springs, Vt......D2 208
Clarendon Station, Ont., Can......C8 153
Clarenville, Newf., Can......D5 152
Claresholm, Alta., Can......D4 148
Clareton, Wyo......B8 213
Claridge, Pa......F2 202
Clarie, coast, Ant......C26 120
Clarinda, Iowa......D2 180
Clarington, Ohio......C7 199
Clarington, Pa......D3 202
Clarion, Iowa......B4 180
Clarion, Pa......D3 202
Clarion, co., Pa......D3 202
Clarion, riv., Pa......D3 202
Clarissa, Minn......D4 187
Clarita, Okla......C5 200
Clark, Colo......A4 171
Clark, Mo......B5 189
Clark, N.J......*B4 194
Clark, Ohio......B6 199
Clark, S. Dak......C8 204
Clark, Wyo......A3 213
Clark, co., Ark......C2 169
Clark, co., Idaho......E6 177
Clark, co., Ill......D6 178
Clark, co., Ind......H6 179
Clark, co., Kans......E4 181
Clark, co., Ky......C5 182
Clark, co., Mo......A6 189
Clark, co., Nev......G6 192
Clark, co., Ohio......C4 199
Clark, co., S. Dak......C8 204
Clark, co., Wash......D3 210
Clark, co., Wis......D3 212
Clark, lake, Alsk......C9 167
Clark, mtn., Mo......D7 189
Clark, mtn., Va......C5 209
Clark Fork, Idaho......A2 177
Clark Fork, riv., Idaho, Mont......B3 177
Clark Hill, res., Ga., S.C......C4 175
Clark Mills, N.Y......*B5 196
Clarkdale, Ariz......C3 168
Clarkdale, Ga......A4 175
Clarke, co., Ala......D2 166
Clarke, co., Ga......C3 175
Clarke, co., Iowa......D4 180
Clarke, co., Miss......C5 188
Clarke, co., Va......B4 209
Clarke, lake, Sask., Can......C2 155
Clarke City, Que., Can......F19 145
Clarkedale, Ark......E8 205
Clarkes Harbour, N.S., Can......F4 151
Clarkesville, Ga......B3 175
Clarkfield, Minn......F3 187
Clarkia, Idaho......C2 177
Clarkrange, Tenn......C8 205
Clarks, La......B3 183
Clarks, Nebr......C8 191
Clarks, riv., Ky......A2 182
Clarks Corners, Conn......B8 172
Clarks Falls, Conn......D9 172
Clarks Fork of the Yellowstone, riv., Wyo., Mont......F7 190
Clarks Green, Pa......*D10 202
Clarks Grove, Minn......G5 187
Clarks Hill, Ind......D4 179
Clarks Hill, S.C......D3 203
Clarks Point, Alsk......D8 167
Clarks Summit, Pa......A9 202
Clarksboro, N.J......D2 194
Clarksburg, Calif......A6 170
Clarksburg, Ont., Can......C4 153
Clarksburg, Ind......F7 179
Clarksburg, Md......B3 173
Clarksburg, Mass......*A1 185
Clarksburg, Mo......C5 189
Clarksburg, N.J......C4 194
Clarksburg, Ohio......C4 199
Clarksburg, Tenn......B3 205
Clarksburg, W. Va......B4, B6 211
Clarksdale, Miss......A3 188
Clarksdale, Mo......B3 189
Clarkson, Ky......C3 182
Clarkson, Miss......B4 188
Clarkson, Nebr......C8 191
Clarkston, Ga......B5 175
Clarkston, Mich......F7 186
Clarkston, Utah......B3 207
Clarkston, Wash......C8 210
Clarksville, Ark......B2 169
Clarksville, N.S., Can......D6 151
Clarksville, Del......C7 173
Clarksville, Idaho......*B2 177
Clarksville, Ind......H6 179
Clarksville, Iowa......B5 180
Clarksville, Md......B4 173
Clarksville, Mich......F5 186
Clarksville, Mo......B7 189
Clarksville, Ohio......C4 199
Clarksville, Tenn......A4 205
Clarksville, Tex......C5 206
Clarksville, Va......E4 209
Clarksville City, Tex......*C5 206
Clarkton, Mo......E8 189
Clarkton, N.C......C5 197
Claryville, Ky......A7 182
Claryville, Mo......D8 189
Clatonia, Nebr......D9 191
Clatskanie, Oreg......A3 201
Clatsop, co., Oreg......A3 201
Claud, Tenn......A4 205
Claude, Tex......B2 206
Claunch, N. Mex......C3 195
Clausthal-Zellerfeld, Ger..B5 61
Clavet, Sask., Can......F2 155
Clawson, Mich......A7 186
Clawson, Utah......D4 207
Claxton, Ga......D5 175
Clay, Ky......C2 182
Clay, N.Y......B4 196
Clay, W. Va......C3, C7 211
Clay,Wyo......A8 213
Clay, co., Ala......B4 166
Clay, co., Ark......A5 169
Clay, co., Fla......B5 174
Clay, co., Ga......E2 175
Clay, co., Ill......E5 178
Clay, co., Ind......F3 179
Clay, co., Iowa......A2 180
Clay, co., Kans......C6 181
Clay, co., Ky......C6 182
Clay, co., Minn......D2 187
Clay, co., Miss......B5 188
Clay, co., Mo......B3 189
Clay, co., Nebr......D7 191
Clay, co., N.C......D2 197
Clay, co., S. Dak......E8 204
Clay, co., Tenn......C8 205
Clay, co., Tex......C3 206
Clay, co., W. Va......C3 211
Clay Center, Kans......C6 181
Clay Center, Nebr......D7 191
Clay Center, Ohio....A2, A4 199
Clay City, Ill......E5 178
Clay City, Ind......F3 179
Clay City, Ky......C6 182
Clay Cross, Eng......A6 56
Clay Springs, Ariz......C5 168
Claycomo, Mo......*B3 189
Claydon, Sask., Can......H1 155
Clayhatchee, Ala......D4 166
Claymont, Del......A7 173
Clayoquot, sound, B.C., Can......E4 149
Claypool, Ariz......D5 168
Claypool, Ind......B6 179
Claysburg, Pa......F5 202
Claysville, Pa......F1 202
Clayton, Ala......D4 166
Clayton, Ont., Can......B8 153
Clayton, Del......B6 173
Clayton, Ga......B3 175
Clayton, Idaho......E4 177
Clayton, Ill......C3 178
Clayton, Ind......E4 179
Clayton, Iowa......B6 180
Clayton, Kans......C3 181
Clayton, La......C4 183
Clayton, Mich......*G6 186
Clayton, Mo......B8, C7 189
Clayton, N.J......D2 194
Clayton, N. Mex......A6 195
Clayton, N.Y......A4, B1 196
Clayton, N.C......B5 197
Clayton, Ohio......*C3 199
Clayton, Okla......C6 200
Clayton, S. Dak......D8 204
Clayton, Tenn......A2 205
Clayton, Wash......B8 210
Clayton, Wis......C1 212
Clayton, co., Ga......C2 175
Clayton, co., Iowa......B6 180
Clayton Lake, Maine......B3 184
Clayville, N.Y......C5 196
Clayville, R.I......B10 172
Cle Elum, Wash......B5 210
Cle Elum, lake, Wash......B4 210
Cle Elum, riv., Wash......B4 210
Clear, cape, Ire......E2 55
Clear, creek, Ariz......C4 168
Clear, creek, Tenn......C9 205
Clear, creek, Wyo......A6 213

INDEX KEY Each place listed in **Bold-faced Type** has its population listed in the Political tables, pages 230 to 280.
Each country, shown in CAPITAL LETTERS, has its population listed in the World Political Information Table, pages 6 to 10.
* Does not appear on map; key shows general location.

Clear, fork, Ohio B5 199
Clear, fork, Tenn. C9 205
Clear, fork, W. Va. D3 211
Clear, fork, W. Va. D6 211
Clear, lake, Calif. C2 170
Clear, lake, Man., Can. D2 150
Clear, lake, Ont., Can. B7 153
Clear, lake, Iowa A4 180
Clear, riv., Alta., Can. A1 148
Clear, stream, N.H. A4 193
Clear Boggy, creek, Okla. C5 200
Clear Creek, Ind. F4 179
Clear Creek, W. Va. D6 211
Clear Creek, co., Colo. B5 171
Clear Fork, W. Va. D3 211
Clear Lake, Iowa A4 180
Clear Lake, Minn. E5 187
Clear Lake, S. Dak. C9 204
Clear Lake, Wis. C1 212
Clear Lake, res., Calif. B3 170
Clear Lake Shores, Tex. F5 206
Clear Spring, Md. A2 173
Clearbrook, Minn. C3 187
Clearco, W. Va. C4 211
Cleare, cape, Alsk. h18 167
Clearfield, Iowa D3 180
Clearfield, Ky. B6 182
Clearfield, Pa. D5 202
Clearfield, S. Dak. D5 204
Clearfield, Utah B3 207
Clearfield, co., Pa. D5 202
Clearlake, Wash. A3 210
Clearmont, Mo. A2 189
Clearmont, Wyo. A6 213
Clearview, Okla. B5 200
Clearview, W. Va. *A4 211
Clearville, Pa. G5 202
Clearwater, Man., Can. E2 150
Clearwater, Fla. E1, E4 174
Clearwater, Idaho C3 177
Clearwater, Kans. E6 181
Clearwater, Minn. E4 187
Clearwater, Nebr. B7 191
Clearwater, S.C. E4 203
Clearwater, Wash. B1 210
Clearwater, co., Idaho C3 177
Clearwater, co., Minn. C3 187
Clearwater, creek, Kans. B4 181
Clearwater, lake, B.C., Can. C7 149
Clearwater, mts., Idaho C2 177
Clearwater, prov. park, Man., Can. C1 150
Clearwater, res., Mo. D7 189
Clearwater, riv., Alta., Can. A5 148
Clearwater, riv., Alta., Can. D3 148
Clearwater, riv., B.C., Can. C7 149
Clearwater, riv., Idaho C2 177
Clearwater, riv., Minn. C3 187
Clearwater Lake, Wis. C4 212
Cleaton, Ky. C2 182
Cleator Moor, Eng. F5 57
Cleburne, Kans. C7 181
Cleburne, Tex. B5, C4 206
Cleburne, co., Ala. B4 166
Cleburne, co., Ark. B3 169
Cleethorpes, Eng. A7 56
Cleeves, Sask., Can. D1 155
Cleghorn, Iowa B2 180
Cleghorn, Wis. D2 212
Clem, Ga. C1 175
Clementon, N.J. D3 194
Clements, Kans. D7 181
Clements, Md. D4 173
Clements, Minn. F3 187
Clementsport, N.S., Can. E4 151
Clementsvale, N.S., Can. E4 151
Clemmons, N.C. A3 197
Clemons, Iowa B4 180
Clemons, N.Y. B7 196
Clemscot, Okla. C4 200
Clemson, S.C. B2 203
Clendenin, W. Va. C3, C6 211
Clendening, res., Ohio B6 199
Cleo, Tex. D3 206
Cleo Springs, Okla. A3 200
Cleona, Pa. F9 202
Clermont, Austl. D8 111
Clermont, Que., Can. B7 154
Clermont, Fla. D5 174
Clermont, Fr. E2 59
Clermont, Ga. B3 175
Clermont, Ind. E5, H7 179
Clermont, Iowa A6 180
Clermont, Ky. C4 182
Clermont, Pa. C5 202
Clermont, co., Ohio C3 199
Clermont-en-Argonne, Fr. E5 59
Clermont-Ferrand, Fr. E5 58
Clermont-l'Hérault, Fr. F5 58
Clervaux, Lux. D6 59
Cleve, see Kleve, Ger.
Clevedon, Eng. C5 56
Cleveland, Ala. A3 166
Cleveland, Ark. B3 169
Cleveland, Fla. F5 174
Cleveland, Ga. B3 175
Cleveland, Kans. B3 181
Cleveland, Minn. F5 187
Cleveland, Miss. B3 188
Cleveland, Mo. C3 189
Cleveland, N. Mex. A4 195
Cleveland, N.Y. B5 196
Cleveland, N.C. B3 197
Cleveland, N. Dak. C6 198
Cleveland, Ohio A6, B2 199
Cleveland, Okla. A5 200
Cleveland, S.C. A2 203
Cleveland, Tenn. D9 205
Cleveland, Tex. D5 206
Cleveland, Utah D5 207
Cleveland, Va. B3 209
Cleveland, Wis. B6 212
Cleveland, co., Ark. D3 169
Cleveland, co., N.C. B2 197
Cleveland, co., Okla. B4 200
Cleveland, hills, Eng. F7 57
Cleveland Heights, Ohio A6, B2 199
Clevelândia, Braz. D2 137
Clever, Mo. D4 189
Cleves, Ohio *C3 199
Clew, bay, Ire. D2 55
Clewiston, Fla. F6 174
Clibreck, mtn., Scot. B4 57
Clichy [-la-Garenne], Fr. C5, g10 58
Clifden, Ire. D1 55
Cliff, N. Mex. E1 195
Cliff Dwellings, ruins, Ariz. A5 168
Clifford, Ont., Can. D4 153
Clifford, Ind. F6 179
Clifford, Mich. E7 186
Clifford, N. Dak. B8 198
Clifford, Pa. C10 202
Clifford, Va. D3 209
Cliffside, B.C., Can. B9 149
Cliffside, N.C. B2, D4 197
Cliffside Park, N.J. D5 194
Clifftop, W. Va. D7 211
Clifton, Ariz. D6 168
Clifton, Colo. B2 171
Clifton, Idaho *G7 177
Clifton, Ill. C6 178
Clifton, Kans. C6 181
Clifton, N.J. B4, D5 194
Clifton, S.C. B4 203
Clifton, Tenn. B4 205
Clifton, Tex. D4 206
Clifton, Va. B4, C5 209
Clifton, Wyo. B8 213
Clifton City, Mo. C4 189
Clifton Forge (Independent City), Va. D3 209
Clifton Heights, Pa. B11 202
Clifton Hill, Mo. B5 189
Clifton Springs, N.Y. C3 196
Cliftonville, Miss. B5 188
Clifty, Tenn. D8 205
Climax, Sask., Can. H1 155
Climax, Colo. B4 171
Climax, Ga. F2 175
Climax, Kans. E7 181
Climax, Mich. F5 186
Climax, Minn. C2 187
Climax Springs, Mo. C4 189
Climbing Hill, Iowa B1 180
Clinch, co., Ga. F4 175
Clinch, mtn., Va. B2 209
Clinch, mts., Tenn. C10 205
Clinch, riv., Tenn. D9 205
Clinch, riv., Va. B2 209
Clinchburg, Va. B3 209
Clincho, Va. B2 209
Clinchfield, Ga. D3 175
Clinchmore, Tenn. C9 205
Clinchport, Va. B2 209
Cline, Tex. E2 206
Cline, falls, Oreg. C5 201
Clines Corners, N. Mex. C4 195
Clingmans Dome, mtn., Tenn. D10 205
Clint, Tex. F1 206
Clinton, Ala. C2 166
Clinton, Ark. B3 169
Clinton, B.C., Can. D7 149
Clinton, Ont., Can. D3 153
Clinton, Conn. D6 172
Clinton, Ga. C3 175
Clinton, Ill. C5 178
Clinton, Ind. E3 179
Clinton, Iowa C7 180
Clinton, Ky. B2 182
Clinton, La. D4 183
Clinton, Maine D3 184
Clinton, Md. C4 173
Clinton, Mass. B4 185
Clinton, Mich. F7 186
Clinton, Minn. E2 187
Clinton, Miss. C3 188
Clinton, Mo. C4 189
Clinton, Mont. D3 190
Clinton, Nebr. B3 191
Clinton, N.J. B3 194
Clinton, N.Y. B5 196
Clinton, N.C. C5 197
Clinton, Ohio *B6 199
Clinton, Okla. B3 200
Clinton, S.C. C4 203
Clinton, Tenn. C9, E11 205
Clinton, Utah B3 207
Clinton, Wis. F5 212
Clinton, co., Ill. E4 178
Clinton, co., Ind. D4 179
Clinton, co., Iowa C7 180
Clinton, co., Ky. D4 182
Clinton, co., Mich. F6 186
Clinton, co., Mo. B3 189
Clinton, co., N.Y. A3 196
Clinton, co., Ohio C4 199
Clinton, co., Pa. D6 202
Clinton, res., N.J. A4 194
Clinton Colden, lake, N.W. Ter., Can. D11 142
Clintonville, Conn. D5 172
Clintonville, Ky. B5 182
Clintonville, Pa. D2 202
Clintonville, W. Va. D4 211
Clintonville, Wis. D5 212
Clintwood, Va. B2 209
Clio, Ala. D4 166
Clio, Iowa D4 180
Clio, La. B6 183
Clio, Mich. E7 186
Clio, S.C. B8 203
Clio, W. Va. C5 211
Clipper, Wash. A3 210
Clipperton, isl., French Polynesia F15 113
Clisham, mtn., Scot. C2 57
Clitherall, Minn. D3 187
Clive, Alta., Can. C4 148
Clive, Iowa *C4 180
Cliza, Bol. C2 135
Clodan, Sask., Can. H1 155
Cloe, Pa. E4 202
Clonakilty, Ire. E2 55
Clonakilty, bay, Ire. E2 55
Cloncurry, Austl. D7 111
Clonmel, Ire. D3 55
Clontarf, Minn. E3 187
Clo-oose, B.C., Can. E5 149
Cloppenburg, Ger. F2 62
Clopton, Ala. D4 166
Cloquet, Minn. D6 187
Cloquet, riv., Minn. C6 187
Closter, N.J. B5, D5 194
Clothier, W. Va. D5 211
Cloud, co., Kans. C6 181
Cloud, bay, N.Z. N15 112
Cloud, mtn., Newf., Can. C3 152
Cloud, peak, Wyo. A5 213
Cloud Chief, Okla. B3 200
Cloud Lake, Fla. *F6 174
Cloudcroft, N. Mex. E4 195
Cloudy, mtn., Alsk. C8 167
Clover, S.C. A5 203
Clover, Va. E4 209
Clover Bottom, Ky. C5 182
Clover Lick, W. Va. C5 211
Cloverdale, Ala. A2 166
Cloverdale, Calif. C2 170
Cloverdale, B.C., Can. B10 149
Cloverdale, Ill. F2 178
Cloverdale, Ind. E4 179
Cloverdale, Oreg. B3 201
Cloverdale, Va. D3 209
Cloverport, Ky. C3 182
Cloverton, Minn. D6 187
Clovis, Calif. D4 170
Clovis, N. Mex. C6 195
Cluanie, lake, Scot. C3 57
Cluj, Rom. B6 68
Clune, Pa. E3 202
Cluny, Alta., Can. D4 148
Cluny, Fr. D6 58
Clusone, It. D5 66
Cluster Springs, Va. E4 209
Clute, Tex. G5 206
Clutier, Iowa B5 180
Clyattville, Ga. F3 175
Clyde, Alta., Can. B4 148
Clyde, N.W. Ter., Can. B19 145
Clyde, Kans. C6 181
Clyde, Mo. A3 189
Clyde, N.Y. B4 196
Clyde, N.C. D3 197
Clyde, N. Dak. A7 198
Clyde, Ohio A5 199
Clyde, Tex. C3 206
Clyde, firth, Scot. E4 57
Clyde, riv., N.S., Can. E4 151
Clyde, riv., Scot. E5 57
Clyde Hill, Wash. *B3 210
Clyde Park, Mont. E6 190
Clydebank, Scot. E4 57
Clymer, N.Y. C1 196
Clymer, Pa. E3 202
Clyo, Ga. D5 175
Cnocmoy, mtn., Scot. E3 57
Cnossus, ruins, Grc. E5 69
Coachella, Calif. F5 170
Coachella, canal, Calif. F6 170
Coahoma, Miss. A3 188
Coahoma, Tex. C2 206
Coahoma, co., Miss. A3 188
Coahuila, state, Mex. B4 129
Coal, co., Okla. C5 200
Coal, creek, Ind. D3 179
Coal, creek, Okla. B6 200
Coal, fork, W. Va. C6 211
Coal, riv., W. Va. C3 211
Coal Bluff, Ind. E3 179
Coal Branch Station, N.B., Can. C4 151
Coal Center, Pa. *F2 202
Coal City, Ill. B5 178
Coal City, Ind. F3 179
Coal Fork, W. Va. C3, C6 211
Coal Grove, Ohio D5 199
Coal Harbour, B.C., Can. D4 149
Coal Hill, Ark. B2 169
Coal Valley, Ala. B2 166
Coal Valley, Ill. D7 180
Coalburn, Scot. E5 57
Coalcomán, Mex. D4, n12 129
Coalcreek, Colo. C5 171
Coaldale, Alta., Can. E4 148
Coaldale, Colo. C5 171
Coaldale, Pa. E10 202
Coalfield, Tenn. C9 205
Coalgate, Okla. C5 200
Coalgood, Ky. D6 182
Coalhurst, Alta., Can. E4 148
Coaling, Ala. B2 166
Coalinga, Calif. D3 170
Coalmont, B.C., Can. E7 149
Coalmont, Colo. A4 171
Coalmont, Ind. F3 179
Coalmont, Tenn. D8 205
Coalport, Pa. E4 202
Coalridge, Mont. B12 190
Coalridge, Ohio C6 199
Coalspur, Alta., Can. C2 148
Coalton, Ill. D4 178
Coalton, Ohio C5 199
Coalton, Okla. B6 200
Coaltown, Pa. *D1 202
Coalville, Eng. B6 56
Coalville, Iowa B3 180
Coalville, Utah C4 207
Coalwood, Mont. E11 190
Coalwood, W. Va. *D3 211
Coamo, P.R. C5 132
Coamo, mun., P.R. C5 132
Coari, Braz. D5 133
Coast, reg., Ken. B6 106
Coast, mts., B.C., Can. E6 142
Coast, ranges, U.S. B3 158
Coastal, plain, N.C., Va. C5 197, E5 209
Coatbridge, Scot. E4 57
Coatepec, Mex. n15 129
Coatepeque, Guat. C2 130
Coatesville, Ind. E4 179
Coatesville, Pa. G10 202
Coaticook, Que., Can. D6 154
Coatney, hill, Conn. B8 172
Coatopa, Ala. C1 166
Coats, Kans. E5 181
Coats, N.C. B5 197
Coats, isl., N.W. Ter., Can. D16 143
Coats Land, reg., Ant. B10 120
Coatsville, Mo. A5 189
Coatzacoalcos (Puerto México), Mex. D6 129
Cobalt, Ont., Can. E9 153
Cobalt, Conn. C6 172
Cobalt, Idaho D4 177
Cobán, Guat. C2 130
Cobar, Austl. E5 112
Cobb, Ga. E3 175
Cobb, Ky. C2 182
Cobb, Wis. F3 212
Cobb, co., Ga. C2 175
Cobb, isl., Md. D4 173
Cobb, riv., Minn. G5 187
Cobble Hill, B.C., Can. B9 149
Cobble Mountain, res., Mass. B2 185
Cobbosseecontee, lake, Maine D2 184
Cobbtown, Ga. D4 175
Cobden, Ont., Can. B8 153
Cobden, Ill. F4 178
Cobequid, mts., N.S., Can. D5 151
Cobh, Ire. E2 55
Cobham, riv., Man., Can. C4 150
Cobija, Bol. B2 135
Cobija, Chile D1 135
Coble, Tenn. B4 205
Cobleskill, N.Y. C6 196
Coboconk, Ont., Can. C6 153
Cobourg, Ont., Can. D6 153
Cobourg, pen., Austl. B5 110
Cobre, Nev. B7 192
Cobun, creek, W. Va. A7 211
Coburg, Austl. *H5 112
Coburg, Ger. C5 61
Coburg, Iowa D2 180
Coburg, Mont. B8 190
Coburg, Oreg. C3 201
Coburn, Pa. E7 202
Coburn, W. Va. A6, B4 211
Coburn, mtn., Maine C2 184
Coburn Gore, Maine C2 184
Coca, Ec. B2 134
Cocanada, see Kakinada, India
Cocentaina, Sp. C5 65
Cochabamba, Bol. C2 135
Cochabamba, dept., Bol. C2 135
Coche, isl., Ven. A5 133
Cocheco, riv., N.H. D4 193
Cochem, Ger. D7 59
Cochetopa, creek, Colo. C4 171
Cochetopa, hills, Colo. C4 171
Cochin, India G6 87
Cochin China, reg., Viet. H6 89
c. 1775 82
Cochise, Ariz. E6 168
Cochise, co., Ariz. F5 168
Cochise Head, mtn., Ariz. E6 168
Cochiti, N. Mex. F5 195
Cochiti, Indian res., N. Mex. F6 195
Cochituate, Mass. D1 185
Cochituate, lake, Mass. D1 185
Cochran, Ga. D3 175
Cochran, co., Tex. C1 206
Cochrane, Alta., Can. D3 148
Cochrane, Ont., Can. E9 153
Cochrane, Wis. D2 212
Cochrane, co., Ont., Can. E9 153
Cochrane, mtn., Arg. D2 136
Cochranton, Pa. C1 202
Cochranville, Pa. G10 202
Cockburn, Austl. F3 112
Cockburn, isl., Ont., Can. C7 186
Cocke, co., Tenn. D10 205
Cockermouth, Eng. F5 57
Cockeysville, Md. B4 173
Cockrell Hill, Tex. B5 206
Cockroach, isl., Vir. Is. f14 132
Cockrum, Miss. A4 188
Coco, riv., Nic. C6 130
Cocoa, Fla. D6 174
Cocoa Beach, Fla. D6 174
Cocoa West, Fla. *D6 174
Cocobeach, Gabon E1 104
Cocolalla, Idaho A2 177
Coconino, co., Ariz. B3 168
Coconino, plat., Ariz. B3 168
Cocopah, Indian res., Mex. E1 168
Cocos, isl., Mariana Is. 115
Cocula, Mex. C4, m12 129
Cocuy, Col. B3 133
Cod, cape, Mass. B7 185
Cod, isl., Newf., Can. g9 152
Codajás, Braz. D5 133
Codajás, lake, Braz. D5 133
Codell, Kans. C4 181
Coden, Ala. E1 166
Coderre, Sask., Can. G2 155
Codesa, Alta., Can. B1 148
Codette, Sask., Can. D3 155
Codigoro, It. E8 66
Codington, co., S. Dak. C8 204
Codó, Braz. B2 138
Codogno, It. B2 67
Codpa, Chile C2 135
Codroipo, It. D8 66
Codroy, Newf., Can. E2 152
Codroy Pond, Newf., Can. D2 152
Codrul, mts., Rom. B6 68
Cody, Nebr. B4 191
Cody, Wyo. A3 213
Codys, N.B., Can. D4 151
Coe Hill, Ont., Can. C7 153
Coelho da Rocha, Braz. *C4 137
Coen, Austl. B7 111
Coesfeld, Ger. B2 61
Coesse, Ind. B7 179
Coetlogon, pass, N. Cal. 115
Coeur d'Alene, Idaho B2 177
Coeur d'Alene, Indian res., Idaho, Wash. B1 177
Coeur d'Alene, lake, Idaho B2 177
Coeur d'Alene, mtn., Idaho D9 210
Coeur d'Alene, mts., Idaho B2 177
Coevorden, Neth. B6 59
Coffee, co., Ala. D3 166
Coffee, co., Ga. E4 175
Coffee, co., Tenn. B5 205
Coffee Creek, Mont. C6 190
Coffee Springs, Ala. D4 166
Coffeen, Ill. D4 178
Coffeeville, Ala. D1 166
Coffeeville, Miss. B4 188
Coffey, Mo. A3 189
Coffey, co., Kans. D8 181
Coffeyville, Kans. E8 181
Coffin, isl., Que., Can. B8 151
Coff's Harbour, Austl. E9 112
Cofield, N.C. A7 197
Cogdell, Ga. E4 175
Coggon, Iowa B6 180
Coghinas, riv., It. D2 67
Cognac, Fr. E3 58
Cogswell, N. Dak. C8 198
Cohagen, Mont. C10 190
Cohansey, creek, N.J. E2 194
Cohasset, Mass. B6, D4 185
Cohasset, Minn. C5 187
Cohocton, N.Y. C3 196
Cohocton, riv., N.Y. C3 196
Cohoe, Alsk. g16 167
Cohoes, N.Y. C7 196
Cohutta, Ga. B2 175
Cohutta, mtn., Ga. B2 175
Coila, Miss. B4 188
Coimbatore, India F6 87
Coimbra, Port. B1 65
Coin, Iowa D2 180
Coín, Sp. D3 65
Coinjock, N.C. A8 197
Coipasa, lake, Bol. C2 135
Coipasa, salt flat, Bol. C2 135
Coire, lake, Scot. B4 57
Cojedes, state, Ven. B4 133
Cojutepeque, Sal. D3 130
Cokato, Minn. E4 187
Coke, co., Tex. D2 206
Cokeburg, Pa. *F1 202
Cokedale, Colo. D6 171
Coker, Ala. B2 166
Cokesbury, N.J. B3 194
Cokesbury, S.C. C3 203
Coketon, W. Va. B5 211
Coketown, W. Va. B2 211
Cokeville, Wyo. C2 213
Colac, Austl. I4 112
Colares, Port. f9 65
Colatina, Braz. E2 138
Colbeck, cape, Ant. B33 120
Colbert, Ga. B3 175
Colbert, Okla. D5 200
Colbert, co., Ala. A2 166
Colborne, Ont., Can. C7 153
Colbún, Chile B2 136
Colburn, Idaho A2 177
Colburn, Ind. C4 179
Colby, Kans. C2 181
Colby, Maine B4 184
Colby, Wis. D3 212
Colbyville, Vt. C3 208
Colchagua, prov., Chile A2 136
Colchester, Conn. C7 172
Colchester, Eng. C8 56
Colchester, Ill. C3 178
Colchester, Vt. B2 208
Colchester, co., N.S., Can. D6 151
Colcord, Okla. A7 200
Cold, lake, Alta., Sask., Can. B5 148, B1 155
Cold, riv., N.H. C4 193
Cold, riv., N.H. D2 193
Cold Fell, mtn., Eng. F6 57
Cold Hollow, mts., Vt. B3 208
Cold Lake, Alta., Can. B5 148
Cold River, N.H. D2 193
Cold Spring, Ky. A7, B5 182
Cold Spring, Minn. E4 187
Cold Spring, N.J. F3 194
Cold Spring, N.Y. *D7 196
Cold Spring, hbr., N.Y. F3 172
Cold Spring, pond, Newf., Can. D3 152
Cold Spring Harbor, N.Y. F3 172
Cold Springs, Okla. C3 200
Cold Stream, pond, Maine C4 184
Colditz, Ger. B7 61
Coldspring, Tex. D5 206
Coldstream, Scot. E6 57
Coldwater, Ont., Can. C5 153
Coldwater, Kans. E4 181
Coldwater, Mich. G5 186
Coldwater, Miss. A4 188
Coldwater, Ohio B3 199
Coldwater, creek, Okla. D3 200
Coldwater, creek, Tex. A1 206
Coldwater, riv., Miss. A3 188
Cole, Okla. B4 200
Cole, co., Mo. C5 189
Cole Camp, Mo. C4 189
Cole Lake, Ont., Can. C5 153
Colebrook, Conn. B4 172
Colebrook, N.H. B1 193
Colebrook River, Conn. B4 172
Coleharbor, N. Dak. B4 198
Coleman, Alta., Can. E3 148
Coleman, P.E.I., Can. C5 151
Coleman, Fla. D4 174
Coleman, Ga. E2 175
Coleman, Md. B5 173
Coleman, Mich. E6 186
Coleman, Okla. C5 200
Coleman, Tex. D3 206
Coleman, Wis. C5 212
Coleman, co., Tex. D3 206
Coleman, riv., Austl. B7 110
Coleman Falls, Va. D3 209
Colerain, N.C. A7 197
Coleraine, Austl. H3 112
Coleraine, Minn. C5 187
Coleraine, N. Ire. C3 55
Coleraine Station, Que., Can. D6 154
Coleridge, Nebr. B8 191
Coleridge, N.C. B4 197
Coleridge, bay, Sol. Is. 115
Coles, Miss. D2 188
Coles, co., Ill. D5 178
Colesberg, S. Afr. D4 107
Colesburg, Iowa B6 180
Colesburg, Ky. C4 182
Colesville, N.J. A3 194
Coleta, Ill. B4 178
Coleville, Sask., Can. F1 155
Coleville, Calif. C4 170
Colfax, Calif. C3 170
Colfax, Sask., Can. H4 155
Colfax, Ill. C5 178
Colfax, Ind. D4 179
Colfax, Iowa C4 180
Colfax, La. C3 183
Colfax, N. Dak. C9 198
Colfax, Wash. C8 210
Colfax, Wis. D2 212
Colfax, co., Nebr. C8 191
Colfax, co., N. Mex. A5 195
Colgan, N. Dak. A2 198
Colgate, Sask., Can. H4 155
Colgate, N. Dak. B8 198
Colico, It. C5 66
Colijnsplaat, Neth. C3 59
Colima, Mex. D4, n12 129
Colima, state, Mex. D4, n12 129
Colinas, Braz. C2 138
Colinet, Newf., Can. E5 152
Colington, N.C. A8 197
Colinton, Alta., Can. B4 148
Coll, isl., Scot. D2 57
Collbran, Colo. B3 171
College, Alsk. C10 167
College Corner, Ohio C3 199
College Gardens, Calif. *D3 170
College Grove, Tenn. B5 205
College Heights, Ark. D4 169
College Heights, S.C. C7 203
College Park, Fla. C5 174
College Park, Ga. B5, C2 175
College Park, Md. C2, C4 173
College Place, Wash. C7 210
College Springs, Iowa D2 180
College Station, Tex. D4 206
Collegedale, Tenn. E10 205
Collegeville, Ind. C3 179
Collegeville, Pa. F11 202
Colleton, co., S.C. F6 203
Colley, Pa. C9 202
Colleyville, Tex. *B5 206
Collie, Austl. F2 111
Collier, co., Fla. F5 174
Collier, bay, Austl. C3 110
Colliers, W. Va. A2 211
Collierville, Tenn. B2 205
Collin, co., Tex. C4 206
Collingdale, Pa. B11 202
Collingswood, N.J. D2 194
Collingsworth, co., Tex. B2 206
Collingwood, Ont., Can. C4 153
Collins, Ark. D4 169
Collins, Ont., Can. E8 153
Collins, Ga. D4 175
Collins, Ind. B7 179
Collins, Iowa C4 180
Collins, Miss. D4 188
Collins, Mo. D4 189
Collins, Mont. C5 190
Collins, Wis. B6 212
Collinston, La. B4 183
Collinsville, Ala. A4 166
Collinsville, Conn. B5 172
Collinsville, Ga. B5 175
Collinsville, Ill. E4 178
Collinsville, Miss. C5 188
Collinsville, Okla. A6 200
Collinsville, Tex. *C4 206
Collinsville, Va. *E6 209
Collinwood, Tenn. B4 205
Collipulli, Chile B2 136
Collis, Minn. E2 187
Collister, Idaho F2 177
Collo, Alg. B6 102
Collyer, Kans. C3 181
Colman, S. Dak. D9 204
Colmar, Fr. C7 58, A3 66
Colmar, Ky. D6 182
Colmar Manor, Md. C2 173
Colmenar de Oreja, Sp. B4 65
Colmenar Viejo, Sp. B4, o17 65
Colmesneil, Tex. D5 206
Colnett, reef, N. Cal. 115
Colo, Iowa B4 180
Cologne (Köln), Ger. C1 61
Cologne, Minn. F5 187
Cologne, N.J. D3 194
Coloma, Mich. F4 186
Coloma, Wis. D4 212
Colomb-Béchar, Alg. C4 102
Colombes, Fr. g10 58
Colombey-les-Belles, Fr. F5 59

INDEX KEY Each place listed in Bold-faced Type has its population listed in the Population tables, pages 230 to 280.
Each country, shown in CAPITAL LETTERS, has its population listed in the World Political Information Table, pages 6 to 10.
* Does not appear on map; key shows general location.

Colombia, Col. C3 133
COLOMBIA, country, S.A. C3 133
Colombia, Great: in 1800's 127
Colombo, Cey. G6 87
Colome, S. Dak. D6 204
Colón, Arg. A5 136
Colón, Cuba D3 131
Colon, Mich. G5 186
Colon, Nebr. D2 191
Colon, N.C. B4 197
Colón, Pan. F8, k11 130
Colón, Archipiélago de (Galápagos Is.), prov., Ec. g5 134
Colon, lake, Man., Can. B4 150
Colona, Colo. C3 171
Colona, Ill. *B3 178
Colonia, N.J. E4 194
Colonia, Ur. E1 137
Colonia Dora, Arg. E3 135
Colonia Las Heras, Arg. D3 136
Colônia Leopoldina, Braz. k6 138
Colonia Mennonita, Par. D4 135
Colonia Paraíso, P.R. B8, f12 132
Colonia Providencia, P.R. D6 132
Colonia Sarmiento, Arg. D3 136
Colonia Suiza, Ur. g8 136
Colonial Beach, Va. C6 209
Colonial Heights, Tenn. *C11 205
Colonial Heights (Independent City), Va. C7, D5 209
Colonias, N. Mex. B5 195
Colonie, N.Y. *C7 196
Colonna, It. h9 67
Colonne, cape, It. E6 67
Colonsay, Sask., Can. F3 155
Colonsay, isl., Scot. D2 57
Colony, Kans. D8 181
Colony, Okla. B3 200
Colony, Wyo. A8 213
Colorado, C.R. E6 130
Colorado, state, U.S. 171
Colorado, co., Tex. E4 206
Colorado, desert, Calif. F6 170
Colorado, nat. mon., Colo. B2 171
Colorado, plat., Ariz. A3 168
Colorado, riv., Arg. B3 136
Colorado, riv., Tex. D3 206
Colorado, riv., U.S. C5 158
Colorado City, Ariz. A3 168
Colorado City, Tex. C2 206
Colorado River, Indian res., Ariz. D1 168
Colorado Springs, Colo. C6 171
Colorados, arch., Cuba D1 131
Colored Hill, W. Va. *D3 211
Coloso, Chile D1 135
Coloso, P.R. B2 132
Coloso Central, P.R. B2 132
Colotepec, Mex. D5 129
Colotlán, Mex. C4, k12 129
Colquechaca, Bol. C2 135
Colquitt, Ga. E2 175
Colquitt, La. B3 183
Colquitt, co., Ga. E3 175
Colrain, Mass. A2 185
Colstrip, Mont. E10 190
Colt, Ark. B5 169
Coltauco, Chile A2 136
Colton, Calif. F3 170
Colton, N.Y. B2 196
Colton, Oreg. B4 201
Colton, S. Dak. D9 204
Colton, Utah D4 207
Colton, Wash. C8 210
Colton, hill, Vt. D4 208
Coltons Point, Md. D4 173
Colts Neck, N.J. C4 194
Colulli, Eth. C5 105
Columbia, Ala. D4 166
Columbia, Conn. C7 172
Columbia, Ill. E3 178
Columbia, Ky. C4 182
Columbia, La. B3 183
Columbia, Miss. D4 188
Columbia, Mo. C5 189
Columbia, N.H. *B1 193
Columbia, N.J. B2 194
Columbia, N.C. B7 197
Columbia, Pa. F9 202
Columbia, S.C. D5 203
Columbia, S. Dak. B7 204
Columbia, Tenn. B4 205
Columbia, Va. D4 209
Columbia, co., Ark. D2 169
Columbia, co., Fla. B4 174
Columbia, co., Ga. C4 175
Columbia, co., N.Y. C7 196
Columbia, co., Oreg. B3 201
Columbia, co., Pa. D9 202
Columbia, co., Wash. C7 210
Columbia, co., Wis. E4 212
Columbia, basin, Wash. C6 210
Columbia, cape, N.W. Ter., Can. A22 118
Columbia, dam, Ala., Ga. D4 166, E1 175
Columbia, lake, B.C., Can. D10 149
Columbia, lake, Conn. C7 172
Columbia, mtn., Alta., Can. C2 148
Columbia, mts., B.C., Can. C7 149
Columbia, mts., Mex. B2 129
Columbia, riv., Can., U.S. G9 142, A3 158
Columbia City, Ind. B6 179
Columbia City, Oreg. B4 201
Columbia Cross Roads, Pa. C8 202
Columbia Falls, Maine D5 184
Columbia Falls, Mont. B2 190
Columbia Heights, Minn. E7 187
Columbia Heights, Wash. *C3 210
Columbia Road, res., S. Dak. B7 204
Columbian Track, Kans. E2 181
Columbiana, Ala. B3 166
Columbiana, Ohio B7 199
Columbiana, co., Ohio B7 199
Columbiaville, Mich. E7 186
Columbine, Colo. A4 171
Columbine, Wyo. B6 213
Columbus, Ark. D2 169
Columbus, Ga. D2 175
Columbus, Ind. F6 179
Columbus, Kans. E9 181
Columbus, Ky. B2 182
Columbus, Miss. B5 188
Columbus, Mont. E7 190
Columbus, Nebr. C8 191
Columbus, N.J. C3 194
Columbus, N. Mex. F2 195
Columbus, N.C. D4 197
Columbus, N. Dak. A3 198
Columbus, Ohio C2, C5 199
Columbus, Pa. C2 202
Columbus, Tex. E4 206
Columbus, Wis. E4 212
Columbus, co., N.C. C5 197
Columbus City, Iowa C6 180
Columbus Grove, Ohio B3 199
Columbus Junction, Iowa C6 180
Colusa, Calif. C2 170
Colusa, co., Calif. C2 170
Colver, Pa. E4 202
Colville, Wash. A8 210
Colville, Indian res., Wash. A6 210
Colville, lake, N.W. Ter., Can. C7 142
Colville, riv., Alsk. B9 167
Colville, riv., Wash. A8 210
Colvin, mtn., Ala. B4 166
Colvos, pass, Wash. D1 210
Colwich, Kans. B5, E6 181
Colwyn, Pa. *G11 202
Colwyn Bay, Wales A4 56
Colyell, creek, La. B6 183
Comacchio, It. B4 67
Comal, Tex. B4 206
Comal, co., Tex. E3 206
Comalapa, Guat. C2 130
Comanche, Okla. C4 200
Comanche, Tex. D3 206
Comanche, co., Kans. E4 181
Comanche, co., Okla. C3 200
Comanche, co., Tex. C3 206
Comarapa, Bol. C3 135
Comayagua, Hond. C4 130
Combahee, riv., S.C. F6 203
Combarbalá, Chile A2 136
Combeaufontaine, Fr. B1 66
Comber, Ont., Can. E2 153
Combermere, Ont., Can. B7 153
Combes, Tex. *F4 206
Combined Locks, Wis. A5 212
Combomune, Moz. B5 107
Combs, Ark. B2 169
Combs, Ky. C6 182
Comer, Ala. C4 166
Comer, Ga. B3 175
Comerio, P.R. C6 132
Comerio, mun., P.R. C6 132
Comertown, Mont. B12 190
Comfort, N.C. B6 197
Comfort, Tenn. D8 205
Comfort, Tex. E3 206
Comfort, W. Va. C3, D6 211
Comfort, pt., La. E6 183
Comfrey, Minn. F4 187
Comilla, Bngl. D9 87
Comines, Bel. D2 59
Comins, Mich. D6 186
Comiso, It. F5 67
Comitán, Mex. D6 129
Comite, riv., La. D4 183
Commack, N.Y. *F3 172
Commentry, Fr. D5 58
Commerce, Calif. *F4 170
Commerce, Ga. B3 175
Commerce, Mo. D8 189
Commerce, Okla. A7 200
Commerce, Tex. C5 206
Commerce City, Colo. B6 171
Commercial Point, Ohio C4 199
Commercy, Fr. C6 58
Commiskey, Ind. G6 179
Committee, bay, N.W. Ter., Can. C15 142
Commonwealth, bay, Ant. C27 120
Como, Que., Can. D8 154
Como, It. B2 67
Como, Miss. A4 188
Como, N.C. A6 197
Como, Tenn. A3 205
Como, lake, It. B2 67
Comobabi, Ariz. E4 168
Comodoro Rivadavia, Arg. D3 136
Comoè, riv., I.C. E4 103
Comoro, is., Afr. f9 107
COMORO ISLANDS, Fr. dep., Afr. f9 107
Comox, B.C., Can. E5 149
Compass Lake, Fla. B1, G3 174
Compeer, Alta., Can. D5 148
Competition, Mo. D5 189
Compiègne, Fr. C5 58
Comptche, Calif. C2 170
Compton, Calif. F2 170
Compton, Que., Can. D6 154
Compton, co., Que., Can. D6 154
Compton, Ill. B4 178
Comstock, Mich. F5 186
Comstock, Minn. D2 187
Comstock, Nebr. C6 191
Comstock, N.Y. B7 196
Comstock, Tex. E2 206
Comstock, Wis. C1 212
Conakry, Guinea E2 103
Conanicut, isl., R.I. C11 172
Conasauga, Tenn. D9 205
Concarneau, Fr. D2 58
Conceição do Norte, Braz. D1 138
Concepción, Arg. E2 135
Concepción, Bol. C3 135
Concepción, Bol. D3 135
Concepción, Chile B2 136
Concepción, Guat. C2 130
Concepción, Pan. F6 130
Concepción, Par. D4 135
Concepcion, Phil. o13 90
Concepcion, Tex. F3 206
Concepción, prov., Chile B2 136
Concepción del Oro, Mex. C4 129
Concepción del Uruguay, Arg. A5 136
Conception, Mo. A3 189
Conception, bay, Newf., Can. E5 152
Conception, pt., Calif. E3 170
Conception Junction, Mo. A3 189
Conchas, Braz. m7 137
Conchas Dam, N. Mex. B5 195
Conchas, res., N. Mex. B5 195
Conche, Newf., Can. C4 152
Conchi, Chile D2 135
Conchillas, Ur. g7 136
Concho, Ariz. C6 168
Concho, co., Tex. D3 206
Conconully, Wash. A6 210
Concord, Calif. B5 170
Concord, Del. C6 173
Concord, Fla. B2 174
Concord, Ga. C2 175
Concord, Ill. D3 178
Concord, Ky. B6 182
Concord, Mass. B5, C2 185
Concord, Mich. F6 186
Concord, Nebr. B9 191
Concord, N.H. D3 193
Concord, N.C. B3 197
Concord, Pa. F6 202
Concord, Tenn. D9, E11 205
Concord, Vt. C5 208
Concord, Va. D4 209
Concord, riv., Mass. A5 185
Concord North, N.C. *B3 197
Concordia, Arg. A5 136
Concordia, Kans. C6 181
Concordia, Mo. C4 189
Concordia, par., La. C4 183
Concrete, N. Dak. A8 198
Concrete, Wash. A4 210
Conda, Idaho G7 177
Conde, Braz. D3 138
Conde, S. Dak. B7 204
Conde [-sur-l'Escaut], Fr. D3 59
Condé [-sur-Marne], Fr. E4 59
Condé-sur-Noireau, Fr. C3 58
Condeúba, Braz. D2 138
Condino, It. D6 66
Condobolin, Austl. F6 112
Condom, Fr. F4 58
Condon, Mont. C3 190
Condon, Oreg. B6 201
Condor, range, Peru B2 134
Cone, Tex. C2 206
Conecuh, co., Ala. D2 166
Conecuh, riv., Ala. D3 166
Conegliano, It. B4 67
Conehatta, Miss. C4 188
Conejos, Colo. D4 171
Conejos, co., Colo. D4 171
Conejos, creek, Colo. D4 171
Conejos, peak, Colo. D4 171
Conemaugh, Pa. F4 202
Conemaugh River, flood control res., Pa. F3 202
Conestee, S.C. B3 203
Conesville, Iowa C6 180
Conesville, Ohio B6 199
Conetoe, N.C. B6 197
Coney, isl., N.Y. E1 196
Conflans, Fr. E5 59
Conflans-Ste. Honorine, Fr. g9 58
Confluence, Ky. C6 182
Confluence, Pa. G3 202
Confolens, Fr. D4 58
Confusion, bay, Newf., Can. C4 152
Confusion, range, Utah D2 207
Congamond, lakes, Conn. A6 172
Congaree, riv., S.C. D6 203
Conger, Minn. G5 187
Conger, mtn., Utah D2 207
Congleton, Eng. A5 56
Congo, Ohio C5 199
Congo, W. Va. A2 211
CONGO, country, Afr. B2 106
Congo, The (Kinshasa), see Zaire, country, Afr.
Congo, French 99
Congo, basin, Zaire A3 106
Congo, riv., Afr. G7 96
Congo Free State 99
Congress, Ariz. C3 168
Congress, Sask., Can. H2 155
Coniclere, Pan. k10 130
Conifer, N.Y. A6, B2 196
Conil, Sp. D2 65
Coniston, Ont., Can. A4, E9 153
Coniston Water, lake, Eng. F5 57
Conjeeveram, see Kancheepuram, India
Conklin, Alta., Can. B5 148
Conklin, Mich. E5 186
Conklin, pt., N.Y. G4 172
Conlen, Tex. A1 206
Conn, lake, Ire. C2 55
Conneaut, Ohio A7 199
Conneaut, creek, Ohio A7 199
Conneaut Lake, Pa. C1 202
Conneautville, Pa. C1 202
Connecticut, state, U.S. 172
Connecticut, riv., U.S. C6 172, B2 185, D2 193
Connell, Wash. C7 210
Connell, mtn., B.C., Can. A1 190
Connellsville, Pa. F2 202
Connelsville, Mo. A5 189
Connemara, mts., Ire. D2 55
Conner, Mont. E7 190
Connersville, Ind. E7 179
Connerville, Okla. C5 200
Conning Towers, Conn. *D8 172
Connoquenessing, Pa. *E1 202
Connors, N.B., Can. B1 151
Connors, Maine B1 151
Conococheague, creek, Md. A2 173
Conover, N.C. B2 197
Conowingo, Md. A5 173
Conowingo, dam, Md. A5 173
Conquest, Sask., Can. F2 155
Conrad, Iowa B5 180
Conrad, Mont. B5 190
Conrad III, crusade of 47
Conran, Mo. E8 189
Conrath, Wis. C2 212
Conroe, Tex. D5 206
Conroy, Iowa C5 180
Consecon, Ont., Can. D7 153
Conselheiro Lafaiete, Braz. F2 138
Consett, Eng. F7 57
Conshohocken, Pa. A11, F11 202
Consolación del Sur, Cuba D2 131
Consort, Alta., Can. C5 148
Constable, N.Y. A2 196
Constableville, N.Y. B5 196
Constance, see Bodensee, lake, Switz.
Constancia Central, P.R. B5 132
Constancia Central, P.R. D4 132
Constanța, Rom. C9 68
Constantia, N.Y. B4 196
Constantina, Sp. D3 65
Constantine, Alg. F10 64, B6 102
Constantine, Mich. G5 186
Constantinople, see Istanbul, Tur.
Constitución, Chile B2 136
Consuegra, Sp. C4 65
Consul, Sask., Can. H1 155
Consumnes, riv., Calif. B6 170
Consumo, P.R. C2 132
Contact, Nev. B7 192
Contai, India G11 88
Contamana, Peru C3 134
Contendas, Braz. D2 138
Content, keys, Fla. H5 174
Continental, Ariz. F5 168
Continental, Ohio A3 199
Continental, divide, Can., U.S. E6 142, B6 158
Continental, peak, Wyo. C4 213
Continental, res., Colo. D3 171
Continental Divide, N. Mex. B1 195
Contoocook, N.H. D3 193
Contoocook, riv., N.H. D3 193
Contra Costa, co., Calif. D2 170
Contraalmirante Cordero, Arg. B3 136
Contratación, Col. B3 133
Contrecoeur, Que., Can. D4 154
Contreras, Mex. h9 129
Contreras, N. Mex. C3 195
Contrexéville, Fr. A1 66
Contumaza, Peru C2 134
Contwoyto, lake, N.W. Ter., Can. C11 142
Convent, La. B6, D5 183
Converse, Ind. C6 179
Converse, La. C2 183
Converse, S.C. B4 203
Converse, co., Wyo. B7 213
Converse, lake, Ala. E1 166
Convoy, Ohio B3 199
Conway, Ark. B3 169
Conway, Iowa D3 180
Conway, Kans. D6 181
Conway, Mass. A2 185
Conway, Miss. C4 188
Conway, Mo. D5 189
Conway, N.H. C4 193
Conway, N.C. A6 197
Conway, N. Dak. A8 198
Conway, Pa. E1 202
Conway, S.C. D9 203
Conway, Tex. B2 206
Conway, Wales A4 56
Conway, co., Ark. B3 169
Conway, lake, N.H. C4 193
Conway Springs, Kans. E6 181
Conway Station, P.E.I., Can. C6 151
Conyers, Ga. B6, C2 175
Conyngham, Pa. *E9 202
Cooch-Behār, India C8 87
Cook, Austl. F5 111
Cook, Ind. B3 179
Cook, Minn. C6 187
Cook, Nebr. D9 191
Cook, co., Ga. E3 175
Cook, co., Ill. B6 178
Cook, co., Minn. A6 187
Cook, cape, B.C., Can. D4 149
Cook, inlet, Alsk. D9 167
Cook, mtn., W. Va. D6 211
Cook, pt., Md. C5 173
Cook, strait, N.Z. N15 112
COOK ISLANDS, N.Z. dep., Oceania H12 113
Cooke, co., Tex. C4 206
Cooke City, Mont. E7 190
Cookeville, Tenn. C8 205
Cooks, Mich. C4 186
Cooks, peak, N. Mex. E2 195
Cooks Falls, N.Y. D5 196
Cooks Harbour, Newf., Can. C4 152
Cooksburg, Pa. D3 202
Cookshire, Que., Can. D6 154
Cookstown, Ont., Can. C5 153
Cookstown, N.J. C3 194
Cooksville, Ill. C5 178
Cooktown, Austl. C8 111
Cookville, Tex. C5 206
Cool Ridge, W. Va. D3 211
Cool Valley, Mo. *C7 189
Cooleemee, N.C. B3 197
Coolgardie, Austl. F3 111
Coolidge, Ariz. E4 168
Coolidge, Ga. E3 175
Coolidge, Kans. D2 181
Coolidge, Tex. D4 206
Coolidge, mtn., S. Dak. D2 204
Coolin, Idaho A2 177
Coolspring, Pa. D3 202
Coolville, Ohio C6 199
Cooma, Austl. H7 112
Coon Rapids, Iowa C3 180
Coon Rapids, Minn. E7 187
Coon Valley, Wis. E2 212
Coonabarabran, Austl. E7 112
Coonamble, Austl. E7 112
Coonoor, India *F6 87
Cooper, Ala. C3 166
Cooper, Conn. D3 172
Cooper, Fla. *F6 174
Cooper, Iowa C3 180
Cooper, Ky. D5 182
Cooper, Maine *D5 184
Cooper, Tex. C5 206
Cooper, co., Mo. C5 189
Cooper, mtn., Alsk. g17 167
Cooper, riv., S.C. E8 203
Cooper Lake, Wyo. D7 213
Co-Operative, Ky. D5 182
Coopers Mills, Maine D3 184
Coopersburg, Pa. E10 202
Cooperstown, N.Y. C6 196
Cooperstown, N. Dak. B7 198
Cooperstown, Pa. D2 202
Cooperstown, Wis. A6 212
Coopersville, Mich. E5 186
Cooperton, Okla. C3 200
Coopertown, Tenn. A5 205
Coos, co., N.H. A4 193
Coos, co., Oreg. D2 201
Coos, riv., Oreg. D3 201
Coos Bay, Oreg. D2 201
Coosa, co., Ala. C3 166
Coosa, riv., Ala., Ga. A4 166
Coosada, Ala. C3 166
Coosawattee, riv., Ga. B2 175
Coosawhatchie, S.C. F6 203
Coosawhatchie, riv., S.C. F5 203
Cootamundra, Austl. G7 112
Cooter, Mo. E8 189
Copacabana, Arg. E2 135
Copacabana, Bol. C2 135
Copainalá, Mex. D6 129
Copake, N.Y. C7 196
Copalis Beach, Wash. B1 210
Copalis Crossing, Wash. B1 210
Copán, Hond. C3 130
Copan, Okla. A6 200
Cope, Colo. B8 171
Cope, S.C. E5 203
Copeland, Fla. G5 174
Copeland, Idaho A2 177
Copeland, Kans. E3 181
Copemish, Mich. D5 186
Copen, W. Va. C4 211
Copenhagen (København), Den. C6 62
Copenhagen, N.Y. B5 196
Copetonas, Arg. B4 136
Copeville, Tex. A6 206
Copiague, N.Y. G3 172
Copiah, co., Miss. D3 188
Copiapó, Chile E1 135
Copinsay, isl., Scot. B6 57
Coplay, Pa. *E11 202
Copparo, It. B3 67
Coppell, Tex. *C4 206
Copper, butte, Wash. A7 210
Copper, mtn., Wyo. B5 213
Copper, mts., Ariz. E2 168
Copper, ridge, Tenn. E11 205
Copper, riv., Alsk. C11 167
Copper Belt, prov., Zambia D4 106
Copper Center, Alsk. C10, g19 167
Copper Cliff, Ont., Can. *E9 153
Copper Harbor, Mich. A3 186
Copper Hill, Va. D2 209
Copper Mountain, B.C., Can. E7 149
Copperas Cove, Tex. D4 206
Copperfield, Nev. B2 192
Copperhill, Tenn. D9 205
Coppermine, N.W. Ter., Can. C9 144
Coppermine, riv., N.W. Ter., Can. C10 142
Coquet, riv., Eng. E7 57
Coquí, P.R. D6 132
Coquille, Oreg. D2 201
Coquimbana, Chile E1 135
Coquimbo, Chile E1 135
Coquimbo, prov., Chile E1 135
Cora, Wyo. C3 213
Corabia, Rom. D7 68
Coracora, Peru E3 134
Coral, Mich. E5 186
Coral, Pa. F3 202
Coral, sea, Pac. O. G9 113
Coral Gables, Fla. F3, G6 174
Coral Rapids, Ont., Can. E9 153
Coralville, Iowa C6 180
Coralville, res., Iowa C6 180
Coram, Mont. B2 190
Coram, N.Y. D4 196
Coraopolis, Pa. A5, F1 202
Corato, It. D6 67
Corazón, Ec. B2 134
Corbeil, Fr. C5 58
Corbeny, Fr. E3 59
Corbett, N.Y. C5 196
Corbetton, Ont., Can. C4 153
Corbie, Fr. C5 58
Corbin, Kans. E6 181
Corbin, Ky. D5 182
Corbin, La. A6 183
Corbin, Mont. D4 190
Corbin City, N.J. E3 194
Corby, Eng. B7 56
Corby, Eng. B7 56
Corcoran, Calif. D4 170
Corcoran, Minn. *E5 187
Corcovado, gulf, Chile C2 136
Cord, Ark. B4 169
Cordaville, Mass. D1 185
Cordele, Ga. E3 175
Cordelia, Calif. B5 170
Cordell (New Cordell), Okla. B3 200
Cordell Hull, glacier, Ant. B34 120
Cordell Hull, res., Tenn. C8 205
Corder, Mo. B4 189
Cordesville, S.C. E8 203
Cordillera, dept., Par. D4 135
Cordillera Central, range, Bol., Col. C2 133, C2 135
Cordillera Occidental, range, Bol., Col. C2 133, C2 135
Cordillera Occidental o de la Costa, range, Peru D3 134
Cordillera Oriental, range, Bol., Col. C3 133, C3 135
Córdoba, Arg. A4 136
Córdoba, Mex. D5, n15 129
Córdoba, Sp. D3 65
Córdoba, prov., Arg. A4 136
Córdoba, dept., Col. B2 133
Cordon, Phil. n13 90
Cordova, Ala. B2 166
Cordova, Alsk. C10, g19 167
Cordova, Ill. B3 178
Cordova, Md. C6 173
Cordova, Mont. C5 190
Cordova, Nebr. *D8 191
Cordova, N.C. C4 197
Córdova, Peru D2 134
Cordova, S.C. E6 203
Cordova, Tenn. B2 205
Cordova, peak, Alsk. C10, g19 167
Cordova Mines, Ont., Can. C7 153
Corea, Maine D5 184
Coreaú, Braz. B2 138
Corella, Sp. A5 65
Corfu, N.Y. C2 196
Corfu, see Kérkira, isl., Grc.
Cori, It. h9 67
Corigliano [Calabro], It. E6 67
Corinna, Maine D3 184
Corinne, Utah B3 207
Corinne, W. Va. D3 211
Corinth, Ga. C2 175
Corinth, see Kórinthos, Grc.
Corinth, Ky. B5 182
Corinth, Maine *D4 184
Corinth, Miss. A5 188
Corinth, N.Y. B7 196
Corinth, N. Dak. A2 198
Corinth, Vt. C4 208
Corinth, W. Va. B5 211
Corinth, bay, Grc. h9 69
Corinth, canal, Grc. h10 69
Corinth, gulf, Grc. C4 69
Corinto, Braz. E2 138
Corinto, Nic. D4 130
Corisco, isl., Afr. E1 104
Cork, Ire. E2 55
Cork, hbr., Ire. E2 55
Cork Station, N.B., Can. D3 151
Corleone, It. F4 67
Corlu, Tur. B6 85
Cormack, mtn., Newf., Can. D4 152
Cormeilles-en-Parisis, Fr. g9 58
Cormoran, reef, Palau Is. 114
Cormorant, Man., Can. B1 150
Cormorant, lake, Man., Can. B1 150
Corn, Okla. B3 200
Corn, creek, Ariz. B5 168
Corn, is., Nic. D6 130
Corn Hill, N.B., Can. D4 151
Corncake, inlet, N.C. D6 197
Cornelia, Ga. B3 175
Cornelius, N.C. B3 197
Cornelius, Oreg. B1 201
Cornell, Ill. C5 178
Cornell, Wis. C2 212
Cornellá, Sp. B6 65
Corner Brook, Newf., Can. D3 152
Cornersville, Tenn. B5 205
Cornerville, Ark. D4 169
Cornfield, Ariz. B6 168
Cornfield, pt., Conn. D7 172
Cornimont, Fr. B2 66
Corning, Ark. A5 169
Corning, Calif. C2 170
Corning, Sask., Can. H4 155
Corning, Iowa D3 180
Corning, Kans. C7 181
Corning, Mo. A2 189
Corning, N.Y. C3 196
Corning, Ohio C5 199
Cornish, Maine E2 184

INDEX KEY Each place listed in **Bold-faced Type** has its population listed in the Population tables, pages 230 to 280.
Each country, shown in CAPITAL LETTERS, has its population listed in the World Political Information Table, pages 6 to 10.
* Does not appear on map; key shows general location.

Cornish, Okla....C4 200
Cornish, Utah....B4 207
Cornish Flat, N.H....D2 193
Cornishville, Ky....C5 182
Corno, mtn., It.....C4 67
Cornplanter, Indian res., Pa.....C3 202
Cornucopia, Oreg....C9 201
Cornucopia, Wis....B2 212
Cornudas, Tex....F1 206
Cornville, Ariz....C4 168
Cornville, Maine....D3 184
Cornwall, Ba. Is....C5 131
Cornwall, Ont., Can....B10 153
Cornwall, P.E.I., Can....*C6 151
Cornwall, Conn....B3 172
Cornwall, Pa....F9 202
Cornwall, Vt....D2 208
Cornwall, Va....C3 209
Cornwall, co., Eng....D3 56
Cornwall Bridge, Conn....B3 172
Cornwall-on-the-Hudson, N.Y....D6 196
Cornwallis, W. Va....B3 211
Cornwallis, isl., N.W. Ter., Can.....B13 142
Cornwell, Fla....E5 174
Cornwells Heights, Pa....A12 202
Coro, Ven....A4 133
Coroatá, Braz....B2 138
Corocoro, Bol....C2 135
Coroico, Bol....C2 135
Corolla, N.C....A8 197
Coromandel, N.Z....L15 112
Coromandel, coast, India....F7 87
Corona, Ala....B2 166
Corona, Calif....F3, F5 170
Corona, N. Mex....C4 195
Corona, S. Dak....B9 204
Coronaca, S.C....C3 203
Coronach, Sask., Can....H3 155
Coronado, Calif....E2, F5 170
Coronation, Alta., Can....C5 148
Coronation, gulf, N.W. Ter., Can.....C10 142
Coronation, isl., Atl. O.....C8 120
Coronda, Arg....A4 136
Coronel, Chile....B2 136
Coronel Brandsen, Arg....B5, g7 136
Coronel Dorrego, Arg....B4 136
Coronel Oviedo, Par....E4 135
Coronel Pringles, Arg....B4 136
Coronel Pringles, Arg....C4 136
Coronel Suárez, Arg....B4 136
Coronela, Cuba....k11 131
Coronie, Sur....A3 139
Corowa, Austl....G6 112
Corozal, Br. Hond....A3 130
Corozal, Col....B2 133
Corozal, P.R....B5 132
Corozal, mun., P.R....B5 132
Corpen, Arg....D3 136
Corps, Fr....E1 66
Corpus Christi, Tex....F4 206
Corral, Chile....B2 136
Corral, Idaho....F4 177
Corral de Almaguer, Sp....C4 65
Corral Viejo, P.R....C4 132
Corrales, Col....B3 133
Corralillo, Cuba....D3 131
Corravillers, Fr....B2 66
Correctionville, Iowa....B2 180
Corregidor, isl., Phil.....o13 90
Correll, Minn....E2 187
Corrente, Braz....D2 138
Correntes, Braz....k5 138
Correntina, Braz....D2 138
Correo, N. Mex....C2 195
Corrib, lake, Ire.....D2 55
Corrientes, Arg....E4 135
Corrientes, prov., Arg....E4 135
Corrientes, cape, Cuba....E1 131
Corrientes, cape, Mex.....C3 129
Corrigan, Tex....D5 206
Corriganville, Md....D2 173
Corrine, key, Fla.....G6 174
Corry, Pa....C2 202
Corryton, Tenn....C10 205
Corse, cape, Fr.....C2 67
Corsica, Pa....D3 202
Corsica, P.R....B2 132
Corsica, S. Dak....D7 204
Corsica, isl., Fr.....C11 64
Corsicana, Tex....C4 206
Corson, S. Dak....D9 204
Corson, co., S. Dak....B4 204
Cortada Central, P.R....D5 132
Cortaro, Ariz....E4 168
Corte, Fr....C2 67
Corte Alto, Chile....C2 136
Corte Madera, Calif....*B5 170
Cortegana, Sp....D2 65
Cortemilia, It....E4 66
Cortes, Sp....D3 65
Cortez, Colo....D2 171
Cortez, Fla....F2 174
Cortez, mts., Nev.....C5 192
Cortina d'Ampezzo, It....C8 66
Cortland, Ill....B5 178
Cortland, Ind....G6 179
Cortland, Nebr....D9 191
Cortland, N.Y....C4 196
Cortland, Ohio....A7 199
Cortland, co., N.Y....C4 196
Cortona, It....C3 67
Coruche, Port....C1 65
Çorum, Tur....B10 85
Corumbá, Braz....B1 137
Corumbá, riv., Braz.....E1 138
Corunna, Ont., Can....E2 153
Corunna, Ind....B7 179
Corunna, Mich....F6 186
Corvallis, Mont....D2 190
Corvallis, Oreg....C1, C3 201
Corvo, isl., Port. (Azores)....g8 102
Corwin, Kans....E5 181
Corwin Springs, Mont....E6 190
Corwith, Iowa....B4 180
Cory, Ind....F3 179
Corydon, Ind....H5 179
Corydon, Iowa....D4 180
Corydon, Ky....C2 182
Coryell, co., Tex....D4 206
Coryville, Pa....C5 202
Cos Cob, Conn....E2 172
Cosalá, Mex....C3 129
Cosby, Mo....B3 189
Cosby, Tenn....D10 205
Coscomatepec, Mex....n15 129
Cosenza, It....E6 67
Cosgrave, Nev....C3 192
Coshocton, Ohio....B6 199
Coshocton, co., Ohio....B6 199
Cosmopolis, Wash....C2 210
Cosmos, Minn....F4 187
Cosne [-sur-Loire], Fr....D5 58
Cossatot, mts., Ark.....C2 169
Cossatot, riv., Ark.....C1 169
Cossonay, Switz....C2 66
Costa Mesa, Calif....F3 170
COSTA RICA, country, N.A....E5 130
in 1800's....127
Costello, Pa....C5 202
Coster, cape, Mare I.....115
Costermansville, see Bukavu, Zaire
Costigan, Maine....C4 184
Costilla, N. Mex....A4 195
Costilla, co., Colo....D5 171
Coswig, Ger....B7 61
Coswig, Ger....B8 61
Cotabato, Phil....D6 90
Cotagaita, Bol....D2 135
Cotahuasi, Peru....D2 134
Cotati, Calif....B5 170
Cote d'Or, ridge, Fr.....D6 58
Côte-St.-Luc, Que., Can....*D9 154
Coteau, N. Dak....A3 198
Coteau, plat., Sask., Can.....G3 155
Coteau Landing, Que., Can....D3 154
Coteaux, Hai....F6 131
Côtes de Fer, Hai....F7 131
Côtes de L'ile de France, mts., Fr.....F3 59
Côtes de Meuse, mts., Fr.....E5 59
Cotesfield, Nebr....C7 191
Cotija, Mex....n12 129
Cotingo, riv., Braz.....C5 133
Coto Laurel, P.R....C4 132
Cotonou, Dah....E5 103
Cotopaxi, Colo....C5 171
Cotopaxi, prov., Ec....B2 134
Cotopaxi, vol., Ec.....B2 134
Cotswold, hills, Eng.....C5 56
Cottage City, Md....*C1 173
Cottage Grove, Minn....E7 187
Cottage Grove, Oreg....D3 201
Cottage Grove, Tenn....A3 205
Cottage Grove, Wis....*E4 212
Cottage Grove, dam, Oreg.....D3 201
Cottage Hills, Ill....*E3 178
Cottageville, S.C....F7 203
Cottageville, W. Va....C3 211
Cottam, Ont., Can....E2 153
Cottbus, Ger....B9 61
Cottel, isl., Newf., Can.....D5 152
Cotter, Ark....A3 169
Cotter, cape, Ant.....B29 120
Cottian Alps, mts., Fr.....E7 58
Cottingham, Eng....A7 56
Cottle, co., Tex....B2 206
Cottle Knob, mtn., W. Va.....C4 211
Cottleville, Mo....A7 189
Cotton, Ga....E2 175
Cotton, Minn....C6 187
Cotton, co., Okla....C3 200
Cotton Center, Tex....B2 206
Cotton Plant, Ark....B4 169
Cotton Town, Ark....B2 169
Cotton Valley, La....B2 183
Cottondale, Ala....B2 166
Cottondale, Fla....B1, G3 174
Cottonport, La....D3 183
Cottonton, Ala....C4 166
Cottontown, Tenn....A5 205
Cottonwood, Ala....D4 166
Cottonwood, Ariz....C3 168
Cottonwood, Calif....B2 170
Cottonwood, Idaho....C2 177
Cottonwood, Minn....F3 187
Cottonwood, Okla....C5 200
Cottonwood, S. Dak....D4 204
Cottonwood, Tex....C3 206
Cottonwood, co., Minn....F3 187
Cottonwood, creek, Wyo.....B4 213
Cottonwood, creek, Wyo.....C2 213
Cottonwood, creek, Wyo.....D2 213
Cottonwood, riv., Kans.....D7 181
Cottonwood, riv., Minn.....F3 187
Cottonwood, wash, Utah....F6 207
Cottonwood Falls, Kans....D7 181
Cotuit, Mass....C7 185
Cotulla, Tex....E3 206
Couchiching, lake, Ont., Can.....C5 153
Couchwood, La....B2 183
Coudekerque-Branche, Fr....B5 58
Couderay, Wis....C2 212
Coudersport, Pa....C5 202
Coudres, isl., Que., Can.....B7 154
Couëron, Fr....D3 58
Cougar, res., Oreg.....C4 201
Coughlan, hbr., Guadalcanal I.....115
Coul, pt., Scot.....E2 57
Coulee, N. Dak....A3 198
Coulee, creek, Wash.....D7 210
Coulee City, Wash....B6 210
Coulee Dam, Wash....B7 210
Coulommiers, Fr....C5 58
Coulonge, riv., Que., Can.....A8 153
Coulsdon [& Purley], Eng....m12 55
Coulter, Man., Can....E1 150
Coulter, Iowa....B4 180
Coulterville, Calif....D3 170
Coulterville, Ill....E4 178
Coulwood, Va....B3 209
Counce, Tenn....B3 205
Council, Ga....F4 175
Council, Idaho....E2 177
Council, Va....B3 209
Council, mtn., Idaho....E2 177
Council Bluffs, Iowa....C2 180
Council Grove, Kans....D7 181
Council Grove, res., Kans.....D7 181
Council Hill, Okla....B6 200
Country Club Hills, Ill....*B6 178
Country Club Hills, Mo....*C7 189
Countryside, Ill....*B6 178
Countyline, Okla....C4 200
Coupar Angus, Scot....D5 57
Coupeville, Wash....A3 210
Coupon, Pa....E4 202
Courantyne, riv., Guy.....A3 139
Courbevoie, Fr....g10 58
Courcelles, Que., Can....D7 154
Courland (Kurisches Haff), lagoon, Sov. Un.....A6 70
Courmayeur, It....D2 66
Coursan, Fr....F5 58
Courtenay, B.C., Can....E5 149
Courtenay, N. Dak....B7 198
Courtland, Ala....A2 166
Courtland, Calif....B6 170
Courtland, Ont., Can....E4 153
Courtland, Kans....C6 181
Courtland, Minn....F4 187
Courtland, Miss....A4 188
Courtland, Va....E5 209
Courtney, Okla....D4 200
Courtrai, see Kortrijk, Bel.
Courtright, Ont., Can....E2 153
Courval, Sask., Can....G2 155
Courville, Que., Can....C9 154
Coushatta, La....B2 183
Coutances, Fr....C3 58
Coutras, Fr....E3 58
Coutts, Alta., Can....E5 148
Couvin, Bel....D4 59
Cove, Ark....C1 169
Cove, Minn....D5 187
Cove, Oreg....B9 201
Cove, Scot....C3 57
Cove, Tex....F5 206
Cove, Utah....B4 207
Cove, Wash....D1 210
Cove, isl., Ont., Can.....B3 153
Cove, pt., Md.....D5 173
Cove City, N.C....B6 197
Cove City, Tex....*D6 206
Covedale, Ohio....D2 199
Covelo, Calif....C2 170
Coventry, Conn....B7 172
Coventry, Eng....B6 56
Coventry, R.I....C10 172
Coventry, Vt....B4 208
Coventry Center, R.I....C10 172
Covered Bridge, N.H.....B2 193
Covert, Mich....F4 186
Covesville, Va....D4 209
Covilhã, Port....B2 65
Covin, Ala....B2 166
Covina, Calif....*E5 170
Covington, Ga....C3 175
Covington, Ind....D3 179
Covington, Ky....A5, A7 182
Covington, La....B7, D5 183
Covington, Mich....B2 186
Covington, Ohio....B3 199
Covington, Okla....A4 200
Covington, Pa....C7 202
Covington, Tenn....B2 205
Covington (Independent City), Va....D3 209
Covington, Wash....D2 210
Covington, co., Ala....D3 166
Covington, co., Miss....D4 188
Cow, creek, Wash.....C7 210
Cow, lake, Oreg.....D9 201
Cow Creek, lakes, Oreg.....D9 201
Cow Head, Newf., Can....D3, k10 152
Cow Knob, mtn., W. Va.....C5 211
Cow Springs, Ariz....A5 168
Cowal, lake, Austl.....F6 112
Cowan, Ind....D7 179
Cowan, Tenn....B5 205
Cowan, lake, Austl.....F3 110
Cowan, lake, Sask., Can.....C2 155
Cowan, riv., Sask., Can.....C2 155
Cowan Knob, mtn., Ark.....B2 169
Cowangie, Austl....G3 112
Cowansville, Que., Can....D5 154
Cowansville, Pa....E2 202
Coward, S.C....D8 203
Coward Springs, Austl....E6 111
Cowarts, Ala....D4 166
Cowden, Ill....D5 178
Cowdenbeath, Scot....D5 57
Cowdrey, Colo....A4 171
Cowee, mts., N.C.....D2 197
Cowell, Ark....B2 169
Cowen, W. Va....C4 211
Cowen, mtn., Mont.....E6 190
Cowes, Eng....D6 56
Coweta, Okla....B6 200
Coweta, co., Ga....C2 175
Cowgill, Mo....B4 189
Cowichan, lake, B.C., Can.....E5 149
Cowichan Station, B.C., Can....B9 149
Cowiche, Wash....C5 210
Cowles, Nebr....D7 191
Cowley, Alta., Can....E3 148
Cowley, Wyo....A4 213
Cowley, co., Kans....E7 181
Cowlic, Ariz....F4 168
Cowlington, Okla....B7 200
Cowlitz, co., Wash....C3 210
Cowlitz, riv., Wash.....C3 210
Cowpasture, riv., Va.....C3 209
Cowpen, mtn., Ga.....B2 175
Cowpens, S.C....A4 203
Cowra, Austl....F7 112
Cowskin, creek, Kans.....B5 181
Cox City, Okla....C4 200
Coxim, Braz....B2 137
Coxipi, riv., Que., Can.....C2 152
Cox's Cove, Newf., Can....D2 152
Coxs Mills, W. Va....B4 211
Coxsackie, N.Y....C7 196
Coy, Ala....D2 166
Coy, Ark....C4 169
Coya, Chile....D2 135
Coyame, Mex....B3 129
Coyanosa, draw, Tex.....D1 206
Coyle, Okla....B4 200
Coyoacán, Mex....h9, n14 129
Coyote, N. Mex....A3 195
Coyote, basin, Colo.....A2 171
Coyville, Kans....E8 181
Cozad, Nebr....D6 191
Cozahome, Ark....A3 169
Cozumel, Mex....C7 129
Cozumel, isl., Mex.....C7 129
Crab, creek, Wash.....B7 210
Crab, creek, Wash.....C6 210
Crab Orchard, Ky....C5 182
Crab Orchard, Nebr....D9 191
Crab Orchard, Tenn....D9 205
Crab Orchard, W. Va....D7 211
Crab Orchard, lake, Ill.....F5 178
Crab Orchard, mts., Tenn.....D9 205
Crabtree, Oreg....C2, C4 201
Crabtree, Pa....F3 202
Crabtree Mills, Que., Can....D4 154
Cracking, riv., Sask., Can.....D4 155
Cracow, Austl....B8 112
Cradle, mtn., Austl.....o15 110
Cradock, S. Afr....D4 107
Crafton, Pa....B5 202
Craftsbury, Vt....B4 208
Craftsbury Common, Vt....B4 208
Cragford, Ala....B4 166
Cragmor, Colo....C6 171
Craig, Alsk....D13, n23 167
Craig, Colo....A3 171
Craig, Iowa....B1 180
Craig, Mo....A2 189
Craig, Mont....C5 190
Craig, Nebr....C9 191
Craig, co., Okla....A6 200
Craig, co., Va....D2 209
Craig, creek, Va.....D2 209
Craig Beach, Ohio....*A7 199
Craig Harbor, N.W. Ter., Can....B23 118
Craighead, co., Ark....B5 169
Craighouse, Scot....E3 57
Craighurst, Ont., Can....C5 153
Craigmont, Idaho....C2 177
Craigmyle, Alta., Can....D4 148
Craigs Road Station, Que., Can....D8 154
Craigsville, Va....C3 209
Craigsville, W. Va....C4 211
Craigville, Ind....C7 179
Craigville, Minn....C5 187
Craik, Sask., Can....F3 155
Crail, Scot....D6 57
Crailsheim, Ger....D5 61
Craiova, Rom....C6 68
Cramerton, N.C....B2 197
Crampel, Alg....C4 102
Cranberry, Pa....D2 202
Cranberry, lake, N.Y.....A6 196
Cranberry Isles, Maine....D4 184
Cranberry Lake, N.Y....A6, B2 196
Cranberry Portage, Man., Can....B1 150
Cranbrook, B.C., Can....E10 149
Cranbury, N.J....C3 194
Cranbury Station, N.J....C4 194
Crandall, Man., Can....D1 150
Crandall, Ga....B2 175
Crandall, Miss....D5 188
Crandall, S. Dak....B8 204
Crandall, Tex....B6 206
Crandon, Wis....C5 212
Crane, Mo....E4 189
Crane, Mont....C12 190
Crane, Oreg....D8 201
Crane, Tex....D1 206
Crane, co., Tex....D1 206
Crane, creek, Ohio....A2 199
Crane, lake, Sask., Can.....G1 155
Crane, lake, Ill.....C3 178
Crane, lake, Minn.....B6 187
Crane, mtn., Oreg.....E6 201
Crane Creek, res., Idaho....E2 177
Crane Hill, Ala....A2 166
Crane Lake, Minn....B6 187
Crane Neck, pt., N.Y.....F4 172
Crane Prairie, res., Oreg.....D5 201
Crane Valley, Sask., Can....H3 155
Cranesville, Pa....C1 202
Cranfield, Miss....D2 188
Cranford, N.J....B4 194
Cransac, Fr....E5 58
Cranston, R.I....B11 172
Crapo, Md....D5 173
Crary, N. Dak....A7 198
Craryville, N.Y....C7 196
Crasna, riv., Rom.....B6 68
Crater, lake, Oreg.....E4 201
Crater, pt., New Britain I.....115
Crater Lake, Oreg....E4 201
Crater Lake, nat. park, Oreg.....E4 201
Craters of the Moon, nat. mon., Idaho....F5 177
Crateús, Braz....C2 138
Crato, Braz....C3 138
Craven, Sask., Can....G3 155
Craven, co., N.C....B6 197
Cravinhos, Braz....k8 137
Crawford, Colo....C3 171
Crawford, Ga....C3 175
Crawford, Maine....*C5 184
Crawford, Miss....B5 188
Crawford, Nebr....B2 191
Crawford, Okla....B2 200
Crawford, co., Ark....B1 169
Crawford, co., Ga....D3 175
Crawford, co., Ill....D6 178
Crawford, co., Ind....H4 179
Crawford, co., Iowa....B2 180
Crawford, co., Kans....E9 181
Crawford, co., Mich....D6 186
Crawford, co., Mo....D6 189
Crawford, co., Ohio....B5 199
Crawford, co., Pa....C1 202
Crawford, co., Wis....E3 212
Crawford, lake, Maine....C5 184
Crawford House, N.H....B4 193
Crawfordsville, Ark....B5 169
Crawfordsville, Ind....D4 179
Crawfordsville, Iowa....C6 180
Crawfordsville, Oreg....C4 201
Crawfordville, Fla....B2 174
Crawfordville, Ga....C4 175
Crawley, Eng....*C7 56
Crayne, Ky....A3 182
Crazy, mts., Mont.....D6 190
Crazy, peak, Mont.....D6 190
Crazy Woman, creek, Wyo.....A6 213
Creagerstown, Md....A3 173
Creal Springs, Ill....F5 178
Creamridge, N.J....C3 194
Crean, lake, Sask., Can.....C2 155
Crediton, Eng....D4 56
Cree, lake, Sask., Can.....E11 142
Creede, Colo....D4 171
Creedmoor, N.C....A5 197
Creek, co., Okla....B5 200
Creekside, Pa....E3 202
Creelman, Sask., Can....H4 155
Creemore, Ont., Can....C4 153
Creighton, Sask., Can....C5 155
Creighton, Mo....C3 189
Creighton, Nebr....B8 191
Creighton, Pa....A6 202
Creighton, S. Dak....C3 204
Creighton Mine, Ont., Can....A3, E9 153
Creil, Fr....C5 58
Crellin, Md....D1 173
Crema, It....B2 67
Cremona, It....B3 67
Crenshaw, Miss....A3 188
Crenshaw, Pa....D4 202
Crenshaw, co., Ala....D3 166
Creola, Ala....E1 166
Creole, La....E2 183
Crépy-en-Valois, Fr....C2 59
Cres, isl., Yugo.....C2 68
Cresaptown, Md....D2 173
Cresbard, S. Dak....B7 204
Crescent, Ga....E5 175
Crescent, Iowa....C2 180
Crescent, Mo....B7 189
Crescent, N.Y....C7 196
Crescent, Okla....B4 200
Crescent, Oreg....D5 201
Crescent, lake, Fla.....C5 174
Crescent, lake, Oreg.....D5 201
Crescent, lake, Wash.....A2 210
Crescent, range, N.H.....B4 193
Crescent Beach, Conn....D8 172
Crescent City, Calif....B1 170
Crescent City, Fla....C5 174
Crescent City, Ill....C6 178
Crescent City Northwest, Calif....*B1 170
Crescent Junction, Utah....E6 207
Crescent Lake, Oreg....D5 201
Crescent Springs, Ky....A7 182
Cresco, Iowa....A5 180
Cresco, Pa....D11 202
Crespo, see Villa Crespo, Arg.
Cresskill, N.J....D5 194
Cresson, Pa....F4 202
Cresson, Tex....B5 206
Cressona, Pa....E9 202
Crest, Fr....E6 58
Crest Hill, Ill....*F2 178
Crested Butte, Colo....C4 171
Cresthill, Va....C5 209
Crestline, Calif....F3 170
Crestline, Nev....F7 192
Crestline, Ohio....B5 199
Creston, B.C., Can....E9 149
Creston, Newf., Can....E4 152
Creston, Ill....B5 178
Creston, Iowa....C3 180
Creston, Mont....B2 190
Creston, Nebr....C8 191
Creston, Ohio....B6 199
Creston, S.C....D6 203
Creston, Tenn....C8 205
Creston, Wash....B7 210
Creston, W. Va....C3 211
Crestone, Colo....D5 171
Crestone, peak, Colo.....D5 171
Crestview, Fla....G2 174
Crestwood, Ill....*B6 178
Crestwood, Ky....A4, B4 182
Crestwood, Mo....*C7 189
Crestwynd, Sask., Can....G3 155
Creswell, N.C....B7 197
Creswell, Oreg....D3 201
Crete, Ill....B6, F3 178
Crete, Nebr....D9 191
Crete, N. Dak....C8 198
Crete, isl., Grc.....E5 69
Crete, sea, Grc.....D5 69
Cretone, It....g9 67
Creuse, riv., Fr.....D4 58
Creutzwald, Fr....C7 58
Creve Coeur, Ill....C4 178
Creve Coeur, Mo....*C7 189
Crevillente, Sp....C5 65
Crewe, Eng....A5 56
Crewe, Va....D4 209
Crewkerne, Eng....D5 56
Criam More, mtn., Scot.....B4 57
Cricket, N.C....A2 197
Cricket, mts., Utah....E2 207
Cridersville, Ohio....B3 199
Crieff, Scot....D5 57
Criffel, mtn., Scot.....F5 57
Criglersville, Va....C4 209
Crikvenica, Yugo....C2 68
Crimea, see Krym, Sov. Un.
Crimmitschau, Ger....C7 61
Crinan, Scot....D3 57
Cripple Creek, Colo....C5 171
Cripple Creek, Va....E1 209
Crisfield, Md....E6 173
Crisp, co., Ga....E3 175
Criss Creek, B.C., Can....D7 149
Crissolo, It....E3 66
Cristal, mts., Gabon....E2 104
Cristalina, Braz....E1 138
Cristobal, C.Z....k11 130
Cristobal Colón, mtn., Col.....A3 133
Crişul Alb, riv., Rom.....B5 68
Crittenden, Ky....B5, B7 182
Crittenden, Va....B6 209
Crittenden, co., Ark....B5 169
Crittenden, co., Ky....A3 182
Crivitz, Ger....E5 62
Crivitz, Wis....C6 212
Crna, riv., Yugo.....E5 68
Črnomelj, Yugo....C2 68
Croatia, reg., Yugo....C2 68
Croche, riv., Que., Can.....A5 154
Crocheron, Md....D5 173
Crocker, Mo....D5 189
Crocker, S. Dak....B8 204
Crockett, Calif....B5 170
Crockett, Tex....D5 206
Crockett, co., Tenn....B2 205
Crockett, co., Tex....D2 206
Crockett Mills, Tenn....B2 205
Crocketville, S.C....F5 203
Crofton, Ky....C2 182
Crofton, Nebr....B8 191
Croghan, N.Y....B5 196
Croix, Fr....D3 59
Croker, cape, Ont., Can.....C4 153
Croker, isl., Austl.....B5 110
Cromarty, Scot....C4 57
Cromer, Man., Can....E1 150
Cromer, Eng....B9 56
Cromona (Haymond), Ky....C7 182
Cromwell, Ala....C1 166
Cromwell, Conn....C6 172
Cromwell, Ind....B6 179
Cromwell, Iowa....C3 180
Cromwell, Ky....C3 182
Cromwell, Minn....D6 187
Cromwell, N.Z....P12 112
Cromwell, Okla....B5 200
Crook, Colo....A8 171
Crook, Eng....F7 57
Crook, co., Oreg....C6 201
Crook, co., Wyo....A8 213
Crooked, creek, Ark.....A3 169
Crooked, creek, Ind.....H7 179
Crooked, creek, Kans.....B7 181
Crooked, creek, Kans.....E3 181
Crooked, creek, Pa.....C7 202
Crooked, isl., Ba. Is.....D6 131
Crooked, lake, Newf., Can.....D3 152
Crooked, lake, Fla.....E5 174
Crooked, lake, Minn.....B7 187
Crooked, riv., B.C., Can.....B6 149
Crooked, riv., Oreg.....C6 201
Crooked Creek, Alsk....C8 167
Crooked Creek, Pa....C7 202
Crooked Creek, res., Pa.....E3 202
Crooked River, Sask., Can....E4 155
Crooks, S. Dak....D9 204
Crookston, Minn....C2 187
Crookston, Nebr....B5 191
Crooksville, Ohio....C5 199
Crookwell, Austl....G7 112
Cropper, Ky....B4 182
Cropsey, Ill....C5 178
Croque, hbr., Newf., Can.....C4 152
Crosby, Eng....*A5 56
Crosby, Minn....D5 187
Crosby, Miss....D2 188
Crosby, N. Dak....A2 198
Crosby, Pa....C5 202
Crosby, Tex....F5 206
Crosby, co., Tex....C2 206
Crosby, mtn., Wyo.....B3 213
Crosbyton, Tex....C2 206
Crosland, Ga....E3 175
Cross, S.C....E7 203
Cross, Tex....D4 206
Cross, co., Ark....B5 169
Cross, cape, S.W. Afr.....B1 107
Cross, creek, W. Va.....B2 211
Cross, isl., Maine....D5 184
Cross, lake, Man., Can.....B3 150
Cross, lake, Man., Can.....C2 150
Cross, lake, La.....B2 183
Cross, lake, Maine....A4 184
Cross, mts., Ark.....C1 169
Cross, riv., Nig.....E6 103
Cross, sound, Alsk.....k21 167
Cross Anchor, S.C....B4 203
Cross Canyon, Ariz....B6 168
Cross City, Fla....C3 174
Cross Creek, N.B., Can....C3 151
Cross Fell, mtn., Eng.....F6 57
Cross Hill, S.C....C4 203
Cross Keys, N.J....D2 194

INDEX KEY Each place listed in **Bold-faced Type** has its population listed in the Population tables, pages 230 to 280.
Each country, shown in CAPITAL LETTERS, has its population listed in the World Political Information Table, pages 6 to 10.
* Does not appear on map; key shows general location.

Cross Lake, Man., Can. B3 150
Cross Mill, N.C. D4 197
Cross Plains, Ind. G7 179
Cross Plains, Tenn. A5 205
Cross Plains, Tex. C3 206
Cross Plains, Wis. E4 212
Cross Roads, Calif. E6 170
Cross Roads Ohio, N.S., Can. D7 151
Cross Timbers, Mo. C4 189
Cross Village, Mich. C5 186
Crossbost, Scot. B2 57
Crossett, Ark. D4 169
Crossfell Edge, mts., Eng. F6 57
Crossfield, Alta., Can. D3 148
Crosslake, Minn. D4 187
Crossroads, N. Mex. D6 195
Crosstown, Mo. D8 189
Crossville, Ala. A4 166
Crossville, Ill. E5 178
Crossville, Tenn. D8 205
Crosswicks, N.J. C3 194
Croswell, Mich. E8 186
Crothersville, Ind. G6 179
Croton, Iowa D6 180
Croton (Hartford), Ohio B5 199
Croton Falls, res., N.Y. D2 172
Croton on Hudson, N.Y. D3, D7 196
Crotone, It. E6 67
Crottendorf, Ger. C7 61
Crouch, Idaho E3 177
Crouse, N.C. B2 197
Crouseville, Maine B4 184
Crow, creek, Colo. A6 171
Crow, creek, Wyo. D8 213
Crow, Indian res., Mont. E9 190
Crow, peak, Mont. D5 190
Crow, riv., Minn. F4 187
Crow Agency, Mont. E9 190
Crow Creek, Indian res., S. Dak. C6 204
Crow Wing, co., Minn. D4 187
Crow Wing, riv., Minn. D4 187
Crowder, Miss. A3 188
Crowder, Okla. B6 200
Crowell, Tex. C3 206
Crowheart, Wyo. B3 213
Crowley, Calif. *D4 170
Crowley, Colo. C7 171
Crowley, La. D3 183
Crowley, Tex. B5 206
Crowley, co., Colo. C7 171
Crowley, lake, Calif. D4 170
Crowleys, ridge, Ark., Mo. E7 189
Crown City, Ohio D5 199
Crown King, Ariz. C3 168
Crown Point, Ind. B3 179
Crown Point, La. C7 183
Crown Point, N.Y. B7 196
Crown Prince, range, Bougainville I. 115
Crownpoint, N. Mex. B1 195
Crows Nest, B.C., Can. E10 149
Crows Nest, Ind. H8 179
Crows Nest, peak, S. Dak. C2 204
Crowsnest, pass, Alta., Can. E3 148
Croydon, Austl. C7 111
Croydon, Eng. E6, m12 55
Croydon, N.H. D2 193
Croydon, Pa. F12 202
Croydon, Utah B4 207
Croydon, mtn., N.H. D2 193
Croydon, peak, N.H. D2 193
Croydon Flat, N.H. D2 193
Crozet, Va. C4 209
Crozier, Ariz. B2 168
Crozier, Va. D5 209
Crozon, Fr. C1 58
Cruachan, mtn., Scot. D3 57
Cruce Magueyes, P.R. B4 132
Crucero, Peru D3 134
Cruces, Cuba D3 131
Crucible, Pa. G2 202
Cruden, Scot. C2 57
Cruger, Miss. B3 188
Crum, W. Va. D2 211
Crummock Water, lake, Eng. F5 57
Crump, Mich. E6 186
Crump, lake, Oreg. E7 201
Crumpton, Md. B6 173
Crumstown, Ind. A5 179
Crusader States 47
Crusades 47
Cruseilles, Fr. C2 66
Cruso, N.C. D3 197
Crutwell, Sask., Can. D2 155
Cruz, cape, Cuba F5 131
Cruz Alta, Arg. A4 136
Cruz Alta, Braz. D2 137
Cruz Bay, Vir. Is. f15 132
Cruz del Eje, Arg. A4 136
Cruz Grande, Chile E1 135
Cruzeiro, Braz. C4 137
Cruzeiro do Sul, Braz. C3 134
Crysler, Ont., Can. B9 153
Crystal, Mich. E6 186
Crystal, Minn. E6 187
Crystal, N.H. A4 193
Crystal, N. Mex. A1 195
Crystal, N. Dak. A8 198
Crystal, bay, Fla. D4 174
Crystal, lake, Conn. B7 172
Crystal, lake, Mich. D4 186
Crystal, lake, N.H. D4 193
Crystal, lake, Vt. B4 208
Crystal, mtn., N.H. B2 193
Crystal, pond, Conn. B8 172
Crystal, riv., Colo. B3 171
Crystal Bay, Nev. D2 192
Crystal Beach, Ont., Can. E5 153
Crystal Beach, Fla. D4 174
Crystal City, Man., Can. E2 150
Crystal City, Mo. B8, C7 189
Crystal City, Tex. E3 206
Crystal Falls, Mich. B2 186
Crystal Hill, Va. E4 209
Crystal Lake, Conn. B7 172
Crystal Lake, Fla. G3 174
Crystal Lake, Ill. A5, E1 178
Crystal Lake, Iowa A4 180
Crystal Lakes, Ohio C3 199
Crystal River, Fla. D4 174
Crystal Springs, Ark. C2, C5 169
Crystal Springs, Sask., Can. E3 155
Crystal Springs, Fla. D4 174
Crystal Springs, Miss. D3 188
Crystal Springs, N. Dak. C6 198
Crystal Valley, Mich. E4 186
Csongrád, Hung. B5 68
Csorna, Hung. B3 68
Cua Rao, Viet. C6 89
Cuajimalpa, Mex. h9 129
Cuando, riv., Ang., Zambia E3 106
Cuangar, Ang. E2 106
Cuango, riv., Ang. C2 106
Cuanza, riv., Ang. C2 106
Cuanza Norte, dist., Ang. C1 106
Cuanza Sul, dist., Ang. D1 106
Cuarto, riv., Arg. A4 136
Cuatro Calles, P.R. D6 132
Cuauhtémoc, Mex. B3 129
Cuautepec, Mex. g9 129
Cuautla [Morelos], Mex. n14 129
Cub Run, Ky. C3 182
Cuba, Ala. C1 166
Cuba, Ill. C3 178
Cuba, Kans. C6 181
Cuba, Mo. C6 189
Cuba, N. Mex. A3 195
Cuba, N.Y. C2 196
Cuba, Ohio C4 199
Cuba, Port. C2 65
CUBA, country, N.A. E4 131
in 1800's 127
Cuba City, Wis. F3 212
Cubal, Ang. D1 106
Cubango, riv., Ang. E2 106
Cubero, N. Mex. B2 195
Cubia, Ang. E3 106
Cucamonga, Calif. F3 170
Cuchara, Colo. D6 171
Cuchara, riv., Colo. D6 171
Cuchillo, N. Mex. D2 195
Cuchivero, riv., Ven. B4 133
Cuchumatanes, mts., Guat. C2 130
Cuckfield, Eng. C7 56
Cúcuta, Col. B3 133
Cudahy, Wis. E2, F6 212
Cuddalore, India F6 87
Cuddapah, India F6 87
Cuddy, mtn., Idaho E2 177
Cudgewa, Austl. H6 112
Cudworth, Sask., Can. E3 155
Cue, Austl. E2 111
Cuéllar, Sp. B3 65
Cuenca, Ec. B2 134
Cuenca, Sp. B4 65
Cuenca, mts., Sp. B4 65
Cuencamé [de Ceniceros], Mex. C4 129
Cuernavaca, Mex. D5, n14 129
Cuero, Tex. E4 206
Cuervo, Cuba k12 131
Cuervo, N. Mex. B5 195
Cuetzalan [del Progreso], Mex. m15 129
Cuevas, Miss. E2 188
Cuevas, Sp. D5 65
Cuglieri, It. D2 67
Cuiabá, Braz. B1 137
Cuiabá, riv., Braz. B1 137
Cuicas, Ven. B3 133
Cuicatlán, Mex. o15 129
Cuilapa, Guat. C2 130
Cuilco, Guat. C2 130
Cuillin, hills, Scot. C2 57
Cuillin, sound, Scot. C2 57
Cuipo, Pan. k10 130
Cuito, riv., Ang. E2 106
Cuíto Cuanavale, Ang. E2 106
Cuitzéo, lake, Mex. n13 129
Cuivre, riv., Mo. B6 189
Culberson, co., Tex. F2 206
Culbertson, Mont. B12 190
Culbertson, Nebr. D5 191
Culcairn, Austl. G6 112
Culdesac, Idaho C2 177
Culebra, P.R. f13 132
Culebra, mun., P.R. f13 132
Culebra, isl., P.R. f13 132
Culebra, peak, Colo. D5 171
Culebrinas, riv., P.R. B2 132
Culebrita, isl., P.R. f14 132
Culhuacán, Mex. h9 129
Culiacán, Mex. C3 129
Culion, Phil. C5 90
Cúllar de Baza, Sp. D4 65
Cullen, La. B2 183
Cullen, Scot. C6 57
Culleoka, Tenn. B5 205
Cullera, Sp. C5 65
Cullison, Kans. E5 181
Cullman, Ala. A3 166
Cullman, co., Ala. A3 166
Culloden, Ga. D2 175
Culloden, pt., N.Y. E9 172
Cullom, Ill. C5 178
Cullowhee, N.C. D3 197
Culoz, Fr. D1 66
Culp Creek, Oreg. D4 201
Culpeper, Ark. B3 169
Culpeper, Va. C5 209
Culpeper, co., Va. C5 209
Culuene, riv., Braz. A2 137
Culver, Ind. B5 179
Culver, Kans. D6 181
Culver, Minn. D6 187
Culver, Oreg. C5 201
Culver City, Calif. F2 170
Culvers, lake, N.J. A3 194
Culverton, Ga. C4 175
Culzean, bay, Scot. E3 57
Cumaná, Ven. A5 133
Cumberland, B.C., Can. E5 149
Cumberland, Ont., Can. A10 153
Cumberland, Ind. E6, H8 179
Cumberland, Iowa C3 180
Cumberland, Ky. D7 182
Cumberland, Md. D2 173
Cumberland, N.C. C5 197
Cumberland, Ohio C6 199
Cumberland, Okla. C5 200
Cumberland, R.I. B11 172
Cumberland, Va. D4 209
Cumberland, Wash. D2 210
Cumberland, Wis. C1 212
Cumberland, co., N.S., Can. D5 151
Cumberland, co., Ill. D5 178
Cumberland, co., Ky. D4 182
Cumberland, co., Maine E2 184
Cumberland, co., N.J. E2 194
Cumberland, co., N.C. B5 197
Cumberland, co., Pa. F7 202
Cumberland, co., Tenn. D8 205
Cumberland, co., Va. D4 209
Cumberland, cape, Espiritu Santo I. 115
Cumberland, isl., Ga. F5 175
Cumberland, lake, Sask., Can. C4 155
Cumberland, lake, Ky. D5 182
Cumberland, mtn., Tenn. C9 205
Cumberland, pen., N.W. Ter., Can. C20 143
Cumberland, plat., Ala., Ky., Tenn. A3 166, C6 182, D7 205
Cumberland, riv., U.S. C11 159
Cumberland, sound, N.W. Ter., Can. C19 143
Cumberland Center, Maine E5 184
Cumberland City, Tenn. A4 205
Cumberland City, res., Pa. G4 202
Cumberland Foreside, Maine E2, E5 184
Cumberland Furnace, Tenn. A4 205
Cumberland Gap, Tenn. C10 205
Cumberland Gap, nat. hist. park, Ky. D6 182
Cumberland Hill, R.I. B11 172
Cumberland House, Sask., Can. D4 155
Cumbres, pass, Colo. D4 171
Cumbrian, mts., Eng. F5 57
Cuming, co., Nebr. C9 191
Cumming, Ga. B2 175
Cumming, Iowa A7 180
Cummings, Kans. A7 181
Cummings, N. Dak. B8 198
Cummington, Mass. B2 185
Cumnock, N.C. B4 197
Cumnock, Scot. E4 57
Cumpas, Mex. A3 129
Çumra, Tur. D9 85
Cunard, W. Va. D7 211
Cunco, Chile B2 136
Cuncumen, Chile A2 136
Cundiff, Ky. D4 182
Cundinamarca, dept., Col. C3 133
Cundys Harbor, Maine E6 184
Cunene, riv., Ang., S.W. Afr. A1 107
Cuneo, It. B1 67
Cuney, Tex. C5 206
Cunnamulla, Austl. D5 112
Cunningham, Kans. E5 181
Cunningham, Ky. A2 182
Cunningham, Tenn. A4 205
Cupar, Sask., Can. G3 155
Cupar, Scot. D6 57
Cupertino, Calif. C5 170
Cuprum, Idaho D2 177
Curaçá, Braz. C3 138
Curaçao, isl., Neth. Antilles A4 133
Curacautín, Chile B2 136
Curacó, riv., Arg. B3 136
Curañilahue, Chile B2 136
Curaray, riv., Ec., Peru B2, B3 134
Curdsville, Ky. C2 182
Curepto, Chile B2 136
Curiapo, Ven. B5 133
Curicó, Chile A2 136
Curicó, prov., Chile A2 136
Curicuriarí, riv., Braz. D4 133
Curimata, riv., Braz. h6 138
Curitiba, Braz. D3 137
Curitibanos, Braz. D2 137
Curlew, Iowa B3 180
Curlew, Wash. A7 210
Curlew, creek, Wash. A7 210
Curlew, lake, Wash. A7 210
Curon Venosta, It. C6 66
Currais Novos, Braz. C3, h5 138
Curralinho, Braz. C5 139
Curran, Ont., Can. B10 153
Curran, Mich. D7 186
Currant, creek, Colo. C5 171
Currant, mtn., Nev. E6 192
Current, riv., Ark., Mo. E6 189
Currie, Minn. F3 187
Currie, Nev. C7 192
Currituck, N.C. A7 197
Currituck, co., N.C. A7 197
Curry, Alsk. C10 167
Curry, co., N. Mex. C6 195
Curry, co., Oreg. E2 201
Curryville, Ga. B1 175
Curryville, Mo. B6 189
Curtea-de-Argeş, Rom. C7 68
Curtice, Ohio A2, A4 199
Curtici, Rom. B5 68
Curtin, Oreg. D3 201
Curtis, Ark. D2 169
Curtis, Mich. B5 186
Curtis, Nebr. D5 191
Curtis, Okla. A2 200
Curtis, isl., Austl. A8 112
Curtiss, Wis. D3 212
Curtisville, Pa. A6, E2 202
Curuá, riv., Braz. D4 139
Curuá do Sul, riv., Braz. C4 139
Curuçá, Braz. B1 138
Čurug, Yugo. C5 68
Curuguaty, Par. D4 135
Curupira, mts., Ven. C5 133
Curuzú Cuatia, Arg. E4 135
Curve, Tenn. B2 205
Curvelo, Braz. E2 138
Curwensville, Pa. E4 202
Curwensville, res., Pa. E4 202
Curwood, mtn., Mich. B2 186
Cusco, Peru D3 134
Cusco, dept., Peru D3 134
Cushing, Iowa B2 180
Cushing, Maine *D3 184
Cushing, Nebr. C7 191
Cushing, Okla. B5 200
Cushing, Tex. D5 206
Cushman, Ark. B4 169
Cushman, Mass. B2 185
Cushman, Mont. D7 190
Cushman, Oreg. D2 201
Cushman, res., Wash. B2 210
Cusick, Wash. A8 210
Cusihuiriachic, Mex. B3 129
Cusset, Fr. D5 58
Cusseta, Ala. C4 166
Cusseta, Ga. D2 175
Custar, Ohio A4 199
Custer, Mich. E4 186
Custer, Mont. D9 190
Custer, N. Dak. B4 198
Custer, Okla. B3 200
Custer, S. Dak. D2 204
Custer, Wash. A3 210
Custer, co., Colo. C5 171
Custer, co., Idaho E4 177
Custer, co., Mont. D11 190
Custer, co., Nebr. C6 191
Custer, co., Okla. B2 200
Custer, co., S. Dak. D2 204
Custer, peak, S. Dak. C2 204
Custer Battlefield, nat. mon., Mont. E9 190
Custer City, Pa. C4 202
Cut Bank, Mont. B4 190
Cut and Shoot, Tex. *D5 206
Cut Knife, Sask., Can. E1 155
Cut Off, La. E5 183
Cut Throat, isl., Newf., Can. A3 152
Cutbank, riv., Alta., Can. B1 148
Cutchogue, N.Y. D4 196
Cutervo, Peru C2 134
Cuthbert, Ga. E2 175
Cutler, Calif. *D4 170
Cutler, Ont., Can. A2 153
Cutler, Ind. D4 179
Cutler, Maine D5 184
Cutler City, Oreg. C3 201
Cutler Ridge, Fla. *G6 174
Cutshin, Ky. C6 182
Cuttack, India D8 87, G10 88
Cutten, Calif. *B1 170
Cuttingsville, Vt. E3 208
Cuttyhunk, isl., Mass. D6 185
Cutzamala, riv., Mex. n13 129
Cuvo, riv., Ang. D1 106
Cuxhaven, Ger. B4 60
Cuyahoga, co., Ohio A6 199
Cuyahoga, riv., Ohio A6 199
Cuyahoga Falls, Ohio A6 199
Cuyahoga Heights, Ohio *A6 199
Cuyama, riv., Calif. E4 170
Cuyamaca, peak, Calif. F5 170
Cuyamungue, N. Mex. F6 195
Cuylerville, N.Y. C3 196
Cuyo, is., Phil. C6 90
Cuyuna, Minn. D5 187
Cuzco, Ind. H4 179
Cwmamman, Wales C4 56
Cybinka, Pol. A9 61
Cyclades, is., Grc. D5 69
Cyclone, Pa. C4 202
Cygnet, Ohio A4 199
Cylinder, Iowa A3 180
Cynthiana, Ind. H2 179
Cynthiana, Ky. B5 182
Cynthiana, Ohio C4 199
Cypress, Ala. C2 166
Cypress, Calif. *F5 170
Cypress, Fla. B1 174
Cypress, Ill. F4 178
Cypress, Tex. F4 206
Cypress, bayou, Ark. B4 169
Cypress, hills, Alta., Can. E5 148
Cypress, hills, Sask., Can. H1 155
Cypress, lake, Sask., Can. H1 155
Cypress, lake, Fla. D5 174
Cypress Hills, prov. park, Sask., Can. H1 155
Cypress Inn, Tenn. B4 205
Cypress River, Man., Can. E2 150
CYPRUS, country, Asia E9 85
Cyrenaica (Barqah), prov., Libya D4 101
in 1st cent. B.C. 44
c. 120 A.D. 45
in 1922-40 53
Cyril, Okla. C3 200
Cyril, riv., Man., Can. B4 150
Cyrus, Minn. E3 187
Cythera, see Kíthira, isl., Grc.
Czar, Alta., Can. C5 148
Czarna, riv., Pol. k14 70
Czarna Przemsza, riv., Pol. g10 70
Czarnków, Pol. B4 70
CZECHOSLOVAKIA, country, Eur. D4 70
in 1922-40 53
after World War II 54
Czersk, Pol. B4 70
Częstochowa, Pol. C5 70
Człuchów, Pol. B4 70

D

Da Lat, Viet. G8 89
Da Nang, Viet. D8 89
Daaquam, Que., Can. C7 154
Daarburuk, Som. D5 105
Dąb, Pol. B3 70
Dab, Pol. g9 70
Dabā, U.A.E. i8 86
Ḍab'ah, Jordan C8 84
Dabakala, I.C. E4 103
Dabarò, Som. D6 105
Dabdab, Libya D2 101
Dabeiba, Col. B2 133
Ďáblice, Czech. n18 70
Dabney, N.C. A5 197
Dabneys, Va. D5 209
Dabola, Guinea D2 103
Dabra-Berhām, Eth. D4 105
Dabra-Mārk'os, Eth. C4 105
Dabra-Tābor, Eth. C4 105
Dąbrowa, Pol. C6 70
Dąbrowa Górnicza, Pol. C5, g10 70
Dąbrowa Grodzieńska, Pol. B7 70
Dacca, Bngl. D9 87, F13 88
Dachau, Ger. D5 60
Dacia: c. 120 A.D. 45
c. 400 A.D. 46
Dacoma, Okla. A3 200
Dacono, Colo. A6 171
Dacula, Ga. C3 175
Dacura, Nic. C6 130
Dacus, Tex. D5 206
Dacusville, S.C. B2 203
Dadanawa, Guy. B3 139
Dadar, Eth. D5 105
Daday, Tur. B9 85
Daddy, creek, Tenn. C9 205
Dade, co., Fla. G6 174
Dade, co., Ga. B1 175
Dade, co., Mo. D4 189
Dade City, Fla. D4 174
Dadeville, Ala. C4 166
Dadeville, Mo. D4 189
Dadu, Pak. D1 88
Dafoe, Sask., Can. F3 155
Dafoe, riv., Man., Can. B4 150
Dagahabur, Eth. D5 105
Dagana, Sen. C1 103
Dagenham, Eng. k13 55
Daggett, Calif. E5 170
Daggett, Mich. C3 186
Daggett, co., Utah C6 207
Dagmar, Mont. B12 190
Dagsboro, Del. C7 173
Dagupan, Phil. n13 90
Dagus Mines, Pa. D4 202
Daguscahonda, Pa. D4 202
Dahan-i-Kashan, Afg. D13 86
Dahan-i-Kusnak, Afg. D11 86
Dahanu, India H4 88
Dahinda Ill. C3 178
Dahlen, N. Dak. A8 198
Dahlgren, Ill. E5 178
Dahlgren, Va. C5 209
Dahlonega, Ga. B3 175
Dahme, Ger. B8 61
DAHOMEY country, Afr. E5 103
Dahshūr, Eg. E3 84
Daigle, Maine A4 184
Daigleville, La. *E6 183
Dailey, Colo. A8 171
Dailey, W. Va. C5 211
Daimiel, Sp. C4 65
Daingerfield, Tex. C5 206
Dairen (Talien), China D9 91
Dairy, Oreg. E5 201
Dairy Valley, Calif. *F2 170
Dairyland, Calif. *F4 170
Dairyland, Wis. B1 212
Daisetta, Tex. D5 206
Daisy, Ark. C2 169
Daisy, Ga. D5 175
Daisy, Okla. C6 200
Daisy (Melville), Tenn. D8, E10 205
Daisy, Wash. A7 210
Daisytown, Pa. *F2 202
Dajabón, Dom. Rep. E8 131
Dajarra, Austl. D6 111
Dakar, Sen. D1 103
Dākhilah, oasis, Eg. D5 101
Dakoro, Niger. C6 103
Dakota, Ill. A4 178
Dakota, Minn. G7 187
Dakota, co., Minn. F5 187
Dakota, co., Nebr. B9 191
Dakota City, Iowa B3 180
Dakota City, Nebr. B9 191
Dakwa, Zaire A4 106
Dalaba, Guinea D2 103
Dalälven, riv., Swe. G6 63
Dalaman, Tur. D7 69
Dalaman, riv., Tur. D7 69
Dalark, Ark. C3 169
Dalarö, Swe. t36 63
Dalay Sayn Shanda, Mong. B4 92
Dalbandin, Pak. C3 87
Dalbeattie, Scot. F5 57
Dalbo, Minn. E5 187
Dalby, Austl. C8 112
Dalby, Swe. C7 62
Dalcahue, Chile C2 136
Dale, Ill. F5 178
Dale, Ind. H4 179
Dale, Okla. B4 200
Dale, Oreg. C8 201
Dale, Pa. *F4 202
Dale, co., Ala. D4 166
Dale Hollow, lake, Tenn. C8 205
Dalemead, Alta., Can. D4 148
Daleview, Mont. B12 190
Daleville, Ala. D4 166
Daleville, Ind. D6 179
Daleville, Miss. C5 188
Dalhart, Tex. A1 206
Dalhousie, N.B., Can. A3 151
Dalhousie, India A5 88
Dalhousie Junction, N.B., Can. A3 151
Dalías, Sp. D4 65
Daliburgh, Scot. C1 57
Daliyat el Karmil, Isr. B7 84
Dalkeith, Fla. B1 174
Dalkeith, Scot. E5 57
Dalkena, Wash. A8 210
Dall, isl., Alsk. n23 167
Dall, mtn., Alsk. f15 167
Dallam, co., Tex. A1 206
Dallas, Ala. B3 166
Dallas, Ga. C2 175
Dallas, Maine *C2 184
Dallas, N.C. B2 197
Dallas, Oreg. C3 201
Dallas, Pa. B8, D10 202
Dallas, S. Dak. D6 204
Dallas, Tex. B5, C4 206
Dallas, W. Va. B2 211
Dallas, Wis. C2 212
Dallas, co., Ala. C2 166
Dallas, co., Ark. D3 169
Dallas, co., Iowa C3 180
Dallas, co., Mo. D4 189
Dallas, co., Tex. B5, C4 206
Dallas Center, Iowa C4 180
Dallas City, Ill. C2 178
Dallastown, Pa. G8 202
Dalmacio Vélez, Arg. A4 136
Dalmally, Scot. D4 57
Dalmatia, Pa. E8 202
Dalmatia, reg., Yugo. D3 68
c. 120 A.D. 45
in 1805 51
in 1922-40 53
Dalmellington, Scot. E4 57
Dalmeny, Sask., Can. E2 155
Dalnyaya, Sov. Un. D11 93
Daloa, I.C. E3 103
Dalroy, Alta., Can. D4 148
Dalry, Scot. E4 57
Dalrymple, mtn., Austl. D8 110
Dalton, Ark. A4 169
Dalton, Ga. B2 175
Dalton, Mass. B1 185
Dalton, Minn. D3 187
Dalton, Mo. B5 189
Dalton, Nebr. C3 191
Dalton, N.H. B3 193
Dalton, N.Y. C3 196
Dalton, Ohio B6 199
Dalton, Pa. C10 202
Dalton City, Ill. D5 178
Dalton Gardens, Idaho B2 177
Daltonganj, India E10 88
Dalwhinnie, Scot. D4 57
Daly City, Calif. B5 170
Daly Waters, Austl. C5 111
Dalzell, S.C. C7 203
Dam, Sur. B4 139
Dam Gamad, Sud. C2 105
Dama, is., Viet. H6 89
Daman, India G4 88
Damanhūr, Eg. C6 101
Damar, Kans. C4 181
Damar, isl., Indon. G7 90
Damar, is., Indon. G7 90
Damara, Cen. Afr. Rep. D3 104
Damariscotta Maine D3 184
Damariscotta, lake, Maine D3 184
Damas, pass, Arg. A2 136
Damascus, Ark. B3 169
Damascus, Ga. E2 175
Damascus, Ga. B2 175
Damascus, Md. B3 173
Damascus, Pa. C11 202
Damascus, (Dimashq), Syr. F11 85
Damascus, Va. B3 209
Damaturu, Nig. D7 103
Damāvand, mtn., Iran D6 86
Damba, Ang. C2 106
Dambidolo, Eth. D3 105
Dâmbovița, riv., Rom. C7 68
D'Ambre, cape, Malag. f9 107
Dame-Marie, cape, Hai. F6 131
Dāmghān, Iran C7 86
Damietta (Dumyāţ), Eg. C3 84, C6 101
Damietta, riv., mouth, Eg. C3 84
Damietta Branch, riv., Eg. D3 84
Dāmiyā, Jordan g13 84
Dammartin-en-Goële, Fr. E2 59
Damme, Ger. B8 59
Damodar, riv., India F10 88

INDEX KEY Each place listed in **Bold-faced Type** has its population listed in the Population tables, pages 230 to 280.
Each country, shown in CAPITAL LETTERS, has its population listed in the World Political Information Table, pages 6 to 10.
* Does not appear on map; key shows general location.

Damoh, India F7 88
Damon, Tex. G4 206
Damongo, Ghana E4 103
Dampier, strait, Bis. Arch. 115
Dampier, strait, Indon. F8 90
Dan, riv., N.C., Va. A4 197, E3 209
Dana, Sask., Can. E3 155
Dana, Ill. C5 178
Dana, Ind. E2 179
Dana, Iowa B3 180
Dana, N.C. D4 197
Dana Point, Calif. *F5 170
Danakil, depression, Eth. C5 105
Danané, I.C. E3 103
Danburg, Ga. C4 175
Danbury, Conn. D3 172
Danbury, Iowa B2 180
Danbury, Nebr. D5 191
Danbury, N.H. C3 193
Danbury, N.C. A3 197
Danbury, Tex. G5 206
Danbury, Wis. B1 212
Danby, Calif. E6 170
Danby, N.Y. C4 196
Danby, Vt. E3 208
Danby Four Corners, Vt. E2 208
Dancy, Ala. B1 166
Dancy, Wis. D4 212
Dancyville, Tenn. B2 205
Dande, riv., Ang. C1 106
Dandenong, Austl. I5 112
Dandridge, Tenn. C10 205
Dandy, Va. A6 209
Dane, Wis. E4 212
Dane, co., Wis. E4 212
Danevang, Tex. E4 206
Danforth, Ill. C6 178
Danforth, Maine C5 184
Danforth, hills, Colo. A2 171
Dāngilā, Eth. C4 105
Dangrek, mts., Thai. E6 89
Dania, Fla. E3, F6 174
Dania, Indian res., Fla. E3, F6 174
Daniel, Wyo. C2 213
Daniels, Md. B4 173
Daniels, co., Mont. B11 190
Daniel's Harbour, Newf., Can. C3 152
Daniels-Rhyne, N.C. *B2 197
Danielson, Conn. B9 172
Danielsville, Ga. B3 175
Danilov, Sov. Un. B2 73
Danilov Grad, Yugo. D4 68
Danjo, isl., Jap. J4 93
Dankhar, India A7 88
Danlí, Hond. C4 130
Dannebrog, Nebr. C7 191
Dannemora, N.Y. A3 196
Dannenberg, Ger. E5 62
Dannevirke, N.Z. N16 112
Dannike, Swe. A7 62
Dans, mtn., Md. D2 173
Dansville, Mich. *F6 186
Dansville, N.Y. C3 196
Dante, Som. C7 105
Dante, S. Dak. D7 204
Dante, Tenn. E11 205
Dante, Va. B2 209
Danube, Minn. F3 187
Danube, riv., Eur. G13 40
Danube, riv. mouths, Eur. G13 40
Danubyu, Bur. D1 89
Danum, New Ire. I. 115
Danvers, Ill. C4 178
Danvers, Mass. A6, C3 185
Danvers, Minn. E3 187
Danville, Ala. A2 166
Danville, Ark. B2 169
Danville, Calif. B6 170
Danville, Que., Can. D5 154
Danville, Ga. D3 175
Danville, Ill. C6 178
Danville, Ind. E4 179
Danville, Iowa D6 180
Danville, Kans. E6 181
Danville, Ky. C5 182
Danville, N.H. E4 193
Danville, Ohio B3 199
Danville, Ohio *C4 199
Danville, Pa. E8 202
Danville, Vt. C4 208
Danville (Independent City), Va. E3 209
Danville, Wash. A7 210
Danville, W. Va. C3, D5 211
Danzig (Gdańsk), Pol. A5 70
Danzig, gulf, Pol. A5 70
Daosa, India D6 88
Daphne, Ala. E2 166
Dapp, Alta., Can. B4 148
Dār al Hamrā, Sau. Ar. I12 85
Dar Chebika, Mor. D2 102
Dar es Salaam, Tan. C6 106
Dar Mazār, Iran G8 86
Dārāb, Iran G7 86
Darabani, Rom. A8 68
Daraj, Libya C2 101
Darasun, Sov. Un. D14 71
Darawah, Eg. D3 84
Darbhanga, India C8 87, D10 88
D'Arbonne, bayou, La. B3 183
Darbun, Miss. D3 188
Darby, Mont. D2 190
Darby, Pa. B11, G11 202
Darby, creek, Ohio C4 199
Darbydale, Ohio *C4 199
Darbyville, Ohio C4 199
D'Arcy Station, Sask., Can. F1 155
Dardanelle, Ark. B2 169
Dardanelle, Calif. C4 170
Dardanelle, res., Ark. B2 169
Dardanelles, strait, Tur. B6 69
Darden, Tenn. B3 205
Dardenne, creek, Mo. A7 189
Dardens, N.C. B7 197
Dare, co., N.C. B8 197
Darende, Tur. C11 85
Daretown, N.J. D2 194
Darfo, It. D6 66
Darfur, Minn. F4 187
Darfur, reg., Sud. C1 105
Dargai, Pak. B5 87
Dargan, Md. B2 173
Darganata, Sov. Un. A11 86
Dargaville, N.Z. K14 112
Darien, Conn. E3 172
Darien, Ga. E5 175
Darien, Wis. F5 212
Darien, mts., Pan. F9 130
Dariense, mts., Nic. D5 130
Darjeeling, India D12 88
Darke, co., Ohio B3 199
Darkharbor, Maine D4 184
Darling, Miss. A3 188
Darling, lake, N. Dak. A4 198
Darling, range, Austl. F2 110
Darling, riv., Austl. E5 112
Darlingford, Man., Can. E2 150
Darlington, Ala. D2 166
Darlington, Eng. C6 55
Darlington, Fla. G3 174
Darlington, Idaho F5 177
Darlington, Ind. D4 179
Darlington, Md. A5 173
Darlington, Mo. A3 189
Darlington, S.C. C8 203
Darlington, Wis. F3 212
Darlington, co., S.C. C8 203
Darlington, cape, Ant. B6 120
Darlove, Miss. B3 188
Darłowo, Pol. A4 70
Darmody, Sask., Can. G2 155
Darmstadt, Ger. D3 61
Darnah (Derna), Libya C4 101
Darnell, La. B4 183
Darnestown, Md. B3 173
Darney, Fr. A2 66
Darnley, cape, Ant. C19 120
Daro, Mala. E4 90
Daroca, Sp. B5 65
Darr, Nebr. D6 191
Darrah, mtn., B.C., Can. A2 190
Darrington, Wash. A4 210
Darrouzett, Tex. A2 206
Darrow, La. B5 183
Darsser, pt., Ger. D6 62
Dart, cape, Ant. B36 120
Dart, riv., Eng. D4 56
Dartford, Eng. *C8 56
Dartford, Wash. D7 210
Dartmoor, moor, Eng. D4 56
Dartmouth, N.S., Can. E6 151
Dartmouth, Eng. D4 56
Dartmouth, Mass. C5 185
Daru, isl., Pap. A7, k11 110
Daruvar, Yugo. C3 68
Darvel, bay, Mala. E5 90
Darwin, Austl. B5 111
Darwin, Calif. D5 170
Darwin, isl., Ec. f5 134
Darya yi Namak, salt lake, Iran D5 86
Daryacheh-i-Namakzar, salt lake, Iran E10 86
Dasē, Eth. C4 105
Dash Point, Wash. D1 210
Dasht, riv., Pak. C3 87
Dasht-i-Daqq-I-Tundi, salt lake, Afg. E10 86
Dasht-i-Lut, plain, Iran E8 86
Dasht-i-Margo, des., Afg. F11 86
Dasht-Kavir, salt des. Iran D7 86
Dashwood, Ont., Can. D3 153
Dasol, bay, Phil. o12 90
Dassel, Minn. E4 187
Date, Ariz. C3 168
Dateland, Ariz. E2 168
Datia, India E7 88
Datil, N. Mex. C2 195
Datto, Ark. A5 169
Datu, cape, Indon., Mala. K8 89
Datze, riv., Ger. E7 62
Daudnagar, India E10 88
Daufuskie, isl., S.C. G6 203
Daufuskie Island, S.C. G6 203
Daugava (Dvina), riv., Sov. Un. C5 72
Daugavpils, Sov. Un. D6 72
Daulatabad, Afg. E11 86
Daulat Yar, Afg. D12 86
Daule, Ec. A2 134
Daule, Ec. B2 134
Daun, Ger. C1 61
Dauphin, Man., Can. D1 150
Dauphin, Pa. F8 202
Dauphin, co., Pa. F8 202
Dauphin, isl., Ala. E1 166
Dauphin, lake, Man., Can. D2 150
Dauphin, riv., Man., Can. D2 150
Dauphiné, former prov., Fr. E6 58
Dauphiny (Dauphiné): c. 1360 48
Daus, Tenn. D8 205
Davangere, India *F6 87
Davant, La. C8, E6 183
Davao, Phil. D7 90
Davao, gulf, Phil. D7 90
Dāvar Panāh, Iran H11 86
Daveluyville, Que., Can. C5 154
Davenport, Calif. C5, D2 170
Davenport, Fla. D5 174
Davenport, Iowa C7, D7 180
Davenport, Nebr. D8 191
Davenport, N.Y. C6 196
Davenport, N. Dak. C8 198
Davenport, Okla. B5 200
Davenport, Wash. B7 210
Davenport Downs, Austl. B3 112
Daventry, Eng. B6 56
Davey, Nebr. E2 191
David, Ky. C7 182
David, Pan. F6 130
David City, Nebr. C8 191
David-Gorodok, Sov. Un. E6 72
Davidson, Sask., Can. F3 155
Davidson, N.C. B3 197
Davidson, Okla. C2 200
Davidson, Tenn. C8 205
Davidson, co., N.C. B3 197
Davidson, co., Tenn. A5 205
Davidson, mts., Alsk. B11 167
Davie, Fla. E3, F6 174
Davie, co., N.C. B3 197
Daviess, co., Ind. G3 179
Daviess, co., Ky. C2 182
Daviess, co., Mo. B3 189
Davin, Sask., Can. G3 155
Davis, Calif. A6, C3 170
Davis, Ill. A4 178
Davis, N.C. C7 197
Davis, Okla. C4 200
Davis, S. Dak. D9 204
Davis, Tex. E3 206
Davis, W. Va. B5 211
Davis, co., Iowa D5 180
Davis, co., Utah C3 207
Davis, bay, Ant. C26 120
Davis, creek, W. Va. C6 211
Davis, dam, Nev. H7 192
Davis, isl., Fla. E2 174
Davis, lake, Oreg. D5 201
Davis, mtn., Pa. G3 202
Davis, mts., Tex. F2 206
Davis, sea, Ant. C22 120
Davis, strait, Can. C21 143
Davis City, Iowa D4 180
Davis Dam, Ariz. B1 168
Davis Inlet, Newf., Can. g9 152
Davis Junction, Ill. A4 178
Davis Station, S.C. D7 203
Davisboro, Ga. D4 175
Davison, Mich. E7 186
Davison, co., S. Dak. D7 204
Davisson, lake, Wash. C3 210
Daviston, Ala. B4 166
Davisville, Mo. D6 189
Davisville, R.I. C11 172
Davle, Czech. o17 70
Davos, Switz. C5 66
Davy, W. Va. D3 211
Dāwā, riv., Eth. E5 105
Dawes, co., Nebr. B2 191
Dawn, Mo. B4 189
Dawn, Tex. B1 206
Dawson, Yukon, Can. D5 144
Dawson, Ga. E2 175
Dawson, Iowa C3 180
Dawson, Minn. F2 187
Dawson, Nebr. D10 191
Dawson, N. Dak. C6 198
Dawson, Pa. F2 202
Dawson, Tex. D4 206
Dawson, co., Ga. B2 175
Dawson, co., Mont. C11 190
Dawson, co., Nebr. D6 191
Dawson, co., Tex. C1 206
Dawson, mtn., B.C., Can. D9 149
Dawson, range, Yukon, Can. D5 142
Dawson, riv., Austl. D8 110
Dawson Creek, B.C., Can. B7 149
Dawson-Lambton, glacier, Ant. B10 120
Dawson Springs, Ky. C2 182
Dawsonville, Ga. B2 175
Dax, Fr. F3 58
Day, Fla. B3 174
Day, co., S. Dak. B8 204
Dayang Bunting, isl., Thai. I3 89
Daykin, Nebr. D8 191
Daylesford, Austl. H5 112
Dayr Abū Sa'īd, Jordan B7 84
Dayr al Balaḩ, Gaza Strip C6 84
Dayr az Zawr, Syr. E13 85
Dayr Dibwān, Jordan h12 84
Dayr Istiyā, Jordan g11 84
Dayrūţ, Eg. D6 101
Daysland, Alta., Can. C4 148
Daysville, Tenn. D9 205
Dayton, Ala. C2 166
Dayton, Idaho G7 177
Dayton, Ind. D4 179
Dayton, Iowa B3 180
Dayton, Ky. A7 182
Dayton, Md. B4 173
Dayton, Minn. E5 187
Dayton, Mont. C2 190
Dayton, Nev. D2 192
Dayton, N.J. C3 194
Dayton, N. Mex. E5 195
Dayton, N.Y. C2 196
Dayton, Ohio C1 199
Dayton, Oreg. B1, B3 201
Dayton, Pa. E3 202
Dayton, Tenn. D8 205
Dayton, Tex. D5, F5 206
Dayton, Va. C4 209
Dayton, Wash. C8 210
Dayton, Wyo. A5 213
Daytona Beach, Fla. C5 174
Dayville, Conn. B9 172
Dayville, Oreg. C7 201
Dazey, N. Dak. B7 198
Dazgir, Iran. C2 86
De Aar, S. Afr. D3 107
Dead, creek, Vt. C2 208
Dead, lake, Sask., Can. B3 155
Dead, lake, Fla. B1 174
Dead, lake, Minn. D3 187
Dead, riv., Maine C2 184
Dead, sea, Isr., Jordan C7 84
Dead Diamond, riv., N.H. A2 193
Dead Indian, peak, Wyo. A3 213
Dead Knoll, mtn., Wyo. C2 213
Dead Man, bay, Fla. C3 174
Deadman, creek, Wash. D7 210
Deadmans, pt., Newf., Can. D5 152
Deadwood, S. Dak. C2 204
Deadwood, res., Idaho E3 177
Deaf Smith, co., Tex. B1 206
Deakin, bay, Ant. C28 120
Deal, Eng. C9 56
Deal, N.J. C4 194
Deal, isl., Md. D6 173
Deal Island, Md. D6 173
Deale, Md. C4 173
Dean, Tenn. C9 205
Dean, chan., B.C., Can. C4 149
Dean, riv., B.C., Can. C4 149
Deán Funes, Arg. A4 136
Deanburg, Tenn. B3 205
Deans, N.J. C3 194
Deanville, W. Va. B4 211
Deanwood, Ga. E4 175
Dearborn, Mich. A7, F7 186
Dearborn, Mo. B3 189
Dearborn, co., Ind. F8 179
Dearg, mtn., Scot. C4 57
Dearing, Ga. C4 175
Dearing, Kans. E8 181
DeArmanville, Ala. B4 166
Deary, Idaho C2 177
Dease, arm, N.W. Ter., Can. C8 142
Dease, strait, N.W. Ter., Can. C11 142
Dease Lake, B.C., Can. D2 149
Death, val., Calif. D5 170
Death Valley, Calif. D5 170
Death Valley, nat. mon., Calif. D5 170
Deatsville, Ala. C3 166
Deauville, Fr. C4 58
Deaver, Wyo. A4 213
De Baca, co., N. Mex. C5 195
Debaltsevo, Sov. Un. q21 72
Debar, Yugo. E5 68
De Bary, Fla. D5 174
Debauch, mtn., Alsk. C8 167
Debden, Sask., Can. D2 155
Debec, N.B., Can. C2 151
De Beque, Colo. B2 171
De Berry, Tex. C5 206
Dębica, Pol. C6 70
Debin, Bul. E7 68
Deblin, Pol. C6 70
Dębno, Pol. B3 70
Debo, lake, Mali C4 103
De Borgia, Mont. C1 190
Deboullie, mtn., Maine B4 184
Debovo, Bul. D7 68
Debrecen, Hung. B5 68
De Cade, lake, La. E5 183
Decamere, Eth. B4 105
Decatur, Ala. A3 166
Decatur, Ark. A1 169
Decatur, Ga. B5, C2 175
Decatur, Ill. D5 178
Decatur, Ind. C8 179
Decatur, Iowa D4 180
Decatur, Mich. F5 186
Decatur, Miss. C4 188
Decatur, Nebr. C9 191
Decatur, Tenn. D9 205
Decatur, Tex. C4 206
Decatur, co., Ga. F2 175
Decatur, co., Ind. F6 179
Decatur, co., Iowa D4 180
Decatur, co., Kans. C3 181
Decatur, co., Tenn. B3 205
Decatur, lake, Ill. D5 178
Decaturville, Tenn. B3 205
Decazeville, Fr. E5 58
Deccan, reg., India E6 87
Deception, lake, Sask., Can. A3 155
Deception, mtn., N.W. Ter., Can. C5 142
Deception, mtn., Wash. B2 210
Decherd, Tenn. B5 205
Děčín, Czech. C3 70
Decize, Fr. D5 58
Decker, Man., Can. D1 150
Decker, Ind. G3 179
Decker, Mont. E10 190
Deckers, Colo. B5 171
Deckerville, Mich. E8 186
Declo, Idaho G5 177
De Cocksdorp, Neth. A4 59
Decorah, Iowa A6 180
Decota, W. Va. D6 211
De Coursey, Ky. A7 182
Dededo, Guam 114
Dedemsvaart, Neth. B6 59
Dedham, Iowa C3 180
Dedham, Mass. B5, D2 185
Dedinovo, Sov. Un. n19 72
Dédougou, Upper Volta D4 103
Dedza, Malawi D5 106
Dee, Oreg. B5 201
Dee, riv., Eng. D5 55
Dee, riv., Scot. C6 57
Dee, riv., Wales D5 55
Deedsville, Ind. C5 179
Deemer, Miss. C4 188
Deemston, Pa. *F1 202
Deep, creek, Del. C6 173
Deep, creek, Mont. C4 190
Deep, creek, Utah C2 207
Deep, creek, Utah F3 207
Deep, creek, Wash. D7 210
Deep, entrance, Eniwetok 114
Deep, fork, Okla. B5 200
Deep, inlet, Newf., Can. g10 152
Deep, riv., N.C. B4 197
Deep Brook, N.S., Can. E4 151
Deep Creek, lake, Md. D1 173
Deep Gap, N.C. A2 197
Deep Gap, pass, N.C. A2 197
Deep Red, run, Okla. C3 200
Deep River, Conn. D7 172
Deep River, Iowa C5 180
Deep Run, N.C. B6 197
Deep Water, W. Va. D6 211
Deepcreek, Wash. D7 210
Deepdale, Man., Can. D1 150
Deephaven, Minn. F5 187
Deepstep, Ga. C4 175
Deepwater, Mo. C4 189
Deepwater, N.J. D1 194
Deepwater, pt., Del. B7 173
Deer, Ark. B2 169
Deer, creek, Ind. C5 179
Deer, creek, Md. A5 173
Deer, creek, Miss. B3 188
Deer, isl., Maine D4 184
Deer, isl., Mass. D3 185
Deer, isl., Miss. E2 188
Deer, lake, Newf., Can. D3 152
Deer, lake, Minn. C5 187
Deer, mtn., Maine C2 184
Deer, peak, Colo. C5 171
Deer, pond, Newf., Can. D4 152
Deer Creek, Ill. C4 178
Deer Creek, Ind. C5 179
Deer Creek, Minn. D3 187
Deer Creek, Okla. A4 200
Deer Creek, res. Ohio C4 199
Deer Flat, res., Idaho F2 177
Deer Grove, Ill. B4 178
Deer Isle, Maine D4 184
Deer Lake, Newf., Can. D3 152
Deer Lodge, Mont. D4 190
Deer Lodge, Tenn. C9 205
Deer Lodge, co., Mont. D3 190
Deer Park, Ala. D1 166
Deer Park, Fla. D6 174
Deer Park, Md. D1 173
Deer Park, N.Y. F3 172
Deer Park, Ohio D2 199
Deer Park, Tex. *E5 206
Deer Park, Wash. B8 210
Deer Park, Wis. C1 212
Deer River, Minn. C5 187
Deer River, N.Y. B5 196
Deer Trail, Colo. B6 171
Deerfield, Ill. A6, E2 178
Deerfield, Kans. E2 181
Deerfield, Mass. A2 185
Deerfield, Mich. G7 186
Deerfield, Mo. D3 189
Deerfield, N.H. D4 193
Deerfield, Ohio A6 199
Deerfield, Wis. E4 212
Deerfield, riv., Mass., Vt. F3 208
Deerfield Beach, Fla. F6 174
Deerfield Street, N.J. D2 194
Deering, Alsk. B7 167
Deering, Mo. E8 189
Deering, N.H. D3 193
Deering, N. Dak. A4 198
Deerton, Mich. B3 186
Deerwood, Minn. D5 187
Deeson, Miss. A3 188
Deeth, Nev. B6 192
Defensa Central, P.R. C6 132
Deferiet, N.Y. A5 196
Defiance, Iowa C2 180
Defiance, Mo. B7 189
Defiance, N. Mex. B1 195
Defiance, Ohio A3 199
Defiance, co., Ohio A3 199
Defiance, mtn., Oreg. B5 201
Deford, Mich. E7 186
De Forest, Wis. E4 212
De Funiak Springs, Fla. G3 174
Degeberga, Swe. C8 62
Degelis, Que., Can. *B9 154
Degerfors, Swe. E8 63
Degerön, Swe. u33 63
Deggendorf, Ger. E7 61
De Graff, Minn. E3 187
De Graff, Ohio B4 199
De Gray, res., Ark. C2 169
Deh Bid, Iran F6 86
Deh-i-Haji, Afg. F12 86
Deh Pāin, Iran G8 86
Deh Titan, Afg. E11 86
Dehak, Iran G10 86
Dehibat, Tun. C7 102
Dehiwala-Mount Lavinia, Cey. *G6 87
Dehra Dun, India B6 88
Deinze, Bel. D3 59
Dej, Rom. B6 68
Dejvice, Czech. n17 70
De Kalb, Ill. B5 178
De Kalb, Miss. C5 188
De Kalb, Mo. B3 189
De Kalb, N.Y. B1 196
De Kalb, Tex. C5 206
De Kalb, co., Ala. A4 166
De Kalb, co., Ga. C2 175
De Kalb, co., Ill. B5 178
De Kalb, co., Ind. B7 179
De Kalb, co., Mo. B3 189
De Kalb, co., Tenn. D8 205
De Kalb Junction, N.Y. B2 196
De Kays, N.J. A4 194
Dekese, Zaire B3 106
Dekoa, Cen. Afr. Rep. D3 104
Del City, Okla. B4 200
Del Mar, Calif. E2 170
Del Monte Heights, Calif. *D3 170
Del Monte Park, Calif. *D3 170
Del Norte, Colo. D4 171
Del Norte, co., Calif. B2 170
Del Paso Heights, Calif. *C3 170
Del Rey Oaks, Calif. *D3 170
Del Rio, Tenn. D10 205
Del Rio, Tex. E2 206
Delacroix, La. E6 183
Delafield, Wis. *E5 212
Delagoa, bay, Moz. C5 107
Delagua, Colo. D6 171
De Lamere, N. Dak. C8 198
Delanco, N.J. C3 194
De Land, Fla. C5 174
De Land, Ill. C5 178
Delaney, Ark. B2 169
Delano, Calif. E4 170
Delano, Minn. E5 187
Delano, Tenn. D9 205
Delano, peak, Utah E3 207
Delano Mines, Nev. B7 192
Delanson, N.Y. C6 196
Delaplaine, Ark. A5 169
Delaronde, lake, Sask., Can. C2 155
Delavan, Ill. C4 178
Delavan, Kans. D7 181
Delavan, Minn. G4 187
Delavan, Wis. F5 212
Delavan Lake, Wis. *F5 212
Delaware, Ark. B2 169
Delaware, Ont., Can. E3 153
Delaware, Iowa B6 180
Delaware, N.J. B2 194
Delaware, Ohio B4 199
Delaware, Okla. A6 200
Delaware, co., Ind. D7 179
Delaware, co., Iowa B6 180
Delaware, co., N.Y. C6 196
Delaware, co., Ohio B4 199
Delaware, co., Okla. A7 200
Delaware, co., Pa. G11 202
Delaware, state, U.S. 173
Delaware, bay, Del. B7 173
Delaware, mts., Tex. F2 206
Delaware, res., Ohio B4 199
Delaware, riv., Del., N.J., N.Y., Pa. C3 194
Delaware, riv., Kans. A7 181
Delaware, water gap, Pa. B2 194
Delaware City, Del. A6 173
Delaware Water Gap, Pa. E11 202
Delbarton, W. Va. D2 211
Delburne, Alta., Can. C4 148
Delcambre, La. E4 183
Delco, N.C. C5 197
Deleau, Man., Can. E1 150
Delémont, Switz. B3 66
De Leon, Tex. C3 206
De Leon Springs, Fla. C5 174
De Léry, Que., Can. D8 154
Delevan, N.Y. C2 196
Delft, Minn. G3 187
Delft, Neth. B4 59
Delfzijl, Neth. A6 59
Delgado, cape, Moz. D7 106
Delger Tsogtuin Hüryee, Mong. A2 92
Delgo, Sud. A3 105
Delhi, Calif. *D3 170
Delhi, Ont., Can. E4 153
Delhi, India C6 87, C6 88
Delhi, Iowa B6 180
Delhi, La. B4 183
Delhi, Minn. F3 187
Delhi, N.Y. C6 196
Delhi, Okla. B2 200
Delia, Alta., Can. D4 148
Delia, Kans. C8 181
Delight, Ark. C2 169
Delisle, Que., Can. A6 154
Delisle, Sask., Can. F2 155
DeLisle, Miss. E4 188
Delitzsch, Ger. B7 61
Dell, Ark. B5 169
Dell, Mont. F4 190
Dell City, Tex. E1 206
Dell Rapids, S. Dak. D9 204
Delle, Fr. B3 66
Dellenbaugh, mtn., Ariz. A2 168
Dellrose, Tenn. B5 205
Dellroy, Ohio B6 199
Dells, gorge, Wis. E4 212
Dellwood, Fla. B1 174
Dellwood, Minn. E6, E7 187
Dellwood, Mo. *C7 189
Dellys, Alg. B5 102
Delmar, Ala. A2 166
Delmar Del. D6 173
Delmar, Iowa C7 180
Delmar, Md. D6 173
Delmar, N.Y. C7 196
Delmas, Sask., Can. E1 155
Delmenhorst, Ger. B4 60
Delmita, Tex. F3 206
Delmont, N.J. E3 194
Delmont, S. Dak. D7 204
Deloit, Iowa B2 180
Delong, Ind. B5 179
Deloraine, Man., Can. E1 150
Deloro, Ont., Can. C7 153
Delos, see Dhílos, isl., Grc.
Delphi, Ind. C4 179
Delphia, Mont. D8 190
Delphos, Kans. C6 181
Delphos, Ohio B3 199
Delray Beach, Fla. F6 174
Delson, **C**ue., Can. D9 154
Delta, Ala. B4 166
Delta, Ont., Can. C8 153
Delta, Colo. C2 171
Delta, Iowa C5 180
Delta, La. B5 183
Delta, Mo. D8 189
Delta, Ohio A4 199
Delta, Pa. G9 202
Delta, Utah D3 207
Delta, co., Colo. C3 171
Delta, co., Mich. C4 186
Delta, co., Tex. C5 206

INDEX KEY Each place listed in **Bold-faced Type** has its population listed in the Population tables, pages 230 to 280. Each country, shown in CAPITAL LETTERS, has its population listed in the World Political Information Table, pages 6 to 10. * Does not appear on map; key shows general location.

Delta, peak, B.C., Can......A3 149
Delta, res., N.Y.......B5 196
Delta Amacuro, ter., Ven......B5 133
Delta Beach, Man., Can...D2 150
Delta City, Miss......B3 188
Deltaville, Va......D6 209
Delton, Mich......F5 186
Delungra, Austl......D8 112
Delvinë, Alb......C3 69
Delyatin, Sov. Un......G5 72
Demaine, Sask., Can......G2 155
Demarcation, bay, Alsk...B11 167
Demarest, N.J......D5 194
Demba, Zaire......C3 106
Demchok, China......A7 88
Demidov, Sov. Un......D8 72
Deming, N. Mex......E2 195
Deming, Wash......A3 210
Demir Kapija, Yugo......E6 68
Demirci, Tur......C7 69
Demmin, Ger......B6 60
Demmitt, Alta., Can......B1 148
Demnat, Mor......I3 64
Demopolis, Ala......C2 166
Demorest, Ga......B3 175
Demorestville, Ont., Can......C7 153
De Mossville, Ky......B7 182
Demotte, Ind......B3 179
Dempster, S. Dak......C9 204
Demyanka, riv., Sov. Un...B8 73
Demyanovka, Sov. Un......C7 73
Den Burg, Neth......A4 59
Den Helder, Neth......B4 59
Den Hoorn, Neth......A4 59
Den Oever, Neth......B5 59
Denain, Fr......D3 59
Denali, Alsk......C10 167
Denare Beach, Sask., Can.C4 155
Denau, Sov. Un......B13 86
Denaud, Fla......F5 174
Denbigh, N. Dak......A5 198
Denbigh, Wales......A4 56
Denbigh, co., Wales......A4 56
Denby, S. Dak......D3 204
Dendermonde, Bel......C4 59
Dendron, Sask., Can......G2 155
Dendron, Va......D6 209
Denezhkin Kamen, mtn., Sov. Un......A5 73
Denham, Ind......B4 179
Denham, Minn......D6 187
Denham Springs, La..A5, D5 183
Denhoff, N. Dak......B5 198
Denholm, Sask., Can......E1 155
Denia, Sp......C6 65
Deniau, Que., Can......B8 154
Deniliquin, Austl......G5 112
Denio, Nev......B3 192
Denison, Iowa......B2 180
Denison, Kans......A7 181
Denison, Tex......C4 206
Denizli, Tur......D7 69
Denman, Nebr......D7 191
Denman, glacier, Ant......C23 120
Denman, glacier tongue, Ant......C23 120
Denmark, N.S., Can......D6 151
Denmark, Iowa......D6 180
Denmark, Kans......C5 181
Denmark, Maine......E2 184
Denmark, S.C......E5 203
Denmark, Tenn......B2 205
Denmark, Wis......A6, D6 212
DENMARK, country, Eur..C3 62
c. 1140...... 47
c. 1360...... 48
in 1721...... 49
in 1810...... 50
in 1815...... 50
in 1914...... 52
Denmark, strait, Arc. O...C17 118
Dennard, Ark......B3 169
Denning, Ark......B2 169
Dennis, Kans......E8 181
Dennis, Mass......C7 185
Dennis, Miss......A5 188
Dennis, hill, Conn......B4 172
Dennis Port, Mass......C7 185
Dennison, Minn......F5 187
Dennison, Ohio......B6 199
Denniston, Va......E4 209
Dennisville, N.J......E3 194
Dennysville, Maine......D5 184
Denpasar, Indon......G5 90
Dent, Minn......D3 187
Dent, co., Mo......D6 189
Denton, Ga......E4 175
Denton, Kans......C8 181
Denton, Md......C6 173
Denton, Mich......A7 186
Denton, Mont......C7 190
Denton, Nebr......D9 191
Denton, N.C......B3 197
Denton, Tenn......D10 205
Denton, Tex......C4 206
Denton, co., Tex......C4 206
Denton, creek, Tex......A5 206
D'Entrecasteaux, is., Pap..k13 110
D'Entrecasteaux, pt., Austl......F2 110
Dentsville, S.C......C6 203
Denver, Colo......B6 171
Denver, Ill......C2 178
Denver, Ind......C5 179
Denver, Iowa......B5 180
Denver, Mo......A3 189
Denver, N.C......B2 197
Denver, Pa......F9 202
Denver, Tenn......A4 205
Denver, W. Va......B5 211
Denver, co., Colo......B6 171
Denver City, Tex......C1 206
Denville, N.J......B4 194
Denzil, Sask., Can......E1 155
Deogahar, India......E11 88
Deolali, India......*E5 87
Deora, Colo......D8 171
De Panne, Bel......C2 59
Depauville, N.Y......A4 196
Depauw, Ind......H5 179
De Pere, Wis......A6, D5 212
Depew, N.Y......C2 196
Depew, Okla......B5 200
Depoe Bay, Oreg......C3 201
Deport, Tex......C5 206
Deposit, N.Y......C5 196
Depot Harbour, Ont., Can......B4 153
Depue, Ill......B4 178
Deputy, Ind......G6 179
DeQueen, Ark......C1 169
Dequen, Que., Can......A5 154
DeQuincy, La......D2 183
Der'a, Syr......F11 85
Dera Ghāzi Khan, Pak......B5 87, B3 88
Dera Ismāil Khan, Pak...B3 88
Derbent, Sov. Un......E3 73
Derbetovka, Sov. Un......I14 72
Derby, Austl......C3 111
Derby, N.B., Can......C4 151
Derby, Colo......*B6 171
Derby, Conn......D4 172
Derby, Eng......B6 56
Derby, Ind......H4 179
Derby, Iowa......D4 180
Derby, Kans......E6 181
Derby, Maine......C4 184
Derby, Miss......E4 188
Derby, N.Y......C2 196
Derby, Ohio......C4 199
Derby, Tex......E3 206
Derby, Vt......B4 208
Derby, Va......B2 209
Derby, co., Eng......A6 56
Derby Junction, N.B., Can......C4 151
Derby Line, Vt......A4 208
Derecske, Hung......B5 68
Derg, lake, Ire......D2 55
De Ridder, La......D2 183
Derik, Tur......D13 85
Derita, N.C......B3 197
Derma, Miss......B4 188
Dermott, Ark......D4 169
Dermott, Tex......C2 206
Derna, see Darnah, Libya
Derniere, isl., La......E5 183
Derravaragh, lake, Ire......D3 55
Derry, La......C3 183
Derry, N.H......E4 193
Derry, N. Mex......E2 195
Derry, Pa......F3 202
Derudeb, Sud......B4 105
DeRuyter, N.Y......C5 196
Derventa, Yugo......C3 68
Derwent, Alta., Can......C5 148
Derwent, Ohio......C6 199
Derwent, riv., Eng......F5 57
Derwent, riv., Eng......F6 57
Derwent, riv., Eng......F7 57
Derwood, Md......B3 173
Des Allemands, La...C6, E5 183
Des Allemands, bayou, La.C6 183
Des Allemands, lake, La.C6, E5 183
Des Arc, Ark......C4 169
Des Arc, Mo......D7 189
Des Arc, bayou, Ark......B4 169
Des Lacs, N. Dak......A4 198
Des Lacs, riv., N. Dak......A4 198
Des Moines, Iowa...A7, C4 180
Des Moines, N. Mex......A6 195
Des Moines, Wash...B3, D1 210
Des Moines, co., Iowa......D6 180
Des Moines, riv., U.S.......B9 159
Des Peres, Mo......B8 189
Des Plaines, Ill......A6 178
Des Plaines, riv., Ill., Wis......B5 178, F2 212
Desaguadero, riv., Arg......A3 136
Desaguadero, riv., Bol......C2 135
Desbiens, Que., Can......A6 154
Desboro, Ont., Can......C4 153
Descalabrado, P.R......C5 132
Descalvado, Braz......k8 137
Deschaillons, Que., Can...C5 154
Deschaillons sur St. Laurent, Que., Can......*C5 154
Deschambault, Que., Can......C6 154
Deschambault Lake, Sask., Can......C4 155
Deschênes, Que., Can...*A9 153
Deschutes, co., Oreg......D5 201
Deschutes, riv., Oreg......B6 201
Desembarcadero Mosquito, P.R......g12 132
Desengaño, cape, Arg......D3 136
Desenzano del Garda, It...D6 66
Deseret, Utah......D3 207
Deseronto, Ont., Can......C7 153
Desert, game range, Nev...G6 192
Desert, mtn., W. Va......C6 211
Desert, peak, Utah......B2 207
Desert, val., Nev......B3 192
Desert Center, Calif......F6 170
Desert Hot Springs, Calif......*F5 170
Deserta Grande, isl., Port. (Madeira Is.)......h12 65
Desha, Ark......B4 169
Desha, co., Ark......D4 169
Deshler, Nebr......D8 191
Deshler, Ohio......A4 199
Deshu, Afg......F11 86
Desio, It......D5 66
Desloge, Mo......D7 189
Desmet, Idaho......B2 177
De Smet, S. Dak......C8 204
Desmochado, Par......E4 135
Desna, riv., Sov. Un......F8 72
Desolación, isl., Chile......h11 136
Desolation, lake, Newf., Can......g9 152
De Soto, Ga......E2 175
De Soto, Ill......F4 178
De Soto, Iowa......C3 180
De Soto, Kans......B8, D9 181
De Soto, Miss......D5 188
De Soto, Mo......C7 189
De Soto, Tex......*C4 206
De Soto, Wis......E2 212
De Soto, co., Fla......E5 174
De Soto, co., Miss......A3 188
De Soto, par., La......B2 183
De Soto City, Fla......E5 174
Despard, W. Va......B7 211
Dessau, Ger......B7 61
Destin, Fla......G2 174
Destrehan, La......C7, E5 183
Desvres, Fr......D9 56
Detlor, Ont., Can......B7 153
Detmold, Ger......B3 61
Detour, Md......A3 173
De Tour, Mich......C6 186
Detour, pt., Mich......C4 186
Detroit, Ala......A1 166
Detroit, Kans......D6 181
Detroit, Maine......D3 184
Detroit, Mich......A8, F7 186
Detroit, Oreg......C4 201
Detroit, Tex......C5 206
Detroit, res., Oreg......C4 201
Detroit, riv., Ont., Can., Mich......F7 186
Detroit Beach, Mich...*G7 186
Detroit Lakes, Minn......D3 187
Dett, Rh......A4 107
Detva, Czech......D5 70
Deuel, co., Nebr......C3 191
Deuel, co., S. Dak......C9 204
Deurne, Bel......C4 59
Deux Freres, isl., Viet......H7 89
Deux Montagnes, co., Que., Can......D3, D8 154
Deux Rivieres, Que., Can......A6 153
Deva, Rom......C6 68
De Valls Bluff, Ark......C4 169
Devarkonda, India......I7 88
Dévaványa, Hung......B5 68
Deventer, Neth......B6 59
Devereux, Ga......C3 175
Deveron, riv., Scot......C6 57
De View, bayou, Ark......B4 169
Devil, pt., Efate I...... 115
Devil River, peak, N.Z.......N14 112
Devils, isl., Fr. Gu......A4 139
Devils, lake, N. Dak......A6 198
Devils, riv., Tex......E2 206
Devils Den, Calif......E4 170
Devils Elbow, Mo......D5 189
Devils Lake, N. Dak......A7 198
Devils Paw, mtn., B.C., Can......k23 167
Devils Postpile, nat. mon., Calif......D4 170
Devils Slide, Utah......B4 207
Devils Tower, Wyo......A8 213
Devils Tower, nat. mon., Wyo......A8 213
Devils Track, lake, Minn...B7 187
Devine, Tex......E3 206
Devizes, Eng......C6 56
Devol, Okla......C3 200
Devoll, riv., Alb......B3 69
Devon, Alta., Can......*C4 148
Devon, Conn......E3 172
Devon, Kans......E9 181
Devon, Mont......B5 190
Devon, co., Eng......E5 56
Devon, isl., N.W. Ter., Can......A15 142
Devondale, Ky......*B4 182
Devonport, Austl......o15 111
Devonport, N.Z......L15 112
Dewalt, Tex......F5 206
Dewar, Iowa......B5 180
Dewar, Okla......B6 200
Dewar Lake, Sask., Can...F1 155
Dewberry, Alta., Can......C5 148
Dewees, inlet, S.C.......F4 203
Dewees, isl., S.C....F4, F8 203
Deweese, Nebr......D7 191
Dewey, Ariz......C3 168
Dewey, Mont......E4 190
Dewey, Okla......A6 200
Dewey, S. Dak......D2 204
Dewey, co., Okla......B2 200
Dewey, co., S. Dak......B4 204
Dewey, res., Ky......C7 182
Dewey Park, Ill......*E4 178
Deweyville, Tex......D6 206
Deweyville, Utah......*B3 207
De Winton, Alta., Can......D3 148
De Witt, Ark......C4 169
Dewitt, Ill......C5 178
De Witt, Iowa......C7 180
De Witt, Mich......F6 186
De Witt, Mo......B4 189
De Witt, Nebr......D9 191
De Witt, Va......D5 209
De Witt, co., Ill......C5 178
De Witt, co., Tex......E4 206
Dewsbury, Eng......A6 56
Dewy Rose, Ga......B4 175
Dexter, Ga......D3 175
Dexter, Iowa......C3 180
Dexter, Kans......E7 181
Dexter, Ky......B3 182
Dexter, Maine......C3 184
Dexter, Mich......F7 186
Dexter, Minn......G6 187
Dexter, Mo......E8 189
Dexter, N. Mex......D5 195
Dexter, N.Y......A4 196
Dexter, Oreg......D4 201
Dexter, lake, Fla......C5 174
Deyhūk, Iran......E8 86
Deyyer, Iran......H5 86
Dezfūl, Iran......E4 86
Dezh Shāhpūr, Iran......D3 86
Dezhnëva, cape, Sov. Un..C21 71
Dha'ain, Sau. Ar......I5 86
Dhahran, see Aẓ Ẓahrān, Sau. Ar.
Dhamtari, India......G8 88
Dhanbad, India......F11 88
D'Hanis, Tex......E3 206
Dhankuta, Nep......D11 88
Dhar, India......F5 88
Dharamjaygarh, India......F9 88
Dharmapuri, India......F6 87
Dharmsala, India......A6 88
Dharwar, India......E6 87
Dhāt al Ḩajj, Sau. Ar......H11 85
Dhaulagiri, peak, Nep......C9 88
Dhekélia, Grc......g11 69
Dhenoúsa, isl., Grc......D5 69
Dhībān, Jordan......G10 85
Dhidhimótikhon, Grc......B6 69
Dhílos (Delos), isl., Grc......D5 69
Dhimitsána, Grc......D4 69
Dholpur, India......D6 88
Dhond, India......H5 88
Dhoraji, India......G3 88
Dhrísta, Grc......g11 69
Dhubri, India......E12 88
Dhulia, India......G5 88
Di Linh, Viet......G8 89
Di Monte Santu, cape, It...D2 67
Día, isl., Grc......E5 69
Diabaig, Scot......C3 57
Diablerets, mtn., Switz......C3 66
Diablo, Calif......*D2 170
Diablo, canyon, Ariz......C4 168
Diablo, dam, Wash......A4 210
Diablo, isl., P.R.......f12 132
Diablo, mtn., Calif......B6 170
Diablo, range, Calif......D3 170
Diablo Heights, C.Z......k11 130
Diagonal, Iowa......D3 180
Dial, Ga......B2 175
Diamante, Arg......A4 136
Diamantina, Braz......E2 138
Diamantina, riv., Austl......D7 110
Diamond, Ont., Can......A8 153
Diamond, Ill......*B5 178
Diamond, La......E6 183
Diamond, Mo......E3 189
Diamond, Ohio......A6 199
Diamond, Oreg......D8 201
Diamond, W. Va......C6 211
Diamond, Wyo......D8 213
Diamond, bay, Epi I...... 115
Diamond, cave, Ark......B2 169
Diamond head, Haw..B4, g10 176
Diamond, lake, Oreg......D4 201
Diamond, mts., Nev......D6 192
Diamond, peak, Idaho......E5 177
Diamond, peak, Oreg......D4 201
Diamond, peak, Wash......C8 210
Diamond, pt., Indon......k11 90
Diamond Bluff, Wis......D1 212
Diamond City, Alta., Can...E4 148
Diamond Harbour, India..F12 88
Diamond Lake, Ill......E2 178
Diamond Point, N.Y......B7 196
Diamond Springs, Calif......C3 170
Diamondville, Wyo......D2 213
Diana, Tenn......B5 205
Diana, W. Va......C4 211
Dianalund, Den......C5 62
Dianópolis, Braz......D1 138
Diapaga, Upper Volta......D5 103
Diapitan, bay, Phil......n14 90
Diaz, Ark......B4 169
Dibaya, Zaire......C3 106
D'Iberville, Miss......E2, E5 188
Diboll, Tex......D5 206
Dibrell, Tenn......D8 205
Dibrugarh, India......C9 87
Dickens, Iowa......A2 180
Dickens, Nebr......D5 191
Dickens, Tex......C2 206
Dickens, co., Tex......C2 206
Dickenson, co., Va......B2 209
Dickerson, Md......B3 173
Dickey, N. Dak......C7 198
Dickey, co., N. Dak......C7 198
Dickeyville, Wis......F3 212
Dickie, Wyo......B4 213
Dickinson, Ala......D2 166
Dickinson, N. Dak......C3 198
Dickinson, Tex......*F5 206
Dickinson, co., Iowa......A2 180
Dickinson, co., Kans......D6 181
Dickinson, co., Mich......B3 186
Dickinson, dam, N. Dak...C2 198
Dickinson Center, N.Y......A2 196
Dickson, Tenn......A4 205
Dickson, co., Tenn......A4 205
Dickson City, Pa......A9, D10 202
Dicle, riv., Tur......D13 85
Didi Alou, New Britain I...... 115
Didsbury, Alta., Can......D3 148
Didwana, India......D5 88
Die, Fr......E6 58
Dieburg, Ger......D3 61
Diefenbaker, lake, Sask. Can......C1 155
Diégo-Suarez (Antsirane), Malag......f9 107
Diégo-Suarez, prov., Malag......f9 107
Diekirch, Lux......E6 59
Diem Zubeir, Sud......D2 105
Diemel, riv., Ger......B3 61
Dien Bien Phu, Viet......B5 89
Diepholz, Ger......B4 60
Dieppe, N.B., Can......C5 151
Dieppe, Fr......C4 58
Dierks, Ark......C1 169
Diessen, Ger......B7 66
Diest, Bel......D5 59
Dieterich, Ill......D5 178
Dietrich, Idaho......G4 177
Dieuze, Fr......F6 59
Diever, Neth......B6 59
Diez, Ger......C3 61
Dif, Som......E5 105
Differdange, Lux......E5 59
Difficult, Tenn......C8 205
Digboi, India......C10 87
Digby, N.S., Can......E4 151
Digby, co., N.S., Can......E4 151
Dighton, Kans......D3 181
Dighton, Mass......C5 185
Dighton, Mich......D5 186
Digne, Fr......E7 58
Digoel, riv., Indon......G10 90
Digoin, Fr......D5 58
Dijon, Fr......D6 58
Dike, Iowa......B5 180
Dikhil, Afars & Is......C5 105
Dikili, Tur......C6 69
Dikili, cape, Tur......B8 69
Dikirnis, Eg......C3 84
Diksmuide, Bel......C2 59
Dikson, Sov. Un......B11 71
Dikwa, Nig......D7 103
Dilaram, Afg......E11 86
Dili, Port. Timor......G7 90
Dilke, Sask., Can......G3 155
Dilkon, Ariz......B5 168
Dill City, Okla......B2 200
Dillard, Ga......B3 175
Dillard, Okla......C4 200
Dillard, Oreg......D3 201
Dille, W. Va......C4 211
Dillenburg, Ger......C3 61
Diller Nebr......D9 191
Dilley, Tex......E3 206
Dilliner, Pa......G2 202
Dilling, Sud......C2 105
Dillingen [an der Donau], Ger......E5 61
Dillingen, Ger......D1 61
Dillingham, Alsk......D8 167
Dillon, Colo......B4 171
Dillon, Mont......E4 190
Dillon, S.C......C9 203
Dillon, co., S.C......C9 203
Dillon, bay, Erromango I...... 115
Dillon, res., Ohio......B5 199
Dillonvale, Ohio......B7 199
Dillsboro, Ind......F7 179
Dillsboro, N.C......D3 197
Dillsburg, Pa......F7 202
Dillwyn, Va......D4 209
Dīlmān, see Shāhpūr, Iran
Dilolo, Zaire......D3 106
Dilworth, Minn......D2 187
Dimashq, see Damascus, Syr.
Dimbelenge, Zaire......C3 106
Dimbokro, I.C......E4 103
Dimitrovgrad, Bul......D7 68
Dimitrovgrad, Yugo......D6 68
Dimmit, co., Tex......E3 206
Dimmitt, Tex......B1 206
Dimock, S. Dak......D8 204
Dimondale, Mich......F6 186
Dinagat, isl., Phil......C7 90
Dinajpur, Bngl......E12 88
Dinan, Fr......C3 58
Dinant, Bel......D4 59
Dinapore, India......E10 88
Dinar, Tur......C8 69
Dinard [-St. Enogat], Fr......C2 58
Dinaric Alps, mts., Yugo...D3 68
Dindigul, India......F6 87
Dinero, Tex......E4 206
Dingalan, bay, Phil......o13 90
Dingelstädt, Ger......B5 61
Dingess, W. Va......D2 211
Dingle, Idaho......G7 177
Dingle, Ire......D1 55
Dingle, bay, Ire......D1 55
Dingmans Ferry, Pa......D12 202
Dingo, Austl......A7 112
Dingolfing, Ger......E7 61
Dinguiraye, Guinea......D2 103
Dingwall, N.S., Can......C9 151
Dingwall, Scot......C4 57
Dinh Lap, Viet......B7 89
Dinkelsbühl, Ger......D5 61
Dinkey Creek, Calif......D4 170
Dinklage, Ger......F2 62
Dinner, pt., Fla......D4 174
Dinorwick, lake, Ont., Can..E5 150
Dinosaur, Colo......A1 171
Dinosaur, prov. park, Alta., Can......D5 148
Dinosaur, nat. mon., Colo., Utah......A1 171, C6 207
Dinsdale, Iowa......B5 180
Dinslaken, Ger...C3 60, B1 61
Dinsmore, Sask., Can......F2 155
Dinsmore, Fla......B5, B6 174
Dinuba, Calif......D4 170
Dinwiddie, Va......D5 209
Dinwiddie, co., Va......D5 209
Dioïla, Mali......D3 103
Dioka, Mali......D2 103
Diourbel, Sen......D1 103
Diphu, pass, China, India..C10 87
Diplo, Pak......E2 88
Dipper Harbour, N.B., Can......D3 151
Dippoldiswalde, Ger......C8 61
Dirēdawā, Eth......D5 105
Diriamba, Nic......E4 130
Dirico, Ang......E3 106
Dirk Hartog, isl., Austl......E1 110
Dirkou, Niger......C7 103
Dirmil, Tur......D7 69
Dirranbandi, Austl......D7 112
Dirty Devil, riv., Utah......E5 207
Disappointment, bay, Ant..C27 120
Disappointment, cape, Ant..D9 120
Disappointment, cape, Wash......C1 210
Disappointment, lake, Austl......D3 110
Disautel, Wash......A6 210
Disentis (Mustèr), Switz...C4 66
Dishman, Wash......D7 210
Dishnā, Eg......D6 101
Disko, Ind......B6 179
Disko, isl., Grnld......C20 118
Disley, Sask., Can......G3 155
Dismal, peak, Va......D2 209
Dismal, swamp, N.C., Va......A7 197, E6 209
Disney, Okla......A6 200
Disputanta, Va......D5 209
Disraeli, Que., Can......D6 154
Diss, Eng......B9 56
Distant, Pa......E3 202
District Heights, Md......C4 173
District of Columbia, U.S..C4 173
Distrito Federal, fed. dist., Mex......D5 129
Distrito Federal, fed. dist., Ven......A4 133
Disūq, Eg......C2 84
Dittlinger, Tex......B4 206
Ditzum, Ger......A7 59
Diu, India......G3 88
Divenié, Con......F2 104
Divernon, Ill......D4 178
Dives-sur-Mer, Fr......C3 58
Divide, Mont......E4 190
Divide, co., N. Dak......A2 198
Divide, peak, Wyo......D5 213
Divinópolis, Braz......F2 138
Divion, Fr......D2 59
Divišov, Czech......o18 70
Divnoye, Sov. Un......D2 73
Divo, I.C......E3 103
Divriği, Tur......C12 85
Dix, Ill......E5 178
Dix, Nebr......C2 191
Dix, dam, Ky......C5 182
Dix, hills, N.Y.......F3 172
Dix, mtn., N.Y.......A7 196
Dix, riv., Ky......C5 182
Dixfield, Maine......D2 184
Dixiana, Ala......B3 166
Dixiana, S.C......D5 203
Dixie, Ala......D3 166
Dixie, Ark......B4 169
Dixie, Ont., Can......E6 153
Dixie, Ga......F3 175
Dixie, Idaho......D3 177
Dixie, La......B2 183
Dixie, Wash......C7 210
Dixie, W. Va......C3, C7 211
Dixie, co., Fla......C3 174
Dixie Inn, La......*B2 183
Dixie Union, Ga......E4 175
Dixmoor, Ill......*F3 178
Dixmont, Maine......*D3 184
Dixon, Calif......A6, C3 170
Dixon, Ill......B4 178
Dixon, Iowa......C7 180
Dixon, Ky......C2 182
Dixon, Mo......D5 189
Dixon, Mont......C2 190
Dixon, Nebr......B9 191
Dixon, N. Mex......A4 195
Dixon, Ohio......B3 199
Dixon, S. Dak......D6 204
Dixon, Wyo......E5 213
Dixon, co., Nebr......B9 191
Dixon, entrance, B.C., Can.B1 149
Dixon Springs, Ill......F5 178
Dixons Mills, Ala......C2 166
Dixonville, Ala......D2 166
Dixonville, Alta., Can......A2 148
Dixonville, Pa......E4 202
Dixville, Que., Can......D6 154
Dixville, peak, N.H.......A4, B1 193
Dixville Notch, N.H......B1 193
Diyālā, Iraq......F15 85, E2 86
Diyarbakir, Tur......D13 85
Dizy-le-Gros, Fr......E4 59
Dizy-Magenta, Fr......E3 59
Dja, riv., Cam......E2 104
Djado, Niger......B7 103
Djafou, Alg......D5 102
Djailolo, Indon......E7 90
Djaja, peak, Indon......F9 90
Djajapura, Indon......F10 90
Djakarta (Jakarta, Batavia), Indon......G3 90
Djakovica, Yugo......D5 68
Djakovo, Yugo......C4 68
Djambala, Con......F2 104
Djambi, Indon......F2 90
Djanet (Ft. Charlet), Alg...E6 102
Djaravica, peak, Yugo......D5 68
Djedeida, Tun......F11 64
Djelfa, Alg......C5 102
Djema, Cen. Afr. Rep......D5 104
Djemadja, isl., Indon......K6 89
Djenné, Mali......D4 103
Djerba, isl., Tun...H12 64, C7 102
Djerid, salt lake, Tun......C6 102
Djibo, Upper Volta......D4 103
Djibouti, Afars & Is......C5 105
Djidjelli, Alg......B6 102
Djolu, Zaire......A3 106
Djouf, basin, Maur., Mali..B3 103
Djougou, Dah......E5 103
Djugu, Zaire......A5 106
Djurdjevac, Yugo......B3 68
Djurjura, mtn., Alg......B5 102
Djursholm, Swe......t36 63
D'Lo, Miss......D4 188
Dmitriyev-Lgovskiy, Sov. Un......E10 72
Dmitriyevka Sov. Un.H12, r21 72
Dmitrov, Sov. Un......C11 72
Dmitrovsk-Orlovskiy, Sov. Un......E10 72

INDEX KEY Each place listed in **Bold-faced Type** has its population listed in the Population tables, pages 230 to 280.
Each country, shown in CAPITAL LETTERS, has its population listed in the World Political Information Table, pages 6 to 10.
* Does not appear on map; key shows general location.

Dnepr, riv., Sov. Un H9 72
Dneprodzerzhinsk, Sov. Un G10 72
Dnepropetrovsk, Sov. Un G10 72
Dnestr, riv., Sov. Un H7 72
Dno, Sov. Un C7 72
Doaktown, N.B., Can C3 151
Doba, Chad D3 104
Dobbinton, Ont., Can C3 153
Dobbs Ferry, N.Y D1 196
Dobbyn, Austl C6 111
Döbeln, Ger B8 61
Doblas, Arg B4 136
Dobo, Indon G8 90
Doboj, Yugo C4 68
Doboy, sound, Ga E5 175
Dobřejovice, Czech o18 70
Dobrich, see Tolbukhin, Bul.
Dobříš, Czech o17 70
Dobrovice, Czech n18 70
Dobrovolsk, Sov. Un A7 70
Dobruja (Dobrudja), reg., Bul., Rom C9 68
in 1914 52
in 1940 53
Dobšiná, Czech D6 70
Dobson, N.C A3 197
Doce, riv., Braz E2 138
Dock Junction, Ga *E5 175
Dockton, Wash D1 210
Doctor Arroyo, Mex C4 129
Doctors, lake, Fla C6 174
Doctors Inlet, Fla C6 174
Doctortown, Ga E5 175
Doddridge, Ark D2 169
Doddridge, co., W. Va B4 211
Dodds, Alta., Can C4 148
Doddsville, Miss B3 188
Dodecanese, prov., Grc D6 69
Dodecanese, is., Grc D6 69
Dodge, Mass B4 185
Dodge, Nebr C9 191
Dodge, N. Dak B3 198
Dodge, Wis D2 212
Dodge, co., Ga D3 175
Dodge, co., Minn G6 187
Dodge, co., Nebr C9 191
Dodge, co., Wis E5 212
Dodge Center, Minn F6 187
Dodge City, Kans E3 181
Dodgeville, Ohio A7 199
Dodgeville, Wis F3 212
Dodoma, Tan C6 106
Dodsland, Sask., Can F1 155
Dodson, La B3 183
Dodson, Mont B8 190
Dodson, Tex B2 206
Doe River, B.C., Can B7 149
Doe Run, Mo D7 189
Doebay, Wash A3 210
Doerun, Ga E3 175
Doetinchem, Neth C6 59
Doeville, Tenn C12 205
Dog, isl., Fla C2 174
Dog, lake, Man., Can D2 150
Dog, riv., Vt C3 208
Dog, rocks, Vir. Is f15 132
Dog Keys, pass, Miss E3 188
Dogiuma, Som E5 105
Dōgo, see Higashi, isl., Jap.
Dogondoutchi, Niger D5 103
Doğubayazit, Tur C15 85
Doha, Qatar I5 86
Dohad, India F5 88
Dohat es Salwa, bay, Sau. Ar I5 86
Doheny, Que., Can B5 154
Doi Inthon, mtn., Thai C3 89
Doire, riv., It D2 66
Dois Irmãos, mts., Braz C2 138
Dojran, lake, Yugo E6 68
Dokkum, Neth A6 59
Doksy, Czech C9 61
Dol [-de-Bretagne], Fr C3 58
Dolak, isl., Indon G9 90
Doland, S. Dak C7 204
Dolavón, Arg C3 136
Dolbeau, Que., Can G18 145
Dole, Fr D6 58
Dolega, Pan F6 130
Doleib Hill, Sud D3 105
Doles, Ga E3 175
Dolgelley, Wales B4 56
Dolgeville, N.Y B6 196
Dolgoprudnyy, Sov. Un n17 72
Dolina, Sov. Un D8 70
Dolinsk (Ochiai), Sov. Un C11 93
Dolinskoye, Sov. Un B9 68
Dolisie, Con F2 104
Dollar Bay, Mich A2 186
Dollard, Sask., Can H1 155
Dollart, bay, Neth A7 59
Dollarville, Mich B5 186
Dolliver, Iowa A3 180
Dolo, Eth E5 105
Dolomita, Ala B3, E4 166
Dolomites, mts., It C7 66
Dolores, Arg B5 136
Dolores, Colo D2 171
Dolores, Guat B3 130
Dolores, Mex B3 129
Dolores, Ur E1 137
Dolores, co., Colo D2 171
Dolores, riv., Colo., Utah C2 171, E7 207
Dolores Hidalgo, Mex m13 129
Dolphin and Union, straits, N.W. Ter., Can C9 142
Dolton, Ill F3 178
Dolton, S. Dak D8 204
Dolzhanskaya, Sov. Un q22 72
Dom Pedrito, Braz E2 137
Domadare, Som E5 105
Domanovići, Yugo D3 68
Domažlice, Czech D2 70
Dombarovskiy, Sov. Un C5 73
Dombås, Nor F3 63
Dombasle [-sur-Meurthe], Fr F6 59
Dombe Grande, Ang D1 106
Dombóvár, Hung B4 68
Domburg, Neth C3 59
Dome, peak, Colo B3 171
Dome, peak, N.W. Ter., Can D7 142
Dome Rock, mts., Ariz D1 168
Domeyko, Chile D2 135
Domeyko, range, Chile D2 135
Domfront, Fr C3 58
Domingo, N. Mex B3 195
Domingo, Indian res., N. Mex G6 195
Dominica, C.R F6 130
DOMINICA, Br. dep., N.A o16 131
Dominica, isl., N.A o16 131
DOMINICAN REPUBLIC, country, N.A F8 131
in 1800's 127
Dominion, N.S., Can C9 151
Dominion, cape, N.W. Ter., Can C18 143
Dominion, lake, Newf., Can h9 152
Dominion City, Man., Can E3 150
Dömitz, Ger B5 60
Dommel, riv., Neth C5 59
Domodedovo, Sov. Un n17 72
Domodossola, It C4 66
Dompierre [-sur-Authie], Fr D9 56
Domremy, Sask., Can E3 155
Domuyo, mtn., Arg B2 136
Domvraína, Grc g9 69
Don, pen., B.C., Can C3 149
Don, riv., Scot C6 57
Don, riv., Sov. Un C1 73
Don Benito, Sp C3 65
Don Martin, lake, Mex B4 129
Dona Ana, N. Mex E3 195
Dona Ana, co., N. Mex E3 195
Donaghadee, N. Ire C4 55
Donald, Ont., Can C6 153
Donald, Oreg B2 201
Donalda, Alta., Can C4 148
Donalds, S.C C3 203
Donaldson, Ark C3 169
Donaldson, Ind B5 179
Donaldson, Minn B2 187
Donaldson, Pa E9 202
Donaldsonville, La B5, D4 183
Donalsonville, Ga E2 175
Donau (Danube), riv., Ger E6 61
Donaueschingen, Ger B4 66
Donauwörth, Ger E5 61
Donavon, Sask., Can F2 155
Doncaster, Eng A6 56
Doncaster, Md D3 173
Dondo, Ang C1 106
Dondo, Moz A5 107
Donegal, Ire C2 55
Donegal, bay, Ire C2 55
Donegal, mts., Ire C2 55
Donelson, Tenn A5, E9 205
Doneraile, S.C C8 203
Donets, riv., Sov. Un G13, q21 72
Donetsk, Sov. Un H11, r20 72
Dong Hoi, Viet D7 89
Dongara, Austl E2 111
Donggala, Indon F5 90
Dongo, Zaire A2 106
Dongola, Ill F4 178
Dongola, Sud B3 105
Dongou, Con E3 104
Donington, Eng B7 56
Doniphan, Kans C8 181
Doniphan, Mo E7 189
Doniphan, Nebr D7 191
Doniphan, co., Kans C8 181
Donji Vakuf, Yugo C3 68
Donkey, creek, Wyo A7 213
Donkin, N.S., Can C10 151
Donley, co., Tex B2 206
Donna, Tex F3 206
Donnacona, Que., Can C6, C8 154
Donnellson, Ill D4 178
Donnellson, Iowa D6 180
Donnelly, Alta., Can B2 148
Donnelly, Idaho E2 177
Donnelly, Minn E2 187
Donnels, Tenn B5 205
Donner, La C5, E5 183
Donner, pass, Calif C3 170
Donnybrook, N. Dak A4 198
Donnybrook Place, Tex *E5 206
Donora, Pa F2 202
Donovan, Ga D4 175
Donovan, Ill C6 178
Donzère, Fr E6 58
Doole, Tex D3 206
Dooley, Mont B12 190
Dooling, Ga D3 175
Doolittle, Mo *D6 189
Dooly, co., Ga D3 175
Doon, Iowa A1 180
Doon, lake, Scot E4 57
Doon, riv., Scot E4 57
Doonerak, mtn., Alsk B9 167
Door, co., Wis D6 212
Dora, Ala B2 166
Dora, Mo E5 189
Dora, N. Mex D6 195
Dora, Oreg D3 201
Dora Baltea, riv., It B1 67
Dorado, P.R B5 132
Dorado, mun., P.R B5 132
Doran, Minn D2 187
Doraville, Ga A5 175
Dorcas, Fla G2 174
Dorcheat, bayou, La B2 183
Dorcheat, creek, Ark D2 169
Dorchester, N.B., Can D5 151
Dorchester, Eng D5 56
Dorchester, Ga E5 175
Dorchester, Iowa A6 180
Dorchester, Nebr D8 191
Dorchester, N.H C3 193
Dorchester, N.J E3 194
Dorchester, S.C E7 203
Dorchester, Wis C3 212
Dorchester, co., Que., Can C7 154
Dorchester, co., Md D5 173
Dorchester, co., S.C E7 203
Dorchester, cape, N.W. Ter., Can C17 143
Dorcyville, La B5 183
Dordogne, riv., Fr E3 58
Dordrecht, Neth C4 59
Dordrecht, S. Afr D4 107
Dore, N. Dak B2 198
Dore, lake, Ont., Can B7 153
Doré, lake, Sask., Can C2 155
Doré, riv., Sask., Can C2 155
Doré Lake, Sask., Can C2 155
Dorena, Mo E8 189
Dorena, Oreg D4 201
Dorena, dam, Oreg D3 201
Dorenlee, Alta., Can C4 148
Dores, Scot C4 57
Dores do Indaiá, Braz E1 138
Dorfen, Ger A8 66
Dorgali, It D2 67
Dori, Upper Volta D4 103
Dorion, Que., Can D3 154
Dormans, Fr E3 59
Dormont, Pa B5 202
Dornbirn, Aus B5 66
Dornie, Scot C3 57
Dornoch, Scot C4 57
Dornoch, firth, Scot C5 57
Dorogobuzh, Sov. Un D9 72
Dorohoi, Rom B8 68
Dorothy, Alta., Can D4 148
Dorothy, Minn C2 187
Dorothy, N.J E3 194
Dorothy, W. Va D6 211
Dorr, Mich F5 186
Dorrance, Kans D5 181
Dorrigo, Austl E9 112
Dorris, Calif B3 170
Dorset, Ont., Can B6 153
Dorset, Minn D3 187
Dorset, Ohio A7 199
Dorset, Vt E2 208
Dorset, co., Eng D5 56
Dorset, mtn., Vt E2 208
Dorset, peak, Vt E2 208
Dorsey, Ill A8 189
Dorsey, Md B4 173
Dorsey, Miss A5 188
Dorsten, Ger B1 61
Dortmund, Ger B2 61
Dortmund Ems, canal, Ger B2 61
Dorton, Ky C7 182
Dörtyol, Tur D11 85
Dorum, Ger E2 62
Doruma, Zaire A4 106
Dorval, Que., Can D8 154
Dos Bahias, cape, Arg C3 136
Dos Bocas, P.R B4 132
Dos Hermanas, Sp D3 65
Dos Palos, Calif D3 170
Dos Rios, Calif C2 170
Doshi, Afg D14 86
Dosquet, Que., Can C6 154
Dosse, riv., Ger E6 62
Dosso, Niger D5 103
Doswell, Va D5 209
Dothan, Ala D4 166
Dothan, W. Va D7 211
Dott, W. Va D3 211
Doty, Wash C2 210
Doty, isl., Wis A5 212
Douai, Fr B5 58
Douala, Cam E1 104
Douarnenez, Fr C1 58
Double, bay, Malaita I 115
Double, mtn., Ala E5 166
Double Bayou, Tex F5 206
Double Mer, lake, Newf., Can A2 152
Double Oak, mtn., Ala E5 166
Double Springs, Ala A2 166
Double Springs, Tenn C8 205
Doublespring, pass, Ida E4 177
Doubletop, peak, Wyo B2 213
Doubs, Md B3 173
Doubs, dept., Fr B2 66
Doubs, riv., Fr., Switz D7 58
Doubtful, sound, N.Z P11 112
Doucette, Tex D5 206
Douds, Iowa D5 180
Doué [-la-Fontaine], Fr D3 58
Douenza, Mali D4 103
Dougherty, Iowa B4 180
Dougherty, Okla C4 200
Dougherty, co., Ga E2 175
Douglas, Alsk D13, k22 167
Douglas, Ariz F6 168
Douglas, Ont., Can B8 153
Douglas, Ga E4 175
Douglas, I. of Man C4 55
Douglas, Mass B4 185
Douglas, Mich F4 186
Douglas, Minn F6 187
Douglas, Nebr D9 191
Douglas, N. Dak B4 198
Douglas, Okla A4 200
Douglas, S. Afr C3 107
Douglas, Wyo C7 213
Douglas, co., Colo B6 171
Douglas, co., Ga C2 175
Douglas, co., Ill D5 178
Douglas, co., Kans D8 181
Douglas, co., Minn E3 187
Douglas, co., Mo E5 189
Douglas, co., Nebr C9 191
Douglas, co., Nev E2 192
Douglas, co., Oreg D3 201
Douglas, co., S. Dak D7 204
Douglas, co., Wash B6 210
Douglas, co., Wis B2 212
Douglas, chan., B.C., Can C3 149
Douglas, lake, Mich C6 186
Douglas, lake, Tenn D10 205
Douglas, mtn., Alsk D9 167
Douglas, pt., Ont., Can C3 153
Douglas Lake, B.C., Can D7 149
Douglas Station, Man., Can E2 150
Douglass, Kans E7 181
Douglass, N.Y B3 196
Douglastown, N.B., Can B4 151
Douglasville, Ala *E2 166
Douglasville, Ga C2 175
Doullens, Fr B5 58
Doumé, Cam E2 104
Douna, Mali D3 103
Dour, Bel D3 59
Dourada, mts., Braz D1 138
Dourado, Braz m7 137
Dourdan, Fr F2 59
Douro (Duero), riv., Port B1 65
Dousman, Wis E5 212
Douthat, Okla A7 200
Douville, Que., Can *B5 154
Douz, Tun C6 102
Dove Creek, Colo D2 171
Dover, Ark B2 169
Dover, Del B6 173
Dover, Eng C9 56
Dover, Fla D4 174
Dover, Ga D5 175
Dover, Idaho A2 177
Dover, Kans D8 181
Dover, Ky B6 182
Dover, Mass D2 185
Dover, Minn G6 187
Dover, Mo B4 189
Dover, N.H D5 193
Dover, N.J B3 194
Dover, N.C B6 197
Dover, Ohio B6 199
Dover, Okla B4 200
Dover, Pa F8 202
Dover, Tenn A4 205
Dover, res., Ohio A3 211
Dover, riv., Alta., Can A4 148
Dover, strait, Eng E7 55
Dover-Foxcroft, Maine C3 184
Dover Plains, N.Y D7 196
Doverel, Ga E2 175
Doverhill, Ind G4 179
Dovesville, S.C C8 203
Dovray, Minn F3 187
Dovrefjell, mts., Nor F3 63
Dow, Okla C6 200
Dow, Ill D3 178
Dow City, Iowa C2 180
Dowa, Malawi D5 106
Dowagiac, Mich G4 186
Dowell, Ill F4 178
Dowelltown, Tenn C8 205
Dowling, lake, Alta., Can D4 148
Dowling Park, Fla B3 174
Downer, Minn D2 187
Downers Grove, Ill *F2 178
Downey, Calif *E4 170
Downey, Idaho G6 177
Downham Market, Eng B8 56
Downieville, Calif C3 170
Downing, Mo A5 189
Downing, Wis C1 212
Downingtown, Pa F10 202
Downpatrick, N. Ire C4 55
Downs, Ala C4 166
Downs, Ill C5 178
Downs, Kans C5 181
Downs, mtn., Wyo B3 213
Downsville, La B3 183
Downsville, N.Y C6 196
Downsville, Wis D2 212
Downton, mtn., B.C., Can C5 149
Dows, Iowa B4 180
Doyle, Calif B3 170
Doyle, Tenn D8 205
Doyle, creek, Kans A6 181
Doyles, Newf., Can E2 152
Doylestown, Ohio B6 199
Doylestown, Pa F11 202
Doyleville, Colo C4 171
Doyline, La B2 183
Doyon, N. Dak A7 198
Dozier, Ala D3 166
Dra, plat., Alg D3 102
Dra, wadi, Mor D3 102
Drabenderhöhe, Ger C2 61
Drachten, Neth A6 59
Dracut, Mass A5 185
Drăgăneşti, Rom C7 68
Draganovo, Bul D7 68
Drăgăşani, Rom C7 68
Dragerton, Utah D5 207
Dragoon, Ariz E5 168
Dragoon, creek, Kans D8 181
Dragör, Den C6 62
Draguignan, Fr F7 58
Drain, Oreg D3 201
Drake, Ariz C3 168
Drake, Sask., Can F3 155
Drake, Colo A5 171
Drake, N. Dak B5 198
Drake, creek, Ky D3 182
Drake, peak, Oreg E6 201
Drake Passage, strait, Ant D6 120
Drakensberg, mts., S. Afr J8 96
Drakes, bay, Calif B5 170
Drakes Branch, Va E4 209
Drakesboro, Ky C2 182
Drakesville, Iowa D5 180
Draketown, Ga C1 175
Dráma, Grc B5 69
Drama, riv., Pol g9 70
Drammen, Nor H4, p28 63
Dramselv, riv., Nor p27 63
Drancy, Fr g10 58
Drangiana: c. 500 B.C. 78
Draper, N.C A4 197
Draper, S. Dak D5 204
Draper, Utah C4 207
Drasco, Ark B4 169
Drau, riv., Aus E6 60
Drava, riv., Yugo B2 68
Draveil, Fr F2 59
Dravograd, Yugo B2 68
Dravosburg, Pa B6 202
Drawsko, Pol B3 70
Drayton, Ont., Can D4 153
Drayton, N. Dak A8 198
Drayton, S.C B4 203
Drayton Plains, Mich F7 186
Drayton Valley, Alta., Can C3 148
Drebkau, Ger B9 61
Drelsdorf, Ger D3 62
Drenthe, prov., Neth B6 59
Dresbach, Minn G7 187
Dresden, Ont., Can E2 153
Dresden, Ger B8 61
Dresden, Kans C3 181
Dresden, Maine *D3 184
Dresden, N.Y *C4 196
Dresden, N. Dak A7 198
Dresden, Ohio B5 199
Dresden, Tenn A3 205
Dresser, Wis C1 212
Dresslerville, Nev E2 192
Dreux, Fr C4 58
Drew, Maine *C4 184
Drew, Miss B3 188
Drew, Oreg E4 201
Drew, co., Ark D4 169
Drewrys Bluff, Va D5 209
Drewryville, Va E5 209
Drews, res., Oreg E6 201
Drewsey, Oreg D8 201
Drewsville, N.H D2 193
Drexel, Mo C3 189
Drexel, Mont C1 190
Drexel, N.C B2 197
Drexel, Ohio C1 199
Drexel Gardens, Ind E5, H7 179
Drezna, Sov. Un n18 72
Driffield, Eng F8 57
Drift, Ky C7 182
Drifton, Pa D10 202
Driftpile, Alta., Can B3 148
Driftwood, Okla A3 200
Driftwood, Pa D5 202
Driftwood, creek, Kans., Nebr B3 181
Driggs, Idaho F7 177
Drin, gulf, Alb B2 69
Drina, riv., Yugo C4 68
Drinkwater, Sask., Can G3 155
Dripping Springs, Tex D3 206
Driscoll, N. Dak C5 198
Driscoll, Tex F4 206
Driskill, mtn., La B3 183
Drissa, Sov. Un D6 72
Driver, Ark B5 169
Driver, Va B6 209
Dröbak, Nor H4, p28 63
Drogheda, Ire D3 55
Drogobych, Sov. Un G4 72
Droitwich, Eng B5 56
Drôme, riv., Fr E6 58
Dronero, It E3 66
Dronfield, Eng A6 56
Dronninglund, Den A4 62
Dropmore, Man., Can D1 150
Druid, Sask., Can F1 155
Druid Hills, Ky *B4 182
Druid Hills, N.C *D3 197
Drulingen, Fr F7 59
Drum, isl., S.C F3 203
Drumbeg Scot B3 57
Drumbo, Ont., Can D4 153
Drumheller, Alta., Can D4 148
Drummond, Idaho E7 177
Drummond, Mont D3 190
Drummond, N.B., Can *B2 151
Drummond, Okla A3 200
Drummond, Wis B2 212
Drummond, co., Que., Can D5 154
Drummond, isl., Mich C7 186
Drummond, lake, Va E6 209
Drummond Island, Mich B7 186
Drummondville, Que., Can D5 154
Drummondville Ouest, Que., Can *D5 154
Drummore, Scot F4 57
Drumright, Okla B5 200
Druzhkovka, Sov. Un q20 72
Drwęca, riv., Pol B5 70
Dry, creek, Kans B6 181
Dry, fork, Mo C6 189
Dry, fork, Mo D6 189
Dry, fork, W. Va B5 211
Dry Branch, Ga D3 175
Dry Creek, La D2 183
Dry Creek, mtn., Nev B5 192
Dry Fork, Va E3 209
Dry Mills, Maine E2, E5 184
Dry Prong, La C3 183
Dry Ridge, Ky B5 182
Dry Run, Pa F6 202
Dry Tortugas, is., Fla H4 174
Dryad, Wash C2 210
Dryberry, lake, Ont., Can E5 150
Drybranch, W. Va C6 211
Dryden, Ont., Can E8 153
Dryden, Maine D2 184
Dryden, Mich F7 186
Dryden, N.Y C4 196
Dryden, Tex D1 206
Dryden, Wash B5 210
Dryfork, W. Va C5 211
Drygalski, ice tongue, Ant B29 120
Drymen, Scot D4 57
Dsalatu, Mong B2 92
Dsamdo, China B11 88
Dschang, Cam D2 104
Duana, pt., Epi I 115
Duane, N.Y A3 196
Duaringa, Austl A7 112
Duart, pt., Scot D3 57
Duarte, Calif *F3 170
Dubach, La B3 183
Dubawnt, lake, N.W. Ter., Can D12 142
Du Bay, res., Wis D4 212
Dubayy, U.A.E I7 86
Dubberly, La B2 183
Dubbo, Austl F7 112
Dubbs, Miss A3 188
Düben, Ger B7 61
Dublin, Ala C3 166
Dublin, Ont., Can D3 153
Dublin, Ga D4 175
Dublin, Ind E7 179
Dublin (Baile Átha Cliath), Ire D3 55
Dublin, Miss A3 188
Dublin, N.H E2 193
Dublin, N.C C5 197
Dublin, Ohio C2 199
Dublin, Pa F11 202
Dublin, Tex C3 206
Dublin, Va D2 209
Dublin Shore, N.S., Can E5 151
Dublon, isl., Truk 114
Dubois, Idaho E6 177
Dubois, Ill E4 178
Dubois, Ind H4 179
Du Bois, Nebr D9 191
Du Bois, Pa D4 202
Dubois, Wyo B3 213
Dubois, co., Ind H4 179
Duboistown, Pa D7 202
Dubossary, Sov. Un H7 72
Dubovka, Sov. Un n18 73
Dubrovka, Sov. Un s31 63
Dubrovnik, Yugo D4 68
Dubuc, Sask., Can G4 155
Dubulu, Zaire A3 106
Dubuque, Iowa B7 180
Dubuque, co., Iowa B7 180
Duchcov, Czech C2 70
Duchesne, Utah C5 207
Duchesne, co., Utah C5 207
Duchess, Austl D6 111
Duchess, Alta., Can D5 148
Du Chien, bayou, Ky B2 182
Ducie, isl., Pac. O H14 113
Duck, N.C A8 197
Duck, creek, Del B7 173
Duck, creek, Nev D7 192
Duck, creek, Ohio C6 199
Duck, creek, Wis A5 212
Duck, lake, Man., Can B2 150
Duck, lake, Maine C4 184
Duck, mtn., Man., Can D1 150
Duck, riv., Tenn B4 205
Duck Bay, Man., Can C1 150
Duck Hill, Miss B4 188
Duck Lake, Sask., Can E2 155
Duck Mountain, prov. park, Sask., Can F5 155
Duck Pond, pt., N.Y E6 172
Duck River, Tenn B4 205
Duck Valley, Indian res., Idaho, Nev G2 177, A5 192
Ducktown, Tenn D9 205
Duckwater, Nev E6 192
Duckwater, peak, Nev E6 192
Ducor, Calif E4 170
Ducos, isl., N. Cal 115
Dudelange, Lux E6 59
Duderstadt, Ger B5 61
Dudhi, India E9 88
Dudinka, Sov. Un C11 71
Dudley, Eng B5 56
Dudley, Ga D3 175
Dudley, Mass B4 185
Dudley, Mo E7 189
Dudley, N.C B5 197
Dudley, Pa F5 202
Dudweiler, Ger D2 61
Due West, S.C C3 203
Duékoué, I.C E3 103
Duenweg, Mo D3 189
Duero (Douro), riv., Sp B3 65
Duff, Sask., Can G4 155
Duff, Ind H3 179
Duff, Nebr B6 191
Duff, Tenn C9 205
Duff, reef, Fiji 114
Duffee, Miss C5 188
Duffer, peak, Nev B3 192
Dufferin, co., Ont., Can C4 153
Duffield, Alta., Can C3 148
Dufftown, Scot C5 57
Duffy, Ohio C7 199
Dufrost, Man., Can E3 150
Dufur, Oreg B5 201
Dug Hill, ridge, Md A4 173
Dugdemona, riv., La B3 183
Dugdown, mtn., Ga C1 175
Dugger, Ind F3 179
Dugi Otok, isl., Yugo C2 68
Dugway, range, Utah C2 207

INDEX KEY Each place listed in **Bold-faced Type** has its population listed in the Population tables, pages 230 to 280.
Each country, shown in CAPITAL LETTERS, has its population listed in the World Political Information Table, pages 6 to 10.
* Does not appear on map; key shows general location.

Duhamel, Que., Can D2 154
Duich, inlet, Scot C3 57
Duisburg, Ger C3 60, B1 61
Duitama, Col B3 133
Duiwelskloof, S. Afr B5 107
Duk Fadiat, Sud D3 105
Duke, Ala B4 166
Duke, Mo D5 189
Duke, (East Duke), Okla C2 200
Duke, isl., Alsk n24 167
Duke Center, Pa C5 202
Duke Ernst, bay, Ant B9 120
Duke of York, isl., Bis. Arch 115
Dukedom, Tenn A3 205
Dukes, co., Mass D6 185
Duki, Pak B4 87
Dukla, pass, Czech., Pol D6 70
Dulce, N. Mex A3 195
Dulce, riv., Arg E3 135
Dülken, Ger C6 59
Dull Center, Wyo B8 213
Dülmen, Ger B2 61
Dulowa, Pol g11 70
Duluth, Ga A5, B2 175
Duluth, Minn D6 187
Dum-Dum, India F12 88
Dūmā, Jordan g12 84
Dumaguete, Phil D6 90
Dumaran, isl., Phil C5 90
Dumas, Ark D4 169
Dumas, Ga D2 175
Dumas, Miss A5 188
Dumas, Tex B2 206
Dumba, Zaire B3 106
Dumbarton, Scot E4 57
Dumbea, N. Cal 115
Dumbea, pass, N. Cal 115
Dumboa, Nig D7 103
Dumfries, Scot E5 57
Dumfries, Va C5 209
Dumfries, co., Scot E5 57
Dumka, India E11 88
Dummer, Sask., Can H3 155
Dummer, N.H *A4 193
Dümmer, lake, Ger F2 62
Dummerston, Vt *F3 208
Dumoine, riv., Que., Can A7 153
Dumont, Iowa B5 180
Dumont, Minn E2 187
Dumont, N.J B5, D5 194
Dumont, Tex C2 206
Dumoulin, cape, N. Cal 115
Dumyāt, see Damietta, Eg.
Dún Laoghaire, Ire D3 55
Dun Seilcheig, lake, Scot C4 57
Dun-sur-Auron, Fr D5 58
Duna (Danube), riv., Czech., Hung B4 68
Dunaföldvár, Hung B4 68
Dunapataj, Hung B4 68
Dunărea (Danube), riv., Rom C8 68
Dunaujváros, Hung B4 68
Dunav (Danube), riv., Yugo C4 68
Dunavant, Kans B7 181
Dunay, Sov. Un E6 93
Dunayevtsy, Sov. Un G6 72
Dunbar, Ky C3 182
Dunbar, Nebr D9, F3 191
Dunbar, Pa G2 202
Dunbar, Scot E6 57
Dunbar, S.C B8 203
Dunbar, W. Va C3, C6 211
Dunbar, Wis C5 212
Dunbarton, N.H D3 193
Dunbarton, co., Scot D4 57
Dunbeath, Scot B5 57
Dunblane, Sask., Can F2 155
Dunblane, Scot D5 57
Dunbridge, Ohio A2 199
Duncan, Ariz E6 168
Duncan, B.C., Can B9, E6 149
Duncan, Ky C5 182
Duncan, Miss A3 188
Duncan, Nebr C8 191
Duncan, Okla C4 200
Duncan, S.C B3 203
Duncan, Wyo B3 213
Duncan, lake, B.C., Can D2 148
Duncan, riv., B.C., Can D9 149
Duncan Falls, Ohio C6 199
Duncannon, Pa F7 202
Duncansby, head, Scot B6 57
Duncansville, Pa F5 202
Duncanville, Tex B5 206
Duncombe, Iowa B4 180
Dundalk, Ont., Can C4 153
Dundalk, Ire C3 55
Dundalk, Md B4, C3 173
Dundalk, bay, Ire D3 55
Dundas, Ont., Can D5 153
Dundas, Ill E5 178
Dundas, Minn F5 187
Dundas, Ohio C5 199
Dundas, Va E4 209
Dundas, co., Ont., Can B9 153
Dundas, isl., B.C., Can B2 149
Dundas, lake, Austl F3 110
Dundas, strait, Austl B5 110
Dundas Harbour, N.W. Ter., Can B16 144
Dundee, Fla D5 174
Dundee (West Dundee), Ill A5, E2 178
Dundee, Iowa B6 180
Dundee, Ky C3 182
Dundee, Mich G7 186
Dundee, Minn G3 187
Dundee, Miss A3 188
Dundee, N.Y C4 196
Dundee, Oreg B1 201
Dundee, Scot D6 57
Dundee, S. Afr C5 107
Dundee, Tex C3 206
Dundee, Wis E5 212
Dundrum, bay, N. Ire C4 55
Dundurn, Sask., Can F2 155
Dundy, co., Nebr D4 191
Dunedin, Fla D4, E1 174
Dunedin, N.Z P13 112
Dunellen, N.J B4 194
Dunfermline, Sask., Can E2 155
Dunfermline, Ill C3 178
Dunfermline, Scot D5 57
Dungannon, Ont., Can D3 153
Dungannon, N. Ire C3 55
Dungannon, Va B2 209
Dungarpur, India F4 88
Dungarvan, Ire D3 55
Dungarvon, riv., N.B., Can C3 151
Dungeness, Wash A2 210
Dungeness, cape, Eng D8 56
Dungeness, riv., Wash B2 210
Dungu, Zaire A4 106
Dunham, Que., Can D5 154
Dunkard, creek, W. Va B4 211
Dunkeld, Scot D5 57
Dunkerque, Fr B5 58
Dunkerton, Iowa B5 180
Dunkirk, Sask., Can G3 155
Dunkirk, Ind D7 179
Dunkirk, see Dunkerque, Fr.
Dunkirk, Mont B5 190
Dunkirk, N.Y C1 196
Dunkirk, Ohio B2 199
Dunklin, co., Mo E7 189
Dunkwa, Ghana E4 103
Dunlap, Ill C4 178
Dunlap, Ind A6 179
Dunlap, Iowa C2 180
Dunlap, Kans D7 181
Dunlap, N. Mex C5 195
Dunlap, Tenn D8 205
Dunlap, lake, Ont., Can B3 153
Dunlo, Pa F4 202
Dunloup, creek, W. Va D7 211
Dunmor, Ky C2 182
Dunmore, Pa A9, D10 202
Dunmore, lake, Vt D2 208
Dunn, N.C B5 197
Dunn, Tex C2 206
Dunn, co., N. Dak B3 198
Dunn, co., Wis D2 212
Dunn Center, N. Dak B3 198
Dunnell, Minn G4 187
Dunnellon, Fla C4 174
Dunnet, bay, Scot B5 57
Dunnet, head, Scot B5 57
Dunnfield, N.J B2 194
Dunning, Nebr C5 191
Dunnsville, Va D6 209
Dunnville, Ont., Can E5 153
Dunnville, Ky C5 182
Dunoon, Scot E4 57
Dunphy, Nev C5 192
Dunrea, Man., Can E2 150
Dunrobin, Ont., Can A8, B8 153
Duns, Scot E6 57
Dunseith, N. Dak A5 198
Dunsmuir, Calif B2 170
Dunstable, Eng C7 56
Dunstable, Mass A5 185
Dunton, Colo D2 171
Duntroon, Ont., Can C4 153
Dunvegan, Scot C2 57
Dunvegan, bay, Scot C2 57
Dunvegan, head, Scot C2 57
Dunville, Newf., Can E5 152
Dunwoody, Ga A5 175
Duong Dong, Viet G5 89
Du Page, co., Ill B5 178
Du Page, riv., Ill F2 178
Duparquet, Que., Can *B2 154
Dupax, Phil n13 90
Duplin, co., N.C C6 197
Dupo, Ill E3 178
Dupont, Colo B6 171
Du Pont, Ga F4 175
Dupont, Ind G6 179
Dupont, Ohio A3 199
Dupont, Pa B9 202
Dupont, S.C B2 203
Du Pont, Wash B3 210
Dupont, bayou, La C7 183
Dupontonia, Tenn *A5 205
Dupree, S. Dak B4 204
Dupuyer, Mont B4 190
Duque de Braganca, Ang C2 106
Duque de Caxias, Braz *C4 137
Duquesne, Pa B6, F2 202
Du Quoin, Ill E4 178
Dūrā, Jordan C7 84
Durán, Ec B2 134
Duran, N. Mex C4 195
Durance, riv., Fr F6 58
Durand, Ga D2 175
Durand, Ill A4 178
Durand, Mich F6 186
Durand, Wis D2 212
Durango, Colo D3 171
Durango, Mex C4 129
Durango, state, Mex C4 129
Durant, Iowa C7 180
Durant, Miss B4 188
Durant, Okla D5 200
Durants Neck, N.C A7 197
Duratón, riv., Sp B4 65
Durazno, Ur E1 137
Durban, Man., Can D1 150
Durban, S. Afr C5 107
Durbin, Fla C6 174
Durbin, N. Dak C8 198
Durbin, W. Va C5 211
Durbin, creek, Fla C6 174
Duren, Ger D6 59, C3 60
Durg, India *D7 87
Durgapur, Bngl E13 88
Dürge, lake, Mong B3 91
Durham, Calif C3 170
Durham, Ont., Can C4 153
Durham, Conn D6 172
Durham, Eng C6 55
Durham, Kans D6 181
Durham, Maine D5 184
Durham, Mo B6 189
Durham, N.H D5 193
Durham, N.C B5 197
Durham, Okla B2 200
Durham, co., Ont., Can C6 153
Durham, co., N.C A5 197
Durham, creek, Pa B2 194
Durham Bridge, N.B., Can C3 151
Durham Downs, Austl C3 112
Durhamville, Tenn B2 205
Durkee, Oreg C9 201
Durmersheim, Ger E3 61
Durness, Scot B4 57
Durness Kyle, bay, Scot B3 57
Durnford, pt., Sp. Sahara E1 102
Duroc, pass, N. Cal 115
Durrells, Newf., Can D4 152
Durrës, Alb B2 69
Dursunbey, Tur C7 69
Duru, Zaire A4 106
D'Urville, cape, Indon F9 90
D'Urville, isl., N.Z N14 112
Duryea, Pa B8, D10 202
Dushanbe, Sov. Un F9 71
Dushaymī, isl., Eg., U.A.R C2 84
Dushore, Pa C9 202
Dusky, sound, N.Z P11 112
Dušníky, Czech n17 70
Duson, La D3 183
Düsseldorf, Ger B1 61
Dustin, Okla B5 200
Dusty, N. Mex D2 195
Dutch, creek, Ark C2 169
Dutch Guiana: c. 1790 126
Dutch Harbor, Alsk E6 167
Dutch John, Utah C6 207
Dutchess, co., N.Y D7 196
Dutchman's Cap, isl., Vir. Is f14 132
Dutchtown, Mo D8 189
Duthie, Idaho B3 177
Dutton, Ala A4 166
Dutton, Ont., Can E3 153
Dutton, Mont C5 190
Dutton, mtn., Utah E3 207
Dutzov, Mo C6 189
Duval, Sask., Can F3 155
Duval, co., Fla B5 174
Duval, co., Tex F3 206
Duvergé, Dom. Rep F8 131
Duvno, Yugo D3 68
Duxbury, Mass B6 185
Duxbury, Vt C3 208
Duyūk, Jordan h12 84
Düzce, Tur B8 85
Dvina (Daugava), riv., Sov. Un D7 72
Dvinskaya, bay, Sov. Un E18 63
Dvůr Králove [nad Labem], Czech C3 70
Dwarka, India F2 88
Dwarka, pt., India F2 88
Dwight, Ill B5 178
Dwight, Kans D7 181
Dwight, Mass B3 185
Dwight, Nebr C8 191
Dwight, N. Dak C9 198
Dworshak, res., Idaho C2 177
Dwyer, Wyo C8 213
Dyakovo, Sov. Un r22 72
Dyaul, isl., Bis. Arch 115
Dyce, Scot C6 57
Dycusburg, Ky A3 182
Dyer, Ark B1 169
Dyer, Ind B2 179
Dyer, Nev F3 192
Dyer, Tenn A3 205
Dyer, co., Tenn A2 205
Dyer, bay, Ont., Can B3 153
Dyer Bay, Ont., Can B3 153
Dyer Brook, Maine B4 184
Dyersburg, Tenn A2 205
Dyersville, Iowa B6 180
Dyess, Ark B5 169
Dyje, riv., Czech D3 70
Dyment, Ont., Can E5 150
Dysart, Sask., Can G3 155
Dysart, Iowa B5 180
Dzamiin Üüde, Mong B4 92
Dzaoudzi, Comoro Is f9 107
Dzerzhinsk, Sov. Un C14 72
Dzerzhinsk, Sov. Un E6 72
Dzerzhinsk, Sov. Un q20 72
Dzhabhan, riv., Mong B3 91
Dzhalal-Abad, Sov. Un E8 73
Dzhambul, Sov. Un E8 73
Dzhankoy, Sov. Un I10 72
Dzhebel, Sov. Un B7 86
Dzhetygara, Sov. Un C6 73
Dzhezkasgen, Sov. Un D7 73
Dzhugdzhur, mts., Sov. Un D16 71
Dzhulfa, Sov. Un C15 85
Dzhusaly, Sov. Un D6 73
Działdowo, Pol B6 70
Działoszyce, Pol C6 70
Dziedzice, Pol h10 70
Dzierżoniów, Pol C4 70
Dzilam González, Mex C7 129
Dzioua, Alg C6 102
Dzitbalché, Mex C6 129
Dzungaria, reg., China B2 91

E

Eads, Colo C8 171
Eads, Tenn B2 205
Eagan, Tenn C10 205
Eagar, Ariz C6 168
Eagle, Alsk C11 167
Eagle, Colo B4 171
Eagle, Nebr D9, E2 191
Eagle, N.Y C2 196
Eagle, W. Va C3, D6 211
Eagle, Wis F5 212
Eagle, co., Colo B4 171
Eagle, cave, Wis E3 212
Eagle, cliff, Mont C1 190
Eagle, creek, Ind E5 179
Eagle, creek, Ky B5 182
Eagle, dam, Ind E4 179
Eagle, key, Fla G6 174
Eagle, lake, Calif B3 170
Eagle, lake, Ont., Can E5 150
Eagle, lake, Maine A4 184
Eagle, lake, Maine B3 184
Eagle, lake, Wis C4 212
Eagle, mtn., Minn A7 187
Eagle, mtn., Tex F1 206
Eagle, peak, Calif B3 170
Eagle, riv., Newf., Can B2 152
Eagle Bend, Minn D3 187
Eagle Bridge, N.Y C7 196
Eagle Butte, S. Dak C4 204
Eagle City, Okla B3 200
Eagle Cliff, mtn., Idaho B3 177
Eagle Creek, Tenn B4 205
Eagle Grove, Iowa B4 180
Eagle Lake, Fla *E5 174
Eagle Lake, Maine A4 184
Eagle Lake, Minn F5 187
Eagle Lake, Tex E4 206
Eagle Mills, Ark D3 169
Eagle Mountain, lake, Tex B5 206
Eagle Nest, N. Mex A4 195
Eagle Nest, res., N. Mex A4 195
Eagle Pass, Tex E2 206
Eagle Point, Oreg E4 201
Eagle River, Alsk g17 167
Eagle River, Mich A2 186
Eagle River, Wis C4 212
Eagle Rock, Va D3 209
Eagle Springs, N.C B4 197
Eagletail, mts., Ariz D2 168
Eagletail, peak, Ariz D2 168
Eaglehill, creek, Sask., Can F2 155
Eagles Mere, Pa D8 202
Eaglesham, Alta., Can B2 148
Eagleton Village, Tenn *D10 205
Eagletown, Okla C7 200
Eagleville, Conn B7 172
Eagleville, Mo A4 189
Eagleville, Pa A10 202
Eagleville, Tenn B5 205
Eakly, Okla B3 200
Ealing, Eng k12 55
Eardley, Que., Can A8 153
Eardley, lake, Man., Can C3 150
Earl, isl., Newf., Can B3 152
Earl Grey, Sask., Can G3 155
Earl Park, Ind C3 179
Earle, Ark B5 169
Earlham, Iowa C3 180
Earlimart, Calif E4 170
Earling, Iowa C2 180
Earling, W. Va D5 211
Earlington, Ky C2 182
Earlsboro, Okla B5 200
Earlton, Kans E8 181
Earlville, Ill B5 178
Earlville, Iowa B6 180
Earlville, N.Y C5 196
Early, Iowa B2 180
Early, co., Ga E2 175
Early Branch, S.C F6 203
Earn, lake, Scot D4 57
Earn, riv., Scot D5 57
Earth, Tex B1 206
Easingwold, Eng F7 57
Easley, S.C B2 203
East, bay, Tex F5 206
East, brook, N.H B4 193
East, cape, Fla G5 174
East, cape, N.Z L17 112
East, cape, P.R e10 132
East, isl., Que., Can B8 151
East, mtn., Mass A1 185
East, pass, Fla C2 175
East, pt., P.E.I., Can C8 151
East, pt., Que., Can B8 152
East, pt., Mass B6 185
East, pt., N.J E2 194
East, pt., N.Y D9 172
East, range, Nev C4 192
East, riv., Ont., Can B5 153
East, riv., N.Y E6 194
East, riv., Wis A6 212
East, riv., Wyo C3 213
East Alamosa, Colo D5 171
East Alburgh, Vt B2 208
East Alliance, Ohio *B6 199
East Alstead, N.H D2 193
East Alton, Ill E3 178
East Andover, Maine D2 184
East Andover, N.H D3 193
East Angus, Que., Can D6 154
East Arlington, Vt E2 208
East Ashtabula, Ohio *A7 199
East Aurora, N.Y C2 196
East Baldwin, Maine E2 184
East Bangor, Pa E11 202
East Bank, La C7 183
East-Bank, W. Va C6 211
East Barnard, Vt D3 208
East Barnet, Vt C4 208
East Barre, Vt C4 208
East Barre, res., Vt C4 208
East Barrington, N.H D4 193
East Bathurst, N.B., Can B4 151
East Baton Rouge, par., La D4 183
East Beckwith, mtn., Colo C3 171
East Bend, N.C A3 197
East Bengal, reg., Bngl E12 88
East Berkshire, Vt B3 208
East Berlin, Conn C6 172
East Berlin, Pa G8 202
East Bernard, Tex E4 206
East Bernstadt, Ky C5 182
East Berwick, Pa *D9 202
East Bethel, Minn *E5 187
East Bethel, Vt D3 208
East Blue Hill, Maine D4 184
East Bonne Terre, Mo D7 189
East Boothbay, Maine E3 184
East Brady, Pa E2 202
East Braintree, Man., Can E4 150
East Braintree, Vt D3 208
East Branch, N.Y D5 196
East Branch, res., N.Y D2 172
East Branch Clarion River, res., Pa C4 202
East Brewster, Mass C7 185
East Brewton, Ala D2 166
East Bridgewater, Mass B6 185
East Brimfield, res., Mass B3 185
East Brookfield, Mass *B3 185
East Brookfield, Vt C3 208
East Brooklyn, Conn *B9 172
East Broughton Station, Que., Can C6 154
East Burke, Vt B5 208
East Butler, Pa E2 202
East Calais, Vt C4 208
East Canaan, Conn A3 172
East Candia, N.H D4 193
East Canon, Colo C5 171
East Canton, Ohio *B6 199
East Carondelet, Ill B8 189
East Carroll, par., La B4 183
East Carver, Mass C6 185
East Chain, Minn G4 187
East Charleston, Vt B5 208
East Chicago, Ind A3 179
East Chicago Heights, Ill *B6 178
East China, sea, China F9 91
East Chop, pt., Mass D6 185
East Cleveland, Ohio B2 199
East Cleveland, Tenn *D9 205
East Clifton, Que., Can D6 154
East Columbia, Tex G4 206
East Columbus, Ind *F6 179
East Concord, Vt C5 208
East Conway, N.H B4 193
East Corinth, Maine C3 184
East Corinth, Vt C4 208
East Cote Blanche, bay, La E4 183
East Coulee, Alta., Can D4 148
East Craftsbury, Vt B4 208
East Dennis, Mass C7 185
East Dereham, Eng B8 56
East Derry, N.H E4 193
East Des Moines, riv., Iowa A3 180
East Detroit, Mich A8 186
East Dixfield, Maine D2 184
East Dixmont, Maine D3 184
East Dorset, Vt E2 208
East Douglas, Mass B4 185
East Dover, Maine C3 184
East Dublin, Ga *D4 175
East Dubuque, Ill A3 178
East Dummerston, Vt F3 208
East Dundee, Ill *A5 178
East Eddington, Maine D4 184
East Ellijay, Ga B2 175
East Ely, Nev D7 192
East End, Vir. Is f16 132
East Enterprise, Ind G8 179
East Fairfield, Vt B3 208
East Fairview, N. Dak B1 198
East Falmouth, Mass C6 185
East Faxon, Pa *D8 202
East Fayetteville, N.C *B5 197
East Feliciana, par., La D4 183
East Flanders, prov., Bel C3 59
East Flat Rock, N.C D3 197
East Flevoland Polder, reg., Neth B5 59
East Florenceville, N.B., Can C2 151
East Franklin, Vt B3 208
East Freetown, Mass C6 185
East Frisian, is., Ger A7 59
East Fultonham, Ohio C5 199
East Gaffney, S.C A4 203
East Galesburg, Ill C3 178
East Gary, Ind A3 179
East Gastonia, N.C *B2 197
East Gate, Nev D3 192
East Georgia, Vt B2 208
East Germany, see Germany, East, country, Eur.
East Glacier Park, Mont B3 190
East Glastonbury, Conn C6 172
East Grafton, N.H C3 193
East Granby, Conn B6 172
East Grand Forks, Minn C2 187
East Granville, Vt C3 208
East Greenbush, N.Y *C7 196
East Greenville, Pa F10 202
East Greenwich, R.I C11 172
East Griffin, Ga *C2 175
East Grinstead, Eng C7 56
East Haddam, Conn D7 172
East Ham, Eng *k13 55
East Hampton, Conn C6 172
East Hampton, N.Y D4 196
East Hardwick, Vt B4 208
East Harpswell, Maine E5 184
East Hartford, Conn B6 172
East Hartland, Conn B5 172
East Haven, Conn D5 172
East Haven, Vt B5 208
East Haverhill, N.H B3 193
East Hazelcrest, Ill *B6 178
East Hebron, N.H C3 193
East Helena, Mont D5 190
East Herkimer, N.Y *B6 196
East Hickory, Pa C3 202
East Highgate, Vt B3 208
East Hills, N.Y *E7 196
East Hodge, La *B3 183
East Holden, Maine D4 184
East Holderness, N.H C3 193
East Islip, N.Y G4 172
East Jordan, N.S., Can F4 151
East Jordan, Mich C5 186
East Juliette, Ga C3 175
East Kelowna, B.C., Can E8 149
East Kent, Conn C3 172
East Kilbride, Scot *E4 57
East Killingly, Conn B9 172
East Kingsford, Mich *C2 186
East Kingston, N.H E4 193
East Lake, N.C B8 197
East Lansdowne, Pa *G11 202
East Lansing, Mich F6 186
East Laport, N.C D3 197
East Las Vegas, Nev G6 192
East Laurinburg, N.C C4 197
East Lebanon, Maine E2 184
East Lee, Mass B1 185
East Lempster, N.H D2 193
East Liberty, Ohio B4 199
East Litchfield, Conn B4 172
East Livermore, Maine D2 184
East Liverpool, Ohio B7 199
East London, S. Afr D4 107
East Longmeadow, Mass B2 185
East Los Angeles, Calif *E4 170
East Lothian, co., Scot E6 57
East Lyme, Conn *D8 172
East Lynn, W. Va C2 211
East Lynn, res., W. Va C2 211
East Lynne, Mo C3 189
East Machias, Maine D5 184
East McKeesport, Pa *F2 202
East Madison, Maine D3 184
East Mansfield, Mass B5 185
East Marion, N.Y E7 172
East Marion, N.C *D4 197
East Massapequa, N.Y *G3 172
East Matunuck, R.I D10 172
East Meadow, N.Y E3 196
East Meredith, N.Y C6 196
East Middlebury, Vt D2 208
East Middletown, N.Y *D6 196
East Millcreek, Utah C4 207
East Millinocket, Maine C4 184
East Millstone, N.J B3 194
East Mobridge, S. Dak B5 204
East Modesto, Calif *D3 170
East Moline, Ill B3 178
East Monroe, Ohio C4 199
East Montpelier, Vt C4 208
East Moriches, N.Y F5 172
East Morris, Conn C4 172
East Naples, Fla F5 174
East Neck, N.Y *D3 196
East New Market, Md C6 173
East Newark, N.J *B4 194
East Newnan, Ga G2 175
East Newport, Maine D3 184
East Nishnabotna, riv., Iowa C2 180
East Northport, N.Y F3 172
East Norwalk, Conn E3 172
East Olympia, Wash C3 210
East Orange, N.J B4 194
East Orange, Vt C4 208
East Orland, Maine D4 184
East Orleans, Mass C8 185
East Otis, Mass B1 185
East Otto, N.Y C2 196
East Palatka, Fla C5 174
East Palestine, Ohio B7 199
East Parsonfield, Maine E2 184
East Patchogue, N.Y F5 172
East Paterson, N.J D5 194
East Peacham, Vt C4 208
East Peoria, Ill C4 178
East Pepperell, Mass A4 185
East Peru, Maine D2 184
East Petersburg, Pa F9 202
East Pine, B.C., Can B7 149
East Pittsburgh, Pa A6 202
East Point, Ga B5, C2 175
East Point, La B2 183
East Poland, Maine D2 184
East Poplar, Sask., Can H3 155
East Portal, Colo B5 171
East Porterville, Calif *D4 170
East Poultney, Vt D2 208
East Prairie, Mo E8 189
East Princeton, Mass B4 185
East Prospect, Pa G8 202
East Providence, R.I B11 172
East Prussia: c. 1866 51
in 1914 52
in 1922-40 53
after World War II 54
East Pryor, mtn., Mont E8 190
East Punjab, state, India B6 88
East Putney, Vt F4 208
East Quogue, N.Y F6 172
East Rainelle, W. Va D4 211
East Randolph, N.Y C2 196
East Randolph, Vt D3 208
East Retford, Eng A7 56
East Ridge, Tenn E10 205
East Rindge, N.H E3 193
East River, Conn D6 172
East River, mtn., Va D1 209

INDEX KEY Each place listed in **Bold-faced Type** has its population listed in the Population tables, pages 230 to 280.
Each country, shown in CAPITAL LETTERS, has its population listed in the World Political Information Table, pages 6 to 10.
* Does not appear on map; key shows general location.

East River Sheet Harbour, N.S., Can. E7 151
East Riverside-Kingshurst, N.B., Can. *D3 151
East Rochester, N.H. D5 193
East Rochester, N.Y. B3 196
East Rochester, Pa. *E1 202
East Rockaway, N.Y. G2 172
East Rockingham, N.C. C4 197
East Rutherford, N.J. D5 194
East Ryegate, Vt. C4 208
East St. John, N.B., Can. D4 151
East St. Johnsbury, Vt. C5 208
East St. Louis, Ill. E3 178
East Salt, creek, Colo. B2 171
East Sandwich, Mass. C7 185
East Sebago, Maine E2 184
East Selkirk, Man., Can. D3 150
East Setauket, N.Y. F4 172
East Shediac, N.B., Can. *C5 151
East Siberian, sea, Sov. Un. B18 71
East Smithfield, Pa. C8 202
East Somerset, Ky. C5 182
East Sparta, Ohio B6 199
East Spencer, N.C. B3 197
East Spokane, Wash. B8, D7 210
East Springfield, N.Y. C6 196
East Springfield, Pa. C1 202
East Stanwood, Wash. A3 210
East Stoneham, Maine D2 184
East Streator, Ill. *B5 178
East Stroudsburg, Pa. D11 202
East Sudbury, Mass. D1 185
East Sullivan, Maine D4 184
East Sullivan, N.H. E2 193
East Sumner, Maine D2 184
East Swanzey, N.H. E2 193
East Syracuse, N.Y. B4 196
East Tawas, Mich. D7 186
East Templeton, Mass. A4 185
East Thermopolis, Wyo. B4 213
East Thetford, Vt. D4 208
East Thomaston, Ga. D2 175
East Tirol, reg., Aus. C8 66
East Tohopekaliga, lake, Fla. D5 174
East Towanda, Pa. C9 202
East Troy, Wis. F5 212
East Tulare, Calif. *D4 170
East Uniontown, Pa. *G2 202
East Vandergrift, Pa. *E2 202
East View, W. Va. *B4 211
East Wakefield, N.H. C4 193
East Wallingford, Vt. E3 208
East Walpole, Mass. D2 185
East Wareham, Mass. C6 185
East Washington, N.H. D3 193
East Washington, Pa. F1 202
East Waterboro, Maine E2 184
East Waterford, Maine D2 184
East Weissport, Pa. *E10 202
East Wellington, B.C., Can. A8 149
East Wenatchee, Wash. B5 210
East Wenatchee Bench, Wash. *B5 210
East Weymouth, Mass. D3 185
East Whittier, Calif. *F4 170
East Willington, Conn. B8 172
East Williston, N.Y. G2 172
East Wilmington, N.C. *C6 197
East Wilton, Maine D2 184
East Windsor Hill, Conn. B6 172
East Wolfeboro, N.H. C4 193
East Woodstock, Conn. B9 172
East Worcester, N.Y. C6 196
Eastaboga, Ala. B3 166
Eastabutchie, Miss. D4 188
Eastborough, Kans. B5 181
Eastbourne, Eng. D8 56
Eastbrook, Maine D4 184
Eastend, Sask., Can. H1 155
Easter, isl., see Rapa Nui, isl., Pac. O.
Easter, mtn., Conn. B3 172
Eastern, prov., Zambia D5 106
Eastern, reg., Ghana E5 103
Eastern, reg., Nig. E6 103
Eastern, reg., Tan. C6 106
Eastern, reg., Ug. A5 106
Eastern, bay, Md. C5 173
Eastern, isl., Newf., Can. C4 152
Eastern, isl., Midway Is. 114
Eastern, pt., Mass. C4 185
Eastern Ghats, range, India E7 87
Eastern Neck, isl., Md. B5 173
Eastern Plain, pt., N.Y. E8 172
Eastford, Conn. B8 172
Eastham, Mass. C8 185
Easthampton, Mass. B2 185
Eastlake, Mich. D4 186
Eastlake, Ohio A6 199
Eastland, Tex. C3 206
Eastland, co., Tex. C3 206
Eastlawn, Mich. *F7 186
Eastleigh, Eng. D6 56
Eastmain, Que., Can. F17 154
Eastman, Que., Can. D5 154
Eastman, Ga. D3 175
Eastman, Wis. E2 212
Easton, Conn. D3 172
Easton, Ill. C4 178
Easton, Kans. B8 181
Easton, Maine B5 184
Easton, Md. C5 173
Easton, Mass. B5 185
Easton, Minn. G5 187
Easton, Mo. B3 189
Easton, N.H. B3 193
Easton, Pa. E11 202
Easton, Wash. B4 210
Easton, res., Conn. E3 172
Eastover, S.C. D6 203
Eastpoint, Fla. C2 174
Eastport, Newf., Can. D5 152
Eastport, Idaho A2 177
Eastport, Maine D6 184
Eastport, N.Y. D4 196
Eastside, Miss. E3 188
Eastside, Oreg. D2 201
Eastside Galesburg, Ill. *C3 178
Eastsound, Wash. A3 210
Eastvale, Pa. *E1 202
Eastville, Va. D7 209
Eastwood, Ky. A4 182
Eaton, Colo. A6 171
Eaton, Ill. D6 178
Eaton, Ind. D7 179
Eaton, Maine C5 184
Eaton, N.Y. C5 196
Eaton, Ohio C3 199
Eaton, Tenn. B2 205
Eaton, co., Mich. F6 186
Eaton Center, N.H. C4 193
Eaton Estates, Ohio *A5 199
Eaton Rapids, Mich. F6 186
Eatonia, Sask., Can. F1 155
Eatons, neck, N.Y. F3 172
Eatons Neck, pt., N.Y. F3 172
Eatonton, Ga. C3 175
Eatontown, N.J. C4 194
Eatonville, Fla. *D5 174
Eatonville, Wash. C3 210
Eau Claire, Mich. G4 186
Eau Claire, Wis. D2 212
Eau Claire, co., Wis. D2 212
Eau Claire, riv., Wis. D2 212
Eau Galle, Wis. D2 212
Eau Gallie, Fla. D6 174
Eau Pleine, riv., Wis. C3 212
Eauze, Fr. F4 58
Ebadon, isl., Kwajalein 114
Ebbw Vale, Wales C4 56
Ebeleben, Ger. B5 61
Ebeltoft, Den. B4 62
Eben Junction, Mich. B4 186
Ebenezer, Sask., Can. F4 155
Ebenezer, Miss. C3 188
Ebenezer, Tenn. E11 205
Ebensburg, Pa. F4 202
Ebermannstadt, Ger. D6 61
Ebersbach, Ger. B9 61
Ebersbach, Ger. E4 61
Eberswalde, Ger. B6 60
Ebingen, Ger. D4 60
Eboli, It. D5 67
Ebolowa, Cam. E2 104
Ebon, atoll, Marshall Is. 115
Ebro, Fla. G3 174
Ebro, Minn. C3 187
Ebro, riv., Sp. B6 65
Eccles, W. Va. D3, D6 211
Eceabat (Maydos), Tur. B6 69
Echague, Phil. n13 90
Echeconnee, creek, Ga. D3 175
Echigawa, Jap. n15 93
Echo, Ala. D4 166
Echo, La. C3 183
Echo, Minn. F3 187
Echo, Oreg. B7 201
Echo, Utah C4 207
Echo, lake, Ont., Can. B7 186
Echo, lake, Maine D2 184
Echo, pond, Vt. B5 208
Echoing, lake, Ont., Can. B5 150
Echoing, riv., Man., Can. B6 150
Echola, Ala. B2 166
Echols, co., Ga. F4 175
Echt, Neth. C5 59
Echt, Scot. C6 57
Echternach, Lux. E6 59
Echuca, Austl. H5 112
Écija, Sp. D3 65
Eckelson, N. Dak. C7 198
Eckerman, Mich. B5 186
Eckernförde, Ger. A4 60
Eckernförder Bucht, bay, Ger. D4 62
Eckert (Orchard City), Colo. C3 171
Eckerty, Ind. H4 179
Eckhart, Md. D2 173
Eckley, Colo. A8 171
Eckley, Pa. E10 202
Eckman, N. Dak. A4 198
Eckman, W. Va. *D3 211
Eckville, Alta. Can. C3 148
Eclectic, Ala. C3 166
Eclipse, Va. B6, E6 209
Econfina, Fla. G3 174
Econfina, riv., Fla. B3 174
Economy, N.S., Can. D6 151
Economy, Ind. E7 179
Economy, Pa. *E1 202
Ecorces, riv., Que., Can. A6 154
Ecorse, Mich. A7 186
Ecru, Miss. A4 188
Ector, Tex. *C4 206
Ector, co., Tex. D1 206
ECUADOR, country, S.A. B2 134
in 1830's 127
Ecum Secum, N.S., Can. E7 151
Ecum Secum Bridge, N.S., Can. E7 151
Eda, Swe. H5 63
Edam, Sask., Can. D1 155
Edam, Neth. B5 59
Eday, isl., Scot. A6 57
Edberg, Alta., Can. C4 148
Edcouch, Tex. F4 206
Edd, Eth. C5 105
Ed Da'ein, Sud. C2 105
Ed Damer, Sud. B3 105
Ed Debba (Well), Sud. B3 105
Eddiceton, Miss. D3 188
Eddington, Maine D4 184
Ed Dueim, Sud. C3 105
Eddy, Mont. C1 190
Eddy, co., N. Mex. E5 195
Eddy, co., N. Dak. B7 198
Eddystone, Pa. B10 202
Eddystone Rocks, reef, English Chan. E4 55
Eddyville, Ill. F5 178
Eddyville, Iowa C5 180
Eddyville, Ky. A3 182
Eddyville, Nebr. C6 191
Ed Dzong, China A13 88
Ede, Neth. B5 59
Ede, Nig. *E5 103
Edea, Cam. E2 104
Eden, Ariz. E6 168
Eden, Austl. H7 112
Eden, Man., Can. D2 150
Eden, Ga. D5 175
Eden, Idaho G4 177
Eden, Maine D4 184
Eden, Md. D6 173
Eden, Miss. C3 188
Eden, Mont. C5 190
Eden, N.Y. C2 196
Eden, S. Dak. B8 204
Eden, Tex. D3 206
Eden, Vt. B3 208
Eden, Wis. E5 212
Eden, Wyo. C3 213
Eden, hill, Conn. D3 172
Eden, riv., Eng. C5 55
Eden, riv., Scot. D5 57
Eden Mills, Vt. B3 208
Eden Valley, Minn. E4 187
Edenborn, Pa. G2 202
Edenderry, Ire. D3 55
Edenton, N.C. A7 197
Edenwold, Sask., Can. G3 155
Edenwold, Tenn. A5, E9 205
Eder, riv., Ger. B4 61
Edesville, Md. B5 173
Edgar, Mont. E8 190
Edgar, Nebr. D8 191
Edgar, Wis. D4 212
Edgar, co., Ill. D6 178
Edgar Springs, Mo. D6 189
Edgard, La. B6, D5 183
Edgartown, Mass. D6 185
Edge, isl., Nor. B12 118
Edgecombe, co., N.C. B6 197
Edgecumbe, cape, Alsk. m21 167
Edgefield, S.C. D4 203
Edgefield, co., S.C. D3 203
Edgeley, Sask., Can. G4 155
Edgeley, N. Dak. C7 198
Edgemere, Idaho A2 177
Edgemere, Md. B5 173
Edgemont, Calif. *F5 170
Edgemont, S. Dak. D2 204
Edgemoor, S.C. B5 203
Edgemoor, Tenn. E11 205
Edgerly, La. D2 183
Edgerton, Alta., Can. C5 148
Edgerton, Kans. D8 181
Edgerton, Minn. G2 187
Edgerton, Mo. B3 189
Edgerton, Ohio A3 199
Edgerton, Wis. F4 212
Edgerton, Wyo. C6 213
Edgewater, Ala. E5 166
Edgewater, Colo. *B5 171
Edgewater, Fla. D6 174
Edgewater, Md. C5 173
Edgewater, N.J. D5 194
Edgewater Gulf Beach, Fla. *G3 174
Edgewater Park, Miss. E2 188
Edgewater Park, N.J. C3 194
Edgewood, B.C., Can. E8 149
Edgewood, Ill. E5 178
Edgewood, Ind. H8 179
Edgewood, Iowa B6 180
Edgewood, Ky. A7 182
Edgewood, Md. B5 173
Edgewood, N. Mex. B3, G6 195
Edgewood, Ohio A7 199
Edgewood, Pa. B6 202
Edgewood, Pa. *E8 202
Edgewood, Tex. *C5 206
Edgewood, Wash. D2 210
Edgeworth, Pa. A5 202
Edgigen, isl., Kwajalein 114
Edhessa, Grc. B4 69
Edina, Minn. E6 187
Edina, Mo. A5 189
Edinboro, Pa. C1 202
Edinburg, Ill. D4 178
Edinburg, Ind. F6 179
Edinburg, Miss. C4 188
Edinburg, N.Y. B6 196
Edinburg, N. Dak. A8 198
Edinburg, Tex. F3 206
Edinburg, Va. C4 209
Edinburgh, Scot. E5 57
Edison, Ga. E2 175
Edison, Nebr. D6 191
Edison, N.J. *B4 194
Edison, Ohio B5 199
Edison, Wash. A3 210
Edisto, isl., S.C. F7 203
Edisto, riv., S.C. E6 203
Edisto Island, S.C. F7, G1 203
Edith, mtn., Mont. D5 190
Edith Ronne Land, reg., Ant. A5 120
Edithburgh, Austl. G1 112
Edmeston, N.Y. C5 196
Edmond, Kans. C4 181
Edmond, Okla. B4 200
Edmonds, Wash. B3 210
Edmondson, Ark. B5 169
Edmonson, co., Ky. C3 182
Edmonston, Md. *C4 173
Edmont, plat., N.C. B3 197
Edmonton, Alta., Can. C4 148
Edmonton, Eng. *k12 55
Edmonton, Ky. C4 182
Edmore, Mich. E5 186
Edmore, N. Dak. A7 198
Edmund, lake, Man., Can. B5 150
Edmunds, Maine D5 184
Edmunds, N. Dak. B7 198
Edmunds, co., S. Dak. B6 204
Edmundson, Mo. *C7 189
Edmundston, N.B., Can. B1 151
Edna, Kans. E8 181
Edna, Tex. E4 206
Edna, W. Va. A7 211
Edna Bay, Alsk. n23 167
Edom: in 13th cent. B.C. 98
Edon, Ohio A3 199
Edouard, lake, Que., Can. B5 154
Edremit, Tur. C6 69
Edremit, gulf, Tur. C6 69
Edsel Ford, ranges, Ant. B34 120
Edson, Alta., Can. C2 148
Edson, Kans. C2 181
Edson, butte, Oreg. E2 201
Eduardo Castex, Arg. B4 136
Eduni, mtn., N.W. Ter., Can. D7 142
Edwall, Wash. B8 210
Edwand, Alta., Can. B4 148
Edward, lake, Zaire B4 106
Edward McDowell, res., N.H. E2 193
Edward VII, pen., Ant. B33 120
Edward VIII, bay, Ant. C18 120
Edwards, Ont., Can. B10 153
Edwards, Colo. B4 171
Edwards, Ill. C4 178
Edwards, Miss. C3 188
Edwards, N.Y. A5, B2 196
Edwards, co., Ill. E5 178
Edwards, co., Kans. E4 181
Edwards, co., Tex. E2 206
Edwards, butte, Oreg. B3 201
Edwards, plat., Tex. D2 206
Edwardsburg, Mich. G4 186
Edwardsport, Ind. G3 179
Edwardsville, Ala. B4 166
Edwardsville, Ill. E4 178
Edwardsville, Kans. B8 181
Edwardsville, Pa. B8 202
Edwin, Ala. D4 166
Edzell, Scot. D6 57
Edziza, peak, B.C., Can. m24 167
Eek, Alsk. C7 167
Eekloo, Bel. C3 59
Eel, riv., Calif. B2 170
Eel, riv., Ind. C5 179
Eel, riv., Ind. F3 179
Eel River Crossing, N.B., Can. *B3 151
Efate, isl., New Hebr. 115
Eferding, Aus. D7 60
Effie, La. C3 183
Effie, Minn. C5 187
Effingham, Ill. D5 178
Effingham, Kans. A7, C8 181
Effingham, N.H. C5 193
Effingham, S.C. C8 203
Effingham, co., Ga. D5 175
Effingham, co., Ill. D5 178
Efland, N.C. A4 197
Eforie, Rom. C9 68
Egadi, is., It. F4 67
Egan, Ga. B5 175
Egan, S. Dak. D9 204
Egan, range, Nev. E7 192
Eganville, Ont., Can. B7 153
Egbert, Wyo. D8 213
Egegik, Alsk. D8 167
Egeland, N. Dak. A6 198
Egeln, Ger. B6 61
Eger, Hung. B5 68
Egersund, Nor. H2 63
Egg, lake, Que., Can. B2 154
Egg, lake, Sask., Can. B3 155
Egg Harbor, Wis. C6 212
Egg Harbor City, N.J. D3 194
Egg Island, pt., N.J. E2 194
Eggebek, Ger. D3 62
Eggenfelden, Ger. E7 61
Egilsstadir, Ice. n25 63
Égletons, Fr. E4 58
Egmond aan Zee, Neth. B4 59
Egmont, bay, P.E.I., Can. C5 151
Egmont, chan., Fla. F1 174
Egmont, cape, N.Z. M14 112
Egmont, key, Fla. F1 174
Egmont, mtn., N.Z. M15 112
Egnar, Colo. D2 171
Egremont, Alta., Can. B4 148
Egremont, Eng. F5 57
Egremont, Mass. B1 185
Eğridir, Tur. D8 85
Eğridir, lake, Tur. C8 85
Egtved, Den. C3 62
Egypt, Ark. B5 169
Egypt, Ga. D5 175
Egypt, Mass. B6, D4 185
Egypt, Miss. B5 188
Egypt, Pa. E10 202
EGYPT, country, Afr. D5 101
in 13th cent. B.C. 98
in 6th cent. B.C. 42
c. 500 B.C. 78
in Alexander's empire 43
c. 120 A.D. 45
in latter 19th cent. 99
in 1914 52
after World War II 83
Ehrenberg, Ariz. D1 168
Ehrenburg, Ger. F2 62
Ehrenfeld, Pa. F4 202
Ehrhardt, S.C. E5 203
Éibar, Sp. A4 65
Eibau, Ger. C9 61
Eibenstock, Ger. C7 61
Eichstätt, Ger. E6 61
Eider, riv., Ger. A4 60
Eidsberg, Nor. H4, p29 63
Eidson, Tenn. C10 205
Eidsvold, Austl. B8 112
Eidsvoll, Nor. G4 63
Eifel, mts., Ger. C1 61
Eigg, isl., Scot. D2 57
Eights, coast, Ant. B3 120
Eighty Eight, Ky. D4 182
Eighty Mile, beach, Austl. C3 110
Eikeren, lake, Nor. p27 63
Eil, Som. D6 105
Eil Malk, isl., Palau Is. 114
Eildon, res., Austl. H6 112
Eilenburg, Ger. B7 61
Ein Gev, Isr. B7 84
Ein Harod, Isr. B7 84
Ein Kerem, Isr. h11 84
Ein Netafim, Isr. E6 84
Ein Scilleme, mtn., Libya E4 101
Einbeck, Ger. B4 61
Eindhoven, Neth. C5 59
Einsiedeln, Switz. B4 66
Eire, see Ireland, country, Eur.
Eirunepé, Braz. C4 134
Eisenach, Ger. C5 61
Eisenberg, Ger. C6 61
Eisenhower, Dwight D., lock, N.Y. A2 196
Eisenhüttenstadt, Ger. A9 61
Eisfeld, Ger. C5 61
Eisleben, Ger. B6 61
Eita, isl., Tarawa 114
Eitorf, Ger. C2 61
Eitzen, Minn. G7 187
Eix, Fr. E5 59
Ejby, Den. C3 62
Ejea de los Caballeros, Sp. A5 65
Ejeda, Malag. h8 107
Ejstrup, Den. C3 62
Ejutla de Crespo, Mex. D5 129
Ekalaka, Mont. E12 190
Ekenäs, Fin. G10 63
Ekeren, Bel. C4 59
Ekhínos, Grc. B5 69
Ekimchan, Sov. Un. D16 71
Eklutna, Alsk. C10, g17 167
Ekoln, lake, Swe. t35 63
Ekron, Ky. C3 182
Eksjö, Swe. I6 63
Ekumaketo, Zaire B3 106
Ekwok, Alsk. D8 167
El Abiod Sidi Cheikh, Alg. H7 64
Elaine, Ark. C5 169
El Aiún, Sp. Sahara D2 102
El Alamein, see Al'Alamayn, Eg.
El Alia, Alg. C6 102
El Alto, P.R. B5 132
Elamanchili, India I9 88
El Amparo, Cuba k11 131
Elamton, Ky. C6 182
Elamville, Ala. D4 166
Eland, Wis. D4 212
El Arahal, Sp. D3 65
El Aricha, Alg. G6 64
El Asnam, Alg. B5 102
Elassón, Grc. C4 69
El 'Atate, mtn., Jordan D7 84
El 'Atrun (Oasis), Sud. B2 105
Elath (Eilat), Isr. E6 84
El 'Aujā, Isr. D6 84
Elâzığ, Tur. C12 85
El Azucar, res., Mex. F3 206
Elba, Ala. D3 166
Elba, Idaho G5 177
Elba, Mich. E7 186
Elba, Minn. F6 187
Elba, Nebr. C7 191
Elba, N.Y. B2 196
Elba, isl., It. C3 67
El Barco, Sp. A2 65
Elbasan, Alb. B3 69
El Baúl, Ven. B4 133
Elbe, riv., Ger. B8 61
Elberfeld, Ind. H3 179
Elberon, Iowa B5 180
Elbert, Colo. B6 171
Elbert, Tex. C3 206
Elbert, co., Colo. B6 171
Elbert, co., Ga. B4 175
Elbert, mtn., Colo. B4 171
Elberta, Ala. E2 166
Elberta, Ga. D3 175
Elberta, Mich. D4 186
Elberta, Utah D4 207
Elberton, Ga. B4 175
Elberton, Wash. C8 210
Elbeuf, Fr. C4 58
Elbigenalp, Aus. B6 66
Elbing, Kans. A6 181
Elbistan, Tur. C11 85
Elbląg, Pol. A5 70
El Bolsón, Arg. C2 136
El Bonillo, Sp. C4 65
El Bordo, Col. C2 133
El Borouj, Mor. H3 64
Elbow, Sask., Can. F2 155
Elbow, lake, Man., Can. B1 150
Elbow, riv., Alta., Can. D3 148
Elbow Lake, Minn. E3 187
Elbridge, N.Y. *B4 196
Elbridge, Tenn. A2 205
El Bur, Som. E6 105
Elburg, Neth. B5 59
El Burgo de Osma, Sp. B4 65
Elburn, Ill. B5 178
Elburz, mts., Iran C5 86
El Cajon, Calif. E2, F5 170
El Callao, Ven. B5 133
El Campo, Tex. E4 206
El Campo North, Tex. *E4 206
El Campo South, Tex. *E4 206
El Capitan, mtn., Mont. D2 190
El Capitan, res., Calif. E2 170
El Carmen, Bol. C4 135
El Carmen, Col. B2 133
El Carre, Eth. D5 105
El Carrizo, Mex. B3 129
El Centro, Calif. F6 170
El Cerrito, Calif. B5 170
El Cerro, Bol. C3 135
El Cerro, P.R. C2 132
El Chaparro, Ven. B4 133
Elche, Sp. C5 65
Elcho, Wis. C4 212
Elco, Ill. F4 178
El Cobre, Cuba k12 131
El Cuervo, butte, N. Mex. G6 195
Eld, isl., Fiji 114
Elda, Sp. C5 65
El Dar el Beda, ruins, Eg. D3 84
Elde, riv., Ger. B5 60
Elderon, Wis. D4 212
Eldersley, Sask., Can. E4 155
Elderton, Pa. E3 202
El Diviso, Col. C2 133
El Djem, Tun. G12 64
Eldon, Iowa D5 180
Eldon, Mo. C5 189
Eldora, Iowa B4 180
El Dorado, Ark. D3 169
Eldorado, Braz. C3 137
Eldorado, Ont., Can. C7 153
Eldorado, Sask., Can. A1 155
Eldorado, Ill. F5 178
El Dorado, Kans. B6, E7 181
Eldorado, Md. C6 173
Eldorado, N.C. B4 197
Eldorado, Ohio C3 199
Eldorado, Okla. C2 200
Eldorado, Tex. D2 206
El Dorado, co., Calif. C3 170
Eldorado, peak, Wash. A4 210
Eldorado Springs, Colo. B5 171
El Dorado Springs, Mo. D3 189
Eldoret, Ken. A6 106
Eldred, Fla. E6 174
Eldred, Ill. D3 178
Eldred, Minn. C2 187
Eldred, Pa. C5 202
Eldridge, Ala. B2 166
Eldridge, Iowa C7, D7 180
Eldridge, Mo. D5 189
Eldridge, N. Dak. C7 198
Eleanor, W. Va. C3 211
Electra, Tex. C3 206
Electra, lake, Colo. D3 171
Electric, peak, Colo. C5 171
Electric, peak, Mont., Wyo. E6 190, A2 213
Electric City, Wash. *B6 210
Electric Mills, Miss. C5 188
Eleele, Haw. B2 176
El Ejemplo Central, P.R. C7 132
Elektrogorsk, Sov. Un. n18 72
Elektrostal', Sov. Un. n18 72
Elephant, butte, N. Mex. D2 195
Elephant, isl., Ant. C7 120
Elephant, mtn., Maine D2 184
Elephant, range, Camb. G5 89
Elephant Butte, res., N. Mex. D2 195
El Escorial, Sp. o16 65
El Espino, P.R. B2 132
Eleusis, see Elevsís, Grc.
Eleuthera, isl., Ba. Is. C5 131
Eleva, Wis. D2 212
Eleven Mile Canyon, res., Colo. C5 171
Eleven Point, riv., Mo. E6 189
Elevsís (Eleusis), Grc. g11 69
Elevsís (Eleusis), gulf, Grc. g11 69
El Faro, P.R. C3 132
El Fasher, Sud. C2 105
El Ferrol, Sp. A1 65
Elfers, Fla. D4 174
Elfin Cove, Alsk. k21 167
Elfrida, Ariz. F6 168
Elfros, Sask., Can. F4 155
El Fud, Eth. D5 105
El Fuerte, Mex. B3 129
El Galhak, Sud. C3 105
El Geteina, Sud. C3 105
Elgin, Ala. A2 166
Elgin, Ariz. F5 168
Elgin, Man., Can. E1 150
Elgin, N.B., Can. D4 151
Elgin, Ill. A5, E2 178
Elgin, Iowa B6 180
Elgin, Kans. E7 181
Elgin, Minn. F6 187
Elgin, Nebr. C7 191
Elgin, Nev. F7 192
Elgin, N. Dak. C4 198
Elgin, Okla. C3 200
Elgin, Oreg. B9 201
Elgin, Pa. C1 202
Elgin, Scot. C5 57
Elgin, S.C. B6 203
Elgin, Tex. D4 206
Elgin, co., Ont., Can. E3 153
Elgol, Scot. C2 57
El Goléa, Alg. C5 102
Elgon, mtn., Ug. A5 106
El Grullo, Mex. n11 129
El Hamurre, Som. D6 105
El Haseke, Syr. D13 85
El Hasîheisa, Sud. C3 105
El Hawata, Sud. C3 105
El Huecú, Arg. B2 136
Eli, Nebr. B4 191
Eliasville, Tex. C3 206
Elida, N. Mex. D6 195
Elida, Ohio B3 199
Elikon (Helicon), mtn., Grc. g9 69
Elila, riv., Zaire B4 106
Elim, Alsk. C7 167
El Indio, Tex. E2 206
Eliot, Maine E2 184

INDEX KEY Each place listed in **Bold-faced Type** has its population listed in the Political tables, pages 230 to 280.
Each country, shown in CAPITAL LETTERS, has its population listed in the World Political Information Table, pages 6 to 10.
* Does not appear on map; key shows general location.

Elista, Sov. Un. D2 73
Elizabeth, Ark. A3 169
Elizabeth, Colo. B6 171
Elizabeth, Ga. A4, C2 175
Elizabeth, Ill. A3 178
Elizabeth, Ind. H6 179
Elizabeth, La. D3 183
Elizabeth, Minn. D2 187
Elizabeth, Miss. B3 188
Elizabeth, N.J. B4, E4 194
Elizabeth, Pa. *F2 202
Elizabeth, W. Va. B3 211
Elizabeth, bay, Ec. g5 134
Elizabeth, cape, Maine E5 184
Elizabeth, cape, Wash. B1 210
Elizabeth, is., Mass. D6 185
Elizabeth City, N.C. A7 197
Elizabethton, Tenn. C11 205
Elizabethtown, Ill. F5 178
Elizabethtown, Ind. F6 179
Elizabethtown, Ky. C4 182
Elizabethtown, N.Y. A7, B3 196
Elizabethtown, N.C. C5 197
Elizabethtown, Pa. F8 202
Elizabethville, Pa. E8 202
El Jadida, Mor. C3 102
El Jebelein, Sud. C3 105
El Jeib, wadi, Jordan G10 85
Elk, Calif. C2 170
Elk, Pol. B7 70
Elk, Wash. A8 210
Elk, Wyo. B2 213
Elk, co., Kans. E7 181
Elk, co., Pa. D4 202
Elk, creek, Okla. B2 200
Elk, creek, S. Dak. C3 204
Elk, isl., Man., Can. D3 150
Elk, mtn., N. Mex. D1 195
Elk, mtn., Wyo. D6 213
Elk, mts., Colo. B3 171
Elk, peak, Mont. D6 190
Elk, riv., B.C., Can. D10 149
Elk, riv., Colo. A4 171
Elk, riv., Kans. E7 181
Elk, riv., Md. A6 173
Elk, riv., Tenn. B5 205
Elk, riv., W. Va. C3 211
Elk, riv., Wis. C3 212
Elk City, Idaho D3 177
Elk City, Kans. E8 181
Elk City, Nebr. D2 191
Elk City, Okla. B2 200
Elk City, res., Kans. E8 181
Elk Creek, Calif. C2 170
Elk Creek, Nebr. D9 191
Elk Creek, Va. E1 209
Elk Falls, Kans. E7 181
Elk Garden, W. Va. B5 211
Elk Grove, Calif. A6, C3 170
Elk Grove Village, Ill. E2 178
Elk Head, mts., Colo. A3 171
Elk Horn, Iowa C2 180
Elk Island, nat. park, Alta., Can. C4 148
Elk Mills, Md. A6 173
Elk Mound, Wis. D2 212
Elk Mountain, N.C. D3 197
Elk Mountain, Wyo. D6 213
Elk Park, N.C. A2, C4 197
Elk Point, Alta., Can. C5 148
Elk Point, S. Dak. E9 204
Elk Ranch, Ark. A2 169
Elk Rapids, Mich. D5 186
Elk River, Idaho C2 177
Elk River, Minn. E5 187
Elk Run Heights, Iowa *B5 180
Elk Springs, Colo. A2 171
Elk Valley, Tenn. C9 205
Elkader, Iowa B6 180
El Kamlin, Sud. B3 105
Elkatawa, Ky. C6 182
El Khandaq, Sud. B3 105
Elkhart, Ill. C4 178
Elkhart, Ind. A6 179
Elkhart Iowa A7 180
Elkhart, Kans. E2 181
Elkhart, Tex. D5 206
Elkhart, co., Ind A6 179
Elkhart, riv., Ind A6 179
Elkhart Lake, Wis. B6, E5 212
Elkhorn, Man., Can. E1 150
Elkhorn, Nebr. D2 191
Elkhorn, Wis. F5 212
Elkhorn, peaks, Idaho F7 177
Elkhorn, ridge, Oreg. C8 201
Elkhorn, riv., Nebr. B7 191
Elkhorn City, Ky. C7 182
Elkhovo, Bul. D8 68
Elkin, N.C. A3 197
Elkins, Ark. B1 169
Elkins, N.H. D3 193
Elkins, N. Mex. D5 195
Elkins, W. Va. C5 211
Elkins Park, Pa. A11 202
Elkland, Mo. D4 189
Elkland, Pa. C7 202
Elkmont, Ala. A3 166
Elkmont, Tenn. D10 205
Elko, B.C., Can. E10 149
Elko, Ga. D3 175
Elko, Nev. C6 192
Elko, S.C. E5 203
Elko, co., Nev. B6 192
Elkol, Wyo. D2 213
Elkridge, Md. B4, C2 173
Elkridge, W. Va. D6 211
Elkton, Fla. C5 174
Elkton, Ky. D2 182
Elkton, Md. A6 173
Elkton, Mich. E7 186
Elkton, Minn. G6 187
Elkton, Oreg. D3 201
Elkton, S. Dak. C9 204
Elkton, Tenn. B5 205
Elkton, Va. C4 209
Elkville, Ill. F4 178
Ellabell, Ga. D5 175
El Lago, Tex. *E5 206
Ellamar, Alsk. g18 167
Ellamore, W. Va. C4 211
Ellaville, Ga. D2 175
Ellef Ringnes, isl., N.W. Ter., Can. B25 118
Ellen, mtn., Utah E5 207
Ellen, mtn., Vt. C3 208
Ellenboro, N.C. B2 197
Ellenboro, W. Va. B3 211
Ellenburg Center, N.Y. A3 196
Ellendale, Del. C7 173
Ellendale, La. C6, E5 183
Ellendale, Minn. G5 187
Ellendale, N. Dak. C7 198
Ellensburg, Wash. C5 210
Ellenton, Fla. E4, F2 174
Ellenton, Ga. E3 175
Ellenton, Pa. C8 202
Ellenville, N.Y. D6 196
Ellenwood, Ga. B5 175
Eller, isl., Kwajalein 114
Ellerbe, N.C. B4 197
Ellershouse, N.S., Can. E6 151
Ellerslie, Ga. D2 175
Ellerslie, Md. D2 173
Ellesmere, isl., N.W. Ter., Can. A22 118
Ellesmere Port, Eng. A5 56
Ellettsville, Ind. F4 179
Ellice, is., Gilbert & Ellice Is. G10 113
Ellichpur, India G6 88
Ellicott City, Md. B4 173
Ellicottville, N.Y. C2 196
Ellijay, Ga. B2 175
Ellington, Conn. B7 172
Ellington, Mo. D7 189
Ellinwood, Kans. D5 181
Elliot, Conn. B8 172
Elliot Knob, mtn., Va. C3 209
Elliott, Ark. D3 169
Elliott, Ill. C5 178
Elliott, Iowa C2 180
Elliott, Md. D5 173
Elliott, N. Dak. C8 198
Elliott, S.C. C7 203
Elliott, co., Ky. B6 182
Elliott, bay, Wash. D1 210
Elliott, key, Fla. G6 174
Elliott, lake, Man., Can. C4 150
Elliot Lake, Ont., Can. A2 153
Ellis, Ark. A3 169
Ellis, Idaho E4 177
Ellis, Kans. D4 181
Ellis, Nebr. D9 191
Ellis, S. Dak. D9 204
Ellis, co., Kans. D4 181
Ellis, co., Okla. A2 200
Ellis, co., Tex. C4 206
Ellis, pond, Maine C2 184
Ellis Pond, Maine D2 184
Ellisburg, N.Y. B4 196
Ellisburg, Pa. C6 202
Ellisdale, N.J. C3 194
Ellisgrove, Ill. E4 178
Ellison Bay, Wis. C6 212
Elliston, Austl. F5 111
Elliston, Newf., Can. D5 152
Elliston, Mont. D4 190
Elliston, Va. D2 209
Ellisville, Miss. D4 188
Ellisville, Mo. B7 189
El Llanito, N. Mex. G5 195
Ellon, Scot. C6 57
Elloree, S.C. D6 203
Ellport, Pa. E1 202
Ellrich, Ger. B5 61
Ells, riv., Alta., Can. A4 148
Ellscott, Alta., Can. B4 148
Ellsinore, Mo. E7 189
Ellston, Iowa D3 180
Ellsworth, Ill. C5 178
Ellsworth, Iowa B4 180
Ellsworth, Kans. D5 181
Ellsworth, Maine D4 184
Ellsworth, Mich. C5 186
Ellsworth, Minn. G3 187
Ellsworth, Nebr. B3 191
Ellsworth, N.H. *C3 193
Ellsworth, Pa. F1 202
Ellsworth, Wis. D1 212
Ellsworth, co., Kans. D5 181
Ellsworth, hill, Conn. B3 172
Ellsworth, mts., Ant. B33 120
Ellsworth, mtn., Conn. B3 172
Ellsworth, lake, Okla. C3 200
Ellwangen, Ger. E5 61
Ellwood City, Pa. E1 202
Elm, creek, Minn. G4 187
Elm, creek, Tex. A5 206
Elm City, N.C. B6 197
Elm Creek, Man., Can. E3 150
Elm Creek, Nebr. D6 191
Elm Grove, Wis. *E5 212
Elm Springs, Ark. A1 169
Elm Springs, S. Dak. C3 204
Elm Springs Colony, S. Dak. D8 204
Elma, Iowa A5 180
Elma, Wash. C2 210
Elmali, Tur. D7 69
El Manteco, Ven. B5 133
Elmdale, Kans. D7 181
Elmdale Village, Mo. *C7 189
El Melik, riv., Sud. B2 105
El Memrhar, Maur. C1 103
Elmendorf, Tex. B4 206
El Mene, Ven. A3 133
Elmer, Mo. B5 189
Elmer, N.J. D2 194
Elmer, Okla. C2 200
Elmer City, Wash. *B7 210
El Mesellemiya, Sud. C3 105
Elmhurst, Ill. B6, F2 178
Elmhurst, Ind. *D6 179
Elmhurst, Pa. A9, D10 202
El Minao, P.R. B6 132
Elmira, Calif. B6 170
Elmira, P.E.I., Can. C7 151
Elmira, Ont., Can. D4 153
Elmira, Mich. C6 186
Elmira, Mo. B3 189
Elmira, N.Y. C4 196
Elmira, Oreg. C3 201
Elmira, W. Va. C4 211
Elmira Heights, N.Y. C4 196
Elmira Southeast, N.Y. *C4 196
El Mirage, Ariz. G1 168
Elmo, Kans. D6 181
Elmo, Mo. A2 189
Elmo, Mont. C2 190
Elmo, Utah D5 207
Elmo, Wyo. D6 213
Elmodel, Ga. E2 175
Elmont, Kans. B6 181
Elmont, N.Y. *G2 172
Elmont, Va. D5 209
El Monte, Calif. *D2 170
El Monte, Calif. F2 170
Elmora (Bakerton), Pa. E4 202
Elmore, Ala. C3 166
Elmore, Minn. G4 187
Elmore, Ohio A4 199
Elmore, co., Ala. C3 166
Elmore, co., Idaho F3 177
Elmore City, Okla. C4 200
El Moro, Colo. D6 171
El Morro, nat. mon., N. Mex. C1 195
El Mraïti (Well), Mali C4 103
El Mreïti (Well), Maur. B3 103
El Mreyer (Well), Maur. B3 103
Elmsdale, N.S., Can. E6 151
Elmsford, N.Y. D2 196
Elmshorn, Ger. B4 60
Elmsville, N.B., Can. D3 151
Elmvale, Ont., Can. C5 153
Elmville, Conn. B9 172
Elmwood, Ont., Can. C3 153
Elmwood, Ill. C4 178
Elmwood, Nebr. D9, E2 191
Elmwood, Wis. D1 212
Elmwood Park, Ill. F2 178
Elmwood Place, Ohio D2 199
Elna, Ky. C7 182
Elne, Fr. F5 58
Elnora, Alta., Can. D4 148
Elnora, Ind. G3 179
El Ocho, P.R. B6 132
El Odaiya, Sud. C2 105
Eloise, Fla. E5 174
Elon College, N.C. A4 197
Elora, Ont., Can. D4 153
Elora, Tenn. B5 205
El Oro, prov., Ec. B2 134
El Oued, Alg. C6 102
El Ouig, Mali C5 103
Eloy, Ariz. E4 168
El Palmito, Mex. B3 129
El Pao, Ven. B5 133
El Paraíso, Hond. D4 130
El Pardo, Sp. o17 65
El Paso, Ark. B3 169
El Paso, Ill. C4 178
El Paso, Tex. E1 206
El Paso, co., Colo. C6 171
El Paso, co., Tex. E1 206
Elphinstone, Man., Can. D1 150
El Polvorín, P.R. B5 132
El Portal, Calif. D4 170
El Portal, Fla. F3 174
El Prado, N. Mex. A4 195
El Pueblo, N. Mex. B4 195
El Puerto de Santa María, Sp. D2 65
El Qaryatein, Syr. E11 85
Elqui, riv., Chile F1 135
Elrama, Pa. F2 202
El Real, Pan. F9 130
El Recreo, Ven. *A4 133
El Reno, Okla. B4 200
El Rio, Calif. E4 170
El Rito, N. Mex. A3 195
El Roboré, Bol. C4 135
Elrod, Ala. B2 166
Elrosa, Minn. E4 187
Elrose, Sask., Can. F1 155
Elroy, Wis. E3 212
Elsa, Tex. F3 206
Elsah, Ill. A8 189
El Salto, Mex. C3 129
EL SALVADOR, country, N.A. D3 130
El Samán, Ven. B4 133
El Sauce, Nic. D4 130
Elsberry, Mo. B7 189
El Segundo, Calif. F2 170
Elsie, Mich. E6 186
Elsie, Nebr. D4 191
Elsie, Oreg. B3 201
Elsinore, Calif. F3, F5 170
Elsinore, Utah E3 207
Elsinore, lake, Calif. F3 170
Elsmere, Del. A6 173
Elsmere, Ky. A7, B5 182
Elsmere, Nebr. B5 191
Elsmore, Kans. E8 181
El Sombrero, Ven. B4 133
Elsterwerda, Ger. B8 61
Elstow, Sask., Can. F2 155
El Tigre, Ven. B5 133
El Tigrito, Ven. B5 133
El Tocuyo, Ven. B4 133
Elton, La. D3 183
Elton, Wis. C5 212
Eltopia, Wash. C7 210
El Toro, Calif. F3 170
El Transito, Chile E1 135
El Triunfo, Hond. D4 130
El Triunfo, Mex. C3 129
Eltville, Ger. C3 61
El Uach, Som. E5 105
Eluru, India E7 87, I8 88
Elva, Man., Can. E1 150
Elva, Tenn. C9 205
El Valle, Ven. *A4 133
Elvas, Port. C2 65
Elvaston, Ill. C2 178
El Verano, Calif. *C2 170
Elverson, Pa. F10 202
Elverum, Nor. G4 63
El Viejo, Nic. D4 130
El Vigía, P.R. B4 132
El Vigía, Ven. B3 133
Elvins, Mo. D7 189
El Volcán, Chile A2 136
El Wak, Ken. A7 106
Elwha, riv., Wash. A2 210
Elwood, Ill. B5 178
Elwood, Ind. D6 179
Elwood, Kans. C9 181
Elwood, Nebr. D6 191
Elwood, N.J. D3 194
Elwood, Utah B3 207
Elwood Park, Fla. E4 174
Ely, Eng. B8 56
Ely, Iowa C6 180
Ely, Minn. C7 187
Ely, Nev. D7 192
Ely, Vt. D4 208
Elyria, Kans. D6 181
Elyria, Nebr. C6 191
Elyria, Ohio A5 199
Elysburg, Pa. E8 202
Elysian, Minn. F5 187
Elzach, Ger. A4 66
Emanuel, co., Ga. D4 175
Emba, Sov. Un. D5 73
Emba, riv., Sov. Un. D5 73
Embarcacion, Arg. D3 135
Embarrass, Minn. C6 187
Embarrass, Wis. D5 212
Embarrass, riv., Ill. E6 178
Embarrass, riv., Wis. D5 212
Embden, N. Dak. C8 198
Embden, pond, Maine D3 184
Embetsu, Jap. D10 93
Embira, riv., Braz. C3 134
Emblem, Wyo. A4 213
Embreeville, Tenn. C11 205
Embreeville Junction, Tenn. *C11 205
Embro, Ont., Can. D4 153
Embrun, Ont., Can. B9 153
Embrun, Fr. E7 58
Embu, Ken. B6 106
Embudo, N. Mex. A4 195
Emden, Ger. B3 60
Emden, Ill. C4 178
Emden, Mo. B6 189
Emelle, Ala. C1 166
Emerado, N. Dak. B8 198
Emerald, Austl. A7 112
Emerson, Ark. D2 169
Emerson, Man., Can. C3 150
Emerson, Ga. B2 175
Emerson, Iowa C2 180
Emerson, Nebr. B9 191
Emerson, N.J. D5 194
Emery, S. Dak. D8 204
Emery, Utah E4 207
Emery, co., Utah E5 207
Emery Mills, Maine E2 184
Emeryville, Calif. *D2 170
Emet, Tur. C7 69
Emi Koussi, vol., Chad B3 104
Emida, Idaho B2 177
Emigrant, Mont. E6 190
Emilia, reg., It. B3 67
Emilia-Romagna, pol. dist., It. E6 66
Emiliano Zapata, Mex. D6 129
Emílio Meyer, Braz. E2 137
Emily, Minn. D5 187
Emily, lake, Minn. E3 187
Emine, cape, Bul. D8 68
Eminence, Ind. E4 179
Eminence, Ky. B4 182
Eminence, Mo. D6 189
Emington, Ill. C5 178
Emirau, isl., Bis. Arch. h13 110
Emirdağ, Tur. C8 85
Emlenton, Pa. D2 202
Emlyn, Ky. D5 182
Emma, Mo. C4 189
Emma, lake, Sask., Can. D3 155
Emmaus, Pa. E11 202
Emmen, Neth. B6 59
Emmendingen, Ger. A3 66
Emmerich, Ger. C3 60
Emmet, Ark. D2 169
Emmet, Nebr. B7 191
Emmet, N. Dak. B4 198
Emmet, co., Iowa A3 180
Emmet, co., Mich. C6 186
Emmetsburg, Iowa A3 180
Emmett, Idaho F2 177
Emmett, Kans. C7 181
Emmett, Mich. F8 186
Emmitsburg, Md. A3 173
Emmons, Minn. G5 187
Emmons, co., N. Dak. C5 198
Emory, Tex. C5 206
Emory, Utah B4 207
Emory, peak, Tex. G2 206
Emory Land, glacier, Ant. B34 120
Empangeni, S. Afr. C5 107
Empedrado, Arg. E4 135
Empire, Ala. B2 166
Empire, Calif. *D3 170
Empire, Colo. B5 171
Empire, Ga. D3 175
Empire, La. E6 183
Empire, Mich. D4 186
Empire, Nev. C2 192
Empire, Ohio B7 199
Empire, Oreg. D2 201
Empoli, It. C3 67
Emporia, Kans. D7 181
Emporia (Independent City), Va. E5 209
Emporium, Pa. D5 202
Empress, Alta., Can. D5 148
Empress Augusta, bay, Bougainville I. 115
Emptinne, Bel. D5 59
Emrick, N. Dak. B6 198
Ems, riv., Ger. A2 61
Ems Jade, canal, Ger. A7 59
Ems Weser, canal, Ger. A3 61
Emsdale, Ont., Can. B5 153
Emsdetten, Ger. A2 61
Emsworth, Pa. A5 202
Ena (Nakatsu), Jap. n16 93
Ena-San, peak, Jap. n16 93
Enard, bay, Scot. B3 57
Encampment, Wyo. D6 213
Encanto, cape, Phil. o13 90
Encarnación, Par. E4 135
Encarnación de Díaz, Mex. m12 129
Enchant, Alta., Can. D4 148
Enchi, Ghana E4 103
Encinal, Tex. E3 206
Encinitas, Calif. F5 170
Encino, N. Mex. C4 195
Encino, Tex. F3 206
Encontrados, Ven. B3 133
Encounter, bay, Austl. G2 112
Endako, B.C., Can. B5 149
Endako, riv., B.C., Can. B5 149
Ende, Indon. G6 90
Endeavor, Pa. C3 202
Endeavor, Wis. E4 212
Endeavour, Sask., Can. E4 155
Endelave, Den. C4 62
Endelave, isl., Den. C4 62
Enderby, B.C., Can. D8 149
Enderby Land, reg., Ant. B18 120
Enderlin, N. Dak. C8 198
Enders, Nebr. D4 191
Enders, res., Nebr. D4 191
Endiang, Alta., Can. D4 148
Endicott, Nebr. D8 191
Endicott, N.Y. C4 196
Endicott, Wash. C8 210
Endicott, mts., Alsk. B9 167
Endless, lake, Maine C4 184
Ene, riv., Peru D3 134
Enebakk, Nor. p29 63
Energy, Ill. *F5 178
Enetai, Wash. *B3 210
Enez, Tur. B6 69
Enfield, Austl. *F6 111
Enfield, N.S., Can. E6 151
Enfield, Conn. B6 172
Enfield, Eng. k12 55
Enfield, Ill. E5 178
Enfield, Maine C4 184
Enfield, N.H. C2 193
Enfield, N.C. A6 197
Enfield, Vt. D4 208
Enfield Center, N.H. C2 193
Engadine, Mich. B5 186
Engaru, Jap. D11 93
Engebi, isl., Eniwetok 114
Engelberg, Switz. C4 66
Engelhard, N.C. B8 197
Engel's, Sov. Un. C3 73
Enghien, Bel. D4 59
Enghien, Fr. g10 58
England, Ark. C4, E6 169
England, reg., U.K. B6 56
c. 1140 47
c. 1360 48
in 1914 52
see also Great Britain
Engle, N. Mex. D2 195
Englee, Newf., Can. C3, h10 152
Englefeld, Sask., Can. E3 155
Englevale, N. Dak. C8 198
Englewood, B.C., Can. D4 149
Englewood, Colo. B6 171
Englewood, Fla. F4 174
Englewood, Ind. *G5 179
Englewood, Kans. E4 181
Englewood, N.J. D5 194
Englewood, Ohio C3 199
Englewood, Oreg. *D2 201
Englewood, S. Dak. C2 204
Englewood, Tenn. D9 205
Englewood Cliffs, N.J. *B4 194
English, Ind. H5 179
English, chan., Eng. F4 55
English, riv., Ont., Can. F14 142
English, riv., Iowa C5 180
English Bay, Alsk. h16 167
English Bazar, India E12 88
English Center, Pa. D7 202
English Creek, N.J. E3 194
English Harbour West, Newf., Can. E4 152
English Lake, Ind. B4 179
Englishtown, N.J. C4 194
Énguera, Sp. C5 65
Enid, Miss. A4 188
Enid, Mont. C12 190
Enid, Okla. A4 200
Enid, res., Miss. A4 188
Enigma, Ga. E3 175
Eniirikku, isl., Bikini 114
Enilda, Alta., Can. B2 148
Eniwetok, isl., Marshall Is. 114
Enka, N.C. D3 197
Enkeldoorn, Rh. A5 107
Enkhuizen, Neth. B5 59
Enköping, Swe. H7, t35 63
Enna, It. F5 67
En Nahud, Sud. C2 105
En Nebk, Syr. E11 85
Ennedi, plat., Chad B4 104
Enngonia, Austl. D5 112
Ennigerloh, Ger. B3 61
Enning, S. Dak. C3 204
Ennis, Ire. D2 55
Ennis, Mont. E5 190
Ennis, Tex. B6, C4 206
Enniscorthy, Ire. D3 55
Enniskillen, N. Ire. C3 55
Ennistymon, Ire. D2 55
Enns, Aus. D7 60
Enns, riv., Aus. D7 60
Ennylabegan, isl., Kwajalein 114
Enoch, Utah F2 207
Enochs, Tex. C1 206
Enochsburg, Ind. F7 179
Enola, Ark. B3 169
Enola, Nebr. C8 191
Enola, Pa. F8 202
Enon, Ala. C4 166
Enon, Ohio C4 199
Enoree, S.C. B4 203
Enoree, riv., S.C. B3 203
Enos, Ind. B3 179
Enosburg Falls, Vt. B3 208
Enrick, riv., Scot. C4 57
Enriquillo, Dom. Rep. G8 131
Enriquillo, lake, Dom. Rep. F8 131
Enschede, Neth. B6 59
Ensenada, Arg. g8 136
Ensenada, Mex. A1 129
Ensenada, N. Mex. A3 195
Ensenada, P.R. D3 132
Enshih, China E6 91
Ensign, Alta., Can. D4 148
Ensign, Kans. E3 181
Ensign, Mich. C4 186
Ensisheim, Fr. B3 66
Ensley, Fla. G2 174
Ensley, Tenn. E8 205
Entebbe, Ug. A5 106
Enterprise, Ala. D4 166
Enterprise, Calif. *B2 170
Enterprise, Ont., Can. C8 153
Enterprise, Iowa A7 180
Enterprise, Kans. D6 181
Enterprise, Miss. C5 188
Enterprise, Oreg. B9 201
Enterprise, Utah B4 207
Enterprise, Utah F2 207
Enterprise, W. Va. A7, B4 211
Entiat, Wash. B5 210
Entiat, mts., Wash. B5 210
Entiat, riv., Wash. B5 210
Entrance, Alta., Can. C2 148
Entraygues, Fr. E5 58
Entre Minho e Douro, reg., Port. B1 65
Entre Rios, see Malema, Moz.
Entre Rios, prov., Arg. A5, f7 136
Entroncamento, Moz. A5 107
Entry, isl., Que., Can. B8 151
Entwistle, Alta., Can. C3 148
Enugu, Nig. E6 103
Enumclaw, Wash. B4 210
Envermeu, Fr. E9 56
Enville, Tenn. B3 205
Enyu, chan., Bikini 114
Enyu, isl., Bikini 114
Enz, riv., Ger. E3 61
Enza, riv., It. E6 66
Enzan, Jap. n17 93
Eola, La. D3 183
Eola, hills, Oreg. C1 201
Eolia, Mo. B6 189
Eoline, Ala. C2 166
Epe, Neth. B5 59
Epéna, Con. E3 104
Épernay, Fr. C5 58
Epes, Ala. C1 166
Ephesus, ruins, Tur. D6 69
Ephraim, Utah D4 207
Ephraim, Wis. C6 212
Ephrata, Pa. F9 202
Ephrata, Wash. B6 210
Epi, isl., New Hebr. 115
Epila, Sp. B5 65
Épinal, Fr. C7 58, A2 66
Épinay [-sur-Seine], Fr. g10 58
Epiphany, S. Dak. D8 204
Epirus, reg., Grc. C3 69
c. 450 B.C. 42
c. 120 A.D. 45
Epoufette, Mich. B5 186
Epperson, Tenn. D9 205
Epping, N.H. D4 193
Epping, N. Dak. A2 198
Eppingen, Ger. D3 61
Epps, La. B4 183
Epsie, Mont. E11 190
Epsom, Ind. G3 179
Epsom, N.H. D4 193
Epsom [& Ewell], Eng. C7 56
Epworth, Iowa B7 180
Equality, Ala. C3 166
Equality, Ill. F5 178
Equator, reg., Zaire A3 106
Equatoria, reg., Sud. D3 105
EQUATORIAL GUINEA, country, Afr. E1 104
Equeurdreville, Fr. C3 58
Equinunk, Pa. C11 202
Erath, La. E3 183
Erath, co., Tex. C3 206
Erba, mtn., Sud. A4 105
Erbach, Ger. D3 61
Erbacon, W. Va. C4 211
Erbendorf, Ger. D7 61
Erciş, Tur. C14 85
Erciyas, mtn., Tur. C10 85
Ercsi, Hung. B4 68
Érd, Hung. B4 68
Erda, Utah C3 207
Erdek, Tur. B6 69
Erdenheim, Pa. A11 202
Erdeni Dzuu, Mong. B5 91
Erding, Ger. D5 60
Erebus, mtn., Ant. B29 120
Erechim, Braz. D2 137

INDEX KEY Each place listed in **Bold-faced Type** has its population listed in the Population tables, pages 230 to 280.
Each country, shown in CAPITAL LETTERS, has its population listed in the World Political Information Table, pages 6 to 10.
* Does not appear on map; key shows general location.

Ereğli, Tur....B8 85
Ereğli, Tur....D10 85
Erepecurú, riv., Braz....C3 139
Eressós, Grc....C5 69
Erétria, see Néa Psará, Grc.
Erft, riv., Ger....D6 59
Erfurt, Ger....C6 61
Ergene, riv., Tur....B6 69
Erhard, Minn....D2 187
Eria, riv., Sp....A2 65
Erice, It....E4 67
Erick, Okla....B2 200
Erickson, Man., Can....D2 150
Ericsburg, Minn....B5 187
Ericson, Nebr....C7 191
Erie, Colo....A5 171
Erie, Ill....B3 178
Erie, Kans....E8 181
Erie, Mich....G7 186
Erie, N. Dak....B8 198
Erie, Pa....B1 202
Erie, co., N.Y....C2 196
Erie, co., Ohio....A5 199
Erie, co., Pa....C1 202
Erie, lake, Can., U.S.....B11 159
Erigavo, Som....C6 105
Eriksdale, Man., Can....D2 150
Erikub, atoll, Marshall Is.....115
Erímanthos, mtn., Grc....D3 69
Erimo, cape, Jap....F11 93
Erin, Ont., Can....D4 153
Erin, Tenn....A4 205
Erin Springs, Okla....C4 200
Eriskay, isl., Scot....C1 57
Erisort, bay, Scot....B2 57
Erithraí, Grc....C4, g10 69
Eritrea, prov., Eth....B4 105
in late 19th cent....99
Erkelenz, Ger....C6 59
Erken, lake, Swe....t36 63
Erlangen, Ger....D6 61
Erlanger, Ky....A5, A7 182
Erma, N.J....F3 194
Ermelino Matarazzo, Braz....*C3 137
Ermelo, Neth....B5 59
Ermelo, S. Afr....C5 107
Ermenek, Tur....D9 85
Ermont, Fr....g10 58
Ernakulam, India....*G6 88
Erne, lake, N. Ire....C3 55
Ernée, Fr....C3 58
Ernest, Pa....E3 202
Ernestina, Arg....g7 136
Ernestville, Tenn....C11 205
Ernfold, Sask., Can....G2 155
Erode, India....*F6 87
Eromanga, Austl....C4 112
Eros, La....B3 183
Er Rahad, Sud....C3 105
Er Rāma, Isr....B7 84
Erriboll, bay, Scot....B4 57
Errigal, mtn., Ire....C2 55
Erris, head, Ire....C1 55
Errol, N.H....B2 193
Errol, isl., La....E7 183
Erromango, isl., New Hebr....115
Er Roseires, Sud....C3 105
Erskine, Alta., Can....C4 148
Erskine, Minn....C3 187
Erstein, Fr....C7 58
Erstfeld, Switz....C4 66
Erving, Mass....A3 185
Erwin, N.C....B5 197
Erwin, S. Dak....C8 204
Erwin, Tenn....C11 205
Erwin, W. Va....B5 211
Erwood, Sask., Can....E4 155
Erzgebirge (Ore), mts., Czech., Ger....C8 61
Erzincan, Tur....C12 85
Erzurum, Tur....C13 85
Esan, cape, Jap....F10 93
Esashi, Jap....D11 93
Esashi, Jap....F10 93
Esbjerg, Den....C2 62
Esbo (Espoo), Fin....A5 72
Esbon, Kans....C5 181
Escada, Braz....k6 138
Escalante, Utah....F4 207
Escalante, des., Utah....F2 207
Escalante, riv., Utah....F4 207
Escalon, Calif....D3 170
Escalón, Mex....B4 129
Escambia, co., Ala....D2 166
Escambia, co., Fla....G1 174
Escanaba, Mich....C3 186
Escanaba, riv., Mich....B3 186
Escatawpa, Miss....E3, E5 188
Escatawpa, riv., Ala., Miss....E5 188
Esch-sur-Alzette, Lux....E5 59
Eschede, Ger....F4 62
Eschenbach, Ger....D6 61
Eschwege, Ger....B5 61
Eschweiler, Ger....C3 60
Escobal, Pan....k11 130
Escobar, Arg....g7 136
Escobas, Tex....F3 206
Escoheag, R.I....C9 172
Escondida, pt., Mex....D5 129
Escondido, Calif....F5 170
Escondido, riv., Nic....D6 130
Escoublac-La-Baule, Fr....D2 58
Escoumains, riv., Que., Can....A8 154
Escuinapa, Mex....C3 129
Escuintla, Guat....C2 130
Escuminac, Que., Can....A3 151
Escuminac, pt., N.B., Can....B5 151
Eseka, Cam....E2 104
Esens, Ger....A7 59
Eşfahān, see Isfahan, Iran
Esgueva, riv., Sp....B3 65
Esh Sheikh Jarrāh, Jordan....m14 84
Esher, Eng....m12 55
Eshimba, Zaire....C3 106
Eshowe, S. Afr....C5 107
Esk, riv., Eng....F5 57
Esk, riv., Scot....E6 57
Eskbank, Sask., Can....G2 155
Eskdale, W. Va....C3, D6 211
Eskifoca, Tur....C6 69
Eskilstuna, Swe....H7, t34 63
Eskimo, lakes, N.W. Ter., Can....C6 142
Eskimo Point, N.W. Ter., Can....D14 144
Eskişehir, Tur....C8 69
Esko, Minn....D6 187
Eskridge, Kans....D7 181
Esla, riv., Sp....B3 65
Eslarn, Ger....D7 61
Eslava, riv., Mex....h9 129
Eslöv, Swe....C7 62
Eşme, Tur....C7 69
Esmeralda, Ven....C4 133
Esmeralda, co., Nev....F4 192
Esmeraldas, Ec....A2 134
Esmeraldas, prov., Ec....A2 134
Esmond, Ill....A5 178
Esmond, N. Dak....A6 198
Esmond, R.I....B10 172
Esmond, S. Dak....C8 204
Esmont, Va....D4 209
Esom Hill, Ga....C1 175
Espada, pt., Col....A3 133
Espanola, Ont., Can....A3 153
Espanola, Fla....C5 174
Espanola, N. Mex....B3 195
Espanola, Wash....D7 210
Espanola, isl., Ec....g6 134
Esparto, Calif....C2 170
Esperance, Austl....F3 111
Esperanza, Arg....A4 136
Esperanza, Miss....A4 188
Esperanza, Tex....F1 206
Esperanza, P.R....g13 132
Espichel, cape, Port....C1 65
Espinal, Col....C3 133
Espinhaço, mts., Braz....E2 138
Espírito Santo, Braz....F2 138
Espírito Santo, state, Braz....F2 138
Espiritu Santo, isl., New Hebr....H10 113
Espita, Mex....C7 129
Espoo, see Esbo, Fin.
Esposende, Port....B1 65
Espy, Pa....D9 202
Espyville Station, Pa....C1 202
Esquatzel Coulee, creek, Wash....C6 210
Esquel, Arg....C2 136
Esquimalt, B.C., Can....B9, E6 149
Esquina, Arg....F4 135
Es Sanamein, Syr....A8 84
Esschen, Bel....C4 59
Essen, Ger....B2 61
Essendon, Austl....*H5 112
Essequibo, riv., Guy....B3 139
Essex, Calif....E6 170
Essex, Ont., Can....E2 153
Essex, Conn....D7 172
Essex, Ill....B5 178
Essex, Iowa....D2 180
Essex, Md....B5 173
Essex, Mo....E8 189
Essex, Mont....B3 190
Essex, N.Y....B3 196
Essex, Vt....B2 208
Essex, co., Ont., Can....E2 153
Essex, co., Eng....C8 56
Essex, co., Mass....A5 185
Essex, co., N.J....B4 194
Essex, co., N.Y....B7 196
Essex, co., Vt....B5 208
Essex, co., Va....D6 209
Essex Fells, N.J....*B4 194
Essex Junction, Vt....C2 208
Essexvale, Rh....B4 107
Essexville, Mich....E7 186
Esslingen, Ger....E4 61
Es Suki, Sud....C3 105
Estaban Echeverría, Arg....*A5 136
Estacada, Oreg....B4 201
Estación Superi, Arg....E2 135
Estados, isl., Arg....h13 136
Estaire, Ont., Can....A4 153
Estância, Braz....D3 138
Estancia, N. Mex....C3 195
Estarreja, Port....B1 65
Estcourt, Que., Can....B8 154
Estcourt, S. Afr....C4 107
Este, It....B3 67
Estelí, Nic....D4 130
Estell Manor, N.J....E3 194
Estella, Sp....A4 65
Estelline, S. Dak....C9 204
Estelline, Tex....B2 206
Estepa, Sp....D3 65
Estepona, Sp....D3 65
Esterhazy, Sask., Can....G4 155
Esternay, Fr....F3 59
Esternberg, Aus....E8 61
Estero, Fla....F5 174
Estero, bay, Calif....E3 170
Estero, isl., Fla....F5 174
Estes Park, Colo....A5 171
Estevan, Sask., Can....H4 155
Estevan, is., B.C., Can....C3 149
Estevan Point, B.C., Can....E4 149
Esther, Alta., Can....D5 148
Esther, Mo....*D7 189
Estherville, Iowa....A3 180
Estherwood, La....D3 183
Estill, Miss....B3 188
Estill, S.C....F5 203
Estill, co., Ky....C6 182
Estill Springs, Tenn....B5 205
Estillfork, Ala....A3 166
Estlin, Sask., Can....G3 155
Esto, Fla....G3 174
Eston, Sask., Can....F1 155
Estonia (S.S.R.), rep., Sov. Un....D5 71
in 1721....49
in 1940....53
after World War II....54
Estrées-St. Denis, Fr....E2 59
Estrêla, Braz....D2 137
Estrêla, mts., Port....B2 65
Estrella, bay, Santa Isabel I....115
Estremadura, reg., Port....C1 65
Estremadura, reg., Sp....C2 65
Estremoz, Port....C2 65
Estrondo, mts., Braz....C1 138, D5 139
Estuary, Sask., Can....G1 155
Esutoru, see Uglegorsk, Sov. Un.
Esztergom, Hung....B4 68
Etah, Grnld....B22 118
Étain, Fr....E5 59
Etamamu, riv., Que., Can....C1 152
Étampes, Fr....C5 58
Etang du Nord, Que., Can....B8 151
Étang Saumatre, lake, Haiti....F7 131
Etaples, Fr....B4 58
Etawa, India....E7 88
Etawah, India....C6 87, D7 88
Eten, isl., Truk....114
Ethan, S. Dak....D8 204
Ethel, Ont., Can....D3 153
Ethel, Miss....B4 188
Ethel, Mo....B5 189
Ethel, Wash....C3 210
Ethel, W. Va....D5 211
Ethelbert, Man., Can....D1 150
Ethelsville, Ala....B1 166
Ethelton, Sask., Can....E3 155
Ether, N.C....B4 197
Ethete, Wyo....B4 213
ETHIOPIA (Abyssinia), country, Afr....F9 97, D4 105
Ethridge, Mont....B5 190
Ethridge, Tenn....B4 205
Etive, inlet, Scot....D3 57
Etlan, Va....C4 209
Etna, Calif....B2 170
Etna, Ind....B6 179
Etna, Maine....D3 184
Etna, N.H....C2 193
Etna, N.Y....C4 196
Etna, Ohio....C5 199
Etna, Pa....B6 202
Etna, Wyo....B2 213
Etna, vol., It....F5 67
Etna Green, Ind....B5 179
Etobicoke, Ont., Can....D5 153
Etolin, isl., Alsk....m23 167
Etolin, strait, Alsk....C6 167
Eton, Ga....B2 175
Etosha, lake, S.W. Afr....A2 107
Etowah, Ark....B5 169
Etowah, Tenn....D9 205
Etowah, co., Ala....A3 166
Etowah, riv., Ga....B2 175
Etra, N.J....C3 194
Etretat, Fr....C4 58
Etta, Miss....A4 188
Et Taiyiba, Isr....B7, f11 84
Ettelbruck, Lux....E6 59
Etter, Tex....B1 206
Etterbeek, Bel....*D4 59
Etters (Goldsboro), Pa....F8 202
Etters Beach, Sask., Can....*F3 155
Ettington, Sask., Can....H2 155
Et Tira, Isr....B6, g10 84
Ettlingen, Ger....E3 61
Ettrick, Va....C7, D5 209
Ettrick, Wis....D2 212
Ettrick, forest, Scot....E5 57
Etumba, Fiji....114
Etzatlán, Mex....m11 129
Etzikom, Alta., Can....E5 148
Etzikom, coulee, Alta., Can....E5 148
Eu, Fr....B4 58
Eubank, Ky....C5 182
Euboea: ca. 450 B.C....42
Eucha, Okla....A7 200
Eucla, Austl....F4 111
Euclid, Minn....C2 187
Euclid, Ohio....A6, B2 199
Euclid, Pa....E2 202
Euclid Center, Mich....*F4 186
Euclid Heights, Ark....*C2 169
Eudora, Ark....D4 169
Eudora, Kans....B8, D8 181
Eudunda, Austl....G2 112
Eufaula, Ala....D4 166
Eufaula, Okla....B6 200
Eufaula, res., Okla....B6 200
Eufola, N.C....B3 197
Eugene, Ind....E3 179
Eugene, Mo....C5 189
Eugene, Oreg....C3 201
Eugenia, pt., Mex....B1 129
Euless, Tex....*B5 206
Eulonia, Ga....E5 175
Eunice, La....D3 183
Eunice, N. Mex....E6 195
Eupen, Bel....D6 59
Euphrates, riv., Asia....F2 86
Eupora Miss....B4 188
Eure, N. C....A7 197
Eure, riv., Fr....C4 58
Eureka, Calif....B1 170
Eureka, Fla....C5 174
Eureka, Ill....C4 178
Eureka, Kans....E7 181
Eureka, Mo....B7 189
Eureka, Mont....B1 190
Eureka, Nev....D6 192
Eureka, N.C....B6 197
Eureka, S.C....D4 203
Eureka, S. Dak....B6 204
Eureka, Utah....D3 207
Eureka, W. Va....B3 211
Eureka, Wis....D5 212
Eureka, co., Nev....D5 192
Eureka Central, P.R....C2 132
Eureka Springs, Ark....A2 169
Euroa, Austl....H5 112
Europe, cont....41
c. 120 A.D....45
c. 400....46
c. 1140....47
c. 1360....48
c. 1721....49
in 1810....50
in 1815....50
in 1914....52
in 1922-40....53
after World War II....54
Euskirchen, Ger....C1 61
Eustis, Fla....D5 174
Eustis, Maine....C2 184
Eustis, Nebr....D5 191
Eutaw, Ala....C2 166
Eutawville, S.C....E7 203
Eutin, Ger....D4 62
Eutsuk, lake, B.C., Can....C4 149
Eva, Ala....A3 166
Eva, Okla....D2 200
Eva, Tenn....A3 205
Evale, Ang....E2 106
Evan, Minn....F4 187
Evangeline, par., La....D3 183
Evanger, Nor....G2 63
Evans, Colo....A6 171
Evans, Ga....C4 175
Evans, La....D2 183
Evans, W. Va....C3 211
Evans, co., Ga....D5 175
Evans, mtn., Colo....B5 171
Evans, mtn., N.Z....O13 112
Evans, strait, N.W. Ter., Can....D16 143
Evans City (Evansburg), Pa....E1 202
Evans Mills, N.Y....A5 196
Evansburgh, Alta., Can....C3 148
Evansdale, Iowa....B5 180
Evansport, Ohio....A3 199
Evanston, Colo....A6 171
Evanston, Ill....A6, E3 178
Evanston, Ky....C6 182
Evanston, Wyo....D2 213
Evansville, Ark....B1 169
Evansville, Ill....E4 178
Evansville, Ind....I2 179
Evansville, Minn....D3 187
Evansville, Miss....A3 188
Evansville, Vt....B4 208
Evansville, Wis....F4 212
Evansville Wyo....C6 213
Evant, Tex....D3 206
Evanton, Scot....C4 57
Evart, Mich....E5 186
Evarts, Ky....D6 182
Eveleth, Minn....C6 187
Even Yehuda, Isr....f10 84
Evening Shade, Ark....A4 169
Everard, lake, Austl....F5 110
Everard, mtn., B.C., Can....D5 149
Everard, ranges, Austl....E5 110
Everest, Kans....C8 181
Everest, peak, Nep....D11 88
Everett, Ont., Can....C5 153
Everett, Mass....C3 185
Everett, Pa....F5 202
Everett, Wash....B3 210
Everett, mtn., Mass....B1 185
Everett, Ga....E5 175
Everettville, W. Va....A7 211
Evergem, Bel....C3 59
Everglades, Fla....G5 174
Everglades, nat. park, Fla....G6 174
Everglades, swamp, Fla....G6 174
Evergreen, Ala....D3 166
Evergreen, Colo....B5 171
Evergreen, La....D3 183
Evergreen, Miss....A5 188
Evergreen, N.C....C5 197
Evergreen, Va....D4 209
Evergreen Park, Ill....F3 178
Everly, Iowa....A2 180
Everman, Tex....*C4 206
Everson, Pa....F2 202
Everson, Wash....A3 210
Everton, Ark....A3 169
Everton, Mo....D4 189
Evesham, Sask., Can....E1 155
Evesham, Eng....B6 56
Évian-les-Bains, Fr....C2 66
Evinayong, Equat. Gui....E1 104
Evington, Va....D3 209
Évora, Port....C2 65
Évreux, Fr....C4 58
Évron, Fr....C3 58
Évros, riv., Tur., Grc....B6 69
Evrótas, riv., Grc....D4 69
Evstratios, isl., Grc....C5 69
Évvoia (Northern), gulf, Grc....C4 69
Évvoia, (Southern), gulf, Grc....g11 69
Évvoia (Euboea), isl., Grc....C4 69
Ewa, Haw....B3, g9 176
Ewa, beach, Haw....g9 176
Ewa Beach, Haw....B3, g9 176
Ewab, is., Indon....G8 90
Ewan, Wash....B8 210
Ewe, bay, Scot....C3 57
Ewell, Md....E5 173
Ewen, Mich....A6 186
Ewing, Ill....E5 178
Ewing, Ky....B6 182
Ewing, Mo....B6 189
Ewing, Nebr....B7 191
Ewing, Va....B1 209
Ewo, Con....F2 104
Exaltación, Bol....B2 135
Excel, Ala....D2 166
Excel, Alta., Can....D5 148
Excello, Mo....B5 189
Excelsior, Minn....F5 187
Excelsior, mtn., Calif....C4 170
Excelsior, mts., Nev....E3 192
Excelsior Springs, Mo....B3, D2 189
Exchange, Pa....D8 202
Exchange, W. Va....C4 211
Excocesa, bay, Dom. Rep....F9 131
Excursion Inlet, Alsk....k22 167
Exe, riv., Eng....D4 56
Executive Committee, range, Ant....B35 120
Exeland, Wis....C2 212
Exeter, Calif....D4 170
Exeter, Ont., Can....D3 153
Exeter, Eng....D4 56
Exeter, Maine....D3 184
Exeter, Mo....E4 189
Exeter, Nebr....D8 191
Exeter, N H....E5 193
Exeter, Pa....B8, D10 202
Exeter, R.I....C10 172
Exeter, riv., N.H....E5 193
Exira, Iowa....C3 180
Exline, Iowa....D5 180
Exmoor, moor, Eng....C4 56
Exmore, Va....D7 209
Exmouth, Eng....D4 56
Exmouth, gulf, Austl....D1 110
Expanse, Sask., Can....H3 155
Experiment, Ga....C2 175
Exploits, bay, Newf., Can....D4 152
Exploits, riv., Newf., Can....D3 152
Export, Pa....F2 202
Exshaw, Alta., Can....D3 148
Extension, B.C., Can....A8 149
Extinct Volcanoes and Lava Beds, Ariz....C6 168
Exuma, sound, Ba. Is....C5 131
Eya, riv., Sov. Un....H12 72
Eyak, Alsk....C10, g19 167
Eyasi, lake, Tan....B5 106
Eye, pen., Scot....B2 57
Eyebrow, Sask., Can....G2 155
Eyehill, creek, Alta., Sask., Can....C5 148, E1 155
Eyemouth, Scot....E6 57
Eylar, mtn., Calif....B6, D3 170
Eynort, inlet, Scot....C1 57
Eyota, Minn....G6 187
Eyre, Austl....F4 111
Eyre, Sask., Can....F1 155
Eyre, lake, Austl....E6 110
Eyre, pen., Austl....F6 110
Ezeiza, Arg....g7 136
Ezine, Tur....C6 69

F

Fabens, Tex....F1 206
Faber, Va....D4 209
Faber, lake, N.W. Ter., Can....D9 142
Fabius, N.Y....C5 196
Fabius San Hilo, pt., Tinian....114
Fåborg, Den....C4 62
Fabriano, It....C4 67
Fabyan, Conn....A9 172
Fabyan House, N.H....B4 193
Facatativá, Col....C3 133
Faceville, Ga....F2 175
Fachi (Well), Niger....C5 104
Fackler, Ala....A4 166
Facpi, pt., Guam....114
Factoryville, Pa....C10 202
Fada, Chad....B4 104
Fada, Mali....C5 103
Fada N'Gourma, Upper Volta....D5 103
Faddeyev, isl., Sov. Un....B17 71
Fadian, pt., Guam....114
Faejö, isl., Den....D5 62
Faemö, isl., Den....D5 62
Faenza, It....B3 67
FAEROE ISLANDS, Dan. dep., Eur....C6 41
Fafan, riv., Eth....D5 105
Fafe, Port....B1 65
Fagaalu, Am. Sam....114
Fagaloa, bay, W. Sam....114
Fagamafute, Am. Sam....114
Făgăraş, Rom....C7 68
Fagatogo, Am. Sam....114
Fågelbro, Swe....t36 63
Fagered, Swe....A6 62
Fagerhult, Swe....B7 62
Fagernes, Nor....G3 63
Fagersta, Swe....G6 63
Fagnano, lake, Arg....h12 136
Faguibine, lake, Mali....C4 103
Fagus, Mo....E7 189
Fahan, inlet, Saipan....114
Fahraj, Iran....H10 86
Fā'id, Eg....D4 84
Failaka, isl., Kuw....G4 86
Fair Bluff, N.C....C4 197
Fair Grove, Mo....D4 189
Fair Haven, Mich....F8 186
Fair Haven, N.J....C4 194
Fair Haven, N.Y....B4 196
Fair Haven, Vt....D2 208
Fair Lawn, N.J....D5 194
Fair Oaks, Calif....A6 170
Fair Oaks, Ga....A5 175
Fair Oaks, Ind....B3 179
Fair Plain, Mich....F4 186
Fair Play, Md....A2 173
Fair Play, Mo....D4 189
Fair Play, S.C....B2 203
Fair Port, Va....D6 209
Fairacres, N. Mex....E3 195
Fairbank, Ariz....F5 168
Fairbank, Iowa....B5 180
Fairbank, Md....C5 173
Fairbanks, Alsk....C10 167
Fairbanks, Fla....C4 174
Fairbanks, Maine....D2 184
Fairborn, Ohio....C3 199
Fairburn, Ga....B4, C2 175
Fairburn, S. Dak....D2 204
Fairbury, Ill....C5 178
Fairbury, Nebr....D8 191
Fairchance, Pa....G2 202
Fairchild, Wis....D3 212
Fairdale, Kans....B8, C9 181
Fairdale, Ky....A4, B4 182
Fairdale, N. Dak....A7 198
Fairdale, Pa....C10 202
Fairfax, Ala....C4 166
Fairfax, Calif....B5, D2 170
Fairfax, Man., Can....E1 150
Fairfax, Iowa....C6 180
Fairfax, Minn....F4 187
Fairfax, Mo....A2 189
Fairfax, Ohio....*C3 199
Fairfax, Okla....A5 200
Fairfax, S.C....F5 203
Fairfax, S. Dak....D7 204
Fairfax, Vt....B2 208
Fairfax, Va....B4, C5 209
Fairfax, co., Va....C5 209
Fairfax Station, Va....B4 209
Fairfield, Ala....B3, E4 166
Fairfield, Austl....*F9 111
Fairfield, Calif....B5, C2 170
Fairfield, Conn....E3 172
Fairfield, Idaho....F4 177
Fairfield, Ill....E5 178
Fairfield, Ind....E8 179
Fairfield, Iowa....C6 180
Fairfield, Ky....C4 182
Fairfield, Maine....D3 184
Fairfield, Mo....C4 189
Fairfield, Mont....C5 190
Fairfield, Nebr....D7 191
Fairfield, N.C....B7 197
Fairfield, N. Dak....B2 198
Fairfield, Ohio....C2 199
Fairfield, Pa....G7 202
Fairfield Tex....D4 206
Fairfield, Vt....B3 208
Fairfield, Wash....B8 210
Fairfield, co., Conn....D3 172
Fairfield, co., Ohio....C5 199
Fairfield, co., S.C....C5 203
Fairford, Ala....D1 166
Fairford, Eng....C6 56
Fairgrove, Mich....E7 186
Fairhaven, Mass....C6 185
Fairhaven, Minn....E4 187
Fairholme, Sask., Can....D1 155
Fairhope, Ala....E2 166
Fairhope, Pa....*F2 202
Fairland, Ind....E6 179
Fairland, Okla....A7 200
Fairlawn, Va....*D2 209
Fairlee, Md....B5 173
Fairlee, Vt....D4 208
Fairlight, Sask., Can....H5 155
Fairmont, Ill....*B5 178
Fairmont, Minn....G4 187
Fairmont, Nebr....D8 191
Fairmont, N.C....C4 197
Fairmont, Okla....A4 200
Fairmont, S.C....B3 203
Fairmont, Wash....*B3 210
Fairmont, W. Va....A7, B4 211
Fairmont City, Ill....B8 189
Fairmont Heights, Md....C2 173
Fairmount, Ga....B2 175
Fairmount, Ill....C6 178
Fairmount, Ind....D6 179
Fairmount, Kans....B8 181
Fairmount, Md....D6 173
Fairmount, N. Dak....C9 198
Fairoaks, Ark....B4 169
Fairoaks, Pa....A5 202
Fairplay, Colo....B5 171
Fairpoint, Ohio....B7 199
Fairpoint, S. Dak....C3 204
Fairport, Iowa....C7 180
Fairport, Mich....C4 186
Fairport, Mo....B3 189
Fairport, N.Y....B3 196
Fairport Harbor, Ohio....A6 199
Fairton, N.J....E2 194
Fairvale, N.B., Can....*D4 151
Fairview, Alta., Can....A1 148
Fairview, Ill....C3 178
Fairview, Ind....G7 179
Fairview, Kans....C8 181
Fairview, Ky....D2 182
Fairview, Mich....D6 186
Fairview, Mo....E3 189
Fairview, Mont....C12 190
Fairview, N.J....D5 194
Fairview, N.J....D3 194
Fairview, N.Y....*D7 196
Fairview, Ohio....B6 199
Fairview, Okla....A3 200
Fairview, Oreg....B4 201
Fairview, Pa....B1 202
Fairview, Pa....*E8 202
Fairview, S. Dak....D9 204
Fairview, Tenn....B4 205
Fairview, Utah....D4 207

INDEX KEY Each place listed in **Bold-faced Type** has its population listed in the Population tables, pages 230 to 280.
Each country, shown in CAPITAL LETTERS, has its population listed in the World Political Information Table, pages 6 to 10.
* Does not appear on map; key shows general location.

Fairview, Wash...*C5 210
Fairview, W. Va...A7, B4 211
Fairview, Wyo...C2 213
Fairview, peak, Nev...D3 192
Fairview, peak, Oreg...D4 201
Fairview Park, Ind...E3 179
Fairview Park, Ohio...B2 199
Fairway, Kans...B9 181
Fairweather, mtn., Alsk...D12 167
Fairy Glen, Sask., Can...D3 155
Faison, N.C...B5 197
Faith, N.C...B3 197
Faith, S. Dak...B3 204
Faithorn, Mich...C3 186
Faix, Tenn...C8 205
Faizābād, Afg...C15 86
Faizabad, India...C7 87, D9 88
Fajardo, P.R...B8, f12 132
Fajardo, mun., P.R...B8, f12 132
Fajardo Central, P.R...B8, f12 132
Fakenham, Eng...B8 56
Fakfak, Indon...F8 90
Fakse, Den...C6 62
Fakse, bay, Den...C6 62
Fakse Ladeplads, Den...C6 62
Faku, China...C10 92
Fal, La...D2 183
Fal, riv., Eng...D3 56
Falabequets, isl., Truk... 114
Falaise, Fr...C3 58
Falalu, isl., Truk... 114
Falas, isl., Truk... 114
Fălciu, Rom...B9 68
Falcon, Ark...D2 169
Falcon, Colo...C6 171
Falcon, Miss...A3 188
Falcon, N.C...B5 197
Falcon, Tex...F3 206
Falcón, state, Ven...A3 133
Falcon, res., Mex., Tex...F3 206
Falcon Heights, Minn...E7 187
Falconer, N.Y...C1 196
Falealili, hbr., W. Sam... 114
Falefa, hbr., W. Sam... 114
Falémé, riv., Mali, Sen...D2 103
Faleshty, Sov. Un...B8 68
Falfurrias, Tex...F3 206
Falher, Alta., Can...B2 148
Falkenberg, Ger...B8 61
Falkenberg, Swe...B6 62
Falkenburg Station, Ont., Can...B5 153
Falkenstein, Ger...C7 61
Falkirk, N. Dak...B4 198
Falkirk, Scot...D5 57
Falkland, B.C., Can...D8 149
FALKLAND ISLANDS, Br. dep., S.A...I4 125
Falkner, Miss...A5 188
Falköping, Swe...H5 63
Falkville, Ala...A3 166
Fall, Ger...B7 66
Fall, riv., Kans...E7 181
Fall Branch, Tenn...C11 205
Fall City, Wash...B4, D2 210
Fall Creek, Wis...D2 212
Fall River, Kans...E7 181
Fall River, Mass...C5 185
Fall River, Wis...E4 212
Fall River, co., S. Dak...D2 204
Fall River, res., Kans...E7 181
Fall River Mills, Calif...B3 170
Fall Rock, Ky...C6 182
Fallbrook, Calif...F5 170
Fallentimber, Pa...E5 202
Falling, creek, Va...C7 209
Falling Rock, creek, W. Va...C6 211
Falling Water, Tenn...E10 205
Falling Waters, W. Va...B7 211
Fallis, Okla...B4 200
Fällnäs, Swe...u35 63
Fallon, Mont...D11 190
Fallon, Nev...D3 192
Fallon, co., Mont...D12 190
Fallriver, Tenn...B4 205
Falls, Pa...A8 202
Falls, co., Tex...D4 206
Falls, riv., Wyo...A2 213
Falls Church (Independent City), Va...C5 209
Falls City, Nebr...D10 191
Falls City, Oreg...C3 201
Falls City, Tex...*E3 206
Falls Creek, Pa...D4 202
Falls of Rough, Ky...C3 182
Falls Village, Conn...B3 172
Fallsburg, Ky...B7 182
Fallston, Md...A5 173
Fallston, N.C...B2 197
Falmouth, N.S., Can...E5 151
Falmouth, Eng...D2 56
Falmouth, Jam...F5 131
Falmouth, Ky...B5 182
Falmouth, Maine...E5, E2 184
Falmouth, Mass...C6 185
Falmouth, Mich...D5 186
Falmouth, Va...C5 209
Falmouth, bay, Eng...D2 56
Falmouth Foreside, Maine...*E5 184
Falmouth Heights, Mass...C6 185
Falo, isl., Truk... 114
False, bay, S. Afr...D2 107
False, cape, Fla...D6 174
False, cape, Va...E7 209
Falster, isl., Den...D5 62
Falsterbo, Swe...C6 62
Fălticeni, Rom...B8 68
Falun, Kans...D6 181
Falun, Swe...G6 63
Famagusta, Cyp...E9 85
Family, lake, Man., Can...C4 150
Famous Ice Beds, Vt...E3 208
Fancher, N.Y...B2 196
Fancy Farm, Ky...B2 182
Fangcheng, China...H5 92
Fanghsien, China...E7 91
Fangshen, China...C8 92
Fannettsburg, Pa...F6 202
Fannin, Miss...C4 188
Fannin, Tex...E4 206
Fannin, co., Ga...B2 175
Fannin, co., Tex...C4 206
Fanning, isl., Pac. O...F12 113
Fannūj, Iran...H9 86
Fanny, mtn., Oreg...B9 201
Fanny Bay, B.C., Can...E5 149
Fannystelle, Man., Can...E3 150
Fano, It...C4 67
Fanö, bay, Den...C2 62
Fanö, isl., Den...C2 62
Fanwood, N.J...*B4 194
Fao, Iraq...G4 86
Fāqūs, Eg...D3 84
Far Hills, N.J...B3 194
Faradje, Zaire...A4 106
Farafangana, Malag...h9 107
Farāfirah, oasis, Eg...D5 101
Farah, Afg...E11 86
Farallon is., Calif...B4 170
Farallón, pt., Mex...n11 129
Farallones, gulf, Calif...B4 170
Faramana, Upper Volta...D4 103
Faranah, Guinea...D2 103
Farber, Mo...B6 189
Fareham, Eng...D6 56
Farewell, cape, Grnld...C19 118
Farewell, cape, N.Z...N14 112
Fargo, Ark...C4 169
Fargo, Ga...F4 175
Fargo, N. Dak...C9 198
Fargo, Okla...A2 200
Fari, Mali...D2 103
Faria, riv., Jordan...g12 84
Faribault, Minn...F5 187
Faribault, co., Minn...G5 187
Faridabad India...*C6 87
Faridpur, Bngl...F12 88
Farilhoes, is., Port...C1 65
Farina, Austl...E2 112
Farina, Ill...E5 178
Farisita, Colo...D5 171
Fāriskūr, Eg...C3 84
Farley, Iowa...B6 180
Farley, Mo...B3 189
Farley, N. Mex...A5 195
Farm, pond, Mass...D2 185
Farmer, Ohio...A3 199
Farmer, S. Dak...D8 204
Farmer City, Ill...C5 178
Farmers, Ky...B6 182
Farmers Exchange, Tenn...B4 205
Farmersburg, Ind...F3 179
Farmersburg, Iowa...B6 180
Farmersville, Ala...C3 166
Farmersville, Calif...*D4 170
Farmersville, Ill...D4 178
Farmersville, Tex...C4 206
Farmerville, La...B3 183
Farmingdale, Maine...D3 184
Farmingdale, N.J...C4 194
Farmingdale, N.Y...G3 172
Farmingdale, S. Dak...D3 204
Farmington, Ark...A1 169
Farmington, Conn...C5 172
Farmington, Del...C6 173
Farmington, Ill...C3 178
Farmington, Iowa...D6 180
Farmington, Maine...D2 184
Farmington, Mich...A7 186
Farmington, Minn...F5 187
Farmington, Mo...D7 189
Farmington, Mont...C4 190
Farmington, N.H...D4 193
Farmington, N. Mex...A1 195
Farmington, N.C...B2 197
Farmington, Pa...G2 202
Farmington, Tenn...B5 205
Farmington, Utah...C4 207
Farmington, Wash...B8 210
Farmington, W. Va...A7 211
Farmington, riv., Conn...B5 172
Farmingville, N.Y...*D4 196
Farmland, Ind...D7 179
Farmville, N.C...B6 197
Farmville, Va...C4 209
Farnam, Nebr...D5 191
Farnams, Mass...A1 185
Farnborough, Eng...C7 56
Farne, is., Eng...C6 57
Farner, Tenn...D9 205
Farnham, Que., Can...D5 154
Farnham, N.Y...C1 196
Farnham, mtn., B.C., Can...D9 149
Farnhamville, Iowa...B3 180
Farnharm, Va...D6 209
Farnhurst, Del...A6 173
Farnumsville, Mass...*B4 185
Faro, Braz...C3 139
Faro, Yukon, Can...*D6 142
Faro, Port...D2 65
Farragut, Iowa...D2 180
Farrar, Iowa...A8 180
Farrar, riv., Scot...C4 57
Farrāshband, Iran...G6 86
Farrel, Miss...A3 188
Farrell, Pa...D1 202
Farrellton, Que., Can...D2 154
Farrerdale, Sask., Can...F3 155
Farris, Okla...C6 200
Farris, lake, Nor...p27 63
Farrukhabad, India...C6 87, D7 88
Fársala, Grc...C4 69
Farsi, Afg...E11 86
Farsö, Den...B3 62
Farson, Iowa...C5 180
Farson, Wyo...C3 213
Farsund, Nor...H2 63
Fårup, Den...B3 62
Farwell, Mich...E6 186
Farwell, Minn...E3 187
Farwell, Nebr...C7 191
Farwell, Tex...B1 206
Fasā, Iran...G6 86
Fasano, It...D6 67
Fassett, Que., Can...D3 154
Fastov, Sov. Un...F7 72
Fatehpur, India...C7 87
Fatsa, Tur...B11 85
Fatuosofia, cape, W. Sam... 114
Fatuvalu, W. Sam... 114
Faucett, Mo...B3 189
Faulk, co., S. Dak...B6 204
Faulkner, co., Ark...B3 169
Faulkton, S. Dak...C6 204
Faunsdale, Ala...C2 166
Fauquembergues, Fr...D10 56
Fauquier, B.C., Can...E8 149
Fauquier, co., Va...C5 209
Fauro, isl., Sol. Is... 115
Faust, Utah...C3 207
Favara, It...F4 67
Faverges, Fr...D2 66
Faversham, Eng...C8 56
Favorita, Fla...C5 174
Fawn, hbr., Fiji... 114
Fawn, lake, Ont., Can...F15 143
Fawn Grove, Pa...*G8 202
Fawnie, range, B.C., Can...C5 149
Faxaflói, bay, Ice...n21 63
Faxon, Okla...C3 200
Faxon, Pa...*D8 202
Faxon, Tenn...A3 205
Fay, Okla...B3 200
Fayd, Sau. Ar...I14 85
Fayal, isl., Port. (Azores)...g8 102
Fayette, Ala...B2 166
Fayette, Ind...E5 179
Fayette, Iowa...B6 180
Fayette, Maine...D2 184
Fayette, Miss...D2 188
Fayette, Mo...B5 189
Fayette, Ohio...A3 199
Fayette, Utah...D4 207
Fayette, co., Ala...B2 166
Fayette, co., Ga...C2 175
Fayette, co., Ill...D4 178
Fayette, co., Ind...E7 179
Fayette, co., Iowa...B6 180
Fayette, co., Ky...B5 182
Fayette, co., Ohio...C4 199
Fayette, co., Pa...G2 202
Fayette, co., Tenn...B2 205
Fayette, co., Tex...E4 206
Fayette, co., W. Va...C3 211
Fayette City, Pa...*F2 202
Fayetteville, Ala...B3 166
Fayetteville, Ark...A1 169
Fayetteville, Ga...C2 175
Fayetteville, Ill...B9 189
Fayetteville, N.Y...B5 196
Fayetteville, N.C...B5 197
Fayetteville, Ohio...C4 199
Fayetteville, Pa...G6 202
Fayetteville, Tenn...B5 205
Fayetteville, W. Va...C3, D7 211
Fayetteville North, N.C...*B5 197
Fays-Billot, Fr...B1 66
Fayville, Mass...D1 185
Faywood, N. Mex...E1 195
Fazzān, see Fezzan, prov., Libya
Fear, cape, N.C...D6 197
Fearn, Scot...C5 57
Feasterville, Pa...A12 202
Feather, riv., Calif...C3 170
Feather Falls, Calif...C3 170
Featherston, Okla...B6 200
Fécamp, Fr...C4 58
Feche, Eth...D4 105
Fédala, Mor...C3 102
Federal, Ont., Can...A9 153
Federal, Wyo...D7 213
Federal Dam, Minn...C4 187
Federal Point, Fla...C5 174
Federalsburg, Md...C6 173
Federation of Malaya, see Malaya, reg., Mala.
Federation of Rhodesia & Nyasaland, see Malawi and Zambia, countries, and Rhodesia, Br. dep., Afr.
Fedora, S. Dak...C8 204
Fedscreek, Ky...C7 182
Feeding Hills, Mass...B2 185
Fefan, isl., Truk... 115
Fehmarn, isl., Ger...D5 62
Feijó, Braz...C3 134
Feilding, N.Z...N15 112
Feira, Zambia...E5 106
Feira de Santana, Braz...D3 138
Felanitx, Sp...C7 65
Felch, Mich...B3 186
Felda, Fla...F5 174
Feldbach, Aus...E7 60
Feldberg, Ger...E7 62
Feldberg, mtn., Ger...B4 66
Feldkirch, Aus...E4 60
Feliciano, P.R...B2 132
Felicity, Ohio...D3 199
Felipe Carrillo Puerto, Mex...D7 129
Felix, cape, N.W. Ter., Can...C13 142
Felixstowe, Eng...C9 56
Felixville, La...D5 183
Fellbach, Ger...E4 61
Fellingsbro, Swe...t33 63
Fellowship, N.J...D3 194
Fellsmere, Fla...E6 174
Felsenthal, Ark...D3 169
Felt, Idaho...F7 177
Felt, Okla...D1 200
Feltham, Eng...*C4 56
Felton, Calif...C5, D2 170
Felton, Del...B6 173
Felton, Ga...C1 175
Felton, Minn...C2 187
Felton, Pa...G8 202
Feltre, It...A3 67
Femund, lake, Nor...F4 63
Fence, Wis...C5 212
Fence, lake, Wis...C4 212
Fence, riv., Mich...B2 186
Fence Lake, N. Mex...C1 195
Fender, Ga...E3 175
Fenelon Falls, Ont., Can...C6 153
Fénérive, Malag...g9 107
Fengchen, China...D5 92
Fengcheng, China...J6 92
Fengchieh, China...I3 92
Fenghsiang, China...G2 92
Fenghsien, China...E6 91
Fengning, China...D7 92
Fengshan, China...C4 93
Fengtu, China...J2 92
Fenick, isl., S.C...G1 203
Fenn, Idaho...D2 177
Fennimore, Wis...F3 212
Fennville, Mich...F4 186
Fenton, Sask., Can...E3 155
Fenton, Iowa...A3 180
Fenton, La...D3 183
Fenton, Mich...F7 186
Fenton, Mo...B8 189
Fentress, Tex...A4 206
Fentress, co., Tenn...C9 205
Fenwick, Ont., Can...D5 153
Fenwick, W. Va...C4 211
Fenwood, Sask., Can...G4 155
Fenyang, China...D7 91, F4 92
Feodosiya, Sov. Un...I10 72
Ferdig, Mont...B5 190
Ferdinand, Idaho...C2 177
Ferdinand, Ind...H4 179
Ferdinandshof, Ger...E7 62
Ferdows, Iran...E9 86
Fère-Champenoise, Fr...F4 59
Ferentino, It...D4 67
Fergana, Sov. Un...E8 73
Fergana, mts., Sov. Un...E8 73
Fergus, Ont., Can...D4 153
Fergus, Mont...C7 190
Fergus, co., Mont...C7 190
Fergus Falls, Minn...D2 187
Ferguson, B.C., Can...D9 149
Ferguson, Iowa...C5 180
Ferguson, Ky...C5 182
Ferguson, Mo...A8, C7 189
Ferguson, W. Va...C2 211
Fériana, Tun...G11 64
Ferintosh, Alta., Can...C4 148
Ferland, Sask., Can...*H2 155
Ferme Neuve, Que., Can...C2 154
Fermeuse, Newf., Can...E5 152
Fermo, It...C4 67
Fermoselle, Sp...B2 65
Fermoy, Ire...D2 55
Fern, Pa...D2 202
Fern Creek, Ky...A4 182
Fern Crest Village, Fla...*F6 174
Fern Park, Fla...D5 174
Fern Ridge, dam, Oreg...C3 201
Fernán-Núñez, Sp...D3 65
Fernandina Beach, Fla...B5, B6 174
Fernandina (Narborough), isl., Ec...g5 134
Fernando de Noronha, ter., Braz...B4 138
Fernando de Noronha, isl., Braz...B4 138
Fernando Póo, reg., Equat. Gui...E1 104
Fernando Póo, isl., Equat. Gui...E1 104
Fernão Veloso, bay, Moz...D7 106
Fernbank, Ala...B1 166
Ferndale, Ark...D5 169
Ferndale, Calif...B1 170
Ferndale, Ky...D6 182
Ferndale, Md...B4 173
Ferndale, Mich...A7 186
Ferndale, Pa...F4 202
Ferndale, Wash...A3 210
Ferney, S. Dak...B7 204
Fernie, B.C., Can...E10 149
Fernley, Nev...D2 192
Fernwood, Idaho...B2 177
Fernwood, Miss...D3 188
Fernwood, N.Y...B4 196
Ferozepore, India...B5 88
Ferrara, It...E7 66, B3 67
Ferreira do Alentejo, Port...C1 65
Ferreira do Zêzere, Port...C1 65
Ferrellsburg, W. Va...C2 211
Ferrelo, cape, Oreg...E2 201
Ferreñafe, Peru...C2 134
Ferriday, La...C4 183
Ferriere, It...E5 66
Ferris, Ill...C2 178
Ferris, Tex...C4, B6 206
Ferris, mts., Wyo...C5 213
Ferrisburg, Vt...C2 208
Ferron, Utah...D4 207
Ferros, Braz...E2 138
Ferrum, Va...E2 209
Ferry, Mich...E4 186
Ferry, co., Wash...A7 210
Ferry, pt., N.J...E4 194
Ferryland, Newf., Can...E5 152
Ferrysburg, Mich...*E4 186
Ferryville, Tun...F11 64
Ferryville, Wis...E2 212
Fertile, Iowa...A4 180
Fertile, Minn...C2 187
Fertilia, It...D2 67
Feshi, Zaire...C2 106
Fessenden, N. Dak...B6 198
Festina, Iowa...A6 180
Festus, Mo...B8, C7 189
Feteşti, Rom...C8 68
Fethiye, Tur...D7 69
Fetisovo, Sov. Un...E4 73
Fettercairn, Scot...D6 57
Feucht, Ger...D6 61
Feuchtwangen, Ger...D5 61
Feudal, Sask., Can...F2 155
Feurs, Fr...E6 58
Feversham, Ont., Can...C4 153
Fez, Mor...G4 64
Fezzan (Fazzān), prov., Libya...D2 101
Ffestiniog, Wales...B4 56
Fianarantsoa, Malag...h9 107
Fianarantsoa, prov., Malag...h9 107
Fianga, Chad...D3 104
Fibre, Mich...B6 186
Ficarolo, It...E7 66
Fich, Eth...D5 105
Fichot, is., Newf., Can...C4 152
Fichtel Gebirge, mts., Ger...C6 61
Ficklin, Ga...C4 175
Ficksburg, S. Afr...C4 107
Fidalgo, isl., Wash...A3 210
Fidelis, Fla...G2 174
Fidenza, It...B3 67
Field, B.C., Can...D9 149
Field, lake, La...E5 183
Fieldale, Va...E3 209
Fielding, Sask., Can...E2 155
Fielding, Utah...B3 207
Fieldon, Ill...D3 178
Fields, Oreg...E8 201
Fieldsboro, N.J...C3 194
Fier, Alb...B2 69
Fierro, N. Mex...E1 195
Fiesole, It...C3 67
Fife, Wash...*B3 210
Fife, co., Scot...D5 57
Fife, lake, Sask., Can...H3 155
Fife Lake, Sask., Can...H3 155
Fife Lake, Mich...D5 186
Fife Ness, cape, Scot...D6 57
Fifield, Wis...C3 212
Fifteen Mile, creek, Wyo...A4 213
Fifteen Mile Falls, res., N.H., Vt...B3 193
5th Cataract (Nile River), Sud...B3 105
Fifty Lakes, Minn...D4 187
Figeac, Fr...E5 58
Figtree, Rh...B4 107
Figueira da Foz, Port...B1 65
Figueras, Sp...A7 65
Figuig, Mor...C4 102
Figure Five, Ark...B1 169
FIJI, country, Oceania... 114
Filbert, W. Va...D3 211
Filchner, cape, Ant...C22 120
Filchner, Ice shelf, Ant...A8 120
File, lake, Man., Can...B1 150
File, riv., Man., Can...B1 150
Filer, Idaho...G4 177
Filer City, Mich...D4 186
Filey, Eng...F8 57
Fili, Grc...g11 69
Filiatrá, Grc...D3 69
Filicudi, isl., It...E5 67
Filingue, Niger...D5 103
Filley, Nebr...D9 191
Fillmore, Calif...E4 170
Fillmore, Sask., Can...H4 155
Fillmore, Ill...D4 178
Fillmore, Ind...E4 179
Fillmore, Mo...A3 189
Fillmore, N.Y...C2 196
Fillmore, N. Dak...A6 198
Fillmore, Okla...C5 200
Fillmore, Utah...E3 207
Fillmore, co., Minn...G6 187
Fillmore, co., Nebr...D8 191
Fimi, riv., Zaire...B2 106
Fina Susu, mtn., Saipan... 114
Finale Emilia, It...E7 66
Finca Marini, P.R...C2 132
Fincastle, Va...C3 209
Finch, Ont., Can...B9 153
Finchley, Eng...*k12 55
Findhorn, Scot...C5 57
Findhorn, riv., Scot...C5 57
Findlater, Sask., Can...G3 155
Findlay, Ill...D5 178
Findlay, Ohio...A4 199
Findley, mtn., B.C., Can...D9 149
Fine, N.Y...A5, B2 196
Finegayan, Guam... 114
Finesville, N.J...B2 194
Fingal, N. Dak...C8 198
Finger, Tenn...B3 205
Fingerville, S.C...A3 203
Fingoe, Moz...A5 107
Finike, Tur...D8 69
Finisterre, cape, Sp...A1 65
Finjasjon, lake, Swe...B7 62
Finke, riv., Austl...E5 110
Finksburg, Md...B4 173
Finland, Minn...C7 187
FINLAND, country, Eur...E12 63
c. 1721... 49
in 1810... 50
in 1914... 51
in 1922-40... 53
after World War II... 54
Finland, gulf, Fin., Sov. Un...H11 63
Finlay, riv., B.C., Can...A5 149
Finlay Forks, B.C., Can...D2 149
Finlayson, Minn...D6 187
Finley, N. Dak...B8 198
Finley, Okla...C6 200
Finley, Tenn...A2 205
Finleyson, Ga...D3 175
Finleyville, Pa...*F1 202
Finmoore, B.C., Can...C6 149
Finn, mtn., Alsk...C8 167
Finnegan, Alta., Can...D4 148
Finney, co., Kans...D3 181
Finschhafen, N. Gui...k12 111
Finspång, Swe...u33 63
Finsteraarhorn, mtn., Switz...C4 66
Finsterwalde, Ger...B8 61
Finzel, Md...D2 173
Fionn, bay, Scot...C3 57
Fiq, Syr...F10 85
Fircrest, Wash...D1 210
Fire, is., N.Y...G4 172
Fire, isl., N.Y...G5 172
Fire Island, inlet, N.Y...G3 172
Firebaugh, Calif...D3 170
Firenze, see Florence, It.
Firenzuola, It...B3 67
Firesteel, S. Dak...B4 204
Firestone, Colo...A6 171
Firmat, Arg...A4 136
Firminy, Fr...E6 58
Firozabad, India...D7 88
Firsovo, Sov. Un...C11 93
1st Cataract (Nile River), Eg...E6 101
First Connecticut, lake, N.H...A2 193
First Roach Pond, lake, Maine...C3 184
Firth, Idaho...F6 177
Firth, Nebr...D9 191
Firūzābād, Iran...G6 86
Fīrūzkūh, Iran...D6 86
Fish, creek, W. Va...C2 211
Fish, riv., Maine...A4 184
Fish, riv., S.W. Afr...C2 107
Fish Cove, pt., Newf., Can...A3 152
Fish Creek, Wis...C6 212
Fish Haven, Idaho...G7 177
Fish River, lake, Maine...B4 184
Fish Springs, range, Utah...D2 207
Fisheating, creek, Fla...F5 174
Fisher, Ark...B5 169
Fisher, Ill...C5 178
Fisher, Minn...C2 187
Fisher, Pa...D3 202
Fisher, W. Va...B5 211
Fisher, co., Tex...C2 206
Fisher, bay, Man., Can...D3 150
Fisher, glacier, Ant...B19 120
Fisher, peak, Va...E2 209
Fisher, riv., Man., Can...D3 150
Fisher, strait, N.W. Ter., Can...D16 143
Fisher Branch, Man., Can...D3 150
Fisherman, isl., Va...B7 209
Fishers, Ind...E5, G8 179
Fishers, isl., N.Y...D5 196
Fishers, lake, N.S., Can...E4 151
Fishers, peak, Colo...D6 171
Fishers Island, sound, Conn., N.Y...D8 172
Fishersville, Va...C4 209
Fishertown, Pa...F4 202
Fisherville, Ont., Can...E5 153
Fisherville, Mass...B4 185
Fishguard, Wales...C3 56
Fishing, bay, Md...D5 173
Fishing, creek, N.C...A6 197
Fishing, creek, S.C...B5 203
Fishing, creek, W. Va...B4 211
Fishing, lake, Man., Can...C4 150
Fishing Creek, Md...D5 173
Fishing Creek, N.J...E3 194
Fishing Creek, res., S.C...B6 203
Fishkill, N.Y...D7 196
Fishkill, creek, N.Y...C1 172
Fishtail, Mont...E7 190
Fishtrap, res., Ky...B2 209
Fishville, La...C3 183
Fisk, Mo...E7 189
Fiskburg, Ky...B5, A7 182
Fiskdale, Mass...B3 185
Fiske, Sask., Can...F1 155
Fiskeville, R.I...C10 172
Fismes, Fr...E3 59
Fitch Bay, Que., Can...D5 154
Fitchburg, Mass...A4 185
Fitchville, Conn...C8 172
Fithian, Ill...C6 178
Fitler, Miss...C2 188
Fittstown, Okla...C5 200
Fitz Roy, Arg...D3 136
Fitz Roy, mtn., Arg...D2 136
Fitzgerald, Ga...E3 175
Fitzhugh, Okla...C5 200
Fitzhugh, sound, B.C., Can...D4 149
Fitzpatrick, Que., Can...B5 154
Fitzroy, Austl...C4 111
Fitzroy, riv., Austl...C3 110
Fitzroy, riv., Austl...D8 110
Fitzroy Harbor, Ont., Can...B8 153
Fitzwilliam, N.H...E2 193
Fitzwilliam, isl., Ont., Can...B3 153
Fitzwilliam Depot, N.H...E2 193
Fiume, see Rijeka, Yugo.
Fiumicino, It...h8 67
Five Islands, N.S., Can...D5 151
Five Points, Ala...B4 166
Five Points, Ind...H8 179
Five Points, N. Mex...G5 195
Fivemile, creek, Wyo...B4 213
Fizi, Zaire...B4 106
Fjärås, Swe...A6 62
Fjärdhundra, Swe...t34 63
Fjerritslev, Den...A3 62
Flag Knob, mtn., Ky...C7 182
Flag Pond, Tenn...C11 205
Flagg, Tex...B1 206
Flagler, Colo...B7 171
Flagler, co., Fla...C5 174
Flagler Beach, Fla...C5 174
Flagstaff, Ariz...B4 168

INDEX KEY Each place listed in **Bold-faced Type** has its population listed in the Population tables, pages 230 to 280.
Each country, shown in CAPITAL LETTERS, has its population listed in the World Political Information Table, pages 6 to 10.
* Does not appear on map; key shows general location.

Flagstaff, lake, Maine C2 184
Flagstaff, lake, Oreg E7 201
Flagtown, N.J. B3 194
Flamand, lake, Que., Can B4 154
Flambeau, res., Wis B3 212
Flambeau, riv., Wis C2 212
Flamborough, head, Eng C6 55
Flaming Gorge, dam, Utah C6 207, D3 213
Flaming Gorge, nat. recreation area, Utah, Wyo D3 213
Flaming Gorge, res., Utah, Wyo B6 207, D3 213
Flanagan, Ill C5 178
Flanders, Ont., Can E5 150
Flanders, Conn C3 172
Flanders, N.J B3 194
Flanders, N.Y F6 172
Flanders, see East Flanders and West Flanders, provs., Bel.
Flanders, former prov., Fr B5 58
Flanders, bay, N.Y F6 172
Flandreau, S. Dak C9 204
Flanigan, Nev C2 192
Flannan, is., Scot A3 55
Flasher, N. Dak C4 198
Flat, Alsk C8 167
Flat, Ky C6 182
Flat, Mo D6 189
Flat, brook, N.J A3 194
Flat, isl., Newf., Can C3 152
Flat, lake, La C5 183
Flat, riv., Mich E5 186
Flat Bay, Newf., Can D2 152
Flat Creek, Ala B2, E4 166
Flat Lick, Ky D6 182
Flat River, Mo D7 189
Flat River, res., R.I C10 172
Flat Rock, Ala A4 166
Flat Rock, Ill E6 178
Flat Rock, Ind F6 179
Flat Rock, Mich F7 186
Flat Rock, N.C D3 197
Flat Rock, Ohio A5 199
Flat Tops, plat., Colo B3 171
Flat Willow, creek, Mont D8 190
Flat Woods, Tenn B4 205
Flatbrookville, N.J A3 194
Flatbush, Alta., Can B3 148
Flatcreek, Tenn B5 205
Flathead, co., Mont B2 190
Flathead, Indian res., Mont C2 190
Flathead, lake, Mont C2 190
Flathead, mts., Mont B2 190
Flathead, riv., B.C., Can., Mont E10 149, B2 190
Flathead, val., Mont C2 190
Flatlands, N.B., Can B3 151
Flatonia, Tex E4 206
Flatrock, creek, Ind F6 179
Flatrock, lake, Man., Can B1 150
Flats, Nebr C4 191
Flattery, cape, Wash A1 210
Flatwood, Ala C2 166
Flatwoods, Ky B7 182
Flatwoods, La C3 183
Flatwoods, W. Va C4 211
Flawil, Switz B5 66
Flaxcombe, Sask., Can F1 155
Flaxton, N. Dak A3 198
Flaxville, Mont B11 190
Fleet, Alta., Can C5 148
Fleet, Eng C7 56
Fleetwood, Eng G5 57
Fleetwood, N.C A2 197
Fleetwood, Pa F10 202
Fleischmanns, N.Y C6 196
Flekkefjord, Nor H2 63
Fleming, Sask., Can G5 155
Fleming, Colo A8 171
Fleming, Ga E5 175
Fleming (Unionville), Pa E6 202
Fleming, co., Ky B6 182
Flemingsburg, Ky B6 182
Flemington, Ga E5 175
Flemington, Mo D4 189
Flemington, N.J B3 194
Flemington, Pa D7 202
Flemington, W. Va B7 211
Flen, Swe t34 63
Flensburg, Ger A4 60, D3 62
Flensburg, Minn E4 187
Flensburg, fjord, Den D3 62
Flers, Fr C3 58
Flesherton, Ont., Can C4 153
Fletcher, Ont., Can E2 153
Fletcher, N.C D3 197
Fletcher, Ohio B3 199
Fletcher, Okla C3 200
Fletcher, Vt B3 208
Fletcher, mtn., Vt B3 208
Fleur de Lys, Newf., Can C3, h10 152
Fleurier, Switz C2 66
Flieden, Ger C4 61
Flin Flon, Man., Can B1 150
Flinders, isl., Austl n15 110
Flinders, is., Austl F5 110
Flinders, range, Austl F6 110
Flinders, riv., Austl C7 110
Flint, Ind A7 179
Flint, Mich E7 186
Flint, Wales A4 56
Flint, co., Wales A4 56
Flint, isl., Pac. O G12 113
Flint, riv., Ga D2 175
Flint, riv., Mich E7 186
Flint, run, W. Va A6 211
Flint City, Ala A3 166
Flint Creek, range, Mont D4 190
Flint Hill, Va C4 209
Flinthill, Mo C7 189
Flintoft, Sask., Can H2 155
Flinton, Ont., Can C7 153
Flintstone, Md D2 173
Flintville, Tenn B5 205
Flipper, pt., Wake Isl 114
Flippin, Ark A3 169
Flippin, Ky D4 182
Flixecourt, Fr D2 59
Flöha, Ger C8 61
Flom, Minn C2 187
Flomaton, Ala D2 166
Flomot, Tex B2 206
Floodwood, Minn D6 187
Flora, Ill E5 178
Flora, Ind C4 179
Flora, Miss C3 188
Flora, N. Dak B6 198
Flora, Oreg B9 201
Flora Vista, N. Mex A1 195
Florahome, Fla C5 174
Floral City, Fla D4 174
Floral Park, Mont *E4 190
Floral Park, N.Y D2 196
Florala, Ala D3 166
Flordell Hills, Mo *C7 189
Florence, Ala A2 166
Florence, Ariz D4 168
Florence, Colo C5 171
Florence, Ind G8 179
Florence (Firenze), It C3 67
Florence, Kans D7 181
Florence, Ky A5, A7 182
Florence, Miss C3 188
Florence, Mo C5 189
Florence, Mont D2 190
Florence, N.J C3 194
Florence, Oreg *D2 201
Florence, S.C C8 203
Florence, S. Dak B8 204
Florence, Tex D4 206
Florence, Vt D2 208
Florence, Wash A3 210
Florence, Wis C5 212
Florence, co., S.C C8 203
Florence, co., Wis C5 212
Florence Junction, Ariz D4 168
Florenceville, N.B., Can C2 151
Florencia, Col C2 133
Florenville, Bel E5 59
Flores, Guat B3 130
Flores, isl., B.C., Can E4 149
Flores, isl., Indon G6 90
Flores, isl., Port. (Azores) g8 102
Flores, sea, Indon G6 90
Floresta, Braz C3 138
Floresville, Tex B4, E3 206
Florey, Tex C1 206
Florham Park, N.J B4 194
Floriano, Braz C2 138
Florianópolis, Braz D3 137
Florida, Cuba E4 131
Florida, Mass A1 185
Florida, Mo B6 189
Florida, N. Mex C3 195
Florida, N.Y D2, D6 196
Florida, Ohio A3 199
Florida [Adentro], P.R B4 132
Florida, Ur E1 137
Florida, state, U.S 174
in 1819-45 163
in 1861 164
Florida, East: c. 1763 162
c. 1790 126
Florida, West: in 1763-67 162
c. 1790 126
Florida, bay, Fla H6 174
Florida, cape, Fla G6 174
Florida, isl., Sol. Is 115
Florida, keys, Fla H6 174
Florida, mts., N. Mex E2 195
Florida, straits, Fla H6 174
Florida City, Fla F3, G6 174
Florien, La C2 183
Florin, Pa *F8 202
Flórina, Grc B3 69
Floris, Iowa D5 180
Floris, Va B4 209
Florissant, Colo C5 171
Florissant, Mo A8 189
Flossmoor, Ill F3 178
Flournoy, Calif C2 170
Flourtown, Pa A11 202
Flovilla, Ga C3 175
Flower, riv., Vt E2 208
Flower Hill, N.Y *E2 196
Flower Station, Ont., Can B8 153
Flowers Cove, Newf., Can C3 152
Floweree, Mont C5 190
Flowery Branch, Ga B3 175
Flowood, Miss C3 188
Floyd, Iowa A5 180
Floyd, N. Mex C6 195
Floyd, Va E2 209
Floyd, co., Ga B1 175
Floyd, co., Ind H6 179
Floyd, co., Iowa A5 180
Floyd, co., Ky C7 182
Floyd, co., Tex B2 206
Floyd, co., Va E2 209
Floyd, riv., Iowa B1 180
Floyd Dale, S.C C9 203
Floydada, Tex C2 206
Floyds, fork, Ky B4 182
Floyds Knobs, Ind H6 179
Floydsburg, Ky A4 182
Fluessenmeer, lake, Neth B5 59
Flumendosa, riv., It E2 67
Flushing, Mich E7 186
Flushing, Ohio B6 199
Fluvanna, Tex C2 206
Fluvanna, co., Va D4 209
Fly Creek, N.Y C6 196
Flying H, N. Mex D4 195
Flynns Lick, Tenn C8 205
Foam Lake, Sask., Can F4 155
Foard, co., Tex B3 206
Foard City, Tex C3 206
Foča, Yugo D4 68
Fochabers, Scot C5 57
Fochimi Hoyoudine (Well), Chad B3 104
Focşani, Rom C8 68
Fogauso, cape, Am. Sam 114
Foggia, It D5 67
Foggo, Nig D6 103
Fogliano, It k9 67
Fogo, Newf., Can D4 152
Fogo, cape, Newf., Can D4 152
Fogo, is., Newf., Can k27 143
Fohnsdorf, Aus E7 60
Föhr, isl., Ger A4 60
Foix, Fr F4 58
Folcroft, Pa *G11 202
Foley, Ala E2 166
Foley, Fla B3 174
Foley, Minn E5 187
Foley, Mo B7 189
Foligno, It C4 67
Folkestone, Eng C9 56
Folkston, Ga F4 175
Folkstone, N.C C6 197
Follansbee, W. Va A4, B2 211
Follett, Tex A2 206
Follonica, It C3 67
Folly, isl., S.C F8 203
Folly Beach, S.C F8, G3 203
Folly Lake, N.S., Can D6 151
Folsom, Calif A6, C3 170
Folsom, La D5 183
Folsom, N.J D3 194
Folsom, N. Mex A6 195
Folsom, W. Va A6, B4 211
Folsomville, Ind H3 179
Fomento, Cuba D4 131
Fond du Lac, Sask., Can E11 144
Fond du Lac, Wis B5, E5 212
Fond du Lac, co., Wis E5 212
Fond du Lac, Indian res., Minn D6 187
Fonda, Iowa B3 180
Fonda, N.Y C6 196
Fonde, Ky D6 182
Fondi, It D4 67
Fonsagrada, Sp A2 65
Fonseca, gulf, Cen. Am D4 130
Fontainebleau, Fr C5 58
Fontana, Calif F3 170
Fontana, Kans D9 181
Fontana, Wis F5 212
Fontana Dam, N.C D2 197
Fontanelle, Iowa C3 180
Fontanelle, Nebr C9 191
Fontanet, Ind E3 179
Fonte Boa, Braz D4 133
Fontenay-le-Comte, Fr D3 58
Fontenay [-sous-Bois], Fr g10 58
Fontenelle, Wyo C2 213
Fontenelle, res., Wyo C2 213
Fonthill, Ont., Can D5 153
Foochow, China F8 91
Foosland, Ill C5 178
Foothills, Alta., Can C2 148
Foothills, B.C., Can C9 149
Footscray, Austl *H5 112
Footville, Wis F4 212
Foping, China H2 92
Forada, Minn E3 187
Foraker, Ohio B4 199
Foraker, Okla A5 200
Forbach, Fr C7 58
Forbes, Austl F7 112
Forbes, Minn C6 187
Forbes, Mo B2 189
Forbes, N.C C4 197
Forbes, N. Dak D7 198
Forbes, mtn., Alta., Can D2 148
Forcados, Nig E6 103
Forcalquier, Fr F6 58
Force, Pa D4 202
Forchheim, Ger D6 61
Ford, Kans E4 181
Ford, Ky C5 182
Ford, Scot D3 57
Ford, co., Ill C5 178
Ford, co., Kans E4 181
Ford, riv., Mich C3 186
Ford City, Calif E4 170
Ford City, Pa E2 202
Fordland, Mo D5 189
Fordlândia, Braz C3 139
Fords Prairie, Wash *C3 210
Fordsville, Ky C3 182
Fordville, N. Dak A8 198
Fordwich, Ont., Can D3 153
Fordwick, Va C3 209
Fordyce, Ark D3 169
Fordyce, Nebr B8 191
Forécariah, Guinea E2 103
Foreman (New Rocky Comfort), Ark D1 169
Foremost, Alta., Can E5 148
Forest, Bel D4 59
Forest, Ont., Can D2 153
Forest, Ind D5 179
Forest, Miss C4 188
Forest, Ohio B4 199
Forest, Tex D5 206
Forest, Va D3 209
Forest, co., Pa C3 202
Forest, co., Wis C5 212
Forest Acres, S.C *D6 203
Forest Center, Minn C7 187
Forest City, Ill C4 178
Forest City, Iowa A4 180
Forest City, Maine C5 184
Forest City, Mo B2 189
Forest City, N.C B2, D4 197
Forest City, Pa C11 202
Forest Dale, Vt D2 208
Forest Green, Mo B5 189
Forest Grove, Oreg B1, B3 201
Forest Heights, Md C1 173
Forest Hill, Ont., Can *E6 153
Forest Hill, La C3 183
Forest Hill, Md A5 173
Forest Hill, Tex *C4 206
Forest Hills, Pa B6 202
Forest Home, Ala D3 166
Forest Homes, Ill *E3 178
Forest Junction, Wis A6 212
Forest Knolls, Calif B5 170
Forest Lake, Mich B4 186
Forest Lake, Minn E6 187
Forest Park, Ga B5 175
Forest Park, Ill F2 178
Forest Park, Okla *B4 200
Forest River, N. Dak A8 198
Forest Station, Maine C5 184
Forest View, Ill *B6 178
Forestburg, Alta., Can C4 148
Forestburg, S. Dak C7 204
Forestdale, R.I B10 172
Forestgrove, Mont D7 190
Forestport, N.Y B5 196
Foreston, Minn E5 187
Foreston, S.C D7 203
Forestville, Conn C5 172
Forestville, N.Y C1 196
Forestville, Pa D1 202
Forestville, Wis D6 212
Forfar, Scot D6 57
Forgan, Sask., Can F2 155
Forgan, Okla A1, D4 200
Forge Village, Mass A5, C1 185
Forges-les-Eaux, Fr C4 58
Forget, Sask., Can H4 155
Forillon, nat. park, Que., Can G20 144
Fork, N.C B3 197
Fork, S.C C9 203
Fork, creek, W. Va D5 211
Fork Mountain, Tenn C9 205
Fork Ridge, Tenn C10 205
Fork River, Man., Can D1 150
Fork Shoals, S.C B3 203
Fork Union, Va D4 209
Forked Deer, Tenn B2 205
Forked River, N.J D4 194
Forkland, Ala C2 166
Forks, Wash B1 210
Forks of Elkhorn, Ky B5 182
Forksville, Pa D8 202
Forlì, It B4 67
Forman, N. Dak C8 198
Formazza, It C4 66
Formby, Eng A4 56
Formello, It g8 67
Formentera, isl., Sp C6 65
Formiga, Braz F1 138
Formosa, Ark B3 169
Formosa, Braz E1 138
Formosa, Ont., Can C3 153
Formosa: c. 1775 82
after World War II 83
see also Taiwan
Formosa, bay, Ken B7 106
Formosa, strait, China G8 91
Formoso, Kans C6 181
Forney, Tex B6, C4 206
Fornovo di Taro, It E6 66
Forres, Scot C5 57
Forrest, Austl F4 111
Forrest, Ill C5 178
Forrest, N. Mex C6 195
Forrest, co., Miss D4 188
Forrest City, Ark B5 169
Forrest Station, Man., Can E2 150
Forreston, Ill A4 178
Forsan, Tex C2 206
Forsayth, Austl C7 111
Forserum, Swe A8 62
Förslövsholm, Swe B6 62
Forst, Ger B9 61
Forsyth, Ga C3 175
Forsyth, Ill D5 178
Forsyth, Mich B3 186
Forsyth, Mo E4 189
Forsyth, Mont D10 190
Forsyth, co., Ga B2 175
Forsyth, co., N.C A3 197
Fort Adams, Miss D2 188
Fort Albany, Ont., Can E9 153
Fort Ann, N.Y B7 196
Fort Apache, Ariz D6 168
Fort Apache, Indian res., Ariz C5 168
Fort-Archambault, Chad D3 104
Fort Ashby, W. Va B6 211
Fort Assiniboine, Alta., Can B3 148
Fort Atkinson, Iowa A6 180
Fort Atkinson, Wis F5 212
Fort Augustus, Scot C4 57
Fort Banya, Ken A6 106
Fort Barnwell, N.C B6 197
Fort Basinger, Fla E5 174
Fort Bayard (Chanchiang), China G7 91
Fort Beaufort, S. Afr D4 107
Fort Belknap, Mont B8 190
Fort Belknap Agency, Mont B8 190
Fort Belknap, Indian res., Mont B8 190
Fort Bellefontaine, Mo A8 189
Fort Bend, co., Tex E5 206
Fort Benning, Ga C5 166
Fort Benton, Mont C6 190
Fort Berthold, Indian res., N. Dak B3 198
Fort Bidwell, Calif B3 170
Fort Bidwell, Indian res., Calif B3 170
Fort Blackmore, Va B2 209
Fort Bragg, Calif C2 170
Fort Branch, Ind H2 179
Fort Bridger, Wyo D2 213
Fort Calhoun, Nebr C9 191
Fort Chadbourne, Tex C2 206
Fort Charlet, see Djanet, Alg.
Fort-Chimo, Que., Can A3 154
Fort Chipewyan, Alta., Can D2 148
Fort Clark, N. Dak B4 198
Fort Cobb, Okla B3 200
Fort Cobb, res., Okla B3 200
Fort Collins, Colo A5 171
Fort Collins West, Colo *A5 171
Fort-Coulonge, Que., Can B8 153
Fort Covington, N.Y A2 196
Fort Crampel, Cen. Afr. Rep D3 104
Fort Crook, Nebr E3 191
Fort-Dauphin, Malag h9 107
Fort Davis, Ala C4 166
Fort Davis, Tex F2 206
Fort Defiance, Ariz B6 168
Fort-de-France, Mart o16 131
Fort Deposit, Ala D3 166
Fort Dick, Calif B1 170
Fort Dodge, Iowa B3 180
Fort Dodge, Kans E4 181
Fort Donelson, nat. military park and cemetery, Tenn A4 205
Fort Duchesne, Utah C6 207
Fort Edward, N.Y B7 196
Fort Erie, Ont., Can E6 153
Fort Fairfield, Maine B5 184
Fort Fitzgerald, Alta., Can D1 148
Fort Flatters, Alg D6 102
Fort Foureau, Cam C2 104
Fort Frances, Ont., Can E7 153
Fort Fraser, B.C., Can B5 149
Fort Frederica, nat. mon., Ga E5 175
Fort Gaines, Ga E1 175
Fort Garland, Colo D5 171
Fort Gay, W. Va C2 211
Fort-George, Que., Can B2 154
Fort George Island, Fla B6 174
Fort Gibson, Okla B6 200
Fort Good Hope, N.W. Ter., Can C7 144
Fort Gouraud, Maur B2 103
Fort Grahame, B.C., Can A5 149
Fort Green, Fla E5 174
Fort Griffin, Tex C3 206
Fort Hall, Idaho F6 177
Fort Hall, Ken B6 106
Fort Hall, Indian res., Idaho F6 177
Fort Hancock, Tex F1 206
Fort Harrison, Mont D4 190
Fort Hill, Pa G3 202
Fort Howard, Md B5 173
Fort Jefferson, nat. mon., Fla H4 174
Fort Jennings, Ohio B3 199
Fort Johnson, N.Y *C6 196
Fort Johnston, Malawi D6 106
Fort Jones, Calif B2 170
Fort Kent, Maine A4 184
Fort Kent Mills, Maine A4 184
Fort Keogh, Mont D11 190
Fort Klamath, Oreg E5 201
Fort Lallemand, Alg C6 102
Fort-Lamy, Chad C3 104
Fort Langley, B.C., Can A10 149
Fort Laperrine (Tamanrasset), Alg E6 102
Fort Laramie, Wyo C8 213
Fort Laramie, nat. mon., Wyo C8 213
Fort Lauderdale, Fla E3, F6 174
Fort Lawn, S.C B6 203
Fort Leavenworth Kans B8, C9 181
Fort Lee, N.J D5 194
Fort Liard, N.W. Ter., Can D8 144
Fort-Liberté, Hai F8 131
Fort Lincoln, N. Dak C5 198
Fort Littleton, Pa F6 202
Fort Loramie, Ohio B3 199
Fort Loudon, Pa G6 202
Fort Loudoun, lake, Tenn D9 205
Fort Lupton, Colo A6 171
Fort Macleod, Alta., Can E4 148
Fort MacMahon, Alg D5 102
Fort Madison, Iowa D6 180
Fort Matanzas, nat. mon., Fla C5 174
Fort McDermitt, Indian res., Nev B4 192
Fort McDowell, Ariz F2 168
Fort McDowell, Indian res., Ariz D4, F3 168
Fort McHenry, nat. mon. and historical shrine, Md C2 173
Fort McKavett, Tex D2 206
Fort McKenzie, Que., Can A2 154
Fort McPherson, N.W. Ter., Can C6 144
Fort Meade, Fla E5 174
Fort Meadow, res., Mass D1 185
Fort Mill, S.C A6 203
Fort Miller, N.Y B7 196
Fort Missoula, Mont D2 190
Fort Mitchell, Ala C4 166
Fort Mitchell, Ky *A5 182
Fort Mitchell, Va E4 209
Fort Mohave, Indian res., Ariz C1 168
Fort Morgan, Ala E1 166
Fort Morgan, Colo A7 171
Fort Motte, S.C D6 203
Fort Munro, Pak C2 88
Fort Myer Heights, Va B5 209
Fort Myers, Fla F5 174
Fort Myers Beach, Fla F5 174
Fort Nelson, B.C., Can D2 149
Fort Norman, N.W. Ter., Can D7 144
Fort Ogden, Fla E5 174
Fort Oglethorpe, Ga B1 175
Fort Payne, Ala A4 166
Fort Peck, Mont B10 190
Fort Peck, dam, Mont B10 190
Fort Peck, Indian res., Mont B11 190
Fort Peck, res., Mont C10 190
Fort Pierce, Fla E6 174
Fort Pierce, inlet, Fla E6 174
Fort Pierre, S. Dak C5 204
Fort Pierre Bordes, see Tin Zaouaten, Alg.
Fort Plain, N.Y C6 196
Fort Polignac, Alg D6 102
Fort Portal, Ug A5 106
Fort Providence, N.W. Ter., Can D9 144
Fort Pulaski, nat. mon., Ga D6 175, G6 203
Fort Qu'Appelle, Sask., Can G4 155
Fort Randall, dam, S. Dak D7 204
Fort Ransom, N. Dak C8 198
Fort Recovery, Ohio B3 199
Fort Resolution, N.W. Ter., Can D10 144
Fort Rice, N. Dak C5 198
Fort Riley, Kans C7 181
Fort Ripley, Minn D4 187
Fort Ritner, Ind G5 179
Fort Robinson, Nebr B2 191
Fort Rock, Oreg D5 201
Fort Rousset, Con F3 104
Fort St. James, B.C., Can B5 149
Fort St. John, B.C., Can A7, E3 149
Fort Sandeman, Pak B4 87
Fort Saskatchewan, Alta., Can C4 148
Fort Scott, Kans E9 181
Fort Selkirk, Yukon, Can D5 144
Fort Severn, Ont., Can D8 153
Fort Shaw, Mont C5 190
Fort Shawnee, Ohio B3 199
Fort Sheridan, Ill A6 178
Fort Shevchenko, Sov. Un E4 73
Fort Sibut, Cen. Afr. Rep D3 104
Fort Smith, Ark B1 169
Fort Smith, N.W. Ter., Can D10 144
Fort Smith, lake, Ark B1 169
Fort Spring, Ky B5 182
Fort Stanton, N. Mex D4 195
Fort Steele, B.C., Can E10 149
Fort Stockton, Tex D1 206
Fort Sumner, N. Mex C5 195
Fort Sumter, nat. mon., S.C F3 203
Fort Supply, Okla A2 200
Fort Supply, res. and dam, Okla A2 200
Fort Thomas, Ariz D6 168
Fort Thomas, Ky A7 182
Fort Thompson, S. Dak C6 204
Fort Totten, N. Dak B7 198
Fort Totten, Indian res., N. Dak B6 198
Fort Towson, Okla C6 200
Fort Valley, Ga D3 175
Fort Vermillion, Alta., Can D1 148
Fort Victoria, Rh B5 107
Fort Walton Beach, Fla G2 174
Fort Washakie, Wyo B4 213
Fort Washington, Md C3 173
Fort Washington, Pa A11 202
Fort Wayne, Ind B7 179
Fort White, Fla C4 174
Fort William, Scot D3 57
Fort William, mtn., Austl B8 112
Fort Wingate, N. Mex B1 195
Fort Worth, Tex B5, C4 206
Fort Wright, Ky A7 182
Fort Yates, N. Dak C5 198
Fort Yukon, Alsk B10 167
Fortaleza, Braz B3 138
Forteau, Newf., Can C3 152
Fortescue, Mo A2 189
Fortescue, N.J E2 194
Fortescue, riv., Austl D2 110
Forth, firth, Scot D6 57
Forth, riv., Scot D4 57
Fortierville, Que., Can C5 154
Fortín Uno, Arg B3 136
Fortine, Mont B2 190
Fortress, mtn., Wyo A3 213
Fortrose, N.Z Q12 112
Fortrose, Scot C4 57
Fortuna, Calif B1 170
Fortuna, Mo C5 189
Fortuna, N. Dak A2 198
Fortuna Ledge, Alsk C7 167
Fortune, Newf., Can E4 152
Fortune, bay, Newf., Can E4 152
Fortune Harbour, Newf., Can D4 152
Fortville, Ind E6 179
Forty Fort, Pa B8, D10 202
Foshan, China B11 91
Foshan, China *G7 91
Foss, Okla B2 200

Foss, dam, Okla B2 200
Fossano, It. B1 67
Fosser, Nor. p29 63
Fossil, Oreg. C6 201
Fossil, Wyo. D2 213
Fossil, lake, Oreg D6 201
Fossombrone, It. C4 67
Fosston, Sask., Can. E4 155
Fosston, Minn. C3 187
Foster, Que., Can. D5 154
Foster, Ky. B5 182
Foster, Mo. C3 189
Foster, Nebr. B8 191
Foster, Okla. C4 200
Foster, Oreg. C4 201
Foster, R.I. B10 172
Foster, Wis. D2 212
Foster, co., N. Dak. B6 198
Foster, riv., Sask., Can A3 155
Foster Brook, Pa. C4 202
Foster City, Mich. C3 186
Foster Village, Haw. g10 176
Fosterburg, Ill. A8 189
Fosters, Ala. B2 166
Fosters, pond, Mass C2 185
Fosters Falls, Va. E2 209
Fosterville, Tenn. B5 205
Fostoria, Ala. C3 166
Fostoria, Iowa A2 180
Fostoria, Kans. C7 181
Fostoria, Mich. E7 186
Fostoria, Ohio A4 199
Fougamou, Gabon F2 104
Fougères, Fr. C3 58
Fouhsin, China C9 91
Fouke, Ark. D2 169
Foula, isl., Scot g9 55
Fouliang, China J7 92
Fouling, China F6 91
Foulness, isl., Eng C8 56
Foulwind, cape, N.Z N13 112
Foum el Hassane, Mor. D3 102
Foumban, Cam. D2 104
Founing, China E8 91
Fount, Ky. D6 182
Fountain, Ala. D2 166
Fountain, Colo. C6 171
Fountain, Fla. B1, G3 174
Fountain, Mich. D4 186
Fountain, Minn. G6 187
Fountain, N.C. *B6 197
Fountain, co., Ind. D3 179
Fountain, creek, Colo C6 171
Fountain, peak, Calif E6 170
Fountain City, Ind. E8 179
Fountain City, Tenn. *C10 205
Fountain City, Wis. D2 212
Fountain Green, Utah D4 207
Fountain Head, Tenn. A5 205
Fountain Hill, Ark. D4 169
Fountain Hill, Pa. E11 202
Fountain Inn, S.C. B3 203
Fountain Run, Ky. D4 182
Fountain Valley, Calif. *F5 170
Fountain Valley School, Colo. C6 171
Fountains, N.C. B6 197
Fountaintown, Ind. E6 179
Fouping, China E6 92
Four Buttes, Mont. B11 190
Four Corners, Oreg. *C4 201
Four Corners, Wyo. A8 213
Four Holes, S.C. E7 203
Four Lakes, Wash. B8, D7 210
Four Mountains, isl., Alsk E6 167
Four Oaks, N.C. B5 197
Four Points, Ga. E2 175
Fourchambault, Fr. D5 58
Fourche, creek, Ark D5 169
Fourche LaFave, riv., Ark C2 169
Fourche Maline, creek, Okla C6 200
Fourchu, N.S., Can. D9 151
Fourmies, Fr. B6 58
Fourmile, Ky. D6 182
Fourmile, creek, Iowa A7 180
Fournier, Ont., Can. B10 153
4th Cataract (Nile River), Sud B3 105
Fourup, isl., Truk 114
Fouta Djallon, mts., Guinea D2 103
Fouyang, China H6 92
Foveaux, strait, N.Z Q11 112
Fowey, Eng. D3 56
Fowler, Calif. D4 170
Fowler, Colo. C6 171
Fowler, Ill. C2 178
Fowler, Ind. C3 179
Fowler, Kans. E3 181
Fowler, Mich. E6 186
Fowlerton, Ind. D6 179
Fowlerton, Tex. E3 206
Fowlerville, Mich. F6 186
Fowlkes, Tenn. B2 205
Fowlstown, Ga. F2 175
Fox, Ark. B3 169
Fox, Mich. C3 186
Fox, Mont. E7 190
Fox, Okla. C4 200
Fox, Oreg. C7 201
Fox, cape, B.C., Can B2 149
Fox, isl., Wash D1 210
Fox, is., Alsk E6 167
Fox, lake, Ill A5 178
Fox, mtn., Nev C2 192
Fox, riv., Ill B5 178
Fox, riv., Iowa, Mo D6 180, A6 189
Fox, riv., Mich B5 186
Fox, riv., Wis D5 212
Fox Chapel, Pa. *F2 202
Fox Creek, Alta., Can. *B2 148
Fox Farm, Wyo. *D8 213
Fox Harbour, Newf., Can. B4 152
Fox Island, Wash. D1 210
Fox Lake, Ill. A5, E2 178
Fox Lake, Wis. E5 212
Fox Point, Wis. E2, E6 212
Fox River Grove, Ill. E2 178
Fox Valley, Sask., Can. G1 155
Foxboro, Ont., Can. C7 153
Foxboro, Mass. B5 185
Foxboro, Wis. B1 212
Foxburg, Pa. D2 202
Foxdale, I. of Man F4 57
Foxe, basin, N.W. Ter., Can C17 143
Foxe, chan., N.W. Ter., Can D17 143
Foxe, pen., N.W. Ter., Can D17 143
Foxford, Sask., Can. D3 155
Foxholm, N. Dak. A4 198
Foxon, Conn. D5 172
Foxpark, Wyo. D6 213
Foxton, N.Z. N15 112
Foxville, Vt. C4 208
Foxwarren, Man., Can. D1 150
Foxworth, Miss. D4 188
Foyil, Okla. A6 200
Foynes, Ire. D2 55
Foz do Iguaçu, Braz. D2 137
Frackville, Pa. E9 202
Fraga, Sp. B6 65
Fraile Muerto, Ur. E2 137
Frametown, W. Va. C4 211
Framingham, Mass. B5, D1 185
França, Braz. D2 138
Franca, Braz. F1 138
Francavilla Fontana, It. D6 67
FRANCE, country, Eur. C4 58
c. 1140 47
c. 1360 48
in 1721 49
in 1804-14 50
in 1815 50
in 1914 52
in 1922-40 53
after World War II 54
Frances, Ky. A3 182
Frances, Wash. C2 210
Francestown, N.H. E3 193
Francesville, Ind. C4 179
Franche-Comté, former prov., Fr. D6 58
Francis, Sask., Can. G4 155
Francis, Mont. D5 190
Francis, Okla. C5 200
Francis, Utah C4 207
Francis, W. Va. A7 211
Francis, lake, N.H A1 193
Francis Case, lake, S. Dak D6 204
Francis Creek, Wis. A6 212
Francis E. Walter, res., Pa D10 202
Francisco, Ind. H3 179
Francistown, Bots. B4 107
Francois, Newf., Can. E3 152
Francois, lake, B.C., Can C5 149
Franconia, N.H. B3 193
Franconville, Fr. g9 58
Francville, Gabon F2 104
Franeker, Neth. A5 59
Frank, W. Va. C5 211
Frankenberg, Ger. B3 61
Frankenberg, Ger. C8 61
Frankenmuth, Mich. E7 186
Frankenthal, Ger. D3 61
Frankewing, Tenn. B5 205
Frankford, Ont., Can. C7 153
Frankford, Del. C7 173
Frankford, Mo. B6 189
Frankford, W. Va. D4 211
Frankfort, Ill. F2 178
Frankfort, Ind. D4 179
Frankfort, Kans. C7 181
Frankfort, Ky. B5 182
Frankfort, Maine D4 184
Frankfort, Mich. D4 186
Frankfort, N.Y. B5 196
Frankfort, Ohio C4 199
Frankfort, S. Afr. C4 107
Frankfort, S. Dak. C7 204
Frankfurt [am Main], Ger. C4 60, C3 61
Frankfurt [an der Oder], Ger. A9 61
Frankische Saale, riv., Ger C4 61
Franklin, Ala. D2 166
Franklin, Ark. A4 169
Franklin, Man., Can. D2 150
Franklin, Conn. C8 172
Franklin, Ga. C1 175
Franklin, Idaho *F2 177
Franklin, Idaho G7 177
Franklin, Ill. D3 178
Franklin, Ind. F5 179
Franklin, Iowa D6 180
Franklin, Kans. E9 181
Franklin, Ky. D3 182
Franklin, La. E4 183
Franklin, Maine D4 184
Franklin, Mass. B5 185
Franklin, Mich. *F7 186
Franklin, Minn. F4 187
Franklin, Mo. B5 189
Franklin, Nebr. D7 191
Franklin, N.H. D3 193
Franklin, N.J. A3 194
Franklin, N.Y. C5 196
Franklin, N.C. D3 197
Franklin, Ohio C3 199
Franklin, Pa. *F4 202
Franklin Pa. D2 202
Franklin, Tenn. B5 205
Franklin, Tex. D4 206
Franklin, Vt. B3 208
Franklin (Independent City), Va. E6 209
Franklin, W. Va. C5 211
Franklin, Wis. F1 212
Franklin, co., Ala. A2 166
Franklin co., Ark. B2 169
Franklin, co., Fla. C2 174
Franklin, co., Ga. B3 175
Franklin, co., Idaho G7 177
Franklin, co., Ill. E5 178
Franklin, co., Ind. F7 179
Franklin, co., Iowa B4 180
Franklin, co., Kans. D8 181
Franklin, co., Ky. B5 182
Franklin, co., Maine C2 184
Franklin, co., Mass. A2 185
Franklin, co., Miss. D3 188
Franklin, co., Mo. C6 189
Franklin, co., Nebr. D7 191
Franklin, co., N.Y. A6 196
Franklin, co., N.C. A5 197
Franklin, co., Ohio B4 199
Franklin, co., Pa. G6 202
Franklin, co., Tenn. B5 205
Franklin, co., Tex. C5 206
Franklin, co., Vt. B2 208
Franklin, co., Va. E3 209
Franklin, co., Wash. C7 210
Franklin, dist., N.W. Ter., Can. B10 144
in 1867 147
Franklin, par., La. B4 183
Franklin, isl., Ont., Can B4 153
Franklin, lake, N.W. Ter., Can C13 142
Franklin, lake, Nev C6 192
Franklin, mts., N.W. Ter., Can C7 142
Franklin, pt., Alsk A8 167
Franklin, res., N.J A3 194
Franklin, straits, N.W. Ter., Can B13 142
Franklin D. Roosevelt, lake, Wash A7 210
Franklin Falls, dam, N.H D3 193
Franklin Falls, res., N.H C3 193
Franklin Grove, Ill. B4 178
Franklin Lakes, N.J. *B4 194
Franklin Mine, Mich. A2 186
Franklin Park, Ill. E2 178
Franklin Park, N.J. C3 194
Franklin Square, N.Y. G2 172
Franklinton, La. D5 183
Franklinton, N.C. A5 197
Franklinville, N.J. D2 194
Franklinville, N.Y. C2 196
Franklinville, N.C. B4 197
Franks, peak, Wyo B3 213
Frankston, Tex. C5 206
Franksville, Wis. F2 212
Frankton, Ind. D6 179
Franktown, Colo. B6 171
Frankville, Ala. D1 166
Frankville, N.S., Can. D8 151
Frankville, Md. D1 173
Frannie, Wyo. A4 213
Franz Josef Land, reg., Sov. Un. B8 71
Frascati, It. D4, h9 67
Fraser, Colo. B5 171
Fraser, Iowa B4 180
Fraser, Mich. *A8 186
Fraser (Great Sandy), isl., Austl B9 112
Fraser, lake, B.C., Can B5 149
Fraser, mtn., B.C., Can C8 149
Fraser, plat., B.C., Can D6 149
Fraser, reach, B.C., Can C3 149
Fraser, riv., B.C., Can C6 149
Fraser Lake, B.C., Can. *B5 149
Fraserburg, S. Afr. D3 107
Fraserburgh, Scot. C7 57
Fraserdale, Ont., Can. E9 153
Fraserwood, Man., Can. D3 150
Frasne, Fr. C2 66
Frauenfeld, Switz. B4 66
Fray Bentos, Ur. E1 137
Frazee, Minn. D3 187
Frazer, Mont. B10 190
Frazeysburg, Ohio B5 199
Frazier, N. Mex. D5 195
Frazier Park, Calif. E4 170
Freda, N. Dak. C4 198
Frederic, Mich. D6 186
Frederic, Wis. C1 212
Frederica, Del. B7 173
Fredericia. Den. C3 62
Frederick, Colo. A6 171
Frederick, Ill. C3 178
Frederick, Md. B3 173
Frederick, Okla. C2 200
Frederick, S. Dak. B7 204
Frederick, co., Md. B3 173
Frederick, co., Va. B4 209
Frederick, sound, Alsk m23 167
Frederick Junction, Md. B3 173
Fredericks Hall, Va. D5 209
Fredericksburg, Ind. H5 179
Fredericksburg, Iowa B5 180
Fredericksburg, Ohio B6 199
Fredericksburg, Pa. F9 202
Fredericksburg, Tex. D3 206
Fredericksburg (Independent City), Va. C5 209
Fredericktown, Mo. D7 189
Fredericktown, Ohio B5 199
Fredericktown, Pa. F1 202
Fredericton, N.B., Can. D3 151
Fredericton Junction, N.B., Can. D3 151
Frederika, Iowa B5 180
Frederiksberg, Den. *C6 62
Frederiksborg, co., Den. C6 62
Frederikshavn, Den. A4 62
Frederikssund, Den. C6 62
Frederiksted, Vir. Is. n14 131, k17 132
Frederiksvaerk, Den. C6 62
Fredonia, Ala. C4 166
Fredonia, Ariz. A3 168
Fredonia, Iowa C6 180
Fredonia, Kans. E8 181
Fredonia, Ky. C1 182
Fredonia, N.Y. C1 196
Fredonia, N. Dak. C6 198
Fredonia, Pa. D1 202
Fredonia, Tex. D3 206
Fredonia, Wis. E6 212
Fredonyer, peak, Calif B3 170
Fredrikstad, Nor. H4, p28 63
Free Soil, Mich. D4 186
Free Union, Va. C4 209
Freeborn, Minn. G5 187
Freeborn, co., Minn. G5 187
Freeburg, Ill. E4 178
Freeburg, Minn. G7 187
Freeburg, Mo. C6 189
Freeburg, Pa. E8 202
Freedom, Calif. C6 170
Freedom, Ind. F4 179
Freedom, Maine D3 184
Freedom, Nebr. D5 191
Freedom, N.H. C4 193
Freedom, Okla. A2 200
Freedom, Pa. E1 202
Freedom, Wis. A5 212
Freedom, Wyo. C1 213
Freehold, N.J. C4 194
Freel, peak, Calif C4 170
Freeland, Mich. E6 186
Freeland, N.C. C5 197
Freeland, Pa. D10 202
Freeland, Tenn. A3 205
Freeland, Wyo. C6 213
Freeland Park, Ind. C3 179
Freelandville, Ind. G3 179
Freels, cape, Newf., Can D5 152
Freeman, Mo. C3 189
Freeman, S. Dak. D8 204
Freeman, Wash. D8 210
Freeman, lake, Ind C4 179
Freemansburg, Pa. E11 202
Freemanspur, Ill. *F5 178
Freemanville, Ala. D2 166
Freemason, is., La E7 183
Freemen, riv., Alta., Can B3 148
Freeport, N.S., Can. E3 151
Freeport, Fla. G3 174
Freeport, Ill. A4 178
Freeport, Iowa A6 180
Freeport, Kans. E6 181
Freeport, Maine E2, E5 184
Freeport, Mich. F5 186
Freeport, Minn. E4 187
Freeport, N.Y. G2 172
Freeport, Ohio B6 199
Freeport, Pa. E2 202
Freeport, Tex. E5, G5 206
Freer, Tex. F3 206
Freestone, co., Tex. D4 206
Freetown, P.E.I., Can. C6 151
Freetown, S.L. E2 103
Freetown, Ind. G5 179
Freetown, N.Y. *D4 196
Freeville, N.Y. C4 196
Freezeout, mts., Wyo C6 213
Fregenal de la Sierra, Sp. C2 65
Fregene, It. h8 67
Freiberg, Ger. C8 61
Freiberger Mulde, riv., Ger B8 61
Freiberg [an der Elbe], Ger. E3 62
Freiburg [im Breisgau], Ger. D3 60, B3 66
Freirina, Chile E1 135
Freising, Ger. E6 61
Freistadt, Aus. D7 60
Freital, Ger. B8 61
Fréjus, Fr. F7 58
Frelighsburg, Que., Can. D5 154
Fremantle, Austl. F2 111
Fremont, Calif. B5, D2 170
Fremont, Ind. A8 179
Fremont, Iowa C5 180
Fremont, Mich. E5 186
Fremont, Mo. E6 189
Fremont, Nebr. C9, D2 191
Fremont, N.H. E4 193
Fremont, N.C. B6 197
Fremont, Ohio A4 199
Fremont, Utah E4 207
Fremont, Wis. D5 212
Fremont, co., Colo. C5 171
Fremont, co., Idaho E7 177
Fremont, co., Iowa D2 180
Fremont, co., Wyo. B4 213
Fremont, isl., Utah B3 207
Fremont, lake, Wyo C3 213
Fremont, peak, Wyo B3 213
Fremont, riv., Utah E4 207
French, creek, Pa C1 202
French, pt., Newf., Can C4 152
French, prairie, Oreg B1 201
French, reefs, N. Cal 115
French, riv., Ont., Can A4 153
French Broad, riv., N.C D3 197
French Broad, riv., Tenn D10 205
French Cameroons, see Cameroon, country, Afr.
French Camp, Calif. B6 170
French Camp, Miss. B4 188
French Congo 99
French Creek, W. Va. C4 211
French Empire, 1804-14 50
French Equatorial Africa, see Central African Rep., Chad, Congo, and Gabon, countries, Afr.
French Frigate, shoal, Haw m14 176
FRENCH GUIANA, dep., S.A. B4 139, 126
French Guinea, see Guinea, country, Afr.
French Gulch, Calif. B2 170
French Lick, Ind. G4 179
French Morocco: *see also* Morocco
French Oceania, see French Polynesia, dep., Oceania
FRENCH POLYNESIA, see Clipperton, Marquesas Is., Society Is., and Tuamotu Arch., Oceania
French River, Minn. D7 187
French Settlement, La. B6, D5 183
FRENCH SOMALILAND, see Afars & Issas, country, Afr.
French Sudan 99
French Sudan, see Mali, country, Afr.
French Togoland, see Togo, country, Afr.
French Ubanghi 99
French Village, N.S., Can. E6 151
French West Africa, see Dahomey, Guinea, Ivory Coast, Mali, Mauritania, Niger, Senegal, and Upper Volta, countries, Afr.
Frenchburg, Ky. C6 182
Frenchglen, Oreg. E8 201
Frenchman, Nev. D3 192
Frenchman, bay, Maine D4 184
Frenchman, creek, Nebr D4 191
Frenchman, hills, Wash C6 210
Frenchman, riv., Sask., Can H1 155
Frenchman Butte, Sask., Can. D1 155
Frenchman Knob, peak, Ky C4 182
Frenchmans Cove, Newf., Can. D2, E4 152
Frenchmans Island, Newf., Can. B4 152
Frenchton, W. Va. C4 211
Frenchtown, Mont. C2 190
Frenchtown, N.J. B2 194
Frenchville, Maine A4 184
Frenchville, Pa. D5 202
Frenda, Alg. G7 64
Freneau, N.J. C4 194
Frenier, La. B6 183
Fresco, riv., Braz D4 139
Freshfield, cape, Ant C28 120
Freshfield, mtn., B.C., Can D9 149
Freshwater, Newf., Can. *E5 152
Freshwater, Eng. D6 56
Fresko, I.C. E3 103
Fresnes-en-Woëvre, Fr. E5 59
Fresnillo, Mex. C4 129
Fresno, Calif. D4 170
Fresno, Ohio B6 199
Fresno, co., Calif. D3 170
Fresno, dam, Mont B7 190
Freudenstadt, Ger. E3 61
Frèvent, Fr. B5 58
Frewsburg, N.Y. C1 196
Freyburg, Ger. B6 61
Freycinet's, pen., Austl o15 110
Freyenstein, Ger. E6 62
Freyung, Ger. E8 61
Friant, Calif. D4 170
Friars Point, Miss. A3 188
Frias, Arg. E2 135
Fribourg, Switz. C3 66
Fribourg, canton, Switz. C3 66
Friday Harbor, Wash. A2 210
Fridley, Minn. E7 187
Fridtjof Nansen, mtn., Ant A32 120
Frieberger Mulde, riv., Ger B8 61
Friedberg, Ger. C3 61
Friedens, Pa. F4 202
Friedland, Ger. B6 60
Friedrichrode, Ger. C5 61
Friedrichshafen, Ger. E4 60
Friedrichskoog, Ger. D2 62
Friedrichstadt, Ger. D3 62
Friedrichsthal, Ger. D2 61
Friend, Kans. D3 181
Friend, Nebr. D8 191
Friend, Oreg. B5 201
Friendship, Ark. C3 169
Friendship, Ind. G7 179
Friendship, Maine E3 184
Friendship, Md. C4 173
Friendship, N.Y. C2 196
Friendship, Ohio D4 199
Friendship, Okla. C2 200
Friendship, Tenn. B2 205
Friendship, Wis. E4 212
Friendsville, Md. D1 173
Friendsville, Tenn. D9, E11 205
Friendswood, Ind. I7 179
Frierson, La. B2 183
Fries, Va. E2 209
Fries Mills, N.J. D2 194
Friesach, Aus. E7 60
Friesack, Ger. F6 62
Friesland, Wis. E4 212
Friesland, prov., Neth. A5 59
Friesland, East: in 1860-70 51
Friesoythe, Ger. A7 59
Frijoles, C.Z. k11 130
Frio, co., Tex. E3 206
Frio, cape, S.W. Afr A1 107
Frio, riv., Tex E3 206
Friona, Tex. B1 206
Fripps, isl., S.C G7 203
Frisches Haff, see Vistula, lagoon, Sov. Un.
Frisco, Colo. B4 171
Frisco, N.C. B8 197
Frisco, Pa. *E1 202
Frisco, Tex. *C4 206
Frisco, mtn., Utah E2 207
Frisco City, Ala. D2 166
Fristoe, Mo. C4 189
Fritch, Tex. B2 206
Fritzlar, Ger. B4 61
Friuli-Venezia Giulia, pol. dist., It. C8 66
Frobisher, Sask., Can. H4 155
Frobisher, bay, N.W. Ter., Can D19 143
Frobisher, lake, Sask., Can B1 155
Frobisher Bay, N.W. Ter., Can. C21 118, D19 145
Frog, lake, Alta., Can C5 148
Frogmore, S.C. G6 203
Frohna, Mo. D8 189
Froid, Mont. B12 190
Frolovo, Sov. Un. D2 73
Fromberg, Mont. E8 190
Frome, Eng. C5 56
Frome, riv., Eng D5 56
Front, range, Colo A5 171
Front Royal, Va. C4 209
Frontenac, Kans. E9 181
Frontenac, Minn. F6 187
Frontenac, Mo. *C7 189
Frontenac, co., Ont., Can. C8 153
Frontenac, co., Que., Can. D7 154
Fronteras, Mex. G6 168
Frontier, Sask., Can. H1 155
Frontier, Wyo. D2 213
Frontier, co., Nebr. D5 191
Frontignan, Fr. F5 58
Frosinone, It. D4 67
Frost, Minn. G5 187
Frost, Tex. C4 206
Frostburg, Md. D2 173
Frostproof, Fla. E5 174
Frouard, Fr. C7 58
Froude, Sask., Can. H4 155
Froya, isl., Nor F3 63
Fruges, Fr. D10 56
Fruita, Colo. B2 171
Fruitdale, Ala. D1 166
Fruitdale, S. Dak. C2 204
Fruitdale, Tex. *C4 206
Fruithurst, Ala. B4 166
Fruitland, Idaho F2 177
Fruitland, Iowa C6 180
Fruitland, Md. D6 173
Fruitland, Mo. D8 189
Fruitland, N. Mex. A1 195
Fruitland, Tenn. B3 205
Fruitland, Utah C5 207
Fruitland Park, Fla. D5 174
Fruitland Park, Miss. E4 188
Fruitport, Mich. E4 186
Fruitvale, B.C., Can. E9 149
Fruitvale, Colo. B2 171
Fruitvale, Idaho E2 177
Fruitvale, Wash. *C5 210
Fruitville, Fla. F2 174
Frunze, Sov. Un. E8 73
Frutal, Braz. E1 138
Fry, Ga. B2 175
Fry Canyon, Utah F5 207
Fryazevo, Sov. Un. n18 72
Fryburg, N. Dak. C2 198
Fryburg, Pa. D3 202
Frýdek-Místek, Czech. D5 70
Frýdlant, Czech. C3 70
Frye, Maine D2 184
Fryeburg, La. B2 183
Fryeburg, Maine D2 184
Fryele, Swe. A8 62
Frys, Sask., Can. H5 155
Fryštát, Czech. h9 70
Fu, China F3 92
Fuan, China K8 92
Fuchin, China B11 91
Fuching, China F8 91
Fuchou, China G6 91
Fuchow, China F8 91
Fuchū, Jap. *I9 93
Fuencarral, Sp. p17 65
Fuente Álamo, Sp. D5 65
Fuente de Cantos, Sp. C2 65
Fuente el Saz, Sp. o17 65
Fuenteovejuna, Sp. C3 65
Fuentes [de Andalucía], Sp. D3 65
Fuentesauco, Sp. B3 65
Fuerfano, peak, N. Mex A2 195
Fuerte, riv., Mex B3 129
Fuerte Olimpo, Par. D4 135
Fuerteventura, isl., Sp. (Can. Is.) m14 65
Fuglebjerg, Den. C5 62
Fuhsien, China E9 92
Fuji, vol., Jap n17, I9 93
Fujieda, Jap. o17 93
Fujimi, Jap. n17 93
Fujinomiya, Jap. n17 93
Fujisawa, Jap. *I9 93
Fujiyoshida, Jap. n17 93
Fūkah, Eg. G6 85
Fukien, prov., China F8 91
Fukou, China G6 92
Fukuchiyama, Jap. I7, n14 93
Fukue, Jap. o16 93
Fukui, Jap. H8 93
Fukuoka, Jap. J5 93
Fukuoka, Jap. F10 93
Fukushima, Jap. H10 93
Fukushima, Jap. I8, n16 93
Fukuyama Jap. I6 93

INDEX KEY Each place listed in **Bold-faced Type** has its population listed in the Population tables, pages 230 to 280
Each country, shown in CAPITAL LETTERS, has its population listed in the World Political Information Table, pages 6 to 10.
* Does not appear on map; key shows general location

Fukuyama, see Matsumae, Jap.
Fulakora, pt., Santa Isabel I. 115
Fulanga, isl., Fiji 114
Fulanga, passage, Fiji 114
Fulda, Ger. C4 61
Fulda, Ind. H4 179
Fulda, Minn. G3 187
Fulda, riv., Ger. C4 61
Fullarton, Ont., Can. D3 153
Fullerton, Calif. F3 170
Fullerton, Ky. B7 182
Fullerton, Nebr. C8 191
Fullerton, N. Dak. C7 198
Fulshear, Tex. F4 206
Fulton, Ala. D2 166
Fulton, Ark. D2 169
Fulton, Calif. A5 170
Fulton, Ill. B3 178
Fulton, Ind. C5 179
Fulton, Kans. D9 181
Fulton, Ky. B2 182
Fulton, Md. B4 173
Fulton, Mich. F5 186
Fulton, Mich. A2 186
Fulton, Miss. A5 188
Fulton, Mo. C6 189
Fulton, N.Y. B4 196
Fulton, Ohio B5 199
Fulton, S. Dak. D8 204
Fulton, Tenn. B2 205
Fulton, co., Ark. A4 169
Fulton, co., Ga. C2 175
Fulton, co., Ill. C3 178
Fulton, co., Ind. B5 179
Fulton, co., Ky. B2 182
Fulton, co., N.Y. B6 196
Fulton, co., Ohio A3 199
Fulton, co., Pa. G5 202
Fultondale, Ala. E4 166
Fultonham, N.Y. C6 196
Fultonville, N.Y. *C6 196
Fultz, Ky. B6 182
Fumay, Fr. C6 58
Funabashi, Jap. n19 93
Funakawa, see Oga, Jap.
Funchal, Port. (Madeira Is.) h12 65, C1 102
Fundación, Col. A3 133
Fundão, Port. B2 65
Fundy, bay, Can. E3 151
Fundy, nat. park, N.B., Can. D4 151
Funhalouro, Moz. B5 107
Funing, bay, China K9 92
Funk, Nebr. D6 191
Funk, isl., Newf., Can. D5 152
Funkley, Minn. C4 187
Funkstown, Md. A2 173
Funter, Alsk. k22 167
Funtua, Nig. D6 103
Fuquay-Varina, N.C. B5 197
Fur, isl., Den. B3 62
Furancungo, Moz. D5 106
Furano, Jap. E11 93
Fūrg, Iran G7 86
Furley, Kans. B5 181
Furlow, Ark. D6 169
Furman, S.C. F5 203
Furmanov, Sov. Un. C13 72
Furmanovka, Sov. Un. E8 73
Furnas, co., Nebr. D6 191
Furnas, res., Braz. C3, k9 137
Furneaux, is., Austl. o15 110
Furness, Sask., Can. D1 155
Furqlus, Syr. E11 85
Fürstenau, Ger. B7 59
Fürstenfeld, Aus. E8 60
Fürstenfeldbruck, Ger. A7 66
Fürstenwalde, Ger. A9 61
Fürth, Ger. D5 61
Furth im Wald, Ger. D7 61
Furu, mtn., Iwo 114
Furukawa, Jap. H8, m16 93
Fusagasugá, Col. C3 133
Fuschl, Aus. B9 66
Fuse, Jap. I7, o14 93
Fushun, China C9 91, D10 92
Fusilier, Sask., Can. F1 155
Füssen, Ger. B6 66
Fusung, China E3 93
Futamata, Jap. o16 93
Futatsune, reef, Iwo 114
Futing, China K9 92
Fuwah, Eg. C2 84
Fuyang, China I8 92
Fuyü, China C2 93
Fuyu, China B9 91
Fuyüan, China B7 93
Fyn, isl., Den. C4 62
Fyne, inlet, Scot. D3 57

G

Gaastra, Mich. B2 186
Gabarouse, N.S., Can. D9 151
Gabela, Ang. D1 106
Gabes, gulf, Tun. C7 102
Gabilan, range, Calif. C6 170
Gąbin, Pol. B5 70
GABON, country, Afr. F2 104
Gaborone, Bots. B4 107
Gabriels, N.Y. B3 196
Gabriola, B.C., Can. A9 149
Gabriola, isl., B.C., Can. A9 149
Gabrovo, Bul. D7 68
Gach Sārān, Iran F5 86
Gackle, N. Dak. C6 198
Gacko, Yugo. D4 68
Gadag, India E6 87
Gadsby, Alta., Can. C4 148
Gadsden, Ala. A3 166
Gadsden, Ariz. E1 168
Gadsden, S.C. D6 203
Gadsden, Tenn. B3 205
Gadsden, co., Fla. B2 174
Gadyach, Sov. Un. F9 72
Găeşti, Rom. C7 68
Gaeta, It. D4 67
Gaeta, gulf, It. D4 67
Gaffney, S.C. A4 203
Gafsa, Tun. G11 64
Gagan, isl., Kwajalein 114
Gagarin, Sov. Un. D10 72
Gage, N. Mex. E1 195
Gage, Okla. A2 200
Gage, co., Nebr. D9 191
Gage, cape, P.E.I., Can. C5 151
Gages Lake, Ill. *A5 178
Gagetown, N.B., Can. D3 151
Gagetown, Mich. E7 186
Gaggenau, Ger. E3 61
Gagi, isl., Sol. Is. 115
Gagliano del Capo, It. E7 67
Gagnoa, I.C. E3 103
Gagny, Fr. g11 58
Gahanna, Ohio C2 199
Gaibandha, Bngl. E12 88
Gail, Tex. C2 206
Gail, riv., Aus. C9 66
Gaildorf, Ger. E4 61
Gaillac, Fr. F4 58
Gaillard, lake, Conn. D5 172
Gaines, Mich. E6 186
Gaines, Pa. C6 202
Gaines, co., Tex. C1 206
Gaines, creek, Okla. C6 200
Gainesboro, Tenn. C8 205
Gainesville, Ala. C1 166
Gainesville, Fla. C4 174
Gainesville, Ga. B3 175
Gainesville, Mo. E5 189
Gainesville, N.Y. C2 196
Gainesville, Tex. C4 206
Gainesville, Va. B4 209
Gainesville Cotton Mills, Ga. *B3 175
Gainesville East, Fla. *C4 174
Gainesville North, Fla. *C4 174
Gainesville West, Fla. *C4 174
Gainsborough, Sask., Can. H5 155
Gainsborough, Eng. A7 56
Gairdner, lake, Austl. F6 110
Gairloch, Scot. C3 57
Gairloch, bay, Scot. C3 57
Gaither, Md. B4 173
Gaithersburg, Md. B3 173
Gakona, Alsk. C10, f19 167
Gala, riv., Scot. E6 57
Galacz, see Galaţi, Rom.
Galahad, Alta., Can. C5 148
Galâla el Baharîya, mts., Eg. E4 84
Galap, Palau Is. 114
Galapagar, Sp. o17 65
Galápagos Islands, see Colón, Archipiélago de, prov., Ec.
Galashiels, Scot. E6 57
Galata, Mont. B5 190
Galaţi, Rom. C9 68
Galatia: c. 50 B.C. 44
c. 120 A.D. 45
Galatia, Ill. F5 178
Galatia, Kans. D5 181
Galatina, It. D7 67
Galax (Independent City), Va. E2 209
Galaxídhion, Grc. C4 69
Galbraith, La. C3 183
Galchutt, N. Dak. C9 198
Galdar, Sp (Can. Is) m14 65
Galdhöpiggen, mtn., Nor. G3 63
Galeana, Mex. A3 129
Galen, Mont. D4 190
Galen, Tenn. C8 205
Galena, Alsk. C8 167
Galena, Ill. A3 178
Galena, Kans. E9 181
Galena, Md. B6 173
Galena, Mo. E4 189
Galena, Ohio B3 199
Galena Park, Tex. F5 206
Galeota, pt., Trin. A5 133
Galera, pt., Chile B2 136
Galera, pt., Trin. A5 133
Galera, riv., It. h8 67
Gales, peak, Oreg. B1 201
Gales Creek, Oreg. B3 201
Gales Ferry, Conn. D8 172
Galesburg, Ill. C3 178
Galesburg, Kans. E8 181
Galesburg, Mich. F5 186
Galesburg, N. Dak. B8 198
Galestown, Md. C6 173
Galesville, Md. C4 173
Galesville, Wis. D2 212
Galeton, Colo. A6 171
Galeton, Pa. C6 202
Galetta, Ont., Can. B8 153
Galiano, isl., B.C., Can. E6 149
Galich, Sov. Un. B2 73
Galicia, reg., Pol. D6 70
in 1914 52
Galicia, reg., Sp. A1 65
Galien, Mich. G4 186
Galilee, R.I. D10 172
Galilee, reg., Isr. B7 84
Galilee, lake, Austl. D8 110
Galilee, Sea of, see Tiberias, lake, Isr.
Galion, Ohio B5 199
Galisteo, N. Mex. B4, G6 195
Galisteo, riv., N. Mex. G6 195
Galiuro, mts., Ariz. E5 168
Galivants Ferry, S.C. C9 203
Galkayu, Som. D6 105
Gallabat, Sud. C4 105
Gallan, head, Scot. B1 57
Gallant, Ala. B3 166
Gallarate, It. B2 67
Gällared, Swe. A8 62
Gallatin, Mo. B4 189
Gallatin, Tenn. A5 205
Gallatin, co., Ill. F5 178
Gallatin, co., Ky. B5 182
Gallatin, co., Mont. E5 190
Gallatin, range, Mont., Wyo. E5 190
Gallatin, riv., Mont. E5 190
Gallatin Gateway, Mont. E5 190
Gallaway, Tenn. B2 205
Galle, Cey. G7 87
Gallego, riv., Sp. A5 65
Gallegos, riv., Arg. E2 136
Gallet, lake, Que., Can. C2 152
Gallia: c. 120 A.D. 45
Gallia, co., Ohio D5 199
Galliate, It. D4 66
Gallicano nel Lazio, It. h9 67
Gallina, N. Mex. A3 195
Gallinas, mts., N. Mex. C2 195
Gallinas, pt., Col. A3 133
Gallion, Ala. C2 166
Gallion, La. B4 183
Gallipoli, It. D6 67
Gallipoli, see Gelibolu, Tur.
Gallipoli, pen., Tur. B6 69
Gallipolis, Ohio D5 199
Gallipolis Ferry, W. Va. C2 211
Gallitzin, Pa. F4 202
Gällivare, Swe. D9 63
Gallman, Miss. D3 188
Gallneukirchen, Aus. E9 61
Gallo, mts., N. Mex. C1 195
Gallo, riv., Sp. B5 65
Galloo, isl., N.Y. B4 196
Galloway, Mo. D4 189
Galloway, Ohio C2 199
Galloway, W. Va. B4 211
Galloway, Wis. D4 212
Galloway, Mull of, head, Scot. F4 57
Gällstad, Swe. A7 62
Gallup, N. Mex. B1 195
Galt, Calif. B6, C3 170
Galt, Ont., Can. D4 153
Galt, Iowa B4 180
Galt, Mo. A4 189
Galten, lake, Swe. t34 63
Galtür, Aus. C6 66
Galty, mts., Ire. D2 55
Galva, Ill. B3 178
Galva, Iowa B2 180
Galva, Kans. D6 181
Galvarino, Chile B2 136
Galves, bank, Mariana Is. 115
Galveston, Ind. C5 179
Galveston, Tex. E5, G5 206
Galveston, co., Tex. E5 206
Galveston, bay, Tex. E5 206
Galveston, isl., Tex. E5 206
Gálvez, Arg. A4 136
Galvin, Wash. C2 210
Galway, Ire. D2 55
Galway, bay, Ire. D2 55
Gamaches, Fr. E9 58
Gamagōri, Jap. *I8 93
Gamaliel, Ark. A3 169
Gamaliel, Ky. D4 182
Gamarra, Col. B3 133
Gamba, Zaire B3 106
Gambaga, Ghana D4 103
Gambēlā, Eth. D3 105
Gambell, Alsk. C5 167
Gamber, Md. B4 173
GAMBIA, country, Afr. D1 103
Gambia, riv., Sen. D2 103
Gambier, Ohio B5 199
Gambo, Newf., Can. D4 152
Gamboma, Con. F3 104
Gambrills, Md. B4 173
Game Lodge, S. Dak. D2 204
Gameleira, Braz. C3, k6 138
Gamerco, N. Mex. B1 195
Gamina, Chile C2 135
Gammertingen, Ger. A5 66
Gammon, riv., Man., Can. D4 150
Gamo-Gofa, reg., Eth. D4 105
Ganado, Ariz. B6 168
Ganado, Tex. E4 206
Ganālē Doryā, riv., Eth. D5 105
Gananoque, Ont., Can. C8 153
Gandajika, Zaire C3 106
Gandamak, Afg. D15 86
Gandara: c. 500 B.C. 78
Gandeeville, W. Va. C3 211
Gander, Newf., Can. D4 152
Gander, lake, Newf., Can. D4 152
Gander, riv., Newf., Can. D4 152
Gander Bay, Newf., Can. D4 152
Gandía, Sp. C5 65
Gandy, Nebr. C5 191
Ganedidalem, Indon. F7 90
Gang, canal, India C4 88
Ganganagar, India *C5 87
Gangapur, India D6 88
Gangaw, Bur. D9 87
Ganges, B.C., Can. B9 149
Ganges, Fr. F5 58
Ganges, Ohio B5 199
Ganges, riv., Bngl., India E11 88
Ganges, riv. mouths, Bngl. G12 88
Gangtok, Sikkim D12 88
Ganju-San, peak, Jap. G10 93
Ganjur, China B8 91
Gannat, Fr. D5 58
Gannet, is., Newf., Can. B3 152
Gannett, Idaho F4 177
Gannett, peak, Wyo. B3 213
Gannon, Md. D2 173
Gannvalley, S. Dak. C7 204
Gano, Ohio C2 199
Ganongga, isl., Sol. Is. 115
Gans, Okla. B7 200
Gansevoort, N.Y. B7 196
Ganta, Lib. E3 103
Gantt, Ala. D3 166
Gantt, S.C. B3 203
Gantt, res., Ala. D3 166
Gantts Quarry, Ala. B3 166
Gao, Mali C5 103
Gaoua, Upper Volta D4 103
Gaoual, Guinea D2 103
Gap, Fr. E7 58
Gap, Pa. G9 202
Gap Mills, W. Va. D4 211
Gapan, Phil. o13 90
Gapland, Md. B2 173
Gara, lake, Ire. D2 55
Garachiné, Pan. F8 130
Garad, Som. D6 105
Garakayo, isl., Palau Is. 114
Garanhuns, Braz. C3, k5 138
Garapan, Saipan 114
Garapan, anchorage, Saipan 114
Garashiyoo, Palau Is. 114
Garautha, India E7 88
Garber, Iowa B6 180
Garber, Okla. A4 200
Garberville, Calif. B2 170
Garça, Braz. C3 137
Garching, Ger. A8 66
Garcia, Colo. D5 171
Garciasville, Tex. F3 206
Gard, riv., Fr. F6 58
Garda, lake, It. B3 67
Gardanne, Fr. F6 58
Gardar, N. Dak. A8 198
Gardelegen, Ger. B5 60
Garden, Ind. F6 179
Garden, Mich. C4 186
Garden, co., Nebr. C3 191
Garden, isl., Mich. C5 186
Garden, riv., Ont., Can. B6 186
Garden City, Ala. A3 166
Garden City, Fla. B6 174
Garden City (Chatham City), Ga. D5 175
Garden City, Idaho F2 177
Garden City, Kans. E3 181
Garden City, La. E4 183
Garden City, Mich. A7 186
Garden City, Minn. F4 187
Garden City, Miss. D2 188
Garden City, Mo. C3 189
Garden City, N.Y. G2 172
Garden City, S. Dak. C8 204
Garden City, Tex. D2 206
Garden City, Utah B4 207
Garden Grove, Calif. *F5 170
Garden Grove, Iowa D4 180
Garden Plain, Kans. B4, E6 181
Garden Prairie, Ill. A5 178
Garden Reach, India *D8 87
Garden Valley, Idaho E3 177
Garden View, Pa. *D7 202
Gardena, Calif. F2 170
Gardena, Idaho F2 177
Gardena, Ill. F2 178
Gardena, N. Dak. A5 198
Gardendale, Ala. B3, E4 166
Gardendale, Tex. E3 206
Gardenton, Man., Can. E3 150
Gardez, Afg. E14 86
Gardi, Ga. E5 175
Gardiner, Maine D3 184
Gardiner, Mont. E6 190
Gardiner, N. Mex. A5 195
Gardiner, Oreg. D2 201
Gardiner, dam, Sask., Can. F2 155
Gardiners, bay, N.Y. E8 172
Gardiners, isl., N.Y. E8 172
Gardiners, pt., N.Y. E8 172
Gardner, Colo. D5 171
Gardner, Fla. E5 174
Gardner, Ill. B5 178
Gardner, Kans. D9 181
Gardner, Mass. A4 185
Gardner, N. Dak. B9 198
Gardner, Tenn. A3 205
Gardner, canal, B.C., Can. C3 149
Gardner, lake, Conn. C8 172
Gardner, lake, Maine D5 184
Gardner, mtn., N.H. B2 193
Gardner Pinnacles, isl., Haw. k14 176
Gardnersville, Ky. B7 182
Gardnerville, Nev. E2 192
Gardo, Som. D6 105
Gardone Riviera, It. D6 66
Gardone Val Trompia, It. D6 66
Gårdstånga, Swe. C7 62
Gardulā, Eth. D4 105
Garesnica, Yugo. C3 68
Garfield, Ark. A2 169
Garfield, Colo. C4 171
Garfield, Ga. D4 175
Garfield, Kans. D4 181
Garfield, Minn. E3 187
Garfield, N.J. D5 194
Garfield, N. Mex. E2 195
Garfield, Wash. B8 210
Garfield, co., Colo. B2 171
Garfield, co., Mont. C9 190
Garfield, co., Nebr. C6 191
Garfield, co., Okla. A4 200
Garfield, co., Utah F4 207
Garfield, co., Wash. C8 210
Garfield, mtn., Mont. F4 190
Garfield, peak, Wyo. C5 213
Garfield Heights, Ohio B2 199
Gargaliánoi, Grc. D3 69
Gargnano, It. D6 66
Garhchiroli, India G8 88
Garibaldi, Braz. D2 137
Garibaldi, Oreg. B3 201
Garibaldi, mtn., B.C., Can. E6 149
Garibaldi, prov. park, B.C., Can. A10, E6 149
Garies, S. Afr. D2 107
Garissa, Ken. B6 106
Garita, N. Mex. B5 195
Garita, P.R. C2 132
Garland, Ala. D3 166
Garland, Ark. D2 169
Garland, Kans. E9 181
Garland, Maine C3 184
Garland, Mont. D11 190
Garland, Nebr. D9 191
Garland, N.C. C5 197
Garland, Pa. C3 202
Garland, Tenn. B2 205
Garland, Tex. B6 206
Garland, Utah B3 207
Garland, Wyo. A4 213
Garland, co., Ark. C2 169
Garmisch-Partenkirchen, Ger. E5 60
Garmouth, Scot. C5 57
Garnavillo, Iowa B6 180
Garneill, Mont. D7 190
Garner, Ark. B4 169
Garner, Iowa A4 180
Garner, N.C. B5 197
Garnet, range, Mont. D3 190
Garnett, Kans. D8 181
Garnett, S.C. F5 203
Garnish, Newf., Can. E4 152
Garonne, riv., Fr. E3 58
Garou, lake, Mali C4 103
Garoua, Cam. D2 104
Garove, isl., Bis. Arch. 115
Garrard, co., Ky. C5 182
Garretson, S. Dak. D9 204
Garrett, Ill. D5 178
Garrett, Ind. B7 179
Garrett, Ky. C7 182
Garrett, Pa. G3 202
Garrett, Wash. *C7 210
Garrett, Wyo. C7 213
Garrett, co., Md. D1 173
Garrett Park, Md. B3 173
Garrettsville, Ohio A6 199
Garrick, Sask., Can. D3 155
Garrison, Iowa B5 180
Garrison, Ky. B6 182
Garrison, Md. B4 173
Garrison, Minn. D5 187
Garrison, Mont. D4 190
Garrison, N.Y. D3, D7 196
Garrison, N. Dak. B4 198
Garrison, Tex. D5 206
Garrison, Utah E1 207
Garrison, dam, N. Dak. B4 198
Garrisonville, Va. C5 209
Garrochales, P.R. B4 132
Garrote, Pan. h11 130
Garrovillas, Sp. C2 65
Garruk, Pak. C4 87
Garry, lake, N.W. Ter., Can. C12 142
Garry, riv., Scot. D5 57
Garryowen, Mont. E9 190
Garske, N. Dak. A7 198
Garstang, Eng. G6 57
Garth, Ala. A3 166
Garthby Station, Que., Can. D6 154
Gartok, China B7 87
Gartz, Ger. E8 62
Garve, Scot. C4 57
Garvellachs, isl., Scot. D2 57
Garvin, Minn. F3 187
Garvin, Okla. D7 200
Garvin, co., Okla. C4 200
Garwin, Iowa B5 180
Garwolin, Pol. C6 70
Garwood, N.J. *B4 194
Garwood, Tex. E4 206
Gary, Ind. A3 179
Gary, Minn. C2 187
Gary, S. Dak. C9 204
Gary, Tex. C5 206
Gary, W. Va. D3 211
Garysburg, N.C. A6 197
Garyville, La. B6, D5 183
Garza, co., Tex. C2 206
Garza Little Elm, res., Tex. A5 206
Garzón, Col. C2 133
Gas, Kans. E8 181
Gas City, Ind. D6 179
Gasconade, Mo. C6 189
Gasconade, co., Mo. C6 189
Gasconade, riv., Mo. C6 189
Gascony, former prov., Fr. E3 58
Gascoyne, N. Dak. C2 198
Gashaka, Cam. D7 103
Gashua, Nig. D7 103
Gasmata, N. Gui. k13 111
Gasparilla, isl., Fla. F4 174
Gaspé, Que., Can. B3 154
Gaspé, pen., Que., Can. B3 154
Gaspé East, co., Que., Can. *B3 154
Gaspé West, co., Que., Can. *B3 154
Gaspésian, prov. park, N.B., Can. B3 154
Gasport, N.Y. B2 196
Gasque, Ala. E2 166
Gassaway, Tenn. B6 205
Gassaway, W. Va. C4 211
Gassetts, Vt. E3 208
Gassol, Nig. E7 103
Gassville, Ark. A3 169
Gaston, Ind. D6 179
Gaston, N.C. A6 197
Gaston, Oreg. B1 201
Gaston, S.C. D5 203
Gaston, co., N.C. B1 197
Gaston, lake, N.C., Va. A6 197
Gastonia, N.C. B2 197
Gastre, Arg. C3 136
Gata, cape, Sp. D4 65
Gata, mts., Sp. B2 65
Gatchina, Sov. Un. s31 63, B8 72
Gate, Okla. A1, D4 200
Gate City, Va. B2 209
Gatehouse of Fleet, Scot. F4 57
Gates, Nebr. C6 191
Gates, N.C. A7 197
Gates, Oreg. C4 201
Gates, Tenn. B2 205
Gates, co., N.C. A7 197
Gates Mills, Ohio *A6 199
Gateshead, Eng. C6 55
Gatesville, Miss. C3 188
Gatesville, N.C. A7 197
Gatesville, Tex. D4 206
Gateway, Colo. C2 171
Gatineau, Que., Can. D2 154
Gatineau, co., Que., Can. C2 154
Gatineau, nat. park, Que., Can. B8 153
Gatineau, riv., Que., Can. D2 154
Gatliff, Ky. D5 182
Gatlinburg, Tenn. D10 205
Gato, Colo. D3 171
Gatooma, Rh. A4 107
Gattman, Miss. B5 188
Gatun, C.Z. k11 130
Gatun, lake, C.Z. k11 130
Gatura, isl., Sol. Is. 115
Gatzke, Minn. B3 187
Gaua, isl., New Hebr. 115
Gauer, lake, Man., Can. A3 150
Gauhati, India C9 87
Gauja, riv., Sov. Un. C5 72
Gauko-Otavi, S.W. Afr. A1 107
Gaul: c. 50 B.C. 44
c. 400 A.D. 46
Gaula, riv., Nor. F4 63
Gauley, riv., W. Va. C3 211
Gauley Bridge, W. Va. C3, D7 211
Gauley Mills, W. Va. C4 211
Gause, Tex. D4 206
Gauss, pen., Grnld. B17 118
Gautier, Miss. E3 188
Gavāter, Iran I10 86
Gávdhos, isl., Grc. E5 69
Gave de Pau, riv., Fr. F3 58
Gave d'Oloron, riv., Fr. F3 58
Gavins Point, dam, Nebr. B8 191
Gaviota, Calif. E3 170
Gävle, Swe. G7 63
Gävlebukten, bay, Swe. G7 63
Gavrilov Posad, Sov. Un. C13 72
Gavrilovka, Sov. Un. G11 72
Gavuvu, New Britain I. 115
Gawler, Austl. G2 112
Gawler, ranges, Austl. F6 110
Gay, Ga. C2 175
Gay, Mich. A2 186
Gay, head, Mass. D6 185
Gay Head, Mass. D6 185
Gaya, India D7 87, E10 88
Gaya, Niger D5 103
Gaylesville, Ala. A4 166
Gaylord, Kans. C5 181
Gaylord, Mich. C6 186
Gaylord, Minn. F4 187
Gaylord, Oreg. E2 201
Gaylordsville, Conn. C3 172
Gayndah, Austl. B8 112
Gays, Ill. D5 178
Gays Mills, Wis. E3 212
Gaysin, Sov. Un. G7 72
Gaysville, Vt. D3 208
Gayville, S. Dak. E8 204
Gaza, Iowa A2 180
Gaza (Ghazzah), Gaza Strip C6 84
Gaza, prov., Moz. B5 107
Gaza Strip, Isr. occ., Asia C6 84
Gazak, Iran H9 86
Gazelle, pen., New Britain I. 115
Gaziantep, Tur. D11 85
Gdańsk, see Danzig, Pol.
Gdov, Sov. Un. B6 72
Gdynia, Pol. A5 70
Gearhart, Oreg. A3 201
Gearhart, mtn., Oreg. E6 201
Geary, N.B., Can. D3 151
Geary, Okla. B3 200
Geary, co., Kans. D7 181
Geauga, co., Ohio A6 199
Gebeit Mines, Sud. A4 105
Gebo, Wyo. B4 213
Gebze, Tur. B7 69
Ged, La. D2 183
Gedaref, Sud. C4 105
Geddes, S. Dak. D7 204
Gedera, Isr. h10 84
Gedern, Ger. C4 61
Gedinne, Bel. E4 59
Gediz, Tur. C7 69
Gediz (Hermus), riv., Tur. C6 69
Gedrosia: c. 500 B.C. 78
Gedser, Den. D5 62
Geel, Bel. C4 59
Geelong, Austl. I5 112
Geelvink, bay, Indon. F9 90
Geeraardsbergen, Bel. D3 59
Geetbets, Bel. D5 59
Geff (Jeffersonville), Ill. E5 178
Geidam, Nig. D7 103
Geiger, Ala. C1 166
Geisenfeld, Ger. E6 61
Geislingen, Ger. E4 61
Geismar, La. B5 183
Geist, res., Ind. E6 179
Geist, res., Pa. D2 194
Geistown, Pa. F4 202
Geita, Tan. B5 106
Gela, It. F5 67

INDEX KEY Each place listed in **Bold-faced Type** has its population listed in the Population tables, pages 230 to 280.
Each country, shown in CAPITAL LETTERS, has its population listed in the World Political Information Table, pages 6 to 10.
* Does not appear on map; key shows general location.

Gelatt, Pa. C10 202
Gelderland, prov., Neth. B5 59
Geldermalsen, Neth. C5 59
Geldern, Ger. C6 59
Geldrop, Neth. C5 59
Gelert, Ont., Can. C6 153
Gelib, Som. E5 105
Gelibolu (Gallipoli), Tur. B6 69
Gelligaer, Wales C4 56
Gellinam, isl., Kwajalein 114
Gelnhausen, Ger. C4 61
Gelsenkirchen, Ger. B2 61
Gelting, Ger. D3 62
Gem, Alta., Can. D4 148
Gem, Kans. C3 181
Gem, W. Va. C4 211
Gem, co., Idaho E2 177
Gem Village, Colo. D3 171
Gemas, Mala. K5 89
Gembloux, Bel. D4 59
Gemena, Zaire A2 106
Gemert, Neth. C5 59
Gemlik, Tur. B7 69
Gemmell, Minn. C4 187
Gemona del Friuli, It. C9 66
Gemünden, Ger. C4 61
Genarp, Swe. C7 62
Gene Autry, Okla. C4 200
Geneina, Sud. C1 105
Genera Villegas, Arg. B4 136
General Acha, Arg. B4 136
General Alvarado, Arg. B5 136
General Alvear, Arg. B5 136
General Alvear, Arg. A3 136
General Belgrano, Arg. B5 136
General Bravo, Mex. G3 206
General Conesa, Arg. C4 136
General La Madrid, Arg. B4 136
General Lavalle, Arg. B5 136
General Madariaga, Arg. B5 136
General Paz, Arg. E4 135
General Pico, Arg. B4 136
General Pinedo, Arg. E3 135
General Roca, Arg. B3 136
General Sarmiento, Arg. g7 136
General Toshevo, Bul. D9 68
General Viamonte, Arg. B4 136
Genesee, Idaho C2 177
Genesee, Mich. E7 186
Genesee, Pa. C6 202
Genesee, co., Mich. E7 186
Genesee, co., N.Y. B2 196
Genesee, riv., N.Y. C2 196
Genesee Depot, Wis. E1 212
Geneseo, Ill. B3 178
Geneseo, Kans. D5 181
Geneseo, N.Y. C3 196
Geneseo, N. Dak. C8 198
Geneva, Ala. D4 166
Geneva, Ga. D2 175
Geneva, Idaho G7 177
Geneva, Ill. B5, F2 178
Geneva, Ind. C8 179
Geneva, Iowa B4 180
Geneva, Ky. C2 182
Geneva, Nebr. D8 191
Geneva, N.Y. C4 196
Geneva, Ohio A7 199
Geneva, Pa. C1 202
Geneva (Genève), Switz. C2 66
Geneva, co., Ala. D4 166
Geneva (Léman), lake, Switz. C2 66
Geneva, lake, Wis. F5 212
Geneva-on-the-Lake, Ohio *A7 199
Genève, see Geneva, Switz.
Genève, canton, Switz. C2 66
Genevia, Ark. C3, D6 169
Genichesk, Sov. Un. H10 72
Genil, riv., Sp. D3 65
Génissiat, Fr. C1 66
Genk, Bel. D5 59
Gennep, Neth. C5 59
Gennevilliers, Fr. g10 58
Genoa, Ark. D2 169
Genoa, Colo. B7 171
Genoa, Ill. A5 178
Genoa (Genova), It. E4 66, B2 67
Genoa, Nebr. C8 191
Genoa, Nev. E2 192
Genoa, N.Y. C4 196
Genoa, Ohio A2, A4 199
Genoa, Tex. E5, F5 206
Genoa, Wis. E2 212
Genoa, republic of: in 1721 49
Genoa, gulf, It. B2 67
Genoa City, Wis. F1, F5 212
Genola, Minn. E4 187
Genola, Utah *C4 207
Genova, see Genoa, It.
Genovesa, isl., Ec. f6 134
Gent, see Ghent, Bel.
Gentbrugge, Bel. C3 59
Genthin, Ger. A7 61
Gentian, Ga. D2 175
Gentilly, Que., Can. C5 154
Gentilly, Fr. g10 58
Gentilly, Minn. C2 187
Gentofte, Den. *C6 62
Gentry, Ark. A1 169
Gentry, Mo. A3 189
Gentry, co., Mo. A3 189
Gentryville, Ind. H3 179
Gentryville, Mo. A3 189
Genzano di Roma, It. h9 67
Geographe, bay, Austl. F2 110
Geographe, chan., Austl. D1 110
Geographic Center of North America, N. Dak. A5 198
Geographic Center of United States, S. Dak. A7 158
Geographical Society, isl., Grnld. B17 118
George, Iowa A2 180
George, N.C. A6 197
George, S. Afr. D3 107
George, co., Miss. E5 188
George, bay, N.S., Can. D8 151
George, hill, Md. D1 173
George, isl., Newf., Can. A3 152
George, isl., Sov. Un. A10 118
George, lake, Austl. G7 112
George, lake, N.S., Can. E4 151
George, lake, Ont., Can. B7 186
George, lake, Fla. C5 174
George, lake, N.Y. B7 196
George, peak, Utah B2 207
George Bryan, coast, Ant. B3 120
George B. Stevenson, res., Pa. D6 202
George V, coast, Ant. C27 120
George River, Que., Can. f8 152
George Town, Ba. Is. D6 131
George Washington Birthplace, nat. mon., Va. C6 209
George West, Tex. E3 206
Georges Mills, N.H. D2 193
Georgesville, Ohio C1 199
Georgetown, Ark. B4 169
Georgetown, Ont., Can. D5 153
Georgetown, P.E.I., Can. C7 151
Georgetown, Cayman Is. F3 131
Georgetown, Colo. B5 171
Georgetown, Conn. D3 172
Georgetown, Del. C7 173
Georgetown, Fla. C5 174
Georgetown, Gam. D2 103
Georgetown, Ga. E1 175
Georgetown, Guy. A3 139
Georgetown, Idaho G7 177
Georgetown, Ill. D6 178
Georgetown, Ind. H6 179
Georgetown, Ky. B5 182
Georgetown, La. C3 183
Georgetown, Maine *E3 184
Georgetown (Fredericktown), Md. B6 173
Georgetown, Mass. A6 185
Georgetown, Minn. C2 187
Georgetown, Miss. D3 188
Georgetown, N.Y. C5 196
Georgetown, Ohio D4 199
Georgetown, Pa. A2 211
Georgetown, S.C. E9 203
Georgetown, Tenn. D9 205
Georgetown, Tex. D4 206
Georgetown, co., S.C. E9 203
Georgeville, Que., Can. D5 154
Georgia, state, U.S. 175
in 18th cent. 162
in 1802 162
in Civil War 164
Georgia, straits, B.C., Can. E5 149
Georgia Center, Vt. B2 208
Georgia Southern, Ga. D5 175
Georgia S.S.R. (Georgian), rep., Sov. Un. E7 71
in 1231 81
c. 1360 48
Georgian, bay, Ont., Can. B3 153
Georgian Bay Island, nat. park, Ont., Can. B3, C5 153
Georgiana, Ala. D3 166
Georgina, riv., Austl. D6 110
Georgsheil, Ger. A7 59
Gera, Ger. C7 61
Gerald, Sask., Can. G5 155
Gerald, Mo. C6 189
Geraldine, Ala. A4 166
Geraldine, Mont. C6 190
Geraldton, Austl. E1 111
Geraldton, Ont., Can. E8 153
Gérardmer, Fr. A2 66
Gerber, Calif. B2 170
Gerbstedt, Ger. B6 61
Gercüş, Tur. D13 85
Gerdine, mtn., Alsk. C9, g15 167
Gerede, Tur. B9 85
Gérgal, Sp. D4 65
Gérin, Que., Can. C4 154
Gering, Nebr. C2 191
Gerlach, Nev. C2 192
Gerlachovka, mtn., Czech. D6 70
German confederation of 1815 51
German East Africa: in late 19th cent. 99
German Federal Republic: in 1950 54
German Kamerun 99
German-Roman empire 47
German Southwest Africa: in 1885 99
German Valley, Ill. A4 178
Germania 44
Germania, N.J. D3 194
Germania, Pa. C6 202
Germansen, lake, B.C., Can. B5 149
Germantown, N.B., Can. D5 151
Germantown, Conn. *D3 172
Germantown, Ill. E4 178
Germantown, Ky. B6 182
Germantown, Md. B3 173
Germantown, Ohio C3 199
Germantown, Tenn. B2 205
Germantown, Wis. E1, E5 212
GERMANY, EAST, country, Eur. B6 60
GERMANY, WEST, country, Eur. C4 60
Germany, reg., Eur. C5 60
c. 120 A.D. 45
in 1812 51
unification of 51
in 1914 52
in 1922-40 53
in 1950 54
Germersheim, Ger. D3 61
Germfask, Mich. B5 186
Germiston, S. Afr. C4 107
Gernrode, Ger. C5 61
Gernsheim, Ger. D3 61
Gero, Jap. n16 93
Gerolzhofen, Ger. D5 61
Gerona, Phil. o13 90
Gerona, Sp. B7 65
Geronimo, Okla. C3 200
Geronimo, Tex. B4 206
Gerrardstown, W. Va. B6 211
Gerrish, N.H. D3 193
Gersfeld, Ger. C4 61
Gersthofen, Ger. E5 61
Gerty, Okla. C5 200
Gervais, Oreg. B2, B4 201
Géryville, Alg. C5 102
Gerze, Tur. B10 85
Geseke, Ger. B3 61
Gesher Haziv, Isr. A7 84
Gessie, Ind. D3 179
Getafe, Sp. B4, p17 65
Gethsémani, Que., Can. h9 152
Gettysburg, Ohio B3 199
Gettysburg, Pa. G7 202
Gettysburg, S. Dak. C6 204
Getúlio Vargas, Braz. D2 137
Getz, ice shelf, Ant. B35 120
Geuda Springs, Kans. E6 181
Gevelsberg, Ger. B2 61
Gex, Fr. C2 66
Geyser, Mont. C6 190
Geyserville, Calif. C2 170
Geyve, Tur. B8 69
Gézenti, Chad A3 104
Ghadir as Sufi (Oasis), Iraq F13 85
Ghagar, res., India E9 88
Ghaggar, riv., India C5 88
GHANA, country, Afr. E4 103
Ghanzi, Bots. B3 107
Ghardaia, Alg. C5 102
Gharyān, Libya C2 101
Ghāt, Libya E2 101
Ghats, Eastern, mts., India E7 87
Ghats, Western, mts., India E5 87
Ghazal, riv., Chad C3 104
Ghaziabad, India *C6 87
Ghazipur, India C7 87
Ghazni, Afg. E14 86
Ghazzah, see Gaza, Gaza Strip
Gheen, Minn. C6 187
Gheens, La. C6, E5 183
Ghent (Gent), Bel. C3 59
Ghent, Ky. B4 182
Ghent, Minn. F3 187
Ghent, N.Y. C7 196
Gheorgheni, Rom. B7 68
Gherla, Rom. B6 68
Ghimir, see Ginir, Eth.
Ghītah, Eg. D3 84
Ghizao, Afg. E13 86
Gholson, Miss. C5 188
Ghost Lake, Alta., Can. *D3 148
Ghudāmis, Libya C1 101
Ghurian, Afg. D10 86
Gi-Paraná, riv., Braz. E2 139
Gia Dinh, Viet. G7 89
Giahel, riv., Som. C6 105
Giamda (Taichao), China E3 91
Giannutri, isl., It. C3 67
Giant, mtn., N.Y. A7 196
Giaveno, It. B1 66
Gibara, Cuba E5 131
Gibbon, Minn. F4 187
Gibbon, Nebr. D7 191
Gibbon, Oreg. B8 201
Gibbonsville, Idaho D5 177
Gibbs, Mo. A5 189
Gibbs, Tenn. A3 205
Gibbsboro, N.J. *D3 194
Gibbstown, La. E2 183
Gibbstown, N.J. D2 194
Gibeon, S.W. Afr. C2 107
Gibraleón, Sp. D2 65
Gibraltar, Gib. D3 65
GIBRALTAR, Br. dep., Eur. D3 65
Gibraltar, Mich. *F7 186
Gibraltar, bay, Sp. D3 65
Gibraltar, pt., Eng. A8 56
Gibraltar, strait, Afr., Eur. G4 64
Gibsland, La. B2 183
Gibson, Ga. C4 175
Gibson, La. C5, E5 183
Gibson, Miss. B5 188
Gibson, Mo. E8 189
Gibson, N.C. C7 197
Gibson, Tenn. B3 205
Gibson, co., Ind. H2 179
Gibson, co., Tenn. A3 205
Gibson, des., Austl. D3 110
Gibson, isl., Md. B5 173
Gibson City, Ill. C5 178
Gibsonburg, Ohio A2, A4 199
Gibsonia, Pa. A6 202
Gibsons, B.C., Can. E6 149
Gibsonton, Fla. E4 174
Gibsonville, N.C. A4 197
Gidam, India H8 88
Giddings, Tex. D4 206
Gideon, Mo. E8 189
Gien, Fr. D5 58
Giessen, Ger. C3 61
Giffard, Que., Can. C9 154
Gifford, Ark. D6 169
Gifford, Fla. E6 174
Gifford, Idaho C2 177
Gifford, Ill. C5 178
Gifford, Pa. C4 202
Gifhorn, Ger. F4 62
Gift, Tenn. B2 205
Gifu, Jap. I8, n15 93
Gig Harbor, Wash. B3, D1 210
Giganta, mts., Mex. B2 129
Gigante, Col. C2 133
Gigha, isl., Scot. E3 57
Gigha, sound, Scot. E3 57
Giglio, isl., It. C3 67
Giguela, riv., Sp. C4 65
Gihon, riv., Vt. B3 208
Gijón, Sp. A3 65
Gijunabena, is., Sol. Is. 115
Gil, isl., B.C., Can. C3 149
Gila, N. Mex. E1 195
Gila, co., Ariz. D5 168
Gila, mts., Ariz. D6 168
Gila, peak, Ariz. D6 168
Gila, riv., Ariz., N. Mex. E2 168, D1 195
Gila, riv., Eth. D3 105
Gila Bend, Ariz. E3 168
Gila Bend, Indian res., Ariz. D3 168
Gila Bend, mts., Ariz. D2 168
Gila Center, Ariz. E1 168
Gila Cliff Dwellings, nat. mon., N. Mex. D1 195
Gila River, Indian res., Ariz. D4 168
Gilbert, Ariz. D4, G2 168
Gilbert, Ark. B3 169
Gilbert, Iowa B4 180
Gilbert, La. B4 183
Gilbert, Minn. C6 187
Gilbert, S.C. D5 203
Gilbert, W. Va. D3 211
Gilbert, is., Gilbert & Ellice Is. G10 113
Gilbert, peak, Wash. C4 210
Gilbert, riv., Austl. C7 110
Gilbert, riv., Newf., Can. B3 152
GILBERT AND ELLICE ISLANDS, Br. dep., Oceania G10 113
Gilbert Plains, Man., Can. D1 150
Gilberton, Pa. *E9 202
Gilbertown, Ala. D1 166
Gilbertsville, Ky. A3 182
Gilbertsville, N.Y. C5 196
Gilbertsville, Pa. F10 202
Gilbertville, Iowa B5 180
Gilbertville, Maine D2 184
Gilbertville, Mass. B3 185
Gilboa, N.H. E2 193
Gilboa, Ohio A4 199
Gilby, N. Dak. A8 198
Gilchrist, Oreg. D5 201
Gilchrist, co., Fla. C4 174
Gilcrest, Colo. A6 171
Gildford, Mont. B6 190
Gilead, Conn. C7 172
Gilead, Maine D2 184
Gilead, Nebr. D8 191
Giles, Tex. B2 206
Giles, co., Tenn. B4 205
Giles, co., Va. D2 209
Gilford, N.H. C4 193
Gilford, isl., B.C., Can. D4 149
Gilford Park, N.J. *D4 194
Gilgandra, Austl. E7 112
Gilgit, Pak. A5 87
Gilgunnia, Austl. F6 112
Gill, Colo. A6 171
Gill, Mass. A3 185
Gillam, Man., Can. A4 150
Gilleleje, Den. B6 62
Gillen, lake, Austl. E3 110
Gillespie, Ill. D4 178
Gillespie, co., Tex. D3 206
Gillespie, dam, Ariz. D3 168
Gillett, Ark. C4 169
Gillett, Fla. F2 174
Gillett, Pa. C8 202
Gillett, Tex. B4 206
Gillett, Wis. D5 212
Gillett Grove, Iowa A2 180
Gillette, Wyo. A7 213
Gillham, Ark. C1 169
Gilliam, La. B2 183
Gilliam, Mo. B4 189
Gilliam, co., Oreg. B6 201
Gillingham, Eng. C8 56
Gillis Point, N.S., Can. C9 151
Gillisburg, Miss. D3 188
Gilluly, Utah D4 207
Gilly, Bel. D4 59
Gilman, Colo. B4 171
Gilman, Conn. C8 172
Gilman, Ill. C6 178
Gilman, Iowa C5 180
Gilman, Minn. E5 187
Gilman, Mont. C4 190
Gilman, Vt. C5 208
Gilman, Wis. C3 212
Gilman City, Mo. A4 189
Gilmanton, N.H. D4 193
Gilmanton, Wis. D2 212
Gilmanton Iron Works, N.H. D4 193
Gilmer, Tex. C5 206
Gilmer, W. Va. C4 211
Gilmer, co., Ga. B2 175
Gilmer, co., W. Va. C4 211
Gilmore, Ark. B5 169
Gilmore, Ga. A5 175
Gilmore, Idaho E5 177
Gilmore City, Iowa B3 180
Gilmour, Ont., Can. C7 153
Gilpin, Ky. C5 182
Gilpin, co., Colo. B5 171
Gilpin, Tex. C2 206
Gilroy, Calif. C6, D3 170
Gilroy, Sask., Can. G2 155
Gilson, Ill. C3 178
Gilsum, N.H. D2 193
Giltner, Nebr. D7 191
Gima, Okinawa 114
Gimli, Man., Can. D3 150
Gingoog, Phil. D7 90
Ginir, Eth. D5 105
Ginosa, It. D6 67
Ginzo, Sp. A2 65
Gioia del Colle, It. D6 67
Gioiosa Ionica, It. E6 67
Girard, Ga. C5 175
Girard, Ill. D4 178
Girard, Kans. E9 181
Girard, La. B4 183
Girard, Ohio A7 199
Girard, Pa. B1 202
Girard, Tex. C2 206
Girardot, Col. C3 133
Girardville, Pa. E9 202
Girdletree, Md. D7 173
Giresun, Tur. B12 85
Giri, riv., Zaire A2 106
Giridih, India E11 88
Girishk, Afg. F12 86
Girna, riv., India G5 88
Giromagny, Fr. D7 58
Girón, Ec. B2 134
Gironde, riv., Fr. E3 58
Giroux, Man., Can. E3 150
Girouxville, Alta., Can. B2 148
Girvan, Scot. E4 57
Girvin, Sask., Can. F3 155
Girvin, Tex. D1 206
Gisborne, N.Z. M17 112
Gisburn, lake, Newf., Can. E4 152
Giscome, B.C., Can. B6 149
Gishu, see Uiju, Kor.
Gislaveds, Swe. A7 62
Gisors, Fr. C4 58
Gitano, Miss. D4 188
Giuba (Juba), riv., Som. E5 105
Giulianova, It. C4 67
Giumbo, Som. F5 105
Giurgiu, Rom. D7 68
Givataim, Isr. g10 84
Give, Den. C3 62
Givet, Fr. B6 58
Givhans, S.C. E1, E7 203
Givors, Fr. E6 58
Givry, isl., Truk 114
Giza (Al Jīzah), Eg. C6 101
Gizhduvan, Sov. Un. A12 86
Gizhiga, Sov. Un. C19 71
Gizo, isl., Sol. Is. 115
Giżycko, Pol. A6 70
Gjinokastër, Alb. B3 69
Gjoa Haven, N.W. Ter., Can. C13 144
Gjövik, Nor. G4 63
Glace Bay, N.S., Can. C10 151
Glacier, B.C., Can. D9 149
Glacier, Wash. A4 210
Glacier, co., Mont. B3 190
Glacier, bay, Alsk. k21 167
Glacier, nat. park, B.C., Can. D9 149
Glacier, nat. park., Mont. B3 190
Glacier, peak, Wash A4 210
Glacier Bay, nat. mon., Alsk. D12 167
Glad Valley, S. Dak. B4 204
Gladbeck, Ger. B1 61
Gladbrook, Iowa B5 180
Glade, Kans. C4 181
Glade, creek, Wash C6 210
Glade, creek, W. Va. D7 211
Glade Park, Colo. B2 171
Glade Spring, Va. B3 209
Glade Valley, N.C. A2 197
Glades, co., Fla. F5 174
Gladeville, Tenn. A5 205
Gladewater, Tex. C5 206
Gladmar, Sask., Can. H3 155
Gladsakse, Den. *C6 62
Gladstone, Austl. A8 112
Gladstone, Austl. F2 112
Gladstone, Man., Can. D2 150
Gladstone, Ill. C3 178
Gladstone, Mich. C3 186
Gladstone, Mo. E2 189
Gladstone, Nebr. D8 191
Gladstone (Peapack-Gladstone), N.J. B3 194
Gladstone, N. Mex. A6 195
Gladstone, N. Dak. C3 198
Gladstone, Oreg. B2, B4 201
Gladstone, Va. D4 209
Gladwin, Mich. E6 186
Gladwin, co., Mich. D6 186
Glady, W. Va. C5 211
Gladys, Va. D3 209
Glåma, riv., Nor. G5, p29 63
Glamis, Sask., Can. F2 155
Glamoč, Yugo. C3 68
Glamorgan, co., Wales C4 56
Glan, lake, Swe. u33 63
Glan, riv., Ger. D2 61
Glancy, Miss. D3 188
Glandorf, Ohio A3 199
Glanshammar, Swe. t33 63
Glärnisch, mtn., Switz. C4 66
Glarus, Switz. B5 66
Glarus, canton, Switz. B5 66
Glasco, Kans. C6 181
Glasco, N.Y. C7 196
Glascock, co., Ga. C4 175
Glasford, Ill. C4 178
Glasgo, Conn. C9 172
Glasgow, Ky. C4 182
Glasgow, Mo. B5 189
Glasgow, Mont. B10 190
Glasgow, Scot. E4 57
Glasgow, Va. D3 209
Glasgow, W. Va. C6 211
Glaslyn, Sask., Can. D1 155
Glasnevin, Sask., Can. H3 155
Glass, Tenn. A2 205
Glass, mts., Tex. D1 206
Glassboro, N.J. D2 194
Glasscock, co., Tex. D2 206
Glassport, Pa. F2 202
Glasston, N. Dak. A8 198
Glastenbury, mtn., Vt. F2 208
Glastonbury, Conn. C6 172
Glastonbury, Eng. C5 56
Glauchau, Ger. C7 61
Glazier, Tex. A2 206
Glazier, lake, Maine A3 184
Glazov, Sov. Un. B4 73
Glazypeau, mtn., Ark. C5 169
Gleason, Tenn. A3 205
Gleason, Wis. C4 212
Gleasondale, Mass. C1 185
Gleichen, Alta., Can. D4 148
Glen, Minn. D5 187
Glen, Mont. E4 190
Glen, N.H. B4 193
Glen, W. Va. C3, C6 211
Glen, canyon, Ariz., Utah G4 207
Glen, lake, Mich. D4 186
Glen Alice, Tenn. D9 205
Glen Allan, Miss. B2 188
Glen Allen, Ala. B2 166
Glen Allen, Va. D5 209
Glen Almond, Que., Can. D2 154
Glen Alpine, N.C. B2, D4 197
Glen Arbor, Mich. D4 186
Glen Avon Heights, Calif. *F5 170
Glen Burnie, Md. B4 173
Glen Campbell, Pa. E4 202
Glen Canyon, dam, Ariz. A4 168
Glen Canyon, nat. recreation area, Ariz., Utah A4 168, F5 207
Glen Carbon, Ill. E4 178
Glen Cove, N.Y. D2 196
Glen Dale, W. Va. B4 211
Glen Dean, Ky. C3 182
Glen Easton, W. Va. B4, C2 211
Glen Echo, Md. C1 173
Glen Elder, Kans. C5 181
Glen Ellen, Calif. B5 170
Glen Ellis, falls, N.H. B4 193
Glen Ellyn, Ill. F2 178
Glen Ewen, Sask., Can. H4 155
Glen Ferris, W. Va. D7 211
Glen Gardner, N.J. B3 194
Glen Haven, Colo. A5 171
Glen Innes, Austl. D8 112
Glen Jean, W. Va. D3, D7 211
Glen Kerr, Sask., Can. G2 155
Glen Lyon, Pa. D9 202
Glen Oaks, Ariz. C3 168
Glen Raven, N.C. A4 197
Glen Riddle, Pa. B10 202
Glen Ridge, Fla. *F6 174
Glen Ridge, N.J. B4 194
Glen Robertson, Ont., Can. B10 153
Glen Rock, N.J. B4, D5 194
Glen Rock, Pa. G8 202
Glen Rose, Tex. C4 206
Glen St. Mary, Fla. B4 174
Glen Ullin, N. Dak. C4 198
Glen White, W. Va. D3 211
Glen Wilton, Va. C3 209
Glenalum, W. Va. D3 211
Glénans, is., Fr. D1 58
Glenarden, Md. *C4 173
Glenavon, Sask., Can. G4 155
Glenbain, Sask., Can. H2 155
Glenbarr, Scot. E3 57
Glenbeulah, Wis. B6 212
Glenboro, Man., Can. E2 150
Glenbrook, Nev. D2 192
Glenburn, Maine *D4 184
Glenburn, N. Dak. A4 198
Glenbush, Sask., Can. D2 155
Glencliff, N.H. C3 193
Glencoe, Ala. B4 166
Glencoe, Ont., Can. E3 153
Glencoe, Ill. A6, E3 178
Glencoe, Ky. B5 182
Glencoe, Md. A4 173
Glencoe, Minn. F4 187
Glencoe, Mo. B7 189
Glencoe, N. Mex. D4 195
Glencoe, Ohio B1 211
Glencoe, Okla. A5 200
Glencoe, val., Scot. D4 57
Glencross, S. Dak. B5 204
Glendale, Ariz. D3, G2 168
Glendale, Ark. D4 169
Glendale, Calif. F2 170
Glendale, Fla. G3 174
Glendale, Idaho G7 177
Glendale, Ky. C4 182
Glendale, Mo. *C7 189
Glendale, Ohio C3, D2 199
Glendale, Oreg. E3 201
Glendale, R.I. B10 172
Glendale, S.C. B4 203
Glendale, Tenn. B5 205
Glendale, Utah F3 207
Glendale, Wis. *E6 212
Glendale Colony, S. Dak. C7 204
Glendale Heights, Ill. *B5 178
Glendevey, Colo. A5 171
Glendive, Mont. C12 190
Glendo, Wyo. C7 213
Glendo, res., Wyo. C7 213
Glendon, Alta., Can. B5 148
Glendora, Calif. F3 170
Glendora, Miss. B3 188
Glenelg, Md. B4 173
Glenelg, Scot. C3 57
Glenella, Man., Can. D2 150
Glenfield, N.Y. B5 196
Glenfield, N. Dak. B7 198
Glenfield, Pa. *E1 202
Glenfinnan, Scot. D3 57
Glenflora, Tex. E4 206
Glengarry, co., Ont., Can. B10 153

INDEX KEY Each place listed in **Bold-faced Type** has its population listed in the Population tables, pages 230 to 280.
Each country, shown in CAPITAL LETTERS, has its population listed in the World Political Information Table, pages 6 to 10.
* Does not appear on map; key shows general location.

Glenham, S. Dak. B5 204
Glenisla, Scot. D5 57
Glenluce, Scot. F4 57
Glenmary, Tenn. C9 205
Glenmont, Ohio B5 199
Glenmora, La. D3 183
Glenmore, Ohio B3 199
Glenmorgan, Austl. C7 112
Glenn, Mich. F4 186
Glenn, co., Calif. C2 170
Glenn Allen, Alsk. f19 167
Glenn Dale, Md. C4 173
Glenn Heights, Tex. *C4 240
Glennie, Mich. D7 186
Glennonville, Mo. E7 189
Glenns Ferry, Idaho G3 177
Glennville, Ga. E5 175
Glenolden, Pa. B11 202
Glenoma, Wash. C3 210
Glenpool, Okla. B5 200
Glenridge, Ill. E4 178
Glenrio, N. Mex. B6 195
Glenrio, Tex. B1 206
Glenrock, Wyo. C7 213
Glens Falls, N.Y. B7 196
Glenshaw, Pa. *E2 202
Glenside, Sask., Can. F2 155
Glenside, Pa. A11 202
Glentana, Mont. B10 190
Glentworth, Sask., Can. H2 155
Glenview, Ill. E2 178
Glenvil, Nebr. D7 191
Glenville, Ala. C4 166
Glenville, Minn. G5 187
Glenville, N.C. D3 197
Glenville, W. Va. C4 211
Glenwood, Ala. D3 166
Glenwood, Ark. C2 169
Glenwood, Newf., Can. D4 152
Glenwood, Fla. C5 174
Glenwood, Ga. D4 175
Glenwood, Ill. *B6 178
Glenwood, Ind. E7 179
Glenwood, Iowa C2 180
Glenwood, Maine *C4 184
Glenwood, Md. B3 173
Glenwood, Mich. F4 186
Glenwood, Minn. E3 187
Glenwood, Mo. A5 189
Glenwood, N.J. A4 194
Glenwood, N. Mex. D1 195
Glenwood, Oreg. A1, B3 201
Glenwood, Utah E4 207
Glenwood, Va. *E3 209
Glenwood, Wash. C4 210
Glenwood, W. Va. C2 211
Glenwood City, Wis. C1 212
Glenwood Park, N.Y. *D6 196
Glenwood Springs, Colo. B3 171
Glenwoodville, Alta., Can. E4 148
Glezen, Ind. H3 179
Glidden, Sask., Can. F1 155
Glidden, Iowa B3 180
Glidden, Wis. B3 212
Glide, Oreg. D3 201
Glifádha, Grc. h11 69
Gliwice, Pol. C5, g9 70
Globe, Ariz. D5 168
Globe, Ky. B6 182
Globino, Sov. Un. G9 72
Głogów, Pol. C3 70
Glorenza, It. A3 67
Glória, Braz. C3 138
Gloria, La. C7 183
Glória de Goitá, Braz. k6 138
Glorieta, N. Mex. B4, F6 195
Glorieuses, is., Afr. f9 107
Glossop, Eng. A6 56
Gloster, Ga. A5 175
Gloster, La. B2 183
Gloster, Miss. D2 188
Glostrup, Den. C6 62
Gloucester, Ont., Can. B9 153
Gloucester, Eng. C5 56
Gloucester, Mass. A6, C4 185
Gloucester, Va. D6 209
Gloucester, co., N.B., Can. B4 151
Gloucester, co., Eng. C5 56
Gloucester, co., N.J. D2 194
Gloucester, co., Va. D6 209
Gloucester, cape, New Britain I. 115
Gloucester City, N.J. D2 194
Glouster, Ohio C5 199
Glover, Mo. D7 189
Glover, N. Dak. C7 198
Glover, Vt. B4 208
Glover, isl., Newf., Can. D3 152
Glovergap, W. Va. A6 211
Gloverville, S.C. E4 203
Gloversville, N.Y. B6 196
Glovertown, Newf., Can. D4 152
Głubczyce, Pol. C4 70
Glubokoye, Sov. Un. D6 72
Głuchołazy, Pol. C4 70
Gluck, S.C. C2 203
Glücksburg, Ger. D3 62
Glückstadt, Ger. E3 62
Gluek, Minn. E3 187
Glukhov, Sov. Un. F9 72
Glussk, Sov. Un. E7 72
Glyndon, Md. B4 173
Glyndon, Minn. D2 187
Glyngöre, Den. B2 62
Glynn, co., Ga. E5 175
Gmunden, Aus. E6 60
Gnadenhutten, Ohio B6 199
Gnesta, Swe. t35 63
Gniezno, Pol. B4 70
Gnjilane, Yugo. D5 68
Gnoien, Ger. E6 62
Goalpara, India D13 88
Goat, isl., Am. Sam. 114
Goat, mtn., Mont. C3 190
Goat Fell, mtn., Scot. E3 57
Goat Rock, dam, Ala., Ga. C4 166, D1 175
Goba, Eth. D5 105
Gobabis, S.W. Afr. B2 107
Gobernador Udaondo, Arg. g7 136
Gobey, Tenn. C9 205
Gobi, des., China, Mong. C5 91
Gobles, Mich. F5 186
Goch, Ger. C3 60
Godar-i-Shah, Afg. G10 86
Godavari, riv., India E6 87
Godda, India E11 88
Goddard, Kans. B5, E6 181
Goderich, Ont., Can. D3 153
Godfrey, Ont., Can. C8 153
Godfrey, Ga. C3 175
Godfrey, Ill. E3 178
Godfrey, crusade of 47
Godhavn, Grnld. C20 118
Godhra, India F4 88
Godley, Ill. *B5 178
Godley, Tex. B5 206
Godoy Cruz, Arg. *A3 136
Gods, lake, Man., Can. B4 150
Gods, riv., Man., Can. A5 150
Gods Lake, Man., Can. B4 150
Godthåb, Grnld. C20 118
Godwin, N.C. B5 197
Godwin Austen, peak, Pak. A6 87
Godwinsville, Ga. D3 175
Goehner, Nebr. D8 191
Goes, Neth. C3 59
Goessel, Kans. D6 181
Goff, Kans. C8 181
Goffs, Calif. E6 170
Goffstown, N.H. D3 193
Gogebic, co., Mich. A5 186
Gogebic, lake, Mich. A5 186
Gogebic, range, Wis. B3 212
Gohfeld, Ger. A3 61
Göhren, Ger. D7 62
Goiana, Braz. C4, h6 138
Goiandira, Braz. E1 138
Goiânia, Braz. B3 137
Goianinha, Braz. h6 138
Goiás, Braz. B2 137
Goiás, state, Braz. D1 138
Goito, It. D6 66
Gojām, reg., Eth. C4 105
Gojō, Jap. o14 93
Göksun, Tur. C11 85
Gokwe, Rh. A4 107
Gol, Nor. G3 63
Golchikha, Sov. Un. B11 71
Golconda, Ill. F5 178
Golconda, Nev. C4 192
Gold, Pa. C6 202
Gold Acres, Nev. C5 192
Gold Bar, Wash. B4 210
Gold Beach, Oreg. E2 201
Gold Bridge, B.C., Can. D6 149
Gold Coast, Austl. E9 111, C9 112
Gold Coast: in 1890 99
see also Ghana
Gold Hill, Ala. C4 166
Gold Hill, N.C. B3 197
Gold Hill, Oreg. E3 201
Gold Point, Nev. F4 192
Gold Point, N.C. *B6 197
Gołdap, Pol. A7 70
Goldbach, Ger. C4 61
Goldberg, Ger. E6 62
Goldboro, N.S., Can. D8 151
Goldbutte, Mont. B5 190
Goldcreek, Mont. D4 190
Golddust, Tenn. B2 205
Golden, B.C., Can. D9 149
Golden, Colo. B5 171
Golden, Idaho D3 177
Golden, Ill. C2 178
Golden, Miss. A5 188
Golden, Mo. E4 189
Golden, N. Mex. B3, G6 195
Golden Beach, Fla. E3 174
Golden City, Mo. D3 189
Golden Ears, prov. park, B.C., Can. E6 149
Golden Gate, bridge, Calif. B5 170
Golden Gate, entrance, Calif. B5 170
Golden Hill, Md. D5 173
Golden Hill, Minn. *F6 187
Golden Hinde, mtn., B.C., Can. E5 149
Golden Horde, Khanate of: c. 1360 48
Golden Lake, Ont., Can. B7 153
Golden Meadow, La. E5 183
Golden Prairie, Sask., Can. G1 155
Golden Spike, nat. historic site, Utah B3 207
Golden Valley, Minn. E6 187
Golden Valley, co., Mont. D7 190
Golden Valley, co., N. Dak. B2 198
Goldendale, Wash. D5 210
Goldengate, Ill. E5 178
Goldenvalley, N. Dak. B3 198
Goldenville, N.S., Can. D7 151
Goldfield, Colo. C5 171
Goldfield, Iowa B4 180
Goldfield, Nev. F4 192
Goldfield, mts., Ariz. G3 168
Goldonna, La. B3 183
Goldpoint, Tenn. E10 205
Goldsand, lake, Man., Can. A1 150
Goldsboro, Md. B6 173
Goldsboro, N.C. B6 197
Goldsmith, Ind. D5 179
Goldsmith, Tex. D1 206
Goldston, N.C. B4 197
Goldthwaite, Tex. D3 206
Golela, S. Afr. C5 107
Goleniów, Pol. B3 70
Goleta, Calif. E4 170
Golf, Ill. *E3 178
Golf Manor, Ohio *D2 199
Golfview, Fla. *F6 174
Goliad, Tex. E4 206
Goliad, co., Tex. E4 206
Golling, Aus. B9 66
Golovin, Alsk. C7 167
Golovnino, Sov. Un. E12 93
Golpāyegān, Iran E5 86
Golspie, Scot. C5 57
Goltry, Okla. A3 200
Golts, Md. B6 173
Golva, N. Dak. C2 198
Golyamo Konare, Bul. D7 68
Goma, Zaire B4 106
Gombari, Zaire A4 106
Gombe, Nig. D7 103
Gomel', Sov. Un. E8 72
Gomera, isl., Port. (Can. Is.) m13 65
Gomez, Fla. E6 174
Gómez Palacio, Mex. B4 129
Gommern, Ger. A6 61
Gonaïves, Hai. F7 131
Gonbad-e Kāvūs, Iran C7 86
Gonda, India C7 87
Gondar, Eth. C4 105
Gondia, India G8 88
Gondola Point, N.B., Can. *D4 151
Gondrecourt-le-Château, Fr. F5 59
Gönen, Tur. B6 69
Gonesse, Fr. g10 58
Gonic, N.H. D5 193
Gonvick, Minn. C3 187
Gonzales, Calif. D3 170
Gonzales, La. B5, D5 183
Gonzales, Tex. E4 206
Gonzales, co., Tex. E4 206
Gonzalez, Fla. G2 174
Gonzalez, Mex. C5 129
González Chaves, Arg. B4 136
Goochland, Va. D5 209
Goochland, co., Va. D5 209
Good Hart, Mich. C5 186
Good Hope, Ga. C3 175
Good Hope, Ill. C3 178
Good Hope, Miss. C4 188
Good Hope, Ohio C4 199
Good Hope, cape, S. Afr. D2 107
Good Hope, mtn., B.C., Can. D5, E3 149
Good Pasture, Colo. C6 171
Good Pine, La. C3 183
Good Spirit Lake, prov. park, Sask., Can. F4 155
Good Thunder, Minn. F4 187
Good Water, Ala. B3 166
Goode, Va. D3 209
Goodell, Iowa B4 180
Goodenough, cape, Ant. C25 120
Gooderham, Ont., Can. C6 153
Goodeve, Sask., Can. F4 155
Goodfellow Terrace, Mo. *C7 189
Goodfield, Ill. C4 178
Goodhue, Minn. F6 187
Goodhue, co., Minn. F6 187
Gooding, Idaho G4 177
Gooding, co., Idaho F4 177
Goodland, Fla. G5 174
Goodland, Ind. C3 179
Goodland, Kans. C2 181
Goodland, Okla. D6 200
Goodlettsville, Tenn. A5, E9 205
Goodman, Miss. C4 188
Goodman, Mo. E3 189
Goodman, Wis. C5 212
Goodnews Bay, Alsk. D7 167
Goodnight, Tex. B2 206
Goodrich, Colo. A6 171
Goodrich, Kans. D9 181
Goodrich, Mich. *F7 186
Goodrich, N. Dak. B5 198
Goodrich, Tex. D5 206
Goodridge, Minn. B3 187
Goodspring, Tenn. B4 205
Goodsprings, Ala. B2 166
Goodsprings, Nev. H6 192
Goodview, Minn. F7 187
Goodwater, Sask., Can. H4 155
Goodwater, Okla. D7 200
Goodwell, Okla. D2 200
Goodwin, Ariz. C3 168
Goodwin, S. Dak. C9 204
Goodwood, S. Afr. *D2 107
Goodyear, Ariz. D3, G1 168
Goole, Eng. A7 56
Goondiwindi, Austl. D8 112
Goor, Neth. B6 59
Goose, bay, Newf., Can. B1 152
Goose, creek, Va. D3 209
Goose, creek, Wyo. A6 213
Goose, isl., B.C., Can. D3 149
Goose, lake, Calif. B3 170
Goose, lake, Man., Can. B1 150
Goose, lake, Sask., Can. F2 155
Goose, lake, Oreg. E6 201
Goose, pond, N.H. C2 193
Goose, riv., Newf., Can. h9 152
Goose Bay, Newf., Can. B1, h9 152
Goose Creek, S.C. E2, F7 203
Goose Creek, res., S.C. E2 203
Goose Egg, Wyo. C6 213
Gooseberry, creek, Wyo. A4 213
Gooselake, Iowa C7 180
Goosport, La. *D2 183
Gopalganj, India D10 88
Goplo, lake, Pol. B5 70
Göppingen, Ger. E4 61
Góra, Pol. C4 70
Góra Kalwaria, Pol. C6 70
Gorakhpur, India C7 87, D9 88
Gorday, Ga. E3 175
Gördes, Tur. C7 69
Gordo, Ala. B2 166
Gordon, Ala. D4 166
Gordon, Ga. D3 175
Gordon, Kans. B6 181
Gordon, Nebr. B3 191
Gordon, Ohio *C3 199
Gordon, Pa. *E9 202
Gordon, Tex. C3 206
Gordon, Wis. B2 212
Gordon, co., Ga. B2 175
Gordon, lake, Alta., Can. A5 148
Gordon Horne, park, B.C., Can. C8 149
Gordonhorne, peak, B.C., Can. D8 149
Gordonsburg, Tenn. B4 205
Gordonsville, Minn. G5 187
Gordonsville, Tenn. C8 205
Gordonsville, Va. C4 209
Gordonville, Mo. D8 189
Gore, N.S., Can. D6 151
Gorē, Eth. D4 105
Gore, N.Z. Q12 112
Gore, Ohio C5 199
Gore, Okla. B6 200
Gore, Va. B4 209
Gore, mtn., Vt. B5 208
Gore, pt., Alsk. h16 167
Gore, range, Colo. B4 171
Gore Bay, Ont., Can. B2 153
Gore Springs, Miss. B4 188
Goree, Tex. C3 206
Goreville, Ill. F5 178
Gorey, Ire. D3 55
Gorgān (Asterabad), Iran C7 86
Gorge High, dam, Wash. A4 210
Gorgona, isl., Col. C2 133
Gorham, Ill. F4 178
Gorham, Kans. D4 181
Gorham, Maine E2, E4 184
Gorham, N. Dak. B2 198
Gorham, N.H. B4 193
Gorham, N.Y. C3 196
Gori, Sov. Un. E2 73
Gorin, Mo. A5 189
Gorinchem, Neth. C5 59
Goris, Sov. Un. C16 85
Gorizia, It. B4 67
Gorki, Sov. Un. D8 72
Gorki (Gor'kiy), Sov. Un. B2 73
Gorkiy, res., Sov. Un. B2 73
Görlev, Den. C5 62
Gorlice, Pol. D6 70
Görlitz, Ger. B9 61
Gorlovka, Sov. Un. G12, q21 72
Gorm, lake, Scot. E2 57
Gorman, Md. D1 173
Gorman, Tenn. A4 205
Gorman, Tex. C3 206
Gormania, W. Va. B5 211
Gormley, Ont., Can. E6 153
Gorna-Dzhumaya, see Blagoevgrad, Bul.
Gorna Oryakhovitsa, Bul. D7 68
Gornji Milanovac, Yugo. C5 68
Gorno-Altaysk, Sov. Un. D11 71
Gornozavodsk, Sov. Un. C10 93
Gorodenka, Sov. Un. G5 72
Gorodishche, Sov. Un. q22 72
Gorodnya, Sov. Un. E8 72
Gorodok, Sov. Un. A5 91
Gorodok, Sov. Un. G4 72
Gorodok, Sov. Un. D7 72
Goroke, Austl. H3 112
Gorong, is., Indon. F8 90
Gorontalo, Indon. E6 90
Gorrie, Ont., Can. D3 153
Gorskoye, Sov. Un. q21 72
Goryn, riv., Sov. Un. F6 72
Gorzów, [Wielkopolski], Pol. B3 70
Gosainthan, peak, Nep. C10 88
Gosford, Austl. F8 112
Goshen, Ala. D3 166
Goshen, Calif. *D4 170
Goshen, N.S., Can. D8 151
Goshen, Conn. B4 172
Goshen, Ind. A6 179
Goshen, Ky. A4 182
Goshen, Mass. B2 185
Goshen, N.H. D2 193
Goshen, N.J. E3 194
Goshen, N.Y. D2, D6 196
Goshen, Oreg. D4 201
Goshen, Utah D4 207
Goshen, Va. D3 209
Goshen, co., Wyo. C8 213
Goshen Hole, sink, Wyo. D8 213
Goshen Springs, Miss. C4 188
Goshute, Indian res., Utah D1 207
Goshute, mts., Nev. C7 192
Goslar, Ger. B5 61
Gosper, co., Nebr. D6 191
Gospić, Yugo. C2 68
Gosport, Ala. D2 166
Gosport, Eng. D6 56
Gosport, Ind. F4 179
Gossburg, Tenn. B5 205
Gossville, N.H. D4 193
Gostivar, Yugo. E5 68
Gostyń, Pol. C4 70
Gostynia, riv., Pol. g9 70
Gostynin, Pol. B5 70
Gotebo, Okla. B3 200
Göteborg, Swe. A5 62, I4 63
Göteborg och Bohus, co., Swe. A5 62
Gotel, mts., Cam. E7 103
Gotemba, Jap. n18 93
Gotha, Ger. C5 61
Gotham, Wis. E3 212
Gothenburg, Nebr. D5 191
Gothic, mesas, Ariz., N. Mex. A6 168, A1 195
Gotland, isl., Swe. I8 63
Gotō, is., Jap. J4 93
Gotse Delchev, Bul. E6 68
Göttingen, Ger. B4 61
Gottwaldov (Zlín), Czech. D4 70
Gouda, Neth. C4 59
Goudeau, La. D3 183
Goudiri, Sen. D2 103
Goudswaard, Neth. C4 59
Gough, Ga. C4 175
Gough, lake, Alta., Can. C4 148
Gouin, res., Que., Can. G17 143
Goulais, riv., Ont., Can. B6 186
Goulburn, Austl. G7 112
Gould, Ark. D4 169
Gould, Que., Can. D6 154
Gould, Colo. A4 171
Gould, Okla. C2 200
Gould City, Mich. B5 186
Gouldbusk, Tex. D3 206
Goulds, Fla. F3 174
Gouldsboro, Maine D4 184
Gouldsboro, Pa. D11 202
Goulimine, Mor. D2 102
Goulvain, cape, N. Cal. 115
Gounamitz, riv., N.B., Can. B2 151
Goundam, Mali C4 103
Gouré, Niger D7 103
Gourma-Rarous, Mali C4 103
Gournay-en-Bray, Fr. C4 58
Gouro, Chad B3 104
Gouverneur, Sask., Can. H2 155
Gouverneur, N.Y. B1 196
Govan, Sask., Can. F3 155
Govan, S.C. E5 203
Gove, Kans. D3 181
Gove, co., Kans. D3 181
Govenlock, Sask., Can. H1 155
Governador, N. Mex. A2 195
Governador Valadares, Braz. *E2 138
Government Camp, Oreg. B5 201
Governor's Harbour, Ba. Is. C5 131
Gowan, Minn. D6 187
Gowan, riv., Man., Can. B4 150
Gowanda, N.Y. C2 196
Gowen, Mich. E5 186
Gowen, Okla. C6 200
Gower, Mo. B3 189
Gowk, Iran G8 86
Gowna, lake, Ire. D3 55
Gowrie, Iowa B3 180
Goya, Arg. E4 135
Goz Béïda, Chad C4 104
Gōz Regeb, Sud. B4 105
Graaff-Reinet, S. Afr. D3 107
Graal-Müritz, Ger. D6 62
Grabill, Ind. B8 179
Grabow, Ger. E5 62
Grabow, bay, Ger. D6 62
Gračac, Yugo. C2 68
Gračanica, Yugo. C4 68
Grace, Idaho G7 177
Grace, Miss. C3 188
Grace, mtn., Mass. A3 185
Grace City, N. Dak. B7 198
Graceham, Md. A3 173
Gracemont, Okla. B3 200
Graceton, Minn. B4 187
Graceville, Fla. G3 174
Graceville, Minn. E2 187
Gracewood, Ga. C4 175
Gracey, Ky. D2 182
Gracias, Hond. C3 130
Graciosa, isl., Port. (Azores) g9 102
Gradačac, Yugo. C4 68
Gradaús, mts., Braz. D4 139
Gradefes, Sp. A3 65
Gradizhsk, Sov. Un. G9 72
Grado, It. D9 66
Grado, Sp. A2 65
Grady, Ark. C4 169
Grady, N. Mex. C6 195
Grady, Okla. C4 200
Grady, co., Ga. F2 175
Grady, co., Okla. C4 200
Gradyville, Ky. C4 182
Gradyville, Pa. B10 202
Graettinger, Iowa A3 180
Grafenau, Ger. E8 61
Graford, Tex. C3 206
Grafton, Austl. D9 112
Grafton, Ont., Can. D6 153
Grafton, Ill. E3 178
Grafton, Iowa A4 180
Grafton, Mass. B4 185
Grafton, Nebr. D8 191
Grafton, N.H. C3 193
Grafton, N.Y. C7 196
Grafton, N. Dak. A8 198
Grafton, Ohio A5 199
Grafton, Vt. E3 208
Grafton, Va. C6 209
Grafton, W. Va. B4, B7 211
Grafton, Wis. E2, E6 212
Grafton, co., N.H. C3 193
Grafton Center, N.H. C3 193
Graham, Ala. B4 166
Graham, Fla. C4 174
Graham, Ga. E4 175
Graham, Ky. C2 182
Graham, Mo. A2 189
Graham, N.C. A4 197
Graham, Okla. C4 200
Graham, Tenn. B4 205
Graham, Tex. C3 206
Graham, Wash. B3 210
Graham, co., Ariz. E5 168
Graham, co., Kans. C4 181
Graham, co., N.C. D2 197
Graham, creek, Ind. G6 179
Graham, isl., B.C., Can. C1 149
Graham, lake, Alta., Can. A3 148
Graham, lake, Maine D4 184
Graham, mtn., Ariz. E6 168
Graham, reach, B.C., Can. C3 149
Graham, riv., B.C., Can. A6 149
Graham Bell, isl., Sov. Un. A8 118
Grahamstown, S. Afr. D4 107
Grahamsville, N.Y. D6 196
Grahamville, S.C. G6 203
Grahn, Ky. B6 182
Graian Alps, mts., Fr., It. D3 66
Grain Valley, Mo. C3 189
Grainfield, Kans. C3 181
Grainger, Alta., Can. D4 148
Grainger, co., Tenn. C10 205
Graingers, N.C. *B6 197
Grainland, Sask., Can. F2 155
Grainola, Okla. A5 200
Grainton, Nebr. D4 191
Grajaú, Braz. C1 138
Grajaú, riv., Braz. B1 138
Grajewo, Pol. B7 70
Gram, Den. C3 62
Gram, isl., Thai. F4 89
Gramada, Bul. D6 68
Gramalote, Col. B3 133
Gramastetten, Aus. E9 61
Grambling, La. B3 183
Gramercy, La. B6 183
Gramling, S.C. A3 203
Grammer, Ind. F6 179
Grammichele, It. F5 67
Grampian, Pa. E4 202
Grampian, mts., Scot. D4 57
Gramsdale, Scot. C1 57
Gramsh, Alb. B3 69
Gramzow, Ger. E8 62
Gran Canaria, isl., Sp. (Can. Is.) n13 65
Gran Chaco, plain, Arg., Par. F3 135
Gran Quivira, nat. mon., N. Mex. C3 195
Gran Sabana, plat., Ven. B5 133
Granada, Colo. C8 171
Granada, Minn. G4 187
Granada, Nic. E5 130
Granada, Sp. D4 65
Granbury, Tex. C4 206
Granby, Que., Can. D5 154
Granby, Colo. A5 171
Granby, Conn. B5 172
Granby, Mass. B2 185
Granby, Mo. E3 189
Granby, Vt. B5 208
Granby, lake, Colo. A5 171
Grand, co., Colo. A4 171
Grand, co., Utah E6 207
Grand, bayou, La. B5 183
Grand, bayou, La. C6 183
Grand, canal, China G7 92
Grand, canyon, Ariz. A3 168
Grand, falls, Maine C5 184
Grand, isl., La. D6 183
Grand, isl., La. E6 183
Grand, isl., Mich. B4 186
Grand, isl., Vt. B2 208
Grand, lake, N.B., Can. D2 151
Grand, lake, N.B., Can. D3 151
Grand, lake, Newf., Can. D3 152
Grand, lake, La. E3 183
Grand, lake, La. E4 183
Grand, lake, La. E6 183
Grand, lake, Maine C5 184
Grand, lake, Mich. C7 186
Grand, lake, Ohio B3 199
Grand, mesa, Colo. C2 171
Grand, riv., Newf., Can. E2 152
Grand, riv., La. D4 183
Grand, riv., Mich. E4 186
Grand, riv., Mo. A3 189
Grand, riv., Ohio A7 199
Grand, riv., S. Dak. B4 204
Grand, val., Colo., Utah B2 171
Grand Atlas, mts., Mor. C3 102
Grand Avenue Park, Wis. *F4 212
Grand Bahama, isl., Ba. Is. B4 131
Grand Bank, Newf., Can. E4 152
Grand-Bassam, I.C. E4 103
Grand Bay, Ala. E1 166
Grand Bay, N.B., Can. D3 151
Grand Beach, Man., Can. D3 150
Grand Beach, Mich. *G4 186
Grand Blanc, Mich. F7 186
Grand Bostonnais, lake, Que., Can. B5 154
Grand-Bourg, Guad. o16 131
Grand Bruit, Newf., Can. E2 152
Grand Cane, La. B2 183
Grand Canyon, Ariz. A3 168
Grand Canyon, nat. mon., Ariz. A3 168
Grand Canyon, nat. park, Ariz. A3 168
Grand Cayman, isl., Cayman Is. F3 131
Grand Centre, Alta., Can. B5 148
Grand Cess, Lib. F3 103
Grand Chenier, La. E3 183
Grand Coteau, La. D3 183
Grand Coulee, Wash. B6 210
Grand Coulee, dam, Wash. B6 210
Grand de Loíza, riv., P.R. B6 132
Grand Erg Occidental, sand dunes, Alg. C5 102
Grand Erg Oriental, sand dunes, Alg. D6 102
Grand-Etang, N.S., Can. C8 151
Grand Falls, N.B., Can. B2 151
Grand Falls, Newf., Can. D4 152
Grand Falls, Minn. B5 187
Grand Falls, lake, Maine C5 184

Grand Forks, B.C., Can....E8 149
Grand Forks, N. Dak....B8 198
Grand Forks, co., N. Dak..B8 198
Grand-Fougeray, Fr....D3 58
Grand Gorge, N.Y....C6 196
Grand Gulf, Miss....C2 188
Grand Harbour, N.B., Can. E3 151
Grand Haven, Mich....E4 186
Grand Hogback, mtn., Colo....B3 171
Grand Island, Nebr....D7 191
Grand Isle, La....E6 183
Grand Isle, Maine....A4 184
Grand Isle, Vt....B2 208
Grand Isle, co., Vt....B2 208
Grand Junction, Colo....B2 171
Grand Junction, Iowa....B3 180
Grand Junction, Mich....F4 186
Grand Junction, Tenn....B2 205
Grand-Lahou, I.C....E3 103
Grand Lake, Colo....A5 171
Grand Lake, La....D2 183
Grand Lake Seboeis, lake Maine....B4 184
Grand Lake Stream, Maine....C5 184
Grand Ledge, Mich....F6 186
Grand-Lieu, lake, Fr....D3 58
Grand Manan, chan., Can., U.S....E3 151
Grand Manan, isl., N.B., Can....E3 151
Grand Marais, Mich....B5 186
Grand Marais, Minn....B7 187
Grand Marsh, Wis....E4 212
Grand Meadow, Minn....G6 187
Grand' Mère, Que., Can....C5 154
Grand Pass, Mo....B4 189
Grand Portage, Minn....A8 187
Grand Portage, Indian res., Minn....B8 187
Grand Prairie, Tex....B5 206
Grand Pre, N.S., Can....D5 151
Grand Rapids, Man., Can....C2 150
Grand Rapids, Mich....F5 186
Grand Rapids, Minn....C5 187
Grand Rapids, N. Dak....C7 198
Grand Rapids, Ohio....A1, A4 199
Grand Ridge, Fla....B1 174
Grand Ridge, Ill....B5 178
Grand River, N.S., Can....D9 151
Grand River, Iowa....D4 180
Grand River, Ohio....*A6 199
Grand Rivers, Ky....A3 182
Grand Ronde, Oreg....B3 201
Grand St. Bernard, pass, Switz., It....D3 66
Grand Saline, Tex....C5 206
Grand Terre, isl., La....E6 183
Grand Teton, mtn., Wyo....B2 213
Grand Teton, nat. park, Wyo....B2 213
Grand Tower, Ill....F4 178
Grand Traverse, co., Mich....D5 186
Grand Traverse, bay, Mich..C5 186
Grand Valley, Ont., Can....D4 153
Grand Valley, Colo....B2 171
Grand Valley, Pa....C2 202
Grand View, Man., Can....D1 150
Grand View, Ind....I4 179
Grand View-on-Hudson, N.Y....*D7 196
Grand Wash, cliffs, Ariz....A2 168
Grande, N. Mex....A6 195
Grande, bay, Arg....E3 136
Grande, hills, Ur....f8 136
Grande, isl., Braz....h5 137
Grande, mts., Mex....G2 206
Grande, riv., Bol....C3 135
Grande, riv., Braz....B2 137
Grande, riv., Braz....D2 138
Grande, riv., Chile....D2 135
Grande, riv., Nic....D5 130
Grande, riv., Pan....k11 130
Grande, riv., P.R....B7 132
Grande, riv. mouth, Ven....B5 133
Grande Anse, N.B., Can....B4 151
Grande Cache, Alta., Can....*C1 148
Grande Catwick, is., Viet....G8 89
Grande de Añasco, riv., P.R..B3 132
Grande de Manatí, riv., P.R..B4 132
Grande de Santiago, riv., Mex....m11 129
Grande Digue, N.B., Can....C5 151
Grande Ligne, Que., Can....D4 154
Grande Miquelon, isl., St. Pierre and Miquelon....E3 152
Grande Prairie, Alta., Can....B1 148
Grande-Rivière, Que., Can....*B3 154
Grande Rivière de la Baleine, riv., Que., Can....A2 154
Grande Ronde, riv., Oreg., Wash....B9 201
Grandes-Bergeronnes, Que., Can....A8 154
Grandes Piles, Que., Can....C5 154
Grandfalls, Tex....D1 206
Grandfather, mtn., N.C....A2 197
Grandfield, Okla....C3 200
Grandin, Mo....E7 189
Grandin, N. Dak....B9 198
Grandmound, Iowa....C7 180
Grândola, Port....C1 65
Grandview, Alta., Can....*C3 148
Grandview, Idaho....G2 177
Grandview, Ill....D6 178
Grandview, Ill....*D4 178
Grandview, Iowa....C6 180
Grandview, Mo....C3, E2 189
Grandview, N.C....D2 197
Grandview, Ohio....C6 199
Grandview, Tenn....D9 205
Grandview, Tex....*C4 206
Grandview, Wash....C6 210
Grandview, Wis....B2 212
Grandview Heights, Ohio....C2 199
Grandville, Mich....F5 186
Grandvilliers, Fr....E1 59
Grandy, Minn....E5 187
Grandy, N.C....A8 197
Grandy, isl., Newf., Can....B4 152
Grangärde, Swe....G6 63
Grange, Ark....B4 169
Grange, Eng....F6 57
Grangeburg, Ala....D4 166
Grangemouth, Scot....D5 57
Granger, Ind....A5 179
Granger, Iowa....A7, C4 180
Granger, Mo....A6 189
Granger, Tex....D4 206
Granger, Wash....C5 210
Granger, Wyo....D3 213
Granges, Fr....A2 66
Grangeville, Idaho....D2 177
Grangeville, La....D5 183
Granite, Colo....B4 171
Granite, Md....B4 173
Granite, Okla....C2 200
Granite, co., Mont....D3 190
Granite, mtn., Ark....D6 169
Granite, mtn., Alsk....B7 167
Granite, mts., Ariz....E2 168
Granite, pass, Wyo....A5 213
Granite, peak, Mont....E7 190
Granite, peak, Nev....B4 192
Granite, peak, Nev....C2 192
Granite, peak, Utah....C2 207
Granite, peak, Utah....E3 207
Granite, peak, Wyo....C4 213
Granite, pt., Newf., Can....C3 152
Granite, range, Nev....C2 192
Granite Canon, Wyo....D7 213
Granite City, Ill....E3 178
Granite Falls, Minn....F3 187
Granite Falls, N.C....B2 197
Granite Falls, Wash....A4 210
Granite Quarry, N.C....B3 197
Graniteville, Mass....C1 185
Graniteville, Mo....D7 189
Graniteville, S.C....D4 203
Graniteville, Vt....C4 208
Granja, Braz....B2 138
Granja de Torrehermosa, Sp....C3 65
Grannis, Ark....C1 169
Grano, N. Dak....A4 198
Granollers, Sp....B7 65
Gransee, Ger....E7 62
Grant, Ala....A3 166
Grant, Colo....B5 171
Grant, Fla....E6 174
Grant, Iowa....C3 180
Grant, Ky....A6 182
Grant, La....D3 183
Grant, Mich....E5 186
Grant, Mont....F3 190
Grant, Nebr....D4 191
Grant, Okla....D6 200
Grant, co., Ark....C3 169
Grant, co., Ind....C6 179
Grant, co., Kans....E2 181
Grant, co., Ky....B5 182
Grant, co., Minn....E2 187
Grant, co., Nebr....C4 191
Grant, co., N. Mex....E1 195
Grant, co., N. Dak....C4 198
Grant, co., Okla....A4 200
Grant, co., Oreg....C7 201
Grant, co., S. Dak....B8 204
Grant, co., Wash....B6 210
Grant, co., W. Va....B5 211
Grant, co., Wis....F3 212
Grant, par., La....C3 183
Grant, mtn., Nev....E3 192
Grant, range, Nev....E6 192
Grant City, Mo....A3 189
Grant Park, Ill....B6 178
Grant Town, W. Va....A7, B4 211
Grantham, Eng....B7 56
Grantham, N.H....D2 193
Grantland, coast, N.W. Ter., Can....A22 118
Granton, Ont., Can....D3 153
Granton, Wis....D3 212
Grantown-on-Spey, Scot....C5 57
Grants, N. Mex....B2 195
Grants Lick, Ky....A7 182
Grants Mills, R.I....A11 172
Grants Pass, Oreg....E3 201
Grantsboro, N.C....B7 197
Grantsburg, Ind....H5 179
Grantsburg, Wis....C1 212
Grantsdale, Mont....D2 190
Grantsville, Md....D1 173
Grantsville, Utah....C3 207
Grantsville, W. Va....C3 211
Grantville, Ga....C2 175
Grantville, Kans....B7 181
Grantville, Pa....F8 202
Grantwood, Mo....*C7 189
Granum, Alta., Can....E4 148
Granville, Fr....C3 58
Granville, Ill....B4 178
Granville, Iowa....B2 180
Granville, Mass....B2 185
Granville, N.Y....B7 196
Granville, N. Dak....A5 198
Granville, Ohio....B5 199
Granville, Tenn....C8 205
Granville, Vt....D3 208
Granville, W. Va....A7 211
Granville, co., N.C....A5 197
Granville, lake, Man., Can..A1 150
Granville Centre, N.S., Can....E4 151
Granville Ferry, N.S., Can..E4 151
Grão Mogol, Braz....E2 138
Grapeland, Tex....D5 206
Grapeview, Wash....B3 210
Grapevine, Ky....C2 182
Grapevine, Tex....B5, C4 206
Grapevine, peak, Nev....F4 192
Gras, lake, N.W. Ter., Can....D10 142
Grasmere, Idaho....G3 177
Grasmere, N.H....D3 193
Grasonville, Md....C5 173
Grass, lake, Ill....A5 178
Grass, riv., Man., Can....B3 150
Grass, riv., N.Y....A2 196
Grass Creek, Wyo....B4 213
Grass Lake, Mich....F6 186
Grass River, prov. park, Man., Can....B1 150
Grass Valley, Calif....C3 170
Grass Valley, Oreg....B6 201
Grasscreek, Ind....C5 179
Grasse, Fr....F7 58
Grasselli, Ala....B3, E4 166
Grassflat, Pa....D5 202
Grassington, Eng....F7 57
Grasslake, Ill....D2 178
Grassrange, Mont....C8 190
Grasston, Minn....E5 187
Grassy, brook, Vt....E3 208
Grassy, lake, La....C5 183
Grassy, mtn., Oreg....D9 201
Grassy Butte, N. Dak....B2 198
Grassy Creek, N.C....A2 197
Grassy Lake, Alta., Can....E5 148
Gråsten, Den....D3 62
Grates Cove, Newf., Can..D5 152
Gratiot, Ohio....C5 199
Gratiot, Wis....F3 212
Gratiot, co., Mich....E6 186
Gratis, Ohio....C3 199
Graton, Calif....*C2 170
Gratz, Pa....E8 202
Graubünden, canton, Switz....C5 66
Graulhet, Fr....F5 58
Gravatá, Braz....C3, k6 138
Grave, creek, W. Va....B2 211
Grave, peak, Idaho....C4 177
Gravelbourg, Sask., Can....H2 155
Gravelines, Fr....D10 56
Gravelly, Ark....C2 169
Gravenhurst, Ont., Can....C5 153
Graves, Ga....E2 175
Graves, S.C....E9 203
Graves, co., Ky....B2 182
Graves, is., Mass....D4 185
Gravesend, Eng....C8 56
Gravesend, bay, N.Y....E5 194
Gravesville, Wis....B6 212
Gravette, Ark....A1 169
Gravina [in Puglia], It....D6 67
Gravity, Iowa....D3 180
Gravois Mills, Mo....C5 189
Grawn, Mich....D5 186
Gray, Sask., Can....G3 155
Gray, Fr....D6 58
Gray, Ga....C3 175
Gray, Iowa....C2 180
Gray, Ky....D6 182
Gray, La....C6 183
Gray, Maine....E2, E5 184
Gray, Okla....D3 200
Gray, Pa....F3 202
Gray, co., Kans....E3 181
Gray, co., Tex....B2 206
Gray Court, S.C....B3 203
Gray Horse, Okla....A5 200
Gray Summit, Mo....B7 189
Grayback, mtn., Oreg....E3 201
Grayland, Wash....C1 210
Grayling, Mich....D6 186
Grayling, Mont....F5 190
Graymoor, Ky....*B4 182
Grayridge, Mo....E8 189
Grays, S.C....F5 203
Grays, hbr., Wash....C1 210
Grays, lake, Idaho....F7 177
Grays, peak, Colo....B5 171
Grays Harbor, co., Wash....B2 210
Grays River, Wash....C2 210
Grayslake, Ill....A5, E2 178
Grayson, Ala....A2 166
Grayson, Sask., Can....G4 155
Grayson, Ga....A6, C3 175
Grayson, Ky....B7 182
Grayson, La....B3 183
Grayson, co., Ky....C3 182
Grayson, co., Tex....C4 206
Grayson, co., Va....E1 209
Graysville, Ala....E4 166
Graysville, Ohio....C6 199
Graysville, Pa....G1 202
Graysville, Tenn....D8 205
Grayville, Ill....E5 178
Graz, Aus....E7 60
Great, basin, U.S....C4 158
Great, bay, N.H....D5 193
Great, bay, N.J....D4 194
Great, chan., India....G9 87
Great, isl., Mass....C7 185
Great, isl., N.C....B7 197
Great, lake, Austl....o15 110
Great, pt., Mass....D7 185
Great, pond, Maine....D3 184
Great, pond, Mass....D3 185
Great, pond, N.Y....E9 172
Great, sand sea, Eg....D5 101
Great, val., U.S., B3 194, G6 202, D9 205, D2 209
Great Abaco, isl., Ba. Is....B5 131
Great Alföld, reg., Hung....B5 68
Great Artesian, basin, Austl....D7 110
Great Australian, bight, Austl....F5 110
Great Barrier, isl., N.Z....L15 112
Great Barrier, reef, Austl....C8 110
Great Barrington, Mass....B1 185
Great Basin, boundary, Nev....B4, E7 192
Great Basin, boundary, Oreg....D7, E5, E8 201
Great Basin, reg., Nev....C3, E3 192
Great Bear, lake, N.W. Ter., Can....C8 142
Great Bend, Kans....D5 181
Great Bend, N. Dak....C9 198
Great Bend, Pa....C10 202
Great Bitter, lake, Eg....D4 84
Great Blue, hill, Mass..B5, D2 185
Great Britain: in 1914.... 52
see also England; Scotland
Great Britain & Northern Ireland, see United Kingdom, country, Eur.
Great Burnt, lake, Newf., Can....D3 152
Great Cacapon, W Va....B6 211
Great Captain, isl., Conn..F2 172
Great Combin, mtn., Switz....D3 66
Great Deer, Sask., Can....E2 155
Great Divide, basin, Wyo..D4 213
Great Dividing, range, Austl....C7 110, E8 112
Great Duck, isl., Ont., Can....B2 153
Great East, pond, Maine....E2 184
Great Egg, bay, N.J....E3 194
Great Egg, inlet, N.J....E3 194
Great Egg Harbor, riv., N.J....D3 194
Great Exuma, isl., Ba. Is....D6 131
Great Falls, Man., Can....D3 150
Great Falls, Mont....C5 190
Great Falls, S.C....B6 203
Great Falls, dam, Tenn....D8 205
Great Guana, cay, Ba. Is....C5 131
Great Hog, neck, N.Y....E7 172
Great Inagua, isl., Ba. Is....E7 131
Great Karroo, plat., S. Afr..D3 107
Great Khan, empire of the.... 81
Great Kills, inlet, N.Y....E5 194
Great Lakes, Ill....E2 178
Great Meadows, N.J....B3 194
Great Mecatina, isl., Que., Can....C2 152
Great Mercury, isl., N.Z....L15 112
Great Miquelon, isl., N.A....m26 143
Great Misery, isl., Mass....C4 185
Great Natuna, isl., Indon....E3 90
Great Neck, N.Y....D2 196
Great Neck Estates, N.Y....*D3 196
Great Neck Plaza, N.Y....*D2 196
Great Nicobar, isl., India....G9 87
Great Paternoster, is., Indon....G5 90
Great Peconic, bay, N.Y....F6 172
Great Pond, Maine....D4 184
Great Quittacus, pond, Mass....C6 185
Great Rann of Kutch, salt flat, India....F2 88
Great River, N.Y....G4 172
Great Sacandaga, lake, N.Y....B6 196
Great Salt, lake, Utah....B3 207
Great Salt, pond, R.I....E10 172
Great Salt Lake, des., Utah....C2 207
Great Salt Plains, dam and res., Okla....A3 200
Great Sand, hills, Sask., Can....G1 155
Great Sand Dunes, nat. mon., Colo....D5 171
Great Sandy, des., Austl....D3 110
Great Sandy, see Fraser, isl., Austl.
Great Sea, reef, Fiji.... 114
Great Seneca, creek, Md....B3 173
Great Slave, lake, N.W. Ter., Can....D10 142
Great Smoky, mts., N.C., Tenn....D2 197, D10 205
Great Smoky Mountains, nat. park, N.C., Tenn. D2 197, D10 205
Great South, bay, N.Y....G4 172
Great South, beach, N.Y....G5 172
Great Stone Face (Old Man of the Mountain), mtn., N.H. B3 193
Great Thatch., isl., Vir. Is..f16 132
Great Victoria, des., Austl..E4 110
Great Village, N.S., Can....D6 151
Great Wall, wall, China....D5 91
Great Wass, isl., Maine....D5 184
Great Whale River, Que., Can....A2 154
Great Yarmouth, Eng....B9 56
Great Zab, riv., Iraq....D14 85
Greater Antilles, is., W.I....B3 124
Greater Khingan, ra., Asia....E15 76
Greater Leech Lake, Indian res., Minn....C4 187
Greathouse, peak, Mont....D7 190
Gredos, mts., Sp....B3 65
GREECE, country, Eur....C4 69
in 7th cent. B.C.... 42
c. 450 B.C.... 42
under Alexander.... 43
c. 120 A.D.... 45
under Byzantines.... 47
in 1950.... 83
Greeley, Colo....A6 171
Greeley, Iowa....B6 180
Greeley, Kans....D8 181
Greeley, Nebr....C7 191
Greeley, Pa....D12 202
Greeley, co., Kans....D2 181
Greeley, co., Nebr....C7 191
Greeleyville, S.C....D8 203
Green, Kans....C7 181
Green, Mich....A5 186
Green, co., Ky....C4 182
Green, co., Wis....F4 212
Green, bay, Mich., Wis....D3 186
Green, is., Sol. Is.... 115
Green, lake, B.C., Can....D7 149
Green, lake, Sask., Can....C2 155
Green, lake, Maine....D4 184
Green, lake, Minn....E4 187
Green, lake, Wis....E5 212
Green, mts., Vt....F2 208
Green, mts., Wyo....D5 213
Green, pond, N.J....A4 194
Green, riv., N.B., Can....B1 151
Green, riv., Colo., Utah, Wyo....E5 207, D3 213
Green, riv., Ill....B4 178
Green, riv., Ky....C2 182
Green, riv., Vt....F3 208
Green, riv., Wash....B3 210
Green, swamp, N.C....C5 197
Green, val., Tex....F2 206
Green Bank, N.J....D3 194
Green Bank, W. Va....C5 211
Green Bay, Va....D4 209
Green Bay, Wis....A6, D6 212
Green Brier, Tenn....A5 205
Green Camp, Ohio....B4 199
Green Castle, Mo....A5 189
Green City, Mo....A5 189
Green Court, Alta., Can....B3 148
Green Cove Springs, Fla....C5, C6 174
Green Creek, N.J....E3 194
Green Forest, Ark....A2 169
Green Garden, Mich....B3 186
Green Grass, S. Dak....B4 204
Green Haven, Md....*B2 173
Green Hill, Ala....A2 166
Green Hill, R.I....D10 172
Green Island, Iowa....B7 180
Green Island, N.Y....*C7 196
Green Isle, Minn....F4 187
Green Knob, mtn., W. Va....C5 211
Green Lake, Sask., Can....C2 155
Green Lake, Wis....E5 212
Green Lake, co., Wis....E4 212
Green Lowther, mtn., Scot..E5 57
Green Mountain, Iowa....B5 180
Green Mountain, res., Colo....B4 171
Green Peter, res., Oreg....C4 201
Green Pond, Ala....B2 166
Green Pond, S.C....F6 203
Green Pond, mtn., N.J....B3 194
Green Ridge, Mo....C4 189
Green River, Utah....E5 207
Green River, Vt....F3 208
Green River, Wyo....D3 213
Green River, lock and dam, Ind., Ky....C2 182
Green River, res., Ky....C4 182
Green River, res., Vt....B3 208
Green Rock, Ill....*B3 178
Green Sea, S.C....C10 203
Green Spring, W. Va....B6 211
Green Springs, Ohio....A4 199
Green Sulphur Springs, W. Va....D4 211
Green Tree, Pa....*F1 202
Green Valley, Ill....C4 178
Green Valley, Minn....F3 187
Green Water Lake, park, Sask., Can....E4 155
Greenacres, Wash....B8, D8 210
Greenacres City, Fla....F6 174
Greenback, Tenn....D9 205
Greenbackville, Va....D7 209
Greenbelt, Md....B4 173
Greenbrier, Ala....A3 166
Greenbrier, Ark....B3 169
Greenbrier, co., W. Va....D4 211
Greenbrier, riv., W. Va....D4 211
Greenburr, Pa....D7 202
Greenbush, Maine....C4 184
Greenbush, Mass....D4 185
Greenbush, Mich....D7 186
Greenbush, Minn....B2 187
Greenbush, Wis....B6 212
Greencastle, Ind....E4 179
Greencastle, Pa....G6 202
Greencreek, Idaho....C2 177
Greendale, Ind....F8 179
Greendale, Mo....*C7 189
Greendale, Wis....F2, F5 212
Greendell, N.J....B3 194
Greene, Iowa....B5 180
Greene, Maine....D2 184
Greene, N.Y....C5 196
Greene, R.I....C10 172
Greene, co., Ala....C1 166
Greene, co., Ark....A5 169
Greene, co., Ga....C3 175
Greene, co., Ill....D3 178
Greene, co., Ind....F3 179
Greene, co., Iowa....B3 180
Greene, co., Miss....D5 188
Greene, co., Mo....D4 189
Greene, co., N.Y....C6 196
Greene, co., N.C....B6 197
Greene, co., Ohio....C4 199
Greene, co., Pa....G1 202
Greene, co., Tenn....C11 205
Greene, co., Va....C4 209
Greeneville, Tenn....C11 205
Greenfield, Calif....D3 170
Greenfield, Ill....D3 178
Greenfield, Ind....E6 179
Greenfield, Iowa....C3 180
Greenfield, Maine....C4 184
Greenfield, Mass....A2 185
Greenfield, Minn....*E5 187
Greenfield, Mo....D4 189
Greenfield, N.H....E3 193
Greenfield, N. Mex....D5 195
Greenfield, Ohio....C4 199
Greenfield, Okla....B3 200
Greenfield, S. Dak....E9 204
Greenfield, Tenn....A3 205
Greenfield, Va....D4 209
Greenfield Wis....*F1 212
Greenfield Hill, Conn....E3 172
Greenfield Park, Que., Can....D9 154
Greenhill, Ind....D3 179
Greenhills, Ohio....D2 199
Greenhorn, mtn., Colo....D6 171
Greenland, Ark....B1 169
Greenland, Mich....A6 186
Greenland, N.H....D5 193
GREENLAND, Dan. dep., N.A....B19 118
Greenland, sea, Arc. O....B15 118
Greenlaw, Scot....E6 57
Greenlawn, N.Y....F3 172
Greenleaf, Kans....C7 181
Greenleaf, Wis....A6, D5 212
Greenlee, co., Ariz....D6 168
Greenmount, Md....A4 173
Greenmountain, N.C....C4 197
Greenock, Pa....F2 202
Greenock, Scot....E4 57
Greenough, Mont....D3 190
Greenport, N.Y....E7 172
Greens, peak, Ariz....C6 168
Greens Farms, Conn....E3 172
Greens Fork, Ind....E7 179
Greensboro, Ala....C2 166
Greensboro, Fla....B2 174
Greensboro, Ga....C3 175
Greensboro, Ind....E7 179
Greensboro, Md....C6 173
Greensboro, N.C....A4 197
Greensboro, Pa....G2 202
Greensboro, Vt....B4 208
Greensboro Bend, Vt....B4 208
Greensburg, Ind....F7 179
Greensburg, Kans....E4 181
Greensburg, Ky....C4 182
Greensburg, La....D5 183
Greensburg, Pa....F2 202
Greenspond, Newf., Can....D5 152
Greensville, co., Va....E5 209
Greentop, Mo....A5 189
Greentown, Ind....D6 179
Greenup, Ill....D5 178
Greenup, Ky....B7 182
Greenup, co., Ky....B6 182
Greenvalley, Wis....D5 212
Greenview, Ill....C4 178
Greenview, W. Va....D5 211
Greenville, Ala....D3 166
Greenville, Calif....B3 170
Greenville, Fla....B3 174
Greenville, Ga....C2 175
Greenville, Ill....E4 178
Greenville, Ind....H6 179
Greenville, Iowa....A2 180
Greenville, Ky....C2 182
Greenville, Lib....F3 103
Greenville, Maine....C3 184
Greenville, Mich....E5 186
Greenville, Miss....B2 188
Greenville, Mo....D7 189
Greenville, N.H....E3 193
Greenville, N.Y....C6 196
Greenville, N.C....B6 197
Greenville, Ohio....B3 199
Greenville, Pa....D1 202
Greenville, R.I....B10 172
Greenville, S.C....B3 203
Greenville, Tex....C4 206
Greenville, W. Va....D4 211
Greenville, Wis....A5 212
Greenville, co., S.C....B3 203
Greenville, chan., B.C., Can....C3 149
Greenville Junction, Maine....C3 184
Greenville North, Miss....*B3 188
Greenwald, Minn....E4 187
Greenwater, prov. park, Sask., Can....E4 155
Greenway, Ark....A5 169
Greenway, Man., Can....E2 150
Greenway, S. Dak....B6 204
Greenwich, Conn....E2 172
Greenwich, Eng....m13 55
Greenwich, Kans....B5 181
Greenwich, N.J....E2 194
Greenwich, N.Y....B7 196
Greenwich, Ohio....A5 199
Greenwich, Utah....E4 207
Greenwich, Va....B4 209
Greenwich, isl., Ant....C6 120
Greenwich, pt., Conn....E2 172
Greenwich Hill, N.B., Can. D3 151
Greenwood, Ala....*B3 166
Greenwood, Ark....B1 169
Greenwood, B.C., Can....E8 149
Greenwood, Del....C6 173
Greenwood, Fla....B1 174
Greenwood, Ind....E5, I8 179
Greenwood, Ky....D5 182
Greenwood, La....B2 183
Greenwood, Miss....B3 188
Greenwood, Mo....E2 189
Greenwood, Nebr....D9, E2 191
Greenwood, N.Y....C3 196
Greenwood, S.C....C3 203
Greenwood, S. Dak....E7 204
Greenwood, Wis....D3 212
Greenwood, co., Kans....E7 181
Greenwood, co., S.C....C3 203

INDEX KEY Each place listed in **Bold-faced Type** has its population listed in the Population tables, pages 230 to 280.
Each country, shown in CAPITAL LETTERS, has its population listed in the World Political Information Tables, pages 6 to 10.
* Does not appear on map; key shows general location.

Greenwood, lake, Ind. G3 179
Greenwood, lake, Minn. C7 187
Greenwood, lake, N.J., N.Y. A4 194
Greenwood, lake, S.C. C4 203
Greenwood Lake, N.Y. *D6 196
Greer, Idaho C2 177
Greer, Mo. E6 189
Greer, S.C. B3 203
Greer, co., Okla. C2 200
Greers Ferry, res., Ark. B3 169
Greetsiel, Ger. A7 59
Gregg, co., Tex. C5 206
Gregory, Mich. F6 186
Gregory, N.C. A7 197
Gregory, S. Dak. D6 204
Gregory, Tex. *F4 206
Gregory, co., S. Dak. D6 204
Gregory, lake, Austl. E6 110
Gregory, range, Austl. C7 110
Gregory, riv., Austl. C6 110
Gregory Bald, mtn., Tenn. D10 205
Greifenhagen, see Gryfino, Pol.
Greifswald, Ger. A6 60
Greifswalder, bay, Ger. D7 62
Greig, N.Y. B5 196
Grein, Aus. D7 60
Greiz, Ger. C7 61
Grelton, Ohio A4 199
Grenå, Den. B4 62
Grenada, Calif. B2 170
Grenada, Miss. B4 188
Grenada, co., Miss. B4 188
GRENADA, Br. dep., N.A. p16 131
Grenada, isl., N.A. p16 131
Grenada, res., Miss. B4 188
Grenade [-sur-Garonne], Fr. F4 58
Grenadines, The, is., Grenada-St. Vincent p16 131
Grenay, Fr. D2 59
Grenchen, Switz. B3 66
Grene, N. Dak. A4 198
Grenfell, Sask., Can. G4 155
Grenloch, N.J. D2 194
Grenoble, Fr. E6 58
Grenola, Kans. E7 181
Grenora, N. Dak. B2 198
Grenville, Que., Can. D3 154
Grenville, N. Mex. A6 195
Grenville, S. Dak. B8 204
Grenville, co., Ont., Can. C9 153
Grenville, cape, Austl. B7 110
Grenville, pt., Wash. B1 210
Gresham, Nebr. C8 191
Gresham, Oreg. B4 201
Gresham, S.C. D9 203
Gresham, Wis. D5 212
Gressitt, Va. D6 209
Gretna, Man., Can. E3 150
Gretna, Fla. B2 174
Gretna, La. C7, E5 183
Gretna, Nebr. C9, E2 191
Gretna, Scot. F5 57
Gretna, Va. E3 209
Greven, Ger. A2 61
Grevená, Grc. B3 69
Grevenbroich, Ger. B1 61
Grevesmühlen, Ger. E5 62
Grey, co., Ont., Can. C4 153
Grey, is., Newf., Can. C4 152
Grey, riv., N.Z. O13 112
Grey Eagle, Minn. E4 187
Greybull, Wyo. A4 213
Greybull, riv., Wyo. A4 213
Greycliff, Mont. E7 190
Greylock, mtn., Mass. A1 185
Greymouth, N.Z. O13 112
Greys, riv., Wyo. C2 213
Greystone, Colo. A2 171
Greystone, Conn. C4 172
Greystone, N.C. A5 197
Greytown, N.Z. N15 112
Greytown, S. Afr. C5 107
Gribbell, isl., B.C., Can. C3 149
Gridley, Calif. C3 170
Gridley, Ill. C5 178
Gridley, Kans. D8 181
Griesheim, Ger. D3 61
Grieskirchen, Aus. D6 60
Griffin, Ark. D3 169
Griffin, Sask., Can. H4 155
Griffin, Ga. C2 175
Griffin, Ind. H2 179
Griffing Park, Tex. *E5 206
Griffins, Conn. B6 172
Griffith, Austl. F8 112
Griffith, Ind. A3 179
Griffith, isl., Ont., Can. C4 153
Griffithsville, W. Va. C3 211
Griffithville, Ark. B4 169
Grifton, N.C. B6 197
Griggs, Okla. D2 200
Griggs, co., N. Dak. B7 198
Griggsville, Ill. D3 178
Grigoriopol, Sov. Un. B9 68
Grim, cape, Austl. o14 110
Grimari, Cen. Afr. Rep. D4 104
Grimes, Ala. D4 166
Grimes, Iowa A7, C4 180
Grimes, Okla. B2 200
Grimes, co., Tex. D5 206
Grimesland, N.C. B6 197
Grimma, Ger. B7 61
Grimmen, Ger. D7 62
Grimms Landing, W. Va. C3 211
Grimsby, Ont., Can. D5 153
Grimsby, Eng. A7 56
Grimsey, isl., Ice. m23 63
Grimshaw, Alta., Can. A2 148
Grimstad, Nor. H3 63
Grimsthorpe, Ont., Can. B2 153
Grind Stone City, Mich. D8 186
Grindsted, Den. C2 62
Grindstone, Maine C4 184
Grindstone, isl., Que., Can. B7 151
Grindstone Island, Que., Can. B8 151
Grinem, isl., Eniwetok 114
Grinnell, Iowa C5 180
Grinnell, Kans. C3 181
Griquatown, S. Afr. C3 107
Gris Nez, cape, Fr. D9 56
Griswold, Man., Can. E1 150
Griswold, Iowa C2 180
Griswoldville, Mass. A2 185
Grizzly, Oreg. C6 201
Grizzly, creek, Colo. A4 171
Grizzly, mtn., Idaho B2 177
Grizzly, mtn., Oreg. C6 201
Grizzly, mtn., Wash. A7 210
Grizzly Bear, mtn., N.W. Ter., Can. C8 142
Groais, isl., Newf., Can. C4 152
Grodekovo, Sov. Un. D5 93
Grodków, Pol. C4 70
Grodno, Sov. Un. E4 72
Grodzisk, Pol. B4 70
Grodzisk Mazowiecki, Pol. m13 70
Groenlo, Neth. B6 59
Groesbeck, Tex. D4 206
Groix, isl., Fr. D2 58
Grójec, Pol. C6 70
Grombalia, Tun. F12 64
Gronau, Ger. A2 61
Gronau, Ger. A4 61
Groningen, Neth. A6 59
Groningen, prov., Neth. A6 59
Gronlid, Sask., Can. D3 155
Groom, Tex. B2 206
Groom Creek, Ariz. C3 168
Groot Vloer, lake, S. Afr. C3 107
Groote Eylandt, isl., Austl. B6 110
Grootfontein, S.W. Afr. A2 107
Gros Morne, mtn., Newf., Can. D3 152
Gros Pate, mtn., Newf., Can. C3 152
Gros Ventre, range, Wyo. B2 213
Gros Ventre, riv., Wyo. B2 213
Groscap, Mich. C6 186
Groslay, Fr. g10 58
Gross, Nebr. B7 191
Gross Ottersleben, Ger. A6 61
Grossbreitenbach, Ger. C6 61
Grosse, isl., Que., Can. B8 151
Grosse Pointe, Mich. A8 186
Grosse Pointe Farms, Mich. *A8 186
Grosse Pointe Park, Mich. A8 186
Grosse Pointe Shores, Mich. *F8 186
Grosse Pointe Woods, Mich. A8 186
Grosse Tete, La. D4 183
Grossenhain, Ger. B8 61
Grosser Arber, mtn., Ger. D8 61
Grosser Plön, lake, Ger. D4 62
Grosser Priel, peak, Aus. E7 60
Grosseto, It. C3 67
Grossevichi, Sov. Un. B9 93
Grossgerau, Ger. D3 61
Grossglockner, mtn., Aus. E6 60
Grossostheim, Ger. D4 61
Grossräschen, Ger. B9 61
Grossröhrsdorf, Ger. B9 61
Grosvenor Dale, Conn. B9 172
Groswater, bay, Newf., Can. A3, g10 152
Groton, Conn. D8 172
Groton, Mass. A4, C1 185
Groton, N.H. C3 193
Groton, N.Y. C4 196
Groton, S. Dak. B7 204
Groton, Vt. C4 208
Grottaferrata, It. h9 67
Grottaglie, It. D6 67
Grottoes, Va. C4 209
Grouard, Alta., Can. B2 148
Grouse (Lost River), Idaho F5 177
Grouse, creek, Kans. E7 181
Grouse, creek, Utah B2 207
Grouse Creek, Utah B2 207
Grouse Creek, mtn., Idaho E5 177
Grouse Creek, mts., Utah B2 207
Grovania, Ga. D3 175
Grove, Maine C5 184
Grove, Okla. A7 200
Grove, pt., Md. B5 173
Grove City, Minn. E4 187
Grove City, Ohio C2, C4 199
Grove City, Pa. D1 202
Grove Hill, Ala. D2 166
Groveland, Calif. D3 170
Groveland, Fla. D5 174
Groveland, Ga. D5 175
Groveland, Mass. A5 185
Groveland, N.Y. C3 196
Groveport, Ohio C2, C5 199
Grover, Colo. A6 171
Grover, N.C. B2 197
Grover, Pa. C8 202
Grover, S.C. E6 203
Grover, S. Dak. C8 204
Grover, Wyo. C2 213
Grover City, Calif. *E3 170
Grover Hill, Ohio A3 199
Grovertown, Ind. B4 179
Groves, Tex. E6 206
Grovespring, Mo. D5 189
Groveton, N.H. A3 193
Groveton, Tex. D5 206
Groveton, Va. B5 209
Grovetown, Ga. C4 175
Groveville, N.J. C3 194
Grow, Tex. C2 206
Growler, peak, Ariz. E2 168
Groznyy, Sov. Un. E3 73
Grubbs, Ark. B4 169
Gruber, lake, Ger. D4 62
Grudovo, Bul. D8 68
Grudziądz, Pol. B5 70
Grues, isl., Que., Can. B7 154
Gruetli, Tenn. D8 205
Gruinard, bay, Scot. C3 57
Grulla, Tex. F3 206
Grünberg, Ger. C3 61
Grundy, Va. B3 209
Grundy, co., Ill. B5 178
Grundy, co., Iowa B5 180
Grundy, co., Mo. A4 189
Grundy, co., Tenn. D8 205
Grundy Center, Iowa B5 180
Grundy Lake, prov. park, Ont., Can. B4 153
Grünstadt, Ger. D3 61
Grunthal, Man., Can. E3 150
Gruver, Iowa A3 180
Gruver, Tex. A2 206
Gruz, Yugo. D4 68
Gryazi, Sov. Un. E12 72
Gryazovets, Sov. Un. B13 72
Gryfice, Pol. B3 70
Gryfino, Pol. B3 70
Grygla, Minn. B3 187
Gstaad, Switz. C3 66
Gu Achi, Ariz. E3 168
Gu Komelik, Ariz. E4 168
Gu Vo, Ariz. E3 168
Gu-Win, Ala. *B2 166
Guacanayabo, gulf, Cuba E5 131
Guadalajara, Mex. C4, m12 129
Guadalajara, Sp. B4 65
Guadalcanal, Sp. C3 65
Guadalcanal, isl., Sol. Is. G9 113
Guadalhorce, riv., Sp. D3 65
Guadalimar, riv., Sp. C4 65
Guadalope, riv., Sp. B5 65
Guadalquivir, riv., Sp. D2 65
Guadalupe, Ariz. G2 168
Guadalupe, Calif. E3 170
Guadalupe, Colo. D4 171
Guadalupe, co., N. Mex. C5 195
Guadalupe, co., Tex. E4 206
Guadalupe, isl., Pac. O. E14 113
Guadalupe, mts., N. Mex. E4 195
Guadalupe, mts., Sp. C3 65
Guadalupe, peak, Tex. E2 206
Guadalupe, riv., Tex. B4 206
Guadalupe [Bravos], Mex. A3 129
Guadalupe Mts., nat. park, N. Mex. E2 206
Guadalupita, N. Mex. A4 195
Guadarrama, mts., Sp. B4 65
Guadarrama, riv., Sp. p17 65
GUADELOUPE, Fr. dep., N.A. n16 131
Guadeloupe, passage, N.A. n16 131
Guadiana, riv., Port. D2 65
Guadiana Alto, riv., Sp. C4 65
Guadiana Menor, riv., Sp. D4 65
Guadiela, riv., Sp. B4 65
Guadix, Sp. D4 65
Guafo, isl., Chile C2 136
Guagua, Phil. o13 90
Guainía, riv., Col. C4 133
Guaira, dept., Par. E4 135
Guajará Mirim, Braz. B2 135
Guajataca, lake, P.R. B3 132
Guajataca, riv., P.R. B3 132
Guajira, see LaGuajira, intendencia, Col.
Gualaceo, Ec. B2 134
Gualala, Calif. C2 170
Gualán, Guat. C3 130
Gualaquiza, Ec. B2 134
Gualeguay, Arg. A5 136
Gualeguaychú, Arg. A5 136
GUAM, U.S. dep., Oceania 114
Guamá, riv., Braz. B1 138
Guamaní Central, P.R. D6 132
Guaminí, Arg. B4 136
Guamúchil, Mex. B3 129
Guanabacoa, Cuba D2 131
Guanábana, P.R. C2 132
Guanabara, state, Brazil h6 137
Guanacaste, mts., C.R. E5 130
Guanahacabibes, gulf, Cuba D1 131
Guanajay, Cuba D2 131
Guanajibo, pt., P.R. C2 132
Guanajibo, riv., P.R. C2 132
Guanajuato, Mex. C4, m13 129
Guanajuato, state, Mex. C4, m13 129
Guanambi, Braz. D2 138
Guanare, Ven. B4 133
Guanche, Pan. h11 130
Guandacol, Arg. E2 135
Guane, Cuba D1 131
Guánica, P.R. D3 132
Guánica, mun., P.R. D3 132
Guánica Central, P.R. D3 132
Guánica, lake, P.R. C3 132
Guanillos del Norte, Chile D1 135
Guaniquilla, pt., P.R. C2 132
Guano, isl., Vir. Is. f16 132
Guano, lake, Oreg. E7 201
Guantánamo, Cuba E6 131
Guapí, Col. C2 133
Guaporé, riv., Bol. B3 135
Guaporé, riv., Braz. E2 139
Guaqui, Bol. C2 135
Guará, Braz. F1 138
Guara, mts., Sp. A5 65
Guarabira, Braz. C3, h6 138
Guaraguao, P.R. C2 132
Guaranda, Ec. B2 134
Guarapuava, Braz. D2 137
Guaraqueçaba, Braz. D3 137
Guaratinguetá, Braz. C3 137
Guarda, Port. B2 65
Guardafui, cape, Som. C7 105
Guardian, W. Va. C4 211
Guareña, Sp. C2 65
Guárico, state, Ven. B4 133
Guárico, riv., Ven. B4 133
Guarujá, Braz. n8 137
Guarulhos, Braz. *C3 137
Guasave, Mex. B3 129
Guasdualito, Ven. B3 133
Guasipati, Ven. B5 133
Guastalla, It. E6 66
Guata, Hond. C4 130
GUATEMALA, country, N.A. C2 130
c. 1790 126
in 1821 127
Guatemala City, Guat. C2 130
Guateque, Col. C3 133
Guatimozín, Arg. A4 136
Guaviare, riv., Col. C3 133
Guaxupé, Braz. C3, k8 137
Guayabal, Cuba E5 131
Guayabal, lake, P.R. C4 132
Guayabero, riv., Col. C3 133
Guayama, P.R. D6 132
Guayama, mun., P.R. D6 132
Guayanés, riv., P.R. C7 132
Guayanilla, P.R. C3 132
Guayanilla, mun., P.R. C3 132
Guayaquil, Ec. B2 134
Guayaquil, gulf, Ec. B1 134
Guayas, prov., Ec. B1 134
Guaymallén, Arg. *A3 136
Guaymas, Mex. B2 129
Guaynabo, P.R. B6 132
Guaynabo, mun., P.R. B6 132
Guazacapán, Guat. C2 130
Gubakha, Sov. Un. B5 73
Gubbio, It. C4 67
Gubin, Pol. B9 61
Gúdar, mts., Sp. B5 65
Gudauta, Sov. Un. A13 85
Gudenå, riv., Den. B3 62
Gudhjem, Den. C8 62
Gudiyatham, India *F6 87
Gudur, India F6 87
Guebwiller, Fr. D7 58
Guecho, Sp. A4 65
Guékédou, Guinea E2 103
Guelma, Alg. B6 102
Guelph, Ont., Can. D4 153
Guelph, N. Dak. C7 198
Güemes, Arg. D2 135
Guenette, Que., Can. C2 154
Guercif, Mor. B4 102
Guéret, Fr. D4 58
Guerette, Maine A4 184
Guerneville, Calif. A4 170
Guernica y Luno, Sp. A4 65
Guernsey, Sask., Can. F3 155
Guernsey, Iowa *C5 180
Guernsey, Wyo. C8 213
Guernsey, co., Ohio B6 199
GUERNSEY, Br. dep., Eur. F5 55
Guerra, Tex. F3 206
Guerrara, Alg. C5 102
Guerrero, state, Mex. D4 129
Gueugnon, Fr. D6 58
Gueydan, La. D3 183
Guffey, Colo. C5 171
Gugegwe, isl., Kwajalein 114
Guguan, isl., Mariana Is. 115
Guiana: see also Dutch Guiana, French Guiana, and Guyana
Guiana, British, see Guyana, country, S.A.
Guiana, French, see French Guiana, dep., S.A.
Guiana, Netherlands (Dutch Guiana), see Surinam, Neth. dep., S.A.
Guiana, highlands, S.A. C4 124
Guide Rock, Nebr. D7 191
Guider, Cam. D2 104
Guidonia, It. D4, h9 67
Guiglo, I.C. E3 103
Guihulngan, Phil. C6 90
Guild, N.H. D2 193
Guild, Tenn. D8 205
Guildford, Eng. C7 56
Guildhall, Vt. B5 208
Guilford, Conn. D6 172
Guilford, Ind. F8 179
Guilford, Maine C3 184
Guilford, Mo. A3 189
Guilford, N.Y. C5 196
Guilford, Vt. F3 208
Guilford, co., N.C. A4 197
Guillestre, Fr. E2 66
Guimarães, Braz. B2 138
Guimarães, Port. B1 65
Guin, Ala. B2 166
Guinea, Va. C5 209
GUINEA, country, Afr. D2 103
Guinea, French, see Guinea, country, Afr.
Guinea, Portuguese, see Portuguese Guinea, dep., Afr.
Guinea, gulf, Afr. F6 96
Güines, Cuba D2 131
Guînes, Fr. D1 59
Guingamp, Fr. C2 58
Guinobatan, Phil. *C6 90
Guion, Ark. B4 169
Guir, cape, Mor. C3 102
Güira de Melena, Cuba D2 131
Güiria, Ven. A5 133
Guisborough, Eng. F7 57
Guise, Fr. C5 58
Guists, creek, Ky. B4 182
Guitiriz, Sp. A2 65
Gujan [-Mestras], Fr. E3 58
Gujarat, state, India D5 87
Gujrānwāla, Pak. B5 87, A5 88
Gujrāt, Pak. B5 87
Gukovo, Sov. Un. *G12 72
Gulbarga, India E6 87, I6 88
Guldborg, Den. D5 62
Gulf, N.C. B4 197
Gulf, co., Fla. C1 174
Gulf Coastal, plain, Ark. C4 169
Gulf Crest, Ala. D1 166
Gulf Hammock, Fla. C4 174
Gulf Shores, Ala. E2 166
Gulf Stream, Fla. *F6 174
Gulfport, Fla. E4, F2 174
Gulfport, Ill. C2 178
Gulfport, Miss. E2, E4 188
Gulgong, Austl. F7 112
Gulkana, Alsk. C10, f19 167
Gull, is., N.Y. E8 172
Gull, isl., N.C. B8 197
Gull, lake, Alta., Can. C4 148
Gull, lake, Minn. D4 187
Gull Lake, Sask., Can. G1 155
Gullivan, bay, Fla. G5 174
Gulliver, Mich. C4 186
Güllük, Tur. D6 69
Gully, Minn. C3 187
Gulu, Ug. A5 106
Gulyantsi, Bul. D7 68
Gulyay-Pole, Sov. Un. H11 72
Gum Spring, mtn., Tenn. D8 205
Gumaca, Phil. p14 90
Gumba, Zaire A3 106
Gumboro, Del. D7 173
Gumel, Nig. D6 103
Gummersbach, Ger. B2 61
Gumu, New Britain I. 115
Gümüşane, Tur. B12 85
Gun Barrel, Tex. *C4 206
Guna, Eth. C4 105
Guna, India E6 88
Guna, mtn., Eth. C4 105
Gunahur, Bougainville I. 115
Gundelfingen, Ger. E5 61
Gungu, Zaire C2 106
Gunisao, lake, Man., Can. C3 150
Gunlock, Utah F2 207
Gunn, Miss. C4 188
Gunnar, Sask., Can. A1 155
Gunn City, Mo. *C3 189
Gunnedah, Austl. E8 112
Gunningsville, N.B., Can. *C5 151
Gunnison, Colo. C4 171
Gunnison, Miss. B3 188
Gunnison, Utah D4 207
Gunnison, co., Colo. C3 171
Gunnison, mtn., Colo. C3 171
Gunnworth, Sask., Can. F1 155
Gunpowder, creek, Ky. A6 182
Gunpowder, neck, Md. B5 173
Gunpowder, riv., Md. B5 173
Gunpowder Falls, riv., Md. A4 173
Gunter, Tex. *C4 206
Guntersville, Ala. A3 166
Guntersville, lake, Ala. A3 166
Guntersville, dam, Ala. A3 166
Gunton, Man., Can. D3 150
Guntown, Miss. A5 188
Guntur, India E7 87
Gunung Api, vol., Indon. G7 90
Gunungsitoli, Indon. L2 89
Günz, riv., Ger. A6 66
Günzburg, Ger. E5 61
Gunzenhausen, Ger. D5 61
Gura-Humorului, Rom. B7 68
Gurabo, P.R. B7 132
Gurabo, mun., P.R. B7 132
Gurabo, riv., P.R. B6 132
Gurdaspur, India A5 88
Gurdon, Ark. D2 169
Gurgan, bay, Iran C6 86
Gurgan, riv., Iran C7 86
Gurguan, pt., Tinian 114
Gurgueia, riv., Braz. C2 138
Gurk, riv., Aus. E7 60
Gurla Mandhata, peak, China B8 88
Gurley, Ala. A3 166
Gurley, Nebr. C3 191
Gurleyville, Conn. B8 172
Gurnee, Ill. E2 178
Gurnet, pt., Mass. B6 185
Gurney, Wis. B3 212
Gurupá, Braz. C4 139
Gurupí, cape, Braz. B1 138
Gurupí, mts., Braz. B1 138
Gurupí, riv., Braz. B1 138
Gur'yev, Sov. Un. D4 73
Gus'-Khrustal'nyy, Sov. Un. D13 72
Gusau, Nig. D6 103
Gusev, Sov. Un. A7 70
Gusher, Utah C6 207
Gusinje, Yugo. D4 68
Gustavus, Alsk. D12, k22 167
Güsten, Ger. B6 61
Gustine, Calif. D3 170
Gustine, Tex. D3 206
Güstrow, Ger. B6 60
Gutau, Aus. E9 61
Gütersloh, Ger. B3 61
Guthrie, Ky. D2 182
Guthrie, Minn. C4 187
Guthrie, N. Dak. A5 198
Guthrie, Okla. B4 200
Guthrie, Tex. C2 206
Guthrie, co., Iowa C3 180
Guthrie Center, Iowa C3 180
Guttenberg, Iowa B6 180
Guttenberg, N.J. D5 194
Guy, Ark. B3 169
Guy, Tex. G4 206
GUYANA, country, S.A. A3 139
Guyandotte, mtn., W. Va. D6 211
Guyandotte riv., W. Va. C2 211
Guyenne, former prov., Fr. E4 58
Guyot, mtn., N.C. D3 197
Guyot, mtn., Tenn. D10 205
Guyra, Austl. E8 112
Guys, Tenn. B3 205
Guys Mills, Pa. C2 202
Guysborough, N.S., Can. D8 151
Guysborough, co., N.S., Can. D8 151
Guyton, Ga. D5 175
Guzman, Mex. F2 175
Gvardeysk, Sov. Un. A6 70
Gwaai, Rh. A4 107
Gwabegar, Austl. E7 112
Gwadar, Pak. C3 87
Gwalior, India C6 87, D7 88
Gwanda, Rh. B4 107
Gwane, Zaire A4 106
Gwelo, Rh. A4 107
Gwin, Miss. B3 188
Gwinn, Mich. B3 186
Gwinner, N. Dak. C8 198
Gwinnett, co., Ga. C2 175
Gwydyr, bay, Alsk. A10 167
Gwynn, Va. D6 209
Gwynne, Alta., Can. C4 148
Gwynneville, Ind. E6 179
Gwynns Falls, riv., Md. C2 173
Gyangtse, China C8 87
Gydan, mts., Sov. Un. C18 71
Gympie, Austl. C9 112
Gyöngyös, Hung. B4 68
Győr, Hung. B3 68
Gypsum, Colo. B4 171
Gypsum, Kans. D6 181
Gypsum, Ohio A5 199
Gypsumville, Man., Can. D2 150
Gyula, Hung. B5 68

H

Ha Arava (Wadi el Araba), depression, Isr., Jordan D7 84
Ha Giang, Viet. A6 89
Ha Ha, bay, Que., Can. C2 152
Ha Tien, Viet. G6 89
Ha Tinh, Viet. C6 89
Haag, Ger. A8 66
Haakon, co., S. Dak. C4 204
Haaksbergen, Neth. B6 59
Haamstede, Neth. C3 59
Haapamäki, Fin. F11 63
Haapsalu, Sov. Un. B4 72
Haarlem, Neth. B4 59
Haarlemmermeer, Neth. B4 59
Hab, riv., Pak. I13 86
Habana (Havana), prov., Cuba h11 131
Habermehl, peak, Ant. B13 120
Habersham, Ga. B3 175
Habersham, co., Ga. B3 175
Haboro, Jap. D10 93
Hachiman, Jap. n15 93
Hachinohe, Jap. F10 93
Hachiōji, Jap. I9, n18 93
Hachita, N. Mex. F1 195
Hacienda, Fla. *F6 174
Hack, mtn., Austl. E2 112
Hackberry, Ariz. B2 168
Hackberry, La. E2 183
Hackberry, Tex. E2 206
Hackberry, creek, Kans. C3 181
Hackensack, Minn. D4 187
Hackensack, N.J. B4, D5 194
Hackensack, riv., N.J. D5 194
Hacker Valley, W. Va. C4 211
Hackett, Ark. B1 169
Hackettstown, N.J. B3 194
Hackleburg, Ala. A2 166
Hackney, Eng. k12 55
Haco, isl., Truk 114
Hacoda, Ala. D3 166
Hadar, Nebr. B8 191
Hadarba, cape, Eg., Sud. A4 105
Haddam, Conn. D6 172
Haddam, Kans. C6 181
Haddam Neck, Conn. C6 172
Haddington, Scot. E6 57
Haddock, Ga. C3 175
Haddon Heights, N.J. D2 194
Haddonfield, N.J. D2 194
Hadejia, Nig. D7 103
Hadera, Isr. B6 84
Haderslev, Den. C3 62
Haderslev, co., Den. C3 62
Hadhramaut, reg., Yemen (Aden) C6 105
Hadim, Tur. D9 85
Haditha, Iraq E14 85
Hadleigh, Eng. B8 56
Hadley, Mass. B2 185
Hadley, Minn. F3 187
Hadley, N.Y. B7 196
Hadley, Pa. D1 202
Hadley, bay, N.W. Ter., Can. B11 142
Hadley, lake, Maine D5 184
Hadlock, Wash. A3 210
Hadlyme, Conn. D7 172
Hadsten, Den. B4 62
Hadsund, Den. B4 62
Hadyai (Ban Hat Yai), Thai. I4 89
Haeju, Kor. G2 93
Haena, Haw. A2 176
Hafford, Sask., Can. E2 155

INDEX KEY Each place listed in **Bold-faced Type** has its population listed in the Population tables, pages 230 to 280.
Each country, shown in CAPITAL LETTERS, has its population listed in the World Political Information Table, pages 6 to 10.
* Does not appear on map; key shows general location.

Hafnarfjördur, Ice...n22 63
Haft Gel, Iran...F4 86
Hafun, cape, Som...C7 105
Hagaman, N.Y...*C6 196
Hagan, Ga...D5 175
Hagari, riv., India...F6 87
Hagarville, Ark...B2 169
Hagemeister, isl., Alsk...D7 167
Hagen, Sask., Can...E3 155
Hagen, Ger...B2 61
Hagenow, Ger...E5 62
Hagerman, Idaho...G4 177
Hagerman, N. Mex...D5 195
Hagermans Corners, Ont., Can...E7 153
Hagerstown, Ind...E7 179
Hagerstown, Md...A2 173
Hagersville, Ont., Can...E4 153
Hagg, mtn., Ant...B5 120
Haggin, mtn., Mont...D3 190
Hagginwood, Calif...*C3 170
Hagi, Jap...I5 93
Hague, Sask., Can...E2 155
Hague, The ('s Gravenhage), see The Hague, Neth.
Hague, N.Y...B7 196
Hague, N. Dak...C6 198
Hague, cape, Fr...C3 58
Haguenau, Fr...C7 58
Hagues, peak, Colo...A5 171
Hahira, Ga...F3 175
Hahnville, La...C6 183
Hai Duong, Viet...B7 89
Haicheng, China...D10 92
Haichow, bay, China...G8 92
Haifa, Isr...B6 84
Haig, lake, Alta., Can...A3 148
Haigerloch, Ger...A4 66
Haigler, Nebr...D4 191
Haikou, China...B9 89
Haiku, Haw...C5 176
Hā'il, Sau. Ar...I14 85
Hailar (Hulun), China...B8 91
Haile, La...B3 183
Hailesboro, N.Y...B1 196
Hailey, Idaho...F4 177
Haileybury, Ont., Can...E9 153
Haileyville, Okla...C6 200
Hailun, China...B10 91
Hailung, China...C10 91
Haimen, China...I9 92
Haina, Haw...C6 176
Hainan: after World War II...83
Hainan, isl., China...C8 89
Hainan, strait, China...B9 89
Hainaut, prov., Bel...D3 59
Haines, Alsk...D12, k22 167
Haines, Oreg...C9 201
Haines City, Fla...D5 174
Haines Falls, N.Y...C6 196
Hainesburg, N.J...B2 194
Hainesport, N.J...D3 194
Hainesville, Ill...*A5 178
Hainesville, N.J...A3 194
Hainichen, Ger...C8 61
Haining, China...I9 92
Haiphong, Viet...B7 89
Hairy Hill, Alta., Can...C5 148
HAITI, country, N.A...F7 131
in 1800's...127
Haiya, Sud...B4 105
Haiyang, China...F9 92
Haiyüan, China...F1 92
Hajdúböszörmeny, Hung...B5 68
Hajduhadház, Hung...B5 68
Hajduki Wielkie, Pol...g9 70
Hajdúnánás, Hung...B5 68
Hajduszoboszló, Hung...B5 68
Hajiabad Kavir, salt flats, Iran...E9 86
Hajiki, cape, Jap...G9 93
Hakalau, Haw...D6 176
Hakâri, Tur...D14 85
Hakodate, Jap...F10 93
Haku-San, peak, Jap...m15 93
Ḥalab, see Aleppo, Syr.
Halabja, Iraq...D2 86
Halaib, Eg...E7 101
Halal, mtn., Eg...D5 84
Halaula, Haw...C6 176
Halawa, Haw...B5 176
Halawa, riv , Haw...g10 176
Halawa Heights, Haw...g10 176
Halberstadt, Ger...B6 61
Halbrite, Sask., Can...H4 155
Halbur, Iowa...C3 180
Haldeman, Ky...B6 182
Halden, Nor...H4 63
Haldimand, co., Ont., Can...E5 153
Hale, Colo...B8 171
Hale, Mich...D7 186
Hale, Mo...B4 189
Hale, co., Ala...C2 166
Hale, co., Tex...B2 206
Hale Center, Tex...B2 206
Haleakala, crater, Haw...C5 176
Haleburg, Ala...D4 166
Haledon, N.J...*B4 194
Haleiwa, Haw...B3, f9 176
Hales Corners, Wis...F1 212
Hales Location, N.H...*B4 193
Halesite, N.Y...*D3 196
Halesowen, Eng...B5 56
Halesworth, Eng...B9 56
Halethorpe, Md...B4, C2 173
Haley, N. Dak...D2 198
Haleyville, Ala...A2 166
Haleyville, N.J...E2 194
Half Moon Bay, Calif...B5 170
Half-moon Bay (Oban), N.Z...Q12 112
Half Way, Mo...D4 189
Halfway, Md...A2 173
Halfway, Oreg...C9 201
Halfway, Wyo...C2 213
Halfway, riv., B.C., Can...A6 149
Ḥalḥūl, Jordan...C7 84
Haliburton, Ont., Can...B6 153
Haliburton, co., Ont., Can...B6 153
Halibut, pt., Mass...A6 185
Halicarnassus, see Bodrum, Tur.
Halifax, N.S., Can...E6 151
Halifax, Eng...A6 56
Halifax, Mass...C6 185
Halifax, N.C...A6 197
Halifax, Pa...F8 202
Halifax, Vt...F3 208
Halifax, Va...E4 209
Halifax, co., N.S., Can...E6 151
Halifax, co., N.C...A6 197
Halifax, co., Va...E4 209
Halifax, bay, Austl...C8 110
Haliimaile, Haw...C5 176
Halileh, cape, Iran...G5 86
Halin, Som...D6 105
Haliri, riv., Iran...H9 86
Halisahar, India...*F12 88
Halkirk, Alta., Can...C4 148
Hall, Ind...E4 179
Hall, Mont...D3 190
Hall, N.Y...C3 196
Hall, co., Ga...B3 175
Hall, co., Nebr...D7 191
Hall, co., Tex...B2 206
Hall, mtn., Wash...A8 210
Hall, pen., N.W. Ter., Can...D19 143
Hall Meadow Brook, res., Conn...B4 172
Hall Summit, La...B2 183
Hall Top, mtn., Tenn...D10 205
Halla San, peak, Kor...J3 93
Halladale, riv., Scot...B5 57
Hallam, Nebr...D9 191
Hallam, peak, B.C., Can...C8 149
Halland, co., Swe...B6 62
Hallandale, Fla...E3, G6 174
Hallands Väderö, isl., Swe...B6 62
Hallboro, Man., Can...D2 150
Halle, Bel...D4 59
Halle, Ger...A3 61
Halle, Ger...B6 61
Halleck, Nev...C6 192
Hallein, Aus...E6 60
Hällestad, Swe...u33 63
Hallett, Okla...A5 200
Hallett, cape, Ant...B30 120
Hallettsville, Tex...E4 206
Halley, Ark...D4 169
Halliday, N. Dak...B3 198
Hallock, Minn...B2 187
Hallowell, Kans...E9 181
Hallowell, Maine...D3 184
Halls, Tenn...B2 205
Halls, stream, N.H...A1 193
Hall's Creek, Austl...C4 111
Halls Crossroads, Tenn...E11 205
Halls Harbour, N.S., Can...D5 151
Halls Summit, Kans...D8 181
Hallsberg, Swe...t33 63
Hallsboro, N.C...C5 197
Hallstead, Pa...C10 202
Hallsville, Mo...B5 189
Hallsville, Ohio...C5 199
Hallsville, Tex...C5 206
Hallton, Pa...D4 202
Halltown, Mo...D4 189
Hallville, Conn...C8 172
Hallwil, lake, Switz...B4 66
Hallwood, Va...D7 209
Halma, Minn...B2 187
Halmahera, isl., Indon...E7 90
Halmstad, Swe...B6 62
Hals, Den...B4 62
Halsell, Ala...C1 166
Halsey, Nebr...C5 191
Halsey, N.J...A3 194
Halsey, Oreg...C3 201
Hälsingborg, Swe...B6 62, I5 63
Hälsö, isl., Swe...A5 62
Halstad, Minn...C2 187
Halstead, Eng...C8 56
Halstead, Kans...A5, E6 181
Haltemprice, Eng...D6 55
Haltern, Ger...B2 61
Haltia, mtn., Fin., Nor...C9 63
Haltom City, Tex...*C4 206
Halton, co., Ont., Can...D5 153
Haltwhistle, Eng...F6 57
Ham, Fr...E3 59
Ham-Nord, Que., Can...D6 154
Ham-Sud, Que., Can...D6 154
Hama (Hamāh), Syr...E11 85
Hamada, Jap...I6 93
Hamadān, Iran...D4 86
Hamāh, see Hama, Syr.
Hamahika, isl., Okinawa...114
Hamakuapoko, Haw...C5 176
Hamamatsu, Jap...I8, o16 93
Hamar, N. Dak...B7 198
Hamar, Nor...G4 63
Hamatombetsu, Jap...D11 93
Hambantota, Cey...G7 87
Hamber, prov. park, B.C., Can...C8 149
Hamberg, N. Dak...B6 198
Hamblen, co., Tenn...C10 205
Hambleton, W. Va...*B5 211
Hamburg, Ark...D4 169
Hamburg, Conn...D7 172
Hamburg, Ger...B5 60, E4 62
Hamburg, Ill...D3 178
Hamburg, Iowa...D2 180
Hamburg, Minn...*F5 187
Hamburg, Miss...D2 188
Hamburg, N.J...A3 194
Hamburg, N.Y...C2 196
Hamburg, Pa...E10 202
Hamburg, S.C...E4 203
Hamburg, Tenn...B3 205
Hamburg, Wis...C4 212
Hamburg, state, Ger...E3 62
Hamburg, mts., N.J...A3 194
Hamden, Conn...D5 172
Hamden, N.Y...C6 196
Hamden, Ohio...C5 199
Hämeenlinna, Fin...G11 63
Hamel, Ill...A9 189
Hamelin, isl., Loyalty Is...115
Hameln, Ger...A4 61
Hamer, Idaho...F6 177
Hamer, S.C...C9 203
Hamersley, plat., Austl...D2 110
Hamersville, Ohio...D4 199
Hamhŭng, Kor...G3 93
Hami (Kumul), China...C3 91
Hamill, S. Dak...D6 204
Hamilton, Ala...A2 166
Hamilton, Alsk...C7 167
Hamilton, Austl...H4 112
Hamilton, Ont., Can...D5 153
Hamilton, Colo...A3 171
Hamilton, Ga...D2 175
Hamilton, Ill...C2 178
Hamilton, Ind...A8 179
Hamilton, Iowa...C5 180
Hamilton, Kans...E7 181
Hamilton, Ky...A6 182
Hamilton, Mass...A6, C4 185
Hamilton, Mich...F4 186
Hamilton, Miss...B5 188
Hamilton, Mo...B4 189
Hamilton, Mont...D2 190
Hamilton, N.Y...C5 196
Hamilton, N.Z...L15 112
Hamilton, N.C...B6 197
Hamilton, N. Dak...A8 198
Hamilton, Ohio...C2, C3 199
Hamilton, Oreg...C7 201
Hamilton, R.I...C11 172
Hamilton, Scot...E4 57
Hamilton, Tex...D3 206
Hamilton, Va...B5 209
Hamilton, Wash...A4 210
Hamilton, co., Fla...B3 174
Hamilton, co., Ill...E5 178
Hamilton, co., Ind...D5 179
Hamilton, co., Iowa...B4 180
Hamilton, co., Kans...E2 181
Hamilton, co., Nebr...D7 191
Hamilton, co., N.Y...B6 196
Hamilton, co., Ohio...C3 199
Hamilton, co., Tenn...D8 205
Hamilton, co., Tex...D3 206
Hamilton, inlet, Newf., Can...A2 152
Hamilton, lake, Ark...C2 169
Hamilton, mtn., Alsk...C8 167
Hamilton, mtn., Nev...D6 192
Hamilton, mtn., N.Y...B6 196
Hamilton, res., Mass...B3 185
Hamilton, sound, Newf., Can...D4 152
Hamilton City, Calif...C2 170
Hamilton Dome, Wyo...B4 213
Hamilton Square (Hamilton Township), N.J...C3 194
Hamina, Fin...G12 63
Hamiota, Man., Can...D1 150
Hamirpur, India...C7 87
Hamirpur, India...B6 88
Hamler, Ohio...A3 199
Hamlet, Ind...B4 179
Hamlet, Nebr...D4 191
Hamlet, N.C...C4 197
Hamlet, N. Dak...A2 198
Hamlet, mtn., Alsk...B6 167
Hamletsburg, Ill...F5 178
Hamlin, Iowa...C3 180
Hamlin, Kans...C8 181
Hamlin, Pa...D11 202
Hamlin, Tex...C2 206
Hamlin, W. Va...C2 211
Hamlin, co., S. Dak...C8 204
Hamlin, lake, Mich...D4 186
Hamm [in Westfalen], Ger...B2 61
Hammamet, gulf, Tun...F12 64
Hammar, Iraq...F3 86
Hammarby, Swe...t35 63
Hammarsjön, lake, Swe...C8 62
Hamme, Bel...C4 59
Hammel, Den...B3 62
Hammelburg, Ger...C4 61
Hammer, S. Dak...B8 204
Hammerfest, Nor...B10 63
Hammersley Fork, Pa...D6 202
Hammersmith, Eng...m12 55
Hammett, Idaho...G3 177
Hammon, Okla...B2 200
Hammonasset, pt., Conn...E6 172
Hammonasset, riv., Conn...D6 172
Hammond, Ill...D5 178
Hammond, Ind...A2 179
Hammond, La...A6, D5 183
Hammond, Minn...F6 187
Hammond, Mont...E12 190
Hammond, N.Y...B1 196
Hammond, Oreg...A3 201
Hammond, Wis...D1 212
Hammond, bay, Mich...C6 186
Hammond East, La...*A6 183
Hammondsport, N.Y...C3 196
Hammondsville, Ohio...A1 211
Hammondville, Ala...*A4 166
Hammonton, N.J...D3 194
Hamneda, Swe...B7 62
Hamoyet, mtn., Eth...B4 105
Hampden, Newf., Can...D3 152
Hampden, Maine...*D4 184
Hampden, Mass...B3 185
Hampden, N.Z...P13 112
Hampden, N. Dak...A7 198
Hampden, co., Mass...B2 185
Hampden Highlands, Maine...D4 184
Hampshire, Ill...A5 178
Hampshire, Tenn...B4 205
Hampshire (Southampton), co., Eng...C6 56
Hampshire, co., Mass...B4 185
Hampshire, co., W. Va...B6 211
Hampstead, N.B., Can...D3 151
Hampstead, Que., Can...*D8 154
Hampstead, Md...A4 173
Hampstead, N.H...E4 193
Hampstead, N.C...C6 197
Hampton, Ark...D3 169
Hampton, N.B., Can...D4 151
Hampton, Conn...B8 172
Hampton, Fla...C4 174
Hampton, Ga...C2 175
Hampton, Ill...D7 180
Hampton, Iowa...B4 180
Hampton, Ky...A3 182
Hampton, Minn...F5 187
Hampton, Nebr...D8 191
Hampton, N.H...E5 193
Hampton, N.J...B3 194
Hampton, N.Y...B7 196
Hampton, Oreg...D6 201
Hampton, S.C...F5 203
Hampton, Tenn...C11 205
Hampton (Independent City), Va...B6, D6 209
Hampton, Wyo...D2 213
Hampton, co., S.C...F5 203
Hampton, butte, Oreg...D6 201
Hampton Bays, N.Y...D4 196
Hampton Beach, N.H...E5 193
Hampton Falls, N.H...E5 193
Hampton Roads, hbr., Va...B6 209
Hampton Roads, bay and tunnel, Va...B7 209
Hampton Springs, Fla...B3 174
Ḥamrā, plat., Libya...D2 101
Hamrarne, strait, Swe...C8 62
Hams, bluff, Vir. Is...h17 132
Hams, fork, Wyo...D2 213
Hamtramck, Mich...A8 186
Hamun-i-Murgho, lake, Pak...H12 86
Hamyang, Kor...I3 93
Han, riv., China...E7 91
Hana, Haw...C6 176
Hanahan, S.C...F2, F7 203
Hanalei, Haw...A2 176
Hanalei, bay, Haw...A2 176
Hanamaki, Jap...*G10 93
Hanamaulu, Haw...B2 176
Hanapepe, Haw...B2 176
Hanau [am Main], Ger...C3 61
Hanceville, Ala...A3 166
Hanceville, B.C., Can...D6 149
Hanchung, China...H2 92
Hancock, Conn...C4 172
Hancock, Iowa...C2 180
Hancock, Maine...D4 184
Hancock, Md...A1 173
Hancock, Mass...A1 185
Hancock, Mich...A2 186
Hancock, Minn...E3 187
Hancock, N.H...E3 193
Hancock, N.Y...D5 196
Hancock, Vt...D3 208
Hancock, W. Va...B6 211
Hancock, Wis...D4 212
Hancock, co., Ga...C3 175
Hancock, co., Ill...C2 178
Hancock, co., Ind...E6 179
Hancock, co., Iowa...A4 180
Hancock, co., Ky...C3 182
Hancock, co., Maine...D4 184
Hancock, co., Miss...E4 188
Hancock, co., Ohio...A4 199
Hancock, co., Tenn...C10 205
Hancock, co., W. Va...A4 211
Hancock, lake, Fla...E5 174
Hancock, pond, Maine...E2 184
Hancocks Bridge, N.J...D2 194
Hand, co., S. Dak...C6 204
Handa, Jap...o15 93
Handa, isl., Scot...B3 57
Handel, Sask., Can...E1 155
Handeni, Tan...C6 106
Handley, W. Va...C6 211
Handsboro, Miss...E2, E4 188
Handsworth, Sask., Can...H4 155
Haney, B.C., Can...A10, E6 149
Hanford, Calif...D4 170
Hanford, N.J...A3 194
Hanford Northwest, Calif...*D4 170
Hangchow, China...E9 91
Hangchow, bay, China...I9 92
Hangelsberg, Ger...A8 61
Hanging Rock, Ohio...D5 199
Hangingstone, riv., Alta., Can...A5 148
Hangö, Fin...H10 63
Hanita, Isr...A7 84
Hankinson, N. Dak...C9 198
Hanks, N. Dak...A2 198
Hanksville, Utah...E5 207
Hanley, Sask., Can...F2 155
Hanley Falls, Minn...F3 187
Hanley Hills, Mo...*A8 189
Hanlontown, Iowa...A4 180
Hann, mtn., Austl...C4 110
Hanna, Alta., Can...D5 148
Hanna, Ind...B4 179
Hanna, Okla...B6 200
Hanna, Utah...C5 207
Hanna, Wyo...D6 213
Hanna City, Ill...C4 178
Hannaford, N. Dak...B7 198
Hannah, N. Dak...A7 198
Hannawa Falls, N.Y...B2 196
Hannibal, Mo...B6 189
Hannibal, N.Y...B4 196
Hannibal, Ohio...C7 199
Hannon, Ala...C4 166
Hannover, Ger...A4 61
Hannover, N. Dak...B4 198
Hannoversch Münden, see Münden, Ger.
Hanöbukten, bay, Swe...J6 63
Hanoi, Viet...B6 89
Hanover: in 1721...49
in 1815...50
in 1866...51
Hanover, Ark...B3 169
Hanover, Ont., Can...C3 153
Hanover, Conn...C8 172
Hanover, Ill...A3 178
Hanover, Ind...G7 179
Hanover, Kans...C7 181
Hanover, Maine...D2 184
Hanover, Mass...B6, E4 185
Hanover, Mich...F6 186
Hanover, Minn...*E5 187
Hanover, Mont...C7 190
Hanover, N.H...C2 193
Hanover, N. Mex...E1 195
Hanover, Ohio...B5 199
Hanover, Pa...G8 202
Hanover, Va...D5 209
Hanover, W. Va...D3 211
Hanover, co., Va...D5 209
Hanover, reg., Ger...B4 60
Hanover, isl., Chile...E2 136
Hanover Park, Ill...*B6 178
Hanoverton, Ohio...B7 199
Hans Lollik, is., Vir. Is...f15 132
Hansboro, N. Dak...A6 198
Hansell, Iowa...B4 180
Hansen, Idaho...G4 177
Hansford, co., Tex...A2 206
Hanska, Minn...F4 187
Hanson, Fla...B3 174
Hanson, Ky...C2 182
Hanson, Mass...B6 185
Hanson, co., S. Dak...D8 204
Hanson, lake, Sask., Can...C4 155
Hansted, see Hanstholm Havn, Den.
Hanstholm Havn (Hansted), Den...A2 62
Hanston, Kans...D4 181
Hantachi, China...A3 93
Hantan, China...F6 92
Hants, co., N.S., Can...D6 151
Hant's Harbour, Newf., Can...D5 152
Hantsport, N.S., Can...D5 151
Haofeng, China...J3 92
Haokang, China...B11 91, C5 93
Haoli, China...B10 91
Hap Hawkins, lake, Mont...F4 190
Haparanda, Swe...E10 63
Hape, New Britain I...115
Hapeville, Ga...B5, C2 175
Happy, Tex...B2 206
Happy Camp, Calif...B2 170
Happy Jack, Ariz...C4 168
Happy Valley, Newf., Can...B1, h9 152
Happy Valley, N. Mex...E5 195
Hapsu, Kor...F4 93
Hapur, India...*C6 87
Ḥaql, Sau. Ar...H10 85
Hague, Fla...C4 174
Hara Usa, lake, Mong...B3 91
Harahan, La...C7 183
Harald, isl., Sov. Un...B32 118
Haralson, Pa...*C2 175
Haralson, co., Ga...C1 175
Hārar, Eth...D5 105
Harardera, Som...E6 105
Hārargē, reg., Eth...D5 105
Harazé, Chad...D4 104
Harbeson, Del...C7 173
Harbin, China...B10 91, D3 93
Harbinger, N.C...A8 197
Harboöre, Den...B2 62
Harbor, Oreg...E2 201
Harbor Beach, Mich...E8 186
Harbor Springs, Mich...C5 186
Harbor View, Ohio...A2 199
Harborcreek, Pa...B2 202
Harborton, Va...D7 209
Harbour Breton, Newf., Can...E4 152
Harbour Buffet, Newf., Can...E4 152
Harbour Deep, Newf., Can...C3 152
Harbour Grace, Newf., Can...E5 152
Harbour Main, Newf., Can...E5 152
Harbour Mille, Newf., Can...E4 152
Harbourton, N.J...C3 194
Harbourville, N.S., Can...D5 151
Harbuck, Tenn...D9 205
Harburg, Ger...E3 62
Harby, Den...C4 62
Harcourt, N.B., Can...C4 151
Harcourt, Iowa...B3 180
Harcuvar, mts., Ariz...D2 168
Harda, India...F6 88
Hardangerfjord, fjord, Nor...H1 63
Hardangerjökelen, mtn., Nor...G2 63
Hardangervidda, mts., Nor...G2 63
Hardaway, Ala...C4 166
Hardee, co., Fla...E5 174
Hardeeville, S.C...G5 203
Hardeman, co., Tenn...B3 205
Hardeman, co., Tex...B3 206
Harden City, Okla...C5 200
Hardenberg, Neth...B6 59
Harderwijk, Neth...B5 59
Hardesty, Okla...D3 200
Hardin, Ill...D3 178
Hardin, Ky...B3 182
Hardin, Mo...B4 189
Hardin, Mont...E9 190
Hardin, co., Ill...F5 178
Hardin, co., Iowa...B4 180
Hardin, co., Ky...C4 182
Hardin, co., Ohio...B4 199
Hardin, co., Tenn...B3 205
Hardin, co., Tex...D5 206
Harding, Mass...B5, D2 185
Harding, Minn...*E4 187
Harding, S. Dak...B2 204
Harding, W. Va...C5 211
Harding, co., N. Mex...B5 195
Harding, co., S. Dak...B2 204
Harding, lake, Ala., Ga...C4 166
Hardinsburg, Ind...H5 179
Hardinsburg, Ky...C3 182
Hardisty, Alta., Can...C5 148
Hardisty, lake, N.W. Ter., Can...D9 142
Hardman, Oreg...B7 201
Hardoi, India...D8 88
Hardtner, Kans...E5 181
Hardwar, India...C7 88
Hardwick, Ga...C3 175
Hardwick, Mass...B3 185
Hardwick, Minn...G2 187
Hardwick, Vt...B4 208
Hardwicke, N.B., Can...B4 151
Hardwood Ridge, mtn., Pa...D11 202
Hardy, Alg...B5 102
Hardy, Ark...A4 169
Hardy, Sask., Can...H3 155
Hardy, Iowa...*B4 180
Hardy, Miss...B4 188
Hardy, Mont...C5 190
Hardy, Nebr...D8 191
Hardy, Okla...A5 200
Hardy, co., W. Va...B6 211
Hare, bay, Newf., Can...C4 152
Hare, hill, Newf., Can...E4 152
Hare Bay, Newf., Can...D4 152
Harelson, La...B5 183
Harfleur, Fr...C4 58
Harford, Pa...C10 202
Harford, co., Md...A5 173
Hargeisa, Som...D5 105
Harghitei, mts., Rom...B7 68
Hargill, Tex...F3 206
Hargrave, Man., Can...E1 150
Hargrave, lake, Man., Can...B2 150
Hargrave, riv., Man., Can...B2 150
Hari, riv., Afg...D10 86
Harihar, India...F6 87
Haringey, Eng...k12 55
Harkers Island, N.C...C7 197
Harkus, isl., Sau. Ar...H4 86
Harlan, Ind...B8 179
Harlan, Iowa...C2 180
Harlan, Kans...C5 181
Harlan, Ky...D6 182
Harlan, co., Ky...D6 182
Harlan, co., Nebr...D6 191
Harlan, res., Nebr...D6 191
Hârlău, Rom...B8 68
Harlech, Wales...B3 56
Harlem, Fla...*F6 174
Harlem, Ga...C4 175
Harlem, Mont...B8 190
Harlem, riv., N.Y...D5 194
Harleton, Tex...C5 206
Harleyville, S.C...E7 203
Harlingen, Neth...A5 59
Harlingen, Tex...F4 206
Harlow, Eng...C8 56
Harlow, N. Dak...A6 198
Harlowton, Mont...D7 190
Härlunda, Swe...B8 62
Harman, W. Va...C5 211
Harmancik, Tur...C7 85
Harmans, Md...B4 173
Harmarville, Pa...A6 202
Harmon, Ill...B4 178
Harmon, La...B2 183
Harmon, Okla...A2 200
Harmon, co., Okla...C2 200
Harmon, creek, W. Va...A2 211
Harmonsburg, Pa...C1 202
Harmony, Ind...E3 179
Harmony, Maine...D3 184
Harmony, Minn...G6 187
Harmony, N.J...B2 194
Harmony, N.C...B3 197
Harmony, Pa...E1 202
Harmony, R.I...B10 172
Harmony, Va...E4 209
Harmonyville, Vt...E3 208
Harms, Tenn...B5 205
Harned, Ky...C3 182
Harnett, co., N.C...B5 197
Harney, Md...A3 173
Harney, co., Oreg...D7 201
Harney, lake, Fla...D6 174
Harney, lake, Oreg...D7 201
Harney, peak, S. Dak...D2 204
Harney, val., Oreg...D8 201
Härnösand, Swe...F8 63
Haro, Sp...A4 65
Haro, cape, Mex...B2 129
Haro, strait B.C., Can...B9 149
Harold, Fla...G2 174
Harper, Iowa...C5 180
Harper, Kans...E5 181
Harper, Lib...F3 103
Harper, Oreg...D9 201
Harper, Tex...D3 206
Harper, Wash...D1 210
Harper, co., Kans...E5 181
Harper, co., Okla...A2 200
Harper, lake, Que., Can...A4 154
Harper, mtn., Alsk...C11 167
Harper Woods, Mich...*F8 186
Harpers Ferry, Iowa...A6 180
Harpers Ferry, W. Va...B7 211
Harpersville, Ala...B3 166

INDEX KEY Each place listed in **Bold-faced Type** has its population listed in the Population tables, pages 230 to 280.
Each country, shown in CAPITAL LETTERS, has its population listed in the World Political Information Table, pages 6 to 10.
* Does not appear on map; key shows general location.

Harperville, Miss.....C4 188
Harpeth, riv., Tenn.....A5 205
Harpster, Ohio.....B4 199
Harptree, Sask., Can.....H3 155
Harquahala, mtn., Ariz.....D2 168
Harquahala, mts., Ariz.....D2 168
Harrah, Okla.....B4 200
Harrah, Wash.....C5 210
Harray, lake, Scot.....A5 57
Harrell, Ark.....D3 169
Harrells, N.C.....*C5 197
Harrellsville, N.C.....*A7 197
Harricanaw, riv., Que., Can.....B2 154
Harrietta, Mich.....D5 186
Harriettsville, Ohio.....C6 199
Harriman, N.Y.....*D6 196
Harriman, Tenn.....D9 205
Harrington, Del.....C6 173
Harrington, Maine.....D5 184
Harrington, S. Dak.....D4 204
Harrington, Wash.....B7 210
Harrington, lake, Maine.....C3 184
Harrington Harbour, Que., Can.....F21 145
Harrington Park, N.J.....C5 194
Harriott, lake, Sask., Can.....A4 155
Harris, Sask., Can.....F2 155
Harris, Iowa.....A2 180
Harris, Kans.....D8 181
Harris, Minn.....E6 187
Harris, Mo.....A4 189
Harris, Okla.....D7 200
Harris, Scot.....D2 57
Harris, Tenn.....A3 205
Harris, co., Ga.....D2 175
Harris, co., Tex.....E5 206
Harris, hill, Mass.....A3 185
Harris, lake, Fla.....D5 174
Harris, sound, Scot.....C1 57
Harris Grove, Va.....A6 209
Harris Hill, N.Y.....*C2 196
Harrisburg, Ark.....B5 169
Harrisburg, Ill.....F5 178
Harrisburg, Mo.....B5 189
Harrisburg, Nebr.....C2 191
Harrisburg, Ohio.....C2 199
Harrisburg, Oreg.....C3 201
Harrisburg, Pa.....F8 202
Harrisburg, S. Dak.....D9 204
Harrismith, S. Afr.....C4 107
Harrison, Ark.....A2 169
Harrison, Ga.....D4 175
Harrison, Idaho.....B2 177
Harrison, Maine.....D2 184
Harrison, Mich.....D6 186
Harrison, Mont.....E5 190
Harrison, Nebr.....B2 191
Harrison, N.J.....D5 194
Harrison, N.Y.....D2 196
Harrison, Ohio.....C3 199
Harrison [Township], Pa.....A7 202
Harrison, S. Dak.....D7 204
Harrison, Tenn.....E10 205
Harrison, co., Ind.....H5 179
Harrison, co., Iowa.....C2 180
Harrison, co., Ky.....B5 182
Harrison, co., Miss.....E4 188
Harrison, co., Mo.....A3 189
Harrison, co., Ohio.....B6 199
Harrison, co., Tex.....C5 206
Harrison, co., W. Va.....B4 211
Harrison, bay, Alsk.....A9 167
Harrison, cape, Newf., Can.....g10 152
Harrison, lake, B.C., Can.....E7 149
Harrison Hot Springs, B.C., Can.....A11 149
Harrison [Township] (Natrona Heights), Pa.....A7, E2 202
Harrison Valley, Pa.....C6 202
Harrisonburg, La.....C4 183
Harrisonburg (Independent City), Va.....C4 209
Harrisonville, Ill.....E3 178
Harrisonville, Md.....B4 173
Harrisonville, Mo.....C3 189
Harrisonville, N.J.....D2 194
Harrisonville, Pa.....G5 202
Harriston, Ont., Can.....D4 153
Harriston, Miss.....D2 188
Harrisville, Mich.....D7 186
Harrisville, Miss.....D3 188
Harrisville, N.H.....E2 193
Harrisville, N.Y.....A5 196
Harrisville, Ohio.....B1 211
Harrisville, Pa.....D1 202
Harrisville, R.I.....B10 172
Harrisville, Utah.....B3 207
Harrisville, W. Va.....B3 211
Harrod, Ohio.....B4 199
Harrods, creek, Ky.....A4 182
Harrodsburg, Ind.....F4 179
Harrodsburg, Ky.....C5 182
Harrogate, Eng.....C6 55
Harrold, S. Dak.....C6 204
Harrop, lake, Man., Can.....C4 150
Harrow, Ont., Can.....E2 153
Harrow, Eng.....k12 55
Harrowby, Man., Can.....D1 150
Harrowsmith, Ont., Can.....C8 153
Harrys, riv., Newf., Can.....D2 152
Harşova, Rom.....C8 68
Harstad, Nor.....C7 63
Hart, Sask., Can.....H3 155
Hart, Mich.....E4 186
Hart, Tex.....B1 206
Hart, co., Ga.....B4 175
Hart, co., Ky.....C4 182
Hart, isl., Md.....B5 173
Hart, isl., N.Y.....B5 194
Hart, lake, Fla.....D5 174
Hart, lake, Oreg.....E7 201
Hart, mtn., Man., Can.....C1 150
Hartell, Alta., Can.....D3 148
Hartfield, Va.....C6 209
Hartford, Ala.....D4 166
Hartford, Ark.....B1 169
Hartford, Conn.....B6 172
Hartford, Ill.....E3 178
Hartford, Iowa.....B7, C4 180
Hartford, Kans.....D8 181
Hartford, Ky.....C3 182
Hartford, Maine.....D2 184
Hartford, Mich.....F4 186
Hartford, N.J.....D3 194
Hartford, N.Y.....B7 196
Hartford, S. Dak.....D9 204
Hartford, Tenn.....D10 205
Hartford, Vt.....D4 208
Hartford, W. Va.....C3 211
Hartford, Wis.....E1, E5 212
Hartford, co., Conn.....B5 172
Hartford City, Ind.....D7 179
Hartha, Ger.....B7 61
Hartington, Nebr.....B8 191
Hartland, N.B., Can.....C2 151
Hartland, Maine.....D3 184
Hartland, Mich.....F7 186
Hartland, Minn.....G5 187
Hartland, N. Dak.....A4 198
Hartland, Vt.....D4 208
Hartland, Wis.....E1, E5 212
Hartland, pt., Eng.....C3 56
Hartland Four Corners, Vt.....D4 208
Hartlepool, Eng.....C6 55
Hartleton, Pa.....*E7 202
Hartley, Iowa.....A2 180
Hartley, Rh.....A5 107
Hartley, Tex.....B1 206
Hartley, co., Tex.....B1 206
Hartline, Wash.....B6 210
Hartly, Del.....B6 173
Hartman, Ark.....B2 169
Hartman, Colo.....C8 171
Hartney, Man., Can.....E1 150
Harts, pond, N.H.....C2 193
Hartsburg, Ill.....C4 178
Hartsburg, Mo.....C5 189
Hartsel, Colo.....B5 171
Hartselle, Ala.....A3 166
Hartsfield, Ga.....E3 175
Hartshorn, Mo.....D6 189
Hartshorne, Okla.....C6 200
Hartsville, Ind.....F6 179
Hartsville, S.C.....C7 203
Hartsville, Tenn.....A5 205
Hartuv, Isr.....h11 84
Hartville, Ohio.....B6 199
Hartville, Mo.....D5 189
Hartville, Wyo.....C8 213
Hartwell, Ga.....B4 175
Hartwell, res., Ga., S.C.....B3 175, C1 203
Hartwick, Iowa.....C5 180
Hartwick, N.Y.....C5 196
Harut, riv., Afg.....E10 86
Harvard, Ill.....A5 178
Harvard, Iowa.....D4 180
Harvard, Mass.....A4, C1 185
Harvard, Nebr.....D7 191
Harvard, mtn., Colo.....C4 171
Harvel, Ill.....D4 178
Harvest, Ala.....A3 166
Harvester, Ill.....*B6 178
Harvey, N.B., Can.....D5 151
Harvey, Ill.....B6, F3 178
Harvey, Iowa.....C5 180
Harvey, La.....C7, E5 183
Harvey, Mich.....B3 186
Harvey, N. Dak.....B6 198
Harvey, co., Kans.....D6 181
Harvey, creek, Pa.....B7 202
Harvey, lake, Pa.....A7 202
Harvey, mtn., Mass., N.Y.....B1 185
Harvey Cedars, N.J.....*D4 194
Harvey Station, N.B., Can.....D3 151
Harveysburg, Ohio.....C3 199
Harveyville, Kans.....D8 181
Harviell, Mo.....E7 189
Harwich, Eng.....C9 56
Harwich, Mass.....C7 185
Harwich Port, Mass.....C7 185
Harwinton, Conn.....B4 172
Harwood, Ont., Can.....C6 153
Harwood, Md.....C4 173
Harwood, Mo.....D3 189
Harwood, N. Dak.....C9 198
Harwood, Tex.....*E4 202
Harwood Heights, Ill.....*B6 178
Harz, mts., Ger.....B5 61
Harzgerode, Ger.....B6 61
Ḩasā, Jordan.....D7 84
Ḩasan Kīādeh, Iran.....C4 86
Hasbrouck Heights, N.J.....D5 194
Hasdo, riv., India.....F9 88
Hase, riv., Ger.....B3 60
Haselünne, Ger.....B3 60
Hashimoto, Jap.....o14 93
Hasi Zegdou, Alg.....D4 164
Haskell, Ark.....C3 169
Haskell, Okla.....B6 200
Haskell, Tex.....C3 206
Haskell, co., Kans.....E3 181
Haskell, co., Okla.....B6 200
Haskell, co., Tex.....C3 206
Haskins, Ohio.....A2, A4 199
Haslach, Aus.....E9 61
Hasle, Den.....C8 62
Haslemere, Eng.....C7 56
Haslet, Tex.....B5 206
Haslev, Den.....C6 62
Hassan, India.....F6 87
Hassayampa, Ariz.....D3 168
Hassayampa, creek, Ariz.....D3 168
Hassayampa, riv., Ariz.....F1 168
Hassell, N.C.....B6 197
Hasselt, Bel.....D5 59
Hasselt, Neth.....B6 59
Hassfurt, Ger.....C5 61
Hassleben, Ger.....E7 62
Hässleholm, Swe.....I5 63
Hassloch, Ger.....D3 61
Hastings, Ont., Can.....C7 153
Hastings, Eng.....D8 56
Hastings, Fla.....C5 174
Hastings, Iowa.....C2 180
Hastings, Mich.....F5 186
Hastings, Minn.....F6, F7 187
Hastings, Nebr.....D7 191
Hastings, N.Z.....M16 112
Hastings, N. Dak.....C7 198
Hastings, Okla.....C3 200
Hastings, Pa.....E4 202
Hastings, W. Va.....A6 211
Hastings, co., Ont., Can.....C7 153
Hastings-on-Hudson, N.Y.....D1 196
Hästveda, Swe.....B7 62
Hasty, Ark.....A2 169
Hasty, Colo.....C8 171
Haswell, Colo.....C7 171
Hat, mtn., Ariz.....E2 168
Hat Creek, Wyo.....C8 213
Hatboro, Pa.....F11 202
Hatch, N. Mex.....E2 195
Hatch, Utah.....F3 207
Hatchechubbee, Ala.....C4 166
Hatchet, creek, Ala.....C3 166
Hatchie, riv., Tenn.....B2 205
Hatchineha, lake, Fla.....D5 174
Hatchville, Mass.....C6 185
Hateg, Rom.....C6 68
Hatfield, Ark.....C1 169
Hatfield, Sask., Can.....F3 155
Hatfield, Ind.....I3 179
Hatfield, Mass.....B2 185
Hatfield, Mo.....A3 189
Hatfield, Pa.....F11 202
Hatfield, Rh.....A5 107
Hathaway, Mont.....D10 190
Hathorne, Mass.....C3 185
Hathras, India.....D7 88
Hatillo, P.R.....B3 132
Hatillo, mun., P.R.....B3 132
Hatley, Ga.....E3 175
Hatley, Wis.....D4 212
Hato Mayor, Dom. Rep.....F9 131
Hato Rey, P.R.....B6 132
Hato Viejo, P.R.....B5 132
Hatta, India.....E7 88
Hattem, Neth.....B6 59
Hatteras, N.C.....B8 197
Hatteras, cape, N.C.....B8 197
Hatteras, inlet, N.C.....B8 197
Hattfjelldal, Nor.....E7 63
Hattiesburg, Miss.....D4 188
Hattieville, Ark.....B3 169
Hattingen, Ger.....*B2 61
Hatton, Ala.....A2 166
Hatton, Ark.....C1 169
Hatton, Sask., Can.....G1 155
Hatton, N. Dak.....B8 198
Hatton Fields, Calif.....*D3 170
Hatvan, Hung.....B4 68
Hatzic, B.C., Can.....A11 149
Haubourdin, Fr.....D3 59
Haubstadt, Ind.....H2 179
Haugan, Mont.....C1 190
Haugen, Wis.....C2 212
Haugesund, Nor.....H1 63
Haughton, La.....B2 183
Hauraki, gulf, N.Z.....L15 112
Hausach, Ger.....A4 66
Hauser, Oreg.....D2 201
Hauser, dam, Mont.....D5 190
Hauser Lake, Idaho.....*B2 177
Haut, isl., Maine.....D4 184
Haut-Rhin, dept., Fr.....B3 66
Haute-Marne, dept., Fr.....B1 66
Haute-Saône, dept., Fr.....B2 66
Haute-Savoie, dept., Fr.....C2 66
Hautes-Alpes, dept., Fr.....E2 66
Hautmont, Fr.....B5 58
Hauula, Haw.....B4, f10 176
Hauzenberg, Ger.....E8 61
Havana, Ala.....C2 166
Havana, Ark.....B2 169
Havana (La Habana), Cuba.....D2, h12 131
Havana, Fla.....B2 174
Havana, Ill.....C3 178
Havana, Kans.....E8 181
Havana, N. Dak.....D8 198
Havana, bay, Cuba.....h12 131
Havant & Waterloo, Eng.....*D6 56
Havasu, creek, Ariz.....A3 168
Havasu, lake, Ariz., Calif.....C1 168, E6 170
Havelberg, Ger.....F6 62
Havelländischer Grosser Haupt, canal, Ger.....F6 62
Havelock, Ont., Can.....C7 153
Havelock, Iowa.....B3 180
Havelock, N.C.....C7 197
Havelock, N. Dak.....C3 198
Haven, Kans.....B4, E6 181
Havensville, Kans.....C7 181
Haverford, Pa.....*F11 202
Haverfordwest, Wales.....C3 56
Haverhill, Eng.....B8 56
Haverhill, Fla.....*F6 174
Haverhill, Kans.....B6 181
Haverhill, Mass.....A5 185
Haverhill, N.H.....B2 193
Haverill, Iowa.....*C5 180
Havering, Eng.....C8 56
Haversham, R.I.....D10 172
Haverstraw, N.Y.....D3, D7 196
Havertown (Llanerch), Pa.....B11 202
Haviland, Kans.....E4 181
Haviland, Ohio.....A3 199
Havířov, Czech.....*D5 70
Havlíčkův Brod, Czech.....D3 70
Havre, see Le Havre, Fr.
Havre, Mont.....B7 190
Havre Aubert, Que., Can.....B8 151
Havre Boucher, N.S., Can.....D8 151
Havre de Grace, Md.....A5 173
Havre St. Pierre, Que., Can.....h9 152
Havza, Tur.....B10 85
Haw, riv., N.C.....B4 197
Haw Knob, mtn., N.C.....D2 197
Haw River, N.C.....A4 197
Hawaii, co., Haw.....D6 176
Hawaii, state, U.S.....176
Hawaiian Gardens, Calif.....*F4 170
Hawarden, Sask., Can.....F2 155
Hawarden, Iowa.....A1 180
Hawdon, lake, Austl.....H2 112
Hawea, lake, N.Z.....P12 112
Hawera, N.Z.....M15 112
Hawes, Ark.....C5 169
Hawes, Eng.....F6 57
Hawes Water, lake, Eng.....F6 57
Hawesville, Ky.....C3 182
Hawi, Haw.....C6 176
Hawick, Scot.....E6 57
Hawk Point, Mo.....C6 189
Hawk Run, Pa.....E5 202
Hawke, bay, N.Z.....M16 112
Hawke, isl., Newf., Can.....B4 152
Hawke, riv., Newf., Can.....B3 152
Hawker, Austl.....E2 112
Hawkesbury, Ont., Can.....B10 153
Hawkesbury, isl., B.C., Can.....C3 149
Hawkestone, Ont., Can.....C5 153
Hawkeye, Iowa.....B6 180
Hawkins, Tex.....*C5 206
Hawkins, Wis.....C3 212
Hawkins, co., Tenn.....C11 205
Hawkinsville, Ga.....D3 175
Hawksbill, mtn., Va.....C4 209
Hawley, Minn.....D2 187
Hawley, Pa.....D11 202
Hawley, Tex.....C3 206
Hawleyville, Conn.....D3 172
Haworth, N.J.....D5 194
Haworth, Okla.....D7 200
Ḩawsh 'Īsá, Eg.....D2 84
Hawthorn, Pa.....D3 202
Hawthorn Woods, Ill.....*A5 178
Hawthorne, Calif.....F2 170
Hawthorne, Fla.....C4 174
Hawthorne, Nev.....E3 192
Hawthorne, N.J.....B4 194
Hawthorne, N.Y.....D2 196
Haxby, Mont.....C10 190
Haxtun, Colo.....A8 171
Hay, Austl.....G5 112
Hay, Wales.....B4 56
Hay, Wash.....C8 210
Hay, isl., Ont., Can.....C4 153
Hay, riv., Austl.....D6 110
Hay, riv., Alta., N.W. Ter., Can.....E9 142
Hay Lakes, Alta., Can.....C4 148
Hay River, N.W. Ter., Can.....D9 144
Hay Springs, Nebr.....B3 191
Hayange, Fr.....C7 58
Hayden, Ala.....B3 166
Hayden, Ariz.....D5 168
Hayden, Colo.....A3 171
Hayden, Fla.....*E4 174
Hayden, Idaho.....*B2 177
Hayden, Ind.....G6 179
Hayden, N. Mex.....B6 195
Hayden, lake, Idaho.....B2 177
Hayden, lake, Maine.....D3 184
Hayden, peak, Idaho.....G2 177
Hayden Junction, Ariz.....E5 168
Hayden Lake, Idaho.....*B2 177
Haydenburg, Tenn.....C8 205
Haydens, Conn.....B6 172
Haydenville, Mass.....B2 185
Haydenville, Ohio.....C5 199
Hayes, La.....D3 183
Hayes, S. Dak.....C4 204
Hayes, co., Nebr.....D4 191
Hayes, mtn., Alsk.....C10 167
Hayes, riv., Man., Can.....B5 150
Hayes & Harlington, Eng.....*C7 56
Hayes Center, Nebr.....D4 191
Hayesville, N.C.....D2 197
Hayesville, Ohio.....B5 199
Hayesville, Oreg.....*C4 201
Hayfield, Man., Can.....E1 150
Hayfield, Iowa.....A4 180
Hayfield, Minn.....G6 187
Hayfield, Va.....B4 209
Hayford, Wash.....D7 210
Hayford, peak, Nev.....G6 192
Hayfork, Calif.....B2 170
Haylow, Ga.....F4 175
Haymana, Tur.....C9 85
Haymarket, Va.....B4, C5 209
Haymock, lake, Maine.....B3 184
Haymond, Ind.....F7 179
Haynau, see Chojnów, Pol.
Hayne, N.C.....B5 197
Haynes, Ark.....C5 169
Haynes, Alta., Can.....C4 148
Haynes, N. Dak.....D3 198
Haynesville, La.....B2 183
Haynesville, Maine.....C5 184
Hayneville, Ala.....C3 166
Hays, Kans.....D4 181
Hays, Mont.....C8 190
Hays, N.C.....A2 197
Hays, co., Tex.....D3 206
Hays Canyon, peak, Nev.....B2 192
Haysi, Va.....B2 209
Haystack, mtn., Nev.....B6 192
Haystack, peak, Utah.....D2 207
Haysville, Ind.....H4 179
Haysville, Kans.....B5 181
Haysville, Tenn.....A5, C7 205
Haysville, Pa.....*E1 202
Hayter, Alta., Can.....C5 148
Hayti, Mo.....E8 189
Hayti, S. Dak.....C8 204
Hayton, Wis.....B6 212
Hayward, Calif.....B5 170
Hayward, Minn.....G5 187
Hayward, Okla.....A4 200
Hayward, Wis.....B2 212
Haywood, Man., Can.....E2 150
Haywood, N.C.....B4 197
Haywood, Okla.....C6 200
Haywood, co., N.C.....D3 197
Haywood, co., Tenn.....B2 205
Hazard, Ky.....C6 182
Hazard, Nebr.....C6 191
Hazardville, Conn.....B6 172
Hazaribagh, India.....E10 88
Hazaripagh, range, India.....F9 88
Hazebrouck, Fr.....B5 58
Hazel, Ky.....B3 182
Hazel, S. Dak.....C8 204
Hazel Crest, Ill.....F3 178
Hazel Dell, Ill.....D5 178
Hazel Green, Ala.....A3 166
Hazel Green, Ky.....C6 182
Hazel Green, Wis.....F3 212
Hazel Hurst, Pa.....C4 202
Hazel Park, Mich.....A8 186
Hazel Patch, Ky.....C5 182
Hazel Run, Minn.....F3 187
Hazelhurst, Wis.....C4 212
Hazelton, B.C., Can.....B4 149
Hazelton, Idaho.....G4 177
Hazelton, Kans.....E5 181
Hazelton, N. Dak.....C5 198
Hazelton, peak, Wyo.....A5 213
Hazelwood, Mo.....*C7 189
Hazelwood, N.C.....D3 197
Hazen, Ark.....C4 169
Hazen, Nev.....D2 192
Hazen N. Dak.....B4 198
Hazen, bay, Alsk.....C6 167
Hazenmore, Sask., Can.....H2 155
Hazlehurst, Ga.....E4 175
Hazlehurst, Miss.....D3 188
Hazlet, Sask., Can.....G1 155
Hazleton, Ind.....H2 179
Hazleton, Iowa.....B6 180
Hazleton, Pa.....E10 202
Hazor, Isr.....h10 84
He Devil, mtn., Idaho.....D2 177
Head Bay d'Espoir, Newf., Can.....E4 152
Head Harbor, isl., Maine.....D5 184
Head of Island, La.....B6 183
Head of the Harbor, N.Y.....*D3 196
Headland, Ala.....D4 166
Headley, mtn., Mont.....C1 190
Headquarters, Idaho.....C3 177
Headrick, Okla.....C2 200
Heads, The, cape, Oreg.....E2 201
Heafford Junction, Wis.....C4 212
Healdsburg, Calif.....A4, C2 170
Healdton, Okla.....C4 200
Healdville, Vt.....E3 208
Healing Springs, Va.....D3 209
Healy, Kans.....D3 181
Healy Fork, Alsk.....C10 167
Heanza, isl., Okinawa.....114
Heard, co., Ga.....C1 175
Hearne, Sask., Can.....G3 155
Hearne, Tex.....D4 206
Hearst, Ont., Can.....E9 153
Hearst, isl., Ant.....C6 120
Heart, lake, Wyo.....A2 213
Heart, riv., Alta., Can.....A2 148
Heart, riv., N. Dak.....C4 198
Heart Butte, Mont.....B4 190
Hearthstone, mtn., Md.....A2 173
Heart's Content, Newf., Can.....E5 152
Heartwell, Nebr.....D7 191
Heartwellville, Vt.....F2 208
Heaters, W. Va.....C4 211
Heath, Mass.....A2 185
Heath, Mont.....C7 190
Heath, Ohio.....B5 199
Heath Springs, S.C.....B6 203
Heatherton, N.S., Can.....D8 151
Heathsville, Va.....D6 209
Heaton, N. Dak.....B6 198
Heavener, Okla.....C7 200
Hebardville, Ga.....*E4 175
Hebbronville, Tex.....F3 206
Hebel, Austl.....D6 112
Heber, Ariz.....C5 168
Heber, Utah.....C4 207
Heber Springs, Ark.....B3 169
Hebert, La.....B4 183
Hebertville, Que., Can.....A6 154
Hébertville Station, Que., Can.....*A6 154
Hebgen, res., Mont.....F5 190
Hebo, Oreg.....B3 201
Hebrides, sea, Scot.....C2 57
Hebron, Newf., Can.....f9 152
Hebron, N.S., Can.....F3 151
Hebron, Conn.....C7 172
Hebron, Ill.....A5 178
Hebron, Ind.....B3 179
Hebron, see Al Khalil, Jordan
Hebron, Ky.....A7 182
Hebron, Maine.....D2 184
Hebron, Md.....D6 173
Hebron, Nebr.....D8 191
Hebron, N.H.....C3 193
Hebron, N. Dak.....C3 198
Hebron, Ohio.....C5 199
Hebron, Tex.....A5 206
Hebron, Va.....D5 209
Hebron, W. Va.....B3 211
Heby, Swe.....t34 63
Hecate, strait, B.C., Can.....F6 142
Hecelchakán, Mex.....C6 129
Hechingen, Ger.....D4 60
Hechtel, Bel.....C5 59
Hecker, Ill.....E4 178
Hecklingen, Ger.....B6 61
Hecla, Man., Can.....D3 150
Hecla, S. Dak.....B7 204
Hecla, isl., Man., Can.....D3 150
Hectanooga, N.S., Can.....E3 151
Hector, Ark.....B3 169
Hector, Minn.....F4 187
Hede, Swe.....F5 63
Hedemora, Swe.....G6 63
Hedensö, Swe.....t34 63
Hedensted, Den.....C3 62
Hedgehog, hill, Conn.....B8 172
Hedgesville, Mont.....D7 190
Hedgesville, W. Va.....B7 211
Hedley, B.C., Can.....E7 149
Hedley, Tex.....B2 206
Hedo, Okinawa.....114
Hedo, pt., Okinawa.....114
Hedon, Eng.....A7 56
Hedrick, Ind.....D2 179
Hedrick, Iowa.....C5 180
Hedwig Village, Tex.....*E5 206
Heek, Ger.....A2 61
Heel, pt., Wake I.....114
Heeney, Colo.....B4 171
Heerde, Neth.....B6 59
Heerenveen, Neth.....B5 59
Heerlen, Neth.....D5 59
Heessen, Ger.....B2 61
Heflin, Ala.....B4 166
Heflin, La.....B2 183
Hefner, lake, Okla.....B4 200
Hegeler, Ill.....*C6 178
Hegins, Pa.....E9 202
Heiberger, Ala.....C2 166
Heide, Ger.....A4 60
Heidelberg, Austl.....*G8 111
Heidelberg, Ger.....D3 61
Heidelberg, Miss.....D5 188
Heidelberg, Pa.....*F1 202
Heidelberg, S. Afr.....D3 107
Heidenau, Ger.....C8 61
Heidenheim, Ger.....E5 61
Heil, N. Dak.....C4 198
Heilbron, S. Afr.....C4 107
Heilbronn, Ger.....D4 61
Heiligenblut, Aus.....B8 66
Heiligenhafen, Ger.....D4 62
Heiligenstadt, Ger.....B5 61
Heilsberg, see Lidzbark Warmiński, Pol.
Heilungkiang, prov., China.....B10 91
Heilwood, Pa.....E4 202
Heimbach, Ger.....D6 59
Heimdal, N. Dak.....B6 198
Heinola, Fin.....G12 63
Heinsberg, Ger.....C6 59
Heinsburg, Alta., Can.....C5 148
Heiskell, Tenn.....E11 205
Heisler, Alta., Can.....C4 148
Heislerville, N.J.....E3 194
Heizer, Kans.....D5 181
Hejaz, pol. div., Sau. Ar.....D7 101
Hekla, peak, Ice.....n23 63
Hekura, isl., Jap.....H8 93
Hel, Pol.....A5 70
Hela, pt., New Britain I.....115
Helagsfjaelet, mtn., Swe.....F5 63
Helbra, Ger.....B6 61
Heldt, Wyo.....C8 213
Helen, Ga.....*B3 175
Helena, Ala.....B3 166
Helena, Ark.....C5 169
Helena, Ga.....D4 175
Helena, Mo.....B3 189
Helena, Mont.....D4 190
Helena, N.Y.....A2 196
Helena, Ohio.....A4 199
Helena, Okla.....A3 200
Helena, S.C.....C4 203
Helensburgh, Scot.....D4 57
Helenwood, Tenn.....C9 205
Helgasjön, lake, Swe.....B8 62
Helgean, riv., Swe.....B8 62
Helgeroa, Nor.....p28 63
Helgoland, bay, Ger.....D2 62
Helgoland, isl., Ger.....D1 62
Helix, Oreg.....B8 201
Hellam, Pa.....G8 202
Hellenthal, Ger.....D6 59
Hellertown, Pa.....E11 202
Hellier, Ky.....*C7 182
Hellín, Sp.....C5 65
Hells, canyon, Idaho, Oreg.....D2 177, B10 201
Hells Canyon, res., Idaho, Oreg.....D2 177, B10 201
Hellville, Malag.....f9 107
Helm, Calif.....D3 170
Helmand, riv., Afg.....F12 86
Helmbrechts, Ger.....C6 61
Helmer, Idaho.....C2 177
Helmer, Ind.....A7 179
Helmeringhausen, S.W. Afr.....C2 107
Helmetta, N.J.....C4 194
Helmond, Neth.....C5 59
Helmsburg, Ind.....F5 179
Helmsdale, Scot.....B5 57
Helmsdale, riv., Scot.....B5 57
Helmsley, Eng.....F7 57
Helmstedt, Ger.....A5 61
Helmville, Mont.....D4 190
Helnaes, isl., Den.....C3 62
Heloise, Tenn.....A2 205
Helotes, Tex.....B3 206
Helper, Utah.....D5 207
Helsingfors, see Helsinki, Fin.
Helsingör, Den.....B6 62
Helsinki, Fin.....G11 63

INDEX KEY Each place listed in Bold-faced Type has its population listed in the Population tables, pages 230 to 280. Each country, shown in CAPITAL LETTERS, has its population listed in the World Political Information Table, pages 6 to 10. * Does not appear on map; key shows general location.

Helston, Eng............D1 56
Heltonville, Ind............G5 179
Helvecia, Arg............A4 136
Helvetia Mines, Pa........D4 202
Hemaruka, Alta., Can.....D5 148
Hematite, Mo............C7 189
Hemau, Ger..............D6 61
Hemel Hempstead, Eng....C7 56
Hemet, Calif.........F4, F5 170
Hemet East, Calif........*F5 170
Hemford, N.S., Can........E5 151
Hemingford, Nebr.........B2 191
Hemingway, S.C..........D9 203
Hemlock, Ind...............D5 179
Hemlock, Mich.............E6 186
Hemlock, N.Y..............C3 196
Hemlock, Ohio..........*C5 199
Hemlock (Eureka), S.C....B5 203
Hemlock, res., Conn.......E3 172
Hemmingford, Que., Can..D4 154
Hemnesberget, Nor.......D5 63
Hemp, Ga.................B2 175
Hempfield, Pa..............*F2 202
Hemphill, Tex............D6 206
Hemphill, co., Tex........B2 206
Hemple, Mo...............B3 189
Hempstead, N.Y..........D2 196
Hempstead, Tex...........D4 206
Hempstead, co., Ark.......D2 169
Hempstead, hbr., N.Y........F2 172
Henager, Ala.............A4 166
Henares, riv., Sp...........B4 65
Hendaye, Fr...............F3 58
Hendek, Tur...............B8 85
Henderson, Ala............D3 166
Henderson, Arg............B4 136
Henderson, Colo...........B6 171
Henderson, Ill............*B3 178
Henderson, Iowa..........C2 180
Henderson, Ky............C2 182
Henderson, Md............B6 173
Henderson, Mich..........E6 186
Henderson, Minn..........F5 187
Henderson, Nebr..........D8 191
Henderson, Nev...........G7 192
Henderson, N.Y...........B4 196
Henderson, N.C...........A5 197
Henderson, Tenn..........B3 205
Henderson, Tex...........C5 206
Henderson, W. Va.........C2 211
Henderson, co., Ky........C2 182
Henderson, co., Ill........C3 178
Henderson, co., N.C.......D3 197
Henderson, co., Tenn......B3 205
Henderson, co., Tex.......C5 206
Henderson, pt., Miss........E2 188
Hendersonville, N.C.......D3 197
Hendersonville, S.C.......F6 203
Hendersonville,
Tenn...............A5, E9 205
Hendon, Sask., Can........E4 155
Hendon, Eng..............k12 55
Hendon, Tenn.............D8 205
Hendricks, Minn..........F2 187
Hendricks, W. Va........*B5 211
Hendricks, co., Ind.......E4 179
Hendrum, Minn............C2 187
Hendry, co., Fla..........F5 174
Henefer, Utah............B4 207
Hengelo, Neth............B6 59
Henghsien, China..........G6 91
Hengshan, China...........F3 92
Hengshan, China...........K5 92
Hengyang, China..........K5 92
Hénin-Liétard, Fr..........D2 59
Henlawson, W. Va.........*D3 211
Henley Harbour, Newf.,
Can.....................B4 152
Henley-on-Thames, Eng....C7 56
Henlopen, cape, Del........C7 173
Hennebont, Fr.............D2 58
Hennef, Ger...............C2 61
Hennepin, Ill.............B4 178
Hennepin, Okla............C4 200
Hennepin, co., Minn.......E5 187
Hennessey, Okla..........A4 200
Henniker, N.H............D3 193
Henning, Ill...............C6 178
Henning, Minn............D3 187
Henning, Tenn............B2 205
Henpan, cape, Buka I........... 115
Henribourg, Sask., Can....D3 155
Henrico, co., Va...........D5 209
Henrietta, Mo.............B4 189
Henrietta, N.Y.............B3 196
Henrietta, N.C.........B2, D4 197
Henrietta, Tex............C3 206
Henrietta Maria, cape, Ont.,
Can.....................D9 153
Henrietta Northeast,
N.Y.....................*B3 196
Henrieville, Utah.........F4 207
Henrique de Carvalho,
Ang.....................C3 106
Henry, Ill................B4 178
Henry, Nebr..............C1 191
Henry, Nev...............B7 192
Henry, S. Dak............C8 204
Henry, Tenn..............A3 205
Henry, Va................E3 209
Henry, co., Ala...........D4 166
Henry, co., Ga............C2 175
Henry, co., Ill............B3 178
Henry, co., Ind...........E7 179
Henry, co., Iowa..........C6 180
Henry, co., Ky............B4 182
Henry, co., Mo............C4 189
Henry, co., Ohio..........A3 199
Henry, co., Tenn..........A3 205
Henry, co., Va............E3 209
Henry, mts., Mont...........B1 190
Henry, mts., Utah...........E5 207
Henry Kater, cape, N.W. Ter.,
Can....................C19 143
Henryetta, Okla...........B6 200
Henrys, fork, Utah, Wyo....B5 207
Henryville, Que., Can.....D4 154
Henryville, Ind.............G6 179
Henryville, Ky.............B5 182
Hensall, Ont., Can........D3 153
Hensel (Canton), N. Dak...A8 198
Henshaw, Ky..............C1 182
Hensler, N. Dak............B4 198
Hensley, Ark...............C3 169
Henslow, cape, Guadalcanal I. 115
Henson, creek, Md...........C1 173
Henteyn Nuruu, mts.,
Mong...................B6 91
Henzada, Bur............E10 87
Hepburn, Sask., Can.......E2 155
Hepburn, Iowa..............D2 180
Hepburn, Ohio..............B4 199
Hephzibah, Ga............C4 175
Hepler, Kans..............E9 181
Heppenheim, Ger...........D3 61
Heppner, Oreg............B7 201
Hepworth, Ont., Can.......C3 153
Heraclea (Heraclea Pontica),
in Asia Minor................ 42
Heraclea,
in Crimea.................... 42
Heraclea,
in Italy...................... 44
Heraclea Pontica (Ereglil,
in Asia Minor)............... 42
Herat, Afg...............D11 86
Herb Lake, Man., Can......B2 150
Herbert, Sask., Can.......G2 155
Herbert, peak, N.Z..........O14 112
Herbertingen, Ger..........A5 66
Herbes, isl., Ala............E5 188
Herbesthal (Lontzen), Bel..D5 59
Herblay, Fr................g9 58
Herblet, lake, Man., Can....B2 150
Herborn, Ger...............C3 61
Hercegnovi, Yugo..........D4 68
Hercegovina, reg., Yugo....D4 68
Herchen, Ger...............C2 61
Herculaneum, Mo.....B8, C7 189
Hercules, Calif...........*C2 170
Herd, Okla.................A5 200
Herdecke, Ger..............B2 61
Heredia, C.R...............E5 130
Hereford, Ariz..............F5 168
Hereford, Colo.............A6 171
Hereford, Eng.............B5 56
Hereford, Md...............A4 173
Hereford, Oreg.............C8 201
Hereford, S. Dak...........C3 204
Hereford, Tex.............B1 206
Hereford, co., Eng.........B5 56
Hereford, inlet, N.J.........E3 194
Herencia, Sp...............C4 65
Herentals, Bel..............C4 59
Herfölge, Den..............C6 62
Herford, Ger..............A3 61
Héricourt, Fr...............B2 66
Herington, Kans...........D7 181
Heriot, S.C.................C7 203
Herisau, Switz..............B5 66
Herkimer, Kans.............C7 181
Herkimer, N.Y.............B6 196
Herkimer, co., N.Y.........B6 196
Herman, Mich..............B2 186
Herman, Minn.............E2 187
Herman, Nebr.............C9 191
Hermann, Mo..............C6 189
Hermano, peak, Colo........D2 171
Hermanos, is., Ven..........A5 133
Hermansville, Mich.........C3 186
Hermantown, Minn..........D6 187
Hermanville, Miss...........D3 188
Hermel, Leb................E11 85
Hermeskeil, Ger.............D1 61
Herminia Central, P.R......C5 132
Herminie, Pa...............F2 202
Hermiston, Oreg...........B7 201
Hermit, is., N. Gui..........h12 110
Hermitage, Ark............D3 169
Hermitage, Newf., Can......E4 152
Hermitage, La.............D4 183
Hermitage, Mo.............D4 189
Hermitage, Tenn............E9 205
Hermitage, Vir. Is..........f16 132
Hermitage, bay, Newf.,
Can.....................E3 152
Hermitage Springs, Tenn...C8 205
Hermleigh, Tex.............C2 206
Hermon, Maine...........*D4 184
Hermon, N.Y...............B2 196
Hermosa, S. Dak...........D2 204
Hermosa Beach, Calif......F2 170
Hermosillo, Mex...........B2 129
Hernád, riv., Hung..........A5 68
Hernandaries, Par..........E5 135
Hernandex, N. Mex.........A3 195
Hernando, Fla.............D4 174
Hernando, Miss............A4 188
Hernando, co., Fla.........D4 174
Herndon, Ga...............D4 175
Herndon, Iowa..............C3 180
Herndon, Kans.............C3 181
Herndon, Ky................D2 182
Herndon, Pa...............E8 202
Herndon, Va...........A4, C5 209
Herndon, W. Va............D3 211
Herne, Ger................B2 61
Herning, Den...............B2 62
Herod, Ga..................E2 175
Herod, pt., N.Y..............F5 172
Heron, Mont................B1 190
Heron Lake, Minn..........G3 187
Herouxville, Que., Can.....C5 154
Herreid, S. Dak............B5 204
Herrenberg, Ger............E3 61
Herrick, Ill................D5 178
Herrick, S. Dak............D6 204
Herrick, creek, B.C., Can....B7 149
Herrick, mtn., Vt............D2 208
Herrick Center, Pa.........C10 202
Herrin, Ill..................F4 178
Herring, bay, Md............C4 173
Herring, run, Md............C2 173
Herring Cove, N.S., Can....E6 151
Herrings, N.Y.............*A5 196
Herrington, Wis............*E2 212
Herrington, lake, Ky.........C5 182
Hersbruck, Ger..............D6 61
Herschel, Sask., Can.......F1 155
Herscher, Ill...............B5 178
Hersey, Mich..............E5 186
Hershey, Nebr.............C5 191
Hershey, Pa...............F8 202
Herstal, Bel.................D5 59
Herten, Ger...............*C7 59
Hertford, Eng...............C7 56
Hertford, N.C..............A7 197
Hertford, co., Eng..........C7 56
Hertford, co., N.C..........A6 197
Hervás, Sp.................B3 65
Hervey, bay, Austl..........B9 112
Hervey Junction, Que.,
Can......................C5 154
Herxheim, Ger..............D3 61
Herzberg, Ger...............B5 61
Herzberg, Ger...............B8 61
Herzberg, Ger...............F6 62
Herzliya, Isr.........B6, g10 84
Herzogenaurach, Ger.......D5 61
Hesdin, Fr.................D10 56
Hesel, Ger..................A7 59
Heshikiya, Okinawa.............. 114
Hespeler, Ont., Can........D4 153
Hesper, Mont...............E8 190
Hesper, N. Dak.............B6 198
Hesperia, Calif............E5 170
Hesperia, Mich............E4 186
Hesperus, Colo.............D2 171
Hesperus, mtn., Colo........D2 171
Hesse, reg., Ger.............C4 60
Hesse-Cassel: *see also*
Hesse-Kassel
Hesse-Darmstadt: in 1867..... 51
Hesse-Kassel: in 1866........ 51
Hessel, Mich................B6 186
Hesselager, Den.............C4 62
Hesselö, isl., Den...........B5 62
Hessen, state, Ger...........C3 61
Hessmer, La...............C3 183
Hesston, Kans.........A5, D6 181
Hester, Okla..............*C2 200
Heston & Isleworth, Eng..*C7 56
Hetland, S. Dak............C8 204
Hetona, Okinawa................ 114
Hettick, Ill.................D3 178
Hettinger, N. Dak..........D3 198
Hettinger, co., N. Dak......C3 198
Hettstedt, Ger..............B6 61
Heuvelton, N.Y.............B1 196
Heves, Hung................B5 68
Heward, Sask., Can.........H4 155
Hewins, Kans...............E7 181
Hewitt, Minn...............D3 187
Hewitt, N.J.................A4 194
Hewitt, Wis.................D3 212
Hewlett Bay Park, N.Y....*E7 196
Hewlett Harbor, N.Y.......*E7 196
Hewlett Neck, N.Y.........*E7 196
Hexham, Eng...............F6 57
Hext, Tex...................D3 206
Heyburn, Idaho.............G5 177
Heyworth, Ill...............C5 178
Hialeah, Fla...........G6, F3 174
Hialeah Gardens, Fla......*G6 174
Hiattville, Kans.............E9 181
Hiawassee, Ga.............B3 175
Hiawatha, Iowa............*C6 180
Hiawatha, Kans............C8 181
Hiawatha, Utah............D4 207
Hibbard, Ind.................B5 179
Hibbing, Minn..............C6 187
Hibernia, N.J..............B4 194
Hibernia: c. 120 A.D.......... 45
Hickiwan, Ariz..............E3 168
Hickman, Del...............C6 173
Hickman, Ky...............B2 182
Hickman, Nebr.............D9 191
Hickman, co., Ky...........B2 182
Hickman, co., Tenn.........B4 205
Hickman's Harbour, Newf.,
Can......................D5 152
Hickok, Kans...............E2 181
Hickory, Ky................B2 182
Hickory, Miss..............C4 188
Hickory, N.C...............B2 197
Hickory, Okla..............C5 200
Hickory, co., Mo...........D4 189
Hickory Corners, Mich......F5 186
Hickory East, N.C.........*B2 197
Hickory Flat, Miss.........A4 188
Hickory Grove, S.C.........B5 203
Hickory Hills, Ill..........*F2 178
Hickory North, N.C........*B2 197
Hickory Plains, Ark.........C4 169
Hickory Ridge, Ark.........B5 169
Hickory Valley, Tenn.......B2 205
Hickory Withe, Tenn........B2 205
Hickox, Ga..................E4 175
Hickson, Ont., Can..........D4 153
Hickson, lake, Sask., Can...A3 155
Hicksville, N.Y..........D3, E7 196
Hicksville, Ohio............A2 199
Hico, Tex..................*D3 206
Hidalgo, Ill.................D5 178
Hidalgo, Tex................F3 206
Hidalgo, co., N. Mex.......F1 195
Hidalgo, co., Tex...........F3 206
Hidalgo, state, Mex...C5, m14 129
Hidalgo del Parral, Mex....B3 129
Hidden Timber, S. Dak......D5 204
Hiddenite, N.C..............B2 197
Hiddensee, isl., Ger.........D7 62
Hideaway Park, Colo........B5 171
Hienghene, N. Cal............ 115
Hierro, isl., Sp. (Can. Is.)....n13 65
Higashi (Dōgo), isl., Jap.....H6 93
Higashimurayama, Jap.....*I9 93
Higbee, Mo.................B5 189
Higden, Ark................B3 169
Higdon, Ala.................A4 166
Higganum, Conn............D6 172
Higgins, Tex...............A2 206
Higgins, lake, Mich..........D6 186
Higgins Millpond, pond,
Md......................C6 173
Higginson, Ark.............B4 169
Higginsport, Ohio..........D4 199
Higginsville, Mo...........B4 189
Higgston, Ga..............*D4 175
High, des., Oreg............D6 201
High, isl., Mich.............C5 186
High, isl., New Hebr............ 115
High, peak, Phil.............o13 95
High Bluff, Man., Can.......D2 150
High Bridge, Ky.............C5 182
High Bridge, N.H............E3 193
High Bridge, N.J...........B3 194
High Falls, res., Wis........C5 212
High Hill, Mo...............C6 189
High Hill, lake, Man., Can...B4 150
High Hill, riv., Alta., Can...A5 148
High Island, Tex.............E5 206
High Knob, mtn., Va.........B4 209
High Knob, mtn., W. Va......C5 211
High Point, N.C............B3 197
High Point, Ohio...........*C3 199
High Point, Wash...........D2 210
High Point, mtn., N.J.......A3 194
High Point, mtn., W. Va.....C5 211
High Prairie, Alta., Can.....B2 148
High Ridge, Conn...........E2 172
High Ridge, Mo..............B7 189
High River, Alta., Can.....D4 148
High Rock, mtn., Md.........D1 173
High Rock, res., N.C.........B3 197
High Rolls-Mountain Park,
N. Mex...................E4 195
High Shoals, Ga.............C3 175
High Spire, Pa...............F8 202
High Springs, Fla...........C4 174
High Veld, plain, S. Afr.....C4 107
High Wycombe,
Eng..............E6 55, C7 56
Highcoal, W. Va.............D6 211
Highest Point in Ala.........B4 166
Highest Point in Alsk........C9 167
Highest Point in Ariz........B4 168
Highest Point in Ark.........B2 169
Highest Point in Calif.......D4 170
Highest Point in Can.........D4 142
Highest Point in Colo........B4 171
Highest Point in Conn........A3 172
Highest Point in Del.........A6 173
Highest Point in Fla..........G3 174
Highest Point in Ga..........B3 175
Highest Point in Haw.........D6 176
Highest Point in Idaho.......E5 177
Highest Point in Ill..........A3 178
Highest Point in Ind..........D8 179
Highest Point in Iowa........A2 180
Highest Point in Kans........C1 181
Highest Point in Ky..........D7 182
Highest Point in La..........B3 183
Highest Point in Maine.......C4 184
Highest Point in Md..........E1 173
Highest Point in Mass........A1 185
Highest Point in Mich........B2 186
Highest Point in Minn........A7 187
Highest Point in Miss........A5 188
Highest Point in Mo..........D7 189
Highest Point in Mont........E7 190
Highest Point in Nebr........C2 191
Highest Point in Nev.........F3 192
Highest Point in N.H.........B4 193
Highest Point in N.J.........A3 194
Highest Point in N. Mex......A4 195
Highest Point in N.Y.........A7 196
Highest Point in N.A.........C9 167
Highest Point in N.C.........D4 197
Highest Point in N. Dak......C2 198
Highest Point in Ohio........B4 199
Highest Point in Okla........D1 200
Highest Point in Oreg........B5 201
Highest Point in Pa..........G3 202
Highest Point in R.I.........B9 172
Highest Point in S.C.........A2 203
Highest Point in S. Dak......D2 204
Highest Point in Tenn.......D10 205
Highest Point in Tex.........E2 206
Highest Point in U.S.........C9 167
Highest Point in Utah........C5 207
Highest Point in Vt..........B3 208
Highest Point in Va..........D1 209
Highest Point in Wash........C4 210
Highest Point in W. Va.......C5 211
Highest Point in Wis.........D4 212
Highest Point in Wyo.........C3 213
Highfalls, N.C...............B4 197
Highgate, Ont., Can.........E3 153
Highgate Center, Vt..........B2 208
Highgate Falls, Vt...........B2 208
Highgate Springs, Vt.........B2 208
Highland, Ark..............C2 169
Highland, Calif.............F3 170
Highland, Fla...............B4 174
Highland, Ill................E4 178
Highland, Ind...............A3 179
Highland, Kans..............C8 181
Highland, Mich..............A7 186
Highland, N.Y...............D7 196
Highland, Ohio..............C4 199
Highland, Wis...............E3 212
Highland, co., Ohio.........C4 199
Highland, co., Va...........C3 209
Highland, lake, Maine........E5 184
Highland, lake, N.H..........E4 208
Highland, peak, Calif.........C4 170
Highland, pt., Fla............G5 174
Highland Beach, Fla.......*F6 174
Highland Beach, Md.......*C5 173
Highland Beach, Okla.....*B4 200
Highland City, Fla........*E5 174
Highland Creek, Ont.
Can......................D5 153
Highland Falls, N.Y.......*D7 196
Highland Grove, Ont.,
Can......................B6 153
Highland Heights, Ky.....*A5 182
Highland Heights, Ohio..*A6 199
Highland Home, Ala.........D3 166
Highland Park, Fla.........*C5 174
Highland Park, Ill........A6, E2 178
Highland Park, Mich........A8 186
Highland Park, N.J..........C4 194
Highland Park, Pa.........*E6 202
Highland Park, Tex..........B5 206
Highland Springs,
Va..................C7, D5 209
Highlands, N.J..............C5 194
Highlands, N.C..............D3 197
Highlands, Tex..............F5 206
Highlands, co., Fla..........E5 174
Highlandville, Iowa..........A6 180
Highlandville, Mo...........*E4 189
Highley Heights, Mo.......*D7 189
Highmore, S. Dak............C6 204
Highpoint, Miss..............B5 188
Highrock, lake, Man., Can....B1 150
Highshoals, N.C..............B2 197
Hightstown, N.J.............C3 194
Highway City, Calif.........*D4 170
Highway Village, Tex.......*F4 206
Highwood, Ill.........A6, E2 178
Highwood, Mont..............C6 190
Highwood, mts., Mont........C6 190
Highwood Baldy, Peak,
Mont.....................C6 190
Highwoods, Ind.............*E5 179
Higley, Ariz..........D4, G2 168
Higüey, Dom. Rep............F9 131
Hiiumaa, isl., Sov. Un........B4 72
Hiko, Nev....................F6 192
Hikone, Jap..................n15 93
Hikurangi, mtn., N.Z.........L17 112
Hiland, Wyo.................B5 213
Hilbert, Wis..........B5, D5 212
Hilda, Alta., Can.............D5 148
Hilda, S.C..................E5 203
Hildburghausen, Ger.........C5 61
Hildebran, N.C.............*B2 197
Hilden, N.S., Can............D6 151
Hilden, Ger...........C3 60, B1 61
Hildesheim, Ger.............A4 61
Hildreth, Nebr...............D6 191
Hiles, Wis....................C5 212
Hilgard, Oreg.................B8 201
Hilger, Mont..................C7 190
Hilham, Tenn..................C8 205
Hill, N.H.....................C3 193
Hill, co., Mont...............B6 190
Hill, co., Tex................D4 206
Hill, lake, Ark................D6 169
Hill Center, N.H..............C3 193
Hill City, Idaho...............F3 177
Hill City, Kans...............C4 181
Hill City, Minn...............D5 187
Hill City, S. Dak.............D2 204
Hill Country Village, Tex..*E3 206
Hillared, Swe.................A7 62
Hillburn, N.Y.................*D6 196
Hillcrest, Ill.................*B4 178
Hillcrest, N.J.................*B2 194
Hillcrest Heights, Fla.....*E5 174
Hillcrest Heights, Md.......C1 173
Hillcrest Mines, Alta.,
Can.......................E3 148
Hillegom, Neth................B4 59
Hiller, Pa....................*F2 202
Hilleröd, Den.................C6 62
Hillesheim, Ger...............C1 61
Hillgrove, Calif..............*F3 170
Hillhead, S. Dak...............B8 204
Hillhouse Addition, Mo.....*D5 189
Hilliard, Alta., Can...........C4 148
Hilliard, Fla..................B5 174
Hilliard, Ohio................C2 199
Hilliards, Pa...................D2 202
Hillier, Ont., Can..............D7 153
Hillingdon, Eng.............k12 55
Hillisburg, Ind................D5 179
Hillman, Mich...............C7 186
Hillman, Minn...............D5 187
Hillmond, Sask., Can.........D1 155
Hillrose, Colo...............A7 171
Hills, Iowa...................C6 180
Hills, Minn...................G2 187
Hills and Dales, Ohio......*B6 199
Hills Creek, res., Oreg.......D4 201
Hillsboro, Ala................A2 166
Hillsboro, Ga..................C3 175
Hillsboro, Ill.................D4 178
Hillsboro, Ind................D3 179
Hillsboro, Iowa..............D6 180
Hillsboro, Kans..............D6 181
Hillsboro, Md................C6 173
Hillsboro, Miss................C4 188
Hillsboro, Mo...........B7, C7 189
Hillsboro, N.H...............D3 193
Hillsboro, N. Mex...........E2 195
Hillsboro, N. Dak............B8 198
Hillsboro, Ohio..............C2 199
Hillsboro, Oreg..........B1, B3 201
Hillsboro, Tenn..............B6 205
Hillsboro, Tex...............C4 206
Hillsboro, Va................*B5 209
Hillsboro, W. Va.............C4 211
Hillsboro, Wis...............E3 212
Hillsboro, co., N.H..........E3 193
Hillsboro, canal, Fla.........F6 174
Hillsboro Beach, Fla.......*F6 174
Hillsboro Lower Village,
N.H.......................D3 193
Hillsboro Upper Village,
N.H.......................D3 193
Hillsborough, Calif.........*B5 170
Hillsborough, N.C............A4 197
Hillsborough, N.B., Can....D5 151
Hillsborough, co., Fla........E4 174
Hillsborough, bay, P.E.I.,
Can.......................C6 151
Hillsborough, bay, Fla........E2 174
Hillsborough, riv., Fla........D4 174
Hillsburgh, Ont., Can.........D4 153
Hillsdale, Ont., Can...........C5 153
Hillsdale, Ill..................B3 178
Hillsdale, Ind.................E3 179
Hillsdale, Kans................D9 181
Hillsdale, Mich...............G6 186
Hillsdale, Mo................*A8 189
Hillsdale, N.J.................C5 194
Hillsdale, N.Y..................C7 196
Hillsdale, Okla................A4 200
Hillsdale, Tenn.................C7 205
Hillsdale, Wis..................C2 212
Hillsdale, Wyo..................D8 213
Hillsdale, co., Mich..........G6 186
Hillsgrove, Pa..................D8 202
Hillside, Colo...................C5 171
Hillside, Ill..................*F2 178
Hillside, N.J..................E4 194
Hillston, Austl..................F5 112
Hillsview, S. Dak.............B6 204
Hillsville, Pa....................D1 202
Hillsville, Va..................E2 209
Hilltonia, Ga..................D5 175
Hilltop, Minn.................*E5 187
Hilltop, W. Va..................D7 211
Hillview, Ill...................D3 178
Hillville, Tenn..................B2 205
Hilo, Haw...............D6, n16 176
Hilo, bay, Haw................D6 176
Hilpoltstein, Ger...............D6 61
Hilpsford, pt., Eng............F5 57
Hilshire Village, Tex......*E5 206
Hilton, Ga......................E1 175
Hilton, N.Y...................B3 196
Hilton Head, isl., S.C.........G6 203
Hiltonhead, S.C.................G6 203
Hiltons, Va.....................B2 209
Hilts, Calif.....................B2 170
Hilversum, Neth..............B5 59
Hima, Ky........................C6 182
Himalaya, mts., Asia.........G11 76
Himeji, Jap....................I7 93
Himes, Wyo.....................A4 213
Himi, Jap.......................H8 93
Himrod, N.Y.....................C4 196
Hinch, mtn., Tenn..............D9 205
Hinchcliffe, Sask., Can.........E4 155
Hinche, Hai......................F7 131
Hinchinbrook, isl., Alsk......g18 167
Hinchinbrook, isl., Austl.....C8 110
Hinckley, Eng.................B6 56
Hinckley, Ill...................B5 178
Hinckley, Maine.................D3 184
Hinckley, Minn................D6 187
Hinckley, Ohio..................A6 199
Hinckley, Utah................D3 207
Hinckley, res., N.Y............B5 196
Hindarabi, isl., Iran...........H6 86
Hindman, Ky..................C7 182
Hindmarsh, lake, Austl........G3 112
Hinds, co., Miss...............C3 188
Hinds, hill, Newf., Can........D3 152
Hinds, lake, Newf., Can.......D3 152
Hindsboro, Ill.................D5 178
Hindsville, Ark..................A2 169
Hindu Kush, mts., Afg.........D14 86
Hindubagh, Pak..................B4 87
Hines, Fla.......................C3 174
Hines, Minn......................C4 187
Hines, Oreg....................D7 201
Hines Creek, Alta., Can......A1 148
Hinesburg, Vt..................C2 208
Hinesburg, pond, Vt...........C2 208
Hinesville, Ga................E5 175
Hingham, Mass...........B6, D3 185
Hingham, Mont................B6 190
Hingham, bay, Mass...........D3 185
Hingoli, India....................H6 88
Hinis, Tur........................C13 85
Hinkle, Miss.....................A5 188
Hinkley, Calif...................E5 170
Hinnom, val., Isr.,
Jordan........................m14 84
Hinnöy, isl., Nor...............C6 63
Hino, Jap.........................I9 93
Hinojosa [del Duque], Sp...C3 65
Hinsdale, Ill...................F2 178
Hinsdale, Mass................B1 185
Hinsdale, Mont...................B9 190
Hinsdale, N.H..................E2 193
Hinsdale, N.Y..................C2 196
Hinsdale, co., Colo............D3 171
Hinton, Alta., Can..............C2 148
Hinton, Iowa....................B1 180
Hinton, Okla....................B3 200
Hinton, W. Va..................D4 211
Hinzir, cape, Tur...............D10 85
Hirado, isl., Jap................J4 93
Hiraiwa, cape, Iwo.................. 114
Hirakata, Jap..................*I7 93
Hiram, Ga.......................C2 175
Hiram, Maine...................E2 184
Hiram, Ohio.....................A6 199
Hiraoka, Jap.....................*I7 93
Hiratsuka, Jap.................n18 93
Hiraya, Jap.......................n14 93
Hirosaki, Jap...................F10 93
Hiroshima, Jap..................I6 93
Hirson, Fr.........................C5 58
Hirtshals, Den....................A3 62
Hisarönü, Tur.....................B9 85
Hiseville, Ky......................C4 182
Hisle, S Dak......................D4 204
Hissar, India.....................C6 87
Hit, Iraq..........................F14 85
Hita, Jap.........................*J5 93
Hitachi, Jap.....................H10 93
Hitchcock, Sask., Can...........H4 155
Hitchcock, Okla.................B3 200
Hitchcock, S. Dak..............C7 204
Hitchcock, Tex..................G5 206
Hitchcock, co., Nebr............D4 191
Hitchin, Eng......................C7 56

INDEX KEY Each place listed in **Bold-faced Type** has its population listed in the Population tables, pages 230 to 280.
Each country, shown in CAPITAL LETTERS, has its population listed in the World Political Information Table, pages 6 to 10.
* Does not appear on map; key shows general location.

Hitchins, Ky..........B7 182
Hitchita, Okla..........B6 200
Hitchland, Tex..........A2 206
Hiteman, Iowa..........C5 180
Hitoyoshi, Jap..........J5 93
Hitra, isl., Nor..........F3 63
Hitterdal, Minn..........D2 187
Hitzacker, Ger..........E5 62
Hivonnait, Arg..........E4 135
Hiwassee, Va..........E2 209
Hiwassee, lake, N.C..........D2 197
Hiwassee, riv., Tenn..........D9 205
Hixson, Tenn..........D8, E10 205
Hixton, Wis..........D3 212
Hjallerup, Den..........A4 62
Hjälmaren, lake, Swe..........H7 63
Hjälmseryd, Swe..........A8 62
Hjo, Swe..........H6 63
Hjörring, Den..........A3 62
Hjörring, co., Den..........A3 62
Hkakabo Razi, mtn., Bur...C10 87
Hlohovec, Czech..........D4 70
Hlomsak, Thai..........D4 89
Ho, China..........F4 92
Hoa Binh, Viet..........B6 89
Hoagland, Ind..........C8 179
Hoai Nhon, Viet..........E8 89
Hoback, riv., Wyo..........B2 213
Hobart, Austl..........o15 111
Hobart, Ind..........A3 179
Hobart, N.Y..........C6 196
Hobart, Okla..........B2 200
Hobbema, Alta., Can..........C4 148
Hobbieville, Ind..........G4 179
Hobbs, Ind..........D6 179
Hobbs, N. Mex..........E6 195
Hobe Sound, Fla..........E6 174
Hoberg, Mo..........*D4 189
Hobgood N.C..........A6 197
Hoboken, Bel..........C4 59
Hoboken, Ga..........E4 175
Hoboken, N.J..........D5 194
Hobro, Den..........B3 62
Höbsögöl Dalay, lake,
Mong..........A5 91
Hobson, Mont..........D7 190
Hobson, Va..........B6 209
Hobson, lake, B.C., Can..........C7 149
Hobson City, Ala..........*B4 166
Hobucken, N.C..........B7 197
Hochfeld, S.W. Afr..........B2 107
Hochfelden, Fr..........F7 59
Hochien, China..........E7 92
Hochih, China..........G6 91
Höchst, Ger..........C3 61
Höchstadt, Ger..........D5 61
Hochuan, China..........I2 92
Hockanum, Conn..........C6 172
Hockenheim, Ger..........D3 61
Hockerville, Okla..........A7 200
Hockessin, Del..........A6 173
Hocking, co., Ohio..........C5 199
Hocking, riv., Ohio..........C5 199
Hockingport, Ohio..........C6 199
Hockinson, Wash..........D3 210
Hockley, Tex..........F4 206
Hockley, co., Tex..........C1 206
Hodgdon Corners, Maine..B5 184
Hodge, La..........B3 183
Hodgeman, co., Kans..........D4 181
Hodgenville, Ky..........C4 182
Hodges, Ala..........A2 166
Hodges, Mont..........D12 190
Hodges, S.C..........C3 203
Hodges, hill, Newf., Can...D4 152
Hodgeville, Sask., Can..........G2 155
Hodgkins, Ill..........*B6 178
Hodgson, Man., Can..........D3 150
Hódmezővásárhely,
Hung..........B5 68
Hodna, lake, Alg..........G9 64
Hodonín, Czech..........D4 70
Hoea, Haw..........C6 176
Hoehne, Colo..........D6 171
Hoek van Holland, Neth....C4 59
Hoensbroek, Neth..........D5 59
Hoeryŏng, Kor..........E4 93
Hoey, Sask., Can..........E3 155
Hof, Ger..........C6 61
Hof, Nor..........p28 63
Hofei, China..........I7 92
Hoffman, Minn..........E3 187
Hoffman, N.C..........B4 197
Hoffman, Okla..........*B6 200
Hoffman Estates, Ill..........E2 178
Hofgeismar, Ger..........B4 61
Höfn, Ice..........n25 63
Hofsjökull, glacier, Ice..........n23 63
Hofuf, Sau. Ar..........I4 86
Hog, hbr., Espiritu Santo I..... 115
Hog, isl., Fla..........C3 174
Hog, isl., Mich..........C5 186
Hog, isl., N.C..........B7 197
Hog, isl., Va..........D7 209
Hog, neck, N.Y..........E7 172
Hog Creek, pt., N.Y..........E8 172
Hogback, mtn., Nebr..........C2 191
Hogback, mtn., S.C..........A3 203
Höganäs, Swe..........B6 62
Hogansburg, N.Y..........A2 196
Hogansville, Ga..........C2 175
Hogback, mtn., Mont..........F4 190
Hogback, mtn., Vt..........C2 208
Hogeland, Mont..........B8 190
Hogem, pass, B.C., Can..........B4 149
Hogsett, W. Va..........C2 211
Hoh, head, Wash..........B1 210
Hoh, riv., Wash..........B1 210
Hohe Tauern, mts., Aus...E6 60
Hohe Venn, plat., Bel.,
Ger..........D6 59
Hohen Solms, La..........B5 183
Hohenwald, Tenn..........B4 205
Hohenzollern: in 1849.......... 51
Hohokus, N.J..........*A4 194
Hohsien, China..........G7 91
Hohwachter, bay, Ger..........D4 62
Hoi An, Viet..........E8 89
Hoi Xuan, Viet..........B6 89
Hoima, Ug..........A5 106
Hoisington, Kans..........D5 181
Höjer, Den..........D2 62
Hokah, Minn..........G7 187
Hoke, co., N.C..........B4 197
Hokes Bluff, Ala..........B4 166
Hoking, China..........F5 91
Hokitika, N.Z..........O13 112
Hokoda, Jap..........m19 93
Holabird, S. Dak..........C6 204
Holap, isl., Truk.......... 114
Holbaek, Den..........C5 62
Holbaek, co., Den..........C5 62
Holbeach, Eng..........B8 56
Holbrook, Ariz..........C5 168
Holbrook, Idaho..........G6 177
Holbrook, Mass..........B5, D3 185
Holbrook, Nebr..........D5 191
Holbrook, N.Y..........*F4 172
Holcomb, Kans..........E3 181
Holcomb, Miss..........B4 188
Holcomb, Mo..........E7 189
Holcomb, Wash..........C2 210
Holcombe, Wis..........C2 212
Holcut, Miss..........A5 188
Holden, Alta., Can..........C4 148
Holden, La..........A6 183
Holden, Mass..........B4 185
Holden, Mo..........C4 189
Holden, Utah..........D3 207
Holden, Vt..........D3 208
Holden, W. Va..........D2 211
Holden Beach, N.C..........*D5 197
Holdenville, Okla..........B5 200
Holderness, N.H..........C3 193
Holdfast, Sask., Can..........G3 155
Holdingford, Minn..........E4 187
Holdrege, Nebr..........D6 191
Hole in the Mountain, peak,
Nev..........C6 192
Holeb, Maine..........C2 184
Hölen, Nor..........p28 63
Holgate, Ohio..........A3 199
Holguín, Cuba..........E5 131
Hollabrunn, Aus..........D8 60
Holladay, Tenn..........B3 205
Holladay, Utah..........C4 207
Holland.......... 48
Holland, Ark..........B3 169
Holland, Man., Can..........E2 150
Holland, Lincolnshire, see
Lincoln, co., Eng.
Holland, Ind..........H3 179
Holland, Iowa..........B5 180
Holland, Ky..........D3 182
Holland, Mass..........B3 185
Holland, Mich..........F4 186
Holland, Minn..........F2 187
Holland, Mo..........E8 189
Holland, N.Y..........C2 196
Holland, Ohio..........A2, A4 199
Holland, Oreg..........E3 201
Holland, Tex..........D4 206
Holland, Va..........E6 209
Holland, isl., Md..........D5 173
Holland, pt., Md..........C4 173
Holland, straits, Md..........D5 173
Holland Center, Ont.,
Can..........C4 153
Holland Patent, N.Y..........B5 196
Hollandale, Minn..........*G5 187
Hollandale, Miss..........B3 188
Hollandale, Wis..........F4 212
Hollansburg, Ohio..........C3 199
Hollenburg, Kans..........C7 181
Holley, N.Y..........B2 196
Holley, Oreg..........C4 201
Holliday, Mo..........B5 189
Holliday, Tex..........C3 206
Hollidaysburg, Pa..........F5 202
Hollins, Ala..........B3 166
Hollins, Va..........D3 209
Hollis, Ark..........C2 169
Hollis, Kans..........C6 181
Hollis, N.H..........E3 193
Hollis, Okla..........C2 200
Hollis Center, Maine..........E2 184
Hollister, Calif..........C6, D3 170
Hollister, Idaho..........G4 177
Hollister, Mo..........E4 189
Hollister, N.C..........A6 197
Hollister, Okla..........C3 200
Hollister, Wis..........C5 212
Hollisterville, Pa..........D11 202
Holliston, Mass..........D1 185
Hollmann, cape, New
Britain I.......... 115
Hollow Rock, Tenn..........A3 205
Holloway, Minn..........E3 187
Holloway, Ohio..........*B6 199
Hollowayville, Ill..........*B4 178
Hollowtop, mtn., Mont..........E4 190
Hollsopple (P.O.), Pa..........F4 202
Hollum, Neth..........A5 59
Holly, Colo..........C8 171
Holly, Mich..........F7 186
Holly Bluff, Miss..........C3 188
Holly Grove, Ark..........C4 169
Holly Hill, Fla..........C5 174
Holly Hill, S.C..........E7 203
Holly Pond, Ala..........A3 166
Holly Ridge, La..........B4 183
Holly Ridge, N.C..........C5 197
Holly Shelter, swamp,
N.C..........C6 197
Holly Springs, Ark..........D3 169
Holly Springs, Ga..........B2 175
Holly Springs, Miss..........A4 188
Holly Springs, N.C..........B5 197
Hollyoak, Del..........A7 173
Hollyvilla, Ky..........*B4 182
Hollyville, Del..........C7 173
Hollywood, Ala..........A4 166
Hollywood, Ariz..........E6 168
Hollywood, Ark..........C2 169
Hollywood, Calif..........F2 170
Hollywood, Fla..........E3, F6 174
Hollywood, Ga..........B3 175
Hollywood, La..........*D2 183
Hollywood, Md..........D4 173
Hollywood, Miss..........A3 188
Hollywood, Mo..........*E7 189
Hollywood, S.C..........F1 203
Hollywood Park, Tex..........*E3 206
Hollywood Ridge Farms,
Fla..........*F6 174
Holman, N. Mex..........A4 195
Holmdel Gardens,
Kans..........A4 181
Holmen, Wis..........E2 212
Holmes, Wyo..........D6 213
Holmes, co., Fla..........G3 174
Holmes, co., Miss..........B3 188
Holmes, co., Ohio..........B6 199
Holmes, mtn., Wyo..........A2 213
Holmes Beach, Fla..........*E4 174
Holmestrand, Nor..........p28 63
Holmesville, Ohio..........B6 199
Holmfield, Man., Can..........E2 150
Holmquist, S. Dak..........B8 204
Holmsbu, Nor..........p28 63
Holmsund, Swe..........F9 63
Holon, Isr..........B6, g10 84
Holopaw, Fla..........D5 174
Holroyd, Austl..........*F8 112
Holsljunga, Swe..........A7 62
Holstebro, Den..........B2 62
Holsted, Den..........C2 62
Holstein: in 1866.......... 51
Holstein, Ont., Can..........C4 153
Holstein, Iowa..........B2 180
Holstein, Mo..........C6 189
Holstein, Nebr..........D7 191
Holston, riv., Tenn..........C11 205
Holston, riv., Va..........B3 209
Holston High Knob, mtn.,
Tenn..........C11 205
Holsworthy, Eng..........D3 56
Holt, Ala..........B2 166
Holt, Fla..........G2 174
Holt, Mich..........F6 186
Holt, Minn..........B2 187
Holt, Mo..........B3 189
Holt, co., Mo..........A2 189
Holt, co., Nebr..........B7 191
Holt, res., Ala..........B2 166
Holter Dam, Mont..........D4 190
Holtland, Tenn..........B5 205
Holton, Ind..........F7 179
Holton, Kans..........A6, C8 181
Holton, Mich..........E4 186
Holtville, Calif..........F6 170
Holtwood, Pa..........G9 202
Holualoa, Haw..........D6 176
Holy, isl., Eng..........C6 55
Holy, isl., Scot..........E3 57
Holy, isl., Wales..........A3 56
Holy Cross, Alsk..........C8 167
Holy Cross, Iowa..........B7 180
Holy Roman Empire: c. 814.. 47
in 1721.......... 49
Holy Trinity, Ala..........C4 166
Holyhead, Wales..........A3 56
Holyoke, Colo..........A8 171
Holyoke, Mass..........B2 185
Holyoke, Minn..........D6 187
Holyoke, range, Mass..........B2 185
Holyrood, Newf., Can..........*E5 152
Holyrood, Kans..........D5 181
Holzkirchen, Ger..........B7 66
Holzminden, Ger..........B4 61
Homalin, Bur..........D9 87
Homberg, Ger..........B1 61
Homberg, Ger..........B4 61
Hombori, Mali..........C4 103
Homburg, Ger..........D2 61
Home, Kans..........C7 181
Home, bay, N.W. Ter.,
Can..........C19 143
Home Corner, Ind..........*C6 179
Home Gardens, Calif..........*F5 170
Home Place, Ind..........E5, H8 179
Homeacre, Pa..........*E2 202
Homécourt, Fr..........C6 58
Homecroft, Ind..........*E5 179
Homedale, Idaho..........F2 177
Homelake, Colo..........D4 171
Homeland, Fla..........E5 174
Homeland, Ga..........F4 175
Homer, Alsk..........D9, h16 167
Homer, Ga..........B3 175
Homer, Ill..........C6 178
Homer, La..........B2 183
Homer, Mich..........F6 186
Homer, Nebr..........B9 191
Homer, N.Y..........C4 196
Homer, Ohio..........B5 199
Homer City, Pa..........E3 202
Homer Youngs, peak, Mont.E3 190
Homerville, Ga..........E4 175
Homestake, Mont..........E4 190
Homestead, Fla..........F3, G6 174
Homestead, Iowa..........C6 180
Homestead, Mont..........B12 190
Homestead, Okla..........A3 200
Homestead, Oreg..........B10 201
Homestead, Pa..........B6 202
Homestead, nat. mon.,
Nebr..........D9 191
Hometown, Ill..........*F3 178
Homewood, Ala..........E4 166
Homewood, Calif..........C3 170
Homewood, Ill..........B6, F3 178
Homewood, Md..........C4 173
Homewood, Miss..........C4 188
Homewood, Pa..........*E1 202
Homeworth, Ohio..........B6 199
Hominy, Okla..........A5 200
Hominy, creek, Okla..........A5 200
Homo, bay, New Hebr.......... 115
Homochitto, riv., Miss..........D2 188
Homosassa, Fla..........D4 174
Homs, Syr..........E11 85
Hon, Ark..........C1 169
Hon Chuoi, isl., Viet..........H6 89
Hon Gay, Viet..........B7 89
Hon Me, isl., Viet..........C6 89
Honaker, Va..........B3 209
Honan, prov., China..........E7 91
c. 750.......... 80
c. 1775.......... 82
Honaunau, Haw..........D6 176
Honda, Col..........B3 133
Honda, bay, Phil..........D5 90
Hondo, N. Mex..........D4 195
Hondo, Tex..........E3 206
Hondo, riv., Br. Hond..........A3 130
Hondo, riv., Mex..........h9 129
HONDURAS, country,
N.A..........C4 130
Honduras, cape, Hond..........B4 130
Honduras, gulf, Br. Hond...B3 130
Honduras, British, see British
Honduras, dep., N.A.
Honea Path, S.C..........C3 203
Hönefoss, Nor..........G4 63
Honeoye Falls, N.Y..........C3 196
Honesdale, Pa..........C11 202
Honey, lake, Calif..........B3 170
Honey Brook, Pa..........F10 202
Honey Creek, Iowa..........C2 180
Honey Creek, Wis..........F1 212
Honey Grove, Pa..........F6 202
Honey Grove, Tex..........C5 206
Honeyford, N. Dak..........A8 198
Honeyville, Utah..........B3 207
Honfleur, Que., Can..........A6 154
Honfleur, Fr..........C4 58
Höng, Den..........C5 62
Honga, riv., Md..........D5 173
HONG KONG, Br. dep.,
Asia..........G7 91
Hongwŏn, Kor..........F3 93
Honiara, Guadalcanal I.......... 115
Honichin Hural, Mong..........C3 92
Honiton, Eng..........D4 56
Honnef, Ger..........C2 61
Hönningen, Ger..........C2 61
Hönö, isl., Swe..........A5 62
Honobia, Okla..........C7 200
Honohina, Haw..........D6 176
Honokaa, Haw..........C6 176
Honokahua, Haw..........B5 176
Honokohau, Haw..........*B5 176
Honolulu, Haw...B4, g10, m16 176
Honolulu, co., Haw....B3, g9 176
Honomu, Haw..........D6 176
Honor, Mich..........D4 186
Honoraville, Ala..........D3 166
Honouliuli, Haw..........g9 176
Honshū, isl., Jap..........I8 93
Honto, see Nevelsk, Sov. Un.
Honuapo, bay, Haw..........D6 176
Hood, Calif..........B6 170
Hood, co., Tex..........C4 206
Hood, canal, Wash..........B2 210
Hood, mtn., Oreg..........B5 201
Hood, pt., Austl..........F2 110
Hood River, Oreg..........B5 201
Hood River, co., Oreg..........B5 201
Hoodoo, Tenn..........B5 205
Hoodoo, peak, Wash..........A5 210
Hoodsport, Wash..........B2 210
Hoogeveen, Neth..........B6 59
Hoogezand, Neth..........A6 59
Hooghly, India..........*D8 87
Hooghly, riv., India..........G11 88
Hookena, Haw..........D6 176
Hooker, Okla..........D3 200
Hooker, S. Dak..........D8 204
Hooker, co., Nebr..........C4 191
Hooker, mtn., Alta., B.C.,
Can..........C8 149
Hookerton, N.C..........B6 197
Hooks, Tex..........*C5 206
Hooksett, N.H..........D4 193
Hookstown, Pa..........*E1 202
Hoolehua, Haw..........B4 176
Hoonah, Alsk..........D12, k22 167
Hoopa Valley, Indian res.,
Calif..........B2 170
Hooper, Colo..........D5 171
Hooper, Nebr..........C9 191
Hooper, Utah..........B3 207
Hooper, Wash..........C7 210
Hooper, creek, Nebr..........E2 191
Hooper, isl., Md..........D5 173
Hooper Bay, Alsk..........C6 167
Hooper, strait, Md..........D5 173
Hoopersville, Md..........D5 173
Hoopeston, Ill..........C6 178
Hooping Harbour, Newf.,
Can..........C3 152
Hoople, N. Dak..........A8 198
Hooppole, Ill..........B4 178
Hoorn, Neth..........B5 59
Hoosac, range, Mass., Vt...A1 185
Hoosac Tunnel, Mass..........A2 185
Hoosic, riv., N.Y.,
Vt..........A1 185, C7 196
Hoosick Falls, N.Y..........C7 196
Hoosier, Sask., Can..........F1 155
Hoover, S. Dak..........B2 204
Hoover, dam, Ariz.,
Nev..........A1 168, G7 192
Hoover, res., Ohio..........B5 199
Hooversville, Pa..........F4 202
Hop, riv., Conn..........C7 172
Hop Bottom, Pa..........C10 202
Hopa, Tur..........B13 85
Hopatcong, N.J..........B3 194
Hopatcong, lake, N.J..........B3 194
Hope, Alsk..........C10, g17 167
Hope, Ark..........D2 169
Hope, B.C., Can..........E7 149
Hope, Idaho..........A2 177
Hope, Ind..........F6 179
Hope, Kans..........D6 181
Hope, Maine..........D3 184
Hope, Mich..........E6 186
Hope, Minn..........G5 187
Hope, N.J..........B3 194
Hope, N. Mex..........E5 195
Hope, N. Dak..........B8 198
Hope, R.I..........C10 172
Hope, isl., B.C., Can..........D4 149
Hope, isl., Nor..........B12 118
Hope, lake, Scot..........B4 57
Hope, mtn., Scot..........B4 57
Hope, pt., Alsk..........B6 167
Hope Hull, Ala..........C3 166
Hope Mills, N.C..........C5 197
Hope Valley, R.I..........C10 172
Hopedale, Newf., Can..........g9 152
Hopedale, Ill..........C4 178
Hopedale, La..........E6 183
Hopedale, Mass..........B4, E1 185
Hopedale, Ohio..........B7 199
Hopeh (Hopei), prov.,
China..........D8 91
Hopelchén, Mex..........D7 129
Hopeman, Scot..........C5 57
Hopes Advance, cape, Que.,
Can..........A2 154
Hopeton, Okla..........A3 200
Hopetoun, Austl..........F3 111
Hopetoun, Austl..........G4 112
Hopetown, S. Afr..........C3 107
Hopeville, Iowa..........D4 180
Hopewell, Ala..........A3 166
Hopewell, N.S., Can..........D7 151
Hopewell, Miss..........D3 188
Hopewell, N.J..........C3 194
Hopewell, Ohio..........C5 199
Hopewell, Pa..........F5 202
Hopewell (Independent City),
Va..........C7, D5 209
Hopewell, W. Va..........*B4 211
Hopewell Cape, N.B., Can. D5 151
Hopewell Junction, N.Y...D7 196
Hopi, buttes, Ariz..........B5 168
Hopi, Indian res., Ariz..........A5 168
Hopkins, Mich..........F5 186
Hopkins, Minn..........E6 187
Hopkins, Mo..........A3 189
Hopkins, S.C..........D6 203
Hopkins, co., Ky..........C2 182
Hopkins, co., Tex..........C5 206
Hopkinsville, Ky..........D2 182
Hopkinton, Iowa..........B6 180
Hopkinton, Mass..........B4, D1 185
Hopkinton, N.H..........D3 193
Hopkinton, N.Y..........A2 196
Hopkinton, R.I..........D9 172
Hopkinton-Everett, res.,
N.H..........D3 193
Hopland, Calif..........C2 170
Hoppo, China..........G6 91
Hopson, Tenn..........C11 205
Hopwood, Pa..........G2 202
Hoquiam, Wash..........C2 210
Hor al Hammar, lake, Iraq.F3 86
Hor Sanniyah, lake, Iraq..........E3 86
Horace, Kans..........D2 181
Horace, N. Dak..........C9 198
Horace, mtn., Alsk..........B10 167
Horatio, Ark..........D1 169
Horatio, S.C..........C6 203
Horažd'ovice, Czech..........D8 61
Horb [am Neckar], Ger..........E3 61
Hörby, Swe..........C7 62
Horconcitos, Pan..........F6 130
Hordio, Som..........C7 105
Hordville, Nebr..........C8 191
Horicon, Wis..........E5 212
Horizon, Sask., Can..........H3 155
Horlick, mts., Ant..........A1 120
Hormigueros, P.R..........C2 132
Hormigueros, mun., P.R...C2 132
Hormuz, isl., Iran..........H8 86
Hormuz, strait, Iran..........H8 86
Horn, Ariz..........E2 168
Horn, Aus..........D7 60
Horn, cape, Chile..........k12 136
Horn, isl., Miss..........E5 188
Horn, lake, Miss..........A3 188
Horn, mtn., Ala..........B3 166
Horn, mts., N.W. Ter., Can.D9 142
Horn, pt., Ice..........m21 63
Horn, pond, Mass..........C2 185
Horn Island, pass, Miss..........E3 188
Horn Lake, Miss..........A3 188
Hornavan, lake, Swe..........D7 63
Hornbeak, Tenn..........A2 205
Hornbeck, La..........C2 183
Hornburg, Ger..........A5 61
Horncastle, Eng..........A7 56
Hornchurch, Eng..........*C8 56
Hornell, N.Y..........C3 196
Hornerstown, N.J..........C3 194
Hornersville, Mo..........E7 189
Horní Litvínov, Czech..........C8 61
Horní Počernice, Czech..n18 70
Hornick, Iowa..........B1 180
Hornings Mills, Ont., Can...C4 153
Hornsby, Tenn..........B3 205
Hornsbyville, Va..........A6 209
Hornsea, Eng..........D6 55
Hornsey, Eng..........*k12 55
Hornslet, Den..........B4 62
Hörnum, Ger..........A5 60
Hořovice, Czech..........D8 61
Horqueta, Par..........D4 135
Horred, Swe..........A6 62
Horrel Hill, S.C..........C6 203
Horry, co., S.C..........D9 203
Horse, creek, Colo..........C7 171
Horse, creek, Wyo..........D8 213
Horse, mtn., N. Mex..........C1 195
Horse, riv., Alta., Can..........A5 148
Horse Branch, Ky..........C3 182
Horse Cave, Ky..........C4 182
Horse Creek, Wyo..........D7 213
Horse Head, lake, N. Dak..B6 198
Horse Heaven, hills, Wash..C6 210
Horse Islands, Newf.
Can..........C4 152
Horse Shoe Bend, Idaho...F2 177
Horse Springs, N. Mex....D1 195
Horseback Knob, hill,
Ohio..........C4 199
Horsefly, B.C., Can..........C7 149
Horsefly, lake, B.C., Can...C7 149
Horseheads, N.Y..........C4 196
Horsens, Den..........C3 62
Horseshoe, cove, Fla..........C3 174
Horseshoe, lake, Man.,
Can..........C4 150
Horseshoe, lake, Ill..........A8 189
Horseshoe, pt., Fla..........C3 174
Horseshoe, res., Ariz..........C4 168
Horseshoe Beach, Fla..........C3 174
Horsham, Austl..........H4 112
Horsham, Eng..........C7 56
Horšovský Tyn, Czech..........D7 61
Horta, Port. (Azores)..........g8 102
Horten, Nor..........H4, p28 63
Hortense, Ga..........E5 175
Horton, Ala..........A3 166
Horton, Iowa..........B5 180
Horton, Kans..........C8 181
Horton, Mo..........D3 189
Horton, Mont..........D10 190
Horton, pt., N.Y..........E7 172
Hortonia, lake, Vt..........D2 208
Hortonville, Wis..........D5 212
Hörve, Den..........C5 62
Hörviken, Swe..........B8 62
Hoschton, Ga..........B3 175
Hosford, Fla..........B2 174
Hoshab, Pak..........H11 86
Hoshan, China..........I7 92
Hoshiarpur, India..........B5 88
Hoskins, Nebr..........B8 191
Hoskins, Oreg..........C3 201
Hosmer, B.C., Can..........E10 149
Hosmer, S. Dak..........B6 204
Hospers, Iowa..........A2 180
Hospet, India..........*E6 87
Hospitalet, Sp..........B7 65
Hosston, La..........B2 183
Hosta, butte, N. Mex..........B1 195
Hoste, isl., Chile..........k12 136
Hostomice, Czech..........o17 70
Hot Creek, range, Nev..........E5 192
Hot Springs, Mont..........C2 190
Hot Springs, see Truth or
Consequences, N. Mex.
Hot Springs, N.C..........C3 197
Hot Springs, S. Dak..........D2 204
Hot Springs, Tex..........E1 206
Hot Springs, Va..........D3 209
Hot Spring, co., Ark..........C2 169
Hot Springs, co., Wyo..........B4 213
Hot Springs, nat. park,
Ark..........C2 169
Hot Springs, peak, Calif....B3 170
Hot Springs, peak, Nev..........B4 192
Hot Springs National Park,
Ark..........C2, C6 169
Hot Sulphur Springs,
Colo..........A4 171
Hotchkiss, Colo..........C3 171
Hötensleben, Ger..........A6 61
Hotevilla, Ariz..........B5 168
Hotien, see Khotan, China
Hoting, Swe..........E7 63
Hotse, China..........G6 92
Hottah, lake, N.W. Ter.,
Can..........C9 142
Hotte, mts., Haiti..........F7 131
Hou, riv., Laos..........B5 89
Houck, Ariz..........B6 168
Houffalize, Bel..........D5 59
Houghton, Mich..........A2 186
Houghton, N.Y..........C2 196
Houghton, S. Dak..........B7 204
Houghton, Wash..........D2 210
Houghton, co., Mich..........B2 186
Houghton, lake, Mich..........D6 186
Houghton, res., S. Dak..........B7 204
Houghton Lake, Mich..........D6 186
Houghton Lake Heights,
Mich..........D6 186
Houilles, Fr..........g9 58
Houlka, Miss..........A4 188
Houlton, Maine..........B5 184
Houltonville, La..........B1 183
Houma, La..........C6, E5 183
Houmt-Souk, Tun..........H12 64
Houndé, Upper Volta..........D4 103
Hounslow, Eng..........m12 55
Hourn, inlet, Scot..........C3 57
Housatonic, Mass..........B1 185
Housatonic, riv., Conn.,
Mass..........D4 172
House, N. Mex..........C6 195
House, range, Utah..........D2 207
House, riv., Alta., Can..........A4 148
House Harbour, Que.,
Can..........B8 151
House Springs, Mo..........B7 189
Houston, Ark..........B3 169
Houston, B.C., Can..........B4 149
Houston, Del..........C6 173
Houston, Fla..........B4 174
Houston, Ind..........F5 179
Houston, Minn..........G7 187
Houston, Miss..........B4 188
Houston, Mo..........D6 189
Houston, Ohio..........B3 199
Houston, Pa..........F1 202
Houston, Tex..........E5, F5 206
Houston, co., Ala..........D4 166
Houston, co., Ga..........D3 175
Houston, co., Minn..........G7 187
Houston, co., Tenn..........A4 205
Houston, co., Tex..........D5 206

Houston Lake, Mo........*B3 189
Houstonia, Mo............C4 189
Houtzdale, Pa.............E5 202
Hove, Eng.................D7 56
Hövelhof, Ger.............B3 61
Hoven, S. Dak.............B6 204
Hovenweep, nat. mon., Colo., Utah....................F6 207
Hoveyzeh, Iran............F4 86
Hovland, Minn.............B7 187
Howar, riv., Sud...........B2 105
Howard, Ala...............B2 166
Howard, Colo..............C5 171
Howard, Ga................D2 175
Howard, Kans..............E7 181
Howard, Miss..............B3 188
Howard, N.Y...............C3 196
Howard, Ohio..............B5 199
Howard, Pa................D6 202
Howard, R.I...............C11 172
Howard, S. Dak............C8 204
Howard, Wis..........A6, D5 212
Howard, co., Ark..........C2 169
Howard, co., Ind..........C5 179
Howard, co., Iowa.........A5 180
Howard, co., Md...........B4 173
Howard, co., Mo...........B5 189
Howard, co., Nebr.........C7 191
Howard, co., Tex..........C2 206
Howard City, Mich.........E5 186
Howard Hanson, flood control res., Wash...............B4 210
Howard Lake, Minn.........E4 187
Howard Prairie, res., Oreg..E4 201
Howards Grove, Wis...B6, E6 212
Howardville, Mo..........*E8 189
Howe, Idaho...............F6 177
Howe, Ind.................A7 179
Howe, Okla................C7 200
Howe, Tex................*C4 206
Howe, cape, Austl.........H7 112
Howe, sound, B.C., Can....E6 149
Howell, Ark...............B4 169
Howell, Ga................F3 175
Howell, Mich..............F7 186
Howell, Tenn..............B5 205
Howell, Utah..............B3 207
Howell, co., Mo...........E6 189
Howells, Nebr.............C8 191
Howes, S. Dak.............C3 204
Howes Mill, Mo............D6 189
Howesville, W. Va.........B5 211
Howey-in-the-Hills, Fla...*D5 174
Howick, Que., Can.........D4 154
Howison, Miss.............E4 188
Howland, Maine............C4 184
Howland, isl., Oceania.....F11 113
Howley, Newf., Can........D3 152
Howley, mtn., Newf., Can......................D2 152
Howrah, India....D8 87, F12 88
Howser, B.C., Can.........D9 149
Howson, peak, B.C., Can...B4 149
Hoxie, Ark................A5 169
Hoxie, Kans...............C3 181
Höxter, Ger...............B4 61
Hoy, isl., Scot............B5 57
Hoya, Ger.................B4 60
Hoyang, China.............G4 92
Hoyerswerda, Ger..........B9 61
Hoylake, Eng..............A4 56
Hoyleton, Ill..............E4 178
Hoyo, mtn., Sp............o17 65
Hoyt, Colo................A6 171
Hoyt, Kans...........B6, C8 181
Hoyt, Okla................B6 200
Hoyt Lakes, Minn..........C6 187
Hoyt Station, N.B., Can....D3 151
Hoytsville, Utah...........C4 207
Hoytville, Ohio............A4 199
Hradec Králové, Czech....C3 70
Hranice, Czech............D4 70
Hriňová, Czech............D5 70
Hron, riv., Czech..........D5 70
Hrubieszów, Pol...........C7 70
Hsi, China................F4 92
Hsiachiang, China.........K6 92
Hsiaching, China..........F6 92
Hsian, China..............E2 93
Hsian, see Sian, China
Hsiang, riv., China.........J5 92
Hsiangfan, China...........H5 92
Hsianghsiang, China.......*K5 92
Hsiangtan, China..F7 91, K5 92
Hsiangyang, China........*H5 92
Hsiapu, China.............K9 92
Hsichang, China...........F5 91
Hsienning China...........J6 92
Hsienyang, China..........G3 92
Hsifeng, China............C11 92
Hsilung, China............G6 91
Hsinchiang, China.........G4 92
Hsinchu, Taiwan...........G9 91
Hsingan, mtn., China.......D7 92
Hsingcheng, China.........D9 92
Hsingshanchen, China......C5 93
Hsingtai, China...........F6 92
Hsinhsiang, China.........G5 92
Hsining, China............D5 91
Hsinkao, mtn., Taiwan.....G9 91
Hsinmin, China..C9 91, C10 92
Hsinning, China...........F7 91
Hsinpin, China............F2 93
Hsintai, China............G7 92
Hsintsai, China...........H6 92
Hsinyang, China...........H6 92
Hsinyeh, China............H5 92
Hsipaw, Bur...............A2 89
Hsiushui, China...........J6 92
Hsüancheng, China..........I8 92
Hsuanhua, China...........C8 91
Hsuchang, China...........H5 92
Hsuchow, see Suchow, China
Hsüi, China...............H8 92
Hsunho, China.............B4 93
Hsüpu, China..............K4 92
Hsüwen, China.............B9 89
Huacho, Peru..............D2 134
Huachuca City, Ariz........F5 168
Huacrachuco, Peru.........C2 134
Huahua, riv., Nic.........C6 130
Huai, riv., China..........E8 91
Huaian, China.............H8 92
Huaian, China.............H8 92
Huailai, China............D6 92
Huailu, N. Cal................. 115
Huainan, China............H7 92
Huaite, China.............E2 93
Huaiyang, China...........H6 92
Huaiyüan, China...........H7 92
Huajuapan de León, Mex..............D5, o15 129
Hualalai, mtn., Haw.......D6 176
Hualapai, mts., Ariz.......C2 168
Hualapai, peak, Ariz.......B2 168
Hualgayoc, Peru...........C2 134
Hualien, Taiwan...........G9 91
Huallaga, riv., Peru.......C2 134
Huallanca, Peru...........C2 134
Hualpai, Indian res., Ariz...B2 168
Huamachuco, Peru..........C2 134
Huamantla, Mex...........n15 129
Huambo, dist., Ang........D2 106
Huancabamba, Peru.........C2 134
Huancané, Peru............E4 134
Huancavelica, Peru........D2 134
Huancavelica, dept., Peru......................D2 134
Huancayo, Peru............D2 134
Huanchaca, Bol............D2 135
Huangan, China.............I6 92
Huangchuan, China.........H6 92
Huangkang, China...........I6 92
Huangmei, China............I6 92
Huangping, China..........K2 92
Huangshih, China...........I6 92
Huangyen, China...........J9 92
Huangyuan, China..........D5 91
Huanjen, China............F2 93
Huanta, Peru..............D3 134
Huánuco, Peru.............C2 134
Huánuco, dept., Peru.......C2 134
Huanuni, Bol..............C2 135
Huara, Chile..............C2 135
Huaral, Peru..............D2 134
Huarás, Peru..............C2 134
Huari, Bol................C2 135
Huariaca, Peru............D2 134
Huarina, Bol..............C2 135
Huarmey, Peru.............D2 134
Huasco, Chile.............E1 135
Huatabampo, Mex...........B3 129
Huatien, China............C10 91
Huatusco, Mex............n15 129
Huauchinango, Mex........m14 129
Huaunta, Nic..............D6 130
Huayllay, Peru............D2 134
Huaytará, Peru............D2 134
Hubbard, Sask., Can........F4 155
Hubbard, Iowa.............B4 180
Hubbard, Minn.............D4 187
Hubbard, Ohio.............A7 199
Hubbard, Oreg........B2, B4 201
Hubbard, Tex..............D4 206
Hubbard, co., Minn........C4 187
Hubbard, lake, Mich........D7 186
Hubbard Creek, res., Tex...C3 206
Hubbard Lake, Mich........D7 186
Hubbards, N.S., Can........E5 151
Hubbardston, Mass.........B3 185
Hubbardston, Mich.........E5 186
Hubbardton, Vt............D2 208
Hubbardton, riv., Vt.......D2 208
Hubbell, Mich.............A2 186
Hubbell, Nebr.............D8 191
Huben, Aus................C8 66
Huberdeau, Que., Can......D3 154
Hubli, India..............E6 87
Huchou, China..............I9 92
Huckleberry, mtn., Oreg....D4 201
Huckleberry, mts., Wash....A8 210
Huddersfield, Eng.........A6 56
Huddleston, Va............C3 209
Huddleston Knob, mtn., Tenn......................C8 205
Hude, Ger.................E2 62
Hudiksvall, Swe...........G7 63
Hudin (Oasis), Som........D6 105
Hudson, Que., Can.....D3, D8 154
Hudson, Colo..............A6 171
Hudson, Fla...............D4 174
Hudson, Ill...............C5 178
Hudson, Ind...............A7 179
Hudson, Iowa..............B5 180
Hudson, Kans..............D5 181
Hudson, Maine.............C4 184
Hudson, Mass.........B4, D1 185
Hudson, Mich..............G6 186
Hudson, N.H...............E4 193
Hudson, N.Y...............C7 196
Hudson, N.C...............B2 197
Hudson, Ohio..............A6 199
Hudson, S. Dak............D9 204
Hudson, Wis...............D1 212
Hudson, Wyo...............C4 213
Hudson, co., N.J..........B4 194
Hudson, bay, Can..........D15 143
Hudson, lake, Okla........A6 200
Hudson, mtn., Maine.......B3 184
Hudson, riv., N.J., N.Y..................A5, D5 194
Hudson, strait, N.W. Ter., Can......................D18 143
Hudson Bay, Sask., Can...E4 155
Hudson Center, N.H........E4 193
Hudson Falls, N.Y.........B7 196
Hudson Heights, Que., Can......................D8 154
Hudson Hope, B.C., Can...A7 149
Hudsonville, Mich.........F5 186
Hudsonville, Miss.........A4 188
Hudspeth, co., Tex........F1 206
Hudwin, lake, Man., Can...C4 150
Hue, Viet.................D7 89
Hueco, mts., Tex..........E1 206
Huedin, Rom...............B6 68
Huehuetenango, Guat.......C2 130
Huejutla, Mex............m14 129
Huelma, Sp................D4 65
Huelva, Sp................D2 65
Huentelauquén, Chile......A2 136
Huércal-Overa, Sp.........D5 65
Huerfano, co., Colo.......D5 171
Huerfano, riv., Colo......D6 171
Huerva, riv., Sp..........B5 65
Huésca, Sp................A5 65
Huéscar, Sp...............D4 65
Huesco, mts., Mex.........F1 206
Huetamo de Núñez, Mex..............D4, n13 129
Huete, Sp.................B4 65
Huetter, Idaho...........*B2 177
Huey, Ill.................*E4 178
Hueytown, Ala.............E4 166
Huff, Ark.................B4 169
Huff, N. Dak..............C5 198
Huffman, Ark..............B6 169
Huffton, S. Dak...........B7 204
Huger, S.C................E3 203
Hugh Butler Lake, res., Nebr......................D5 191
Hughenden, Austl..........D7 111
Hughes, Alsk..............B9 167
Hughes, Ark...............C5 169
Hughes, Austl.............F4 111
Hughes, co., Okla.........B5 200
Hughes, co., S. Dak.......C5 204
Hughes, range, B.C., Can......................E10 149
Hughes, riv., Man., Can...A1 150
Hughes, riv., W. Va.......B3 211
Hughes Springs, Tex......*C5 206
Hughestown, Pa..........*D10 202
Hughesville, Md...........C4 173
Hughesville, Mo...........C4 189
Hughesville, Mont.........C6 190
Hughesville, Pa...........D8 202
Hughson, Calif...........*D3 170
Hugo, Colo................B7 171
Hugo, Minn................E7 187
Hugo, Okla................C6 200
Hugoton, Kans.............E2 181
Huhohaote (Kweisui), China..........C7 91, D4 92
Huichang, China...........F8 91
Huichapan, Mex...........m14 129
Hüichŏn, Kor..............F3 93
Huila, dist., Ang..........E1 106
Huila, dept., Col..........C2 133
Huili, China..............F5 91
Huimin, China.............F7 92
Huinan, China.............E3 93
Huitzuco, Mex............n14 129
Huixtla, Mex..............D6 129
Huiyang, China............G7 91
Huizen, Neth..............B5 59
Hukou, China..............J7 92
Hukuntsi, Bots............B3 107
Hulah, Okla...............A5 200
Hulah, res., Okla..........A5 200
Hulan, China.............B10 91
Hulbert, Ark..............B5 169
Hulbert, Mich.............B6 186
Hulbert, Okla.............B6 200
Hulberton, N.Y............B2 196
Hulda, Isr...........C6, h10 84
Huleh, lake, Isr...........A7 84
Hulett, Wyo...............A8 213
Hulin, China..............C6 93
Hull, Que., Can...........D2 154
Hull, Eng.................A7 56
Hull, Ga.................*B3 175
Hull, Ill..................D2 178
Hull, Iowa................A1 180
Hull, Mass...........B6, D3 185
Hull, co., Que., Can......D2 154
Hull, riv., Eng............G8 57
Hulls Cove, Maine.........D4 184
Hulmeville, Pa..........*F12 202
Hulst, Neth...............C4 59
Hulun, see Hailar, China
Hulun Nor, lake, China....B8 91
Hulutao, China............D9 92
Hulwān, Eg................E3 84
Humacao, P.R..............C7 132
Humacao, mun., P.R. C7, g11 132
Humahuaca, Arg............D2 135
Humaitá, Braz.............D1 139
Humansdorp, S. Afr........D3 107
Humansville, Mo...........D4 189
Humarock, Mass............E4 185
Humbe, Ang................E1 106
Humber, riv., Eng..........A7 56
Humbermouth, Newf., Can......................D3 152
Humbird, Wis..............D3 212
Humble, Tex..........E5, F5 206
Humble City, N. Mex.......E6 195
Humboldt, Ariz............C3 168
Humboldt, Sask., Can......E3 155
Humboldt, Ill.............D5 178
Humboldt, Iowa............B3 180
Humboldt, Kans............E8 181
Humboldt, Minn............B1 187
Humboldt, Nebr...........D10 191
Humboldt, Nev.............C3 192
Humboldt, S. Dak..........D8 204
Humboldt, Tenn............B3 205
Humboldt, co., Calif.......B2 170
Humboldt, co., Iowa.......B3 180
Humboldt, co., Nev........B3 192
Humboldt, range, Nev......C3 192
Humboldt, riv., Nev.......C3 192
Hume, res., Austl..........G6 112
Hume, Ill.................D6 178
Hume, Mo..................C3 189
Hume, N.Y.................C2 196
Hume, Va..................C5 209
Humenné, Czech............D6 70
Humeston, Iowa............D4 180
Hummels Wharf, Pa.........E8 202
Hummelstown, Pa..........*F8 202
Humnoke, Ark..............C4 169
Humpata, Ang..............E1 106
Humphrey, Ark.............C4 169
Humphrey, Idaho...........E6 177
Humphrey, Nebr............C8 191
Humphreys, La.............C5 183
Humphreys, Mo.............A4 189
Humphreys, Okla...........C2 200
Humphreys, co., Miss......B3 188
Humphreys, co., Tenn......A4 205
Humphreys, mtn., Calif....D4 170
Humphreys, peak, Ariz.....B4 168
Humpolec, Czech...........D3 70
Humptulips, Wash..........B2 210
Hūn, Libya................D3 101
Hunan, prov., China.......F7 91
Hunchun, China...........C11 91
Hundested, Den............C5 62
Hundred, W. Va............B4 211
Hunedoara, Rom............C6 68
Hünfeld, Ger..............C4 61
HUNGARY, country, Eur....B4 68
c. 1140......................... 47
c. 1294......................... 81
c. 1360......................... 48
in 1721......................... 49
in 1810......................... 50
in 1922-40...................... 53
after World War II.............. 54
see also Austria-Hungary
Hunger, mtn., Vt..........C8 208
Hungerford, Austl.........D5 112
Hŭnghae, Kor..............H4 93
Hungnam, Kor..............G3 93
Hungry Horse, Mont........B2 190
Hungshui, riv., China......G6 91
Huningue, Fr..............B3 66
Hunker, Pa...............*F2 202
Hunnewell, Kans...........E6 181
Hunnewell, Mo.............B6 189
Hunsrück, mts., Ger........D2 61
Hunstanton, Eng...........B8 56
Hunt, Ariz................C6 168
Hunt, Ark.................B2 169
Hunt, co., Tex............C4 206
Hunt, mtn., Yukon, Can....D7 148
Hunt, mtn., Wyo...........A5 213
Hunte, riv., Ger...........B4 60
Hunter, Ark...............B4 169
Hunter, Kans..............C5 181
Hunter, Mo................E7 189
Hunter, N.Y...............C6 196
Hunter, N. Dak............B8 198
Hunter, Okla..............A4 200
Hunter, Tex..........A4, E3 206
Hunter, cape, Guadalcanal I... 115
Hunter, is., Austl........o14 110
Hunter, isl., B.C., Can....D3 149
Hunter, mtn., N.Y.........C6 196
Hunterdon, co., N.J.......B3 194
Hunters, Wash.............A7 210
Hunters, hot springs, Oreg......................E6 201
Hunters Creek Village, Tex.....................*E5 206
Hunters River, P.E.I., Can..C6 151
Huntersfield, mtn., N.Y....C6 196
Huntersville, N.C..........B3 197
Huntersville, W. Va.......C4 211
Huntertown, Ind...........B7 179
Hunting, creek, Md........C4 173
Hunting, isl., S.C.........G7 203
Hunting Valley, Ohio.....*A6 199
Huntingburg, Ind..........H4 179
Huntingdon, B.C., Can...B10 149
Huntingdon, Que., Can.....D3 154
Huntingdon, Eng...........B7 56
Huntingdon, Pa............F6 202
Huntingdon, Tenn..........A3 205
Huntingdon, co., Que., Can......................D3 154
Huntingdon, co., Eng......B7 56
Huntingdon, co., Pa.......F5 202
Huntingdon, isl., Newf., Can......................B3 152
Huntington, Ark...........B1 169
Huntington, Ind...........C7 179
Huntington, Mass..........B2 185
Huntington, N.Y..........*B2 194
Huntington (P.O.), N.Y. D3, E7 196
Huntington, Oreg..........C9 201
Huntington, Tex...........D5 206
Huntington, Utah..........D5 207
Huntington, Vt............C3 208
Huntington, W. Va.........C2 211
Huntington, co., Ind......C6 179
Huntington, bay, N.Y......F3 172
Huntington Bay, N.Y......*E7 196
Huntington Beach, Calif...F5 170
Huntington Beach (East Neck), N.Y.................*E7 196
Huntington Center, Vt.....C3 208
Huntington Park, Calif....F4 170
Huntington Station, N.Y...F3 172
Huntington Woods, Mich..A7 186
Huntingtown, Md...........C4 173
Huntland, Tenn............B5 205
Huntleigh, Mo............*C7 189
Huntley, Ill...............A5 178
Huntley, Minn.............G4 187
Huntley, Mont.............E8 190
Huntley, Nebr.............D6 191
Huntley, Wyo..............D8 213
Huntly, Scot..............C6 57
Hunts Point, N.S., Can....F5 151
Hunts Point, Wash........*B3 210
Huntsville, Ala............A3 166
Huntsville, Ark............A2 169
Huntsville, Ont., Can......B5 153
Huntsville, Ind............E6 179
Huntsville, Ky............C3 182
Huntsville, Mo............B5 189
Huntsville, Ohio.........*B4 199
Huntsville, Tenn..........C9 205
Huntsville, Tex...........D5 206
Huntsville, Utah..........B4 207
Huntsville, Wash..........C7 210
Hunucmá, Mex..............C7 129
Huon, gulf, N. Gui.........k12 110
Hupeh (Hupei), prov., China......................E7 91
Hurd, cape, Ont., Can.....B3 153
Hurdland, Mo..............A5 189
Hurdsfield, N. Dak.........B6 198
Hurffville, N.J...........D2 194
Hurley, Miss..............E5 188
Hurley, Mo................E4 189
Hurley, N. Mex............E1 195
Hurley, N.Y...............D6 196
Hurley, S. Dak............D8 204
Hurley, Va................B3 209
Hurley, Wis...............B3 212
Hurleyville, N.Y..........D6 196
Hurliness, Scot...........B5 57
Hurlock, Md...............C6 173
Huron, Calif.............*D3 170
Huron, Ind................G4 179
Huron, Kans...............C8 181
Huron, Ohio...............A5 199
Huron, S. Dak.............C7 204
Huron, co., Ont., Can.....D3 153
Huron, co., Mich..........E7 186
Huron, co., Ohio..........A5 199
Huron, lake, Can., U.S....B11 159
Huron, mts., Mich..........B3 186
Huron, riv., Mich..........A6 186
Huron, riv., Ohio..........A5 199
Hurricane, Utah...........F2 207
Hurricane, W. Va..........C2 211
Hurricane, cliffs, Ariz....A2 168
Hurricane, creek, Ark.....C3 169
Hurricane, creek, Ga......E4 175
Hurricane, mtn., Tenn.....C9 205
Hurricane Deck, Mo.......*C5 189
Hurricane Mills, Tenn.....B4 205
Hurst, Ill.................F4 178
Hurst, Tex...............*C4 206
Hurstville, Austl........*G8 112
Hürth, Ger................C1 61
Hurtsboro, Ala............C4 166
Hurup, Den................B2 62
Huşi, Rom.................B9 68
Huskvarna, Swe.............I6 63
Huson, Mont...............C2 190
Hussar, Alta., Can........D4 148
Hussein-Dey, Alg.........*B5 102
Husser, La................D5 183
Hustburg, Tenn............B4 205
Husted, Colo..............C6 171
Hustisford, Wis...........E5 212
Hustle, Va................C5 209
Hustler, Wis.............*E3 212
Hustontown, Pa............F5 202
Hustonville, Ky...........C5 182
Husum, Ger................A4 60
Husum, Wash...............D4 210
Hutch, isl., S.C...........G1 203
Hutch, mtn., Ariz..........C4 168
Hutchins, Tex.............B5 206
Hutchinson, Kans.....A4, D6 181
Hutchinson, Minn..........F4 187
Hutchinson, co., S. Dak...D8 204
Hutchinson, co., Tex......B2 206
Hutchinsons, isl., Fla.....E6 174
Hutsonville, Ill...........D6 178
Huttig, Ark...............D3 169
Hutto, Tex................D4 206
Hutton, La................C2 183
Hutton, Md................D1 173
Hutton Valley, Mo.........E6 189
Huttonsville, W. Va.......C5 211
Huu, Indon................G5 90
Ḥuwwārah, Jordan..........g12 84
Huxford, Ala..............D2 166
Huxley, Alta., Can........D4 148
Huxley, Iowa..............C4 180
Huy, Bel..................D5 59
Huyton-with-Roby, Eng...*A5 56
Hvalpsund, Den............B3 62
Hvidbjerg, Den............B2 62
Hvide Sande, Den..........C2 62
Hvitsten, Nor.............p28 63
Hvittingfoss, Nor.........p28 63
Hwang Ho (Yellow), riv., China...........D8 91, F4 92
Hwangling, China..........D6 91
Hweitseh, China...........F5 91
Hyak, Wash................B4 210
Hyampom, Calif............B2 170
Hyannis, Mass.............C7 185
Hyannis, Nebr.............C4 191
Hyannis Port, Mass........C7 185
Hyas, Sask., Can..........F4 155
Hyatts, Ohio..............B4 199
Hyattstown, Md............B3 173
Hyattsville, Md......C1, C4 173
Hyattville, Wyo...........A5 213
Hybart, Ala...............D2 166
Hyco, riv., Va.............E4 209
Hydaburg, Alsk.....D13, n23 167
Hyde, co., N.C............B7 197
Hyde, co., S. Dak.........C6 204
Hyde Park, Guy............A3 139
Hyde Park, N.Y............D7 196
Hyde Park, Pa...........*F10 202
Hyde Park, Utah...........B4 207
Hyde Park, Vt.............B3 208
Hyden, Austl..............F2 111
Hyden, Ky.................C6 182
Hyder, Alsk.........D13, n24 167
Hyder, Ariz...............E2 168
Hyderabad, India...E6 87, I7 88
Hyderābād, Pak...C4 87, E2 88
Hydetown, Pa..............C2 202
Hydeville, Vt.............D2 208
Hydra, see Ídhra, isl., Grc.
Hydraulic, B.C., Can......C7 149
Hydro, Okla...............B3 200
Hye, Tex..................D3 206
Hyères, Fr................F7 58
Hyères, is., Fr............F7 58
Hyesanjin, Kor............F4 93
Hygiene, Colo.............A5 171
Hylo, Alta., Can..........B4 148
Hylton, Tex...............C2 206
Hyman, S.C................D8 203
Hyman, Tex................C2 206
Hymel, La.................B6 183
Hymera, Ind...............F3 179
Hyndman, Pa...............G4 202
Hyndman, peak, Idaho......F4 177
Hyner, Pa.................D6 202
Hyŏpchŏn, Kor..............I4 93
Hypoluxo, Fla............*F6 174
Hyrcania: c. 500 B.C........... 78
Hyrum, Utah...............B4 207
Hyrynsalmi, Fin...........E13 63
Hysham, Mont..............D9 190
Hythe, Alta., Can.........B1 148
Hythe, Eng................C9 56

I

Iablès, dunes, Alg.........D4 102
Iaeger, W. Va.............D3 211
Ialomița, riv., Rom........C8 68
Iamonia, lake, Fla.........B2 174
Iantha, Mo................D3 189
Iaşi, Rom.................B8 68
Iatan, Mo.................B3 189
Iates, pt., Guam................ 114
Iatt, lake, La.............C3 183
Iba, Phil.................o12 90
Ibanad, Nig...............E5 103
Ibagué, Col...............C2 133
Ibanda, Ug................B5 106
Ibapah, Utah..............C2 207
Ibar, riv., Yugo...........D5 68
Ibaraki, Jap..............o14 93
Ibarra, Ec................A2 134
Ibbenbüren, Ger...........A2 61
Iberá, lake, Arg...........E4 135
Iberia, Mo................C5 189
Iberia, Ohio..............B5 199
Iberia, par., La...........E4 183
Iberville, Que., Can......D4 154
Iberville, La........B5, D4 183
Iberville, co., Que., Can......................D4 154
Iberville, par., La.........D4 183
Ibi, Nig..................E6 103
Ibiá, Braz................E1 138
Ibiapaba, mts., Braz.......B2 138
Ibicuí, riv., Braz..........D2 137
Ibicuy, Arg..........A5, f7 136
Ibiraputa, riv., Braz......E1 137
Ibitinga, Braz............C3 137
Ibiza, Sp.................C6 65
Ibiza, isl., Sp............C6 65
Ibo, Moz..................D7 106
Iboki, New Britain I............ 115
Ibu, Okinawa.................... 114
Iburg, Ger................A3 61
Ica, Peru.................D2 134
Ica, dept., Peru...........D2 134
Içá, riv., Braz............D4 133
Icacal, Pan...............k10 130
Icacos, isl., P.R..........B8 132
Içana, riv., Braz..........C4 133
Ice, mtn., B.C., Can.......B7 149
Ice, pond, Pa.............A1 194
Ice Harbor, dam, Wash......A8 201
Iceberg, pt., N.W. Ter., Can......................B23 118
ICELAND, country, Eur....n23 63
Ichalkaranji, India.......*E5 87
Ichang, China.............I4 92
Icheng, China.............I5 92
Ichi Banare, isl., Okinawa...... 114
Ichihara, Jap............*I10 93
Ichikawa, Jap.............n18 93
Ichinomiya, Jap...........n15 93
Ichinoseki, Jap...........G10 93
Ichnya, Sov. Un...........F9 72
Ichuan, China.............H4 92
Ichun, China.............B11 91
Ichun, China..............K6 92
Ickesburg, Pa.............F7 202
Icó, Braz.................C3 138
Icy, strait, Alsk.........k22 167
Ida, La...................A2 183
Ida, Mich.................G7 186
Ida, co., Iowa............B2 180
Ida, lake, Minn...........E3 187
Ida, mtn., Grc.............E5 69
Ida Grove, Iowa...........B2 180
Idabel, Okla..............D7 200
Idah, Nig.................E6 103
Idaho, state, U.S................ 177
Idaho, co., Idaho..........D3 177
Idaho City, Idaho.........F3 177
Idaho Falls, Idaho........F6 177
Idaho Springs, Colo.......B5 171
Idalia, Colo..............B8 171
Idalou, Tex...............C2 206
Idamay, Ky................C6 182
Idana, Kans...............C6 181
Idanha, Oreg..............C4 201
Idanha-a-Nova, Port.......C2 65
Idar-Oberstein, Ger........D2 61
Idaville, Ind..............C4 179
Idaville, Oreg............B3 201
Idd Abu Sufyan (Well), Sud......................B2 105
Iddan, Som................D6 105
'Idd el Ghanam, Sud.......C1 105
Iddesleigh, Alta., Can....D5 148
Ideal, Ga.................D2 175

INDEX KEY
Each place listed in Bold-faced Type has its population listed in the Population tables, pages 230 to 280.
Each country, shown in CAPITAL LETTERS, has its population listed in the World Political Information Table, pages 6 to 10.
* Does not appear on map; key shows general location.

Ideal, S. Dak. D6 204
Idehan, des., Libya D2 101
Idehan Marzūq, dunes, Libya E2 101
Ider, Ala. A4 166
Idetown, Pa. B7 202
Idfīnā, Eg. C2 84
Idfū, Eg. E6 101
Ídhra, Grc. D4 69
Ídhra (Hydra), isl., Grc. D4 69
Idi, Indon. E1, m11 90
Idiofa, Zaire C2 106
Idkū, Eg. C2 84
Idkū lake, Eg. C2 84
Idlewild, Tenn. A3 205
Idleyld Park, Oreg. D3 201
Idlib, Syr. E11 85
Idnah, Jordan C6 84
Idrigill, pt., Scot. C2 57
Idrija, Yugo. B2 68
Idritsa, Sov. Un. C7 72
Idro, lake, It. D6 66
Ie, isl., Okinawa 114
Ieper (Ypres), Bel. D2 59
Ierápetra, Grc. E5 69
Ierissós, Grc. B4 69
Iesi, It. C4 67
Ifakara, Tan. C6 106
Ife, Nig. E5 103
Iférouane, Niger C6 103
Ifni (city), see Sidi Ifni, Mor.
Iganga, Ug. A5 106
Igaraçu, Braz. h6 138
Igara Paraná, riv., Col. D3 133
Igarapava, Braz. F1 138
Igarapé Açu, Braz. B1 138
Igarapé Mirí, Braz. C5 139
Igarka, Sov. Un. C11 71
Iğdir, Tur. C15 85
Iglesias, It. E2 67
Igloo, S. Dak. D2 204
Ignacio, Colo. D3 171
Iğneada, Tur. B6 69
Igny, Fr. h9 58
Igoumenítsa, Grc. C3 69
Igra, Sov. Un. B4 73
Iguaçu, cataracts, Braz D2 137
Iguaçu, riv., Braz D2 137
Iguala, Mex. D5, n14 129
Igualada, Sp. B6 65
Igualdad Central, P.R. B2 132
Iguape, Braz. C3 137
Iguatemí, riv., Braz C2 137
Iguatu, Braz. C3 138
Iguidi, sand dunes, Alg., Maur D3 102
Igurin, isl., Eniwetok 114
Iha, Okinawa 114
Ihlen, Minn. G2 187
Ihosy, Malag. h9 107
Ihsien, China D9 92
Ihsien, China F8 92
Ihsien, China G7 92
Ihsing, China I8 92
Iida, Jap. I8, n16 93
Iide-San, peak, Jap. H9 93
Iijima, Jap. n16 93
Iisalmi, Fin. F12 63
Iizuka, Jap. *J5 93
Ijamsville, Md. B3 173
Ijebu Ode, Nig. E5 103
IJmuiden, Neth. B4 59
IJssel, riv., Neth. B6 59
IJsselmeer, see Zuider Zee, Neth.
Ijuí, Braz. D2 137
Ijuí, riv., Braz D2 137
Ikaalinen, Fin. G10 63
Ikaría, isl., Grc. D6 69
Ikast, Den. B3 62
Ikeda, Jap. o14 93
Ikela, Zaire B3 106
Ikere, Nig. E6 103
Ikhtiman, Bul. D6 68
Iki, isl., Jap J4 93
Ila, Ga. B3 175
Ilagan, Phil. B6 90
Ilan (Sanhsing), China B10 91
Ilan, Taiwan *G9 91
Ilanz, Switz. C5 66
Iława, Pol. B5 70
Ilbunga, Austl. E6 111
Ilchester, Md. B4 173
Ilderton, Ont., Can. D3 153
Ile-à-la-Crosse, Sask., Can. B1, B2 155
Ile-a-la-Crosse, lake, Sask., Can. B2 155
Ile-de-France, former prov., Fr. C5 58
Ile de France, hills, Fr F3 59
Île-de-Montreal et Île-Jésus, co. Que., Can. *D4 154
Île-Perrot, Que., Can. D8 154
Îles-de-la-Madeleine, co., Que., Can. *B8 151
Ilesha, Nig. E5 103
Ilfeld, N. Mex. B4 195
Ilford, Man., Can. A4 150
Ilford, Eng. *C8 56
Ilfracombe, Eng. C3 56
Ilgin, Tur. C8 85
Ilhavo, Port. B1 65
Ilhéus, Braz. D3 138
Ili, Sov. Un. E9 73
Ili, riv., Sov. Un. E9 73
Iliamna, Alsk. D6 167
Iliamna, lake, Alsk. D6 167
Iliamna, vol., Alsk. D9, g15 167
Iliff, Colo. A7 171
Iligan, Phil. *D6 90
Ilikí, lake, Grc. g10 69
Ilinskaya, Sov. Un. I13 72
Iliodhrómia, isl., Grc. C4 69
Ilion, N.Y. B5 196
Ilkeston, Eng. B6 56
Ilkhan Empire: in 1294 81
Ilkley, Eng. G7 57
Illampu, mtn., Bol. C2 135
Illana, bay, Phil. D6 90
Illapel, Chile A2 136
Ille [-sur-la-Têt], Fr. F5 58
Iller, riv., Ger. D5 60
Illiers, Fr. C4 58
Illinois, state, U.S. 178
Illinois, bayou, Ark. B2 169
Illinois, peak, Idaho, Mont. B3 177
Illinois, riv., Ill. B5 178
Illinois, riv., Ark., Okla. A7 200
Illinois, riv., Oreg. E3 201
Illinois City, Ill. B3 178
Illiopolis, Ill. D4 178
Illkirch-Graffenstaden, Fr. F7 59
Illmo, Mo. D8 189
Illo, Nig. D5 103
Íllora, Sp. D4 65
Illyrian Provinces: in 1810 50
Illyricum: in 1st cent. B.C. 44
Ilmen, lake, Sov. Un. B8 72
Ilmenau, Ger. C5 61
Ilmenau, riv., Ger. B5 60
Ilo, Peru E3 134
Iloilo, Phil. C6 90
Ilorin, Nig. E5 103
Ilovaysk, Sov. Un. r21 72
Ilovlinskaya, Sov. Un. D2 73
Ilubabor, reg., Eth. D3 105
Ilwaco, Wash. C1 210
Ilwaki, Indon. G7 90
Iłża, Pol. C6 70
Im Amguel, Alg. E6 102
Imabari, Jap. I6 93
Imambaba, Sov. Un. C11 86
Iman, Sov. Un. E16 71
Iman, riv., Sov. Un. D7 93
Imari, Jap. *J4 93
Imazu, Jap. n15 93
Imbābah, Eg. *C6 101
Imbabura, prov., Ec. A2 134
Imbler, Oreg. B9 201
Imboden, Ark. A4 169
Ime mtn., Scot. D4 57
Imgyt, marsh, Sov. Un. B8 73
Imías, Cuba E6 131
Imienpo, China D4 93
Imilac, Chile D2 135
Imlay, Nev. C3 192
Imlay City, Mich. E7 186
Imlaystown, N.J. C3 194
Immeln, lake, Swe. B8 62
Immenstadt, Ger. E5 60
Immokalee, Fla. F5 174
Imnaha, Oreg. B10 201
Imnaha, riv., Oreg. B10 201
Imogene, Iowa D2 180
Imola, It. B3 67
Imotski, Yugo. D3 68
Imperatriz, Braz. C1 138
Imperia, It. C2 67
Imperial, Calif. F6 170
Imperial, Sask., Can. F3 155
Imperial, Mo. B8, C7 189
Imperial, Nebr. D4 191
Imperial, Pa. B5 202
Imperial, Tex. D1 206
Imperial, co., Calif. F6 170
Imperial, diversion dam, Ariz. E1 168
Imperial, val., Calif. F6 170
Imperial Beach, Calif. *F5 170
Imphal, India D9 87
Imroz (Ímbros), isl., Tur. B5 69
Imst, Aus. E5 60
Imus, Phil. o13 90
'Imwās, Jordan h11 84
In Ahmar (Well), Maur. C3 103
In Alay, Mali C4 103
In Azaoua (Oasis), Niger B6 103
In Belbel, Alg. D5 102
In Beriem (Well), Mali C4 103
In Gall, Niger C6 103
In Guezzam (Oasis), Alg. F5 102
In Salah, Alg. D5 102
Ina, Jap. n16 93
Ina, Ill. E5 178
Ina, riv., Pol. B3 70
Inajá, Braz. C3 138
Inawatan, Indon. F8 90
Iñapari, Peru D4 134
Inarajan, Guam 114
Inarajan, bay, Guam 114
Inari, Fin. C12 63
Inari, lake, Fin. C12 63
Inatori, Jap. o18 93
Inavale, Nebr. D7 191
Inawashiro, lake, Jap. H10 93
Inazawa, Jap. n15 93
Inca, Sp. C7 65
Incastro, riv., It. h9 67
Ince, cape, Tur. A10 85
İncesu, Tur. C10 85
Inchard, bay, Scot. B3 57
Inchelium, Wash. A7 210
Inchŏn, Kor. H3 93
Indaal, inlet, Scot. E2 57
Indalsälven, riv., Swe. F7 63
Indan, Phil. o14 90
Indang, Phil. o13 90
Indaw, Bur. D10 87
Indefatigable, see Santa Cruz, isl., Ec.
Independence, Calif. D4 170
Independence, Ind. D3 179
Independence, Iowa B6 180
Independence, Kans. E8 181
Independence, Ky. A7, B5 182
Independence, La. D5 183
Independence, Minn. *F5 187
Independence, Miss. A4 188
Independence, Mo. B3, E2 189
Independence, Ohio B2 199
Independence Oreg. C1, C3 201
Independence, Va. E1 209
Independence, Wis. D2 212
Independence, co., Ark. B4 169
Independence, mts., Nev. C5 192
Independence Hill, Ind. *B3 179
Independencia, Bol. C2 135
Inderagiri, riv., Indon. F2 90
Inderborskiy, Sov. Un. D4 73
Index, Wash. B4 210
INDIA, country, Asia D6 87
c. 250 B.C. 79
c. 400 A.D. 79
Indiahoma, Okla. C3 200
Indialantic, Fla. *D6 174
Indian, bay, Fla. D4 174
Indian, creek, Ind. H5 179
Indian, creek, Md. C4 173
Indian, creek, Ohio C3 199
Indian, creek, S. Dak. B2 204
Indian, creek, Tenn. B3 205
Indian, creek, W. Va. D4 211
Indian, isl., N.C. B7 197
Indian, lake, Mich. C4 186
Indian, lake, N.Y. B6 196
Indian, lake, Ohio B4 199
Indian, mtn., Conn. B3 172
Indian, ocean, Asia I8 76
Indian, peak, Utah E2 207
Indian, peak, Wyo. A3 213
Indian, pond, Maine B3 184
Indian, pond, Maine C2 184
Indian, pond, Maine D3 184
Indian, riv., Ont., Can. B7 153
Indian, riv., Del. C7 173
Indian, riv., Fla. D6 174
Indian, riv., Mich. B4 186
Indian, riv., N.Y. A5 196
Indian, rock, Wash. C5 210
Indian, stream, N.H. A1 193
Indian Agency, Colo. D3 171
Indian Bay, Man., Can. E4 150
Indian Brook, N.S., Can. C9 151
Indian Creek, Fla. *G6 174
Indian Gap, Tex. D3 206
Indian Grave, mtn., Ga. C2 175
Indian Head, Sask., Can. G4 155
Indian Head, Md. C3 173
Indian Head Park, Ill. *B6 178
Indian Hill, Ohio D2 199
Indian Hills, Ky. *B4 182
Indian Lake, N.Y. B6 196
Indian Mound, Tenn. A4 205
Indian Pass, Fla. C1 174
Indian Prairie, canal, Fla. E5 174
Indian River (village), Maine D5 184
Indian River, Mich. C6 186
Indian River, co., Fla. E6 174
Indian River, bay, Del. C7 173
Indian Rocks Beach, Fla. E1 174
Indian Springs, Ga. C3 175
Indian Springs, Ind. G4 179
Indian Springs, Nev. G6 192
Indian Trail, N.C. B3 197
Indian Valley, Idaho E2 177
Indian Valley, Va. E2 209
Indian Village, Kans. E8 181
Indian Wells, Ariz. B5 168
Indiana, Pa. E3 202
Indiana, state, U.S. 179
Indiana, co., Pa. E3 202
Indianapolis, Ind. E5, H8 179
Indianola, Ill. D6 178
Indianola, Iowa C4 180
Indianola, Miss. B3 188
Indianola, Nebr. D5 191
Indianola, Okla. B6 200
Indiantown, Fla. E6 174
Indiera Alta, P.R. C3 132
Indiga, Sov. Un. B18 41
Indigirka, riv., Sov. Un. C17 71
Indio, Calif. F5 170
Indio, riv., Pan. k10 130
Indio, riv., Pan. k12 130
Indispensable, strait, Sol. Is. 115
Indochina, French, see Cambodia, Laos, and Vietnam, countries, Asia
Indochina, reg., Asia H13 76, B5 89
INDONESIA, country, Asia F6 90, 83
Indore, India D6 87, F5 88
Indravati, riv., India H8 88
Indus, Minn. B5 187
Indus, riv., Pak. C4 87
Indus, riv. mouths, Pak. D4 87
Industrial, S.C. B6 203
Industry, Calif. *F4 170
Industry, Ill. C3 178
Industry, Kans. C6 181
Industry, Pa. *E1 202
Ine, Jap. n14 93
Inebolu, Tur. B9 85
Inez, Ky. C7 182
Inez, Tex. E4 206
Infanta, Phil. o12 90
Infanta, Phil. o13 90
Infantas, Col. B3 133
Infantes, Sp. C4 65
Infiesto, Sp. A3 65
Ingá, Braz. h6 138
Ingalls, Ark. D3 169
Ingalls, Ind. E6 179
Ingalls, Kans. E3 181
Ingalls, Mich. C3 186
Ingelheim, Ger. D3 61
Ingende, Zaire B2 106
Ingeniero Jacobacci, Arg. C3 136
Ingeniero Luiggi, Arg. B4 136
Ingenika, riv., B.C., Can. A5 149
Ingenio, P.R. B6 132
Inger, Minn. C5 187
Ingersheim, Fr. A3 66
Ingersoll, Ont., Can. D4 153
Ingersoll, Okla. A3 200
Ingham, Austl. C8 111
Ingham, co., Mich. F6 186
Ingham, peak, Utah B2 207
Ingleside, Md. B6 173
Ingleside, Nebr. D7 191
Ingleside, Tex. F4 206
Inglewood, Austl. D8 112
Inglewood, Calif. F2 170
Inglewood, Ont., Can. D5 153
Inglewood, Nebr. *C9 191
Inglewood, N.Z. M15 112
Inglewood, Tenn. E9 205
Inglis, Man., Can. D1 150
Ingold, N.C. C5 197
Ingolf, Ont., Can. E4 150
Ingolstadt, Ger. E6 61
Ingomar, Miss. A4 188
Ingomar, Mont. D9 190
Ingomar, Pa. A5 202
Ingonish, N.S., Can. C5 151
Ingornachoix, bay, Newf., Can. C3 152
Ingraham, lake, Fla. G5 174
Ingram, Pa. B5 202
Ingram, Wis. C3 212
Ingrid Christensen, coast, Ant. C21 120
Ingul, riv., Sov. Un. H9 72
Ingulets, riv., Sov. Un. H9 72
Inhambane, Moz. B6 107
Inhambane, prov., Moz. B5 107
Inhambane, bay, Moz. B6 107
Inhambupe, Braz. D3 138
Inhaminga, Moz. A6 107
Inharrime, Moz. B6 107
Inhuçu, Braz. B2 138
Inhumas, Braz. B3 137
Iniesta, Sp. C5 65
Ining, see Kuldja, China
Inírida, riv., Col. C4 133
Inishbofin, isl., Ire. D1 55
Inishtrahull, isl., Ire. C3 55
Inishturk, isl., Ire. D1 55
Injasuti, peak, Bas., S. Afr. D4 107
Injune, Austl. B7 112
Inkerman, N.B., Can. B5 151
Inkom, Idaho G6 177
Inkster, Mich. A7 186
Inkster, N. Dak. A8 198
Inland, sea, Jap. I6 93
Inlet, N.Y. B6 196
Inlet, pt., N.Y. E7 172
Inman, Ga. C2 175
Inman, Kans. D6 181
Inman, Nebr. B7 191
Inman, S.C. A3 203
Inman Mills, S.C. *A3 203
Inn, riv., Aus., Ger., Switz. D6 60, E8 61
Innamincka, Austl. E7 111
Inner, sound, Scot. C3 57
Inner Mongolia, auton. reg., China C8 91
Innerleithen, Scot. E5 57
Innisfail, Austl. C8 111
Innisfail, Alta., Can. C4 148
Innisfree, Alta., Can. C5 148
Innokentyevskiy, Sov. Un. B10 93
Innsbruck, Aus. E5 60
Inola, Okla. A6 200
Inongo, Zaire B2 106
Inowrocław, Pol. B5 70
I-n-Rabir, Alg. E6 102
Insch, Scot. C6 57
Insein, Bur. E10 87
Insinger, Sask., Can. F4 155
Inspiration, Ariz. D5 168
Institute, W. Va. C3 211
Instow, Sask., Can. H1 155
Inta, Sov. Un. C8 71
Intake, Mont. C12 190
Intercession City, Fla. D5 174
Intercity, Wash. *B3 210
Interior, S. Dak. D4 204
Interior, Va. D2 209
Interlachen, Fla. C5 174
Interlaken, N.J. *C4 194
Interlaken, N.Y. C4 196
Interlaken, Switz. C3 66
International Falls, Minn. B5 187
International Peace Garden, park, Man., Can. E1 150
Intersection, mtn., B.C., Can. C8 149
Intervale, N.H. B4 193
Intiyaco, Arg. E3 135
Intracoastal, waterway, La., Tex. E3 183, E5 206
Inubō, cape, Jap. I10 93
Inútil, bay, Chile h12 136
Inuvik, N.W. Ter., Can. C6 145
Inver Grove, Minn. E7 187
Inveraray, Scot. D3 57
Inverbervie, Scot. D6 57
Invercargill, N.Z. Q12 112
Inverell, Austl. D8 112
Invergarry, Scot. C4 57
Invergordon, Scot. C4 57
Invermay, Sask., Can. F4 155
Invermere, B.C., Can. D9 149
Inverness, Ala. C4 166
Inverness, Calif. B4, C2 170
Inverness, N.S., Can. C8 151
Inverness, Que., Can. C6 154
Inverness, Fla. D4 174
Inverness, Miss. B3 188
Inverness, Mont. B6 190
Inverness, Scot. C4 57
Inverness, co., N.S., Can. C8 151
Inverness, co., Scot. C3 57
Invisible, mtn., Idaho F5 177
Inwood, Man., Can. D3 150
Inwood, Ont., Can. E3 153
Inwood, Ind. B5 179
Inwood, Iowa A1 180
Inwood, N.Y. E2 196
Inwood, W. Va. B6 211
Inyan Kara, mtn., Wyo. A8 213
Inyanga, Rh. A5 107
Inyankara, creek, Wyo. A8 213
Inyo, co., Calif. D5 170
Inyo, mtn., Calif. D5 170
Inyokern, Calif. E5 170
Inza, Sov. Un. E16 72
Inzano, lake, B.C., Can. B5 149
Ioánnina, Grc. C3 69
Ioka, Utah C5 207
Iokanga, Sov. Un. D18 63
Iola, Ill. E5 178
Iola, Kans. E8 181
Iola, Wis. D4 212
Iona, N.S., Can. D9 151
Iona, Idaho F7 177
Iona, Minn. G3 187
Iona, N.J. D2 194
Iona, S. Dak. D6 204
Iona, isl., Scot. D2 57
Ione, Calif. C3 170
Ione, Colo. A6 171
Ione, Nev. E4 192
Ione, Oreg. B7 201
Ione, Wash. A8 210
Ionia: c. 450 B.C. 42
Ionia, Iowa A5 180
Ionia, Kans. C5 181
Ionia, Mich. F5 186
Ionia, Mo. C4 189
Ionia, co., Mich. F5 186
Ionian, is., Grc. C3 69
Ionian, sea, Grc. C2 69
Ios, isl., Grc. D5 69
Iosco, co., Mich. D7 186
Iosegun, riv., Alta., Can. B2 148
Iosegun Lake, Alta., Can. B2 148
Iota, La. D3 183
Iowa, La. D2 183
Iowa, state, U.S. 180
Iowa, co., Iowa C5 180
Iowa, co., Wis. E3 212
Iowa, lake, Iowa A3 180
Iowa, riv., Iowa C6 180
Iowa City, Iowa C6 180
Iowa Falls, Iowa B4 180
Iowa Park, Tex. C3 206
Ipameri, Braz. E1 138
Ipava, Ill. C3 178
Ipel, riv., Czech D5 70
Iphigenia, sound, Alsk. n23 167
Ipiales, Col. C2 133
Ipin, China F5 91
Ipirá, Braz. D3 138
Ipoh, Mala. J4 89
Ipoly, riv., Hung. B4 68
Ippy, Cen. Afr. Rep. D4 104
Ipsala, Tur. B6 69
Ipswich, Austl. C9 112
Ipswich, Eng. B9 56
Ipswich, Mass. A6 185
Ipswich, S. Dak. B6 204
Ipswich, riv., Mass. A5 185
Ipu, Braz. B2 138
Ipueiras, Braz. B2 138
Iquique, Chile D1 135
Iquitos, Peru B3 134
Ira, Iowa C4 180
Ira, Tex. C2 206
Ira, Vt. D2 208
Iraan, Tex. D2 206
Iracoubo, Fr. Gu. A4 139
Iráklion (Candia), Grc. E5 69
Irala, Par. E5 135
IRAN (Persia), country, Asia E6 86, 83
Iran, mts., Indon., Mala E4 90
Iran, plat., Iran E7 86
Irapa, Ven. A5 133
Irapuato, Mex. C4, m13 129
IRAQ, country, Asia F14 85, E2 86, 83
Irasburg, Vt. B4 208
Irasville, Vt. C3 208
Irbid, Jordan B7 84
Irbil, Iraq D15 85
Irbit, Sov. Un. B6 73
Irebu, Zaire B2 106
Iredell, Tex. *D4 206
Iredell, co., N.C. B3 197
Ireland, Ind. H3 179
Ireland, Tex. D4 206
IRELAND (Eire), country, Eur. D3 55
c. 1922 53
in 1950 54
Irene, S. Dak. D8 204
Irerrer, riv., Alg. E6 102
Ireton, Iowa B1 180
Irgiz, Sov. Un. D6 73
Irgiz, riv., Sov. Un. D6 73
Irharhar, riv., Alg. D6 102
Iri, Kor. I3 93
Irian, see Indonesia, country, Asia
Iriga, Phil. C6 90
Iringa, Tan. C6 106
Iriomote, isl., Ryūkyū Is. G9 91
Irion, co., Tex. D2 206
Iriri, riv., Braz C4 139
Irish, mtn., Nev F6 192
Irish, sea, Ire. D4 55
Irish Free State 53
Irkutsk, Sov. Un. D13 71
Irma, Alta., Can. C5 148
Irmino, Sov. Un. q21 72
Irmo, S.C. C5 203
Iron, Minn. C6 187
Iron, co., Mich. B2 186
Iron, co., Mo. D7 189
Iron, co., Utah F2 207
Iron, co., Wis. B3 212
Iron, mtn., Ariz. C3 168
Iron, mts., Tenn., Va. E1 209
Iron Belt, Wis. B3 212
Iron City, Ga. E2 175
Iron City, Tenn. B4 205
Iron Gate, Mo. *D3 189
Iron Gate, Va. D3 209
Iron Gate, gorge, Rom., Yugo. C6 68
Iron Lightning, S. Dak. B4 204
Iron Mountain, Mich. C2 186
Iron Mountain, Mo. D7 189
Iron Mountain, Wyo. D7 213
Iron Ridge, Wis. E5 212
Iron River, Mich. B2 186
Iron River, Wis. B2 212
Iron Springs, Ariz. C3 168
Irondale, Ala. E5 166
Irondale, Mo. D7 189
Irondale, Ohio B7 199
Irondequoit, N.Y. B3 196
Irons, Mich. D5 186
Ironside, Que., Can. A9 153
Ironside, Oreg. C9 201
Ironspot, Ohio C5 199
Ironton, Minn. D5 187
Ironton, Mo. D7 189
Ironton, Ohio D5 199
Ironwood, Mich. A5 186
Iroquois, Ont., Can. C9 153
Iroquois, Ill. C6 178
Iroquois, S. Dak. C8 204
Iroquois, co., Ill. C6 178
Iroquois, riv., Ill., Ind. C3 179
Iroquois Falls, Ont., Can. *E9 153
Irrawaddy, riv., Bur. D10 87
Irricana, Alta., Can. D4 148
Irrigon, Oreg. B7 201
Irt, riv., Eng. F5 57
Irthing, riv., Eng. F6 57
Irtysh, Sov. Un. C8 73
Irtysh, riv., Sov. Un. B8 73
Irumu, Zaire A4 106
Irún, Sp. A5 65
Irvine, Alta., Can. E5 148
Irvine, Fla. C4 174
Irvine, Ky. C6 182
Irvine, Pa. C3 202
Irvine, Scot. E4 57
Irvine, riv., Scot. E4 57
Irvines Landing, B.C., Can. E5 149
Irving, Ill. D4 178
Irving, Oreg. C3 201
Irving, Tex. B5 206
Irvington, Ala. E1 166
Irvington, Ill. E4 178
Irvington, Ky. C3 182
Irvington, Nebr. D3 191
Irvington, N.J. E4 194
Irvington, N.Y. D1 196
Irvington, Va. D6 209
Irvona, Pa. E4 202
Irwin, Idaho F7 177
Irwin, Iowa C2 180
Irwin, Pa. F2 202
Irwin, S.C. *B6 203
Irwin, co., Ga. E3 175
Irwindale, Calif. *E4 170
Irwinton, Ga. D3 175
Irwinville, Ga. E3 175
Isa, Nig. D6 103
Isa, Okinawa 114
Isaac, lake, B.C., Can. C7 149
Isaacs Harbour, N.S., Can. D8 151
Isabel, Kans. E5 181
Isabel, S. Dak. B4 204
Isabel, mtn., Wyo. C2 213
Isabela, Phil. *D6 90
Isabela, P.R. A2 132
Isabela, mun., P.R. B2 132
Isabela (Albermarle), isl., Ec. g5 134
Isabella, Man., Can. D1 150
Isabella, Ga. E3 175
Isabella, Minn. C7 187
Isabella, Okla. A3 200
Isabella, Pa. G2 202
Isabella, Tenn. D9 205
Isabella, co., Mich. E6 186
Isabella, lake, Minn. C7 187
Isabella, mts., Nic. D5 130
Isaccea, Rom. C9 68
Isafjörđur, Ice. m21 63
Isahaya, Jap. J5 93
Isaka, Zaire B2 106
Isanga, Zaire B3 106
Isangi, Zaire A3 106
Isanti, Minn. E5 187
Isanti, co., Minn. E5 187
Isar, riv., Ger. E7 61
Isarco, riv., It. A3 67
'Īsawīyah, Jordan h12, m14 84
Isbergues, Fr. D2 59
Isbister, riv., Man., Can. C4 150
Ischia, isl., It. D4 67
Ischua, N.Y. C2 196
Iscia Baidoa, Som. E5 105
Ise, Jap. I8 o15 93
Ise, riv., Ger. F4 62
Isel, riv., Aus. E6 60
Iselin, N.J. B4 194
Iselin, Pa. E3 202
Isen, riv., Ger. A8 66
Iseo, lake, It. B3 67
Isère, dept., Fr. D1 66
Isère, riv., Fr. E6 58
Iserlohn, Ger. B2 61
Isernia, It. D5 67
Iseyin, Nig. E5 103
Isezaki, Jap. H9, m18 93
Isfahan (Eşfahān), Iran E5 86
Ishan, China G6 91
Ishawooa, Wyo. A3 213
Ishikawa, Okinawa 114
Ishim, Sov. Un. B7 73
Ishim, riv., Sov. Un. B8 73

INDEX KEY Each place listed in **Bold-faced Type** has its population listed in the Population tables, pages 230 to 280.
Each country, shown in CAPITAL LETTERS, has its population listed in the World Political Information Table, pages 6 to 10.
* Does not appear on map; key shows general location.

Ishimbay, Sov. Un........C5 73
Ishinomaki, Jap........G10 93
Ishioka, Jap........m19 93
Ishkashim Afg........C15 86
Ishpeming, Mich........B3 186
Isigny-sur-Mer, Fr........C3 58
Isil-Kul, Sov. Un........C8 73
Isiolo, Ken........A6 106
Isiro, Zaire........A4 106
Isisford, Austl........B5 112
İskenderun (Alexandretta), Tur........D11 85
Isker, riv., Bul........D6 68
İskilip, Tur........B10 85
Iskwatikan, lake, Sask., Can........B3 155
Isla Cabellos, Ur........E1 137
Isla Cristina, Sp........D2 65
Islāmābād, Pak........B5 87
Islamorada, Fla........H6 174
Island, Ky........C2 182
Island, co., Wash........A3 210
Island, beach, N.J........D4 194
Island, dam, Ala........B3 166
Island, lake, Man., Can........C4 150
Island, pond, N.H........E4 193
Island, pond, Vt........B5 208
Island Brook, Que., Can........D6 154
Island City, Oreg........B8 201
Island Falls, Sask., Can........B4 155
Island Falls, Maine........B4 184
Island Grove, Fla........C4 174
Island Heights, N.J........D4 194
Island Lake, Man., Can........C4 150
Island Lake, Ill........*A5 178
Island Lake, riv., Man., Can........B4 150
Island No. 40, isl., Tenn........E8 205
Island Park, Idaho........E7 177
Island Park, N.Y........*E3 196
Island Park, R.I........C12 172
Island Park, res., Idaho........E7 177
Island Pond, Vt........B5 208
Islay, Alta., Can........C5 148
Islay, isl., Scot........E2 57
Isle, Minn........D5 187
Isle, riv., Fr........E4 58
Isle au Haut, Maine........D4 184
sle aux Morts, Newf., Can........E2 152
Isle La Motte, Vt........B2 208
Isle Maligne, Que., Can........A6 154
ISLE OF MAN, Br. dep., Eur........C4 55
Isle of Palms, S.C........F3 203
Isle of Pines, isl., N. Cal........115
Isle of Wight, Va........B6, E6 209
Isle of Wight, co., Eng........D6 56
Isle of Wight, co., Va........E6 209
Isle of Wight, bay, Md........D7 173
Isle of Wight, isl., Eng........E6 55
Isle Pierre, B.C., Can........C6 149
Isle Royale, isl., Mich........A2 186
Isle Royale, nat. park, Mich........A2 186
Isle Verte, Que., Can........A8 154
Islesboro, Maine........D4 184
Islesford, Maine........D4 184
Islet, isl., Eniwetok........114
Isleta, N. Mex........C3 195
Isleta, Indian res., N. Mex........C3 195
Isleton, Calif........B6, C3 170
Islington, Eng........C7 56
Islington, Mass........D2 185
Ismailia (Al Ismā'īlīyah, Eg........D4 84
Ismā'īlīah, canal, Eg........D3 84
Ismay, Mont........D12 190
Isnā, Eg........D6 101
Isoka, Zambia........D5 106
Isola, Miss........B3 188
Isola Capo Rizzuto, It........E6 67
Isola della Scala, It........D7 66
Isole Pelagie, isl., It........B2 101
Isparta, Tur........D8 85
İspir, Tur........B13 85
ISRAEL, country, Asia........C6 84
c. 1950........83
Israel, riv., N.H........B3 193
Issano Landing, Guy........A3 139
Issaquah, Wash........B3, D2 210
Issaquena, co., Miss........C2 188
Issia, I.C........E3 103
Issoire, Fr........E5 58
Issoudun, Fr........D4 58
Issue, Md........D4 173
Issy [-les-Moulineaux], Fr........g10 58
Issyk-kul, lake, Sov. Un........E9 73
Istachatta, Fla........D4 174
İstanbul, Tur........B7 69, B7 85
Istiaía, Grc........C4 69
sto, mtn., Alsk........B11 167
Istokpoga, lake, Fla........E5 174
Istranca, mts., Tur........B6 69
Istres, Fr........F6 58
Istrian, pen., Yugo........C1 68
Itá, Par........E4 135
Itabaiana, Braz........C3, h6 138
Itabaiana, Braz........E4 137
Itabaianinha, Braz........D3 138
Itabapoana, riv., Braz........C4 137
Itaberaba, Braz........D2 138
Itaberaí, Braz........B3 137
Itabira, Braz........E2 138
Itaboraí, Braz........C4, h6 137
Itabuna, Braz........D3 138
Itacaiunas, riv., Braz........D4 139
Itacoatiara, Braz........C3 139
Itaeté, Braz........D2 138
Itaguaçu, Braz........E2 138
Itagüí, Col........B2 133
Itaituba, Braz........C3 139
Itajaí, Braz........D3 137
Itala, Som........E6 105
Italian Somaliland........99
Italy, Tex........C4 206
ITALY, country, Eur........C4 67
in 7th cent. B.C........42
in 1st cent. B.C........44
in 120 A.D........45
c. 400........46
unification of........51
in 1914........52
in 1922-40........53
after World War II........54
Italy Cross, N.S., Can........E5 151
Itamaraca, isl., Braz........h6 138
Itami, Jap........o14 93
Itanhaém, Braz........n8 137
Itapecuru, riv., Braz........B2 138
Itapecuru-Mirim, Braz........B2 138
Itapemirim, Braz........C4 137
Itaperuna, Braz........C4 137
Itapetininga, Braz........C3, m7 137
Itapeva, Braz........C3 137
Itapi, riv., Braz........C3 139
Itapicuru, riv., Braz........D3 138
Itapipoca, Braz........B3 138
Itápolis, Braz........k7 137
Itaporanga, Braz........C3 138
Itapua, dept., Par........E4 135
Itaqui, Braz........D1 137
Itararé, Braz........C3 137
Itararé, riv., Braz........C3 137
Itaretama, Braz........C3, g5 138
Itarsi, India........F6 88
Itasca, Ill........E2 178
Itasca, Tex........C4 206
Itasca, co., Minn........C5 187
Itasca, lake, Minn........C3 187
Itatiaya, peak, Braz........h5 137
Itatiba, Braz........m8 137
Itatinga, Braz........m7 137
Itaúna, Braz........F2 138
Itawamba, co., Miss........A5 188
Itéa, Grc........C4 69
Itecoal, riv., Braz........C3 139
Ithaca, Mich........E6 186
Ithaca, Nebr........E2 191
Ithaca, N.Y........C4 196
Ithaca, see Itháki, isl., Grc.
Itháki, Grc........C3 69
Itháki (Ithaca), isl., Grc........C3 69
Itigi, Tan........C5 106
Itimbiri, riv., Zaire........A3 106
Itirapina, Braz........m8 137
Itō, Jap........o18 93
Itoko, Zaire........B3 106
Itoman, Okinawa........114
Itsmina, Col........B2 133
Itta Bena, Miss........B3 188
Itú, Braz........C3, m8 137
Itu, China........F8 92
Ituango, Col........B2 133
Ituiutaba, Braz........B3 137
Itumbiara, Braz........B3 137
Ituna, Sask., Can........F4 155
Itung, China........C10 91
Ituxí, riv., Braz........C4 139
Ityāy al Bārūd, Eg........D3 84
Itzehoe, Ger........B4 60
Iuka, Ill........E5 178
Iuka, Kans........E5 181
Iuka, Miss........A5 188
Iva, S.C........C2 203
Iva, W. Sam........114
Ivaí, riv., Braz........C2 137
Ivalo, Fin........C12 63
Ivangrad, Yugo........D4 68
Ivanhoe, Austl........F5 112
Ivanhoe, Calif........*D4 170
Ivanhoe, Minn........F2 187
Ivanhoe, N.C........C5 197
Ivanhoe, Va........D2 209
Ivanić Grad, Yugo........C3 68
Ivano-Frankovsk, Sov. Un........G5 72
Ivanovichi, Sov. Un........D7 93
Ivanovka, Sov. Un........q21 72
Ivanovka, Sov. Un........A4 93
Ivanovo, Sov. Un........B2 73
Ivanteyevka, Sov. Un........n17 72
Ivato, Malag........g9 107
Ivaylovgrad, Bul........E8 68
Ivdel, Sov. Un........A6 73
Ivesdale, Ill........D5 178
Ivigtut, Grnld........C19 118
Ivinheima, riv., Braz........C2 137
Ivins, Utah........F2 207
Ivohibe, Malag........h9 107
Ivor, Va........E6 209
IVORY COAST, country, Afr........E3 103
Ivoryton, Conn........D7 172
Ivösjön, lake, Swe........B6 63
Ivrea, It........B1 67
Ivry, Que., Can........C3 154
Ivry-sur-Seine, Fr........g10 58
Ivy, Tenn........D9 205
Ivy, Va........C4 209
Ivy, mtn., Conn........B4 172
Ivyland, Pa........*F11 202
Ivyton, Ky........C7 182
Ivywild, Colo........C6 171
Iwaki, Jap........*H10 93
Iwakuni, Jap........I6 93
Iwamizawa, Jap........E10 93
Iwamurada, Jap........m17 93
Iwanai, Jap........E10 93
Iwaya, Jap........o14 93
Iwo, Nig........E5 103
Iwo, isl., Pac. O........114
Iwŏn, Kor........F4 93
Ixelles, Bel........*D4 59
Ixiamas, Bol........B2 135
Ixmiquilpan, Mex........m14 129
Ixtacalco, Mex........h9 129
Ixtapalapa, Mex........h9 129
Ixtlán de Juárez, Mex........o15 129
Ixtlán del Río, Mex........C4, m11 129
Iyang, China........J5 92
Izabal, lake, Guat........C3 130
Izamal, Mex........C7 129
Izard, co., Ark........A4 169
Izegem, Bel........D3 59
Izhevsk, Sov. Un........B4 73
Izmail, Sov. Un........I7 72
İzmir (Smyrna), Tur........C6 69, C6 85
İzmir, bay, Tur........C6 69
İzmit (Kocaeli), Tur........B7 69
İznik, Tur........B7 69
İznik, lake, Tur........B7 69
Izra', Syr........B8 84
Izu, isl., Pac. O........D18 113
Izúcar de Matamoros, Mex........n14 129
Izuhara, Jap........I4 93
Izumi, Jap........*I7 93
Izumi-Sano, Jap........*I7 93
Izumo, Jap........I6 93
Izyum Sov. Un........G11 72

J

Jabal ad Durūz, mtn., Syr........F11 85
Jabal Al Uwaynat, mtn., Sud........A2 105
Jabal Ash Sham, mtn., Oman........D2 87
Jabal Raḍwa, mtn., Sau. Ar........E7 101
Jabal Ramm, mtn., Jordan........E7 84
Jabal Shār, mtn., Sau. Ar........H10 85
Jabal Razih, mtn., Yemen (Ṣan'ā')........B5 105
Jabalón, riv., Sp........C4 65
Jabalpur, India........D6 87, F7 88
Jablonec [nad Nisou], Czech........C3 70
Jablonná, Czech........o17 70
Jabłonna, Pol........k13 70
Jablunkov, pass, Czech........D5 70
Jaboatão, Braz........C4, k6 138
Jaboticabal, Braz........C3, k7 137
Jabrin, isl., Iran........H5 86
Jabwat, isl., Marshall Is........115
Jaca, Sp........A5 65
Jacala [de Ledesma], Mex........m14 129
Jácana, P.R........C5 132
Jacaraci, Braz........D2 138
Jacaré, riv., Braz........D2 138
Jacareí, Braz........m9 137
Jacarèzinho, Braz........C3 137
Jachal, Arg........F2 135
Jáchymov, Czech........C2 70
Jacinto, Miss........A5 188
Jacinto City, Tex........F5 206
Jack, co., Tex........C3 206
Jack, mtn., Mont........D4 190
Jack, mtn., Va........C3 209
Jack, mtn., Wash........A5 210
Jackfish, lake, Sask., Can........D1 155
Jackfork, mtn., Okla........C6 200
Jackhead Harbour, Man., Can........D3 150
Jackman, Maine........C2 184
Jackman Station, Maine........C2 184
Jacks, mtn., Pa........E6 202
Jacks, peak, Utah........D3 207
Jacks Creek, Tenn........B3 205
Jacksboro, Tenn........C9 205
Jacksboro, Tex........C3 206
Jackson, Ala........D2 166
Jackson, Calif........C3 170
Jackson, Ga........C3 175
Jackson, Ky........C6 182
Jackson, La........D4 183
Jackson, Maine........D3 184
Jackson, Mich........F6 186
Jackson, Minn........G4 187
Jackson, Miss........C3 188
Jackson, Mo........D8 189
Jackson, Mont........E3 190
Jackson, Nebr........B9 191
Jackson, N.H........B4 193
Jackson, N.J........C4 194
Jackson, N.C........A6 197
Jackson, Ohio........C3 199
Jackson, R.I........C10 172
Jackson, S.C........E4 203
Jackson, Tenn........B3 205
Jackson, Wis........E1, E5 212
Jackson, Wyo........B2 213
Jackson, co., Ala........A3 166
Jackson, co., Ark........B4 169
Jackson, co., Colo........A4 171
Jackson, co., Fla........B1 174
Jackson, co., Ga........B3 175
Jackson, co., Ill........F4 178
Jackson, co., Ind........G5 179
Jackson, co., Iowa........B7 180
Jackson, co., Kans........C8 181
Jackson, co., Ky........C5 182
Jackson, co., Mich........F6 186
Jackson, co., Minn........G3 187
Jackson, co., Miss........E5 188
Jackson, co., Mo........C3 189
Jackson, co., N.C........D3 197
Jackson, co., Ohio........C5 199
Jackson, co., Okla........C2 200
Jackson, co., Oreg........E4 201
Jackson, co., S. Dak........D4 204
Jackson, co., Tenn........C8 205
Jackson, co., Tex........E4 206
Jackson, co., W. Va........C3 211
Jackson, co., Wis........D3 212
Jackson, par., La........B3 183
Jackson, dam, Ala........D1 166
Jackson, lake, Fla........B2 174
Jackson, lake, Fla........E5 174
Jackson, lake, Ga........C3 175
Jackson, lake, Wyo........B2 213
Jackson, mtn., Maine........D2 184
Jackson, mtn., N.H........B4 193
Jackson, mts., Nev........B3 192
Jackson, riv., Va........D3 209
Jackson Center, Ohio........B3 199
Jackson Center, Pa........D1 202
Jackson Hill, Ind........F3 179
Jackson Junction, Iowa........A5 180
Jackson's Arm, Newf., Can........D3 152
Jacksons Gap, Ala........C4 166
Jacksonboro, S.C........F1, F7 203
Jacksonburg, W. Va........A6, B4 211
Jacksonport, Ark........B4 169
Jacksonville, Ala........B4 166
Jacksonville, Ark........C3, D6 169
Jacksonville, Fla........B5, B6 174
Jacksonville, Ga........E3 175
Jacksonville, Ill........D3 178
Jacksonville, Iowa........C2 180
Jacksonville, Maine........D5 184
Jacksonville, Mo........B5 189
Jacksonville, N.C........C6 197
Jacksonville, Ohio........C5 199
Jacksonville, Oreg........E4 201
Jacksonville, Tex........D5 206
Jacksonville, Vt........F3 208
Jacksonville Beach, Fla........B5, B6 174
Jacmel, Hai........F7 131
Jaco, isl., Indon........G7 90
Jacob Lake, Ariz........A3 168
Jacobabad, Pak........C2 88
Jacobina, Braz........D2 138
Jacobson, Minn........C5 187
Jacobstown, N.J........C3 194
Jacobsville, Mich........B2 186
Jacoby, La........D4 183
Jacomino, Cuba........h12 131
Jacques Cartier, co., Que., Can........D8 154
Jacques Cartier, mtn., Que., Can........G19 143
Jacques Cartier, riv., Que., Can........B6 154
Jacquet, riv., N.B., Can........B3 151
Jacquet River, N.B., Can........B4 151
Jacquinot, bay, New Britain I........115
Jacuí, Braz........k8 137
Jacuí, riv., Braz........D2 137
Jacuípe, riv., Braz........D3 138
Jacuitiba, Braz........m8 137
Jacumba, Calif........F5 170
Jacundá, riv., Braz........C4 139
Jaddi, cape, Pak........I11 86
Jade, Ger........A8 59
Jade, bay, Ger........E2 62
Jadhamiyah, Sau. Ar........I14 85
Jādū, Libya........C2 101
Jaegerspris, Den........C5 62
Jaeggevarre, mtn., Nor........C8 63
Jaén, Peru........C2 134
Jaén, Sp........D4 65
Jaffa, cape, Austl........H2 112
Jaffna, Cey........G7 87
Jaffrey, N.H........E2 193
Jaffrey Center, N.H........E2 193
Jafura Dahana, des., Sau. Ar........I4 86
Jagadhri, India........B6 88
Jagatai, empire of........81
Jagdalpur, India........H9 88
Jagin, riv., Iran........H9 86
Jagok, lake, China........B12 88
Jagst, riv., Ger........D4 61
Jaguarão, Braz........E2 137
Jaguariaíva, Braz........C3 137
Jagüey Grande, Cuba........D3 131
Jahrom, Iran........G6 86
Jahra, Kuw........G3 86
Jaicós, Braz........C2 138
Jaipur, India........C6 87, D5 88
Jaisalmer, India........D3 88
Jajce, Yugo........C3 68
Jajpur, India........G11 88
Jakarta, see Djakarta, Indon.
Jakin, Ga........E2 175
Jakobstad, Fin........F10 63
Jal, N. Mex........E6 195
Jalaigai, pt., Guam........114
Jalālābād, Afg........D15 86
Jalapa, Guat........C3 130
Jalapa Enríquez, Mex........D5, n15 129
Jalaun, India........D7 88
Jalca Grande, Peru........C2 134
Jaleswar, India........D10 88
Jalgaon, India........G5 88
Jalisco, Mex........m11 129
Jalisco, state, Mex........C4, m12 129
Jalna, India........H5 88
Jalón, riv., Sp........B5 65
Jalor, India........E4 88
Jalpa, Mex........C4, m12 129
Jalpaiguri, India........D12 88
Jalpan, Mex........C5, m14 129
Jālū, Libya........D4 101
Jālū, oasis, Libya........D4 101
Jaluit, atoll, Marshall Is........115
Jamachim, riv., Braz........D3 139
Jamaica, Iowa........C3 180
Jamaica, N.Y........E2 196
Jamaica, Vt........E3 208
JAMAICA, country, N.A........F5 131
Jamaica, bay, N.Y........E2 196
Jamaica, chan., W.I........G6 131
Jamalpur, India........*C8 87
Jamalpur, Bngl........E12 88
Jamdena, isl., Indon........G8 90
James, Ga........D3 175
James, bay, Ont., Can........F16 143
James, isl., Md........C5 173
James, isl., S.C........F8 203
James, lake, Ind........A7 179
James, lake, N.C........B2 197
James, pt., Md........C5 173
James, range, Austl........D5 110
James, riv., Alta., Can........D3 148
James, riv., Mo........E4 189
James, riv., N. Dak........C7 198
James, riv., S. Dak........C7 204
James, riv., Va........D5 209
James City, N.C........B6 197
James City, Pa........C4 202
James City, co., Va........D6 209
James Craik, Arg........A4 136
James Creek (Marklesburg), Pa........E5 202
James Island, B.C., Can........B9 149
James River, bay, Va........B7 209
James Ross, isl., Ant........C7 120
James Ross, strait, N.W. Ter., Can........C13 142
Jamesburg, N.J........C4 194
Jameson, Mo........A3 189
Jamesport, Mo........B4 189
Jamesport, N.Y........F6 172
Jamestown, Ala........A4 166
Jamestown, Austl........F2 112
Jamestown, Calif........D3 170
Jamestown, Ont., Can........E8 153
Jamestown, Colo........A5 171
Jamestown, Ill........E4 178
Jamestown, Ind........E4 179
Jamestown, Kans........C6 181
Jamestown, Ky........D4 182
Jamestown, La........B2 183
Jamestown, Mo........C5 189
Jamestown, N.Y........C1 196
Jamestown, N.C........B4 197
Jamestown, N. Dak........C7 198
Jamestown, Ohio........C4 199
Jamestown, Pa........D1 202
Jamestown, R.I........D11 173
Jamestown, S.C........E8 203
Jamestown, Tenn........C9 205
Jamestown, Va........A6 209
Jamestown, res., N. Dak........B7 198
Jamesville, N.Y........*C4 196
Jamesville, N.C........B7 197
Jamesville, Va........D7 209
Jamieson, Fla........B2 174
Jamieson, Oreg........C9 201
Jamiltepec, Mex........D5 129
Jamison, Nebr........B6 191
Jammā'īn, Jordan........g11 84
Jammer, bay, Den........A3 62
Jammu, India........B5 87, A5 88
Jammu and Kashmir, disputed reg., India, Pak........A6 87
Jamnagar, India........D5 87, F3 88
Jampur, Pak........C3 88
Jamsah, Eg........D6 101
Jamshedpur, India........D8 87, F11 88
Jämshög, Swe........B8 62
Jamul, Calif........F5 170
Jamuna, riv., Bngl........E12 88
Jamundá, riv., Braz........C3 139
Jan, lake, Sask., Can........C4 155
Jan Mayen, isl., Atl. O........B15 118
Jandula, riv., Sp........C4 65
Jane, Mo........E3 189
Jane Lew, W. Va........B4 211
Janesville, Calif........B3 170
Janesville, Iowa........B5 180
Janesville, Minn........F5 187
Janesville, Wis........F4 212
Janeville, N.B., Can........B4 151
Jangain, isl., Sol. Is........115
Jangipur, India........E12 88
Janīn, Jordan........B7 84
Janiuay, Phil........*C6 90
Janos, Mex........A3 129
Jánoshalma, Hung........B4 68
Janow, Man., Can........E4 150
Janów Lubelski, Pol........C7 70
Jansen, Sask., Can........F3 155
Jansen, Nebr........D8 191
Januária, Braz........E2 138
Jaoho (Tuanshantzu), China........B11 91
Jaozari, Afg........D13 86
JAPAN, country, Asia........H9 93
c. 750 A.D........80
c. 1294........81
c. 1775........82
after World War II........83
Japan, sea, Asia........G6 93
Japaratuba, Braz........D3 138
Japen, isl., Indon........F9 90
Jappa, Bougainville I........115
Japtan, isl., Eniwetok........114
Japurá, riv., Braz........D4 133
Japvo, peak, India........C9 87
Jaqué, Pan........G8 130
Jara, peak, China........E5 91
Jarablus, Syr........D11 85
Jaraguá, Braz........B3 137
Jaraguá do Sul, Braz........D3 137
Jaral [del Progreso], Mex........m13 129
Jarales, N. Mex........C3 195
Jarama, riv., Sp........B4 65
Jarash, Jordan........B7 84
Jarbalo, Kans........B8 181
Jarbidge, Nev........B6 192
Jardim de Angicos, Braz........g6 138
Jardim do Seridó, Braz........C3 138
Jardine, Mont........E6 190
Jardines de la Reina, is., Cuba........E4 131
Jardinópolis, Braz........k8 137
Jarí, riv., Braz........B4 139
Järlåsa, Swe........t35 63
Järna, Swe........t35 63
Jarnac, Fr........E3 58
Jarny, Fr........E5 59
Jarocin, Pol........C4 70
Jarosław, Pol........C7 70
Jaroso, Colo........D5 171
Jarrahi, riv., Iran........F4 86
Jarratt, Va........E5 209
Jarrell, Tenn........A3 205
Jarrettsville, Md........A5 173
Jarrow, Alta., Can........C5 148
Jarvie, Alta., Can........B3 148
Jarvis, Ont., Can........E4 153
Jarvis, isl., Oceania........G12 113
Jarvisburg, N.C........A8 197
Jasień, Pol........B10 61
Jāsk, Iran........I8 86
Jask, bay, Iran........I8 86
Jasło, Pol........D6 70
Jasmin, Sask., Can........F4 155
Jason, isl., Ant........C7 120
Jasonville, Ind........F3 179
Jasper, Ala........B2 166
Jasper, Ark........A2 169
Jasper, Alta., Can........C1 148
Jasper, Ont., Can........C9 153
Jasper, Fla........B4 174
Jasper, Ga........B2 175
Jasper, Ind........H4 179
Jasper, Minn........G2 187
Jasper, Mo........D3 189
Jasper, N.Y........C3 196
Jasper, Ohio........C4 199
Jasper, Tenn........D8 205
Jasper, Tex........D6 206
Jasper, co., Ga........C3 175
Jasper, co., Ill........D5 178
Jasper, co., Ind........B3 179
Jasper, co., Iowa........C4 180
Jasper, co., Miss........C4 188
Jasper, co., Mo........D3 189
Jasper, co., S.C........G5 203
Jasper, co., Tex........D6 206
Jasper, nat. park, Alta., Can........C1 148
Jastarnia, Pol........A5 70
Jastrzębia Góra, Pol........A5 70
Jastrzębie, Pol........h9 70
Jászapáti, Hung........B5 68
Jászberény, Hung........B4 68
Jat Poti, Afg........F12 86
Jath, India........I5 88
Jati, Pak........E2 88
Jatibonico, Cuba........E4 131
Játiva, Sp........C5 65
Jaú, Braz........C3, m7 137
Jaú, riv., Braz........D5 133
Jauaperí, riv., Braz........C5 133
Jauca, P.R........D5 132
Jauja, Peru........D2 134
Jaumave, Mex........C5 129
Jaunpur, India........E9 88
Java, S. Dak........B6 204
Java, Va........E3 209
Java, isl., Indon........G3 90
Java, sea, Indon........G4 90
Javaés, riv., Braz........E5 139
Jávea, Sp........C6 65
Jawhar, India........H4 88
Jawor, Pol........C4 70
Jaworzno, Pol........g10 70
Jay, Fla........G2 174
Jay, Maine........D2 184
Jay, N.Y........B11 196
Jay, Okla........A7 200
Jay, co., Ind........D7 179
Jay, peak, Vt........B3 208
Jay Em, Wyo........C8 213
Jayanga, Peru........C2 134
Jayess, Miss........D3 188
Jaynes, Ariz........E4 168
Jayton, Tex........C2 206
Jayuya, P.R........C4 132
Jayuya, mun., P.R........C4 132
Jean, Nev........H6 192
Jeanerette, La........E4 183
Jeannette, Pa........F2 202
Jebba, Nig........E5 103
Jebel Aulia, Sud........B3 105
Jebel Akhdhar, mts., Oman........D2 87
Jebel Marra, mtn., Sud........C1 105
Jebel Neba, mtn., Jordan........C7 84
Jebel Toubkal, mtn., Mor........C3 102
Jedburg, S.C........E1 203
Jedburgh, Scot........E6 57
Jeddito, Ariz........B5 168
Jeddo, Mich........E8 186
Jędrzejów, Pol........C6 70
Jeetze, riv., Ger........E5 62
Jeff, Ky........C6 182
Jeff Davis, co., Ga........E4 175
Jeff Davis, co., Tex........F2 206
Jeffers, Minn........F3 187
Jeffers, Mont........E5 190
Jefferson, Ala........C2 166
Jefferson, Ark........C3 169
Jefferson, Colo........B5 171
Jefferson, Ga........B3 175
Jefferson, Iowa........B3 180
Jefferson, La........C7 183
Jefferson, Maine........D3 184
Jefferson, Md........B2 173
Jefferson, Mass........B4 185
Jefferson, N.H........B4 193
Jefferson, N.J........D2 194
Jefferson, N.Y........C6 196
Jefferson, N.C........A2 197
Jefferson, Ohio........A7 199
Jefferson, Okla........A4 200
Jefferson, Oreg........C1, C4 201
Jefferson, Pa........*F2 202
Jefferson, S.C........B7 203
Jefferson, S. Dak........E9 204
Jefferson, Tex........C5 206
Jefferson, Wis........E5 212
Jefferson, co., Ala........B3 166
Jefferson, co., Ark........C3 169
Jefferson, co., Colo........B5 171

INDEX KEY Each place listed in **Bold-faced Type** has its population listed in the Population tables, pages 230 to 280.
Each country, shown in CAPITAL LETTERS, has its population listed in the World Political Information Table, pages 6 to 10.
* Does not appear on map; key shows general location.

Jefferson, co., Fla......B3 174
Jefferson, co., Ga......C4 175
Jefferson, co., Idaho......F6 177
Jefferson, co., Ill......E5 178
Jefferson, co., Ind......G7 179
Jefferson, co., Iowa......C6 180
Jefferson, co., Kans......C8 181
Jefferson, co., Ky......B4 182
Jefferson, co., Miss......D2 188
Jefferson, co., Mo......C7 189
Jefferson, co., Mont......D4 190
Jefferson, co., Nebr......D8 191
Jefferson, co., N.Y......A5 196
Jefferson, co., Ohio......B7 199
Jefferson, co., Okla......C4 200
Jefferson, co., Oreg......C5 201
Jefferson, co., Pa......D3 202
Jefferson, co., Tenn......C10 205
Jefferson, co., Tex......E5 206
Jefferson, co., Wash......B2 210
Jefferson, co., W. Va......B7 211
Jefferson, co., Wis......E5 212
Jefferson, par., La......E5 183
Jefferson, hill, Ky......A4 182
Jefferson, mtn., Idaho......E7 177
Jefferson, mtn., Nev......E5 192
Jefferson, mtn., Oreg......C5 201
Jefferson City, Mo......C5 189
Jefferson City, Mont......D4 190
Jefferson City, Tenn......C10 205
Jefferson Davis, co.,
Miss......D4 188
Jefferson Davis, par., La..D3 183
Jefferson Heights, La....*E5 183
Jefferson Island, La......E4 183
Jefferson Island, Mont......E5 190
Jeffersontown, Ky....A4, B4 182
Jeffersonville, Ga......D3 175
Jeffersonville, Ind......H6 179
Jeffersonville, Ky......C6 182
Jeffersonville, N.Y......D6 196
Jeffersonville, Ohio......C4 199
Jeffersonville, Vt......B3 208
Jeffrey, W. Va......D3, D5 211
Jeffreys, creek, S.C......C8 203
Jehol, see Chengte, China
Jehossee, isl., S.C......G1 203
Jejui-Guazú, riv., Par......D4 135
Jēkabpils, Sov. Un......C5 72
Jekyll, isl., Ga......E5 175
Jelenia Góra, Pol......C3 70
Jelgav, Sov. Un......C4 72
Jellico, Tenn......C9 205
Jelling, Den......C3 62
Jelm, Wyo......D6 213
Jelm, mtn., Wyo......D7 213
Jelöy, isl., Nor......p28 63
Jemez, dam, N. Mex......G5 195
Jemez, Indian res.,
N. Mex......B2, F5 195
Jemez, riv., N. Mex......G5 195
Jemez Pueblo,
N. Mex......B3, F5 195
Jemez Springs,
N. Mex......B3, F5 195
Jemison, Ala......C3 166
Jemo, isl., Marshall Is...... 115
Jemseg, N.B., Can......D3 151
Jemtland, Maine......A4 184
Jena, Ger......C6 61
Jena, La......C3 183
Jenbach, Aus......B7 66
Jenera, Ohio......B4 199
Jenkins, Ky......C7 182
Jenkins, Minn......D4 187
Jenkins, co., Ga......D5 175
Jenkinsburg, Ga......C2 175
Jenkinsville, S.C......C5 203
Jenkintown, Pa......A11, F11 202
Jenks, Okla......A6 200
Jenner, Alta., Can......D5 148
Jenners, Pa......F3 202
Jennie, Ark......D4 169
Jennings, Fla......B3 174
Jennings, Kans......C3 181
Jennings, La......D3 183
Jennings, Md......D1 173
Jennings, Mich......D5 186
Jennings, Mo......A8 189
Jennings, Okla......A5 200
Jennings, co., Ind......G6 179
Jenny Jump, mtn., N.J......B3 194
Jenny Lake, Wyo......B2 213
Jenny Lind, Ark......B1 169
Jensen, Utah......C6 207
Jensen Beach, Fla......E6 174
Jenshou, China......C11 87
Jeptha Knob, peak, Ky......B4 182
Jequié, Braz......D2 138
Jequitinhonha, riv., Braz......E2 138
Jerauld, co., S. Dak......C7 204
Jérémie, Hai......F6 131
Jeremoabo, Braz......D3 138
Jerez de la Frontera, Sp....D2 65
Jerez de los Caballeros,
Sp......C2 65
Jericho, Ark......B5 169
Jericho, Austl......A6 112
Jericho, see Arīḥā, Jordan
Jericho, N.Y......*F2 172
Jericho, Utah......D3 207
Jericho, Vt......B3 208
Jericho, Va......*E6 209
Jericho Center, Vt......C3 208
Jerico Springs, Mo......D4 189
Jermyn, Pa......C10 202
Jermyn, Tex......C3 206
Jerome, Ariz......C3 168
Jerome, Ark......D4 169
Jerome, Fla......F5 174
Jerome, Idaho......G4 177
Jerome, Ill......*D4 178
Jerome, Iowa......D4 180
Jerome, Mich......F6 186
Jerome, Mo......D5 189
Jerome, Pa......F4 202
Jerome, Va......C4 209
Jerome, co., Idaho......G4 177
Jerome Park, res., N.Y......D6 194
Jeromesville, Ohio......B5 199
Jerris, inlet, B.C., Can......D6 149
Jersey, Ga......C3 175
Jersey, Tenn......E10 205
JERSEY, Br. dep., Eur......F5 55
Jersey, co., Ill......D3 178
Jersey, mtn., Idaho......E3 177
Jersey City, N.J......B4, E5 194
Jersey Shore, Pa......D7 202
Jerseyville, Ont., Can......D4 153
Jerseyville, Ill......D3 178
Jerumenha, Braz......C2 138
Jerusalem, Ark......B3 169
Jerusalem, Isr......C7, h11 84
Jerusalem, Jordan....C7, h11 84
Jerusalem, Ohio......C6 199
Jerusalem, kingdom of...... 47
Jervis, bay, Austl......G8 112
Jesenik, Czech......C4 70
Jessamine, co., Ky......C5 182
Jessen, Ger......B7 61
Jessie, N. Dak......B7 198
Jessieville, Ark......C2 169
Jessnitz, Ger......B7 61
Jessore, Bngl......F12 88
Jessup (Winton), Pa......A9 202
Jessup, lake, Fla......D5 174
Jessups, Md......B4 173
Jesterville, Md......D6 173
Jesup, Ga......E5 175
Jesup, Iowa......B5 180
Jesús Carranza, Mex......D5 129
Jesus del Monte, Cuba...h12 131
Jesús María, Arg......A4 136
Jet, Okla......A3 200
Jetersville, Va......D4 209
Jetmore, Kans......D4 181
Jetson, Ky......C3 182
Jette, Bel......D4 59
Jeumont, Fr......D4 59
Jever, Ger......B3 60
Jewel Cave, nat. mon.,
S. Dak......D2 204
Jewell, Iowa......B4 180
Jewell, Kans......C5 181
Jewell, Ohio......A3 199
Jewell, Oreg......B3 201
Jewell, co., Kans......C5 181
Jewell Ridge, Va......B3 209
Jewett, Ill......D5 178
Jewett, Ohio......B6 199
Jewett, Tex......D4 206
Jewett, lake, Sask., Can......A3 155
Jewett City, Conn......C9 172
Jeypore, India......H9 88
Jeziorna, Pol......m14 70
Jhal, Pak......C1 88
Jhal Jhao, Pak......C4 87
Jhalrapatan, India......E6 88
Jhang Maghiāna, Pak......B4 88
Jhansi, India......C6 87, E7 88
Jhawāni, Nep......D10 88
Jhelum, Pak......B5 87
Jhelum, riv., Pak......B5 87
Jhunjhunu, India......C5 88
Jiachan, China......B8 88
Jibhalanta (Uliassutai),
Mong......B4 91
Jicarilla Apache, Indian res.,
N. Mex......A2 195
Jičín, Czech......C3 70
Jifnā, Jordan......h11 84
Jiggalong, Austl......D3 111
Jigger, La......B4 183
Jiggitai, lake, China......A8 87
Jiggs, Nev......C6 192
Jihchao, China......G8 92
Jihlava, Czech......D3 70
Jijigā, Eth......D5 105
Jijia, riv., Rom......B8 68
Jijona, Sp......C5 65
Jilf Al Kabir, plat.,
Eg......E5 101
Jiloca, riv., Sp......B5 65
Jílové, Czech......o17 70
Jim Falls, Wis......C2 212
Jim Hogg, co., Tex......F3 206
Jim Thorpe (Mauch Chunk),
Pa......E10 202
Jim Wells, co., Tex......F3 206
Jim Woodruff, dam, Fla......F2 175
Jimā, Eth......D4 105
Jimā, reg., Eth......D4 105
Jimbolia, Rom......C5 68
Jimena, Sp......D3 65
Jiménez, Mex......B4 129
Jināḥ, Eg......D6 101
Jindřichův Hradec,
Czech......D3 70
Jinja, Ug......A5 106
Jinotega, Nic......D5 130
Jinotepe, Nic......E4 130
Jipijapa, Ec......B1 134
Jiquilisco, Sal......D3 130
Jiquilpan de Juárez,
Mex......n12 129
Jirgā, Eg......D6 101
Jirgalanta (Kobdo),
Mong......B3 91
Jirkov, Czech......C8 61
Jisr esh Shughur, Syr......E11 85
Jiul, riv., Rom......C6 68
Jiyānklīs, Eg......C2 84
Jizān, Sau. Ar......B5 105
Jo Daviess, co., Ill......A3 178
Joanna, S.C......C4 203
João Pessoa, Braz....C4, h6 138
Joaquin, Tex......*D6 206
Joaquín V. González, Arg....E3 136
Job, W. Va......C5 211
Job, peak, Nev......D3 192
Jobos, P.R......D6 132
Jobstown, N.J......C3 194
Jocotepec, Mex......m12 129
Jodar, Sp......D4 65
Jodhpur, India....C5 87, D4 88
Jodie, W. Va......C7 211
Jodoigne, Bel......D4 59
Joe Batts Arm, Newf.,
Can......D4 152
Joelton, Tenn......E9 205
Joensuu, Fin......F13 63
Joes, Colo......B8 171
Joes, brook, Vt......C4 208
Joes, creek, W. Va......D6 211
Joeuf, Fr......C6 58
Joffre, mtn., B.C., Can......D10 149
Joggins, N.S., Can......D5 151
Jogipet, India......I7 88
Jogjakarta, Indon......G4 90
Johannesburg, Calif......E5 170
Johannesburg, Mich......D6 186
Johannesburg, S. Afr......C4 107
John, isl., Ont., Can......B8 186
John, pass, Fla......F5 174
John Day, Oreg......C8 201
John Day, dam, Wash......D5 210
John Day, riv., Oreg......C6 201
John F. Kennedy Space
Center, Fla......D6 174
John H. Kerr, dam,
N.C., Va......A5 197, E4 209
John Long, mts., Mont......D3 190
John Martin, res., Colo......C7 171
John Redmond, res., Kans..C2 189
John Sevier, Tenn......E11 205
John W. Flannagan, res.,
Va......B2 209
Johns, Ala......E4 166
Johns, isl., S.C......F7 203
Johns, pass, Fla......E1 174
Johns Island, S.C......F2, F7 203
Johnsburg, Ill......E2 178
Johnsburg, N.Y......B7 196
Johnsburg, Wis......B5 212
Johnson, Ariz......E5 168
Johnson, Ark......A1 169
Johnson, Ind......H2 179
Johnson, Kans......E2 181
Johnson, Nebr......D10 191
Johnson, Vt......B3 208
Johnson, Wash......C8 210
Johnson, co., Ark......B2 169
Johnson, co., Ga......D4 175
Johnson, co., Ill......F5 178
Johnson, co., Ind......F5 179
Johnson, co., Iowa......C6 180
Johnson, co., Kans......D9 181
Johnson, co., Ky......C7 182
Johnson, co., Mo......C4 189
Johnson, co., Nebr......D9 191
Johnson, co., Tenn......C12 205
Johnson, co., Tex......C4 206
Johnson, co., Wyo......A6 213
Johnson City, N.Y......C5 196
Johnson City, Tenn......C11 205
Johnson City, Tex......D3 206
Johnson City Southeast,
Tenn......*C11 205
Johnson Creek, Wis......E5 212
Johnsonburg, N.J......B3 194
Johnsonburg, Pa......D4 202
Johnsondale, Calif......D4 170
Johnsons Grove, Tenn......B2 205
Johnsonville, S.C......D9 203
Johnsonville, Tenn......A4 205
Johnston, Iowa......A7 180
Johnston, R.I......B11 172
Johnston, S.C......D4 203
Johnston, co., N.C......B5 197
Johnston, co., Okla......C5 200
Johnston, isl.,
Oceania......E11 113, n14 176
Johnston, key, Fla......H5 174
Johnston City, Ill......F5 178
Johnston Island, U.S. dep.,
Oceania......E11 113, n14 176
Johnstone, strait, B.C., Can.D4 149
Johnston's, pt., Scot......E3 57
Johnstons Station, Miss......D3 188
Johnstown, Colo......A6 171
Johnstown, Nebr......B5 191
Johnstown, N.Y......B6 196
Johnstown, N. Dak......A8 198
Johnstown, Ohio......B5 199
Johnstown, Pa......F4 202
Johnsville, Md......A3 173
Johntown, Tex......C5 206
Johnville, Que., Can......D6 154
Johor, pol. div., Mala......K5 89
Johor Baharu, Mala......L5 89
Joice, Iowa......A4 180
Joigny, Fr......D5 58
Joiner, Ark......B5 169
Joinville, Braz......D3 137
Joinville, Fr......C6 58
Joinville, isl., Ant......C7 180
Jojutla, Mex......n14 129
Jokaj, hbr., Ponape...... 114
Jokaj, isl., Ponape...... 114
Jokkmokk, Swe......D8 63
Joliet, Ill......B5, F2 178
Joliet, Mont......E8 190
Joliette, Que., Can......C4 154
Joliette, N. Dak......A8 198
Joliette, co., Que., Can......C3 154
Jolley, Iowa......B3 180
Jolly, Tex......C3 206
Jolo, Phil......D6 90
Jolo, isl., Phil......D6 90
Jomalig, isl., Phil......o14 90
Jonas Ridge, N.C......B2, C4 197
Jonava, Sov. Un......A8 70
Jones, La......B4 183
Jones, Md......B4 173
Jones, Okla......B4 200
Jones, Phil......n13 90
Jones, Tenn......B2 205
Jones, co., Ga......C3 175
Jones, co., Iowa......B6 180
Jones, co., Miss......D4 188
Jones, co., N.C......B6 197
Jones, co., S. Dak......D5 204
Jones, co., Tex......C3 206
Jones, beach, N.Y......G2 172
Jones, sound, N.W. Ter.,
Can......B23 118
Jones Mill, Ark......C3, D6 169
Jones Mill, Tenn......A3 205
Jones Mills, Pa......F3 202
Jonesboro, Ark......B5 169
Jonesboro, Ga......C2 175
Jonesboro, Ill......F4 178
Jonesboro, Ind......D6 179
Jonesboro, La......B3 183
Jonesboro, Maine......D5 184
Jonesboro, Tenn......C11 205
Jonesburg, Mo......C6 189
Jonesport, Maine......D5 184
Jonestown, Miss......C3 188
Jonestown, Miss......A3 188
Jonestown, Pa......F9 202
Jonesville, Ill......B4 178
Jonesville, Ind......F6 179
Jonesville, La......C4 183
Jonesville, Mich......G6 186
Jonesville, N.C......A3 197
Jonesville, S.C......B4 203
Jonesville, Vt......C3 208
Jonesville, Va......B2 209
Jongkha Dzong, China...C10 88
Jönköping, Swe......A8 62
Jönköping, co., Swe......A8 62
Jonquière, Que., Can......A6 154
Jonuta, Mex......D6 129
Jonzac, Fr......E3 58
Joplin, Mo......D3 189
Joplin, Mont......B6 190
Joppa, Ala......A3 166
Joppa, Ill......F5 178
Jordan, Ala......D1 166
Jordan, Ark......A3 169
Jordan, Ky......B2 182
Jordan, Minn......F5 187
Jordan, Mont......C10 190
Jordan, N.Y......B4 196
JORDAN, country, Asia..G11 85
Jordan, creek, Pa......B1 194
Jordan, dam, Ala......C3 166
Jordan, lake, Ala......C3 166
Jordan, lake, N.S., Can......E4 151
Jordan, riv., Asia......B7 84
Jordan, riv., Utah......C4 207
Jordan Valley, Oreg......E9 201
Jorhat, India......C9 87
Jornada del Muerto, des.,
N. Mex......E3 195
Jörns, Swe......E9 63
Jos, Nig......E6 103
José Batlle y Ordóñez,
Ur......E1 137
José de San Martín, Arg...C2 136
Joseph, Oreg......B9 201
Joseph, Utah......E3 207
Joseph, lake, Ont., Can......B5 153
Joseph Bonaparte, gulf,
Austl......B4 110
Joseph City, Ariz......C5 168
Josephine, Tex......*C4 206
Josephine, co., Oreg......E3 201
Josephville, Mo......A7 189
Joshua, Tex......B5 206
Joshua Tree, nat. mon.,
Calif......F6 170
Jost Van Dyke, is., Vir. Is......f15 132
Jostedalsbre, glacier, Nor...G2 63
Jotunheimen, mts., Nor......G3 63
Joubert, S. Dak......D7 204
Jourdanton, Tex......E3 206
Joussard, Alta., Can......B3 148
Joux, lake, Switz......C2 66
Jouy-en-Josas, Fr......g9 58
Jovellanos, Cuba......D3 131
Joy, Ill......B3 178
Joyce, La......C3 183
Joyuda, P.R......C2 132
J. Percy Priest, res.,
Tenn......E9 205
Juab, co., Utah......D2 207
Juan Aldama, Mex......C4 129
Juan de Fuca, strait,
Wash......A1 210
Juan Díaz, Pan......k12 130
Juan E. Barra, Arg......B4 136
Juan Fernández, is.,
Pac. O......I17 113
Juan Lacaze, Ur......g8 136
Juana Díaz, P.R......C4 132
Juana Díaz, mun., P.R......C5 132
Juanita, Colo......D3 171
Juanita, N. Dak......B7 198
Juanita Central, P.R......B6 132
Juanjui, Peru......C2 134
Juárez, Arg......B5 136
Juárez, Mex......A3 129
Juárez, Mex......D5 129
Juaso, Ghana......E4 103
Juàzeiro, Braz......C2 138
Juàzeiro do Norte,
Braz......C3 138
Juba, Sud......E3 105
Jubbah, Sau. Ar......I13 85
Jubillee, lake, Newf., Can..D4 152
Júcar, riv., Sp......C5 65
Júcaro, Cuba......E4 131
Juchipila, riv., Mex......m12 129
Juchipila, Mex......m12 129
Juchitán [de Zaragoza],
Mex......D6 129
Jucuapa, Sal......D3 130
Jud, N. Dak......C7 198
Juda, Wis......F4 212
Judaea...... 44
Judah, Alta., Can......A2 148
Judayyidat 'Ar'ar (Oasis),
Sau. Ar......G13 85
Juddah, Sau. Ar......A4 105
Judds Bridge, Conn......C3 172
Jude, isl., Newf., Can......E4 152
Judean, hills, Isr., Jordan...C7 84
Judenburg, Aus......E7 60
Judique, N.S., Can......D8 151
Judith, isl., N.C......B7 197
Judith, mts., Mont......C7 190
Judith, peak, Mont......C7 190
Judith, riv., Mont......C7 190
Judith Basin, co., Mont...C6 190
Judith Gap, Mont......D7 190
Judith Neck, pt., R.I......D11 172
Judson, Ind......E3 179
Judson, Minn......F4 187
Judson, N. Dak......C4 198
Judsonia, Ark......B4 169
Judyville, Ind......D3 179
Juelsminde, Den......C4 62
Juian, China......K9 92
Juigalpa, Nic......D5 130
Juist, Ger......A6 59
Juist, isl., Ger......B3 60
Juiz de Fora, Braz.....C4, g6 137
Jujuy, Arg......D2 135
Jujuy, prov., Arg......D2 135
Jukao, China......H9 92
Jukkasjärvi, Swe......D9 63
Julesburg, Colo......A8 171
Juliaca, Peru......E3 134
Juliaetta, Idaho......C2 177
Julian, Calif......F5 170
Julian, Nebr......*D7 191
Julian, N.C......B4 197
Julian, W. Va......C3, D5 211
Julian Alps, mts., Yugo......C2 68
Julianehåb, Grnld......C19 118
Jülich, Ger......D6 59
Juliette, Ga......C3 175
Julimes, Mex......B3 129
Julio de Castilhos, Braz...D2 137
Julita, Swe......t34 63
Juliustown, N.J......C3 194
Jullundur, India...B6 87, B5 88
Jumas, riv., Braz......C2 139
Jumbo, peak, Nev......G7 192
Jumento, is., Ba. Is......D6 131
Jumet, Bel......D4 59
Jumilla, Sp......C5 65
Jumna, riv., India......E8 88
Jump, riv., Wis......C2 212
Jumping Branch, W. Va...D4 211
Jumullong Manglo, mtn.,
Guam...... 114
Junagadh,
India......D5 87, G3 88
Junan, China......H6 92
Juncos, P.R......C7 132
Juncos, mun., P.R......C7 132
Juncos Central, P.R......C7 132
Junction, Ill......F5 178
Junction, Ohio......A3 199
Junction, Tex......D3 206
Junction, Utah......E3 207
Junction City, Ark......D3 169
Junction City, Ga......D2 175
Junction City, Kans......C7 181
Junction City, Ky......C5 182
Junction City, La......B3 183
Junction City, Mo......*D7 189
Junction City, Ohio......C5 199
Junction City, Oreg......C3 201
Junction City, Wis......D4 212
Jundah, Austl......B4 112
Jundiaí, Braz......C3, m8 137
June in Winter, lake, Fla......E5 174
June Lake, Calif......D4 170
June Park, Fla......*D6 174
Juneau, Alsk......D13, k22 167
Juneau, Wis......E5 212
Juneau, co., Wis......E3 212
Junee, Austl......G6 112
Jungcheng, China......F10 92
Jungchiang, China......L3 92
Jungfrau, mtn., Switz......C3 66
Junghsien, China......F6 91
Junglinster, Lux......E6 59
Jungyün, China......G7 91
Juniata, Nebr......D7 191
Juniata, co., Pa......E6 202
Juniata, riv., Pa......E6 202
Juniata Terrace, Pa......E6 202
Junín, Arg......A4 136
Junín, Peru......D2 134
Junín, dept., Peru......D2 134
Junín, lake, Peru......D2 134
Junín de los Andes, Arg...B2 136
Junior, W. Va......C5 211
Junior, lake, Maine......C4 184
Juniper, N.B., Can......C2 151
Juniper, Ga......D2 175
Juniper, flat, Oreg......B6 201
Junipero Serra, peak, Calif..D3 170
Junius, S. Dak......C8 204
Juno, Tex......D2 206
Juno Beach, Fla......*F6 174
Junor, Sask., Can......D2 155
Juntura, Oreg......D8 201
Jupiter, Fla......F6 174
Jupiter, inlet, Fla......F6 174
Jupiter, isl., Fla......E6 174
Jupiter Inlet Colony,
Fla......*F6 174
Juquiá, Braz......C3, n8 137
Jur, riv., Sud......D2 105
Jura, dept., Fr......C1 66
Jura, isl., Scot......D3 57
Jura, mts., Switz., Fr......C1 66
Jura, sound, Scot......E3 57
Jurbarkas, Sov. Un......A7 70
Jurby, head, I. of Man......F4 57
Jurf ad Darāwīsh, Jordan..D7 84
Juriti, Braz......C3 139
Juruá, riv., Braz......C4 134
Juruena, riv., Braz......D3 139
Jussey, Fr......B1 66
Justice, Ill......*B6 178
Justiceburg, Tex......C2 206
Justin, Tex......A5, C4 206
Justo Daract, Arg......A3 136
Jutaí, riv., Braz......B4 134
Jüterbog, Ger......B8 61
Jutiapa, Guat......C3 130
Juticalpa, Hond......C4 130
Jutland, pen., Den......B3 62
Juwain, Afg......F10 86
Jūymand, Iran......D9 86
Južna Morava, riv., Yugo..D5 68
Jyderup, Den......C5 62
Jyekundo (Yüshu), China..E4 91
Jyväskylä, Fin......F11 63

K

Ka Lae (South Cape), cape,
Haw......E6 176
Kaaawa, Haw......f10 176
Kaala, peak, Haw......f9 176
Kaalaea, Haw......g10 176
Kaalualu, bay, Haw......E6 176
Kabaena, isl., Indon......G6 90
Kabala, S.L......E2 103
Kabale, Ug......B5 106
Kabalo, Zaire......C4 106
Kabambare, Zaire......B4 106
Kabankalan, Phil......*D6 90
Kabarnet, Ken......A6 106
Kabba, Nig......E6 103
Kabelstation, Sur......B3 139
Kabenga, Zaire......C4 106
Kabetogama, lake, Minn......B5 187
Kabinda, Zaire......C3 106
Kabir Kuh, mts., Iran......E3 86
Kabompo, riv., Zambia......D3 106
Kabong, Mala......E4 90
Kabongo, Zaire......C4 106
Kaboudia, cape, Tun......G12 64
Kabul, Afg......D14 86
Kabul, riv., Afg......D14 86
Kabwe, Zambia......D4 106
Kačák, riv., Czech......n17 70
Kachek, China......C9 89
Kachess, res., Wash......B4 210
Kachuga, Sov. Un......D13 71
Kackley, Kans......C6 181
Kadaň, Czech......C8 61
Kade, Ghana......E4 103
Kadet, chan., Ger......D6 62
Kadinhan, Tur......C9 85
Kadiri, India......F6 87
Kadiyevka,
Sov. Un......G12, q21 72
Kadoka, S. Dak......D4 204
Kadoma, Jap......*I6 93
Kadugli, Sud......C2 105
Kaduna, Nig......D6 103
Kaduna, riv., Nig......D6 103
Kaea, cape, Haw......C5 176
Kaédi, Maur......C2 103
Kaélé, Cam......C2 104
Kaena, pt., Haw......C4 176
Kaena, pt., Haw......B3, f8 176
Kaeryŏng, Kor......H4 93
Kaesŏng, Kor......G3 93
Kāf, Sau. Ar......C7 101
Kafanchan, Nig......E6 103
Kaffrine, Sen......D1 103
Kafia Kingi, Sud......D1 105
Kafkaf, New Ire. I...... 115
Kafr ad Dawwār,
Eg......C2 84
Kafr 'Ammār, Eg......E3 84
Kafr ash Shaykh,
Eg......C2 84
Kafr az Zayyāt, Eg......D2 84
Kafr Dā'ūd, Eg......D2 84
Kafr Mālik, Jordan......h12 84
Kafr Qaddūm, Jordan......g11 84
Kafr Qāsim, Isr......g10 84
Kafr Ṣaqr, Eg......D3 84
Kafr Zībād, Jordan......g11 84
Kafue, Zambia......E4 106
Kafue, riv., Zambia......D4 106
Kagan, Sov. Un......B12 86
Kaganovich, Sov. Un......E12 72
Kagawong, Ont., Can......B2 153
Kagera, riv., Tan......B5 106
Kağizman, Tur......B14 85
Kagman, mtn., Saipan...... 114
Kagoshima, Jap......K5 93
Kagoshima, bay, Jap......K5 93
Kagul, Sov. Un......C9 68
Kahajan, riv., Indon......F4 90
Kahakuloa, Haw......B5 176
Kahaluu, Haw......D6 176
Kahaluu, Haw......g10 176
Kahama, Tan......B5 106
Kahana, Haw......B4, f10 176
Kahemba, Zaire......C2 106
Kahira, Okinawa...... 114
Kahla, Ger......C6 61
Kahnūj, Iran......H8 86
Kahlotus, Wash......C7 210
Kahoka, Mo......A6 189
Kahoolawe, isl., Haw......C5 176
Kahua, Haw......C6 176
Kahuku, Haw......B4, f10 176
Kahuku, pt., Haw......B4 176
Kahului, Haw......C5 176
Kahului Bay, Haw......C5 176
Kaiama, Nig......E5 103
Kaiapoi, N.Z......O14 112
Kaiba, isl., Sov. Un......C10 93
Kaibab, Ariz......A3 168

Kaibab, plat., Ariz..........A3 168
Kaibito, Ariz..............A4 168
Kaieteur, fall, Guy..........A3 139
Kaifeng, China..........G6 92
Kaihsien, China..........E6 91
Kaihua, China..............J8 92
Kaikoura, N.Z............O14 112
Kailai, New Britain I.......... 115
Kailas, range, China......C11 88
Kailu, China................C9 92
Kailua, Haw..............g11 176
Kailua-Kona, Haw.........D6 176
Kaimana, Indon..............F8 90
Kaimare, Pap...............k11 111
Kaimu, Haw..................D7 176
Kainaliu, Haw...............D6 176
Kainan, Jap.....................I7 93
Kaintira, India.............G10 88
Kaiparowits, plat., Utah.....F4 207
Kaiping, China..............D10 92
Kaipokok, bay, Newf.,
Can..........................g10 152
Kaiserslautern, Ger.......D2 61
Kaišiadorys, Sov. Un.......A8 70
Kaitaia, N.Z...............K14 112
Kaitangata, N.Z............Q12 112
Kaithal, India...............C6 88
Kaiton, New Britain I.......... 115
Kaitung, China............B10 92
Kaiwi, chan., Haw.........B4 176
Kaiyüan, China..............E2 93
Kaizuka, Jap................o14 93
Kajaani, Fin................E12 63
Kajakai, res., Afg..........E12 86
Kajiado, Ken.................B6 106
Kajikazawa, Jap.............n17 93
Kaka, Sud......................C3 105
Kakagi, lake, Ont., Can......E5 150
Kakamas, S. Afr..............C3 107
Kakamega, Ken...............A5 106
Kamamigahara, Jap.........*I7 93
Kake, Alsk..........D13, m23 167
Kakegawa, Jap...............o17 93
Kaketsa, mtn., B.C., Can..E6 142
Kakhovka, Sov. Un...........H9 72
Kakhovka, res., Sov. Un....H9 72
Kakinada, India....E7 87, I9 88
Kakisa, lake, N.W. Ter.,
Can............................D9 142
Kakogawa, Jap...............*I7 93
Kakumaa, Ken...............A5 106
Kakwa, riv., Alta., Can.....B1 148
Kāl Gūsheh, Iran..............F9 86
Kalabagh, Pak.................B5 87
Kalabakan, Mala...............E5 90
Ka abana, Mali.................D3 103
Kalābishah, Eg................E6 101
Kalabo, Zambia...............D3 106
Kalach, Sov. Un...............C2 73
Kalach [-na-Donu,
Sov. Un.......................G14 72
Kaladar, Ont., Can............C7 153
Kalahari, des., Bots..........B3 107
Kalahari Gemsbok, nat.
park, S. Afr..................C3 107
Kalaheo, Haw..................B2 176
Kalai-Khumb, Sov. Un...B15 86
Kalai-Mor, Sov. Un.........D11 86
Kālak, Iran.......................I9 86
Kalama, Wash.................C3 210
Kalámai, Grc....................D4 69
Kalamazoo, Mich..............F5 186
Kalamazoo, co., Mich.......F5 186
Kalamazoo, riv., Mich.......F5 186
Kalambo, falls, Tan.,
Zambia..........................C5 106
Kalampáka, Grc................C3 69
Kalankala (Well), Niger....C7 105
Kalaotoa, isl., Indon.........G6 90
Kalapana, Haw..................D7 176
Kalat, Pak........................C4 87
Kalāt-i-Ghilzai, Afg.........E13 86
Kalāteh Minār, Iran..........D10 86
Kalaupapa, Haw................B5 176
Kalávrita, Grc....................C4 69
Kalbā, U.A.E......................I8 86
Kalecik, Tur......................B9 85
Kaleden, B.C., Can............E8 149
Kalehe, Zaire....................B4 106
Kalem, Miss......................C4 188
Kalemi, Zaire.....................C4 106
Kalemona, New Britain I........ 115
Kaleva, Mich....................D4 186
Kalewa, Bur......................D9 87
Kalgalaksha, Sov. Un.......E16 63
Kalgan (Changkiakou),
China.............................C7 91
Kalgary, Tex......................C2 206
Kalgin, isl., Alsk...............g16 167
Kalgoorlie, Austl...............F3 111
Kali Sindh, riv., India.......E6 88
Kalida, Ohio....................*B3 199
Kalima, Zaire.....................B4 106
Kálimnos, Grc...................D6 69
Kálimnos, isl., Grc...........D6 69
Kalinin, Sov. Un...............B1 73
Kaliningrad (Königsberg),
Sov. Un.............A6 70, D3 72
Kaliningrad, Sov. Un....*C11 72
Kaliningrad, reg., Sov. Un. A6 70
Kalinkovichi, Sov. Un........E7 72
Kalispel, Indian res., Wash. A8 210
Kalispell, Mont.................B2 190
Kalisz, Pol........................C5 70
Kaliua, Tan.......................C5 106
Kalixälven, riv., Swe........D10 63
Kalīyā, Jordan....................h13 84
Kalkan, Tur........................D7 69
Kalkaska, Mich.................D5 186
Kalkaska, co., Mich............D5 186
Kalkfeld, S.W. Afr..............B2 107
Kalkrand, S.W. Afr.............B2 107
Kållerstad, Swe.................A7 62
Kallithéa, Grc....................h11 69
Kallsjön, lake, Swe...........F5 63
Kalmalo, Nig......................D6 103
Kalmar, Swe.......................I7 63
Kalmar, Swe.....................t35 63
Kalmar, Swe.......................I7 63
Kalmarsund, sound, Swe....I7 63
Kalmykovo, Sov. Un..........D4 73
Kalo, Iowa..........................B3 180
Kalocsa, Hung....................B4 68
Kalohi, chan., Haw............C4 176
Kalomo, Zambia..................E4 106
Kalona, Iowa.....................C6 180
Kalone, peak, B.C., Can....C4 149
Kalpi, India.........................D7 88
Kalskag, Alsk......................C7 167
Kaltag, Alsk........................C8 167
Kaluaaha, Haw.....................B5 176
Kaluga, Sov. Un.................D11 72
Kalundborg, Den..................C5 62
Kalush, Sov. Un..................G5 72
Kałuszyn, Pol.......................B6 70
Kalvehave, Den....................C6 62
Kalvesta, Kans......................D3 181
Kalvsjön, lake, Swe............A7 62
Kalyan, India.......................H4 88
Kama, Zaire..........................B4 106
Kama, res., Sov. Un............B5 73
Kama, riv., Sov. Un.............B4 73
Kama, rock, Iwo..................... 114
Kamadia (Well), Niger.......B7 103
Kamaing, Bur.....................C10 87
Kamaishi, Jap...................G10 93
Kamakou, Haw.....................B5 176
Kamakura, Jap....................n18 93
Kamaniskeg, lake, Ont.,
Can...................................B7 153
Kamaran, isl., Asia..............B5 105
Kamarhati, India.............*F12 88
Kamarod, Pak........................C3 87
Kamas, Utah.........................C4 207
Kamatsi, lake, Sask., Can..A4 155
Kamba, pt., Fiji........................ 114
Kambara, isl., Fiji..................... 114
Kambove, Zaire...................D4 106
Kamchatka, pen., Sov.
Un.....................................D18 71
Kamela, Oreg......................B8 201
Kamen-na-Obi, Sov. Un. C10 73
Kamenets-Podol'skiy,
Sov. Un...............................G6 72
Kamenjak, cape, Yugo......C1 68
Kamenka, Sov. Un..............G7 72
Kamensk-Shakhtinskiy,
Sov. Un...............................G13 72
Kamensk-Ural'skiy,
Sov. Un...............................B6 73
Kamenz, Ger.........................B9 61
Kameoka, Jap.......................n14 93
Kamet, peak, India..............B7 88
Kami, isl., Jap......................I4 93
Kamiah, Idaho....................C2 177
Kamiak, mtn., Wash............C8 210
Kamichli, Syr......................D13 85
Kamień Pomorski, Pol.......B3 70
Kamina, Zaire.......................C4 106
Kamioka, Jap......................m16 93
Kamloops, B.C., Can..........D7 149
Kamooloa, Haw.....................f9 176
Kamondorski, Calif.............*D3 170
Kamori-Yama, peak, Jap......I6 93
Kamouraska, Que., Can...B8 154
Kamouraska, co., Que.,
Can......................................B8 154
Kampa Dzong, China.......C12 88
Kampala, Ug.......................A5 106
Kampar, Mala........................J4 89
Kampar, riv., Indon.............E2 90
Kampen, Neth.......................B5 59
Kampeska, lake, S. Dak.....C8 204
Kamphaeng Phet, Thai......D3 89
Kampot, Camb.....................G6 89
Kampsville, Ill....................D3 178
Kampungbaru, Indon.........E6 90
Kamrar, Iowa.......................B4 180
Kamsack, Sask., Can..........F5 155
Kamuchawie, lake, Sask.,
Can.......................................A4 155
Kamuela (Waimea), Haw..C6 176
Kamuli, Ug............................A5 106
Kamyshebakha, Sov. Un..q21 72
Kamyshin, Sov. Un..............C3 73
Kamyshlov, Sov. Un............B6 73
Kan, riv., China.....................K6 92
Kana, Okinawa........................ 114
Kanab, Utah..........................F3 207
Kanab, creek, Ariz................A3 168
Kanabec, co., Minn.............E5 187
Kanaga, isl., Alsk..................E4 167
Kanaiwa, Jap..........................H8 93
Kanala, N. Cal.......................... 115
Kananaskis, riv., Alta.,
Can.......................................D3 148
Kanapou, bay, Haw...............C5 176
Kanarraville, Utah..................F2 207
Kanash, Sov. Un.....................B3 73
Kanaskat, Wash.....................D2 210
Kanathea, isl., Fiji.................... 114
Kanauga, Ohio.......................D5 199
Kanauj, India..........................D7 88
Kanawha, Iowa.....................B4 180
Kanawha, co., W. Va.........C3 211
Kanawha, riv., W. Va...........C3 211
Kanayama, Jap.....................n16 93
Kanazawa, Jap.......................H8 93
Kanchanaburi, Thai...............E3 89
Kancheepuram
(Conjeeveram), India.......F7 87
Kanchenjunga, peak,
Nep.......................................D11 88
Kanchou, China.......................F7 91
Kanchrapara, India.........*F12 88
Kandagach, Sov. Un...........D5 73
Kandahār, Afg.......................F12 86
Kandahar, Sask., Can.......F3 155
Kandalaksha, Sov. Un.....D15 63
Kandalakshskaya, bay,
Sov. Un..............................D15 63
Kandangan, Indon...............F5 90
Kandavu, isl., Fiji.................... 114
Kandel, Ger..........................D3 61
Kandersteg, Switz...............C3 66
Kandi, Dah............................D5 103
Kandıra, Tur..........................B8 69
Kandiyohi, Minn.................E4 187
Kandiyohi, co., Minn..........E3 187
Kandla, India.........................F3 88
Kandreho, Malag..................g9 107
Kandy, Cey..........................G7 87
Kane, Ill..................................D3 178
Kane, Pa..................................C4 202
Kane, Wyo...........................A4 213
Kane, co., Ill...........................B5 178
Kane, co., Utah......................F3 207
Kane, basin, Arc. O............B21 118
Kaneohe, Haw.........B4, g10 176
Kaneohe, bay, Haw............f10 176
Kanevskaya, Sov. Un.....H12 72
Kangal, Tur...........................C11 85
Kangaroo, isl., Austl...........G6 110
Kangean, is., Indon..............G5 90
Kanggye, Kor........................F3 93
Kangha, bay, Kor................H3 93
Kangley, Ill...........................B5 178
Kangnŭng, Kor.......................H4 93
Kango, Gabon........................E2 104
Kangoku, rock, Iwo.................... 114
Kangpao, China....................D6 92
Kangting, China.....................E5 91
Kani, Bur..................................A1 89
Kani, I.C..................................E3 103
Kaniama, Zaire......................C3 106
Kanin, cape, Sov. Un..........B17 40
Kanjiža, Yugo...........................B5 68
Kankakee, Ill..........................B6 178
Kankakee, co., Ill..................B6 178
Kankakee, riv., Ill.,
Ind......................B5 178, B4 179
Kankan, Guinea.....................D3 103
Kanker, India..........................G8 88
Kånna, Swe............................B7 62
Kannan, China.........................C1 93
Kannapolis, N.C.................B3 197
Kannata Valley, Sask.,
Can.......................................*G3 155
Kano, Nig..................................D6 103
Kanona, Zambia.....................D5 106
Kanopolis, Kans......................D5 181
Kanopolis, res., Kans.............D5 181
Kanorado, Kans.......................C1 181
Kanosh, Utah............................E3 207
Kanoya, Jap.................................K5 93
Kanpur, India.......C7 87, D8 88
Kanpur Cantonment,
India....................................*D8 88
Kanrach, Pak.............................C4 87
Kansas, Ala..............................B2 166
Kansas, Ill..................................D6 178
Kansas, Ohio............................A4 199
Kansas, Okla...............................A7 200
Kansas, state, U.S...................... 181
Kansas, riv., Kans..................C7 181
Kansas City, Kans.....B9, C9 181
Kansas City, Mo..........B3, E2 189
Kansasville, Wis.......................F1 212
Kansk, Sov. Un.........................D12 71
Kansŏng, Kor...........................G4 93
Kansu, prov., China................D5 91
Kantang, Thai...........................I3 89
Kantunilkín, Mex....................C7 129
Kanuma, Jap.........................*H9 93
Kanye, Bots...............................B4 107
Kanyŭ, China............................G8 92
Kao Tao, is., Viet.....................B7 89
Kaoan, China.............................J6 92
Kaohsiung, Taiwan..................G9 91
Kaolack, Sen...............................D1 103
Kaouar, oases, Niger...............C7 103
Kaoyao, China..............................G7 91
Kaoyu, China................................H8 92
Kaoyu, lake, China......................H8 92
Kapaa, Haw.................................A2 176
Kapandrition, Grc.......................g11 69
Kapanga, Zaire.............................C3 106
Kapapa, isl., Haw.....................g10 176
Kapapala, Haw.............................D6 176
Kapenguria, Ken..........................A6 106
Kapfenberg, Aus..........................E7 60
Kapiri Mposhi, Zambia...............D4 106
Kapit, Mala......................................E4 90
Kaplan, La.....................................D3 183
Kaplice, Czech..............................E9 61
Kapoeta, Sud..................................E3 105
Kapoho, Haw..................................D7 176
Kaposvár, Hung.............................B3 68
Kaposvar, creek, Sask...............G4 155
Kappa, Ill...*C4 178
Kapsan, Kor..F4 93
Kapterko (Well), Chad.................B4 104
Kapuas, riv., Indon.........................F4 90
Kapulena, Haw....................................C6 176
Kapuskasing, Ont., Can...............E9 153
Kapustin Yar, Sov. Un..................D3 73
Kaputar, mtn., Austl......................E8 112
Kapuvár, Hung.....................................B3 68
Kara, Sov. Un.......................................C9 71
Kara, mtn., Tur..................................D9 85
Kara, sea, Sov. Un..........................B9 71
Kara-Bogaz-Gol, Sov. Un...E4 73
Kara-Bogaz-Gol, gulf,
Sov. Un...E4 73
Kara Kum, des., Sov. Un...............E5 73
Kara Shahr (Yenki),
China...C2 91
Kara Tau, range, Sov. Un..............E7 73
Kara-Tyube, Sov. Un........................D4 73
Karabük, Tur......................................B9 85
Karaburun, Tur..C6 69
Karachev, Sov. Un.............................E10 72
Karāchi, Pak..D4 87
Karaga, Sov. Un....................................D19 71
Karaganda, Sov. Un...........................D8 73
Karagin, isl., Sov. Un.....................D19 71
Karaisali, Tur.......................................D10 85
Karakas, Sov. Un................................D10 73
Karakelong, isl., Indon...................E7 90
Karakoram, pass, India,
Pak...A6 87
Karakoram, range, Asia.................A6 87
Karaköse, Tur......................................C14 85
Karakul, Sov. Un..................................B11 86
Karamai, China....................................B1 91
Karaman, Tur..D9 85
Karamea, N.Z......................................N14 112
Karamea, bight, N.Z........................N13 112
Karamürsel, Tur.......................................B7 69
Karand, Iran...D3 86
Karapınar, Tur..D9 85
Karas, mts., S.W. Afr........................C2 107
Karasu, Sov. Un.......................................C6 73
Karasu, Tur...B8 69
Karasuk, Sov. Un...................................C9 73
Karatal, riv., Sov. Un...........................D9 73
Karatas, cape, Tur...............................D10 85
Karatsu, Jap..J4 93
Karaul Keldy, Sov. Un.......................D5 73
Karauli, India...D6 88
Karawanken, mts., Aus.,
Yugo..........................E7 60, B2 68
Karbalā', Iraq...F15 85
Karcag, Hung...B5 68
Karczew, Pol..m14 70
Kardhítsa, Grc...C3 69
Karema, Tan..C5 106
Karesuando, Swe...C10 63
Kargasok, Sov. Un.......................................B10 73
Kargil, India..B6 87
Kargopol, Sov. Un..A12 72
Karguiri, Niger...D7 103
Kariaí, Grc...B5 69
Karibib, S.W. Afr...B2 107
Karikal, India...F6 87
Karikari, cape, N.Z.......................................K14 112
Karima, Sud...B3 105
Karimata, arch., Indon.................................F3 90
Karimundjawa, is., Indon...........................G4 90
Karin, Som...C6 105
Karisimbi, vol., Rwanda,
Zaire...B4 106
Káristos, Grc...C5 69
Kariya, Jap...*I8 93
Kārīz, Iran..D10 86
Karkar, isl., N. Gui...h12 110
Karkaralinsk, Sov. Un..D9 73
Karkinitskiy, bay, Sov. Un..............................I9 72
Karkur, Isr...B7 84
Karl-Marx-Stadt, see
Chemnitz, Ger.
Karlobag, Yugo...C2 68
Karlovac, Yugo...C2 68
Karlóvasi, Grc..D6 69
Karlsbad, Czech...C2 70
Karlshamn, Swe...I6 63
Karlskoga, Swe...H6 63
Karlskrona, Swe..I6 63
Karlsruhe, Ger...D3 61
Karlsruhe, N. Dak..A5 198
Karlstad, Minn..B2 187
Karlstad, Swe..H5 63
Karlstadt, Ger...D4 61
Karluk, Alsk...D9 167
Karmutzen, mtn., B.C.,
Can..D4 149
Karnak, Ill..F5 178
Karnal, India..*C6 87
Karnes, co., Tex...E4 206
Karnes City, Tex...E4 206
Karns City, Pa...E2 202
Kärnten, state, Aus...C9 66
Karoi, Rh..A4 107
Karonga, Malawi..C5 106
Karora, Sud..B4 105
Karow, Ger...E6 62
Kárpathos, isl., Grc...E6 69
Karpenísion, Grc...C3 69
Karpinsk, Sov. Un...*D8 71
Kars, Tur...B14 85
Karsakpay, Sov. Un..D7 73
Karshi, Sov. Un...F9 71
Karshinskiy, Sov. Un..D4 73
Karstädt, Ger...E5 62
Kartal, Tur...B7 69
Kartaly, Sov. Un...C6 73
Karthaus, Pa..D5 202
Kartuzy, Pol..A5 70
Karup, Den..B3 62
Karup Å, riv., Den...B3 62
Karur, India..*F6 87
Karval, Colo..C7 171
Karvia, Fin..F10 63
Karviná, Czech..D5 70
Karwar, India..F5 87
Kås, Den...A3 62
Kas, Sud..C1 105
Kaş, Tur..D7 85
Kas Kong, Camb..G5 89
Kasaan, Alsk..n23 167
Kasai, reg., Zaire..B3 106
Kasai, riv., Afr...G8 96
Kasaji, Zaire...D3 106
Kasama, Zambia...D5 106
Kasanga, Tan...C5 106
Kasaoka, Jap..I6 93
Kasaragod, India...F5 87
Kasba, India...E11 88
Kasba, lake, N.W. Ter.,
Can...D12 142
Kasba Tadla, Mor..C3 102
Kasempa, Zambia..D4 106
Kasenga, Zaire...D4 106
Kasese, Ug..A5 106
Kāshān, Iran...E5 86
Kashegelok, Alsk..C8 167
Kashgar (Sufu), China...F10 71
Kashima, Jap...n19 93
Kashipur, India..C7 88
Kashira, Sov. Un...D12 72
Kashirka, riv., Sov. Un...D12 72
Kashiwa, Jap..*n18 93
Kashiwazaki, Jap...H9 93
Kâshmar, Iran..D9 86
Kashmir: c. 250 B.C... 79
c. 750 A.D... 80
c. 1775 A.D... 82
after World War II.. 83
see also Jammu and
Kashmir
Kashmor, Pak..C2 88
Kasilof, Alsk...C9, g16 167
Kasimov, Sov. Un..C2 73
Kaskaskia, Ill..F4 178
Kaskaskia, riv., Ill..D5 178
Kaskö, Fin..F9 63
Kaslo, B.C., Can...E9 149
Kasongo, Zaire..B4 106
Kasongo-Lunda, Zaire...B2 106
Kásos, isl., Grc...E6 69
Kasota, Minn..F5 187
Kassala, Sud..B4 105
Kassala, reg., Sud...B4 105
Kassandra, gulf, Grc...B4 69
Kassel, Ger..B4 61
Kasserine, Tun...G11 64
Kasson, Minn..F6 187
Kastamonu, Tur...B9 85
Kastélli, Grc...E4 69
Kastellórizo, isl., Grc..D7 69
Kastoría, Grc..B3 69
Kastro, Tur...B5 69
Kástron, Grc...C5 69
Kasugai, Jap...*n15 93
Kasukabe, Jap...n18 93
Kasumi, Jap..I7 93
Kasumiga-Ura, bay, Jap...H10 93
Kasungu, Malawi..D5 106
Kasūr, Pak..B5 87, B5 88
Katahdin, mtn., Maine..C4 184
Katako-Kombe, Zaire...B3 106
Katalla, Alsk...C11 167
Katanga, reg., Zaire...C3 106
Katanning, Austl...F2 111
Katata, Jap..n14 93
Katerini, Grc...B4 69
Kates Needle, mtn., B.C.,
Can...m24 167
Katha, Bur..D10 87
Katherine, Austl..B5 111
Kathleen, Fla...D4 174
Kathryn, N. Dak...C8 198
Kathryn, Alta., Can...D4 148
Kathua, India..A5 88
Katihar, India..E11 88
Katimik, lake, Man., Can..C2 150
Katiola, I.C..E3 103
Katire, Sud...E3 105
Katmai, mtn., Alsk..D9 167
Katmai, nat. mon., Alsk..D9 167
Katmai, vol., Alsk..D9 167
Katmandu, Nep..D10 88
Katni, India..F8 88
Katokhí, Grc..C3 69
Katombe, Zaire..C3 106
Katonah, N.Y..A5 194
Katoomba, Austl..F8 112
Katoúna, Grc...C3 69
Katowice (Stalinogród),
Pol..C5, g10 70
Katrinah, mtn., Eg...D6 101
Katrine, lake, Scot..D4 57
Katrineholm, Swe...H7, u34 63
Katsina, Nig...D6 103
Katsina Ala, riv., Nig...E6 103
Katsuyama, Jap...m15 93
Kattegat, chan., Eur..I4 63
Katwijk aan Zee, Neth..B4 59
Katy, Tex...F4 206
Kau, desert, Haw..D6 176
Kauai, co., Haw..B2 176
Kauai, chan., Haw...B3 176
Kauai, isl., Haw...A2 176
Kaufbeuren, Ger...E5 60
Kaufman, Tex..C4 206
Kaufman, co., Tex..C4 206
Kauhajoki, Fin...F10 63
Kauhava, Fin...F10 63
Kaukau Veld, plain, Bots.,
S.W. Afr...B3 107
Kaukauna, Wis...A5, D5 212
Kaulakahi, chan., Haw...A2 176
Kauliranta, Fin..D10 63
Kaumakani, Haw..B2 176
Kaumalapau, Haw...C5 176
Kauna, pt., Haw...D6 176
Kaunakakai, Haw..B4 176
Kaunas, Sov. Un...A7 70, D4 72
Kaupo, Haw..C5 176
Kaura Namoda, Nig...D6 103
Kaut, New Ire. I... 115
Kautokeino, Nor...C10 63
Kavacha, Sov. Un...C19 71
Kavajë, Alb...B2 69
Kavali, India..F6 87
Kavála, Grc...B5 69
Kavála, gulf, Grc...B5 69
Kavar, Iran...G6 86
Kavarna, Bul...D9 68
Kavieng, New Ire. I.. 115
Kävlinge, Swe...C7 62
Kawachi, Jap..*I7 93
Kawada, Okinawa... 114
Kawagama, lake, Ont.,
Can..B6 153
Kawagoe, Jap..n18 93
Kawaguchi, Jap..n18 93
Kawaihae, Haw...C6 176
Kawaihae, bay, Haw...C6 176
Kawaihoa, pt., Haw...B1 176
Kawaikini, peak, Haw..A2 176
Kawailoa, Haw...f9 176
Kawailoa Beach, Haw..f9 176
Kawambwa, Zambia..C4 106
Kawanishi, Jap..*I6 93
Kawardha, India...F8 88
Kawasaki, Jap..I9, n18 93
Kawbar, Jordan...h11 84
Kawela, Haw..B5 176
Kawhia, hbr., N.Z...M15 112
Kawich, range, Nev..F5 192
Kawinaw, lake, Man., Can..C2 150
Kawkareik, Bur..D3 89
Kawkawlin, Mich..E7 186
Kawm Hamādah, Eg..D2 84
Kawm Umbū, Eg..E6 101
Kawnipi, lake, Ont., Can...B7 187
Kay, co., Okla..A4 200
Kaya, Upper Volta...D4 103
Kayangel, is., Palau Is... 114
Kaycee, Wyo...B6 213
Kayenta, Ariz..A5 168
Kayes, Con..F2 104
Kayes, Mali...D2 103
Kayford, W. Va..C3, D6 211
Kayjay, Ky...D6 182
Kaylor, S. Dak..D8 204
Kayseri, Tur..C10 85
Kaysville, Utah...B4 207
Kayville, Sask., Can..H3 155
Kazachye, Sov. Un..B16 71
Kazakevichevo, Sov. Un...B7 93
Kazakh S.S.R., rep.,
Sov. Un..E9 71
Kazakh, hills, Sov. Un..D7 73
Kazan', Sov. Un..B3 73
Kazan, riv., N.W. Ter.,
Can..D12 142
Kazanlŭk, Bul..D7 68
Kazbek, mtn., Sov. Un...E2 73
Kāzerūn, Iran...G5 86
Kazhim, Sov. Un...A4 73
Kazi-Magomed, Sov. Un..E3 73
Kâzim Pasa (Saray),
Tur...C15 85
Kazimierz, Pol...C6 70
Kazincbarcika, Hung...A5 68
Kazumba, Zaire..C3 106
Kdyně, Czech...D8 61
Ké-Macina, Mali..D3 103
Kéa, Grc...D5 69
Kéa, isl., Grc..D5 69
Keaau, Haw..D6 176
Keahole, pt., Haw..D5 176
Kealaikahiki, chan., Haw..C5 176
Kealakekua, Haw...D6 176
Kealakekua, bay, Haw...D6 176
Kealia, Haw...D6 176
Kealia, Haw...A2 176
Keams Canyon, Ariz..B5 168
Keanae, Haw..C5 176
Keansburg, N.J...C4 194
Keaoi, isl., Haw...D6 176
Kearney, Ont., Can...B5 153
Kearney, Mo...B3, D2 189
Kearney, Nebr...D6 191
Kearney, Wyo...A6 213
Kearney, co., Nebr...D7 191
Kearneysville, W. Va..B7 211
Kearns, Utah...C3 207
Kearny, Ariz..D5 168
Kearny, N.J..B4 194
Kearny, co., Kans...D2 181
Kearsarge, Mich...A2 186
Kearsarge, N.H..B4 193
Kearsarge, mtn., N.H...D3 193
Keatchie, La...B2 183
Keating, Oreg..C9 201
Keatley, Sask., Can..E2 155
Keats, Kans...C7 181
Keauhou, Haw...D6 176
Keawakapu, Haw...C5 176
Keawekaheka, pt., Haw..D6 176
Kebbi, Nig..D5 103
Kebili, Tun...H11 64
Kebnekaise, mtn., Swe..D8 63
Kebock, head, Scot...B2 57
Kechi, Kans..B5, E6 181
Kecskemét, Hung...B4 68
Kedah, pol. div., Mala...J4 89
Kedainiai, Sov. Un..A8 70
Keddie, Calif...B3 170
Kedges, straits, Md...D5 173
Kedgwick, N.B., Can..B2 151
Kedgwick, riv., N.B., Can..B2 151
Kediri, Indon..*G4 90
Kedleston, Sask., Can...G3 155
Kédougou, Sen...D2 103
Kedron, Ark...C3 169
Keedysville, Md...B2 173
Keefers, B.C., Can..D7 149
Keefeton, Okla...B6 200
Keegan, Maine..A5 184
Keego Harbor, Mich...A7 186
Keei, Haw...D6 176
Keele, peak, N.W. Ter., Can..D6 142
Keeler, Sask., Can...G3 155
Keeler, Calif..D5 170
Keeline, Wyo..C8 213
Keeling, Tenn...B2 205
Keeling, Va...E3 209
Keels, Newf., Can..D5 152
Keelung, see Chilung, Taiwan
Keene, Calif..E4 170
Keene, Ont., Can...C6 153
Keene, Ky..C5 182
Keene, Nebr..D6 191
Keene, N.H...E2 193
Keene, N.Y..A7, B3 196
Keene, N. Dak...B3 198
Keene, Ohio..B6 199
Keene, Tex..B5 206
Keeneland, Ky...*B4 182
Keene Valley, N.Y..A7, B3 196
Keenesburg, Colo..A6 171
Keeney Knob, mtn., W. Va...D4 211
Keensburg, Ill...E6 178
Keeseville, N.Y...B3 196
Keetmanshoop, S.W. Afr...C2 107
Keewatin, Ont., Can...E4 150
Keewatin, Minn..C5 187
Keewatin, dist., N.W. Ter.,
Can...D14 144
in 1867.. 147
Keewatin, riv., Man., Can..A1 150
Keezletown, Va...C4 209
Kefallinía (Cephalonia),
isl., Grc..C3 69

INDEX KEY Each place listed in **Bold-faced Type** has its population listed in the Population tables, pages 230 to 280.
Each country, shown in CAPITAL LETTERS, has its population listed in the World Political Information Tables, pages 6 to 10.
* Does not appear on map; key shows general location.

Keflavík, Ice...o21 63
Kegaska, Que., Can...h9 152
Kegonsa, lake, Wis...F4 212
Kegueur Terbi, mtn., Chad...A3 104
Keheili, Sud...B3 105
Kehl, Ger...E2 61
Kehsi Mansam, Bur...B2 89
Keighley, Eng...D6 55
Keilberg, mtn., Czech...C8 61
Keimoes, S. Afr...C3 107
Keiser, Ark...B5 169
Keitele, lake, Fin...F11 63
Keith, Austl...H3 112
Keith, Scot...C6 57
Keith, co., Nebr...C4 191
Keithley Creek, B.C., Can...C7 149
Keithsburg, Ill...B3 178
Keitum, Ger...D2 62
Keizer, Oregon...*C4 201
Kejimkujik, lake, N.S., Can...E4 151
Kejimkujik, nat. park, N.S., Can...E4 151
Kekaha, Haw...B2 176
Kekoskee, Wis...*E5 212
Kelantan, pol. div., Mala...J4 89
Kelantan, riv., Mala...J5 89
Keldron, S. Dak...B4 204
Kelfield, Sask., Can...F1 155
Kelford, N.C...A6 197
Kelheim, Ger...E6 61
Kelibia, Tun...F12 64
Kelif, Sov. Un...C13 86
Kelkit, riv., Tur...B11 85
Kell, Ill...E5 178
Kellé, Con...F2 104
Kellenhusen, Ger...D5 62
Keller, Tex...B5 206
Keller, Va...D7 209
Keller, Wash...A7 210
Keller, lake, Sask., Can...A2 155
Kellerman, Ala...B2 166
Kellerton, Iowa...D3 180
Kellerville, Ill...D3 178
Kellet, cape, N.W. Ter., Can...B7 142
Kellettville, Pa...C3 202
Kelley, Iowa...C4 180
Kelleys, isl., Ohio...A5 199
Kelleys Island, Ohio...A5 199
Kelliher, Sask., Can...F4 155
Kelliher, Minn...C4 187
Kellmünz, Ger...A6 66
Kellnersville, Wis...A6, D6 212
Kelloe, Man., Can...D1 150
Kellogg, Idaho...B2 177
Kellogg, Iowa...C5 180
Kellogg, Minn...F6 187
Kells, range, Scot...E4 57
Kelly, Ky...D2 182
Kelly, La...C3 183
Kelly, N. Mex...C2 195
Kelly, Wyo...B2 213
Kelly Brook, mtn., Maine...A3 184
Kelly Lake, Minn...C5 187
Kellyton, Ala...C3 166
Kellytown, Ga...C2 175
Kellyville, N.H...D2 193
Kellyville, Okla...B5 200
Kellyville, Tex...C5 206
Kelmė, Sov. Un...A7 70
Kélo, Chad...D3 104
Kelowna, B.C., Can...E8 149
Kelsey, Alta., Can...C4 148
Kelsey, lake, Man., Can...D5 155
Kelsey Bay, B.C., Can...D4 149
Kelso, Calif...E6 170
Kelso, Mo...D8 189
Kelso, N. Dak...B8 198
Kelso, Scot...E6 57
Kelso, Wash...C3 210
Kelso Station, Sask., Can...H5 155
Keltie, cape, Ant...C26 120
Keltonburg, Tenn...D8 205
Keltys, Tex...*D5 206
Keluang Mala...K5 89
Kelvington, Sask., Can...E4 155
Kelwood, Man., Can...D2 150
Kem, Sov. Un...E16 63
Kem, riv., Sov. Un...E15 63
Kembé, Cen. Afr. Rep...E4 104
Kemerovo, Sov. Un...B11 73
Kemi, Fin...E11 63
Kemijärvi, Fin...D12 63
Kemijärvi, lake, Fin...D12 63
Kemme, Libya...E3 101
Kemmerer, Wyo...D2 213
Kemnath, Ger...D6 61
Kemnay, Man., Can...E1 150
Kemp, Okla...D5 200
Kemp, Tex...C4 206
Kemp, coast, Ant...C18 120
Kemp, lake, Tex...C3 206
Kemp City, Okla...*D5 200
Kempen, Ger...C6 59
Kemper, S.C...C9 203
Kemper, co., Miss...C5 188
Kempner, Tex...D3 206
Kempsey, Austl...E9 112
Kempshall, mtn., N.Y...A6 196
Kempten, Ger...E5 60
Kempton, Ill...C5 178
Kempton, Ind...D5 179
Kempton, N. Dak...B8 198
Kemptville, Ont., Can...B9 153
Kenadsa, Alg...C4 102
Kenai, Alsk...C9, g16 167
Kenai, mts., Alsk...h16 167
Kenai, pen., Alsk...h16 167
Kenamu, riv., Newf., Can...B1 152
Kenansville, Fla...E6 174
Kenansville, N.C...C6 197
Kenaston, Sask., Can...F2 155
Kenaston, N. Dak...A3 198
Kenbridge, Va...E4 209
Kendal, Eng...C5 55
Kendal, Sask., Can...G4 155
Kendall, Fla...F3 174
Kendall, Kans...E2 181
Kendall, N.Y...B2 196
Kendall, Wis...E3 212
Kendall, co., Ill...B5 178
Kendall, co., Tex...E3 206
Kendall Park, N.J...C3 194
Kendallville, Ind...B7 179
Kendari, Indon...F6 90
Kendrapara, India...G11 88
Kendrick, Fla...C4 174
Kendrick, Idaho...C2 177
Kendrick, Okla...B5 200
Kenduskeag, Maine...D4 184
Kenedy, Tex...E4 206
Kenedy, co., Tex...F4 206
Kenefic, Okla...C5 200
Kenel, S. Dak...B5 204
Kenema, S.L...E2 103
Kenesaw, Nebr...D7 191
Keng Kabao, Laos...D6 89
Keng Tung, Bur...C10 87
Kenge, Zaire...B2 106
Kenhardt, S. Afr...C3 107
Kenhorst, Pa...*F10 202
Kéniéba, Mali...D2 103
Kenilworth, Eng...B6 56
Kenilworth, Ill...E3 178
Kenilworth, N.J...*B4 194
Kenilworth, Utah...D5 207
Kenimekh, Sov. Un...A12 86
Kenitra, Mor...C3 102
Kenly, N.C...B5 197
Kenmare, Ire...E2 55
Kenmare, N. Dak...A3 198
Kenmare, riv., Ire...E1 55
Kenmore, N.Y...C2 196
Kenna, N. Mex...D6 195
Kenna, W. Va...C3 211
Kenneday, peak, Wyo...D6 213
Kennan, Wis...C3 212
Kennard, Ind...E6 179
Kennard, Nebr...C9, D2 191
Kennard, Tex...D5 206
Kennebago, lake, Maine...C2 184
Kennebec, S. Dak...D6 204
Kennebec, co., Maine...D3 184
Kennebec, riv., Maine...D3 184
Kennebunk, Maine...E2 184
Kennebunkport, Maine...E2 184
Kennedale, Tex...B5 206
Kennedy, Ala...B2 166
Kennedy, Sask., Can...G4 155
Kennedy, Minn...B2 187
Kennedy, Nebr...B5 191
Kennedy, N.Y...C1 196
Kennedy, cape, Fla...D6 174
Kennedy, lake, Sask., Can...D4 155
Kennedy, mtn., B.C., Can...C12 167
Kennedy, mtn., Yukon, Can...D5 142
Kennedyville, Md...B6 173
Kenner, La...C7, E5 183
Kennesaw, Ga...A4, B2 175
Kennet, riv., Eng...C6 56
Kennetcook, N.S., Can...D6 151
Kenneth, Minn...G2 187
Kenneth City, Fla...*E4 174
Kennett, Mo...E7 189
Kennett Square, Pa...G10 202
Kennewick, Wash...C6 210
Kenney, Ill...C4 178
Kenney, dam, B.C., Can...C5 149
Kennington Cove, N.S., Can...D10 151
Kennisis, lake, Ont., Can...B6 153
Kennydale, Wash...D2 210
Keno, Oreg...E5 201
Kénogami, Que., Can...A6 154
Kenogami, lake, Que., Can...A6 154
Kenora, Ont., Can...E7 153
Kenora, co., Ont., Can...E7 153
Kenosha, Wis...F2, F6 212
Kenosha, co., Wis...F5 212
Kenova, W. Va...C2 211
Kensal, N. Dak...B7 198
Kensett, Ark...B4 169
Kensett, Iowa...A4 180
Kensico, res., N.Y...D2 196
Kensington, P.E.I., Can...C6 151
Kensington, Conn...C5 172
Kensington, Kans...C4 181
Kensington, Md...*B3 173
Kensington, Minn...E3 187
Kensington, N.H...E5 193
Kensington, N.Y...*F2 172
Kensington, Ohio...B7 199
Kensington & Chelsea, Eng...m12 55
Kensington Park, Fla...*E4 174
Kent, Ala...C4 166
Kent, Conn...C3 172
Kent, Ind...G6 179
Kent, Iowa...D3 180
Kent, Minn...D2 187
Kent, Ohio...A4 199
Kent, Oreg...B6 201
Kent, Tex...F2 206
Kent, Wash...B3, D2 210
Kent, co., N.B., Can...C4 151
Kent, co., Ont., Can...E2 153
Kent, co., Eng...C8 56
Kent, co., Del...B6 173
Kent, co., Md...B5 173
Kent, co., Mich...E5 186
Kent, co., R.I...C10 172
Kent, co., Tex...C2 206
Kent, isl., Del...B7 173
Kent, isl., Md...C5 173
Kent, pt., Md...C5 173
Kent, riv., Eng...F6 57
Kent Bridge, Ont., Can...E2 153
Kent City, Mich...E5 186
Kent Junction, N.B., Can...C4 151
Kentau, Sov. Un...E7 73
Kentland, Ind...C3 179
Kenton, Man., Can...E1 150
Kenton, Del...B6 173
Kenton, Mich...B2 186
Kenton, Ky...A7 182
Kenton, Ohio...B4 199
Kenton, Okla...D1 200
Kenton, Tenn...A2 205
Kenton, co., Ky...B5 182
Kents Store, Va...D4 209
Kentucky, state, U.S...182
in 1778-92...162
during Civil War...164
Kentucky, dam, Ky...A3 182
Kentucky, lake, Ky., Tenn...D1 182
Kentucky, ridge, Ky...D6 182
Kentucky, riv., Ky...B5 182
Kentville, N.S., Can...D5 151
Kentwood, La...D5 183
Kenvil, N.J...B3 194
Kenville, Man., Can...D1 150
Kenvir, Ky...D6 182
Kenwood, Okla...A7 200
KENYA, country, Afr...A6 106
Kenya, mtn., Ken...B6 106
Kenyon, Minn...F6 187
Kenyon, R.I...D10 172
Keo, Ark...C4, E6 169
Keokea, Haw...C5 176
Keokuk, Iowa...D6 180
Keokuk, co., Iowa...C5 180
Keokuk, lock and dam, Iowa...D6 180
Keoma, Alta., Can...D4 148
Keonjhargarh, India...G10 88
Keosauqua, Iowa...D6 180
Keota, Colo...A6 171
Keota, Iowa...C6 180
Keota, Okla...B7 200
Kep, Camb...G6 89
Kępno, Pol...C5 70
Keppel, Sask., Can...E2 155
Kepsut, Tur...C7 69
Kerala, state, India...F6 87
Kerang, Austl...G4 112
Keratsinion, Grc...h11 69
Kerby, Oreg...E3 201
Kerch', Sov. Un...I11 72
Kerch, strait, Sov. Un...I11 72
Kerema, Pap...k12 111
Keremeos, B.C., Can...E8 149
Kerempe, cape, Tur...A9 85
Kerens, Tex...C4 206
Kerhonkson, N.Y...D6 196
Kericho, Ken...B6 106
Kerintji, mtn., Indon...F2 90
Kerkennah, is., Tun...C7 102
Kerkhoven, Minn...E3 187
Kérkira, Grc...C2 69
Kérkira (Corfu), isl., Grc...C2 69
Kerkrade, Neth...D6 59
Kermadec, is., Pac. O...I11 113
Kerman, Calif...*D4 170
Kermān, Iran...F8 86
Kermanshah, Iran...D3 86
Kermit, N. Dak...A2 198
Kermit, Tex...D1 206
Kermit, W. Va...D2 211
Kermode, mtn., B.C., Can...C2 149
Kern, co., Calif...E4 170
Kern, riv., Calif...E4 170
Kernersville, N.C...A3 197
Kernville, Calif...E4 170
Kernville, Oreg...C3 201
Kerpen, Ger...C1 61
Kerr, co., Tex...D3 206
Kerr, lake, Fla...C5 174
Kerrera, isl., Scot...D3 57
Kerrick, Minn...D6 187
Kerrick, Tex...A1 206
Kerrobert, Sask., Can...F1 155
Kerrville, Tex...D3 206
Kersey, Colo...A6 171
Kersey, Pa...D4 202
Kershaw, Mont...C6 190
Kershaw, S.C...B6 203
Kershaw, co., S.C...C6 203
Kersley, B.C., Can...C6 149
Kerteminde, Den...C4 62
Kerulen, riv., Mong...B7 91
Kerza, Alg...D4 102
Keşan, Tur...B6 69
Kesarya (Sdot Yam), Isr...B6 84
Kesennuma, Jap...G10 93
Keshena, Wis...D5 212
Kesley, Iowa...B5 180
Kestenga, Sov. Un...E14 63
Keswick, Ont., Can...C5 153
Keswick, Eng...F5 57
Keswick, Iowa...C5 180
Keswick, Va...C4 209
Keszthely, Hung...B3 68
Ket, riv., Sov. Un...B10 73
Keta, Ghana...E5 103
Ketapang, Indon...F3 90
Ketchikan, Alsk...D13, n24 167
Ketchum, Idaho...F4 177
Ketchum, Okla...A6 200
Ketona, Ala...E5 166
Ketrzyn Mazowiecki, Pol...A6 70
Kettering, Eng...B7 56
Kettering, Ohio...C3 199
Kettle, creek, Pa...C6 202
Kettle, riv., B.C., Can., Wash...E8 149
Kettle, riv., Minn...D6 187
Kettle Falls, Wash...A7 210
Kettle Falls, nat. park, Wash...A8 210
Kettle River, Minn...D6 187
Kettle River, range, Wash...A7 210
Kettleman City, Calif...E4 170
Kettlersville, Ohio...*B3 199
Kettlewell, Eng...F6 57
Kettwig, Ger...B1 61
Kęty, Pol...D5, h10 70
Ketzin, Ger...A7 61
Keuka, lake, N.Y...C3 196
Keuterville, Idaho...C2 177
Kevil, Ky...A2 182
Kevin, Mont...B5 190
Kewanee, Ill...B4 178
Kewanee, Miss...C5 188
Kewanee, Mo...E8 189
Kewanna, Ind...B5 179
Kewaskum, Wis...E5 212
Kewaunee, Wis...D6 212
Kewaunee, co., Wis...D6 212
Keweenaw, co., Mich...A2 186
Keweenaw, bay, Mich...B2 186
Keweenaw, pt., Mich...A3 186
Keweenaw Bay, Mich...B2 186
Key Junction, Ont., Can...B4 153
Key Largo, Fla...G6 174
Key West, Fla...H5 174
Key West, Iowa...B7 180
Keya Paha, co., Nebr...B6 191
Keya Paha, riv., Nebr., S. Dak...D6 204
Keyapaha, S. Dak...D5 204
Keyes, Calif...*D4 170
Keyes, Man., Can...D2 150
Keyes, Okla...D2 200
Keyesport, Ill...E4 178
Keyhole, res., Wyo...A8 213
Keymar, Md...A3 173
Keynsham, Eng...C5 56
Keyport, N.J...C4 194
Keysburgh, Ky...D2 182
Keyser, W. Va...B6 211
Keystone, Ind...C7 179
Keystone, Iowa...C5 180
Keystone, Nebr...C4 191
Keystone, Okla...*A5 200
Keystone, S. Dak...D2 204
Keystone, W. Va...D3 211
Keystone, peak, Ariz...F4 168
Keystone, res., Okla...A5 200
Keystone Heights, Fla...C4 174
Keysville, Fla...E4 174
Keysville, Ga...C4 175
Keysville, Va...D4 209
Keytesville, Mo...B5 189
Kezar, lake, Maine...D2 184
Kezar, pond, Maine...D2 184
Kezar Falls, Maine...E2 184
Kezhma, Sov. Un...D13 71
Kežmarok, Czech...D6 70
Kfar Ata, Isr...B7 84
Kfar Blum, Isr...A7 84
Kfar Monash, Isr...f10 84
Kfar Sava, Isr...B6, g10 84
Kfar Vitkin, Isr...B6 84
Kfar Yona, Isr...f10 84
Khabab, Syr...A8 84
Khabarovsk, Sov. Un...E16 71, B7 93
Khabīs, see Shahdād, Iran
Khachmas, Sov. Un...E3 73
Khadar Khel, Afg...E14 86
Khairpur, Pak...D2 88
Khalafābād, Iran...F4 86
Khalij Surt, see Sidra, gulf, Libya
Khalkí (Chalke), isl., Grc...D6 69
Khalkidhikí, pen., Grc...B4 69
Khalkís, Grc...C4, g11 69
Khambhaliya, India...D4 87
Khamgaon, India...G6 88
Khan, The Great, empire of...81
Khān az Zabīb, Jordan...C8 84
Khān Yūnis, Gaza Strip...C6 84
Khanabad, Afg...C14 86
Khanaqin, Iraq...D2 86
Khanderi, is., India...H4 88
Khandwa, India...G6 88
Khānewāl, Pak...B3 88
Khanh An, Viet...H6 89
Khanh Hung, Viet...H6 89
Khaniá, Grc...E4 69
Khaniá, gulf, Grc...E4 69
Khanka, lake, China, Sov. Un...D6 93
Khanpur, Pak...C5 87
Khanty-Mansiysk, Sov. Un...A7 73
Kharagpur, India...D8 87, F11 88
Kharan Kalat, Pak...G12 86
Kharānaq, Iran...E7 86
Kharg, isl., Iran...G5 86
Khargon, India...G5 88
Khariar, India...G9 88
Khārijah, oasis, Eg...D6 101
Kharkov, Sov. Un...G11 72
Kharmanli, Bul...E7 68
Kharovsk, Sov. Un...B13 72
Kharr, wadi, Sau. Ar...G14 85
Khartoum, Sud...B3 105
Khartoum, reg., Sud...B3 105
Khartoum North, Sud...B3 105
Khartsyzsk, Sov. Un...q21 72
Khasavyurt, Sov. Un...E3 73
Khash, Afg...F11 86
Khāsh, Iran...G10 86
Khashuri, Sov. Un...A14 85
Khasi, hills, India...C9 87
Khaskovo Bul...E7 68
Khatanga, Sov. Un...B13 71
Khatanga, riv., Sov. Un...B13 71
Khemmarat, Thai...D6 89
Khenchela, Alg...B6 102
Khenifra, Mor...C3 102
Kherson, Sov. Un...H9 72
Kheta, riv., Sov. Un...B12 71
Khilchipur, India...E6 88
Khilok, Sov. Un...D14 71
Khimki, Sov. Un...n17 72
Khíos, Grc...C6 69
Khíos (Chios), isl., Grc...C5 69
Khisfin, Syr...B7 84
Khiva, Sov. Un...E9 73
Khlebarovo, Bul...D8 68
Khmelnik, Sov. Un...G6 72
Khmel'nitskiy, Sov. Un...G6 72
Khmer empire (Kambujadesa)...81
Khochniyé, Syr...A7 84
Khodzheyli, Sov. Un...E5 73
Khokhropar, Pak...E3 88
Kholm, Sov. Un...C8 72
Kholmsk, Sov. Un...E17 71
Khon Kaen, Thai...D5 89
Khonak, Afg...D13 86
Khong, Laos...E6 89
Khong, riv., Laos...E7 89
Khong Sedone, Laos...E6 89
Khoper, riv., Sov. Un...C2 73
Khor, riv., Sov. Un...C7 93
Khor Anghar, Afars & Is...C5 105
Khora Sfakíon, Grc...E5 69
Khorinsk, Sov. Un...A6 91
Khorog, Sov. Un...F10 71
Khorol, Sov. Un...G9 72
Khorramābād, Iran...E4 86
Khorramshahr, Iran...F4 86
Khotan (Hotien), China...A6 87
Khotan, riv., China...A7 87
Khotin, Sov. Un...G6 72
Khrisoúpolis, Grc...B5 69
Khrom-Tau, Sov. Un...C5 73
Khu Khan, Thai...E6 89
Khulna, Bngl...D8 87
Khunzakh, Sov. Un...A16 85
Khurda, India...G10 88
Khurja, India...C6 88
Khushab, Pak...A4 88
Khust, Sov. Un...G4 72
Khuzdar, Pak...C4 87
Khvāf, Iran...D10 86
Khvor, Iran...E7 86
Khvormūj, Iran...G5 86
Khvoy, Iran...B2 86
Khyber, pass, Afg., Pak...B5 87
Kia, Santa Isabel I...115
Kia, isl., Fiji...114
Kialing, riv., China...E6 91
Kiamichi, mtn., Okla...C6 200
Kiamichi, riv., Okla...C6 200
Kiamika, Que., Can...C2 154
Kiamika, riv., Que., Can...C2 154
Kiana, Alsk...B7 167
Kiangsi, prov., China...F7 91
Kiangsu, prov., China...E9 91
Kiani, lake, P.R...g12 132
Kiantajärvi, lake, Fin...E13 63
Kiaohsien, China...F9 92
Kiask, lake, Man., Can...A3 150
Kiawah, isl., S.C...F7 203
Kibangou, Con...F2 104
Kibau, Tan...C6 106
Kiberege, Tan...C6 106
Kiblah, Ark...D2 169
Kibombo, Zaire...B4 106
Kibondo, Tan...B5 106
Kibwezi, Ken...B6 106
Kičevo, Yugo...E5 68
Kickapoo, Kans...A8 181
Kickapoo, Tex...D5 206
Kickapoo, creek, Ill...C4 178
Kickapoo, riv., Wis...E3 212
Kickapoo Settlements, Indian res., Kans...B2 189
Kicking Horse, pass, Alta., B.C., Can...D2 148
Kidal, Mali...C5 103
Kidapawan, Phil...*D7 90
Kidder, Mo...B3 189
Kidder, S. Dak...B8 204
Kidder, co., N. Dak...C6 198
Kidderminster, Eng...B5 56
Kidira, Sen...D2 103
Kidnappers, cape, N.Z...M16 112
Kidron, val., Jordan...m14 84
Kidsgrove, Eng...A5 56
Kidugalo, Tan...C6 106
Kidwelly, Wales...C3 56
Kief, N. Dak...B5 198
Kiefer, Okla...B5 200
Kiel, Ger...A5 60, D4 62
Kiel, Wis...B5, E5 212
Kiel, bay, Ger...A5 60
Kiel, canal, Ger...B4 60
Kielce, Pol...C6 70
Kiester, Minn...G5 187
Kieta, Bougainville I...115
Kiev, Sov. Un...F8 72
Kifisiá, Grc...g11 69
Kifissós, riv., Grc...g11 69
Kifissós (Cephisus), riv., Grc...g9 69
Kifri, Iraq...D2 86
Kifta, Maur...C2 103
Kigali, Rwanda...B5 106
Kiği, Tur...C13 85
Kiglapait, mtn., Newf., Can...g9 152
Kigoma, Tan...B4 106
Kihei, Haw...C5 176
Kiholo, bay, Haw...D6 176
Kii, strait, Jap...J7 93
Kikinda, Yugo...C5 68
Kikongo, Zaire...B2 106
Kikori, Pap...k11 111
Kikwit, Zaire...C2 106
Kila, Mont...B2 190
Kilauea, Haw...A2 176
Kilauea, crater, Haw...D6 176
Kilbourne, Ill...C3 178
Kilbourne, La...B4 183
Kilbourne, Ohio...B5 199
Kilbrannan, sound, Scot...E3 57
Kilburn, N.B., Can...C2 151
Kilchoan, Scot...D2 57
Kilchrenan, Scot...D3 57
Kilchu, Kor...F4 93
Kildare, Que., Can...C4 154
Kildare, Ire...D3 55
Kildare, Okla...A4 200
Kildare, cape, P.E.I., Can...C6 151
Kildeer, Ill...*A5 178
Kilembe, Zaire...C2 106
Kilgore, Idaho...E7 177
Kilgore, Nebr...B5 191
Kilgore, Tex...C5 206
Kilgore East, Tex...*C5 206
Kili, isl., Marshall Is...115
Kilifi, Ken...B6 106
Kilimanjaro, mtn., Tan...B6 106
Kilinailau, isl., Sol. Is...115
Kilis, Tur...D11 85
Kiliya, Sov. Un...I7 72
Kilkee, Ire...D2 55
Kilkenny, Ire...D3 55
Kilkenny, Minn...F5 187
Kilkís, Grc...B4 69
Kill Devil Hills, N.C...*A6 197
Kill Van Kull, chan., N.Y...E5 194
Killala, Ire...C2 55
Killaloe Station, Ont., Can...B7 153
Killaly, Sask., Can...G4 155
Killam, Alta., Can...C5 148
Killarney, Man., Can...E2 150
Killarney, Ire...D2 55
Killarney, W. Va...D3 211
Killarney, prov. park, Ont., Can...A3 153
Killbuck, Ohio...B6 199
Killdeer, Sask., Can...H2 155
Killdeer, N. Dak...B3 198
Killdeer, mts., N. Dak...B3 198
Killduff, Iowa...C5 180
Killeen, Tex...D4 206
Killen, Ala...A2 166
Killian, La...B6 183
Killian, S.C...C6 203
Killiecrankie, pass, Scot...D4 57
Killin, Scot...D4 57
Killinek, isl., Newf., Can...F8 152
Killington, peak, Vt...D3 208
Killingworth, Conn...D6 172
Killíni, Grc...D3 69
Killmalie, Scot...D3 57
Kilmanagh, Mich...E7 186
Kilmarnock, Scot...E4 57
Kilmarnock, Va...D6 209
Kilmatinde, Tan...C5 106
Kilmelfort, Scot...D3 57
Kilmichael, Miss...B4 188
Kilmonivaig, Scot...D4 57
Kiln, Miss...E4 188
Kilosa, Tan...C6 106
Kilrush, Ire...D2 55
Kilsyth, Scot...E4 57
Kilwa, Zaire...C4 106
Kilwa [Kivinje], Tan...C6 106
Kilworthy, Ont., Can...C5 153
Kim, Colo...D7 171
Kimamba, Tan...C6 106
Kimball, Minn...E4 187
Kimball, Nebr...C2 191
Kimball, S. Dak...D7 204
Kimball, W. Va...*D3 211
Kimball, co., Nebr...C2 191
Kimball, mtn., Alsk...C11 167
Kimballton, Iowa...C2 180
Kimbe, bay, Bis. Arch...115
Kimberley, B.C., Can...E9 149
Kimberley, S. Afr...C3 107
Kimberlin Heights, Tenn...E12 205
Kimberly, Ala...B3 166
Kimberly, Idaho...G4 177
Kimberly, Minn...D5 187
Kimberly, Oreg...C7 201
Kimberly, W. Va...D6 211
Kimberly, Wis...A5 212
Kimble, co., Tex...D3 206
Kimbles, Pa...D11 202
Kimbolton, Ohio...B6 199
Kimbrough, Ala...C2 166
Kimchaek (Sŏngjin), Kor...F4 93
Kimch'on, Kor...*H4 93
Kími, Grc...C5 69
Kimiwan, lake, Alta., Can...B2 148
Kimmell, Ind...B6 179
Kimmins, Tenn...B4 205
Kimmswick, Mo...B8 189
Kimowin, riv., Sask., Can...A6 148
Kimry, Sov. Un...C11 72
Kin, Okinawa...114
Kinabalu, mtn., Mala...D5 90
Kinadodo, New Ire. I...115
Kinard, Fla...B1 174
Kinards, S.C...C4 203
Kinbasket, lake, B.C., Can...D8 149
Kinbrace, Scot...B5 57
Kinbrae, Minn...G3 187
Kinburn, Ont., Can...B8 153
Kincaid, Sask., Can...H2 155
Kincaid, Ill...D4 178
Kincaid, Kans...D8 181
Kincaid Knob, mtn., W. Va...A7 211
Kincardine, Ont., Can...C3 153
Kincardine, co., Scot...D6 57
Kinchafonee, riv., Ga...E2 175
Kinde, Mich...E8 186
Kinder, La...D3 183
Kinderhook, Ill...D2 178
Kinderhook, N.Y...C7 196
Kindersley, Sask., Can...F1 155
Kindia, Guinea...D2 103
Kindred, N. Dak...C8 198
Kindu [-Port Empain], Con. K...B4 106
Kineo, mtn., Maine...C3 184
Kineshma, Sov. Un...B2 73
King, Ont., Can...E6 153
King, N.C...A3 197
King, Wis...D4 212
King, co., Tex...C2 206
King, co., Wash...B4 210
King, isl., Austl...n14, G7 110
King, isl., Bur...F3 89

INDEX KEY Each place listed in **Bold-faced Type** has its population listed in the Population tables, pages 230 to 280. Each country, shown in CAPITAL LETTERS, has its population listed in the World Political Information Table, pages 6 to 10. * Does not appear on map; key shows general location.

King, isl., B.C., Can C4 149
King, mtn., Oreg D8, E3 201
King, sound, Austl C3 110
King and Queen C. H., Va D6 209
King and Queen, co., Va D6 209
King Christian IX Land, reg., Grnld C18 118
King Christian X Land, reg., Grnld B17 118
King City, Calif D3 170
King City, Mo A3 189
King Cove, Alsk E7 167
King Ferry, N.Y C4 196
King Frederik VI, coast, Grnld C19 118
King Frederik VIII Land, reg., Grnld B17 118
King George, Va C5 209
King George, co., Va C5 209
King George, isl., Ant C7 120
King George, mtn., B.C., Can D10 149
King George, sound, Austl F2 110
King George IV, lake, Newf., Can D3 152
King Hill, Idaho F3 177
King Lear, peak, Nev B3 192
King Leopold, range, Austl C4 110
King William, Va D5 209
King William, co., Va D5 209
King William, isl., N.W. Ter., Can C13 142
King William's Town, S. Afr D4 107
Kingaroy, Austl C8 112
Kingfield, Maine D2 184
Kingfisher, Okla B4 200
Kingfisher, co., Okla B4 200
Kingman, Ariz B1 168
Kingman, Alta., Can C4 148
Kingman, Ind E3 179
Kingman, Kans B3, E5 181
Kingman, Maine C4 184
Kingman, co., Kans E5 181
Kings, Ill A4 178
Kings, Miss C3 188
Kings, co., Calif D4 170
Kings, co., N.B., Can D4 151
Kings, co., N.S., Can E5 151
Kings, co., P.E.I., Can C7 151
Kings, co., (Brooklyn borough), N.Y E1 196
Kings, peak, Calif B1 170
Kings, peak, Utah C5 207
Kings, riv., Ark A2 169
Kings, riv., Calif D4 170
Kings, riv., Nev B3 192
Kings Canyon, Colo A4 171
Kings Canyon, nat. park, Calif D4 170
Kings Creek, S.C A5 203
Kings Gardens, Kans A4 181
King's Lynn, Eng B8 56
Kings Mill, Tex B2 206
Kings Mills, Ohio C2, C3 199
Kings Mountain, Ky C5 182
Kings Mountain, N.C B2 197
Kings Park, N.Y D3 196
Kings Point, Newf., Can D3 152
Kings Point, N.Y F1 172
Kings Valley, Oreg C3 201
Kingsbridge, Eng D4 56
Kingsburg, Calif D4 170
Kingsbury, Ind A4 179
Kingsbury, Maine *C3 184
Kingsbury, Tex B4 206
Kingsbury, co., S. Dak C8 204
Kingsclear, N.B., Can D3 151
Kingscote, Austl G6 111
Kingsdale, Minn D6 187
Kingsdown, Kans E4 181
Kingsey Falls, Que., Can D5 154
Kingsford, Mich C2 186
Kingsford Heights, Ind *B4 179
Kingsgate, B.C., Can E9 149
Kingshill, Vir. Is k17 132
Kingsland, Ark D3 169
Kingsland, Ga F5 175
Kingsland, Tex D3 206
Kingsley, Iowa B2 180
Kingsley, Ky *B4 182
Kingsley, Mich D5 186
Kingsley, dam, Nebr C4 191
Kingsmere, lake, Sask., Can C2 155
Kingsport, Tenn C11 205
Kingston, Ark A2 169
Kingston, Austl H2 112
Kingston, N.S., Can E5 151
Kingston, Ont., Can C8 153
Kingston, Ga B2 175
Kingston, Idaho B2 177
Kingston, Ill A5 178
Kingston, Jam G5 131
Kingston, Ky C5 182
Kingston, Md D6 173
Kingston, Mass C6 185
Kingston, Mich E7 186
Kingston, Minn E4 187
Kingston, Mo B3 189
Kingston, N.H E4 193
Kingston, N.J C3 194
Kingston, N. Mex E2 195
Kingston, N.Y D6 196
Kingston, Ohio C5 199
Kingston, Okla D5 200
Kingston, Pa B8, D10 202
Kingston, R.I D10 172
Kingston, Tenn D9 205
Kingston, Utah E3 207
Kingston, W. Va D3, D6 211
Kingston, Wis E4 212
Kingston Mines, Ill *C4 178
Kingston upon Thames, Eng m12 55
Kingston Springs, Tenn A4 205
Kingstown, St. Vincent p16 131
Kingstree, S.C D8 203
Kingsville, Ont., Can E2 153
Kingsville, Mo C3 189
Kingsville, Ohio A7 199
Kingsville, Tex F4 206
Kingswood, Ky C3 182
Kington, Eng B4 56
Kingurutik, lake, Newf., Can g9 152
Kingussie, Scot C4 57
Kingwa, Que., Can D17 145
Kingwood, W. Va B5 211
Kinistino, Sask., Can E3 155
Kinkala, Con. B F2 104
Kinkora, P.E.I., Can C6 151
Kinley, Sask., Can E2 155
Kinloch, Mo A8 189
Kinloch Hourn, Scot C3 57
Kinlochewe, Scot C3 57
Kinmount, Ont., Can C6 153
Kinmundy, Ill E5 178
Kinnaird, B.C., Can E9 149
Kinnairds, head, Scot C7 57
Kinnelon, N.J B4 194
Kinney, Minn *C6 187
Kinney, co., Tex E2 206
Kinomoto, Jap n15 93
Kinosaki, Jap I7 93
Kinpoku, peak, Jap G9 93
Kinrooi, Bel C5 59
Kinross, P.E.I., Can C7 151
Kinross, Iowa *C6 180
Kinross, Scot D5 57
Kinross, co., Scot D5 57
Kinsale, Ire E2 55
Kinsale, Va C6 209
Kinsella, Alta., Can C5 148
Kinsey, Ala D4 166
Kinsey, Mont D11 190
Kinshasa, Zaire B2 106
Kinsley, Kans E4 181
Kinsman, Ill *B5 178
Kinsman, Ohio A7 199
Kinston, Ala D3 166
Kinston, N.C B6 197
Kinta, Okla B6 200
Kintampo, Ghana E4 103
Kintinku, Tan C6 106
Kintore, Scot C6 57
Kintyre, N. Dak C6 198
Kinuso, Alta., Can B3 148
Kinyangiri, Tan B5 106
Kinyeti, mtn., Sud E3 105
Kinzig, riv., Ger C4 61
Kinzig, riv., Ger E2 61
Kinzua, Oreg C6 201
Kioa, isl., Fiji 114
Kiona, Wash C6 210
Kiowa, Colo B6 171
Kiowa, Kans E5 181
Kiowa, Okla C6 200
Kiowa, co., Colo C8 171
Kiowa, co., Kans E4 181
Kiowa, co., Okla C2 200
Kiowa, creek, Colo B6 171
Kiowa, creek, Okla A1 200
Kipahigan, lake, Man., Sask., Can B1 150
Kipahulu, Haw C5 176
Kiparissia, Grc D3 69
Kiparissia, gulf, Grc D3 69
Kipili, Tan C5 106
Kipini, Ken B7 106
Kipling, Mich C3 186
Kipling, Sask., Can G4 155
Kipnuk, Alsk C7 167
Kipp, Kans D6 181
Kipton, Ohio A5 199
Kiptopeke, Va B7, D7 209
Kipushi, Zaire D4 106
Kirakira, San Cristobal I 115
Kirby, Ark C2 169
Kirby, Mont E10 190
Kirby, Ohio *B4 199
Kirby, Tex *E3 206
Kirby, Wyo B4 213
Kirbyville, Tex D6 206
Kirchdorf, Ger D5 62
Kirchhain [im Bezirk Kassel], Ger C3 61
Kirchhain [Niederlausitz], Ger B8 61
Kirchheim [unter Teck], Ger E4 61
Kirchheimbolanden, Ger D3 61
Kirchhunden, Ger B3 61
Kirdāsah, Eg G3 84
Kirensk, Sov. Un D13 71
Kirghiz S.S.R., rep., Sov. Un E10 71
Kirghiz, steppe, Sov. Un E9 76
Kirgiz, range, Sov. Un E8 73
Kiri, Zaire B2 106
Kirikkale, Tur *C9 85
Kirin (Chilin), China C10 91
Kirin, prov., China C9 91
Kirinian, isl., Eniwetok 114
Kirk, Colo B8 171
Kirk, Oreg E5 201
Kırkağaç, Tur C6 85
Kirkby, Eng *A5 56
Kirkby Lonsdale, Eng F6 57
Kirkby Stephen, Eng F6 57
Kirkcaldy, Alta., Can D4 148
Kirkcaldy, Scot D5 57
Kirkcolm, Scot F3 57
Kirkcudbright, Scot F4 57
Kirkcudbright, co., Scot E4 57
Kirkcudbright, bay, Scot F4 57
Kirkee, India *E5 87
Kirkella, Man., Can D1 150
Kirkenes, Nor C14 63
Kirkersville, Ohio C5 199
Kirkfield, Ont., Can C6 153
Kirkintilloch, Scot E4 57
Kirkland, Ariz C3 168
Kirkland, Ga E4 175
Kirkland, Ill A5 178
Kirkland, Tenn B5 205
Kirkland, Tex B2 206
Kirkland, Wash B3, D2 210
Kirkland Junction, Ariz C3 168
Kirkland Lake, Ont., Can E9 153
Kirklareli, Tur B6 69
Kirklin, Ind D5 179
Kirkman, Iowa C2 180
Kirkmansville, Ky C2 182
Kirkoswald, Eng F6 57
Kirkpatrick, lake, Alta., Can D5 148
Kirkpatrick, mtn., Ant A29 120
Kirksey, Ky B3 182
Kirksey, S.C C3 203
Kirksville, Ky C5 182
Kirksville, Mo A5 189
Kirkton, Ont., Can D3 153
Kirkūk, Iraq D2 86
Kirkville, Iowa C5 180
Kirkwall, Scot B6 57
Kirkwood, Del A6 173
Kirkwood, Ill C3 178
Kirkwood, Mo B7 189
Kirkwood, N.Y C5 196
Kirkwood, Pa G9 202
Kirkwood, S. Afr D4 107
Kirley, S. Dak C4 204
Kirn, Ger D2 61
Kiron, Iowa B2 180
Kirov, Sov. Un B3 73
Kirova, bay, Sov. Un B4 86
Kirovabad, Sov. Un E3 73
Kirovabad, Sov. Un C14 86
Kirovakan, Sov. Un B15 85
Kirovgrad, Sov. Un B6 73
Kirovograd, Sov. Un G9 72
Kirovsk, Sov. Un D15 63
Kirriemuir, Alta., Can D5 148
Kirriemuir, Scot D5 57
Kirsanov, Sov. Un E14 72
Kırşehir, Tur C10 85
Kirthar, range, Pak C4 87
Kirtland, N. Mex A1 195
Kirtland Hills, Ohio *A6 199
Kirtley, Wyo C8 213
Kiruna, Swe D9 63
Kirundu, Zaire B4 106
Kirvin, Tex *D4 206
Kirwin, Kans C4 181
Kirwin, res., Kans C4 181
Kiryū, Jap H9, m18 93
Kisaki, Tan C6 106
Kisalaya, Nic C5 130
Kisanga, Zaire C4 106
Kisangani, Zaire A4 106
Kisarazu, Jap n18 93
Kisbey, Sask., Can H4 155
Kiselëvsk, Sov. Un C11 73
Kisengi, Zaire D3 106
Kisengwa, Zaire C4 106
Kisenyi, Rwanda B4 106
Kishanganj, India D11 88
Kishangarh, India C5 87
Kishi, Nig E5 103
Kishinëv, Sov. Un B9 68, H7 72
Kishiwada, Jap o14 93
Kishon, riv., Isr B7 84
Kishorganj, Bngl D9 87
Kishorn, inlet, Scot C3 57
Kisii, Ken B5 106
Kisiju, Tan C6 106
Kisiwa, creek, Kans A4 181
Kisiwani, Tan B6 106
Kiska, isl., Alsk E3 167
Kiskatinaw, riv., B.C., Can B7 149
Kiskitto, lake, Man., Can B2 150
Kiskittogisu, lake, Man., Can B2 150
Kiskőrös, Hung B4 68
Kiskundorozsma, Hung B5 68
Kiskunfélegyhaza, Hung B4 68
Kiskunhalas, Hung B4 68
Kiskunmajsa, Hung B4 68
Kislovodsk, Sov. Un E2 73
Kismet, Kans E3 181
Kiso-Sammyaku, mts., Jap n16 93
Kissee Mills, Mo E4 189
Kisseynew, lake, Man., Can B1 150
Kissidougou, Guinea E2 103
Kissimmee, Fla D5 174
Kissimmee, lake, Fla E5 174
Kissimmee, riv., Fla E5 174
Kissimmee Park, Fla D5 174
Kississing, Man., Can B1 150
Kississing, lake, Man., Can B1 150
Kississing, riv., Man., Can B1 150
Kistigan, lake, Man., Can B5 150
Kistler, Pa *F6 202
Kistler, W. Va D3, D5 211
Kistna, riv., India E6 87
Kistrand, Nor B11 63
Kisújszállás, Hung B5 68
Kisumu, Ken A5 106
Kisvárda, Hung A6 68
Kit Carson, Colo C8 171
Kit Carson, co., Colo B8 171
Kita, Iwo 114
Kita, Mali D3 103
Kita-iwo (Kita-Iō) (San Alessandro), isl., Kazan-retto 115
Kitaibaraki, Jap *H10 93
Kitakyūshū, Jap J5 93
Kitale, Ken A5 106
Kitamaki, Jap m17 93
Kitami, Jap E11 93
Kitangari, Tan D6 106
Kitano, pt., Iwo 114
Kitchener, Ont., Can D4 153
Kite, Ga D4 175
Kitega, Burundi B5 106
Kitgum, Ug A5 106
Kíthira, Grc D4 69
Kíthira (Cythera), isl., Grc D4 69
Kíthnos, isl., Grc D5 69
Kiti, pt., Ponape 114
Kitimat, B.C., Can B3 149
Kitsap, co., Wash B3 210
Kitscoty, Alta., Can C5 148
Kittanning, Pa E2 202
Kittatinny, mts., N.J A3 194
Kittery, Maine E2 184
Kittery Point, Maine E2 184
Kittilä, Fin D11 63
Kittitas, Wash C5 210
Kittitas, co., Wash B5 210
Kittitas, val., Wash B5 210
Kittrell, N.C A5 197
Kitts, Ky D6 182
Kittson, co., Minn B2 187
Kittyhawk, bay, N.C A8 197
Kitty Hawk, N.C A8 197
Kitui, Ken B6 106
Kitwe, Zambia D4 106
Kitzbühel, Aus E6 60
Kitzingen, Ger D5 61
Kitzmiller, Md D1 173
Kiungshan, China C9 89
Kivalina, Alsk B7 167
Kivu, reg., Zaire B4 106
Kivu, lake, Zaire B4 106
Kiwalik, Alsk B7 167
Kiyan, Okinawa 114
Kiyiu, lake, Sask., Can F1 155
Kizel, Sov. Un B5 73
Kizil, riv., Tur B10 85
Kizlyar, Sov. Un E3 73
Kizyl-Arvat, Sov. Un F8 71
Kjakan, Nor C10 63
Kjellerup, Den B3 62
Kjelvik, Nor B12 63
Kladno, Czech C3, n17 70
Klagenfurt, Aus E7 60
Klagetoh, Ariz B6 168
Klaipėda, see Memel, Sov. Un.
Klamath, co., Oreg E5 201
Klamath, mts., Oreg E2 201
Klamath, riv., Calif., Oreg B2 170
Klamath Agency, Oreg E5 201
Klamath Falls, Oreg E5 201
Klamath Glen, Calif B1 170
Klammamett, India I8 88
Klang, Mala K4 89
Klanxbull, Ger D2 62
Klarälven, riv., Swe G5 63
Klatovy, Czech D2 70
Klawock, Alsk D13, n23 167
Kleberg, Tex *C4 206
Kleberg, co., Tex F4 206
Klecany, Czech n17 70
Kleena Kleene, B.C., Can D5 149
Klein, Mont D8 190
Kleinburg, Ont., Can E6 153
Klemme, Iowa A4 180
Klerksdorp, S. Afr C4 107
Kletnya, Sov. Un E9 72
Kletsk, Sov. Un E6 72
Kleve, Ger C6 59
Klickitat, Wash D4 210
Klickitat, co., Wash D5 210
Klickitat, creek, Wash D5 210
Klickitat, riv., Wash C4 210
Klimovsk, Sov. Un n17 72
Klin, Sov. Un C11 72
Klinaklini, riv., B.C., Can D5 149
Kline, Colo D2 171
Kline, S.C E5 203
Klingenthal, Ger C7 61
Klintsy, Sov. Un E9 72
Klippan, Swe B7 62
Klitmöller, Den A2 62
Ključ, Yugo C3 68
Kłobuck, Pol C5 70
Klock, Ont., Can A6 153
Kłodnica, riv., Pol g9 70
Klodzko, Pol C4 70
Klondike, Tenn E11 205
Klondike, Tex C5 206
Klondike, reg., Yukon, Can D5 142
Klostermansfeld, Ger B6 61
Klosterneuburg, Aus D8 60
Kloten, N. Dak B7 198
Klötze, Ger F5 62
Klotzsche, Ger B8 61
Klotzville, La B5 183
Kluane, lake, Yukon, Can D5 142
Kluczbork, Pol C5 70
Klucze, Pol g11 70
Klukwan, Alsk k22 167
Klütz, Ger E5 62
Klyazma, riv., Sov. Un B2 73
Klyuchevskaya, vol., Sov. Un D18 71
Knapp, creek, W. Va C5 211
Knap, pt., Scot E3 57
Knapp, Wis D1 212
Knaresborough, Eng F7 57
Knee, lake, Man., Can B4 150
Knee, lake, Sask., Can B2 155
Knesebeck, Ger F4 62
Knezha, Bul D7 68
Knickerbocker, Tex D2 206
Knierim, Iowa B3 180
Knife, riv., N. Dak B3 198
Knife River, Minn D7 187
Knifley, Ky C4 182
Knight, Wyo D2 213
Knight, inlet, B.C., Can D5 149
Knightdale, N.C B5 197
Knighton, Wales B4 56
Knights Landing, Calif C3 170
Knightstown, Ind E6 179
Knightsville, Ind E3 179
Knin, Yugo C3 68
Knippa, Tex E3 206
Knislinge, Swe B8 62
Knittelfeld, Aus E7 60
Knob, creek, Ky A4 182
Knob Lick, Ky C4 182
Knob Lick, Mo D7 189
Knob Noster, Mo C4 189
Knobel, Ark A5 169
Knobly, mtn., W. Va B5 211
Knobsville, Pa F6 202
Knokke, Bel C3 59
Knokmealdown, mts., Ire D2 55
Knops, pond, Mass C1 185
Knott, Tex C2 206
Knott, co., Ky C6 182
Knotts Island, N.C A8 197
Knottsville, Ky C3 182
Knowles, Okla A1, D4 200
Knowlton, Que., Can D5 154
Knowlton, Wis D4 212
Knox, Ill C3 178
Knox, Ind B4 179
Knox, N. Dak A6 198
Knox, Pa D2 202
Knox, co., Ill B3 178
Knox, co., Ind G3 179
Knox, co., Ky D6 182
Knox, co., Maine D4 184
Knox, co., Mo A5 189
Knox, co., Nebr B8 191
Knox, co., Ohio B5 199
Knox, co., Tenn C10 205
Knox, co., Tex C3 206
Knox, cape, B.C., Can B1 149
Knox, coast, Ant C23 120
Knox, creek, Ky., Va D2 211
Knox, is., Marshall Is 115
Knox City, Mo A5 189
Knox City, Tex C3 206
Knox Dale, Pa D3 202
Knoxville, Ala C2 166
Knoxville, Ark B2 169
Knoxville, Ga D3 175
Knoxville, Ill C3 178
Knoxville, Iowa C4 180
Knoxville, Md B2 173
Knoxville, Miss D2 188
Knoxville, Mo B3 189
Knoxville, Pa C7 202
Knoxville, Tenn D10, E11 205
Knysna, S. Afr D3 107
Knyszyn, Pol B7 70
Ko Vayo, Ariz E3 168
Kobdo, see Jirgalanta, Mong.
Kobdo, riv., Mong B3 91
Kōbe, Jap I7, o14 93
Kobelyaki, Sov. Un G10 72
København, see Copenhagen, Den.
Köbenhavn, co., Den C6 62
Koblenz, Ger C2 61
Kobona, Sov. Un r32 63
Kobrin, Sov. Un E5 72
Kobroor, isl., Indon G8 90
Kobuk, Alsk B8 167
Kobuk, riv., Alsk B8 167
Kobuleti, Sov. Un B13 85
Kocába, riv., Czech o17 70
Kocaeli, see İzmit, Tur.
Kočani, Yugo E6 68
Kočevje, Yugo C2 68
Koch, peak, Mont E5 190
Kochel, Ger B7 66
Kochel, lake, Ger B7 66
Kocher, riv., Ger D4 61
Kōchi, Jap J6 93
Kochiu, China G5 91
Kock, Pol C7 70
Kodaira, Jap *I9 93
Kodak, Ky C6 182
Kodiak, Alsk D9 167
Kodiak, isl., Alsk D9 167
Kodok, Sud D3 105
Koes, S.W. Afr C2 107
Kofa, mts., Ariz D2 168
Koffiefontein, S. Afr C4 107
Koforidua, Ghana E4 103
Kōfu, Jap I9, n17 93
Koga, Jap m18 93
Koganei, Jap *I7 93
Köge, Den C6 62
Köge, bay, Den C6 62
Kogilnik, riv., Sov. Un B9 68
Kohala, Haw C6 176
Kohala, mts., Haw C6 176
Kohāt, Pak B5 87
Kohatk, Ariz E3 168
Kohima, India C9 87
Kohler, Wis B6, E6 212
Kohls Ranch, Ariz C4 168
Kohlu, Pak C4 87
Kohtla-Järve, Sov. Un B6 72
Koiaris, Bougainville I 115
Köinge, Swe A6 62
Koje, isl., Kor I4 93
Kojima, Jap *I6 93
Koka (Xanthus), riv., Tur D7 69
Kokadjo, lake, Maine C3 184
Kokand, Sov. Un E8 73
Kokand, Khanate of: c. 1775 82
Kokanee Glacier, park, B.C., Can E9 149
Kokchetav, Sov. Un C7 73
Kokkola, Fin F10 63
Koko, Nig D5 103
Koko, head, Haw B4 176
Koko Nor (Tsinghai), lake, China D4 91
Kokomo (Recen), Colo B4 171
Kokomo, Haw C5 176
Kokomo, Ind D5 179
Kokomo, Miss D3 188
Kokopo, N. Gui h13 111
Kokos, is., Indon K1 89
Kokrines, Alsk C9 167
Koksilah, B.C., Can B9 149
Kokstad, S. Afr D4 107
Kokubunji, Jap *I9 93
Kola, Sov. Un C15 63
Kola, pen., Sov. Un D17 63
Kolan, China E4 92
Kolar Gold Fields, India F6 87
Kolarovgrad (Shumen), Bul *D8 68
Kolárovo, Czech E4 70
Kolayat, India D4 88
Kolbäck, Swe t34 63
Kolbano, Indon H6 90
Kolbio, Som F5 105
Kolbuszowa, Pol C6 70
Kolchugino, Sov. Un C12 72
Kolczewo, Pol E8 62
Kolda, Sen D2 103
Koldewey, isl., Grnld B16 118
Kolding, Den C3 62
Kole, Zaire B3 106
Koleč, Czech n17 70
Kolezhma, Sov. Un E16 63
Kolguyev, isl., Sov. Un C7 71
Kolhapur, India E5 87, I5 88
Koliganek, Alsk D8 167
Kolimbine, riv., Maur C2 103
Kolín, Czech C3 70
Kolin, La C3 183
Kolin, Mont C7 190
Kölleda, Ger B6 61
Köln, see Cologne, Ger.
Kolno, Pol B6 70
Koło, Pol B5 70
Koloa, Haw B2 176
Kolob, canyon, Utah F2 207
Kołobrzeg, Pol A3 70
Kolokani, Mali D3 103
Kolola Springs, Miss B5 188
Kolombangara, isl., Sol. Is 115
Kolomna, Sov. Un B1 73
Kolomyya, Sov. Un G5 72
Kolonodale, Indon F6 90
Kolpashevo, Sov. Un B10 73
Kolpino, Sov. Un s31 63
Kolva, riv., Sov. Un A5 73
Kolwa, Pak C3 87
Kolwezi, Zaire D4 106
Kolyberovo, Sov. Un n18 72
Kolyma, riv., Sov. Un C18 71
Kom Vo, Ariz F3 168
Komádi, Hung B5 68
Komadugu, riv., Nig D6 103
Komaki, Jap *I8 93
Komalu, New Ire. I 115
Komandorskiye, is., Sov. Un D19 71
Komarno, Man., Can D3 150
Komárno, Czech E5 70
Komarno, Sov. Un D7 70
Komarno, marsh, Sov. Un B10 73
Komárom, Hung B4 68
Komatipoort, S. Afr C5 107
Komatke, Ariz G2 168
Komatsu, Jap H8 93
Komatsushima, Jap I7 93
Komelik, Ariz F4 168
Kominato, Jap n19 93
Komló, Hung B4 68
Kommunarsk, Sov. Un G12, q21 72
Komodo, isl., Indon G5 90
Komono, Con F2 104
Komoran, isl., Indon G9 90
Komotiní, Grc B5 69
Kompong Cham, Camb F6 89
Kompong Chhnang, Camb F6 89
Kompong Kleang, Camb F6 89
Kompong Som, bay, Camb G6 89
Kompong Speu, Camb G6 89
Kompong Thom, Camb F6 89
Komrat, Sov. Un H7 72
Komsomol'sk, Sov. Un D16 71
Kōnan, Jap n15 93
Konawa, Okla C5 200
Kondoa, Tan B6 106
Kondopoga, Sov. Un F16 63
Kong, reg., I.C E4 103
Kong, isl., Camb G5 89
Kongeå, riv., Den C2 62
Kongju, Kor H3 93
Kongmoon (Chiangmen), China G7 91
Kongolo, Zaire C4 106
Kongsberg, N. Dak B5 198
Kongsberg, Nor H3, p27 63
Kongsmark, Den C2 62
Kongsvinger, Nor G5 63
Königs Wusterhausen, Ger A8 61
Königsberg, see Kaliningrad, Sov. Un.
Königsbrück, Ger B8 61
Königshofen, Ger C5 61
Königslutter, Ger A5 61
Königstein, Ger C4 61
Konin, Pol B5 70
Konispol, Alb C3 69
Kónitsa, Grc B3 69
Konjic, Yugo D3 68
Könnern, Ger B6 61
Konosha, Sov. Un A13 72
Konotop, Sov. Un F9 72
Końskie, Pol C6 70
Konstantinovka, Sov. Un q20 72
Konstanz, Ger E4 60
Konta, India I8 88
Kontagora, Nig D6 103
Kontcha, Cam D2 104
Kontich, Bel C4 59
Kontiomäki, Fin E13 63
Kontum, Viet E8 89

INDEX KEY Each place listed in **Bold-faced Type** has its population listed in the Population tables, pages 230 to 280.
Each country, shown in CAPITAL LETTERS, has its population listed in the World Political Information Table, pages 6 to 10.
* Does not appear on map; key shows general location.

Konya, Tur. D9 85
Konyang, Kor. I3 93
Konzhakovskiy Kamen, mtn., Sov. Un. B5 73
Koochiching, co., Minn. B4 187
Koolau, range, Haw g10 176
Koontz Lake, Ind. B5 179
Koosharem, Utah E4 207
Kooskia, Idaho C3 177
Kootenai, Idaho A2 177
Kootenai, co., Idaho B2 177
Kootenai, riv., Mont B1 190
Kootenay, lake, B.C., Can E9 149
Kootenay, nat. park, B.C., Can D9 149
Kootenay, riv., B.C., Can E10 149
Kópasker, Ice m24 63
Kopervik, Nor H1 63
Kopet, mts., Sov. Un B7 86
Kopeysk, Sov. Un B6 73
Köping, Swe H6, t33 63
Koppány, riv., Hung B4 68
Koppel, Pa E1 202
Koprivnica, Yugo B3 68
Kopychintsy, Sov. Un G5 72
K'orähē, Eth D5 105
Koraluk, riv., Newf., Can g9 152
Koram, Eth C4 105
Korarou, lake, Mali C4 103
Korba, Tun F12 64
Korbach, Ger B3 61
Korbu, mtn., Mala J4 89
Korçë, Alb B3 69
Korčula, isl., Yugo D3 68
Kordofan, reg., Sud C2 105
KOREA, NORTH, country, Asia F4 93
KOREA, SOUTH, country, Asia H4 93
Korea, reg., Asia 93
c. 1775 82
after World War II 83
Korea, bay, China D9 91
Korea, strait, Kor I4 93
Korets, Sov. Un F6 72
Korhogo, I.C E3 103
Kori, creek, Pak D4 87, F2 88
Kórinthos (Corinth), Grc. D4, h9 69
Kōriyama, Jap H10 93
Korkino, Sov. Un *D9 71
Korla, see Kuerhlo, China
Kormatiki, cape, Cyp E9 85
Körmend, Hung B3 68
Kornat, isl., Yugo D2 68
Korner, Mont B4 190
Korneuburg, Aus D8 60
Kornwestheim, Ger E4 61
Koro, isl., Fiji 114
Koromo, Jap n16 93
Koronis, lake, Minn E4 187
Koropí, Grc h11 69
Koror, isl., Palau Is 114
Korosten, Sov. Un F7 72
Korotoyak, Sov. Un F12 72
Korovin, vol., Alsk E5 167
Korsakov (Otomari), Sov. Un C11 93
Korsör, Den C5 62
Kōrti, Sud B3 105
Kortrijk (Courtrai), Bel D3 59
Korumburra, Austl I5 112
Koryak, mts., Sov. Un C19 71
Kós, Grc D6 69
Kós, isl., Grc D6 69
Koschagyl, Sov. Un D6 74
Kościan, Pol B4 70
Kościerzyna, Pol A4 70
Kosciusko, Miss B4 188
Kosciusko, co., Ind B6 179
Kosciusko, mtn., Austl H7 112
Koshan, China B11 91
Koshigaya, Jap n8 93
Koshiki, isl., Jap K4 93
Koshkonong, Mo E6 189
Koshkonong, lake, Wis F5 212
Kosi, riv., India C8 87
Košice, Czech D6 70
Košíře, Czech n17 70
Koskaecodde, lake, Newf., Can D4 152
Kosŏng, Kor G4 93
Kosovska Mitrovica, Yugo D5 68
Kosse, Tex D4 206
Kösslarn, Ger A9 66
Kossol, passage, Palau Is 114
Kossol, reef, Palau Is 114
Kossuth, Miss A5 188
Kossuth, co., Iowa A3 180
Kostelec, Czech n18 70
Kostelec nad Černými Lesy, Czech o18 70
Kosti, Sud C3 105
Kostroma, Sov. Un B2 73
Kostrzyń, Pol B3 70
Koszalin, Pol A4 70
Kőszeg, Hung B3 68
Kot-i-Ashru, Afg D14 86
Kota, India E5 88
Kota Baharu, Mala I5 89
Kota Kinabalu, Mala D5 90
Kotabaru, Indon F5 90
Kotatengah, Indon L4 89
Kotel, Bul D8 68
Kotelnich, Sov. Un B3 73
Kotelnikovskiy, Sov. Un D2 73
Kotelny, isl., Sov. Un B16 71
Köthen, Ger B6 61
Kotido, Ug A5 106
Kotka, Fin G12 63
Kotlas, Sov. Un C7 71
Kotlik, Alsk C7 167
Kotonkoro, Nig D6 103
Kotor, Yugo D4 68
Kotor, bay, Yugo D4 68
Kotor Varoš, Yugo C3 68
Kotovsk, Sov. Un E13 72
Kotovsk, Sov. Un H7 72
Kotovskoye, Sov. Un B9 68
Kotri, Pak E2 88
Kottagudem, India *E7 87
Kottayam, India *G6 87
Kotte, Cey *G6 87
Kotung, China B3 93
Kotzebue, Alsk B7 167
Kotzebue, sound, Alsk B7 167
Kötzting, Ger D7 61
Kouango, Cen. Afr. Rep D4 104
Kouchibouguac, nat. park, N.B., Can C5 151
Kouchibouguacis, riv., N.B., Can C4 151
Koudougou, Upper Volta D4 103
Koula-Moutou, Gabon F2 104
Koulikoro, Mali D3 103
Kounradskiy, Sov. Un D9 73
Kountze, Tex D5 206
Koupangtzu, China D9 92
Kourémalé, Mali D3 103
Kouri, isl., Okinawa 114
Kourou, Fr. Gu A4 139
Kouroussa, Guinea D3 103
Koutiala, Mali D3 103
Kouts, Ind B3 179
Kouvola, Fin G12 63
Kovel, Sov. Un F5 72
Kovik, Que., Can A2 154
Kovrov, Sov. Un B2 73
Kowloon, Hong Kong G7 91
Kowŏn, Kor G3 93
Koyuk, Alsk C7 167
Koyukuk, Alsk C8 167
Kozan, Tur D10 85
Kozáni, Grc B3 69
Kozelsk, Sov. Un D10 72
Kozienice, Pol C6 70
Koźle, Pol C5 70
Kozloduy, Bul D6 68
Kōzu, isl., Jap I9 93
Kożuchów, Pol C3 70
Kpandu, Ghana E5 103
Kra, isth., Thai G3 89
Kraemer, La C6 183
Kragerö, Nor H3 63
Kragujevac, Yugo D5 68
Krakow, Ger E6 62
Kraków, Pol C5 70
Krakower, lake, Ger E6 62
Kraljevo, Yugo D5 68
Královské Vinohrady, Czech n17 70
Kralupy [nad Vltavou], Czech n17 70
Králův Dvůr, Czech o17 70
Kramatorsk, Sov. Un G11, q20 72
Kramer, Ind D3 179
Kramer, N. Dak A5 198
Kramer Junction, Calif E5 170
Kranídhion, Grc D4 69
Kranj, Yugo B2 68
Kranzburg, S. Dak C9 204
Krasburg, S.W. Afr C2 107
Kraslice, Czech C2 70
Krasnaya Sloboda, Sov. Un D2 73
Kraśnik Lubelski, Pol C7 70
Krasnoarmeysk, Sov. Un F15 72
Krasnoarmeysk, Sov. Un G15 72
Krasnoarmeyskaya, Sov. Un I12 72
Krasnodar, Sov. Un I12 72
Krasnodon, Sov. Un q22 72
Krasnogorsk, Sov. Un B11 93
Krasnograd, Sov. Un G10 72
Krasnokamsk, Sov. Un B5 73
Krasnoselye, Sov. Un G9 72
Krasnoslobodsk, Sov. Un D14 72
Krasnotur'insk, Sov. Un B6 73
Krasnoufimsk, Sov. Un B5 73
Krasnovishersk, Sov. Un A5 73
Krasnovodsk, Sov. Un E4 73
Krasnoyarsk, Sov. Un D12 71
Krasnoye Selo, Sov. Un s31 63
Krasnoznamenskiy, Sov. Un C7 73
Krasnystaw, Pol C7 70
Krasnyy Kholm, Sov. Un B11 72
Krasnyy Kut, Sov. Un C3 73
Krasnyy Liman, Sov. Un q20 72
Krasnyy Luch, Sov. Un q21 72
Krasnyy Sulin, Sov. Un H13 72
Krasnyy Yar, Sov. Un F15 72
Kratie, Camb F7 89
Kratovo, Yugo D6 68
Krause, pt., Vir. Is k17 132
Krebs, Okla C6 200
Krefeld, Ger B1 61
Kremenchug, Sov. Un G9 72
Kremenchug, res., Sov. Un G9 72
Kremenets, Sov. Un F5 72
Kremennaya, Sov. Un p21 72
Kremikovtsi, Bul D6 68
Kremlin, Mont B6 190
Kremlin, Okla A4 200
Kremmling, Colo A4 171
Krems, Aus D7 60
Kreole, Miss *E3 188
Kresgeville, Pa E10 202
Kress, Tex B2 206
Kreuzlingen, Switz B5 66
Kribi, Cam E1 104
Krichev, Sov. Un E8 72
Kriens, Switz B4 66
Krilon, cape, Sov. Un D11 93
Krilon, pen., Sov. Un C11 93
Krishnagar, India F12 88
Krishnagiri, India F6 87
Kristiansand, Nor H2 63
Kristianstad, Swe I6 63
Kristianstad, co., Swe B7 62
Kristiansund, Nor F2 63
Kristinestad, Fin F9 63
Kriva Palanka, Yugo D6 68
Krivorozhye, Sov. Un q21 72
Krivoy Rog, Sov. Un H9 72
Križevci, Yugo B3 68
Krk, isl., Yugo C2 68
Krka, riv., Yugo D3 68
Krnov, Czech C4 70
Krogsered, Swe A6 62
Krokeaí, Grc D4 69
Krokstadelva, Nor p28 63
Krolevets, Sov. Un F9 72
Kroměříž, Czech D4 70
Kromy, Sov. Un E10 72
Kronach, Ger C6 61
Kronau, Sask., Can G3 155
Kronoberg, co., Swe B8 62
Kronshtadt, Sov. Un B7 72
Kroonstad, S. Afr C4 107
Kröpelin, Ger D5 62
Kropotkin, Sov. Un I13 72
Krosno, Pol D6 70
Krosno Odrzańskie, Pol B3 70
Krotoszyn, Pol C4 70
Krotz Springs, La D4 183
Krško, Yugo C2 68
Kruger, nat. park, S. Afr B5 107
Krugersdorp, S. Afr C4 107
Krujë, Alb B2 69
Krum, Tex *C4 206
Krumbach, Ger A6 66
Krumovgrad, Bul E7 68
Krung Thep, see Bangkok, Thai.
Krusenstern Rock, reef, Haw m12 176
Kruševac, Yugo D5 68
Kruševo, Yugo E5 68
Kruszwica, Pol B5 70
Krydor, Sask., Can E2 155
Krym (Crimea), pen., Sov. Un I10 72
Krymskaya, Sov. Un I11 72
Krynica, Pol D6 70
Krynki, Pol B7 70
Ksar es Souk, Mor C4 102
Ktípas, mtn., Grc g10 69
Ku Lao Cham, isl., Viet E8 89
Ku Lao Re, isl., Viet E8 89
Kuakue, bay, Loyalty Is 115
Kuala Dungun, Mala J5 89
Kuala-Kerau, Mala K5 89
Kuala Lipis, Mala J5 89
Kuala Lumpur, Mala K4 89
Kuala Terengganu, Mala J5 89
Kualakurun, Indon F4 90
Kualapuu, Haw B4 176
Kuan, China F6 92
Kuandang, Indon E6 90
Kuangan, China I2 92
Kuangchang, China K7 92
Kuanghua, China H4 92
Kuangnan, China G6 91
Kuangte, China I8 92
Kuangyüan, China H1 92
Kuantan, Mala K5 89
Kuanti, China E4 93
Kuantien, China F2 93
Kuanyün, China G8 92
Kuaua, N. Cal 115
Kuba, Sov. Un E3 73
Kublai Khan, dominions of 81
Kuchen, China H7 92
Kucheng, China H4 92
Kuchêng, see Chitai, China
Kuching, Mala E4 90
Kuchino, isl., Jap K4 93
Kuchino Erabu, isl., Jap K5 93
Kudat, Mala D5 90
Kudus, Indon *G4 90
Kudymkar, Sov. Un B4 73
Kueichi, China J7 92
Kueichih, China I7 92
Kueilin, China F7 91
Kueisui, see Huhehot, China
Kueite, China D5 91
Kueiyang, China F6 91
Kuerhlo (Korla), China C2 91
Kufstein, Aus E6 60
Kuge, Jap n14 93
Kuh, cape, Iran I8 86
Kūh-e-Bīzak, mtn., Iran D10 86
Kūh-e-Bozqush, mts., Iran C3 86
Kūh-e-Sahand, mtn., Iran C3 86
Kuh-i-Alwand, mtn., Iran D4 86
Kuh-i-Birg, mtn., Iran H10 86
Kuh-i-Bizak, mtn., Iran D10 86
Kuh-i-Furgun, mtn., Iran H8 86
Kuh-i-Garrah, mtn., Iran F5 86
Kuh-i-Gireh, mtn., Iran H8 86
Kuh-i-Gugird, mts., Iran D6 86
Kuh-i-Hormuz, mtn., Iran H7 86
Kuh-i-Huzar, mtn., Iran G8 86
Kuh-i-Istin, mtn., Iran F10 86
Kuh-i-Kharman, mtn., Iran G6 86
Kuh-i-Kurkhud, mtn., Iran C8 86
Kuh-i-Kuru, mtn., Iran D5 86
Kuh-i-Mazar, mtn., Afg E13 86
Kuh-i-Murghum, mtn., Iran E8 86
Kuh-i-Naibandan, mtn., Iran E8 86
Kuh-i-Nila, mtn., Iran E5 86
Kuh-i-Rahmand, mtn., Iran D4 86
Kuh-i-Ran, mtn., Iran H9 86
Kuh-i-Saguch, mtn., Iran F8 86
Kuh-i-Surkh, mts., Iran D9 86
Kuh-i-Tafrish, mtn., Iran C5 86
Kūhpāyēh, Iran E6 86
Kuhsan, Afg D10 86
Kuji, Jap F10 93
Kuju-San, peak, Jap J5 93
Kukaiau, Haw C6 176
Kukawa, Nig D7 103
Kukës, Alb A3 69
Kuki, Jap m18 93
Kuku, pt., Wake I 114
Kukuihaele, Haw C6 176
Kula, Bul D6 68
Kula, Haw C5 176
Kula, Tur C7 69
Kula, Yugo C4 68
Kula, gulf, Sol. Is 115
Kuldja (Ining), China C10 73
Kulebaki, Sov. Un D14 72
Kulhakangri, peak, China C13 88
Kuling, China J7 92
Kulltorp, Swe A7 62
Kulm, N. Dak C7 198
Kulmbach, Ger C6 61
Kulpmont, Pa E9 202
Kulu, isl., Alsk m22 167
Kulun, China C9 92
Kulunda, Sov. Un C9 73
Kulunda, lake, Sov. Un C9 73
Kumagaya, Jap m18 93
Kumai, Indon F4 90
Kumak, N. Cal 115
Kumamoto, Jap J5 93
Kumanovo, Yugo D5 68
Kumasi, Ghana E4 103
Kumbakonam, India F6 87
Kumbo, Cam E7 103
Kŭmchŏn, Kor H4 93
Kŭmhae, Kor D10 91
Kŭmhwa, Kor G3 93
Kumi, Ug A5 106
Kumihama, Jap n14 93
Kumkale, Tur C6 69
Kumla, Swe H6, t33 63
Kummerower, lake, Ger E6 62
Kŭmsŏng, Kor G3 93
Kumukahi, cape, Haw D7 176
Kumyan, China C8 89
Kuna, Idaho F2 177
Kunar, Afg D15 86
Kunar, riv., Pak., Afg D15 86, A5 87
Kunckle, Pa A8 202
Kundar, riv., Pak B2 88
Kundūz, Afg C14 86, A4 87
Kungchuling, China E2 93
Kunghit, isl., B.C., Can C2 149
Kungrad, Sov. Un E5 73
Kungsbacka, Swe A6 62
Kungsörs, Swe t34 63
Kungu, Zaire A2 106
Kungur, Sov. Un B5 73
Kunia, Haw g9 176
Kunkletown, Pa B2 194
Kunlun, mts., China D3 91
Kunming, China C11 87, F5 91
Kunsan, Kor I3 93
Kunszentmárton, Hung B5 68
Kuntu, China B9 92
Künzelsau, Ger D4 61
Kuolayarvi, Sov. Un D13 63
Kuop (Royalists), is., Truk 114
Kuopio, Fin F12 63
Kuoyang, China H7 92
Kupa, riv., Yugo C2 68
Kupang, Indon H6 90
Kupindal, New Britain I 115
Kupino, Sov. Un C9 73
Kupk, Ariz F3 168
Kupreanof, isl., Alsk m23 167
Kupyansk, Sov. Un G11 72
Kur, riv., Sov. Un B7 93
Kura, riv., Sov. Un E3 73
Kurakhovka, Sov. Un q20 72
Kurashiki, Jap *I6 93
Kurdikos-Naumiestis, Sov. Un A7 70
Kurdistan: in 1914 52
in 1921 53
Kŭrdzhali, Bul E7 68
Kure, Jap I6 93
Kure Beach, N.C *D6 197
Kure, isl., Haw k12 176
Kuressaare, Sov. Un B4 72
Kureyka, riv., Sov. Un C12 71
Kurgaldzhino, Sov. Un C8 73
Kurgan, Sov. Un B7 73
Kuri, India D3 88
Kuria, isl., Gilbert Is 115
Kurigram, Bngl E12 88
Kuril, is., Sov. Un E17 71
Kuril, strait, Sov. Un D18 71
Ku-ring-gai, Austl *F8 112
Kurisches Haff, see Courland lagoon, Sov. Un.
Kurkhera, India G8 88
Kurmuk, Sud C3 105
Kurnool, India E6 87
Kuro, isl., Jap K4 93
Kuroki, Sask., Can F4 155
Kurovskoye, Sov. Un n18 72
Kurow, N.Z P13 112
Kursk, Sov. Un F11 72
Kuršumlija, Yugo D5 68
Kurtalan, Tur D13 85
Kurthwood, La C2 183
Kurtistown, Haw D6 176
Kurtz, Ind G5 179
Kuruman, S. Afr C3 107
Kurume, Jap J5 93
Kurunegala, Cey G7 87
Kuşadası, Tur D6 69
Kusakaki, isl., Jap K4 93
Kusatsu, Jap n14 93
Kusel, Ger D2 61
Kushchevskaya, Sov. Un H12 72
Kushevat, Sov. Un C9 71
Kushiro, Jap E12 93
Kushka, Sov. Un F9 71
Kushmurun, Sov. Un C6 73
Kushmurun, lake, Sov. Un C6 73
Kushva, Sov. Un B5 73
Kuskokwim, bay, Alsk D7 167
Kuskokwim, mts., Alsk C8 167
Kuskokwim, riv., Alsk C8 167
Kussia, Bougainville I 115
Kustanay, Sov. Un C6 73
Küsten, canal, Ger B7 59
Kut, isl., Thai G5 89
Kut al Hai, Iraq E3 86
Kut al Imara, Iraq E2 86
Kütahya, Tur C7 69
Kutaisi, Sov. Un A14 85
Kutaka, isl., Okinawa 114
Kutaradja, Indon J1 89, k11 90
Kutatjane, Indon K2 89
Kutch, Colo C7 171
Kutch, gulf, India D4 87
Kutë, Alb B2 69
Kutina, Yugo C3 68
Kutlay, Sov. Un D4 73
Kutná Hora, Czech D3 70
Kutno, Pol B5 70
Kuto, N. Cal 115
Kuttawa, Ky A3 182
Kutu, Zaire B2 106
Kutua, pt., Truk 114
Kutum, Sud C1 105
Kuty, Sov. Un A7 68
Kutztown, Pa E10 202
Kuusamo, Fin E13 63
Kuwait, Kuw G3 86
KUWAIT, country, Asia G3 86
Kuwana, Jap I8, n15 93
Kuyang, Mong D4 92
Kuybyshev, Sov. Un B9 73
Kuybyshev, Sov. Un C4 73
Kuybyshev, res., Sov. Un D8 73
Kuyto Ozero, lake, Sov. Un E14 63
Kuyüan, China G2 92
Kuznetsk, Sov. Un C3 73
Kuznetsova, Sov. Un C10 93
Kuzomen, Sov. Un D17 63
Kvarner, gulf, Yugo C2 68
Kwa Mashu, S. Afr *C5 107
Kwa Mtoro, Tan C6 106
Kwajalein, atoll, Marshall Is 115
Kwajalong, isl., Kwajalein 114
Kwakoegron, Sur A3 139
Kwale, Ken B6 106
Kwale, Nig E6 103
Kwamouth, Zaire B2 106
Kwangchow, bay, China B9 89
Kwangju, Kor I3 93
Kwango, riv., Zaire C2 106
Kwangsi Chuang, auton. reg., China G6 91
Kwangtung, prov., China G7 91
Kwanmo, mtn., Kor F4 93
Kwatisore, Indon F8 90
Kweichow, prov., China F6 91
Kweichu, see Kweiyang, China
Kweihsien, China G6 91
Kweisui, see Huhohaote, China
Kwidzyń, Pol B5 70
Kwigillingok, Alsk D7 167
Kwiguk, Alsk C7 167
Kwilu, riv., Zaire B2 106
Kwohsien, China D7 91
Kyabé, Chad D3 104
Kyabra, creek, Austl B4 112
Kyaiklat, Bur E10 87
Kyaikto, Bur D2 89
Kyakhta, Sov. Un D13 71
Kyangin, Bur E10 87
Kyaring, lake, China B8 87
Kyaring, lake, China E4 91
Kyaukpadaung, Bur C1 89
Kyaukpyu, Bur E9 87
Kyaukse, Bur B2 89
Kybartai, Sov. Un A7 70
Kyelang, India A6 88
Kyje, Czech n18 70
Kyle, Sask., Can G1 155
Kyle, Scot C3 57
Kyle, S. Dak D3 204
Kyle, Tex E4 206
Kyles Ford, Tenn C10 205
Kylestrome, Scot B3 57
Kyll, riv., Ger D1 61
Kyllburg, Ger D6 59
Kynuna, Austl D7 111
Kyōga, cape, Jap I7 93
Kyoga, lake, Ug A5 106
Kyŏmipo, Kor *G2 93
Kyŏngju, Kor I4 93
Kyŏngsŏng, Kor F4 93
Kyōto, Jap I7, n14 93
Kyrenia, Cyp E9 85
Kyritz, Ger B6 60
Kyrkjebö, Nor G1 63
Kyrock, Ky C3 182
Kyshtym, Sov. Un B6 73
Kyuquot, B.C., Can D4 149
Kyuquot, sound, B.C., Can E4 149
Kyuroku, isl., Jap F9 93
Kyūshū, isl., Jap J5 93
Kyustendil, Bul D6 68
Kyzyl, Sov. Un D12 71
Kyzyl-Kiya, Sov. Un E8 73
Kyzylkum, des., Sov. Un E6 73
Kzyl-Orda, Sov. Un E7 73

L

Laa, Aus D8 60
Laaber, riv., Ger E7 61
Laage, Ger E6 62
La Almunia de Dona Godina, Sp B5 65
Laasphe, Ger C3 61
La Asunción, Ven A5 133
Laau, pt., Haw B4 176
Labadie, Mo C7 189
Labadieville, La C5, E5 183
La Baie, Que., Can C5 154
La Banda, Arg E3 135
La Barca, Mex C4, m12 129
La Barge, Wyo C2 213
Labé, Guinea D2 103
Labe (Elbe), riv., Czech C3 70
Labelle, Que., Can C3 154
Labelle, co., Que., Can C2 154
La Belle, Fla F5 174
La Belle, Mo A6 189
Labette, Kans E8 181
Labette, co., Kans E8 181
Labin, Yugo C2 68
Labinsk, Sov. Un E7 71
La Bisbal, Sp B7 65
Labo, Phil o14 90
Labo, mtn., Phil o14 90
La Boca, C.Z m11 130
La Boca, P.R B4 132
Laboe, Ger D4 62
La Bolt, S. Dak B9 204
Labouheyre, Fr E3 58
Laboulaye, Arg A4 136
Labrador, reg., Newf., Can g8 152, 147
Labrador, sea, Newf., Can A3, g10 152
Labrador City, Newf., Can H8 152
Lábrea, Braz D4 139
La Broquerie, Man., Can E3 150
Labuan, isl., Mala D5 90
Labuha, Indon F7 90
Labuhanbilik, Indon K4 89
Labuk, bay, Mala D5 90
Lac a Beauce, Que., Can B5 154
Lac à l'Eau-Claire, lake, Que., Can A2 154
Lac au Saumon, Que., Can *B3 154
Lac aux Brochets, Que., Can B5 154
Lac aux Sables, Que., Can C5 154
Lac Baker, N.B., Can B1 151
Lac Beauport, Que., Can C6 154
Lac Bouchette, Que., Can A5 154
Lac-Brome, Que., Can *D5 154
Lac Carre, Que., Can C3 154
Lac Chat, Que., Can B5 154
Lac Court Oreilles, lake, Wis C2 212
Lac Court Oreilles, Indian res., Wis C2 212
Lac des Allemands, lake, La C6 183
Lac des Commissaires, lake, Que., Can A5 154
Lac des Deux Montagnes, lake, Que., Can B8 154
Lac du Bonnet, Man., Can D3 150
Lac du Flambeau, Wis C4 212
Lac du Flambeau, Indian res., Wis C3 212
Lac Edouard, Que., Can B5 154
Lac-Etchemin, Que., Can C7 154
Lac Forbes, lake, Que., Can C3 154
Lac-Frontière, Que., Can C7 154
Lac Hal Hal, lake, Que., Can A7 154
Lac Ile-à-la-Crosse, lake, Sask., Can B2 155
Lac Joseph, lake, Newf., Can h8 152
Lac La Belle, Wis *E5 212
Lac la Biche, Alta., Can B5 148
Lac la Croix, lake, Minn B6 187
Lac la Plonge, lake, Sask., Can B2 155
Lac la Ronge, lake, Sask., Can B3 155
Lac La Ronge, prov. park, Sask., Can C5 155
Lac Masson, Que., Can C3 154
Lac Mégantic, Que., Can D7 154
Lac qui Parle, co., Minn F2 187
Lac qui Parle, lake, Minn E2 187
Lac qui Parle, riv., Minn F2 187
Lac Saguay, Que., Can C2 154
Lac St. Jean, lake, Que., Can A5 154
Lac-St. Jean-Est, Que. Can A6 154
Lac-St.-Jean-Est., co., Que., Can A6 154
Lac-St. Jean-Ouest, Que., Can A6 154
Lac-St. Jean-Ouest, co., Que., Can A6 154
Lac Sainte Marie, Que., Can D2 154
Lac Vert, Sask., Can E3 155
La Cabaña, Cuba h12 131
Lacadena, Sask., Can G1 155
L'Acadie, Que., Can D4 154
La Calera, Chile A2 136
Lacamp, La C3 183
La Capelle, Fr E3 59
La Carlota, Arg A4 136
La Carlota, Phil *C6 90
La Carolina, Sp C4 65
Laccadive, is., India F5 87
La Ceiba, Hond C4 130
La Ceiba, Ven B3 133
La Ceja, Col B2 133
La Center, Ky A2 182
La Center, Wash *D3 210
Lacey, Wash B3 210
Laceys Spring, Ala A3 166
Laceyville, Pa C9 202
La Chambre, Fr D2 66
La Charité, Fr D5 58
La Charqueada, Ur E2 137

INDEX KEY Each place listed in **Bold-faced Type** has its population listed in the Population tables, pages 230 to 280.
Each country, shown in CAPITAL LETTERS, has its population listed in the World Political Information Table, pages 6 to 10.
* Does not appear on map; key shows general location.

La Châtre, Fr. D5 58
La Chaux-de-Fonds, Switz. B2 66
Lachine, Que., Can. D4, D9 154
Lachine, Mich. C7 186
La Chorrera, Pan. F8, m11 130
Lachute, Que., Can. D3 154
La Cienega, N. Mex. F6 195
La Ciotat, Fr. F6 58
La Cisa, pass., It. B3 67
Lackawanna, N.Y. C2 196
Lackawanna, co., Pa. D10 202
Lackawaxen, Pa. D12 202
Laclede, Idaho A2 177
Laclede, Ill. E5 178
Laclede, Mo. B4 189
Laclede, co., Mo. D5 189
La Cocha, Arg. E2 135
Lacolle, Que., Can. D4 154
La Colorado, Mex. B2 129
Lacomb, Oreg. C2, C4 201
Lacombe, Alta., Can. C4 148
Lacombe, La. B7, D6 183
Lacombe, bayou, La. B7 183
Lacon, Ill. B4 178
Lacona, Iowa C4 180
Lacona, N.Y. B4 196
La Conception Station, Que., Can. C3 154
Laconia, N.H. C4 193
Laconia, Tenn. B2 205
Laconia, gulf, Grc. D4 69
La Conner, Wash. A3 210
Lacoochee, Fla. D4 174
La Coruña, Sp. A1 65
La Coste, Tex. *E3 206
Lacota, Mich. F4 186
La Courneuve, Fr. g10 58
Lacreek, lake, S. Dak. D4 204
La Crescent, Minn. G7 187
La Crosse, Ark. A4 169
La Crosse, Fla. C4 174
La Crosse, Ind. B4 179
La Crosse, Kans. D4 181
La Crosse, Va. E4 209
Lacrosse, Wash. C8 210
La Crosse, Wis. E2 212
La Crosse, co., Wis. E2 212
La Crosse, riv., Wis. E3 212
La Cruz, Col. C2 133
La Cruz, Mex. C3 129
La Cuesta, P.R. B3 132
La Cueva, N. Mex. B4 195
Lacy-Lakeview, Tex. *D4 206
La Cygne, Kans. D9 181
Ladakh: c. 1775 82
Ladd, Ill. B4 178
Ladder, creek, Kans. D2 181
Laddonia, Mo. B6 189
Ladgasht, Pak. C3 87
Ladies, isl., S.C. G6 203
Ladispoli, It. h8 67
Lādīz, Iran G10 86
Ladner, B.C., Can. A10, E6 149
Ladner, S. Dak. B2 204
Ladnun, India D5 88
Ladoga, Ind. E4 179
Ladoga, lake, Sov. Un. A8 72
Ladonia, Tex. C5 206
Ladora, Iowa C5 180
La Dorada, Col. B3 133
La Due, Mo. C4 189
Ladue, Mo. *C7 189
Lady Lake, Fla. D5 174
Lady Laurier, mtn., B.C., Can. A6 149
Lady Newnes, ice shelf, Ant. B29 120
Ladybank, Scot. D5 57
Ladybrand, S. Afr. C4 107
Ladysmith, B.C., Can. B9, E6 149
Ladysmith, S. Afr. C4 107
Ladysmith, Wis. C2 212
Lae, N. Gui. k12 111
Lae, atoll, Marshall Is. 115
Laerdal, Nor. G2 63
Laesö, isl., Den. A4 62
La Esperanza, Cuba k12 131
La Esperanza, Cuba D2 131
La Esperanza, Hond. C3 130
La Esperanza, P.R. B6 132
La Estrada, Sp. A1 65
La Estrella, Bol. C3 135
La Farge, Wis. E3 212
La Fargeville, N.Y. A5, B1 196
Lafayette, Ala. C4 166
Lafayette, Calif. *D2 170
Lafayette, Colo. B5 171
La Fayette, Ga. B1 175
La Fayette, Ill. B4 178
Lafayette, Ind. D4 179
La Fayette, Ky. D2 182
Lafayette, La. D3 183
Lafayette, Minn. F4 187
Lafayette, N.J. A3 194
Lafayette, N.Y. C4 196
Lafayette, Ohio C4 199
Lafayette, Oreg. B1, B3 201
LaFayette, R.I. C11 172
Lafayette, Tenn. C7 205
Lafayette, co., Ark. D2 169
Lafayette, co., Fla. C3 174
Lafayette, co., Miss. A4 188
Lafayette, co., Mo. C4 189
Lafayette, co., Wis. F3 212
Lafayette, par., La. D3 183
Lafayette, mtn., N.H. B3 193
Lafayette Central, P.R. D6 132
Lafayette Southwest, La. *D3 183
Lafayette Springs, Miss. A4 188
Lafe, Ark. A5 169
La Fère, Fr. E3 59
La Feria, Tex. F4 206
La Ferté-Bernard, Fr. C4 58
La Ferté-Macé, Fr. C3 58
La Ferté-sous-Jouarre, Fr. C5 58
Lafferty, Ohio B6 199
Lafia, Nig. E6 103
Lafiagi, Nig. E6 103
Lafleche, Sask., Can. H2 155
La Flèche, Fr. D3 58
La Follette, Tenn. C9 205
La Fontaine, Ind. C6 179
Lafontaine, Kans. E8 181
Lafourche, La. C6, E5 183
Lafourche, par., La. E5 183
Lafourche, bayou, La. E5 183
La France, S.C. B2 203
Lafrenais, lake, Que., Can. A4 154
La Garita, Colo. D4 171
Lagarto, Pan. k10 130
Lage, Ger. B3 61
Lågen, riv., Nor. G3, p27 63
Lagg, Scot. E3 57
Laggan, bay, Scot. E2 57
Laggan, lake, Scot. D4 57
Laghouat, Alg. C5 102
La Gloria, Col. B3 133
Lagny, Fr. C5 58
Lago, mtn., Wash. A5 210
Lago Argentino, Arg. E2 136
Lago Buenos Aires, Arg. D2 136
Lago Posadsa, Arg. D2 136
Lago Viedma, Arg. D2 136
Lagôa, Port. D1 65
Lagos, Chile B2 136
Lagos, Nig. E5 103
Lagos, Port. D1 65
Lagos Colony: in 1898 99
Lagos de Moreno, Mex. C4, m13 129
La Grand' Combe, Fr. E6 58
La Grande, Oreg. B8 201
La Grande-Rivière, riv., Que., Can. B2 154
La Grange, Ark. C5 169
La Grange, Austl. C3 111
La Grange, Fla. D6 174
La Grange, Ga. C1 175
La Grange, Ill. B6, F2 178
Lagrange, Ind. A7 179
La Grange, Ky. B4 182
La Grange, Maine C4 184
La Grange, Mo. A6 189
La Grange, N.C. B6 197
Lagrange, Ohio A5 199
La Grange, Tenn. B2 205
La Grange, Tex. E4 206
Lagrange, Wyo. D8 213
Lagrange, co., Ind. A7 179
La Grange Park, Ill. F2 178
Lagro, Ind. C6 179
Lagrue, bayou, Ark. C4 169
La Guadeloupe, Que., Can. D7 154
La Guaira, Ven. A4 133
La Guardia, Sp. B1 65
La Guajira (Guajira), intendencia, Col. A3 133
Laguna, Ariz. E1 168
Laguna, Braz. D3 137
Laguna, N. Mex. B2 195
Laguna, dam, Ariz. E1 168
Laguna, Indian res., N. Mex. C2 195
Laguna Beach, Calif. F5 170
Laguna Madre, lagoon, Tex. F4 206
Lagunillas, Bol. C3 135
Lagunillas, Ven. A3 133
La Habana, see Havana, Cuba
La Habra, Calif. F3 170
Lahad Datu, Mala. D5 90
Lahaina, Haw. C5 176
La Harpe, Ill. C3 178
La Harpe, Kans. E8 181
Lahasusu, see Tungchiang, China
Lahat, Indon. F2 90
La Have, N.S., Can. E5 151
Lahave, riv., N.S., Can. E5 151
La Have Island, N.S., Can. E5 151
La Haye-Descartes, Fr. D4 58
Laheria Sarai, India D10 88
Laḩij, Yemen (Aden) C5 105
Lahn, riv., Ger. C3 61
Laholm, Swe. B7 62
Laholmsbukten, bay, Swe. B6 62
Lahoma, Okla. A3 200
Lahontan, res., Nev. D2 192
Lahore, Pak. B5 87, B5 88
Lahore Cantonment, Pak. *B5 88
Lahr, Ger. D3 60
Lahri, Pak. C2 88
Lahti, Fin. G11 63
La Huaca, Peru B1 134
La Huerta, N. Mex. E5 195
Laï, Chad D3 104
Lai Chau, Viet. A5 89
Laichow, bay, China F8 92
Laide, Scot. C3 57
Laidon, lake, Scot. D4 57
Laie, Haw. B4, f10 176
Laifeng, China J3 92
Laigle, Fr. C4 58
Laihka, Bur. B2 89
Laingsburg, Mich. F6 186
Laingsburg, S. Afr. D3 107
Lair, Ky. B5 182
Laird, Sask., Can. E2 155
Laird, Colo. A8 171
Lairg, Scot. B4 57
Laiwui, Indon. F7 90
Laiyang, China F9 92
Laiyüan, China E6 92
La Jara, Colo. D5 171
La Jara, N. Mex. A3 195
Lajas, P.R. C2 132
Lajas, mun., P.R. C2 132
Lajes, Braz. D2 137
La Jolla, pt., Calif. E2 170
Lajord, Sask., Can. G3 155
La Jose (Newburg), Pa. E4 202
Lajosmizse, Hung. B4 68
Lajoya, N. Mex. C3 195
La Joya, Peru E3 134
La Junta, Colo. D7 171
Lak, riv., Ken. A7 106
Lake, La. B6 183
Lake, Mich. E5 186
Lake, Miss. C4 188
Lake, co., Calif. C2 170
Lake, co., Colo. B4 171
Lake, co., Fla. D5 174
Lake, co., Ill. A6 178
Lake, co., Ind. B3 179
Lake, co., Mich. E5 186
Lake, co., Minn. C7 187
Lake, co., Mont. C2 190
Lake, co., Ohio A6 199
Lake, co., Oreg. E6 201
Lake, co., S. Dak. C8 204
Lake, co., Tenn. A2 205
Lake, reg., Tan. B5 106
Lake, dist., Eng. C5 55
Lake, fork, Colo. C3 171
Lake, mtn., Wyo. D6 213
Lake, range, Nev. C2 192
Lake, swamp, S.C. D8 203
Lake Alfred, Fla. D5 174
Lake Alma, Sask., Can. H3 155
Lake Andes, S. Dak. D7 204
Lake Annis, N.S., Can. E4 151
Lake Ariel, Pa. D11 202
Lake Arrowhead, Calif. E5, F3 170
Lake Arthur, La. D3 183
Lake Arthur, N. Mex. E5 195
Lake Benton, Minn. F2 187
Lake Beulah, Wis. F1 212
Lake Buena Kista, Fla. *D5 174
Lake Bluff, Ill. A6, E2 178
Lake Bonaparte, N.Y. A5 196
Lake Bronson, Minn. B2 187
Lake Brown, Austl. F2 111
Lake Bruce, Ind. B5 179
Lake Butler, Fla. B4 174
Lake Carey, Pa. C10 202
Lake Cargelligo, Austl. F6 112
Lake Carmel, N.Y. *D7 196
Lake Chance, creek, Utah F4 207
Lake Charles, La. D2 183
Lake Chelan, nat. recr. area, Wash. A5 210
Lake City, Ark. B5 169
Lake City, Calif. B3 170
Lake City, Colo. C3 171
Lake City, Fla. B4 174
Lake City, Ga. *C2 175
Lake City, Iowa B3 180
Lake City, Kans. E5 181
Lake City, Mich. D5 186
Lake City, Minn. F6 187
Lake City, Pa. B1 202
Lake City, S.C. D8 203
Lake City, S. Dak. B8 204
Lake City, Tenn. C9 205
Lake Clear Junction, N.Y. B6 196
Lake Como, Pa. C11 202
Lake Cormorant, Miss. A3 188
Lake Cowichan, B.C., Can. B8 149
Lake Crystal, Minn. F4 187
Lake Delton, Wis. E4 212
Lake Elmo, Minn. *E7 187
Lake Elmore, Vt. B3 208
Lake End, La. C2 183
Lake Entiat, res., Wash. B5 210
Lake Erie Beach, N.Y. *C1 196
Lake Forest, Ill. A6, E2 178
Lake Fork, Ill. D4 178
Lake Fork, riv., Utah C5 207
Lake Fort Gibson, res., Okla. A6 200
Lake Geneva, Wis. F5 212
Lake George, Colo. C5 171
Lake George, Mich. E6 186
Lake George, N.Y. B7 196
Lake Greeson, res., Ark. C2 169
Lake Hamilton, Fla. *D5 174
Lake Havasu City, Ariz. C1 168
Lake Helen, Fla. D5 174
Lake Hiawatha, N.J. B4 194
Lake Holloway, Fla. *D5 174
Lake Hubert, Minn. D4 187
Lake Hughes, Calif. E4 170
Lake Huntington, N.Y. D6 196
Lake in the Hills, Ill. *A5 178
Lake Itasca, Minn. C3 187
Lake Jackson, Tex. G5 206
Lake James, Ind. A7 179
Lake Katrine, N.Y. *D6 196
Lake Leelanau, Mich. D5 186
Lake Lemon, res., Ind. F5 179
Lake Lenore, Sask., Can. E3 155
Lake Lillian, Minn. F4 187
Lake Linden, Mich. A2 186
Lake Lindsey, Fla. D4 174
Lake Lotawana, Mo. *C3 189
Lake Louise, Alta., Can. D2 148
Lake Luzerne, N.Y. B7 196
Lake Madge, Sask., Can. F5 155
Lake Manawa, Iowa C2 180
Lake Mary, Fla. D5 174
Lake McDonald, Mont. B3 190
Lake Mead, nat. recreation area, Ariz., Nev. A1 168, H7 192
Lake Merwin, res., Wash. D3 210
Lake Metigoshe, N. Dak. A5 198
Lake Mills, Iowa A4 180
Lake Minchumina, Alsk. C9 167
Lake Mohawk, N.J. *A3 194
Lake Nebagamon, Wis. B2 212
Lake Norden, S. Dak. C8 204
Lake Norman, res., N.C. B3 197
Lake Odessa, Mich. F5 186
Lake of the Rivers, lake, Sask., Can. H3 155
Lake of the Woods, co., Minn. B4 187
Lake of the Woods, lake, Ont., Can., Minn. E7 153, A4 187
Lake Orion, Mich. F7 186
Lake Oswego, Oreg. B2, B4 201
Lake O' the Pines, res., Tex. C5 206
Lake Ouachita, res., Ark. C2 169
Lake Ozark, Mo. C5 189
Lake Park, Fla. F6 174
Lake Park, Ga. F3 175
Lake Park, Iowa A2 180
Lake Park, Minn. D2 187
Lake Placid, Fla. E5 174
Lake Placid, N.Y. A7, B3 196
Lake Pleasant, N.Y. B6 196
Lake Pontchartrain Causeway, La. B7 183
Lake Preston, S. Dak. C8 204
Lake Providence, La. B4 183
Lake River, Ont., Can. D9 153
Lake Ronkonkoma, N.Y. F4 172
Lake St. John East, co., Que., Can. A6 154
Lake St. John West, co., Que., Can. A5 154
Lake Shore, Fla. B5 174
Lake Shore, Minn. *D4 187
Lake Stevens, Wash. A3 210
Lake Success, N.Y. D2 196
Lake Superior, prov. park, Ont., Can. E8 153
Lake Tawakoni, res., Tex. C4 206
Lake Tomahawk, Wis. C4 212
Lake Toxaway, N.C. D3 197
Lake Traverse, Ont., Can. B6 153
Lake Tschida, dam, N. Dak. C4 198
Lake Valley, Sask., Can. G2 155
Lake View, Iowa B2 180
Lake View, Miss. E8 205
Lake View, S.C. C9 203
Lake Villa, Ill. E2 178
Lake Village, Ark. D4 169
Lake Village, Ind. B3 179
Lake Waccamaw, N.C. C5 197
Lake Wales, Fla. E5 174
Lake Wallula, Wash. C7 210
Lake Williams, N. Dak. B6 198
Lake Wilson, Minn. G3 187
Lake Winola, Pa. A8 202
Lake Worth, Fla. F6 174
Lake Worth, inlet, Fla. F6 174
Lake Worth Village, Tex. *C4 206
Lake Zurich, Ill. E2 178
Lakecreek, Oreg. E4 201
Lakefield, Ont., Can. C6 153
Lakefield, Minn. G3 187
Lakefork, Idaho E2 177
Lakehurst, N.J. C4 194
Lakeland, Fla. D5 174
Lakeland, Ga. E3 175
Lakeland Village, Calif. *F5 170
Lakemba, isl., Fiji 114
Lakemba, passage, Fiji 114
Lakemills, Wis. E5 212
Lakemont, Pa. F5 202
Lakemore, Ohio A6 199
Lakenan, Mo. B6 189
Lakeport, Calif. C2 170
Lakeshore, Miss. E4 188
Lakeside, Ariz. C6 168
Lakeside, Calif. E2, F5 170
Lakeside, Iowa B2 180
Lakeside, Nebr. B3 191
Lakeside, N.J. A4 194
Lakeside, Ohio A5 199
Lakeside, Oreg. D2 201
Lakeside, mts., Utah C3 207
Lakeside Park, Ky. A7 182
Lakesville, Md. D5 173
Laketon, Ind. C6 179
Laketown, Utah B4 207
Lakeview, Calif. F3 170
Lakeview, Idaho B2 177
Lakeview, Mich. *F5 186
Lakeview, Mich. E5 186
Lakeview, Mont. F5 190
Lakeview, Ohio B4 199
Lakeview, Oreg. E6 201
Lakeview, Tex. B2 206
Lakeview, Tex. *E6 206
Lakeview, Utah C4 207
Lakeville, Conn. B3 172
Lakeville, Ind. A5 179
Lakeville, Mass. C6 185
Lakeville, Minn. F5 187
Lakeville, N.Y. C3 196
Lakeville, Ohio *A7 199
Lakewood, Calif. *E4 170
Lakewood, Colo. B5 171
Lakewood, Maine D3 184
Lakewood, Mich. *F5 186
Lakewood, N.J. C4 194
Lakewood, N. Mex. E5 195
Lakewood, N.Y. C1 196
Lakewood, Ohio A6, B2 199
Lakewood, Tex. *E5 206
Lakewood, Wash. A3 210
Lakewood, Wis. C5 212
Lakhi, Afg. F12 86
Lakhimpur, India C8 88
Lakhpat, India F2 88
Lakhtinskiy, Sov. Un. r31 63
Lakin, Kans. E2 181
Lakoleh, Ken. A7 106
Lakota, Iowa A3 180
Lakota, N. Dak. A7 198
Laksefjord, fjord, Nor. B12 63
Lala, Manus I. 115
La Laguna, Sp. (Can. Is.) m13 65
Lalambut, cape, New Ire. I. 115
Lālī, Iran E4 86
La Libertad, Guat. B2 130
La Libertad, Sal. D3 130
La Libertad, dept., Peru C2 134
La Ligua, Chile A2 136
Lalín, Sp. A1 65
La Línea, Sp. D3 65
La Lisa, Cuba k11 131
Lalitpur, India E7 88
Lalo, pt., Tinian 114
La Loche, Sask., Can. B1 155
La Loma, N. Mex. B4 195
La Louvière, Bel. D4 59
La Luz, N. Mex. E4 195
La Machine, Fr. D5 58
La Maddalena, It. D2 67
La Madeleine, Fr. D3 59
La Madera, N. Mex. A3 195
Lama-Kara, Togo E5 103
Lamalanga (Mission), Pentecost I. 115
La Malbaie, Que., Can. B7 154
Lamaline, Newf., Can. E4 152
Lamar, Ark. B2 169
Lamar, Colo. C8 171
Lamar, Miss. A4 188
Lamar, Mo. D3 189
Lamar, Nebr. D4 191
Lamar, Okla. B5 200
Lamar, Pa. D6 202
Lamar, S.C. C7 203
Lamar, co., Ala. B1 166
Lamar, co., Ga. C2 175
Lamar, co., Miss. D4 188
Lamar, co., Tex. C5 206
Lamarche, Fr. A1 66
La Marque, Tex. G5 206
Lamartine, Que., Can. B7 154
Lamas, Peru C2 134
Lamasco, Ky. A3 182
Lamb, co., Tex. B1 206
Lamb, pt., Ambrim I. 115
Lamballe, Fr. C2 58
Lambaréné, Gabon F2 104
Lambasa, Fiji 114
Lambatip, Malekula I. 115
Lambayeque, Peru C2 134
Lambayeque, dept., Peru C2 134
Lambert, Ill. F2 178
Lambert, Miss. A3 188
Lambert, Mont. C12 190
Lambert, Okla. A3 200
Lambert, cape, New Britain I. 115
Lambert, glacier, Ant. B19 120
Lambert Lake, Maine C5 184
Lamberton, Minn. F3 187
Lambertville, Mich. *G7 186
Lambertville, N.J. C3 194
Lambeth, Ont., Can. E3 153
Lambeth, Eng. m12 55
Lambourn, Eng. C6 56
Lambrecht, Ger. D3 61
Lambro, riv., It. D5 66
Lambrook, Ark. C5 169
Lambsburg, Va. E2 209
Lambton, Que., Can. D6 154
Lambton, co., Ont., Can. E2 153
Lambtor, cape, N.W. Ter., Can. B8 142
Lambumbu, hbr., Malekula I. 115
Lamdessar Timur, Indon. G8 90
Lame Deer, Mont. E10 190
Lamego, Port. B2 65
Lamèque, N.B., Can. B5 151
La Mére et L'Enfant, mtn., Viet. F8 89
La Mesa, Calif. E2 170
La Mesa, N. Mex. E3 195
Lamesa, Tex. C2 206
Lameshur, Vir. Is. f16 132
Lamía, Grc. C4 69
La Minerve, Que., Can. C3 154
Lamlash, Scot. E3 57
Lammermuir, hills, Scot. E6 57
Lamoil, isl., Truk 114
La Moille, Ill. B4 178
Lamoille, Nev. C6 192
Lamoille, co., Vt. B3 208
Lamoille, riv., Vt. B3 208
La Moine, riv., Ill. C3 178
Lamon, bay, Phil. C6, o13 90
Lamona, Wash. B7 210
Lamoni, Iowa D4 180
Lamont, Calif. E4 170
Lamont, Alta., Can. C4 148
Lamont, Fla. B3 174
Lamont, Idaho F7 177
Lamont, Iowa B6 180
Lamont, Kans. D7 181
Lamont, Okla. A4 200
Lamont, Wash. B8 210
Lamont, Wyo. C5 213
La Monte, Mo. C4 189
La Motte, Iowa B7 180
La Motte, isl., Vt. B2 208
La Moure, N. Dak. C7 198
La Moure, co., N. Dak. C7 198
Lampa, Peru E3 134
Lampang, Thai. C3 89
Lampasas, Tex. D3 206
Lampasas, co., Tex. D3 206
Lampedusa, isl., It. G13 64
Lampertheim, Ger. D3 61
Lampeter, Wales B3 56
Lamphun, Thai. C3 89
Lampman, Sask., Can. H4 155
Lamu, Ken. B7 106
La Mure, Fr. E6 58
Lamussong, New Ire. I. 115
Lamy, N. Mex. B4, G6 195
Lanagan, Mo. E3 189
Lanai, isl., Haw. C4 176
Lanai City, Haw. C5 176
Lanaihale, Haw. C5 176
Lanak La, pass, China, India B6 87
Lanark, Ill. A4 178
Lanark, Scot. E5 57
Lanark, W. Va. D3, D7 211
Lanark, co., Ont., Can. B8 153
Lanark, co., Scot. E4 57
Lancashire, co., Eng. A5 56
Lancaster, Calif. E4 170
Lancaster, N.B., Can. D3 151
Lancaster, Ont., Can. B10 153
Lancaster, Eng. C5 55
Lancaster, Kans. C8 181
Lancaster, Ky. C5 182
Lancaster, Mass. B4 185
Lancaster, Minn. B2 187
Lancaster, Mo. A5 189
Lancaster, N.H. B3 193
Lancaster, N.Y. C2 196
Lancaster, Ohio C5 199
Lancaster, Pa. F9 202
Lancaster, S.C. B6 203
Lancaster, Tenn. C8 205
Lancaster, Tex. B5 206
Lancaster, Va. D6 209
Lancaster, Wis. F3 212
Lancaster, co., Nebr. D9 191
Lancaster, co., Pa. G9 202
Lancaster, co., S.C. B6 203
Lancaster, co., Va. D6 209
Lancaster, sound, N.W. Ter., Can. B15 142
Lancaster Mills, S.C. *B6 203
Lance, creek, Wyo. C8 213
Lance Creek, Wyo. B8 213
Lancer, Sask., Can. G1 155
Lancer, Ky. C7 182
Lanchi, China J8 92
Lanchou, China D5 91
Lanciano, It. C5 67
Lancing, Tenn. C9 205
Łańcut, Pol. C7 70
Land between the Lakes, recr. area, Ky., Tenn. B3 182, A4 205
Land O' Lakes, Wis. B4 212
Landa, N. Dak. A5 198
Landaff, N.H. B3 193
Landana, Ang. C1 106
Landau [an der Isar], Ger. E7 61
Landau [in der Pfalz], Ger. D3 61
Landeck, Aus. E5 60
Landen, Bel. D5 59
Lander, Wyo. C4 213
Lander, co., Nev. C4 192
Landerneau, Fr. C1 58
Landes, W. Va. C5 211
Landes, heath, Fr. E3 58
Landess, Ind. C6 179
Landine, bay, Loyalty Is. 115
Landing, lake, Man., Can. B3 150
Landis, Sask., Can. E1 155
Landis, N.C. B3 197
Landisburg, Pa. F7 202
Landisville, Pa. *F11 202
Landivisiau, Fr. C2 58
Lando, S.C. B5 203
Landover Hills, Md. *C4 173
Landrum, S.C. A3 203
Land's End, cape, Eng. D2 56
Landsberg, Ger. D5 60
Landshut, Ger. E7 61
Landskrona, Swe. C6 62
Landsman, creek, Colo. B8 171
Landsort, Swe. u35 63
Landusky, Mont. C8 190
Lane, Ill. C5 178
Lane, Kans. D8 181
Lane, Nev. D7 192
Lane, S.C. D8 203
Lane, S. Dak. C7 204
Lane, Tenn. A2 205
Lane, co., Kans. D3 181
Lane, co., Oreg. D4 201
Laneburg, Ark. D2 169
La Negra, Chile D1 135
Lanesboro, Iowa B3 180
Lanesboro, Mass. A1 185
Lanesboro, Minn. G7 187
Lanesboro, Pa. C10 202
Lanesville, Ind. H6 179
Lanett, Ala. C4 166
Lanfine, Alta., Can. D5 148
Lanford, S.C. B4 203
Lang, Sask., Can. H3 155
Lang Son, Viet. B7 89
Langå, Den. B3 62
Langa Langa, Zaire B2 106
Langadhás, Grc. B4 69
Langak, lake, China B8 88
Langbank, Sask., Can. G4 155
Langchung, China I2 92
Langdale, Ala. C4 166
Langdale, dam, Ala., Ga. D1 175
Langdon, Alta., Can. D4 148
Langdon, Iowa A2 180
Langdon, Kans. E5 181
Langdon, Mo. A2 189
Langdon, N.H. D2 193
Langdon, N. Dak. A7 198
L'Ange Gardien, Que., Can. C9 154
Langeac, Fr. E5 58
Langeland, isl., Den. D4 62
Langelands Belt, strait, Den. D4 62
Langell, val., Oreg. E5 201
Langeloth, Pa. F1 202
Langen, Ger. D3 61
Langenau, Ger. E5 61
Langenburg, Sask., Can. G5 155
Langensalza, Ger. B5 61
Langenselbold, Ger. C4 61
Langenthal, Switz. B3 66
Langenzenn, Ger. D5 61
Langeoog, Ger. A7 59
Langeoog, isl., Ger. B3 60
Langesund, Nor. H3, p27 63
Langevin, Que., Can. C7 154
Langford, B.C., Can. B9 149
Langford, S. Dak. B8 204
Långhalsen, lake, Swe. u34 63
Langham, Sask., Can. E2 155
Länghem, Swe. A7 62
Langholm, Scot. E5 57

INDEX KEY Each place listed in **Bold-faced Type** has its population listed in the Population tables, pages 230 to 280.
Each country, shown in CAPITAL LETTERS, has its population listed in the World Political Information Table, pages 6 to 10.
* Does not appear on map; key shows general location.

Langhorne, Pa....F12 **202**
Långhundra, Swe....t36 **63**
Langjökull, glacier, Ice....n22 **63**
Langkawi, isl., Mala....I3 **89**
Langkha Tuk, mtn., Thai...H3 **89**
Langlade, co., Wis....C4 **212**
Langley, Ark....C2 **169**
Langley, B.C., Can....A10 **149**
Langley, Ky....C7 **182**
Langley, Okla....A6 **200**
Langley, S.C....D4 **203**
Langley, Wash....A3 **210**
Langley Park, Md....C1 **173**
Langleyville, Ill....D4 **178**
Langlois, Oreg....E2 **201**
Langnau in Emmental, Switz....C3 **66**
Langogne, Fr....E5 **58**
Langon, Fr....E3 **58**
Langöy, isl., Nor....C6 **63**
Langreo, Sp....A3 **65**
Langres, Fr....D6 **58**
Langres, plat., Fr....D6 **58**
Langruth, Man., Can....D2 **150**
Langsa, Indon....E1, m11 **90**
Langstaff, Ont., Can....E6 **153**
Langston, Ala....A3 **166**
Langston, Okla....B4 **200**
Langton, Ont., Can....E4 **153**
Langtry, Tex....E2 **206**
Languedoc, former prov., Fr....F5 **58**
L'Anguille, riv., Ark....B5 **169**
Lanham, Md....C4 **173**
Lanham, Nebr....D9 **191**
Lanhsi, China....C3 **93**
Lanier, co., Ga....E3 **175**
Lanigan, Sask., Can....F3 **155**
Lanigan, creek, Sask., Can..F3 **155**
Lanín, vol., Arg....B2 **136**
Lankin, N. Dak....A8 **198**
Lanklaar, Bel....C5 **59**
Lannion, Fr....C2 **58**
Lannon, Wis....E1 **212**
L'Annonciation, Que., Can....C3 **154**
Lanoka Harbor, N.J....D4 **194**
Lanoraie, Que., Can....D4 **154**
Lansdale, Pa....F11 **202**
Lansdowne, Ont., Can....C8 **153**
Lansdowne, Md....B4, C2 **173**
Lansdowne, Pa....B11, G11 **202**
L'Anse, Mich....B2 **186**
L'Anse, Indian res., Mich..B2 **186**
L'Anse-au-Clair, Newf., Can....C3 **152**
L'Anse-au-Loup, Newf., Can....C3 **152**
L'Anse-au-Meadow, Newf., Can....C4 **152**
L'Anse-St. Jean, Que., Can....A7 **154**
Lansford, N. Dak....A4 **198**
Lansford, Pa....E10 **202**
Lansing, Ill....B6, F3 **178**
Lansing, Iowa....A6 **180**
Lansing, Kans....B8 **181**
Lansing, Mich....F6 **186**
Lansing, N.C....A2 **197**
Lansing, Ohio....B1 **211**
Lansing, W. Va....D7 **211**
Lanslebourg, Fr....D2 **66**
Lanta, isl., Thai....I3 **89**
Lantana, Fla....F6 **174**
Lantern, hill, Conn....D9 **172**
Lantry, S. Dak....C4 **204**
Lantsang, China....G4 **91**
Lantz, W. Va....C4 **211**
Lanús, Arg....*g7 **136**
Lanusei, It....E2 **67**
Lanuvio, It....h9 **67**
Lanzarote, isl., Sp. (Can. Is)....m15 **65**
Lao Kay, Viet....A5 **89**
Laoag, Phil....B6 **90**
Laon, Fr....C5 **58**
Laona, Wis....C5 **212**
La Oroya, Peru....D2 **134**
LAOS, country, Asia....C5 **89**
Laotto, Ind....B7 **179**
Lap, isl., Truk.... **114**
Lapa, Braz....D3 **137**
Lapai, Dyaul I.... **115**
La Palma, Ariz....E4 **168**
La Palma, Pan....F8 **130**
La Palma, Sp....D2 **65**
La Pampa, prov., Arg....B3 **136**
La Paragua, Ven....B5 **133**
La Passe, Ont., Can....B8 **153**
La Patrie, Que., Can....D6 **154**
La Paz, Arg....A5 **136**
La Paz, Arg....A3 **136**
La Paz, Bol....C2 **135**
La Paz, Col....A3 **133**
La Paz, Hond....C4 **130**
Lapaz, Ind....B5 **179**
La Paz, Mex....C2 **129**
La Paz, Mex....C4 **129**
La Paz, dept., Bol....C2 **135**
La Pedrera Col....D4 **133**
Lapeer, Mich....E7 **186**
Lapeer, co., Mich....E7 **186**
Lapel, Ind....D6 **179**
La Pica, P.R....C3 **132**
La Piedad, Mex....m12 **129**
Lapine, Ala....D3 **166**
La Pine, Oreg....D5 **201**
Laplace, La....B6 **183**
Lapland, reg., Eur....C12 **63**
La Plant, S. Dak....B5 **204**
La Plata: c. 1790.... **126**
La Plata, Arg....A5, g8 **136**
La Plata, Col....C2 **133**
La Plata, Md....C4 **173**
La Plata, Mo....A5 **189**
Laplata, N. Mex....A1 **195**
La Plata, co., Colo....D3 **171**
La Plata, mts., Colo....D2 **171**
La Plata, peak, Colo....B4 **171**
La Plata, riv., Arg....B5 **136**
La Platte, Nebr....E3 **191**
La Platte. riv. Vt....C2 **208**
La Playa, P.R....B2 **132**
La Plonge, lake, Sask., Can...B2 **155**
La Pobla de Lillet, Sp....A6 **65**
La Pocatière, Que., Can....B7 **154**
La Poile, bay, Newf., Can...E2 **152**
Lapointe, Que., Can....B8 **154**
Lapoint, Utah....C6 **207**
La Pointe, Wis....B3 **212**
La Pola, Sp....A3 **65**
La Porte, Calif....C3 **170**
Laporte, Sask., Can....F1 **155**
Laporte, Colo....A5 **171**
La Porte, Ind....A4 **179**
Laporte, Minn....C4 **187**
Laporte, Pa....D9 **202**
La Porte, Tex....F5 **206**
La Porte, co., Ind....A4 **179**
La Porte City, Iowa....B5 **180**
Läppe, Swe....t33 **63**
Lappeenranta, Fin....G13 **63**
La Prairie, Que., Can....D4 **154**
La Prairie, Minn....C5 **187**
Laprairie, co., Que., Can..D4 **154**
Laprida, Arg....B4 **136**
La Providence, Que., Can....*D5 **154**
La Pryor, Tex....E3 **206**
Lâpseki, Tur....B6 **85**
Laptev, sea, Sov. Un....B15 **71**
Łapy, Pol....C7 **65**
La Puebla, Sp....C7 **65**
La Puebla de Montalbán, Sp....C3 **65**
La Puente, Calif....*E4 **170**
La Puente, N. Mex....A3 **195**
La Purísima, Mex....B2 **129**
La Push, Wash....B1 **210**
Lapwai, Idaho....C2 **177**
Laqiya Arba'in (Well), Sud....B2 **105**
La Quiaca, Arg....D2 **135**
L'Aquila, It....C4 **67**
Lār, Iran....H7 **86**
Lara, state, Ven....A3 **133**
Larache, Mor....G3 **64**, B3 **102**
Larak, isl., Iran....H8 **86**
Laramie, Wyo....D7 **213**
Laramie, co., Wyo....D8 **213**
Laramie, basin, Wyo....C6 **213**
Laramie, mts., Colo., Wyo....C7 **213**
Laramie, peak, Wyo....C7 **213**
Laramie, riv., Wyo....D7 **213**
La Rangu, Sud....E2 **105**
Laranjeiras, Braz....D3 **138**
Laranjeiras do Sul, Braz...D2 **137**
Larantuka, Indon....G6 **90**
Larch, riv., Que., Can....A12 **154**
Larche, pass, Fr., It....E2 **66**
Larchmont, N.Y....D2 **196**
Larchwood, Iowa....A1 **180**
Lardeau, B.C., Can....D9 **149**
Lardo, Idaho....E2 **177**
L'Ardoise, N.S., Can....D9 **151**
Laredo, Mo....A4 **189**
Laredo, Mont....B7 **190**
Laredo, Sp....A4 **65**
Laredo, Tex....F3 **206**
Laredo, sound, B.C., Can...C3 **149**
La Réole, Fr....E3 **58**
Lares, P.R....B3 **132**
Lares, mun., P.R....B3 **132**
Largeau, Chad....B3 **104**
Largentière, Fr....E6 **58**
Largo, Fla....E1, E4 **174**
Largo, canyon, N. Mex....A2 **195**
Largo, key, Fla....G6 **174**
Largs, Scot....E4 **57**
Lariat, Colo....D4 **171**
Lariat, Tex....B1 **206**
La Ricamarie, Fr....E6 **58**
Larimer, co., Colo....A5 **171**
Larimore, N. Dak....B8 **198**
Larino, It....D5 **67**
La Rioja, Arg....E2 **135**
La Rioja, Cuba....E5 **131**
La Rioja, prov., Arg....E2 **135**
Lárisa, Grc....C4 **69**
La Riviere, Man., Can....E2 **150**
Lark, N. Dak....C4 **198**
Lark Harbour, Newf., Can....D2 **152**
Lārkāna, Pak....D2 **88**
Larkinburg, Kans....A7 **181**
Larkinsville, Ala....A3 **166**
Larkspur, Calif....B5 **170**
Larkspur, Colo....B6 **171**
Larksville, Pa....B8 **202**
Larnaca, Cyp....E9 **85**
Larne, N. Ire....C4 **55**
Larned, Kans....D4 **181**
La Robla, Sp....A3 **65**
La Roche-sur-Foron, Fr....C2 **66**
La Roche-sur-Yon, Fr....D3 **58**
La Rochelle, Fr....D3 **58**
La Roda, Sp....C4 **65**
La Romana, Dom. Rep....F9 **131**
La Ronge, Sask., Can....B3 **155**
La Ronge, lake, Sask., Can..B3 **155**
Larose, La....E5 **183**
Larrabee, Iowa....B2 **180**
Larrabee, Maine....D5 **184**
Larrys River, N.S., Can....D8 **151**
Larsen, ice shelf, Ant....C7 **120**
Larsen Bay, Alsk....D9 **167**
Larslan, Mont....B10 **190**
Larsmont, Minn....D7 **187**
Larson, N. Dak....B3 **198**
Larto, La....C4 **183**
La Rue, Ohio....B4 **199**
Larue, co., Ky....C4 **182**
Laruns, Fr....F3 **58**
Larvik, Nor....H4, p28 **63**
Larwill, Ind....B6 **179**
La Sal, Utah....E6 **207**
La Sal, mts., Utah....E6 **207**
La Salle, Man., Can....E3 **150**
La Salle, Que., Can....D9 **154**
La Salle, Colo....A6 **171**
La Salle, Ill....B4 **178**
La Salle, Minn....F4 **187**
La Salle, co., Ill....B5 **178**
La Salle, co., Tex....E3 **206**
La Salle, par., La....C3 **183**
Las Animas, Colo....C7 **171**
Las Animas, co., Colo....D6 **171**
Las Anod, Som....D6 **105**
Las Arenas, P.R....C2 **132**
La Sarre, Que., Can....E9 **153**
Lasauses, Colo....D5 **171**
Lasberg, Aus....E9 **61**
Las Cabras, Chile....A2 **136**
Lascahobas, Hai....F8 **131**
Lascano, Ur....E2 **137**
Lascassas, Tenn....B5 **205**
L'Ascension, Que., Can....A6 **154**
La Scie, Newf., Can....D4 **152**
Las Coloradas, Arg....B2 **136**
Las Cruces, N. Mex....E3 **195**
La Serena, Chile....E1 **135**
La Seyne [-sur-Mer], Fr....F6 **58**
Las Flores, Arg....B5 **136**
Las Flores, P.R....C5 **132**
Lashburn, Sask., Can....D1 **155**
Lashio, Bur....D10 **87**
La Sierra, Calif....F3 **170**
Łask, Pol....C5 **70**
Las Lajas, Arg....B2 **136**
Las Lomitas, Arg....D3 **135**
Las Mareas, P.R....D6 **132**
Las Marías, P.R....B3 **132**
Las Marías, mun., P.R....C2 **132**
Las Matas [de Farfán], Dom. Rep....F8 **131**
Las Nutrias, N. Mex....C3 **195**
La Solana, Sp....C4 **65**
Las Palmas, Pan....F7 **130**
Las Palmas, P.R....D2 **132**
Las Palmas, P.R....D6 **132**
Las Palmas [de Gran Canaria], Sp. (Can. Is.)....D1 **102**
Las Palomas, N. Mex....D2 **195**
La Spezia, It....B2 **67**
Las Piedras, P.R....D6 **132**
Las Piedras, Ur....E1 **137**
Las Piedras, mun., P.R....C7 **132**
Las Piñas, P.R....B7 **132**
Las Pipinas, Arg....B5 **136**
Las Plumas, Arg....C3 **136**
Las Rosas, Arg....A4 **136**
Las Rozas de Madrid, Sp..p17 **65**
Lassen, co., Calif....B3 **170**
Lassen, peak, Calif....B3 **170**
Lassen Volcanic, nat. park, Calif....B3 **170**
Lasso, mtn., Tinian.... **114**
L'Assomption, Que., Can..D4 **154**
L'Assomption, co., Que., Can....D4 **154**
Last Chance, creek, Utah...F4 **207**
Last Mountain, lake, Sask., Can....F3 **155**
Las Tablas, N. Mex....A3 **195**
Las Tablas, Pan....G7 **130**
Las Termas, Arg....E3 **135**
Lastoursville, Gabon....F2 **104**
Lastrup, Ger....B7 **59**
Lastrup, Minn....D4 **187**
Las Varillas, Arg....A4 **136**
Las Vegas, Nev....G6 **192**
Las Vegas (city), N. Mex..B4 **195**
Las Vegas (town), N. Mex....*B4 **195**
Las Vegas, P.R....C2 **132**
Las Vigas, Mex....n15 **129**
Las Villas, prov., Cuba....D3 **131**
La Tabatière, Que., Can....C2 **152**
Latacunga, Ec....B2 **134**
La Tagua, Col....D3 **133**
Latah, Wash....B8 **210**
Latah, co., Idaho....C2 **177**
Latah, creek, Wash....B8 **210**
Latakia (Al Lādhiqīyah), Syr....E10 **85**
Laterrière, Que., Can....A6 **154**
La Teste-de-Buch, Fr....E3 **58**
Latexo, Tex....D5 **206**
Latham, Ala....D2 **166**
Latham, Ill....D4 **178**
Latham, Kans....E7 **181**
Latheron, Scot....B5 **57**
Lathrop, Calif....B6 **170**
Lathrop, Mich....*B3 **186**
Lathrop, Mo....B3 **189**
Lathrop Wells, Nev....G5 **192**
Lathrup Village, Mich....*A7 **186**
Latimer, Iowa....B4 **180**
Latimer, Kans....D7 **181**
Latimer, co., Okla....C6 **200**
Latin America: c. 1790.... **126**
after independence.... **127**
Latina, It....D4, k9 **67**
Latium, reg., It....C4 **67**
La Toma, Ec....B2 **134**
Laton, Calif....D4 **170**
Latonia Lakes, Ky....*A5 **182**
Latour, Mo....C3 **189**
La Tour-du-Pin, Fr....E6 **58**
La Tremblade, Fr....E3 **58**
Latrobe, Pa....F3 **202**
Latrūn, Jordan....C6, h10 **84**
Latta, S.C....C9 **203**
Lattimer Mines, Pa....E10 **202**
Lattimore, N.C....B2 **197**
Lattingtown, N.Y....*F2 **172**
Latty, Ohio....A3 **199**
La Tuque, Que., Can....B5 **154**
Latur, India....H6 **88**
Latvia: in 1940.... **53**
after World War II.... **54**
Latvia (S.S.R.), rep., Sov. Un....D5 **71**
Lau, New Britain I.... **115**
Lau, Nig....E7 **103**
Lau, is., Fiji.... **114**
Lauchhammer, Ger....B8 **61**
Laud, Ind....B7 **179**
Lauda, Ger....D4 **61**
Lauder, Man., Can....E1 **150**
Lauder, Scot....E6 **57**
Lauderdale, Minn....E7 **187**
Lauderdale, Miss....C5 **188**
Lauderdale, co., Ala....A2 **166**
Lauderdale, co., Miss....C5 **188**
Lauderdale, co., Tenn....B2 **205**
Lauderdale-by-the-Sea, Fla....*F6 **174**
Lauenburg, Ger....E4 **62**
Lauf, Ger....D6 **61**
Laufen, Ger....B8 **66**
Lauffen, Ger....D4 **61**
Laughery, creek, Ind....F7 **179**
Laughlin, peak, N. Mex....A5 **195**
Laughlintown, Pa....F3 **202**
Lauingen, Ger....E5 **61**
Laulau, Saipan.... **114**
Laulii, Am. Sam.... **114**
Launceston, Austl....o15 **111**
Launceston, Eng....D3 **56**
La Unión, Arg....B3 **136**
La Unión, Chile....C2 **136**
La Unión, Col....C2 **133**
La Unión, Mex....D4, o13 **129**
La Union, N. Mex....F3 **195**
La Unión, Peru....C2 **134**
La Unión, Sal....D4 **130**
La Unión, Sp....D5 **65**
Laupahoehoe, Haw....D6 **176**
Laupheim, Ger....D4 **60**
Laura, Austl....C7 **111**
Laura, Sask., Can....F2 **155**
Laura, Ohio....C3 **199**
Laurbjerg, Den....B3 **62**
Laurel, Ont., Can....D4 **153**
Laurel, Del....C6 **173**
Laurel, Fla....E4 **174**
Laurel, Ind....E7 **179**
Laurel, Iowa....C5 **180**
Laurel, Md....B4 **173**
Laurel, Miss....D4 **188**
Laurel, Mont....E8 **190**
Laurel, Nebr....B8 **191**
Laurel, N.Y....F6 **172**
Laurel, Va....D5 **209**
Laruel, Wash....D4 **210**
Laurel, co., Ky....C5 **182**
Laurel, creek, W. Va....D6 **211**
Laurel, fork, W. Va....C5 **211**
Laurel, mtn., W. Va....B5 **211**
Laurel, riv., Del....C6 **173**
Laurel, riv., Ky....D5 **182**
Laurel Bay, S. Car....G6 **203**
Laurel Bloomery, Tenn...C12 **205**
Laurel Fork, Va....E2 **209**
Laurel Hill, Fla....G2 **174**
Laurel Hill, N.C....C4 **197**
Laurel Hollow, N.Y....*E7 **196**
Laurel Park, N.C....*D3 **197**
Laurel Run, Pa....B8 **202**
Laurel Springs, N.J....*D3 **194**
Laureldale, N.J....D3 **194**
Laureldale, Pa....F10 **202**
Laureles, Ur....E1 **137**
Laurelton, Pa....E7 **202**
Laurelville, Ohio....C5 **199**
Laurelwood Academy, Oreg....B1 **201**
Laurence Harbor, N.J....C4 **194**
Laurencekirk, Scot....D6 **57**
Laurens, Iowa....B3 **180**
Laurens, S.C....B3 **203**
Laurens, co., Ga....D4 **175**
Laurens, co., S.C....C4 **203**
Laurentides, Que., Can....D4 **154**
Laurentides, prov. park, Que., Can....B6 **154**
Lauria Inferiore, It....D5 **67**
Laurie, isl., Atl. O....C8 **120**
Laurie, lake, Man., Can....A1 **150**
Laurie, riv., Man., Can....A1 **150**
Laurier, Man., Can....D2 **150**
Laurierville, Que., Can....C6 **154**
Laurin, Mont....E4 **190**
Laurinburg, N.C....C4 **197**
Laurium, Mich....A2 **186**
Laurot, is., Indon....F5 **90**
Lausanne, Switz....C2 **66**
Lauscha, Ger....C6 **61**
Lausitzer, mts., Czech., Ger....C9 **61**
Laut, isl., Indon....F5 **90**
Lautaro, Chile....B2 **136**
Lauterbach, Ger....C4 **61**
Lauterecken, Ger....D2 **61**
Lauthala, is., Fiji.... **114**
Lauzon, Que., Can....C6, C9 **154**
Lauzon, lake, Ont., Can....B8 **186**
Lava, flow, N. Mex....B2 **195**
Lava Bed, Idaho....F4, F5, F6 **177**
Lava Beds, Nev....C3 **192**
Lava Beds, nat. mon., Calif..B3 **170**
Lava Hot Springs, Idaho..G6 **177**
Lavaca, Ark....C1 **166**
Lavaca, Ark....B1 **169**
Lavaca, co., Tex....E4 **206**
Laval, Que., Can....D4 **154**
Laval, Fr....C3 **58**
Laval, co., Que., Can....*D4 **154**
Laval-des-Rapides, Que., Can....*D4 **154**
Lavalle, Arg....A3 **136**
La Valle, Wis....E3 **212**
Lavallette, N.J....D4 **194**
Lavalley, Colo....D5 **171**
Lavaltrie, Que., Can....D4 **154**
Lavant, riv., Aus....E7 **60**
Lavant Station, Ont., Can..B8 **153**
Lavaur, Fr....F4 **58**
Lavaveix-les-Mines, Fr....D5 **58**
Laveen, Ariz....G2 **168**
La Vega, Dom. Rep....F8 **131**
La Vega, Ven....*A4 **133**
La Vela, Ven....A4 **133**
Lavelanet, Fr....F4 **58**
Lavello, It....D5 **67**
La Vérendrye, prov. park, Que., Can....B2 **154**
La Vergne, Tenn....A5, E9 **205**
La Verkin, Utah....F2 **207**
La Verne, Calif....F3 **170**
Laverne, Okla....A2 **200**
La Vernia, Tex....B4, E3 **206**
Laverton, Austl....E3 **111**
La Veta, Colo....D5 **171**
Laviana, Sp....A3 **65**
La Victoria, Ven....A4 **133**
Lavieille, lake, Ont., Can....B6 **153**
La Villa, Tex....*F4 **206**
Lavina, Mont....D8 **190**
Lavinia, Tenn....B3 **205**
La Vista, Nebr....D3 **191**
Lavon, Tex....A6 **206**
Lavon, res., Tex....A6 **201**
Lavongai, New Hanover I.... **115**
Lavonia, Ga....B3 **175**
Lavoy, Alta., Can....C5 **148**
Lavras, Braz....C3 **137**
Lavras da Mangabeira, Braz....C3 **138**
Lavras do Sul, Braz....E2 **137**
Lávrion, Grc....D5 **69**
Lawai, Haw....B2 **176**
Lawen, Oreg....D8 **201**
Lawers, mtn., Scot....D4 **57**
Lawford, lake, Man., Can..B3 **150**
Lawit, mtn., Mala....J5 **89**
Lawler, Iowa....A5 **180**
Lawler, Minn....D5 **187**
Lawn, Newf., Can....E4 **152**
Lawn, Pa....F8 **202**
Lawn, Tex....C3 **206**
Lawndale, Calif....*F4 **170**
Lawndale, Minn....D2 **187**
Lawndale, N.C....B2 **197**
Lawnside, N.J....*D2 **194**
Lawogan, New Ire. I.... **115**
Lawra, Ghana....D4 **103**
Lawrence, Ind....E5, H8 **179**
Lawrence, Kans....B7, D8 **181**
Lawrence, Mass....A5 **185**
Lawrence, Mich....F4 **186**
Lawrence, Miss....C4 **188**
Lawrence, Nebr....D7 **191**
Lawrence, N.Y....G2 **172**
Lawrence, N.Z....P12 **112**
Lawrence, Okla....C5 **200**
Lawrence, Pa....F1 **202**
Lawrence, co., Ala....A2 **166**
Lawrence, co., Ark....A4 **169**
Lawrence, co., Ill....E6 **178**
Lawrence, co., Ind....G4 **179**
Lawrence, co., Ky....B7 **182**
Lawrence, co., Miss....D3 **188**
Lawrence, co., Mo....D4 **189**
Lawrence, co., Ohio....D5 **199**
Lawrence, co., Pa....D1 **202**
Lawrence, co., S. Dak....C2 **204**
Lawrence, co., Tenn....B4 **205**
Lawrence, lake, Ont., Can..A5 **187**
Lawrence Park, Pa....*B1 **202**
Lawrence Station, N.B., Can....D2 **151**
Lawrenceburg, Ind....F8 **179**
Lawrenceburg, Ky....B5 **182**
Lawrenceburg, Tenn....B4 **205**
Lawrenceport, Ind....G5 **179**
Lawrencetown, N.S., Can..E4 **151**
Lawrenceville, Que., Can..D5 **154**
Lawrenceville, Ga....A6, C3 **175**
Lawrenceville, Ill....E6 **178**
Lawrenceville, N.J....C3 **194**
Lawrenceville, N.Y....A2 **196**
Lawrenceville, Pa....C7 **202**
Lawrenceville, Va....E5 **209**
Laws, Calif....D4 **170**
Lawshe, Ohio....D4 **199**
Lawson, Ark....D3 **169**
Lawson, Sask., Can....G2 **155**
Lawson, Mo....B3 **189**
Lawsonville, N.C....A3 **197**
Lawtell, La....D3 **183**
Lawtey, Fla....B4 **174**
Lawton, Cuba....h12 **131**
Lawton, Iowa....B1 **180**
Lawton, Ky....B6 **182**
Lawton, Mich....F5 **186**
Lawton, N. Dak....A7 **198**
Lawton, Okla....C3 **200**
Lawton, W. Va....D4, D7 **211**
Lawyersville, N.Y....C6 **196**
Laxford, bay, Scot....B3 **57**
Lay, Colo....A3 **171**
Lay, cape, Viet....D7 **89**
Lay, dam, Ala....C3 **166**
Lay, lake, Ala....C3 **166**
Layland, W. Va....D7 **211**
Layman, Va....D2 **209**
Laysan, isl., Haw....k13 **176**
Layton, Utah....B4 **207**
Laytonsville, Md....B3 **173**
Lazdijai, Sov. Un....A7 **70**
Lazear, Colo....C3 **171**
Lazy Lake, Fla....*F6 **174**
Lea, co., N. Mex....D6 **195**
Leach, Okla....A7 **200**
Leachville, Ark....B5 **169**
Leacross, Sask., Can....D5 **155**
Lead, S. Dak....C2 **204**
Lead, hill, Mo....D5 **189**
Lead, mtn., Maine....D4 **184**
Lead Hill, Ark....A3 **169**
Lead Mountain, ponds, Maine....D4 **184**
Leadbetter, pt., Wash....C1 **210**
Leader, Sask., Can....G1 **155**
Leader, riv., Scot....E6 **57**
Leadhills, Scot....E5 **57**
Leadington, Mo....*D7 **189**
Leadore, Idaho....E5 **177**
Leadpoint, Wash....A8 **210**
Leadville, Colo....B4 **171**
Leadwood, Mo....D7 **189**
Leaf, Miss....D5 **188**
Leaf, lake, Sask., Can....D4 **155**
Leaf, riv., Miss....D4 **188**
Leaf River, Ill....A4 **178**
League City, Tex....*E5 **206**
Leake, co., Miss....C4 **188**
Leakesville, Miss....D5 **188**
Leakey, Tex....E3 **206**
Leaksville, N.C....A4 **197**
Leal, N. Dak....B7 **198**
Lealman, Fla....E2 **174**
Leamington, Ont., Can....E2 **153**
Leamington, Eng....B6 **56**
Leamington, Utah....D3 **207**
Leapwood, Tenn....B3 **205**
Learned, Miss....C3 **188**
Leary, Ga....E2 **175**
Leasburg, Mo....C6 **189**
Leasburg, N.C....A4 **197**
Leaside, Ont., Can....E6 **153**
Leask, Sask., Can....E2 **155**
Leatherwood, Ky....C6 **182**
Leatherwood, creek, W. Va..C7 **211**
Leavenworth, Ind....H5 **179**
Leavenworth, Kans....B8, C9 **181**
Leavenworth, Wash....B5 **210**
Leavenworth, co., Kans....C8 **181**
Leavittsburg, Ohio....A7 **199**
Leawood, Kans....D9 **181**
Łeba, Pol....A4 **70**
Lebam, Wash....C2 **210**
Lebanon, Conn....C8 **172**
Lebanon, Del....B6 **173**
Lebanon, Ill....E4 **178**
Lebanon, Ind....D5 **179**
Lebanon, Kans....C5 **181**
Lebanon, Ky....C4 **182**
Lebanon, Mo....D5 **189**
Lebanon, Nebr....D5 **191**
Lebanon, N.H....C2 **193**
Lebanon, N.J....B3 **194**
Lebanon, Ohio....C3 **199**
Lebanon, Okla....D5 **200**
Lebanon, Oreg....C4, D2 **201**
Lebanon, Pa....F9 **202**
Lebanon, S. Dak....B6 **204**
Lebanon, Tenn....A5 **205**
Lebanon, Va....B3 **209**
LEBANON, country, Asia..E10 **85**
Lebanon, co., Pa....F9 **202**
Lebanon Junction, Ky....C4 **182**
Lebec, Calif....E4 **170**
Lebedin, Sov. Un....F10 **72**
Lebedyan, Sov. Un....E12 **72**
Le Blanc, Fr....D4 **58**
Le Blanc-Mesnil, Fr....g10 **58**
Lebo, Zaire....A3 **106**
Lebo, Kans....D8 **181**
Lebo, Mont....D6 **190**
Lębork, Pol....A4 **70**
Le Bourg-d'Oisans, Fr....D2 **66**
Le Bourget, Fr....g10 **58**
Le Bouscat, Fr....E3 **58**
Lebret, Sask., Can....G4 **155**
Lebrija, Sp....D2 **65**
Lebu, Chile....B2 **136**
Lebyazhye, Sov. Un....B7 **73**
Le Cateau, Fr....B5 **58**
Lecce, It....D7 **67**
Lecco, It....B2 **67**
Le Center, Minn....F5 **187**
Lech, riv., Ger....E5 **61**
Le Chambon-Feugerolles, Fr....E6 **58**
Le Château, Fr....E3 **58**
Lechbruck, Ger....B6 **66**
Le Chesnay, Fr....g9 **58**
Le Chesne, Fr....E4 **59**
Leck, Ger....D2 **62**
Le Claire, Iowa....C7, D7 **180**
Leclercville, Que., Can....C6 **154**
Lecompte, La....C3 **183**
Lecompton, Kans....B7, C8 **181**
Léconi, Gabon....F2 **104**
Le Conte, mtn., Tenn....D10 **205**
Le Coteau, Fr....D6 **58**
Le Creusot, Fr....D6 **58**
Le Croisic, Fr....D2 **58**
Le Crotoy, Fr....D9 **56**
Lectoure, Fr....F4 **58**
Łeczyca, Pol....B5 **70**
Ledbetter, N.C....C4 **197**
Ledbury, Eng....B5 **56**
Ledčice, Czech....n17 **70**
Ledeberg, Bel....C3 **59**
Ledesma, Arg....D3 **135**
Ledesma, Sp....B3 **65**
Ledford, Ill....F5 **178**
Ledger, Mont....B5 **190**
Ledgewood, N.J....B3 **194**
Ledo, India....C10 **87**
Ledoux, N. Mex....B4 **195**
Leduc, Alta., Can....C4 **148**
Leduck, isl., Vir. Is....f16 **132**
Ledyard, Conn....D8 **172**
Ledyard, Iowa....A3 **180**
Lee, Fla....B3 **174**
Lee, Ill....B5 **178**
Lee, Maine....C4 **184**
Lee, Mass....B1 **185**
Lee, Nev....C6 **192**
Lee, N.H....D4 **193**
Lee, Tenn....D8 **205**
Lee, co., Ala....C4 **166**

INDEX KEY Each place listed in **Bold-faced Type** has its population listed in the Population tables, pages 230 to 280.
Each country, shown in CAPITAL LETTERS, has its population listed in the World Political Information Table, pages 6 to 10
* Does not appear on map; key shows general location.

Lee, co., Ark. C5 169
Lee, co., Fla. F5 174
Lee, co., Ga. E2 175
Lee, co., Ill. B4 178
Lee, co., Iowa D6 180
Lee, co., Ky. C6 182
Lee, co., Miss. A5 188
Lee, co., N.C. B4 197
Lee, co., S.C. C7 203
Lee, co., Tex. D4 206
Lee, co., Va. B1 209
Lee, creek, Ark., Okla. B1 169, B7 200
Lee, lake, Miss. B2 188
Lee, riv., Ire. E2 55
Lee Center, Ill. B4 178
Lee Park, Pa. B8 202
Lee Pope, Ga. D3 175
Lee Vining, Calif. D4 170
Leech, lake, Sask., Can. F4 155
Leech, lake, Minn. C4 187
Leechburg, Pa. E2 202
Leechville, N.C. B7 197
Leedey, Okla. B2 200
Leeds, Ala. B3, E5 166
Leeds, Eng. A6 56
Leeds, Mass. B2 185
Leeds, N. Dak. A6 198
Leeds, S.C. B5 203
Leeds, Utah F2 207
Leeds, co., Ont., Can. C8 153
Leeds Point, N.J. E4 194
Leeds Village, Que., Can. C6 154
Leedy, Miss. A5 188
Leek, Eng. A5 56
Leelanau, co., Mich. D5 186
Leelanau, lake, Mich. C5 186
Leeper, Mo. D7 189
Leeper, Pa. D3 202
Leer, Ger. B3 60
Lee's Summit, Mo. C3, E2 189
Leesburg, Ala. A4 166
Leesburg, Fla. D5 174
Leesburg, Ga. E2 175
Leesburg, Ind. B6 179
Leesburg, Miss. C4 188
Leesburg, N.J. E3 194
Leesburg, Ohio C4 199
Leesburg, Va. B5 209
Leesport, Pa. *F9 202
Leesville, Ind. G5 179
Leesville, La. C2 183
Leesville, Ohio B6 199
Leesville, S.C. D4 203
Leesville, Tex. B4, E4 206
Leesville, lake, Va. D3 209
Leetes Island, Conn. D6 172
Leeton, Mo. C4 189
Leetonia, Ohio B7 199
Leetsdale, Pa. A5 202
Leeuwarden, Neth. A5 59
Leeuwin, cape, Austl. F2 110
Leeville, La. E5 183
Leeward Islands, see Antigua, Montserrat, St. Kitts-Nevis-Anguilla, and Virgin Is. (Br.), Br. deps., N.A.
Lefebvre, Que., Can. B8 154
Le Ferriere, It. h9 67
Lefevre, pt., Lifou I. 115
Leflore, Okla. C7 200
Leflore, co., Miss. B3 188
Le Flore, co., Okla. C7 200
Lefor, N. Dak. C3 198
Lefors, Tex. B2 206
Le François, Mart. o16 131
Lefroy, Ont., Can. C5 153
Lefroy, lake, Austl. F3 110
Legal, Alta., Can. C4 148
Leganés, Sp. p17 65
Legau, Ger. E5 60
Legazpi, Phil. C6 90
Leghorn (Livorno), It. C3 67
Legion, Tex. *E3 206
Legnago, It. D7 66
Legnano, It. B2 67
Legnica, Pol. C4 70
Le Gore, Md. A3 173
Le Grand, Calif. D3 170
Le Grand, Iowa B5 180
Leh, India B6 87
Le Havre, Fr. C4 58
Lehi, Utah C4 207
Lehigh, Iowa B3 180
Lehigh, Kans. D6 181
Lehigh, Okla. C5 200
Lehigh, co., Pa. E10 202
Lehigh Acres, Fla. F5 174
Lehighton, Pa. E10 202
Lehman, Pa. B7 202
Lehman Caves, nat. mon., Nev. E7 192
Lehr, N. Dak. C6 198
Lehrte, Ger. A4 61
Lehua, isl., Haw. A1 176
Leiah, Pak. B5 87
Leibnitz, Aus. E7 60
Leicester, Eng. D6 55, B6 57
Leicester, Mass. B4 185
Leicester, N.Y. C3 196
Leicester, Vt. D2 208
Leicester, co., Eng. B6 56
Leicester Junction, Vt. D2 208
Leichhardt, Austl. *F8 112
Leichhardt, riv., Austl. C7 110
Leiden, Neth. B4 59
Leigh, Eng. *A5 56
Leigh, Nebr. C8 191
Leigh Creek, Austl. E6 112
Leighton, Ala. A2 166
Leighton, Iowa *C5 180
Leili, isl., Sol. Is. 115
Leinan, Sask., Can. G2 155
Leine, riv., Ger. A4 61
Leipalingis, Sov. Un. A7 70
Leipers Fork, Tenn. B5 205
Leipsic, Del. B6 173
Leipsic, Ohio A4 199
Leipsic, riv., Del. B6 173
Leipzig, Sask., Can. E1 155
Leipzig, Ger. B7 61
Leiria, Port. C1 65
Leisnig, Ger. B7 61
Leiston, Eng. B9 56
Leisure City, Fla. F3 174
Leitches Creek, N.S., Can. C9 151
Leitchfield, Ky. C3 182
Leiter, Wyo. A6 213
Leiters Ford, Ind. B5 179
Leitersburg, Md. A2 173
Leith, N. Dak. C4 198
Leith, Pa. *G2 202
Leitha, riv., Aus. E8 60
Lejunior, Ky. D6 182
Lek, riv., Neth. C4 59
Leka, isl., Nor. E4 63
Le Kef, Tun. B6 102
Le Kreider, Alg. C5 102
Leksands, Swe. G6 63
Leksula, Indon. F7 90
Lekumbi, pt., Fiji 114
Lela, Tex. B2 206
Leland, Ill. B5 178
Leland, Iowa A4 180
Leland, Mich. C5 186
Leland, Miss. B3 188
Leland, Oreg. E3 201
Leland, Wash. B3 210
Leland Grove, Ill. *D4 178
Leleiwi, pt., Haw. D7 176
Leleque, Arg. C2 136
Lelia Lake, Tex. B2 206
Leloaloa, Am. Sam. 114
Le Locle, Switz. B2 66
Lelom, reef, Truk 114
Le Loup, Kans. D8 181
Lelystad, Neth. B5 59
Lem, peak, Idaho E5 177
Léman, see Geneva, lake, Switz.
Le Mans, Fr. D4 58
Le Marin, Mart. o16 131
Le Mars, Iowa B1 180
Lemasters, Pa. G6 202
Lembach, Fr. F7 59
Lembak, Indon. F2 90
Lemberg, Sask., Can. G4 155
Leme, Braz. m8 137
Lemelerveld, Neth. B6 59
Lemery, Phil. p13 90
Lemgo, Ger. A3 61
Lemhi, Idaho E5 177
Lemhi, co., Idaho E4 177
Lemhi, pass, Idaho, Mont. E5 177
Lemhi, range, Idaho E5 177
Lemhi, riv., Idaho E5 177
Lemieux, Que., Can. C5 154
Lemitar, N. Mex. C3 195
Lemmer, Neth. B5 59
Lemmon, S. Dak. B3 204
Lemmon, mtn., Ariz. E5 168
Lemnos, see Límnos, isl., Grc.
Lemon, isl., S.C. G6 203
Lemon Fair, riv., Vt. D2 208
Lemon Grove, Calif. E2, F5 170
Lemons, Mo. A4 189
Lemont, Ill. B5, F2 178
Lemont, Pa. E6 202
Lemonweir, riv., Wis. E3 212
Lemoore, Calif. D4 170
Le Moule, Guad. n16 131
Le Moyen, La. D3 183
Le Moyne, Que., Can. *D4 154
Lemoyne, Nebr. C4 191
Lemoyne, Ohio A2 199
Lemoyne, Pa. *F8 202
Lempster, N.H. D2 193
Lemsford, Sask., Can. G1 155
Lemvig, Den. B2 62
Lena, Ill. A4 178
Lena, La. C3 183
Lena, Miss. C4 188
Lena, Sp. A3 65
Lena, Wis. D5 212
Lena, riv., Sov. Un. C15 71
Lenapah, Okla. A6 200
Lenawee, co., Mich. G6 186
Lençóis, Braz. D2 138
Lend, Aus. B9 66
Lendinara, It. D7 66
Lenexa, Kans. D9 181
Leney, Sask., Can. E2 155
Lengby, Minn. C3 187
Lengede, Ger. A5 61
Lengeh, Iran H7 86
Lenger, Sov. Un. E7 73
Lengerich, Ger. A2 61
Lenhartsville, Pa. E10 202
Leninabad, Sov. Un. E7 73
Leninakan, Sov. Un. E2 73
Leningrad, Sov. Un. H14, s31 63, B8 72
Lenino, Sov. Un. n17 72
Leninogorsk, Sov. Un. C10 73
Leninsk, Sov. Un. G15 72
Leninsk-Kuznetskiy, Sov. Un. C11 73
Lenk, Switz. C3 66
Lenne, riv., Ger. B2 61
Lennep, Mont. D6 190
Lennox, Calif. *E4 170
Lennox, S. Dak. D9 204
Lennox, isl., Chile k12 136
Lennox and Addington, co., Ont., Can. B7 153
Lennoxville, Que., Can. D6 154
Leno, It. D6 66
Lenoir, N.C. B2 197
Lenoir, co., N.C. B6 197
Lenoir City, Tenn. D9 205
Lenora, Kans. C4 181
Lenora, Okla. A2 200
Lenorah, Tex. C2 206
Lenore, Man., Can. E1 150
Lenore, Idaho C2 177
Lenore, lake, Sask., Can. E3 155
Lenore, lake, Wash. B6 210
Lenox, Ga. E3 175
Lenox, Iowa D3 180
Lenox, Mass. B1 185
Lenox, Mo. D6 189
Lenox, Tenn. A2 205
Lenox, Va. *B7 209
Lenox Dale, Mass. B1 185
Lens, Fr. B5 58
Lentner, Mo. B5 189
Lenwood, Calif. *E5 170
Lenzburg, Ill. B9 189
Lenzen, Ger. E5 62
Leo, Ind. B7 179
Léo, Upper Volta D4 103
Leo, Wyo. C6 213
Leoben, Aus. E7 60
Léogane, Hai. F7 131
Leola, Ark. C3 169
Leola, S. Dak. B7 204
Leoma, Tenn. B4 205
Leominster, Eng. B5 56
Leominster, Mass. A4 185
Leon, Iowa D4 180
Leon, Kans. E7 181
León, Mex. C4, m13 129
Leon, N.Y. C1 196
León, Nic. D4 130
Leon, Okla. D4 200
León, Sp. A3 65
Leon, W. Va. C3 211
Leon, co., Fla. B2 174
Leon, co., Tex. D4 206
Leon, kingdom of Sp. 47
León, reg., Sp. B3 65
Leon Valley, Tex. *E3 206
Leona, Kans. C8 181
Leona, Tex. D5 206
Leonard, Ont., Can. A10 153
Leonard, Mich. F7 186
Leonard, Minn. C3 187
Leonard, Mo. B5 189
Leonard, N. Dak. C8 198
Leonard, Tex. C4 206
Leonardo, N.J. C4 194
Leonardsville, N.Y. C5 196
Leonardtown, Md. D4 173
Leonardville, N.B., Can. E2 151
Leonardville, Kans. C7 181
Leonberg, Ger. E4 61
Leone, bay, Am. Sam. 114
Leonfelden, Aus. E9 61
Leonforte, It. F5 67
Leongatha, Austl. I5 112
Leonia, Fla. G3 174
Leonia, N.J. B5, D5 194
Leonídhion, Grc. D4 69
Leonora, Austl. E3 111
Leonville, La. D4 183
Leopold, Mo. D8 189
Léopold II, lake, Zaire B2 106
Leopold and Astrid, coast, Ant. C21 120
Leopoldina, Braz. C4, g6 137
Leopoldsburg, Bel. C5 59
Leopoldville, reg., Zaire B2 106
Leora, Mo. E7 189
Leota, Minn. G2 187
Leoti, Kans. D2 181
Leoville, Sask., Can. D2 155
Leoville, Kans. C3 181
Leovo, Sov. Un. H7 72
Lepanto, Ark. B5 169
Lepe, Sp. D2 65
Lepel, Sov. Un. D7 72
Leper Settlement, Haw. B5 176
Le Petit-Quevilly, Fr. C4 58
Lepihué, Chile C2 136
L'Épiphanie, Que., Can. D4 154
Le Plessis-Belleville, Fr. E2 59
Le Plessis-Robinson, Fr. g10 58
Lepontine Alps, mts., Switz. C4 66
Le Portel, Fr. D9 56
Lepreau, N.B., Can. D3 151
Lepreau, pt., N.B., Can. D3 151
Lepsy, Sov. Un. D9 73
Le Puy [-en-Velay], Fr. E5 58
Le Quesnoy, Fr. D3 59
Lequrie, Okla. B6 200
Le Raincy, Fr. g11 58
Le Raysville, Pa. C9 202
Lercara Friddi, It. F4 67
Léré, Chad D2 104
Lérida, Sp. B6 65
Lerma, Sp. A4 65
Lerma, riv., Mex. m13 129
Lermoos, Aus. B6 66
Lerna, Ill. D5 178
Léros, isl., Grc. D6 69
Leross, Sask., Can. F4 155
Leroux, wash, Ariz. B5 168
Leroy, Ala. D2 166
Leroy, Sask., Can. F3 155
Le Roy, Ill. C5 178
Le Roy, Ind. B3 179
Le Roy, Iowa D4 180
Le Roy, Kans. D8 181
Le Roy, Mich. D5 186
Le Roy, Minn. G6 187
Leroy, Mont. C7 190
Le Roy, N.Y. C3 196
Le Roy, N. Dak. A8 198
Leroy, Ohio A6 199
Le Roy, Pa. C8 202
Le Roy, Wyo. D2 213
Lerum, Swe. A6 62
Lerwick, Scot. g10 55
Lery, lake, La. C8 183
Les Cayes, Hai. F7 131
Les Cèdres, Que., Can. *D3 154
Les Diablerets, Switz. C3 66
Les Éboulements, Que., Can. B7 154
Les Échelles, Fr. D1 66
Les Escoumins, Que., Can. A8 154
Les Étroits, Que., Can. B9 154
Les Fonds, Que., Can. C8 154
Lesh, Alb. B2 69
Leshara, Nebr. D2 191
Les Haudères, Switz. C3 66
Lesina, lake, It. D5 67
Lesko, Pol. D7 70
Leskovac, Yugo. D5 68
Leslie, Ark. B3 169
Leslie, Ga. E2 175
Leslie, Idaho F5 177
Leslie, Mich. F6 186
Leslie, W. Va. C4 211
Leslie, co., Ky. C6 182
Leslie Station, Sask., Can. F4 155
Leslieville, Alta., Can. C3 148
Les Lilas, Fr. g10 58
Lesneven, Fr. C1 58
Lesogorsk (Nayoshi), Sov. Un. B11 93
LESOTHO, country, Afr. C4 107
Lesozavodsk, Sov. Un. D6 93
Lesparre [-Médoc], Fr. E3 58
Les Ponts-de-Cé, Fr. D3 58
Les Sables-d'Olonne, Fr. D3 58
Lesser Antilles, is., W.I. B4 124
Lesser Khingan, ra., China B10 91
Lesser Slave, lake, Alta., Can. B3 148
Lessines, Bel. D3 59
Lesslie, S.C. B6 203
Lester, Ala. A2 166
Lester, Iowa A1 180
Lester, W. Va. D6 211
Lester Prairie, Minn. F4 187
Lesterville, Mo. D7 189
Lesterville, S. Dak. D8 204
Lestock, Sask., Can. F3 155
Le Sueur, Minn. F5 187
Le Sueur, co., Minn. F5 187
Lésvos (Lesbos), isl., Grc. C6 69
Leszno, Pol. C4 70
Le Tarf, Alg. F2 67
Letart Falls, Ohio D6 199
Letcher, S. Dak. D7 204
Letcher, co., Ky. C7 182
Le Teil, Fr. E6 58
Letellier, Man., Can. E3 150
Letha, Idaho F2 177
Lethbridge, Alta., Can. E4 148
Lethbridge, Newf., Can. D5 152
Le Thillot, Fr. B2 66
Letiahau, riv., Bech. B3 107
Leticia, Col. D4 133
Letohatchee, Ala. C3 166
Letona, Ark. B4 169
Le Touquet-Paris-Plage, Fr. D9 56
Letpadan, Bur. D1 89
Le Tréport, Fr. B4 58
Letterkenny, Ire. C3 55
Letts, Ind. F6 179
Letts, Iowa C6 180
Lettsworth, La. D4 183
Leucadia, Calif. *F5 170
Leucas, see Levkás, isl., Grc.
Leupp, Ariz. B5 168
Leupp Corners, Ariz. B5 168
Leushinskiy Tuman, lake, Sov. Un. B6 73
Leutkirch, Ger. B6 66
Leuven (Louvain), Bel. D4 59
Leuze, Bel. D3 59
Levack, Ont., Can. *E9 153
Levádhia, Grc. C4, g9 69
Levallois-Perret, Fr. C5, g10 58
Levan, Utah D4 207
Levanger, Nor. F4 63
Levanna, mtn., It. B1 67
Levant, Kans. C2 181
Levant, Maine D4 184
Levasy, Mo. *B3 189
Levelland, Tex. C1 206
Leven, Scot. D6 57
Leveque, cape, Austl. C3 110
Leverett, Mass. B2 185
Levering, Mich. C6 186
Leverkusen, Ger. B1 61
Levey, Iowa A7 180
Levi, W. Sam. 114
Levice, Czech. D5 70
Levie, Fr. D2 67
Le Vigan, Fr. F5 58
Levin, N.Z. N15 112
Lévis, Que., Can. C6, C9 154
Levis, co., Que., Can. C6 154
Levisa, fork, Ky. C7 182
Lévithos, isl., Grc. D6 69
Levittown, N.Y. G2 172
Levkás, Grc. C3 69
Levkás (Leucas), isl., Grc. C3 69
Lévktra, Grc. g10 69
Levoča, Czech. D6 70
Levskigrad, Bul. D7 68
Levuka, Fiji 114
Levy, N. Mex. A5 195
Levy, co., Fla. C4 174
Levy, lake, Fla. C4 174
Lewarae, N.C. *C4 197
Lewellen, Nebr. C3 191
Lewes, Del. C7 173
Lewes, Eng. D8 56
Lewis, Ind. F3 179
Lewis, Iowa C2 180
Lewis, Kans. E4 181
Lewis, Mo. C4 189
Lewis, N.Y. A7, B3 196
Lewis, Wis. C1 212
Lewis, co., Idaho C2 177
Lewis, co., Ky. B6 182
Lewis, co., Mo. A6 189
Lewis, co., N.Y. B5 196
Lewis, co., Tenn. B4 205
Lewis, co., Wash. C3 210
Lewis, co., W. Va. C4 211
Lewis, creek, Vt. C2 208
Lewis, hill, Newf., Can. D2 152
Lewis, lake, Wyo. A2 213
Lewis, mtn., Nev. C5 192
Lewis, range, Can., U.S. G10 142, B3 190
Lewis, riv., Wash. C4 210
Lewis, riv., Wyo. A2 213
Lewis and Clark, co., Mont. C4 190
Lewis and Clark, cavern, Mont. D5 190
Lewis and Clark Lake, res., Nebr. B8 191
Lewis Center, Ohio B4 199
Lewis-Clark, lake, S. Dak. E8 204
Lewis Gardens, Va. *D5 209
Lewis Run, Pa. C4 202
Lewis Smith, lake, Ala. B2 166
Lewis with Harris, isl., Scot. B2 57
Lewisberry, Pa. F8 202
Lewisburg, Ky. D3 182
Lewisburg, La. D3 183
Lewisburg, Ohio C3 199
Lewisburg, Pa. E8 202
Lewisburg, Tenn. B5 205
Lewisburg, W. Va. D4 211
Lewisham, Eng. C7 56
Lewisport, Ky. C3 182
Lewisporte, Newf., Can. D4 152
Lewiston, Idaho C2 177
Lewiston, Maine D2, D5 184
Lewiston, Mich. D6 186
Lewiston, Minn. G7 187
Lewiston, N.Y. B1 196
Lewiston, N.C. A6 197
Lewiston, Utah B4 207
Lewiston, peak, Utah C3 207
Lewiston Orchards, Idaho C2 177
Lewistown, Ill. C3 178
Lewistown, Md. A3 173
Lewistown, Mo. A6 189
Lewistown, Mont. C7 190
Lewistown, Pa. E6 202
Lewisville, Ark. D2 169
Lewisville, N.B., Can. C5 151
Lewisville, Idaho F6 177
Lewisville, Ind. E7 179
Lewisville, Minn. G4 187
Lewisville, Ohio C6 199
Lewisville, Pa. G10 202
Lewisville, Tex. A5, C4 206
Lewvan, Sask., Can. G3 155
Lexa, Ark. C5 169
Lexie, Miss. D3 188
Lexington, Ala. A2 166
Lexington, Ark. B4 169
Lexington, Ga. C3 175
Lexington, Ill. C5 178
Lexington, Ind. G6 179
Lexington, Ky. B5 182
Lexington, Mass. B5, C2 185
Lexington, Mich. E8 186
Lexington, Minn. *E5 187
Lexington, Miss. B3 188
Lexington, Mo. B4 189
Lexington, Nebr. D6 191
Lexington, N.Y. C6 196
Lexington, N.C. B2 197
Lexington, Ohio B3 199
Lexington, Okla. B4 200
Lexington, Oreg. B7 201
Lexington, S.C. D5 203
Lexington, Tenn. B3 205
Lexington, Tex. D4 206
Lexington (Independent City), Va. D3 209
Lexington, Wash. C3 210
Lexington, co., S.C. D5 203
Lexington Park, Md. D5 173
Leyba, N. Mex. B4 195
Leyburn, Eng. F7 57
Leyden, Mass. *A2 185
Leyland, Alta., Can. C2 148
Leyond, riv., Man., Can. D3 150
Leysdown, Eng. C8 56
Leyte, isl., Phil. C6 89
Leyton, Eng. *k13 55
Leżajsk, Pol. C7 70
Lézignan [-Corbières], Fr. F5 58
Lezirias, reg., Port. f10 65
Lgov, Sov. Un. F10 72
Lhasa, China F3 91
Lhatse Dzong, China C11 88
L'Hay-les-Roses, Fr. g10 58
Lhokseumawe, Indon. J2 89
Lhoksukon, Indon. J2 89
Li, China J4 92
Lianga, bay, Phil. D7 90
Liancheng, China D5 92
Liang East, mtn., Mala. K4 89
Liangshan, China I2 92
Liangyang, China G7 91
Liao, China F5 92
Liao, riv., China C10 92
Liaocheng, China F6 92
Liaoning, prov., China C9 91
Liaotung, bay, China D9 92
Liaotung, pen., China E10 92
Liaoyang, China D10 92
Liaoyuan, China C9 91
Liard, riv., B.C., N.W. Ter., Can. E7 142
Liart, Fr. E4 59
Liathach, mtn., Scot. C3 57
Lib, isl., Marshall Is. 115
Líbano, Col. C3 133
Libau, Man., Can. D3 150
Libby, Mont. B1 190
Libčice, Czech. n17 70
Liběchov, Czech. n17 70
Libenge, Zaire A2 106
Liberal, Kans. E3 181
Liberal, Mo. D3 189
Liberec, Czech. C3 70
Liberia, C.R. E5 130
LIBERIA, country, Afr. E2 103
Libertad, Ven. B4 133
Liberty, Sask. Can. F3 155
Liberty, Idaho G7 177
Liberty, Ill. D2 178
Liberty, Ind. E8 179
Liberty, Kans. E8 181
Liberty, Ky. C5 182
Liberty, Maine D3 184
Liberty, Miss. D3 188
Liberty, Mo. B3, E2 189
Liberty, Nebr. D9 191
Liberty, N.Y. D6 196
Liberty, N.C. B4 197
Liberty, Pa. *F2 202
Liberty, Pa. C7 202
Liberty, S.C. B2 203
Liberty, Tenn. C8 205
Liberty, Tex. D5, F5 206
Liberty, Wash. B5 210
Liberty, co., Fla. B2 174
Liberty, co., Ga. E5 175
Liberty, co., Mont. B5 190
Liberty, co., Tex. D5 206
Liberty Center, Ind. C7 179
Liberty Center, Iowa C4 180
Liberty Center, Ohio A3 199
Liberty Corner, N.J. B3 194
Liberty Grove, Md. A5 173
Liberty Hill, S.C. C6 203
Liberty Hill, Tenn. C10 205
Liberty Lake, Wash. D8 210
Liberty Mills, Ind. B6 179
Libertytown, Md. B3 173
Libertyville, Ill. A6, E2 178
Libertyville, Iowa D5 180
Libiron, isl., Eniwetok 114
Liblar, Ger. C1 61
Libmanan, Phil. *C6 90
Libourne, Fr. E3 58
Libramont, Bel. E5 59
Libreville, Gabon E1 104
Libušin, Czech. n17 70
LIBYA, country, Afr. D2 101
in 7th cent. B.C. 42
in 1922-40 53
Libyan, des., Libya D8 96
Libyan, plat., Eg., Libya C4 101
Licantén, Chile B2 136
Licata, It. F4 67
Lice, Tur. C13 85
Licenza, It. g9 67
Lichfield, Eng. B6 56
Lichiang, China F5 91
Liching, China F8 92
Lichtenburg, S. Afr. C4 107
Lichtenfels, Ger. C6 61
Lichtenstein, Ger. C7 61
Lick, creek, Ky. A7 182
Lick, creek, Tenn. C11 205
Licking, Mo. D6 189
Licking, co., Ohio B5 199
Licking, creek, Md., Pa. A1 173
Licking, riv., Ky. B7 182
Licosa, cape, It. D5 67
Lida, Nev. F4 192
Lida, Sov. Un. E5 72
Lida, lake, Minn. D3 187
Liddel, riv., Eng. E6 57
Lidderdale, Iowa B3 180
Lidgerwood, N. Dak. C8 198
Lidice, Czech. C3, n17 70
Lidingö, Swe. H8, t36 63
Lidköping, Swe. H5 63
Lido di Roma, It. h8 67
Lidzbark Warmiński, Pol. A6 70
Liebenthal, Sask., Can. G1 155
Liebenthal, Kans. D4 181
Lieberose, Ger. B9 61
LIECHTENSTEIN, country, Eur. B5 66
Liège, Bel. D5 59
Liège, prov., Bel. D5 59
Liege, riv., Alta., Can. A4 148
Lieksa, Fin. F14 63
Lienen, Ger. A2 61
Lienhua, China K5 92
Lienyunchiang, China G8 92
Lienz, Aus. E6 60
Liepāja, Sov. Un. C3 72
Lier, Bel. C4 59
Lierneux, Bel. D5 59
Liestal, Switz. B3 66
Liévin, Fr. D2 59
Lievre, riv., Que., Can. D2 154
Lièvres, isl., Que., Can. B8 154
Liffey, riv., Ire. D3 55
Lifford, Ire. C3 55
Lifou, isl., Loyalty Is. 115
Ligao, Phil. *C6 90
Lighthouse, inlet, S.C. G3 203
Lighthouse, pt., Fla. C2 174
Lighthouse, pt., La. E3 183
Lighthouse, pt., Mich. C5 186
Lighthouse Point, Fla. *F6 174
Lightning, creek, Wyo. B8 213
Lightning Ridge, Austl. D6 112
Lignite, N. Dak. A3 198
Lignum, Va. C5 209
Ligny-en-Barrois, Fr. F5 59
Ligonha, riv., Moz. A6 107
Ligonier, Ind. B6 179
Ligonier, Pa. F3 202
Ligovo, Sov. Un. s31 63
Liguan, cape, New Britain I. 115
Liguria, reg., It. B2 67
Ligurian, sea, It. C2 67
Ligurian Apennines, mts., It. E4 66
Lihir, isl., Bis. Arch. 115

INDEX KEY Each place listed in **Bold-faced Type** has its population listed in the Population tables, pages 230 to 280. Each country, shown in CAPITAL LETTERS, has its population listed in the World Political Information Table, pages 6 to 10.
* Does not appear on map; key shows general location.

Lihua, China F5 91
Lihue, Haw. B2 176
Likasi, Zaire D4 106
Likely, Calif. B3 170
Likhoslavl, Sov. Un. C10 72
Likiep, atoll, Marshall Is. 115
Likino-Dulevo, Sov. Un. n18 72
Lilbourn, Mo. E8 189
L'Île-Rousse, Fr. C2 67
Lilesville, N.C. C4 197
Liling, China K5 92
Lillburn, Ga. A5 175
Lille, Fr. B5 58, D3 59
Lille, Maine A4 184
Lille Belt, strait, Den. C3 62
Lillehammer, Nor. G4 63
Lillers, Fr. D2 59
Lillesand, Nor. H3 63
Lilleström, Nor. H4, p29 63
Lillian, Ala. E2 166
Lillian, Tex. B5 206
Lillie, La. B3 183
Lillie, glacier tongue, Ant. B29 120
Lillington, N.C. B5 197
Lillinonah, res., Conn. C3 172
Lillis, Kans. C7 181
Lillooet, B.C., Can. D7 149
Lillooet, range, B.C., Can. E7 149
Lillooet, riv., B.C., Can. D6 149
Lilly, Ga. D3 175
Lilly, Pa. F4 202
Lilly, fork, W. Va. C7 211
Lilly Grove, W. Va. *D3 211
Lilongwe, Malawi D5 106
Lily, Ky. C5 182
Lily, S. Dak. B8 204
Lily, Wis. C5 212
Lim, riv., Yugo. D4 68
Lima, Ill. C2 178
Lima, Mont. F4 190
Lima, N.Y. C3 196
Lima, Ohio B3 199
Lima, Par. D4 135
Lima, Peru D2 134
Lima, dept., Peru D2 134
Lima, res., Mont. F4 190
Lima, riv., Port. B1 65
Lima Duarte, Braz. C4, g6 137
Lima Ringmo, lake, China A9 88
Limanowa, Pol. D6 70
Limassol, Cyp. E9 85
Limay, riv., Arg. B3 136
Limay Mahuida, Arg. B3 136
Limbach, Ger. C7 61
Limbé, Hai. F7 131
Limburg, Ger. C3 61
Limburg, prov., Bel. D5 59
Limburg, prov., Neth. D5 59
Lime, Colo. C6 171
Lime, Oreg. C9 201
Lime, creek, Iowa A4 180
Lime City, Ohio A2 199
Lime Rock, Conn. B3 172
Lime Springs, Iowa A5 180
Lime Village, Alsk. C8 167
Limedale, Ind. E4 179
Limeil-Brévannes, Fr. h10 58
Limeira, Braz. C3, m8 137
Limerick, Sask., Can. H2 155
Limerick, Ire. D2 55
Limerick, Maine E2 184
Limestone, Ark. B2 169
Limestone, Fla. E5 174
Limestone, Maine B5 184
Limestone, N.Y. C2 196
Limestone, Pa. D3 202
Limestone, Tenn. C11 205
Limestone, co., Ala. A2 166
Limestone, co., Tex. D4 206
Limestone, bay, Man., Can. C2 150
Limestone, pt., Man., Can. C2 150
Limestone, riv., Man., Can. A4 150
Limeton, Va. C4 209
Limfjorden, fjord, Den. B3 62
Limington, Maine E2 184
Limko, China C8 89
Limkong, China B9 89
Limmen, bight, Austl. B6 110
Límni, Grc. C4 69
Límnos (Lemnos), isl., Grc. C5 69
Limoeiro, Braz. C3, h6 138
Limoeiro do Norte, Braz. C3 138
Limoges, Ont., Can. B9 153
Limoges, Fr. E4 58
Limon, Colo. B7 171
Limón, C.R. F6 130
Limón, Hond. C5 130
Limón, riv., P.R. B4 132
Limones, P.R. C7 132
Limousin, former prov., Fr. E4 58
Limousin, plat., Fr. E4 58
Limoux, Fr. F5 58
Limpopo, riv., Afr. B5 107
Līnah, Sau. Ar. H14 85
Linares, Chile B2 136
Linares, Col. C2 133
Linares, Mex. C5 129
Linares, Sp. C4 65
Linares, prov., Chile B2 136
Linaro, cape, It. C3 67
Linchiang, China F3 93
Linching, China F6 92
Lincoln, Ala. B3 166
Lincoln, Arg. A4 136
Lincoln, Ark. B1 169
Lincoln, Calif. C3 170
Lincoln, Ont., Can. *D5 153
Lincoln, Del. C7 173
Lincoln, Eng. A7 56
Lincoln, Idaho F6 177
Lincoln, Ill. C4 178
Lincoln, Ind. C5 179
Lincoln, Iowa B5 180
Lincoln, Kans. C5 181
Lincoln, Ky. C6 182
Lincoln, Maine C4 184
Lincoln, Mass. C2 185
Lincoln, Mich. D7 186
Lincoln, Minn. D4 187
Lincoln, Mo. C4 189
Lincoln, Mont. D4 190
Lincoln, Nebr. D9, E2 191
Lincoln, N.H. B3 193
Lincoln, N. Mex. D4 195
Lincoln, Pa. *F2 202
Lincoln, R.I. B11 172
Lincoln, Tenn. B5 205
Lincoln, Vt. C2 208
Lincoln, Va. B5 209
Lincoln, Wash. B7 210
Lincoln, co., Ark. D4 169
Lincoln, co., Ont., Can. D5 153
Lincoln, co., Colo. C7 171
Lincoln, co., Eng. A7 56
Lincoln, co., Ga. C4 175
Lincoln, co., Idaho G4 177
Lincoln, co., Kans. C5 181
Lincoln, co., Ky. C5 182
Lincoln, co., Maine D3 184
Lincoln, co., Minn. F2 187
Lincoln, co., Miss. D3 188
Lincoln, co., Mo. B6 189
Lincoln, co., Mont. B1 190
Lincoln, co., Nebr. D5 191
Lincoln, co., Nev. F6 192
Lincoln, co., N. Mex. D4 195
Lincoln, co., N.C. B1 197
Lincoln, co., Okla. B5 200
Lincoln, co., Oreg. C3 201
Lincoln, co., S. Dak. D9 204
Lincoln, co., Tenn. B5 205
Lincoln, co., Wash. B7 210
Lincoln, co., W. Va. C2 211
Lincoln, co., Wis. C4 212
Lincoln, co., Wyo. C2 213
Lincoln, par., La. B3 183
Lincoln, mtn., Colo. B4 171
Lincoln, rock, Wash. B5 210
Lincoln, sea, Arc. O. A20 118
Lincoln, tomb, Ill. D4 178
Lincoln, wolds, Eng. A7 56
Lincoln Center, Maine C4 184
Lincoln City, Ind. H4 179
Lincoln City, Oreg. C3 201
Lincoln Heights, Ohio D2 199
Lincoln Park, Colo. *C5 171
Lincoln Park, Ga. D2 175
Lincoln Park, Mich. A7 186
Lincoln Park, N.J. B4 194
Lincolnshire, Ill. *A6 178
Lincolnshire, Ky. *B4 182
Lincolnton, Ga. C4 175
Lincolnton, N.C. B2 197
Lincolnville, Kans. D7 181
Lincolnville, Maine D3 184
Lincolnville, S.C. E2 203
Lincolnwood, Ill. E3 178
Lincroft, N.J. C4 194
L'Incudine, mtn., Fr. D2 67
Lind, Wash. C7 210
Linda, Calif. *C3 170
Lindale, Ga. B1 175
Lindale, Tex. C5 206
Lindau, Ger. E4 60
Lindbergh, Alta., Can. C5 148
Lindbergh, Wyo. D8 213
Linden, Ala. C2 166
Linden, Ind. D4 179
Linden, Iowa C3 180
Linden, Mich. F7 186
Linden, N.J. E4 194
Linden, N.C. B5 197
Linden, Pa. D7 202
Linden, Tenn. B4 205
Linden, Tex. C5 206
Linden, Wis. F3 212
Lindenhafen, New Britain I. 115
Lindenhurst, Ill. *A5 178
Lindenhurst, N.Y. G3 172
Lindenwold, N.J. D3 194
Linderöd, Swe. C7 62
Lindesberg, Swe. H6 63
Lindhos, Grc. D7 69
Lindi, Tan. C6 106
Lindi, riv., Zaire A4 106
Lindlar, Ger. B2 61
Lindome, Swe. A6 62
Lindon, Colo. B7 171
Lindon, Utah C4 207
Lindow, Ger. F6 62
Lindrith, N. Mex. A2 195
Lindsay, Calif. D4 170
Lindsay, Ont., Can. C6 153
Lindsay, Mont. C11 190
Lindsay, Nebr. C8 191
Lindsay, Okla. C4 200
Lindsborg, Kans. D6 181
Lindsey, Ohio A4 199
Lindstrom, Minn. E6 187
Lindy, Nebr. B8 191
Lineboro, Md. A4 173
Linefork, Ky. C7 182
Linesville, Pa. C1 202
Lineville, Ala. B4 166
Lineville, Iowa D4 180
Linfen, China F4 92
Linganore, creek, Md. B3 173
Lingayen, Phil. B6, n13 90
Lingayen, gulf, Phil. n13 90
Lingen, Ger. B3 60
Lingga, arch., Indon. F2 90
Lingle, Wyo. C8 213
Linglestown, Pa. F8 202
Lingling (Yungchow), China F7 91
Lingo, N. Mex. D6 195
Lingshan, China G6 91
Linguére, Sen. C1 103
Lingwu, China E6 91
Lingyüan, China D8 92
Linhai, China J9 92
Linhares, Braz. E2 138
Linho, China C8 92
Linhsi, China D8 92
Linhsia, China D5 91
Lini, China G8 92
Liniere, Que., Can. C7 154
Linju, China G5 92
Linköping, Swe. H6 63
Linlithgow, Scot. E5 57
Linn, Kans. C6 181
Linn, Mo. C6 189
Linn, Tex. F3 206
Linn, co., Iowa B6 180
Linn, co., Kans. D9 181
Linn, co., Mo. B4 189
Linn, co., Oreg. C4 201
Linn Creek, Mo. C5 189
Linn Grove, Ind. C7 179
Linn Grove, Iowa B2 180
Linneus, Maine B5 184
Linneus, Mo. B4 189
Linnhe, inlet, Scot. D3 57
Linntown, Pa. *E6 202
Lino Lakes, Minn. *E5 187
Lins, Braz. C3 137
Lintan, China E5 91
Linthicum Heights, Md. B4 173
Lintien, China C2 93
Lintlaw, Sask., Can. E4 155
Linton, Que., Can. B5 154
Linton, Ga. C4 175
Linton, Ind. F3 179
Linton, Ky. D2 182
Linton, N. Dak. C5 198
Linton, Tenn. A4 205
Lintung, China B8 92
Linville, N.C. A2, C4 197
Linville, Va. C4 209
Linwood, Ala. D4 166
Linwood, Ont., Can. D4 153
Linwood, Ga. B2 175
Linwood, Ga. B1 175
Linwood, Iowa C7, D7 180
Linwood, Kans. B8 181
Linwood, Mass. B4 185
Linwood, Mich. E7 186
Linwood, Nebr. C9 191
Linwood, N.J. E3 194
Linwood, N.C. B3 197
Linworth, Ohio C2 199
Linyü, China D8 92
Linz, Aus. D7 60
Lions, La. B6 183
Lions, gulf, Fr. F6 58
Lions Bay, B.C., Can. *E6 149
Lions Head, Ont., Can. C3 153
Lionville, Pa. F10 202
Lipa, Phil. C6, p13 90
Lipan, Tex. C3 206
Lipari, It. E5 67
Lipari, isl., It. E5 67
Lipetsk, Sov. Un. C1 73
Lipik, Yugo. C3 68
Liping, China F6 91
Lipkany, Sov. Un. A8 68
Lipno, Pol. B5 70
Lipova, Rom. B5 68
Lippe, riv., Ger. B3 61
Lippstadt, Ger. B3 61
Lipscomb, Ala. B3, E4 166
Lipscomb, Tex. A2 206
Lipscomb, co., Tex. A2 206
Lipsos, isl., Grc. D6 69
Lipton, Sask., Can. G4 155
Lipu, China G7 91
Lira, Ug. A5 106
Lircay, Peru D3 134
Liri, riv., It. D4 67
Liria, Sp. C5 65
Lisafa, Zaire B2 106
Lisala, Zaire A3 106
Lisboa, see Lisbon, Port.
Lisbon, Iowa C6 180
Lisbon, La. B3 183
Lisbon, Maine D2, D5 184
Lisbon, Md. B3 173
Lisbon, N.H. B3 193
Lisbon, N.Y. A1 196
Lisbon, N. Dak. C8 198
Lisbon, Ohio B7 199
Lisbon (Lisboa), Port. C1, f9 65
Lisbon Center, Maine D5 184
Lisbon Falls, Maine D5, E2 184
Lisburn, N. Ire. C3 55
Lisburn, cape, Espiritu Santo I. 115
Lisburne, cape, Alsk. B6 167
Lisco, Nebr. C3 191
Liscomb, N.S., Can. D7 151
Liscomb, Iowa B4 180
Lishih, China F4 92
Lishu, China E2 93
Lishui, China F8 91
Lishukou, China D5 93
Lisianski, isl., Haw. k13 176
Lisichansk, Sov. Un. q21 72
Lisieux, Sask., Can. H3 155
Lisieux, Fr. C4 58
Liskeard, Eng. D3 56
Liski, Sov. Un. F12 72
Lisle, Ont., Can. C5 153
Lisle, Ill. F2 178
L'Isle, Fr. B2 66
L'Islet, Que., Can. B7 154
L'Islet, co., Que., Can. B7 154
L'Islet-sur-Mer, Que., Can. *B7 154
Lisman, Ala. C1 166
Lismore, Austl. D9 112
Lismore, N.S., Can. D7 151
Lismore, Minn. G3 187
Lismore, isl., Scot. D3 57
Listafjord, fjord, Nor. H2 63
Lister, B.C., Can. E9 149
Lister, mtn., Ant. B28 120
Listie, Pa. F3 202
Listonburg, Pa. G3 202
Listowel, Ont., Can. D4 153
Listowel, Ire. D2 55
Litchfield, Calif. B3 170
Litchfield, Conn. B4 172
Litchfield, Ill. D4 178
Litchfield, Mich. F6 186
Litchfield, Minn. E4 187
Litchfield, Nebr. C6 191
Litchfield, N.H. E4 193
Litchfield, co., Conn. B3 172
Litchfield Park, Ariz. G1 168
Litchville, N. Dak. C7 198
Liteň, Czech. o17 70
Lithgow, Austl. F8 112
Lithia Springs, Ga. B4 175
Lithinon, cape, Grc. E5 69
Lithonia, Ga. B5, C2 175
Lithopolis, Ohio *C2 199
Lithuania (S.S.R.), rep., Sov. Un. D5 71
c. 1360 48
in 1721 49
in 1940 53
Lititz, Pa. F9 202
Litókhoron, Grc. B4 69
Litoměřice, Czech. C3 70
Litomyšl, Czech. D4 70
Litslena, Swe. t35 63
Little, lake, La. E5 183
Little, mtn., Wyo. D5 213
Little, riv., Ark. B5 169
Little, riv., Ark., Okla. D1 169, C8 200
Little, riv., Conn. C6 172
Little, riv., Ga. C3 175
Little, riv., Ga. C4 175
Little, riv., Ga. E3 175
Little, riv., Ky. D2 182
Little, riv., La. C3 183
Little, riv., N.C. B4 197
Little, riv., S.C. C3 203
Little, riv., Tenn. E11 205
Little, riv., Va. E2 209
Little Acres, Ariz. D5 168
Little Alföld, reg., Hung. B3 68
Little Andaman, isl., India F9 87
Little Antietam, creek, Md. A2 173
Little Arkansas, riv., Kans. A4 181
Little Bahama, bank, Ba. Is. B4 131
Little Bay Islands, Newf., Can. D4 152
Little Beaver, creek, Colo. B8 171
Little Beaver, creek, Kans. C2 181
Little Belt, mts., Mont. D6 190
Little Bighorn, riv., Mont., Wyo. E9 190
Little Birch, W. Va. C4 211
Little Bitter, lake, Eg. D4 84
Little Black, riv., Maine A3 184
Little Blue, riv., Ind. H5 179
Little Blue, riv., Kans., Nebr. C7 181, D8 191
Little Bow, riv., Alta., Can. D4 148
Little Britain, Ont., Can. C6 153
Little Brook, N.S., Can. E3 151
Little Bullhead, Man., Can. D3 150
Little Cadotte, riv., Alta., Can. A2 148
Little Canada, Minn. *E5 187
Little Carpathians, mts., Czech. D4 70
Little Catalina, Newf., Can. D5 152
Little Cayman, isl., Cayman Is. F3 131
Little Cedar, Iowa A5 180
Little Cedar, riv., Iowa A5 180
Little Chief, Okla. A5 200
Little Chute, Wis. A5, D5 212
Little City, Okla. *C5 200
Little Coal, riv., W. Va. C3, D5 211
Little Colorado, riv., Ariz. A4 168
Little Compton, R.I. C12 172
Little Creek, Del. B7 173
Little Creek, peak, Utah F3 207
Little Current, Ont., Can. B3 153
Little Cypress, creek, Tex. F4 206
Little Deer Isle, Maine D4 184
Little Lake des Allemands, lake, La. C6 183
Little Diomede, isl., Alsk. B6 167
Little Dry, creek, Mont. C10 190
Little Eagle, S. Dak. B5 204
Little Egg, harbor, N.J. D4 194
Little Egg, inlet, N.J. E4 194
Little Falls, Minn. E4 187
Little Falls, N.J. B4 194
Little Falls, N.Y. B6 196
Little Ferry, N.J. D5 194
Little Fishing, creek, W. Va. A6 211
Little Fork, riv., Minn. B5 187
Little Frog, mtn., Tenn. D9 205
Little Grand, lake, Newf., Can. D3 152
Little Gunpowder Falls, riv., Md. A4 173
Little Harbour Deep, Newf., Can. C3 152
Little Hocking, Ohio C6 199
Little Humboldt, riv., Nev. B4 192
Little Inagua, isl., Ba. Is. E7 131
Little Kanawha, riv., W. Va. B3, C3 211
Little Laramie, riv., Wyo. D7 213
Little Lynches, riv., S.C. C7 203
Little Makin, isl., Gilbert Is. 115
Little Manatee, riv., Fla. F2 174
Little Manitou, lake, Sask., Can. F3 155
Little Marais, Minn. C7 187
Little Mazarn, creek, Ark. D5 169
Little Meadows, Pa. C9 202
Little Mecatina, isl., Que., Can. C2 152
Little Mecatina, riv., Que., Can. h9 152
Little Miami, riv., Ohio C3 199
Little Minch, chan., Scot. C2 57
Little Miquelon, isl., N.A. m26 143
Little Missouri, riv., Ark. D2 169
Little Missouri, riv., U.S. A7 158
Little Moose, mtn., N.Y. B6 196
Little Mountain, S.C. C5 203
Little Muddy, creek, N. Dak. A2 198
Little Muddy, riv., Ill. E4 178
Little Ocmulgee, riv., Ga. D3 175
Little or Gray, riv., Newf., Can. E3 152
Little Orleans, Md. A1 173
Little Osage, riv., Kans., Mo. E9 181, D3 189
Little Otter, creek, Vt. C2 208
Little Owyhee, riv., Nev. B5 192
Little Paternoster, isl., Indon. F5 90
Little Patuxent, riv., Md. B4 173
Little Peconic, bay, N.Y. E7 172
Little Pee Dee, riv., S.C. C9 203
Little Pend Oreille, riv., Wash. A8 210
Little Pigeon, riv., Ind. I3 179
Little Pine, creek, Pa. D7 202
Little Pipe, creek, Md. A3 173
Little Playgreen, lake, Man., Can. B2 150
Little Powder, riv., Mont., Wyo. F11 190, A7 213
Little Prairie, B.C., Can. B7 149
Little Rann of Kutch, salt flat, India F3 88
Little Red, riv., Ark. B4 169
Little River, Ala. D2 166
Little River, N.S., Can. E3 151
Little River, Kans. D5 181
Little River, S.C. D10 203
Little River, co., Ark. D1 169
Little River, inlet, N.C. D5 197
Little River, inlet, S.C. D10 203
Little River, res., Vt. C3 208
Little Rock, Ark. C3, D6 169
Little Rock, Iowa A2 180
Little Rock, Ky. B5 182
Little Rock, S.C. C9 203
Little Rock, riv., Iowa A2 180
Little Sable, pt., Mich. E4 186
Little Sachigo, lake, Ont., Can. B5 150
Little St. Bernard, pass, Fr., It. D2 66
Little Salt, lake, Utah F3 207
Little Sandy, creek, Wyo. C3 213
Little Sandy, riv., Ky. B7 182
Little Satilla, riv., Ga. E4 175
Little Sauk, Minn. E4 187
Little Sebago, lake, Maine E4 184
Little Sevier, riv., Utah F3 207
Little Silver, N.J. C4 194
Little Sioux, Iowa C1 180
Little Sioux, riv., Iowa B2 180
Little Smoky, riv., Alta., Can. B2 148
Little Smoky, val., Nev. D5 192
Little Snake, riv., Colo., Wyo. A2 171, D5 213
Little Spokane, riv., Wash. B8 210
Little Suamico, Wis. D5 212
Little Sugar, riv., N.H. D2 193
Little Tallapoosa, riv., Ala., Ga. B4 166, C1 175
Little Tenmile, creek, W. Va. A6 211
Little Tennessee, riv., Tenn. D9 205
Little Tucson, Ariz. F4 168
Little Turtle, lake, Ont., Can. B6 187
Little Valley, Calif. B3 170
Little Valley, N.Y. C2 196
Little Vermillion, riv., Ill. E2 179
Little Wabash, riv., Ill. E5 178
Little West, fork, Tenn. A4 205
Little White, riv., Ont., Can. B7 186
Little White, riv., S. Dak. D4 204
Little Wolf, riv., Wis. D4 212
Little Wood, riv., Idaho F4 177
Little York, Ill. B3 178
Little York, Ind. G6 179
Little Zab, riv., Iraq E15 85
Littlefield, Ariz. A2 168
Littlefield, Tex. C1 206
Littlefork, Minn. B5 187
Littlehampton, Eng. D7 56
Littlelot, Tenn. B4 205
Littleport, Iowa B6 180
Littlerock, Wash. C2 210
Littlestown, Pa. G7 202
Littleton, Ala. E4 166
Littleton, Colo. B6 171
Littleton, Ill. C3 178
Littleton, Maine B5 184
Littleton, Mass. C1 185
Littleton, N.H. B3 193
Littleton, N.C. A6 197
Littleton, W. Va. B4, C2 211
Littleton Common, Mass. C1 185
Littleville, Ala. *A2 166
Lithuhi, Tan. D5 106
Liu Panshan, mts., China G2 92
Liu Pen Shan, mts., China K2 92
Liuan, China E6 92
Liucheng, China G6 91
Liuchou, China G6 91
Liucura, Chile B2 136
Liuho, China E2 93
Liupa, China E6 91
Liuyang, China J5 92
Live Oak, Calif. C3 170
Live Oak, Calif. *D2 170
Live Oak, Fla. B4 174
Live Oak, co., Tex. E3 206
Livelong, Sask., Can. D1 155
Lively, Ont., Can. A3 153
Livengood, Alsk. B10 167
Livenza, riv., It. B8 66
Livermore, Calif. B6 170
Livermore, Colo. A5 171
Livermore, Iowa B3 180
Livermore, Ky. C2 182
Livermore, Maine D2 184
Livermore, peak, Tex. F2 206
Livermore Falls, Maine D2 184
Livermore Falls, N.H. C3 193
Liverpool, N.S., Can. E5 151
Liverpool, Eng. A5 56
Liverpool, N.Y. B4 196
Liverpool, Pa. E7 202
Liverpool, Tex. G5 206
Liverpool, W. Va. C3 211
Liverpool, bay, N.W. Ter., Can. B7 142
Liverpool, bay, Eng. A4 56
Liverpool North, Ohio *B7 199
Livinda, riv., Congo, Gabon E2 104
Livingston, Ala. C1 166
Livingston, Calif. D3 170
Livingston, Guat. C3 130
Livingston, Ill. E4 178
Livingston, Ky. C5 182
Livingston, La. A6, D5 183
Livingston, Mont. E6 190
Livingston, N.J. *B4 194
Livingston, N.Y. C7 196
Livingston, S.C. D5 203
Livingston, Tenn. C8 205
Livingston, Tex. D5 206
Livingston, Wis. F3 212
Livingston, co., Ill. C5 178
Livingston, co., Ky. A3 182
Livingston, co., Mich. F6 186
Livingston, co., Mo. B4 189
Livingston, co., N.Y. C3 196
Livingston, par., La. D5 183
Livingston Manor, N.Y. D6 196
Livingstone, Zambia E4 106
Livingstone, range, Alta., Can. D10 149
Livingstone Cove, N.S., Can. D8 151
Livingstonia, Malawi D5 106
Livno, Yugo. D3 68
Livny, Sov. Un. E11 72
Livona, N. Dak. C5 198
Livonia: in 1721 49
Livonia, Ind. G5 179
Livonia, La. D4 183
Livonia, Mich. A7, F7 186
Livonia, Mo. A5 189
Livonia, N.Y. C3 196
Livorno, see Leghorn, It.
Livramento, Braz. E1 137
Livry-Gargan, Fr. g11 58
Liwale, Tan. C6 106
Liyang, China I8 92
Lizard, creek, Iowa B3 180
Lizard, pt., Eng. E2 56
Lizard Head, pass, Colo. D3 171
Lizard Head, peak, Wyo. C3 213
Lizella, Ga. D3 175
Lizemores, W. Va. C3, C7 211
Lizotte, Que., Can. A5 154
Lizton, Ind. E4 179
Ljubljana, Yugo. B2 68
Ljubuški, Yugo. D3 68
Ljungby, Swe. I5 63
Ljusdal, Swe. G7 63
Ljusterö, Swe. t36 63
Llandilo, Wales C4 56
Llandovery, Wales C4 56
Llandrindod Wells, Wales B4 56
Llandudno, Wales A4 56
Llanelly, Wales C3 56
Llanerch, see Havertown, Pa.
Llanes, Sp. A3 65
Llanfyllin, Wales B4 56
Llangefni, Wales A3 56
Llangollen, Wales B4 56
Llangynog, Wales B4 56
Llanidloes, Wales B4 56
Llano, N. Mex. A4 195
Llano, Tex. D3 206
Llano, co., Tex. D3 206
Llano Estacado, plain, Tex. C1 206
Llano Estacado, plat., N. Mex., Tex. C6 195
Llanos, plains, Col., Ven. C4 124
Llanquihue, lake, Chile C2 136
Llanquihue, prov., Chile C2 136
Llanrwst, Wales A4 56
Llata, Peru C2 134
Llaves, N. Mex. A3 195
Llerena, Sp. C2 65
Llerena, pt., C.R. F6 130
Lleyn, pen., Wales B3 56
Llico, Chile A2 136
Llivia, Sp. F4 58
Llobregat, riv., Sp. B6 65
Llorana, mtn., Pan. h11 130
Lloyd, Fla. B2 174
Lloyd, Ky. B7 182
Lloyd, Mont. B7 190
Lloyd, neck, N.Y. F3 172
Lloyd, pt., N.Y. F2 172
Lloyd Harbor, N.Y. *F3 172
Lloyd Place, Va. *E6 209
Lloydminster, Alta., Sask., Can. C5 148, D1 155
Lluchmayor, Sp. C7 65
Llullaillaco, vol., Chile D2 135
Loa, riv., Chile D2 135
Loa, Utah E4 207
Loachapoka, Ala. C4 166

Loami, Ill...D4 178
Loange, riv., Zaire...C2 106
Lobatse, Bots...C4 107
Löbau, Ger...B9 61
Lobaye, riv., Cen. Afr. Rep...E3 104
Lobelville, Tenn...B4 205
Lobenstein, Ger...C6 61
Lobería, Arg...B5 136
Lobito, Ang...D1 106
Lobnya, Sov. Un...m17 72
Lobo, Phil...p13 90
Lobo, Tex...F2 206
Lobos, Arg...B5, g7 136
Lobos, isl., P.R....f12 132
Lobos de Tierra, isl., Peru..C1 134
Lobster, lake, Maine...C3 184
Lobstick, lake, Newf., Can...g8 152
Loburg, Ger...A7 61
Loc Ninh, Viet...G7 89
Locarno, Switz...C4 66
Locate, Mont...D11 190
Loch Arbour, N.J...*C4 194
Loch Lynn Heights, Md...D1 173
Loch Maree, lake, Scot...C3 57
Loch Raven, Md...*B4 173
Loch Raven, res., Md...B4 173
Loch Torridon, lake, Scot...C3 57
Lochaline, Scot...D3 57
Lochbroom, Scot...B4 55
Lochcarron, Scot...C3 57
Lochdonhead, Scot...D3 57
Lochearnhead, Scot...D4 57
Lochem, Neth...B6 59
Loches, Fr...D4 58
Lochgilphead, Scot...D3 57
Lochiel, Ariz...F5 168
Loching, China...J9 92
Lochinver, Scot...B3 57
Lochmaben, Scot...E5 57
Lochmere, N.H...D3 193
Lochnagar, mtn., Scot...D5 57
Lochranza, Scot...E3 57
Lochsa, riv., Idaho...C3 177
Lochuan, China...G3 92
Lochy, lake, Scot...D4 57
Lock Haven, Pa...D7 202
Lock Springs, Mo...B4 189
Lockbourne, Ohio...C2 199
Locke, Ind...B5 179
Locke, N.Y...C4 196
Locke, Tenn...B1, E8 205
Locke Mills, Maine...D2 184
Lockeford, Calif...B6 170
Lockeport, N.S., Can...F4 151
Lockerbie, Scot...E5 57
Lockesburg, Ark...D1 169
Lockhart, Ala...D3 166
Lockhart, Minn...C2 187
Lockhart, S.C...B5 203
Lockhart, Tex...A4, E4 206
Lockland, Ohio...A7 182
Lockney, Tex...B2 206
Lockport, Man., Can...D3 150
Lockport, Ill...B5, F2 178
Lockport, Ky...B5 182
Lockport, La...C6, E5 183
Lockport, N.Y...B2 196
Lockport Station, La...C6 183
Lockridge, Iowa...C6 180
Lockwood, Sask., Can...F3 155
Lockwood, Mo...D4 189
Lockwood, W. Va...C3, C7 211
Locminé, Fr...D2 58
Loco, Okla...C4 200
Loco Hills, N. Mex...E6 195
Locumba, Peru...E3 134
Locust, N.J...C4 194
Locust, creek, Mo...B4 189
Locust, fork, Ala...B3 166
Locust, pt., Md...B5 173
Locust Bayou, Ark...D3 169
Locust Grove, Ga...C2 175
Locust Grove, Md...B6 173
Locust Grove, Okla...A6 200
Locust Hill, Ont., Can...E7 153
Locust Valley, N.Y...F2 172
Lod (Lydda), Isr...C6, h10 84
Loda, Ill...C5 178
Löderup, Swe...C8 62
Lodève, Fr...F5 58
Lodeynoye Pole, Sov. Un..A9 72
Lodge, S.C...E6 203
Lodge, creek, Can., Mont...H1 155, B7 190
Lodge Grass, Mont...E9 190
Lodgepole, Nebr...C3 191
Lodgepole, S. Dak...B3 204
Lodgepole, creek, Nebr., Wyo...C3 191, D8 213
Lodhran, Pak...C3 88
Lodi, Calif...B6, C3 170
Lodi, Zaire...B3 106
Lodi, It...D5 66
Lodi, N.J...B4 194
Lodi, N.Y...C4 196
Lodi, Ohio...A5 199
Lodi, Wis...B3 209
Lodi, Wis...E4 212
Lodja, Zaire...B3 106
Lodore, canyon, Colo...A2 171
Lods, Fr...B2 66
Lodwar, Ken...A6 106
Łódź, Pol...C5 70
Loeches, Sp...p18 65
Loei, Thai...D3 89
Loelli (Well), Sud...D3 105
Loeriesfontein, S. Afr...D2 107
Lofer, Aus...B8 66
Lofgreen, Utah...C3 207
Lofoten, is., Nor...C5 63
Lofton, Ga...C1 175
Loftus, Eng...F8 57
Log Lane Village, Colo...A7 171
Logan (Hanaford), Ill...F5 178
Logan, Iowa...C2 180
Logan, Kans...C4 181
Logan, Mont...E5 190
Logan, N. Mex...B6 195
Logan, N. Dak...A4 198
Logan, Ohio...C5 199
Logan, Okla...A1, D4 200
Logan, Utah...B4 207
Logan, W. Va...D3, D5 211
Logan, co., Ark...B2 169
Logan, co., Colo...A7 171
Logan, co., Ill...C4 178
Logan, co., Kans...D2 181
Logan, co., Ky...D3 182
Logan, co., Nebr...C5 191
Logan, co., N. Dak...C6 198
Logan, co., Ohio...B4 199
Logan, co., Okla...B4 200
Logan, co., W. Va...D3 211
Logan, mtn., Yukon, Can...D4 142
Logan, mtn., Wash...A5 210
Logan, pass, Mont...B3 190
Logan Lake, B.C., Can...*D7 149
Logan Martin, lake, Ala...B3 166
Logandale, Nev...G7 192
Logansport, Ind...C5 179
Logansport, Ky...C3 182
Logansport, La...C2 183
Loganton, Pa...D7 202
Loganville, Ga...C3 175
Loganville, Pa...G8 202
Loganville, Wis...E3 212
Loggieville, N.B., Can...*C4 151
Logone, riv., Chad...D3 104
Logroño, Sp...A4 65
Logrosán, Sp...C3 65
Løgstør, Den...B3 62
Løgumkloster, Den...C2 62
Lohals, Den...C4 62
Lohardaga, India...F10 88
Lohman, Mont...B7 190
Loho, China...H6 92
Lohr, Ger...D4 61
Lohrville, Iowa...B3 180
Loi Mai, mtn., Bur...B2 89
Loire, riv., Fr...D3 58
Lois, Tenn...B5 205
Loíza, P.R...B7 132
Loíza, mun., P.R...B7 132
Loíza Aldea, P.R...B7 132
Loja, Ec...B2 134
Loja, Sp...D3 65
Loja, prov., Ec...B2 134
Lojar, cape, Indon...F5 90
Lokandu, Zaire...B4 106
Lokeren, Bel...C3 59
Lokhvitsa, Sov. Un...F9 72
Lokichar, Ken...A6 106
Lokichoggio, Ken...A5 106
Lokitaung, Ken...A6 106
Løkken, Den...A3 62
Lokoja, Nig...E6 103
Lokoro, riv., Zaire...B3 106
Lokossa, Dah...E5 103
Lokwei, China...C9 89
Lol, riv., Sud...D2 105
Lola, Ky...A3 182
Lola, mtn., Calif...C3 170
Lolland, isl., Den...D5 62
Lollar, Ger...C3 61
Lollie (Minter), Ga...D4 175
Lolo, Mont...D2 190
Lolo, pass, Idaho...C4 177
Lolo Hot Springs, Mont...D2 190
Lolobau, isl., Bis. Arch...115
Lom, Bul...D6 68
Loma, Colo...B2 171
Loma, Mont...C6 190
Loma, Nebr...C9 191
Loma, N. Dak...A7 198
Loma, mts., Guinea, S.L...E2 103
Lomami, riv., Zaire...B3 106
Loman, Minn...B5 187
Lomas, Peru...E3 134
Lomas de Zamora, Arg...A5, g7 136
Lomax, Ala...C3 166
Lomax, Ill...C2 178
Lombard, Ill...F2 178
Lombardy, reg., It...B2 67
c. 814...47
in 1815...50
in 1859...51
Lombez, Fr...F4 58
Lomblen, isl., Indon...G6 90
Lombok, isl., Indon...G5 90
Lombok, strait, Indon...G5 90
Lomé, Togo...E5 103
Lomela, Zaire...B3 106
Lomela, riv., Zaire...B3 106
Lometa, Tex...D3 206
Lomira, Wis...E5 212
Lomita, Calif...*F4 170
Lommel, Bel...C5 59
Lomond, Alta., Can...D4 148
Lomond, Newf., Can...D3 152
Lomond, lake, Scot...D4 57
Lomonosov, Sov. Un...s30 63
Lomonosovskaya, Sov. Un...C7 73
Lompoc, Calif...E3 170
Łomża, Pol...B7 70
Lonaconing, Md...D2 173
Loncoche, Chile...B2 136
Londesborough, Ont., Can...D3 153
London, Ark...B2 169
London, Ont., Can...E3 153
London, Eng...E6, k12 55
London, Ky...C5 182
London, Ohio...C4 199
London, Tex...D3 206
London Mills, Ill...C3 178
Londonbridge, Va...*E6 209
Londonderry, N.S., Can...D6 151
Londonderry, N.H...E4 193
Londonderry, N. Ire...C3 55
Londonderry, Ohio...C5 199
Londonderry, Vt...E3 208
Londonderry, cape, Austl...B4 110
Londonderry, isl., Chile...k11 136
Londrina, Braz...C2 137
Lone, mtn., S. Dak...B2 204
Lone Elm, Kans...D8 181
Lone Grove, Okla...C4 200
Lone Jack, Mo...*C3 189
Lone Mountain, Tenn...C10 205
Lone Oak, Ky...A2 182
Lone Oak, S.C...*B4 203
Lone Oak, Tex...C5 206
Lone Pine, Calif...D4 170
Lone Rock, Sask., Can...D1 155
Lone Rock, Iowa...A3 180
Lone Rock, Wis...E3 212
Lone Star, S.C...D6 203
Lone Star, Tex...*C5 206
Lone Tree, Iowa...C6 180
Lone Tree, creek, Colo...A6 171
Lone Wolf, Okla...C2 200
Lonejack, Mo...C3 189
Lonely, Tenn...A4 205
Lonely, isl., Ont., Can...B3 153
Lonepine, Mont...C2 190
Lonerock, Oreg...B7 201
Lonetree, Wyo...D2 213
Long, co., Ga...E5 175
Long, bay, N.C...D5 197
Long, beach, N.Y...E7 172
Long, beach, N.Y...G2 172
Long, isl., Ba. Is...D6 131
Long, isl., N.S., Can...E3 151
Long, isl., Maine...D4 184
Long, isl., Mass...D3 185
Long, isl., N. Gui...k12 110
Long, isl., N.Y...F3 172, D3 196
Long, isl., Sol. Is...115
Long, key, Fla...H6 174
Long, lake, N.B., Can...B3 151
Long, lake, La...E5 183
Long, lake, Maine...A4 184
Long, lake, Maine...D2 184
Long, lake, Mich...C7 186
Long, lake, Mich...D5 186
Long, lake, Minn...D4 187
Long, lake, N.Y...B6 196
Long, lake, N. Dak...C6 198
Long, lake, Wash...D1 210
Long, lake, Wis...C2 212
Long, mtn., N.H...A4 193
Long, pond, Fla...C4 174
Long, pond, Maine...C2 184
Long, pond, Maine...C3 184
Long, pond, Mass...C6 185
Long, strait, Sov. Un...B20 71
Long Barn, Calif...C3 170
Long Beach, Calif...F2, F4 170
Long Beach, Ind...A4 179
Long Beach, Minn...E3 187
Long Beach, Miss...E2, E4 188
Long Beach, N.Y...E2, E3 196
Long Beach, Wash...C1 210
Long Beach Resort, Fla...*G3 174
Long Bottom, Ohio...C6 199
Long Branch, Ont., Can...E6 153
Long Branch, N.J...C5 194
Long Cliff, Ind...C5 179
Long Creek, Oreg...C7 201
Long Creek, mtn., Wyo...C5 213
Long Eaton, Eng...B6 56
Long Eddy, N.Y...D5 196
Long Grove, Ill...*A5 178
Long Grove, Iowa...C7 180
Long Harbour, Newf., Can...E5 152
Long Hill, Conn...D4 172
Long Island, Kans...C4 181
Long Island, Maine...*E5 184
Long Island, Tenn...*C11 205
Long Island, Va...D3 209
Long Island, sound, Conn., N.Y...E5 172, D3 196
Long Key, Fla...H6 174
Long Lake, Ill...*A5 178
Long Lake, Mich...D7 186
Long Lake, Minn...*F5 187
Long Lake, N.Y...B6 196
Long Lake, Wis...C5 212
Long Lane, Mo...D5 189
Long Park, Colo...C2 171
Long Pine, Nebr...B6 191
Long Point, N.S., Can...B8 151
Long Point, Ill...B5 178
Long Pond, Newf., Can...E5 152
Long Pond, Maine...C2 184
Long Prairie, Minn...E4 187
Long Range, mts., Newf., Can...D3, E2 152
Long Rapids, Mich...C7 186
Long Ridge, Conn...E2 172
Long Run, W. Va...B4, B6 211
Long Savannah, Tenn...E10 205
Long Valley, Ariz...C4 168
Long Valley, N.J...B3 194
Long Valley Junction, Utah...F3 207
Long View, Ky...C4 182
Long Xuyen, Viet...G6 89
Longa, riv., Ang...D1 106
Longá, riv., Braz...B2 138
Longbenton, Eng...*C6 55
Longboat, inlet, Fla...F1 174
Longboat, key, Fla...E4 174
Longboat Key, Fla...F2 174
Longbranch, Wash...B3 210
Longcreek, S.C...B1 203
Longdale, Okla...A3 200
Longford, Ire...D3 55
Longford, Kans...C6 181
Longford Mills, Ont., Can..C5 153
Longhurst, N.C...A5 197
Longiram, Indon...F5 90
Longisland, N.C...B3 197
Longlake, S. Dak...B6 204
Longleaf, La...C3 183
Longmeadow, Mass...B2 185
Longmont, Colo...A5 171
Longport, N.J...E3 194
Longreach, Austl...A5 112
Longridge, Eng...G6 57
Longs, peak, Colo...A5 171
Longstreet, La...B2 183
Longton, Kans...E7 181
Longtown, Eng...E6 57
Longtown, Mo...D8 189
Longueau, Fr...E2 59
Longueuil, Que., Can...D4, D9 154
Longuyon, Fr...C6 58
Longvale, Calif...C2 170
Longvalley, S. Dak...D4 204
Longview, Alta., Can...D3 148
Longview, Ill...D5 178
Longview, Miss...B5 188
Longview, N.C...B2 197
Longview, Tex...C5 206
Longview, Wash...C3 210
Longville, La...D2 183
Longville, Minn...D4 187
Longwood, Fla...*D5 174
Longwood, Mo...C4 189
Longwood, N.C...C5 197
Longwood Park, N.C...*C4 197
Longwoods, Md...C5 173
Longwy, Fr...C6 58
Loning, China...G4 92
Lonkin, Bur...C10 87
Lonoke, Ark...C4, D6 169
Lonoke, co., Ark...C4 169
Lons-le-Saunier, Fr...D6 58
Lonsdal, Nor...D6 63
Lonsdale, Ark...C3 169
Lonsdale, Ont., Can...C7 153
Lonsdale, Minn...F5 187
Lonsdale, R.I...B11 172
Looe, Eng...D3 56
Loogootee, Ind...G4 179
Lookeba, Okla...B3 200
Lookout, Calif...B3 170
Lookout, Ky...C7 182
Lookout, Okla...A2 200
Lookout, W. Va...C4, D7 211
Lookout, Wyo...D7 213
Lookout, cape, N.C...C7 197
Lookout, mtn., Oreg...C6 201
Lookout, mtn., Tenn...D8 205
Lookout, pass, Idaho, Mont...C1 190
Lookout, pt., Mich...D7 186
Lookout, ridge, Alsk...B8 167
Lookout Heights, Ky...*A5 182
Lookout Mountain, Tenn..E10 205
Lookout Mountain, ridge, Ala., Ga., Tenn...A4 166
Lookout Point, res., Oreg...D4 201
Looma, Alta., Can...C4 148
Loomis, Sask., Can...H1 155
Loomis, Nebr...D6 191
Loomis, S. Dak...D7 204
Loomis, Wash...A6 210
Loon, creek, Sask., Can...F3 155
Loon, lake, Alta., Can...A3 148
Loon, lake, Maine...B3 184
Loon, riv., Alta., Can...A3 148
Loon, riv., Man., Can...A1 150
Loon Bay, Newf., Can...D4 152
Loon Lake, Wash...A8 210
Loon Lake, mts., N.Y...B3 196
Loon Straits, Man., Can...D3 150
Loonhaunt, lake, Ont., Can...B5 187
Loop, Tex...C1 206
Loop, creek, W. Va...D6 211
Loop, head, Ire...D1 55
Loos, Fr...D3 59
Loosahatchie, riv., Tenn...B2 205
Loose Creek, Mo...C6 189
Looxahoma, Miss...A4 188
Lop Nor, lake, China...D3 91
Lopatka, cape, Sov. Un...D18 71
Lopei, China...C5 93
Lopevi, isl., New Hebr...115
Lopez, Pa...D9 202
Lopez, Phil...p14 90
Lopez, cape, Gabon...F1 104
Lopez, isl., Wash...A3 210
Loping, China...J7 92
Lopori, riv., Zaire...A3 106
Lopphavet, sea, Nor...B9 63
Lora, Sp...D3 65
Lora, riv., Afg...B3 87
Lorado, W. Va...D3, D6 211
Lorain, Ohio...A5 199
Lorain, Pa...*F4 202
Lorain, co., Ohio...A5 199
Loraine, Ill...C2 178
Loraine, N. Dak...A4 198
Loraine, Tex...C2 206
Loralai, Pak...B2 88
Loramie, res., Ohio...B3 199
Loranger, La...D5 183
Lorca, Sp...D5 65
Lord Howe, is., Pac. O...I9 113
Lordsburg, N. Mex...E1 195
Lore City, Ohio...C6 199
Loreauville, La...D4 183
Loreburn, Sask., Can...F2 155
Lorena, Braz...C3 137
Lorengau, Manus I...115
Lorentz, W. Va...C4 211
Lorenzo, Idaho...F7 177
Lorenzo, Nebr...C2 191
Lorenzo, Tex...C2 206
Loreto, Arg...E3 135
Loreto, Braz...C1 138
Loreto, Col...D3 133
Loreto, It...C4 67
Loreto, Mex...B2 129
Loreto, Par...D4 135
Loreto, dept., Peru...C3 134
Loretta, Kans...D4 181
Loretta, Wis...C3 212
Lorette, Man., Can...E3 150
Loretteville, Que., Can...C6, C8 154
Loretto, Fla...C6 174
Loretto, Ky...C4 182
Loretto, Mich...C3 186
Loretto, Minn...*E5 187
Loretto, Nebr...C7 191
Loretto, Pa...A4 202
Loretto, Tenn...B4 205
Lorica, Col...B2 133
Lorida, Fla...E5 174
Lorient, Fr...D2 58
L'Orignal, Ont., Can...B10 153
Lorimor, Iowa...C3 180
Loring, Mont...B9 190
Loris, S.C...C10 203
Lorlie, Sask., Can...G4 155
Lorman, Miss...D2 188
Lorne, firth, Scot...D3 57
Lorne Park, Ont., Can...E6 153
Lorneville, Ont., Can...C5 153
Lörrach, Ger...E3 60
Lorraine, Kans...D5 181
Lorraine, N.Y...B5 196
Lorraine, plat., Fr...F6 59
Lorraine, former prov., Fr..C6 58
c. 1360...48
in 1721...49
in 1871...51
in 1940...53
Lorsch, Ger...D3 61
Lorton, Nebr...*D9 191
Lorup, Ger...B7 59
Los Alamitos, Calif...*F5 170
Los Alamos, Calif...E3 170
Los Alamos, N. Mex...*B3 195
Los Alamos, N. Mex...B4 195
Los Alamos, co., N. Mex..B3 195
Los Altos, Calif...C5 170
Los Altos Hills, Calif...*D3 170
Los Amates, Guat...C3 130
Los Amigos Privados, Cuba...k11 131
Los Andes, Chile...A2 136
Los Angeles, Calif...E4, F2 170
Los Ángeles, Chile...B2 136
Los Angeles, co., Calif...E4, F2 170
Los Angeles, aqueduct, Calif...E4 170
Losantville (Bronson), Ind...D7 179
Los Banos, Calif...D3 170
Los Barrios, Sp...D3 65
Los Blancos, Arg...D3 135
Los Caños Central, P.R...B4 132
Los Cerrillos, Arg...A3 136
Los Ebanos, Tex...F3 206
Los Fresnos, Tex...F4 206
Los Gatos, Calif...C5, D2 170
Loshan, China...F5 91
Loshan, China...H6 92
Los Herreras, Mex...G3 206
Lošinj, isl., Yugo...C2 68
Los Llanos, P.R...C5 132
Los Lunas, N. Mex...C3 195
Los Mochis, Mex...B3 129
Los Molinos, Calif...B2 170
Los Muertos, P.R...B4 132
Los Negros, isl., Bis. Arch...115
Losombo, Zaire...A2 106
Los Palacios, Cuba...C2 131
Los Palacios, Sp...D3 65
Los Pinos, Cuba...k11 131
Los Pinos, N. Mex...A3 195
Los Pinos, riv., Colo...D3 171
Los Pozos, Chile...E1 135
Los Rábanos, P.R...C3 132
Los Ranchos de Albuquerque, N. Mex...G5 195
Los Reyes, Mex...D4, n12 129
Los Reyes [la Paz], Mex...h10 129
Los Reyes, is., Bis. Arch...115
Los Ríos, prov., Ec...B2 134
Los Santos, Pan...G7 130
Los Santos, Sp...C2 65
Los Sarmientos, Arg...E2 135
Los Sauces, Chile...B2 136
Lossiemouth, Scot...C5 57
Lössnitz, Ger...C7 61
Lossuk, New Ire. I...115
Lost, creek, Wyo...C4 213
Lost, peak, Utah...F2 207
Lost, riv., Ind...G4 179
Lost, riv., Minn...C3 187
Lost, riv., Wash...A5 210
Lost, riv., W. Va...B6 211
Lost Cabin, Wyo...B5 213
Lost City, W. Va...C6 211
Lost Creek, W. Va...B4 211
Lost Hills, Calif...E4 170
Lost Nation, Iowa...C7 180
Lost Ranger, peak, Colo...A4 171
Lost River, W. Va...C6 211
Lost River, range, Idaho...E5 177
Lost River Glacial, caverns, N.H...B3 193
Lost Springs, Kans...D7 181
Lost Springs, Wyo...C8 213
Lost Trail, pass, Idaho, Mont...D5 177, E2 190
Lostant, Ill...B4 178
Los Taques, Ven...A3 133
Los Teques, Ven...A4 133
Lostine, Oreg...B9 201
Los Trujillos, N. Mex...C3 195
Lostwood, N. Dak...A3 198
Los Vilos, Chile...A2 136
Lot, Ponape...114
Lot, hbr., Ponape...114
Lot, riv., Fr...E4 58
Lota, Chile...B2 136
Lotawana, lake, Mo...E2 189
Lotbinière, Que., Can...C6 154
Lotbinière, co., Que., Can...C6 154
Lothair, Ky...C6 182
Lothair, Mont...B5 190
Loting, China...A9 89
Loto, Zaire...B3 106
Lotofaga, W. Sam...114
Lötschberg, tunnel, Switz...C3 66
Lott, Tex...D4 206
Lotung, Taiwan...G9 91
Lou, isl., Bis. Arch...115
Louann, Ark...D3 169
Loudima, Con...F2 104
Loudon, N.H...D4 193
Loudon, Tenn...D9 205
Loudon, co., Tenn...D9 205
Loudonville, Ohio...B5 199
Loudoun, co., Va...B5 209
Loudun, Fr...D4 58
Louga, Sen...C1 103
Loughborough, Eng...B6 56
Lougheed, Alta., Can...C5 148
Loughman, Fla...D5 174
Loughrea, Ire...D2 55
Louin, Miss...C4 188
Louis VII, crusade of...47
Louis IX, crusade of...47
Louis XIV, point, N.W. Ter., Can...F16 143
Louis Gentil, Mor...C3 102
Louis Trichardt, S. Afr...B4 107
Louisa, Ky...B7 182
Louisa, Va...C5 209
Louisa, co., Iowa...C6 180
Louisa, co., Va...D5 209
Louisa, lake, Fla...D5 174
Louisbourg, N.S., Can...D10 151
Louisburg, Kans...D9 181
Louisburg, Minn...E2 187
Louisburg, Mo...D4 189
Louisburg, N.C...A5 197
Louisdale, N.S., Can...D8 151
Louise, Ga...C2 175
Louise, Miss...C3 188
Louise, Tex...E4 206
Louise, W. Va...B2 211
Louise, isl., B.C., Can...C2 149
Louise, lake, Alsk...f18 167
Louiseville, Que., Can...C5 154
Louisiade, arch., Pap...G9 113
Louisiana, Mo...B6 189
Louisiana, state, U.S...183
in 1812...163
during Civil War...164
Louisiana, pt., La...E2 183
Louisville, Ala...D4 166
Louisville, Colo...B5 171
Louisville, Ga...C4 175
Louisville, Ill...E5 178
Louisville, Kans...C7 181
Louisville, Ky...A4, B4 182
Louisville, Miss...B4 188
Louisville, Nebr...D9, E3 191
Louisville, N.Y...A2 196
Louisville, Ohio...B6 199
Louisville, Tenn...D9, E11 205
Loukhi, Sov. Un...D15 63
Loulé, Port...D1 65
Louny, Czech...C2 70
Loup, co., Nebr...C6 191
Loup, riv., Que., Can...B8 154
Loup, riv., Que., Can...C4 154
Loup, riv., Nebr...C8 191
Loup City, Nebr...C7 191
Lourdes, Newf., Can...D2 152
Lourdes, Que., Can...C4 154
Lourdes, Que., Can...C6 154
Lourdes, Fr...F3 58
Lourenço Marques, Moz..C5 107
Lourenço Marques, prov., Moz...C5 107
Loures, Port...f9 65
Lousã, Port...B1 65
Lousana, Alta., Can...C4 148
Louth, Eng...A8 56
Loutrá Aidhipsoú, Grc...C4 69
Loutrákion, Grc...h9 69
L'Outre, bayou, La...B3 183
Louvain, see Leuven, Bel.
Louvale, Ga...D2 175
Louviers, Colo...B6 171
Louviers, Fr...C4 58
Louzi, Zaire...B1 106
Lovat, riv., Sov. Un...C8 72
Love, Sask., Can...D3 155
Love, co., Okla...D4 200
Love, pt., Md...B5 173
Lovech, Bul...D7 68
Lovelaceville, Ky...A2 182
Lovelady, Tex...D5 206
Loveland, Colo...A5 171
Loveland, Iowa...C2 180
Loveland, Ohio...C1, D2 199
Loveland, Okla...C3 200
Loveland, pass, Colo...B5 171
Loveland Park, Ohio...C2, C3 199
Lovell, Maine...D2 184
Lovell, Okla...A4 200
Lovell, Wyo...A4 213
Lovelock, Nev...C3 192
Lovely, Ky...C7 182
Loverna, Sask., Can...F1 155
Loves Park, Ill...A4 178
Lovett, Ga...D4 175
Lovett, Ind...G6 179
Lovettsville, Va...B5 209
Lovewell, pond, Maine...D2 184
Lovewell, res., Kans...C5 181
Lovick, Ala...E5 166
Lovilia, Iowa...C5 180
Loving, N. Mex...E6 195
Loving, co., Tex...D1 206
Lovingston, Va...D4 209
Lovington, Ill...D5 178
Lovington, Iowa...A7 180
Lovington, N. Mex...E6 195
Lovisa, Fin...G12 63

INDEX KEY Each place listed in **Bold-faced Type** has its population listed in the Population tables, pages 230 to 280.
Each country, shown in CAPITAL LETTERS, has its population listed in the World Political Information Table, pages 6 to 10.
* Does not appear on map; key shows general location.

Lovosice, Czech....C9 61
Low, Que., Can....D2 154
Low, see Tuamotu, arch., Fr. Polynesia
Low, cape, N.W. Ter., Can....D15 143
Low, pen., B.C., Can....E5 149
Low Moor, Iowa....C7 180
Low Tatra, mts., Czech....D5 70
Lowa, Zaire....B4 106
Lowakai, Manus I....115
Lowden, Iowa....C7 180
Lowe Farm, Man., Can....E3 150
Lowell, Ark....A1 169
Lowell, Ind....B3 179
Lowell, Mass....A5, C2 185
Lowell, Mich....F5 186
Lowell, Nebr....D7 191
Lowell, N.C....B2 197
Lowell, Ohio....C6 199
Lowell, Oreg....D4 201
Lowell, Vt....B4 208
Lowell, Wash....*B3 210
Lowell, W. Va....D4 211
Lowell, Wis....*E5 212
Lowell, isl., Mass....C4 185
Lowell, mts., Vt....B4 208
Lowellville, Ohio....A7 199
Lower, lake, Nev....B2 192
Lower Arrow, lake, B.C., Can....E8 149
Lower Bank, N.J....D3 194
Lower Brule, S. Dak....C6 204
Lower Brule, Indian res., S. Dak....C5 204
Lower Burrell, Pa....*E2 202
Lower Cabot, Vt....C4 208
Lower Canada: 1792-1840....146
Lower Caraquet, N.B., Can....*B5 151
Lower East Pubnico, N.S., Can....F4 151
Lower Egypt: in 7th cent. B.C.....42
Lower Giuba, dist., Som....E5 105
Lower Hutt, N.Z....*N15 112
Lower Island Cove, Newf., Can....D5 152
Lower Lake, Calif....C2 170
Lower Marlboro, Md....C4 173
Lower Matecumbe, key, Fla....H6 174
Lower Monumental, res., Wash....C7 210
Lower New York, bay, N.Y.....E1, E2 196
Lower Paia, Haw....C5 176
Lower Peach Tree, Ala....D2 166
Lower Red, lake, Minn....C3 187
Lower Salem, Ohio....C6 199
Lower Southampton, N.B., Can....D2 151
Lower Village, Vt....C3 208
Lower West Pubnico, N.S., Can....F4 151
Lowes, Ky....A2 182
Lowestoft, Eng....B9 56
Lowgap, Ark....A2 169
Lowgap N.C....A3 197
Łowicz, Pol....B5 70
Lowland, N.C....B7 197
Lowman, Idaho....E3 177
Lowmansville, Ky....C7 182
Lowmoor, Va....D3 209
Lowndes, Mo....D7 189
Lowndes, co., Ala....C3 166
Lowndes, co., Ga....F3 175
Lowndes, co., Miss....B5 188
Lowndesboro, Ala....C3 166
Lowndesville, S.C....C2 203
Lowry, Minn....E3 187
Lowry, S. Dak....B6 204
Lowry City, Mo....C4 189
Lowrys, S.C....B5 203
Lowryville, Tenn....B3 205
Lowville, N.Y....B5 196
Loxley, Ala....E2 166
Loxton, Austl....G3 112
Loyal, Okla....B3 200
Loyal, Wis....D3 212
Loyalist, Alta., Can....D5 148
Loyall, Ky....D6 182
Loyalsock, creek, Pa....D8 202
Loyalton, Calif....C3 170
Loyalton, S. Dak....B6 204
Loyalty, is., Pac. O....H10 113
Loyang, China....G5 92
Loysburg, Pa....F5 202
Loysville, Pa....F7 202
Lozeau, Mont....C2 190
Loznica, Yugo....C4 68
Lozovatka, Sov. Un....G9 72
Lozovaya, Sov. Un....G11 72
Lozoya, canal, Sp....o17 65
Lualaba (Congo), riv., Zaire....B4 106
Lualualei, Haw....g9 176
Lua Makika, mtn., Haw....C5 176
Luampa, Zambia....E3 106
Luan, riv., China....C8 91
Luana, Iowa....A6 180
Luana, riv., Zaire....B4 106
Luanda, Ang....C1 106
Luanda, dist., Ang....C1 106
Luang Prabang, Laos....C5 89
Luanguinga, riv., Ang., Zambia....D3 106
Luanshya, Zambia....D4 106
Luarca, Sp....A2 65
Luashi, Zaire....D3 106
Lubaczów, Pol....C7 70
Lubań, Pol....C3 70
Lubang, Phil....p13 90
Lubang, is., Phil....C6 90
Lubao, Phil....o13 90
Lubartów, Pol....C7 70
Lubawa, Pol....B5 70
Lübbecke, Ger....A3 61
Lübben, Ger....B8 61
Lübbenau, Ger....B8 61
Lubbock, Tex....C2 206
Lubbock, co., Tex....C2 206
Lubec, Maine....D6 184
Lübeck, Ger....B5 60, E4 62
Lübeck, bay, Ger....B5 60
Lubefu, Zaire....B3 106
Lubero, Zaire....B4 106
Lubicon, lake, Alta., Can....A3 148
Lubilash, riv., Zaire....C3 106
Lubin, Pol....C4 70
Lublin, Pol....C7 70
Lublin, Wis....C3 212
Lubliniec, Pol....C5 70
Lubny, Sov. Un....F9 72
Lubrín, Sp....D4 65
Lubsko, Pol....C3 70
Lübtheen, Ger....E5 62
Lubudi, Zaire....C4 106
Lubudi, riv., Zaire....D3 106
Lubue, Zaire....B2 106
Lubumbashi, Zaire....D4 106
Lubutu, Zaire....B4 106
Lucama, N.C....B5 197
Lucan, Ont., Can....D3 153
Lucan, Minn....F3 187
Lucania, mtn., Yukon, Can....D4 142
Lucas, Iowa....C4 180
Lucas, Kans....C5 181
Lucas, Ky....D3 182
Lucas, Mich....D5 186
Lucas, Ohio....B5 199
Lucas, S. Dak....D6 204
Lucas, co., Iowa....C4 180
Lucas, co., Ohio....A4 199
Lucas, channel, Ont., Can....B3 153
Lucasville, Ohio....D5 199
Lucca, It....C3 67
Lucca, N. Dak....C8 198
Luce, co., Mich....B5 186
Luce, bay, Scot....F4 57
Lucea, Jam....F4 131
Lucedale, Miss....E5 188
Lucena, Phil....C6, p13 90
Lucena, Sp....D3 65
Lucena del Cid, Sp....B5 65
Lučenec, Czech....D5 70
Lucera, It....D5 67
Lucerne, Calif....C2 170
Lucerne, Colo....A6 171
Lucerne, Ind....C5 179
Lucerne, Mo....A4 189
Lucerne (Luzern), Switz....B4 66
Lucerne, Wyo....B4 213
Lucerne, lake, Switz....C4 66
Lucerne Valley, Calif....E5 170
Lucernemines, Pa....E3 202
Lucero, Cuba....h12 131
Luceville, Que., Can....A9 154
Luchi, China....J4 92
Luchou, China....F6 91
Lüchow, Ger....F5 62
Luchuan, China....G7 91
Lucien, Miss....D3 188
Lucien, Okla....A4 200
Lucile, Ga....E2 175
Lucile, Idaho....D2 177
Lucin, Utah....B2 207
Lucinda, Pa....D3 202
Lucipara, is., Indon....G7 90
Lucira, Ang....D1 106
Luck, N.C....D3 197
Luck, Wis....C1 212
Luckau, Ger....B8 61
Luckenwalde, Ger....A8 61
Luckey, Ohio....A2, A4 199
Lucknow, Ont., Can....C3 153
Lucknow, India....C7 87, D8 88
Lucky Lake, Sask., Can....G2 155
Lucky Peak, res., Idaho....F3 177
Lucky Strike, Alta., Can....E5 148
Luçon, Fr....D3 58
Lucy, La....B6 183
Lucy, Tenn....E8 205
Luda Kamchiya, riv., Bul....D8 68
Ludden, N. Dak....C7 198
Ludell, Kans....C3 181
Lüdenscheid, Ger....B2 61
Lüderitz, S.W. Afr....C2 107
Lüderitz, bay, S.W. Afr....C1 107
Ludgate, Ont., Can....B4 153
Ludhiana, India....B6 87, B5 88
Lüdinghausen, Ger....B2 61
Ludington, Mich....E4 186
Ludlow, Calif....E5 170
Ludlow, N.B., Can....C3 151
Ludlow, Colo....D6 171
Ludlow, Eng....B5 56
Ludlow, Ill....C5 178
Ludlow, Ky....A7 182
Ludlow, Maine....B4 184
Ludlow, Mass....B3 185
Ludlow, Miss....C4 188
Ludlow, Mo....B4 189
Ludlow, Pa....C4 202
Ludlow, S. Dak....B2 204
Ludlow, Vt....E3 208
Ludlow, mtn., Vt....E3 208
Ludlow Falls, Ohio....C3 199
Ludowici, Ga....E5 175
Ludvika, Swe....G6 63
Ludwigs, canal, Ger....D6 61
Ludwigsburg, Ger....E4 61
Ludwigshafen, Ger....D3 61
Ludwigslust, Ger....B5 60
Luebo, Zaire....C3 106
Lueders, Tex....C3 206
Luepa, Ven....B5 133
Lufkin, Tex....D5 206
Lufuna, Zaire....C2 106
Luga, Sov. Un....B7 72
Luga, riv., Sov. Un....B7 72
Lugagnano Val d'Adra, It....E5 66
Lugan, riv., Sov. Un....q22 72
Luganchik, riv., Sov. Un....q22 72
Lugano, Switz....C4 66
Lugau, Ger....C7 61
Lugela, riv., Moz....A6 107
Lugenda, riv., Moz....D6 106
Lugert, Okla....C2 200
Lugh Ferrandi, Som....E5 105
Lugnaquillia, mtn., Ire....D3 55
Lugo, It....B3 67
Lugo, Sp....A2 65
Lugoff, S.C....C6 203
Lugoj, Rom....C5 68
Lugovoy, Sov. Un....E8 73
Luho, China....E5 91
Luichow, China....G6 91
Luichow, pen., China....G7 91
Luing, isl., Scot....D3 57
Luís Correia, Braz....B2 138
Luís Gomes, Braz....C3 138
Luis Lopez, N. Mex....D3 195
Luitpold, mtn., N. Gui....k12 110
Luiza, Zaire....C3 106
Luján, Arg....g7 136
Lujan [de Cuyo], Arg....A3 136
Lukachukai, Ariz....A6 168
Luke, Md....D1 173
Lukenie, riv., Zaire....B2 106
Lukeville, Ariz....F3 168
Lukolela, Zaire....B2 106
Lukovit, Bul....D7 68
Lukow, Pol....C7 70
Lukoyanov, Sov. Un....D15 72
Lukuga, riv., Zaire....C4 106
Lukulu, Zambia....D3 106
Lula, Ga....B3 175
Lula, Miss....A3 188
Lula, Okla....C5 200
Luleå, Swe....E10 63
Luleälven, riv., Swe....D9 63
Luling, La....C7 183
Luling, Tex....B4, E4 206
Lulu, Fla....B4 174
Lulua, riv., Zaire....C3 106
Luluabourg, Zaire....C3 106
Lulung, China....E8 92
Lum, Mich....E7 186
Lumba, Zaire....A2 106
Lumber, riv., N.C....C5 197
Lumber Bridge, N.C....C4 197
Lumber City, Ga....E4 175
Lumberport, W. Va....A6, B4 211
Lumberton, Miss....D4 188
Lumberton, N.J....D3 194
Lumberton, N. Mex....A3 195
Lumberton, N.C....C5 197
Lumbo, Moz....D7 106
Lumby, B.C., Can....D8 149
Luminao, reef, Guam....114
Lumpkin, Ga....D2 175
Lumpkin, co., Ga....B2 175
Lumsden, Newf., Can....D5 152
Lumsden, Sask., Can....G3 155
Lumsden, N.Z....P12 112
Lumsden, Scot....C6 57
Lumut, mtn., Indon....F6 90
Lumut, pt., Indon....F3 90
Luna, N. Mex....D1 195
Luna, co., N. Mex....E2 195
Luna Pier (Lakewood), Mich....G7 186
Lunan, bay, Scot....D6 57
Lund, Idaho....G7 177
Lund, Nev....E6 192
Lund, Swe....J5 63
Lund, Utah....E2 207
Lunda, dist., Ang....C2 106
Lundale, W. Va....D3, D5 211
Lundar, Man., Can....D2 150
Lundazi, Zambia....D5 106
Lundbreck, Alta., Can....E3 148
Lundby, Den....C5 62
Lundby, Swe....t34 63
Lundell, Ark....C5 169
Lunderskov, Den....C3 62
Lundu, Mala....E3 90
Lundy, isl., Eng....C3 56
Lune, riv., Eng....F6 57
Lüneburg, Ger....B5 60
Lunel, Fr....F6 58
Lünen, Ger....B2 61
Lunenburg, N.S., Can....E5 151
Lunenburg, Mass....A4 185
Lunenburg, Vt....C5 208
Lunenburg, Va....E4 209
Lunenburg, co., N.S., Can....E5 151
Lunenburg, co., Va....E4 209
Lunéville, Fr....C7 58
Lung, China....G2 92
Lungchen, China....B3 93
Lungchi, China....G8 91
Lungchüan, China....J8 92
Lungchuchai, China....H4 92
Lunghsi, China....E5 91
Lungkou, China....F9 92
Lungping, China....F6 92
Lungtsin, China....G6 91
Lungué-Bungo, riv., Ang., Zambia....D3 106
Luni, riv., India....E3 88
Luning, Nev....B3 192
Lunino, Sov. Un....E15 72
Lunyama, Zaire....C4 106
Lup, Thai....D5 89
Lupani, Rh....A4 107
Lupei, China....B9 92
Lupeni, Rom....C6 68
Lupin, see Manchouli, China
Lupton, Ariz....B6 168
Lupton, Mich....D6 186
Lupton City, Tenn....E10 205
Lupus, Mo....C5 189
Luque, Par....E4 135
Luquillo, P.R....B8, f12 132
Luquillo, mun., P.R....B8, f12 132
Luquillo, mts., P.R....B7 132
Luray, Kans....C5 181
Luray, Mo....A6 189
Luray, S.C....F5 203
Luray, Tenn....B3 205
Luray, Va....C4 209
Lure, Fr....D7 58
Lurgan, N. Ire....C3 55
Luribay, Bol....C2 135
Lurín, Peru....D2 134
Lúrio, Moz....D7 106
Lúrio, riv., Moz....D6 106
Lurton, Ark....B2 169
Lusaka, Zambia....E4 106
Lusambo, Zaire....B3 106
Lusby, Md....D5 173
Luscar, Alta., Can....C2 148
Luseland, Sask., Can....E1 155
Lushan, China....H5 92
Lushnjë, Alb....B2 69
Lushoto, Tan....B6 106
Lushton, Nebr....D8 191
Lüshun, see Port Arthur, China
Lusignan, Fr....D4 58
Lusk, Tex....C3 206
Lusk, Wyo....C8 213
Lustre, Mont....B11 190
Luta, see Rota, isl., Mariana Is.
Lutcher, La....B6, D5 183
Lutesville, Mo....D8 189
Luther, Mich....D5 186
Luther, Mont....E7 190
Luther, Okla....B4 200
Luthersville, Ga....C2 175
Lutherville, Md....B4 173
Luti, Choiseul I....115
Luting, China....F5 91
Lütjenburg, Ger....D4 62
Luton, Eng....C7 56
Luton, Iowa....B1 180
Lutsen, Minn....B6 187
Lutsk, Sov. Un....F5 72
Luttrell, Tenn....C10 205
Lutts, Tenn....B4 205
Lutugino, Sov. Un....q22 72
Lutz, Fla....D4 174
Lützow-Holm, bay, Ant....C16 120
Luverne, Ala....D3 166
Lu Verne, Iowa....B3 180
Luverne, Minn....G2 187
Luverne, N. Dak....B8 198
Luvua, riv., Zaire....C4 106
Luwingu, Zambia....D5 106
Luwuk, Indon....F6 90
Luxapalila, creek, Ala....B2 166
Luxembourg, Lux....E6 59
LUXEMBOURG, country, Eur....E6 59
Luxembourg, prov., Bel....E5 59
Luxemberg, Iowa....B6 180
Luxemburg, Wis....D6 212
Luxemburg, duchy of:
c. 1360....48
c. 1867....51
in 1940....53
Luxeuil-les-Bains, Fr....D7 58
Luxomni, Ga....A5 175
Luxor, see Al Uqşur, Eg.
Luxora, Ark....B6 169
Luyanó, Cuba....h12 131
Luz, Braz....E1 138
Luza, riv., Sov. Un....A3 73
Luzern, see Lucerne, Switz.
Luzern, canton, Switz....B4 66
Luzerne, Mich....D6 186
Luzerne, Pa....B8 202
Luzerne, co., Pa....D9 202
Lužnice, riv., Czech....D3 70
Luzon, isl., Phil....B6, o13 90
Lvov, Sov. Un....G5 72
Lwanhsien, China....D8 91
Lwow, see Lvov, Sov. Un.
Lwówek Śląski, Pol....C3 70
Lyall, mtn., N.Z....P11 112
Lyallpur, Pak....B5 87, B4 88
Lyaskovets, Bul....D7 68
Lybster, Scot....B5 57
Lycan, Colo....D8 171
Lychen, Ger....E7 62
Lycia: c. 450 B.C....42
c. 120 A.D....45
Lycksele, Swe....E8 63
Lycoming, N.Y....B4 196
Lycoming, co., Pa....D7 202
Lycoming, creek, Pa....D7 202
Lyden, N. Mex....A3 195
Lydenburg, S. Afr....C5 107
Lydia, S.C....C7 203
Lydia Mills, S.C....*C4 203
Lydick, Ind....A5 179
Lyell, isl., B.C., Can....C2 149
Lyell, mtn., Alta., B.C., Can....D2 148
Lyerly, Ga....B1 175
Lyford, Ind....E3 179
Lyford, Tex....F4 206
Lygnern, lake, Swe....A6 62
Lykens, Pa....E8 202
Lykesland, S.C....D6 203
Lyle, Minn....G6 187
Lyle, Wash....D4 210
Lyles, Tenn....B4 205
Lyleton, Man., Can....E1 150
Lyman, Miss....E2, E4 188
Lyman, Nebr....C1 191
Lyman, N.H....B3 193
Lyman, Okla....A5 200
Lyman, S.C....B3 203
Lyman, S. Dak....D6 204
Lyman, Utah....E4 207
Lyman, Wash....A3 210
Lyman, Wyo....D2 213
Lyman, co., S. Dak....D6 204
Lyman, res., Ariz....C6 168
Lyme, N.H....C2 193
Lyme, bay, Eng....D4 56
Lyme Center, N.H....C2 193
Lymington, Eng....D6 56
Łyna, riv., Pol., Sov. Un....B6 70
Lynas, pt., Wales....A3 56
Lynbrook, N.Y....G2 172
Lynch, Ky....D7 182
Lynch, Md....B5 173
Lynch, Nebr....B7 191
Lynch Station, Va....D3 209
Lynchburg, Ohio....C4 199
Lynchburg, S.C....C7 203
Lynchburg, Tenn....B5 205
Lynchburg (Independent City), Va....D3 209
Lynches, riv., S.C....D8 203
Lynd, Minn....F3 187
Lynde, pt., Conn....D7 172
Lyndeboro, N.H....E3 193
Lynden, Wash....A3 210
Lyndhurst, Ont., Can....C8 153
Lyndhurst, N.J....D5 194
Lyndhurst, Ohio....B2 199
Lyndon, Ill....B4 178
Lyndon, Kans....D8 181
Lyndon, Ky....A4 182
Lyndon, Vt....B4 208
Lyndon Center, Vt....B4 208
Lyndon Station, Wis....E4 212
Lyndonville, N.Y....B2 196
Lyndonville, Vt....B5 208
Lyndora, Pa....E2 202
Lyngby (Lyngby-Tårbaek), Den....C6 62
Lynhurst, Ind....H7 179
Lynn, Ala....A2 166
Lynn, Ark....A4 169
Lynn, Ind....D8 179
Lynn, Mass....B6, C3 185
Lynn, Pa....C10 202
Lynn, co., Tex....C2 206
Lynn, canal, Alsk....k22 167
Lynn, lake, W. Va....B5 211
Lynn Gardens, Tenn....*C11 205
Lynn Grove, Ky....B3 182
Lynn Haven, Fla....G3 174
Lynn Lake, Man., Can....A1, C4 150
Lynndyl, Utah....D3 207
Lynne, Fla....C5 174
Lynnfield, Mass....C3 185
Lynnhaven Roads, hbr., Va....B7 209
Lynnport, Pa....E10 202
Lynnview, Ky....*B4 182
Lynnville, Ind....H3 179
Lynnville, Iowa....C5 180
Lynnville, Ky....B2 182
Lynnville, Tenn....B5 205
Lynnwood, Pa....*F2 202
Lynnwood, Wash....*B3 210
Lynton, Eng....C4 56
Lynwood, Calif....F2 170
Lynxville, Wis....E2 212
Lyö, isl., Den....C4 62
Lyon, Fr....E6 58
Lyon, Miss....A3 188
Lyon, co., Iowa....A1 180
Lyon, co., Kans....D7 181
Lyon, co., Ky....C1 182
Lyon, co., Minn....F3 187
Lyon, co., Nev....D2 192
Lyon, mtn., N.Y....B3 196
Lyon, riv., Scot....D4 57
Lyon Mountain, N.Y....A3 196
Lyonnais, former prov., Fr....E6 58
Lyons, Colo....A5 171
Lyons, Ga....D4 175
Lyons, Ill....F3 178
Lyons, Ind....G3 179
Lyons, Kans....D5 181
Lyons, Mich....F6 186
Lyons, Nebr....C9 191
Lyons, N.J....B3 194
Lyons, N.Y....B4 196
Lyons, Ohio....A3 199
Lyons, Oreg....C4 201
Lyons, S. Dak....D9 204
Lyons, Tex....D4 206
Lyons, Wis....F1 212
Lyons, creek, Kans....D7 181
Lyons Falls, N.Y....B5 196
Lyra, reef, Bis. Arch....115
Lys, riv., Bel., Fr....D2, D3 59
Lysá, Czech....n18 70
Lysaya Gora, Sov. Un....G8 72
Lysekil, Swe....H4 63
Lysite, Wyo....B5 213
Lyster Station, Que., Can....C6 154
Lys'va, Sov. Un....B5 73
Lytham, Eng....A5 56
Lytle, Tex....E3 206
Lytton, B.C., Can....D7 149
Lytton, Iowa....B3 180
Lyubar, Sov. Un....G6 72
Lyubertsy, Sov. Un....n17 72

M

Ma'ād, Jordan....B7 84
Maalaea, Haw....C5 176
Maalaea, bay, Haw....C5 176
Ma'ale Aqrabim (Scorpion Pass), pass, Isr....D7 84
Ma'ān, Jordan....G10 85
Maanshan, China....I8 92
Maas, riv., Neth....C5 59
Maaseik, Bel....C5 59
Maastricht, Neth....D5 59
Mabana, Wash....A3 210
Mabank, Tex....C4 206
Mabber, cape, Som....D6 105
Mabel, Minn....G7 187
Mabel, lake, B.C., Can....D8 149
Mabelvale, Ark....D5 169
Maben, Ala....E4 166
Maben, Miss....B4 188
Maberly, Ont., Can....C8 153
Mabie, W. Va....C5 211
Mabiri, cape, Bougainville I....115
Mablethorpe, Eng....A8 56
Mableton, Ga....A4 175
Mabo, hbr., Malaita I....115
Mabote, Moz....B5 107
Mabou, N.S., Can....C8 151
Mabrous (Well), Niger....B7 103
Mabscott, W. Va....D3, D7 211
Mabton, Wash....C5 210
Macachín, Arg....B4 136
Macaé, Braz....C4 137
Macaíba, Braz....g6 138
Macalelon, Phil....P14 90
MacAlpine, lake, N.W. Ter., Can....C12 142
Macamic, Que., Can....*E9 153
Macao, Macao....G7 91
MACAO, Port. dep., Asia....G7 91
Macapá, Braz....B4 139
Macará, Ec....B2 134
MacArthur, W. Va....*D3 211
Macas, Ec....B2 134
Macau, Braz....C3 138
Macbeth, S.C....E8 203
Macbride, Iowa....C6 180
Macbride, lake, Ill....B2 178
Maccan, N.S., Can....D5 151
Maccarese, It....h8 67
Macclenny, Fla....B4 174
Macclesfield, Eng....A5 56
Macclesfield, N.C....B6 197
Maccluer, gulf, Indon....F8 90
MacCorkle, W. Va....C3 211
Macdhui, mtn., Scot....C5 57
Macdona, Tex....B3 206
MacDonald, W. Va....D3, D7 211
Macdonald, lake, Austl....D4 110
Mac Donald, range, B.C., Can....E10 149
Macdonalton, Pa....G4 202
Macdonnell, ranges, Austl....D5 110
Macduff, Scot....C6 57
Macedon, N.Y....B3 196
Macedon: c. 450 B.C....42
under Alexander....43
Macedonia, Iowa....C2 180
Macedonia, Ohio....A6, B2 199
Macedonia, reg., Yugo., Grc....B4 69
c. 50 B.C....44
c. 120 A.D....45
c. 400 A.D....46
in 1922-40....53
Maceió, Braz....C3, k6 138
Macenta, Guinea....E3 103
Maceo, Ky....C3 182
Macerata, It....C4 67
Maces, bay, N.B., Can....D3 151
Macfarlan, W. Va....B3 211
MacGillicuddy's Reeks, mts., Ire....E2 55
MacGregor, Man., Can....E2 150
Mach, Pak....C1 88
Machachi, Ec....B2 134
Machado, Braz....C3, k9 137
Machakos, Ken....B6 106
Machala, Ec....B2 134
Machanao, mtn., Guam....114
Machar, lake, Ont., Can....B5 153
Macheke, Rh....A5 107
Macheng, China....I6 92
Machete Central, P.R....D6 132
Machias, Maine....D5 184
Machias, N.Y....C2 196
Machias, bay, Maine....D5 184
Machias, lakes, Maine....C5 184
Machias, riv., Maine....B4 184
Machias, riv., Maine....D5 184
Machiasport, Maine....D5 184
Machichi, riv., Man., Can....A6 150
Machico, Port. (Madeira Is)....h12 65
Machida, Jap....*n18 93
Machiques, Ven....A3 133
Machrihanish, Scot....E3 57
Machu Picchu, Peru....D3 134
Machynlleth, Wales....B4 56
Macia, Moz....C5 107
Măcin, Rom....C9 68
Mačiya: c. 500 B.C....78
Mack, Colo....B2 171
Mackay, Austl....D8 111
Mackay, Idaho....F5 177
Mackay, lake, Austl....D4 110
MacKay, lake, N.W. Ter., Can....D10 142
Mackay, riv., Alta., Can....A4 148
Mackenna, Arg....A4 136
Mackenzie, dist., N.W. Ter., Can....D10 144
MacKenzie, bay, Ant....C20 120
Mackenzie, bay, N.W. Ter., Can....C5 142
Mackenzie, mts., N.W. Ter., Can....D6 142
Mackenzie, riv., N.W. Ter., Can....C6 142
Mackey, Ind....*H3 179
Mackeys, N.C....B7 197

INDEX KEY Each place listed in **Bold-faced Type** has its population listed in the Population tables, pages 230 to 280.
Each country, shown in CAPITAL LETTERS, has its population listed in the World Political Information Tables, pages 6 to 10.
* Does not appear on map; key shows general location.

Mackeys Station, Ont., Can ... A7 153
Mackeyville, Pa ... D7 202
Mackinac, co., Mich ... B5 186
Mackinac, bridge, Mich ... C6 186
Mackinac, isl., Mich ... C6 186
Mackinac, straits, Mich ... C6 186
Mackinac Island, Mich ... C6 186
Mackinaw, Ill ... C4 178
Mackinaw, riv., Ill ... C4 178
Mackinaw City, Mich ... C6 186
Mackinnon Road, Ken ... B6 106
Macklin, Sask., Can ... E1 155
Macks Creek, Mo ... D5 189
Macksburg, Iowa ... C3 180
Macksburg, Ohio ... C6 199
Macksville, Kans ... E5 181
Mackville, Ky ... C4 182
Mackville, Vt ... C4 208
Mackville, Wis ... A5 212
Maclean, Austl ... D9 112
Maclear, S. Afr ... D4 107
MacLeod Lake, B.C., Can ... E2 149
MacNutt, Sask., Can ... F5 155
Maco, Bol ... B2 135
Macocola, Ang ... C2 106
Macomb, Ill ... C3 178
Macomb, Okla ... B4 200
Macomb, co., Mich ... F8 186
Mâcon, Fr ... D6 58
Macon, Ga ... D3 175
Macon, Ill ... D5 178
Macon, Miss ... B5 188
Macon, Mo ... B5 189
Macon, Nebr ... D7 191
Macon, N.C ... A5 197
Macon, Tenn ... B2 205
Macon, co., Ala ... C4 166
Macon, co., Ga ... D2 175
Macon, co., Ill ... D5 178
Macon, co., Mo ... B5 189
Macon, co., N.C ... D2 197
Macon, co., Tenn ... C7 205
Macon, bayou, Ark ... D4 169
Macon, bayou, La ... B4 183
Macoun, Sask., Can ... H4 155
Macoun, lake, Sask., Can ... A4 155
Macoupin, co., Ill ... D4 178
Macouria, Fr. Gu ... B4 139
Macovane, Moz ... B6 107
Macquarie, isl., Pac. O ... D28 120
Macquarie, riv., Austl ... E6 112
Mac-Robertson, coast, Ant ... C19 120
Macroom, Ire ... E2 55
Macrorie, Sask., Can ... F2 155
Mac Tier, Ont., Can ... B5 153
Macuelizo, Hond ... C3 130
Macungie, Pa ... E10 202
Macwahoc, Maine ... C4 184
Macy, Ind ... C5 179
Macy, Nebr ... B9 191
Mad, lake, Idaho ... D8 210
Mad, riv., Calif ... B2 170
Mad, riv., N.H ... C3 193
Mad, riv., Ohio ... C4 199
Mad, riv., Vt ... C3 208
Ma'dabā, Jordan ... C7 84
Madaba, Tan ... C6 106
Madagascar: in 1896 ... 99
see also Malagasy Republic
Madagascar, isl., Afr ... g9 107
Madame, isl., N.S., Can ... D9 151
Madang, N. Gui ... k12 111
Madaoua, Niger ... D6 103
Madaripur, Bngl ... F13 88
Madawaska, Ont., Can ... B7 153
Madawaska, Maine ... A4 184
Madawaska, co., N.B., Can ... B1 151
Madawaska, lake, Maine ... B4 184
Madawaska, riv., Ont., Can ... B7 153
Madawaska, riv., N.B., Que., Can ... B9 154
Madaya, Bur ... A2 89
Madbury, N.H ... D5 193
Madden, Miss ... C4 188
Madden, lake, Pan ... k11 130
Madden Dam, C.Z ... k11 130
Maddock, N. Dak ... B6 198
Maddox, Md ... D4 173
Madeira, Ohio ... D2 199
Madeira, isl., Port. (Madeira Is.) ... h11 **65,** C1 102
Madeira, riv., Braz ... D2 139
Madeira Is., reg., Atl. O ... h11 **65,** C1 102
Madelia, Minn ... F4 187
Madeline, Calif ... B3 170
Madeline, isl., Wis ... B3 212
Madera, Calif ... D3 170
Madera, Mex ... B3 129
Madera, Pa ... E5 202
Madera, co., Calif ... D4 170
Maderia Beach, Fla ... *E4 174
Madhupur, India ... E11 88
Madhya Pradesh, state, India ... D6 87
Madill, Okla ... C5 200
Madimba, Zaire ... C2 106
Madinat ash Sha'b, Yemen (Aden) ... E10 97
Madingou, Con ... F2 104
Madison, Ala ... A3 166
Madison, Ala ... C3 166
Madison, Ark ... B5 169
Madison, Sask., Can ... F1 155
Madison, Conn ... D6 172
Madison, Fla ... B3 174
Madison, Ga ... C3 175
Madison, Ill ... E3 178
Madison, Ind ... G7 179
Madison, Kans ... D7 181
Madison, Maine ... D3 184
Madison, Md ... C5 173
Madison, Minn ... E2 187
Madison, Miss ... C3 188
Madison, Mo ... B5 189
Madison, Nebr ... C8 191
Madison, N.H ... C4 193
Madison, N.J ... B4 194
Madison, N.Y ... C5 196
Madison, N.C ... A4 197
Madison, Ohio ... A6 199
Madison, S.C ... B1 203
Madison, S. Dak ... D8 204
Madison, Tenn ... A5, E9 205
Madison, Va ... C4 209
Madison, W. Va ... C3, D5 211
Madison, Wis ... E4 212
Madison, co., Ala ... A3 166
Madison, co., Ark ... B2 169
Madison, co., Fla ... B3 174
Madison, co., Ga ... B3 175
Madison, co., Idaho ... F7 177
Madison, co., Ill ... E4 178
Madison, co., Ind ... D6 179
Madison, co., Iowa ... C3 180
Madison, co., Ky ... C5 182
Madison, co., Miss ... C3 188
Madison, co., Mo ... D7 189
Madison, co., Mont ... E4 190
Madison, co., Nebr ... C8 191
Madison, co., N.Y ... C5 196
Madison, co., N.C ... C3 197
Madison, co., Ohio ... C4 199
Madison, co., Tenn ... B3 205
Madison, co., Tex ... D5 206
Madison, co., Va ... C4 209
Madison, par., La ... B4 183
Madison, range, Mont ... E5 190
Madison, riv., Mont., Wyo ... E5 **190,** A2 213
Madison College, Tenn ... E9 205
Madison Heights, Mich ... *F7 186
Madison Heights, Va ... D3 209
Madison Lake, Minn ... F5 187
Madisonburg, Pa ... E6 202
Madisonville, Ky ... C2 182
Madisonville, La ... B7, D5 183
Madisonville, Tenn ... D9 205
Madisonville, Tex ... D5 206
Madiun, Indon ... *G4 90
Madjene, Indon ... F5 90
Madoc, Ont., Can ... C7 153
Madoc, Mont ... B11 190
Madon, riv., Fr ... A2 66
Madona, Sov. Un ... C6 72
Madonna di Campiglio, It ... C6 66
Madras, India ... F7 87
Madras, Oreg ... C5 201
Madre, mts., Guat., Mex ... C2 **130,** D6 129
Madre, mts., Phil ... B6 90
Madre de Dios, dept., Peru ... D3 134
Madre de Dios, isl., Chile ... E1 136
Madre de Dios, riv., Bol., Peru ... B2 135
Madre del Sur, mts., Mex ... o13 129
Madre Occidental, mts., Mex ... C3 129
Madre Oriental, mts., Mex ... C5 129
Madrid, Ala ... D4 166
Madrid, Iowa ... A7, C4 180
Madrid, Maine ... D2 184
Madrid, Nebr ... D4 191
Madrid, N. Mex ... B3, G6 195
Madrid, N.Y ... A2 196
Madrid, Sp ... B4, p17 65
Madridejos, Sp ... C4 65
Madrūsah, Libya ... E2 101
Madugula, India ... I9 88
Madura, isl., Indon ... G4 90
Madurai, India ... G6 87
Mae Hong Son, Thai ... C3 89
Maebashi, Jap ... H9, m18 93
Maelamun, mtn., Thai ... E3 89
Maella, Sp ... B6 65
Maengsan, Kor ... G3 93
Maes, N. Mex ... B5 195
Maeser, Utah ... C6 207
Maesteg, Wales ... C4 56
Maestra, mts., Cuba ... E5 131
Maevatanana, Malag ... g9 107
Mafeking, Man., Can ... C1 150
Mafeking, S. Afr ... C4 107
Maffra, Austl ... H6 112
Mafra, Braz ... D3 137
Mafra, Port ... C1 65
Maga, mtn., Tinian ... 114
Magadan, Sov. Un ... D18 71
Magadi, Ken ... B6 106
Magadi, lake, Ken ... B6 106
Magaguadavic, lake, N.B., Can ... D2 151
Magalia, Calif ... C3 170
Magallanes, see Punta Arenas, Chile
Magallanes, prov., Chile ... E2, h11 136
Magallanes, strait, Chile ... h11 136
Maganga, Zaire ... A4 106
Magangué, Col ... B3 133
Maganja da Costa, Moz ... A6 107
Magaria, Niger ... D6 103
Magat, riv., Phil ... n13 90
Magazine, Ark ... B2 169
Magazine, mtn., Ark ... B2 169
Magdalen Islands, co., Que., Can ... B8 151
Magdalena, Arg ... B5, g8 136
Magdalena, Bol ... B3 135
Magdalena, Mex ... A2 129
Magdalena, N. Mex ... C2 195
Magdalena, dept., Col ... A3 133
Magdalena, isl., Chile ... C2 136
Magdalena, isl., Mex ... C2 129
Magdalena, lake, Mex ... m11 129
Magdalena, plain, Mex ... C2 129
Magdalena, riv., Col ... B3 133
Magdalena, riv., Mex ... h9 129
Magdalo, Phil ... o13 90
Magdeburg, Ger ... A6 61
Magdiel, Isr ... g10 84
Magé, Braz ... h6 137
Magee, Miss ... D4 188
Magelang, Indon ... G4 87
Magenta, It ... B2 67
Maggia, riv., Switz ... C4 66
Maggie, Va ... D2 209
Maggie, creek, Nev ... C5 192
Maggiore, lake, It., Switz ... C4 66
Maghāghah, Eg ... D6 101
Magic, res., Idaho ... F4 177
Magic City, Tex ... B2 206
Magicienne, bay, Saipan ... 114
Maglaj, Yugo ... C4 68
Maglić, Yugo ... D5 68
Maglie, It ... D7 67
Magna, Utah ... C3 207
Magness, Ark ... B4 169
Magnet, Ark ... C3 169
Magnet, Man., Can ... D2 150
Magnet, Nebr ... B8 191
Magnet Cove, Ark ... C6 169
Magnetawan, Ont., Can ... B5 153
Magnetawan, riv., Ont., Can ... B4 153
Magnetic Springs, Ohio ... B4 199
Magnitogorsk, Sov. Un ... C5 73
Magnolia, Ark ... D2 169
Magnolia, Del ... B7 173
Magnolia, Ill ... B4 178
Magnolia, Iowa ... C2 180
Magnolia, Ky ... C4 182
Magnolia, Md ... B5 173
Magnolia, Minn ... G2 187
Magnolia, Miss ... D3 188
Magnolia, N.J ... D2 194
Magnolia, N.C ... C5 197
Magnolia, Ohio ... B6 199
Magnolia, Tex ... D5 206
Magnolia Springs, Ala ... E2 166
Magoari, cape, Braz ... B1 138
Magoffin, co., Ky ... C6 182
Magog, Que., Can ... D5 154
Magothy, riv., Md ... B4 173
Magou, Niger ... D5 103
Magoúla, Grc ... g11 69
Magpie, Que., Can ... h8 152
Magpie, riv., Que., Can ... h8 152
Magrath, Alta., Can ... E4 148
Magruder, mtn., Nev ... F4 192
Magude, Moz ... B5 107
Magwe, Bur ... D9 87
Maha Sarakham, Thai ... D5 89
Mahābād, Iran ... C2 86
Mahabo, Malag ... h8 107
Mahaffey, Pa ... E4 202
Mahagi, Zaire ... A5 106
Mahaicony, Guy ... A3 139
Mahakam, riv., Indon ... F5 90
Mahalapye, Bots ... B4 107
Mahameru, mtn., Indon ... G4 90
Mahanadi, riv., India ... G10 88
Mahanayim, Isr ... m14 84
Mahanoro, Malag ... g9 107
Mahanoy City, Pa ... E9 202
Maharashtra, state, India ... D5 87
Mahaska, Kans ... C6 181
Mahaska, co., Iowa ... C5 180
Mahbubnagar, India ... I7 88
Mahdia, Tun ... B7 102
Mahe, India ... F6 87
Mahenge, Tan ... C6 106
Mahgara, isl., Eg ... C2 84
Mahi. riv., India ... F4 88
Mahia, pen., N.Z ... M16 112
Mahigani, Bngl ... E12 88
Mahitahi, N.Z ... O12 112
Mahnomen, Minn ... C3 187
Mahnomen, co., Minn ... C3 187
Mahogany, mtn., Oreg ... D9 201
Mahogany, peak, Nev ... B2 192
Mahomet, Ill ... C5 178
Mahón, Sp ... C8 65
Mahone Bay, N.S., Can ... E5 151
Mahoning, co., Ohio ... B7 199
Mahoosuc, range, Maine, N.H ... D1 **184,** B4 193
Mahopac, N.Y ... D3, D7 196
Mahto, S. Dak ... B5 204
Mahtomedi, Minn ... E7 187
Mahtowa, Minn ... D6 187
Mahukona, Haw ... C6 176
Mahunda, Moz ... D6 106
Mahur, isl., Bis. Arch ... 115
Mahuta, Tan ... D6 106
Mahuva, India ... G3 88
Mahwah, N.J ... A4 194
Mai, isl., New Hebr ... 115
Maiana, isl., Gilbert Is ... 115
Maîche, Fr ... B2 66
Maicurú, riv., Braz ... C4 139
Maida, N. Dak ... A7 198
Maidani, cape, Iran ... I9 86
Maiden, N.C ... B2 197
Maiden Rock, Wis ... D1 212
Maidenhead, Eng ... C7 56
Maidstone, Sask., Can ... D1 155
Maidstone, Eng ... C8 56
Maidstone, lake, Vt ... B5 208
Maidsville, W. Va ... B5 211
Maiduguri, Nig ... D7 103
Maihar, India ... E8 88
Maikala, range, India ... F8 88
Maiko, riv., Zaire ... B4 106
Maikoor, isl., Indon ... G8 90
Maili, pt., Haw ... g9 176
Maillard, Que., Can ... B7 154
Maillot, Alg ... F9 64
Maimāna, Afg ... D12 86
Main, pass, La ... E6 183
Main, riv., Ger ... C3, D4 61
Main-a-Dieu, N.S., Can ... C10 151
Main Brook, Newf., Can ... *C3 152
Main Centre, Sask., Can ... G2 155
Main Topsail, mtn., Newf., Can ... D3 152
Mainburg, Ger ... E6 61
Maine, N.Y ... C4 196
Maine, former prov., Fr ... C3 58
Maine, state, U.S ... 184
in 17th cent ... 162
Maïné-Soroa, Niger ... D7 103
Mainesburg, Pa ... C7 202
Mainland, see Pomona, isl., Scot.
Mainland, isl., Scot ... g10 55
Mainland, riv., Man., Can ... C4 150
Maintirano, Malag ... g8 107
Mainz, Ger ... D3 61
Maipó, vol., Arg., Chile ... A2 136
Maipú, Arg ... B5 136
Maiquetía, Ven ... A4 133
Maira, riv., It ... E3 66
Maire, strait, Arg ... h12 136
Mairiporã, Braz ... m8 137
Mairum, Pak ... G11 86
Maisi, cape, Cuba ... E6 131
Maison-Carrée, Alg ... *B5 102
Maisons-Alfort, Fr ... g10 58
Maisons-Laffitte, Fr ... g9 58
Mait, Dyaul ... 115
Mait, Som ... C6 105
Maitland, Austl ... F8 112
Maitland, N.S., Can ... D6 151
Maitland, Ont., Can ... C9 153
Maitland (Lake Maitland), Fla ... *D5 174
Maitland, Mo ... A2 189
Maize, Kans ... B5 181
Maizuru, Jap ... I7, n14 93
Majagual, Col ... B3 133
Majestic, Ky ... C7 182
Māji, Eth ... D4 105
Majijo, peak, Ponape ... 114
Major, Sask., Can ... F1 155
Major, co., Okla ... A3 200
Majorca: c. 1721 ... 49
Majorsville, W. Va ... B2 211
Majra, Afg ... D12 86
Majunga, Malag ... g9 107
Majunga, prov., Malag ... g9 107
Majuro, atoll, Marshall Is ... 115
Makah, Indian res., Wash ... A1 210
Makaha, pt., Haw ... A2 176
Makalado, Zaire ... A4 106
Mak'alē, Eth ... C4 105
Makanalua, pen., Haw ... B5 176
Makanda, Ill ... F4 178
Makapala, Haw ... C6 176
Makapuu, pt., Haw ... B4 176
Makarov (Shirutoru), Sov. Un ... B11 93
Makarska, Yugo ... D3 68
Makassar (Macassar), strait, Indon ... F5 90
Makat, Sov. Un ... D4 73
Makawao, Haw ... C5 176
Makaweli, Haw ... B2 176
Mak'dalā, Eth ... C4 105
Makena, Haw ... C5 176
Makeni, S.L ... E2 103
Makenzen, see Orlyak, Bul.
Makeyevka, Sov. Un ... G11, q20 72
Makgadikgadi Pan, lake, Bots ... B4 107
Makhachkala, Sov. Un ... E3 73
Makharadze, Sov. Un ... B14 85
Makhfar al Quwayrah, Jordan ... E7 84
Makhlata, Bul ... D7 68
Makin, isl., Gilbert Is ... F10 113
Makinak, Man., Can ... D2 150
Makinsk, Sov. Un ... C8 73
Makkah, see Mecca, Sau. Ar.
Makkinga, Neth ... B6 59
Makkovik, Newf., Can ... g10 152
Makkum, Neth ... A5 59
Makó, Hung ... B5 68
Makokou, Gabon ... E2 104
Makongai, isl., Fiji ... 114
Makoti, N. Dak ... B4 198
Makoua, Con ... F3 104
Maków, Pol ... B6 70
Makran, range, Pak ... H12 86
Makri, India ... H8 88
Maktar, Tun ... G11 64
Makteir, sand dunes, Maur ... B3 103
Mākū, Iran ... B2 86
Makumbi, Zaire ... C3 106
Makura, isl., New Hebr ... 115
Makurazaki, Jap ... K5 93
Makurdi, Nig ... E6 103
Makushin, vol., Alsk ... E6 167
Mal, bay, Ire ... D2 55
Mal Abrigo, Ur ... E1 137
Malabar, Fla ... D6 174
Malabar, coast, India ... F5 87
Malacca, strait, Asia ... K4 89
Malad City, Idaho ... G6 177
Malafede, riv., It ... h8 67
Málaga, Col ... B3 133
Malaga, N.J ... D2 194
Malaga, N. Mex ... E5 195
Málaga, Sp ... D3 65
Málaga, bay, Sp ... D3 65
Malagash, N.S., Can ... D6 151
MALAGASY REPUBLIC, country, Afr ... h9 107
Malagón, Sp ... C4 65
Malaimbandy, Malag ... h9 107
Malaita, isl., Sol. Is ... G9 113
Malakal, Sud ... D3 105
Malakat, Mussau I ... 115
Malakoff, Fr ... g10 58
Malakoff, Tex ... C4 206
Malalbergo, It ... E7 66
Malang, Indon ... G4 90
Malange, Ang ... C2 106
Malange, dist., Ang ... C2 106
Malanzán, Arg ... A3 136
Mälaraspö, Swe ... t35 63
Mälaren (Malar), lake, Swe ... t34 63
Malargüe, Arg ... B3 136
Malartic, Que., Can ... *E9 153
Malasiqui, Phil ... *o13 90
Malaspina, Arg ... C3 136
Malaspina, glacier, Alsk ... D11 167
Malatya, Tur ... C12 85
MALAWI, country, Afr ... D5 106
Malay, pen., Asia ... I13 76
Malaya, reg., Mala ... J4 **89,** D2 90
in 1950 ... 83
Malaya Uzen, riv., Sov. Un ... D3 73
Malaya Vishera, Sov. Un ... B9 72
Malaybalay, Phil ... D7 90
Malāyer, Iran ... D4 86
MALAYSIA, country, Asia ... E2, E4 90
Malazgirt, Tur ... C14 85
Malbaie, riv., Que., Can ... B7 154
Malbon, Austl ... D7 111
Malbork, Pol ... A5 70
Malchin, Ger ... B6 60
Malchow, Ger ... E6 62
Malcolm, Austl ... E3 111
Malcolm, Nebr ... D9 191
Malcom, Iowa ... C5 180
Malden, Mass ... C3 185
Malden, Mo ... E8 189
Malden, Wash ... B8 210
Malden, W. Va ... C6 211
Malden, isl., Pac. O ... G12 113
MALDIVES, country, Asia ... I10 77
Maldon, Eng ... C8 56
Maldonado, Ur ... E2 137
Malè, It ... C6 66
Male, Maldives ... I10 76
Maléa, cape, Grc ... D4 69
Malegaon, India ... G5 88
Malekula, isl., New Hebr ... 115
Malema (Entre Rios), Moz ... D6 106
Malemba-Nkulu, Zaire ... C4 106
Malendok, isl., Bis. Arch ... 115
Maler-Kotla, India ... B5 88
Malesherbes, Fr ... C5 58
Malesus, Tenn ... B3 205
Malha (Well), Sud ... B2 105
Malheur, co., Oreg ... D9 201
Malheur, lake, Oreg ... D8 201
Malheur, riv., Oreg ... D9 201
Mali, Guinea ... D2 103
MALI, country, Afr ... C4 103
Mali, isl., Fiji ... 114
Maligne, lake, Alta., Can ... C2 148
Malin, Oreg ... E5 201
Malin, Sov. Un ... F7 72
Malin, head, Ire ... C3 55
Malinau, Indon ... E5 90
Malindi, Ken ... B7 106
Malinec, Czech ... D5 70
Malinmore, head, Ire ... C2 55
Malino, Sov. Un ... n18 72
Malinta, Ohio ... A3 199
Maliwun, Bur ... G3 89
Maljamar, N. Mex ... E6 195
Malkangiri, India ... H8 88
Malkara, Tur ... B6 69
Malko Tŭrnovo, Bul ... E8 68
Mallaig, Scot ... D3 57
Mallard, Iowa ... B3 180
Mallawī, Eg ... D6 101
Malleco, prov., Chile ... B2 136
Mallersdorf, Ger ... E7 61
Malles Venosta, It ... C6 66
Mallet Creek, Ohio ... A6 199
Malletts, bay, Vt ... B2 208
Mallorca, is., Sp ... C7 65
Mallory, W. Va ... *D3 211
Mallorytown, Ont., Can ... C9 153
Mallow, Ire ... D2 55
Malmbäck, Swe ... A8 62
Malmberget, Swe ... D9 63
Malmédy, Bel ... D6 59
Malmesbury, S. Afr ... D2 107
Malmköping, Swe ... t34 63
Malmo, Minn ... D5 187
Malmo, Nebr ... C9, D1 191
Malmö, Swe ... C7 **62,** J5 63
Malmöhus, co., Swe ... C7 62
Malmyzh, Sov. Un ... B8 93
Malo, isl., New Hebr ... 115
Maloarkhangelsk, Sov. Un ... E11 72
Maloelap, atoll, Marshall Is ... 115
Maloja, pass, Switz ... C5 66
Malolos, Phil ... o13 90
Malone, Ont., Can ... C7 153
Malone, Fla ... B1 174
Malone, N.Y ... A2 196
Malone, Wash ... C2 210
Maloneyville, Tenn ... E11 205
Malonton, Man., Can ... D3 150
Małopiana, riv., Pol ... f9 70
Malott, Wash ... A6 210
Maloy, Iowa ... D3 180
Maloyaroslavets, Sov. Un ... D11 72
Malpeque, bay, P.E.I., Can ... C6 151
Malpura, India ... D5 88
Malsch, Ger ... E3 61
Malshaya Uzen, riv., Sov. Un ... D3 73
Malta, Idaho ... G5 177
Malta, Ill ... B5 178
Malta, Mont ... B9 190
Malta, Ohio ... C6 199
MALTA, country, Eur ... F14 64
Malta Bend, Mo ... B4 189
Maltahohe, S.W. Afr ... B2 107
Malton, Ont., Can ... E6 153
Malton, Eng ... C6 55
Malumteken, New Ire. I ... 115
Malung, Swe ... G5 63
Malvern, Ala ... D4 166
Malvern, Ark ... C3, D6 169
Malvern, Eng ... B5 56
Malvern, Iowa ... C2 180
Malvern, Ohio ... B6 199
Malvern, Pa ... A10, F10 202
Malverne, N.Y ... G2 172
Malwood, Ont., Can ... A9 153
Mam Soul, mtn., Scot ... C3 57
Mamala, bay, Haw ... g10 176
Mamanutha, is., Fiji ... 114
Mamanguape, Braz ... C3, h6 138
Mamantel, Mex ... D6 129
Mamaroneck, N.Y ... D2 196
Mamba, Jap ... m17 93
Mambasa, Zaire ... A4 106
Mamberamo, riv., Indon ... F9 90
Mamers, Fr ... C4 58
Mamers, N.C ... B5 197
Mameyes, P.R ... B7 132
Mamfe, Cam ... E6 103
Mamie, N.C ... A8 197
Mamiña, Chile ... D2 135
Mammoth, Ariz ... E5 168
Mammoth, Utah ... D3 207
Mammoth, W. Va ... C3, C6 211
Mammoth Cave, nat. park, Ky ... C3 182
Mammoth Lake, Calif ... D4 170
Mammoth Spring, Ark ... A4 169
Mamolo, isl., Fiji ... 114
Mamonovo, Sov. Un ... A5 70
Mamoré, riv., Bol., Braz ... B2 135
Mamou, Guinea ... D2 103
Mamou, La ... D3 183
Mampawah, Indon ... E3 90
Mampong, Ghana ... E4 103
Mamry, lake, Pol ... A6 70
Mamudju, Indon ... F5 90
Man, I.C ... E3 103
Man, W. Va ... D3, D5 211
Man, Isle of, see Isle of Man, Br. dep., Eur.
Man, riv., Sask., Can ... D4 155
Mana, Fr. Gu ... A4 139
Mana, Haw ... A2 176
Manabí, prov., Ec ... B1 134
Manacapuru, Braz ... D5 133
Manacor, Sp ... C7 65
Manado, Indon ... E6 90
Managua, Nic ... D4 130
Managua, lake, Nic ... D4 130
Manahawkin, N.J ... D4 194
Manakara, Malag ... h9 107
Manakin-Sabot, Va ... D5 209
Manalapan, Fla ... *F6 174
Manalapan, N.J ... C4 194
Manam, is., N. Gui ... h12 110
Manama, Bahrain ... H5 86
Mañana, Pan ... F8 130
Manana, isl., Haw ... g11 176
Mananara, Malag ... g9 107
Mananara, riv., Malag ... h9 107
Mananjary, Malag ... h9 107
Manantenina, Malag ... h9 107
Manantico, creek, N.J ... E3 194
Manaoba, isl., Sol. Is ... 115
Manapire, riv., Ven ... B4 133
Manapla, Phil ... *C6 90
Manas (Suilai), China ... C2 91
Manasarowar, lake, China ... B9 88
Manasquan, N.J ... C4 194
Manasquan, riv., N.J ... C4 194
Manass, riv., China ... C2 91
Manassa, Colo ... D5 171
Manassas, Ga ... D4 175
Manassas, Va ... B4, C5 209
Manassas Park, Va ... *C5 209
Manatee, co., Fla ... E4 174
Manatee, riv., Fla ... E4 174
Manatí, P.R ... B5 132
Manatí, mun., P.R ... B5 132
Manaus, Braz ... C3 139
Manavgat, Tur ... D8 85
Manawa, Wis ... D5 212
Manawan, lake, Sask., Can ... B4 155
Mancelona, Mich ... D5 186
Mancha, reg., Sp ... C4 65
Mancha Real, Sp ... D4 65
Manchac, bayou, La ... B5 183
Manchaug, Mass ... B4 185
Manchester, Conn ... B6 172
Manchester, Eng ... D5 **55,** A5 56
Manchester, Ga ... D2 175
Manchester, Ill ... D3 178
Manchester, Iowa ... B6 180
Manchester, Kans ... C6 181
Manchester, Ky ... C6 182
Manchester, Maine ... D3 184
Manchester, Md ... A4 173
Manchester, Mass ... A6, C4 185
Manchester, Mich ... F6 186
Manchester, Mo ... B7 189
Manchester, N.H ... E4 193
Manchester, N.Y ... C3 196
Manchester, Ohio ... D4 199
Manchester, Okla ... A3 200
Manchester, Pa ... F8 202
Manchester, S. Dak ... C8 204
Manchester, Tenn ... B5 205
Manchester, Vt ... E2 208
Manchester Center, Vt ... E2 208
Manchester Depot, Vt ... E2 208
Manchouli (Lupin), China ... B8 91
Manchuria, reg., China ... B10 91
c. 1775 ... 82
Mancos, Colo ... D2 171

INDEX KEY Each place listed in **Bold-faced Type** has its population listed in the Population tables, pages 230 to 280.
Each country, shown in CAPITAL LETTERS, has its population listed in the World Political Information Table, pages 6 to 10.
* Does not appear on map; key shows general location.

Mancos, riv., Colo......D2 171
Mandabe, Malag......h8 107
Mandaguari, Braz......C2 137
Mandal, Afg......E10 86
Mandal, Nor......H2 63
Mandalay, Bur...D10 87, B2 89
Mandali, Iraq......E2 86
Mandalya, gulf, Tur......D6 69
Mandan, N. Dak......C5 198
Mandar, gulf, Indon......F5 90
Mandara, mts., Cam......C2 104
Mandarah, Eg......C2 84
Mandaree, N. Dak......B3 198
Mandarin, Fla......B5, C6 174
Mandera, Ken......A7 106
Manderfeld, Bel......D6 59
Manderfield, Utah......E3 207
Manderson, S. Dak......D3 204
Manderson, Wyo......A5 213
Mandeville, Ark......D2 169
Mandeville, Que., Can......C4 154
Mandeville, La......B7, D5 183
Mandimba, Moz......D6 106
Mandla, India......F8 88
Mándra, Grc......C4, g11 69
Mandritsara, Malag......g9 107
Mandsaur, India......E5 88
Manduria, It......D6 67
Mandvi, India......F2 88
Manell, chan., Guam...... 114
Manes, Mo......D5 189
Manfalūț, Eg......D6 101
Manfred, N. Dak......B6 198
Manfredonia, It......D5 67
Manfredonia, gulf, It......D6 67
Manga, Braz......D2 138
Mangalia, Rom......D9 68
Mangalore, India......F5 87
Mangaratiba, Braz......h5 137
Mangas, mtn., N. Mex......D1 195
Mangatarem, Phil......o13 90
Mangham, La......B4 183
Mangla, Pak......B5 87
Mango, isl., Fiji...... 114
Mangoky, riv., Malag......h8 107
Mangole, isl., Indon......F7 90
Mangonia Park, Fla......*F6 174
Mangotsfield, Eng......C5 56
Mangualde, Port......B2 65
Manguéni, plat., Niger......B7 103
Mangum, Okla......C2 200
Mangyshlak, pen., Sov. Un.E4 73
Manhasset, N.Y......F2 172
Manhattan, Ill......*B6 178
Manhattan, Ind......E4 179
Manhattan, Kans......C7 181
Manhattan, Mont......E5 190
Manhattan, Nev......E4 192
Manhattan, isl., N.Y......D6 194
Manhattan Beach, Calif....F2 170
Manheim, Pa......F9 202
Manheim, W. Va......B5 211
Manhica, Moz......C5 107
Manhuaçu, Braz......F2 138
Mani, P.R......C2 132
Maniagassa, isl., Saipan...... 114
Maniago, It......C8 66
Manicoré, Braz......D2 139
Manicouagane, riv., Que., Can......F19 143
Manigotagan, Man., Can......D3, D5 150
Manigotagan, lake, Man., Can......D4 150
Manigotagan, riv., Man., Can......D3 150
Manihiki, is., Pac. O......G11 113
Manika E Sofala, prov., Moz......A5 107
Manila, Ariz......C5 168
Manila, Ark......B5 169
Manila, Phil......C6, o13 90
Manila, Utah......C6 207
Manila, bay, Phil......C6, o13 90
Manilla, Austl......E8 112
Manilla, Ind......E6 179
Manilla, Iowa......C2 180
Manisa, Tur......C6 69
Manistee, Mich......D4 186
Manistee, co., Mich......D4 186
Manistee, riv., Mich......D5 186
Manistique, Mich......C4 186
Manistique, lake, Mich......B5 186
Manistique, riv., Mich......B4 186
Manito, Ill......C4 178
Manito, lake, Sask., Can......E1 155
Manitoba, prov., Can...... 150
in 1867...... 147
Manitoba, lake, Man., Can..D2 150
Manitou, Man., Can......E2 150
Manitou, Okla......C3 200
Manitou, isl., Mich......A3 186
Manitou, lakes, Ont., Can....E5 150
Manitou, riv., Ont., Can......E5 150
Manitou Beach, Sask., Can......F3 155
Manitou Springs, Colo......C6 171
Manitoulin, co., Ont., Can.B2 153
Manitoulin, isl., Ont., Can..B2 153
Manitowaning, Ont., Can..B3 153
Manitowoc, Wis......B6, D6 212
Manitowoc, co., Wis......D6 212
Manitowoc, riv., Wis......B6 212
Maniwaki, Que., Can......C2 154
Maniya (Oasis), Iraq......G14 85
Manizales, Col......B2 133
Manja, Malag......h8 107
Manjacaze, Moz......B5 107
Manjra, riv., India......E6 87
Mankato, Kans......C5 181
Mankato, Minn......F5 187
Mankono, I.C......E3 103
Mankota, Sask., Can......H2 155
Mankoya, Zambia......D3 106
Manley Hot Springs, Alsk......B9 167
Manley, Nebr......E3 191
Manlius, Ill......B4 178
Manlius, N.Y......C5 196
Manlléu, Sp......A7 65
Manly, Iowa......A4 180
Manly, N.C......B4 197
Manlyville, Tenn......A3 205
Manmad, India......G5 88
Mann, ranges, Austl......E5 110
Mannar, Cey......G6 87
Mannar, gulf, India......G6 87
Mannboro, Va......D5 209
Mannford, Okla......*A5 200
Mannheim, Ger......D3 61
Manning, Ark......C3 169
Manning, Iowa......C2 180
Manning, N. Dak......B3 198
Manning, Oreg......A1 201
Manning, S.C......D7 203
Manning, strait, Sol. Is...... 115
Mannington, Ky......C2 182
Mannington, W. Va....A7, B4 211
Manns, creek, W. Va......C7 211
Manns Choice, Pa......G4 202
Manns Harbor, N.C......B8 197
Mannsville, N.Y......B4 196
Mannsville, Okla......C5 200
Mannu, riv., It......E2 67
Mannville, Alta., Can......C5 148
Manö, isl., Den......C2 62
Manokin, Md......D6 173
Manokin, riv., Md......D6 173
Manokotak, Alsk......D8 167
Manokwari, Indon......F8 90
Manombo, Malag......h8 107
Manomet, Mass......C6 185
Manomet, hill, Mass......C6 185
Manomet, pt., Mass......C6 185
Manono, Zaire......C4 106
Manono, isl., W. Sam...... 114
Manor, Sask., Can......H4 155
Manor, Ga......E4 175
Manor, Pa......*F2 202
Manor, Tex......D4 206
Manor, Wash......D3 210
Manorhaven, N.Y......*E3 196
Manorville, N.Y......D4 196
Manorville, Pa......E2 202
Manosque, Fr......F6 58
Manotick, Ont., Can......B9 153
Manouane, lake, Que., Can......B2 154
Manpojin, Kor......F3 93
Manresa, Sp......B6 65
Mansa, Zambia......D4 106
Mansa Konko, Gam......D1 103
Månsarp, Swe......A8 62
Manseau, Que., Can......C5 154
Mansel, isl., N.W. Ter., Can......D16 143
Mansfield, Ark......B1 169
Mansfield, Austl......H6 112
Mansfield, Conn......B7 172
Mansfield, Eng......A6 56
Mansfield, Ga......C3 175
Mansfield, Ill......C5 178
Mansfield, La......B2 183
Mansfield, Mass......B5 185
Mansfield, Mo......D5 189
Mansfield, Ohio......B5 199
Mansfield, Pa......C7 202
Mansfield, S. Dak......B7 204
Mansfield, Tenn......A3 205
Mansfield, Tex......B5 206
Mansfield, Wash......B6 210
Mansfield, flood control res., Ind......E3 179
Mansfield, mtn., Vt......B3 208
Mansfield Center, Conn....B8 172
Mansfield Depot, Conn....B7 172
Mansfield Hollow, flood control res., Conn......B8 172
Mansfield Southeast, Ohio......*B5 199
Manso ou das Mortes, riv., Braz......A2 137
Manson, Iowa......B3 180
Manson, Wash......B5 210
Manson, riv., B.C., Can....B6 149
Manson Creek, B.C., Can..B5 149
Mansonville, Que., Can....D5 154
Mansura, La......C3 183
Mant, hbr., Ponape...... 114
Mant, is., Ponape...... 114
Manta, Ec......B1 134
Mantachie, Miss......A5 188
Mantador, N. Dak......C9 198
Mantagao, riv., Man., Can..D3 150
Mantario, Sask., Can......F1 155
Mantaro, riv., Peru......D3 134
Mantas, Niger......C5 103
Manteca, Calif......D3, B6 170
Mantee, Miss......B4 188
Manteno, Ill......B6 178
Manteo, N.C......B8 197
Manter, Kans......E2 181
Mantes [-la-Jolie], Fr......C4 58
Manthani, India......H7 88
Manti, Utah......D4 207
Mantilla, Cuba......k12 131
Mantiqueira, mts., Braz....C4 137
Mantoloking, N.J......C4 194
Manton, Mich......D5 186
Mantorville, Minn......F6 187
Mantua (Mantova), It......D6 66, B3 67
Mantua, N.J......D2 194
Mantua, Ohio......A6 199
Mantua, Utah......B4 207
Manú, Peru......D3 134
Manuel Alves, riv., Braz....C1 138
Manuel Benavides, Mex....B4 129
Manuel F. Mantilla, Arg....E4 135
Manuelito, N. Mex......B1 195
Manui, isl., Indon......F6 90
Manukau, N.Z......L15 112
Manukau, hbr., N.Z......L15 112
Manumuskin, N.J......E3 194
Manuro, pt., Efate I...... 115
Manus, isl., Bis. Arch...... 115
Manvel, N. Dak......A8 198
Manvel, Tex......F5 206
Manville, N.J......B3 194
Manville, R.I......B11 172
Manville, Wyo......C8 213
Many, La......C2 183
Many Farms, Ariz......A6 168
Manyara, lake, Tan......B6 106
Manyas, lake, Tur......B6 69
Manyberries, Alta., Can....E5 148
Manych, canal, Sov. Un....H14 72
Manych, lake, Sov. Un....H14 72
Manych, riv., Sov. Un......D2 73
Manyoni, Tan......C5 106
Manzala, lake, Eg......C3 84
Manzanares, Sp......C4 65
Manzanares, canal, Sp....p17 65
Manzanares, riv., Sp....o17 65
Manzanillo, Cuba......E5 131
Manzanillo, Mex......D4, n11 129
Manzanillo, P.R......D4 132
Manzanita, Oreg......B3 201
Manzano, N. Mex......C3 195
Manzano, peak, N. Mex....C3 195
Manzanola, Colo......C7 171
Manziana, It......g8 67
Manzil, Jordan......C8 84
Manzil Bu Ruguaybah, Tun......*F12 64
Mao, Chad......C3 104
Maoming, China......G7 91
Mapai, Moz......B5 107
Mapastepec, Mex......D6 129
Mapaville, Mo......C7 189
Mapes, N. Dak......A7 198
Mapia, is., Indon......E8 90
Mapiri, Bol......C2 135
Maple, Ont., Can......E6 153
Maple, Tex......C1 206
Maple, riv., Iowa......B2 180
Maple, riv., N. Dak......C8 198
Maple Bluff, Wis......E4 212
Maple Creek, Sask., Can..H1 155
Maple Grove, Minn......*E5 187
Maple Heights, Ohio......B2 199
Maple Hill, Kans......C7 181
Maple Hill, N.C......C6 197
Maple Lake, Minn......E5 187
Maple Mount, Ky......C2 182
Maple Park, Ill......*B5 178
Maple Plain, Minn......*E5 187
Maple Rapids, Mich......E6 186
Maple Shade, N.J......D2 194
Maple Valley, Wash......D2 210
Maplebay, Minn......C2 187
Maples, Ind......B8 179
Maplesville, Ala......C3 166
Mapleton, Iowa......B2 180
Mapleton, Kans......D9 181
Mapleton, Maine......B4 184
Mapleton, Minn......G5 187
Mapleton, N. Dak......C8 198
Mapleton, Oreg......C3 201
Mapleton, Utah......C4 207
Mapleton Depot, Pa......E6 202
Mapleview, Minn......*G6 187
Mapleville, R.I......B10 172
Maplewood, La......D2 183
Maplewood, Maine......E2 184
Maplewood, Minn......E7 187
Maplewood, Mo......B8 189
Maplewood, N.J......B4 194
Mapuera, riv., Braz......C3 139
Ma'qalā', Sau. Ar......H3 86
Maqnāh, Sau. Ar......H10 85
Maquela do Zombo, Ang....C2 106
Maquinchao, Arg......C3 136
Maquoketa, Iowa......B7 180
Maquoketa, riv., Iowa......B7 180
Maquon, Ill......C3 178
Mar, mts., Braz......D3 137
Mar de Espanha, Braz......g6 137
Mar del Plata, Arg......B5 136
Mar Menor, lagoon, Sp......D5 65
Mar Negro, P.R......D5 132
Marabá, Braz......D5 139
Maracá, isl., Braz......B4 139
Maracai, lake, Braz......D4 133
Maracaibo, Ven......A3 133
Maracaibo, lake, Ven......B3 133
Maracaju, Braz......C1 137
Maracay, Ven......A4 133
Maracayo, P.R......B3 132
Marādah, Libya......D3 101
Maradi, Niger......D6 103
Marāgheh, Iran......C3 86
Maragogi, Braz......k6 138
Maragogipe, Braz......D3 138
Marais des Cygnes (Osage), riv., Kans......D8 181
Marajó, isl., Braz......C5 139
Maraki, isl., Gilbert Is...... 115
Maralal, Ken......A6 106
Maramasike, isl., Sol. Is...... 115
Maramasike, pass, Sol. Is...... 115
Maramec, Okla......A5 200
Marana, Ariz......E4 168
Marand, Iran......B2 86
Marandellas, Rh......A5 107
Maranguape, Braz......B3 138
Maranhão, state, Braz......B1 138
Marano, lagoon, It......D9 66
Maranoa, riv., Austl......C7 112
Marañón, riv., Peru......B2 134
Marans, Fr......D3 58
Maraș, Tur......D11 85
Mărășești, Rom......C8 68
Maratha Empire: c. 1775...... 82
Marathon, Ont., Can......E8 153
Marathon, Fla......H5 174
Marathón, Grc......g11 69
Marathon, Iowa......B3 180
Marathon, N.Y......C4 196
Marathon, Tex......D1, F2 206
Marathon, Wis......D4 212
Marathon, co., Wis......D4 212
Maratua, isl., Indon......E5 90
Marau, isl., Sol. Is...... 115
Marau, sound, Sol. Is...... 115
Maravatío, Mex......n13 129
Marāwah, Libya......F3 85
Marbella, Sp......D3 65
Marble, Ark......A2 169
Marble, Colo......B3 171
Marble, Minn......C5 187
Marble, N.C......D2 197
Marble, canyon, Ariz......A4 168
Marble Bar, Austl......D2 111
Marble Canyon, Ariz......A4 168
Marble City, Okla......B7 200
Marble Cliff, Ohio......C2 199
Marble Dale, Conn......C3 172
Marble Falls, Tex......D3 206
Marble Hall, S. Afr......B4 107
Marble Hill, Mo......D8 189
Marble Mountain, N.S., Can......D8 151
Marble Rock, Iowa......B5 180
Marblehead, Ill......D2 178
Marblehead, Mass.....B6, C4 185
Marblehead, Ohio......A5 199
Marblehill, Ga......B2 175
Marblemount, Wash......A4 210
Marbleton, Que., Can......D6 154
Marbleton, Wyo......C2 213
Marburg, Ger......C3 60
Marbury, Ala......C3 166
Marbury, Md......C3 173
Marcala, Hond......C4 130
Marcaria, It......D6 66
Marcelin, Sask., Can......E2 155
Marceline, Ill......C2 178
Marceline, Mo......B5 189
Marcella, Ark......B4 169
Marcellus, Mich......G5 186
Marcellus, N.Y......C4 196
March, Eng......B8 56
Marchand, Man., Can......E3 150
Marchand, Mor......H3 64
Marche, Ark......D5 169
Marche, former prov., Fr..D4 58
Marche-en-Famenne, Bel..D5 59
Marchena, Sp......D3 65
Marchena, isl., Ec......f5 134
Marches, reg., It......C4 67
Marchwell, Sask., Can......G5 155
Marco, Fla......G5 174
Marco, Ind......G3 179
Marco, La......C3 183
Marcola, Oreg......C4 201
Marcos Juárez, Arg......A4 136
Marcus, Iowa......B2 180
Marcus, S. Dak......C3 204
Marcus, Wash......A7 210
Marcus Baker, mtn., Alsk..g18 167
Marcus Hook, Pa......G11 202
Marcy, mtn., N.Y......A7 196
Marcy Colony, S. Dak......D8 204
Mardān, Pak......B5 87
Mardela Springs, Md......D6 173
Mardin, Tur......D13 85
Mare, isl., Loyalty Is...... 115
Marechal Deodoro, Braz......C3, k6 138
Marengo, Sask., Can......F1 155
Marengo, Ill......A5 178
Marengo, Ind......H5 179
Marengo, Iowa......C5 180
Marengo, Ohio......B3 199
Marengo, Wis......B3 212
Marengo, co., Ala......C2 166
Marenisco, Mich......A5 186
Marennes, Fr......E3 58
Maretz, Fr......D3 59
Mareuil-sur-Ourcq, Fr......E3 59
Mareyevka, Sov. Un......C7 73
Marfa, Tex......F2 206
Marfork, W. Va......D3, D6 211
Marfrance, W. Va......C4 211
Marganets, Sov. Un......H10 72
Margão, India......E5 87
Margaree, N.S., Can......C8 151
Margaree Harbour, N.S., Can......C8 151
Margaret, Ala......B3 166
Margaret, Man., Can......E2 150
Margaret, Tex......B3 206
Margaretsville, N.S., Can......D4 151
Margaretville, N.Y......C6 196
Margarita, isl., Ven......A5 133
Margate, Eng......C9 56
Margate, Fla......*F6 174
Margate, N.J......E3 194
Margelan, Sov. Un......E8 73
Margerum, Ala......A1 166
Margherita, Som......E5 105
Margherita, lake, Eth......D4 105
Margherita, mtn., Ug., Zaire......A5 106
Marghi, Afg......D13 86
Margiana: c. 500 B.C...... 78
Margie, Minn......B5 187
Margny-lès-Compiègne, Fr......E2 59
Margo, Sask., Can......F4 155
Margona Village, Mo......*C7 189
Margrethe, lake, Mich......D6 186
Marguerite, bay, Ant......C6 120
Marguerite, riv., Que., Can......h8 152
Mari, lake, Sask., Can......B4 155
Maria, Que., Can......A4 151
Maria, isl., Austl......o15 110
Maria, riv., Arg......E2 135
Maria Chiquita, Pan......k11 130
Maria Grande, Arg......A5 136
Maria Grande, Pan......k11 130
Maria la Baja, Col......B2 133
Maria Luisa, Cuba......k12 131
Maria Stein, Ohio......B3 199
Maria Van Diemen, cape, N.Z......K11 112
Mariager, Den......B3 62
Mariager, fjord, Den......B4 62
Marian, lake, Fla......E5 174
Mariana, is., Pac. O......E8 113
Marianao, Cuba......D2, k11 131
Marianna, Ark......C5 169
Marianna, Fla......B1 174
Marianna, Pa......*F3 202
Mariano Moreno, Arg......B3 136
Mariánské Lázně, Czech....D2 70
Mariapolis, Man., Can......E2 150
Marias, pass, Mont......B3 190
Mariato, pt., Pan......G7 130
Mariaville, Maine......D4 184
Maribel, N.C......B7 197
Maribel, Wis......A6 212
Maribo, Den......D5 62
Maribo, co., Den......D5 62
Maribor, Yugo......B2 68
Maricá, Braz......h6 137
Maricaban, isl., Phil......p13 90
Maricao, P.R......C3 132
Maricao, mun., P.R......C3 132
Maricopa, Ariz......D3 168
Maricopa, Calif......E4 170
Maricopa, co., Ariz....D3, F1 168
Maricopa, Indian res., Ariz......E3 168
Maridi, Sud......E2 105
Marié, riv., Braz......D4 133
Marie Byrd Land, reg., Ant......B36 120
Marie-Galante, isl., Guad..o16 131
Mariedam, Swe......u33 63
Mariefred, Swe......t35 63
Mariehamn, Fin......G8 63
Mariembourg, Bel......D4 59
Mariemont, Ohio......D2 199
Marienberg, Ger......C8 61
Mariental, S.W. Afr......B2 107
Marienthal, Kans......D2 181
Marienville, Pa......D3 202
Maries, co., Mo......C6 189
Mariestad, Swe......H5 63
Marietta, Fla......B6 174
Marietta, Ga......A5, C2 175
Marietta, Ill......C3 178
Marietta, Minn......E2 187
Marietta, Miss......A5 188
Marietta, Ohio......C6 199
Marietta, Okla......D4 200
Marietta, Pa......F8 202
Marietta, S.C......A2 203
Marietta, Wash......A3 210
Marietta East, Ga......*C2 175
Marieville, Que., Can......D4 154
Mariinsk, Sov. Un......B11 73
Marijampole, Sov. Un......A7 70
Marília, Braz......C3 137
Marín, Sp......A1 65
Marin, co., Calif......C2 170
Marina, Calif......C6 170
Marina di Ravenna, It......E8 66
Marine, Ill......E4 178
Marine City, Mich......F8 186
Marine on St. Croix, Minn......E6, E8 187
Marinette, Wis......C6 212
Marinette, co., Wis......C5 212
Maringa, riv., Zaire......A3 106
Maringouin, La......D4 183
Marinha Grande, Port......C1 65
Marino, It......h9 67
Marinovka, Sov. Un......r21 72
Marion, Ala......C2 166
Marion, Ark......B5 169
Marion, Austl......*G2 112
Marion, Conn......C5 172
Marion, Ill......F5 178
Marion, Ind......C6 179
Marion, Iowa......B6 180
Marion, Kans......D6 181
Marion, Ky......A3 182
Marion, La......B3 183
Marion, Mass......C6 185
Marion, Mich......D5 186
Marion, Miss......C5 188
Marion, Mont......B2 190
Marion, Nebr......D5 191
Marion, N.Y......B3 196
Marion, N.C......B2, D4 197
Marion, N. Dak......C7 198
Marion, Ohio......B4 199
Marion, Oreg......C2 201
Marion, Pa......G6 202
Marion, S.C......C9 203
Marion, S. Dak......D8 204
Marion, Va......B3 209
Marion, Wis......D5 212
Marion, co., Ala......A2 166
Marion, co., Ark......A3 169
Marion, co., Fla......C4 174
Marion, co., Ga......D2 175
Marion, co., Ill......E5 178
Marion, co., Ind......E5 179
Marion, co., Iowa......C4 180
Marion, co., Kans......D6 181
Marion, co., Ky......C4 182
Marion, co., Miss......D4 188
Marion, co., Mo......B6 189
Marion, co., Ohio......B4 199
Marion, co., Oreg......C4 201
Marion, co., S.C......C9 203
Marion, co., Tenn......D8 205
Marion, co., Tex......C5 206
Marion, co., W. Va......B4 211
Marion, lake, S.C......E7 203
Marion Center, Pa......E3 202
Marion Heights, Pa......*E9 202
Marion Junction, Ala......C2 166
Marion Station, Md......D6 173
Marionville, Mo......D4 189
Mariposa, Calif......D4 170
Mariposa, co., Calif......D3 170
Mariposa, Chile......B2 136
Maris Town, Miss......C3 188
Mariscal Estigarribia, Par..D3 135
Marismas, marshes, Sp...D2 65
Marissa, Ill......E4 178
Maritime Alps, mts., Fr., It......E7 58
Maritsa, riv., Bul......D7 68
Mariupol, see Zhdanov, Sov. Un.
Mariveles, Phil......o13 90
Marjan, see Wazi Khwa, Afg.
Mark, Ill......B4 178
Markaryd, Swe......I5 63
Markdale, Ont., Can......C4 153
Marked Tree, Ark......B5 169
Markerwaard Polder, reg., Neth......B5 59
Markesan, Wis......E5 212
Market Drayton, Eng......B5 56
Market Harborough, Eng..B7 56
Market Rasen, Eng......A7 56
Market Weighton, Eng......G8 57
Markham, Ont., Can...D5, E7 153
Markham, Ill......F3 178
Markham, Tex......E4 206
Markham, Va......C5 209
Markham, mtn., Ant......A28 120
Markhana, Afg......D13 86
Marki, Pol......k14 70
Markinch, Sask., Can......G3 155
Markkleeberg, Ger......B7 61
Markland, Ind......G8 179
Markland, lock & dam, Ind., Ky......G7 179, B5 182
Markle, Ind......C7 179
Markleeville, Calif......C4 170
Markleville, Ind......E6 179
Markleysburg, Pa......G3 202
Markneukirchen, Ger......C7 61
Markópoulon, Grc......h11 69
Markovka, Sov. Un......G12 72
Markovo, Sov. Un......C20 71
Markranstädt, Ger......B7 61
Marks, Miss......A3 188
Marksboro, N.J......B3 194
Marksville, La......C3 183
Marktheidenfeld, Ger......D4 61
Marktredwitz, Ger......D7 61
Markville, Minn......D6 187
Marl, Ger......*C3 60
Marland, Okla......A4 200
Marlbank, Ont., Can......C7 153
Marlboro, Alta., Can......C2 148
Marlboro, Conn......C7 172
Marlboro, Mass......B4, D1 185
Marlboro, N.H......E2 193
Marlboro, N.J......C4 194
Marlboro, N.Y......D6 196
Marlboro, Vt......F3 208
Marlboro, co., S.C......B8 203
Marlborough, Eng......C6 56
Marlborough, Guy......A3 139
Marlborough, Mo......*C7 189
Marle, Fr......E3 59
Marlette, Mich......E7 186
Marley, Md......B4 173
Marlin, Tex......D4 206
Marlin (Krupp), Wash......B7 210
Marlinton, W. Va......C4 211
Marlow, Ala......E2 166
Marlow, Ga......D5 175
Marlow, Ger......D6 62
Marlow, N.H......D2 193
Marlow, Okla......C4 200
Marlowe, W. Va......B7 211
Marlton, N.J......D3 194
Marly-le-Roi, Fr......g9 58
Marmaduke, Ark......A5 169
Marmande, Fr......E4 58
Marmara, sea, Tur......B7 85
Marmara, isl., Tur......B6 69
Marmaris, Tur......D7 69
Marmarth, N. Dak......C2 198
Marmelos, riv., Braz......D2 139
Marmet, W. Va......C3, C6 211
Marmolada, mtn., It......C7 66
Marmora, Ont., Can......C7 153
Marmora, N.J......E3 194
Marmora, peak, It......D2 67
Marnay, Fr......B1 66
Marne, Ger......E3 62
Marne, Iowa......C2 180
Marne, Mich......E5 186
Marne, dept., Fr......F4 59
Marne, riv., Fr......C5 58
Marne au Rhin, canal, Fr..F6 59
Maro, reef, Haw......k13 176
Maroa, Ill......C5 178
Maroantsetra, Malag......g9 107
Maromokotro, mtn., Malag..f9 107
Maroni, riv., Sur., Fr. Gu..B4 139
Maroua, Cam......C2 104
Marovoay, Malag......g9 107
Marpi, mtn., Saipan...... 114
Marpi, pt., Saipan...... 114
Marpo, pt., Tinian...... 114
Marquam, Oreg......B2, B4 201
Marquand, Mo......D7 189
Marquês de Valença, Braz......C4, h6 137
Marquesas, is., Fr. Polynesia......G13 113
Marquesas, keys, Fla......H4 174
Marquette, Man., Can......D3 150
Marquette, Iowa......*A6 180
Marquette, Kans......D6 181
Marquette, Mich......B3 186
Marquette, Nebr......D8 191
Marquette, co., Mich......B3 186
Marquette, co., Wis......E4 212
Marquette Heights, Ill...*C4 178
Marquez, Tex......D4 206
Marquis, Sask., Can......G3 155
Marquise, Fr......D9 56
Marrakech, Mor......I3 64, C3 102

Marree, Austl. E6 111
Marrero, La. C7 183
Marrickville, Austl. *F8 112
Marromeu, Moz. A6 107
Marroqui, pt., Sp. D3 65
Marrowbone, Ky. D4 182
Mars, Pa. E1 202
Mars, hill, Maine B5 184
Mars, riv., Que., Can. A7 154
Mars Hill, Ind. E5, H7 179
Mars Hill, Maine B5 184
Mars Hill, N.C. D3 197
Marsa Al Burayqah, Libya C3 101
Marsá Sūsah, Libya C4 101
Marsabit, Ken. A6 106
Marsala, It. F4 67
Marscot, mtn., Santa Isabel I. 115
Marsden, Sask., Can. E1 155
Marseillan, Fr. F5 58
Marseille, Fr. F6 58
Marseille-en-Beauvaisis, Fr E1 59
Marseilles, Ill. B5 178
Marsh, Mont. D12 190
Marsh, fork, W. Va. D6 211
Marsh, isl., La. E4 183
Marsh, lake, Minn. E2 187
Marsh, peak, Utah C6 207
Marsh Harbour, Ba. Is. B5 131
Marsh Hill, Pa. D8 202
Marshall, Ark. B3 169
Marshall, Sask., Can. D1 155
Marshall, Ill. D6 178
Marshall, Ind. E3 179
Marshall, Lib. E2 103
Marshall, Mich. F6 186
Marshall, Minn. F3 187
Marshall, Mo. B4 189
Marshall, N.C. D3 197
Marshall, N. Dak. B3 198
Marshall, Okla. A4 200
Marshall, Tex. C5 206
Marshall, Va. C5 209
Marshall, Wash. D7 210
Marshall, Wis. E4 212
Marshall, Wyo. C7 213
Marshall, co., Ala. A3 166
Marshall, co., Ill. B4 178
Marshall, co., Ind. B5 179
Marshall, co., Iowa C4 180
Marshall, co., Kans. C7 181
Marshall, co., Ky. B3 182
Marshall, co., Minn. B2 187
Marshall, co., Miss. A4 188
Marshall, co., Okla. C5 200
Marshall, co., S. Dak. B8 204
Marshall, co., Tenn. B5 205
Marshall, co., W. Va. B4 211
Marshall, is., Pac. O. F10 113
Marshall Hall, Md. C3 173
Marshall Northeast, Tex. *C5 206
Marshallberg, N.C. C7 197
Marshalls Creek, Pa. D11 202
Marshallton, Del. A6 173
Marshallton, Pa. *E8 202
Marshalltown, Iowa B5 180
Marshallville, Ga. D3 175
Marshallville, Ohio B6 199
Marshes Siding, Ky. D5 182
Marshfield, Ind. D3 179
Marshfield, Mass. B6, E4 185
Marshfield, Mo. D5 189
Marshfield, Vt. C4 208
Marshfield, Wis. D3 212
Marshfield Hills, Mass. B6, E4 185
Marshville, N.C. C3 197
Marshyhope, creek, Del., Md. C6 173
Marsing, Idaho F2 177
Marske-by-the-Sea, Eng. F7 57
Marsland, Nebr. B2 191
Marstal, Den. D4 62
Marsteller, Pa. E4 202
Marston, Mo. E8 189
Marston, N.C. C3 197
Marstons Mills, Mass. C7 185
Mart, Tex. D4 206
Martaban, Bur. E10 87
Martaban, gulf, Bur. E10 87
Martapura, Indon. F4 90
Martel, Fla. C4 174
Martel, Fr. E4 58
Martelange, Bel. E5 59
Martell, Nebr. D9 191
Martell, Wis. D1 212
Martelle, Iowa B6 180
Martensdale, Iowa C4 180
Martensville, Sask., Can. *E2 155
Martha, Okla. C2 200
Martha's Vineyard, isl., Mass. D6 185
Marthasville, Mo. C6 189
Marthaville, La. C2 183
Martí, Cuba E5 131
Martigny-Ville, Switz. C3 66
Martigues, Fr. F6 58
Martin, Ga. B3 175
Martin, Ky. C7 182
Martin, Mich. F5 186
Martin, N. Dak. B5 198
Martin, Ohio A2 199
Martin, S.C. E5 203
Martin, S. Dak. D4 204
Martin, Tenn. A3 205
Martin, co., Fla. E6 174
Martin, co., Ind. G4 179
Martin, co., Ky. C7 182
Martin, co., Minn. G4 187
Martin, co., N.C. B6 197
Martin, co., Tex. C2 206
Martin, dam, Ala. C4 166
Martin, lake, Ala. C4 166
Martina [Franca], It. D6 67
Martindale, Que., Can. D2 154
Martindale, Tex. A4 206
Martinez, Calif. B5, C2 170
Martínez, Cuba D2 131
Martinez, Ga. C4 175
Martinez East, Calif. *C2 170
MARTINIQUE, Fr. dep., N.A. o16 131
Martinique, passage, N.A. o16 131
Martins, pond, Mass. C2 185
Martins Creek, N.J. B2 194
Martins Creek, Pa. B2 194
Martins Ferry, Ohio B7 199
Martins Pond, Mass. C2 185
Martinsburg, Ind. H5 179
Martinsburg, Iowa C5 180
Martinsburg, Mo. B6 189
Martinsburg, Nebr. B9 191
Martinsburg, N.Y. B5 196
Martinsburg, Ohio B5 199
Martinsburg, Pa. F5 202
Martinsburg, W. Va. B7 211
Martinsdale, Mont. D6 190
Martinsville, Ill. D6 178
Martinsville, Ind. F5 179
Martinsville, Miss. D3 188
Martinsville, Mo. A3 189
Martinsville, N.J. B3 194
Martinsville, Ohio C4 199
Martinsville (Independent City), Va. E3 209
Martinton, Ill. C6 178
Martinville, Ark. B3 169
Martinville, Que., Can. D6 154
Martling, Ala. A3 166
Martofte, Den. C4 62
Martos, Sp. D4 65
Martre, lake, N.W. Ter., Can. D9 142
Martwick, Ky. C2 182
Marty, S. Dak. F7 204
Maru, bay, Sol. Is. 115
Maruchak, Afg. D11 86
Maruf, Afg. F13 86
Marugame, Jap. I6 93
Marum, Neth. A6 59
Marumsco, creek, Md. D6 173
Marun, riv., Iran F4 86
Marunga, hbr., San Cristobal I. 115
Marvast, Iran F7 86
Marvejols, Fr. E5 58
Marvel, Ala. B2 166
Marvel, Colo. D2 171
Marvell, Ark. C5 169
Marvin, S. Dak. B9 204
Marvin Terrace, Mo. *C7 189
Marvindale, Pa. C4 202
Marvine, mtn., Utah E4 207
Marvyn, Ala. C4 166
Marwayne, Alta., Can. C5 148
Mary, Sov. Un. F9 71
Mary, lake, Minn. E3 187
Mary, lake, Miss. D2 188
Mary Esther, Fla. *G2 174
Mary Ridge, Mo. *C7 189
Maryborough, Austl. H4 112
Maryborough, Austl. B9 112
Marydel, Md. B6 173
Maryfield, Sask., Can. H5 155
Maryland, state, U.S. 173
in 18th cent. 162
Maryland, pt., Md. D3 173
Maryland Heights, Mo. A8 189
Maryland Line, Md. A4 173
Maryport, Eng. C5 55
Marys, peak, Oreg. C3 201
Marys, riv., Nev. A6 192
Mary's Harbour, Newf., Can. B4 152
Mary's Igloo, Alsk. B6 167
Marystown, Newf., Can. E4 152
Marysvale, Utah E3 207
Marysville, Calif. C3 170
Marysville, B.C., Can. E10 149
Marysville, N.B., Can. D3 151
Marysville, Ont., Can. C7 153
Marysville, Idaho E7 177
Marysville, Iowa C5 180
Marysville, Kans. C7 181
Marysville, Mich. F8 186
Marysville, Mont. D4 190
Marysville, Ohio B4 199
Marysville, Pa. F8 202
Marysville, Wash. A3 210
Marytown, W. Va. D3 211
Marytown, Wis. B5 212
Maryville, Ill. A9 189
Maryville, Mo. A3 189
Maryville, Tenn. D10, E11 205
Marzūq, Libya D2 101
Masai Steppe, plat., Tan. B6 106
Masaka, Ug. B5 106
Masalembo-Besar, isl., Indon. G5 90
Masalog, pt., Tinian 114
Masan, Kor. I4 93
Masardis, Maine B4 184
Masaryktown, Fla. D4 174
Masasi, Tan. D6 106
Masatepe, Nic. E4 130
Masaya, Nic. E4 130
Masbate, Phil. C6 90
Mascara, Alg. G7 64, B5 102
Mascoma, lake, N.H. C2 193
Mascoma, riv., N.H. C2 193
Mascot, Nebr. D6 191
Mascot, Tenn. C10, E12 205
Mascotte, Fla. *D5 174
Mascota, Mex. m11 129
Mascouche, Que., Can. D4 154
Mascoutah, Ill. E4 178
Masefau, bay, Am. Sam. 114
Masefield, Sask., Can. H2 155
Maseru, Leso. C4 107
Mashaki, Afg. E14 86
Masham, Eng. F7 57
Mashapaug, pond, Conn. A8 172
Mashhad, see Meshed, Iran
Mashīz, Iran G8 86
Mashkel, riv., Iran H11 86
Mashonaland, reg., Rh. A5 107
Mashpee, Mass. C7 185
Masi-Manimba, Zaire B2 106
Masindi, Ug. A5 106
Masira, isl., Oman D2 87
Masisea, Peru C3 134
Masisi, Zaire B4 106
Masjed Soleymān, Iran F4 86
Mask, lake, Ire. D2 55
Maskell, Nebr. B9 191
Maskinonge, Que., Can. C4 154
Maskinonge, co., Que., Can. C4 154
Masnières, Fr. D3 59
Mason, Ill. E5 178
Mason, Mich. F6 186
Mason, N.H. E3 193
Mason, Ohio C2, C3 199
Mason, Okla. B5 200
Mason, Tenn. B2 205
Mason, Tex. D3 206
Mason, W. Va. B2 211
Mason, Wis. B2 212
Mason, Wyo. C2 213
Mason, co., Ill. C4 178
Mason, co., Ky. B6 182
Mason, co., Mich. D4 186
Mason, co., Tex. D3 206
Mason, co., Wash. B2 210
Mason, co., W. Va. C3 211
Mason City, Ill. C4 178
Mason City, Iowa A4 180
Mason City, Nebr. C6 191
Masonhall, Tenn. A2 205
Masons, N.H. A3 193
Masontown, Pa. G2 202
Masontown, W. Va. B5 211
Masonville, Ark. D4 169
Masonville, Colo. A5 171
Masonville, N.Y. C5 196
Mass, Mich. A6 186
Massa, It. B3 67
Massa Marittima, It. C3 67
Massaade, Syr. A7 84
Massabesic, lake, N.H. E4 193
Massac, co., Ill. F5 178
Massachusetts, state, U.S. 185
in 17th cent. 162
in Revolutionary War 162
in 1820 163
Massachusetts, bay, Mass. B6 185
Massacre, bay, Am. Sam. 114
Massacre, lake, Nev. B2 192
Massaemett, mtn., Mass. A2 185
Massafra, It. D6 67
Massakory, Chad C3 104
Massangena, Moz. B5 107
Massanutten, mtns., Va. C4 209
Massapê, Braz. B2 138
Massapeag, Conn. D8 172
Massapequa, N.Y. G3 172
Massapequa Park, N.Y. *E3 196
Massapoag, pond, Mass. E2 185
Massasecum, N.H. D3 193
Massaua, Eth. B4 105
Massena, Iowa C3 180
Massena, N.Y. A2 196
Masset, B.C., Can. C1 149
Masset, inlet, B.C., Can. C1 149
Massey, Ont., Can. A2 153
Massey, Md. B6 173
Massif Central, mts., Fr. E5 58
Massif de Tarazit, plat., Niger B6 103
Massillon, Ohio B6 199
Massinga, Moz. B6 107
Massive, mtn., Colo. B4 171
Masson, Que., Can. D2 154
Massy, Fr. h10 58
Masten, Del. C6 173
Masters, Colo. A6 171
Masterton, N.Z. N15 112
Mastic Beach, N.Y. *F5 172
Mastuj, Pak. k17 86
Mastung, Pak. C1 88
Mastūrah, Sau. Ar. E7 101
Masuda, Jap. I5 93
Masulipatam, India E7 87
Masuria, reg., Pol. B6 70
Masury, Ohio A7 199
Masuya, Okinawa 114
Mata, Zaire C3 106
Mata Armilla, Arg. D2 136
Mata de São João, Braz. D3 138
Matabeleland, reg., Rh. A4 107
Mataboor, Indon. F9 90
Matachewan, Ont., Can. E9 153
Matadi, Zaire C1 106
Matador, Sask., Can. G2 155
Matador, Tex. C2 206
Matafotufotu, cape, W. Sam. 114
Matagalpa, Nic. D5 130
Matagorda, Tex. E5 206
Matagorda, co., Tex. E5 206
Matagorda, bay, Tex. E4 206
Matagorda, isl., Tex. E4 206
Matagorda, pen., Tex. E5 206
Matak, isl., Indon. K7 89
Matam, Sen. C2 103
Matamã, Eth. C4 105
Matamoras, Pa. D12 202
Matamoros, Mex. B5 129
Matamoros [de la Laguna], Mex. B4 129
Ma'tan, Libya D2 101
Ma'tan as Sarra (Well), Libya E4 101
Ma'tan Bishārah (Well), Libya E4 101
Ma'tan Rāshidah (Oasis), Libya H3 85
Matanalem, cape, New Hanover I. 115
Matane, Que., Can. G19 145
Matane, co., Que., Can. *B3 154
Matanuska, riv., Alsk. g18 167
Matanuska, val., Alsk. g17 167
Matanzas, Cuba D3 131
Matanzas, prov., Cuba D3 131
Matanzas, inlet, Fla. C5 174
Matapan, cape, Grc. D4 69
Matapedia, co., Que., Can. *B3 154
Matara, Cey. G7 87
Mataram, Indon. G5 90
Matarani, Peru E3 134
Matarka, Mor. H5 64
Mataró, Sp. B7 65
Mataso, isl., New Hebr. 115
Matatiele, S. Afr. D4 107
Matautu, W. Sam. 114
Matawan, N.J. C4 194
Matawin, res., Que., Can. C4 154
Matawin, riv., Que., Can. C4 154
Matehuala, Mex. C4 129
Mateko, Zaire B2 106
Matera, It. D6 67
Mátészalka, Hung. B6 68
Mateur, Tun. F11 64
Matewan, W. Va. D2 211
Matfield Green, Kans. D7 181
Mathelo, Pak. D2 88
Mather, Man., Can. E2 150
Mather, Pa. G1 202
Mather, Wis. D3 212
Mather, peak, Wyo. A5 213
Matherville, Ill. B3 178
Matherville, Miss. D5 188
Matheson, Colo. B7 171
Matheson Island, Man., Can. D3 150
Mathews, Ala. C3 166
Mathews, La. C6, E5 183
Mathews, Va. D6 209
Mathews, co., Va. D6 209
Mathews, lake, Calif. F3 170
Mathias, W. Va. C6 211
Mathias Point, Va. C5 209
Mathis, Tex. E4 206
Mathiston, Miss. B4 188
Mathura, India C6 87, D6 88
Matiakouali, Upper Volta D5 103
Matinecock, N.Y. *D3 196
Matinenda, lake, Ont., Can. B8 186
Matinicus, Maine E4 184
Matinicus, isl., Maine E4 184
Matjan, is., Indon. G6 90
Matlock, Eng. A6 56
Matlock, Iowa A2 180
Mato Grosso, Braz. B4 135
Mato Grosso, state, Braz. B4 135
Matoaca, Va. C7 209
Matoaka, W. Va. D3 211
Matong, New Britain I. 115
Matozinhos, Port. B1 65
Maṭraḥ, Oman D2 87
Matrosovo, Sov. Un. B11 93
Maṭrūḥ, Eg. G6 85
Matsqui, B.C., Can. B10 149
Matsubara, Jap. *I7 93
Matsudo, Jap. *n18 93
Matsue, Jap. I6 93
Matsuida, Jap. m17 93
Matsumae, Jap. F10 93
Matsumoto, Jap. H8, m16 93
Matsuyama, Jap. J6 93
Matsuzaka, Jap. I8, o15 93
Matsuzaki, Jap. o17 93
Mattamiscontis, lake, Maine C4 184
Mattamuskeet, lake, N.C. B7 197
Mattancheri, India G6 87
Mattapoisett, Mass. C6 185
Mattaponi, riv., Va. D5 209
Mattawa, Ont., Can. A6 153
Mattawa, Wash. *C6 210
Mattawamkeag, Maine C4 184
Mattawamkeag, lake, Maine C4 184
Mattawamkeag, riv., Maine C4 184
Mattawana, Pa. E6 202
Matterhorn, mtn., Nev. B6 192
Matterhorn, mtn., Switz. D3 66
Matteson, Ill. F3 178
Matthew Town, Ba. Is. E7 131
Matthews, Ga. C4 175
Matthews, Ind. D7 179
Matthews, Mo. E8 189
Matthews, N.C. B3 197
Matthews, mtn., Mo. D7 189
Mattituck, N.Y. D4 196
Mattoon, Ill. D5 178
Mattoon, Wis. C4 212
Mattson, Miss. A3 188
Matucana, Peru D2 134
Matuku, isl., Fiji 114
Matun, Afg. E14 86
Matundu, Zaire A3 106
Matunuck, R.I. D10 172
Maturín, Ven. B5 133
Mau, Fiji 114
Mau, India E9 88
Maúa, Moz. D6 106
Mauban, Phil. o13 90
Maubeuge, Fr. B5 58
Maubin, Bur. D1 89
Mauch Chunk, see Jim Thorpe, Pa.
Mauchline, Scot. E4 57
Mauckport, Ind. H5 179
Maud, Ohio C2, C3 199
Maud, Okla. B5 200
Maud, Scot. C6 57
Maud, Tex. C5 206
Maudlow, Mont. D5 190
Maués, Braz. C3 139
Maues Guaçu, riv., Braz. C3 139
Maug (Mougu), is., Mariana Is. 115
Maugani, India E8 88
Maugansville, Md. A2 173
Maughold, head, I. of Man F4 57
Maui, co., Haw. B5 176
Maui, isl., Haw. C5 176
Mauk, Ga. D2 175
Mauldin, S.C. *B3 203
Maule, prov., Chile B2 136
Mauléon-Soule, Fr. F3 58
Maumee, Ohio A2, A4 199
Maumee, bay, Ohio A2 199
Maumee, riv., Ind., Ohio B8 179, A4 199
Maun, Bots. A3 107
Mauna Kea, vol., Haw. D6 176
Mauna Loa, vol., Haw. D6 176
Maunabo, P.R. C7 132
Maunabo, mun., P.R. C7 132
Maunaloa, Haw. B4 176
Maunalua, bay, Haw. g11 176
Maungdaw, Bur. D9 87
Maunie, Ill. E5 178
Maupin, Oreg. B5 201
Maurepas, La. B6 183
Maurepas, lake, La. D5 183
Maurertown, Va. C4 209
Maurice, Iowa B1 180
Maurice, La. D3 183
Maurice, S. Dak. C2 204
Maurice, riv., N.J. E2 194
Mauricetown, N.J. E3 194
Mauriceville, Tex. D2 183
Maurier, pt., Que., Can. C2 152
Maurine, S. Dak. B3 204
MAURITANIA, country, Afr. C2 103
Maury, N.C. B6 197
Maury, co., Tenn. B4 205
Maury, isl., Wash. D1 210
Maury City, Tenn. B2 205
Mauryan empire 79
Mauston, Wis. E3 212
Mauterndorf, Aus. E6 60
Mauwee, peak, Conn. C3 172
Maverick, Ariz. D6 168
Maverick, co., Tex. E2 206
Mavinga, Ang. E3 106
Mawer, Sask., Can. G2 155
Mawkmai, Bur. B2 89
Mawlaik, Bur. D9 87
Max, Nebr. D4 191
Max, N. Dak. B4 198
Max Meadows, Va. E2 209
Maxbass, N. Dak. A4 198
Maxcanú, Mex. C6 129
Maxeys, Ga. C3 175
Maxie, Miss. E4 188
Maxinkuckee, lake, Ind. B5 179
Maxstone, Sask., Can. H2 155
Maxton, N.C. C4 197
Maxville, Ont., Can. B10 153
Maxville, Fla. B4 174
Maxville, Mont. D3 190
Maxwell, Calif. C2 170
Maxwell, Ind. E6 179
Maxwell, Iowa A7, C4 180
Maxwell, Nebr. C5 191
Maxwell, N. Mex. A5 195
Maxwell, Tenn. B5 205
Maxwell Colony, S. Dak. D8 204
May, Idaho E5 177
May, Okla. A2 200
May, Tex. D3 206
May, cape, N.J. C13 159
May, isl., Scot. D6 57
May, mtn., Alta., Can. B1 148
May Park, Oreg. *B8 201
May Pen, Jam. G5 131
Maya, mts., Br. Hond. B3 130
Mayaguana, isl., Ba. Is. D7 131
Mayaguana, passage, Ba. Is. D7 131
Mayagüez, P.R. C2 132
Mayagüez, mun., P.R. C2 132
Mayagüez, bay, P.R. C2 132
Mayama, Con. B. F2 104
Mayarí, Cuba E6 131
Maybank, Miss. D4 188
Maybee, Mich. F7 186
Maybell, Colo. A2 171
Mayberry, Md. A3 173
Maybole, Scot. E4 57
Maybrook, N.Y. D6 196
Maydi, Yemen B5 105
Maydos, see Eceabat, Tur.
Mayen, Ger. C2 61
Mayenne, Fr. C3 58
Mayenne, riv., Fr. D3 58
Mayer, Ariz. C3 168
Mayersville, Miss. C2 188
Mayerthorpe, Alta., Can. C3 148
Mayes, co., Okla. A6 200
Mayesville, S.C. D7 203
Mayetta, Kans. B6, C8 181
Mayetta, N.J. D4 194
Mayfair, Sask., Can. E2 155
Mayfield, Kans. E6 181
Mayfield, Ky. B2 182
Mayfield, N.Y. B6 196
Mayfield, Ohio *C3 199
Mayfield, Ohio *A6 199
Mayfield, Pa. C10 202
Mayfield, Utah D4 207
Mayfield, Wash. C3 210
Mayfield Heights, Ohio A6 199
Mayflower, Ark. C3 169
Mayflower, Tex. D6 206
Mayhew, Miss. B5 188
Mayhill, N. Mex. E4 195
Maykain, Sov. Un. C9 73
Mayking, Ky. C7 182
Maykop, Sov. Un. *E6 71
Mayland, Tenn. C8 205
Maymont, Sask., Can. E2 155
Maymyo, Bur. D10 87
Maynard, Ark. A5 169
Maynard, Iowa B6 180
Maynard, Ky. D3 182
Maynard, Mass. B5, C1 185
Maynard, Minn. F3 187
Maynard, Ohio B1 211
Maynardville, Tenn. C10 205
Mayne, isl., B.C., Can. B9 149
Maynooth, Ont., Can. B7 153
Mayo, Fla. B3 174
Mayo, Md. C4 173
Mayo, S.C. A4 203
Mayo, mts., Ire. C2 55
Mayo, riv., Arg. D2 136
Mayo, Yukon, Can. D5 144
Mayodan, N.C. A4 197
Mayon, vol., Phil. C6 90
Mayotte, isl., Comoro Is. f9 107
Mayoumba, Gabon F2 104
Maypearl, Tex. *C4 206
Mayport, Fla. B5, B6 174
Mayrhofen, Aus. B7 66
Mays, Ind. E7 179
Mays Landing, N.J. E3 194
Mays Lick, Ky. B6 182
Mayse, res., Tex. D6 200
Maysville, Ala. A3 166
Maysville, Ark. A1 169
Maysville, Ga. B3 175
Maysville, Ind. G3 179
Maysville, Iowa D7 180
Maysville, Ky. B6 182
Maysville, Mo. B3 189
Maysville, N.C. C6 197
Maysville, Okla. C4 200
Maysville, W. Va. B5 211
Maytown, Ala. *B2 166
Mayuram, India *F6 87
Mayview, Mo. B4 189
Mayville, Mich. E7 186
Mayville, N.J. E3 194
Mayville, N.Y. C1 196
Mayville, N. Dak. B8 198
Mayville, Oreg. B6 201
Mayville, Wis. E5 212
Maywood, Calif. F2 170
Maywood, Ill. F2 178
Maywood, Ind. H7 179
Maywood, Mo. B6 189
Maywood, Nebr. D5 191
Maywood, N.J. D5 194
Mayyat Yarqah (Oasis), Eg. E5 84
Maza, Arg. B4 136
Maza, N. Dak. A6 198
Mazabuka, Zambia E4 106
Mazagão, Braz. C4 139
Mazamet, Fr. F5 58
Mazán, Arg. E2 135
Mazapil, Mex. C4 129
Mazar-i-Sharif, Afg. C13 86
Mazara del Vallo, It. F4 67
Mazāri 'an Nūbānī, Jordan g11 84
Mazarn, creek, Ark. C5 169
Mazarredo, Arg. D3 136
Mazarrón, Sp. D5 65
Mazaruni, riv., Guy. A2 139
Mazatenango, Guat. C2 130
Mazatlán, Mex. C3 129
Mazatzal, mts., Ariz. C4 168
Mazatzal, peak, Ariz. C4 168
Mažeikiai, Sov. Un. C4 72
Mazenod, Sask., Can. H2 155
Mazeppa, Minn. F6 187
Mazgirt, Tur. C12 85
Mazie, Okla. A6 200
Mazomanie, Wis. E4 212
Mazon, Ill. B5 178
Mazzarino, It. F5 67
Mbabane, Swaz. C5 107
Mbaïki, Cen. Afr. Rep. E3 104
Mbala, Zambia C5 106
Mbale, Ug. A5 106
Mbalmayo, Cam. E2 104
Mbamba Bay, Tan. D5 106
Mbandaka, Zaire A2 106
Mbarara, Ug. B5 106
M'bari, riv., Cen. Afr. Rep. D4 104
Mbatiki, isl., Fiji 114
Mbenga, isl., Fiji 114
Mbenga, pass, Fiji 114
Mbeya, Tan. C5 106
M'Bour, Sen. D1 103
Mbout, Maur. C2 103
Mbuk, isl., Bis. Arch. 115
Mbuji Mayi, Zaire G4 104
Mbulia, isl., Fiji 114
Mbulo, isl., Sol. Is. 115
Mburucuyá, Arg. E4 135
Mbya, bay, Fiji 114
McAdam, N.B., Can. D2 151
McAdams, Miss. B4 188
McAdenville, N.C. *B2 197
McAdoo, Pa. E9 202
McAdoo, Tex. C2 206
McAfee, Miss. C4 188
McAfee, N.J. A3 194
McAfee, peak, Nev. B5 192
McAlester, Okla. C6 200
McAlester, lake, Okla. B6 200
McAlister, N. Mex. C6 195
McAlisterville, Pa. E7 202
McAllen, Tex. F3 206
McAllister, Mont. E5 190
McAlmont, Ark. D6 169
McAlpin, Fla. B4 174
McAlpine, lock & dam, Ind., Ky. H6 179, A4 182
McAndrews, Ky. C7 182
McArthur, Ohio C5 199
McAuley, Man., Can. D1 150
McBain, Mich. D5 186
McBaine, Mo. C5 189
McBean, Ga. C5 175
McBee, S.C. C7 203
McBride, B.C., Can. C7 149
McBride, Mich. *E5 186
McBride, Mo. D8 189
McCabe, Mont. B12 190
McCall, Idaho E2 177
McCall, La. B5, D4 183

INDEX KEY Each place listed in **Bold-faced Type** has its population listed in the Population tables, pages 230 to 280.
Each country, shown in CAPITAL LETTERS, has its population listed in the World Political Information Table, pages 6 to 10.
* Does not appear on map; key shows general location.

McCall Creek, Miss.......D3 188
McCalla, Ala.......E4 166
McCallsburg, Iowa.......B4 180
McCamey, Tex.......D1 206
McCammon, Idaho.......G6 177
McCanna, N. Dak.......A8 198
McCarthy, Alsk.......C11 167
McCartney, mtn., Mont.......E4 190
McCartys, N. Mex.......B2 195
McCaskill, Ark.......D2 169
McCauley, isl., B.C., Can.......C2 149
McCaulley, Tex.......C2 206
McCaysville, Ga.......B2 175
McChesneytown, Pa.......*F3 202
McClain, co., Okla.......C4 200
McClave, Colo.......C8 171
McCleary, Wash.......B2 210
McClelland, Ark.......B4 169
McClelland, Iowa.......C2 180
McClellanville, S.C.......E9 203
McClintock, chan., N.W. Ter., Can.......B12 142
McClintock, mtn., Ant.......A28 120
McCloud, Calif.......B2 170
McClure, Ill.......F4 178
McClure, Ohio.......A4 199
McClure, Pa.......E7 202
McClure, Va.......B2 209
McClure, lake, Calif.......F1 192
McClusky, N. Dak.......B5 198
McColl, S.C.......B8 203
McComas, W. Va.......D3 211
McComb, Miss.......D3 188
McComb, Ohio.......A4 199
McConaughy, lake, Nebr.......C3 191
McCondy, Miss.......B5 188
McCone, co., Mont.......C11 190
McConnell, Ill.......A4 178
McConnell, Tenn.......A3 205
McConnells, S.C.......B5 203
McConnellsburg, Pa.......G6 202
McConnellstown, Pa.......F5 202
McConnelsville, Ohio.......C6 199
McCook, Ill.......*B6 178
McCook, Nebr.......D5 191
McCook, co., S. Dak.......D8 204
McCook Lake, S. Dak.......E9 204
McCool, Miss.......B4 188
McCool Junction, Nebr.......D8 191
McCoole, Md.......D2 173
McCord, Sask., Can.......H2 155
McCordsville, Ind.......E6 179
McCormick, S.C.......D3 203
McCormick, co., S.C.......D3 203
McCoy, Colo.......B4 171
McCoysville, Pa.......F6 202
McCracken, Kans.......D4 181
McCracken, co., Ky.......A2 182
McCreary, Man., Can.......D2 150
McCreary, co., Ky.......D5 182
McCredie, Mo.......C6 189
McCrory, Ark.......B4 169
McCulloch, co., Tex.......D3 206
McCulloh, Ala.......C4 166
McCullom Lake, Ill.......*A5 178
McCullough, Ala.......D2 166
McCullough, mtn., Nev.......H6 192
McCullough, range, Nev.......B1 168
McCullum, Ala.......B2 166
McCune, Kans.......E8 181
McCurtain, Okla.......B7 200
McCurtain, co., Okla.......C7 200
McCutchenville, Ohio.......B4 199
McDade, Tex.......D4 206
McDaniel, Md.......C5 173
McDavid, Fla.......G2 174
McDermitt, Nev.......B4 192
McDermott, Ohio.......D4 199
McDonald, Kans.......C2 181
McDonald, Miss.......C4 188
McDonald, N. Mex.......D6 195
McDonald, Ohio.......A7 199
McDonald, Pa.......B5 202
McDonald, Tenn.......D9, E11 205
McDonald, co., Mo.......E3 189
McDonald, creek, Mont.......C8 190
McDonough, Ga.......C2 175
McDonough, N.Y.......C5 196
McDonough, co., Ill.......C3 178
McDougal, Ark.......A5 169
McDougal, mtn., Wyo.......C2 213
McDowell, Ky.......C7 182
McDowell, Va.......C3 209
McDowell, co., N.C.......D4 197
McDowell, co., W. Va.......D3 211
McDowell, mtn., Ariz.......G2 168
McDowell, peak, Ariz.......F2 168
McDuffie, co., Ga.......C4 175
McElhattan, Pa.......D7 202
McElroy, creek, W. Va.......A6 211
McEwen, Tenn.......A4 205
McFadden, Wyo.......D6 213
McFaddin, Tex.......E4 206
McFall, Mo.......A3 189
McFarlan, N.C.......C3 197
McFarland, Calif.......E4 170
McFarland, Kans.......C7 181
McFarland, Mich.......B3 186
McFarland, Wis.......*E4 212
McGaha, Ky.......C4 182
McGaheysville, Va.......C4 209
McGee, Sask., Can.......F1 155
McGehee, Ark.......D4 169
McGill, Nev.......D7 192
McGillivray, lake, Que., Can.......A7 153
McGillivray Falls, B.C., Can.......D6 149
McGivney, N.B. Can.......C3 151
McGrath, Alsk.......C8 167
McGrath, Minn.......D5 187
McGraw, N.Y.......C4 196
McGraws, W. Va.......D3 211
McGregor, Iowa.......A6 180
McGregor, Minn.......D5 187
McGregor, N. Dak.......A3 198
McGregor, Tex.......D4 206
McGregor, lake, Alta., Can.......D4 148
McGregor, riv., B.C., Can.......B7 149
McGrew, Nebr.......C2 191
McGuffey, Ohio.......B4 199
McGuire, mtn., Idaho.......D4 177
McHenry, Ill.......A5, E2 178
McHenry, Ky.......C3 182
McHenry, Md.......D1 173
McHenry, Miss.......E4 188
McHenry, N. Dak.......B7 198
McHenry, co., Ill.......A5 178
McHenry, co., N. Dak.......A5 198
McHue, Ark.......B4 169
McIndoe Falls, Vt.......C4 208
McIntire, Iowa.......A5 180
McIntosh, Ala.......D1 166
McIntosh, Ont., Can.......E5 150
McIntosh, Fla.......C4 174
McIntosh, Ga.......E5 175
McIntosh, Minn.......C3 187
McIntosh, N. Mex.......C3 195
McIntosh, S. Dak.......B4 204
McIntosh, co., Ga.......E5 175
McIntosh, co., N. Dak.......C6 198
McIntosh, co., Okla.......B6 200
McIntosh, lake, Sask., Can.......B3 155
McIntosh, run, Md.......D4 173
McIntyre, Ga.......D3 175
McIntyre, Pa.......E3 202
McIntyre, creek, Ohio.......B1 211
McKague, Sask., Can.......E4 155
McKean, Pa.......C1 202
McKean, co., Pa.......C4 202
McKee, Ky.......C6 182
McKee City, N.J.......E3 194
McKees Rocks, Pa.......B5, F1 202
McKeesport, Pa.......B6, F2 202
McKenney, Va.......E5 209
McKenzie, Ala.......D3 166
McKenzie, N. Dak.......C5 198
McKenzie, Tenn.......A3 205
McKenzie, co., N. Dak.......B2 198
McKenzie, pass, Oreg.......C4 201
McKenzie, riv., Oreg.......C4 201
McKenzie Bridge, Oreg.......C4 201
McKerrow, Ont., Can.......A3 153
McKinley, Ala.......C2 166
McKinley, Maine.......D4 184
McKinley, Minn.......C6 187
McKinley, Wyo.......C7 213
McKinley, co., N. Mex.......B1 195
McKinley, mtn., Alsk.......C9 167
McKinley Park, Alsk.......C10 167
McKinleyville, Calif.......B1 170
McKinney, Ky.......C5 182
McKinney, Tex.......C4 206
McKinney, lake, Kans.......E2 181
McKinnon, Wyo.......D3 213
McKittrick, Calif.......E4 170
McKittrick, Mo.......C6 189
McKittrick Summit, mtn., Calif.......E4 170
McKnight, lake, Man., Can.......A1 150
McLain, Miss.......D5 188
McLaughlin, Alta., Can.......C5 148
McLaughlin, S. Dak.......B5 204
McLaughlin, riv., Man., Can.......C3 150
McLaurin, Miss.......D4 188
McLean, Sask., Can.......G3 155
McLean, Ill.......C4 178
McLean, Nebr.......B8 191
McLean, Tex.......B2 206
McLean, Va.......A5 209
McLean, co., Ill.......C5 178
McLean, co., Ky.......C2 182
McLean, co., N. Dak.......B4 198
McLean, mtn., Maine.......A4 184
McLeansboro, Ill.......E5 178
McLemore, Okla.......*B4 200
McLemoresville, Tenn.......B3 205
McLennan, Alta., Can.......B2 148
McLennan, co., Tex.......D4 206
McLeod, Mont.......E6 190
McLeod, N. Dak.......C8 198
McLeod, co., Minn.......F4 187
McLeod, lake, B.C., Can.......B6 149
McLeod, riv., Alta., Can.......C2 148
McLoud, Okla.......B4 200
McLoughlin, mtn., Oreg.......E4 201
McLouth, Kans.......B7, C8 181
McMahon, Sask., Can.......G2 155
McMasterville, Que., Can.......*D4 154
McMechen, W. Va.......B2, B4 211
McMichael, creek, Pa.......B2 194
McMillan, Mich.......B5 186
McMillan, Tenn.......E12 205
McMillan, lake, N. Mex.......E5 195
McMillan Manor, Calif.......*E4 170
McMinn, co., Tenn.......D9 205
McMinnville, Oreg.......B1, B3 201
McMinnville, Tenn.......D8 205
McMorran, Sask., Can.......F1 155
McMullen, co., Tex.......E3 206
McMurdo, Ant.......B29 120
McMurdo, sound, Ant.......B29 120
McMurray, Alta., Can.......A5 148
McMurray, Wash.......A3 210
McNab, Ark.......D2 169
McNair, Miss.......E2 188
McNair, Tex.......*E5 206
McNairy, Tenn.......B3 205
McNairy, co., Tenn.......B3 205
McNary, Ariz.......C6 168
McNary, La.......D3 183
McNary, Tex.......F1 206
McNeal, Ariz.......F6 168
McNeal, Fla.......B1 174
McNeil, Ark.......D2 169
McNeil, Tex.......D4 206
McNeil, isl., Wash.......D1 210
McNeill, Miss.......E4 188
McNeill, mtn., B.C., Can.......B2 149
McNutt, isl., N.S., Can.......F4 151
McPhail, riv., Man., Can.......C3 150
McPherson, Kans.......D6 181
McPherson, co., Kans.......D6 181
McPherson, co., Nebr.......C4 191
McPherson, co., S. Dak.......B6 204
McQuady, Ky.......C3 182
McQueeney, Tex.......B4 206
McRae, Ark.......B4 169
McRae, Ga.......D4 175
McRoberts, Ky.......C7 182
McSherrystown, Pa.......G7 202
McTaggart, Sask., Can.......H3 155
McTavish, Man., Can.......E3 150
McVeigh, Ky.......C7 182
McVeytown, Pa.......F6 202
McVille, N. Dak.......B7 198
McWilliams, Ala.......D2 166
Mchinja, Tan.......C6 106
Mchinji, Malawi.......D5 106
Mdandu, Tan.......C5 106
Mea Shearim, Isr.......m14 84
Meacham, Sask., Can.......E3 155
Meacham, Oreg.......B8 201
Mead, Colo.......A6 171
Mead, Nebr.......C9, D2 191
Mead, Okla.......D5 200
Mead, Wash.......B8, D7 210
Mead, lake, Nev.......G7 192
Meade, Kans.......E3 181
Meade, co., Kans.......E3 181
Meade, co., Ky.......C3 182
Meade, co., S. Dak.......C3 204
Meade, peak, Idaho.......G7 177
Meaden, peak, Colo.......A3 171
Meador, Ky.......D3 182
Meadow, S. Dak.......B3 204
Meadow, Tex.......C1 206
Meadow, Utah.......E3 207
Meadow, creek, W. Va.......D7 211
Meadow, mtn., Md.......D1 173
Meadow, riv., W. Va.......C4 211
Meadow, val., Nev.......F7 192
Meadow Bridge, W. Va.......D4, D7 211
Meadow Creek, Idaho.......A2 177
Meadow Creek, W. Va.......D4, D7 211
Meadow Grove, Nebr.......B8 191
Meadow Lake, Sask., Can.......B1 155
Meadow Park, Fla.......F6 174
Meadow Valley, wash, Nev.......F7 192
Meadowbrook, W. Va.......A7 211
Meadowdale, Wyo.......C8 213
Meadowlands, Minn.......C6 187
Meadowlands, Pa.......F1 202
Meadowlands, S. Afr.......*C4 107
Meadows, Idaho.......E2 177
Meadows, N.H.......B4 193
Meadowview, Va.......B3 209
Meadville, Miss.......D3 188
Meadville, Mo.......B4 189
Meadville, Pa.......C1 202
Meaford, Ont., Can.......C4 153
Meagher, co., Mont.......D6 190
Meaghers Grant, N.S., Can.......E6 151
Mealy, mts., Newf., Can.......B2 152
Meandarra, Austl.......C7 112
Meander Creek, res., Ohio.......A7 199
Means, Ky.......C6 182
Mearim, riv., Braz.......C1 138
Mears, Mich.......E4 186
Meath Park, Sask., Can.......D3 155
Meaux, Fr.......C5 58
Mebane, N.C.......A4 197
Mecca, Calif.......F5 170
Mecca, Ind.......E3 179
Mecca (Makkah), Sau. Ar.......A4 105
Mechanic Falls, Maine.......D2 184
Mechanicsburg, Ill.......*D4 178
Mechanicsburg, Ind.......D5 179
Mechanicsburg, Ohio.......B4 199
Mechanicsburg, Pa.......F7 202
Mechanicsville, Iowa.......C6 180
Mechanicsville, Md.......D4 173
Mechanicsville, Va.......D5 209
Mechanicsville, Vt.......C2 208
Mechanicville, N.Y.......C7 196
Mechant, lake, La.......E4 183
Mechelen, Bel.......C4 59
Mecheria, Alg.......C4 102
Meck, isl., Kwajalein.......114
Mecklenburg, co., N.C.......B3 197
Mecklenburg, co., Va.......E4 209
Mecklenburg, reg., Ger.......B5 60
Mecklenburg, state, Ger.......E5 60
Mecklenburg, bay, Ger.......D5 62
Mecklenburg Schwerin: in 1867.......51
Meckling, S. Dak.......E8 204
Meconta, Moz.......D6 106
Mecosta, Mich.......E5 186
Mecosta, co., Mich.......E5 186
Mecox, bay, N.Y........F7 172
Mecúfi, Moz.......D7 106
Medak, India.......H7 88
Medan, Indon.......K3 89, E1, m11 90
Médanos, Arg.......B4, f7 136
Medanosa, pt., Arg.......D3 136
Medart, Fla.......B2 174
Medaryville, Ind.......B4 179
Meddybemps, Maine.......C5 184
Meddybemps, lake, Maine.......C5 184
Médéa, Alg.......B5 102
Medellín, Col.......B2 133
Medemblik, Neth.......B5 59
Medenine, Tun.......C7 102
Méderdra, Maur.......C1 103
Medfield, Mass.......D2 185
Medford, Mass.......B5, C3 185
Medford, Minn.......F5 187
Medford, N.J.......D3 194
Medford, Okla.......A4 200
Medford, Oreg.......E4 201
Medford, Wis.......C3 212
Medford Lakes, N.J.......D3 194
Medford Station, N.Y.......F5 172
Medgidia, Rom.......C9 68
Media: c. 500 B.C.......43
under Alexander.......47
Media, Ill.......C3 178
Media, Pa.......B10, G11 202
Median kingdom: 612-550 B.C.......42
Mediapolis, Iowa.......C6 180
Medias, Rom.......B7 68
Medical Lake, Wash.......B8, D7 210
Medicina, It.......E7 66
Medicine, creek, Mo.......B4 189
Medicine, creek, Nebr.......D5 191
Medicine Bow, Wyo.......D6 213
Medicine Bow, peak, Wyo.......D6 213
Medicine Bow, range, Colo., Wyo.......A4 171, D6 213
Medicine Bow, riv., Wyo.......D6 213
Medicine Hat, Alta., Can.......D5 148
Medicine Lake, Mont.......B12 190
Medicine Lodge, Kans.......E5 181
Medicine Lodge, riv., Kans.......E5 181
Medicine Park, Okla.......C3 200
Medill, Mo.......A6 189
Medina, Minn.......*E5 187
Medina, N.Y.......B2 196
Medina, N. Dak.......C6 198
Medina, Ohio.......A6 199
Medina (Al Madīnah), Sau. Ar.......E7 101
Medina, Tenn.......B3 205
Medina, Tex.......E3 206
Medina, Wash.......D2 210
Medina, co., Ohio.......A6 199
Medina, co., Tex.......E3 206
Medina de Ríoseco, Sp.......B3 65
Medina del Campo, Sp.......B3 65
Medina Sidonia, Sp.......D3 65
Medinilla, isl., Mariana Is.......115
Mediterranean, sea.......E10 64, E6 85
Medium, lake, Iowa.......A3 180
Medjerda, riv., Tun., Alg.......G10 64
Medjez-el-Bab, Tun.......F11 64
Medley, Fla.......*G6 174
Mednogorsk, Sov. Un.......C5 73
Medomak, Maine.......D3 184
Medon, Tenn.......B3 205
Medora, Man., Can.......E1 150
Medora, Ill.......D3 178
Medora, Ind.......G5 179
Medora, Kans.......A4, D6 181
Medora, N. Dak.......C2 198
Medstead, Sask., Can.......D1 155
Meductic, N.B., Can.......D2 151
Meduxnekeag, riv., N.B., Can., Maine.......B5 184
Medveditsa, riv., Sov. Un.......C2 73
Medvezhegorsk, Sov. Un.......F16 63
Medvezhi, is., Sov. Un.......B19 71
Medway, Maine.......C4 184
Medway, Mass.......B5, E1 185
Medzhibozh, Sov. Un.......G6 72
Meehan, Miss.......C5 188
Meekatharra, Austl.......E2 111
Meeker, Colo.......A3 171
Meeker, Okla.......B5 200
Meeker, co., Minn.......E4 187
Meelpaeg, lake, Newf., Can.......D3 152
Meerane, Ger.......C7 61
Meerle, Bel.......C4 59
Meerut, India.......C6 87, C6 88
Meerut Cantonment, India.......*C6 88
Meeteetse, Wyo.......A4 213
Meeting, lake, Sask., Can.......D2 155
Meeting Creek, Alta., Can.......C4 148
Mēgā, Eth.......E4 105
Megali, canal, Grc.......g10 69
Megalópolis, Grc.......D4 69
Megantic, co., Que., Can.......C6 154
Mégantic, lake, Que., Can.......D7 154
Megantic, mtn., Que., Can.......D6 154
Megapode, cape, Santa Isabel I.......115
Mégara, Grc.......C4, g10 69
Megargel, Ala.......D2 166
Megargel, Tex.......C3 206
Meggett, S.C.......F1, F7 203
Megunticook, mtn., Maine.......D3 184
Mehar, Pak.......C4 87
Meherpur, Pak.......F12 88
Meherrin, Va.......D4 209
Meherrin, riv., Va.......E4 209
Mehkar, India.......G6 88
Mehoopany, Pa.......C9 202
Mehsana, India.......F4 88
Mehun-sur-Yèvre, Fr.......D5 58
Meiganga, Cam.......D2 104
Meigs, Ga.......E2 175
Meigs, co., Ohio.......C5 199
Meigs, co., Tenn.......D9 205
Meihsien, China.......G8 91
Meiktila, Bur.......D10 87
Meilap, Ponape.......114
Meilleur, lake, Que., Can.......A4 154
Meiners Oaks, Calif.......*E4 170
Meiningen, Ger.......C5 61
Meiringen, Switz.......C4 66
Meissen, Ger.......B8 61
Meitan, China.......K2 92
Mejicana, mtn., Arg.......E2 135
Mejillones, Chile.......D1 135
Mejit, isl., Marshall Is.......115
Mékambo, Gabon.......E2 104
Mekerrhane, lake, Alg.......D5 102
Mekhtar, Pak.......B2 88
Mekinac, lake, Que., Can.......B5 154
Mekinock, N. Dak.......A8 198
Meknès, Mor.......H4 64, C3 102
Mekong, riv., Asia.......B10 87, E6 89
Mekoryuk, Alsk.......C6 167
Melaka, Mala.......K5 89
in 1641-1824.......K6 82
Melaka, pol. div., Mala.......K5 89
Mélambes, Grc.......E5 69
Melaval, Sask., Can.......H2 155
Melba, Idaho.......F2 177
Melber, Ky.......A2 182
Melbern, Ohio.......A3 199
Melbeta, Nebr.......C2 191
Melbourne, Ark.......A4 169
Melbourne, Austl.......H5 112
Melbourne, Ont., Can.......E3 153
Melbourne, Fla.......D6 174
Melbourne, Iowa.......C4 180
Melbourne, Ky.......A7 182
Melbourne, Mo.......A4 189
Melbourne, Wash.......C2 210
Melbourne Beach, Fla.......D6 174
Melbourne Village, Fla.......*D6 174
Melcher, Iowa.......C4 180
Meldorf, Ger.......D3 62
Meldrim, Ga.......D5 175
Meldrum Bay, Ont., Can.......B1 153
Meleb, Man., Can.......D3 150
Melekeiok, Palau.......114
Melekess, Sov. Un.......*C3 73
Melenki, Sov. Un.......D13 72
Melfa, Va.......*D7 209
Melfi, Chad.......C3 104
Melfi, It.......D5 67
Melfort, Sask., Can.......E3 155
Meli, bay, New Hebr.......115
Melilla, Sp. dep., Afr.......G5 64
Melipilla, Chile.......A2 136
Melita, Man., Can.......E1 150
Melito di Porto Salvo, It.......F5 67
Melitopol', Sov. Un.......H10 72
Mella, riv., It.......D6 66
Melle, Fr.......D3 58
Melle, Ger.......A3 61
Mellen, Wis.......B3 212
Mellette, S. Dak.......B7 204
Mellette, co., S. Dak.......D4 204
Mellit, Sud.......C2 105
Mellott, Ind.......D3 179
Mellow Valley, Ala.......B4 166
Mellrichstadt, Ger.......C5 61
Mellville, R.I.......C11 172
Mellwood, Ark.......C5 169
Melmore, Ohio.......A4 199
Mělník, Czech.......n18 70
Melo, Ur.......E2 137
Melocheville, Que., Can.......D8 154
Melouprey, Camb.......F6 89
Melrhir, salt lake, Alg.......C6 102
Melrose, N.B., Can.......C6 151
Melrose, N.S., Can.......D7 151
Melrose, Conn.......B6 172
Melrose, Fla.......C4 174
Melrose, Iowa.......D4 180
Melrose, La.......C3 183
Melrose, Mass.......B5, C3 185
Melrose, Minn.......E4 187
Melrose, Mont.......E4 190
Melrose, N. Mex.......C6 195
Melrose, Ohio.......A3 199
Melrose, Wis.......D2 212
Melrose Park, Ill.......F2 178
Melrose Park, N.Y.......*C4 196
Melsetter, Rh.......A5 107
Melstone, Mont.......D9 190
Melstrand, Mich.......B4 186
Melsungen, Ger.......B4 61
Melton Hill, res., Tenn.......D9 205
Melton Mowbray, Eng.......B7 56
Melun, Fr.......C5 58
Melvaig, Scot.......C3 57
Melvern, Kans.......D8 181
Melvich, Scot.......B5 57
Melville, Sask., Can.......G4 155
Melville, La.......D4 183
Melville, Mont.......D7 190
Melville, N. Dak.......B6 198
Melville, bay, Grnld.......B21 118
Melville, cape, Austl.......B7 110
Melville, isl., Austl.......B5 110
Melville, isl., N.W. Ter., Can.......A10 142
Melville, lake, Newf., Can.......B2 152
Melville, pen., N.W. Ter., Can.......C16 142
Melvin, Ala.......D1 166
Melvin, Ill.......C5 178
Melvin, Iowa.......A2 180
Melvin, Ky.......C7 182
Melvin, Tex.......D3 206
Melvin Village, N.H.......C4 193
Melvindale, Mich.......*A7 186
Melvine, Tenn.......D8 205
Mélykút, Hung.......B4 68
Memba, Moz.......D7 106
Memel (Klaipeda), Sov. Un.......D3 72
Memeland: in 1922-1940.......53
Memmingen, Ger.......E5 60
Memphis, Fla.......F2 174
Memphis, Ind.......H6 179
Memphis, Mich.......F8 186
Memphis, Mo.......A5 189
Memphis, Nebr.......E2 191
Memphis, Tenn.......B1, E8 205
Memphis, Tex.......B2 206
Memphiș, ruins, Eg.......D6 101
Memphremagog, lake, Que., Can., Vt.......B4 208
Memramcook, N.B., Can.......C5 151
Mena, Ark.......C1 169
Menahga, Minn.......D3 187
Menai, strait, Wales.......A3 56
Ménaka, Mali.......C5 103
Menam, see Chao Phraya, riv., Thai.
Menan, Idaho.......F7 177
Menands, N.Y.......C7 196
Menard, Tex.......D3 206
Menard, co., Ill.......C4 178
Menard, co., Tex.......D3 206
Menasha, Wis.......A5, D5 212
Menche, Guat.......B2 130
Mendawi, riv., Indon.......F4 90
Mende, Fr.......E5 58
Menden, Ger.......B2 61
Mendenhall, Miss.......D4 188
Menderes (Scamander), riv., Tur.......C6 69
Mendes, Ga.......E5 175
Méndez, Mex.......B5 129
Mendham, Sask., Can.......G1 155
Mendham, N.J.......B3 194
Mendip, hills, Eng.......C5 56
Mendjalutung, Indon.......E5 90
Mendocino, Calif.......C2 170
Mendocino, co., Calif.......C2 170
Mendon, Ill.......C2 178
Mendon, Mass.......E1 185
Mendon, Mich.......F5 186
Mendon, Mo.......B4 189
Mendon, Ohio.......B3 199
Mendon, Utah.......B4 207
Mendon, Vt.......D3 208
Mendota, Calif.......D3 170
Mendota, Ill.......B4 178
Mendota, Tex.......B2 206
Mendota, lake, Wis.......E4 212
Mendota Heights, Minn.......*F5 187
Mendoza, Arg.......A3 136
Mendoza, Pan.......k11 130
Mendoza, prov., Arg.......A3 136
Menemen, Tur.......C6 69
Menen, Bel.......D3 59
Menfi, It.......F4 67
Mengcheng, China.......H7 92
Menggala, Indon.......F3 90
Menglien, China.......G4 91
Mengtzu, China.......G5 91
Menifee, Ark.......B3 169
Menifee, co., Ky.......C6 182
Menihek, lakes, Newf., Can.......g8 152
Menindee, Austl.......F4 112
Menifee, Ark.......B3 169
Menindee, lake, Austl.......F4 112
Meningie, Austl.......G2 112
Menlo, Ga.......B1 175
Menlo, Iowa.......C3 180
Menlo, Kans.......C3 181
Menlo, Wash.......C2 210
Menlo Park, Calif.......B5 170
Menlo Park, N.J.......B4 194
Menno, S. Dak.......D8 204
Meno, Okla.......A3 200
Menoken, N. Dak.......C5 198
Menola, N.C.......A6 197
Menominee, Mich.......C3 186
Menominee, co., Mich.......C3 186
Menominee, co., Wis.......C5 212
Menominee, riv., Mich., Wis.......C3 186, C6 212
Menomonee, riv., Wis.......E1 212
Menomonee Falls, Wis.......E1, E5 212
Menomonie, Wis.......D2 212
Menorca, isl., Sp.......B7 65
Mentana, It.......g9 67
Mentawai, is., Indon.......F1 90
Mentmore, N. Mex.......B1 195
Menton, Fr.......F7 58
Mentone, Ala.......A4 166
Mentone, Ind.......B5 179
Mentone, Tex.......D1, F2 206
Mentor, Ky.......A7 182
Mentor, Minn.......C2 187
Mentor, Ohio.......A6 199
Mentor, Tenn.......E11 205
Mentor-on-the-Lake, Ohio.......A6 199
Menzies, Austl.......E3 111
Meoqui, Mex.......B3 129
Meota, Sask., Can.......D1 155
Meppel, Neth.......B6 59
Meppen, Ger.......B3 60
Mequellarë, Alb.......B3 69
Mequon, Wis.......E2 212
Mer Rouge, La.......B4 183
Merabéllo, gulf, Grc.......E5 69
Meramec, riv., Mo.......C7 189
Merano, It.......A3 67
Merasheen, Newf., Can.......E4 152
Merasheen, isl., Newf., Can.......E4 152
Merauke, Indon.......G10 90
Meraux, La.......C7 183
Merca, Som.......E5 105
Mercara, India.......F6 87
Merced, Calif.......D3 170
Merced, co., Calif.......D3 170
Merced, riv., Calif.......D3 170
Mercedes, Arg.......A3 136
Mercedes, Arg.......A5, g7 136
Mercedes, Arg.......E4 135
Mercedes, Tex.......F4 206
Mercedes, Ur.......E1 137
Mercedita Central, P.R.......C4 132
Mercer, Maine.......D3 184
Mercer, Mo.......A4 189
Mercer, N. Dak.......B5 198
Mercer, Ohio.......B3 199
Mercer, Pa.......D1 202
Mercer, Tenn.......B2 205
Mercer, Wis.......B3 212
Mercer, co., Ill.......B3 178
Mercer, co., Ky.......C5 182
Mercer, co., Mo.......A4 189
Mercer, co., N.J.......C3 194
Mercer, co., N. Dak.......B4 198
Mercer, co., Ohio.......B3 199
Mercer, co., Pa.......D1 202
Mercer, co., W. Va.......D3 211
Mercer, isl., Wash.......D2 210
Mercer Island, Wash.......B3, D2 210
Mercersburg, Pa.......G6 202

INDEX KEY Each place listed in **Bold-faced Type** has its population listed in the Population tables, pages 230 to 280.
Each country, shown in CAPITAL LETTERS, has its population listed in the World Political Information Table, pages 6 to 10.
* Does not appear on map; key shows general location.

Mercerville, N.J. C3 194
Mercês, Braz. g6 137
Merchantville, N.J. *D2 194
Mercier, Que., Can. *D4 154
Mercier, Kans. C8 181
Mercoal, Alta., Can. C2 148
Mercury, Nev. G5 192
Mercury, Tex. D3 206
Mercury, bay, N.Z. L15 112
Mercy, cape, N.W. Ter., Can. C20 143
Merdjayoun, Leb. F10 85
Meredith, Colo. B4 171
Meredith, N.H. C3 193
Meredith, lake, Colo. C7 171
Meredith Center, N.H. C3 193
Meredosia, Ill. D3 178
Merefa, Sov. Un. G11 72
Meregh, Som. E6 105
Merepoint, Maine E5 184
Mergui, Bur. F10 87
Mergui, arch., Bur. F10 87
Merid, Sask., Can. F1 155
Mérida, Mex. C7 129
Mérida, Sp. C2 65
Mérida, Ven. B3 133
Mérida, state, Ven. B3 133
Meriden, Conn. C5 172
Meriden, Iowa B2 180
Meriden, Kans. B7, C8 181
Meriden, Minn. F5 187
Meriden, N.H. C2 193
Meriden, Wyo. D8 213
Meridian, Ga. E5 175
Meridian, Idaho F2 177
Meridian, Miss. C5 188
Meridian, N.Y. B4 196
Meridian, Okla. B4 200
Meridian, Pa. *E2 202
Meridian, Tex. D4 206
Meridian Hills, Ind. *E5 179
Meridiano, Arg. B4 136
Meridianville, Ala. A3 166
Merigold, Miss. B3 188
Merigomish, N.S., Can. D7 151
Merino, Colo. A7 171
Merino Village, Mass. B4 185
Meriwether, co., Ga. C2 175
Merizo, port, Guam 114
Merkarvia, Fin. G9 63
Merkel, Tex. C2 206
Merkinė, Sov. Un. A8 70
Merksem, Bel. C4 59
Merksplas, Bel. C4 59
Merkus, cape, New Britain I. 115
Merlebach, Fr. E6 59
Merlin, Ont., Can. E2 153
Merlin, Oreg. E3 201
Merlo, Arg. g7 136
Mermentau, La. D3 183
Mermentau, riv., La. E2 183
Mern, Den. C6 62
Merna, Nebr. C6 191
Merna, Wyo. C2 213
Merom, Ind. F2 179
Meron, mtn., Isr. A7 84
Merowe, Sud. B3 105
Merriam, Kans. B8 181
Merrick, N.Y. G2 172
Merrick, co., Nebr. C7 191
Merrick, mtn., Scot. E4 57
Merrickville, Ont., Can. C9 153
Merricourt, N. Dak. C7 198
Merrifield, Minn. D4 187
Merrifield, Va. B5 209
Merrill, Iowa B1 180
Merrill, Mich. E6 186
Merrill, Miss. E5 188
Merrill, Oreg. E5 201
Merrill, Wis. C4 212
Merrillan, Wis. D3 212
Merrillville, Ind. B3 179
Merrimac, Ky. C4 182
Merrimac, Mass. A5 185
Merrimac, Wis. E4 212
Merrimack, N.H. E4 193
Merrimack, co., N.H. D3 193
Merrimack, riv., Mass., N.H. A5 185, D3 193
Merrimacport, Mass. A5 185
Merriman, Nebr. B4 191
Merrimon, N.C. C7 197
Merrionette Park, Ill. *F3 178
Merritt, B.C., Can. D7 149
Merritt, N.C. B7 197
Merritt, res., Nebr. B5 191
Merritt Island, Fla. D6 174
Merritt-Peck Colonies, Calif. *D4 170
Merriwa, Austl. F8 112
Merriweather, Mich. A5 186
Merrow, Conn. B7 172
Merry Hill, N.C. A7 197
Merry Oaks, N.C. B4 197
Merrymeeting, lake, N.H. D4 193
Merryville, La. D2 183
Mers-el-Kebir, Alg. G6 64
Mersa Fatma, Eth. B5 105
Merseburg, Ger. B6 61
Mersey, riv., Eng. A5 56
Mershon, Ga. E4 175
Mersin, Tur. D10 85
Mersing, Mala. K5 89
Merthyr Tydfil, Wales C4 56
Merti, Ken. A6 106
Mértola, Port. D2 65
Merton, Wis. E1 212
Merton, Eng. C7 56
Mertz, glacier, Ant. C27 120
Mertzon, Tex. D2 206
Méru, Fr. C5 58
Meru, Ken. A6 106
Meru, mtn., Tan. B6 106
Merundung, isl., Indon. K8 89
Merville, Fr. D2 59
Mervin, Sask., Can. D1 155
Merwin, Mo. C3 189
Méry [-sur-Seine], Fr. F3 59
Merzifon, Tur. B10 85
Merzig, Ger. E6 59
Mesa, Ariz. D4, G2 168
Mesa, Colo. B2 171
Mesa, co., Colo. C2 171
Mesa, peak, Colo. D4 171
Mesa De Maya, plat., Colo. D7 171
Mesa Verde, nat. park, Colo. D2 171
Mesabi, range, Minn. C5 187
Mesagne, It. D6 67
Mescalero, N. Mex. D4 195
Mescalero Apache, Indian res., N. Mex. D4 195
Meschede, Ger. B3 61
Mesegon, isl., Truk 114
Mesena, Ga. C4 175
Meservey, Iowa *B4 180
Meshcherskoye, Sov. Un. n17 72
Meshchovsk, Sov. Un. D10 72
Meshed (Mashhad), Iran C9 86
Meshkovskaya, Sov. Un. G13 72
Meshomasic, mtn., Conn. C6 172
Meshoppen, Pa. C9 202
Meshra'er Req, Sud. D2 105
Mesic, N.C. B7 197
Mesick, Mich. D5 186
Mesilinka, riv., B.C., Can. A5 149
Mesilla, N. Mex. E3 195
Mesita, Colo. D5 171
Meskéné, Syr. D12 85
Mesocco, Switz. C5 66
Mesológion, Grc. C3 69
Mesopotamia: under Alexander 43
in 115-117 A.D. 45
Mesquita, Braz. *C4 137
Mesquite, Nev. G7 192
Mesquite, N. Mex. E3 195
Mesquite, Tex. B6 206
Messalonskee, lake, Maine D3 184
Messina, It. E5 67
Messina, S. Afr. B5 107
Messina, strait, It. E5 67
Messini, Grc. D3 69
Messini, gulf, Grc. D4 69
Messkirch, Ger. B5 66
Mesta, riv., Bul. E6 68
Mestre, It. B4 67
Mesudiye, Tur. B11 85
Meszah, peak, B.C., Can. k24 167
Meta, Mo. C5 189
Meta, dept., Col. C3 133
Meta, riv., Col., Ven. B4 133
Métabetchouan, Que., Can. A6 154
Métabetchouan, riv., Que., Can. A5 154
Metairie, La. C7 183
Metaline, Wash. A8 210
Metaline Falls, Wash. A8 210
Metalton, Ark. A2 169
Metamora, Ill. C4 178
Metamora, Ind. F7 179
Metamora, Mich. F7 186
Metamora, Ohio A4 199
Metán, Arg. E3 135
Metangula, Moz. D5 106
Metapán, Sal. C3 130
Metaponto, It. D6 67
Metarica, Moz. D6 106
Metarma, cape, Eg. E4 84
Metascouac, lake, Que., Can. B6 154
Metasville, Ga. C4 175
Metcalf, Ga. F3 175
Metcalf, Ill. D6 178
Metcalfe, Ont., Can. B9 153
Metcalfe, Miss. B2 188
Metcalfe, co., Ky. D4 182
Metchosin, B.C., Can. B9 149
Metedeconk, riv., N.J. C4 194
Meteghan, N.S., Can. E3 151
Meteghan River, N.S., Can. E3 151
Meteghan Station, N.S., Can. E3 151
Meteor, crater, Ariz. C4 168
Methóni, Grc. D3 69
Methow, Wash. A5 210
Methuen, Mass. A5 185
Methven, Scot. D5 57
Methy, lake, Sask., Can. B1 155
Metiskow, Alta., Can. C5 148
Metković, Yugo. D3 68
Metlakatla, Alsk. D13, n14 167
Meto, Ark. D6 169
Meto, bayou, Ark. C4, D6 169
Metolius, Oreg. C5 201
Metonga, lake, Wis. C4 212
Metropolis, Ill. F5 178
Metropolitan, Mich. B2 186
Métsovon, Grc. C3 69
Metten, Ger. E7 61
Mettewee, riv., N.Y., Vt. E2 208
Metter, Ga. D4 175
Mettet, Bel. D4 59
Mettingen, Ger. A2 61
Mettmann, Ger. B1 61
Metuchen, N.J. B4 194
Metulla, Isr. A7 84
Metz, Fr. C7 58
Metz, Ind. A8 179
Metz, Mich. C7 186
Metz, Mo. D3 189
Metzeral, Fr. B3 66
Metzger, Oreg. B2 201
Meudon, Fr. g9 58
Meulaboh, Indon. J2 89
Meung [-sur-Loire], Fr. D4 58
Meureudoe, Indon. J2 89
Meurthe, riv., Fr. F6 59
Meurthe-et-Moselle, dept., Fr. F6 59
Meuse, dept., Fr. E5 59
Meuse, hills, Fr. C6 58
Meuse, riv., Bel., Fr. C6 58, D5 59, A1 66
Meuselwitz, Ger. B7 61
Mexcala, riv., Mex. n12 129
Mexia, Ala. D2 166
Mexia, Tex. D4 206
Mexicali, Mex. A1 129
Mexican Hat, Utah F6 207
Mexican Springs, N. Mex. B1 195
Mexico, Ind. C5 179
Mexico, Ky. A3 182
Mexico, Maine D2 184
Mexico, Mo. B6 189
Mexico, N.Y. B4 196
Mexico, Pa. E7 202
MEXICO, country, N.A. 129
c. 1790 126
in 1821-24 127
México, state, Mex. D5, n14 129
Mexico, gulf, N.A. E9 159
Mexico City, Mex. D5, h9, n14 129
Meyādīn, Syr. E13 85
Meyers Chuck, Alsk. n23 167
Meyersdale, Pa. G3 202
Meyronne, Sask., Can. H2 155
Meyssac, Fr. E4 58
Mèze, Fr. F5 58
Mezen, Sov. Un. B17 41
Mezen, riv., Sov. Un. C17 40
Mezenc, mtn., Fr. E6 58
Mezenskaya, bay, Sov. Un. B16 40
Mezhdurechensk, Sov. Un. *D11 71
Meziadin, lake, B.C., Can. A3 149
Mézières, Fr. E4 59
Mezőkövesd, Hung. B5 68
Mezőtur, Hung. B5 68
Mezquital, Mex. C4 129
Mezzana, It. C6 66
Mezzolombardo, It. C7 66
Mga, Sov. Un. s32 63
Mga, riv., Sov. Un. s32 63
Mglin, Sov. Un. E9 72
Mhor, lake, Scot. C4 57
Mhow, India F5 88
Miahuatlán, Mex. D5 129
Miajadas, Sp. C3 65
Miajlar, India D3 88
Miami, Ariz. D5 168
Miami, Man., Can. E2 150
Miami, Fla. F3, G6 174
Miami, Ind. C5 179
Miami, Mo. B4 189
Miami, N. Mex. A5 195
Miami, Okla. A7 200
Miami, Rh. A4 107
Miami, Tex. B2 206
Miami, W. Va. D6 211
Miami, co., Ind. C5 179
Miami, co., Kans. D9 181
Miami, co., Ohio B3 199
Miami, canal, Fla. F6 174
Miami, riv., Ohio C3 199
Miami Beach, Fla. F3, G6 174
Miami Shores, Fla. F3, G6 174
Miami Springs, Fla. F3, G6 174
Miamisburg, Ohio C3 199
Miamitown, Ohio D2 199
Miāndasht, Iran C8 86
Miandrivazo, Malag. g9 107
Miāneh, Iran C3 86
Mianus, res., Conn., N.Y. E2 172
Mianus, riv., Conn., N.Y. A5 194
Mianwali, Pak. A3 88
Miarinarivo, Malag. g9 107
Miass, Sov. Un. C6 73
Miass, riv., Sov. Un. B6 73
Miasteczko Śląskie, Pol. f9 70
Miastko, Pol. A4 70
Mica, Wash. B8, D8 210
Mica, peak, Idaho D8 210
Micá, riv., Rom. B7 68
Micanopy, Fla. C4 174
Micay, Col. C2 133
Micco, Fla. E6 174
Miccosukee, Fla. B2 174
Miccosukee, lake, Fla. B2 174
Michael, lake, Newf., Can. A2 152
Michalovce, Czech. D6 70
Michałów, Pol. k13 70
Michaud, pt., N.S., Can. D9 151
Michel, B.C., Can. E10 149
Michel, lake, Newf., Can. C3 152
Michelson, mtn., Alsk. B11 167
Michendorf, Ger. A8 61
Michiana Shores, Ind. *A4 179
Michichi, Alta., Can. D4 148
Michie, Tenn. B3 205
Michigamme, Mich. B2 186
Michigamme, lake, Mich. B2 186
Michigan, N. Dak. A7 198
Michigan, state, U.S. 186
Michigan, creek, Colo. A4 171
Michigan, isl., Wis. B3 212
Michigan, lake, U.S. B10 159
Michigan, prairie, Wash. C7 210
Michigan Center, Mich. F6 186
Michigan City, Ind. A4 179
Michigan City, Miss. A4 188
Michigantown, Ind. D5 179
Michikamau, lake, Newf., Can. g8 152
Michoacán, state, Mex. D4, n13 129
Michurin, Bul. D8 68
Michurinsk, Sov. Un. C2 73
Mickleyville, Ind. H7 179
Micoud, St. Lucia p16 131
Micro, N.C. B5 197
Midai, isl., Indon. K7 89
Midale, Sask., Can. H4 155
Midas, Idaho A2 177
Middelburg, Neth. C3 59
Middelfart, Den. C3 62
Middelharnis, Neth. C4 59
Middelkerke, Bel. C2 59
Middle, Iowa C6 180
Middle, isl., New Hebr. 115
Middle, riv., B.C., Can. B5 149
Middle, riv., Iowa C3 180
Middle, riv., Minn. B2 187
Middle Alkali, lake, Calif. B2 192
Middle Andaman, isl., India F9 87
Middle Brook, Newf., Can. D4 152
Middle Bushkill, creek, Pa. A2 194
Middle Congo, see Congo country, Afr.
Middle Granville, N.Y. B7 196
Middle Ground, isl., Midway Is. 114
Middle Haddam, Conn. C6 172
Middle Island, N.Y. F5 172
Middle Island, creek, W. Va. B3 211
Middle Lake, Sask., Can. E3 155
Middle Loup, riv., Nebr. C5 191
Middle Musquodoboit, N.S., Can. D6 151
Middle Nodaway, riv., Iowa C3 180
Middle Park, basin, Colo. A4 171
Middle Patuxent, riv., Md. B4 173
Middle Point, Ohio B3 199
Middle Raccoon, riv., Iowa C3 180
Middle Ridge, mts., Newf., Can. D4 152
Middle River, Md. *B5 173
Middle River, Minn. B2 187
Middle Stewiacke, N.S., Can. D6 151
Middle Valley, N.J. B3 194
Middle Water, Tex. B1 206
Middleboro, Mass. C6 185
Middlebourne, W. Va. B4 211
Middlebranch, Ohio B6 199
Middlebro, Man., Can. E4 150
Middlebrook, Va. C3 209
Middleburg, Fla. B5 174
Middleburg, Ky. C5 182
Middleburg, N.Y. C6 196
Middleburg, N.C. A5 197
Middleburg, Ohio B3 199
Middleburg, Pa. E7 202
Middleburg, S. Afr. D4 107
Middleburg, Tenn. B2 205
Middleburg, Va. C5 209
Middleburgh Heights, Ohio B2 199
Middlebury, Conn. C4 172
Middlebury, Ind. A6 179
Middlebury, Vt. C2 208
Middlebury, riv., Vt. D2 208
Middlefield, Conn. C6 172
Middlefield, Mass. B1 185
Middlefield, Ohio A6 199
Middleford, Del. C6 173
Middleport, N.Y. B2 196
Middleport, Ohio C5 199
Middleport, Pa. *E9 202
Middlesboro, Ky. D6 182
Middlesex, Br. Hond. B3 130
Middlesex, N.J. B4 194
Middlesex, N.Y. C3 196
Middlesex, N.C. B5 197
Middlesex, Vt. C3 208
Middlesex, co., Ont., Can. D3 153
Middlesex, co., Conn. D6 172
Middlesex, co., Mass. A5 185
Middlesex, co., N.J. C4 194
Middlesex, co., Va. D6 209
Middlesex Fells, res., Mass. C3 185
Middleton, N.S., Can. E4 151
Middleton, Eng. *A5 56
Middleton, Ga. B4 175
Middleton, Idaho F2 177
Middleton, Mass. A5, C3 185
Middleton, Mich. E6 186
Middleton, N.H. D4 193
Middleton, Tenn. B3 205
Middleton, Wis. E4 212
Middleton, isl., Alsk. D10 167
Middletown, Calif. C2 170
Middletown, Conn. C6 172
Middletown, Del. B6 173
Middletown, Ill. C4 178
Middletown, Ind. D6 179
Middletown, Iowa D6 180
Middletown, Ky. A4 182
Middletown, Md. B2 173
Middletown, Mo. B6 189
Middletown, N.J. C4 194
Middletown, N.Y. D6 196
Middletown, N.C. B7 197
Middletown, Ohio C3 199
Middletown, Pa. F8 202
Middletown, R.I. C11 172
Middletown, Va. B4 209
Middletown Springs, Vt. E2 208
Middleville, Ont., Can. B8 153
Middleville, Mich. F5 186
Middleville, N.J. A3 194
Middleville, N.Y. B6 196
Midelt, Mor. H4 64
Midfield, Ala. E4 166
Midgic, N.B., Can. D5 151
Midhurst, Ont., Can. C5 153
Midian: in 13th cent. B.C. 98
Midkiff, W. Va. C2 211
Midland, Ark. B1 169
Midland, Calif. F6 170
Midland, Ont., Can. C5 153
Midland, Ind. F3 179
Midland, La. D3 183
Midland, Md. D2 173
Midland, Mich. E6 186
Midland, N.C. B3 197
Midland, Ohio C4 199
Midland, Pa. E1 202
Midland, Pa. *F1 202
Midland, S. Dak. C4 204
Midland, Tex. D1 206
Midland, Va. C5 209
Midland, co., Mich. E6 186
Midland, co., Tex. D1 206
Midland, basin, Colo. A2 171
Midland City, Ala. D4 166
Midland Park, Kans. B5 181
Midland Park, N.J. B4 194
Midland Park, S.C. F2 203
Midlandvale, Alta., Can. D4 148
Midleton, Ire. E2 55
Midlothian, Ill. F3 178
Midlothian, Md. D2 173
Midlothian, Tex. B5, C4 206
Midlothian, Va. C6, D5 209
Midlothian, co., Scot. E5 57
Midnapore, Alta., Can. D3 148
Midnapur, India F11 88
Midnight, Miss. B3 188
Midongy du Sud, Malag. h9 107
Midsayap, Phil. *D6 90
Midstate Mill (Amerotron Mill), N.C. *C4 197
Midvale, Idaho E2 177
Midvale, Ohio B6 199
Midvale, Utah C4 207
Midville, Ga. D4 175
Midway, Ala. C4 166
Midway, B.C., Can. E8 149
Midway, Fla. B2 174
Midway, Ky. B5 182
Midway, Pa. G7 202
Midway, Tenn. C11 205
Midway, Utah C4 207
Midway, Wash. D2 210
Midway, is., Oceania 114
Midway, range, B.C., Can. E8 149
MIDWAY ISLANDS, U.S. dep., Oceania 114
Midway Park, N.C. C6 197
Midwest, Wyo. B6 213
Midwest City, Okla. B4 200
Midyat, Tur. D13 85
Midye, Tur. B7 85
Miechów, Pol. C6 70
Miechowice, Pol. g9 70
Międzychód, Pol. B3 70
Miedzyrzec, Pol. C7 70
Międzyrzecz, Pol. B3 70
Międzyrzecz, Pol. g10 70
Międzyzdroje, Pol. B3 70
Mielec, Pol. C6 70
Mien, lake, Swe. B8 62
Mienia, riv., Pol. m14 70
Mienning, China F5 91
Mienyang, China I5 92
Mieres, Sp. A3 65
Miesbach, Ger. B7 66
Mīeso, Eth. D5 105
Mifflin, Pa. E7 202
Mifflin, Tenn. B3 205
Mifflin, co., Pa. E6 202
Mifflinburg, Pa. E7 202
Mifflintown, Pa. E7 202
Mifflinville, Pa. D9 202
Migdal, Isr. B7 84
Migdal Ashqelon, Isr. C6 84
Migennes, Fr. D5 58
Migiurtinia, dist., Som. D6 105
Migliarino, It. E7 66
Mignon, Ala. B3 166
Miguel Alves, Braz. B2 138
Miguel Auza, Mex. C4 129
Mihai-Viteazu, Rom. C9 68
Mihara, Jap. *I6 93
Mijares, riv., Sp. B5 65
Mijdaḥah, Yemen (Aden) C6 105
Mikado, Sask., Can. F4 155
Mikado, Mich. D7 186
Mikana, Wis. C2 206
Mikasa, Jap. *E10 93
Mikhaylov, Sov. Un. D12 72
Mikhaylovgrad, Bul. D6 68
Mikhaylovka, Sov. Un. C2 73
Mikhaylovka, Sov. Un. H10 72
Mikhaylovskiy, Sov. Un. C9 73
Mikindani, Tan. D7 106
Mikkalo, Oreg. B6 201
Mikkeli, Fin. G12 63
Mikołów, Pol. g9 70
Míkonos, isl., Grc. D5 69
Mikope, Zaire C3 106
Mikulczyce, Pol. g9 70
Mikulov, Czech. D4 70
Mikura, isl., Jap. J9 93
Mil Koh, mtn., Afg. E10 86
Mila, Va. D6 209
Milaca, Minn. E5 187
Milagro, Arg. A3 136
Milam, W. Va. C5 211
Milam, co., Tex. D4 206
Milan, Que., Can. D6 154
Milan, Ga. D3 175
Milan, Ill. B3 178
Milan, Ind. F7 179
Milan (Milano), It. D5 66, B2 67
Milan, Kans. E6 181
Milan, Mich. F7 186
Milan, Minn. E3 187
Milan, Mo. A4 189
Milan, N.H. A4 193
Milan, N. Mex. B2 195
Milan, Ohio A5 199
Milan, Pa. C8 202
Milan, Tenn. B3 205
Milan, Wash. B8 210
Milan, Wis. D3 212
Milano, see Milan, It.
Milano, Tex. D4 206
Milâs, Tur. D6 69
Milazzo, It. E5 67
Milbank, S. Dak. B9 204
Milbanke, sound, B.C., Can. C3 149
Milbridge, Maine D5 184
Milburn, Ky. B2 182
Milburn, Nebr. C6 191
Milburn, Okla. C5 200
Milburn, W. Va. D6 211
Milden, Sask., Can. F2 155
Mildenhall, Eng. B8 56
Mildmay, Ont., Can. C3 153
Mildred, Sask., Can. D2 155
Mildred, Kans. D8 181
Mildred, Mont. D12 190
Mildred, Pa. D9 202
Mildura, Austl. G4 112
Miléai, Grc. C4 69
Miles, Austl. C8 112
Miles, Iowa B7 180
Miles, Tex. D2 206
Miles, mtn., Vt. C5 208
Miles City, Mont. D11 190
Milesburg, Pa. E6 202
Milestone, Sask., Can. H3 155
Milesville, S. Dak. C4 204
Miletus, ruins, Tur. D6 69
Milevsko, Czech. D9 61
Miley, S.C. F5 203
Milfay, Okla. B5 200
Milford, Calif. B3 170
Milford, Conn. E4 172
Milford, Del. C7 173
Milford, Ill. C6 178
Milford, Ind. B6 179
Milford, Iowa A2 180
Milford, Kans. C7 181
Milford, Ky. B5 182
Milford, Maine D4 184
Milford, Mass. B4, E1 185
Milford, Mich. A6, F7 186
Milford, Mo. D3 189
Milford, Nebr. D8 191
Milford, N.H. E3 193
Milford, N.J. B2 194
Milford, N.Y. C6 196
Milford, Ohio C3 199
Milford, Pa. D12 202
Milford, Tex. *C4 206
Milford, Utah E3 207
Milford, Va. C5 209
Milford, res., Kans. C6 181
Milford Center, Ohio B4 199
Milford Haven, Wales C2 56
Milford Station, N.S., Can. D6 151
Milhurst, N.J. C4 194
Miliana, Alg. B5 102
Milicz, Pol. C4 70
Miling, Austl. F2 111
Milipe, pt., Malekula I. 115
Milk, riv., Alta., Can. E5 148
Milk, riv., Mont. B8 190
Milk River, Alta., Can. E4 148
Mill, brook, Vt. B5 208
Mill, creek, Ind. F4 179
Mill, creek, Kans. C6 181
Mill, creek, Kans. D7 181
Mill, creek, N.J. D4 194
Mill, creek, Ohio B4 199
Mill, creek, Tenn. E9 205
Mill, creek, W. Va. C3 211
Mill, riv., Mass. D1 185
Mill City, Nev. C3 192
Mill City, Oreg. C4 201
Mill City, Pa. A8 202
Mill Creek, Ind. A4 179
Mill Creek, Mont. D4 190
Mill Creek, Okla. C5 200
Mill Creek, Pa. F6 202
Mill Creek, W. Va. C5 211
Mill Creek, falls, Oreg. E4 201
Mill Grove, Mo. A4 189
Mill Hall, Pa. D7 202
Mill Iron, Mont. E12 190
Mill Plain, Conn. D2 172
Mill Point, W. Va. C4 211
Mill River, Mass. B1 185
Mill Run, Pa. G3 202
Mill Shoals, Ill. E5 178
Mill Spring Mo. D7 189
Mill Stream, Austl. D2 111
Mill Valley, Calif. B5, D2 170
Mill Village, N.S., Can. E5 151
Mill Village, Pa. C2 202
Milladore, Wis. D4 212
Millard, Ky. C7 182
Millard, Mo. A5 189
Millard, Nebr. D3 191
Millard, co., Utah D2 207
Millarton, N. Dak. C7 198
Millau, Fr. E5 58
Millbank, Ont., Can. D4 153
Millboro, S. Dak. D6 204
Millboro, Va. D3 209
Millbrae, Calif. B5 170
Millbrook, Ala. C3 166
Millbrook, Ont., Can. C6 153
Millbrook, Mich. E5 186
Millbrook, N.Y. D7 196
Millbrook, N.C. B5 197
Millburn, Ill. E2 178
Millburn, N.J. B4 194
Millbury, Mass. B4 185
Millbury, Ohio A2 199
Millcreek, Ill. F4 178

INDEX KEY Each place listed in **Bold-faced Type** has its population listed in the Population tables, pages 230 to 280. Each country, shown in CAPITAL LETTERS, has its population listed in the World Political Information Table, pages 6 to 10. * Does not appear on map; key shows general location.

Millcreek, Mo. D7 189
Milldale, Conn. C5 172
Mille, atoll, Marshall Is. 115
Mille lac, Indian res., Minn D5 187
Mille Lacs, co., Minn. D5 187
Mille Lacs, lake, Minn D5 187
Mille-Vaches, pt., Que., Can A8 154
Milledgeville, Ga. C3 175
Milledgeville, Ill. B4 178
Milledgeville, Tenn. B3 205
Millen, Ga. D5 175
Miller, Kans. D8 181
Miller, Miss. A4 188
Miller, Mo. *D4 189
Miller, Nebr. D6 191
Miller, Ohio D5 199
Miller, S. Dak. C7 204
Miller, co., Ark. D2 169
Miller, co., Ga. E2 175
Miller, co., Mo. C5 189
Miller, flat, Oreg C5 201
Miller, mtn., Alsk C11 167
Miller, peak, Ariz F5 168
Miller Dale Colony, S. Dak. C6 204
Miller Place, N.Y. F5 172
Miller Run, riv., Vt B4 208
Millerovo, Sov. Un. G13 72
Millers, Md. A4 173
Millers, riv., Mass A3 185
Millers Falls, Mass. A3 185
Millers Ferry, Ala. C2 166
Millers Ferry, res., Ala C2 166
Millersburg, Ind. A6 179
Millersburg, Iowa C5 180
Millersburg, Ky. B5 182
Millersburg, Mich. C6 186
Millersburg, Ohio B6 199
Millersburg, Pa. E8 202
Millersport, Ohio C5 199
Millerstown, Pa. E7 202
Millersview, Tex. D3 206
Millersville, Ind. H8 179
Millersville, Pa. F9 202
Millerton, N.B., Can. C4 151
Millerton, Iowa D4 180
Millerton, N.Y. D7 196
Millerton, Okla. D6 200
Millerton, Pa. C8 202
Millertown, Newf., Can. D3 152
Millertown Junction, Newf., Can. D3 152
Millerville, Ala. B4 166
Millerville, Minn. D3 187
Milles Iles, riv., Que., Can D8 154
Millet, Alta., Can. C4 148
Millett, S.C. E4 203
Millett, Tex. E3 206
Millgrove, Ind. D7 179
Millhaven, Ga. D5 175
Millheim, Pa. E7 202
Millhousen, Ind. F7 179
Millicent, Austl. H3 112
Millicent, Alta., Can. D5 148
Milligan, Fla. G2 174
Milligan, Nebr. D8 191
Milligan College, Tenn. C11 205
Milliken, Colo. A6 171
Millikin, La. B4 183
Millington, Md. B6 173
Millington, Mich. E7 186
Millington, N.J. *B3 194
Millington, Oreg. D2 201
Millington, Tenn. B2 205
Millinocket, Maine C4 184
Millinocket, lake, Maine B4 184
Millinocket, lake, Maine C4 184
Millis, Mass. B5, D2 185
Millom, Eng. F5 57
Millport, Ala. B1 166
Millport, Pa. C5 202
Millport, Scot. E4 57
Millrift, Pa. D12 202
Millry, Ala. D1 166
Mills, Nebr. B6 191
Mills, N. Mex. A5 195
Mills, Pa. C6 202
Mills, Utah D3 207
Mills, Wyo. C6 213
Mills, co., Iowa C2 180
Mills, co., Tex. D3 206
Mills, lake, N.W. Ter., Can D9 142
Millsboro, Del. C7 173
Millsboro, Pa. G1 202
Millstadt, Ill. E3 178
Millston, Wis. D3 212
Millstone, Conn. D8 172
Millstone, N.J. B3 194
Millstone, riv., N.J C3 194
Milltown, Ala. B4 166
Milltown, N.B., Can. D2 151
Milltown, Newf., Can. E4 152
Milltown, Ind. H5 179
Milltown, Ky. C4 182
Milltown, Maine C5 184
Milltown, Mont. D3 190
Milltown, N.J. C4 194
Milltown, S. Dak. D8 204
Milltown, Wis. C1 212
Millvale, Pa. B6 202
Millville, N.B., Can. C2 151
Millville, Del. C7 173
Millville, Ky. B5 182
Millville, Mass. B4 185
Millville, N.J. E2 194
Millville, Ohio *C2 199
Millville, Pa. D9 202
Millville, W. Va. B7 211
Millwood, Va. B4 209
Millwood, Wash. D8 210
Millwood, W. Va. C3 211
Millwood, res., Ark C5 206
Milmay, N.J. E3 194
Milner, B.C., Can. A10 149
Milner, Colo. A3 171
Milner, Ga. C2 175
Milner, dam, Idaho G5 177
Milner Ridge, Man., Can. D3 150
Milnesand, N. Mex. D6 195
Milnor, N. Dak. C8 198
Milo, Alta., Can. D4 148
Milo, Iowa C4 180
Milo, Maine C4 184
Milo, Mo. D3 189
Milo, Tenn. D8 205
Milolii, Haw. D6 176
Mílos, isl., Grc D5 69
Milparinka, Austl. D3 112
Milpitas, Calif. B6 170
Milroy, Ind. F7 179
Milroy, Minn. F3 187
Milroy, Pa. E6 202
Milstead, Ga. B6, C3 175
Miltenberg, Ger. D4 61
Milton, N.S., Can. E5 151
Milton, Conn. B3 172
Milton, Del. C7 173
Milton, Fla. G2 174
Milton, Ill. A8 189
Milton, Ill. D3 178
Milton, Ind. E7 179
Milton, Iowa D5 180
Milton, Kans. E6 181
Milton, Ky. B4 182
Milton, La. D3 183
Milton, Mass. B5, D3 185
Milton, N.H. D5 193
Milton, N.Y. D7 196
Milton, N.Z. Q12 112
Milton, N.C. A4 197
Milton, N. Dak. A7 198
Milton, Pa. D8 202
Milton, Utah B4 207
Milton, Vt. B2 208
Milton, Wash. D1 210
Milton, W. Va. C2 211
Milton, Wis. F5 212
Milton, res., Colo A6 171
Milton, res., Ohio A7 199
Milton-Freewater, Oreg. B8 201
Milton Junction, Wis. F5 212
Milton Mills, N.H. D5 193
Milton West, Ont., Can. D5 153
Miltona, Minn. D3 187
Miltona, lake, Minn D3 187
Miltonvale, Kans. C6 181
Milverton, Ont., Can. D4 153
Milwaukee, N.C. A6 197
Milwaukee, Wis. E2, E6 212
Milwaukee, co., Wis. E5 212
Milwaukee, riv., Wis E2 212
Milwaukie, Oreg. B2, B4 201
Mimbres, N. Mex. E2 195
Mimbres, mts., N. Mex D2 195
Mimico, Ont., Can. D5, E6 153
Miminegash, P.E.I., Can. *C5 151
Mimizan, Fr. E3 58
Mimoň, Czech. C9 61
Mimongo, Gabon F2 104
Mims, Fla. D6 174
Mina, Nev. E3 192
Mina, S. Dak. B7 204
Mināb, Iran H8 86
Minago, riv., Man., Can B2 150
Minam, Oreg. B9 201
Minamata, Jap. J5 93
Minami, Iwo 114
Minami-iwo (Minami-Iō) (San Augustino) isl., Kazan-retto 115
Minas, Cuba E5 131
Minas, Ur. E1 137
Minas, basin, N.S., Can D5 151
Minas, chan., N.S., Can D5 151
Minas de Oro, Hond. C4 130
Minas de Ríotinto, Sp. D2 65
Minas Gerais, state, Braz. B4, g6, k8 137
Minatare, Nebr. C2 191
Minatitlán, Mex. D6 129
Minato, Jap. n18 93
Minbu, Bur. D9 87
Minburn, Alta., Can. C5 148
Minburn, Iowa C3 180
Minch, chan., Scot B3 57
Minchin, China D5 91
Mincio, riv., It D6 66
Minco, Okla. B4 200
Mindanao, isl., Phil D7 90
Mindanao, sea, Phil D6 90
Mindel, riv., Ger A6 66
Mindelheim, Ger. A6 66
Mindemoya, Ont., Can. B2 153
Minden, Ont., Can. C6 153
Minden, Ger. A3 61
Minden, Iowa C2 180
Minden, La. B2 183
Minden, Nebr. D7 191
Minden, Nev. E2 192
Minden, W. Va. D3, D7 211
Minden City, Mich. E8 186
Mindenmines, Mo. D3 189
Mindoro, Wis. D2 212
Mindoro, isl., Phil C6 90
Mindoro, strait, Phil C6 90
Mine Centre, Ont., Can. E5 150
Mine La Motte, Mo. D7 189
Minechoag, mtn., Mass B3 185
Minehead, Eng. C4 56
Mineiros, Braz. B2 137
Mineola, Iowa C2 180
Mineola, N.Y. D2, D3, E7 196
Mineola, Tex. C5 206
Miner, Mo. E8 189
Miner, Mont. E6 190
Miner, co., S. Dak. D8 204
Mineral, Ill. B4 178
Mineral, Va. C5 209
Mineral, Wash. C3 210
Mineral, co., Colo. D4 171
Mineral, co., Mont. C1 190
Mineral, co., Nev. E3 192
Mineral, co., W. Va. B6 211
Mineral, mts., Utah E3 207
Mineral City, Ohio B6 199
Mineral Hills, Mich. B2 186
Mineral del Oro, Mex. n13 129
Mineral Park, Tenn. E10 205
Mineral Point, Mo. D7 189
Mineral Point, Wis. F3 212
Mineral Springs, Ark. D2 169
Mineral Wells, Miss. A4 188
Mineral Wells, Tex. C3 206
Mineral'nyye Vody, Sov. Un. *E2 73
Minersville, Ohio C6 199
Minersville, Pa. E9 202
Minersville, Utah E3 207
Minerva, N.Y. B7 196
Minerva, Ohio B6 199
Minerva Park, Ohio *C5 199
Minervino Murge, It. D6 67
Minetto, N.Y. B4 196
Mineville, N.Y. A7 196
Mingan, Que., Can. F20 145
Mingan, passage, Que., Can h8 152
Mingchiang, China A7 89
Mingechaur, res., Sov. Un E3 73
Mingenew, Austl. E2 111
Mingo, Iowa C4 180
Mingo, co., W. Va. D2 211
Mingo, creek, S.C D9 203
Mingo Junction, Ohio B7 199
Mingoyo, Tan. D6 106
Mingshui, China C2 93
Mingshui, China C4 91
Minho, riv., Port B1 65
Minicoy, isl., India G5 87
Minidoka, Idaho G5 177
Minidoka, co., Idaho G5 177
Minidoka, dam, Idaho G5 177
Minier, Ill. C4 178
Miniota, Man., Can. D1 150
Minipi, lake, Newf., Can h9 152
Minisink, isl., N.J A3 194
Minitonas, Man., Can. C1 150
Mink Creek, Idaho *G7 177
Minna, Nig. E6 103
Minna, bluff, Ant B29 120
Minne Maud, creek, Utah D5 207
Minneapolis, Kans. C6 181
Minneapolis, Minn. E7, F5 187
Minneapolis, N.C. C1 197
Minnedosa, Man., Can. D2 150
Minnedosa, riv., Man., Can D1 150
Minnehaha, co., S. Dak. D9 204
Minneiska, Minn. F7 187
Minneola, Fla. *D5 174
Minneola, Kans. E4 181
Minneota, Minn. F3 187
Minnesota, state, U.S. 187
in 1849 163
Minnesota, riv., Minn F3 187
Minnesota Lake, Minn. G5 187
Minnetonka, Minn. *F5 187
Minnetonka, lake, Minn F5 187
Minnewanka, lake, Alta., Can D3 148
Minnewaska, lake, Minn E3 187
Minnewaukan, N. Dak. A6 198
Mino, Jap. n15 93
Miño, riv., Sp A1 65
Minoa, N.Y. *B4 196
Minocqua, Wis. C4 212
Minokamo, Jap. n15 93
Minong, Wis. B2 212
Minonk, Ill. C4 178
Minooka, Ill. B5 178
Minor Hill, Tenn. B4 205
Minorca: in 1721 49
Minot, Mass. D4 185
Minot, N. Dak. A4 198
Minsen, Ger. A7 59
Minsk, Sov. Un. E6 72
Mińsk Mazowiecki, Pol. B6, m15 70
Minster, Ohio B3 199
Minter, Ala. C2 166
Minter City, Miss. B3 188
Minto, Alsk. C10 167
Minto, Man., Can. E1 150
Minto, N.B., Can. C3 151
Minto, N. Dak. A8 198
Minto, lake, Que., Can A2 154
Minton, Sask., Can. H3 155
Minturn, Ark. B4 169
Minturn, Colo. B4 171
Minturn, Maine D4 184
Minturno, It. D4 67
Minūf, Eg. D2 84
Minusinsk, Sov. Un. D12 71
Minvoul, Gabon E2 104
Minyā al Qamḥ, Eg. D3 84
Minya Konka, peak, China F5 91
Mio, Mich. D6 186
Miola, Pa. D3 202
Miquelon, cape, St. Pierre and Miquelon E3 152
Mira, La. B2 183
Mira, Port. B1 65
Mira, riv., Port D1 65
Mira Gut, N.S., Can. C10 151
Mira Loma, Calif. *F3 170
Miracle Hot Springs, Calif. E4 170
Mirador, Braz. C2 138
Miraflores, Col. C3 133
Miraflores, Peru E3 134
Miraflores, locks, C.Z m11 130
Miragoâne, Hai. F7 131
Miraj, India I5 88
Miramar, Cuba h11 131
Miramar, Fla. E3 174
Miramichi, bay, N.B., Can B4 151
Miranda, Braz. C1 137
Miranda, Col. C2 133
Miranda, S. Dak. C7 204
Miranda, state, Ven. A4 133
Miranda, riv., Braz C1 137
Miranda de Ebro, Sp. A4 65
Miranda do Douro, Port. B2 65
Mirande, Fr. F4 58
Mirandela, Port. B2 65
Mirando City, Tex. F3 206
Mirandola, It. E7 66
Mirassol, Braz. C3 137
Mirebalais, Hai. F7 131
Mirecourt, Fr. C7 58
Mirepoix, Fr. F4 58
Mirgorod, Sov. Un. G9 72
Miri, Mala. E4 90
Mirialguda, India I7 88
Miriam Vale, Austl. B8 112
Mirond, lake, Sask., Can B4 155
Mirow, Ger. E6 62
Mirpur Khās, Pak. E2 88
Mirror, Alta., Can. C4 148
Mirror Lake, N.H. C4 193
Miryang, Kor. I4 93
Mirzapur, India C7 87, E9 88
Misaki, see Miura, Jap.
Misakubo, Jap. n16 93
Misantla, Mex. D5, n15 129
Misburg, Ger. A4 61
Miscoe, hill, Mass E1 185
Miscou, isl., N.B., Can B5 151
Miscouche, P.E.I., Can. C6 151
Misenheimer, N.C. B3 197
Mishan, China D6 93
Mishawaka, Ind. A5 179
Mishicot, Wis. A6, D6 212
Mishima, Jap. I9, n17 93
Misiones, prov., Arg. E4 135
Misiones, dept., Par. E4 135
Miskitos, is., Nic C6 130
Miskolc, Hung. A5 68
Misoöl, isl., Indon F7 90
Mispillion, riv., Del C7 173
Misquamicut, R.I. D9 172
Miṣr al Jadīdah, Eg. D3 84
Misrātah, Libya C3 101
Misrātah, cape, Libya H14 64
Missaukee, co., Mich. D5 186
Missaukee, lake, Mich D5 186
Missinaibi, riv., Ont., Can G16 143
Mission, Kans. *B9 181
Mission, S. Dak. D5 204
Mission, Tex. F3 206
Mission, Indian res., Calif F5 170
Mission, range, Mont C3 190
Mission City, B.C., Can. A10, E6 149
Mission Hill, S. Dak. E8 204
Mission Hills, Kans. B9 181
Mission Ridge, S. Dak. C5 204
Missisquoi, co., Que., Can. D4 154
Missisquoi, bay, Vt A2 208
Missisquoi, riv., Vt B3 208
Mississagi, riv., Ont., Can B7 186
Mississagi, strait, Ont., Can C7 186
Mississauga, Ont., Can. D5 E6 153
Mississinewa, res., Ind C6 179
Mississinewa, riv., Ind C6 179
Mississippi, co., Ark. B5 169
Mississippi, co., Mo. E8 189
Mississippi, state, U.S. 188
in 1817 163
in Civil War 164
Mississippi, delta, La E6 183
Mississippi, lake, Ont., Can B6 153
Mississippi, riv., U.S D9 159
Mississippi, sound, Miss E5 188
Mississippi City, Miss. E2, E4 188
Missoula, Mont. D2 190
Missoula, co., Mont. D2 190
Missoula Southwest, Mont. *D2 190
Missour, Mor. C4 102
Missouri, state, U.S. 189
in 1821 163
in Civil War 164
Missouri, buttes, Wyo A8 213
Missouri, riv., U.S B8 158
Missouri City, Mo. E2 189
Missouri City, Tex. F5 206
Missouri Coteau, hills, N. Dak B4 198
Missouri Valley, Iowa C2 180
Mistaken, pt., Newf., Can E5 152
Mistassini, Que., Can. *G18 145
Mistassini, lake, Que., Can B2 154
Mistastin, lake, Newf., Can g9 152
Mistelbach [an der Zaya], Aus. D8 60
Misti, vol., Peru E3 134
Miston, Tenn. A2 205
Mistretta, It. F5 67
Mīt Fāris, Eg. C3 84
Mīt Ghamr, Eg. D3 84
Mita, pt., Mex C3 129
Mitaka, Jap. *I9 93
Mitake, Jap. I8, n16 93
Mitcham, Eng. *m12 55
Mitchell, Ala. C4 166
Mitchell, Austl. C6 112
Mitchell, Ont., Can. D3 153
Mitchell, Ga. C4 175
Mitchell, Ill. A8 189
Mitchell, Ind. G5 179
Mitchell, Iowa A5 180
Mitchell, La. C2 183
Mitchell, Nebr. C2 191
Mitchell, Oreg. C6 201
Mitchell, S. Dak. D7 204
Mitchell, co., Ga. E2 175
Mitchell, co., Iowa A5 180
Mitchell, co., Kans. C5 181
Mitchell, co., N.C. C4 197
Mitchell, co., Tex. C2 206
Mitchell, dam, Ala C3 166
Mitchell, isl., La E6 183
Mitchell, lake, Ala C3 166
Mitchell, lake, Mich D5 186
Mitchell, mtn., N.C D4 197
Mitchell, riv., Austl C7 110
Mitchellsburg, Ky. C5 182
Mitchellville, Iowa A8, C4 180
Mitchellville, Tenn. A5 205
Mitchelstown, Ire. D2 55
Mitilíni (Mytilene), Grc. C6 69
Mitishto, riv., Man., Can B2 150
Mitla, pass, Eg E4 84
Mito, Jap. H10, m19 93
Mitre, mtn., N.Z N15 112
Mitsinjo, Malag. g9 107
Mittelland, canal, Ger B5 60
Mittenwald, Ger. B7 66
Mittersill, Aus. B8 66
Mitterteich, Ger. D7 61
Mittl Isar, canal, Ger A7 66
Mittweida, Ger. C7 61
Mitú, Col. C3 133
Mitūbis, Eg. C2 84
Mitumba, mts., Zaire C4 106
Mitwaba, Zaire C4 106
Mitzic, Gabon E2 104
Miura (Misaki), Jap. n18 93
Mixcoac, Mex. h9 129
Mixquiahuala, Mex. m14 129
Mixteco, riv., Mex o14 129
Miyake, isl., Jap I9 93
Miyako, Jap. G10 93
Miyakonojō, Jap. K5 93
Miyan Kaleh, pen., Iran C6 86
Miyata, Jap. *J5 93
Miyazaki, Jap. K5 93
Miyazu, Jap. n14 93
Mizdah, Libya C2 101
Mize, Miss. D4 188
Mizil, Rom. C8 68
Mizpah, Minn. C4 187
Mizpah, Mont. D11 190
Mizpah, N.J. E3 194
Mizpah, creek, Mont E11 190
Mizque, Bol. C2 135
Mjölby, Swe. H6 63
Mjösa, lake, Nor G4 63
Mkalama, Tan. B5 106
Mkushi, Zambia D4 106
Mladá Boleslav, Czech. C3, n18 70
Mlanje, Malawi E6 106
Mljet, isl., Yugo D3 68
Mnichovo Hradiště, Czech. C9 61
Mo, Nor. D6 63
Moa, isl., Indon G7 90
Moab: in 13th cent. B.C. 98
Moab, Utah E6 207
Moala, isl., Fiji 114
Moamba, Moz. C5 107
Moanda, Gabon F2 104
Moapa, Nev. G7 192
Moapa River, Indian res., Nev G7 192
Moar, lake, Man., Ont., Can C4 150
Moark, Ark. A5 169
Moaula, Haw. D6 176
Moba, Zaire C4 106
Mobara, Jap. n19 93
Mobaye, Cen. Afr. Rep. E4 104
Mobeetie, Tex. B2 206
Moberly, Mo. B5 189
Mobile, Ala. E1 166
Mobile, Ariz. D3 168
Mobile, Newf., Can. E5 152
Mobile, co., Ala. E1 166
Mobile, bay, Ala E1 166
Mobile, riv., Ala E1 166
Mobridge, S. Dak. B5 204
Mobula, Zaire A4 106
Moca, Dom. Rep. F8 131
Moca, P.R. B2 132
Moca, mun., P.R. B2 132
Mocajuba, Braz. C5 139
Moçambique, Moz. E7 106
Moçambique, prov., Moz. D6 106
Moçâmedes, Ang. E1 106
Mocamedes, dist., Ang. E1 106
Mocanagua, Pa. D9 202
Moccasin, Ariz. A3 168
Moccasin, Mont. C7 190
Mocha, isl., Chile B2 136
Mochudi, Bots. B4 107
Mocímboa da Praia, Moz. D7 106
Möckeln, lake, Swe B8 62
Mocksville, N.C. B3 197
Moclips, Wash. B1 210
Mocoa, Col. C2 133
Mocóca, Braz. C3, k8 137
Mocomoco, Bol. C2 135
Mocorito, Mex. B3 129
Moctezuma, Mex. B3 129
Moctezuma, riv., Mex m14 129
Mocuba, Moz. A6 107
Modale, Iowa C2 180
Modane, Fr. D2 66
Mode, Ill. D5 178
Model, Colo. D6 171
Model, Tenn. A4 205
Model, res., Colo D6 171
Modena, It. B3 67
Modena, duchy of: in 1815 50
in 1860 51
Modena, Mo. A4 189
Modena, N.Y. D6 196
Modena, Pa. *G10 202
Modena, Utah F2 207
Modena, Wis. D2 212
Modeste, La. B5 183
Modesto, Calif. D3 170
Modesto, Ill. D4 178
Modjokerto, Indon. *G4 90
Modlin, Pol. B6, k13 70
Mödling, Aus. D8 60
Modoc, Ga. D4 175
Modoc, Ind. D7 179
Modoc, Kans. D2 181
Modoc, co., Calif. B3 170
Modoc Point, Oreg. E5 201
Modřany, Czech. o17 70
Moe, Austl. *I5 112
Moen, isl., Truk 114
Moengo, Sur. A4 139
Moenkopi, Ariz. A4 168
Moenkopi, wash, Ariz A5 168
Moerbeke, Bel. C3 59
Moers, Ger. B1 61
Moffat, Colo. C5 171
Moffat, Scot. E5 57
Moffat, co., Colo. A2 171
Moffat, railroad tunnel, Colo B5 171
Moffett, Okla. B7 200
Moffit, N. Dak. C5 198
Moga, Zaire B4 106
Mogadiscio, Som. E6 105
Mogador, Mor. C3 102
Mogadore, Ohio A6 199
Mogaung, Bur. C10 87
Mogfog, Guam 114
Mogi das Cruzes, Braz. C3, m8 137
Mogi Guaçu, riv., Braz k8 137
Mogi Mirim, Braz. m8 137
Mogielnica, Pol. C6 70
Mogilëv, Sov. Un. E8 72
Mogilev-Podolskiy, Sov. Un. G6 72
Mogilno, Pol. B4 70
Mogincual, Moz. A7 107
Mogocha, Sov. Un. D14 71
Mogochin, Sov. Un. B10 73
Mogok, Bur. D10 87
Mogollon, N. Mex. D1 195
Mogollon, plat., Ariz C4 168
Mogote, Colo. D4 171
Mogotes, pt., Arg B5 136
Mogpog, Phil. p13 90
Moguer, Sp. D2 65
Mogul empire: c. 1690 82
c. 1775 82
Mohács, Hung. C4 68
Mohaleshoek, Leso. D4 107
Mohall, N. Dak. A4 198
Mohammed, cape, Eg I10 85
Mohave, co., Ariz. B1 168
Mohave, lake, Ariz B1 168
Mohave, mts., Ariz C1 168
Mohawk, Ariz. E2 168
Mohawk, Mich. A2 186
Mohawk, N.Y. C5 196
Mohawk, lake, N.J A3 194
Mohawk, mtn., Conn B3 172
Mohawk, riv., N.H B1 193
Mohawk, riv., N.Y C6 196
Mohegan, Conn. D8 172
Mohican, riv., Ohio B5 199
Mohicanville, res., Ohio B5 199
Mohler, Wash. B7 210
Mohnton, Pa. F10 202
Mohon, Fr. C6 58
Mohoro, Tan. C6 106
Mohulu, Zaire B4 106
Moiese, Mont. C2 190
Moindu, N. Cal. 115
Moinesti, Rom. B8 68
Mointy, Sov. Un. D8 73
Moira, N.Y. A2 196
Moisie, Que., Can. h8 152
Moisie, riv., Que., Can h8 152
Moissac, Fr. E4 58
Moïssala, Chad D3 104
Moita, Port. f10 65
Mojave, Calif. E4 170
Mojave, desert, Calif E5 170
Mojave, riv., Calif E5 170
Mojo, Eth. D4 105
Mokameh, India E10 88
Mokami, hill, Newf., Can g9 152
Mokane, Mo. C6 189
Mokapu, pen., Haw g10 176
Mokapu, pt., Haw g11 176
Mokelumne, riv., Calif C3 170
Mokelumne Hill, Calif. C3 170
Mokena, Ill. F2 178
Mokepa, Zaire A4 106
Mokhotlong, Leso. C4 107
Mokolo, Cam. C2 104
Mokolo, Zaire A2 106
Mokpo, Kor. I3 93
Moksha, riv., Sov. Un C2 73
Moku Manu, isl., Haw g11 176
Mokuleia, Haw. B3, f9 176
Mol, Bel. C5 59
Mol, Yugo. C5 68
Mola [di Bari], It. D6 67
Molalla, Oreg. B4 201
Molanosa, Sask., Can. C3 155
Moláoi, Grc. D4 69
Molasses, pond, Maine D4 184
Mold, Wales A4 56
Moldava, reg., Rom. B8 68
Moldavia (S.S.R.), rep., Sov. Un. E5 71
c. 1360 48
in 1922-40 53
Molde, Nor. F2 63
Moldova, riv., Rom B8 68
Moldoveanu, mtn., Rom C7 68
Môle St. Nicolas, Hai. F7 131
Moledet, Isr. B7 84
Molena, Ga. C2 175
Molenbeek-St. Jean, Bel. *D4 59
Molengraaff, mts., Indon F5 90
Molepolole, Bots. B4 107
Molfetta, It. D6 67

Molina, Chile B2 136
Molina, Colo B2 171
Molina de Aragón, Sp B5 65
Molina de Segura, Sp C5 65
Moline, Ill B3 178
Moline, Kans E7 181
Moline, Mich F5 186
Moline, Ohio A2 199
Moline Acres, Mo *C7 189
Molinella, It E7 66
Molino, Fla G2 174
Molinos, Arg E2 135
Moliro, Zaire C5 106
Moliterno, It D5 67
Möll, riv., Aus C9 66
Mölle, Swe B6 62
Mollendo, Peru E3 134
Mollusk, Va D6 209
Mölndal, Swe I5 63
Molochansk, Sov. Un H10 72
Molodechno, Sov. Un D6 72
Molokai, isl., Haw B5 176
Molokini, isl., Haw C5 176
Molopo, riv., Bots., S. Afr C3 107
Molotovskoye, Sov. Un I13 72
Moloundou, Cam E3 104
Mols, isl., Den B4 62
Molsheim, Fr F7 59
Molson, Man., Can D3 150
Molson, Wash A6 210
Molson, lake, Man., Can B3 150
Molson, riv., Man., Can B3 150
Molt, Mont E8 190
Molteno, S. Afr D4 107
Moltke, cape, Bougainville I. 115
Molucca, is., Indon F7 90
Molucca, passage, Indon E7 90
Molucca, sea, Indon E7 90
Molus, Ky D6 182
Moma, Moz A6 107
Momauguin, Conn D5 172
Mombango, Zaire A3 106
Mombasa, Ken B6 106
Mombetsu, Jap D11 93
Momboyo, riv., Zaire B3 106
Momchilgrad, Bul E7 68
Momence, Ill B6 178
Momi, Fiji 114
Mominabad, India H6 88
Momostenango, Guat C2 130
Mompono, Zaire A3 106
Mompog, pass, Phil p14 90
Mompós, Col B3 133
Mön, isl., Den C6 62
Mon Louis, Ala E1 166
Mona, Mont B12 190
Mona, Utah D4 207
Mona, isl., P.R e10 132
Mona, passage, W.I F9 131
Mona ó Carreta, pt., C.R F6 130
Mona Vatu, mtn., Fiji 114
Monaca, Pa E1 202
Monaco, Monaco F7 58
MONACO, country, Eur F7 58
Monadhliath, mts., Scot C4 57
Monadnock, mtn., N.H E2 193
Monagas, state, Ven B5 133
Monaghan, S.C B3 203
Monahans, Tex D1 206
Monango, N. Dak C7 198
Monarch, Alta., Can E4 148
Monarch, Mont C6 190
Monarch (Monarch Mills), S.C B4 203
Monarch, mtn., B.C., Can D5 149
Monarch, pass, Colo C4 171
Monashee, mts., B.C., Can D8 149
Monastir, Tun B7 102
Monastyrshchina, Sov. Un D8 72
Monção, Braz B1 138
Moncayo, mtn., Sp B5 65
Monchegorsk, Sov. Un D15 63
Mönchen-Gladbach, Ger C6 59, C3 60
Monchique, Port D1 65
Monchique, mts., Port D1 65
Moncks Corner, S.C E7 203
Monclo, W. Va D3, D5 211
Monclova, Mex B4 129
Monclova, Ohio A1 199
Moncton, N.B., Can C5 151
Moncure, N.C B4 197
Mond, lake, Aus B9 66
Mondamin, Iowa C1 180
Mondego, cape, Port B1 65
Mondego, riv., Port B1 65
Mondoñedo, Sp A2 65
Mondorf-les-Bains, Lux E6 59
Mondovì, It B1 67
Mondovi, Wis D2 212
Monee, Ill B6 178
Monegaw Springs, Mo C4 189
Monemvasia, Grc D4 69
Monero, N. Mex A3 195
Monessen, Pa F2 202
Moneta, Va D3 209
Moneta, Wyo B5 213
Monett, Mo E4 189
Monetta, S.C D4 203
Monette, Ark B5 169
Money, Miss B3 188
Monfalcone, It B4 67
Monforte de Lemos, Sp A2 65
Mong Hpayak, Bur B3 89
Mong Hsat, Bur B3 89
Mong Mit, Bur D10 87
Mong Nai, Bur A3 89
Mong Pan, Bur B3 89
Monga, Con. K A3 106
Mongala, riv., Zaire A3 106
Mongalla, Sud D3 105
Monges, is., Ven A3 133
Monghyr, India C8 87, E11 88
Mongo, Chad C3 104
Mongo, Ind A7 179
Mongolia, Ont., Can E7 153
MONGOLIA, country, Asia B5 91
Outer Mongolia 82
c. 1775 82
c. 1950 83
Mongolia, plat., Mong B6 91
Mongu, Zambia E3 106
Monhegan, isl., Maine E3 184
Moniaive, Scot E5 57
Monico, Wis C4 212
Monida, Mont F4 190
Monida, pass, Idaho F4 190
Monie, Md D6 173
Moniquirá, Col B3 133
Moniteau, co., Mo C5 189
Monito, isl., P.R e10 132
Monitor, Alta., Can D5 148
Monitor, Oreg B2 201
Monitor, Wash B5 210
Monitor, range, Nev E5 192
Monitor, val., Nev E5 192
Monkey River, Br. Hond B3 130
Monkira, Austl B3 112
Monkman, pass, B.C., Can B7 149
Monkoto, Zaire B3 106
Monkton, Ont., Can D3 153
Monkton, Vt C2 208
Monmouth, Ill C3 178
Monmouth, Iowa B7 180
Monmouth, Maine D2 184
Monmouth, Oreg C1, C3 201
Monmouth, Wales C5 56
Monmouth, co., N.J C4 194
Monmouth, co., Wales C5 56
Monmouth, mtn., B.C., Can D6 149
Monmouth, peak, Oreg C3 201
Monmouth Beach, N.J C5 194
Monmouth Junction, N.J C3 194
Monnikendam, Neth B5 59
Monnow, riv., Eng C5 56
Mono, co., Calif D4 170
Mono, isl., Sol. Is 115
Mono, lake, Calif D4 170
Mono, pt., Nic E6 130
Mono Lake, Calif D4 170
Monocacy, riv., Md B3 173
Monolith, Calif E4 170
Monomonac, lake, Mass., N.H A3 185
Monomoy, isl., Mass C7 185
Monomoy, pt., Mass C7 185
Monon, Ind C4 179
Monona, Iowa A6 180
Monona, Wis E4 212
Monona, co., Iowa B2 180
Monona, lake, Wis E4 212
Monongah, W. Va A7, B4 211
Monongahela, Pa F2 202
Monongahela, riv., Pa., W. Va B5 211
Monongalia, co., W. Va B4 211
Monopoli, It D6 67
Monor, Hung B4 68
Monóvar, Sp C5 65
Monoville, Tenn C8 205
Monowi, Nebr B7 191
Monowice, Pol g10 70
Monreale, It E4 67
Monroe, Ark C4 169
Monroe, Conn D4 172
Monroe, Ga C3 175
Monroe, Ind C8 179
Monroe, Iowa C4 180
Monroe, La B3 183
Monroe, Maine D3 184
Monroe, Mich G7 186
Monroe, Nebr C8 191
Monroe, N.H B2 193
Monroe, N.J A3 194
Monroe, N.Y D2, D6 196
Monroe, N.C C3 197
Monroe, Ohio *C3 199
Monroe, Okla C7 200
Monroe, Oreg C3 201
Monroe, S. Dak D8 204
Monroe, Tenn C8 205
Monroe, Utah E3 207
Monroe, Va D3 209
Monroe, Wash B4 210
Monroe, Wis F4 212
Monroe, co., Ala D2 166
Monroe, co., Ark C4 169
Monroe, co., Fla H5 174
Monroe, co., Ga D3 175
Monroe, co., Ill E3 178
Monroe, co., Ind F4 179
Monroe, co., Iowa D5 180
Monroe, co., Ky D4 182
Monroe, co., Mich G7 186
Monroe, co., Miss B5 188
Monroe, co., Mo B5 189
Monroe, co., N.Y B3 196
Monroe, co., Ohio C6 199
Monroe, co., Pa D11 202
Monroe, co., Tenn D9 205
Monroe, co., W. Va D4 211
Monroe, co., Wis E3 212
Monroe Bridge, Mass A2 185
Monroe Center, Ill A5 178
Monroe City, Ind G3 179
Monroe City, Mo B6 189
Monroeton, Pa C9 202
Monroeville, Ala D2 166
Monroeville, Ind C8 179
Monroeville, N.J D2 194
Monroeville, Ohio A5 199
Monroeville, Pa *F2 202
Monrovia, Calif F2 170
Monrovia, Ind E5 179
Monrovia, Kans C8 181
Monrovia, Lib E2 103
Mons, Bel D3 59
Möns Klint, isl., Den D6 62
Monsanto, Ill B8 189
Monschau, Ger D6 59
Monselice, It D7 66
Monserrate Central, P.R B4 132
Monson, Maine C3 184
Monson, Mass B3 185
Mont Alto, Pa G6 202
Mont Belvieu, Tex E5, F5 206
Mont Carmel, Que., Can B8 154
Mont Cenis, pass, Fr., It D2 66
Mont Cenis, tunnel, Fr., It D2 66
Mont Clare, Pa A10 202
Mont-de-Marsan, Fr F3 58
Mont Ida, Kans D8 181
Mont-Joli, Que., Can A9 154
Mont Laurier, Que., Can C2 154
Mont Rolland, Que., Can D3 154
Mont Royal, Que., Can *D9 154
Mont-St. Martin, Fr C6 58
Mont-St. Michel, Fr C3 58
Mont Tremblant, Que., Can C3 154
Mont Tremblant, prov. park, Que., Can C5 154
Mont Vernon, N.H E3 193
Montabaur, Ger C2 61
Montagnana, It D7 66
Montagu, hbr., New Britain I. 115
Montague, Calif B2 170
Montague, P.E.I., Can C7 151
Montague, Mass A2 185
Montague, Mich E4 186
Montague, Mont C6 190
Montague, Tex C4 206
Montague, co., Tex C4 206
Montague, isl., Alsk D10 167
Montague, isl., Mex A2 129
Montague, peak, Alsk g18 167
Montague City, Mass A2 185
Montalbán, Sp B5 65
Montalegre, Port B2 65
Montalto, mtn., It E5 67
Montalvo, Calif *E4 170
Montana, Alsk f17 167
Montana, Ark B2 169
Montana, state, U.S 190
Montánchez, Sp C2 65
Montandon, Pa E8 202
Montargis, Fr D5 58
Montataire, Fr E2 59
Montauban, Que., Can C5 154
Montauban, Fr E4 58
Montauban-les-Mines, Que., Can C5 154
Montauk, Mo D6 189
Montauk, N.Y E9 172
Montauk, hbr., N.Y E9 172
Montauk, pt., N.Y E9 172
Montbard, Fr D6 58
Montbéliard, Fr D7 58
Montblanch, Sp B6 65
Montbrison, Fr E6 58
Montcalm, co., Que., Can C3 154
Montcalm, co., Mich E5 186
Montcalm, peak, Fr F4 58
Montceau-les-Mines, Fr D6 58
Montcerf, Que., Can C1 154
Montchanin [-les-Mines], Fr D6 58
Montclair (Monte Vista), Calif *E5 170
Montclair, N.J B4 194
Montcoal, W. Va D3, D6 211
Montcornet, Fr E4 59
Montdidier, Fr C5 58
Monte Alegre, Braz C2 137
Monte Alegre, Braz C4 139
Monte Azul, Braz E2 138
Monte Bello, is., Austl D2 110
Monte Carmelo, Braz E1 138
Monte Caseros, Arg A5 136
Monte Coman, Arg A3 136
Monte Cristo, Bol B3 135
Monte Gargano, pen., It D5 67
Monte Ne, Ark A1 169
Monte Patria, Chile A2 136
Monte Plata, Dom. Rep F9 131
Monte Porzio Catone, It h9 67
Monte Quemado, Arg E3 135
Monte Sano, mts., Ala A3 166
Monte Sant'Angelo, It D5 67
Monte Santo, Braz D3 138
Monte Vista, Colo D4 171
Monteagle, Tenn D8 205
Monteagudo, Arg D2 137
Montebello, Calif F2 170
Montebello, Que., Can D3 154
Montebello, P.R B4 132
Montebello, Va D3 209
Montebelluna, It D8 66
Montecatini Terme, It C3 67
Montecelio, It g9 67
Montecristi, Dom. Rep F8 131
Montecristi, Ec B1 134
Montecristo, isl., It C3 67
Montefrío, Sp D3 65
Montego Bay, Jam F5 131
Montegut, La E5 183
Monteiro, Braz C3 138
Monteith, mtn., B.C., Can B6 149
Montelavar, Port F9 65
Montélimar, Fr E6 58
Montell, Tex E2 206
Montellano, Sp D3 65
Montello, Nev B7 192
Montello, Wis E4 212
Montemor-o-Novo, Port C1 65
Montemorelos, Mex B5 129
Montenegro, Braz D2 137
Montenegro, reg., Yugo D4 68
in 1721 49
in 1810 50
after World War I 53
Montepuez, Moz D6 106
Montepulciano, It C3 67
Montereau, Fr C5 58
Monterey, Ala D3 166
Monterey, Calif C6, D3 170
Monterey, Ind B4 179
Monterey, Ky B5 182
Monterey, Mass B1 185
Monterey, Tenn C8 205
Monterey, Va C3 209
Monterey, co., Calif D3 170
Monterey, bay, Calif D3 170
Monterey Park, Calif *E4 170
Montería, Col B2 133
Monteros, Arg E2 135
Monterotondo, It g9 67
Monterrey, Mex B4 129
Montes Claros, Braz E2 138
Montesano, Wash C2 210
Montevallo, Ala B3 166
Montevarchi, It C3 67
Montevideo, Minn F3 187
Montevideo, Ur E1 137
Monteview, Idaho F6 177
Montevue, Md B3 173
Montezuma, Ga D2 175
Montezuma, Ind E3 179
Montezuma, Iowa C5 180
Montezuma, Kans E3 181
Montezuma, N. Mex B4 195
Montezuma, Ohio B3 199
Montezuma, Tenn B3 205
Montezuma, co., Colo D2 171
Montezuma, creek, Utah F6 207
Montezuma, peak, Ariz D3 168
Montezuma Castle, nat. mon., Ariz C4 168
Montezuma Creek, Utah F6 207
Montfort, Que., Can D3 154
Montfort, Wis F3 212
Montfort-sur-Meu, Fr C3 58
Montgomery, Ala C3 166
Montgomery, Ga E5 175
Montgomery, Ill F1 178
Montgomery, Ind G3 179
Montgomery, La C3 183
Montgomery, Mass B2 185
Montgomery, Mich G6 186
Montgomery, Minn F5 187
Montgomery, N.Y D6 196
Montgomery, Ohio *C3 199
Montgomery, Pak B4 88
Montgomery, Pa D8 202
Montgomery, Vt B3 208
Montgomery, Wales B4 56
Montgomery, W. Va C3, C6 211
Montgomery, co., Ala C3 166
Montgomery, co., Ark C2 169
Montgomery, co., Ga D4 175
Montgomery, co., Ill D4 178
Montgomery, co., Ind D4 179
Montgomery, co., Iowa C2 180
Montgomery, co., Kans E8 181
Montgomery, co., Ky B6 182
Montgomery, co., Md B3 173
Montgomery, co., Miss B4 188
Montgomery, co., Mo C6 189
Montgomery, co., N.Y C6 196
Montgomery, co., N.C B4 197
Montgomery, co., Ohio C3 199
Montgomery, co., Pa F10 202
Montgomery, co., Tenn A4 205
Montgomery, co., Tex D5 206
Montgomery, co., Va D2 209
Montgomery, co., Wales B4 56
Montgomery Center, Vt B3 208
Montgomery City, Mo C6 189
Montgomery Creek, Calif B3 170
Monthermé, Fr E5 59
Monthey, Switz C2 66
Monthois, Fr E4 59
Monticello, Ark D4 169
Monticello, Fla B3 174
Monticello, Ga C3 175
Monticello, Ill C5 178
Monticello, Ind C4 179
Monticello, Iowa B6 180
Monticello, Ky D5 182
Monticello, Maine B5 184
Monticello, Minn E5 187
Monticello, Miss D3 188
Monticello, Mo A6 189
Monticello, N. Mex D2 195
Monticello, N.Y D6 196
Monticello, Utah F6 207
Monticello, Wis F4 212
Montier, Mo E6 189
Montier-en-Der, Fr F4 59
Montiers-sur-Saulx, Fr F5 59
Montigny-Lencoup, Fr F3 59
Montigny-lès-Metz, Fr E6 59
Montijo, Port C1, f10 65
Montijo, Sp C2 65
Montilla, Sp D3 65
Montivilliers, Fr C3 58
Montluçon, Fr D5 58
Montmagny, Que., Can C7 154
Montmagny, co., Que., Can C7 154
Montmartre, Sask., Can G4 155
Montmédy, Fr E5 59
Montmélian, Fr E2 66
Montmirail, Fr F3 59
Montmorenci, Ind D3 179
Montmorenci, S.C D4 203
Montmorency, Que., Can C6, C9 154
Montmorency, Fr g10 58
Montmorency, co., Mich C6 186
Montmorency, riv., Que., Can B6 154
Montmorency No. 1, co., Que., Can B6 154
Montmorency No. 2, co., Que., Can C7 154
Montmorillon, Fr D4 58
Montney, B.C., Can A7 149
Monto, Austl B8 112
Montone, riv., It B3 67
Montoro, Sp C3 65
Montour, Idaho F2 177
Montour, Iowa C5 180
Montour, co., Pa D8 202
Montour Falls, N.Y C4 196
Montoursville, Pa D8 202
Montowese, Conn D5 172
Montoya, N. Mex B5 195
Montpelier, Idaho G7 177
Montpelier, Ind C7 179
Montpelier, Iowa C7 180
Montpelier, La D5 183
Montpelier, Miss B5 188
Montpelier, N. Dak C7 198
Montpelier, Ohio A3 199
Montpelier, Vt C3 208
Montpelier Station, Va C4 209
Montpellier, Que., Can D2 154
Montpellier, Fr F5 58
Montreal, Que., Can D4, D9 154
Montreal, Wis B3 212
Montreal, lake, Sask., Can C3 155
Montreal, riv., Sask., Can C3 155
Montreal Lake, Sask., Can C3 155
Montreal Nord, Que., Can D9 154
Montreat, N.C f10 197
Montreuil, Fr g10 58, F2 59
Montreuil-sur-Mer, Fr B4 58
Montreux, Switz C2 66
Montrose, Ala E2 166
Montrose, Ark D4 169
Montrose, Colo C3 171
Montrose, Ga D3 175
Montrose, Ill D5 178
Montrose, Iowa D6 180
Montrose, Kans C5 181
Montrose, Mich E7 186
Montrose, Miss C4 188
Montrose, Mo C4 189
Montrose, Pa C10 202
Montrose, Scot D6 57
Montrose, S. Dak D8 204
Montrose, co., Colo C2 171
Montross, Va C6 209
Montrouge, Fr g10 58
Montserrat, Mo C4 189
MONTSERRAT, Br. dep., N.A n15 131
Montserrat, isl., N.A n15 131
Montserrat, peak, Sp B6 65
Montvale, N.J C5 194
Montvale, Va D3 209
Montville, Conn D8 172
Montville, Mass B1 185
Montville, N.J B4 194
Montzen, Bel D5 59
Monument, Colo B6 171
Monument, Kans C2 181
Monument, N. Mex E6 195
Monument, Oreg C7 201
Monument, Pa D6 202
Monument, peak, Colo B3 171
Monument, peak, Idaho G4 177
Monument Beach, Mass C6 185
Monument Valley, ruins, Ariz A5 168
Monywa, Bur D10 87
Monza, It D5 66, B2 67
Monze, Zambia E4 106
Monzón, Peru C2 134
Monzón, Sp B6 65
Moodus, Conn D7 172
Moodus, res., Conn C7 172
Moody, Maine E2 184
Moody, Mo E6 189
Moody, Tex D4 206
Moody, co., S. Dak C9 204
Moody Beach, Maine E2 184
Mooers, N.Y A3 196
Mooers Forks, N.Y A3 196
Moon, lake, Miss A3 188
Moon Run, Pa B5 202
Moonachie, N.J *B4 194
Moonta, Austl F6 111
Moor Lake Station, Ont., Can A7 153
Moora, Austl F2 111
Moorabbin, Austl *G8 111
Moorcroft, Wyo A8 213
Moore, Idaho F5 177
Moore, Mont D7 190
Moore, Okla B4 200
Moore, S.C B3 203
Moore, Tex E3 206
Moore, Utah D4 207
Moore, W. Va B5 211
Moore, co., N.C B4 197
Moore, co., Tenn B5 205
Moore, co., Tex B2 206
Moore, res., N.H., Vt B3 193, C5 208
Moore Haven, Fla F5 174
Moorefield, Ont., Can D4 153
Moorefield, Ky B6 182
Moorefield, Nebr D5 191
Moorefield, W. Va B6 211
Moorefield, riv., W. Va C5 211
Mooreland, Ind E7 179
Mooreland, Okla A2 200
Moorepark, Man., Can D2 150
Moores Corner, Mass B3 185
Moores Hill, Ind F7 179
Moores Mills, N.B., Can D2 151
Mooresburg, Tenn C10 205
Moorestown, Mich D5 186
Moorestown, N.J D3 194
Mooresville, Ind E5 179
Mooresville, Mo B4 189
Mooresville, N.C B3 197
Mooresville, Tenn B5 205
Mooreton, N. Dak C9 198
Mooreville, Miss A5 188
Moorewood, Okla B2 200
Moorhead, Iowa C2 180
Moorhead, Minn D2 187
Moorhead, Miss B3 188
Moorhead, Mont E11 190
Mooring, Tenn A2 205
Mooringsport, La B2 183
Moorland, Iowa B3 180
Moorman, Ky C2 182
Moorpark, Calif E4 170
Moors, The, moors, Scot F4 57
Moosburg, Ger E6 61
Moose, Wyo B2 213
Moose, creek, Wyo D2 213
Moose, isl., Man., Can D3 150
Moose, lake, B.C., Can C1 148
Moose, lake, Man., Can B1 150
Moose, mtn., Sask., Can H4 155
Moose, mtn., N.H C2 193
Moose, pond, Maine D3 184
Moose, riv., Ont., Can F16 143
Moose, riv., Maine C2 184
Moose, riv., N.H B4 193
Moose, riv., N.Y B5 196
Moose, riv., Vt B5 208
Moose Creek, Ont., Can B10 153
Moose Jaw, Sask., Can C1, G3 155
Moose Lake, Man., Can C1 150
Moose Lake, Minn D6 187
Moose Lake, res., Wis B3 212
Moose Mountain, creek, Sask., Can H4 155
Moose Mountain, prov. park, Sask., Can H4 155
Moose Pass, Alsk C10, g17 167
Moose River, Maine C2 184
Moosehead, lake, Maine C3 184
Mooseheart, Ill B5, F1 178
Moosehorn, Man., Can D2 150
Moosejaw, creek, Sask., Can G3 155
Mooseleuk, stream, Maine B4 184
Mooselookmeguntic, lake, Maine D2 184
Moosic, Pa B9 202
Moosic, mts., Pa A9 202
Moosilauke, mtn., N.H B3 193
Moosomin, Sask., Can G5 155
Moosonee, Ont., Can E9 153
Moosup, Conn C9 172
Moosup Valley, R.I C9 172
Mopang, lakes, Maine D5 184
Mopeia, Moz A6 107
Mopti, Mali D4 103
Moquegua, Peru E3 134
Moquegua, dept., Peru E3 134
Mór, Hung B4 68
Mor, isl., Truk 114
Mora, Cam C2 104
Mora, Ga E4 175
Mora, Minn E5 187
Mora, N. Mex B4 195
Mora, P.R B2 132
Mora, Sp C4 65
Mora, Swe G6 63
Mora, co., N. Mex A5 195
Mora, riv., N. Mex B5 195
Mora de Ebro, Sp B6 65
Moraca, riv., Yugo D4 68
Morada, Calif *D3 170
Morada Nova, Braz C3 138
Moradabad, India C6 87, C7 88
Morafenobe, Malag g8 107
Morag, Pol B5 70
Moraine, Ohio *C3 199
Morales, Guat C3 130
Morales, Mex k13 129
Morales, Tex E4 206
Moramanga, Malag g9 107
Moran, Ind D4 179
Moran, Kans E8 181
Moran, Mich B6 186
Moran, Tex C3 206
Moran, Va D4 209
Moran, Wyo B2 213
Morann, Pa E5 202
Morant Bay, Jam G5 131
Morat, lake, Scot D3 57
Morat, lake, Switz C3 66
Morata de Tajuña, Sp p18 65
Moratalla, Sp C5 65
Morattico, Va *D6 209
Moratuwa, Cey *G6 87
Morava, riv., Czech D4 70
Morava, riv., Yugo C5 68
Moravia, Iowa D5 180
Moravia, N.Y C4 196
Moravia, reg., Czech D4 70
c. 1360 48
in 1721 49
in 1815-71 51
in 1914 52
Morawhanna, Guy A3 139
Moray, co., Scot C5 57
Moray, firth, Scot C5 57
Moraya, Bol D2 135
Morbach, Ger D2 61
Morcenx, Fr E3 58
Morden, Man., Can E2 150
Morden, N.S., Can D5 151
More, mtn., Scot C1 57
More, mtn., Scot D3 57
More, mtn., Scot D4 57
More Assynt, mtn., Scot B4 57
Moreau, riv., S. Dak B3 204
Moreauville, La C4 183
Morecambe [& Heysham], Eng F6 57
Morecambe, bay, Eng C5 55
Moree, Austl D7 112
Morehead, Ky B6 182
Morehead City, N.C C7 197
Morehouse, Mo E8 189
Morehouse, par., La B4 183
Moreland, Ark B3 169
Moreland, Ga C2 175
Moreland, Idaho F6 177
Moreland, Ky C5 182
Moreland Hills, Ohio *A6 199
Morelia, Mex D4, n13 129
Morell, P.E.I., Can C7 151
Morella, Sp B5 65
Morelos, state, Mex D5, n14 129

INDEX KEY Each place listed in **Bold-faced Type** has its population listed in the Population tables, pages 230 to 260.
Each country, shown in CAPITAL LETTERS, has its population listed in the World Political Information Table, pages 6 to 10.
* Does not appear on map; key shows general location.

Morelos, dam, Ariz.........E1 168
Morena, mts., Sp.........C3 65
Morenci, Ariz........D6 168
Morenci, Mich........G6 186
Moresby, isl., B.C., Can.........C2 149
Moreton, bay, Austl.........C9 112
Moreton, isl., Austl.........C9 112
Moreton-in-Marsh, Eng........C6 56
Moretown, Vt........C3 208
Moreuil, Fr........E2 59
Morewood, Ont., Can........B9 153
Morey, peak, Nev.........E5 192
Morez, Fr........D7 58
Morgan, Austl........G2 112
Morgan, Ga........E2 175
Morgan, Ky........B5 182
Morgan, Minn........F4 187
Morgan, Mont........B9 190
Morgan, Tex........C4 206
Morgan, Utah........B4 207
Morgan, Vt........B4 208
Morgan, co., Ala........A3 166
Morgan, co., Colo........A7 171
Morgan, co., Ga........C3 175
Morgan, co., Ill........D3 178
Morgan, co., Ind........F5 179
Morgan, co., Ky........C6 182
Morgan, co., Mo........C5 189
Morgan, co., Ohio........C6 199
Morgan, co., Tenn........C9 205
Morgan, co., Utah........B4 207
Morgan, co., W. Va........B6 211
Morgan, isl., S.C.........G6 203
Morgan, pt., Conn.........E5 172
Morgan Center, Vt........B5 208
Morgan City, La........C5, E4 183
Morgan City, Miss........B3 188
Morgan Hill, Calif........C6, D3 170
Morgana, S.C........D3 203
Morganfield, Ky........C2 182
Morganton, Ark........B3 169
Morganton, Ga........B2 175
Morganton, N.C........B2 197
Morgantown, Ind........F5 179
Morgantown, Ky........C3 182
Morgantown, Miss........D4 188
Morgantown, Pa........F10 202
Morgantown, W. Va........A7, B5 211
Morganville, Ga........B1 175
Morganville, Kans........C6 181
Morganville, N.J........C4 194
Morganza, La........D4 183
Morges, Switz........C2 66
Morgex, It........D3 66
Morghāb, Iran........F6 86
Morgusaia, isl., Sol. Is.........115
Mori, Jap........E10 93
Moriah, N.Y........A7 196
Moriah, mtn., Nev.........D7 192
Moriah, mtn., N.H.........B4 193
Moriarty, N. Mex........C3 195
Morice, lake, B.C., Can.........B4 149
Morice, riv., B.C., Can.........B4 149
Moriches, bay, N.Y.........F5 172
Moriguchi, Jap........*o14 93
Morin Heights, Que., Can........D3 154
Morinville, Alta., Can........C4 148
Morioka, Jap........G10 93
Morrisset-Station, Que., Can........C7 154
Moriyama, Jap........*I8 93
Morjärv, Swe........D10 63
Morkill, riv., B.C., Can.........C7 149
Mörkö, Swe........t35 63
Morlaix, Fr........C2 58
Morland, Kans........C3 181
Morley, Alta., Can........D3 148
Morley, Eng........A6 56
Morley, Mich........E5 186
Morley, Mo........D8 189
Morley, N.Y........A2 196
Morman, peak, Nev.........G7 192
Mormon Lake, Ariz........C4 168
Morning Sun, Iowa........C6 180
Morning View, Ky........A7 182
Morningside, Md........C4 173
Morningside, Minn........*F5 187
Morningside, S. Dak........C7 204
Mornington, isl., Chile........D1 136
Moro, Ark........C5 169
Moro, Ill........A8 189
Moro, Oreg........B6 201
Moro, creek, Ark.........D3 169
Moro, gulf, Phil.........D6 90
Morobay, Ark........D3 169
Morobe, N. Gui........k12 111
Morocco, Ind........C3 179
MOROCCO, country, Afr........C3 102
before 1911........99
after World War II........54
Morococha, Peru........D2 134
Morogoro, Tan........C6 106
Moroleón, Mex........m13 129
Morombe, Malag........h8 107
Morón, Cuba........D4 131
Morón de la Frontera, Sp........D3 65
Morona, riv., Peru........B2 134
Morondava, Malag........h8 107
Moroni, Utah........D4 207
Morong, Phil........o13 90
Morotai, isl., Indon.........E7 90
Moroto, Ug........A5 106
Morovis, P.R........B5 132
Morovis, mun., P.R........B5 132
Morozovsk, Sov. Un........D2 73
Morpeth, Ont., Can........E3 153
Morpeth, Eng........E7 57
Morphou, Cyp........E9 85
Morral, Ohio........B4 199
Morrice, Mich........*F6 186
Morrill, Kans........C8 181
Morrill, Nebr........C2 191
Morrill, co., Nebr........C2 191
Morrilton, Ark........B3 169
Morrin, Alta., Can........B4 148
Morrinhos, Braz........E1 138
Morrinsville, N.Z........L15 112
Morris, Ala........B3 166
Morris, Man., Can........E3 150
Morris, Conn........C4 172
Morris, Ga........E2 175
Morris, Ill........B5 178
Morris, Ind........F7 179
Morris, Minn........E3 187
Morris, N.Y........C5 196
Morris, Okla........B6 200
Morris, co., Kans........D7 181
Morris, co., N.J........B3 194
Morris, co., Tex........C5 206
Morris, isl., S.C.........F8 203
Morris, mtn., N.Y.........A6 196
Morris Chapel, Tenn........B3 205
Morris Jesup, cape, Grnld.........A18 118
Morris Plains, N.J........B4 194
Morris Run, Pa........C7 202
Morrisburg, Ont., Can........C9 153
Morrisdale, Pa........E5 202
Morrison, Colo........B5 171
Morrison, Ill........B4 178
Morrison, Mo........C6 189
Morrison, Okla........A4 200
Morrison, Tenn........D8 205
Morrison, Wis........A6 212
Morrison, co., Minn........D4 187
Morrison City, Tenn........C11 205
Morrisonville, Ill........D4 178
Morriston, Fla........C4 174
Morristown, Ariz........D3, F1 168
Morristown, Ind........E6 179
Morristown, Minn........F5 187
Morristown, N.J........B4 194
Morristown, N.Y........B1 196
Morristown, S. Dak........B4 204
Morristown, Tenn........C10 205
Morristown, Vt........B3 208
Morristown, nat. historical park, N.J.........B3 194
Morrisville, Mo........D4 189
Morrisville, N.Y........C5 196
Morrisville, Pa........F12 202
Morrisville, Vt........B3 208
Morrisville, Va........B5 209
Morrito, Nic........E5 130
Morro, Ec........B1 134
Morro Bay, Calif........E3 170
Morro do Chapéu, Braz........E2 138
Morropón, Peru........C2 134
Morrosquillo, gulf, Col.........B2 133
Morrow, Ga........B5, C2 175
Morrow, La........D3 183
Morrow, Ohio........C3 199
Morrow, co., Ohio........B5 199
Morrow, co., Oreg........B7 201
Morrowville, Kans........C6 181
Morse, Sask., Can........G2 155
Morse, La........D3 183
Morse, Tex........A2 206
Morse, Wis........B3 212
Morse, res., Ind.........D5 179
Morse Bluff, Nebr........C9 191
Morse Mill, Mo........B7 189
Morses, creek, N.J.........E4 194
Morshansk, Sov. Un........C2 73
Mortagne [-au-Perche], Fr........C4 58
Mortara, It........B2 67
Morteau, Fr........D7 58
Morteros, Arg........A4 136
Mortlach, Sask., Can........G2 155
Morton, Ill........C4 178
Morton, Minn........F4 187
Morton, Miss........C4 188
Morton, Pa........*G11 202
Morton, Tex........C1 206
Morton, Wash........C4 210
Morton, Wyo........B4 213
Morton, co., Kans........E2 181
Morton, co., N. Dak........C4 198
Morton Grove, Ill........F3 178
Mortons Gap, Ky........C2 182
Morup, Swe........B6 62
Moruya, Austl........G8 112
Morvan, mts., Fr.........D6 58
Morven, Ga........F3 175
Morven, N.C........C3 197
Morven, mtn., Scot.........B5 57
Morvern, Scot........D3 57
Morvi, India........F3 88
Moryakovskiy Zaton, Sov. Un........B10 73
Morye, Sov. Un........r32 63
Mosalsk, Sov. Un........D10 72
Mosbach, Ger........D4 61
Mosby, Mo........D2 189
Mosby, Mont........D9 190
Mosca, Colo........D5 171
Moscarello, riv., It.........k9 67
Moscos, is., Bur.........E2 89
Moscow, Ark........C4 169
Moscow, Idaho........C2 177
Moscow, Ind........F6 179
Moscow, Iowa........C6 180
Moscow, Kans........E2 181
Moscow, Ohio........D3 199
Moscow, Pa........B9 202
Moscow (Moskva), Sov. Un........D11, n17 72
principality of: c. 1360........48
Moscow, Tenn........B2 205
Moscow, Vt........C3 208
Moscow Mills, Mo........C7 189
Mosel, riv., Ger.........C2 61
Moseley, Va........D5 209
Moselle, Miss........D4 188
Moselle, dept., Fr........E6 59
Moselle, riv., Fr.........C7 58
Moser River, N.S., Can........E7 151
Moses, lake, Wash.........B6 210
Moses Coulee, canyon, Wash.........B6 210
Moses Lake, Wash........B6 210
Mosgiel, N.Z........P13 112
Mosher, S. Dak........D5 204
Mosherville, N.S., Can........D6 151
Moshi, Tan........B6 106
Moshupa, Bots........B4 107
Mosier, Oreg........B5 201
Mosinee, Wis........D4 212
Mosjöen, Nor........E5 63
Moskee, Wyo........A8 213
Moskva, see Moscow, Sov. Un.
Moskva, riv., Sov. Un.........n17 72
Moso, isl., New Hebr.........115
Mosonmagyaróvár, Hung........B3 68
Mosquera, Col........C2 133
Mosquero, N. Mex........B6 195
Mosquito, Newf., Can........E5 152
Mosquito, creek, Iowa........C2 180
Mosquito, lagoon, Fla.........D6 174
Mosquito Coast, reg., Hond., Nic........D6 130
Mosquito Creek, res., Ohio........A7 199
Mosquitos, gulf, Pan.........F7 130
Moss, Miss........D4 188
Moss, Nor........H4, p28 63
Moss, Tenn........C8 205
Moss, mtn., Ark.........C3 169
Moss Glen, falls and chasm, Vt.........B3 208
Moss Landing, Calif........C6 170
Moss Point, Miss........E3, E5 188
Moss Vale, Austl........G8 112
Mossaka, Con........F3 104
Mossbank, Sask., Can........H3 155
Mossel Bay, S. Afr........D3 107
Mossendjo, Con........F2 104
Mossleigh, Alta., Can........D4 148
Mossoró, Braz........C3 138
Mossville, Ark........B2 169
Mossy, riv., Man., Can.........D2 150
Mossy, river, Sask., Can.........C4 155
Mossy Head, Fla........G2 174
Mossyrock, Wash........C3 210
Most, Czech........C2 70
Mostaganem, Alg........B5 102
Mostar, Yugo........D3 68
Móstoles, Sp........p17 65
Mosul, Iraq........D14 85
Mota, isl., New Hebr.........115
Motagua, riv., Guat.........C3 130
Motala, Swe........H6 63
Motatán, Ven........B3 133
Mothe, isl., Fiji........114
Motherwell [& Wishaw], Scot........E5 57
Motihari, India........D10 88
Motilla del Palancar, Sp........C5 65
Motley, Minn........D4 187
Motley, co., Tex........B2 206
Moto, see Oshima, Jap.
Moto, mtn., Iwo........114
Motombo-Mukulu, Zaire........C3 106
Motril, Sp........D4 65
Motrul, riv., Rom.........C6 68
Motsa, Isr........h11 84
Mott, N. Dak........C3 198
Motueka, N.Z........N14 112
Motuhora, N.Z........M16 112
Motul [de Felipe Carrillo Puerto], Mex........C7 129
Motupe, Peru........C2 134
Moturiki, isl., Fiji........114
Mouchoir, passage, Ba. Is.........E8 131
Moúdhros (Mudros), Grc........C5 69
Moudjéria, Maur........C2 103
Moudon, Switz........C2 66
Mougu, see Maug, is., Mariana Is.
Moulins, Fr........D5 58
Moúlki, Grc........g10 69
Moulmein, Bur........E10 87, D2 89
Moulouya, riv., Mor.........C4 102
Moulton, Ala........A2 166
Moulton, Iowa........D5 180
Moulton, Tex........*E4 206
Moultonboro, N.H........C4 193
Moultonville, N.H........C4 193
Moultrie, Ga........E3 175
Moultrie, co., Ill........D5 178
Moultrie, lake, S.C.........E7 203
Mound, Minn........F5 187
Mound Bayou, Miss........B3 188
Mound City, Ill........F4 178
Mound City, Kans........D9 181
Mound City, Mo........A2 189
Mound City, S. Dak........B5 204
Mound City Group, nat. mon., Ohio........C4 199
Mound Valley, Kans........E8 181
Moundou, Chad........D3 104
Moundridge, Kans........D6 181
Mounds, Ill........F4 178
Mounds, Okla........B5 200
Mounds View, Minn........*E5 187
Moundsville, W. Va........B2, B4 211
Moundville, Ala........C2 166
Moundville, Mo........D3 189
Mounier, mtn., Fr.........E7 58
Mount Abu, India........E4 88
Mount Airy, Ga........B3 175
Mount Airy, Md........B3 173
Mount Airy, N.J........C3 194
Mount Airy, N.C........A3 197
Mount Airy, Tenn........D8 205
Mount Airy, Va........E3 209
Mount Albert, Ont., Can........C5 153
Mount Andrew, Ala........D4 166
Mount Angel, Oreg........B2, B4 201
Mount Arlington, N.J........B3 194
Mount Assiniboine, prov. park, B.C., Can.........D10 149
Mount Auburn, Ill........D4 178
Mount Auburn, Iowa........B5 180
Mount Ayr, Ind........C3 179
Mount Ayr, Iowa........D3 180
Mount Baldy, Calif........F3 170
Mount Barker, Austl........G2 112
Mount Berry, Ga........B1 175
Mount Bethel, N.J........B3 194
Mount Blanc, tunnel, Fr., It.........D2 66
Mount Blanchard, Ohio........B4 199
Mount Brydges, Ont., Can........E3 153
Mount Calvary, Wis........B5, E5 212
Mount Carmel, Ala........C3 166
Mount Carmel, Newf., Can........E5 152
Mount Carmel, Conn........D5 172
Mount Carmel, Fla........G2 174
Mount Carmel, Ill........E6 178
Mount Carmel, Ind........F8 179
Mount Carmel, N. Dak........A7 198
Mount Carmel, Ohio........D2 199
Mount Carmel, Pa........E9 202
Mount Carmel, S.C........C2 203
Mount Carmel, Utah........F3 207
Mount Carmel Junction, Utah........F3 207
Mount Carroll, Ill........A4 178
Mount Cenis, pass, Fr.........E7 58
Mount Clemens, Mich........A8, F8 186
Mount Clinton, Va........C4 209
Mount Cory, Ohio........B4 199
Mount Crawford, Va........C4 209
Mount Croghan, S.C........B7 203
Mount Darwin, Rh........A5 107
Mount Desert, isl., Maine........D4 184
Mount Dora, Fla........D5 174
Mount Dora, N. Mex........A6 195
Mount Eaton, Ohio........B6 199
Mount Eden, Ky........B4 182
Mount Edgecumbe, Alsk........m22 167
Mount Elgin, Ont., Can........E4 153
Mount Enterprise, Tex........D5 206
Mount Ephraim, N.J........*D2 194
Mount Erie, Ill........E5 178
Mount Etna, Ind........C6 179
Mount Etna, Iowa........C3 180
Mount Forest, Ont., Can........D4 153
Mount Gambier, Austl........H3 112
Mount Gilead, N.C........B4 197
Mount Gilead, Ohio........B5 199
Mount Hamilton, Calif........C6 170
Mount Healthy, Ohio........D2 199
Mount Hebron, Calif........B2 170
Mount Hermon, La........D5 183
Mount Heron, Va........B3 209
Mount Holly, Ark........D3 169
Mount Holly, N.J........D3 194
Mount Holly, N.C........B2 197
Mount Holly, S.C........E2, E7 203
Mount Holly, Vt........E3 208
Mount Holly Springs, Pa........F7 202
Mount Hood, Oreg........B5 201
Mount Hope, Ala........A2 166
Mount Hope, Austl........F5 112
Mount Hope, Ont., Can........D5 153
Mount Hope, Conn........B8 172
Mount Hope, Kans........B4, E6 181
Mount Hope, N.J........B3 194
Mount Hope, W. Va........D3, D7 211
Mount Hope, Wis........F3 212
Mount Hope, riv., Conn.........B8 172
Mount Horeb, Wis........E4 212
Mount Ida, Ark........C2 169
Mount Idaho, Idaho........C2 177
Mount Isa, Austl........D6 111
Mount Jackson, Va........C4 209
Mount Jewett, Pa........C4 202
Mount Joy, Iowa........D7 180
Mount Joy, Pa........F9 202
Mount Judea, Ark........B2 169
Mount Juliet, Tenn........A5 205
Mount Kisco, N.Y........D3, D7 196
Mount Laurel, N.J........D3 194
Mount Lebanon, Pa........F1 202
Mount Lookout, W. Va........D7 211
Mount Magnet, Austl........E2 111
Mount McKinley, nat. park, Alsk.........C9 167
Mount Meigs, Ala........C3 166
Mount Misery, pt., N.Y.........F4 172
Mount Montgomery, Nev........F3 192
Mount Morgan, Austl........A8 112
Mount Moriah, Mo........A4 189
Mount Morris, Ill........A4 178
Mount Morris, Mich........E7 186
Mount Morris, N.Y........C3 196
Mount Morris, Pa........G1 202
Mount Olive, Ala........B3, E4 166
Mount Olive, Ark........B3 169
Mount Olive, Ill........D4 178
Mount Olive, Miss........D4 188
Mount Olive, N.C........B5 197
Mount Olive, Tenn........E11 205
Mount Oliver, Pa........B6 202
Mount Olivet, Ky........B5 182
Mount Orab, Ohio........C4 199
Mount Penn, Pa........*F10 202
Mount Pinson, Ala........*B3 166
Mount Pisgah, Va........C4 209
Mount Pleasant, Ark........B4 169
Mount Pleasant, Del........A6 173
Mount Pleasant, Fla........B2 174
Mount Pleasant, Iowa........D6 180
Mount Pleasant, Md........B3 173
Mount Pleasant, Mich........E6 186
Mount Pleasant, Miss........A4 188
Mount Pleasant, N.J........B2 194
Mount Pleasant, N.C........B2 197
Mount Pleasant, Ohio........B1 211
Mount Pleasant, Pa........F2 202
Mount Pleasant, S.C........E3, F8 203
Mount Pleasant, Tenn........B4 205
Mount Pleasant, Tex........C5 206
Mount Pleasant, Utah........D4 207
Mount Pocono, Pa........D11 202
Mount Prospect, Ill........A6, E2 178
Mount Pulaski, Ill........C4 178
Mount Rainier, Md........C1 173
Mount Rainier, nat. park, Wash.........C4 210
Mount Revelstoke, nat. park, B.C., Can.........D8 149
Mount Robson, prov. park, B.C., Can.........C8 149
Mount Royal, N.J........D2 194
Mount Rushmore, nat. mem., S. Dak.........D2 204
Mount Savage, Md........D2 173
Mount Shasta, Calif........B2 170
Mount Sidney, Va........C4 209
Mount Solon, Va........C3 209
Mount Sterling, Ala........C1 166
Mount Sterling, Ill........D3 178
Mount Sterling, Ky........B6 182
Mount Sterling, Ohio........C4 199
Mount Stewart, P.E.I., Can........C7 151
Mount Storm, W. Va........B5 211
Mount Summit, Ind........D7 179
Mount Tabor, Vt........E3 208
Mount Uniacke, N.S., Can........E6 151
Mount Union, Iowa........C6 180
Mount Union, Pa........F6 202
Mount Upton, N.Y........C5 196
Mount Vernon, Ala........D1 166
Mount Vernon, Ark........B3 169
Mount Vernon, Ga........D4 175
Mount Vernon, Ill........E5 178
Mount Vernon, Ind........I2 179
Mount Vernon, Iowa........C6 180
Mount Vernon, Ky........C5 182
Mount Vernon, Maine........D3 184
Mount Vernon, Md........D6 173
Mount Vernon, Mo........D4 189
Mount Vernon, N.Y........*C2 196
Mount Vernon, N.Y........D2 196
Mount Vernon, Ohio........B5 199
Mount Vernon, Oreg........C7 201
Mount Vernon, S. Dak........D7 204
Mount Vernon, Tenn........D9 205
Mount Vernon, Tex........C5 206
Mount Vernon, Wash........A3 210
Mount Victory, Ohio........B4 199
Mount Viso, mtn., It.........E3 66
Mount Washington, Ky........A4, B4 182
Mount Washington, N.H........B4 193
Mount Wolf, Pa........F8 202
Mount Zion, Ga........C1 175
Mount Zion, Ill........*D5 178
Mountain, N. Dak........A8 198
Mountain, W. Va........B4 211
Mountain, Wis........C5 212
Mountain, lake, Sask., Can.........B3 155
Mountain Ash, Ky........D5 182
Mountain Brook, Ala........E5 166
Mountain City, Ga........B3 175
Mountain City, Nev........B6 192
Mountain City, Tenn........C12 205
Mountain Creek, Ala........C3 166
Mountain Dale, N.Y........D6 196
Mountain Grove, Ont., Can........C8 153
Mountain Grove, Mo........D5 189
Mountain Home, Ark........A3 169
Mountain Home, Idaho........F3 177
Mountain Home, Tex........D3 206
Mountain Home, Utah........C5 207
Mountain Home or Needle, mts., Utah........E2 207
Mountain Iron, Minn........C6 187
Mountain Lake, Minn........G4 187
Mountain Lake Park, Md........D1 173
Mountain Lakes, N.J........B4 194
Mountain Nile, see Bahr el Jèbel, riv., Sud.
Mountain Park, Alta., Can........C2 148
Mountain Park, Okla........C3 200
Mountain Pine, Ark........C2, C5 169
Mountain Point, Alsk........n24 167
Mountain Valley, Ark........C2 169
Mountain View, Ark........B3 169
Mountain View, Calif........B5 170
Mountain View, Alta., Can........E4 148
Mountain View, Colo........*B5 171
Mountain View, Ga........*C2 175
Mountain View, Idaho........*F2 177
Mountain View, Mo........D6 189
Mountain View, Okla........B3 200
Mountain View, Wyo........*C6 213
Mountain View, Wyo........D2 213
Mountain Village, Alsk........C7 167
Mountainair, N. Mex........C3 195
Mountainburg, Ark........B1 169
Mountainhome, Pa........D11 202
Mountainside, N.J........B4 194
Mountainview, Haw........D6 176
Mountforest, Mich........E6 186
Mountlake Terrace, Wash........*B3 210
Mountrail, co., N. Dak........A3 198
Mounts, bay, Eng.........D2 56
Mountville, Ga........C2 175
Mountville, Pa........*F9 202
Mountville, S.C........C4 203
Moura, Braz........D5 133
Moura, Port........C2 65
Mourdi, depression, Chad........B4 104
Mourmelon-le-Grand, Fr........E4 59
Mourne, mts., N. Ire.........F2 57
Mouscron, Bel........D3 59
Mouse Island, Newf., Can........E2 152
Mousie, Ky........C7 182
Moûtiers [-Tarentaise], Fr........E7 58
Mouton, isl., N.S., Can.........F5 151
Mouy, Fr........E2 59
Moville, Iowa........B1 180
Mowbullan, mtn., Austl.........C8 112
Moweaqua, Ill........D5 178
Mower, co., Minn........G6 187
Mowich, Oreg........D5 201
Mowrystown, Ohio........C4 199
Moxahala, Ohio........C5 199
Moxee City, Wash........C5 210
Moxico, dist., Ang........D3 106
Moxie, pond, Maine........C3 184
Moxley, Ga........D4 175
Moyālē, Eth........E4 105
Moyale, Ken........A6 106
Moyamba, S.L........E2 103
Moyers, Okla........C6 200
Moyeuvre-Grande, Fr........E6 59
Moyie, range, B.C., Can.........E9 149
Moyie Springs, Idaho........A2 177
Moyobamba, Peru........C2 134
Moyock, N.C........A7 197
Moyuta, Guat........C2 130
MOZAMBIQUE, Port. dep., Afr........B5 107
Mozambique, chan., Afr.........g8 107
Mozart, Sask., Can........F3 155
Mozdok, Sov. Un........E2 73
Mozhaysk, Sov. Un........D11 72
Mozyr, Sov. Un........E7 72
Mpanda, Tan........C5 106
Mpika, Zambia........D5 106
Mporokoso, Zambia........C5 106
Mpouia, Con........F3 104
Mpulungu, Zambia........C5 106
Mpwapwa, Tan........C6 106
Mrągowo, Pol........B6 70
M'Raïer, Alg........C6 102
Mrewa, Rh........A5 107
Mšec, Czech........n16 70
Mšené, Czech........n17 70
M'Sila, Alg........B5 102
Msta, riv., Sov. Un.........D14 40
Mstislavl, Sov. Un........D8 72
Mtakuja, Tan........C5 106
Mtoko, Rh........A5 107
Mtorashanga, Rh........A5 107
Mtsensk, Sov. Un........E11 72
Mtubatuba, S. Afr........C5 107
Mtwara, Tan........D7 106
Muang Fang, Thai........C3 89
Muang Hot, Thai........C3 89
Muang Nan, Thai........C4 89
Muari, cape, Pak.........I13 86
Mubi, Nig........D7 103
Mucajaí, riv., Braz.........C5 133
Much Wenlock, Eng........B5 56
Mücheln, Ger........B6 61
Muchkap, Sov. Un........F14 72
Muck, isl., Scot.........D2 57
Muckalee, creek, Ga.........D2 175
Muckleshoot, Indian res., Wash.........D2 210
Mucuburi, Moz........D6 106
Mucuri, Braz........E3 138
Mucuri, riv., Braz.........E2 138
Mucusso, Ang........E3 106
Mud, creek, Ala.........E4 166
Mud, creek, Ga.........B5 175
Mud, creek, Iowa........A7 180
Mud, creek, Okla.........C4 200
Mud, lake, Maine........A4 184
Mud, lake, Minn.........C5 187
Mud, lake, Nev.........B2 192
Mud, lake, Nev.........C2 192
Mud, riv., Minn.........B3 187
Mud, riv., W. Va.........C2 211
Mud Butte, S. Dak........C3 204
Mud Lake, Idaho........F6 177
Mud Lick, creek, Ky.........A6 182
Mudanya, Tur........B7 69
Mudawwarah, Jordan........E8 84
Muddo Gashi, Ken........A6 106
Muddy, Ill........F5 178
Muddy, creek, Colo.........A4 171
Muddy, creek, Kans.........B7 181
Muddy, creek, Ky.........D2 182
Muddy, creek, Wyo.........B4 213
Muddy, creek, Wyo.........C6 213
Muddy, creek, Wyo.........D2 213
Muddy, creek, Wyo.........D5 213
Muddy, fork, Ind.........A3 182
Muddy, lake, Sask., Can.........E1 155
Muddy, mtn., Wyo.........C6 213
Muddy, mts., Nev.........G7 192
Muddy, peak, Nev.........G7 192
Muddy, riv., Utah........E4 207
Muddy Boggy, creek, Okla.........C6 200
Muddy Creek, mtn., Ark.........C2 169
Müden, Ger........F4 62
Mudgee, Austl........F7 112
Mudjatik, riv., Sask., Can.........A2 155
Mudon, Bur........E10 87
Mudros, see Moúdhros, Grc.
Mudugh, dist., Som........D6 105
Mueda, Mos........D6 106
Muenster, Sask., Can........E3 155
Muenster, Tex........C4 206
Mueo, N. Cal........115
Mueo, pass, N. Cal.........115
Muertos, isl., P.R.........D4 132
Mufu, pt., Santa Isabel I.........115
Mufulira, Zambia........D4 106
Mugallala, creek, Austl.........D6 112
Mugía, Sp........A1 65
Muğla, Tur........D7 69
Muglad, Sud........C2 105
Mugodzhary, mts., Sov. Un.........D5 73
Mugulo, Pap........k11 111
Mugwump, lake, Oreg.........E7 201
Muhammad Qol, Sud........A4 105
Muhammadābād, Iran........C9 86
Muheza, Tan........C6 106
Muhinga, Burundi........B5 106
Mühlacker, Ger........E3 61
Mühldorf, Ger........D6 60
Muhlenberg, co., Ky........C2 182
Mühlhausen, Ger........B5 61
Mühlig-Hoffmann, mts., Ant.........B13 120

INDEX KEY Each place listed in **Bold-faced Type** has its population listed in the Population tables, pages 230 to 280.
Each country, shown in CAPITAL LETTERS, has its population listed in the World Political Information Table, pages 6 to 10.
* Does not appear on map; key shows general location.

Muhutwe, Tan. B5 106
Mui, isl., Eniwetok 114
Mui Bai Bung, pt., Viet. H6 89
Mui Ron, cape, Viet. C7 89
Mui Vung Tau, cape, Viet. G7 89
Muir, Mich. E6 186
Muir Woods, nat. mon., Calif. B5 170
Muirkirk, Md. B4 173
Muirkirk, Scot. E4 57
Mukachëvo, Sov. Un. G4 72
Mukah, Mala. E4 90
Mukden (Shenyang), China C9 91, D10 92
Mukeru, Palau 114
Mukho, Kor. H4 93
Mukilteo, Wash. B3 210
Mukutawa, riv., Man., Can. C3 150
Mukwonago, Wis. F1, F5 212
Mula, Sp. C5 65
Mulas, pt., P.R. g13 132
Mulat, isl., Yugo. C2 68
Mulberry, Ark. B1 169
Mulberry, Calif. *C3 170
Mulberry, Fla. E4 174
Mulberry, Ind. D4 179
Mulberry, Kans. E9 181
Mulberry, Ohio C3 199
Mulberry, Tenn. B5 205
Mulberry, fork, Ala. B3 166
Mulberry, mtn., Ark. B3 169
Mulberry, riv., Ark. B2 169
Mulberry Grove, Ill. E4 178
Mulchén, Chile B2 136
Mulde, riv., Ger. B7 61
Muldoon, Tex. E4 206
Muldraugh, Ky. C4 182
Muldrow, Okla. B7 200
Mule, creek, Kans. E4 181
Mule Creek, N. Mex. D1 195
Mule Creek, Wyo. B8 213
Mulegé, Mex. B2 129
Muleng, China D5 93
Muleng, riv., China D6 93
Muleshoe, Tex. B1 206
Mulga, Ala. B3, E4 166
Mulgrave, N.S., Can. D8 151
Mulgrave, isl., Austl. B7 110
Mulhacén, mtn., Sp. D4 65
Mulhall, Okla. A4 200
Mülheim [an der Ruhr], Ger. B1 61
Mulhouse, Fr. D7 58, B3 66
Muliama, New Ire. I. 115
Mulino, Oreg. B2, B4 201
Mulitapuili, cape, W. Sam. 114
Mull, head, Scot. B6 57
Mull, isl., Scot. D2 57
Mull, sound, Scot. D2 57
Mullaghareirk, mts., Ire. D2 55
Mullan, Idaho B3 177
Mullan, pass, Mont. D4 190
Mullen, Nebr. B4 191
Mullens, W. Va. D3 211
Müller, mts., Indon. E4 90
Mullet, key, Fla. F1 174
Mullet, lake, Mich. C6 186
Mullet, pen., Ire. C1 55
Mullet, riv., Wis. B6 212
Mullewa, Austl. E2 111
Müllheim, Ger. E3 60
Mullica, riv., N.J. D3 194
Mullica Hill, N.J. D2 194
Mulliken, Mich. F6 186
Mullin, Tex. D3 206
Mullingar, Ire. D3 55
Mullins, S.C. C9 203
Mullinville, Kans. E4 181
Müllrose, Ger. A9 61
Mulobezi, Zambia E4 106
Mulseryd, Swe. A7 62
Multān, Pak. B5 87, B3 88
Multnomah, co., Oreg. B4 201
Mulvane, Kans. E6 181
Mulvihill, Man., Can. D2 150
Mumbwa, Zambia D4 106
Mummy, range, Colo. A5 171
Mun, riv., Thai. D5 89
Muna, Mex. C7 129
Münchberg, Ger. C6 61
München, see Munich, Ger.
Muncie, Ind. D7 179
Muncy, Pa. D8 202
Muncy Valley, Pa. D8 202
Mundare, Alta., Can. C4 148
Munday, Tex. C3 206
Mundelein, Ill. A5, E2 178
Münden, Ger. B4 61
Munden, Kans. C6 181
Mundi Mundi, Vella Lavella I. 115
Mundua, isl., Bis. Arch. 115
Munford, Ala. B4 166
Munford, Tenn. B2 205
Munfordville, Ky. C4 182
Mungana, Austl. C7 111
Mungari, Moz. A5 107
Mungbere, Zaire A4 106
Munger, Mich. E7 186
Mungindi, Austl. D7 112
Munhall, Pa. B6 202
Munich (München), Ger. D5 60, A7 66
Munich, N. Dak. A7 198
Munising, Mich. B4 186
Munith, Mich. F6 186
Munjor, Kans. D4 181
Munnsville, N.Y. C5 196
Muñoz, Phil. o13 90
Muñoz Gamero, pen., Chile h11 136
Munsan, Kor. H3 93
Munsey Park, N.Y. *E3 196
Münsingen, Ger. E4 61
Munson, Alta., Can. D4 148
Munson, Fla. G2 174
Munson, Pa. E5 202
Munsonville, N.H. D2 193
Munster, Fr. C7 58
Munster, Ger. B5 60
Munster, Ind. A2 179
Münster [in Westfalen], Ger. B2 61
Münstereifel, Ger. C1 61
Munsungan, lake, Maine B3 184
Muntenia, reg., Rom. C7 68
Muntok, Indon. F3 90
Munuscong, lake, Mich. B6 186
Muong Hou Nua, Laos A4 89
Muong Hou Tai, Laos A4 89
Muong Hun Xieng Hung, Laos B5 89
Muong Lane, Laos C5 89
Muong May, Laos E7 89
Muong Phalane, Laos D6 89
Muong Sing, Laos B4 89
Muong Soui, Laos C5 89
Muong Sung, Laos B5 89
Muonio, Fin. D10 63
Muonio, riv., Fin. D10 63
Muqdadiyah, Iraq E2 86
Mur, riv., Aus. E7 60
Mura, riv., Yugo. B3 68
Murakami, Jap. G9 93
Murano, It. D8 66
Murashi, Sov. Un. B3 73
Murat, Fr. E5 58
Murat, mtn., Tur. C7 69
Murat, riv., Tur. C13 85
Murau, Aus. E7 60
Muravera, It. E2 67
Muravyevo, Sov. Un. C11 93
Mürcheh Khvort, Iran E5 86
Murchison, N.Z. N14 112
Murchison, falls, Ug. A5 106
Murchison, riv., Austl. E2 110
Murcia, Sp. C5 65
Murcia, reg., Sp. C5 65
Murcki, Pol. g10 70
Murdab, bay, Iran C4 86
Murderkill, riv., Del. B7 173
Murdo, S. Dak. D5 204
Murdock, Fla. F4 174
Murdock, Kans. B4, E6 181
Murdock, Minn. E3 187
Murdock, Nebr. E2 191
Muresul, riv., Rom. B7 68
Muret, Fr. F4 58
Murfreesboro, Ark. C2 169
Murfreesboro, N.C. A6 197
Murfreesboro, Tenn. B5 205
Murgha Kibzai, Pak. B4 87, B2 88
Murghab, riv., Afg. D12 86
Murgon, Austl. C8 112
Muri, Nig. E7 103
Muriaé, Braz. C4 137
Murici, Braz. k6 138
Muriel, lake, Alta., Can. B5 148
Müritz, lake, Ger. B6 60
Murmansk, Sov. Un. C15 63
Murnau, Ger. B7 66
Murom, Sov. Un. B2 73
Muroran, Jap. E10 93
Muros, Sp. A1 65
Muroto, cape, Jap. J7 93
Murphy, Idaho F2 177
Murphy, Mo. B7 189
Murphy, N.C. D2 197
Murphy, Oreg. E3 201
Murphy, isl., S.C. E9 203
Murphy, lake, B.C., Can. C7 149
Murphysboro, Ill. F4 178
Murphytown, W. Va. B3 211
Murray, Idaho B3 177
Murray, Iowa C4 180
Murray, Ky. B3 182
Murray, Nebr. D10, E3 191
Murray, Utah C4 207
Murray, co., Ga. B2 175
Murray, co., Minn. F3 187
Murray, co., Okla. C4 200
Murray, head, P.E.I., Can. C7 151
Murray, lake, Okla. C4 200
Murray, lake, S.C. C5 203
Murray, riv., Austl. G2 112
Murray, riv., B.C., Can. B7 149
Murray Bridge, Austl. G2 112
Murray City, Ohio C5 199
Murray Harbour, P.E.I., Can. D7 151
Murray River, P.E.I., Can. C7 151
Murraysville, W. Va. B3 211
Murrayville, B.C., Can. B10 149
Murrayville, Ga. B3 175
Murrayville, Ill. D3 178
Murrells, inlet, S.C. D10 203
Murrells Inlet, S.C. D9 203
Murrhardt, Ger. E4 61
Murrieta, Calif. F5 170
Murrumbidgee, riv., Austl. G5 112
Murrupula, Moz. A6 107
Murrysville, Pa. B7 202
Murska Sobota, Yugo. B3 68
Murtaugh, Idaho G4 177
Murtle, lake, B.C., Can. C8 149
Murua, is., Pap. k13 110
Murud, India H4 88
Murwillumbah, Austl. D9 112
Mürz, riv., Aus. E7 60
Murzynowo, Pol. F8 62
Mürzzuschlag, Aus. E7 60
Muş, Tur. C13 85
Musa Qal'a, Afg. E12 86
Musala, isl., Indon. L3 89
Musala, peak, Bul. D6 68
Musan, Kor. E4 93
Musangoi, Zaire C3 106
Musāsh as Sirr (Oasis), Eg. D5 84
Musashino, Jap. *I9 93
Muscat, Oman D2 87
Muscat & Oman, see Oman, country, Asia
Muscatatuck, riv., Ind. G5 179
Muscatine, Iowa C6 180
Muscatine, co., Iowa C6 180
Muscle Shoals, Ala. A2 166
Musclow, mtn., B.C., Can. C4 149
Muscoda, Wis. E3 212
Muscogee, co., Ga. D2 175
Musconetcong, mtn., N.J. B2 194
Musconetcong, riv., N.J. B3 194
Muscotah, Kans. A7, C8 181
Muse, Okla. C7 200
Muse, Pa. F1 202
Musgrave, ranges, Austl. E5 110
Musgrave Harbour, Newf., Can. D5 152
Musgravetown, Newf., Can. D5 152
Mushāsh Abū Khawf (Oasis), Eg. E6 84
Mushie, Zaire B2 106
Mushin, Nig. E5 103
Mushketovo, Sov. Un. r20 72
Musi, riv., Indon. F2 90
Muskeget, chan., Mass. D7 185
Muskeget, isl., Mass. D7 185
Muskego, Wis. F1 212
Muskego, lake, Wis. F1 212
Muskegon, Mich. E4 186
Muskegon, co., Mich. E4 186
Muskegon, lake, Mich. E4 186
Muskegon, riv., Mich. D4 186
Muskegon Heights, Mich. E4 186
Muskingum, co., Ohio B6 199
Muskingum, riv., Ohio C6 199
Muskö, Swe. u36 63
Muskogee, Okla. B6 200
Muskogee, co., Okla. B6 200
Muskoka, co., Ont., Can. B5 153
Muskoka, lake, Ont., Can. C5 153
Muskrat, creek, Wyo. B5 213
Muskwa, riv., Alta., Can. A3 148
Musmâr, Sud. B4 105
Musoma, Tan. B5 106
Musquacook, lakes, Maine B3 184
Musquaro, lake, Que., Can. h9 152
Musquash, N.B., Can. D3 151
Musquash, mtn., Maine C5 184
Musquodoboit Harbour, N.S., Can. E6 151
Mussau, isl., Bis. Arch. 115
Musselburgh, Scot. E5 57
Musselshell, Mont. D8 190
Musselshell, co., Mont. D8 190
Musselshell, riv., Mont. D9 190
Mussende, Ang. D2 106
Mussidan, Fr. E4 58
Mussoorie, India B6 88
Mustafa Kemalpaşa, Tur. B7 85
Mustang, Okla. B4 200
Mustang, draw, Tex. C1 206
Musters, lake, Arg. D3 136
Mustinka, riv., Minn. E2 187
Mustvee, Sov. Un. B6 72
Musumusu, W. Sam. 114
Muswellbrook, Austl. F8 112
Mūt, Eg. D5 101
Mut, Tur. D9 85
Mutá, pt., Braz. D3 138
Mutan, riv., China D4 93
Mutanchiang, China C10 91, D4 93
Mutarara, Moz. A5 107
Mutayyin, Yemen (Ṣan'ā'). B5 105
Mutcho, pt., Saipan 114
Mutena, Zaire C3 106
Mutok, hbr., Ponape 114
Mutsu, bay, Jap. F10 93
Mutton, mts., Oreg. C5 201
Mutton Bay, Que., Can. C2, h10 152
Muttontown, N.Y. *F2 172
Mutual, Okla. A2 200
Mutupina, pt., Bougainville I. 114
Mutzig, Fr. F7 59
Muxima, Ang. C1 106
Muynak, Sov. Un. E5 73
Muyunkum, des., Sov. Un. E7 73
Muz Tagh, mtn., China F11 71
Muzaffargarh, Pak. B3 88
Muzaffarnagar, India *C6 88
Muzaffarpur, India C8 87, D10 88
Muzambinho, Braz. k8 137
Muzon, cape, Alsk. n23 167
Mwambo, Tan. D7 106
Mwanza, Tan. B5 106
Mwaya, Tan. C5 106
Mweka, Zaire B3 106
Mwene-Ditu, Zaire C3 106
Mwenga, Zaire B4 106
Mweru, lake, Zaire, Zambia C4 106
Mwimba, Zaire C3 106
Mwinilunga, Zambia D3 106
My Tho, Viet. G7 89
Myakka, riv., Fla. E4 174
Myakka City, Fla. E4 174
Myaungmya, Bur. D1 89
Mycenae, ruins, Grc. D4 69
Myers, Mont. D9 190
Myers, S.C. F3 203
Myerstown, Pa. F9 202
Myersville, Md. A2 173
Myingyan, Bur. D10 87
Myitkyina, Bur. C10 87
Myitnge, riv., Bur. B2 89
Myjava, Czech. D4 70
Mylo, N. Dak. A6 198
Mymensingh, Bngl. D9 87, E13 88
Myn-Aral, Sov. Un. D8 73
Mynard, Nebr. E3 191
Myrick, Miss. D5 188
Myrnam, Alta., Can. C5 148
Myrtle, Man., Can. E3 150
Myrtle, Ont., Can. C6 153
Myrtle, Minn. G5 187
Myrtle, Miss. A4 188
Myrtle, Mo. E6 189
Myrtle, Va. B6 209
Myrtle Beach, Conn. E4 172
Myrtle Beach, S.C. D10 203
Myrtle Creek, Oreg. D3 201
Myrtle Grove, Fla. G2 174
Myrtle Point, Oreg. D2 201
Myrtlewood, Ala. C2 166
Mysen, Nor. p29 63
Mysia: c. 450 B.C. 42
Myślenice, Pol. D5 70
Myślibórz, Pol. B3 70
Mysłowice, Pol. g10 70
Mysore, India F6 87
Mysore, state, India F6 87
c. 1775 82
Mystic, Conn. D9 172
Mystic, Ga. E3 175
Mystic, Iowa D5 180
Mystic, lakes, Mass. C2 185
Mytilene, see Mitilíni, Grc.
Mytishchi, Sov. Un. n17 72
Myton, Utah C5 207
Mže, riv., Czech. D8 61
Mzimba, Malawi D5 106
Mzuzu, Malawi D5 106

N

Na Cham, Viet. A7 89
Na Puu Kulua, paek, Haw. D6 176
Naab, riv., Ger. D7 61
Naalehu, Haw. D6 176
Na'an, Isr. h10 84
Naantali, Fin. G10 63
Naas, Ire. D3 55
Nabadwip, India *D8 87
Nabberu, lake, Austl. E3 110
Nabburg, Ger. D7 61
Nabesna, Alsk. C11 167
Nabeul, Tun. B7 102
Nabnasset, Mass. *A5 185
Naboomspruit, S. Afr. B4 107
Nabq, Eg. H10 85
Nabua, Phil. *C6 90
Nābulus, Jordan B7, g12 84
Nacala, Moz. D7 106
Nacaome, Hond. D4 130
Nacfa, Eth. B4 105
Naches, Wash. C5 210
Nachingwea, Tan. D6 106
Nachod, Czech. C4 70
Nacimiento, Chile B2 136
Nacimiento, res., Calif. E3 170
Nackawic, N.B., Can. *C2 151
Nacmine, Alta., Can. D4 148
Naco, Ariz. F6 168
Nacogdoches, Tex. D5 206
Nacogdoches, co., Tex. D5 206
Nacozari, Mex. A3 129
Nadarzyn, Pol. m13 70
Nadeau, Mich. C3 186
Naden, hbr., B.C., Can. B1 149
Nadiad, India F4 88
Nadir, Vir. Is. f15 132
Nadlac, Rom. B5 68
Nadvornaya, Sov. Un. G5 72
Nady, Ark. D4 169
Naesŏng, Kor. H4 93
Naestved, Den. C5 62
Naf, Idaho G5 177
Nafada, Nig. D7 103
Nafishah, Eg. D4 84
Nafutan, mtn., Saipan 114
Nafutan, pt., Saipan 114
Naga, Phil. C6 90
Naga, hills, Bur., India C10 87
Nagano, Jap. H9 93
Nagaoka, Jap. H9 93
Nagapattinam, India F6 87
Nagar-Parkar, Pak. E3 88
Nagarote, Nic. D4 130
Nagasaki, Jap. J4 93
Nagaur, India C5 88
Nagcarlan, Phil. o13 90
Nagchhu Dzong, China E3 91
Nageezi, N. Mex. A2 195
Nagelê, Eth. D4 105
Nagercoil, India G6 87
Naggar, India A6 88
Nago, Okinawa 114
Nago, bay, Okinawa 114
Nagog, pond, Mass. C1 185
Nagold, Ger. E3 61
Nagoya, Jap. I8, n15 93
Nagpur, India D6 87, G7 88
Nags Head, N.C. B8 197
Naguabo, P.R. C8, g12 132
Naguabo, mun., P.R. C7, g11 132
Naguilian, Phil. n13 90
Nagykanizsa, Hung. B3 68
Nagykőrös, Hung. B4 68
Naha, Okinawa 114
Nahalat Yehuda, Isr. h10 84
Nahant, Mass. C3 185
Nahariya, Isr. A7 84
Nahe, riv., Ger. D2 61
Nahma, Mich. C4 186
Nahmakanta, lake, Maine C3 184
Nahr al Khābūr, riv., Syr. E13 85
Nahr el Harir, riv., Syr. B7 84
Nahuel Huapí, Arg. C2 136
Nahuel Huapí, lake, Arg. C2 136
Nahuel Niyeu, Arg. C3 136
Nahuelquir, Arg. C3 136
Nahunta, Ga. E5 175
Naiau, isl., Fiji 114
Naic, Phil. o13 90
Naicam, Sask., Can. E3 155
Naihati, India *F12 88
Naila, Ger. C6 61
Nain, Newf., Can. g9 152
Nā'īn, Iran E6 86
Naingoro, pass, Fiji 114
Naini-Tal, India C7 88
Nairai, isl., Fiji 114
Nairn, Scot. C5 57
Nairn, co., Scot. C5 57
Nairn, riv., Scot. C4 57
Nairobi, Ken. B6 106
Naivasha, Ken. B6 106
Najibabad, India C7 88
Najin, Kor. E5 93
Nakadōri, isl., Jap. J4 93
Nakagusuku, bay, Okinawa 114
Nakalau, Fiji 114
Nak'amet, Eth. D4 105
Nakaminto, Jap. m19 93
Nakamura, Jap. J6 93
Nakanai, mts., New Britain I. 115
Nakano, isl., Jap. L4 93
Nakatsu, Jap. J5 93
Nakatsu, see Ena, Jap.
Nakaushi, Okinawa 114
Nakchak, China B9 88
Nakety, bay, Loyalty Is. 115
Nakhichevan na Arakse, Sov. Un. F3 73
Nakhodka, Sov. Un. E6 93
Nakhon Pathom, Thai. F4 89
Nakhon Ratchasima, Thai. E5 89
Nakhon Sawan, Thai. E4 89
Nakhon Si Thammarat, Thai. H3 89
Nakhrachi, Sov. Un. B7 73
Nakina, N.C. C5 197
Nakiri, Jap. o15 93
Nakło, Pol. B4 70
Naknek, Alsk. D8 167
Naknek, lake, Alsk. D8 167
Nakorokoro, pt., Fiji 114
Nakskov, Den. D5 62
Nakuru, Ken. B6 106
Nakusp, B.C., Can. D9 149
Nal, riv., Pak. H12 86
Nal'chik, Sov. Un. E2 73
Nallen, W. Va. C4, D7 211
Nalón, riv., Sp. A2 65
Naloto, Fiji 114
Nālūt, Libya C2 101
Nam (Tengri), lake, China E3 91
Nam Dinh, Viet. B7 89
Namai, bay, Palau Is. 114
Namaka, Alta., Can. D4 148
Namakan, lake, Minn. B6 187
Namangan, Sov. Un. E8 73
Namanock, isl., N.J. A3 194
Namanyere, Tan. C5 106
Namapa, Moz. D6 106
Namasgali, Ug. A5 106
Namatanai, New Ire. I. 115
Nambe, N. Mex. B4, F6 195
Nambe, Indian res., N. Mex. F6 195
Nambour, Austl. C9 112
Namcha Barwa, mtn., China F4 91
Nämdö, isl., Swe. t36 63
Namekagon, lake, Wis. B2 212
Namekagon, riv., Wis. B2 212
Nametil, Moz. A6 107
Namew, lake, Man., Sask., Can. B1 150, C5 155
Namib, des., S.W. Afr. B1 107
Namiquipa, Mex. B3 129
Namlea, Indon. F7 90
Namoi, riv., Austl. E7 112
Namoli, Fiji 114
Namorik, atoll, Marshall Is. 115
Nampa, Alta., Can. A2 148
Nampa, Idaho F2 177
Nampala, Mali C3 103
Nampo, see Chinnampo, Kor.
Nampula, Moz. A6 107
Namsen, riv., Nor. E4 63
Namsos, Nor. E4 63
Namu, atoll, Marshall Is. 115
Namu, isl., Bikini 114
Namua, isl., W. Sam. 114
Namur, Bel. D4 59
Namur, Que., Can. D3 154
Namur, prov., Bel. D4 59
Namur, isl., Kwajalein 114
Namuruputh, Sud. E4 105
Namutoni, S. W. Afr. A2 107
Namwala, Zambia E4 106
Namwŏn, Kor. I3 93
Namysłów, Pol. C4 70
Nan, riv., Thai. C4 89
Nan Chao (T'ai) Empire: c. 750 80
Nan Shan, mts., China D4 91
Nana, riv., Cen. Afr. Rep. D3 104
Nanafalia, Ala. C2 166
Nanaimo, B.C., Can. A8, E5 149
Nanakuli, Haw. B3, g9 176
Nanam, Kor. F4 93
Nanango, pt., Choiseul I. 115
Nanao, Jap. H8 93
Nanatsu, isl., Jap. H8 93
Nanawan, riv., Man., Can. C3 150
Nance, co., Nebr. C7 191
Nanchang, China I4 92
Nanchang, China J6 92
Nancheng, China K7 92
Nanchuan, China J2 92
Nanchung, China I2 92
Nancy, Fr. C7 58, F6 59
Nancy, Ky. C5 182
Nancy, creek, Ga. A5 175
Nanda Devi, peak, India B7 88
Nander, India H6 88
Nandurbar, India G5 88
Nanduri, Fiji 114
Nanfeng, China K7 92
Nang Rong, Thai. E5 89
Nanga-Eboko, Cam. E2 104
Nanga Parbat, peak, India A5 87
Nangis, Fr. F3 59
Nani, Afg. E14 86
Nanjemoy, Md. D3 173
Nankapenparam, reef, Ponape 114
Nankin, Ohio B5 199
Nanking, China E8 91, H8 92
Nankipooh, Ga. D2 175
Nankou, pass, China D7 92
Nankung, China F6 92
Nannine, Austl. E2 111
Nanning, China G6 91
Nanoose Bay, B.C., Can. A8 149
Nanping, China K8 92
Nansemond, Va. B6 209
Nansemond, co., Va. E6 209
Nansemond, riv., Va. B6 209
Nansio, Tan. B5 106
Nanson, N. Dak. A6 198
Nantasket Beach, Mass. B6 185
Nantel, Que., Can. C3 154
Nanterre, Fr. g9 58
Nantes, Fr. D3 58
Nanteuil-le-Haudouin, Fr. E2 59
Nanticoke, Ont., Can. E4 153
Nanticoke, Md. D6 173
Nanticoke, Pa. B7, D10 202
Nanticoke, riv., Del., Md. D6 173
Nantien, China J9 92
Nanton, Alta., Can. D4 148
Nantua, Fr. D6 58
Nantucket, Mass. D7 185
Nantucket, co., Mass. D7 185
Nantucket, isl., Mass. D7 185
Nantucket, sound, Mass. C7 185
Nantung, China H9 92
Nantuxent, pt., N.J. E2 194
Nantwich, Eng. A5 56
Nanty Glo, Pa. F4 202
Nanuet, N.Y. D1 196
Nanuku, passage, Fiji 114
Nanuku, reef, Fiji 114
Nanyang, China H5 92
Nanyuki, Ken. A6 106
Nao, cape, Sp. C6 65
Naoli, riv., China C6 93
Naoma, W. Va. D6 211
Naomi, lake, Pa. A2 194
Náousa, Grc. B4 69
Napa, Calif. B5, C2 170
Napa, co., Calif. C2 170
Napa, riv., Calif. A5 170
Napadogan, N.B., Can. C3 151
Napakiak, Alsk. C7 167
Napakfok, bay, Newf., Can. f9 152
Napamute, Alsk. C8 167
Napanee, Ont., Can. C8 153
Napanoch, N.Y. D6 196
Napatree, pt., R.I. D9 172
Napavine, Wash. C3 210
Nape, Laos C6 89
Napeague, bay, N.Y. E8 172
Napeague, beach, N.Y. F8 172
Naper, Nebr. B6 191
Naperville, Ill. B5, F2 178
Napier, N.Z. M16 112
Napier, mts., Ant. C18 120
Napier Field, Ala. *D4 166
Napierville, Que., Can. D4 154
Napierville, co., Que., Can. D4 154
Napinka, Man., Can. E1 150
Naplate, Ill. *B5 178
Naples, Fla. F5 174
Naples, Idaho A2 177
Naples, Ill. D3 178
Naples (Napoli), It. D5 67
Naples, Maine E2 184
Naples, N.Y. C3 196
Naples, S. Dak. C8 204
Naples, Tex. C5 206
Naples, Utah C6 207
Naples, kingdom of: c. 1360 48
in 1714-35 49
in 1806-13 50
Naples, bay, It. D5 67
Napo, prov., Ec. B2 134
Napo, riv., Ec. B2 134
Napoleon, Ind. F7 179
Napoleon, Mo. B3 189
Napoleon, N. Dak. C6 198
Napoleon, Ohio A3 199
Napoleon's march on Moscow 50
Napoleonville, La. C5, E4 183
Napoli, see Naples, It.
Naponee, Nebr. D6 191
Napoopoo, Haw. D6 176
Nappanee, Ind. B5 179
Napton, Mo. B4 189
Naqura, Leb. A7 84
Nara, Jap. o14 93
Nara, Mali C3 103
Nara, canal, Pak. E2 88
Nara Vista, N. Mex. B6 195
Naracoorte, Austl. H3 112
Narage, isl., Bis. Arch. 115
Narai, Jap. n16 93
Naramata, B.C., Can. E8 149
Naranja, Fla. F3, G6 174

INDEX KEY Each place listed in **Bold-faced Type** has its population listed in the Population tables, pages 230 to 280.
Each country, shown in CAPITAL LETTERS, has its population listed in the World Political Information Table, pages 6 to 10.
* Does not appear on map; key shows general location.

Naranjito, P.R. B6 132
Naranjito, mun., P.R. B5 132
Nararu, mtn., Fiji 114
Narashino, Jap. *I10 93
Narata, Fiji 114
Nārāyanganj, Bngl. F13 88
Narayanpet, India I6 88
Narbada, riv., India F7 88
Narberth, Pa. B11, F11 202
Narberth, Wales C3 56
Narbonne, Fr. F5 58
Narborough, see Fernandina, isl., Ec.
Narcisse, Man., Can. D3 150
Narcoossee, Fla. D5 174
Nardin, Okla. A4 200
Nardò, It. D7 67
Nares, pt., Ont., Can. B4 153
Narew, riv., Pol. B6 70
Nariño, dept., Col. C2 133
Narita, Jap. n19 93
Narka, Kans. C6 181
Naro-Fominsk, Sov. Un. D11 72
Narodnaya, mtn., Sov. Un. C9 71
Narok, Ken. B6 106
Narrabri, Austl. E7 112
Narragansett, R.I. D11 172
Narragansett, bay, R.I. C11 172
Narraguagus, riv., Maine D5 184
Narrandera, Austl. G6 112
Narraway, riv., Alta., B.C., Can. B1 148, B8 149
Narrogin, Austl. F2 111
Narromine, Austl. F7 112
Narrows, Va. D2 209
Narrows, strait, N.Y. E5 194
Narrows, strait, Vir. Is. f16 132
Narrows, strait, Wash. D1 210
Narrowsburg, N.Y. D5 196
Narsinghpur, India F7 88
Naruna, Va. D3 209
Narva, Sov. Un. B7 72
Narvik, Nor. C7 63
Naryan Mar, Sov. Un. C8 71
Naryilco, Austl. D3 112
Naryn, Sov. Un. E9 73
Naryn, riv., Sov. Un. E9 73
Nasa Manned, spacecraft center, Tex. F5 206
Nasala, Fiji 114
Nasarawa, Nig. E6 103
Nasca, Peru D3 134
Naschitti, N. Mex. A1 195
Nase, Jap. F10 91
Naseby, N.Z. P13 112
Nash, N. Dak. A8 198
Nash, Okla. A3 200
Nash, Tex. C5 206
Nash, co., N.C. A6 197
Nash, pt., Wales C4 56
Nash, stream, N.H. A4 193
Nash Creek, N.B., Can. B3 151
Nashawena, isl., Mass. D6 185
Nashoba, Okla. C6 200
Nashoba, hill, Mass. C1 185
Nashotah, Wis. *E5 212
Nashua, Iowa B5 180
Nashua, Minn. D2 187
Nashua, Mont. B10 190
Nashua, N.H. E4 193
Nashua, riv., Mass., N.H. B4 185, E3 193
Nashville, Ark. D2 169
Nashville, Ga. E3 175
Nashville, Ill. E4 178
Nashville, Ind. F5 179
Nashville, Kans. E5 181
Nashville, Mich. F5 186
Nashville, N.C. B6 197
Nashville, Ohio B5 199
Nashville, Tenn. A5, E9 205
Nashwaak, riv., N.B., Can. C3 151
Nashwaaksis, N.B., Can. C3 151
Nashwauk, Minn. C5 187
Našice, Yugo. C4 68
Nasielsk, Pol. B6 70
Näsijärvi, lake, Fin. G10 63
Nasik, India E5 87, G4 88
Nasir, Sud. D3 105
Nāsiri, see Ahvāz, Iran
Naskaupi, riv., Newf., Can. g9 152
Naslini, Ariz. B6 168
Nason, Ill. E4 178
Nasonville, R.I. B10 172
Nass, riv., B.C., Can. B3 149
Nassau, Ba. Is. C5 131
Nassau, Minn. E2 187
Nassau, N.Y. C7 196
Nassau, country of: in 1866 51
Nassau, co., Fla. B5 174
Nassau, co., N.Y. E7 196
Nassau, gulf, Chile k12 136
Nassau, pt., N.Y. F7 172
Nassau, range, Indon. F9 90
Nassau, riv., Fla. B6 174
Nassau, sound, Fla. B5 174
Nassauville, Fla. B5, B6 174
Nassawadox, Va. D7 209
Nassawango, creek, Md. D7 173
Nasser, lake, Eg., Sud. E6 101
Nässjö, Swe. I6 63
Nasugbu, Phil. o13 90
Nasukoin, mtn., Mont. B2 190
Natá, Pan. F7 130
Natagaima, Col. C2 133
Natal, Braz. C3, g6 138
Natal, B.C., Can. E10 149
Natal, prov., S. Afr. C5 107
Natalbany, La. D5 183
Natalia, Tex. E3 206
Natanes, plat., Ariz. D5 168
Natashquan, Que., Can. F20 145
Natashquan, riv., Que., Can. h9 152
Natawahunan, lake, Man., Can. B3 150
Natchaug, riv., Conn. B8 172
Natchez, Miss. D2 188
Natchitoches, La. C2 183
Natchitoches, par., La. C2 183
Natewa, bay, Fiji 114
Nathalie, Va. E4 209
Nathilau, pt., Fiji 114
Nathoula, isl., Fiji 114
Nathrop, Colo. C4 171
Natick, Mass. B5, D2 185
Natimuk, Austl. H3 112
Nation, lakes, B.C., Can. B5 149
National, Wash. C3 210
National, W. Va. A7, B4 211
National City, Calif. E2, F5 170
National City, Ill. *E3 178
National City, Mich. D7 186
National Garden, Fla. C5 174
National Park, N.J. *D2 194
Natitingou, Dah. D5 103
Natividade, Braz. D1 138
Natívitas, Mex. h9 129
Natoma, Kans. C4 181
Natron, lake, Tan. B6 106
Natrona, co., Wyo. C6 213
Natrona Heights, Pa. A7, E2 202
Nattarö, isl., Swe. u36 63
Nattaung, mtn., Bur. C2 89
Nattaway, riv., Que., Can. B2 154
Natuna, isl., Indon. E3 90
Natural, bridge, Utah F3 207
Natural, bridge, Va. D3 209
Natural Bridge, Ala. A2 166
Natural Bridge, N.Y. A5 196
Natural Bridge, Va. D3 209
Natural Bridges, nat. mon., Utah F6 207
Natural Steps, Ark. D5 169
Naturaliste, cape, Austl. F2 110
Naturita, Colo. C2 171
Naubinway, Mich. B5 186
Naucalpan de Juárez, Mex. h9 129
Nauders, Aus. E5 60
Naudville, Que., Can. *A6 154
Nauen, Ger. B6 60
Naugatuck, Conn. D4 172
Naugatuck, riv., Conn. C4 172
Naughton, Ont., Can. A3 153
Naumburg [an der Saale], Ger. B6 61
Naumburg [in Hessen], Ger. B4 61
Nauna, isl., Bis. Arch. 115
Naunhof, Ger. B7 61
Naupe, Peru C2 134
NAURU, country, Oceania G10 113
Naushon, isl., Mass. D6 185
Nautla, Mex. C5, m15 129
Nauvoo, Ala. B2 166
Nauvoo, Ill. C2 178
Nauwigewauk, N.B., Can. D4 151
Nava, lake, Sp. A3 65
Nava del Rey, Sp. B3 65
Navahermosa, Sp. C3 65
Navajo, Ariz. B6 168
Navajo, co., Ariz. B5 168
Navajo, Indian res., Ariz. A4 168
Navajo, Indian res., N. Mex. C2 195
Navajo, mtn., Ariz. A5 168
Navajo, mtn., Utah F5 207
Navajo, nat. mon., Ariz. A5 168
Navajo, res., Colo., N. Mex. D3 171, A2 195
Navajo, riv., Colo. D3 171
Navalcarnero, Sp. B3, p16 65
Navalmoral de la Mata, Sp. C3 65
Navan, Ont., Can. A10, B9 153
Navarin, cape, Sov. Un. C20 71
Navarino, Wis. D5 212
Navarino, isl., Chile k12 136
Navarre, Ohio B6 199
Navarre, reg., Sp. A5 65
c. 1140 47
c. 1360 48
Navarro, Arg. B5, g7 136
Navarro, co., Tex. D4 206
Navas de Tolosa, Sp. C4 65
Navasota, Tex. D4 206
Navassa, N.C. C5 197
Navassa, isl., W.I. F6 131
Nave, isl., Scot. E2 57
Nävekvarn, Swe. u34 63
Naver, lake, Scot. B4 57
Naver, riv., Scot. B4 57
Navesink, N.J. C4 194
Navia, Arg. A3 136
Navia, riv., Sp. A2 65
Navidad, Chile A2 136
Navina, Okla. B4 200
Naviti, isl., Fiji 114
Navojoa, Mex. B3 129
Navola, Fiji 114
Navolato, Mex. C3 129
Navotas, Phil. *o13 90
Návpaktos, Grc. C3 69
Návplion, Grc. D4 69
Navrongo, Ghana D4 103
Navsari, India G4 88
Navy Yard City, Wash. *B3 210
Nawābshāh, Pak. C4 87, D2 88
Nawada, India E10 88
Náxos, Grc. D5 69
Náxos, isl., Grc. D5 69
Nay, Fr. F3 58
Näy Band, Iran E8 86
Näy Band, cape, Iran H6 86
Nayarit, state, Mex. C4, m11 129
Naylor, Ga. F3 175
Naylor, Mo. E7 189
Nayoro, Jap. D11 93
Naytahwaush, Minn. C3 187
Nazaka, Okinawa 114
Nazaré, Braz. D3 138
Nazaré, Port. C1 65
Nazaré da Mata, Braz. h6 138
Nazareth, Isr. B7 84
Nazareth, Ky. C4 182
Nazareth, Pa. E11 202
Nazareth, Tex. B1 206
Nazas, Mex. B4 129
Naze, cape, Nor. I2 63
Naze, headland, Eng. C9 56
Nāzerābād, Iran H11 86
Nāzīk, Iran B2 86
Nazilli, Tur. D7 69, D7 85
Naziya, Sov. Un. s32 63
Nazko, riv., B.C., Can. C6 149
Nazreth (Adāmā), Eth. D4 105
Nazyvayevsk, Sov. Un. B8 73
Ncheu, Malawi D5 106
Ndai, isl., Sol. Is. 115
Ndala, Tan. B5 106
Ndélé, Cen. Afr. Rep. D4 104
N'Dende, Gabon F2 104
Ndjolé, Gabon F2 104
Ndola, Zambia D4 106
Ndravuni, isl., Fiji 114
Ndriol, Rambutyo I. 115
Ndua, N. Cal. 115
Néa Kokkiniá, Grc. h11 69
Néa Palátia, Grc. g11 69
Néa Psará (Erétria), Grc. g11 69
Neagh, lake, N. Ire. C3 55
Neah Bay, Wash. A1 210
Neal, Kans. E7 181
Neápolis, Grc. D4 69
Neápolis, Grc. E5 69
Near, is., Alsk. E2 167
Near Eastern kingdoms: in 612–550 B.C. 42
Neath, Wales C4 56
Neavitt, Md. C5 173
Neba, Jap. n16 93
Neba, isl., N. Cal. 115
Nebel, riv., Ger. E6 62
Nebine, creek, Austl. D6 112
Nebish, Minn. C4 187
Nebit-Dag, Sov. Un. B7 86
Nebo, Ill. D3 178
Nebo, Ky. C2 182
Nebo, La. C3 183
Nebo, mtn., Utah D4 207
Nebraska, Ind. F7 179
Nebraska, state, U.S. 191
Nebraska City, Nebr. D10, F3 191
Nebužely, Czech. n18 70
Necedah, Wis. D3 212
Nechako, mts., B.C., Can. C5 149
Nechako, riv., B.C., Can. C5 149
Neche, N. Dak. A8 198
Neches, riv., Tex. D5 206
Nechí, Col. B3 133
Nechí, riv., Col. B3 133
Neck City, Mo. D3 189
Neckar, riv., Ger. D3 61
Necker, isl., Haw. m15 176
Necochea, Arg. B5 136
Neder Rijn, riv., Neth. C5 59
Nederburgh, cape, Indon. F6 90
Nederland, Colo. B5 171
Nederland, Tex. E6 206
Nee, res., Colo. C8 171
Needham, Mass. D2 185
Needham Heights, Mass. D2 185
Needle, mtn., Wyo. A3 213
Needle or Mountain Home, mts., Utah E2 207
Needles, Calif. E6 170
Needmore, Ga. F4 175
Needmore, Ind. G4 179
Needmore, Pa. G5 202
Needville, Tex. E5, F4 206
Neeley, Idaho G6 177
Neeley, Miss. D5 188
Neelin, Man., Can. E2 150
Neels Gap, Ga. B3 175
Neelyville, Mo. E7 189
Ñeembucu, dept., Par. E4 135
Neenah, Wis. A5, D5 212
Neepawa, Man., Can. D2 150
Neerpelt, Bel. C5 59
Neeses, S.C. D5 203
Neffs, Ohio B7 199
Neffsville, Pa. F9 202
Negaunee, Mich. B3 186
Negeri Sembilan, pol. div., Mala. K5 89
Negev, reg., Isr. D6 84
Negley, Ohio B7 199
Negley, Tex. C5 206
Negoiu, mtn., Rom. C7 68
Negombo, Cey. G6 87
Negotin, Yugo. C6 68
Negra, range, Peru C2 134
Negrais, cape, Bur. E9 87
Negreira, Sp. A1 65
Négrine, Alg. G10 64
Negrita, C.R. E6 130
Negro, mtn., Md. D1 173
Negro, riv., Arg. B3 136
Negro, riv., Bol. B3 135
Negro, riv., Braz. B1 137
Negro, riv., Braz. D2 137
Negro, riv., S.A. D4 124
Negro, riv., Ur. E1 137
Negros, isl., Phil. D6 90
Negru-Vodă, Rom. D9 68
Neguac, N.B., Can. B4 151
Nehalem, Oreg. B3 201
Nehalem, riv., Oreg. B3 201
Nehawka, Nebr. D10, E3 191
Nehbandān, Iran F10 86
Neheim-Hüsten, Ger. B2 61
Nehue, bay, Loyalty Is. 115
Neichiang, China F5 91
Neiden, Nor. C13 63
Neidpath, Sask., Can. G2 155
Neihart, Mont. D6 190
Neihsiang, China H5 92
Neihuang, China G6 92
Neilburg, Sask., Can. E1 155
Neill, pt., Wash. D1 210
Neillsville, Wis. D3 212
Neisse, riv., Ger., Pol. B9 61
Neiva, Col. C2 133
Nejdek, Czech. C7 61
Nekoma, Kans. D4 181
Nekoma, N. Dak. A7 198
Nekoosa, Wis. D4 212
Neksö, Den. A3 70
Nelagoney, Okla. A5 200
Nelbi, Sen. C2 103
Nelidovo, Sov. Un. C9 72
Neligh, Nebr. B7 191
Nell, isl., Kwajalein 114
Nellore, India F7 87
Nellysford, Va. D4 209
Nelma, Sov. Un. C9 93
Nelson, Ariz. B2 168
Nelson, B.C., Can. E9 149
Nelson, Ga. B2 175
Nelson, Ill. B4 178
Nelson, Ky. C2 182
Nelson, Mo. C4 189
Nelson, Nebr. D7 191
Nelson, Nev. H7 192
Nelson, N.H. E2 193
Nelson, N.Z. N14 112
Nelson, Pa. C7 202
Nelson, Wis. D1 212
Nelson, co., Ky. C4 182
Nelson, co., N. Dak. B7 198
Nelson, co., Va. D4 209
Nelson, riv., Man., Can. A4 150
Nelson Forks, B.C., Can. D2 149
Nelson House, Man., Can. B2 150
Nelson Miramichi, N.B., Can. *C4 151
Nelsonville, Ohio C5 199
Nelspruit, S. Afr. C5 107
Néma, Maur. C3 103
Nemacolin, Pa. G2 202
Nemadji, riv., Minn., Wis. D6 187, B1 212
Nemaha, Iowa B2 180
Nemaha, Nebr. D10 191
Nemaha, co., Kans. C7 181
Nemaha, co., Nebr. D10 191
Nemaha, riv., Nebr. D10 191
Nemakščiai, Sov. Un. A7 70
Neman, Sov. Un. A7 70
Neman, riv., Sov. Un. E5 72
Nemeiben, lake, Sask., Can. B3 155
Nemi, lake, It. h9 67
Nemo, S. Dak. C2 204
Nemours, Alg. B4 102
Nemours, Fr. C5 58
Nemunas, riv., Sov. Un. A6 70
Nemuro, Jap. E12 93
Nemuro, strait, Jap. E12 93
Nenagh, Ire. D2 55
Nenana, Alsk. C10 167
Nene, riv., Eng. B8 56
Nenzel, Nebr. B4 191
Neodesha, Kans. E8 181
Neoga, Ill. D5 178
Neola, Iowa C2 180
Neola, Utah C5 207
Neon, Ky. C7 182
Neopit, Wis. D5 212
Neosho, Mo. E3 189
Neosho, Wis. E5 212
Neosho, co., Kans. E8 181
Neosho, riv., Kans., Okla. E8 181
Neosho Falls, Kans. D8 181
Neosho Rapids, Kans. D8 181
NEPAL, country, Asia D10 88
c. 400 A.D. 79
c. 1775 82
Nepaug, res., Conn. B5 172
Nepean, cape, Tetipari I. 115
Nepewassi, lake, Ont., Can. A4 153
Nephi, Utah D4 207
Nepomuk, Czech. D8 61
Neponset, Ill. B4 178
Neponset, riv., Mass. D2 185
Nepton, Ky. B6 182
Neptune, Sask., Can. H3 155
Neptune, N.J. C4 194
Neptune Beach, Fla. B5, B6 174
Neptune City, N.J. *C4 194
Nequasset, Maine E3 184
Nera, riv., It. C4 67
Nérac, Fr. E4 58
Nerâne, Syr. A7 84
Nerchinsk, Sov. Un. D14 71
Nerekhta, Sov. Un. C13 72
Neretva, riv., Yugo. D3 68
Neris, riv., Sov. Un. A8 70
Nerja, Sp. D4 65
Nero, La. C8, E6 183
Nerpichye, Sov. Un. B12 93
Nerstrand, Minn. F5 187
Nerva, Sp. D2 65
Nes op Ameland, Neth. A5 59
Nes Ziona, Isr. h10 84
Nesbit, Miss. A3 188
Nesbitt, Man., Can. E2 150
Nesco, N.J. D3 194
Nesconset, N.Y. F4 172
Nescopeck, Pa. D9 202
Nesebŭr, Bul. D8 68
Neshaminy, creek, Pa. C2 194
Neshanic, riv., N.J. C3 194
Neshanic Station, N.J. B3 194
Nesher, Isr. B7 84
Neshkoro, Wis. E4 212
Neshoba, Miss. C4 188
Neshoba, co., Miss. C4 188
Neskaupstaður, Ice. n26 63
Neskowin, Oreg. B3 201
Nesle, Fr. E2 59
Nesmith, S.C. D8 203
Nesodden, Nor. p28 63
Nespelem, Wash. A7 210
Nesquehoning, Pa. E10 202
Ness, co., Kans. D3 181
Ness, lake, Scot. C4 57
Ness City, Kans. D4 181
Nesselwang, Ger. B6 66
Nesslau, Switz. B5 66
Nessmersiel, Ger. A7 59
Nesterov, Sov. Un. A7 70
Nesterov, Sov. Un. C7 70
Nestoria, Mich. B2 186
Nestórion, Grc. B3 69
Nestorville, W. Va. B5 211
Néstos, riv., Grc. B5 69
Nesvizh, Sov. Un. E6 72
Netanya, Isr. B6, f10 84
Netarts, Oreg. B3 201
Netawaka, Kans. C8 181
Netcong, N.J. B3 194
Netherhill, Sask., Can. F1 155
NETHERLANDS, country, Eur. B5 59
c. 1815 50
in 1922-40 53
after World War II 54
Netherlands, Austrian: c. 1721 49
Netherlands, United: c. 1721 49
Netherlands Guiana, see Surinam, Neth. dep., S.A.
Netherlands Indies, see Indonesia, country, Asia
Netherlands New Guinea, see Indonesia, country, Asia
Nethy Bridge, Scot. C5 57
Netolice, Czech. D9 61
Netrakona, Bngl. E13 88
Nett, lake, Minn. B5 187
Nett Lake, Minn. B5 187
Nettie, W. Va. C4 211
Nettilling, lake, N.W. Ter., Can. C18 143
Nettleton, Miss. A5 188
Nettleton, Mo. B4 189
Nettuno, It. k9 67
Netvořice, Czech. o18 70
Netzahualcóyotl, Mex. *n14 129
Neu-Isenburg, Ger. C3 61
Neu-Ulm, Ger. D5 60
Neubeckum, Ger. B3 61
Neubert, Tenn. D10, E11 205
Neubrandenburg, Ger. B6 60
Neuburg, Ger. E6 61
Neuchâtel, Switz. C2 66
Neuchâtel, canton, Switz. C2 66
Neuchâtel, lake, Switz. C2 66
Neudorf, Sask., Can. G4 155
Neuenkirchen, Ger. E3 62
Neuenrade, Ger. B2 61
Neuerburg, Ger. E6 59
Neufchâteau, Bel. E5 59
Neufchâteau, Fr. C6 58
Neufchâtel-en-Bray, Fr. C4 58
Neufchâtel [-sur-Aisne], Fr. E4 59
Neufelden, Aus. D6 60
Neugersdorf, Ger. C9 61
Neuhaldensleben, Ger. B5 60
Neuharlingersiel, Ger. A7 59
Neuhaus, Ger. B3 61
Neuhaus, Ger. C6 61
Neuhaus, Ger. E6 62
Neuilly [-sur-Marne], Fr. g11 58
Neuilly [-sur-Seine], Fr. g10 58
Neukirchen am Grossvenediger, Aus. B8 66
Neumarkt, see Šroda Śląska, Pol.
Neumarkt [in der Oberpfalz], Ger. D6 61
Neumarkt-Sankt Veit, Ger. A8 66
Neumünster, Ger. A4 60, D3 62
Neunburg vorm Wald, Ger. D7 61
Neunkirchen, Aus. E8 60
Neunkirchen, Ger. D2 61
Neuquén, Arg. B3 136
Neuquén, prov., Arg. B3 136
Neuquén, riv., Arg. B3 136
Neurara, Chile D2 135
Neuruppin, Ger. B6 60
Neuse, riv., N.C. B5 197
Neusiedler, lake, Aus. E8 60
Neuss, Ger. B1 61
Neustadt, Ont., Can. C3 153
Neustadt a Rübenberge, Ger. F3 62
Neustadt [an der Aisch], Ger. D5 61
Neustadt [an der Dosse], Ger. B6 60
Neustadt [an der Orla], Ger. C6 61
Neustadt an der Waldnaab, Ger. D7 61
Neustadt [an der Weinstrasse], Ger. D3 61
Neustadt [bei Coburg], Ger. C6 61
Neustadt-Glewe, Ger. E5 62
Neustadt [im Schwarzwald], Ger. B4 66
Neustadt [in Holstein], Ger. D4 62
Neustadt [in Sachsen], Ger. B9 61
Neustadt [Kreis Marburg], Ger. C4 61
Neustrelitz, Ger. B6 60
Neuville, Que., Can. C6, C8 154
Neuville-lés-Dieppe, Fr. E9 56
Neuwerk, isl., Ger. E2 62
Neuwied, Ger. C2 61
Neva, Tenn. C12 205
Neva, riv., Sov. Un. s31 63
Nevada, Iowa B4 180
Nevada, Mo. D3 189
Nevada, Ohio B4 199
Nevada, state, U.S. 192
Nevada, co., Ark. D2 169
Nevada, co., Calif. C3 170
Nevada, mts., Sp. D4 65
Nevada City, Calif. C3 170
Nevada Mills, Ind. A7 179
Nevado, mtn., Arg. B3 136
Nevado Chaupi Orko, mtn., Bol. B2 135
Nevado del Huila, mtn., Col. C2 133
Neve Sha'anan, Isr. m14 84
Nevel, Sov. Un. C7 72
Nevelsk (Honto), Sov. Un. C10 93
Nevers, Fr. D5 58
Neversink, res., N.Y. D6 196
Neversink, riv., N.Y. D6 196
Neves, Braz. *C4 137
Nevesinje, Yugo. D4 68
Neville, Sask., Can. H2 155
Néville, Fr. E8 56
Nevils, Ga. D5 175
Nevin, Wales B3 56
Nevinnomyssk, Sov. Un. E2 73
Nevinville, Iowa C3 180
Nevis, Minn. D4 187
Nevis, bay, Scot. C3 57
Nevis, isl., St. Kitts-Nevis n15 131
Nevis, mtn., Scot. D4 57
Nevşehir, Tur. C10 85
New, inlet, Fla. C2 174
New, inlet, N.C. D6 197
New, riv., Ariz. F1 168
New, riv., N.Z. P12 112
New, riv., N.C. C6 197
New, riv., Va., W. Va. D2 209, C3 211
New Agat, Guam 114
New Albany, N.S., Can. E4 151
New Albany, Ind. H6 179
New Albany, Kans. E8 181
New Albany, Miss. A4 188
New Albany, Ohio C2 199
New Albany, Pa. C9 202
New Albin, Iowa A6 180
New Alexandria, Pa. *F3 202
New Almelo, Kans. C3 181
New Alsace, Ind. F7 179
New Amsterdam, Guy. A3 139
New Athens, Ill. E4 178
New Athens, Ohio B6 199
New Auburn, Minn. F4 187
New Auburn, Wis. C2 212
New Augusta, Miss. D4 188
New Babylonian empire 42
New Baden, Ill. E4 178
New Baltimore, Mich. F8 186
New Baltimore, N.Y. C6 196
New Baltimore, Ohio G4 199
New Baltimore, Pa. G4 202
New Bedford, Ill. B4 178
New Bedford, Mass. C6 185
New Berlin, Fla. B6 174
New Berlin, Ill. D4 178
New Berlin, N.Y. C5 196
New Berlin, Pa. E8 202
New Berlin, Tex. B4 206
New Berlin, Wis. E1 212
New Berlinville, Pa. *F10 202
New Bern, N.C. B6 197
New Bethlehem, Pa. D3 202
New Blaine, Ark. B2 169
New Bloomfield, Mo. C5 189
New Bloomfield (Bloomfield), Pa. F7 202
New Bloomington, Ohio B4 199
New Boston, Ill. B3 178
New Boston, Iowa D6 180
New Boston, Mass. B1 185
New Boston, Mich. A7 186
New Boston, N.H. E3 193
New Boston, Ohio D3 199
New Boston, Tex. C5 206
New Braintree, Mass. B3 185
New Braunfels, Tex. A4, E3 206
New Bremen, N.Y. B5 196
New Bremen, Ohio B3 199
New Bridge, Oreg. C9 201
New Brigden, Alta., Can. D5 148
New Brighton, Minn. *E5 187
New Brighton, Pa. E1 202
New Britain, Conn. C5 172
New Britain, Pa. *F11 202
New Britain, isl., Bis. Arch. 115
New Brockton, Ala. D4 166
New Brunswick, N.J. C4 194
New Brunswick, prov., Can. C3 151
New Buffalo, Mich. G4 186
New Burlington, Ohio C4 199
New Burnside, Ill. F5 178
NEW CALEDONIA, Fr. dep., Oceania 115
New Cambria, Kans. D6 181
New Cambria, Mo. B5 189
New Canaan, Conn. E3 172
New Canton, Ill. D2 178
New Canton, Va. D4 209
New Carlisle, Que., Can. A4 151
New Carlisle, Ind. A4 179
New Carlisle, Ohio C3 199
New Carthage (Cartagena), Sp. 44
New Castile, reg., Sp. C4 65
New Castle, Ala. B3, E5 166
New Castle, Colo. B3 171
New Castle, Del. A6 173
New Castle, Ind. E7 179
New Castle, Ky. B4 182
New Castle, N.H. D5 193
New Castle, Pa. D1 202
New Castle, Va. D2 209
New Castle, co., Del. A6 173
New Castle Northwest, Pa. *D1 202

INDEX KEY Each place listed in **Bold-faced Type** has its population listed in the Population tables, pages 230 to 280.
Each country, shown in CAPITAL LETTERS, has its population listed in the World Political Information Table, pages 6 to 10.
* Does not appear on map; key shows general location.

New Chicago, Ind.........A3 179
New City, N.Y........D3, D7 196
New Columbia, Pa..........D8 202
New Concord, Ky..........B3 182
New Concord, Ohio.........C6 199
New Cumberland, Pa......F8 202
New Cumberland, W. Va..........A2, A4 211
New Cumnock, Scot.........E4 57
New Dayton, Alta., Can....E4 148
New Delhi, India..C6 87, C6 88
New Denmark, N.B., Can..C2 151
New Denver, B.C., Can....E9 149
New Diggings, Wis.........F3 212
New Douglas, Ill.........*E4 178
New Durham, N.H.........D4 193
New Eagle, Pa..........*F2 202
New Edinburg, Ark.........D3 169
New Effington, S. Dak.....B9 204
New Egypt, N.J..........C3 194
New Ellenton, S.C........*E4 203
New Empire, Nev..........D2 192
New England, N. Dak......C3 198
New Enterprise, Pa........F5 202
New Era, Mich............E4 186
New Fairfield, Conn.......D3 172
New Florence, Mo.........C6 189
New Florence, Pa..........F3 202
New Franken, Wis..........D6 212
New Franklin, Mo.........B5 189
New Freedom, Pa..........G8 202
New Galilee, Pa...........E1 202
New Galloway, Scot........E4 57
New Georgia, isl., Sol. Is........ 115
New Germany, N.S., Can..E5 151
New Glarus, Wis...........F4 212
New Glasgow, N.S., Can..D7 151
New Gloucester, Maine...........D5, E2 184
New Goshen, Ind...........E3 179
New Granada: c. 1790....... 126
in 1831............ 127
New Grenada, Pa..........F5 202
New Gretna, N.J..........D4 194
New Guinea, isl., Oceania........F9 90, G8 113
New Guinea, Netherlands, see Indonesia, country, Asia
NEW GUINEA, TERRITORY OF, Austl. trust., Oceania..........h12 111
New Hamburg, Ont., Can..D4 153
New Hampshire, state, U.S... 193
New Hampton, Iowa.......A5 180
New Hampton, Mo.........A3 189
New Hampton, N.H........C3 193
New Hanover, Ill..........B8 189
New Hanover, co., N.C.....C6 197
New Hanover, isl., Bis. Arch.. 115
New Harbor, Maine.........E3 184
New Harbour, Newf., Can..E5 152
New Harmony, Ind.........H2 179
New Harmony, Utah........*F2 207
New Hartford, Conn.......B5 172
New Hartford, Iowa.......B5 180
New Hartford, N.Y.........*B5 196
New Haven, Conn..........D5 172
New Haven, Ill.............F5 178
New Haven, Ind...........B7 179
New Haven, Iowa..........A5 180
New Haven, Ky............C4 182
New Haven, Mich...........F8 186
New Haven, Mo............C6 189
New Haven, N.Y...........B4 196
New Haven, Ohio..........A5 199
New Haven, Vt.............C2 208
New Haven, W. Va.........C3 211
New Haven, Wyo...........A8 213
New Haven, co., Conn......D4 172
New Haven, hbr., Conn....D5 172
New Haven, riv., Vt.......C2 208
New Hazelton, B.C., Can..B4 149
NEW HEBRIDES, Fr. and Br. dep., Oceania.......... 115
New Hebrides, is., Oceania...........H10 113
New Hill, N.C............B5 197
New Holland, Ga...........B3 175
New Holland, Ill...........C4 178
New Holland, Ohio.........C4 199
New Holland, Pa...........F9 202
New Holland, S. Dak.......D7 204
New Holstein, Wis.....B6, E5 212
New Hope, Ala............A3 166
New Hope, Ky.............C4 182
New Hope, Minn..........*E5 187
New Hope, Pa............F12 202
New Hope, S.C............C8 203
New Hope, mtn., Ala.......E4 166
New Hradec, N. Dak.......B3 198
New Hudson, Mich.........A6 186
New Hyde Park, N.Y.......G2 172
New Iberia, La............D4 183
New Ipswich, N.H..........E3 193
New Ireland, isl., Bis. Arch... 115
New Jersey, state, U.S....... 194
New Johnsonville, Tenn..A4 205
New Kensington, Pa...A7, E2 202
New Kent, Va.............D6 209
New Kent, co., Va..........D6 209
New Knoxville, Ohio.......B3 199
New Lebanon, Ind..........F3 179
New Lebanon, N.Y.........C7 196
New Lebanon, Ohio......*C3 199
New Leipzig, N. Dak......C4 198
New Lenox, Ill.........B6, F2 178
New Lexington, Ala........B2 166
New Lexington, Ohio.......C5 199
New Liberty, Ky...........B5 182
New Lima, Okla............B5 200
New Limerick, Maine.......B5 184
New Lisbon, Ind...........E7 179
New Lisbon, N.J..........D3 194
New Lisbon, Wis..........E3 212
New Liskeard, Ont., Can...E9 153
New London, Conn........D8 172
New London, Ind..........D5 179
New London, Iowa.........D6 180
New London, Minn..........E4 187
New London, Mo...........B6 189
New London, N.H..........D3 193
New London, N.C..........B3 197
New London, Ohio.........A5 199
New London, Wis..........D5 212
New London, co., Conn....C8 172
New Lothrop, Mich.........E6 186
New Lowell, Ont., Can.....C5 153
New Madison, Ohio........C3 199
New Madrid, Mo...........E8 189
New Madrid, co., Mo.......E8 189
New Malden, Eng.......*m11 55
New Marion, Ind..........F7 179
New Market, Ala..........A3 166
New Market, Ind..........E4 179
New Market, Iowa.........D3 180
New Market, Md...........B3 173
New Market, Minn.........F5 187
New Market, Tenn........C10 205
New Market, Va...........C4 209
New Marlboro, Mass.......B1 185
New Marshfield, Ohio......C5 199
New Martinsville, W. Va...B4 211
New Matamoras, Ohio......C6 199
New Meadows, Idaho.......E2 177
New Melle, Mo............C7 189
New Mexico, state, U.S....... 195
New Miami, Ohio..........C3 199
New Middleton, Tenn......C7 205
New Middletown, Ind......H5 179
New Middletown, Ohio...*B7 199
New Milford, Conn........C3 172
New Milford, N.J..........D5 194
New Milford, Ohio........A6 199
New Milford, Pa..........C10 202
New Mills, N.B., Can......B3 151
New Milton, W. Va.........B4 211
New Minden, Ill...........E4 178
New Monmouth, N.J........C4 194
New Munich, Minn.........E4 187
New Munster, Wis..........F1 212
New Norfolk, Austl.........o15 111
New Norway, Alta., Can...C4 148
New Offenburg, Mo.........D7 189
New Orleans, La.......C7, E5 183
New Osgoode, Sask., Can..E4 155
New Oxford, Pa............G7 202
New Palestine, Ind.........E6 179
New Paltz, N.Y............D6 196
New Paris, Ind............B6 179
New Paris, Ohio...........C3 199
New Paris, Pa.............F4 202
New Pekin, Ind............G5 179
New Perlican, Newf., Can..E5 152
New Philadelphia, Ohio...B6 199
New Philadelphia (Silver Creek), Pa..........E9 202
New Pine Creek, Calif......B3 170
New Pine Creek, Oreg......E6 201
New Plymouth, Idaho.......F2 177
New Plymouth, N.Z........M15 112
New Plymouth, Ohio.......C5 199
New Point, Ind............F7 179
New Point, Mo.............A2 189
New Point Comfort, pt., Va.D6 209
New Port Richey, Fla......D4 174
New Portland, Maine.......D2 184
New Prague, Minn..........F5 187
New Preston, Conn.........C3 172
New Providence, Iowa.....B4 180
New Providence, N.J.....*B4 194
New Providence, Pan.......k11 130
New Providence, Pa........G9 202
New Providence, Tenn.....A4 205
New Providence, isl., Ba. Is.C5 131
New Quay, Wales..........B3 56
New Raymer, Colo..........A7 171
New Richland, Minn........G5 187
New Richmond, Que., Can..............A4 151
New Richmond, Ind........D4 179
New Richmond, Ohio.......D3 199
New Richmond, Wis........C1 212
New Riegel, Ohio..........A4 199
New River, Ariz...........D3 168
New River, Tenn...........C9 205
New River, gorge, W. Va...D7 211
New River, inlet, N.C......C6 197
New Road, N.S., Can......E6 151
New Roads, La............D4 183
New Rochelle, N.Y....D2, D3 196
New Rockford, N. Dak.....B6 198
New Rocky Comfort, Ark.*D1 169
New Ross, N.S., Can......E5 151
New Ross, Ind............E4 179
New Ross, Ire.............D3 55
New Salem, Ill............D3 178
New Salem, Ind............E7 179
New Salem, Kans..........E7 181
New Salem, Mass..........A3 185
New Salem, N. Dak........C4 198
New Salisbury, Ind.........H5 179
New Sarpy, La............C7 183
New Sharon, Iowa.........C5 180
New Sharon, Maine........D2 184
New Shrewsbury, N.J......*C4 194
New Siberian, see Novosibirskiye, is., Sov. Un.
New Site, Miss............A5 188
New Smyrna Beach, Fla...C6 174
New South Wales, state, Austl................F8 111
New Square, N.Y.........*D6 196
New Straitsville, Ohio....C5 199
New Sweden, Maine........B4 184
New Tazewell, Tenn.....C10 205
New Toronto, Ont., Can...........D5, E6 153
New Town, N. Dak.........B3 198
New Trenton, Ind..........F8 179
New Ulm, Minn............F4 187
New Ulm, Tex.............E4 206
New Underwood, S. Dak...C3 204
New Vienna, Iowa.........B6 180
New Vienna, Ohio.........C4 199
New Village, N.J..........B2 194
New Vineyard, Maine.....D2 184
New Virginia, Iowa........C4 180
New Washington, Ind......G6 179
New Washington, Ohio.....B5 199
New Waterford, N.S., Can.C9 151
New Waterford, Ohio.......B7 199
New Waverly, Ind..........C5 179
New Waverly, Tex..........D5 206
New Westminster, B.C., Can............A10, E6 149
New Whiteland, Ind........E5 179
New Wilmington, Pa.......D1 202
New Windsor, Ill..........B3 178
New Windsor, Md..........A3 173
New Windsor, N.Y.........*D6 196
New Woodstock, N.Y.......C5 196
New World, isl., Newf., Can..........D4 152
New Year, lake, Nev........B2 192
New York, N.Y.......D1, E7 196
New York, state, U.S...... 196
New York, co., N.Y.........D1 196
New York Mills, Minn......D3 187
New York Mills, N.Y.....*B5 196
NEW ZEALAND, country, Oceania..........P15 112
New Zealand Dependencies, see Cook Is., Tokelau Is.
New Zion, S.C.............D7 203
Newala, Tan...............D6 106
Newald, Wis..............C5 212
Newark, Ark..............B4 169
Newark, Calif.............B5 170
Newark, Del..............A6 173
Newark, Eng..............A7 56
Newark, Ill................B5 178
Newark, Md...............D7 173
Newark, Mo...............B6 189
Newark, N.J..........B4, E4 194
Newark, N.Y..............B3 196
Newark, Ohio.............B5 199
Newark, S. Dak...........B8 204
Newark, Tex..............A5 206
Newark, bay, N.J..........E5 194
Newark Valley, N.Y........C4 196
Newaygo, Mich............E5 186
Newaygo, co., Mich........E5 186
Newberg, Oreg........B1, B4 201
Newbern, Ala..............C2 166
Newbern, Ill...............D3 178
Newbern, Tenn.............A2 205
Newberry, Calif............E5 170
Newberry, Fla..............C4 174
Newberry, Ind.............G3 179
Newberry, Mich............B5 186
Newberry, S.C.............C4 203
Newberry, co., S.C........C4 203
Newborn, Ga..............C3 175
Newboro, Ont., Can.......C8 153
Newbridge, Ire.............D2 55
Newbrook, Alta., Can......B4 148
Newburg, Iowa.............C5 180
Newburg, Md..............D4 173
Newburg, Mo..............D6 189
Newburg, N. Dak..........A5 198
Newburg, Pa...............F7 202
Newburg, W. Va...........B5 211
Newburgh, Ont., Can......C8 153
Newburgh, Ind.............I13 173
Newburgh, Maine...........D3 184
Newburgh, N.Y.............D6 196
Newburgh, Scot............C6 57
Newburg Center, Maine...D4 184
Newburgh Heights, Ohio..B2 199
Newbury, Ont., Can........E3 153
Newbury, Eng..............C6 56
Newbury, Mass...........*A6 185
Newbury, N.H..............D2 193
Newbury, Vt...............C4 208
Newburyport, Mass........A6 185
Newcastle, Austl...........F8 112
Newcastle, Calif...........C3 170
Newcastle, N.B., Can......C4 151
Newcastle, Ont., Can......D6 153
Newcastle, Ire.............D2 55
Newcastle, Maine..........D3 184
Newcastle, Nebr...........B9 191
Newcastle, Okla...........B4 200
Newcastle, S. Afr..........C4 107
Newcastle, Tex............C3 206
Newcastle, Utah...........F2 207
Newcastle, Wyo...........B8 213
Newcastle Bridge, N.B., Can.............C3 151
Newcastle Emlyn, Wales..B3 56
Newcastle Mine, Alta., Can.............D4 148
Newcastle-under-Lyme, Eng..........A5 56
Newcastle upon Tyne, Eng............C6 55
Newcastle Waters, Austl...C5 111
Newcomb, N. Mex.........A1 195
Newcomb, N.Y............B6 196
Newcomb, Tenn............C9 205
Newcomerstown, Ohio.....B6 199
Newdale, Man., Can.......D1 150
Newdale, Idaho............F7 177
Newdegate, Austl..........F2 111
Newell, Ala...............B4 166
Newell, Ark...............D3 169
Newell, Iowa..............B2 180
Newell, Pa...............*G2 202
Newell, S. Dak............C2 204
Newell, W. Va.......A2, A4 211
Newellton, La.............B4 183
Newfane, N.Y..............B2 196
Newfane, Vt...............F3 208
Newfield, Maine...........E2 184
Newfield, N.J..............D2 194
Newfields, N.H.............D5 193
Newfolden, Minn...........B2 187
Newfound, gap, Tenn..........D10 205
Newfound, lake, N.H.........C3 193
Newfoundland, N.J.......A4 194
Newfoundland, Pa........D11 202
Newfoundland, prov., Can.......... 152
in 1867.......... 147
Newfoundland, mts., Utah.........B2 207
Newgate, B.C., Can.......E10 149
Newgulf, Tex............*E5 206
Newhall, Calif.........E4, F2 170
Newhall, Iowa.............C6 180
Newhall, Maine............E4 184
Newhall, W. Va............D3 211
Newham, Eng..............k13 55
Newhebron, Miss..........D4 188
Newhope, Ark..............C2 169
Newington, Conn..........C6 172
Newington, Ga.............D5 175
Newington, N.H............D5 193
Newington, Va.............B5 209
Newkirk, N. Mex...........B5 195
Newkirk, Okla..............A4 200
Newland, N.C.........A2, C4 197
Newland, Va...............C6 209
Newllano, La..............C2 183
Newlon, W. Va.............C4 211
Newman, Calif.............D3 170
Newman, Ill................D6 178
Newman, Kans.............B7 181
Newman, lake, Wash.......B8 210
Newman Grove, Nebr......C8 191
Newmans, lake, Fla........C4 174
Newmanstown, Pa..........F9 202
Newmarket, Ont., Can......C5 153
Newmarket, Eng............B8 56
Newmarket, N.H............D5 193
Newnan, Ga................C2 175
Newnata, Ark..............B3 169
Newnham, Eng.............C5 56
Newport, Ark..............B4 169
Newport, Del..............A6 173
Newport, Eng..............B5 56
Newport, Eng..............D6 56
Newport, Fla..............B2 174
Newport, Ind..............E3 179
Newport, Ky..........A5, A7 182
Newport, Maine...........D3 184
Newport, Mich.............G7 186
Newport, Minn.............E7 187
Newport, Nebr.............B6 191
Newport, N.H..............D2 193
Newport, N.J...............E2 194
Newport, N.Y..............B5 196
Newport, N.C..............C7 197
Newport, Ohio.............C6 199
Newport, Oreg.............C3 201
Newport, Pa...............F7 202
Newport, R.I..............D11 172
Newport, S.C..............B5 203
Newport, Tenn............D10 205
Newport, Tex..............C3 206
Newport, Vt...............B4 208
Newport, Va...............D2 209
Newport, Wales............C5 56
Newport, Wash.............A8 210
Newport, co., R.I.........C11 172
Newport Beach, Calif..........F3, F5 170
Newport Center, Vt........B4 208
Newport News (Independent City), Va......B6, E6 209
Newport Station, N.S., Can.........E5 151
Newquay, Eng.............D2 56
Newry, Maine..............D2 184
Newry, N. Ire..............C3 55
Newry, S.C................B2 203
Newsite, Ala...............B4 166
Newsom, Tenn.............E9 205
Newsoms, Va...............E5 209
Newton, Ala...............D4 166
Newton, Ga................E2 175
Newton, Ill.................E5 178
Newton, Iowa..............C4 180
Newton, Kans........A5, D6 181
Newton, Mass.........B5, D2 185
Newton, Miss..............C4 188
Newton, N.H...............E4 193
Newton, N.J...............A3 194
Newton, N.C...............B2 197
Newton, Tex...............D6 206
Newton, Utah..............B4 207
Newton, W. Va.............C3 211
Newton, Wis...............B6 212
Newton, co., Ark..........B2 169
Newton, co., Ga...........C3 175
Newton, co., Ind..........B3 179
Newton, co., Miss.........C4 188
Newton, co., Mo...........E3 189
Newton, co., Tex..........D6 206
Newton Abbot, Eng.........D4 56
Newton Falls, N.Y......A6, B2 196
Newton Falls, Ohio........A7 199
Newton Grove, N.C........B5 197
Newton Hamilton, Pa......F6 202
Newton Junction, N.H.....E4 193
Newton Stewart, Scot......F4 57
Newtonville, Ont., Can....D6 153
Newtonville, Ind...........H4 179
Newtonville, N.J..........D3 194
Newtown, Newf., Can......D5 152
Newtown, Conn............D3 172
Newtown, Ind..............D3 179
Newtown, Mo..............A4 189
Newtown, Ohio........C3, D2 199
Newtown, Pa.............F12 202
Newtown, Va...............D5 209
Newtown [& Llanllwchaiarn], Wales...........B4 56
Newtown Square, Pa......D2 194
Newtownabbey, N. Ire.....F3 57
Newtownards, N. Ire......C4 55
Newville, Ala..............D4 166
Newville, Pa...............F7 202
Newville, W. Va...........C4 211
Ney, Ohio..................A3 199
Ney, lake, Ont., Can.......B5 150
Neya, Sov. Un..............B2 73
Neye, isl., Guam.......... 114
Neyriz, Iran...............G7 86
Neyshābūr, Iran............C9 86
Nez Perce, co., Idaho......C2 177
Nezhin, Sov. Un............F8 72
Nezperce, Idaho...........C2 177
Nezpique, bayou, La........D3 183
Ngabang, Indon............E3 90
Ngabé, Con................F3 104
Ngala, Nig.................D7 103
Ngaloa, bay, Fiji.......... 114
Ngaloa, hbr., Fiji.......... 114
Ngamea, isl., Fiji.......... 114
Ngami, lake, Bots..........B3 107
N'Gaoundéré, Cam..........D2 104
Ngara, Tan.................B5 106
Ngardmau, Palau, Is......... 114
Ngaruangl, reef, Palau Is.... 114
Ngaruawahia, N.Z.........L15 112
Ngatapa, N.Z..............M16 112
Ngau, isl., Fiji............. 114
Ngele Levu, isl., Fiji....... 114
Ngemelis, is., Palau Is...... 114
Ngesebus, isl., Palau Is..... 114
Ngidinga, Zaire............C2 106
Ngong, Ken................B6 106
Ngoring Nor, lake, China...E4 91
Ngounié, riv., Gabon......F2 104
Nguigmi, Niger............D7 103
Nguna, isl., New Hebr...... 115
Nguru, Nig.................D7 103
Nha Trang, Viet............F8 89
Nhill, Austl................H3 112
Niafounke, Mali............C4 103
Niagara, N. Dak...........B8 198
Niagara, Wis...............C5 212
Niagara, co., N.Y..........B2 196
Niagara, cave, Minn......G6 187
Niagara Falls, Ont., Can..............D5 153
Niagara Falls, N.Y.........B1 196
Niagara-on-the-Lake, Ont., Can..............D5 153
Niamey, Niger.............D5 103
Niangara, Zaire............A4 106
Niangua, Mo...............D5 189
Niantic, Conn..............D8 172
Niantic, Ill.................D4 178
Niarada, Mont..............C2 190
Niassa, prov., Moz.........D6 106
Nibe, Den..................B3 62
NICARAGUA, country, N.A..............D5 130
Nicaragua, lake, Nic........E5 130
Nicastro, It.................E6 67
Nicatous, lake, Maine.......C4 184
Nice, Fr....................F7 58
Niceville, Fla..............G2 174
Nichinan (Obi), Jap.........K5 93
Nichicun, lake, Que., Can...............B2 154
Nicholas, co., Ky...........B6 182
Nicholas, co., W. Va.......C4 211
Nicholas, chan., Cuba......D3 131
Nicholasville, Ky...........C5 182
Nicholls, Ga................E4 175
Nichols, Conn..............E4 172
Nichols, Iowa...............C6 180
Nichols, Mo................D4 189
Nichols, N.Y................C4 196
Nichols, S.C................C9 203
Nichols Hills, Okla.........B4 200
Nicholson, Ga.............*B3 175
Nicholson, Miss............E4 188
Nicholson, Pa..............C10 202
Nicholson, riv., Austl.......C6 110
Nicholville, N.Y............A2 196
Nickajack, lake, Tenn......D8 205
Nickelsville, Va.............B2 209
Nickerie, riv., Sur..........A3 139
Nickerson, Kans........A3, D5 181
Nickerson, Nebr............C9 191
Nickerson, hill, Conn......D7 172
Nickleville, Pa..............D2 202
Nicobar, is., India..........G9 87
Nicodemus, Kans...........C4 181
Nicola, B.C., Can...........D7 149
Nicola, riv., B.C., Can.....D7 149
Nicolet, Que., Can..........C5 154
Nicolet, co., Que., Can.....C5 154
Nicolet, lake, Mich.........B6 186
Nicolet, riv., Que., Can....C5 154
Nicoll, pt., N.Y..........G4 172
Nicollet, Minn..............F4 187
Nicollet, co., Minn.........F4 187
Nicolls' Town, Ba. Is.......C4 131
Nicoma Park, Okla.........B4 200
Nicosia, Cyp................E9 85
Nicosia, It..................F5 67
Nicotera, It.................E5 67
Nicoya, C.R................E5 130
Nicoya, gulf, C.R..........F5 130
Nicoya, pen., C.R..........F5 130
Nictaux Falls, N.S., Can...E4 151
Nicuadala, Moz............A6 107
Nida, riv., Pol............C6 70
Nidan, rock, Iwo........... 114
Nidd, riv., Eng............F7 57
Nidda, Ger..................C4 61
Nidda, riv., Ger............C4 61
Nidzica, Pol................B6 70
Niebüll, Ger................D2 62
Niederbronn-les-Bains, Fr.................F7 59
Niedermarsberg, Ger.......B3 61
Niedersachsen (Lower Saxony), state, Ger........A4 61
Nielsville, Minn............C2 187
Niemodlin, Pol..............C4 70
Nienburg, Ger...............B4 60
Niers, riv., Ger............C6 59
Nierstein, Ger..............D3 61
Niesky, Ger................B9 61
Nieszawa, Pol..............B5 70
Niete, mtn., Lib...........E3 103
Nietleben, Ger.............B6 61
Nieuw Amsterdam, Sur....A3 139
Nieuw Nickevie, Sur.......A3 139
Nieuweroord, Neth.........B6 59
Nieuwpoort, Bel............C2 59
Nigadoo, N.B., Can.......B4 151
Niğde, Tur.................D10 85
Nigei, isl., B.C., Can......D4 149
NIGER, country, Afr.......C6 103
Niger, riv., Afr............E6 96
Niger, riv., mouths, Nig....F6 103
Niger Coast: in 1884......... 99
NIGERIA, country, Afr.....E6 103
Nigg, Scot..................C5 57
Nighthawk, Wash..........A6 210
Nightingale, isl., Viet......B7 89
Nigríta, Grc................B4 69
Nihing, riv., Pak..........H11 86
Nihoa, isl., Haw..........m15 176
Nii, isl., Jap...............I9 93
Niigata, Jap................H9 93
Niihama, Jap...............J6 93
Niihau, isl., Haw..........B1 176
Niijimahon, Jap............o18 93
Niimi, Jap..................I6 93
Nijar, Sp...................D4 65
Nijkerk, Neth...............B5 59
Nijmegen, Neth.............C5 59
Nikaia, Grc................*C4 69
Nikep, Md..................D2 173
Nikishka, Alsk..............g16 167
Nikitinka, Sov. Un..........D9 72
Nikitovka, Sov. Un..........q21 72
Nikki, Dah..................E5 103
Nikko, Jap..................H9 93
Nikolayev, Sov. Un.........H9 72
Nikolayevsk, Sov. Un.......D17 71
Nikolayevskiy, Sov. Un. . .F15 72
Nikolsk, Sov. Un............B3 73
Nikolski, Alsk...............E6 167
Nikonovskoye, Sov. Un.....n18 72
Nikopol, Bul................D7 68
Nikopol', Sov. Un..........H10 72
Nīksar, Tur.................B11 85
Nīkshahr, Iran..............H10 86
Nikšić, Yugo................D4 68
Niland, Calif................F6 170
Nile, N.Y...................C2 196
Nile, riv., Eg., Sud........E6 101
Niles, Ill...................E2 178
Niles, Kans.................D6 181
Niles, Mich.................G4 186
Niles, Ohio.................A7 199
Nilópolis, Braz............*C4 137
Nilvange, Fr.................E6 59
Nilwood, Ill.................D4 178
Nimaj, India.................E5 88
Nimba, mtn., Guinea.......E3 103
Nîmes, Fr...................F6 58
Nimmons, Ark...............A5 169
Nimpkish, riv., B.C., Can...D4 149
Nimrod, glacier, Ant.......A29 120
Nimrod, res., Ark...........C2 169
Nimule, Sud.................E3 105
Ninaview, Colo..............D7 171
Nine Mile, creek, Kans......B8 181
Nine Mile, pt., Mich........C6 186
Nine Mile Falls, Wash......D7 210
Ninette, Man., Can..........E2 150
Ninety Mile, beach, Austl....I6 112
Ninety Six, S.C.............C3 203
Nineveh, Ind................F5 179
Nineveh, Pa.................G1 202
Nineveh, ruins, Iraq........D14 85
Ninga, Man., Can............E2 150
Ningan, China..............C10 91
Ningchiang, China...........H2 92
Ningchin, China.............F6 92
Ningching, China............F4 91
Ningerh, China.............D11 87
Ninghai, China..............J9 92
Ninghsien, China............D6 91
Ninghsien, see Ningpo, China
Ninghua, China..............K7 92
Ningming, China............A7 89
Ningpo (Ninghsien), China.................F9 91
Ningsia, see Yinchuan, China
Ningsia Hui, auton. reg., China.................D6 91
Ningte, China...............K8 92
Ningtu, China...............K6 92
Ningwu, China..............E5 92
Ninh Binh, Viet.............B6 89
Ninilchik, Alsk.........C9, g16 167
Ninnekah, Okla..............C4 200
Ninnescah, riv., Kans.......E6 181
Ninnis, glacier, Ant........C27 120
Ninole, Haw.................D6 176
Ninove, Bel..................D4 59
Nioaque, Braz...............C1 137
Niobe, N. Dak...............A3 198
Niobrara, Nebr..............B7 191
Niobrara, co., Wyo..........B8 213
Niobrara, creek, Wyo......C8 213
Niobrara, riv., Nebr........B7 191
Nioki, Zaire..................B2 106
Nioro, Mali..................C3 103
Nioro, Sen...................D1 103
Niort, Fr.....................D3 58
Niota, Ill.....................C2 178
Niota, Tenn..................D9 205
Niotaze, Kans................E7 181
Nipawin, Sask., Can........D4 155
Nipawin, prov. park, Sask., Can..............C3 155
Nipishish, lake, Newf., Can.g9 152
Nipisiguit, bay, N.B., Can...B4 151
Nipisiguit, riv., N.B., Can...B3 151
Nipissing, co., Ont., Can..A5 153
Nipissing, lake, Ont., Can..A5 153

INDEX KEY Each place listed in **Bold-faced Type** has its population listed in the Population tables, pages 230 to 280.
Each country, shown in CAPITAL LETTERS, has its population listed in the World Political Information Table, pages 6 to 10.
* Does not appear on map; key shows general location.

Nipissing Junction, Ont., Can. A5 153
Nipomo, Calif. E3 170
Nippers Harbour, Newf., Can. D4 152
Nipple, mtn., Colo D2 171
Nipton, Calif. E6 170
Niquelândia, Braz. A3 137
Niquero, Cuba E5 131
Nirasaki, Jap. n17 93
Nirmal, India H7 88
Nirmali, India D11 88
Niš, Yugo. D5 68
Nisa, Port. C2 65
Nisava, riv., Yugo D6 68
Nishi, Iwo 114
Nishino, isl., Pac. O E8 113
Nishinomiya, Jap. *I7 93
Nishio, Jap. o15 93
Nishnabotna, riv., Iowa D2 180
Nisiros, isl., Grc D6 69
Nisko, Pol. C7 70
Nisland, S. Dak. C2 204
Nisqually, riv., Wash C3 210
Nissan, riv., Swe B7 62
Nissum, fjord, Den B2 62
Nisswa, Minn. D4 187
Nistowiak, lake, Sask., Can B3 155
Nisula, Mich. B2 186
Niterói, Braz. C4, h6 137
Nith, riv., Scot E5 57
Nitra, Czech. D5 70
Nitra, riv., Czech D5 70
Nitro, W. Va. C3 211
Nitta Yuma, Miss. B3 188
Nittenau, Ger. D7 61
Nivelles, Bel. D4 59
Nivernais, former prov., Fr. D5 58
Nivernais, hills, Fr D5 58
Niverville, Man., Can. E3 150
Nivskiy, Sov. Un. D15 63
Niwka, Pol. g10 70
Niwot, Colo. A5 171
Nixa, Mo. D4 189
Nixburg, Ala. C3 166
Nixon, Nev. D2 192
Nixon, Tex. E4, B4 206
Nizam, dominions of: c.1775 82
Nizamabad, India H7 88
Nizamsagar, lake, India H6 88
Nizhmozero, Sov. Un. E17 63
Nizhne-Chirskaya, Sov. Un. G14 72
Nizhne-Kolymsk, Sov. Un. C19 71
Nizhneudinsk, Sov. Un. D12 71
Nizhneye, Sov. Un. q21 72
Nizhniy Lomov, Sov. Un. E14 72
Nizhniy Tagil, Sov. Un. B5 73
Nizhnyaya Tunguska, riv., Sov. Un C12 71
Nizmennyy, cape, Sov. Un E7 93
Nizza Monferrato, It. E4 66
Njombe, Tan. C5 106
Njurunda, Swe. F7 63
Nkai, Rh. A4 107
Nkana, Zambia *C4 106
Nkangsamba, Cam. E1 104
Nkhata Bay, Malawi D5 106
Nkota Kota, Malawi D5 106
No Mans Land, isl., Mass D6 185
No Point, pt., Md D5 173
No Wood, Wyo. B5 213
Noakhali, Bngl. F13 88
Noank, Conn. D9 172
Noasca, It. D3 66
Noatak, Alsk. B7 167
Noatak, riv., Alsk B7 167
Nobel, Ont., Can. B4 153
Nobeoka, Jap. J5 93
Noble, Ga. B1 175
Noble, Ill. E5 178
Noble, La. C2 183
Noble, Okla. B4 200
Noble, co., Ind. B7 179
Noble, co., Ohio C6 199
Noble, co., Okla. A4 200
Noble Lake, Ark. C4 169
Nobleboro, Maine D3 184
Nobleford, Alta., Can. E4 148
Nobles, co., Minn. G3 187
Noblesville, Ind. D5 179
Nobleton, Fla. D4 174
Noboribetsu, Jap. E10 93
Nobscot, hill, Mass B5 185
Nocatee, Fla. E5 174
Nochixtlán, Mex. o15 129
Nocona, Tex. C4 206
Nodaway, Iowa D3 180
Nodaway, co., Mo. A3 189
Nodaway, riv., Iowa, Mo D2 180, A2 189
Node, Wyo. C8 213
Nodoa, China C8 89
Noel, Mo. E3 189
Noelville, Ont., Can. A4 153
Noemfoor, isl., Indon F8 90
Nogal, N. Mex. D4 195
Nogal, riv., Som D6 105
Nogales, Ariz. F5 168
Nogales, Mex. A2 129
Nogales, Mex. n15 129
Nogara, It. D7 66
Nōgata, Jap. J5 93
Nogent-en-Bassigny, Fr. C6 58
Nogent-le-Rotrou, Fr. C4 58
Nogent [-sur-Marne], Fr. g10 58
Nogent [-sur-Seine], Fr. C5 58
Noginsk, Sov. Un. B1 73
Nogoa, riv., Austl B6 112
Nogoyá, Arg. A5 136
Nogueira, Sp. A2 65
Nohar, India C5 88
Noheji, Jap. F10 93
Nohly, Mont. C12 190
Noho, China B2 93
Noire, riv., Que., Can A7 153
Noirmoutier, isl., Fr D2 58
Noisy-le-Sec, Fr. g10 58
Nojima, cape, Jap I9 93
Nok Kundi, Pak. G11 86
Nokomis, Sask., Can. F3 155
Nokomis, Fla. E4 174
Nokomis, Ill. D4 178
Nokomis, lake, Wis C4 212
Nokrek, peak, India E13 88
Nola, Ark. C2 169
Nola, Cen. Afr. Rep. E3 104
Nola, It. D5 67
Nola, Miss. D3 188
Nolan, Tex. C2 206
Nolan, W. Va. D2 211
Nolan, co., Tex. C2 206
Nolensville, Tenn. B5 205
Nolin, res., Ky C3 182
Nolin, riv., Ky C3 182
Nolinsk, Sov. Un. B3 73
Noma, Fla. G3 174
Noma, cape, Jap K5 93
Nome, Alsk. C6 167
Nome, N. Dak. C8 198
Nomeny, Fr. F6 59
Nominingue, Que., Can. C2 154
Nonacho, lake, N.W. Ter., Can D11 142
Nonconnah, Tenn. E8 205
Nonconnah, creek, Tenn E8 205
Nondalton, Alsk. C8 167
Nonesuch, riv., Maine E4 184
Nong Khai, Thai. D5 89
Nongoma, S. Afr. C5 107
Nonni, riv., China B9 91, B2 93
Nonoava, Mex. B3 129
Nonout, isl., Gilbert Is 115
Noodle, Tex. C2 206
Nooksack, Wash. A3 210
Nooksack, riv., Wash A3 210
Noonan, N. Dak. A2 198
Noordwijk-Binnen, Neth. B4 59
Noorvik, Alsk. B7 167
Nooseneck, R. I. C10 172
Nootka, isl., B.C., Can E4 149
Nootka, sound, B.C., Can E4 149
Nopal, Tex. E4 206
Noquebay, lake, Wis C6 212
Nóqui, Ang. C1 106
Nora, Sask., Can. E4 155
Nora, Ill. A4 178
Nora, Ind. H8 179
Nora, Nebr. D8 191
Nora, Swe. H6 63
Nora Springs, Iowa A5 180
Noranda, Que., Can. B2 154
Norbeck, S. Dak. B6 204
Norborne, Mo. B4 189
Norbourne Estates, Ky. *B4 182
Norcatur, Kans. C3 181
Norco, Calif. *F5 170
Norco, La. B6, D5 183
Norcross, Ga. A5, C2 175
Norcross, Minn. E2 187
Nord, canal, Fr D3 59
Nord, dept., Fr. D3 59
Nord, mts., Hai F7 131
Nordborg, Den. C3 62
Nordby, Den. C2 62
Nordby, Den. C4 62
Nordegg, Alta., Can. C2 148
Nordegg, riv., Alta., Can C2 148
Norden, Ger. B3 60
Norden, Nebr. B5 191
Nordenham, Ger. B4 60
Norderney, Ger. A7 59
Norderney, isl., Ger A7 59
Norderstedt, Ger. *E4 62
Nordfjora, fjord, Nor G1 63
Nordhausen, Ger. B5 61
Nordheim, Tex. *E4 206
Nordhorn, Ger. B3 60
Nordland, Wash. A3 210
Nördlingen, Ger. E5 61
Nordmaling, Swe. F8 63
Nordman, Idaho A2 177
Nordreisa, Nor. C9 63
Nordrhein-Westfalen (North Rhine-Westphalia), state, Ger. B2 61
Nordstrand, isl., Ger A4 60
Nordvik, Sov. Un. B14 71
Norene, Tenn. A5 205
Norfield, Miss. D3 188
Norfolk, Conn. B4 172
Norfolk, Mass. B5 185
Norfolk, Nebr. B8 191
Norfolk, N.Y. A2 196
Norfolk (Independent City), Va. B7, E6 209
Norfolk, co., Ont., Can. E4 153
Norfolk, co., Eng. B9 56
Norfolk, co., Mass. B5 185
Norfolk, is., Oceania H10 113
NORFOLK ISLAND, Austl. dep., Oceania H10 113
Norfork, Ark. A3 169
Norfork, lake, Ark A3 169
Norge, Okla. C4 200
Norias, Tex. F4 206
Noril'sk, Sov. Un. C11 71
Norland, Ont., Can. C6 153
Norlina, N.C. A5 197
Norma, N.J. E2 194
Norma, N. Dak. A4 198
Norma, Tenn. C9 205
Normal, Ala. A3 166
Normal, Ill. C5 178
Norman, Ark. C2 169
Norman, Ind. G5 179
Norman, Nebr. D7 191
Norman, N.C. B3 197
Norman, Okla. B4 200
Norman, co., Minn. C2 187
Norman, isl., Vir. Is F16 132
Norman, riv., Austl C7 110
Norman Park, Ga. E3 175
Norman Wells, N.W. Ter., Can. C7 144
Normanby, riv., Austl B7 110
Normandin, Que., Can. *G18 145
Normandy, former prov., Fr. C3 58
Normandy, Mo. A8 189
Normandy, Tenn. B5 205
Normandy, hills, Fr C3 58
Normandy Beach, N.J. C4 194
Normandy Park, Wash. *B3 210
Normangee, Tex. D4 206
Normanna, Tex. E4 206
Normanton, Austl. C7 111
Normantown, Ga. D4 175
Nornalup, Austl. F2 111
Norphlet, Ark. D3 169
Norquay, Sask., Can. F4 155
Ñorquincó, Arg. C2 136
Norra Värmdö, Swe. t36 63
Norrahammar, Swe. A8 62
Nörre Åby, Den. C3 62
Nörre Alslev, Den. D5 62
Nörresundby, Den. A3 62
Norridge, Ill. *B6 178
Norridgewock, Maine D3 184
Norris, Ill. C3 178
Norris, Mont. E5 190
Norris, S.C. B2 203
Norris, S. Dak. D4 204
Norris, Tenn. C9 205
Norris, dam, Tenn C9 205
Norris, lake, Tenn C10 205
Norris Arm, Newf., Can. D4 152
Norris City, Ill. F5 178
Norris Point, Newf., Can. D3 152
Norristown, Pa. A10, F11 202
Norrisville, Md. A4 173
Norrköping, Swe. H7, u34 63
Norrtälje, Swe. H8, t36 63
Norseman, Austl. F3 111
Norte, chan., Braz B4 139
Norte, range, Braz E3 139
Norte de Santander, dept., Col. B3 133
North, S.C. D5 203
North, Va. D6 209
North, brook, Vt B3 208
North, cape, Malekula I 115
North, cape, N.Z. K14 112
North, cape, Nor B11 63, A12 118
North, cape, P.R. e10 132
North, chan., Ont., Can A2 153
North, chan., N. Ire C3 55
North, creek, Ga B5 175
North, inlet, S.C E9 203
North, isl., New Hebr 115
North, isl., N.Z L14 112
North, isl., S.C E9 203
North, is., La E7 183
North, mtn., Pa D9 202
North, mtn., Va., W. Va C4 209
North, pass, La E7 183
North, plains, N. Mex C1 195
North, pt., Md B5 173
North, pt., Md C5 173
North, pt., Mich D7 186
North, pt., Pentecost I 115
North, pond, Maine D3 184
North, pond, Mass D1 185
North, riv., Ala B2 166
North, riv., Newf., Can B3 152
North, riv., Fla C6 174
North, riv., Mass E4 185
North, riv., Vt F3 208
North, riv., Va D3 209
North, sea, Eur D8 40
North, sound, Scot A6 57
North Abington, Mass. B6, E3 185
North Adams, Mass. A1 185
North Adams, Mich. G6 186
North Albany, Oreg. C1 201
North Amherst, Mass. B2 185
North Amity, Maine C5 184
North Andaman, isl., India F9 87
North Andover, Mass. A5 185
North Anna, riv., Va C5 209
North Anson, Maine D3 184
North Apollo, Pa. E2 202
North Arapaho, peak, Colo A5 171
North Arlington, N.J. D5 194
North Atlanta, Ga. B5 175
North Attleboro, Mass. C5 185
North Augusta, Ont., Can. C9 153
North Augusta, S.C. D4 203
North Aurora, Ill. F1 178
North Baltimore, Ohio A4 199
North Barrackpore, India *F12 88
North Battle Mountain, Nev. C5 192
North Bangor, N.Y. A2 196
North Battleford, Sask., Can. E1 155
North Bay, Ont., Can. A5, E9 153
North Bay, Fla. *G6 174
North Beach, Md. C4 173
North Belle Vernon, Pa. *F2 202
North Bellingham, Mass. E1 185
North Bellmore, N.Y. *G2 172
North Belmont, N.C. B2 197
North Bend, B.C., Can. E7 149
North Bend, Nebr. C9 191
North Bend, Ohio D1 199
North Bend, Oreg. D2 201
North Bend, Pa. D6 202
North Bend, Wash. B4 210
North Bend, Wis. D2 212
North Bennington, Vt. F2 208
North Bergen, N.J. D5 194
North Berwick, Maine E2 184
North Berwick, Scot. D6 57
North Billerica, Mass. A5, C2 185
North Bloomfield, Ohio A7 199
North Bonneville, Wash. D4 210
North Borneo (Sabah), reg. Mala. D5 90
North Brabant, prov., Neth. C4 59
North Braddock, Pa. F2 202
North Bradford, Maine C4 184
North Bradley, Mich. E6 186
North Branch, Mich. E7 186
North Branch, Minn. E6 187
North Branch, N.J. B3 194
North Branford, Conn. D5 172
North Bridgton, Maine D2 184
North Brook, Ont., Can. C7 153
North Brookfield, Mass. B3 185
North Brooksville, Maine D4 184
North Brother, mtn., Maine C4 184
North Buena Vista, Iowa B7 180
North Cacapon, riv., W. Va B6 211
North Calais, Vt. C4 208
North Caldwell, N.J. B4 194
North Canadian, riv., Okla A1 200
North Canton, Conn. B5 172
North Canton, Ga. B2 175
North Canton, Ohio B6 199
North Cape, Wis. F1 212
North Cape May, N.J. F3 194
North Carolina, state, U.S. 197
in 1800-50 163
in 1865 164
North Carver, Mass. C6 185
North Cascades, nat. park, Wash A4 210
North Catasauqua, Pa. *E11 202
North Charleroi, Pa. *F2 202
North Charleston, S.C. F2, F8 203
North Charlestown, N.H. D2 193
North Chelmsford, Mass. A5 185
North Chicago, Ill. A6, E2 178
North Chillicothe, Ill. C4 178
North Clarendon, Vt. D3 208
North Cohasset, Mass. D4 185
North Cohocton, N.Y. C3 196
North College Hill, Ohio D2 199
North Collins, N.Y. C2 196
North Conway, N.H. B4 193
North Corbin, Ky. D5 182
North Coventry, Conn. B7 172
North Creek, N.Y. B7 196
North Dakota, state, U.S. 198
North Danville, Vt. C4 208
North Dartmouth, Mass. C6 185
North Derby, Vt. A4 208
North Dighton, Mass. C5 185
North Dixmont, Maine D3 184
North Dorset, Vt. E2 208
North Downs, hills, Eng C8 56
North East, Md. A6 173
North East, Pa. B2 202
North East, isl., Nor A12 118
North East, is., Truk 114
North East Carry, Maine C3 184
North Eastham, Mass. C8 185
North Easton, Mass. B5 185
North Edmonton, Alta., Can. C4 148
North Egremont, Mass. B1 185
North English, Iowa C5 180
North Enid, Okla. A4 200
North Esk, riv., Scot D6 57
North Fabius, riv., Mo A6 189
North Fairfield, Ohio A5 199
North Falmouth, Mass. C6 185
North Ferrisburg, Vt. C2 208
North Fond du Lac, Wis. B5, E5 212
North Fork, Calif. D4 170
North Fork, Idaho D5 177
North Fork Republican, riv., Colo A8 171
North Foster, R.I. B10 172
North Fox, isl., Mich C5 186
North Franklin, Conn. C8 172
North Freedom, Wis. E4 212
North Frisian, is., Ger A4 60
North Fryeburg, Maine D2 184
North Galiano, B.C., Can. B9 149
North Gamboa, C.Z. k11 130
North Gower, Ont., Can. B9 153
North Grafton, Mass. B4 185
North Granby, Conn. B5 172
North Gray, Maine E5 184
North Grosvenor Dale, Conn. B9 172
North Guilford, Conn. D6 172
North Guilford, Maine C3 184
North Haledon, N.J. *B4 194
North Hampton, N.H. E5 193
North Hampton, Ohio C4 199
North Hanover, Mass. E3 185
North Harpswell, Maine E4 184
North Hartland, Vt. D4 208
North Hartland, res., Vt D4 208
North Hartsville, S.C. *C7 203
North Hatfield, Mass. B2 185
North Hatley, Que., Can. D6 154
North Haven, Conn. D5 172
North Haven, Maine D4 184
North Haverhill, N.H. B2 193
North Havre, Mont. B7 190
North Head, N.B., Can. E3 151
North Henderson, Ill. B3 178
North Henderson, N.C. *A5 197
North Hero, Vt. B2 208
North Highlands, Calif. *C3 170
North Holland (Noordholland), prov., Neth. B4 59
North Holston, Va. B3 209
North Horn, lake, Tenn E8 205
North Hornell, N.Y. *C3 196
North Horr, Ken. A6 106
North Hudson, N.Y. B7 196
North Hudson, Wis. *D1 212
North Hyde Park, Vt. B3 208
North Industry, Ohio B6 199
North Irwin, Pa. *F2 202
North Islesboro, Maine D4 184
North Java, N.Y. C2 196
North Jay, Maine D2 184
North Judson, Ind. B4 179
North Kamloops, B.C., Can. D7 149
North Kansas City, Mo. E2 189
North Kennebunk Port, Maine E2 184
North Kingstown, R.I. C11 172
North Kingsville, Ohio A7 199
North Korea, see Korea, North, country, Asia
North La Junta, Colo. C7 171
North Lake, Mich. B3 186
North Lake, Wis. E1 212
North Laramie, riv., Wyo C7 213
North Las Vegas, Nev. G6 192
North Lawrence, N.Y. A2 196
North Lemmon, S. Dak. D3 198
North Lewisburg, Ohio B4 199
North Liberty, Ind. A5 179
North Liberty, Iowa C6 180
North Lima, Ohio B7 199
North Little Rock, Ark. C3, D6 169
North Loon, mtn., Idaho D3 177
North Loup, Nebr. C7 191
North Loup, riv., Nebr B5 191
North Lubec, Maine D5 184
North Madison, Conn. D6 172
North Magnetic Pole, Can A11 142
North Mamm, peak, Colo B3 171
North Manchester, Ind. C6 179
North Manitou, isl., Mich C4 186
North Mankato, Minn. F4 187
North Merrick, N.Y. *G2 172
North Miami, Fla. F3, G6 174
North Miami, Okla. A7 200
North Miami Beach, Fla. E3 174
North Middleboro, Mass. C6 185
North Middletown, Ky. B5 182
North Monmouth, Maine D2 184
North Montpelier, Vt. C4 208
North Muskegon, Mich. E4 186
North New Hyde Park, N.Y. *E7 196
North New Portland, Maine D2 184
North New River, canal, Fla F6 174
North Newcastle, Maine D3 184
North Newport, N.H. D2 193
North Newton (Bethel College), Kans. A5 181
North Norwich, N.Y. C5 196
North Ogden, Utah B4 207
North Olmsted, Ohio B1 199
North Orange, Mass. A3 185
North Oxford, Mass. B4 185
North Pacific, ocean D11 133
North Palisade, mtn., Calif D4 170
North Palm Beach, Fla. *F6 174
North Park, basin, Colo A4 171
North Parsonfield, Maine E2 184
North Pekin, Ill. *C4 178
North Pelham, N.Y. *E7 196
North Peninsula, Fla. *C5 174
North Penobscot, Maine D4 184
North Perry, Maine C5 184
North Pitcher, N.Y. C5 196
North Plain, Conn. D7 172
North Plainfield, N.J. B4 194
North Plains, Oreg. A1, B3 201
North Platte, Nebr. C5 191
North Platte, riv., U.S B7 158
North Pleasanton, Tex. *E2 206
North Plymouth, Mass. *C6 185
North Pole, Arc. O 118
North Pomfret, Vt. D4 208
North Portal, Sask., Can. H4 155
North Powder, Oreg. B9 201
North Pownal, Maine E5 184
North Pownal, Vt. F2 208
North Prairie, Wis. F5 212
North Providence, R.I. B11 172
North Pyramid, peak, N. Mex E1 195
North Quincy, Ill. *D2 178
North Range Corner, N.S., Can. E4 151
North Reading, Mass. C3 185
North Richland Hills, Tex. *C4 206
North Ridgeville, Ohio A5, B1 199
North Rim, Ariz. A3 168
North River Bridge, N.S., Can. C9 151
North Riverside, Ill. *B6 178
North Robinson, Ohio B5 199
North Rochester, N.H. D5 193
North Ronaldsay, isl., Scot A5 55
North Rose, N.Y. B4 196
North Royalton, Ohio B2 199
North Rustico, P.E.I., Can. C6 151
North Sacramento, Calif. A6 170
North St. Paul, Minn. E7 187
North Salem, Ind. E4 179
North Salem, N.H. E4 193
North Salt Lake, Utah C4 207
North Sandwich, N.H. C4 193
North Santee, riv., S.C E9 203
North Saskatchewan, riv., Alta., Sask., Can F10 142
North Scituate, Mass. D4 185
North Scituate, R.I. B10 172
North Searsmont, Maine D3 184
North Sherburne, Vt. D3 208
North Shoshone, peak, Nev D4 192
North Shreveport, La. *B2 183
North Shrewsbury, Vt. D3 208
North Sioux City, S. Dak. E9 204
North Springfield, Pa. C1 202
North Springfield, Vt. E3 208
North Springfield, flood control res., Vt E3 208
North Star, Ohio B3 199
North Stonington, Conn. D9 172
North Stradbroke, isl., Austl C9 112
North Stratford, N.H. A3, B1 193
North Sudbury, Mass. C1 185
North Sunderland, Eng. E7 57
North Sutton, N.H. D3 193
North Swansea, Mass. C5 185
North Sydney, Austl. *F9 111
North Sydney, N.S., Can. C9 151
North Syracuse, N.Y. B4 196
North Tarrytown, N.Y. D2, D3 196
North Terre Haute, Ind. E3 179
North Thetford, Vt. D4 208
North Thompson, riv., B.C., Can D8 149
North Tolsta, Scot. B2 57
North Tonawanda, N.Y. B2 196
North Troy, Vt. B4 208
North Truchas, peak, N. Mex B4 195
North Tunbridge, Vt. D4 208
North Turlock, Calif. *D3 170
North Turner, mtn., Maine C4 184
North Twin, lake, Newf., Can D3 152
North Twin, lake, Wis B4 212
North Tyne, riv., Eng E6 57
North Uist, isl., Scot C1 57
North Umpqua, riv., Oreg D4 201
North Uvalde, Tex. E3 206
North Uxbridge, Mass. B4 185
North Valley Stream, N.Y. *E3 196
North Vancouver, B.C., Can. A10, E6 149
North Vandergrift, Pa. *E2 202
North Vassalboro, Maine D3 184
North Vernon, Ind. F6 179
North Versailles, Pa. *F2 202
North Vietnam, see Vietnam, North, country, Asia
North Virginia Beach, Va. *E7 209
North Wabasca, lake, Alta., Can A3 148
North Waldoboro, Maine D3 184
North Wales, Pa. F11 202
North Walpole, N.H. D2 193
North Walsham, Eng. B9 56
North Warren, Maine D3 184
North Warren, Pa. C3 202
North Washington, Iowa A5 180
North Waterford, Maine D2 184
North Weare, N.H. D3 193
North Webster, Ind. B6 179
North West, harbor, N.Y E7 172
North-West Frontier, reg., Pak. A3 88
North West River, Newf., Can. B1, h9 152
North West Upsalquitch, riv., N.B., Can B2 151
North Westchester, Conn. C7 172
North Western, prov., Zambia D4 106
North Westminster (Gageville), Vt. E4 208
North Westport, Mass. C5 185
North Weymouth, Mass. D3 185
North Wilbraham, Mass. B3 185
North Wildwood, N.J. F3 194
North Wilkesboro, N.C. A2 197
North Wilmington, Mass. C2 185
North Windham, Conn. B8 172
North Windham, Maine E2, E4 184
North Woodstock, Conn. B9 172
North Woodstock, N.H. B3 193
North Yarmouth, Maine E5 184
North York, Ont., Can. D5, E6 153
North York, Pa. G8 202
North York, moors, Eng C6 55
North Zanesville, Ohio *C5 199
North Zulch, Tex. D4 206
Northallerton, Eng. F7 57
Northam, Austl. F2 111
Northam, Eng. C3 56
Northampton, Austl. E1 111
Northampton, Eng. D6 55, B7 56
Northampton, Mass. B2 185
Northampton, Pa. E11 202
Northampton, co., Eng. B7 56
Northampton, co., N.C. A6 197
Northampton, co., Pa. E11 202
Northampton, co., Va. D7 209

Northboro, Iowa....D2 180
Northboro, Mass....B4 185
Northbridge, Mass....B4 185
Northbrook, Ill....E2 178
Northcarrollton, Miss....B4 188
Northcrest, Calif....*B1 170
Northeast, cape, Alsk....C6 167
Northeast, pass, La....E7 183
Northeast, pond, N.H....D5 193
Northeast, point, Newf., Can....B4 152
Northeast, riv., Md....A6 173
Northeast Foreland, pt., Grnld....A16 118
Northeast Harbor, Maine..D4 184
Northeast New Guinea, reg., N. Gui....k12 111
Northeast Polder, reg., Neth....B5 59
Northeast Providence, chan., Ba. Is....C5 131
Northeastern Polder (Noordoostelijke Polder), reg., Neth....B5 59
Northeim, Ger....B5 61
Northern, prov., Malawi...D5 106
Northern, prov., Zambia...D5 106
Northern, reg., Ghana....E4 103
Northern, reg., Ken....A6 106
Northern, reg., Nig....D6 103
Northern, reg., Sud....B3 105
Northern, reg., Tan....B6 106
Northern, reg., Ug....A5 106
Northern, head, N.B., Can....E3 151
Northern Arm, Newf., Can.D4 152
Northern Cheyenne, Indian res., Mont....E10 190
Northern Dvina, riv., Sov. Un....C7 71
Northern German confederation.... 51
Northern Indian, lake, Man., Can....A3 150
Northern Ireland, reg., U.K....C3 55, 54
Northern Light, lake, Ont., Can....A7 187
Northern Sporades, is., Grc....C5 69
Northern Territory, ter., Austl....C5 111
Northfield, B.C., Can....A9 149
Northfield, Conn....C4 172
Northfield, Ill....*E3 178
Northfield, Maine....D5 184
Northfield, Mass....A3 185
Northfield, Minn....F5 187
Northfield, N.H....D3 193
Northfield, N.J....E3 194
Northfield, Ohio....B2 199
Northfield, Tex....B2 206
Northfield, Vt....C3 208
Northfield, Wis....D2 212
Northfield, mts., Vt....C3 208
Northfield Center, Vt....C3 208
Northfield Falls, Vt....C3 208
Northford, Conn....D5 172
Northgate, Sask., Can....H4 155
Northgate, N. Dak....A3 198
Northlake, Ill....*F2 178
Northland, Mich....B3 186
Northmoor, Mo....E2 189
Northome, Minn....C4 187
Northport, Ala....B2 166
Northport, Maine....D4 184
Northport, Mich....C5 186
Northport, Nebr....C2 191
Northport, N.Y....D3 196
Northport, Wash....A8 210
Norths, highland, Ant....C25 120
Northside, N.C....A5 197
Northstar, Mich....E6 186
Northumberland, N.H....A3 193
Northumberland, Pa....E8 202
Northumberland, co., N.B., Can....B3 151
Northumberland, co., Ont., Can....C7 153
Northumberland, co., Pa...E8 202
Northumberland, co., Va..D6 209
Northumberland, is., Austl....D9 110
Northumberland, strait, Can....C5 151
Northvale, N.J....C5 194
Northview, Mo....D4 189
Northville, Conn....C3 172
Northville, Mich....A7 186
Northville, N.Y....B6 196
Northville, S. Dak....B7 204
Northwest, cape, Austl....D1 110
Northwest, highlands, Scot.C3 57
Northwest Polder, reg., Neth....B5 59
Northwest Providence, chan., Ba. Is....B4 131
Northwest St. Augustin, riv., Que., Can....C2 152
Northwest Territories, ter., Can....C13 144
Northwestern, dist., Alsk..B7 167
Northwich, Eng....A5 56
Northwood, Iowa....A4 180
Northwood, N.H....D4 193
Northwood, N. Dak....B8 198
Northwood Center, N.H...D4 193
Northwood Narrows, N.H..D4 193
Northwood Ridge, N.H....D4 193
Northwoods, Mo....*C7 189
Norton, N.B., Can....D4 151
Norton, Eng....F8 57
Norton, Kans....C4 181
Norton, Mass....C5 185
Norton, Ohio....A6 199
Norton, Rh....A5 107
Norton, Tex....D2 206
Norton, Vt....A5 208
Norton (Independent City), Va....B2 209
Norton, W. Va....C5 211
Norton, co., Kans....C4 181
Norton, bay, Alsk....C7 167
Norton, pond, Vt....B5 208
Norton, res., Kans....C4 181
Norton, res., Mass....B12 172
Norton, sound, Alsk....C6 167
Nortons Corner, Ariz..D4, G2 168
Nortonville, Kans....A7, C8 181
Nortonville, Ky....C2 182
Nortonville, N. Dak....C7 198
Nortorf, Ger....D3 62
Norvegia, cape, Ant....B11 120
Norvell, Ark....B5 169
Norvello, Va....E4 209
Norvelt, Pa....*F3 202
Norwalk, Calif....*F4 170
Norwalk, Conn....E3 172
Norwalk, Iowa....A7, C4 180
Norwalk, Ohio....A5 199
Norwalk, Wis....E3 212
Norwalk, is., Conn....E3 172
Norwalk, riv., Conn....E3 172
Norway, Iowa....C6 180
Norway, Kans....C6 181
Norway, Maine....D2 184
Norway, Mich....C3 186
Norway, Oreg....D2 201
Norway, S.C....E5 203
NORWAY, country, Eur....E5 63
c. 1140.... 47
c. 1360.... 48
in 1810.... 50
in 1815.... 50
in 1914.... 52
Norway, isl., Viet....B7 89
Norway, lake, Minn....E3 187
Norway House, Man., Can....C3 150
Norwegian, sea, Eur....B6 40
Norwell, Mass....D4 185
Norwich, Ont., Can....E4 153
Norwich, Conn....C8 172
Norwich, Eng....B9 56
Norwich, Kans....E6 181
Norwich, N.Y....C5 196
Norwich, N. Dak....A5 198
Norwich, Vt....D4 208
Norwichtown, Conn....C8 172
Norwood, Ont., Can....C7 153
Norwood, Colo....C2 171
Norwood, Ga....C4 175
Norwood, La....D4 183
Norwood, Mass....B5, D2 185
Norwood, Minn....F5 187
Norwood, Mo....D5 189
Norwood, N.J....C5 194
Norwood, N.Y....A2 196
Norwood, N.C....B3 197
Norwood, Ohio....D2 199
Norwood, Pa....B11 202
Norwoodville, Iowa....A7 180
Norwottock, mtn., Mass....B2 185
Nosbonsing, lake, Ont., Can....A5 153
Noshiro, Jap....F10 93
Nösjön, lake, Swe....A6 62
Noss, head, Scot....B6 57
Nossa Senhora das Dores, Braz....D3 138
Nossen, Ger....B8 61
Nosy-bé, isl., Malag....f9 107
Notasulga, Ala....C4 166
Notch, peak, Utah....D2 207
Notch Hill, B.C., Can....D8 149
Noteć, riv., Pol....B3 70
Notikewin, Alta., Can....A2 148
Notikewin, riv., Alta., Can....A2 148
Noto, It....F5 67
Noto, gulf, It....F5 67
Noto, isl., Jap....H8 93
Notodden, Nor....H3 63
Notre Dame, N.B., Can....C5 151
Notre Dame, bay, Newf., Can....D4 152
Notre Dame, mts., Que., Can....D6 154
Notre Dame [de la Salette], Que., Can....D2 154
Notre Dame de Lourdes, Man., Can....E2 150
Notre-Dame-de-Rimouski, Que., Can....A9 154
Notre Dame [des Bois], Que., Can....D6 154
Notre-Dame-du-Lac, Que., Can....B9 154
Notre Dame du Laus, Que., Can....C2 154
Notre Dame Junction, Newf., Can....D4 152
Nottawa, Ont., Can....C4 153
Nottawasaga, bay, Ont., Can....C4 153
Nottaway, riv., Que., Can..F17 143
Nottely, lake, Ga....B2 175
Nottingham, Eng....B6 56
Nottingham, N.H....D4 193
Nottingham, co., Eng....A7 56
Nottingham, isl., N.W. Ter., Can....D17 143
Nottoway, Va....D4 209
Nottoway, co., Va....D4 209
Nottoway, riv., Va....E5 209
Notukeu, creek, Sask., Can.H2 155
Notus, Idaho....F2 177
Nouadhibou, Maur....B1 103
Nouakchott, Maur....C1 103
Nouméa, N. Cal.... 115
Nouna, Upper Volta....D4 103
Noupoort, S. Afr....D3 107
Noutonice, Czech....n17 70
Nouvelle-Anvers, Zaire....A2 106
Nouzonville, Fr....C6 58
Nova, Ohio....A5 199
Nova Chaves, Ang....D3 106
Nova Cruz, Braz....C3, h6 138
Nova Freixo, Moz....D6 106
Nova Friburgo, Braz...C4, h6 137
Nova Gaia, Ang....D2 106
Nova Granada, Braz....C3 137
Nova Iguaçu, Braz....h6 137
Nova Lima, Braz....F2 138
Nova Lisboa, Ang....D2 106
Nova Lusitania, Moz....A5 107
Nova Mambone, Moz....B6 107
Nova Russas, Braz....B2 138
Nova Scotia, prov., Can....E6 151
Nova Sofala, Moz....B5 107
Nova Soure, Braz....D3 138
Nova Varoš, Yugo....D4 68
Nova Venécia, Braz....E2 138
Nova Zagora, Bul....D8 68
Novar, Ont., Can....B5 153
Novara, It....D4 66, B2 67
Novato, Calif....B5, C2 170
Novaya Astrakhan, Sov. Un....p21 72
Novaya Ladoga, Sov. Un..A9 72
Novaya Lyalya, Sov. Un...B6 73
Novaya Odessa, Sov. Un..H8 72
Novaya Sibir, isl., Sov. Un....B17 71
Novaya Zemlya, is., Sov. Un....B8 71
Nové Mesto [nad Váhom], Czech....D4 70
Nové Strašeci, Czech....C8 61
Nové Zámky, Czech....E5 70
Novelda, Sp....C5 65
Novelty, Mo....A5 189
Novgorod, Sov. Un....B8 72
Novgorod-Severskiy, Sov. Un....E9 72
Novi, Mich....A7 186
Novi Ligure, It....B2 67
Novi Pazar, Bul....D8 68
Novi Pazar, Yugo....D5 68
Novi Sad, Yugo....C4 68
Novice, Tex....D3 206
Novigrad, Yugo....C2 68
Novinger, Mo....A5 189
Novo-Annenskiy, Sov. Un....C2 73
Novo Kazalinsk, Sov. Un..D6 73
Novo Mesto, Yugo....C2 68
Novo Redondo, Ang....D1 106
Novo-Selo, Bul....C6 68
Novo-Troitsk, Sov. Un....*D8 71
Novoaydar, Sov. Un....G12, q21 72
Novocherkassk, Sov. Un....H13 72
Novoekonomicheskoye, Sov. Un....q20 72
Novograd-Volynskiy, Sov. Un....F6 72
Novogrudok, Sov. Un....E5 72
Novokurovka, Sov. Un....B7 93
Novokuybyshevsk, Sov. Un....*D7 71
Novokuznetsk, Sov. Un...D11 71
Novomirgorod, Sov. Un....G8 72
Novomoskovsk, Sov. Un...C1 73
Novomoskovsk, Sov. Un..G10 72
Novopokrovskaya, Sov. Un....I13 72
Novorossiysk, Sov. Un....I11 72
Novoshakhtinsk, Sov. Un....H12 72
Novosibirsk, Sov. Un....B10 73
Novosibirskiye (*New Siberian*), *is., Sov. Un*....B17 71
Novosil, Sov. Un....E11 72
Novoukrainka, Sov. Un....G8 72
Novouzensk, Sov. Un....C3 73
Novoyeniseyskaya, Sov. Un....B11 93
Novozybkov, Sov. Un....E8 72
Nový Bohumín, Czech....D5 70
Nový Bydžov, Czech....C3 70
Novy Jičín, Czech....D5 70
Novyy Donbass, Sov. Un.q21 72
Novyy Oskol, Sov. Un....F11 72
Novyy Port, Sov. Un....C10 71
Novyy Vasyugan, Sov. Un....B9 73
Novyye Senzhary, Sov. Un....G10 72
Nowa Sól, Pol....C3 70
Nowagród, Pol....B10 61
Nowata, Okla....A6 200
Nowata, co., Okla....A6 200
Nowe Warpno, Pol....B3 70
Nowlin, S. Dak....C4 204
Nowogard, Pol....B3 70
Nowood, creek, Wyo....A5 213
Nowra, Austl....G8 112
Nowshera, Pak....*B5 87
Nowy Dwor, Pol....k13 70
Nowy Sacz, Pol....D6 70
Nowy Targ, Pol....D6 70
Nowy Tomyśl, Pol....B4 70
Noxapater, Miss....C4 188
Noxen, Pa....A7, D9 202
Noxon, Mont....C1 190
Noxon, res., Mont....C1 190
Noxontown, pond, Del....B6 173
Noxubee, co., Miss....B5 188
Noxubee, riv., Miss....B5 188
Noxville, Tex....D3 206
Noya, Sp....A1 65
Noyack, bay, N.Y....E7 172
Noyes, Minn....B1 187
Noyon, Fr....C5 58
Nsanje, Malawi....E6 106
Nsawam, Ghana....E4 103
Nsukka, Nig....E6 103
Nu Mine, Pa....E3 202
Nuanetsi, Rh....B5 107
Nubansit, lake, N.H....E2 193
Nuberg, Ga....B4 175
Nubian, des., Sud....A3 105
Ñuble, prov., Chile....B2 136
Nuckolls, co., Nebr....D7 191
Nucla, Colo....C2 171
Nueces, co., Tex....F4 206
Nueces, riv., Tex....E3 206
Nueltin, lake, N.W. Ter., Can....D13 142
Nueva Casas Grandes, Mex....A3 129
Nueva Esparta, state, Ven.A5 133
Nueva Esparta, is., Ven....A5 133
Nueva Gerona, Cuba....E2 131
Nueva Imperial, Chile....B2 136
Nueva Lubecka, Arg....C2 136
Nueva Palmira, Ur....E1 137
Nueva Rosita, Mex....B4 129
Nueva San Salvador, Sal..D3 130
Nueve de Julio, Arg....B4 136
Nuevitas, Cuba....E5 131
Nuevo, gulf, Arg....C4 136
Nuevo Guerrero, Mex....F3 206
Nuevo Laredo, Mex....B5 129
Nuevo León, state, Mex....B4 129
Nuevo Mundo, mtn., Bol...D2 135
Nugget, Wyo....D2 213
Nugima, New Hanover I.... 115
Nuits [-St. Georges], Fr....D6 58
Nukha, Sov. Un....*E3 73
Nukheila (Merga) (Well), Sud....B2 105
Nukualofa, Tonga....H11 113
Nukumanu, is., Sol. Is.... 115
Nukus, Sov. Un....E5 73
Nulato, Alsk....C8 167
Nules, Sp....C5 65
Nullarbor, Austl....F5 111
Nullarbor, plain, Austl....F4 110
Numa, Iowa....D5 180
Numan, Nig....E7 103
Numazu, Jap....I9, n17 93
Nuna Nuna, Bougainville I... 115
Nunaka Valley, Alsk....g17 167
Nunawading, Austl....*H5 112
Nunda, N.Y....C3 196
Nunda, S. Dak....C8 204
Nuneaton, Eng....B6 56
Nunez, Ga....D4 175
Nungan, China....C10 91
Nunica, Mich....E4 186
Nunivak, isl., Alsk....C6 167
Nunkiang, China....B10 91
Nunn, Colo....A6 171
Nunnelly, Tenn....B4 205
Nunukan Timur, isl., Indon....E5 90
Nuoro, It....D2 67
Nuquí, Col....B2 133
Nuremberg (Nürnberg), Ger....D6 61
Nuremberg, Pa....E9 202
Nuri, Mex....B3 129
Nurmes, Fin....F13 63
Nürnberg, see Nuremberg, Ger.
Nurrari, lakes, Austl....E5 110
Nursery, Tex....E4 206
Nürtingen, Ger....E4 61
Nusaybin, Tur....D13 85
Nushagak, Alsk....D8 167
Nushki, Pak....C4 87
Nusle, Czech....n17 70
Nussi, Bougainville I.... 115
Nut, lake, Sask., Can....E4 155
Nut Mountain, Sask., Can....E4 155
Nuthe, riv., Ger....A8 61
Nuthegan, riv., Vt....B5 208
Nutley, N.J....B4, D5 194
Nutrioso, Ariz....D6 168
Nuttby, mtn., N.S., Can....D6 151
Nutter Fort, W. Va....B4, 6 211
Nutting Lake, Mass....C2 185
Nuuanu Pali, pass, Haw...g10 176
Nuutele, isl., W. Sam.... 114
Nuutoi, cape, W. Sam.... 114
Nuwara Eliya, Cey....G7 87
Nuwaybi'al Muzayyinah, Eg....H10 85
Nuyaka, Okla....B5 200
Nuzvid, India....I8 88
Nvalat, Isr....C6, h10 84
Nyac, Alsk....C8 167
Nyack, N.Y....D1, D3 196
Nyala, Sud....C1 105
Nyamandhlovu, Rh....A4 107
Nyamtumbo, Tan....D6 106
Nyandoma, Sov. Un....A13 72
Nyanza, Rwanda....B4 106
Nyanza, reg., Ken....A5 106
Nyasa, lake, Afr....H9 96
Nyasaland, see Malawi, country, Afr.
Nyborg, Den....C4 62
Nybro, Swe....I6 63
Nye, Mont....E7 190
Nye, co., Nev....E5 192
Nyeland Acres, Calif....*E4 170
Nyeri, Ken....B6 106
Nyimba, Zambia....D5 106
Nyíregyháza, Hung....B5 68
Nyköbing [på Falster], Den....D5 62
Nyköbing [på Mors], Den..B2 62
Nyköbing [på Sjaelland], Den....C5 62
Nyköping, Swe....H7, u34 63
Nylstroom, S. Afr....B4 107
Nymagee, Austl....F6 112
Nymburk, Czech....C3, n19 70
Nymindegab, Den....C2 62
Nynäshamn, Swe....H7, u35 63
Nyngan, Austl....E6 112
Nyong, riv., Cam....E2 104
Nyonga, Tan....C5 106
Nýřany, Czech....D2 70
Nýrsko, Czech....D8 61
Nysa, Pol....C4 70
Nysa, riv., Pol....C4 70
Nyssa, Oreg....D9 201
Nysted, Den....D5 62
Nyunzu, Zaire....C4 106
Nzega, Tan....B5 106
N'Zérékoré, Guinea....E3 103

O

Oa, Mull of, head, Scot....E2 57
Oacoma, S. Dak....D6 204
Oahe, dam, S. Dak....C5 204
Oahe, res., S. Dak....C5 204
Oahu, isl., Haw....B4 176
Oak, Nebr....D8 191
Oak, isl., Wis....B3 212
Oak, lake, Man., Can....E1 150
Oak, mtn., Ga....D2 175
Oak Bay, N.B., Can....D2 151
Oak Bluffs, Mass....D6 185
Oak City, N.C....B6 197
Oak City, Utah....D3 207
Oak Creek, Colo....A4 171
Oak Creek, Wis....F2 212
Oak Creek, canyon, Ariz....C4 168
Oak Forest, Ill....F3 178
Oak Grove, Ky....D2 182
Oak Grove, La....B4 183
Oak Grove, Mich....F7 186
Oak Grove, Mo....*B3 189
Oak Grove, Oreg....B2, B4 201
Oak Grove, S.C....C8 203
Oak Grove, Va....C6 209
Oak Harbor, Ohio....A4 199
Oak Harbor, Wash....A3 210
Oak Hill, Fla....D6 174
Oak Hill, Mich....D4 186
Oak Hill, Mo....C6 189
Oak Hill, Ohio....D5 199
Oak Hill, Tenn....E9 205
Oak Hill, W. Va....D3, D7 211
Oak Island, Minn....A4 187
Oak Lake, Man., Can....E1 150
Oak Lawn, Ill....B6, F3 178
Oak Orchard, Del....C7 173
Oak Park, Ga....D4 175
Oak Park, Ill....B6, F3 178
Oak Park, Mich....A7 186
Oak Point, Man., Can....D2 150
Oak Ridge, La....B4 183
Oak Ridge, Mo....D8 189
Oak Ridge, N.C....A4 197
Oak Ridge, Pa....D3 202
Oak Ridge, Tenn....C9 205
Oak Ridges, Ont., Can....E6 153
Oak River, Man., Can....D1 150
Oak Vale, Miss....D4 188
Oak Valley, Kans....E7 181
Oak View, Calif....*E4 170
Oakalla, Tex....D4 206
Oakboro, N.C....B3 197
Oakbrook Terrace, Ill....*F2 178
Oakburn, Man., Can....D1 150
Oakdale, Calif....D3 170
Oakdale, Conn....D8 172
Oakdale, Ill....E4 178
Oakdale, La....D3 183
Oakdale, Mass....B4 185
Oakdale, Nebr....B8 191
Oakdale, N.Y....G4 172
Oakdale, Pa....B5 202
Oakdale, Tenn....D9 205
Oakengates, Eng....B5 56
Oakes, N. Dak....C7 198
Oakesdale, Wash....B8 210
Oakey, Austl....C8 112
Oakfield, Ga....E3 175
Oakfield, Maine....B4 184
Oakfield, N.Y....B2 196
Oakfield, Tenn....B3 205
Oakfield, Wis....E5 212
Oakford, Ill....C4 178
Oakford, Ind....D5 179
Oakford, Pa....A12, F12 202
Oakgrove, Ark....A2 169
Oakham, Eng....B7 56
Oakham, Mass....B3 185
Oakhill, Kans....C6 181
Oakhurst, N.J....C4 194
Oakhurst, Okla....A5 200
Oakland, Ala....A2 166
Oakland, Ark....A3 169
Oakland, Calif....B5, D2 170
Oakland, Ont., Can....D4 153
Oakland, Fla....*D5 174
Oakland, Ill....D5 178
Oakland, Iowa....C2 180
Oakland, Ky....C3 182
Oakland, Maine....D3 184
Oakland, Md....D1 173
Oakland, Miss....A4 188
Oakland, Mo....*C7 189
Oakland, Nebr....C9 191
Oakland, N.J....A4 194
Oakland, N.C....D3 197
Oakland, Okla....C5 200
Oakland, Oreg....D3 201
Oakland, Pa....*D1 202
Oakland, Pa....C10 202
Oakland, R.I....B10 172
Oakland, Tenn....B2 205
Oakland, co., Mich....F7 186
Oakland City, Ind....H3 179
Oakland Park, Fla....E3, F6 174
Oaklandon, Ind....H8 179
Oaklawn, Kans....B5 181
Oaklawn, La....B8 183
Oakley, Idaho....G5 177
Oakley, Kans....C3 181
Oakley, Mich....E6 186
Oakley, Miss....C3 188
Oakley, N.C....*D3 197
Oakley, S.C....E7 203
Oakley, Utah....C4 207
Oaklyn, N.J....*D2 194
Oakman, Ala....B2 166
Oakman, Ga....B2 175
Oakmont, Pa....A6, E2 202
Oakner, Man., Can....D1 150
Oakridge, Oreg....D4 201
Oaks, Okla....A7 200
Oaks, Pa....A10 202
Oakton, Ky....B2 182
Oakton, Va....B4 209
Oaktown, Ind....G3 179
Oakvale, W. Va....D4 211
Oakview, Mo....*B3 189
Oakville, Man., Can....E2 150
Oakville, Ont., Can....D5 153
Oakville, Conn....C4 172
Oakville, Iowa....C6 180
Oakville, Ind....D7 179
Oakville, Mo....B8 189
Oakville, Va....D4 209
Oakville, Wash....C2 210
Oakway, S.C....B1 203
Oakwood, Ga....B3 175
Oakwood, Ill....C6 178
Oakwood, Mo....B6 189
Oakwood, N. Dak....A8 198
Oakwood (Oakwood Village), Ohio....*B2 199
Oakwood, Ohio....C3 199
Oakwood, Ohio....A3 199
Oakwood, Okla....B3 200
Oakwood, Pa....*D1 202
Oakwood, Tex....D5 206
Oakwood, Va....B3 209
Oamaru, N.Z....P13 112
Ōami, Jap....n19 93
Oasis, Nev....B7 192
Oasis, Utah....D3 207
Oatman, Ariz....C1 168
Oats, S.C....C7 203
Oaxaca, Mex....D5 129
Oaxaca, state, Mex....D5 129
Ob, riv., Sov. Un....C9 71
Obama, Jap....n14 93
Oban, see Half-moon Bay, N.Z.
Oban, Scot....D3 57
Oban Station, Sask., Can..E1 155
O'Bannon, Ky....A4 182
Obbia, Som....D6 105
Obed, Alta., Can....C2 148
Obed, riv., Tenn....C9 205
Obeh, Afg....D11 86
Oberá, Arg....E4 135
Oberammergau, Ger....B7 66
Oberdrauburg, Aus....C8 66
Oberhausen, Ger....B1 61
Oberkirch, Ger....E3 61
Oberlin, Kans....C3 181
Oberlin, La....D3 183
Oberlin, Ohio....A5 199
Obernai, Fr....C7 58
Obernburg, Ger....D4 61
Oberon, N. Dak....B6 198
Oberösterreich (Upper Austria), state, Aus....E9 61
Oberstaufen, Ger....B6 66
Oberstdorf, Ger....E5 60
Obert, Nebr....B8 191
Oberursel, Ger....C3 61
Oberwald, Switz....C4 66
Obetz, Ohio....C2, C5 199
Obi, see Nichinan, Jap.
Obiam, cape, Saipan.... 114
Obiam, inlet, Saipan.... 114
Óbidos, Braz....C3 139
Obihiro, Jap....E11 93
Obion, Tenn....A2 205
Obion, co., Tenn....A2 205
Obion, creek, Ky....B2 182
Obion, riv., Tenn....A2 205
Oblong, Ill....D6 178
Obluchye, Sov. Un....E16 71
Obo, Cen. Afr. Rep....D5 104
Obock, Afars & Is....C5 105
Öbör Sumun, Mong....B5 91
Oborniki, Pol....B4 70
Oboyan, Sov. Un....F11 72
O'Brien, Fla....B4 174
O'Brien, Oreg....E3 201
O'Brien, co., Iowa....A2 180
Observation, isl., Fla....F6 174
Observation, peak, Calif....B3 170
Obsidian, Idaho....F4 177
Obskaya, bay, Sov. Un....C10 71
Obuasi, Ghana....E4 103
Obubra, Nig....E6 103
Ocala, Fla....C4 174
Ocampo, Arg....E4 135
Ocampo, Mex....B3 129
Ocaña, Col....B3 133
Ocaña, Sp....C4 65
Occidental Calif....B4 170
Occoquan, Va....C5 209
Occum, Conn....C8 172
Ocean, co., N.J....D4 194
Ocean, isl., Gilbert Is.... 115
Ocean Beach, N.Y....G4 172
Ocean Bluff, Mass....B6, E4 185
Ocean City, Md....D7 173
Ocean City, N.J....E3 194
Ocean City, Wash....B1 210

INDEX KEY Each place listed in **Bold-faced Type** has its population listed in the Population tables, pages 230 to 280.
Each country, shown in CAPITAL LETTERS, has its population listed in the World Political Information Table, pages 6 to 10.
* Does not appear on map; key shows general location.

Ocean Drive Beach, S.C. D10 203
Ocean Falls, B.C., Can. C4 149
Ocean Gate, N.J. D4 194
Ocean Grove, N.J. C4 194
Ocean Park, Wash. C1 210
Ocean Ridge, Fla. *F6 174
Ocean Springs, Miss. E3, E5 188
Ocean View, Del. C7 173
Ocean View, N.J. E3 194
Oceana, W. Va. D3 211
Oceana, co., Mich. E4 186
Oceanlake, Oreg. *C3 201
Oceano, Calif. *E3 170
Oceanport, N.J. C4 194
Oceanside, Calif. F5 170
Oceanside, N.Y. *G2 172
Oceanville, N.J. E4 194
Oceanway, Fla. B6 174
Ochakov, Sov. Un. H8 72
Ochamchire, Sov. Un. A13 85
Ocheda, lake, Minn. G3 187
Ochelata, Okla. A6 200
Ocheyedan, Iowa A2 180
Ocheyedan, mound, Iowa A2 180
Ocheyedan, riv., Iowa A2 180
Ochiai, see Dolinsk, Sov. Un.
Ochil, hills, Scot. D5 57
Ochiltree, co., Tex. A2 206
Ochir, Mong. B6 92
Ochlocknee, Ga. F2 175
Ochlockonee, riv., Fla., Ga. F2 175
Ochoco, res., Oreg. C6 201
Ocholt, Ger. A7 59
Ochopee, Fla. G5 174
Ochre River, Man., Can. D2 150
Ochsenfurt, Ger. D5 61
Ochtrup, Ger. A2 61
Ocilla, Ga. E3 175
Ockelbo, Swe. G7 63
Öckerö, isl., Swe. A5 62
Ocmulgee, nat. mon., Ga. D3 175
Ocmulgee, riv., Ga. D3 175
Ocna Sibiului, Rom. C7 68
Ocnele-Mari, Rom. C7 68
Ocoee, Fla. D5 174
Ocoee, Tenn. D9 205
Ocoee, lake, Tenn. D9 205
Ocoña, Peru E3 134
Oconee, Ga. D4 175
Oconee, Ill. D4 178
Oconee, co., Ga. C3 175
Oconee, co., S.C. B1 203
Oconee, riv., Ga. D4 175
Oconomowoc, Wis. E5 212
Oconto, Nebr. C6 191
Oconto, Wis. D6 212
Oconto, co., Wis. D5 212
Oconto, riv., Wis. D5 212
Oconto Falls, Wis. D5 212
Ocós, Guat. C1 130
Ocotal, Nic. D4 130
Ocotepeque, Hond. C3 130
Ocotillo, Ariz. G2 168
Ocotlán, Mex. C4, m12 129
Ocracoke, N.C. B8 197
Ocracoke, inlet, N.C. B7 197
Ocracoke, isl., N.C. B8 197
Ocros, Peru D2 134
Octoraro, creek, Md., Pa. G9 202
Octavia, Nebr. C8 191
Ocumare del Tuy, Ven. A4 133
Ocussi, reg., Port. Timor G6 90
Oda, Ghana E4 103
Odanah, Wis. B3 212
Odawara, Jap. n18 93
Odda, Nor. G2 63
Odder, Den. C4 62
Oddur, Som. E5 105
Odebolt, Iowa B2 180
Odei, riv., Man., Can. A3 150
Odell, Ill. B5 178
Odell, Nebr. D9 191
Odell, Tex. B3 206
Odell, lake, Oreg. D5 201
Odem, Tex. F4 206
Odemira, Port. D1 65
Ödemis, Tur. C6 69
Oden, Ark. C2 169
Odendaalsrus, S. Afr. C4 107
Odensala, Swe. t35 63
Odensback, Swe. t33 63
Odense, Den. C4 62
Odense, co., Den. C4 62
Odense Å, riv., Den. C4 62
Odenton, Md. B4 173
Odenville, Ala. B3 166
Odenwald, mts., Ger. D3 61
Oder (Odra), riv., Ger., Pol. B7 60, B3 70
Oder-Spree, canal, Ger. A9 61
Odessa, Ont., Can. C8 153
Odessa, Sask., Can. G4 155
Odessa, Del. B6 173
Odessa, Fla. D4 174
Odessa, Minn. E2 187
Odessa, Mo. C4 189
Odessa, Nebr. D6 191
Odessa, N.Y. C4 196
Odessa, Sov. Un. H8 72
Odessa, Tex. D1 206
Odessa, Wash. B7 210
Odienné, I.C. E3 103
Odin, Ill. E4 178
Odin, Kans. D5 181
Odin, Minn. G4 187
Odin, mtn., B.C., Can. D8 149
Odivelas, Port. f9 65
Odobești, Rom. C8 68
Odon, Ind. G4 179
O'Donnell, Tex. C2 206
Odorhei, Rom. B7 68
Odum, Ga. E4 175
Odweina, Som. D6 105
Odzi, Rh. A5 107
Oebisfelde, Ger. A5 61
Oeiras, Braz. C2 138
Oeiras, Port. f9 65
Oelde, Ger. B3 61
Oella, Md. B4 173
Oelrichs, S. Dak. D2 204
Oelsnitz, Ger. C7 61
Oelsnitz [im Vogtland], Ger. C7 61
Oelwein, Iowa B6 180
Oesede, Ger. A3 61
Ofahoma, Miss. C4 188
O'Fallon, Ill. E4 178
O'Fallon, Mo. A7 189
O'Fallon, creek, Mont. D12 190
Offenbach, Ger. C3 61
Offenburg, Ger. E2 61
Offerle, Kans. E4 181
Offerman, Ga. E4 175
Oficina Avanzada, Chile D2 135
Oficina Pepita, Chile D2 135
Oficina Rosario, Chile D2 135
Oficina San Gregorio, Chile D2 135
Ōfunato, Jap. G10 93
Oga (Funakawa), Jap. G9 93
Ōgaki, Jap. I8, n15 93
Ogallah, Kans. D4 181
Ogallala, Nebr. C4 191
Ogasawara, see Bonin Islands, Jap.
Ogbomosho, Nig. E5 103
Ogden, Ark. D1 169
Ogden, Ill. C6 178
Ogden, Iowa B3 180
Ogden, Kans. C7 181
Ogden, Utah A4 207
Ogden, mtn., Alsk. k23 167
Ogden Dunes, Ind. *A3 179
Ogdensburg, N.J. A3 194
Ogdensburg, N.Y. A1 196
Ogdensburg, Pa. C8 202
Ogeechee, riv., Ga. D4 175
Ogema, Sask., Can. H3 155
Ogema, Minn. C3 187
Ogema, Wis. C3 212
Ogemaw, Ark. D2 169
Ogemaw, co., Mich. D6 186
Ogilvie, Minn. E5 187
Ogilvie, range, Yukon, Can. D5 142
Oglala, S. Dak. D3 204
Ogle, co., Ill. A4 178
Oglesby, Ill. B4 178
Oglesby, Tenn. E9 205
Oglethorpe, Ga. D2 175
Oglethorpe, co., Ga. C3 175
Oglethorpe, mtn., Ga. B2 175
Oglio, riv., It. D5 66
Ogoja, Nig. E6 103
Ogoki, riv., Ont., Can. E8 153
Ogooué, riv., Gabon F2 104
Ogrodzieniec, Pol. g11 70
Ogulin, Yugo. C2 68
Ogunquit, Maine E2 184
Ogurchinskiy, isl., Sov. Un. B6 86
Ohakune, N.Z. M15 112
Ōhara, Jap. n19 93
Ohatchee, Ala. B3 166
Ohaton, Alta., Can. C4 148
O'Higgins, prov., Chile A2 136
Ohio, Colo. C4 171
Ohio, Ill. B4 178
Ohio, N.Y. B6 196
Ohio, state, U.S. 199
Ohio, co., Ind. G7 179
Ohio, co., Ky. C3 182
Ohio, co., W. Va. A4 211
Ohio, peak, Colo. C3 171
Ohio, riv., U.S. C11 159
Ohio Brush, creek, Ohio D4 199
Ohio City, Ohio B3 199
Ohiopyle, Pa. G3 202
Ohiowa, Nebr. D8 191
Ohoopee, Ga. D4 175
Ohoopee, riv., Ga. D4 175
Ohopoho, S.W. Afr. A1 107
Ohrdruf, Ger. C5 61
Ohře, riv., Czech. n17 70
Ohrid, Yugo. E5 68
Ohrigstad, S. Afr. B5 107
Öhringen, Ger. D4 61
Oiapoque, riv., Braz. B4 139
Oich, riv., Scot. B4 57
Oignon, riv., Fr. B1 66
Oil, creek, Pa. D2 202
Oil Center, N. Mex. E6 195
Oil City, La. B2 183
Oil City, Miss. C3 188
Oil City, Pa. D2 202
Oil Spring, Indian res., N.Y. C2 196
Oil Springs, Ont., Can. E2 153
Oil Trough, Ark. B4 169
Oildale, Calif. E4 170
Oilmont, Mont. B5 190
Oilton, Okla. A5 200
Oilton, Tex. F3 206
Oise, dept., Fr. E2 59
Oise, canal, Fr. E3 59
Oise, riv., Fr. C5 58
Oiseau, riv., Man., Can. D4 150
Oisemont, Fr. E9 56
Ōita, Jap. J5 93
Oiticica, Braz. C2 138
Oizulo, Moz. D6 106
Ojai, Calif. E4 170
Ojinaga, Mex. B4 129
Ojo Caliente, N. Mex. A3 195
Ojo de Agua, Arg. E3 135
Ojo Feliz, N. Mex. A4 195
Ojocaliente, Mex. C4 129
Ojos del Salado, mtn., Arg. F4 124
Ojus, Fla. E3, G6 174
Oka, Que., Can. D3, D8 154
Oka, riv., Sov. Un. B2 73
Okaba, Indon. G9 90
Okabena, Minn. G3 187
Okahandja, S.W. Afr. B2 107
Okak, isl., Newf., Can. g9 152
Okaloosa, co., Fla. u15 174
Okanagan, lake, B.C., Can. D8 149
Okanagan, range, B.C., Can. E7 149
Okanagan Center, B.C., Can. D8 149
Okanagan Falls, B.C., Can. E8 149
Okanagan Landing, B.C., Can. D8 149
Okanogan, Wash. A6 210
Okanogan, co., Wash. A6 210
Okanogan, riv., Wash A6 210
Okapilco, creek, Ga. E3 175
Okāra, Pak. B4 87
Okarche, Okla. B4 200
Okatibbee, creek, Miss. C5 188
Okatoma, creek, Miss. D4 188
Okaton, S. Dak. D5 204
Okauchee, Wis. *E5 212
Okaukuejo, S.W. Afr. A2 107
Okawville, Ill. E4 178
Okay, Ark. D2 169
Okay, Okla. B6 200
Okaya, Jap. H9, m17 93
Okayama, Jap. I6 93
Okazaki, Jap. o16 93
O'Kean, Ark. A5 169
Okeana, Ohio C1 199
Okęcie, Pol. m13 70
Okeechobee, Fla. E6 174
Okeechobee, co., Fla. E6 174
Okeechobee, lake, Fla. F6 174
Okeelanta, Fla. F6 174
Okeene, Okla. A3 200
Okefenokee, swamp, Ga. F4 175
Okehampton, Eng. D3 56
Okemah, Okla. B5 200
Oker, riv., Ger. A5 61
Okesa, Okla. A5 200
Oketo, Kans. C7 181
Okfuskee, co., Okla. B5 200
Okha, India F2 88
Okha, Sov. Un. D17 71
Okhotsk, Sov. Un. D17 71
Okhotsk, sea, Sov. Un. D17 71
Okinawa, isl., Japan 114
Oklahoma, Pa. *E2 202
Oklahoma, state, U.S. 200
Oklahoma, co., Okla. B4 200
Oklahoma City, Okla. B4 200
Oklawaha, Fla. C5 174
Oklawaha, riv., Fla. C5 174
Oklee, Minn. C3 187
Okmulgee, Okla. B6 200
Okmulgee, co., Okla. B6 200
Okoboji, Iowa A2 180
Okobojo, creek, S. Dak. C5 204
Okolona, Ark. C2 169
Okolona, Ky. A4 182
Okolona, Miss. B5 188
Okome, Swe. A6 62
Okondja, Gabon F2 104
Okotoks, Alta., Can. D4 148
Okovanggo, riv., Ang., S.W. Afr. A2 107
Okovanggo, swamps, Bots A3 107
Okreek, S. Dak. D5 204
Oktaha, Okla. B6 200
Oktibbeha, co., Miss. B5 188
Oktyabrsk, Sov. Un. *D7 71
Oktyabrskiy, Sov. Un. C4 73
Okuniew, Pol. k14 70
Okushiri, isl., Jap. E9 93
Ola, Ark. B2 169
Ola, Idaho E2 177
Olaa (Keaau), Haw. *D6 176
Ólafsfjördur, Ice. m23 63
Ólafsvík, Ice. n21 63
Olalla, Wash. D1 210
Olamon, Maine C4 184
Olancha, Calif. D4 170
Olancha, peak, Calif. D4 170
Olanchito, Hond. C4 130
Öland, isl., Swe. I7 63
Olanta, Pa. E4 202
Olanta, S.C. D8 203
Olar, S.C. E5 203
Olascoaga, Arg. B4 136
Olathe, Colo. C3 171
Olathe, Kans. D9 181
Olavarría, Arg. B4 136
Oława, Pol. C4 70
Olazagutia, Sp. A4 65
Olberg, Ariz. D4, H3 168
Olbernhau, Ger. C8 61
Olbia, It. D2 67
Olcott, N.Y. B2 196
Olcott, W. Va. C3, C6 211
Old, chan., Sask., Can. D4 155
Old Bahama, chan., Cuba D4 131
Old Bennington, Vt. F2 208
Old Bight, Ba. Is. C6 131
Old Bridge, N.J. C4 194
Old Brookville, N.Y. *F2 172
Old Castile, reg., Sp. B4 65
Old Faithful, Wyo. A2 213
Old Faithful, geyser, Wyo. A2 213
Old Field, N.Y. F4 172
Old Field, pt., N.Y. F4 172
Old Forge, N.Y. B6 196
Old Forge, Pa. A9, D10 202
Old Fort, N.C. D4 197
Old Greenwich, Conn. E2 172
Old Harbor, Alsk. D9 167
Old Harbor, pt., R.I. E10 172
Old Head of Kinsale, head, Ire. E2 55
Old Hickory, Tenn. A5, E9 205
Old Hickory, res., Tenn. A5, E9 205
Old Lyme, Conn. D7 172
Old Man, mtn., Newf., Can. D3 152
Old Man of the Mountain (Great Stone Face), mtn., N.H. B3 193
Old Marissa, Ill. B9 189
Old Meldrum, Scot. C6 57
Old Mines, Mo. C7 189
Old Monroe, Mo. A7, C7 189
Old Mystic, Conn. D9 172
Old Orchard Beach, Maine E2, E5 184
Old Perlican, Newf., Can. D5 152
Old Point Comfort, pt., Va. B7 209
Old Rhodes, key, Fla. G6 174
Old River, lake, Ark. D6 169
Old Saybrook, Conn. D7 172
Old Speck, mtn., Maine D2 184
Old Tampa, bay, Fla. E2 174
Old Tappan, N.J. *B4 194
Old Tati, Bots. B4 107
Old Topsail, inlet, N.C. C6 197
Old Town, Ark. D2 169
Old Town, Fla. C4 174
Old Town, Maine D4 184
Old Washington, Ohio B6 199
Old Westbury, N.Y. *F2 172
Old Wives, lake, Sask., Can. G3 155
Oldbury, Eng. *B6 56
Oldeani, Tan. B6 106
Olden, Tex. C3 206
Oldenburg, Ind. F7 179
Oldenburg [in Holstein], Ger. A5 60
Oldenburg [in Oldenburg], Ger. B4 60, E2 62
Oldenzaal, Neth. B6 59
Oldham, Eng. A5 56
Oldham, S. Dak. C8 204
Oldham, co., Ky. B4 182
Oldham, co., Tex. B1 206
Oldman, riv., Alta., Can. E4 148
Oldmans, creek, N.J. D2 194
Olds, Alta., Can. D3 148
Olds, Iowa C6 180
Oldsmar, Fla. E4 174
Oldtown, Idaho A2 177
Oldtown, Md. D2 173
Oldwick, N.J. B3 194
Olean, Mo. C5 189
Olean, N.Y. C2 196
O'Leary Station, P.E.I., Can. C5 151
Olecko, Pol. A7 70
Oleiros, Sp. A1 65
Olekma, riv., Sov. Un. D15 71
Olekminsk, Sov. Un. C15 71
Olenek, riv., Sov. Un. C14 71
Olentangy, riv., Ohio B5 199
Oléron, isl., Fr. E3 58
Oleśnica, Pol. C4 70
Olesno, Pol. C5 70
Olex, Oreg. B6 201
Oley, Pa. F10 202
Olga, N. Dak. A7 198
Olga, Sov. Un. E7 93
Olga, mtn., Vt. F3 208
Ölgod, Den. C2 62
Olgopol, Sov. Un. G7 72
Olhão, Port. D2 65
Olifants, riv., S. Afr. B5 107
Olímpia, Braz. F1 138
Olimpo, dept., Par. D4 135
Olin, Iowa B6 180
Olinda, Braz. C4, k6 138
Olite, Sp. A5 65
Oliva, Sp. C5 65
Oliva de la Frontera, Sp. C2 65
Olivais, Port. f9 65
Olive, Mont. E11 190
Olive Branch, Miss. A4 188
Olive Hill, Ky. B6 182
Olivehill, Tenn. B3 205
Olivehurst, Calif. C3 170
Oliveira, Braz. F2 138
Olivenza, Sp. C2 65
Oliver, Ala. A2 166
Oliver, B.C., Can. E8 149
Oliver, Colo. C3 171
Oliver, Ga. D5 175
Oliver, Pa. G2 202
Oliver, Wis. B1 212
Oliver, co., N. Dak. B4 198
Oliver Springs, Tenn. C9 205
Olives, mtn., Jordan h12, m14 84
Olivet, Ill. D6 178
Olivet, Kans. D8 181
Olivet, Md. D5 173
Olivet, Mich. F6 186
Olivet, S. Dak. D8 204
Olivette, Mo. *C7 189
Olivia, Minn. F4 187
Olivia, N.C. B4 197
Olivier, La. E4 183
Olivone, Switz. C4 66
Öljaren, lake, Swe. t34 63
Olkusz, Pol. g11 70
Olla, La. C3 183
Ollague, Chile D2 135
Ollagüe, vol., Bol. D2 135
Ollan, is., Truk 114
Ollie, Iowa C5 180
Ollie, Mont. D12 190
Ollita, range, Arg. F2 135, A2 136
Olmito, Tex. F4 206
Olmitz, Kans. D5 181
Olmos, Peru C2 134
Olmos Park, Tex. B3 206
Olmstead, Ark. C3 169
Olmstead, Ky. D2 182
Olmsted, Ill. F4 178
Olmsted, co., Minn. G6 187
Olmsted Falls, Ohio B1 199
Olmstedville, N.Y. B7 196
Olney, Ill. E5 178
Olney, Md. B3 173
Olney, Mo. B6 189
Olney, Mont. B2 190
Olney, Tex. C3 206
Olney Springs, Colo. C7 171
Olofströms, Swe. B8 62
Oloh, Miss. D4 188
Olomono, cape, W. Sam. 114
Olomouc, Czech. D4 70
Olongapo, Phil. *C6 90
Oloron Ste. Marie, Fr. F3 58
Olot, Sp. A7 65
Olowalu, Haw. C5 176
Olpe, Ger. B2 61
Olpe, Kans. D7 181
Olsburg, Kans. C7 181
Olshany, Sov. Un. F10 72
Olst, Neth. B6 59
Olsztyn, Pol. B6 70
Olten, Switz. B3 66
Oltenia, reg., Rom. C6 68
Oltenita, Rom. C8 68
Olton, Tex. B1 206
Oltu, Tur. B13 85
Olu Malau, is., Sol. Is. 115
Oluei, pt., Bougainville I. 115
Olustee, Fla. B4 174
Olustee, Okla. C2 200
Olvenstedt, Ger. A6 61
Olvera, Sp. D3 65
Olvey, Ark. A3 169
Olympia, Ky. B6 182
Olympia, Wash. B3 210
Olympia, ruins, Grc. D3 69
Olympia Fields, Ill. *B6 178
Olympia Village, Mo. *C7 189
Olympic, mts., Wash B2 210
Olympic, nat. park., Wash B2 210
Olympus, mtn., Grc. B4 69
Olympus, mtn., Ky. B6 182
Olumpus, mtn., Wash B2 210
Olyphant, Pa. A9, D10 202
Olyutorskiy, cape, Sov. Un. D20 71
Olza, riv., Czech. h9 70
Om, riv., Sov. Un. B9 73
Om Ager, Eth. C4 105
Oma, Miss. D3 188
Omae, cape, Jap. o17 93
Omagh, N. Ire. C3 55
Omaguas, Peru B3 134
Omaha, Ark. A2 169
Omaha, Ga. D1 175
Omaha, Ill. F5 178
Omaha, Nebr. C9, D3 191
Omaha, Tex. *C5 206
Omaha, Indian res., Nebr. B9 191
Omak, Wash. A6 210
Omak, lake, Wash. A6 210
OMAN, country, Asia D2 87
Oman, gulf, Asia D2 87
Oman, Trucial, see United Arab Emirates, country, Asia
Omar, W. Va. D3, D5 211
Omarama, N.Z. P12 112
Omaruru, S.W. Afr. B2 107
Omas, Peru D2 134
Omboue, Gabon F1 104
Ombrone, riv., It. C3 67
Omdurman, Sud. B3 105
Ōme, Jap. *I9 93
Omega, Ga. E3 175
Omega, N. Mex. C1 195
Omega, Ohio C5 199
Omega, Okla. B3 200
Omemee, Ont., Can. C6 153
Omemee, N. Dak. A5 198
Omeo, Austl. H6 112
Omer, Mich. D7 186
Ometepe, isl., Nic. E5 130
Ometepec, Mex. D5 129
Omigawa, Jap. n19 93
Ominato, Jap. F10 93
Omineca, mts., B.C., Can. A4 149
Omineca, riv., B.C., Can. A5 149
Ōmiya, Jap. I9, n18 93
Ommen, Neth. B6 59
Omø, isl., Den. C5 62
Omo, riv., Eth. D4 105
Omolon, riv., Sov. Un. C18 71
Ompompanoosuc, riv., Vt. D4 208
Omro, Wis. D5 212
Omsk, Sov. Un. C8 73
Ōmuta, Jap. J5 93
Ona, Fla. E5 174
Onaga, Kans. C7 181
Onaka, S. Dak. B6 204
Onalaska, Wash. C3 210
Onalaska, Wis. E2 212
Onamia, Minn. D5 187
Onancock, Va. D7 209
Onarga, Ill. C5 178
Onawa, Iowa B1 180
Onawa, Maine C3 184
Onawa, lake, Maine C3 184
Onaway, Idaho C2 177
Onaway, Mich. C6 186
Onchiota, N.Y. B3 196
Onda, Sp. C5 65
Ondangua, S.W. Afr. A2 107
Ondava, riv., Czech. D6 70
Ondo, Nig. E5 103
Öndör Haan, Mong. A4 92
100 Mile House, B.C., Can. C7 149
150 Mile House, B.C., Can. C7 149
Oneata, isl., Fiji 114
Oneco, Conn. C9 172
Oneco, Fla. E4, F2 174
Onega, Sov. Un. F18 63
Onega, lake, Sov. Un. G16 63
Onega, riv., Sov. Un. C15 40
Oneida, Ill. B3 178
Oneida, Iowa B6 180
Oneida, Kans. C8 181
Oneida, Ky. C6 182
Oneida, N.Y. B5 196
Oneida, Ohio C3 199
Oneida, Tenn. C9 205
Oneida, Wis. A5 212
Oneida, co., Idaho G6 177
Oneida, co., N.Y. B5 196
Oneida, co., Wis. C4 212
Oneida, lake, N.Y. B5 196
Oneida Castle, N.Y. *B5 196
O'Neill, Nebr. B7 191
Onekama, Mich. D4 186
Onemak, isl., Kwajalein 114
Oneonta, Ala. B3 166
Oneonta, N.Y. C5 196
Onezhskaya, bay, Sov. Un. E17 63
Ong, Nebr. D8 191
Ongin, Mong. B5 91
Ongin, riv., Mong. B5 91
Onida, S. Dak. C5 204
Onilahy, riv., Malag. h8 107
Onitsha, Nig. E6 103
Onley, Va. D7 209
Only, Tenn. B4 205
Onna, Okinawa 114
Ōno, Jap. n15 93
Ono, isl., Fiji 114
Onoda, Jap. *J5 93
Onomichi, Jap. I6 93
Onondaga, Mich. F6 186
Onondaga, co., N.Y. C4 196
Onondaga, Indian res., N.Y. C4 196
Onota, lake, Mass. B1 185
Onoville, N.Y. C2 196
Onoway, Alta., Can. C3 148
Onsala, Swe. A5 62
Onset, Mass. C6 185
Onslow, Austl. D2 111
Onslow, Iowa B6 180
Onslow, co., N.C. C6 197
Onslow, bay, N.C. C6 197
Onsong, Kor. E4 93
Onsted, Mich. F6 186
Ontake-San, peak, Jap. n16 93
Ontario, Calif. E5, F3 170
Ontario, Ind. A7 179
Ontario, Iowa B4 180
Ontario, N.Y. B3 196
Ontario, Ohio B5 199
Ontario, Oreg. C10 201
Ontario, Wis. E3 212
Ontario, prov., Can. 153
in 1867 147
Ontario, co., Ont., Can. C5 153
Ontario, co., N.Y. C3 196
Ontario, lake, U.S., Can. B12 159
Onteniente, Sp. C5 65
Ontonagon, Mich. A5 186
Ontonagon, co., Mich. A5 186
Ontonagon, Indian res., Mich. A5 186
Ontong Java, is., Sol. Is. 115
Onward, Ind. C5 179
Oodnadatta, Austl. E6 111
Ookala, Haw. C6 176
Ooldea, Austl. F5 111
Oolitic, Ind. G4 179
Oologah, Okla. A6 200
Oologah, dam, Okla. A6 200
Oologah, res., Okla. A6 200
Ooltewah, Tenn. D8, E10 205
Ooltgensplaat, Neth. C4 59
Oostburg, Neth. C3 59
Oostburg, Wis. E6 212
Oosterend, Neth. A4 59
Oosterend, Neth. A5 59
Oosterhout, Neth. C4 59
Oostmahorn, Neth. A6 59
Oostvoorne, Neth. C4 59
Ootacamund, India F6 87
Ootsa, lake, B.C., Can. C4 149
Ootsa Lake, B.C., Can. C4 149
Opaeula Camp, Haw. f9 176
Opal, Alta., Can. C4 148
Opal, S. Dak. C3 204
Opal, Wyo. D2 213
Opal Cliffs, Calif. *D2 170
Opala, Zaire B3 106
Opa-locka, Fla. F3 174
Opalton, Austl. A4 112
Opatów, Pol. C6 70
Opava, Czech. D4 70
Opdal, Nor. F3 63
Opelika, Ala. C4 166
Opelousas, La. D3 183
Open, bay, Bis. Arch. 115
Opeongo, lake, Ont., Can. B6 153
Opeongo, riv., Ont., Can. B6 153
Opheim, Mont. B10 190
Ophir, Alsk. C8 167
Ophir, Oreg. E2 201
Ophir, Utah *C3 207
Ophir, mtn., Mala K5 89
Opihikao, Haw. D7 176
Opochka, Sov. Un. C7 72
Opoczno, Pol. C6 70
Opole, Pol. C4 70
Opole Lubelskie, Pol. C6 70
Opotiki, N.Z. M16 112
Opp, Ala. D3 166
Oppelo, Ark. B3 169
Opportunity, Wash. B8, D8 210
Optic Lake, Man., Can. C5 155
Optima, Okla. D3 200

INDEX KEY Each place listed in **Bold-faced Type** has its population listed in the Population tables, pages 230 to 280.
Each country, shown in CAPITAL LETTERS, has its population listed in the World Political Information Table, pages 6 to 10.
* Does not appear on map; key shows general location.

Oputo, Mex. G6 168
Oquawka, Ill. C3 178
Oquossoc, Maine D2 184
Ora, Ind. B4 179
Ora, It. C7 66
Ora, Miss. D4 188
Ora, S.C. B4 203
Oracle, Ariz. E5 168
Oradea, Rom. B5 68
Oradell, N.J. D5 194
Oradell, res., N.J. D5 194
Orai, India E7 88
Oraibi, Ariz. B5 168
Oraibi, wash, Ariz. A5 168
Oral, S. Dak. D2 204
Oralabor, Iowa A7 180
Oran, Alg. G6 64, B4 102
Orán, Arg. D3 135
Oran, Iowa B5 180
Oran, Mo. D8 189
Orange, Austl. F7 112
Orange, Calif. F3 170
Orange, Conn. D4 172
Orange, Fr. E6 58
Orange, Ind. E7 179
Orange, Mass. A3 185
Orange, N.H. C3 193
Orange, N.J. B4 194
Orange, Ohio *A6 199
Orange, Tex. D6 206
Orange, Vt. C4 208
Orange, Va. C4 209
Orange, co., Calif. F5 170
Orange, co., Fla. D5 174
Orange, co., Ind. G4 179
Orange, co., N.Y. D6 196
Orange, co., N.C. A4 197
Orange, co., Tex. D6 206
Orange, co., Vt. D3 208
Orange, co., Va. C4 209
Orange, bay, Newf., Can. C3 152
Orange, cape, Braz. B4 139
Orange, cliffs, Utah E5 207
Orange, lake, Fla. C4 174
Orange, riv., S.W. Afr., S. Afr. C2 107
Orange Beach, Ala. E2 166
Orange City, Fla. D5 174
Orange City, Iowa B1 180
Orange Cove, Calif. *D4 170
Orange Free State, prov., S. Afr. C4 107
Orange Grove, Miss. E3, E5 188
Orange Grove, Tex. F4 206
Orange Lake, Fla. C4 174
Orange Park, Fla. B5, C6 174
Orange Walk, Br. Hond. A3 130
Orangeburg, S.C. E6 203
Orangeburg, co., S.C. E6 203
Orangedale, N.S., Can. D8 151
Orangeville, Ont., Can. D4 153
Orangeville, Ill. A4 178
Orangeville, Utah D4 207
Orani, Phil. o13 90
Oranienbaum, Ger. B7 61
Oranienburg, Ger. B6 60
Oranje, canal, Neth. B6 59
Oranje, mts., Indon. F9 90
Oranjemund, S.W. Afr. C2 107
Orăştie, Rom. C6 68
Oraviţa, Rom. C5 68
Orba, riv., It. E4 66
Orbetello, It. C3 67
Orbey, Fr. A3 66
Orbigo, riv., Sp. A3 65
Orbisonia, Pa. F6 202
Orbost, Austl. H7 112
Örby, Swe. A6 62
Orcas, isl., Wash. A3 210
Orchard, Colo. A6 171
Orchard, Idaho F2 177
Orchard, Iowa A5 180
Orchard, Nebr. B7 191
Orchard Beach, Md. *B4 173
Orchard Homes, Mont. D2 190
Orchard Lake, Mich. *F7 186
Orchard Mesa, Colo. *B2 171
Orchard Park, N.Y. C2 196
Orchard Valley, Wyo. D8 213
Orchards, Wash. D3 210
Orchies, Fr. D3 59
Orchila, isl., Ven. A4 133
Orcotuna, Peru D2 134
Orcutt, Calif. E3 170
Orcutts, Conn. B7 172
Ord, Nebr. C7 191
Ordale, Sask., Can. D2 155
Ordenes, Sp. A1 65
Orderville, Utah F3 207
Ording, Ger. D2 62
Ordoqui, Arg. B4 136
Ordos, des., China D6 91
Ordot, Guam 114
Ordoz, mtn., China E2 92
Ordu, Tur. B11 85
Orduña, Sp. A4 65
Ordville, Nebr. C2 191
Ordway, Colo. C7 171
Ordzhonikidze, Sov. Un. E2 73
Ore, mts., see Erzgebirge, Czech., Ger.
Ore City, Tex. C5 206
Oreana, Idaho F2 177
Oreana, Nev. C3 192
Oreba, isl., Kwajalein 114
Örebro, Swe. H6, t33 63
Oregon, Ill. A4 178
Oregon, Mo. B2 189
Oregon, Ohio A2, A4 199
Oregon, Wis. F4 212
Oregon, state, U.S. 201
in 1846-48 163
Oregon, co., Mo. E6 189
Oregon, inlet, N.C. B8 197
Oregon Caves, nat. mon., Oreg. E3 201
Oregon City, Oreg. B2, B4 201
Öregrund, Swe. G8 63
Orehoved, Den. D5 62
Orekhov, Sov. Un. H10 72
Orekhovo-Zuyevo, Sov. Un. B1 73
Orël, Sov. Un. E11 72
Orem, Utah C4 207
Orenburg, Sov. Un. C5 73
Orense, Sp. A2 65
Orestes, Ind. D6 179
Orestiás, Grc. B6 69
Öresund (The Sound), strait, Den., Swe. C6 62
Orford, N.H. C2 193
Orford, cape, New Britain I. 115
Orford, mtn., Que., Can. D5 154
Orfordness, cape, Eng. B9 56
Orfordville, N.H. C2 193
Orfordville, Wis. F4 212
Organ, N. Mex. E3 195
Organ, cave, W. Va. D4 211
Organ Pipe Cactus, nat. mon., Ariz. E3 168
Orgaz, Sp. C4 65
Orgelet, Fr. C1 66
Orgeyev, Sov. Un. H7 72
Orhon, riv., Mong. B5 91
Orick, Calif. B1 170
Orient, Ill. F5 178
Orient, Iowa C3 180
Orient, Maine C5 184
Orient, N.Y. E7 172
Orient, Ohio C2, C4 199
Orient, S. Dak. C6 204
Orient, Wash. A7 210
Orient, harbor, N.Y. E7 172
Orient, pt., N.Y. E8 172
Orienta, Okla. A3 200
Oriental, N.C. B7 197
Oriental, reg., Zaire A4 106
Oriente, prov., Cuba E11 131
Orihuela, Sp. C5 65
Orillia, Ont., Can. C5 153
Orin, Wyo. C7 213
Orinda, Calif. *D2 170
Orinoco, riv., Ven. B5 133
Oriole, Md. D6 173
Orion, Alta., Can. E5 148
Orion, Ill. B3 178
Orion, Phil. o13 90
Oriska, N. Dak. C8 198
Oriskany, N.Y. B5 196
Oriskany, Va. D3 209
Oriskany Falls, N.Y. C5 196
Orissa, state, India E7 87
Oristano, It. E2 67
Oristano, gulf, It. E2 67
Oriva, Wyo. A7 213
Orivesi, lake, Fin. F13 63
Orizaba, Mex. D5, n15 129
Orkdal, Nor. F3 63
Örkelljunga, Swe. B7 62
Orkla, riv., Nor. F4 63
Orkney, Sask., Can. H2 155
Orkney, co., Scot. A5 57
Orkney, is., Scot. A5 57
Orla, Tex. E2 206
Orland, Calif. C2 170
Orland, Ind. A7 179
Orland, Maine D4 184
Orland Park, Ill. F2 178
Orlando, Fla. D5 174
Orlando, Okla. A4 200
Orleães, Braz. D3 137
Orléanais, former prov., Fr. D4 58
Orleans, Calif. B2 170
Orleans, Ont., Can. A9 153
Orléans, Fr. D4 58
Orleans, Ind. G5 179
Orleans, Iowa A2 180
Orleans, Mass. C7 185
Orleans, Minn. B2 187
Orleans, Nebr. D6 191
Orleans, Vt. B4 208
Orleans, co., N.Y. B2 196
Orleans, co., Vt. B4 208
Orleans, par., La. E6 183
Orléans, isl., Que., Can. C6 154
Orlinda, Tenn. A5 205
Orlovo, Sov. Un. B11 93
Orlyak, Bul. D8 68
Orman, dam, S. Dak. C2 204
Ormara, Pak. C3 87
Ormiston, Sask., Can. H3 155
Ormoc, Phil. *C6 90
Ormond Beach, Fla. C5 174
Ormsby, Ont., Can. C7 153
Ormsby, Minn. G4 187
Ormsby, co., Nev. *D2 192
Ormskirk, Eng. A5 56
Ormstown, Que., Can. D3 154
Ornans, Fr. B2 66
Orne, riv., Fr. C3 58
Orneta, Pol. A6 70
Ornö, Swe. t36 63
Ornö, isl., Swe. t36 63
Örnsköldsvik, Swe. F8 63
Orö, isl., Den. C5 62
Oro Grande, Calif. E5 170
Orocovis, P.R. C5 132
Orocovis, mun., P.R. C5 132
Orocué, Col. C3 133
Orofino, Idaho C2 177
Orogrande, Idaho D3 177
Orogrande, N. Mex. E3 195
Oromocto, N.B., Can. D3 151
Oromocto, lake, N.B., Can. D3 151
Orono, Ont., Can. D6 153
Orono, Maine D4 184
Orono, Minn. *E5 187
Oronoco, Minn. F6 187
Oronogo, Mo. D3 189
Oronoque, Conn. E4 172
Oronsay, isl., Scot. D2 57
Oronsay, passage, Scot. D2 57
Oroquieta, Phil. D6 90
Orós, Braz. C3 138
Orosei, gulf, It. D2 67
Orosháza, Hung. B5 68
Orote, pen., Guam 114
Orovada, Nev. B4 192
Oroville, Calif. C3 170
Oroville, Wash. A6 210
Orpha, Wyo. C7 213
Orpington, Eng. m13 55
Orr, Minn. B6 187
Orr, N. Dak. A8 198
Orr, Okla. C4 200
Orrick, Mo. B3 189
Orrin, N. Dak. A5 198
Orrington, Maine D4 184
Orrs Island, Maine E3, E5 184
Orrstown, Pa. F6 202
Orrum, N.C. C5 197
Orrville, Ala. C2 166
Orrville, Ohio B6 199
Orsa, Swe. G6 63
Orsainville, Que., Can. C9 154
Orsay, Fr. F2 59
Orsha, Sov. Un. D8 72
Orsières, Switz. C3 66
Orsino, Fla. D6 174
Orsk, Sov. Un. C5 73
Orson, Pa. C11 202
Orşova, Rom. C6 68
Ørsted, Den. B4 62
Örsundsbro, Swe. t35 63
Orta, lake, It. D4 66
Ortegal, cape, Sp. A1 65
Orthez, Fr. F3 58
Ortigueira, Sp. A2 65
Orting, Wash. B3 210
Ortisei, It. C7 66
Ortiz, Colo. D4 171
Ortiz, Mex. B2 129
Ortiz, mts., N. Mex. G6 195
Ortley, S. Dak. B8 204
Ortona a Mare, It. C5 67
Ortonville, Mich. F7 186
Ortonville, Minn. E2 187
Orukuizu, isl., Palau Is. 114
Oruro, Bol. C2 135
Oruro, dept., Bol. C2 135
Orvieto, It. C4 67
Orviston, Pa. D6 202
Orwell, N.Y. B5 196
Orwell, Ohio A7 199
Orwell, Vt. D2 208
Orwigsburg, Pa. E9 202
Oryakhovo, Bul. D6 68
Orysa, Tenn. B2 205
Orzesze, Pol. g9 70
Osa, pen., C.R. B8 130
Osage, Sask., Can. H4 155
Osage, Iowa A5 180
Osage, Minn. D3 187
Osage, Okla. A5 200
Osage, W. Va. *B5 211
Osage, Wyo. B8 213
Osage, co., Kans. D8 181
Osage, co., Mo. C6 189
Osage, co., Okla. A5 200
Osage, creek, Ark. A2 169
Osage, fork, Mo. D5 189
Osage, riv., Mo. C5 189
Osage Beach, Mo. C5 189
Osage City, Kans. D8 181
Osage City, Mo. C5 189
Ōsaka, Jap. I7, o14 93
Osaka, Jap. n16 93
Ōsaka, bay, Jap. o14 93
Osaka, mtn., Iwo 114
Osakis, Minn. E3 187
Osakis, lake, Minn. E3 187
Osam, riv., Bul. D7 68
Osawatomie, Kans. D9 181
Osborn, Mo. B3 189
Osborne, Kans. C5 181
Osborne, Pa. *E1 202
Osborne, co., Kans. C5 181
Osburn, Idaho B3 177
Osby, Swe. B7 62
Oscar, La. D4 183
Osceola, Ark. B6 169
Osceola, Ind. A5 179
Osceola, Iowa C4 180
Osceola, Mo. C4 189
Osceola, Nebr. C8 191
Osceola, Pa. C7 202
Osceola, S. Dak. C8 204
Osceola, Tex. C4 206
Osceola, Wis. C1 212
Osceola, co., Fla. E5 174
Osceola, co., Iowa A2 180
Osceola, co., Mich. E5 186
Osceola Mills, Pa. E5 202
Oschatz, Ger. B8 61
Oschersleben, Ger. A6 61
Oscoda, Mich. D7 186
Oscoda, co., Mich. D6 186
Oscuro, N. Mex. E3 195
Osek, Czech. C8 61
Oselki, Sov. Un. r31 63
Osgood, Ind. F7 179
Osgood, Mo. A4 189
Osgoode Station, Ont., Can. B9 153
Osh, Sov. Un. E10 73
Oshamambe, Jap. E10 93
Oshawa, Ont., Can. D6 153
Oshima (Moto), Jap. o18 93
Ō Shima, isl., Jap. I9 93
Oshkosh, Nebr. C3 191
Oshkosh, Wis. B5, D5 212
Oshogbo, Nig. E5 103
Oshoto, Wyo. A8 213
Oshwe, Zaire B2 106
Osijek, Yugo. C4 68
Osilinka, riv., B.C., Can. A5 149
Osinniki, Sov. Un. *D11 71
Osipovichi, Sov. Un. E7 72
Oskaloosa, Iowa C5 180
Oskaloosa, Kans. B7, C8 181
Oskaloosa, Mo. D3 189
Oskarshamn, Swe. I7 63
Oskol, riv., Sov. Un. G11 72
Osler, Sask., Can. E2 155
Oslo, Fla. E6 174
Oslo, Minn. B1 187
Oslo, Nor. H4, p28 63
Oslofjord, fjord, Nor. H4 63
Osma, Sp. B4 65
Osmanabad, India H6 88
Osmancık, Tur. B10 85
Osmaneli, Tur. B7 69
Osmaniye, Tur. D11 85
Osmond, Nebr. B8 191
Osnabrock, N. Dak. A7 198
Osnabrück, Ger. A3 61
Osório, Braz. D2 137
Osorno, Chile C2 136
Osorno, prov., Chile C2 136
Osov, Czech. o17 70
Osoyoos, B.C., Can. E8 149
Osoyoos, lake, B.C., Can., Wash. A6 210
Ospika, riv., B.C., Can. A6 149
Osprey, Fla. E4 174
Oss, Neth. C5 59
Ossabaw, isl., Ga. E5 175
Ossabaw, sound, Ga. E6 175
Osseo, Minn. E6 187
Osseo, Wis. D2 212
Ossian, Ind. C7 179
Ossian, Iowa A6 180
Ossineke, Mich. D7 186
Ossining, N.Y. D3, D7 196
Ossipee, N.H. C4 193
Ossipee, lake, N.H. C4 193
Ossipee, mts., N.H. C4 193
Ossokmanuan, lake, Newf., Can. h8 152
Ost, Kans. B4 181
Östanå, Swe. t36 63
Ostashkov, Sov. Un. C9 72
Oste, riv., Ger. E3 62
Osteen, Fla. D5 174
Ostend, Bel. C2 59
Osterburg, Ger. F5 62
Osterburg, Pa. F4 202
Osterode, Ger. B5 61
Östersund, Swe. F6 63
Osterville, Mass. C7 185
Osterwieck, Ger. B5 61
Ostia Antica, It. h8 67
Ostiglia, It. D7 66
Ostrach, Ger. B5 66
Ostrander, Minn. G6 187
Ostrander, Ohio B4 199
Östratorp, Swe. C7 62
Ostrava, Czech. D5 70
Ostróda, Pol. B5 70
Ostrog, Sov. Un. F6 72
Ostrogozhsk, Sov. Un. F12 72
Ostrołęka, Pol. B6 70
Ostrov, Czech. C2 70
Ostrov, Rom. C8 68
Ostrov, Sov. Un. C7 72
Ostrów, Pol. B6 70
Ostrów Lubelski, Pol. C7 70
Ostrów [Wielkopolski], Pol. C4 70
Ostrowiec, Pol. C6 70
Ostrzeszów, Pol. C4 70
Ostuni, It. D6 67
Ōsumi, is., Jap. K5 93
Ōsumi (Van Diemen), strait, Jap. K5 93
Osuna, Sp. D3 65
Oswayo, Pa. C5 202
Oswegatchie, N.Y. A5 196
Oswegatchie, riv., N.Y. B1 196
Oswego, Ill. B5, F1 178
Oswego, Kans. E8 181
Oswego, Mont. B11 190
Oswego, N.Y. B4 196
Oswego, S.C. C7 203
Oswego, co., N.Y. B4 196
Oswego, riv., N.Y. B4 196
Oswestry, Eng. B4 56
Oświęcim, Pol. C5, g10 70
Osyka, Miss. D3 188
Ota, Jap. m18 93
Otago, harbor, N.Z. P13 112
Otago, pen., N.Z. P13 112
Ōtaki, Jap. n19 93
Otaki, N.Z. N15 112
Otar, Sov. Un. E9 73
Otaru, Jap. E10 93
Otaru, bay, Jap. E10 93
Otava, riv., Czech. D8 61
Otavalo, Ec. A2 134
Otavi, S.W. Afr. A2 107
Otchinjau, Ang. E1 106
Oteen, N.C. D3 197
Otego, Kans. C5 181
Otego, N.Y. C5 196
Otero, co., Colo. D7 171
Otero, co., N. Mex. E3 195
Othello, Wash. C6 210
Otho, Iowa B3 180
Óthris, mts., Grc. C4 69
Oti, riv., Ghana E5 103
Otis, Colo. A8 171
Otis, Ind. A4 179
Otis, Kans. D4 181
Otis, Mass. B1 185
Otis, N. Mex. E5 195
Otis, res., Mass. B1 185
Otis Orchards, Wash. D8 210
Otisco, Ind. G6 179
Otisco, Minn. G5 187
Otisco, N.Y. C4 196
Otisville, Mich. E7 186
Otjiwarongo, S.W. Afr. B2 107
Otley, Iowa C4 180
Oto, Iowa B2 180
Otočac, Yugo. C2 68
Otoe, Nebr. D9, E3 191
Otoe, co., Nebr. D9 191
Otomari, see Korsakov, Sov. Un.
Otradnoye, Sov. Un. s31 63
Otranto, It. D7 67
Otsego, Mich. F5 186
Otsego, co., Mich. C6 186
Otsego, co., N.Y. C5 196
Otsego, lake, N.Y. C6 196
Otsego Lake, Mich. D6 186
Ōtsu, Jap. o14 93
Otta, isl., Truk 114
Ottarp, Swe. C6 62
Ottauquechee, riv., Vt. D3 208
Ottawa, Ont., Can. A9, B9 153
Ottawa, Ill. B5 178
Ottawa, Kans. D8 181
Ottawa, Ohio A3 199
Ottawa, W. Va. D5 211
Ottawa, co., Kans. C6 181
Ottawa, co., Mich. F4 186
Ottawa, co., Ohio A4 199
Ottawa, co., Okla. A7 200
Ottawa, is., N.W. Ter., Can. E16 143
Ottawa, riv., Ont., Que., Can. G17 143
Ottawa, riv., Ohio A2 199
Ottawa Hills, Ohio A2, A4 199
Ottawa Lake, Mich. G7 186
Otter, Mont. E10 190
Otter, brook, N.H. F2 193
Otter, creek, Utah E4 207
Otter, creek, Vt. C2 208
Otter, isl., S.C. G1 203
Otter, lake, Sask., Can. B3 155
Otter, riv., Alta., Can. A2 148
Otter, riv., Eng. D4 56
Otter, riv., Va. D3 209
Otter Brook, res., N.H. E2 193
Otter Creek, Fla. C4 174
Otter Creek, Maine D4 184
Otter Lake, Ont., Can. B5 153
Otter Lake, Mich. E7 186
Otter Lake, N.Y. B5 196
Otter River, Mass. A3 185
Otter Tail, co., Minn. D3 187
Otter Tail, lake, Minn. D3 187
Otter Tail, riv., Minn. D2 187
Otterbein, Ind. D3 179
Otterberg, Ger. D2 61
Otterburn, Eng. E6 57
Otterburn, Park, Que., Can. *D4 154
Otterburne, Man., Can. E3 150
Otterndorf, Ger. E3 62
Ottersburg, Ger. E3 62
Ottertail, Minn. D3 187
Otterup, Den. C4 62
Otterville, Ont., Can. E4 153
Otterville, Iowa B6 180
Otterville, Mo. C4 189
Otthon, Sask., Can. F4 155
Ottignies, Bel. D4 59
Ottilien, reef, Bis. Arch. 115
Öttingen, Ger. E5 61
Otto, Wyo. A4 213
Ottokee, Ohio A3 199
Ottoman empire: in 1815 50
in 1914 52
Ottone, It. E5 66
Ottosen, Iowa B3 180
Ottoville, Ohio B3 199
Ottsville, Pa. F11 202
Ottumwa, Iowa C5 180
Ottumwa, Kans. D8 181
Ottumwa, S. Dak. C4 204
Otukamamoan, lake, Ont., Can. A6 187
Oturkpo, Nig. E6 103
Otuzco, Peru C2 134
Otway, N.C. C7 197
Otway, cape, Austl. I4 112
Otway, sound, Chile h11 136
Otwell, Ark. B5 169
Otwell, Ind. H3 179
Otwock, Pol. m14 70
Ötztal Alps, mts., Aus., It. A3 67
Ouachita, co., Ark. D3 169
Ouachita, par., La. B3 183
Ouachita, mts., Okla. C6 200
Ouachita, riv., Ark. D3 169
Ouachita, riv., La. B3 183
Ouaddaï, reg., Chad C4 104
Ouadi Rimé, riv., Chad C3 104
Ouagadougou, Upper Volta D4 103
Ouahigouya, Upper Volta D4 103
Ouaka, riv., Cen. Afr. Rep. D4 104
Ouakoro, Mali D3 103
Oualata, Maur. C3 103
Ouallam, Niger D5 103
Ouanda Djallé, Cen. Afr. Rep. D1 105
Ouarane, sand dunes, Maur. B3 103
Ouargla, Alg. C6 102
Ouchina (Well), Mali C5 103
Ouddorp, Neth. C3 59
Oude-Pekela, Neth. A7 59
Oudenaarde, Bel. D3 59
Oudtshoorn, S. Afr. D3 107
Oued Zem, Mor. H3 64
Oueiba (Well), Chad B4 104
Ouelle, I.C. E4 103
Ouesso, Con. E3 104
Ouezzane, Mor. C3 102
Ougarta, Alg. D4 102
Oughter, lake, Ire. D3 55
Ouidah, Dah. E5 103
Oujda, Mor. C4 102
Oulchy-le-Château, Fr. E3 59
Oullins, Fr. E6 58
Oulu, Fin. E11 63
Oulujärvi, lake, Fin. E12 63
Oum Chalouba, Chad B4 104
Oum el Asel (Oasis), Mali B4 103
Oum Hadjer, Chad C3 104
Ounasjoki, riv., Fin. D11 63
Ounianga Kébir, Chad B4 104
Ouray, Colo. C3 171
Ouray, Utah C6 207
Ouray, co., Colo. C3 171
Ouray, mtn., Colo. C4 171
Ouri, Chad A3 104
Ouricurí, Braz. C2 138
Ourinhos, Braz. C3 137
Ourique, Port. D1 65
Ouro Fino, Braz. C3, m8 137
Ouro Prêto, Braz. F2 138
Ourthe, riv., Bel. D5 59
Ourukaen, isl., Bikini 114
Ouse, riv., Eng. D6 55
Outagamie, co., Wis. D5 212
Outat el Hadj, Mor. H5 64
Outer, isl., Que., Can. C2 152
Outer, isl., Wis. A3 212
Outer Hebrides, is., Scot. C1 57
Outer Mongolia: *see also* Mongolia
Outer Santa Barbara, chan., Calif. F4 170
Outes, Sp. A1 65
Outing, Minn. D5 187
Outjo, S.W. Afr. B2 107
Outlook, Sask., Can. F2 155
Outlook, Mont. B12 190
Outlook, Wash. C5 210
Outlying Islands (U.S.), see Baker, Howland, Jarvis, Johnston and Sand, Midway Is., Palmyra, Wake
Outpost, mtn., Alsk. B9 167
Outreau, Fr. B4 58
Outremont, Que., Can. D9 154
Ouville-la-Rivière, Fr. E8 56
Ouyen, Austl. G4 112
Ouzinkie, Alsk. D9 167
Ovada, It. E4 66, B2 67
Oval, Pa. D7 202
Ovalau, isl., Fiji 114
Ovalle, Chile A2 136
Ovando, Mont. C3 190
Ovar, Port. B1 65
Overath, Ger. C2 61
Overbrook, Kans. D8 181
Overbrook, Okla. C4 200
Overflowing, riv., Man., Sask., Can. C1 150, D5 155
Overgaard, Ariz. C5 168
Overijsche, Bel. D4 59
Overijssel, prov., Neth. B6 59
Overisel, Mich. F4 186
Overland, Mo. A8 189
Overland Park, Kans. B9 181
Overlea, Md. B4, C3 173
Overly, N. Dak. A5 198
Overstreet, Fla. B1, H3 174
Overton, Nebr. D6 191
Overton, Nev. G7 192
Overton, Tex. C5 206
Overton, co., Tenn. C8 205
Övertorneå, Swe. D10 63
Ovett, Miss. D4 188
Ovid, Colo. A8 171
Ovid, Idaho G7 177
Ovid, Mich. E6 186
Ovid, N.Y. C4 196
Oviedo, Fla. D5 174
Oviedo, Sp. A3 65
Ovilla, Tenn. B4 205
Ovruch, Sov. Un. F7 72
Owaneco, Ill. D4 178
Owanka, S. Dak. C3 204
Owasco, lake, N.Y. C4 196
Owasso, Okla. A6 200
Owatonna, Minn. F5 187
Owego, N.Y. C4 196
Owen, Wis. D3 212
Owen, co., Ind. F4 179
Owen, co., Ky. B5 182
Owen, lake, Wis. B2 212
Owen, mtn., Colo. C3 171
Owen, mtn., N.Z. N14 112
Owen, sound, Ont., Can. C4 153
Owen Sound, Ont., Can. C4 153
Owen Stanley, range, Pap. k12 110
Owendale, Mich. E7 186
Owens, N.C. *B5 197
Owens, creek, Md. A3 173
Owens, lake, Calif. D4 170
Owens, riv., Calif. D4 170
Owens Cross Roads, Ala. A3 166
Owensboro, Ky. C3 182
Owensboro East, Ky. *C3 182
Owensboro West, Ky. *C3 182
Owensburg, Ind. G4 179
Owensville, Ark. C3, C6 169
Owensville, Ind. H2 179
Owensville, Mo. C6 189
Owensville, Ohio C3 199
Owenton, Ky. B5 182
Owerri, Nig. E6 103
Owikeno, lake, B.C., Can. D4 149
Owings, Md. C4 173
Owingsville, Ky. B6 182
Owl, creek, Wyo. B4 213
Owl Creek, mts., Wyo. B4 213
Owls Head, Maine D3 184
Owosso, Mich. E6 186
Owsley, co., Ky. C6 182
Owyhee, Nev. B5 192
Owyhee, co., Idaho G2 177
Owyhee, dam, Oreg. D9 201
Owyhee, mts., Idaho G2 177
Owyhee, res., Oreg. D9 201
Owyhee, riv., Idaho, Nev., Oreg. E9 201
Öxabäck, Swe. A6 62

NDEX KEY Each place listed in **Bold-faced Type** has its population listed in the Population tables, pages 230 to 280.
Each country, shown in CAPITAL LETTERS, has its population listed in the World Political Information Table, pages 6 to 10.
* Does not appear on map; key shows general location.

Oxbow, Sask., Can........H4 155
Oxbow, Maine........B4 184
Oxbow, dam, Idaho........E2 177
Oxbow, res., Idaho, Oreg........C10 201
Oxelösund, Swe........u35 63
Oxford, Ala........B4 166
Oxford, Ark........A4 169
Oxford, N.S., Can........D6 151
Oxford, Conn........*D4 172
Oxford, Eng........C6 56
Oxford, Fla........D4 174
Oxford, Ga........C3 175
Oxford, Idaho........G7 177
Oxford, Ind........C3 179
Oxford, Iowa........C6 180
Oxford, Kans........E6 181
Oxford, La........C2 183
Oxford, Maine........D2 184
Oxford, Md........C5 173
Oxford, Mass........B4 185
Oxford, Mich........F7 186
Oxford, Miss........A4 188
Oxford, Nebr........D6 191
Oxford, N.J........B3 194
Oxford, N.Y........C5 196
Oxford, N.C........A5 197
Oxford, Ohio........C3 199
Oxford, Pa........G10 202
Oxford, Wis........E4 212
Oxford, co., Ont., Can........D4 153
Oxford, co., Eng........C6 56
Oxford, co., Maine........D2 184
Oxford, lake, Man., Can........B4 150
Oxford House, Man., Can........B4 150
Oxford Junction, N.S., Can........D6 151
Oxford Junction, Iowa........C7 180
Oxley, Ark........B3 169
Oxly, Mo........E7 189
Oxnard, Calif........E4 170
Oxus, see Amu Darya, riv., Afg., Sov. Un.
Oyama, Jap........m18 93
Oyem, Gabon........E2 104
Oyen, Alta., Can........D5 148
Oyens, Iowa........B1 180
Øyeren, lake, Nor........p29 63
Oykell, riv., Scot........C4 57
Oykell Bridge, Scot........C4 57
Oymyakon, Sov. Un........C17 71
Oyo, Nig........E5 103
Oyonnax, Fr........D6 58
Oyster, keys, Fla........G6 174
Oyster Bay, N.Y........D3, F7 196
Oyster Bay Cove, N.Y........*F2 172
Ozamiz, Phil........D6 90
Ozan, Ark........D2 169
Ozark, Ala........D4 166
Ozark, Ark........B2 169
Ozark, Mich........B6 186
Ozark, Mo........D4 189
Ozark, co., Mo........E5 189
Ozark, escarpment, Ark., Mo........E7 189
Ozark, plat., Okla..A1 169, A7 200
Ozark, res., Ark........B1 169
Ozarks, lake, Mo........C5 189
Ożarowice, Pol........g10 70
Ozaukee, co., Wis........E6 212
Ozawkie, Kans........B7 181
Ózd, Hung........A5 68
Ozena, Miss........E4 188
Ozero Imandra, lake, Sov. Un........D15 63
Ozette, lake, Wash........A1 210
Ozieri, It........D2 67
Ozona, Fla........E1 174
Ozona, Tex........D2 206
Ozorków, Pol........C5 70
Ōzu, Jap........J6 93
Ozuluama, Mex........C5, m15 129

P

Pa, China........E7 92
Paaba, isl., N. Cal........115
Paan, China........E4 91
Paar, riv., Ger........E6 61
Paarl, S. Afr........D2 107
Paauhau, Haw........C6 176
Paauilo, Haw........C6 176
Pabbay, isl., Scot........C1 57
Pabianice, Pol........C5 70
Pablo, Mont........C2 190
Pābna, Bngl........E12 88
Pacaás Novos, mts., Braz..E2 139
Pacajá, riv., Braz........C4 139
Pacajá Grande, riv., Braz..C4 139
Pacaraima, mts., Braz., Ven........C5 133
Pacasmayo, Peru........C2 134
Pace, Fla........G2 174
Pace, Miss........B3 188
Pachai, China........K2 92
Pachaug, pond, Conn........C9 172
Pacheco, Calif........*D2 170
Pachmarhi, India........F7 88
Pachuca [de Soto], Mex........C5, m14 129
Pachung, China........I2 92
Pachuta, Miss........C5 188
Pacific, B.C., Can........B3 149
Pacific, Mo........B7, C7 189
Pacific, Wash........D2 210
Pacific, co., Wash........C2 210
Pacific, creek, Wyo........C3 213
Pacific, ocean........113
Pacific, ranges, B.C., Can..D4 149
Pacific City, Oreg........B3 201
Pacific Grove, Calif...C5, D3 170
Pacific Junction, Iowa....C2 180
Pacifica, Calif........*D2 170
Pack Monadnock, mtn., N.H........E3 193
Packard, mtn., Mass........B3 185
Packwaukee, Wis........E4 212
Packwood, Iowa........C5 180
Pacolet, S.C........B4 203
Pacolet, riv., S.C........A4 203
Pacolet Mills, S.C........B4 203
Pacolet Park, S.C........*B4 203
Pacora, Pan........k12 130
Pacov, Czech........D10 61
Pacquet, Newf., Can........C4 152
Pactola, res., S. Dak........C2 204
Pactolus, N.C........B6 197
Paczków, Pol........C4 70
Padagī, Iran........F10 86
Padang, Indon........F2 90
Padang Endau, Mala........K5 89
Padangpandjang, Indon....F2 90
Padangsidempuan, Indon........E1, m11 90
Padauiri, riv., Braz........C5 133
Paddling, lake, Sask., Can..E2 155
Paddockwood, Sask., Can........D3 155
Paddy Knob, mtn., Va., W. Va........C5 211
Paden, Miss........A5 188
Paden, Okla........B5 200
Paden City, W. Va........B4 211
Paderborn, Ger........B3 61
Padilla, Bol........C3 135
Padilla, creek, N. Mex........D5 195
Padova, see Padua, It.
Padre, isl., Tex........F4 206
Padre Island, nat. seashore, Tex........F4 206
Padroni, Colo........A7 171
Padstow, Eng........D3 56
Padua (Padova), It. D7 66, B3 67
Paducah, Ky........A2 182
Paducah, Tex........B2 206
Padwa, India........H9 88
Paektu-san, peak, China, Kor........E4 93
Paektu-san, see Changpai, mts., China
Paepaealeia, cape, W. Sam....114
Paeroa, N.Z........L15 112
Paestum, ruins, It........D5 67
Pag, isl., Yugo........C2 68
Pagai Selatan, isl., Indon..F2 90
Pagai Utara, isl., Indon....F2 90
Pagan, isl., Mariana Is........115
Pagat, pt., Guam........114
Pagatan, Indon........F4 90
Pagato, riv., Sask., Can....A4 155
Page, Ariz........A4 168
Page, Nebr........B7 191
Page, N. Dak........B8 198
Page, Okla........C7 200
Page, W. Va........C3, D6 211
Page, co., Iowa........D2 180
Page, co., Va........C4 209
Page City, Kans........C2 181
Pagedale, Mo........*C7 189
Pageland, S.C........B7 203
Paglia, mtn., Switz........C5 66
Pagny [-sur-Moselle], Fr....F6 59
Pago, bay, Guam........114
Pago, pt., Guam........114
Pago Pago, Am. Sam........114
Pago Pago, hbr., Am. Sam....114
Pagoda, peak, Colo........A3 171
Pagosa Springs, Colo........D3 171
Paguate, N. Mex........B2 195
Pahala, Haw........D6 176
Pahang, pol. div., Mala....K5 89
Pahang, riv., Mala........K5 89
Paharpur, Pak........A3 88
Pahoa, Haw........D7 176
Pahokee, Fla........F6 174
Pahra, Afg........D10 86
Pahranagat, range, Nev....F6 192
Pahrump, Nev........G5 192
Pahute, mesa, Nev........F5 192
Pahute, peak, Nev........B2 192
Paia, Haw........C5 176
Paicheng, China........B10 92
Paichuan, China........C3 93
Paiho, China........H4 92
Päijänne, lake, Fin........G11 63
Pailingmiao, China........D4 92
Pailo, Tenn........D8 205
Paincourt, Ont., Can........E2 153
Paincourtville, La........B5 183
Paine Oeste, mtn., Chile....E2 136
Painesville, Ohio........A6 199
Painesville Northeast, Ohio........*A6 199
Paint, Pa........*F4 202
Paint, creek, Ohio........C4 199
Paint, creek, W. Va........D6 211
Paint, lake, Man., Can....B3 150
Paint, mtn., W. Va........D6 211
Paint, riv., Mich........B2 186
Paint Bank, Va........D2 209
Paint Lick, Ky........C5 182
Paint Rock, Ala........A3 166
Paint Rock, Tex........D3 206
Painted Desert, Ariz........A4 168
Painted Post, N.Y........C3 196
Painted Rock, res., Ariz....E2 168
Painter, Va........D7 209
Paintsville, Ky........C7 182
Paisley, Ont., Can........C3 153
Paisley, Fla........D5 174
Paisley, Oreg........E6 201
Paisley, Scot........E4 57
Paita, N. Cal........115
Paita, Peru........C1 134
Paiyin, China........D5 91
Paja, Pan........m11 130
Pajala, Swe........D10 63
Pajaro, Calif........*D3 170
Pajaros (Uracas), isl., Mariana Is........115
Pajero, riv., Calif........C6 170
Pajon, pt., Guam........114
Pak, isl., Bis. Arch........115
Pakanbaru, Indon........E2 90
Pakaraima, mts., Guy........A2 139
Pakenham, Ont., Can........B8 153
Pakhoi, China........G6 91
PAKISTAN, country, Asia........C4 87, 83
Pakli, China........C8 89
Pakokku, Bur........D10 87
Pakowki, lake, Alta., Can....E5 148
Pakra, riv., Yugo........C3 68
Paks, Hung........B4 68
Pakse, Laos........E6 89
Pala, Chad........D3 104
Palabong, New Ire. I........115
Palacios, Tex........E4 206
Palafrugell, Sp........B7 65
Palagruza, is., Yugo........D3 68
Palaiokhóra, Grc........E4 69
Palaión Fáliron, Grc........h11 69
Palaiseau, Fr........h9 58
Palamás, Grc........C4 69
Palamós, Sp........B7 65
Palana, Sov. Un........D18 71
Palanga, Sov. Un........D3 72
Palanpur, India........E4 88
Palapag, Phil........C7 90
Palapye, Bots........B4 107
Palas de Rey, Sp........A2 65
Palatinate: c. 1360........48
Palatinate, Bavarian........51
Palatine, Ill........A5, E2 178
Palatine Bridge, N.Y....*C6 196
Palatka, Fla........C5 174
Palau (Pelew), is., Pac. O........114
Palauig, Phil........o12 90
Palauli, W. Sam........114
Palauli, bay, W. Sam........114
Palawan, isl., Phil........C5 90
Palayamcottai, India....*G6 87
Palazzolo Acreide, It........F5 67
Palco, Kans........C4 181
Palembang, Indon........F2 90
Palena, riv., Chile........C2 136
Palencia, Sp........A3 65
Palenque, ruins, Mex........B1 130
Palenville, N.Y........C6 196
Palermo, It........E4 67
Palermo, Maine........D3 184
Palermo, N.J........E3 194
Palermo, N. Dak........A3 198
Palestine, Ark........C5 169
Palestine, Ill........D6 178
Palestine, Ohio........B3 199
Palestine, Tex........D5 206
Palestine, W. Va........B3 211
PALESTINE (Gaza Strip), see Gaza Strip, Isr. occ., Asia
Palestine, reg., Asia........C7 84
c. 120 A.D........45
in 1922–40........53
Palestine Potash Company, Jordan........h13 84
Palestrina, It........h9 67
Paletwa, Bur........D9 87
Palezgir Chauki, Pak........B2 88
Palghat, India........F6 87
Palgrave, Ont., Can........D5 153
Palhoça, Braz........D3 137
Pali, India........E4 88
Palidoro (Baebiana), It......h8 67
Palikea, mtn., Haw........g9 176
Palikir, pass, Ponape........114
Palikir, pt., Ponape........114
Palimé, Togo........E5 103
Palisade, Colo........B2 171
Palisade, Minn........D5 187
Palisade, Nebr........D4 191
Palisade, Nev........C5 192
Palisades, Idaho........F7 177
Palisades, Wash........B6 210
Palisades, cliffs, N.J........D5 194
Palisades Park, N.J........D5 194
Paliseul, Bel........E5 59
Palitana, India........G3 88
Palk, strait, Cey., India....G6 87
Pall Mall, Tenn........C9 205
Pallasovka, Sov. Un........D3 73
Palling, B.C., Can........B5 149
Palliser, cape, N.Z........N15 112
Palm Bay, Fla........D6 174
Palm Beach, Fla........F6 174
Palm Beach, co., Fla........F6 174
Palm Beach Shores, Fla..*F6 174
Palm Desert, Calif........*F5 170
Palm Harbor, Fla........E1 174
Palm Springs, Calif........F5 170
Palm Springs, Fla........F6 174
Palm Valley, Fla........C6 174
Palma, Moz........D7 106
Palma, isl., Sp. (Can. Is.)..m13 65
Palma, riv., Braz........D1 138
Palma [de Mallorca], Sp...C7 65
Palma del Río, Sp........D3 65
Palma Soriano, Cuba........E5 131
Palmares, Braz........C3, k6 138
Palmas, Braz........D2 137
Palmas, cape, I.C........F3 103
Palmas Altas, P.R........B4 132
Palmas de Monte Alto, Braz........D2 138
Palmdale, Calif........E4 170
Palmdale, Fla........F5 174
Palmeirin Has, pt., Ang....C1 106
Palmeira, Braz........D3 137
Palmeira dos Índios, Braz........C3, k5 138
Palmer, Alsk........C10, g17 167
Palmer, Sask., Can........H2 155
Palmer, Ill........D4 178
Palmer, Iowa........B3 180
Palmer, Kans........C6 181
Palmer, Mass........B3 185
Palmer, Mich........B3 186
Palmer, Miss........D4 188
Palmer, Nebr........C7 191
Palmer, Tenn........D8 205
Palmer, Tex........B6 206
Palmer, Wash........D2 210
Palmer Heights, Pa........*E11 202
Palmer Lake, Colo........B6 171
Palmerston, Ont., Can....D4 153
Palmerston, N.Z........P13 112
Palmerston North, N.Z...N15 112
Palmersville, Tenn........A3 205
Palmerton, Pa........E10 202
Palmerville, Austl........C7 111
Palmetto, Fla........E4, F2 174
Palmetto, Ga........C2 175
Palmetto, La........D4 183
Palmi, It........E5 67
Palmira, Col........C2 133
Palmira, Cuba........D3 131
Palmira, Ec........B2 134
Palms, Mich........E8 186
Palms, is., S.C........F8 203
Palmyra, Ill........D4 178
Palmyra, Ind........H5 179
Palmyra, Iowa........B7 180
Palmyra, Maine........D3 184
Palmyra, Mo........B6 189
Palmyra, Nebr........D9, F2 191
Palmyra, N.J........C2 194
Palmyra, N.Y........B3 196
Palmyra, N.C........A6 197
Palmyra, Pa........F8 202
Palmyra, Syr........E12 85
Palmyra, Tenn........A4 205
Palmyra, Va........D4 209
Palmyra, Wis........F5 212
Palmyra, isl., Oceania....F12 113
Palmyras, pt., India........G11 88
Palni, India........*F6 87
Palo, Iowa........B6 180
Palo (Alsium), It........h8 67
Palo, Mich........E6 186
Palo Alto, Calif........B5, D2 170
Palo Alto, Pa........*E9 202
Palo Alto, co., Iowa........A3 180
Palo Blanco, P.R........B4 132
Palo Duro, canyon, Tex....B2 206
Palo Pinto, Tex........C3 206
Palo Pinto, co., Tex........C3 206
Palo Seco, P.R........B2 132
Palo Verde, Ariz........D3, G1 168
Palo Verde, Calif........F6 170
Paloduro, Tex........B2 206
Paloich, Sud........C3 105
Palomar, mtn., Calif........F5 170
Palomas, mts., Ariz........D2 168
Palombara Sabina, It........g9 67
Palominos, isl., P.R........f12 132
Palopo, Indon........F6 90
Palos, cape, Sp........D5 65
Palos Heights, Ill........*F3 178
Palos Hills, Ill........*F2 178
Palos Park, Ill........F2 178
Palos Verdes Estates, Calif........*F2 170
Palourde, lake, La........E4 183
Palouse, Wash........C8 210
Palouse, riv., Wash........C7 210
Palpa, Peru........D3 134
Pålsboda, Swe........t33 63
Palua, Ven........B5 133
Palung, China........D4 91
Pama, N. Cal........115
Pama, Upper Volta........D5 103
Pambrun, Sask., Can........H2 155
Pamdenec, N.B., Can....*D3 151
Pamekasan, Indon........G4 90
Pamiers, Fr........F4 58
Pamir, mts., Sov. Un........F10 71
Pamlico, co., N.C........B7 197
Pamlico, riv., N.C........B7 197
Pamlico, sound, N.C........B7 197
Pampa, Tex........B2 206
Pampa Grande, Bol........C3 135
Pampa Peñon, Chile........D2 135
Pampanga, riv., Phil........o13 90
Pampas, Peru........D3 134
Pampas, reg., Arg........G4 124
Pampilhosa do Botão, Port........B1 65
Pamplico, S.C........D8 203
Pamplin, Va........D4 209
Pamplona, Col........B3 133
Pamplona, Sp........A5 65
Pamunkey, riv., Va........D5 209
Pana, Ont., Can........B10 153
Pana, Ill........D4 178
Panaca, Nev........F7 192
Panacea, Fla........B2 174
Panache, lake, Ont., Can........A3 153
Panagyurishte, Bul........D7 68
Panaitan, isl., Indon........G2 90
Panama, Ill........D4 178
Panama, Iowa........C2 180
Panama, Nebr........D9 191
Panama, N.Y........C1 196
Panama, Okla........B7 200
PANAMA, country, N.A....F7 130
Panama, bay, Pan........B8 130
Panama, canal, C.Z....F8, k11 130
Panama, gulf, Pan........F8 130
Panama Canal Zone, see Canal Zone, U.S. dep., N.A.
Panama City, Fla........G3 174
Panama City, Pan....F8, m11 130
Panama City Beach, Fla..*G3 174
Panama Isthmus: in 1800's....127
Panamint, range, Calif....D5 170
Panao, Peru........C2 134
Panarea, isl., It........E5 67
Panay, isl., Phil........C6 90
Pancake, range, Nev........E5 192
Pančevo, Yugo........C5 68
Pancoastburg, Ohio........C4 199
Pandale, Tex........D2 206
Pandharpur, India........I5 88
Pandhurna, India........G7 88
Pando, New Britain I........115
Pando, Ur........E1 137
Pando, dept., Bol........B2 135
Pandora, Ohio........B4 199
Pandora, Tex........B4, E4 206
Pandu, Zaire........A2 106
Panelas, Braz........k6 138
Panet, Que., Can........C7 154
Panevežys, Sov. Un........D5 72
Panfilov, Sov. Un........E9 73
Pangala, Con........F2 104
Pangburn, Ark........B4 169
Pangfou, China........H7 92
Pangi, Zaire........B4 106
Panginay, Phil........o13 90
Pangkalanbuun, Indon....F4 90
Pangkalangresik, Indon....F2 90
Pangkalpinang, Indon....F3 90
Pangkong, lake, China....B6 87
Pangman, Sask., Can........H3 155
Pangnirtung, N.W. Ter., Can........C19 145
Pangong, lake, India........B6 87
Pangsau, pass, Bur........C10 87
Panguitch, Utah........F3 207
Panhandle, Tex........B2 206
Paniau, mtn., Haw........B1 176
Panihati, India........*F12 88
Panipat, India........C6 88
Paniqui, Phil........o13 90
Panjang, isl., Viet........H5 89
Panjao, Afg........D13 86
Panjgur, Pak........C3 87
Panjim, India........E5 87
Panjpai, Pak........G13 86
Pankshin, Nig........E6 103
Panmunjom, Kor........H3 93
Panna, India........E8 88
Panola, Ala........C1 166
Panola, co., Miss........A3 188
Panola, co., Tex........C5 206
Panora, Iowa........C3 180
Panshan, China........D9 92
Panshih, China........E2 93
Panshun, China........*G7 91
Pantar, isl., Indon........G6 90
Pantego, N.C........B7 197
Pantelleria, It........F3 67
Pantelleria, isl., It........F3 67
Panther, creek, Ky........C2 182
Pantin, Fr........g10 58
Panton, Vt........C2 208
Pantsyan, China........C5 92
Pánuco, Mex........C5, k14 129
Pánuco, riv., Mex........k14 129
Panulcillo, Chile........F1 135
Panzi, Zaire........C2 106
Panzós, Guat........C3 130
Pão de Acúçar, Braz........C3 138
Paochang, China........D6 92
Paocheng, China........H2 92
Paochi, China........G2 92
Paoching, China........C6 93
Paokang, China........I4 92
Paokuotu, China........C9 92
Paola, It........E6 67
Paola, Kans........D9 181
Paoli, Colo........A8 171
Paoli, Ind........G5 179
Paoli, Okla........C4 200
Paoli, Pa........A10 202
Paonia, Colo........C3 171
Paoshan, China........F4 91
Paote, China........E4 92
Paoti, China........E7 92
Paoting (Tsingyüan), China........E6 92
Paotou, China........D4 92
Paoua, Cen. Afr. Rep........D3 104
Paoying, China........H8 92
Pap, mtn., Scot........D3 57
Papa, Haw........D6 176
Pápa, Hung........B3 68
Papaaloa, Haw........D6 176
Papagayo, gulf, C.R........E5 130
Papago, Indian res., Ariz....E3 168
Papaikou, Haw........D6 176
Papal States (States of the Church): in 9th cent........47
c. 1360........48
c. 1721........49
c. 1815........50
in 1860........51
Papalaulelei, cape, W. Sam....114
Papantla, Mex........C5, m15 129
Papatele, mtn., Am. Sam....114
Papaya, Phil........o13 90
Papeete, Fr. Polynesia....H13 113
Papenburg, Ger........B3 60
Paphos, Cyp........E9 85
Papialou, is., Bis. Arch........115
Papigi, see Parigi, Indon.
Papillion, Nebr........C9, E3 191
Papillion, creek, Nebr........E3 191
Papineau, co., Que., Can..D2 154
Papineau, lake, Ont., Can....B7 153
Papineauville, Que., Can..D2 154
Paposo, Chile........E1 135
PAPUA, Austl. dep., Oceania........k12 111
Papua, gulf, N. Gui........k11 110
Papudo, Chile........A2 136
Papulu, New Britain I........115
Papun, Bur........E10 87
Paquette, Que., Can........D6 154
Paquetville, N.B., Can....B4 151
Pará, see Belém, Braz.
Pará, state, Braz........B1 138
Pará, riv., Braz........B1 138
Parabel, Sov. Un........B10 73
Paracale, Phil........o14 90
Paracatu, Braz........E1 138
Paracatu, riv., Braz........E1 138
Paracel, is., China........B4 90
Parachinar, Pak........E15 86
Paraćin, Yugo........D5 68
Paracurú, Braz........B3 138
Parade, S. Dak........B4 204
Paradis, La........C6 183
Paradise, Calif........C3 170
Paradise, Calif........*D3 170
Paradise, Kans........C5 181
Paradise, Mich........B5 186
Paradise, Mont........C2 190
Paradise, Pa........F9 202
Paradise Hill, Sask., Can..D1 155
Paradise Hills, N. Mex.B3, G5 195
Paradise Valley, Ariz........G2 168
Paradise Valley, Alta., Can........C5 148
Paradise Valley, Nev........B4 192
Paradox, Colo........C2 171
Paragon, Ind........F4 179
Paragonah, Utah........F3 207
Paragould, Ark........A5 169
Paragua, riv., Ven........B5 133
Paraguaçu, riv., Braz........D3 138
Paraguaçu Paulista, Braz........C2 137
Paraguai, riv., Braz........B1 137
Paraguaná, pen., Ven........A4 133
Paraguarí, Par........E4 135
Paraguarí, dept., Par........E4 135
PARAGUAY, country, S.A........D4 135
c. 1790........126
in 1811–70........127
Paraguay, riv., Par........D4 135
Paraíba, state, Braz....C3, h6 138
Paraíba, riv., Braz........C4 137
Paraíba do Sul, Braz........h6 137
Paraíso, Mex........D6 129
Paraisópolis, Braz........C3 137
Parakhino Poddubye, Sov. Un........B9 72
Parakou, Dah........E5 103
Paraloma, Ark........D1 169
Param, isl., Ponape........114
Paramaribo, Sur........A3 139
Paramé, Fr........C3 58
Paramirim, Braz........D2 138
Paramithiá, Grc........C3 69
Paramonga, Peru........D2 134
Paramount, Calif........*E4 170
Paramount, Md........A2 173
Paramus, N.J........*B4 194
Paraná, Arg........A4 136
Paranã, Braz........D1 138
Paraná, state, Braz........C2 137
Paraná, riv., Arg., Braz........E4 135, C2 137
Paraná, riv., Braz........D1 138
Paranaguá, Braz........D3 137
Paranaíba, Braz........B2 137
Paranaíba, riv., Braz........B2 137
Paranam, Sur........A3 139
Paranapanema, riv., Braz..C2 137
Paranatinga, riv., Braz........E3 139
Parangaba, Braz........*B3 138
Paraopeba, Braz........E1 138
Parapeti, riv., Bol........C3 135
Paratinga, Braz........D2 138
Paray-le-Monial, Fr........D6 58
Parbati, riv., India........E6 88
Parbhani, India........H6 88
Parchim, Ger........B5 60
Parchment, Mich........F5 186
Parczew, Pol........C7 70
Pardeeville, Wis........E4 212
Pardess Hanna, Isr........B6 84
Pardo, riv., Braz........C2 137
Pardo, riv., Braz........C3 137
Pardo, riv., Braz........E2 138
Pardoe, Pa........D1 202
Pardoo, Austl........D2 111
Pardubice, Czech........C3 70
Parecis, mts., Braz........E2 139
Paredes de Nava, Sp........A3 65
Parent, Que., Can........G18 145
Parepare, Indon........F5 90
Parfúri, Moz........B5 107
Párga, Grc........C3 69
Pargolovo, Sov. Un........r31 63
Parguera, P.R........D2 132
Parhams, La........C4 183
Paria, gulf, Ven........A5 133
Paria, pen., Ven........A5 133
Paria, riv., Ariz., Utah....F4 207
Pariaguán, Ven........B5 133
Paricutín, vol., Mex........n12 129
Parigi, Indon........F6 90
Parika, Guy........A3 139
Parima, mts., Braz........C5 133
Pariñas, pt., Peru........B1 134
Parintins, Braz........C3 139
Paris, Ark........B2 169
Paris, Ont., Can........D4 153
Paris, Fr........C5, g10 58
Paris, Idaho........G7 177
Paris, Ill........D6 178
Paris, Ky........B5 182
Paris, Maine........D2 184
Paris, Md........C4 173
Paris, Mich........E5 186
Paris, Miss........A4 188
Paris, Mo........B5 189
Paris, Tenn........A3 205
Paris, Tex........C5 206
Paris, Va........B5 209
Paris, peak, Idaho........G7 177
Paris Crossing, Ind........G6 179
Parishville, N.Y........A2 196
Parisville, Que., Can........C5 154
Park, Kans........C3 181
Park, co., Colo........B5 171
Park, co., Mont........E6 190

INDEX KEY Each place listed in **Bold-faced Type** has its population listed in the Population tables, pages 230 to 280.
Each country, shown in CAPITAL LETTERS, has its population listed in the World Political Information Table, pages 6 to 10.
* Does not appear on map; key shows general location.

Park, co., Wyo. A3 213
Park, plat., Colo. D6 171
Park, range, Colo., Wyo. B4 171, D5 213
Park City, Ill. *A6 178
Park City, Kans. B5 181
Park City, Ky. C3 182
Park City, Mont. E8 190
Park City, Utah C4 207
Park Court, Alta., Can. C3 148
Park Falls, Wis. C3 212
Park Forest, Ill. F3 178
Park Grove, Mont. B10 190
Park Hall, Md. D5 173
Park Head, Ont., Can. C3 153
Park Hill, Ont., Can. D3 153
Park Hill, Okla. B7 200
Park Hills, Ky. A7 182
Park Place, Oreg. B2 201
Park Rapids, Minn. D3 187
Park Ridge, Ill. A6, E2 178
Park Ridge, N.J. C5 194
Park Ridge, Wis. *D4 212
Park Ridge Manor, Ill. *A6 178
Park River, N. Dak. A8 198
Park Valley, Utah B2 207
Park View, N. Mex. A3 195
Parkbeg, Sask., Can. G2 155
Parkdale, Ark. D4 169
Parkdale, P.E.I., Can. C6 151
Parkdale, Colo. C5 171
Parkdale, Oreg. B5 201
Parke, co., Ind. E3 179
Parker, Ariz. C1 168
Parker, Colo. B6 171
Parker, Fla. G3 174
Parker, Idaho F7 177
Parker, Kans. D8 181
Parker, Pa. D2 202
Parker, S. Dak. D8 204
Parker, Va. C5 209
Parker, Wash. C5 210
Parker, co., Tex. C4 206
Parker, dam, Ariz., Calif. C1 168
Parker, peak, S. Dak. D2 204
Parker City, Ind. D7 179
Parker Dam, Calif. E6 170
Parker Head, Maine E6 184
Parkers Prairie, Minn. D3 187
Parkersburg, Ill. E5 178
Parkersburg, Iowa B5 180
Parkersburg, N.C. C5 197
Parkersburg, W. Va. B3 211
Parkerton, Wyo. C7 213
Parkertown, N.J. D4 194
Parkerview, Sask., Can. F4 155
Parkerville, Kans. D7 181
Parkes, Austl. F7 112
Parkesburg, Pa. G10 202
Parkfield, Calif. E3 170
Parkin, Ark. B5 169
Parkland, Alta., Can. D4 148
Parkland, Wash. E1 210
Parkman, Sask., Can. H5 155
Parkman, Maine C3 184
Parkman, Ohio A6 199
Parkman, Wyo. A5 213
Parks, La. D4 183
Parks, Nebr. D4 191
Parkside, Sask., Can. D2 155
Parkside, Ky. *B4 182
Parkside, Pa. *G11 202
Parksley, Va. D7 209
Parkston, S. Dak. D8 204
Parksville, B.C., Can. E5 149
Parksville, N.Y. D6 196
Parksville, S.C. D3 203
Parkton, Md. A4 173
Parkton, N.C. C4 197
Parkview, Ohio *A6 199
Parkville, Md. B4, C3 173
Parkville, Mo. B3, E2 189
Parkville, Pa. *G8 202
Parkway, Mo. *C6 189
Parkway Village, Ky. *B4 182
Parla, Sp. p17 65
Parlakimedi, India H10 88
Parlier, Calif. D4 170
Parlin, Colo. C4 171
Parma, Idaho F2 177
Parma, It. E6 66, B3 67
Parma, Mich. F6 186
Parma, Mo. E8 189
Parma, Ohio A6, B2 199
Parma, duchy of: in 1860 51
Parma, riv., It. E6 66
Parma Heights, Ohio B2 199
Parmachenee, lake, Maine C2 184
Parmele, N. C. B6 197
Parmelee, S. Dak. D4 204
Parmer, co., Tex. B1 206
Parnaguá, Braz. D2 138
Parnaíba, Braz. B2 138
Parnaíba, riv., Braz. B2 138
Parnassós, mtn., Grc. C4 69
Parnell, Iowa C6 180
Parnell, Mo. A3 189
Párnis Óros, mtn., Grc. g11 69
Pärnu, Sov. Un. B5 72
Parole, Md. C4 173
Paron, Ark. C3 169
Paropamisus, range, Afg. D12 86
Páros, Grc. D5 69
Páros, isl., Grc. D5 69
Parowan, Utah F3 207
Parr, Ind. B3 179
Parral, Chile B2 136
Parramatta, Austl. *F9 111
Parramore, isl., Va. D7 209
Parran, Nev. D3 192
Parras de la Fuente, Mex. B4 129
Parrett, riv., Eng. C5 56
Parrish, Ala. B2 166
Parrish, Fla. E4, F2 174
Parrish, Wis. C4 212
Parrott, Ga. E2 175
Parrott, Va. D2 209
Parrottsville, Tenn. C10 205
Parrs, ridge, Md. B3 173
Parrsboro, N.S., Can. D5 151
Parry, Sask., Can. H3 155
Parry, cape, N.W. Ter., Can. B8 142
Parry, isl., Ont., Can. B4 153
Parry, isl., Eniwetok 114
Parry, is., N.W. Ter., Can. B25 118
Parry, mtn., B.C., Can. C3 149
Parry Sound, Ont., Can. B4, F9 153
Parry Sound, co., Ont., Can. B5 153
Parsberg, Ger. D6 61
Parshall, Colo. A4 171
Parshall, N. Dak. B3 198
Parsnip, riv., B.C., Can. B6 149
Parsons, Kans. E8 181
Parsons, Tenn. B3 205
Parsons, W. Va. B5 211
Parson's Pond, Newf., Can. C3, h10 152
Parsonsburg, Md. D7 173
Partabgarh, India E5 88
Partabpur, India H8 88
Parthenay, Fr. D3 58
Parthenen, Aus. C6 66
Parthenon, Ark. B2 169
Parthia: c. 500 B.C. 78
c. 335 B.C. 43
c. 260 B.C. 43
Parthian empire: c. 50 B.C. 44
c. 120 A.D. 45
Partinico, It. E4 67
Partlow, Va. C5 209
Partoun, Utah D2 207
Partridge, Kans. B4, E5 181
Partridgeberry, hills, Newf., Can. D4 152
Parvan, Afg. D11 86
Pas-de-Calais, dept., Fr. D2 59
Pasadena, Calif. E4, F2 170
Pasadena, Newf., Can. D3 152
Pasadena, Md. B4 173
Pasadena, Tex. F5 206
Pasadena Hills, Mo. *C7 189
Pasadena Park, Mo. *C7 189
Pasaje, Ec. B2 134
Pasay, Phil. C6, o13 90
Pasayton, riv., B.C., Can., Wash. A5 210
Pascagoula, Miss. E3, E5 188
Pascagoula, bay, Miss. E3 188
Pascagoula, riv., Miss. E5 188
Paşcani [-Gară], Rom. B8 68
Pasco, Wash. C6 210
Pasco, co., Fla. D4 174
Pasco, dept., Peru D3 134
Pasco West, Wash. *C6 210
Pascoag, R.I. B10 172
Pascoag, res., R.I. B9 172
Pascola, Mo. E8 189
Pascualitos, Mex. F6 170
Paseley, cape, Austl. F3 110
Pasewalk, Ger. B7 60
Pashkovo, Sov. Un. B5 93
Pasig, Phil. o13 90
Pastęk, Pol. A5 70
Pasni, Pak. C3 87
Paso de los Indios, Arg. C3 136
Paso de los Libres, Arg. E4 135
Paso de los Toros, Ur. E1 137
Paso del Limay, Arg. C2 136
Paso Río Mayo, Arg. D2 136
Paso Robles (El Paso de Robles), Calif. E3 170
Pasqua, Sask., Can. G3 155
Pasque, isl., Mass. D6 185
Pasquia, hills, Sask., Can. D4 155
Pasquia, riv., Sask., Man., Can. C1 150, D5 155
Pasquo, Tenn. E9 205
Pasquotank, co., N.C. A7 197
Pasrur, Pak. A5 88
Pass Christian, Miss. E2, E4 188
Passaconaway, mtn., N.H. C4 193
Passadumkeag, Maine C4 184
Passadumkeag, mtn., Maine C4 184
Passaic, N.J. B4, D5 194
Passaic, co., N.J. A4 194
Passaic, riv., N.J. B4 194
Passau, Ger. E8 61
Passekeag, N.B., Can. D4 151
Passero, cape, It. F5 67
Passo Fundo, Braz. D2 137
Passos, Braz. F1 138
Passumpsic, Vt. C4 208
Passumpsic, riv., Vt. C4 208
Pastaza, prov., Ec. B2 134
Pastaza, riv., Ec., Peru B2 134
Pastillo, P.R. D5 132
Pasto, Col. C2 133
Pasto Viejo Central, P.R. C7 132
Pastora, peak, Ariz. A6 168
Pastura, N. Mex. C5 195
Pasuruan, Indon. G4 90
Pasweigin, Sask., Can. F4 155
Patagonia, Ariz. F5 168
Patan, India F4 88
Patan, Nep. D10 88
Patapedia, riv., N.B., Can. B2 151
Patapsco, Md. A4 173
Patapsco, res., Md. B4 173
Patapsco, riv., Md. B4 173
Pataskala, Ohio C5 199
Pataz, Peru C2 134
Patchewollock, Austl. G4 112
Patchogue, N.Y. D4 196
Patea, N.Z. M15 112
Pateley Bridge, Eng. F7 57
Patéras, mtn., Grc. g10 69
Paterno, It. F5 67
Pateros, Wash. A6 210
Paterson, N.J. B4, D5 194
Paterson, Wash. D6 210
Patesville, Ky. C3 182
Pathankot, India A5 88
Pathfinder, res., Wyo. C6 213
Pathfork, Ky. D6 182
Pathlow, Sask., Can. E3 155
Pati, pt., Guam 114
Patiala, India B6 87, B6 88
Patiali, India D7 88
Patillas, P.R. C6 132
Patillas, mun., P.R. C6 132
Patmos, Ark. D2 169
Pátmos, isl., Grc. D6 69
Patna, India C8 87, E10 88
Patnanongan, isl., Phil. o14 90
Patoka, Ill. E4 178
Patoka, Ind. H2 179
Patoka, riv., Ind. H2 179
Paton, Iowa B3 180
Patos, Braz. C3 138
Patos de Minas, Braz. E1 138
Pátrai (Patras), Grc. C3 69
Pátrai, gulf, Grc. C3 69
Patras, see Pátrai, Grc.
Patricia, Alta., Can. D5 148
Patricia, Tex. C1 206
Patrick, S.C. B7 203
Patrick, co., Va. E2 209
Patrick, port, Aneityum I. 115
Patrick Springs, Va. E2 209
Patricksburg, Ind. F4 179
Patriot, Ind. G8 179
Patrocínio, Braz. E1 138
Patroon, Tex. D6 206
Patsaliga, creek, Ala. D3 166
Patsville, Nev. B6 192
Pattani, Thai. I4 89
Pattaquattie, hill, Mass. B3 185
Patten, Maine C4 184
Pattenburg, N.J. B2 194
Patterson, Ark. B4 169
Patterson, Calif. B6 170
Patterson, Ga. E4 175
Patterson, Idaho E5 177
Patterson, Ill. D3 178
Patterson, Iowa C4 180
Patterson, Kans. E4 181
Patterson, La. E4 183
Patterson, Mo. D7 189
Patterson, N.Y. D7 196
Patterson, Va. B3 209
Patterson, creek, W. Va. B5 211
Patterson Gardens, Mich. *G7 186
Patterson Knob, mtn., Tenn. E9 205
Patteson, passage, New Hebr. 115
Pattison, Miss. D3 188
Patton, Mo. D7 189
Patton, Pa. E4 202
Pattonsburg, Mo. A3 189
Pattutto, mtn., B.C., Can. A3 149
Patu, Braz. C3 138
Patuakhali, Bngl. F13 88
Patuca, riv., Hond. C5 130
Patung, China I4 92
Patuxent, riv., Md. B3 173
Patzau, Wis. B1 212
Pátzcuaro, Mex. D4, n13 129
Pátzcuaro, lake, Mex. n13 129
Patzicía, Guat. C2 130
Patzún, Guat. C2 130
Pau, Fr. F3 58
Pau dos Ferros, Braz. C3 138
Paucarbamba, Peru D3 134
Paucartambo, riv., Peru D3 134
Paudalho, Braz. C3, h6 138
Paugh Lake, Ont., Can. B7 153
Pauillac, Fr. E3 58
Pauk, Bur. D9 87
Paul, Idaho G5 177
Paul, isl., Newf., Can. g9 152
Paul, stream, Vt. B5 208
Paul Smiths, N.Y. B2 196
Paul Spur, Ariz. F6 168
Paulden, Ariz. C3 168
Paulding, Mich. A6 186
Paulding, Miss. C4 188
Paulding, Ohio A3 199
Paulding, co., Ga. C2 175
Paulding, co., Ohio A3 199
Paulette, Miss. B5 188
Paulina, N.J. B3 194
Paulina, Oreg. C7 201
Paulina, mts., Oreg. D5 201
Paulina, peak, Oreg. D5 201
Pauline, Kans. B6 181
Pauline, Nebr. D7 191
Pauline, S.C. B4 203
Pauline, mtn., B.C., Alta., Can. C1 148, C8 149
Paulins, kill, N.J. A3 194
Paulistana, Braz. C2 138
Paull, lake, Sask., Can. A3 155
Paull, riv., Sask., Can. B3 155
Paullina, Iowa B2 180
Paulo Afonso, falls, Braz. C3 138
Pauloff Harbor, Alsk. E7 167
Pauls Valley, Okla. C4 200
Paulsboro, N.J. D2 194
Paungde, Bur. E10 87
Paupack, Pa. D11 202
Pauuma, isl., New Hebr. 115
Pauwela, Haw. C5 176
Pavia, It. D5 66, B2 67
Pavilion, N.Y. C2 196
Pavilion, key, Fla. G5 174
Pavillion, Wyo. B4 213
Pavlodar, Sov. Un. C9 73
Pavlof, vol., Alsk. D7 167
Pavlograd, Sov. Un. G10 72
Pavlovo, Sov. Un. D14 72
Pavlovsk, Sov. Un. s31 63
Pavlovsk, Sov. Un. F13 72
Pavlovskaya, Sov. Un. H13 72
Pavlovskiy Posad, Sov. Un. n18 72
Pavo, Ga. F3 175
Pavonia, Ohio B5 199
Paw Creek, N.C. B3 197
Paw Paw, Mich. F5 186
Paw Paw, W. Va. B6 211
Paw Paw, riv., Mich. F4 186
Paw Paw Lake, Mich. *F4 186
Pawcatuck, Conn. D9 172
Pawhuska, Okla. A5 200
Pawlet, Vt. E2 208
Pawleys Island, S.C. E9 203
Pawling, N.Y. D7 196
Pawłowicze, Pol. h9 70
Pawnee, Ill. D4 178
Pawnee, Okla. A5 200
Pawnee, Tex. E4 206
Pawnee, co., Kans. D4 181
Pawnee, co., Nebr. D9 191
Pawnee, co., Okla. A5 200
Pawnee, creek, Colo. A7 171
Pawnee, riv., Kans. D3 181
Pawnee City, Nebr. D9 191
Pawnee Rock, Kans. D5 181
Pawpaw, Ill. B5 178
Pawpaw, creek, W. Va. A7 211
Pawtuckaway, pond, N.H. D4 193
Pawtucket, R.I. B11 172
Pawtucket, res., R.I. B11 176
Pax, W. Va. D6 211
Paxico, Kans. C7 181
Paxoí, isl., Grc. C3 69
Paxtang, Pa. *F8 202
Paxton, Fla. G3 174
Paxton, Ill. C5 178
Paxton, Ind. F3 179
Paxton, Mass. B4 185
Paxton, Nebr. C4 191
Paxtonville, Pa. E7 202
Paxville, S.C. D7 203
Payen, China C3 93
Payenhala, China A10 92
Payette, Idaho E2 177
Payette, co., Idaho E2 177
Payette, lake, Idaho E2 177
Payette, riv., Idaho F2 177
Payintala, see Tungliao, China
Payne, Ga. D3 175
Payne, Ohio A3 199
Payne, co., Okla. A5 200
Payne, lake, Que., Can. A2 154
Payne Bay, Que., Can. A2 154
Paynes, Miss. B3 188
Paynes Creek, Calif. B3 170
Paynesville, Mich. A6 186
Paynesville, Minn. E4 187
Paynesville, Mo. B7 189
Payneville, Ky. C3 182
Paynton, Sask., Can. E1 155
Paysandú, Ur. E1 137
Payson, Ariz. C4 168
Payson, Ill. D2 178
Payson, Okla. B5 200
Payson, Utah C4 207
Paz, bay, Mex. C2 129
Pazardzhik, Bul. D7 68
Pazin, Yugo. C1 68
Pe Ell, Wash. C2 210
Pea, riv., Ala. D3 166
Pea Patch, isl., Del. D1 194
Pea Ridge, Ark. A1 169
Peabody, Kans. A6, D6 181
Peabody, Mass. A6, C3 185
Peabody, riv., N.H. B4 193
Peace, riv., Alta., B.C., Can. A2 148
Peace, riv., Fla. E5 174
Peace Dale, R.I. D11 172
Peace River, Alta., Can. A2 148
Peach, co., Ga. D3 175
Peach Creek, W. Va. D5 211
Peach Orchard, Ark. A5 169
Peach Orchard Knob, peak, Ky. C3 182
Peach Springs, Ariz. B2 168
Peacham, Vt. C4 208
Peache, pt., Mass. C4 185
Peachland, B.C., Can. E8 149
Peachland, N.C. C3 197
Peacock, Mich. D5 186
Peacock, pt., Wake I. 114
Peak, S.C. C5 203
Peak Hill, Austl. E2 111
Peaked, mtn., Maine B4 184
Peale, isl., Wake I. 114
Peale, mtn., Utah E6 207
Pear Ridge, Tex. E2 183
Pearce, Ariz. F6 168
Pearce, Alta., Can. E4 148
Pearcy, Ark. C2, D5 169
Pearisburg, Va. D2 209
Pearl, Ill. D3 178
Pearl, Miss. C3 188
Pearl, hbr., Haw. B4, g10 176
Pearl, riv., Miss. C3 188
Pearl and Hermes, reef, Haw. k12 176
Pearl Beach, Mich. *F8 186
Pearl City, Haw. B4, g10 176
Pearl City, Ill. A4 178
Pearl River, La. D6 183
Pearl River, N.Y. D1 196
Pearl River, co., Miss. E4 188
Pearland, Tex. F5 206
Pearlington, Miss. E4 188
Pearsall, Tex. E3 206
Pearsoll, peak, Oreg. E3 201
Pearson, Ark. B3 169
Pearson, Ga. E4 175
Peary Land, reg., Grnld. A18 118
Pease, Minn. E5 187
Peasleeville, N.Y. B3 196
Peavine, Tenn. C9 205
Pebane, Moz. A6 107
Pebworth, Ky. C6 182
Peć, Yugo. D5 68
Peçanha, Braz. E2 138
Pecatonica, Ill. A4 178
Pecatonica, riv., Wis. F3 212
Pechenga, Sov. Un. C14 63
Pechora, riv., Sov. Un. B18 40
Peck, Idaho C2 177
Peck, Kans. E6 181
Peck, Mich. E8 186
Peckerwood, lake, Ark. C4 169
Peckham, Okla. A4 200
Peckville (Blakely), Pa. A9 202
Peconic, N.Y. E7 172
Peconic, riv., N.Y. F6 172
Pecos, N. Mex. B4, F6 195
Pecos, Tex. D1, F2 206
Pecos, co., Tex. D1 206
Pecos, riv., N. Mex., Tex. E5 195, D1 206
Pécs, Hung. B4 68
Peculiar, Mo. C3 189
Pedasí, Pan. G7 130
Peddocks, isl., Mass. D3 185
Pedra Azul, Braz. E2 138
Pedraza, see Ciudad Bolivia, Ven.
Pedregal, Pan. F6 130
Pedregal, Pan. k12 130
Pedregal, Ven. A3 133
Pedreiras, Braz. B2 138
Pedricktown, N.J. D2 194
Pedro, S. Dak. C3 204
Pedro Afonso, Braz. C1 138
Pedro Avelino, Braz. C3 138
Pedro de Valdivia, Chile D2 135
Pedro Juan Caballero, Par. D4 135
Pedro Luro, Arg. B4 136
Pedro Miguel, C.Z. k11 130
Pedro Velho, Braz. h6 138
Pee Dee, riv., N.C., S.C. D9 203
Peebinga, Austl. G3 112
Peebles, Sask., Can. G4 155
Peebles, Ohio D4 199
Peebles, Scot. E5 57
Peebles, co., Scot. E5 57
Peekaboo, mtn., Maine C5 184
Peekskill, N.Y. D3, D7 196
Peel, N.B., Can. C2 151
Peel, I. of Man F4 57
Peel, co., Ont., Can. D5 153
Peel, riv., N.W. Ter., Can. C5 142
Peel, sound, N.W. Ter., Can. B13 142
Peel Fell, mtn., Scot. E6 57
Peene, riv., Ger. B6 60
Peer, Bel. C5 59
Peerless, Mont. B11 190
Peerless, lake, Alta., Can. A3 148
Peers, Alta., Can. C3 148
Peesane, Sask., Can. E4 155
Peetz, Colo. A7 171
Peever, S. Dak. B9 204
Pefferlaw, Ont., Can. C5 153
Pegan, hill, Mass. D2 185
Pegasus, bay, N.Z. O14 112
Pegau, Ger. B7 61
Peggs, Okla. A6 200
Peggy, Tex. E3 206
Pegnitz, Ger. D6 61
Pego, Sp. C5 65
Pegram, Tenn. A4 205
Pegu, Bur. E10 87
Pegu Yona, mts., Bur. C1 89
Pehčevo, Yugo. E6 68
Pehuajo, Arg. B4 136
Pei, China G7 92
Pei, China G7 92
Peian, China B10 91
Peiho, cape, New Britain I. 115
Peilintzu, see Suihuan, China
Peine, Ger. A5 61
Peiping, see Peking, China
Peipus, lake, Sov. Un. B6 72
Peixe, Braz. D1 138
Pejepscot, Maine E2, E5 184
Pekalongan, Indon. G3 90
Pekan, Mala. K5 89
Pekia, China A8 88
Pekin, Ill. C4 178
Pekin (New Pekin), Ind. G5 179
Pekin, N. Dak. B7 198
Peking (Peiping), China D8 91, E7 92
Pelagie, is., It. G13 64
Pélagos, isl., Grc. C5 69
Pelahatchie, Miss. C4 188
Pelaihari, Indon. F4 90
Pelat, mtn., Fr. E7 58
Pelee, isl., Ont., Can. F2 153
Peleliu, isl., Palau Is. 114
Pelham, Ala. B3 166
Pelham, Ont., Can. *D5 153
Pelham, Ga. E2 175
Pelham, Mass. B3 185
Pelham, N.H. E4 193
Pelham, N.Y. *E7 196
Pelham, N.C. A4 197
Pelham, S.C. B3 203
Pelham, Tenn. D8 205
Pelham Manor, N.Y. D1 196
Pelhřimov, Czech. D3 70
Pelican, Alsk. k21 167
Pelican, La. C2 183
Pelican, bay, Man., Can. C1 150
Pelican, lake, Man., Can. C1 150
Pelican, lake, Sask., Can. B4 155
Pelican, lake, Minn. B6 187
Pelican, lake, Minn. D3 187
Pelican, lake, Minn. D3 187
Pelican, lake, Minn. D4 187
Pelican, lake, Minn. E5 187
Pelican, lake, Wis. C4 212
Pelican, mts., Alta., Can. B4 148
Pelican Lake, Wis. C4 212
Pelican Narrows, Sask., Can. B4 155
Pelican Rapids, Man., Can. C1 150
Pelican Rapids, Minn. D2 187
Pelion, S.C. D5 203
Pell City, Ala. B3 166
Pella, Iowa C5 180
Pellejas Central, P.R. C4 132
Pellice, riv., It. E3 66
Pellston, Mich. C6 186
Pellville, Ky. C3 182
Pellworm, isl., Ger. A4 60
Pelly, Sask., Can. F5 155
Pelly, lake, N.W. Ter., Can. C12 142
Pelly, mts., Yukon, Can. D6 142
Pelly, riv., Yukon, Can. D6 142
Pelly Crossing, Yukon, Can. D5 144
Peloncillo, mts., Ariz., N. Mex. E6 168, E1 195
Peloponnesos, reg., Grc. D4 69
Pelotas, Braz. E2 137
Pelotas, riv., Braz. D2 137
Pelto, lake, La. E5 183
Pelzer, S.C. B3 203
Pelzer North, S.C. *B3 203
Pemadumcook, lake, Maine C3 184
Pemanggil, isl., Mala. K6 89
Pemaquid, Maine E3 184
Pematangsiantar, Indon. K3 89
Pemba, Zambia E4 106
Pemba, isl., Tan. B6 106
Pemberton, B.C., Can. D6 149
Pemberton, N.J. D3 194
Pemberton, Ohio B3 199
Pemberville, Ohio A2, A4 199
Pembina, N. Dak. A8 198
Pembina, co., N. Dak. A8 198
Pembina, mts., N. Dak. A7 198
Pembina, riv., Alta., Can. C3 148
Pembina, riv., Man., Can. E2 150
Pembine, Wis. C6 212
Pembroke, Ont., Can. B7, E10 153
Pembroke, Fla. *G6 174
Pembroke, Ga. D5 175
Pembroke, Ky. D2 182
Pembroke, Maine D5 184
Pembroke, Mass. B6 185
Pembroke, N.H. D4 193
Pembroke, N.Y. C2 196
Pembroke, N.C. C4 197
Pembroke, Va. D2 209
Pembroke, Wales C3 56
Pembroke, co., Wales C3 56
Pembroke Pines, Fla. *F6 174
Pembuang, riv., Indon. F4 90
Pemigewasset, riv., N.H. C3 193
Pemiscot, co., Mo. E8 189
Pemmican Portage, Sask., Can. D4 155
Pemuco, Chile B2 136
Pen Argyl, Pa. E11 202
Pen-y-Ghent, mtn., Eng. F6 57
Peña Negra, mts., Sp. A2 65
Peña Roya, mtn., Sp. B5 65
Penablanca, N. Mex. B3, F5 195
Penacook, N.H. D3 193
Penafiel, Port. B1 65
Peñafiel, Sp. B3 65
Peñalara, mtn., Sp. B4 65
Penalosa, Kans. E5 181
Penamacor, Port. B2 65
Penápolis, Braz. C2 137
Peñaranda de Bracamonte, Sp. B3 65
Peñarroya-Pueblonuevo, Sp. C3 65
Peñas, cape, Sp. A3 65
Penas, gulf, Chile D2 136
Penasco, N. Mex. A4 195
Penasse, Minn. A4 187
Penawawa, Wash. C8 210
Penbrook, Pa. F8 202
Pence, Ind. D2 179
Penchi, China C9 91
Penck, cape, Ant. C21 120
Penck, trough, Ant. B12 120
Pend Oreille, Idaho A2 177
Pend Oreille, co., Wash. A8 210
Pend Oreille, lake, Idaho A2 177
Pend Oreille, riv., Wash. A8 210
Pendelikón (Pentelicus), mtn., Grc. g11 69
Pendembu, S.L. E2 103
Pender, Nebr. B9 191
Pender, co., N. C. C6 197
Pender Island, B.C., Can. B9 149
Pendergrass, Ga. B3 175
Pendle Hill, mtn., Eng. G6 57
Pendleton, Ind. E6 179
Pendleton, Oreg. B8 201
Pendleton, S.C. B2 203
Pendleton, co., Ky. B5 182
Pendleton, co., W. Va. C5 211
Pendroy, Mont. B4 190
Penebscot, bay, Maine D4 184
Penedo, Braz. D3 138
Penetanguishene, Ont., Can. C5 153
Penfield, Ga. C3 175
Penfield, Ill. C6 178
Penfield, Pa. D4 202
Pengan, China I2 92
Penganga, riv., India H6 88
Penge, Zaire C3 106
Pengibu, isl., Indon. L7 89
Penglai, China B9 92
Pengshui, China J3 92
Penguin, is., Newf., Can. E3 152
Penhold, Alta., Can. C4 148
Penhook, Va. E3 209

INDEX KEY Each place listed in **Bold-faced Type** has its population listed in the Population tables, pages 230 to 280. Each country, shown in CAPITAL LETTERS, has its population listed in the World Political Information Table, pages 6 to 10.
* Does not appear on map; key shows general location.

Peniche, Port....C1 65
Penicuik, Scot....E5 57
Peninsula, Minn....E7 187
Peninsula, Ohio....A6 199
Penitas, Tex....F3 206
Penitente, mts., Braz....C1 138
Penitentiary, mtn., Ala....A2 166
Penn, Sask., Can....D2 155
Penn, N. Dak....A6 198
Penn Grove, Calif....B5 170
Penn Hills, Pa....*F2 202
Penn Yan, N.Y....C3 196
Pennall, mtn., Utah....F5 207
Pennant, pt., N.S., Can....E6 151
Pennant Station, Sask., Can....G1 155
Pennask, mtn., B.C., Can....E7 149
Penndel, Pa....*F12 202
Penne, It....C4 67
Pennellville, N.Y....B4 196
Penneshaw, Austl....G1 112
Penney Farms, Fla....C5 174
Pennfield, N.B., Can....D3 151
Penniac, N.B., Can....C3 151
Pennine Alps, mts., It., Switz....C3 66
Pennine Chain, mts., Eng....C5 55
Pennington, Ala....C1 166
Pennington, N.J....C3 194
Pennington, co., Minn....B2 187
Pennington, co., S. Dak....D2 204
Pennington Gap, Va....B2 209
Pennock, Minn....E3 187
Penns Grove, N.J....D2 194
Pennsauken, N.J....D2 194
Pennsboro, W. Va....B4 211
Pennsburg, Pa....F11 202
Pennsuco, Fla....F3 174
Pennsville, N.J....D1 194
Pennsville, Ohio....C6 199
Pennsylvania, state, U.S....202
c. 1776....162
during Civil War....164
Pennsylvania Furnace, Pa....E5 202
Pennville, Ind....D7 179
Penny, B.C., Can....C7 149
Penny Highland, mts., N.W. Ter., Can....C19 143
Penobscot, Maine....D4 184
Penobscot, co., Maine....C4 184
Penobscot, lake, Maine....C4 184
Penobscot, riv., Maine....C4 184
Penobsquis, N.B., Can....D4 151
Penokee, Kans....C4 181
Penong, Austl....F5 111
Penonomé, Pan....F7 130
Penrith, Austl....F8 112
Penrith, Eng....F6 57
Penrose, Colo....C5 171
Pensacola, Fla....G2 174
Pensacola, Okla....A6 200
Pensacola, dam, Okla....A6 200
Pensacola, mts., Ant....A8 120
Pensaukee, Wis....D6 212
Pense, Sask., Can....G3 155
Pentagon, mtn., Mont....C3 190
Pentecost, Miss....B3 188
Pentecost, isl., New Hebr....115
Pentecoste, Braz....B3 138
Pentelicus, see Pendelikón, mtn., Grc.
Penticton, B.C., Can....E8 149
Pentland, firth, Scot....B5 57
Pentland, hills, Scot....E5 57
Penton, Miss....A3 188
Penton, N.J....D2 194
Pentwater, Mich....E4 186
Peñuelas, P.R....C4 132
Peñuelas, mun., P.R....C4 132
Penwell, Tex....D1 206
Penza, Sov. Un....C3 73
Penzance, Ariz....C5 168
Penzance, Sask., Can....F3 155
Penzance, Eng....D2 56
Penzberg, Ger....E5 60
Penzhino, Sov. Un....C19 71
Penzlin, Ger....E7 62
Peoa, Utah....C4 207
Peoples, Ky....C5 182
Peoria, Ariz....D3, G1 168
Peoria, Ill....C4 178
Peoria, Miss....D3 188
Peoria, Ohio....B4 199
Peoria, co., Ill....C4 178
Peoria Heights, Ill....C4 178
Peotone, Ill....B6 178
Pep, N. Mex....D6 195
Pepacton, res., N.Y....C6 196
Pepeekeo, Haw....D6 176
Pepin, Wis....D1 212
Pepin, co., Wis....D2 212
Pepin, lake, Wis....D1 212
Pepper Pike, Ohio....*B2 199
Pepperell, Mass....A4 185
Pepperton, Ga....C3 175
Peqin, Alb....B2 69
Pequabuck, Conn....C5 172
Pequannock, N.J....B4 194
Pequawket, mtn., N.H....B4 193
Pequení, riv., Pan....k12 130
Pequest, riv., N.J....B3 194
Pequirí, riv., Braz....B1 137
Pequirí, riv., Braz....C2 137
Pequop, Nev....B7 192
Pequot Lakes, Minn....D4 187
Perak, pol. div., Mala....J4 89
Perak, isl., Indon....J2 89
Perak, riv., Mala....J4 89
Perakhóra (Loutrakion-Perakhora), Grc....g9 69
Perales de Tajuña, Sp....p18 65
Peralta, N. Mex....C3 195
Percé, Que., Can....*B3 154
Perchas, P.R....B3 132
Percival, Iowa....D2 180
Percy, Fr....C3 58
Percy, Ill....E4 178
Percy, Miss....B3 188
Percy, N.H....A4 193
Perdido, Ala....D2 166
Perdido, bay, Fla....G1 174
Perdido, mtn., Sp....A6 65
Perdido, riv., Fla....G1 174
Perdue, Sask., Can....E2 155
Pere Marquette, riv., Mich....E4 186
Pereira, Col....C2 133
Pereira Barreto, Braz....C2 137
Perekop, Sov. Un....H9 72
Perené, riv., Peru....D3 134
Pereslavl-Zalesskiy, Sov. Un....C12 72
Pereyaslav-Khmelnitskiy, Sov. Un....F8 72
Perez, Phil....o13 90
Pergamino, Arg....A4 136
Pergine Valsugana, It....A3 67
Perham, Maine....B4 184
Perham, Minn....D3 187
Péribonca, Que., Can....A5 154
Perico, Tex....A1 206
Périgueux, Fr....E4 58
Perijá, mts., Ven....B3 133
Perim, isl., Yemen (Aden)....C5 105
Peristérion, Grc....*C4 69
Perkasie, Pa....F11 202
Perkins, Que., Can....D2 154
Perkins, Ga....D5 175
Perkins, Mich....C3 186
Perkins, Okla....B4 200
Perkins, co., Nebr....D4 191
Perkins, co., S. Dak....B3 204
Perkinston, Miss....E4 188
Perkinstown, Wis....C3 212
Perkinsville, Vt....E3 208
Perkiomen, creek, Pa....C2 194
Perla, Ark....C3, D6 169
Perlas, arch., Pan....F8 130
Perlas, lagoon, Nic....D6 130
Perleberg, Ger....B5 60
Perley, Minn....C2 187
Perlis, pol. div., Mala....I4 89
Perm', Sov. Un....B5 73
Perma, Mont....C2 190
Përmet, Alb....B3 69
Pernambuco, state, Braz....C3, k6 138
Pernell, Okla....C4 200
Pernik, Bul....D6 68
Péronne, Fr....C5 58
Perot, bayou, La....C7 183
Perote, Ala....D4 166
Perpignan, Fr....F5 58
Perquimans, co., N.C....A7 197
Perrin, Tex....C3 206
Perrin, Va....D6 209
Perrine, Fla....F3, G6 174
Perrineville, N.J....C4 194
Perris, Calif....F3, F5 170
Perros-Guirec, Fr....C2 58
Perrot, isl., Que., Can....D8 154
Perry, Ark....B3 169
Perry, Fla....B3 174
Perry, Ga....D3 175
Perry, Ill....D3 178
Perry, Iowa....C3 180
Perry, Kans....B7, C8 181
Perry, La....E3 183
Perry, Maine....D5 184
Perry, Mich....F6 186
Perry, Mo....B6 189
Perry, N.Y....C3 196
Perry, Ohio....A6 199
Perry, Okla....A4 200
Perry, S.C....D5 203
Perry, Utah....B3 207
Perry, co., Ala....C2 166
Perry, co., Ark....C3 169
Perry, co., Ill....E4 178
Perry, co., Ind....H4 179
Perry, co., Ky....C6 182
Perry, co., Miss....D4 188
Perry, co., Mo....D8 189
Perry, co., Ohio....C5 199
Perry, co., Pa....F7 202
Perry, co., Tenn....B4 205
Perry, peak, Mass....B1 185
Perry, res., Kans....B7, C8 181
Perry, stream, N.H....A1 193
Perry Hall, Md....B5 173
Perrydale, Oreg....B3, C1 201
Perrygo Place, Wis....*F4 212
Perryman, Md....B5 173
Perryopolis, Pa....*F2 202
Perry's Victory and International Peace Memorial, nat. mon., Ohio....A5 199
Perrysburg, N.Y....C2 196
Perrysburg, Ohio....A2, A4 199
Perrysville, Ind....D3 179
Perrysville, Ohio....B5 199
Perryton, Tex....A2 206
Perryvale, Alta., Can....B4 148
Perryville, Alsk....D8 167
Perryville, Ark....B3 169
Perryville, Ky....C5 182
Perryville, La....B3 183
Perryville, Md....A5 173
Perryville, Mo....D8 189
Perryville, R.I....D10 172
Perryville, Tenn....B3 205
Persan, Fr....E2 59
Persepolis, ruins, Iran....G6 86
Pershing (East Germantown), Ind....E7 179
Pershing, Iowa....C5 180
Pershing, Mo....C6 189
Pershing, co., Nev....C3 192
Persia, Iowa....C2 180
Persia: c. 325 B.C....43
c. 120 A.D....45
in 1907-18....52
in 1922-40....53
see also Iran
Persia, Tenn....C10 205
Persian, gulf, Asia....H5 86
Persian empire: c. 500 B.C....78
Persimmon Grove, Ky....A7 182
Persis: c. 500 B.C....78
Person, co., N.C....A5 197
Perstorps, Swe....B7 62
Pertek, Tur....C12 85
Perth, Austl....F2 111
Perth, N.B., Can....C2 151
Perth, Ont., Can....C8 153
Perth, Kans....E6 181
Perth, N. Dak....A6 198
Perth, Scot....D5 57
Perth, co., Ont., Can....D3 153
Perth, co., Scot....D5 57
Perth Amboy, N.J....B4, E4 194
Perthshire, Miss....B3 188
Pertuis, Fr....F6 58
Pertuis Breton, bay, Fr....D3 58
Peru, Ill....B4 178
Peru, Ind....C5 179
Peru, Iowa....C4 180
Peru, Kans....E7 181
Peru, Mass....B1 185
Peru, Nebr....D10 191
Peru, N.Y....B3 196
Peru, Vt....E3 208
PERU, country, S.A....D3 134
in 1542....126
in 1824–1929....127
Perugia, It....C4 67
Peruque, Mo....A7 189
Péruwelz, Bel....D3 59
Pervomaysk, Sov. Un....G8 72
Pervomaysk, Sov. Un....q21 72
Pervoural'sk, Sov. Un....B6 73
Pesaro, It....C4 67
Pescadero, Calif....C5, D2 170
Pescara, It....C5 67
Pescara, riv., It....C4 67
Peschanyy, cape, Sov. Un....B10 93
Peshastin, Wash....B5 210
Peshāwar, Pak....B5 87
Peshkopi, Alb....B3 69
Peshtera, Bul....D7 68
Peshtigo, Wis....C6 212
Peshtigo, riv., Wis....C5 212
Peski, Sov. Un....C7 73
Peski, Sov. Un....F14 72
Peski, Sov. Un....n18 72
Peso da Régua, Port....B2 65
Pesotum, Ill....D5 178
Pesqueira, Braz....C3, k5 138
Petaca, N. Mex....A4 195
Petah Tiqwa, Isr....B6, g10 84
Petal, Miss....D4 188
Petaluma, Calif....B5, C2 170
Pétange, Lux....E5 59
Petare, Ven....*A4 133
Petatlán, Mex....D4 129
Petauke, Zambia....D5 106
Petawawa, Ont., Can....B7 153
Petawawa, riv., Ont., Can....A7 153
Petenwell, res., Wis....D4 212
Peter, isl., Vir. Is....f16 132
Peter Dana Point, Maine....C5 184
Peter Pond, lake, Sask., Can....B1 155
Peter The Great, bay, Sov. Un....E5 93
Peterborough, Austl....F2 112
Peterborough, Ont., Can....C6 153
Peterborough, Eng....B7 56
Peterborough (Peterboro), N.H....E3 193
Peterborough, co., Ont., Can....C6 153
Petergof, see Petrodvorets, Sov. Un.
Peterhead, Scot....C7 57
Peterman, Ala....D2 166
Peters, creek, W. Va....C7 211
Peters, mtn. Va., W. Va....D4 211
Peters Landing, Tenn....B4 205
Petersburg, Alsk....D13, m23 167
Petersburg, Ill....C4 178
Petersburg, Ind....H3 179
Petersburg, Ky....A6 182
Petersburg, Mich....G7 186
Petersburg, Nebr....C7 191
Petersburg, N.J....E3 194
Petersburg, N.Y....C7 196
Petersburg, N. Dak....A8 198
Petersburg, Ohio....B7 199
Petersburg, Pa....E5 202
Petersburg, Tenn....B5 205
Petersburg, Tex....C2 206
Petersburg (Independent City), Va....C7, D5 209
Petersburg, W. Va....C5 211
Petersburg Junction, N.Y....A1 185
Petersdorf, Ger....D5 62
Petersfield, Man., Can....D3 150
Petersfield, Eng....D7 56
Petersham, Mass....B3 185
Peterson, Iowa....B2 180
Peterson, Minn....G7 187
Peterstown, W. Va....D4 211
Petersville, Ky....B6 182
Petilia Policastro, It....E6 67
Pétionville, Hai....F7 131
Petit, lake, La....C8 183
Petit Bois, isl., Miss....E5 188
Petit-Etang, N.S., Can....C9 151
Petit-Goâve, Hai....F7 131
Petit Jean, mtn., Ark....B3 169
Petit Jean, mtn., Ark....C2 169
Petit Rocher, N.B., Can....B4 151
Petitcodiac, N.B., Can....D4 151
Petitcodiac, riv., N.B., Can....C5 151
Petite Amite, riv., La....B6 183
Petite-de-Grat, N.S., Can....D9 151
Petite Lieure, riv., Que., Can....A5 154
Petite Miquelon, isl., St. Pierre and Miquelon....E3 152
Petite Riviere Bridge, N.S., Can....E5 151
Petitjean, Mor....G4 64
Peto, Mex....C7 129
Petorca, Chile....A2 136
Petoskey, Mich....C6 186
Petrey, Ala....D3 166
Petrich, Bul....E6 68
Petrie, reef, N. Cal....115
Petrified, forest, N. Dak....B2 198
Petrified, forest, S. Dak....D2 204
Petrified Forest, nat. park, Ariz....B6 168
Petrified Wood, park, S. Dak....B3 204
Petrikov, Sov. Un....E7 72
Petrinja, Yugo....C3 68
Petrodvorets, Sov. Un....s30 63
Petrohué, Chile....C2 136
Petrokrepost, Sov. Un....s32 63, B8 72
Petrolândia, Braz....C3 138
Petroleum, Ind....C7 179
Petroleum, co., Mont....C8 190
Petrolia, Ont., Can....E2 153
Petrolia, Kans....E8 181
Petrolia, Pa....D2 202
Petrolia, Tex....B3 206
Petrolina, Braz....C2 138
Petropavlovsk, Sov. Un....C7 73
Petropavlovskiy, Sov. Un....D3 73
Petropavlovsk [-Kamchatskiy], Sov. Un....D18 71
Petrópolis, Braz....C4, h6 137
Petros, Tenn....C9 205
Petroşeni, Rom....C6 68
Petrovgrad, see Zrenjanin, Yugo.
Petrovsk, Sov. Un....E15 72
Petrovsk-Zabaykalskiy, Sov. Un....D13 71
Petrovskoye, Sov. Un....D2 73
Petrozavodsk, Sov. Un....A10 72
Petterill, riv., Eng....F6 57
Pettibone, N. Dak....B6 198
Pettigrew, Ark....B2 169
Pettingell, peak, Colo....B5 171
Pettis, co., Mo....C4 189
Pettisville, Ohio....A3 199
Pettus, Tex....E4 206
Petty Harbour, Newf., Can....E5 152
Petukhovo, Sov. Un....B7 73
Pevely, Mo....B8 189
Pewamo, Mich....E6 186
Pewaukee, Wis....E1, E5 212
Pewaukee, lake, Wis....E1 212
Pewee Valley, Ky....A4, B4 182
Peyton, Colo....B6 171
Pézenas, Fr....F5 58
Pfaffenhofen, Ger....E6 61
Pfarrkirchen, Ger....E7 61
Pfeifer, Kans....D4 181
Pforzheim, Ger....E3 61
Pfunds, Aus....C6 66
Pfungstadt, Ger....D3 61
Phalodi, India....D4 88
Phaltan, India....I5 88
Phan Rang, Viet....G8 89
Phan Thiet, Viet....G8 89
Phangan, isl., Thai....H4 89
Pharoah, Okla....B5 200
Pharr, Tex....F3 206
Phatthalung, Thai....I4 89
Pheba, Miss....B5 188
Phelps, Ky....C7 182
Phelps, N.Y....C3 196
Phelps, Wis....B4 212
Phelps, co., Mo....D6 189
Phelps, co., Nebr....D6 191
Phelps, lake, N.C....B7 197
Phelps City, Mo....A2 189
Phenix, Va....D4 209
Phenix City, Ala....C4 166
Phet Buri, Thai....F3 89
Phetchabun, Thai....D4 89
Phichit, Thai....D4 89
Phil Campbell, Ala....A2 166
Philadelphia, Miss....C4 188
Philadelphia, Mo....B6 189
Philadelphia, N.Y....A5 196
Philadelphia, Pa....B11, G11 202
Philadelphia, Tenn....D9 205
Philadelphia, co., Pa....G11 202
Philbrook, Minn....D4 187
Philip, crusade of....47
Philip, S. Dak....C4 204
Philipp, Miss....B3 188
Philippeville, Bel....D4 59
Philippi, W. Va....B4 211
Philippine, is., Phil....B6 90
Philippine, sea, Phil....A6, o14 90
PHILIPPINES, country, Asia....B6 90
in 1946....83
Philippolis, S. Afr....D4 107
Philipsburg, Mont....D3 190
Philipsburg, Pa....E5 202
Philipsville, Ont., Can....C8 153
Philleo, lake, Wash....D7 210
Phillip, isl., Austl....I5 112
Phillippy, Tenn....A2 205
Phillips, Maine....D2 184
Phillips, Nebr....D7 191
Phillips, Okla....C5 200
Phillips, Tex....B2 206
Phillips, Wis....C3 212
Phillips, co., Ark....C5 169
Phillips, co., Colo....A8 171
Phillips, co., Kans....C4 181
Phillips, co., Mont....B8 190
Phillips, brook, N.H....A4, B1 193
Phillipsburg, Que., Can....D4 154
Phillipsburg, Ga....*E3 175
Phillipsburg, Kans....C4 181
Phillipsburg, Mo....D5 189
Phillipsburg, N.J....B2 194
Phillipsburg, Ohio....*C3 199
Phillipsdale, R.I....B11 172
Phillipston, Mass....A3 185
Phillipstown, Ill....*E5 178
Phillipsville, N.C....*D3 197
Philmont, N.Y....C7 196
Philo, Ill....C5 178
Philo (Taylorsville), Ohio....C6 199
Philomath, Oreg....C3 201
Philpott, res., Va....E2 209
Philrich, Tex....*B2 206
Phippen, Sask., Can....E1 155
Phippsburg, Colo....A4 171
Phippsburg, Maine....E6 184
Phitsanulok, Thai....D4 89
Phlox, Wis....C4 212
Phnom Penh, Camb....G6 89
Phoebus, Va....B6 209
Phoenicia, N.Y....C6 196
Phoenix, Ariz....D3, G2 168
Phoenix, Ill....F3 178
Phoenix, Md....A4 173
Phoenix, Mich....A2 186
Phoenix, N.Y....B4 196
Phoenix, Oreg....E4 201
Phoenix, is., Pac. O....G11 113
Phoenixville, Conn....B8 172
Phoenixville, Pa....A10, F10 202
Phong Saly, Laos....B5 89
Phrae, Thai....C4 89
Phu Cuong, Viet....G7 89
Phu Lai Leng, mtn., Laos....C6 89
Phu Quoc, isl., Viet....G6 89
Phu Vinh, Viet....H7 89
Phuket, Thai....I3 89
Phuket, isl., Thai....I3 89
Phuoc Le, Viet....G7 89
Phutthaisong, Thai....E5 89
Piaanu, pass, Truk....114
Piacenza, It....D5 66, B2 67
Pialba, Austl....B9 112
Pianosa, isl., It....C3 67
Pianosa, isl., It....C5 67
Piapot, Sask., Can....H1 155
Piaseczno, Pol....m14 70
Piatra-Neamț, Rom....B8 68
Piatt, co., Ill....D5 178
Piauí, state, Braz....C2 138
Piauí, mts., Braz....C2 138
Piauí, riv., Braz....C2 138
Piave, riv., It....D8 66
Piazza Armerina, It....F5 67
Pibor, riv., Sud....D3 105
Pibor Post, Sud....D3 105
Pibroch, Alta., Can....B4 148
Pic de Tio, mtn., Guinea....E3 103
Pic du Midi d'Ossau, mtn., Fr....F3 58
Pic Tousidé, mtn., Chad....A3 104
Picabo, Idaho....F4 177
Picacho, Ariz....E4 168
Picacho, N. Mex....D4 195
Picard, Que., Can....B8 154
Picardy (Picardie), former prov., Fr....C5 58
Picayune, Miss....E4 188
Piccadilly, Newf., Can....D2 152
Piceance, creek, Colo....B2 171
Pichan, see Shanshan, China
Pichanal, Arg....D3 135
Picher, Okla....A7 200
Pichilemu, Chile....A2 136
Pichincha, prov., Ec....B2 134
Pick City, N. Dak....B4 198
Pickard, pt., Mass....C4 185
Pickardville, Alta., Can....B4 148
Pickardville, N. Dak....B5 198
Pickaway, co., Ohio....C4 199
Pickens, Ark....D4 169
Pickens, Miss....C4 188
Pickens, Okla....C6 200
Pickens, S.C....B2 203
Pickens, W. Va....C4 211
Pickens, co., Ala....B1 166
Pickens, co., Ga....B2 175
Pickens, co., S.C....B2 203
Pickensville, Ala....B1 166
Pickerel, Ont., Can....B4 153
Pickerel, Wis....C5 212
Pickerel, lake, Wis....C4 212
Pickerel, riv., Ont., Can....B4 153
Pickering, Ont., Can....D5 153
Pickering, Eng....F8 57
Pickering, Mo....A3 189
Pickerington, Ohio....C2, C5 199
Picketberg, S. Afr....D2 107
Pickett, co., Tenn....C8 205
Pickford, Mich....B6 186
Pickleville, Utah....B4 207
Pickrell, Nebr....D9 191
Pickstown, S. Dak....E7 204
Pickwick, Minn....G7 187
Pickwick, lake, Ala., Miss., Tenn....A1 166
Pickwick Dam, Tenn....B3 205
Pickwick Landing, dam, Tenn....A5 188
Pico, isl., Port. (Azores)....g8 102
Pico Rivera, Calif....*E4 170
Picos, Braz....C2 138
Pictograph Rocks, Ariz....D2 168
Picton, Ont., Can....D7 153
Picton, N.Z....N15 112
Pictou, N.S., Can....D7 151
Pictou, co., N.S., Can....D7 151
Pictou, isl., N.S., Can....D7 151
Pictou Landing, N.S., Can....D7 151
Picture, gorge, Oreg....C7 201
Picture Butte, Alta., Can....E4 148
Picture Rocks, Pa....D8 202
Pictured, cave, Wis....E2 212
Picuí, Braz....h5 138
Picún-Leufú, Arg....B3 136
Pidurutalagala, peak, Cey....G7 87
Pie Town, N. Mex....C1 195
Piedade, Braz....m8 137
Piedmont, Ala....B4 166
Piedmont, Calif....B5 170
Piedmont, Que., Can....D3 154
Piedmont, Kans....E7 181
Piedmont, Mo....D7 189
Piedmont, Okla....B4 200
Piedmont, S.C....B3 203
Piedmont, S. Dak....C2 204
Piedmont, W. Va....B5 211
Piedmont, Wyo....E2 213
Piedmont, reg., It....B1 67
in 1721....49
in 1860....51
Piedmont, res., Ohio....B6 199
Piedmont, upland, U.S....C2 197, E3 209
Piedra Negra, pt., Mex....D5 129
Piedra Sola, Ur....E1 137
Piedrabuena, Sp....C3 65
Piedras, pt., Arg....B5 136
Piedras, riv., Pan....k12 130
Piedras, riv., Peru....D3 134
Piedras Blancas, pt., Calif....E3 170
Piedras Negras, Guat....B2 130
Piedras Negras, Mex....B4 129
Piekiełko, Pol....k13 70
Pieksämäki, Fin....F12 63
Piélagos, Sp....A4 65
Pielisjarvi, lake, Fin....F13 63
Piendamó, Col....C2 133
Pienkuan, China....E4 92
Piennes, Fr....E5 59
Pierce, Colo....A6 171
Pierce, Fla....E5 174
Pierce, Idaho....C3 177
Pierce, Nebr....B8 191
Pierce, Tenn....A3 205
Pierce, W. Va....B5 211
Pierce, co., Ga....E4 175
Pierce, co., Nebr....B8 191
Pierce, co., N. Dak....A5 198
Pierce, co., Wash....C3 210
Pierce, co., Wis....D1 212
Pierce, lake, Man., Can....B5 150
Pierce, lake, Fla....E5 174
Pierce, pond, Maine....C2 184
Pierce City, Mo....E3 189
Piercefield, N.Y....A6, B2 196
Pierces, N.J....E3 194
Pierceton, Ind....B6 179
Pierceville, Kans....E3 181
Piercy, Calif....C2 170
Piermont, N.H....C2 193
Piermont, N.Y....D6 196
Pierowall, Scot....A6 57
Pierpont, Ohio....A7 199
Pierpont, S. Dak....B8 204
Pierre, S. Dak....C5 204
Pierre, bayou, Miss....D3 188
Pierre Part, La....C5 183
Pierrefitte-sur-Aire, Fr....F5 59
Pierrefitte [-sur-Seine], Fr....g10 58
Pierrefonds, Que., Can....D8 154
Pierreville, Que., Can....C5 154
Pierron, Ill....E4 178
Pierson, Man., Can....E1 150
Pierson, Fla....C5 174
Pierson, Iowa....B2 180
Pierson, Mich....*E5 186
Pierz, Minn....E4 187
Piešt'any, Czech....D4 70
Piet Retief, S. Afr....C5 107
Pietermaritzburg, S. Afr....C5 107
Pietersburg, S. Afr....B4 107
Pietrasanta, It....C3 67
Pieve di Cadore, It....A4 67
Pigeon, Mich....E7 186
Pigeon, bay, Man., Can....C3 150
Pigeon, creek, Ala....D3 166
Pigeon, creek, Ind....H3 179
Pigeon, lake, Alta., Can....C3 148
Pigeon, mtn., Ga....B1 175
Pigeon, pt., Calif....D2 170
Pigeon, pt., Can., U.S....A8 187
Pigeon, riv., Man., Can....C3 150
Pigeon, riv., Can., U.S....A7 187
Pigeon, riv., Ind....A6 179
Pigeon, riv., N. Car., Tenn....D3 197
Pigeon, riv., Wis....B6 212
Pigeon Cove, Mass....A6 185
Pigeon Falls, Wis....D2 212
Pigeon Forge, Tenn....D10 205
Pigeon River, Minn....A7 187
Pigg, riv., Va....E3 209
Piggott, Ark....A5 169
Pigüé, Arg....B4 136
Piirai, isl., Eniwetok....114
Pijijiapan, Mex....D6 129
Pike, Ark....C2 169
Pike, N.H....B2 193
Pike, N.Y....C2 196
Pike, co., Ala....D4 166
Pike, co., Ark....C2 169
Pike, co., Ga....C2 175
Pike, co., Ill....D3 178
Pike, co., Ind....H3 179
Pike, co., Ky....C7 182
Pike, co., Miss....D3 188
Pike, co., Mo....B6 189
Pike, co., Ohio....C4 199
Pike, co., Pa....D11 202
Pike, riv., Wis....C5 212
Pike Rigg, mtn., Eng....F6 57
Pike Road, N.C....B7 197
Pikes, beach, N.Y....F6 172
Pikes, peak, Colo....C5 171
Pikes Rock, mts., Pa....C3 202
Pikesville, Md....B4, C2 173

Piketon, Ohio C4 199
Pikeview, Colo C6 171
Pikeville, Ky C7 182
Pikeville, N.C B6 197
Pikeville, Tenn D8 205
Pikwitonei, Man., Can B3 150
Piła, Pol B4 70
Pilar, Braz C3, k6 138
Pilar, N. Mex A4 195
Pilar, Par E4 135
Pilar de Goiás, Braz A3 137
Pilar [do Sul], Braz m8 137
Pilatus, peak, Switz C4 66
Pilcomayo, riv., Par D4 135
Pilger, Sask., Can E3 155
Pilger, Nebr B8 191
Pilgrim Knob, Va B3 209
Pilibhit, India C7 88
Pilica, riv., Pol C5 70
Pillager, Minn D4 187
Pillar, pt., Calif B5 170
Pillaro, Ec B2 134
Pilley's Island, Newf., Can D4 152
Pillow, (Uniontown), Pa E8 202
Pillsbury, N. Dak B8 198
Pilos, Grc D3 69
Pilot, peak, Nev B7 192
Pilot, peak, Nev E4 192
Pilot, peak, Wyo A3 213
Pilot, range, N.H A4 193
Pilot Butte, Sask., Can G3 155
Pilot Grove, Mo C5 189
Pilot Knob, Mo D7 189
Pilot Knob, mtn., Ark B2 169
Pilot Knob, mtn., Ark C1 169
Pilot Knob, mtn., Idaho D3 177
Pilot Mound, Man., Can E2 150
Pilot Mound, Iowa B3 180
Pilot Mountain, N.C A3 197
Pilot Point, Alsk D8 167
Pilot Point, Tex C4 206
Pilot Rock, Oreg B8 201
Pilot Station, Alsk C7 167
Pilottown, La E6 183
Pilsen, Wis A6 212
Pilvo, Sov. Un A11 93
Pima, Ariz E6 168
Pima, co., Ariz E3 168
Pimba, Austl F6 111
Piña, Pan k10 130
Pinal, co., Ariz E4, H2 168
Pinal, mts., Ariz D5 168
Pinang, Mala J4 89
Pinang, pol. div., Mala J4 89
Pinang, isl., Mala J4 89
Pinar del Río, Cuba D2 131
Pinar del Río, prov., Cuba D2 131
Pinarbaşi, Tur C11 85
Pinas, Arg A3 136
Pincher Creek, Alta., Can E4 148
Pincher Station, Alta., Can E4 148
Pinckard Ala D4 166
Pinckney, Mich F7 186
Pinckney, isl., S.C G6 203
Pinckneyville, Ill E4 178
Pinckneyville, Miss D2 188
Pinconning, Mich E7 186
Pińczów, Pol C6 70
Pindall, Ark A3 169
Pindamonhangaba, Braz C3 137
Pindaré, riv., Braz B1 138
Pindus, mts., Grc C3 69
Pine, Ariz C4 168
Pine, Colo B5 171
Pine, Mo E6 189
Pine, co., Minn D6 187
Pine, cape, Newf., Can E5 152
Pine, creek, Nev C5 192
Pine, creek, Pa D7 202
Pine, creek, Wash B8 210
Pine, key, Fla F1 174
Pine, lake, Ind A4 179
Pine, lake, Minn D3 187
Pine, lake, Wis C4 212
Pine, mtn., Conn B5 172
Pine, mtn., Ga D2 175
Pine, mtn., Ky., Tenn D6 182, C9 205
Pine, mtn., Okla C6 200
Pine, mtn., Oreg D6 201
Pine, mtn., Wyo D3 213
Pine, ridge, Nebr B2 191
Pine, riv., Alta., Can B4 148
Pine, riv., B.C., Can B6 149
Pine, riv., Man., Can D1 150
Pine, riv., Mich D7 186
Pine, riv., N.H C4 193
Pine, riv., Wis C4 212
Pine Apple, Ala D3 166
Pine Bank, Pa G1 202
Pine Barrens, forest, N.J D3 194
Pine Beach, N.J *D4 194
Pine Bluff, Ark C3 169
Pine Bluff Southeast, Ark *C3 169
Pine Bluffs, Wyo D8 213
Pine Bush, N.Y D6 196
Pine Castle, Fla D5 174
Pine City, Ark C4 169
Pine City, Minn E6 187
Pine City, Wash B8 210
Pine Creek, Austl B5 111
Pine Creek, gorge, Pa C7 202
Pine Creek, res., Okla C6 200
Pine Falls, Man., Can D3 150
Pine Forest, Tex *D5 206
Pine Forest, range, Nev B3 192
Pine Grove, Ga E4 175
Pine Grove, La D5 183
Pine Grove, Pa E9 202
Pine Grove, W. Va A6, B4 211
Pine Grove Mills, Pa E6 202
Pine Hall, N.C A3 197
Pine Hill, Ala D2 166
Pine Hill, Austl A6 112
Pine Hill, Ky C5 182
Pine Hill, N.J D3 194
Pine Hill, N.Y *C6 196
Pine Hills, Fla D5 174
Pine Island, Minn F6 187
Pine Island, sound, Fla F4 174
Pine Knot, Ky D5 182
Pine Lake, Ga A5 175
Pine Lawn, Mo A8 189
Pine Level, Ala C3 166
Pine Level, N.C B5 197
Pine Lodge, N. Mex D4 195
Pine Meadow, Conn B5 172
Pine Mountain, Ga D2 175
Pine Orchard, Conn D5 172
Pine Park, Ga F2 175
Pine Plains, N.Y D7 196
Pine Point, Maine E2, E5 184
Pine Prairie, La D3 183
Pine Ridge, Ark C2 169
Pine Ridge, Miss D2 188
Pine Ridge, S. Dak D3 204
Pine Ridge, Indian res., S. Dak D3 204
Pine River, Man., Can D1 150
Pine River, Minn D4 187
Pine Spring, Minn *E6 187
Pine Swamp Knob, mtn., W. Va B5 211
Pine Valley, Calif F5 170
Pine Valley, N.H E3 193
Pine Valley, N.J *D3 194
Pine Village, Ind D3 179
Pinebluff, N.C B4 197
Pinebluff, lake, Sask., Can C4 155
Pinebur, Miss D4 188
Pinecreek, Minn B3 187
Pinecrest, Calif C3 170
Pineda, Fla D6 174
Pinedale, Ariz C5 168
Pinedale, Wyo C3 213
Pinega, Sov. Un C17 41
Pinehouse Lake, Sask., Can B2 155
Pinehurst, Ga D3 175
Pinehurst, Idaho B2 177
Pinehurst, Mass C2 185
Pinehurst, N.C B4 197
Pinehurst, Tex *D6 206
Pinehurst, Wash B3 210
Pineland, S.C F5 203
Pineland, Tex D6 206
Pinellas, co., Fla E4 174
Pinellas, pt., Fla F2 174
Pinellas Park, Fla E1, E4 174
Pineora, Ga D5 175
Pineridge, S.C *D5 203
Pinerolo, It B1 67
Piñeros, isl., P.R B8 132
Pinery, prov. park, Ont., Can D3 153
Pinetop, Ariz C6 168
Pinetops, N.C B6 197
Pinetown, N.C B7 197
Pinetta, Fla B3 174
Pineview, Ga D3 175
Pineville, Ky D6 182
Pineville, La C3 183
Pineville, Mo E3 189
Pineville, N.C B3 197
Pineville, S.C E7 203
Pineville, W. Va D3 211
Pineville Junction, La *C3 183
Pinewald, N.J D4 194
Pinewood, Minn C3 187
Pinewood, S.C D7 203
Piney, Man., Can E4 150
Piney, buttes, Mont C10 190
Piney, creek, Mo D5 189
Piney, creek, W. Va D7 211
Piney, fork, W. Va A6 211
Piney Flats, Tenn C11 205
Piney Fork, Ohio B7 199
Piney Park, Mo *C6 189
Piney Point, Tex *E5 206
Piney View, W. Va D7 211
Piney Woods, Miss C3 188
Pingchiang, China J5 92
Pingchuan, China D8 92
Pinghsiang, China K5 92
Pingliang, China G2 92
Pinglo, China G7 91
Pinglo, China E2 92
Pingnan, China G7 91
Pingree, Idaho F6 177
Pingree, N. Dak B7 198
Pingree Grove, Ill *A5 178
Pingting, China F5 92
Pingtingshan, China H5 92
Pingtu, China F8 92
Pingtung, Taiwan *G9 91
Pingwu, China E5 91
Pinhal, Braz C3, m8 137
Pinhal Novo, Port f10 65
Pinheiro, Braz B1 138
Pinhel, Port B2 65
Pinhsien, China D3 93
Pini, isl., Indon E1 90
Piniós (Peneus), riv., Grc C4 69
Pink, cliffs, Utah F3 207
Pink Hill, N.C B6 197
Pinkham, Sask., Can F1 155
Pinkstaff, Ill E6 178
Pinnacle, Ark C3, D5 169
Pinnacle, N.C A3 197
Pinnacle, butte, Wyo B3 213
Pinnacle, mtn., Mo B7 189
Pinnacle, mtn., N.Y B6 196
Pinnacles, nat. mon., Calif D3 170
Pinnaroo, Austl G3 112
Pinneberg, Ger E3 62
Pinnebog, Mich E7 186
Pinó Hachado, pass, Arg B2 136
Pinola, Miss D4 188
Pinole, Calif B5 170
Pinon, Ariz A5 168
Pinon, N. Mex E4 195
Pinopolis, S.C E7 203
Pinopolis, dam, S.C E8 203
Pinos, Cuba h12 131
Pinos, Mex C4 129
Pinos, isl., Cuba E2 131
Pinos, mtn., Calif E4 170
Pinos, pt., Calif D3 170
Pinos Altos, N. Mex E1 195
Pinos-Puente, Sp D4 65
Pinoso, Sp C5 65
Pinotpandian, Phil o13 90
Pinsk, Sov. Un E6 72
Pinsk, marshes, Sov. Un E6 72
Pinson, Ala E5 166
Pinson, Tenn B3 205
Pinta, isl., Ec f5 134
Pintados, Chile D2 135
Pintendre, Que., Can C9 154
Pinto, Md D2 173
Pinto, Sp p17 65
Pinto, butte, Sask., Can H2 155
Pinto, creek, Sask., Can H2 155
Pintura, Utah F2 207
Pintwater, range, Nev G6 192
Pinware, riv., Newf., Can C3 152
Pinzolo, It C6 66
Pinzón, isl., Ec g5 134
Pioche, Nev F7 192
Piombino, It C3 67
Pioneer, Iowa B3 180
Pioneer, La B4 183
Pioneer, Ohio A3 199
Pioneer, mts., Idaho F5 177
Pioneer, mts., Mont E3 190
Pioneer Mine, B.C., Can D6 149
Piopolis, Que., Can D7 154
Piotrków [Trybunalski], Pol C5 70
Piove di Sacco, It D8 66
Pipe, Wis B5 212
Pipe, creek, Ind D6 179
Pipe, creek, Ohio B1 211
Pipe Spring, nat. mon., Ariz A3 168
Pipe Stem, creek, N. Dak B6 198
Piper, Kans B8 181
Piper City, Ill C5 178
Piperi, isl., Grc C5 69
Pipers Gap, Va E2 209
Piperville, Ont., Can A10 153
Pipestem, W. Va D4 211
Pipestone, Man., Can E1 150
Pipestone, Minn G2 187
Pipestone, co., Minn F2 187
Pipestone, creek, Man., Sask., Can E1 150, G5 155
Pipestone, nat. mon., Minn G2 187
Pipestone, pass, Mont E4 190
Pipmuacan, res., Que., Can B2 154
Piqua, Kans E8 181
Piqua, Ohio B3 199
Piracanjuba, Braz E1 138
Piracicaba, Braz C3, m8 137
Piracicaba, riv., Braz m8 137
Piraçununga, Braz C3, k8 137
Piracuruca, Braz B2 138
Piraeus, see Piraiévs, Grc.
Piraiévs (Piraeus), Grc D4, h11 69
Pirajú, Braz C3 137
Pirajuí, Braz C3 137
Piramida, mtn., Sov. Un D12 71
Piran, Yugo C1 68
Piranga, Braz F2 138
Piranhas, Braz C3 138
Pirapóra, Braz E2 138
Pireway, N.C C5 197
Pírgos, Grc D3 69
Piriápolis, Ur E1 137
Pirin, mts., Bul E6 68
Piripiri, Braz B2 138
Pirmasens, Ger D2 61
Pirna, Ger C8 61
Pirot, Yugo D6 68
Pirtleville, Ariz F6 168
Piru, Indon F7 90
Piryatin, Sov. Un F9 72
Pis, isl., Truk 114
Pisa, It C3 67
Pisagua, Chile C1 135
Piscataqua, riv., N.H., Maine D5 193
Piscataquis, co., Maine C3 184
Piscataquis, riv., Maine C3 184
Piscataquog, riv., N.H D3 193
Piscataway, creek, Md C4 173
Pisciotta, It D5 67
Pisco, Peru D2 134
Piseco, lake, N.Y B6 196
Pisek, Czech D3 70
Pisek, N. Dak A8 198
Pisgah, Ala A4 166
Pisgah, Iowa C2 180
Pisgah, Md C3 173
Pisgah, mtn., Vt F3 208
Pisgah, mtn., Wyo B8 213
Pisgah Forest, N.C D3 197
Pishin, Pak B1 88
Pishin Lora, riv., Pak C4 87
Pishukan, cape, Pak I11 86
Pisia, riv., Pol m12 70
Pisidia: c. 450 B.C. 42
c. 325 B.C. 43
c. 120 A.D. 45
Pisinimo, Ariz E3 168
Pismo Beach, Calif E3 170
Pisogne, It D6 66
Pistal River, Oreg E2 201
Pisticci, It D6 67
Pistoia, It C3 67
Pistolet, bay, Newf., Can C4 152
Pisuerga, riv., Sp A3 65
Pisz, Pol B6 70
Pita, Guinea D2 103
Pitalito, Col C2 133
Pitangui, Braz E2 138
Pitcairn, Pa *F2 202
PITCAIRN, Br. dep., Oceania H14 113
Piteå, Swe E9 63
Piteälven, riv., Swe E9 63
Pitești, Rom C7 68
Pithiviers, Fr C5 58
Piti, Guam 114
Pitkas Point, Alsk C7 167
Pitkin, Colo C4 171
Pitkin, La D3 183
Pitkin, co., Colo B4 171
Pitlochry, Scot D5 57
Pitman, N.J D2 194
Pito, Pan F9 130
Pitreville, La D3 183
Pitrufquén, Chile B2 136
Pitsburg, Ohio C3 199
Pitt, Minn B4 187
Pitt., co., N.C B6 197
Pitt, cape, Mbulo I 115
Pitt, isl., B.C., Can C3 149
Pittman Center, Tenn D10 205
Pitts, Ga E3 175
Pittsboro, Ind E5 179
Pittsboro, Miss B4 188
Pittsboro, N.C B4 197
Pittsburg, Calif B5 170
Pittsburg, Ill F5 178
Pittsburg, Ind C4 179
Pittsburg, Kans E9 181
Pittsburg, Ky C5 182
Pittsburg, N.H A1 193
Pittsburg, Okla C6 200
Pittsburg, Oreg B3 201
Pittsburg, Tex C5 206
Pittsburg, co., Okla C6 200
Pittsburg East, Calif *D3 170
Pittsburg West, Calif *D3 170
Pittsburgh, Pa B6, F2 202
Pittsfield, Ill D3 178
Pittsfield, Maine D3 184
Pittsfield, Mass B1 185
Pittsfield, N.H D4 193
Pittsfield, Pa C3 202
Pittsfield, Vt D3 208
Pittsford, Mich G6 186
Pittsford, N.Y B3 196
Pittsford, Vt D2 208
Pittsford Mills, Vt D2 208
Pittston, Pa B8, D10 202
Pittstown, N.J B3 194
Pittsview, Ala C4 166
Pittsville, Md D7 173
Pittsville, Mo C4 189
Pittsville, Wis D3 212
Pittsylvania, co., Va E3 209
Pitzuwo, China E10 92
Piuka, Jap D11 93
Piura, Peru C1 134
Piura, dept., Peru C1 134
Piute, co., Utah E3 207
Piute, peak, Calif E4 170
Piuthān, Nep C9 88
Piva, riv., Yugo D4 68
Pixley, Calif E4 170
Piyang, China H5 92
Piz Kesch, mtn., Switz C5 66
Pizzo, It E6 67
Placentia, Calif *F3 170
Placentia, Newf., Can E5 152
Placentia, bay, Newf., Can E4 152
Placer, Oreg E3 201
Placer, co., Calif C3 170
Placerville, Calif C3 170
Placerville, Colo C2 171
Placerville, Idaho F3 177
Placetas, Cuba D4 131
Placid, lake, Fla E5 174
Placid, lake, N.Y B3 196
Placida, Fla F4 174
Placitas, N. Mex B3, G5 195
Plain, Wis E3 212
Plain City, Ohio B4 199
Plain City, Utah B3 207
Plain Dealing, La B2 183
Plainfield, Conn C9 172
Plainfield, Ga D3 175
Plainfield, Ill B5, F2 178
Plainfield, Ind E5 179
Plainfield, Iowa B5 180
Plainfield, Mass A2 185
Plainfield, N.H C2 193
Plainfield, N.J B4 194
Plainfield, Tenn *D10 205
Plainfield, Vt C4 208
Plainfield, Wis D4 212
Plains, Ga D2 175
Plains (West Plains), Kans E3 181
Plains, Mont C2 190
Plains, Pa B8 202
Plains, Tex C1 206
Plainsboro, N.J C3 194
Plainview, Ark C2 169
Plainview, Minn F6 187
Plainview, Nebr B8 191
Plainview, N.Y *G3 172
Plainview, S. Dak C3 204
Plainview, Tex B2 206
Plainville, Conn C5 172
Plainville, Ill D2 178
Plainville, Ind G3 179
Plainville, Kans C4 181
Plainville, Mass B5 185
Plainwell, Mich F5 186
Plaisance, Que., Can D2 154
Plaisance, Hai F7 131
Plaisance-du-Gers, Fr F4 58
Plaisted, Maine A4 184
Plaistow, N.H E4 193
Plamondon, Alta., Can B4 148
Planá, Czech D7 61
Planada, Calif *D3 170
Planaltina, Braz E1 138
Plandome, N.Y *F2 172
Plandome Heights, N.Y *F2 172
Plankinton, S. Dak D7 204
Plano, Ill B5 178
Plano, Iowa D4 180
Plano, Tex A6, C4 206
Plant City, Fla D4 174
Plantagenet, Ont., Can B9 153
Plantation, Fla *F6 174
Plantersville, Ala C3 166
Plantersville, Miss A5 188
Plantersville, S.C D9 203
Plantsite, Ariz D6 168
Plantsville, Conn C5 172
Plaquemine, La B5, D4 183
Plaquemine Southwest, La *D4 183
Plaquemines, par., La E6 183
Plasencia, Sp B2 65
Plaster Rock, N.B., Can C2 151
Plastun, Sov. Un D8 93
Plasy, Czech D8 61
Plata Central, P.R B2 132
Plate Cove West, Newf., Can D5 152
Platea, Pa C1 202
Plateau City, Colo B3 171
Platina, Calif B2 170
Platinum, Alsk D7 167
Platner, Colo A7 171
Plato, Sask., Can F1 155
Plato, Col B3 133
Plato, Mo D5 189
Platt, nat. park., Okla C5 200
Platte, S. Dak D7 204
Platte, co., Mo B3 189
Platte, co., Nebr C8 191
Platte, co., Wyo C7 213
Platte, riv., Iowa, Mo D3 180, B3 189
Platte, riv., Minn E4 187
Platte, riv., Nebr D6 191
Platte Center, Nebr C8 191
Platte City, Mo B3, D1 189
Plattenville, La B5 183
Platter, Okla D5 200
Platteville, Colo A6 171
Platteville, Wis F3 212
Plattling, Ger E7 61
Plattsburg, Mo B3 189
Plattsburgh, N.Y A3 196
Plattsmouth, Nebr C10, E3 191
Plattsville, Ont., Can D4 153
Plattville, Ill B5 178
Plaucheville, La D4 183
Plauen, Ger C7 61
Plauer, lake, Ger E6 62
Plave, riv., Ger A7 61
Playa de Fajardo (Puerto Real), P.R B8, f12 132
Playa de Guayanés, P.R C7 132
Playa de Guayanilla, P.R C3 132
Playa de Humacao (Punta Santiago), P.R C8, g12 132
Playa de Marianao, Cuba h11 131
Playa de Naguabo, P.R C8, g12 132
Playa de Ponce, P.R D4 132
Playa Grande, P.R B2 132
Playa Salinas, P.R D3 132
Playa Sardinera, P.R B8, f12 132
Playgreen, lake, Man., Can B2 150
Plaza, N. Dak A4 198
Plazuela Central, P.R B4 132
Pleasant, bay, Que., Can B8 151
Pleasant, bay, Maine D5 184
Pleasant, lake, Ariz D3 168
Pleasant, lake, Maine C5 184
Pleasant, mtn., Va D3 209
Pleasant, pt., Rendova I 115
Pleasant, pond, Maine B4 184
Pleasant, pond, Maine C3 184
Pleasant, pond, N.H D4 193
Pleasant, riv., Maine C3 184
Pleasant Bay, N.S., Can C9 151
Pleasant Beach, Wash D1 210
Pleasant City, Ohio C6 199
Pleasant Dale, Nebr D9 191
Pleasant Gap, Pa E6 202
Pleasant Garden, N.C B4 197
Pleasant Grove, Ala E4 166
Pleasant Grove, Miss A3 188
Pleasant Grove, Utah C4 207
Pleasant Hill, Ala C3 166
Pleasant Hill, Calif *D3 170
Pleasant Hill, Ill D3 178
Pleasant Hill, Iowa *C4 180
Pleasant Hill, La C2 183
Pleasant Hill, Miss A4 188
Pleasant Hill, Mo C3 189
Pleasant Hill, N. Mex C6 195
Pleasant Hill, Ohio B3 199
Pleasant Hill, S.C B6 203
Pleasant Hill, Tenn *D8 205
Pleasant Hill, Va *E6 209
Pleasant Hills, Pa *F2 202
Pleasant Hope, Mo D4 189
Pleasant Lake, Ind A7 179
Pleasant Lake, Mass C7 185
Pleasant Lake, N. Dak A6 198
Pleasant Mills, Ind C8 179
Pleasant Mount, Pa C11 202
Pleasant Plain, Iowa C6 180
Pleasant Plains, Ark B4 169
Pleasant Plains, Ill D4 178
Pleasant Pond, Maine C3 184
Pleasant Prairie, Wis F2 212
Pleasant Ridge, Mich *A7 186
Pleasant Shade, Tenn C8 205
Pleasant Valley, Conn B5 172
Pleasant Valley, Iowa D7 180
Pleasant Valley, Md A3 173
Pleasant Valley, Mo *B3 189
Pleasant Valley, N.Y D7 196
Pleasant Valley, Oreg C9 201
Pleasant Valley, Va B4 209
Pleasant View, Colo D2 171
Pleasant View, Ill C3 178
Pleasant View, Ind I8 179
Pleasant View, Ky D5 182
Pleasant View, Tenn A4 205
Pleasant View, Utah B3 207
Pleasantdale, Sask., Can E3 155
Pleasanton, Calif B6 170
Pleasanton, Iowa D4 180
Pleasanton, Kans D9 181
Pleasanton, Nebr D6 191
Pleasanton, N. Mex D1 195
Pleasanton, Tex E3 206
Pleasants, co., W. Va B3 211
Pleasantville, Ind G3 179
Pleasantville, Iowa C4 180
Pleasantville, N.J E3 194
Pleasantville, N.Y A5 194, D3 196
Pleasantville, Ohio C5 199
Pleasantville, Pa C2 202
Pleasure Beach, Conn *E4 172
Pleasure Ridge Park, Ky A4 182
Pleasureville, Ky B4 182
Plebo, Lib F3 103
Pledger, Tex G4 206
Pleiku, Viet F7 89
Plenita, Rom C6 68
Plenty, Sask., Can F1 155
Plentywood, Mont B12 190
Plesetsk, Sov. Un C7 71
Plessis, N.Y A5, B1 196
Plessisville, Que., Can C6 154
Pleszew, Pol C4 70
Pletcher, Ala C3 166
Pletipi, lake, Que., Can B2 154
Plettenberg, Ger B2 61
Plettenberg, La D4 183
Pleven, Bul D7 68
Plevna, Kans E5 181
Plevna, Mo B5 189
Plevna, Mont D12 190
Pliny, range, N.H B4 193
Pljevlja, Yugo D4 68
Plochingen, Ger E4 61
Plock, Pol B5 70
Ploërmel, Fr D2 58
Ploiești, Rom C8 68
Plomárion, Grc C6 69
Plomb du Cantal, mtn., Fr E5 58
Plombières-les-Bains, Fr B2 66
Plomosa, mts., Ariz D1 168
Plön, Ger D4 62
Płońsk, Pol B6 70
Plougastel [-Daoulas], Fr C1 58
Plovdiv, Bul D7 68
Plover, Iowa B3 180
Plover, Wis D4 212
Plover, riv., Wis D4 212
Plum, Pa *F2 202
Plum, bayou, Ark D6 169
Plum, creek, Nebr B5 191
Plum, creek, Nebr D5 191
Plum, isl., Mass A6 185
Plum, isl., N.Y E8 172
Plum Branch, S.C D3 203
Plum City, Wis D1 212
Plum Coulee, Man., Can E3 150
Plum Gut, strait, N.Y E8 172
Pluma, S. Dak C2 204
Plumas, Man., Can D2 150
Plumas, co., Calif B3 170
Plumerville, Ark B3 169
Plummer, Idaho B2 177
Plummer, Minn C2 187
Plumsteadville, Pa F11 202
Plumtree, Rh B4 107
Plumwood, Ohio B4 199
Plunkett, Sask., Can F3 155
Plunkettville, Okla C7 200
Plush, Oreg E7 201
Plymouth, Conn C4 172
Plymouth, Eng D3 56
Plymouth, Fla D5 174
Plymouth, Ill C3 178
Plymouth, Ind B5 179
Plymouth, Iowa A4 180
Plymouth, Maine D3 184
Plymouth, Mass C6 185
Plymouth, Mich A7, F7 186
Plymouth, Minn *F5 187
Plymouth, Montserrat n15 131
Plymouth, Nebr D9 191
Plymouth, N.H C3 193
Plymouth, N.C B7 197
Plymouth, Ohio B5 199
Plymouth, Pa B8, D10 202
Plymouth, Utah B3 207
Plymouth, W. Va C3 211
Plymouth, Wis B6, E6 212
Plymouth, co., Iowa B1 180
Plymouth, co., Mass C6 185
Plymouth, bay, Mass C6 185
Plymouth, rock, Mass C6 185
Plymouth Union, Vt D3 208
Plymouth Village, Ky *B4 182
Plympton, N.S., Can E4 151
Plympton, Mass C6 185
Plymptonville, Pa *D5 202
Plzeň, Czech D2 70
Pô, Upper Volta D4 103
Po, riv., It D7 66
Po, riv., Va C5 209
P'o Hai, state: c. 750 80
Poai, China G5 92
Poamoho, riv., Haw f9 176
Pobé, Dah E5 103

INDEX KEY Each place listed in **Bold-faced Type** has its population listed in the Population tables, pages 230 to 280.
Each country, shown in CAPITAL LETTERS, has its population listed in the World Political Information Table, pages 6 to 10.
* Does not appear on map; key shows general location.

Pobedino, Sov. Un........B11 93
Poblado Cerrillos, P.R.....C4 132
Poblado Cerro Gordo, P.R. B5 132
Poblado Mediania Alta, P.R.........B7 132
Poblado Paso Seco, P.R....D5 132
Poblado Sabalos, P.R.....C2 132
Poca, W. Va.........C3 211
Pocahontas, Ark.........A5 169
Pocahontas, Ill.........E4 178
Pocahontas, Iowa.........B3 180
Pocahontas, Tenn.........B3 205
Pocahontas, Va.......B3, D1 209
Pocahontas, co., Iowa.....B3 180
Pocahontas, co., W. Va...C4 211
Pocasset, Mass.........C6 185
Pocasset, Okla.........B4 200
Pocatalico, riv., W. Va.....C3 211
Pocatello, Idaho.........G6 177
Pochep, Sov. Un.........E9 72
Pochutla, Mex.........D5 129
Pocitos, Arg.........D2 135
Pocklington, reef, Sol. Is......... 115
Pocola, Okla.........B7 200
Pocomoke, riv., Md.........D7 173
Pocomoke, sound, Md.......E6 173
Pocomoke City, Md.......D6 173
Poconé, Braz.........B1 137
Pocono, lake, Pa.........A1 194
Pocono, mts., Pa.........E11 202
Pocono Pines, Pa.........D11 202
Poços de Caldas, Braz. C3, k8 137
Pocotalico, W. Va.........C3 211
Pocotopaug, lake, Conn.....C6 172
Pocumtuck, mtn., Mass.....A2 185
Podbořany, Czech.........C8 61
Podgorica, see Titograd, Yugo.
Podhořany, Czech.........n17 70
Podkamennaya Tunguska, riv., Sov. Un.........C12 71
Podmokly, Czech.........C3 70
Podol'sk, Sov. Un.........B1 73
Podor, Sen.........C2 103
Podporozhye, Sov. Un.....G16 63
Poel, isl., Ger.........E5 62
Pofadder, S. Afr.........C2 107
Poge, cape, Mass.........D7 185
Poggibonsi, It.........C3 67
Pöggstall, Aus.........D7 60
Pogradec, Alb.........B3 69
Pogranichnoye, Sov. Un..A11 93
Pohai, see Chihli, gulf, China
Pohang, Kor.........H4 93
Pohopoco, creek, Pa.......B1 194
Pohsien, China.........H6 92
Pohue, bay, Haw.........E6 176
Poinsett, co., Ark.........B5 169
Poinsett, lake, Fla.........D6 174
Poinsett, lake, S. Dak.......C8 204
Poinsette, S. Dak.........C8 204
Point, lake, N.W. Ter., Can.........C10 142
Point Arena, Calif.........C2 170
Point Baker, Alsk.........m23 167
Point Cedar, Ark.......C2, D5 169
Point Clear, Ala.........E2 166
Point Comfort, Tex.......*E4 206
Point Edward, Ont., Can...D2 153
Point Hope, Alsk.........B6 167
Point Imperial, mtn., Ariz.........A4 168
Point Judith, R.I.........D11 172
Point Lay, Alsk.........B7 167
Point Leamington, Newf., Can.........D4 152
Point Lookout, Md.........D5 173
Point Lookout, Mo.........E4 189
Point Marion, Pa.........F2 202
Point of Rocks, Md.........B2 173
Point of Rocks, Wyo.......D4 213
Point Pelee, nat. park, Ont., Can.........F2 153
Point Pleasant, N.J.......C4 194
Point Pleasant, Pa.........F11 202
Point Pleasant, Va.........D1 209
Point Pleasant, W. Va.....C2 211
Point Pleasant Beach, N.J. C4 194
Point Reyes, nat. seashore, Calif.........C2 170
Point Reyes Station, Calif.........B5 170
Point Roberts, Wash.........A2 210
Point Sapin, N.B., Can.......C5 151
Point Washington, Fla.......G3 174
Pointe a la Hache, La.......E6 183
Pointe-à-Pitre, Guad.......n16 131
Pointe-au-Baril-Station, Ont., Can.........B4 153
Pointe-au-Pic, Que., Can...B7 154
Pointe-aux-Trembles, Que., Can.........D9 154
Pointe Bleue, Que., Can....A5 154
Pointe-Claire, Que., Can.........D4, D8 154
Pointe Coupee, par., La...D4 183
Pointe-des-Cascades, Que., Can.........D8 154
Pointe du Bois, Man., Can.........D4 150
Pointe du Chene, N.B., Can.........C5 151
Pointe du Lac, Que., Can...C5 154
Pointe-Gatineau, Que., Can.........D2 154
Pointe Noire, Con.........F2 104
Pointe Verte, N.B., Can...B4 151
Poirino, It.........E3 66
Poison, creek, Wyo.........B5 213
Poisson Blanc, lake, Que., Can.........C2 154
Poissy, Fr.........C4 58
Poitiers, Fr.........D4 58
Poitou, former prov., Fr....D3 58
Poix, Fr.........E9 56
Poix-Terron, Fr.........E4 59
Pojo, Bol.........C3 135
Pojoaque, N. Mex.........B3 195
Pojoaque, Indian res., N. Mex.........F6 195
Pok, Ponape......... 114
Pokaran, India.........D3 88
Pokataroo, Austl.........D7 112
Pokegama, lake Minn.......C5 187
Pokegamma, lake, Wis......C2 212
Pokhra, Nep.........C9 88
Poko, Zaire.........A4 106
Poko, mtn., Alsk.........B7 167
Pokotu, China.........B9 91
Pokrov, Sov. Un.........n19 72
Pokrovskoye, Sov. Un....H12 72
Polacca, Ariz.........B5 168
Polān, Iran.........I10 86
Poland, N.Y.........B5 196
Poland, Ohio.........*A7 199
POLAND, country, Eur.....C5 70
c. 1140......... 47
c. 1360......... 48
in 1721......... 49
in 1815......... 50
in 1914......... 52
in 1922-40......... 53
after World War II......... 54
Poland Spring, Maine.....D2 184
Polar, Tex.........C2 206
Polar, Wis.........C5 212
Polar, caves, N.H.........C3 193
Polaris, Mont.........E3 190
Polavaram, India.........I8 88
Polbain, Scot.........B3 57
Polch, Ger.........C2 61
Polcura, Chile.........B2 136
Pole, mtn., Wyo.........D7 213
Polebridge, Mont.........B2 190
Polecat, creek, Okla.......B5 200
Polenia, bay, Erromango I......... 115
Polesella, It.........E7 66
Polessk, Sov. Un.........A6 70
Polevskoy, Sov. Un.........B6 73
Polgar, Hung.........B5 68
Poli, Cam.........D2 104
Poli, China.........B11 91
Policastro, gulf, It.........E5 67
Police, Pol.........B3 70
Poligny, Fr.........D6 58
Polikhnitos, Grc.........C6 69
Polillo, Phil.........o13 90
Polillo, isl., Phil.........o13 90
Polillo, is., Phil.......C6, o14 90
Polillo, strait, Phil.........o14 90
Polis, Cyp.........E9 85
Polish, mtn., Md.........D3 173
Políyiros, Grc.........B4 69
Polk, Nebr.........C8 191
Polk, Ohio.........B5 199
Polk, Pa.........D2 202
Polk, Tenn.........A2 205
Polk, co., Ark.........C1 169
Polk, co., Fla.........E5 174
Polk, co., Ga.........C1 175
Polk, co., Iowa.........C4 180
Polk, co., Minn.........C2 187
Polk, co., Mo.........D4 189
Polk, co., Nebr.........C8 191
Polk, co., N.C.........D4 197
Polk, co., Oreg.........C3 201
Polk, co., Tenn.........D9 205
Polk, co., Tex.........D5 206
Polk, co., Wis.........C1 212
Polk City, Fla.........D5 174
Polk City, Iowa.......A7, C4 180
Polkan, mtn., Sov. Un.......C12 71
Polkton, N.C.........B3 197
Polkville, Miss.........C4 188
Pollachi, India.........*F6 87
Pollard, Ala.........D2 166
Pollard, Ark.........A5 169
Pollards Point, Newf., Can. D3 152
Pollensa, Sp.........C7 65
Pollock, Idaho.........D2 177
Pollock, La.........C3 183
Pollock, Mo.........A4 189
Pollock, S. Dak.........B5 204
Pollocksville, N.C.........B6 197
Pollockville, Alta., Can.....D5 148
Polo, Ill.........B4 178
Polo, Mo.........B3 189
Polochic, riv., Guat.........C3 130
Pologi, Sov. Un.........H11 72
Polonnoye, Sov. Un.........F6 72
Polotsk, Sov. Un.........D7 72
Polson, Mont.........C2 190
Poltava, Sov. Un.........G10 72
Poltimore, Que., Can.......D2 154
Polunochnoye, Sov. Un.....A6 73
Polvadera, N. Mex.........C3 195
Polwarth, Sask., Can.......D2 155
Polyanovgrad, Bul.........D8 68
Polyarnyy, Sov. Un.........C15 63
Pomabamba, Peru.........C2 134
Pomarão, Port.........D2 65
Pomaria, S.C.........C4 203
Pomasau, Manus I......... 115
Pomba, riv., Braz.........g6 137
Pombal, Braz.........C3 138
Pombal, Port.........C1 65
Pombetsu, Jap.........E11 93
Pomerania, reg., Pol.........B4 70
c. 1867......... 51
Pomeranian, bay, Pol.......D8 62
Pomerene, Ariz.........E5 168
Pomeroy, Iowa.........B3 180
Pomeroy, N. Ire.........F2 57
Pomeroy, Ohio.........C5 199
Pomeroy, Pa.........*G10 202
Pomeroy, Wash.........C8 210
Pomezia, It.........h9 67
Pomfret, Conn.........B9 172
Pomfret, Md.........C3 173
Pomfret Vt.........D3 208
Pomio, New Britain I......... 115
Pomme de Terre, flood control res., Mo.........D4 189
Pomme de Terre, riv., Minn.........E3 187
Pomme de Terre, riv., Mo..D4 189
Pomoho, Haw.........f9 176
Pomona, Calif.......E5, F3 170
Pomona, Kans.........D8 181
Pomona, Mo.........E6 189
Pomona, N.J.........E3 194
Pomona (Mainland), isl., Scot.........A5 55
Pomona, res., Kans.........D8 181
Pomona Park, Fla.........C5 174
Pomonkey, Md.........C3 173
Pomorie, Bul.........D8 68
Pompano Beach, Fla...E3, F6 174
Pompeii, ruins, It.........D5 67
Pompeyevka, Sov. Un.......B5 93
Pompeys Pillar, Mont.......E9 190
Pompton Lakes, N.J.......A4 194
Pompton Plains, N.J.......B4 194
Pomquet, N.S., Can.........D8 151
Ponaganset, lake, R.I......B10 172
Ponape, Ponape......... 114
Ponape, isl., Caroline Is......... 114
Ponask, lake, Ont., Can......B5 150
Ponask, riv., Ont., Can......B5 150
Ponass, lake, Sask., Can.....E3 155
Ponca, Nebr.........B9 191
Ponca, creek, Nebr., S. Dak. D6 204
Ponca, Indian res., Nebr.....B7 191
Ponca City, Okla.........A4 200
Ponce, P.R.........C4 132
Ponce, mun., P.R.........C4 132
Ponce de Leon, Fla.........G3 174
Ponce de Leon, bay, Fla.....G5 174
Ponce de Leon, inlet, Fla....C6 174
Poncha, pass, Colo.........C4 171
Poncha Springs, Colo.......C4 171
Ponchatoula, La.......B6, D5 183
Pond, creek, Colo.........C7 171
Pond, creek, Ky.........A4 182
Pond, creek, Okla.........B3 200
Pond, fork, W. Va.........D3 211
Pond, lake, Newf., Can.......C3 152
Pond, riv., Ky.........C2 182
Pond Inlet, N.W. Ter., Can.........B17 145
Pondcreek, Okla.........A4 200
Pondera, co., Mont.........B4 190
Ponderay, Idaho.........A2 177
Ponderosa, N. Mex....B3, F5 195
Pondfork, Mo.........E5 189
Pondicherry, India.........F6 87
Pondosa, Calif.........B3 170
Pondosa, Oreg.........B9 201
Ponds, isl., Newf., Can.......B4 152
Pone, isl., Md.........D5 173
Poneloya, Nic.........D4 130
Ponemah, Minn.........B4 187
Ponemah, N.H.........E3 193
Ponerihuen, N. Cal......... 115
Poneto, Ind.........C7 179
Ponferrada, Sp.........A2 65
Pongo de Manseriche, gorge, Peru.........B2 134
Pongoma, Sov. Un.........E16 63
Ponhook, lake, N.S., Can.....E4 151
Ponkapog, pond, Mass.......D3 185
Ponoka, Alta., Can.........C4 148
Ponoy, Sov. Un.........D19 63
Ponoy, riv., Sov. Un.........D18 63
Pons, Fr.........E3 58
Ponsford, Minn.........D3 187
Pont-à-Mousson, Fr.........C7 58
Pont-de-Roide, Fr.........B2 66
Pont-l'Abbé, Fr.........D2 58
Pont-Rouge, Que., Can.........C6, C8 154
Pont-St. Esprit, Fr.........E6 58
Pont-Ste. Maxence, Fr.......E2 59
Pont Viau, Que., Can.....*D8 154
Ponta Delgada, Port. (Azores).........h9 102
Ponta de Pedras, Braz.......C5 139
Ponta Grossa, Braz.........D2 137
Ponta Porã, Braz.........C1 137
Pontal, Braz.........k7 137
Pontarlier, Fr.........D7 58
Pontchartrain, lake, La.......D5 183
Ponte de Sôr, Port.........C1 65
Ponte di Legno, It.........C6 66
Ponte Nova, Braz.........F2 138
Ponte Vedra Beach, Fla.........B5, B6 174
Pontedera, It.........C3 67
Pontefract, Eng.........A6 56
Ponteix, Sask., Can.........H2 155
Pontevedra, Sp.........A1 65
Pontiac, Ill.........C5 178
Pontiac, Mich.........A7, F7 186
Pontiac, S.C.........C6 203
Pontiac, co., Que., Can.....A7 153
Pontianak, Indon.........F3 90
Pontine, is., It.........D4 67
Pontivy, Fr.........C2 58
Pontoise, Fr.........C5 58
Pontoon Beach, Ill.........*E3 178
Pontoosuc, lake, Mass.......B1 185
Pontotoc, Miss.........A4 188
Pontotoc, Okla.........C5 200
Pontotoc, Tex.........D3 206
Pontotoc, co., Miss.........A4 188
Pontotoc, co., Okla.........C5 200
Pontremoli, It.........B2 67
Pontresina, Switz.........C5 66
Pontrilas, Sask., Can.........D3 155
Pontus: in 1st cent. B.C......... 44
c. 120 A.D......... 45
c. 400 A.D......... 46
Pontypool, Ont., Can.........C6 153
Pontypool, Wales.........C4 56
Pontypridd, Wales.........C4 56
Pony, Mont.........E5 190
Ponza, isl., It.........D4 67
Poole, Eng.........D6 56
Poole, Ky.........C2 182
Poole, Nebr.........D7 191
Pooler, Ga.........D5 175
Pooles, isl., Md.........B5 173
Poolesville, Md.........B3 173
Pooleville, Okla.........C4 200
Poolewe, Scot.........C3 57
Pooley, isl., B.C., Can.......C3 149
Poolville, Tex.........C4 206
Poona, India.......E5 87, H4 88
Poona Cantonment, India. *H4 88
Pooncarie, Austl.........F4 112
Poopó, Bol.........C2 135
Poopó, lake, Bol.........C2 135
Poor Knights, is., N.Z.......K15 112
Popasnaya, Sov. Un.........q21 72
Popayán, Col.........C2 133
Pope, Ala.........C2 166
Pope, Man., Can.........D1 150
Pope, Miss.........A4 188
Pope, co., Ark.........B2 169
Pope, co., Ill.........F5 178
Pope, co., Minn.........E3 187
Popejoy, Iowa.........B4 180
Poperinge, Bel.........D2 59
Popham, pt., Ont., Can.......B3 153
Popham Beach, Maine.......E3 184
Poplar, Calif.........*D4 170
Poplar, Mont.........B11 190
Poplar, N.C.........C4 197
Poplar, Wis.........B2 212
Poplar, isl., Md.........C5 173
Poplar, mtn., Ky.........D5 182
Poplar, riv., Man., Can.......C3 150
Poplar, riv., Sask., Can......H2 155
Poplar, riv., Mont.........B11 190
Poplar Bluff, Mo.........E7 189
Poplar Branch, N.C.........A8 197
Poplar Creek, Miss.........B4 188
Poplar Grove, Ark.........C5 169
Poplar Grove, Ill.........A5 178
Poplar Plains, Ky.........B6 182
Poplar Point, Man., Can....D3 150
Poplarfield, Man., Can.....D3 150
Poplarville, Miss.........E4 188
Popocatepetl, vol., Mex.....n14 129
Popokabaka, Zaire.........C2 106
Popovka, Sov. Un.........H11 72
Popovo, Bul.........D8 68
Poppel, Bel.........C5 59
Popple, riv., Wis.........C5 212
Poquetanuck, Conn.........D8 172
Poquonock, Conn.........B6 172
Poquonock Bridge, Conn..D8 172
Poquoson, Va.........B6, D6 209
Porbandar, India.........G2 88
Porcher, isl., B.C., Can.......C2 149
Porcuna, Sp.........D3 65
Porcupine, S. Dak.........D3 204
Porcupine, cape, Newf., Can.........B3 152
Porcupine, mtn., Man., Sask., Can.........C1 150, E5 155
Porcupine, mts., Mich.........A5 186
Porcupine, riv., Alsk., Yukon, Can.........C4 142
Porcupine Plain, Sask., Can.........E4 155
Pordenone, It.....D8 66, B4 67
Poreč, Yugo.........C1 68
Pori, Fin.........G9 63
Porjus, Swe.........D8 63
Porkhov, Sov. Un.........C7 72
Porlamar, Ven.........A5 133
Porlo, New Britain I......... 115
Pornic, Fr.........D2 58
Poroma, Bol.........C2 135
Poronaysk (Shikuka), Sov. Un.........B11 93
Porong, riv., Camb.........F6 89
Porpoise, bay, Ant.........C26 120
Porrentruy, Switz.........B3 66
Porsangerfjord, fjord, Nor.........B12 63
Porsgrunn, Nor.........p27 63
Port Adelaide, Austl.........G2 112
Port Alberni, B.C., Can.....E5 149
Port Alexander, Alsk.........D13, m22 167
Port Alfred, Que., Can.....A7 154
Port Alfred, S. Afr.........D4 107
Port Alice, B.C., Can.......D4 149
Port Allegany, Pa.........C5 202
Port Allen, La.........B5, D4 183
Port Angeles, Wash.........A2 210
Port Angeles East, Wash.........*A2 210
Port Anson, Newf., Can....D4 152
Port Antonio, Jam.........F5 131
Port Aransas, Tex.........F4 206
Port Arthur (Lüshun), China.........D9 91
Port Arthur, Tex.........E6 206
Port Augusta, Austl.........F6 111
Port-au-Persil, Que., Can.........B8 154
Port au Port, Newf., Can...D2 152
Port au Port, bay, Newf., Can.........D2 152
Port au Port, pen., Newf., Can.........D2 152
Port-au-Prince, Hai.........F7 131
Port Austin, Mich.........D8 186
Port Barre, La.........D4 183
Port Bergé, Malag.........g9 107
Port Blair, India (Andaman Is.).........F9 87
Port Blakely, Wash.........D1 210
Port Blandford, Newf., Can.........D4 152
Port Bolivar, Tex.......E5, G5 206
Port Borden, P.E.I., Can....C6 151
Port Burwell, Ont., Can....E4 153
Port Byron, Ill.........B3 178
Port Byron, N.Y.........B4 196
Port Carbon, Pa.........*E9 202
Port Carling, Ont., Can.....B5 153
Port Carson, Pa.........E9 202
Port Cartier, Que., Can.......h8 152
Port Chalmers, N.Z.........P13 112
Port Charlotte, Fla.........*F4 174
Port Chester, N.Y.........D2, D3, E7 196
Port Chicago, Calif.........B5 170
Port Chilkoot, Alsk.........D12 167
Port Clements, B.C., Can.........C1 149
Port Clinton, Ohio.........A5 199
Port Clyde, N.S., Can.........F4 151
Port Clyde, Maine.........E3 184
Port Colborne, Ont., Can...E5 153
Port Colden, N.J.........B3 194
Port Coquitlam, B.C., Can.........A10, E6 149
Port Crane, N.Y.........C5 196
Port Credit, Ont., Can.........D5, E6 153
Port-Daniel-Station, Que., Can.........A5 151
Port-de-Bouc, Fr.........F6 58
Port-de-Paix, Hai.........F7 131
Port Deposit, Md.........A5 173
Port Dickinson, N.Y.......C5 196
Port Dickson, Mala.........K4 89
Port Douglas, Austl.........C8 111
Port Dover, Ont., Can.......E4 153
Port Eads, La.........E6 183
Port Edward, B.C., Can.....B2 149
Port Edwards, Wis.........D4 212
Port Elgin, N.B., Can.......C5 151
Port Elgin, Ont., Can.......C3 153
Port Elizabeth, N.J.........E3 194
Port Elizabeth, S. Afr......D4 107
Port Ellen, Scot.........E2 57
Port Erin, I of Man.........F4 57
Port Essington, B.C., Can.........B3 149
Port Ewen, N.Y.........D7 196
Port Fairy, Austl.........I4 112
Port-Francqui, Zaire.........B3 106
Port Gamble, Wash.........B3 210
Port Gamble, Indian res., Wash.........B3 210
Port-Gentil, Gabon.........F1 104
Port George, N.S., Can.....D4 151
Port Gibson, Miss.........D3 188
Port Glasgow, Scot.........E4 57
Port Graham, Alsk.....D9, h16 167
Port Greville, N.S., Can....D5 151
Port Hammond, B.C., Can.........A10 149
Port Harcourt, Nig.........F6 103
Port Hardy, B.C., Can.......D4 149
Port Harrison, Que., Can...A2 154
Port Hastings, N.S., Can....D8 151
Port Hawkesbury, N.S., Can.........D8 151
Port Hedland, Austl.........D2 111
Port Heiden, Alsk.........D8 167
Port Henry, N.Y.........A7 196
Port Hill, P.E.I., Can.........C6 151
Port Homer, Ohio.........A2 211
Port Hood, N.S., Can.........C8 151
Port Hope, Ont., Can.......D6 153
Port Hope, Mich.........E8 186
Port Hope Simpson, Newf., Can.........B3 152
Port Hueneme, Calif.........E4 170
Port Huron, Mich.........F8 186
Port Isabel, Tex.........F4 206
Port Jackson, bay, Austl.....F8 112
Port Jefferson, N.Y.........D3 196
Port Jefferson, Ohio.........B3 199
Port Jefferson Station, N.Y.........*D3 196
Port Jervis, N.Y.........D6 196
Port Kent, N.Y.........B3 196
Port Lavaca, Tex.........E4 206
Port Leyden, N.Y.........B5 196
Port Lincoln, Austl.........F6 111
Port Loko, S.L.........E2 103
Port Loring, Ont., Can.......B5 153
Port-Louis, Fr.........D2 58
Port Ludlow, Wash.........B3 210
Port Macquarie, Austl.......E9 112
Port Maitland, N.S., Can....F3 151
Port Maitland, Ont., Can....E5 153
Port Maria, Jam.........F5 131
Port Matilda, Pa.........E5 202
Port Mayaca, Fla.........F6 174
Port Medway, N.S., Can......E5 151
Port Menier, Que., Can......k8 152
Port Moller, Alsk.........D7 167
Port Monmouth, N.J.........C4 194
Port Moody, B.C., Can.........A10, E6 149
Port Moresby, Pap.........k12 111
Port Morien, N.S., Can.....C10 151
Port Morris, N.J.........B3 194
Port Mouton, N.S., Can......F5 151
Port Murray, N.J.........B3 194
Port Musgrave, bay, Austl.........B7 110
Port Neches, Tex.........E6 206
Port Nelson, Man., Can.........A5, C5 150
Port Nolloth, S. Afr.........C2 107
Port Norris, N.J.........E2 194
Port O'Connor, Tex.........E4 206
Port of Ness, Scot.........B2 57
Port-of-Spain, Trin.........A5 133
Port Orange, Fla.........C6 174
Port Orchard, Wash.........B3, D1 210
Port Orford, Oreg.........E2 201
Port Penn, Del.........A6 173
Port Perry, Ont., Can.......C6 153
Port Phillip, bay, Austl.........G7, n14 110
Port Pirie, Austl.........F1 112
Port Radium, N.W. Ter., Can.........C9 144
Port Reading, N.J.........E4 194
Port Renfrew, B.C., Can....E5 149
Port Republic, N.J.........D4 194
Port Republic, Va.........C4 209
Port Rexton, Newf., Can.........D5 152
Port Richey, Fla.........D4 174
Port Rowan, Ont., Can.....E4 153
Port Royal, Ky.........B4 182
Port Royal, Pa.........E7 202
Port Royal, S.C.........G6 203
Port Royal, Tenn.........A4 205
Port Royal, Va.........C5 209
Port Royal, isl., S.C.........G6 203
Port Royal, sound, S.C.......G6 203
Port Said (Būr Sa'īd), Eg.......C4 84, G9 85, C6 101
Port St. Joe, Fla.......C1, H3 174
Port St. Johns, S. Afr.......D4 107
Port-St. Louis [-du-Rhône], Fr.........F6 58
Port Sanilac, Mich.........E8 186
Port Saunders, Newf., Can.........C3, h10 152
Port Sewall, Fla.........E6 174
Port Shepstone, S. Afr.....D5 107
Port Simpson, B.C., Can.........B2 149
Port Stanley, Ont., Can....E3 153
Port Stephens, bay, Austl....F9 112
Port Sudan, Sud.........B4 105
Port Sulphur, La.........E6 183
Port-sur-Saône, Fr.........B2 66
Port Talbot, Wales.........C4 56
Port Tampa, Fla.........*E4 174
Port Tobacco, Md.........C3 173
Port Townsend, Wash.......A3 210
Port Union, Newf., Can....D5 152
Port Union, Ohio.........C2 199
Port-Vendres, Fr.........F5 58
Port Vila, see Vila, Efate I
Port Vincent, La.......B6, D5 183
Port Vue, Pa.........*F2 202
Port Wakefield, Austl.......G2 112
Port Washington, N.Y.....D2 196
Port Washington, Ohio.....B6 199
Port Washington, Wis......E6 212
Port Washington North, N.Y.........*E7 196
Port Wentworth, Ga.........D5 175
Port William, Ohio.........C4 199
Port William, Scot.........F4 57
Port Wing, Wis.........B2 212
Portachuelo, Bol.........C3 135
Portadown, N. Ire.........C3 55
Portage, Alsk.........g17 167
Portage, P.E.I., Can.........C5 151
Portage, Ind.........A3 179
Portage, Maine.........B4 184
Portage, Mich.........F5 186
Portage, Mont.........C5 190
Portage, Ohio.........*A4 199
Portage, Pa.........F4 202
Portage, Utah.........B3 207
Portage, Wis.........E4 212
Portage, co., Ohio.........A6 199
Portage, co., Wis.........D4 212
Portage, bay, Man., Can......D2 150
Portage, head, Wash.........A1 210
Portage, isl., N.B., Can......B5 151
Portage, lake, Maine.........B4 184
Portage, river, Ohio.........A4 199
Portage Des Sioux, Mo.....A8 189
Portage la Prairie, Man., Can.........D5, E2 150
Portage Lake, Maine.......*B4 184
Portageville, Mo.........E8 189
Portageville, N.Y.........C2 196
Portal, Ariz.........F6 168
Portal, Ga.........D5 175
Portal, N. Dak.........A3 198
Portalegre, Port.........C2 65
Portales, N. Mex.........C6 195
Portarlington, Ire.........D3 55
Portaskaig, Scot.........E2 57
Portel, Braz.........C4 139
Porteña, Arg.........A4 136
Porter, Ala.........B2, E4 166
Porter, Ind.........A3 179
Porter, Maine.........E2 184
Porter, Minn.........F2 187
Porter, Okla.........B6 200
Porter, Tex.........D5 206
Porter, Wash.........C2 210
Porter, co., Ind.........B3 179
Porter, lake, Sask., Can......A2 155
Porter Corners, N.Y.........B7 196
Porterdale, Ga.........C3 175
Portersville, Pa.........E1 202
Porterville, Calif.........D4 170
Porterville, Miss.........C5 188
Porthcawl, Wales.........C4 56
Portia, Ark.........A4 169
Portici, It.........E2 68
Portillo, Cuba.........F5 131
Portimão, Port.........D1 65
Portis, Kans.........C5 181
Portland, Ark.........D4 169
Portland, Austl.........I3 112
Portland, Ont., Can.........C8 153
Portland, Colo.........C5 171
Portland, Conn.........C6 172
Portland, Eng.........D5 56
Portland, Fla.........G3 174
Portland, Ind.........D8 179
Portland, Maine.......E2, E5 184
Portland, Mich.........F6 186
Portland, Mo.........C6 189
Portland, N.Y.........C1 196
Portland, N. Dak.........B8 198
Portland, Ohio.........C6 199
Portland, Oreg.........B2, B4 201
Portland, Pa.........E11 202
Portland, Tenn.........A5 205
Portland, Tex.........F4 206
Portland, canal, Alsk., B.C., Can.........B3 149

INDEX KEY Each place listed in **Bold-faced Type** has its population listed in the Population tables, pages 230 to 280.
Each country, shown in CAPITAL LETTERS, has its population listed in the World Political Information Table, pages 6 to 10.
* Does not appear on map; key shows general location.

Portland, inlet, B.C., Can...B2 149
Portland, promontory, Que., Can...A2 154
Portland Bill, pt., Eng...D5 56
Portland Mills, Pa...D4 202
Portlandville, N.Y...C6 196
Portlaoighise, Ire...D3 55
Portmadoc, Wales...B3 56
Portmahomack, Scot...C5 57
Portnahaven, Scot...E2 57
Portneuf, Que., Can...C6 154
Portneuf, co., Que., Can...C5 154
Portneuf-sur-Mer, Que., Can...A8 154
Pôrto, Port...B1 65
Pôrto Alegre, Braz...E2 137
Pôrto Alexandre, Ang...E1 106
Pôrto Amboim, Ang...D1 106
Pôrto Amélia, Moz...D7 106
Pôrto Calvo, Braz...C3, k6 138
Pôrto de Moz, Braz...C4 139
Pôrto de Mós, Port...C1 65
Pôrto Esperança, Braz...B1 137
Pôrto Feliz, Braz...C3, m8 137
Pôrto Garibaldi, It...E8 66
Pôrto Guaíra, Braz...C2 137
Pôrto Mendes, Braz...C2 137
Pôrto Murtinho, Braz...D4 135
Pôrto Nacional, Braz...D1 138
Porto-Novo, Dah...E5 103
Porto Santo, isl., Port. (*Madeira Is.*)...g12 65
Pôrto Seguro, Braz...E3 138
Porto Torres, It...D2 67
Pôrto União, Braz...D2 137
Porto-Vecchio, Fr...D2 67
Pôrto Velho, Braz...D2 139
Portobelo, Pan...F8, h11 130
Portoferraio, It...C3 67
Portofino, It...B2 67
Portogruaro, It...B4 67
Portola, Calif...C3 170
Portomaggiore, It...B3 67
Portoscuso, It...E2 67
Portoviejo, Ec...B1 134
Portpatrick, Scot...F3 57
Portree, Scot...C2 57
Portreeve, Sask., Can...G1 155
Portrush, N. Ire...E2 57
Portsmouth, Dominica...o16 131
Portsmouth, Eng...D6 56
Portsmouth, Iowa...C2 180
Portsmouth, N.H...D5 193
Portsmouth, Ohio...D5 199
Portsmouth, R.I...C12 172
Portsmouth, (Independent City), Va...B6, E6 209
Portsoy, Scot...C6 57
PORTUGAL, country, Eur...C1 65
c. 1140... 47
c. 1360... 48
in 1815... 50
in 1914... 52
Portugal Cove South, Newf., Can...E5 152
Portugalete, Sp...A4 65
Portugalia, Ang...C3 106
Portuguesa, state, Ven...B4 133
Portuguesa, riv., Ven...B4 133
Portuguese East Africa: in 1885... 99
see also Mozambique
PORTUGUESE GUINEA, dep., Afr...D1 103, 99
PORTUGUESE TIMOR, dep., Asia...G7 90
Portuguese West Africa... 99
see also Angola
Portville, N.Y...C2 196
Porum, Okla...B6 200
Porvenir, Chile...h11 136
Porz, Ger...C2 61
Posadas, Arg...E4 135
Posadas, Sp...D3 65
Poschiavo, Switz...C6 66
Posen, Ill...F3 178
Posen, Mich...C7 186
Posen, see Poznan, Pol.
Posey, co., Ind...H2 179
Poseyville, Ind...H2 179
Poshekhonye-Volodarsk, Sov. Un...B12 72
Poso, Indon...F6 90
Poso, lake, Indon...F6 90
Posse, Braz...D1 138
Pössneck, Ger...C6 61
Post, Oreg...C6 201
Post, Tex...C2 206
Post Falls, Idaho...B2 177
Post Mills, Vt...D4 208
Postmasburg, S. Afr...C3 107
Postojna, Yugo...C2 68
Poston, S.C...D9 203
Postville, Iowa...A6 180
Potaro Landing, Guy...A3 133
Potato Creek, S. Dak...D4 204
Potchefstroom, S. Afr...C4 107
Poteau, Okla...B7 200
Poteau, mtn., Ark., Okla...C7 200
Poteau, riv., Ark., Okla...B7 200
Poteet, Tex...E3 206
Potenza, It...D5 67
Potenza, riv., It...C4 67
Potgietersrus, S. Afr...B4 107
Poth, Tex...E3 206
Potholes, res., Wash...B6 210
Poti, Sov. Un...*E7 71
Poti, riv., Braz...C2 138
Potiskum, Nig...D7 103
Potlatch, Idaho...C2 177
Poto, Peru...D4 134
Potocho, China...A11 88
Potomac, Ill...C6 178
Potomac, Md...B3 173
Potomac, Mont...D3 190
Potomac, riv., Md., Va., W. Va...C12 159, A1, D4 173
Potomac Heights, Md...C3 173
Potomac Park, Md...*D2 173
Potosí, Bol...C2 135
Potosi, Mo...D7 189
Potosi, Wis...F3 212
Potosí, dept., Bol...D2 135
Potrerillos, Chile...E2 135
Potrerillos, Hond...C4 130
Potro, mtn., Arg...E2 135
Potsdam, Ger...A8 61
Potsdam, N.Y...A2 196
Potsdam, Ohio...C3 199
Pott, isl., N. Cal... 115
Pottawatomie, co., Kans...C7 181
Pottawatomie, co., Okla...B5 200
Pottawatomie, creek, Kans...D8 181
Pottawatomie, Indian res., Kans...C8 181
Pottawattamie, co., Iowa...C2 180
Pottawattamie Park, Ind...*A4 179
Potter, Ark...C1 169
Potter, Kans...A8, C8 181
Potter, Nebr...C2 191
Potter, Wis...B6 212
Potter, co., Pa...C6 202
Potter, co., S. Dak...B6 204
Potter, co., Tex...B2 206
Potter Hill, R.I...D9 172
Potter Place, N.H...D3 193
Potter Valley, Calif...C2 170
Potters Mills, Pa...E6 202
Pottersdale, Pa...D5 202
Pottersville, Mo...E5 189
Pottersville, N.J...B3 194
Pottersville, N.Y...B7 196
Potterville, Ga...D2 175
Potterville, Mich...*F6 186
Potts, creek, Va., W. Va...D2 209
Potts, mtn., Va...D2 209
Potts Camp, Miss...A4 188
Pottsboro, Tex...*C4 206
Pottstown, Pa...F10 202
Pottsville, Ark...B2 169
Pottsville, Pa...E9 202
Potwin, Kans...B6, E6 181
Pouce Coupé, B.C., Can...B7 149
Pouch Cove., Newf., Can...E5 152
Poughkeepsie, Ark...A4 169
Poughkeepsie, N.Y...D7 196
Poulan, Ga...E3 175
Poulo Condore, is., Viet...H7 89
Poulsbo, Wash...B3 210
Poultney, Vt...D2 208
Poultney, riv., Vt...E2 208
Pound, Va...B2 209
Pound, Wis...C5 212
Pound, gap, Va...A2 209
Pouso Alegre, Braz...C3, m9 137
Pouxeux, Fr...A2 66
Povenets, Sov. Un...F16 63
Poverty, bay, N.Z...M17 112
Póvoa de Varzim, Port...B1 65
Povorino, Sov. Un...C2 73
Povorotnyy, cape, Sov. Un...E6 93
Povungnituk, Que., Can...E17 145
Powassan, Ont., Can...A5 153
Poway, Calif...F5 170
Powder, riv., Mont., Wyo...B6 213
Powder, riv., Oreg...C9 201
Powder River, Wyo...B6 213
Powder River, co., Mont...E11 190
Powder River, pass, Wyo...A5 213
Powder Springs, Ga...A4 175
Powderhorn, Colo...C3 171
Powderville, Mont...E11 190
Powe, Mo...E7 189
Powell, Mo...E3 189
Powell, Ohio...B4 199
Powell, Pa...C8 202
Powell, Tenn...E11 205
Powell, Tex...C4 206
Powell, Wyo...A4 213
Powell, co., Ky...C6 182
Powell, co., Mont...D4 190
Powell, lake, Ariz., Utah...A5 168
Powell, mtn., Colo...B4 171
Powell, mtn., N. Mex...B1 195
Powell, mtn., Tenn...C10 205
Powell, riv., Tenn., Va...C10 205
Powell Butte, Oreg...C5 201
Powell Creek, Austl...C5 111
Powell Park, basin, Colo...A2 171
Powell River, B.C., Can...E5 149
Powellsville, N.C...A7 197
Powellton, W. Va...C3, D6 211
Powellville, Md...D7 173
Powelton, Ga...C4 175
Powelton, Pa...E5 202
Power, Mont...C5 190
Power, W. Va...A4, B2 211
Power, co., Idaho...G6 177
Powers, Mich...C3 186
Powers, Oreg...E2 201
Powers Lake, N. Dak...A3 198
Powersville, Mo...A4 189
Powerview, Man., Can...*D3 150
Poweshiek, co., Iowa...C5 180
Powhatan, Ala...B2, E4 166
Powhatan, Ark...A4 169
Powhatan, La...C2 183
Powhatan, Va...D5 209
Powhatan, co., Va...D5 209
Powhatan Point, Ohio...C7 199
Powhattan, Kans...C8 181
Pownal, Maine...E5 184
Pownal, Vt...F2 208
Pownal Center, Maine...E5 184
Pownal Center, Vt...F2 208
Poy Sippi, Wis...D4 212
Poya, pass, N. Cal... 115
Poyang, China...J7 92
Poyang, lake, China...J7 92
Poyarkovo, Sov. Un...B4 93
Poyen, Ark...C3 169
Poygan, lake, Wis...D5 212
Poynette, Wis...E4 212
Poza Rica, Mex...*C5 129
Požarevac, Yugo...C5 68
Poznań, Pol...B4 70
Poznan, prov., Pol...A9 61
Pozo Almonte, Chile...D2 135
Pozo Redondo, mts., Ariz...E3 168
Pozoblanco, Sp...C3 65
Pozuelo de Alarcon, Sp...p17 65
Pozuzo, Peru...D2 134
Pozzallo, It...F5 67
Pozzuoli, It...D5 67
Prachatice, Czech...E9 61
Prachin Buri, Thai...E4 89
Prachuap Khiri Khan, Thai...G3 89
Praco, Ala...E4 166
Practicos, pt., Cuba...E5 131
Prade Ranch, Tex...E3 206
Prades, Fr...F5 58
Prado, basin, Calif...F3 170
Praestö, Den...C6 62
Praestö, co., Den...C5 62
Praga, Pol...k14 70
Prague (Praha), Czech...C3, n17 70
Prague, Nebr...C9 191
Prague, Okla...B5 200
Praha, see Prague, Czech.
Prahran, Austl...*H5 112
Praia, C.V. Is...*E3 97
Prainha, Braz...C4 139
Prairie, Ala...C2 166
Prairie, Miss...B5 188
Prairie, co., Ark...C4 169
Prairie, co., Mont...D11 190
Prairie, bayou, Ark...D6 169
Prairie, riv., Minn...C5 187
Prairie City, Ill...C3 178
Prairie City, Iowa...C4 180
Prairie City, Oreg...C8 201
Prairie City, S. Dak...B3 204
Prairie Creek, Ind...F2 179
Prairie Dog, creek, Kans., Nebr...C3 181, E6 191
Prairie Dog Town, fork, Okla...C2 200
Prairie du Chien, Wis...E2 212
Prairie du Rocher, Ill...E3 178
Prairie du Sac, Wis...E4 212
Prairie Farm, Wis...C2 212
Prairie Grove, Ark...B1 169
Prairie Hill, Mo...B5 189
Prairie Home, Mo...C5 189
Prairie Home, Nebr...E2 191
Prairie Point, Miss...B5 188
Prairie River, Sask., Can...E4 155
Prairie View, Ark...B2 169
Prairie View, Kans...C4 181
Prairie View, Tex...*D5 206
Prairie Village, Kans...*D9 181
Prairieburg, Iowa...*B6 180
Prairieton, Ind...F3 179
Prairieville, La...B5 183
Pralognan-la-Vanoise, Fr...D2 66
Pran Buri, Thai...F3 89
Praszka, Pol...C5 70
Prata, Braz...E1 138
Prathersville, Mo...*B3 189
Prato, It...C3 67
Prats-de-Mollo, Fr...F5 58
Pratt, Kans...E5 181
Pratt, W. Va...*C3 211
Pratt, co., Kans...E5 181
Prattsburg, N.Y...C3 196
Prattsville, Ark...C3 169
Prattsville, N.Y...C6 196
Prattville, Ala...C3 166
Prattville, Mich...G6 186
Prattville, Okla...*A5 200
Pratum, Oreg...C2 201
Pravdinsk (Friedland), Sov. Un...A6 70
Pravia, Sp...A2 65
Prawle, pt., Eng...D4 56
Pray, Mont...E6 190
Preble, Ind...C7 179
Preble, co., Ohio...C3 199
Predazzo, It...C7 66
Preeceville, Sask., Can...F4 155
Preetz, Ger...D4 62
Pregel, riv., Sov. Un...A6 70
Pregnall, S.C...E7 203
Prelate, Sask., Can...G1 155
Premont, Tex...F3 206
Prémontré, Fr...E3 59
Prenter, W. Va...C3, D6 211
Prentice, Wis...C3 212
Prentiss, Maine...C4 184
Prentiss, Miss...D4 188
Prentiss, N.C...*D3 197
Prentiss, co., Miss...A5 188
Prenzlau, Ger...B6 60
Přerov, Czech...D4 70
Prescott, Ariz...C3 168
Prescott, Ark...D2 169
Prescott, Ont., Can...C9 153
Prescott, Iowa...C3 180
Prescott, Kans...D9 181
Prescott, Mich...D7 186
Prescott, Oreg...A4 201
Prescott, Wash...C7 210
Prescott, Wis...D1 212
Prescott, co., Ont., Can...B10 153
Presho, S. Dak...D5 204
Presidencia Roque Sáenz Peña, Arg...E3 135
Presidente Epitácio, Braz...C2 137
Presidente Hayes, dept., Par...D4 135
Presidente Prudente, Braz...C2 137
Presidential, range, N.H...B4 193
Presidents, isl., Tenn...E8 205
Presidio, Tex...G2 206
Presidio, co., Tex...F2 206
Preslav, Bul...D8 68
Prešov, Czech...D6 70
Presque Isle, Maine...B4 184
Presque Isle, Mich...C7 186
Presque Isle, Wis...B4 212
Presque Isle, co., Mich...C6 186
Pressath, Ger...D6 61
Pressmens Home, Tenn...C10 205
Prestatyn, Wales...A4 56
Presteigne, Wales...B4 56
Přeštice, Czech...D8 61
Preston, Austl...*G8 111
Preston, Ont., Can...D4 153
Preston, Conn...C9 172
Preston, Eng...A5 56
Preston, Ga...D2 175
Preston, Idaho...G7 177
Preston, Iowa...B7 180
Preston, Kans...E5 181
Preston, Ky...B6 182
Preston, Md...C6 173
Preston, Minn...G6 187
Preston, Miss...C5 188
Preston, Mo...D4 189
Preston, Okla...B6 200
Preston, Wash...D2 210
Preston, co., W. Va...B5 211
Preston, peak, Calif...B2 170
Preston Park, Pa...C11 202
Prestonsburg, Ky...C7 182
Prestonville, Ky...B4 182
Prestrud, inlet, Ant...B33 120
Prestwick, Ala...D2 166
Prestwick, Scot...E4 57
Presumpscot, riv., Maine...E4 184
Preti, mtn., It...C8 66
Preto, riv., Braz...h6 137
Prêto, riv., Braz...D2 138
Prêto, riv., Braz...C2 139
Pretoria, S. Afr...C4 107
Pretty Boy, res., Md...A4 173
Pretty Prairie, Kans...B4, E5 181
Préveza, Grc...C3 69
Prewitt, N. Mex...B2 195
Prewitt, res., Colo...A7 171
Prey Veng, Camb...G6 89
Pribilof, is., Alsk...D5 167
Priboj, Yugo...D4 68
Příbram, Czech...D3 70
Price, Que., Can...*B3 154
Price, Md...B6 173
Price, Tex...C5 206
Price, Utah...D5 207
Price, co., Wis...C3 212
Pr ce, isl., B.C., Can...C3 149
Pr ce, riv., Utah...D5 207
Price Hill, W. Va...D3, D7 211
Pricedale, Miss...D3 188
Priceville, Ont., Can...C4 153
Prichard, Ala...E1 166
Prichard, W. Va...C2 211
Priddy, Tex...D3 206
Prides Crossing, Mass...C4 185
Priego, Sp...D3 65
Prienai, Sov. Un...A7 70
Prieska, S. Afr...C3 107
Priest, lake, Idaho...A2 177
Priest Rapids, dam, Wash...C6 210
Priest Rapids, res., Wash...C6 210
Priest River, Idaho...A2 177
Priestly, mtn., B.C., Can...B3 149
Prijedor, Yugo...C3 68
Prijepolje, Yugo...D4 68
Prikumsk, Sov. Un...E2 73
Prilep, Yugo...E5 68
Priluki, Sov. Un...F9 72
Prim, pt., P.E.I., Can...C6 151
Primate, Sask., Can...E1 155
Primera, Tex...*F4 206
Primero, riv., Arg...A4 136
Primghar, Iowa...A2 180
Primolano, It...D7 66
Primorsk, Sov. Un...G13 63
Primorsk (Fischhausen), Sov. Un...A6 70
Primorsko-Akhtarsk, Sov. Un...H12 72
Primrose, Nebr...C7 191
Primrose, Pa...*E9 202
Primrose, R.I...B10 172
Primrose, lake, Sask., Can...B1 155
Prince, Sask., Can...E1 155
Prince, Nev...F7 192
Prince, co., P.E.I., Can...C5 151
Prince, inlet, S.C...F4 203
Prince, lake, Va...B6 209
Prince Albert, Sask., Can...D3 155
Prince Albert, nat. park, Sask., Can...C2 155
Prince Albert, sound, N.W. Ter., Can...B10 142
Prince Alfred, cape, N.W. Ter., Can...B8 142
Prince Charles, isl., N.W. Ter., Can...C17 143
Prince Charles, mts., Ant...B19 120
Prince Charles Foreland, pt., Nor...B14 118
Prince Edward, co., Ont., Can...C7 153
Prince Edward, co., Va...D4 209
Prince Edward Island, prov., Can...C6 151
Prince Edward Island, nat. park, P.E.I., Can...C6 151
Prince Frederick, Md...C4 173
Prince George, B.C., Can...C6 149
Prince George, Va...C7, D5 209
Prince George, co., Va...D5 209
Prince Georges, co., Md...C4 173
Prince Harald, coast, Ant...B16 120
Prince of Wales, cape, Alsk...B6 167
Prince of Wales, isl., Alsk...n23 167
Prince of Wales, isl., Austl...B7 110
Prince of Wales, isl., N.W. Ter., Can...B13 142
Prince of Wales, strait, N.W. Ter., Can...B9 142
Prince Olav, coast, Ant...C17 120
Prince Patrick, isl., N.W. Ter., Can...B27 118
Prince Regent, inlet, N.W. Ter., Can...B14 142
Prince Rupert, B.C., Can...B2 149
Prince William, N.B., Can...D2 151
Prince William, co., Va...C5 209
Prince William, sound, Alsk...g18 167
Prince's Lakes, Ind...*F5 179
Princes Risborough, Eng...C7 56
Princesa Isabel, Braz...C3 138
Princess Anne, Md...D6 173
Princess Astrid, coast, Ant...B13 120
Princess Charlotte, bay, Austl...B7 110
Princess Martha, coast, Ant...B11 120
Princess Ragnhild, coast, Ant...B15 120
Princess Royal, isl., B.C., Can...C3 149
Princeton, Ala...A3 166
Princeton, Ark...D3 169
Princeton, Calif...C2 170
Princeton, B.C., Can...E7 149
Princeton, Newf., Can...D5 152
Princeton, Ont., Can...D4 153
Princeton, Fla...F3, G6 174
Princeton, Idaho...C2 177
Princeton, Ill...B4 178
Princeton, Ind...H2 179
Princeton, Iowa...C7 180
Princeton, Kans...D8 181
Princeton, Ky...C2 182
Princeton, Maine...C5 184
Princeton, Mass...B4 185
Princeton, Mich...B3 186
Princeton, Minn...E5 187
Princeton, Mo...A4 189
Princeton, N.J...C3 194
Princeton, N.C...B5 197
Princeton, Oreg...D8 201
Princeton, S.C...B3 203
Princeton, W. Va...D3 211
Princeton, Wis...E4 212
Princeton, mtn., Colo...C4 171
Princeton Junction, N.J...C3 194
Princeville, Que., Can...C6 154
Princeville, Ill...C4 178
Princeville, N.C...B6 197
Principe, chan., B.C., Can...C3 149
Principe, isl., São Tomé & Principe...E1 104
Prineville, Oreg...C6 201
Prineville, res., Oreg...C6 201
Prineville Southeast, Oreg...*C6 201
Pringle, Pa...*D10 202
Pringle, S. Dak...D2 204
Prinsburg, Minn...F3 187
Prinzapolca, Nic...D6 130
Prinzapolca, riv., Nic...D6 130
Prior Lake, Minn...F5 187
Priozersk, Sov. Un...G14 63
Pripyat (Pripet), riv., Sov. Un...E7 72
Prishib, Sov. Un...B4 86
Priština, Yugo...D5 68
Pritchard, isl., S.C...G7 203
Pritchardville, S.C...G6 203
Pritchett, Colo...D8 171
Pritchett, Tex...C5 206
Pritzerbe, Ger...F6 62
Pritzwalk, Ger...B6 60
Privas, Fr...E6 58
Privert, lake, Que., Can...g8 152
Privolnoye, Sov. Un...H9 72
Prizren, Yugo...D5 68
Prizzi, It...F4 67
Probolinggo, Indon...G4 90
Procious, W. Va...C7 211
Procter, B.C., Can...E9 149
Proctor, Colo...A8 171
Proctor, Ky...C6 182
Proctor, Minn...D6 187
Proctor, Mont...C2 190
Proctor, Nev...C7 192
Proctor, Okla...B7 200
Proctor, Tex...D3 206
Proctor, Vt...D2 208
Proctor, W. Va...C1 211
Proctorsville, Vt...E3 208
Proctorville, N.C...C4 197
Proctorville, Ohio...D5 199
Proddatur, India...*F6 87
Proença-a-Nova, Port...C2 65
Progreso, Hond...C4 130
Progreso, Mex...C7 129
Progress, Miss...D3 188
Prohner, bay, Ger...D7 62
Project City, Calif...B2 170
Prokhladnyy, Sov. Un...E3 73
Prokop'yevsk, Sov. Un...D11 71
Prokuplje, Yugo...D5 68
Prole, Iowa...B7 180
Proletarsk, Sov. Un...*G12 72
Proletarskaya, Sov. Un...H13 72
Prome, Bur...E10 87
Promise City, Iowa...D4 180
Promontory, mts., Utah...B3 207
Pronsfeld, Ger...D6 59
Prony, bay, N. Cal... 115
Prophetstown, Ill...B4 178
Propriá, Braz...D3 138
Prorer, bay, Ger...D7 62
Prorva, Sov. Un...D4 73
Proskurov, see Khmelnitsky, Sov. Un.
Prosna, riv., Pol...C5 70
Prośnica, riv., Pol...A3 70
Prosotsáni, Grc...B4 69
Prospect, N.S., Can...E6 151
Prospect, Conn...C5 172
Prospect, Ky...A4 182
Prospect, Ohio...B4 199
Prospect, Oreg...E4 201
Prospect, Pa...E1 202
Prospect, Tenn...B5 205
Prospect, Va...D4 209
Prospect, hill, Mass...D6 185
Prospect, hill, Mass...D2 185
Prospect, hill, Oreg...C1 201
Prospect Harbor, Maine...D4 184
Prospect Hill, N.C...A4 197
Prospect Park, N.J...B4 194
Prospect Park, Pa...B11 202
Prospect Plains, N.J...C4 194
Prosper, N. Dak...C9 198
Prosperity, S.C...C4 203
Prosser, Nebr...D7 191
Prosser, Wash...C6 210
Prostějov, Czech...D4 70
Prostki, Pol...B7 70
Protection, Kans...E4 181
Protem, Mo...E5 189
Protivin, Iowa...A5 180
Proton Station, Ont., Can...C4 153
Prouts Neck, Maine...E5 184
Provadiya, Bul...D8 68
Provadiya, riv., Bul...D8 68
Provencal, La...C2 183
Provence, former prov., Fr...F7 58
c. 1360... 48
Providence, Fla...C4 174
Providence, Ky...C2 182
Providence, R.I...B11 172
Providence, Tenn...*A5 205
Providence, Utah...B4 207
Providence, co., R.I...B10 172
Providence Bay, Ont., Can...B2 153
Providence Forge, Va...D5 209
Providencia, isl., Col...D7 130
Province, lake, Maine, N.H...C5 193
Provincetown, Mass...B7 185
Proving Ground, Ill...A3 178
Provins, Fr...C5 58
Provo, Ark...C1 169
Provo, S. Dak...D2 204
Provo, Utah...C4 207
Provo, riv., Utah...C4 207
Provolt, Oreg...E3 201
Provost, Alta., Can...C5 148
Prowers, co., Colo...D8 171
Proyecto St. Just, P.R...B7 132
Prozor, Yugo...D3 68
Pruden, Tenn...C10 205
Prudence, isl., R.I...C11 172
Prudence Island, R.I...C11 172
Prudentópolis, Braz...D2 137
Prudenville, Mich...D6 186
Prud'homme, Sask., Can...E3 155
Prudnik, Pol...C4 70
Prue, Okla...A5 200
Prüm, Ger...C3 60
Prussia: c. 1140... 47
c. 1721... 49
in 1810... 50
in 1815... 50
c. 1866... 51
Prussia, East: c. 1866... 51
in 1914... 52
in 1922–40... 53
after World War II... 54
Prussia, Rhine province of... 51
Prussia, West... 51
Pruszków, Pol...B6, m13 70
Prut, riv., Sov. Un...H7 72
Pruzhany, Sov. Un...E5 72
Prydz, bay, Ant...C20 120
Pryor, Colo...D6 171
Pryor, Mont...E8 190
Pryor (Pryor Creek), Okla...A6 200
Pryor, mts., Mont...E8 190
Pryorsburg, Ky...B2 182
Przasnysz, Pol...B6 70
Przedbórz, Pol...C5 70
Przemsza, riv., Pol...g10 70
Przemyśl, Pol...D7 70
Przeworsk, Pol...C7 70
Przewóz, Pol...B9 61
Przhevalsk, Sov. Un...E9 73
Psakhná, Grc...C4 69
Psará, isl., Grc...C5 69
Psary, Pol...g10 70
Psel, riv., Sov. Un...G9 72
Pskov, Sov. Un...C7 72
Pskov, lake, Sov. Un...B6 72
Pszczyna, Pol...D5, h9 70
Pszczynka, riv., Pol...h9 70
Ptarmigan, mtn., Wyo...A3 213
Ptich, riv., Sov. Un...E7 72
Ptolemaic kingdom: c. 325 B.C... 43
Ptolemaís, Grc...B3 69
Ptolemies kingdom: c. 1st cent. B.C... 44
Ptuj, Yugo...B2 68
Pu, China...G6 92
Puako, Haw...D6 176
Pualapa, Espiritu Santo I... 115
Puán, Arg...B4 136
Puapua, W. Sam... 114
Pucallpa, Peru...C3 134
Pucheng, China...K8 92
Puck, Pol...A5 70
Puckaway, lake, Wis...E4 212
Puckett, Miss...C4 188
Pudasjärvi, Fin...E12 63
Pudozh, Sov. Un...A11 72
Pudukkottai, India...*F6 87
Puebla, Mex...D5, n14 129

INDEX KEY Each place listed in **Bold-faced Type** has its population listed in the Population tables, pages 230 to 280.
Each country, shown in CAPITAL LETTERS, has its population listed in the World Political Information Table, pages 6 to 10.
* Does not appear on map; key shows general location.

Puebla, state, Mex....D5, n14 129
Puebla de Don Fadrique, Sp.........D4 65
Puebla del Caramiñal, Sp.A1 65
Pueblito de Ponce, P.R....B3 132
Pueblo, Colo..............C6 171
Pueblo, co., Colo...........C6 171
Pueblo Colorado, wash, Ariz..............B6 168
Pueblo Hundido, Chile....E2 135
Pueblo Nuevo, Pan.......m11 130
Pueblo Nuevo, P.R.........B3 132
Pueblo Nuevo, Ven.........A4 133
Pueblo, pass, N. Cal.......... 115
Puebloviejo, Ec............B2 134
Puembut, N. Cal............ 115
Puembut, pass, N. Cal.......... 115
Puente Alto, Chile..........B2 136
Puente Ceso, Sp..........A1 65
Puente-Genil, Sp..........D3 65
Puenteareas, Sp...........A1 65
Puentedeume, Sp...........A1 65
Puerco, riv., Ariz............B6 168
Puerto Acosta, Bol..........C2 135
Puerto Alegre, Bol..........B3 135
Puerto Alvaro Obregón, Mex.........................D6 129
Puerto Armuelles, Pan....F6 130
Puerto Arroyo Verde, Arg..C3 136
Puerto Asién, Chile.........D2 136
Puerto Asís, Col.............C2 133
Puerto Ayacucho, Ven.....B4 133
Puerto Baquerizo, Ec........g6 134
Puerto Barrios, Guat.......C3 130
Puerto Belgrano, Arg.......B4 136
Puerto Bermúdez, Peru....D3 134
Puerto Berrío, Col...........B3 133
Puerto Bolívar, Ec...........B2 134
Puerto Cabello, Ven.........A4 133
Puerto Cabezas, Nic.........C6 130
Puerto Carreño, Col.........B4 133
Puerto Casado, Par.........D4 135
Puerto Chicama, Peru.......C2 134
Puerto Colombia, Col........A3 133
Puerto Constanza, Arg.......f7 136
Puerto Cortés, Hond.........C4 130
Puerto Cumarebo, Ven.......A4 133
Puerto de Cabras, Sp. (Can. Is.)...............m15 65
Puerto de la Cruz, Sp. (Can. Is)...................m13 65
Puerto de la Paloma, Ur...E2 137
Puerto de Luna, N. Mex...C5 195
Puerto del Son, Sp..........A1 65
Puerto Deseado, Arg........D3 136
Puerto Eten, Peru............C2 134
Puerto Guaraní, Par.........D4 135
Puerto Heath, Bol.............B2 135
Puerto Iguazú, Arg...........E5 135
Puerto Jobos, P.R............D6 132
Puerto la Cruz, Ven..........A5 133
Puerto Leguízamo, Col.....D3 133
Puerto Madryn, Arg..........C3 136
Puerto Maldonado, Peru....D4 134
Puerto Manatí, Cuba.........E5 131
Puerto México, see Coatzacoalcos, Mex.
Puerto Mineral, Arg..........E4 135
Puerto Montt, Chile.........C2 136
Puerto Morazán, Nic.........D4 130
Puerto Natales, Chile..E2, h11 136
Puerto Ordaz, Ven.............B5 133
Puerto Padre, Cuba...........E5 131
Puerto Páez, Ven..............B4 133
Puerto Peñasco, Mex........A2 129
Puerto Pinasco, Par..........D4 135
Puerto Piramides, Arg.......C4 136
Puerto Plata, Dom. Rep.....F8 131
Puerto Princesa, Phil........D5 90
Puerto Real, P.R...............C2 132
Puerto Real, see Playa de Fajardo, P.R.
Puerto Real, Sp.................D2 65
PUERTO RICO, U.S. dep., N.A............................ 132
in 1800's.......................... 127
Puerto Sastre, Par..........D4 135
Puerto Siles, Bol.............B2 135
Puerto Suârez, Bol...........C4 135
Puerto Sucre, Bol.............B2 135
Puerto Supe, Peru............D2 134
Puerto Tejada, Col............C2 133
Puerto Vallarta, Mex..C3, m11 129
Puerto Varas, Chile...........C2 136
Puerto Victoria, Peru.........C3 134
Puerto Viejo, C.R..............F6 130
Puerto Villamizar, Col........B3 133
Puerto Visser, Arg..............D3 136
Puerto Wilches, Col............B3 133
Puertollano, Sp................C3 65
Pugachev, Sov. Un.............C3 73
Pugal, India.........................C4 88
Puget, sound, Wash...........B3 210
Puget Island, Wash............C2 210
Puget-Théniers, Fr..............F7 58
Pughtown, W. Va..................A2 211
Pugwash, N. S., Can............D6 151
Puhi, Haw............................B2 176
Puhsi, China.........................B2 93
Puigcerdá, Sp.......................A6 65
Pujehun, S.L.........................E2 103
Pujilí, Ec..............................B2 134
Pukalani, Haw......................C5 176
Pukchŏng, Kor.......................F4 93
Pukë, Alb..............................A2 69
Pukeamaru, mtn., N.Z.........L17 112
Pukeashun, mtn., B.C., Can.D8 149
Pukekohe, N.Z......................L15 112
Pukou, China.........................H8 92
Pukwana, S. Dak.................D6 204
Pul-i-Khumri, Afg.................D14 86
Pula, It...................................E2 67
Pula, Yugo..............................C1 68
Pulacayo, Bol.........................D2 135
Pulantien, China..D9 91, E9 92
Pulaski, Ga..............................D5 175
Pulaski, Ill...............................F4 178
Pulaski, Iowa..........................D5 180
Pulaski, Miss..........................C4 188
Pulaski, N.Y.............................B4 196
Pulaski, Tenn...........................B4 205
Pulaski, Va...............................D2 209
Pulaski, Wis..............................D5 212
Pulaski, co., Ark........................C3 169
Pulaski, co., Ga..........................D3 175
Pulaski, co., Ill...........................F4 178
Pulaski, co., Ind..........................B4 179
Pulaski, co., Ky...........................C5 182
Pulaski, co., Mo...........................D5 189
Pulaski, co., Va............................D2 209
Puławy, Pol....................................C6 70
Pull, pt., Vir. Is.........................h17 132
Pullman, Mich..................................F4 186
Pullman, Wash...............................C8 210
Pullman, W. Va...............................B4 211
Pulog, mtn., Phil...........................n13 90
Pulozero, Sov. Un...........................C15 63
Pułtusk, Pol......................................B6 70
Puluntai, China...A9 87, D3 91
Puluntohai, see Bulun Tokhoi, China
Pume, pass, N. Cal.......................... 115
Pume, pen., N. Cal.......................... 115
Pumphrey, Md...............................C2 173
Pumpkin, buttes, Wyo.....................B7 213
Pumpkin, creek, Mont.....................E11 190
Pumpville, Tex..................................E2 206
Puna, Bol...C2 135
Puná, isl., Ec..................................B1 134
Punakha, Bhu..................................D12 88
Punaluu, Haw.....................................f10 176
Punat, Yugo...C2 68
Punata, Bol...C2 135
Punchaw, B.C., Can..............................C6 149
Pungo, N.C...B7 197
Pungo, lake, N.C...................................B7 197
Pungsan, Kor...F4 93
Pungsan, Kor...H4 93
Punjab, reg., India, Pak...B5 87
Punnichy, Sask., Can..........F3 155
Puno, Peru...........................E3 134
Puno, dept., Peru..................E3 134
Punta, N. Mex.......................C3 195
Punta, mtn., P.R..................C4 132
Punta Alta, Arg.......................B4 136
Punta Arenas, Chile..........h11 136
Punta de Díaz, Chile.............E1 135
Punta de Piedras, Ven.......A5 133
Punta de Vacas, Arg..........A3 136
Punta del Este, pt., Ur.........F2 137
Punta Fijo, Ven.....................A3 133
Punta Gorda, Br. Hond.........B3 130
Punta Gorda, Fla..................F4 174
Punta Moreno, Peru.............C2 134
Puntarenas, C.R.....................E5 130
Punto Fijo, Ven.....................A3 133
Puntzi, lake, B.C., Can..........C5 149
Punxsutawney, Pa..................E4 202
Puposky, Minn.........................C4 187
Puquio, Peru..........................D3 134
Puquios, Chile.........................E2 135
Pur, riv., Sov. Un.................C10 71
Puranpur, India.......................C8 88
Purasa, New Ire. I.................... 115
Purcell, Mo...............................D3 189
Purcell, Okla.............................B4 200
Purcell, mts., Mont....................B1 190
Purcell, mts., B.C., Can...........E9 149
Purcellville, Va..........................B5 209
Purdham, hill, Ark.....................D6 169
Purdin, Mo...............................B4 189
Purdum, Nebr...............................B5 191
Purdy, Mo.................................E4 189
Purdy, Va.....................................E5 209
Purépero, Mex............................n12 129
Purgatoire, riv., Colo.................D7 171
Purgatory, peak, Colo..................D5 171
Puri, India...................................H10 88
Purina, bay, N. Cal......................... 115
Puritan, Mich.................................A5 186
Purmerend, Neth...............................B4 59
Purna, riv., India...............................H6 88
Purnea, India..E11 88
Purple Springs, Alta., Can.E5 148
Purpula, mtn., Sov. Un......D14 71
Pursat, Camb...........................F4 89
Pursglove, W. Va...................B4 211
Purulia, India..........................F11 88
Purús, riv., Braz., Peru...............D3 134, D2 139
Purvis, Miss............................D4 188
Purvis, Va..................................B6 209
Puryear, Tenn...........................A3 205
Puryŏng, Kor................................F4 93
Pusan, Kor..................................I4 93
Pushaw, lake, Maine.................D4 184
Pushkin, Sov. Un..........................B8 72
Pushkino, Sov. Un..C11, m17 72
Pushmataha, Ala.........................C1 166
Pushmataha, co., Okla.......C6 200
Pushthrough, Newf., Can..E3 152
Püspökladány, Hung..........B5 68
Pustelnik, Pol.....................k14 70
Pustunich, Mex....................D6 129
Pustynnove, Sov. Un...........B16 72
Putah, creek, Calif...............A5 170
Putao, Bur.............................C10 87
Puteaux, Fr...............................g9 58
Putien, China............................F8 91
Putilovo, Sov. Un....................s32 63
Puting, cape, Indon................F4 90
Putivl, Sov. Un.........................F9 72
Putlitz, Ger................................E6 62
Putnam, Ala..............................C1 166
Putnam, Conn.............................B9 172
Putnam, Okla...............................B3 200
Putnam, Tex..................................C3 206
Putnam, co., Fla.........................C5 174
Putnam, co., Ga..........................C3 175
Putnam, co., Ill............................B4 178
Putnam, co., Ind..........................E4 179
Putnam, co., Mo..........................A4 189
Putnam, co., N.Y..........................D7 196
Putnam, co., Ohio........................B3 199
Putnam, co., Tenn.......................C8 205
Putnam, co., W. Va......................C3 211
Putnam Station, N.Y......................B7 196
Putnamville, Ind.............................E4 179
Putnamville, Vt...............................C3 208
Putney, Ga.......................................E2 175
Putney, S. Dak..................................B7 204
Putney, Vt..F3 208
Putney, W. Va...........................C3, C6 211
Putre, Chile.......................................C2 135
Puttalam, Cey....................................G6 87
Putte, Neth..C4 59
Püttlingen, Ger....................................D1 61
Putumayo, riv., Col., Peru..D3 133
Pütürge, Tur.......................................C12 85
Puu Kainapuaa, mtn., Haw.f10 176
Puu Kalena, mtn., Haw.....g9 176
Puu Keahiakahoe, mtn., Haw.......................g10 176
Puu Konahuanui, mtn., Haw.......................g10 176
Puu Waawaa, peak, Haw...D6 176
Puukolii, Haw...................C5 176
Puulavesi, lake, Fin...........G12 63
Puunene, Haw.....................C5 176
Puurs, Bel............................C4 59
Puxico, Mo.........................E7 189
Puy de Dome, mtn., Fr.......E5 58
Puy de Sancy, mtn., Fr.......E5 58
Puyallup, Wash...........B3, D2 210
Puyallup, riv., Wash...........C3 210
Puyang, China......................G6 92
Puyehue, Chile.....................C2 136
Puyo, Ec...............................B2 134
Puzim, cape, Iran................I10 86
Pweto, Zaire........................C4 106
Pwllheli, Wales.....................B3 56
Pyapon, Bur.........................E10 87
Pyasina, riv., Sov. Un.......B12 71
Pyatigorsk, Sov. Un............E2 73
Pyatt, Ark.............................A3 169
Pyavzero, lake, Sov. Un...D14 63
Pyhäjärvi, lake, Fin............G10 63
Pyinbugyi, Bur.......................F3 89
Pyinmana, Bur.......................E10 87
Pyland, Miss..........................B4 188
Pyles, fork, W. Va.................A6 211
Pymatuning, res., Pa.............C1 202
Pyŏngchang, Kor....................H4 93
Pyongtaek, Kor.....................*H3 93
Pyŏngyang, Kor.....................G2 93
Pyote, Tex..............................D1 206
Pyramid, lake, Nev..................C2 192
Pyramid, mtn., B.C., Can......E7 142
Pyramid, mts., N. Mex...........E1 195
Pyramid, peak, Wyo...............B2 213
Pyramid Lake, Indian res., Nev.......................C2 192
Pyramids, ruins, Eg...........D6 101
Pyrenees, mts., Fr, Sp................G8 40, A5 65
Pyrites, N.Y.............................B2 196
Pyrmont, Ind...........................D4 179
Pyrzyce, Pol.............................B3 70
Pysht, Wash............................A1 210
Pyskowice, Pol...........................g9 70
Pytalovo, Sov. Un......................C6 72
Pyu, Bur....................................E10 87

Q

Qabātiyah, Jordan.........B7 84
Qābis, Tun.....................C7 102
Qadīmah, Sau. Ar..........A4 105
Qais, isl., Iran.................H6 86
Qala Āhangarān, Afg.................D12 86, B4 87
Qal'a Bist., Afg..............F12 86
Qal'a-i-Ghor (Taiwara), Afg.............................E12 86
Qal'a Nau, Afg..................D11 86
Qal'a Salih, Iraq..................F3 86
Qal'a Shaharak, Afg.........D12 86
Qal'a Sharqat, Iraq............E14 85
Qal'a Sikar, Iraq..................F3 86
Qalamshāh, Eg....................H8 85
Qal'at al Mu'azzam, Sau. Ar................................I11 85
Qaliya, cape, Kuw................G4 86
Qalqīlyah, Jordan.........B6, g10 84
Qalyūb, Eg............................D3 84
Qamīnīs, Libya.....................C4 101
Qana, Leb..............................A7 84
Qārah, Eg...............................H6 85
Qareh Dāgh, mtn., Iran........B2 86
Qaru, isl., Sau. Ar..............G4 86
Qārūn, lake Eg...................D6 101
Qaryat al 'Ulyā, Sau. Ar....H3 86
Qaşr al Kharānah, Jordan..........................G11 85
Qaşr Bānī Walīd, Libya.....C2 101
QATAR, country, Asia..I5 86, 83
Qatia, Eg.................................E8 85
Qattah, Eg...............................D2 84
Qattara (Quaţţārah), depression, Eg................................D5 101
Qāyen, Iran............................E9 86
Qazvīn, Iran..............................C4 86
Qeshm, Iran.............................H8 86
Qeshm, isl., Iran.....................H7 86
Qila Saifullah, Pak...................B2 88
Qinā, Eg....................................D6 101
Qiryat Anavim, Isr.......C7, h11 84
Qiryat Hayim, Isr....................B7 84
Qiryat Ono, Isr........................g10 84
Qiumbele, Ang........................C2 106
Qizil Jilga, India......................A6 87
Qizil Unzun, riv., Iran..........C4 86
Qom, Iran.................................D5 86
Quabbin, res., Mass...............B3 185
Quaco, head, N.B., Can........D4 151
Quaddick, res., Conn............B9 172
Quakenbrück, Ger...................B3 60
Quaker City, Ohio...................C6 199
Quaker Hill, Conn...................D8 172
Quakertown, N.J.......................B3 194
Quakertown, Pa......................F11 202
Qualicum Beach, B.C., Can................................E5 149
Quality, Ky.................................C3 182
Quamba, Minn..........................E5 187
Quan Long, Viet........................H6 89
Quanah, Tex..............................B3 206
Quang Ngai, Viet.........................E8 89
Quang Tri, Viet.............................D7 89
Quannapowite, lake, Mass..C2 185
Quantico, Md................................D6 173
Quantico, Va.................................C5 209
Quapaw, Okla..............................A7 200
Qu'Appelle, Sask., Can.....G4 155
Qu'Appelle, riv., Sask., Can...................................G4 155
Quaraí, Braz.............................E1 137
Quarai, N. Mex........................C3 195
Quaraí, riv., Braz....................E1 137
Quarryville, N.B., Can...........C4 151
Quarryville, Pa..........................G9 202
Quartu Sant'Elena, It...............E2 67
Quartz, mtn., Oreg..................D4 201
Quartz Hill, Calif...................*E4 170
Quartz Mountain, Oreg.........E6 201
Quartzsite, Ariz......................D1 168
Quasqueton, Iowa...................B6 180
Quassapaug, pond, Conn...C4 172
Quatsino, sound, B.C., Can.D3 149
Quaţţārah, see Qattara, depression, Eg.
Quay, N. Mex........................C6 195
Quay, Okla.............................A5 200
Quay, co., N. Mex..................C6 195
Qūchān, Iran.............................C9 86
Que Que, Rh...............................A4 107
Quealy, Wyo...............................D3 213
Quebec, Que., Can..........C6, 9 154
Quebec, co., Que., Can....B6 154
Quebec, prov., Can................... 154
in 1867.................................. 147
Quebec-Ouest, Que., Can...................................*C9 154
Quebeck, Tenn...........................D8 205
Quebradillas, P.R........................B3 132
Quebradillas, mun., P.R.....B3 132
Quechee, Vt..................................D4 208
Quecreek, Pa................................F3 202
Quedlinburg, Ger...........................B6 61
Queen, cape, N.W. Ter., Can..................................D17 143
Queen Anne, Md........................C6 173
Queen Annes, co., Md..............B5 173
Queen Bess, mtn., B.C., Can..D5 149
Queen Carola, hbr., Buka I.......... 115
Queen Charlotte, B.C., Can...C1 149
Queen Charlotte, cape, N. Cal. 115
Queen Charlotte, is., B.C., Can..C1 149
Queen Charlotte, mts., B.C., Can..C1 149
Queen Charlotte, sound, B.C., Can..........................F7 142
Queen Charlotte, strait, B.C., Can.......................D4 149
Queen City, Mo..........................A5 189
Queen City, Tex.........................*C5 206
Queen Creek, Ariz.........................G3 168
Queen Fabiola, mts., Ant..B17 120
Queen Mary, coast, Ant...C22 120
Queen Maud, gulf, N.W. Ter., Can...........................C12 142
Queen Maud, range, Ant..A31 120
Queen Maud Land, reg., Ant................................B14 120
Queen Shoals, W. Va.........C6 211
Queen Victoria, sea, Arc. O...........................A11 118
Queens, borough and co., N.Y.......................................D2 196
Queens, co., N.B., Can.....D4 151
Queens, co., N.S., Can.....E4 151
Queens, co., P.E.I., Can....C6 151
Queens, chan., Austl.............B4 110
Queens, sound, B.C., Can..D3 149
Queensborough, Ont., Can.......................................C7 153
Queensland, Ga........................E3 175
Queensland, state, Austl..D7 111
Queensport, N.S., Can.......D8 151
Queenstown, Austl..................o15 111
Queenstown, Alta., Can.......D4 148
Queenstown, N.B., Can.......D3 151
Queenstown, Guy.....................A3 139
Queenstown, Md........................C5 173
Queenstown, N.Z....................P12 112
Queenstown, S. Afr.................D4 107
Queets, Wash..............................B1 210
Queguay, Ur.................................E1 137
Queguay Grande, riv., Ur..E1 137
Queimadas, Braz.........................D3 138
Queixadas, Braz..........................E2 138
Quela, Ang....................................C2 106
Quelimane, Moz..........................A6 107
Quemado, N. Mex........................C1 195
Quemado, Tex...............................E2 206
Quemado de Güines, Cuba...D3 131
Quemú Quemú, Arg....................B4 136
Quenemo, Kans.............................D8 181
Quentin, Miss.................................D3 188
Quequén, Arg................................B5 136
Querétaro, Mex...............C4, m13 129
Querétaro, state, Mex.....................................C4, m13 129
Querfurt, Ger..................................B6 61
Quesada, Sp.....................................D4 65
Quesnel, B.C., Can........C6 149
Quesnel, lake, B.C., Can.....C7 149
Quesnel, riv., B.C., Can........C6 149
Questa, N. Mex......................A4 195
Quetena, Bol............................D2 135
Quetico, prov. park, Ont., Can.......................................E8 153
Quetta, Pak..........B4 87, B1 88
Quezaltenango, Guat............C2 130
Quezaltepeque, Sal...............D3 130
Quezon City, Phil........C6, o13 90
Qui Nhon, Viet.........................F8 89
Quiani, riv., Braz......................D5 133
Quibala, Ang...............................D1 106
Quibdó, Col...................................B2 133
Quibell, Ont., Can.........................E5 150
Quiberon, Fr...................................D2 58
Quiberon, pen., Fr..........................D2 58
Quicksburg, Va................................C4 209
Quidnessett, R.I..........................C11 172
Quidnick, R.I...............................C10 172
Quidnick, res., R.I.....................C10 172
Quietus, Mont..............................E10 190
Quiindy, Par.....................................E4 135
Quijotoa, Ariz..............................*E3 168
Quilá, Mex...C3 129
Quilan, cape, Chile........................C2 136
Quilcene, Wash.................................B3 210
Quilengues, Ang...............................D1 106
Quill, lakes, Sask., Can.................F3 155
Quill Lake, Sask., Can................E3 155
Quillaga, Chile..................................D2 135
Quillan, Fr...F5 58
Quillota, Chile....................................A2 136
Quilmes, Arg.......................................g7 136
Quilon, India......................................G6 87
Quilpie, Austl......................................C5 112
Quilpué, Chile.....................................A2 136
Quimby, Iowa......................................B2 180
Quimby, Maine..........................B4 184
Quimilí, Arg.................................E3 135
Quimper, Fr.....................................D1 58
Quimperlé, Fr..................................D2 58
Quinaby, Oreg......................B4, C1 201
Quinault, Wash..............................B2 210
Quinault, Indian res., Wash.B1 210
Quinault, lake, Wash.................B2 210
Quinault, riv., Wash....................B1 210
Quincy, Calif....................................C3 170
Quincy, Fla.......................................B2 174
Quincy, Ill..D2 178
Quincy, Ind..F4 179
Quincy, Kans......................................E7 181
Quincy, Ky...B6 182
Quincy, Mass..........................B5, D3 185
Quincy, Mich....................................G6 186
Quincy, Miss.......................................B5 188
Quincy, Mo...C4 189
Quincy, N.H..C3 193
Quincy, Ohio......................................B4 199
Quincy, Oreg.......................................A3 201
Quincy, Pa...G6 202
Quincy, Wash......................................B6 210
Quincy, bay, Mass.................................D3 185
Quinebaug, Conn...............................A9 172
Quinebaug, riv., Conn.......................C8 172
Quines, Arg...A3 136
Quinhagak, Alsk.....................................D7 167
Quinlan, Okla..A2 200
Quinlan, Tex...C4 206
Quinn, S. Dak..D3 204
Quinn, riv., Nev...B4 192
Quinn Canyon, range, Nev..F6 192
Quinnesec, Mich.....................................C3 186
Quinnipiac, riv., Conn........................D5 172
Quinnville, R.I...B11 172
Quintana de la Serena, Sp..C3 65
Quintana Roo, ter., Mex...D7 129
Quintanar, Sp...C4 65
Quinter, Kans..C3 181
Quintero, Chile...A2 136
Quinton, Sask., Can...............................F3 155
Quinton, Ky...D5 182
Quinton, N.J...D2 194
Quinton, Okla...B6 200
Quinwood, W. Va.....................................C4 211
Quipapá, Braz...............................C3, k6 138
Quipungo, Ang...D1 106
Quirauk, mtn., Md..................................A2 173
Quirindi, Austl..E8 112
Quiriquire, Ven...B5 133
Quirke, lake, Ont., Can..........................B8 186
Quiroga, Sp...A2 65
Quiros, cape, Espiritu Santo I. 115
Quirpon, isl., Newf., Can......C4 152
Quispamsis, N.B., Can...*D4 151
Quissanga, Moz..........................D7 106
Quita Sueño Bank, shoals, Caribbean Sea.................C7 130
Quitaque, Tex..............................B2 206
Quitman, Ark..................................B3 169
Quitman, Ga.....................................F3 175
Quitman, La.......................................B3 183
Quitman, Miss....................................C5 188
Quitman, Mo...A2 189
Quitman, Tex...C5 206
Quitman, co., Ga.................................E1 175
Quitman, co., Miss..............................A3 188
Quitman, mts., Tex.............................F1 206
Quito, Ec...B2 134
Quixadá, Braz..B3 138
Quixéramobim, Braz...............................C3 138
Quilin, Mo...E7 189
Quogue, N.Y..*D4 196
Quoi, isl., Truk....................................... 114
Quonochontaug, R.I...........................D10 172
Quonset Point, R.I..............................C11 172
Quorn, Austl..F2 112
Quoyness, Scot...B5 57
Qūş, Eg...D6 101
Quşrah, Jordan..g12 84

R

Raab, riv., Aus..............E7 60
Raabs, Aus.......................D7 60
Raahe, Fin.........................E11 63
Raalte, Neth.......................B6 59
Raanana, Isr......................g10 84
Raasay, isl., Scot.............C3 57
Rab, isl., Yugo..................C2 68
Raba, Indon.......................G5 90
Rába (Raab), riv., Hung.....B3 68
Rabastens, Fr.....................F4 58
Rabat, Mor...............G3 64, C3 102
Rabaul, N. Gui.......................G9 113
Rabbit, creek, S. Dak...........B3 204
Rabbit Ears, pass, Colo........A4 171
Rabbit Hash, Ky.......................A6 182
Rabbit Lake, Sask., Can...D2 155
Rabch, riv., Iran....................I9 86
Rabun, Ala...............................D2 166
Rabun, co., Ga........................B3 175
Rabun, gap, Ga.........................B3 175
Rabun Bald, mtn., Ga..............B3 175
Råby, Swe...................................u34 63
Rača Kragujevačka, Yugo..C5 68
Racoon, creek, Del...................A7 173
Raccoon, creek, Ohio..............D5 199
Raccoon, riv., Iowa..................C3 180
Raccourci, isl., La...................D4 183
Race, cape, Newf., Can.........E5 152
Race, pt., Mass.........................B7 185
Race, pt., N.Y...........................D8 172
Race, strait, N.Y........................E8 172
Raceland, Ky...............................B7 182
Raceland, La....................C6, E5 183
Racepond, Ga..................................F4 175
Rach Gia, Viet.................................G6 89
Rachaya, Leb.....................................F10 85
Racibórz, Pol.......................................C5 70
Racine, Minn......................................G6 187
Racine, Mo..E3 189
Racine, Ohio......................................D6 199
Racine, W. Va..............................C3, D6 211
Racine, Wis...............................F2, F6 212
Racine, co., Wis...................................F5 212
Racine, dam, Ohio, W. Va..C3 211
Račinĕves, Czech..........................n17 70
Rackwick, Scot..................................B5 57
Raco, Mich...B6 186
Rădăuti, Rom.....................................B7 68
Radcliff, Ky...C4 182
Radcliff, Ohio.....................................C5 199
Radcliffe, Iowa..................................B4 180
Råde, Nor..p28 63
Radeberg, Ger.....................................B8 61
Radebeul, Ger.....................................B8 61
Radersburg, Mont..............................D5 190
Radford (Independent City), Va...D2 209
Radisson, Sask., Can.......................E2 155
Radisson, Wis..C2 212
Radium, Kans..D5 181
Radium, Minn..B2 187
Radium Hot Springs, B.C., Can...D9 149
Radium Springs, N. Mex...E3 195
Radley, Kans...E9 181
Radnice, Czech..D8 61
Radnor, Pa...*G11 202
Radnor, co., Wales......................................B4 56
Radnor, forest, Wales..............................B4 56
Radom, Pol...C6 70
Radomir, Bul..D6 68
Radomsko, Pol...C5 70
Radomyshl, Sov. Un.................................F7 72
Radoviš, Yugo...E6 68
Radstadt, Aus...E6 60
Radville, Sask., Can...............................H3 155
Radway, Alta., Can.................................B4 148
Radzionków, Pol..g9 70
Radzymin, Pol..k14 70
Radzyń, Pol...C7 70
Rae, N.W. Ter., Can..............................D9 144
Rae, strait, N.W. Ter., Can...C13 142
Rae Bareli, India.....................................D8 88
Raeford, N.C...C4 197
Raesfeld, Ger..B1 61
Raeville, Nebr..C7 191
Rafaela, Arg..A4 136
Rafaḥ, Gaza Strip.......................................C6 84
Rafaï, Cen. Afr. Rep..................................D4 104
Raft River, mts., Utah..........................B2 207
Raga, Sud..D2 105
Raga Tsangpo, riv., China.C11 88
Ragan, Nebr..D6 191
Ragay, Phil..p14 90
Ragay, gulf, Phil..................................p14 90
Ragged, isl., Maine..............................E4 184
Ragged, lake, Maine............................C3 184
Ragged Top, mtn., Wyo.......................D7 213
Ragland, Ala...B3 166
Raglesville, Ind...G4 179
Ragley, La...D2 183
Rago, Kans..E5 181
Ragsdale, Ind...G3 179
Ragunda, Swe..F7 63
Ragusa, It...F5 67
Rahab el Berdi, Sud....................................C1 105
Rahden, Ger..F2 62
Rahīmyār Khan, Pak.......................C3 88
Rahway, N.J...................................B4, E4 194
Rahway, riv., N.J...............................E4 194
Raichur, India....................................E6 87
Raiford, Fla..B4 174
Raigarh, India.......................................G9 88
Railroad, val., Nev............................E6 192
Rainbow, Conn..B6 172

Rainbow, Mont....C5 190
Rainbow, falls, Tenn....D10 205
Rainbow, lake, Maine....C3 184
Rainbow, res., Wis....C4 212
Rainbow Bridge, nat. mon., Utah....F5 207
Rainbow City, Ala....*A3 166
Rainbow Lake, Alta., Can....*D1 148
Rainelle, W. Va....D4 211
Raines, Ga....E3 175
Rainier, Oreg....A4 201
Rainier, Wash....C3 210
Rainier, mtn., Wash....C4 210
Rains, co., Tex....C5 206
Rainsboro, Ohio....C4 199
Rainsville, Ala....A4 166
Rainy, lake, Ont., Can., Minn....B5 187
Rainy, riv., Ont., Can., Minn....B4 187
Rainy River, Ont., Can....B4 187
Rainy River, co., Ont., Can....E7 153
Raipur, India....D7 87, G8 88
Ra'is, Sau. Ar....E7 101
Raisin, Tex....E4 206
Raja, cape, Indon....K2 89
Rajah Buayan, Phil....D7 90
Rajahmundry, India....E7 87, I8 88
Rajapalayam, India....G6 87
Rajasthan, state, India....C5 87
Rajkot, India....D5 87, F3 88
Rajmahal, India....E11 88
Rajnandgaon, India....G8 88
Rajpipla, India....G4 88
Rajput States: c. 1775.... 82
Rājshāhi, Bngl....D8 87, E12 88
Rake, Iowa....A4 180
Rakhov, Sov. Un....A7 68
Rakkestad, Nor....p29 63
Rakovník, Czech....C2 70
Rakvere, Sov. Un....B6 72
Raleigh, Newf., Can....C4 152
Raleigh, Fla....C4 174
Raleigh, Ill....F5 178
Raleigh, Ind....E7 179
Raleigh, Miss....C4 188
Raleigh, N.C....B5 197
Raleigh, N. Dak....C4 198
Raleigh, Tenn....B2, E8 205
Raleigh, W. Va....D7 211
Raleigh, co., W. Va....D3 211
Raleigh, bay, N.C....C7 197
Raley, Alta., Can....E4 148
Ralik Chain, is., Marshall Is.... 115
Rallaouia (Wells), Maur....B2 103
Ralls, Tex....C2 206
Ralls, co., Mo....B6 189
Ralph, Ala....B2 166
Ralph, Mich....B3 186
Ralph, S. Dak....B2 204
Ralphton, Pa....F3 202
Ralston, Iowa....B3 180
Ralston, Nebr....D3 191
Ralston, Okla....A5 200
Ralston, Pa....D8 202
Ralston, Tenn....A3 205
Ralston, Wyo....A4 213
Ralston, val., Nev....E4 192
Ram, head, Vir. Is....f16 132
Ram, riv., Alta., Can....C3 148
Rām Allāh, Jordan....C7, h11 84
Rama, Sask., Can....F4 155
Rama, Nic....D5 130
Ramada, bay, New Georgia I.... 115
Ramah, Colo....B6 171
Ramah, N. Mex....B1 195
Ramapo, mts., N.J....A4 194
Ramapo, riv., N.J....A4 194
Ramat Gan, Isr....B6, g10 84
Ramat Hakovesh, Isr....g10 84
Ramat Hasharon, Isr....g10 84
Ramban, India....B6 87
Rambervillers, Fr....C7 58
Rambi, isl., Fiji.... 114
Rambouillet, Fr....C4 58
Rambutyo, isl., Bis. Arch.... 115
Ramea, Newf., Can....E3 152
Ramea, is., Newf., Can....E3 152
Ramenskoye, Sov. Un....D12, n18 72
Ramer, Ala....C3 166
Ramer, Tenn....B3 205
Rameshk, Iran....H9 86
Ramganga, riv., India....D7 88
Rāmhormoz, Iran....F4 86
Ramhurst, Ga....B2 175
Ramirez, Tex....F3 206
Ramiriquí, Col....B3 133
Ramirito, Tex....F3 206
Ramle, Isr....C6, h10 84
Ramnäs, Swe....t34 63
Râmnicu-Sărat, Rom....C8 68
Râmnicu-Vâlcea, Rom....C7 68
Ramona, Calif....F5 170
Ramona, Kans....D6 181
Ramona, Okla....A6 200
Ramona, S. Dak....C8 204
Ramos, isl., Sol. Is.... 115
Rampart, Alsk....B9 167
Rampart, range, Colo....B5 171
Rampur, India....C6 87, C7 88
Rampur, India....G9 88
Ramsay, Mich....A5 186
Ramsay, Mont....E4 190
Ramsayville, Ont., Can....A9 153
Ramseur, N.C....B4 197
Ramsey, Eng....B7 56
Ramsey, Ill....D4 178
Ramsey, I. of Man....F4 57
Ramsey, N.J....A4 194
Ramsey, co., Minn....E5 187
Ramsey, co., N. Dak....A7 198
Ramsgate, Eng....C9 56
Ramshorn, mtn., Wyo....B3 213
Ramshorn, peak, Mont....E5 190
Ramu, riv., N. Gui....k11 110
Ranaghat, India....F12 88
Ranburne, Ala....B4 166
Rancagua, Chile....A2 136
Ranchcreek, Mont....E11 190
Rancherie, rock, Oreg....C6 201
Ranchester, Wyo....A5 213
Ranchi, India....D8 87, F10 88
Rancho Cordova, Calif....*C3 170
Ranchos de Taos, N. Mex....A4 195
Ranco, Chile....C2 136
Ranco, lake, Chile....C2 136
Rancocas, N.J....C3 194
Rancocas, creek, N.J....C3 194
Rand, Colo....A4 171
Rand, W. Va....C6 211
Randalia, Iowa....B6 180
Randall, Iowa....B4 180
Randall, Kans....C5 181
Randall, Minn....D4 187
Randall, co., Tex....B2 206
Randallstown, Md....B4 173
Randers, Den....B4 62
Randers, co., Den....B4 62
Randle, Wash....C4 210
Randleman, N.C....B4 197
Randlett, Okla....C3 200
Randlett, Utah....C6 207
Randolph, Ariz....E4 168
Randolph, Iowa....D2 180
Randolph, Maine....D3 184
Randolph, Mass....B5, D3 185
Randolph, Miss....A4 188
Randolph, Nebr....B8 191
Randolph, N.H....B4 193
Randolph, N.Y....C2 196
Randolph, Ohio....A6 199
Randolph, Utah....B4 207
Randolph, Vt....D3 208
Randolph, Wis....E4 212
Randolph, co., Ala....B4 166
Randolph, co., Ark....A4 169
Randolph, co., Ga....E2 175
Randolph, co., Ill....E4 178
Randolph, co., Ind....D7 179
Randolph co., Mo....B5 189
Randolph co., N.C....B4 197
Randolph, co., W. Va....C5 211
Randolph Center, Vt....D3 208
Randolph Field, Tex....E3 206
Random, isl., Newf., Can....D5 152
Random Lake, Wis....E6 212
Randow, riv., Ger....B7 60
Randsburg, Calif....E5 170
Randwick, Austl....*F9 111
Ranfurly, Alta., Can....C5 148
Rangaunu, bay, N.Z....K14 112
Rangeley, Maine....D2 184
Rangeley, lake, Maine....D2 184
Rangely, Colo....A2 171
Ranger, Ga....B2 175
Ranger, Tex....C3 206
Ranger, W. Va....C2 211
Ranger, lake, N. Mex....D6 195
Rangiora, N.Z....O14 112
Rangitata, riv., N.Z....O13 112
Rangoon, Bur....E10 87, D2 89
Rangpur, Bngl....E12 88
Rangsum (Tungpu), China....E4 91
Ranier, Minn....B5 187
Raniganj, India....D8 87
Rankin, Ill....C6 178
Rankin, Pa....*F2 202
Rankin, Tex....D2 206
Rankin, co., Miss....C4 188
Rann of Kutch, swamp, India....D4 87
Rannes, Austl....B8 112
Rannoch, lake, Scot....D4 57
Ranshaw, Pa....*E9 202
Ransom, Ill....B5 178
Ransom, Kans....D4 181
Ransom, Pa....A8 202
Ransom, co., N. Dak....C8 198
Ransomville, N.Y....B2 196
Ranson, W. Va....B7 211
Rantauparapat, Indon....K3 89
Rantoul, Ill....C5 178
Rantoul, Kans....D8 181
Rantowles, S.C....F2 203
Ranum, Den....B3 62
Raon [-l'Etape], Fr....A2 66
Raoui, sand dunes, Alg....D4 102
Raoult, cape, New Britain I.... 115
Rapa Nui (Easter), isl., Pac. O....H15 113
Rapallo, It....B2 67
Rapelje, Mont....E7 190
Raphine, Va....D3 209
Rapid, riv., Minn....B4 187
Rapid City, Man., Can....D1 150
Rapid City, Mich....D5 186
Rapid City, S. Dak....C2 204
Rapid River, Mich....C4 186
Rapidan, Va....C4 209
Rapides, La....C3 183
Rapides, par., La....C3 183
Rappahannock, co., Va....C4 209
Rappahannock, riv., Va....C5 209
Rappahannock Academy, Va....C5 209
Raquette, lake, N.Y....B6 196
Raquette, riv., N.Y....B2 196
Raquette Lake, N.Y....B6 196
Rarden, Ohio....D4 199
Rardin, Ill....D5 178
Raritan, Ill....C3 178
Raritan, N.J....B3 194
Raritan, bay, N.J....C4 194
Raritan, riv., N.J....C4 194
Rarous (Well), Niger....C6 103
Ras al Bidiya, cape, Sau. Ar....H4 86
Ra's al Khaymah, U.A.E....I7 86
Ra's al Milh, cape, Libya....F5 85
Ra's al Tīn, cape, Libya....F4 85
Ra's al 'Ushsh, Eg....C4 84
Ra's an Naqb, Jordan....E7 84
Ras at Tanura, cape, Sau. Ar....H5 86
Ras el 'Ain, Syr....D13 85
Ras el Hadd, cape, Oman....D2 87
Ras en Naqura, cape, Leb....A6 84
Ras Madraka, cape, Oman....E2 87
Rasa, pt., Arg....C4 136
Rasar, Tenn....D10 205
Rasbokil, Swe....t35 63
Rāsdajan, mtn., Eth....C4 105
Raseiniai, Sov. Un....A7 70
Rashad, Sud....C3 105
Rashīd, see Rosetta, Eg.
Rashkov, Sov. Un....B9 68
Rasht, Iran....C4 86
Raška, Yugo....D5 68
Raška, riv., Yugo....D5 68
Raso, cape, Arg....C4 136
Raso, cape, Braz....B5 139
Raspberry, peak, Ark....C1 169
Rasskazovo, Sov. Un....E13 72
Rastatt, Ger....E3 61
Rastede, Ger....A8 59
Raszyn, Pol....m13 70
Rat, isl., Bis. Arch.... 115
Rat, is., Alsk....E3 167
Rat, lake, Man., Can....A2 150
Rat, riv., Man., Can....A2 150
Rat, riv., Man., Can....E3 150
Rat Buri, Thai....F3 89
Ratak Chain, is., Marshall Is.... 115
Ratangarh, India....E5 88
Ratcliff, Ark....B2 169
Ratekau, Ger....E4 62
Rathbun, Iowa....D5 180
Rathbun, res., Iowa....D5 180
Rathdrum, Idaho....B2 177
Rathenow, Ger....B6 60
Rathlin, isl., N. Ire....C3 55
Rathwell, Man., Can....E2 150
Ratingen, Ger....B1 61
Ratlam, India....F5 88
Ratnagiri, India....I4 88
Ratner, Sask., Can....D3 155
Raton, N. Mex....A5 195
Raton, mesa, Colo....D6 171
Raton, pass, Colo....D6 171
Ratónes, is., P.R....D5 132
Rattan, Okla....C6 200
Rattenberg, Aus....E5 68
Rattlesnake, creek, Kans....E4 181
Rattlesnake, creek, Ohio....C4 199
Rattlesnake, creek, Wash....C6 210
Rattlesnake, flat, Wash....C7 210
Rattlesnake, hills, Wash....C6 210
Rattlesnake, mtn., Conn....C5 172
Rattlesnake, range, Wyo....C5 213
Rattling Brook, Newf., Can....D3 152
Rattray, head, Scot....C7 57
Rättvik, Swe....G6 63
Ratzeburg, Ger....E4 62
Ratzeburger, lake, Ger....E4 62
Raub, Ind....C3 179
Raub, N. Dak....B3 198
Rauch, Arg....B5 136
Raue, isl., Nor....p28 63
Raufarhöfn, Ice....m25 63
Rauland, Nor....H2 63
Rauma, Fin....G9 63
Raus, Tenn....B5 205
Rausu-Dake, peak, Jap....D12 93
Rautalampi, Fin....F12 63
Rauville, S. Dak....B8 204
Rava-Russkaya, Sov. Un....F2 72
Ravalli, Mont....C2 190
Ravalli, co., Mont....D2 190
Ravanna, Mo....A4 189
Rāvar, Iran....F8 86
Raven, Va....B3 209
Raven, headland, Ire....B1 56
Raven Park, basin, Colo....A2 171
Raven Rock, N.J....C2 194
Ravena, N.Y....C7 196
Ravendale, Calif....B3 170
Ravenden, Ark....A4 169
Ravenden Springs, Ark....A4 169
Ravenel, S.C....F1 203
Ravenglass, Eng....F5 57
Ravenna, It....B4 67
Ravenna, Ky....C6 182
Ravenna, Mich....E5 186
Ravenna, Nebr....C7 191
Ravenna, Ohio....A6 199
Ravenna, Tex....*C4 206
Ravensburg, Ger....E4 60
Ravenscrag, Sask., Can....H1 155
Ravenscroft, Tenn....D8 205
Ravensdale, Wash....D2 210
Ravensthorpe, Austl....F3 111
Ravenswood, Ind....H8 179
Ravenswood, W. Va....C3 211
Ravensworth, Ont., Can....B5 153
Ravenwood, Mo....A3 189
Ravi, riv., Pak....B4 88
Ravia, Okla....C5 200
Ravinia, S. Dak....D7 204
Rawa Mazowiecka, Pol....C6 70
Rāwalpindi, Pak....B5 87
Rawalpindi Cantonment, Pak....*B5 87
Rawdon, Que., Can....C4 154
Rawhide, creek, Wyo....C8 213
Rawhide, lake, Ont., Can....B8 186
Rawicz, Pol....C4 70
Rawlings, Md....D2 173
Rawlings, Va....E5 209
Rawlinna, Austl....F4 111
Rawlins, Wyo....D5 213
Rawlins, co., Kans....C2 181
Rawlins, hills, Wyo....C5 213
Rawson, Arg....C3 136
Rawson, Arg....g6 136
Rawson, N. Dak....B2 198
Rawson, Ohio....B4 199
Rawsonville, Vt....E3 208
Ray, Ariz....D5 168
Ray, Ind....A8 179
Ray, Minn....B5 187
Ray, N. Dak....A2 198
Ray, co., Mo....B3 189
Ray, cape, Newf., Can....E2 152
Ray-Aleksandrovka, Sov. Un....q20 72
Ray City, Ga....E3 175
Raya, isl., Indon....J1 89
Rayagada, India....H9 88
Raybon, Ga....E5 175
Raychikhinsk, Sov. Un....B4 93
Raygorodka, Sov. Un....q22 72
Rayland, Ohio....B2 211
Rayle, Ga....C4 175
Raymilton, Pa....D2 202
Raymond, Calif....D4 170
Raymond, Alta., Can....E4 148
Raymond, Ga....C2 175
Raymond, Ill....D4 178
Raymond, Iowa....*B5 180
Raymond, Kans....D5 181
Raymond, Maine....E2, 4 184
Raymond, Minn....E3 187
Raymond, Miss....C3 188
Raymond, Mont....B12 190
Raymond, Nebr....D9 191
Raymond, N.H....D4 193
Raymond, S. Dak....C8 204
Raymond, Wash....C2 210
Raymond of Toulouse, crusade of.... 47
Raymondville, Mo....D6 189
Raymondville, N.Y....A2 196
Raymondville, Tex....F4 206
Raymore, Sask., Can....F3 155
Raymore, Mo....C3 189
Rayne, La....D3 183
Raynesford, Mont....C6 190
Raynham, Mass....C5 185
Raynham Center, Mass....C5 185
Rayón, Mex....B2 129
Rayong, Thai....F4 89
Raystown, branch, Pa....F5 202
Raytown, Ga....C4 175
Raytown, Mo....E2 189
Rayville, La....B4 183
Rayville, Mo....B3 189
Razan, Iran....D4 86
Razgrad, Bul....D8 68
Razlog, Bul....E6 68
Razmak, Pak....B4 87
Razorback, mtn., B.C., Can....D5 149
Ré, isl., Fr....D3 58
Rea, Mo....A3 189
Reader, Ark....D2 169
Reader, W. Va....A6, B4 211
Reader, lake, Man., Can....C1 150
Readfield, Maine....D3 184
Reading, Eng....C7 56
Reading, Kans....D8 181
Reading, Mass....A5, C3 185
Reading, Mich....G6 186
Reading, Minn....G3 187
Reading, Ohio....C3, D2 199
Reading, Pa....F10 202
Reading, Vt....E3 208
Reading Center, N.Y....C4 196
Readland, Ark....D4 169
Readlyn, Sask., Can....H3 155
Readlyn, Iowa....B5 180
Readsboro, Vt....F3 208
Readstown, Wis....E3 212
Readyville, Tenn....B5 205
Reagan, Tenn....B3 205
Reagan, co., Tex....D2 206
Reagan Wells, Tex....E3 206
Real, co., Tex....E3 206
Real, range, Bol....C2 135
Realicó, Arg....B4 136
Realitos, Tex....F3 206
Ream, Camb....G5 89
Reamstown, Pa....F9 202
Reardan, Wash....B8 210
Reasnor, Iowa....C4 180
Reata, Mex....B4 129
Reaville, N.J....C3 194
Rebecca, Ga....E3 175
Rebersburg, Pa....E7 202
Rebiana (Oasis), Libya....E4 101
Rebiano, sand sea, Libya....E3 101
Reboly, Sov. Un....F14 63
Rebun, isl., Jap....D10 93
Recalde, Arg....B4 136
Recanati, It....C4 67
Recherche, arch., Austl....F3 110
Rechitsa, Sov. Un....E8 72
Recife, Braz....C4, k6 138
Recinto, Chile....B2 136
Recklinghausen, Ger....B2 61
Recluse, Wyo....A7 213
Recogne, Bel....E5 59
Reconnaissance, mtn., Guam.... 114
Reconquista, Arg....E4 135
Recovery, Ga....F2 175
Recreo, Arg....E2 135
Rector, Ark....A5 169
Red, creek, Miss....E4 188
Red, isl., Newf., Can....E4 152
Red, mtn., Ala....B3 166
Red, mtn., Calif....B2 170
Red, mtn., Mont....C4 190
Red, peak, Colo....B4 171
Red, riv., Man., Can....E3 150
Red, riv., Ky....C6 182
Red, riv., Tenn....A4 205
Red, riv., U.S....D9 159
Red, riv., Viet....B6 89
Red, sea, Afr., Asia....D9 96
Red Bank, N.J....C4 194
Red Bank, S.C....D5 203
Red Bank, Tenn....D8, E10 205
Red Banks, Miss....A4 188
Red Bay, Ala....A1 166
Red Bay, Newf., Can....C3, h10 152
Red Bird, creek, Ky....C6 182
Red Bluff, Calif....B2 170
Red Bluff, res., Tex....E2 206
Red Boiling Springs, Tenn....C8 205
Red Bud, Ill....E4 178
Red Cedar, lake, Wis....C2 212
Red Cedar, riv., Wis....D2 212
Red Cliff, Wis....B3 212
Red Cliff, Indian res., Wis....B3 212
Red Cloud, Nebr....D7 191
Red Creek, N.Y....B4 196
Red Deer, Alta., Can....C4 148
Red Deer, lake, Man., Can....C1 150
Red Deer, riv., Alta., Sask., Can....D5 148
Red Deer, riv., Man., Sask., Can....E4 155
Red Elm, S. Dak....B4 204
Red Feather Lakes, Colo....A5 171
Red Hill, Pa....*F11 202
Red Hook, N.Y....D7 196
Red House, Va....D4 209
Red House, W. Va....C3 211
Red Indian, lake, Newf., Can....D3 152
Red Jacket, W. Va....D2 211
Red Key, Ind....D7 179
Red Lake, co., Minn....C2 187
Red Lake, Indian res., Minn....B3 187
Red Lake, riv., Minn....C2 187
Red Lake Falls, Minn....C2 187
Red Level, Ala....D3 166
Red Lick, Miss....D3 188
Red Lion, Pa....G8 202
Red Lodge, Mont....E7 190
Red Mountain, Calif....E5 170
Red Mountain, pass, Colo....D3 171
Red Oak, Ga....B5 175
Red Oak, Iowa....D2 180
Red Oak, N.C....A6 197
Red Oak, Okla....C6 200
Red Oak, Tex....B5 206
Red Oak, Va....E4 209
Red Pass, B.C., Can....C8 149
Red Pheasant, Sask., Can....E1 155
Red Rapids, N.B., Can....C2 151
Red River, co., Tex....C5 206
Red River, par., La....B2 183
Red River of the North, riv., Minn., N. Dak....B9 198
Red Rock, Ariz....E4 168
Red Rock, Mont....F4 190
Red Rock, Tex....E4 206
Red Rock, lake, Iowa....B9 159
Red Rock, res., Iowa....D5 180
Red Rock, riv., Mont....F4 190
Red Scaffold, S. Dak....C4 204
Red Shirt, S. Dak....D3 204
Red Springs, N.C....C4 197
Red Sucker, lake, Man., Can....B5 150
Red Sucker, riv., Man., Can....B5 150
Red Table, mtn., Colo....B4 171
Red Tank, C.Z....k11 130
Red Wharf, bay, Wales....A3 56
Red Willow, Alta., Can....C4 148
Red Willow, co., Nebr....D5 191
Red Willow, creek, Colo....A8 171
Red Willow, creek, Nebr....D5 191
Red Willow, riv., B.C., Can....B7 149
Red Wing, Colo....D5 171
Red Wing, Minn....F6 187
Redang, Lux....E5 59
Redang, isl., Mala....J5 89
Redbay, Fla....G3 174
Redberry, lake, Sask., Can....E2 155
Redbird, Nebr....B7 191
Redbird, Okla....A6 200
Redbridge, Eng....k13 55
Redby, Minn....C4 187
Redcliff, Alta., Can....D5 148
Redcliff, Colo....B4 171
Redcloud, peak, Colo....D3 171
Reddell, La....D3 183
Reddick, Fla....C4 174
Reddick, Ill....B5 178
Redding, Calif....B2 170
Redding, Conn....D3 172
Redding, Iowa....D3 180
Redding Ridge, Conn....D3 172
Reddish Knob, mtn., Va....C3 209
Redditch, Eng....B6 56
Rede, riv., Eng....E6 57
Redenção, Braz....B3 138
Redeye, riv., Minn....D3 187
Redeyef, Tun....G11 64
Redfield, Ark....C3 169
Redfield Iowa....C3 180
Redfield, Kans....E9 181
Redfield, N.Y....B5 196
Redfield, S. Dak....C7 204
Redford, N.Y....A3 196
Redford, Tex....G2 206
Redgranite, Wis....D4 212
Redgut, bay, Ont., Can....B6 187
Redhouse, Ky....C5 182
Redig, S. Dak....B2 204
Redington, Nebr....C2 191
Redington Beach, Fla....*E4 174
Redington Shores, Fla....*E4 174
Redlake, Minn....C3 187
Redlands, Calif....E5, F3 170
Redlawn, Va....E4 209
Redmesa, Colo....D2 171
Redmon, Ill....D6 178
Redmond, Oreg....C5 201
Redmond, Utah....E4 207
Redmond, Wash....C2 210
Rednitz, riv., Ger....D6 61
Redon, Fr....D2 58
Redonda, isl., B.C., Can....D5 149
Redondela, Sp....A1 65
Redondo, Port....C2 65
Redondo, Wash....D1 210
Redondo, peak, N. Mex....F5 195
Redondo Beach, Calif....F2 170
Redore, Minn....C6 187
Redoubt, vol., Alsk....g15 167
Redowl, S. Dak....C3 204
Redrock, Ark....B2 169
Redrock, N. Mex....E1 195
Redrock, Okla....A4 200
Redruth, Eng....D2 56
Redstone, B.C., Can....C6 149
Redstone, Colo....B3 171
Redstone, Mont....B12 190
Redstone, N.H....B4 193
Redtop, Mo....D4 189
Redvale, Colo....C2 171
Redvers, Sask., Can....H5 155
Redwater, Alta., Can....C4 148
Redwater, creek, Mont....C11 190
Redwine, Ky....B6 182
Redwood, Miss....C3 188
Redwood, N.Y....A5, B1 196
Redwood, co., Minn....F3 187
Redwood, nat. park, Calif....B2 170
Redwood, riv., Minn....F3 187
Redwood City, Calif....B5, D2 170
Redwood Falls, Minn....F3 187
Redwood Valley, Calif....C2 170
Ree, lake, Ire....D3 55
Ree Heights, S. Dak....C6 204
Reece, Kans....E7 181
Reece City, Ala....*A3 166
Reed, Okla....C2 200
Reed, lake, Man., Can....B1 150
Reed City, Mich....E5 186
Reeder, N. Dak....C3 198
Reedley, Calif....D4 170
Reedpoint, Mont....E7 190
Reeds, Mo....*D3 189
Reeds, peak, N. Mex....D2 195
Reeds Ferry, N.H....E4 193
Reeds Lake, Mich....F5 186
Reeds Spring, Mo....E4 189
Reedsburg, Wis....E3 212
Reedsport, Oreg....D2 201
Reedsville, Ohio....C6 199
Reedsville, Pa....E6 202
Reedsville, W. Va....B5 211
Reedsville, Wis....A6, D6 212
Reedville, Va....D6 209
Reedy, W. Va....C3 211
Reedy, creek, W. Va....C3 211
Reedy, lake, Fla....E5 174
Reedy, riv., S.C....C3 203
Reef, pt., N.Z....K14 112
Reefton, N.Z....O13 112
Reelfoot, lake, Tenn....A2 205
Reelsville, Ind....E4 179
Reengus, India....D5 88
Reere, isl., Bikini.... 114
Rees, Ohio....C2 199
Reese, Mich....E7 186
Reese, Utah....B3 207
Reese, riv., Nev....D4 192
Reese Village, Tex....*C2 206
Reeseville, Wis....E5 212
Reesville, Ohio....C4 199
Reeth, Eng....F7 57
Reeves, co., Tex....D1 206
Reeves, mts., Austl....F7 112
Reevesville, Ill....F5 178
Reevesville, S.C....E6 203
Reform, Ala....B1 166
Reform, Miss....B4 188
Refresco, Chile....E2 135
Reftele, Swe....A7 62
Refugio, Tex....E4 206
Refugio, co., Tex....E4 206
Rega, riv., Pol....B3 70
Regan, N. Dak....B5 198
Regen, Ger....E8 61
Regen, riv., Ger....D6 60
Regensburg, Ger....D7 61
Regent, Man., Can....E1 150
Regent, N. Dak....C3 198
Reger, Mo....A4 189
Reggane, Alg....D5 102
Reggio di Calabria, It....E5 67
Reggio nell'Emilia, It....E6 66, B3 67
Reghin, Rom....B7 68
Regina, Sask., Can....G3 155
Regina, Mont....C9 190
Regina, N. Mex....A3 195
Regina Beach, Sask., Can....G3 155
Register, Ga....D5 175
Regla, Cuba....h12 131
Regna, Swe....u33 63
Reguengos de Monsaraz, Port....C2 65
Rehau, Ger....C7 61
Rehna, Ger....E5 62
Rehoboth, Mass....C5 185
Rehoboth, N. Mex....B1 195
Rehoboth, S.W. Afr....B2 107
Rehoboth, bay, Del....C7 173
Rehoboth Beach, Del....C7 173
Rehovot, Isr....C6, h10 84

INDEX KEY Each place listed in **Bold-faced Type** has its population listed in the Political tables, pages 230 to 280. Each country, shown in CAPITAL LETTERS, has its population listed in the World Political Information Table, pages 6 to 10. * Does not appear on map; key shows general location.

Reï Bouba, Cam..........D2 **104**
Reichenbach, Ger..........C7 **61**
Reichenbach, Ger..........A4 **66**
Reid, lake, Sask., Can..........G1 **155**
Reid, mtn., Alsk..........n24 **167**
Reidland, Ky..........A2 **182**
Reids Grove, Md..........C6 **173**
Reidsville, Ga..........D4 **175**
Reidsville, N.C..........A4 **197**
Reidville, S.C..........B3 **203**
Reigate, Eng..........C7 **56**
Reims, Fr..........C6 **58,** E4 **59**
Rein, bay, New Britain I.......... **115**
Reina Adelaida, arch., Chile..........E2 **136**
Reinbeck, Iowa..........B5 **180**
Reindeer, isl., Man., Can..........C3 **150**
Reindeer, lake, Sask., Can..........A4 **155**
Reindeer, riv., Sask., Can..........B4 **155**
Reinfeld, Ger..........E4 **62**
Reinosa, Mex..........B5 **129**
Reinosa, Sp..........A3 **65**
Reipetown, Nev..........D6 **192**
Reisterstown, Md..........B4 **173**
Reit im Winkl, Ger..........B8 **66**
Reitz, S. Afr..........C4 **107**
Rekarne, Swe..........t34 **63**
Reliance, N.W. Ter., Can..........D11 **144**
Reliance, S. Dak..........D6 **204**
Reliance, Tenn..........D9 **205**
Reliance, Wyo..........D3 **213**
Relizane, Alg..........B5 **102**
Rémada, Tun..........C7 **102**
Remagen, Ger..........C2 **61**
Remanso, Braz..........C2 **138**
Remarkable, pt., Espiritu Santo I.......... **115**
Rembert, S.C..........C6 **203**
Rembertów, Pol..........B6, k14 **70**
Rembrandt, Iowa..........B2 **180**
Remecó, Arg..........B4 **136**
Remedios, Cuba..........D4 **131**
Remedios, Pan..........F7 **130**
Remer, Minn..........C5 **187**
Remerton, Ga..........F3 **175**
Remington, Ind..........C3 **179**
Remington, Va..........C5 **209**
Remiremont, Fr..........C7 **58**
Remlap, Ala..........B3 **166**
Remmel, dam, Ark..........D6 **169**
Rems, riv., Ger..........E4 **61**
Remscheid, Ger..........B2 **61**
Remsen, Iowa..........B2 **180**
Remsen, N.Y..........B5 **196**
Remus, Mich..........E5 **186**
Renault, Alg..........F7 **64**
Renault, Ill..........E3 **178**
Rencona, N. Mex..........B4, G6 **195**
Rencontre East, Newf., Can..........E4 **152**
Rendova, hbr., Rendova I.......... **115**
Rendova, isl., Sol. Is.......... **115**
Rendsburg, Ger..........A4 **60**
Rendville, Ohio..........C5 **199**
Renews, Newf., Can..........E5 **152**
Renforth, N.B., Can..........*D4 **151**
Renfrew, Ont., Can..........B8 **153**
Renfrew, S.C..........B2 **203**
Renfrew, co., Ont., Can..........B7 **153**
Renfrew, co., Scot..........E4 **57**
Renfrow, Okla..........A4 **200**
Rengo, Chile..........A2 **136**
Reni, Sov. Un..........C9 **68**
Renick, Mo..........B5 **189**
Renick (Falling Springs), W. Va..........D4 **211**
Renk, Sud..........C3 **105**
Renmark, Austl..........G3 **112**
Rennell, isl., Sol. Is.......... **115**
Renner, S. Dak..........D9 **204**
Renner, Tex..........A5 **206**
Rennerod, Ger..........C3 **61**
Rennert, N.C..........C4 **197**
Rennes, Fr..........C3 **58**
Rennick, bay, Ant..........C29 **120**
Rennie, Man., Can..........E4 **150**
Reno, Ill..........E4 **178**
Reno, Kans..........B8 **181**
Reno, Nev..........D2 **192**
Reno, Pa..........D2 **202**
Reno, co., Kans..........E5 **181**
Reno, hill, Wyo..........C6 **213**
Reno, lake, Minn..........E3 **187**
Renohill, Wyo..........B6 **213**
Renous, N.B., Can..........C4 **151**
Renous, riv., N.B., Can..........C3 **151**
Renovo, Pa..........D6 **202**
Renown, Sask., Can..........F3 **155**
Rensselaer, Ind..........C3 **179**
Rensselaer, N.Y..........C7 **196**
Rensselaer, co., N.Y..........C7 **196**
Rensselaer Falls, N.Y..........B1 **196**
Rensselaerville, N.Y..........C6 **196**
Rentiesville, Okla..........B6 **200**
Renton, Wash..........B3, D2 **210**
Rentz, Ga..........D4 **175**
Renville, Minn..........F3 **187**
Renville, co., Minn..........F3 **187**
Renville, co., N. Dak..........A4 **198**
Renwick, Iowa..........B4 **180**
Repton, Ala..........D2 **166**
Republic, Kans..........C6 **181**
Republic, Mo..........D4 **189**
Republic, Ohio..........A4 **199**
Republic, Pa..........G2 **202**
Republic, Wash..........A7 **210**
Republic, co., Kans..........C6 **181**
Republican, riv., U.S..........B7 **158**
Republican City, Nebr..........D6 **191**
Repulse Bay, N.W. Ter., Can..........C15 **144**
Requa, Calif..........B1 **170**
Requena, Sp..........C5 **65**
Rerik, Ger..........D5 **62**
Reşadiye, Tur..........D6 **69**
Rescue, Va..........B6, E6 **209**
Reserve, Sask., Can..........E4 **155**
Reserve, Kans..........C8 **181**
Reserve, La..........B6 **183**
Reserve, Mont..........B12 **190**
Reserve, N. Mex..........D1 **195**
Reserve, Wis..........C2 **212**
Reshef, Isr..........g10 **84**
Resina, It..........D5 **67**
Resistencia, Arg..........E4 **135**
Reşiţa, Rom..........C5 **68**
Resko, Pol..........B3 **70**
Resolute, N.W. Ter., Can..........B14 **144**
Resolution, isl., N.W. Ter., Can..........D20 **143**
Resolution, pt., Tanna I.......... **115**
Rest Haven, Ga..........*B2 **175**
Resthaven, mtn., Alta., Can..........C1 **148**
Restigouche, co., N.B., Can..........B2 **151**
Restigouche, riv., N.B., Can..........B2 **151**
Reston, Man., Can..........E1 **150**
Reszel, Pol..........A6 **70**
Retalhuleu, Guat..........C2 **130**
Retamito, Arg..........A3 **136**
Rethel, Fr..........C6 **58**
Réthimnon, Grc..........E5 **69**
Reti, Pak..........C2 **88**
Retie, Bel..........C5 **59**
Retlaw, Alta., Can..........D4 **148**
Retsil, Wash..........D1 **210**
Retsof, N.Y..........C3 **196**
Reubens, Idaho..........*C2 **177**
Reus, Sp..........B6 **65**
Reusens, Va..........D3 **209**
Reutlingen, Ger..........E4 **61**
Reutte, Aus..........E5 **60**
Reva, S. Dak..........B2 **204**
Revda, Sov. Un..........B5 **73**
Revel, Fr..........F5 **58**
Revelo, Ky..........D5 **182**
Revelstoke, B.C., Can..........D8 **149**
Reventazón, Peru..........C1 **134**
Revenue, Sask., Can..........E1 **155**
Revere, Mass..........C3 **185**
Revere, Minn..........F3 **187**
Revere, Mo..........A6 **189**
Reverie, Tenn..........B2 **205**
Revigny, Fr..........F4 **59**
Revillagigedo, isl., Alsk..........n24 **167**
Revillagigedo, is., Mex..........D2 **129**
Revillo, S. Dak..........B9 **204**
Revin, Fr..........E4 **59**
Revivim, Isr..........C6 **84**
Revloc, Pa..........F4 **202**
Řevnice, Czech..........o17 **70**
Rew, Pa..........C4 **202**
Rewa, Fiji.......... **114**
Rewa, India..........E8 **88**
Reward, Sask., Can..........E1 **155**
Rewari, India..........C6 **88**
Rewey, Wis..........F3 **212**
Rex, Ga..........B5 **175**
Rex, mtn., Ant..........B5 **120**
Rexburg, Idaho..........F7 **177**
Rexford, Kans..........C3 **181**
Rexford, Mont..........B1 **190**
Rexford, N.Y..........C7 **196**
Rexroat, Okla..........C4 **200**
Rexton, N.B., Can..........C5 **151**
Rexton, Mich..........B5 **186**
Reydell, Ark..........C4 **169**
Reydon, Okla..........B2 **200**
Reyes, pt., Calif..........C2 **170**
Reykjavík, Ice..........n22 **63**
Reynaud, Sask., Can..........E3 **155**
Reyno, Ark..........A5 **169**
Reynolds, Ga..........D2 **175**
Reynolds, Ill..........B3 **178**
Reynolds, Ind..........C4 **179**
Reynolds, Mo..........D6 **189**
Reynolds, Nebr..........D8 **191**
Reynolds, N. Dak..........B8 **198**
Reynolds, co., Mo..........D6 **189**
Reynolds Corners, Ohio..........*A2 **199**
Reynolds Knob, mtn., W. Va..........C5 **211**
Reynoldsburg, Ohio..........C2, C5 **199**
Reynoldsville, Pa..........D4 **202**
Rezā'īyeh, Iran..........C2 **86**
Rezat, riv., Ger..........D5 **61**
Rezé, Fr..........D3 **58**
Rēzekne, Sov. Un..........C6 **72**
Rezeni, Sov. Un..........B9 **68**
Rhaetian Alps, mts., Switz..........C5 **66**
Rhame, N. Dak..........C2 **198**
Rhazâlé, Syr..........B8 **84**
Rhea, co., Tenn..........D9 **205**
Rheda, Ger..........B3 **61**
Rheden, Neth..........B6 **59**
Rhein, Sask., Can..........F4 **155**
Rhein (Rhine), riv., Ger..........C6 **59**
Rheine, Ger..........A2 **61**
Rheinhausen, Ger..........B1 **61**
Rheinkamp, Ger..........B7 **58**
Rheinland-Pfalz (Rhineland-Palatinate), state, Ger..........D2 **61**
Rheinsberg, Ger..........E6 **62**
Rheinwaldhorn, mtn., Switz..........C5 **66**
Rhenen, Neth..........C5 **59**
Rheydt, Ger..........C6 **59**
Rhin, canal, Ger..........F6 **62**
Rhinau, Fr..........F6 **62**
Rhine, Ga..........E3 **175**
Rhine, confederation of the.......... **51**
Rhine, province of Prussia.......... **51**
Rhine, riv., Eur..........C2 **61**
Rhinebeck, N.Y..........D7 **196**
Rhineland, Mo..........C6 **189**
Rhineland, reg., Ger..........C3 **60**
Rhinelander, Wis..........C4 **212**
Rhinow, Ger..........F6 **62**
Rhode Island, state, U.S.......... **172**
Rhodell, W. Va..........D3 **211**
Rhodes, Iowa..........C4 **180**
Rhodes, Mich..........E6 **186**
Rhodes: c. 450 B.C.......... **42**
c. 50 B.C.......... **44**
c. 1360 A.D.......... **48**
after World War II.......... **54**
Rhodes, see Ródhos, isl., Grc.
Rhodes, peak, Idaho..........C4 **177**
Rhodes Point, Md..........E5 **173**
RHODESIA, country, Afr..........A4 **107**
Rhodesia and Nyasaland, Fed. of, see Malawi, Rhodesia, and Zambia, countries, Afr.
Rhodhiss, N.C..........B2 **197**
Rhodope, mts., Bul..........E7 **68**
Rhome, Tex..........A5 **206**
Rhondda, Wales..........C4 **56**
Rhône, riv., Switz..........C3 **66**
Rhyl, Wales..........A4 **56**
Riacho de Santana, Braz..........D2 **138**
Rialto, Calif..........*F3 **170**
Rialto, Tenn..........B2 **205**
Rianjo, Sp..........A1 **65**
Rib, mtn., Wis..........D4 **212**
Rib, riv., Wis..........C3 **212**
Rib Lake, Wis..........C3 **212**
Ribadavia, Sp..........A1 **65**
Ribadeo, Sp..........A2 **65**
Ribadesella, Sp..........A3 **65**
Ribas do Rio Pardo, Braz..........C2 **137**
Ribávè, Moz..........D6 **106**
Ribble, riv., Eng..........G6 **57**
Ribe, Den..........C2 **62**
Ribe, co., Den..........C2 **62**
Ribeauvillé, Fr..........C7 **58**
Ribeira do Pombal, Braz..........D3 **138**
Ribeirão Bonito, Braz..........m7 **137**
Ribeirão Branco, Braz..........n7 **137**
Ribeirão Prêto, Braz..........C3, k8 **137**
Ribera, It..........F4 **67**
Ribérac, Fr..........E4 **58**
Riberalta, Bol..........B2 **135**
Ribnitz, Ger..........D6 **62**
Ribstone, Alta., Can..........C5 **148**
Říčany, Czech..........o18 **70**
Riccione, It..........B4 **67**
Rice, Calif..........E6 **170**
Rice, Minn..........E4 **187**
Rice, Tex..........*C4 **206**
Rice, Va..........D4 **209**
Rice, co., Kans..........D5 **181**
Rice, co., Minn..........F5 **187**
Rice, creek, Minn..........E7 **187**
Rice, lake, Ont., Can..........C6 **153**
Rice, lake, Minn..........C3 **187**
Rice, lake, Minn..........D5 **187**
Rice Lake, Wis..........C2 **212**
Riceboro, Ga..........E5 **175**
Rices Landing, Pa..........G1 **202**
Riceton, Sask., Can..........G3 **155**
Riceville, Iowa..........A5 **180**
Riceville, Tenn..........D9 **205**
Rich, Miss..........A3 **188**
Rich, Mor..........H4 **64**
Rich, co., Utah..........B4 **207**
Rich, mtn., Ark., Okla..........C1 **169**
Rich, mtn., Va..........B3 **209**
Rich Creek, Va..........D2 **209**
Rich Fountain, Mo..........C6 **189**
Rich Hill, Mo..........C3 **189**
Rich Lake, Alta., Can..........B5 **148**
Rich Mountain, Ark..........C1 **169**
Rich Square, N.C..........A6 **197**
Richard, Sask., Can..........E2 **155**
Richard, crusade of.......... **47**
Richard City, Tenn..........D8 **205**
Richards, Mo..........D3 **189**
Richards, Tex..........D5 **206**
Richards, lake, Ariz..........C5 **168**
Richard's Harbour, Newf., Can..........E3 **152**
Richards Spur, Okla..........C3 **200**
Richardson, Sask., Can..........G3 **155**
Richardson, Ky..........C7 **182**
Richardson, Tex..........B6 **206**
Richardson, co., Nebr..........D10 **191**
Richardson, lakes, Maine..........D2 **184**
Richardson, mts., Yukon, Can..........C5 **142**
Richardton, N. Dak..........C3 **198**
Richburg, N.Y..........C2 **196**
Richburg, S.C..........B5 **203**
Richdale, Alta., Can..........D5 **148**
Richelieu, co., Que., Can..........D4 **154**
Richey, Mont..........C11 **190**
Richfield, Calif..........C2 **170**
Richfield, Idaho..........F4 **177**
Richfield, Kans..........E2 **181**
Richfield, Minn..........E7 **187**
Richfield, Nebr..........E3 **191**
Richfield, N.C..........B3 **197**
Richfield, Pa..........E7 **202**
Richfield, Utah..........E3 **207**
Richfield, Wis..........E1 **212**
Richfield Springs, N.Y..........C5 **196**
Richford, N.Y..........C4 **196**
Richford, Vt..........B3 **208**
Richibucto, N.B., Can..........C5 **151**
Richland, Ga..........D2 **175**
Richland, Ind..........I3 **179**
Richland, Iowa..........C6 **180**
Richland, Mo..........D5 **189**
Richland, Mont..........B10 **190**
Richland, Nebr..........C8 **191**
Richland, N.J..........E3 **194**
Richland, N.Y..........B4 **196**
Richland, Oreg..........C9 **201**
Richland, Pa..........*F9 **202**
Richland, S. Dak..........E9 **204**
Richland, Wash..........C6 **210**
Richland, co., Ill..........E5 **178**
Richland, co., Mont..........C12 **190**
Richland, co., N. Dak..........C9 **198**
Richland, co., Ohio..........B5 **199**
Richland, co., S.C..........D6 **203**
Richland co., Wis..........E3 **212**
Richland, par., La..........B4 **183**
Richland, creek, Ill..........B9 **189**
Richland, creek, Tenn..........B5 **205**
Richland Balsam, mtn., N.C..........D3 **197**
Richland Center, Wis..........E3 **212**
Richland Hills, Tex..........*C4 **206**
Richland Springs, Tex..........D3 **206**
Richlands, N.C..........C6 **197**
Richlands, Va..........B3 **209**
Richlandtown, Pa..........F11 **202**
Richlawn, Ky..........*B4 **182**
Richlea, Sask., Can..........F1 **155**
Richmond, Austl..........D7 **111**
Richmond, Calif..........B5, D2 **170**
Richmond, Ont., Can..........B9 **153**
Richmond, P.E.I., Can..........C6 **151**
Richmond, Que., Can..........D5 **154**
Richmond, Eng..........F7 **57**
Richmond, Eng..........*m11 **55**
Richmond, Ill..........A5, D1 **178**
Richmond, Ind..........E8 **179**
Richmond, Iowa..........C6 **180**
Richmond, Kans..........D8 **181**
Richmond, Ky..........C5 **182**
Richmond, Maine..........D3, D6 **184**
Richmond, Mass..........B1 **185**
Richmond, Mich..........F8 **186**
Richmond, Minn..........E4 **187**
Richmond, Mo..........B4 **189**
Richmond, N.H..........E2 **193**
Richmond, N.Z..........N14 **112**
Richmond, Ohio..........A1 **211**
Richmond, S. Afr..........C5 **107**
Richmond, S. Afr..........D3 **107**
Richmond, Tenn..........B5 **205**
Richmond, Tex..........E5, F4 **206**
Richmond, Utah..........B4 **207**
Richmond, Vt..........C3 **208**
Richmond (Independent City), Va..........C7, D5 **209**
Richmond (Staten Island), borough and co., N.Y..........E1 **196**
Richmond, co., N.S., Can..........D9 **151**
Richmond, co., Que., Can..........D5 **154**
Richmond, co., Ga..........C4 **175**
Richmond, co., N.C..........B4 **197**
Richmond, co., Va..........D6 **209**
Richmond Beach, Wash..........B3 **210**
Richmond Dale, Ohio..........C5 **199**
Richmond Heights, Fla..........F3 **174**
Richmond Heights, Mo..........B8 **189**
Richmond Heights, Ohio..........*A6 **199**
Richmond Heights, Va..........C7 **209**
Richmond Hill, Ont., Can..........E6, D5 **153**
Richmond Hill, N.C..........*A4 **197**
Richmondville, N.Y..........C6 **196**
Richmound, Sask., Can..........G1 **155**
Richthofen, mtn., Colo..........A5 **171**
Richton, Miss..........D5 **188**
Richton Park, Ill..........*B6 **178**
Richvalley, Ind..........C6 **179**
Richview, Ill..........E4 **178**
Richville, Mich..........E7 **186**
Richville, Minn..........D3 **187**
Richville, N.Y..........B1 **196**
Richville, Vt..........E2 **208**
Richwood, Ga..........D3 **175**
Richwood, Ky..........A7 **182**
Richwood, Ohio..........B4 **199**
Richwood, W. Va..........C4 **211**
Richwoods, Mo..........C7 **189**
Ricketts, Iowa..........B2 **180**
Rickman, Tenn..........C8 **205**
Rickreall, Oreg..........C1, C3 **201**
Rico, Colo..........D2 **171**
Rico, mts., Colo..........D2 **171**
Riddle, Idaho..........G2 **177**
Riddle, N.C..........A7 **197**
Riddle, Oreg..........E3 **201**
Riddle, mtn., Oreg..........D8 **201**
Riddlesburg, Pa..........F5 **202**
Riderwood, Ala..........C1 **166**
Ridge, mtn., Va..........B2 **209**
Ridge, res., N.J..........A3 **194**
Ridge Farm, Ill..........D6 **178**
Ridge Spring, S.C..........D4 **203**
Ridgebury, Conn..........D2 **172**
Ridgecrest, Calif..........*E5 **170**
Ridgecrest, N.C..........D4 **197**
Ridgedale, Sask., Can..........D3 **155**
Ridgedale, Mo..........E4 **189**
Ridgefield, Conn..........D3 **172**
Ridgefield, N.J..........D5 **194**
Ridgefield, Wash..........*D3 **210**
Ridgefield Park, N.J..........B4, D5 **194**
Ridgeland, Miss..........C3 **188**
Ridgeland, S.C..........G6 **203**
Ridgeland, Wis..........C2 **212**
Ridgeley, W. Va..........B6 **211**
Ridgely, Md..........C6 **173**
Ridgely, Tenn..........A2 **205**
Ridgeside, Tenn..........E10 **205**
Ridgetop, Tenn..........A5 **205**
Ridgetown, Ont., Can..........E3 **153**
Ridgeview, S. Dak..........B5 **204**
Ridgeview, W. Va..........C3, D5 **211**
Ridgeville, Man., Can..........E3 **150**
Ridgeville, Ga..........E5 **175**
Ridgeville, Ind..........D7 **179**
Ridgeville, Md..........B3 **173**
Ridgeville, S.C..........E1, E7 **203**
Ridgeville Corners, Ohio..........A3 **199**
Ridgeway, Ont., Can..........E5 **153**
Ridgeway, Iowa..........A6 **180**
Ridgeway, Mich..........F7 **186**
Ridgeway, Mo..........A4 **189**
Ridgeway, Ohio..........B4 **199**
Ridgeway, S.C..........C6 **203**
Ridgeway, Va..........E3 **209**
Ridgeway, Wis..........F3 **212**
Ridgeway, branch, N.J..........C4 **194**
Ridgewood, N.J..........B4 **194**
Ridgway, Colo..........C3 **171**
Ridgway, Ill..........F5 **178**
Ridgway, Mont..........E12 **190**
Ridgway, Pa..........D4 **202**
Riding Mountain, nat. park, Man., Can..........D1 **150**
Ridley Park, Pa..........B11 **202**
Ridott, Ill..........A4 **178**
Ridotta Capuzzo, Libya..........C4 **101**
Ried, Aus..........D6 **60**
Riegelsville, N.J..........B2 **194**
Riegelsville, Pa..........B2 **194**
Rienza, riv., It..........C7 **66**
Rienzi, Miss..........A5 **188**
Riesa, Ger..........B8 **61**
Riesel, Tex..........D4 **206**
Rieth, Oreg..........B8 **201**
Rieti, It..........C4 **67**
Riffe, Wash..........C3 **210**
Riffle, W. Va..........C4 **211**
Rifle, Colo..........B3 **171**
Rifle, riv., Mich..........D6 **186**
Rifle Gap, res., Colo..........B3 **171**
Rift Valley, reg., Ken..........A6 **106**
Riga (Rīga), Sov. Un..........C5 **72**
Riga, gulf, Sov. Un..........C4 **72**
Rigaud, Que., Can..........D3 **154**
Rigby, Idaho..........F7 **177**
Riggins, Idaho..........D2 **177**
Rigi, mtn., Switz..........B4 **66**
Rigili, isl., Eniwetok.......... **114**
Rigo, Pap..........k12 **111**
Rigolet, Newf., Can..........A2, g10 **152**
Riihimäki, Fin..........G11 **63**
Rijeka (Fiume), Yugo..........C2 **68**
Rijssen, Neth..........B6 **59**
Rikers, isl., N.Y..........D6 **194**
Riley, Ind..........F3 **179**
Riley, Kans..........C7 **181**
Riley, Ky..........C4 **182**
Riley, co., Kans..........C7 **181**
Riley, mtn., N. Mex..........F3 **195**
Rillito, Ariz..........E4 **168**
Rilly-la-Montagne, Fr..........E4 **59**
Rimbey, Alta., Can..........C3 **148**
Rimbo, Swe..........t36 **63**
Rimersburg, Pa..........D2 **202**
Rimini, It..........B4 **67**
Rimini, Mont..........D4 **190**
Rimouski, Que., Can..........A9 **154**
Rimouski, co., Que., Can..........A9 **154**
Rimouski, prov. park, Que., Can..........A9 **154**
Rimouski, riv., Que., Can..........A9 **154**
Rimouski-Est, Que., Can..........A9 **154**
Rimrock, Ariz..........C4 **168**
Rimrock, lake, Wash..........C4 **210**
Rinard, Iowa..........B3 **180**
Rinchhen Ling, China..........F3 **91**
Rincon, Ga..........D5 **175**
Rincon, N. Mex..........E2 **195**
Rincón, P.R..........B1 **132**
Rincón, mun., P.R..........B2 **132**
Rincón de Romos, Mex..........k12 **129**
Rinconada, Arg..........D2 **135**
Rinconado, N. Mex..........A4 **195**
Rindge, N.H..........E2 **193**
Rindjani, peak, Indon..........G5 **90**
Riner, Va..........D2 **209**
Rineyville, Ky..........C3 **182**
Ringana, Choiseul I.......... **115**
Ringe, Den..........C4 **62**
Ringelheim, Ger..........A5 **61**
Ringgold, Ga..........B1 **175**
Ringgold, La..........B2 **183**
Ringgold, Md..........A2 **173**
Ringgold, Nebr..........C5 **191**
Ringgold, Tex..........C4 **206**
Ringgold, Va..........E3 **209**
Ringgold, co., Iowa..........D3 **180**
Ringgold, is., Fiji.......... **114**
Ringim, Nig..........D6 **103**
Ringköbing, Den..........B2 **62**
Ringköbing, co., Den..........B2 **62**
Ringköbing, fjord, Den..........C2 **62**
Ringling, Mont..........D6 **190**
Ringling, Okla..........C4 **200**
Ringoes, N.J..........C3 **194**
Ringold, Okla..........C6 **200**
Ringos Mills, Ky..........B6 **182**
Ringsaker, Nor..........G4 **63**
Ringsjön, lake, Swe..........C7 **62**
Ringso, isl., Swe..........u35 **63**
Ringsted, Den..........C5 **62**
Ringsted, Iowa..........A3 **180**
Ringvassöy, isl., Nor..........C8 **63**
Ringwood, N.J..........A4 **194**
Ringwood, Okla..........A3 **200**
Riñihue, Chile..........B2 **136**
Rinteln, Ger..........A4 **61**
Rio, Fla..........E6 **174**
Rio, Ill..........B3 **178**
Rio, W. Va..........B6 **211**
Rio, Wis..........E4 **212**
Rio Arriba, co., N. Mex..........A2 **195**
Río Balsas, Mex..........D5, o14 **129**
Rio Blanco, Colo..........B3 **171**
Río Blanco, P.R..........C7, g11 **132**
Rio Blanco, co., Colo..........B2 **171**
Rio Branco, Braz..........C4 **134**
Rio Branco, Ur..........E2 **137**
Rio Branco, ter., Braz..........C5 **133**
Rio Branco do Sul, Braz..........D3 **137**
Rio Bravo del Norte, see Rio Grande, riv., U.S., Mex.
Río Bueno, Chile..........C2 **136**
Río Caribe, Ven..........A5 **133**
Rio Chama, riv., N. Mex..........A3 **195**
Río Chico, Ven..........A4 **133**
Rio Claro, Braz..........C3, m8 **137**
Río Colorado, Arg..........B4 **136**
Río Cuarto, Arg..........A4 **136**
Rio de Janeiro, Braz..........C4, h6 **137**
Rio de Janeiro, state, Braz..........C4, h6 **137**
Río de Jesús, Pan..........G7 **130**
Río de Oro, Col..........B3 **133**
Río de Oro, Sp. overseas prov., Afr..........E2 **102**
Rio Dell, Calif..........B1 **170**
Río Gallegos, Arg..........E3, h12 **136**
Río Grande, Arg..........h12 **136**
Rio Grande, Braz..........E2 **137**
Río Grande, Mex..........C4 **129**
Rio Grande, N.J..........E3 **194**
Río Grande, Nic..........D6 **130**
Rio Grande, Ohio..........D5 **199**
Río Grande, P.R..........B7 **132**
Rio Grande, co., Colo..........D4 **171**
Río Grande, mun., P.R..........B7, f11 **132**
Rio Grande, res., Colo..........D3 **171**
Rio Grande (Rio Bravo del Norte), riv., U.S., Mex..........B4 **129**
Rio Grande City, Tex..........F3 **206**
Rio Grande do Norte, state, Braz..........C3, g6 **138**
Rio Grande do Sul, state, Braz..........E2 **137**
Río Hato, Pan..........F7 **130**
Río Hondo, Mex..........h9 **129**
Rio Hondo, Tex..........F4 **206**
Rio Hondo, riv., N. Mex..........D4 **195**
Río Jueyes, P.R..........C5 **132**
Río Llano Central, P.R..........B3 **132**
Rio Linda, Calif..........*C3 **170**
Rio Maior, Port..........C1 **65**
Río Martin, Mor..........G4 **64**
Río Mulato, Bol..........C2 **135**
Río Muni, reg., Equat. Gui..........E1 **104**
Rio Negro, Braz..........D3 **137**
Río Negro, prov., Arg..........C3 **136**
Rio Pardo, Braz..........D2 **137**
Rio Pardo de Minas, Braz..........E2 **138**
Río Penasco, riv., N. Mex..........E5 **195**
Río Piedras, P.R..........B6 **132**
Rio Pomba, Braz..........g6 **137**
Río Primero, Arg..........A4 **136**
Río Pueblo, N. Mex..........A4 **195**
Rio Puerco, riv., N. Mex..........B3 **195**
Rio Salado, riv., N. Mex..........C2 **195**
Río Seco, Chile..........D1 **135**
Río Tercero, Arg..........A4 **136**
Rio Verde, Braz..........B2 **137**
Río Verde, Mex..........m13 **129**
Rio Vista, Calif..........B6, C3 **170**
Riobamba, Ec..........B2 **134**
Ríohacha, Col..........A3 **133**
Rioja, Peru..........C2 **134**
Riom, Fr..........E5 **58**
Rion, S.C..........C5 **203**
Rionero in Vulture, It..........D5 **67**
Ríosucio [Caldas dept.], Col..........B2 **133**
Ríosucio [Choco dept.], Col..........B2 **133**
Ripley, Calif..........F6 **170**
Ripley, Ont., Can..........C3 **153**
Ripley, Eng..........A6 **56**
Ripley, Ill..........C3 **178**
Ripley, Maine..........D3 **184**
Ripley, Miss..........A5 **188**
Ripley, N.Y..........C1 **196**
Ripley, Ohio..........D4 **199**
Ripley, Okla..........A5 **200**
Ripley, Tenn..........B2 **205**
Ripley, W. Va..........C3 **211**
Ripley, co., Ind..........F7 **179**
Ripley, co., Mo..........E7 **189**
Riplinger, Wis..........D3 **212**
Ripogenus, lake, Maine..........C3 **184**
Ripoll, Sp..........A7 **65**
Ripon, Calif..........B6 **170**
Ripon, Que., Can..........D2 **154**
Ripon, Eng..........C6 **55**
Ripon, Wis..........E5 **212**
Rippey, Iowa..........C3 **180**
Rippowam, riv., Conn., N.Y..........A5 **194**
Ripton, Vt..........D2 **208**
Ririe, Idaho..........F7 **177**
Ririna, cape, Epi I.......... **115**
Risco, Mo..........E8 **189**
Rishiri, isl., Jap..........D10 **93**
Rishon le-Zion, Isr..........C6, h10 **84**
Rising City, Nebr..........C8 **191**
Rising Star, Tex..........C3 **206**
Rising Sun, Ind..........G8 **179**
Rising Sun, Md..........A5 **173**
Risingsun, Iowa..........A7 **180**
Risingsun, Ohio..........A4 **199**
Risle, riv., Fr..........C4 **58**
Rison, Ark..........D3 **169**
Risör, Nor..........H3 **63**
Ritchey, Mo..........E3 **189**
Ritchie, co., W. Va..........B3 **211**
Ritidian, pt., Guam.......... **115**
Ritter, Oreg..........C7 **201**
Ritter, mtn., Calif..........D4 **170**
Rittman, Ohio..........B6 **199**
Ritzville, Wash..........B7 **210**
Riva, It..........B3 **67**
Rivadavia, Arg..........A3 **136**
Rivadavia, Arg..........B4 **136**
Rivadavia, Arg..........D3 **135**
Rivadavia, Chile..........E1 **135**
Rivanna, riv., Va..........D4 **209**
Rivas, Nic..........E5 **130**
Rive-de-Gier, Fr..........E6 **58**

River Bourgeois, N.S., Can....D9 151
River Cess, Lib....E3 103
River Edge, N.J....D5 194
River Falls, Ala....D3 166
River Falls, Wis....D1 212
River Falls, dam, Ala....D3 166
River Forest, Ill....F2 178
River Grove, Ill....F2 178
River Hebert, N.S., Can....D5 151
River Hills, Wis....E2 212
River John, N.S., Can....D6 151
River Jordan, B.C., Can....B8 149
River Oaks, Tex....*C4 206
River of Ponds, Newf., Can....C3 152
River Rouge, Mich....A8, F7 186
River Sioux, Iowa....C2 180
River View, Ala....C4 166
Rivera, Arg....B4 136
Rivera, Ur....E1 137
Riverbank, Calif....D3 170
Riverdale, Calif....D4 170
Riverdale, Ga....*C2 175
Riverdale, Ill....F3 178
Riverdale, Kans....E6 181
Riverdale, Md....C2, C4 173
Riverdale, Nebr....D6 191
Riverdale, N.J....B4 194
Riverdale, N. Dak....B4 198
Riverdale, Utah....*B4 207
Rivergaro, It....E5 66
Riverhead, N.Y....D4 196
Riverhurst, Sask., Can....G2 155
Riverina, reg., Austl....G4 112
Riverland Terrace, S.C....F2 203
Riverport, N.S., Can....E5 151
Rivers, Man., Can....D1 150
Rivers, inlet, B.C., Can....D4 149
Riversdale, N.S., Can....D6 151
Riverside, Ala....B3 166
Riverside, Calif....F3, F5 170
Riverside, Colo....B5 171
Riverside, Conn....E2 172
Riverside, Ga....E3 175
Riverside, Ill....F2 178
Riverside, Iowa....C6 180
Riverside, Md....D3 173
Riverside, Mo....*B3 189
Riverside, N.J....C3 194
Riverside, N.Y....*C3 196
Riverside, Oreg....D8 201
Riverside, Pa....E8 202
Riverside, R.I....B11 172
Riverside, Utah....B3 207
Riverside, Wash....A6 210
Riverside, Wyo....D6 213
Riverside, co., Calif....F5 170
Riverside, res., Colo....A6 171
Riverside-Albert, N.B., Can....*D5 151
Riverton, Ala....A1 166
Riverton, Man., Can....D3 150
Riverton, Conn....B4 172
Riverton, Ill....D4 178
Riverton, Iowa....D2 180
Riverton, Kans....E9 181
Riverton, Minn....D4 187
Riverton, Nebr....D7 191
Riverton, N.J....C2 194
Riverton, N.Z....Q12 112
Riverton, Oreg....D2 201
Riverton, Utah....C4 207
Riverton, Vt....C3 208
Riverton, Va....C4 209
Riverton, W. Va....C5 211
Riverton, Wyo....B4 213
Riverview, Fla....B6 174
Riverview, Fla....E2 174
Riverview, Mich....A7 186
Riverview, Mo....*C7 189
Riverview, dam, Ala., Ga....C4 166
Riverview-Heights, N.B., Can....*C5 151
Riverville, Va....D4 209
Rives, Mo....E8 189
Rives, Tenn....A2 205
Rives Junction, Mich....F6 186
Rivesaltes, Fr....F5 58
Rivesville, W. Va....A7, B4 211
Riviera, Tex....F4 206
Rivière à la Baleine, Que., Can....E19 143
Riviera Beach, Fla....F6 174
Riviera Beach, Md....*B4 173
Rivière-à-Pierre, Que., Can....C5 154
Rivière-Bleue, Que., Can....B8 154
Rivière de Rupert, riv., Que., Can....B2 154
Riviere des Prairies, Que., Can....*D9 154
Rivière-du Loup, Que., Can....B8 154
Riviere du Loup, co., Que., Can....B8 154
Riviere du Milieu, Que., Can....B5 154
Riviere du Moulin, Que., Can....A6 154
Riviere Ouelle, Que., Can....B7 154
Rivière-Raquette, Que., Can....C7 154
Rivière-Trois-Pistoles, Que., Can....A8 154
Rivière Verte, N.B., Can....B1 151
Rivière-Verte, Que., Can....B8 154
Rivulet, Mont....C2 190
Rixford, Pa....C4 202
Riyadh (Ar Riyāḍ), Sau. Ar....I3 86
Rize, Tur....B13 85
Rizokarpaso, Cyp....E10 85
Rjukan, Nor....H3 63
Roachdale, Ind....E4 179
Road Town, Vir. Is....m14 131, f16 132
Roads, Ohio....C5 199
Roadstown, N.J....E2 194
Roan, plat., Colo....B2 171
Roan, plat., Utah....D6 207
Roan High Knob, mtn., N.C., Tenn....C11 205
Roan Mountain, Tenn....C11 205
Roane, co., Tenn....D9 205
Roane, co., W. Va....C3 211
Roann, Ind....C6 179
Roanne, Fr....D6 58
Roanoke, Ala....B4 166
Roanoke, Ill....C4 178
Roanoke, Ind....C7 179
Roanoke, La....D3 183
Roanoke, Tex....A5 206
Roanoke (Independent City), Va....D3 209
Roanoke, W. Va....C4 211
Roanoke, co., Va....D2 209
Roanoke, isl., N.C....B8 197
Roanoke, pt., N.Y....F6 172
Roanoke, riv., N.C., Va....E4 209
Roanoke Rapids, N.C....A6 197
Roanoke Rapids, lake, N.C., Va....E5 209
Roanoke Rapids Lake, res., N.C....A6 197
Roaring, fork, Colo....B4 171
Roaring Branch, Pa....C8 202
Roaring Spring, Pa....F5 202
Roaring Springs, Tex....C2 206
Roark, Ky....C6 182
Roatán, Hond....B4 130
Rob Roy, isl., Sol. Is....115
Roba, Ala....C4 166
Robards, Ky....C2 182
Robāṭ-E Khān, Iran....E8 86
Robb, Alta., Can....C2 148
Robbin, Minn....B1 187
Robbins, Ill....F3 178
Robbins, N.C....B4 197
Robbins, Tenn....C9 205
Robbinsdale, Minn....E5, E6 187
Robbinston, Maine....C5 184
Robbinsville, N.J....C3 194
Robbinsville, N.C....D2 197
Robbs, Ill....F5 178
Robeline, La....C2 183
Roberdel, N.C....*C4 197
Robersonville, N.C....B6 197
Robert, La....A7, D5 183
Robert, cape, Ont., Can....A2 153
Robert English, coast, Ant....B4 120
Robert Lee, Tex....D2 206
Robert of Normandy, crusade of....47
Robert S. Kerr, lake, Okla....B6 200
Roberta, Ga....D2 175
Roberts, Idaho....F6 177
Roberts, Ill....C5 178
Roberts, Miss....C4 188
Roberts, Mont....E7 190
Roberts, Wis....D1 212
Roberts, co., S. Dak....B8 204
Roberts, co., Tex....B2 206
Roberts, mtn., Alsk....C6 167
Roberts, mtn., Wyo....C3 213
Roberts, pt., Wash....A2 210
Robert's Arm, Newf., Can....D4 152
Roberts Creek, mtn., Nev....D5 192
Robertsdale, Ala....E2 166
Robertsdale, Pa....F5 202
Robertson, S. Afr....D2 107
Robertson, Wyo....D2 213
Robertson, co., Ky....B5 182
Robertson, co., Tenn....A5 205
Robertson, co., Tex....D4 206
Robertson, bay, Ant....B29 120
Robertson, lake, Que., Can....C2 152
Roberstonville, Que., Can....C6 154
Robertsport, Lib....E2 103
Robertstown, Ga....B3 175
Robertsville, Conn....B4 172
Roberval, Que., Can....A5 154
Robeson, co., N.C....C4 197
Robesonia, Pa....*F9 202
Robin Hood's Bay, Eng....F8 57
Robinette, Oreg....E1 177
Robins, Iowa....B6 180
Robins, Ohio....C6 199
Robins, isl., N.Y....F7 172
Robinson, Ill....D6 178
Robinson, Kans....C8 181
Robinson, N. Dak....B6 198
Robinson, Pa....F3 202
Robinson, Tex....*D4 206
Robinson, fork, W. Va....A6 211
Robinson, fork, W. Va....C7 211
Robinson, mtn., Ark....A1 169
Robinson's, Newf., Can....D2 152
Robinsons, Maine....B5 184
Robinsonville, Miss....A3 188
Robinvale, Austl....G4 112
Roblin, Man., Can....D1 150
Roblin, riv., Man., Can....A5 150
Robsart, Sask., Can....H1 155
Robson, B.C., Can....E9 149
Robson, mtn., B.C., Can....C8, E3 149
Robstown, Tex....F4 206
Roby, Mo....D5 189
Roby, Tex....C2 206
Roca, Nebr....F2 191
Roca, cape, Port....f9 65
Rocafuerte, Ec....B1 134
Rocafuerte, Peru....B2 134
Rocanville, Sask., Can....G5 155
Rocas, is., Braz....B4 138
Rocca Massima, It....h9 67
Roccastrada, It....C3 67
Rocha, Ur....E2 137
Rochdale, Eng....A5 56
Rochdale, Mass....B4 185
Rochdale, N.Y....*D7 196
Roche Harbor, Wash....A2 210
Roche-Percee, Sask., Can....H4 155
Rochechouart, Fr....E4 58
Rochefort, Bel....D5 59
Rochefort, Fr....E3 58
Rochelaise Central, P.R....C2 132
Rochelle, Ga....E3 175
Rochelle, Ill....B4 178
Rochelle, La....C3 183
Rochelle, Tex....D3 206
Rochelle Park, N.J....D5 194
Rocheport, Mo....C5 189
Rochester, Alta., Can....B4 148
Rochester, Eng....C8 56
Rochester, Ill....D4 178
Rochester, Ind....B5 179
Rochester, Iowa....C6 180
Rochester, Ky....C3 182
Rochester, Mass....C6 185
Rochester, Mich....F7 186
Rochester, Minn....F6 187
Rochester, N.H....D5 193
Rochester, N.Y....B3 196
Rochester, Ohio....A5 199
Rochester, Pa....E1 202
Rochester, Tex....C3 206
Rochester, Vt....D3 208
Rochester, Wash....C2 210
Rochester, Wis....F1 212
Rochester, mtn., Vt....D3 208
Rochfort Bridge, Alta., Can....C3 148
Rochikarai, isl., Bikini....114
Rochlitz, Ger....B7 61
Rociada, N. Mex....B4 195
Rock, Kans....E7 181
Rock, Mich....B3 186
Rock, co., Minn....G2 187
Rock, co., Nebr....B6 191
Rock, co., Wis....F4 212
Rock, creek, Ill....B4 178
Rock, creek, Kans....B4 181
Rock, creek, Md....B3 173
Rock, creek, Nebr....E1 191
Rock, creek, Nev....C5 192
Rock, creek, Wash....D5 210
Rock, creek, Wash....E8 210
Rock, creek, Wyo....D6 213
Rock, isl., Fla....C3 174
Rock, isl., Wis....C6 212
Rock, lake, Man., Can....E2 150
Rock, lake, Wash....B8 210
Rock, mtn., Ala....B2 166
Rock, mtn., Colo....D3 171
Rock, riv., Ill., Wis....B3 178, E5 212
Rock, riv., Iowa, Minn....A1 180, G2 187
Rock, riv., Wash....B8 210
Rock Bay, B.C., Can....D5 149
Rock Bluff, Fla....B2 174
Rock Creek, B.C., Can....A6 210
Rock Creek, Kans....B7 181
Rock Creek, Minn....E6 187
Rock Creek, Ohio....A7 199
Rock Creek, butte, Oreg....C8 201
Rock Elm, Wis....D1 212
Rock Falls, Ill....B4 178
Rock Falls, Iowa....A4 180
Rock Hall, Md....B5 173
Rock Hill, Mo....*C7 189
Rock Hill, S.C....B6 203
Rock Island, Que., Can....D5 154
Rock Island, Ill....B3 178
Rock Island, Wash....B5 210
Rock Island, co., Ill....B3 178
Rock Point, Ariz....A6 168
Rock Point, Md....D4 173
Rock Port, Mo....A2 189
Rock Rapids, Iowa....A1 180
Rock River, Wyo....D7 213
Rock Run, Ala....A4 166
Rock Springs, Mont....D10 190
Rock Springs, Wis....E4 212
Rock Springs, Wyo....D3 213
Rock Valley, Iowa....A1 180
Rockaway, N.J....B3 194
Rockaway, Oreg....B3 201
Rockaway, beach, N.Y....E5 194
Rockaway, inlet, N.Y....E5 194
Rockaway Beach, Mo....E4 189
Rockbridge, Ill....D3 178
Rockbridge, Ohio....C5 199
Rockbridge, co., Va....D3 209
Rockcastle, co., Ky....C5 182
Rockcastle, riv., Ky....C5 182
Rockcliffe Park, Ont., Can....*A9 153
Rockdale, Austl....G8 112
Rockdale, Ill....B5, F2 178
Rockdale, Iowa....B7 180
Rockdale, Tenn....B4 205
Rockdale, Tex....D4 206
Rockdale, co., Ga....C3 175
Rockefeller, plat., Ant....B36 120
Rocker, Mont....E4 190
Rockerville, S. Dak....D2 204
Rockfall, Conn....C6 172
Rockfield, Ind....C4 179
Rockfield, Ky....D3 182
Rockfield, Wis....E1 212
Rockford, Ala....C3 166
Rockford, Ill....A4 178
Rockford, Iowa....A5 180
Rockford, Mich....E5 186
Rockford, Minn....E5 187
Rockford, Ohio....B3 199
Rockford, Tenn....D10, E11 205
Rockford, Wash....B8 210
Rockford Bay, Idaho....D8 210
Rockglen, Sask., Can....H3 155
Rockham, S. Dak....C7 204
Rockhampton, Austl....A8 112
Rockhaven, Sask., Can....E1 155
Rockhill Furnace, Pa....F6 202
Rockholds, Ky....D5 182
Rockingham, Ga....E4 175
Rockingham, Mo....B4 189
Rockingham, N.C....C4 197
Rockingham, Vt....E3 208
Rockingham, co., N.H....D4 193
Rockingham, co., N.C....A4 197
Rockingham, co., Va....C4 209
Rocklake, N. Dak....A6 198
Rockland, Ont., Can....B9 153
Rockland, Idaho....G6 177
Rockland, Maine....D3 184
Rockland, Mass....B6, E3 185
Rockland, Mich....A6 186
Rockland, N.Y....D6 196
Rockland, co., N.Y....D6 196
Rockledge, Fla....D6 174
Rockledge, Ga....D4 175
Rockledge, Pa....A11 202
Rocklin, Calif....*C3 170
Rockmart, Ga....C1 175
Rockport, Ark....D6 169
Rockport, Ill....D2 178
Rockport, Ind....I3 179
Rockport, Ky....C3 182
Rockport, Maine....D3 184
Rockport, Mass....A6 185
Rockport, Miss....D3 188
Rockport, N.J....B3 194
Rockport, Tex....E4 206
Rockport, Wash....A4 210
Rocks, Md....A5 173
Rocksprings, Tex....D2 206
Rockstone, Guy....A3 139
Rockton, Ill....A4 178
Rockton, Pa....D4 202
Rockvale, Colo....C5 171
Rockvale, Tenn....B5 205
Rockville, Conn....B7 172
Rockville, Ind....E3 179
Rockville, Md....B3 173
Rockville, Minn....E4 187
Rockville, Mo....C3 189
Rockville, Nebr....C7 191
Rockville, Utah....F2 207
Rockville Centre, N.Y....E3 196
Rockwall, Tex....B6, C4 206
Rockwall, co., Tex....C4 206
Rockwell, Iowa....B4 180
Rockwell, N.C....B3 197
Rockwell City, Iowa....B3 180
Rockwood, Ala....A2 166
Rockwood, Ont., Can....D4 153
Rockwood, Ill....F4 178
Rockwood, Maine....C3 184
Rockwood, Mich....F7 186
Rockwood, Pa....G3 202
Rockwood, Tenn....D9 205
Rockwood, Tex....D3 206
Rocky, Okla....B2 200
Rocky, bay, Newf. Can....B4 152
Rocky, lake, Man., Can....B1 150
Rocky, lake, Maine....D5 184
Rocky, mtn., Mont....C4 190
Rocky, mts., N.A....A4 158
Rocky, pt., N.Y....E7 172
Rocky, pt., N.Y....F2 172
Rocky, riv., Alta., Can....C2 148
Rocky, riv., N.C....B3 197
Rocky, riv., Ohio....B2 199
Rocky, riv., S.C....C2 203
Rocky Boys, Indian res., Mont....B7 190
Rocky Comfort, Mo....E3 189
Rocky Coulee, creek, Wash....B6 210
Rocky Ford, Colo....C7 171
Rocky Ford, Ga....D5 175
Rocky Fork, lake, Ohio....C4 199
Rocky Gap, Va....D1 209
Rocky Harbour, Newf., Can....D3 152
Rocky Hill, Conn....C6 172
Rocky Hill, Ky....C3 182
Rocky Hill, N.J....C3 194
Rocky Mount, N.C....B6 197
Rocky Mount, Va....D3 209
Rocky Mountain, nat. park, Colo....A5 171
Rocky Mountain House, Alta., Can....C3 148
Rocky Point, Idaho....B2 177
Rocky Point, N.Y....F5 172
Rocky Point, N.C....C6 197
Rocky Ridge, Ohio....*A4 199
Rocky Ripple, Ind....H8 179
Rocky River, Ohio....A6, B2 199
Rocky River, Tenn....*D8 205
Rocky Top, mtn., Oreg....C4 201
Rockyford, Alta., Can....D4 148
Rockygrove, Pa....D2 202
Rockyhock, N.C....A7 197
Rockypoint, Wyo....A7 213
Roda, Va....B2 209
Rodach, Ger....C5 61
Rodanthe, N.C....B8 197
Rödby, Den....D5 62
Rödby Havn, Den....D5 62
Roddickton, Newf., Can....C3, h10 152
Rödding, Den....C3 62
Roddy, Tenn....D9 205
Rodeo, N. Mex....F1 195
Roder, riv., Ger....B8 61
Roderfield, W. Va....*D3 211
Roderick, isl., B.C., Can....C3 149
Röderkro, Den....C3 62
Rodessa, La....B1 183
Rodewisch, Ger....C7 61
Rodez, Fr....E5 58
Ródhos, Grc....D7 69
Ródhos (Rhodes), isl., Grc....D6 69
Roding, Ger....D7 61
Rodinga, Austl....D5 111
Rodman, Iowa....A3 180
Rodman, S.C....B5 203
Rodnei, mts., Rom....B7 68
Rodney, Ont., Can....E3 153
Rodney, Miss....D2 188
Rodney, pond, Newf., Can....D4 152
Rodney Village, Del....B6 173
Roduco, N.C....A7 197
Roe, Ark....C4 169
Roebling, N.J....C3 194
Roebourne, Austl....D2 111
Roebuck, S.C....B4 203
Roebuck, bay, Austl....C3 110
Roeland Park, Kans....B9 181
Roer, riv., Ger....D6 59
Roermond, Neth....C5 59
Roes Welcome, sound, N.W. Ter., Can....D15 142
Roeselare, Bel....D3 59
Roetgen, Ger....D6 59
Roff, Okla....C5 200
Rogachev, Sov. Un....E8 72
Roganville, Tex....D6 206
Rogatica, Yugo....D4 68
Roger, lake, Conn....D7 172
Roger Mills, co., Okla....B2 200
Rogers, Ark....A1 169
Rogers, Conn....B9 172
Rogers, Minn....E5 187
Rogers, Nebr....C9 191
Rogers, N. Mex....D6 195
Rogers, N. Dak....B7 198
Rogers, Ohio....B7 199
Rogers, Tex....D4 206
Rogers, co., Okla....A6 200
Rogers, mtn., Va....B3 209
Rogers, pass, Mont....C4 190
Rogers City, Mich....C7 186
Rogerson, Idaho....G4 177
Rogersville, Ala....A2 166
Rogersville, N.B., Can....C4 151
Rogersville, Mo....D4 189
Rogersville, Pa....G1 202
Rogersville, Tenn....C10 205
Roggen, Colo....A6 171
Rogoźno, Pol....B4 70
Rogue, riv., Oreg....E2 201
Rogue River, Oreg....E3 201
Rogue River, range, Oreg....E2 201
Rohnert Park, Calif....*C2 170
Rohnerville, Calif....*B1 170
Rohrersville, Md....B2 173
Rohri, canal, Pak....D2 88
Rohtak, India....*C6 88
Rohwer, hbr., Ark....D4 169
Roi, isl., Kwajalein....114
Roi Et, Thai....D5 89
Roig Central, P.R....C7 132
Roissy-en-France, Fr....g11 58
Roj, isl., Ponape....114
Rojas, Arg....A4 136
Rojo, cape, P.R....n13 131, D2 132
Rokan, riv., Indon....L4 89
Rokeby, Sask., Can....F4 155
Rokel, riv., S.L....E2 103
Rokitno, Sov. Un....F6 72
Rokycany, Czech....D2 70
Roland, Ark....C3 169
Roland, Man., Can....E3 150
Roland, Iowa....B4 180
Roland, Okla....B7 200
Roland, lake, Md....C2 173
Rolesville, N.C....B5 197
Rolette, N. Dak....A6 198
Rolette, co., N. Dak....A6 198
Rolfe, Iowa....B3 180
Rolfsö, isl., Nor....B10 63
Roll, Ariz....E2 168
Roll, Ind....C7 179
Roll, Okla....B2 200
Rolla, B.C., Can....B7 149
Rolla, Kans....E2 181
Rolla, Mo....D6 189
Rolla, N. Dak....A6 198
Rolle, Switz....C2 66
Rolleville, Ba. Is....D6 131
Rolling, fork, Ark....C1 169
Rolling Fields, Ky....*B4 182
Rolling Fork, Miss....C3 188
Rolling Fork, riv., Ky....C4 182
Rolling Hills, Calif....*E4 170
Rolling Hills, Kans....B5 181
Rolling Hills Estates, Calif....*E4 170
Rolling Meadows, Ill....*B6 178
Rolling Prairie, Ind....A4 179
Rollingbay, Wash....D1 210
Rollingstone, Minn....F7 187
Rollins, Mont....C2 190
Rollinsford, N.H....D5 193
Roma, Austl....C7 112
Roma, see Rome, It.
Roma, Tex....F3 206
Romain, cape, S.C....F9 203
Romaine, riv., Que., Can....h9 152
Roman, Rom....B8 68
Roman empire: c. 120 A.D....45
c. 400 A.D....46
Roman Nose, mtn., Md....D1 173
Roman Nose, mtn., Oreg....D3 201
Roman Republic: in 1st cent. B.C....44
ROMANIA, country, Eur....B7 68
see also Rumania
Romano, cape, Fla....G5 174
Romano, isl., Cuba....D5 131
Romans [-sur-Isère], Fr....E6 58
Romanzof, cape, Alsk....C6 167
Romanzof, mts., Alsk....B11 167
Romayor, Tex....D5 206
Rombauer, Mo....E7 189
Rome, Ga....B1 175
Rome, Ill....*E5 178
Rome, Ill....C4 178
Rome, Ind....I4 179
Rome, Iowa....D6 180
Rome (Roma), It....D4, h9 67
Rome, ancient city plan....45
Rome, diocese of....46
Rome, Miss....B3 188
Rome, Mo....E5 189
Rome, N.Y....B5 196
Rome, Ohio....*C5 199
Rome, Pa....C9 202
Rome City, Ind....B7 179
Romema, Isr....m14 84
Romeo, Colo....D4 171
Romeo, Mich....F7 186
Romeoville, Ill....F2 178
Romero, Tex....B1 206
Romeville, La....B6 183
Romford, Conn....C3 172
Romford, Eng....k13 55
Romilly [-sur-Seine], Fr....C5 58
Rominger, N.C....A2 197
Romita, Mex....m13 129
Romney, Ind....D4 179
Romney, W. Va....B6 211
Romny, Sov. Un....F9 72
Römö, isl., Den....C2 62
Romona, Ind....F4 179
Romorantin, Fr....D4 58
Rompin, riv., Mala....K5 89
Romsdalsfjord, fjord, Nor....F2 63
Romsey, Eng....D6 56
Romulus, Mich....A7 186
Romulus, N.Y....C4 196
Romurikku, isl., Bikini....114
Ron, Viet....D7 89
Rona, isl., Scot....C2 57
Ronald, Wash....B4 210
Ronan, Mont....C2 190
Roncador, mts., Braz....E4 139
Roncador, reef, Sol. Is....115
Roncador Bank, shoals, Caribbean Sea....D8 130
Ronceverte, W. Va....D4 211
Ronciglione, It....C4 67
Ronda, N.C....A3 197
Ronda, Sp....D3 65
Rönde, Den....B4 62
Rondeau, prov. park, Ont., Can....E3 153
Rondo, Ark....C5 169
Rondônia, ter., Braz....E2 139
Rondout, Ill....E2 178
Roneys Point, W. Va....B2 211
Rong, isl., Camb....G5 89
Rongelab, atoll, Marshall Is....115
Rongerick, atoll, Marshall Is....F10 113
Ronkiti, Ponape....114
Ronkiti, hbr., Ponape....114
Ronkonkoma, N.Y....F4 172
Ronkonkoma, lake, N.Y....F4 172
Rönne, Den....C8 62
Ronne, entrance, Ant....B4 120
Rönne, riv., Swe....B6 62
Ronse, Bel....D3 59
Ronuro, riv., Braz....F4 139
Roodepoort-Maraisburg, S. Afr....*C4 107
Roodeschool, Neth....A6 59
Roodhouse, Ill....D3 178
Roof, butte, Ariz....A6 168
Rooks, co., Kans....C4 181
Roopville, Ga....C1 175
Roorkee, India....*C6 88
Roosendaal, Neth....C4 59
Roosevelt, Ariz....D4 168
Roosevelt, Minn....B3 187
Roosevelt (Jersey Homesteads), N.J....C4 194
Roosevelt, N.Y....G2 172
Roosevelt, Okla....C2 200
Roosevelt, Tex....D2 206
Roosevelt, Utah....C5 207
Roosevelt, Wash....D5 210
Roosevelt, co., Mont....B11 190
Roosevelt, co., N. Mex....C6 195
Roosevelt, isl., Ant....B32 120
Roosevelt, riv., Braz....D2 139
Roosevelt Campobello, international park, N.B., Can....E3 151
Roosevelt Park, Mich....E4 186
Root, riv., Minn....G7 187
Root, riv., Wis....F2 212
Ropczyce, Pol....C6 70
Roper, N.C....B7 197
Roper, riv., Austl....B5 110
Ropesville, Tex....C1 206
Roque Bluffs, Maine....D5 184
Roquefort, Fr....E3 58
Roques, is., Ven....A4 133
Roques, pt., Cuba....h11 131
Roquetas, Sp....B6 65
Rora, head, Scot....B5 57
Roraima, mtn., Ven....B5 133
Rorke, lake, Man., Can....B5 150
Rorketon, Man., Can....D2 150
Röros, Nor....F4 63
Rorowana, bay, Bougainville I....115
Rorschach, Switz....B5 66
Rosa, La....D3 183
Rosa, mtn., Switz....D3 66
Rosa, pt., Mex....B3 129
Rosa Morada, Mex....k11 129
Rosaire, Que., Can....C7 154
Rosales, Phil....o13 90
Rosalia, Kans....E7 181
Rosalia, Wash....B8 210
Rosalie, Nebr....B9 191
Rosalind, Alta., Can....C4 148
Rosamond, Calif....E4 170
Rosamond, Ill....D4 178
Rosario, Arg....A4 136
Rosário, Braz....B2 138
Rosario, Mex....C3 129
Rosario, Par....D4 135
Rosario, Phil....p13 90
Rosario, P.R....C2 132
Rosario, Ur....E1 137
Rosario de la Frontera, Arg....E3 135
Rosário do Sul, Braz....E2 137

INDEX KEY Each place listed in **Bold-faced Type** has its population listed in the Population tables, pages 230 to 280.
Each country, shown in CAPITAL LETTERS, has its population listed in the World Political Information Table, pages 6 to 10.
* Does not appear on map; key shows general location.

Rosário Oeste, Braz....A1 137
Rosario Tala, Arg....A5 136
Rosati, Mo....C6 189
Rosboro, Ark....C2 169
Rosburg, Wash....C2 210
Roscoe, Ill....A4 178
Roscoe, Minn....E4 187
Roscoe, Mo....D4 189
Roscoe, Mont....E7 190
Roscoe, Nebr....C4 191
Roscoe, N.Y....D6 196
Roscoe, Pa....F2 202
Roscoe, S. Dak....B6 204
Roscoe, Tex....C2 206
Roscommon, Ire....D2 55
Roscommon, Mich....D6 186
Roscommon, co., Mich....D6 186
Roscrea, Ire....D3 55
Rose, Nebr....B6 191
Rose, Okla....A6 200
Rose, mtn., Nev....D2 192
Rose, peak, Ariz....D6 168
Rose Blanche, Newf., Can....E2 152
Rose Bud, Ark....B3 169
Rose City, Mich....D6 186
Rose Creek, Minn....G6 187
Rose Hill, Ill....D5 178
Rose Hill, Iowa....C5 180
Rose Hill, Kans....E6 181
Rose Hill, Miss....C4 188
Rose Hill, Va....B1 209
Rose Lynn, Alta., Can....D5 148
Rose Prairie, B.C., Can....A7 149
Rose Valley, Sask., Can....E4 155
Rose Valley, Pa....*G11 202
Roseau, Dominica....o16 131
Roseau, Minn....B3 187
Roseau, co., Minn....B3 187
Roseau, riv., Man., Can....E3 150
Roseau, riv., Minn....B2 187
Rosebery, B.C., Can....D9 149
Roseboro, N.C....C5 197
Rosebud, Alta., Can....D4 148
Rosebud, Mo....C6 189
Rosebud, Mont....D10 190
Rosebud, S. Dak....D5 204
Rosebud, Tex....D4 206
Rosebud, co., Mont....D10 190
Rosebud, creek, Mont....E10 190
Rosebud, Indian res., S. Dak....D5 204
Rosebud, riv., Alta., Can....D4 148
Roseburg, Oreg....D3 201
Rosebush, Mich....E6 186
Rosedale, B.C., Can....A11 149
Rosedale, Fla....*E4 174
Rosedale, Ind....E3 179
Rosedale, La....*D4 183
Rosedale, Md....C3 173
Rosedale, Miss....B2 188
Rosedale, Tenn....C9 205
Rosedale, Wash....D1 210
Rosedale, W. Va....C4 211
Rosedale Abbey, Eng....F8 57
Rosedale Station, Alta., Can....D4 148
Roseglen, N. Dak....B4 198
Rosehill, N.C....C5 197
Roseisle, Man., Can....E2 150
Roseland, Calif....*C2 170
Roseland, Fla....E6 174
Roseland, Ind....A5 179
Roseland, La....D5 183
Roseland, Nebr....D7 191
Roseland, N.J....*B4 194
Roseland, Ohio....B5 199
Roselawn, Ind....B3 179
Roselle, Ill....E2 178
Roselle, N.J....E4 194
Roselle Park, N.J....E4 194
Rosemark, Tenn....B2 205
Rosemary, Alta., Can....D4 148
Rosemead, Calif....*F2 170
Rosemère, Que., Can....D8 154
Rosemont, Ill....*A6 178
Rosemont, Md....*C2 173
Rosemont, N.J....C3 194
Rosemount, Minn....F5 187
Rosenberg, Tex....E5, F4 206
Rosendael, Fr....B5 58
Rosendale, Mo....A3 189
Rosendale, N.Y....*D6 196
Rosendale, Wis....E5 212
Roseneath, Ont., Can....C6 153
Rosenfeld, Man., Can....E3 150
Rosenhayn, N.J....E2 194
Rosenheim, Ger....E6 60
Rosepine, La....D2 183
Roseray, Sask., Can....G1 155
Roseto, Pa....E11 202
Roseton, N.Y....D6 196
Rosetown, Sask., Can....F1 155
Rosetta (Rashīd), Eg....C6 101
Rosetta, Miss....D2 188
Rosetta, riv. mouth, Eg....C2 84
Rosevear, Alta., Can....C2 148
Roseville, Calif....C3 170
Roseville, Ill....C3 178
Roseville, Mich....A8 186
Roseville, Minn....E7 187
Roseville, Ohio....C5 199
Roseville, Va....C5 209
Rosewood, Ohio....B4 199
Rosewood Heights, Ill....*E3 178
Rosh Ha'ayin, Isr....g10 84
Rosh Pina, Isr....B7 84
Rosharon, Tex....G5 206
Rosheim, Fr....F7 59
Rosholt, S. Dak....B9 204
Rosholt, Wis....D4 212
Rosiclare, Ill....F5 178
Rosie, Ark....B4 169
Rosier, Ga....D4 175
Rosières-en-Santerre, Fr....E2 59
Rosignol, Guy....A3 139
Rosine, Ky....C3 182
Roşiorii-de-Vede, Rom....C7 68
Roskilde, Den....C6 62
Roskilde, co., Den....C6 62
Roslavl, Sov. Un....E9 72
Roslin, Tenn....C9 205
Roslyn, N.Y....*E3 196
Roslyn, S. Dak....B8 204
Roslyn, Wash....B4 210
Roslyn Estates, N.Y....*F2 172
Roslyn Harbor, N.Y....*F2 172
Roslyn Heights, N.Y....F2 172
Rosman, N.C....D3 197
Rosny-sous-Bois, Fr....g10 58
Ross, Calif....*C2 170
Ross, Minn....B3 187
Ross, N.Z....O13 112
Ross, N. Dak....A3 198
Ross, Ohio....C2, C3 199
Ross, co., Ohio....C4 199
Ross, dam, Wash....A4 210
Ross, ice shelf, Ant....A32 120
Ross, isl., Ant....B29 120
Ross, isl., Bur....F3 89
Ross, isl., Man., Can....B3 150
Ross, lake, Wash....A4 210
Ross, mtn., N.Z....N15 112
Ross, sea, Ant....B31 120
Ross and Cromarty, co., Scot....C4 57
Ross Barnett, res., Miss....C3 188
Ross Fork, Mont....C7 190
Ross Lake, Nat. recreation Area, Wash....A5 210
Ross-on-Wye, Eng....C5 56
Rossano, It....E6 67
Rossburg, Ohio....B3 199
Rossburn, Man., Can....D1 150
Rosseau, Ont., Can....B5 153
Rosseau, Mich....A6 186
Rossel, cape, Uea I.... 115
Rossel, isl., Sol. Is.... 115
Rossendale, Man., Can....E2 150
Rosser, Tex....B6 206
Rossford, Ohio....A2, A4 199
Rossie, N.Y....B1 196
Rossignol, lake, N.S., Can....E4 151
Rossiter, Pa....E4 202
Rossland, B.C., Can....E9 149
Rosslau, Ger....B7 61
Rosslyn Farms, Pa....*F1 202
Rosso, Maur....C1 103
Rossosh, Sov. Un....F12 72
Rosston, Ark....D2 169
Rosston, Okla....A2 200
Rossville, Ga....B1 175
Rossville, Ill....C6 178
Rossville, Ind....D4 179
Rossville, Iowa....A6 180
Rossville, Kans....C8 181
Rossville, Tenn....B2 205
Rossway, N.S., Can....E4 151
Rosthern, Sask., Can....E2 155
Rostock, Ger....A6 60, D6 62
Rostov, Sov. Un....C12 72
Rostov [-na-Donu], Sov. Un....H12 72
Roşul, pass, Rom....C6 68
Roswell, Ga....A5, B2 175
Roswell, Idaho....F2 177
Roswell, N. Mex....D5 195
Roswell, S. Dak....C8 204
Rota, Sp....D2 65
Rota (Luta), isl., Mariana Is.... 115
Rotan, Tex....C2 206
Rotenburg, Ger....B4 60
Rotenburg [an der Fulda], Ger....B4 61
Roth, Ger....D6 61
Roth, N. Dak....A5 198
Rothaar, mts., Ger....B3 61
Rothbury, Eng....E7 57
Rothbury, Mich....E4 186
Rothenbach, Ger....D6 61
Rothenburg [in der Lausitz], Ger....B9 61
Rothenburg ob der Tauber, Ger....D5 61
Rother, riv., Eng....D8 56
Rotherham, Eng....A6 56
Rothesay, N.B., Can....D4 151
Rothesay, Scot....E3 57
Rothsay, Minn....D2 187
Rothschild, Wis....D4 212
Rothsville, Pa....F9 202
Rothville, Mo....B4 189
Rothwell, N.B., Can....C3 151
Roto, Austl....F5 112
Rotondella, It....D6 67
Rotorua, N.Z....M16 112
Rott, riv., Ger....E8 61
Rottenburg, Ger....E3 61
Rottenmann, Aus....E7 60
Rotterdam, Neth....C4 59
Rotterdam, N.Y....*C6 196
Rotterdam Junction, N.Y....C6 196
Rottumeroog, isl., Neth....A6 59
Rottweil, Ger....G4 60
Rotuma, isl., Pac. O....G10 113
Roubaix, Fr....B5 58, D3 59
Roudnice [nad Labem], Czech....n17 70
Rouen, Fr....C4 58
Rouge, riv., Que., Can....D3 154
Rougemont, Fr....B2 66
Rougemont, N.C....A5 197
Rough, riv., Ky....C3 182
Rough River, res., Ky....C3 182
Rougon, La....D4 183
Rouleau, Sask., Can....G3 155
Roulette, Pa....C5 202
Round, isl., Miss....E3 188
Round, lake, Ont., Can....B7 153
Round, lake, Wis....B2 212
Round, mtn., Austl....E9 112
Round Bay, Md....B4 173
Round Harbour, Newf., Can....D4 152
Round Hill, Alta., Can....C4 148
Round Hill, N.S., Can....E4 151
Round Island, passage, Fiji.... 114
Round Lake, Ill....E2 178
Round Lake, Minn....G3 187
Round Lake, N.Y....C7 196
Round Lake Beach, Ill....*E2 178
Round Lake Heights, Ill....*A5 178
Round Lake Park, Ill....*E2 178
Round Mound, mtn., Kans....D4 181
Round Mountain, Nev....E4 192
Round Mountain, Tex....D3 206
Round Oak, Ga....C3 175
Round Pond, Ark....B5 169
Round Pond, Maine....E3 184
Round Rock, Ariz....A6 168
Round Rock, Tex....D4 206
Round Top Hill, mtn., Mass....B1 185
Round Valley, Indian res., Calif....C2 170
Round Valley, res., N.J....B3 194
Roundhead, Ohio....B4 199
Roundlake, Miss....A3 188
Roundup, Mont....D8 190
Roura, Fr. Gu....B5 139
Rourkela, India....*D8 87
Rousay, isl., Scot....A5 57
Rouses Point, N.Y....A3 196
Rouseville, Pa....D2 202
Rousseau, Mich....A6 186
Routon, Tenn....A3 205
Routt, co., Colo....A3 171
Rouville, co., Que., Can....D4 154
Rouyn, Que., Can....*E9 153
Rouzerville, Pa....G6 202
Rovaniemi, Fin....D11 63
Rovato, It....B2 67
Roven'ki, Sov. Un....G12, q22 72
Rover, Ark....C2 169
Rover, Tenn....B5 205
Rovereto, It....B3 67
Rovigo, It....B3 67
Rovinj, Yugo....C1 68
Rovno, Sov. Un....F6 72
Rovnoye, Sov. Un....F16 72
Rowan, Iowa....B4 180
Rowan, co., Ky....B6 182
Rowan, co., N.C....B2 197
Rowan, lake, Ont., Can....E5 153
Rowan Mills, N.C....*B3 197
Rowans Ravine, prov. park, Sask., Can....G3 155
Rowayton, Conn....E3 172
Rowe, Mass....A2 185
Rowe, N. Mex....B4, G6 195
Rowena, S. Dak....D9 204
Rowena, Tex....D2 206
Rowesville, S.C....E6 203
Rowland, Ky....C5 182
Rowland, N.C....C4 197
Rowland, Pa....D11 202
Rowlesburg, W. Va....B5 211
Rowlett, Tex....*C4 206
Rowletts, Ky....C4 182
Rowley, Alta., Can....D4 148
Rowley, Iowa....B6 180
Rowley, Mass....A6 185
Rox, Nev....G7 192
Roxabell, Ohio....C4 199
Roxana, Del....D7 173
Roxana, Ill....*C3 178
Roxas, Phil....C6 90
Roxboro, N.C....A5 197
Roxboro, lake, N.C....A5 197
Roxburgh, N.Z....P12 112
Roxburgh, co., Scot....E6 57
Roxbury, Conn....C3 172
Roxbury, Kans....D6 181
Roxbury, Maine....D2 184
Roxbury, N.H....E2 193
Roxbury, N.Y....C6 196
Roxbury, Vt....C3 208
Roxbury Falls, Conn....C3 172
Roxie, Miss....D2 188
Roxobel, N.C....A6 197
Roxton, Tex....C5 206
Roxton Falls, Que., Can....D5 154
Roxton Pond, Que., Can....D5 154
Roy, Fla....C5 174
Roy, Mont....C8 190
Roy, N. Mex....B5 195
Roy, Utah....B3 207
Roy Brown, Nev....D4 192
Roy Hill, Austl....D2 111
Royal, Ark....C2, C5 169
Royal, Fla....D4 174
Royal, Iowa....A2 180
Royal, Nebr....B7 191
Royal, N.C....B7 197
Royal, gorge, Colo....C5 171
Royal, riv., Maine....E5 184
Royal Center, Ind....C4 179
Royal Mills, N.C....A5 197
Royal Niger Company.... 99
Royal Oak, B.C., Can....B9 149
Royal Oak, Md....C5 173
Royal Oak, Mich....A7, E7 186
Royalists, see Kuop, is., Truk
Royalties, Alta., Can....D3 148
Royalton, Ill....F4 178
Royalton, Ind....H7 179
Royalton, Ky....C6 182
Royalton, Minn....E4 187
Royalton, Pa....*F8 202
Royalton, Vt....D3 208
Royalton, Wis....D5 212
Royalty, Tex....D1 206
Royan, Fr....E3 58
Roye, Fr....C5 58
Royersford, Pa....F10 202
Royse City, Tex....C4 206
Royston, Ga....B3 175
Roysville, Lib....E2 103
Rozay-en-Brie, Fr....F2 59
Rozel, Kans....D4 181
Rozet, Wyo....A7 213
Rožňava, Czech....D6 70
Rtishchevo, Sov. Un....C2 73
Ruac, isl., Truk.... 114
Ruaha, Tan....C6 106
Ruaha, riv., Tan....C6 106
Ruanda-Urundi, see Rwanda and Burundi, countries, Afr.
Ruapehu, mtn., N.Z....M15 112
Rub'al Khali, des., Sau. Ar....A6 105
Rubezhnoye, Sov. Un....p21 72
Rubidoux, Calif....F3 170
Rubinéia, Braz....C2 137
Rubonia, Fla....F2 174
Rubtsovsk, Sov. Un....C10 73
Ruby, Alsk....C8 167
Ruby, La....C3 183
Ruby, S.C....B7 203
Ruby, lake, Nev....C6 192
Ruby, mts., Nev....C6 192
Ruby, range, Colo....C3 171
Ruby, range, Mont....E4 190
Ruby Valley, Nev....C6 192
Ruby Valley, Indian res., Nev....C6 192
Rubys Inn, Utah....F3 207
Ruchi, isl., Eniwetok.... 114
Rucker, Tenn....B5 205
Rūd Sar, Iran....C5 86
Ruda Śląska, Pol....*C5 70
Ruda, riv., Pol....g9 70
Rudbar, Afg....F11 86
Rudd, Iowa....A5 180
Ruddell, Sask., Can....E2 155
Ruddles Mills, Ky....B5 182
Rüdesheim, Ger....C3 60
Rudha Hunish, isl., Scot....C2 57
Rudköbing, Den....D4 62
Rudnichnyy, Sov. Un....B4 73
Rudnyy, Sov. Un....*D9 71
Rudolf, lake, Ken....A6 106
Rudolph, Ohio....A4 199
Rudolph, Tex....F4 206
Rudolph, isl., Sov. Un....A8 118
Rudolstadt, Ger....C6 61
Rudyard, Mich....B6 186
Rudyard, Mont....B6 190
Rue, Fr....D9 56
Rueil-Malmaison, Fr....g9 58
Ruelle [-sur-Touvre], Fr....E4 58
Rufa'a, Sud....C3 105
Rufe, Okla....C6 200
Ruffec, Fr....D4 58
Ruffin, N.C....A4 197
Ruffin, S.C....E6 203
Rufiji, riv., Tan....C6 106
Rufina Central, P.R....C3 132
Rufino, Arg....A4 136
Rufisque, Sen....D1 103
Rufus, Oreg....B6 201
Rufus Woods, lake, Wash....A6 210
Rugby, Eng....B6 56
Rugby, N. Dak....A6 198
Rugeley, Eng....B6 56
Rügen, isl., Ger....A6 60
Rugged, mtn., B.C., Can....D4 149
Rugozero, Sov. Un....E15 63
Ruhla, Ger....C5 61
Ruhland, Ger....B8 61
Ruhr, riv., Ger....B3 61
Rui, Afg....D13 86
Ruidosa, Tex....F2 206
Ruidoso, N. Mex....D4 195
Ruidoso Downs, N. Mex....D4 195
Ruislip-Northwood, Eng....*C7 56
Ruiz, Mex....m11 129
Ruiiyoru, isl., Eniwetok.... 114
Rukoji, isl., Bikini.... 114
Rukoji, pass, Bikini.... 114
Rukuruku, bay, Fiji.... 114
Rukwa, lake, Tan....C5 106
Rule, Tex....C3 206
Ruleton, Kans....C2 181
Ruleville, Miss....B3 188
Rulo, Nebr....D10 191
Rum, creek, W. Va....D5 211
Rum, isl., Ba. Is....D6 131
Rum, isl., Scot....D2 57
Rum, riv., Minn....E5 187
Rum, sound, Scot....D2 57
Rum Jungle, Austl....B5 111
Ruma, Yugo....C4 68
Rumaitha, Iraq....F2 86
Rumania (Romania): in 1914.... 52
in 1922–40.... 53
after World War II.... 54
Rumbek, Sud....D2 105
Rumbley, Md....D6 173
Rumburk, Czech....C9 61
Rumely, Mich....B3 186
Rumford, Maine....D2 184
Rumford, R.I....B11 172
Rumford, S. Dak....D2 204
Rumford Corner, Maine....D2 184
Rumilly, Fr....D1 66
Rummerfield, Pa....C9 202
Rumney, N.H....C3 193
Rumney Depot, N.H....C3 193
Rumoe, Jap....E10 93
Rump, mtn., Maine....C1 184
Rumpi, Malawi....D5 106
Rumsey, Alta., Can....D4 148
Rumsey, Ky....C2 182
Rumson, N.J....C4 194
Runcorn, Eng....A5 56
Runge, Tex....E4 206
Rungwa, Tan....C5 106
Runnells, Iowa....A7, C4 180
Runnels, co., Tex....D3 206
Runnemede, N.J....D2 194
Running, creek, Colo....B6 171
Runnymede, Sask., Can....F5 155
Runtu, S.W. Afr....A2 107
Rupanco, Chile....C2 136
Rupat, isl., Indon....L4 89
Rupert, Idaho....G5 177
Rupert, Vt....E2 208
Rupert, W. Va....D4 211
Rupert, riv., Que., Can....B2 154
Rupert House, Que., Can....B2 154
Rupununi, riv., Guy....B3 139
Rural Hall, N.C....A2 197
Rural Retreat, Va....B3, E1 209
Rurrenabaque, Bol....B2 135
Rurui, cape, Jap....D13 93
Rusagonis, N.B., Can....D3 151
Rusapi, Rh....A5 107
Ruse, Bul....D7 68
Rusera, India....E11 88
Rush, Colo....C6 171
Rush, Ire....D3 55
Rush, Ky....B7 182
Rush, co., Ind....E6 179
Rush, co., Kans....D4 181
Rush, creek, Colo....D7 171
Rush, creek, Nebr....C3 191
Rush, creek, Ohio....B4 199
Rush, creek, Okla....C4 200
Rush, lake, Minn....D3 187
Rush, lake, Minn....E6 187
Rush, lake, Wis....E5 212
Rush, riv., Wis....D1 212
Rush, val., Utah....C3 207
Rush Center, Kans....D4 181
Rush City, Minn....E6 187
Rush Hill, Mo....B6 189
Rush Lake, Sask., Can....G2 155
Rush Springs, Okla....C4 200
Rushden, Eng....B7 56
Rushford, Minn....G7 187
Rushford, N.Y....C2 196
Rushmere, Va....B6 209
Rushmore, Minn....G3 187
Rushsylvania, Ohio....B4 199
Rushville, Ill....C3 178
Rushville, Ind....E7 179
Rushville, Mo....B2 189
Rushville, Nebr....B3 191
Rushville, N.Y....C3 196
Rushville, Pa....C9 202
Rusk, Tex....D5 206
Rusk, co., Tex....C5 206
Rusk, co., Wis....C2 212
Ruskin, Fla....E4, F2 174
Ruskin, Nebr....D8 191
Ruskin, Tenn....A4 205
Ruso, N. Dak....B5 198
Russas, Braz....B3 138
Russell, Ark....B4 169
Russell, Man., Can....D1 150
Russell, Ont., Can....B9, B10 153
Russell, Fla....C6 174
Russell, Iowa....C4 180
Russell, Kans....D5 181
Russell, Ky....B7 182
Russell, Mass....B2 185
Russell, Minn....F3 187
Russell, N.Y....B2 196
Russell, N.Z....K15 112
Russell, N. Dak....A5 198
Russell, Okla....C2 200
Russell, Pa....C3 202
Russell, co., Ala....C4 166
Russell, co., Ont., Can....B9 153
Russell, co., Kans....D5 181
Russell, co Ky....C4 182
Russell, co., Va....B3 209
Russell, fork, Ky....C7 182
Russell, is., Sol. Is.... 115
Russell, lake, Alta., Can....A3 148
Russell, lake, Man., Can....A1 150
Russell, mtn., Alsk....f15 167
Russell Gardens, N.Y....*E3 196
Russell Konda, India....H10 88
Russell Springs, Kans....D2 181
Russell Springs, Ky....C4 182
Russells Point, Ohio....*B4 199
Russellton, Pa....*E2 202
Russellville, Ala....A2 166
Russellville, Ark....B2 169
Russellville, Ill....E6 178
Russellville, Ind....E4 179
Russellville, Ky....D3 182
Russellville, Mo....C5 189
Russellville, Ohio....D4 199
Russellville, S.C....E8 203
Russellville, Tenn....C10 205
Rüsselsheim, Ger....D3 61
Russia, Ohio....B3 199
Russia: in 1914.... 52
see also Soviet Union
Russian, riv., Calif....C2 170
Russiaville, Ind....D5 179
Russum, Miss....D2 188
Rustad, Minn....D2 187
Rustavi, Sov. Un....*E7 71
Rustburg, Va....D3 209
Rustico, P.E.I., Can....C6 151
Ruston, La....B3 183
Ruston, Wash....B3, D1 210
Ruszow, Pol....B10 61
Rutana, Burundi....B5 106
Rutba, Iraq....F13 85
Rutchenkovo, Sov. Un....r20 72
Rute, Sp....D3 65
Ruteng, Indon....G6 90
Ruth, Mich....E8 186
Ruth, Miss....D3 188
Ruth, Nev....D7 192
Ruth, N.C....D4 197
Ruthenia, reg., Sov. Un....D7 70
in 1914.... 52
in 1939.... 53
Rutherford, Calif....A5 170
Rutherford, N.J....B4, D5 194
Rutherford, Tenn....A3 205
Rutherford, co., N.C....B2 197
Rutherford, co., Tenn....B5 205
Rutherford, fork, Tenn....A3 205
Rutherfordton, N.C....B2, D4 197
Rutherglen, Ont., Can....A5 153
Rutherglen, Scot....E4 57
Rutheron, N. Mex....A3 195
Ruthilda, Sask., Can....F1 155
Ruthin, Wales....A4 56
Ruthton, Minn....F2 187
Ruthven, Ala....D2 166
Ruthven, Iowa....A3 180
Rüti, Switz....B4 66
Rutland, B.C., Can....E8 149
Rutland, Ill....C4 178
Rutland, Iowa....B3 180
Rutland, Mass....B4 185
Rutland, N. Dak....C8 198
Rutland, Ohio....C5 199
Rutland (Roseville), Pa....C8 202
Rutland, S. Dak....C9 204
Rutland, Vt....D3 208
Rutland, co., Eng....B7 56
Rutland, co., Vt....D2 208
Rutland Station, Sask., Can....E1 155
Rutledge, Ala....D3 166
Rutledge, Ga....C3 175
Rutledge, Minn....D6 187
Rutledge, Mo....A5 189
Rutledge, Tenn....C10 205
Rutshuru, Zaire....B4 106
Rutter, Ont., Can....A4 153
Ruunitto, isl., Eniwetok.... 114
Ruvo [di Puglia], It....D6 67
Ruvuma, riv., Moz., Tan....D6 106
Ruwandiz, Iraq....C2 86
Ruweiha, ruins, Jordan....D7 84
Ruwenzori, mts., Ug., Zaire....A5 106
Ruza, Sov. Un....D11 72
Ruzayevka, Sov. Un....C3 73
Ružomberok, Czech....D5 70
RWANDA, country, Afr....B4 106
Ry, Den....B3 62
Ryan, Iowa....B6 180
Ryan, Okla....C4 200
Ryan, creek, Ala....A3 166
Ryan, peak, Idaho....F4 177
Ryan Park, Wyo....D6 213
Ryazan', Sov. Un....C1 73
Ryazhsk, Sov. Un....E13 72
Rybatskoye, Sov. Un....s31 63
Rybinsk (Shcherbakov), Sov. Un....B1 73
Rybinsk, res., Sov. Un....B1 73
Rybnik, Pol....C5, g9 70
Rybnitsa, Sov. Un....B9 68
Rycroft, Alta., Can....B1 148
Ryde, Austl....*F8 112
Ryde, Eng....D6 56
Ryder, N. Dak....B4 198
Ryderwood, Wash....C2 210
Rye, Ark....D4 169
Rye, Colo....D6 171
Rye, Eng....D8 56
Rye, N.H....D5 193
Rye, N.Y....D2, D3 196
Rye, lake, N.Y....A5 194
Rye Beach, N.H....E5 193
Rye Patch, dam, Nev....C3 192
Rye Patch, res., Nev....C3 192
Ryeå, riv., Den....A3 62
Ryegate, Mont....D7 190
Ryegate, Vt....C4 208
Ryerson, Sask., Can....H5 155
Rygge, Nor....p28 63
Ryley, Alta., Can....C4 148
Rylsk, Sov. Un....F10 72
Rynda, Sov. Un....C17 63
Ryomgård, Den....B4 62
Rypin, Pol....B5 70
Ryūkyū, is., Asia....F10 91
RYŪKYŪ ISLANDS (Southern), U.S. occ., Asia....F10 91
Rządza, riv., Pol....k14 70
Rzepin, Pol....B3 70
Rzeszów, Pol....C6 70
Rzhev, Sov. Un....C10 72

S

Saa, Maramasike I.... 115
Saale, riv., Ger....B6 61
Saaler, bay, Ger....D6 62
Saalfeld, Ger....C6 61
Saalfelden, Aus....B8 66
Saar, state, Ger....E6 59, 53
Saar, riv., Ger....E6 59
Saarbrücken, Ger....D1 61
Saarburg, Ger....E6 59
Saaremaa, isl., Sov. Un....B4 72
Saarlouis, Ger....D1 61
Saavedra, Arg....B4 136
Saavedra, Chile....B2 136
Sabá, Hond....C4 130
Šabac, Yugo....C4 68
Sabadell, Sp....B7 65
Sabael, N.Y....B6 196
Sab'ah, mtn., Libya....D3 101
Sabalana, is., Indon....G5 90
Sabana, P.R....B8, f12 132
Sabana de la Mar, Dom. Rep....F9 131
Sabana Grande, P.R....C3 132
Sabana Grande, mun., P.R....C3 132
Sabana Llana, P.R....C5 132
Sabana Seca, P.R....B6 132
Sabanagrande, Hond....D4 130
Sabanalarga, Col....A3 133
Sabang, Indon....k11 90

Sabará, Braz. E2 138
Sabarmati, riv., India F4 88
Sabaskong, bay, Ont., Can. E4 150
Sabasṭiyah, Jordan f11 84
Sabattus, Maine D2 184
Sabattus, pond, Maine D2 184
Sabaudia, It. D4 67
Sabbathday, pond, Maine D5 184
Sabderat, Eth. B4 105
Sabetha, Kans. C8 181
Sabhah, Libya D2 101
Sabillasville, Md. A3 173
Sabin, Minn. D2 187
Sabina, Ohio C4 199
Sabinal, Tex. E3 206
Sabinas, Mex. B4 129
Sabinas Hidalgo, Mex. B4 129
Sabine, Tex. E6 206
Sabine, W. Va. D3 211
Sabine, co., Tex. D6 206
Sabine, par., La. C2 183
Sabine, lake, La., Tex. E2 183
Sabine, mtn., Ant. B29 120
Sabine, pass, La. E2 183
Sabine, riv., La., Tex. C2 **183**, D6 206
Sabine Pass, Tex. E6 206
Sabinópolis, Braz. E2 138
Sabinoso, N. Mex. B5 195
Sabinsville, Pa. C6 202
Sable, cape, N.S., Can. H19 143
Sable, cape, Fla. G5 174
Sable, isl., N.S., Can. H21 143
Sable Island, cape, N.S., Can. F4 151
Sable River, N.S., Can. F4 151
Sablé [-sur-Sarthe], Fr. D3 58
Sabon Birni, Nig. D6 103
Sabor, riv., Port. B2 65
Sabrina, coast, Ant. C24 120
Sabula, Iowa B7 180
Sabula, Mo. D7 189
Sabula, Pa. D4 202
Sabzawar, Afg. E11 86
Sabzevār, Iran C8 86
Sac, co., Iowa B2 180
Sac and Fox, Indian res., Iowa C5 180
Sac and Fox, Indian res., Kans., Nebr. B2 189
Sac City, Iowa B2 180
Sacaba, Bol. C2 135
Sacajawea, lake, Wash. C7 210
Sacajawea, peak, Oreg. B9 201
Sacand Fox, Indian res., Kans. E10 191
Sacandaga, lake, N.Y. B6 196
Sacaton, Ariz. D4 168
Sacavém, Port. f9 65
Sacavem, riv., Port. f9 65
Sachem Head, Conn. D6 172
Sachigo, lake, Ont., Can. C5 150
Sachigo, riv., Ont., Can. B6 150
Sachse, Tex. B6 206
Sachsen, former state, Ger. B8 61
Sachsen-Anhalt (Saxony-Anhalt), former state, Ger. B6 61
Sacile, It. D8 66
Sackets Harbor, N.Y. B4 196
Sackville, N.B., Can. D5 151
Saclay, Fr. h9 58
Saco, Ala. D4 166
Saco, Maine E2, E4 184
Saco, Mont. B9 190
Saco, riv., Maine, N.H. B4 193
Sacramento, Calif. A6, C3 170
Sacramento, Ky. C2 182
Sacramento, co., Calif. C3 170
Sacramento, mts., N. Mex. E4 195
Sacramento, riv., Calif. C3 170
Sacramento, riv., N. Mex. E4 195
Sacramento, val., Calif. C2 170
Sacre-Coeur-Saguenay, Que., Can. A8 154
Sacred Heart, Minn. F3 187
Sacrofano, It. g8 67
Sacul, Tex. D5 206
Sá da Bandeira, Ang. D1 106
Ṣad'dah, Yemen B5 105
Saddle, isl., New Hebr. 115
Saddle, mtn., Colo. C5 171
Saddle, mtn., Oreg. B3 201
Saddle, mts., Wash. C6 210
Saddle, riv., N.J. D5 194
Saddle Ball, mtn., Mass. A1 185
Saddle Brook, N.J. *A4 194
Saddle Bunch, keys, Fla. H5 174
Saddle River, N.J. *A4 194
Saddle Rock, N.Y. *G2 172
Saddleback, mtn., Ariz. F1 168
Saddleback, mtn., Maine B4 184
Saddleback, mtn., Maine D2 184
Saddlestring, Wyo. A6 213
Sadieville, Ky. B5 182
Sadiya, India C10 87
Sado, isl., Jap. G9 93
Sado, riv., Port. C1 65
Sadorus, Ill. D5 178
Sadská, Czech. n18 70
Saeby, Den. A4 62
Saegertown, Pa. C1 202
Saeki, Jap. J5 93
Saengchŏn, Kor. G3 93
Safad, Isr. B7 84
Safata, bay, W. Sam. 114
Safatulafei, W. Sam. 114
Safety Harbor, Fla. E2, E4 174
Saffell, Ark. B4 169
Safford, Ala. C2 166
Safford, Ariz. E6 168
Saffordville, Kans. D7 181
Saffron Walden, Eng. B8 56
Safi, Mor. C3 102
Safīdābeh, Iran F10 86
Safonovo, Sov. Un. D9 72
Safranbolu, Tur. B9 85
Safune, W. Sam. 114
Safune, bay, W. Sam. 114
Sag Harbor, N.Y. D4 196
Sag Sag, New Britain I. 115
Saga, Jap. J5 93
Sagadahoc, co., Maine E3 184
Sagaing, Bur. D10 87
Sagami, sea, Jap. n18 93
Sagamihara, Jap. *n18 93
Sagamore, Mass. C6 185
Sagamore, Pa. E3 202
Sagamore Hills, Ohio B2 199
Sagån, riv., Swe. t34 63
Saganaga, lake, Ont., Can., Minn. A6, B8 187
Sagaponack, N.Y. F7 172
Sagar, India F7 88
Sagara, Fiji 114
Sagara, Jap. o17 93
Sagay, Phil. *D6 90
Sage, Wyo. D2 213
Saginaw, Ala. B3 166
Saginaw, Mich. E7 186
Saginaw, Oreg. D3 201
Saginaw, Tex. B5 206
Saginaw, co., Mich. E6 186
Saginaw, bay, Mich. E7 186
Sagiz, Sov. Un. D4 73
Sagiz, riv., Sov. Un. D5 73
Sagle, Idaho A2 177
Saglek, bay, Newf., Can. f9 152
Sagola, Mich. B2 186
Sagra, mtn., Sp. D4 65
Sagua de Tánamo, Cuba E6 131
Sagua la Grande, Cuba D3 131
Saguache, Colo. C4 171
Saguache, co., Colo. C4 171
Saguache, creek, Colo. C4 171
Saguaro, nat. mon., Ariz. E4 168
Saguenay, co., Que., Can. A8 154
Saguenay, riv., Que., Can. A7 154
Saguia el Hamra (Sekia el Hamra), Sp. overseas prov., Afr. D2 102
Sagunto, Sp. C5 65
Saha, Manus I. 115
Saḥāb, Jordan C8 84
Sahagún, Col. B2 133
Sahara, des., Afr. D5 96
Saharan Atlas, mts., Alg. C5 102
Saharanpur, India C6 **87**, C6 88
Ṣahrajat al Kubrá, Eg. D3 84
Sahuaripa, Mex. B3 129
Sahuarita, Ariz. F5 168
Sahuaro, res., Ariz. G3 168
Sahuayo, Mex. m12 129
Saïda, Alg. G7 64
Saida (Sidon), Leb. F10 85
Sa'īdābād, Iran G7 86
Saidpur, Bngl. C8 87
Saigō, Jap. H6 93
Saigon, Viet. G7 89
Saikhoa Ghat, India F4 91
Sail, rock, Vir. Is. f14 132
Sailor Springs, Ill. E5 178
Saimaa, lake, Fin. G13 63
St. Abb's, head, Scot. E6 57
St. Adelphe, Que., Can. C5 154
St. Adolphe, Que., Can. D6 154
St. Affrique, Fr. F5 58
St. Agapit, Que., Can. C6 154
St. Agatha, Maine A4 184
St. Aimé, Que., Can. D5 154
St. Alban, Que., Can. C5 154
St. Alban's, Newf., Can. E4 152
St. Albans, Eng. C7 56
St. Albans, Maine D3 184
St. Albans, Vt. B2 208
St. Albans, W. Va. C3 211
St. Albans, bay, Vt. B2 208
St. Albans, head, Eng. D5 56
St. Albans Bay, Vt. B2 208
St. Albert, Alta., Can. C4 148
St. Alexandre, Que., Can. B8 154
St. Alexandre, Que., Can. D4 154
St. Alexis des Monts, Que., Can. C4 154
St. Alphonse, Que., Can. D5 154
St. Amand, Fr. D3 59
St. Amand-Mont-Rond, Fr. D5 58
St. Amant, La. B6 183
St. Amarin, Fr. B3 66
St. Ambroise, Que., Can. A6 154
St. Anaclet, Que., Can. A9 154
St. Andre, N.B., Can. *B1 151
St. Andre, cape, Malag. g8 107
St. André [de Kamouraska], Que., Can. B8 154
St. Andrews, N.B., Can. D2 151
St. Andrew's, Newf., Can. E2 152
St. Andrews, Scot. D6 57
St. Andrews, Tenn. B6 205
St. Andrew, bay, Fla. G3 174
St. Andrews, bay, Scot. D6 57
St. Andrews, sound, Ga. F5 175
St. Andrews East, Que., Can. D3 154
St. Anicet, Que., Can. D3 154
St. Ann, Mo. *A8 189
St. Anna, Wis. B6 212
St. Anne, Ill. B6 178
St. Anns, N.S., Can. C9 151
St. Ann's Bay, Jam. F5 131
St. Anselme, N.B., Can. *C5 151
St. Anselme, Que., Can. C7 154
St. Ansgar, Iowa A5 180
St. Anthony, Newf., Can. C4 152
St. Anthony, Idaho F7 177
St. Anthony, Ind. H4 179
St. Anthony, Iowa B4 180
St. Anthony, Minn. *F5 187
St. Anthony, N. Dak. C5 198
St. Antoine, Que., Can. C6, C8 154
St. Antoine, Que., Can. D5 154
St. Antoine de Kent, N.B., Can. C5 151
St. Antoine des Laurentides, Que., Can. *D3 154
St. Antonin, Que., Can. B8 154
St. Apollinaire, Que., Can. C6, D8 154
St. Arnaud, Austl. H4 112
St. Arsène, Que., Can. B8 154
St. Athanase, Que., Can. B8 154
St. Aubert, Que., Can. B7 154
St. Augustin, Que., Can. D8 154
St. Augustin, riv., Que., Can. C2 152
St. Augustin-de-Québec, Que., Can. C8 154
St. Augustin-Saguenay, Que., Can. C2 152
St. Augustine, Fla. C5, C7 174
St. Austell, Eng. D3 56
St. Avold, Fr. C7 58
St. Barbe, is., Newf., Can. C4 152
St. Barnabé-Sud, Que., Can. D5 154
St. Barnabe Nord, Que., Can. C5 154
St. Barthélémy, Que., Can. C4 154
St. Barthélemy, isl., Guad. n15 131
St. Basile, N.B., Can. B1 151
St. Basile [de Portneuf], Que., Can. C6 154
St.-Basile-le-Grand, Que., Can. *D4 154
St. Bees, head, Eng. C5 55
St. Benedict, Sask., Can. E3 155
St. Benedict, Iowa A3 180
St. Benedict, Kans. C7 181
St. Benedict, Oreg. B2 201
St. Benoît, Que., Can. D8 154
St. Benoît-Labre, Que., Can. C7 154
St. Bernard, Ala. A3 166
St. Bernard, Que., Can. C6 154
St. Bernard, La. C8, E6 183
St. Bernard, Nebr. C8 191
St. Bernard, Ohio D2 199
St. Bernard, par., La. E6 183
St. Bernice, Ind. E2 179
St. Bethlehem, Tenn. A4 205
St. Bonaventure, Que., Can. D5 154
St. Boswells, Sask., Can. G2 155
St. Brendan's, Newf., Can. D5 152
St. Bride, mtn., Alta., Can. D3 148
St. Bride's, Newf., Can. E4 152
St. Brides, bay, Wales C2 56
St. Brieuc, Fr. C2 58
St. Brieux, Sask., Can. E3 155
St. Bruno, Que., Can. *B8 154
St. Calais, Fr. D4 58
St. Calixte, Que., Can. D4 154
St. Camille, Que., Can. C7 154
St. Casimir, Que., Can. *C5 154
St. Catharine, Ky. C4 182
St. Catharine, lake, Vt. E2 208
St. Catharines, Ont., Can. D5 153
St. Catherines, isl., Ga. E5 175
St. Catherines, pt., Eng. D6 56
St. Catherines, sound, Ga. E5 175
St. Célestin, Que., Can. C5 154
St. Césaire, Que., Can. D4 154
St. Chamond, Fr. E6 58
St. Charles, Ark. C4 169
St. Charles, Idaho G7 177
St. Charles, Ill. B5, F1 178
St. Charles, Iowa C4 180
St. Charles, Ky. C2 182
St. Charles, Mich. E6 186
St. Charles, Minn. G6 187
St. Charles, Mo. A7, C7 189
St. Charles, S. Dak. D6 204
St. Charles, Va. B2 209
St. Charles, co., Mo. C7 189
St. Charles, par., La. E5 183
St. Charles, cape, Newf., Can. B4 152
St. Charles [de Bellechasse], Que., Can. C7 154
St. Chély-d'Apcher, Fr. E5 58
St. Chrysostome, Que., Can. D4 154
St. Clair, Ga. C4 175
St. Clair, Mich. F8 186
St. Clair, Minn. F5 187
St. Clair, Mo. C6 189
St. Clair, Pa. E9 202
St. Clair, co., Ala. B3 166
St. Clair, co., Ill. E3 178
St. Clair, co., Mich. F8 186
St. Clair, co., Mo. C4 189
St. Clair, lake, Ont., Can., Mich. E2 **153**, F8 186
St. Clair, riv., Ont., Can., Mich. E2 **153**, F8 186
St. Clair Shores, Mich. A8 186
St. Claire, Que., Can. C7 154
St. Clairsville, Ohio B7 199
St. Claude, Man., Can. E2 150
St. Claude, Que., Can. D6 154
St. Claude [-sur-Bienne], Fr. D6 58
St. Clément, Que., Can. B8 154
St. Cloud, Fla. D5 174
St. Cloud, Fr. g9 58
St. Cloud, Minn. E4 187
St. Cloud, Wis. B5, E5 212
St. Côme, Que., Can. C4 154
St. Constant, Que., Can. D9 154
St. Croix, N.B., Can. D2 151
St. Croix, Ind. H4 179
St. Croix, co., Wis. C1 212
St. Croix, isl., Vir. Is. n14 **131**, k17 132
St. Croix, lake, Wis. D1 212
St. Croix, riv., N.B., Can. D2 151
St. Croix, riv., Maine C5 184
St. Croix, riv., Minn., Wis. E6 187
St. Croix, stream, Maine B4 184
St. Croix Falls, Wis. C1 212
St. Cuthbert, Que., Can. C4 154
St. Cyprien, Que., Can. B8 154
St. Cyrille [de L'Islet], Que., Can. B7 154
St. Cyrille [de Wendover], Que., Can. D5 154
St. Damase, Que., Can. D4 154
St. Damase-des-Aulnaies, Que., Can. B7 154
St. Damien, Que., Can. C4 154
St. Damien, Que., Can. C7 154
St. David, Ariz. F5 168
St. David, Que., Can. C9 154
St. David, Ill. C3 178
St. David, Maine A4 184
St. David's, Newf., Can. D2 152
St. David's, Wales C2 56
St. David's, head, Wales C2 56
St. Denis, Que., Can. B8 154
St. Denis, Que., Can. D4 154
St. Denis, Fr. C5, g10 58
St. Didace, Que., Can. C4 154
St. Dié, Fr. C7 58
St. Dizier, Fr. C6 58
St. Dominique, Que., Can. D5 154
St. Dominique, Que., Can. D8 154
St. Donat-de-Montcalm, Que., Can. C3 154
St. Donatus, Iowa B7 180
St. Édouard, Que., Can. D4, E9 154
St. Edward, Nebr. C8 191
St. Eleanors, P.E.I., Can. C6 151
St. Éleuthere, Que., Can. B8 154
St. Elias, cape, Alsk. D11 167
St. Elias, mtn., Alsk. C11 167
St. Elias, mts., Alsk., Yukon, Can. C11 167
St. Elie, Fr. Gu. B4 139
St. Elizabeth, Mo. C5 189
St. Elmo, Ala. E1 166
St. Elmo, Ill. D5 178
St. Éloi, Que., Can. A8 154
St. Émile, Que., Can. D3 154
St. Ephrem, Que., Can. C7 154
St. Esprit, Que., Can. D4 154
St. Etienne, Que., Can. C9 154
St. Étienne, Que., Can. E8 154
St. Étienne, Fr. E6 58
St. Eusèbe, Que., Can. B9 154
St. Eustache, Que., Can. D4, D8 154
St. Eustache sur le Lac, Que., Can. D8 154
St. Eustatius, isl., Neth. Antilles n15 131
St. Fabien, Que., Can. A9 154
St. Félix-de-Valois, Que., Can. C4 154
St. Ferdinand, Que., Can. C6 154
St. Féréol, Que., Can. B7 154
St. Fidèle, Que., Can. B7 154
St. Fintan's, Newf., Can. D2 152
St. Flavien, Que., Can. C6 154
St. Florent [-sur-Cher], Fr. D5 58
St. Florian, Ala. A2 166
St. Flour, Fr. E5 58
St. Fortunat, Que., Can. D6 154
St. Francis, Ark. A5 169
St. Francis, Kans. C2 181
St. Francis, Maine A4 184
St. Francis, Minn. E5 187
St. Francis, S. Dak. D4 204
St. Francis, Wis. E2 212
St. Francis, co., Ark. B5 169
St. Francis, cape, Newf., Can. E5 152
St. Francis, lake, Que., Can. D6 154
St. Francis, riv., Que., Can., Maine B9 **154**, A3 184
St. Francis, riv., Que., Can. D5 154
St. Francis, riv., Mo. E7 189
St. Francisville, Ill. E6 178
St. Francisville, La. D4 183
St. Francois, Que., Can. C7 154
St. Francois, co., Mo. D7 189
St. Francois de Madawaska, N.B., Can. *B1 151
St. Francois [du-Lac], Que., Can. C5 154
St. Francois Xavier, Que., Can. D5 154
St. Frédéric, Que., Can. C7 154
St. Froid, lake, Maine B4 184
St. Gabriel, La. B5 183
St. Gabriel [-de-Brandon], Que., Can. C4 154
St. Gall, Switz. B5 66
St. Gaudens, Fr. F4 58
St. Gédéon-de-Beauce, Que., Can. D7 154
St. George, Austl. D7 112
St. George, N.B., Can. D3 151
St. George, Ont., Can. D4 153
St. George, Ga. F4 175
St. George, Kans. C7 181
St. George, Maine D3 184
St. George, Mo. *C7 189
St. George, S.C. E6 203
St. George, Utah F2 207
St. George, Va. C4 209
St. George, cape, Newf., Can. D2 152
St. George, cape, Fla. C1 174
St. George, cape, N. Gui. h13 110
St. George, cape, New Ire. I. 115
St. George, isl., Alsk. D6 167
St. George, isl., Fla. C2 174
St. George Island, Md. D5 173
St.-Georges, Bel. D5 59
St. George's, Newf., Can. D2 152
St. Georges, Que., Can. C5 154
St. Georges, Que., Can. C6 154
St. Georges, Del. A6 173
St. Georges, Fr. Gu. B5 139
St. George's, Grenada p16 131
St. Georges, bay, Newf., Can. D2 152
St. George's, chan., New Britain I. 115
St. George's, chan., Ire. E3 55
St. Georges Ouest, Que., Can. *C7 154
St. Gerard, Que., Can. D6 154
St. Germain, Que., Can. B8 154
St. Germain, forest, Fr. g9 58
St. Germain [de Grantham], Que., Can. D5 154
St. Germain-en-Laye, Fr. g9 58
St. Gervais, Que., Can. C7 154
St. Gervais-les-Bains, Fr. D2 66
St. Gilles, Bel. *D4 59
St. Gilles. Que., Can. C6 154
St. Gilles [-du-Gard], Fr. F6 58
St. Gilles [-sur-Vie], Fr. D3 58
St. Girons, Fr. F4 58
St. Gobain, Fr. C5 58
St. Gotthard, tunnel, Switz. C4 66
St. Govan's, head, Wales C3 56
St. Gregoire, Que., Can. C5 154
St. Gregor, Sask., Can. E3 155
St. Gregory, mtn., Newf., Can. D2 152
St. Guillaume, Que., Can. D5 154
St. Hedwig, Tex. *E3 206
St. Helen, lake, Mich. D6 186
St. Helena, Calif. A5, C2 170
St. Helena, Nebr. B8 191
ST. HELENA, Br. dep., Afr. H5 97
St. Helena, par., La. D5 183
St. Helena, bay, S. Afr. D2 107
St. Helena, isl., S.C. G6 203
St. Helena, sound, S.C. G7 203
St. Helens, Eng. A5 56
St. Helens, Oreg. B4 201
St. Helens, mtn., Wash. C3 210
St. Helier, Jersey F5 55
St. Henri, Que., Can. C6, C9 154
St. Henry, Ohio B3 199
St. Hermas, Que., Can. D8 154
St. Herménégilde, Que., Can. D6 154
St. Hilaire, N.B., Can. *B1 151
St. Hilaire, Que., Can. D7 154
St. Hilaire, Minn. B2 187
St. Hilaire Est, Que., Can. D4 154
St. Hilarion, Que., Can. B7 154
St. Honore, Que., Can. *A6 154
St. Honoré, Que., Can. D7 154
St. Honoré-de-Témiscouata, Que., Can. B8 154
St.-Hubert, Bel. D5 59
St. Hubert-de-Témiscouata, Que., Can. B8 154
St. Hugues, Que., Can. D5 154
St. Hyacinthe, Que., Can. D5 154
St. Hyacinthe, co., Que., Can. D4 154
St. Ignace, Mich. C6 186
St. Ignatius, Mont. C2 190
St. Ignatius Mission, Guy. B3 139
St. Inigoes, Md. D5 173
St. Irenee, Que., Can. B7 154
St. Isidore, Que., Can. E8 154
St. Isidore-d'Auckland, Que., Can. D6 154
St. Isidore-de-Prescott, Ont., Can. B10 153
St. Ives, Eng. B7 56
St. Ives, Eng. D2 56
St. Jacob, Ill. E4 178
St. Jacobs, Ont., Can. D4 153
St. Jacques, N.B., Can. *B1 151
St. Jacques, Que., Can. D4 154
St. Jacques-le-Mineur, Que., Can. E9 154
St. James, Ark. B4 169
St. James, La. C6 183
St. James, Mich. C5 186
St. James, Minn. G4 187
St. James, Mo. D6 189
St. James, N.Y. F4 172
St. James, par., La. D5 183
St. James, Nebr. B8 191
St. James, cape, B.C., Can. F6 142
St. James, is., Vir. Is. f15 132
St. James City, Fla. F4 174
St. Janvier, Que., Can. D4, D8 154
St. Jean, Que., Can. D4 154
St. Jean, co., Que., Can. D4 154
St. Jean, riv., Que., Can. A7 154
St. Jean-Baptiste, Man., Can. E3 150
St. Jean Chrysostome, Que., Can. C9 154
St. Jean-d'Angély, Fr. E3 58
St. Jean de Dieu, Que., Can. A8 154
St. Jean-de-Luz, Fr. F3 58
St. Jean de Matha, Que., Can. C4 154
St. Jean [-de-Maurienne], Fr. D2 66
St. Jean Eudes, Que., Can. *A7 154
St. Jean-Port-Joli, Que., Can. B7 154
St. Jérôme, Que., Can. D3 154
St. Jo, Tex. C4 206
St. Joachim, Que., Can. B7 154
St. Joachim, Que., Can. D5 154
St. Joe, Ark. A3 169
St. Joe, Idaho B2 177
St. Joe, Ind. B8 179
St. Joe, riv., Idaho B3 177
Saint John, N.B., Can. D3 151
St. John, Ind. B3 179
St. John, Kans. E5 181
St. John, Maine A4 184
St. John, Mo. *A8 183
St. John, N. Dak. A6 198
St. John, Utah C3 207
St. John, Wash. B8 210
St. John, co., N.B., Can. D4 151
St. John, bay, Newf., Can. C3 152
St. John, cape, Newf., Can. D4 152
St. John, isl., Newf., Can. C3 152
St. John, isl., Vir. Is. f16 132
St. John, lake, Newf., Can. D4 152
St. John, riv., Can., Maine C2 **151**, B3 184
St. John the Baptist, par., La. D5 183
St. John's, Antigua n16 131
St. Johns, Ariz. C6 168
St. John's, Newf., Can. E5 152
St. Johns, Ill. E4 178
St. Johns, Mich. F6 186
St. Johns, Ohio B3 199
St. Johns, co., Fla. C5 174
St. Johns, riv., Fla. B5 174
St. Johns River, entrance, Fla. B6 174
St. Johnsbury, Vt. *C4 208
St. Johnsbury Center, Vt. C4 208
St. Johnsville, N.Y. B6 196
St. Jones, riv., Del. B6 173
St. Joseph, N.B., Can. D5 151
St. Joseph, Dominica o16 131
St. Joseph, Ill. C5 178
St. Joseph, La. C4 183
St. Joseph, Mich. F4 186
St. Joseph, Minn. E4 187
St. Joseph, Mo. B3 189
St. Joseph, Tenn. B4 205
St. Joseph, co., Ind. A5 179
St. Joseph, co., Mich. G5 186
St. Joseph, bay, Fla. C1 174
St. Joseph, isl., Ont., Can. B7 186
St. Joseph, isl., Mich. B6 186
St. Joseph, isl., Tex. E4 206
St. Joseph, lake, Ont., Can. E8 153
St. Joseph, lake, Que., Can. C8 154
St. Joseph, pt., Fla. H3 174
St. Joseph, riv., Ind., Mich., Ohio B8 **179**, F5 **186**, A3 199
St. Joseph-de-Beauce, Que., Can. C7 154
St. Joseph de Sorel, Que., Can. *C4 154
St. Joseph-du-Lac, Que., Can. D8 154
St. Joseph's, Newf., Can. E5 152
St. Josephs, sound, Fla. E1 174
St. Jovite, Que., Can. C3 154
St. Jovite Station, Que., Can. C3 154
St. Jude, Que., Can. D5 154
St. Jude Acres, Mo. *D7 189
St. Junien, Fr. E4 58
St. Just, Eng. D2 56
St. Just-en-Chaussée, Fr. E2 59
St. Keverne, Eng. D2 56
St. Kilda, Austl. *H5 112
St. Kitts, isl., St. Kitts-Nevis n15 131
ST. KITTS-NEVIS, Br. dep., N.A. n15 131
St. Lambert, Que., Can. C6 154
St. Lambert, Que., Can. D9 154
St. Landry, La. D3 183
St. Landry, par., La. D3 183
St. Laurent, Man., Can. D3 150
St. Laurent, Que., Can. D9 154
St. Laurent, Fr. Gu. A4 139
St. Laurent-Blangy, Fr. D2 59
St. Laurent-de-la-Salanque, Fr. F5 58
St. Laurent-du-Jura, Fr. C1 66
St. Lawrence, Austl. D8 111
St. Lawrence, Newf., Can. E4 152
St. Lawrence, Pa. *F10 202
St. Lawrence, S. Dak. C7 204
St. Lawrence, co., N.Y. A6 196
St. Lawrence, cape, N.S., Can. B9 151
St. Lawrence, gulf, Can. G20 143
St. Lawrence, isl., Alsk. C5 167
St. Lawrence, riv., Ont., Que., Can., N.Y. G19 143
St. Lazare, Man., Can. D1 150
St. Lazare, Que., Can. D8 154
St. Leo, Fla. D4 174
St. Leo, Minn. F2 187
St. Léon, Que., Can. C5 154
St. Leon, Ind. F8 179
St. Léon [de Chicoutimi], Que., Can. A6 154
St. Léonard, N.B., Can. B2 151
St. Léonard, Que., Can. C6 154
St. Leonard, Md. D4 173
St. Leonard [d'Aston], Que., Can. C5 154

INDEX KEY Each place listed in **Bold-faced Type** has its population listed in the Population tables, pages 230 to 280.
Each country shown in CAPITAL LETTERS has its population listed in the World Political Information Table, pages 6 to 10.
* Does not appear on map; key shows general location.

St. Léonard [-de-Noblat], Fr. E4 58
St. Lewis, riv., Newf., Can. B3 152
St. Lewis, sound, Newf., Can. B4 152
St. Liboire, Que., Can. D5 154
St. Libory, Ill. E4 178
St. Libory, Nebr. C7 191
St. Lô, Fr. C3 58
St. Louis, P.E.I., Can. C5 151
St. Louis, Que., Can. D5 154
St. Louis, Sask., Can. E3 155
St. Louis, Mich. E6 186
St. Louis (Independent City), Mo. B8, C7 189
St. Louis, Okla. B5 200
St. Louis, Sen. C1 103
St. Louis, co., Minn. C6 187
St. Louis, co., Mo. C7 189
St. Louis, bay, Miss. E2 188
St. Louis, lake, Que., Can. D8 154
St. Louis, riv., Minn. D6 187
St. Louis-de-Gonzaque, Que., Can. E8 154
St. Louis de Kent, N.B., Can. C5 151
St. Louis-du-Ha-Ha, Que., Can. B9 154
St. Louis Park, Minn. E6 187
St. Louisville, Ohio B5 199
St. Loup-sur-Semouse, Fr. B2 66
St. Lucas, Iowa A6 180
ST. LUCIA, Br. dep., N.A. p16 131
St. Lucia, cape, S. Afr. C5 107
St. Lucia, chan., N.A. o16 131
St. Lucia, isl., N.A. p16 131
St. Lucie, Fla. E6 174
St. Lucie, co., Fla. E6 174
St. Lucie, canal, Fla E6 174
St. Lucie, inlet, Fla. E6 174
St. Ludger, Que., Can. D7 154
St. Magloire, Que., Can. C8 154
St. Magnus, bay, Scot. g10 55
St. Maixent-l'Ecole, Fr. D3 58
St. Malachie, Que., Can. C7 154
St. Malo, Fr. C2 58
St. Malo, gulf, Fr. C2 58
St. Mandé, Fr. g10 58
St. Marc, Que., Can. D4 154
St. Marc, Hai. F7 131
St.-Marc [-des-Carrières], Que., Can. C5 154
St. Marcel, Que., Can. C7 154
St. Marcellin, Fr. E6 58
St. Margaret, bay, Newf., Can. C3 152
St. Margarets, Md. B5 173
St. Margaret's Hope, Scot. B6 57
St. Maries, Idaho B2 177
St. Mark, Kans. B5 181
St. Marks, Fla. B2 174
St. Martin, Minn. *E4 187
St. Martin, Ohio *C4 199
St. Martin, par., La. D4 183
St. Martin, isl., Mich. C4 186
St. Martin, isl., Fr., Neth. Ant. m15 131
St. Martin, lake, Man., Can. D2 150
St. Martin, riv., Md. D7 173
St. Martin-Boulogne, Fr. D9 56
St. Martin [-de-Ré], Fr. D3 58
St. Martin-de-Tours, Que., Can. D7 154
St. Martin Station, Man., Can. D2, D5 150
St. Martins, N.B., Can. D4 151
St. Martinville, La. D4 183
St. Martory, Fr. F4 58
St. Mary, Ky. C4 182
St. Mary, par., La. E4 183
St. Mary, bay, N.S., Can. E3 151
St. Mary, cape, N.S., Can. E3 151
St. Mary, riv., Alta., Can. E4 148
St. Mary, riv., B.C., Can. E2 148
St. Mary-of-the-Woods, Ind. E2 179
St. Mary's, Newf., Can. E5 152
St. Marys, Ont., Can. D3 153
St. Marys, Ga. F5 175
St. Marys, Ind. A5 179
St. Marys, Kans. C7 181
St. Marys, Mo. D8 189
St. Marys, Ohio B3 199
St. Marys, Pa. D4 202
St. Marys, W. Va. B3 211
St. Marys, co., Md. D4 173
St. Mary's, bay, Newf., Can. E5 152
St. Mary's, cape, Newf., Can. E4 152
St. Marys, entrance, Fla. B5 174
St. Marys, riv., N.S., Can. D8 151
St. Marys, riv., Fla., Ga. F5 175
St. Marys, riv., Ind., Ohio B3 199
St. Marys, riv., Md. D5 173
St. Marys, riv., Mich. B6 186
St. Marys Point, Minn. *F6 187
St. Mathieu, Que., Can. A9 154
St. Mathieu, Que., Can. E9 154
St. Matthew, isl., Alsk. C5 167
St. Matthew, isl., Bur. H3 89
St. Matthews, Ky. A4, B4 182
St. Matthews, S.C. D6 203
St. Maur-des-Fossés, Fr. g10 58, F2 59
St. Maurice, Que., Can. C5 154
St. Maurice, Switz. C3 66
St. Maurice, co., Que., Can. C4 154
St. Maurice, riv., Que., Can. B4, C5 154
St. Maxime, Que., Can. C6 154
St. Meinrad, Ind. H4 179
St. Méthode, Que., Can. C6 154
St. Michael, Alsk. C7 167
St. Michael, Alta., Can. C4 148
St. Michael, Minn. E5 187
St. Michael, N. Dak. B7 198
St. Michael, Pa. *F4 202
St. Michaels, Ariz. B6 168
St. Michaels, Md. C5 173
St. Michaels, bay, Newf., Can. B4 152
St. Michel, Que., Can. C7 154
St. Michel, Que., Can. E9 154
St. Michel, Fr. E4 59
St.-Michel-de-l'Atalaye, Hai. F7 131
St. Michel [-de-Maurienne], Fr. D2 66
St. Michel des Saints, Que., Can. C4 154
St. Mihiel, Fr. C6 58
St. Modeste, Que., Can. B8 154
St. Moritz, Switz. C5 66
St. Nazaire, Que., Can. A6 154
St. Nazaire, Que., Can. C7 154
St. Nazaire, Que., Can. D5 154
St. Nazaire, Fr. D2 58
St. Nazianz, Wis. B6, D6 212
St. Neots, Eng. B7 56
St. Nerée, Que., Can. C7 154
St. Nicholas, Que., Can. C8 154
St. Nicolas-de-Port, Fr. F6 59
St. Noël, Que., Can. *B3 154
St. Norbert, Man., Can. E3 150
St. Norbert [d'Arthabaska], Que., Can. C6 154
St. Odilon, Que., Can. C7 154
St. Olaf, Iowa B6 182
St. Olof, Swe. C8 62
St. Omer, Fr. B5 58
St. Onge, S. Dak. C2 204
St.-Ouen, Fr. g10 58
St. Ours, Que., Can. D4 154
St. Pacôme, Que., Can. B8 154
St. Pamphile, Que., Can. C8 154
St. Paris, Ohio B4 199
St. Pascal, Que., Can. B8 154
St. Patrick, lake, Que., Can. A7 153
St. Paul, Ark. B2 169
St. Paul, Alta., Can. B5 148
St. Paul, Que., Can. C7 154
St. Paul, Ind. F6 179
St. Paul, Iowa *D6 180
St. Paul, Kans. E8 181
St. Paul, Minn. E7, F5 187
St. Paul, Mo. A7 189
St. Paul, Nebr. C7 191
St. Paul, Oreg. B1 201
St. Paul, S.C. D7 203
St. Paul, Va. B2 209
St. Paul, isl., Alsk. D5 167
St. Paul, isl., N.S., Can. B9 151
St. Paul, riv., Newf., Que., Can. C3 152
St. Paul, riv., Lib. E3 103
St. Paul-de-la-Croix, Que., Can. B8 154
St. Paul-du-Nord, Que., Can. A8 154
St. Paul Park, Minn. F6, F7 187
St. Paulin, Que., Can. C4 154
St. Pauls, N.C. C5 197
St. Peter, Ill. E5 178
St. Peter, Kans. C3 181
St. Peter, Minn. F5 187
St. Peter, Mont. C5 190
St. Peter Port, Guernsey F5 55
St. Peters, N.S., Can. D9 151
St. Peters, Ind. F7 179
St. Peters, Mo. A7, C7 189
St. Peters Bay, P.E.I., Can. C7 151
St. Petersburg, Fla. E2, E4 174
St. Petersburg, Pa. D2 202
St. Petersburg Beach, Fla. F1 174
St. Philemon, Que., Can. C7 154
St. Philip, Ind. I2 179
St. Philip and St. James, bay, Espiritu Santo I. 115
St. Philippe, Que., Can. D4, D9 154
St. Philippe-de-Néri, Que., Can. B8 154
St. Phillips, Mont. D12 190
St. Phillips, isl., S.C. G6 203
St. Pie, Que., Can. D5 154
St. Pierre, Que., Can. C7 154
St. Pierre, Mart. o16 131
St. Pierre, St. Pierre and Miquelon E3 152
St. Pierre, isl., St. Pierre and Miquelon E3 152
St. Pierre-Jolys, Man., Can. C5 154
ST. PIERRE AND MIQUELON, Fr. dep., N.A. E3 152
St. Pierre-d'Albigny, Fr. D2 66
St. Pierre-en-Port, Fr. E8 56
St. Pierre-Jolys, Man., Can. E3 150
St. Pierre [les Becquets], Que., Can. C5 154
St. Pius, N. Dak. C3 198
St. Placide, Que., Can. D7 154
St. Pol [-de-Léon], Fr. C2 58
St. Pol-sur-Mer, Fr. C2 59
St. Pol [-sur-Ternoise], Fr. B5 58
St. Pourçain [-sur-Sioule], Fr. D5 58
St. Prime, Que., Can. A5 154
St. Prosper, Que., Can. C5 154
St. Prosper-de-Dorchester, Que., Can. C7 154
St. Quentin, N.B., Can. B2 151
St. Quentin, Fr. C5 58, E3 59
St. Raphaël, Que., Can. C7 154
St. Raphaël, Fr. F7 58
St. Raymond, Que., Can. C6 154
St. Redempteur, Que., Can. C9 154
St. Rédempteur, Que., Can. D3 154
St. Regis, Mont. C1 190
St. Regis, riv., N.Y. A2 196
St. Regis Falls, N.Y. A2 196
St. Regis Park, Ky. *C4 182
St. Rémi, Que., Can. D4, E9 154
St. Remi, Que., Can. D6 154
St. Rémi-d'Amherst, Que., Can. C3 154
St. Robert, Mo. *D5 189
St. Roch, Que., Can. D4 154
St. Roch-des-Aulnaies, Que., Can. B7 154
St. Romuald, Que., Can. C6, C9 154
St. Rose, La. C7 183
St. Samuel, Que., Can. D7 154
St. Sauveur-des-Monts, Que., Can. D3 154
St. Sébastien-de-Beauce, Que., Can. D7 154
St. Sebastien, cape, Malag. f9 107
St. Servan [-sur-Mer], Fr. C3 58
St. Sever, Fr. F3 58
St. Sévérin, Que., Can. C6 154
St. Shotts, Newf., Can. E5 152
St. Siméon, Que., Can. B8 154
St. Siméon, Fr. F3 59
St. Simon-de-Rimouski, Que., Can. A8 154
St. Simons, isl., Ga. E5 175
St. Simons, sound, Ga. E5 175
St. Simons Island, Ga. E5 175
St. Sixte, Que., Can. D2 154
St. Stephen, N.B., Can. D2 151
St. Stephen, S.C. E8 203
St. Stephen, Wyo. C4 213
St. Stephens, Ala. D1 166
St. Stephens, Minn. *E4 187
St. Sylvestre, Que., Can. C6 154
St. Tammany, La. B8, D6 183
St. Tammany, par., La. D5 183
St. Theodore, Que., Can. C4 154
St. Théophile, Que., Can. D7 154
St. Thomas, Ont., Can. E3 153
St. Thomas, Que., Can. C4 154
St. Thomas, Mo. C5 189
St. Thomas, N. Dak. A8 198
St. Thomas, Pa. G6 202
St. Thomas, isl., Vir. Is. f15 132
St. Timothee, Que., Can. E8 154
St. Tite, Que., Can. C5 154
St. Tite-des-Caps, Que., Can. B7 154
St. Tropez, Fr. F7 58
St. Ubald, Que., Can. C5 154
St. Ulric, Que., Can. *A2 154
St. Urbain, Que., Can. E8 154
St. Urbain-de-Charlevoix, Que., Can. B7 154
St. Valère, Que., Can. C5 154
St. Valerien, Que., Can. D5 154
St. Valéry-en-Caux, Fr. E8 56
St. Valéry-sur-Somme, Fr. B4 58
St. Vallier, Que., Can. C7 154
St. Vallier, Fr. E6 58
St. Victor [de Beauce], Que., Can. C7 154
St. Vincent, Minn. B1 187
ST. VINCENT, Br. dep., N.A. p16 131
St. Vincent, cape, Malag. h8 107
St. Vincent, cape, Port. D1 65
St. Vincent, gulf, Austl. G2 112
St. Vincent, isl., Fla. C1 174
St. Vincent, isl., N.A. p16 131
St. Vincent, pass, N. Cal. 115
St. Vincent, passage, N.A. p16 131
St. Vincent's, Newf., Can. E5 152
St.-Vith, Bel. D6 59
St. Vrain, N. Mex. C6 195
St. Walburg, Sask., Can. D1 155
St. Wendells, Ind. H2 179
St. Williams, Ont., Can. E4 153
St. Xavier, Mont. E9 190
St. Yrieix-la-Perche, Fr. E4 58
St. Zacharie, Que., Can. C7 154
Ste. Agathe, Man., Can. E3 150
Ste. Agathe, Que., Can. C6 154
Ste. Agathe-des-Monts, Que., Can. C3 154
Ste. Agnes-de-Dundee, Que., Can. D3 154
Ste. Anne, Que., Can. D4 154
Ste. Anne, Guad. n16 131
Ste. Anne, riv., Que., Can. C6 154
Ste. Anne-de-Beaupré, Que., Can. B7 154
Ste. Anne [de Bellevue], Que., Can. D8 154
Ste. Anne-de-la-Pérade, Que., Can. C5 154
Ste Anne-de-Madawaska, N.B., Can. B2 151
Ste. Anne des Chenes, Man., Can. E3 150
Ste.-Anne-des-Monts, Que., Can. *B3 154
Ste. Apolline-de-Patton, Que., Can. C7 154
Ste. Barbe, Que., Can. D3 154
Ste. Beatrix, Que., Can. C4 154
Ste. Blandine, Que., Can. A9 154
Ste. Brigide, Que., Can. D4 154
Ste. Brigitte, Que., Can. C5 154
Ste. Catherine, Que., Can. C6, C8 154
Ste. Cécile, Que., Can. D7 154
Ste. Clothilde, Que., Can. D5 154
Ste. Croix, Que., Can. C6, D8 154
Ste. Croix, Switz. C2 66
Ste. Edwige, Que., Can. D6 154
Ste. Élizabeth, Que., Can. C4 154
Ste. Émelie, Que., Can. C4 154
Ste. Eulalie, Que., Can. C5 154
Ste. Euphémie, Que., Can. C7 154
Ste. Famille, Que., Can. C7 154
Ste. Famille d'Aumond, Que., Can. C2 154
Ste. Felicite, Que., Can. *A2 154
Ste. Flore, Que., Can. C5 154
Ste. Foy Que., Can. C9 154
Ste. Foy-la-Grande, Fr. E4 58
Ste. Francoise, Que., Can. A8 154
Ste. Genevieve, Que., Can. C5 154
Ste. Genevieve, Mo. D7 189
Ste. Genevieve, co., Mo. D7 189
Ste. Germaine-Station, Que., Can. C7 154
Ste. Gertrude, Que., Can. C5 154
Ste. Helène, Que., Can. B8 154
Ste. Henédine, Que., Can. C7 154
Ste. Julienne, Que., Can. D4 154
Ste. Justine, Que., Can. D3 154
Ste. Louise, Que., Can. B7 154
Ste. Lucie, Que., Can. C7 154
Ste. Madeleine, Que., Can. D4 154
Ste. Marguerite, Que., Can. C7 154
Ste. Marguerite, Que., Can. D3 154
Ste. Marguerite, riv., Que., Can. A7 154
Ste. Marguerite-Nord-Est, riv., Que., Can A7 154
Ste. Marie, Que., Can. C5 154
Ste. Marie, Ill. E5 178
Ste. Marie, cape, Malag. i8 107
Ste. Marie, isl., Malag. g9 107
Ste. Marie-aux-Mines, Fr. A3 66
Ste. Marie-de-Beauce, Que., Can. C6 154
Ste. Marie-sur-Me, N.B., Can. B5 151
Ste. Martine, Que., Can. D4, E8 154
Ste. Mélanie, Que., Can. C4 154
Ste. Menehould, Fr. C6 58
Ste. Monique, Que., Can. C5 154
Ste. Perpétue, Que., Can. C5 154
Ste. Perpétue-de-L'Islet, Que., Can. B8 154
Ste. Petronille, Que., Can. C9 154
Ste. Philomène, Que., Can. D4, E8 154
Ste. Rosalie, Que., Can. *D5 154
Ste. Rose, Que., Can. D4 154
Ste. Rose, Guad. n16 131
Ste. Rose-du-Dégelé, Que., Can. B9 154
Ste. Rose du Lac, Man., Can. D2 150
Ste. Sabine, Que., Can. C7 154
Ste. Savine, Fr. C6 58
Ste. Scholastique, Que., Can. D3, D8 154
Ste. Sophie, Que., Can. C5 154
Ste. Sophie, Que., Can. D4 154
Ste. Thècle, Que., Can. C5 154
Ste. Thérèse, Que., Can. D4 154
Ste. Thèrèse-Ouest, Que., Can. *D4 154
Ste. Thérèse-de-Blainville, Que., Can. D8 154
Ste. Veronique, Que., Can. C3 154
Saintes, Fr. E3 58
Saintonge, former prov., Fr. E3 58
Saipan, chan., Saipan 114
Saipan, isl., Mariana Is. 114
Sa'ir, Jordan C7 84
Saiyidabad, Afg. D14 86
Sajama, mtn., Bol. C2 135
Saka, China C10 88
Saka, Ken. B6 106
Sakai, Jap. o14 93
Sakaide, Jap. *I6 93
Sakākā, Sau. Ar. H13 85
Sakakawea, lake, N. Dak. B3 198
Sakania, Zaire D4 106
Sakar, isl., Bis., Arch 115
Sakaraha, Malag. h8 107
Sakarya, riv., Tur. B8 85
Sakashita, Jap. n16 93
Sakata, Jap. G9 93
Sakchu, Kor. F2 93
Sakhalin: after World War II 83
Sakhalin, isl., Sov. Un. D17 71
Šakiai, Sov. Un. A7 70
Sakimotobu, Okinawa 114
Sakishima, is., Ryukyu Is. G9 91
Sakon Nakhon, Thai. D5 89
Sakonnet, R.I. D12 172
Sakonnet, riv., R.I. D12 172
Sak'ot'ā, Eth. C4 105
Sakripe, Lib. E3 103
Sakskōbing, Den. D5 62
Sakti, China A9 88
Sakti, India F9 88
Sal, pt., Calif. E3 170
Sal, riv., Sov. Un. D2 73
Sala, Swe. H7, t34 63
Sala Consilina, It. D5 67
Sala-y-Gomez, isl., Pac. O. H16 113
Saladas, Arg. E4 135
Saladillo, Arg. B5 136
Salado, riv., Arg. A3 136
Salado, riv., Arg. B5 136
Salado, riv., Arg. C3 136
Salado, riv., Arg. E3 135
Salado, riv., Mex. B4 129
Salaga, Ghana E4 103
Salajar, isl., Indon. G6 90
Salamá, Guat. C4 130
Salamá, Hond. C4 130
Salamanca, Chile A2 136
Salamanca, Mex. m13 129
Salamanca, N.Y. C2 196
Salamanca, Sp. B3 65
Salamat, riv., Chad C3 104
Salamaua, N. Gui. k12 111
Salamina, Col. B2 133
Salamís, Grc. D4, h11 69
Salamís, isl., Grc. h10 69
Salamonia, Ind. D8 179
Salamonie, res., Ind. C6 179
Salamonie, riv., Ind. C7 179
Salas, Sp. A2 65
Salatiga, Indon. *G4 90
Salavat, Sov. Un. *D8 71
Salaverry, Peru C2 134
Salavina, Arg. E3 135
Salawati, isl., Indon. F8 90
Salcedo, Ec. B2 134
Saldanha, S. Afr. D2 107
Saldus, Sov. Un. C4 72
Sale, Austl. I6 112
Sale, Eng. *A5 56
Salé, Mor. C3 102
Sale City, Ga. E2 175
Sale Creek, Tenn. D8 205
Salealua, bay, W. Sam. 114
Salekhard, Sov. Un. C9 71
Salem, Ala. C4 166
Salem, Ark. A4 169
Salem, Conn. D7 172
Salem, Fla. C3 174
Salem, Ill. E5 178
Salem, India F6 87
Salem, Ind. G5 179
Salem, Iowa D6 180
Salem, Ky. A3 182
Salem, Maine D2 184
Salem, Mass. A6, C3 185
Salem, Mich. A7 186
Salem, Mo. D6 189
Salem, Nebr. D10 191
Salem, N.H. E4 193
Salem, N.J. D2 194
Salem, N. Mex. E2 195
Salem, N.Y. B7 196
Salem, Ohio B7 199
Salem, Oreg. C1, C4 201
Salem, S.C. B2 203
Salem, S. Dak. D8 204
Salem, Utah C4 207
Salem (Independent City), Va. D2 209
Salem, W. Va. B4, B6 211
Salem, Wis. F1 212
Salem, co., N.J. D2 194
Salem, creek, Ohio A1 211
Salem, fork, W. Va. B6 211
Salem, pond, Vt. B4 208
Salem, riv., N.J. D2 194
Salem Depot, N.H. *E4 193
Salem Heights, Oreg. *C4 201
Salemburg, N.C. B5 197
Salemi, It. F4 67
Salen, Scot. D3 57
Salerno, Fla. E6 174
Salerno, It. D5 67
Salerno, gulf, It. D5 67
Sales, pt., Eng. C8 56
Salesville, Ohio *C6 199
Salfit, Jordan B7, g11 84
Salford, Eng. A5 56
Salgótarján, Hung. A4 68
Salgueiro, Braz. C3 138
Salida, Calif. *D3 170
Salida, Colo. C5 171
Salies-de-Béarn, Fr. F3 58
Salihli, Tur. C7 69
Salima, Malawi D5 106
Salin, Bur. B1 89
Salina, Kans. D6 181
Salina, Okla. A6 200
Salina, Utah E4 207
Salina, isl., It. E5 67
Salina Cruz, Mex. D5 129
Salina Springs, Ariz. A6 168
Salinas, Braz. E2 138
Salinas, Calif. C6, D3 170
Salinas, Ec. B1 134
Salinas, P.R. D5 132
Salinas, mun., P.R. C5 132
Salinas, bay, P.R. D2 132
Salinas, cape, Sp. C7 65
Salinas, pampa, Arg. A3 136
Salinas, peak, N. Mex. D3 195
Salinas, pt., Ang. D1 106
Salinas, pt., Peru D2 134
Salinas, pt., P.R. B6 132
Salinas, riv., Calif. D3 170
Salinas de Garcí Mendoza, Bol. C2 135
Salinas Grandes, salt flat, Arg. E3 135
Saline, La. B3 183
Saline, Mich. F7 186
Saline, co., Ark. C3 169
Saline, co., Ill. F5 178
Saline, co., Kans. D6 181
Saline, co., Mo. B4 189
Saline, co., Nebr. D8 191
Saline, bayou, La. B3 183
Saline, riv., Ark. C1 169
Saline, riv., Ark. D3 169
Saline, riv., Ill. F5 178
Saline, riv., Kans. C4 181
Salineno, Tex. F3 206
Salineville, Ohio B7 199
Salinópolis, Braz. B1 138
Salins-les-Bains, Fr. D6 58
Salisbury, N.B., Can. C4 151
Salisbury, Conn. B3 172
Salisbury, Eng. C6 56
Salisbury, Md. D6 173
Salisbury, Mass. A6 185
Salisbury, Mo. B5 189
Salisbury, N.H. D3 193
Salisbury, N.C. B3 197
Salisbury, Pa. G3 202
Salisbury, Rh. A5 107
Salisbury, Vt. D2 208
Salisbury, isl., N.W. Ter., Can. D17 143
Salisbury, plain, Eng. C6 56
Salisbury Beach, Mass. A6 185
Salisbury Center, N.Y. B6 196
Salisbury West, N.C. *B3 197
Salix, Iowa B1 180
Salkehatchie, riv., S.C. E5 203
Salkum, Wash. C3 210
Salladasburg, Pa. D7 202
Sallanches, Fr. D2 66
Salley, S.C. D5 203
Salliqueló, Arg. B4 136
Sallis, Miss. B4 188
Sallisaw, Okla. B7 200
Salm, isl., Sov. Un. B9 118
Salmo, B.C., Can. E9 149
Salmon, Idaho D5 177
Salmon, mtn., N.H. A2 193
Salmon, mts., Calif. B2 170
Salmon, peak, Tex. E2 206
Salmon, res., N.Y. B5 196
Salmon, riv., B.C., Can. B6 149
Salmon, riv., N.B., Can. B2 151
Salmon, riv., Idaho D3 177
Salmon, riv., N.Y. A3 196
Salmon Arm, B.C., Can. D8 149
Salmon Bay, Que., Can. C3, h10 152
Salmon Creek, Wash. D3 210
Salmon Falls, N.H. D5 193
Salmon Falls, creek, Nev. B7 192
Salmon Falls, riv., Idaho G4 177
Salmon Falls, riv., N.H., Maine D5 193
Salmon Valley, B.C., Can. D8 149
Salmon Gums, Austl. F3 111
Salmon River, mts., Idaho D3 177
Salo, Fin. G10 63
Salo, It. D6 66
Salol, Minn. B3 187
Salome, Ariz. D2 168
Salon, riv., Fr. B1 66
Salon-de-Provence, Fr. F6 58
Salonika (Thessaloníki), Grc. B4 69
Salonika, gulf, Grc. B4 69
Salonta, Rom. B5 68
Salpi, lake, It. D6 67
Salsacate, Arg. A3 136
Salsette, isl., India H4 88
Salsk, Sov. Un. D2 73
Salsomaggiore, It. B2 67
Salt, basin, Tex. E2 206
Salt, creek, Ind. G5 179
Salt, creek, Kans. A3 181
Salt, creek, Nebr. E2 191
Salt, creek, Ohio C5 199
Salt, creek, Wyo. B6 213
Salt, fork, Okla. A3 200
Salt, fork, Okla. C2 200
Salt, isl., Vir. Is. f16 132
Salt, lake, Austl. D1 110
Salt, lake, Sask., Can. D5 155
Salt, lake, Haw. g10 176
Salt, lake, N. Mex. E5 195
Salt, marsh, Kans. D5 181
Salt, pt., Calif. C2 170
Salt, riv., Ariz. D4 168
Salt, riv., Ky. C4 182
Salt, riv., Mo. A5 189
Salt Cay, isl., Turks & Caicos Is. f14 132
Salt Fork, Okla. A4 200
Salt Fork, creek, Kans. E4 181
Salt Fork of Arkansas, riv., Okla. A4 200
Salt Lake, co., Utah C4 207
Salt Lake City, Utah C4 207
Salt Lick, Ky. B6 182
Salt Peter, cave, Ga. B2 175
Salt River, Ky. C4 182
Salt River, Indian res., Ariz. G2 168
Salt River, mts., Ariz. G2 168
Salt River, range, Wyo. C2 213
Salt-Spring, isl., B.C., Can. E6 149
Salt Springs, Fla. C5 174
Salt Wells, Nev. D3 192
Salta, Arg. D2 135
Salta, prov., Arg. D2 135
Saltash, Eng. D3 56
Saltburn-by-the-Sea, Eng. F8 57
Saltcoats, Sask., Can. F4 155
Saltcoats, Scot. E4 57
Salter Path, N.C. C7 197
Salters, S.C. D8 203
Saltese, Mont. C1 190
Saltfjord, fjord, Nor. D6 63
Saltholm, isl., Den. C6 62
Saltillo, Ind. G5 179
Saltillo Mex. B4 129
Saltillo, Miss. A5 188
Saltillo, Pa. F5 202

INDEX KEY Each place listed in **Bold-faced Type** has its population listed in the Population tables, pages 230 to 280.
Each country, shown in CAPITAL LETTERS, has its population listed in the World Political Information Table, pages 6 to 10.
* Does not appear on map; key shows general location.

Saltillo, Tenn.....B3 205
Salto, Braz.....m8 137
Salto, Ur.....E1 137
Salto Grande, Braz.....C2 137
Salton, sea, Calif.....F6 170
Saltonstall, lake, Conn.....D5 172
Saltpond, Ghana.....E4 103
Saltrou, Hai.....F7 131
Saltsburg, Pa.....F3 202
Saltsjöbaden, Swe.....t36 63
Saltville, Va.....B3 209
Saluafata, hbr., W. Sam..... 114
Salud, Pan.....k10 130
Saluda, N.C.....D4 197
Saluda, S.C.....C4 203
Saluda, Va.....D6 209
Saluda, co., S.C.....C4 203
Saluda, dam, S.C.....C4 203
Saluda, riv., S.C.....C3 203
Salur, India.....H9 88
Saluvia, Pa.....F5 202
Saluzzo, It.....B1 67
Salvador, Braz.....D3 138
Salvador, Sask., Can.....E1 155
Salvador, El, see El Salvador, country, N.A.
Salvador, lake, La.....E5 183
Salvage, Newf., Can.....D5 152
Salvage, is., Port.....m14 65
Salvatierra, Mex.....m13 129
Salvisa, Ky.....C5 182
Salween, riv., Bur.....D10 87
Salyany, Sov. Un.....F3 73
Salyersville, Ky.....C6 182
Salym, marsh, Sov. Un.....B8 73
Salzach, riv., Aus., Ger.....A8 66
Salzburg, Aus.....E6 60, B9 66
Salzburg, state, Aus.....B8 66
Salzgitter, Ger.....A5 61
Salzwedel, Ger.....B5 60
Sam Neua, Laos.....B5 89
Sam Rayburn, res., Tex.....D5 206
Sama, China.....C8 89
Sama, Sp.....A3 65
Samaipata, Bol.....C3 135
Samalá, riv., Guat.....C2 130
Samālūt, Eg.....D6 101
Samaná, Dom. Rep.....F9 131
Samaná, bay, Dom. Rep.....F9 131
Samana, isl., Ba. Is.....D7 131
Samaniego, Col.....C2 133
Samannūd, Eg.....D3 84
Samar, isl., Phil.....C7 90
Samara, riv., Sov. Un.....C4 73
Samarai, Pap.....m13 111
Samarga, Sov. Un.....C9 93
Samaria, Idaho.....G6 177
Samarinda, Indon.....F5 90
Samarkand, Sov. Un.....F9 71
Samarra, Iraq.....D2 86
Samata, W. Sam..... 114
Sambalpur, India.....G9 88
Sambar, cape, Indon.....F4 90
Sambas, Indon.....E3 90
Sambava, Malag.....f10 107
Sambhal, India.....C7 88
Sambhar, India.....C5 88
Sambonifacio, It.....D7 66
Sambor, Sov. Un.....G4 72
Samborombón, bay, Arg.....B5 136
Sambre, riv., Bel.....D4 59
Samburg, Tenn.....A2 205
Samchŏnpo, Kor.....*I4 93
Same, Tan.....B6 106
Samedan, Switz.....C5 66
Samit, Camb.....G5 89
Sammamish, lake, Wash.....D2 210
Samnorwood, Tex.....B2 206
Samnū, Libya.....D2 101
Samo, New Ire. I..... 115
Samoa, Calif.....B1 170
Samoa, American, see American Samoa, U.S. dep., Oceania
Samokov, Bul.....D6 68
Sámos, isl., Grc.....D6 69
Samoset, Fla.....F2 174
Samosir, isl., Indon.....K3 89
Samothráki, isl., Grc.....B5 69
Sampacho, Arg.....A4 136
Sampit, Indon.....F4 90
Sampson, co., N.C.....B5 197
Sampwe, Zaire.....C4 106
Samrong, Camb.....E5 89
Samsö, isl., Den.....C4 62
Samsö Belt, strait, Den.....C4 62
Samson, Ala.....D3 166
Samsun, Tur.....B11 85
Samtown, La.....*C3 183
Samtredia, Sov. Un.....A14 85
Samū', Jordan.....C7 84
Samui, isl., Thai.....H4 89
Samut Sakhon, Thai.....F4 89
Samwari, Pak.....C1 88
San, Mali.....D4 103
San, riv., Camb.....F7 89
San, riv., Pol.....C7 70
San Acacia, N. Mex.....C3 195
San Acacio, Colo.....D5 171
San Agustín, Arg.....A3 136
San Agustín, Col.....C2 133
San Agustín, cape, Phil.....D7 90
San Alessandro, see Kita-iwo, isl., Kazan-retto Is.
San Ambrosio, isl., Pac. O.....H17 113
San Andreas, Calif.....C3 170
San Andrés, Col.....D7 130
San Andrés, isl., Col.....D7 130
San Andres, mts., N. Mex.....E3 195
San Andres, peak, N. Mex.....E3 195
San Andrés de Giles, Arg.....g7 136
San Andrés Tetepilco, Mex.....h9 129
San Andrés [Totoltepec], Mex.....h9 129
San Andrés Tuxtla, Mex.....D5 129
San Angelo, Tex.....D2 206
San Anselmo, Calif.....B5 170
San Antonio, Arg.....D2 135
San Antonio, Chile.....A2 136
San Antonio, Chile.....E1 135
San Antonio, Fla.....D4 174
San Antonio, N. Mex.....D3 195
San Antonio, Phil.....o13 90
San Antonio, P.R.....A2 132
San Antonio, Tex.....B3, E3 206
San Antonio, bay, Tex.....E4 206
San Antonio, cape, Arg.....B5 136
San Antonio, cape, Cuba.....E1 131
San Antonio, peak, Calif.....F3 170
San Antonio, riv., Tex.....B4 206
San Antonio Abad, Sp.....C6 65
San Antonio de Areco, Arg.....g7 136
San Antonio de los Baños, Cuba.....D2 131
San Antonio de los Cobres, Arg.....D2 135
San Antonio Oeste, Arg.....C4 136
San Antonito, N. Mex.....G5 195
San Ardo, Calif.....D3 170
San Augustine, Tex.....D5 206
San Augustine, co., Tex.....D5 206
San Augustino, see Minami-iwo, isl., Kazan-retto, Is.
San Bartolomeo [in Galdo], It.....D5 67
San Benedetto del Tronto, It.....C4 67
San Benito, Tex.....F4 206
San Benito, co., Calif.....D3 170
San Benito, mtn., Calif.....D3 170
San Benito, riv., Calif.....C6 170
San Bernardino, Calif.....E5, F3 170
San Bernardino, co., Calif. E5 170
San Bernardino, mts., Calif.....F3 170
San Bernardino, riv., Mex.....G6 168
San Bernardo, Chile.....A2 136
San Blas, Mex.....m11 129
San Blas, cape, Fla.....H3 174
San Blas, mts., Pan.....F8 130
San Blas, riv., Guat.....B2 130
San Borja, Bol.....B2 135
San Borja, riv., Mex.....h9 129
San Bruno, Calif.....B5, D2 170
San Candido, It.....C8 66
San Carlos, Arg.....A3 136
San Carlos, Ariz.....D5 168
San Carlos, Calif.....B5 170
San Carlos, Chile.....B2 136
San Carlos, Mex.....B4 129
San Carlos, Nic.....E5 130
San Carlos, Phil.....C6 90
San Carlos, Phil.....o13 90
San Carlos, Ur.....E2 137
San Carlos, Ven.....C4 133
San Carlos, Ven.....B4 133
San Carlos, Indian res., Ariz.....D5 168
San Carlos, res., Ariz.....D5 168
San Carlos [de Bariloche], Arg.....C2 136
San Carlos [del Zulia], Ven.....B3 133
San Cataldo, It.....F4 67
San Clemente, Calif.....F5 170
San Clemente, Sp.....C4 65
San Clemente, isl., Calif.....F4 170
San Cristóbal, Arg.....A4 136
San Cristóbal, Dom. Rep.....F8 131
San Cristóbal, N. Mex.....A4 195
San Cristóbal, Pan.....F7 130
San Cristóbal, Ven.....B3 133
San Cristóbal, isl., Sol. Is.....G9 113
San Cristóbal (Chatham), isl., Ec.....g6 134
San Daniele del Friuli, It.....C9 66
San Diego, Calif.....E2, F5 170
San Diego, Tex.....F3 206
San Diego, co., Calif.....F5 170
San Diego, cape, Arg.....h12 136
San Diego, riv., Calif.....E2 170
San Dimas, Calif.....*F5 170
San Dimas, Mex.....C3 129
San Donà di Piave, It.....B4 67
San Elizario, Tex.....F1 206
San Enrique, Arg.....B4 136
San Estanislao, Par.....D4 135
San Esteban, Hond.....C5 130
San Fabian, Phil.....n13 90
San Felice sul Panaro, It.....E7 66
San Felipe, Chile.....A2 136
San Felipe, N. Mex.....B3, G5 195
San Felipe, Tex.....*E4 206
San Felipe, Ven.....A4 133
San Felipe, Indian res., N. Mex.....G5 195
San Felipe, pt., Mex.....A2 129
San Feliu de Guixols, Sp.....B7 65
San Felix, isl., Pac. O.....H17 113
San Fernando, Arg.....A5, g7 136
San Fernando, Calif.....F2 170
San Fernando, Chile.....A2 136
San Fernando, Mex.....C5 129
San Fernando, Phil.....o13 90
San Fernando, Phil.....B6, n13 90
San Fernando, Sp.....D2 65
San Fernando, Trin.....A5 133
San Fernando de Apure, Ven.....B4 133
San Fernando de Atabapo, Ven.....C4 133
San Fernando de Henares, Sp.....p17 65
San Fidel, N. Mex.....B2 195
San Francisco, Arg.....A4 136
San Francisco, Calif.....B5, D2 170
San Francisco, Col.....C2 133
San Francisco, Sal.....D3 130
San Francisco, co., Calif.....D2 170
San Francisco, bay, Calif.....B5 170
San Francisco, cape, Ec.....A1 134
San Francisco, mts., Ariz.....B4 168
San Francisco, pass, Arg.....E2 135
San Francisco, riv., Arg.....D2 135
San Francisco, riv., N. Mex.....D1 195
San Francisco Central, P.R.....D3 132
San Francisco de Borja, Mex.....B3 129
San Francisco de Macorís, Dom. Rep.....F8 131
San Francisco del Oro, Mex.....B3 129
San Francisco del Rincón, Mex.....m13 129
San Gabriel, Calif.....F2 170
San Gabriel, Ec.....A2 134
San Gabriel, mts., Calif.....F2 170
San Gabriel, pt., Mex.....B2 129
San Gabriel Chilac, Mex.....D5, n15 129
San Germán, P.R.....C2 132
San Germán, mun., P.R.....C2 132
San Gil, Col.....B3 133
San Gimignano, It.....C3 67
San Giovanni in Fiore, It.....E6 67
San Giovanni in Persiceto, It.....E7 66
San Gorgonio, mtn., Calif.....E5 170
San Gregorio, Calif.....C5 170
San Gregorio Atlapulco, Mex.....h9 129
San Ignacio, Bol.....B2 135
San Ignacio, Bol.....C3 135
San Ignacio, Mex.....B2 129
San Ignacio, Par.....E4 135
San Ildefonso, N. Mex.....B3, F6 195
San Ildefonso, Sp.....B3 65
San Ildefonso, cape, Phil.....n14 90
San Ildefonso, Indian res., N. Mex.....F6 195
San Ildefonso, pen., Phil.....B6, n14 90
San Isidro, Arg.....g7 136
San Jacinto, Calif.....F4, F5 170
San Jacinto, Nev.....B7 192
San Jacinto, co., Tex.....D5 206
San Jacinto, peak, Calif.....F5 170
San Jacinto, riv., Tex.....F5 206
San Jaime, Arg.....A5 136
San Javier, Arg.....A5 136
San Javier, Bol.....C3 135
San Javier, Chile.....B2 136
San Javier, riv., Arg.....E4 135, A4 136
San Jerónimo [Aculco Lldice], Mex.....h9 129
San Jeronimo, mts., Col.....B2 133
San Joaquin, Calif.....*D3 170
San Joaquin, Par.....D4 135
San Joaquin, co., Calif.....C3 170
San Joaquin, riv., Calif.....D3 170
San Joaquin, val., Calif.....D3 170
San Jon, N. Mex.....B6 195
San Jorge, isl., Sol. Is..... 115
San Jose, Ariz.....E6 168
San José, Bol.....C3 135
San Jose, Br. Hond.....B3 130
San Jose, Calif.....C6, D3 170
San José, C.R.....F5 130
San José, Guat.....D2 130
San Jose, Ill.....C4 178
San Jose, N. Mex.....B4 195
San Jose, Phil.....o13 90
San Jose, Phil.....o13 90
San Jose, Phil.....C6 90
San José, Ur.....E1 137
San José, isl., Mex.....B2 129
San Jose, riv., B.C., Can.....D7 149
San Jose, riv., Ur.....g8 136
San José Boquerón, Arg.....E3 135
San José de Feliciano, Arg.....A5 136
San José de los Molinos, Peru.....D2 134
San José del Cabo, Mex.....C3 129
San José del Guaviare, Col.....C3 133
San Jose [del Monte], Phil.....o13 90
San Juan, Arg.....A3 136
San Juan, Colo.....D6 171
San Juan, Dom. Rep.....F8 131
San Juan, N. Mex.....E2 195
San Juan, Pan.....k11 130
San Juan, Phil.....p13 90
San Juan, Phil.....n13 90
San Juan, P.R.....B6 132
San Juan, Tex.....F3 206
San Juan, Ven.....A4 133
San Juan, co., Colo.....D3 171
San Juan, co., N. Mex.....A1 195
San Juan, co., Utah.....F5 207
San Juan, co., Wash.....A3 210
San Juan, mun., P.R.....B6 132
San Juan, prov., Arg.....A3 136
San Juan, isl., Wash.....A2 210
San Juan, mts., Colo.....D3 171
San Juan, passage, P.R.....B8 132
San Juan, riv., Arg.....A3 136
San Juan, riv., B.C., Can.....B8 149
San Juan, riv., Col.....D3 171
San Juan, riv., Nic.....E6 130
San Juan, riv., U.S.....C5 158
San Juan Bautista, Calif.....C6 170
San Juan Bautista, Par.....E4 135
San Juan Capistrano, Calif.....F5 170
San Juan de Aragón, Mex.....h9 129
San Juan de Colón, Ven.....B3 133
San Juan de los Lagos, Mex.....m12 129
San Juan de los Morros, Ven.....B4 133
San Juan del Norte, Nic.....E6 130
San Juan del Río, Mex.....m13 129
San Juan del Sur, Nic.....E5 130
San Juan Ixtayoapan, Mex.....h10 129
San Juan Nepomuceno, Col.....B2 133
San Juan y Martínez, Cuba.....D2 131
San Julián, Arg.....D3 136
San Justo, Arg.....A4 136
San Leandro, Calif.....B5 170
San Lorenzo, Arg.....A4 136
San Lorenzo, Calif.....*D3 170
San Lorenzo, Ec.....A2 134
San Lorenzo, Hond.....D4 130
San Lorenzo, N. Mex.....E2 195
San Lorenzo, P.R.....C7 132
San Lorenzo, Ven.....B3 133
San Lorenzo, mun., P.R.....C7 132
San Lorenzo del Escorial, Sp.....B3, o16 65
San Lorenzo Tezonco, Mex.....h9 129
San Lucas, Bol.....D2 135
San Lucas, Mex.....C3 129
San Luis, Arg.....A3 136
San Luis, Ariz.....E3 168
San Luis, Ariz.....E1 168
San Luis, Colo.....D5 171
San Luis, Cuba.....h12 131
San Luis, Cuba.....E6 131
San Luis, Guat.....B3 130
San Luis, Mex.....A2 129
San Luis, N. Mex.....B2 195
San Luis, prov., Arg.....A3 136
San Luis, creek, Colo.....C5 171
San Luis, pass, Tex.....G5 206
San Luis, peak, Colo.....D4 171
San Luis, pt., Calif.....E3 170
San Luis, riv., Mex.....h9 129
San Luis, val., Colo.....D4 171
San Luis de la Paz, Mex.....m13 129
San Luis Jilotepeque, Guat.....C3 130
San Luis Obispo, Calif.....E3 170
San Luis Obispo, co., Calif.....E3 170
San Luis Potosí, Mex.....C4, k13 129
San Luis Potosí, state, Mex.....C4, k13 129
San Manuel, Ariz.....E5 168
San Marco [in Lamis], It.....D5 67
San Marcos, Col.....B2 133
San Marcos, Guat.....C2 130
San Marcos, Tex.....A4, E4 206
San Marcos, riv., Tex.....A4 206
San Marcos de Colón, Hond.....D4 130
San Marino, Calif.....F2 170
San Marino, San Marino.....C4 67
SAN MARINO, country, Eur.....C4 67
San Martín, Arg.....A3 136
San Martín, Arg.....g7 136
San Martin, Calif.....C6 170
San Martín, Col.....C3 133
San Martín, dept., Peru.....C2 134
San Martín de la Vega, Sp.....p17 65
San Martín de Los Andes, Arg.....C2 136
San Martino dei Calvi, It.....D5 66
San Martino di Castrozza, It.....C7 66
San Mateo, Calif.....B5 170
San Mateo, Fla.....C5 174
San Mateo, N. Mex.....B2 195
San Mateo, Sp.....B6 65
San Mateo, Ven.....B5 133
San Mateo, co., Calif.....D2 170
San Mateo, cape, Ec.....B1 134
San Mateo, mts., N. Mex.....D2 195
San Mateo Xalpa, Mex.....h9 129
San Matias, Bol.....C4 135
San Matías, gulf, Arg.....C4 136
San Miguel, Ariz.....F4 168
San Miguel, Calif.....E3 170
San Miguel, N. Mex.....E3 195
San Miguel, Pan.....F8 130
San Miguel, Sal.....D3 130
San Miguel, co., Colo.....D2 171
San Miguel, co., N. Mex.....B4 195
San Miguel, isl., Calif.....E3 170
San Miguel, mts., Colo.....D2 171
San Miguel, riv., Colo.....C2 171
San Miguel de Allende, Mex.....m13 129
San Miguel del Padrón, Cuba.....*h12 131
San Narciso, Phil.....p14 90
San Narciso, Phil.....o13 90
San Nicholas, Phil.....o13 90
San Nicolás, Arg.....A4 136
San Nicolas, Phil.....n13 90
San Nicolas, isl., Calif.....F4 170
San Nicolás [Totolapan], Mex.....h9 129
San Onofre, Col.....B2 133
San Pablo, Calif.....B5 170
San Pablo, Colo.....D5 171
San Pablo, Phil.....o13 90
San Pablo, bay, Calif.....B5 170
San Patricio, N. Mex.....D4 195
San Patricio, co., Tex.....E4 206
San Patricio, bayou, La.....C2 183
San Pedro, Arg.....A5, f7 136
San Pedro, Arg.....D3 135
San Pedro, Bol.....B3 135
San Pedro, Bol.....C2 135
San Pedro, Chile.....D2 135
San Pedro, Cuba.....k11 131
San Pedro, Par.....D4 135
San Pedro, Tex.....*F4 206
San Pedro, peaks, N. Mex.....A3 195
San Pedro, riv., Ariz.....E5 168
San Pedro, riv., Mex.....C4 129
San Pedro, riv., Mex.....G1 195
San Pedro de Atacama, Chile.....D2 135
San Pedro de las Colonias, Mex.....B4 129
San Pedro de Lloc, Peru.....C2 134
San Pedro de Macorís, Dom. Rep.....F9 131
San Pedro Martir, mts., Mex.....A1 129
San Pedro Sula, Hond.....C3 130
San Perlita, Tex.....*F4 206
San Pierre, Ind.....B4 179
San Pietro, isl., It.....E2 67
San Quintin, Phil.....o13 90
San Rafael, Arg.....A3 136
San Rafael, Calif.....B5, D2 170
San Rafael, N. Mex.....B2 195
San Rafael, Ven.....A3 133
San Rafael, mts., Calif.....E4 170
San Rafael, riv., Utah.....D5 207
San Rafael, swell, Utah.....E5 207
San Rafael, val., Utah.....E5 207
San Rafael del Norte, Nic.....D4 130
San Rafael Knob, mtn., Utah.....E5 207
San Ramón, Peru.....D2 134
San Ramon, Ur.....g9 136
San Remo, It.....C1 67
San Roque, Sp.....D3 65
San Rosendo, Chile.....B2 136
San Saba, Tex.....D3 206
San Saba, co., Tex.....D3 206
San Salvador, Arg.....A5 136
San Salvador, Sal.....D3 130
San Salvador (Watling), isl., Ba. Is.....C6 131
San Salvador (Santiago), isl., Ec.....g5 134
San Sebastián, P.R.....B3 132
San Sebastián, Sp.....A4 65
San Sebastián, mun., P.R.....B3 132
San Sebastián, cape, Arg.....h12 136
San Sebastián de los Reyes, Sp.....o17 65
San Sepolcro, It.....C4 67
San Severo, It.....D5 67
San Simeon, Calif.....E3 170
San Simon, Ariz.....E6 168
San Simon, creek, Ariz.....E6 168
San Valentin, mtn., Chile.....D2 136
San Vicente, Col.....C3 133
San Vicente, Sal.....D3 130
San Vicente Central, P.R.....B5 132
San Vicente de Alcántara, Sp.....C2 65
San Vicente de Baracaldo, Sp.....A4 65
San Vicente de la Barquera, Sp.....A3 65
San Vito al Tagliamento, It.....B4 67
San Xavier, Indian res., Ariz.....E4 168
San Ygnacio, Tex.....F3 206
San'ā', Yemen (Ṣan'ā').....B5 105
Sanaga, riv., Cam.....E2 104
Sanagha, riv., Con.....E3 104
Sanak, isl., Alsk.....E7 167
Sanana, isl., Indon.....F7 90
Sanandaj, Iran.....D3 86
Sanarate, Guat.....C2 130
Sanariapo, Ven.....B4 133
Sanborn, Iowa.....A2 180
Sanborn, Minn.....F3 187
Sanborn, N. Dak.....C7 198
Sanborn, Wis.....B3 212
Sanborn, co., S. Dak.....D7 204
Sanbornton, N.H.....D3 193
Sanbornville, N.H.....C4 193
Sancerre, Fr.....D5 58
Sanchan, China.....B3 93
Sánchez, Dom. Rep.....F9 131
Sánchez Román, Mex.....C4, m12 129
Sanchiang, China.....L3 92
Sanchor, India.....E3 88
Sancti Spíritus, Cuba.....E4 131
Sanctuary, Sask., Can.....G1 155
Sand, creek, Colo.....A7 171
Sand, creek, Ind.....F6 179
Sand, creek, Kans.....A5 181
Sand, creek, Wyo.....B7 213
Sand, isl., Haw.....g10 176
Sand, isl., Midway Is..... 114
Sand, isl., Wis.....B3 212
Sand, islet, Midway Is..... 114
Sand, lake, Ont., Can.....D4 150
Sand, riv., Alta., Can.....B5 148
Sand, riv., Minn.....D6 187
Sand Brook, N.J.....C3 194
Sand Creek, Mont.....C11 190
Sand Creek, Okla.....A3 200
Sand Creek, Wis.....C2 212
Sand Cut, Fla.....F6 174
Sand Fork (Layopolis), W. Va.....C4 211
Sand Hill, Mass.....D4 185
Sand Hill, riv., Newf., Can.....B3 152
Sand Hill, riv., Minn.....C2 187
Sand Lake, Mich.....E5 186
Sand Point, Alsk.....D7 167
Sand Point, Ont., Can.....B8 153
Sand Springs, Mont.....C9 190
Sand Springs, Okla.....A5 200
Sanda, Jap.....o14 93
Sanda, isl., Scot.....E3 57
Sandakan, Mala.....D5 90
Sandal, bay, Lifou I..... 115
Sandani, Tan.....C6 106
Sanday, isl., Scot.....A6 57
Sanday, sound, Scot.....A6 57
Sandborn, Ind.....G3 179
Sandcoulee, Mont.....C5 190
Sande, Nor.....p28 63
Sandefjord, Nor.....p28 63
Sanders, Ariz.....B6 168
Sanders, Idaho.....B2 177
Sanders, Ky.....B5 182
Sanders, Mont.....D9 190
Sanders, co., Mont.....C1 190
Sanderson, Tex.....D1 206
Sandersville, Ga.....D4 175
Sandersville, Miss.....D4 188
Sandfly, lake, Sask., Can.....B2 155
Sandfontein, S.W. Afr.....B2 107
Sandhammaren, cape, Swe.....C8 62
Sandhill, Miss.....C4 188
Sandia, Peru.....D4 134
Sandia, Tex.....E4 206
Sandia, Indian res., N. Mex.....B3, G5 195
Sandia, peak, N. Mex.....G5 195
Sandia Park, N. Mex.....G5 195
Sandikli, Tur.....C8 69
Sandila, India.....D8 88
Sandilands, Man., Can.....E3 150
Sandlick, creek, W. Va.....D6 211
Sandnes, Nor.....H1 63
Sandoa, Zaire.....C3 106
Sandomierz, Pol.....C6 70
Sandon, B.C., Can.....E9 149
Sandoná, Col.....C2 133
Sandoval, Ill.....E4 178
Sandoval, N. Mex.....B3, G5 195
Sandoval, co., N. Mex.....B2 195
Sandoway, Bur.....E9 87
Sandown, Eng.....D6 56
Sandown, N.H.....E4 193
Sandpoint, Idaho.....A2 177
Sands, Mich.....B3 186
Sands, key, Fla.....F3 174
Sands, pt., N.Y.....F2 172
Sands Point, N.Y.....F2 172
Sandspit, B.C., Can.....C2 149
Sandston, Va.....C7 209
Sandstone, Austl.....E2 111
Sandstone, Minn.....D6 187
Sandstone, W. Va.....D4, D7 211
Sandusky, Mich.....E8 186
Sandusky, N.Y.....C2 196
Sandusky, Ohio.....A5 199
Sandusky, co., Ohio.....A5 199
Sandusky, bay, Ohio.....A5 199
Sandusky, riv., Ohio.....A4 199
Sandusky South, Ohio.....*A5 199
Sandvig, Den.....C8 62
Sandviken, Swe.....G7 63
Sandwich, Ill.....B5 178
Sandwich, Mass.....C7 185
Sandwich, N.H.....C4 193
Sandwich, bay, Newf., Can.....B3 152
Sandwich, range, N.H.....C3 193
Sandwith, Sask., Can.....D1 155
Sandy, Oreg.....B4 201
Sandy, Pa.....*D4 202
Sandy, Utah.....C4 207
Sandy, brook, Conn.....A4 172
Sandy, cape, Austl.....B9 112
Sandy, creek, Ohio.....B6 199
Sandy, creek, Wyo.....C3 213
Sandy, des., Austl.....C5 110
Sandy, hook, N.J.....C5 194
Sandy, isl., S.C.....D9 203
Sandy, lake, Newf., Can.....D3 152
Sandy, lake, Ont., Can.....D8 153
Sandy, lake, Minn.....D5 187
Sandy, neck, Mass.....C7 185
Sandy, pt., R.I.....E10 172
Sandy, pond, Mass.....C2 185
Sandy ridge, Va.....B3 209
Sandy, riv., Maine.....D2 184
Sandy Bay, mtn., Maine.....C2 184
Sandy Creek, N.Y.....B4 196
Sandy Hill, Vt.....C3 208
Sandy Hook, Conn.....D3 172
Sandy Hook, Ky.....B6 182
Sandy Hook, Md.....B2 173
Sandy Hook, Miss.....D4 188
Sandy Hook, Mo.....*C5 189
Sandy Lake, Man., Can.....D1 150
Sandy Lake, Pa.....D1 202
Sandy Point, Maine.....D4 184
Sandy Ridge, N.C.....A3 197
Sandy Springs, Ga.....A5 175
Sandy Springs, S.C.....B2 203
Sandybeach, lake, Ont., Can.....E5 150
Sandyville, Iowa.....*C4 180
Sandyville, W. Va.....C3 211
Sanfjället, mtn., Swe.....F5 63
Sanford, Ala.....*D3 166
Sanford, Man., Can.....E3 150
Sanford, Colo.....D5 171
Sanford, Fla.....D5 174
Sanford, Ind.....E2 179
Sanford, Maine.....E2 184
Sanford, Mich.....E6 186
Sanford, Miss.....D4 188
Sanford, N.C.....B4 197
Sanford, Tex.....B2 206
Sanford, mtn., Alsk.....C11, f19 167
Sang-i-Masha, Afg.....E13 86
Sangabar, Afg.....D12 86
Sangallan, isl., Peru.....D2 134
Sangamner, India.....H5 88

INDEX KEY Each place listed in **Bold-faced Type** has its population listed in the Population tables, pages 230 to 280. Each country shown in CAPITAL LETTERS has its population listed in the World Political Information Table pages 6 to 10.
* Does not appear on map; key shows general location.

Sangamon, co., Ill. D4 178
Sangamon, riv., Ill. C3 178
Sangatte, Fr. D9 56
Sangélima, Cam E2 104
Sanger, Calif D4 170
Sanger, N. Dak B5 198
Sanger, Tex C4 206
Sangerhausen, Ger B6 61
Sangerville, Maine C3 184
Sanggau, Indon E4 90
Sangju, Kor H4 93
Sangli, India *E5 87
Sangonera, riv., Sp D5 65
Sangre de Cristo, range, Colo D5 171
Sangre de Cristo, range, N. Mex B4 195
Sangro, riv., It D5 67
Sangrur, India B5 88
Sangudo, Alta., Can C3 148
Sangue, riv., Braz E3 139
Sangüesa, Sp A5 65
Sanguinara, riv., It h8 67
Sangwin, Lib E3 103
Sanhsing, see Ilan, China
Sanibel, Fla F4 174
Sanibel, isl., Fla F4 174
Sanilac, co., Mich E8 186
Sanish, N. Dak B3 198
Sanitz, Ger D6 62
Sanjō, Jap H9 93
Sankarani, riv., Guinea, Mali D3 103
Sankertown, Pa *F4 202
Sankt Anton [am Arlberg], Aus B6 66
Sankt Blasien, Ger B4 66
S[ank]t. Gallen, canton, Switz B5 66
Sankt Georgen [im Attergau], Aus B9 66
Sankt Goarshausen, Ger C2 61
Sankt Johann [in Tirol], Aus B8 66
Sankt Michaelisdonn, Ger E3 62
Sankt Pölten, Aus D7 60
Sankt Veit [an der Glan], Aus E7 60
Sankt Wendel, Ger D2 61
Sankuru, riv., Zaire B3 106
Sanlúcar [de Barrameda], Sp D2 65
Sanmenhsia, China G4 92
Sânnicolaul-Mare, Rom B5 68
Sannois, Fr g10 58
Sano, Jap *H9 93
Sanok, Pol D7 70
Sanpete, co., Utah D4 207
Sanpoil, riv., Wash A7 210
Sanquhar, Scot E5 57
Sansanné-Mango, Togo D5 103
Sanshui, China G7 91
Sansom Park Village, Tex *C4 206
Sant' Angelo Romano, It g9 67
Sant' Antioco, isl., It E2 67
Sant' Eufemia, gulf, It E5 67
Santa, Idaho B2 177
Santa, Peru C2 134
Santa, riv., Peru C2 134
Santa Ana, Bol B2 135
Santa Ana, Bol C2 135
Santa Ana, Calif F3, F5 170
Santa Ana, Ec B1 134
Santa Ana, Mex A2 129
Santa Ana, N. Mex G5 195
Santa Ana, Peru D3 134
Santa Ana, Sal D3 130
Santa Ana, Ven B5 133
Santa Ana, Indian res., N. Mex B3, G5 195
Santa Ana, isl., Sol. Is 115
Santa Ana, mts., Calif F3 170
Santa Ana, riv., Calif F3 170
Santa Anita, Mex h9 129
Santa Anna, Tex D3 206
Santa Bárbara, Braz m8 137
Santa Bárbara, Braz E2 138
Santa Barbara, Calif E4 170
Santa Bárbara, Chile B2 136
Santa Bárbara, Hond C4 130
Santa Bárbara, Mex B3 129
Santa Barbara, co., Calif E3 170
Santa Barbara, chan., Calif E4 170
Santa Barbara, isl., Calif F4 170
Santa Bárbara Central, P.R C4 132
Santa Catalina, Arg D2 135
Santa Catalina, Chile E2 135
Santa Catalina, gulf, Calif F5 170
Santa Catalina, isl., Calif F4 170
Santa Catalina, mts., Ariz E5 168
Santa Catarina, state, Braz D2 137
Santa Catarina, isl., Braz D3 137
Santa Clara, Calif C6, D3 170
Santa Clara, Cuba D4 131
Santa Clara, N.Y A2 196
Santa Clara, Ur E2 137
Santa Clara, Utah F2 207
Santa Clara, co., Calif D3 170
Santa Clara, val., Calif C6 170
Santa Claus, Ga *D4 175
Santa Claus, Ind H4 179
Santa Coloma de Farnés, Sp B7 65
Santa Coloma de Gramanet, Sp B7 65
Santa Croce, cape, It F5 67
Santa Cruz, Arg E3 136
Santa Cruz, Ariz G2 168
Santa Cruz, Bol C3 135
Santa Cruz, Braz C3, h6 138
Santa Cruz, Calif C5, D2 170
Santa Cruz, Chile A2 136
Santa Cruz, C.R E5 130
Santa Cruz, N. Mex B3 195
Santa Cruz, Phil p13 90
Santa Cruz, Phil o12 90
Santa Cruz, Phil o13 90
Santa Cruz, co., Ariz F5 168
Santa Cruz, co., Calif D2 170
Santa Cruz, dept., Bol C3 135
Santa Cruz, prov., Arg D3 136
Santa Cruz, isl., Calif F4 170
Santa Cruz (Indefatigable), isl., Ec g5 134
Santa Cruz, is., Pac. O G10 113
Santa Cruz, mts., Calif C5 170
Santa Cruz, riv., Ariz E4 168
Santa Cruz Barillas, Guat C2 130
Santa Cruz de la Palma, Sp. (Can. Is.) m13 65, D1 102
Santa Cruz de la Zarza, Sp C4 65
Santa Cruz de Tenerife, Sp. (Can. Is.) m13 65, D1 102
Santa Cruz del Quiché, Guat C2 130
Santa Cruz del Sur, Cuba E5 131
Santa Cruz do Rio Pardo, Braz C3 137
Santa Cruz do Sul, Braz D2 137
Santa Elena, Ec B1 134
Santa Elena, Tex F3 206
Santa Elena, Ven C5 133
Santa Eugenia [de Ribeira], Sp A1 65
Santa Eulalia del Río, Sp C6 65
Santa Fe, Arg A4 136
Santa Fé, Cuba E2 131
Santa Fe, Mex h9 129
Santa Fe, N. Mex B4, F6 195
Santa Fe, Ohio B3 199
Santa Fe, Tenn B4 205
Santa Fe, co., N. Mex B3 195
Santa Fe, prov., Arg A4 136
Santa Fé, isl., Ec g5 134
Santa Fe, riv., N. Mex F6 195
Santa Fe Baldy, mtn., N. Mex B4 195
Santa Fe Springs, Calif *F2 170
Santa Filomena, Braz C1 138
Santa Inés, isl., Chile h11 136
Santa Inés Ahuatempan, Mex n14 129
Santa Isabel, Arg B3 136
Santa Isabel, Chile D2 135
Santa Isabel, Equat. Gui E1 104
Santa Isabel, P.R D5 132
Santa Isabel, mun., P.R D5 132
Santa Isabel, isl., Sol. Is 115
Santa Isabel de Siguas, Peru E3 134
Santa Juana Central, P.R C6 132
Santa Lucía, Cuba E6 131
Santa Lucía, Ur E1 137
Santa Lucia, range, Calif E3 170
Santa Margarita, Calif E3 170
Santa Margarita, isl., Mex C2 129
Santa María, Arg E2 135
Santa Maria, Braz D2 137
Santa Maria, Calif E3 170
Santa Maria, Phil o13 90
Santa María, P.R g13 132
Santa Maria, Tex *F4 206
Santa Maria, isl., Port. (Azores) h9 102
Santa María, isl., Ec g5 134
Santa Maria, mts., Ariz C3 168
Santa Maria, riv., Ariz C2 168
Santa María, riv., Mex m14 129
Santa María, riv., Mex G2 195
Santa María, riv., Pan F7 130
Santa Maria [Capua Vetere], It D5 67
Santa María del Oro, Mex B3 129
Santa Maria di Leuca, cape, It E7 67
Santa Maria Madalena, Braz C4 137
Santa Marta, Col A3 133
Santa Marta, Sp C2 65
Santa Marta, mts., Col A3 133
Santa Monica, Calif F2 170
Santa Paula, Calif E4 170
Santa Quitéria, Braz B2 138
Santa Rita, Braz k8 137
Santa Rita, Braz C4, h6 138
Santa Rita, Guam 114
Santa Rita, Mont B4 190
Santa Rita, N. Mex E1 195
Santa Rita, Ven A3 133
Santa Rita, mts., Pan k11 130
Santa Rita Park, Calif D3 170
Santa Rosa, Arg A3 136
Santa Rosa, Arg A4 136
Santa Rosa, Arg B4 136
Santa Rosa, Bol B2 135
Santa Rosa, Braz k8 137
Santa Rosa, Braz D2 137
Santa Rosa, Calif A5, C2 170
Santa Rosa, Col B2 133
Santa Rosa, Ec B2 134
Santa Rosa, Mo B3 189
Santa Rosa, N. Mex C5 195
Santa Rosa Phil o13 90
Santa Rosa, Tex *F4 206
Santa Rosa, co., Fla G2 174
Santa Rosa, isl., Calif G2 170
Santa Rosa, mtn., Guam 114
Santa Rosa, range, Nev B4 192
Santa Rosa, reef, Mariana Is 115
Santa Rosa Beach, Fla G2 174
Santa Rosa de Aguán, Hond C5 130
Santa Rosa de Copán, Hond C3 130
Santa Rosalía, Mex B2 129
Santa Rosalía, pt., Mex B2 129
Santa Susana, Calif *E4 170
Santa Teresa Gallura, It D2 67
Santa Ursula, Mex h9 129
Santa Vitória do Palmar, Braz E2 137
Santa Ynez, Calif E3 170
Santafé, Sp D4 65
Santai, China E6 91
Santan, Ariz G2 168
Santan, mtn., Ariz G3 168
Santana, Braz D2 138
Santana, Port. (Madeira Is.) h12 65
Santana do Ipanema, Braz C3 138
Santander, Col C2 133
Santander, Sp A4 65
Santander, dept., Col B3 133
Santander, mts., Col B3 133
Santander Jiménez, Mex C5 129
Santanoni, peak, N.Y A6 196
Santanópole, Braz C3 138
Santañy, Sp C7 65
Santaquin, Utah C4 207
Santarém, Braz C4 139
Santarém, Port C1 65
Santaren, chan., W.I C4 131
Santee, Nebr B8 191
Santee, S.C *E7 203
Santee, dam, S.C E7 203
Santee, Indian res., Nebr B8 191
Santee, riv., S.C E8 203
Santiago, Bol C2 135
Santiago, Braz D2 137
Santiago, Chile A2 136
Santiago, Dom. Rep F8 131
Santiago, Mex C3 129
Santiago, Pan F7 130
Santiago, Par E4 135
Santiago, Phil n13 90
Santiago, Sp A1 65
Santiago, prov., Chile A2 136
Santiago, cape, Phil p13 90
Santiago, isl., Phil n12 90
Santiago, isl., P.R C8 132
Santiago, see San Salvador, isl., Ec.
Santiago, peak, Calif F3 170
Santiago, peak, Tex E1, G2 206
Santiago, riv., Peru B2 134
Santiago de Cao, Peru C2 134
Santiago de Cuba, Cuba E6 131
Santiago del Estero, Arg E3 135
Santiago del Estero, prov., Arg E3 135
Santiago Ixcuintla, Mex C3, m11 129
Santiago Morona, prov., Ec B2 134
Santiago Papasquiaro, Mex B3 129
Santiago Tepalcatlalpan, Mex h9 129
Santiam, riv., Oreg C2 201
Santipur, India F12 88
Santisteban del Puerto, Sp C4 65
Santo, Tex C3 206
Santo Amaro, Braz D3 138
Santo Amaro, isl., Braz m8 137
Santo André, Braz *C3 137
Santo Angelo, Braz D2 137
Santo Antônio, Braz C3, h6 138
Santo Antônio de Jesus, Braz D3 138
Santo António do Zaire, Ang C1 106
Santo Domingo, Dom. Rep F9 131
Santo Domingo, Nic D5 130
Santo Domingo, Phil B6 90
Santo Domingo, Indian res., N. Mex G6 195
Santo Domingo de la Calzada, Sp A4 65
Santo Domingo de los Colorados, Ec B2 134
Santo Domingo Pueblo, N. Mex B3, F5 195
Santo Tomas, N. Mex E5 195
Santo Tomás, Peru D3 134
Santo Tomas, Ven B5 133
Santo Tomé, Arg E4 135
Santo Tomé de Guayana, Ven B5 133, A2 139
Santoña, Sp A4 65
Santos, Braz C3, m8 137
Santos Dumont, Braz C4, g6 137
Santuao, China K8 92
Santuc, S.C B4 203
Sanvic, Fr C4 58
Sanyati, riv., Rh A4 107
Sanza Pombo, Ang C2 106
São Bento do Sul, Braz D3 137
São Bento do Una, Braz k5 138
São Bernardo [do Campo], Braz C3, m8 137
São Borja, Braz D1 137
São Caetano do Sul, Braz *C3 137
São Carlos, Braz C3, m8 137
São Cristovão, Braz D3 138
São Domingos, Braz D1 138
São Fidélis, Braz C4 137
São Francisco, Braz E2 138
São Francisco, Braz C5 133
São Francisco, riv., Braz C3 138
São Francisco do Sul, Braz D3 137
São Gabriel, Braz E2 137
São Gonçalo, Braz *C4 137
São Gotardo, Braz E1 138
São Jerônimo, Braz D2 137
São Jerônimo, mts., Braz B2 137
São João, isl., Braz B2 138
São João da Barra, Braz C4 137
São João da Boa Vista, Braz C3, k8 137
São João das Lampas, Port f9 65
São João de Meriti, Braz *C4 137
São João del Rei, Braz C4, g5 137
São João do Cariri, Braz C3, h5 138
São João do Piauí, Braz C2 138
São João Nepomuceno, Braz C4, g6 137
São Joaquim, Braz D3 137
São Jorge, isl., Port. (Azores) g8 102
São José de Mipibú, Braz h6 138
São José do Rio Pardo, Braz k8 137
São José do Rio Prêto, Braz C3 137
São José dos Campos, Braz C3, m9 137
São José dos Pinhais, Braz D3 137
São Leopoldo, Braz D2 137
São Lourenco, Braz C3 137
São Lourenço, riv., Braz B1 137
São Lourenço do Sul, Braz E2 137
São Luís, Braz B2 138
São Luís do Quitunde, Braz k6 138
São Luís Gonzaga, Braz D2 137
São Manuel, Braz C3, m7 137
São Mateus, Braz E3 138
São Miguel, isl., Port. (Azores) h9 102
São Miguel Arcanjo, Braz m8 137
São Miguel dos Campos, Braz k5 138
São Paulo, Braz C3, m8 137
São Paulo, state, Braz C3, m8 137
São Paulo de Olivença, Braz D4 133
São Pedro, Braz m8 137
São Pedro do Piauí, Braz C2 138
São Raimundo Nonato, Braz C2 138
São Roque, Braz m8 137
São Roque, cape, Braz C3 138
São Salvador, Ang C1 106
São Sebastião, cape, Moz B6 107
São Sebastião, isl., Braz C3 137
São Sebastião do Paraíso, Braz C3 137
São Simão, Braz C3, k8 137
São Tomé, Sao Tomé & Principe E1 104
São Tomé, isl., São Tomé & Principe E1 104
SÃO TOMÉ & PRINCIPE, Port. dep., Afr E1 104
São Vicente, Braz C3 137
São Vicente, Port. (Madeira Is.) h11 65
Saône, riv., Fr D6 58
Saorre, mtn., N.W. Ter., Can D16 143
Saoura, riv., Alg D4 102
Sápai, Grc B5 69
Sapatu, isl., Viet H8 89
Sapele, Nig E6 103
Sapello, N. Mex B4 195
Sapelo, isl., Ga E5 175
Sapelo, sound, Ga E5 175
Saponac, Maine C4 184
Saposoa, Peru C2 134
Sapozhok, Sov. Un E13 72
Sappa, creek, Nebr., Kans C3 181
Sappemeer, Neth A6 59
Sapphire, mts., Mont D3 190
Sappho, Wash A1 210
Sappington, Mo B8 189
Sappington, Mont E5 190
Sapporo, Jap E10 93
Sappurai Sho, see Supply, reef, Mariana Is.
Sapri, It D5 67
Sapulpa, Okla B5 200
Saqqārah, Eg E3 84
Saqqez, Iran C3 86
Saquarema, Braz C4, h6 137
Sar-e Yazd, Iran F7 86
Šar Planina, mts., Yugo D5 68
Sara, dune, Libya E4 101
Sara, riv., Chad, Cen. Afr. Rep D3 104
Sara Buri, Thai E4 89
Sara Kaeo, Thai F5 89
Sarābīyūm, Eg D4 84
Sarafand, Isr h10 84
Saragosa, Tex D1, F2 206
Saragosa, Ala B2 166
Saragosa, Pan k11 130
Saragossa (Zaragoza), Sp B5 65
Saraguro, Ec B2 134
Sarah, Miss A3 188
Sarajevo, Yugo D4 68
Saraland, Ala E1 166
Saran', Sov. Un D8 73
Saranac, Mich F5 186
Saranac, N.Y A3 196
Saranac, lakes, N.Y A6 196
Saranac, riv., N.Y B3 196
Saranac Inn, N.Y B3 196
Saranac Lake, N.Y B3 196
Saranap, Calif *B5 170
Sarande, Alb C2 69
Sarandí del Yí, Ur E1 137
Sarandí Grande, Ur E1 137
Sarangani, bay, Phil D6 90
Sarangpur, India F6 88
Saransk, Sov. Un C3 73
Sarapul, Sov. Un B4 73
Sarasota, Fla E4, F2 174
Sarasota, co., Fla E4 174
Sarasota, bay, Fla E4 174
Sarata, Sov. Un B9 68
Saratoga, Ark D2 169
Saratoga, Calif C5 170
Saratoga, Ind D8 179
Saratoga, Iowa A5 180
Saratoga, N.C B6 197
Saratoga, Tex D5 206
Saratoga, Wyo D6 213
Saratoga, co., N.Y B7 196
Saratoga, lake, N.Y C7 196
Saratoga Palace, Va *E6 209
Saratoga Springs, N.Y B7 196
Saratov, Sov. Un C3 73
Saravane, Laos E7 89
Sarawak, reg., Mala E4 90
c. 1950 83
Saray, Tur B6 69
Saray, see Kâzim Paşa, Tur.
Sarayköy, Tur D7 69
Sarbāz, Iran H10 86
Sarben, Nebr C4 191
Sárbogárd, Hung B4 68
Sarca, riv., It D6 66
Sarcelles, Fr g10 58
Sarcoxie, Mo D3 189
Sarda, riv., India C8 88
Sardalas, Libya D2 101
Sardinia, Ind F6 179
Sardinia, Ohio C4 199
Sardinia, isl., It D2 67
Sardinia, kingdom of: in 1720 49
in 1810 50
in 1815 50
c. 1860 51
Sardis, Ala C3 166
Sardis, B.C., Can B11 149
Sardis, Ga D5 175
Sardis, Ky B6 182
Sardis, Miss A4 188
Sardis, Ohio C7 199
Sardis, Okla C6 200
Sardis, Tenn B3 205
Sardis, dam, Miss A4 188
Sardis, res., Miss A4 188
Sardo, Eth C5 105
Sarektjakko, mtn., Swe D7 63
Sarepta, La B2 183
Sarepta, Miss A4 188
Sargans, Switz B5 66
Sargeant, Minn G6 187
Sargent, Ga C2 175
Sargent, Nebr C6 191
Sargent, co., N. Dak C8 198
Sargents, Colo C4 171
Sargodha, Pak A4 88
Sarhad, Afg k17 86
Sar-i-Pul, Afg C12 86
Sārī, Iran C6 86
Sária, isl., Grc E6 69
Sarigan (Sariguan), isl., Mariana Is 115
Sariguan, see Sarigan, isl., Mariana Is.
Sarikamiş, Tur B14 85
Sarine, riv., Switz C3 66
Sariñena, Sp B5 65
Sarita, Tex F4 206
Sariwŏn, Kor G2 93
Sark, isl., Guernsey F5 55
Sarkişla, Tur C11 85
Şarköy, Tur B6 69
Sarlat, Fr E4 58
Sarles, N. Dak A7 198
Särna, Swe G5 63
Sarnen, Switz C4 66
Sarnen, lake, Switz C4 66
Sarnia, Ont., Can E2 153
Sarny, Sov. Un F6 72
Särö, Swe A5 65
Sarona, Wis C2 212
Saronic, gulf, Grc D4 69
Saronno, It B2 67
Saronville, Nebr D8 191
Saros, gulf, Tur B6 69
Sárospatak, Hung A5 68
Sarova, Sov. Un D14 72
Sarpsborg, Nor p29 63
Sarpy, co., Nebr C9 191
Sarre-Union, Fr F7 59
Sarrebourg, Fr F7 58
Sarreguemines, Fr C7 58
Sarria, Sp A2 65
Sarsfield, Ont., Can A10 153
Sarstedt, Ger A4 61
Sarstún, riv., Guat C3 130
Sartell, Minn E4 187
Sartène, Fr D2 67
Sarthe, riv., Fr D3 58
Sartrouville, Fr g9 58
Sarufutsu, Jap D11 93
Sarus, see Seyhan, riv., Tur.
Sárvár, Hung B3 68
Sarvestān, Iran G6 86
Sary-Ishikotrau, des., Sov. Un D9 73
Sary-Ozek, Sov. Un E9 73
Sarybyevo, Sov. Un o18 72
Sarysu, riv., Sov. Un D7 73
Sarzana, It B2 67
Sasabe, Ariz F4 168
Sasaginnigak, lake, Man., Can D4 150
Sasakwa, Okla C5 200
Sasalaguan, mtn., Guam 114
Sasaram, India E10 88
Sasebo, Jap J4 93
Saskatchewan, prov., Can 155
in 1867 147
Saskatchewan, riv., Sask., Can F12 142
Saskatoon, Sask., Can E2 155
Saskeram, riv., Sask., Can D5 155
Sasovo, Sov. Un C2 73
Saspamco, Tex B4 206
Sass, cape, New Ire. I 115
Sassafras, mtn., S.C A2 203
Sassafras, riv., Md B5 173
Sassandra, I.C E3 103
Sassandra, riv., I.C E3 103
Sassanian empire 46
Sassari, It D2 67
Sassenberg, Ger B3 61
Sasser, Ga E2 175
Sassnitz, Ger A6 60
Sasso Marconi, It E7 66
Sassuolo, It E6 66
Sastre, Arg A4 136
Sasuri, Kor F3 93
Sasykkol, lake, Sov. Un D10 73
Satah, mtn., B.C., Can C5 149
Satalo, W. Sam 114
Satanta, Kans E3 181
Satapuala, W. Sam 114
Satara, India I4 88
Satartia, Miss C3 188
Sataua, bay, W. Sam 114
Satellite Beach, Fla *D6 174
Säter, Swe G6 63
Saticoy, Calif E4 170
Satilla, riv., Ga E4 175
Satipo, Peru D3 134
Satka, Sov. Un B5 73
Satmala, range, India H7 88
Satna, India E8 88
Sátoraljaújhely, Hung A5 68
Satpura, range, India G5 88
Sätrabrunn, Swe t34 63
Satrup, Ger D3 62
Satsop, Wash B2 210
Satsuma, Ala E1 166
Satsuma, Fla C5 174
Sattahip, Thai F4 89
Sattler, Tex A4 206
Satu Mare, Rom B6 68
Satun, Thai I4 89
Satupaitea, W. Sam 114
Saturna, isl., B.C., Can E6 149
Satus, creek, Wash C5 210
Sauce, Arg A5 136
Sauceda, mts., Ariz E3 168
Saucier, Miss E4 188
Saucillo, Mex B3 129
Sauda, Nor H2 63
SAUDI ARABIA, country, Asia G7 77, 83
Saugatuck, Conn E3 172
Saugatuck, Mich F4 186
Saugatuck, riv., Conn D3 172
Saugerties, N.Y C7 196
Saugus, Calif F2 170
Saugus, Mass B5, C3 185
Saugus, riv., Mass C3 185
Sauk, co., Wis E4 212
Sauk, riv., Minn E4 187
Sauk, riv., Wash A4 210
Sauk Centre, Minn E4 187
Sauk City, Wis E4 212
Sauk Rapids, Minn E4 187
Sauk Village, Ill *B6 178
Saukville, Wis E6 212
Saulgrub, Ger B7 66
Saulnierville, N.S., Can E3 151
Saulsbury, Tenn B2 205
Saulston, N.C B6 197
Sault-au-Mouton, Que., Can A8 154
Sault Ste. Marie, Ont., Can E8 153
Sault Ste. Marie, Mich B6 186
Saumlakki, Indon G8 90
Saumur, Fr D3 58
Saunders, co., Nebr C9 191
Saunderstown, R.I C11 172
Saundersville, Tenn E9 205
Saunemin, Ill C5 178
Saurashtra, pen., India D4 87
Sausalito, Calif B5, D2 170
Sauveterre, Fr E5 58
Sava, riv., Yugo C4 68
Savage, Md B4 173
Savage, Minn F5, F6 187
Savage, Miss A3 188
Savage, Mont C12 190
Savage, riv., Md D1 173
Savage River, res., Md D1 173
Savaii, isl., W. Sam 114
Savalan, mtn., Iran B3 86
Savalou, Dah E5 103
Savanna, Ill A3 178
Savanna, Okla C6 200
Savanna-la-Mar, Jam F4 131
Savannah, Ga D5 175
Savannah, Mo B3 189
Savannah, N.Y B4 196
Savannah, Ohio B5 199
Savannah, Tenn B3 205
Savannah, lake, Md D6 173
Savannah, riv., Ga., S.C F5 203
Savannah Beach, Ga D6 175
Savannakhet, Laos D6 89
Savé, Dah E5 103
Save, riv., Moz B5 107
Sāveh, Iran B4 86
Săveni, Rom B8 68
Saverne, Fr C7 58
Saverton, Mo B6 189
Savery, Wyo D5 213
Savigliano, It B1 67

INDEX KEY Each place listed in **Bold-faced Type** has its population listed in the Population tables, pages 230 to 280.
Each country, shown in CAPITAL LETTERS, has its population listed in the World Political Information Table, pages 6 to 10.
* Does not appear on map; key shows general location.

Savigny [-sur-Orgel], Fr. F2 59
Savo, isl., Sol. Is. 115
Savo, riv., It. h9 67
Savoie, dept., Fr. D2 66
Savona, B.C., Can. D7 149
Savona, It. B2 67
Savona, N.Y. C3 196
Savonburg, Kans. E8 181
Savonlinna, Fin. G13 63
Savoonga, Alsk. C5 167
Savoy, Ill. *C5 178
Savoy, Mass. A1 185
Savoy, Mont. B8 190
Savoy, former prov., Fr. E7 58
c. 1360 48
in 1721 49
in 1860 51
Savran, Sov. Un. G8 72
Sävsjö, Swe. A8 62
Savu, is., Indon. B3 110
Savu, sea, Indon. G6 90
Savur, Tur. D13 85
Savusavu, bay, Fiji 114
Saw, Bur. D9 87
Saw Mill, riv., N.Y. D6 194
Sawankhalok, Thai. D3 89
Sawatch, range, Colo. B4 171
Sawbill Landing, Minn. C7 187
Sawda, mtn., Libya D3 101
Sawe, Indon. L2 89
Sawhāj, Eg. D6 101
Sawknah, Libya D3 101
Sawmill, Ariz. B6 168
Sawnee, mtn., Ga. B2 175
Sawtooth, mts., Idaho E3 177
Sawtooth, ridge, Wash. A5 210
Sawyer, Kans. E5 181
Sawyer, Mich. G4 186
Sawyer, Minn. D6 187
Sawyer, N. Dak. A4 198
Sawyer, Okla. C6 200
Sawyer, co., Wis. C2 212
Sawyer, lake, Wash. D2 210
Sawyerville, Que., Can. D6 154
Sawyerville, Ill. *D4 178
Saxe, Va. E4 209
Saxis, Va. D7 209
Saxman, W. Va. C4 211
Saxmundham, Eng. B9 56
Saxon, S.C. B4 203
Saxon, W. Va. D3, D6 211
Saxon, Wis. B3 212
Saxon duchies: in 1867 51
Saxonburg, Pa. E2 202
Saxony, reg., Ger. C6 60
in 9th cent. 47
in 1721 49
in 1815 50
in 1867 51
Saxony, kingdom of 51
Saxton, Ky. D5 182
Saxton, Pa. F5 202
Saxtons, riv., Vt. E3 208
Saxtons River, Vt. E3 208
Say, Niger D5 103
Sayabec, Que., Can. G19 145
Sayaboury, Laos C4 89
Sayán, Peru D2 134
Sayan, mts., Sov. Un. D12 71
Saybrook, Ill. C5 178
Saybrook Point, Conn. D7 172
Sayle, Mont. E11 190
Saylorsburg, Pa. E11 202
Sayner, Wis. B4 212
Sayr Usa, Mong. C6 91
Sayre, Ala. B3 166
Sayre, Okla. B2 200
Sayre, Pa. C8 202
Sayreton, Ala. B3, E4 166
Sayreville, N.J. C4 194
Sayula, Mex. D4, n12 129
Sayula, lake, Mex. n12 129
Sayville, N.Y. G4 172
Sazan, isl., Alb. B2 69
Sázava, Czech. o18 70
Sázava, riv., Czech. o18 70
Sazliyka, riv., Bul. D7 68
Scafell Pike, mtn., Eng. F5 57
Scalby, Eng. F8 57
Scales Mound, Ill. A3 178
Scalp Level, Pa. F4 202
Scaly, N.C. D3 197
Scammon, Kans. E9 181
Scammon Bay, Alsk. C6 167
Scandia, Alta., Can. D4 148
Scandia, Kans. C6 181
Scandia, Minn. E8 187
Scandinavia, Wis. D4 212
Scanlon, Minn. D6 187
Scansano, It. C3 67
Scanterbury Man., Can. D3 150
Scantic, Conn. B6 172
Scanzano, It. D6 67
Scapa, Alta., Can. D4 148
Scapa Flow, bay, Scot. B5 57
Scapegoat, mtn., Mont. C4 190
Scappoose, Oreg. B4 201
Scarba, isl., Scot. D3 57
Scarboro, Ga. D5 175
Scarboro, Maine E2, E5 184
Scarborough, Ont., Can. E7 153
Scarborough, Eng. C6 55
Scarbro, W. Va. D7 211
Scarp, isl., Scot. B1 57
Scarsdale, N.Y. D2 196
Scarth, Man., Can. E1 150
Scarville, Iowa A4 180
Scauri, It. F4 67
Sceaux, Fr. g10 58
Scenic, S. Dak. D3 204
Sceptre, Sask., Can. G1 155
Sceui Ghimira, Eth. D4 105
Schaal, lake, Ger. E4 62
Schaefferstown, Pa. F9 202
Schaerbeek, Bel. *D4 59
Schaffer, Mich. C3 186
Schaffhausen, Switz. B4 66
Schaffhausen, canton, Switz. B4 66
Schagen, Neth. B4 59
Schaghticoke, N.Y. C7 196
Schaller, Iowa B2 180
Schärding, Aus. E8 61
Scharhörn, isl., Ger. E2 62
Schaumberg, Ill. E2 178
Schefferville (Knob Lake), Que., Can. B3 154
Schefield, N. Dak. C3 198
Schell City, Mo. C3 189
Schell Creek, range, Nev. E7 192
Schellbourne, Nev. D7 192
Schellsburg, Pa. F4 202
Schenectady, N.Y. C7 196
Schenectady, co., N.Y. C6 196
Schenefeld, Ger. D3 62
Schenevus, N.Y. C6 196
Schererville, Ind. B3 179
Scherfede, Ger. B4 61
Schertz, Tex. B4 206
Scheveningen, Neth. B4 59
Schiedam, Neth. C4 59
Schiermonnikoog, isl., Neth. A6 59
Schifferstadt, Ger. D3 61
Schiller Park, Ill. E2 178
Schilpario, It. C6 66
Schiltigheim, Fr. C7 58
Schio, It. B3 67
Schkeuditz, Ger. B7 61
Schladming, Aus. E6 60
Schlater, Miss. B3 188
Schlei, inlet, Ger. D3 62
Schleicher, co., Tex. D2 206
Schleiz, Ger. C6 61
Schleswig, Ger. A4 60
in 1866 51
Schleswig, Iowa B2 180
Schleswig-Holstein, reg., Ger. A4 60
Schleswig-Holstein, state, Ger. D4 62
Schley, Va. D6 209
Schley, co., Ga. D2 175
Schlitz, Ger. C4 61
Schlüchtern, Ger. C4 61
Schmalkalden, Ger. C5 61
Schmölln, Ger. C7 61
Schneeberg, Ger. C7 61
Schneeberg, mtn., Ger. C6 61
Schneider, Ind. B3 179
Schoenchen, Kans. D4 181
Schofield, Wis. D4 212
Schofield Barracks, Haw. g9 176
Schoharie, N.Y. C6 196
Schoharie, co., N.Y. C6 196
Schoharie, creek, N.Y. C6 196
Scholle, N. Mex. C3 195
Scholls, Oreg. B2 201
Schönbach, Aus. D7 60
Schönebeck, Ger. A6 61
Schöneck, Ger. C7 61
Schongau, Ger. E5 60
Schöningen, Ger. A5 61
Schoodic, lake, Maine C4 184
Schoolcraft, Mich. F5 186
Schoolcraft, co., Mich. B4 186
Schooley, mtn., N.J. B3 194
Schoonhoven, Neth. C4 59
Schopfheim, Ger. B3 66
Schorndorf, Ger. E4 61
Schoten, Bel. C4 59
Schötmar, Ger. A3 61
Schouten, is., Indon. F9 90
Schram City, Ill. D4 178
Schramberg, Ger. D4 60
Schriever, La. C6, E5 183
Schrobenhausen, Ger. E6 61
Schroeder, Minn. B6, C8 187
Schroon, lake, N.Y. B7 196
Schroon Lake, N.Y. B7 196
Schuchk, Ariz. E4 168
Schuchuli, Ariz. E3 168
Schulenburg, Tex. E4 206
Schuler, Alta., Can. D5 148
Schulte, Kans. B5 181
Schulter, Okla. B6 200
Schurz, Nev. E3 192
Schüttorf, Ger. A2 61
Schuyler, Nebr. C8 191
Schuyler, Va. D4 209
Schuyler, co., Ill. C3 178
Schuyler, co., Mo. A5 189
Schuyler, co., N.Y. C4 196
Schuyler Lake, N.Y. C5 196
Schuylerville, N.Y. B7 196
Schuylkill, co., Pa. E9 202
Schuylkill, riv., Pa. A11 202
Schuylkill Haven, Pa. E9 202
Schwabach, Ger. D6 61
Schwäbisch Gmünd, Ger. E4 61
Schwäbisch Hall, Ger. D4 61
Schwäbische Alb, plat., Ger. E4 61
Schwabmünchen, Ger. A6 66
Schwandorf, Ger. D7 61
Schwaner, mts., Indon. F4 90
Schwarmstedt, Ger. F3 62
Schwarze Elster, riv., Ger. B8 61
Schwarzenbach [an der sächsischen Saale], Ger. C6 61
Schwarzenbek, Ger. E4 62
Schwarzenberg, Ger. C7 61
Schwarzenfeld, Ger. D7 61
Schwarzheide, Ger. B8 61
Schwaz, Aus. E5 60
Schwedt, Ger. B7 60
Schweinfurt, Ger. C5 61
Schwenksville, Pa. *F10 202
Schwenningen, Ger. D4 60
Schwerin, Ger. B5 60
Schweriner, lake, Ger. E5 62
Schwetzingen, Ger. D3 61
Schwyz, Switz. B4 66
Schwyz, canton, Switz. B4 66
Schyan, riv., Que., Can. A7 153
Sciacca, It. F4 67
Science Hill, Ky. C5 182
Scilla, glacier, Ant. C19 120
Scilly, is., Eng. F3 55
Scio, N.Y. C3 196
Scio, Ohio B6 199
Scio, Oreg. C2, C4 201
Sciota, Ill. C3 178
Scioto, co., Ohio D4 199
Scioto, riv., Ohio B4 199
Scioto Furnace, Ohio D5 199
Sciotodale, Ohio *D5 199
Scipio, Ind. F6 179
Scipio, Utah D3 207
Scitico, Conn. B6 172
Scituate, Mass. B6, D4 185
Scituate, res., R.I. B10 172
Scobey, Mont. B11 190
Scofield, Utah D4 207
Scollard, Alta., Can. D4 148
Scooba, Miss. C5 188
Scopus, mtn., Jordan m14 84
Scoresbysund, Grnld. B17 118
Scotch Plains, N.J. B4 194
Scotia, Calif. B1 170
Scotia, Nebr. C7 191
Scotia, N.Y. C7 196
Scotia, S.C. F5 203
Scotland, Ark. B3 169
Scotland, Ont., Can. D4 153
Scotland, Conn. C8 172
Scotland, Ga. D4 175
Scotland, Ind. G4 179
Scotland, N.H. E2 193
Scotland, Pa. G6 202
Scotland, S. Dak. D8 204
Scotland, reg., U.K. D4 57
c. 1140 47
c. 1721 49
Scotland, co., Mo. A5 189
Scotland, co., N.C. C4 197
Scotland Neck, N.C. A6 197
Scotlandville, La. A5, D4 183
Scotrun, Pa. D11 202
Scotsburn, N.S., Can. D7 151
Scotsguard, Sask., Can. H1 155
Scotstown, Que., Can. D6 154
Scott, Ark. C3, D6 169
Scott, Sask., Can. E1 155
Scott, Ga. D4 175
Scott, La. D3 183
Scott, Miss. B2 188
Scott, Ohio B3 199
Scott, co., Ark. C1 169
Scott, co., Ill. D3 178
Scott, co., Ind. G6 179
Scott, co., Iowa C7 180
Scott, co., Kans. D3 181
Scott, co., Ky. B5 182
Scott, co., Minn. F5 187
Scott, co., Miss. C4 188
Scott, co., Mo. D8 189
Scott, co., Tenn. C9 205
Scott, co., Va. B2 209
Scott, cape, B.C., Can. D3 149
Scott, glacier, Ant. A34 120
Scott, glacier, Ant. C23 120
Scott, glacier tongue, Ant. C23 120
Scott, is., Ant. C30 120
Scott, is., B.C., Can. D3 149
Scott, mtn., Idaho E3 177
Scott, mtn., Okla. C3 200
Scott, mtn., Oreg. E4 201
Scott, peak, Idaho E6 177
Scott, range, Ant. C18 120
Scott City, Kans. D3 181
Scott City, Mo. D8 189
Scott Township, Penn. *F1 202
Scottdale, Ga. B5 175
Scottdale, Pa. F2 202
Scottish, sea, Scot. D2 57
Scottland, Ill. D6 178
Scotts, Mich. F5 186
Scotts, mtn., N.J. B2 194
Scotts Bluff, co., Nebr. C2 191
Scotts Bluff, nat. mon., Nebr. C2 191
Scotts Hill, N.C. C6 197
Scotts Hill, Tenn. B3 205
Scotts Mills, Oreg. B4, C2 201
Scottsbluff, Nebr. C2 191
Scottsboro, Ala. A3 166
Scottsburg, Ind. G6 179
Scottsburg, Oreg. D3 201
Scottsburg, Va. E4 209
Scottsdale, Ariz. D4, G2 168
Scottsville, Ark. B2 169
Scottsville, Kans. C6 181
Scottsville, Ky. D3 182
Scottsville, N.Y. B3 196
Scottsville, Va. D4 209
Scottville, Ill. D3 178
Scottville, Mich. E4 186
Scourie, Scot. B3 57
Scout Lake, Sask., Can. H3 155
Scraggly, lake, Maine B4 184
Scranton, Ark. B2 169
Scranton, Iowa B3 180
Scranton, Kans. D8 181
Scranton, Ky. C6 182
Scranton, N.Y. *C2 196
Scranton, N.C. B7 197
Scranton, N. Dak. C2 198
Scranton, Pa. A9, D10 202
Scranton, S.C. D8 203
Scraper, Okla. A7 200
Screven, Ga. E4 175
Screven, co., Ga. D5 175
Scribner, Nebr. C9 191
Scridain, bay, Scot. D2 57
Scrolls, caves, Jordan C7 84
Scullville, N.J. E3 194
Scunthorpe, Eng. A7 56
Scuol (Schuls), Switz. C6 66
Scurry, co., Tex. C2 206
Scusciuban, Som. C7 105
Scutari, lake, Alb. A2 69
Scyrene, Ala. D2 166
Sdom, Isr. C7 84
Sea Bright, N.J. C5 194
Sea Cliff, N.Y. F2 172
Sea Girt, N.J. C4 194
Sea Island, Ga. E5 175
Sea Isle City, N.J. E3 194
Sea View, Mass. E4 185
Seaboard, N.C. A6 197
Seábra, Braz. C3 134
Seabrook, Del. B7 173
Seabrook, N.H. E5 193
Seabrook, Tex. F5 206
Seabrook, isl., S.C. F7 203
Seabrook Farms, N.J. *E2 194
Seadrift, Tex. E4 206
Seaford, Del. C6 173
Seaford, N.Y. G3 172
Seaford, Va. A6 209
Seaforth, Ont., Can. D3 153
Seaforth, Minn. F3 187
Seagoville, Tex. B6 206
Seagram, lake, Sask., Can. E1 155
Seagrave, Ont., Can. C6 153
Seagraves, Tex. C1 206
Seagrove, N.C. B4 197
Seaham, Eng. F7 57
Seahurst, Wash. D1 210
Seal, lake, Newf., Can. g9 152
Seal Beach, Calif. *F2 170
Seal Cove, N.B., Can. E3 151
Seal Cove, Newf., Can. D3 152
Seal Cove, Maine D4 184
Seal Harbor, Maine D4 184
Seal Rock, Oreg. C2 201
Seale, Ala. C4 166
Sealevel, N.C. C7 197
Sealston, Va. C5 209
Sealy, Tex. E4 206
Seama, N. Mex. B2 195
Seaman, Ohio D4 199
Seanor, Pa. F4 202
Searchlight, Nev. H7 192
Searcy, Ark. B4 169
Searcy, co., Ark. B3 169
Searight, Ala. D3 166
Searles, Ala. B2 166
Searles, Minn. F4 187
Searles, lake, Calif. E5 170
Sears, Mich. E5 186
Sears, falls, Nebr. B5 191
Searsboro, Iowa C5 180
Searsburg, Vt. F3 208
Searsport, Maine D4 184
Searston, Newf., Can. E2 152
Seaside, Calif. C6 170
Seaside, Oreg. B3 201
Seaside Heights, N.J. D4 194
Seaside Park, N.J. D4 194
Seat Pleasant, Md. C2, C4 173
Seatack, Va. *E7 209
Seaton, Eng. D4 56
Seaton, Ill. B3 178
Seattle, Wash. B3, D1 210
Seaview, Wash. C1 210
Seaville, N.J. E3 194
Seba Beach, Alta., Can. C3 148
Sebáco, Nic. D4 130
Sebago, lake, Maine E2 184
Sebago Lake, Maine E2 184
Sebasco Estates, Maine E6 184
Sebastian, Fla. E6 174
Sebastian, co., Ark. B1 169
Sebastian, cape, Oreg. E2 201
Sebastian, inlet, Fla. E6 174
Sebastián Vizcaíno, bay, Mex. B2 129
Sebasticook, lake, Maine D3 184
Sebastopol, Calif. A5, C2 170
Sebastopol, Miss. C4 188
Sebatik, isl., Indon. E5 90
Sebec, Maine C3 184
Sebec, lake, Maine C3 184
Sebeka, Minn. D3 187
Sebeş, Rom. C6 68
Sebewaing, Mich. E7 186
Şebinkarahisar, Tur. B12 85
Šebnitz, Ger. C9 61
Seboeis, Maine C4 184
Seboeis, riv., Maine B4 184
Seboois, lake, Maine C4 184
Seboomook, lake, Maine C3 184
Seboruco, P.R. C4 132
Sebou, riv., Mor. G4 64
Seboyeta, N. Mex. B2 195
Sebree, Ky. C2 182
Sebrell, Va. E5 209
Sebring, Fla. E5 174
Sebring, Ohio B6 199
Sebringville, Ont., Can. D3 153
Secaucus, N.J. D5 194
Secchia, riv., It. B3 67
Sechelt, B.C., Can. E6 149
Sechura, Peru C1 134
Sechura, bay, Peru C1 134
Seco, Ky. C7 182
Second, lake, N.H. A2 193
2nd Cataract (Nile River), Sud. A2 105
Second Mesa, Ariz. B5 168
Secor, Ill. C4 178
Secretan, Sask., Can. G2 155
Secretary, Md. C6 173
Secretary, isl., N.Z. P11 112
Section, Ala. A4 166
Secunderabad, India E6 87, I7 88
Secunderabad Cantonment, India *I7 88
Security, Colo. C6 171
Sedalia, Alta., Can. D5 148
Sedalia, Colo. B6 171
Sedalia, Ind. D4 179
Sedalia, Ky. B2 182
Sedalia, Mo. C4 189
Sedalia (Midway), Ohio C4 199
Sedan, Fr. C6 58
Sedan, Kans. E7 181
Sedan, Minn. E3 187
Sedan, N. Mex. A6 195
Sedbergh, Eng. F6 57
Sédérog, Niger C5 103
Sedgewick, Alta., Can. C5 148
Sedgewickville, Mo. D8 189
Sedgwick, Ark. B5 169
Sedgwick, Colo. A8 171
Sedgwick, Kans. B5, E6 181
Sedgwick, Maine D4 184
Sedgwick, co., Colo. A8 171
Sedgwick, co., Kans. E6 181
Sedgewick, mtn., N. Mex. B1 195
Sédhiou, Sen. D1 103
Sedlčany, Czech. D9 61
Sedley, Sask., Can. G3 155
Sedley, Va. E6 209
Sedona, Ariz. C4 168
Sedro Woolley, Wash. A3 210
Seebe, Alta., Can. D3 148
Seeber, riv., Man., Can. B5 150
Seeber, riv., Ont., Can. C5 150
Seebert, W. Va. C4 211
Seehausen, Ger. F5 62
Seeheim, S.W. Afr. C2 107
Seeis, S.W. Afr. B2 107
Seekonk, Mass. C5 185
Seeley, Calif. F6 170
Seeley Lake, Mont. C3 190
Seeleys Bay, Ont., Can. C8 153
Seelow, Ger. F8 62
Seely, Wyo. A8 213
Seelyville, Ind. F3 179
Seelyville, Pa. C11 202
Sées, Fr. C4 58
Seesen, Ger. B5 61
Sefadu, S.L. E2 103
Seferihisar, Tur. C6 69
Sefid, riv., Iran C4 86
Segamat, Mala. K5 89
Segesta, ruins, It. F4 67
Segezha, Sov. Un. F16 63
Seglora, Swe. A6 62
Sego, Utah D6 207
Segorbe, Sp. C5 65
Ségou, Mali D3 103
Segovia, Sp. B3 65
Segovia, Tex. D3 206
Segovia or Wanks, see Coco, riv., Nic.
Segozero, lake, Sov. Un. F15 63
Segre, Fr. D3 58
Segre, riv., Sp. B6 65
Segreganset, Mass. C5 185
Seguedine (Well), Niger B7 103
Séguéla, I.C. E3 103
Seguin, Tex. B4, E4 206
Seguin Falls, Ont., Can. B5 153
Seguine, pt., N.Y. E4 194
Segundo, Colo. D6 171
Segura, riv., Sp. C5 65
Sehkūheh, Iran F10 86
Sehore, India F6 88
Sehwan, Pak. D1 88
Seibert, Colo. B8 171
Seibo, Dom. Rep. F9 131
Seiling, Okla. A3 200
Seille, riv., Fr. F6 59
Seinäjoki, Fin. F10 63
Seine, bay, Fr. C3 58
Seine, riv., Fr. C4 58
Seine-et-Marne, dept., Fr. F2 59
Seine-et-Oise, dept., Fr. F2 59
Seine Maritime, dept., Fr. E9 56
Seis de Septiembre, Arg. g7 136
Seistan, reg., Iran, Afg. F10 86
Seixal, Port. f9 65
Sejerby, Den. C5 62
Sejerö, bay, Den. C5 62
Sekenke, Tan. B5 106
Seki, Jap. o15 93
Sekiu, Wash. A1 210
Sekondi-Takoradi, Ghana F4 103
Selah, Wash. C5 210
Selangor, pol. div., Mala. K4 89
Selanovtsi, Bul. D7 68
Selapiu, isl., Bis. Arch. 115
Selaru, isl., Indon. G8 90
Selatan, cape, Indon. F4 90
Selatpandjang, Indon. L5 89
Selawik, Alsk. B7 167
Selawik, lake, Alsk. B7 167
Selb, Ger. C7 61
Selbu, Nor. F4 63
Selby, Eng. A6 56
Selby, S. Dak. B5 204
Selbyville, Del. D7 173
Selbyville, W. Va. C4 211
Selde, Den. B3 62
Selden, Kans. C3 181
Selden, N.Y. *E3 196
Seldovia, Alsk. D9, h16 167
Selenge, riv., Mong. B5 91
Selenicë, Alb. B2 69
Selenter, lake, Ger. D4 62
Sélestat, Fr. C7 58
Seletytengiz, lake, Sov. Un. C8 73
Seleucid kingdom 43
Selfridge, N. Dak. C5 198
Selibaby, Maur. C2 103
Selidovka, Sov. Un. q20 72
Seligenstadt, Ger. C3 61
Seliger, lake, Sov. Un. C9 72
Seligman, Ariz. B3 168
Seligman, Mo. E4 189
Selima (Oasis), Sud. A2 105
Selinsgrove, Pa. E8 202
Selinunte, ruins, It. F4 67
Selizharovo, Sov. Un. C9 72
Seljuk, kingdom of Iconium 47
Selkirk, Man., Can. D3 150
Selkirk, Ont., Can. E5 153
Selkirk, Kans. D2 181
Selkirk, Scot. E6 57
Selkirk, co., Scot. E5 57
Selkirk, mts., B.C., Can. D9 149
Selkirk, mts., Idaho A2 177
Selleck, Wash. B4, D2 210
Seller, lake, Man., Can. B4 150
Sellers, Ala. C3 166
Sellers, S.C. C9 203
Sellersburg, Ind. H6 179
Sellersville, Pa. F11 202
Sells, Ariz. F4 168
Selm, Ger. B2 61
Selma, Ala. C2 166
Selma, Ark. D4 169
Selma, Calif. D4 170
Selma, Ind. D7 179
Selma, N.C. B5 197
Selma, Oreg. E3 201
Selmah, N.S., Can. D6 151
Selman, Okla. A2 200
Selmer, Tenn. B3 205
Selsey, Eng. D7 56
Selsey Bill, pt., Eng. D7 56
Selukwe, Rh. A5 107
Selva, Arg. E3 135
Selvas, forests, S.A. D4 124
Selvin, Ind. H3 179
Selway, riv., Idaho C3 177
Selwyn, Austl. D7 111
Selwyn, lake, N.W. Ter., Can. D12 142
Selwyn, mtn., B.C., Can. B6 149
Selwyn, range, Yukon, Can. D6 142
Selwyn, strait, New Hebr. 115
Selz, N. Dak. B6 198
Seman, Ala. C3 166
Seman, riv., Alb. B2 69
Semans, Sask., Can. F3 155
Semarang, Indon. G4 90
Semenovka, Sov. Un. E9 72
Seminary, Miss. D4 188
Seminoe, mts., Wyo. C6 213
Seminoe, res., Wyo. D6 213
Seminoe Dam, Wyo. C6 213
Seminole, Ala. E2 166
Seminole, Okla. B5 200
Seminole, Tex. C1 206
Seminole, co., Fla. D5 174
Seminole, co., Ga. F2 175
Seminole, co., Okla. B5 200
Seminole, Indian res., Fla. F6 174
Semipalatinsk, Sov. Un. C10 73
Semitau, Indon. E4 90
Semiyarskoye, Sov. Un. C9 73
Semliki, riv., Zaire A5 106
Semmens, lake, Man., Can. B4 150
Semmering, pass, Aus. E7 60
Semnān, Iran D6 86
Semora, N.C. A4 197
Semoy, riv., Bel. E5 59
Sempacher, lake, Switz. B4 66
Semur-en-Auxois, Fr. D6 58
Sen, riv., Camb. F6 89
Sena, N. Mex. B4 195
Sena, cape, New Ire. I. 115
Sena Madureira, Braz. C4 134
Senachwine, lake, Ill. B4 178
Senador Pompeu, Braz. C3 138
Senanga, Zambia E3 106
Senate, Sask., Can. H1 155
Senath, Mo. E7 189
Senatobia, Miss. A4 188
Sendai, Jap. G10 93
Sendai (Kagoshima pref.), Jap. K5 93
Sendai, bay, Jap. G10 93
Seneca, Ariz. D5 168
Seneca, Ill. B5 178
Seneca, Kans. C7 181
Seneca, Mo. E3 189
Seneca, Nebr. B5 191
Seneca, N. Mex. A6 195
Seneca, Oreg. C8 201
Seneca, Pa. D2 202
Seneca, S.C. B2 203
Seneca, S. Dak. B6 204
Seneca, Wis. E3 212
Seneca, co., N.Y. C4 196
Seneca, co., Ohio A4 199
Seneca, lake, N.Y. C4 196
Seneca, mtn., N.Y. C2 196
Seneca Falls, N.Y. C4 196
Seneca Gardens, Ky. *B4 182
Senecaville, Ohio C6 199
Senecaville, res., Ohio C6 199
Seneffe, Bel. D4 59
SENEGAL, country, Afr. D2 103
in 1885 99
Sénégal, riv., Maur., Sen. C2 103
Senekal, S. Afr. C4 107
Seney, Mich. B5 186
Senftenberg, Ger. B9 61
Senga Hill, Zambia C5 106
Senguerr, riv., Arg. D3 136
Senhor do Bonfim, Braz. D2 138
Senhōshi, Jap. D10 93
Senigallia, It. C4 67
Senj, Yugo. C2 68
Senja, isl., Nor. C7 63
Senlac, Sask., Can. E1 155
Senlis, Fr. C5 58
Sennār, Sud. C3 105
Senneterre, Que., Can. B2 154
Senneville, Que., Can. *D4 154
Senoia, Ga. C2 175
Sens, Fr. C5 58
Senta, Yugo. C5 68

INDEX KEY Each place listed in **Bold-faced Type** has its population listed in the Population tables, pages 230 to 280.
Each country, shown in CAPITAL LETTERS, has its population listed in the World Political Information Table, pages 6 to 10.
* Does not appear on map; key shows general location.

Sentery, Zaire C4 106
Sentinel, Ariz. E2 168
Sentinel, Okla. B2 200
Sentinel, butte, N. Dak. C2 198
Sentinel, peak, B.C., Can. B6 149
Sentinel Butte, N. Dak. C2 198
Senzu, Jap. n17 93
Seo de Urgel, Sp. A6 65
Seoni, India F7 88
Seoul (Sŏul), Kor. H3 93
Separ, N. Mex. E1 195
Sepi, Santa Isabel I. 115
Sepik, riv., New Gui. h11 110
Sępolno, Pol. B4 70
Sept-Îles (Seven Islands), Que., Can. B3 154
Sepulga, riv., Ala. D3 166
Sequatchie, Tenn. D8 205
Sequatchie, co., Tenn. D8 205
Sequatchie, riv., Tenn. D8 205
Sequim, Wash. A2 210
Sequoia, nat. park, Calif. D4 170
Sequoia National Park, Calif. D4 170
Sequoyah, co., Okla. B7 200
Serafimovich, Sov. Un. D2 73
Serafina, N. Mex. B4 195
Seraing, Bel. D5 59
Serakhs, Sov. Un. C10 86
Serampur, India *F12 88
Serang, Indon. G3 90
Serasan, isl., Indon. K8 89
Serbia, reg., Yugo. D5 68
c. 1140 47
c. 1360 48
in 1721 49
in 1914 52
Serdobsk, Sov. Un. E15 72
Sered, Czech. D4 70
Şereflikoçhisar, Tur. C9 85
Seremban, Mala. K4 89
Serengeti, plain, Tan. B5 106
Serenje, Zambia D5 106
Serenli, Som. E5 105
Sergeant, Pa. C4 202
Sergeant Bluff, Iowa B1 180
Sergeantsville, N.J. C3 194
Sergipe, state, Braz. D3 138
Seria, Bru. E4 90
Sérifos, Grc. D5 69
Sérifos, isl., Grc. D5 69
Seringapatam, India F6 87
Serinháem, Braz. k6 138
Serles, Tenn. B3 205
Sermaize, Fr. F4 59
Sernyy Zavod, Sov. Un. B9 86
Seroei, Indon. F9 90
Serón, Sp. D4 65
Serov, Sov. Un. B6 73
Serowe, Bots. B4 107
Serpa, Port. D2 65
Serpentine, lakes, Austl. E4 110
Serpukhov, Sov. Un. C1 73
Serra Negra, Braz. m8 137
Serra Talhada, Braz. C3 138
Sérrai, Grc. B4 69
Serrana Bank, shoals, Caribbean Sea C7 130
Serranilla Bank, shoals, Col. C8 130
Serres, Fr. E1 66
Serrezuela, Arg. A3 136
Serrinha, Braz. D3 138
Serro, Braz. E2 138
Sertã, Port. C1 65
Sertânia, Braz. C3 138
Serua, isl., Indon. G8 90
Serule, Bots. B4 107
Sérvia, Grc. B4 69
Servia, Ind. C6 179
Sese, is., Ug. B5 106
Sesheke, Zambia E3 106
Sésia, riv., It. D4 66
Sesoko, isl., Okinawa 114
Sesoko, Okinawa 114
Sesser, Ill. E4 178
Sessums, Miss. B5 188
Sesto [Fiorentino], It. C3 67
Sesto San Giovanni, It. D5 66
Šeštokai, Sov. Un. A7 70
Sestri Levante, It. B2 67
Sestriere, It. E2 66
Sestroretsk, Sov. Un. A7 72
Setana, Jap. E9 93
Setauket, N.Y. F4 172
Sète, Fr. F5 58
Sete Lagoas, Braz. E4 138
Sete Quedas, falls, Braz. C2 137
Seth, W. Va. C3, D6 211
Seth Ward, Tex. *B2 206
Sétif, Alg. B6 102
Seto, Jap. I8, n16 93
Seton Portage, B.C., Can. D6 149
Settat, Mor. C3 102
Setté-Cama, Gabon F1 104
Settee, lake, Sask., Can. B4 155
Setting, lake, Man., Can. B2 150
Settle, Eng. F6 57
Setúbal, Port. C1 65
Setúbal, bay, Port. C1 65
Seul, lake, Ont., Can. E8 153
Seul Choix, pt., Mich. C5 186
Sevan, lake, Sov. Un. E3 73
Sevastopol, Sov. Un. I9 72
Seven Devils, mts., Idaho. D2 177
Seven Hills, Ohio *A6 199
Seven Islands, see Sept-Îles, Que., Can.
Seven Islands, bay, Newf., Can. f9 152
Seven Mile, Ohio C3 199
Seven Mile, beach, N.J. E3 194
Seven Mile Corner, S. Dak. D4 204
Seven Persons, Alta., Can. E5 148
Seven Sisters, Tex. E3 206
Seven Sisters, mtn., B.C., Can. B3 149
Sevenoaks, Eng. C8 56
Sevensprings, N.C. B6 197
70 Mile House, B.C., Can. D7 149
Severance, Colo. A6 171
Severance, Kans. C8 181
Severka, riv., Sov. Un. n18 72
Severn, Md. B4 173
Severn, N.C. A6 197
Severn, Va. D6 209
Severn, mouth, Eng. C5 56
Severn, riv., Ont., Can. D8 153
Severn, riv., Eng. B5 56
Severn, riv., Md. B4 173
Severna Park, Md. B4 173
Severnaya Zemlya, reg., Sov. Un. B11 71
Severodonetsk, Sov. Un. q21 72
Severodvinsk, Sov. Un. E18 63
Severomorsk, Sov. Un. C15 63
Severy, Kans. E7 181
Sevier, Utah E3 207
Sevier, co., Ark. D1 169
Sevier, co., Tenn. D10 205
Sevier, co., Utah E4 207
Sevier, des., Utah D3 207
Sevier, lake, Utah E2 207
Sevier, riv., Utah D3 207
Sevierville, Tenn. D10 205
Sevilla, Col. C2 133
Sevilla, see Seville, Sp.
Seville, Fla. C5 174
Seville, Ga. E3 175
Seville, Ohio A6 199
Seville (Sevilla), Sp. D3 65
Sevlievo, Bul. D7 68
Sevogle, riv., N.B., Can. B3 151
Sevran, Fr. g11 58
Sèvre, riv., Fr. D3 58
Sèvre Niortaise, riv., Fr. D3 58
Sèvres, Fr. g9 58
Sewal, Iowa D4 180
Sewanee, Tenn. B6 205
Seward, Alsk. C10, g17 167
Seward, Ill. A4 178
Seward, Kans. D5 181
Seward, Nebr. D8 191
Seward, Okla. B4 200
Seward, Pa. F3 202
Seward, co., Kans. E3 181
Seward, co., Nebr. D8 191
Seward, pen., Alsk. B7 167
Seward Roads, chan., Midway Is. 114
Sewaren, N.J. E4 194
Sewell, Chile A2 136
Sewell, N.J. D2 194
Sewickley, Pa. A5, E1 202
Sewickley Heights, Pa. *E1 202
Sexsmith, Alta., Can. B1 148
Sextonville, Wis. E3 212
Seydişehir, Tur. D8 85
Seydisfjördur, Ice. n25 63
Seyhan (Sarus), riv., Tur. C10 85
Seym, riv., Sov. Un. F9 72
Seymchan, Sov. Un. C18 71
Seymour, Austl. H5 112
Seymour, Conn. D4 172
Seymour, Ind. G6 179
Seymour, Iowa D4 180
Seymour, Mo. D5 189
Seymour, Tenn. D10, E12 205
Seymour, Tex. C3 206
Seymour, Wis. A5, D5 212
Seymour, inlet, B.C., Can. D4 149
Seymour, lake, Vt. B4 208
Seymour, range, B.C., Can. B8 149
Seymourville, La. B5 183
Sézanne, Fr. C5 58
Sezimbra, Port. C1 65
Sezze, It. D4 67
Sfântul-Gheorghe, Rom. C7 68
Sfax, Tun. G12 64, C7 102
Sgarbhbreac, mtn., Scot. E2 57
's Gravenhage, see The Hague, Neth.
Sgurr Mor, mtn., Scot. E3 57
Sha, China K7 92
Shabalē, riv., Eth. D5 105
Shabani, Rh. B5 107
Shabbona, Ill. B5 178
Shabunda, Zaire B4 106
Shabwah, Yemen (Aden). B6 105
Shackelford, co., Tex. C3 206
Shackleton, Sask., Can. G1 155
Shackleton, ice shelf, Ant. C22 120
Shade, riv., Ohio C5 199
Shadehill, S. Dak. B3 204
Shadehill, dam, S. Dak. B3 204
Shadehill, res., S. Dak. B3 204
Shades, creek, Ala. E4 166
Shades, mtn., Ala. E4 166
Shadeville, Ohio C2 199
Shadrinsk, Sov. Un. B6 73
Shady Dale, Ga. C3 175
Shady Cove, Oreg. E4 201
Shady Grove, Ala. D3 166
Shady Grove, Fla. B3 174
Shady Grove, Ky. A3, C2 182
Shady Side, Md. C4 173
Shady Spring, W. Va. D3 211
Shady Valley, Tenn. C12 205
Shadygrove, Pa. G6 202
Shadypoint, Okla. B7 200
Shadyside, Ohio C7 199
Shafer, butte, Idaho F2 177
Shafer, lake, Ind. C4 179
Shafter, Calif. E4 170
Shafter, Nev. C7 192
Shafter, Tex. p12 206
Shaftesbury, Eng. D5 56
Shaftsbury, Vt. E2 208
Shaftsbury Center, Vt. F2 208
Shag Harbour, N.S., Can. F4 151
Shageluk, Alsk. C8 167
Shagwong, pt., N.Y. E9 172
Shah, riv., Iran C5 86
Shāh Fulādi, mtn., Afg. D13 86
Shahdād (Khabīs), Iran F8 86
Shahdadkot, Pak. D1 88
Shahgarh, India D2 88
Shaḥḥāt, Libya C4 101
Shahi, isl., Iran C2 86
Shahjahanpur, India D7 88
Shahjui, Afg. E13 86
Shahpur, India I6 88
Shāhpūr (Dīlmān), Iran B2 86
Shahpur, Pak. C4 87
Shahpura, India E5 88
Shahr-e Bābak, Iran F7 86
Shahrezā, Iran E5 86
Shāhrūd, Iran C7 86
Shahsavār, Iran C5 86
Shaib al Qur, wadi, Sau. Ar. G13 85
Shaib Hub, riv., Iraq G14 85
Shaikh Shu'aib, isl., Iran H6 86
Shaker Heights, Ohio A6, B2 199
Shakhrisyabz, Sov. Un. B13 86
Shakhty, Sov. Un. H13 72
Shakhtërsk, Sov. Un. *G12 72
Shakhunya, Sov. Un. B3 73
Shaki, Nig. E5 103
Shakopee, Minn. F5 187
Shakotan, cape, Jap. E10 93
Shaktoolik, Alsk. C7 167
Shalath, B.C., Can. D6 149
Shaler, Pa. *E2 202
Shalimar, Fla. G2 174
Shallmar, Md. D1 173
Shallotte, N.C. D5 197
Shallotte, inlet, N.C. D5 197
Shallow Lake, Ont., Can. C3 153
Shallow Water, Kans. D3 181
Shallowater, Tex. C1 206
Shamattawa, Man., Can. B5 150
Shambat, Sud. B3 105
Shambaugh, Iowa D2 180
Shambe, Sud. D3 105
Shamīl, Iran H8 86
Shamokin, Pa. E8 202
Shamokin Dam, Pa. E8 202
Shamrock, Sask., Can. G2 155
Shamrock, Fla. C3 174
Shamrock, La. C2 183
Shamrock, Okla. B5 200
Shamrock, Tex. B2 206
Shamva, Rh. A5 107
Shanchung, Taiwan *G9 91
Shandaken, N.Y. C6 196
Shandon, Calif. E3 170
Shandon, Ohio C2 199
Shanesville, Ohio *B6 199
Shang, China H3 92
Shangchiu, China G6 92
Shanghai, China E9 91, I9 92
Shangjao, China J8 92
Shangnan, China H4 92
Shangshui, China H6 92
Shangssu, China A7 89
Shangtu, China D5 92
Shaniko, Oreg. B6 201
Shannock, R.I. D10 172
Shannon, Ga. B1 175
Shannon, Ill. A4 178
Shannon, Miss. A5 188
Shannon, Tex. C3 206
Shannon, co., Mo. D6 189
Shannon, co., S. Dak. D3 204
Shannon, bay, Ire. E2 55
Shannon, isl., Grnld. B16 118
Shannon, lake, Wash. A4 210
Shannon, riv., Ire. D2 55
Shannon City, Iowa D3 180
Shannontown, S.C. *D7 203
Shanshan (Pichan), China C3 91
Shansi, prov., China D7 91
Shantar, is., Sov. Un. D16 71
Shantung, prov., China D8 91
Shantung, pen., China D9 91, F9 92
Shanwa, Tan. B5 106
Shaohsing, China E9 91, I9 92
Shaokuan, China G7 91
Shaopo, China H8 92
Shaowu, China K7 92
Shaoyang, China F7 91, K4 92
Shap, Eng. F6 57
Shapinsay, isl., Scot. A6 57
Shapio, lake, Newf., Can. g9 152
Shapki, Sov. Un. s32 63
Shapleigh, Maine E2 184
Sharafkhāneh, Iran B2 86
Sharangad, Mong. B2 92
Sharasume (Chenghwa), China B2 91
Sharbot Lake, Ont., Can. C8 153
Shari, Jap. E12 93
Sharita, cape, Oman H8 86
Shark, bay, Austl. E1 110
Shark, pt., Fla. G5 174
Sharkey, co., Miss. C3 188
Sharkh, Oman D2 87
Sharon, Conn. B3 172
Sharon, Ga. C4 175
Sharon, Kans. E5 181
Sharon, Mass. B5, E2 185
Sharon, Miss. C4 188
Sharon, N.H. E3 193
Sharon, N.Y. C6 196
Sharon, N. Dak. B8 198
Sharon, Okla. A2 200
Sharon, Pa. D1 202
Sharon, S.C. B5 203
Sharon, Tenn. A3 205
Sharon, Vt. D4 208
Sharon, W. Va. D6 211
Sharon, Wis. F5 212
Sharon Grove, Ky. D2 182
Sharon Hill, Pa. B11 202
Sharon Springs, Kans. D2 181
Sharon Springs, N.Y. C6 196
Sharonville, Ohio D2 199
Sharp, co., Ark. A4 169
Sharp Top, mtn., Ark. C2 169
Sharpe, lake, Man., Can. B5 150
Sharpe, lake, S. Dak. B8 159
Sharpes, Fla. D6 174
Sharples, W. Va. D3, D5 211
Sharps Chapel, Tenn. C10 205
Sharpsburg, Iowa D3 180
Sharpsburg, Ky. B6 182
Sharpsburg, Md. B2 173
Sharpsburg, N.C. B6 197
Sharpsburg, Pa. B6 202
Sharpsville, Ind. D5 179
Sharpsville, Pa. D1 202
Sharptown, Md. C6 173
Sharptown, N.J. D2 194
Sharya, Sov. Un. B3 73
Shāshamani, Eth. D4 105
Shashi, riv., Bots., Rh. B4 107
Shashke, Sov. Un. C7 73
Shashih, China E7 91
Shasta, co., Calif. B3 170
Shasta, lake, Calif. B2 170
Shasta, mtn., Calif. B2 170
Shastsk, Sov. Un. D13 72
Shatney, mtn., N.H. A1 193
Shatra, Iraq F3 86
Shattuck, Okla. A2 200
Shattuckville, Mass. A2 185
Shatura, Sov. Un. D12 72
Shauck, Ohio B5 199
Shaunavon, Sask., Can. H1 155
Shavano Park, Tex. *E3 206
Shavers, fork, W. Va. C5 211
Shaw, Minn. C6 187
Shaw, Miss. B3 188
Shaw, Oreg. C2 201
Shaw, W. Va. B5 211
Shawa, reg., Eth. D4 105
Shawanaga, Ont., Can. B4 153
Shawangunk, mts., N.Y. D6 196
Shawano, Wis. D5 212
Shawano, co., Wis. D5 212
Shawano, lake, Wis. D5 212
Shawatun, China D9 92
Shawboro, N.C. A7 197
Shawbridge, Que., Can. D3 154
Shawhan, Ky. B5 182
Shawinigan, Que., Can. C5 154
Shawinigan Sud, Que., Can. C5 154
Shawmut, Ala. C4 166
Shawmut, Maine D3 184
Shawmut, Mont. D7 190
Shawnee, Colo. C5 204
Shawnee, Kans. B8 181
Shawnee, Ohio C5 199
Shawnee, Okla. B5 200
Shawnee, Wyo. C8 213
Shawnee, co., Kans. D8 181
Shawneetown, Ill. F5 178
Shawnigan Lake, B.C., Can. B9 149
Shawsheen, riv., Mass. C2 185
Shawsville, Md. A4 173
Shawsville, Va. D2 209
Shawville, Que., Can. B8 153
Shayang, China I5 92
Shchëkino, Sov. Un. D11 72
Shchëlkovo, Sov. Un. n18 72
Shcherbakov, see Rybinsk, Sov. Un.
Shchetovo, Sov. Un. q22 72
Shchigry, Sov. Un. F11 72
Shchors, Sov. Un. F8 72
Shchuchinsk, Sov. Un. C8 73
Shchurovo, Sov. Un. n18 72
Sheboygan, Wis. B6, E6 212
Sheboygan, co., Wis. E6 212
Sheboygan, riv., Wis. B6 212
Sheboygan Falls, Wis. B6, E6 212
Shebshi, mts., Nig. E7 103
Shechichen, China H5 92
Shedd, Oreg. C3 201
Shedden, Ont., Can. E3 153
Shediac, N.B., Can. C5 151
Sheelin, lake, Ire. D3 55
Sheenjek, riv., Alsk. B11 167
Sheep, mtn., Ariz. E1 168
Sheep, mtn., Wyo. A5 213
Sheep, mtn., Wyo. B2 213
Sheep, peak, Nev. G6 192
Sheep, range, Nev. G6 192
Sheeps Haven, mtn., Mass. A1 185
Sheerness, Alta., Can. D5 148
Sheerness, Eng. C8 56
Sheet Harbour, N.S., Can. E7 151
Sheffield, Ala. A2 166
Sheffield, Eng. A6 56
Sheffield, Ill. B4 178
Sheffield, Iowa B4 180
Sheffield, Mass. B1 185
Sheffield, N.Z. O14 112
Sheffield, Ohio A5 199
Sheffield, Pa. C3 202
Sheffield, Tex. D2 206
Sheffield, Vt. B4 208
Sheffield, lake, Newf., Can. D3 152
Sheffield Lake, Ohio A5 199
Shefford, co., Que., Can. D5 154
Sheguiandah, Ont., Can. B3 153
Sheho, Sask., Can. F4 155
Shehsien, China J8 92
Sheikh, Som. D6 105
Shekar Dzong, China C11 88
Shekhūpura, Pak. B5 88
Shelbiana, Ky. C7 182
Shelbina, Mo. B5 189
Shelburn, Ind. F3 179
Shelburn, Oreg. C2, C4 201
Shelburne, N.S., Can. F4 151
Shelburne, Ont., Can. C4 153
Shelburne, Mass. A2 185
Shelburne, N.H. B4 193
Shelburne, Vt. C2 208
Shelburne, co., N.S., Can. F4 151
Shelburne, pond, Vt. C2 208
Shelburne Falls, Mass. A2 185
Shelburne Falls, Vt. C2 208
Shelby, Ala. B3 166
Shelby, Ind. B3 179
Shelby, Iowa C2 180
Shelby, Mich. E4 186
Shelby, Miss. B3 188
Shelby, Mont. B5 190
Shelby, Nebr. C8 191
Shelby, N.C. B2 197
Shelby, Ohio B5 199
Shelby, co., Ala. B3 166
Shelby, co., Ill. D5 178
Shelby, co., Ind. E6 179
Shelby, co., Iowa C2 180
Shelby, co., Ky. B4 182
Shelby, co., Mo. B5 189
Shelby, co., Ohio B3 199
Shelby, co., Tenn. B2 205
Shelby, co., Tex. D5 206
Shelby City, Ky. C5 182
Shelbyville, Ill. D5 178
Shelbyville, Ind. E6 179
Shelbyville, Ky. B4 182
Shelbyville, Mo. B5 189
Shelbyville, Tenn. B5 205
Sheldahl, Iowa A7 180
Sheldon, Ill. C6 178
Sheldon, Iowa A2 180
Sheldon, Mo. D3 189
Sheldon, N. Dak. C8 198
Sheldon, S.C. F6 203
Sheldon, Tex. F5 206
Sheldon, Vt. B3 208
Sheldon, Wis. C3 212
Sheldon Springs, Vt. B3 208
Sheldonville, Mass. B5 185
Shelekhov, gulf, Sov. Un. D18 71
Shelikof, strait, Alsk. D9 167
Shell, creek, Wyo. A5 213
Shell, lake, Minn. D3 187
Shell, lake, Wis. C2 212
Shell, riv., Man., Can. D1 150
Shell Beach, Calif. *E2 170
Shell Beach, La. E6 183
Shell Creek, Tenn. C11 205
Shell Lake, Sask., Can. D2 155
Shell Lake, Wis. C2 212
Shell Rock, Iowa B5 180
Shellbrook, Sask., Can. D2 155
Shelley, Idaho F6 177
Shellman, Ga. E2 175
Shellman Bluff, Ga. E5 175
Shellmouth, Man., Can. D1 150
Shellrock, riv., Iowa B5 180
Shellsburg, Iowa B6 180
Shelly, Minn. C2 187
Shelter, isl., N.Y. E7 172
Shelter Island, N.Y. D4 196
Shelter Island Heights, N.Y. E7 172
Shelton, Conn. D4 172
Shelton, Nebr. D7 191
Shelton, S.C. C5 203
Shelton, Wash. B2 210
Shemogue, N.B., Can. C5 151
Shenandoah, Iowa D2 180
Shenandoah, Pa. E9 202
Shenandoah, Va. C4 209
Shenandoah, co., Va. C4 209
Shenandoah, mtn., Va. C3 209
Shenandoah, nat. park, Va. C4 209
Shenandoah, riv., Va. B5 209
Shenandoah, val., Va. C4 209
Shenandoah Heights, Pa. *E9 202
Shenandoah Tower, mtn., Va., W. Va. C5 211
Shenango River, res., Ohio, Pa. D1 202
Shenchiu, China H6 92
Shendi, Sud. B3 105
Shenipsit, lake, Conn. B7 172
Shenmu, China D7 91
Shensi, prov., China D6 91
Shentsa Dzong, China B12 88
Shenyang, see Mukden, China
Sheopur, India E6 88
Shepard, Alta., Can. D4 148
Shepard, N. Dak. B7 198
Shepardsville, Ind. E3 179
Shepaug, dam, Conn. D4 172
Shepaug, riv., Conn. C3 172
Shepetovka, Sov. Un. F6 72
Shepherd, Mich. E6 186
Shepherd, Mont. D8 190
Shepherd, Tex. D5 206
Shepherd Brook, mtn., Maine B3 184
Shepherdstown, W. Va. B7 211
Shepherdsville, Ky. A4, C4 182
Shepp, Tenn. B2 205
Shepparton, Austl. H5 112
Sheppey, isl., Eng. C8 56
Sheppton, Pa. E9 202
Shepton Mallet, Eng. C5 56
Sherard, Miss. A3 188
Sherborn, Mass. D2 185
Sherborne, Eng. D5 56
Sherbrooke, N.S., Can. D8 151
Sherbrooke, Que., Can. C2, D6 154
Sherbrooke, co., Que., Can. D5 154
Sherbrooke, lake, N.S., Can. E5 151
Sherburn, Minn. G4 187
Sherburne, N.Y. C5 196
Sherburne, co., Minn. E5 187
Sherburne Center, Vt. D3 208
Shereik, Sud. B3 105
Shereshevo, Sov. Un. B8 70
Shergarh, India D4 88
Sheridan, Ark. C3 169
Sheridan, Colo. B5 171
Sheridan, Ill. B5 178
Sheridan, Ind. D5 179
Sheridan, Ky. A3 182
Sheridan, Maine B4 184
Sheridan, Mich. E5 186
Sheridan, Mo. A3 189
Sheridan. Mont. E4 190
Sheridan, Oreg. B3 201
Sheridan, Wyo. A6 213
Sheridan, co., Kans. C3 181
Sheridan, co., Mont. B12 190
Sheridan, co., Nebr. B3 191
Sheridan, co., N. Dak. B5 198
Sheridan, co., Wyo. A5 213
Sheridan, mtn., Wyo. A2 213
Sheridan Lake, Colo. C8 171
Sheringham, Eng. B9 56
Sherkaly, Sov. Un. C9 71
Sherman, Conn. C3 172
Sherman, Maine C4 184
Sherman, Miss. A5 188
Sherman, Mo. B7 189
Sherman, N. Mex. E2 195
Sherman, N.Y. C1 196
Sherman, S. Dak. D9 204
Sherman, Tex. C4 206
Sherman, co., Kans. C2 181
Sherman, co., Nebr. C6 191
Sherman, co., Oreg. B6 201
Sherman, co., Tex. A2 206
Sherman, mtn., Ark. A2 169
Sherman, res., Nebr. C7 191
Sherman Mills, Maine C4 184
Sherman Station, Maine C4 184
Sherpur, Bngl. E12 88
Sherrard, Ill. B3 178
Sherridon, Man., Can. B1 150
Sherrill, Ark. C4 169
Sherrill, N.Y. B5 196
Sherrodsville, Ohio B6 199
's Hertogenbosch, Neth. C5 59
Sherwood, Ark. C3, D6 169
Sherwood, Mich. *F5 186
Sherwood, Miss. B4 188
Sherwood, N. Dak. A4 198
Sherwood, Ohio A3 199
Sherwood, Okla. C7 200
Sherwood, Oreg. B2 201
Sherwood, Tenn. B6 205
Sherwood, Tex. D2 206
Sherwood Park, Alta., Can. C4 148
Sheshebee, Minn. D5 187
Shetek, lake, Minn. F3 187
Shetland, is., Scot. g10 55
Shetucket, riv., Conn. C8 172
Shevlin, Minn. C3 187
Sheyenne, N. Dak. B6 198
Sheyenne, riv., N. Dak. C8 198
Shfaram, Isr. B7 84
Shfayim, Isr. g10 84
Shiant, is., Scot. C2 57
Shiawassee, co., Mich. F6 186
Shibarghan, Afg. C12 86
Shibata, Jap. G9 93
Shibetsu, Jap. D11 93
Shibin al Kawm, Eg. D3 84
Shibin al Qanāṭir, Eg. D3 84
Shichito, isl., Pac. O. D8 113
Shickley, Nebr. D8 191
Shickshinny, Pa. D9 202
Shideler, Ind. D7 179
Shidler, Okla. A5 200
Shiel, lake, Scot. D3 57
Shieldaig, Scot. C3 57
Shields, Kans. D3 181
Shields, N. Dak. C4 198
Shihchiachuang, China E6 92
Shihchüan, China H3 92
Shihmen, China J4 92
Shihshou, China J5 92
Shihtaokuo, China F10 92
Shihtsuishan, China D6 91, E2 92
Shikārpur, Pak. C4 87, D2 88
Shikoku, isl., Jap. J6 93
Shikuka, see Poronaysk, Sov. Un.
Shilka, Sov. Un. D14 71
Shilla, peak, India A7 88
Shillington, Pa. F10 202
Shillong, India C9 87
Shiloh, Ark. *B3 169
Shiloh, Ga. D2 175
Shiloh, Ill. B9 189
Shiloh, N.J. E2 194
Shiloh, N.C. A7 197
Shiloh, Ohio C3 199
Shiloh, Ohio B5 199
Shiloh, Tenn. A4 205
Shiloh, nat. military park and cemetery, Tenn. B3 205
Shimabara, Jap. J5 93
Shimada, Jap. o7 93
Shimanovsk, Sov. Un. D15 71
Shimizu, Jap. I9, n17 93
Shimo, isl., Jap. J5 93
Shimoda, Jap. o17 93

Shimodate, Jap...m18 93
Shimoga, India...F6 87
Shimonoseki, Jap...I5 93
Shimotsuma, Jap...m18 93
Shin, lake, Scot...B4 57
Shin Pond, Maine...B4 184
Shinall, mtn., Ark...D5 169
Shindlar, S. Dak...D9 204
Shiner, Tex...E4 206
Shinewell, Okla...D7 200
Shingbwiyang, Bur...C10 87
Shinglehouse, Pa...C5 202
Shingleton, Mich...B4 186
Shingū, Jap...J7 93
Shinjō, Jap...G10 93
Shinkolobwe, Zaire...D4 106
Shinnecock, bay, N.Y...F6 172
Shinnston, W. Va...A7, B4 211
Shinshiro, Jap...o16 93
Shinyanga, Tan...B5 106
Shio, cape, Jap...J7 93
Shiocton, Wis...A5, D5 212
Shiogama, Jap...G10 93
Shiojiri, Jap...m16 93
Shioya, cape, Jap...H10 93
Ship, isl., Miss...E5 188
Ship Bottom, N.J...D4 194
Ship Cove, Newf., Can...E4 152
Ship Harbour, N.S., Can...E7 151
Ship Island, pass., Miss...E2 188
Ship Rock, mtn., N. Mex...A6 168
Shipiskan, lake, Newf., Can...g9 152
Shipka, pass, Bul...D7 68
Shipki, pass, India...B7 88
Shipman, Sask., Can...D3 155
Shipman, Ill...D3 178
Shipman, Va...D4 209
Shippegan, N.B., Can...B5 151
Shippegan, isl., N.B., Can...B5 151
Shippensburg, Pa...F6 202
Shippenville, Pa...D3 202
Shiprock, N. Mex...A1 195
Shipshewana, Ind...A6 179
Shir Kuh, mtn., Iran...F7 86
Shirabad, Sov. Un...C13 86
Shiraz, Iran...G6 86
Shirbin, Eg...C8 85
Shire, riv., Malawi, Moz...E5 106
Shire Nor, China...E3 91
Shiremanstown, Pa...*F8 202
Shiretoko, cape, Jap...D12 93
Shireza, Pak...C4 87
Shiriya, cape, Jap...F10 93
Shirley, Ark...B3 169
Shirley, Ill...C4 178
Shirley, Ind...E6 179
Shirley, Mass...A4 185
Shirley, Mont...D11 190
Shirley, W. Va...A6 211
Shirley Center, Mass...A4 185
Shirley Mills, Maine...C3 184
Shirleysburg, Pa...F6 202
Shirotori, Jap...n15 93
Shirutoru, see Makarov, Sov. Un.
Shishaldin, vol., Alsk...E7 167
Shishido, Jap...m19 93
Shishmaref, Alsk...B6 167
Shively, Ky...A4, B4 182
Shivers, Miss...D4 188
Shivpuri, India...E6 88
Shivwits, Utah...F2 207
Shizuoka, Jap...I9, o17 93
Shkodër, Alb...A2 69
Shkotovo, Sov. Un...E6 93
Shoal, creek, Tenn...B4 205
Shoal, lake, Ont., Can...B6 187
Shoal, lake, Ont., Can...E4 150
Shoal, lakes, Man., Can...D3 150
Shoal, riv., Man., Can...C1 150
Shoal Harbour, Newf., Can...D5 152
Shoal Lake, Man., Can...D1 150
Shoals, Ind...G4 179
Shoalwater, cape, Wash...C1 210
Shobankazgan, Sov. Un...E6 73
Shobonier, Ill...E4 178
Shoe, pt., Newf., Can...D5 152
Shoe Cove, Newf., Can...D4 152
Shoeheel, creek, S.C...B9 203
Shoemakersville, Pa...E10 202
Shola, lake, Eth...D4 105
Sholapur, India...E6 87, I5 88
Sholes, Nebr...B8 191
Shona, isl., Scot...D3 57
Shongopovi, Ariz...B5 168
Shonkin, Mont...C6 190
Shonto, Ariz...A5 168
Shooks, Minn...C4 187
Shooting Creek, N.C...D2 197
Shop Spring, Tenn...A5 205
Shore Acres, Calif...*B5 170
Shoreacres, B.C., Can...E9 149
Shoreacres, Tex...*E5 206
Shoreham, Mich...F4 186
Shoreham, N.Y...F5 172
Shoreham, Vt...D2 208
Shoreview, Minn...*F5 187
Shorewood, Ill...*B5 178
Shorewood, Minn...*F5 187
Shorewood, Wis...E2, E6 212
Shorewood Hills, Wis...*E4 212
Short, creek, Ohio...B1 211
Short, mtn., Tenn...B6 205
Short, mtn., Tenn...C10 205
Short Beach, Conn...D5 172
Short Creek, W. Va...B2 211
Short Falls, N.H...D4 193
Short Mountain, res., Okla...B1 169
Shorter, Ala...C4 166
Shorterville, Ala...D4 166
Shortland, isl., Sol. Is... 115
Shorts Creek, Va...E2 209
Shortsville, N.Y...C3 196
Shoshone, Calif...H5 192
Shoshone, Colo...B3 171
Shoshone, Idaho...G4 177
Shoshone, co., Idaho...B3 177
Shoshone, basin, Wyo...B4 213
Shoshone, falls, Idaho...G4 177
Shoshone, mtn., Nev...G5 192
Shoshone, mts., Nev...E4 192
Shoshone, range, Nev...C4 192
Shoshone, riv., Wyo...A4 213
Shoshong, Bots...B4 107
Shoshoni, Wyo...B4 213
Shostka, Sov. Un...F9 72
Shou, China...H7 92
Shouldice, Alta., Can...D4 148
Shoultes, Wash...*A3 210
Shouns, Tenn...C12 205
Shoup, Idaho...D4 177
Show Low, Ariz...C5 168
Showak, Sud...C4 105
Showell, Md...D7 173
Shpola, Sov. Un...G8 72
Shreve, Ohio...B5 199
Shreveport, La...B2 183
Shrewsbury, Eng...B5 56
Shrewsbury, Mass...B4 185
Shrewsbury, Mo...*C7 189
Shrewsbury, N.J...C4 194
Shrewsbury, Pa...G8 202
Shrewsbury, riv., N.J...C5 194
Shropshire, co., Eng...B5 56
Shrub Oak, N.Y...*D7 196
Shuangcheng, China...B10 91, D3 93
Shuangchiang, China...G4 91
Shuangshan, China...E1 93
Shuangyang, China...E2 93
Shuangyashan, China...B11 91
Shubenacadie, N.S., Can...D6 151
Shubert, Nebr...D10 191
Shubrā al Khayma, Eg...D3 84
Shubrā Khīt, Eg...C2 84
Shubuta, Miss...D5 188
Shucheng, China...I7 92
Shueyville, Iowa...*C6 180
Shu'fāt, Jordan...h11 84
Shuford, Miss...A4 188
Shujabad, Pak...C3 88
Shuksan, mtn., Wash...A4 210
Shulan, China...D3 93
Shulaps, peak, B.C., Can...D6 149
Shulerville, S.C...E8 203
Shullsburg, Wis...F3 212
Shumagin, isl., Alsk...E7 167
Shuman House, Alsk...B11 167
Shumaykh, Libya...I13 64
Shumen, Bul...D8 68
Shumerlya, Sov. Un...B3 73
Shumikha, Sov. Un...B6 73
Shunan, China...J8 92
Shūnat Nimrin, Jordan...h13 84
Shunchang, China...K7 92
Shungnak, Alsk...B8 167
Shunk, Pa...C8 202
Shunner Fell, mtn., Eng...F6 57
Shunning, China...G4 91
Shuo, China...E4 92
Shuqrā', Yemen (Aden)...C6 105
Shuqualak, Miss...C5 188
Shur, riv., Iran...D5 86
Shur, riv., Iran...E7 86
Shur, riv., Iran...F8 86
Shur, riv., Iran...H7 86
Shūrāb, Iran...G10 86
Shūrāb, Iran...G10 86
Shuri, Okinawa... 114
Shūsh, Iran...E4 86
Shushan, N.Y...B7 196
Shusht el Maghara, mtn., Eg...D5 84
Shūshtar, Iran...E4 86
Shuswap, lake, B.C., Can...D8 149
Shuswap, riv., B.C., Can...D8 149
Shutesbury, Mass...B3 185
Shuwaykah, Jordan...f11 84
Shuya, Sov. Un...B2 73
Shūzenji, Jap...o17 93
Shwebo, Bur...D10 87
Shwegyin, Bur...G2 89
Si, riv., China...G7 91
Siāh Band Koh, mtn., Afg...E11 86
Siahan, range, Iran, Pak...H11 86
Siālkot, Pak...B5 87, A5 88
Sialum, N. Gui...k12 111
Siam: c. 1775... 82
see also Thailand
Siam, gulf, Asia...G4 89
Sian (Hsian), China...E6 91
Siantan, isl., Indon...K6 89
Siasconset, Mass...D8 185
Siátista, Grc...B3 69
Siau, isl., Indon...E7 90
Šiauliai, Sov. Un...D4 72
Sibay, Sov. Un...C5 73
Sibbald, Alta., Can...D5 148
Šibenik, Yugo...D2 68
Šibert, Ky...C6 182
Siberut, isl., Indon...F1 90
Sibi, Pak...C4 87
Sibiti, Con...F2 104
Sibiu, Rom...C7 68
Sibley, Ill...C5 178
Sibley, Iowa...A2 180
Sibley, La...B2 183
Sibley, Miss...D2 188
Sibley, Mo...E3 189
Sibley, co., Minn...F4 187
Sibolga, Indon...L3 89
Sibsagar, India...C9 87
Sibu, Mala...E4 90
Sibuatan, mtn., Indon...K3 89
Sibutu, isl., Phil...E5 90
Sibuyan, sea, Phil...C6 90
Sicamous, B.C., Can...D8 149
Sicapoo, mtn., Phil...B6 90
Sichomovi, Ariz...B5 168
Sicilies, Two, kingdom of the:
in 1815... 50
in 1860... 51
Sicily: in 7th cent. B.C... 42
c. 120 A.D... 45
c. 1140... 47
c. 1360... 48
in 1714-35... 49
in 1810... 50
in 1860... 51
Sicily, isl., It...F4 67
Sicily Island, La...C4 183
Sicklerville, N.J...D3 194
Sico, riv., Hond...C5 130
Sicuaní, Peru...D3 134
Sidādah, Libya...C2 101
Sidāmo, reg., Eth...E4 105
Sideling, hill, Md., W. Va...A1 173
Sideling Hill, creek, Md., Pa...A1 173
Sidell, Ill...D6 178
Siderno Marina, It...E6 67
Sídheros, cape, Grc...E6 69
Sidhirókastron, Grc...B4 69
Sidi Abd el Hakem, Alg...D5 102
Sidi Abdalkah Ben Ali, Alg...D5 102
Sīdī Barrānī, Eg., U.A.R...G5 85
Sidi bel Abbès, Alg...B4 102
Sidi Bennour, Mor...H2 64, C3 102
Sidi bou Haous, Alg...H8 64
Sidi Hadjed Dine, Alg...C5 102
Sidi Ifni, Mor...D2 102
Sīdī Sālīm, Eg., U.A.R...C2 84
Sidikalang, Indon...m11 90
Sidlaw, hills, Scot...D5 57
Sidley, mtn., Ant...B36 120
Sidmouth, Eng...D4 56
Sidnaw, Mich...B2 186
Sidney, Ark...A4 169
Sidney, B.C., Can...B9, E6 149
Sidney, Man., Can...E2 150
Sidney, Ill...C5 178
Sidney, Ind...B6 179
Sidney, Iowa...D2 180
Sidney, Maine...D3 184
Sidney, Mont...C12 190
Sidney, Nebr...C3 191
Sidney, N.Y...C5 196
Sidney, Ohio...B3 199
Sidney Center, N.Y...C5 196
Sidney Lanier, lake, Ga...B2 175
Sidon, Ark...B4 169
Sidon, see Saida, Leb.
Sidon, Miss...B3 188
Sidonia, Tenn...A3 205
Sidra (Khalīj Surt), gulf, Libya...C3 101
Siedlce, Pol...B7 70
Sieg, riv., Ger...C3 60
Siegburg, Ger...C2 61
Siegen, Ger...C3 61
Sieglar, Ger...C2 61
Siem Reap, Camb...F5 89
Siemens, cape, Mussau I... 115
Siemianowice Śląskie, Pol...g10 70
Siemiatycze, Pol...B7 70
Siena, It...C3 67
Sieper, La...C3 183
Sieradz, Pol...C5 70
Siero, Sp...A3 65
Sierpc, Pol...B5 70
Sierra, co., Calif...C3 170
Sierra, co., N. Mex...E2 195
Sierra Ancha, mts., Ariz...D4 168
Sierra Blanca, Tex...F1 206
Sierra Blanca, mtn., Tex...F1 206
Sierra Blanca, peak, N. Mex...D4 195
Sierra City, Calif...C3 170
Sierra Colorada, Arg...C3 136
Sierra Del Hueso, mts., Mex...F1 206
Sierra Diablo, mts., Tex...F2 206
Sierra Estrella, mts., Ariz...G1 168
Sierra Gordo, Chile...D2 135
SIERRA LEONE, country, Afr...E2 103
in 1898... 99
Sierra Madre, Calif...F2 170
Sierra Madre, mts., Wyo...D6 213
Sierra Mojada, Mex...B4 129
Sierra Nevada, mts., Calif...D4 170
Sierra Vieja, mts., Tex...F2 206
Sierra Vista, Ariz...F5 168
Sierraville, Calif...C3 170
Sierre, Switz...C3 66
Siesta, key, Fla...E4 174
Siewierz, Pol...g10 70
Sífnos, isl., Grc...D5 69
Sifton, Man., Can...D1 150
Sigean, Fr...F5 58
Sigel, Ill...D5 178
Sigel, Pa...D3 202
Sighet, Rom...B6 68
Sighişoara, Rom...B7 68
Sighty Crag, mtn., Eng...E6 57
Sigli, Indon...J1 89
Siglufjördur, Ice...m23 63
Sigmaringen, Ger...A5 66
Signakhi, Sov. Un...B15 85
Signal, mtn., Va...B4 209
Signal, peak, Ariz...D1 168
Signal, peak, Utah...F2 207
Signal Hill, Calif...*E4 170
Signal Mountain, Tenn...D8, E10 205
Sigourney, Iowa...C5 180
Sigsig, Ec...B2 134
Sigtuna, Swe...t35 63
Siguatepeque, Hond...C4 130
Sigüenza, Sp...B4 65
Siguiri, Guinea...D3 103
Sigurd, Utah...E4 207
Siirt, Tur...D13 85
Sikar, India...D5 88
Sikasso, Mali...D3 103
Sikes, La...B3 183
Sikeston, Mo...E8 189
Sikhote Alin, mts., Sov. Un...D7 93
Sikiá, Grc...B4 69
Síkinos, isl., Grc...D5 69
Sikionía, Grc...C4 69
SIKKIM, country, Asia...D12 88
Siklós, Hung...C4 68
Sil, riv., Sp...A2 65
Sil Nakya, Ariz...E4 168
Silandro, It...A3 67
Silang, Phil...o13 90
Silao, Mex...m13 129
Silas, Ala...D1 166
Silat adh Dhahr, Jordan...f11 84
Silay, Phil...*C6 90
Silchar, India...D9 87
Sile, N. Mex...F5 195
Şile, Tur...B7 69
Siler City, N.C...B4 197
Silerton, Tenn...B3 205
Silesia, Md...C4 173
Silesia, Mont...E8 190
Silesia, reg., Pol...C4 70
c. 1360... 48
c. 1721... 49
in 1815-71... 51
in 1922-40... 53
Siletz, Oreg...C3 201
Silex, Mo...B6 189
Silgarhi Doti, Nep...C8 88
Silhuas, Peru...C2 134
Silica, Ohio...A1 199
Silifke, Tur...D9 85
Siliguri, India...D12 88
Silistra, Bul...C8 68
Silivri, Tur...B7 69
Siljan, Nor...p27 63
Siljan, lake, Swe...G6 63
Silkeborg, Den...B3 62
Sillery, Que., Can...C9 154
Silloth, Eng...F5 57
Siloam, Ga...C3 175
Siloam Springs, Ark...A1 169
Siloam Springs, Mo...E5 189
Silsbee, Tex...D5 206
Silsby, lake, Man., Can...B4 150
Silt, Colo...B3 171
Silton, Sask., Can...G3 155
Siltou (Well), Chad...B3 104
Siluria, Ala...B3 166
Šilutė, Sov. Un...A6 70
Silva, Mo...D7 189
Silva, N. Dak...A6 198
Silva Jardim, Braz...h6 137
Silva Pôrto, Ang...D2 106
Silver, S.C...D7 203
Silver, creek, Ill...B9 189
Silver, creek, Ind...H6 179
Silver, creek, Nebr...D2 191
Silver, creek, Oreg...D7 201
Silver, lake, Ont., Can...E4 150
Silver, lake, Iowa...A3 180
Silver, lake, Maine...C3 184
Silver, lake, Nev...B5 192
Silver, lake, N.H...C4 193
Silver, lake, N.H...E2 193
Silver, lake, Oreg...D6 201
Silver, lake, Oreg...D7 201
Silver, lake, Wash...D7 210
Silver Bank, passage, Ba. Is...E8 131
Silver Bay, Minn...C7 187
Silver Bay, N.Y...B7 196
Silver Bell, Ariz...E4 168
Silver Bow, co., Mont...E4 190
Silver Bow Park, Mont...*D4 190
Silver City, C.Z...k11 130
Silver City, Iowa...C2 180
Silver City, Miss...B3 188
Silver City, Nev...D2 192
Silver City, N. Mex...E1 195
Silver City, S. Dak...C2 204
Silver City, Utah...D3 207
Silver Cliff, Colo...C5 171
Silver Creek, Ga...B1 175
Silver Creek, Miss...D3 188
Silver Creek, Mo...*D3 189
Silver Creek, Nebr...C8 191
Silver Creek, N.Y...C1 196
Silver Gate, Mont...E6 190
Silver Grove, Ky...A7 182
Silver Lake, Ind...B6 179
Silver Lake, Kans...C8 181
Silver Lake, Mass...C2 185
Silver Lake, Minn...F4 187
Silver Lake, N.H...C4 193
Silver Lake, Ohio...*A6 199
Silver Lake, Oreg...D6 201
Silver Lake, Wis...F1, F5 212
Silver Peak, range, Nev...F4 192
Silver Point, Tenn...C8 205
Silver River, mtn., Newf., Can...D3 152
Silver Run, Md...A3 173
Silver Sands, Alta., Can...*B4 148
Silver Spring, Md...C1, C3 173
Silver Springs, Fla...C4 174
Silver Springs, Nev...D2 192
Silver Springs, N.Y...C2 196
Silver Star, Mont...E4 190
Silver Star, mtn., Wash...A5 210
Silverbow, Mont...E4 190
Silverdale, Kans...E7 181
Silverdale, Pa...*F11 202
Silverdale, Wash...B3, D1 210
Silverhill, Ala...E2 166
Silverlake, Wash...C3 210
Silverpeak, Nev...F4 192
Silverstreet, S.C...C4 203
Silverthrone, mtn., B.C., Can...D4 149
Silvertip, mtn., Mont...C3 190
Silverton, B.C., Can...E9 149
Silverton, Colo...D3 171
Silverton, Idaho...B3 177
Silverton, N.J...C4 194
Silverton, Ohio...D2 199
Silverton, Oreg...B4, C2 201
Silverton, Tex...B2 206
Silverwood, N.B., Can...*D3 151
Silves, Port...D1 65
Silvia, Col...C2 133
Silvis, Ill...B3 178
Silwān, Jordan...h11, m14 84
Simanggang, Mala...E4 90
Simav, Tur...C7 69
Simav, riv., Tur...C7 69
Simberi, isl., Bis. Arch... 115
Simbo, isl., Sol. Is... 115
Simcoe, Ont., Can...E4 153
Simcoe, co., Ont., Can...C5 153
Simcoe, N. Dak...A5 198
Simcoe, creek, Wash...C5 210
Simcoe, lake, Ont., Can...C5 153
Simcoe, mts., Wash...C5 210
Simdega, India...F10 88
Simeulue, isl., Indon...K1 89
Simferopol', Sov. Un...I10 72
Simi, Calif...*E4 170
Simi, isl., Grc...D6 69
Similkameen, riv., B.C., Can...E7 149
Simití, Col...B3 133
Simla, Colo...B6 171
Simla, India...B6 87
Simleul-Silvaniei, Rom...B6 68
Simmern, Ger...D2 61
Simmesport, La...D4 183
Simmie, Sask., Can...H1 155
Simmons, Mo...D5 189
Simms, Mont...C5 190
Simnasho, Oreg...C5 201
Simonette, riv., Alta., Can...B1 148
Simonhouse, lake, Man., Can...B1 150
Simonstorp, Swe...u34 63
Simonsville, Vt...E3 208
Simoom Sound, B.C., Can...D4 149
Simpang Kiri, riv., Indon...K2 89
Simplico Mendes, Braz...C2 138
Simplon, pass, Switz...C4 66
Simpson, Sask., Can...F3 155
Simpson, Ill...F5 178
Simpson, Kans...C6 181
Simpson, La...C2 183
Simpson, Minn...G6 187
Simpson, Mont...B6 190
Simpson, N.C...B6 197
Simpson, Pa...C11 202
Simpson, W. Va...B7 211
Simpson, co., Ky...D3 182
Simpson, co., Miss...D4 188
Simpson, creek, W. Va...B7 211
Simpson, des., Austl...E6 110
Simpson, pen., N.W. Ter., Can...C15 142
Simpsonville, Ky...B4 182
Simpsonville, S.C...B3 203
Simrishamn, Swe...J6 63
Sims, Ill...E5 178
Sims, Ind...D6 179
Sims, N.C...B5 197
Sims, stream, N.H...A4, B1 193
Sims Chapel, Ala...D1 166
Simsboro, La...B3 183
Simsbury, Conn...B5 172
Simtustus, lake, Oreg...C5 201
Simunjan, Mala...E4 90
Sinabang, Indon...K2 89
Sinai, S. Dak...C8 204
Sinai, pen., Eg...E5 84
Sinai: in 13th cent. B.C... 98
Sinaia, Rom...C7 68
Sinajana, Guam... 114
Sinaloa, Mex...B3 129
Sinaloa, state, Mex...C3 129
Sinanju, Kor...G2 93
Sinarū, Eg...E2 84
Sināwan, Libya...C2 101
Sinawi, Afg...D15 86
Sinçé, Col...B2 133
Sincelejo, Col...B2 133
Sinclair, Man., Can...E1 150
Sinclair, Maine...A4 184
Sinclair, Wyo...D5 213
Sinclair's, bay, Scot...B5 57
Sinclairville, N.Y...C1 196
Sind, reg., Pak...C4 87
c. 1775... 82
Sind, riv., India...D7 88
Sindal, Den...A4 62
Sindara, Gabon...F2 104
Sindelfingen, Ger...E3 61
Sindirgi, Tur...C7 69
Sinelnikovo, Sov. Un...G10 72
Sines, Port...D1 65
Singa, Sud...C3 105
Singapore, Singapore...L5 89
SINGAPORE, country, Asia...L5 89
Singapore, strait, Asia...L5 89
Singaradja, Indon...G5 90
Singen, Ger...B4 66
Singer, La...D2 183
Singers Glen, Va...C4 209
Singhampton, Ont., Can...C4 153
Singida, Tan...B5 106
Singitic, gulf, Grc...B4 69
Singkawang, Indon...L8 89
Singkep, isl., Indon...F2 90
Singkil, Indon...E1, m11 90
Singleton, Austl...F8 112
Singu, Bur...B1 89
Sinhsien, China...D7 91
Sinhŭng, Kor...F3 93
Siniscola, It...D2 67
Sinj, Yugo...D3 68
Sinjil, Jordan...g12 84
Sinkat, Sud...B4 105
Sinkiang: c. 1950... 83
Sinkiang Uighur, prov., China...C2 91
Sinking, creek, Ky...C3 182
Sinking Spring, Ohio...C4 199
Sinking Spring, Pa...*F9 202
Sinks Grove, W. Va...D4 211
Sinnamahoning, Pa...D5 202
Sinnamahoning, creek, Pa...D5 202
Sinnamary, Fr. Gu...A4 139
Sinnūris, Eg...E2 84
Sinoia, Rh...A5 107
Sinop, Tur...A10 85
Sint-Amandsberg, Bel...C3 59
Sint Jacobiparochie, Neth...A5 59
Sint-Lenaarts, Bel...C4 59
Sint-Niklaas, Bel...C4 59
Sint-Truiden, Bel...D5 59
Sintaluta, Sask., Can...G4 155
Sintang, Indon...E4 90
Sinton, Tex...E4 206
Sintra, Port...f9 65
Sinú, riv., Col...B2 133
Sinŭiju, Kor...F2 93
Sinyavino, Sov. Un...s32 63
Sinzig, Ger...C2 61
Sion, Switz...C3 66
Sioux, co., Iowa...A1 180
Sioux, co., Nebr...B2 191
Sioux, co., N. Dak...C4 198
Sioux Center, Iowa...A1 180
Sioux City, Iowa...B1 180
Sioux Falls, S. Dak...D9 204
Sioux Lookout, Ont., Can...E8 153
Sioux Rapids, Iowa...B2 180
Sipanok, chan., Sask., Can...D4 155
Sipiwesk, lake, Man., Can...B3 150
Siple, mtn., Ant...B36 120
Sipolilo, Rh...A5 107
Sipsey, Ala...B2 166
Sipsey, fork, Ala...A2 166
Sipsey, riv., Ala...B2 166
Sipul, New Britain I... 115
Sipura, isl., Indon...F1 90
Siquirres, C.R...E6 130
Siquisique, Ven...A4 133
Sir Abu Nu'air, isl., Sau. Ar...I7 86
Sir Alexander, mtn., B.C., Can...C7 149
Sir Douglas, mtn., Alta., B.C., Can...D3 148
Sir Edward Pellew Group, is., Austl...C6 110
Sir Francis Drake's Channel, strait, Vir. Is...f16 132
Sir James McBrien, mtn., N.W. Ter., Can...D7 142
Sir Sandford, mtn., B.C., Can...D9 149
Sir Wilfrid, mtn., Que...C2 154
Sir Wilfrid Laurier, mtn., B.C., Can...C8 149
Siracusa, see Syracuse, It.
Sirājganj, Bngl...D8 87
Sirdar, B.C., Can...E9 149
Siren, Wis...C1 212
Siret, Rom...B8 68
Siretul, riv., Rom...B8 68
Sirḥān, wadi, Libya...G3 85
Sīrīk, Iran...H8 86
Sirmione, It...D6 66
Sirnai, isl., Grc...D6 69
Sironj, India...C6 88
Síros, Grc...D5 69
Síros, isl., Grc...D5 69
Sirpur, India...H7 88
Sirri, isl., Iran...I7 86
Sirsa, India...C5 88
Sirte (Surt), Libya...C3 101
Širvintos, Sov. Un...A8 70
Sisak, Yugo...C3 68
Sisaket, Thai...E6 89
Sisib, lake, Man., Can...C2 150
Sisipuk, lake, Man., Sask., Can...B5 155, B1 150
Siskiyou, co., Calif...B2 170
Siskiyou, mts., Calif., Oreg...F3 201
Siskiyou, pass, Oreg...E4 201
Sisophon, Camb...F5 89
Sisquoc, Calif...E3 170
Sisseton, S. Dak...B8 204
Sisseton, Indian res., N. Dak., S. Dak...D8 198
Sisson Branch, res., N.B., Can...B2 151
Sissonville, W. Va...C3 211
Sister Bay, Wis...C6 212
Sisterdale, Tex...E3 206
Sisteron, Fr...E6 58
Sisters, Oreg...C5 201
Sistersville, W. Va...B4 211
Sitapur, India...D8 88
Siteki, Swaz...C5 107
Sitía, Grc...E6 69
Sitionuevo, Col...A3 133
Sitka, Alsk...D12, m22 167
Sitka, Ark...A4 169
Sitka, Kans...E4 181
Sitka, nat. mon., Alsk...D12 167
Sitka, sound, Alsk...m22 167
Sitkum, Oreg...D3 201
Sittang, riv., Bur...E10 87
Sittard, Neth...D5 59
Sítto da Abadia, Braz...A3 137
Sittwe, Bur...D9 87
Siutu, W. Sam... 114
Sivas, Tur...C11 85
Siverek, Tur...D12 85
Sivrihisar, Tur...C8 85
Siwah (Oasis), Eg...D5 101

INDEX KEY Each place listed in **Bold-faced Type** has its population listed in the Population tables, pages 230 to 280.
Each country, shown in CAPITAL LETTERS, has its population listed in the World Political Information Table, pages 6 to 10.
* Does not appear on map; key shows general location.

Siwalik, range, India, Nep. C8 88
Siwana, India E4 88
Six Mile, S.C. B2 203
Sixmile, creek, Fla. C6 174
Sixmile, lake, La. E4 183
Sixteen Island Lake, Que., Can. D3 154
6th Cataract (Nile River), Sud. B3 105
Sizerville, Pa. C5 202
Sjaelland, isl., Den. C5 62
Sjenica, Yugo. D5 68
Sjöbo, Swe. C7 62
Skaelskör, Den. C5 62
Skaerbaek, Den. C2 62
Skagen, Den. A4 62
Skagen, cape, Den. A4 62
Skagerrak, chan., Eur. I3 63
Skagit, co., Wash. A4 210
Skagit, riv., Wash. A4 210
Skagway, Alsk. D12, k22 167
Skälderviken, bay, Swe. B6 62
Skamania, Wash. D3 210
Skamania, co., Wash. D4 210
Skamokawa, Wash. C2 210
Skanderborg, Den. B3 62
Skanderborg, co., Den. C3 62
Skaneateles, N.Y. C4 196
Skaneateles, lake, N.Y. C4 196
Skanee, Mich. B2 186
Skanör, Swe. C6 62
Skantzoura, isl., Grc. C5 69
Skara, Swe. H5 63
Skarkar, Afg. C15 86
Skarven, lake, Swe. t35 63
Skawa, riv., Pol. h11 70
Skawina, Pol. D5 70
Skedee, Okla. A5 200
Skeena, mts., B.C., Can. A3 149
Skeena, riv., B.C., Can. B3 149
Skegness, Eng. A8 56
Skeldon, Guy. A3 139
Skeleton, lake, Ont., Can. B5 153
Skellefteå, Swe. E9 63
Skellefteälven, riv., Swe. E8 63
Skellytown, Tex. B2 206
Skelton, W. Va. D7 211
Skene, Miss. B3 188
Skhimatárion, Grc. g11 69
Skiathos, isl., Grc. C4 69
Skiatook, Okla. A5 200
Skibbereen, Ire. E2 55
Skibby, Den. C5 62
Skiddaw, mtn., Eng. F5 57
Skidegate, B.C., Can. C2 149
Skidegate, inlet, B.C., Can. C2 149
Skidmore, Mo. A2 189
Skidmore, Tex. E4 206
Skien, Nor. H3, p27 63
Skierniewice, Pol. C6 70
Skiff, Alta., Can. E5 148
Skihist, mtn., B.C., Can. D7 149
Skikda, Alg. F10 64, B6 102
Skillet, fork, Ill. E5 178
Skillman, N.J. C3 194
Skipperville, Ala. D4 166
Skipton, Eng. G7 57
Skiros, Grc. C5 69
Skiros, isl., Grc. C5 69
Skive, Den. B3 62
Skjern, Den. C2 62
Skjern Å, riv., Den. C2 62
Skoczów, Pol. h9 70
Škofja Loka, Yugo. B2 68
Skokie, Ill. A6, E3 178
Skokomish, Indian res., Wash. B2 210
Skole, Sov. Un. D7 70
Skönnarbo, Swe. u33 63
Skópelos, isl., Grc. C4 69
Skopin, Sov. Un. E12 72
Skopje, Yugo. D5 68
Skörping, Den. B3 62
Skotovataya, Sov. Un. q20 72
Skotselv, Nor. p27 63
Skövde, Swe. H5 63
Skovorodino, Sov. Un. D15 71
Skowhegan, Maine D3 184
Skownan, Man., Can. D2 150
Skradin, Yugo. D2 68
Skull Valley, Ariz. C3 168
Skull Valley, Indian res., Utah C3 207
Skuna, riv., Miss. B4 188
Skunk, riv., Iowa C6 180
Skurup, Swe. C7 62
Skvira, Sov. Un. G7 72
Skwentna, riv., Alsk. g15 167
Skwierzyna, Pol. B3 70
Sky Manor, N.J. C4 194
Skye, isl., Scot. C2 57
Skykomish, Wash. B4 210
Skykomish, riv., Wash. B4 210
Skyland, N.C. D3 197
Skylight, Ky. A4 182
Skyline, Ala. A3 166
Skyline, Minn. *F4 187
Skyring, lake, Chile E2 136
Skyway, bridge, Fla. E4 174
Slade, Ky. C6 182
Sladesville, N.C. B7 197
Slagelse, Den. C5 62
Slagle, La. C2 183
Slamet, vol., Indon. G3 90
Slangerup, Den. C6 62
Slănic-Prahova, Rom. C7 68
Slaný, Czech. n17 70
Slapy, Czech. o17 70
Slate, W. Va. B3 211
Slate Run, Pa. D6 202
Slate Spring, Miss. B4 188
Slater, Colo. A3 171
Slater, Iowa A7, C4 180
Slater, Mo. B4 189
Slater, S.C. A3 203
Slater, Wyo. D8 213
Slatersville, R.I. B10 172
Slatina, Rom. C7 68
Slatington, Pa. E10 202
Slaton, Tex. C2 206
Slätthög, Swe. A8 62
Slaughter, La. D4 183
Slaughter Beach, Del. C7 173
Slaughters, Ky. C2 182
Slave, riv., Alta., Can. D10 142
Slave Lake, Alta., Can. B3 148
Slavgorod, Sov. Un. C9 73
Slavonia, reg., Yugo. C3 68
Slavonska Pozega, Yugo. C3 68
Slavsk, Sov. Un. A6 70
Slavyanoserbsk, Sov. Un. q21 72
Slavyansk, Sov. Un. G11, q20 72
Slavyansk-na-Kubani, Sov. Un. I12 72
Sławków, Pol. g10 70
Slawno, Pol. A4 70
Slayden, Miss. A4 188
Slayden, Tenn. *A4 205
Slayton, Minn. G3 187
Sleaford, Eng. A7 56
Sleat, pt., Scot. C2 57
Sleat, sound, Scot. C3 57
Sled, lake, Sask., Can. C2 155
Sledge, Miss. A3 188
Sleeper, Mo. D5 189
Sleeping Bear, pt., Mich. D4 186
Sleepy, pt., Fiji 114
Sleepy Creek, W. Va. B6 211
Sleepy Eye, Minn. F4 187
Sleetmute, Alsk. C8 167
Sliabh Gaoil, mtn., Scot. E3 57
Slick, Okla. B5 200
Slick Rock, Colo. C2 171
Slickville, Pa. F2 202
Slide, mtn., N.Y. D6 196
Slidell, La. B8, D6 183
Sliderock, mtn., Mont. D3 190
Sligo, Ire. C2 55
Sligo, Pa. D3 202
Sligo, bay, Ire. C2 55
Slim, buttes, S. Dak. B2 204
Slinger, Wis. E1, E5 212
Slippery Rock, Pa. D1 202
Sliven, Bul. D8 68
Slivenec, Czech. n17 70
Sloan, Iowa B1 180
Sloan, Nev. H6 192
Sloan, N.Y. *C2 196
Sloans Valley, Ky. D5 182
Sloat, Calif. C3 170
Sloatsburg, N.Y. A4 194
Slobodskoy, Sov. Un. B4 73
Slobozia, Rom. C8 68
Slocan, B.C., Can. E9 149
Slocan, lake, B.C., Can. E9 149
Slocomb, Ala. D4 166
Slocum, R.I. C10 172
Slonim, Sov. Un. E5 72
Slope, co., N. Dak. C2 198
Slough, Eng. C7 56
Slovac, Ark. C4 169
Slovakia, reg., Czech. D5 70
Slovan, Pa. F1 202
Slovenia, reg., Yugo. C2 68
Słubice, Pol. A9 61
Sluch, riv., Sov. Un. F6 72
Slunj, Yugo. C2 68
Słupa, riv., Pol. A4 70
Słupca, Pol. B4 70
Słupsk (Stolp), Pol. A4 70
Slutsk, Sov. Un. E6 72
Slyne, head, Ire. D1 55
Slyudyanka, Sov. Un. D13 71
Smackover, Ark. D3 169
Smackover, creek, Ark. D2 169
Smålandsfarvandet, bay, Den. C5 62
Small, pt., Maine E6 184
Small Point, Maine E6 184
Smara, Sp. Sahara D2 102
Smarr, Ga. D3 175
Smarts, mtn., N.H. C2 193
Smartt, Tenn. D8 205
Smeaton, Sask., Can. D3 155
Smečno, Czech. n17 70
Smederevo, Yugo. C5 68
Smela, Sov. Un. G8 72
Smeltertown, Tex. E1 206
Smelterville, Idaho B2 177
Smethport, Pa. C5 202
Smíchov, Czech. n17 70
Smicksburg, Pa. E3 202
Smidovich, Sov. Un. B6 93
Smiley, Sask., Can. F1 155
Smiley, Tex. B4, E4 206
Smith, Alta., Can. B3, D1 148
Smith, Nev. E2 192
Smith, co., Kans. C5 181
Smith, co., Miss. C4 188
Smith, co., Tenn. C8 205
Smith, co., Tex. C5 206
Smith, bay, Alsk. A9 167
Smith, cape, Ont., Can. B3 153
Smith, isl., Ant. C6 120
Smith, isl., Md., Va. D5 173, D6 209
Smith, isl., Va. D7 209
Smith, peak, Idaho A2 177
Smith, pt., N.S., Can. D6 151
Smith, pt., Mass. D7 185
Smith, pt., Va. D6 209
Smith, riv., Mont. D5 190
Smith, riv., Va. E2 209
Smith, sound, Arc. O. B22 118
Smith, sound, B.C., Can. D4 149
Smith Center, Kans. C5 181
Smith Mills, Ky. C2 182
Smith Mountain, lake, Va. D3 209
Smith River, Calif. B1 170
Smith Town, Ky. D5 182
Smithboro, Ill. E4 178
Smithburg, W. Va. B4, B6 211
Smithdale, Miss. D3 188
Smithers, B.C., Can. B4 149
Smithers, W. Va. C3, C6 211
Smithfield, Ill. C3 178
Smithfield, Ky. *B4 182
Smithfield, Maine D3 184
Smithfield, Mo. D3 189
Smithfield, Nebr. D6 191
Smithfield, N.C. B5 197
Smithfield, Ohio B7 199
Smithfield, Pa. G2 202
Smithfield, Tex. B5 206
Smithfield, Utah B4 207
Smithfield, Va. B6, E6 209
Smithfield, W. Va. A6 211
Smithland, Iowa B2 180
Smithland, Ky. A3 182
Smithland, Tex. C5 206
Smithmill, Pa. E5 202
Smithonia, Ga. B3 175
Smiths, Ala. C4 166
Smiths Cove, N.S., Can. E4 151
Smiths Falls, Ont., Can. C8 153
Smiths Ferry, Idaho E2 177
Smiths Grove, Ky. C3 182
Smiths Lake, N. Mex. B1 195
Smithsburg, Md. A2 173
Smithshire, Ill. C3 178
Smithton, Ark. D2 169
Smithton, Austl. o15 111
Smithton, Ill. E4 178
Smithton, Mo. C4 189
Smithton, Pa. *F2 202
Smithtown, N.H. E5 193
Smithtown, N.C. *A3 197
Smithtown, N.Y. F4 172
Smithtown, bay, N.Y. F4 172
Smithville, Ark. A4 169
Smithville, Ga. E2 175
Smithville, Ind. F4 179
Smithville, Miss. A5 188
Smithville, Mo. B3, D2 189
Smithville, N.J. E4 194
Smithville, N.J. D3 194
Smithville, Ohio B6 199
Smithville, Okla. C7 200
Smithville, Tenn. D8 205
Smithville, Tex. D4 206
Smithville, W. Va. B3 211
Smithville Flats, N.Y. C5 196
Smithwick, S. Dak. D2 204
Smoaks, S.C. E6 203
Smock, Pa. *G2 202
Smoke Bend, La. B5 183
Smoke Creek, Nev. C2 192
Smoke Creek, des., Nev. C2 192
Smokerun, Pa. E5 202
Smokey Dome, mtn., Idaho F4 177
Smoky, cape, Austl. E9 112
Smoky, cape, N.S., Can. C9 151
Smoky, mts., Idaho F4 177
Smoky, riv., Alta., Can. B1 148
Smoky Hill, riv., Kans. D5 181
Smoky Junction, Tenn. C9 205
Smoky Lake, Alta., Can. B4 148
Smöla, isl., Nor. F2 63
Smolan, Kans. D6 181
Smolensk, Sov. Un. D8 72
Smolyan, Bul. E7 68
Smoot, Wyo. C2 213
Smooth Rock Falls, Ont., Can. *E9 153
Smoothstone, lake, Sask., Can. C2 155
Smoothstone, riv., Sask., Can. B2 155
Smoots, creek, Kans. B4 181
Smyadovo, Bul. D8 68
Smyley, cape, Ant. B4 120
Smyre, N.C. *B2 197
Smyrna, Del. B6 173
Smyrna, Ga. A5, C2 175
Smyrna, N.Y. C5 196
Smyrna, S.C. A5 203
Smyrna, Tenn. B5 205
Smyrna, see İzmir, Tur.
Smyrna, riv., Del. B6 173
Smyrna Mills, Maine B4 184
Smyth, co., Va. B3 209
Snaefell, mtn., I of Man F4 57
Snake, creek, Nebr. B2 191
Snake, falls, Nebr. B5 191
Snake, lake, Sask., Can. B2 155
Snake, mtn., Vt. C2 208
Snake, range, Nev. E7 192
Snake, riv., Minn. B1 187
Snake, riv., Minn. D5 187
Snake, riv., Oreg. C9 201
Snake, riv., U.S. B4 158
Snake, riv., Wash. C8 210
Snake Indian, riv., Alta., Can. C1 148
Snake River, plain, Idaho F2 177
Snake River, range, Idaho, Wyo. F7 177
Snares, is., N.Z. R11 112
Sneads, Fla. B2 174
Sneads Ferry, N.C. C6 197
Snedsted, Den. B2 62
Sneedville, Tenn. C10 205
Sneek, Neth. A5 59
Snelling, S.C. E5 203
Snezhnoye, Sov. Un. q21 72
Snezhnvy, peak, Sov. Un. D14 71
Sniardwy, lake, Pol. B7 70
Snipe, keys, Fla. H5 174
Snipe, lake, Alta., Can. B2 148
Snizort, bay, Scot. C2 57
Snöhetta, mtn., Nor. F3 63
Snohomish, Wash. B3 210
Snohomish, co., Wash. A4 210
Snomac, Okla. B5 200
Snoqualmie, Wash. B4 210
Snoqualmie, pass, Wash. B4 210
Snov, riv., Sov. Un. F8 72
Snover, Mich. E8 186
Snow, Okla. C6 200
Snow, mtn., Calif. C2 170
Snow, mtn., Maine C2 184
Snow, peak, Wash. A7 210
Snow Camp, N.C. B4 197
Snow Hill, Ala. D2 166
Snow Hill, Ark. D3 169
Snow Hill, Md. D7 173
Snow Hill, N.C. B6 197
Snow Lake, Ark. C5 169
Snow Road Station, Ont., Can. C8 153
Snow Shoe, Pa. D6 202
Snow Water, lake, Nev. C7 192
Snowball, Ark. B3 169
Snowbank, lake, Minn. B7 187
Snowden, Sask., Can. D3 155
Snowdon, mtn., Wales A3 56
Snowdon, mts., Wales A4 56
Snowdoun, Ala. C3 166
Snowflake, Ariz. C5 168
Snowflake, Man., Can. E2 150
Snowking, mtn., Wash. A4 210
Snowmass, Colo. B4 171
Snowmass, mtn., Colo. B3 171
Snowshoe, lake, Maine B4 184
Snowshoe, peak, Mont. B1 190
Snowville, Utah B3 207
Snowville, Va. D2 209
Snowy, mtn., N.Y. B6 196
Snowyside, peak, Idaho F4 177
Snyatyn, Sov. Un. A7 68
Snyder, Ark. D4 169
Snyder, Colo. A7 171
Snyder, Nebr. C9 191
Snyder, Okla. C3 200
Snyder, Tex. C2 206
Snyder, co., Pa. E7 202
Snyder Knob, mtn., W. Va. C5 211
Snydertown, Pa. *E8 202
Soai Rieng, Camb. G6 89
Soalala, Malag. g9 107
Soap Lake, Wash. B6 210
Soar, riv., Eng. B6 56
Soatá, Col. B3 133
Soay, isl., Scot. C2 57
Sobat, riv., Sud. D3 105
Soběslav, Czech. D9 61
Sobieski, Minn. *E4 187
Sobieski, Wis. D5 212
Sobinka, Sov. Un. D13 72
Sobota Rimavská, Czech. D6 70
Sobral, Braz. B2 138
Sobti (Well), Mali B4 103
Söby, Den. D4 62
Sochaczew, Pol. B6 70
Soche, see Yarkand, China
Sochi, Sov. Un. *E6 71
Social Circle, Ga. C3 175
Social Hill, Ark. D6 169
Society, is., Fr. Polynesia H12 113
Society Hill, S.C. B8 203
Socorro, Braz. m8 137
Socorro, Col. B3 133
Socorro, N. Mex. C3 195
Socorro, co., N. Mex. C3 195
Socotra, isl., Yemen (Aden) H8 76
Socrum, Fla. D4 174
Socuéllamos, Sp. C4 65
Soda Creek, B.C., Can. C6 149
Soda Springs, Idaho G7 177
Sodankylä, Fin. D12 63
Sodaville, Oreg. C4 201
Soddy, Tenn. D8, E10 205
Söderala, Swe. G7 63
Söderhamn, Swe. G7 63
Söderköping, Swe. H7 63
Södertälje, Swe. t35 63
Sodiri, Sud. C2 105
Sodo, Eth. D4 105
Sodus, N.Y. B3 196
Sodus Point, N.Y. B4 196
Soest, Ger. B3 61
Sofádhes, Grc. C4 69
Sofia (Sofiya), Bul. D6 68
Sofia, riv., Malag. g9 107
Sofiya, see Sofia, Bul.
Sofiyevka, Sov. Un. G9 72
Sofre, Pan. F7 130
Sofu-Gan, isl. Pac. O. E8 113
Sogamoso, Col. B3 133
Sogdiana: c. 500 B.C. 78
in 329 B.C. 43
c. 750 A.D. 80
Sögel, Ger. B7 59
Sognefjord, fjord, Nor. G1 63
Söğüt, Tur. C8 69
Sohagpur, India F8 88
Sohano, Zoller Is. 115
Soignies, Bel. D4 59
Sointula, B.C., Can. D4 149
Soissons, Fr. C5 58
Sōka, Jap. *I9 93
Sokal, Sov. Un. F5 72
Sokch'o, Kor. G4 93
Söke, Tur. D6 69
Sokhondo, mtn., Sov. Un. E14 71
Sokhta Chinar, Afg. D13 86
Sokol, Sov. Un. B13 72
Sokółka, Pol. B7 70
Sokolo, Mali D3 103
Sokolov, Czech. C7 61
Sokołow, Pol. B7 70
Sokoto, Nig. D6 103
Sol-Iletsk, Sov. Un. C5 73
Soła, riv., Pol. h10 70
Solana, Fla. *F4 174
Solander, isl., N.Z. Q11 112
Solano, N. Mex. B5 195
Solano, Phil. n13 90
Solano, co., Calif. C2 170
Solbad Hall [in Tirol], Aus. E5 60
Soldatna, Alsk. g16 167
Soldier, Iowa C2 180
Soldier, Kans. C8 181
Soldier, Ky. B6 182
Soldier, key, Fla. F3 174
Soldier Pond, Maine A4 184
Soldier Summit, Utah D4 207
Soldiers Grove, Wis. E3 212
Soledad, Calif. D3 170
Soledad, Col. A3 133
Soledad, Ven. B5 133
Soleduck, riv., Wash. B1 210
Solen, N. Dak. C5 198
Solent, chan., Eng. D6 56
Solesmes, Fr. D3 59
Solihull, Eng. B6 56
Solikamsk, Sov. Un. B5 73
Soliman, Tun. F12 64
Solimões (Amazon), riv., Braz., Peru B4 134
Solingen, Ger. B2 61
Sollas, Scot. C1 57
Sollefteå, Swe. F7 63
Sóller, Sp. C7 65
Soller Central, P.R. B3 132
Sollihögda, Nor. p28 63
Sollum, gulf, Eg. G5 85
Sollyu-Bong, mts., Kor. G2 93
Solna, Swe. H7, t36 63
Solok, Indon. F2 90
Solomea, W. Sam. 114
Solomon, Ariz. E6 168
Solomon, Kans. D6 181
Solomon, riv., Kans. C6 181
SOLOMON ISLANDS, Br. dep., Oceania 115
Solomons, Md. D5 173
Solon, Iowa C6 180
Solon, Maine D3 184
Solon, Ohio A6 199
Solon Mills, Ill. D2 178
Solon Springs, Wis. B2 212
Solonika, see Thessaloniki, Grc.
Solothurn, Switz. B3 66
Solothurn, canton, Switz. B3 66
Solovyevsk, Sov. Un. D15 71
Solsberry, Ind. F4 179
Solsgirth, Man., Can. D1 150
Solta, isl., Yugo. D3 68
Soltau, Ger. B4 60
Solun, China A9 92
Solvang, Calif. *E3 170
Solvay, N.Y. B4 196
Sölvesborg, Swe. B8 62
Solway, Minn. C3 187
Solway, firth, Eng., Scot. F5 57
Solwezi, Zambia D4 106
Soma, Tur. C6 69
SOMALIA, country, Afr. E5 105
see also Somalia
Somaliland: in 1889 99
after World War II 83
see also Somalia
Somaliland, British 99
Somaliland, French, see Afars & Is., Fr., dep., Afr.
Sombor, Yugo. C4 68
Sombra, Ont., Can. E2 153
Sombrerete, Mex. C4 129
Sombrero, chan., India G9 87
Somerdale, N.J. D2 194
Somers, Conn. B7 172
Somers, Iowa B3 180
Somers, Mont. B2 190
Somers, Wis. F2, F6 212
Somers Point, N.J. E3 194
Somerset, Man., Can. E2 150
Somerset, Colo. C3 171
Somerset, Ind. C6 179
Somerset, N.J. C4 194
Somerset, Kans. D9 181
Somerset, Ky. C5 182
Somerset, Md. *C3 173
Somerset, Mass. C5 185
Somerset, Ohio C3 199
Somerset, Pa. F3 202
Somerset, Tex. B3 206
Somerset, Wis. C1 212
Somerset, co., Eng. C5 56
Somerset, co., Maine C2 184
Somerset, co., Md. D6 173
Somerset, co., N.J. B3 194
Somerset, co., Pa. G3 202
Somerset, isl., N.W. Ter., Can. B14 142
Somerset, res., Vt. E3 208
Somerset East, S. Afr. D4 107
Somersville, Conn. B7 172
Somersworth, N.H. D5 193
Somerton, Ariz. E1 168
Somervell, co., Tex. C4 206
Somerville, Ala. A3 166
Somerville, Ind. H3 179
Somerville, Mass. B5, D3 185
Somerville, N.J. B3 194
Somerville, Ohio C3 199
Somerville, Tenn. B2 205
Somerville, Tex. D4 206
Someşul, riv., Rom. B6 68
Somme, dept., Fr. E2 59
Somme, riv., Fr. B4 58
Sommepy, Fr. E4 59
Sömmerda, Ger. B6 61
Sommesous, Fr. F4 59
Somonauk, Ill. B5 178
Somosomo, strait, Fiji 114
Somoto, Nic. D4 130
Sompeta, India H10 88
Somuncurá, plat., Arg. C3 136
Son, riv., India E9 88
Son La, Viet. B5 89
Son Tay, Viet. B6 89
Soná, Pan. F7 130
Sŏnchŏn, Kor. G2 88
Soncino, It. D5 66
Sönd, riv., Den. D3 62
Sönder Omme, Den. C2 62
Sönderborg, Den. D3 62
Sönderborg, co., Den. D3 62
Sönderho, Den. C2 62
Sondershausen, Ger. B5 61
Söndervig, Den. B2 62
Sondheimer, La. B4 183
Sondrio, It. A2 67
Sonestown, Pa. D8 202
Song, Nig. E7 103
Song Cau, Viet. F8 89
Songarh, India G4 88
Sŏngchŏn, Kor. G3 93
Songea, Tan. D6 106
Sŏngjin, see Kimchaek, Kor.
Songkhla, Thai. I4 89
Songololo, Zaire C1 106
Songt'an, Kor. H3 93
Sonhat, India F9 88
Sonmiani, Pak. C4 87
Sonmiani, bay, Pak. I12 86
Sonneberg, Ger. C6 61
Sonnette, Mont. E11 190
Sonningdale, Sask., Can. E2 155
Sono, riv., Braz. C1 138
Sonobe, Jap. n14 93
Sonoita, Ariz. F5 168
Sonoita, Mex. A2 129
Sonoma, Calif. B5, C2 170
Sonoma, Tex. *C4 206
Sonoma, co., Calif. C2 170
Sonoma, peak, Nev. C4 192
Sonoma, range, Nev. C4 192
Sonora, Ariz. D4 168
Sonora, Calif. D3 170
Sonora, Ky. C4 182
Sonora, Ohio C6 199
Sonora, Tex. D2 206
Sonora, state, Mex. B2 129
Sonora, riv., Mex. G5 168
Sonoraville, Ga. B2 175
Sonpur, India G9 88
Sonqor, Iran D3 86
Sonsón, Col. B2 133
Sonsonate, Sal. D3 130
Sontag, Miss. D3 188
Sonyea, N.Y. C3 196
Soo, locks, Mich. B6 186
Soochow (Suchou), China E9 91
Sooke, B.C., Can. B9, E6 149
Sopchoppy, Fla. B2 174
Soper, Okla. C6 200
Soperton, Ga. D4 175
Sophia, N.C. B4 197
Sophia, W. Va. D3 211
Sopot, Pol. A5 70
Sopris, Colo. D6 171
Sopron, Hung. B3 68
Soquel, Calif. C6 170
Sôr, riv., Port. C1 65
Sør Rondane, mts., Ant. B15 120
Sora, It. D4 67
Sorak-San, peak, Kor. G4 93
Sorata, Bol. C2 135
Sorbas, Sp. D4 65
Sorel, Que., Can. C4 154
Sorell, cape, Austl. o15 110
Sorento, Ill. E4 178
Soresina, It. B2 67
Soria, Sp. B4 65
Soriano, Ur. f7 136
Sorö, Den. C5 62
Sorö, co., Den. C5 62
Sorocaba, Braz. C3, m8 137
Sorochinsk, Sov. Un. C4 73
Soroco, P.R. B8, f12 132
Soroki, Sov. Un. G7 72
Sorong, Indon. F8 90
Soroti, Ug. A5 106
Söröy, isl., Nor. B10 63
Sorraia, riv., Port. C1 65
Sorrento, Fla. D5 174
Sorrento, It. D5 67
Sorrento, La. B6, D5 183
Sorris Sorris, S. W. Afr. B1 107
Sorsogon, Phil. C6 90
Sortavala, Sov. Un. G14 63
Sorum, S. Dak. B3 204
Sörumsand, Nor. p29 63
Sosan, Kor. H3 93
Sosnovka, Sov. Un. E13 72
Sosnowiec, Pol. C5, g10 70
Soso, Miss. D4 188
Sottern, lake, Swe. t33 63
Sotteville-lès-Rouen, Fr. C4 58
Souanké, Con. E2 104
Soubré, I.C. E3 103
Soucook, riv., N.H. D4 193
Soudan, Minn. C6 187
Souderton, Pa. F11 202
Souflíon, Grc. B6 69
Soufriere, St. Lucia p16 131
Souhegan, riv., N.H. E3 193
Souk Ahras, Alg. F10 64
Souk-el Arba, Tun. F11 64
Sŏul, see Seoul, Kor.
Soulac [-sur-Mer], Fr. E3 58
Soulanges, co., Que., Can. D3 154
Sound Beach, N.Y. *F5 172
Sound View, Conn. D7 172
Sources, mtn., Bas., S. Afr. C4 107
Sourdnahunk, lake, Maine B3 184
Soure, Braz. C5 139
Soure, Port. B1 65
Souris, Man., Can. E1 150
Souris, N. Dak. A5 198
Souris, riv., Man., Sask., Can., N. Dak. G12 142
Souris East, P.E.I., Can. C7 151

INDEX KEY Each place listed in **Bold-faced Type** has its population listed in the Population tables, pages 230 to 280. Each country, shown in CAPITAL LETTERS, has its population listed in the World Political Information Table, pages 6 to 10.
* Does not appear on map: key shows general location.

Sourlake, Tex. D5 206
Sourland, mtn., N.J. C3 194
Sous, riv., Mor. C3 102
Sousa, Braz. C3 138
Soustons, Fr. F3 58
South, cape, N.Z. Q11 112
South, cape, Nor. B13 118
South, isl., New Hebr. 115
South, isl., N.Z. O12 112
South, isl., S.C. E9 203
South, isl., Truk 114
South, mtn., Idaho G2 177
South, mtn., Md. A2 173
South, mtn., N. Mex. G6 195
South, mtn., Pa. B2 194
South, mts., N.C. B2 197
South, pass, Kwajalein 114
South, pass, La. F6 183
South, pass, Wyo. C4 213
South, pt., Newf., Can. C4 152
South, pt., Mich. D7 186
South, pt., Pentecost I. 115
South, riv., Ont., Can. B5 153
South, riv., Ga. B5 175
South, riv., Iowa C4 180
South, riv., Md. C4 173
South, riv., N.C. C5 197
South Acton, Mass. C1 185
South Acworth, N.H. D2 193
South Addison, Maine D5 184
SOUTH AFRICA, country, Afr. C3 107
South African Republic (Transvaal) 99
South Amboy, N.J. C4 194
South Amboy Junction, N.J. E4 194
South America, cont. 125
South Amherst, Ohio A5 199
South Andaman, isl., India F9 87
South Anna, riv., Va. D5 209
South Apopka, Fla. *D5 174
SOUTH ARABIA, see Southern Yemen, Asia
South Ashburnham, Mass. A4 185
South Ashfield, Mass. A2 185
South Aulatsivik, isl., Newf., Can. g9 152
South Australia, state, Austl. E5 111
South Baker, Oreg. C9 201
South Barnstead, N.H. D4 193
South Barre, Mass. B3 185
South Barre, Vt. C3 208
South Barrington, Ill. *A5 178
South Bay, Fla. F6 174
South Bellingham, Mass. B5 185
South Belmar, N.J. C4 194
South Belmont, N.C. *B2 197
South Beloit, Ill. A4 178
South Bend, Ind. A5 179
South Bend, Nebr. E2 191
South Bend, Tex. C3 206
South Bend, Wash. C2 210
South Bennettsville, S.C. *B8 203
South Bentinck Arm, chan., B.C., Can. C4 149
South Berwick, Maine E2 184
South Bethlehem, N.Y. C7 196
South Bloomfield, Ohio C5 199
South Boardman, Mich. D5 186
South Boise, Idaho *F2 177
South Bolton, Que., Can. D5 154
South Boston (Independent City), Va. E4 209
South Bound Brook, N.J. B3 194
South Branch, Newf., Can. E2 152
South Branch, lake, Maine C4 184
South Branch, mtn., W. Va. B6 211
South Bristol, Maine E3 184
South Britain, Conn. D4 172
South Broadway, Wash. *C5 210
South Brook, Newf., Can. *D3 152
South Brookfield, N.S., Can. E5 151
South Bruny, isl., Austl. o15 110
South Burlington, Vt. C2 208
South Byfield, Mass. A6 185
South Byron, N.Y. B2 196
South Canaan, Pa. C11 202
South Carolina, state, U.S. 203
in 1779-81 162
during Civil War 164
South Carver, Mass. C6 185
South Central, dist., Alsk. C10 167
South Charleston, Ohio C4 199
South Charleston, W. Va. C6 211
South Charlestown, N.H. D2 193
South Chatham, Mass. C7 185
South Chatham, N.H. B4 193
South Chelmsford, Mass. C1 185
South Chicago Heights, Ill. F3 178
South China, Maine D3 184
South China, sea, Asia H14 76
South Cle Elum, Wash. B5 210
South Clement, creek, Md. D4 173
South Cleveland, Tenn. *D9 205
South Clinton, Tenn. *C9 205
South Coatesville, Pa. *G10 202
South Coffeyville, Okla. A6 200
South Colby, Wash. D1 210
South Colton, N.Y. B2 196
South Congaree, S.C. *D5 203
South Connellsville, Pa. G2 202
South Corning, N.Y. *C3 196
South Dakota, state, U.S. 204
South Danbury, N.H. D3 193
South Danville, N.H. E4 193
South Dartmouth, Mass. C6 185
South Dayton, N.Y. C1 196
South Daytona, Fla. C5 174
South Deer Isle, Maine D4 184
South Deerfield, Mass. B2 185
South Deerfield, N.H. D4 193
South Dennis, N.J. E3 194
South Dorset, Vt. E2 208
South Downs, hills, Eng. D7 56
South Dum Dum, India *F12 88
South Duxbury, Mass. B6 185
South Easton, Mass. B5 185
South Effingham, N.H. C5 193
South Elgin, Ill. E2 178
South Eliot, Maine *E2 184
South El Monte, Calif. *E5 170
South Elwood, Ind. D6 179
South English, Iowa C5 180
South Erradale, Scot. C3 57
South Esk, riv., Scot. D6 57
South Essex, Mass. A6 185
South Euclid, Ohio *B2 199
South Fabius, riv., Mo. A5 189
South Fallsburg, N.Y. D6 196
South Farmingdale, N.Y. *E7 196
South Fayetteville, N.C. *B5 197
South Flevoland Polder, reg., Neth. B5 59
South Floral Park, N.Y. *G2 172
South Fork, Sask., Can. H1 155
South Fork, Colo. D4 171
South Fork, Pa. F4 202
South Fork, res., Wash. B4 210
South Fork Republican, riv., Colo. B8 171
South Fort George, B.C., Can. C6 149
South Fort Mitchell, Ky. *A7 182
South Fort Smith, Ark. B1 169
South Foster, R.I. B10 172
South Fox, isl., Mich. C5 186
South Freeport, Maine E5 184
South Fulton, Tenn. A3 205
South Gamboa, C.Z. k11 130
South Gastonia, N.C. *B2 197
South Gate, Calif. F2 170
South Georgia, isl., Atl. O. D9 120
South Gifford, Mo. A5 189
South Glastonbury, Conn. C6 172
South Glens Falls, N.Y. *B7 196
South Grand, riv., Mo. C3 189
South Greenfield, Mo. D4 189
South Greensburg, Pa. *F2 202
South Greenwood, S.C. C3 203
South Groveland, Mass. A5 185
South Hadley, Mass. B2 185
South Hadley Falls, Mass. B2 185
South Hamilton, Mass. A6, C3 185
South Hampton, N.H. E5 193
South Hanover, Mass. E4 185
South Harpswell, Maine E5 184
South Harriman, Tenn. *D9 205
South Haven, Kans. E6 181
South Haven, Mich. F4 186
South Heart, N. Dak. C2 198
South Heart, riv., Alta., Can. B2 148
South Heights, Pa. *E1 202
South Henderson, N.C. *A5 197
South Hero, Vt. B2 208
South Hill, Va. E4 209
South Hingham, Mass. B6 185
South Holland, Ill. *A6 178
South Holland, prov., Neth. B4 59
South Holston, lake, Tenn., Va. C11 205, B2 209
South Hooksett, N.H. D4 193
South Houston, Tex. F5 206
South Humboldt, riv., Nev. C6 192
South Huntington, N.Y. *E7 196
South Hutchinson, Kans. A4 181
South Indian Lake, Man., Can. A2 150
South International Falls, Minn. B5 187
South Jacksonville, Ill. D3 178
South Jordan, Utah C3 207
South Junction, Man., Can. E4 150
South Junction, Oreg. C5 201
South Kent, Conn. C3 172
South Killingly, Conn. B9 172
South Kingston, N.H. E4 193
South Korea, see Korea, South, country, Asia
South Laguna, Calif. *F5 170
South Lake Tahoe, Calif. E2 192
South Lancaster, Mass. B4 185
South Lansing, N.Y. C4 196
South Lebanon, Maine E2 184
South Lebanon, Ohio C3 199
South Lee, Mass. B1 185
South Liberty, Maine D3 184
South Lincoln, Vt. C3 208
South Londonderry, Vt. E3 208
South Loup, riv., Nebr. C6 191
South Lubec, Maine D5 184
South Lunenburg, Vt. C5 208
South Lyme, Conn. D8 172
South Lyndeboro, N.H. E3 193
South Lyon, Mich. A6, F7 186
South Magnetic Pole, Ant. C26 120
South Manitou, isl., Mich. C4 186
South Mansfield, La. B2 183
South Marsh, isl., Md. D5 173
South Medford, Oreg. *E4 201
South Meriden, Conn. C5 172
South Merrimack, N.H. E3 193
South Miami, Fla. F3, G6 174
South Middleboro, Mass. C6 185
South Milford, Ind. A7 179
South Milford, Mass. B4 185
South Mills, N.C. A7 197
South Milwaukee, Wis. F2, F6 212
South Modesto, Calif. *D3 170
South Molton, Eng. C4 56
South Monroe, Mich. *G7 186
South Montrose, Pa. C10 202
South Mountain, Pa. G7 202
South Naknek, Alsk. D8 167
South Natick, Mass. D2 185
South Natuna, is., Indon. E3 90
South New Berlin, N.Y. C5 196
South New River, canal, Fla. E3 174
South Newburg, Maine D4 184
South Newbury, N.H. D3 193
South Newbury, Vt. C4 208
South Newfane, Vt. F3 208
South Northfield, Vt. C3 208
South Nyack, N.Y. C6 194
South Ogden, Utah B4 207
South Orange, N.J. B4 194
South Orkney, is., Atl. O. C8 120
South Oroville, Calif. *C3 170
South Orrington, Maine D4 184
South Otselic, N.Y. C5 196
South Oyster, bay, N.Y. G3 172
South Paris, Maine D2 184
South Park, Calif. *C2 170
South Pasadena, Calif. F2 170
South Pass City, Wyo. C4 213
South Peacham, Vt. C4 208
South Pekin, Ill. C4 178
South Peninsula, Fla. *C5 174
South Penobscot, Maine D4 184
South Pittsburg, Tenn. D8 205
South Plainfield, N.J. B4 194
South Platte, riv., Colo., Nebr. A7 171, C4 191
South Point, Ohio D5 199
South Pole, Ant. A 120
South Pomfret, Vt. D3 208
South Porcupine, Ont., Can. E9 153
South Portland, Maine E2, E5 184
South Portsmouth, Ky. B7 182
South Pottstown, Pa. *F10 202
South Poultney, Vt. E2 208
South Prairie, Wash. B3 210
South Queensferry, Scot. E5 57
South Range, Mich. A2 186
South Range, Wis. B2 212
South Reading, Vt. E3 208
South Renovo, Pa. D6 202
South River, Newf., Can. *E5 152
South River, Ont., Can. B5 153
South River, N.J. C4 194
South Rockwood, Mich. *F7 186
South Ronaldsay, isl., Scot. B6 57
South Roxana, Ill. *E3 178
South Royalston, Mass. A3 185
South Royalton, Vt. D3 208
South Russell, Ohio *A6 199
South Ryegate, Vt. C4 208
South St. Paul, Minn. E7, F5 187
South Salem, Ohio C4 199
South Salisbury, N.C. *B3 197
South Salt Lake, Utah C4 207
South San Francisco, Calif. B5 170
South San Gabriel, Calif. *F2 170
South Saskatchewan, riv., Alta., Sask., Can. F11 142
South Seaville, N.J. E3 194
South Shetland, is., Ant. C6 120
South Shields, Eng. C6 55
South Shore, Ky. *B7 182
South Shore, Mo. A7 189
South Shore, S. Dak. B9 204
South Side Place, Tex. F5 206
South Sioux City, Nebr. B9 191
South Slocan, B.C., Can. E9 149
South Solon, Ohio C4 199
South Spencer, Mass. B3 185
South Sterling, Pa. D11 202
South Strafford, Vt. D4 208
South Streator, Ill. *B5 178
South Suburban, India *D8 87
South Superior, Wyo. D4 213
South Sutton, N.H. D3 193
South Swansea, Mass. C5 185
South Taft, Calif. *E4 170
South Tamworth, N.H. C4 193
South Toms River, N.J. *D4 194
South Torrington, Wyo. C8 213
South Tucson, Ariz. E5 168
South Tunnel, Tenn. A5 205
South Turlock, Calif. *D3 170
South Twin, lake, Newf., Can. D4 152
South Twin, mtn., N.H. B3 193
South Tyne, riv., Eng. F6 57
South Uist, isl., Scot. C1 57
South Uniontown, Pa. *G2 202
South Ventana Cone, mtn., Calif. D3 170
South Vienna, Ohio C4 199
South Vietnam, see Vietnam, South, country, Asia
South View, Alta., Can. *B4 148
South Wabasca, lake, Alta., Can. B4 148
South Wadesboro, N.C. C3 197
South Wallingford, Vt. E3 208
South Walpole, Mass. E2 185
South Wareham, Mass. C6 185
South Waterford, Maine D2 184
South Waverly, Pa. C8 202
South Wayne, Wis. F4 212
South Weare, N.H. D3 193
South Webster, Ohio D5 199
South Wellfleet, Mass. C8 185
South Wellington, B.C., Can. A9 149
SOUTH WEST AFRICA, U. N. mand., Afr. B2 107
South West City, Mo. E3 189
South West Fargo, N. Dak. C9 198
South West Harbor, Maine D4 184
South Westbury, N.Y. *G2 172
South Weymouth, Mass. D3 185
South Whitley, Ind. B6 179
South Williamson, Ky. C5 182
South Williamsport, Pa. D7 202
South Willington, Conn. B7 172
South Wilmington, Ill. B5 178
South Windham, Conn. C8 172
South Windham, Maine E2, E4 184
South Windsor, Conn. B6 173
South Wisconsin Rapids, Wis. *D4 212
South Wolfeboro, N.H. C4 193
South Woodbury, Vt. C4 208
South Woodstock, Conn. B9 172
South Woodstock, Vt. D3 208
South Worthington, Mass. B2 185
South Yarmouth, Mass. C7 185
South Yuba, Calif. *C3 170
South Zanesville, Ohio C5 199
Southall, Eng. *C7 56
Southampton, Ont., Can. C3 153
Southampton, N.S., Can. D5 151
Southampton, Eng. D6 56
Southampton, Mass. B2 185
Southampton, N.Y. D4 196
Southampton, co., Va. E5 209
Southampton, beach, N.Y. F7 172
Southampton, cape, N.W. Ter., Can. D16 143
Southampton, isl., N.W. Ter., Can. D16 143
Southard, N.J. C4 194
Southard, Okla. A3 200
Southaven, Miss. A3 188
Southboro, Mass. B4, D1 185
Southbranch, Mich. D7 186
Southbridge, Mass. B3 185
Southbury, Conn. D4 172
Southeast, pass, La. E6 183
Southeastern, dist., Alsk. D12 167
Southend-on-Sea, Eng. C8 56
Southern, prov., Malawi E5 106
Southern, prov., Zambia E4 106
Southern, reg., Ken. B6 106
Southern, reg., Tan. D6 106
Southern, uplands, Scot. E4 57
Southern Alps, mts., N.Z. O13 112
Southern Cross, Austl. F2 111
Southern Cross, Mont. D3 190
Southern Highlands, reg., Tan. C5 106
Southern Indian, lake, Man., Can. A2 150
Southern Pines, N.C. B4 197
Southern Rhodesia, see Rhodesia, country, Afr.
Southern Ute, Indian res., Colo. D3 171
Southern View, Ill. *D4 178
Southern Yemen, see Yemen (Aden), country, Asia
Southey, Sask., Can. G3 155
Southfield, Mass. B1 185
Southfield, Mich. *F7 186
Southgate, Eng. *C7 56
Southgate, Ky. A7 182
Southgate, Mich. *F7 186
Southington, Conn. C5 172
Southlake, Tex. *C4 206
Southland, Tex. C2 206
Southmag, Ont., Can. B4 153
Southminster, Eng. C8 56
Southmont, N.C. B3 197
Southmont, Pa. *F4 202
Southold, N.Y. D4 196
Southport, Conn. E3 172
Southport, Eng. A4 56
Southport, Fla. G3 174
Southport, Ind. E5, I8 179
Southport, N.C. D5 197
Southside, N.C. B2 197
Southside, Tenn. A4 205
Southville, Mass. D1 185
Southwark, Eng. C7 56
Southwest, Pa. F2 202
Southwest, cape, Que., Can. B7 151
Southwest, cape, Vir. Is. k17 132
Southwest, chan., Fla. E4 174
Southwest, head, N.B., Can. E3 151
Southwest, pass, La. E3 183
Southwest, pass, La. F6 183
Southwest, pt., R.I. E10 172
Southwest Greensburg, Pa. *F2 202
Southwest Harbor, Maine D4 184
Southwest Wausau, Wis. *D4 212
Southwestern, mts., Va. C4 209
Southwick, Mass. B2 185
Southwold, Eng. B9 56
Soverato, It. E6 67
Sovereign, Sask., Can. F2 155
Sovetsk (Tilsit), Sov. Un. A6 70, D3 72
Sovetskaya Gavan, Sov. Un. E16 71, B10 93
Soviet Socialist Republics, Union of 53
see also Soviet Union
SOVIET UNION, (U.S.S.R.), country, Eur., Asia 71
in 1922-40 53
see also Russia
Soweto, S. Afr. *C4 107
Soya, cape, Jap. D10 93
Sozopol, Bul. D8 68
Spa, Bel. D5 59
Spadra, Ark. B2 169
SPAIN, country, Eur. 65
in 1st cent. B.C. 44
c. 120 A.D. 45
c. 400 46
in 1713 49
in 1808-13 50
in 1814 50
in 1922-40 53
Spalding, Austl. F2 112
Spalding, Sask., Can. E3 155
Spalding, Eng. B7 56
Spalding, Idaho C2 177
Spalding, Nebr. C7 191
Spalding, co., Ga. C2 175
Spanaway, Wash. B3 210
Spangle, Wash. B8, D7 210
Spangler, Pa. E4 202
Spaniard's Bay, Newf., Can. E5 152
Spanish, Ont., Can. A2 153
Spanish, peak, Oreg. C7 201
Spanish Equatorial Region, see Equatorial Guinea, country, Afr.
Spanish Fork, Utah C4 207
Spanish Fort, Tex. C4 206
Spanish Guinea, see Equatorial Guinea, country, Afr.
Spanish Morocco: *see also* Morocco
Spanish Possessions in North Africa, see Ceuta, Melilla, dep., Afr.
Spanish Ranch, Calif. C3 170
SPANISH SAHARA, dep., Afr. E2 102
Spanish Town, Jam. G5 131
Spanishburg, W. Va. D3 211
Sparenberg, Tex. C2 206
Sparkill, N.Y. C5 194
Sparkman, Ark. D3 169
Sparks, Ga. E3 175
Sparks, Nebr. B5 191
Sparks, Nev. D2 192
Sparks, Okla. B5 200
Sparksville, Ky. C4 182
Sparland, Ill. B4 178
Sparlingville, Mich. *E8 186
Sparr, Fla. C4 174
Sparreholm, Swe. t34 63
Sparrow Lake, Ont., Can. C5 153
Sparrows Point, Md. B5 173
Sparta, Ga. C4 175
Sparta, see Spárti, Grc.
Sparta, Ill. E4 178
Sparta, Ky. B5 182
Sparta, Mich. E5 186
Sparta, Mo. E4 189
Sparta, N.J. A3 194
Sparta, N.C. A2 197
Sparta, Ohio B5 199
Sparta, Oreg. C9 201
Sparta, Tenn. D8 205
Sparta, Wis. E3 212
Sparta, mts., N.J. B3 194
Spartanburg, Ind. D8 179
Spartanburg, S.C. B4 203
Spartanburg, co., S.C. B4 203
Spartansburg, Pa. C2 202
Spárti (Sparta), Grc. D4 69
Spas-Demensk, Sov. Un. D10 72
Spassk-Dalniy, Sov. Un. E16 71
Spassk-Ryazanskiy, Sov. Un. D13 72
Spaulding, Ala. E4 166
Spaulding, Okla. B5 200
Spavinaw, Okla. A6 200
Spavinaw, creek, Ark., Okla. A7 200
Spean Bridge, Scot. D4 57
Spear, N.C. C4 197
Spear, cape, Newf., Can. E5 152
Spearfish, S. Dak. C2 204
Spearhill, Man., Can. D2 150
Spearman, Tex. A2 206
Spearsville, La. B3 183
Spearville, Kans. E4 181
Spectacle, pond, Maine D4 184
Speculator, N.Y. B6 196
Spedden, Alta., Can. B5 148
Spednik, lake, N.B., Can. D2 151
Speed, Ind. H6 179
Speed, Kans. C4 181
Speed, N.C. B6 197
Speedway, Ind. E5, H7 179
Speedwell, Tenn. C10 205
Speedwell, Va. E1 209
Speer, Wyo. D8 213
Speers, Sask., Can. E2 155
Speers, Pa. *F2 202
Speight, Ky. C7 182
Speigner, Ala. C3 166
Spelter, W. Va. B7 211
Spenard, Alsk. g17 167
Spencer, Idaho E6 177
Spencer, Ind. F4 179
Spencer, Iowa A2 180
Spencer, Mass. B4 185
Spencer, Nebr. B7 191
Spencer, N.Y. C4 196
Spencer, N.C. B3 197
Spencer, Ohio A5 199
Spencer, Okla. *B4 200
Spencer, S. Dak. D8 204
Spencer, Tenn. D8 205
Spencer, Va. E2 209
Spencer, W. Va. C3 211
Spencer, Wis. D3 212
Spencer, co., Ind. H4 179
Spencer, co., Ky. B4 182
Spencer, cape, Alsk. k21 167
Spencer, gulf, Austl. F6 110
Spencer, lake, Maine C2 184
Spencer, pond, Maine C3 184
Spencerport, N.Y. B3 196
Spencers Island, N.S., Can. D5 151
Spencerville, Ind. B8 179
Spencerville, Md. B4 173
Spencerville, Ohio B3 199
Spences Bridge, B.C., Can. D7 149
Spennymoor, Eng. F7 57
Sperkhiós, riv., Grc. C4 69
Sperling, Man., Can. E3 150
Sperrin, mts., N. Ire. C3 55
Sperry, Iowa D6 180
Sperry, Okla. A6 200
Sperryville, Va. C4 209
Spesutie, isl., Md. B5 173
Spey, riv., Scot. C5 57
Speyer, Ger. D3 61
Spiceland, Ind. E7 179
Spicer, Minn. E4 187
Spickard, Mo. A4 189
Spider, lake, Wis. B2 212
Spiekeroog, Ger. A7 59
Spiekeroog, isl., Ger. B3 60
Spigno Monferrato, It. E4 66
Spillville, Iowa A6 180
Spilsby, Eng. A8 56
Spinazzola, It. D6 67
Spindale, N.C. B2 197
Spink, S. Dak. E9 204
Spink, co., S. Dak. C7 204
Spink Colony, S. Dak. C7 204
Spirit, lake, Iowa A2 180
Spirit, lake, Wash. C3 210
Spirit, res., Wis. C4 212
Spirit Lake, Idaho B2 177
Spirit Lake, Iowa A2 180
Spirit River, Alta., Can. B1 148
Spiritwood, Sask., Can. D2 155
Spiritwood, N. Dak. C7 198
Spiro, Okla. B7 200
Spišská Nová Ves, Czech. D6 70
Spithead, roadstead, Eng. D6 56
Spitsbergen, see Svalbard, Nor. dep., Nor.
Spittal, Aus. E6 60
Spivey, Kans. E5 181
Split, Yugo. D3 68
Split, cape, N.S., Can. D5 151
Split, lake, Man., Can. A4 150
Splügen, Switz. C5 66
Splügen, pass, Switz. C5 66
Spofford, N.H. E2 193
Spofford, Tex. E2 206
Spofford, lake, N.H. E2 193
Spokane, Wash. B8, D7 210
Spokane, co., Wash. B8 210
Spokane, mtn., Wash. B8 210
Spokane, riv., Wash. B7 210
Spoleto, It. C4 67
Spondin, Alta., Can. D5 148
Spoon, riv., Ill. C3 178
Spooner, Wis. C2 212
Spooner, lake, Wis. C1 212
Sporades, is., Grc. D6 68
Spotswood, N.J. C4 194
Spotsylvania, Va. C5 209
Spotsylvania, co., Va. C5 209
Spotted, isl., Newf., Can. B4 152
Spotted Horse, Wyo. A7 213
Spöttrup, Den. B2 62
Spottsville, Ky. C2 182
Spragge, Ont., Can. A2 153
Sprague, Ala. C3 166
Sprague, Man., Can. E4 150
Sprague, Nebr. D9 191
Sprague, Wash. B8 210
Sprague, W. Va. D7 211
Sprague, lake, Wash. B7 210
Sprague, riv., Oreg. E5 201
Sprague River, Oreg. E5 201
Spragueville, Iowa B7 180
Spragueville, N.Y. A5, B1 196
Spragueville, R.I. B10 172
Sprakensehl, Ger. F4 62
Spray, N.C. A4 197
Spray, Oreg. C7 201
Spreckels, Calif. C6 170
Spree, riv., Ger. B9 61
Spremberg, Ger. B9 61
Sprigg, W. Va. D2 211
Spring, Tex. F5 206
Spring, brook, Pa. B9 202
Spring, creek, Ga. F2 175
Spring, isl., S.C. G6 203
Spring, lake, Ill., Iowa B3 178
Spring, mts., Nev. G6 192
Spring, riv., Ark. A4 169
Spring, riv., Mo. D3 189
Spring Arbor, Mich. F6 186
Spring Brook, N. Dak. A2 198
Spring Canyon, Utah D5 207
Spring City, Pa. F10 202
Spring City, Tenn. D9 205
Spring City, Utah D4 207
Spring Coulee, Alta., Can. E4 148

INDEX KEY Each place listed in **Bold-faced Type** has its population listed in the Population tables, pages 230 to 280.
Each country shown in CAPITAL LETTERS, has its population listed in the World Political Information Table pages 6 to 10.
* Does not appear on map: key shows general location.

Spring Creek, N.C. D3 197
Spring Creek, Pa. C2 202
Spring Creek, Tenn. B3 205
Spring Dale, W. Va. D4 211
Spring Garden, Ala. B4 166
Spring Green, Wis. E3 212
Spring Grove, Ill. E2 178
Spring Grove, Ind. E8 179
Spring Grove, Minn. G7 187
Spring Grove, Pa. G8 202
Spring Hill, Ark. D2 169
Spring Hill, Que., Can. D6 154
Spring Hill, Iowa B7 180
Spring Hill, Kans. D9 181
Spring Hill, Pa. *F4 202
Spring Hill, Tenn. B5 205
Spring Hill Junction, N.S., Can. D5 151
Spring Hope, N.C. B5 197
Spring Lake, Fla. D4 174
Spring Lake, Mich. E4 186
Spring Lake, N.J. C4 194
Spring Lake, N.C. B4 197
Spring Lake, Utah D4 207
Spring Lake Heights, N.J. C4 194
Spring Lake Park, Minn. *E5 187
Spring Lick, Ky. C3 182
Spring Mills, Pa. E6 202
Spring Mills, S.C. *B6 203
Spring Place, Ga. B2 175
Spring Valley, Ala. A2 166
Spring Valley, Sask., Can. H3 155
Spring Valley, Ill. B4 178
Spring Valley, Minn. G6 187
Spring Valley, N.Y. D1 196
Spring Valley, Ohio C3 199
Spring Valley, Tex. *E5 206
Spring Valley, Va. E1 209
Spring Valley, Wis. D1 212
Springbok, S. Afr. C2 107
Springboro, Ohio C3 199
Springboro, Pa. C1 202
Springbrook, Ont., Can. C7 153
Springbrook, Iowa B7 180
Springbrook, Wis. C2 212
Springdale, Ark. A1 169
Springdale, Newf., Can. D3 152
Springdale, Mont. E6 190
Springdale, Ohio D2 199
Springdale, Oreg. B4 201
Springdale, Pa. A7, E2 202
Springdale, S.C. *D5 203
Springdale, Utah F3 207
Springdale, Wash. A8 210
Springe, Ger. A4 61
Springer, N. Mex. A5 195
Springer, Okla. C4 200
Springerton, Ill. E5 178
Springerville, Ariz. C6 168
Springfield, Ark. B3 169
Springfield, N.B., Can. D4 151
Springfield, N.S., Can. E5 151
Springfield, Ont., Can. E4 153
Springfield, Colo. D8 171
Springfield, Fla. G3 174
Springfield, Ga. D5 175
Springfield, Idaho F6 177
Springfield Ill. D4 178
Springfield, Ky. C4 182
Springfield, La. B6, D5 183
Springfield, Maine C4 184
Springfield, Mass. B3 185
Springfield, Mich. *F5 186
Springfield, Minn. F4 187
Springfield, Mo. D4 189
Springfield, Nebr. C9, E3 191
Springfield, N.H. C2 193
Springfield, N.J. *B4 194
Springfield, Ohio C4 199
Springfield, Oreg. C4 201
Springfield, Pa. *G11 202
Springfield, S.C. D5 203
Springfield, S. Dak. E8 204
Springfield, Tenn. A5 205
Springfield, Vt. E4 208
Springfield, Va. B5 209
Springfield, W. Va. B6 211
Springfield, lake, Ill. D4 178
Springfield Place, Mich. *F5 186
Springfontein, S. Afr. D4 107
Springhill, Ala. D4 166
Springhill, N.S., Can. D5 151
Springhill, La. A2 183
Springhouse, B.C., Can. D6 149
Springlee, Ky. *B6 182
Springport, Mich. F6 186
Springs, S. Afr. C4 107
Springside, Sask., Can. F4 155
Springsure, Austl. B7 112
Springvale, Austl. A3 112
Springvale, Ga. E2 175
Springvale, Maine E2 184
Springview, Nebr. B6 191
Springville, Ala. B3 166
Springville, Ind. E4 179
Springville, Iowa B6 180
Springville, La. B6, D5 183
Springville, Miss. A4 188
Springville, N.Y. C2 196
Springville, Pa. C10 202
Springville, Tenn. A3 205
Springville, Utah C4 207
Springwater, Sask., Can. F1 155
Springwater, N.Y. C3 196
Spruce, fork, W. Va. D5 211
Spruce, mtn., Ariz. C3 168
Spruce, mtn., Nev. C7 192
Spruce, riv., Sask., Can. D3 155
Spruce Brook, Newf., Can. D2 152
Spruce Creek, Pa. E5 202
Spruce Grove, Alta., Can. C4 148
Spruce Knob, mtn., W. Va. C5 211
Spruce Lake, Sask., Can. D1 155
Spruce Pine, Ala. A2 166
Spruce Pine, N.C. C4 197
Spruce Run, res., N.J. B3 194
Spruce Woods, prov. park, Man., Can. E2 150
Sprucedale, Ont., Can. B5 153
Spud, rock, Ariz. E5 168
Spungabera, Moz. B5 107
Spur, Tex. C2 206
Spurfield, Alta., Can. B3 148
Spurgeon, Ind. H3 179
Spurr, mtn., Alsk. g15 167
Spy Hill, Sask., Can. G5 155
Sqamish, Wash. E6 149
Squa Pan, Maine B4 184
Squam, lake, N.H. C4 193
Squam, mts., N.H. C3 193
Squapan, lake, Maine B4 184
Square, lake, Maine A4 184
Square Butte, Mont. C6 190
Square Islands, Newf., Can. B4, h11 152
Squattack, Que., Can. B9 154
Squaw, hill, Wyo. D7 213
Squaw, peak, Mont. C2 190
Squaw Cap, mtn., N.B., Can. B3 151
Squaw Lake, Minn. C4 187
Squaw Rapids, Sask., Can. D4 155
Squibnocket, pt., Mass. D6 185
Squillace, gulf, It. E6 67
Squires, Mo. E5 189
Squirrel, Idaho E7 177
Srbobran, Yugo. C4 68
Sredne-Kolymsk, Sov. Un. C18 71
Śrem, Pol. B4 70
Sremska Mitrovica, Yugo. C4 68
Sremski Karlovci, Yugo. C4 68
Sretensk, Sov. Un. D14 71
Srinagar, India B5 87
Środa, Pol. B4 70
Środa Śląska, Pol. C4 70
Ssu, China H7 92
Ssu-chan, China B2 93
Ssumao, China G5 91
Ssŭnan, China K3 92
Ssuping, China C9 91
Ssushui, China G7 92
Staatsburg, N.Y. D7 196
Stab, Ky. C5 182
Stacy, N.C. C7 197
Stacyville, Iowa A5 180
Stacyville, Maine C4 184
Stade, Ger. B4 60
Stadskanaal, Neth. B6 59
Stadthagen, Ger. A4 61
Stadtkyll, Ger. D6 59
Stadtlohn, Ger. B1 61
Stadtroda, Ger. C6 61
Staffa, isl., Scot. D2 57
Staffin, Scot. C2 57
Stafford, Conn. B7 172
Stafford, Eng. B5 56
Stafford, Kans. E5 181
Stafford, Nebr. B7 191
Stafford, N.Y. C2 196
Stafford, Ohio C6 199
Stafford, Okla. B2 200
Stafford, Tex. *F5 206
Stafford, Va. C5 209
Stafford, co., Eng. B5 56
Stafford, co., Kans. D5 181
Stafford, co., Va. C5 209
Stafford Springs, Conn. B7 172
Stafford Springs, Miss. D5 188
Staffordsville, Ky. C7 182
Staffordville, Conn. B7 172
Staffordville, N.J. D4 194
Staines, Eng. C7 56
Stains, Fr. g10 58
Stairs, mtn., N.H. B4 193
Stålboga, Swe. t34 63
Staley, N.C. B4 197
Stalingrad, see Volgograd, Sov. Un.
Stalinogród, see Katowice, Pol.
Stall Lake, Man., Can. B2 150
Stallo, Miss. C4 188
Stalwart, Sask., Can. F3 155
Stalwart, Mich. B6 186
Stambaugh, Mich. B2 186
Stamford, Conn. E2 172
Stamford, Eng. B7 56
Stamford, Nebr. D6 191
Stamford, N.Y. C6 196
Stamford, S. Dak. D4 204
Stamford, Tex. C3 206
Stamford, Vt. F2 208
Stamping Ground, Ky. B5 182
Stampried, S.W. Afr. B2 107
Stamps, Ark. D2 169
Stanaford, W. Va. D3, D7 211
Stanardsville, Va. C4 209
Stanberry, Mo. A3 189
Stanchfield, Minn. E5 187
Standard, Alta., Can. D4 148
Standard, La. C3 183
Standerton, S. Afr. C4 107
Standing Rock, Ala. B4 166
Standing Rock, N. Mex. B1 195
Standing Rock, Indian res., S. Dak. B4 204
Standish, Maine E2 184
Standish, Mass. E4 185
Standish, Mich. E7 186
Standish, N.Y. A3 196
Stanfield, Ariz. E3 168
Stanfield, N.C. *B3 197
Stanfield, Oreg. B7 201
Stanford, Ill. C4 178
Stanford, Ind. F4 179
Stanford, Ky. C5 182
Stanford, Mont. C6 190
Stangelville, Wis. A6, D6 212
Stanger, S. Afr. C5 107
Stanhope, Que., Can. D6 154
Stanhope, Eng. F6 57
Stanhope, Iowa B4 180
Stanhope, N.J. B3 194
Staniard Creek, Ba. Is. C5 131
Stanislaus, co., Calif. D3 170
Stanisławów, Pol. k15 70
Stanke Dimitrov, Bul. D6 68
Stanley, N.B., Can. C3 151
Stanley, Eng. C6 56
Stanley, Falk. Is. I5 124
Stanley, Idaho E4 177
Stanley, Kans. D9 181
Stanley, Ky. C2 182
Stanley, N. Mex. B4, G6 195
Stanley, N.C. B2 197
Stanley, N. Dak. A3 198
Stanley, Okla. C6 200
Stanley, Va. C4 209
Stanley, Wis. D3 212
Stanley, co., S. Dak. C5 204
Stanley, falls, Zaire A4 106
Stanley, port, Malekula I. 115
Stanley Corner, S. Dak. D8 204
Stanleytown, Va. E3 209
Stanleyville, N.C. *A3 197
Stanly, co., N.C. B3 197
Stanmore, Alta., Can. D5 148
Stann Creek, Br. Hond. B3 130
Stanovoi, mts., Sov. Un. D15 76
Stans, Switz. C4 66
Stanstead, co., Que., Can. D5 154
Stanthorpe, Austl. D8 112
Stanton, Ala. C3 166
Stanton, Calif. *F3 170
Stanton, Iowa D2 180
Stanton, Ky. C6 182
Stanton, Mich. E5 186
Stanton, Miss. D2 188
Stanton, Mo. C6 189
Stanton, Nebr. C8 191
Stanton, N.J. B3 194
Stanton, N. Dak. B4 198
Stanton, Tenn. B2 205
Stanton, Tex. C2 206
Stanton, co., Kans. E2 181
Stanton, co., Nebr. C8 191
Stantonsburg, N.C. B6 197
Stantonville, Tenn. B3 205
Stanwood, Iowa C6 180
Stanwood, Mich. E5 186
Stanwood, Wash. A3 210
Staplehurst, Nebr. D8 191
Staples, Minn. D4 187
Staples, Tex. A4 206
Stapleton, Ala. E2 166
Stapleton, Ga. C4 175
Stapleton, Nebr. C5 191
Star, Miss. C3 188
Star, N.C. B4 197
Star, Tex. D3 206
Star, lake, Minn. D3 187
Star, peak, Nev. C3 192
Star City, Ark. D4 169
Star City, Sask., Can. E3 155
Star City, Ind. C4 179
Star City, W. Va. B5 211
Star Junction, Pa. *F2 202
Star Prairie, Wis. C1 212
Stará Boleslav, Czech. n18 70
Stara Zagora, Bul. D7 68
Starachowice, Pol. C6 70
Staraya Russa, Sov. Un. C8 72
Starbuck, Man., Can. E3 150
Starbuck, Minn. E3 187
Starbuck, Wash. C7 210
Starbuck, isl., Pac. O. G12 113
Starford, Pa. E4 202
Stargard, Pol. B3 70
Stargo, Ariz. D6 168
Staritsa, Sov. Un. C10 72
Stark, Kans. E8 181
Stark, N.H. A4 193
Stark, co., Ill. B4 178
Stark, co., N. Dak. C3 198
Stark, co., Ohio B6 199
Starke, Fla. C4 174
Starke, co., Ind. B4 179
Starkey, Oreg. B8 201
Starkey, Va. D3 209
Starks, La. D2 183
Starks, Maine D3 184
Starksboro, Vt. C2 208
Starkville, Colo. D6 171
Starkville, Miss. B5 188
Starkville, N.Y. C6 196
Starkweather, N. Dak. A7 198
Starlight, Pa. C11 202
Starnberg, Ger. B7 66
Starobelsk, Sov. Un. G12 72
Starodub, Sov. Un. E9 72
Starogard, Pol. B5 70
Starokonstantinov, Sov. Un. G6 72
Starominskaya, Sov. Un. H12 72
Starr, S.C. C2 203
Starr, co., Tex. F3 206
Starr, mtn., Tenn. D9 205
Starrking, N.H. B4 193
Starrucca, Pa. C11 202
Start, bay, Eng. D4 56
Start, pt., Eng. D4 56
Startex, S.C. B3 203
Startup, Wash. B4 210
Starvation, res., Utah C5 207
Starý Plzenec, Czech. D8 61
Stary Sącz, Pol. D6 70
Staryy Oskol, Sov. Un. F11 72
Stassfurt, Ger. B6 61
Staszów, Pol. C6 70
State Center, Iowa B4 180
State College, Miss. B5 188
State College, Pa. E6 202
State Line, Ind. D2 179
State Line, Mass. B1 185
State Line, Miss. D5 188
State Line, N.H. E2 193
State Line, Pa. G6 202
State Road, Maine B4 184
State Road, N.C. A3 197
Staten, isl., N.Y. E1 196
Staten Island, see Richmond, borough and co., N.Y.
Statenville, Ga. F3 175
Statesboro, Ga. D5 175
Statesville, N.C. B3 197
Statham, Ga. C3 175
Stathelle, Nor. p27 63
Station No. 6, Sud. A3 105
Statue of Liberty, nat. mon., N.Y. E5 196
Staufen, Ger. B3 66
Staunton, Ill. D4 178
Staunton, Ind. F3 179
Staunton (Independent City), Va. C3 209
Stavanger, Nor. H1 63
Stave, lake, B.C., Can. A11 149
Staveley, Eng. A6 56
Stavelot, Bel. D5 59
Stavely, Alta., Can. D4 148
Stavenhagen, Ger. E6 62
Stavenisse, Neth. C4 59
Staveren, Neth. B5 59
Staves, Ark. C3 169
Stavropol, Sov. Un. I14 72
Stawell, Austl. H4 112
Stayner, Ont., Can. C4 153
Stayton, Oreg. C2, C4 201
Stead, N. Mex. A6 195
Steamboat, Nev. D2 192
Steamboat, mtn., Mont. C4 190
Steamboat, mtn., Wyo. D4 213
Steamboat Canyon, Ariz. B6 168
Steamboat Rock, Iowa B4 180
Steamboat Springs, Colo. A4 171
Stearns, Ky. D5 182
Stearns, co., Minn. E4 187
Stebbins, Alsk. C7 167
Steblev, Sov. Un. G8 72
Štěchovice, Czech. o17 70
Stecker, Okla. C3 200
Stecoah, N.C. D2 197
Stedman, N.C. B5 197
Steele, Ala. B3 166
Steele, Mo. E8 189
Steele, N. Dak. C6 198
Steele, co., Minn. F5 187
Steele, co., N. Dak. B8 198
Steele, mtn., Wyo. D6 213
Steele City, Nebr. D8 191
Steeleville, Ill. E4 178
Steelton, Pa. F8 202
Steelville, Mo. D6 189
Steen, Minn. G2 187
Steenbergen, Neth. C4 59
Steenburg, Ont., Can. C7 153
Steens, Miss. B5 188
Steens, mtn., Oreg. E8 201
Steenwijk, Neth. B6 59
Steep Falls, Maine E2 184
Steep Rock, Man., Can. D2 150
Steep Rock Lake, Ont., Can. E8 153
Sheephill, lake, Sask., Can. B4 155
Ştefăneşti, Rom. B8 68
Stefanie, lake, Eth. E4 105
Stege, Den. D6 62
Steger, Ill. B6, F3 178
Steilacoom, Wash. E1 210
Stein, Ger. D6 61
Steinach, Aus. B7 66
Steinauer, Nebr. D9 191
Steinbach, Man., Can. E3 150
Steinbach-Hallenberg, Ger. C5 61
Steinfort, Lux. E5 59
Steinhatchee, Fla. C3 174
Steinhatchee, riv., Fla. C3 174
Steinhausen, S.W. Afr. B2 107
Steinhuder, lake, Ger. F3 62
Steinkjer, Nor. E4 63
Stella, Ont., Can. C8 153
Stella, Ky. E3 182
Stella, Mo. E3 189
Stella, Nebr. D10 191
Stella, mtn., It. C5 66
Stellarton, N.S., Can. D7 151
Stem, N.C. A5 197
Stenay, Fr. E5 59
Stendal, Ger. B5 60
Stendal, Ind. H3 179
Stenen, Sask., Can. F4 155
Stengårdshult, Swe. A7 62
Stenness, lake, Scot. A5 57
Stensele, Swe. E7 63
Stepanakert, Sov. Un. F3 73
Stepenitz, riv., Ger. E5 62
Stephan, S. Dak. C6 204
Stephen, Minn. B2 187
Stephens, Ark. D2 169
Stephens, Ga. C3 175
Stephens, co., Ga. B3 175
Stephens, co., Okla. C4 200
Stephens, co., Tex. C3 206
Stephens, passage, Alsk. m23 167
Stephens City, Va. B4 209
Stephens Knob, mtn., Ky. D5 182
Stephensburg, N.J. B3 194
Stephenson, Mich. C3 186
Stephenson, co., Ill. A4 178
Stephensport, Ky. C3 182
Stephenville, Newf., Can. D2 152
Stephenville, Tex. C3 206
Stephenville Crossing, Newf., Can. D2 152
Stepnoy, Sov. Un. D3 73
Stepnyak, Sov. Un. C8 73
Steps, pt., Am. Sam. 114
Steptoe, Nev. D7 192
Steptoe, Wash. B8 210
Steptoe, creek, Nev. E7 192
Sterco, Alta., Can. C2 148
Sterkstroom, S. Afr. D4 107
Sterley, Tex. B2 206
Sterling, Alsk. g16 167
Sterling, Colo. A7 171
Sterling, Conn. C9 172
Sterling, Idaho F6 177
Sterling, Ill. B4 178
Sterling, Ind. D3 179
Sterling, Kans. D5 181
Sterling, Mass. B4 185
Sterling, Mich. D6 186
Sterling, Nebr. D9 191
Sterling, N. Dak. C5 198
Sterling, Okla. C3 200
Sterling, Utah D4 207
Sterling, Va. A4, B5 209
Sterling, co., Tex. D2 206
Sterling, isl., Sol. Is. 115
Sterling, res., Colo. A7 171
Sterling City, Tex. D2 206
Sterling Run, Pa. D5 202
Sterlington, La. B3 183
Sterlitamak, Sov. Un. C5 73
Sternberg, Ger. E5 62
Šternberk, Czech. D4 70
Sterrett, Ala. B3 166
Štětl, Czech. C9 61
Stetson, Maine D3 184
Stetson, mtn., Maine C5 184
Stetsonville, Wis. C3 212
Stettin (Szczecin), Pol. E8 62, B3 70
Stettin, lagoon, Ger., Pol. E8 62
Stettler, Alta., Can. C4 148
Steuben, Maine D5 184
Steuben, Mich. B4 186
Steuben, Wis. E3 212
Steuben, co., Ind. A7 179
Steuben, co., N.Y. C3 196
Steubenville, Ohio B7 199
Steve, Ark. C2 169
Stevenage, Eng. C7 56
Stevens, N.J. C3 194
Stevens, N. Mex. D1 195
Stevens, co., Kans. E2 181
Stevens, co., Minn. E2 187
Stevens, co., Wash. A8 210
Stevens, pass, Wash. B4 210
Stevens, peak, Idaho, Mont. C1 190
Stevens Creek, dam, Ga. C4 175
Stevens Point, Wis. D4 212
Stevens Pottery, Ga. D3 175
Stevens Village, Alsk. B10 167
Stevenson, Ala. A4 166
Stevenson, Conn. D4 172
Stevenson, Wash. D4 210
Stevenson, lake, Man., Can. C3 150
Stevenson, riv., Man., Can. C4 150
Stevensville, Md. C5 173
Stevensville, Mich. F4 186
Stevensville, Mont. D2 190
Steveston, B.C., Can. A9 149
Steward, Ill. B4 178
Stewardson, Ill. D5 178
Stewart, Ala. C2 166
Stewart, B.C., Can. E2 149
Stewart, Minn. F4 187
Stewart, Miss. B4 188
Stewart, Nev. D2 192
Stewart, Ohio C6 199
Stewart, Tenn. A4 205
Stewart, co., Ga. D2 175
Stewart, co., Tenn. A4 205
Stewart, isl., N.Z. Q11 112
Stewart, mtn., Ariz. G3 168
Stewart, riv., Yukon, Can. D5 142
Stewart Manor, N.Y. *E7 196
Stewart Valley, Sask., Can. G2 155
Stewarton, Scot. E4 57
Stewartstown, N.H. B1 193
Stewartstown, Pa. G8 202
Stewartsville, Ala. B3 166
Stewartsville, Ind. H2 179
Stewartsville, Mo. B3 189
Stewartsville, N.J. B2 194
Stewartville, Minn. G6 187
Stewiacke, N.S., Can. D6 151
Steynsburg, S. Afr. D4 107
Steyr, Aus. D7 60
Stibnite, Idaho E3 177
Stickney, Ill. *B6 178
Stickney, S. Dak. D7 204
Stigler, Okla. B6 200
Stikine, mts., B.C., Can. E7 142
Stikine, riv., B.C., Can. E6 142
Stiles, Tex. D2 206
Stilesville, Ind. E4 179
Stilis, Grc. C4 69
Still Pond, Md. B5 173
Still River, Mass. B4 185
Stillaguamish, riv., Wash. A4 210
Stillman Valley, Ill. A4 178
Stillmore, Ga. D4 175
Stillwater, B.C., Can. E5 149
Stillwater, Minn. E6, E8 187
Stillwater, Nev. D3 192
Stillwater, N.J. A3 194
Stillwater, N.Y. C7 196
Stillwater, Okla. A4 200
Stillwater, Pa. D9 202
Stillwater, R.I. B10 172
Stillwater, co., Mont. E7 190
Stillwater, range, Nev. D3 192
Stillwater, res., N.Y. B5 196
Stillwell, Ga. D5 175
Stillwell, Ind. A4 179
Stilson, Ga. D5 175
Stilwell, Kans. D9 181
Stilwell, Okla. B7 200
Stimson, mtn., Mont. B3 190
Stinchar, riv., Scot. E4 57
Stine, mtn., Mont. E3 190
Stinesville, Ind. F4 179
Stinnett, Tex. B2 206
Stinson Lake, N.H. C3 193
Štip, Yugo. E6 68
Stirling, Alta., Can. E4 148
Stirling, Ont., Can. C7 153
Stirling, Que., Can. B5 154
Stirling, N.J. B4 194
Stirling, Scot. D5 57
Stirling, co., Scot. D4 57
Stirling City, Calif. C3 170
Stirrat, W. Va. D3 211
Stirum, N. Dak. C8 198
Stissing, mtn., N.Y. B2 172
Stites, Idaho C2 177
Stittsville, Ont., Can. B9 153
Stjördal, Nor. F4 63
Stoa Pikt, Ariz. E3 168
Stobnica, Pol. E8 62
Stockbridge, Ga. C2 175
Stockbridge, Mass. B1 185
Stockbridge, Mich. F6 186
Stockbridge, Vt. D3 208
Stockbridge, Wis. B5, D5 212
Stockbridge, Indian res., Wis. D5 212
Stockdale, Ohio D5 199
Stockdale, Pa. *F2 202
Stockdale, Tex. B4, E4 206
Stockerau, Aus. D8 60
Stockertown, Pa. E11 202
Stockett, Mont. C5 190
Stockham, Nebr. D8 191
Stockholm, Sask., Can. G4 155
Stockholm, Maine A4 184
Stockholm, N.J. A3 194
Stockholm, S. Dak. B9 204
Stockholm, Swe. H8, t36 63
Stockholm, Wis. D1 212
Stockhorn, mtn., Switz. C3 66
Stockland, Ill. C6 178
Stockport, Eng. A5 56
Stockport, Iowa D6 180
Stockport, Ohio C6 199
Stockton, Ala. E2 166
Stockton, Calif. B6, D3 170
Stockton, Man., Can. E2 150
Stockton, Ga. F4 175
Stockton, Ill. A3 178
Stockton, Kans. C4 181
Stockton, Md. D7 173
Stockton, Minn. *F7 187
Stockton, Mo. D4 189
Stockton, N.J. C3 194
Stockton, N.Y. C1 196
Stockton, Utah C3 207
Stockton, isl., Wis. B3 212
Stockton, res., Mo. D4 189
Stockton Springs, Maine D4 184
Stockville, Nebr. D5 191
Stockwell, Ind. D4 179
Stod, Czech. D8 61
Stoddard, N.H. D2 193
Stoddard, Wis. E2 212
Stoddard, co., Mo. E8 189
Stoeckl, mtn., B.C., Can. A2 149
Stoke Centre, Que., Can. D6 154
Stoke-on-Trent, Eng. A5 56
Stokes, N.C. B6 197
Stokes, co., N.C. A3 197
Stokesdale, N.C. A4 197
Stokesley, Eng. F7 57
Stokke, Nor. p28 63
Stolac, Yugo. D3 68
Stolberg, Ger. C3 60
Stolbovaya, Sov. Un. n17 72
Stollberg, Ger. C7 61
Stolp, see Słupsk, Pol.
Stolzenau, Ger. F3 62
Stone, Eng. B5 56
Stone, Idaho G6 177
Stone, Ky. C7 182
Stone, co., Ark. B3 169
Stone, co., Miss. E4 188
Stone, co., Mo. E4 189
Stone, mtn., Ga. C2 175
Stone, mtn., Vt. B5 208
Stone, mts., N. Car. A2 197
Stone, mts., Tenn. C12 205
Stone City, Colo. C6 171
Stone City, Iowa B6 180
Stone Corral, lake, Oreg. E7 201
Stone Harbor, N.J. E3 194
Stone Lake, Wis. C2 212
Stone Mountain, Ga. B5, C2 175
Stone Park, Ill. *F2 178
Stonebluff, Ind. D3 179
Stoneboro, Pa. D1 202
Stoneboro, S.C. B6 203
Stonefort, Ill. F5 178
Stonega, Va. B2 209
Stoneham, Colo. A7 171
Stoneham, Mass. C3 185
Stonehaven, N.B., Can. B4 151
Stonehaven, Scot. D6 57
Stonehenge, Austl. B4 112
Stoner, Colo. D2 171
Stones River, nat. military park and cemetery, Tenn. B5 205
Stoneville, Miss. B3 188
Stoneville, N.C. A4 197
Stoneville, S. Dak. C3 204
Stonewall, Man., Can. D3 150
Stonewall, Ga. B4 175
Stonewall, La. B2 183
Stonewall, Miss. C5 188

INDEX KEY Each place listed in **Bold-faced Type** has its population listed in the Population tables, pages 230 to 280. Each country, shown in CAPITAL LETTERS, has its population listed in the World Political Information Table, pages 6 to 10.
* Does not appear on map: key shows general location.

Stonewall, Okla....C5 200
Stonewall, Tex....D3 206
Stonewall, co., Tex....C2 206
Stonewood, W. Va....*B4 211
Stoney, isl., Newf., Can....B4 152
Stoney Creek, Ont., Can....D5 153
Stonington, Colo....D8 171
Stonington, Conn....D9 172
Stonington, Ill....D4 178
Stonington, Maine....D4 184
Stonington, Mich....C4 186
Stono, inlet, S.C....F8 203
Stono, riv., S.C....F2 203
Stony, brook, N.J....C3 194
Stony, creek, Va....D5 209
Stony, isl., N.Y....B4 196
Stony, lake, Ont., Can....C6 153
Stony, riv., W. Va....B5 211
Stony Beach, Sask., Can....G3 155
Stony Brook, N.Y....F4 172
Stony Brook, hbr., N.Y....F4 172
Stony Creek, Conn....D5 172
Stony Creek, N.Y....B7 196
Stony Creek, Va....E5 209
Stony Mountain, Man., Can....D3 150
Stony Plain, Alta., Can....C3 148
Stony Point, N.Y....A5 194
Stony Point, N.C....B2 197
Stony Rapids, Sask., Can....E11 144
Stony Ridge, Ohio....A2 199
Stonyford, Calif....C2 170
Stör, riv., Ger....B4 60
Stora Luleträsk, lake, Swe....D8 63
Stora Sundby, Swe....t34 63
Storå, riv., Den....B2 62
Storavan, lake, Swe....E8 63
Storden, Minn....F3 187
Store Belt, strait, Den....C4 62
Store-Heddinge, Den....C6 62
Storey, co., Nev....D2 192
Storfjord, fjord, Nor....F2 63
Storkerson, cape, N.W. Ter., Can....B11 142
Storkow, Ger....A8 61
Storla, S. Dak....D7 204
Storm, lake, Iowa....B2 180
Storm, mtn., Alsk....h16 167
Storm Lake, Iowa....B2 180
Stormont, co., Ont., Can....B9 153
Stornoway, Sask., Can....F4 155
Stornoway, Scot....B2 57
Storozhinets, Sov. Un....G5 72
Storr, mtn., Scot....C2 57
Storrs, Conn....B7 172
Storsjö, Swe....F5 63
Storsjön, lake, Swe....F6 63
Storthoaks, Sask., Can....H5 155
Storuman, lake, Swe....E6 63
Story, Wyo....A6 213
Story, co., Iowa....B4 180
Story City, Iowa....B4 180
Story Prairie, Ohio....*A4 199
Stotesbury, Mo....D3 189
Stotts City, Mo....D4 189
Stottville, N.Y....C7 196
Stouffville, Ont., Can....D5, E7 153
Stoughton, Sask., Can....H4 155
Stoughton, Mass....B5, E3 185
Stoughton, Wis....F4 212
Stour, riv., Eng....C8 56
Stour, riv., Eng....C9 56
Stour, riv., Eng....D5 56
Stourbridge, Eng....B5 56
Stourport-on-Severn, Eng....B5 56
Stout, Iowa....B5 180
Stout (Rome), Ohio....D4 199
Stoutland, Mo....D5 189
Stoutsville, Mo....B6 189
Stoutsville, Ohio....C2 199
Stovall, Ga....D2 175
Stovall, Miss....A3 188
Stovall, N.C....A5 197
Stove Creek, Sask., Can....E4 155
Stover, Miss....A3 188
Stover, Mo....C5 189
Stövring, Den....B3 62
Stow, Maine....D2 184
Stow, Mass....B4, C1 185
Stow, Ohio....A6 199
Stow, creek, N.J....E2 194
Stowe [Township], Pa....*F1 202
Stowe, Pa....F10 202
Stowe, Vt....C3 208
Stowmarket, Eng....B8 56
Stoy, Ill....D6 178
Stoyoma, mtn., B.C., Can....D7 149
Stoystown, Pa....F4 202
Strabane, N. Ire....C3 55
Strabane, Pa....F1 202
Strachur, Scot....D3 57
Strader, La....B7 183
Strafford, Mo....D4 189
Strafford, N.H....D4 193
Strafford, Vt....D4 208
Strafford, co., N.H....D4 193
Straffordville, Ont., Can....E4 153
Straight, Okla....D3 200
Strakonice, Czech....D2 70
Straldzha, Bul....D8 68
Stralsund, Ger....A6 60
Strandburg, S. Dak....B9 204
Strandby, Den....A4 62
Strandquist, Minn....B2 187
Strang, Nebr....D8 191
Strang, Okla....A6 200
Stranger, creek, Kans....B8 181
Strangford, lake, N. Ire....C4 55
Strängnäs, Swe....t35 63
Strångsjö, Swe....u34 63
Stranraer, Sask., Can....F1 155
Stranraer, Scot....F3 57
Strasbourg, Sask., Can....G3 155
Strasbourg, Fr....C7 58, F7 59
Strasburg, Colo....B6 171
Strasburg, Ger....E7 62
Strasburg, Ill....D5 178
Strasburg, Mo....C3 189
Strasburg, N. Dak....C5 198
Strasburg, Ohio....B6 199
Strasburg, Pa....G9 202
Strasburg, Va....C4 209
Strass, Aus....B7 66
Strasswalchen, Aus....B9 66
Stratford, Calif....D4 170
Stratford, Ont., Can....D4 153
Stratford, Conn....E4 172
Stratford, Iowa....B4 180
Stratford, N.H....A3 193
Stratford, N.J....D2 194
Stratford, N.Y....B6 196
Stratford, N.Z....M15 112
Stratford, Okla....C5 200
Stratford, S. Dak....B7 204
Stratford, Tex....A1 206
Stratford, Wis....D3 212
Stratford, pt., Conn....E4 172
Stratford Center, Que., Can....D6 154
Stratford-on-Avon, Eng....B6 56
Stratham, N.H....D5 193
Strathaven, Scot....E4 57
Strathclair, Man., Can....D1 150
Strathcona, Ont., Can....C8 153
Strathcona, Minn....B2 187
Strathlorne, N.S., Can....C8 151
Strathmere, N.J....E3 194
Strathmoor Village, Ky....*B4 182
Strathmore, Calif....D4 170
Strathmore, Alta., Can....D4 148
Strathcona, prov. park, B.C., Can....E5 149
Strathroy, Ont., Can....E3 153
Strattanville, Pa....D3 202
Stratton, Colo....B8 171
Stratton, Maine....C2 184
Stratton, Nebr....D4 191
Stratton, Ohio....B7 199
Stratton, mtn., Vt....E3 208
Straubing, Ger....E7 61
Straubville, N. Dak....C8 198
Straughn, Ind....E7 179
Strausberg, Ger....F7 62
Strausstown, Pa....F9 202
Straw, Mont....D7 190
Strawberry, Ark....B4 169
Strawberry, mtn., Oreg....C8 201
Strawberry, mts., Oreg....C8 201
Strawberry, pt., Mass....B6 185
Strawberry, res., Utah....C4 207
Strawberry, riv., Ark....A4 169
Strawberry, riv., Utah....C5 207
Strawberry Daniels, pass, Utah....C4 207
Strawberry Plains, Tenn....C10 205
Strawberry Point, Iowa....B6 180
Strawn, Ill....C5 178
Strawn, Kans....D8 181
Strawn, Tex....C3 206
Strážnice, Czech....D4 70
Streamstown, Alta., Can....C5 148
Streamwood, Ill....*A5 178
Streator, Ill....B5 178
Streeter, N. Dak....C6 198
Streeter, Tex....D3 206
Streetman, Tex....D4 206
Streetsville, Ont., Can....E6 153
Strehaia, Rom....C6 68
Strelka, Sov. Un....C13 71
Stresa, It....D4 66
Stretford, Eng....*A5 56
Stribling, Tenn....A4 205
Stříbro, Czech....D2 70
Strichen, Scot....C6 57
Strimón, gulf, Grc....B4 69
Strimón, riv., Grc....B4 69
Stringer, Miss....D4 188
Stringtown, Colo....B4 171
Stringtown, Ky....B5 182
Stringtown, Miss....B3 188
Stringtown, Okla....C5 200
Strofádhes, isl., Grc....D3 69
Stroh, Ind....A7 179
Stroma, isl., Scot....B5 57
Stromboli, isl., It....E5 67
Strome, Alta., Can....C4 148
Strome Ferry, Scot....C3 57
Stromness, Scot....B5 57
Stromsburg, Nebr....C8 191
Stronach, Mich....D4 186
Stroner, Wyo....A7 213
Strong, Ark....D3 169
Strong, Maine....D2 184
Strong, riv., Miss....C4 188
Strong City, Kans....D7 181
Strong City, Okla....B2 200
Strongfield, Sask., Can....F2 155
Stronghurst, Ill....C3 178
Strongs, Mich....B6 186
Strongsville, Ohio....A6, B2 199
Stronsay, firth, Scot....A6 57
Stronsay, isl., Scot....A6 57
Strontian, Scot....D3 57
Stroud, Eng....C5 56
Stroud, Okla....B5 200
Stroudsburg, Pa....E11 202
Struble, Iowa....B1 180
Struer, Den....B2 62
Struga, Yugo....E5 68
Strum, Wis....D2 212
Struma, riv., Bul....E6 68
Strumble, head, Wales....B2 56
Strumica, Yugo....E6 68
Strunk, Ky....D5 182
Struthers, Ohio....A7 199
Stryama, riv., Bul....D7 68
Stryker, Mont....B2 190
Stryker, Ohio....A3 199
Strykersville, N.Y....C2 196
Stryy, Sov. Un....G4 72
Stryy, riv., Sov. Un....D7 70
Strzegom, Pol....C4 70
Strzelce, Pol....C5 70
Strzelce Krajenskie, Pol....B3 70
Strzelecki, creek, Austl....D3 112
Strzelin, Pol....C4 70
Strzelno, Pol....B5 70
Strzemieszyce, Pol....g10 70
Stuart, Fla....E6 174
Stuart, Iowa....C3 180
Stuart, Nebr....B6 191
Stuart, Okla....C5 200
Stuart, Va....E2 209
Stuart, lake, B.C., Can....B5 149
Stuart, mtn., Wash....B4 210
Stuart, range, Austl....E5 110
Stuart, riv., B.C., Can....B6 149
Stuarts Draft, Va....C3 209
Stub, hill, N.H....A2 193
Stubbeköbing, Den....D6 62
Studley, Kans....C3 181
Stull, Kans....B7 181
Stull, lake, Ont., Can....B5 150
Stull, riv., Man., Can....B5 150
Stump, lake, N. Dak....B7 198
Stump Creek, Pa....D4 202
Stumptown, W. Va....C4 211
Stumpy Point, N.C....B8 197
Stung Treng, Camb....F6 89
Stupart, riv., Man., Can....B4 150
Stupino, Sov. Un....D12 72
Stura, riv., It....D3 66
Sturbridge, Mass....B3 185
Sturgeon, Mo....B5 189
Sturgeon, bay, Man., Can....C3 150
Sturgeon, lake, Alta., Can....B2 148
Sturgeon, riv., Sask., Can....D2 155
Sturgeon, riv., Mich....B4 186
Sturgeon Bay, Wis....D6 212
Sturgeon Falls, Ont., Can....A5 153
Sturgeon Lake, Minn....D6 187
Sturgeon Landing, Sask., Can....C5 155
Sturgeon-weir, riv., Sask., Can....C4 155
Sturgis, Sask., Can....F4 155
Sturgis, Ky....C2 182
Sturgis, Mich....G5 186
Sturgis, Miss....B4 188
Sturgis, S. Dak....C2 204
Sturt, creek, Austl....C4 110
Sturtevant, Wis....F2, F6 212
Stutsman, co., N. Dak....B6 198
Stutterheim, S. Afr....D4 107
Stuttgart, Ark....C4 169
Stuttgart, Ger....E4 61
Stuttgart, Kans....C4 181
Styr, riv., Sov. Un....F5 72
Styria, reg., Aus....E7 60
Su, China....H7 92
Suakin, Sud....B4 105
Subi-Besar, isl., Indon....K8 89
Subiaco, Ark....B2 169
Subic, Phil....C6, o13 90
Subic, bay, Phil....o13 90
Sublett, range, Idaho....G6 177
Sublette, Ill....B4 178
Sublette, Kans....E3 181
Sublette, co., Wyo....C2 213
Sublimity, Oreg....C2, C4 201
Subotica, Yugo....B4 68
Sucarnoochee, Miss....C5 188
Sucarnoochee, creek, Ala., Miss....C5 188
Succasunna, N.J....B3 194
Success, Ark....A5 169
Success, Sask., Can....G1 155
Success, mtn., N.H....B4 193
Suceava, Rom....B8 68
Suceava, riv., Rom....B8 68
Sucha, Pol....D5 70
Suchan, Sov. Un....E6 93
Suchdol, Czech....n17 70
Suches, Ga....B2 175
Suchitoto, Sal....D3 130
Suchocin, Pol....k13 70
Suchou, see Soochow, China
Suchow (Hsuchow), China....E8 91
Suck, riv., Ire....D2 55
Sucre, Bol....C2 135
Sucre, state, Ven....A5 133
Suçuapara, Braz....B3 137
Sucuriú, riv., Braz....B2 137
Sucy-en-Brie, Fr....g11 58
Süd-Nord, canal, Ger....B7 59
Sudan, Tex....B1 206
SUDAN, country, Afr....C2 105
Sudan, French....99
see also Mali
Sudbury, Ont., Can....A4, E9 153
Sudbury, Eng....B8 56
Sudbury, Mass....B5, D1 185
Sudbury, Vt....D2 208
Sudbury, co., Ont., Can....A3 153
Sudbury, res., Mass....D1 185
Sudbury, riv., Mass....B5 185
Sudd, swamp, Sud....D3 105
Süderbrarup, Ger....D3 62
Sudetes, mts., Pol....C4 70
Sudlersville, Md....B6 173
Sudogda, Sov. Un....D13 72
Sudzha, Sov. Un....F10 72
Sueca, Sp....C5 65
Suez (As Suways), Eg....C6 101
Suez, canal, Eg....C6 101
Suez, gulf, Afr....D6 101
Suffern, N.Y....D1, D2, D6 196
Suffield, Alta., Can....D5 148
Suffield, Conn....B6 172
Suffolk, Mont....C7 190
Suffolk (Independent City), Va....B6, E6 209
Suffolk (East Suffolk, West Suffolk), co., Eng....B8 56
Suffolk, co., Mass....B5 185
Suffolk, co., N.Y....D3 196
Sufu, see Kashgar, China
Sugar, creek, Ind....F6 179
Sugar, creek, Ind....E3 179
Sugar, creek, Pa....C8 202
Sugar, isl., Mich....B6 186
Sugar, mtn., Mich....A2 186
Sugar, riv., N.H....D2 193
Sugar, riv., Wis....F4 212
Sugar City, Colo....C7 171
Sugar City, Idaho....F7 177
Sugar Creek, Mo....E2 189
Sugar Grove, Ark....B2 169
Sugar Grove, Ill....*B5 178
Sugar Grove, N.C....A2 197
Sugar Grove, Ohio....C5 199
Sugar Grove, Va....B3, E1 209
Sugar Grove, W. Va....C5 211
Sugar Hill, Ga....B2 175
Sugar Hill, N.H....B3 193
Sugar Land, Tex....E5, F4 206
Sugar Notch, Pa....B8 202
Sugar Run, Pa....C9 202
Sugar Tree, Tenn....B3 205
Sugar Valley, Ga....B1 175
Sugarcreek, Ohio....*B6 199
Sugargrove, Pa....C3 202
Sugarloaf, hill, Ohio....A6 199
Sugarloaf, mtn., Maine....C2 184
Sugarloaf, mtn., Md....B3 173
Sugarloaf, mtn., Mont....C4 190
Sugarloaf, mtn., N.H....A4, B1 193
Sugarloaf, mtn., Okla....B7 200
Sugden, Okla....C4 200
Suget, pass, China, India....A6 87
Suggi, lake, Sask., Can....C4 155
Suggsville, Ala....D2 166
Sugluk, Que....A2 154
Şuḩār, Oman....D2 87
Suhl, Ger....C5 61
Sui, China....G6 92
Suiattle, riv., Wash....A4 210
Suichi, China....B9 89
Suichiang, China....F7 91
Suichuan, China....F7 91
Suichung, China....D9 92
Suifenho, China....C11 91
Suihsien, China....E7 91
Suihua (Peilintzu), China....B10 91
Suileng, China....C3 93
Suilu, China....A7 89
Suining, China....E6 91
Suipacha, Arg....g7 136
Suipacha, Bol....D2 135
Suipin, China....C5 93
Suippes, Fr....E4 59
Suir, riv., Ire....D3 55
Suisun City, Calif....B5 170
Suita, Jap....*o14 93
Suite, China....D7 91
Suiter, Va....D1 209
Suitland, Md....C2 173
Suitung, China....C9 92
Sukabumi, Indon....G3 90
Sukadana, Indon....F3 90
Sukhona, riv., Sov. Un....D16 40
Sukhumi, Sov. Un....*E7 71
Sukkur, Pak....C4 87, D2 88
Sukunka, riv., B.C., Can....B7 149
Sul, chan., Braz....C5 139
Sula, Mont....E3 190
Sula, isl., Indon....F6 90
Sula, riv., Sov. Un....F9 72
Sulaiman, range, Pak....C2 88
Sulęcin, Pol....B3 70
Sulei, isl., Sol. Is....115
Sulina, Rom....C9 68
Sulingen, Ger....F2 62
Sulitjelma, mtn., Swe....D7 63
Suliwula, mtn., China....D4 91
Sullana, Peru....B1 134
Sulligent, Ala....B1 166
Sullivan, Ill....D5 178
Sullivan, Ind....F3 179
Sullivan, Ky....C2 182
Sullivan, Mo....C6 189
Sullivan, N.H....D2 193
Sullivan, Ohio....A5 199
Sullivan, Wis....E5 212
Sullivan, co., Ind....F3 179
Sullivan, co., Mo....A4 189
Sullivan, co., N.H....D2 193
Sullivan, co., N.Y....D6 196
Sullivan, co., Pa....D8 202
Sullivan, co., Tenn....C11 205
Sullivan, isl., Bur....G2 89
Sullivan, lake, Alta., Can....D5 148
Sullivans Island, S.C....F3 203
Sully, Iowa....C5 180
Sully, co., S. Dak....C5 204
Sulmona, It....C4 67
Sulphide, Ont., Can....C7 153
Sulphur, Ky....B4 182
Sulphur, La....D2 183
Sulphur, Okla....C5 200
Sulphur, fork, Tenn....A4 205
Sulphur, see Iwo, isl., Kazan-retto
Sulphur, riv., Ark....D2 169
Sulphur, riv., Alta., Can....C1 148
Sulphur Rock, Ark....B4 169
Sulphur South, La....*D2 183
Sulphur Spring, val., Ariz....E6 168
Sulphur Springs, Ark....A1 169
Sulphur Springs, Ind....D7 179
Sulphur Springs, Mo....B8 189
Sulphur Springs, Ohio....B5 199
Sulphur Springs, Tex....C5 206
Sulphurdale, Utah....E3 207
Sultan, Wash....B4 210
Sultanabad, India....H7 88
Sultanabad, see Arāk, Iran
Sultanpur, India....D9 88
Sulu, arch., Phil....D6 90
Sulu, riv., China....C4 91
Sulu, sea, Phil....D5 90
Suluq, Libya....C4 101
Sulzbach, Ger....D2 61
Sulzbach-Rosenberg, Ger....D6 61
Sulzberger, bay, Ant....B33 120
Sumach, Wash....*C5 210
Sumas, Wash....A3 210
Sumatra, Fla....B2 174
Sumatra, Mont....D9 190
Sumatra: c. 750 A.D....80
c. 1775....82
after World War II....83
Sumatra, isl., Indon....E2 90
Sumava Resorts, Ind....B3 179
Sumay, Guam....114
Sumba, isl., Indon....G5 90
Sumbar, riv., Sov. Un....B7 86
Sumbawa, Indon....G5 90
Sumbawanga, Tan....C5 106
Sumbay, Peru....E3 134
Sumburgh, pt., Scot....h10 55
Sümeg, Hung....B3 68
Sumenep, Indon....G4 90
Sumgait, Sov. Un....A4 86
Sumiton, Ala....B2 166
Summan, des., Sau. Ar....H3 86
Summer, isl., Mich....C4 186
Summer, lake, Oreg....E6 201
Summer Hill, Ill....D3 178
Summer Lake, Oreg....E6 201
Summer Shade, Ky....D4 182
Summerberry, Sask., Can....G4 155
Summerberry, riv., Man., Can....C1 150
Summerdale, Ala....E2 166
Summerfield, Fla....C4 174
Summerfield, Ill....*E4 178
Summerfield, Kans....C7 181
Summerfield, La....B3 183
Summerfield, Mo....C6 189
Summerfield, N.C....A4 197
Summerfield, Ohio....C6 199
Summerford, Newf., Can....D4 152
Summerland, B.C., Can....E8 149
Summerland Key, Fla....H5 174
Summers, co., W. Va....D4 211
Summerside, P.E.I., Can....C6 151
Summersville, Ky....C4 182
Summersville, Mo....D6 189
Summersville, W. Va....C4, C7 211
Summersville, res., W. Va....C4, C7 211
Summerton, S.C....D7 203
Summertown, Ga....D4 175
Summertown, Tenn....B4 205
Summerville, Ga....B1 175
Summerville, Oreg....B8 201
Summerville, Pa....D3 202
Summerville, S.C....E2, E7 203
Summit, Ark....A3 169
Summit, Calif....F3 170
Summit, C.Z....k11 130
Summit, Ill....F2 178
Summit, Miss....D3 188
Summit, N.J....B4 194
Summit, Oreg....C3 201
Summit, R.I....C10 172
Summit, S. Dak....B8 204
Summit, Tenn....E10 205
Summit, Utah....F3 207
Summit, co., Colo....B4 171
Summit, co., Ohio....A6 199
Summit, co., Utah....C4 207
Summit, lake, Iowa....C3 180
Summit, mtn., Nev....D5 192
Summit, mtn., N.Z....N16 112
Summit, peak, Colo....D4 171
Summit Hill, Pa....E10 202
Summit Lake, Indian res., Nev....B2 192
Summit Point, W. Va....B7 211
Summit Station, Ohio....C2 199
Summitville, Colo....D4 171
Summitville, Ind....D6 179
Summitville, Tenn....B6 205
Summum, Ill....C3 178
Sumner, Ga....E3 175
Sumner, Ill....E6 178
Sumner, Iowa....B5 180
Sumner, Mich....E6 186
Sumner, Miss....B3 188
Sumner, Mo....B4 189
Sumner, Nebr....D6 191
Sumner, Okla....A4 200
Sumner, Wash....B3 210
Sumner, co., Kans....E6 181
Sumner, co., Tenn....A5 205
Sumner, strait, Alsk....m23 167
Sumoto, Jap....I7 93
Šumperk, Czech....D4 70
Sumpter, Oreg....C8 201
Sumrall, Miss....D4 188
Sumter, Ga....E2 175
Sumter, S.C....D7 203
Sumter, co., Ala....C1 166
Sumter, co., Fla....D4 174
Sumter, co., Ga....D2 175
Sumter, co., S.C....D7 203
Sumter, fort, S.C....F3 203
Sumterville, Ala....C1 166
Sumy, Sov. Un....F10 72
Sun, La....D6 183
Sun, riv., Mont....C4 190
Sun City, Fla....F2 174
Sun City, Kans....E5 181
Sun Prairie, Wis....E4 212
Sun River, Mont....C5 190
Sun Valley, Idaho....F4 177
Suna, Tan....C5 106
Sunagawa, Jap....E10 93
Sunapee, N.H....D2 193
Sunapee, lake, N.H....D2 193
Sunapee, mtn., N.H....D2 193
Sunart, inlet, Scot....D3 57
Sunbright, Tenn....C9 205
Sunburg, Minn....E3 187
Sunburst, Mont....B5 190
Sunbury, Ill....B5 178
Sunbury, N.C....A7 197
Sunbury, Ohio....B5 199
Sunbury, Pa....E8 202
Sunbury, co., N.B., Can....D3 151
Sunchales, Arg....A4 136
Suncho Corral, Arg....E3 135
Sunchŏn, Kor....G2 93
Sunchŏn, Kor....I3 93
Suncook, N.H....D4 193
Suncook, ponds, N.H....D4 193
Sunda, strait, Indon....G3 90
Sundance, Wyo....A8 213
Sundance, mtn., Wyo....A8 213
Sundance Beach, Alta., Can....*C3 148
Sundarbans, swamp, Bngl., India....G12 88
Sunday, strait, Austl....C3 110
Sundbyberg, Swe....t35 63
Sunderland, Ont., Can....C5 153
Sunderland, Eng....C6 55
Sunderland, Md....C4 173
Sunderland, Mass....B2 185
Sunderland, Vt....E2 208
Sundown, Man., Can....E3 150
Sundown, Tex....C1 206
Sundre, Alta., Can....D3 148
Sundridge, Ont., Can....B5 153
Sunds, Den....B3 62
Sundsvall, Swe....F7 63
Sunfield, Mich....F5 186
Sunflower, Ariz....D4 168
Sunflower, Miss....B3 188
Sunflower, co., Miss....B3 188
Sunflower, mtn., Kans....C2 181
Sunflower, riv., Miss....B3 188
Sungai Petani, Mala....J4 89
Sungaiguntung, Indon....E2 90
Sungari, res., China....E3 93
Sungari, riv., China....C5 93
Sungchiang, China....I9 92
Sunghsien, China....E7 91
Sungkan, China....J2 92
Sungtao, China....J3 92
Sungurlu, Tur....B10 85
Sunland Gardens, Fla....*E6 174
Sunland Park, N. Mex....F3 195
Sunlight, creek, Wyo....A3 213
Sunman, Ind....F7 179
Sunne, Swe....H5 63
Sunny Acres, Ky....*A7 182
Sunny South, Ala....D2 166
Sunnybrae, N.S., Can....D7 151
Sunnybrook, Alta., Can....C3 148
Sunnydale, Kans....B5 181
Sunnyland, Fla....F2 174
Sunnymead, Calif....*F5 170
Sunnynook, Alta., Can....D5 148
Sunnyside, Newf., Can....E5 152
Sunnyside, Fla....G3 174
Sunnyside, Ill....*A5 178
Sunnyside, Utah....D5 207
Sunnyside, Wash....C5 210
Sunnyslope, Alta., Can....D4 148
Sunnyvale, Calif....B5 170
Sunnyvale, Tex....*A6 206
Sunnyview, S. Dak....C9 204
Sunol, Calif....B6 170
Sunol, Nebr....C3 191
Sunray, Tex....B2 206
Sunrise, Tex....*D4 206
Sunrise, Wyo....C8 213
Sunrise, mtn., N.J....A3 194
Sunrise Heights, Mich....*F5 186
Sunset, La....D3 183
Sunset, Maine....D4 184
Sunset, Tex....C4 206
Sunset, Utah....*B3 207
Sunset, hill, Conn....B8 172
Sunset Crater, nat. mon., Ariz....B4 168
Sunset Hills, Mo....*C7 189
Sunshine, Austl....*H5 112
Sunshine, Fla....F2 174
Sunshine, Maine....D4 184
Sunshine, Wyo....A3 213
Sunspot, N. Mex....E4 195
Suntar, Sov. Un....C14 71
Suntaug, lake, Mass....C3 185
Suntrana, Alsk....C10 167
Sunyani, Ghana....E4 103
Suo, sea, Jap....J5 93
Suoyarvi, Sov. Un....F15 63
Supai, Ariz....A3 168
Superb, Sask., Can....F1 155
Superior, Ariz....D4 168
Superior, Colo....B5 171
Superior, Iowa....A3 180
Superior, Mont....C2 190
Superior, Nebr....D7 191
Superior, Wis....B1 212
Superior, Wyo....D4 213
Superior, lake, U.S., Can....A10 159
Suphan Buri, Thai....E4 89
Supi Oidak, Ariz....F4 168
Supply, N.C....C5 197
Supply (Sappural Sho), reef, Mariana Is....115

INDEX KEY Each place listed in **Bold-faced Type** has its population listed in the Population tables, pages 230 to 280.
Each country, shown in CAPITAL LETTERS, has its population listed in the World Political Information Table, pages 6 to 10.
* Does not appear on map; key shows general location.

Suq ash Shuyukh, Iraq....F3 86
Suquamish, Wash........B3 210
Şūr, Oman..............D2 87
Şūr Bāhir, Jordan........k11 84
Sura, riv., Sov. Un..........C3 73
Surabaja, Indon...........G4 90
Surakarta, Indon..........G4 90
Surakhany, Sov. Un.........E4 73
Šurany, Czech.............D5 70
Surat, Austl..............C7 112
Surat, India.......D5 87, G4 88
Surat Thani, Thai..........H3 89
Suratgarh, India...........C4 88
Surazh, Sov. Un...........E9 72
Surbiton, Eng...........*C7 56
Suresnes, Fr..............g9 58
Suretamati, mtn., Vanua Lava I.............. 115
Suretka, C.R..............F6 130
Surette Island, N.S., Can..............F4 151
Surf City, N.J............D4 194
Surf City, N.C...........*C6 197
Surfside, Fla.............F3 174
Surgères, Fr...............D3 58
Surgoinsville, Tenn.......C11 205
Surgut, Sov. Un...........C10 71
Suri, India................F11 88
Suriapet, India.............I7 88
Suribachi, mtn., Iwo............ 114
Surigao, Phil..............D7 90
SURINAM (Netherlands Guiana), Neth. dep., S.A...............B3 139
Suriname, riv., Sur..........B3 139
Suring, Wis...............D5 212
Surkhan Darya, riv., Sov. Un...............C13 86
Surprise, Ariz............G1 168
Surprise, Nebr............C8 191
Surrency, Ga..............E4 175
Surrey, N.B., Can.........*D5 151
Surrey, N. Dak............A4 198
Surrey, Wash..............B10 149
Surrey, co., Eng............C7 56
Surry, Maine..............D4 184
Surry, N.H................D2 193
Surry, Va...............B5, D6 209
Surry, co., N.C............A3 197
Surry, co., Va.............D6 209
Surry Mountain, res., N.H..D2 193
Surt, see Sirte, Libya
Sürüç, Tur................D12 85
Surud Ad, mtn., Som.........C6 105
Suruga, bay, Jap............o17 93
Surveyor, W. Va............D6 211
Surville, cape, San Cristobal............... 115
Susa, It....................B1 67
Sušac, isl., Yugo...........D3 68
Sūsah, Tun...............B7 102
Sušak, Yugo................C2 68
Susak, isl., Yugo...........C2 68
Susanino, Sov. Un..........s31 63
Susank, Kans..............D5 181
Susanville, Calif..........B3 170
Susiana: c. 500 B.C............. 78
Sušice, Czech...............D2 70
Susitna, Alsk..............g16 167
Susitna, riv., Alsk.........C10 167
Susquehanna, Pa...........C10 202
Susquehanna, co., Pa....C10 202
Susquehanna, riv., Md., N.Y., Pa......A5 173, C4 196, E8 202
Susques, Arg...............D2 135
Sussex, N.B., Can..........D4 151
Sussex, N.J................A3 194
Sussex, Va.................E5 209
Sussex, Wis...............E1 212
Sussex, Wyo...............B6 213
Sussex, co., Del...........C6 173
Sussex, co., Eng............D7 56
Sussex, co., N.J...........A3 194
Sussex, co., Va............E5 209
Sussex Corner, N.B., Can...............D4 151
Susua, P.R.................C3 132
Susung, China...............I7 92
Susurluk, Tur..............C7 69
Sutbcliffe, Nev.............D2 192
Sutherland, Iowa...........B2 180
Sutherland, Nebr...........C4 191
Sutherland, S. Afr..........D3 107
Sutherland, Va..........C7, D5 209
Sutherland, co., Scot.........B4 57
Sutherland, res. and canal system, Nebr..............D5 191
Sutherland Springs, Tex....B4 206
Sutherlin, Oreg............D3 201
Sutlej, riv., India, Pak.......B4 88
Sutter, Calif.............*C3 170
Sutter, co., Calif..........C3 170
Sutter Creek, Calif.........C3 170
Suttle, Ala.................C2 166
Sutton, Alsk...............g17 167
Sutton, Ark................D2 169
Sutton, Que., Can..........D5 154
Sutton, Eng..............m12 55
Sutton, Nebr..............D8 191
Sutton, N.H...............D3 193
Sutton, N. Dak.............B7 198
Sutton, Vt.................B4 208
Sutton, W. Va.............C4 211
Sutton, co., Tex...........D2 206
Sutton, res., W. Va..........C4 211
Sutton Coldfield, Eng.......B6 56
Sutton in Ashfield, Eng....A6 56
Sutton West, Ont., Can....C5 153
Suttons Bay, Mich..........D5 186
Suttsu, Jap................E10 92
Sūüjiin Hudag, Mong.......A2 92
Suva, Fiji................... 114
Suva, hbr., Fiji................ 114
Süveydiye, Tur.............D10 85
Suwa, Jap.................m17 93
Suwałki, Pol...............A7 70
Suwanee, Ga..............B2 175
Suwannee, Fla.............C3 174
Suwannee, co., Fla........B3 174
Suwannee, riv., Fla., Ga.....F4 175
Suwannee, sound, Fla.......C3 174
Suwanoochee, creek, Ga.....F4 175
Suwanose, isl., Jap..........L4 93
Şuwaylih, Jordan...........B7 84
Şuwaymah, Jordan.........h13 84
Suwŏn, Kor..............*H3 93
Suyo, Peru.................B1 134
Suzu, cape, Jap.............H8 93
Suzuka, Jap..............o15 93
Suzuka-Sammyaku, mts., Jap..............o15 93
Suzzara, It..................E6 66
SVALBARD, Nor. dep., Eur......................B13 118
Svalbard, is., Nor..........B13 118
Svärtagård, Swe...........u35 63
Svartån, riv., Swe...........t34 63
Svartisen, mtn., Nor........D6 63
Svatovo, Sov. Un...........G12 72
Svedala, Swe...............C7 62
Sveg, Swe...................F6 63
Svendborg, Den.............C4 62
Svendborg, co., Den........C4 62
Svene, Nor..................p27 63
Svenljunga, Swe............A7 62
Svensen, Oreg..............A3 201
Svenstrup, Den.............B3 62
Sverdlovsk, Sov. Un.......q22 72
Sverdlovsk, Sov. Un.......B6 73
Sverdrup, is., N.W. Ter., Can......................B25 118
Svetlaya, Sov. Un...........C9 93
Svicha, riv., Sov. Un........D8 70
Svilajnac, Yugo.............C5 68
Svilengrad, Bul..............E8 68
Svindal, Nor................p29 63
Svinninge, Den..............C5 62
Svir, riv., Sov. Un.........A10 72
Svirstroy, Sov. Un...........A9 72
Svishtov, Bul................D7 68
Svitavy, Czech..............D4 70
Svobodnyy, Sov. Un.......D15 71
Svobodnyy, cape, Sov. Un...................C11 93
Svyatoy, cape, Sov. Un....B16 71
Swadlincote, Eng............B6 56
Swaffham, Eng..............B8 56
Swain, co., N.C............D2 197
Swain, reefs, Austl..........D9 110
Swains, isl., Pac. O.........G11 113
Swainsboro, Ga............D4 175
Swakopmund, S.W. Afr....B1 107
Swale, riv., Eng.............C6 55
Swaledale, Iowa............B4 180
Swalwell, Alta., Can........D4 148
Swamp, riv., N.Y............C2 172
Swampscott, Mass....B6, C3 185
Swan, Iowa.................C4 180
Swan, creek, Ohio...........A2 199
Swan, falls, Idaho...........F2 177
Swan, hills, Alta., Can......................B2 148
Swan, is., Hond.............B6 130
Swan, lake, Man., Can......C1 150
Swan, lake, Maine...........D4 184
Swan, lake, Nebr............C3 191
Swan, lake, Wash...........D2 210
Swan, peak, Mont............C3 190
Swan, range, Mont...........B3 190
Swan, riv., Austl.............F2 110
Swan, riv., Man., Can.......D1 150
Swan, riv., Sask., Can.......E4 155
Swan Creek, Ill..............C3 178
Swan Hill, Austl.............G4 112
Swan Hills, Alta., Can.......................B3 148
Swan Lake, Man., Can......E2 150
Swan Lake, Idaho...........G6 177
Swan Lake, Miss............B3 188
Swan Lake, Mont............C3 190
Swan River, Man., Can.....C1 150
Swan River, Minn...........C5 187
Swan Valley, Idaho.........F7 177
Swanage, Eng...............D6 56
Swandale, W. Va......C7, C4 211
Swanington, Ind............C3 179
Swannanoa, N.C...........D3 197
Swanquarter, N.C...........B7 197
Swans, isl., Maine...........D4 184
Swans Island, Maine........D4 184
Swansboro, N.C.............C6 197
Swansea, Ont., Can......*E6 153
Swansea, Ill................B9 189
Swansea, Mass.............C5 185
Swansea, S.C...............D5 203
Swansea, Wales............C4 56
Swansea, bay, Wales........C4 56
Swanson, Sask., Can........F2 155
Swanson Lake, res., Nebr......................D4 191
Swanton, Md................D1 173
Swanton, Nebr.............D8 191
Swanton, Ohio..............A4 199
Swanton, Vt................B2 208
Swanville, Minn............E4 187
Swanzey, N.H..............E2 193
Swarthmore, Pa...........B10 202
Swartswood, N.J............A3 194
Swartswood, lake, N.J.......A3 194
Swartz, La..................B4 183
Swartz Creek, Mich..........F7 186
Swatara, Minn..............D5 187
Swatow, China.............G8 91
Swayzee, Ind...............C6 179
SWAZILAND, country, Afr...................C5 107, 99
Swea City, Iowa............A3 180
Sweatman, Miss.............B4 188
Swedeborg, Mo.............D5 189
Swedeburg, Nebr...........E2 191
Swedeland, Pa.............A11 202
SWEDEN, country, Eur.......F7 63
c. 1140...................... 47
c. 1360...................... 48
c. 1721...................... 49
in 1815...................... 50
in 1914...................... 52
Swedesboro, N.J...........D2 194
Sweeny, Tex...............G4 206
Sweet, Idaho................F2 177
Sweet Briar, Va.............D3 209
Sweet Grass, co., Mont....E7 190
Sweet Hall, Va..............D6 209
Sweet Home, Ark.....C3, D6 169
Sweet Home, Oreg..........C4 201
Sweet Home, Tex............E4 206
Sweet Springs, Mo.........C4 189
Sweet Springs, W. Va.......D4 211
Sweet Valley, Pa............D9 202
Sweet Water, Ala...........C2 166
Sweet Water, canyon, Utah....................D6 207
Sweetgrass, Mont...........B5 190
Sweetsburg, Que., Can....D5 154
Sweetsers, Ind..............C6 179
Sweetwater, Fla..........*G6 174
Sweetwater, Idaho..........C2 177
Sweetwater, Okla...........B2 200
Sweetwater, Tenn..........D8 205
Sweetwater, Tex............C2 206
Sweetwater, co., Wyo.......D3 213
Sweetwater, riv., Wyo.......C4 213
Swenson, Tex...............C2 206
Swepsonville, N.C..........A4 197
Swider, riv., Pol............m14 70
Świdnica, Pol..............C4 70
Świdnik, Pol................m14 70
Świdwin, Pol................B3 70
Świebodzice, Pol............C4 70
Świebodzin, Pol.............B3 70
Świecie, Pol................B5 70
Świętochłowice, Pol.........g9 70
Świetokrzyskie, mts., Pol....C6 70
Swift, Minn.................B3 187
Swift, co., Minn............E3 187
Swift, creek, N.C............B6 197
Swift, creek, Va.............C6 209
Swift, res., Wash............C3 210
Swift, riv., N.H..............C4 193
Swift, riv., N.H..............B4 193
Swift Current, Sask., Can..........................G2 155
Swift Diamond, riv., N.H....B2 193
Swifton, Ark................B4 169
Swiftown, Miss..............B3 188
Swiftwater, N.H.............B3 193
Swinburne, cape, N.W. Ter., Can....................B13 142
Swindle, isl., B.C., Can......C3 149
Swindon, Eng...............C6 56
Swink, Colo................C7 171
Swinomish, Indian res., Wash......................A3 210
Świnoujście, Pol............A3 70
Swisher, Iowa...............C6 180
Swisher, co., Tex...........B2 206
Swiss, W. Va..........C3, C7 211
Swiss Confederation: c. 1360...................... 48
Swisshome, Oreg...........C3 201
Swissvale, Pa..............B6 202
Switz City, Ind..............F3 179
Switzer, W. Va..............D5 211
Switzerland, Fla............C6 174
Switzerland, S.C............G5 203
SWITZERLAND, country, Eur........................C4 66
in 1721...................... 49
in 1815...................... 50
see also Swiss Confederation
Switzerland, co., Ind........G7 179
Swords, Ga..................C3 175
Swoyersville, Pa.....B8, D10 202
Sycamore, Ala...............B3 166
Sycamore, Ga...............E3 175
Sycamore, Ill...............B5 178
Sycamore, Kans.............E8 181
Sycamore, Mo..............E5 189
Sycamore, Ohio.............B4 199
Sycamore, S.C..............E5 203
Sycamore, creek, Tenn.......A4 205
Sycamore, creek, W. Va.....*C7 211
Sycamore Hills, Mo.......*C7 189
Sychevka, Sov. Un.........D10 72
Syców, Pol..................C4 70
Sydenham, Ont., Can.......C8 153
Sydney, Austl.............F8 112
Sydney, N.S., Can..........C9 151
Sydney, N. Dak.............C7 198
Sydney Mines, N.S., Can.........................C9 151
Sykeston, N. Dak...........B6 198
Sykesville, Md..............B4 173
Sykesville, N.J..............C3 194
Sykesville, Pa..............D4 202
Syktyvkar, Sov. Un.........C8 71
Sylacauga, Ala..............B3 166
Sylamore, Ark..............B3 169
Sylhet, Bngl................D9 87
Sylling, Nor................p28 63
Sylt, isl., Ger...............D2 62
Sylva, N.C.................D3 197
Sylvan, Oreg...............B2 201
Sylvan, Pa..................G6 202
Sylvan, lake, Ind............B7 179
Sylvan Beach, N.Y..........B5 196
Sylvan Grove, Kans.........C5 181
Sylvan Hills, Ark............D6 169
Sylvan Lake, Alta., Can....C3 148
Sylvan Lake, Mich.........*F7 186
Sylvan Shores, Fla........*D5 174
Sylvan Springs, Ala......*B3 166
Sylvania, Ala...............A4 166
Sylvania, Sask., Can.......E3 155
Sylvania, Ga...............D5 175
Sylvania, Ky................A3 182
Sylvania, Ohio........A1, A4 199
Sylvania, Pa...............C8 202
Sylvarena, Miss............C4 188
Sylvester, Ga..............E3 175
Sylvester, Tex..............C2 206
Sylvester, W. Va.........*C3 211
Sylvester, mtn., Newf., Can.......................D4 152
Sylvia, Kans................E5 181
Sylvia, Tenn................A4 205
Symerton, Ill..............*B5 178
Symmes, creek, Ohio........D5 199
Symsonia, Ky...............A2 182
Syosset, N.Y................F2 172
Syr Darya, riv., Sov. Un....E7 73
Syracuse, Ind...............B6 179
Syracuse (Siracusa), It.....F5 67
Syracuse, Kans.............E2 181
Syracuse, Mo...............C5 189
Syracuse, Nebr.........D9, F3 191
Syracuse, N.Y..............B4 196
Syracuse, Ohio.............D6 199
Syracuse, Utah.............B3 207
SYRIA, country, Asia.....E12 85
in 7th cent. B.C................ 44
in 1st cent. B.C................ 46
c. 120 A.D...................... 45
in 1920-21..................... 53
after World War II............ 83
Syriam, Bur................D2 89
Sysladobsis, lake, Maine...C4 184
Sysola, riv., Sov. Un........A4 73
Syzran', Sov. Un...........C3 73
Szabadszállás, Hung........B4 68
Szamos, riv., Hung..........A6 68
Szamotuły, Pol..............B4 70
Szarvas, Hung..............B5 68
Szczakowa, Pol.............g10 70
Szczebrzeszyn, Pol.........C7 70
Szczecin, see Stettin, Pol.
Szczecinek, Pol.............B4 70
Szczuczyn Białostocki, Pol.........................B7 70
Szczytno, Pol...............B6 70
Szechwan, prov., China....E5 98
Szeged, Hung...............B5 61
Székesfehérvár, Hung.....B4 68
Szekszárd, Hung............B4 68
Szengen, China.............G6 91
Szentendre, Hung...........B4 68
Szentes, Hung..............B5 68
Szigetvár, Hung.............B3 68
Szolnok, Hung..............B5 68
Szombathely, Hung.........B3 68
Szprotawa, Pol..............C3 70
Sztum, Pol..................B5 70
Szubin, Pol.................B4 70
Szydłowiec, Pol.............C6 70
Szymanów, Pol.............m12 70

T

Taal, Phil..................p13 90
Taal, lake, Phil.............p13 90
Tab, Ind.....................D3 179
Tabaco, Phil..............*C6 90
Ţābah, Sau. Ar..............I14 85
Tabar, isl., Bis. Arch.......... 115
Tabar, is., Bis. Arch........... 115
Ţabas, Iran...................E8 86
Ţabas, Iran..................E10 86
Tabasco, state, Mex.........D6 129
Tabatinga, mts., Braz.......D2 138
Tabayoc, mtn., Phil.........n13 90
Tabbys, peak, Utah..........C3 207
Tabelbala, Alg..............D4 102
Taber, Alta., Can...........E4 148
Taberg, N.Y.................B5 196
Tabernacle, N.J.............D3 194
Tabernas, Sp................D4 65
Tabernash, Colo.............B5 171
Taberville, Mo..............C4 189
Tabik, isl., Kwajalein......... 114
Tabiona, Utah..............C5 207
Tablas, cape, Chile.........A2 136
Tablas, isl., Phil............C6 90
Table, bay, Newf., Can.......B3 152
Table, bay, S. Afr...........D2 107
Table, head, Newf., Can.....B4 152
Table, mtn., Ariz............E5 168
Table, mtn., Newf., Can.....E2 152
Table Grove, Ill.............C3 178
Table Rock, Nebr...........D9 191
Table Top, mtn., Ariz........E3 168
Tablónes, P.R.........C8, g12 132
Taboada, Sp.................A2 65
Tábor, Czech................D3 70
Tabor, Iowa.................D2 180
Tabor, Minn................B2 187
Tabor, S. Dak..............E8 204
Tabor, mtn., Isr.............B7 84
Tabor City, N.C............C5 197
Tabora, Tan.................C5 106
Tabou, I.C...................F3 103
Tabriz, Iran..................B3 86
Tabūk, Sau. Ar..............D7 101
Tabusintac, riv., N.B., Can.........................B4 151
Tacámbaro de Codallos, Mex.........................n13 129
Tacheng, China.............E7 92
Tachie, riv., B.C., Can.......B5 149
Tachiiwa, pt., Iwo............. 114
Tachikawa, Jap............n18 93
Táchira, state, Ven..........B3 133
Tachov, Czech...............D7 61
Tacloban, Phil...............C6 90
Tacna, Ariz...................E1 168
Tacna, Peru..................E3 134
Tacna, dept., Peru..........E3 134
Tacoma, Colo.................D3 171
Tacoma, Wash..........B3, D1 210
Tacoma Park, S. Dak........B7 204
Taconic, Conn...............A3 172
Taconic, range, Mass........A1 185
Taconite, Minn............*C5 187
Taconite Harbor, Minn..................B6, C8 187
Tacoronte, Sp. (Can. Is.)...............m13 65
Tacuarembó, Ur.............E1 137
Tacuatí, Par..................D4 135
Tacuba, Mex.................h9 129
Tacubaya, Mex...............h9 129
Tad, W. Va...................C6 211
Tademait, plat., Alg..........D5 102
Tadent, riv., Alg.............E6 102
Tadjoura, Afars & Is.........C5 105
Tadoule, lake, Man., Can....C5 150
Tadoussac, Que., Can.......A8 154
Tadzhik, S.S.R., rep., Sov. Un..........................E7 73
Taegu, Kor...................I4 93
Taejŏn, Kor..................H3 93
Taeyudong, Kor...............F2 93
Tafalla, Sp....................A5 65
Tafí Viejo, Arg...............E2 135
Taft, Calif....................E4 170
Taft, Fla......................D5 174
Taft, La.......................B6 183
Taft, Okla.....................B6 200
Taft, Oreg....................C3 201
Taft, Tenn....................B5 205
Taft, Tex......................F4 206
Taft Heights, Calif........*E4 170
Taft Southwest, Tex.......*F4 206
Taftsville, Vt................D4 208
Taftville, Conn...............C8 172
Tagāb, Afg..................D14 86
Tagachan, pt., Guam.......... 114
Taganrog, Sov. Un..........H12 72
Taganrog, gulf, Sov. Un....H12 72
Tagawa, Jap.................*G9 93
Tagbilaran, Phil..............D6 90
Taghrīfat, Libya..............D3 101
Tagliamento, riv., It.........C8 66
Tagolo, pt., Phil.............D6 90
Tagouranet (Well), Maur...C3 103
Taguan, pt., Guam............. 114
Taguatinga, Braz.............D1 138
Taguchi, Jap.................n16 93
Tagus, N. Dak...............A4 198
Tagus, see Tajo, riv., Sp.
Tagus, see Tejo, riv., Port.
Tahan, mtn., Mala............J5 89
Tahat, mtn., Alg.............E5 102
Tahiti, isl., Society Is......H13 113
Tahlequah, Okla.............B7 200
Tahoe, lake, Calif., Nev.....C3 170
Tahoe City, Calif............C3 170
Tahoe Valley, Calif...........C3 170
Tahoka, Tex.................C2 206
Taholah, Wash...............B1 210
Tahoma, Calif................C3 170
Tahona, Okla.................B7 200
Tahoua, Niger................D6 103
Tahsien, China................I2 92
Tahsis, B.C., Can..........*E4 149
Ţahtā, Eg.....................D6 101
Tahtsa, lake, B.C., Can......C4 149
Tahtsa, peak, B.C., Can.....C4 149
Tahuya, Wash................B2 210
Tai, China....................E5 92
Taï, I.C.......................E3 103
Tai, lake, China..............I9 92
Taian, China.................D10 92
Taian, China..................F7 92
Taiban, N. Mex...............C5 195
Taichao, see Giamda, China
Taichintala, China...........B9 92
Taichou, China..............H8 92
Taichung, Taiwan............G9 91
Taihape, N.Z................M15 112
Taikang, China...............C2 93
Taiku, China..................F5 92
Tailagoin, mts., Mong........C6 91
Tailai, China..................C1 93
Tailem Bend, Austl...........G2 112
Tailevu, pt., Fiji............... 114
Tain, Scot.....................C4 57
Tainan, Taiwan..............G9 91
Taining, China................K7 92
Taipei, Taiwan...............G9 91
Taiping, Mala................J4 89
Taipingon, pt., Rota I......... 115
Taipu, Braz...................g6 138
Taira, Jap....................H10 93
Taishun, China...............K8 92
Taitao, pen., Chile..........D1 136
Taitiarato, Pap..............k11 111
T'aitung, Taiwan.............G9 91
Taivalkoski, Fin..............E13 63
TAIWAN, country (Nationalist China), Asia........G9 91
see also Formosa
Taiwan, isl., Asia...........G9 91
Taiwara, see Qala'i-Ghor, Afg.
Taiyuan, China....D7 91, F5 92
Ta'izz, Yemen (San'ā').......C5 105
Tajarhī, Libya................E2 101
Tajimi, Jap.............I8, n16 93
Tajique, N. Mex..............C3 195
Tajo (Tagus), riv., Sp........C3 65
Tajumulco, peak, Guat.......C2 130
Tajuña, riv., Sp..............B4 65
Tājūrā', Libya................C2 101
Tak, Thai.....................D3 89
Taka, atoll, Marshall Is....... 115
Taka Banare, isl., Okinawa........................ 114
Takabba, Ken.................A7 106
Takada, Jap..................H9 93
Takaka, N.Z..................N14 112
Takamatsu, Jap..............I7 93
Takaoka, Jap.................H8 93
Takarazuka, Jap............*I7 93
Takasago, Jap..............*I7 93
Takasaki, Jap...........H9, m17 93
Takata, Jap...................H9 93
Takatō, Jap...................n17 93
Takatsuki, Jap...............*I7 93
Takaw, Bur....................B3 89
Takayama, Jap.......H8, m16 93
Takazē, riv., Eth.............C4 105
Takefu, Jap..................n15 93
Takeo, Camb..................G6 89
Tākestān, Iran................C4 86
Takht-i-Sulaiman, mtn., Iran............................C5 86
Takhta-Bazar, Sov Un...D11 86
Takhta-Kupyr, Sov. Un....E6 73
Takihara, Jap.................o15 93
Takilma, Oreg.................E3 201
Takingeun, Indon..............J2 89
Takla, lake, B.C., Can........B5 149
Takla Makan, des., China..........................F11 76
Taklakhar, China.............B8 88
Takoma Park, Md............C1 173
Takotna, Alsk.................C8 167
Takouchen, China.............D7 92
Taku, China...................E7 92
Takua Pa, Thai................H3 89
Takut, Bur....................A3 89
Ţalā, Eg.......................D2 84
Tala, Mex....................m12 129
Tala, Ur.......................E1 137
Talaga, Phil...................p13 90
Talagante, Chile..............A2 136
Talai, China...................C3 92
Talakan, Sov. Un.............B6 93
Talakmau, mtn., Indon.......E2 90
Talala, Okla..................A6 200
Talamanca, mts., C.R.........F6 130
Talanga, Hond.................C4 130
Talanquera, pt., Cuba......h12 131
Talara, Peru...................B1 134
Talas, Sov. Un................E8 73
Talasea, N. Gui...............k9 111
Talaud, is., Indon............E7 90
Talavera de la Reina, Sp............................C3 65
Talbert, Ky....................C6 182
Talbiya, Isr...................m14 84
Talbot, Ind....................D3 179
Talbot, Oreg...................C1 201
Talbot, co., Ga...............D2 175
Talbot, co., Md...............C5 173
Talbot, isl., Fla..............B5 174
Talbot, lake, Man., Can.....B2 150
Talbotton, Ga.................D2 175
Talca, Chile...................B2 136
Talca, prov., Chile............B2 136
Talcahuano, Chile............B2 136
Talcher, India.................G10 88
Talco, Tex....................C5 206
Talcott, W. Va................D4 211
Talcottville, Conn.............B7 172
Talcottville, N.Y..............B5 196
Taldy-Kurgan, Sov. Un.........................D9 73
Talence, Fr....................E3 58
Talent, Oreg..................E4 201
Talha, Chad...................A4 104
Tali, China.....................F5 91
Tali, China.....................E6 91
Tali Post, Sud.................D3 105
Taliabu, isl., Indon...........F6 90
Taliaferro, co., Ga...........C4 175
Talien, see Dairen, China
Talihina, Okla.................C6 200
Talim, isl., Phil..............o13 90
Tāliqān, Afg.......C14 86, A4 87
Tālisay, Phil..................o14 90
Talish, mts., Iran, Sov. Un.........................B4 86
Talitsa, Sov. Un................B6 73
Täljeån, riv., Swe.............t33 63
Talkeetna, Alsk...........C9, f16 167
Talkeetna, mts., Alsk........f17 167
Ţalkhā, Eg......................C3 84
Talking Rock, Ga..............B2 175
Tallaboa, P.R...................D4 132
Talladega, Ala.................B3 166
Talladega, co., Ala............B3 166
Talladega, mts., Ala...........B3 166
Talladega Springs, Ala.......B3 166
Tallahala, creek, Miss........D4 188
Tallahassee, Fla..............B2 174
Tallahatchie, co., Miss.......B3 188
Tallahatchie, riv., Miss.......B3 188
Tallangatta, Austl..............H6 112
Tallant, Okla....................A5 200
Tallapoosa, Ga.................C1 175
Tallapoosa, Mo..................E8 189
Tallapoosa, co., Ala...........C4 166
Tallapoosa, riv., Ala...........C3 166
Tallard, Fr......................E2 66
Tallassee, Ala..................C4 166
Tallevast, Fla....................F2 174
Tallinn, Sov. Un...............B5 72
Tallmadge, Ohio...............A6 199
Tallula, Ill......................D4 178
Tallula, Miss....................C2 188
Tallulah, La....................B4 183
Tallulah Falls, Ga............*B3 175
Ţallūzā, Jordan..................f12 84
Talmage, Sask., Can...........H4 155
Talmage, Kans...................C6 181
Talmage, Nebr.................D9 191
Talmage, Utah...................C5 207
Talnoye, Sov. Un................G8 72
Talo, mtn., Eth.................C4 105
Talodi, Sud......................C3 105
Talofofo, Guam.................... 114
Talofofo, bay, Guam............. 114
Taloga, Okla...................A3 200
Talomaco, Espiritu Santo I.......................... 115
Talon, lake, Ont., Can........A5 153
Talowah, Miss...................D4 188

Talpa, N. Mex. A4 195
Talpa, Tex. D3 206
Talpa de Allende, Mex. m11 129
Talquin, lake, Fla. B2 174
Talsi, Sov. Un. C4 72
Taltal, Chile E1 135
Tam Ky, Viet. E8 89
Tama, Iowa C5 180
Tama, co., Iowa B5 180
Tamaha, Okla. B7 200
Tamalameque, Col. B3 133
Tamale, Ghana E4 103
Tamalpais, mtn., Calif. B5 170
Taman, Sov. Un. I11 72
Tamanar, Mor. C3 102
Tamano, Jap. I6 93
Tamanrasset, see Fort Laperrine, Alg.
Tamanrasset, riv., Alg. E5 102
Tamaqua, Pa. E10 202
Tamar, riv., Eng. D3 56
Tamarack, Idaho E2 177
Tamarack, Minn. D5 187
Tamarite, Sp. B6 65
Tamaroa, Ill. E4 178
Tamassee, S.C. B1 203
Tamatave, Malag. g9 107
Tamatave, prov., Malag. g9 107
Tamaulipas, state, Mex. C5 129
Tamazula de Gordiano, Mex. n12 129
Tamazunchale, Mex. C5, m14 129
Tambach, Ken. A6 106
Tambacounda, Sen. D2 103
També, Braz. C3, h6 138
Tambelan, is., Indon. E3 90
Tambellaga (Well), Niger C6 103
Tambo, Austl. B6 112
Tambo, riv., Peru D3 134
Tambo, riv., Peru E3 134
Tambo Grande, Peru B1 134
Tambov, Sov. Un. C2 73
Tambralinga: c. 750 80
c. 1294 81
Tambre, riv., Sp. A1 65
Tambura, Sud. D2 105
Tamchakett, Maur. C2 103
Tamdy-Bulak, Sov. Un. E6 73
Tame, Col. B3 133
Tamega, riv., Port. B2 65
Tamel Aike, Arg. D2 136
Tamerlane, dominions of 81
Tamgue, mtn., Guinea D2 103
Tamiahua, Mex. C5, m15 129
Tamiahua, lagoon, Mex. C5 129
Tamiami, canal, Fla. G6 174
Tamiao, China C4 92
Tamil Nadu, state, India F6 87
Tamina, Tex. D5 206
Taming, China F6 92
Tamiš, riv., Yugo. C5 68
Tamms, Ill. F4 178
Ţammūn, Jordan B7, f12 84
Tamo, Ark. C4 169
Tamola, Miss. C5 188
Tamora, Nebr. D8 191
Tamora, Ponape 114
Tamoroi, Ponape 114
Tampa, Fla. E2, E4 174
Tampa, Kans. D6 181
Tampa, bay, Fla. E4 174
Tampasak, Mala. D5 90
Tampere, Fin. G10 63
Tampico, Ill. B4 178
Tampico, Ind. G6 179
Tampico, Mex. C5, k15 129
Tampico, Mont. B10 190
Tams, W. Va. D3 211
Tamuning, Guam 114
Tamworth, Austl. E8 112
Tamworth, Ont., Can. C7 153
Tamworth, Eng. B6 56
Tamworth, N.H. C4 193
Tana, Chile C2 135
Tana, lake, Eth. C4 105
Tana, riv., Ken. B7 106
Tanabe, Jap. J7 93
Tanacross, Alsk. C11 167
Tanaelv, riv., Fin. C11 63
Tanafjord, fjord, Nor. B13 63
Tanaga, isl., Alsk. E4 167
Tanahbala, isl., Indon. F1 90
Tanahgrogot, Indon. F5 90
Tanahmasa, isl., Indon. F1 90
Tanakpur, India C8 88
Tanami, Austl. D4 111
Tanana, Alsk. B9 167
Tanana, riv., Alsk. C11 167
Tananarive, Malag. g9 107
Tananarive, prov., Malag. g9 107
Tanapag, Saipan 114
Tanapag, hbr., Saipan 114
Tanaro, riv., It. B2 67
Tanauan, Phil. o13 90
Tanaunella, It. D2 67
Tanavuso, pt., Fiji 114
Tancheng, China G8 92
Tanchŏn, Kor. F4 93
Tancook Island, N.S., Can. E5 151
Tanda, India D9 88
Tăndărei, Rom. C8 68
Tandil, Arg. B5 136
Tandjung, Indon. F5 90
Tandjungbalai, Indon. E1, m11 90
Tandjungpandan, Indon. F3 90
Tandjungselor, Indon. E5 90
Tando-Adam, Pak. E2 88
Tandou, lake, Austl. F3 112
Tanega, isl., Jap. K5 93
Tanega, strait, Jap. K5 93
Taney, co., Mo. E4 189
Taneycomo, lake, Mo. E5 189
Taneytown, Md. A3 173
Taneyville, Mo. E4 189
Tanezrouft, des., Alg., Mali E4 102
Tanga, Tan. C6 106
Tanga, reg., Tan. C6 106
Tangancícuaro [de Arista], Mex. n12 129
Tanganyika, see Tanzania, country, Afr.
Tanganyika, lake, Afr. C4 106
Tangent, Oreg. C3, D1 201
Tangerhütte, Ger. A6 61
Tangermünde, Ger. B5 60
Tangho, China H5 92
Tangier, N.S., Can. E7 151
Tangier, Ind. E3 179
Tangier, Mor. B3 102
Tangier, Va. D7 209
Tangier, isl., Va. D6 209
Tangier, sound, Md. D6 173
Tangipahoa, La. D5 183
Tangipahoa, par., La. D5 183
Tangipahoa, riv., La. D5 183
Tangra, lake, China B8 87
Tangshan, China E8 92
Tangshan, China G7 92
Tangtu, China I8 92
Tanguiéta, Dah. D5 103
Tanguisson, pt., Guam 114
Tangwang, riv., China B10 91
Tangyang, China I4 92
Tangyüan, China C4 93
Tanhsien, China C8 89
Tanimbar, is., Indon. G8 90
Taninges, Fr. C2 66
Tank, Pak. A3 88
Tank, cape, Iran I9 86
Tanna, isl., New Hebr. 115
Tännäs, Swe. F5 63
Tanner, Ala. A3 166
Tanner, W. Va. C4 211
Tanner, mtn., B.C., Can. E8 149
Tannersville, N.Y. *C6 196
Tannis, bay, Den. A4 62
Tannu-Ola, mts., Sov. Un., Mong. A3 91
Tanout, Niger C6 103
Tanque Verde, Ariz. *E5 168
Tanta, Eg. D3 84
Tantallon, Sask., Can. G5 155
Tantoyuca, Mex. m14 129
Tanum, Swe. H4 63
Tanza, Phil. o13 90
TANZANIA, country, Afr. C5 106
Tao, riv., China B9 91
Taoan, China B10 92
Taoerhshan, China B9 92
Taohsien, China F7 91
Taokou, China G6 92
Taolin, China D5 92
Taopi, Minn. G6 187
Taormina, It. F5 67
Taos, N. Mex. A4 195
Taos, co., N. Mex. A4 195
Taos Pueblo, N. Mex. A4 195
Taoudenni, Mali B4 103
Taourirt, Mor. C4 102
Taoyüan, China J4 92
Tapa Shan, mtn., China I4 92
Tapacari, Bol. C2 135
Tapachula, Mex. E6 129
Tapaga, cape, W. Sam. 114
Tapajós, riv., Braz. D3 139
Tapak, Ponape 114
Tapak, isl., Ponape 114
Tapaktuan, Indon. m11 90
Tapalqué, Arg. B4 136
Tapanahoni, riv., Sur. B3 139
Tapanshang, China C8 92
Tapanui, N.Z. P12 112
Tapauá, riv., Braz. C4 134
Taperoá, Braz. h5 138
Tapirapé, riv., Braz. E4 139
Tapis, mtn., Mala. K5 89
Tapotchau, mtn., Saipan 114
Tappahannock, Va. D6 209
Tappan, N.Y. D1 196
Tappan, res., Ohio B6 199
Tappen, N. Dak. C6 198
Tappita, Lib. E3 103
Tapti, riv., India D5 90
Tapuaenuku, mtn., N.Z. O14 112
Tapuhsing, China E4 91
Tapurucuara, Braz. D4 133
Taputapu, cape, Am. Sam. 114
Taquara, Braz. D2 137
Taquara, mts., Braz. E2 137
Taquarí, riv., Braz. B1 137
Taquarí, riv., Braz. D2 137
Taquaritinga, Braz. k7 137
Taquaritinga do Norte, Braz. h5 138
Tar, riv., N.C. B5 197
Tara, Ont., Can. C3 153
Tara, Sov. Un. B8 73
Tara, riv., Sov. Un. B9 73
Tara, riv., Yugo. D4 68
Tarabuco, Bol. C3 135
Tarabulus (Tripoli), Leb. E10 85
Ţarābulus, see Tripoli, Libya
Ţarābulus, see Tripolitania, prov., Libya
Tarague, Guam 114
Tarakan, Indon. E5 90
Tarakliya, Sov. Un. C9 68
Tarancón, Sp. B4 65
Taransay, isl., Scot. C1 57
Taranto, It. D6 67
Taranto, gulf, It. D6 67
Tarapaca, Col. D4 133
Tarapacá, prov., Chile C2 135
Tarapoto, Peru C2 134
Tarare, Fr. E6 58
Tarascon, Fr. F6 58
Tarata, Bol. C2 135
Tarata, Peru E3 134
Tarauacá, riv., Braz. C3 134
Tarawa, New Britain I. 115
Tarawa, isl., Gilbert Is. 115
Tarawera, N.Z. M16 112
Tarazona, Sp. B5 65
Tarazona, Sp. C5 65
Tarbagatay, range, Sov. Un. D10 73
Tarbat Ness, pt., Scot. C5 57
Tarbelville, Vt. E3 208
Tarbert, Scot. C2 57
Tarbert, Scot. E3 57
Tarbert, inlet, Scot. E3 57
Tarbert, East, inlet, Scot. C2 57
Tarbert, West, inlet, Scot. C1 57
Tarbes, Fr. F4 58
Tarbet, Scot. D4 57
Tarboro, Ga. F5 175
Tarboro, N.C. B6 197
Tarbū, Libya D3 101
Tarcento, It. C9 66
Tarcoola, Austl. F5 111
Taree, Austl. E9 112
Tarentum, Ala. D4 166
Tarentum, Pa. A7, E2 202
Tarfaya, Mor. D2 102
Tarfside, Scot. D6 57
Targhee, pass, Idaho, Mont. E7 177
Tărgovişte, Rom. C7 68
Târgul-Frumos, Rom. B8 68
Târgul-Jiu, Rom. C6 68
Târgul-Neamt, Rom. B8 68
Târgul-Ocna, Rom. B8 68
Târgul-Săcuesc, Rom. B8 68
Tarhūnah, Libya C2 101
Tarifa, Sp. D3 65
Tariffville, Conn. B5 172
Tarigtig, pt., Phil. n14 90
Tarija, Bol. D3 135
Tarija, dept., Bol. D3 135
Tarik, isl., Truk 114
Tarim Darya, riv., China E11 76
Taritai, isl., Tarawa 114
Tarkiln, R.I. B10 172
Tarkiln, hill, Maine E4 184
Tarkio, Mo. A2 189
Tarkio, Mont. C2 190
Tarkwa, Ghana E4 103
Tarlac, Phil. B6, o13 90
Tarland, Scot. C6 57
Tarlton, Ohio C5 199
Tarm, Den. C2 62
Tarma, Peru D2 134
Tarn, riv., Fr. F4 58
Tarna, riv., Hung. B5 68
Tărnava, riv., Rom. B7 68
Tărnăveni, Rom. B7 68
Tarnobrzeg, Pol. C6 70
Tarnopol, Sask., Can. E3 155
Tarnov, Nebr. C8 191
Tarnów, Pol. C6 70
Tarnowskie Góry, Pol. C5, g9 70
Taro, riv., It. B2 67
Tārom, Iran G7 86
Taroom, Austl. B7 112
Taroudant, Mor. C3 102
Tarp, Ger. D3 62
Tarpley, Tex. E3 206
Tarpon Springs, Fla. D4 174
Tarquí, Peru B2 134
Tarquinia, It. C3 67
Tarragona, Sp. B6 65
Tarrant, Ala. B3, E4 166
Tarrant, co., Tex. C4 206
Tarrasa, Sp. B7 65
Tárrega, Sp. B6 65
Tarryall, Colo. B5 171
Tarryall, creek, Colo. B5 171
Tarryall, mts., Colo. B5 171
Tarrytown, Ga. D4 175
Tarrytown, N.Y. D2, D7 196
Târs, Den. A4 62
Tarshiha, Isr. A7 84
Tarso Ahon, mtn., Chad A3 104
Tarsus, Tur. D10 85
Tartagal, Arg. D3 135
Tartu, Sov. Un. B6 72
Tartuguan, pt., Guam 114
Tartūs, Syr. E10 85
Tarut, isl., Sau. Ar. H5 86
Tarutung, Indon. K3 89
Tarutao, isl., Thai. I3 89
Tarver, Ga. F4 175
Tarves, Scot. C6 57
Tarya, riv., Bol. D3 135
Tasawāh, Libya D2 101
Tascosa, Tex. B1 206
Taseko, lake, B.C., Can. D6 149
Taseko, mtn., B.C., Can. D6 149
Taseko, riv., B.C., Can. D6 149
Tashauz, Sov. Un. E5 73
Tashigong, China A7 88
Tashkent, Sov. Un. E7 73
Tashkumyr, Sov. Un. E8 73
Tashkurghan, Afg. C13 86
Tåsinge, isl., Den. C4 62
Taskan, Sov. Un. C18 71
Taşköprü, Tur. B10 85
Tasman, bay, N.Z. N14 112
Tasman, pen., Austl. o15 110
Tasman, sea, Austl. H8 112
Tasmania, state, Austl. o15 111
Tassili-n-Ajjer, plat., Alg. D6 102
Tassili oua-n-Ahaggar, plat., Alg. E6 102
Tasso, Tenn. D9 205
Taswell, Ind. H4 179
Tata, Hung. B4 68
Tatabánya, Hung. B4 68
Tatamagouche, N.S., Can. D6 151
Tatamy, Pa. *E11 202
Tatar, strait, Sov. Un. C10 93
Tatarbunary, Sov. Un. C9 68
Tatarsk, Sov. Un. B9 73
Tatau, isl., Bis. Arch. 115
Tate, Sask., Can. F3 155
Tate, Ga. B2 175
Tate, co., Miss. A4 188
Tateville, Ky. D5 182
Tateyama, Jap. I9, n18 93
Tathlina, lake, N.W. Ter., Can. D9 142
Tatien, China L7 92
Tatitlek, Alsk. C10, g18 167
Tatla, lake, B.C., Can. C5 149
Tatlayoka Lake, B.C., Can. D5 149
Tatnam, cape, Man., Can. C5 150
Tatra, mts., Pol., Czech. D5 70
Tatsumi, reef, Mariana Is. 115
Tatta, Pak. E1 88
Tattershall, Eng. A7 56
Tattnall, co., Ga. D4 175
Tatuí, Braz. C3, m8 137
Tatuk, lake, B.C., Can. C5 149
Tatum, N. Mex. D6 195
Tatum, S.C. B8 203
Tatum, Tex. *C5 206
Tatumville, Tenn. A2 205
Tatung, China C7 91, D5 92
Tatung, China I7 92
Tatvan, Tur. C14 85
Tau, isl., Thai. G3 89
Tauá, Braz. C2 138
Taubaté, Braz. C3 137
Tauber, riv., Ger. D4 61
Tauberbischofsheim, Ger. D4 61
Taucha, Ger. B7 61
Tauern, tunnel, Aus. C9 66
Taum Sauk, mtn., Mo. D7 189
Taung, S. Afr. C3 107
Taungdwingyi, Bur. D10 87
Taunggyi, Bur. D10 87
Taunton, Eng. C4 56
Taunton, Mass. C5 185
Taunton, Minn. F2 187
Taunton, N.J. D3 194
Taunton, riv., Mass. C5 185
Taunus, mts., Ger. C3 61
Taupo, lake, N.Z. M15 112
Taurage, Sov. Un. D4 72
Tauranga, N.Z. L16 112
Taurianova, It. E6 67
Taurus, mts., Tur. D8 85
Tauste, Sp. B5 65
Tauu, is., Sol. Is. 115
Tavalo, New Britain I. 115
Tavares, Fla. D5 174
Tavas, Tur. D7 69
Tavda, Sov. Un. B7 73
Tavda, riv., Sov. Un. B6 73
Tavernier, Fla. G6 174
Taveuni, isl., Fiji 114
Taviche, Mex. D5 129
Tavira, Port. D2 65
Tavistock, Ont., Can. D4 153
Tavistock, Eng. D3 56
Tavolzhan, Sov. Un. C9 73
Tavoy, Bur. F10 87
Tavoy, isl., Bur. F3 89
Tavoy, pt., Bur. F3 89
Tavşanli, Tur. C7 69
Taw, riv., Eng. D4 56
Tawas, lake, Mich. D7 186
Tawas City, Mich. D7 186
Tawatinaw, Alta., Can. B4 148
Tawe, riv., Wales C4 56
Tawi Tawi, is., Phil. D6 90
Tawi Tawi, isl., Phil. D6 90
Ţāwurghā', Libya C3 101
Taxco de Alarcón, Mex. n14 129
Tay, firth, Scot. D5 57
Tay, lake, Scot. D4 57
Tay, riv., Scot. D5 57
Tayabamba, Peru C2 134
Tayabas, bay, Phil. p13 90
Tayāsīr, Jordan f12 84
Taycheedah, Wis. B5 212
Tayga, Sov. Un. B11 73
Taylor, Ariz. C5 168
Taylor, Ark. D2 169
Taylor, Miss. A4 188
Taylor, Nebr. C6 191
Taylor, N. Dak. C3 198
Taylor, Pa. A9, D10 202
Taylor, Tex. D4 206
Taylor, Wis. D2 212
Taylor, co., Fla. B3 174
Taylor, co., Ga. D2 175
Taylor, co., Iowa D3 180
Taylor, co., Ky. C4 182
Taylor, co., Tex. C3 206
Taylor, co., W. Va. B4 211
Taylor, co., Wis. C3 212
Taylor, mtn., Idaho E4 177
Taylor, mtn., N.Z. O13 112
Taylor, ridge, Ga. B1 175
Taylor, riv., Colo. C4 171
Taylor Knob, mtn., Tenn. E9 205
Taylor Lake Village, Tex. *E5 206
Taylor Mill, Ky. A7 182
Taylor Park, res., Colo. C4 171
Taylor Springs, Ill. D4 178
Taylors, S.C. B3 203
Taylors, isl., Md. D5 173
Taylors Falls, Minn. E6 187
Taylors Island, Md. D5 173
Taylorsport, Ky. A7 182
Taylorsville, Ga. B2 175
Taylorsville, Ind. F6 179
Taylorsville, Ky. B4 182
Taylorsville, Miss. D4 188
Taylorsville, N.C. B2 197
Taylorville, Ill. D4 178
Taymā', Sau. Ar. D7 101
Taymouth, N.B., Can. C3 151
Taymyr, lake, Sov. Un. B13 71
Taymyr, pen., Sov. Un. B12 71
Tayncha, Sov. Un. C7 73
Tayport, Scot. D6 57
Taytay, Phil. C5 90
Taytsy, Sov. Un. s31 63
Tayü, China F7 91
Tayug, Phil. n13 90
Tayung, China J4 92
Taz, riv., Sov. Un. C11 71
Taza, Mor. C4 102
Tazerbo (Oasis), Libya D4 101
Tazewell, Ga. D2 175
Tazewell, Tenn. C10 205
Tazewell, Va. B3 209
Tazewell, co., Ill. C4 178
Tazewell, co., Va. B3 209
Tazovskaya, bay, Sov. Un. C7 118
Tazrouk, Alg. E6 102
Tchepone, Laos D7 89
Tchibanga, Gabon F2 104
Tchula, Miss. B3 188
Tczew, Pol. A5 70
Te, China F7 92
Te Anau, lake, N.Z. P11 112
Te Awamutu, N.Z. M15 112
Te Kuiti, N.Z. M15 112
Te Moak, Indian Res., Nev. C6 192
Te Waewae, bay, N.Z. Q11 112
Tea, S. Dak. D9 204
Tea, creek, Sask., Can. C2 155
Teacheys, N.C. C5 197
Teague, Tex. D4 206
Teanaway, Wash. B5 210
Teaneck, N.J. D5 194
Teangue, Scot. C3 57
Teapa, Mex. D6 129
Teasdale, Utah E4 207
Teaticket, Mass. C6 185
Tebbetts, Mo. C6 189
Tebicuary, riv., Par. E4 135
Tebingtinggi, Indon. E1, m11 90
Tecalitlán, Mex. n12 129
Tecate, Mex. F5 170
Teche, bayou, La. D4 183
Techirghiol, Rom. C9 68
Tecka, Arg. C2 136
Teckla, Wyo. B7 213
Tecolotito, N. Mex. B4 195
Tecolutla, riv., Mex. m15 129
Tecomán, Mex. n12 129
Tecopa, Calif. E5 170
Tecpan de Galeana, Mex. D4 129
Tecuala, Mex. C3 129
Tecuci, Rom. C8 68
Tecumseh, Ont., Can. E2 153
Tecumseh, Kans. B7 181
Tecumseh, Mich. F7 186
Tecumseh, Nebr. D9 191
Tecumseh, Okla. B5 200
Tecumseh, mtn., N.H. C3 193
Ted, Som. E5 105
Tedrow, Ohio A3 199
Tedzhen, Sov. Un. C10 86
Teegarden, Ind. B5 179
Teema, Okinawa 114
Tees, Alta., Can. C4 148
Tees, riv., Eng. C6 55
Teesside, Eng. C6 55
Teeswater, Ont., Can. D3 153
Tefa, isl., Bis. Arch. 115
Tefé, Braz. D5 133
Tefé, lake, Braz. C2 139
Tefé, riv., Braz. B4 134
Tefenni, Tur. D7 69
Tefft, Ind. B4 179
Tegal, Indon. *G3 90
Tegarden, Okla. A3 200
Tegelen, Neth. C6 59
Tegern, lake, Ger. B7 66
Tegucigalpa, Hond. C4 130
Teguise, Sp. (Can. Is.) m15 65
Tehachapi, Calif. E4 170
Tehama, Calif. *B3 170
Tehama, co., Calif. B2 170
Teheran (Tehrān), Iran D5 86
Tehri, India B7 88
Tehsing, China J7 92
Tehtsin, China F4 91
Tehua, China F8 91
Tehuacán, Mex. D5, n15 129
Tehuantepec, Mex. D5 129
Tehuantepec, gulf, Mex. D6 129
Tehuantepec, isth., Mex. D6 129
Tehuitzingo, Mex. n14 129
Teide, peak, Sp. (Can. Is.) m13 65
Teifi, riv., Wales B3 56
Teigen, Mont. C8 190
Teignmouth, Eng. D4 56
Teiteiripucchi, isl., Eniwetok 114
Tejo (Tagus), riv., Port. C1 65
Tekamah, Nebr. C9 191
Tekapo, lake, N.Z. O13 112
Tekax de Alvaro Obregón, Mex. C7 129
Tekeli, Sov. Un. E9 73
Tekirdağ, Tur. B6 69
Tekkali, India H10 88
Tekoa, Wash. B8 210
Tekonsha, Mich. F5 186
Tekro (Well), Chad B4 104
Tel Abiad, Syr. D12 85
Tel 'Afar, Iraq D14 85
Tel Aviv-Yafo, Isr. B6, g10 84
Tel el Farama, ruins, Eg. C4 84
Tel Mond, Isr. B6 84
Tela, Hond. C4 130
Telavi, Sov. Un. E3 73
Telde, Sp. (Can. Is.) m14 65
Telegraph, Tex. D3 206
Telegraph Creek, B.C., Can. D2 149
Telén, Arg. B3 136
Teleneshty, Sov. Un. B9 68
Teleorman, riv., Rom. C7 68
Telephone, Tex. C4 206
Telerhteba, mtn., Alg. E6 102
Telescope, peak, Calif. D5 170
Telfair, co., Ga. E4 175
Telford, Eng. B5 56
Telford, Pa. F11 202
Telford, Tenn. C11 205
Telfs, Aus. B7 66
Télimélé, Guinea D2 103
Telkalakh, Syr. E11 85
Telkwa, B.C., Can. B4 149
Tell, Jordan g11 84
Tell, Tex. B2 206
Tell City, Ind. I4 179
Teller, Alsk. B6 167
Teller, co., Colo. C5 171
Telli, lake, China B2 91
Tellico Plains, Tenn. D9 205
Telluride, Colo. D3 171
Telocaset, Oreg. B9 201
Telogia, Fla. B2 174
Telok Anson, Mala. J4 89
Teloloapan, Mex. D5, n14 129
Telos, lake, Maine B3 184
Telsen, Arg. C3 136
Telukbetung, Indon. G3 90
Tema, Ghana E5 103
Temax, Mex. C7 129
Tembo, Zaire C2 106
Temecula, Calif. F5 170
Temerloh-Mentekab, Mala. K5 89
Temir-Tau, Sov. Un. C8 73
Témiscamingue, co., Que., Can. A6 153
Témiscouata, co., Que., Can. B9 154
Témiscouata, lake, Que., Can. B9 154
Temora, Austl. G6 112
Temósachic, Mex. B3 129
Tempe, Ariz. D4, G2 168
Tempe Downs, Austl. D5 111
Temperance, Mich. G7 186
Temperance, riv., Minn. C8 187
Temperanceville, Va. D7 209
Tempio Pausania, It. D2 67
Tempiute, Nev. F6 192
Temple, Ga. C1 175
Temple, Mich. D5 186
Temple, N.H. E3 193
Temple, N. Dak. A2 198
Temple, Okla. C3 200
Temple, Pa. F10 202
Temple, Tex. D4 206
Temple City, Calif. *E4 170
Temple Hill, Ky. D4 182
Temple Terrace, Fla. E2 174
Templeton, Ind. C3 179
Templeton, Iowa C3 180
Templeton, Mass. A3 185
Templeton, Pa. E3 202
Templeville, Md. B6 173
Templin, Ger. B6 60
Templow, Tenn. A5 205
Tempoal, riv., Mex. m14 129
Temryuk, Sov. Un. I11 72
Temuco, Chile B2 136
Temuka, N.Z. P13 112
Temvik, N. Dak. C5 198
Ten Degree, chan., India G9 87
Ten Mile, S.C. F2, F7 203
Ten Mile, Tenn. D9 205
Ten Mile, lake, Newf., Can. C3 152
Ten Sleep, Wyo. A5 213
Ten Thousand, is., Fla. G5 174
Tena, Ec. B2 134
Tenafly, N.J. B5, D5 194
Tenaha, Tex. D5 206
Tenakee Springs, Alsk. D12, m22 167
Tenali, India *E7 87
Tenancingo [de Degollado], Mex. D5, n14 129
Tenango del Valle, Mex. n14 129
Tenant, mtn., N.Y. B6 196
Tenants Harbor, Maine E3 184
Tenasserim, Bur. F3 89
Tenasserim, riv., Bur. F3 89
Tenay, Fr. E6 58
Tenbridge, Tenn. E10 205
Tenby, Wales C3 56
Tench, isl., Bis. Arch. 115
Tendal, La. B4 183
Tende, Fr. E7 58
Tendelti, Sud. C3 105
Tendoy, Idaho E5 177
Tendoy, mts., Mont. F4 190
Tendre, mtn., Switz. C2 66
Ténéré, des., Niger B7 103
Tenerife, isl., Sp. (Can. Is.) m13 65
Ténès, Alg. B5 102
Ténès, cape, Alg. F7 64
Teng, China G7 92
Tengchung, China F4 91
Tenggol, isl., Mala. J5 89
Tengiz, lake, Sov. Un. C7 73
Tengkou, China E2 92
Tengrela, I.C. D3 103
Tenian, see Tinian, isl., Mariana Is.
Tenino, Wash. C3 210
Tenke, Zaire D4 106
Tenkiller Ferry, res., Okla. B6 200
Tenkodogo, Upper Volta D4 103
Tenmile, creek, W. Va. B6 211
Tenmile, lake, Minn. D4 187
Tennant, Iowa C2 180
Tennant Creek, Austl. C5 111
Tennent, N.J. C4 194
Tennessee, Ill. C3 178

INDEX KEY Each place listed in **Bold-faced Type** has its population listed in the Population tables, pages 230 to 280.
Each country, shown in CAPITAL LETTERS, has its population listed in the World Political Information Table, pages 6 to 10.
* Does not appear on map: key shows general location.

Tennessee, state, U.S. 205
in 1796 162
in Civil War 164
Tennessee, pass, Colo B4 171
Tennessee, riv., U.S. D10 159
Tennessee City, Tenn A4 205
Tennessee Ridge, Tenn A4 205
Tennga, Ga B2 175
Tennille, Ga D4 175
Tenniya, Okinawa 114
Tennyson, Ind H3 179
Tenosique, Mex D6 129
Tensas, par., La B4 183
Tensas, riv., La B4 183
Tensed, Idaho B2 177
Tenstrike, Minn C4 187
Tenterfield, Austl D9 112
Teocaltiche, Mex C4, m12 129
Teófilo Otoni, Braz E2 138
Tepa, Indon G7 90
Tepalcatepec, Mex n12 129
Tepalcatepec, riv., Mex n12 129
Tepatitlán [de Morelos], Mex C4, m12 129
Tepelenë, Alb B3 69
Tepepan, Mex h9 129
Tepic, Mex C4, m11 129
Teplice, Czech C2 70
Tepoca, cape, Mex A2 129
Tequila, Mex m12 129
Ter-Apel, Neth B7 59
Téra, Niger D5 103
Teramo, It C4 67
Tercan, Tur C13 85
Terceira, isl., Port. (Azores) g9 102
Tercero, riv., Arg A4 136
Terebovlya, Sov. Un G5 72
Terekty, Sov. Un D7 73
Terence Bay, N.S., Can E6 151
Terengganu, pol. div., Mala J5 89
Tererro, N. Mex F6 195
Teresina, Braz C2 138
Teresópolis, Braz C4, h6 137
Terewah, lake, Austl D6 112
Tergnier, Fr E3 59
Terhune, Ind D5 179
Teri Nam, lake, China B8 87
Teriberka, Sov. Un C16 63
Terlingua, Tex E1, G2 206
Terlingua, creek, Tex G2 206
Terlton, Okla A5 200
Termet (Well), Niger C7 103
Termez, Sov. Un F9 71
Termini Imerese, It F4 67
Términos, lagoon, Mex D6 129
Termoli, It C5 67
Ternate, Indon E7 90
Ternate, isl., Indon E7 90
Terneuzen, Neth C3 59
Terney, Sov. Un D8 93
Terni, It C4 67
Ternopol', Sov. Un G5 72
Terpeniye, bay, Sov. Un B11 93
Terra Alta, W. Va B5 211
Terra Nova, Newf., Can D4 152
Terra Nova, nat. park, Newf., Can D4 152
Terrace, B.C., Can B3 149
Terrace, Minn E3 187
Terrace, mts., Utah B2 207
Terrace Park, Ohio *A7 182
Terracina, It D4 67
Terral, Okla D4 200
Terrasson, Fr E4 58
Terraville, S. Dak C2 204
Terre Haute, Ind F3 179
Terre Hill, Pa F9 202
Terrebonne, Que., Can D4, D9 154
Terrebonne, Oreg C5 201
Terrebonne, co., Que., Can D3 154
Terrebonne, par., La E5 183
Terrebonne, bay, La E5 183
Terrebonne, bayou, La E5 183
Terrell, Tex C4 206
Terrell, co., Ga E2 175
Terrell, co., Tex D1 206
Terrell Hills, Tex B4 206
Terrenceville, Newf., Can E4 152
Terreton, Idaho F6 177
Terrible, mtn., Switz B3 66
Terril, Iowa A3 180
Terry, Miss C3 188
Terry, Mont D11 190
Terry, co., Tex C1 206
Terry, peak, S. Dak C2 204
Terrytown, Nebr C2 191
Terryville, Conn C4 172
Tersakkan, riv., Sov. Un C7 73
Terschelling, isl., Neth A5 59
Terskey Alat, range, Sov. Un E9 73
Teruel, Col C2 133
Teruel, Sp B5 65
Terwagne, Bel D5 59
Tes, riv., Mong B4 91
Tes Nos Pes, Ariz A6 168
Tešanj, Yugo C3 68
Tescott, Kans C6 181
Teshekpuk, lake, Alsk A9 167
Teshio, Jap D10 93
Teslin, Yukon, Can D6 144
Teslin, lake, B.C., Yukon, Can D6 142
Tessalit, Mali B5 103
Tessaoua, Niger D6 103
Tessenei, Eth B4 105
Tessier, Sask., Can F2 155
Tessin, Ger D6 62
Test, riv., Eng C6 56
Testigos, is., Ven A5 133
Tesuque, N. Mex B4, F6 195
Tesuque, Indian res., N. Mex F6 195
Tesuque Pueblo, N. Mex F6 195
Tetachuk, lake, B.C., Can C5 149
Tetagouche, riv., N.B., Can B4 151
Tetbury, Eng C5 56
Tete, Moz A5 107
Tete, prov., Moz A5 107
Tête-à-la-Baleine, Que., Can C2 152
Tete Jaune Cache, B.C., Can C8 149
Teterow, Ger B6 60
Teteven, Bul D7 68
Tetipari, isl., Sol. Is 115
Tetlin, Alsk C11 167
Teton, Idaho F7 177
Teton, co., Idaho F7 177
Teton, co., Mont C4 190
Teton, co., Wyo B2 213
Teton, mts., Wyo B2 213
Teton, riv., Mont C5 190
Tetonia, Idaho F7 177
Tetouan, Mor B3 102
Tetovo, Yugo D5 68
Tetrino, Sov. Un D18 63
Tetu, China B3 93
Tetu, lake, Ont., Can D4 150
Tetyukhe-Pristan, Sov. Un D7 93
Teuchern, Ger B7 61
Teuco, riv., Arg D3 135
Téul de González Ortega, Mex m12 129
Teulada, It E2 67
Teulon, Man., Can D3 150
Teure, isl., Jap D10 93
Teutonic Knights, lands of 48
Teutopolis, Ill D5 178
Tevere (Tiber), riv., It C4 67
Teviot, riv., Scot E6 57
Tevriz, Sov. Un B8 73
Tewkesbury, Eng C5 56
Tewksbury, Mass A5, C2 185
Texa, isl., Scot E2 57
Texada, isl., B.C., Can E5 149
Texanna, Okla B6 200
Texarkana, Ark D1 169
Texarkana, Tex C5 206
Texarkana, lake, Tex C5 206
Texas, Md B4 173
Texas, state, U.S 206
in 1845 163
during Civil War 164
Texas, co., Mo D5 189
Texas, co., Okla D3 200
Texas, pt., Tex E2 183
Texas City, Tex E5, G5 206
Texcaltitlán, Mex n14 129
Texcoco, Mex n14 129
Texcoco, lake, Mex h9 129
Texel, isl., Neth A4 59
Texhoma, Okla D2 200
Texhoma, Tex A2 206
Texico, N. Mex C6 195
Texline, Tex A1 206
Texola, Okla B2 200
Texoma, lake, Okla., Tex D5 200
Texon, Tex D2 206
Teziutlán, Mex D5, n15 129
Tezpur, India C9 87
Tezzeron, lake, B.C., Can B5 149
Tha Hin, Thai E4 89
Thabeikkyin, Bur A2 89
Thacker, W. Va D2 211
Thackeray, Ill E5 178
Thackerville, Okla D4 200
THAILAND, country, Asia E4 89
after World War II 83
see also Siam
Thakhek, Laos D6 89
Thal, Pak B5 87
Thale, Ger B6 61
Thalia, Tex C3 206
Thalwil, Switz B4 66
Thame, Eng C7 56
Thames, N.Z L15 112
Thames, firth, N.Z L15 112
Thames, riv., Ont., Can E3 153
Thames, riv., Conn D8 172
Thames, riv., Eng C6 56
Thames, riv., mouth, Eng C8 56
Thamesville, Ont., Can E3 153
Thamīlat Suwaylimah (Oasis), Eg D6 84
Thana, India *E5 87
Thane, Alsk k22 167
Thanglha, mts., China E2 91
Thanh Hoa, Viet C6 89
Thanjavur, India F6 87
Thann, Fr D7 58
Thannhausen, Ger A6 66
Thano Bula Khan, Pak E1 88
Thaon [-les-Vosges], Fr C7 58
Thar or Indian, des., India E2 88
Tharad, India E3 88
Thargomindah, Austl C4 112
Tharrawaddy, Bur E10 87
Thásos, Grc B5 69
Thásos, isl., Grc B5 69
Thatch, isl., Vir. Is f15 132
Thatcher, Ariz E6 168
Thatcher, Colo D6 171
Thatcher, Idaho G7 177
Thaton, Bur E10 87
Thawville, Ill C5 178
Thaxton, Miss A4 188
Thayer, Ill D4 178
Thayer, Ind B3 179
Thayer, Iowa C3 180
Thayer, Kans E8 181
Thayer, Mo E6 189
Thayer, Nebr D8 191
Thayer, W. Va D7 211
Thayer, co., Nebr D8 191
Thayer Junction, Wyo D4 213
Thayetmyo, Bur C1 89
Thayne, Wyo C1 213
Thazi, Bur B2 89
The Cheviot, mtn., Eng E6 57
The Dalles (Dalles City), Oreg B5 201
The Dome, mtn., Vt F2 208
The Father, mtn., N. Gui k13 110
The Forks, Maine C3 184
The Gap, Ariz A4 168
The Hague ('s Gravenhage), Neth B4 59
The Hollow, Va E2 209
The Hummocks, R.I C12 172
The Pas, Man., Can C1 150
The Peak, N.C A2 197
The Pinnacle, mtn., Conn B5 172
The Plains, Ohio C5 199
The Plains, Va C5 209
The Range, N.B., Can C4 151
The Rock, Ga D2 175
The Rockies, mtn., Wash C3 210
The Slot, strait, Sol. Is 115
The Springs, N.Y E8 172
The Twins, peaks, Alta., Can C2 148
The Village, Okla B4 200
The Weirs (Weirs Beach), N.H C4 193
Theadville, Miss D5 188
Thealka, Ky C7 182
Theba, Ariz E3 168
Thebes, Ill F4 178
Thebes, ruins, Eg D6 101
Thebes, see Thívai, Grc.
Thedford, Ont., Can D3 153
Thedford, Nebr C5 191
Thelan, N. Dak C2 198
Thelma, N.C A6 197
Thelon, riv., N.W. Ter., Can D12 142
Thenon, Fr E4 58
Theodore, Ala E1 166
Theodore, Austl B8 112
Theodore, Sask., Can F4 155
Theodore Roosevelt, lake, Ariz D5 168
Theodore Roosevelt, nat. mem. park, N. Dak B2 198
Theodosia, Mo E5 189
Thérain, riv., Fr E2 59
Theresa, N.Y A5, B1 196
Theresa, Wis E5 212
Theressa, Fla C4 174
Therien, Alta., Can B5 148
Thérmon, Grc C3 69
Thermopolis, Wyo B4 213
Thessalon, Ont., Can E9 153
Thessalon, riv., Ont., Can B7 186
Thessaloníki, see Salonika, Grc.
Thessaly, reg., Grc C4 69
Theta, Tenn B4 205
Thetford, Eng B8 56
Thetford, Vt D4 208
Thetford Center, Vt D4 208
Thetford Mines, Que., Can C6 154
Thibar, Tun F11 64
Thibaudeau, Man., Can A4 150
Thibodaux, La C6, E5 183
Thicket Portage, Man., Can B3 150
Thickwood, hills, Sask., Can E2 155
Thida, Ark B4 169
Thief, lake, Minn B3 187
Thief, riv., Minn B2 187
Thief River Falls, Minn B2 187
Thielson, mtn., Oreg D4 201
Thiene, It D7 66
Thiensville, Wis E2, E6 212
Thiers, Fr E5 58
Thiès, Sen D1 103
Thika, Ken B6 106
Thimbles, The, is., Conn E6 172
Thimbu, Bhu D12 88
Thio, Eth C5 105
Thio, N. Cal 115
Thionville, Fr C7 58
Thíra, isl., Grc D5 69
Third, lake, N.H A2 193
3rd Cataract (Nile River), Sud A3 105
Thirsk, Eng F7 57
Thirty One Mile, lake, Que., Can C2 154
Thisted, Den B2 62
Thisted, co., Den B2 62
Thistle, Utah D4 207
Thíthia, isl., Fiji 114
Thívai (Thebes), Grc C4, g10 69
Thog Jalung, China A8 88
Thok Daurakpa, China A10 88
Tholen, Neth C4 59
Thomas, Md C5 173
Thomas, Okla B3 200
Thomas, S. Dak C8 204
Thomas, Wash D2 210
Thomas, W. Va B5 211
Thomas, co., Ga F3 175
Thomas, co., Kans C2 181
Thomas, co., Nebr C5 191
Thomas, creek, Fla B6 174
Thomas, range, Utah D2 207
Thomasboro, Ill C5 178
Thomaston, Ala C2 166
Thomaston, Conn C4 172
Thomaston, Ga D2 175
Thomaston, Maine D3 184
Thomaston, N.Y *E3 196
Thomaston, Tex E4 206
Thomaston, flood control res., Conn C4 172
Thomasville, Ala D2 166
Thomasville, Ga F3 175
Thomasville, Mo E6 189
Thomasville, N.C B3 197
Thomasville, Tenn A4 205
Thomlinson, mtn., B.C., Can B4 149
Thompson, Man., Can B3 150
Thompson, Conn *B9 172
Thompson, Iowa A4 180
Thompson, Mich C4 186
Thompson, Mo B5 189
Thompson, N. Dak B8 198
Thompson, Ohio A6 199
Thompson, Pa C10 202
Thompson, Utah E6 207
Thompson, isl., Mass D3 185
Thompson, lake, Maine D2 184
Thompson, peak, Calif B2 170
Thompson, peak, N. Mex F6 195
Thompson, res., Oreg E5 201
Thompson, riv., B.C., Can D7 149
Thompson, riv., Iowa, Mo C3 180, A4 189
Thompson Falls, Mont C1 190
Thompsons, creek, Miss D5 188
Thompsons Station, Tenn B5 205
Thompsontown, Pa E7 202
Thompsonville, Conn A6 172
Thompsonville, Ill *F5 178
Thompsonville, Mich D5 186
Thomson, Ga C4 175
Thomson, Ill B3 178
Thomson, riv., Austl B4 112
Thomson's Falls, Ken A6 106
Thon Buri, Thai F4 89
Thonon-les-Bains, Fr C2 66
Thor, Iowa B3 180
Thorburn, N.S., Can D7 151
Thoreau, N. Mex B1 195
Thorhild, Alta., Can B4 148
Thorn, see Toruń, Pol.
Thornbury, Ont., Can C4 153
Thornbury, Pa *F1 202
Thorndale, Ont., Can D3 153
Thorndale, Tex D4 206
Thorndike, Maine D3 184
Thorndike, Mass B3 185
Thorne, Nev E3 192
Thorne, N. Dak A6 198
Thornfield, Mo E5 189
Thornhill, Man., Can E2 150
Thornhill, Ont., Can D5, E6 153
Thornhill, Scot E5 57
Thornton, Ark D3 169
Thornton, Calif B6 170
Thornton, Ont., Can C5 153
Thornton, Colo *B6 171
Thornton, Idaho F7 177
Thornton, Ill *F3 178
Thornton, Iowa B4 180
Thornton, Miss B3 188
Thornton, Tex D4 206
Thornton, Wash B8 210
Thornton, W. Va A7 211
Thornton, Wyo A8 213
Thorntown, Ind D4 179
Thornville, Ohio C5 199
Thornwood, W. Va C5 211
Thorny, mtn., Mo D6 189
Thorofare, N.J D2 194
Thorold, Ont., Can D5 153
Thorp, Wash B5 210
Thorp, Wis D3 212
Thorpe, W. Va D3 211
Thorsby, Ala C3 166
Thorsby, Alta., Can C3 148
Thouars, Fr D3 58
Thousand, is., N.Y A4, B1 196
Thousand Lake, mtn., Utah E4 207
Thousand Oaks, Calif *E4 170
Thousand Ship's, bay, Santa Isabel I 115
Thousand Spring, creek, Nev B7 192
Thrace: c. 450 B.C 42
c. 1st cent. B.C 44
c. 120 A.D 45
c. 400 A.D 46
Thrall, Kans D7 181
Thrapston, Eng B7 56
Three Bridges, N.J B3 194
Three Fingered Jack, mtn., Oreg C5 201
Three Forks, Mont E5 190
Three Hills, Alta., Can D4 148
Three Kings, is., N.Z K14 112
Three Lakes, Wis C4 212
Three Mile Bay, N.Y A4 196
Three Mile Plains, N.S., Can D5 151
Three Oaks, Mich G4 186
Three Points, cape, Ghana F4 103
Three Rivers, Mass B3 185
Three Rivers, Mich G5 186
Three Rivers, Miss E5 188
Three Rivers, N. Mex D3 195
Three Rivers, Tex E3 206
Three Rock Cove, Newf., Can D2 152
Three Sisters, mts., Oreg C5 201
Three Springs, Pa F6 202
Threepoint, lake, Man., Can B2 150
Throckmorton, Tex C3 206
Throckmorton, co., Tex C3 206
Throop, Pa A9 202
Thuir, Fr F5 58
Thule, Grnld B21 118
Thule, mtn., N.W. Ter., Can B17 143
Thun, Switz C3 66
Thun, lake, Switz C3 66
Thunder, bay, Mich C7 186
Thunder, butte, S. Dak B4 204
Thunder, hills, Sask., Can C2 155
Thunder Bay, Ont., Can E8 153
Thunder Bay, co., Ont., Can E8 153
Thunder Bay, riv., Mich C7 186
Thunder Butte, S. Dak B4 204
Thunder Butte, creek, S. Dak B3 204
Thunder Hawk, S. Dak B4 204
Thunderbird, lake, Okla B4 200
Thunderbolt, Ga D5 175
Thungsong, Thai H3 89
Thurgau, canton, Switz B4 66
Thüringen, former state, Ger C6 61
Thuringer Wald, mts., Ger C5 61
Thuringia, reg., Ger C5 60
Thurles, Ire D3 55
Thurlow, dam, Ala C4 166
Thurman, Iowa D2 180
Thurmont, Md A3 173
Thurrock, Eng *C8 56
Thursday, isl., Austl B7 110
Thurso, Que., Can D2 154
Thurso, Scot B5 57
Thurso, riv., Scot B5 57
Thurston, Nebr B9 191
Thurston, Ohio C5 199
Thurston, co., Nebr B9 191
Thurston, co., Wash C3 210
Thurston, isl., Ant B2 120
Thuvu, Fiji 114
Thwaites, ice tongue, Ant B1 120
Thysville, Zaire C1 106
Tiahuanaco, Bol C2 135
Tianna, beach, N.Y F6 172
Tiaong, Phil p13 90
Tiaret, Alg B5 102
Tibagi, Braz C2 137
Tibagi, riv., Braz C2 137
Tibasti, des., Libya E3 101
Tibati, Cam D2 104
Tibbie, Ala D1 166
Tiber, res., Mont B5 190
Tiber, see Tevere, riv., It.
Tiberias, Isr B7 84
Tiberias (Sea of Galilee), lake, Isr B7 84
Tibesti, reg., Chad A3 104
Tibesti Massif, plat., Chad A3 104
Tibet, prov., China E3 91
c. 750 A.D 80
c. 1294 81
c. 1775 82
after World War II 83
Tibet, plat., China B10 88
Tibnine, Leb A7 84
Tibooburra, Austl D4 112
Tiburón, isl., Mex B2 129
Tice, Fla F5 174
Tichborne, Ont., Can C8 153
Tichinane (Well), Maur C2 103
Tichit, Maur C3 103
Tichnor, Ark C4 169
Ticino, canton, Switz C4 66
Ticino, riv., It., Switz C4, D4 66
Tickfaw, La D5 183
Tickfaw, riv., La D5 183
Ticomán, Mex g9 129
Ticonderoga, N.Y B7 196
Ticonic, Iowa B2 180
Ticul, Mex C7 129
Tide Head, N.B., Can B3 151
Tidikelt, reg., Alg D5 102
Tidioute, Pa C3 202
Tidjikja, Maur C2 103
Tie Plant, Miss B4 188
Tie Siding, Wyo D7 213
Tiehling, China C9 91, C10 92
Tiel, Neth C5 59
Tiel, Sen D1 103
Tielmes de Tajuña, Sp p18 65
Tielt, Bel C3 59
Tien Shan, mts., Asia E10 76
Tien Yen, Viet B7 89
Tienchen, China D6 92
Tienchiang, China I2 92
Tienen, Bel D4 59
Tienmen, China I5 92
Tienpai, China G7 91
Tienpao, China G6 91
Tienshui, China E6 91
Tientsin, China D8 91, E7 92
Tierp, Swe G7 63
Tierra Amarilla, Chile E1 135
Tierra Amarilla, N. Mex A3 195
Tierra Blanca, Mex D5, n15 129
Tierra del Fuego, ter., Arg h12 136, 127
Tierra del Fuego, isl., Arg., Chile h12 136
Tietar, riv., Sp C3 65
Tietê, Braz C3, m8 137
Tietê, riv., Braz C2 137
Tieton, Wash C5 210
Tieton, dam, Wash C4 210
Tieton, riv., Wash C4 210
Tiff City, Mo E3 189
Tiffany, Colo D3 171
Tiffany, mtn., Wash A6 210
Tiffin, Iowa C6 180
Tiffin, Ohio A4 199
Tiffin, riv., Ohio A3 199
Tiflis, Sov. Un E2 73
Tift, co., Ga E3 175
Tifton, Ga E3 175
Tiftona, Tenn *D8 205
Tigard, Oreg B2 201
Tiger, Ga B3 175
Tiger, Wash A8 210
Tigerton, Wis D4 212
Tigerville, S.C A3 203
Tighnabruaich, Scot E3 57
Tigil, Sov. Un D18 71
Tignall, Ga C4 175
Tignére, Cam D2 104
Tignish, P.E.I., Can C5 151
Tigre, Arg g7 136
Tigre, reg., Eth C4 105
Tigre, isl., Viet D7 89
Tigre, riv., Peru B2 134
Tigres, pen., Ang E1 106
Tigrett, Tenn B2 205
Tigri, Afg D15 86, B5 87
Tigris, riv., Asia E2 86
Tiguabos, Cuba E6 131
Tihuatlán, Mex m15 129
Tijeras, N. Mex G5 195
Tijī, Libya C2 101
Tijuana, Mex A1 129
Tijucas, Braz D3 137
Tikal, ruins, Guat B3 130
Tikamgarh, India E7 88
Tikhoretsk, Sov. Un I13 72
Tikhvin, Sov. Un B9 72
Tikrit, Iraq E14 85
Tiksi, Sov. Un B15 71
Tilamuta, Indon E6 90
Tilburg, Neth C5 59
Tilbury, Ont., Can E2 153
Tilcara, Arg D2 135
Tilden, Ill E4 178
Tilden, Miss A5 188
Tilden, Nebr B8 191
Tilden, Tex E3 206
Tilemsi, val., Mali C5 103
Tilford, S. Dak C2 204
Tilghman, Md C5 173
Tilghman, isl., Md C5 173
Tiline, Ky A3 182
Tillabéri, Niger D5 103
Tillamook, Oreg B3 201
Tillamook, co., Oreg B3 201
Tillar, Ark D4 169
Tillatoba, Miss B4 188
Tillberga, Swe t34 63
Tiller, Oreg E4 201
Tillery, lake, N.C B3 197
Tilley, Alta., Can D5 148
Tillman, S.C G5 203
Tillman, co., Okla C2 200
Tillson, N.Y D6 196
Tillsonburg, Ont., Can E4 153
Tillyfourie, Scot C6 57
Tilos, isl., Grc D6 69
Tilpa, Austl E5 112
Tilremt, Alg C5 102
Tilsit, see Sovetsk, Sov. Un.
Tilston, Man., Can E1 150
Tilting, Newf., Can D4 152
Tilton, Ga B2 175
Tilton, Ill C6 178
Tilton, N.H D3 193
Tiltonsville, Ohio B7 199
Tim, Sov. Un F11 72
Tim Ford, lake, Tenn B5 205
Timaná, Col C2 133
Timaru, N.Z P13 112
Timashevskaya, Sov. Un I12 72
Timbalier, bay, La E5 183
Timbalier, isl., La E5 183
Timbaúba, Braz h6 138
Timber, Oreg B3 201
Timber Lake, S. Dak B4 204
Timbered Knob, mtn., Mo E5 189
Timberlake, N.C A5 197
Timberlake, Ohio *A6 199
Timberville, Va C4 209
Timblin, Pa E3 202
Timbo, Ark B3 169
Timbuktu, see Tombouctou, Mali
Timerzit, Mor C4 102
Times Beach, Mo *C7 189
Timewell (Mound Station), Ill C3 178
Timimoun, Alg D5 102
Timiskaming, co., Ont., Can E9 153
Timiskaming, co., Que., Can A6 153
Timiskaming Station, Que., Can G17 145
Timişoara, Rom C5 68
Timken, Kans D4 181
Timmendorfer Strand [an die Ostsee], Ger E4 62
Timmins, Ont., Can E9 153
Timmonsville, S.C C8 203
Timms, hill, Wis C3 212
Timnath, Colo A6 171
Timonium, Md B4 173
Timor, Portuguese, see Portuguese Timor, dep., Asia
Timor, isl., Indon G6 90
Timor, sea, Indon G7 90
Timpas, Colo D7 171
Timpson, Tex D5 206
Timrå, Swe F7 63
Timsâh, lake, Eg D4 84
Timur, dominions of 81
Tin Amzi, riv., Alg E6 102
Tin City, N.C C6 197
Tin Rerhoh (Oasis), Alg E5 102
Tin Zaouaten (Fort Pierre Bordes), Alg E5 102
Tina, Mo B4 189
Tina, bay, Eg C4 84

INDEX KEY Each place listed in **Bold-faced Type** has its population listed in the Population tables, pages 230 to 280. Each country, shown in CAPITAL LETTERS, has its population listed in the World Political Information Table, pages 6 to 10.
* Does not appear on map; key shows general location.

Tinajas Altas, mts., Ariz., N. Mex E1 168
Tinaquillo, Ven B4 133
Tindouf, Alg D3 102
Tineo, Sp A2 65
Tinghert, plat., Alg., Libya D7 102
Tinghsien, China E6 92
Tinghsin, China C4 91
Tinghsing, China E6 92
Tingjegaon, Nep C9 88
Tinglev, Den D3 62
Tingley, Iowa D3 180
Tingmerkpuk, mtn., Alsk B7 167
Tingo María, Peru C2 134
Tingpien, China F2 92
Tingri Dzong, China C11 88
Tingsryd, Swe B8 62
Tingwick, Que., Can D6 154
Tingwon, is., Bis. Arch 115
Tingyüanying, China E1 92
Tinian, Tinian 114
Tinian, hbr., Tinian 114
Tinian (Tenian), isl., Mariana Is 115
Tinkisso, riv., Guinea D2 103
Tinley Park, Ill F3 178
Tinnie, N. Mex D4 195
Tinniswood, mtn., B.C., Can D6 149
Tinogasta, Arg E2 135
Tínos, Grc D5 69
Tínos, isl., Grc D5 69
Tinputts, hbr., Bougainville I 115
Tinquipaya, Bol C2 135
Tinrhert, plat., Alg D5 102
Tinsley, Miss C3 188
Tinsman, Ark D3 169
Tinsukia, India C10 87
Tintah, Minn D2 187
Tintigny, Bel E5 59
Tintina, Arg E3 135
Tintinara, Austl G3 112
Tinton Falls, N.J C4 194
Tioga, Ill C2 178
Tioga, La C3 183
Tioga, N. Dak A3 198
Tioga, Pa C7 202
Tioga, Tex *C4 206
Tioga, W. Va C4 211
Tioga, co., N.Y C4 196
Tioga, co., Pa C7 202
Tioga, riv., N.Y., Pa C7 202
Tiogue, lake, R.I C10 172
Tioman, isl., Mala K6 89
Tiona, Pa C3 202
Tione di Trento, It C6 66
Tionesta, Pa C3 202
Tionesta, creek, Pa C3 202
Tionesta Creek, res., Pa D3 202
Tioughnioga, riv., N.Y C4 196
Tip Top, Ky C6 182
Tip Top, hill, Ont., Can E8 153
Tipler, Wis C5 212
Tiplersville, Miss A5 188
Tipp City, Ohio C3 199
Tippah, co., Miss A5 188
Tippah, creek, Miss A4 188
Tippecanoe, Ind B5 179
Tippecanoe, co., Ind D4 179
Tippecanoe, riv., Ind C4 179
Tipperary, Ire D2 55
Tippett, Nev D7 192
Tippo, Miss B3 188
Tipton, Calif D4 170
Tipton, Ind D5 179
Tipton, Iowa C6 180
Tipton, Kans C5 181
Tipton, Mo C5 189
Tipton, Okla C2 200
Tipton, co., Ind D5 179
Tipton, co., Tenn B2 205
Tipton, mtn., Ariz B1 168
Tiptonville, Tenn A2 205
Tiptop, Va B3, E1 209
Tiran, isl., Sau. Ar I10 85
Tirana, see Tiranë, Alb.
Tiranë (Tirana), Alb B2 69
Tirano, It A3 67
Tiraque Chico, Bol C2 135
Tiraspol', Sov. Un H7 72
Tirat Carmel, Isr B6 84
Tirat Zvi, Isr B7 84
Tire, Tur C6 69
Tire Hill, Pa F4 202
Tirebolu, Tur B12 85
Tiree, isl., Scot D2 57
Tirenno (Well), Chad A3 104
Tîrgu Mureş, Rom B7 68
Tiriro, Guinea D3 103
Tírnavos, Grc C4 69
Tiro, Ohio B5 199
Tirol, state, Aus B7 66
Tirol, reg., Aus E5 60
Tirschenreuth, Ger D7 61
Tirso, riv., It D2 67
Tirstrup, Den B4 62
Tiruchirappalli, India F6 87
Tirunelveli, India G6 87
Tiruppur, India *F6 87
Tisa, riv., Yugo C5 68
Tisaren, lake, Swe t33 63
Tisch Mills, Wis A6 212
Tisdale, Sask., Can E3 155
Tishomingo, Miss A5 188
Tishomingo, Okla C5 200
Tishomingo, co., Miss A5 188
Tiskilwa, Ill B4 178
Tisnaren, lake, Swe u33 63
Tista, riv., India D12 88
Tisvildeleje, Den B6 62
Tisza, riv., Hung B5 68
Tiszafüred, Hung B5 68
Tiszakécske, Hung B5 68
Titagarh, India *F12 88
Titicaca, lake, Bol., Peru C2 135
Titicus, Conn D3 172
Titicus, res., N.Y D2 172
Titograd, Yugo D4 68
Titonka, Iowa A3 180
Titov Veles, Yugo E5 68
Titovo Užice, Yugo D4 68
Titule, Zaire A4 106
Titus, co., Tex C5 206
Titusville, Fla D6 174
Titusville, N.J C3 194
Titusville, Pa C2 202
Tiuggi, is., Mala K6 89
Tiumpan, head, Scot B2 57
Tivaouane, Sen C1 103
Tiverton, N.S., Can E3 151
Tiverton, Ont., Can C3 153
Tiverton, Eng D4 56
Tiverton, R.I C12 172
Tiverton Four Corners, R.I C12 172
Tivoli, It D4, h9 67
Tivoli, N.Y C7 196
Tivoli, Tex E4 206
Tixtla, Mex o14 129
Tizapán, Mex h9 129
Tizi Ouzou, Alg B5 102
Tizimín, Mex C7 129
Tiznit, Mor D3 102
Tjeukemeer, lake, Neth B5 59
Tjilatjap, Indon G3 90
Tjina, cape, Indon G2 90
Tjirebon, Indon G3 90
Tlacolula, Mex D5 129
Tlacotalpan, Mex D5 129
Tlacotepec, Mex o14 129
Tláhuac, Mex h9 129
Tlahualilo de Zaragoza, Mex B4 129
Tlalnepantla, Mex g9 129
Tlalnepantla, riv., Mex g9 129
Tlalpan, Mex h9 129
Tlalpujahua, Mex n13 129
Tlaltenco, Mex h9 129
Tlapa, Mex o14 129
Tlapacoyan, Mex n15 129
Tlapaneco, riv., Mex o14 129
Tlaquepaque, Mex m12 129
Tlaxcala, Mex D5, n14 129
Tlaxcala, state, Mex D5, n14 129
Tlaxco, Mex n14 129
Tlaxiaco, Mex D5 129
Tlemcen, Alg G6 64, C4 102
Tlemcès (Well), Niger C5 103
Tłuszcz, Pol k14 70
Tmassah', Libya D3 101
To, isl., Jap I9 93
To Bong, Viet F8 89
Toa Alta, P.R B6 132
Toa Alta, mun., P.R B5 132
Toa Baja, P.R B5 132
Toa Baja, mun., P.R B6 132
Toadlena, N. Mex A1 195
Toano, Va D6 209
Toast, N.C A3 197
Toay, Arg B4 136
Toba, Jap o15 93
Toba, inlet, B.C., Can D5 149
Toba, lake, Indon m11 90
Toba, riv., B.C., Can D5 149
Tobacco Root, mts., Mont E5 190
Tobago, isl., Trin A5 133
Tobago, is., Vir. Is f15 132
Tobarra, Sp C5 65
Tobaru, Okinawa 114
Tobermory, Ont., Can B3 153
Tobermory, Scot D2 57
Tobi, isl., Jap G9 93
Tobias, Nebr D8 191
Tobin, lake, Sask., Can D4 155
Tobin, mtn., Nev C4 192
Tobins Harbor, Mich A2 186
Tobinsport, Ind I4 179
Tobique, riv., N.B., Can B2 151
Tobol, Sov. Un C6 73
Tobol, riv., Sov. Un C6 73
Tobolsk, Sov. Un B7 73
Tobruk, see Ţubruq, Libya
Tobushi, pt., Iwo 114
Toby, mtn., Mass B2 185
Tobyhanna, Pa D11 202
Tocantinópolis, Braz C1 138
Tocantins, riv., Braz C1 138
Toccoa, Ga B3 175
Toccoa Falls, Ga B3 175
Toccopola, Miss A4 188
Toce, riv., It C4 66
Tochcha, lake, B.C., Can B5 149
Tochigi, Jap H9, m18 93
Tocito, N. Mex A1 195
Tocoa, Hond C4 130
Tocopilla, Chile D1 135
Tocorpuri, hill, Bol D2 135
Tocra, see Tūkrah, Libya
Tocsin, Ind C7 179
Tocumwal, Austl G5 112
Tocuyo, riv., Ven A4 133
Tod Park, Utah C3 207
Todd, co., Ky D2 182
Todd, co., Minn D4 187
Todd, co., S. Dak D5 204
Todd, fork, Ohio C4 199
Todd, riv., Austl D6 110
Toddville, Md D5 173
Toddy, pond, Maine D4 184
Todi, It C4 67
Tödi, mtn., Switz C4 66
Todoga, cape, Jap G11 93
Todos os Santos, bay, Braz D3 138
Todos Santos, Bol C2 135
Todos Santos, Mex C2 129
Todtnau, Ger B3 66
Toe, head, Scot C1 57
Toecane, N.C C4 197
Tofield, Alta., Can C4 148
Tofino, B.C., Can E5 149
Tofte, Minn B6, C8 187
Toftlund, Den C3 62
Toga, Va D4 209
Togiak, Alsk D7 167
Togian, is., Indon F6 90
Togo, Sask., Can F5 155
TOGO, country, Afr E5 103, 99
Tohakum, peak, Nev C2 192
Tohatchi, N. Mex B1 195
Tohickon, creek, Pa C2 194
Tohopekaliga, lake, Fla D5 174
Toi, cape, Jap K5 93
Toimi, Minn C7 187
Toivola, Mich B2 186
Toivola, Minn C6 187
Toiyabe, range, Nev E4 192
Toiyabe Dome, mtn., Nev E4 192
Tokaj, Hung A5 68
Tokar, Sud B4 105
Tokara, is., Jap L4 93
Tokara, strait, Jap K5 93
Tokat, Tur B11 85
Tokeland, Wash C2 210
TOKELAU ISLANDS, N.Z. dep., Oceania G11 113
Tokenon, Kor G3 93
Toki, Jap *I8 93
Toki, pt., Wake I 114
Tokio, Ark C2 169
Tokio, N. Dak B7 198
Tokio, Tex C1 206
Tokmak, Sov. Un E9 73
Tokorozawa, Jap *I9 93
Tokoto, China D4 92
Tokuchi, Okinawa 114
Tokuno, isl., Ryukyu Is F10 91
Tokushima, Jap I7 93
Tokuyama, Jap J6 93
Tōkyō, Jap I9 93
Tōkyō, bay, Jap n18 93
Tol, isl., Truk 114
Tolbukhin (Dobrich), Bul D8 68
Toleak, pt., Wash B1 210
Toledo, Ont., Can C8 153
Toledo, Cuba k11 131
Toledo, Ill D5 178
Toledo, Iowa B5 180
Toledo, Ohio A2, A4 199
Toledo, Oreg C3 201
Toledo, Phil *C6 90
Toledo, Sp C3 65
Toledo, Wash C3 210
Toledo, mts., Sp C3 65
Toledo Bend, res., La., Tex C2 183
Toler, Ky C7 182
Tolg, Swe A8 62
Tolga, Alg C6 102
Tolima, dept., Col C2 133
Tolima, vol., Col C2 133
Tolimán, Mex m14 129
Tolken, lake, Swe A6 62
Tolland, Conn B7 172
Tolland, co., Conn B7 172
Tollense, lake, Ger E7 62
Tollense, riv., Ger E7 62
Tollesboro, Ky B6 182
Tolleson, Ariz G1 168
Tollette, Ark D2 169
Tolley, N. Dak A4 198
Tollhouse, Calif D4 170
Tolloche, Arg E3 135
Tolmezzo, It A4 67
Tolmin, Yugo B1 68
Tolna, Hung B4 68
Tolna, N. Dak B7 198
Tolo, gulf, Indon F6 90
Tolocolme, peak, Ponape 114
Tolono, Ill D5 178
Tolosa, Sp A4 65
Tolovana Park, Oreg B3 201
Tolsta, head, Scot B2 57
Tolstoi, Man., Can E3 150
Tolstoy, S. Dak B6 204
Toltec, Ariz E4 168
Toltec, Colo D6 171
Tolten, Chile B2 136
Tolú, Col B2 133
Tolu, Ky A3 182
Toluca, Ill B4 178
Toluca, Mex D5, n14 129
Tolun, China C8 91
Tolyatti, Sov. Un E7 71
Tom, Okla D7 200
Tom, mtn., Conn C3 172
Tom Bean, Tex *C4 206
Tom Green, co., Tex D2 206
Tom Nevers, head, Mass D7 185
Tomah, Wis E3 212
Tomahawk, Wis C4 212
Tomahawk, lake, Wis C4 212
Tomakomai, Jap E10 93
Tomakovka, Sov. Un H10 72
Tomales, Calif B4 170
Tomar, Port C1 65
Tomari, Sov. Un C11 93
Tomaszów Lubelski, Pol C7 70
Tomaszow Mazowiecki, Pol C6 70
Tomatlán, Mex D3, n11 129
Tomato, Ark B6 169
Tomave, Bol D2 135
Tombador, mts., Braz D2 138
Tomball, Tex D5 206
Tombigbee, riv., Ala., Miss B5 188
Tombouctou (Timbuktu), Mali C4 103
Tombstone, Ariz F5 168
Tomé, Chile B2 136
Tome, N. Mex C3 195
Tomelilla, Swe C7 62
Tomelloso, Sp C4 65
Tomichi, creek, Colo C4 171
Tomini, gulf, Indon E6 90
Tomintoul, Scot C5 57
Tomkins Cove, N.Y D3, D7 196
Tommot, Sov. Un D15 71
Tomnolen, Miss B4 188
Tomo, riv., Col B4 133
Tompkins, Newf., Can E2 152
Tompkins, Sask., Can G1 155
Tompkins, co., N.Y C4 196
Tompkinsville, Ky D4 182
Tompkinsville, Md D4 173
Toms, riv., N.J C4 194
Toms Creek, Va B2 209
Toms River, N.J D4 194
Tomsk, Sov. Un B11 73
Tonalá, Mex D6 129
Tonalea, Ariz A5 168
Tonasket, Wash A6 210
Tonawanda, N.Y B2 196
Tonawanda, Indian res., N.Y B2 196
Tonbridge, Eng C8 56
Tondano, Indon E6 90
Tönder, Den D2 62
Tönder, co., Den C2 62
Toney, Ala A3 166
Tong, isl., Bis. Arch 115
TONGA, country, Oceania H11 113
Tonganoxie, Kans B8, C8 181
Tongareva, isl., Pac. O G12 113
Tongduch'ŏn, Kor H3 93
Tongeren, Bel D5 59
Tongjoson, bay, Kor G3 93
Tongking: c. 1775 82
Tongoa, isl., New Hebr 115
Tongoi, Chile F1 135
Tongue, Scot B4 57
Tongue, riv., Mont., Wyo E10 190
Tongue, Kyle of, bay, Scot B4 57
Tongue River, Indian res., Mont E10 190
Tonica, Ill B4 178
Tónichi, Mex B3 129
Tonj, Sud D2 105
Tonk Raj, India C6 87, D5 88
Tonka Bay, Minn *F5 187
Tonkawa, Okla A4 200
Tonkin, reg., Viet B6 89
Tonkin, gulf, Asia C7 89
Tonle Sap, lake, Camb C2 89
Tonneins, Fr E4 58
Tonnerre, Fr D5 58
Tönning, Ger D2 62
Tonoloway, ridge, Md A1 173
Tonopah, Nev E4 192
Tonosí, Pan G7 130
Tonpah, Ariz D3 168
Tönsberg, Nor H4, p28 63
Tontitown, Ark A1 169
Tonto, natural bridge, Ariz C4 168
Tonto, nat. mon., Ariz D4 168
Tonto Basin, Ariz D4 168
Tontogany, Ohio A1 199
Tonton, Phil n13 90
Tony, Wis C3 212
Tooele, Utah C3 207
Tooele, co., Utah C2 207
Tool, Tex *C4 206
Toole, co., Mont B5 190
Toombs, co., Ga D4 175
Toomsboro, Ga D3 175
Toomsuba, Miss C5 188
Toone, Tenn B3 205
Toowoomba, Austl C8 112
Top, pond, Newf., Can E3 152
Topawa, Ariz F4 168
Topaz, Calif C4 170
Topeka, Ind A6 179
Topeka, Kans B6, C8 181
Topinabee, Mich C6 186
Topki, Sov. Un B11 73
Topley, B.C., Can B4 149
Toplica, riv., Yugo D5 68
Topock, Ariz C1 168
Topol'čany, Czech D5 70
Topólia, Grc g10 69
Topolnitsa, riv., Bul D7 68
Topolobampo, Mex B3 129
Topolovgrad, Bul D8 68
Toponas, Colo A4 171
Topozero, lake, Sov. Un E14 63
Toppenish, Wash C5 210
Toppenish, ridge, Wash C5 210
Topsfield, Maine C5 184
Topsfield, Mass A6 185
Topsham, Maine E3, E5 184
Topsham, Vt C4 208
Topsy, Tenn B4 205
Topton, Miss C5 188
Topton, Pa F10 202
Toquerville, Utah F2 207
Toquima, range, Nev E4 192
Tor, bay, Eng D4 56
Torbali, Tur C6 69
Torbat-e-Heydariyeh, Iran D9 86
Torbat-e-Jām, Iran D10 86
Torbay, Newf., Can E5 152
Torbay, Eng D4 56
Torbert, mtn., Alsk g15 167
Torbreck, mtn., Austl H5 112
Torbrook, N.S., Can E5 151
Torcello, It D8 66
Torch, lake, Mich D5 186
Torch, riv., Sask., Can D4 155
Torekov, Swe B6 62
Torez, Sov. Un q21 72
Torgau, Ger B7 61
Torhout, Bel C3 59
Tori, isl., Jap J4 93
Toride, Jap n19 93
Torino, see Turin, It.
Torit, Sud E3 105
Toriu, New Britain I 115
Torko, Bougainville I 115
Tórmes, riv., Sp B2 65
Tornado, mtn., Alta., B.C., Can E10 149
Torneälven, riv., Swe D10 63
Torneträsk, lake, Swe C9 63
Torngat, mts., Newf., Que., Can f8 152
Tornillo, Tex F1 206
Tornio, Fin E11 63
Tornquist, Arg B4 136
Toro, La C2 183
Toro, Sp B3 65
Torö, Swe u35 63
Toro, mtn., P.R B7 132
Toro, peak, Calif F5 170
Toro Negro, riv., P.R B4 132
Toroi, Mong C4 92
Törökszentmiklos, Hung B5 68
Toronto, Ont., Can D5, E6 153
Toronto, Iowa C7 180
Toronto, Kans E8 181
Toronto, Ohio B7 199
Toronto, S. Dak C9 204
Toronto, res., Kans E7 181
Toropets, Sov. Un C8 72
Tororo, Ug A5 106
Torote, riv., Sp o18 65
Torquay, Sask., Can H4 155
Torrance, Calif F2 170
Torrance, Ont., Can C5 153
Torrance, co., N. Mex C3 195
Torre Annunziata, It D5 67
Torre de Cerredo, mtn., Sp A3 65
Torre del Greco, It D5 67
Torre Pacheco, Sp D5 65
Torredonjimeno, Sp D4 65
Torrejón de Ardoz, Sp p18 65
Torrejoncillo, Sp C2 65
Torrelavega, Sp A3 65
Torremaggiore, It D5 67
Torrens, lake, Austl F6 110
Torrente, Sp C5 65
Torreón, Mex B4 129
Torreon, N. Mex C3 195
Tôrres, Braz D3 137
Torres, is., New Hebr 115
Torres, strait, Austl., Pap A7, k11 110
Tôrres Novas, Port C1 65
Tôrres Vedras, Port C1 65
Torrevieja, Sp D5 65
Torrey, Utah E4 207
Torriglia, It E5 66
Törring, Den C3 62
Torrington, Alta., Can D4 148
Torrington, Conn B4 172
Torrington, Eng D3 56
Torrington, Wyo C8 213
Torrinha, Braz m7 137
Torrowangee, Austl E3 112
Torrox, Sp D4 65
Tors Cove, Newf., Can E5 152
Torshälla, Swe t34 63
Tórshavn, Den. (Faeroe Is.) C6 41
Tortilla Flat, Ariz D4 168
Tortola, isl., Vir. Is m14 131, f16 132
Tortona, It B2 67
Tortosa, Sp B6 65
Tortosa, cape, Sp B6 65
Tortue, isl., Hai E7 131
Tortuga, isl., Ven A4 133
Tortugas, N. Mex E3 185
Ţorūd, Iran D7 86
Toruń, Pol B5 70
Toruńlubuski, Pol A10 61
Torup, Swe B7 62
Tory, isl., Ire C2 55
Tory Hill, Ont., Can C6 153
Torysa, riv., Czech D6 70
Torzhok, Sov. Un C10 72
Tosno, Sov. Un B8 72
Tosson Hill, mtn., Eng E7 57
Tostado, Arg E3 135
Toston, Mont D5 190
Tosya, Tur B10 85
Toszek, Pol g9 70
Totagatic, riv., Wis B2 212
Totana, Sp D5 65
Toteng, Bots B3 107
Toterose, lake, Wash A6 210
Totkomlós, Hung B5 68
Totnes, Eng D4 56
Toto, Ang C1 106
Toto, Guam 114
Tōtōmi, sea, Jap o16 93
Totonicapán, Guat C2 130
Totorapalca, Bol C2 135
Totowa, N.J B4 194
Totoya, isl., Fiji 114
Totson, mtn., Alsk C8 167
Tottenham, Austl F6 112
Tottenham, Ont., Can C5 153
Tottenham, Eng k12 55
Tottori, Jap I7 93
Totz, Ky D6 182
Touba, I. C E3 103
Touba, Sen D1 103
Touchet, Wash C7 210
Touchet, riv., Wash C7 210
Touchwood, lake, Man., Can B4 150
Toufourine (Oasis), Mali B4 103
Tougaloo, Miss C3 188
Tougan, Upper Volta D4 103
Touggourt, Alg C6 102
Touhy, Nebr C9 191
Toul, Fr C6 58
Touléplou, I. C E3 103
Toulon, Fr F6 58
Toulon, Ill B4 178
Toulon, Nev C3 192
Toulouse, Fr F4 58
Toummo (Oasis), Niger B7 103
Toungo, Nig E7 103
Toungoo, Bur E10 87
Tounin, Alg F7 64
Touraine, former prov., Fr D4 58
Tourcoing, Fr B5 58, D3 59
Tourlaville, Fr C3 58
Tournai, Bel D3 59
Tournon [-sur-Rhône], Fr E6 58
Tournus, Fr D6 58
Touros, Braz C3 138
Tours, Fr D4 58
Tourville, Que., Can B8 154
Toussaint, creek, Ohio A2 199
Toutle, riv., Wash C3 210
Tova, reef, Fiji 114
Toval, New Britain I 115
Tovar, Ven B3 133
Tovey (Humphrey), Ill D4 178
Tow, Tex D3 206
Towaco, N.J B4 194
Towada, lake, Jap F10 93
Towanda, Ill C5 178
Towanda, Kans B6, E7 181
Towanda, Pa C9 202
Towanda, creek, Pa C8 202
Towang, India C9 87
Towaoc, Colo D2 171
Tower, Mich C6 186
Tower, Minn C6 187
Tower, rock, Am. Sam 114
Tower City, N. Dak C8 198
Tower City, Pa E8 202
Tower Hamlets, Eng k12 55
Tower Hill, Ill D5 178
Town, creek, Md D2 173
Town, hill, Md., Pa A1 173
Town and Country, Mo *C7 189
Town Creek, Ala A2 166
Town of Pines, Ind *A4 179
Towner, Colo C8 171
Towner, N. Dak A5 198
Towner, co., N. Dak A6 198
Townley, Ala B2 166
Towns, Ga D4 175
Towns, co., Ga B3 175
Townsend, Del B6 173
Townsend, Ga E5 175
Townsend, Mass A4 185
Townsend, Mont D5 190
Townsend, Tenn D10 205
Townsend, Va D7 209
Townshend, Vt E3 208
Townshend, res., Vt E3 208
Townsville, Austl C8 111
Townsville, N.C A5 197
Townville, Pa C2 202
Townville, S.C B2 203
Towson, Md B4, C2 173
Towuti, lake, Indon F6 90
Towyn, Wales B3 56
Toxey, Ala D1 166
Toy, Nev C3 192
Toyah, Tex F2 206
Toyahvale, Tex F2 206
Toyama, Jap H8 93
Toyama, bay, Jap H8 93
Toyohara, see Yuzhno-Sakhalinsk, Sov. Un.
Toyohashi, Jap I8, o16 93
Toyohira, Jap *E10 93
Toyokawa, Jap o16 93
Toyonaka, Jap o14 93
Toyota, Jap n16 93
Tozeur, Tun C6 102
Trabancos, riv., Sp B3 65
Traben-Trarbach, Ger D2 61
Trabzon, Tur B12 85
Tracadie, N.B., Can B5 151
Tracadie, N.S., Can D8 151
Tracadie, riv., N.B., Can B4 151
Tracy, Calif B6, D3 170
Tracy, N.B., Can D3 151
Tracy, Conn C5 172
Tracy, Iowa C5 180
Tracy, Ky D4 182
Tracy, Minn F3 187
Tracy, Mo B3, D1 189
Tracy, brook, Md C4 173
Tracy City, Tenn D8 205
Tracy-le-Mont, Fr E3 59
Tracyton, Wash D1 210
Trade, Tenn C12 205
Trade, lake, Sask., Can B4 155
Tradesville, S.C B6 203
Tradewater, riv., Ky C2 182
Trading Post, Kans D9 181
Traer, Iowa B5 180
Traer, Kans C3 181
Trafalgar, Ind F5 179
Trafford, Pa B7 202
Trafford, lake, Fla F5 174
Traiguén, Chile B2 136
Trail, B.C., Can E9 149
Trail, Minn C3 187
Trail, Oreg E4 201
Trail, ridge, Ga F4 175
Trail City, S. Dak B5 204
Trail Creek, Ind A4 179
Trailer Estates, Fla *E4 174
Traill, co., N. Dak B8 198
Traill, isl., Grnld B17 118
Trainer, Pa *G11 202
Traipu, Braz C3 138
Trairí, riv., Braz h6 138
Tralee, Ire D2 55
Trammel, Va B2 209
Tramping, lake, Sask., Can E1 155
Tramping Lake, Sask., Can E1 155
Tranås, Swe H6 63

INDEX KEY Each place listed in **Bold-faced Type** has its population listed in the Population tables pages 230 to 280.
Each country shown in CAPITAL LETTERS has its population listed in the World Political Information Table, pages 6 to 10.
* Does not appear on map; key shows general location.

Trancas, Arg E2 135
Trancoso, Port B2 65
Tranebjerg, Den C4 62
Tranemo, Swe A7 62
Trang, Thai I3 89
Trangan, isl., Indon G8 90
Trani, It D6 67
Tranquillity, Calif D3 170
Trans-Ili Alatau, mts., Sov. Un E9 73
Transfer, Pa D1 202
Transjordan, see also Jordan 53
Transvaal, prov., S. Afr B4 107, 99
Transylvania, La B4 183
Transylvania, co., N.C D3 197
Transylvania, reg., Rom B6 68
c. 1721 49
Transylvanian Alps, mts., Rom C6 68
Trap, mtn., Ark D5 169
Trapani, It E4 67
Trapiche, Guat B2 130
Trappe, Md C5 173
Trappe, Pa *F11 202
Trappe, creek, Md D7 173
Trapper, peak, Idaho D4 177
Trapper, peak, Mont E2 190
Traralgon, Austl I6 112
Traryd, Swe B7 62
Trás-os-Montes, reg., Port B2 65
Trasimeno, lake, It C4 67
Trask, Mo E6 189
Traskwood, Ark C3 169
Trat, Thai F5 89
Traun, lake, Aus E6 60
Traun, riv., Aus D7 60
Traunik, Mich B4 186
Traunstein, Ger E6 60
Trave, riv., Ger E4 62
Travelers Rest, S.C B3 203
Travers, Alta., Can D4 148
Travers, res., Alta., Can D4 148
Traverse, co., Minn E2 187
Traverse, isl., Mich A2 186
Traverse, lake, Minn E2 187
Traverse City, Mich D5 186
Travis, co., Tex D4 206
Travnik, Yugo C3 68
Tray, mtn., Ga B3 175
Tre Teste, riv., It h9 67
Treadway, Tenn C10 205
Treadway, lake, Ill C3 178
Treasure, co., Mont D9 190
Treasure Island, Fla *E4 174
Treasury, is., Sol. Is 115
Trebbia, riv., It E5 66
Trebel, riv., Ger E6 62
Třebíč, Czech D3 70
Trebinje, Yugo D4 68
Trebišov, Czech D6 70
Treble, mtn., B.C., Can B3 149
Třeboň, Czech D3 70
Treece, Kans E9 181
Tregaron, Wales B4 56
Tregarva, Sask., Can G3 155
Trego, Mont B2 190
Trego, Wis C2 212
Trego, co., Kans D4 181
Tréguier, Fr C2 58
Treherne, Man., Can E2 150
Treig, lake, Scot D4 57
Treinta y Tres, Ur E2 137
Treis, Ger C2 61
Trélazé, Fr D3 58
Trelew, Arg C3 136
Trelleborg, Swe J5 63
Tremadoc, bay, Wales B3 56
Tremblant, mtn., Que., Can C3 154
Tremblay [-lès-Gonesse], Fr g11 58
Trembleur, lake, B.C., Can B5 149
Tremiti, is., It C5 67
Tremont, Ill C4 178
Tremont, Miss A5 188
Tremont, Pa E9 202
Tremont City, Ohio B4 199
Tremonton, Utah B3 207
Třemošná, Czech D8 61
Tremp, Sp A6 65
Trempealeau, Wis D2 212
Trempealeau, co., Wis D2 212
Trempealeau, riv., Wis D2 212
Trenary, Mich B4 186
Trenche, riv., Que., Can B5 154
Trenčín, Czech D5 70
Trenque Lauquén, Arg B4 136
Trent, Ger D7 62
Trent, Oreg D4 201
Trent, S. Dak D9 204
Trent, Tex C2 206
Trent, riv., Eng A7 56
Trent, riv., N.C B6 197
Trent Woods, N.C *B6 197
Trentino: c. 1866 51
in 1914 52
in 1922-40 53
Trentino-Alto Adige, pol. dist., It C7 66
Trento, It C7 66, A3 67
Trenton, Ala A3 166
Trenton, N.S., Can D7 151
Trenton, Ont., Can C7 153
Trenton, Fla C4 174
Trenton, Ga B1 175
Trenton, Ill E4 178
Trenton, Ky D2 182
Trenton, Mich B7, F7 186
Trenton, Mo A4 189
Trenton, Nebr D4 191
Trenton, N.J C3 194
Trenton, N.C B6 197
Trenton, N. Dak A2 198
Trenton, Ohio C3 199
Trenton, S.C D4 203
Trenton, Tenn B3 205
Trenton, Tex C4 206
Trenton, Utah B4 207
Trentwood, Wash *B8 210
Trepassey, Newf., Can E5 152
Trepassey, bay, Newf., Can E5 152
Tres Algarrobos, Arg B4 136
Tres Arboles, Ur E1 137
Tres Arroyos, Arg B4 136
Tres Cerros, Arg D3 136
Trés Corações, Braz C3 137
Tres Esquinas, Col C2 133
Três Lagoas, Braz C2 137
Tres Lomas, Arg B4 136
Tres Marías, is., Mex C3 129
Três Marias, res., Braz B3 137
Tres Piedras, N. Mex A4 195
Tres Pinos, Calif C6 170
Tres Puntas, cape, Arg D3 136
Tres Ritos, N. Mex A4 195
Tresckow, Pa E10 202
Tresle Creek, Idaho A2 177
Treuchtlingen, Ger E5 61
Treuenbrietzen, Ger A7 61
Treutlen, co., Ga D4 175
Treviglio, It B2 67
Treviño, Sp A4 65
Treviso, It D8 66, B4 67
Trevor, Wis F1 212
Trevorton, Pa E8 202
Trevose, head, Eng D2 56
Treynor, Iowa C2 180
Treysa, Ger C4 61
Trezevant, Tenn A3 205
Trhové Sviny, Czech E9 61
Tri Lakes, Ind *B7 179
Triadelphia, W. Va A4, B2 211
Triadelphia, res., Md B3 173
Triangle, Va C5 209
Triangle Lake, Oreg C3 201
Triaucourt, Fr F5 59
Tribbet, Miss B3 188
Tribbey, Okla B4 200
Tribune, Sask., Can H4 155
Tribune, Kans D2 181
Trichur, India F6 87
Tridell, Utah C6 207
Trident, Mont E5 190
Trident, peak, Nev B3 192
Trier, Ger D1 61
Trieste, It B4 67
Trieste, gulf, It B4 67
Trigg, co., Ky D2 182
Triglav, mtn., Yugo B1 68
Trigo, mts., Ariz D1 168
Trigueros, Sp D2 65
Tríkkala (Tricca), Grc C3 69
Trilby, Fla D4 174
Trilla, Ill D5 178
Trimble, Colo D3 171
Trimble, Mo B3 189
Trimble, Ohio *C5 199
Trimble, Tenn A2 205
Trimble, co., Ky B4 182
Trimble, isl., Wash D1 210
Trimont, Minn G4 187
Trimountain, Mich A2 186
Trinchera, Colo D6 171
Trinchera, creek, Colo D5 171
Trinchera, peak, Colo D5 171
Trincomalee, Cey G7 87
Tring-Jonction, Que., Can C7 154
Trinidad, Bol B3 135
Trinidad, Calif *B1 170
Trinidad, Colo D6 171
Trinidad, Cuba E4 131
Trinidad, Tex C4 206
Trinidad, Ur E1 137
Trinidad, bay, Pan k11 130
Trinidad, isl., Arg B4 136
Trinidad, isl., Trin A5 133
TRINIDAD & TOBAGO, country, N.A A5 133
Trinité, Mart o16 131
Trinity, Ala A2 166
Trinity, Newf., Can D5 152
Trinity, N.C B4 197
Trinity, Tex D5 206
Trinity, co., Calif B2 170
Trinity, co., Tex D5 206
Trinity, bay, Newf., Can D5 152
Trinity, isl., Alsk D9 167
Trinity, mtn., Idaho F3 177
Trinity, mtn., Nev C3 192
Trinity, mts., Calif B2 170
Trinity, range, Nev C3 192
Trinity, riv., Calif B2 170
Trinity, riv., Tex D5 206
Trinity Center, Calif B2 170
Trinity Springs, Ind G4 179
Trino, It B2 67
Trinway, Ohio B5 199
Trio, S.C E8 203
Trion, Ga B1 175
Triplett, Mo B4 189
Tripoli, Iowa B5 180
Tripoli, see Tarabulus, Leb.
Tripoli (Țarābulus), Libya C2 101
Tripoli, Wis C4 212
Trípolis, Grc D4 69
Tripolitania: c. 1914 52
in 1922-40 53
Tripolitania (Țarābulus), prov., Libya C2 101
Tripp, S. Dak D8 204
Tripp, co., S. Dak D6 204
Trischen, isl., Ger A4 60
Triste, gulf, Ven A4 133
Tritle, mtn., Ariz C3 168
Triumph, La E6 183
Triune, Tenn B5 205
Triunfo, Braz C3 138
Trivandrum, India G6 87
Trnava, Czech D4 70
Trobriand, is., Pap k13 110
Trochu, Alta., Can D4 148
Trogir, Yugo D3 68
Trögstad, Nor p29 63
Trois-Pistoles, Que., Can A8 154
Trois Rivières, Que., Can C5 154
Trois-Saumons, Que., Can B7 154
Troisdorf, Ger C2 61
Troisvierges, Lux D6 59
Troitsk, Sov. Un C6 73
Troitskoye, Sov. Un B8 93
Trolldalen, Nor p28 63
Trollhättan, Swe H5 63
Trombetas, riv., Braz C3 139
Trombley, Mich B3 186
Trombudo [Central], Braz D3 137
Tromper, bay, Ger D7 62
Tromsö, Nor C8 63
Trona, Calif E5 170
Tronador, mtn., Arg C2 136
Trondheim, Nor F4 63
Trondheimsfjord, fjord, Nor F3 63
Troodos, mtn., Cyp E9 65
Troon, Scot E4 57
Tropea, It E5 67
Trophy, mtn., B.C., Can D8 149
Tropic, Utah F3 207
Trosa, Swe u35 63
Trosky, Minn G2 187
Trossachs, Sask., Can H3 155
Trotters, N. Dak B2 198
Trotwood, Ohio C1 199
Trough Creek, Pa F5 202
Troup, Tex C5 206
Troup, co., Ga C1 175
Trousdale, Kans E4 181
Trousdale, co., Tenn A5 205
Trousers, lake, N.B., Can B2 151
Trout, La C3 183
Trout, creek, Fla B6 174
Trout, lake, B.C., Can D9 149
Trout, lake, N.W. Ter., Can D8 142
Trout, lake, Ont., Can A5 153
Trout, lake, Minn B6 187
Trout, lake, Wis B4 212
Trout, peak, Wyo A3 213
Trout, riv., Alta., Can A3 148
Trout, riv., Vt B3 208
Trout Creek, Ont., Can B5 153
Trout Creek, Mich A6 186
Trout Creek, Mont C1 190
Trout Creek, Utah D2 207
Trout Creek, pass, Colo C5 171
Trout Dale, Va B3, E1 209
Trout Lake, Mich B5 186
Trout Lake, Wash D4 210
Trout River, Newf., Can D2 152
Trout Run, Pa D7 202
Troutdale, Maine C3 184
Troutdale, Oreg *B4 201
Troutman, Ga E2 175
Troutman, N.C B3 197
Troutville, Va D3 209
Trouville, Fr C4 58
Trowbridge, Eng C5 56
Troy, Ala D4 166
Troy, Idaho C2 177
Troy, Ill E4 178
Troy, Ind H4 179
Troy, Iowa D5 180
Troy, Kans C8 181
Troy, Mich *F7 186
Troy, Miss A5 188
Troy, Mo C7 189
Troy, Mont B1 190
Troy, N.H E2 193
Troy, N.Y C7 196
Troy, N.C B4 197
Troy, Ohio B3 199
Troy, Okla C5 200
Troy, Oreg B9 201
Troy, Pa C8 202
Troy, S.C D3 203
Troy, S. Dak B9 204
Troy, Tenn A2 205
Troy, Vt B4 208
Troy, W. Va B4 211
Troy, peak, Nev E6 192
Troy, ruins, Tur C6 69
Troy Grove, Ill B4 178
Troy Mills, Iowa B6 180
Troyes, Fr C6 58
Trstenik, Yugo D5 68
Traux, Sask., Can H3 155
Trubchevsk, Sov. Un E9 72
Truc Giang, Viet G7 89
Truchas, N. Mex A4 195
Trucial Coast, see United Arab Emirates, country, Asia
Trucial States, see United Arab Emirates, country, Asia
Truckee, Calif C3 170
Truckee, riv., Nev D2 192
Truesdale, Iowa *B2 180
Truesdale, Mo *C6 189
Truitt, peak, Yukon, Can D6 142
Trujillo, Hond C4 130
Trujillo, N. Mex B5 195
Trujillo, Peru C2 134
Trujillo, Sp C3 65
Trujillo, Ven B3 133
Trujillo, state, Ven B3 133
Trujillo Alto, P.R B6 132
Trujillo Alto, mun., P.R B6 132
Truk, is., Caroline Is 114
Truman, Minn G4 187
Trumann, Ark B5 169
Trumansburg, N.Y C4 196
Trumbauersville, Pa *F11 202
Trumbull, Conn E4 172
Trumbull, Nebr D7 191
Trumbull, co., Ohio A7 199
Trumbull, mtn., Ariz A2 168
Trŭn, Bul D6 68
Truro, N.S., Can D6 151
Truro, Eng D2 56
Truro, Iowa C4 180
Truro, Mass C7 185
Truscott, Tex C3 206
Trussville, Ala B3, E5 166
Truth or Consequences, N. Mex D2 195
Trutnov, Czech C3 70
Truxton, Ariz B2 168
Truxton, Mo B6 189
Truxton, N.Y C4 196
Tryon, Nebr C5 191
Tryon, N.C D4 197
Tryon, Okla B5 200
Trysil, Nor G5 63
Trzcianka, Pol B4 70
Trzebiatowo, Pol A3 70
Trzebinia, Pol C5, g10 70
Trzebnica, Pol C4 70
Tsagaan Hamar, Mong C2 92
Tsala Apopka, lake, Fla D4 174
Tsane, Bots B3 107
Tsang, China E7 92
Tsanghsien, China E7 92
Tsangpo (Brahmaputra), riv., China C8 87
Tsaratanana, Malag g9 107
Tsau, Bots B3 107
Tsavo, Ken B6 106
Tschetter Colony, S. Dak D8 204
Tschida, lake, N. Dak C4 198
Tselinograd (Akmolinsk), Sov. Un C8 73
Tsetsey Suma, Mong C1 92
Tshabong, Bots C3 107
Tshela, Zaire B1 106
Tshikapa, Zaire C3 106
Tshilongo, Zaire D4 106
Tshimbo, Zaire C4 106
Tshofa, Zaire C4 106
Tshuapa, riv., Zaire B3 106
Tsiafojavona, mtn., Malag g9 107
Tsihombe, Malag i9 107
Tsimlyansk, res., Sov. Un D2 73
Tsinan (Chinan), China D8 91
Tsinghai, prov., China D4 91
Tsinghai, see Koko Nor, lake, China
Tsingmai, China C8 89
Tsingtao (Chingtao), China D9 91, F9 92
Tsingyüan, see Paoting, China
Tsinling Shan, mts., China E6 91
Tsintsabis, S.W. Afr A2 107
Tsiroanomandidy, Malag g9 107
Tsis, isl., Truk 114
Tsitsutl, peak, B.C., Can C5 149
Tsivory, Malag h9 107
Tskhakaya, Sov. Un A14 85
Tskhinvali, Sov. Un E2 73
Tsna, riv., Sov. Un C2 73
Tsodilo, mtn., Bots A3 107
Tsoshui, China H3 92
Tsu, Jap I8, o15 93
Tsu-Shima, isl., Jap I4 93
Tsuchiura, Jap H10, m19 93
Tsugaru, strait, Jap F10 93
Tsukan, isl., Okinawa 114
Tsulukidze, Sov. Un A14 85
Tsumeb, S.W. Afr A2 107
Tsumis, S.W. Afr B2 107
Tsunami, Okinawa 114
Tsunghua, China G7 92
Tsunhua, China D7 92
Tsuni, China K2 92
Tsurikake, Jap E9 93
Tsuruga, Jap I8, n15 93
Tsuruoka, Jap G9 93
Tsushima, Jap n15 93
Tsushima, strait, Jap I4 93
Tsuyama, Jap I7 93
Tsuyung, China F5 91
Túa, riv., Port B2 65
Tual, Indon G8 90
Tualatin, Oreg *B4 201
Tualatin, riv., Oreg B1 201
Tuam, Ire D2 55
Tuamotu (Low), arch., Fr. Polynesia H13 113
Tuangku, isl., Indon K2 89
Tuanshantzu, see Jaoho, China
Tuapse, Sov. Un *E6 71
Tuasivi, cape, W. Sam 114
Tuatapere, N.Z Q11 112
Tuath, bay, Scot D2 57
Tuba City, Ariz A4 168
Tubac, Ariz F4 168
Tubarão, Braz D3 137
Tūbās, Jordan B7, f12 84
Tuberose, Sask., Can G1 155
Tübingen, Ger E4 61
Tubre, It C6 66
Țubruq (Tobruk), Libya C4 101
Tucacas, Ven A4 133
Tucannon, canyon, Wash C8 210
Tucannon, riv., Wash C8 210
Tucano, Braz D3 138
Tuchola, Pol B4 70
Tuchüan, China B9 92
Tuckahoe, N.J E3 194
Tuckahoe, N.Y D1 196
Tuckahoe, creek, Md C6 173
Tuckahoe, riv., N.J E3 194
Tucker, Ark C4 169
Tucker, Ga A5 175
Tucker, Miss D4 188
Tucker, Tex D5 206
Tucker, co., W. Va B5 211
Tucker, isl., N.J D4 194
Tuckerman, Ark B4 169
Tuckernuck, isl., Mass D7 185
Tuckerton, N.J D4 194
Tucson, Ariz E5 168
Tucumán, Arg E2 135
Tucumán, prov., Arg E2 135
Tucumcari, N. Mex B6 195
Tucumcari, mtn., N. Mex B6 195
Tucupita, Ven B5 133
Tucuruí, Braz C5 139
Tuczna, riv., Pol m13 70
Tucznobaby, Pol g10 70
Tudela, Sp A5 65
Tufi, Pap k12 111
Tug, fork, W. Va., Ky C2 211
Tugaloo, lake, Ga., S.C B1 203
Tugaske, Sask., Can G2 155
Tuguegarao, Phil B6 90
Tuho, N. Cal 115
Tuho, cape, N. Cal 115
Tuira, riv., Pan F9 130
Tukangbesi, is., Indon G6 90
Tūkrah (Tocra), Libya C4 101
Tuktoyaktuk, N.W. Ter., Can C6 144
Tukums, Sov. Un C4 72
Tukuyu, Tan C5 106
Tukwila, Wash D1 210
Tukzar, Afg D13 86
Țūl Karm, Jordan B7, f11 84
Tula, Mex C5 129
Tula, Miss A4 188
Tula, Sov. Un C1 73
Tulagi, Florida I 115
Tulalip, Indian res., Wash A3 210
Tulancingo, Mex C5, m14 129
Tulare, Calif D4 170
Tulare, S. Dak C7 204
Tulare, co., Calif D4 170
Tularosa, N. Mex D3 195
Tularosa, val., N. Mex E3 195
Tulcán, Ec A2 134
Tulcea, Rom C9 68
Tulchin, Sov. Un G7 72
Tule River, Indian res., Calif E4 170
Tuléar, Malag h8 107
Tulelake, Calif B3 170
Tuli, Rh B4 107
Tulia, Tex B2 206
Tullahassee, Okla B6 200
Tullahoma, Tenn B5 205
Tullamore, Ire D3 55
Tulle, Fr E4 58
Tullins, Fr E6 58
Tulln, Aus D8 60
Tullos, La C3 183
Tully, Austl C8 111
Tully, N.Y C4 196
Tullytown, Pa *F2 202
Țulmaythah, Libya F3 85
Tuloma, riv., Sov. Un C15 63
Tulot, Ark B5 169
Tulsa, Okla A6 200
Tulsa, co., Okla B6 200
Tulu Wallel, mtn., Eth D3 105
Tuluá, Col C2 133
Tulufan, see Turfan, China
Tulun, Sov. Un D13 71
Tulyehualco, Mex h9 129
Tuma, riv., Nic D5 130
Tumaco, Col C2 133
Tumaco, bay, Col C2 133
Tumacacori, Ariz F4 168
Tumacacori, nat. mon., Ariz F4 168
Tumatumari, Guy A3 139
Tumba, Swe t35 63
Tumba, lake, Zaire B2 106
Tumbarumba, Austl G7 112
Tumbaya, Arg D2 135
Tumbes, Peru B1 134
Tumbes, dept., Peru B1 134
Tumble, mtn., Mont E6 190
Tumbling Shoals, Ark B3 169
Tumen, China C10 91
Tumen, riv., China E4 93
Tumeremo, Ven B5 133
Tumkur, India F6 87
Tumnin, riv., Sov. Un A10 93
Tumon, bay, Guam 114
Tump, range, Wyo D2 213
Tumtum, Wash B8 210
Tumu, Ghana D4 103
Tumucumaque, mts., Braz B4 139
Tumurisk, sand dunes, Iran D8 86
Tumut, Austl G7 112
Tumwater, Wash B3 210
Tunas, pt., P.R D7 132
Tunas de Zaza, Cuba E4 131
Tunaycha, lake, Sov. Un C11 93
Tunb, isl., Iran H7 86
Tunbridge, Vt D4 208
Tunbridge Wells, Eng C8 56
Tunchi, China J8 92
Tunduru, Tan D6 106
Tundzha, riv., Bul D8 68
Tung Nghia, Viet *G8 89
Tunga, China F7 92
Tunga, riv., India E6 87
Tungan, China G8 91
Tungcheng, China I7 92
Tungchiang, China I7 92
Tungchiang (Lahasusu), China C6 93
Tunghai, China E8 91
Tungho, China C4 93
Tunghsiang, China J7 92
Tunghsing, China G6 91
Tunghua, China F2 93
Tungjen, China K3 92
Tungkuan, China G4 92
Tungkuang, China F7 92
Tungla, Nic D5 130
Tungliao (Payintala), China C10 92
Tungning, China D5 93
Tungpei, China B10 91
Tungping, China G7 92
Tungpu, see Rangsum, China
Tungsheng, China E3 92
Tungsunitewang, China C6 92
Tungtai, China H9 92
Tungting, lake, China J5 92
Tungtzu, China J2 92
Tungurahua, prov., Ec B2 134
Tunhua, China C10 91
Tuni, India I9 88
Tunica, Miss A3 188
Tunica, co., Miss A3 188
Tuninga, riv., Braz D5 133
Tunis, Tun F11 64, B7 102
Tunis, gulf, Tun F12 64
Tunis Mills, Md C5 173
TUNISIA, country, Afr B6 102
Tunja, Col B3 133
Tunk, lake, Maine D4 184
Tunkhannock, Pa C10 202
Tunkí, Nic D5 130
Tunnel Hill, Ga B1 175
Tunnel Springs, Ala D2 166
Tunnelton, Ind G5 179
Tunnelton, W. Va B5 211
Tunnibuli, Santa Isabel I 115
Tunö, isl., Den C4 62
Tuntatuliak, Alsk C7 167
Tununak, Alsk C6 167
Tunungayualok, isl., Newf., Can g9 152
Tunuyán, Arg A3 136
Tunuyán, riv., Arg A3 136
Tuolumne, Calif D3 170
Tuolumne, co., Calif C4 170
Tuolumne, riv., Calif D3 170
Tupã, Braz C2 137
Tupelo, Ark B4 169
Tupelo, Miss A5 188
Tupelo, Okla C5 200
Tupiza, Bol D2 135
Tupman, Calif E4 170
Tupper, B.C., Can B7 149
Tupper, lake, N.Y A6 196
Tupper Lake, N.Y A6, B2 196
Tuppers Plains, Ohio C6 199
Tupperville, Ont., Can E2 153
Tupungato, Arg A3 136
Tupungato, mtn., Arg A3 136
Túquerres, Col C2 133
Țūr, Jordan m14 84
Tura, India E13 88
Tura, Sov. Un C13 71
Tura, riv., Sov. Un B6 73
Tūrān, Iran D8 86
Turan, lowland, Sov. Un E5 73
Turbaco, Col A2 133
Turbat, Pak C3 87
Turbeville, S.C D7 203
Turbo, Col B2 133
Turbotville, Pa D8 202
Turčiansky Svätý Martin, Czech D5 70
Turda, Rom B6 68
Turek, Pol B5 70
Turfan (Tulufan), China C2 91
Turfan, depression, China E11 71
Turgay, Sov. Un D6 73
Turgay, riv., Sov. Un D6 73
Tŭrgovishte, Bul D8 68
Turgutlu, Tur C6 69
Turi, Sov. Un B5 72
Turi, pt., Braz B2 138
Turia, riv., Sp C5 65
Turiaçu, Braz B1 138
Turiaçu, riv., Braz B1 138
Turin, Alta., Can E4 148
Turin, Ga C2 175
Turin, Iowa B2 180
Turin (Torino), It D3 66, B1 67
Turin, N.Y B5 196
Turinsk, Sov. Un B6 73
Turiy Rog, Sov. Un D5 93
Turiyā, riv., Sov. Un F5 72
Turk Mine, Rh A4 107
Turka, Sov. Un G4 72
Turkestan, Sov. Un E7 73
Turkestan: in 1914 52
Túrkeve, Hung B5 68
Turkey, N.C C5 197
Turkey, Tex B2 206
TURKEY, country, Asia, Eur C10 85
after World War I 53
after World War II 54
Turkey, creek, Nebr D8 191
Turkey, creek, Okla A3 200
Turkey, pt., Md B5 173
Turkey, riv., Iowa B6 180
Turkmen S.S.R., rep., Sov. Un E5 73
Turks, is., Turks & Caicos Is E8 131

TURKS & CAICOS ISLANDS, Br. dep., N.A. E8 131
Turks Island, passage, Ba. Is E8 131
Turku, Fin G10 63
Turkwel, riv., Ken A6 106
Turley, Okla A6 200
Turlock, Calif D3 170
Turmus 'Ayyā, Jordan B7 84
Turnbull, mtn., Ariz D5 168
Turneffe, is., Br. Hond B4 130
Turner, Kans B8 181
Turner, Maine D2 184
Turner, Mich D7 186
Turner, Mont B8 190
Turner, Oreg C2, C4 201
Turner, co., Ga E3 175
Turner, co., S. Dak D8 204
Turner, mtn., Conn C2 172
Turner Valley, Alta., Can D3 148
Turners, Tenn A5 205
Turners Falls, Mass A2 185
Turnersville, Tex D4 206
Turnerville, Wyo C2 213
Turney, Mo B3 189
Turnhout, Bel C4 59
Turnor, lake, Sask., Can B1 155
Turnov, Czech C3 70
Tŭrnovo, Bul D7 68
Turnu-Măgurele, Rom D7 68
Turnu-Severin, Rom C6 68
Turö, isl., Den C4 62
Turon, Kans E5 181
Turpin, Okla D3 200
Turrell, Ark B5 169
Turret, peak, Ariz C4 168
Turriff, Scot C6 57
Turtkul, Sov. Un E6 73
Turtle, bay, Espíritu Santo I 115
Turtle, lake, Sask., Can D1 155
Turtle, mts., Man., Can., N. Dak A5 198
Turtle, riv., Ont., Can E5 150
Turtle Creek, N.B., Can D5 151
Turtle Creek, Pa B6 202
Turtle Lake, N. Dak B5 198
Turtle Lake, Wis C1 212
Turtle Mountain, Indian res., N. Dak A6 198
Turtle Mountain, prov. park, Man., Can E1 150
Turtle River, Minn C4 187
Turtleford, Sask., Can D1 155
Turton, S. Dak B7 204
Turugart, pass, China, Sov. Un E9 73
Turukhansk, Sov. Un C11 71
Turvo, riv., Braz m7 137
Tuscaloosa, Ala B2 166
Tuscaloosa, co., Ala B2 166
Tuscaloosa, dam, Ala B2 166
Tuscany, reg., It C3 67
in 1721 49
in 1815 50
in 1860 51
Tuscarawas, co., Ohio B6 199
Tuscarawas, riv., Ohio B6 199
Tuscarora, Nev B5 192
Tuscarora, Indian, res., N.Y B2 196
Tuscarora, mts., Nev C5 192
Tuscarora, mts., Pa F6 202
Tuscola, Ill D5 178
Tuscola, Miss C4 188
Tuscola, Tex C3 206
Tuscola, co., Mich E7 186
Tusculum, ruins, It h9 67
Tuscumbia, Ala A2 166
Tuscumbia, Mo C5 189
Tushan, China L2 92
Tushihkou, China D6 92
Tushka, Okla C5 200
Tuskahoma, Okla C6 200
Tuskegee, Ala C4 166
Tuskegee Institute, Ala C4 166
Tusket, N.S., Can F4 151
Tustin, Calif F3 170
Tustin, Mich D5 186
Tustumena, lake, Alsk g16 167
Tūt, Iran E7 86
Tutamoe, mtn., N.Z K14 112
Tutayev, Sov. Un C12 72
Tuthill, S. Dak D4 204
Tuticorin, India G6 87
Tutrakan, Bul C8 68
Tuttle, Idaho G4 177
Tuttle, N. Dak B5 198
Tuttle, Okla B4 200
Tuttle, lake, Iowa, Minn A3 180
Tuttle Creek, dam, Kans C7 181
Tuttle Creek, res., Kans C7 181
Tuttlingen, Ger E4 60
Tutubu, Tan C5 106
Tutuila, isl., Am. Sam 114
Tututalak, mtn., Alsk B7 167
Tutwiler, Miss A3 188
Tuve, Swe A5 62
Tuvu, Fiji 114
Tuvutha, isl., Fiji 114
Tuxedo, N.C D3 197
Tuxedo Park, N.Y D2, D6 196
Tuxford, Sask., Can G3 155
Tuxpan, Mex C3, m11 129
Tuxpan, Mex C5, m15 129
Tuxpan, Mex n12 129
Tuxpan, riv., Mex m15 129
Tuxtepec, Mex n15 129
Tuxtepec, riv., Mex n15 129
Tuxtla, Mex D6 129
Túy, Sp A1 65
Tuy Hoa, Viet F8 89
Tuyen Quang, Viet B6 89
Tuymazy, Sov. Un C4 73
Tuyün, China K2 92
Tuz, lake, Tur C9 85
Tuz Khurmatli, Iraq D2 86
Tuzigoot, nat. mon., Ariz C3 168
Tuzla, Yugo C4 68
Tuzlu, salt lake, Iran D4 86
Twaiyya, Sau. Ar I13 85
Tweed, Ont., Can C7 153
Tweed, riv., Scot E5 57
Tweedsmuir, prov. park, B.C., Can C4 149
Tweedy, mtn., Mont D6 190
Twelve Mile, Ind C5 179
Twelvepole, creek, W. Va C2 211
Twentymile, creek, W. Va C3 211
Twentynine Palms, Calif E5 170
Twickenham, Eng *m11 55
Twig, Minn D6 187
Twiggs, co., Ga D3 175
Twillingate, Newf., Can D4 152
Twillingate, dist., Newf., Can D4 152
Twillingate, is., Newf., Can D4 152
Twin, buttes, Oreg C4 201
Twin, creek, Ohio C3 199
Twin, lakes, Conn A3 172
Twin, lakes, Iowa B3 180
Twin, lakes, Maine C4 184
Twin, mts., Wyo D7 213
Twin, peaks, Idaho E4 177
Twin Bridges, Mont E4 190
Twin Brooks, S. Dak B9 204
Twin City (Summit and Graymont), Ga D4 175
Twin Falls, Idaho G4 177
Twin Falls, co., Idaho G4 177
Twin Lake, Mich E4 186
Twin Lakes, Calif *D2 170
Twin Lakes, Colo B4 171
Twin Lakes, Ga F3 175
Twin Lakes, Wis F1 212
Twin Lakes, mtn., N.Y B6 196
Twin Mountain, N.H B3 193
Twin Rocks, Pa F4 202
Twin Valley, Minn C2 187
Twining, Mich D7 186
Twinsburg, Ohio A6 199
Twinton, Tenn C8 205
Twisp, Wash A5 210
Two Butte, creek, Colo D8 171
Two Buttes, Colo D8 171
Two Creeks, Man., Can D1 150
Two Guns, Ariz B4 168
Two Harbors, Minn C7 187
Two Hills, Alta., Can C5 148
Two Mile, beach, N.J F3 194
Two Prairie, bayou, Ark D6 169
Two Rivers, Wis B6, D6 212
Two Rivers, riv., Minn B1 187
Two Sicilies, kingdom of the:
in 1815 50
in 1860 51
Twodot, Mont D6 190
Twoforks, riv., Sask., Can C2 155
Ty Ty, Ga E3 175
Tyachev, Sov. Un A6 68
Tyaskin, Md D6 173
Tyborön, Den B2 62
Tyborön, canal, Den B2 62
Tychy, Pol g9 70
Tye, Tex *C3 206
Tye River, Va D4 209
Tygart, lake, W. Va B5, 7 211
Tygart River, falls, W. Va A7 211
Tygart Valley, riv., W. Va A7, B4 211
Tygarts, creek, Ky B7 182
Tyger, riv., S.C B4 203
Tygh Valley, Oreg B5 201
Tyhee, Idaho G6 177
Tyler, Ala C3 166
Tyler, Minn F2 187
Tyler, Mo E8 189
Tyler, Pa D4 202
Tyler, Tex C5 206
Tyler, Wash D6 210
Tyler, co., Tex D5 206
Tyler, co., W. Va B4 211
Tyler, branch, Vt B3 208
Tylersville, Pa E7 202
Tylerton, Md E5 173
Tylertown, Miss D3 188
Tymochtee, creek, Ohio B4 199
Týn nad Vltavou, Czech D9 61
Tyndall, Man., Can D3 150
Tyndall, S. Dak E8 204
Tyndinskiy, Sov. Un D15 71
Tyndrum, Scot D4 57
Tyne, riv., Eng C5 55
Tyne, riv., Scot E6 57
Tyne Valley, P.E.I., Can C6 151
Týnec, Czech o18 70
Tynemouth, Eng C6 55
Tyner, Sask., Can G1 155
Tyner, Ind B5 179
Tyner, Ky C6 182
Tyner, N.C A7 197
Tyner, Tenn D8, E10 205
Tyngsboro, Mass A5 185
Tynset, Nor F4 63
Tyonek, Alsk C9, g16 167
Tyre (Sur), Leb A7 84
Tyringham, Mass B1 185
Tyro, Ark D4 169
Tyro, Kans E8 181
Tyrol, reg., Aus: c. 1721 49
see also Tirol
Tyrone, Colo D6 171
Tyrone, Ky B5 182
Tyrone, Mo D6 189
Tyrone, N. Mex E1 195
Tyrone, Okla D3 200
Tyrone, Pa E5 202
Tyronza, Ark B5 169
Tyrrell, co., N.C B7 197
Tyrrell, lake, Austl G4 112
Tyrrhenian, sea, It D3 67
Tyson, Vt E3 208
Tyukalinsk, Sov. Un B8 73
Tyuleniy, isl., Sov. Un B12 93
Tyumen, Sov. Un B7 73
Tyvan, Sask., Can G4 155
Tzekwei, China E7 91
Tzukung, China F5 91
Tzuli, China J4 92
Tzupo, China F7 92
Tzuyang, China G7 92
Tzuyang, China H3 92
Tzuyuan, China K4 92

U

U, cape, Ponape 114
Uarai, pass, N. Cal 115
Uardere, Eth D6 105
Uatumã, riv., Braz C3 139
Uaupés, Braz D4 133
Uaupés, riv., Braz C4 133
Ubá, Braz C4, g6 137
Ubaíra, Braz D3 138
Ubaitaba, Braz D3 138
Ubanghi, French 99
Ubangi, riv., Afr A2 106
Ubangi-Shari, see Central African Republic, country, Afr.
Ubatche, N. Cal 115
Ubaye, riv., Fr E2 66
Ube, Jap I5 93
Ubeda, Sp C4 65
Uberaba, Braz E1 138
Uberlândia, Braz E1 138
Überlingen, Ger E4 60
Ubiaja, Nig E6 103
Ubly, Mich E8 186
Ubombo, S. Afr C5 107
Uborka, Sov. Un D7 93
Ubort, riv., Sov. Un F6 72
Ubrique, Sp D3 65
Ubundi, Zaire F5 104
Ucayali, riv., Peru C3 134
Uccen Jargga, mtn., Nor C8 63
Uccle, Bel D4 59
Uch-Aral, Sov. Un D10 73
Uchisa, Peru C2 134
Uchiura, bay, Jap E10 93
Ücker, riv., Ger B6 60
Ucluelet, B.C., Can E5 149
Ucon, Idaho F7 177
Ucross, Wyo A6 213
Udaipur, India D5 87, E4 88
Udall, Kans E6 181
Udall, Mo E5 189
Udaquiola, Arg B5 136
Uddevalla, Swe H4 63
Uden, Neth C5 59
Udgir, India H6 88
Udhampur, India B6 87
Udine, It A4 67
Udjung Pandang, Indon G5 90
Udon Thani, Thai D5 89
Udot, isl., Truk 114
Uea, isl., Loyalty Is 115
Ueckermünde, Ger B7 60
Ueda, Jap H9, m17 93
Uegoa, N. Cal 115
Uehling, Nebr C9 191
Uélé, riv., Zaire A3 106
Uelen, Sov. Un C22 71
Uelkal, Sov. Un C21 71
Uelzen, Ger B5 60
Uen, isl., N. Cal 115
Ueno, Jap o15 93
Uetersen, Ger E3 62
Ufa, Sov. Un C5 73
Uffenheim, Ger D5 61
Ugab, riv., S.W. Afr B2 107
Ugalla, riv., Tan C5 106
UGANDA, country, Afr A5 106
Ugashik, Alsk D8 167
Ugashik, lakes, Alsk D8 167
Ugie, riv., Scot C7 57
Ugil, isl., Sol. Is 115
Ugines, Fr D2 66
Uglegorsk (Esutoru), Sov. Un B11 93
Uglich, Sov. Un B1 73
Ugra, riv., Sov. Un D10 72
Ugŭrchin, Bul D7 68
Uh, riv., Czech., Sov. Un D7 70
Uherské Hradiště, Czech D4 70
Uhlava, riv., Czech D8 61
Uhrichsville, Ohio B6 199
Uhrinĕves, Czech n18 70
Uhu, Malaita I 115
Uie, bay, N. Cal 115
Uig, Scot B2 57
Uig, Scot C2 57
Uíge, dist., Ang C2 106
Uijec, isl., Truk 114
Uijŏngbu, Kor *H3 93
Uiju (Gishu), Kor C9 91
Uil, Sov. Un D4 73
Uil, riv., Sov. Un D4 73
Uinamarca, lake, Bol., Peru C2 135
Uinta, co., Wyo D2 213
Uintah, Utah *B4 207
Uintah, co., Utah D6 207
Uintah, mts., Utah C5 207
Uintah and Ouray, Indian res., Utah D5 207
Uitenhage, S. Afr D4 107
Uithuizen, Neth A6 59
Uitoe, pass, N. Cal 115
Ujae, atoll, Marshall Is 115
Ujelang, isl., Marshall Is F9 113
Uji, Jap *I7 93
Uji, isl., Jap K4 93
Ujidomai, Okinawa 114
Ujiji, Tan B4 106
Ujjain, India D6 87, F5 88
Uka, Okinawa 114
Uka, Sov. Un D19 71
Ukerewe, isl., Tan B5 106
Ukhta, Sov. Un C8 71
Ukhta, Sov. Un E14 63
Ukiah, Calif C2 170
Ukiah, Oreg B8 201
Ukmergė, Sov. Un D5 72
Ukraine (S.S.R.), rep., Sov. Un E5 71
c. 1950 54
Ulaan Goom, Mong B3 91
Ulalu, isl., Truk 114
Ulan Bator (Urga), Mong B6 91
Ulan-Ude, Sov. Un D13 71
Ulawa, isl., Sol. Is 115
Ulchin, Kor H4 93
Ulcinj, Yugo E4 68
Uldza, riv., Mong B7 91
Ulen, Ind D5 179
Ulen, Minn C2 187
Ulfborg, Den B2 62
Ulhasnagar, India *H4 88
Uliassutai, see Jibhalanta, Mong.
Ulifauro, pass, Truk 114
Ulindi, riv., Zaire B4 106
Ulithi, is., Pac. O F8 113
Ulla, Sov. Un D7 72
Ulla, riv., Sp A1 65
Ulladulla, Austl G8 112
Ullapool, Scot C3 57
Ullared, Swe A6 62
Ullin, Ill F4 178
Ullswater, lake, Eng F6 57
Ullŭng, isl., Kor H5 93
Ulm, Ark C4 169
Ulm, Ger E4 61
Ulm, Mont C5 190
Ulm, Wyo A6 213
Ulman, Mo C5 189
Ulmer, mtn., Ant B4 120
Ulmers, S.C E5 203
Ulricehamn, Swe I5 63
Ulsan, Kor I4 93
Ülsen, Ger B6 59
Ulster, Pa C8 202
Ulster, co., N.Y D6 196
Ulu, mtn., Tur B7 69
Ulugh Muztagh, mtn., China A8 87
Ulva, isl., Scot D2 57
Ulverston, Eng C5 55
Ulverstone, Austl o15 111
Ulyanovka, Sov. Un s31 63
Ul'yanovsk, Sov. Un C3 73
Ulysses, Kans E2 181
Ulysses, Nebr C8 191
Ulysses (Lewisville), Pa C6 202
Ulzburg, Ger E3 62
Uman', Sov. Un G8 72
Uman isl., Truk 114
Umarkot, Pak E2 88
Umatac, bay, Guam 114
Umatilla, Fla D5 174
Umatilla, Oreg B7 201
Umatilla, co., Oreg B8 201
Umatilla, Indian res., Oreg B8 201
Umatilla, lake, Oreg., Wash B6 201
Umatilla, riv., Oreg B7 201
Umbagog, lake, N.H A4, B2 193
Umbria, reg., It C4 67
Umbuzeiro, Braz C3, h6 138
Umcolcus, lake, Maine B4 184
Umeå, Swe F9 63
Umeälven, riv., Swe E8 63
Umhausen, Aus B6 66
Umiat, Alsk B9 167
Umm al Maradim, isl., Sau. Ar G4 86
Umm el Fahm, Isr B7 84
Umm el Nabâyil, cape, Eg C2 84
Umm Keddada, Sud C2 105
Umm Khunān, Eg E3 84
Umm Ruwāba, Sud C3 105
Umnak, isl., Alsk E6 167
Umpire, Ark C1 169
Umpqua, Oreg D3 201
Umpqua, riv., Oreg D3 201
Umptanum, ridge, Wash C5 210
Umsaskis, lake, Maine B3 184
Umtali, Rh A5 107
Umtata, S. Afr D4 107
Umtingalu, New Britain I 115
Umuahia, Nig E6 103
Umvuma, Rh A5 107
Umzinto, S. Afr D5 107
Una, Tenn E9 205
Una, riv., Braz k6 138
Una, riv., Yugo C2 68
Unadilla, Ga D3 175
Unadilla, Nebr F2 191
Unadilla, N.Y C5 196
Unadilla, riv., N.Y C5 196
Unaka, mts., N.C., Tenn C4 197
Unalakleet, Alsk C7 167
Unalaska, Alsk E6 167
Unalaska, isl., Alsk E6 167
Unango, Moz D6 106
'Unayzah, Sau. Ar *D8 101
Uncas, Okla A5 200
Uncasville, Conn D8 172
Uncía, Bol C2 135
Uncompahgre, butte, Colo C2 171
Uncompahgre, mts., Colo C3 171
Uncompahgre, peak, Colo C3 171
Uncompahgre, plat., Colo C2 171
Uncompahgre, riv., Colo C3 171
Undaga, isl., Bis. Arch 115
Underhill, Vt B3 208
Underhill Center, Vt B3 208
Underwood, Ala B3 166
Underwood, Ind G6 179
Underwood, Iowa C2 180
Underwood, Minn D3 187
Underwood, N. Dak B4 198
Underwood, Wash D4 210
Undu, cape, Fiji 114
Unea, isl., Bis. Arch 115
Unecha, Sov. Un E9 72
Unezhma, Sov. Un F17 63
Unga, Alsk D7 167
Ungarie, Austl F6 112
Ungava, bay, N.W. Ter., Can A3 154
Unggi, Kor E5 93
Unhošt', Czech n17 70
União, Braz B2 138
União da Vitória, Braz D2 137
União dos Palmares, Braz C3, k6 138
Unicoi, Tenn C11 205
Unicoi, co., Tenn C11 205
Unicoi, mts., N.C D2 197
Unicoi, mts., Tenn D9 205
Unije, isl., Yugo C2 68
Unimak, isl., Alsk E7 167
Unimak, pass, Alsk E6 167
Union, Ark A4 169
Union, Ill A5 178
Union, Ind H3 179
Union, Iowa B4 180
Union, Ky A5 182
Union, La B5, D5 183
Union, Maine D3 184
Union, Miss C4 188
Union, Mo C6 189
Union, Nebr D10, E3 191
Union, N.H D4 193
Union, N.J B4 194
Union, N.C A6 197
Union, N. Dak A8 198
Union, Ohio *C3 199
Union, Okla B4 200
Union, Oreg B9 201
Union, S.C B4 203
Union, Wash B2 210
Union, W. Va D4 211
Union, co., Ark D3 169
Union, co., Fla B4 174
Union, co., Ga B2 175
Union, co., Ill F4 178
Union, co., Iowa C8 180
Union, co., Ky C1 182
Union, co., Miss A4 188
Union, co., N.J B4 194
Union, co., N. Mex A6 195
Union, co., N.C B3 197
Union, co., Ohio B4 199
Union, co., Oreg B8 201
Union, co., Pa E7 202
Union, co., S.C B4 203
Union, co., S. Dak E9 204
Union, co., Tenn C10 205
Union, par., La B3 183
Union, lake, N.J E2 194
Union, riv., Maine D4 184
Union Bay, B.C., Can E5 149
Union Beach, N.J C4 194
Union Bridge, Md A3 173
Union Center S. Dak C3 204
Union Center, Wis E3 212
Union City, Calif B5 170
Union City, Ga B4, C2 175
Union City, Ind D8 179
Union City, Mich F5 186
Union City, N.J B5 194
Union City, Ohio *B3 199
Union City, Pa C2 202
Union City, Tenn A2 205
Union Creek, Oreg E4 201
Union Dale, Pa C11 202
Unión de Reyes, Cuba D3 131
Unión de Tula, Mex m11 129
Union Flat, creek, Wash C8 210
Union Furnace, Ohio C5 199
Union Gap, Wash C5 210
Union Grove, Wis F1, F5 212
Union Hall, Va D3 209
Union Mills, Ind B4 179
Union Mills, Md A3 173
Union of South Africa, see South Africa, country, Afr.
Union of Soviet Socialist Republics, see Soviet Union, country, Eur., Asia
Union Pier, Mich G4 186
Union Point, Man., Can E3 150
Union Point, Ga C3 175
Union Springs, Ala C4 166
Union Springs, N.Y C4 196
Union Star, Mo B3 189
Union Village, R.I B10 172
Union Village, Vt D4 208
Union Village, res., Vt C2 193
Uniondale, Ind C7 179
Uniondale, N.Y *G2 172
Uniontown, Ala C2 166
Uniontown, Ind H4 179
Uniontown, Kans E9 181
Uniontown, Ky C2 182
Uniontown, Md A3 173
Uniontown, Mo D8 189
Uniontown, Ohio B6 199
Uniontown, Pa G2 202
Uniontown, Wash C8 210
Unionville, Ont., Can D5, E7 153
Unionville, Conn B5 172
Unionville, Ga *E3 175
Unionville, Ill B4 178
Unionville, Iowa D5 180
Unionville, Maine D5 184
Unionville, Mich E7 186
Unionville, Mo A4 189
Unionville, N.C B3 197
Unionville, Ohio A7 199
Unionville, Tenn B5 205
Unionville, Va C5 209
Unionville Center, Ohio B4 199
Unisan, Phil p13 90
United, Pa F3 202
UNITED ARAB EMIRATES, country, Asia G8 77
United Arab Republic, see Egypt, country, Afr.
UNITED KINGDOM OF GREAT BRITAIN AND NORTHERN IRELAND, country, Eur 55
in 1810 50
United Nations Headquarters, N.Y D6 194
United Netherlands: c. 1721 49
United Pueblos, Indian res., N. Mex A3 195
UNITED STATES, country, N.A 160
during revolution 162
in 1775-1800 162
in 1800-50 163
during Civil War 164
United States, westward expansion of 163
U.S. Air Force Academy, Colo C6 171
U.S. Naval Ammunition Depot, Nev E3 192
Unity, Sask., Can E1 155
Unity, Ill F4 178
Unity, Maine D3 184
Unity, N.H D2 193
Unity, Oreg C8 201
Unity, Wis D3 212
Unity, dam, Oreg C8 201
Unityville, S. Dak D8 204
Universal, Ind E3 179
Universal City, Tex B4 206
Universales, mts., Sp B5 65
University, Miss A4 188
University City, Mo A8, C7 189
University Heights, Ohio B2 199
University Park, Iowa C5 180
University Park, Md *C4 173
University Park, N. Mex E3 195
University Park, Tex B5 206
Unlingen, Ger A5 66
Unna, Ger B2 61
Unnen, lake, Swe B7 62
Unsan, Kor G2 93
Unsernherrn, Ger E6 61
Unst, isl., Scot g10 55
Unstrut, riv., Ger B5 61
Unterwalden, canton, Switz C4 66
Unuk, riv., B.C., Can A2 149
Unuwhao, mtn., N.Z K14 112
Unwin, Sask., Can E1 155
Ünye, Tur B11 85
Unzha, riv., Sov. Un B2 73
Uondo, Eth D4 105
Uorra Ilu, Eth C4 105
Upalco, Utah C5 207
Upemba, lake, Zaire C4 106
Upernavik, Grnld B20 118
Upham, N. Dak A5 198
Upia, riv., Col C3 133
Upington, S. Afr C3 107
Upland, Calif E5, F3 170
Upland, Ind D7 179
Upland, Nebr D7 191
Upland, Pa *G11 202
Upolu, isl., W. Sam 114
Upolu, pt., Haw C6 176
Upper, reg., Ghana D4 103
Upper Ammonoosuc, riv., N.H A4 193
Upper Arlington, Ohio C2, B4 199
Upper Arrow, lake, B.C., Can D8 149
Upper Black Eddy, Pa E11 202
Upper Blackville, N.B., Can C4 151
Upper Brookville, N.Y *D3 196
Upper Canada 146
Upper Darby, Pa B11, G11 202
Upper Fairmount, Md D6 173
Upper Falls, Md B5 173
Upper Frenchville, Maine A4 184
Upper Gagetown, N.B., Can D3 151
Upper Ganges, canal, India C6 88
Upper Giuba, dist., Som E5 105
Upper Gloucester, Maine D5, E2 184
Upper Humber, riv., Newf., Can D3 152
Upper Indian Pond, lake, Newf., Can D3 152
Upper Iowa, riv., Iowa A5 180
Upper Island Cove, Newf., Can E5 152
Upper Jay, N.Y B3 196
Upper Kapuas, mts., Indon., Mala E4 90
Upper Kent, N.B., Can C2 151

INDEX KEY Each place listed in **Bold-faced Type** has its population listed in the Population tables pages 230 to 280.
Each country shown in CAPITAL LETTERS has its population listed in the World Political Information Table, pages 6 to 10.
* Does not appear on map; key shows general location.

Upper Klamath, lake, Oreg E4 201
Upper Lough Erne, lake, N. Ire C3 55
Upper Marlboro, Md C4 173
Upper Musquodoboit, N.S., Can D7 151
Upper New York, bay, N.J., N.Y. E5 194
Upper Nile, reg., Sud D3 105
Upper Nyack, N.Y *D7 196
Upper Red, lake, Minn B4 187
Upper Sackville, N.B., Can D5 151
Upper Saddle River, N.J A4 194
Upper Sandusky, Ohio B4 199
Upper Seal, lake, Que., Can E18 142
Upper Silesia, reg., Pol g9 70
Upper Strasburg, Pa F6 202
Upper Tract, W. Va C5 211
UPPER VOLTA, country, Afr D4 103
Upper Wilson, pond, Maine C3 184
Upper Wood Harbour, N.S., Can F4 151
Upperco, Md A4 173
Upperville, Va C5 209
Uppsala, Swe H7, t35 63
Upsala, Minn E4 187
Upsalquitch, N.B., Can B3 151
Upshur, co., Tex C5 206
Upshur, co., W. Va C4 211
Upson, co., Ga D2 175
Upson, Wis B3 212
Upton, Que., Can D5 154
Upton, Ky C4 182
Upton, Maine D1 184
Upton, Mass B4, D1 185
Upton, Mo D5 189
Upton, Utah C4 207
Upton, Wyo A8 213
Upton, co., Tex D1 206
Urabá, gulf, Col B2 133
Uracas, see Pajaros, isl., Mariana Is.
Uracoa, Ven B5 133
Urakawa, Jap E11 93
Ural, Mont B1 190
Ural, mts., Sov. Un C5 73
Ural, riv., Sov. Un C5 73
Ural'sk, Sov. Un C4 73
Urandí, Braz D2 138
Urania, La C3 183
Uranium City, Sask., Can A1 155
Uraricoera, riv., Braz C5 133
Urasi, cove, Malaita I 115
Uravan, Colo C2 171
Urawa, Jap I9, n18 93
Urbana, Ark D3 169
Urbana, Ill C5 178
Urbana, Ind C6 179
Urbana, Iowa B6 180
Urbana, Md B3 173
Urbana, Mo D4 189
Urbana, N. Dak C7 198
Urbana, Ohio B4 199
Urbancrest, Ohio C2 199
Urbandale, Iowa A7, C4 180
Urbank, Minn D3 187
Urbanna, Va D6 209
Urbino, It C4 67
Urcos, Peru D3 134
Urdaneta, Phil o13 90
Urdy, is., Bis. Arch 115
Urdzhar, Sov. Un D10 73
Ure, riv., Eng F7 57
Ureparapara, isl., New Hebr 115
Ures, Mex B2 129
Urfa, Tur D12 85
Urga, see Ulan Bator, Mong.
Urga Sov. Un E5 73
Urgench, Sov. Un E6 73
Urgun, Afg E14 86
Urgut, Sov. Un B13 86
Uri, canton, Switz C4 66
Uriah, Ala D2 166
Uribia, Col A3 133
Urich, Mo C4 189
Urique, Mex B3 129
Uritsk, Sov. Un s31 63
Urk, Neth B5 59
Urla, Tur C6 69
Urmi, riv., Sov. Un B6 93
Urmia, salt lake, Iran C2 86
Uroyan, mts., P.R. C3 132
Urr, riv., Scot F5 57
Urrao, Col B2 133
Ursa, Ill C2 178
Ursatyevskaya, Sov. Un E7 73
Ursina, Pa G3 202
Ursine, Nev F7 192
Uruapan, Mex D4, n13 129
Urubamba, Peru D3 134
Urubamba, riv., Peru C3 134
Urubú, riv., Braz C3 139
Urucará, Braz C3 139
Uruçuí, Braz C3 139
Urucuia, riv., Braz E1 138
Uruguai, riv., Braz D2 137
Uruguaiana, Braz E1 137
URUGUAY, country, S.A. E1 137
in 1814-28 127
Uruguay, riv., Arg., Ur A5 136
Urukthapel, isl., Palau Is 114
Urumchi (Wulumuchi), China C2 91
Urungu, riv., China B2 91
Uruno, pt., Guam 114
Urusha, Sov. Un D15 71
Uryupinsk, Sov. Un C2 73
Urzhum, Sov. Un B3 73
Urziceni, Rom C8 68
Usak, Tur C7 69
Usakos, S.W. Afr B2 107
Usedom, Ger E7 62
Usedom, isl., Ger E8 62
Ush-Tobe, Sov. Un D9 73
Ushaki, Sov. Un s32 63
Usher, Fla C4 174
Ushi, pt., Tinian 114
Ushturinan Kuh, mtn., Iran E4 86
Ushuaia, Arg h12 136
Usingen, Ger C3 61
Usk, B.C., Can B3 149
Usk, Wash A8 210
Üsküdar, Tur B7 69, B7 85
Uslar, Ger B4 61
Uslava, riv., Czech D8 61
Usman, Sov. Un E12 72
Usol'ye-Sibirskoye, Sov. Un D13 71
Uspallata, pass, Arg., Chile A3 136
Uspenskiy, Sov. Un D8 73
Usquepaugh, R.I C10 172
Ussel, Fr E5 58
Ussuri, riv., China, Sov. Un C7 93
Ussuriysk, Sov. Un E16 71, E6 93
Ust-Aldan, Sov. Un C15 71
Ust-Bolsheretsk, Sov. Un D18 71
Ust-Ishim, Sov. Un B8 73
Ust-Kamchatsk, Sov. Un D19 71
Ust'-Kamenogorsk, Sov. Un C10 73
Ust-Kut, Sov. Un D13 71
Ust-Maya, Sov. Un C16 71
Ust-Olenek, Sov. Un B14 71
Ust-Srednikan, Sov. Un C18 71
Ust-Tsilma, Sov. Un C8 71
Ust-Tym, Sov. Un B9 73
Ust-Tyrma, Sov. Un A5 93
Ust-Urt, plat., Sov. Un E5 73
Ust-Usa, Sov. Un C8 71
Uster, Switz B4 66
Ústí nad Labem, Czech C3 70
Ustica, isl., It E4 67
Ustka, Pol A4 70
Ustyuzhna, Sov. Un B11 72
Usulután, Sal D3 130
Utah, state, U.S. 207
in 1850 163
Utah, co., Utah C4 207
Utah, lake, Utah C4 207
Utajärvi, Fin E12 63
Ute, Iowa B2 180
Ute, creek, N. Mex A6 195
Ute Mountain, Indian res., Colo D2 171
Utete, Tan C6 106
Utica (North Utica), Ill B4 178
Utica, Ind H6 179
Utica, Kans D3 181
Utica, Ky C2 182
Utica, Mich A8, F7 186
Utica, Miss C3 188
Utica, Mo B4 189
Utica, Mont D6 190
Utica, Nebr D8 191
Utica, N.Y B5 196
Utica, Ohio B5 199
Utica, Okla D5 200
Utica, Pa D2 202
Utica, S.C *B1 203
Utica, S. Dak E8 204
Utiel, Sp C5 65
Utik, lake, Man., Can B4 150
Utikuma, lake, Alta., Can B3 148
Utirik, atoll, Marshall Is 115
Utleyville, Colo D7 171
Utö, isl., Swe u36 63
Utopia, Tex E3 206
Utopia, lake, N.B., Can D3 151
Utrata, riv., Pol m13 70
Utrecht, Neth B5 59
Utrecht, prov., Neth B5 59
Utrera, Sp D3 65
Utsjoki, Fin C12 63
Utsunomiya, Jap H9 93
Uttar Pradesh, state, India C6 87
Uttaradit, Thai D4 89
Utterson, Ont., Can B5 153
Uttoxeter, Eng B6 56
Utuado, P.R B4 132
Utuado, mun., P.R B4 132
Utulei, Am. Sam 114
Uusikaupunki, Fin G9 63
Uvada, Utah F1 207
Uvalda, Ga D4 175
Uvalde, Tex E3 206
Uvalde, co., Tex E3 206
Úvaly, Czech n18 70
Uvarovo, Sov. Un E14 72
Uvat, Sov. Un B7 73
Uverite, pt., Fiji 114
Uvinza, Tan C5 106
Uvira, Zaire B4 106
Uwharrie, riv., N.C B4 197
Uwajima, Jap J6 93
Uxbridge, Ont., Can C5 153
Uxbridge, Eng k12 55
Uxbridge, Mass B4 185
Uyak, Alsk D9 167
Uyuni, Bol D2 135
Uyuni, salt flat, Bol D2 135
Uzbek S.S.R., rep., Sov. Un E9 71
Uzès, Fr E6 58
Uzh, riv., Sov. Un F7 72
Uzhgorod, Sov. Un G4 72
Uzlovaya, Sov. Un E11 72
Uzunköprü, Tur B6 69

V

Vaal, riv., S. Afr C4 107
Vaals, Neth D5 59
Vaasa, Fin F9 63
Vác, Hung B4 68
Vaca, key, Fla H5 174
Vaca, pt., P.R f13 132
Vaca, pt., P.R g12 132
Vacaria, Braz D2 137
Vacaville, Calif B6, C2 170
Vaccina, riv., It h8 67
Vacha, Ger C5 61
Vacherie, La B6 183
Vacia Talega, pt., P.R B7 132
Vader, Wash C3 210
Vadis, W. Va B4 211
Vadito, N. Mex A4 195
Vadnais Heights, Minn *F5 187
Vado, N. Mex E3 195
Vadsö, Nor B13 63
Vaduz, Liech B5 66
Vagay, Sov. Un B7 73
Vagnhärad, Swe u35 63
Vagos, Port B1 65
Váh, riv., Czech D4 70
Vaholi, bay, New Georgia I 115
Vaiden, Miss B4 188
Vaigai, riv., India G6 87
Vaigalu, W. Sam 114
Vaihingen [an der Enz], Ger E3 61
Vail, Ariz E5 168
Vail, Iowa B2 180
Vail, lake, Scot D4 57
Vail Homes, N.J *C4 194
Vailele, bay, W. Sam 114
Vails, N.J B2 194
Vaitele, bay, W. Sam 114
Vakfikebir (Büyükliman), Tur B12 85
Vakhrushev, Sov. Un B11 93
Val Barrette, Que., Can C2 154
Val-David, Que., Can C3 154
Val-d'Or, Que., Can E9 153
Val Marie, Sask., Can H2 155
Val Morin, Que., Can C3 154
Val Racine, Que., Can D6 154
Val Verde, co., Tex E2 206
Valais, canton, Switz C3 66
Valatie, N.Y C7 196
Valcartier Village, Que., Can C6, C8 154
Valcheta, Arg C3 136
Valcourt, Que., Can D5 154
Valdagno, It D7 66
Valday, Sov. Un C9 72
Valday, hills, Sov. Un C9 72
Valdemarsvik, Swe H7 63
Valdemorillo, Sp o16 65
Valdepeñas, Sp C4 65
Valders, Wis B6, D6 212
Valdes, isl., B.C., Can A9 149
Valdés, pen., Arg C4 136
Valdese, N.C B2 197
Valdez, Alsk C10, g18 167
Valdez, Colo D6 171
Valdilecha, Sp p18 65
Valdivia, Chile B2 136
Valdivia, Col B2 133
Valdivia, prov., Chile B2 136
Valdobbiadene, It D7 66
Valdosta, Ga F3 175
Våle, Nor p28 63
Vale, Oreg D9 201
Vale, S. Dak C2 204
Vale, Tenn A3 205
Valeene, Ind H5 179
Valemount, B.C., Can C8 149
Valença, Braz D3 138
Valença, Port A1 65
Valença do Piauí, Braz C2 138
Valence, Fr E6 58
Valencia, Ariz G1 168
Valencia, Pa E2 202
Valencia, Sp C2 65
Valencia, Sp C5 65
Valencia, Ven A4 133
Valencia, co., N. Mex C1 195
Valencia, reg., Sp C5 65
Valencia, isl., Ire E1 55
Valenciennes, Fr B5 58
Valentigney, Fr D7 58
Valentine, Ariz B2 168
Valentine, Mont C8 190
Valentine, Nebr B5 191
Valentine, Tex F2 206
Valera, Ven B3 133
Valga, Sov. Un *B5 72
Valhalla, N.Y D3, D7 196
Valhalla, mts., B.C., Can E2 148
Valhermoso Springs, Ala A3 166
Valier, Ill E4 178
Valier, Mont B4 190
Valier, Pa E3 202
Valjevo, Yugo C4 68
Valka, Sov. Un C6 72
Valkeakoski, Fin G11 63
Valkenswaard, Neth C5 59
Valki, Sov. Un G10 72
Vall de Uxó, Sp C5 65
Valladolid, Ec B2 134
Valladolid, Mex C7 129
Valladolid, Sp B3 65
Vallauris, Fr F7 58
Valle de Bravo, Mex n13 129
Valle de la Pascua, Ven B4 133
Valle de Santiago, Mex m13 129
Valle del Cauca, dept., Col C2 133
Valle Grande, Bol C3 135
Valle Grande, mts., N. Mex F5 195
Vallecas, Sp B4, p17 65
Vallecito, Colo D3 171
Vallecito, res., Colo D3 171
Vallecitos, N. Mex A3 195
Valledupar, Col A3 133
Vallée Jonction, Que., Can C7 154
Vallejo, Calif B5, C2 170
Vallenar, Chile E1 135
Valles Mines, Mo C7 189
Valletta, Malta G14 64
Valley, Nebr C9, D2 191
Valley, Wash A8 210
Valley, Wyo A3 213
Valley, co., Idaho E3 177
Valley, co., Mont B10 190
Valley, co., Nebr C6 191
Valley, creek, Ala E4 166
Valley, riv., Man., Can D1 150
Valley Bend, W. Va C4 211
Valley Brook, Okla *B4 200
Valley Center, Kans B5, E6 181
Valley Centre, Sask., Can F2 155
Valley City, Ill D3 178
Valley City, N. Dak C8 198
Valley City, Ohio A6 199
Valley Cottage, N.Y D1 196
Valley Falls, Kans B7, C8 181
Valley Farms, Ariz E4 168
Valley Forge, Pa A10 202
Valley Grove, W. Va A4, B2 211
Valley Head, Ala A4 166
Valley Head, W. Va C4 211
Valley Lee, Md D4 173
Valley Mills, Ind H7 179
Valley Mills, Tex D4 206
Valley Park, Miss C3 188
Valley Park, Mo B7 189
Valley Spring, Tex D3 206
Valley Springs, Ark A3 169
Valley Springs, S. Dak D9 204
Valley Station, Ky A4 182
Valley Stream, N.Y E2 196
Valley View, Ill *A5 179
Valley View, Ky C5 182
Valley View, Ohio *A6 199
Valley View, Pa E8 202
Valley View, Tex C4 206
Valleyfield, Newf., Can D5 152
Valleyfield, Que., Can D3, E8 154
Valleyford, Wash B8, D8 210
Valleyview, Alta., Can B2 148
Valleyview, B.C., Can *D7 149
Valli di Comacchio, lake, It E8 66
Valliant, Okla C6 200
Vallo della Lucania, It D5 67
Vallonia, Ind G5 179
Vallorbe, Switz C2 66
Valls, Sp B6 65
Vallscreek, W. Va D3 211
Valmeyer, Ill E3 178
Valmiera, Sov. Un C5 72
Valmont, Que., Can C5 154
Valmontone, It h9 67
Valmy, Nev C4 192
Valognes, Fr C3 58
Valois, Que., Can D8 154
Valois, N.Y C4 196
Valona, see Vlorë, Alb.
Valparai, India *F6 87
Valparaiso, Sask., Can E3 155
Valparaíso, Chile A2 136
Valparaiso, Fla G2 174
Valparaiso Ind B3 179
Valparaiso, Mex C4 129
Valparaiso, Nebr C9 191
Valparaíso, prov., Chile A2 136
Valpe, Espiritu Santo I 115
Valréas, Fr E6 58
Valsch, cape, Indon G9 90
Valua, isl., New Hebr 115
Value, Miss C3 188
Valuyki, Sov. Un F12 72
Valverde, Dom. Rep F8 131
Valverde del Camino, Sp D2 65
Valyermo, Calif F3 170
Vambu, isl., Bis. Arch 115
Vamdrup, Den C3 62
Vamori, Ariz F4 168
Van, Tex C5 206
Van, Tur C14 85
Van, W. Va D6 211
Van, lake, Tur C14 85
Van Alstyne, Tex C4 206
Vananda, Mont D10 190
Van-Bruyssel, Que., Can B5 154
Van Buren, Ark B1 169
Van Buren, Ind C6 179
Vanburen, Ky C4 182
Van Buren, Maine A5 184
Van Buren, Mo E6 189
Vanburen, Ohio A4 199
Van Buren, co., Ark B3 169
Van Buren, co., Iowa D5 180
Van Buren, co., Mich F4 186
Van Buren, co., Tenn D8 205
Vance, Miss A3 188
Vance, S.C E7 203
Vance, Tex E2 206
Vance, co., N.C A5 197
Vanceboro, Maine C5 184
Vanceboro, N.C B6 197
Vanceburg, Ky B6 182
Vancleave, Miss E5 188
Vancouver, B.C., Can A9, E6 149
Vancouver, Wash D3 210
Vancouver, isl., B.C., Can E4 149
Vancouver, ranges, B.C., Can D4 149
Vandalia, Ill E4 178
Vandalia, Mo B6 189
Vandalia, Mont B10 190
Vandalia, Ohio *C3 199
Vandemere, N.C B7 197
Vander Wagen, N. Mex B1 195
Vanderbilt, Mich C6 186
Vanderbilt, Pa F2 202
Vanderbilt, Tex E4 206
Vanderbilt, peak, N. Mex E1 195
Vanderburgh, co., Ind H2 179
Vandergrift, Pa E2 202
Vanderhoof, B.C., Can C5 149
Vanderpool, Tex E3 206
Vandervoort, Ark C1 169
Van Diemen, cape, Austl B5 110
Van Diemen, gulf, Austl B5 110
Vandiver, Ala B3 166
Vandling, Pa C11 202
Vanduser, Mo E8 189
Vandyne, Wis B5 212
Vanegas, Mex C4 129
Vänern, lake, Swe H5 63
Vänersborg, Swe H5 63
Van Etten, N.Y C4 196
Vanga, Ken B6 106
Vånga, Swe B8 62
Vangaindrano, Malag h9 107
Vanguard, Sask., Can H2 155
Vanguna, isl., Sol. Is 115
Van Hill, Tenn C11 205
Van Hiseville, N.J C4 194
Van Horn, Tex F2 206
Van Horne, Iowa B5 180
Vanier, Ont., Can A9 153
Vankleek Hill, Ont., Can B10 153
Van Kull, kill, N.J E5 194
Van Lear, Ky C7 182
Vanleer, Tenn A4 205
Vanlue, Ohio B4 199
Van Meter, Iowa C4 180
Vanna, Ga B3 175
Vanndale, Ark B5 169
Vannes, Fr D2 58
Van Norman, Mont C10 190
Vanoss, Okla C4 200
Van Rees, mts., Indon F9 90
Vanrhynsdorp, S. Afr D2 107
Vansant, Va B3 209
Vanscoy, Sask., Can F2 155
Vantage, Sask., Can H2 155
Van Tassell, Wyo C8 213
Vanua Lava, isl., New Hebr 115
Vanua Levu, isl., Fiji 114
Vanua Mbalavu, isl., Fiji 114
Vanua Vatu, isl., Fiji 114
Vanves, Fr g10 58
Van Vleck, Tex G4 206
Van Vleet, Miss B5 188
Van Wert, Ga C1 175
Van Wert, Iowa D4 180
Van Wert, Ohio B3 199
Van Wert, co., Ohio B3 199
Van Winkle, Miss C3 188
Van Wyck, S.C B6 203
Van Wyksvlei, S. Afr D3 107
Van Yen, Viet B6 89
Van Zandt, co., Tex C5 206
Vanzant, Mo E5 189
Vārāhi, India F3 88
Varallo, It D4 66
Varangerfjord, fjord, Nor B14 63
Varano, lake, It D5 67
Varaždin, Yugo B3 68
Varazze, It B2 67
Varberg, Swe I5 63
Vardaman, Miss B4 188
Vardar, riv., Yugo E5 68
Varde, Den C2 62
Vardenis, Sov. Un B15 85
Vardö, Nor B14 63
Varel, Ger B4 60
Varella, cape, Viet F8 89
Varena, Sov. Un A8 70
Varennes, Que., Can D4, D9 154
Vareš, Yugo C4 68
Varese, It D4 66, B2 67
Varginha, Braz C3 137
Vári, Grc h11 69
Varilla, Chile D1 135
Varina, Iowa B3 180
Varina, Va C7 209
Varkaus, Fin F12 63
Varna, Bul D8 68
Varna, Ont., Can D3 153
Varna, Ill B4 178
Varna, co., Bul D8 68
Varnado, La D6 183
Värnamo, Swe I6 63
Varnell, Ga *B2 175
Varner, Kans B4 181
Varney, Ont., Can C4 153
Varney, Mont E5 190
Varnsdorf, Czech C3 70
Varnville, S.C F5 203
Väröbacka, Swe A6 62
Várpalota, Hung B4 68
Vars, Ont., Can A10 153
Varysburg, N.Y C2 196
Varzi, It E5 66
Varzuga, riv., Sov. Un D17 63
Vashon, Wash B3, D1 210
Vashon, isl., Wash D1 210
Vashon, pt., Wash D1 210
Vasilkov, Sov. Un F8 72
Vaslui, Rom B8 68
Vass, N.C B4 197
Vassar, Man., Can E4 150
Vassar, Kans D8 181
Vassar, Mich E7 186
Vassouras, Braz h6 137
Västerås, Swe H7, t34 63
Västerhaninge, Swe t36 63
Västervik, Swe I7 63
Vasto, It C5 67
Vasyugan, riv., Sov. Un B9 73
Vaternish, pt., Scot C2 57
Vathí, Grc D6 69
Vatia, pt., Fiji 114
VATICAN CITY, country, Eur D4, h8 67
Vaticano, cape, It E5 67
Vatilau, isl., Sol. Is 115
Vatomandry, Malag g9 107
Vatra-Dornei, Rom B7 68
Vättern, lake, Swe H6 63
Vatu Leile, isl., Fiji 114
Vatu Vara, isl., Fiji 114
Vaucluse, S.C D4 203
Vaucouleurs, Fr F5 59
Vaud, canton, Switz C2 66
Vaudreuil, Que., Can D3, D8 154
Vaudreuil, co., Que., Can D3 154
Vaughan, Ont., Can *D5 153
Vaughan, Miss C3 188
Vaughan, N.C A6 197
Vaughan, W. Va C7 211
Vaughn, Mont C5 190
Vaughn, N. Mex C4 195
Vaughn, Oreg C3 201
Vaughns Gap, Tenn E9 205
Vaughnsville, Ohio B3 199
Vaupés, comisaría, Col C3 133
Vaupés, riv., Col C3 133
Vauvillers, Fr B2 66
Vauxhall, Alta., Can D4 148
Vavoua, I.C E3 103
Vawn, Sask., Can D1 155
Vaxholm, Swe t36 63
Växjö, Swe I6 63
Våxtorp, Swe B7 62
Vay, Idaho A2 177
Vaygach, isl., Sov. Un C8 71
Vayland, S. Dak C7 204
Veachland, Ky B4 182
Veadeiros, plat., Braz D1 138
Vealmoor, Tex C2 206
Veazie, Maine D4 184
Veberöd, Swe C7 62
Veblen, S. Dak B8 204
Vechta, Ger F2 62
Vechte, riv., Ger B6 59
Veckholm, Swe t35 63
Vecsés, Hung B4 68
Vedado, Cuba h11 131
Vedea, riv., Rom C7 68
Vederslöv, Swe B8 62
Vedia, Arg A4 136
Veedersburg, Ind D3 179
Veendam, Neth A6 59
Vega, Tex B1 206
Vega, isl., Nor E4 63
Vega Alta, P.R B5 132
Vega Alta, mun., P.R B5 132
Vega Baja, P.R B5 132
Vega Baja, mun., P.R B5 132
Vegreville, Alta., Can C4 148
Veguita, N. Mex C3 195
Veinticinco de Mayo, Arg A3 136
Veinticinco de Mayo, Arg B3 136
Veinticinco de Mayo, Arg B4 136
Veisali, Guadalcanal I 115
Vejen, Den C3 62
Vejer, Sp D3 65
Vejle, Den C3 62
Vejle, co., Den C3 62
Vejprty, Czech C2 70
Vela, cape, Col A3 133
Velarde, N. Mex A4 195
Velasco, Tex E5 206
Velbert, Ger B2 61
Velda, Mo *C7 189
Velda Village Hills, Mo *C7 189
Velden, Ger A8 66
Velebit, mts., Yugo C2 68
Velestínon, Grc C4 69
Vélez, Col B3 133
Vélez-Blanco, Sp D4 65
Vélez-Málaga, Sp D3 65
Vélez-Rubio, Sp D4 65
Velgast, Ger D6 62
Velhas, riv., Braz E2 138
Velika, riv., Yugo E5 68
Velikaya, riv., Sov. Un C7 72
Velikiye Ustyug, Sov. Un C7 71
Velikiye Luki, Sov. Un C8 72
Vélingara, Sen D2 103
Velizh, Sov. Un D8 72
Velké Meziříčí, Czech D4 70
Vella, gulf, Sol. Is 115
Vella Lavella, isl., Sol. Is 115
Velletri, It D4, h9 67
Vellinge, Swe C7 62
Vellore, India F6 87
Velma, Okla C4 200
Velpen, Ind H3 179
Velsen, Neth B4 59
Velsk, Sov. Un C16 41
Veltrusy, Czech n17 70
Velva, N. Dak A5 198
Velvary, Czech n17 70
Vemb, Den B2 62
Ven, isl., Swe C6 62
Venaco, Fr C2 67
Venado Tuerto, Arg A4 136
Venango, Nebr D3 191
Venango, Pa C1 202
Venango, co., Pa D2 202
Vendée, hills, Fr D3 58
Vendôme, Fr D4 58
Vendrell, Sp B6 65
Venedocia, Ohio B3 199
Veneta, Oreg C3 201

Veneta, lagoon, It........D8 66
Venetia: in 1815........ 50
in 1866........ 51
Venetian Alps, mts., It....A4 67
Venetian Village, Ill......*A6 178
Venetie, Alsk........B10 167
Veneto, reg., It........A3 67
Venev, Sov. Un........D12 72
Venezia, see Venice, It.
VENEZUELA, country, S.A........B4 133
in 1830........ 127
Venezuela, gulf, Ven.......A3 133
Veniaminof, mtn., Alsk....D8 167
Venice, Alta., Can........B4 148
Venice, Fla........E4 174
Venice, Ill........E3 178
Venice (Venezia), It........D8 66, B4 67
Venice, La........E6 183
Venice, Nebr........D2 191
Venice, Ohio........A5 199
Venice, Utah........E4 207
Venice, republic of: c. 1360........ 48
in 1721........ 49
Venice, gulf, It........B4 67
Vénissieux, Fr........E6 58
Venkatapuram, India......H8 88
Venlo, Neth........C6 59
Venn, Sask., Can........F3 155
Vennachar, Ont., Can.....B7 153
Veno, isl., Den........B2 62
Venssimo Sarmento, Ang........C3 106
Vent, Aus........C6 66
Venta, riv., Sov. Un........C3 72
Ventana, Ariz........E3 168
Venter, riv., Aus........B6 66
Ventimiglia, It........C1 67
Ventnor, Ont., Can........C9 153
Ventnor, Eng........D6 56
Ventnor City, N.J........E4 194
Venton, Md........D6 173
Ventoux, mtn., Fr........E6 58
Ventspils, Sov. Un........C3 72
Ventuari, riv., Ven........C4 133
Ventura, Calif........E4 170
Ventura, Iowa........A4 180
Ventura, co., Calif........E4 170
Venturia, N. Dak........D6 198
Venus, Fla........E5 174
Venus, Pa........D3 202
Venus, Tex........B5 206
Venustiano Carranza, Mex........D6 129
Vera, Arg........E3 135
Vera, Okla........A6 200
Vera, Sp........D5 65
Vera, Tex........C3 206
Vera Cruz, Ind........C7 179
Veracruz, Mex......D5, n15 129
Veracruz, state, Mex........C5, m15 129
Veranopolis, Braz........D2 137
Veraval, India........G3 88
Verbania, It........D4 66
Verbena, Ala........C3 166
Vercelli, It........B2 67
Vercheres, Que., Can....D4 154
Vercheres, co., Que., Can........D4 154
Verda, Ky........D6 182
Verde, isl., Phil........p13 90
Verde, riv., Ariz........C4 168
Verde, riv., Braz....A1 137, E3 139
Verde, riv., Braz........B2 137
Verde, riv., Braz........C2 137
Verde, riv., Mex........m14 129
Verde, riv., Par........D4 135
Verde Grande, riv., Mex...m12 129
Verde Island Passage, strait, Phil........p13 90
Verdel, Nebr........B7 191
Verden, Ger........B4 60
Verden, Okla........B3 200
Verdi, Minn........F2 187
Verdi, Nev........D2 192
Verdi, peak, Nev........C6 192
Verdigre, Nebr........B7 191
Verdigris, Okla........A6 200
Verdigris, riv., Kans., Okla........E8 181, A6 200
Verdon, Nebr........D10 191
Verdon, S. Dak........B7 204
Verdun, Que., Can........D9 154
Verdun, Fr........C6 58
Verdunville, W. Va.....*D2 211
Vereeniging, S. Afr.....C4 107
Verendrye, N. Dak........A5 198
Vergara, Sp........A4 65
Vergara, Ur........E2 137
Vergas, Minn........D3 187
Vergennes, Ill........F4 178
Vergennes, Vt........C2 208
Verigin, Sask., Can........F4 155
Verín, Sp........B2 65
Verkhne-Kolymsk, Sov. Un........C18 71
Verkhneye, Sov. Un........G12, q21 72
Verkhniy Baskunchak, Sov. Un........D3 73
Verkhniy Ufaley, Sov. Un........B6 73
Verkhnyaya Tunguska, riv., Sov. Un........D12 71
Verkhoyansk, Sov. Un.....C16 71
Verkhoyansk, mts., Sov. Un........C15 71
Verlo, Sask., Can........G1 155
Vermejo Park, N. Mex.....A5 195
Vermilion, Alta., Can......C5 148
Vermilion, Ill........D6 178
Vermilion, Ohio........A5 199
Vermilion, co., Ill........C6 178
Vermilion, par., La........E3 183
Vermilion, bay, La........E3 183
Vermilion, iron range, Minn........C6 187
Vermilion, lake, Minn......C6 187
Vermilion, hills, Sask., Can........G2 155
Vermilion, pass, Alta., Can........D2 148
Vermilion, riv., Alta., Can........C5 148
Vermilion, riv., Ill., Ind........B5 178, D2 179
Vermilion, riv., La........E3 183
Vermilion, riv., Minn........B6 187
Vermilion, riv., Ohio........A5 199
Vermilion Bay, Ont., Can........E5 150
Vermillion Heights, Ill...*C6 178
Vermillion-on-the-Lake, Ohio........*A5 199
Vermillion, Kans........C7 181
Vermillion, S. Dak........E9 204
Vermillion, Utah........E4 207
Vermillion, co., Ind........E3 179
Vermillion, bluffs, Colo......A2 171
Vermillion, riv., Que., Can........B4 154
Vermont, Ill........C3 178
Vermont, state, U.S........ 208
Vermontville, Mich........F5 186
Vernal, Utah........C6 207
Vernalis, Calif........B6 170
Verndale, Minn........D3 187
Verne, Wyo........D2 213
Verner, Ont., Can........A4 153
Verneuil, Fr........C4 58
Verneuk Pan, lake, S. Afr...D3 107
Vernon, Ala........B1 166
Vernon, Ariz........C6 168
Vernon, B.C., Can........D8 149
Vernon, Calif........*F4 170
Vernon, Colo........B8 171
Vernon, Conn........B7 172
Vernon, Del........C6 173
Vernon, Fla........G3 174
Vernon, Fr........C4 58
Vernon, Ill........E4 178
Vernon, Ind........G6 179
Vernon, Mich........*F6 186
Vernon, N.J........A4 194
Vernon, N.Y........*B5 196
Vernon, Okla........B6 200
Vernon, Tenn........B4 205
Vernon, Tex........B3 206
Vernon, Utah........C3 207
Vernon, Vt........F3 208
Vernon, co., Mo........D3 189
Vernon, co., Wis........E3 212
Vernon, par., La........C2 183
Vernon, creek, Ind........G6 179
Vernon, lake, Ont., Can.....B5 153
Vernon Bridge, P.E.I., Can........C7 151
Vernon Center, Minn........G4 187
Vernon Hill, Va........E3 209
Vernon River, P.E.I., Can........C7 151
Vernon Valley, N.Y.....*D3 196
Vernonia, Oreg........B3 201
Vero Beach, Fla........E6 174
Véroia, Grc........B4 69
Verona, Ont., Can........C8 153
Verona, Ill........B5 178
Verona, It........D7 66, B3 67
Verona, Ky........A7 182
Verona, Miss........A5 188
Verona, Mo........E4 189
Verona, N.J........B4 194
Verona, N.C........C6 197
Verona, N. Dak........C7 198
Verona, Ohio........C3 199
Verona, Pa........B6 202
Verona, Tenn........B5 205
Verona, Wis........F4 212
Verona Park, Mich.....*F5 186
Verónica, Arg........g8 136
Verret, lake, La........E4 183
Verrières-le-Buisson, Fr........h10 58
Versailles, Conn........C8 172
Versailles, Fr........C5, g9 58, F2 59
Versailles, Ill........D3 178
Versailles, Ind........F7 179
Versailles, Ky........B5 182
Versailles, Mo........C5 189
Versailles, Ohio........B3 199
Versailles, Pa........*F2 202
Verse, Wyo........B7 213
Versmold, Ger........A3 61
Versoix, Switz........C2 66
Verte, isl., Que., Can.....A8 154
Verte, riv., Que., Can.....B8 154
Vertedero, P.R........C5 132
Vertentes, riv., Braz........E4 139
Verton, Fr........D9 56
Vertou, Fr........D3 58
Vertus, Fr........F4 59
Verviers, Bel........D5 59
Vervins, Fr........C5 58
Verwood, Sask., Can.......H3 155
Verzenay, Fr........C6 58
Veseleyville, N. Dak.....A8 198
Veselí nad Lužnicí, Czech........D9 61
Veseloye, Sov. Un........H10 72
Vesey, Tex........C5 206
Vesoul, Fr........D7 58
Vesper, Kans........C5 181
Vesper, Wis........D4 212
Vesta, C.R........F6 130
Vesta, Minn........F3 187
Vesta, Nebr........D9 191
Vestaburg, Mich........E6 186
Vestal Center, N.Y........C4 196
Vestavia Hills, Ala........E4 166
Vestby, Nor........p29 63
Vesterålen, is., Nor........C6 63
Vesterö Havn, Den........A4 62
Vesteröya, isl., Nor........p28 63
Vestervig, Den........B2 62
Vestmannaeyjar, Ice........o22 63
Vestry, Miss........E5 188
Vesuvius, Va........D3 209
Vesuvius, vol., It........D5 67
Vesyegonsk, Sov. Un.....B11 72
Veszprém, Hung........B3 68
Vésztő, Hung........B5 68
Veteran, Alta., Can........C5 148
Veteran, Wyo........D8 213
Vetlanda, Swe........I6 63
Vetluga, riv., Sov. Un........B3 73
Vetluzhskiy, Sov. Un........B3 73
Vetovo, Bul........D8 68
Vetren, Bul........D7 68
Veurne, Bel........C2 59
Vevay, Ind........G7 179
Vevey, Switz........C2 66
Veynes, Fr........E6 58
Veyo, Utah........F2 207
Vézère, riv., Fr........E4 58
Vezirköprü, Tur........B10 85
Viacha, Bol........C2 135
Viadana, It........B3 67
Viamonte, Arg........A4 136
Vian, Okla........B7 200
Viana, Braz........B2 138
Viana del Bollo, Sp........A2 65
Viana do Alentejo, Port....C1 65
Viana do Castelo, Port......B1 65
Vianen, Neth........C5 59
Vianópolis, Braz........E1 138
Viar, riv., Sp........D3 65
Viareggio, It........C3 67
Vibank, Sask., Can........G4 155
Vibo Valentia, It........E6 67
Viborg, Den........B3 62
Viborg, S. Dak........D8 204
Viborg, co., Den........B3 62
Viburnum, Mo........D6 189
Vic [-en Bigorre], Fr........F4 58
Vic [-sur-Seille], Fr........F6 59
Vicálvaro, Sp........p17 65
Vicco, Ky........C6 182
Vicente, pt., Calif........F2 170
Vicente López, Arg.......*A5 136
Vicenza, It........D7 66, B3 67
Viceroy, Sask., Can........H3 155
Vich, Sp........B7 65
Vichada, comisaría, Col....C3 133
Vichuga, Sov. Un........C13 72
Vichuquén, Chile........A2 136
Vichy, Fr........D5 58, 53
Vichy, Mo........C6 189
Vici, Okla........A2 200
Vick, La........C3 183
Vickery, Ohio........A5 199
Vickery, Tex........B5 206
Vicksburg, Ind........F3 179
Vicksburg, Mich........F5 186
Vicksburg, Miss........C3 188
Vicksburg, nat. mil. park, Miss........C3 188
Viçosa, Braz........C3, k5 138
Viçosa, Braz........F2 138
Viçosa do Ceará, Braz........B2 138
Vicovaro, It........g9 67
Victor, Colo........C5 171
Victor, Idaho........F7 177
Victor, Iowa........C5 180
Victor, Mont........D2 190
Victor, S. Dak........B9 204
Victor Harbor, Austl........G2 112
Victor Mills, S.C........*B3 203
Victoria, Arg........A4 136
Victoria, Cam........F6 103
Victoria, B.C., Can........B9 149
Victoria, Newf., Can........E5 152
Victoria, P.E.I., Can........C6 151
Victoria, Chile........B2 136
Victoria, Hong Kong........G7 91
Victoria, Ill........B3 178
Victoria, Kans........D4 181
Victoria, Miss........A4 188
Victoria, Mo........C7 189
Victoria, Phil........o13 90
Victoria, P.R........B2 132
Victoria, Tenn........D8 205
Victoria, Tex........E4 206
Victoria, Va........E4 209
Victoria, co., N.B., Can....B2 151
Victoria, co., N.S., Can....C9 151
Victoria, co., Ont., Can....C6 153
Victoria, co., Tex........E2 206
Victoria, dist., B.C., Can....E6 149
Victoria, state, Austl........G7 112
Victoria, falls, Rh........H8 96
Victoria, isl., N.W. Ter., Can........B10 142
Victoria, lake, Austl........F3 112
Victoria, lake, Newf., Can........D3 152
Victoria, lake, Afr........G9 96
Victoria, mtn., Pap........k12 110
Victoria, reef, Bis. Arch........ 115
Victoria, riv., Austl........C5 110
Victoria, riv., Newf., Can...D3 152
Victoria, strait, N.W. Ter., Can........C13 142
Victoria Beach, Man., Can........D3 150
Victoria Central, P.R........B2 132
Victoria de las Tunas, Cuba........E5 131
Victoria Falls, Rh........A4 107
Victoria Harbour, Ont., Can........C5 153
Victoria Land, reg., Ant........B29 120
Victoria Mine, Ont., Can........A3 153
Victoria Point, Bur........F10 87
Victoria River Downs, Austl........C5 111
Victoria Road, Ont., Can........C6 153
Victoria West, S. Afr......D3 107
Victoriaville, Que., Can....C6 154
Victorica, Arg........B3 136
Victorino de la Plaza, Arg........B4 136
Victorville, Calif........E5 170
Victory, N.Y........*B7 196
Victory, Wis........E2 212
Victory Gardens, N.J....*B3 194
Victory Heights, N.Y.....*C4 196
Vicuña, Chile........F1 135
Vida, Mont........C11 190
Vidal, Calif........E6 170
Vidalia, Ga........D4 175
Vidalia, La........C4 183
Vidette, Ga........C4 175
Vidin, Bul........D6 68
Vidor, Tex........D5 206
Vidora, Sask., Can........H1 155
Viechtach, Ger........D7 61
Viedma, Arg........C4 136
Vielsalm, Bel........D5 59
Vienenburg, Ger........B5 61
Vienna (Wien), Aus........D8 60
Vienna, Ont., Can........E4 153
Vienna, Ga........D3 175
Vienna, Ill........F5 178
Vienna, Md........D6 173
Vienna, Mo........C6 189
Vienna, N.J........B3 194
Vienna, S. Dak........C8 204
Vienna, Va........B4, C5 209
Vienna, W. Va........B3 211
Vienne, Fr........E6 58
Vienne, riv., Fr........D4 58
Vientiane, Laos........D5 89
Vieques, P.R........g13 132
Vieques, mun., P.R........g13 132
Vieques, isl., P.R........g13 132
Vieques, sound, P.R........g13 132
Viernheim, Ger........D3 61
Viersen, Ger........C6 59
Vierzon, Fr........D5 58
Viesca, Mex........B4 129
Vieste, It........D6 67
VIETNAM, NORTH, country, Asia........C6 89
VIETNAM, SOUTH, country, Asia........F8 89
Vietnam, reg., Asia........D8 89, 83
Viewfield, S. Dak........C3 204
Vigan, Phil........*B6 90
Viger, Que., Can........B8 154
Vigevano, It........B2 67
Vignola, It........E7 66
Vigo, Sp........A1 65
Vigo, co., Ind........F3 179
Vigsö, bay, Den........A2 62
Vihowa, Pak........B5 87, B3 88
Vijayapuri, India........*E6 87
Vijayavada, India........E7 87
Vík, Ice........o23 63
Vikenara, cape, Santa Isabel I........ 115
Vikesund, Nor........p27 63
Viking, Alta., Can........C5 148
Viking, Minn........B2 187
Vikramasingapuram, India........*G6 87
Vila, New Hebr........ 115
Vila Cabral, Moz........D6 106
Vila da Feira, Port........B1 65
Vila da Ponte, Ang........D2 106
Vila de Aljustrel, Ang.....D2 106
Vila de João Belo, Moz.....C5 107
Vila de Manica, Moz........A5 107
Vila de Rei, Port........C1 65
Vila do Conde, Port........B1 65
Vila Fontes, Moz........A6 107
Vila Franca de Xira, Port........C1 65
Vila Gago Coutinho, Ang........D3 106
Vila General Machado, Ang........D2 106
Vila João de Almeida, Ang........E1 106
Vila Junqueiro, Moz........A6 107
Vila Luso, Ang........D2 106
Vila Macedo de Cavaleiros, Ang........D2 106
Vila Marechal Carmona, Ang........C2 106
Vila Mariano Machado, Ang........D1 106
Vila Nova de Fozcoa, Port........B2 65
Vila Nova de Gaia, Port......B1 65
Vila Nova de Milfontes, Port........D1 65
Vila Nova de Seles, Ang........D1 106
Vila Pereira d'Eça, Ang.....E2 106
Vila Pery, Moz........A5 107
Vila Real, Port........B2 65
Vila Real de Santo António, Port........D2 65
Vila Robert Williams, Ang........D2 106
Vila Salazar, Ang........C1 106
Vila Serpa Pinto, Ang......D2 106
Vila Teixeira da Silva, Ang........D2 106
Vila Teixeira de Sousa, Ang........D3 106
Vila Vasco de Gama, Moz........D5 106
Vila Viçosa, Port........C2 65
Vila Vila, Bol........C2 135
Vilaine, riv., Fr........D2 58
Vilanculos, Moz........B6 107
Vilas, Colo........D8 171
Vilas, S. Dak........C8 204
Vilas, co., Wis........B4 212
Vildbjerg, Den........B2 62
Vildo, Tenn........B2 205
Vileyka, Sov. Un........D6 72
Vilhelmina, Swe........E7 63
Viljandi, Sov. Un........B5 72
Vilkaviškis, Sov. Un........A7 70
Vilkovo, Sov. Un........I7 72
Villa Acuña, Mex........B4 129
Villa Ahumada, Mex........A3 129
Villa Alhucemas, Mor.....G5 64
Villa Angela, Arg........E3 135
Villa Aroma, Bol........C2 135
Villa Bella, Bol........B2 135
Villa Cisneros, Sp. Sahara........E1 102
Villa Colón, C.R........F5 130
Villa Constitución, Arg.....A4 136
Villa Crespo, Arg........A4 136
Villa Cuauhtémoc, Mex....k15 129
Villa de Cura, Ven........A4 133
Villa de Guadalupe Hidalgo, Mex........h9 129
Villa del Rosario, Arg......A4 136
Villa Dolores, Arg........A3 136
Villa Federal, Arg........A5 136
Villa García, Mex........k13 129
Villa Grove, Colo........C5 171
Villa Grove, Ill........D5 178
Villa Hayes, Par........E4 135
Villa Huidobro, Arg........A4 136
Villa Iris, Arg........B4 136
Villa María, Arg........A4 136
Villa Montes, Bol........D3 135
Villa Nueva, Arg........A4 136
Villa Obregón, Mex........h9 129
Villa Oliva, Par........E4 135
Villa Park, Ill........F2 178
Villa Pedro Montoya, Mex........m14 129
Villa Pérez, P.R........C3 132
Villa Ranchaero, S. Dak...C3 204
Villa Rica, Ga........C2 175
Villa Ridge, Ill........F4 178
Villa Ridge, Mo........C7 189
Villa Unión, Arg........E2 135
Villa Unión, Mex........C3 129
Villa Valeria, Arg........A4 136
Villablino, Sp........A2 65
Villacañas, Sp........C4 65
Villacarrillo, Sp........C4 65
Villach, Aus........E6 60
Villacidro, It........E2 67
Villafamés, Sp........B5 65
Villafranca, It........B3 67
Villafranca de los Barros, Sp........C2 65
Villafranca del Bierzo, Sp........A2 65
Villafranca del Panadés, Sp........B6 65
Villafranca di Verona, It...D6 66
Villagarcía de Arosa, Sp...A1 65
Village, Ark........D2 169
Village, Va........D6 209
Village, creek, Ala........E4 166
Village Springs, Ala........B3 166
Villaggio Duca degli Abruzzi, Som........E6 105
Villaguay, Arg........A5 136
Villahermosa, Mex........D6 129
Villajoyosa, Sp........C5 65
Villalba, P.R........C5 132
Villalba, Sp........A2 65
Villalba, mun., P.R........C4 132
Villaldama, Mex........B4 129
Villalón, Cuba........k11 131
Villalonga, Arg........B4 136
Villalpando, Sp........B3 65
Villamartín, Sp........D3 65
Villamil, Ec........g5 134
Villanueva, Col........A3 133
Villanueva, N. Mex........B4 195
Villanueva de Córdoba, Sp........C3 65
Villanueva de la Serena, Sp........C3 65
Villanueva del Arzobispo, Sp........C4 65
Villanueva [del Río y Minas], Sp........D3 65
Villanueva y Geltrú, Sp.....B6 65
Villaputzu, It........E2 67
Villard, Minn........E3 187
Villard-Bonnot, Fr........E6 58
Villarreal, Sp........C5 65
Villarrica, Chile........B2 136
Villarrica, Par........E4 135
Villarrobledo, Sp........C4 65
Villarrubia, Sp........C4 65
Villas, N.J........E3 194
Villaverde, Sp........p17 65
Villavicencio, Col........C3 133
Villaviciosa, Sp........A3 65
Villazón, Bol........D2 135
Villazón, Bol........D3 135
Villé, Fr........A3 66
Ville-de Tracy, Que., Can........C4 154
Ville Marie, Que., Can.....E9 153
Ville Platte, La........D3 183
Ville St. Georges, Que., Can........C7 154
Villefranche [-de-Rouergue], Fr........E5 58
Villefranche [-sur-Saône], Fr........E6 58
Villegreen, Colo........D7 171
Villejuif, Fr........g10 58
Villemomble, Fr........g10 58
Villena, Sp........C5 65
Villenaux-la-Grande, Fr....F3 59
Villeneuve-le-Roi, Fr......h10 58
Villeneuve-St. Georges, Fr........h10 58
Villeneuve-sur-Lot, Fr......E4 58
Villeneuve-sur-Yonne, Fr........C5 58
Villepinte, Fr........g11 58
Villeroy, Que., Can........C6 154
Villers-Bretonneux, Fr......E2 59
Villers-Cotterets, Fr........C5 58
Villers-Outréaux, Fr........D3 59
Villerupt, Fr........C6 58
Villeta, Par........E4 135
Villeurbanne, Fr........E6 58
Villia, Grc........g10 69
Villiers-St. Georges, Fr....F3 59
Villingen, Ger........D4 60
Villisca, Iowa........D3 180
Vilna, Alta., Can........B5 148
Vilnius, Sov. Un........D5 72
Vilonia, Ark........B3 169
Vilppula, Fin........F11 63
Vils, riv., Ger........E7 61
Vils, riv., Ger........D6 61
Vilsbiburg, Ger........E7 61
Vilseck, Ger........D6 61
Vilshofen, Ger........E8 61
Vilvoorde, Bel........D4 59
Vilyuy, riv., Sov. Un........C15 71
Vilyuysk, Sov. Un........C15 71
Vimianzo, Sp........A1 65
Vimmerby, Swe........I6 63
Vimperk, Czech........D2 70
Vina, Ala........A1 166
Vina, Calif........C2 170
Viña del Mar, Chile........A2 136
Vinalhaven, Maine........D4 184
Vinalhaven, isl., Maine......D4 184
Vinaroz, Sp........B6 65
Vincennes, Fr........g10 58
Vincennes, Ind........G2 179
Vincennes, bay, Ant........C24 120
Vincent, Ala........B3 166
Vincent, Ark........E8 205
Vincent, Iowa........B3 180
Vincent, La........D2 183
Vincent, Ohio........C6 199
Vincent, Tex........C2 206
Vincentown, N.J........D3 194
Vinces, Ec........B2 134
Vinchina, Arg........E2 135
Vinco, Okla........B4 200
Vindelälven, riv., Swe........E8 63
Vinderup, Den........B2 62
Vindex, Md........D1 173
Vindhya, mts., India........F5 88
Vine Grove, Ky........C4 182
Vinegar, hill, Oreg........C8 201
Vineland, Fla........D5 174
Vineland, N.J........E2 194
Vinemont, Ala........A3 166
Vineyard, sound, Mass......D6 185
Vineyard Haven (Tisbury), Mass........D6 185
Vingåker, Swe........t33 63
Vinh, Viet........C6 89
Vinh Loi, Viet........H6 89
Vinh Long, Viet........G6 89
Vinh Yen, Viet........B6 89
Vinhais, Port........B2 65
Vining, Kans........C6 181
Vining, Minn........D3 187
Vinita, Okla........A6 200
Vinita Park, Mo........*C7 189
Vinkovci, Yugo........C4 68
Vinnitsa, Sov. Un........G7 72
Vinson, Okla........C2 200
Vinson Massif, mtn., Ant...B4 120
Vinton, Iowa........B5 180
Vinton, La........D2 183
Vinton, Ohio........D5 199
Vinton, Va........D3 209
Vinton, co., Ohio........C5 199
Vintondale, Pa........F4 202
Viola, Ark........A4 169
Viola, Del........B6 173
Viola, Idaho........C1 177
Viola, Ill........B3 178
Viola, Kans........E6 181
Viola, Tenn........B6, D8 205
Viola, Wis........E3 212
Viola, Wyo........C2 213
Violet, La........C8 183
Vipiteno, It........C7 66
Vir-Pazar, Yugo........D4 68
Virden, Man., Can........E1 150
Virden, Ill........D4 178
Virden, N. Mex........E1 195
Vire, Fr........C3 58
Vire, riv., Fr........C3 58
Virgelle, Mont........B6 190
Virgenes, cape, Arg........E3 136
Virgil, Kans........E7 181
Virgil, N.Y........C4 196
Virgil, S. Dak........C7 204
Virgilina, Va........E4 209
Virgin, Utah........F2 207
Virgin, mts., Ariz., Nev...G7 192
Virgin, riv., Ariz., Utah...G2 207
Virgin Gorda, isl., Vir. Is........m14 131
VIRGIN ISLANDS, Br. dep., N.A........f16 132
Virgin Islands, nat. park, Vir. Is........f16 132
VIRGIN ISLANDS OF THE U.S., dep., N.A........f15 132
Virginia, Idaho........G6 177
Virginia, Ill........D3 178
Virginia, Minn........C6 187
Virginia, Nebr........D9 191
Virginia, S. Afr........*C4 107
Virginia, state, U.S........ 209
in 17th cent........ 162
in Revolutionary War........ 162
in Civil War........ 164
Virginia, peak, Nev........D2 192
Virginia Beach (Independent City), Va........B7, E7 209

INDEX KEY Each place listed in **Bold-faced Type** has its population listed in the Population tables, pages 230 to 280.
Each country, shown in CAPITAL LETTERS, has its population listed in the World Political Information Table, pages 6 to 10.
* Does not appear on map; key shows general location.

Virginia City, Mont........E5 190
Virginia City, Nev.........D2 192
Virginia Gardens, Fla....*G6 174
Viroflay, Fr................g9 58
Viroqua, Wis.............E3 212
Virovitica, Yugo............C3 68
Virrat, Fin..................F10 63
Virserum, Swe................I6 63
Virton, Bel...................E5 59
Virú, Peru....................C2 134
Virudhunagar, India......*G6 87
Vis, Yugo.....................D3 68
Vis, isl., Yugo..............D3 68
Visakhapatnam,
India............E7 87, I9 88
Visalia, Calif..............D4 170
Visalia, Ky...................A7 182
Visayan, sea, Phil..........C6 90
Visby, Swe....................I8 63
Visconde do Rio Branco,
Braz.......................C4 137
Viscount, Sask., Can......F3 155
Viscount Melville, sound,
N.W. Ter., Can..............B11 142
Višegrad, Yugo...............D4 68
Viseu, Braz..................B1 138
Viseu, Port...................B2 65
Vishera, riv., Sov. Un.......A5 73
Višlanda, Swe................B8 62
Viso, Guadalcanal I............ 115
Viso, mtn., It.......E3 66, B1 67
Visoko, Yugo..................D4 68
Visonau, Fiji.................... 114
Visp, Switz...................C3 66
Vista, Calif................F5 170
Vista, Man., Can..............D1 150
Vista, Mo....................D4 189
Vistula (Frisches Haff),
lagoon, Sov. Un.............A5 70
Visuvisu, pt., New
Georgia I........................ 115
Vita, Man., Can...............E3 150
Vital, S. Dak..................D4 204
Vitanovak, Yugo...............D5 68
Vitarte, Peru...............D2 134
Vitebsk, Sov. Un.............D8 72
Viterbo, It...................C4 67
Viti Levu, bay, Fiji............. 114
Viti Levu, isl., Fiji.............. 114
Vitim, Sov. Un................D14 71
Vitim, riv., Sov. Un.........D14 71
Vitor, Peru...................E3 134
Vitória, Braz................F2 138
Vitória, Braz..................k5 138
Vitoria, Sp...................A4 65
Vitória da Conquista,
Braz........................D2 138
Vitória [de Santo Antão],
Braz..................C3, k6 138
Vitória do Mearim, Braz...B2 138
Vitré, Fr......................C3 58
Vitry-le-Francois, Fr.........C6 58
Vitry [-sur-Seine], Fr.......g10 58
Vittel, Fr......................C6 58
Vittoria, Ont., Can............E4 153
Vittoria, It...................F5 67
Vittorio Veneto, It............B4 67
Vitu, is., Bis. Arch.............. 115
Vivero, Sp.....................A2 65
Vivian, La....................B2 183
Vivian, S. Dak.................D5 204
Vivian, W. Va..................D3 211
Vivoratá, Arg..................B5 136
Viwa, isl., Fiji.................. 114
Vizcaíno, des., Mex..........B2 129
Vizcaíno, mts., Mex..........B2 129
Vize, Tur......................B6 69
Vizianagram,
India...........E7 87, H9 88
Vizille, Fr.....................E6 58
Viziru, Rom....................C8 68
Vizzini, It.....................F5 67
Vlaardingen, Neth...........C4 59
Vladimir, Sov. Un............B2 73
Vladimir Volynskiy,
Sov. Un.......................F5 72
Vladimiro-Aleksandrovskoye,
Sov. Un.......................E6 93
Vladimirovka, Sov. Un........D3 73
Vladivostok,
Sov. Un.........E16 71, E6 93
Vlasenica, Yugo...............C4 68
Vlašim, Czech..................D9 61
Vlasotince, Yugo...............D6 68
Vlčany, Czech..................D4 70
Vlieland, Neth.................A5 59
Vlieland, isl., Neth...........A4 59
Vlissingen, Neth...............C3 59
Vlkava, Czech..................n18 70
Vlkava, riv., Czech...........n18 70
Vlorë (Valona), Alb..........B2 69
Vlotho, Ger.....................A3 61
Vltava, riv., Czech...........n17 70
Voca, Tex.......................D3 206
Volcano, is., Jap................ 115
Vodlozero, lake, Sov. Un....F17 63
Vodňany, Czech.................D9 61
Voeune Sai, Camb..............F7 89
Vogelkop, pen., Indon........F8 90
Voghera, It.....................B2 67
Voh, N. Cal....................... 115
Vohenstrauss, Ger.............D7 61
Vohipeno, Malag...............h9 107
Voi, Ken........................B6 106
Void, Fr.........................F5 59
Voiron, Fr.......................E6 58
Voitsberg, Aus..................E7 60
Voivïs, lake, Grc..............C4 69
Vojens, Den.....................C3 62
Vokhma, Sov. Un................B3 73
Volary, Czech...................E8 61
Volborg, Mont..................E11 190
Volcano, isl., Phil............o13 90
Volchansk, Sov. Un............F11 72
Volga, Iowa....................B6 180
Volga, S. Dak................C9 204
Volga, W. Va....................B4 211
Volga, plat., Sov. Un..........C3 73
Volga, riv., Sov. Un...........C3 73
Volgograd (Stalingrad),
Sov. Un.......................D2 73
Volgograd, res., Sov. Un....D3 73
Volin, S. Dak..................E8 204
Volkach, Ger....................D5 61
Volkhov, Sov. Un...............B9 72
Volkhov, riv., Sov. Un.........B8 72
Völklingen, Ger...............D1 61
Volkovysk, Sov. Un.............E5 72
Vollenhove, Neth...............B5 59
Volney, Va.......................E1 209
Volnovakha, Sov. Un..........H11 72
Volo, Ill.........................E2 178
Volochayevka Vtoraya,
Sov. Un.......................B7 93
Volochisk, Sov. Un.............G6 72
Volodarskiy, Sov. Un..........s31 63
Volodarskoye, Sov. Un.........C7 73
Vologda, Sov. Un.............B1 73
Volokolamsk, Sov. Un.........C10 72
Vólos, Grc.....................C4 69
Vólos, gulf, Grc...............C4 69
Vol'sk, Sov. Un................C3 73
Volta, see Upper Volta,
country, Afr.
Volta, reg., Ghana..............E5 103
Volta, lake, Ghana............E4 103
Volta, riv., Ghana.............E4 103
Volta Noire, riv.,
Upper Volta...................D4 103
Volta Redonda, Braz..C4, h5 137
Voltaire, N. Dak..............A5 198
Volterra, It......................C3 67
Voltri, It..........................B2 67
Volturno, riv., It...............D5 67
Voluntown, Conn..............C9 172
Volusia, co., Fla..............C5 174
Volzhskiy, Sov. Un..........G15 72
Vona, Colo......................B8 171
Vonda, Sask., Can.............E2 155
Von Frank, mtn., Alsk.......C8 167
Vónitsa, Grc......................C3 69
Vonore, Tenn...................D9 205
Von Ormy, Tex....................B3 206
Voorheesville, N.Y..........*C7 196
Vopnafjörður, Ice...............n25 63
Vorarlberg, state, Aus.........B5 66
Vordingborg, Den...............C5 62
Vorkuta, Sov. Un..............C9 71
Vorona, riv., Sov. Un.........E14 72
Voronezh, Sov. Un.............C1 73
Voronezh, riv., Sov. Un......E12 72
Voronya, riv., Sov. Un........C16 63
Voroshilovgrad,
Sov. Un.............G12, g22 72
Vorskla, riv., Sov. Un........G10 72
Vosburg, S. Afr..................D3 107
Vosges, dept., Fr.................A2 66
Vosges, mts., Fr.................C7 58
Voskresensk, Sov. Un.......n18 72
Voss, N. Dak....................A8 198
Voss, Nor..........................G2 63
Vossburg, Miss....................D5 188
Vostochnyy, Sov. Un............B11 93
Vostok, isl., Pac. O...........G12 113
Votaw, Tex........................D5 206
Votice, Czech......................D9 61
Votkinsk, Sov. Un...............B4 73
Vouga, riv., Port.................B1 65
Vouliagméni, Grc.................h11 69
Vouvray, Fr........................D4 58
Vouziers, Fr........................C6 58
Voyageurs, nat. park, Minn.B5 187
Vozhega, Sov. Un.................A13 72
Voznesensk, Sov. Un.............H8 72
Voznesenskoye, Sov. Un.........A8 93
Voznesenye, Sov. Un............A10 72
Vrå, Den............................A3 62
Vrå, Swe............................B7 62
Vraňany, Czech....................n17 70
Vranje, Yugo........................D5 68
Vratsa, Bul..........................D6 68
Vrbas, Yugo.........................C4 68
Vrchlabí, Czech.....................C3 70
Vrede, S. Afr........................C4 107
Vreden, Ger..........................A1 61
Vredenburgh, Ala...............D2 166
Vrena, Swe..........................u34 63
Vriezenveen, Neth.................B6 59
Vrigstad, Swe.......................A8 62
Vršac, Yugo..........................C5 68
Vršovice, Czech.....................n17 70
Vrútky, Czech........................D5 70
Vryburg, S. Afr......................C3 107
Vryheid, S. Afr......................C5 107
Všetaty, Czech.......................n18 70
Vsetín, Czech.........................D5 70
Vsevidof, mtn., Alsk.............E6 167
Vsevolozhskiy, Sov. Un..........r31 63
Vücha, riv., Bul....................E7 68
Vukovar, Yugo........................C4 68
Vulcan, Alta., Can...............D4 148
Vulcan, Mich..........................C3 186
Vulcan, Mo.............................D7 189
Vulcano, isl., It.....................E5 67
Vŭlchedrŭm, Bul.....................D6 68
Vung Tau, Viet......................G7 89
Vuoloyarvi, Sov. Un.................r31 63
Vuya, pt., Fiji........................ 114
Vyartsilya, Sov. Un..................F14 63
Vyatka, riv., Sov. Un..............B4 73
Vyatskiye Polyany, Sov.
Un.....................................B4 73
Vyazemskiy, Sov. Un................C7 93
Vyazma, Sov. Un.....................D10 72
Vyazma, riv., Sov. Un.............n18 72
Vyazniki, Sov. Un....................C14 72
Vyborg, Sov.
Un...............G13 63, A7 72
Vygozero, lake, Sov. Un........F16 63
Vyksa Sov. Un........................D14 72
Vyritsa, Sov. Un......................s31 63
Vÿrovka, riv., Czech...............n19 70
Vyshniy Volochëk,
Sov. Un..............................C10 72
Vyškov, Czech..........................D4 70
Vysočany, Czech.......................n17 70
Vysoká u Mělnika,
Czech................................n18 70
Vysoké Mýto, Czech.................D4 70
Vysoké Tatry, Czech.................D6 70
Vyšší Brod, Czech.....................E9 61
Vytegra, Sov. Un......................A11 72

W

Wa, Ghana............................D4 103
WaKeeney, Kans....................C4 181
Waal, riv., Neth......................C5 59
Waalwijk, Neth........................C5 59
Wabamun, Alta., Can................C3 148
Wabamun, lake, Alta.,
Can....................................C3 148
Wabana (Bell Island),
Newf., Can..........................E5 152
Wabasca, riv., Alta.,
Can....................................A3 148
Wabash, Ark...........................C5 169
Wabash, Ind..........................C6 179
Wabash, Nebr.........................E2 191
Wabash, co., Ill.....................E6 178
Wabash, co., Ind...................C6 179
Wabash, riv., U.S..................C10 159
Wabasha, Minn.......................F6 187
Wabasha, co., Minn................F6 187
Wabasso, Fla...........................E6 174
Wabasso, Minn........................F3 187
Wabaunsee, Kans.......................C7 181
Wabaunsee, co., Kans...............D7 181
Wabbaseka, Ark.......................C4 169
Wabek, N. Dak...........................B4 198
Wabeno, Wis.............................C5 212
Wabigoon, Ont., Can...................E5 150
Wabigoon, lake, Ont.,
Can.......................................E5 150
Wabigoon, riv., Ont., Can.......E5 150
Wabowden, Man.,
Can............................B2, D5 150
Wąbrzeźno, Pol..........................B5 70
Wabuska, Nev.............................D2 192
Waccamaw, riv., N.C.,
S.C.......................................D5 197
Waccasassa, bay, Fla.............C4 174
Wachapreague, Va....................D7 209
Wachusett, mtn., Mass............B4 185
Wachusett, res., Mass.............B4 185
Wacissa, Fla...............................B3 174
Waco, Ga..................................C1 175
Waco, Nebr................................D8 191
Waco, N.C..................................B2 197
Waco, Tex...................................D4 206
Waconda, lake, Kans..............C5 181
Waconia, Minn............................F5 187
Wad Medani, Sud........................C3 105
Waddān, Libya...............................D3 101
Waddān, mtn., Libya................D3 101
Waddell, Ariz..........................D3, G1 168
Wadden, sea, Neth......................A5 59
Waddington, N.Y.........................A2 196
Waddington, mtn., B.C.,
Can..................................D5, E2 149
Waddy, Ky.....................................B4 182
Waddy, lake, Sask., Can............A4 155
Wade, N.C......................................B5 197
Wade, Okla....................................D5 200
Wade, mtn., Ant.........................A30 120
Wadena, Sask., Can.....................F4 155
Wadena, Iowa...............................B6 180
Wadena, Minn..............................D3 187
Wadena, co., Minn........................D4 187
Wädenswil, Switz............................B4 66
Wadesboro, La.................................B6 183
Wadesboro, N.C.............................C3 197
Wadesville, Ind.................................H2 179
Wadham, is., Newf., Can...............D5 152
Wadhams, N.Y..........................A7, B3 196
Wadhwan, India...............................F3 88
Wadi el Joz, Jordan.........................m14 84
Wadi Sirhān, val.,
Sau. Ar.....................................C7 101
Wading, riv., N.J.............................D3 194
Wading River, N.J..............................D4 194
Wading River, N.Y..............................D4 194
Wadley, Ala....................................B4 166
Wadley, Ga.......................................D4 175
Wadmalaw, isl., S.C..........................G2 203
Wadowice, Pol...........................D5, h10 70
Wadsworth, Ala....................................C3 166
Wadsworth, Ill....................................E2 178
Wadsworth, Kans...........................B8, C9 181
Wadsworth, Nev.....................................D2 192
Wadsworth, Ohio.................................A4 199
Waelder, Tex.......................................E4 206
Wagener, S.C......................................D5 203
Wager, bay, N.W. Ter.,
Can..C15 142
Wagga, Sud...B4 105
Wagga Wagga, Austl................................G6 112
Waggoner, Ill.......................................D4 178
Wagina, isl., Sol. Is............................. 115
Waging [am See], Ger..............................B8 66
Waginger, lake, Ger...............................E6 60
Wagner, Mont...B8 190
Wagner, S. Dak......................................D7 204
Wagon Mound, N. Mex.............................A5 195
Wagon Wheel Gap, Colo.............................D4 171
Wagoner, Ariz...C3 168
Wagoner, Okla..B6 200
Wagoner, co., Okla.....................................B6 200
Wagontire, Oreg...D7 201
Wagram, N.C...C4 197
Wągrowiec, Pol...B4 70
Wah Wah, mts., Utah.....................................E2 207
Wahai, Indon...F7 90
Wahiawa, Haw.....................................B3, f9 176
Wahkiakum, co., Wash...................................C2 210
Wahkon, Minn...D5 187
Wahneta, Fla..*E5 174
Wahoo, Nebr..C9, D2 191
Wahoo, creek, Nebr..E1 191
Wahpeton, Iowa..*A2 180
Wahpeton, N. Dak...C9 198
Wahsatch, Utah...B4 207
Waia, isl., Fiji.. 114
Waiakoa, Haw...*C5 176
Waialee, Haw...f9 176
Waialua (Waialua Mill),
Haw..B3, f9 176
Waialua, bay, Haw..f9 176
Waianae, Haw...B3, g9 176
Waianae, mts., Haw...g9 176
Waiawa, riv., Haw..g10 176
Waiblingen, Ger...E4 61
Waidhofen, Aus..D7 60
Waidhofen [an der Ybbs],
Aus...E7 60
Waigeo, isl., Indon...E8 90
Waihee, Haw...C5 176
Waikabubak, Indon..G5 90
Waikalo, Indon..G5 90
Waikane, Haw...g10 176
Waikapu, Haw..C5 176
Waikari, N.Z...O14 112
Waikato, riv., N.Z...L15 112
Waikawa, N.Z...Q12 112
Waikerie, Austl..G2 112
Waikii, Haw..D6 176
Waikiki, beach, Haw...g10 176
Waikangilala, isl., Fiji... 114
Wailea, Haw...D6 176
Wailua (Wailua Houselots),
Haw..A2 176
Wailuku, Haw...C5 176
Wailuku, riv., Haw...D6 176
Waimanalo, Haw...B4, g11 176
Waimanalo, bay, Haw..g11 176
Waimate, N.Z..P13 112
Waimea, Haw...f9 176
Waimea, Haw...B2 176
Wainganga, riv., India..G7 88
Waingapu, Indon...G6 90
Waini, pt., Guy..A3 139
Wainunu, bay, Fiji.. 114
Wainwright, Alsk..A8 167
Wainwright, Alta., Can..C5 148
Wainwright, Ohio..B6 199
Wainwright, Okla..B6 200
Waiohinu, Haw...D6 176
Waipahu, Haw..B3, g9 176
Waipara, N.Z..O14 112
Waipawa, N.Z..M16 112
Waipio, Haw..C6 176
Waipio Acres, Haw...g9 176
Waipukurau, N.Z..N16 112
Wairoa, N.Z..M16 112
Waitaki, riv., N.Z..P13 112
Waitara, N.Z..M15 112
Waite, Maine..C5 184
Waite Hill, Ohio..*A6 199
Waite Park, Minn...E4 187
Waiteville, W. Va..D4 211
Waits, riv., Vt..C4 208
Waits River, Vt...C4 208
Waitsburg, Wash..C7 210
Waitsfield, Vt...C3 208
Waitville, Sask., Can...E3 155
Waiwo, Indon..F8 90
Wajima, Jap..H8 93
Wajir, Ken...A7 106
Waka, Zaire..A3 106
Waka, Tex..A2 206
Wakamatsu, Jap...H9 93
Wakarusa, Ind..A5 179
Wakarusa, Kans...D8 181
Wakarusa, riv., Kans...D8 181
Wakasa, bay, Jap..I7 93
Wakatipu, lake, N.Z..P12 112
Wakatomika, creek, Ohio...B5 199
Wakaw, Sask., Can..E3 155
Wakaya, isl., Fiji... 114
Wakayama, Jap...I7, o14 93
Wake, co., N.C...B5 197
Wake, isl., Oceania.. 114
Wake Forest, N.C...B5 197
WAKE ISLAND, U.S. dep.,
Oceania... 114
Wake Village, Tex...*C5 206
Wakefield, Que., Can...D2 154
Wakefield, Eng...A6 56
Wakefield, Kans...C6 181
Wakefield, Mass...A5, C3 185
Wakefield, Mich...A5 186
Wakefield, Nebr..B9 191
Wakefield, N.H...C4 193
Wakefield, Ohio...D4 199
Wakefield, R.I..D11 172
Wakefield, Va...E6 209
Wakeham Bay, Que.,
Can...D18 145
Waken, Ohio...A5 199
Wakeman, Ohio...A5 199
Wakenda, Mo..B4 189
Wakita, Okla...A4 200
Wakkanai, Jap...D10 93
Wakkerstroom, S. Afr..C5 107
Wakomata, lake, Ont.,
Can...B7 186
Wakonda, S. Dak...E8 204
Wakopa, Man., Can..E2 150
Wakpala, S. Dak..B5 204
Wakuach, lake, Que.,
Can...g8 152
Wakulla, Fla...B2 174
Wakulla, co., Fla...B2 174
Wakwekobi, lake, Ont.,
Can..B7 186
Walachia, reg., Rom...C7 68
Walagā, reg., Eth..D4 105
Walang, India...C10 87
Walbourg, Fr..F7 59
Walbridge, Ohio...A2 199
Wałbrzych, Pol...C4 70
Walchen, lake, Ger...B7 66
Walcott, Ark..A5 169
Walcott, Iowa...C7 180
Walcott, N. Dak..C9 198
Walcott, Wyo...D6 213
Wałcz, Pol...B4 70
Waldbröl, Ger...C2 61
Waldeck: in 1867.. 51
Waldeck, Sask., Can...G2 155
Walden, Colo..A4 171
Walden, N.Y..D6 196
Walden, Vt...C4 208
Walden, pond, Mass..C2 185
Walden, ridge, Tenn...D8 205
Walden Heights, Vt...C4 208
Waldenburg, Ark...B5 169
Waldheim, Sask., Can..E2 155
Waldheim, Ger...B8 61
Waldkappel, Ger..B4 61
Waldkirchen, Ger...E8 61
Waldmünchen, Ger..D7 61
Waldo, Ark...D2 169
Waldo, B.C., Can..E10 149
Waldo, Fla..C4 174
Waldo, Kans..C5 181
Waldo, N. Mex...G6 195
Waldo, Ohio...B4 199
Waldo, co., Maine..D3 184
Waldo, hills, Oreg...C2 201
Waldo, lake, Mass..E3 185
Waldo, lake, Oreg..D4 201
Waldoboro, Maine..D3 184
Waldorf, Md...C4 173
Waldorf, Minn...G5 187
Waldport, Oreg...C2 201
Waldron, Ark...C1 169
Waldron, Sask., Can..G4 155
Waldron, Ind...F6 179
Waldron, Kans...E5 181
Waldron, Mich...G6 186
Waldron, Mo..E1 189
Waldsassen, Ger...C7 61
Waldshut, Ger..E4 60
Waldwick, N.J...A4 194
Wales, Alsk...B6 167
Wales, Mass..B3 185
Wales, Minn...C7 187
Wales, N. Dak..A7 198
Wales, Tenn...B4 205
Wales, Utah..D4 207
Wales, reg.,
U.K.......................................D5 55, B4 56
Waleska, Ga..B2 175
Walford Station, Ont.,
Can..A2 153
Walgett, Austl...E7 112
Walgreen, coast, Ant..B2 120
Walhachin, B.C., Can..D7 149
Walhalla, Mich...E4 186
Walhalla, N. Dak...A8 198
Walhalla, S.C..B1 203
Walhonding, riv., Ohio...B5 199
Walikale, Zaire...B4 106
Walker, Iowa...B6 180
Walker, Kans...D4 181
Walker, La...A6 183
Walker, Minn...C4 187
Walker, Mo..D3 189
Walker, S. Dak..B4 204
Walker, co., Ala..B2 166
Walker, co., Ga...B1 175
Walker, co., Tex...D5 206
Walker, creek, Wyo..C7 213
Walker, lake, Man.,
Can..B3 150
Walker, lake, Nev..E3 192
Walker, mtn., Ga...B3 175
Walker, mtn., Va..D1 209
Walker, rim, Oreg..D5 201
Walker River, Indian res.,
Nev..E3 192
Walker Springs, Ala..D2 166
Walkersville, Md...B3 173
Walkersville, W. Va...C4 211
Walkerton, Ont., Can...C3 153
Walkerton, Ind...B5 179
Walkertown, N.C..A3 197
Walkerville, Mich..E4 186
Walkerville, Mont...D4 190
Wall, Pa..*F2 202
Wall, S. Dak...D3 204
Wall, lake, Iowa...B4 180
Wall Lake, Iowa...B2 180
Walla Walla, Wash...C7 210
Walla Walla, co., Wash...C7 210
Walla Walla, riv., Wash..C7 210
Wallace, Ala...D2 166
Wallace, N.S., Can..D6 151
Wallace, Idaho...B3 177
Wallace, Kans..D2 181
Wallace, Mich...C3 186
Wallace, Nebr...D4 191
Wallace, N.Y...C3 196
Wallace, N.C..C5 197
Wallace, S. Dak..B8 204
Wallace, Va...B3 209
Wallace, W. Va...A6, B4 211
Wallace, co., Kans..D2 181
Wallace, creek, Wyo...C5 213
Wallaceburg, Ont.,
Can..E2 153
Wallacetown, Ont., Can...E3 153
Wallachia: in 1242... 81
c. 1360... 48
Wallagrass, Maine..A4 184
Wallal Downs, Austl..C3 111
Walland, Tenn..D10 205
Wallaroo, Austl..F6 111
Wallasey, Eng...A4 56
Wallaston, cape, N.W. Ter.,
Can...B9 142
Walldürn, Ger..D4 61
Walled Lake, Mich..A7 186
Wallen, Ind..B7 179
Wallen, lake, Switz...B5 66
Wallenpaupack, lake, Pa...D11 202
Waller, Tex...D5 206
Waller, co., Tex..E4 206
Wallerville, Miss..A5 188
Walling, mtn., Mass..B1 185
Wallingford, Conn...D5 172
Wallingford, Eng..C6 56
Wallingford, Iowa..A3 180
Wallingford, Vt...E3 208
Wallington, N.J...D5 194
Wallis, Tex..E4 206
Wallkill, N.Y..D6 196
Wallkill, riv., N.Y..D6 196
Wallo, reg., Eth...C4 105
Walloomsac, riv., Vt..F2 208
Walloon, lake, Mich...C6 186
Wallowa, Oreg...B9 201
Wallowa, co., Oreg..B9 201
Wallowa, mts., Oreg..B9 201
Wallpack Center, N.J...A3 194
Walls, Miss...A3 188
Wallsburg, Utah..C4 207
Wallsend, Eng...C6 55
Wallula, Wash...C7 210
Wallum, lake, R.I..A9 172
Wallville, Md...D4 173
Walney, isl., Eng...C5 55
Walnut, Calif...*F3 170
Walnut, Ill...B4 178
Walnut, Iowa..C2 180
Walnut Kans...E8 181
Walnut, Miss...A5 188
Walnut, N.C..C3 197
Walnut, creek, Kans...D4 181
Walnut, hill, Mass...B2 185
Walnut, mtn., Conn..B4 172
Walnut, riv., Kans...E7 181
Walnut Bottom, Pa..F7 202
Walnut Canyon, nat. mon.,
Ariz..B4 168
Walnut Cove, N.C...A3 197
Walnut Creek, Calif..B5 170
Walnut Grove, Ala..A3 166
Walnut Grove, Calif...B6 170
Walnut Grove, Minn..F3 187
Walnut Grove, Miss..C4 188
Walnut Grove, Mo..D4 189
Walnut Heights, Calif...*B5 170
Walnut Hill, Ark..D2 169
Walnut Hill, Fla...G1 174
Walnut Hill, Maine..E5 184
Walnut Ridge, Ark...A5 169
Walnut Springs, Tex...*C4 206
Walnutport, Pa..E10 202
Walpole, Sask., Can...H5 155
Walpole, Mass...B5, E2 185
Walpole, N.H...D2 193
Walsall, Eng..B5 56
Walsenburg, Colo..D6 171
Walsh, Alta., Can...E5 148
Walsh, Colo..D8 171
Walsh, co., N. Dak...A8 198
Walsingham, cape, N.W. Ter.,
Can...C20 143
Walsrode, Ger...F3 62
Walston, Pa...E4 202
Walter Bathurst, cape,
N.W. Ter., Can...B17 143
Walter F. George, dam, Ala.,
Ga...D4 166
Walter F. George, res., Ala.,
Ga...D4 166
Walterboro, S.C..F6 203
Walterhill, Tenn..B5 205
Walters, Minn...G5 187
Walters, Okla..C3 200
Walters, Va..E6 209
Walters Falls, Ont., Can..C4 153
Waltershausen, Ger..C5 61
Waltersville, Miss..C3 188
Walterville, Oreg...C4 201
Walthall, Miss..B4 188
Walthall, co., Miss..D3 188
Waltham, Maine..D4 184
Waltham, Mass...B5, D2 185
Waltham, Minn..G6 187
Waltham, Mont...C6 190
Waltham Forest,
Eng...K12 55, C7 56
Waltham Station, Que.,
Can..B8 153
Walthamstow, Eng..*k12 55
Walthill, Nebr...B9 191
Walthourville, Ga..E5 175
Waltman, Wyo..B5 213
Walton, Ont., Can...D3 153
Walton, N.S., Can..D6 151
Walton, Fla...E6 174
Walton, Ind...C5 179
Walton, Kans...A5, D6 181
Walton, Ky...A7, B5 182
Walton, Nebr..E2 191
Walton, N.Y..C5 196
Walton, W. Va...C3 211
Walton, co., Fla..G3 174
Walton, co., Ga...C3 175
Walton Hills, Ohio..*A6 199
Walton & Weybridge,
Eng..m12 55
Waltonville, Ill...E4 178
Waltreak, Ark...C2 169
Walum, N. Dak...B7 198
Walvis Bay, S. Afr...B1 107
Walworth, N.Y..B3 196
Walworth, Wis...F5 212
Walworth, co., S. Dak..B5 204
Walworth, co., Wis...F5 212
Wama, Afg...D15 86
Wamac, Ill..E4 178
Wamba, Zaire..A4 106
Wamba, Nig...E6 103
Wamba, riv., Zaire..C2 106
Wamego, Kans...C7 181
Wamesit, Mass..A5, C2 185

Wamgumbaug, lake, Conn....B7 172
Wami, riv., Tan....C6 106
Wamic, Oreg....B5 201
Wampsville, N.Y....B5 196
Wampum, Pa....E1 202
Wamsutter, Wyo....D4 213
Wana, Pak....A2 88
Wanaaring, Austl....D5 112
Wanakena, N.Y....A6 196
Wanamaker, Ind....E6, H8 179
Wanamassa, N.J....C4 194
Wanamie, Pa....D9 202
Wanamingo, Minn....F6 187
Wanan, China....K6 92
Wanapitei, riv., Ont., Can....A4 153
Wanapum, res., Wash....B6 210
Wanaque, N.J....A4 194
Wanaque, res., N.J....A4 194
Wanatah, Ind....B4 179
Wanawana, isl., Sol. Is.... 115
Wanblee, S. Dak....D4 204
Wanchese, N.C....B8 197
Wanda, Minn....F3 187
Wanderer, bay, Guadalcanal I.... 115
Wandering River, Alta., Can....B4 148
Wando, Kor....I3 93
Wando, S.C....E8, F3 203
Wando, riv., S.C....F8 203
Wandoan, Austl....C7 112
Wandsworth, Eng....m12 55
Wanette, Okla....C4 200
Wanganui, N.Z....M15 112
Wangaratta, Austl....H6 112
Wangava, isl., Fiji.... 114
Wangching, China....C10 91
Wangen, Ger....B5 66
Wangerooge, isl., Ger....B3 60
Wangkuei, China....C3 93
Wanham, Alta , Can....B1 148
Wanhsien, China....D6 91
Wanhsien, China....I3 92
Wanilla, Miss....D3 188
Wanipigow, riv., Man., Can....D4 150
Wankie, Rh....A4 107
Wankie, nat. park, Rh....A4 107
Wann, Nebr....E2 191
Wann, Okla....A6 200
Wannaska, Minn....B3 187
Wanne-Eickel, Ger....*C7 59
Wanoni, bay, San Cristobal I.... 115
Wansreck, riv., Eng....E6 57
Wanstead & Woodford, Eng....*C8 56
Wantagh, N.Y....G2 172
Wantsai, China....J6 92
Wanup, Ont., Can....A4 153
Wapakoneta, Ohio....B3 199
Wapanucka, Okla....C5 200
Wapato, Wash....C5 210
Wapawekka, hills, Sask., Can....C3 155
Wapawekka, lake, Sask., Can....C3 155
Wapella, Sask., Can....G5 155
Wapella, Ill....C5 178
Wapello, Iowa....C6 180
Wapello, co., Iowa....C5 180
Wapisu, lake, Man., Can....B2 150
Wapiti, pass., B.C., Can....B7 149
Wapiti, range, Wyo....A3 213
Wapiti, riv., B.C., Alta., Can....B1 148, B7 149
Wappapello, Mo....E7 189
Wappapello, res., Mo....D7 189
Wapping, Conn....B6 172
Wappinger, creek, N.Y....B1 172
Wappingers Falls, N.Y....D7 196
Wapsipinicon, riv., Iowa....B5 180
Wapske, N.B., Can....B5 184
Wapus, lake, Sask., Can....A4 155
Wapwallopen, Pa....D9 202
Wāqid, Eg....D2 84
Waqqāş, Jordan....B7 84
Waquoit, Mass....C6 185
War, W. Va....D3 211
War Eagle, W. Va....D3 211
War Eagle, creek, Ark....A2 169
Warabi, Jap....*I10 93
Waramaug, lake, Conn....C3 172
Warangal, India....E6 87, H7 88
Warangoi, New Britain I.... 115
Warba, Minn....C5 187
Warburg, Alta., Can....C3 148
Warburg, Ger....B4 61
Warburton, Austl....H5 112
Warburton, riv., Austl....C2 112
Ward, Ala....C1 166
Ward, Ark....B4 169
Ward, S.C....D4 203
Ward, S. Dak....C9 204
Ward, W. Va....C6 211
Ward, co., N. Dak....A4 198
Ward, co., Tex....D1 206
Ward, mtn., Mont....D2 190
Ward Ridge, Fla....*C1 174
Wardān, Eg....D2 84
Wardell, Mo....E8 189
Warden, Wash....C6 210
Warden Junction, Alta., Can....C4 148
Wardensville, W. Va....B6 211
Warder, lake, Ger....E4 62
Wardha, India....G7 88
Wardlow, Alta., Can....D5 148
Wardner, B.C., Can....E10 149
Wardner, Idaho....B2 177
Wardsboro, Vt....E3 208
Wardville, La....*C3 183
Wardville, Okla....C5 200
Ware, Iowa....B3 180
Ware, Mass....B3 185
Ware, co., Ga....E4 175
Ware, riv., Mass....B3 185
Ware Center, Mass....B3 185
Ware Shoals, S.C....C3 203
Wareagle, Ark....A2 169
Wareham, Eng....D5 56
Wareham, Mass....C6 185
Warehouse Point, Conn....B6 172
Waren, Ger....B6 60
Waren, Indon....F9 90
Warendorf, Ger....B2 61
Waresboro, Ga....E4 175
Waretown, N.J....D4 194
Warfield, B.C., Can....*E9 149
Warfield, Ky....C7 182
Warfield, Va....E5 209
Warfordsburg, Pa....G5 202
Warin, Ger....E5 62
Waring, Tex....E3 206
Wark, Eng....E6 57
Warkworth, Ont., Can....C7 153
Warkworth, N.Z....L15 112
Warland, Mont....B1 190
Warley, Eng....B6 56
Warm Beach, Wash....A3 210
Warm Lake, Idaho....E3 177
Warm River, Idaho....E7 177
Warm Springs, Ark....A4 169
Warm Springs, Ga....D2 175
Warm Springs, Nev....E5 192
Warm Springs, Oreg....C5 201
Warm Springs, Va....C3 209
Warm Springs, Indian res., Oreg....C5 201
Warm Springs, res., Oreg....D8 201
Warman, Sask., Can....E2 155
Warmbad, S. Afr....B4 107
Warmbad, S. W. Afr....C2 107
Warminster, Eng....C5 56
Warminster, Pa....*F11 202
Warmsprings, Mont....D4 190
Warnemünde, Ger....A6 60
Warner, Alta., Can....E4 148
Warner, N.H....D3 193
Warner, Ohio....C6 199
Warner, Okla....B6 200
Warner, S. Dak....B7 204
Warner, mtn., Mass....B1 185
Warner, mtn., Oreg....E7 201
Warner, mts., Calif., Oreg....F6 201
Warner Robins, Ga....D3 175
Warner Springs, Calif....F5 170
Warnerton, La....D5 183
Warnes, Bol....C3 135
Warnow, riv., Ger....B6 60
Warpath, riv., Man., Can....C2 150
Warr Acres, Okla....B4 200
Warracknabeal, Austl....H4 112
Warragul, Austl....I5 112
Warren, Ark....D3 169
Warren, Austl....E6 112
Warren, Ont., Can....A4 153
Warren, Conn....C3 172
Warren, Idaho....D3 177
Warren, Ill....A4 178
Warren, Ind....C7 179
Warren, Maine....D3 184
Warren, Mass....B3 185
Warren, Mich....A8, F7 186
Warren, Minn....B2 187
Warren, Mont....E8 190
Warren, N.H....C3 193
Warren, N.Y....C6 196
Warren, Ohio....A7 199
Warren, Oreg....B4 201
Warren, Pa....C3 202
Warren, R.I....C12 172
Warren, Tex....D5 206
Warren, Vt....C3 208
Warren, co., Ga....C4 175
Warren, co., Ill....C3 178
Warren, co., Ind....D3 179
Warren, co., Iowa....C4 180
Warren, co., Ky....C3 182
Warren, co., Miss....C3 188
Warren, co., Mo....C6 189
Warren, co., N.J....B3 194
Warren, co., N.Y....B7 196
Warren, co., N.C....A5 197
Warren, co., Ohio....C3 199
Warren, co., Pa....C3 202
Warren, co., Tenn....D8 205
Warren, co., Va....C4 209
Warren, peaks, Wyo....A8 213
Warren Center, Pa....C9 202
Warren Park, Ind....H8 179
Warrendale, Pa....A5 202
Warrens, Wis....D3 212
Warrensburg, Ill....D4 178
Warrensburg, Mo....C4 189
Warrensburg, N.Y....B7 196
Warrensburg, Tenn....C10 205
Warrensville Heights, Ohio....B2 199
Warrensville, Pa....D8 202
Warrenton, Ga....C4 175
Warrenton, Mo....C6 189
Warrenton, N.C....A5 197
Warrenton, Oreg....A3 201
Warrenton, S. Afr....C3 107
Warrenton, Va....C5 209
Warrentown, Ky....B5 182
Warrenville, Conn....B8 172
Warrenville, Ill....F2 178
Warrenville, S.C....D4 203
Warri, Nig....E6 103
Warrick, co., Ind....H3 179
Warrington, Eng....D5 55
Warrington, Fla....G2 174
Warrior, Ala....B3 166
Warrior, mtn., Md....D2 173
Warrior, res., Ala....C2 166
Warriors Mark, Pa....E5 202
Warrnambool, Austl....I4 112
Warroad, Minn....B3 187
Warsaw, Ont., Can....C6 153
Warsaw, Ill....C2 178
Warsaw, Ind....B6 179
Warsaw, Ky....B5, B6 182
Warsaw, Mo....C4 189
Warsaw, N.Y....C2 196
Warsaw, N.C....B5 197
Warsaw, N. Dak....A8 198
Warsaw, Ohio....B5 199
Warsaw (Warszawa), Pol....B6, m14 70
Warsaw, Va....D6 209
Warsaw, grand duchy of.... 50
Warson Woods, Mo....*C7 189
Warspite, Alta., Can....B4 148
Warstein, Ger....B3 61
Warszawa, see Warsaw, Pol.
Warta, Pol....C5 70
Warta, riv., Pol....B5 70
Wartburg, Tenn....C9 205
Warth, Aus....B6 66
Warthen, Ga....C4 175
Wartime, Sask., Can....F1 155
Wartrace, Tenn....B5 205
Warwick, Austl....D9 112
Warwick, Ont., Can....D3 153
Warwick, Que , Can....D6 154
Warwick, Eng....B6 56
Warwick, Ga....E3 175
Warwick, Md....B6 173
Warwick, Mass....A3 185
Warwick, N.Y....D2, D6 196
Warwick, N. Dak....B7 198
Warwick, Okla....B5 200
Warwick, Pa....F10 202
Warwick, R.I....C11 172
Warwick, dam, Ga....E2 175
Wasatch, co., Utah....C4 207
Wasatch, mts., Utah....C4 207
Wasco, Calif....E4 170
Wasco, Oreg....B6 201
Wasco, co., Oreg....B5 201
Waseca, Sask., Can....D1 155
Waseca, Minn....F5 187
Waseca, co., Minn....F5 187
Wash, The, bay, Eng....B8 56
Washabaugh, co., S. Dak....D4 204
Washademoak, lake, N.B., Can....D4 151
Washago, Ont., Can....C5 153
Washakie, co., Wyo....B5 213
Washakie Needles, mtn., Wyo....B3 213
Washburn, Ill....C4 178
Washburn, Iowa....B5 180
Washburn, Maine....B4 184
Washburn, Mo....E4 189
Washburn, N. Dak....B4 198
Washburn, Wis....B3 212
Washburn, co., Wis....C2 212
Washburn, mtn., Wyo....A2 213
Washington, Ark....D2 169
Washington, Conn....C3 172
Washington, D.C....C1, C3 173
Washington, Ga....C4 175
Washington, Ill....C4 178
Washington, Ind....G3 179
Washington, Iowa....C6 180
Washington, Kans....C6 181
Washington, Ky....B6 182
Washington, La....D3 183
Washington, Mass....B1 185
Washington, Miss....D2 188
Washington. Mo....C6 189
Washington, Nebr....D2 191
Washington, N.H....D2 193
Washington, N.J....B3 194
Washington, N.C....B6 197
Washington, Okla....B4 200
Washington, Pa....F1 202
Washington, Tenn....D9 205
Washington, Utah....F2 207
Washington, Vt....C4 208
Washington, Va....C4 209
Washington, W. Va....B3 211
Washington, state, U.S.... 210
Washington, co., Ala....D1 166
Washington, co., Ark....A1 169
Washington, co., Colo....B7 171
Washington, co., Fla....G3 174
Washington, co., Ga....C4 175
Washington, co., Idaho....E2 177
Washington, co., Ill....E4 178
Washington, co., Ind....G5 179
Washington, co., Iowa....C6 180
Washington, co., Kans....C6 181
Washington, co., Ky....C4 182
Washington, co., Maine....D5 184
Washington, co., Md....A2 173
Washington, co., Minn....E6 187
Washington, co., Miss....B3 188
Washington, co., Mo....D7 189
Washington, co., Nebr....C9 191
Washington, co., N.Y....B7 196
Washington, co., N.C....B7 197
Washington, co., Ohio....C6 199
Washington, co., Okla....A6 200
Washington, co., Oreg....B3 201
Washington, co., Pa....F1 202
Washington, co., R.I....D10 172
Washington, co., Tenn....C11 205
Washington, co., Tex....D4 206
Washington, co., Utah....F2 207
Washington, co., Vt....C3 208
Washington, co., Va....B3 209
Washington, co., Wis....E5 212
Washington, par., La....D5 183
Washington, cape, Fiji.... 114
Washington, isl., Pac. O....F12 113
Washington, isl., Wis....C6 212
Washington, lake, Fla....D6 174
Washington, lake, Minn....E4 187
Wishington, lake, Miss....B2 188
Washington, lake, Wash....D2 210
Washington, mon., Md....C1 173
Washington, mtn., N.H....B4 193
Washington Bald, mtn., Maine....D2 151
Washington Court House, Ohio....C4 199
Washington Crossing, N.J....C3 194
Washington Depot, Conn....C3 172
Washington Heights, N.Y....*D6 196
Washington North, Pa....*F1 202
Washington Park, Ill....E3 178
Washington Terrace, Utah....B4 207
Washington West, Pa....*F1 202
Washingtonville, N.Y....*D6 196
Washingtonville, Pa....D8 202
Washir, Afg....E11 86
Washita, co., Okla....B2 200
Washita, riv., Okla....B3 200
Washoe, Nev....D2 192
Washoe, co., Nev....C2 192
Washougal, Wash....D3 210
Washow, bay, Man., Can....D3 150
Washta, Iowa....B2 180
Washtenaw, co., Mich....F7 186
Washtucna, Wash....C7 210
Washunga, Okla....*A5 200
Wasigny, Fr....E4 59
Wasilków, Pol....B7 70
Wasilla, Alsk....C10, g17 167
Waskada, Man., Can....E1 150
Waskaiowaka, lake, Man., Can....A3 150
Waskatenau, Alta., Can....B4 148
Waskesiu, lake, Sask., Can....D2 155
Waskigomog, lake, Ont., Can....B5 153
Waskish, Minn....B4 187
Waskom, Tex....C5 206
Wasque, pt., Mass....D7 185
Wass, lake, Man., Can....C4 150
Wassaw, sound, Ga....E6 175
Wassenaar, Neth....B4 59
Wasseralfingen, Ger....E5 61
Wasserburg am Inn, Ger....A8 66
Wasserkuppe, mtn., Ger....C4 61
Wassokeag, lake, Maine....C3 184
Wasson, Ill....F5 178
Wassuk, range, Nev....E3 192
Wassy-sur-Blaise, Fr....F4 59
Wasta, S. Dak....C3 204
Wataga, Ill....B3 178
Watampone, Indon....F6 90
Wataroa, N.Z....O13 112
Watatic, mtn., Mass....A4 185
Watauga, S. Dak....B4 204
Watauga, Tenn....C11 205
Watauga, Tex....*C4 206
Watauga, co., N.C....A2 197
Watauga, res., Tenn....C12 205
Watch Hill, R.I....D9 172
Watchaug, pond, R.I....D10 172
Watchet, Eng....C4 56
Watchung, N.J....*B4 194
Water, isl., Vir. Is....f15 132
Water Proof, La....C4 182
Water Valley, Ky....B2 182
Water Valley, Miss....A4 188
Water Valley, Tex....D2 206
Water View, Va....D6 209
Water Village, N.H....C4 193
Waterboro, Maine....E2 184
Waterbury, Conn....C4 172
Waterbury, Nebr....B9 191
Waterbury, Vt....C3 208
Waterbury, riv., Vt....C3 208
Waterbury Center, Vt....C3 208
Waterdown, Ont., Can....D5 153
Wateree, S.C....D6 203
Wateree, res., S.C....C6 203
Wateree, riv., S.C....D6 203
Waterflow, N. Mex....A1 195
Waterford, Ont., Can....E4 153
Waterford, Conn....D8 172
Waterford, Ind....A4 179
Waterford, Ire....D3 55
Waterford, Ky....A4 182
Waterford, Miss....A4 188
Waterford, N.Y....C7 196
Waterford, Ohio....C6 199
Waterford, Pa....C2 202
Waterford, Pa....F6 202
Waterford, Va....B5 209
Waterford, Wis....F1, F5 212
Waterford Mills, Ind....A6 179
Waterford Works, N.J....D3 194
Waterhen, lake, Man., Can....C2 150
Waterloo, Ala....A1 166
Waterloo, Ark....D2 169
Waterloo, Bel....D4 59
Waterloo, Ont., Can....D4 153
Waterloo, Que., Can....D5 154
Waterloo, Ill....E3 178
Waterloo, Ind....B7 179
Waterloo, Iowa....B5 180
Waterloo, Kans....B4 181
Waterloo, Mont....E4 190
Waterloo, Nebr....D2 191
Waterloo, N.Y....C4 196
Waterloo, Oreg....C4 201
Waterloo, S.L....E2 103
Waterloo, S.C....C3 203
Waterloo, Wis....E5 212
Waterloo, co., Ont., Can....D4 153
Waterman, Ill....B5 178
Waterport, N.Y....B2 196
Waters, Mich....D6 186
Watersmeet, Mich....A6 186
Waterton, riv., Alta., Can....E4 148
Waterton-Glacier International Peace Park, Can., U.S....A5 160
Waterton Lakes, nat. park, Alta., Can....E3 148
Waterton Park, Alta., Can....E4 148
Watertown, Conn....C4 172
Watertown, Fla....B4 174
Watertown, Mass....D2 185
Watertown, Minn....*F5 187
Watertown, N.Y....B5 196
Watertown, Ohio....C6 199
Watertown, S. Dak....C8 204
Watertown, Tenn....A5 205
Watertown, Wis....E5 212
Waterville, N.S., Can....D5 151
Waterville, Que., Can....*D6 154
Waterville, Iowa....A6 180
Waterville, Kans....C7 181
Waterville, Maine....D3 184
Waterville, Minn....F5 187
Waterville, N.H....C3 193
Waterville, N.Y....C5 196
Waterville, Ohio....A1, A4 199
Waterville, Pa....D7 202
Waterville, Vt....B3 208
Waterville, Wash....B5 210
Watervliet, Bel....C3 59
Watervliet, Mich....F4 186
Watervliet, N.Y....C7 196
Waterways, Alta., Can....A5 148
Watford, Ont., Can....E3 153
Watford, Eng....C7 56
Watford City, N. Dak....B2 198
Watha, N.C....C6 197
Wathena, Kans....C9 181
Watino, Alta., Can....B2 148
Watkins, Iowa....C6 180
Watkins, Minn....E4 187
Watkins Glen, N.Y....C4 196
Watkinsville, Ga....C3 175
Watlam, China....A9 89
Watling, see San Salvador, isl., Ba. Is.
Watonga, Okla....B3 200
Watonwan, co., Minn....F4 187
Watonwan, riv., Minn....F4 187
Watou, Bel....D2 59
Watova, Okla....A6 200
Watrous, Sask., Can....F3 155
Watrous, N. Mex....B5 195
Watsa, Zaire....A4 106
Watseka, Ill....C6 178
Watson, Ark....D4 169
Watson, Sask., Can....E3 155
Watson, Ill....D5 178
Watson, Ind....A4 182
Watson, Minn....E3 187
Watson, Mo....A2 189
Watson Lake, Yukon, Can....D7 144
Watsontown, Pa....D8 202
Watsonville, Calif....C6, D3 170
Watten, Fr....D10 56
Watten, lake, Scot....B5 57
Wattenberg, Colo....A6 171
Wattensaw, bayou, Ark....C4 169
Wattenscheid, Ger....*C7 59
Wattis, Utah....D5 207
Watton, Eng....B8 56
Watton, Mich....B2 186
Wattrelos, Fr....B5 58
Watts, Okla....A7 200
Watts Bar, dam, Tenn....D9 205
Watts Bar, lake, Tenn....D9 205
Watts Bar Dam, Tenn....D9 205
Wattsburg, Pa....B2 202
Wattsville, Ala....B3 166
Wattsville, S.C....B4 203
Wattwil, Switz....B5 66
Watu, Zaire....B3 106
Watuppa, pond, Mass....C5 185
Wau, Sud....D2 105
Waubamick, Ont., Can....B4 153
Waubaushene, Ont., Can....C5 153
Waubay, S. Dak....B8 204
Waubay, lake, S. Dak....B8 204
Waubun, Minn....C3 187
Wauchope, Sask., Can....H5 155
Wauchula, Fla....E5 174
Waucoma, Iowa....A5 180
Wauconda, Ill....E2 178
Waugh, mtn., Idaho....D4 177
Waukau, Wis....E5 212
Waukee, Iowa....C4 180
Waukeenah, Fla....B3 174
Waukegan, Ill....A6, E2 178
Waukesha, Wis....E1, F5 212
Waukesha, co., Wis....E5 212
Waukomis, Okla....A4 200
Waukon, Iowa....A6 180
Wauna, Wash....D1 210
Waunakee, Wis....E4 212
Wauneta, Nebr....D4 191
Waupaca, Wis....D4 212
Waupaca, co., Wis....D5 212
Waupun, Wis....E5 212
Wauregan, Conn....C9 172
Waurika, Okla....C4 200
Wausa, Nebr....B8 191
Wausau, Fla....G3 174
Wausau, Wis....D4 212
Wausaukee, Wis....C6 212
Wauseon, Ohio....A3 199
Waushara, co., Wis....D4 212
Wautoma, Wis....D4 212
Wauwatosa, Wis....E1 212
Wauzeka, Wis....E3 212
Wave Hill, Austl....C5 111
Waveland, Ind....E3 179
Waveland, Miss....E1, E4 188
Waveney, riv., Eng....B9 56
Waverley, Austl....*F8 112
Waverley, N.S., Can....E6 151
Waverley, Mass....D2 185
Waverly, Ala....C4 166
Waverly, Ark....E8 205
Waverly, Fla....*E5 174
Waverly, Ga....E5 175
Waverly, Ill....D4 178
Waverly, Ind....E5 179
Waverly, Iowa....B5 180
Waverly, Kans....D8 181
Waverly, Ky....C2 182
Waverly, La....B4 183
Waverly, Minn....E5 187
Waverly, Mo....B4 189
Waverly, Nebr....D9, E2 191
Waverly, N.Y....C4 196
Waverly, Ohio....C5 199
Waverly, Tenn....A4 205
Waverly, Va....D5 209
Waverly, W. Va....B3 211
Waverly Hall, Ga....D2 175
Wavnoka, Okla....A3 200
Wavre, Bel....D4 59
Wāw al Kabīr, Libya....D3 101
Wāw an Nāmūs (Well), Libya....E3 101
Wawaka, Ind....B7 179
Wawanesa, Man., Can....E2 150
Wawasee, lake, Ind....B6 179
Wawayanda, lake, N.J....A4 194
Wawayanda, mtn., N.J., N.Y....A4 194
Waweig, N.B., Can....D2 151
Wawk Hudunik, Colo....E3 168
Wawota, Sask., Can....H4 155
Waxahachie, Tex....B5, C4 206
Waxhaw, N.C....C3 197
Waxweiler, Ger....D6 59
Way, Miss....C3 188
Way, is., Viet....H5 89
Wayagamac, lake, Que., Can....B5 154
Wayan, Idaho....G7 177
Waycross, Ga....E4 175
Wayland, Iowa....C6 180
Wayland, Ky....C7 182
Wayland, Mass....D2 185
Wayland, Mich....F5 186
Wayland, Mo....A6 189
Wayland, N.Y....C3 196
Wayland Springs, Tenn....B4 205
Waymart, Pa....C11 202
Wayne, Alta., Can....D4 148
Wayne, Ill....E2 178
Wayne, Kans....C6 181
Wayne, Mich....A7 186
Wayne, Nebr....B8 191
Wayne, N.J....E6 196
Wayne, N.Y....C3 196
Wayne, Ohio....A4 199
Wayne, Okla....C4 200
Wayne, Pa....A10, F11 202
Wayne, W. Va....C2 211
Wayne, co., Ga....E5 175
Wayne, co., Ill....E5 178
Wayne, co., Ind....E7 179
Wayne, co., Iowa....D4 180
Wayne, co., Ky....D5 182
Wayne, co., Mich....F7 186
Wayne. co., Miss....D5 188
Wayne, co., Mo....D7 189
Wayne, co., Nebr....B8 191
Wayne, co., N.Y....B3 196
Wayne, co., N.C....B5 197
Wayne, co., Ohio....B6 199
Wayne, co., Pa....C11 202
Wayne, co., Tenn....B4 205
Wayne, co., Utah....E4 207
Wayne, co., W. Va....C2 211
Wayne City, Ill....E5 178
Waynesboro, Ga....C4 175
Waynesboro, Miss....D5 188
Waynesboro, Pa....G6 202
Waynesboro, Tenn....B4 205
Waynesboro (Independent City), Va....C4 209
Waynesburg, Ky....C5 182
Waynesburg, Ohio....B6 199
Waynesburg, Pa....G1 202
Waynesfield, Ohio....*B4 199
Waynesville, Ga....E5 175
Waynesville, Ill....C4 178
Waynesville, Mo....D5 189
Waynesville, N.C....D3 197
Waynesville, Ohio....C3 199
Waynetown, Ind....D3 179
Wayside, Kans....E8 181
Wayside, Miss....B2 188
Wayside, Tex....B2 206
Wayside, Wis....A6 212
Wayzata, Minn....*F5 187
Wazi Khwa (Marjan), Afg....E14 86
We, isl., Indon....J1 89
Weakley, co., Tenn....A3 205
Weare, N.H....D3 193
Weatherby, Mo....B3 189
Weatherford, Okla....B3 200
Weatherford, Tex....C4 206
Weatherly, Pa....E10 202
Weathersfield, Vt....*E4 208
Weatogue, Conn....B5 172
Weaubleau, Mo....D4 189
Weaver, Ala....B4 166
Weaver, lake, Man., Can....C3 150
Weaver, mts., Ariz....C3 168
Weaversford, N.C....A2 197
Weaverville, Calif....B2 170
Weaverville, N.C....D3 197
Webatuck, creek, N.Y....B2 172
Webb, Ala....D4 166
Webb, Sask., Can....G1 155
Webb, Iowa....B2 180
Webb, Miss....B3 188
Webb, Tex....F3 206
Webb, co., Tex....F3 206
Webb, hill, Mass....B3 185
Webb, lake, Maine....D2 184
Webb City, Ark....B2 169
Webb City, Mo....D3 189
Webb City, Okla....A5 200

INDEX KEY Each place listed in **Bold-faced Type** has its population listed in the Population tables, pages 230 to 280.
Each country, shown in CAPITAL LETTERS, has its population listed in the World Political Information Table, pages 6 to 10.
* Does not appear on map; key shows general location.

Webber, Kans ... C5 181
Webber, lake, Man., Can ... B5 150
Webbers Falls, Okla ... B6 200
Webberville, Mich ... F6 186
Webbville, Ky ... B7 182
Webbwood, Ont., Can ... A3 153
Weber, Utah ... B4 207
Weber, co., Utah ... B3 207
Weber, mtn., B.C., Can ... B3 149
Weber City, Va ... *B2 209
Weberville, Alta., Can ... A2 148
Webi Shebeli, riv., Som ... E5 105
Webster, Alta., Can ... B1 148
Webster, Fla ... D4 174
Webster, Iowa ... C5 180
Webster, Maine ... D2 184
Webster, Mass ... B4 185
Webster, Minn ... F5 187
Webster, Mont ... D12 190
Webster, N.H ... D3 193
Webster, N.Y ... B3 196
Webster, N. Dak ... A7 198
Webster, Ohio ... B3 199
Webster, Pa ... F2 202
Webster, S. Dak ... B8 204
Webster, Tex ... F5 206
Webster, Wis ... C1 212
Webster, co., Ga ... D2 175
Webster, co., Iowa ... B3 180
Webster, co., Ky ... C2 182
Webster, co., Miss ... B4 188
Webster, co., Mo ... D5 189
Webster, co., Nebr ... D7 191
Webster, co., W. Va ... C4 211
Webster, par., La ... B2 183
Webster, res., Kans ... C4 181
Webster City, Iowa ... B4 180
Webster Groves, Mo ... B8 189
Webster Mills, Pa ... G5 202
Webster Springs (Addison), W. Va ... C4 211
Websterville, Vt ... C4 208
Wecota, S. Dak ... B6 204
Weda, Indon ... E7 90
Weddell, sea, Ant ... B8 120
Wedderburn, Oreg ... E2 201
Wedgefield, S.C ... D6 203
Wedgeport, N.S., Can ... F4 151
Wedowee, Ala ... B4 166
Wedron, Ill ... B5 178
Weed, Calif ... B2 170
Weed, N. Mex ... E4 195
Weed Heights, Nev ... D2 192
Weedon, Que., Can ... D6 154
Weedpatch, hill, Ind ... F5 179
Weedsport, N.Y ... B4 196
Weedville, Pa ... D5 202
Weehawken, N.J ... D5 194
Weekapaug, R.I ... D9 172
Weekes, Sask., Can ... E4 155
Weeks (Weeks Island), La ... E4 183
Weeksbury, Ky ... C7 182
Weekstown, N.J ... D3 194
Weeksville, N.C ... A7 197
Weems, Va ... D6 209
Weener, Ger ... A7 59
Weeping Water, Nebr ... D9, E3 191
Weeping Water, creek, Nebr ... E3 191
Weert, Neth ... C5 59
Weesp, Neth ... B5 59
Weferlingen, Ger ... A6 61
Wegdahl, Minn ... F3 187
Weggs, cape, Que., Can ... D18 143
Wegorzewo, Pol ... A6 70
Węgrów, Pol ... B7 70
Wei-Chou, isl., China ... B8 89
Weichang China ... C8 91
Weida, Ger ... C7 61
Weiden, Ger ... D7 61
Weidenau, Ger ... C3 61
Weidman, Mich ... E6 186
Weifang, China ... D8 91
Weihai, China ... D9 91, F10 92
Weihsi, China ... F4 91
Weilburg, Ger ... C3 61
Weilheim, Ger ... E5 60
Weimar, Ger ... C6 61
Weimar, Tex ... E4 206
Weinan, China ... E6 91
Weinböhla, Ger ... B8 61
Weiner, Ark ... B5 169
Weinert, Tex ... C3 206
Weingarten, Ger ... D3 61
Weinheim, Ger ... D3 61
Weining, China ... F5 91
Weinsberg, Ger ... D4 61
Weippe, Idaho ... C3 177
Weir, Que., Can ... D3 154
Weir, Kans ... E9 181
Weir, Ky ... C2 182
Weir, Miss ... B4 188
Weir, lake, Fla ... C5 174
Weir, riv., Man., Can ... A4 150
Weir River, Man., Can ... A4 150
Weirdale, Sask., Can ... D3 155
Weirsdale, Fla ... D5 174
Weirton, W. Va ... A2, A4 211
Weiser, Idaho ... E2 177
Weiser, riv., Idaho ... E2 177
Weishan, lake, China ... G7 92
Weisner, mtn., Ala ... A4 166
Weiss, res., Ala ... A4 166
Weisse Elster, riv., Ger ... B7 61
Weissen, lake, Aus ... C9 66
Weissenburg [in Bayern], Ger ... D5 61
Weissenfels, Ger ... B6 61
Weissenhorn, Ger ... A6 66
Weissert, Nebr ... C6 191
Weisshorn, mtn., Switz ... C3 66
Weisswasser, Ger ... B9 61
Weitchpec, Calif ... B2 170
Weitra, Aus ... E9 61
Wejherowo, Pol ... A5 70
Wekusko, lake, Man., Can ... B2 150
Welaka, Fla ... C5 174
Welborn, Kans ... B8 181
Welch, Okla ... A6 200
Welch, Tex ... C1 206
Welch, W. Va ... D3 211
Welcome, La ... B6 183
Welcome, Minn ... G4 187
Weld, Maine ... D2 184
Weld, co., Colo ... A6 171
Welda, Kans ... D8 181
Welden, Ger ... E5 61
Weldon, Ill ... C5 178
Weldon, Iowa ... D4 180
Weldon, N.C ... A6 197
Weldon, Tex ... D5 206
Weldon Spring, Mo ... A7 189
Weldona, Colo ... A7 171
Weleetka, Okla ... B5 200
Welford, Austl ... B4 112
Welkom, S. Afr ... C4 107
Welland, Ont., Can ... E5 153
Welland, co., Ont., Can ... D5 153
Welland, riv., Eng ... D6 55, B7 56
Wellandport, Ont., Can ... D5 153
Wellborn, Fla ... B4 174
Wellborn, Tex ... D4 206
Wellersburg, Pa ... G4 202
Welles, hbr., Midway Is ... 114
Wellesley, Ont., Can ... D4 153
Wellesley, Mass ... B5, D2 185
Wellesley, is., Austl ... C6 110
Wellesley Hills, Mass ... D2 185
Wellfleet, Mass ... C7 185
Wellfleet, Nebr ... D5 191
Wellford, S.C ... B3 203
Wellin, Bel ... D5 59
Welling, Okla ... B7 200
Wellingborough, Eng ... B7 56
Wellington, Ala ... B4 166
Wellington, B.C., Can ... A8 149
Wellington, Ont., Can ... *D7 153
Wellington, Colo ... A5 171
Wellington, Eng ... B5 56
Wellington, Eng ... D4 56
Wellington, Ill ... C6 178
Wellington, Kans ... E6 181
Wellington, Ky ... *B4 182
Wellington, Maine ... C3 184
Wellington, Mo ... B4 189
Wellington, Nev ... E2 192
Wellington, N.Z ... N15 112
Wellington, Ohio ... A5 199
Wellington, Tex ... B2 206
Wellington, Utah ... D5 207
Wellington, co., Ont., Can ... D4 153
Wellington, chan., N.W. Ter., Can ... A14 142
Wellington, isl., Chile ... D2 136
Wellington Station, N.S., Can ... E6 151
Wellington Station, P.E.I., Can ... C5 151
Wellman, Iowa ... C6 180
Wellman, Tex ... C1 206
Wellpinit, Wash ... B8 210
Wells, B.C., Can ... C7 149
Wells, Eng ... C5 56
Wells, Kans ... C6 181
Wells, Maine ... E2 184
Wells, Mich ... C3 186
Wells, Minn ... G5 187
Wells, Nev ... B7 192
Wells, N.Y ... B6 196
Wells, Tex ... D5 206
Wells, Vt ... E2 208
Wells, co., Ind ... C7 179
Wells, co., N. Dak ... B6 198
Wells, lake, Austl ... E3 110
Wells, lake, Man., Can ... A1 150
Wells, riv., Vt ... C4 208
Wells Beach, Maine ... E2 184
Wells Gray, prov. park, B.C., Can ... C8 149
Wells [-next-the-sea], Eng ... B8 56
Wells River, Vt ... C4 208
Wells Tannery, Pa ... F5 202
Wellsboro, Ind ... B4 179
Wellsboro, Pa ... C7 202
Wellsburg, Iowa ... B5 180
Wellsburg, N.Y ... C4 196
Wellsburg, N. Dak ... B6 198
Wellsburg, W. Va ... A4, B2 211
Wellsford, Kans ... E4 181
Wellston, Mich ... D5 186
Wellston, Mo ... A8 189
Wellston, Ohio ... C5 199
Wellston, Okla ... B4 200
Wellsville, Kans ... D8 181
Wellsville, Mo ... B6 189
Wellsville, N.Y ... C3 196
Wellsville, Ohio ... B7 199
Wellsville, Pa ... F8 202
Wellsville, Utah ... B4 207
Wellton, Ariz ... E1 168
Wellwood, Man., Can ... D2 150
Wels, Aus ... D7 60
Welsford, N.B., Can ... D3 151
Welsh, La ... D3 183
Welshpool, Wales ... B4 56
Welton, Iowa ... C7 180
Welty, Okla ... B5 200
Welwyn, Sask., Can ... G5 155
Welwyn Garden City, Eng ... k12 55
Welzow, Ger ... B9 61
Wem, Eng ... B5 56
Wema, Zaire ... B3 106
Wembere, riv., Tan ... B5 106
Wembley, Alta., Can ... B1 148
Wembley, Eng ... *k11 55
Wemding, Ger ... E5 61
Wenasoga, Miss ... A5 188
Wenatchee, Wash ... B5 210
Wenatchee, lake, Wash ... B5 210
Wenatchee, mts., Wash ... B5 210
Wenatchee, riv., Wash ... B5 210
Wenceslau Braz, Braz ... C3 137
Wenchang, China ... C9 89
Wenchi, Ghana ... E4 103
Wenchow, China ... F9 91, K9 92
Wenchüan, China ... B8 91
Wendel, Calif ... B3 170
Wendel, W. Va ... B7 211
Wendell, Idaho ... G4 177
Wendell, Mass ... A3 185
Wendell, Minn ... D2 187
Wendell, N.H ... D2 193
Wendell, N.C ... B5 197
Wenden, Ariz ... D2 168
Wendover, Utah ... C1 207
Wendover, Wyo ... C8 213
Wenham, Mass ... A6, C3 185
Wenham, lake, Mass ... C3 185
Wenham, swamp, Mass ... C3 185
Wenlock, riv., Austl ... B7 110
Wennington, Eng ... F6 57
Wenona, Ill ... B4 178
Wenona, Md ... D6 173
Wenonah, N.J ... D2 194
Wenshan, China ... G5 91
Wensum, riv., Eng ... D7 55
Wentworth, Austl ... G3 112
Wentworth, N.S., Can ... D6 151
Wentworth, Mo ... E3 189
Wentworth, N.H ... C3 193
Wentworth, N.C ... A4 197
Wentworth, S. Dak ... C8 204
Wentworth, Wis ... B2 212
Wentworth, co., Ont., Can ... D4 153
Wentworth, lake, N.H ... C4 193
Wentzville, Mo ... C7 189
Weogufka, mtn., Ala ... C3 166
Weohyakapka, lake, Fla ... E5 174
Weona, Ark ... B5 169
Weott, Calif ... B2 170
Wepener, S. Afr ... C4 107
Werbomont, Bel ... D5 59
Werdau, Ger ... C7 61
Werder, Ger ... A7 61
Werdohl, Ger ... B2 61
Werfen, Aus ... E6 60
Werl, Ger ... B2 61
Wernberg, Ger ... D7 61
Werne [an der Lippe], Ger ... B2 61
Werner, N. Dak ... B3 198
Wernersville, Pa ... *F9 202
Werneuchen, Ger ... B6 60
Wernigerode, Ger ... B5 61
Werra, riv., Ger ... C5 61
Wertach, riv., Ger ... D5 60
Wertheim, Ger ... D4 61
Wertingen, Ger ... E5 61
Wervik, Bel ... D3 59
Wesco, Mo ... D6 189
Wesconnett, Fla ... B6 174
Wesel, Ger ... B1 61
Weser, canal, Ger ... B4 60
Weser, riv., Ger ... A4 61
Weskan, Kans ... D2 181
Weslaco, Tex ... F3 206
Weslaco North, Tex ... *F3 206
Weslemkoon, lake, Ont., Can ... C7 153
Wesley, Ark ... A2 169
Wesley, Ga ... D4 175
Wesley, Iowa ... A4 180
Wesley, Maine ... D5 184
Wesleyville, Newf., Can ... D5 152
Wesleyville, Pa ... B2 202
Wessel, is., Austl ... B6 110
Wesselburen, Ger ... D2 62
Wessington, S. Dak ... C7 204
Wessington Springs, S. Dak ... C7 204
Wesson, Ark ... D3 169
Wesson, Miss ... D3 188
West, Miss ... B4 188
West, Tex ... D4 206
West, bay, La ... E6 183
West, bay, Tex ... G5 206
West, butte, Mont ... B5 190
West, cape, Guadalcanal I ... 115
West, fork, W. Va ... D6 211
West, ice shelf, Ant ... C21 120
West, isl., Mass ... C6 185
West, lake, Maine ... C4 184
West, mtn., N.Y ... B6 196
West, mtn., Vt ... B5 208
West, riv., N.S., Can ... D7 151
West, riv., Mass ... E1 185
West, riv., Vt ... E3 208
West, spit, Eniwetok ... 114
West Acton, Mass ... C1 185
West Alexander, Pa ... F1 202
West Alexandria, Ohio ... C3 199
West Allis, Wis ... E2 212
West Alton, N.H ... C4 193
West Arichat, N.S., Can ... D8 151
West Athens, Maine ... D3 184
West Auburn, Mass ... B4 185
West Augusta, Va ... C3 209
West Ausdale, Ohio ... *B5 199
West Baden Springs, Ind ... G4 179
West Baldwin, Maine ... E2 184
West Barnet, Vt ... C4 208
West Barnstable, Mass ... C7 185
West Barrington, R.I ... B11 172
West Bath, Maine ... *E6 184
West Bathurst, N.B., Can ... B4 151
West Baton Rouge, par., La ... D4 183
West Battle, lake, Minn ... D3 187
West Bay, N.S., Can ... D8 151
West Belmar, N.J ... *C4 194
West Bend, Sask., Can ... F4 155
West Bend, Iowa ... B3 180
West Bend, Wis ... E5 212
West Bengal, state, India ... F11 88
West Benson, Nebr ... D3 191
West Berkshire, Vt ... B3 208
West Bethel, Maine ... D2 184
West Blocton, Ala ... B2 166
West Bloomfield, N.Y ... C3 196
West Bolton, Vt ... C3 208
West Bountiful, Utah ... *C4 207
West Bowdoin, Maine ... D5 184
West Boylston, Mass ... B4 185
West Branch, Iowa ... C6 180
West Branch, Mich ... D6 186
West Branch, res., Conn ... A4 172
West Branch, res., N.Y ... D2 172
West Brattleboro, Vt ... F3 208
West Brentwood, N.H ... E4 193
West Bridgewater, Mass ... B5 185
West Bridgewater, Vt ... D3 208
West Brimfield, Mass ... B3 185
West Bromwich, Eng ... B6 56
West Brookfield, Mass ... B3 185
West Brooklyn, Ill ... B4 178
West Brownsville, Pa ... *F2 202
West Burke, Vt ... B5 208
West Burlington, Iowa ... D6 180
West Buxton, Maine ... E2 184
West Cache, creek, Okla ... C3 200
West Caldwell, N.J ... *B4 194
West Camp, N.Y ... C7 196
West Campton, N.H ... C3 193
West Canaan, N.H ... C2 193
West Canada, creek, N.Y ... B6 196
West Cape May, N.J ... F3 194
West Carroll, par., La ... B4 183
West Carrollton, Ohio ... C3 199
West Carry, pond, Maine ... C2 184
West Carthage, N.Y ... B5 196
West Castleton, Vt ... D2 208
West Charleston, Vt ... B4 208
West Chazy, N.Y ... A3 196
West Cheshire, Conn ... C5 172
West Chester, Iowa ... C6 180
West Chester, Ohio ... C2 199
West Chester, Pa ... G10 202
West Chesterfield, N.H ... E1 193
West Chicago, Ill ... F2 178
West Chop, pt., Mass ... D6 185
West City, Ill ... E5 178
West Claremont, N.H ... D2 193
West Clarkston, Wash ... *C8 210
West Coffeyville, Kans ... E8 181
West College Corner, Ind ... E8 179
West Columbia, S.C ... D5 203
West Columbia, Tex ... E5, G4 206
West Concord, Mass ... B5, C1 185
West Concord, Minn ... F6 187
West Concord, N.C ... *B3 197
West Conshohocken, Pa ... A11 202
West Cornwall, Conn ... B3 172
West Cornwall, Vt ... D2 208
West Cote Blanche, bay, La ... E4 183
West Covina, Calif ... F3 170
West Creek, N.J ... D4 194
West Crossett, Ark ... D4 169
West Cumberland, Maine ... E2, E5 184
West Cummington, Mass ... B2 185
West Danby, N.Y ... C4 196
West Danville, Vt ... C4 208
West Decatur, Pa ... E5 202
West Derry, Pa ... *F3 202
West Des Moines, Iowa ... A7, C4 180
West Dudley, Mass ... B4 185
West Dummerston, Vt ... F3 208
West Duxbury, Mass ... B6 185
West Easton, Pa ... *E11 202
West Elizabeth, Pa ... *F2 202
West Elk, mts., Colo ... C3 171
West Elk, peak, Colo ... C3 171
West Elmira, N.Y ... *C4 196
West Elwood, Ind ... D6 179
West Eminence, Mo ... D6 189
West Emma, creek, Kans ... D6 181
West End, Ark ... *C3 169
West End, Ba. Is ... B4 131
West End, Fla ... *C4 174
West End, N.C ... B4 197
West End, N.Y ... *C2 196
West End Anniston, Ala ... *B4 166
West Enfield, Maine ... C4 184
West Enosburg, Vt ... B3 208
West Epping, N.H ... D4 193
West Fairlee, Vt ... D4 208
West Fairview, Pa ... *F8 202
West Falmouth, Mass ... C6 185
West Fargo, N. Dak ... C9 198
West Farmington, Maine ... D2 184
West Farmington, Ohio ... A7 199
West Feliciana, par., La ... D4 183
West Flanders, prov., Bel ... C3 59
West Florida: in 1763-67 ... 162
c. 1790 ... 126
West Fork, Ark ... B1 169
West Fork, res., Ohio ... D1 199
West Fork, riv., W. Va ... B4 211
West Forks, Maine ... *C3 184
West Frankfort, Ill ... F5 178
West Friendship, Md ... B4 173
West Frisian, is., Neth ... A4 59
West Gardiner, Maine ... *D3 184
West Germany, see Germany, West, country, Eur.
West Glacier, Mont ... B3 190
West Glens Falls, N.Y ... *B7 196
West Glocester, R.I ... B9 172
West Glover, Vt ... B4 208
West Gorham, Maine ... E4 184
West Goshen, Conn ... B3 172
West Gouldsboro, Maine ... D4 184
West Granby, Conn ... B5 172
West Granville, Mass ... B2 185
West Gravenhurst, Ont., Can ... C5 153
West Green, Ga ... E4 175
West Greene, Ala ... C1 166
West Groton, Mass ... A4 185
West Groton, Vt ... C4 208
West Grove, Iowa ... D5 180
West Grove, Pa ... G10 202
West Gulfport, Miss ... *E4 188
West Halifax, Vt ... F3 208
West Ham, Eng ... *C8 56
West Hamlin, W. Va ... C2 211
West Hampstead, N.H ... E4 193
West Hanover, Mass ... E3 185
West Harrison, Ind ... F8 179
West Hartford, Conn ... B6 172
West Hartford, Vt ... D4 208
West Hartland, Conn ... A5 172
West Hatfield, Mass ... B2 185
West Haven, Conn ... D5 172
West Haverstraw, N.Y ... *D7 196
West Hazleton, Pa ... E9 202
West Helena, Ark ... C5 169
West Hickory, Pa ... C3 202
West Hill, res., Mass ... D1 185
West Hollywood, Calif ... *F2 170
West Hollywood, Fla ... E3 174
West Homestead, Pa ... *F2 202
West Hopkinton, N.H ... D3 193
West Indies, is., N.A ... 131
West Jefferson, N.C ... A2 197
West Jefferson, Ohio ... C1, C4 199
West Jonesport, Maine ... D5 184
West Jordan, Utah ... C4 207
West Junction, Tenn ... B1, E8 205
West Kankakee, Ill ... B6 178
West Kennebunk, Maine ... E2 184
West Kingston, R.I ... D10 172
West La Crosse, Wis ... *E2 212
West Lafayette, Ind ... D4 179
West Lafayette, Ohio ... B6 199
West Las Vegas, N. Mex ... B4 195
West Lawn, Pa ... F9 202
West Lebanon, Ind ... D3 179
West Lebanon, Maine ... E2 184
West Lebanon, N.H ... C2 193
West Lebanon, Pa ... *F9 202
West Leechburg, Pa ... *E2 202
West Leisenring, Pa ... G2 202
West Leyden, N.Y ... B5 196
West Liberty, Ill ... E5 178
West Liberty, Iowa ... C6 180
West Liberty, Ky ... C6 182
West Liberty, Ohio ... B4 199
West Liberty, W. Va ... B2 211
West Lima, Wis ... E3 212
West Lincoln, Nebr ... E1 191
West Lincoln, Vt ... C2 208
West Linn, Oreg ... B2, B4 201
West Long Branch, N.J ... C4 194
West Lorne, Ont., Can ... E3 153
West Lothian, co., Scot ... E5 57
West Louisville, Ky ... C2 182
West Lubec, Maine ... D5 184
West Manchester, Ohio ... C3 199
West Mansfield, Ohio ... B4 199
West Mayfield, Pa ... *E1 202
West Medway, Mass ... B5, E1 185
West Melbourne, Fla ... *D6 174
West Memphis, Ark ... B5 169
West Methow, riv., Wash ... A5 210
West Miami, Fla ... F3 174
West Middlesex, Pa ... D1 202
West Middleton, Ind ... D5 179
West Mifflin, Pa ... F2 202
West Milan, N.H ... A4 193
West Milford, N.J ... A4 194
West Milford, W. Va ... B4 211
West Milton, Ohio ... C3 199
West Milton, Pa ... D8 202
West Milwaukee, Wis ... E2 212
West Mineral, Kans ... E9 181
West Monroe, La ... B3 183
West Monterey, Pa ... D2 202
West Muncie, Ind ... D7 179
West Musquash, lake, Maine ... C5 184
West Mystic, Conn ... *D9 172
West New Guinea, see Indonesia, country, Asia
West New York, N.J ... D5 194
West Newbury, Mass ... A6 185
West Newbury, Vt ... C4 208
West Newfield, Maine ... E2 184
West Newton, Ind ... I7 179
West Newton, Pa ... F2 202
West Nicholson, Rh ... B4 107
West Nishnabotna, riv., Iowa ... C2 180
West Norriton, Pa ... *F11 202
West Nottingham, N.H ... D4 193
West Olive, Mich ... F4 186
West Orange, Mass ... A3 185
West Orange, N.J ... B4 194
West Orange, Tex ... *D6 206
West Ossipee, N.H ... C4 193
West Palm Beach, Fla ... F6 174
West Panama City Beach, Fla ... G3 174
West Paris, Maine ... D2 184
West Park, N.Y ... D7 196
West Paterson, N.J ... *B4 194
West Pawlet, Vt ... E2 208
West Pearl, riv., La ... D6 183
West Pelzer, S.C ... B3 203
West Pembroke, Maine ... D5 184
West Pensacola, Fla ... G2 174
West Peru, Maine ... D2 184
West Peterborough, N.H ... E3 193
West Petersburg, Alsk ... m23 167
West Pittsburg, Pa ... E1 202
West Pittston, Pa ... B8 202
West Plains, Mo ... E6 189
West Point, Ala ... A3 166
West Point, Ark ... B4 169
West Point, Calif ... C3 170
West Point, Ga ... D1 175
West Point, Ill ... C2 178
West Point, Iowa ... D6 180
West Point, Ky ... C4 182
West Point, Miss ... B5 188
West Point, Nebr ... C9 191
West Point, N.Y ... D3, D7 196
West Point, Utah ... *B3 207
West Point, Va ... D6 209
West Point, mtn., Alsk ... C11 167
West Portsmouth, Ohio ... D4 199
West Prairie, riv., Alta., Can ... B2 148
West Pubnico, N.S., Can ... F4 151
West Punjab, reg., Pak ... B3 88
West Quoddy Head, cape, Maine ... D6 184
West Reading, Pa ... F10 202
West Redding, Conn ... D3 172
West Richland, Wash ... *C6 210
West Rindge, N.H ... E2 193
West River, Md ... C4 173
West Road, riv., B.C., Can ... C5 149
West Roag, bay, Scot ... B1 57
West Rockingham, N.C ... *C4 197
West Rumney, N.H ... C3 193
West Rupert, Vt ... E2 208
West Rutland, Vt ... D2 208
West Rye, N.H ... D5 193
West St. Modeste, Newf., Can ... C3 152
West St. Paul, Minn ... E7 187
West Salem, Ill ... E5 178
West Salem, Ohio ... B5 199
West Salem, Wis ... E2 212
West Sayville, N.Y ... G4 172
West Scarboro, Maine ... E2, E4 184
West Seboois, Maine ... C4 184
West Seneca, N.Y ... *C2 196
West Shefford, Que., Can ... D5 154
West Siberian, plain, Sov. Un ... A7 73
West Simsbury, Conn ... B5 172
West Slope, Oreg ... B4 201
West Somerset, Ky ... C5 182
West Spanish, peak, Colo ... D6 171
West Spitsbergen, isl., Nor ... A13 118
West Springfield, Mass ... B2 185
West Springfield, N.H ... D2 193
West Stafford, Conn ... B7 172
West Sterling, Ill ... *B4 178
West Stewartstown, N.H ... A1 193
West Stockbridge, Mass ... B1 185
West Suffield, Conn ... B6 172
West Sullivan, Maine ... D4 184
West Sumner, Maine ... D2 184
West Sunbury, Pa ... E2 202
West Swanzey, N.H ... E2 193
West Tarbert, bay, Scot ... C1 57
West Terre Haute, Ind ... F3 179
West Thornton, N.H ... C3 193
West Tisbury, Mass ... D6 185
West Topsham, Vt ... C4 208
West Townsend, Mass ... A4 185
West Townshend, Vt ... E3 208
West Union, Ill ... D6 178
West Union, Iowa ... B6 180
West Union, Ohio ... D4 199
West Union, S.C ... B1 203
West Union, W. Va ... B4, B6 211
West Unity, Ohio ... A3 199
West University Place, Tex ... F5 206
West Upton, Mass ... B4, D1 185
West Valley, N.Y ... C2 196
West Vancouver, Wash ... A9, E6 210
West Van Lear, Ky ... C7 182
West View, Ohio ... B2 199
West View, Pa ... A5 202
West View Park, Tenn ... *C11 205
West Virginia, state, U.S ... 211
West Walker, riv., Calif., Nev ... E2 192
West Wardsboro, Vt ... E3 208
West Wareham, Mass ... C6 185
West Warren, Mass ... B3 185
West Warwick, R.I ... C10 172
West Wenatchee, Wash ... *B5 210
West Willington, Conn ... B7 172
West Wilton, N.H ... E3 193
West Winfield, N.Y ... C5 196
West Winfield, Pa ... E2 202
West Winter Haven, Fla ... *D5 174
West Woodstock, Vt ... D3 208
West Wyalong, Austl ... F6 112

INDEX KEY Each place listed in **Bold-faced Type** has its population listed in the Population tables, pages 230 to 280. Each country, shown in CAPITAL LETTERS, has its population listed in the World Political Information Table, pages 6 to 10. * Does not appear on map; key shows general location.

West Wyoming, Pa. B8 202
West Yarmouth, Mass. C7 185
West Yellowstone, Mont. F5 190
West York, Ill. D6 178
West York, Pa. G8 202
West Yuma, Ariz. *E1 168
Westalton, Mo. A8 189
Westbank, B.C., Can. E8 149
Westbay, Fla. G3 174
Westboro, Mo. A2 189
Westboro, Wis. C3 212
Westborough, Mass. B4, D1 185
Westbourne, Man., Can. D2 150
Westbourne, Tenn. C9 205
Westbrook, Conn. D7 172
Westbrook, Maine E2, E5 184
Westbrook, Minn. F3 187
Westbrook, Tex. C2 206
Westbrookville, N.Y. D6 196
Westbury, N.Y. G2 172
Westby, Mont. B12 190
Westby, Wis. E3 212
Westchester, Ill. *B6 178
Westchester, co., N.Y. D7 196
Westcliffe, Colo. C5 171
Westconnaug, res., R.I. B10 172
Westcreek, Colo. B5 171
Westend, Calif. E5 170
Wester Schelde, chan., Neth C3 59
Westerham, Sask., Can. G1 155
Westerkappeln, Ger. A2 61
Westerland, Ger. A4 60
Westerly, R.I. D9 172
Western, Nebr. D8 191
Western, prov., Zambia E3 106
Western, reg., Ghana E4 103
Western, reg., Nig. E5 103
Western, reg., Tan. C5 106
Western, reg., Ug. E5 106
Western, downs, Eng. E5 55
Western, isl., Newf., Can. C4 152
Western Australia, state, Austl. D3 111
Western Ghats, range, India E5 87
Western Grove, Ark. A3 169
WESTERN SAMOA, country, Oceania 114
Western Springs, Ill. F2 178
Westernport, Md. D2 173
Westerstede, Ger. A7 59
Westervelt, Ill. D5 178
Westerville, Nebr. C6 191
Westerville, Ohio B5 199
Westerwald, mts., Ger. C2 61
Westfall, Kans. D5 181
Westfall, Oreg. D9 201
Westfield, N.B., Can. D3 151
Westfield, Ill. D6 178
Westfield, Ind. D5 179
Westfield, Iowa B1 180
Westfield, Maine B5 184
Westfield, Mass. B2 185
Westfield, N.J. B4 194
Westfield, N.Y. C1 196
Westfield, N.C. A3 197
Westfield, N. Dak. C5 198
Westfield, Pa. C6 202
Westfield, Vt. B4 208
Westfield, Wis. E4 212
Westfield, riv., Mass. B2 185
Westfir, Oreg. D4 201
Westford, Conn. B8 172
Westford, Mass. C1 185
Westford, Vt. B2 208
Westgate, Fla. F6 174
Westgate, Iowa B6 180
Westhampton, N.Y. F6 172
Westhampton, beach, N.Y. G6 172
Westhampton Beach, N.Y. D4 196
Westhoff, Tex. E4 206
Westhope, N. Dak. A4 198
Westkapelle, Bel. C3 59
Westkapelle, Neth. C3 59
Westlake, La. D2 183
Westlake, Ohio B1 199
Westlake, Oreg. D2 201
Westley, Calif. B6 170
Westline, Pa. C4 202
Westlink, Kans. B5 181
Westlock, Alta., Can. B4 148
Westmeath, Ont., Can. B8 153
Westminster, Calif. *F5 170
Westminster, Colo. B5 171
Westminster, city of, Eng. k11 55
Westminster, Md. A4 173
Westminster, Mass. A4 185
Westminster, S.C. B1 203
Westminster, Vt. E4 208
Westminster Station, Vt. E4 208
Westminster West, Vt. E3 208
Westmont, Ill. F2 178
Westmont, N.J. D2 194
Westmont, Pa. F4 202
Westmoreland, Kans. C7 181
Westmoreland, N.H. E2 193
Westmoreland, Tenn. A5 205
Westmoreland, co., Pa. F2 202
Westmoreland, co., Va. C6 209
Westmoreland Depot, N.H. D2 193
Westmorland, Calif. F6 170
Westmorland, co., N.B., Can. C5 151
Westmount, Que., Can. *D9 154
Weston, Ont., Can. E6 153
Weston, Colo. D6 171
Weston, Conn. E3 172
Weston, Ga. E2 175
Weston, Idaho G7 177
Weston, Ill. C5 178
Weston, Maine C5 184
Weston, Mass. D2 185
Weston, Mo. B3, D1 189
Weston, Nebr. C9 191
Weston, Ohio A4 199
Weston, Oreg. B8 201
Weston, Vt. E3 208
Weston, W. Va. B4 211
Weston, Wyo. A7 213
Weston, co., Wyo. B8 213
Weston-super-Mare, Eng. C5 56
Westover, Ala. B3 166
Westover, Md. D6 173
Westover, Pa. E4 202
Westover, W. Va. A7, B5 211
Westphalia, Ind. G3 179
Westphalia, Kans. D8 181
Westphalia, Mich. F6 186
Westphalia, Mo. C5 189
Westphalia, reg., Ger. C3 60
in 1810 50
in 1860's 51
Westpoint, Ind. D3 179
Westpoint, Tenn. B4 205
Westport, Newf., Can. D3, k10 152
Westport, N.S., Can. E3 151
Westport, Ont., Can. C8 153
Westport, Conn. E3 172
Westport, Ind. F6 179
Westport, Ire. D2 55
Westport, Ky. A4, B4 182
Westport, Mass. C5 185
Westport, Minn. E3 187
Westport, N.H. E2 193
Westport, N.Y. A7, B3 196
Westport, N.Z. N13 112
Westport, Oreg. A3 201
Westport, S. Dak. B7 204
Westport, Tenn. B3 205
Westport, Wash. C1 210
Westport Point, Mass. C5 185
Westray, firth, Scot. A5 57
Westray, isl., Scot. A5 57
Westrhauderfehn, Ger. A7 59
Westside, Iowa B2 180
Westterschelling, Neth. A5 59
Westville, N.S., Can. D7 151
Westville, Fla. G3 174
Westville, Ill. C6 178
Westville, Ind. A4 179
Westville, N.H. E4 193
Westville, N.J. D2 194
Westville, Ohio B4 199
Westville, Okla. B7 200
Westville, Pa. D4 202
Westville, S.C. C6 203
Westville, res., Mass. B3 185
Westwater, Utah D6 207
Westway, Conn. B7 172
Westwego, La. C7, E5 183
Westwold, B.C., Can. D8 149
Westwood, Calif. B3 170
Westwood, Kans. B9 181
Westwood, Ky. B7 182
Westwood, Mass. B5, D2 185
Westwood, N.J. B4, D5 194
Westwood Lakes, Fla. F3 174
Westworth, Tex. *C4 206
Wet, mts., Colo. C5 171
Wetar, isl., Indon. G7 90
Wetaskiwin, Alta., Can. C4 148
Wethersfield, Conn. C6 172
Wetmore, Colo. C5 171
Wetmore, Kans. C8 181
Wetmore, Mich. B4 186
Wetonka, S. Dak. B7 204
Wettingen, Switz. B4 66
Wetumka, Okla. B5 200
Wetumpka, Ala. C3 166
Wetzel, co., W. Va. B4 211
Wetzlar, Ger. C3 61
Wevelgem, Bel. D3 59
Wever, Iowa D6 180
Wewahitchka, Fla. B1 174
Wewak, N. Gui. h11 111
Wewela, S. Dak. D6 204
Wewoka, Okla. B5 200
Wexford, Ire. D3 55
Wexford, co., Ire. B1 56
Wexford, co., Mich. D5 186
Weyakwin, lake, Sask., Can. C3 155
Weyanoke, La. D4 183
Weyauwega, Wis. D5 212
Weyburn, Sask., Can. H4 155
Weyerhauser, Wis. C2 212
Weyers Cave, Va. C4 209
Weymouth, N.S., Can. E4 151
Weymouth [& Melcombe Regis], Eng. D5 56
Weymouth, Mass. B6, D3 185
Weymouth, bay, Eng. D5 56
Whakatane, N.Z. L16 112
Whalan, Minn. G7 187
Whaley, pond, N.Y. C2 172
Whaleysville, Md. D7 173
Whaleyville, Va. E6 209
Whangarei, N.Z. K15 112
Whangarei, hbr., N.Z. K15 112
Whappen Rig, mtn., Scot. E5 57
Wharfe, riv., Eng. D6 55
Wharton, N.J. B3 194
Wharton, Ohio B4 199
Wharton, Pa. C5 202
Wharton, Tex. E4 206
Wharton, W. Va. D6 211
Wharton, co., Tex. E4 206
Wharton West, Tex. *E4 206
What Cheer, Iowa C5 180
Whatcom, co., Wash. A4 210
Whatcom, lake, Wash. A3 210
Whately, Mass. B2 185
Whatley, Ala. D2 166
Wheat Ridge, Colo. B5 171
Wheatcroft, Ky. C2 182
Wheatfield, Ind. B3 179
Wheatland, Calif. C3 170
Wheatland, Ind. G3 179
Wheatland, Iowa C7 180
Wheatland, Mo. D4 189
Wheatland, N. Dak. C8 198
Wheatland, Okla. B4 200
Wheatland, Pa. *D1 202
Wheatland, Wyo. C8 213
Wheatland, co., Mont. D7 190
Wheatley, Ark. C4 169
Wheatley, Ont., Can. E2 153
Wheaton, Ill. B5, F2 178
Wheaton, Kans. C7 181
Wheaton, Md. B3 173
Wheaton, Minn. E2 187
Wheaton, Mo. E3 189
Wheelbarrow, peak, Nev. F5 192
Wheeler, Ala. A2 166
Wheeler, Ill. D5 178
Wheeler, Ind. A3 179
Wheeler, Kans. C2 181
Wheeler, Miss. A5 188
Wheeler, Mont. B10 190
Wheeler, Oreg. B3 201
Wheeler, Tex. B2 206
Wheeler, Wis. C2 212
Wheeler, co., Ga. D4 175
Wheeler, co., Nebr. C7 191
Wheeler, co., Oreg. C6 201
Wheeler, co., Tex. B2 206
Wheeler, dam, Ala. A2 166
Wheeler, peak, Calif. C4 170
Wheeler, peak, Nev. E7 192
Wheeler, peak, N. Mex. A4 195
Wheeler, res., Ala. A2 166
Wheelersburg, Ohio D5 199
Wheeless, Okla. D1 200
Wheeling, Ill. E2 178
Wheeling, Mo. B4 189
Wheeling, W. Va. A4, B2 211
Wheeling, creek, W. Va. B2 211
Wheelock, N. Dak. A2 198
Wheelock, Vt. B4 208
Wheelock, mtn., Vt. B4 208
Wheelwright, Ky. C7 182
Wheelwright, Mass. B3 185
Whelen Springs, Ark. D2 169
Whernside, mtn., Eng. F6 57
Whickham, Eng. F7 57
Whidbey, isl., Wash. A3 210
Whigham, Ga. F2 175
Whipholt, Minn. C4 187
Whippany, N.J. B4 194
Whipple, W. Va. D7 211
Whirlwind, reef, Bis. Arch. 115
Whiskey, peak, Wyo. C5 213
Whiskey Chitto, creek, La. C2 183
Whiskey Gap, Alta., Can. E4 148
Whitacres, Conn. A6 172
Whitaker, Pa. *F2 202
Whitakers, N.C. A6 197
Whitbourne, Newf., Can. E5 152
Whitby, Ont., Can. D6 153
Whitby, Eng. C6 55
Whitchurch, Eng. B5 56
Whitchurch-Stouffville, Ont., Can. *D5 153
Whitcomb, mtn., N.H. A4 193
White, Ga. B2 175
White, S. Dak. C9 204
White, co., Ark. B4 169
White, co., Ga. B3 175
White, co., Ill. E5 178
White, co., Ind. C4 179
White, co., Tenn. D8 205
White, bay, Newf., Can. D3 152
White, butte, N. Dak. C2 198
White, isl., Nor. A11 118
White, lake, Ont., Can. B8 153
White, lake, La. E3 183
White, mts., Calif., Nev. F3 192
White, mts., N.H. B3 193
White, pass, B.C., Can., U.S. E5 142
White, riv., Ariz. D5 168
White, riv., Ark., Mo. E4 189
White, riv., Colo., Utah C6 207
White, riv., Ind. H3 179
White, riv., Mich. E4 186
White, riv., Nebr., S. Dak. A3 191
White, riv., Nev. E6 192
White, riv., Tex. C2 206
White, riv., Vt. D3 208
White, riv., Wash. B4 210
White, riv., Wash. B5 210
White, sea, Sov. Un. E17 63
White Bear, Sask., Can. G1 155
White Bear, is., Newf., Can. A3 152
White Bear, lake, Newf., Can. A2 152
White Bear, riv., Newf., Can. E3 152
White Bear Beach, Minn. E7 187
White Bear Lake, Minn. E5, E7 187
White Bird, Idaho D2 177
White Bluff, Tenn. A4 205
White Breast, creek, Iowa C4 180
White Butte, S. Dak. B3 204
White Canyon, Utah F5 207
White Cap, mtn., Maine C3 184
White Carpathians, mts., Czech D4 70
White Castle, La. B5, D4 183
White City, Sask., Can. *G3 155
White City, Fla. E6 174
White City, Kans. D7 181
White Clay, creek, Del., Pa. A6 173
White Clay, creek, Nebr., S. Dak. B3 191
White Cliffs, Austl. E4 112
White Cloud, Kans. C8 181
White Cloud, Mich. E5 186
White Cone, Ariz. B5 168
White Coomb, mtn., Scot. E5 57
White Deer, Tex. B2 206
White Earth, Minn. C3 187
White Earth, N. Dak. A3 198
White Earth, Indian res., Minn. C3 187
White Earth, lake, Minn. C3 187
White Face, mtn., Vt. B3 208
White Fathers, N.Y. B6 196
White Fish, pt., Wis. D6 212
White Fox, Sask., Can. D3 155
White Gull, creek, Sask., Can. D3 155
White Gull, lake, Que., Can. g8 152
White Hall, Ala. C3 166
White Hall, Ga. C3 175
White Hall, Ill. D3 178
White Hall, Md. A4 173
White Hall, S.C. F6 203
White Haven, Pa. D10 202
White Heath, Ill. C5 178
White Horse, N.J. C3 194
White Horse Beach, Mass. C6 185
White House Station, N.J. B3 194
White Knob, mts., Idaho F5 177
White Lake, Ont., Can. B8 153
White Lake, S. Dak. D7 204
White Lake, Wis. C5 212
White Mesa, natural bridge, Ariz. A4 168
White Mills, Pa. C11 202
White Mountain, Alsk. C7 167
White Mountain, peak, Calif. D4 170
White Nile, see Bahr el Abyad, riv., Sud.
White Oak, Ga. E5 175
White Oak, N.C. C5 197
White Oak, Ohio D2 199
White Oak, Okla. A6 200
White Oak, Pa. *F2 202
White Oak, S.C. C5 203
White Oak, Tex. *C5 206
White Oak, lake, Ark. D2 169
White Oak, mtn., Ark. C2 169
White Owl, S. Dak. C3 204
White Pigeon, Mich. G5 186
White Pine, Mich. A5 186
White Pine, Tenn. C10 205
White Pine, co., Nev. D6 192
White Plains, Ala. B4 166
White Plains, Ga. C3 175
White Plains, Ky. C2 182
White Plains, Md. C4 173
White Plains, N.Y. D2, D3, D7 196
White Plains, N.C. A3 197
White Pond, S.C. E5 203
White River, S. Dak. D5 204
White River, plat., Colo. B3 171
White River Junction, Vt. D4 208
White Rock, B.C., Can. B10, E6 149
White Rock, R.I. D9 172
White Rock, S.C. C5 203
White Rock, S. Dak. B9 204
White Rocks, mtn., Ky. D6 182
White Russia: after World War II 54
White Salmon, Wash. D4 210
White Salmon, riv., Wash. D4 210
White Sands, nat. mon., N. Mex. E3 195
White Settlement, Tex. *C4 206
White Springs, Fla. B4 174
White Stone, Va. D6 209
White Sulphur Springs, Mont. D6 190
White Sulphur Springs, W. Va. D4 211
White Swan, Wash. C5 210
White Tank, mts., Ariz. G1 168
White Volta, riv., Ghana E4 103
White Woman, creek, Kans. D2 181
Whiteadder, riv., Scot. E6 57
Whiteclay, Nebr. B3 191
Whiteday, creek, W. Va. A7 211
Whitecourt, Alta., Can. B3 148
Whitedeer, Pa. D8 202
Whiteface, Tex. C1 206
Whiteface, mtn., N.Y. B3 196
Whiteface, riv., Minn. C6 187
Whitefield, N.H. B3 193
Whitefield, Okla. B6 200
Whitefish, Ont., Can. A3 153
Whitefish, Mont. B2 190
Whitefish, bay, Ont., Can. A4 187
Whitefish, bay, Mich. B6 186
Whitefish, lake, Ont., Can. A8 187
Whitefish, lake, Minn. D4 187
Whitefish, pt., Wis. D6 212
Whitefish, range, Mont. B2 190
Whitefish, riv., Mich. B4 186
Whitefish Bay, Wis. E2 212
Whitefish Falls, Ont., Can. A3 153
Whitefish Point, Mich. B6 186
Whiteflat, Tex. B2 206
Whiteford, Md. A5 173
Whitefox, riv., Sask., Can. D3 155
Whitehall, La. B6, D5 183
Whitehall, Mich. E4 186
Whitehall, Mont. E4 190
Whitehall, N.Y. B7 196
Whitehall, Ohio C2 199
Whitehall, Pa. *F1 202
Whitehall, Wis. D2 212
Whitehall, res., Mass. D1 185
Whitehaven, Eng. C5 55
Whitehaven, Md. D6 173
Whitehaven, Tenn. E8 205
Whitehead, Ala. A2 166
Whitehorn, pt., Wash. A3 210
Whitehorse, Yukon, Can. D5 144
Whitehorse, S. Dak. B5 204
Whitehouse, Ohio A1, A4 199
Whitehouse, Scot. C6 57
Whiteland, Ind. *E5 179
Whitelaw, Alta., Can. A1 148
Whitelaw, Wis. B6 212
Whiteleysburg, Del. C6 173
Whiteman, mts., New Britain I. 115
Whitemouth, Man., Can. E4 150
Whitemouth, lake, Man., Can. E4 150
Whitemouth, riv., Man., Can. E4 150
Whitemud, riv., Alta., Can. A2 148
Whiteoak, Tenn. B4 205
Whiteoak, creek, Ohio D4 199
Whiteoak, creek, Tenn. A4 205
Whiteoak, swamp, N.C. C6 197
Whitepine, Mont. C1 190
Whiteriver, Ariz. D6 168
Whiterocks, Utah C6 207
Whites, Miss. B5 188
Whites, Wash. B2 210
Whites, creek, Tenn. E9 205
Whites Brook, N.B., Can. B2 151
Whites City, N. Mex. E5 195
Whites Creek, Tenn. E9 205
Whitesail, lake, B.C., Can. C4 149
Whitesand, bay, Eng. D3 56
Whitesand, riv., Sask., Can. F4 155
Whitesbog, N.J. D3 194
Whitesboro, N.J. E3 194
Whitesboro, N.Y. *B5 196
Whitesboro, Okla. C7 200
Whitesboro, Tex. C4 206
Whitesburg, Ga. C2 175
Whitesburg, Ky. C7 182
Whiteshell, prov. park, Man., Can. D4 150
Whiteshield, mtn., B.C., Alta., Can. C8 149
Whiteside, Mo. B6 189
Whiteside, Tenn. D8 205
Whiteside, co., Ill. B3 178
Whiteson, Oreg. B1, B3 201
Whitestone, Ga. B2 175
Whitestone, lake, Man., Can. A3 150
Whitestown, Ind. D5 179
Whitesville, Ky. C3 182
Whitesville, N.Y. C3 196
Whitesville, W. Va. D6 211
Whiteswan, lakes, Sask., Can. C3 155
Whitetail, Mont. B11 190
Whiteville, N.C. C5 197
Whiteville, Tenn. B2 205
Whitewater, Man., Can. E1 150
Whitewater, Colo. C2 171
Whitewater, Kans. B6, E6 181
Whitewater, Mo. D8 189
Whitewater, Mont. B9 190
Whitewater, Wis. F5 212
Whitewater, bay, Fla. G6 174
Whitewater, riv., Ind. F7 179
Whitewater, riv., Kans. B6 181
Whitewater Baldy, mtn., N. Mex. D1 195
Whitewood, Sask., Can. G4 155
Whitewood, S. Dak. C2 204
Whitewright, Tex. C4 206
Whitfield, Ala. C1 166
Whitfield, co., Ga. B2 175
Whitfield Estate, Fla. F2 174
Whitham, Mo. B4 189
Whithorn, Scot. F4 57
Whiting, Ind. A3 179
Whiting, Iowa B1 180
Whiting, Kans. A7, C8 181
Whiting, Maine D5 184
Whiting, N.J. D4 194
Whiting, Vt. D2 208
Whiting, Wis. D4 212
Whiting Bay, Scot. E3 57
Whitingham, Vt. F3 208
Whitingham, res., Vt. F3 208
Whitinsville, Mass. B4 185
Whitkow, Sask., Can. E2 155
Whitla, Alta., Can. E5 148
Whitlash, Mont. B5 190
Whitley, co., Ind. B6 179
Whitley, co., Ky. D5 182
Whitley City, Ky. D5 182
Whitlock, Tenn. A3 205
Whitman, Mass. B6, E5 185
Whitman, Nebr. B4 191
Whitman, N. Dak. A7 198
Whitman, Wyo. C8 213
Whitman, co., Wash. B8 210
Whitmans, pond, Mass. D3 185
Whitmell, Va. E3 209
Whitmer, W. Va. C5 211
Whitmire, S.C. C4 203
Whitmore, Haw. f9 176
Whitmore, mts., Ant. A2 119
Whitmore Lake, Mich. A6 186
Whitnel, N.C. B2 197
Whitney, Ont., Can. B6 153
Whitney, Idaho G7 177
Whitney, Nebr. B2 191
Whitney, Oreg. C8 201
Whitney, Pa. F3 202
Whitney, S.C. B4 203
Whitney, Tex. D4 206
Whitney, mtn., Calif. D4 170
Whitney Point, N.Y. C5 196
Whitneyville, Maine D5 184
Whitsett, N.C. A4 197
Whitstable, Eng. C9 56
Whitt, Tex. C4 206
Whittaker, Mich. B6 186
Whittemore, Iowa A3 180
Whittemore, Mich. D7 186
Whitten, Iowa B4 180
Whittier, Alsk. C10, g17 167
Whittier, Calif. F2, F4 170
Whittier, N.C. D3 197
Whittlesey, Eng. B7 56
Whittlesey, mtn., Wis. B3 212
Whitwell, Tenn. D8 205
Wholdaia, lake, N.W. Ter., Can. D12 142
Whonock, B.C., Can. A10 149
Whyalla, Austl. F6 111
Whycocomagh, N.S., Can. D8 151
Wiarton, Ont., Can. C3 153
Wiay, isl., Scot. C1 57
Wibaux, Mont. D12 190
Wibaux, co., Mont. D12 190
Wiborg, Ky. D5 182
Wichita, Kans. B5, E6 181
Wichita, co., Kans. D2 181
Wichita, co., Tex. B3 206
Wichita, mtn., Okla. C2 200
Wichita, mts., Okla. C3 200
Wichita Falls, Tex. C3 206
Wick, Scot. B5 57
Wickatunk, N.J. C4 194
Wicked, pt., Ont., Can. D7 153
Wickenburg, Ariz. D3 168
Wickes, Ark. C1 169
Wickes, Mont. D4 190
Wickett, Tex. D1 206
Wickham, Que., Can. *D5 154
Wickiup, res., Oreg. D5 201
Wickliffe, Ky. A2 182
Wickliffe, Ohio A6, B2 199
Wicklow, Ire. D3 55
Wicklow, mts., Ire. D3 55
Wicksville, S. Dak. C3 204
Wicomico, co., Md. D6 173
Wicomico, riv., Md. D4 173
Wicomico, riv., Md. D6 173
Wiconisco, Pa. E8 202
Wide, bay, New Britain I. 115
Wide, passage, Eniwetok 114
Wide Ruin, Ariz. B6 168
Widemouth, W. Va. D3 211
Widen, W. Va. C4, C7 211
Widener, Ark. B5 169
Widnes, Eng. A5 56
Widuchowo, Pol. E8 62
Wiebelskirchen, Ger. D2 61
Wiedenbrück, Ger. B3 61
Wieliczka, Pol. C6 70
Wielka Wieś, Pol. A5 70
Wieluń, Pol. C5 70
Wien, see Vienna, Aus.
Wiener Neustadt, Aus. E8 60
Wieprz, riv., Pol. C7 70
Wieprzówka, riv., Pol. h10 70
Wiergate, Tex. D6 206
Wiesau, Ger. D7 61
Wiesbaden, Ger. C3 61
Wiesenburg, Ger. A7 61
Wiesental, Ger. D3 61
Wiesloch, Ger. D3 61
Wigan, Eng. A5 56
Wiggins, Colo. A6 171
Wiggins, Miss. E4 188
Wiggins, peak, Wyo. B3 213
Wight, isl., Eng. D6 56
Wigton, Eng. F5 57
Wigtown, Scot. F4 57
Wigtown, co., Scot. F4 57
Wigtown, bay, Scot. F4 57
Wiheish, isl., Eg. C2 84
Wijhe, Neth. B6 59
Wikieup, Ariz. C2 168
Wikwemikong, Ont., Can. B3 153
Wil, Switz. B5 66
Wilamette Summit, mtn., Oreg. D4 201
Wilbarger, co., Tex. B3 206
Wilber, Nebr. D9 191
Wilberforce, Ont., Can. B6 153
Wilberforce, Ohio C4 199
Wilbraham, Mass. *B3 185
Wilbur, Oreg. D3 201
Wilbur, Wash. B7 210
Wilbur Park, Mo. *C7 189
Wilburn, Ark. B4 169
Wilburton, Okla. C6 200
Wilcannia, Austl. E4 112
Wilcox, Sask., Can. G3 155
Wilcox, Fla. C4 174
Wilcox, Nebr. D6 191
Wilcox, Pa. C4 202
Wilcox, co., Ala. D2 166
Wilcox, riv., Mass. B1 185
Wilcox, co., Ga. E3 175
Wild, brook, Vt. B4 208
Wild, riv., N.H. B4 193
Wild Cherry, Ark. A3 169
Wild Horse, Colo. C8 171
Wild Horse, creek, Wyo. A7 213
Wild Horse, res., Nev. B6 192
Wild Rice, N. Dak. C9 198
Wild Rice, riv., Minn. C2 187
Wild Rice, riv., N. Dak. C8 198
Wild Rose, Wis. D4 212
Wilda, La. C3 183
Wildbad, Ger. E3 61
Wildcat, Okla. B6 200
Wildcat, creek, Ind. D4 179
Wildcat, hill, Sask., Can. D4 155
Wildcat Top, mtn., Tenn. D10 205
Wilden, Pa. *E11 202
Wilder, Idaho F2 177

INDEX KEY Each place listed in **Bold-faced Type** has its population listed in the Political tables, pages 230 to 280.
Each country, shown in CAPITAL LETTERS, has its population listed in the World Political Information Table, pages 6 to 10.
* Does not appear on map; key shows general location.

Wilder, Tenn. ... C8 205
Wilder, Vt. ... D4 208
Wilder, dam, N.H. ... C2 193
Wildersville, Tenn. ... B3 205
Wildervank, Neth. ... A6 59
Wilderville, Oreg. ... E3 201
Wildeshausen, Ger. ... F2 62
Wildhorse, creek, Okla. ... C4 200
Wildnest, lake, Sask., Can. ... C4 155
Wildomar, Calif. ... F3 170
Wildorado, Tex. ... B1 206
Wildrose, N. Dak. ... A2 198
Wildspitze, mtn., Aus. ... C6 66
Wildsville, La. ... C4 183
Wildwood, Alta., Can. ... C3 148
Wildwood, Fla. ... D4 174
Wildwood, N.J. ... F3 194
Wildwood Crest, N.J. ... F3 194
Wiley, Colo. ... C8 171
Wilhelm, mtn., N. Gui. ... k12 110
Wilhelm-Pieck-Stadt Guben, Ger. ... B9 61
Wilhelm II, coast, Ant. ... C22 120
Wilhelmina, mtn., Indon. ... F9 90
Wilhelmina, mts., Sur. ... B3 139
Wilhelmshaven, Ger. ... B4 60, E2 62
Wilkau, Ger. ... C7 61
Wilkes, co., Ga. ... C4 175
Wilkes, co., N.C. ... A2 197
Wilkes, isl., Wake I. ... 114
Wilkes-Barre, Pa. ... B8, D10 202
Wilkes Land, reg., Ant. ... B25 120
Wilkesboro, N.C. ... A2 197
Wilkesboro, flood control res., N.C. ... A2 197
Wilkeson, Wash. ... B3 210
Wilkesville, Ohio ... C5 199
Wilkie, Sask., Can. ... E1 155
Wilkin, co., Minn. ... D2 187
Wilkins, Nev. ... B7 192
Wilkinsburg, Pa. ... B6, F2 202
Wilkinson, Ind. ... E6 179
Wilkinson, Miss. ... D2 188
Wilkinson, W. Va. ... D3 211
Wilkinson, co., Ga. ... D3 175
Wilkinson, co., Miss. ... D2 188
Will, co., Ill. ... B6 178
Willacoochee, Ga. ... E3 175
Willacy, co., Tex. ... F4 206
Willamette, riv., Oreg. ... C3 201
Willamina, Oreg. ... B3 201
Willapa, Wash. ... C2 210
Willapa, bay, Wash. ... C1 210
Willapa, hills, Wash. ... C2 210
Willard, Colo. ... A7 171
Willard, Kans. ... C8 181
Willard, Ky. ... B7 182
Willard, Mo. ... D4 189
Willard, Mont. ... D12 190
Willard, N. Mex. ... C3 195
Willard, N.Y. ... C4 196
Willard, N.C. ... C6 197
Willard, Ohio ... A5 199
Willard, Utah ... B3 207
Willard, Wis. ... D3 212
Willard, stream, Vt. ... B5 208
Willards, Md. ... D7 173
Willcox, Ariz. ... E6 168
Willemstad, Neth. ... C4 59
Willemstad, Neth. Antilles ... A4 133
Willernie, Minn. ... E7 187
Willesden, Eng. ... *k12 55
Willet, N.Y. ... C5 196
Willette, Tenn. ... C8 205
Willey House, N.H. ... B4 193
William, lake, Man., Can. ... C2 150
William Creek, Austl. ... E6 111
Williams, Ariz. ... B3 168
Williams, Calif. ... C2 170
Williams, Ind. ... G4 179
Williams, Iowa ... B4 180
Williams, Minn. ... B4 187
Williams, Mont. ... B4 190
Williams, S.C. ... E6 203
Williams, co., N. Dak. ... A2 198
Williams, co., Ohio ... A3 199
Williams, cape, Ant. ... C29 120
Williams, mtn., Okla. ... C7 200
Williams, riv., Ariz. ... C1 168
Williams, riv., Vt. ... E3 208
Williams, riv., W. Va. ... C4 211
Williams Bay, Wis. ... F5 212
Williams Lake, B.C., Can. ... C6, E3 149
Williamsburg, Ont., Can. ... C9 153
Williamsburg, Ind. ... E8 179
Williamsburg, Iowa ... C5 180
Williamsburg, Kans. ... D8 181
Williamsburg, Ky. ... D5 182
Williamsburg, Md. ... C6 173
Williamsburg, Mass. ... B2 185
Williamsburg, Mich. ... D5 186
Williamsburg, N. Mex. ... D2 195
Williamsburg, Ohio ... C3 199
Williamsburg, Pa. ... F5 202
Williamsburg (Independent City), Va. ... D6 209
Williamsburg, W. Va. ... D4 211
Williamsburg, co., S.C. ... D8 203
Williamsfield, Ill. ... C3 178
Williamson, Ga. ... C2 175
Williamson, Ill. ... A9 189
Williamson, Iowa ... C4 180
Williamson, N.Y. ... B3 196
Williamson, W. Va. ... D2 211
Williamson, co., Ill. ... F5 178
Williamson, co., Tenn. ... B5 205
Williamson, co., Tex. ... D4 206
Williamson, head, Ant. ... C28 120
Williamsport, Newf., Can. ... C3 152
Williamsport, Ind. ... D3 179
Williamsport, Md. ... A2 173
Williamsport, Ohio ... C4 199
Williamsport, Pa. ... D7 202
Williamsport, Tenn. ... B4 205
Williamston, Mich. ... F6 186
Williamston, N.C. ... B6 197
Williamston, S.C. ... B3 203
Williamstown, Ont., Can. ... B10 153
Williamstown, Kans. ... B7 181
Williamstown, Ky. ... B5 182
Williamstown, Mass. ... A1 185
Williamstown, Mo. ... A6 189
Williamstown, N.J. ... D3 194
Williamstown, N.Y. ... B5 196
Williamstown, Ohio ... B4 199
Williamstown, Pa. ... E8 202
Williamstown, Vt. ... C3 208
Williamstown, W. Va. ... B3 211
Williamsville, Ill. ... D4 178
Williamsville, Miss. ... B4 188
Williamsville, Mo. ... E7 189
Williamsville, N.Y. ... C2 196
Williamsville, Vt. ... F3 208
Williaumez, pen., New Britain I. ... 115
Williford, Ark. ... A4 169
Williford, Fla. ... C4 174
Willimantic, Conn. ... C8 172
Willimantic, riv., Conn. ... B7 172
Willingboro, N.J. ... *C3 194
Willingdon, Alta., Can. ... C4 148
Willis, Kans. ... C8 181
Willis, Mich. ... A7 186
Willis, Okla. ... D5 200
Willis, Tex. ... D5 206
Willis, Va. ... E2 209
Willis, isl., Newf., Can. ... D5 152
Willis Beach, Nebr. ... B9 191
Willis Creek, res., Ohio ... B6 199
Willis Wharf, Va. ... D7 209
Willisburg, Ky. ... C4 182
Williston, Fla. ... C4 174
Williston, N.C. ... C7 197
Williston, N. Dak. ... A2 198
Williston, Ohio ... A2 199
Williston, S. Afr. ... D3 107
Williston, S.C. ... E5 203
Williston, Tenn. ... B2 205
Williston, Vt. ... C2 208
Williston Basin, reg., Mont., N. Dak. ... B11 190, A1 198
Williston Park, N.Y. ... G2 172
Willisville, Ark. ... D2 169
Willisville, Ill. ... F4 178
Willits, Calif. ... C2 170
Willmar, Minn. ... E3 187
Willmar Station, Sask., Can. ... H4 155
Willmore Wilderness, prov. park Alta., B.C., Can. ... C1 148
Willoughby, Austl. ... *F8 112
Willoughby, Ohio ... A6 199
Willoughby, lake, Vt. ... B4 208
Willoughby Hills, Ohio ... A6 199
Willow, Alsk. ... g16 167
Willow, Ark. ... C3 169
Willow, Okla. ... B2 200
Willow, creek, Utah ... D6 207
Willow, creek, Wyo. ... B6 213
Willow, res., Wis. ... C3 212
Willow, riv., B.C., Can. ... C6 149
Willow Branch, Ind. ... E6 179
Willow Bunch, Sask., Can. ... H3 155
Willow City, N. Dak. ... A5 198
Willow City, Tex. ... D3 206
Willow Creek, Mont. ... E5 190
Willow Grove, Pa. ... A11, F11 202
Willow Hill, Ill. ... E5 178
Willow Hill, Pa. ... F6 202
Willow Island, Nebr. ... D5 191
Willow Lake, S. Dak. ... C8 204
Willow Ranch, Calif. ... B3 170
Willow River, Minn. ... D6 187
Willow Springs, Ill. ... F2 178
Willow Springs, Mo. ... E6 189
Willowbrook, Sask., Can. ... F4 155
Willowbunch, lake, Sask., Can. ... H3 155
Willowcreek, Oreg. ... C9 201
Willowdale, Ont., Can. ... E6 153
Willowgrove, Del. ... B6 173
Willowick, Ohio ... B2 199
Willowmore, S. Afr. ... D3 107
Willows, Calif. ... C2 170
Willows, Sask., Can. ... H3 155
Wills, creek, W. Va. ... C6 211
Wills, hill, Mass. ... C3 185
Wills, mtn., Md. ... D2 173
Wills Creek, res., Ohio ... A3 211
Wills Point, Tex. ... *C5 206
Willsboro, N.Y. ... B3 196
Willshire, Ohio ... B3 199
Wilma, Fla. ... B2 174
Wilmar, Ark. ... D4 169
Wilmer, Ala. ... E1 166
Wilmer, Tex. ... B6 206
Wilmerding, Pa. ... B6 202
Wilmersdorf, Ger. ... E7 62
Wilmette, Ill. ... A6, E3 178
Wilmington, Del. ... A6 173
Wilmington, Ill. ... B5 178
Wilmington, Mass. ... A5, C2 185
Wilmington, N.Y. ... B3 196
Wilmington, N.C. ... C6 197
Wilmington, Ohio ... C4 199
Wilmington, Vt. ... F3 208
Wilmington, lake, Fla. ... E6 174
Wilmont, Minn. ... G3 187
Wilmore, Kans. ... E4 181
Wilmore, Ky. ... C5 182
Wilmot, Ark. ... D4 169
Wilmot, Kans. ... E7 181
Wilmot, N.H. ... D3 193
Wilmot, Ohio ... B6 199
Wilmot, S. Dak. ... B9 204
Wilmot Flat, N.H. ... D3 193
Wilmot Station, N.S., Can. ... E4 151
Wilmurt, N.Y. ... B6 196
Wilno, Ont., Can. ... B7 153
Wilrijk, Bel. ... C4 59
Wilsall, Mont. ... E6 190
Wilsey, Kans. ... D7 181
Wilson, Ark. ... B5 169
Wilson, Conn. ... B6 172
Wilson, Fla. ... D6 174
Wilson, Kans. ... D5 181
Wilson, La. ... D4 183
Wilson, Mich. ... C3 186
Wilson, N.Y. ... B2 196
Wilson, N.C. ... B5 197
Wilson, Okla. ... C4 200
Wilson, Pa. ... E11 202
Wilson, Tex. ... C2 206
Wilson, Wyo. ... B2 213
Wilson, co., Kans. ... E8 181
Wilson, co., N.C. ... B5 197
Wilson, co., Tenn. ... A5 205
Wilson, co., Tex. ... E3 206
Wilson, creek, Wash. ... B5 210
Wilson, creek, Wash. ... B6 210
Wilson, dam, Ala. ... A2 166
Wilson, lake, Ala. ... A2 166
Wilson, mtn., Ariz. ... B1 168
Wilson, mtn., Calif. ... F2 170
Wilson, mtn., Colo. ... D3 171
Wilson, mtn., Nev. ... E7 192
Wilson, mtn., Oreg. ... B5 201
Wilson, pond, Maine ... C3 184
Wilson, res., Kans. ... C5 181
Wilson, riv., Austl. ... C4 112
Wilson, strait, Sol. Is. ... 115
Wilson Creek, Wash. ... B6 210
Wilson Mills (Lincoln Plantation), Maine ... D1 184
Wilson Mills, N.C. ... B5 197
Wilsons, Va. ... D5 209
Wilson's, promontory, Austl. ... I6 112
Wilsons Beach, N.B., Can. ... E3 151
Wilsonville, Ala. ... B3 166
Wilsonville, Conn. ... A9 172
Wilsonville, Ill. ... D4 178
Wilsonville, Ky. ... A4 182
Wilsonville, Nebr. ... D5 191
Wilsonville, Oreg. ... B2 201
Wilstedt, Ger. ... E3 62
Wilster, Ger. ... B3 62
Wilton, Ala. ... B3 166
Wilton, Ark. ... D1 169
Wilton, Conn. ... E3 172
Wilton, Maine ... D2 184
Wilton, Minn. ... C3 187
Wilton, N.H. ... E3 193
Wilton, N.Y. ... B7 196
Wilton, N. Dak. ... B5 198
Wilton, Wis. ... E3 212
Wilton Junction (Wilton), Iowa ... C6 180
Wilton Manor, Fla. ... *F6 174
Wiltz, Lux. ... E5 59
Wiluna, Austl. ... E3 111
Wimapedi, riv., Man., Can. ... B2 150
Wimauma, Fla. ... E4 174
Wimbledon, Eng. ... m12 55
Wimbledon, N. Dak. ... B7 198
Wimborne, Alta., Can. ... D4 148
Wimborne, Eng. ... D6 56
Wimico, lake, Fla. ... C1 174
Winagami, lake, Alta., Can. ... B2 148
Winamac, Ind. ... B4 179
Winburg, S. Afr. ... C4 107
Winburne, Pa. ... E5 202
Wincheck, pond, R.I. ... C9 172
Winchell, mtn., Mass. ... B2 185
Winchendon, Mass. ... A3 185
Winchendon Springs, Mass. ... A3 185
Winchester, Ark. ... D4 169
Winchester, Calif. ... F3 170
Winchester, Ont., Can. ... B9 153
Winchester, Eng. ... C6 56
Winchester, Idaho ... C2 177
Winchester, Ill. ... D3 178
Winchester, Ind. ... D8 179
Winchester, Kans. ... B7 181
Winchester, Ky. ... C5 182
Winchester, Mass. ... C2 185
Winchester, Miss. ... D5 188
Winchester, Mo. ... A6 189
Winchester, N.H. ... E2 193
Winchester, Ohio ... D4 199
Winchester, Tenn. ... B5 205
Winchester (Independent City), Va. ... B4 209
Winchester Bay, Oreg. ... D2 201
Winchester Center, Conn. ... B4 172
Wind, lake, Wis. ... F1 212
Wind, riv., Wash. ... D4 210
Wind, riv., Wyo. ... B7 213
Wind, riv., Wyo. ... B3 213
Wind Cave, nat. park., S. Dak. ... D2 204
Wind Lake, Wis. ... F5 212
Wind Ridge, Pa. ... G1 202
Wind River, Wyo. ... C4 213
Wind River, basin, Wyo. ... B4 213
Wind River, Indian res., Wyo. ... B3 213
Wind River, peak, Wyo. ... C3 213
Wind River, range, Wyo. ... B3 213
Windber, Pa. ... F4 202
Winder, Ga. ... C3 175
Windermere, B.C., Can. ... D10 149
Windermere, Ont., Can. ... B5 153
Windermere, Conn. ... B7 172
Windermere, Eng. ... C5 55
Windermere, lake, Eng. ... F6 57
Windfall, Ind. ... D6 179
Windgap, Pa. ... E11 202
Windham, Conn. ... C8 172
Windham, Mont. ... C6 190
Windham, N.H. ... E4 193
Windham, N.Y. ... C6 196
Windham, Ohio ... A6 199
Windham, co., Conn. ... B8 172
Windham, co., Vt. ... F3 208
Windhoek, S.W. Afr. ... B2 107
Windigo, riv., Que., Can. ... B4 154
Windigo Lake, Ont., Can. ... E8 153
Winding Stair, mtn., Okla. ... C6 200
Windmere, Ill. ... *A5 178
Windmill, pt., Va. ... D6 209
Windom, Kans. ... D6 181
Windom, Minn. ... G3 187
Windom, peak, Colo. ... D3 171
Windorah, Austl. ... B4 112
Window Rock, Ariz. ... B6 168
Windsbach, Ger. ... D5 61
Windsheim, Ger. ... D5 61
Windsor, Calif. ... A5 170
Windsor, Newf., Can. ... D4 152
Windsor, N.S., Can. ... E5 151
Windsor, Ont., Can. ... E1 153
Windsor, Que., Can. ... D5 154
Windsor, Colo. ... A6 171
Windsor, Conn. ... B6 172
Windsor, Eng. ... C7 56
Windsor, Ill. ... D5 178
Windsor, Mass. ... A1 185
Windsor, Mo. ... C4 189
Windsor, N.J. ... C3 194
Windsor, N.Y. ... *C5 196
Windsor, N.C. ... B7 197
Windsor, N. Dak. ... C6 198
Windsor, Pa. ... G8 202
Windsor, S.C. ... E4 203
Windsor, Vt. ... E4 208
Windsor, Va. ... B6, E6 209
Windsor, co., Vt. ... D3 208
Windsor Heights, Iowa ... A7 180
Windsor Locks, Conn. ... B6 172
Windsorville, Conn. ... B6 172
Windthorst, Sask., Can. ... G4 155
Windthorst, Tex. ... C3 206
Windward, passage, W.I. ... F6 131
Windward Islands, see Dominica, Grenada, St. Lucia, and St. Vincent, Br. dep., N.A.
Windy, W. Va. ... B3 211
Windy, lake, Sask., Can. ... C4 155
Windy, peak, Wash. ... A6 210
Windy, pt., Newf., Can. ... C4 152
Windy Hill, S.C. ... *C8 203
Windy Hills, Ky. ... *B4 182
Wine, isl., La. ... E5 183
Winefred, lake, Alta., Can. ... B5 148
Winefred, riv., Alta., Can. ... B5 148
Winfall, N.C. ... A7 197
Winfield, Ala. ... B2 166
Winfield, Alta., Can. ... C3 148
Winfield, Ill. ... *B5 178
Winfield, Iowa ... C6 180
Winfield, Kans. ... E7 181
Winfield, Md. ... B3 173
Winfield, Mo. ... A7, C7 189
Winfield, Pa. ... E8 202
Winfield, Tenn. ... C9 205
Winfield, W. Va. ... C3 211
Winfred, S. Dak. ... D8 204
Wing, Ala. ... D3 166
Wing, Ark. ... C2 169
Wing, N. Dak. ... B5 198
Wing, riv., Minn. ... D3 187
Wingate, Eng. ... F7 57
Wingate, Ind. ... D3 179
Wingate, Md. ... D5 173
Wingate, N.C. ... C3 197
Wingate, Pa. ... E6 202
Wingdale, N.Y. ... D7 196
Winger, Minn. ... C3 187
Wingham, Ont., Can. ... D3 153
Wingo, Ky. ... B2 182
Winifred, Mont. ... C7 190
Winifreda, Arg. ... B4 136
Winifrede, W. Va. ... D6 211
Winigan, Mo. ... A5 189
Winisk, riv., Ont., Can. ... D8 153
Wink, Tex. ... D1 206
Winkelman, Ariz. ... E5 168
Winkle, Ohio ... C4 199
Winkler, Man., Can. ... E3 150
Winkler, co., Tex. ... D1 206
Winlaw, B.C., Can. ... E9 149
Winlock, Wash. ... C3 210
Winn, par., La. ... C3 183
Winn, Maine ... C4 184
Winn, Mich. ... E6 186
Winnabow, N.C. ... C5 197
Winneba, Ghana ... E4 103
Winnebago, Ill. ... A4 178
Winnebago, Minn. ... G4 187
Winnebago, Nebr. ... B9 191
Winnebago, Wis. ... B5 212
Winnebago, co., Ill. ... A4 178
Winnebago, co., Iowa ... A4 180
Winnebago, co., Wis. ... D5 212
Winnebago, Indian res., Nebr. ... B9 191
Winnebago, lake, Wis. ... E5 212
Winneconne, Wis. ... D5 212
Winnemucca, Nev. ... C4 192
Winnemucca, lake, Nev. ... C2 192
Winner, S. Dak. ... D6 204
Winneshiek, co., Iowa ... A6 180
Winnetka, Ill. ... A6, E3 178
Winnetoon, Nebr. ... B8 191
Winnett, Mont. ... C8 190
Winnfield, La. ... C3 183
Winnibigoshish, lake, Minn. ... C4 187
Winnie, Tex. ... *E5 206
Winnifred, Alta., Can. ... E5 148
Winning Pool, Austl. ... D1 111
Winnipeg, Man., Can. ... E3 150
Winnipeg, lake, Man., Can. ... C3 150
Winnipeg, riv., Man., Can. ... D4 150
Winnipeg Beach, Man., Can. ... D3 150
Winnipegosis, Man., Can. ... D2 150
Winnipegosis, lake, Man., Can. ... C2 150
Winnipesaukee, lake, N.H. ... C4 193
Winnisquam, N.H. ... C3 193
Winnisquam, lake, N.H. ... C3 193
Winnsboro, La. ... B4 183
Winnsboro, S.C. ... C5 203
Winnsboro, Tex. ... C5 206
Winnsboro Mills, S.C. ... *C5 203
Winokur, Ga. ... E4 175
Winona, Ind. ... B4 179
Winona, Kans. ... C2 181
Winona, Mich. ... B2 186
Winona, Minn. ... F7 187
Winona, Miss. ... B4 188
Winona, Mo. ... E6 189
Winona, Wash. ... C8 210
Winona, W. Va. ... C4, D7 211
Winona, co., Minn. ... F7 187
Winona Lake, Ind. ... B6 179
Winona Lakes, N.Y. ... *D6 196
Winooski, Vt. ... C2 208
Winooski, riv., Vt. ... C3 208
Winschoten, Neth. ... A7 59
Winsen, Ger. ... E4 62
Winsford, Eng. ... A5 56
Winside, Nebr. ... B8 191
Winslow, Ariz. ... C5 168
Winslow, Ark. ... B1 169
Winslow, Ill. ... A4 178
Winslow, Ind. ... H3 179
Winslow, Maine ... D3 184
Winslow, Nebr. ... C9 191
Winslow, N.J. ... D3 194
Winslow, Wash. ... D1 210
Winsted, Conn. ... B4 172
Winsted, Minn. ... F4 187
Winston, Fla. ... D4 174
Winston, Mo. ... B3 189
Winston, Mont. ... D5 190
Winston, N. Mex. ... D2 195
Winston, Oreg. ... D3 201
Winston, co., Ala. ... A2 166
Winston, co., Miss. ... B4 188
Winston-Salem, N.C. ... A3 197
Winstonville, Miss. ... B3 188
Winsum, Neth. ... A6 59
Winter, Sask., Can. ... E1 155
Winter, Wis. ... C3 212
Winter Beach, Fla. ... E6 174
Winter Garden, Fla. ... D5 174
Winter Harbor, Maine ... D4 184
Winter Harbour, B.C., Can. ... D3 149
Winter Haven, Fla. ... D5 174
Winter Park, Colo. ... B5 171
Winter Park, Fla. ... D5 174
Winter Rim, mts., Oreg. ... E6 201
Winterberg, Ger. ... B3 61
Wintering, lake, Man., Can. ... B3 150
Winterpock, Va. ... D5 209
Winterport, Maine ... D4 184
Winters, Calif. ... A6, C2 170
Winters, Tex. ... D3 206
Winterset, Iowa ... C3 180
Wintersville, Ohio ... B7 199
Winterswijk, Neth. ... C6 59
Winterthur, Switz. ... B4 66
Winterton, Newf., Can. ... E5 152
Winterville, Ga. ... C3 175
Winterville, Maine ... B4 184
Winterville, Miss. ... B2 188
Winterville, N.C. ... B6 197
Winthrop, Ark. ... D1 169
Winthrop, Iowa ... B6 180
Winthrop, Maine ... D3 184
Winthrop, Mass. ... B6, D3 185
Winthrop, Minn. ... F4 187
Winthrop, Mo. ... B2 189
Winthrop, N.Y. ... A2 196
Winthrop, Wash. ... A5 210
Winthrop, lake, Mass. ... D1 185
Winthrop Harbor, Ill. ... A6, D2 178
Winton, Austl. ... D7 111
Winton, Minn. ... C7 187
Winton, N.C. ... A7 197
Wintzenheim, Fr. ... A3 66
Winyah, bay, S.C. ... E9 203
Wiota, Iowa ... C3 180
Wirral, N.B., Can. ... D3 151
Wirt, Minn. ... C5 187
Wirt, Okla. ... C4 200
Wirt, co., W. Va. ... B3 211
Wirtz, Va. ... D3 209
Wisbech, Eng. ... B8 56
Wiscasset, Maine ... D3 184
Wisconsin, state, U.S. ... 212
Wisconsin, lake, Wis. ... E4 212
Wisconsin, riv., Wis. ... E3 212
Wisconsin Dells, Wis. ... E4 212
Wisconsin Rapids, Wis. ... D4 212
Wisdom, Mont. ... E3 190
Wise, N.C. ... A5 197
Wise, Va. ... B2 209
Wise, co., Tex. ... C4 206
Wise, co., Va. ... B2 209
Wise River, Mont. ... E4 190
Wiseman, Alsk. ... B9 167
Wiseton, Sask., Can. ... F2 155
Wishart, Sask., Can. ... F3 155
Wishaw, Scot. ... E5 57
Wishek, N. Dak. ... C6 198
Wishram, Wash. ... D5 210
Wisla, riv., Pol. ... B5 70
Wisloka, riv., Pol. ... D6 70
Wismar, Ger. ... B5 60
Wismar, Guy. ... A3 139
Wismar, bay, Ger. ... D5 62
Wisner, La. ... C4 183
Wisner, Nebr. ... C9 191
Wissant, Fr. ... D9 56
Wissembourg, Fr. ... C7 58
Wissmann Pool, lake, Zaire ... B2 106
Wissota, lake, Wis. ... D2 212
Wister, Okla. ... C7 200
Wister, lake, Okla. ... C7 200
Witbank, S. Afr. ... C4 107
Witch Lake, Mich. ... B2 186
Witchekan, lake, Sask., Can. ... D2 155
Witham, Eng. ... C8 56
Witham, riv., Eng. ... A7 56
Withamsville, Ohio ... D2 199
Withee, Wis. ... D3 212
Witherbee, N.Y. ... A7 196
Withernsea, Eng. ... A8 56
Witherspoon, mtn., Alsk. ... g18 167
Withlacoochee, riv., Fla., Ga. ... B3 174
Withrow, Wash. ... B6 210
Witless Bay, Newf., Can. ... E5 152
Witney, Eng. ... C6 56
Witry-lès-Reims, Fr. ... E4 59
Witt, Ill. ... D4 178
Witt, Tenn. ... C10 205
Witten, Ger. ... B2 61
Witten, S. Dak. ... D5 204
Witten, lake, Ger. ... D3 62
Wittenberg, Ger. ... B7 61
Wittenberg, Wis. ... D4 212
Wittenberge, Ger. ... B5 60
Wittenheim, Fr. ... B3 66
Wittingen, Ger. ... B5 60
Wittlich, Ger. ... D1 61
Wittman, Md. ... C5 173
Wittmann, Ariz. ... D3, F1 168
Wittmund, Ger. ... A7 59
Wittstock, Ger. ... B6 60
Wittvlei, S.W. Afr. ... B2 107
Witzenhausen, Ger. ... B4 61
Wiveliscombe, Eng. ... C4 56
Wiville, Ark. ... B4 169
Wiwŏn, Kor. ... F3 93
Wixom, Mich. ... A7 186
Wixom, lake, Mich. ... E6 186
Wkra, riv., Pol. ... B6 70
Włocławek, Pol. ... B5 70
Włodawa, Pol. ... C7 70
Włoszczowa, Pol. ... C5 70
Woburn, Que., Can. ... D7 154
Woburn, Mass. ... B5, C2 185
Woden, Iowa ... A4 180
Woerden, Neth. ... B4 59
Wohlthat, mts., Ant. ... B14 120
Woito, Ont., Can. ... B7 153
Wokam, isl., Indon. ... G8 90
Woking, Alta., Can. ... B1 148
Woking, Eng. ... C7 56
Wokingham, Eng. ... C7 56
Wolbach, Nebr. ... C7 191
Wolcott, Colo. ... B4 171
Wolcott, Conn. ... C5 172
Wolcott, Ind. ... C3 179
Wolcott, N.Y. ... B4 196
Wolcott, Vt. ... B4 208
Wolcottville, Ind. ... E7 179
Woldegk, Ger. ... E7 62
Wolf, Wyo. ... A5 213
Wolf, creek, Iowa ... B5 180
Wolf, creek, Mich. ... D7 186
Wolf, creek, Mont. ... C7 190
Wolf, creek, Okla. ... A2 200
Wolf, creek, W. Va. ... D7 211
Wolf, isl., Que., Can. ... B8 151
Wolf, isl., Ec. ... f5 134
Wolf, lake, Ill. ... F3 178
Wolf, mtn., Alsk. ... B9 167
Wolf, riv., Miss., Tenn. ... A4 188
Wolf, riv., Wis. ... E4 188
Wolf, riv., Wis. ... D5 212
Wolf Creek, Mont. ... C4 190
Wolf Creek, Oreg. ... E3 201
Wolf Creek, pass, Colo. ... D4 171
Wolf Island, Mo. ... E8 189
Wolf Lake, Ill. ... F4 178
Wolf Lake, Mich. ... E4 186
Wolf Lake, Minn. ... D3 187
Wolf Point, Mont. ... B11 190
Wolf Run, Ohio ... A1 211
Wolfe, Sask., Can. ... E1 155
Wolfe, co., Que., Can. ... D6 154
Wolfe, co., Ky. ... C6 182
Wolfe City, Tex. ... C4 206
Wolfeboro, N.H. ... C4 193
Wolfeboro Center, N.H. ... C4 193
Wolfeboro Falls, N.H. ... C4 193
Wolfen, Ger. ... B7 61
Wolfenbüttel, Ger. ... A5 61
Wolfestown, Que., Can. ... D6 154
Wolfhagen, Ger. ... B4 61
Wolfflake, Ind. ... B7 179
Wolford, N. Dak. ... A6 198
Wolfratshausen, Ger. ... B7 66
Wolfsberg, Aus. ... E7 60
Wolfsburg, Ger. ... B5 60
Wolfville, N.S., Can. ... D5 151
Wolgast, Ger. ... A6 60
Wolhusen, Switz. ... B4 66
Wolin, Pol. ... E8 62
Wolin, isl., Pol. ... E8 62
Wollaston, isl., Chile ... k12 136

INDEX KEY Each place listed in **Bold-faced Type** has its population listed in the Population tables, pages 230 to 280. Each country, shown in CAPITAL LETTERS, has its population listed in the World Political Information Table, pages 6 to 10.
* Does not appear on map; key shows general location.

Wollaston, lake, Sask., Can. E12 142
Wollongong, Austl. G8 112
Wolmaransstad, S. Afr. C4 107
Wolmirstedt, Ger. A6 61
Wołomin, Pol. k14 70
Wołow, Pol. C4 70
Wolseley, Sask., Can. G4 155
Wolseth, N. Dak. A4 198
Wolsey, S. Dak. C7 204
Wolsztyn, Pol. B4 70
Wolverhampton, Eng. B5 56
Wolverine, Mich. C6 186
Wolverine, riv., B.C., Can. B7 149
Wolverine Lake, Mich. *F7 186
Wolverton, Eng. B7 56
Wolverton, Minn. D2 187
Womack Hill, Ala. D1 166
Womelsdorf, Pa. F9 202
Women, lake, Minn. D4 187
Wonalancet, N.H. C4 193
Wonder, Oreg. E3 201
Wonder Lake, Ill. A5, E2 178
Wonewoc, Wis. E3 212
Wonisule, Espiritu Santo I. 115
Wŏnju, Kor. *H3 93
Wonowon, B.C., Can. A7 149
Wŏnsan, Kor. G3 93
Wonthaggi, Austl. I5 112
Wood, N.C. A5 197
Wood, Pa. F5 202
Wood, S. Dak. D5 204
Wood, co., Ohio A4 199
Wood, co., Tex. C5 206
Wood, co., W. Va. B3 211
Wood, co., Wis. D3 212
Wood, lake, Sask., Can. B4 155
Wood, mtn., Sask., Can. H2 155
Wood, mtn., Mont. E7 190
Wood, pond, Maine C2 184
Wood, riv., B.C., Can. C8 149
Wood, riv., Sask., Can. H2 155
Wood, riv., Wyo. B3 213
Wood Buffalo, nat. park, Alta., N.W. Ter., Can. E10 144
Wood Dale, Ill. E2 178
Wood End, pt., Mass. B7 185
Wood Lake, Minn. F3 187
Wood Lake, Nebr. B5 191
Wood Lynne, N.J. *D2 194
Wood Mountain, Sask., Can. H2 155
Wood-Ridge, N.J. D5 194
Wood River, Ill. E3 178
Wood River, Nebr. D7 191
Wood River Junction, R.I. D10 172
Wood Village, Oreg. *B4 201
Woodall, mtn., Miss. A5 188
Woodard, N.C. B7 197
Woodberry, Ark. D3 169
Woodbine, Ga. F5 175
Woodbine, Ill. A3 178
Woodbine, Iowa C2 180
Woodbine, Kans. D7 181
Woodbine, Ky. D5 182
Woodbine, Md. B3 173
Woodbine, N.J. E3 194
Woodboro, Wis. C4 212
Woodbourne, N.Y. D6 196
Woodbridge, Calif. B6 170
Woodbridge, Ont., Can. D5, E6 153
Woodbridge, Conn. D4 172
Woodbridge, Eng. B9 56
Woodbridge, N.J. B4, E4 194
Woodbridge, Va. C5 209
Woodburn, Ind. B8 179
Woodburn, Iowa C4 180
Woodburn, Ky. D3 182
Woodburn, Oreg. B2, B4 201
Woodbury, Conn. C4 172
Woodbury, Ga. D2 175
Woodbury, Ky. C3 182
Woodbury, N.J. D2 194
Woodbury, Pa. F5 202
Woodbury, Tenn. B5 205
Woodbury, Vt. C4 208
Woodbury, co., Iowa B1 180
Woodbury, mtn., Vt. C4 208
Woodbury Heights, N.J. *D2 194
Woodcliff, Ga. D5 175
Woodcliff, lake, N.J. C5 194
Woodcliff Lake, N.J. C5 194
Woodfibre, B.C., Can. E6 149
Woodford, S.C. D5 203
Woodford, co., Ill. C4 178
Woodford, co., Ky. B5 182
Woodhull, Ill. B3 178
Woodhull, N.Y. C3 196
Woodinville, Wash. B 210
Woodlake, Calif. D4 170
Woodlake, Tex. D5 206
Woodland, Ala. B4 166
Woodland, Calif. A6, C3 170
Woodland, Ga. D2 175
Woodland, Ill. C6 178
Woodland, Maine *B4 184
Woodland, Maine C5 184
Woodland, Mich. F5 186
Woodland, Miss. B4 188
Woodland, N.C. A6 197
Woodland, Pa. E4 202
Woodland, Wash. D3 210
Woodland Beach, Mich. *G7 186
Woodland Mills, Tenn. A2 205
Woodland Park, Colo. C5 171
Woodlawn, Ont., Can. A8 153
Woodlawn, Ill. E4 178
Woodlawn, Ky. A2 182
Woodlawn, Md. C2 173
Woodlawn, Ohio D2 199
Woodlawn, Tenn. A4 205
Woodlawn, Va. E2 209
Woodlawn Beach, N.Y. C2 196
Woodlawn Park, Ky. *B4 182
Woodleaf, N.C. B3 197
Woodman, N.H. C5 193
Woodmere, N.Y. *G2 172
Woodmont, Conn. E4 172
Woodmoor, Md. C2 173
Woodport, N.J. B3 194
Woodridge, Man., Can. E3 150
Woodridge, N.Y. *D6 196
Woodroffe, mtn., Austl. E5 110
Woodrow, Ark. B3 169
Woodrow, Sask., Can. H2 155
Woodruff, Ariz. C5 168
Woodruff, Kans. C4 181
Woodruff, S.C. B3 203
Woodruff, Utah B4 207
Woodruff, Wis. C4 212
Woodruff, co., Ark. B4 169
Woodruff Place, Ind. *H8 179
Woods, co., Okla. A3 200
Woods, lake, Austl. C5 110
Woods, lake, Ont., Can., Minn. E7 153, A4 187
Woods, lake, Tenn. B5 205
Woods Cross, Utah C4 207
Woods Hole, Mass. C6 185
Wood's Island, Newf., Can. D2 152
Woodsboro, Md. A3 173
Woodsboro, Tex. E4 206
Woodsburgh, N.Y. *E6 196
Woodsdale, N.C. A5 197
Woodsfield, Ohio C6 199
Woodside, Austl. I6 112
Woodside, Calif. *D2 170
Woodside, Del. B6 173
Woodside, Mont. D2 190
Woodside, Utah D5 207
Woodson, Ark. C3 169
Woodson, Ill. D3 178
Woodson, Tex. C3 206
Woodson, co., Kans. E8 181
Woodson Terrace, Mo. *C7 189
Woodstock, Ala. B2 166
Woodstock, N.B., Can. C2 151
Woodstock, Ont., Can. D4 153
Woodstock, Conn. B9 172
Woodstock, Ga. B2 175
Woodstock, Ill. A5 178
Woodstock, Md. B4 173
Woodstock, Minn. F2 187
Woodstock, N.H. C3 193
Woodstock, Ohio B4 199
Woodstock, Vt. D3 208
Woodstock, Va. C4 209
Woodstock Valley, Conn. B8 172
Woodston, Kans. C4 181
Woodstown, N.J. D2 194
Woodsville, N.H. B2 193
Woodville, Austl. *G2 112
Woodville, Calif. *D4 170
Woodville, Ont., Can. C6 153
Woodville, Fla. B2 174
Woodville, Ga. C3 175
Woodville, Idaho F6 177
Woodville, Ky. A2 182
Woodville, Mass. D1 185
Woodville, Miss. D2 188
Woodville, N.Z. N15 112
Woodville, N.C. A6 197
Woodville, Ohio A2, A4 199
Woodville (New Woodville), Okla. D5 200
Woodville, R.I. D9 172
Woodville, Tex. D5 206
Woodville, Wis. D1 212
Woodward, Ala. B3, E4 166
Woodward, Iowa C4 180
Woodward, Okla. A2 200
Woodward, co., Okla. A2 200
Woodwards Cove, N.B., Can. E3 151
Woodway, Tex. *D4 206
Woodway, Va. B2 209
Woodworth, La. C3 183
Woodworth, N. Dak. B6 198
Woody, riv., Sask., Man., Can. C1 150, E5 155
Wool Market, Miss. E2, E5 188
Woody Point, Newf., Can. D3 152
Wooldridge, Mo. C5 189
Wooler, Eng. E6 57
Woolford, Md. C5 173
Woolper, creek, Ky. A6 182
Woolrich, Pa. D7 202
Woolsey, Nev. C3 192
Woolsey, peak, Ariz. D3 168
Woolstock, Iowa B4 180
Woolwich, Eng. m13 55
Woolwich, Maine E6 184
Woomera, Austl. F6 111
Woonsocket, R.I. A10 172
Woonsocket, S. Dak. C7 204
Woonsocket, hill, R.I. B10 172
Woonsocket, res., R.I. B10 172
Wooramel, Austl. E1 111
Wooster, Ark. B3 169
Wooster, Ohio B6 199
Woosung, China B10 92
Worbis, Ger. B5 61
Worcester, Eng. B5 56
Worcester, Mass. B4 185
Worcester, N.Y. C6 196
Worcester, S. Afr. D2 107
Worcester, Vt. C3 208
Worcester, co., Eng. B5 56
Worcester, co., Md. D7 173
Worcester, co., Mass. A3 185
Worcester, range, Vt. C3 208
Worden, Ill. E4 178
Worden, Mont. E8 190
Worden, Oreg. E5 201
Wordens, pond, R.I. D10 172
Wordsworth, Sask., Can. H4 155
Workington, Eng. C5 55
Worksop, Eng. A6 56
Workum, Neth. B5 59
Worland, Mo. C3 189
Worland, Wyo. A5 213
Worley, Idaho B2 177
Wormerveer, Neth. B4 59
Wormleysburg, Pa. *F8 202
Worms, Ger. D3 61
Worms, Nebr. C7 191
Woronoco, Mass. B2 185
Worth, Ill. *B5 178
Worth, Mo. A3 189
Worth, co., Ga. E3 175
Worth co., Iowa A4 180
Worth, co., Mo. A3 189
Wortham, Tex. D4 206
Worthing, Eng. D7 56
Worthing, S. Dak. D9 204
Worthington, Ont., Can. A3 153
Worthington, Fla. C4 174
Worthington, Ind. F4 179
Worthington, Iowa B6 180
Worthington, Ky. B7 182
Worthington, Mass. B2 185
Worthington, Minn. G3 187
Worthington, Mo. A5 189
Worthington, Ohio B4, C2 199
Worthington, Pa. E2 202
Worthington, W. Va. A7 211
Worthington, mts., Nev. F6 192
Worthington, peak, Nev. F6 192
Worthington Knob, mtn., Tenn. D8 205
Worthville, Ky. B4 182
Worthville, N.C. B4 197
Worton, Md. B5 173
Wostok, Alta., Can. C4 148
Wotho, atoll, Marshall Is. 115
Wotje, atoll, Marshall Is. 115
Wotton, Que., Can. D6 154
Wounded Knee, S. Dak. D3 204
Wowon, isl., Indon. F6 90
Woźniki, Pol. f10 70
Wrangel, isl., Sov. Un. B21 71
Wrangell, Alsk. D13, m23 167
Wrangell, isl., Alsk. m24 167
Wrangell, mtn., Alsk. f19 167
Wrangell, mts., Alsk. C11 167
Wrath, cape, Scot. B3 57
Wray, Colo. A8 171
Wray, Ga. E3 175
Wren, Ohio B3 199
Wrens, Ga. C4 175
Wrenshall, Minn. D6 187
Wrentham, Alta., Can. E4 148
Wrentham, Mass. B5 185
Wrexham, Wales A5 56
Wriezen, Ger. B7 60
Wright, Ala. A2 166
Wright, Iowa C5 180
Wright, Kans. E4 181
Wright, Minn. D5 187
Wright, co., Iowa B4 180
Wright, co., Minn. E4 187
Wright, co., Mo. D5 189
Wright, mtn., Mont. C4 190
Wright Brothers, nat. memorial, N.C. A8 197
Wright City, Mo. C6 189
Wright City, Okla. C6 200
Wrightstown, N.J. C3 194
Wrightstown, Wis. A6, D5 212
Wrightsville, Ark. C3, D6 169
Wrightsville, Ga. D4 175
Wrightsville, Pa. F8 202
Wrightsville, res., Vt. C3 208
Wrightsville Beach, N.C. C6 197
Wrightwood, Calif. E5, F3 170
Wrigley, gulf, Ant. B36 120
Wrigley, Tenn. B4 205
Wrocław (Breslau), Pol. C4 70
Wrocław, prov., Pol. B10 61
Wrong, lake, Man., Can. C3 150
Wrottesley, cape, N.W. Ter., Can. B8 142
Wroxeter, Ont., Can. D3 153
Wroxton, Sask., Can. F5 155
Września, Pol. B4 70
Wschowa, Pol. C4 70
Wu, riv., China J3 92
Wu Chin Shan, mtn., China C8 89
Wuchan, China A2 93
Wuchang, China D3 93
Wuch'i, Taiwan G9 91
Wuchou, China G7 91
Wuchuan, China D4 92
Wuchuan, China J3 92
Wufeng, China D4 92
Wuhan, China E7 91, I6 92
Wuho, China H7 92
Wuhsi, China E9 91
Wuhu, China I8 92
Wui, China F6 92
Wukang, China K4 92
Wukari, Nig. E6 103
Wulanhaote, China A10 92
Wulumuchi, see Urumchi, China
Wümme, riv., Ger. E3 62
Wunsiedel, Ger. C6 61
Wunstorf, Ger. A4 61
Wuntho, Bur. D10 87
Wupatki, nat. mon., Ariz. B4 168
Wuppertal, Ger. B2 61
Würm, lake, Ger. E5 60
Württemberg, reg., Ger. D4 60
in 1810 50
in 1815 50
in 1871 51
Wurtsboro, N.Y. D6 196
Wurzach, Ger. B5 66
Würzburg, Ger. D4 61
Wurzen, Ger. B7 61
Wushan, China I3 92
Wuskwatim, lake, Man., Can. B2 150
Wusu, China C1 91
Wusung, China I9 92
Wutu, China E6 91
Wuwei, China D5 91
Wuwei, China I7 92
Wuyuan, China D3 92
Wuyün, China B10 91
Wyaconda, Mo. A6 189
Wyaconda, riv., Mo. A6 189
Wyalusing, Pa. C9 202
Wyandot, co., Ohio B4 199
Wyandotte, Mich. A7, F7 186
Wyandotte, Okla. A7 200
Wyandotte, co., Kans. C9 181
Wyandra, Austl. C5 112
Wyanet, Ill. B4 178
Wyarno, Wyo. A6 213
Wyatt, Ind. A5 179
Wyatt, Mo. E8 189
Wyckoff, N.J. *A4 194
Wyco, W. Va. D3 211
Wye, riv., Eng. C5 56
Wye Mills, Md. C5 173
Wyebridge, Ont., Can. C5 153
Wyesocking, bay, N.C. B7 197
Wyevale, Ont., Can. C5 153
Wyeville, Wis. D3 212
Wygiełzów, Pol. g10 70
Wykoff, Minn. G6 187
Wylie, Tex. *C4 206
Wylliesburg, Va. E4 209
Wylzysk, Pol. B4 70
Wyman, Iowa C6 180
Wyman, lake, Maine C3 184
Wyman Dam, Maine C3 184
Wymark, Sask., Can. G2 155
Wymondham, Eng. B9 56
Wymore, Nebr. D9 191
Wyndham, Austl. C4 111
Wyndmere, N. Dak. C8 198
Wynnburg, Tenn. A2 205
Wynne, Ark. B5 169
Wynne Wood, Okla. C4 200
Wynona, Okla. A5 200
Wynoochee, riv., Wash. B2 210
Wynot, Nebr. B8 191
Wynyard, Sask., Can. F3 155
Wyocena, Wis. E4 212
Wyodak, Wyo. A7 213
Wyola, Mont. E9 190
Wyoming, Ont., Can. E2 153
Wyoming, Del. B6 173
Wyoming, Ill. B4 178
Wyoming, Iowa B6 180
Wyoming, Mich. *F5 186
Wyoming, Minn. E6 187
Wyoming, N.Y. C2 196
Wyoming, Ohio D2 199
Wyoming, Pa. B8 202
Wyoming, R.I. C10 172
Wyoming, state, U.S. 213
Wyoming, co., N.Y. C2 196
Wyoming, co., Pa. D9 202
Wyoming, co., W. Va. D3 211
Wyoming, basin, Wyo. D3 213
Wyoming, peak, Wyo. C2 213
Wyoming, range, Wyo. B2 213
Wyomissing, Pa. F10 202
Wyomissing Hills, Pa. *F10 202
Wyre, riv., Eng. G6 57
Wysokie Mazowieckie, Pol. B7 70
Wyszków, Pol. B6 70
Wythe, co., Va. E1 209
Wytheville, Va. E1 209
Wytopitlock, Maine C4 184
Wyvis, mtn., Scot. C4 57

X

Xánthi, Grc. B5 69
Xanthus, see Koka, riv., Tur.
Xapecó, riv., Braz. D2 137
Xau, lake, Bots. B3 107
Xapurí, Braz. D4 134
Xauen, Mor. B3 102
Xavantes, mts., Braz. E5 139
Xavier, Kans. B8 181
Xbonil, Mex. D6 129
Xcalak, Mex. D7 129
Xenia, Ill. E5 178
Xenia, Ohio C4 199
Xieng Khouang, Laos C5 89
Xilitla, Mex. m14 129
Xingú, riv., Braz. C4 139
Xique-Xique, Braz. D2 138
Xochimilco, Mex. h9, n14 129

Y

Yaak, Mont. B1 190
Yaan, China F5 91
Yabbenohr, isl., Kwajalein 114
Yablis, Nic. C5 130
Yablonovy, mts., Sov. Un. D14 71
Yabucoa, P.R. C7 132
Yabucoa, mun., P.R. C7 132
Ya'bud, Jordan B7 84
Yachats, Oreg. C2 201
Yaco, riv., Braz. C4 134
Yacolt, Wash. D3 210
Yacuiba, Bol. D3 135
Yadkin, co., N.C. A3 197
Yadkin, riv., N.C. B3 197
Yadkin Valley, N.C. A2 197
Yadkinville, N.C. A3 197
Yagi, Jap. o14 93
Yaguachi, Ec. B2 134
Yaguajay, Cuba D4 131
Yaguas, riv., Peru B3 134
Yahk, B.C., Can. E9 149
Yahuma, Zaire A3 106
Yainax, butte, Oreg. E5 201
Yaizu, Jap. o17 93
Yakima, Wash. C5 210
Yakima, co., Wash. C5 210
Yakima, Indian res., Wash. C4 210
Yakima, ridge, Wash. C5 210
Yakima, riv., Wash. C5 210
Yakima, val., Wash. C5 210
Yakoma, Zaire A3 106
Yaku, isl., Jap. K5 93
Yakutat, Alsk. D12 167
Yakutat, bay, Alsk. D12 167
Yakutsk, Sov. Un. C15 71
Yalaha, Fla. D5 174
Yale, B.C., Can. E7 149
Yale, Ill. D5 178
Yale, Iowa C3 180
Yale, Mich. E8 186
Yale, Okla. A5 200
Yale, S. Dak. C8 204
Yale, Va. E5 209
Yale, mtn., Colo. C4 171
Yale, res., Wash. D3 210
Yalesville, Conn. D5 172
Yalinga, Cen. Afr. Rep. D4 104
Yalobusha, co., Miss. A4 188
Yalova, Tur. B7 69
Yalta, Sov. Un. I10 72
Yalu, China B9 91
Yalu, riv., China, Kor. D11 92
Yalung, riv., China E5 91
Yalutorovsk, Sov. Un. B7 73
Yalvaç, Tur. C8 85
Yama, Sov. Un. q21 72
Yamachiche, Que., Can. C5 154
Yamagata, Jap. G10 93
Yamaguchi, Jap. I5 93
Yamal, pen., Sov. Un. B9 71
Yamantau, mtn., Sov. Un. C5 73
Yamaska, Que., Can. C5 154
Yamaska, co., Que., Can. C5 154
Yamato, Jap. n18 93
Yambio, Sud. E2 105
Yambol, Bul. D8 68
Yamdrok, lake, China C9 87
Yamethin, Bur. D10 87
Yamhill, Oreg. B1 201
Yamhill, co., Oreg. B3 201
Yamkino, Sov. Un. n18 72
Yamma Yamma, lake, Austl. C3 112
Yampa, Colo. A4 171
Yampa, plat., Colo., Utah A1 171
Yampa, riv., Colo. A2 171
Yamparaez, Bol. C2 135
Yamsay, mtn., Oreg. E5 201
Yamsk, Sov. Un. D18 71
Yamunanagar, India *B6 88
Yana, riv., Sov. Un. C16 71
Yanam, India E7 87, I9 88
Yanao, Austl. H3 112
Yanaoca, Peru D3 134
Yanbu', Sau. Ar. E7 101
Yancey, co., N.C. C4 197
Yanceyville, N.C. A4 197
Yande, pass, N. Cal. 115
Yanfolila, Mali D3 103
Yang, China H2 92
Yangambi, Zaire A3 106
Yangasa Cluster, is., Fiji 114
Yangchiang, China G7 91
Yangchou, China E8 91
Yangchuan, China *D7 91
Yangchun, China G7 91
Yangeshiri, isl., Jap. D10 93
Yangi-Yul, Sov. Un. E7 73
Yangmingshan, Taiwan *G9 91
Yangtze, riv., China H9 92
Yangyang, Kor. G4 93
Yankeetown, Fla. C4 174
Yankeetown, Ind. I3 179
Yankton, S. Dak. E8 204
Yankton, co., S. Dak. D8 204
Yankton, Indian res., S. Dak. D7 204
Yanonge, Zaire A3 106
Yantic, Conn. C8 172
Yantley, Ala. C1 166
Yantra, riv., Bul. D7 68
Yanush, Okla. C6 200
Yao, Chad C3 104
Yao, Jap. *o14 93
Yaosca, Nic. D5 130
Yaoundé, Cam. E2 104
Yap, isl., Pac. O. F8 113
Yaphank, N.Y. F5 172
Yaque del Norte, riv., Dom. Rep. F8 131
Yaqui, riv., Mex. B3 129
Yar, Sov. Un. B4 73
Yaracuy, state, Ven. A4 133
Yaraka, Austl. B5 112
Yarbo, Ala. D1 166
Yarda, well, Chad B3 104
Yardley, Pa. F12 202
Yardville, N.J. C3 194
Yarí, riv., Col. C3 133
Yariga-Take, peak, Jap. H8 93
Yaritagua, Ven. A4 133
Yarkand (Soche), China F10 71
Yarker, Ont., Can. C8 153
Yarkon, riv., Isr. B6, g10 84
Yarkovo, Sov. Un. B7 73
Yarmouth, N.S., Can. F3 151
Yarmouth, Iowa C6 180
Yarmouth, Maine E2, E5 184
Yarmouth, Mass. C7 185
Yarmouth, co., N.S., Can. F4 151
Yarmūk, riv., Jordan, Syr. B7 84
Yarnell, Ariz. C3 168
Yarnema, Sov. Un. F18 63
Yaroslavl', Sov. Un. B1 73
Yarovskoye, marsh, Sov. Un. B8 73
Yarraden, Austl. B7 111
Yarram, Austl. I6 112
Yarrow Point, Wash. *B3 210
Yarrowsburg, Md. B2 173
Yartsevo, Sov. Un. D9 72
Yarumal, Col. B2 133
Yasana, Zaire A4 106
Yasawa, isl., Fiji 114
Yasawa Group, is., Fiji 114
Yashi, Nig. D6 103
Yasinovataya, Sov. Un. q20 72
Yasinya, Sov. Un. A7 68
Yasothon, Thai. E6 89
Yata, Bol. B2 135
Yate, N. Cal. 115
Yates, co., N.Y. C3 196
Yates Center, Kans. E8 181
Yates City, Ill. C3 178
Yatesboro, Pa. E3 202
Yatesville, Ga. D2 175
Yathata, isl., Fiji 114
Yathkyed, lake, N.W. Ter., Can. D13 142
Yatsuga-Take, peak, Jap. H9 93
Yatsushiro, Jap. J5 93
Yatsushiro, sea, Jap. K4 93
Yaṭṭah, Jordan C7 84
Yatung, China D12 88
Yauca, Peru E3 134
Yauco, P.R. C3 132
Yauco, mun., P.R. C3 132
Yauco, riv., P.R. C3 132
Yauli, Peru D2 134
Yaupi, Ec. B2 134
Yauri, Peru D3 134
Yautepec, Mex. n14 129
Yauyos, Peru D2 134
Yavapai, co., Ariz. C3 168
Yavarí, riv., Braz., Peru B3 134
Yavne, Isr. C6, h9 84
Yavneel, Isr. B7 84
Yavorov, Sov. Un. G4 72
Yawata, isl., Truk 114
Yawatahama, Jap. J6 93
Yawhee, plat., Oreg. E5 201
Yawngseng, Bur. A3 89
Yazd (Yezd), Iran F7 86
Yazd, reg., Iran F6 86
Yazd-e Khvāst, Iran F6 86
Yazdan, Iran E10 86
Yazoo, co., Miss. C3 188
Yazoo, riv., Miss. C3 188
Yazoo City, Miss. C3 188
Ybbs, riv., Aus. D7 60
Yding Skovhöj, hill, Den. B3 62
Ye, Bur. E10 87
Yeadon, Pa. B11 202
Yeager, Okla. B5 200
Yeagertown, Pa. E6 202
Yebbi Bou, Chad A3 104
Yeccla, isl., Sol. Is. 115
Yecla, Sp. C5 65
Yeddo, Ind. D3 179
Yefremov, Sov. Un. E12 72
Yegendybulak, Sov. Un. D9 73
Yegor'yersk, Sov. Un. B1 73
Yeguas, pt., P.R. C7 132
Yeharnu, is., Sol. Is. 115
Yehpaishou, China D8 92
Yei, Sud. E3 105
Yelan, Sov. Un. F14 72
Yelan-Kolenovskiy, Sov. Un. F13 72
Yelanskoye, Sov. Un. C15 71
Yelets, Sov. Un. C1 73
Yélimané, Mali C2 103
Yell, co., Ark. B2 169
Yell, isl., Scot. g10 55
Yellandalpad, India I8 88
Yelleq, mtn., Eg. D5 84
Yellow, creek, Tenn. A4 205
Yellow, lake, Wis. C1 212
Yellow, see Hwang Ho, riv., China
Yellow, riv., Fla. G2 174
Yellow, riv., Ga. A6 175
Yellow, riv., Ind. B4 179
Yellow, riv., Wis. D3 212
Yellow, sea, China D9 91
Yellow Bluff, Ala. D2 166
Yellow Creek, Sask., Can. E3 155
Yellow Grass, Sask., Can. H3 155
Yellow Jacket, Colo. D2 171
Yellow Jacket, mts., Idaho D4 177
Yellow Medicine, co., Minn. F2 187
Yellow Pine, Ala. D1 166
Yellow Pine, Idaho E3 177
Yellow Springs, Md. B3 173
Yellow Springs, Ohio C4 199
Yellowhead, pass, B.C., Alta., Can. F9 142
Yellowknife, N.W. Ter., Can. D10 142
Yellowstone, co., Mont. D8 190
Yellowstone, lake, Wyo. A2 213
Yellowstone, nat. park, Idaho, Mont., Wyo. A1 213

INDEX KEY Each place listed in **Bold-faced Type** has its population listed in the Population tables, pages 230 to 280.
Each country, shown in CAPITAL LETTERS, has its population listed in the World Political Information Table, pages 6 to 10.
* Does not appear on map; key shows general location.

Yellowstone, riv., Mont., Wyo....C12 190, A2 213
Yellowstone National Park (part), co., Wyo...A2 213
Yellowstone Park, Wyo...A2 213
Yellowtail, res., Mont., Wyo...E8 190
Yellville, Ark...A3 169
Yelm, Wash...C3 210
Yelnya, Sov. Un...D9 72
Yéltes, riv., Sp...B2 65
Yelvington, Ky...C3 182
Yelwa, Nig...D5 103
Yemanzhelinsk, Sov. Un...C6 73
Yemasse, S.C...F6 203
YEMEN (Aden), country, Asia...E10 97, C6 105
YEMEN (San'ā'), country, Asia...H7 77, 83
Yen, riv., China...G8 92
Yen Bay, Viet...B6 89
Yena, Sov. Un...D14 63
Yenakiyevo, Sov. Un...G12, q21 72
Yenan, China...D6 91
Yenangyat, Bur...B1 89
Yenangyaung, Bur...B1 89
Yencheng, China...H5 92
Yencheng, China...H9 92
Yenchi, China...C10 91
Yendi, Ghana...E4 103
Yendua, isl., Fiji...114
Yenice, riv., Tur...B9 85
Yenisey, riv., Sov. Un...C11 71
Yeniseysk, Sov. Un...D12 71
Yenshan, China...E7 92
Yenshih, China...G5 92
Yenshou, China...D4 93
Yenta, riv., Alsk...f16 167
Yeo, lake, Austl...E3 110
Yeoman, Ind...C4 179
Yeotmal, India...G7 88
Yeovil, Eng...D5 56
Yerània Óri, mtn., Grc...g10 69
Yerba Buena, Chile...E1 135
Yerevan, Sov. Un...E2 73
Yerington, Nev...E2 192
Yerkéhida (Well), Niger...B7 103
Yermo, Calif...E5 170
Yermolayevo, Sov. Un...C5 73
Yerres, Fr...h10 58
Yerres, riv., Fr...F2 59
Yerseke, Neth...C4 59
Yershov, Sov. Un...C3 73
Yerupaja, mtn., Peru...D2 134
Yesilova, Tur...D7 69
Yeso, N. Mex...C5 195
Yessentuki, Sov. Un...E2 73
Yessey, Sov. Un...C13 71
Yeste, Sp...C4 65
Yetter, Iowa...B3 180
Yeu, isl., Fr...D2 58
Yevlakh, Sov. Un...E3 73
Yevpatoriya, Sov. Un...I9 72
Yeysk, Sov. Un...H12 72
Yezd, see Yazd, Iran
Yi, riv., Ur...E1 137
Yiannitsá, Grc...B4 69
Yiaros, isl., Grc...D5 69
Yila Vasco de Gama, Moz...D5 106
Yin Shan, mtn., China...D4 92
Yinchuan (Ningsia), China...E2 92
Ying, China...E5 92
Yingkou, China...D10 92
Yingshang, China...H7 92
Yingtak, China...G7 91
Yioúra, isl., Grc...C5 69
Yirol, Sud...D3 105
Yithion, Grc...D4 69
Ylig, bay, Guam...114
Ylikitka, lake, Fin...D13 63
Ymers, isl., Grnld...B17 118
Ymir, B.C., Can...E9 149
Yoakum, Tex...E4 206
Yoakum, co., Tex...C1 206
Yockanookany, riv., Miss...C4 188
Yocona, riv., Miss...A4 188
Yoder, Colo...C6 171
Yoder, Ind...C7 179
Yoder, Kans...B4 181
Yoder, Wyo...D8 213
Yoe, Pa...*G8 202
Yoho, nat. park, B.C., Can...D9 149
Yoichi, Jap...E10 93
Yojoa, lake, Hond...C3 130
Yokadouma, Cam...E2 104
Yokkaichi, Jap...I8, o15 93
Yoko, Cam...D2 104
Yokoate, isl., Jap...L4 93
Yokohama, Jap...I9, n18 93
Yokoshiba, Jap...n19 93
Yokosuka, Jap...I9, n18 93
Yokosuka, Jap...o16 93
Yokote, Jap...G10 93
Yokun Seat, mtn., Mass...B1 185
Yola, Nig...E7 103
Yolaina, mts., Nic...E5 130
Yolo, co., Calif...C2 170
Yolyn, W. Va...D5 211
Yom, riv., Thai...C4 89
Yomakyo, mtn., Bur...C2 89
Yona, Guam...114
Yonago, Jap...I6 93
Yoncalla, Oreg...D3 201
Yonezawa, Jap...H10 93
Yŏngan, Kor...F4 93
Yonges Island, S.C...G1, F7 203
Yŏnghŭng, Kor...G3 93
Yŏngil, bay, Kor...H4 93
Yonkers, N.Y...D1, D3, E7 196
Yonne, riv., Fr...D5 58
Yorba Linda, Calif...*F5 170
York, Ala...C1 166
York, Austl...F2 111
York, Ont., Can...D5 153
York, Eng...D6 55
York, Maine...E2 184
York, Nebr...D8 191
York, N. Dak...A6 198
York, Pa...G8 202
York, S.C...B5 203
York, co., N.B., Can...C3 151
York, co., Ont., Can...D5 153
York, co., Eng...A6 56
York, co., Maine...E2 184
York, co., Nebr...D8 191
York, co., Pa...G8 202
York, co., S.C...A5 203
York, co., Va...D6 209
York, pt., Newf., Can...C4 152
York, riv., Ont., Can...B7 153
York, riv., Va...D6 209
York Beach, Maine...E2 184
York Factory, Man., Can...A5, C5 150
York Harbor, Maine...E2 184
York Haven, Pa...F8 202
York Springs, Pa...F7 202
York Wolds, hills, Eng...C6 55
Yorke, pen., Austl...F6 110
Yorklyn, Del...A6 173
Yorkshire, N.Y...C2 196
Yorkton, Sask., Can...F4 155
Yorktown, Ark...C4 169
Yorktown, Ind...D6 179
Yorktown, Iowa...D2 180
Yorktown, N.J...D2 194
Yorktown, N.Y...*D7 196
Yorktown, Tex...E4 206
Yorktown, Va...A6, D6 209
Yorktown Heights, N.Y...A5 194
Yorktown Manor, R.I...C11 172
Yorkville, Ill...B5 178
Yorkville, N.Y...B5 196
Yorkville, Ohio...B7 199
Yorkville, Tenn...A2 205
Yoro, Hond...C4 130
Yoseki, Zaire...A3 106
Yosemite, Ky...C5 182
Yosemite, nat. park, Calif...D4 170
Yosemite National Park, Calif...D4 170
Yoshiwara, Jap...n17 93
Yoshkar-Ola, Sov. Un...B3 73
Yost, Utah...B2 207
Yŏsu, Kor...I3 93
Yotala, Bol...C2 135
Youbou, B.C., Can...B8 149
Youghal, Ire...D3 55
Youghal, bay, Ire...E3 55
Youghiogheny, res., Md...D1 173
Youghiogheny, riv., Md., Pa...D1 173
Youghiogheny River, res., Pa...G3 202
Youkounkoun, Guinea...D2 103
Young, Ariz...C5 168
Young, Austl...G7 112
Young, Sask., Can...F3 155
Young, Ur...E1 137
Young, co., Tex...C3 206
Young America, Ind...C5 179
Young America, Minn...*F5 187
Young Harris, Ga...B3 175
Youngs Creek, Ind...H4 179
Youngs Point, Ont., Can...C6 153
Youngstown, Alta., Can...D5 148
Youngstown, Fla...B1, G3 174
Youngstown, Ind...F3 179
Youngstown, N.Y...B1 196
Youngstown, Ohio...A7 199
Youngstown, Pa...*F3 202
Youngsville, La...D3 183
Youngsville, N. Mex...A3 195
Youngsville, N.C...A5 197
Youngsville, Pa...C2 202
Youngstown, Ariz...G1 168
Youngwood, Pa...F2 202
Yountville, Calif...A5 170
Yovo, isl., Sol. Is...115
Yozgat, Tur...C10 85
Ypacaraí, Par...E4 135
Ypané, riv., Par...D4 135
Ypres, see Ieper, Bel.
Ypsilanti, N. Dak...C7 198
Ypsilanti, Mich...A6, F7 186
Yreka, Calif...B2 170
Ysabel, chan., Bis. Arch...115
Ysleta, Tex...F1 206
Yssingeaux, Fr...E6 58
Ystad, Swe...J5 63
Ythan, riv., Scot...C6 57
Yü, China...E6 92
Yü, riv., China...G6 91
Yüan, riv., China...J4 92
Yüanan, China...I4 92
Yuanchiang, China...G5 91
Yüanling, China...J4 92
Yüanshih, China...F7 92
Yuba, co., Calif...C3 170
Yuba, riv., Calif...C3 170
Yuba City, Calif...C3 170
Yūbari, Jap...E10 93
Yubi, cape, Mor...D2 102
Yucatán, state, Mex...C7 129
Yucatán, chan., Mex...C7 129
Yucca, Ariz...C1 168
Yucca, mtn., Nev...G5 192
Yucca Valley, Calif...E5 170
Yücheng, China...F7 92
Yuchi, China...K8 92
Yüehyang, China...J5 92
Yug, riv., Sov. Un...A3 73
YUGOSLAVIA, country, Eur...C3 68
in 1922–40...53
after World War II...54
Yühuan, China...J9 92
Yukhnov, Sov. Un...D10 72
Yukon, Fla...B5, B6 174
Yukon, Okla...B4 200
Yukon, Pa...*F2 202
Yukon, W. Va...D3 211
Yukon, ter., Can...D5 144, 147
Yukon, riv., Alsk., Yukon, Can...B9 167
Yuksekkum, Tur...D7 69
Yulee, Fla...B5, B6 174
Yuli, Nig...E7 103
Yülin, China...C8 89
Yülin, China...E3 92
Yuma, Ariz...E1 168
Yuma, Colo...A8 171
Yuma, Mich...D5 186
Yuma, co., Ariz...D1 168
Yuma, co., Colo...A8 171
Yuma, des., Ariz...E1 168
Yuma, Indian res., Calif...F6 170
Yumari, peak, Ven...C4 133
Yumbi, Zaire...B4 106
Yumen, China...B4 91
Yunabaru, Okinawa...114
Yüncheng, China...G4 92
Yúnes, riv., P.R...B4 132
Yungan, China...F8 91, L7 92
Yungas, mts., Bol...C2 135
Yungay, Chile...B2 136
Yungay, Peru...C2 134
Yungchi, China...G4 92
Yungching, China...*D5 91
Yungchow, see Lingling, China
Yungera, Austl...G4 112
Yunghsiu, China...J6 92
Yungnien, China...F6 92
Yungshou, China...G2 92
Yungshun, China...J3 92
Yungsui, China...J3 92
Yünho, China...J8 92
Yünhsiao, China...G8 91
Yünhsien, China...G5 91
Yunhsien, China...H4 92
Yünnan, plat., China...F5 91
Yünnan, prov., China...G5 91
Yunta, Austl...F2 112
Yurécuaro, Mex...m12 129
Yurimaguas, Peru...C2 134
Yurino, Sov. Un...C16 72
Yuriria, Mex...m13 129
Yurochi, isl., Bikini...114
Yuryev-Polskiy, Sov. Un...C12 72
Yuryevets, Sov. Un...C14 72
Yuscarán, Hond...D4 130
Yüshan, China...J8 92
Yüshih, China...G6 92
Yushkozero, Sov. Un...E15 63
Yüshu, see Jyekundo, China
Yüta, China...F8 91
Yutan, Nebr...C9, D2 191
Yütien, China...E7 92
Yütu, China...F8 91
Yuty, Par...E4 135
Yutzu, China...F5 92
Yüwang, China...F2 92
Yuyang, China...J3 92
Yüyao, China...I9 92
Yüyü, China...D5 92
Yuzha, Sov. Un...C13 72
Yuzhno-Sakhalinsk (Toyohara), Sov. Un...C11 93
Yuzhnoye, Sov. Un...C11 93
Yverdon, Switz...C2 66
Yvetot, Fr...C4 58
Ywathit, Bur...C2 89

Z

Zaandam, Neth...B4 59
Ząbkowice, Pol...C4 70
Ząbkowice, Pol...g10 70
Zābol, Iran...F10 86
Zābolī, Iran...H10 86
Zabrze, Pol...C5, g9 70
Zacapa, Guat...C3 130
Zacapu, Mex...n13 129
Zacatecas, Mex...C4 129
Zacatecas, state, Mex...C4, m12 129
Zacatecoluca, Sal...D3 130
Zachary, La...D4 183
Zachun, Ger...E5 62
Zack, Ark...B3 169
Zacoalco [de Torres], Mex...C4, m12 129
Zacualpan, Mex...m14 129
Zacualtipán, Mex...m14 129
Zadar, Yugo...C2 68
Zadonsk, Sov. Un...E12 72
Za'farānah, Eg...H9 85
Zafra, Sp...C2 65
Żagań, Pol...C3 70
Zaghouan, Tun...B7 102
Zagorá, Grc...C4 69
Zagora, Mor...C3 102
Zagorsk, Sov. Un...B1 73
Zagreb, Yugo...C2 68
Zagros, mts., Iran...E3 86
Zagyva, riv., Hung...B5 68
Zāhedān, Iran...G10 86
Zahl, N. Dak...A2 198
Zahle, Leb...F10 85
Zahna, Ger...B7 61
ZAIRE, country, Afr...B3 106
Zaire, prov., Ang...C1 106
Zaječar, Yugo...D6 68
Zakataly, Sov. Un...B16 85
Zákinthos, Grc...D3 69
Zákinthos (Zante), isl., Grc...D3 69
Zakopane, Pol...D5 70
Zakroczym, Pol...k13 70
Zala, riv., Hung...B3 68
Zalaegerszeg, Hung...B3 68
Zalamea de la Serena, Sp...C3 65
Zalamea la Real, Sp...D2 65
Zalău, Rom...B6 68
Zaleski, Ohio...C5 199
Zalewo, Pol...B5 70
Zalingei, Sud...C1 105
Zaliv, bay, Sov. Un...B4 118
Zalma, Mo...D7 189
Zaltan, mts., Libya...D3 101
Zaltbommel, Neth...C5 59
Zama, Miss...C4 188
Zambezi, riv., Afr...H8 96
Zambezia, prov., Moz...A6 107
ZAMBIA, country, Afr...D4 106
Zamboanga, Phil...D6 90
Zambrano, Col...B3 133
Zambrów, Pol...B7 70
Zamora, Ec...B2 134
Zamora, Mex...C4, m12 129
Zamora, Sp...B3 65
Zamora, riv., Ec...B2 134
Zamość, Pol...C7 70
Zampa, pt., Okinawa...114
Zamsar, China...B13 88
Zamzam, wadi, Libya...C2 101
Zanaga, Con...F2 104
Zandvoort, Neth...B4 59
Zanesfield, Ohio...*B4 199
Zanesville, Ind...C7 179
Zanesville, Ohio...C6 199
Zanja Blanca, P.R...C5 132
Zanjān, Iran...C4 86
Zanzibar, Tan...C6 106
Zanzibar, see Tanzania, country, Afr.
Zanzibar, isl., Afr...C6 106
Zaouiet Tahtania, Alg...C4 102
Zap, N. Dak...B4 198
Zapadna Morava, riv., Yugo...D5 68
Zapala, Arg...B2 136
Zapallar, Arg...E4 135
Zapata, Tex...F3 206
Zapata, co., Tex...F3 206
Zapata, pen., Cuba...D3 131
Zapatoca, Col...B3 133
Zaporozh'ye, Sov. Un...H10 72
Zapotillo, Ec...B1 134
Zapotitlán, Mex...h9 129
Zara, Tur...C11 85
Zaragoza, Col...B3 133
Zaragoza, Mex...B4, m13 129
Zaragoza, Mex...m13 129
Zaragoza, see Saragossa, Sp.
Zarand, Iran...F8 86
Zárate, Arg...A5, g7 136
Zaraysk, Sov. Un...D12 72
Zaraza, Ven...B4 133
Zardalu, Pak...B1 88
Zardeh Kuh, mtn., Iran...E5 86
Zarembo, isl., Alsk...m23 167
Zarephath, N.J...B3 194
Zaria, Nig...D6 103
Zarnekow, Ger...E7 62
Zarnowiec, Pol...A5 70
Zarqa, Eg...C3 84
Zarrentin, Ger...E4 62
Zaruma, Ec...B2 134
Zarumilla, Peru...B1 134
Żary, Pol...C3 70
Żary, Pol...g9 70
Zarzal, Col...C2 133
Zasenbeck, Ger...F4 62
Zashiversk, Sov. Un...C17 71
Zasieki, Pol...C3 70
Zásmuky, Czech...o19 70
Zastavna, Sov. Un...A7 68
Zastron, S. Afr...D4 107
Žatec, Czech...C2 70
Zator, Pol...h10 70
Zavala, co., Tex...E3 206
Zavalla, Tex...D5 206
Zavitaya, Sov. Un...D15 71
Zavodo-Petrovskiy, Sov. Un...B7 73
Zawiercie, Pol...C5, g10 70
Zawīlah, Libya...D3 101
Zāwiyat Masūs, Libya...C4 101
Zayon, New Britain I...115
Zaysan, Sov. Un...E11 71
Zaysan Nor, lake, Sov. Un...E11 71
Zaza, riv., Cuba...D4 131
Zbraslav, Czech...o17 70
Zdice, Czech...o16 70
Zdolbunov, Sov. Un...F6 72
Zduńska Wola, Pol...C5 70
Zealandia, Sask., Can...F2 155
Zealandia, bank, Mariana Is...115
Zearing, Iowa...B4 180
Zeba, Mich...B2 186
Zeballos, B.C., Can...D4 149
Zebdāni, Syr...F11 85
Zebrzydowice, Pol...h9 70
Zebulon, Ga...C2 175
Zebulon, Ky...C7 182
Zebulon, N.C...B5 197
Zeebrugge, Bel...C3 59
Zeeland, Mich...F4 186
Zeeland, N. Dak...D6 198
Zeeland, prov., Neth...C3 59
Zeerust, S. Afr...C4 107
Zegrze, Pol...k14 70
Zehdenick, Ger...B6 60
Zeidab, Sud...B3 105
Zeigler, Ill...F4 178
Zeila, Som...C5 105
Zeist, Neth...B5 59
Zeitz, Ger...B7 61
Zekiah, swamp, Md...C4 173
Zelechów, Pol...C6 70
Zelee, cape, Malaita I...115
Zelënodol'sk, Sov. Un...B3 73
Zelenogorsk, Sov. Un...r30 63, A7 72
Železná Ruda [Mestys], Czech...D8 61
Zelienople, Pa...E1 202
Zell, S. Dak...C7 204
Zell am Ziller, Aus...B7 66
Zella-Mehlis, Ger...C5 61
Zeller, lake, Aus...B8 66
Zellwood, Fla...D5 174
Zelma, Sask., Can...F3 155
Zelzate, Bel...C3 59
Zemetchino, Sov. Un...E14 72
Zémio, Cen. Afr. Rep...D5 104
Zena, Okla...A7 200
Zenda, Kans...E5 181
Zenica, Yugo...C3 68
Zenith, Ill...E5 178
Zenith, Kans...E5 181
Zenith, Wash...D1 210
Zenobia, peak, Colo...A2 171
Zenon Park, Sask., Can...D4 155
Zenoria, La...C3 183
Zeona, S. Dak...B3 204
Žepče, Yugo...C4 68
Zephyr, Tex...D3 206
Zephyr Cove, Nev...E2 192
Zephyrhills, Fla...D4 174
Zerbst, Ger...B7 61
Zerka, riv., Jordan...B7 84
Zermatt, Switz...C3 66
Zernez, Switz...C6 66
Zeta, riv., Yugo...D4 68
Zeulenroda, Ger...C6 61
Zeven, Ger...E3 62
Zevenaar, Neth...C6 59
Zevgolatió, Grc...D3 69
Zeway, lake, Eth...D4 105
Zeya, Sov. Un...D15 71
Zeya, riv., Sov. Un...D15 71
Zezere, riv., Port...B2 65
Zgierz, Pol...C5 70
Zgorzelec, Pol...B10 61
Zhangiz-Tobe, Sov. Un...D10 73
Zharkamys, Sov. Un...D5 73
Zhdanov (Mariupol), Sov. Un...H11 72
Zhidachov, Sov. Un...D8 70
Zhigansk, Sov. Un...C15 71
Zhigulevsk, Sov. Un...C3 73
Zhilaya Kosa, Sov. Un...D4 73
Zhilevo, Sov. Un...o18 72
Zhitomir, Sov. Un...F7 72
Zhizdra, Sov. Un...E10 72
Zhmerinka, Sov. Un...G7 72
Zhob, riv., Pak...B2 88
Zhukovka, Sov. Un...E9 72
Zhukovskiy, Sov. Un...n18 72
Zia Pueblo, Indian res., N. Mex...F5 195
Ziā'ābād, Iran...D4 86
Zibā', Sau. Ar...I10 85
Ziebach, co., S. Dak...C4 204
Ziel, mtn., Austl...D5 110
Zielona Góra, Pol...C3 70
Zierikzee, Neth...C3 59
Ziesar, Ger...A7 61
Ziftá, Eg...D3 84
Zigey, Chad...C3 104
Ziguinchor, Sen...D1 103
Zikhron Ya'aqov, Isr...B6 84
Zile, Tur...B10 85
Žilina, Czech...D5 70
Ziling (Goring), lake, China...B12 88
Zillah, Libya...D3 101
Zillah, Wash...C5 210
Ziller, riv., Aus...B7 66
Zilwaukee, Mich...E7 186
Zima, Sov. Un...D13 71
Zimapán, Mex...C5, m14 129
Zimba, Zambia...E4 106
Zimmerman, La...C3 183
Zimmerman, Minn...E5 187
Zimnicea, Rom...D7 68
Zinc, Ark...A3 169
Zincville, Okla...A7 200
Zindajan, Afg...D10 86
Zinder, Niger...D6 103
Zingst, Ger...D6 62
Zion, Ill...A6, D2 178
Zion, Md...A6 173
Zion, N.J...C3 194
Zion, S.C...C9 203
Zion, nat. park, Utah...F3 207
Zionsville, Ind...E5, G7 179
Zionville, N.C...A2 197
Zipaquirá, Col...B3 133
Zippori, Isr...B7 84
Zirándaro, Mex...n13 129
Zirkel, mtn., Colo...A4 171
Zirndorf, Ger...D5 61
Zistersdorf, Aus...D8 60
Zitácuaro, Mex...n13 129
Zittau, Ger...C9 61
Žižkov, Czech...n17 70
Zlatograd, Bul...E7 68
Zlatoust, Sov. Un...B5 73
Zlin, see Gottwaldov, Czech.
Zlitan, Libya...H14 64
Złoczew, Pol...C5 70
Zlonice, Czech...n17 70
Złotoryja, Pol...C3 70
Złotów, Pol...B4 70
Zlynka, Sov. Un...E8 72
Zmeinogorsk, Sov. Un...C10 73
Znamenka, Sov. Un...G9 72
Żnin, Pol...B4 70
Znojmo, Czech...D4 70
Zoar, Ohio...*B6 199
Zolfo Springs, Fla...E5 174
Zoller, is., Sol. Is...115
Zolochev, Sov. Un...G5 72
Zolotonosha, Sov. Un...G9 72
Zolotoy, cape, Sov. Un...C9 93
Zomba, Malawi...E6 106
Zomergem, Bel...C3 59
Zona, La...D5 183
Zongo, Zaire...A2 106
Zonguldak, Tur...B8 85
Zonza, riv., Pol...k14 70
Zook Spur, Iowa...A7 180
Zörbig, Ger...B7 61
Zorita, Sp...C3 65
Zorritos, Peru...B1 134
Zortman, Mont...C8 190
Zossen, Ger...A8 61
Zottegem, Bel...D3 59
Zouar, Chad...A3 104
Zoutkamp, Neth...A6 59
Zrenjanin (Petrovgrad), Yugo...C5 68
Zrmanja, riv., Yugo...C2 68
Zschopau, Ger...C8 61
Zubtsov, Sov. Un...C10 72
Zuehl, Tex...B4 206
Zuénoula, I.C...E3 103
Zuera, Sp...B5 65
Zug, Switz...B4 66
Zug, canton, Switz...B4 66
Zug, lake, Switz...B4 66
Zugdidi, Sov. Un...A13 85
Zugspitze, mtn., Ger...B6 66
Zuhreh, riv., Iran...F5 86
Zuider Zee (IJsselmeer), sea, Neth...B5 59
Zuidhorn, Neth...A6 59
Zulia, state, Ven...B3 133
Zülpich, Ger...C1 61
Zulueta, Cuba...D4 131
Zumbo, Moz...A5 107
Zumbro, riv., Minn...F6 187
Zumbro Falls, Minn...F6 187
Zumbrota, Minn...F6 187
Zumpango [de Ocampo], Mex...n14 129
Zungeru, Nig...E6 103
Zuni, N. Mex...B1 195
Zuni, Va...B5 209
Zuni, Indian res., N. Mex...B1 195
Zuni, mts., N. Mex...B1 195
Zuni, res., Ariz...C6 168
Zuni, riv., Ariz., N. Mex...C6 168, C1 195
Zurich, Ont., Can...D3 153
Zurich, Kans...C4 181
Zurich, Switz...B4 66
Zürich, canton, Switz...B4 66
Zürich, lake, Switz...B4 66
Zuru, Nig...D6 103
Zusam, riv., Ger...E5 61
Zutphen, Neth...B6 59
Zuwārah, Libya...C2 101
Zuwayā, Jordan...C7 84
Zuyevka, Sov. Un...B4 73
Zvenigorodka, Sov. Un...G8 72
Zvolen, Czech...D5 70
Zvornik, Yugo...C4 68
Zwartsluis, Neth...B6 59
Zweibrücken, Ger...D2 61
Zweisimmen, Switz...C3 66
Zwenkau, Ger...B7 61
Zwettl, Aus...D7 60
Zwickau, Ger...C6 60
Zwickauer Mulde, riv., Ger...C7 61
Zwiesel, Ger...D8 61
Zwingle, Iowa...B7 180
Zwolle, La...C2 183
Zwolle, Neth...B6 59
Zylks, La...A1 183
Żyrardów, Pol...B6, m12 70
Zyryanovsk, Sov. Un...D10 73
Żywiec, Pol...D5 70

INDEX KEY Each place listed in **Bold-faced Type** has its population listed in the Population tables, pages 230 to 280.
Each country, shown in CAPITAL LETTERS, has its population listed in the World Political Information Table, pages 6 to 10.
* Does not appear on map; key shows general location.

ANSWERS TO QUESTIONS

The answers on this page are organized according to the sections of the atlas. Each answer is followed by the number of the page in the atlas on which the answer can be found.

HOW TO GET THE MOST OUT OF THE WORLD BOOK ATLAS

HOW TO FIND PLACES ON MAPS (page XII)

1. Page 135
2. Page 44
3. Page 88
4. Western (67)
5. East (204)
6. Miramichi River (151)
7. Allen County (181)
8. Southwest (171)
9. South Island (112)
10. Chile (135)

HOW TO FIND DIRECTIONS ON MAPS (page XIV)

1. New Orleans (160-161)
2. Japan (77)
3. Washington, D.C. (173)
4. North (148)
5. West (97)
6. Melbourne (112)
7. Greenland (118)
8. Northeast (125)
9. Northeast (199)
10. Northeast (160, 161)

HOW TO FIND DISTANCES ON MAPS (page XVI)

1. Annapolis, Md. (173)
2. 95 miles (101)
3. 145 miles (112)
4. Sioux City to Fort Dodge (180)
5. 110 miles (67)
6. 460 miles (89)
7. 770 miles (92)
8. Copenhagen to Oslo, 295 miles; Oslo to Stockholm, 250 miles; Stockholm to Helsinki, 240 miles (63)
9. 200 miles (131)
10. Vancouver to Edmonton (144,145)

HOW TO UNDERSTAND SYMBOLS ON MAPS (page XVII)

1. Increasing (181)
2. El Centro, Sacramento, San Bernardino (170)
3. Ottawa (178)
4. Vientiane, Laos, and Phnom Penh, Cambodia (89)
5. Mauna Loa (176)
6. Coconino County (168)
7. Milan (67)
8. Cape Breton Highlands National Park (151)
9. Minneapolis (187)
10. Eldorado (206)

HOW TO UNDERSTAND POPULATIONS (page XVIII)

1. 166,800 (230-241)
2. Soviet Union (11)
3. 6,494,000,000 (11)
4. Taipei (230-241)
5. Plumtree (107)
6. Istanbul (85)
7. Davao (90)
8. Manchester (230-241)
9. Chicago (161; 246-280)
10. Hilo (176)

HOW TO PRONOUNCE NAMES OF CITIES (page XIX)*

1. The first *(BRAY mun)*
2. Szombathely *(SOHM bawt hay)*
3. The last *(KRAHS nuh YAHRSK)*
4. Four *(ED in BUR uh)*
5. The first, D *(juh KAHR tuh)*
6. *(EE say)*
7. One *(PRAHG)*
8. *(SAHN tah KROOS); (SUN tuh muh REE uh)*
9. *(PING DOONG)*
10. *(SAY toh); (TRWAH); (VAHT un shite)*

*All answers in this section are found on pages 230 through 241.

HOW TO UNDERSTAND ABBREVIATIONS AND FOREIGN TERMS ON MAPS (page XX)*

1. mountain
2. Prince Edward Island
3. hill or mountain
4. creek or crater
5. Japanese
6. Topolnitsa is a river in Bulgaria.
7. harbor or port
8. stream
9. ridge or mountain
10. Spanish

*All answers in this section are found on pages XX and 1.

EUROPE (page 39)

1. Iceland and Malta (40)
2. Italy (40)
3. Switzerland (58)
4. Austria (72)
5. Pyrenees (65)
6. Second largest (11)
7. West Germany (6-10)
8. Madrid (41)
9. Sangatte (56)
10. Budapest (41)
11. Caspian Sea (73)
12. Copenhagen (62)
13. France (44)
14. Belgium (50 and 59)
15. Ottoman Empire (52)
16. Yugoslavia (53)
17. 1938 (53)
18. Russia (54)
19. Spain (54)
20. Switzerland (6-10)

ASIA (page 75)

1. Russia (76)
2. New Delhi (87)
3. Israel and Lebanon (85)
4. Russia and Mongolia (77)
5. Nepal (88)
6. Indonesia (90)
7. Honshū (93)
8. Black Sea (85)
9. India (11)
10. Turkey (77)
11. 2,241,000,000 (11)
12. Burma (87)
13. Iran (282-391)
14. Luzon, Philippines (90)
15. 38° parallel (83)
16. Iraq (45; 77)
17. Afghanistan and Pakistan (87)
18. Thirteenth Century (81)
19. Nara (80)
20. 1258 (81)

AFRICA (page 95)

1. Indian Ocean (96)
2. South Africa (97)
3. Algeria (97)
4. North (96)
5. Addis Ababa (97)
6. Victoria (96)
7. Tanzania (106)
8. Morocco (97)
9. Lesotho (97)
10. Red Sea (101)
11. Madagascar (96)
12. Nile (96)
13. Asia (11)
14. Sudan (97)
15. 373,000,000 (11)
16. Liberia (100)
17. Great Britain (100)
18. Ethiopia (99)
19. Between 20° North and 22° South Latitude (99)
20. Morocco (102)

AUSTRALIA, NEW ZEALAND, AND PACIFIC ISLANDS (page 109)

1. Canberra (111)
2. Wellington (112)
3. Indian Ocean (110)
4. New Guinea (113)
5. Mariana Islands (113)
6. Wake (113)
7. Queensland (110)
8. 13,000,000 (11)
9. Colorado (6-10)
10. Victoria (6-10)
11. Indonesia (113)
12. 2,936,000 (6-10)
13. Indonesia (113)
14. West (113)
15. France (113)
16. Two (112)
17. Hawaii (176)
18. Solomon Islands (115)
19. Solomon Islands (115)
20. Marshall Islands (115)

POLAR REGIONS (page 117)

1. Iceland (118)
2. Thule, Greenland (118)
3. South America (120)
4. Larger (11)
5. Europe (118)
6. Peary (119)
7. 1909 (119)
8. Amundsen (121)
9. 1911 (121)
10. *Nautilus* (119)

LATIN AMERICA (page 123)

1. Mexico (128)
2. Dominican Republic (131)
3. Brasília (125)
4. Panama (130)
5. Chile (125)
6. Bolivia (125)
7. California (129)
8. Recife (125; 145)
9. Titicaca (135)
10. Argentina (136)
11. Brazil (11)
12. Brazil (125)
13. Colombia (125)
14. 56,179,000 (6-10)
15. Southeast (130)
16. Portugal (126)
17. Puerto Rico (127)
18. 1848 (127)
19. Surinam (128)
20. Uruguay (137)

CANADA (page 141)

1. Prince Edward Island (144, 145)
2. Lake Winnipeg (144, 145)
3. Winnipeg (150)
4. Ontario (145)
5. Montreal (145)
6. Mt. Logan (144)
7. Hudson Bay (142, 143)
8. Ontario (144, 145)
9. Winnipeg (142, 143)
10. Alberta (144, 145)
11. Ontario (6-10)
12. Prince Edward Island (6-10)
13. 22,516,000 (6-10)
14. Yukon (144)
15. Manitoba (142, 143)
16. Lower Canada (146)
17. Hudson's Bay Company (146)
18. Nova Scotia (147)
19. Newfoundland (147)
20. April, 1813 (146)

UNITED STATES (page 157)

1. Alaska (160, 161)
2. Alabama (160, 161)
3. Erie (158, 159)
4. Louisiana (158, 159)
5. Rocky Mountains (158, 159)
6. Alaska (167)
7. Chicago (160, 161)
8. Russia (160, 161)
9. Michigan and Pennsylvania (158, 159)
10. Canada (11)
11. Kentucky, Virginia, North Carolina, Georgia, Alabama, Mississippi, Arkansas, Missouri (160, 161)
12. Rhode Island (6-10)
13. New Jersey (6-10)
14. Lincoln, Nebraska (6-10)
15. Illinois (10)
16. Nauvoo (163)
17. Vermont (162)
18. Mexico (163)
19. Pennsylvania (164)
20. Missouri (164)

POPULATION (page 229)*

1. Moscow, Rome, Madrid
2. 9 million
3. 7 million
4. 3 million
5. Leningrad
6. West Berlin
7. Cairo
8. 141,575
9. Paris
10. Stockholm

*All answers in this section are found on pages 230 through 241.